Presented To:

By:

Date:

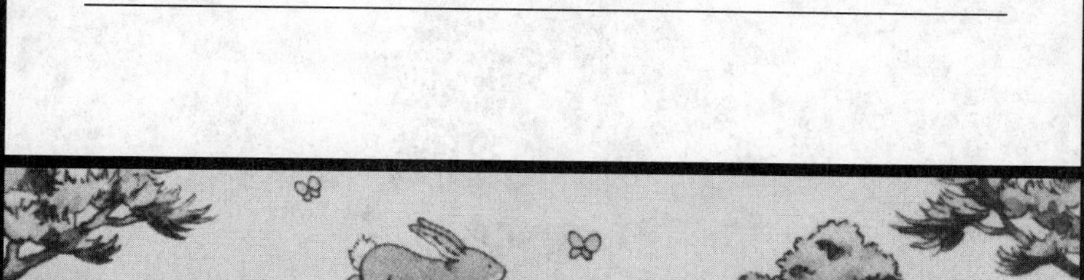

Holy Bible

with Deuterocanonicals/Apocrypha

Interconfessional Illustrated Edition

Contemporary English Version

Holy Bible

with Deuterocanonicals/Apocrypha

Interconfessional Illustrated Edition

Contemporary English Version

AMERICAN BIBLE SOCIETY
NEW YORK

THE HOLY BIBLE

with Deuterocanonicals/Apocrypha

Interconfessional Illustrated Edition

CONTEMPORARY ENGLISH VERSION

Quotation Rights for the *Contemporary English Version*

Illustrations by Lynn Adams

ISBN 1-58516-173-X
Printed in the United States of America
Eng. Bible CEV053P-109815
ABS-10/07-7, 500-32, 500-RRD 1 (5)

Welcome to the Contemporary English Version

Languages are spoken before they are written. And far more communication is done through the spoken word than through the written word. In fact, more people *hear* the Bible read than read it for themselves. Traditional translations of the Bible count on the *reader's* ability to understand a *written* text. But the *Contemporary English Version* differs from all other English Bibles—past and present—in that it takes into consideration the needs of the *hearer,* as well as those of the reader, who may not be familiar with traditional biblical language.

The *Contemporary English Version* has been described as a "user-friendly" and a "mission-driven" translation that can be *read aloud* without stumbling, *heard* without misunderstanding, and *listened to* with enjoyment and appreciation, because the language is contemporary and the style is lucid and lyrical.

The *Contemporary English Version* invites you to *read,* to *hear,* to *understand* and to *share*

the Word of God now
as never before!

The Contemporary English Version

Translation it is that opens the window, to let in the light; that breaks the shell, that we may eat the kernel; that puts aside the curtain, that we may look into the most holy place; that removes the cover of the well, that we may come by the water ("The Translators to the Reader," King James Version, 1611).

The most important document in the history of the English language is the *King James Version* of the Bible. To measure its spiritual impact on the English speaking world would be more impossible than counting the grains of sand along the ocean shores. Historically, many Bible translators have attempted in some measure to *retain the form* of the *King James Version.* But the translators of the *Contemporary English Version* of the Bible have diligently sought to *capture the spirit* of the *King James Version* by following certain principles set forth by its translators in the document "The Translators to the Reader," which was printed in the earliest editions.

This is the Word of God, which we translate

Accuracy, beauty, clarity, and dignity—all of these can and must be achieved in the translation of the Bible. After all, as the translators of the *King James Version* stated, "This is the Word of God, which we translate."

Every attempt has been made to produce a text that is faithful to the *meaning* of the original. In order to assure the *accuracy* of the *Contemporary English Version,* the Old Testament was translated directly from the Hebrew and Aramaic texts published by the United Bible Societies (*Biblia Hebraica Stuttgartensia,* fourth edition corrected). And the New Testament was translated directly from the Greek text published by the United Bible Societies (third edition corrected and compared with the fourth revised edition).

The drafts in their earliest stages were sent for review and comment to a number of biblical scholars, theologians, and educators representing a wide variety of church traditions. In addition, drafts were sent for review and comment to all English-speaking Bible Societies and to more than forty United Bible Societies translation consultants around the world. Final approval of the text was given by the American Bible Society Board of Trustees on the recommendation of its Translations Subcommittee.

We desire that the Scripture . . . may be understood

That the Scripture may be understood even by ordinary people was a primary goal of the translators of the *King James Version.* And they raised the question,

"What can be more available thereto than to deliver God's book unto God's people in a tongue which they understand?" Martin Luther also did his translation for the common people, and he established the following guidelines:

> We do not have to inquire of the literal Latin, how we are to speak German . . . Rather we must inquire about this of the mother in the home, the children on the street, the common man in the marketplace. *We must be guided by their language, the way they speak, and do our translating accordingly.*

Today more people *hear* the Bible read aloud then read it for themselves! And statistics released by the National Center for Education indicate that "almost half of U.S. adults have very limited reading and writing skills." If this is the case, a contemporary translation must be a text that an inexperienced reader can *read aloud* without stumbling, that someone unfamiliar with traditional biblical terminology can *hear without misunderstanding,* and that everyone can *listen to with enjoyment* because the style is lucid and lyrical.

In order to attain these goals of clarity, beauty, and dignity, the translators of the *Contemporary English Version* carefully studied every word, phrase, clause, and paragraph of the original. Then, with equal care, they struggled to discover the best way to translate the text, so that it would be suitable both for *private* and *public* reading, and for *memorizing.* The result is an English text that is enjoyable and easily understood by the vast majority of English speakers, regardless of their religious or educational background.

In the *hearing* of a translation, even the inclusion of a simple word like "and" can make a significant difference. Matthew 2.9 of the *Contemporary English Version* reads as follows: "The wise men listened to what the king said and then left. *And* the star they had seen in the east went on ahead of them until it stopped over the place where the child was."

"And" at the beginning of the second sentence assists both the person who reads the text aloud and those who must depend upon hearing it read. Like all other punctuation marks, the period after "left" is silent, and so the text without "And" could possibly be *heard* as, "The wise men listened to what the king said and then left the star they had seen in the east." However, as the text now stands, the oral reader must pause briefly for a breath before "And," which will signal the hearer that a new sentence has begun.

As another example, try reading the following two sentences aloud: "You yourselves admit, then, that you agree with what your ancestors did" and "for it was better with me then than now." Both suffer from potential tongue twisters ("admit, then, that" and "then than"). But the first is doubly difficult because it consists of a lengthy series of unaccented syllables that do not allow the reader to take a breath. In the *Contemporary English Version* every attempt has been made to avoid these and other kinds of constructions that could possibly prove problematic for oral reading.

According to the rules of English grammar, the pronoun *he* must refer back to *God* in the following sentence: "The other, however, rebuked him saying, 'Don't you fear *God?* You received the same sentence *he* did.' " But the reference is actually to Jesus, who is mentioned earlier in the passage. Traditional translations assume that the reader can study the printed text and finally figure out the meaning, but the *Contemporary English Version* is concerned equally with the reader and the *hearer.* And in many situations, the hearer may have only *one* chance to understand what is read aloud.

In poetry, the *appearance of the text on the page* is important, since in oral reading there is a tendency to stress the last word on a line and to pause momentarily before going to the next line, especially if the second line is indented. Compare the three following examples, where the lines of the same text have been broken improperly (left column) and properly (right column):

<table>
<tr><td>He brought me out into a broad
    place.
With the loyal you show yourself
    loyal.
The Lord my God lights up
    my darkness.</td><td>He brought me out
    into a broad place.
With the loyal
    you show yourself loyal.
The Lord my God
    lights up my darkness.</td></tr>
</table>

No fault is to be found with the translation itself. Yet there is a significant difference in the *appearance* of the text on the page, because the lines on the right have been *measured,* in order to prevent unfortunate runovers. In this form, the text not only looks better on the page, but it is easier to read and memorize, and it avoids such disastrous combinations as "He brought me out into a broad" or "With the loyal you show yourself" or "The Lord my God lights up." Moreover, both formats require exactly the same amount of lines.

The first translation in the history of the English Bible to develop a text with measured poetry lines is the *Contemporary English Version,* in which the translators have consciously created a text that will not suffer from unfortunate line breaks when published in double columns. *Accuracy* is the main concern of translators, but it must be realized that in the translation of biblical poetry, what the reader *sees* is what will be *said,* and what others will *hear.* This means that lines improperly broken can easily lead to a misunderstanding of the text, especially for those who must depend upon *hearing* the Scriptures read.

Hebrew poetry has its own systems of sound, rhyme, and rhythm, as well as a *form* that involves much repetition. It is impossible in English to retain the sounds, rhymes, and rhythms of the Hebrew text, but traditional translations have attempted to reproduce the frequent repetition, in which a second line will repeat or expand, either negatively or positively, the thoughts of the previous line. However, this repetition is often ineffective for those English speakers who are unaccustomed to the poetic style of the biblical authors. And so, the translators of the *Contemporary English Version* have followed the example of Martin Luther in the translation of poetry:

Whoever would speak German *must not use Hebrew style*. Rather he must see to it—once he understands the Hebrew author—that he concentrates on the *sense* of the text, asking himself, "Pray tell, what do the Germans say in such a situation?" Once he has the German words to serve his purpose, let him drop the Hebrew words and *express the meaning freely* in the best German he knows.

The qualities that many critics value most in modern poetry are effortless *economy* and *exactness* of language. It is hoped that readers will discover similar features in the poetry of the *Contemporary English Version*, which strives for beauty and dignity, as much as for accuracy and clarity. In this translation, the poetry often requires fewer lines than do traditional translations, but the *integrity, intent,* and *impact* of the original are consistently maintained. Note, for example, the rendering of Job 38.14,15:

Early dawn outlines the hills
like stitches on clothing
or sketches on clay.
But its light is too much
for those who are evil,
and their power is broken.

Whenever the contents of two or more verses have been joined together and rearranged in the poetic sections of the *Contemporary English Version*, this is signaled by an asterisk (*) before the first verse number in the series.

In everyday speech, "gender generic" or "inclusive" language is used, because it sounds most natural to people today. This means that where the biblical languages require masculine nouns or pronouns when both men and women are intended, this intention must be reflected in translation, though the English *form* may be very different from that of the original. The Greek text of Matthew 16.24 is literally, "If anyone wants to follow me, *he* must deny *himself* and take up *his* cross and follow me." The *Contemporary English Version* shifts to a form which is still accurate, and at the same time more effective in English: "If any of *you* want to be my followers, *you* must forget about *yourself*. *You* must take up *your* cross and follow me."

Variety of translations is profitable

The translators of the *King James Version* said, ". . . variety of translations is profitable for the finding out of the sense of the Scriptures" and "We affirm and avow that the very meanest translation of the Bible in English, set forth by men of our profession . . . contains the Word of God, nay is the Word of God." They even stated, "No cause therefore why the Word translated should be denied to be the Word, or forbidden to be current, notwithstanding that some imperfections and blemishes may be noted in the setting forth of it."

Each English translation is, in its own right, the Word of God, yet each translation serves to meet the needs of a different audience. In this regard, the *Contemporary English Version* should be considered a *companion*—the *mission* arm—of traditional translations, because it takes seriously the words of the apostle Paul that "faith comes by *hearing*."

It has pleased God in his divine providence

Translating the Bible may be compared to living the life of faith. God has not given us all the answers for our pilgrim journey, but we have been provided with all that we need to know in order to be saved. As the translators of the *King James Version* observed:

> . . . it has pleased God in His divine providence here and there to scatter those words and sentences of that difficulty and doubtfulness, not in doctrinal points that concern salvation (for in such it has been vouched that the Scriptures are plain), but in matters of less moment, that fearfulness would better beseem us than confidence . . .
>
> For as it is a fault of incredulity, to doubt of those things that are evident; so to determine of such things that the Spirit of God has left (even in the mind of the judicious) questionable, can be no less than presumption.

Bible translators do not have the privilege and luxury of working from the original manuscripts of either the Old or New Testament. Indeed, there are numerous difficult passages where decisions must be made concerning what word or words actually belong in the text, and what these words may, in fact, mean. At such places, the best a translator can do is to give what seems to be one possible meaning for the difficult text and to indicate this by a note, which was also what the King James translators did: ". . . so diversity of signification and sense in the margin, where the text is not clear, must needs be good; yea, is necessary, as we are persuaded." Fortunately, these "words and sentences of that difficulty and doubtfulness" do not in any way leave unclear the central message of the Bible or any of its major doctrines.

Having and using as great helps as were needful

The translators of the *Contemporary English Version* have not created new or novel interpretations of the text. Rather, it was their goal to express mainstream interpretations of the text in current, everyday English. To do so required *listening* carefully to each word of the biblical text, to the way in which English is spoken today, to the remarks of their reviewers, and especially to the Spirit of God. Once again the comments of the translators of the *King James Version* are appropriate:

> Neither did we think much to consult the translators or commentators . . . but neither did we disdain to revise that which we had done, and to bring to the anvil that which we had hammered; but having and using as great helps as were needful, and fearing no reproach for slowness, nor

coveting praise for expedition, we have at the length, through the good hand of the Lord upon us, brought forth the work to that pass that you see.

Accordingly, the translators of the *Contemporary English Version* are indebted to all translators and biblical scholars who have gone before them and have made it possible to understand something of the languages, cultures, and history of biblical times. And, together with the apostle Paul, they confess: *We don't have the right to claim that we have done anything on our own. God gives us what it takes to do all that we do.* (2 Corinthians 3.5)

Offer praise to God our Savior because of our Lord Jesus Christ! (Jude 24,25)

A Note on the Deuterocanonicals/Apocrypha

In the earliest editions of the *King James Version,* the books of the Bible were divided into three sections: Old Testament, Apocrypha,* and New Testament. "Apocrypha" comes from a Greek word meaning "hidden" and is used of those books, or parts of books, that are not included in the Hebrew Scriptures, but are found in early Christian versions of the Old Testament. These books are largely of Jewish origin and for the most part were written before the destruction of the temple by the Romans in A.D. 70. They were gradually interspersed among the other books of the Septuagint, which is the Greek translation of the Hebrew Scriptures, begun in Alexandria Egypt about 250 B.C.

The Jewish Community recognizes as authoritative only the Hebrew Scriptures. But the status of the Apocrypha remains in dispute among Christians. Martin Luther published this collection after the Old Testament in his 1534 edition of the Bible and referred to it as the "Apocrypha." Though it had been in all earlier English versions, the Puritans began dropping it from printings of the Geneva Bible by 1600.

The Roman Catholic Church includes many of these same books plus expanded editions of Esther and Daniel, and refers to these as the "Deuterocanonicals," meaning a second collection of books accepted as canonical (authoritative) at a later date. Most Orthodox Churches include these books, as well as 3 and 4 Maccabees, and Psalm 151. In this edition of the *Contemporary English Version,* this larger collection of books is included between the Old and New Testaments.

* In the Apocrypha were: 1 Esdras, 2 Esdras, Tobit, Judith, Rest of Esther, Wisdom of Solomon, Ecclesiasticus (Wisdom of Sirach), Baruch, Song of the Three Children, Bel and the Dragon, Prayer of Manasseh, Susanna, 1 Maccabees, 2 Maccabees.

Contents

OLD TESTAMENT

DEUTEROCANONICALS/APOCRYPHA

NEW TESTAMENT

Alphabetical Listing
with Abbreviations

OLD TESTAMENT

Amos	Am	941	Judges	Jg	239
1 Chronicles	1 Ch	413	1 Kings	1 K	346
2 Chronicles	2 Ch	445	2 Kings	2 K	379
Daniel	Dn	906	Lamentations	Lm	845
Deuteronomy	Dt	164	Leviticus	Lv	97
Ecclesiastes	Ec	686	Malachi	Ml	992
Esther	Es	513	Micah	Mic	957
Exodus	Ex	54	Nahum	Nh	965
Ezekiel	Ez	853	Nehemiah	Ne	495
Ezra	Ezra	483	Numbers	Nu	125
Genesis	Gn	1	Obadiah	Ob	952
Habakkuk	Hb	969	Proverbs	Pr	653
Haggai	Hg	978	Psalms	Ps	554
Hosea	Ho	923	Ruth	Ru	270
Isaiah	Is	702	1 Samuel	1 S	275
Jeremiah	Jr	774	2 Samuel	2 S	313
Job	Job	522	Song of Songs	Sgs	695
Joel	Jl	936	Zechariah	Zec	980
Jonah	Jon	954	Zephaniah	Zep	973
Joshua	Js	208			

DEUTEROCANONICALS/APOCRYPHA

Baruch	Ba	1126	4 Maccabees	4 Macc	1280
Bel and the Dragon	Bel	1141	Prayer of Manasseh	Man	1233
1 Esdras	1 Esd	1213	Psalm 151	Ps 151	1235
2 Esdras	2 Esd	1248	Sirach	Si	1064
Esther (Greek)	Gk Est	1032	Song of the Three Hebrews	Az/ S of 3 H	1135
Judith	Jdt	1015	Susanna	Su	1138
Letter of Jeremiah	Let Jer	1132	Tobit	Tb	999
1 Maccabees	1 Macc	1144	Wisdom of Solomon	Ws	1046
2 Maccabees	2 Macc	1182			
3 Maccabees	3 Macc	1236			

NEW TESTAMENT

Acts	Ac	1451	Mark	Mk	1344
Colossians	Col	1551	Matthew	Mt	1299
1 Corinthians	1 Co	1508	1 Peter	1 P	1597
2 Corinthians	2 Co	1524	2 Peter	2 P	1603
Ephesians	Eph	1540	Philemon	Phm	1576
Galatians	Ga	1534	Philippians	Phil	1546
Hebrews	He	1578	Revelation	Rev	1616
James	Jas	1592	Romans	Ro	1491
John	Jn	1418	1 Thessalonians	1 Th	1556
1 John	1 Jn	1607	2 Thessalonians	2 Th	1560
2 John	2 Jn	1612	1 Timothy	1 Ti	1563
3 John	3 Jn	1613	2 Timothy	2 Ti	1569
Jude	Jd	1614	Titus	Titus	1573
Luke	Lk	1372			

OTHER ABBREVIATIONS

Circa (around)	c.
Old Testament	OT
New Testament	NT
Septuagint	LXX

The
OLD TESTAMENT

About the Old Testament

The Old Testament is a collection of 39 books written in Hebrew, with a few chapters written in Aramaic. These books are arranged in five groups in English Bibles:

(1) The Pentateuch. The name means "five books," and this group is made up of Genesis, Exodus, Leviticus, Numbers, and Deuteronomy. The group is sometimes called the "Law of Moses" or the "Torah," a Hebrew word referring to God's "law" or "teachings."

(2) The Historical Books. This group is made up of Joshua, Judges, Ruth, 1 and 2 Samuel, 1 and 2 Kings, 1 and 2 Chronicles, Ezra, Nehemiah, and Esther. Together, the Pentateuch and Historical books tell the history of Israel two times. The books of Genesis through 2 Kings tell the history the first time, while the books of 1 Chronicles through Nehemiah tell it the second time from a somewhat different point of view.

(3) The Poetic Books. This group is sometimes called the "Wisdom Books," and it contains Job, Psalms, Proverbs, Ecclesiastes, and the Song of Songs. Lamentations is also one of the poetic books, but in English Bibles it follows Jeremiah, because Jeremiah has often been thought to be its author.

(4) The Major Prophets are the longer books that contain the messages of the prophets Isaiah, Jeremiah, Ezekiel, and Daniel.

(5) The Minor Prophets are the shorter books that contain the messages of the prophets Hosea, Joel, Amos, Obadiah, Jonah, Micah, Nahum, Habakkuk, Zephaniah, Haggai, Zechariah, and Malachi.

GENESIS

ABOUT THIS BOOK

The name "Genesis" comes from a Greek word meaning "beginning." And this is a book of beginnings, because it talks about the beginning of the universe, the beginning of the human race, and the beginning of the people of Israel.

The first part of Genesis (1–11) tells about creation and the human race up to the time of Abraham. Everything God created was good, but the first two human beings, Adam and Eve, disobeyed him and brought evil into the world. People became so sinful that God decided to send a flood to kill everyone except a man named Noah and his family. They worshiped God, and so God told them to build a large boat to save themselves and a few of each kind of animals and birds. After the flood people again spread out over the earth, and most of them stopped worshiping God.

The rest of the book of Genesis (12–50) contains the story of Abram and his family. God chose them to be the beginning of his own special people. God also changed Abram's name to Abraham, and the name of Abram's wife Sarai to Sarah. Abraham and his wife Sarah had no children, but God promised that they would have a child and that their descendants would someday have their own land and be a blessing for all nations.

Abraham and Sarah moved to Canaan, the land that God had promised to give their descendants. Abraham and Sarah had a son, Isaac, when they were very old. Isaac later had two sons, Jacob and Esau. As the book concludes, Jacob's twelve sons and their families are living in Egypt. One of these brothers, Joseph, had become the governor of Egypt. But Joseph knew that God would someday keep his promise to his people:

> *Before Joseph died, he told his brothers, "I won't live much longer. But God will take care of you and lead you out of Egypt to the land he promised Abraham, Isaac, and Jacob."*
>
> *(50.24)*

A QUICK LOOK AT THIS BOOK

- The Story of Creation (1.1—2.25)
- The First Sin and the First Murder (3.1—4.16)
- Descendants of Adam before the Flood (4.17—5.32)
- Noah and the Flood (6.1—9.28)
- The Descendants of Noah and the Tower of Babel (10.1—11.32)
- The Lord Chooses Abram (12.1-20)
- Abram and Lot (13.1—14.24)
- The Lord's Promises to Abram (15.1-21)
- Abram, Hagar, and Ishmael (16.1-16)
- God Changes Abram's Name to Abraham and Promises Him a Son (17.1—18.15)
- Abraham, Lot, Sodom, and Gomorrah (18.16—19.38)
- Abraham, Sarah, and Isaac (20.1—23.20)
- Rebekah, a Wife for Isaac (24.1-67)
- The Death of Abraham (25.1-18)

- Isaac and His Family (25.19—28.9)
- Jacob and His Family (28.10—35.29)
- Esau and His Family (36.1-43)
- Joseph Is Sold by His Brothers as a Slave (37.1-36)
- Judah and Tamar (38.1-30)
- Joseph in Egypt (39.1—41.57)
- Joseph and His Brothers (42.1—45.28)
- Jacob and His Family Go to Egypt (46.1—47.31)
- Jacob Blesses His Family and Dies (48.1—50.14)
- Joseph Dies (50.15-26)

The Story of Creation

1 In the beginning God
created the heavens
and the earth.[a]
2 The earth was barren,
with no form of life;[b]
it was under a roaring ocean
covered with darkness.
But the Spirit of God[c]
was moving over the water.

The First Day

3 God said, "I command light to shine!"
And light started shining. 4 God looked at
the light and saw that it was good. He separated light from darkness 5 and named the
light "Day" and the darkness "Night."
Evening came and then morning—that was
the first day.[d]

The Second Day

6 God said, "I command a dome to separate the water above it from the water below it." 7 And that's what happened. God
made the dome 8 and named it "Sky."
Evening came and then morning—that was
the second day.

The Third Day

9 God said, "I command the water under the sky to come together in one place,
so there will be dry ground." And that's
what happened. 10 God named the dry
ground "Land," and he named the water
"Ocean." God looked at what he had done
and saw that it was good.
11 God said, "I command the earth to
produce all kinds of plants, including fruit
trees and grain." And that's what happened. 12 The earth produced all kinds of
vegetation. God looked at what he had
done, and it was good. 13 Evening came
and then morning—that was the third
day.

The Fourth Day

14 God said, "I command lights to appear in the sky and to separate day from
night and to show the time for seasons,
special days, and years. 15 I command them
to shine on the earth." And that's what
happened. 16 God made two powerful
lights, the brighter one to rule the day and
the other[e] to rule the night. He also made
the stars. 17 Then God put these lights
in the sky to shine on the earth, 18 to rule
day and night, and to separate light from
darkness. God looked at what he
had done, and it was good. 19 Evening
came and then morning—that was the
fourth day.

The Fifth Day

20 God said, "I command the ocean to
be full of living creatures, and I command
birds to fly above the earth." 21 So God
made the giant sea monsters and all the
living creatures that swim in the ocean. He
also made every kind of bird. God looked at

[a] **1.1** *the heavens and the earth*: "The heavens and the earth" stood for the universе. [b] **1.1,2** *In . . . life*: Or "When God began to create the heavens and the earth, the earth was barren with no form of life." [c] **1.2** *the Spirit of God*: Or "a mighty wind." [d] **1.5** *the first day*: A day was measured from evening to evening. [e] **1.16** *the brighter . . . the other*: The sun and the moon. But they are not called by their names, because in Old Testament times some people worshiped the sun and the moon as though they were gods.

1.3 2 Macc 7.28; 2 Co 4.6. **1.6-8** 2 P 3.5.

what he had done, and it was good. 22 Then he gave the living creatures his blessing —he told the ocean creatures to live everywhere in the ocean and the birds to live everywhere on earth. 23 Evening came and then morning—that was the fifth day.

The Sixth Day

24 God said, "I command the earth to give life to all kinds of tame animals, wild animals, and reptiles." And that's what happened. 25 God made every one of them. Then he looked at what he had done, and it was good.

26 God said, "Now we will make humans, and they will be like us. We will let them rule the fish, the birds, and all other living creatures."

27 So God created humans to be like himself; he made men and women. 28 God gave them his blessing and said:

> Have a lot of children! Fill the earth with people and bring it under your control. Rule over the fish in the ocean, the birds in the sky, and every animal on the earth.
>
> 29 I have provided all kinds of fruit and grain for you to eat. 30 And I have given the green plants as food for everything else that breathes. These will be food for animals, both wild and tame, and for birds.

31 God looked at what he had done. All of it was very good! Evening came and then morning—that was the sixth day.

2 So the heavens and the earth and everything else were created.

The Seventh Day

2 By the seventh day God had finished his work, and so he rested. 3 God blessed the seventh day and made it special because on that day he rested from his work.

4 That's how God created the heavens and the earth.

The Garden of Eden

When the LORD God made the heavens and the earth, 5 no grass or plants were growing anywhere. God had not yet sent any rain, and there was no one to work the land. 6 But streams[f] came up from the ground and watered the earth.

7 The LORD God took a handful of soil and made a man.[g] God breathed life into the man, and the man started breathing. 8 The LORD made a garden in a place called Eden, which was in the east, and he put the man there.

9 The LORD God placed all kinds of beautiful trees and fruit trees in the garden. Two other trees were in the middle of the garden. One of the trees gave life—the other gave the power to know the difference between right and wrong.

10 From Eden a river flowed out to water the garden, then it divided into four rivers. 11 The first one is the Pishon River that flows through the land of Havilah, 12 where pure gold, rare perfumes, and precious stones are found. 13 The second is the Gihon River that winds through Ethiopia.[h] 14 The Tigris River that flows east of Assyria is the third, and the fourth is the Euphrates River.

15 The LORD God put the man in the Garden of Eden to take care of it and to look after it. 16 But the LORD told him, "You may eat fruit from any tree in the garden, 17 except the one that has the power to let you know the difference between right and wrong. If you eat any fruit from that tree, you will die before the day is over!"

18 The LORD God said, "It isn't good for the man to live alone. I need to make a suitable partner for him." 19-20 So the LORD took some soil and made animals and birds. He brought them to the man to see what names he would give each of them. Then the man named the tame animals and the birds and the wild animals. That's how they got their names.

[f]**2.6** *streams*: Or "mist." [g]**2.7** *man*: In Hebrew "man" comes from the same word as "soil."
[h]**2.13** *Ethiopia*: The Hebrew text has "Cush," which was a region south of Egypt that included parts of the present countries of Ethiopia and Sudan.

1.26 Ws 2.23; Si 17.3, 4; 1 Co 11.7. **1.27,28** Gn 5.1, 2. **1.27** Mt 19.4; Mk 10.6.
2.2,3 Ex 20.11. **2.2** He 4.4, 10. **2.7** Ws 15.8, 11; 1 Co 15.45. **2.9** Rev 2.7; 22.2, 14.

None of these was the right kind of partner for the man. 21 So the LORD God made him fall into a deep sleep, and he took out one of the man's ribs. Then after closing the man's side, 22 the LORD made a woman out of the rib.

The LORD God brought her to the man,
23 and the man exclaimed,

"Here is someone like me!
She is part of my body,
my own flesh and bones.
She came from me, a man.
So I will name her Woman!"[i]

24 That's why a man will leave his own father and mother. He marries a woman, and the two of them become like one person.
25 Although the man and his wife were both naked, they were not ashamed.

The First Sin

3 The snake was sneakier than any of the other wild animals that the LORD God had made. One day it came to the woman and asked, "Did God tell you not to eat fruit from any tree in the garden?"
2 The woman answered, "God said we could eat fruit from any tree in the garden,
3 except the one in the middle. He told us not to eat fruit from that tree or even to touch it. If we do, we will die."
4 "No, you won't!" the snake replied.
5 "God understands what will happen on the day you eat fruit from that tree. You will see what you have done, and you will know the difference between right and wrong, just as God does."
6 The woman stared at the fruit. It looked beautiful and tasty. She wanted the wisdom that it would give her, and she ate some of the fruit. Her husband was there with her, so she gave some to him, and
he ate it too. 7 Right away they saw what they had done, and they realized they were naked. Then they sewed fig leaves together to make something to cover themselves.
8 Late in the afternoon a breeze began
to blow, and the man and woman heard the LORD God walking in the garden. They were frightened and hid behind some trees.

The Trouble with Sin

9 The LORD called out to the man and asked, "Where are you?"
10 The man answered, "I was naked, and when I heard you walking through the garden, I was frightened and hid!"
11 "How did you know you were naked?" God asked. "Did you eat any fruit from that tree in the middle of the garden?"
12 "It was the woman you put here with me," the man said. "She gave me some of the fruit, and I ate it."
13 The LORD God then asked the woman, "What have you done?"
"The snake tricked me," she answered. "And I ate some of that fruit."
14 So the LORD God said to the snake:

"Because of what you have done,
you will be the only animal
to suffer this curse—
For as long as you live,
you will crawl on your stomach
and eat dirt.
15 You and this woman
will hate each other;
your descendants and hers
will always be enemies.
One of hers will strike you
on the head,
and you will strike him
on the heel."

16 Then the LORD said to the woman,

"You will suffer terribly
when you give birth.
But you will still desire
your husband,
and he will rule over you."

17 The LORD said to the man,

"You listened to your wife
and ate fruit from that tree.
And so, the ground

[i]**2.23** *a man . . . woman*: In Hebrew the words "man" and "woman" are similar.
2.24 Mt 19.5; Mk 10.7, 8; 1 Co 6.16; Eph 5.31. **3.1** Ws 2.24; Rev 12.9; 20.2.
3.13 2 Co 11.3; 1 Ti 2.14. **3.15** Rev 12.17. **3.17,18** He 6.8.

will be under a curse
because of what you did.
As long as you live,
you will have to struggle
to grow enough food.
18 Your food will be plants,
but the ground will produce
thorns and thistles.
19 You will have to sweat
to earn a living;
you were made out of soil,
and you will once again
turn into soil."

20 The man Adam[j] named his wife Eve[k] because she would become the mother of all who live.

21 Then the LORD God made clothes out of animal skins for the man and his wife.

22 The LORD said, "These people now know the difference between right and wrong, just as we do. But they must not be allowed to eat fruit from the tree that lets them live forever." 23 So the LORD God sent them out of the Garden of Eden, where they would have to work the ground from which the man had been made. 24 Then God put winged creatures at the entrance to the garden and a flaming, flashing sword to guard the way to the life-giving tree.

Cain Murders Abel

4 Adam[l] and Eve had a son. Then Eve said, "I'll name him Cain because I got[m] him with the help of the LORD." 2 Later she had another son and named him Abel.

Abel became a sheep farmer, but Cain farmed the land. 3 One day, Cain gave part of his harvest to the LORD, 4 and Abel also gave an offering to the LORD. He killed the first-born lamb from one of his sheep and gave the LORD the best parts of it. The LORD was pleased with Abel and his offering, 5 but not with Cain and his offering. This made Cain so angry that he could not hide his feelings.

6 The LORD said to Cain:

What's wrong with you? Why do you have such an angry look on your face? 7 If you had done the right thing, you would be smiling.[n] But you did the wrong thing, and now sin is waiting to attack you like a lion. Sin wants to destroy you, but don't let it!

8 Cain said to his brother Abel, "Let's go for a walk."[o] And when they were out in a field, Cain killed him.

9 Afterwards the LORD asked Cain, "Where is Abel?"

"How should I know?" he answered. "Am I supposed to look after my brother?"

10 Then the LORD said:

Why have you done this terrible thing? You killed your own brother, and his blood flowed onto the ground. Now his blood is calling out for me to punish you. 11 And so, I'll put you under a curse. Because you killed Abel and made his blood run out on the ground, you will never be able to farm the land again. 12 If you try to farm the land, it won't produce anything for you. From now on, you'll be without a home, and you'll spend the rest of your life wandering from place to place.

13 "This punishment is too hard!" Cain said. 14 "You're making me leave my home and live far from you.[p] I will have to wander about without a home, and just anyone could kill me."

15 "No!"[q] the LORD answered. "Anyone who kills you will be punished seven times worse than I am punishing you." So the LORD put a mark on Cain to warn everyone not to kill him. 16 But Cain had to go far from the LORD and live in the Land of Wandering,[r] which is east of Eden.

[j]**3.20** *The man Adam*: In Hebrew "man" and "Adam" are the same. [k]**3.20** *Eve*: In Hebrew "Eve" sounds like "living." [l]**4.1** *Adam*: See the note at 3.20. [m]**4.1** *Cain . . . got*: In Hebrew "Cain" sounds like "got." [n]**4.7** *you would be smiling*: Or "I would have accepted your offering."
[o]**4.8** *Cain said to his brother Abel, "Let's . . . walk*: Most ancient translations; Hebrew "Cain spoke to his brother Abel." [p]**4.14** *live . . . you*: At this time it was believed that the LORD was with his people only in their own land. [q]**4.15** *No*: Three ancient translations; Hebrew "Very well!"
[r]**4.16** *Wandering*: The Hebrew text has "Nod," which means "wandering."

3.22 Rev 22.14. **4.4** He 11.4. **4.8** Ws 10.3; Mt 23.35; Lk 11.51; 1 Jn 3.12.
4.10 He 12.24.

More and More People

17 Later, Cain and his wife had a son
named Enoch. At the time Cain was building a town, and so he named it Enoch after
his son. 18 Then Enoch had a son named
Irad, who had a son named Mehujael, who
had a son named Methushael, who had a
son named Lamech.
19 Lamech married Adah, then Zillah.
20-21 Lamech and Adah had two sons, Jabal
and Jubal. Their son Jabal was the first to
live in tents and raise sheep and goats.
Jubal was the first to play harps and
flutes.
22 Lamech and Zillah had a son named
Tubal Cain who made tools out of bronze
and iron. They also had a daughter, whose
name was Naamah.
23 One day, Lamech said to his two
wives, "A young man wounded me, and I
killed him. 24 Anyone who tries to get even
with me will be punished ten times more
than anyone who tries to get even with
Cain."
25 Adam and his wife had another son.
They named him Seth, because they said,
"God has given[s] us a son to take the place
of Abel, who was killed by his brother
Cain." 26 Later, Seth had a son and named
him Enosh.
About this time people started worshiping the LORD.[t]

Descendants of Adam

5 1-2 God created men and women to be
like himself. He gave them his blessing
and called them human beings. This is a
list of the descendants of Adam, the first
man:
3-4 When Adam was one hundred thirty,
he had a son who was just like him, and he
named him Seth. Adam had more children
5 and died at the age of nine hundred
thirty.
6 When Seth was one hundred five, he
had a son named Enosh. 7 Seth had more
children 8 and died at the age of nine hundred twelve.
9 When Enosh was ninety, he had a son
named Kenan. 10 Enosh had more children
11 and died at the age of nine hundred five.
12 When Kenan was seventy, he had a
son named Mahalalel. 13 Kenan had more
children 14 and died at the age of nine hundred ten.
15 When Mahalalel was sixty-five, he
had a son named Jared. 16 Mahalalel had
more children 17 and died at the age of
eight hundred ninety-five.
18 When Jared was one hundred sixty-
two, he had a son named Enoch. 19 Jared
had more children 20 and died at the age of
nine hundred sixty-two.
21 When Enoch was sixty-five, he had a
son named Methuselah, 22 and during the
next three hundred years he had more children. Enoch truly loved God, 23-24 and God
took him away at the age of three hundred
sixty-five.
25 When Methuselah was one hundred
eighty-seven, he had a son named Lamech.
26 Methuselah had more children 27 and
died at the age of nine hundred sixty-nine.
28 When Lamech was one hundred
eighty-two, he had a son. 29 Lamech said,
"I'll name him Noah because he will give
us comfort,[u] as we struggle hard to make a
living on this land that the LORD has put
under a curse." 30 Lamech had more children 31 and died at the age of seven hundred seventy-seven.
32 After Noah was five hundred years
old, he had three sons and named them
Shem, Ham, and Japheth.

The LORD Will Send a Flood

6 1-2 More and more people were born,
until finally they spread all over the
earth. Some of their daughters were so
beautiful that supernatural beings[v] came
down and married the ones they wanted.
3 Then the LORD said, "I won't let my life-

[s]**4.25** *Seth . . . given*: In Hebrew "Seth" sounds like "given." [t]**4.26** *worshiping the LORD*: Or "worshiping in the name of the LORD." [u]**5.29** *Noah . . . comfort*: In Hebrew "Noah" sounds like "comfort." [v]**6.1,2** *supernatural beings*: Or "angels."

5.1,2 Gn 1.27, 28; Mt 19.4; Mk 10.6. **5.23,24** Si 44.16; 49.14; He 11.5; Jd 14. **6.1-4** Job 1.6; 2.1.

giving breath remain in anyone forever.[w] No one will live for more than one hundred twenty years."[x]

4 The children of the supernatural beings who had married these women became famous heroes and warriors. They were called Nephilim and lived on the earth at that time and even later.

5 The LORD saw how bad the people on earth were and that everything they thought and planned was evil. 6 He was very sorry that he had made them, 7 and he said, "I'll destroy every living creature on earth! I'll wipe out people, animals, birds, and reptiles. I'm sorry I ever made them."

8 But the LORD was pleased with Noah, 9 and this is the story about him. Noah was the only person who lived right and obeyed God. 10 He had three sons: Shem, Ham, and Japheth.

11-12 God knew that everyone was terribly cruel and violent. 13 So he told Noah:

> Cruelty and violence have spread everywhere. Now I'm going to destroy the whole earth and all its people. 14 Get some good lumber and build a boat. Put rooms in it and cover it with tar inside and out. 15 Make it four hundred fifty feet long, seventy-five feet wide, and forty-five feet high. 16 Build a roof[y] on the boat and leave a space of about eighteen inches between the roof and the sides.[z] Make the boat three stories high and put a door on one side.
>
> 17 I'm going to send a flood that will destroy everything that breathes! Nothing will be left alive. 18 But I solemnly promise that you, your wife, your sons, and your daughters-in-law will be kept safe in the boat.[a]
>
> 19-20 Bring into the boat with you a male and a female of every kind of animal and bird, as well as a male and a female of every reptile. I don't want them to be destroyed. 21 Store up enough food both for yourself and for them.

22 Noah did everything the LORD told him to do.

The Flood

7 The LORD told Noah:

> Take your whole family with you into the boat, because you are the only one on this earth who pleases me. 2 Take seven pairs of every kind of animal that can be used for sacrifice[b] and one pair of all others. 3 Also take seven pairs of every kind of bird with you. Do this so there will always be animals and birds on the earth. 4 Seven days from now I will send rain that will last for forty days and nights, and I will destroy all other living creatures I have made.

5-7 Noah was six hundred years old when he went into the boat to escape the flood, and he did everything the LORD had told him to do. His wife, his sons, and his daughters-in-law all went inside with him. 8-9 He obeyed God and took a male and a female of each kind of animal and bird into the boat with him. 10 Seven days later a flood began to cover the earth.

11-12 Noah was six hundred years old when the water under the earth started gushing out everywhere. The sky opened like windows, and rain poured down for forty days and nights. All this began on the seventeenth day of the second month of the year. 13 On that day Noah and his wife went into the boat with their three sons, Shem, Ham, and Japheth, and their wives. 14 They took along every kind of animal, tame and wild, including the birds. 15 Noah took a male and a female of every living creature with him, 16 just as God had told him to do. And when they were all in the boat, God closed the door.

[w] **6.3** *I won't . . . forever*: One possible meaning for the difficult Hebrew text. [x] **6.3** *No one . . . years*: Or "In fact, they will all be destroyed in about one hundred years" (that is, at the time of the flood). [y] **6.16** *roof*: Or "window." [z] **6.16** *leave . . . sides*: One possible meaning for the difficult Hebrew text. [a] **6.18** *boat*: One possible meaning for the difficult Hebrew text of verse 18. [b] **7.2** *animal . . . for sacrifice*: Hebrew "clean animals." Animals that could be used for sacrifice were called "clean," and animals that could not be used were called "unclean."

6.4 Nu 13.33; Si 16.7; Ba 3.26. **6.4-7** 3 Macc 2.4. **6.5-8** Mt 24.37; Lk 17.26; 1 P 3.20. **6.9** Si 44.17, 18; 2 P 2.5. **6.22** He 11.7. **7.5-7** Mt 24.38, 39; Lk 17.27. **7.11,12** 2 P 3.6.

17-18 For forty days the rain poured down without stopping. And the water became deeper and deeper, until the boat started floating high above the ground. 19-20 Finally, the mighty flood was so deep that even the highest mountain peaks were almost twenty-five feet below the surface of the water. 21 Not a bird, animal, reptile, or human was left alive anywhere on earth. 22-23 The LORD destroyed everything that breathed. Nothing was left alive except Noah and the others in the boat. 24 A hundred fifty days later, the water started going down.

The Water Goes Down

8 God did not forget about Noah and the animals with him in the boat. So God made a wind blow, and the water started going down. 2 God stopped up the places where the water had been gushing out from under the earth. He also closed up the sky, and the rain stopped. 3 For one hundred fifty days the water slowly went down. 4 Then on the seventeenth day of the seventh month of the year, the boat came to rest somewhere in the Ararat mountains. 5 The water kept going down, and the mountain tops could be seen on the first day of the tenth month.

6-7 Forty days later Noah opened a window to send out a raven, but it kept flying around until the water had dried up. 8 Noah wanted to find out if the water had gone down, and he sent out a dove. 9 Deep water was still everywhere, and the dove could not find a place to land. So it flew back to the boat. Noah held out his hand and helped it back in.

10 Seven days later Noah sent the dove out again. 11 It returned in the evening, holding in its beak a green leaf from an olive tree. Noah knew that the water was finally going down. 12 He waited seven more days before sending the dove out again, and this time it did not return.

13 Noah was now six hundred one years old. And by the first day of that year, almost all the water had gone away. Noah made an opening in the roof of the boat[c] and saw that the ground was getting dry. 14 By the twenty-seventh day of the second month, the earth was completely dry.

15 God said to Noah, 16 "You, your wife, your sons, and your daughters-in-law may now leave the boat. 17 Let out the birds, animals, and reptiles, so they can mate and live all over the earth." 18 After Noah and his family had gone out of the boat, 19 the living creatures left in groups of their own kind.

The LORD's Promise for the Earth

20 Noah built an altar where he could offer sacrifices to the LORD. Then he offered on the altar one of each kind of animal and bird that could be used for a sacrifice.[d] 21 The smell of the burning offering pleased God, and he said:

Never again will I punish the earth for the sinful things its people do. All of them have evil thoughts from the time they are young, but I will never destroy everything that breathes, as I did this time.

22 As long as the earth remains,
there will be planting
and harvest,
cold and heat;
winter and summer,
day and night.

God's Promise to Noah

9 God said to Noah and his sons:

I am giving you my blessing. Have a lot of children and grandchildren, so people will live everywhere on this earth. 2 All animals, birds, reptiles, and fish will be afraid of you. I have placed them under your control, 3 and I have given them to you for food. From now on, you may eat them, as well as the green plants that you have always eaten. 4 But life is in the blood, and you must not eat any meat that still has blood in it. 5-6 I created humans to be like me, and I will punish any animal or person that takes a human life.

[c]**8.13** *made . . . boat*: One possible meaning for the difficult Hebrew text. [d]**8.20** *animal . . . sacrifice*: See the note at 7.2.

7.22,23 3 Macc 2.4. **9.1** Gn 1.28. **9.4** Lv 7.26, 27; 17.10-14; 19.26; Dt 12.5-19, 23, 24; 15.23. **9.5,6** Gn 1.26; Ex 20.13.

If an animal kills someone, that animal must die. And if a person takes the life of another, that person must be put to death.

7 I want you and your descendants to have many children, so people will live everywhere on earth.

8 Again, God said to Noah and his sons:

9 I am going to make a solemn promise to you and to everyone who will live after you. 10 This includes the birds and the animals that came out of the boat. 11 I promise every living creature that the earth and those living on it will never again be destroyed by a flood.

12-13 The rainbow that I have put in the sky will be my sign to you and to every living creature on earth. It will remind you that I will keep this promise forever. 14 When I send clouds over the earth, and a rainbow appears in the sky, 15 I will remember my promise to you and to all other living creatures. Never again will I let floodwaters destroy all life. 16 When I see the rainbow in the sky, I will always remember the promise that I have made to every living creature. 17 The rainbow will be the sign of that solemn promise.

Noah and His Family

18 Noah and his sons, Shem, Ham, and Japheth, came out of the boat. Ham later had a son named Canaan. 19 All people on earth are descendants of Noah's three sons.

20 Noah farmed the land and was the first to plant a vineyard. 21 One day he got drunk and was lying naked in his tent. 22 Ham entered the tent and saw him naked, then went back outside and told his brothers. 23 Shem and Japheth put a robe over their shoulders and walked backwards into the tent. Without looking at their father, they placed it over his body.

24 When Noah woke up and learned what his youngest son had done, 25 he said,

"I now put a curse on Canaan!
He will be the lowest slave
of his brothers.
26 I ask the LORD my God
to bless Shem
and make Canaan his slave.
27 I pray that the LORD
will give Japheth
more and more[e] land
and let him take over
the territory of Shem.
May Canaan be his slave."

28 Noah lived three hundred fifty years after the flood 29 and died at the age of nine hundred fifty.

The Descendants of Noah

10 After the flood Shem, Ham, and Japheth had many descendants.

The Descendants of Japheth

2-5 Japheth's descendants had their own languages, tribes, and land. They were Gomer, Magog, Madai, Javan, Tubal, Meshech, and Tiras.

Gomer was the ancestor of Ashkenaz, Riphath, and Togarmah.

Javan was the ancestor of Elishah, Tarshish, Kittim, and Dodanim,[f] who settled along the coast.

The Descendants of Ham

6-20 Ham's descendants had their own languages, tribes, and land. They were Ethiopia,[g] Egypt, Put, and Canaan.

Cush[h] was the ancestor of Seba, Havilah, Sabtah, Raamah, and Sabteca.

Raamah was the ancestor of Sheba and Dedan.

Cush was also the ancestor of Nimrod, a mighty warrior whose strength came from the LORD. Nimrod is the reason for the saying, "You hunt like Nimrod with the strength of the LORD!" Nimrod first ruled in Babylon, Erech, and Accad, all of[i] which

[e]**9.27** *more and more*: In Hebrew "Japheth" sounds like "more and more." [f]**10.2-5** *Dodanim*: Most Hebrew manuscripts; some Hebrew manuscripts and one ancient translation have "Rodanim." [g]**10.6-20** *Ethiopia*: See the note at 2.13. [h]**10.6-20** *Cush*: See the note at 2.13. [i]**10.6-20** *and Accad, all of*: Or "Accad, and Calneh."

9.7 Gn 1.28.

were in Babylonia.[j] From there Nimrod went to Assyria and built the great city of Nineveh. He also built Rehoboth-Ir and Calah, as well as Resen, which is between Nineveh and Calah.

Egypt was the ancestor of Ludim, Anamim, Lehabim, Naphtuhim, Pathrusim, Casluhim, and Caphtorim, the ancestor of the Philistines.[k]

Canaan's sons were Sidon and Heth. He was also the ancestor of the Jebusites, the Amorites, the Girgashites, the Hivites, the Arkites, the Sinites, the Arvadites, the Zemarites, and the Hamathites.

Later the Canaanites spread from the territory of Sidon and went as far as Gaza in the direction of Gerar. They also went as far as Lasha in the direction of Sodom, Gomorrah, Admah, and Zeboiim.

The Descendants of Shem

21-31 Shem's descendants had their own languages, tribes, and land. He was the older brother of Japheth and the ancestor of the tribes of Eber.

Shem was the ancestor of Elam, Asshur, Arpachshad, Lud, and Aram.

Aram was the ancestor of Uz, Hul, Gether, and Mash.

Arpachshad was the father of Shelah and the grandfather of Eber, whose first son was named Peleg,[l] because it was during his time that tribes divided up the earth. Eber's second son was Joktan.

Joktan was the ancestor of Almodad, Sheleph, Hazarmaveth, Jerah, Hadoram, Uzal, Diklah, Obal, Abimael, Sheba, Ophir, Havilah, and Jobab. Their land reached from Mesha in the direction of Sephar, the hill country in the east.

32 This completes the list of Noah's descendants. After the flood their descendants became nations and spread all over the world.

The Tower of Babel

11 At first everyone spoke the same language, 2 but after some of them moved from the east[m] and settled in Babylonia,[n] 3-4 they said:

> Let's build a city with a tower that reaches to the sky! We'll use hard bricks and tar instead of stone and mortar. We'll become famous, and we won't be scattered all over the world.

5 But when the LORD came down to look at the city and the tower, 6 he said:

> These people are working together because they all speak the same language. This is just the beginning. Soon they will be able to do anything they want. 7 Come on! Let's go down and confuse them by making them speak different languages—then they won't be able to understand each other.

8-9 So the people had to stop building the city, because the LORD confused their language and scattered them all over the earth. That's how the city of Babel[o] got its name.

The Descendants of Shem

10-11 Two years after the flood, when Shem was one hundred, he had a son named Arpachshad. He had more children and died at the age of six hundred. This is a list of his descendants:

12 When Arpachshad was thirty-five, he had a son named Shelah. 13 Arpachshad had more children and died at the age of four hundred thirty-eight.

14 When Shelah was thirty, he had a son named Eber. 15 Shelah had more children and died at the age of four hundred thirty-three.

16 When Eber was thirty-four, he had a son named Peleg. 17 Eber had more children and died at the age of four hundred sixty-four.

18 When Peleg was thirty, he had a son named Reu. 19 Peleg had more children

[j] **10.6-20** *Babylonia*: The Hebrew text has "Shinar," another name for Babylonia.
[k] **10.6-20** *Casluhim, and Caphtorim, the ancestor of the Philistines*: Hebrew "Caphtorim, and Casluhim, the ancestor of the Philistines." The Philistines were from Caphtor (see Jeremiah 47.4; Amos 9.7), better known as Crete. [l] **10.21-31** *Peleg*: In Hebrew "Peleg" means "divided."
[m] **11.2** *from the east*: Or "to the east." [n] **11.2** *Babylonia*: See the note at 10.6-20.
[o] **11.8,9** *Babel*: In Hebrew "Babel" sounds like "confused."

and died at the age of two hundred thirty-
nine.
20 When Reu was thirty-two he had a
son named Serug. 21 Reu had more children and died at the age of two hundred
thirty-nine.
22 When Serug was thirty, he had a son
named Nahor. 23 Serug had more children
and died at the age of two hundred thirty.
24 When Nahor was twenty-nine, he
had a son named Terah. 25 Nahor had more
children and died at the age of one hundred forty-eight.

The Descendants of Terah

26-28 After Terah was seventy years old,
he had three sons: Abram, Nahor, and Haran, who became the father of Lot. Terah's
sons were born in the city of Ur in
Chaldea,[p] and Haran died there before the
death of his father. The following is the
story of Terah's descendants.
29-30 Abram married Sarai, but she was
not able to have any children. And Nahor
married Milcah, who was the daughter of
Haran and the sister of Iscah.
31 Terah decided to move from Ur to the
land of Canaan. He took along Abram and
Sarai and his grandson Lot, the son of Haran. But when they came to the city of Haran,[q] they decided to settle there instead.
32 Terah lived to be two hundred five years
old and died in Haran.

The LORD Chooses Abram

12 The LORD said to Abram:
Leave your country, your family,
and your relatives and go to the land
that I will show you. 2 I will bless you
and make your descendants into a
great nation. You will become famous
and be a blessing to others. 3 I will
bless anyone who blesses you, but I
will put a curse on anyone who puts a
curse on you. Everyone on earth will
be blessed because of you.[r]
4-5 Abram was seventy-five years old
when the LORD told him to leave the city of
Haran. He obeyed and left with his wife
Sarai, his nephew Lot, and all the possessions and slaves they had gotten while in
Haran.
When they came to the land of Canaan,
6 Abram went as far as the sacred tree of
Moreh in a place called Shechem. The
Canaanites were still living in the land at
that time, 7 but the LORD appeared to
Abram and promised, "I will give this land
to your family forever." Abram then built an
altar there for the LORD.
8 Abram traveled to the hill country east
of Bethel and camped between Bethel and
Ai, where he built another altar and worshiped the LORD. 9 Later, Abram started out
toward the Southern Desert.

Abram in Egypt

10-11 The crops failed, and there was no
food anywhere in the land. So Abram and
his wife Sarai went to live in Egypt for a
while. But just before they got there, he
said, "Sarai, you are really beautiful!
12 When the Egyptians see how lovely you
are, they will murder me because I am your
husband. But they won't kill you. 13 Please
save my life by saying that you are my
sister."
14 As soon as Abram and Sarai arrived in
Egypt, the Egyptians noticed how beautiful
she was. 15 The king's[s] officials told him
about her, and she was taken to his house.
16 The king was good to Abram because of
Sarai, and Abram was given sheep, cattle,
donkeys, slaves, and camels.
17 Because of Sarai, the LORD struck the
king and everyone in his palace with terrible diseases. 18 Finally, the king sent for
Abram and said to him, "What have you
done to me? Why didn't you tell me Sarai
was your wife? 19 Why did you make me
believe she was your sister? Now I've married her. Take her and go! She's your wife."
20 So the king told his men to let Abram
and Sarai take their possessions and leave.

[p] **11.26-28** *Ur in Chaldea*: Chaldea was a region at the head of the Persian Gulf. Ur was on the main trade routes from Mesopotamia to the Mediterranean Sea. [q] **11.31** *Haran*: About 550 miles northwest of Ur. [r] **12.3** *Everyone . . . you*: Or "Everyone on earth will ask me to bless them as I have blessed you." [s] **12.15** *The king's*: The Hebrew text has "Pharaoh's," a Hebrew word sometimes used for the king of Egypt.

12.1 Ac 7.2, 3; He 11.8. **12.3** Ga 3.8. **12.7** Ac 7.5; Ga 3.16. **12.13** Gn 20.2; 26.7.

Abram and Lot Separate

13 Abram and Sarai took everything they owned and went to the Southern Desert. Lot went with them.

2 Abram was very rich. He owned many cattle, sheep, and goats, and had a lot of silver and gold. 3 Abram moved from place to place in the Southern Desert. And finally, he went north and set up his tents between Bethel and Ai, 4 where he had earlier camped and built an altar. There he worshiped the LORD.

5 Lot, who was traveling with him, also had sheep, goats, and cattle, as well as his own family and slaves. 6-7 At this time the Canaanites and the Perizzites were living in the same area, and so there wasn't enough pastureland left for Abram and Lot with all of their animals. Besides this, the men who took care of Abram's animals and the ones who took care of Lot's animals started quarreling.

8 Abram said to Lot, "We are close relatives. We shouldn't argue, and our men shouldn't be fighting one another. 9 There is plenty of land for you to choose from. Let's separate. If you go north, I'll go south; if you go south, I'll go north."

10 This happened before the LORD had destroyed the cities of Sodom and Gomorrah. And when Lot looked around, he saw there was plenty of water in the Jordan Valley. All the way to Zoar the valley was as green as the garden of the LORD or the land of Egypt. 11 So Lot chose the whole Jordan Valley for himself, and as he started toward the east, he and Abram separated. 12 Abram stayed in the land of Canaan. But Lot settled near the cities of the valley and put up his tents not far from Sodom, 13 where the people were evil and sinned terribly against the LORD.

Abram Moves to Hebron

14 After Abram and Lot had gone their separate ways, the LORD said to Abram:

> Look around to the north, south, east, and west. 15 I will give you and your family all the land you can see. It will be theirs forever! 16 I will give you more descendants than there are specks of dust on the earth, and someday it will be easier to count the specks of dust than to count your descendants. 17 Now walk back and forth across the land, because I am giving it to you.

18 Abram took down his tents and went to live near the sacred trees of Mamre at Hebron, where he built an altar in honor of the LORD.

Abram Rescues Lot

14 About this time, King Amraphel of Babylonia,[t] King Arioch of Ellasar, King Chedorlaomer of Elam, and King Tidal of Goiim 2 attacked King Bera of Sodom, King Birsha of Gomorrah, King Shinab of Admah, King Shemeber of Zeboiim, and the king of Bela, also known as the city of Zoar. 3-4 King Chedorlaomer and his allies had ruled these last five kings for twelve years, but in the thirteenth year the kings rebelled and came together in Siddim Valley, which is now covered by the southern part of the Dead Sea.

5 A year later King Chedorlaomer and his allies attacked and defeated the Rephaites in Ashteroth-Karnaim, the Zuzites in Ham, and the Emites in Shaveh-Kiriathaim. 6 They also defeated the Horites in the hill country of Edom,[u] as far as El-Paran, near the desert.

7 They went back to the city of Enmishpat, better known as Kadesh. Then they captured all the land that belonged to the Amalekites, and they defeated the Amorites who were living in Hazazon-Tamar.

8-9 At Siddim Valley, the armies of the kings of Sodom, Gomorrah, Admah, Zeboiim, and Bela fought the armies of King Chedorlaomer of Elam, King Tidal of Goiim, King Amraphel of Babylonia, and King Arioch of Ellasar. The valley 10 was full of tar pits, and when the troops from Sodom and Gomorrah started running away, some of them fell into the pits. Others escaped to the hill country. 11 Their en-

[t] **14.1** *Babylonia*: See the note at 10.6-20.

[u] **14.6** *Edom*: The Hebrew text has "Seir," another name for Edom.

13.10 Gn 2.10. **13.15** Ac 7.5.

emies took everything of value from Sodom and Gomorrah, including their food supplies. [12] They also captured Abram's nephew Lot, who lived in Sodom. They took him and his possessions and then left.

[13] At this time Abram the Hebrew was living near the oaks that belonged to Mamre the Amorite. Mamre and his brothers Eshcol and Aner were Abram's friends. Someone who had escaped from the battle told Abram [14] that his nephew Lot had been taken away. Three hundred eighteen of Abram's servants were fighting men, so he took them and followed the enemy as far north as the city of Dan.

[15] That night, Abram divided up his troops, attacked from all sides, and won a great victory. But some of the enemy escaped to the town of Hobah north of Damascus, [16] and Abram went after them. He brought back his nephew Lot, together with Lot's possessions and the women and everyone else who had been captured.

Abram Is Blessed by Melchizedek

[17] Abram returned after he had defeated King Chedorlaomer and the other kings. Then the king of Sodom went to meet Abram in Shaveh Valley, which is also known as King's Valley.

[18] King Melchizedek of Salem was a priest of God Most High. He brought out some bread and wine [19] and said to Abram:

"I bless you in the name
of God Most High,
Creator of heaven and earth.
[20] All praise belongs
to God Most High
for helping you defeat
your enemies."

Then Abram gave Melchizedek a tenth of everything.

[21] The king of Sodom said to Abram, "All I want are my people. You can keep everything else."

[22] Abram answered:

The LORD God Most High made the heavens and the earth. And I have promised him [23] that I won't keep anything of yours, not even a sandal strap or a piece of thread. Then you can never say that you are the one who made me rich. [24] Let my share be the food that my men have eaten. But Aner, Eshcol, and Mamre went with me, so give them their share of what we brought back.

The LORD's Promise to Abram

15 Later the LORD spoke to Abram in a vision, "Abram, don't be afraid! I will protect you and reward you greatly."

[2] But Abram answered, "LORD All-Powerful, you have given me everything I could ask for, except children. And when I die, Eliezer of Damascus will get all I own.[v] [3] You have not given me any children, and this servant of mine will inherit everything."

[4] The LORD replied, "No, he won't! You will have a son of your own, and everything you have will be his." [5] Then the LORD took Abram outside and said, "Look at the sky and see if you can count the stars. That's how many descendants you will have." [6] Abram believed the LORD, and the LORD was pleased with him.

The LORD Makes Another Promise to Abram

[7] The LORD said to Abram, "I brought you here from Ur in Chaldea, and I gave you this land."

[8] Abram asked, "LORD God, how can I know the land will be mine?"

[9] Then the LORD told him, "Bring me a three-year-old cow, a three-year-old female goat, a three-year-old ram, a dove, and a young pigeon."

[10] Abram obeyed the LORD. Then he cut[w] the animals in half and laid the two halves of each animal opposite each other on the ground. But he did not cut the doves and pigeons in half. [11] And when

[v] **15.2** *And . . . own*: One possible meaning for the difficult Hebrew text. [w] **15.10** *cut*: In Hebrew "cut" sounds something like "agreement." What follows shows that the LORD is making an agreement with Abram.

14.18-20 He 7.1-10. **15.5** Ro 4.18; He 11.12. **15.6** 1 Macc 2.52; Ro 4.3; Ga 3.6; Jas 2.23.

birds came down to eat the animals, Abram
chased them away.
12 As the sun was setting, Abram fell
into a deep sleep, and everything became
dark and frightening. 13-15 Then the LORD
said:

Abram, you will live to an old age
and die in peace.
But I solemnly promise that your
descendants will live as foreigners in a
land that doesn't belong to them. They
will be forced into slavery and abused
for four hundred years. But I will terribly punish the nation that enslaves
them, and they will leave with many
possessions.
16 Four generations later,[x] your descendants will return here and take
this land, because only then will the
people who live here[y] be so sinful that
they deserve to be punished.

17 Sometime after sunset, when it was
very dark, a smoking cooking pot[z] and a
flaming fire went between the two halves of
each animal. 18 At that time the LORD made
an agreement with Abram and told him:

I will give your descendants the
land east of the Shihor River[a] on the
border of Egypt as far as the Euphrates
River. 19 They will possess the land of
the Kenites, the Kenizzites, the Kad-
monites, 20 the Hittites, the Perizzites,
the Rephaites, 21 the Amorites, the
Canaanites, the Girgashites, and the
Jebusites.

Hagar and Ishmael

16 Abram's wife Sarai had not been
able to have any children. But she
owned a young Egyptian slave woman
named Hagar, 2 and Sarai said to Abram,
"The LORD has not given me any children.
Sleep with my slave, and if she has a child,
it will be mine."[b] Abram agreed, 3 and
Sarai gave him Hagar to be his wife. This
happened after Abram had lived in the
land of Canaan for ten years. 4 Later, when
Hagar knew she was going to have a baby,
she became proud and was hateful to
Sarai.
5 Then Sarai said to Abram, "It's all your
fault![c] I gave you my slave woman, but she
has been hateful to me ever since she
found out she was pregnant. You have done
me wrong, and you will have to answer to
the LORD for this."
6 Abram said, "All right! She's your
slave, and you can do whatever you want
with her." But Sarai began treating Hagar
so harshly that she finally ran away.
7 Hagar stopped to rest at a spring in the
desert on the road to Shur. While she was
there, the angel of the LORD came to her
8 and asked, "Hagar, where have you come
from, and where are you going?"

She answered, "I'm running away from
Sarai, my owner."
9 The angel said, "Go back to Sarai and
be her slave. 10-11 I will give you a son, who
will be called Ishmael,[d] because I have
heard your cry for help. And later I will give
you so many descendants that no one will
be able to count them all. 12 But your son
will live far from his relatives; he will be
like a wild donkey, fighting everyone, and
everyone fighting him."
13 Hagar thought, "Have I really seen
God and lived to tell about it?"[e] So from
then on she called him, "The God Who
Sees Me."[f] 14 That's why people call the
well between Kadesh and Bered, "The Well
of the Living One Who Sees Me."[g]

[x] **15.16** *Four generations later*: This may refer to the "four hundred years" of verses 13-15.
[y] **15.16** *people who live here*: The Hebrew text has "Amorites," a name sometimes used of the people who lived in Palestine before the Israelites.
[z] **15.17** *smoking cooking pot*: One possible meaning for the difficult Hebrew text. The smoke and fire represent the presence of the LORD.
[a] **15.18** *Shihor River*: See Joshua 13.2-7.
[b] **16.2** *Sleep . . . mine*: It was the custom for a wife who could not have children to let her husband sleep with one of her slave women. The children of the slave would belong to the wife.
[c] **16.5** *It's . . . fault*: Or "I hope you'll be punished for what you did to me!"
[d] **16.10,11** *Ishmael*: In Hebrew "Ishmael" sounds like "God hears."
[e] **16.13** *Have . . . it*: One possible meaning for the difficult Hebrew text.
[f] **16.13** *The God Who Sees Me*: Or "The God I Have Seen."
[g] **16.14** *The Well . . . Me*: Or "Beer-Lahai-Roi" (see 25.11).

15.12 Job 4.13, 14. **15.13-15 a** Ex 1.1-14; Ac 7.6; **b** Ex 12.40, 41; Ac 7.7. **15.18** Ac 7.5.

15-16 Abram was eighty-six years old when Hagar gave birth to their son, and he named him Ishmael.

God's Promise to Abraham

17 Abram was ninety-nine years old when the LORD appeared to him again and said, "I am God All-Powerful. If you obey me and always do right, 2 I will keep my solemn promise to you and give you more descendants than can be counted." 3 Abram bowed with his face to the ground, and God said:

4-5 I promise that you will be the father of many nations. That's why I now change your name from Abram to Abraham.[h] 6 I will give you a lot of descendants, and in the future they will become great nations. Some of them will even be kings.

7 I will always keep the promise I have made to you and your descendants, because I am your God and their God. 8 I will give you and them the land in which you are now a foreigner. I will give the whole land of Canaan to your family forever, and I will be their God.

9 Abraham, you and all future members of your family must promise to obey me. 10-11 As the sign that you are keeping this promise, you must circumcise every man and boy in your family. 12-13 From now on, your family must circumcise every baby boy when he is eight days old. You must even circumcise any man or boy you have as a slave, both those born in your homes and those you buy from foreigners. This will be a sign that my promise to you will last forever. 14 Any man who isn't circumcised hasn't kept his promise to me and cannot be one of my people.

15 Abraham, your wife's name will now be Sarah instead of Sarai. 16 I will bless her, and you will have a son by her. She will become the mother of nations, and some of her descendants will even be kings.

17 Abraham bowed with his face to the ground and thought, "I am almost a hundred years old. How can I become a father? And Sarah is ninety. How can she have a child?" So he started laughing. 18 Then he asked God, "Why not let Ishmael[i] inherit what you have promised me?"

19 But God answered:

No! You and Sarah will have a son. His name will be Isaac,[j] and I will make an everlasting promise to him and his descendants.

20 I have heard what you asked me to do for Ishmael, and so I will also bless him with many descendants. He will be the father of twelve princes, and I will make his family a great nation. 21 But your son Isaac will be born about this time next year, and the promise I am making to you and your family will be for him and his descendants forever.

22 God finished speaking to Abraham and then left.

23-27 On that same day Abraham obeyed God by circumcising Ishmael. Abraham was also circumcised, and so were all other men and boys in his household, including his servants and slaves. He was ninety-nine years old at the time, and his son Ishmael was thirteen.

The LORD Promises Abraham a Son

18 One hot summer afternoon Abraham was sitting by the entrance to his tent near the sacred trees of Mamre, when the LORD appeared to him. 2 Abraham looked up and saw three men standing nearby. He quickly ran to meet them, bowed with his face to the ground, 3 and said, "Please come to my home where I can serve you. 4 I'll have some water brought, so you can wash your feet, then you can rest under the tree. 5 Let me get you some

[h] **17.4,5** *Abraham*: In Hebrew "Abraham" sounds like "father of many nations." [i] **17.18** *Ishmael*: Ishmael was the son of Sarah's slave Hagar (see 16.1-16). [j] **17.19** *Isaac*: In Hebrew "Isaac" sounds like "laugh."

16.15,16 Ga 4.22. **17.4,5** Ro 4.17. **17.7** Lk 1.55. **17.8** Ac 7.5. **17.10,11** Ac 7.8; Ro 4.11. **18.2 a** He 13.2.

food to give you strength before you leave. I would be honored to serve you."

"Thank you very much," they answered. "We accept your offer."

6 Abraham quickly went to his tent and said to Sarah, "Hurry! Get a large sack of flour and make some bread." 7 After saying this, he rushed off to his herd of cattle and picked out one of the best calves, which his servant quickly prepared. 8 He then served his guests some yogurt and milk together with the meat.

While they were eating, he stood near them under the trees, 9 and they asked, "Where is your wife Sarah?"

"She is right there in the tent," Abraham answered.

10 One of the guests was the LORD, and he said, "I'll come back about this time next year, and when I do, Sarah will already have a son."

Sarah was behind Abraham, listening at the entrance to the tent. 11 Abraham and Sarah were very old, and Sarah was well past the age for having children. 12 So she laughed and said to herself, "Now that I am worn out and my husband is old, will I really know such happiness?"[k]

13 The LORD asked Abraham, "Why did Sarah laugh? Does she doubt that she can have a child in her old age? 14 I am the LORD! There is nothing too difficult for me. I'll come back next year at the time I promised, and Sarah will already have a son."

15 Sarah was so frightened that she lied and said, "I didn't laugh."

"Yes, you did!" he answered.

Abraham Prays for Sodom

16 When the three men got ready to leave, they looked down toward Sodom, and Abraham walked part of the way with them.

17 The LORD said to himself, "I should tell Abraham what I am going to do, 18 since his family will become a great and powerful nation that will be a blessing to all other nations on earth.[l] 19 I have chosen him to teach his family to obey me forever and to do what is right and fair. Then I will give Abraham many descendants, just as I promised."

20 The LORD said, "Abraham, I have heard that the people of Sodom and Gomorrah are doing all kinds of evil things. 21 Now I am going down to see for myself if those people really are that bad. If they aren't, I want to know about it."

22 The men turned and started toward Sodom. But the LORD stayed with Abraham, 23 who asked, "LORD, when you destroy the evil people, are you also going to destroy those who are good? 24 Wouldn't you spare the city if there are only fifty good people in it? 25 You surely wouldn't let them be killed when you destroy the evil ones. You are the judge of all the earth, and you do what is right."

26 The LORD replied, "If I find fifty good people in Sodom, I will save the city to keep them from being killed."

27 Abraham answered, "I am nothing more than the dust of the earth. Please forgive me, LORD, for daring to speak to you like this. 28 But suppose there are only forty-five good people in Sodom. Would you still wipe out the whole city?"

"If I find forty-five good people," the LORD replied, "I won't destroy the city."

29 "Suppose there are just forty good people?" Abraham asked.

"Even for them," the LORD replied, "I won't destroy the city."

30 Abraham said, "Please don't be angry, LORD, if I ask you what you will do if there are only thirty good people in the city."

"If I find thirty," the LORD replied, "I still won't destroy it."

31 Then Abraham said, "I don't have any right to ask you, LORD, but what would you do if you find only twenty?"

"Because of them, I won't destroy the city," was the LORD's answer.

32 Finally, Abraham said, "Please don't get angry, LORD, if I speak just once more.

[k] **18.12** *know such happiness*: Either the joy of making love or the joy of having children.
[l] **18.18** *that will be . . . on earth*: Or "and all other nations on earth will ask me to bless them as I have blessed his family."

18.10 Ro 9.9. **18.12** 1 P 3.6. **18.14** Lk 1.37.

Suppose you find only ten good people there."

"For the sake of ten good people," the LORD told him, "I still won't destroy the city."

33 After speaking with Abraham, the LORD left, and Abraham went back home.

The Evil City of Sodom

19 That evening the two angels[m] arrived in Sodom, while Lot was sitting near the city gate.[n] When Lot saw them, he got up, bowed down low, 2 and said, "Gentlemen, I am your servant. Please come to my home. You can wash your feet, spend the night, and be on your way in the morning."

They told him, "No, we'll spend the night in the city square." 3 But Lot kept insisting, until they finally agreed and went home with him. He baked some bread,[o] cooked a meal, and they ate.

4 Before Lot and his guests could go to bed, every man in Sodom, young and old, came and stood outside his house 5 and started shouting, "Where are your visitors? Send them out, so we can have sex with them!"

6 Lot went outside and shut the door behind him. 7 Then he said, "Friends, please don't do such a terrible thing! 8 I have two daughters who have never been married. I'll bring them out, and you can do what you want with them. But don't harm these men. They are guests in my home."

9 "Don't get in our way," the crowd answered. "You're an outsider. What right do you have to order us around? We'll do worse things to you than we're going to do to them."

The crowd kept arguing with Lot. Finally, they rushed toward the door to break it down. 10 But the two angels in the house reached out and pulled Lot safely inside. 11 Then they struck everyone in the crowd blind, and none of them could even find the door.

12-13 The two angels said to Lot, "The LORD has heard many terrible things about the people of Sodom, and he has sent us here to destroy the city. Take your family and leave. Take every relative you have in the city, as well as the men your daughters are going to marry."

14 Lot went to the men who were engaged to his daughters and said, "Hurry and get out of here! The LORD is going to destroy this city." But they thought he was joking, and they laughed at him.

15 Early the next morning the two angels tried to make Lot hurry and leave. They said, "Take your wife and your two daughters and get out of here as fast as you can! If you don't, every one of you will be killed when the LORD destroys the city." 16 At first, Lot just stood there. But the LORD wanted to save him. So the angels took Lot, his wife, and his two daughters by the hand and led them out of the city. 17 When they were outside, one of the angels said, "Run for your lives! Don't even look back. And don't stop in the valley. Run to the hills, where you will be safe."

18-19 Lot answered, "You have done us a great favor, sir. You have saved our lives, but please don't make us go to the hills. That's too far away. The city will be destroyed before we can get there, and we will be killed when it happens. 20 There's a town near here. It's only a small place, but my family and I will be safe, if you let us go there."

21 "All right, go there," he answered. "I won't destroy that town. 22 Hurry! Run! I can't do anything until you are safely there."

The town was later called Zoar[p] because Lot had said it was small.

Sodom and Gomorrah Are Destroyed

23 The sun was coming up as Lot reached the town of Zoar, 24 and the LORD sent burning sulfur down like rain on Sodom and Gomorrah. 25 He destroyed

[m] **19.1** *two angels*: The two men of 18.22. [n] **19.1** *near the city gate*: In a large area where the people would gather for community business and for meeting with friends. [o] **19.3** *bread*: The Hebrew text has "bread without yeast," which could be fixed quickly when guests came without warning. [p] **19.22** *Zoar*: In Hebrew "Zoar" sounds like "small."

19.5-8 Jg 19.22-24. **19.11** 2 K 6.18. **19.16** 2 P 2.7, 8. **19.24,25** 3 Macc 2.5; Mt 10.15; 11.23, 24; Lk 10.12; 17.29; 2 P 2.6; Jd 7.

those cities and everyone who lived in
them, as well as their land and the trees
and grass that grew there.
26 On the way, Lot's wife looked back
and was turned into a block of salt.
27 That same morning Abraham got up
and went to the place where he had stood
and spoken with the LORD. 28 He looked
down toward Sodom and Gomorrah and
saw smoke rising from all over the land—it
was like a flaming furnace.
29 When God destroyed the cities of the
valley where Lot lived, he remembered his
promise to Abraham and saved Lot from
the terrible destruction.

Moab and Ammon

30 Lot was afraid to stay on in Zoar. So
he took his two daughters and moved to a
cave in the hill country. 31 One day his
older daughter said to her sister, "Our
father is old, and there are no men anywhere for us to marry. 32 Let's get our
father drunk! Then we can sleep with him
and have children." 33 That night they got
their father drunk, and the older daughter
got in bed with him, but he was too drunk
even to know she was there.
34 The next day the older daughter said
to her sister, "I slept with my father last
night. We'll get him drunk again tonight, so
you can go to bed with him, and we can
each have a child." 35 That night they got
their father drunk, and this time the
younger sister slept with him. But once
again he was too drunk even to know she
was there.
36 That's how Lot's two daughters had
their children. 37 The older daughter
named her son Moab,[q] and he is the ancestor of the Moabites. 38 The younger daughter named her son Benammi,[r] and he is
the ancestor of the Ammonites.

Abraham and Sarah at Gerar

20 Abraham moved to the Southern
Desert, where he settled between
Kadesh and Shur. Later he went to Gerar,
and while there 2 he told everyone that his
wife Sarah was his sister. So King Abimelech of Gerar had Sarah brought to him.
3 But God came to Abimelech in a dream
and said, "You have taken a married
woman, and for this you will die!"
4-5 Abimelech said to the Lord, "Don't
kill me! I haven't slept with Sarah. Didn't
they say they were brother and sister? I am
completely innocent."
6 God spoke to Abimelech in another
dream and said:

> I know you are innocent. That's
> why I kept you from sleeping with
> Sarah and doing anything wrong.
> 7 Her husband is a prophet. Let her go
> back to him, and his prayers will save
> you from death. But if you don't return
> her, you and all your people will die.

8 Early the next morning Abimelech
sent for his officials, and when he told
them what had happened, they were frightened. 9 Abimelech then called in Abraham
and said:

> Look what you've done to us! What
> have I ever done to you? Why did you
> make me and my nation guilty of such
> a terrible sin? 10 What were you think-
> ing when you did this?

11 Abraham answered:

> I did it because I didn't think any of
> you respected God, and I was sure that
> someone would kill me to get my wife.
> 12 Besides, she is my half sister. We
> have the same father, but different
> mothers. 13 When God made us leave
> my father's home and start wandering, I
> told her, "If you really love me, you will
> tell everyone that I am your brother."

14 Abimelech gave Abraham some
sheep, cattle, and slaves. He sent Sarah
back 15 and told Abraham that he could
settle anywhere in his country. 16 Then he
said to Sarah, "I have given your brother a
thousand pieces of silver as proof to everyone that you have done nothing wrong."[s]
17-18 Meanwhile, God had kept Abimelech's wife and slaves from having chil-

[q] **19.37** *Moab*: In Hebrew "Moab" sounds like "from (my) father." [r] **19.38** *Benammi*: In Hebrew "Benammi" means "son of my relative." [s] **20.16** *as proof . . . wrong*: One possible meaning for the difficult Hebrew text.

19.26 Ws 10.7; Lk 17.32. **20.2** Gn 12.13; 26.7.

dren. But Abraham prayed, and God let them start having children again.

Sarah Has a Son

21 The LORD was good to Sarah and kept his promise. 2 Although Abraham was very old, Sarah had a son exactly at the time God had said. 3 Abraham named his son Isaac, 4 and when the boy was eight days old, Abraham circumcised him, just as the LORD had commanded.

5 Abraham was a hundred years old when Isaac was born, 6 and Sarah said, "God has made me laugh.[t] Now everyone will laugh with me. 7 Who would have dared to tell Abraham that someday I would have a child? But in his old age, I have given him a son."

8 The time came when Sarah no longer had to nurse Isaac,[u] and on that day Abraham gave a big feast.

Hagar and Ishmael Are Sent Away

9-10 One day, Sarah noticed Hagar's son Ishmael[v] playing,[w] and she said to Abraham, "Get rid of that Egyptian slave woman and her son! I don't want him to inherit anything. It should all go to my son."[x]

11 Abraham was worried about Ishmael. 12 But God said, "Abraham, don't worry about your slave woman and the boy. Just do what Sarah tells you. Isaac will inherit your family name, 13 but the son of the slave woman is also your son, and I will make his descendants into a great nation."

14 Early the next morning Abraham gave Hagar an animal skin full of water and some bread. Then he put the boy on her shoulder and sent them away.

They wandered around in the desert near Beersheba, 15 and after they had run out of water, Hagar put her son under a bush. 16 Then she sat down a long way off, because she could not bear to watch him die. And she cried bitterly.

17 When God heard the boy crying, the angel of God called out to Hagar from heaven and said, "Hagar, why are you worried? Don't be afraid. I have heard your son crying. 18 Help him up and hold his hand, because I will make him the father of a great nation." 19 Then God let her see a well. So she went to the well and filled the skin with water, then gave some to her son.

20-21 God blessed Ishmael, and as the boy grew older, he became an expert with his bow and arrows. He lived in the Paran Desert, and his mother chose an Egyptian woman for him to marry.

A Peace Treaty

22 About this time Abimelech and his army commander Phicol said to Abraham, "God blesses everything you do! 23 Now I want you to promise in the name of God that you will always be loyal to me and my descendants, just as I have always been loyal to you in this land where you have lived as a foreigner." 24 And so, Abraham promised.

25 One day, Abraham told Abimelech, "Some of your servants have taken over one of my wells."

26 "This is the first I've heard about it," Abimelech replied. "Why haven't you said something before? I don't have any idea who did it." 27 Abraham gave Abimelech some sheep and cattle, and then the two men made a peace treaty.

28 Abraham separated seven female lambs from his flock of sheep, 29 and Abimelech asked, "Why have you done this?"

30 Abraham told him, "I want you to accept these seven lambs as proof that I dug this well." 31 So they called the place Beersheba,[y] because they made a treaty there.

[t] **21.6** *God has made me laugh*: In Hebrew "Isaac" sounds like "laugh." [u] **21.8** *no longer had to nurse Isaac*: In ancient Israel mothers nursed their children until they were about three years old. Then there was a family celebration. [v] **21.9,10** *Ishmael*: The son of Abraham and Hagar, who was Sarah's slave woman (see 16.1-16). [w] **21.9,10** *playing*: Hebrew; one ancient translation "playing with her son Isaac." [x] **21.9,10** *Get rid . . . son*: When Abraham accepted Ishmael as his son, it gave Ishmael the right to inherit part of what Abraham owned. But slaves who were given their freedom lost the right to inherit such property. [y] **21.31** *Beersheba*: Meaning "Well of Good Fortune" or "Peace Treaty Well."

21.2 He 11.11. **21.4** Gn 17.12; Ac 7.8. **21.9,10** Ga 4.29, 30. **21.12** Ro 9.7, 8; He 11.17, 18. **21.22** Gn 26.26.

32 When the treaty was completed, Abimelech and his army commander Phicol went back to the land of the Philistines. 33 Abraham planted a tamarisk tree[z] in Beersheba and worshiped the eternal LORD God. 34 Then Abraham lived a long time as a foreigner in the land of the Philistines.

The LORD Tells Abraham To Offer Isaac as a Sacrifice

22 Some years later God decided to test Abraham, so he spoke to him.

Abraham answered, "Here I am, LORD."

2 The LORD said, "Go get Isaac, your only son, the one you dearly love! Take him to the land of Moriah, and I will show you a mountain where you must sacrifice him to me on the fires of an altar." 3 So Abraham got up early the next morning and chopped wood for the fire. He put a saddle on his donkey and left with Isaac and two servants for the place where God had told him to go.

4 Three days later Abraham looked off in the distance and saw the place. 5 He told his servants, "Stay here with the donkey, while my son and I go over there to worship. We will come back."

6 Abraham put the wood on Isaac's shoulder, but he carried the hot coals and the knife. As the two of them walked along, 7-8 Isaac said, "Father, we have the coals and the wood, but where is the lamb for the sacrifice?"

"My son," Abraham answered, "God will provide the lamb."

The two of them walked on, and 9 when they reached the place that God had told him about, Abraham built an altar and placed the wood on it. Next, he tied up his son and put him on the wood. 10 He then took the knife and got ready to kill his son. 11 But the LORD's angel shouted from heaven, "Abraham! Abraham!"

"Here I am!" he answered.

12 "Don't hurt the boy or harm him in any way!" the angel said. "Now I know that you truly obey God, because you were willing to offer him your only son."

13 Abraham looked up and saw a ram caught by its horns in the bushes. So he took the ram and sacrificed it in place of his son.

14 Abraham named that place "The LORD Will Provide." And even now people say, "On the mountain of the LORD it will be provided."[a]

15 The LORD's angel called out from heaven a second time:

> 16 You were willing to offer the LORD your only son, and so he makes you this solemn promise, 17 "I will bless you and give you such a large family, that someday your descendants will be more numerous than the stars in the sky or the grains of sand along the beach. They will defeat their enemies and take over the cities where their enemies live. 18 You have obeyed me, and so you and your descendants will be a blessing to all nations on earth."

19 Abraham and Isaac went back to the servants who had come with him, and they returned to Abraham's home in Beersheba.

The Children of Nahor

20-23 Abraham's brother Nahor had married Milcah, and Abraham was later told that they had eight sons. Uz was their firstborn; Buz was next, and then there was Kemuel who became the father of Aram; their other five sons were: Chesed, Hazo, Pildash, Jidlaph, and Bethuel, who became the father of Rebekah. 24 Nahor also had another wife.[b] Her name was Reumah, and she had four sons: Tebah, Gaham, Tahash, and Maacah.

Sarah's Death and Burial

23 1-2 When Sarah was one hundred twenty-seven years old, she died in Kiriath-Arba, better known as Hebron, in the land of Canaan. After Abraham had

[z]**21.33** *tamarisk tree*: A tall shade tree that has deep roots and needs little water. [a]**22.14** *The LORD Will Provide . . . it will be provided*: Or "The LORD Will Be Seen . . . the LORD will be seen" or "It (a ram) Will Be Seen . . . it (a ram) will be seen." [b]**22.24** *another wife*: This translates a Hebrew word for a woman who was legally bound to a man, but without the full privileges of a wife.

22.1-13 Ws 10.5; Si 44.20; 4 Macc. 7.13, 14; 13.12; He 11.17-19. **22.2** 2 Ch 3.1. **22.9** Jas 2.21. **22.10** 4 Macc 16.20. **22.16,17** He 6.13, 14. **22.17** He 11.12. **22.18** Ac 3.25.

mourned for her, 3 he went to the Hittites
and said, 4 "I live as a foreigner in your
land, and I don't own any property where I
can bury my wife. Please let me buy a piece
of land."

5-6 "Sir," they answered, "you are an important man. Choose the best place to bury
your wife. None of us would refuse you a
resting place for your dead."

7 Abraham bowed down 8 and replied,
"If you are willing to let me bury my wife
here, please ask Zohar's son Ephron 9 to
sell me Machpelah Cave at the end of his
field. I'll pay what it's worth, and all of you
can be witnesses."

10 Ephron was sitting there near the city
gate, when Abraham made this request,
and he answered, 11 "Sir, the whole field,
including the cave, is yours. With my own
people as witnesses, I freely give it to you as
a burial place for your dead."

12 Once again, Abraham bowed down
13 and said to Ephron, "In front of these
witnesses, I offer you the full price, so I can
bury my wife. Please accept my offer."

14-15 "But sir," the man replied, "the
property is worth only four hundred pieces
of silver. Why should we haggle over such a
small amount? Take the land. It's yours."

16-18 Abraham accepted Ephron's offer
and paid him the four hundred pieces of
silver in front of everyone at the city gate.
That's how Abraham got Ephron's property
east of Hebron,[c] which included the field
with all of its trees, as well as Machpelah
Cave at the end of the field. 19 So Abraham
buried his wife Sarah in Machpelah Cave
that was in the field 20 he had bought from
the Hittites.

A Wife for Isaac

24 Abraham was now a very old man.
The LORD had made him rich, and
he was successful in everything he did.
2 One day, Abraham called in his most
trusted servant and said to him, "Solemnly
promise me 3 in the name of the LORD, who
rules heaven and earth, that you won't
choose a wife for my son Isaac from the
people here in the land of Canaan. 4 Instead, go back to the land where I was born
and find a wife for him from among my
relatives."

5 But the servant asked, "What if the
young woman I choose refuses to leave
home and come here with me? Should I
send Isaac there to look for a wife?"

6 "No!" Abraham answered. "Don't ever
do that, no matter what. 7 The LORD who
rules heaven brought me here from the
land where I was born and promised that
he would give this land to my descendants
forever. When you go back there, the LORD
will send his angel ahead of you to help you
find a wife for my son. 8 If the woman refuses to come along, you don't have to keep
this promise. But don't ever take my son
back there." 9 So the servant gave Abraham
his word that he would do everything he
had been told to do.

10 Soon after that, the servant loaded
ten of Abraham's camels with valuable
gifts. Then he set out for the city in northern Syria,[d] where Abraham's brother Nahor lived.

11 When he got there, he let the camels
rest near the well outside the city. It was
late afternoon, the time when the women
came out for water. 12 The servant prayed:

> You, LORD, are the God my master
> Abraham worships. Please keep your
> promise to him and let me find a wife
> for Isaac today. 13 The young women of
> the city will soon come to this well for
> water, 14 and I'll ask one of them for a
> drink. If she gives me a drink and then
> offers to get some water for my camels,
> I'll know she is the one you have
> chosen and that you have kept your
> promise to my master.

15-16 While he was still praying, a beautiful unmarried young woman came by with
a water jar on her shoulder. She was Rebekah, the daughter of Bethuel, the son of

[c] **23.16-18** *Hebron*: The Hebrew text has "Mamre," a place just north of Hebron.
[d] **24.10** *northern Syria*: The Hebrew text has "Aram-Naharaim," probably referring to the land around the city of Haran (see also "Paddan-Aram" in 25.20; 28.2, 6; 31.18, 20; 33.18; 35.23-26; 46.8-15; and "Paddan" in 48.7).
23.4 He 11.9, 13; Ac 7.16.

Abraham's brother Nahor and his wife Milcah. Rebekah walked past Abraham's servant, then went over to the well, and filled her water jar. When she started back, 17 Abraham's servant ran to her and said, "Please let me have a drink of water."

18 "I'll be glad to," she answered. Then she quickly took the jar from her shoulder and held it while he drank. 19-20 After he had finished, she said, "Now I'll give your camels all the water they want." She quickly poured out water for them, and she kept going back for more, until his camels had drunk all they wanted. 21 Abraham's servant did not say a word, but he watched everything Rebekah did, because he wanted to know for certain if this was the woman the LORD had chosen.

22 The servant had brought along an expensive gold ring and two large gold bracelets. When Rebekah had finished bringing the water, he gave her the ring for her nose[e] and the bracelets for her arms. 23 Then he said, "Please tell me who your father is. Does he have room in his house for me and my men to spend the night?"

24 She answered, "My father is Bethuel, the son of Nahor and Milcah. 25 We have a place where you and your men can stay, and we also have enough straw and feed for your camels."

26 Then the servant bowed his head and prayed, 27 "I thank you, LORD God of my master Abraham! You have led me to his relatives and kept your promise to him."

28 Rebekah ran straight home and told her family everything. 29-30 Her brother Laban heard her tell what the servant had said, and he saw the ring and the bracelets she was wearing. So Laban ran out to Abraham's servant, who was standing by his camels at the well. 31 Then Laban said, "The LORD has brought you safely here. Come home with me. There's no need for you to keep on standing outside. I have a room ready for you in our house, and there's also a place for your camels."

32 Abraham's servant went home with Laban, where Laban's servants unloaded his camels and gave them straw and feed. Then they brought water into the house, so Abraham's servant and his men could wash their feet. 33 After that, they brought in food. But the servant said, "Before I eat, I must tell you why I have come."

"Go ahead and tell us," Laban answered.

34 The servant explained:

I am Abraham's servant. 35 The LORD has been good to my master and has made him very rich. He has given him many sheep, goats, cattle, camels, and donkeys, as well as a lot of silver and gold, and many slaves. 36 Sarah, my master's wife, didn't have any children until she was very old. Then she had a son, and my master has given him everything. 37 I solemnly promised my master that I would do what he said. And he told me, "Don't choose a wife for my son from the women in this land of Canaan. 38 Instead, go back to the land where I was born and find a wife for my son from among my relatives."

39 I asked my master, "What if the young woman refuses to come with me?"

40 My master answered, "I have always obeyed the LORD, and he will send his angel to help you find my son a wife from among my own relatives. 41 But if they refuse to let her come back with you, then you are freed from your promise."

42 When I came to the well today, I silently prayed, "You, LORD, are the God my master Abraham worships, so please lead me to a wife for his son 43 while I am here at the well. When a young woman comes out to get water, I'll ask her to give me a drink. 44 If she gives me a drink and offers to get some water for my camels, I'll know she is the one you have chosen."

45 Even before I had finished praying, Rebekah came by with a water jar on her shoulder. When she had filled the jar, I asked her for a drink. 46 She quickly lowered the jar from her shoulder and said, "Have a drink. Then I'll get water for your camels." So I drank, and after that she got some water for

[e]**24.22** *ring for her nose*: Nose-rings were popular jewelry items, as were earrings.

my camels. 47 I asked her who her
father was, and she answered, "My
father is Bethuel the son of Nahor and
Milcah." Right away I put the ring in
her nose and the bracelets on her
arms. 48 Then I bowed my head and
gave thanks to the God my master
Abraham worships. The LORD had led
me straight to my master's relatives,
and I had found a wife for his son.

49 Now please tell me if you are
willing to do the right thing for my
master. Will you treat him fairly, or do
I have to look for another young
woman?

50 Laban and Bethuel answered, "The
LORD has done this. We have no choice in
the matter. 51 Take Rebekah with you; she can
marry your master's son, just as the LORD
has said." 52 Abraham's servant bowed
down and thanked the LORD. 53 Then he
gave clothing, as well as silver and gold jewelry, to Rebekah. He also gave expensive
gifts to her brother and her mother.

54 Abraham's servant and the men with
him ate and drank, then spent the night
there. The next morning they got up, and
the servant told Rebekah's mother and
brother, "I would like to go back to my master now."

55 "Let Rebekah stay with us for a week
or ten days," they answered. "Then she
may go."

56 But he said, "Don't make me stay any
longer. The LORD has already helped me
find a wife for my master's son. Now let us
return."

57 They answered, "Let's ask Rebekah
what she wants to do." 58 They called her
and asked, "Are you willing to leave with
this man right now?"

"Yes," she answered.

59 So they agreed to let Rebekah and an
old family servant woman[f] leave immediately with Abraham's servant and his men.
60 They gave Rebekah their blessing and
said, "We pray that God will give you many
children and grandchildren and that he
will help them defeat their enemies." 61 Afterwards, Rebekah and the young women
who were to travel with her prepared to
leave. Then they got on camels and left
with Abraham's servant and his men.

62 At that time Isaac was living in the
southern part of Canaan near a place
called "The Well of the Living One Who
Sees Me."[g] 63-65 One evening he was walking out in the fields, when suddenly he saw
a group of people approaching on camels.
So he started toward them. Rebekah saw
him coming; she got down from her camel,
and asked, "Who is that man?"

"He is my master Isaac," the servant answered. Then Rebekah covered her face
with her veil.[h]

66 The servant told Isaac everything that
had happened.

67 Isaac took Rebekah into the tent[i]
where his mother had lived before she
died, and Rebekah became his wife. He
loved her and was comforted over the loss
of his mother.

Abraham Marries Keturah

25 Abraham married Keturah, 2 and
they had six sons: Zimran, Jokshan, Medan, Midian, Ishbak, and Shuah.
3 Later, Jokshan became the father of
Sheba and Dedan, and when Dedan grew
up, he had three sons: Asshurim, Le-
tushim, and Leummim. 4 Midian also had
five sons: Ephah, Epher, Hanoch, Abida,
and Eldaah.

5-6 While Abraham was still alive, he
gave gifts to the sons of Hagar and Keturah.
He also sent their sons to live in the east
far from his son Isaac, and when Abraham
died, he left everything to Isaac.

The Death of Abraham

7-8 Abraham died at the ripe old age of
one hundred seventy-five. 9-10 His sons

[f]**24.59** *old family servant woman*: Probably Deborah, who had taken care of Rebekah from the time she was born (see 35.8). [g]**24.62** *Who Sees Me*: Or "I Have Seen." [h]**24.63-65** *covered . . . veil*: Since the veiling of a bride was part of the wedding ceremony, this probably means that she was willing to become the wife of Isaac. [i]**24.67** *took . . . tent*: This shows that Rebekah is now the wife of Isaac and the successor of Sarah as the leading woman in the tribe.

25.9,10 Gn 23.3-18.

Isaac and Ishmael buried him east of Hebron[j] in Machpelah Cave that was part of
the field Abraham had bought from Ephron
son of Zohar the Hittite. Abraham was
buried there beside his wife Sarah. 11 God
blessed Isaac after this, and Isaac moved to
a place called "The Well of the Living One
Who Sees Me."[k]

Ishmael's Descendants

12 Ishmael was the son of Abraham and
Hagar, the slave woman of Sarah. 13 Ishmael had twelve sons, in this order: Nebaioth, Kedar, Adbeel, Mibsam, 14 Mishma, Dumah, Massa, 15 Hadad, Tema, Jetur, Naphish, and Kedemah. 16 Each of
Ishmael's sons was a tribal chief, and a village was named after each of them.

17-18 Ishmael had settled in the land
east of his brothers, and his sons[l] settled
everywhere from Havilah to Shur, east of
Egypt on the way to Asshur.[m] Ishmael was
one hundred thirty-seven when he died.

The Birth of Esau and Jacob

19 Isaac was the son of Abraham, 20 and
he was forty years old when he married Rebekah, the daughter of Bethuel. She was
also the sister of Laban, the Aramean from
northern Syria.[n]

Almost twenty years later, 21 Rebekah
still had no children. So Isaac asked the
LORD to let her have a child, and the LORD
answered his prayer.

22 Before Rebekah gave birth, she knew
she was going to have twins, because she
could feel them inside her, fighting each
other. She thought, "Why is this happening to me?" Finally, she asked the LORD
why her twins were fighting, 23 and he told
her:

"Your two sons will become
two separate nations.[o]
The younger of the two
will be stronger,
and the older son
will be his servant."

24 When Rebekah gave birth, 25 the first
baby was covered with red hair, so he was
named Esau.[p] 26 The second baby grabbed
on to his brother's heel, so they named him
Jacob.[q] Isaac was sixty years old when they
were born.

Esau Sells His Rights as the First-Born Son

27 As Jacob and Esau grew older, Esau
liked the outdoors and became a good
hunter, while Jacob settled down and became a shepherd. 28 Esau would take the
meat of wild animals to his father Isaac,
and so Isaac loved him more, but Jacob was
his mother's favorite son.

29 One day, Jacob was cooking some
stew, when Esau came home hungry 30 and
said, "I'm starving to death! Give me some
of that red stew right now!" That's how
Esau got the name "Edom."[r]

31 Jacob replied, "Sell me your rights as
the first-born son."[s]

32 "I'm about to die," Esau answered.
"What good will those rights do me?"

33 But Jacob said, "Promise me your
birthrights, here and now!" And that's what
Esau did. 34 Jacob then gave Esau some
bread and some of the bean stew, and when
Esau had finished eating and drinking, he
just got up and left, showing how little he
thought of his rights as the first-born.

Isaac and Abimelech

26 Once during Abraham's lifetime,
the fields had not produced enough
grain, and now the same thing happened.
So Isaac went to King Abimelech of the
Philistines in the land of Gerar, 2 because
the LORD had appeared to Isaac and said:

[j]**25.9,10** *Hebron*: See the note at 23.16-18. [k]**25.11** *The Well . . . Sees Me*: Or "Beer-Lahai-Roi." (see 16.14). [l]**25.17,18** *sons*: Or "descendants." [m]**25.17,18** *Havilah to Shur . . . Asshur*: The exact location of these places is not known. [n]**25.20** *northern Syria*: See the note at 24.10. [o]**25.23** *two separate nations*: Or "two nations always in conflict." [p]**25.25** *Esau*: In Hebrew "Esau" sounds like "hairy." [q]**25.26** *Jacob*: In Hebrew "Jacob" sounds like "heel." [r]**25.30** *Edom*: In Hebrew "Edom" sounds like "red." [s]**25.31** *rights . . . son*: The first-born son inherited the largest amount of property, as well as the leadership of the family.

25.23 Ro 9.11, 12. **25.33** He 12.16.

Isaac, stay away from Egypt! I will show you where I want you to go. 3 You will live there as a foreigner, but I will be with you and bless you. I will keep my promise to your father Abraham by giving this land to you and your descendants.

4 I will give you as many descendants as there are stars in the sky, and I will give your descendants all of this land. They will be a blessing to every nation on earth,[t] 5 because Abraham did everything I told him to do.

6 Isaac moved to Gerar 7 with his beautiful wife Rebekah. He was afraid that someone might kill him to get her, and so he told everyone that Rebekah was his sister. 8 After Isaac had been there a long time, King Abimelech looked out a window and saw Isaac hugging and kissing Rebekah. 9 Abimelech called him in and said, "Rebekah must be your wife! Why did you say she is your sister?"

"Because I thought someone would kill me," Isaac answered.

10 "Don't you know what you've done?" Abimelech exclaimed. "If someone had slept with her, you would have made our whole nation guilty!" 11 Then Abimelech warned his people that anyone who even touched Isaac or Rebekah would be put to death.

12 Isaac planted grain and had a good harvest that same year. The LORD blessed him, 13 and Isaac was so successful that he became very rich. 14 In fact, the Philistines were jealous of the large number of sheep, goats, and slaves that Isaac owned, 15 and they stopped up the wells that Abraham's servants had dug before his death. 16 Finally, Abimelech said, "Isaac, I want you to leave our country. You have become too powerful to stay here."

17 Isaac left and settled in Gerar Valley, 18 where he cleaned out those wells that the Philistines had stopped up. Isaac also gave each of the wells the same name[u] that Abraham had given to them. 19 While his servants were digging in the valley, they found a spring-fed well. 20 But the shepherds of Gerar Valley quarreled with Isaac's shepherds and claimed the water belonged to them. So the well was named "Quarrel," because they had quarreled with Isaac.

21 Isaac's servants dug another well, and the shepherds also quarreled about it. So that well was named "Jealous." 22 Finally, they dug one more well. There was no quarreling this time, and the well was named "Lots of Room," because the LORD had given them room and would make them very successful.

23 Isaac went on to Beersheba, 24 where the LORD appeared to him that night and told him, "Don't be afraid! I am the God who was worshiped by your father Abraham, my servant. I will be with you and bless you, and because of Abraham I will give you many descendants." 25 Isaac built an altar there and worshiped the LORD. Then he set up camp, and his servants started digging a well.

26 Meanwhile, Abimelech had left Gerar and was taking his advisor Ahuzzath and his army commander Phicol to see Isaac. 27 When they arrived, Isaac asked, "Why are you here? Didn't you send me away because you hated me?"

28 They answered, "We now know for certain that the LORD is with you, and we have decided there needs to be a peace treaty between you and us. So let's make a solemn agreement 29 not to harm each other. Remember, we have never hurt you, and when we sent you away, we let you go in peace. The LORD has truly blessed you."

30 Isaac gave a big feast for them, and everyone ate and drank. 31 Early the next morning Isaac and the others made a solemn agreement, then he let them go in peace.

32 Later that same day Isaac's servants came and said, "We've struck water!" 33 So Isaac named the well Shibah,[v] and the town is still called Beersheba.[w]

[t]**26.4** *They . . . on earth*: Or "All nations on earth will ask me to bless them." [u]**26.18** *gave . . . same name*: By doing this Isaac claimed ownership of the wells. [v]**26.33** *Shibah*: In Hebrew "Shibah" sounds something like "good luck" and "promise." [w]**26.33** *Beersheba*: Meaning "Well of Good Fortune" or "Peace Treaty Well."

26.3,4 Gn 22.16-18. **26.7** Gn 12.13; 20.2. **26.26** Gn 21.22.

Esau's Foreign Wives

34 When Esau was forty, he married Judith the daughter of Beeri the Hittite and Basemath the daughter of Elon the Hittite. 35 But these two women brought a lot of grief to his parents Isaac and Rebekah.

Isaac Blesses Jacob

27 After Isaac had become old and almost blind, he called in his firstborn son Esau, who asked him, "Father, what can I do for you?"

2 Isaac replied, "I am old and might die at any time. 3 So take your bow and arrows, then go out in the fields, and kill a wild animal. 4 Cook some of that tasty food that I love so much and bring it to me. I want to eat it once more and give you my blessing before I die."

5 Rebekah had been listening, and as soon as Esau left to go hunting, 6 she said to Jacob, "I heard your father tell Esau 7 to kill a wild animal and cook some tasty food for your father before he dies. Your father said this because he wants to bless your brother with the LORD as his witness. 8 Now, my son, listen carefully to what I want you to do. 9 Go and kill two of your best young goats and bring them to me. I'll cook the tasty food that your father loves so much. 10 Then you can take it to him, so he can eat it and give you his blessing before he dies."

11 "My brother Esau is a hairy man," Jacob reminded her. "And I am not. 12 If my father touches me and realizes I am trying to trick him, he will put a curse on me instead of giving me a blessing."

13 Rebekah insisted, "Let his curse fall on me! Just do what I say and bring me the meat." 14 So Jacob brought the meat to his mother, and she cooked the tasty food that his father liked. 15 Then she took Esau's best clothes and put them on Jacob. 16 She also covered the smooth part of his hands and neck with goatskins 17 and gave him some bread and the tasty food she had cooked.

18 Jacob went to his father and said, "Father, here I am."

"Which one of my sons are you?" his father asked.

19 Jacob replied, "I am Esau, your firstborn, and I have done what you told me. Please sit up and eat the meat I have brought. Then you can give me your blessing."

20 Isaac asked, "My son, how did you find an animal so quickly?"

"The LORD your God was kind to me," Jacob answered.

21 "My son," Isaac said, "come closer, where I can touch you and find out if you really are Esau." 22 Jacob went closer. His father touched him and said, "You sound like Jacob, but your hands feel hairy like Esau's." 23 And so Isaac blessed Jacob, thinking he was Esau.

24 Isaac asked, "Are you really my son Esau?"

"Yes, I am," Jacob answered.

25 So Isaac told him, "Serve me the wild meat, and I can give you my blessing."

Jacob gave him some meat, and he ate it. He also gave him some wine, and he drank it. 26 Then Isaac said, "Son, come over here and kiss me." 27 While Jacob was kissing him, Isaac caught the smell of his clothes and said:

"The smell of my son
is like a field
the LORD has blessed.
28 God will bless you, my son,
with dew from heaven
and with fertile fields,
rich with grain and grapes.
29 Nations will be your servants
and bow down to you.
You will rule over your brothers,
and they will kneel
at your feet.
Anyone who curses you
will be cursed;
anyone who blesses you
will be blessed."

30 Right after Isaac had given Jacob his blessing and Jacob had gone, Esau came back from hunting. 31 He cooked the tasty food, brought it to his father, and said, "Father, please sit up and eat the meat I

27.27-29 He 11.20. **27.29** Gn 12.3.

have brought you, so you can give me your blessing."

32 "Who are you?" Isaac asked.

"I am Esau, your first-born son."

33 Isaac started trembling and said, "Then who brought me some wild meat right before you came in? I ate it and gave him a blessing that cannot be taken back."

34 Esau cried loudly and begged, "Father, give me a blessing too!"

35 Isaac answered, "Your brother tricked me and stole your blessing."

36 Esau replied, "My brother deserves the name Jacob,[x] because he has already cheated me twice. The first time he cheated me out of my rights as the first-born son, and now he has cheated me out of my blessing." Then Esau asked his father, "Don't you still have any blessing left for me?"

37 "My son," Isaac answered, "I have made Jacob the ruler over you and your brothers, and all of you will be his servants. I have also promised him all the grain and grapes that he needs. There's nothing left that I can do for you."

38 "Father," Esau asked, "don't you have more than one blessing? You can surely give me a blessing too!" Then Esau started crying again.

39 So his father said:

"Your home will be far
from that fertile land,
where dew comes down
from the heavens.
40 You will live by the power
of your sword
and be your brother's slave.
But when you decide to be free,
you will break loose."

41 Esau hated his brother Jacob because he had stolen the blessing that was supposed to be his. So he said to himself, "Just as soon as my father dies, I'll kill Jacob."

42 When Rebekah found out what Esau planned to do, she sent for Jacob and told him, "Son, your brother Esau is just waiting for the time when he can kill you.
43 Now listen carefully and do what I say. Go to the home of my brother Laban in Haran
44 and stay with him for a while. When Esau stops being angry
45 and forgets what you have done to him, I'll send for you to come home. Why should I lose both of my sons on the same day?"[y]

46 Rebekah later told Isaac, "Those Hittite wives of Esau are making my life miserable! If Jacob marries a Hittite woman, I'd be better off dead."

Isaac's Instructions to Jacob

28 Isaac called in Jacob, then gave him a blessing, and said:

Don't marry any of those Canaanite women.
2 Go at once to your mother's father Bethuel in northern Syria[z] and choose a wife from one of the daughters of Laban, your mother's brother.
3 I pray that God All-Powerful will bless you with many descendants and let you become a great nation.
4 May he bless you with the land he gave Abraham, so that you will take over this land where we now live as foreigners.
5 Isaac then sent Jacob to stay with Rebekah's brother Laban, the son of Bethuel the Aramean.

Esau Marries the Daughter of Ishmael

6 Esau found out that his father Isaac had blessed Jacob and had warned him not to marry any of the Canaanite women. He also learned that Jacob had been sent to find a wife in northern Syria[z]
7 and that he had obeyed his father and mother.
8 Esau already had several wives, but he realized at last how much his father hated the Canaanite women.
9 So he married Ishmael's daughter Mahalath, who was the sister of Nebaioth[a] and the granddaughter of Abraham.

[x]**27.36** *Jacob*: In Hebrew "Jacob" sounds like "cheat." [y]**27.45** *lose . . . day*: Esau would be hunted down as a murderer if he killed Jacob, and so Rebekah would lose both of her sons. [z]**28.2,6** *northern Syria*: See the note at 24.10. [a]**28.9** *Nebaioth*: Ishmael's oldest son (see 25.13).

27.36 Gn 25.29-34. **27.38** He 12.17. **27.39,40** He 11.20. **27.40** Gn 36.8; 2 K 8.20. **27.42** Ws 10.10. **28.4** Gn 17.4-8.

Jacob's Dream at Bethel

10 Jacob left the town of Beersheba and started out for Haran. 11 At sunset he stopped for the night and went to sleep, resting his head on a large rock. 12 In a dream he saw a ladder[b] that reached from earth to heaven, and God's angels were going up and down on it.

13 The LORD was standing beside the ladder[c] and said:

> I am the LORD God who was worshiped by Abraham and Isaac. I will give to you and your family the land on which you are now sleeping. 14 Your descendants will spread over the earth in all directions and will become as numerous as the specks of dust. Your family will be a blessing to all people.[d]
>
> 15 Wherever you go, I will watch over you, then later I will bring you back to this land. I won't leave you—I will do all I have promised.

16 Jacob woke up suddenly and thought, "The LORD is in this place, and I didn't even know it." 17 Then Jacob became frightened and said, "This is a fearsome place! It must be the house of God and the ladder[e] to heaven."

18 When Jacob got up early the next morning, he took the rock that he had used for a pillow and stood it up for a place of worship. Then he poured olive oil on the rock to dedicate it to God, 19 and he named the place Bethel.[f] Before that it had been named Luz.

20 Jacob solemnly promised God, "If you go with me and watch over me as I travel, and if you give me food and clothes 21 and bring me safely home again, you will be my God. 22 This rock will be your house, and I will give back to you a tenth of everything you give me."

Jacob Arrives at Laban's Home

29 As Jacob continued on his way to the east, 2 he looked out in a field and saw a well where shepherds took their sheep for water. Three flocks of sheep were lying around the well, which was covered with a large rock. 3 Shepherds would roll the rock away when all their sheep had gathered there. Then after the sheep had been watered, the shepherds would roll the rock back over the mouth of the well.

4 Jacob asked the shepherds, "Where are you from?"

"We're from Haran," they answered.

5 Then he asked, "Do you know Nahor's grandson Laban?"

"Yes we do," they replied.

6 "How is he?" Jacob asked.

"He's fine," they answered. "And here comes his daughter Rachel with the sheep."

7 Jacob told them, "Look, the sun is still high up in the sky, and it's too early to bring in the rest of the flocks. Water your sheep and take them back to the pasture."

8 But they replied, "We can't do that until they all get here, and the rock has been rolled away from the well."

9 While Jacob was still talking with the men, his cousin Rachel came up with her father's sheep. 10 When Jacob saw her and his uncle's sheep, he rolled the rock away and watered the sheep. 11 He then kissed Rachel and started crying because he was so happy. 12 He told her that he was the son of her aunt Rebekah, and she ran and told her father about him.

13 As soon as Laban heard the news, he ran out to meet Jacob. He hugged and kissed him and brought him to his home, where Jacob told him everything that had happened. 14 Laban said, "You are my nephew, and you are like one of my own family."

Jacob Marries Leah and Rachel

After Jacob had been there for a month, 15 Laban said to him, "You shouldn't have to work without pay, just because you are a relative of mine. What do you want me to give you?"

[b]**28.12** *ladder*: Or "stairway." [c]**28.13** *the ladder*: Or "Jacob" or "the stairway" (see the note at 28.12). [d]**28.14** *Your family . . . people*: Or "All people will ask me to bless them as I have blessed your family." [e]**28.17** *ladder*: See the note at 28.12. [f]**28.19** *Bethel*: In Hebrew "Bethel" means "House of God."

28.10 Ws 10.10. **28.12** Jn 1.51. **28.13** Gn 13.14, 15. **28.14** Gn 12.3; 22.18.

16-17 Laban had two daughters. Leah was older than Rachel, but her eyes didn't sparkle,[g] while Rachel was beautiful and had a good figure. 18 Since Jacob was in love with Rachel, he answered, "If you will let me marry Rachel, I'll work seven years for you."

19 Laban replied, "It's better for me to let you marry Rachel than for someone else to have her. So stay and work for me." 20 Jacob worked seven years for Laban, but the time seemed like only a few days, because he loved Rachel so much.

21 Jacob said to Laban, "The time is up, and I want to marry Rachel now!" 22 So Laban gave a big feast and invited all their neighbors. 23 But that evening he brought Leah to Jacob, who married her and spent the night with her. 24 Laban also gave Zilpah to Leah as her servant woman.

25 The next morning Jacob found out that he had married Leah, and he asked Laban, "Why did you do this to me? Didn't I work to get Rachel? Why did you trick me?"

26 Laban replied, "In our country the older daughter must get married first. 27 After you spend this week[h] with Leah, you may also marry Rachel. But you will have to work for me another seven years."

28-30 At the end of the week of celebration, Laban let Jacob marry Rachel, and he gave her his servant woman Bilhah. Jacob loved Rachel more than he did Leah, but he had to work another seven years for Laban.

31 The LORD knew that Jacob loved Rachel more than he did Leah, and so he gave children to Leah, but not to Rachel. 32 Leah gave birth to a son and named him Reuben,[i] because she said, "The LORD has taken away my sorrow. Now my husband will love me more than he does Rachel." 33 She had a second son and named him Simeon,[j] because she said, "The LORD has heard that my husband doesn't love me." 34 When Leah's third son was born, she said, "Now my husband will hold me close." So this son was named Levi.[k] 35 She had one more son and named him Judah,[l] because she said, "I'll praise the LORD!"

Problems between Rachel and Leah

30 Rachel was very jealous of Leah for having children, and she said to Jacob, "I'll die if you don't give me some children!"

2 But Jacob became upset with Rachel and answered, "Don't blame me! I'm not God."

3 "Here, take my servant Bilhah," Rachel told him. "Have children by her, and I'll let them be born on my knees to show that they are mine."

4 Then Rachel let Jacob marry Bilhah, 5 and they had a son. 6 Rachel named him Dan,[m] because she said, "God has answered my prayers. He has judged me and given me a son." 7 When Bilhah and Jacob had a second son, 8 Rachel said, "I've struggled hard with my sister, and I've won!" So she named the boy Naphtali.[n]

9 When Leah realized she could not have any more children, she let Jacob marry her servant Zilpah, 10 and they had a son. 11 "I'm really lucky," Leah said, and she named the boy Gad.[o] 12 When they had another son, 13 Leah exclaimed, "I'm happy now, and all the women will say how happy I am." So she named him Asher.[p]

Love Flowers

14 During the time of the wheat harvest, Reuben found some love flowers[q] and took them to his mother Leah. Rachel asked Leah for some of them, 15 but Leah said, "It's bad enough that you stole my

[g] **29.16,17** *but her eyes didn't sparkle*: Or "and her eyes sparkled." [h] **29.27** *this week*: The wedding feast lasted for seven days (see Judges 14.12, 17). [i] **29.32** *Reuben*: In Hebrew "Reuben" means, "Look, a son!" [j] **29.33** *Simeon*: In Hebrew "Simeon" sounds like "someone who hears." [k] **29.34** *hold me close . . . Levi*: In Hebrew "Levi" sounds like "hold (someone) close." [l] **29.35** *Judah*: In Hebrew "Judah" sounds like "praise." [m] **30.6** *Dan*: In Hebrew "Dan" means "judge." [n] **30.8** *Naphtali*: In Hebrew "Naphtali" means "struggle" or "contest." [o] **30.11** *Gad*: In Hebrew "Gad" means "lucky." [p] **30.13** *Asher*: In Hebrew "Asher" means "happy." [q] **30.14** *love flowers*: Also called "mandrakes," a flowering plant that was thought to give sexual powers.

husband! Now you want my son's love flowers too."

"All right," Rachel answered. "Let me have the flowers, and you can sleep with Jacob tonight."

16 That evening when Jacob came in from the fields, Leah told him, "You're sleeping with me tonight. I hired you with my son's love flowers."

They slept together that night, 17 and God answered Leah's prayers by giving her a fifth son. 18 Leah shouted, "God has rewarded me for letting Jacob marry my servant," and she named the boy Issachar.[r]

19 When Leah had another son, 20 she exclaimed, "God has given me a wonderful gift, and my husband will praise me for giving him six sons." So she named the boy Zebulun.[s] 21 Later, Leah had a daughter and named her Dinah.

22-23 Finally, God remembered Rachel—he answered her prayer by giving her a son. "God has taken away my disgrace," she said. 24 "I'll name the boy Joseph,[t] and I'll pray that the LORD will give me another son."

Jacob and Laban

25 After Joseph was born, Jacob said to Laban, "Release me from our agreement[u] and let me return to my own country. 26 You know how hard I've worked for you, so let me take my wives and children and leave."

27-28 But Laban told him, "If you really are my friend, stay on, and I'll pay whatever you ask. I'm sure[v] the LORD has blessed me because of you."

29 Jacob answered:

> You've seen how hard I've worked for you, and you know how your flocks and herds have grown under my care. 30 You didn't have much before I came, but the LORD has blessed everything I have ever done for you. Now it's time for me to start looking out for my own family.

31 "How much do you want me to pay you?" Laban asked.

Then Jacob told him:

> I don't want you to pay me anything. Just do one thing, and I'll take care of your sheep and goats. 32 Let me go through your flocks and herds and take the sheep and goats that are either spotted or speckled[w] and the black lambs. That's all you need to give me. 33 In the future you can easily find out if I've been honest. Just look and see if my animals are either spotted or speckled, or if the lambs are black. If they aren't, they've been stolen from you.

34 "I agree to that," was Laban's response. 35 Before the end of the day, Laban had separated his spotted and speckled animals and the black lambs from the others and had put his sons in charge of them. 36 Then Laban made Jacob keep the rest of the sheep and goats at a distance of three days' journey.

37 Jacob cut branches from some poplar trees and from some almond and evergreen trees. He peeled off part of the bark and made the branches look spotted and speckled. 38 Then he put the branches where the sheep and goats would see them[x] while they were drinking from the water trough. The goats mated there 39 in front of the branches, and their young were spotted and speckled.

40 Some of the sheep that Jacob was keeping for Laban were already spotted. And when the others were ready to mate, he made sure that they faced in the direction of the spotted and black ones. In this way, Jacob built up a flock of sheep for him-

[r] **30.18** *Issachar*: In Hebrew "Issachar" sounds like "reward." [s] **30.20** *Zebulun*: In Hebrew "Zebulun" sounds like "give" and "praise." [t] **30.24** *Joseph*: In Hebrew "Joseph" sounds like "take away" and "add." [u] **30.25** *Release . . . agreement*: Jacob had agreed to work seven years for each of Laban's two daughters (see 29.18). [v] **30.27,28** *I'm sure*: The Hebrew text means to find out by some kind of magic, such as fortunetelling. [w] **30.32** *spotted or speckled*: In ancient times sheep were usually white, and goats were usually black or dark brown; only a few sheep would have black spots, and only a few goats would have white spots. [x] **30.38** *would see them*: It was believed by some that what sheep and goats saw at the time of breeding would determine the color of their young.

self and did not put them with the other sheep.

41 When the stronger sheep were mating near the drinking place, Jacob made sure that the spotted branches were there. 42 But he would not put out the branches when the weaker animals were mating. So Jacob got all of the healthy animals, and Laban got what was left. 43 Jacob soon became rich and successful. He owned many sheep, goats, camels, and donkeys, as well as a lot of slaves.

Jacob Runs from Laban

31 Jacob heard that Laban's sons were complaining, "Jacob is now a rich man, and he got everything he owns from our father." 2 Jacob also noticed that Laban was not as friendly as he had been before. 3 One day the LORD said, "Jacob, go back to your relatives in the land of your ancestors, and I will bless you."

4 Jacob sent for Rachel and Leah to meet him in the field where he kept his sheep, 5 and he told them:

Your father isn't as friendly with me as he used to be, but the God my ancestors worshiped has been on my side. 6 You know that I have worked hard for your father 7 and that he keeps cheating me by changing my wages time after time. But God has protected me. 8 When your father said the speckled sheep would be my wages, all of them were speckled. And when he said the spotted ones would be mine, all of them were spotted. 9 That's how God has taken sheep and goats from your father and given them to me.

10 Once, when the flocks were mating, I dreamed that all the rams were either spotted or speckled. 11 Then God's angel called me by name. I answered, 12 and he said, "Notice that all the rams are either spotted or speckled. I know everything Laban is doing to you, 13 and I am the God you worshiped at Bethel,[y] when you poured olive oil on a rock and made a promise to me. Leave here right away and return to the land where you were born."

14 Rachel and Leah said to Jacob:

There's nothing left for us to inherit from our father. 15 He treats us like foreigners and has even cheated us out of the bride price[z] that should have been ours. 16 Now do whatever God tells you to do. Even the property God took from our father and gave to you really belongs to us and our children.

17 Then Jacob, his wives, and his children got on camels and left 18 for the home of his father Isaac in Canaan. Jacob took all of the flocks, herds, and other property that he had gotten in northern Syria.[a]

19 Before Rachel left, she stole the household idols[b] while Laban was out shearing his sheep.

20 Jacob tricked Laban the Aramean[c] by not saying that he intended to leave. 21 When Jacob crossed the Euphrates River and headed for the hill country of Gilead, he took with him everything he owned.

Laban Catches Up with Jacob

22 Three days later Laban found out that Jacob had gone. 23 So he took some of his relatives along and chased after Jacob for seven days, before catching up with him in the hill country of Gilead. 24 But God appeared to Laban in a dream that night and warned, "Don't say a word to Jacob. Don't make a threat or a promise."

25 Jacob had set up camp in the hill country of Gilead, when Laban and his relatives came and set up camp in another

[y]**31.13** *you . . . Bethel*: Or "who appeared to you at Bethel." [z]**31.15** *bride price*: Usually the husband-to-be paid a bride price to the father of the bride. But Jacob didn't pay Laban a bride price for either Rachel or Leah. Instead he was tricked into working fourteen years to get the bride he loved. So there was no money for either of Laban's daughters. [a]**31.18** *northern Syria*: See the note at 24.10. [b]**31.19** *household idols*: These were thought to protect the household from danger. It is also possible that the person who had them would inherit the family property. [c]**31.20** *the Aramean*: Meaning someone from northern Syria (see the note at 24.10).
31.13 Gn 28.18-22.

part of the hill country. Laban went to Jacob [26] and said:

Look what you've done! You've tricked me and run off with my daughters like a kidnapper. [27] Why did you sneak away without telling me? I would have given you a going-away party with singing and with music on tambourines and harps. [28] You didn't even give me a chance to kiss my own grandchildren and daughters good-by. That was really foolish. [29] I could easily hurt you, but the God your father worshiped has warned me not to make any threats or promises.

[30] I can understand why you were eager to return to your father, but why did you have to steal my idols?

[31] Jacob answered, "I left secretly because I was afraid you would take your daughters from me by force. [32] If you find that any one of us has taken your idols, I'll have that person killed. Let your relatives be witnesses. Show me what belongs to you, and you can take it back." Jacob did not realize that Rachel had stolen the household idols.

[33] Laban searched the tents of Jacob, Leah, and the two servant women,[d] but did not find the idols. Then he started for Rachel's tent. [34] She had already hidden them in the cushion she used as a saddle and was sitting on it. Laban searched everywhere and did not find them. [35] Rachel said, "Father, please don't be angry with me for not getting up; I am having my period." Laban kept on searching, but still did not find the idols.

[36] Jacob became very angry and said to Laban:

What have I done wrong? Have I committed some crime? Is that why you hunted me down? [37] After searching through everything I have, did you find anything of yours? If so, put it here, where your relatives and mine can see it. Then we can decide what to do.

[38] In all the twenty years that I've worked for you, not one of your sheep or goats has had a miscarriage, and I've never eaten even one of your rams. [39] If a wild animal killed one of your sheep or goats, I paid for it myself. In fact, you demanded the full price, whether the animal was killed during the day or at night.[e] [40] I sweated every day, and I couldn't sleep at night because of the cold.

[41] I had to work fourteen of these twenty long years to earn your two daughters and another six years to buy your sheep and goats. During that time you kept changing my wages. [42] If the fearsome God[f] worshiped by Abraham and my father Isaac had not been on my side, you would have sent me away without a thing. But God saw my hard work, and he knew the trouble I was in, so he helped me. Then last night he told you how wrong you were.

Jacob and Laban Make an Agreement

[43] Laban said to Jacob, "Leah and Rachel are my daughters, and their children belong to me. All these sheep you are taking are really mine too. In fact, everything you have belongs to me. But there is nothing I can do to keep my daughters and their children. [44] So I am ready to make an agreement with you, and we will pile up some large rocks here to remind us of the agreement."

[45] After Jacob had set up a large rock, [46] he told his men to get some more rocks and pile them up next to it. Then Jacob and Laban ate a meal together beside the rocks. [47] Laban named the pile of rocks Jegar Sahadutha.[g] But Jacob named it Galeed.[h] [48] Laban said to Jacob, "This pile of rocks will remind us of our agreement." That's why the place was named Galeed. [49] Laban also said, "This pile of rocks means that the LORD will watch us both while we are apart from each

[d] **31.33** *two servant women*: Bilhah and Zilpah (see 30.4, 9). [e] **31.39** *you demanded . . . night*: A shepherd was not responsible for sheep and goats killed by wild animals, if the shepherd could supply proof of how they were killed. [f] **31.42** *fearsome God*: One possible meaning for the difficult Hebrew text. [g] **31.47** *Jegar Sahadutha*: In Aramaic "Jegar Sahadutha" means "a pile of rocks to remind us." [h] **31.47** *Galeed*: In Hebrew "Galeed" means "a pile of rocks to remind us."

other." So the place was also named Mizpah.[i]

50 Then Laban said:

If you mistreat my daughters or marry other women, I may not know about it, but remember, God is watching us! 51-52 Both this pile of rocks and this large rock have been set up between us as a reminder. I must never go beyond them to attack you, and you must never go beyond them to attack me. 53 My father Nahor, your grandfather Abraham, and their ancestors all worshiped the same God, and he will make sure that we each keep the agreement.

Then Jacob made a promise in the name of the fearsome God[j] his father Isaac had worshiped. 54 Jacob killed an animal and offered it as a sacrifice there on the mountain, and he invited his men to eat with him. After the meal they spent the night on the mountain. 55 Early the next morning, Laban kissed his daughters and his grandchildren good-by, then he left to go back home.

Jacob Gets Ready To Meet Esau

32 As Jacob was on his way back home, some of God's angels came and met him. 2 When Jacob saw them, he said, "This is God's camp." So he named the place Mahanaim.[k]

3 Jacob sent messengers on ahead to Esau, who lived in the land of Seir, also known as Edom. 4 Jacob told them to say to Esau, "Master, I am your servant! I have lived with Laban all this time, 5 and now I own cattle, donkeys, and sheep, as well as many slaves. Master, I am sending these messengers in the hope that you will be kind to me."

6 When the messengers returned, they told Jacob, "We went to your brother Esau, and now he is heading this way with four hundred men."

7 Jacob was so frightened that he divided his people, sheep, cattle, and camels into two groups. 8 He thought, "If Esau attacks one group, perhaps the other can escape."

9 Then Jacob prayed:

You, LORD, are the God who was worshiped by my grandfather Abraham and by my father Isaac. You told me to return home to my family, and you promised to be with me and make me successful. 10 I don't deserve all the good things you have done for me, your servant. When I first crossed the Jordan, I had only my walking stick, but now I have two large groups of people and animals. 11 Please rescue me from my brother. I am afraid he will come and attack not only me, but my wives and children as well. 12 But you have promised that I would be a success and that someday it will be as hard to count my descendants as it is to count the stars in the sky.

13 After Jacob had spent the night there, he chose some animals as gifts for Esau: 14-15 two hundred female goats and twenty males, two hundred female sheep and twenty males, thirty female camels with their young, forty cows and ten bulls, and twenty female donkeys and ten males.

16 Jacob put servants in charge of each herd and told them, "Go ahead of me and keep a space between each herd." 17 Then he said to the servant in charge of the first herd, "When Esau meets you, he will ask whose servant you are. He will want to know where you are going and who owns those animals in front of you. 18 So tell him, 'They belong to your servant Jacob, who is coming this way. He is sending them as a gift to his master Esau.' "

19 Jacob also told the men in charge of the second and third herds and those who followed to say the same thing when they met Esau. 20 And Jacob told them to be sure to say that he was right behind them. Jacob hoped the gifts would make Esau friendly, so Esau would be glad to see him when they met. 21 Jacob's men took the gifts on ahead of him, but he spent the night in camp.

[i]**31.49** *Mizpah*: In Hebrew "Mizpah" sounds like "a place from which to watch." [j]**31.53** *fearsome God*: See the note at 31.42. [k]**32.2** *Mahanaim*: In Hebrew "Mahanaim" means "two camps."
32.12 Gn 22.17.

Jacob's Name Is Changed to Israel

22-23 Jacob got up in the middle of the
night and took his wives, his eleven children, and everything he owned across to
the other side of the Jabbok River for safety.
24 Afterwards, Jacob went back and spent
the rest of the night alone.

A man came and fought with Jacob until
just before daybreak. 25 When the man
saw that he could not win, he struck
Jacob on the hip and threw it out of
joint. 26 They kept on wrestling until the
man said, "Let go of me! It's almost daylight."

"You can't go until you bless me," Jacob
replied.

27 Then the man asked, "What is your
name?"

"Jacob," he answered.

28 The man said, "Your name will no
longer be Jacob. You have wrestled with
God and with men, and you have won.
That's why your name will be Israel."[l]

29 Jacob said, "Now tell me your name."

"Don't you know who I am?" he asked.
And he blessed Jacob.

30 Jacob said, "I have seen God face to
face, and I am still alive." So he named the
place Peniel.[m] 31 The sun was coming up
as Jacob was leaving Peniel. He was limp-
ing because he had been struck on the hip,
32 and the muscle on his hip joint had been
injured. That's why even today the people
of Israel don't eat the hip muscle of any
animal.

Jacob Meets Esau

33 Later that day Jacob met Esau
coming with his four hundred men.
So Jacob had his children walk with their
mothers. 2 The two servant women, Zilpah
and Bilhah, together with their children
went first, followed by Leah and her children, then by Rachel and Joseph. 3 Jacob
himself walked in front of them all, bowing
to the ground seven times as he came near
his brother.

4 But Esau ran toward Jacob and
hugged and kissed him. Then the two
brothers started crying.

5 When Esau noticed the women and
children he asked, "Whose children are
these?"

Jacob answered, "These are the ones the
LORD has been kind enough to give to me,
your servant."

6 Then the two servant women and
their children came and bowed down to
Esau. 7 Next, Leah and her children came
and bowed down; finally, Joseph and
Rachel also came and bowed down.

8 Esau asked Jacob, "What did you
mean by these herds I met along the road?"

"Master," Jacob answered, "I sent them
so that you would be friendly to me."

9 "But, brother, I already have plenty,"
Esau replied. "Keep them for yourself."

10 "No!" Jacob said. "Please accept
these gifts as a sign of your friendship for
me. When you welcomed me and I saw
your face, it was like seeing the face of
God. 11 Please accept these gifts I brought
to you. God has been good to me, and I
have everything I need." Jacob kept insisting until Esau accepted the gifts.

12 "Let's get ready to travel," Esau said.
"I'll go along with you."

13 But Jacob answered, "Master, you
know traveling is hard on children, and I
have to look after the sheep and goats
that are nursing their young. If my
animals travel too much in one day, they
will all die. 14 Why don't you go on ahead
and let me travel along slowly with the
children, the herds, and the flocks.
We can meet again in the country of
Edom."

15 Esau replied, "Let me leave some of
my men with you."

"You don't have to do that," Jacob answered. "I am happy, simply knowing that
you are friendly to me."

16 So Esau left for Edom. 17 But Jacob
went to Succoth,[n] where he built a house
for himself and set up shelters for his ani-

[l]**32.28** *Israel*: In Hebrew one meaning of "Israel" is "a man who wrestles with God."
[m]**32.30** *Peniel*: In Hebrew "Peniel" means "face of God." [n]**33.17** *Succoth*: In Hebrew "Succoth" means "shelters."

32.22,23 Ws 10.12. **32.24-26** Ho 12.3, 4. **32.28** Gn 35.9-11. **32.29** Jg 13.17, 18.

mals. That's why the place is called Succoth.

Jacob Arrives at Shechem

18 After leaving northern Syria,[o] Jacob arrived safely at Shechem in Canaan and set up camp outside the city. 19 The land where he camped was owned by the descendants of Hamor, the father of Shechem. So Jacob paid them one hundred pieces of silver[p] for the property, 20 then he set up his tents and built an altar there to honor the God of Israel.

Dinah Is Raped

34 Dinah, the daughter of Jacob and Leah, went to visit some of the women who lived there. 2 She was seen by Hamor's son Shechem, the leader of the Hivites, and he grabbed her and raped her. 3 But Shechem was attracted to Dinah, so he told her how much he loved her. 4 He even asked his father to get her for his wife.

5 Meanwhile, Jacob heard what had happened. But his sons were out in the fields with the cattle, so he did not do anything at the time. 6 Hamor arrived at Jacob's home 7 just as Jacob's sons were coming in from work. When they learned that their sister had been raped, they became furiously angry. Nothing is more disgraceful than rape, and it should not be tolerated in Israel.

8 Hamor said to Jacob and his sons:

> My son Shechem really loves Dinah. Please let him marry her. 9 Why don't you start letting your families marry into our families and ours marry into yours? 10 You can share this land with us. Move freely about until you find the property you want; then buy it and settle down here.

11 Shechem added, "Do this favor for me, and I'll give whatever you want. 12 Ask anything, no matter how expensive. I'll do anything, just let me marry Dinah."

13 Jacob's sons wanted to get even with Shechem and his father because of what had happened to their sister. 14 So they tricked them by saying:

> You're not circumcised![q] It would be a disgrace for us to let you marry Dinah now. 15 But we will let you marry her, if you and the other men in your tribe get circumcised. 16 Then your families can marry into ours, and ours can marry into yours, and we can live together like one nation. 17 But if you don't agree to get circumcised, we'll take Dinah and leave this place.

18 Hamor and Shechem liked what was said. 19 Shechem was the most respected person in his family, and he was so in love with Dinah that he hurried off to get everything done. 20 The two men met with the other leaders of their city and told them:

> 21 These people really are friendly. Why not let them move freely about until they find the property they want? There's enough land here for them and for us. Then our families can marry into theirs, and theirs can marry into ours.
>
> 22 We have to do only one thing before they will agree to stay here and become one nation with us. Our men will have to be circumcised like their men. 23 Just think! We'll get their property, as well as their flocks and herds. All we have to do is to agree, and they will live here with us.

24 Every grown man followed this advice and got circumcised.

Dinah's Brothers Take Revenge

25 Three days later the men who had been circumcised were still weak from pain. So Simeon and Levi,[r] two of Dinah's brothers, attacked with their swords and killed every man in town, 26 including Hamor and Shechem. Then they took Dinah and left. 27 Jacob's other sons came

[o]**33.18** *northern Syria*: See the note at 24.10. [p]**33.19** *pieces of silver*: Or "lambs" or "cattle." [q]**34.14** *You're not circumcised*: Israelite boys were circumcised when they were eight days old, and no uncircumcised man could be part of the people of Israel. [r]**34.25** *Simeon and Levi*: Dinah's full brothers.

33.19 Js 24.32; Jn 4.5.

and took everything they wanted. All this was done because of the horrible thing that had happened to their sister. 28 They took sheep, goats, donkeys, and everything else that was in the town or the fields. 29 After taking everything of value from the houses, they dragged away the wives and children of their victims.

30 Jacob said to Simeon and Levi, "Look what you've done! Now I'm in real trouble with the Canaanites and Perizzites who live around here. There aren't many of us, and if they attack, they'll kill everyone in my household."

31 They answered, "Was it right to let our own sister be treated that way?"

Jacob Returns to Bethel

35 God told Jacob, "Return to Bethel, where I appeared to you when you were running from your brother Esau. Make your home there and build an altar for me."

2 Jacob said to his family and to everyone else who was traveling with him:

> Get rid of your foreign gods! Then make yourselves acceptable to worship God and put on clean clothes. 3 Afterwards, we'll go to Bethel. I will build an altar there for God, who answered my prayers when I was in trouble and who has always been at my side.

4 So everyone gave Jacob their idols and their earrings,[s] and he buried them under the oak tree near Shechem.

5 While Jacob and his family were traveling through Canaan, God terrified the people in the towns so much that no one dared bother them. 6 Finally, they reached Bethel, also known as Luz. 7 Jacob built an altar there and called it "God of Bethel," because that was the place where God had appeared to him when he was running from Esau. 8 While they were there, Rebekah's personal servant Deborah[t] died. They buried her under an oak tree and called it "Weeping Oak."

God Blesses Jacob at Bethel

9-11 After Jacob came back to the land of Canaan, God appeared to him again. This time he gave Jacob a new name and blessed him by saying:

> I am God All-Powerful, and from now on your name will be Israel[u] instead of Jacob. You will have many children. Your descendants will become nations, and some of the men in your family will even be kings. 12 I will give you the land that I promised Abraham and Isaac, and it will belong to your family forever.

13 After God had gone, 14 Jacob set up a large rock, so that he would remember what had happened there. Then he poured wine and olive oil on the rock to show that it was dedicated to God, 15 and he named the place Bethel.[v]

Benjamin Is Born

16 Jacob and his family had left Bethel and were still a long way from Ephrath, when the time came for Rachel's baby to be born. 17 She was having a rough time, but the woman who was helping her said, "Don't worry! It's a boy." 18 Rachel was at the point of death, and right before dying, she said, "I'll name him Benoni."[w] But Jacob called him Benjamin.[x]

19 Rachel was buried beside the road to Ephrath, which is also called Bethlehem. 20 Jacob set up a tombstone over her grave, and it is still there. 21 Jacob, also known as Israel, traveled to the south of Eder Tower, where he set up camp.

22 During their time there, Jacob's oldest son Reuben slept with Bilhah, who was one of Jacob's other wives.[y] And Jacob found out about it.

[s] **35.4** *earrings*: These would have had symbols of foreign gods on them. [t] **35.8** *Deborah*: See 24.59 and the note there. [u] **35.9-11** *Israel*: See the note at 32.28. [v] **35.15** *Bethel*: See the note at 28.19. [w] **35.18** *Benoni*: In Hebrew "Benoni" means "Son of my Sorrow." [x] **35.18** *Benjamin*: In Hebrew "Benjamin" can mean "Son at my Right Side" (the place of power). [y] **35.22** *other wives*: See the note at 22.24. Bilhah had been Rachel's servant woman (see 29.28-30).

35.1 Gn 28.11-17. **35.9-11** Gn 32.28. **35.9-12** Gn 17.4-8. **35.14,15** Gn 28.18, 19. **35.22** Gn 49.4.

Jacob's Twelve Sons

23-26 Jacob had twelve sons while living in northern Syria.[z] His first-born Reuben was the son of Leah, who later gave birth to Simeon, Levi, Judah, Issachar, and Zebulun. Leah's servant Zilpah had two sons: Gad and Asher.

Jacob and his wife Rachel had Joseph and Benjamin. Rachel's servant woman Bilhah had two more sons: Dan and Naphtali.

Isaac Dies

27 Jacob went to his father Isaac at Hebron, also called Mamre or Kiriath-Arba, where Isaac's father Abraham had lived as a foreigner. 28-29 Isaac died at the ripe old age of one hundred eighty, then his sons Esau and Jacob buried him.

Esau's Family

36 Esau, also known as Edom, had many descendants. 2 He married three Canaanite women: The first was Adah, the daughter of Elon the Hittite; the second was Oholibamah, the daughter of Anah and the granddaughter of Zibeon the Hivite; 3 the third was Basemath, who was Ishmael's daughter and Nebaioth's sister.

4-5 Esau and his three wives had five sons while in Canaan. Adah's son was Eliphaz; Basemath's son was Reuel; Oholibamah's three sons were Jeush, Jalam, and Korah.

6 Esau took his children and wives, his relatives and servants, his animals and possessions he had gotten while in Canaan, and moved far from Jacob. 7 He did this because the land was too crowded and could not support him and his brother with their flocks and herds. 8 That's why Esau made his home in the hill country of Seir.

9-14 Esau lived in the hill country of Seir and was the ancestor of the Edomites. Esau had three wives: Adah, Basemath, and Oholibamah. Here is a list of his descendants: Esau and Adah had a son named Eliphaz, whose sons were Teman, Omar, Zepho, Gatam, and Kenaz. Timna was the other wife[a] of Esau's son Eliphaz, and she had a son named Amalek.

Esau and Basemath had a son named Reuel, whose sons were Nahath, Zerah, Shammah, and Mizzah.

Esau and Oholibamah had three sons: Jeush, Jalam, and Korah.

Chiefs and Leaders in Edom

15 Esau and Adah's oldest son was Eliphaz, and the clans that descended from him were Teman, Omar, Zepho, Kenaz, 16 Korah, Gatam, and Amalek. These and Esau's other descendants lived in the land of Edom.

17 The clans that descended from Esau and Basemath's son Reuel were Nahath, Zerah, Shammah, and Mizzah.

18 The clans that descended from Esau and Oholibamah the daughter of Anah were Jeush, Jalam, and Korah. 19 All of these clans descended from Esau, who was known as Edom.

20 Seir was from the Horite tribe that had lived in Edom before the time of Esau. The clans that had descended from him were Lotan, Shobal, Zibeon, Anah, 21 Dishon, Ezer, and Dishan.

22 Lotan's sons were Hori and Heman; his sister was Timna.

23 Shobal's sons were Alvan, Manahath, Ebal, Shepho, and Onam.

24 Zibeon's sons were Aiah and Anah—the same Anah who found an oasis[b] in the desert while taking the donkeys of his father out to pasture.

25 Anah's children were Dishon and Oholibamah.

26 Dishon's sons were Hemdan, Eshban, Ithran, and Cheran.

27 Ezer's sons were Bilhan, Zaavan, and Akan.

28 Dishan's sons were Uz and Aran.

29 The clans of the Horites were Lotan, Shobal, Zibeon, Anah, 30 Dishon, Ezer, and Dishan, and they lived in the land of Seir.

31-39 Before there were kings in Israel,

[z]**35.23-26** *northern Syria*: See the note at 24.10. [a]**36.9-14** *other wife*: See the note at 22.24. [b]**36.24** *an oasis*: One possible meaning for the difficult Hebrew text.
35.27 Gn 13.18. **36.2** Gn 26.34. **36.3** Gn 28.9.

the following kings ruled Edom one after another:

Bela son of Beor from Dinhabah;
Jobab son of Zerah from Bozrah;
Husham from the land of Teman;
Hadad son of Bedad from Avith (Bedad had defeated the Midianites in Moab);
Samlah from Masrekah;
Shaul from the city of Rehoboth on the Euphrates River;
Baalhanan son of Achbor;
Hadar from the city of Pau (his wife Mehetabel was the daughter of Matred and the granddaughter of Mezahab).

40 The clans that descended from Esau took their names from their families and the places where they lived. They are Timna, Alvah, Jetheth, 41 Oholibamah, Elah, Pinon, 42 Kenaz, Teman, Mibzar, 43 Magdiel, and Iram. These clans descended from Esau, who was known as Edom, the father of the Edomites. They took their names from the places where they settled.

Joseph and His Brothers

37 Jacob lived in the land of Canaan, where his father Isaac had lived, 2 and this is the story of his family.

When Jacob's son Joseph was seventeen years old, he took care of the sheep with his brothers, the sons of Bilhah and Zilpah.[c] But he was always telling his father all sorts of bad things about his brothers.

3 Jacob loved Joseph more than he did any of his other sons, because Joseph was born after Jacob was very old. Jacob had given Joseph a fancy coat[d] 4 to show that he was his favorite son, and so Joseph's brothers hated him and would not be friendly to him.

5 One day, Joseph told his brothers what he had dreamed, and they hated him even more. 6 Joseph said, "Let me tell you about my dream. 7 We were out in the field, tying up bundles of wheat. Suddenly my bundle stood up, and your bundles gathered around and bowed down to it."

8 His brothers asked, "Do you really think you are going to be king and rule over us?" Now they hated Joseph more than ever because of what he had said about his dream.

9 Joseph later had another dream, and he told his brothers, "Listen to what else I dreamed. The sun, the moon, and eleven stars bowed down to me."

10 When he told his father about this dream, his father became angry and said, "What's that supposed to mean? Are your mother and I and your brothers all going to come and bow down in front of you?" 11 Joseph's brothers were jealous of him, but his father kept wondering about the dream.

Joseph Is Sold and Taken to Egypt

12 One day when Joseph's brothers had taken the sheep to a pasture near Shechem, 13 his father Jacob said to him, "I want you to go to your brothers. They are with the sheep near Shechem."

"Yes, sir," Joseph answered.

14 His father said, "Go and find out how your brothers and the sheep are doing. Then come back and let me know." So he sent him from Hebron Valley.

Joseph was near Shechem 15 and wandering through the fields, when a man asked, "What are you looking for?"

16 Joseph answered, "I'm looking for my brothers who are watching the sheep. Can you tell me where they are?"

17 "They're not here anymore," the man replied. "I overheard them say they were going to Dothan."

Joseph left and found his brothers in Dothan. 18 But before he got there, they saw him coming and made plans to kill him. 19 They said to one another, "Look, here comes the hero of those dreams! 20 Let's kill him and throw him into a pit and say that some wild animal ate him.

[c]**37.2** *Bilhah and Zilpah*: See 30.1-13. [d]**37.3,23** *fancy coat*: Or "a coat of many colors" or "a coat with long sleeves."
37.11 Ac 7.9.

Then we'll see what happens to those dreams."

21 Reuben heard this and tried to protect Joseph from them. "Let's not kill him," he said. 22 "Don't murder him or even harm him. Just throw him into a dry well out here in the desert." Reuben planned to rescue Joseph later and take him back to his father.

23 When Joseph came to his brothers, they pulled off his fancy coat[d] 24 and threw him into a dry well.

25 As Joseph's brothers sat down to eat, they looked up and saw a caravan of Ishmaelites coming from Gilead. Their camels were loaded with all kinds of spices that they were taking to Egypt. 26 So Judah said, "What will we gain if we kill our brother and hide his body? 27 Let's sell him to the Ishmaelites and not harm him. After all, he is our brother." And the others agreed.

28 When the Midianite merchants came by, Joseph's brothers took him out of the well, and for twenty pieces of silver they sold him to the Ishmaelites[e] who took him to Egypt.

29 When Reuben returned to the well and did not find Joseph there, he tore his clothes in sorrow. 30 Then he went back to his brothers and said, "The boy is gone! What am I going to do?"

31 Joseph's brothers killed a goat and dipped Joseph's fancy coat in its blood. 32 After this, they took the coat to their father and said, "We found this! Look at it carefully and see if it belongs to your son."

33 Jacob knew it was Joseph's coat and said, "It's my son's coat! Joseph has been torn to pieces and eaten by some wild animal."

34 Jacob mourned for Joseph a long time, and to show his sorrow he tore his clothes and wore sackcloth.[f] 35 All of Jacob's children came to comfort him, but he refused to be comforted. "No," he said, "I will go to my grave, mourning for my son." So Jacob kept on grieving.

36 Meanwhile, the Midianites had sold Joseph in Egypt to a man named Potiphar, who was the king's[g] official in charge of the palace guard.

Judah and Tamar

38 About that time Judah left his brothers in the hill country and went to live near his friend Hirah in the town of Adullam. 2 While there he met the daughter of Shua, a Canaanite man. Judah married her, 3 and they had three sons. He named the first one Er; 4 she named the next one Onan. 5 The third one was born when Judah was in Chezib, and she named him Shelah.

6 Later, Judah chose Tamar as a wife for Er, his oldest son. 7 But Er was very evil, and the LORD took his life. 8 So Judah told Onan, "It's your duty to marry Tamar and have a child for your brother."[h]

9 Onan knew the child would not be his,[i] and when he had sex with Tamar, he made sure that she would not get pregnant. 10 The LORD wasn't pleased with Onan and took his life too.

11 Judah did not want the same thing to happen to his son Shelah, and he told Tamar, "Go home to your father and live there as a widow until my son Shelah is grown." So Tamar went to live with her father.

12 Some years later Judah's wife died, and he mourned for her. He then went with his friend Hirah to the town of Timnah, where his sheep were being sheared. 13 Tamar found out that her father-in-law

[d]**37.3,23** *fancy coat*: Or "a coat of many colors" or "a coat with long sleeves."
[e]**37.28** *Midianite . . . Ishmaelites*: According to 25.1, 2, 12 both the Midianites and the Ishmaelites were descendants of Abraham, and in Judges 8.22-24 the two names are used of the same people. It is possible that in this passage "Ishmaelite" has the meaning "nomadic traders," while "Midianite" refers to their ethnic origin. [f]**37.34** *sackcloth*: A rough dark-colored cloth made from goat or camel hair and used to make grain sacks. It was worn in times of trouble or sorrow. [g]**37.36** *the king's*: See the note at 12.15. [h]**38.8** *It's your duty . . . child . . . brother*: If a man died without having children, his brother was to marry the dead man's wife and have a child, who was to be considered the child of the dead brother (see Deuteronomy 25.5, 6). [i]**38.9** *the child . . . not be his*: When Judah died, Onan would get his dead brother's share of the inheritance, but if his dead brother had a son, the inheritance would go to him instead.
37.28 Ws 10.13; Ac 7.9.

Judah was going to Timnah to shear his
sheep. 14 She also realized that Shelah was
now a grown man, but she had not been allowed to marry him. So she decided to
dress in something other than her widow's
clothes and to cover her face with a veil.
After this, she sat outside the town of
Enaim on the road to Timnah.

15 When Judah came along, he did not
recognize her because of the veil. He
thought she was a prostitute 16 and asked
her to sleep with him. She asked, "What
will you give me if I do?"

17 "One of my young goats," he answered.

"What will you give me to keep until you
send the goat?" she asked.

18 "What do you want?" he asked in
return.

"The ring on that cord around your
neck," was her reply. "I also want the special walking stick[j] you have with you." He
gave them to her, they slept together, and
she became pregnant.

19 After returning home, Tamar took off
the veil and dressed in her widow's clothes
again.

20 Judah had his friend Hirah take a
goat to the woman, so he could get back
the ring and walking stick, but she wasn't
there. 21 Hirah asked the people of Enaim,
"Where is the prostitute who sat along the
road outside your town?"

"There's never been one here," they
answered.

22 Hirah went back and told Judah, "I
couldn't find the woman, and the people of
Enaim said no prostitute had ever been
there."

23 "If you couldn't find her, we'll just let
her keep the things I gave her," Judah answered. "And we'd better forget about the
goat, or else we'll look like fools."

24 About three months later someone
told Judah, "Your daughter-in-law Tamar
has behaved like a prostitute, and now
she's pregnant!"

"Drag her out of town and burn her to
death!" Judah shouted.

25 As Tamar was being dragged off, she
sent someone to tell her father-in-law, "The
man who gave me this ring, this cord, and
this walking stick is the one who got me
pregnant."

26 "Those are mine!" Judah admitted.
"She's a better person than I am, because I
broke my promise to let her marry my son
Shelah." After this, Judah never slept with
her again.

27-28 Tamar later gave birth to twins. But
before either of them was born, one of
them stuck a hand out of her womb. The
woman who was helping tied a red thread
around the baby's hand and explained,
"This one came out first."

29 Right away his hand went back in,
and the other child was born first. The
woman then said, "What an opening you've
made for yourself!" So they named the
baby Perez.[k] 30 When the brother with the
red thread came out, they named him
Zerah.[l]

Joseph and Potiphar's Wife

39 The Ishmaelites took Joseph to
Egypt and sold him to Potiphar, the
king's[m] official in charge of the palace
guard. 2-3 So Joseph lived in the home of
Potiphar, his Egyptian owner.

Soon Potiphar realized that the LORD
was helping Joseph to be successful in
whatever he did. 4 Potiphar liked Joseph
and made him his personal assistant,
putting him in charge of his house and all
of his property. 5 Because of Joseph, the
LORD began to bless Potiphar's family and
fields. 6 Potiphar left everything up to
Joseph, and with Joseph there, the only decision he had to make was what he wanted
to eat.

Joseph was well-built and handsome,
7 and Potiphar's wife soon noticed him.
She asked him to make love to her, 8 but he
refused and said, "My master isn't worried

[j]**38.18** *ring . . . walking stick*: The ring was shaped like a cylinder and could be rolled over soft clay as a way of sealing special documents. The walking stick was probably a symbol of power and the sign of leadership in the tribe, though it may have been a shepherd's rod. [k]**38.29** *Perez*: In Hebrew "Perez" sounds like "opening." [l]**38.30** *Zerah*: In Hebrew "Zerah" means "bright," probably referring to the red thread. [m]**39.1; 40.1-3** *the king's*: See the note at 12.15.

39.2,3 Ac 7.9. **39.7-12** 4 Macc. 2.2.

about anything in his house, because he has placed me in charge of everything he owns. 9 No one in my master's house is more important than I am. The only thing he hasn't given me is you, and that's because you are his wife. I won't sin against God by doing such a terrible thing as this." 10 She kept begging Joseph day after day, but he refused to do what she wanted or even to go near her.

11 One day, Joseph went to Potiphar's house to do his work, and none of the other servants were there. 12 Potiphar's wife grabbed hold of his coat and said, "Make love to me!" Joseph ran out of the house, leaving her hanging onto his coat.

13 When this happened, 14 she called in her servants and said, "Look! This Hebrew has come just to make fools of us. He tried to rape me, but I screamed for help. 15 And when he heard me scream, he ran out of the house, leaving his coat with me."

16 Potiphar's wife kept Joseph's coat until her husband came home. 17 Then she said, "That Hebrew slave of yours tried to rape me! 18 But when I screamed for help, he left his coat and ran out of the house."

19 Potiphar became very angry 20 and threw Joseph in the same prison where the king's prisoners were kept.

While Joseph was in prison, 21 the LORD helped him and was good to him. He even made the jailer like Joseph so much that 22 he put him in charge of the other prisoners and of everything that was done in the jail. 23 The jailer did not worry about anything, because the LORD was with Joseph and made him successful in all that he did.

Joseph Tells the Meaning of the Prisoners' Dreams

40 1-3 While Joseph was in prison, both the king's[m] personal servant[n] and his chief cook made the king angry. So he had them thrown into the same prison with Joseph. 4 They spent a long time in prison, and Potiphar, the official in charge of the palace guard, made Joseph their servant.

5 One night each of the two men had a dream, but their dreams had different meanings. 6 The next morning, when Joseph went to see the men, he could tell they were upset, 7 and he asked, "Why are you so worried today?"

8 "We each had a dream last night," they answered, "and there is no one to tell us what they mean."

Joseph replied, "Doesn't God know the meaning of dreams? Now tell me what you dreamed."

9 The king's personal servant told Joseph, "In my dream I saw a vine 10 with three branches. As soon as it budded, it blossomed, and its grapes became ripe. 11 I held the king's cup and squeezed the grapes into it, then I gave the cup to the king."

12 Joseph said:

> This is the meaning of your dream. The three branches stand for three days, 13 and in three days the king will pardon you. He will make you his personal servant again, and you will serve him his wine, just as you used to do.
>
> 14 But when these good things happen, please don't forget to tell the king about me, so I can get out of this place. 15 I was kidnapped from the land of the Hebrews, and here in Egypt I haven't done anything to deserve being thrown in jail.

16 When the chief cook saw that Joseph had given a good meaning to the dream, he told Joseph, "I also had a dream. In it I was carrying three breadbaskets stacked on top of my head. 17 The top basket was full of all kinds of baked things for the king, but birds were eating them."

18 Joseph said:

> This is the meaning of your dream. The three baskets are three days, 19 and in three days the king will cut off your head. He will hang your body on a pole, and birds will come and peck at it.

20 Three days later, while the king was celebrating his birthday with a dinner for

[m] **39.1; 40.1-3** *the king's*: See the note at 12.15. [n] **40.1-3** *personal servant*: The Hebrew text has "cup bearer," an important and trusted official in the royal court, who personally served wine to the king.

39.21 Ac 7.9. **40.19** 3 Macc. 6.34.

his officials, he sent for his personal servant and the chief cook. [21] He put the personal servant back in his old job [22] and had the cook put to death.

Everything happened just as Joseph had said it would, [23] but the king's personal servant completely forgot about Joseph.

Joseph Interprets the King's Dreams

41 Two years later the king[o] of Egypt dreamed he was standing beside the Nile River. [2] Suddenly, seven fat, healthy cows came up from the river and started eating grass along the bank. [3] Then seven ugly, skinny cows came up out of the river and [4] ate the fat, healthy cows. When this happened, the king woke up.

[5] The king went back to sleep and had another dream. This time seven full heads of grain were growing on a single stalk. [6] Later, seven other heads of grain appeared, but they were thin and scorched by the east wind. [7] The thin heads of grain swallowed the seven full heads. Again the king woke up, and it had only been a dream.

[8] The next morning the king was upset. So he called in his magicians and wise men and told them what he had dreamed. None of them could tell him what the dreams meant.

[9] The king's personal servant said:

Now I remember what I was supposed to do. [10] When you were angry with me and your chief cook, you threw us both in jail in the house of the captain of the guard. [11] One night we both had dreams, and each dream had a different meaning. [12] A young Hebrew, who was a servant of the captain of the guard, was there with us at the time. When we told him our dreams, he explained what each of them meant, [13] and everything happened just as he said it would. I got my job back, and the cook was put to death.

[14] The king sent for Joseph, who was quickly brought out of jail. He shaved, changed his clothes, and went to the king.

[15] The king said to him, "I had a dream, yet no one can explain what it means. I am told that you can interpret dreams."

[16] "Your Majesty," Joseph answered, "I can't do it myself, but God can give a good meaning to your dreams."

[17] The king told Joseph:

I dreamed I was standing on the bank of the Nile River. [18] I saw seven fat, healthy cows come up out of the river, and they began feeding on the grass. [19] Next, seven skinny, bony cows came up out of the river. I have never seen such terrible looking cows anywhere in Egypt. [20] The skinny cows ate the fat ones. [21] But you couldn't tell it, because these skinny cows were just as skinny as they were before. Right away, I woke up.

[22] I also dreamed that I saw seven heads of grain growing on one stalk. The heads were full and ripe. [23] Then seven other heads of grain came up. They were thin and scorched by a wind from the desert. [24] These heads of grain swallowed the full ones. I told my dreams to the magicians, but none of them could tell me the meaning of the dreams.

[25] Joseph replied:

Your Majesty, both of your dreams mean the same thing, and in them God has shown what he is going to do. [26] The seven good cows stand for seven years, and so do the seven good heads of grain. [27] The seven skinny, ugly cows that came up later also stand for seven years, as do the seven bad heads of grain that were scorched by the east wind. The dreams mean there will be seven years when there won't be enough grain.

[28] It is just as I said—God has shown what he intends to do. [29] For seven years Egypt will have more than enough grain, [30] but that will be followed by seven years when there won't be enough. The good years of plenty will be forgotten, and everywhere in Egypt people will be starving. [31] The

[o]**41.1,37** *the king*: See the note at 12.15.
41.8 Dn 2.2.

famine will be so bad that no one will
remember that once there had been
plenty. 32 God has given you two
dreams to let you know that he has
definitely decided to do this and that
he will do it soon.
33 Your Majesty, you should find
someone who is wise and will know
what to do, so that you can put him in
charge of all Egypt. 34 Then appoint
some other officials to collect one-fifth
of every crop harvested in Egypt during the seven years when there is
plenty. 35 Give them the power to collect the grain during those good years
and to store it in your cities. 36 It can
be stored until it is needed during the
seven years when there won't be
enough grain in Egypt. This will keep
the country from being destroyed because of the lack of food.

Joseph Is Made Governor over Egypt

37 The king[o] and his officials liked this
plan. 38 So the king said to them, "No
one could possibly handle this better
than Joseph, since the Spirit of God is
with him."
39 The king told Joseph, "God is the one
who has shown you these things. No one
else is as wise as you are or knows as much
as you do. 40 I'm putting you in charge of
my palace, and everybody will have to obey
you. No one will be over you except me.
41 You are now governor of all Egypt!"
42 Then the king took off his royal ring
and put it on Joseph's finger. He gave him
fine clothes to wear and placed a gold
chain around his neck. 43 He also let him
ride in the chariot next to his own, and
people shouted, "Make way for Joseph!" So
Joseph was governor of Egypt.
44 The king told Joseph, "Although I'm
king, no one in Egypt is to do anything
without your permission." 45 He gave
Joseph the Egyptian name Zaphenath
Paneah. And he let him marry Asenath, the
daughter of Potiphera, a priest in the city of
Heliopolis.[p] Joseph traveled all over Egypt.
46 Joseph was thirty when the king
made him governor, and he went everywhere for the king. 47 For seven years there
were big harvests of grain. 48 Joseph collected and stored up the extra grain in the
cities of Egypt near the fields where it was
harvested. 49 In fact, there was so much
grain that they stopped keeping record, because it was like counting the grains of
sand along the beach.
50 Joseph and his wife had two sons before the famine began. 51 Their first son
was named Manasseh, which means, "God
has let me forget all my troubles and my
family back home." 52 His second son was
named Ephraim, which means "God has
made me a success[q] in the land where I
suffered."[r]
53 Egypt's seven years of plenty came to
an end, 54 and the seven years of famine
began, just as Joseph had said. There was
not enough food in other countries, but all
over Egypt there was plenty. 55 When the
famine finally struck Egypt, the people
asked the king for food, but he said, "Go to
Joseph and do what he tells you to do."
56 The famine became bad everywhere
in Egypt, so Joseph opened the storehouses
and sold the grain to the Egyptians. 57 People from all over the world came to Egypt,
because the famine was severe in their
countries.

Joseph's Brothers Go to Egypt To Buy Grain

42 When Jacob found out there was
grain in Egypt, he said to his sons,
"Why are you just sitting here, staring at
one another? 2 I have heard there is grain
in Egypt. Now go down and buy some, so
we won't starve to death."
3 Ten of Joseph's brothers went to Egypt
to buy grain. 4 But Jacob did not send
Joseph's younger brother Benjamin with
them; he was afraid that something might

[o]**41.1,37** *the king*: See the note at 12.15. [p]**41.45** *Heliopolis*: The Hebrew text has "On," which is better known by its Greek name "Heliopolis." [q]**41.52** *God has made me a success*: Or "God has given me children." [r]**41.52** *Ephraim . . . suffered*: In Hebrew "Ephraim" actually means either "fertile land" or "pastureland."

41.40 Ac 7.10. **41.42** Dn 5.29. **41.54** Ac 7.11. **41.55** Jn 2.5. **42.2** Ac 7.12.

happen to him. 5 So Jacob's sons joined
others from Canaan who were going to
Egypt because of the terrible famine.
6 Since Joseph was governor of Egypt
and in charge of selling grain, his brothers
came to him and bowed with their faces to
the ground. 7-8 They did not recognize
Joseph, but right away he knew who they
were, though he pretended not to know. Instead, he spoke harshly and asked, "Where
do you come from?"

"From the land of Canaan," they answered. "We've come here to buy grain."
9 Joseph remembered what he had
dreamed about them and said, "You're
spies! You've come here to find out where
our country is weak."
10 "No sir," they replied. "We're your
servants, and we have only come to
buy grain. 11 We're honest men, and we
come from the same family—we're not
spies."
12 "That isn't so!" Joseph insisted.
"You've come here to find out where our
country is weak."
13 But they explained, "Sir, we come
from a family of twelve brothers. The
youngest is still with our father in Canaan,
and one of our brothers is dead."
14 Joseph replied:

It's just like I said. You're spies,
15 and I'm going to find out who you
really are. I swear by the life of the
king that you won't leave this place until your youngest brother comes here.
16 Choose one of you to go after your
brother, while the rest of you stay here
in jail. That will show whether you are
telling the truth. But if you are lying, I
swear by the life of the king that you
are spies!

17 Joseph kept them all under guard for
three days, 18 before saying to them:

Since I respect God, I'll give you a
chance to save your lives. 19 If you are
honest men, one of you must stay here
in jail, and the rest of you can take the
grain back to your starving families.
20 But you must bring your youngest
brother to me. Then I'll know that you
are telling the truth, and you won't be
put to death.

Joseph's brothers agreed 21 and said to
one another, "We're being punished because of Joseph. We saw the trouble he was
in, but we refused to help him when he
begged us. That's why these terrible things
are happening."
22 Reuben spoke up, "Didn't I tell you
not to harm the boy? But you wouldn't listen, and now we have to pay the price for
killing him."
23 They did not know that Joseph could
understand them, since he was speaking
through an interpreter. 24 Joseph turned
away from them and cried, but soon he
turned back and spoke to them again.
Then he had Simeon tied up and taken
away while they watched.

Joseph's Brothers Return to Canaan

25 Joseph gave orders for his brothers'
grain sacks to be filled with grain and for
their money[s] to be put in their sacks. He
also gave orders for them to be given food
for their journey home. After this was
done, 26 they each loaded the grain on
their donkeys and left.
27 When they stopped for the night, one
of them opened his sack to get some grain
for his donkey, and right away he saw his
moneybag. 28 "Here's my money!" he told
his brothers. "Right here in my sack."

They were trembling with fear as they
stared at one another and asked themselves, "What has God done to us?"
29 When they returned to the land of
Canaan, they told their father Jacob everything that had happened to them:

30 The governor of Egypt was rude
and treated us like spies. 31 But we told
him, "We're honest men, not spies.
32 We come from a family of twelve
brothers. The youngest is still with our
father in Canaan, and the other is
dead."

33 Then the governor of Egypt told
us, "I'll find out if you really are hon-

[s]**42.25** *money*: Probably in the form of small pieces of silver and/or other precious or semi-precious metals; there were no coins or paper money at this time.

42.9 Gn 37.5-10. **42.22** Gn 37.21, 22.

est. Leave one of your brothers here with me, while you take the grain to your starving families. 34 But bring your youngest brother to me, so I can be certain that you are honest men and not spies. After that, I'll let your other brother go free, and you can stay here and trade."

35 When the brothers started emptying their sacks of grain, they found their moneybags in them. They were frightened, and so was their father Jacob, 36 who said, "You have already taken my sons Joseph and Simeon from me. And now you want to take away Benjamin! Everything is against me."

37 Reuben spoke up, "Father, if I don't bring Benjamin back, you can kill both of my sons. Trust me with him, and I will bring him back."

38 But Jacob said, "I won't let my son Benjamin go down to Egypt with the rest of you. His brother is already dead, and he is the only son I have left.[t] I am an old man, and if anything happens to him on the way, I'll die from sorrow, and all of you will be to blame."

Joseph's Brothers Return to Egypt with Benjamin

43 The famine in Canaan got worse, 2 until finally, Jacob's family had eaten all the grain they had bought in Egypt. So Jacob said to his sons, "Go back and buy some more grain."

3-5 Judah replied, "The governor strictly warned us that we would not be allowed to see him unless we brought our youngest brother with us. If you let us take Benjamin along, we will go and buy grain. But we won't go without him!"

6 Jacob asked, "Why did you cause me so much trouble by telling the governor you had another brother?"

7 They answered, "He asked a lot of questions about us and our family. He wanted to know if you were still alive and if we had any more brothers. All we could do was answer his questions. How could we know he would tell us to bring along our brother?"

8 Then Judah said to his father, "Let Benjamin go with me, and we will leave right away, so that none of us will starve to death. 9 I promise to bring him back safely, and if I don't, you can blame me as long as I live. 10 If we had not wasted all this time, we could already have been there and back twice."

11 Their father said:

If Benjamin must go with you, take the governor a gift of some of the best things from our own country, such as perfume, honey, spices, pistachio nuts, and almonds.[u] 12 Also take along twice the amount of money for the grain, because there must have been some mistake when the money was put back in your sacks. 13 Take Benjamin with you and leave right away.

14 When you go in to see the governor, I pray that God All-Powerful will be good to you and that the governor will let your other brother and Benjamin come back home with you. If I must lose my children, I suppose I must.

15 The brothers took the gifts, twice the amount of money, and Benjamin. Then they hurried off to Egypt. When they stood in front of Joseph, 16 he saw Benjamin and told the servant in charge of his house, "Take these men to my house. Slaughter an animal and cook it, so they can eat with me at noon."

17 The servant did as he was told and took the brothers to Joseph's house. 18 But on the way they got worried and started thinking, "We are being taken there because of the money that was put back in our sacks last time. He will arrest us, make us his slaves, and take our donkeys."

19 So when they arrived at Joseph's house, they said to the servant in charge, 20 "Sir, we came to Egypt once before to buy grain. 21 But when we stopped for the night, we each found in our grain sacks the exact amount we had paid. We have

[t]**42.38** *only son I have left*: Jacob had only two sons by Rachel, his favorite wife. [u]**43.11** *honey, spices, pistachio nuts, and almonds*: Some of these foods were still available in Canaan, but the main food was bread, and there was no grain to make bread.

brought that money back, 22 together with enough money to buy more grain. We don't know who put the money in our sacks."

23 "It's all right," the servant replied. "Don't worry. The God you and your father worship must have put the money there, because I received your payment in full." Then he brought Simeon out to them.

24 The servant took them into Joseph's house and gave them water to wash their feet. He also tended their donkeys. 25 The brothers got their gifts ready to give to Joseph at noon, since they had heard they were going to eat there.

26 When Joseph came home, they gave him the gifts they had brought, and they bowed down to him. 27 After Joseph had asked how they were, he said, "What about your elderly father? Is he still alive?"

28 They answered, "Your servant our father is still alive and well." And again they bowed down to Joseph.

29 When Joseph looked around and saw his brother Benjamin, he said, "This must be your youngest brother, the one you told me about. God bless you, my son."

30 Right away he rushed off to his room and cried because of his love for Benjamin. 31 After washing his face and returning, he was able to control himself and said, "Serve the meal!"

32 Joseph was served at a table by himself, and his brothers were served at another. The Egyptians sat at yet another table, because Egyptians felt it was disgusting to eat with Hebrews. 33 To the surprise of Joseph's brothers, they were seated in front of him according to their ages, from the oldest to the youngest. 34 They were served food from Joseph's table, and Benjamin was given five times as much as each of the others. So Joseph's brothers drank with him and had a good time.

The Missing Cup

44 1-2 Later, Joseph told the servant in charge of his house, "Fill the men's grain sacks with as much as they can hold and put their money in the sacks. Also put my silver cup in the sack of the youngest brother." The servant did as he was told.

3 Early the next morning, the men were sent on their way with their donkeys. 4 But they had not gone far from the city when Joseph told the servant, "Go after those men! When you catch them, say, 'My master has been good to you. So why have you stolen his silver cup? 5 Not only does he drink from his cup, but he also uses it to learn about the future. You have done a terrible thing.' "

6 When the servant caught up with them, he said exactly what Joseph had told him to say. 7 But they replied, "Sir, why do you say such things? We would never do anything like that! 8 We even returned the money we found in our grain sacks when we got back to Canaan. So why would we want to steal any silver or gold from your master's house? 9 If you find that one of us has the cup, then kill him, and the rest of us will become your slaves."

10 "Good!" the man replied, "I'll do what you have said. But only the one who has the cup will become my slave. The rest of you can go free."

11 Each of the brothers quickly put his sack on the ground and opened it. 12 Joseph's servant started searching the sacks, beginning with the one that belonged to the oldest brother. When he came to Benjamin's sack, he found the cup. 13 This upset the brothers so much that they began tearing their clothes in sorrow. Then they loaded their donkeys and returned to the city.

14 When Judah and his brothers got there, Joseph was still at home. So they bowed down to Joseph, 15 who asked them, "What have you done? Didn't you know I could find out?"

16 "Sir, what can we say?" Judah replied. "How can we prove we are innocent? God has shown that we are guilty. And now all of us are your slaves, especially the one who had the cup."

17 Joseph told them, "I would never punish all of you. Only the one who was caught with the cup will become my slave. The rest of you are free to go home to your father."

Judah Pleads for Benjamin

[18] Judah went over to Joseph and said:
Sir, you have as much power as the king[v] himself, and I am only your slave. Please don't get angry if I speak.
[19] You asked us if our father was still alive and if we had any more brothers.
[20] So we told you, "Our father is a very old man. In fact, he was already old when Benjamin was born. Benjamin's brother is dead. Now Benjamin is the only one of the two brothers who is still alive, and our father loves him very much."
[21] You ordered us to bring him here, so you could see him for yourself.
[22] We told you that our father would die if Benjamin left him. [23] But you warned us that we could never see you again, unless our youngest brother came with us. [24] So we returned to our father and reported what you had said.
[25] Later our father told us to come back here and buy more grain. [26] But we answered, "We can't go back to Egypt without our youngest brother. We will never be let in to see the governor, unless he is with us."
[27] Sir, our father then reminded us that his favorite wife had given birth to two sons. [28] One of them was already missing and had not been seen for a long time. My father thinks the boy was torn to pieces by some wild animal, [29] and he said, "I am an old man. If you take Benjamin from me, and something happens to him, I will die of a broken heart."
[30] That's why Benjamin must be with us when I go back to my father. He loves him so much [31] that he will die if Benjamin doesn't come back with me. [32] I promised my father that I would bring him safely home. If I don't, I told my father he could blame me the rest of my life.
[33] Sir, I am your slave. Please let me stay here in place of Benjamin and let him return home with his brothers.
[34] How can I face my father if Benjamin isn't with me? I couldn't bear to see my father in such sorrow.

Joseph Tells His Brothers Who He Is

45 Since Joseph could no longer control his feelings in front of his servants, he sent them out of the room. When he was alone with his brothers, he told them, "I am Joseph." [2] Then he cried so loudly that the Egyptians heard him and told about it in the king's[v] palace.
[3] Joseph asked his brothers if his father was still alive, but they were too frightened to answer. [4] Joseph told them to come closer to him, and when they did, he said:
Yes, I am your brother Joseph, the one you sold into Egypt. [5] Don't worry or blame yourselves for what you did. God is the one who sent me ahead of you to save lives.
[6] There has already been a famine for two years, and for five more years no one will plow fields or harvest grain. [7] But God sent me on ahead of you to keep your families alive and to save you in this wonderful way.
[8] After all, you weren't really the ones who sent me here—it was God. He made me the highest official in the king's court and placed me over all Egypt.
[9] Now hurry back and tell my father that his son Joseph says, "God has made me ruler of Egypt. Come here as quickly as you can. [10] You will live near me in the region of Goshen with your children and grandchildren, as well as with your sheep, goats, cattle, and everything else you own. [11] I will take care of you there during the next five years of famine. But if you don't come, you and your family and your animals will starve to death."
[12] All of you, including my brother Benjamin, can tell by what I have said that I really am Joseph. [13] Tell my father about my great power here in

[v]**44.18; 45.2; 46.5-7** *the king*: See the note at 12.15.
45.1 Ac 7.13. **45.9-11** Ac 7.14.

Egypt and about everything you have
seen. Hurry and bring him here.
14 Joseph and Benjamin hugged each
other and started crying. 15 Joseph was still
crying as he kissed each of his other brothers. After this, they started talking with
Joseph.
16 When it was told in the palace that
Joseph's brothers had come, the king and
his officials were happy. 17 So the king said
to Joseph:

> Tell your brothers to load their
> donkeys and return to Canaan.
> 18 Have them bring their father and
> their families here. I will give them the
> best land in Egypt, and they can eat
> and enjoy everything that grows on
> it. 19 Also tell your brothers to take
> some wagons from Egypt for their
> wives and children to ride in. And be
> sure to have them bring their father.
> 20 They can leave their possessions
> behind, because they will be given the
> best of everything in Egypt.

21 Jacob's sons agreed to do what the
king had said. And Joseph gave them wagons and food for their trip home, just as the
king had ordered. 22 Joseph gave some new
clothes to each of his brothers, but to Benjamin he gave five new outfits and three
hundred pieces of silver. 23 To his father he
sent ten donkeys loaded with the best
things in Egypt, and ten other donkeys
loaded with grain and bread and other food
for the return trip. 24 Then he sent his
brothers off and told them, "Don't argue on
the way home!"
25 Joseph's brothers left Egypt, and
when they arrived in Canaan, 26 they told
their father that Joseph was still alive and
was the ruler of Egypt. But their father was
so surprised that he could not believe
them. 27 Then they told him everything
Joseph had said. When he saw the wagons
Joseph had sent, he felt much better 28 and
said, "Now I can believe you! My son
Joseph must really be alive, and I will get to
see him before I die."

Jacob and His Family Go to Egypt

46 Jacob packed up everything he
owned and left for Egypt. On the
way he stopped near the town of Beersheba
and offered sacrifices to the God his father
Isaac had worshiped. 2 That night, God
spoke to him and said, "Jacob! Jacob!"
"Here I am," Jacob answered.
3 God said, "I am God, the same God
your father worshiped. Don't be afraid to go
to Egypt. I will give you so many descendants that one day they will become a nation. 4 I will go with you to Egypt, and later
I will bring your descendants back here.
Your son Joseph will be at your side when
you die."
5-7 Jacob and his family set out from
Beersheba and headed for Egypt. His sons
put him in the wagon that the king[v] had
sent for him, and they put their small children and their wives in the other wagons. Jacob's whole family went to Egypt, including
his sons, his grandsons, his daughters, and
his granddaughters. They took along their
animals and everything else they owned.
8-15 When Jacob went to Egypt, his children who were born in northern Syria[w]
also went along with their families.

Jacob and his wife Leah had a total of
thirty-three children, grandchildren, and
great-grandchildren, but two of their grandchildren had died in Canaan.

> Their oldest son Reuben took his
> sons Hanoch, Pallu, Hezron, and
> Carmi.
>
> Their son Simeon took his sons Je-
> muel, Jamin, Ohad, Jachin, Zohar, and
> Shaul, whose mother was a Canaanite.
>
> Their son Levi took his sons Ger-
> shon, Kohath, and Merari.
>
> Their son Judah took his sons She-
> lah, Perez, and Zerah. Judah's sons Er
> and Onan had died in Canaan. Judah's
> son Perez took his sons Hezron and
> Hamul.
>
> Their son Issachar took his sons
> Tola, Puvah, Jashub,[x] and Shimron.

[v]**44.18; 45.2; 46.5-7** *the king*: See the note at 12.15. [w]**46.8-15** *northern Syria*: See the note at 24.10. [x]**46.8-15** *Jashub*: The Samaritan Hebrew Text and one ancient translation; the Standard Hebrew Text "Iob."

46.5-7 Ac 7.15.

Their son Zebulun took his sons
Sered, Elon, and Jahleel.
Their daughter Dinah also went.
16-18 Jacob and Zilpah, the servant
woman Laban had given his daughter
Leah, had a total of sixteen children,
grandchildren, and great-grandchildren.
Their son Gad took his sons
Ziphion, Haggi, Shuni, Ezbon, Eri,
Arodi, and Areli.
Their son Asher took his sons Im-
nah, Ishvah, Ishvi, and Beriah, who
took his sons, Heber and Malchiel.
Serah, the daughter of Asher, also
went.
19-22 Jacob and Rachel had fourteen
children and grandchildren.
Their son Joseph was already in
Egypt, where he had married Asenath,
daughter of Potiphera, the priest of
Heliopolis.[y] Joseph and Asenath had
two sons, Manasseh and Ephraim.
Jacob and Rachel's son Benjamin
took his sons Bela, Becher, Ashbel,
Gera, Naaman, Ehi, Rosh, Muppim,
Huppim, and Ard.
23-25 Jacob and Bilhah, the servant
woman Laban had given his daughter
Rachel, had seven children and grandchildren.
Their son Dan took his son
Hushim.
Their son Naphtali took his sons
Jahzeel, Guni, Jezer, and Shillem.
26 Sixty-six members of Jacob's family
went to Egypt with him, not counting
his daughters-in-law. 27 Jacob's two grandsons who were born there made it a total of
seventy members of Jacob's family in
Egypt.
28 Jacob had sent his son Judah ahead
of him to ask Joseph to meet them in
Goshen. 29 So Joseph got in his chariot and
went to meet his father. When they met,
Joseph hugged his father around the neck
and cried for a long time. 30 Jacob said to
Joseph, "Now that I have seen you and
know you are still alive, I am ready to die."
31 Then Joseph said to his brothers and
to everyone who had come with them:
I must go and tell the king[z] that you
have arrived from Canaan. 32 I will tell
him that you are shepherds and that
you have brought your sheep, goats,
cattle, and everything else you own.
33 The king will call you in and ask
what you do for a living. 34 When he
does, be sure to say, "We are shepherds. Our families have always raised
sheep." If you tell him this, he will let
you settle in the region of Goshen.
Joseph wanted them to say this to the
king, because the Egyptians did not like to
be around anyone who raised sheep.

47 1-2 Joseph took five of his brothers
to the king and told him, "My
father and my brothers have come from
Canaan. They have brought their sheep,
goats, cattle, and everything else they own
to the region of Goshen."
Then he introduced his brothers to the
king, 3 who asked them, "What do you do
for a living?"
"Sir, we are shepherds," was their answer. "Our families have always raised
sheep. 4 But in our country all the pastures
are dried up, and our sheep have no grass
to eat. So we, your servants, have come
here. Please let us live in the region of
Goshen."
5 The king said to Joseph, "It's good that
your father and brothers have arrived. 6 I
will let them live anywhere they choose in
the land of Egypt, but I suggest that they
settle in Goshen, the best part of our
land. I would also like for your finest shepherds to watch after my own sheep and
goats."
7 Then Joseph brought his father Jacob
and introduced him to the king. Jacob gave
the king his blessing, 8 and the king asked
him, "How old are you?"
9 Jacob answered, "I have lived only a
hundred thirty years, and I have had to
move from place to place. My parents and
my grandparents also had to move from
place to place. But they lived much longer,
and their life was not as hard as mine."
10 Then Jacob gave the king his blessing
once again and left. 11 Joseph obeyed the

[y]**46.19-22** *Heliopolis*: See the note at 41.45.
46.19-22 Gn 41.50-52. **46.27** Ac 7.14.

[z]**46.31** *the king*: See the note at 12.15.

king's orders and gave his father and brothers some of the best land in Egypt near the
city of Rameses. 12 Joseph also provided
food for their families.

A Famine in Egypt

13 The famine was bad everywhere in
Egypt and Canaan, and the people were
suffering terribly. 14 So Joseph sold them
the grain that had been stored up, and he
put the money[a] in the king's treasury.
15 But when everyone had run out of
money, the Egyptians came to Joseph and
demanded, "Give us more grain! If you
don't, we'll soon be dead, because our
money's all gone."
16 "If you don't have any money," Joseph
answered, "give me your animals, and I'll
let you have some grain." 17 From then on,
they brought him their horses and donkeys
and their sheep and goats in exchange for
grain.

Within a year Joseph had collected
every animal in Egypt. 18 Then the people
came to him and said:

> Sir, there's no way we can hide the
> truth from you. We are broke, and we
> don't have any more animals. We have
> nothing left except ourselves and our
> land. 19 Don't let us starve and our
> land be ruined. If you'll give us grain
> to eat and seed to plant, we'll sell our-
> selves and our land to the king.[b] We'll
> become his slaves.

20 The famine became so severe that
Joseph finally bought every piece of land in
Egypt for the king 21 and made everyone
the king's slaves,[c] 22 except the priests. The
king gave the priests a regular food allowance, so they did not have to sell their
land. 23 Then Joseph said to the people,
"You and your land now belong to the king.
I'm giving you seed to plant, 24 but one-
fifth of your crops must go to the king. You
can keep the rest as seed or as food for
your families."
25 "Sir, you have saved our lives!" they
answered. "We are glad to be slaves of the
king." 26 Then Joseph made a law that one-
fifth of the harvest would always belong to
the king. Only the priests did not lose their
land.

Jacob Becomes an Old Man

27 The people of Israel made their home
in the land of Goshen, where they became
prosperous and had large families. 28 Jacob
himself lived there for seventeen years, before dying at the age of one hundred forty-
seven. 29 When Jacob knew he did not have
long to live, he called in Joseph and said,
"If you really love me, you must make a
solemn promise not to bury me in Egypt.
30 Instead, bury me in the place where my
ancestors are buried."

"I will do what you have asked," Joseph
answered.
31 "Will you give me your word?" Jacob
asked.

"Yes, I will," Joseph promised. After this,
Jacob bowed down and prayed at the head
of his bed.

Jacob Blesses Joseph's Two Sons

48 Joseph was told that his father Jacob had become very sick. So
Joseph went to see him and took along his
two sons, Manasseh and Ephraim. 2 When
Joseph arrived, someone told Jacob, "Your
son Joseph has come to see you." Jacob sat
up in bed, but it took almost all his
strength.
3 Jacob told Joseph:

> God All-Powerful appeared to me at
> Luz in the land of Canaan, where he
> gave me his blessing 4 and promised, "I
> will give you a large family with many
> descendants that will grow into a na-
> tion. And I am giving you this land that
> will belong to you and your family
> forever."

5 Then Jacob went on to say:

> Joseph, your two sons Ephraim and
> Manasseh were born in Egypt, but I
> accept them as my own, just as
> Reuben and Simeon are mine. 6 Any

[a] **47.14** *money*: See the note at 42.25. [b] **47.19** *the king*: See the note at 12.15.
[c] **47.21** *made . . . slaves*: One ancient translation and the Samaritan Hebrew Text; the Standard Hebrew Text "made everyone move to the cities."
47.29,30 Gn 49.29-32; 50.6. **48.3,4** Gn 28.13, 14.

children you have later will be considered yours, but their inheritance will come from Ephraim and Manasseh.
7 Unfortunately, your mother Rachel died in Canaan after we had left northern Syria[d] and before we reached Bethlehem.[e] And I had to bury her along the way.
8-10 Jacob was very old and almost blind. He did not recognize the two boys, and so he asked Joseph, "Who are these boys?"

Joseph answered, "They are my sons. God has given them to me here in Egypt."

"Bring them to me," Jacob said. "I want to give them my blessing." Joseph brought the boys to him, and he hugged and kissed them.

11 Jacob turned to Joseph and told him, "For many years I thought you were dead and that I would never see you again. But now God has even let me live to see your children."
12 Then Joseph made his sons move away from Jacob's knees,[f] and Joseph bowed down in front of him with his face to the ground.

13 After Joseph got up, he brought his two sons over to Jacob again. He led his younger son Ephraim to the left side of Jacob and his older son Manasseh to the right.
14 But before Jacob gave them his blessing, he crossed his arms, putting his right hand on the head of Ephraim and his left hand on the head of Manasseh.
15 Then he gave Joseph his blessing and said:

> My grandfather Abraham and my father Isaac worshiped the LORD God. He has been with me all my life,
> 16 and his angel has kept me safe. Now I pray that he will bless these boys and that my name and the names of Abraham and Isaac will live on because of them. I ask God to give them many children and many descendants as well.

17 Joseph did not like it when he saw his father place his right hand on the head of the younger son. So he tried to move his father's right hand from Ephraim's head and place it on Manasseh.
18 Joseph said, "Father, you have made a mistake. This is the older boy. Put your right hand on him."

19 But his father said, "Son, I know what I am doing. It's true that Manasseh's family will someday become a great nation. But Ephraim will be even greater than Manasseh, because his descendants will become many great nations."

20 Jacob told him that in the future the people of Israel would ask God's blessings on one another by saying, "I pray for God to bless you as much as he blessed Ephraim and Manasseh." Jacob put Ephraim's name first to show that he would be greater than Manasseh.
21 After that, Jacob said, "Joseph, you can see that I won't live much longer. But God will be with you and will lead you back to the land he promised our family long ago.
22 Meanwhile, I'm giving you the hillside[g] I captured from the Amorites."

Jacob Blesses His Sons

49 *1 Jacob called his sons together and said:

My sons, I am Jacob,
your father Israel.
2 Come, gather around,
as I tell your future.

3 Reuben, you are my oldest,
born at the peak of my powers;
you were an honored leader.
4 Uncontrollable as a flood,
you slept with my wife
and disgraced my bed.
And so you no longer deserve
the place of honor.

5 Simeon and Levi,
you are brothers,
each a gruesome sword.
6 I never want to take part
in your plans or deeds.
You slaughtered people
in your anger,

[d]**48.7** *northern Syria*: See the note at 24.10. [e]**48.7** *Bethlehem*: The Hebrew text has "Ephrath, that is, Bethlehem." [f]**48.12** *move . . . Jacob's knees*: The two boys were placed either on or between Jacob's knees, as a sign that he had accepted them as his sons. [g]**48.22** *the hillside*: Or "a larger share than your brothers, the land."

48.7 Gn 35.16-19. **48.20** He 11.21.

and you crippled cattle
for no reason.
7 Now I place a curse on you
because of
your fierce anger.
Your descendants
will be scattered
among the tribes of Israel.

8 Judah, you will be praised
by your brothers;
they will bow down to you,
as you defeat your enemies.
9 My son, you are a lion
ready to eat your victim!
You are terribly fierce;
no one will bother you.
10 You will have power and rule
until nations obey you[h]
and come bringing gifts.
11 You will tie your donkey
to a choice grapevine
and wash your clothes
in wine from those grapes.
12 Your eyes are darker than wine,
your teeth whiter than milk.

13 Zebulun, you will settle
along the seashore
and provide safe harbors
as far north as Sidon.

14 Issachar, you are a strong donkey
resting in the meadows.[i]
15 You found them so pleasant
that you worked too hard
and became a slave.

16 Dan,[j] you are the tribe
that will bring justice
to Israel.
17 You are a snake that bites
the heel of a horse,
making its rider fall.

18 Our LORD, I am waiting
for you to save us.

19 Gad,[k] you will be attacked,
then attack your attackers.

20 Asher, you will eat food
fancy enough for a king.

21 Naphtali, you are a wild deer
with lovely fawns.[l]

22 Joseph, you are a fruitful vine
growing near a stream
and climbing a wall.[m]
23 Enemies attacked with arrows,
refusing to show mercy.
24 But you stood your ground,
swiftly shooting back
with the help of Jacob's God,
the All-Powerful One—
his name is the Shepherd,
Israel's mighty rock.[n]
25 Your help came from the God
your father worshiped,
from God All-Powerful.
God will bless you with rain
and streams from the earth;
he will bless you
with many descendants.
26 My son, the blessings I give
are better than the promise
of ancient mountains
or eternal hills.[o]
Joseph, I pray these blessings
will come to you,
because you are the leader
of your brothers.

27 Benjamin, you are a fierce wolf,
destroying your enemies
morning and evening.

28 These are the twelve tribes of Israel, and this is how Jacob gave each of them their proper blessings.

[h] **49.10** *until . . . you*: One possible meaning for the difficult Hebrew text. [i] **49.14** *resting . . . meadows*: One possible meaning for the difficult Hebrew text. [j] **49.16** *Dan*: In Hebrew "Dan" means "justice" or "judgment." [k] **49.19** *Gad*: In Hebrew "Gad" sounds like "attack." [l] **49.21** *with lovely fawns*: Or "speaking lovely words." [m] **49.22** *wall*: One possible meaning for the difficult Hebrew text. [n] **49.24** *mighty rock*: The Hebrew text has "rock," which is sometimes used in poetry to compare the LORD to a mountain where his people can run for protection from their enemies. [o] **49.26** *eternal hills*: One possible meaning for the difficult Hebrew text.

49.9 Nu 24.9; Rev 5.5.

Jacob's Death

29-31 Jacob told his sons:

Soon I will die, and I want you to bury me in Machpelah Cave. Abraham bought this cave as a burial place from Ephron the Hittite, and it is near the town of Mamre in Canaan. Abraham and Sarah are buried there, and so are Isaac and Rebekah. I buried Leah there too. 32 Both the cave and the land that goes with it were bought from the Hittites.

33 When Jacob had finished giving these instructions to his sons, he lay down on his bed and died.
50
1 Joseph started crying, then leaned over to hug and kiss his father.

2 Joseph gave orders for Jacob's body to be embalmed, 3 and it took the usual forty days.

The Egyptians mourned seventy days for Jacob. 4 When the time of mourning was over, Joseph said to the Egyptian leaders, "If you consider me your friend, please speak to the king[p] for me. 5 Just before my father died, he made me promise to bury him in his burial cave in Canaan. If the king will give me permission to go, I will come back here."

6 The king answered, "Go to Canaan and keep your promise to your father."

7-9 When Joseph left Goshen with his brothers, his relatives, and his father's relatives to bury Jacob, many of the king's highest officials and even his military chariots and cavalry went along. The Israelites left behind only their children, their cattle, and their sheep and goats.

10 After crossing the Jordan River and reaching Atad's threshing place, Joseph had everyone mourn and weep seven days for his father. 11 The Canaanites saw this and said, "The Egyptians are in great sorrow." Then they named the place "Egypt in Sorrow."[q]

12 So Jacob's sons did just as their father had instructed. 13 They took him to Canaan and buried him in Machpelah Cave, the burial place Abraham had bought from Ephron the Hittite.

14 After the funeral, Joseph, his brothers, and everyone else returned to Egypt.

Joseph's Promise to His Brothers

15 After Jacob died, Joseph's brothers said to each other, "What if Joseph still hates us and wants to get even with us for all the cruel things we did to him?"

16 So they sent this message to Joseph:

Before our father died, 17 he told us, "You did some cruel and terrible things to Joseph, but you must ask him to forgive you."

Now we ask you to please forgive the terrible things we did. After all, we serve the same God that your father worshiped.

When Joseph heard this, he started crying.

18 Right then, Joseph's brothers came and bowed down to the ground in front of him and said, "We are your slaves."

19 But Joseph told them, "Don't be afraid! I have no right to change what God has decided. 20 You tried to harm me, but God made it turn out for the best, so that he could save all these people, as he is now doing. 21 Don't be afraid! I will take care of you and your children." After Joseph said this, his brothers felt much better.

Joseph's Death

22 Joseph lived in Egypt with his brothers until he died at the age of one hundred ten. 23 Joseph lived long enough to see Ephraim's children and grandchildren. He also lived to see the children of Manasseh's son Machir, and he welcomed them into his family. 24 Before Joseph died, he told his brothers, "I won't live much longer. But God will take care of you and lead you out of Egypt to the land he promised Abraham, Isaac, and Jacob. 25 Now promise me that you will take my body with you when God leads you to that land."

26 So Joseph died in Egypt at the age of one hundred ten; his body was embalmed and put in a coffin.

[p] **50.4** *the king*: See the note at 12.15. [q] **50.11** *Egypt in Sorrow*: Or "Abel-Mizraim."

49.29-31 a Gn 23.3-20; **b** Gn 25.9, 10; **c** Gn 35.28, 29. **49.33** Ac 7.15. **50.5** Gn 47.29-31. **50.13** Ac 7.16. **50.25** Ex 13.19; Js 24.32; He 11.22.

EXODUS

ABOUT THIS BOOK

The title "Exodus" comes from a Greek word meaning "going out," and this book tells how the Lord set his people Israel free from slavery and brought them out of Egypt.

The book of Exodus teaches that the Lord is the one true God and the ruler of all creation. And when the Lord decides to do something, no one can stop him.

Exodus can be divided into three parts. Most of the events in the first part (1–13) take place in Egypt, where the people of Israel had been made slaves by the king. The Lord heard their cries for help and chose Moses to set them free. Moses was an Israelite who had been adopted by an Egyptian princess.

When Moses demanded that the Israelites be set free, the king refused. And so the Lord told Moses to bring ten disasters on Egypt. These disasters have often been called "the ten plagues." Finally, the king let the Israelites leave Egypt.

The second part of the book (14–18) includes events that happened while the people of Israel were on their way to Mount Sinai, God's holy mountain. The king of Egypt quickly changed his mind about setting them free, and he ordered his army to capture them. But the Lord protected Israel and destroyed the Egyptian army. Then, as the Israelites traveled through the desert, the Lord provided food and water for them.

The final part of Exodus (19–40) takes place at Mount Sinai, where the Lord appeared to Moses. The Lord gave him the Ten Commandments, as well as laws for worship, sacrifice, and everyday life, and instructions on making the sacred tent and its furnishings, the altars, and the priestly clothes. But this part also tells how the people made an idol and disobeyed the first of the Ten Commandments:

> *"I am the LORD your God, the one who brought you out of Egypt where you were slaves.*
> *"Do not worship any god except me."*
> *(20.2, 3)*

A QUICK LOOK AT THIS BOOK

- The People of Israel Become Slaves (1.1-22)
- Moses Is Born and Grows Up (2.1-25)
- God Sends Moses To Speak to the King of Egypt (3.1—6.30)
- The First Nine Disasters (7.1—10.29)
- The Last Disaster and the First Passover (11.1—13.22)
- The People Cross the Red Sea (14.1—15.21)
- Moses Leads the People to Mount Sinai (15.22—18.27)
- The Ten Commandments and Other Laws (19.1—24.18)
- Instructions for the Sacred Tent, Its Furnishings, and the Sacred Chest (25.1—27.21)
- Instructions for the Priests, Sacrifices, and the Sabbath (28.1—31.18)
- The People Make an Idol (32.1-35)
- The Lord Makes Promises, Renews His Agreement, and Gives More Laws to Israel (33.1—35.3)

- Offerings and Gifts for the Sacred Tent and the Priestly Clothes (35.4—36.7)
- Skilled Workers Make the Sacred Tent and Its Furnishings (36.8—38.31)
- The Priestly Clothes Are Made (39.1-31)
- The Sacred Tent Is Set Up (39.32—40.38)

The People of Israel Suffer

1 1-5 When Jacob went to Egypt, his son Joseph was already there. So Jacob took his eleven other sons and their families. They were: Reuben, Simeon, Levi, Judah, Issachar, Zebulun, Benjamin, Dan, Naphtali, Gad, and Asher. Altogether, Jacob had seventy children, grandchildren, and great-grandchildren[a] who went with him.

6 After Joseph, his brothers, and everyone else in that generation had died, 7 the people of Israel became so numerous that the whole region of Goshen was full of them.

8 Many years later a new king came to power. He did not know what Joseph had done for Egypt, 9 and he told the Egyptians:

> There are too many of those Israelites in our country, and they are becoming more powerful than we are. 10 If we don't outsmart them, their families will keep growing larger. And if our country goes to war, they could easily fight on the side of our enemies and escape from Egypt.

11 The Egyptians put slave bosses in charge of the people of Israel and tried to wear them down with hard work. Those bosses forced them to build the cities of Pithom and Rameses,[b] where the king[c] could store his supplies. 12 But even though the Israelites were mistreated, their families grew larger, and they took over more land. Because of this, the Egyptians hated them worse than before 13 and made them work so hard 14 that their lives were miserable. The Egyptians were cruel to the people of Israel and forced them to make bricks and to mix mortar and to work in the fields.

15 Finally, the king called in Shiphrah and Puah, the two women who helped the Hebrew[d] mothers when they gave birth. 16 He told them, "If a Hebrew woman gives birth to a girl, let the child live. If the baby is a boy, kill him!"

17 But the two women were faithful to God and did not kill the boys, even though the king had told them to. 18 The king called them in again and asked, "Why are you letting those baby boys live?"

19 They answered, "Hebrew women have their babies much quicker than Egyptian women. By the time we arrive, their babies are already born." 20-21 God was good to the two women because they truly respected him, and he blessed them with children of their own.

The Hebrews kept increasing 22 until finally, the king gave a command to everyone in the nation, "As soon as a Hebrew boy is born, throw him into the Nile River! But you can let the girls live."

Moses Is Born

2 A man from the Levi tribe married a woman from the same tribe, 2 and she later had a baby boy. He was a beautiful child, and she kept him inside for three months. 3 But when she could no longer keep him hidden, she made a basket out of

[a] **1.1-5** *seventy children . . . great-grandchildren*: See Genesis 46.8-27. [b] **1.11** *Pithom and Rameses*: This is the only mention of Pithom in the Bible; its exact location is unknown, though it was probably in the northern Delta of Egypt. Rameses is the famous Delta city that was the home of Rameses II; its exact location is also unknown. [c] **1.11** *the king*: The Hebrew text has "Pharaoh," a Hebrew word sometimes used for the title of the king of Egypt. [d] **1.15** *Hebrew*: An earlier term for "Israelite."

1.1-5 Gn 46.8-27. **1.7** Ac 7.17. **1.8** Ac 7.18. **1.10** 3 Macc 3.24; Ac 7.19. **1.22** Ac 7.19. **2.2** Ac 7.20; He 11.23.

reeds and covered it with tar. She put him in the basket and placed it in the tall grass along the edge of the Nile River. 4 The baby's older sister[e] stood off at a distance to see what would happen to him.

5 About that time one of the king's[f] daughters came down to take a bath in the river, while her servant women walked along the river bank. She saw the basket in the tall grass and sent one of the young women to pull it out of the water. 6 When the king's daughter opened the basket, she saw the baby and felt sorry for him because he was crying. She said, "This must be one of the Hebrew babies."

7 At once the baby's older sister came up and asked, "Do you want me to get a Hebrew woman to take care of the baby for you?"

8 "Yes," the king's daughter answered.

So the girl brought the baby's mother, 9 and the king's daughter told her, "Take care of this child, and I will pay you."

The baby's mother carried him home and took care of him. 10 And when he was old enough, she took him to the king's daughter, who adopted him. She named him Moses[g] because she said, "I pulled him out of the water."

Moses Escapes from Egypt

11 After Moses had grown up, he went out to where his own people were hard at work, and he saw an Egyptian beating one of them. 12 Moses looked around to see if anyone was watching, then he killed the Egyptian and hid his body in the sand.

13 When Moses went out the next day, he saw two Hebrews fighting. So he went to the man who had started the fight and asked, "Why are you beating up one of your own people?"

14 The man answered, "Who put you in charge of us and made you our judge? Are you planning to kill me, just as you killed that Egyptian?"

This frightened Moses because he was sure that people must have found out what had happened. 15 When the king[h] heard what Moses had done, the king wanted to kill him. But Moses escaped and went to the land of Midian.

One day, Moses was sitting there by a well, 16 when the seven daughters of Jethro, the priest of Midian,[i] came up to water their father's sheep and goats. 17 Some shepherds tried to chase them away, but Moses came to their rescue and watered their animals. 18 When Jethro's daughters returned home, their father asked, "Why have you come back so early today?"

19 They answered, "An Egyptian rescued us from the shepherds, and he even watered our sheep and goats."

20 "Where is he?" Jethro asked. "Why did you leave him out there? Invite him to eat with us."

21 Moses agreed to stay on with Jethro, who later let his daughter Zipporah marry Moses. 22 And when she had a son, Moses said, "I will name him Gershom,[j] since I am a foreigner in this country."

23 After the death of the king of Egypt, the Israelites still complained because they were forced to be slaves. They cried out for help, 24 and God heard their loud cries. He did not forget the promise he had made to Abraham, Isaac, and Jacob, 25 and because he knew what was happening to his people, he felt sorry for them.

God Speaks to Moses

3 One day, Moses was taking care of the sheep and goats of his father-in-law Jethro, the priest of Midian, and Moses decided to lead them across the desert to Sinai,[k] the holy mountain. 2 There an an-

[e]**2.4** *older sister*: Miriam, the sister of Moses and Aaron. [f]**2.5** *the king's*: See the note at 1.11. [g]**2.10** *Moses*: In Hebrew "Moses" sounds like "pull out." [h]**2.15** *the king*: See the note at 1.11. [i]**2.16** *Jethro, the priest of Midian*: Hebrew "the priest of Midian." But see 3.1; 4.18; 18.1, 2-4 where his name is given. In the Hebrew of verse 18 he is spoken of as "Reuel," which may have been the name of the tribe to which Jethro belonged. [j]**2.22** *Gershom*: In Hebrew "Gershom" sounds like "foreigner." [k]**3.1** *Sinai*: The Hebrew text has "Horeb," another name for Sinai.

2.10 3 Macc 3.24; Ac 7.21. **2.11-14** Ac 7.23-28. **2.11** He 11.24. **2.15** Ac 7.29; He 11.27. **2.24** Gn 15.13-15. **3.2-10** Ac 7.30-34.

gel of the LORD appeared to him from a
burning bush. Moses saw that the bush was
on fire, but it was not burning up. 3 "This is
strange!" he said to himself. "I'll go over
and see why the bush isn't burning up."
4 When the LORD saw Moses coming
near the bush, he called him by name, and
Moses answered, "Here I am."
5 God replied, "Don't come any closer.
Take off your sandals—the ground where
you are standing is holy. 6 I am the God
who was worshiped by your ancestors Abraham, Isaac, and Jacob."
Moses was afraid to look at God, and so
he hid his face.
7 The LORD said:
I have seen how my people are suffering as slaves in Egypt, and I have
heard them beg for my help because of
the way they are being mistreated. I
feel sorry for them, 8 and I have come
down to rescue them from the Egyptians.
I will bring my people out of Egypt
into a country where there is good
land, rich with milk and honey. I will
give them the land where the Canaanites, Hittites, Amorites, Perizzites, Hivites, and Jebusites now live. 9 My
people have begged for my help, and I
have seen how cruel the Egyptians are
to them. 10 Now go to the king! I am
sending you to lead my people out of
his country.
11 But Moses said, "Who am I to go to
the king and lead your people out of
Egypt?"
12 God replied, "I will be with you. And
you will know that I am the one who sent
you, when you worship me on this mountain after you have led my people out of
Egypt."[l]
13 Moses answered, "I will tell the people of Israel that the God their ancestors
worshiped has sent me to them. But what
should I say, if they ask me your name?"
14-15 God said to Moses:
I am the eternal God. So tell them
that the LORD,[m] whose name is "I
Am," has sent you. This is my name
forever, and it is the name that people
must use from now on.
16 Call together the leaders of Israel
and tell them that the God who was
worshiped by Abraham, Isaac, and Jacob has appeared to you. Tell them I
have seen how terribly they are being
treated in Egypt, 17 and I promise to
lead them out of their troubles. I will
give them a land rich with milk and
honey, where the Canaanites, Hittites,
Amorites, Perizzites, Hivites, and Jebusites now live.
18 The leaders of Israel will listen to
you. Then you must take them to the
king of Egypt and say, "The LORD God
of the Hebrews has appeared to us. Let
us walk three days into the desert,
where we can offer a sacrifice to him."
19 But I know that the king of Egypt
won't let you go unless something
forces him to. 20 So I will use my
mighty power to perform all kinds of
miracles and strike down the Egyptians. Then the king will send you
away.
21 After I punish the Egyptians,
they will be so afraid of you that they
will give you anything you want.
You are my people, and I will let
you take many things with you when
you leave the land of Egypt. 22 Every
Israelite woman will go to her
Egyptian neighbors or to any Egyptian
woman living in her house. She
will ask them for gold and silver
jewelry and for their finest clothes.
The Egyptians will give them to
you, and you will put these fine things
on your sons and daughters. You will
carry all this away when you leave
Egypt.

[l] **3.12** *I will be with you . . . out of Egypt*: Or "I will be with you. This bush is a sign that I am the one sending you, and it is a promise that you will worship me on this mountain after you have led my people out of Egypt." [m] **3.14,15** *LORD*: The Hebrew text has "Yahweh," which is usually translated "LORD" in the CEV. Since it seems related to the word translated "I am," it may mean "I am the one who is" or "I will be what I will be" or "I am the one who brings into being."

3.13 Ex 6.2, 3. **3.14,15** Rev 1.4, 8. **3.21,22** Ex 12.35, 36. **3.21** Ws 10.17.

The LORD Gives Great Power to Moses

4 Moses asked the LORD, "Suppose everyone refuses to listen to my message, and no one believes that you really appeared to me?"

2 The LORD answered, "What's that in your hand?"

"A walking stick," Moses replied.

3 "Throw it down!" the LORD commanded. So Moses threw the stick on the ground. It immediately turned into a snake, and Moses jumped back.

4 "Pick it up by the tail!" the LORD told him. And when Moses did this, the snake turned back into a walking stick.

5 "Do this," the LORD said, "and the Israelites will believe that you have seen me, the God who was worshiped by their ancestors Abraham, Isaac, and Jacob."

6 Next, the LORD commanded Moses, "Put your hand inside your shirt." Moses obeyed, and when he took it out, his hand had turned white as snow—like someone with leprosy.[n]

7 "Put your hand back inside your shirt," the LORD told him. Moses did so, and when he took it out again, it was as healthy as the rest of his body.

8-9 Then the LORD said, "If no one believes either of these miracles, take some water from the Nile River and pour it on the ground. The water will immediately turn into blood."

10 Moses replied, "I have never been a good speaker. I wasn't one before you spoke to me, and I'm not one now. I am slow at speaking, and I can never think of what to say."

11 But the LORD answered, "Who makes people able to speak or makes them deaf or unable to speak? Who gives them sight or makes them blind? Don't you know that I am the one who does these things? 12 Now go! When you speak, I will be with you and give you the words to say."

13 Moses begged, "LORD, please send someone else to do it."

14 The LORD became irritated with Moses and said:

What about your brother Aaron, the Levite? I know he is a good speaker. He is already on his way here to visit you, and he will be happy to see you again. 15-16 Aaron will speak to the people for you, and you will be like me, telling Aaron what to say. I will be with both of you as you speak, and I will tell each of you what to do. 17 Now take this walking stick and use it to perform miracles.

Moses Returns to Egypt

18 Moses went to his father-in-law Jethro and asked, "Please let me return to Egypt to see if any of my people are still alive."

"All right," Jethro replied. "I hope all goes well."

19 But even before this, the LORD had told Moses, "Leave the land of Midian and return to Egypt. Everyone who wanted to kill you is dead." 20 So Moses put his wife and sons on donkeys and headed for Egypt, holding the walking stick that had the power of God.

21 On the way the LORD said to Moses:

When you get to Egypt, go to the king and work the miracles I have shown you. But I will make him so stubborn that he will refuse to let my people go. 22 Then tell him that I have said, "Israel is my first-born son,
23 and I commanded you to release him, so he could worship me. But you refused, and now I will kill your first-born son."

Zipporah's Son Is Circumcised

24 One night while Moses was in camp, the LORD was about to kill him. 25 But Zipporah[o] circumcised her son with a flint knife. She touched his[p] legs with the skin she had cut off and said, "My dear son, this blood will protect you."[q] 26 So the LORD did not harm Moses. Then Zipporah said, "Yes,

[n] **4.6** *leprosy*: The word translated "leprosy" was used for many different kinds of skin diseases.
[o] **4.25** *Zipporah*: The wife of Moses (see 2.16-21). [p] **4.25** *his*: Either Moses or the boy.
[q] **4.25** *My dear son . . . you*: Or "My dear husband, you are a man of blood" (meaning Moses).
4.23 Ex 12.29.

my dear, you are safe because of this circumcision."[r]

Aaron Is Sent To Meet Moses

27 The LORD sent Aaron to meet Moses in the desert. So Aaron met Moses at Mount Sinai[s] and greeted him with a kiss. 28 Moses told Aaron what God had sent him to say; he also told him about the miracles God had given him the power to perform.

29 Later they brought together the leaders of Israel, 30 and Aaron told them what the LORD had sent Moses to say. Then Moses worked the miracles for the people, 31 and everyone believed. They bowed down and worshiped the LORD because they knew that he had seen their suffering and was going to help them.

Moses and Aaron Go to the King of Egypt

5 Moses and Aaron went to the king[t] of Egypt and told him, "The LORD God says, 'Let my people go into the desert, so they can honor me with a celebration there.' "

2 "Who is this LORD and why should I obey him?" the king replied. "I refuse to let you and your people go!"

3 They answered, "The LORD God of the Hebrews, has appeared to us. Please let us walk three days into the desert where we can offer sacrifices to him. If you don't, he may strike us down with terrible troubles or with war."

4-5 The king said, "Moses and Aaron, why are you keeping these people from working? Look how many you are keeping from doing their work. Now everyone get back to work!"

6 That same day the king gave orders to his slave bosses and to the men directly in charge of the Israelite slaves. He told them:

7 Don't give the slaves any more straw[u] to put in their bricks. Force them to find their own straw wherever they can, 8 but they must make the same number of bricks as before. They are lazy, or else they would not beg me to let them go and sacrifice to their God. 9 Make them work so hard that they won't have time to listen to these lies.

10 The slave bosses and the men in charge of the slaves went out and told them, "The king says he will not give you any more straw. 11 Go and find your own straw wherever you can, but you must still make as many bricks as before."

12 The slaves went all over Egypt, looking for straw. 13 But the slave bosses were hard on them and kept saying, "Each day you have to make as many bricks as you did when you were given straw." 14 The bosses beat the men in charge of the slaves and said, "Why didn't you force the slaves to make as many bricks yesterday and today as they did before?"

15 Finally, the men in charge of the slaves went to the king and said, "Why are you treating us like this? 16 No one brings us any straw, but we are still ordered to make the same number of bricks. We are beaten with whips, and your own people are to blame."

17 The king replied, "You are lazy—nothing but lazy! That's why you keep asking me to let you go and sacrifice to your LORD. 18 Get back to work! You won't be given straw, but you must still make the same number of bricks."

19 The men knew they were in deep trouble when they were ordered to make the same number of bricks each day. 20 After they left the king, they went to see Moses and Aaron, who had been waiting for them. 21 Then the men said, "We hope the LORD will punish both of you for making the king and his officials hate us. Now they even have an excuse to kill us."

The LORD's Promise to Moses

22 Moses left them and prayed, "Our LORD, why have you brought so much trouble on your people? Is that why you sent me here? 23 Ever since you told me to speak to the king,[v] he has caused nothing

[r] **4.26** *you are . . . circumcision*: Or "you are a man of blood." [s] **4.27** *Mount Sinai*: Hebrew "the mountain of God." [t] **5.1** *the king*: See the note at 1.11. [u] **5.7** *straw*: The straw made the mud bricks stronger and kept them from shrinking, cracking, or losing their shape. [v] **5.23** *the king*: See the note at 1.11.

but trouble for these people. And you haven't done a thing to help."

6 The LORD God told Moses:

Soon you will see what I will do to the king. Because of my mighty power, he will let my people go, and he will even chase them out of his country.

2 My name is the LORD.[w] 3 But when I appeared to Abraham, Isaac, and Jacob, I came as God All-Powerful and did not use my name. 4 I made an agreement and promised them the land of Canaan, where they were living as foreigners. 5 Now I have seen how the people of Israel are suffering because of the Egyptians, and I will keep my promise.

6 Here is my message for Israel: "I am the LORD! And with my mighty power I will punish the Egyptians and free you from slavery. 7 I will accept you as my people, and I will be your God. Then you will know that I was the one who rescued you from the Egyptians. 8 I will bring you into the land that I solemnly promised Abraham, Isaac, and Jacob, and it will be yours. I am the LORD!"

9 When Moses told this to the Israelites, they were too discouraged and mistreated to believe him.

10 Then the LORD told Moses 11 to demand that the king of Egypt let the Israelites leave. 12 But Moses replied, "I'm not a powerful speaker. If the Israelites won't listen to me, why should the king of Egypt?" 13 But the LORD sent Aaron and Moses with a message for the Israelites and for the king; he also ordered Aaron and Moses to free the people from Egypt.

Family Record of Aaron and Moses

14 The following men were the heads of their ancestral clans:

The sons of Reuben, Jacob's[x] oldest son, were Hanoch, Pallu, Hezron, and Carmi.

15 The sons of Simeon were Jemuel, Jamin, Ohad, Jachin, Zohar, and Shaul, the son of a Canaanite woman.

16 Levi lived to be one hundred thirty-seven; his sons were Gershon, Kohath, and Merari.

17 Gershon's sons were Libni and Shimei.

18 Kohath lived to be one hundred thirty-three; his sons were Amram, Izhar, Hebron, and Uzziel.

19 Merari's sons were Mahli and Mushi. All of the above were from the Levi tribe.

20 Amram lived to be one hundred thirty-seven. He married his father's sister Jochebed, and they had two sons, Aaron and Moses.

21 Izhar's sons were Korah, Nepheg, and Zichri.

22 Uzziel's sons were Mishael, Elzaphan, and Sithri.

23 Aaron married Elisheba. She was the daughter of Amminadab and the sister of Nahshon; they had four sons, Nadab, Abihu, Eleazar, and Ithamar.

24 Korah's sons were Assir, Elkanah, and Abiasaph.

25 Aaron's son Eleazar married one of Putiel's daughters, and their son was Phinehas. This ends the list of those who were the heads of clans in the Levi tribe.

26 The LORD had commanded Aaron and Moses to lead every family and tribe of Israel out of Egypt, 27 and so they ordered the king of Egypt to set the people of Israel free.

The LORD Commands Moses and Aaron To Speak to the King

28 When the LORD spoke to Moses in the land of Egypt, 29 he said, "I am the LORD. Tell the king[y] of Egypt everything I say to you."

30 But Moses answered, "You know I am a very poor speaker, and the king will never listen to me."

[w] **6.2** *My name is the LORD*: See the note at 3.14, 15. [x] **6.14** *Jacob*: The Hebrew text has "Israel," Jacob's name after God renamed him. [y] **6.29; 7.8,9,14; 8.1** *the king*: See the note at 1.11.

6.2,3 Gn 17.1; 28.3; 35.9-11; Ex 3.13-15. **6.16-19** Nu 3.17-20; 26.57, 58; 1 Ch 6.16-19.

7 The LORD said:
I am going to let your brother
Aaron speak for you. He will tell your
message to the king, just as a prophet
speaks my message to the people.
2 Tell Aaron everything I say to you,
and he will order the king to let my
people leave his country. 3-4 But I will
make the king so stubborn that he
won't listen to you. He won't listen
even when I do many terrible things to
him and his nation. Then I will bring a
final punishment on Egypt, and the
king will let Israel's families and tribes
go. 5 When this happens, the Egyptians will know that I am the LORD.
6 Moses and Aaron obeyed the LORD
7 and spoke to the king. At the time, Moses
was eighty years old, and Aaron was eighty-
three.

A Stick Turns into a Snake

8-9 The LORD said, "Moses, when the
king[y] asks you and Aaron to perform a miracle, command Aaron to throw his walking
stick down in front of the king, and it will
turn into a snake."
10 Moses and Aaron went to the king
and his officials and did exactly as the
LORD had commanded—Aaron threw the
stick down, and it turned into a snake.
11 Then the king called in the wise men
and the magicians, who used their secret
powers to do the same thing—12 they threw
down sticks that turned into snakes. But
Aaron's snake swallowed theirs. 13 The king
behaved just as the LORD had said and
stubbornly refused to listen.

The Nile River Turns into Blood

14 The LORD said to Moses:
The Egyptian king[y] stubbornly
refuses to change his mind and let
the people go. 15 Tomorrow morning
take the stick that turned into a snake,
then wait beside the Nile River for
the king. 16 Tell him, "The LORD God
of the Hebrews sent me to order you
to release his people, so they can
worship him in the desert. But
until now, you have paid no attention.
17 "The LORD is going to do something to show you that he really is the
LORD. I will strike the Nile with this
stick, and the water will turn into
blood. 18 The fish will die, the river will
stink, and none of you Egyptians will
be able to drink the water."
19 Moses, then command Aaron to
hold his stick over the water. And
when he does, every drop of water in
Egypt will turn into blood, including
rivers, canals, ponds, and even the water in buckets and jars.
20 Moses and Aaron obeyed the LORD.
Aaron held out his stick, then struck the
Nile, as the king and his officials watched.
The river turned into blood, 21 the fish
died, and the water smelled so bad that
none of the Egyptians could drink it. Blood
was everywhere in Egypt.
22 But the Egyptian magicians used
their secret powers to do the same thing.
The king did just as the LORD had said—he
stubbornly refused to listen. 23 Then he
went back to his palace and never gave it a
second thought. 24 The Egyptians had to
dig holes along the banks of the Nile for
drinking water, because water from the
river was unfit to drink.

Frogs

8 25 Seven days after the LORD had
struck the Nile, 1 he said to Moses:
Go to the palace and tell the king[y]
of Egypt that I order him to let my people go, so they can worship me. 2 If he
refuses, I will cover his entire country
with frogs. 3 Warn the king that the
Nile will be full of frogs, and from
there they will spread into the royal
palace, including the king's bedroom
and even his bed. Frogs will enter the
homes of his officials and will find
their way into ovens and into the bowls
of bread dough. 4 Frogs will be crawling
on everyone—the king, his officials,
and every citizen of Egypt.
5 Moses, now command Aaron to

[y]**6.29; 7.8,9,14; 8.1** *the king*: See the note at 1.11.
7.3,4 Ac 7.36. **7.14-24** Ws 11.6-8. **7.17** Rev 16.4.

hold his stick over the water. Then frogs will come from all rivers, canals, and ponds in Egypt, and they will cover the land.

6 Aaron obeyed, and suddenly frogs were everywhere in Egypt. 7 But the magicians used their secret powers to do the same thing.

8 The king sent for Moses and Aaron and told them, "If you ask the LORD to take these frogs away from me and my people, I will let your people go and offer sacrifices to him."

9 "All right," Moses answered. "You choose the time when I am to pray for the frogs to stop bothering you, your officials, and your people, and for them to leave your houses and be found only in the river."

10 "Do it tomorrow!" the king replied.

"As you wish," Moses agreed. "Then everyone will discover that there is no god like the LORD, 11 and frogs will no longer be found anywhere, except in the Nile."

12 After Moses and Aaron left the palace, Moses begged the LORD to do something about the frogs he had sent as punishment for the king. 13 The LORD listened to Moses, and frogs died everywhere—in houses, yards, and fields. 14 The dead frogs were placed in piles, and the whole country began to stink. 15 But when the king saw that things were now better, he again did just as the LORD had said and stubbornly refused to listen to Moses and Aaron.

Gnats

16 The LORD said to Moses, "Command Aaron to strike the ground with his walking stick, and everywhere in Egypt the dust will turn into gnats." 17 They obeyed, and when Aaron struck the ground with the stick, gnats started swarming on people and animals. In fact, every speck of dust in Egypt turned into a gnat. 18 When the magicians tried to use their secret powers to do this,[z] they failed, and gnats stayed on people and animals.

19 The magicians told the king,[a] "God has done this." But, as the LORD had said, the king was too stubborn to listen.

Flies

20 The LORD said to Moses:

Early tomorrow morning, while the king[a] is on his way to the river, go and say to him, "The LORD commands you to let his people go, so they can worship him. 21 If you don't, he will send swarms of flies to attack you, your officials, and every citizen of your country. Houses will be full of flies, and the ground will crawl with them.

22-23 "The LORD's people in Goshen won't be bothered by flies, but your people in the rest of the country will be tormented by them. That's how you will know that the LORD is here in Egypt. This miracle will happen tomorrow."

24 The LORD kept his promise—the palace and the homes of the royal officials swarmed with flies, and the rest of the country was infested with them as well. 25 Then the king sent for Moses and Aaron and told them, "Go sacrifice to your God, but stay here in Egypt."

26 "That's impossible!" Moses replied. "Any sacrifices we offer to the LORD our God would disgust the Egyptians, and they would stone us to death. 27 No indeed! The LORD has ordered us to walk three days into the desert before offering sacrifices to him, and that's what we have to do."

28 Then the king told him, "I'll let you go into the desert to offer sacrifices, if you don't go very far. But in the meantime, pray for me."

29 "Your Majesty," Moses replied, "I'll pray for you as soon as I leave, and by tomorrow the flies will stop bothering you, your officials, and the citizens of your country. Only make sure that you're telling the truth this time and that you really intend to let our people offer sacrifices to the LORD."

30 After leaving the palace, Moses prayed, 31 and the LORD answered his prayer. Not a fly was left to pester the king,

[z] **8.18** *to do this*: Or "to get rid of the gnats."
8.19 Lk 11.20.

[a] **8.19,20; 9.1,10,13** *the king*: See the note at 1.11.

his officials, or anyone else in Egypt. [32] But the king turned stubborn again and would not let the people go.

Dead Animals

9 The LORD sent Moses with this message for the king[a] of Egypt:

The LORD God of the Hebrews commands you to let his people go, so they can worship him. [2] If you keep refusing, [3] he will bring a terrible disease on your horses and donkeys, your camels and cattle, and your sheep and goats. [4] But the LORD will protect the animals that belong to the people of Israel, and none of theirs will die. [5] Tomorrow is the day the LORD has set to do this.

[6] It happened the next day—all of the animals belonging to the Egyptians died, but the Israelites did not lose even one. [7] When the king found out, he was still too stubborn to let the people go.

Sores

[8] The LORD said to Moses and Aaron:

Take a few handfuls of ashes from a stove and have Moses throw them into the air. Be sure the king is watching. [9] The ashes will blow across the land of Egypt, causing sores to break out on people and animals.

[10] So they took a few handfuls of ashes and went to the king.[a] Moses threw them into the air, and sores immediately broke out on the Egyptians and their animals. [11] The magicians were suffering so much from the sores, that they could not even come to Moses. [12] Everything happened just as the LORD had told Moses—he made the king too stubborn to listen to Moses and Aaron.

Hailstones

[13] The LORD told Moses to get up early the next morning and say to the king:[a]

The LORD God of the Hebrews commands you to let his people go, so they can worship him! [14] If you don't, he will send his worst plagues to strike you, your officials, and everyone else in your country. Then you will find out that no one can oppose the LORD. [15] In fact, he could already have sent a terrible disease and wiped you from the face of the earth. [16] But he has kept you alive, just to show you his power and to bring honor to himself everywhere in the world.

[17] You are still determined not to let the LORD's people go. [18] All right. At this time tomorrow, he will bring on Egypt the worst hailstorm in its history. [19] You had better give orders for every person and every animal in Egypt to take shelter. If they don't, they will die.

[20] Some of the king's officials were frightened by what the LORD had said, and they hurried off to make sure their slaves and animals were safe. [21] But others paid no attention to his threats and left their slaves and animals out in the open.

[22] Then the LORD told Moses, "Stretch your arm toward the sky, so that hailstones will fall on people, animals, and crops in the land of Egypt." [23-24] Moses pointed his walking stick toward the sky, and hailstones started falling everywhere. Thunder roared, and lightning flashed back and forth, striking the ground. This was the worst storm in the history of Egypt. [25] People, animals, and crops were pounded by the hailstones, and bark was stripped from trees. [26] Only Goshen, where the Israelites lived, was safe from the storm.

[27] The king sent for Moses and Aaron and told them, "Now I have really sinned! My people and I are guilty, and the LORD is right. [28] We can't stand any more of this thunder and hail. Please ask the LORD to make it stop. Your people can go—you don't have to stay in Egypt any longer."

[29] Moses answered, "As soon as I leave the city, I will lift my arms in prayer. When the thunder and hail stop, you will know that the earth belongs to the LORD. [30] But I am certain that neither you nor your officials really fear the LORD God."

[31] Meanwhile, the flax and barley crops had been destroyed by the storm because they were ready to ripen. [32] But the wheat

[a]**8.19,20; 9.1,10,13** *the king*: See the note at 1.11.

9.10 Rev 16.2. **9.16** 3 Macc 2.6; Ro 9.17. **9.23,24** Rev 8.7; 16.21.

crops[b] ripen later, and they were not damaged.

33 After Moses left the royal palace and the city, he lifted his arms in prayer to the LORD, and the thunder, hail, and drenching rain stopped. 34 When the king realized that the storm was over, he disobeyed once more. He and his officials were so stubborn 35 that he refused to let the Israelites go. This was exactly what the LORD had said would happen.

Locusts

10 The LORD said to Moses:

Go back to the king.[c] I have made him and his officials stubborn, so that I could work these miracles. 2 I did this because I want you to tell your children and your grandchildren about my miracles and about my harsh treatment of the Egyptians. Then all of you will know that I am the LORD.

3 Moses and Aaron went to the king and told him that the LORD God of the Hebrews had said:

How long will you stubbornly refuse to obey? Release my people so they can worship me. 4 Do this by tomorrow, or I will cover your country with so many locusts[d] 5 that you won't be able to see the ground. Most of your crops were ruined by the hailstones, but these locusts will destroy what little is left, including the trees. 6 Your palace, the homes of your officials, and all other houses in Egypt will overflow with more locusts than have ever been seen in this country.

After Moses left the palace, 7 the king's officials asked, "Your Majesty, how much longer is this man going to be a troublemaker? Why don't you let the people leave, so they can worship the LORD their God? Don't you know that Egypt is a disaster?"

8 The king had Moses and Aaron brought back, and he said, "All right, you may go and worship the LORD your God. But first tell me who will be going."

9 "Everyone, young and old," Moses answered. "We will even take our sheep, goats, and cattle, because we want to hold a celebration in honor of the LORD."

10 The king replied, "The LORD had better watch over you on the day I let you leave with your families! You're up to no good. 11 Do you want to worship the LORD? All right, take only the men and go." Then Moses and Aaron were chased out of the palace.

12 The LORD told Moses, "Stretch your arm toward Egypt. Swarms of locusts will come and eat everything left by the hail."

13 Moses held out his walking stick, and the LORD sent an east wind that blew across Egypt the rest of the day and all that night. By morning, locusts 14 were swarming everywhere. Never before had there been so many locusts in Egypt, and never again will there be so many. 15 The ground was black with locusts, and they ate everything left on the trees and in the fields. Nothing green remained in Egypt—not a tree or a plant.

16 At once the king sent for Moses and Aaron. He told them, "I have sinned against the LORD your God and against you. 17 Forgive me one more time and ask the LORD to stop these insects from killing every living plant."

18 Moses left the palace and prayed. 19 Then the LORD sent a strong west wind[e] that swept the locusts into the Red Sea.[f] Not one locust was left anywhere in Egypt, 20 but the LORD made the king so stubborn that he still refused to let the Israelites go.

Darkness

21 The LORD said to Moses, "Stretch your arm toward the sky, and everything will be covered with darkness thick enough to touch." 22 Moses stretched his arm toward the sky, and Egypt was covered with

[b] **9.32** *wheat crops*: The Hebrew text mentions two kinds of wheat. [c] **10.1** *the king*: See the note at 1.11. [d] **10.4** *locusts*: A type of grasshopper that comes in swarms and causes great damage to crops. [e] **10.19** *west wind*: The Hebrew text has "wind from the sea," referring to the Mediterranean Sea (see verse 13). [f] **10.19** *Red Sea*: Hebrew *yam suph*, here referring to the Gulf of Suez, since the term is extended to include the northwestern arm of the Red Sea (see also the note at 13.18).

10.14,15 Rev 9.2, 3. **10.21-23** Ws 17.1-21. **10.22** Ps 105.28; Rev 16.10.

darkness for three days. 23 During that time, the Egyptians could not see each other or leave their homes, but there was light where the Israelites lived.

24 The king[g] sent for Moses and told him, "Go worship the LORD! And take your families with you. Just leave your sheep, goats, and cattle."

25 "No!" Moses replied. "You must let us offer sacrifices to the LORD our God, 26 and we won't know which animals we will need until we get there. That's why we can't leave even one of them here."

27 This time the LORD made the king so stubborn 28 that he said to Moses, "Get out and stay out! If you ever come back, you're dead!"

29 "Have it your way," Moses answered. "You won't see me again."

Moses Warns the Egyptians That the LORD Will Kill Their First-Born Sons

11 The LORD said to Moses:

I am going to punish the king[g] of Egypt and his people one more time. Then the king will gladly let you leave his land, so that I will stop punishing the Egyptians. He will even chase you out. 2 Now go and tell my people to ask their Egyptian neighbors for gold and silver jewelry.

3 So the LORD made the Egyptians greatly respect the Israelites, and everyone, including the king and his officials, considered Moses an important leader.

4 Moses went to the king and said:

I have come to let you know what the LORD is going to do. About midnight he will go through the land of Egypt, 5 and wherever he goes, the first-born son in every family will die. Your own son will die, and so will the son of the lowest slave woman. Even the first-born males of cattle will die. 6 Everywhere in Egypt there will be loud crying. Nothing like this has ever happened before or will ever happen again.

7 But there won't be any need for the Israelites to cry. Things will be so quiet that not even a dog will be heard barking. Then you Egyptians will know that the LORD is good to the Israelites, even while he punishes you. 8 Your leaders will come and bow down, begging me to take my people and leave your country. Then we will leave.

Moses was very angry; he turned and left the king.

9 What the LORD had earlier said to Moses came true. He had said, "The king of Egypt won't listen. Then I will perform even more miracles." 10 So the king of Egypt saw Moses and Aaron work miracles, but the LORD made him stubbornly refuse to let the Israelites leave his country.

The Passover

12 Some time later the LORD said to Moses and Aaron:

2 This month[h] is to be the first month of the year for you. 3 Tell the people of Israel that on the tenth day of this month the head of each family must choose a lamb or a young goat for his family to eat. 4-5 If any family is too small to eat the whole animal, they must share it with their next-door neighbors. Choose either a sheep or a goat, but it must be a one-year-old male that has nothing wrong with it. And it must be large enough for everyone to have some of the meat.

6 Each family must take care of its animal until the evening of the fourteenth day of the month, when the animals are to be killed. 7 Some of the blood must be put on the two doorposts and above the door of each house where the animals are to be eaten. 8 That night the animals are to be roasted and eaten, together with bitter herbs and thin bread made without yeast. 9 Don't eat the meat raw or boiled. The entire animal, including its head, legs, and insides, must be roasted. 10 Eat what you want that night, and the next morning burn

[g] **10.24; 11.1** *The king*: See the note at 1.11. [h] **12.2** *This month*: Abib (also called Nisan), the first month of the Hebrew calendar, from about mid-March to mid-April.

12.1-13 Lv 23.4, 5; Nu 9.1-5; 28.16; Dt 16.1, 2.

whatever is left. 11 When you eat the meal, be dressed and ready to travel. Have your sandals on, carry your walking stick in your hand, and eat quickly. This is the Passover Festival in honor of me, your LORD.

12 That same night I will pass through Egypt and kill the first-born son in every family and the first-born male of all animals. I am the LORD, and I will punish the gods of Egypt. 13 The blood on the houses will show me where you live, and when I see the blood, I will pass over you. Then you won't be bothered by the terrible disasters I will bring on Egypt.

14 Remember this day and celebrate it each year as a festival in my honor. 15 For seven days you must eat bread made without yeast. And on the first of these seven days, you must remove all yeast from your homes. If you eat anything made with yeast during this festival, you will no longer be part of Israel. 16 Meet together for worship on the first and seventh days of the festival. The only work you are allowed to do on either of these two days is that of preparing the bread.

17 Celebrate this Festival of Thin Bread as a way of remembering the day that I brought your families and tribes out of Egypt. And do this each year. 18 Begin on the evening of the fourteenth day of the first month by eating bread made without yeast. Then continue this celebration until the evening of the twenty-first day. 19 During these seven days no yeast is allowed in anyone's home, whether they are native Israelites or not. If you are caught eating anything made with yeast, you will no longer be part of Israel. 20 Stay away from yeast, no matter where you live. No one is allowed to eat anything made with yeast!

21 Moses called the leaders of Israel together and said:

Each family is to pick out a sheep and kill it for Passover. 22 Make a brush from a few small branches of a hyssop plant and dip the brush in the bowl that has the blood of the animal in it. Then brush some of the blood above the door and on the posts at each side of the door of your house. After this, everyone is to stay inside.

23 During that night the LORD will go through the country of Egypt and kill the first-born son in every Egyptian family. He will see where you have put the blood, and he will not come into your house. His angel that brings death will pass over and not kill your first-born sons.

24-25 After you have entered the country promised to you by the LORD, you and your children must continue to celebrate Passover each year. 26 Your children will ask you, "What are we celebrating?" 27 And you will answer, "The Passover animal is killed to honor the LORD. We do these things because on that night long ago the LORD passed over the homes of our people in Egypt. He killed the first-born sons of the Egyptians, but he saved our children from death."

After Moses finished speaking, the people of Israel knelt down and worshiped the LORD. 28 Then they left and did what Moses and Aaron had told them to do.

Death for the First-Born Sons

29 At midnight the LORD killed the first-born son of every Egyptian family, from the son of the king[i] to the son of every prisoner in jail. He also killed the first-born male of every animal that belonged to the Egyptians.

30 That night the king, his officials, and everyone else in Egypt got up and started crying bitterly. In every Egyptian home, someone was dead.

The People of Israel Escape from Egypt

31 During the night the king[i] sent for Moses and Aaron and told them, "Get your

[i] **12.29,31** *the king*: See the note at 1.11.

12.14-20 Ex 23.15; 34.18; Lv 23.6-8; Nu 28.17-25; Dt 16.3-8. **12.23** He 11.28.
12.29 Ex 4.22, 23.

people out of my country and leave us alone! Go and worship the LORD, as you have asked. 32 Take your sheep, goats, and cattle, and get out. But ask your God to be kind to me."

33 The Egyptians did everything they could to get the Israelites to leave their country fast. They said, "Please hurry and leave. If you don't, we will all be dead." 34 So the Israelites quickly made some bread dough and put it in pans. But they did not mix any yeast in the dough to make it rise. They wrapped cloth around the pans and carried them on their shoulders.

35 The Israelites had already done what Moses had told them to do. They had gone to their Egyptian neighbors and asked for gold and silver and for clothes. 36 The LORD had made the Egyptians friendly toward the people of Israel, and they gave them whatever they asked for. In this way they carried away the wealth of the Egyptians when they left Egypt.

37 The Israelites walked from the city of Rameses to the city of Succoth. There were about six hundred thousand of them, not counting women and children. 38 Many other people went with them as well, and there were also a lot of sheep, goats, and cattle. 39 They left Egypt in such a hurry that they did not have time to prepare any food except the bread dough made without yeast. So they baked it and made thin bread.

40-41 The LORD's people left Egypt exactly four hundred thirty years after they had arrived. 42 On that night the LORD kept watch for them, and on this same night each year Israel will always keep watch in honor of the LORD.

Instructions for Passover

43 The LORD gave Moses and Aaron the following instructions for celebrating Passover:

No one except Israelites may eat the Passover meal.

44 Your slaves may eat the meal if they have been circumcised, 45 but no foreigners who work for you are allowed to have any.

46 The entire meal must be eaten inside, and no one may leave the house during the celebration.

No bones of the Passover lamb may be broken. 47 And all Israelites must take part in the meal.

48 If anyone who isn't an Israelite wants to celebrate Passover with you, every man and boy in that family must first be circumcised. Then they may join in the meal, just like native Israelites. No uncircumcised man or boy may eat the Passover meal! 49 This law applies both to native Israelites and to those foreigners who live among you.

50 The Israelites obeyed everything the LORD had commanded Moses and Aaron to tell them. 51 And on that same day the LORD brought Israel's families and tribes out of Egypt.

Dedication of the First-Born

13 The LORD said to Moses, 2 "Dedicate to me the first-born son of every family and the first-born males of your flocks and herds. These belong to me."

The Festival of Thin Bread

3-4 Moses said to the people:

Remember this day in the month of Abib.[j] It is the day when the LORD's mighty power rescued you from Egypt, where you were slaves. Do not eat anything made with yeast. 5 The LORD promised your ancestors that he would bring you into the land of the Canaanites, Hittites, Amorites, Hivites, and Jebusites. It is a land rich with milk and honey.

Each year during the month of Abib, celebrate these events in the following way: 6 For seven days you are to eat bread made without yeast, and on the seventh day you are to celebrate a

[j] **13.3,4** *Abib*: Or Nisan, the first month of the Hebrew calendar, from about mid-March to mid-April.

12.35,36 Ex 3.21, 22. **12.40,41** Gn 15.13-15; Ga 3.17. **12.46** Nu 9.12; Jn 19.36. **13.2** Nu 3.11-13; Lk 2.23.

festival in honor of the LORD. 7 During
those seven days, you must not eat
anything made with yeast or even have
yeast anywhere near your homes.
8 Then on the seventh day you must
explain to your children that you do
this because the LORD brought you out
of Egypt.
9 This celebration will be like wearing a sign on your hand or on your
forehead, because then you will pass
on to others the teaching of the LORD,
whose mighty power brought you out
of Egypt. 10 Celebrate this festival each
year at the same time.
11 The LORD will give you the land
of the Canaanites, just as he promised
you and your ancestors. 12 From then
on, you must give him every first-born
son from your families and every first-
born male from your animals, because
these belong to him. 13 You can save
the life of a first-born donkey[k] by sacrificing a lamb; if you don't, you must
break the donkey's neck. You must
save every first-born son.
14 In the future your children will
ask what this ceremony means. Explain it to them by saying, "The LORD
used his mighty power to rescue us
from slavery in Egypt. 15 The king[l]
stubbornly refused to set us free, so
the LORD killed the first-born male of
every animal and the first-born son of
every Egyptian family. This is why we
sacrifice to the LORD every first-born
male of every animal and save every
first-born son."
16 This ceremony will serve the
same purpose as a sign on your hand
or on your forehead to tell how the
LORD's mighty power rescued us from
Egypt.

The LORD Leads His People

17 After the king[l] had finally let the people go, the LORD did not lead them through
Philistine territory,[m] though that was the
shortest way. God had said, "If they are attacked, they may decide to return to
Egypt." 18 So he led them around through
the desert and toward the Red Sea.[n]
The Israelites left Egypt, prepared for
battle.
19 Moses had them take along the bones
of Joseph, whose dying words had been,
"God will come to your rescue, and when
he does, be sure to take along my bones."
20 The people of Israel left Succoth and
camped at Etham at the border of Egypt
near the desert. 21-22 During the day the
LORD went ahead of his people in a thick
cloud, and during the night he went ahead
of them in a flaming fire. That way the
LORD could lead them at all times, whether
day or night.

The Israelites Cross the Red Sea

14 At Etham the LORD said to Moses:
2 Tell the people of Israel to
turn back and camp across from Pi-
Hahiroth near Baal-Zephon, between
Migdol and the Red Sea.[o] 3 The king[p]
will think they were afraid to cross the
desert and that they are wandering
around, trying to find another way to
leave the country. 4 I will make the
king stubborn again, and he will try to
catch you. Then I will destroy him and
his army. People everywhere will praise

[k] **13.13** *donkey*: This was the only "unclean" animal that had to be saved; the first-born of all "clean" animals (sheep, goats, cattle) had to be sacrificed. Donkeys were important because they were the basic means of transportation. [l] **13.15,17** *The king*: See the note at 1.11.
[m] **13.17** *Philistine territory*: The shortest land route from the Nile Delta to Canaan; it was the southern section of the major road that led to Megiddo and then on to Mesopotamia by way of Asia Minor. [n] **13.18** *Red Sea*: Hebrew *yam suph* "Sea of Reeds," one of the marshes or fresh water lakes, near the eastern part of the Nile Delta. This identification is based on Exodus 13.17—14.9, which lists the towns on the route of the Israelites before crossing the sea. In the Greek translation of the Scriptures made about 200 B.C., the "Sea of Reeds" was named "Red Sea." [o] **14.2** *Red Sea*: Hebrew *hayyam* "the Sea," understood as *yam suph*, "Sea of Reeds" (see also the note at 13.18). [p] **14.3** *The king*: See the note at 1.11.
13.12 Ex 34.19, 20; Lk 2.23. **13.19** Gn 50.25; Js 24.32. **13.21,22** Ws 10.17, 18; 18.3.

me for my victory, and the Egyptians
will know that I really am the LORD.

The Israelites obeyed the LORD and camped where he told them.

5 When the king of Egypt heard that the Israelites had finally left, he and his officials changed their minds and said, "Look what we have done! We let them get away, and they will no longer be our slaves."

6 The king got his war chariot and army ready. 7 He commanded his officers in charge of his six hundred best chariots and all his other chariots to start after the Israelites. 8 The LORD made the king so stubborn that he went after them, even though the Israelites proudly[q] went on their way. 9 But the king's horses and chariots and soldiers caught up with them while they were camping by the Red Sea near Pi-Hahiroth and Baal-Zephon.

10 When the Israelites saw the king coming with his army, they were frightened and begged the LORD for help. 11 They also complained to Moses, "Wasn't there enough room in Egypt to bury us? Is that why you brought us out here to die in the desert? Why did you bring us out of Egypt anyway? 12 While we were there, didn't we tell you to leave us alone? We had rather be slaves in Egypt than die in this desert!"

13 But Moses answered, "Don't be afraid! Be brave, and you will see the LORD save you today. These Egyptians will never bother you again. 14 The LORD will fight for you, and you won't have to do a thing."

15 The LORD said to Moses, "Why do you keep calling out to me for help? Tell the Israelites to move forward. 16 Then hold your walking stick over the sea. The water will open up and make a road where they can walk through on dry ground. 17 I will make the Egyptians so stubborn that they will go after you. Then I will be praised because of what happens to the king and his chariots and cavalry. 18 The Egyptians will know for sure that I am the LORD."

19 All this time God's angel had gone ahead of Israel's army, but now he moved behind them. A large cloud had also gone ahead of them, 20 but now it moved between the Egyptians and the Israelites. The cloud gave light to the Israelites, but made it dark for the Egyptians, and during the night they could not come any closer.

21 Moses stretched his arm over the sea, and the LORD sent a strong east wind that blew all night until there was dry land where the water had been. The sea opened up, 22 and the Israelites walked through on dry land with a wall of water on each side.

23 The Egyptian chariots and cavalry went after them. 24 But before daylight the LORD looked down at the Egyptian army from the fiery cloud and made them panic. 25 Their chariot wheels got stuck,[r] and it was hard for them to move. So the Egyptians said to one another, "Let's leave these people alone! The LORD is on their side and is fighting against us."

26 The LORD told Moses, "Stretch your arm toward the sea—the water will cover the Egyptians and their cavalry and chariots." 27 Moses stretched out his arm, and at daybreak the water rushed toward the Egyptians. They tried to run away, but the LORD drowned them in the sea. 28 The water came and covered the chariots, the cavalry, and the whole Egyptian army that had followed the Israelites into the sea. Not one of them was left alive. 29 But the sea had made a wall of water on each side of the Israelites; so they walked through on dry land.

30 On that day, when the Israelites saw the bodies of the Egyptians washed up on the shore, they knew that the LORD had saved them. 31 Because of the mighty power he had used against the Egyptians, the Israelites worshiped him and trusted him and his servant Moses.

The Song of Moses

15 Moses and the Israelites sang this song in praise of the LORD:

I sing praises to the LORD
for his great victory!

[q]**14.8** *proudly*: Or "victoriously." [r]**14.25** *stuck*: The Samaritan Hebrew text and two ancient translations; Hebrew "came off."

14.21-28 3 Macc 2.7. **14.22** 1 Co 10.1, 2; He 11.29. **15.1** Rev 15.3. **15.1-21** 3 Macc 2.8. **15.1-27** 3 Macc 6.4.

He has thrown the horses
and their riders
into the sea.
2 The LORD is my strength,
the reason for my song,
because he has saved me.
I praise and honor the LORD—
he is my God and the God
of my ancestors.
3 The LORD is his name,
and he is a warrior!
4 He threw the chariots and army
of Egypt's king[s]
into the Red Sea,[t]
and he drowned the best
of the king's officers.
5 They sank to the bottom
just like stones.

6 With the tremendous force
of your right arm, our LORD,
you crushed your enemies.
7 What a great victory was yours,
as you defeated everyone
who opposed you.
Your fiery anger wiped them out,
as though they were straw.
8 You were so furious
that the sea piled up
like a wall,
and the ocean depths
curdled like cheese.

9 Your enemies boasted
that they would
pursue and capture us,
divide up our possessions,
treat us as they wished,
then take out their swords
and kill us right there.
10 But when you got furious,
they sank like lead,
swallowed by ocean waves.

11 Our LORD, no other gods
compare with you—
Majestic and holy!
Fearsome and glorious!
Miracle worker!
12 When you signaled
with your right hand,
your enemies were swallowed
deep into the earth.

13 The people you rescued
were led by your powerful love
to your holy place.
14 Nations learned of this
and trembled—
Philistines shook with horror.
15 The leaders of Edom and of Moab
were terrified.
Everyone in Canaan fainted,
16 struck down by fear.
Our LORD, your powerful arm
kept them still as a rock
until the people you rescued
for your very own
had marched by.

17 You will let your people settle
on your chosen mountain,
where you built your home
and your temple.
18 Our LORD, you will rule forever!

The Song of Miriam

19 The LORD covered the royal Egyptian
cavalry and chariots with the sea, after the
Israelites had walked safely through on dry
ground. 20 Miriam the sister of Aaron was a
prophet. So she took her tambourine and
led the other women out to play their tambourines and to dance. 21 Then she sang to
them:

"Sing praises to the LORD
for his great victory!
He has thrown the horses
and their riders into the sea."

Bitter Water at Marah

22 After the Israelites left the Red Sea,[t]
Moses led them through the Shur Desert
for three days, before finding water. 23 They
did find water at Marah, but it was bitter,
which is how that place got its name.[u]
24 The people complained and said,
"Moses, what are we going to drink?"

[s] **15.4** *Egypt's king*: See the note at 1.11. [t] **15.4,22** *Red Sea*: See the note at 13.18.
[u] **15.23** *Marah . . . name*: In Hebrew "Marah" means "bitter."
15.2 Ps 118.14; Is 12.2.

[25] Moses asked the LORD for help, and
the LORD told him to throw a piece of wood
into the water. Moses did so, and the water
became fit to drink.

At Marah the LORD tested his people
and also gave them some laws and teachings. [26] Then he said, "I am the LORD your
God, and I cure your diseases. If you obey
me by doing right and by following my laws
and teachings, I won't punish you with the
diseases I sent on the Egyptians."

[27] Later the Israelites came to Elim,
where there were twelve springs and seventy palm trees. So they camped there.

The LORD Sends Food from Heaven

16 On the fifteenth day of the second
month after the Israelites had escaped from Egypt, they left Elim and
started through the western edge of the
Sinai Desert[v] in the direction of Mount
Sinai. [2] There in the desert they started
complaining to Moses and Aaron, [3] "We
wish the LORD had killed us in Egypt.
When we lived there, we could at least sit
down and eat all the bread and meat we
wanted. But you have brought us out here
into this desert, where we are going to
starve."

[4] The LORD said to Moses, "I will send
bread[w] down from heaven like rain. Each
day the people can go out and gather only
enough for that day. That's how I will see if
they obey me. [5] But on the sixth day of
each week they must gather and cook twice
as much."

[6] Moses and Aaron told the people,
"This evening you will know that the LORD
was the one who rescued you from Egypt.
[7] And in the morning you will see his glorious power, because he has heard your complaints against him. Why should you grumble to us? Who are we?"

[8] Then Moses continued, "You will
know it is the LORD when he gives you
meat each evening and more than enough
bread each morning. He is really the one
you are complaining about, not us—we are
nobodies—but the LORD has heard your
complaints."

[9] Moses turned to Aaron and said,
"Bring the people together, because the
LORD has heard their complaints."

[10] Aaron was speaking to them, when
everyone looked out toward the desert and
saw the bright glory of the LORD in a cloud.
[11] The LORD said to Moses, [12] "I have heard
my people complain. Now tell them that
each evening they will have meat and each
morning they will have more than enough
bread. Then they will know that I am the
LORD their God."

[13] That evening a lot of quails came and
landed everywhere in the camp, and the
next morning dew covered the ground.
[14] After the dew had gone, the desert was
covered with thin flakes that looked like
frost. [15] The people had never seen anything like this, and they started asking each
other, "What is it?"[x]

Moses answered, "This is the bread that
the LORD has given you to eat. [16] And he
orders you to gather about two quarts for
each person in your family—that should be
more than enough."

[17] They did as they were told. Some
gathered more and some gathered less,
[18] according to their needs, and none was
left over.

[19] Moses told them not to keep any
overnight. [20] Some of them disobeyed, but
the next morning what they kept was stinking and full of worms, and Moses was
angry.

[21] Each morning everyone gathered as
much as they needed, and in the heat of
the day the rest melted. [22] However, on the
sixth day of the week, everyone gathered
enough to have four quarts, instead of two.
When the leaders reported this to Moses,
[23] he told them that the LORD had said,
"Tomorrow is the Sabbath, a sacred day of
rest in honor of me. So gather all you want

[v] **16.1** *the western edge of the Sinai Desert*: Hebrew "the Sin Desert." [w] **16.4** *bread*: This was something like a thin wafer, and it was called "manna," which in Hebrew means, "What is it?"
[x] **16.15** *What is it*: See the note at 16.4.

15.25 Si 38.5. **16.4** Ws 16.20-29; Jn 6.31. **16.15** 1 Co 10.3. **16.18** 2 Co 8.15.
16.23 Ex 20.8-11.

to bake or boil, and make sure you save
enough for tomorrow."
24 The people obeyed, and the next
morning the food smelled fine and had no
worms. 25 "You may eat the food," Moses
said. "Today is the Sabbath in honor of the
LORD, and there won't be any of this food
on the ground today. 26 You will find it
there for the first six days of the week, but
not on the Sabbath."
27 A few of the Israelites did go out to
look for some, but there was none. 28 Then
the LORD said, "Moses, how long will you
people keep disobeying my laws and teachings? 29 Remember that I was the one who
gave you the Sabbath. That's why on the
sixth day I provide enough bread for two
days. Everyone is to stay home and rest on
the Sabbath." 30 And so they rested on the
Sabbath.
31 The Israelites called the bread
manna.[y] It was white like coriander seed
and delicious as wafers made with honey.
32 Moses told the people that the LORD had
said, "Store up two quarts of this manna,
because I want future generations to see
the food I gave you during the time you
were in the desert after I rescued you from
Egypt."
33 Then Moses told Aaron, "Put some
manna in a jar and store it in the place of
worship for future generations to see."
34 Aaron followed the LORD's instructions and put the manna in front of the sacred chest for safekeeping. 35-36 The Israelites ate manna for forty years, before
they came to the border of Canaan that was
a settled land.[z]

The LORD Gives Water from a Rock

(Numbers 20.1-13)

17 The Israelites left the desert and
moved from one place to another
each time the LORD ordered them to. Once
they camped at Rephidim,[a] but there was
no water for them to drink.
2 The people started complaining to
Moses, "Give us some water!"
Moses replied, "Why are you complaining to me and trying to put the LORD to the
test?"
3 But the people were thirsty and kept
on complaining, "Moses, did you bring us
out of Egypt just to let us and our families
and our animals die of thirst?"
4 Then Moses prayed to the LORD,
"What am I going to do with these people?
They are about to stone me to death!"
5 The LORD answered, "Take some of the
leaders with you and go ahead of the rest of
the people. Also take along the walking
stick you used to strike the Nile River,
6 and when you get to the rock at Mount
Sinai,[b] I will be there with you. Strike the
rock with the stick, and water will pour out
for the people to drink." Moses did this
while the leaders watched.
7 The people had complained and tested
the LORD by asking, "Is the LORD really with
us?" So Moses named that place Massah,
which means "testing" and Meribah, which
means "complaining."

Israel Defeats the Amalekites

8 When the Israelites were at Rephidim,
they were attacked by the Amalekites. 9 So
Moses told Joshua, "Have some men ready
to attack the Amalekites tomorrow. I will
stand on a hilltop, holding this walking
stick that has the power of God."
10 Joshua led the attack as Moses had
commanded, while Moses, Aaron, and Hur
stood on the hilltop. 11 The Israelites out-
fought the Amalekites as long as Moses
held up his arms, but they started losing
whenever he had to lower them. 12 Finally,
Moses was so tired that Aaron and Hur got
a rock for him to sit on. Then they stood
beside him and supported his arms in the
same position until sunset. 13 That's how
Joshua defeated the Amalekites.
14 Afterwards, the LORD said to Moses,

[y] **16.31** *manna*: See the note at 16.4. [z] **16.35,36** *land*: The Hebrew text adds, "An omer is one tenth of an ephah." In the CEV "omer" is usually translated "two quarts." [a] **17.1** *Rephidim*: The last stopping place for the Israelites between the Red Sea and Mount Sinai; the exact location is not known. [b] **17.6** *Sinai*: The Hebrew text has "Horeb," another name for Sinai.

16.31 Nu 11.7-9. **16.33** He 9.4. **16.35,36** Js 5.11, 12. **17.1-7** Nu 20.2-13. **17.14** Dt 25.17-19; 1 S 15.2-9.

The six days of creation

Genesis 1.1-31

Noah prepares for the flood

Genesis 6 – 9

"Write an account of this victory and read it to Joshua. I want the Amalekites to be forgotten forever."

15 Moses built an altar and named it "The LORD Gives Me Victory." 16 Then Moses explained, "This is because I depended on the LORD.[c] But in future generations, the LORD will have to fight the Amalekites again."

Jethro Visits Moses

18 Jethro was the priest of Midian and the father-in-law of Moses. And he heard what the LORD God had done for Moses and his people, after rescuing them from Egypt.

2-4 In the meantime, Moses had sent his wife Zipporah and her two sons to stay with Jethro, and he had welcomed them. Moses was still a foreigner in Midian when his first son was born, and so Moses said, "I'll name him Gershom."[d]

When his second son was born, Moses said, "I'll name him Eliezer,[e] because the God my father worshiped has saved me from the king of Egypt."[f]

5-6 While Israel was camped in the desert near Mount Sinai,[g] Jethro sent Moses this message: "I am coming to visit you, and I am bringing your wife and two sons."

7 When they arrived, Moses went out and bowed down in front of Jethro, then kissed him. After they had greeted each other, they went into the tent, 8 where Moses told him everything the LORD had done to protect Israel against the Egyptians and their king. He also told him how the LORD had helped them in all of their troubles.

9 Jethro was so pleased to hear this good news about what the LORD had done, 10 that he shouted, "Praise the LORD! He rescued you and the Israelites from the Egyptians and their king. 11 Now I know that the LORD is the greatest God, because he has rescued Israel from their arrogant enemies." 12 Jethro offered sacrifices to God. Then Aaron and Israel's leaders came to eat with Jethro there at the place of worship.

Judges Are Appointed
(Deuteronomy 1.9-18)

13 The next morning Moses sat down at the place where he decided legal cases for the people, and everyone crowded around him until evening. 14 Jethro saw how much Moses had to do for the people, and he asked, "Why are you the only judge? Why do you let these people crowd around you from morning till evening?"

15 Moses answered, "Because they come here to find out what God wants them to do. 16 They bring their complaints to me, and I make decisions on the basis of God's laws."

17 Jethro replied:

> That isn't the best way to do it. 18 You and the people who come to you will soon be worn out. The job is too much for one person; you can't do it alone. 19 God will help you if you follow my advice. You should be the one to speak to God for the people, 20 and you should teach them God's laws and show them what they must do to live right.
>
> 21 You will need to appoint some competent leaders who respect God and are trustworthy and honest. Then put them over groups of ten, fifty, a hundred, and a thousand. 22 These judges can handle the ordinary cases and bring the more difficult ones to you. Having them to share the load will make your work easier. 23 This is the way God wants it done. You won't be under nearly as much stress, and everyone else will return home feeling satisfied.

24 Moses followed Jethro's advice. 25 He chose some competent leaders from every tribe in Israel and put them over groups of ten, fifty, a hundred, and a thousand. 26 They served as judges, deciding the easy

[c] **17.16** *This . . . LORD*: One possible meaning for the difficult Hebrew text. [d] **18.2-4** *Gershom*: See the note at 2.22. [e] **18.2-4** *Eliezer*: In Hebrew "Eliezer" means "God has helped me." [f] **18.2-4** *saved . . . Egypt*: See 2.1-15. [g] **18.5,6** *Mount Sinai*: Hebrew "the mountain of God."

18.2-4 Ex 2.21, 22; Ac 7.29. **18.11** 3 Macc 2.3.

cases themselves, but bringing the more difficult ones to Moses.

27 After Moses and his father-in-law Jethro had said good-by to each other, Jethro returned home.

At Mount Sinai

19 1-2 The Israelites left Rephidim.[h] Then two months after leaving Egypt, they arrived at the desert near Mount Sinai, where they set up camp at the foot of the mountain.

3 Moses went up the mountain to meet with the LORD God, who told him to say to the people:

4 You saw what I did in Egypt, and you know how I brought you here to me, just as a mighty eagle carries its young. 5 Now if you will faithfully obey me, you will be my very own people. The whole world is mine, 6 but you will be my holy nation and serve me as priests.

Moses, that is what you must tell the Israelites.

7 After Moses went back, he reported to the leaders what the LORD had said, 8 and they promised, "We will do everything the LORD has commanded." So Moses told the LORD about this.

9 The LORD said to Moses, "I will come to you in a thick cloud and let the people hear me speak to you. Then they will always trust you." Again Moses reported to the people what the LORD had told him.

10 Once more the LORD spoke to Moses:

Go back and tell the people that today and tomorrow they must get themselves ready to meet me. They must wash their clothes 11 and be ready by the day after tomorrow, when I will come down to Mount Sinai, where all of them can see me.

12 Warn the people that they are forbidden to touch any part of the mountain. Anyone who does will be put to death, 13 either with stones or arrows, and no one must touch the body of a person killed in this way. Even an animal that touches this mountain must be put to death. You may go up the mountain only after a signal is given on the trumpet.

14 After Moses went down the mountain, he gave orders for the people to wash their clothes and make themselves acceptable to worship God. 15 He told them to be ready in three days and not to have sex in the meantime.

The LORD Comes to Mount Sinai

16 On the morning of the third day there was thunder and lightning. A thick cloud covered the mountain, a loud trumpet blast was heard, and everyone in camp trembled with fear. 17 Moses led them out of the camp to meet God, and they stood at the foot of the mountain.

18 Mount Sinai was covered with smoke because the LORD had come down in a flaming fire. Smoke poured out of the mountain just like a furnace, and the whole mountain shook. 19 The trumpet blew louder and louder. Moses spoke, and God answered him with thunder.

20 The LORD came down to the top of Mount Sinai and told Moses to meet him there. 21 Then he said, "Moses, go and warn the people not to cross the boundary that you set at the foot of the mountain. They must not cross it to come and look at me, because if they do, many of them will die. 22 Only the priests may come near me, and they must obey strict rules before I let them. If they don't, they will be punished."

23 Moses replied, "The people cannot come up the mountain. You warned us to stay away because it is holy."

24 Then the LORD told Moses, "Go down and bring Aaron back here with you. But the priests and people must not try to push their way through, or I will rush at them like a flood!"

25 After Moses had gone back down, he told the people what the LORD had said.

[h] **19.1,2** *Rephidim*: See the note at 17.1.

19.5,6 1 P 2.9. **19.5** Dt 4.20; 7.6; 14.2; 26.18; Titus 2.14. **19.6** Rev 1.6; 5.10. **19.12,13** He 12.18-20. **19.16** Rev 4.5. **19.16-18** Dt 4.11, 12.

The Ten Commandments
(Deuteronomy 5.1-21)

20 God said to the people of Israel:
2 I am the LORD your God, the
one who brought you out of Egypt
where you were slaves.
3 Do not worship any god except me.
4 Do not make idols that look like
anything in the sky or on earth or in
the ocean under the earth. 5 Don't bow
down and worship idols. I am the LORD
your God, and I demand all your love.
If you reject me, I will punish your
families for three or four generations.
6 But if you love me and obey my laws,
I will be kind to your families for thousands of generations.
7 Do not misuse my name.[i] I am
the LORD your God, and I will punish
anyone who misuses my name.
8 Remember that the Sabbath Day
belongs to me. 9 You have six days
when you can do your work, 10 but the
seventh day of each week belongs to
me, your God. No one is to work on
that day—not you, your children, your
slaves, your animals, or the foreigners
who live in your towns. 11 In six days I
made the sky, the earth, the oceans,
and everything in them, but on the
seventh day I rested. That's why I
made the Sabbath a special day that
belongs to me.
12 Respect your father and your
mother, and you will live a long time in
the land I am giving you.
13 Do not murder.
14 Be faithful in marriage.
15 Do not steal.
16 Do not tell lies about others.
17 Do not want anything that belongs to someone else. Don't want anyone's house, wife or husband, slaves,
oxen, donkeys or anything else.

The People Are Afraid
(Deuteronomy 5.23-33)

18 The people trembled with fear when
they heard the thunder and the trumpet
and saw the lightning and the smoke coming from the mountain. They stood a long
way off 19 and said to Moses, "If you speak
to us, we will listen. But don't let God speak
to us, or we will die!"
20 "Don't be afraid!" Moses replied.
"God has come only to test you, so that
by obeying him you won't sin." 21 But
when Moses went near the thick cloud
where God was, the people stayed a long
way off.

Idols and Altars

22 The LORD told Moses to say to the
people of Israel:
With your own eyes, you saw me
speak to you from heaven. 23 So you
must never make idols of silver or gold
to worship in place of me.[j]
24 Build an altar out of earth, and
offer on it your sacrifices[k] of sheep,
goats, and cattle. Wherever I choose to
be worshiped, I will come down to
bless you. 25 If you ever build an altar
for me out of stones, do not use any
tools to chisel the stones, because that
would make the altar unfit. 26 And
don't build an altar that requires steps;
you might expose yourself when you
climb up.

[i]**20.7** *misuse my name*: Probably includes breaking promises, telling lies after swearing to tell the truth, using the LORD's name as a curse word or a magic formula, and trying to control the LORD by using his name. [j]**20.23** *in place of me*: Or "together with me." [k]**20.24** *sacrifices*: The Hebrew text mentions two types of sacrifices: Sacrifices to please the LORD (traditionally called "whole burnt offerings") and sacrifices to ask the LORD's blessing (traditionally called "peace offerings").

20.4,5 Ex 34.17; Lv 19.4; 26.1; Dt 4.15-18; 27.14-26. **20.5,6** Ex 34.6, 7; Nu 14.18; Dt 7.9, 10. **20.7** Lv 19.12. **20.8** Ex 16.23-30; 31.12-15. **20.9,10** Ex 23.12; 31.14, 15; 34.21; 35.2; Lv 23.3. **20.11** Gn 2.1-3; Ex 31.17. **20.12 a** Dt 27.14-26; Mt 15.4; 19.19; Mk 7.10; 10.19; Lk 18.20; Eph 6.2; **b** Eph 6.3. **20.13** Gn 9.5, 6; Lv 24.17; Mt 5.21; 19.18; Mk 10.19; Lk 18.20; Ro 13.9; Jas 2.11. **20.14** Lv 20.10; Mt 5.27; 19.18; Mk 10.19; Lk 18.20; Ro 13.9; Jas 2.11. **20.15** Lv 19.11; Mt 19.18; Mk 10.19; Lk 18.20; Ro 13.9. **20.16** Ex 23.1; Mt 19.18; Mk 10.19; Lk 18.20. **20.17** Ro 7.7; 13.9. **20.18,19** He 12.18, 19. **20.25** Dt 27.5-7; Js 8.30-32.

Hebrew Slaves

(Deuteronomy 15.12-18)

21 The LORD gave Moses the following laws for his people:

2 If you buy a Hebrew slave, he must remain your slave for six years. But in the seventh year you must set him free, without cost to him. 3 If he was single at the time you bought him, he alone must be set free. But if he was married at the time, both he and his wife must be given their freedom. 4 If you give him a wife, and they have children, only the man himself must be set free; his wife and children remain the property of his owner.

5 But suppose the slave loves his wife and children so much that he won't leave without them. 6 Then he must stand beside either the door or the doorpost at the place of worship,[l] while his owner punches a small hole through one of his ears with a sharp metal rod. This makes him a slave for life.

7 A young woman who was sold by her father doesn't gain her freedom in the same way that a man does. 8 If she doesn't please the man who bought her to be his wife, he must let her be bought back.[m] He cannot sell her to foreigners; this would break the contract he made with her. 9 If he selects her as a wife for his son, he must treat her as his own daughter.

10 If the man later marries another woman, he must continue to provide food and clothing for the one he bought and to treat her as a wife. 11 If he fails to do any of these things, she must be given her freedom without cost.

Murder and Other Violent Crimes

The LORD said:

12 Death is the punishment for murder. 13 But if you did not intend to kill someone, and I, the LORD, let it happen anyway, you may run for safety to a place that I have set aside. 14 If you plan in advance to murder someone, there's no escape, not even by holding on to my altar.[n] You will be dragged off and killed.

15 Death is the punishment for attacking your father or mother.

16 Death is the punishment for kidnapping. If you sell the person you kidnapped, or if you are caught with that person, the penalty is death.

17 Death is the punishment for cursing your father or mother.

18 Suppose two of you are arguing, and you hit the other with either a rock or your fist, without causing a fatal injury. If the victim has to stay in bed, 19 and later has to use a stick when walking outside, you must pay for the loss of time and do what you can to help until the injury is completely healed. That's your only responsibility.

20 Death is the punishment for beating to death any of your slaves. 21 However, if the slave lives a few days after the beating, you are not to be punished. After all, you have already lost the services of that slave who was your property.

22 Suppose a pregnant woman suffers a miscarriage[o] as the result of an injury caused by someone who is fighting. If she isn't badly hurt, the one who injured her must pay whatever fine her husband demands and the judges approve. 23 But if she is seriously injured, the payment will be life for life, 24 eye for eye, tooth for tooth, hand for hand, foot for foot, 25 burn for burn, cut for cut, and bruise for bruise.

26 If you hit one of your slaves and cause the loss of an eye, the slave must be set free. 27 The same law applies if you knock out a slave's tooth—the slave goes free.

28 A bull that kills someone with its horns must be killed and its meat

[l] **21.6** *at the place of worship*: The Hebrew text has "in the presence of God," which probably refers to the place where God was worshiped. [m] **21.8** *bought back*: Either by her family or by another Israelite who wanted to marry her. [n] **21.14** *altar*: As a rule, anyone who ran to the altar was safe from the death penalty, until proven guilty. [o] **21.22** *suffers a miscarriage*: Or "gives birth before her time."

21.2-6 Lv 25.39-46. **21.12** Lv 24.17. **21.13** Nu 35.10-34; Dt 19.1-13; Js 20.1-9. **21.16** Dt 24.7. **21.17** Lv 20.9; Mt 15.4; Mk 7.10. **21.24** Lv 24.19, 20; Dt 19.19-21; Mt 5.38.

destroyed, but the owner of the bull isn't responsible for the death.

29 Suppose you own a bull that has been in the habit of attacking people, but you have refused to keep it fenced in. If that bull kills someone, both you and the bull must be put to death by stoning. 30 However, you may save your own life by paying whatever fine is demanded. 31 This same law applies if the bull gores someone's son or daughter. 32 If the bull kills a slave, you must pay the slave owner thirty pieces of silver for the loss of the slave, and the bull must be killed by stoning.

33 Suppose someone's ox or donkey is killed by falling into an open pit that you dug or left uncovered on your property. 34 You must pay for the dead animal, and it becomes yours.

35 If your bull kills someone else's, yours must be sold. Then the money from your bull and the meat from the dead bull must be divided equally between you and the other owner.

36 If you refuse to fence in a bull that is known to attack others, you must pay for any animal it kills, but the dead animal will belong to you.

Property Laws

The LORD said:

22 If you steal an ox and slaughter or sell it, you must replace it with five oxen; if you steal a sheep and slaughter it or sell it, you must replace it with four sheep. 2-4 But if you cannot afford to replace the animals, you must be sold as a slave to pay for what you have stolen. If you steal an ox, donkey, or sheep, and are caught with it still alive, you must pay the owner double.

If you happen to kill a burglar who breaks into your home after dark, you are not guilty. But if you kill someone who breaks in during the day, you are guilty of murder.

5 If you allow any of your animals to stray from your property and graze[p] in someone else's field or vineyard, you must repay the damage from the best part of your own harvest of grapes and grain.

6 If you carelessly let a fire spread from your property to someone else's, you must pay the owner for any crops or fields destroyed by the fire.

7 Suppose a neighbor asks you to keep some silver or other valuables, and they are stolen from your house. If the thief is caught, the thief must repay double. 8 But if the thief isn't caught, some judges[q] will decide if you are the guilty one.

9 Suppose two people claim to own the same ox or donkey or sheep or piece of clothing. Then the judges[r] must decide the case, and the guilty person will pay the owner double.

10 Suppose a neighbor who is going to be away asks you to keep a donkey or an ox or a sheep or some other animal, and it dies or gets injured or is stolen while no one is looking. 11 If you swear with me as your witness that you did not harm the animal, you do not have to replace it. Your word is enough. 12 But if the animal was stolen while in your care, you must replace it. 13 If the animal was attacked and killed by a wild animal, and you can show the remains of the dead animal to its owner, you do not have to replace it.

14 Suppose you borrow an animal from a neighbor, and it gets injured or dies while the neighbor isn't around. Then you must replace it. 15 But if something happens to the animal while the owner is present, you do not have to replace it. If you had leased the animal, the money you paid the owner will cover any harm done to it.

Laws for Everyday Life

The LORD said:

16 Suppose a young woman has never been married and isn't engaged. If a man talks her into having sex, he must pay the bride price[s] and marry her. 17 But if her father refuses to let her marry the man, the bride price must still be paid.

[p]**22.5** *graze*: Or "eat everything." [q]**22.8** *some judges*: Or "I." [r]**22.9** *the judges*: Or "I."
[s]**22.16** *bride price*: It was the custom for a man to pay his wife's family a bride price before the actual wedding ceremony took place.
22.16,17 Dt 22.28, 29.

18 Death is the punishment for witchcraft.

19 Death is the punishment for having sex with an animal.

20 Death is the punishment for offering sacrifices to any god except me.

21 Do not mistreat or abuse foreigners who live among you. Remember, you were foreigners in Egypt.

22 Do not mistreat widows or orphans. 23 If you do, they will beg for my help, and I will come to their rescue. 24 In fact, I will get so angry that I will kill your men and make widows of their wives and orphans of their children.

25 Don't charge interest when you lend money to any of my people who are in need. 26 Before sunset you must return any coat taken as security for a loan, 27 because that is the only cover the poor have when they sleep at night. I am a merciful God, and when they call out to me, I will come to help them.

28 Don't speak evil of me[t] or of the ruler of your people.

29 Don't fail to give me the offerings of grain and wine that belong to me.[u]

Dedicate to me your first-born sons 30 and the first-born of your cattle and sheep. Let the animals stay with their mothers for seven days, then on the eighth day give them to me, your God.

31 You are my chosen people, so don't eat the meat of any of your livestock that was killed by a wild animal. Instead, feed the meat to dogs.

Equal Justice for All

The LORD said:

23 Don't spread harmful rumors or help a criminal by giving false evidence.

2 Always tell the truth in court, even if everyone else is[v] dishonest and stands in the way of justice. 3 And don't favor the poor, simply because they are poor.

4 If you find an ox or a donkey that has wandered off, take it back where it belongs, even if the owner is your enemy.

5 If a donkey is overloaded and falls down, you must do what you can to help, even if it belongs to someone who doesn't like you.[w]

6 Make sure that the poor are given equal justice in court. 7 Don't bring false charges against anyone or sentence an innocent person to death. I won't forgive you if you do.

8 Don't accept bribes. Judges are blinded and justice is twisted by bribes.

9 Don't mistreat foreigners. You were foreigners in Egypt, and you know what it is like.

Laws for the Sabbath

The LORD said:

10 Plant and harvest your crops for six years, 11 but let the land rest during the seventh year. The poor are to eat what they want from your fields, vineyards, and olive trees during that year, and when they have all they want from your fields, leave the rest for wild animals.

12 Work the first six days of the week, but rest and relax on the seventh day. This law is not only for you, but for your oxen, donkeys, and slaves, as well as for any foreigners among you.

13 Make certain that you obey everything I have said. Don't pray to other gods or even mention their names.

Three Annual Festivals

(Exodus 34.18-26; Deuteronomy 16.1-17)

The LORD said:

14 Celebrate three festivals each year in my honor.

[t]**22.28** *me*: Or "your judges." [u]**22.29** *Don't fail . . . me*: One possible meaning for the difficult Hebrew text. [v]**23.2** *everyone else is*: Or "the authorities are." [w]**23.5** *you*: One possible meaning for the difficult Hebrew text of verse 5.

22.18 Dt 18.10, 11. **22.19** Lv 18.23; 20.15, 16; Dt 27.14-26. **22.20** Dt 17.2-7. **22.21,22** Ex 23.9; Lv 19.33, 34; Dt 24.17, 18; 27.14-26. **22.25** Lv 25.35-38; Dt 15.7-11; 23.19, 20. **22.26,27** Dt 24.10-13. **22.28** Ac 23.5. **22.31** Lv 17.15. **23.1** Ex 20.16; Lv 19.11, 12; Dt 5.20. **23.3** Lv 19.15. **23.4,5** Dt 22.1-4. **23.6-8** Lv 19.15; Dt 16.18, 19. **23.9** Ex 22.21; Lv 19.33, 34; Dt 24.17, 18; 27.14-26. **23.10,11** Lv 25.1-7. **23.12** Ex 20.9-11; 31.15; 34.21; 35.2; Lv 23.3; Dt 5.13, 14.

15 Celebrate the Festival of Thin Bread
by eating bread made without yeast, just as
I have commanded.[x] Do this at the proper
time during the month of Abib,[y] because it
is the month when you left Egypt. And
make certain that everyone brings the
proper offerings.
16 Celebrate the Harvest Festival[z] each
spring when you start harvesting your
wheat, and celebrate the Festival of Shelters[a]
each autumn when you pick your fruit.
17 Your men must come to these three
festivals each year to worship me.
18 Do not offer bread made with yeast
when you sacrifice an animal to me. And
make sure that the fat of the animal is
burned that same day.
19 Each year bring the best part of your
first harvest to the place of worship.
Don't boil a young goat in its mother's
milk.

A Promise and a Warning

The LORD said:
20 I am sending an angel to protect you
and to lead you into the land I have ready
for you. 21 Carefully obey everything the angel says, because I am giving him complete
authority, and he won't tolerate rebellion.
22 If you faithfully obey him, I will be a
fierce enemy of your enemies. 23 My angel
will lead you into the land of the Amorites,
Hittites, Perizzites, Canaanites, Hivites,
and Jebusites, and I will wipe them out.
24 Don't worship their gods or follow their
customs. Instead, destroy their idols and
shatter their stone images.
25 Worship only me, the LORD your God!
I will bless you with plenty of food and water and keep you strong. 26 Your women will
give birth to healthy children, and everyone
will live a long life.
27 I will terrify those nations and make
your enemies so confused that they will
run from you. 28 I will make the Hivites,
Canaanites, and Hittites panic as you approach. 29 But I won't do all this in the first
year, because the land would become poor,
and wild animals would be everywhere.
30 Instead, I will force out your enemies little by little and give your nation time to
grow strong enough to take over the land.
31 I will see that your borders reach
from the Red Sea[b] to the Euphrates River
and from the Mediterranean Sea to the
desert. I will let you defeat the people who
live there, and you will force them out of
the land. 32 But you must not make any
agreements with them or with their gods.
33 Don't let them stay in your land. They
will trap you into sinning against me and
worshiping their gods.

The People Agree To Obey God

24 The LORD said to Moses, "Come up
to me on this mountain. Bring
along Aaron, as well as his two sons Nadab
and Abihu, and seventy of Israel's leaders.
They must worship me at a distance, 2 but
you are to come near. Don't let anyone else
come up."
3 Moses gave the LORD's instructions to
the people, and they promised, "We will do
everything the LORD has commanded!"
4 Then Moses wrote down what the LORD
had said.
The next morning Moses got up early.
He built an altar at the foot of the mountain and set up a large stone for each of the
twelve tribes of Israel. 5 He also sent some
young men to burn offerings and to sacrifice bulls as special offerings[c] to the LORD.
6 Moses put half of the blood from the animals into bowls and sprinkled the rest on
the altar. 7 Then he read aloud the LORD's
commands and promises, and the people

[x]**23.15** *as I have commanded*: See 12.14-20. [y]**23.15** *Abib*: See the note at 12.2.
[z]**23.16** *Harvest Festival*: Traditionally called the "Festival of Weeks" and known in New Testament times as "Pentecost." [a]**23.16** *Festival of Shelters*: The Hebrew text has "Festival of Ingathering" (so also in 34.22), which was the final harvesting of crops and fruits before the autumn rains began. But the usual name was "Festival of Shelters." [b]**23.31** *Red Sea*: Hebrew *yam suph*, here referring to the Gulf of Aqaba, since the term is extended to include the northeastern arm of the Red Sea (see also the note at 13.18). [c]**24.5** *special offerings*: Often translated "peace offerings," which were to make peace between God and his people, who ate certain parts of the sacrificed animal.
23.15 Ex 12.14-20; Lv 23.6-8; Nu 28.17-25. **23.16** **a** Lv 23.15-21; Nu 28.26-31; **b** Lv 23.39-43. **23.19** Dt 26.2; Ex 34.26; Dt 14.21.

shouted, "We will obey the LORD and do
everything he has commanded!"
8 Moses took the blood from the bowls
and sprinkled it on the people. Next, he
told them, "With this blood the LORD
makes his agreement with you."
9 Moses and Aaron, together with Nadab
and Abihu and the seventy leaders, went
up the mountain 10 and saw the God of Israel. Under his feet was something that
looked like a pavement made out of sapphire,[d] and it was as bright as the sky.
11 Even though these leaders of Israel
saw God, he did not punish them. So they
ate and drank.

Moses on Mount Sinai

12 The LORD said to Moses, "Come up
on the mountain and stay here for a while.
I will give you the two flat stones on which
I have written the laws that my people
must obey." 13 Moses and Joshua his assistant got ready, then Moses started up the
mountain to meet with God.
14 Moses had told the leaders, "Wait
here until we come back. Aaron and Hur
will be with you, and they can settle any arguments while we are away."
15 When Moses went up on Mount
Sinai, a cloud covered it, 16 and the bright
glory of the LORD came down and stayed
there. The cloud covered the mountain
for six days, and on the seventh day the
LORD told Moses to come into the cloud.
17-18 Moses did so and stayed there forty
days and nights. To the people, the LORD's
glory looked like a blazing fire on top of the
mountain.

The Sacred Tent
(Exodus 35.4-9)

25 The LORD said to Moses:
2 Tell everyone in Israel who
wants to give gifts that they must bring
them to you. 3 Here is a list of what you are
to collect: Gold, silver, and bronze; 4 blue,
purple, and red wool; fine linen; goat hair;
5 tanned ram skins; fine leather; acacia
wood; 6 olive oil for the lamp; sweet-
smelling spices to mix with the oil for dedicating the tent and ordaining the priests;
7 and onyx[e] stones for the sacred vest and
the breastpiece. 8 I also want them to build
a special place where I can live among my
people. 9 Make it and its furnishings exactly
like the pattern I will show you.

The Sacred Chest
(Exodus 37.1-9)

The LORD said to Moses:
10 Tell the people to build a chest of acacia wood forty-five inches long, twenty-
seven inches wide, and twenty-seven
inches high. 11 Cover it inside and out with
pure gold and put a gold edging around the
lid. 12 Make four gold rings and fasten one
of them to each of the four legs of the
chest. 13 Make two poles of acacia wood.
Cover them with gold 14 and put them
through the rings, so the chest can be carried by the poles. 15 Don't ever remove the
poles from the rings. 16 When I give you
the Ten Commandments written on two
flat stones, put them inside the chest.
17 Cover the lid of the chest with pure
gold. 18-19 Then hammer out two winged
creatures of pure gold and fasten them to
the lid at the ends of the chest. 20 The
creatures must face each other with their
wings spread over the chest. 21 Inside it
place the two flat stones with the Ten Commandments and put the gold lid on top
of the chest. 22 I will meet you there[f] between the two creatures and tell you what
my people must do and what they must
not do.

The Table for the Sacred Bread
(Exodus 37.10-16)

The LORD said:
23 Make a table of acacia wood thirty-six
inches long, eighteen inches wide, and
twenty-seven inches high. 24-25 Cover it
with pure gold and put a gold edging

[d]**24.10** *sapphire*: A precious stone, blue in color. [e]**25.7** *onyx*: A precious stone with bands of different colors. [f]**25.22** *I will meet you there*: It was believed that God had his earthly throne on the lid of the sacred chest.

24.8 a Mt 26.28; Mk 14.24; Lk 22.20; 1 Co 11.25; He 10.29; **b** He 9.19, 20.
24.17,18 Dt 9.9-11. **25.17** He 9.5.

around it with a border three inches wide.[g] 26 Make four gold rings and attach one to each of the legs 27-28 near the edging. The poles for carrying the table are to be placed through these rings and are to be made of acacia wood covered with gold. 29-30 The table is to be kept in the holy place, and the sacred loaves of bread must always be put on it. All bowls, plates, jars, and cups for wine offerings are to be made of pure gold and set on this table.

The Lampstand

(Exodus 37.17-24)

The LORD said:

31 Make a lampstand of pure gold. The whole lampstand, including its decorative flowers, must be made from a single piece of hammered gold 32 with three branches on each of its two sides. 33 There are to be three decorative almond blossoms on each branch 34 and four on the stem. 35 There must also be a blossom where each pair of branches comes out from the stem. 36 The lampstand, including its branches and decorative flowers, must be made from a single piece of hammered pure gold. 37 The lamp on the top and those at the end of each of its six branches must be made so as to shine toward the front of the lampstand. 38 The tongs and trays for taking care of the lamps are to be made of pure gold. 39 The lampstand and its equipment will require seventy-five pounds of pure gold, 40 and they must be made according to the pattern I showed you on the mountain.

Curtains and Coverings for the Sacred Tent

(Exodus 36.8-19)

The LORD said to Moses:

26 Furnish the sacred tent with curtains made from ten pieces of the finest linen. They must be woven with blue, purple, and red wool and embroidered with figures of winged creatures. 2 Make each piece fourteen yards long and two yards wide 3 and sew them together into two curtains with five sections each. 4-6 Put fifty loops of blue cloth along one of the wider sides of each curtain, then fasten the two curtains at the loops with fifty gold hooks.

7-8 As the material for the tent, use goat hair to weave eleven sections fifteen yards by two yards each. 9 Sew five of the sections together to make one panel. Then sew the other six together to make a second panel, and fold the sixth section double over the front of the tent. 10 Put fifty loops along one of the wider sides of each panel 11 and fasten the two panels at the loops with fifty bronze hooks. 12-13 The panel of goat hair will be a yard longer than the tent itself, so fold half a yard of the material behind the tent and on each side as a protective covering. 14 Make two more coverings—one with ram skins dyed red and the other with fine leather.

The Framework for the Sacred Tent

(Exodus 36.20-34)

The LORD said:

15 Build a framework of acacia wood for the walls of the sacred tent. 16 Each frame is to be fifteen feet high and twenty-seven inches wide 17 with two wooden pegs near the bottom. 18-21 Place two silver stands under each frame with sockets for the pegs, so the frames can be joined together. Twenty of these frames are to be used along the south side and twenty more along the north. 22 For the back wall along the west side use six frames 23-24 with two more at the southwest and northwest corners. Make certain that these corner frames are joined from top to bottom. 25 Altogether, this back wall will have eight frames with two silver stands under each one.

26-27 Make five crossbars for each of the wooden frames, 28 with the center crossbar running the full length of the wall. 29 Cover the frames and the crossbars with gold and attach gold rings to the frames to run the crossbars through. 30 Then set up the tent in the way I showed you on the mountain.

[g] **25.24,25** *a gold edging . . . wide*: Or "a gold edging around it three inches wide."
25.29,30 Lv 24.5-8. **25.40** Ac 7.44; He 8.5.

The Curtain inside the Sacred Tent
(Exodus 36.35-38)

The LORD said:

31-33 Make a curtain to separate the holy place from the most holy place. Use fine linen woven with blue, purple, and red wool, and embroidered with figures of winged creatures. Cover four acacia wood posts with gold and set them each on a silver stand. Then fasten gold hooks to the posts and hang the curtain there.

34 Inside the most holy place, you must put the sacred chest that has the place of mercy on its lid.[h] 35 Outside the curtain put the table for the sacred bread on the right side and the gold lampstand on the left.

36 For the entrance to the tent, use a piece of fine linen woven with blue, purple, and red wool and embroidered with fancy needlework. 37 Cover five acacia wood posts with gold and set them each on a bronze stand. Then put gold hooks on the posts and hang the curtain there.

The Altar for Offering Sacrifices
(Exodus 38.1-7)

The LORD said to Moses:

27 Use acacia wood to build an altar seven and a half feet square and four and a half feet high, 2 and make each of the four top corners stick up like the horn of a bull. Then cover the whole altar with bronze, including the four horns. 3 All the equipment for the altar must also be made of bronze—the pans for the hot ashes, the shovels, the sprinkling bowls, the meat forks, and the fire pans. 4-5 Midway up the altar build a ledge around it, and cover the bottom half of the altar with a decorative bronze grating. Then attach a bronze ring beneath the ledge at the four corners of the altar. 6-7 Cover two acacia wood poles with bronze and put them through the rings for carrying the altar. 8 Construct the altar in the shape of an open box, just as you were shown on the mountain.

The Courtyard around the Sacred Tent
(Exodus 38.9-20)

The LORD said:

9-15 Surround the sacred tent with a courtyard one hundred fifty feet long on the south and north and seventy-five feet wide on the east and west. Use twenty bronze posts on bronze stands for the south and north and ten for the west. Then hang a curtain of fine linen on the posts along each of these three sides by using silver hooks and rods.

Place three bronze posts on each side of the entrance at the east and hang a curtain seven and a half yards wide on each set of posts. 16 Use four more of these posts for the entrance way, then hang on them an embroidered curtain of fine linen ten yards long and woven with blue, purple, and red wool.

17-18 The curtains that surround the courtyard must be two and a half yards high and are to be hung from the bronze posts with silver hooks and rods. 19 The rest of the equipment for the sacred tent must be made of bronze, including the pegs for the tent and for the curtain surrounding the courtyard.

The Oil for the Lamp in the Holy Place
(Leviticus 24.1-4)

The LORD said to Moses:

20 Command the people of Israel to supply you with the purest olive oil. Do this so the lamp will keep burning 21 in front of the curtain that separates the holy place from the most holy place, where the sacred chest is kept. Aaron and his sons are responsible for keeping the lamp burning every night in the sacred tent. The Israelites must always obey this command.

[h] **26.34** *place of mercy on its lid*: It was believed that God had his earthly throne on the lid of the sacred chest, and from this place he showed mercy to his people.

26.31-33 He 6.19; 9.3-5.

The Clothes for the High Priest
(Exodus 39.1-7)

The LORD *said to Moses:*

28 Send for your brother Aaron and his sons Nadab, Abihu, Eleazar, and Ithamar. They are the ones I have chosen from Israel to serve as my priests. 2 Make Aaron some beautiful clothes that are worthy of a high priest. 3 Aaron is to be dedicated as my high priest, and his clothes must be made only by persons who possess skills that I have given them. 4 Here are the items that need to be made: a breastpiece, a priestly vest, a robe, an embroidered shirt, a turban, and a sash. These sacred clothes are to be made for your brother Aaron and his sons who will be my priests. 5 Only gold and fine linen, woven with blue, purple, and red wool, are to be used for making these clothes.

The Vest for the High Priest
(Exodus 39.2-7)

The LORD *said:*

6-8 The entire priestly vest must be made of fine linen skillfully woven with blue, purple, and red wool, and decorated with gold. It is to have two shoulder straps to support it and a sash that fastens around the waist.

9-12 Put two onyx[i] stones in gold settings, then attach one to each of the shoulder straps. On one of these stones engrave the names of Israel's first six sons in the order of their birth. And do the same with his remaining six sons on the other stone. In this way Aaron will always carry the names of the tribes of Israel when he enters the holy place, and I will never forget my people.

13-14 Attach two gold settings to the shoulder straps and fasten them with two braided chains of pure gold.

The Breastpiece for the High Priest
(Exodus 39.8-21)

The LORD *said:*

15 From the same costly material make a breastpiece for the high priest to use in learning what I want my people to do. 16 It is to be nine inches square and folded double 17 with four rows of three precious stones: In the first row put a carnelian, a chrysolite, and an emerald; 18 in the second row a turquoise, a sapphire, and a diamond; 19 in the third row a jacinth, an agate, and an amethyst; 20 and in the fourth row a beryl, an onyx, and a jasper.[j] Mount the stones in delicate gold settings 21 and engrave on each of them the name of one of the twelve tribes of Israel.

22-25 Attach two gold rings to the upper front corners of the breastpiece and fasten them with two braided gold chains to gold settings on the shoulder straps. 26 Attach two other gold rings to the lower inside corners next to the vest 27 and two more near the bottom of the shoulder straps right above the sash. 28 Then take a blue cord and tie the two lower rings on the breastpiece to those on the vest. This will keep the breastpiece in place.

29 In this way Aaron will have the names of the twelve tribes of Israel written on his heart each time he enters the holy place, and I will never forget my people. 30 He must also wear on his breastpiece the two small objects[k] that he uses to receive answers from me.

The Other High-Priestly Clothes
(Exodus 39.22-26, 30, 31)

The LORD *said:*

31 Under his vest Aaron must wear a robe of blue wool 32 with an opening in the center for his head. Be sure to bind the material around the collar to keep it from

[i]**28.9-12** *onyx*: See the note at 25.7. [j]**28.20** *jasper*: The stones mentioned in verses 17-20 are of different colors: *carnelian* is deep red or reddish white; *chrysolite* is olive green; *emerald* is green; *turquoise* is blue or blue green; *sapphire* is blue; *diamond* is colorless or white; *jacinth* is reddish orange; *agate* has circles of brown and white; *amethyst* is deep purple; *beryl* is green or bluish green; *onyx* has bands of different colors; and *jasper* is usually green or clear.
[k]**28.30** *two small objects*: The Hebrew text has "urim and thummim," which may have been made of wood, stone, or metal, and were used in some way to receive answers from God.
28.30 Nu 27.21; Dt 33.8; Ezra 2.63; Ne 7.65.

raveling. 33-34 Along the hem of the robe
weave pomegranates[l] of blue, purple, and
red wool with a gold bell between each of
them. 35 If Aaron wears these clothes when
he enters the holy place as my high priest,
the sound of the bells will be heard, and his
life will not be in danger.

36 On a narrow strip of pure gold engrave the words: "Dedicated to the LORD."
37 Fasten it to the front of Aaron's turban
with a blue cord, 38 so he can wear it on his
forehead. This will show that he will take
on himself the guilt for any sins the people
of Israel commit in offering their gifts to
me, and I will forgive them.

39 Make Aaron's robe and turban of fine
linen and decorate his sash with fancy
needlework.

The Clothes for the Other Priests
(Exodus 39.27-29)

40 Since Aaron's sons are priests, they
should also look dignified. So make robes,
sashes, and special caps for them. 41 Then
dress Aaron and his sons in these clothes,
pour olive oil on their heads, and ordain
them as my priests.

42 Make linen shorts for them that reach
from the waist down to the thigh, so they
won't expose themselves. 43 Whenever they
enter the sacred tent or serve at the altar or
enter the holy place, they must wear these
shorts, or else they will be guilty and die.
This same rule applies to any of their descendants who serve as priests.

Instructions for Ordaining Priests
(Leviticus 8.1-36)

The LORD said to Moses:

29 When you ordain one of Aaron's
sons as my priest, choose a young
bull and two rams that have nothing wrong
with them. 2 Then from your finest flour
make three batches of dough without yeast.
Shape some of it into larger loaves, some
into smaller loaves mixed with olive oil,
and the rest into thin wafers brushed with
oil. 3 Put all of this bread in a basket and
bring it when you come to sacrifice the
three animals to me.

4 Bring Aaron and his sons to the entrance of the sacred tent and have them
wash themselves. 5 Dress Aaron in the
priestly shirt, the robe that goes under the
sacred vest, the vest itself, the breastpiece,
and the sash. 6 Put on his turban with its
narrow strip of engraved gold 7 and then
ordain him by pouring olive oil on his head.

8 Next, dress Aaron's sons in their special shirts 9 and caps and their sashes,[m]
then ordain them, because they and their
descendants will always be priests.

10 Lead the bull to the entrance of the
sacred tent, where Aaron and his sons will
lay their hands on its head. 11 Kill the bull
near my altar in front of the tent. 12 Use a
finger to smear some of its blood on each of
the four corners of the altar and pour out
the rest of the blood on the ground next to
the altar. 13 Then take the fat from the animal's insides, as well as the lower part of
the liver and the two kidneys with their fat,
and send them up in smoke on the altar.
14 But the meat, the skin, and the food still
in the bull's stomach must be burned outside the camp as an offering to ask forgiveness for the sins of the priests.[n]

15 Bring one of the rams to Aaron and
his sons and have them lay their hands on
its head. 16 Kill the ram and splatter its
blood against all four sides of the altar.
17 Cut up the ram, wash its insides and
legs, and lay all of its parts on the altar, including the head. 18 Then make sure that
the whole animal goes up in smoke with a
smell that pleases me.

19 Bring the other ram to Aaron and his
sons and have them lay their hands on its
head. 20 Kill the ram and place some of its
blood on Aaron's right ear lobe, his right
thumb, and the big toe of his right foot. Do
the same for each of his sons and splatter
the rest of the blood against the four sides

[l] **28.33,34** *pomegranates*: A bright red fruit that looks like an apple. [m] **29.9** *their sashes*: One ancient translation; Hebrew "the sashes of Aaron and his sons." [n] **29.14** *for the sins of the priests*: When a sacrifice for the forgiveness of sins was made for someone other than priests, the part that was not burned on the altar could be eaten by the priests (see Leviticus 5.13; 6.26).

28.33,34 Si 45.9. **29.18** Eph 5.2; Phil 4.18.

of the altar. 21 Then take some of the blood from the altar, mix it with the oil used for ordination, and sprinkle it on Aaron and his clothes, and also on his sons and their clothes. This will show that they and their clothes have been dedicated to me.

22 This ram is part of the ordination service. So remove its right hind leg,[o] its fat tail, the fat on its insides, as well as the lower part of the liver and the two kidneys with their fat. 23 Take one loaf of each kind of bread[p] from the basket, 24 and put this bread, together with the meat, into the hands of Aaron and his sons. Then they will lift it all up[q] to show that it is dedicated to me. 25 After this, the meat and bread are to be placed on the altar and sent up in smoke with a smell that pleases me.

26 You may eat the choice ribs from this second ram, but you must first lift them up[q] to show that this meat is dedicated to me.

27-28 In the future, when anyone from Israel offers the ribs and a hind leg of a ram either to ordain a priest or to ask for my blessing, the meat belongs to me, but it may be eaten by the priests. This law will never change.

29-30 After Aaron's death, his priestly clothes are to be handed down to each descendant who succeeds him as high priest, and these clothes must be worn during the seven-day ceremony of ordination.

31 Boil the meat of the ordination ram in a sacred place, 32 then have Aaron and his sons eat it together with the three kinds of bread[r] at the entrance to the sacred tent. 33 At their ordination, a ceremony of forgiveness was performed for them with this sacred food, and only they have the right to eat it. 34 If any of the sacred food is left until morning, it must be burned up.

35 Repeat this ordination ceremony for Aaron and his sons seven days in a row, just as I have instructed you. 36 Each day you must offer a bull as a sacrifice for sin and as a way of purifying the altar. In addition, you must smear the altar with olive oil to make it completely holy. 37 Do this for seven days, and the altar will become so holy that anyone who touches it will become holy.

Daily Sacrifices

(Leviticus 6.8-13; Numbers 28.1-8)

The LORD said:

38 Each day you must sacrifice two lambs a year old, 39 one in the morning and one in the evening. 40-41 With each lamb offer two pounds of your finest flour mixed with a quart of pure olive oil, and also pour out a quart of wine as an offering. The smell of this sacrifice on the fires of the altar will be pleasing to me. 42-43 You and your descendants must always offer this sacrifice on the altar at the entrance to the sacred tent.

People of Israel, I will meet and speak with you there, and my shining glory will make the place holy. 44 Because of who I am, the tent will become sacred, and Aaron and his sons will become worthy to serve as my priests. 45 I will live among you as your God, 46 and you will know that I am the LORD your God, the one who rescued you from Egypt, so that I could live among you.

The Altar for Burning Incense

(Exodus 37.25-28)

The LORD said to Moses:

30 Build an altar of acacia wood where you can burn incense. 2 Make it eighteen inches square and thirty-six inches high, and make each of its four corners stick up like the horn of a bull. 3 Cover it with pure gold and put a gold edging around it. 4 Then below the edging on opposite sides attach two gold rings through which you can put the poles for carrying the altar. 5 These poles are also to be made of acacia wood covered with gold.

6 Put the altar in front of the inside curtain of the sacred tent. The chest with the place of mercy[s] is kept behind that curtain, and I will talk with you there. 7-8 From now on, when Aaron tends the lamp each

[o] **29.22** *right hind leg*: This was usually given to the officiating priest (see Leviticus 7.33).
[p] **29.23** *each kind of bread*: See verses 2, 3.
[q] **29.24,26** *lift it all up*: Or "wave it all."
[r] **29.32** *three kinds of bread*: See verses 2, 3.
[s] **30.6** *place of mercy*: See the note at 26.34.

morning and evening, he must burn sweet-smelling incense to me on the altar. 9 Burn only the proper incense on the altar and never use it for grain sacrifices or animal sacrifices or drink offerings. 10 Once a year Aaron must purify the altar by smearing on its four corners[t] the blood of an animal sacrificed for sin, and this practice must always be followed. The altar is sacred because it is dedicated to me.

The Money for the Sacred Tent

11 The LORD said to Moses:

12 Find out how many grown men there are in Israel and require each of them to pay me to keep him safe from danger while you are counting them. 13-15 Each man over nineteen, whether rich or poor, must pay me the same amount of money, weighed according to the official standards. 16 This money is to be used for the upkeep of the sacred tent, and because of it, I will never forget my people.

The Large Bronze Bowl

(Exodus 38.8)

17 The LORD said to Moses:

18-21 Make a large bronze bowl and a bronze stand for it. Then put them between the altar for sacrifice and the sacred tent, so the priests can wash their hands and feet before entering the tent or offering a sacrifice on the altar. Each priest in every generation must wash himself in this way, or else he will die right there.

The Oil for Dedication and Ordination

(Exodus 37.29)

22 The LORD said to Moses:

23-25 Mix a gallon of olive oil with the following costly spices: twelve pounds of myrrh, six pounds of cinnamon, six pounds of cane, and twelve pounds of cassia. Measure these according to the official standards. Then use this sacred mixture 26 for dedicating the tent and chest, 27 the table with its equipment, the lampstand with its equipment, the incense altar with all its utensils, 28 the altar for sacrifices, and the large bowl with its stand. 29 By dedicating them in this way, you will make them so holy that anyone who even touches them will become holy.

30 When you ordain Aaron and his sons as my priests, sprinkle them with some of this oil, 31 and say to the people of Israel: "This oil must always be used in the ordination service of a priest. It is holy because it is dedicated to the LORD. 32 So treat it as holy! Don't ever use it for everyday purposes or mix any for yourselves. 33 If you do, you will no longer belong to the LORD's people."

The Sweet-Smelling Incense

34-35 Mix equal amounts of the costly spices stacte, onycha, galbanum, and pure frankincense, then add salt to make the mixture pure and holy. 36 Pound some of it into powder and sprinkle it in front of the sacred chest, where I meet with you. Be sure to treat this incense as something very holy. 37 It is truly holy because it is dedicated to me, so don't ever make any for yourselves. 38 If you ever make any of it to use as perfume, you will no longer belong to my people.

The LORD Chooses Bezalel and Oholiab

(Exodus 35.30—36.1)

31 The LORD said to Moses:

2 I have chosen Bezalel[u] from the Judah tribe to make the sacred tent and its furnishings. 3-5 Not only have I filled him with my Spirit, but I have given him wisdom and made him a skilled craftsman who can create objects of art with gold, silver, bronze, stone, and wood. 6 I have appointed Oholiab[v] from the tribe of Dan to work with him, and I have also given skills to those who will help them make everything exactly as I have commanded you: 7-11 the sacred tent with its furnishings, the sacred chest with its place of mercy, the table with all that is on it, the lamp with its equipment, the incense altar, the altar for

[t] **30.10** *four corners*: See 27.2; 30.2. [u] **31.2** *Bezalel*: Hebrew "Bezalel, son of Uri and grandson of Hur." [v] **31.6** *Oholiab*: Hebrew "Oholiab son of Ahisamach."

30.10 3 Macc 1.11. **30.13** Ex 38.25, 26. **30.18-21** Ex 38.8. **30.22-38** Ex 37.29.

sacrifices with its equipment, the bronze bowl with its stand, the beautiful priestly clothes for Aaron and his sons, the oil for dedication and ordination services, and the sweet-smelling incense for the holy place.

Laws for the Sabbath

12-13 Moses told the Israelites that the LORD had said:

The Sabbath belongs to me. Now I command you and your descendants to always obey the laws of the Sabbath. By doing this, you will know that I have chosen you as my own. 14-15 Keep the Sabbath holy. You have six days to do your work, but the Sabbath is mine, and it must remain a day of rest. If you work on the Sabbath, you will no longer be part of my people, and you will be put to death.

16 Every generation of Israelites must respect the Sabbath. 17 This day will always serve as a reminder, both to me and to the Israelites, that I made the heavens and the earth in six days, then on the seventh day I rested and relaxed.

18 When God had finished speaking to Moses on Mount Sinai, he gave him the two flat stones on which he had written all of his laws with his own hand.

The People Make an Idol To Worship

(Deuteronomy 9.6-29)

32 After the people saw that Moses had been on the mountain for a long time, they went to Aaron and said, "Make us an image of a god who will lead and protect us. Moses brought us out of Egypt, but nobody knows what has happened to him."

2 Aaron told them, "Bring me the gold earrings that your wives and sons and daughters are wearing." 3 Everybody took off their earrings and brought them to Aaron, 4 then he melted them and made an idol in the shape of a young bull.

All the people said to one another, "This is the god who brought us out of Egypt!"

5 When Aaron saw what was happening, he built an altar in front of the idol and said, "Tomorrow we will celebrate in honor of the LORD." 6 The people got up early the next morning and killed some animals to be used for sacrifices and others to be eaten. Then everyone ate and drank so much that they began to carry on like wild people.

7 The LORD said to Moses:

Hurry back down! Those people you led out of Egypt are acting like fools. 8 They have already stopped obeying me and have made themselves an idol in the shape of a young bull. They have bowed down to it, offered sacrifices, and said that it is the god who brought them out of Egypt. 9 Moses, I have seen how stubborn these people are, 10 and I'm angry enough to destroy them, so don't try to stop me. But I will make your descendants into a great nation.

11 Moses tried to get the LORD God to change his mind:

Our LORD, you used your mighty power to bring these people out of Egypt. Now don't become angry and destroy them. 12 If you do, the Egyptians will say that you brought your people out here into the mountains just to get rid of them. Please don't be angry with your people. Don't destroy them!

13 Remember the solemn promise you made to Abraham, Isaac, and Jacob. You promised that someday they would have as many descendants as there are stars in the sky and that you would give them land.

14 So even though the LORD had threatened to destroy the people, he changed his mind and let them live.

15-16 Moses went back down the mountain with the two flat stones on which God had written all of his laws with his own hand, and he had used both sides of the stones.

17 When Joshua heard the noisy shouts

31.14,15 Ex 20.8-11; 23.12; 34.21; 35.2; Lv 23.3; Dt 5.12-14. **31.17** Ex 20.11.
32.1 Ac 7.40. **32.4** 1 K 12.28; Ac 7.41. **32.6** 1 Co 10.7. **32.11-14** Nu 14.13-19.
32.13 Gn 22.16, 17; Gn 17.8.

of the people, he said to Moses, "A battle must be going on down in the camp."

18 But Moses replied, "It doesn't sound like they are shouting because they have won or lost a battle. They are singing wildly!"

19 As Moses got closer to the camp, he saw the idol, and he also saw the people dancing around. This made him so angry that he threw down the stones and broke them to pieces at the foot of the mountain.
20 He melted the idol the people had made, and he ground it into powder. He scattered it in their water and made them drink it.
21 Moses asked Aaron, "What did these people do to harm you? Why did you make them sin in this terrible way?"

22 Aaron answered:

Don't be angry with me. You know as well as I do that they are determined to do evil. 23 They even told me, "That man Moses led us out of Egypt, but now we don't know what has happened to him. Make us a god to lead us." 24 Then I asked them to bring me their gold earrings. They took them off and gave them to me. I threw the gold into a fire, and out came this bull.

25 Moses knew that the people were out of control and that it was Aaron's fault. And now they had made fools of themselves in front of their enemies. 26 So Moses stood at the gate of the camp and shouted, "Everyone who is on the LORD's side come over here!"

Then the men of the Levi tribe gathered around Moses, 27 and he said to them, "The LORD God of Israel commands you to strap on your swords and go through the camp, killing your relatives, your friends, and your neighbors."

28 The men of the Levi tribe followed his orders, and that day they killed about three thousand men. 29 Moses said to them, "You obeyed the LORD and did what was right, and so you will serve as his priests for the people of Israel. It was hard for you to kill your own sons and brothers, but the LORD has blessed you and made you his priests today."

30 The next day Moses told the people, "This is a terrible thing you have done. But I will go back to the LORD to see if I can do something to keep this sin from being held against you."

31 Moses returned to the LORD and said, "The people have committed a terrible sin. They have made a gold idol to be their god.
32 But I beg you to forgive them. If you don't, please wipe my name out of your book."[w]

33 The LORD replied, "I will wipe out of my book the name of everyone who has sinned against me. 34 Now take my people to the place I told you about, and my angel will lead you. But when the time comes, I will punish them for this sin."

35 So the LORD punished the people of Israel with a terrible disease for talking Aaron into making the gold idol.

The LORD Tells Israel To Leave Mount Sinai

33 The LORD said to Moses:

You led the people of Israel out of Egypt. Now get ready to lead them to the land I promised their ancestors Abraham, Isaac, and Jacob. 2-3 It is a land rich with milk and honey, and I will send an angel to force out those people who live there—the Canaanites, the Amorites, the Hittites, the Perizzites, the Hivites, and the Jebusites. I would go with my people, but they are so rebellious that I would destroy them before they get there.

4-5 Even before the LORD said these harsh things, he had told Moses, "These people really are rebellious, and I would kill them at once, if I went with them. But tell them to take off their fancy jewelry, then I'll decide what to do with them." So the people started mourning, 6 and after leaving Mount Sinai,[x] they stopped wearing fancy jewelry.

[w] **32.32** *your book*: The people of Israel believed that the LORD kept a record of the names of his people, and anyone whose name was removed from that book no longer belonged to the LORD.
[x] **33.6** *Mount Sinai*: The Hebrew text has "Mount Horeb," another name for Sinai.
32.32 Ps 69.28; Rev 3.5. **33.1** **a** Gn 12.7; **b** Gn 26.3; **c** Gn 28.13.

The LORD Is with His People

[7] Moses used to set up a tent far from camp. He called it the "meeting tent," and whoever needed some message from the LORD would go there. [8] Each time Moses went out to the tent, everyone would stand at the entrance to their own tents and watch him enter. [9-11] Then they would bow down because a thick cloud would come down in front of the tent, and the LORD would speak to Moses face to face, just like a friend. Afterwards, Moses would return to camp, but his young assistant Joshua[y] would stay at the tent.

The LORD Promises To Be with His People

[12] Moses said to the LORD, "I know that you have told me to lead these people to the land you promised them. But you have not told me who my assistant will be. You have said that you are my friend and that you are pleased with me. [13] If this is true, let me know what your plans are, then I can obey and continue to please you. And don't forget that you have chosen this nation to be your own."

[14] The LORD said, "I will go with you and give you peace."

[15] Then Moses replied, "If you aren't going with us, please don't make us leave this place. [16] But if you do go with us, everyone will know that you are pleased with your people and with me. That way, we will be different from the rest of the people on earth."

[17] So the LORD told him, "I will do what you have asked, because I am your friend and I am pleased with you."

[18] Then Moses said, "I pray that you will let me see you in all of your glory."

[19] The LORD answered:

All right. I am the LORD, and I show mercy and kindness to anyone I choose. I will let you see my glory and hear my holy name, [20] but I won't let you see my face, because anyone who sees my face will die. [21] There is a rock not far from me. Stand beside it, [22] and before I pass by in all of my shining glory, I will put you in a large crack in the rock. I will cover your eyes with my hand until I have passed by. [23] Then I will take my hand away, and you will see my back. You will not see my face.

The Second Set of Commandments

(Deuteronomy 10.1-5)

34 One day the LORD said to Moses, "Cut two flat stones like the first ones I made, and I will write on them the same commandments that were on the two you broke. [2] Be ready tomorrow morning to come up Mount Sinai and meet me at the top. [3] No one is to come with you or to be on the mountain at all. Don't even let the sheep and cattle graze at the foot of the mountain." [4] So Moses cut two flat stones like the first ones, and early the next morning he carried them to the top of Mount Sinai, just as the LORD had commanded.

[5] The LORD God came down in a cloud and stood beside Moses there on the mountain. God spoke his holy name, "the LORD."[z] [6] Then he passed in front of Moses and called out, "I am the LORD God. I am merciful and very patient with my people. I show great love, and I can be trusted. [7] I keep my promises to my people forever, but I also punish anyone who sins. When people sin, I punish them and their children, and also their grandchildren and great-grandchildren."

[8] Moses quickly bowed down to the ground and worshiped the LORD. [9] He prayed, "LORD, if you really are pleased with me, I pray that you will go with us. It is true that these people are sinful and rebellious, but forgive our sin and let us be your people."

A Promise and Its Demands

(Exodus 23.14-19; Deuteronomy 7.1-5; 16.1-17)

[10] The LORD said:

I promise to perform miracles for you that have never been seen anywhere on earth. Neighboring nations will stand in fear and know that I was

[y]**33.9-11** *Joshua*: Hebrew "Joshua son of Nun." [z]**34.5** *the LORD*: See the note at 3.14, 15.

33.19 Ro 9.15. **34.6,7** Ex 20.5, 6; Nu 14.18; Dt 5.9, 10; 7.9, 10.

the one who did these marvelous things. [11] I will force out the Amorites, the Canaanites, the Hittites, the Perizzites, the Hivites, and the Jebusites, but you must do what I command you today. [12] Don't make treaties with any of those people. If you do, it will be like falling into a trap. [13] Instead, you must destroy their altars and tear down the sacred poles[a] they use in the worship of the goddess Asherah. [14] I demand your complete loyalty—you must not worship any other god! [15] Don't make treaties with the people there, or you will soon find yourselves worshiping their gods and taking part in their sacrificial meals. [16] Your men will even marry their women and be influenced to worship their gods.

[17] Don't make metal images of gods.

[18] Don't fail to observe the Festival of Thin Bread in the month of Abib.[b] Obey me and eat bread without yeast for seven days during Abib, because that is the month you left Egypt.

[19] The first-born males of your families and of your flocks and herds belong to me.

[20] You can save the life of a first-born donkey[c] by sacrificing a lamb; if you don't, you must break the donkey's neck. You must save every first-born son.

Bring an offering every time you come to worship.

[21] Do your work in six days and rest on the seventh day, even during the seasons for plowing and harvesting. [22] Celebrate the Harvest Festival[d] each spring when you start harvesting your wheat, and celebrate the Festival of Shelters[e] each autumn when you pick your fruit.

[23] Your men must come to worship me three times a year, because I am the LORD God of Israel. [24] I will force the nations out of your land and enlarge your borders. Then no one will try to take your property when you come to worship me these three times each year.

[25] When you sacrifice an animal on the altar, don't offer bread made with yeast. And don't save any part of the Passover meal for the next day.

[26] I am the LORD your God, and you must bring the first part of your harvest to the place of worship.

Don't boil a young goat in its mother's milk.

[27] The LORD told Moses to put these laws in writing, as part of his agreement with Israel. [28] Moses stayed on the mountain with the LORD for forty days and nights, without eating or drinking. And he wrote down the Ten Commandments, the most important part of God's agreement with his people.

Moses Comes Down from Mount Sinai

[29] Moses came down from Mount Sinai, carrying the Ten Commandments. His face was shining brightly because the LORD had been speaking to him. But Moses did not know at first that his face was shining. [30] When Aaron and the others looked at Moses, they saw that his face was shining, and they were afraid to go near him. [31] Moses called out for Aaron and the leaders to come to him, and he spoke with them. [32] Then the rest of the people of Israel gathered around Moses, and he gave them the laws that the LORD had given him on Mount Sinai.

[33] The face of Moses kept shining, and after he had spoken with the people, he covered his face with a veil. [34] Moses would always remove the veil when he went into the sacred tent to speak with the LORD. And when he came out, he would tell the people everything the LORD had told him to say. [35] They could see that his face was still

[a]**34.13** *sacred poles*: Or "trees," used as symbols of Asherah, the goddess of fertility.
[b]**34.18** *Abib*: See the note at 12.2. [c]**34.20** *donkey*: See the note at 13.13. [d]**34.22** *Harvest Festival*: See the note at 23.16. [e]**34.22** *Festival of Shelters*: See the note at 23.16.

34.13 Dt 16.21. **34.17** Ex 20.4; Lv 19.4; Dt 5.8; 27.14-26. **34.18** Ex 12.14-20; Lv 23.6-8; Nu 28.16-25. **34.19** Ex 13.2. **34.20** Ex 13.13. **34.21** Ex 20.9, 10; 23.12; 31.14, 15; 35.2; Lv 23.3; Dt 5.13, 14. **34.22** **a** Lv 23.15-21; Nu 28.26-31; **b** Lv 23.39-43. **34.25** Ex 12.10. **34.26** **a** Dt 26.2; **b** Dt 14.21. **34.29-35** 2 Co 3.7-16.

shining. So after he had spoken with them, he would put the veil back on and leave it on until the next time he went to speak with the LORD.

Laws for the Sabbath

35 Moses called together the people of Israel and told them that the LORD had said:

2 You have six days in which to do your work. But the seventh day must be dedicated to me, your LORD, as a day of rest. Whoever works on the Sabbath will be put to death. 3 Don't even build a cooking fire at home on the Sabbath.

Offerings for the Sacred Tent

(Exodus 25.1-9; 35.10-19)

4 Moses told the people of Israel that the LORD had said:

5 I would welcome an offering from anyone who wants to give something. You may bring gold, silver, or bronze; 6 blue, purple, or red wool; fine linen; goat hair; 7 tanned ram skin or fine leather; acacia wood; 8 olive oil for the lamp; sweet-smelling spices for the oil of dedication and for the incense; or 9 onyx[f] stones or other gems for the sacred vest and breastpiece.

10 If you have any skills, you should use them to help make what I have commanded: 11 the sacred tent with its covering and hooks, its framework and crossbars, and its post and stands; 12 the sacred chest with its carrying poles, its place of mercy, and the curtain in front of it; 13 the table with all that goes on it, including the sacred bread; 14 the lamp with its equipment and oil; 15 the incense altar with its carrying poles and sweet-smelling incense; the ordination oil; the curtain for the entrance to the sacred tent; 16 the altar for sacrifices with its bronze grating, its carrying poles, and its equipment; the large bronze bowl with its stand; 17 the curtains with the posts and stands that go around the courtyard; 18 the pegs and ropes for the tent and the courtyard; 19 and the finely woven priestly clothes for Aaron and his sons.

Gifts for the LORD

20 Moses finished speaking, and everyone left. 21 Then those who wanted to bring gifts to the LORD, brought them to be used for the sacred tent, the worship services, and the priestly clothes. 22 Men and women came willingly and gave all kinds of gold jewelry such as pins, earrings, rings, and necklaces. 23 Everyone brought their blue, purple, and red wool, their fine linen, and their cloth made of goat hair, as well as their ram skins dyed red and their fine leather. 24 Anyone who had silver or bronze or acacia wood brought it as a gift to the LORD.

25 The women who were good at weaving cloth brought the blue, purple, and red wool and the fine linen they had made. 26 And the women who knew how to make cloth from goat hair were glad to do so.

27 The leaders brought different kinds of jewels to be sewn on the special clothes and the breastpiece for the high priest. 28 They also brought sweet-smelling spices to be mixed with the incense and olive oil that were for the lamps and for ordaining the priests. 29 Moses had told the people what the LORD wanted them to do, and many of them decided to bring their gifts.

Bezalel and Oholiab

(Exodus 31.1-11)

30 Moses said to the people of Israel:

The LORD has chosen Bezalel[g] of the Judah tribe. 31-33 Not only has the LORD filled him with his Spirit, but he has given him wisdom and made him a skilled craftsman who can create objects of art with gold, silver, bronze, stone, and wood. 34 The LORD is urging him and Oholiab[h] from the tribe of

[f]**35.9** *onyx*: See the note at 25.7. [g]**35.30** *Bezalel*: See the note at 31.2. [h]**35.34** *Oholiab*: Hebrew "Oholiab son of Ahisamach."

35.2 Ex 20.8-11; 23.12; 31.14, 15; 34.21; Lv 23.3; Dt 5.12-14.

Dan to teach others. 35 And he has given them all kinds of artistic skills, including the ability to design and embroider with blue, purple, and red wool and to weave fine linen.

36 The LORD has given to Bezalel, Oholiab, and others the skills needed for building a place of worship, and they will follow the LORD's instructions.

2 Then Moses brought together these workers who were eager to work, 3 and he gave them the money that the people of Israel had donated for building the place of worship. In fact, so much money was being given each morning, 4 that finally everyone stopped working 5 and said, "Moses, there is already more money than we need for what the LORD has assigned us to do." 6 So Moses sent word for the people to stop giving, and they did. 7 But there was already more than enough to do what needed to be done.

The Curtains and Coverings for the Sacred Tent

(Exodus 26.1-14)

8-9 The skilled workers got together to make the sacred tent and its linen curtains woven with blue, purple, and red wool and embroidered with figures of winged creatures. Each of the ten panels was fourteen yards long and two yards wide, 10 and they were sewn together to make two curtains with five panels each. 11-13 Then fifty loops of blue cloth were put along one of the wider sides of each curtain, and the two curtains were fastened together at the loops with fifty gold hooks.

14-15 As the material for the tent, goat hair was used to weave eleven sections fifteen yards by two yards each. 16 These eleven sections were joined to make two panels, one with five and the other with six sections. 17 Fifty loops were put along one of the wider sides of each panel, 18 and the two panels were fastened at the loops with fifty bronze hooks. 19 Two other coverings were made—one with fine leather and the other with ram skins dyed red.

The Framework for the Sacred Tent

(Exodus 26.15-30)

20 Acacia wood was used to build the framework for the walls of the sacred tent. 21 Each frame was fifteen feet high and twenty-seven inches wide 22-26 with two wooden pegs near the bottom. Then two silver stands were placed under each frame with sockets for the pegs, so they could be joined together. Twenty of these frames were used along the south side and twenty more along the north. 27 Six frames were used for the back wall along the west side 28-29 with two more at the southwest and northwest corners. These corner frames were joined from top to bottom. 30 Altogether, along the back wall there were eight frames with two silver stands under each of them.

31-33 Five crossbars were made for each of the wooden frames, with the center crossbar running the full length of the wall. 34 The frames and crossbars were covered with gold, and gold rings were attached to the frames to run the crossbars through.

The Inside Curtain for the Sacred Tent

(Exodus 26.31-37)

35 They made the inside curtain[i] of fine linen woven with blue, purple, and red wool, and embroidered with figures of winged creatures. 36 They also made four acacia wood posts and covered them with gold. Then gold rings were fastened to the posts, which were set on silver stands.

37 For the entrance to the tent, they used a curtain of fine linen woven with blue, purple, and red wool and embroidered with fancy needlework. 38 They made five posts, covered them completely with gold, and set them each on a gold-covered bronze stand. Finally, they attached hooks for the curtain.

The Sacred Chest

(Exodus 25.10-22)

37 Bezalel built a chest of acacia wood forty-five inches long, twenty-seven inches wide, and twenty-seven inches high. 2 He covered it inside and out with pure

[i] **36.35** *inside curtain*: Separating the holy place from the most holy place.

gold and put a gold edging around the top.
3 He made four gold rings and fastened one
of them to each of the four legs of the
chest. 4 Then he made two poles of acacia
wood, covered them with gold, 5 and put
them through the rings, so the chest could
be carried by the poles.
6 The entire lid of the chest, which was
also covered with pure gold, was the place
of mercy.[j] 7-9 On each of the two ends of
the chest he made a winged creature of
hammered gold. They faced each other,
and their wings covered the place of
mercy.

The Table for the Sacred Bread
(Exodus 25.23-30)

10 Bezalel built a table of acacia wood
thirty-six inches long, eighteen inches
wide, and twenty-seven inches high.
11-12 He covered it with pure gold and put a
gold edging around it with a border three
inches wide.[k] 13 He made four gold rings
and attached one to each of the legs 14 near
the edging. The poles for carrying the table
were placed through these rings 15 and
were made of acacia wood covered with
gold. 16 Everything that was to be set on the
table was made of pure gold—the bowls,
plates, jars, and cups for wine offerings.

The Lampstand
(Exodus 25.31-40)

17 Bezalel made a lampstand of pure
gold. The whole lampstand, including its
decorative flowers, was made from a single
piece of hammered gold, 18 with three
branches on each of its two sides. 19 There
were three decorative almond blossoms on
each branch 20 and four on the stem.
21 There was also a blossom where each
pair of branches came out from the stem.
22 The lampstand, including its branches
and decorative flowers, was made from a
single piece of hammered pure gold.
23-24 The lamp and its equipment, including the tongs and trays, were made of about
seventy-five pounds of pure gold.

The Altar for Burning Incense
(Exodus 30.1-5)

25 For burning incense, Bezalel made an
altar of acacia wood. It was eighteen inches
square and thirty-six inches high with each
of its four corners sticking up like the horn
of a bull. 26 He covered it with pure gold
and put a gold edging around it. 27 Then
below the edging on opposite sides he attached two gold rings through which he
put the poles for carrying the altar.
28 These poles were also made of acacia
wood and covered with gold.

The Oil for Dedication and the Incense
(Exodus 30.22-38)

29 Bezalel mixed the oil for dedication
and the sweet-smelling spices for the
incense.

The Altar for Offering Sacrifices
(Exodus 27.1-8)

38 Bezalel built an altar of acacia
wood for offering sacrifices. It was
seven and a half feet square and four and a
half feet high 2 with each of its four corners
sticking up like the horn of a bull, and it
was completely covered with bronze. 3 The
equipment for the altar was also made of
bronze—the pans for the hot ashes, the
shovels, the meat forks, and the fire pans.
4 Midway up the altar he built a ledge
around it and covered the bottom half of
the altar with a decorative bronze grating.
5 Then he attached a bronze ring beneath
the ledge at the four corners to put the
poles through. 6 He covered two acacia
wood poles with bronze and 7 put them
through the rings for carrying the altar,
which was shaped like an open box.

The Large Bronze Bowl
(Exodus 30.18-21)

8 Bezalel made a large bowl and a stand
out of bronze from the mirrors of the
women who helped at the entrance to the
sacred tent.

[j] **37.6** *place of mercy*: See the note at 26.34. [k] **37.11,12** *a gold edging . . . wide*: Or "a gold edging around it three inches wide."

37.29 Ex 30.22-38. **38.8** Ex 30.18.

The Courtyard around the Sacred Tent
(Exodus 27.9-19)

9-17 Around the sacred tent Bezalel built
a courtyard one hundred fifty feet long on
the south and north and seventy-five feet
wide on the east and west. He used twenty
bronze posts on bronze stands for the south
and north and ten for the west. Then he
hung a curtain of fine linen on the posts
along each of these three sides by using silver hooks and rods. He placed three bronze
posts on each side of the entrance at the
east and hung a curtain seven and a half
yards wide on each set of posts.
18-19 For the entrance to the courtyard,
Bezalel made a curtain ten yards long,
which he hung on four bronze posts that
were set on bronze stands. This curtain
was the same height as the one for the rest
of the courtyard and was made of fine linen
embroidered and woven with blue, purple,
and red wool. He hung the curtain on
the four posts, using silver hooks and
rods. 20 The pegs for the tent and for the
curtain around the tent were made of
bronze.

The Sacred Tent

21-23 Bezalel had worked closely with
Oholiab,[l] who was an expert at designing
and engraving, and at embroidering blue,
purple, and red wool. The two of them
completed the work that the LORD had
commanded.

Moses made Aaron's son Ithamar responsible for keeping record of the metals
used for the sacred tent. 24 According to
the official weights, the amount of gold
given was two thousand two hundred nine
pounds, 25 and the silver that was collected
when the people were counted[m] came to
seven thousand five hundred fifty pounds.
26 Everyone who was counted paid the required amount, and there was a total of
603,550 men who were twenty years old or
older.
27 Seventy-five pounds of the silver were
used to make each of the one hundred
stands for the sacred tent and the curtain.
28 The remaining fifty pounds of silver were
used for the hooks and rods and for covering the tops of the posts.
29 Five thousand three hundred pounds
of bronze were given. 30 And it was used to
make the stands for the entrance to the
tent, the altar and its grating, the equipment for the altar, 31 the stands for the
posts that surrounded the courtyard, including those at the entrance to the courtyard, and the pegs for the tent and the
courtyard.

Making the Priestly Clothes
(Exodus 28.1-14)

39 Beautiful priestly clothes were
made of blue, purple, and red wool
for Aaron to wear when he performed his
duties in the holy place. This was done
exactly as the LORD had commanded
Moses.
2-3 The entire priestly vest was made of
fine linen, woven with blue, purple, and
red wool. Thin sheets of gold were hammered out and cut into threads that were
skillfully woven into the vest. 4-5 It had two
shoulder straps to support it and a sash
that fastened around the waist. 6 Onyx[n]
stones were placed in gold settings, and
each one was engraved with the name of
one of Israel's sons. 7 Then these were attached to the shoulder straps of the vest, so
the LORD would never forget his people.
Everything was done exactly as the LORD
had commanded Moses.

The Breastpiece
(Exodus 28.15-30)

8 The breastpiece was made with the
same materials and designs as the priestly
vest. 9 It was nine inches square and folded
double 10 with four rows of three precious
stones: A carnelian, a chrysolite, and an
emerald were in the first row; 11 a
turquoise, a sapphire, and a diamond were
in the second row; 12 a jacinth, an agate,
and an amethyst were in the third row;

[l] **38.21-23** *Bezalel . . . Oholiab*: Hebrew "Bezalel son of Uri and grandson of Hur of the Judah tribe had worked closely with Oholiab son of Ahisamach from the tribe of Dan." [m] **38.25** *counted*: See 30.11-16; Numbers 1. [n] **39.6** *Onyx*: See the note at 25.7.

38.25,26 Ex 30.11-16. **38.26** Mt 17.24.

13 and a beryl, an onyx, and a jasper[o] were in the fourth row. They were mounted in a delicate gold setting, 14 and on each of them was engraved the name of one of the twelve tribes of Israel.

15-18 Two gold rings were attached to the upper front corners of the breastpiece and fastened with two braided gold chains to gold settings on the shoulder straps. 19 Two other gold rings were attached to the lower inside corners next to the vest, 20 and two more near the bottom of the shoulder straps right above the sash. 21 To keep the breastpiece in place, a blue cord was used to tie the two lower rings on the breastpiece to those on the vest. These things were done exactly as the LORD had commanded Moses.

The Clothes for the Priests
(Exodus 28.31-43)

22 The priestly robe was made of blue wool 23 with an opening in the center for the head. The material around the collar was bound so as to keep it from raveling. 24-26 Along the hem of the robe were woven pomegranates[p] of blue, purple, and red wool with a bell of pure gold between each of them. This robe was to be worn by Aaron when he performed his duties.

27-29 Everything that Aaron and his sons wore was made of fine linen woven with blue, purple, and red wool, including their robes and turbans, their fancy caps and underwear, and even their sashes that were embroidered with needlework.

30 "Dedicated to the LORD" was engraved on a narrow strip of pure gold, 31 which was fastened to Aaron's turban. These things were done exactly as the LORD had commanded Moses.

The Work Is Completed
(Exodus 35.10-19)

32 So the people of Israel finished making everything the LORD had told Moses to make. 33 Then they brought it all to Moses: the sacred tent and its equipment, including the hooks, the framework and crossbars, and its posts and stands; 34 the covering of tanned ram skins and fine leather; the inside curtain; 35 the sacred chest with its carrying poles and the place of mercy; 36 the table with all that goes on it, including the sacred bread; 37 the lampstand of pure gold, together with its equipment and oil; 38 the gold-covered incense altar; the ordination oil and the sweet-smelling incense; the curtain for the entrance to the tent; 39 the bronze altar for sacrifices with its bronze grating, its carrying poles, and its equipment; the large bronze bowl with its stand; 40 the curtain with its posts and cords, and its pegs and stands that go around the courtyard; everything needed for the sacred tent; 41 and the finely woven priestly clothes for Aaron and his sons.

42-43 When Moses saw that the people had done everything exactly as the LORD had commanded, he gave them his blessing.

The LORD's Tent Is Set Up

40 The LORD said to Moses:

2 Set up my tent on the first day of the year[q] 3 and put the chest with the Ten Commandments behind the inside curtain[r] of the tent. 4 Bring in the table and set on it those things that are made for it. Also bring in the lampstand and attach the lamps to it. 5 Then place the gold altar of incense in front of the sacred chest and hang a curtain at the entrance to the tent. 6 Set the altar for burning sacrifices in front of the entrance to my tent. 7 Put the large bronze bowl between the tent and the altar and fill the bowl with water. 8 Surround the tent and the altar with the wall of curtains and hang the curtain that was made for the entrance.

9 Use the sacred olive oil to dedicate the tent and everything in it to me. 10 Do the same thing with the altar for offering sacrifices and its equipment 11 and with the bowl and its stand. 12 Bring Aaron and his sons to

[o]**39.13** *jasper*: For the stones mentioned in verses 10-13, see the note at 28.20.
[p]**39.24-26** *pomegranates*: See the note at 28.33, 34. [q]**40.2** *first day of the year*: See the note at 12.2. [r]**40.3** *inside curtain*: Separating the holy place from the most holy place.

the entrance of the tent and have them wash themselves. 13 Dress Aaron in the priestly clothes, then use the sacred olive oil to ordain him and dedicate him to me as my priest. 14 Put the priestly robes on Aaron's sons 15 and ordain them in the same way, so they and their descendants will always be my priests.

16 Moses followed the LORD's instructions. 17 And on the first day of the first month[s] of the second year, the sacred tent was set up. 18 The posts, stands, and framework were put in place, 19 then the two layers of coverings were hung over them. 20 The stones with the Ten Commandments written on them were stored in the sacred chest, the place of mercy[t] was put on top of it, and the carrying poles were attached. 21 The chest was brought into the tent and set behind the curtain in the most holy place. These things were done exactly as the LORD had commanded Moses.

22 The table for the sacred bread was put along the north wall of the holy place, 23 after which the bread was set on the table. 24 The lampstand was put along the south wall, 25 then the lamps were attached to it there in the presence of the LORD. 26 The gold incense altar was set up in front of the curtain, 27 and sweet-smelling incense was burned on it. These things were done exactly as the LORD had commanded Moses.

28 The curtain was hung at the entrance to the sacred tent. 29 Then the altar for offering sacrifices was put in front of the tent, and animal sacrifices and gifts of grain were offered there. 30 The large bronze bowl was placed between the altar and the entrance to the tent. It was filled with water, 31 then Moses and Aaron, together with Aaron's sons, washed their hands and feet. 32 In fact, they washed each time before entering the tent or offering sacrifices at the altar. These things were done exactly as the LORD had commanded Moses.

33 Finally, Moses had the curtain hung around the courtyard.

The Glory of the LORD

34 Suddenly the sacred tent was covered by a thick cloud and filled with the glory of the LORD. 35 And so, Moses could not enter the tent. 36 Whenever the cloud moved from the tent, the people would break camp and follow; 37 then they would set up camp and stay there, until it moved again. 38 No matter where the people traveled, the LORD was with them. Each day his cloud was over the tent, and each night a fire could be seen in the cloud.

[s]**40.17** *first month*: See the note at 12.2.
[t]**40.20** *place of mercy*: See the note at 26.34.
40.34 1 K 8.10, 11; Is 6.4; Ez 43.4, 5; Rev 15.8.

LEVITICUS

ABOUT THIS BOOK

Leviticus tells how the Lord continued to give laws and instructions to Moses. The book's name is related to the word "Levite," a term referring to a person who belonged to the tribe of Levi. Levites were to be special servants of the Lord at the sacred tent, and the priests came from one of the Levite families. Much of the book deals with the responsibilities of the priests and other Levites, for example, sacrifices, gifts to the Lord, and religious festivals. But this book also contains laws about what animals could be used for food, what materials could be used for clothing, and how to care for the poor.

Most of the book is made up of laws, but it has a few stories telling what happened when the people or priests obeyed or disobeyed God's instructions. God was quick to punish those who rebelled, but he also made this promise to those who would obey him:

> *"I will walk with you—I will be your God, and you will be my people. I am the LORD your God, and I rescued you from Egypt, so that you would never again be slaves. I have set you free; now walk with your heads held high."*
>
> *(26.12, 13)*

A QUICK LOOK AT THIS BOOK

- Laws about Sacrifices (1.1—7.38)
- Ordaining the Priests (8.1-36)
- Aaron's First Sacrifices (9.1-24)
- Two Priests Are Killed (10.1-20)
- Laws about What Is Clean and Unclean (11.1—15.33)
- Laws about the Great Day of Forgiveness (16.1-34)
- Laws on Various Subjects (17.1—20.27)
- Rules for Priests To Follow (21.1—22.33)
- Instructions for Religious Festivals (23.1—25.55)
- Blessings and Punishments (26.1-46)
- Laws about Promises and Offerings to the Lord (27.1-34)

---

1 1-3 The LORD spoke to Moses from the sacred tent and gave him instructions for the community of Israel to follow when they offered sacrifices.

Sacrifices To Please the LORD

The LORD said:

Sacrifices to please me[a] must be completely burned on the bronze altar.[b]

[a] **1.1-3** *Sacrifices to please me*: These sacrifices have traditionally been called "whole burnt offerings" because the whole animal was burned on the altar. A main purpose of such sacrifices was to please the LORD with the smell of the sacrifice, and so in the CEV they are often called "sacrifices to please the LORD." [b] **1.1-3** *bronze altar*: This altar for offering sacrifices was in front of the entrance to the sacred tent; it was made of acacia wood covered with bronze. A smaller altar for offering incense was inside the tent; it was made of acacia wood covered with gold.

Bulls or rams or goats[c] are the animals to be used for these sacrifices. If the animal is a bull, it must not have anything wrong with it. Lead it to the entrance of the sacred tent, and I will let you know if it is[d] acceptable to me. 4 Lay your hand on its head, and I will accept the animal as a sacrifice for taking away your sins.

5 After the bull is killed in my presence, some priests from Aaron's family will offer its blood to me by splattering it against the four sides of the altar.

6 Skin the bull and cut it up, 7 while the priests pile wood on the altar fire to make it start blazing. 8-9 Wash the bull's insides and hind legs, so the priests can lay them on the altar with the head, the fat, and the rest of the animal. A priest will then send all of it up in smoke with a smell that pleases me.

10 If you sacrifice a ram or a goat, it must not have anything wrong with it. 11 Lead the animal to the north side of the altar, where it is to be killed in my presence. Then some of the priests will splatter its blood against the four sides of the altar.

12-13 Cut up the animal and wash its insides and hind legs. A priest will put these parts on the altar with the head, the fat, and the rest of the animal. Then he will send all of it up in smoke with a smell that pleases me.

14 If you offer a bird for this kind of sacrifice, it must be a dove or a pigeon. 15 A priest will take the bird to the bronze altar, where he will wring its neck and put its head on the fire. Then he will drain out its blood on one side of the altar, 16 remove the bird's craw with what is in it,[e] and throw them on the ash heap at the east side of the altar.[f] 17 Finally, he will take the bird by its wings, tear it partially open,[g] and send it up in smoke with a smell that pleases me.

Sacrifices To Give Thanks to the LORD

The LORD said:

2 When you offer sacrifices to give thanks to me,[h] you must use only your finest flour. Put it in a dish, sprinkle olive oil and incense on the flour, 2 and take it to the priests from Aaron's family. One of them will scoop up the incense together with a handful of the flour and oil. Then, to show that the whole offering belongs to me, the priest will lay this part on the bronze altar and send it up in smoke with a smell that pleases me. 3 The rest of this sacrifice is for the priests; it is very holy because it was offered to me.

4 If you bake bread in an oven for this sacrifice, use only your finest flour, but without any yeast. You may make the flour into a loaf mixed with olive oil, or you may make it into thin wafers and brush them with oil.

5 If you cook bread in a shallow pan for this sacrifice, use only your finest flour. Mix it with olive oil, but do not use any yeast. 6 Then break the bread into small pieces and sprinkle them with oil. 7 If you cook your bread in a pan with a lid on it, you must also use the finest flour mixed with oil.

8 You may prepare sacrifices to give thanks in any of these three ways. Bring your sacrifice to a priest, and he will take it to the bronze altar. 9 Then, to show that the whole offering belongs to me, the priest will lay part of it on the altar and send it up in smoke with a smell that pleases me. 10 The rest of this sacrifice is for the priests; it is very holy because it was offered to me.

11 Yeast and honey must never be burned on the altar, so don't ever mix either of these in a grain sacrifice. 12 You may offer either of them separately,[i] when you present the first part of your harvest to

[c] **1.1-3** *goats*: Hebrew "male goats." [d] **1.1-3** *if it is*: Or "if you are." [e] **1.16** *with what is in it*: One possible meaning for the difficult Hebrew text. [f] **1.16** *ash heap at the east side of the altar*: Ashes were piled here, then once a day they were taken to the ash heap outside the camp (see 4.11, 12; 6.10, 11). [g] **1.17** *tear it partially open*: Or "tear it open without pulling off the wings." [h] **2.1** *sacrifices to give thanks to me*: These sacrifices have traditionally been called "grain offerings." A main purpose of such sacrifices was to thank the LORD with a gift of grain, and so in the CEV they are sometimes called "sacrifices to give thanks to the LORD." [i] **2.12** *You . . . separately*: One possible meaning for the difficult Hebrew text.

me, but they must never be burned on the altar.

13 Salt is offered when you make an agreement with me, so sprinkle salt on these sacrifices.

14 Freshly cut grain, either roasted or coarsely ground,[j] must be used when you offer the first part of your grain harvest. 15 You must mix in some olive oil and put incense on top, because this is a grain sacrifice. 16 A priest will sprinkle all of the incense and some of the grain and oil on the altar and send them up in smoke to show that the whole offering belongs to me.

Sacrifices To Ask the LORD's Blessing

The LORD said:

3 When you offer sacrifices to ask my blessing,[k] you may offer either a bull or a cow, but there must be nothing wrong with the animal. 2 Lead it to the entrance of the sacred tent, lay your hand on its head, and have it killed there. A priest from Aaron's family will splatter its blood against the four sides of the altar.

3 Offer all of the fat on the animal's insides, 4 as well as the lower part of the liver and the two kidneys with their fat. 5 Some of the priests will lay these pieces on the altar and send them up in smoke with a smell that pleases me, together with the sacrifice that is offered to please me.[l]

6 Instead of a bull or a cow, you may offer any sheep or goat that has nothing wrong with it. 7 If you offer a sheep, you must present it to me at the entrance to the sacred tent. 8 Lay your hand on its head and have it killed there. A priest will then splatter its blood against the four sides of the altar.

9 Offer the fat on the tail, the tailbone, and the insides, 10 as well as the lower part of the liver and the two kidneys with their fat. 11 One of the priests will lay these pieces on the altar and send them up in smoke as a food offering for me.

12 If you offer a goat, you must also present it to me 13 at the entrance to the sacred tent. Lay your hand on its head and have it killed there. A priest will then splatter its blood against the four sides of the altar.

14 Offer all of the fat on the animal's insides, 15 as well as the lower part of the liver and the two kidneys with their fat. 16 One of the priests will put these pieces on the altar and send them up in smoke as a food offering with a smell that pleases me.

All fat belongs to me. 17 So you and your descendants must never eat any fat or any blood, not even in the privacy of your own homes.[m] This law will never change.

Sacrifices for Sin

(Leviticus 6.24-30)

4 The LORD told Moses 2 to say to the community of Israel:

Offer a sacrifice to ask forgiveness when you sin by accidentally doing something I have told you not to do.

When the High Priest Sins

The LORD said:

3 When the high priest sins, he makes everyone else guilty too. And so, he must sacrifice a young bull that has nothing wrong with it. 4 The priest will lead the bull to the entrance of the sacred tent, lay his hand on its head, and kill it there. 5 He will take a bowl of the blood inside the tent, 6 dip a finger in the blood, and sprinkle some of it seven times toward the sacred chest behind the curtain. 7 Then, in my presence, he will smear some of the blood on each of the four corners of the incense altar, before pouring out the rest at the foot of the bronze altar[n] near the entrance to the tent.

8-10 The priest will remove the fat from the bull, just as he does when he sacrifices a bull to ask my blessing.[o] This includes

[j] **2.14** *either . . . ground*: Or "roasted and coarsely ground." [k] **3.1** *sacrifices to ask my blessing*: These sacrifices have traditionally been called "peace offerings" or "offerings of well-being." A main purpose was to ask for the LORD's blessing, and so in the CEV they are sometimes called "sacrifices to ask the LORD's blessing." [l] **3.5** *sacrifice . . . to please me*: See the note at 1.1-3. [m] **3.17** *not even . . . homes*: Or "no matter where you live." [n] **4.7** *incense altar . . . bronze altar*: See the note at 1.1-3. [o] **4.8-10** *to ask my blessing*: See the note at 3.1.

the fat on the insides, as well as the lower part of the liver and the two kidneys with their fat. He will then send it all up in smoke.

11-12 The skin and flesh of the bull, together with its legs, insides, and the food still in its stomach, are to be taken outside the camp and burned on a wood fire near the ash heap.[p]

When the Whole Nation Sins

The LORD said:

13 When the nation of Israel disobeys me without meaning to, the whole nation is still guilty. 14 Once you realize what has happened, you must sacrifice a young bull to ask my forgiveness. Lead the bull to the entrance of the sacred tent, 15 where your tribal leaders will lay their hands on its head, before having it killed in my presence.

16 The priest will take a bowl of the animal's blood inside the sacred tent, 17 dip a finger in the blood, and sprinkle some of it seven times toward the sacred chest behind the curtain. 18 Then, in my presence, he must smear some of the blood on each of the four corners of the incense altar, before pouring out the rest at the foot of the bronze altar[q] near the entrance to the tent. 19-21 After this, the priest will remove the fat from the bull and send it up in smoke on the altar. Finally, he will burn its remains outside the camp, just as he did with the other bull. By this sacrifice the sin of the whole nation will be forgiven.

When a Tribal Leader Sins

The LORD God said:

22 Any tribal leader who disobeys me without meaning to is still guilty. 23 As soon as the leader realizes what has happened, he must sacrifice a goat[r] that has nothing wrong with it. 24 This is a sacrifice for sin. So he will lay his hand on the animal's head, before having it killed in my presence at the north side of the bronze altar. 25 The priest will dip a finger in the blood, smear some of it on each of the four corners of the altar, and pour out the rest at the foot of the altar. 26 Then he must send all of the fat up in smoke, just as he does when a sacrifice is offered to ask my blessing.[s] By this sacrifice the leader's sin will be forgiven.

When Ordinary People Sin

The LORD said:

27 When any of you ordinary people disobey me without meaning to, you are still guilty. 28 As soon as you realize what you have done, you must sacrifice a female goat that has nothing wrong with it. 29 Lead the goat to the north side of the bronze altar and lay your hand on its head, before having it killed. 30 Then a priest will dip a finger in the blood; he will smear some of it on each of the four corners of the altar and pour out the rest at the foot of the altar. 31 After this, the priest will remove all of the fat, just as he does when an animal is sacrificed to ask my blessing.[s] The priest will then send the fat up in smoke with a smell that pleases me. This animal is sacrificed so that I will forgive you ordinary people when you sin.

32 If you offer a lamb instead of a goat as a sacrifice for sin, it must be a female that has nothing wrong with it. 33 Lead the lamb to the altar and lay your hand on its head, before having it killed. 34 The priest will dip a finger in the blood, smear some of it on each of the four corners of the altar, and pour out the rest at the foot of the altar. 35 After this, all of the fat must be removed, just as when an animal is sacrificed to ask my blessing. Then the priest will send it up in smoke to me, together with a food offering, and your sin will be forgiven.

The LORD said:

5 If you refuse to testify in court about something you saw or know has happened, you have sinned and can be punished.

2 You are guilty and unfit to worship me, if you accidentally touch the dead body of any kind of unclean animal.

[p]**4.11,12** *ash heap*: See the note at 1.16. [q]**4.18** *incense altar . . . bronze altar*: See the note at 1.1-3. [r]**4.23** *goat*: See the note at 1.1-3. [s]**4.26,31** *sacrifice . . . blessing*: See the note at 3.1.
4.27-31 Nu 15.27, 28.

[3] You are guilty if you find out that you have accidentally touched any waste that comes from a human body.

[4] You are guilty the moment you realize that you have made a hasty promise to do something good or bad.

[5] As soon as you discover that you have committed any of these sins, you must confess what you have done. [6] Then you must bring a female sheep or goat to me as the price for your sin. A priest will sacrifice the animal, and you will be forgiven.

[7] If you are poor and cannot afford to bring an animal, you may bring two doves or two pigeons. One of these will be a sacrifice to ask my forgiveness, and the other will be a sacrifice to please me.

[8] Give both birds to the priest, who will offer one as a sacrifice to ask my forgiveness. He will wring its neck without tearing off its head, [9] splatter some of its blood on one side of the bronze altar, and drain out the rest at the foot of the altar. [10] Then he will follow the proper rules for offering the other bird as a sacrifice to please me.

You will be forgiven when the priest offers these sacrifices as the price for your sin.

[11] If you are so poor that you cannot afford doves or pigeons, you may bring two pounds of your finest flour. This is a sacrifice to ask my forgiveness, so don't sprinkle olive oil or sweet-smelling incense on it. [12] Give the flour to a priest, who will scoop up a handful and send it up in smoke together with the other offerings. This is a reminder that all of the flour belongs to me. [13] By offering this sacrifice, the priest pays the price for any of these sins you may have committed. The priest gets the rest of the flour, just as he does with grain sacrifices.

Sacrifices To Make Things Right

(Leviticus 7.1-10)

[14-15] The LORD told Moses what the people must do to make things right when they find out they have cheated the LORD without meaning to:

If this happens, you must either sacrifice a ram that has nothing wrong with it or else pay the price of a ram with the official money used by the priests. [16] In addition, you must pay what you owe plus a fine of twenty percent. Then the priest will offer the ram as a sacrifice to make things right, and you will be forgiven.

[17-19] If you break any of my commands without meaning to, you are still guilty, and you can be punished. When you realize what you have done, you must either bring to the priest a ram that has nothing wrong with it or else pay him for one. The priest will then offer it as a sacrifice to make things right, and you will be forgiven.

Other Sins That Need Sacrifices or Payments

(Numbers 5.5-10)

6 [1-3] The LORD told Moses what the people must do when they commit other sins against the LORD:

You have sinned if you rob or cheat someone, if you keep back money or valuables left in your care, or if you find something and claim not to have it.

[4] When this happens, you must return what doesn't belong to you [5] and pay the owner a fine of twenty percent. [6-7] In addition, you must either bring to the priest a ram that has nothing wrong with it or else pay him for one. The priest will then offer it as a sacrifice to make things right, and you will be forgiven for what you did wrong.

Daily Sacrifices

(Exodus 29.38-43; Numbers 28.1-8)

[8-9] The LORD told Moses to tell Aaron and his sons how to offer the daily sacrifices that are sent up in smoke to please the LORD:[t]

You must put the animal for the sacrifice on the altar in the evening and let it stay there all night. But make sure the fire keeps burning. [10] The next morning you will dress in your priestly clothes, including your linen underwear. Then clean away the ashes left by the sacrifices and pile them beside the altar. [11] Change into your everyday clothes, take the ashes outside the

[t] **6.8,9** *to please the LORD*: See the note at 1.1-3.
6.1-7 Nu 5.5-8.

camp, and pile them in the special place.[u]

12 The fire must never go out, so put wood on it each morning. After this, you are to lay an animal on the altar next to the fat that you sacrifice to ask my blessing.[v] Then send it all up in smoke to me.

13 The altar fire must always be kept burning—it must never go out.

Sacrifices To Give Thanks to the LORD

The LORD said:

14 When someone offers a sacrifice to give thanks to me,[w] the priests from Aaron's family must bring it to the front of the bronze altar, 15 where one of them will scoop up a handful of the flour and oil, together with all the incense on it. Then, to show that the whole offering belongs to me, he will lay all of this on the altar and send it up in smoke with a smell that pleases me. 16-17 The rest of it is to be baked without yeast and eaten by the priests in the sacred courtyard of the sacred tent. This bread is very holy, just like the sacrifices for sin or for making things right, and I have given this part to the priests from what is offered to me on the altar.

18 Only the men in Aaron's family are allowed to eat this bread, and they must go through a ceremony to be made holy before touching it.[x] This law will never change.

When Priests Are Ordained

19 The LORD spoke to Moses 20 and told him what sacrifices the priests must offer on the morning and evening of the day they are ordained:

It is the same as the regular morning and evening sacrifices—a pound of flour 21 mixed with olive oil and cooked in a shallow pan. The bread must then be crumbled into small pieces[y] and sent up in smoke with a smell that pleases me. 22-23 Each of Aaron's descendants who is ordained as a priest must perform this ceremony and make sure that the bread is completely burned on the altar. None of it may be eaten!

Sacrifices for Sin

(*Leviticus 4.1*, 2)

24 The LORD told Moses 25 how the priests from Aaron's family were to offer the sacrifice for sin:

This sacrifice is very sacred, and the animal must be killed in my presence at the north side of the bronze altar. 26 The priest who offers this sacrifice must eat it in the sacred courtyard of the sacred tent, 27 and anyone or anything that touches the meat will be holy.[z] If any of the animal's blood is splattered on the clothes of the priest, they must be washed in a holy place. 28 If the meat was cooked in a clay pot, the pot must be destroyed,[a] but if it was cooked in a bronze pot, the pot must be scrubbed and rinsed with water.

29 This sacrifice is very holy, and only the priests may have any part of it. 30 None of the meat may be eaten from the sacrifices for sin that require blood to be brought into the sacred tent.[b] These sacrifices must be completely burned.

Sacrifices To Make Things Right

(*Leviticus 5.14-19*)

The LORD said:

7 The sacrifice to make things right is very sacred. 2 The animal must be killed in the same place where the sacrifice to please me[c] is killed, and the animal's blood must be splattered against the four sides of the bronze altar. 3 Offer all of the animal's fat, including the fat on its tail and on its insides, 4 as well as the lower part of the liver and the two kidneys with their fat. 5 One of the priests will lay these pieces on the altar and send them up in smoke to me. 6 This sacrifice for making

[u] **6.11** *ashes . . . in the special place*: See the note at 1.16. [v] **6.12** *sacrifice to ask my blessing*: See the note at 3.1. [w] **6.14** *a sacrifice to give thanks to me*: See the note at 2.1. [x] **6.18** *and they . . . touching it*: One possible meaning for the difficult Hebrew text. [y] **6.21** *crumbled . . . pieces*: One possible meaning for the difficult Hebrew text. [z] **6.27** *that touches . . . holy*: One possible meaning for the difficult Hebrew text. [a] **6.28** *clay pot . . . destroyed*: Juice from the meat cannot be completely cleaned from a clay pot. [b] **6.30** *that require blood . . . tent*: See 4.1-21. [c] **7.2** *sacrifice to please me*: See the note at 1.1-3.

things right is very holy. Only the priests may eat it, and they must eat it in a holy place.[d]

7 The ceremony for this sacrifice and the one for sin are just alike, and the meat may be eaten only by the priest who performs this ceremony of forgiveness.

8 In fact, the priest who offers a sacrifice to please me[e] may keep the skin of the animal, 9 just as he may eat the bread from a sacrifice to give thanks to me.[f] 10 All other grain sacrifices—with or without olive oil in them—are to be divided equally among the priests of Aaron's family.

Sacrifices To Ask the LORD's Blessing

The LORD said:

11 Here are the instructions for offering a sacrifice to ask my blessing:[g] 12 If you offer it to give thanks, you must offer some bread together with it. Use the finest flour to make three kinds of bread without yeast—two in the form of loaves mixed with olive oil and one in the form of thin wafers brushed with oil. 13 You must also make some bread with yeast. 14 Give me one loaf or wafer from each of these four kinds of bread, after which they will belong to the priest who splattered the blood against the bronze altar.

15 When you offer an animal to ask a blessing from me or to thank me, the meat belongs to you, but it must be eaten the same day. 16 It is different with the sacrifices you offer when you make me a promise or voluntarily give me something. The meat from those sacrifices may be kept and eaten the next day, 17-18 but any that is left must be destroyed. If you eat any after the second day, your sacrifice will be useless and unacceptable, and you will be both disgusting and guilty.

19 Don't eat any of the meat that touches something unclean. Instead, burn it. The rest of the meat may be eaten by anyone who is clean and acceptable to me. 20-21 But don't eat any of this meat if you have become unclean by touching something unclean from a human or an animal or from any other creature. If you do, you will no longer belong to the community of Israel.

22 The LORD told Moses 23 to say to the people:

Don't eat the fat of cattle, sheep, or goats. 24 If one of your animals dies or is killed by some wild animal, you may do anything with its fat except eat it. 25 If you eat the fat of an animal that can be used as a sacrifice to me, you will no longer belong to the community of Israel. 26 And no matter where you live, you must not eat the blood of any bird or animal, 27 or you will no longer belong to the community of Israel.

28 The LORD also told Moses 29-30 to say to the people of Israel:

If you want to offer a sacrifice to ask my blessing, you must bring the part to be burned and lay it on the bronze altar. But you must first lift up[h] the choice ribs with their fat to show that the offering is dedicated to me. 31 A priest from Aaron's family will then send the fat up in smoke, but the ribs belong to the priests. 32-33 The upper joint of the right hind leg is for the priest who offers the blood and the fat of the animal. 34 I have decided that the people of Israel must always give the choice ribs and the upper joint of the right hind leg to Aaron's descendants 35 who have been ordained as priests to serve me. 36 This law will never change. I am the LORD!

37 These are the ceremonies for sacrifices to please the LORD, to give him thanks, and to ask his blessing or his forgiveness, as well as the ceremonies for those sacrifices that demand a payment and for the sacrifices that are offered when priests are ordained. 38 While Moses and the people of Israel were in the desert at Mount Sinai, the LORD commanded them to start offering these sacrifices.

[d]**7.6** *holy place*: The courtyard of the sacred tent (see 6.16, 17). [e]**7.8** *sacrifice to please me*: See the note at 1.1-3. [f]**7.9** *sacrifice to give thanks to me*: See the note at 2.1. [g]**7.11** *sacrifice to ask my blessing*: See the note at 3.1. [h]**7.29,30** *lift up*: Or "wave."

7.26,27 Gn 9.4; Lv 17.10-14; 19.26; Dt 12.5-19, 23, 24; 15.23.

The Ceremony for Ordaining Priests

(Exodus 29.1-37)

8 The LORD said to Moses:

2 Send for Aaron and his sons, as well as their priestly clothes, the oil for ordination, the bull for the sin offering, the two rams, and a basket of bread made without yeast. 3 Then bring the whole community of Israel together at the entrance to the sacred tent.

4 Moses obeyed the LORD, and when everyone had come together, 5 he said, "We are here to follow the LORD's instructions."

6 After Moses told Aaron and his sons to step forward, he had them wash themselves. 7 He put the priestly shirt and robe on Aaron and wrapped the sash around his waist. Then he put the sacred vest on Aaron and fastened it with the finely woven belt. 8 Next, he put on Aaron the sacred breastpiece that was used in learning what the LORD wanted his people to do. 9 He placed the turban on Aaron's head, and on the front of the turban was the narrow strip of thin gold as a sign of his dedication to the LORD.

10 Moses then dedicated the sacred tent and everything in it to the LORD by sprinkling them with some of the oil for ordination. 11 He sprinkled the bronze altar seven times, and he sprinkled its equipment, as well as the large bronze bowl and its base. 12 He also poured some of the oil on Aaron's head to dedicate him to the LORD. 13 At last, Moses dressed Aaron's sons in their shirts, then tied sashes around them and put special caps on them, just as the LORD had commanded.

14 Moses led out the bull that was to be sacrificed for sin, and Aaron and his sons laid their hands on its head. 15 After it was killed, Moses dipped a finger in the blood and smeared some of it on each of the four corners of the bronze altar, before pouring out the rest at the foot of the altar. This purified the altar and made it a fit place for offering the sacrifice for sin. 16 Moses then took the fat on the bull's insides, as well as the lower part of the liver and the two kidneys with their fat, and sent them up in smoke on the altar fire. 17 Finally, he took the skin and the flesh of the bull, together with the food still in its stomach, and burned them outside the camp, just as the LORD had commanded.

18 Moses led out the ram for the sacrifice to please the LORD.[i] After Aaron and his sons had laid their hands on its head, 19 Moses killed the ram and splattered its blood against the four sides of the altar. 20-21 Moses had the animal cut up, and he washed its insides and hind legs. Then he laid the head, the fat, and the rest of the ram on the altar and sent them up in smoke with a smell that pleased the LORD. All this was done just as the LORD had commanded.

22 Moses led out the ram for the ceremony of ordination. Aaron and his sons laid their hands on its head, 23 and it was killed. Moses smeared some of its blood on Aaron's right earlobe, some on his right thumb, and some on the big toe of his right foot. 24 Moses did the same thing for Aaron's sons, before splattering the rest of the blood against the four sides of the altar. 25 He took the animal's fat tail, the fat on its insides, and the lower part of the liver and the two kidneys with their fat, and the right hind leg. 26 Then he took from a basket some of each of the three kinds of bread[j] that had been made without yeast and had been dedicated to the LORD.

27 Moses placed the bread on top of the meat and gave it all to Aaron and his sons, who lifted it up[k] to show that it was dedicated to the LORD. 28 After this, Moses placed it on the fires of the altar and sent it up in smoke with a smell that pleased the LORD. This was part of the ordination ceremony. 29 Moses lifted up[k] the choice ribs of the ram to show that they were dedicated to the LORD. This was the part that the LORD had said Moses could have.

30 Finally, Moses sprinkled the priestly clothes of Aaron and his sons with some of

[i] **8.18** *sacrifice to please the LORD*: See the note at 1.1-3. [j] **8.26** *three kinds of bread*: Made from the finest wheat flour; olive oil was mixed into part of the dough, and some of it was made into thin wafers brushed with oil (see Exodus 29.2, 3). [k] **8.27,29** *lifted it up*: See the note at 7.29, 30.

the oil for ordination and with some of the blood from the altar. So Aaron and his sons, together with their priestly clothes, were dedicated to the LORD.

31 Moses said to Aaron and his sons:

The LORD told me that you must boil this meat at the entrance to the sacred tent and eat it there with the bread. 32 Burn what is left over 33 and stay near the entrance to the sacred tent until the ordination ceremony ends seven days from now. 34 We have obeyed the LORD in everything that has been done today, so that your sins may be forgiven.[l] 35 The LORD has told me that you must stay near the entrance to the tent for seven days and nights, or else you will die.

36 Aaron and his sons obeyed everything that the LORD had told Moses they must do.

The First Sacrifices Offered by Aaron and His Sons

9 Eight days later Moses called together Aaron, his sons, and Israel's leaders. 2 Then he said to Aaron:

Find a young bull and a ram that have nothing wrong with them. Offer the bull to the LORD as a sacrifice for sin and the ram as a sacrifice to please him.[m]

3 Tell the people of Israel that they must offer sacrifices as well. They must offer a goat[n] as a sacrifice for sin, and a bull and a ram as a sacrifice to please the LORD. The bull and the ram must be a year old and have nothing wrong with them. 4 Then the people must offer a bull and a ram as a sacrifice to ask the LORD's blessing[o] and also a grain sacrifice[p] mixed with oil. Do this, because the LORD will appear to you today.

5 After the animals and the grain had been brought to the front of the sacred tent, and the people were standing there in the presence of the LORD, 6 Moses said:

The LORD has ordered you to do this, so that he may appear to you in all of his glory. 7 Aaron, step up to the altar and offer the sacrifice to please the LORD, then offer the sacrifices for the forgiveness of your sins and for the sins of the people, just as the LORD has commanded.

8 Aaron stepped up to the altar and killed the bull that was to be the sacrifice for his sins. 9 His sons brought him the blood. He dipped a finger in it, smeared some on the four corners of the bronze altar, and poured out the rest at its foot. 10 But he sent up in smoke the fat, the kidneys, and the lower part of the liver, just as the LORD had commanded Moses. 11 Then Aaron burned the skin and the flesh outside the camp.

12 After Aaron had killed the ram that was sacrificed to please the LORD, Aaron's sons brought him the blood, and he splattered it against all four sides of the altar. 13 They brought him each piece of the animal, including the head, and he burned them all on the altar. 14 He washed the insides and the hind legs and also sent them up in smoke.

15 Next, Aaron sacrificed the goat for the sins of the people, as he had done with the sacrifice for his own sins. 16 And so, he burned this sacrifice on the altar in the proper way. 17 He also presented the grain sacrifice and burned a handful of the flour on the altar as part of the morning sacrifice.

18 At last, he killed the bull and the ram as a sacrifice to ask the LORD's blessing on the people. Aaron's sons brought him the blood, and he splattered it against the four sides of the altar. 19 His sons placed all the fat, as well as the kidneys and the lower part of the liver 20 on top of the choice ribs. 21 Then Aaron burned the fat on the altar and lifted up[q] the ribs and the right hind leg to show that these were dedicated to the LORD. This was done just as the LORD had instructed Moses.

[l] **8.34** *forgiven*: One possible meaning for the difficult Hebrew text of verse 34. [m] **9.2** *sacrifice to please him*: See the note at 1.1-3. [n] **9.3** *goat*: See the note at 1.1-3. [o] **9.4** *to ask the LORD's blessing*: See the note at 3.1. [p] **9.4** *grain sacrifice*: To give thanks to the LORD (see the note at 2.1). [q] **9.21** *lifted up*: See the note at 7.29, 30.

9.7 He 7.27. **9.18** Lv 3.1-11.

22 Aaron held out his hand and gave the people his blessing, before coming down from the bronze altar where he had offered the sacrifices. 23 He and Moses went into the sacred tent, and when they came out, they gave the people their blessing. Then the LORD appeared to the people in all of his glory. 24 The LORD sent fiery flames that burned up everything on the altar, and when everyone saw this, they shouted and fell to their knees to worship the LORD.

Nadab and Abihu

10 Nadab and Abihu were two of Aaron's sons, but they disobeyed the LORD by burning incense to him on a fire pan, when they were not supposed to.[r] 2 Suddenly the LORD sent fiery flames and burned them to death. 3 Then Moses told Aaron that this was exactly what the LORD had meant when he said:

"I demand respect
from my priests,
and I will be praised
by everyone!"

Aaron was speechless.

4 Moses sent for Mishael and Elzaphan, the two sons of Aaron's uncle Uzziel. Then he told them, "Take these two dead relatives of yours outside the camp far from the entrance to the sacred tent." 5 So they dragged the dead men away by their clothes.

6 Then Moses told Aaron and his other two sons, Eleazar and Ithamar:

Don't show your sorrow by messing up your hair and tearing your priestly clothes, or the LORD will get angry. He will kill the three of you and punish everyone else. It's all right for your relatives, the people of Israel, to mourn for those he destroyed by fire. 7 But you are the LORD's chosen priests, and you must not leave the sacred tent, or you will die.

Aaron and his two sons obeyed Moses.

8 The LORD said to Aaron:

9 When you or your sons enter the sacred tent, you must never drink beer or wine. If you do, you will die right there! This law will never change. 10 You must learn the difference between what is holy and what isn't holy and between the clean and the unclean. 11 You must also teach the people of Israel everything that I commanded Moses to say to them.

12 Moses told Aaron and his two sons, Eleazar and Ithamar:

The grain sacrifice that was offered to give thanks to the LORD[s] is very holy. So make bread without yeast from the part that wasn't sent up in smoke and eat it beside the altar. 13 The LORD has said that this belongs to you and your sons, and that it must be eaten in a holy place. 14-15 But the choice ribs and the hind leg that were lifted up[t] may be eaten by your entire family, as long as you do so in an acceptable place.[u] These parts are yours from the sacrifices that the people offer to ask the LORD's blessing.[v] This is what the LORD has commanded, and it will never change.

16 When Moses asked around and learned that the ram for the sin sacrifice had already been burned on the altar, he became angry with Eleazar and Ithamar and said, 17 "Why didn't you eat the meat from this sacrifice in an acceptable place? It is very holy, and the LORD has given you this sacrifice to remove Israel's sin and guilt. 18 Whenever an animal's blood isn't brought into the sacred tent, I commanded you to eat its meat in an acceptable place, but you burned it instead."

19 Their father Aaron replied, "Today two of my sons offered the sacrifice for sin and the sacrifice to please the LORD, and look what has happened to me! Would the LORD have approved if I had eaten the sacrifice for sin?"

20 Moses was satisfied with Aaron's reply.

[r] **10.1** *when they . . . to*: One possible meaning for the difficult Hebrew text. [s] **10.12** *grain sacrifice . . . to give thanks to the LORD*: See the note at 2.1. [t] **10.14,15** *lifted up*: See the note at 7.29, 30. [u] **10.14,15** *acceptable place*: See 6.24-30. [v] **10.14,15** *to ask the LORD's blessing*: See the note at 3.1.

9.22 Nu 6.22-26. **10.12,13** Lv 6.14-18. **10.14,15** Lv 7.29-34. **10.17** Lv 6.24-26.

Clean and Unclean Animals
(Deuteronomy 14.3-21)

11 The LORD told Moses and Aaron
2 to say to the community of Israel:
You may eat 3 any animal that has divided hoofs and chews the cud.[w] 4-8 But
you must not eat animals such as camels,
rock badgers, and rabbits that chew the
cud but don't have divided hoofs. And you
must not eat pigs—they have divided hoofs,
but don't chew the cud. All of these animals are unclean,[x] and you are forbidden
even to touch their dead bodies.
9-12 You may eat anything that lives in
water and has fins and scales. But it would
be disgusting for you to eat anything else
that lives in water, and you must not even
touch their dead bodies.
13-19 Eagles, vultures, buzzards, crows,
ostriches, hawks, sea gulls, owls, pelicans,
storks, herons, hoopoes,[y] and bats are also
disgusting, and you are forbidden to eat any
of them.
20-23 The only winged insects you may
eat are locusts, grasshoppers, and crickets.
All other winged insects that crawl are too
disgusting for you to eat.
24-28 Don't even touch the dead bodies
of animals that have divided hoofs but
don't chew the cud. And don't touch the
dead bodies of animals that have paws. If
you do, you must wash your clothes, but
you are still unclean until evening.
29-30 Moles, rats, mice, and all kinds of
lizards are unclean. 31 Anyone who touches
their dead bodies or anything touched by
their dead bodies becomes unclean until
evening. 32 If something made of wood,
cloth, or leather touches one of their dead
bodies, it must be washed, but it is still unclean until evening. 33 If any of these animals is found dead in a clay pot, the pot
must be broken to pieces, and everything in
it becomes unclean. 34 If you pour water
from this pot on any food, that food becomes unclean, and anything drinkable in
the pot becomes unclean.
35 If the dead body of one of these animals touches anything else, including
ovens and stoves, that thing becomes unclean and must be destroyed. 36 A spring or
a cistern where one of these dead animals
is found is still clean, but anyone who
touches the animal becomes unclean. 37 If
the dead body of one of these animals is
found lying on seeds that have been set
aside for planting, the seeds remain clean.
38 But seeds that are soaking in water become
unclean, if the dead animal is found in the
water.
39 If an animal that may be eaten happens to die, and you touch it, you become
unclean until evening. 40 If you eat any of
its meat or carry its body away, you must
wash your clothes, but you are still unclean
until evening.
41-42 Don't eat any of those disgusting
little creatures that crawl or walk close to
the ground. 43 If you eat any of them, you
will become just as disgusting and unclean
as they are. 44 I am the LORD your God, and
you must dedicate yourselves to me and be
holy, just as I am holy. Don't become disgusting by eating any of these unclean
creatures. 45 I brought you out of Egypt so
that I could be your God. Now you must
become holy, because I am holy!
46-47 I have given these laws so that you
will know what animals, birds, and fish are
clean and may be eaten, and which ones
are unclean and may not be eaten.

What Women Must Do after Giving Birth

12 The LORD told Moses 2 to say to the
community of Israel:
If a woman gives birth to a son, she
is unclean for seven days, just as she is

[w] **11.3** *chews the cud*: Some animals that eat grass and leaves have more than one stomach and chew their food a second time after it has been partly digested in the first stomach. This partly digested food is called the "cud." [x] **11.4-8** *unclean*: In the Old Testament "clean" and "unclean" refer to whatever makes a person, animal, or object acceptable or unacceptable to God. For example, a person became unclean by eating certain foods, touching certain objects, and having certain kinds of diseases or bodily discharges. [y] **11.13-19** *Eagles . . . hoopoes*: Some of the birds in this list are difficult to identify.

11.1-23 4 Macc 5.26. **11.1-47** 4 Macc 1.34. **11.44** Lv 19.2; 1 P 1.16.

during her monthly period. 3 Her son must be circumcised on the eighth day, 4 but her loss of blood keeps her from being completely clean for another thirty-three days. During this time she must not touch anything holy or go to the place of worship. 5 Any woman who gives birth to a daughter is unclean for two weeks, just as she is during her period. And she won't be completely clean for another sixty-six days.

6 When the mother has completed her time of cleansing, she must come to the front of the sacred tent and bring to the priest a year-old lamb as a sacrifice to please me[z] and a dove or a pigeon as a sacrifice for sin. 7 After the priest offers the sacrifices to me, the mother will become completely clean from her loss of blood, whether her child is a boy or a girl. 8 If she cannot afford a lamb, she can offer two doves or two pigeons, one as a sacrifice to please me and the other as a sacrifice for sin.

Skin Diseases

13 The LORD told Moses and Aaron to say to the people:

2 If sores or boils or a skin rash should break out and start spreading on your body, you must be brought to Aaron or to one of the other priests. 3 If the priest discovers that the hair in the infected area has turned white and that the infection seems more than skin deep, he will say, "This is leprosy[a]—you are unclean."

4 But if the infected area is white and only skin deep, and if the hair in it hasn't turned white, the priest will order you to stay away from everyone else for seven days. 5 If the disease hasn't spread by that time, he will order you to stay away from everyone else for another seven days. 6 Then if the disease hasn't gotten any worse or spread, the priest will say, "You are clean. It was only a sore. After you wash your clothes, you may go home."

7 However, if the disease comes back, you must return to the priest. 8 If it is discovered that the disease has started spreading, he will say, "This is leprosy—you are unclean."

9 Any of you with a skin disease must be brought to a priest. 10 If he discovers that the sore spot is white with pus and that the hair around it has also turned white, 11 he will say, "This is leprosy. You are unclean and must stay away from everyone else." 12-13 But if the disease has run its course and only the scars remain, he will say, "You are clean." 14-15 If the sores come back and turn white with pus, he will say, "This is leprosy—you are unclean."

16-17 However, if the sores heal and only white spots remain, the priest will say, "You are now clean."

18-19 If you have a sore that either swells or turns reddish-white after it has healed, then you must show it to a priest. 20 If he discovers that the hair in the infected area has turned white and that the infection seems more than skin deep, he will say, "This is leprosy—you are unclean." 21 But if the white area is only on the surface of the skin and hasn't gotten any worse, and if the hair in it hasn't turned white, he will have you stay away from everyone else for seven days.

22 If the sore begins spreading during this time, the priest will say, "You are unclean because you have a disease." 23 But if it doesn't spread, and only a scar remains, he will say, "You are now clean."

24 If you have a burn that gets infected and turns red or reddish-white, 25 a priest must examine it. Then if he discovers that the hair in the infected area has turned white and that the infection seems more than skin deep, he will say, "The burn has turned into leprosy, and you are unclean." 26 But if the priest finds that the hair in the infected area hasn't turned white and that the sore is only skin deep and it is healing, he will have you stay away from everyone else for seven days. 27 On the seventh day the priest will examine you again, and if the infection is spreading, he will say, "This is leprosy—you are unclean." 28 However, if the infection hasn't spread and has begun to heal, and if only a scar remains, he will

[z] **12.6** *sacrifice to please me*: See the note at 1.1-3.

[a] **13.3** *leprosy*: The word translated "leprosy" was used for many different kinds of skin diseases.

12.3 Gn 17.12, 13; Lk 2.21. **12.8** Lk 2.24.

say, "Only a scar remains from the burn, and you are clean."

29 If you have a sore on your head or chin, 30 it must be examined by a priest. If the infection seems more than skin deep, and the hair in it has thinned out and lost its color, he will say, "This is leprosy—you are unclean." 31 On the other hand, if he discovers that the itchy spot is only skin deep, but that the hair still isn't healthy, he will order you to stay away from everyone else for seven days. 32 By that time, if the itch hasn't spread, if the hairs seem healthy, and if the itch is only skin deep, 33 you must shave off the hairs around the infection, but not those on it. Then the priest will tell you to stay away from everyone else for another seven days. 34 By that time, if the itch hasn't spread and seems no more than skin deep, he will say, "You are clean; now you must wash your clothes."

35-36 Later, if the itch starts spreading, even though the hair is still healthy, the priest will say, "You are unclean." 37 But if he thinks you are completely well, he will say, "You are clean."

38 If white spots break out on your skin, 39 but the priest discovers that it is only a rash, he will say, "You are clean."

40-41 If you become bald on any part of your head, you are still clean. 42-43 But if a priest discovers that a reddish-white sore has broken out on the bald spot and looks like leprosy, he will say, 44 "This is leprosy—you are unclean."

45 If you ever have leprosy, you must tear your clothes, leave your hair uncombed, cover the lower part of your face, and go around shouting, "I'm unclean! I'm unclean!" 46 As long as you have the disease, you are unclean and must live alone outside the camp.

47-50 If a greenish or reddish spot[b] appears anywhere on any of your clothing or on anything made of leather, you must let the priest examine the clothing or the leather. He will put it aside for seven days, 51 and if the mildew has spread in that time, he will say, "This is unclean 52 because the mildew has spread." Then he will burn the clothing or the piece of leather.

53 If the priest discovers that the mildew hasn't spread, 54 he will tell you to wash the clothing or leather and put it aside for another seven days, 55 after which he will examine it again. If the spot hasn't spread, but is still greenish or reddish, the clothing or leather is unclean and must be burned. 56 But if the spot has faded after being washed, he will tear away the spot. 57 Later, if the spot reappears elsewhere on the clothing or the leather, you must burn it. 58 Even if the spot completely disappears after being washed, it must be washed again before it is clean.

59 These are the rules for deciding if clothing is clean or unclean after a spot appears on it.

The Ceremony for People Healed of Leprosy

14 The LORD told Moses to say to the people:

2-3 After you think you are healed of leprosy,[c] you must ask for a priest to come outside the camp and examine you. And if you are well, 4 he will have someone bring out two live birds that are acceptable for sacrifice, together with a stick of cedar wood, a piece of red yarn, and a branch from a hyssop plant. 5 The priest will have someone kill one of the birds over a clay pot of spring water. 6 Then he will dip the other bird, the cedar, the red yarn, and the hyssop in the blood of the dead bird. 7 Next, he will sprinkle you seven times with the blood and say, "You are now clean." Finally, he will release the bird and let it fly away.

8 After this you must wash your clothes, shave your entire body, and take a bath before you are completely clean. You may move back into camp, but you must not enter your tent for seven days. 9 Then you must once again shave your head, face, and eyebrows, as well as the hair on the rest of your body. Finally, wash your clothes and take a bath, and you will be completely clean.

[b]**13.47-50** *spot*: The Hebrew word translated "spot" and "mildew" in verses 47-59 is the same one translated "leprosy" earlier in the chapter. [c]**14.2,3** *leprosy*: See the note at 13.3.

14.2,3 Mt 8.4; Mk 1.44; Lk 5.14; 17.14.

[10] On the eighth day you must bring to the priest two rams and a year-old female lamb that have nothing wrong with them; also bring a half pint of olive oil and six pounds of your finest flour mixed with oil. [11] Then the priest will present you and your offerings to me at the entrance to my sacred tent. [12] There he will offer one of the rams, together with the pint of oil, as a sacrifice to make things right.[d] He will also lift them up[e] to show that they are dedicated to me. [13] This sacrifice is very holy. It belongs to the priest and must be killed in the same place where animals are killed as sacrifices for sins and as sacrifices to please me.[f]

[14] The priest will smear some of the blood from this sacrifice on your right ear lobe, some on your right thumb, and some on the big toe of your right foot. [15] He will then pour some of the olive oil into the palm of his left hand, [16] dip a finger of his right hand into the oil, and sprinkle some of it seven times toward the sacred tent. [17] Next, he will smear some of the oil on your right ear lobe, some on your right thumb, and some on the big toe of your right foot, [18-20] and pour the rest of the oil from his palm on your head. Then he will offer the other two animals—one as a sacrifice for sin and the other as a sacrifice to please me, together with a grain sacrifice. After this you will be completely clean.

[21] If you are poor and cannot afford to offer this much, you may offer a ram as a sacrifice to make things right, together with a half pint of olive oil and two pounds of flour mixed with oil as a grain sacrifice. The priest will then lift these up[g] to dedicate them to me. [22] Depending on what you can afford, you must also offer either two doves or two pigeons, one as a sacrifice for sin and the other as a sacrifice to please me. [23] The priest will offer these to me in front of the sacred tent on the eighth day.

[24-25] The priest will kill this ram for the sacrifice to make things right, and he will lift it up[g] with the olive oil in dedication to me. Then he will smear some of the blood on your right ear lobe, some on your right thumb, and some on the big toe of your right foot.

[26] The priest will pour some of the olive oil into the palm of his left hand, [27] then dip a finger of his right hand in the oil and sprinkle some of it seven times toward the sacred tent. [28] He will smear some of the oil on your right ear lobe, some on your right thumb, and some on the big toe of your right foot, just as he did with the blood of the sacrifice to make things right. [29-31] And he will pour the rest of the oil from his palm on your head.

Then, depending on what you can afford, he will offer either the doves or the pigeons together with the grain sacrifice. One of the birds is the sacrifice for sin, and the other is the sacrifice to please me. After this you will be completely clean.

[32] These are the things you must do if you have leprosy and cannot afford the usual sacrifices to make you clean.

When Mildew Is in a House

[33] The LORD told Moses and Aaron to say to the people:

[34] After I have given you the land of Canaan as your permanent possession, here is what you must do, if I ever put mildew[h] on the walls of any of your homes. [35] First, you must say to a priest, "I think mildew is on the wall of my house."

[36] The priest will reply, "Empty the house before I inspect it, or else everything in it will be unclean."

[37] If the priest discovers greenish or reddish spots that go deeper than the surface of the walls, [38] he will have the house closed for seven days. [39] Then he will return and check to see if the mildew has spread. [40-41] If so, he will have someone scrape the plaster from the walls, remove the filthy stones, then haul everything off and dump it in an unclean place outside the town. [42] Afterwards the wall must be repaired with new stones and fresh plaster.

[d] **14.12** *sacrifice to make things right*: See 7.1-10. [e] **14.12** *lift them up*: See the note at 7.29, 30. [f] **14.13** *sacrifices to please me*: See the note at 1.1-3. [g] **14.21,24,25** *lift these up*: See the note at 7.29, 30. [h] **14.34** *mildew*: The Hebrew word translated "mildew" is the same one translated "leprosy" and "spot" in chapter 13.

43 If the mildew appears a second time,
44 the priest will come and say, “This house
is unclean. It’s covered with mildew that
can’t be removed.” 45 Then he will have the
house torn down and every bit of wood,
stone, and plaster hauled off to an unclean
place outside the town. 46 Meanwhile, if
any of you entered the house while it was
closed, you will be unclean until evening.
47 And if you either slept or ate in the
house, you must wash your clothes.

48 On the other hand, if the priest discovers that mildew hasn’t reappeared after
the house was newly plastered, he will say,
“This house is clean—the mildew has
gone.” 49 Then, to show that the house is
now clean, he will get two birds, a stick of
cedar wood, a piece of red yarn, and a
branch from a hyssop plant and bring them
to the house. 50 He will kill one of the birds
over a clay pot of spring water 51-52 and let
its blood drain into the pot. Then he will
dip the cedar, the hyssop, the yarn, and the
other bird into the mixture of blood and
water. Next, he will sprinkle the house
seven times with the mixture, then the
house will be completely clean. 53 Finally,
he will release the bird and let it fly away,
ending the ceremony for purifying the
house.

54-57 These are the things you must do if
you discover that you are unclean because
of an itch or a sore, or that your clothing or
house is unclean because of mildew.

Sexual Uncleanness

15 The LORD told Moses and Aaron
2 to say to the community of Israel:
Any man with an infected penis is unclean, 3 whether it is stopped up or keeps
dripping. 4 Anything that he rests on or sits
on is also unclean, 5-7 and if you touch either these or him, you must wash your
clothes and take a bath, but you still remain unclean until evening.

8 If you are spit on by the man, you
must wash your clothes and take a bath,
but you still remain unclean until evening.
9-10 Any saddle or seat on which the man
sits is unclean. And if you touch or carry either of these, you must wash your clothes
and take a bath, but you still remain unclean until evening. 11 If the man touches
you without first washing his hands, you
must wash your clothes and take a bath,
but you still remain unclean until evening.
12 Any clay pot that he touches must be destroyed, and any wooden bowl that he
touches must be washed.

13 Seven days after the man gets well,
he will be considered clean, if he washes
his clothes and takes a bath in spring water.
14 On the eighth day he must bring either
two doves or two pigeons to the front of my
sacred tent and give them to a priest.
15 The priest will offer one of the birds as a
sacrifice for sin and the other as a sacrifice
to please me,[i] then I will consider the man
completely clean.

16 Any man who has a flow of semen
must take a bath, but he still remains unclean until evening. 17 If the semen
touches anything made of cloth or leather,
these must be washed, but they still remain
unclean until evening. 18 After having sex,
both the man and the woman must take a
bath, but they still remain unclean until
evening.

19 When a woman has her monthly period, she remains unclean for seven days,
and if you touch her, you must take a bath,
but you remain unclean until evening.
20-23 Anything that she rests on or sits on is
also unclean, and if you touch either of
these, you must wash your clothes and take
a bath, but you still remain unclean until
evening. 24 Any man who has sex with her
during this time becomes unclean for
seven days, and anything he rests on is also
unclean.

25 Any woman who has a flow of blood
outside her regular monthly period is unclean until it stops, just as she is during her
monthly period. 26 Anything that she rests
on or sits on during this time is also unclean, just as it would be during her period.
27 If you touch either of these, you must
wash your clothes and take a bath, but you
still remain unclean until evening.

28 Seven days after the woman gets well,
she will be considered clean. 29 On the
eighth day, she must bring either two doves

[i] **15.15** *sacrifice to please me*: See the note at 1.1-3.

or two pigeons to the front of my sacred tent and give them to a priest. 30 He will offer one of the birds as a sacrifice for sin and the other as a sacrifice to please me; then I will consider the woman completely clean.

31 When any of you are unclean, you must stay away from the rest of the community of Israel. Otherwise, my sacred tent will become unclean, and the whole nation will die.

32-33 These are the things you men must do if you become unclean because of an infected penis or if you have a flow of semen. And these are the things you women must do when you become unclean either because of your monthly period or an unusual flow of blood. This is also what you men must do if you have sex with a woman who is unclean.

The Great Day of Forgiveness

16 1-2 Two of Aaron's sons had already lost their lives for disobeying the LORD,[j] so the LORD told Moses to say to Aaron:

I, the LORD, appear in a cloud over the place of mercy on the sacred chest, which is behind the inside curtain[k] of the sacred tent. And I warn you not to go there except at the proper time. Otherwise, you will die!

3 Before entering this most holy place, you must offer a bull as a sacrifice for your sins[l] and a ram as a sacrifice to please me.[m] 4 You will take a bath and put on the sacred linen clothes, including the underwear, the robe, the sash, and the turban. 5 Then the community of Israel will bring you a ram and two goats, both of them males. The goats are to be used as sacrifices for sin, and the ram is to be used as a sacrifice to please me.

6 Aaron, you must offer the bull as a sacrifice of forgiveness for your own sins and for the sins of your family. 7 Then you will lead the two goats into my presence at the front of the sacred tent, 8 where I will show you[n] which goat will be sacrificed to me and which one will be sent into the desert to the demon Azazel.[o] 9 After you offer the first goat as a sacrifice for sin, 10 the other one must be presented to me alive, before you send it into the desert to take away the sins of the people.

11 You must offer the bull as a sacrifice to ask forgiveness for your own sins and for the sins of your family. 12 Then you will take a fire pan of live coals from the bronze altar, together with two handfuls of finely ground incense, into the most holy place. 13 There you will present them to me by placing the incense on the coals, so that the place of mercy will be covered with a cloud of smoke. Do this, or you will die right there! 14 Next, use a finger to sprinkle some of the blood on the place of mercy, which is on the lid of the sacred chest; then sprinkle blood seven times in front of the chest.

15 Aaron, you must next sacrifice the goat for the sins of the people, and you must sprinkle its blood inside the most holy place, just as you did with the blood of the bull. 16 By doing this, you will take away the sins that make both the most holy place and the people of Israel unclean. Do the same for the sacred tent, which is here among the people. 17 Only you are allowed in the sacred tent from the time you enter until the time you come out. 18 After leaving the tent, you will purify the bronze altar by smearing each of its four corners with some of the blood from the bull and from the goat. 19 Use a finger to sprinkle the altar seven times with the blood, and it will be completely clean from the sins of the people.

20 After you have purified the most holy place, the sacred tent, and the bronze altar, you must bring the live goat to the front of the tent. 21 There you will lay your hands on its head, while confessing every sin the people have committed, and you will appoint someone to lead the goat into the

[j] **16.1,2** *lost . . . disobeying the LORD*: See 10.1, 2. [k] **16.1,2** *inside curtain*: That separated the holy place from the most holy place. [l] **16.3** *for your sins*: See 4.3-12. [m] **16.3** *sacrifice to please me*: See the note at 1.1-3. [n] **16.8** *I will show you*: The Hebrew text has "you must cast lots to find out." Pieces of wood or stone (called "lots") were used to find out what God wanted his people to do. [o] **16.8** *Azazel*: It was believed that a demon named Azazel lived in the desert.

16.1,2 3 Macc 1.11; He 6.19. **16.3** He 9.7. **16.15** He 9.12.

desert, so that it can take away their sins.
22 Finally, this goat that carries the heavy
burden of Israel's sins must be released
deep in the desert.
23-24 Aaron, after this you must go inside
the sacred tent, take a bath, put on your
regular priestly clothes, and leave there the
clothes you put on before entering the most
holy place. Then you will come out and
offer sacrifices to please me and sacrifices
for your sins and for the sins of the people. 25 The fat from these sacrifices for sin
must be sent up in smoke on the bronze
altar.
26 The one who led the goat into the
desert and sent it off to the demon Azazel
must take a bath and wash his clothes before coming back into camp. 27 The remains of the bull and the goat whose blood
was taken into the most holy place must be
taken outside the camp and burned. 28 And
whoever does this must take a bath and
change clothes before coming back into
camp.

The LORD told Moses to say to the people:
29 On the tenth day of the seventh
month[p] of each year, you must go without
eating to show sorrow for your sins, and no
one, including foreigners who live among
you, is allowed to work. 30 This is the day
on which the sacrifice for the forgiveness of
your sins will be made in my presence,
31 and from now on, it must be celebrated
each year. Go without eating and make this
a day of complete rest just like the Sabbath.
32 The high priest must offer the sacrifices
for cleansing from sin, while wearing the
sacred linen clothes. 33 He will offer these
sacrifices for the most holy place, the sacred tent, the bronze altar, all the priests,
and for the whole community. 34 You must
celebrate this day each year—it is the Great
Day of Forgiveness[q] for all the sins of the
people of Israel.
Moses did exactly as the LORD had commanded.

Where To Offer Sacrifices

17 The LORD told Moses 2 to tell
Aaron, his sons, and everyone else
in Israel:
3-4 Whenever you kill any of your cattle,
sheep, or goats as sacrifices to me, you
must do it at the entrance to the sacred
tent. If you don't, you will be guilty of pouring out blood, and you will no longer belong
to the community of Israel. 5 And so, when
you sacrifice an animal to ask my blessing,[r]
it must not be done out in a field, 6 but in
front of the sacred tent. Then a priest can
splatter its blood against the bronze altar
and send its fat up in smoke with a smell
that pleases me. 7 Don't ever turn from me
again and offer sacrifices to goat-demons.
This law will never change.
8 Remember! No one in Israel, including foreigners, is to offer a sacrifice anywhere 9 except at the entrance to the sacred tent. If you do, you will no longer
belong to my people.

Do Not Eat Blood

The LORD said:
10 I will turn against any of my people
who eat blood. This also includes any foreigners living among you. 11 Life is in the
blood, and I have given you the blood
of animals to sacrifice in place of your
own. 12 That's also why I have forbidden
you to eat blood. 13 Even if you should
hunt and kill a bird or an animal, you
must drain out the blood and cover it with
soil.
14 The life of every living creature is in
its blood. That's why I have forbidden you
to eat blood and why I have warned you
that anyone who does will no longer belong
to my people.
15 If you happen to find a dead animal
and eat it, you must take a bath and wash
your clothes, but you are still unclean until
evening. 16 If you don't take a bath, you will
suffer for what you did wrong.

[p] **16.29** *seventh month*: Tishri (also called Ethanim), the seventh month of the Hebrew calendar, from about mid-September to mid-October. [q] **16.34** *Great Day of Forgiveness*: Traditionally known as the Day of Atonement. [r] **17.5; 19.5** *sacrifice . . . to ask my blessing*: See the note at 3.1.

16.21,22 Tb 8.3. **16.23** Ez 44.19. **16.27** He 13.11. **16.29-34** Lv 23.26-32; Nu 29.7-11. **17.10** Gn 9.4; Lv 7.26, 27; 19.26; Dt 12.5-19, 23, 24; 15.23. **17.11** He 9.22.

Forbidden Sex

18 The LORD told Moses 2 to tell the people of Israel:

I am the LORD your God! 3 So don't follow the customs of Egypt where you used to live or those of Canaan where I am bringing you. 4 I am the LORD your God, and you must obey my teachings. 5 Obey them and you will live. I am the LORD.

6 Don't have sex with any of your close relatives, 7 especially your own mother. This would disgrace your father. 8 And don't disgrace him by having sex with any of his other wives. 9 Don't have sex with your sister or stepsister, whether you grew up together or not. 10 Don't disgrace yourself by having sex with your granddaughter 11 or half sister 12-13 or a sister of your father or mother. 14 Don't disgrace your uncle by having sex with his wife. 15 Don't have sex with your daughter-in-law 16 or sister-in-law. 17 And don't have sex with the daughter or granddaughter of any woman that you have earlier had sex with. You may be having sex with a relative, and that would make you unclean. 18 As long as your wife is alive, don't cause trouble for her by taking one of her sisters as a second wife.

19 When a woman is having her monthly period, she is unclean, so don't have sex with her.

20 Don't have sex with another man's wife—that would make you unclean.

21 Don't sacrifice your children on the altar fires to the god Molech. I am the LORD your God, and that would disgrace me.

22 It is disgusting for a man to have sex with another man.

23 Anyone who has sex with an animal is unclean.

24 Don't make yourselves unclean by any of these disgusting practices of those nations that I am forcing out of the land for you. They made themselves 25 and the land so unclean, that I punished the land because of their sins, and I made it vomit them up. 26-27 Now don't do these sickening things that make the land filthy. Instead, obey my laws and teachings. 28 Then the land won't become sick of you and vomit you up, just as it did them. 29-30 If any of you do these vulgar, disgusting things, you will be unclean and no longer belong to my people. I am the LORD your God, and I forbid you to follow their sickening way of life.

Moral and Religious Laws

19 The LORD told Moses 2 to say to the community of Israel:

I am the LORD your God. I am holy, and you must be holy too! 3-4 Respect your father and your mother, honor the Sabbath, and don't make idols or images. I am the LORD your God.

5 When you offer a sacrifice to ask my blessing,[r] be sure to follow my instructions. 6 You may eat the meat either on the day of the sacrifice or on the next day, but you must burn anything left until the third day. 7 If you eat any of it on the third day, the sacrifice will be disgusting to me, and I will reject it. 8 In fact, you will be punished for not respecting what I say is holy, and you will no longer belong to the community of Israel.

9 When you harvest your grain, always leave some of it standing along the edges of your fields and don't pick up what falls on the ground. 10 Don't strip your grapevines clean or gather the grapes that fall off the vines. Leave them for the poor and for those foreigners who live among you. I am the LORD your God.

11 Do not steal or tell lies or cheat others.

12 Do not misuse my name by making

[r] **17.5; 19.5** *sacrifice . . . to ask my blessing*: See the note at 3.1.

18.5 Ne 9.29; Ez 18.9; 20.11-13; Lk 10.28; Ro 10.5; Ga 3.12. **18.8** Lv 20.11; Dt 22.30; 27.14-26. **18.9** Lv 20.17; Dt 27.14-26. **18.12-14** Lv 20.19, 20. **18.15** Lv 20.12. **18.16** Lv 20.21. **18.17** Lv 20.14; Dt 27.14-26. **18.19** Lv 20.18. **18.20** Lv 20.10. **18.21** Lv 20.1-5. **18.22** Lv 20.13. **18.23** Ex 22.19; Lv 20.15, 16; Dt 27.14-26. **19.2** Lv 11.44, 45; 1 P 1.16. **19.3,4** **a** Ex 20.12; Dt 5.16; **b** Ex 20.8; Dt 5.12; **c** Lv 26.1; **d** Ex 20.23; 34.17; Dt 17.2-7. **19.9,10** Lv 23.22; Dt 24.19-22. **19.11** **a** Ex 20.15; Dt 5.19; **b** Ex 20.16; Dt 5.20. **19.12** Ex 20.7; Dt 5.11; Mt 5.33.

promises you don't intend to keep. I am the LORD your God.

13 Do not steal anything or cheat anyone, and don't fail to pay your workers at the end of each day.[s]

14 I am the LORD your God, and I command you not to make fun of the deaf or to cause a blind person to stumble.

15 Be fair, no matter who is on trial—don't favor either the poor or the rich.

16 Don't be a gossip, but never hesitate to speak up in court, especially if your testimony can save someone's life.[t]

17 Don't hold grudges. On the other hand, it's wrong not to correct someone who needs correcting. 18 Stop being angry and don't try to take revenge. I am the LORD, and I command you to love others as much as you love yourself.

19 Breed your livestock animals only with animals of the same kind, and don't plant two kinds of seed in the same field or wear clothes made of different kinds of material.

20 If a man has sex with a slave woman who is promised in marriage to someone else, he must pay a fine, but they are not to be put to death. After all, she was still a slave at the time.[u] 21-22 The man must bring a ram to the entrance of the sacred tent and give it to a priest, who will then offer it as a sacrifice to me, so the man's sins will be forgiven.

23 After you enter the land, you will plant fruit trees, but you are not to eat any of their fruit for the first three years. 24 In the fourth year the fruit must be set apart, as an expression of thanks 25 to me, the LORD God. Do this, and in the fifth year, those trees will produce an abundant harvest of fruit for you to eat.

26 Don't eat the blood of any animal.

Don't practice any kind of witchcraft.

27-28 I forbid you to shave any part of your head or beard or to cut and tattoo yourself as a way of worshiping the dead.

29 Don't let your daughters serve as temple prostitutes—this would bring disgrace both to them and the land.

30 I command you to respect the Sabbath and the place where I am worshiped.

31 Don't make yourselves disgusting to me by going to people who claim they can talk to the dead.

32 I command you to show respect for older people and to obey me with fear and trembling.

33 Don't mistreat any foreigners who live in your land. 34 Instead, treat them as well as you treat citizens and love them as much as you love yourself. Remember, you were once foreigners in the land of Egypt. I am the LORD your God.

35-36 Use honest scales and don't cheat when you weigh or measure anything.

I am the LORD your God. I rescued you from Egypt, 37 and I command you to obey my laws.

Penalties for Disobeying God's Laws

20 The LORD told Moses 2 to say to the community of Israel:

Death by stoning is the penalty for any citizens or foreigners in the country who sacrifice their children to the god Molech. 3 They have disgraced both the place where I am worshiped and my holy name, and so I will turn against them and no longer let them belong to my people. 4 Some of you may let them get away with human sacrifice, 5 but not me. If any of you worship Molech, I will turn against you and your entire family, and I will no longer let you belong to my people.

6 I will be your enemy if you go to someone who claims to speak with the dead, and

[s] 19.13 *to pay . . . end of each day*: Day laborers needed their wages to buy food for their evening meal, which was the main meal of the day. [t] 19.16 *but never . . . someone's life*: One possible meaning for the difficult Hebrew text. [u] 19.20 *time*: One possible meaning for the difficult Hebrew text of verse 20.

19.13 Dt 24.14, 15. **19.14** Dt 27.14-26. **19.15** Ex 23.6-8; Dt 16.19. **19.17** Mt 18.15. **19.18** Mt 5.43; 19.19; 22.39; Mk 12.31; Lk 10.27; Ro 13.9; Ga 5.14; Jas 2.8. **19.19** Dt 22.9-11. **19.26 a** Gn 9.4; Lv 7.26, 27; 17.10-14; Dt 12.5-19, 23, 24; 15.23; **b** Dt 18.10, 11. **19.27,28** Lv 21.5; Dt 14.1. **19.29** Dt 23.17. **19.30** Lv 26.2. **19.31** Dt 18.10, 11; 1 S 28.1-3; 2 K 23.4; Is 8.19. **19.33,34** Ex 22.21; Dt 24.17, 18; 27.14-26. **19.35,36** Dt 25.13-16; Pr 20.10; Ez 45.10.

I will destroy you from among my people. 7 Dedicate yourselves to me and be holy because I am the LORD your God. 8 I have chosen you as my people, and I expect you to obey my laws.

9 If you curse your father or mother, you will be put to death, and it will be your own fault.

10 If any of you men have sex with another man's wife, both you and the woman will be put to death.

11 Having sex with one of your father's wives disgraces him. So both you and the woman will be put to death, just as you deserve. 12 It isn't natural to have sex with your daughter-in-law, and both of you will be put to death, just as you deserve. 13 It's disgusting for men to have sex with one another, and those who do will be put to death, just as they deserve. 14 It isn't natural for a man to marry both a mother and her daughter, and so all three of them will be burned to death. 15-16 If any of you have sex with an animal, both you and the animal will be put to death, just as you deserve.

17 If you marry one of your sisters, you will be punished, and the two of you will be disgraced by being openly forced out of the community. 18 If you have sex with a woman during her monthly period, both you and the woman will be cut off from the people of Israel. 19 The sisters of your father and mother are your own relatives, and you will be punished for having sex with any of them. 20 If you have sex with your uncle's wife, neither you nor she will ever have any children. 21 And if you marry your sister-in-law, neither of you will ever have any children.[v]

22 Obey my laws and teachings. Or else the land I am giving you will become sick of you and throw you out. 23 The nations I am chasing out did these disgusting things, and I hated them for it, so don't follow their example. 24 I am the LORD your God, and I have promised you their land that is rich with milk and honey. I have chosen you to be different from other people. 25 That's why you must make a difference between animals and birds that I have said are clean and unclean[w]—this will keep you from becoming disgusting to me. 26 I am the LORD, the holy God. You have been chosen to be my people, and so you must be holy too.

27 If you claim to receive messages from the dead, you will be put to death by stoning, just as you deserve.

Instructions for Priests

21 The LORD gave Moses these instructions for Aaron's sons, the priests:

Touching a dead body will make you unclean. So don't go near a dead relative, 2 except your mother, father, son, daughter, brother, 3 or an unmarried sister, who has no husband to take care of her. 4 Don't make yourself unclean by attending the funeral of someone related to you by marriage.[x] 5 Don't shave any part of your head or trim your beard or cut yourself to show that you are mourning. 6 I am the LORD your God, and I have chosen you alone to offer sacrifices of food to me on the altar. That's why you must keep yourselves holy. 7 Don't marry a divorced woman or a woman who has served as a temple prostitute. You are holy, 8 because I am holy. And so, you must be treated with proper respect, since you offer food sacrifices to me, the God of holiness.

9 If any of you priests has a daughter who disgraces you by serving as a temple prostitute, she must be burned to death.

10 If you are the high priest, you must not mess up your hair or tear your clothes

[v]**20.21** *And . . . children*: According to Deuteronomy 25.5, 6 a man was supposed to marry his brother's widow if his brother had died without having children. Otherwise, such marriages were forbidden (see also Matthew 22.23-33; Mark 12.18-27; Luke 20.27-40). [w]**20.25** *clean and unclean*: See the note at 11.4-8. [x]**21.4** *marriage*: One possible meaning for the difficult Hebrew text of verse 4.

20.9 Ex 21.17; Mt 15.4; Mk 7.10. **20.10** Ex 20.14; Lv 18.20; Dt 5.18. **20.11** Lv 18.8; Dt 22.30; 27.14-26. **20.12** Lv 18.15. **20.13** Lv 18.22. **20.14** Lv 18.17; Dt 27.14-26. **20.15,16** Ex 22.19; Lv 18.23; Dt 27.14-26. **20.17** Lv 18.9; Dt 27.14-26. **20.18** Lv 18.19. **20.19,20** Lv 18.12-14. **20.21** Lv 18.16. **21.5** Lv 19.27, 28; Dt 14.1.

in order to mourn for the dead. 11 Don't make yourself unclean by going near a dead body, not even that of your own father or mother. 12 If you leave the sacred place to attend a funeral, both you and the sacred place become unclean, because you are the high priest.

13 If you are the high priest, you must marry only a virgin 14 from your own tribe. Don't marry a divorced woman or any other woman who has already had sex, including a temple prostitute. 15 In this way, your descendants will be qualified to serve me. Remember—I am the LORD, and I have chosen you.

16 The LORD told Moses 17-18 to say to Aaron:

No descendant of yours can ever serve as my priest if he is blind or lame, if his face is disfigured, if one leg is shorter than the other, 19 if either a foot or a hand is crippled, 20 if he is a hunchback or a dwarf, if an eye or his skin is diseased, or if his testicles have been damaged. 21 These men may not serve as my priests and burn sacrifices to me. 22 They may eat the food offerings presented to me, 23 but they may not enter the sacred place or serve me at the altar. Remember—I am the LORD, the one who makes a priest holy.

24 Moses told all of this to Aaron, his sons, and the people of Israel.

The Offerings Are Holy

22 The LORD told Moses 2 to say to Aaron and his sons:

I am the LORD God, and I demand that you honor my holy name by showing proper respect for the offerings brought to me by the people of Israel. 3 If any of you are unclean when you accept an offering for me, I will no longer let you serve as a priest. 4 None of you may take part in the sacred meals while you have a skin disease or an infected penis, or after you have been near a dead body or have had a flow of semen, 5 or if you have touched an unclean creature of any sort, including an unclean person. 6-7 Once you are unclean, you must take a bath, but you still cannot eat any of the sacred food until evening. 8 I command you not to eat anything that is killed by a wild animal or dies a natural death. This would make you unclean. 9 Obey me, or you will die on duty for disgracing the place of worship. Remember—I am the LORD, the one who makes a priest holy.

10 Only you priests and your families may eat the food offerings; these are too sacred for any of your servants. 11 However, any slave that you own, including those born into your household, may eat this food. 12 If your daughter marries someone who isn't a priest, she can no longer have any of this food. 13 But if she returns to your home, either widowed or divorced, and has no children, she may join in the meal. Only members of a priestly family can eat this food, 14 and anyone else who accidentally does so, must pay for the food plus a fine of twenty percent.

15 I warn you not to treat lightly the offerings that are brought by the people of Israel. 16 Don't let them become guilty of eating this sacred food. Remember—I am the LORD, the one who makes these offerings holy.

Acceptable Sacrifices

17 The LORD told Moses 18 to tell Aaron and his sons and everyone else the rules for offering sacrifices. He said:

The animals that are to be completely burned on the altar 19-20 must have nothing wrong with them, or else I won't accept them. Bulls or rams or goats[y] are the animals to be used for these sacrifices.

21 When you offer a sacrifice to ask my blessing,[z] there must be nothing wrong with the animal. This is true, whether the sacrifice is part of a promise or something you do voluntarily. 22 Don't offer an animal that is blind or injured or that has an infection or a skin disease. 23 If one of your cattle or lambs has a leg that is longer or shorter than the others, you may offer it voluntarily, but not as part of a promise. 24 As long as you live in this land, don't offer an animal with injured testicles. 25 And don't bring me animals you bought from a foreigner. I won't accept them, because

[y]**22.19,20** *goats*: See the note at 1.1-3. [z]**22.21** *sacrifice to ask my blessing*: See the note at 3.1.
22.19,20 Dt 17.1.

they are no better than one that has something wrong with it.

26 The LORD told Moses to say:

27 Newborn cattle, sheep, or goats must remain with their mothers for seven days, but on the eighth day, you may send them up in smoke to me, and I will accept the offering. 28 Don't sacrifice a newborn animal and its mother on the same day.

29 When you offer a sacrifice to give thanks[a] to me, you must do it in a way that is acceptable. 30 Eat all of the meat that same day and don't save any for the next day. I am the LORD your God!

31 Obey my laws and teachings—I am the LORD. 32-33 I demand respect from the people of Israel, so don't disgrace my holy name. Remember—I am the one who chose you to be priests and rescued all of you from Egypt, so that I would be your LORD.

Religious Festivals

23 The LORD told Moses 2 to say to the community of Israel:

I have chosen certain times for you to come together and worship me.

3 You have six days when you can do your work, but the seventh day of each week is holy because it belongs to me. No matter where you live, you must rest on the Sabbath and come together for worship. This law will never change.

Passover and the Festival of Thin Bread

(Numbers 28.16-25)

The LORD said:

4-5 Passover is another time when you must come together to worship me, and it must be celebrated on the evening of the fourteenth day of the first month[b] of each year.

6 The Festival of Thin Bread begins on the fifteenth day of that same month; it lasts seven days, and during this time you must honor me by eating bread made without yeast. 7 On the first day of this festival you must rest from your work and come together for worship. 8 Each day of this festival you must offer sacrifices. Then on the final day you must once again rest from your work and come together for worship.

Offering the First Part of the Harvest

9 The LORD told Moses 10 to say to the community of Israel:

After you enter the land I am giving you, the first bundle of wheat from each crop must be given to me. So bring it to a priest 11 on the day after the Sabbath. He will lift it up[c] in dedication to me, and I will accept you. 12 You must also offer a sacrifice to please me.[d] So bring the priest a one-year-old lamb that has nothing wrong with it 13 and four pounds of your finest flour mixed with olive oil. Then he will place these on the bronze altar and send them up in smoke with a smell that pleases me. Together with these, you must bring a quart of wine as a drink offering. 14 I am your God, and I forbid you to eat any new grain or anything made from it until you have brought these offerings. This law will never change.

The Harvest Festival

(Numbers 28.26-31)

The LORD said:

15 Seven weeks after you offer this bundle of grain, each family must bring another offering of new grain. 16 Do this exactly fifty days later, which is the day following the seventh Sabbath. 17 Bring two loaves of bread to be lifted up[e] in dedication to me. Each loaf is to be made with yeast and with four pounds of the finest flour from the first part of your harvest.

18 At this same time, the entire community of Israel must bring seven lambs that are a year old, a young bull, and two rams. These animals must have nothing wrong

[a]**22.29** *sacrifice to give thanks*: See 7.12. [b]**23.4,5** *first month*: Abib (also called Nisan), the first month of the Hebrew calendar, from about mid-March to mid-April. [c]**23.11** *lift it up*: See the note at 7.29, 30. [d]**23.12** *sacrifice to please me*: See the note at 1.1-3. [e]**23.17** *lifted up*: See the note at 7.29, 30.

23.3 Ex 20.8-10; 23.12; 31.14, 15; 34.21; 35.2; Dt 5.12-14. **23.4,5** Ex 12.1-13; Dt 16.1, 2. **23.6-8** Ex 12.14-20; 23.15; 34.18; Dt 16.3-8. **23.15-21** Ex 23.16; 34.22; Dt 16.9-12.

with them, and they must be offered as a sacrifice to please me.[f] You must also offer the proper grain and wine sacrifices with each animal.[g] 19 Offer a goat[h] as a sacrifice for sin, and two rams a year old as a sacrifice to ask my blessing.[i] 20 The priest will lift up[j] the rams together with the bread in dedication to me. These offerings are holy and are my gift to the priest. 21 This is a day of celebration and worship, a time of rest from your work. You and your descendants must obey this law.

22 When you harvest your grain, always leave some of it standing around the edges of your fields and don't pick up what falls on the ground. Leave it for the poor and for those foreigners who live among you. I am the LORD your God!

The Festival of Trumpets
(Numbers 29.1-6)

23 The LORD told Moses 24-25 to say to the people of Israel:

The first day of the seventh month[k] must be a day of complete rest. Then at the sound of the trumpets, you will come together to worship and to offer sacrifices on the altar.

The Great Day of Forgiveness
(Numbers 29.7-11)

26 The LORD God said to Moses:

27 The tenth day of the seventh month[k] is the Great Day of Forgiveness.[l] It is a solemn day of worship; everyone must go without eating to show sorrow for their sins, and sacrifices must be burned. 28 No one is to work on that day—it is the Great Day of Forgiveness, when sacrifices will be offered to me, so that I will forgive your sins. 29 I will destroy anyone who refuses to go without eating. 30-31 None of my people are ever to do any work on that day—not now or in the future. And I will wipe out those who do! 32 This is a time of complete rest just like the Sabbath, and everyone must go without eating from the evening of the ninth to the evening of the tenth.

The Festival of Shelters
(Numbers 29.12-40)

33 The LORD told Moses 34 to say to the community of Israel:

Beginning on the fifteenth day of the seventh month,[m] and continuing for seven days, everyone must celebrate the Festival of Shelters in honor of me. 35 No one is to do any work on the first day of the festival—it is a time when everyone must come together for worship. 36 For seven days, sacrifices must be offered on the altar. The eighth day is also to be a day of complete rest, as well as a time of offering sacrifices on the altar and of coming together for worship.

37 I have chosen these festivals as times when my people must come together for worship and when animals, grain, and wine are to be offered on the proper days. 38 These festivals must be celebrated in addition to the Sabbaths and the times when you offer special gifts or sacrifices to keep a promise or as a voluntary offering.

39 Remember to begin the Festival of Shelters on the fifteenth day of the seventh month after you have harvested your crops. Celebrate this festival for seven days in honor of me and don't do any work on the first day or on the day following the festival. 40 Pick the best fruit from your trees[n] and cut leafy branches to use during the time of this joyous celebration in my honor. 41 I command you and all of your descendants to celebrate this festival during the seventh month of each year. 42 For seven days every Israelite must live in a shelter, 43 so future generations will know that I made their ancestors live in shelters when I brought them out of Egypt. I am the LORD your God.

[f]**23.18** *sacrifice to please me*: See the note at 1.1-3. [g]**23.18** *proper grain . . . animal*: See Numbers 15.1-16. [h]**23.19** *goat*: See the note at 1.1-3. [i]**23.19** *sacrifice to ask my blessing*: See the note at 3.1. [j]**23.20** *lift up*: See the note at 7.29, 30. [k]**23.24,25,27** *seventh month*: See the note at 16.29. [l]**23.27** *Great Day of Forgiveness*: See the note at 16.34. [m]**23.34** *seventh month*: See the note at 16.29. [n]**23.40** *best fruit from your trees*: One possible meaning for the difficult Hebrew text.

23.22 Lv 19.9, 10; Dt 24.19-22. **23.26-32** Lv 16.29-34. **23.33-36** Dt 16.13-15.

44 This is how Moses instructed the people of Israel to celebrate the LORD's festivals.

Caring for the Lamps
(Exodus 27.20, 21)

24 The LORD told Moses 2 to say to the community of Israel:

You must supply the purest olive oil for the lamps in the sacred tent, so they will keep burning. 3-4 Aaron will set up the gold lampstand in the holy place of the sacred tent. Then he will light the seven lamps that must be kept burning there in my presence, every night from now on. This law will never change.

The Sacred Bread

The LORD said:

5 Use your finest flour to bake twelve loaves of bread about four pounds each, 6 then take them into the sacred tent and lay them on the gold table in two rows of six loaves. 7 Alongside each row put some pure incense that will be sent up by fire in place of the bread as an offering to me. 8 Aaron must lay fresh loaves on the table each Sabbath, and priests in all generations must continue this practice as part of Israel's agreement with me. 9 This bread will always belong to Aaron and his family; it is very holy because it was offered to me, and it must be eaten in a holy place.[o]

Punishment for Cursing the LORD

10-11 Shelomith, the daughter of Dibri from the tribe of Dan, had married an Egyptian, and they had a son. One day their son got into a fight with an Israelite man in camp and cursed the name of the LORD. So the young man was dragged off to Moses, 12 who had him guarded while everyone waited for the LORD to tell them what to do.

13 Finally, the LORD said to Moses:

14 This man has cursed me! Take him outside the camp and have the witnesses lay their hands on his head. Then command the whole community of Israel to stone him to death. 15-16 And warn the others that everyone else who curses me will die in the same way, whether they are Israelites by birth or foreigners living among you.

17 Death is also the penalty for murder, 18 but the killing of an animal that belongs to someone else requires only that the animal be replaced. 19 Personal injuries to others must be dealt with in keeping with the crime— 20 a broken bone for a broken bone, an eye for an eye, or a tooth for a tooth. 21 It's possible to pay the owner for an animal that has been killed, but death is the penalty for murder. 22 I am the LORD your God, and I demand equal justice both for you Israelites and for those foreigners who live among you.

23 When Moses finished speaking, the people did what the LORD had told Moses, and they stoned to death the man who had cursed the LORD.

The Seventh Year
(Deuteronomy 15.1-11)

25 When Moses was on Mount Sinai, the LORD told him 2 to say to the community of Israel:

After you enter the land that I am giving you, it must be allowed to rest one year out of every seven. 3 You may raise grain and grapes for six years, 4 but the seventh year you must let your fields and vineyards rest in honor of me, your LORD. 5 This is to be a time of complete rest for your fields and vineyards, so don't harvest anything they produce. 6-7 However, you and your slaves and your hired workers, as well as any domestic or wild animals, may eat whatever grows on its own.

The Year of Celebration

The LORD said to his people:

8 Once every forty-nine years 9 on the tenth day of the seventh month,[p] which is

[o]**24.9** *holy place*: The courtyard of the sacred tent (see 6.16, 17). [p]**25.9** *seventh month*: See the note at 16.29.

24.5,6 Ex 25.30. **24.9** Mt 12.4; Mk 2.26; Lk 6.4. **24.17** Ex 21.12. **24.20** Ex 21.23-25; Dt 19.19-21; Mt 5.38. **24.22** Nu 15.15, 16. **25.1-7** Ex 23.10, 11.

also the Great Day of Forgiveness,[q] trumpets are to be blown everywhere in the land. 10 This fiftieth year[r] is sacred—it is a time of freedom and of celebration when everyone will receive back their original property, and slaves will return home to their families. 11 This is a year of complete celebration, so don't plant any seed or harvest what your fields or vineyards produce. 12 In this time of sacred celebration you may eat only what grows on its own.

13 During this year, all property must go back to its original owner. 14-15 So when you buy or sell farmland, the price is to be determined by the number of crops it can produce before the next Year of Celebration. Don't try to cheat. 16 If it is a long time before the next Year of Celebration, the price will be higher, because what is really being sold are the crops that the land can produce. 17 I am the LORD your God, so obey me and don't cheat anyone.

18-19 If you obey my laws and teachings, you will live safely in the land and enjoy its abundant crops. 20 Don't ever worry about what you will eat during the seventh year when you are forbidden to plant or harvest. 21 I will see to it that you harvest enough in the sixth year to last for three years. 22 In the eighth year you will live on what you harvested in the sixth year, but in the ninth year you will eat what you plant and harvest in the eighth year.

23 No land may be permanently bought or sold. It all belongs to me—it isn't your land, and you only live there for a little while.

24 When property is being sold, the original owner must be given the first chance to buy it.

25 If any of you Israelites become so poor that you are forced to sell your property, your closest relative must buy it back, 26 if that relative has the money. Later, if you can afford to buy it, 27 you must pay enough to make up for what the present owner will lose on it before the next Year of Celebration, when the property would become yours again. 28 But if you don't have the money to pay the present owner a fair price, you will have to wait until the Year of Celebration, when the property will once again become yours.

29 If you sell a house in a walled city, you have only one year in which to buy it back. 30 If you don't buy it back before that year is up, it becomes the permanent property of the one who bought it, and it will not be returned to you in the Year of Celebration. 31 But a house out in a village may be bought back at any time just like a field. And it must be returned to its original owner in the Year of Celebration. 32 If any Levites own houses inside a walled city, they will always have the right to buy them back. 33 And any houses that they do not buy back will be returned to them in the Year of Celebration, because these homes are their permanent property among the people of Israel. 34 No pastureland owned by the Levi tribe can ever be sold; it is their permanent possession.

Help for the Poor

The LORD said:

35 If any of your people become poor and unable to support themselves, you must help them, just as you are supposed to help foreigners who live among you. 36-37 Don't take advantage of them by charging any kind of interest or selling them food for profit. Instead, honor me by letting them stay where they now live. 38 Remember—I am the LORD your God! I rescued you from Egypt and gave you the land of Canaan, so that I would be your God.

39 Suppose some of your people become so poor that they have to sell themselves and become your slaves. 40 Then you must treat them as servants, rather than as slaves. And in the Year of Celebration they are to be set free, 41 so they and their children may return home to their families and property. 42 I brought them out of Egypt to be my servants, not to be sold as slaves.

[q] **25.9** *Great Day of Forgiveness*: See the note at 16.34. [r] **25.10** *fiftieth year*: The year following seven periods of seven years.

25.35 Dt 15.7, 8. **25.36,37** Ex 22.25; Dt 23.19, 20. **25.39-46** Ex 21.2-6; Dt 15.12-18.

43 So obey me, and don't be cruel to the poor.

44 If you want slaves, buy them from other nations 45 or from the foreigners who live in your own country, and make them your property. 46 You can own them, and even leave them to your children when you die, but do not make slaves of your own people or be cruel to them.

47 Even if some of you Israelites become so much in debt that you must sell yourselves to foreigners in your country, 48 you still have the right to be set free by a relative, such as a brother 49 or uncle or cousin, or some other family member. In fact, if you ever get enough money, you may buy your own freedom 50 by paying your owner for the number of years you would still be a slave before the next Year of Celebration. 51-52 The longer the time until then, the more you will have to pay. 53 And even while you are the slaves of foreigners in your own country, your people must make sure that you are not mistreated. 54 If you cannot gain your freedom in any of these ways, both you and your children will still be set free in the Year of Celebration. 55 People of Israel, I am the LORD your God, and I brought you out of Egypt to be my own servants.

Blessings for Obeying the LORD

The LORD said:

26 I am the LORD your God! So don't make or worship any sort of idols or images. 2 Respect the Sabbath and honor the place where I am worshiped, because I am the LORD.

3 Faithfully obey my laws, 4 and I will send rain to make your crops grow and your trees produce fruit. 5 Your harvest of grain and grapes will be so abundant, that you won't know what to do with it all. You will eat and be satisfied, and you will live in safety. 6 I will bless your country with peace, and you will rest without fear. I will wipe out the dangerous animals and protect you from enemy attacks. 7 You will chase and destroy your enemies, 8 even if there are only five of you and a hundred of them, or only a hundred of you and ten thousand of them. 9 I will treat you with such kindness that your nation will grow strong, and I will also keep my promises to you. 10 Your barns will overflow with grain each year. 11 I will live among you and never again look on you with disgust. 12 I will walk with you—I will be your God, and you will be my people. 13 I am the LORD your God, and I rescued you from Egypt, so that you would never again be slaves. I have set you free; now walk with your heads held high.

Punishment for Disobeying the LORD

The LORD said:

14-15 If you disobey me and my laws, and if you break our agreement, 16 I will punish you terribly, and you will be ruined. You will be struck with incurable diseases and with fever that leads to blindness and depression. Your enemies will eat the crops you plant, 17 and I will turn from you and let you be destroyed by your attackers. You will even run at the very rumor of attack. 18 Then, if you still refuse to obey me, I will punish you seven times for each of your sins, 19 until your pride is completely crushed. I will hold back the rain, so the sky above you will be like iron, and the ground beneath your feet will be like copper. 20 All of your hard work will be for nothing—and there will be no harvest of grain or fruit.

21 If you keep rebelling against me, I'll punish you seven times worse, just as your sins deserve! 22 I'll send wild animals to attack you, and they will gobble down your children and livestock. So few of you will be left that your roads will be deserted.

23 If you remain my enemies after this, 24 I'll remain your enemy and punish you even worse. 25 War will break out because you broke our agreement, and if you escape to your walled cities, I'll punish you with horrible diseases, and you will be captured by your enemies. 26 You will have such a shortage of bread, that ten women will be able to bake their bread in the same oven.

26.1 **a** Lv 19.3, 4; **b** Ex 20.4; Dt 5.8; 16.21, 22; 29.16-18. **26.3-5** Dt 11.13-15; 28.1-14. **26.12** 2 Co 6.16. **26.14-33** Dt 28.15-68.

Each of you will get only a few crumbs, and you will go hungry.

27 Then if you don't stop rebelling, 28 I'll really get furious and punish you terribly for your sins! 29 In fact, you will be so desperate for food that you will eat your own children. 30 I'll destroy your shrines and tear down your incense altars, leaving your dead bodies piled on top of your idols. And you will be disgusting to me. 31 I'll wipe out your towns and your places of worship and will no longer be pleased with the smell of your sacrifices. 32 Your land will become so desolate that even your enemies who settle there will be shocked when they see it. 33 After I destroy your towns and ruin your land with war, I'll scatter you among the nations.

34-35 While you are prisoners in foreign lands, your own land will enjoy years of rest and refreshment, as it should have done each seventh year when you lived there. 36-37 In the land of your enemies, you will tremble at the rustle of a leaf, as though it were a sword. And you will become so weak that you will stumble and fall over each other, even when no one is chasing you. 38 Many of you will die in foreign lands, 39 and others of you will waste away in sorrow as the result of your sins and the sins of your ancestors.

40-41 Then suppose you realize that I turned against you and brought you to the land of your enemies because both you and your ancestors had stubbornly sinned against me. If you humbly confess what you have done and start living right, 42 I'll keep the promise I made to your ancestors Abraham, Isaac, and Jacob. I will bless your land 43 and let it rest during the time that you are in a foreign country, paying for your rebellion against me and my laws.

44 No matter what you have done, I am still the LORD your God, and I will never completely reject you or become absolutely disgusted with you there in the land of your enemies. 45 While nations watched, I rescued your ancestors from Egypt so that I would be their God. Yes, I am your LORD, and I will never forget our agreement.

46 Moses was on Mount Sinai when the LORD gave him these laws and teachings for the people of Israel.

Making Promises to the LORD

27 The LORD told Moses 2 to say to the community of Israel:

If you ever want to free someone who has been promised to me, 3-7 you may do so by paying the following amounts, weighed according to the official standards:

fifty pieces of silver for men
ages twenty to sixty,
and thirty pieces for women;
twenty pieces of silver
for young men
ages five to twenty,
and ten pieces
for young women;
fifteen pieces of silver for men
ages sixty and above
and ten pieces for women;
five pieces of silver for boys
ages one month to five years,
and three pieces for girls.

8 If you have promised to give someone to me and can't afford to pay the full amount for that person's release, you will be taken to a priest, and he will decide how much you can afford.

9 If you promise to sacrifice an animal to me, it becomes holy, and there is no way you can set it free. 10 If you try to substitute any other animal, no matter how good, for the one you promised, they will both become holy and must be sacrificed. 11 Donkeys are unfit for sacrifice, so if you promise me a donkey,[s] you must bring it to the priest, 12 and let him determine its value. 13 But if you want to buy it back, you must pay an additional twenty percent.

14 If you promise a house to me, a priest will set the price, whatever the condition of the house. 15 But if you decide to buy it back, you must pay an additional twenty percent.

16 If you promise part of your family's

[s] **27.11** *Donkeys . . . donkey*: The Hebrew text has "If you promise me an unclean animal," which probably refers to a donkey (see Exodus 13.13; 34.20).

26.42 **a** Gn 28.13, 14; **b** Gn 26.3, 4; **c** Gn 17.7, 8. **26.44** 3 Macc 6.15.

land to me, its value must be determined by the bushels of seed needed to plant the land, and the rate will be ten pieces of silver for every bushel of seed. 17 If this promise is made in the Year of Celebration,[t] the land will be valued at the full price. 18 But any time after that, the price will be figured according to the number of years before the next Year of Celebration. 19 If you decide to buy back the land, you must pay the price plus an additional twenty percent, 20 but you cannot buy it back once someone else has bought it. 21 When the Year of Celebration comes, the land becomes holy because it belongs to me, and it will be given to the priests.

22 If you promise me a field that you have bought, 23 its value will be decided by a priest, according to the number of years before the next Year of Celebration, and the money you pay will be mine. 24 However, on the next Year of Celebration, the land will go back to the family of its original owner. 25 Every price will be set by the official standards.

Various Offerings

The LORD said:

26 All first-born animals of your flocks and herds are already mine, and so you cannot promise any of them to me. 27 If you promise me a donkey,[u] you may buy it back by adding an additional twenty percent to its value. If you don't buy it back, it can be sold to someone else for whatever a priest has said it is worth.

28 Anything that you completely dedicate to me must be completely destroyed.[v] It cannot be bought back or sold. Every person, animal, and piece of property that you dedicate completely is only for me. 29 In fact, any humans who have been promised to me in this way must be put to death.

30 Ten percent of everything you harvest is holy and belongs to me, whether it grows in your fields or on your fruit trees. 31 If you want to buy back this part of your harvest, you may do so by paying what it is worth plus an additional twenty percent.

32 When you count your flocks and herds, one out of ten of every newborn animal[w] is holy and belongs to me, 33 no matter how good or bad it is. If you substitute one animal for another, both of them become holy, and neither can be bought back.

34 Moses was on Mount Sinai when the LORD gave him these laws for the people of Israel.

[t]**27.17** *Year of Celebration*: See 25.8-34. [u]**27.27** *donkey*: See the note at verse 11.
[v]**27.28** *completely dedicate . . . completely destroyed*: In order to show that something belonged completely to the LORD and could not be used by anyone else, it was destroyed. This law most often applied to towns and people captured in war (see Joshua 6.16, 17). [w]**27.32** *one out of ten of every newborn animal*: Or "one out of every ten animals."
27.28 Nu 18.14. **27.30-33** Nu 18.21; Dt 14.22-29.

NUMBERS

ABOUT THIS BOOK

The book of Numbers continues the history of the people of Israel after they escaped from Egypt, and it tells what happened during the forty years when the Israelites lived in the desert on their journey from Mount Sinai to Canaan. This book is named "Numbers" because it begins with Moses counting the Israelites to find out the number of people in each of Israel's twelve tribes.

Numbers can be divided into three parts. In the first part (1.1—10.10) the Lord has Moses count the people, and then he gives Moses instructions for setting up Israel's camp and for assigning the Levites their duties. This part ends with everyone celebrating Passover and offering sacrifices to the Lord.

The second part (10.11—21.20) includes events that happened while the Israelites were on their way to Moab, a nation living east of the Jordan River. This was a very difficult journey through the desert, and the people often complained and even rebelled against Moses and against God. The Israelites refused to enter Canaan after hearing about the nations that lived there, and so the Lord punished the Israelites by making them remain in the desert for forty years. This part of Numbers ends with the people camped in Moab near Mount Pisgah.

The third part of the book (21.21—36.13) begins with the Israelites conquering the land just east of the Jordan River, from the border with Moab in the south to Lake Galilee in the north. Then the king of Moab hired the foreign prophet Balaam to curse the people of Israel. But the Lord told Balaam to bless the Israelites, and Balaam obeyed.

The Israelites prepared to cross the Jordan River and conquer the land of Canaan, although some of the people decided to settle east of the Jordan River. The Israelites were counted a second time, then the Lord appointed Joshua to be Israel's next leader and chose other leaders to help Joshua divide the land among the tribes. The book concludes with the Lord giving the Israelites more laws.

Numbers is about people who were rebellious and discouraged and who refused to believe that the Lord would take care of them. But the book also shows how the Lord protected them in war and gave them food and water in the barren desert. The Lord wanted the Israelites to realize that he did not want them to be destroyed; he wanted to bless them, just as Aaron prayed:

"I pray that the Lord
will bless and protect you,
and that he will show you mercy
and kindness.
May the Lord be good to you
and give you peace."
(6.24-26)

A QUICK LOOK AT THIS BOOK

The People of Israel Are Counted

1 The people of Israel had left Egypt and were living in the Sinai Desert. Then on the first day of the second month[a] of the second year, Moses was in the sacred tent when the LORD said:

2-3 I want you and Aaron to find out how many people are in each of Israel's clans and families. And make a list of all the men twenty years and older who are able to fight in battle.
4-15 The following twelve family leaders, one from each tribe, will help you:

Elizur son of Shedeur
from Reuben,
Shelumiel son of Zurishaddai
from Simeon,
Nahshon son of Amminadab
from Judah,
Nethanel son of Zuar
from Issachar,
Eliab son of Helon
from Zebulun,
Elishama son of Ammihud
from Ephraim,
Gamaliel son of Pedahzur
from Manasseh,
Abidan son of Gideoni
from Benjamin,
Ahiezer son of Ammishaddai
from Dan,
Pagiel son of Ochran
from Asher,
Eliasaph son of Deuel
from Gad,
and Ahira son of Enan
from Naphtali.

16-17 Moses and Aaron, together with these twelve tribal leaders, 18 called together the people that same day. They were counted according to their clans and families. Then Moses and the others listed the names of the men twenty years and older, 19 just as the LORD had commanded.
20-46 The number of men from each tribe who were at least twenty years old and strong enough to fight in Israel's army was as follows:

46,500 from Reuben,
the oldest son of Jacob,[b]

---

[a] **1.1** *second month*: Ziv, the second month of the Hebrew calendar, from about mid-April to mid-May. [b] **1.20-46** *Jacob*: The Hebrew text has "Israel," Jacob's name after God renamed him.
1.1-46 Nu 26.1-51.

59,300 from Simeon,
45,650 from Gad,
74,600 from Judah,
54,400 from Issachar,
57,400 from Zebulun,
40,500 from Ephraim,
32,200 from Manasseh,
35,400 from Benjamin,
62,700 from Dan,
41,500 from Asher,
53,400 from Naphtali.

The total number of men registered by Moses, Aaron, and the twelve leaders was 603,550.

47 But those from the Levi tribe were not included 48 because the LORD had said to Moses:

49 When you count the Israelites, do not include those from the Levi tribe. 50-51 Instead, give them the job of caring for the sacred tent, its furnishings, and the objects used for worship. They will camp around the tent, and whenever you move, they will take it down, carry it to the new camp, and set it up again. Anyone else who tries to go near it must be put to death.

52 The rest of the Israelites will camp in their own groups and under their own banners. 53 But the Levites will camp around the sacred tent to make sure that no one goes near it and makes me furious with the Israelites.

54 The people of Israel did everything the LORD had commanded.

Instructions for Setting Up Israel's Camp

2 The LORD told Moses and Aaron 2 how the Israelites should arrange their camp:

Each tribe must set up camp under its own banner and under the flags of its ancestral families. These camps will be arranged around the sacred tent, but not close to it.

3-4 Judah and the tribes that march with it must set up camp on the east side of the sacred tent, under their own banner. The 74,600 troops of the tribe of Judah will be arranged by divisions and led by Nahshon son of Amminadab. 5-6 On one side of Judah will be the tribe of Issachar, with Nethanel son of Zuar as the leader of its 54,400 troops. 7-8 On the other side will be the tribe of Zebulun, with Eliab son of Helon as the leader of its 57,400 troops. 9 These 186,400 troops will march into battle first.

10-11 Reuben and the tribes that march with it must set up camp on the south side of the sacred tent, under their own banner. The 46,500 troops of the tribe of Reuben will be arranged by divisions and led by Elizur son of Shedeur. 12-13 On one side of Reuben will be the tribe of Simeon, with Shelumiel son of Zurishaddai as the leader of its 59,300 troops. 14-15 On the other side will be the tribe of Gad, with Eliasaph son of Deuel as the leader of its 45,650 troops. 16 These 151,450 troops will march into battle second.

17 Marching behind Reuben will be the Levites, arranged in groups, just as they are camped. They will carry the sacred tent and their own banners.

18-19 Ephraim and the tribes that march with it must set up camp on the west side of the sacred tent, under their own banner. The 40,500 troops of the tribe of Ephraim will be arranged by divisions and led by Elishama son of Ammihud. 20-21 On one side of Ephraim will be the tribe of Manasseh, with Gamaliel son of Pedahzur as the leader of its 32,200 troops. 22-23 On the other side will be the tribe of Benjamin, with Abidan son of Gideoni as the leader of its 35,400 troops. 24 These 108,100 troops will march into battle third.

25-26 Dan and the tribes that march with it must set up camp on the north side of the sacred tent, under their own banner. The 62,700 troops of the tribe of Dan will be arranged by divisions and led by Ahiezer son of Ammishaddai. 27-28 On one side of Dan will be the tribe of Asher, with Pagiel son of Ochran as the leader of its 41,500 troops. 29-30 On the other side will be the tribe of Naphtali with Ahira son of Enan as the leader of its 53,400 troops. 31 These 157,600 troops will march into battle last.

32 So all the Israelites in the camp were counted according to their ancestral families. The troops were arranged by divisions and totaled 603,550. 33 The only Israelites

not included were the Levites, just as the
LORD had commanded Moses.
34 Israel did everything the LORD had
told Moses. They arranged their camp according to clans and families, with each
tribe under its own banner. And that was
the order by which they marched into
battle.

The Sons of Aaron

3 When the LORD talked with Moses on
Mount Sinai, 2 Aaron's four sons,
Nadab, Abihu, Eleazar, and Ithamar, 3 were
the ones to be ordained as priests. 4 But the
LORD killed Nadab and Abihu in the Sinai
Desert when they used fire that was unac-
ceptable[c] in their offering to the LORD.[d]
And because Nadab and Abihu had no
sons, only Eleazar and Ithamar served as
priests with their father Aaron.

The Duties of the Levites

5 The LORD said to Moses:
6 Assign the Levi tribe to Aaron the
priest. They will be his assistants 7 and
will work at the sacred tent for him
and for all the Israelites. 8 The Levites
will serve the community by being responsible for the furnishings of the
tent. 9 They are assigned to help Aaron
and his sons, 10 who have been appointed to be priests. Anyone else who
tries to perform the duties of a priest
must be put to death.
11-13 Moses, I have chosen these
Levites from all Israel, and they will
belong to me in a special way. When I
killed the first-born sons of the Egyptians, I decided that the first-born sons
in every Israelite family and the first-
born males of their flocks and herds
would be mine.[e] But now I accept
these Levites in place of the first-born
sons of the Israelites.

The Levites Are Counted

14 In the Sinai Desert the LORD said to
Moses, 15 "Now I want you to count the
men and boys in the Levi tribe by families
and by clans. Include every one at least a
month old." 16 So Moses obeyed and
counted them.
17 Levi's three sons, Gershon, Kohath,
and Merari, had become the heads of their
own clans. 18 Gershon's sons were Libni
and Shimei. 19 Kohath's sons were Amram,
Izhar, Hebron, and Uzziel. 20 And Merari's
sons were Mahli and Mushi. These were
the sons and grandsons of Levi, and they
had become the leaders of the Levite clans.
21 The two Gershon clans were the Lib-
nites and Shimeites, 22 and they had seven
thousand five hundred men and boys at
least one month old. 23 The Gershonites
were to camp on the west side of the sacred
tent, 24 under the leadership of Eliasaph
son of Lael. 25 Their duties at the tent included taking care of the tent itself, along
with its outer covering, the curtain for the
entrance, 26 the curtains hanging inside
the courtyard around the tent, as well as
the curtain and ropes for the entrance to
the courtyard and its altar. The Gershonites
were responsible for setting these things up
and taking them down.
27 The four Kohath clans were the Am-
ramites, Izharites, Hebronites, and the
Uzzielites, 28 and they had eight thousand
six hundred[f] men and boys at least one
month old. 29 The Kohathites were to camp
on the south side of the sacred tent, 30 under the leadership of Elizaphan son of
Uzziel. 31 Their duties at the tent included
taking care of the sacred chest, the table
for the sacred bread, the lampstand, the altars, the objects used for worship, and the
curtain in front of the most holy place. The
Kohathites were responsible for setting
these things up and taking them down.
32 Eleazar son of Aaron was the head of
the Levite leaders, and he made sure that
the work at the sacred tent was done.
33 The two Merari clans were the Mah-
lites and the Mushites, 34 and they had six
thousand two hundred men and boys at
least one month old. 35 The Merarites were

[c] **3.4** *fire that was unacceptable*: One possible meaning for the difficult Hebrew text. [d] **3.4** *the LORD killed Nadab and Abihu . . . to the LORD*: See Leviticus 10.1, 2. [e] **3.11-13** *When I killed . . . mine*: See Exodus 13.1, 2, 11-16. [f] **3.28** *eight thousand six hundred*: Hebrew; some manuscripts of one ancient translation "eight thousand three hundred."

3.2 Nu 26.60. **3.4** Lv 10.1, 2; Nu 26.61. **3.11-13** Ex 13.2.

to camp on the north side of the sacred tent, under the leadership of Zuriel son of Abihail. 36-37 Their duties included taking care of the tent frames and the pieces that held the tent up: the bars, the posts, the stands, and its other equipment. They were also in charge of the posts that supported the courtyard, as well as their stands, tent pegs, and ropes. The Merari clans were responsible for setting these things up and taking them down.

38 Moses, Aaron, and his sons were to camp in front of the sacred tent, on the east side, and to make sure that the Israelites worshiped in the proper way. Anyone else who tried to do the work of Moses and Aaron was to be put to death.

39 So Moses and Aaron obeyed the LORD and counted the Levites by their clans. The total number of Levites at least one month old was twenty-two thousand.

The Levites Are Accepted as Substitutes for the First-Born Sons

40 The LORD said to Moses, "Make a list and count the first-born sons at least one month old in each of the Israelite families. 41 They belong to me, but I will accept the Levites as substitutes for them, and I will accept the Levites' livestock as substitutes for the Israelites' first-born livestock."

42 Moses obeyed the LORD and counted the first-born sons; 43 there were 22,273 of them.

44 Then the LORD said, 45 "The Levites will belong to me and will take the place of the first-born sons; their livestock will take the place of the Israelites' first-born livestock. 46 But since there are more first-born sons than Levites, the extra two hundred seventy-three men and boys must be bought back from me. 47 For each one, you are to collect five pieces of silver, weighed according to the official standards. 48 This money must then be given to Aaron and his sons."

49 Moses collected the silver from the extra two hundred seventy-three first-born men and boys, 50 and it amounted to one thousand three hundred sixty-five pieces of silver, weighed according to the official standards. 51 Then he gave it to Aaron and his sons, just as the LORD had commanded.

The Duties of the Kohathite Clans

4 The LORD told Moses and Aaron: 2-3 Find out how many men between the ages of thirty and fifty are in the four Levite clans of Kohath. Count only those who are able to work at the sacred tent.

4 The Kohathites will be responsible for carrying the sacred objects used in worship at the sacred tent. 5 When the Israelites are ready to move their camp, Aaron and his sons will enter the tent and take down the curtain that separates the sacred chest from the rest of the tent. They will cover the chest with this curtain, 6 and then with a piece of fine leather, and cover it all with a solid blue cloth. After this they will put the carrying poles in place.

7 Next, Aaron and his sons will use another blue cloth to cover the table for the sacred bread.[g] On the cloth they will place the dishes, the bowls for incense, the cups, the jugs for wine, as well as the bread itself. 8 They are to cover all of this with a bright red cloth, and then with a piece of fine leather, before putting the carrying poles in place.

9 With another blue cloth they will cover the lampstand, along with the lamps, the lamp snuffers, the fire pans, and the jars of oil for the lamps. 10 All of this will then be covered with a piece of fine leather and placed on a carrying frame.

11 The gold incense altar[h] is to be covered with a blue cloth, and then with a piece of fine leather, before its carrying poles are put in place.

12 Next, Aaron and his sons will take blue cloth and wrap all the objects used in worship at the sacred tent. These will need

[g] **4.7** *sacred bread*: This bread was offered to the LORD and was a symbol of his presence in the sacred tent. It was put out on a special table and was replaced with fresh bread each Sabbath (Leviticus 24.5-9). [h] **4.11** *gold incense altar*: This altar for offering incense was inside the sacred tent; it was made of acacia wood covered with gold. A large altar for offering sacrifices was in front of the entrance to the tent; it was made of acacia wood covered with bronze (see verse 13).

to be covered with a piece of fine leather, then placed on a carrying frame.

13 They are to remove the ashes from the bronze altar and cover it with a purple cloth. 14 On that cloth will be placed the utensils used at the altar, including the fire pans, the meat forks, the shovels, and the sprinkling bowls. All of this will then be covered with a piece of fine leather, before the carrying poles are put in place.

15 When the camp is ready to be moved, the Kohathites will be responsible for carrying the sacred objects and the furnishings of the sacred tent. But Aaron and his sons must have already covered those things so the Kohathites won't touch them and die.

16 Eleazar son of Aaron the priest will be in charge of the oil for the lamps, the sweet-smelling incense, the grain for the sacrifices, and the olive oil used for dedications and ordinations. Eleazar is responsible for seeing that the sacred tent, its furnishings, and the sacred objects are taken care of.

17-20 The Kohathites must not go near or even look at the sacred objects until Aaron and his sons have covered those objects. If they do, their entire clan will be wiped out. So make sure that Aaron and his sons go into the tent with them and tell them what to carry.

The Duties of the Gershonite Clans

21 The LORD said to Moses:

22-23 Find out how many men between the ages of thirty and fifty are in the two Levite clans of Gershon. Count only those who are able to work at the sacred tent.

24 The Gershonites will be responsible 25 for carrying the curtains of the sacred tent, its two outer coverings,[i] the curtain for the entrance to the tent, 26 the curtains hanging around the courtyard of the tent, and the curtain and ropes for the entrance to the courtyard. The Gershonites are to do whatever needs to be done to take care of these things, 27 and they will carry them wherever Aaron and his sons tell them to.

28 These are the duties of the Gershonites at the sacred tent, and Ithamar son of Aaron will make sure they do their work.

The Duties of the Merarite Clans

29-30 The LORD said:

Moses, find out how many men between thirty and fifty are in the two Levite clans of Merari, but count only those who are able to work at the sacred tent.

31 The Merarites will be responsible for carrying the frames of the tent and its other pieces, including the bars, the posts, the stands, 32 as well as the posts that support the courtyard, together with their stands, tent pegs, and ropes. The Merarites are to be told exactly what objects they are to carry, 33 and Ithamar son of Aaron will make sure they do their work.

The Levites Are Counted Again

34-49 Moses, Aaron, and the other Israelite leaders obeyed the LORD and counted the Levi tribe by families and clans, to find out how many men there were between the ages of thirty and fifty who could work at the sacred tent. There were two thousand seven hundred fifty Kohathites, two thousand six hundred thirty Gershonites, and three thousand two hundred Merarites, making a total of eight thousand five hundred eighty. Then they were all assigned their duties.

People Are Sent Outside the Camp

5 The LORD told Moses 2-3 to say to the people of Israel, "Put out of the camp everyone who has leprosy[j] or a bodily discharge or who has touched a dead body. Now that I live among my people, their camp must be kept clean."

4 The Israelites obeyed the LORD's instructions.

The Penalty for Committing a Crime
(Leviticus 6.1-7)

5 The LORD told Moses 6 to say to the community of Israel:

If any of you commit a crime against

[i] **4.25** *two outer coverings*: See Exodus 26.14. [j] **5.2,3** *leprosy*: The word translated "leprosy" was used for many different kinds of skin diseases.
5.5-8 Lv 6.1-7.

someone, you have sinned against me. 7 You must confess your guilt and pay the victim in full for whatever damage has been done, plus a fine of twenty percent. 8 If the victim has no relative who can accept this money, it belongs to me and will be paid to the priest. In addition to that payment, you must take a ram for the priest to sacrifice so your sin will be forgiven.

9-10 When you make a donation to the sacred tent, that money belongs only to the priest, and each priest will keep what is given to him.

A Suspicious Husband

11 The LORD told Moses 12-14 to say to the people of Israel:

Suppose a man becomes jealous and suspects that his wife has been unfaithful, but he has no proof. 15 He must take his wife to the priest, together with two pounds of ground barley as an offering to find out if she is guilty. No olive oil or incense is to be put on that offering.

16 The priest is to have the woman stand at my altar, 17 where he will pour sacred water into a clay jar and stir in some dust from the floor of the sacred tent. 18-22 Next, he will remove her veil, then hand her the barley offering, and say, "If you have been faithful to your husband, this water won't harm you. But if you have been unfaithful, it will bring down the LORD's curse—you will never be able to give birth to a child, and everyone will curse your name."

Then the woman will answer, "If I am guilty, let it happen just as you say."

23 The priest will write these curses on special paper and wash them off into the bitter water, 24 so that when the woman drinks this water, the curses will enter her body. 25 He will take the barley offering from her and lift it up[k] in dedication to me, the LORD. Then he will place it on my altar 26 and burn part of it as a sacrifice. After that, the woman must drink the bitter water.

27 If the woman has been unfaithful, the water will immediately make her unable to have children, and she will be a curse among her people. 28 But if she is innocent, her body will not be harmed, and she will still be able to have children.

29-30 This is the ceremony that must take place at my altar when a husband suspects that his wife has been unfaithful. The priest must have the woman stand in my presence and carefully follow these instructions. 31 If the husband is wrong, he will not be punished; but if his wife is guilty, she will be punished.

Rules for Nazirites

6 The LORD told Moses 2 to say to the people of Israel:

If any of you want to dedicate yourself to me by vowing to become a Nazirite, 3 you must no longer drink any wine or beer or use any kind of vinegar. Don't drink grape juice or eat grapes or raisins—4 not even the seeds or skins.

5 Even the hair of a Nazirite is sacred to me, and as long as you are a Nazirite, you must never cut your hair.

6 During the time that you are a Nazirite, you must never go close to a dead body, 7-8 not even that of your father, mother, brother, or sister. That would make you unclean. Your hair is the sign that you are dedicated to me, so remain holy.

9 If someone suddenly dies near you, your hair is no longer sacred, and you must shave it seven days later during the ceremony to make you clean. 10 Then on the next day, bring two doves or two pigeons to the priest at the sacred tent. 11 He will offer one of the birds as a sacrifice for sin and the other as a sacrifice to please me.[l] You will then be forgiven for being too near a dead body, and your hair will again become sacred. 12 But the dead body made you unacceptable, so you must make another vow

[k]**5.25** *lift it up*: Or "wave it." [l]**6.11** *sacrifice to please me*: This sacrifice has traditionally been called a "whole burnt offering," because the whole animal was burned on the altar. A main purpose of such a sacrifice was to please the LORD with the smell of the sacrifice, and so in the CEV it is often called "a sacrifice to please the LORD."

6.3 Lk 1.15.

to become a Nazirite and be dedicated
once more. Finally, a year-old ram must be
offered as the sacrifice to make things
right.
13 When you have completed your
promised time of being a Nazirite, go to the
sacred tent 14 and offer three animals that
have nothing wrong with them: a year-old
ram as a sacrifice to please me, a year-old
female lamb as a sacrifice for sin, and a
full-grown ram as a sacrifice to ask my
blessing.[m] 15 Wine offerings and grain sacrifices must also be brought with these animals. Finally, you are to bring a basket of
bread made with your finest flour and olive
oil, but without yeast. Also bring some thin
wafers brushed with oil.
16 The priest will take these gifts to my
altar and offer them, so that I will be
pleased and will forgive you. 17 Then he
will sacrifice the ram and offer the wine,
grain, and bread.
18 After that, you will stand at the entrance to the sacred tent, shave your head,
and put the hair in the fire where the priest
has offered the sacrifice to ask my blessing.
19 Once the meat from the ram's shoulder has been boiled, the priest will take it,
along with one loaf of bread and one wafer
brushed with oil, and give them to you.
20 You will hand them back to the priest,
who will lift them up[n] in dedication to me.
Then he can eat the meat from the ram's
shoulder, its choice ribs, and its hind leg,
because this is his share of the sacrifice.
After this, you will no longer be a Nazirite
and will be free to drink wine.
21 These are the requirements for
Nazirites. However, if you can afford to offer more, you must do so.

The Blessing for the People

22 The LORD told Moses, 23 "When
Aaron and his sons bless the people of Israel, they must say:

24 I pray that the LORD
will bless and protect you,
25 and that he will show you mercy
and kindness.
26 May the LORD be good to you
and give you peace."

27 Then the LORD said, "If Aaron and his
sons ask me to bless the Israelites, I will
give them my blessing."

The Leaders Bring Gifts to the Sacred Tent

7 When Moses had finished setting up
the sacred tent, he dedicated it to the
LORD, together with its furnishings, the altar, and its equipment. 2 Then the twelve
tribal leaders of Israel, the same men who
had been in charge of counting the
people,[o] came to the tent 3 with gifts for
the LORD. They brought six strong carts
and twelve oxen—one ox from each leader
and a cart from every two.
4 The LORD said to Moses, 5 "Accept
these gifts, so the Levites can use them
here at the sacred tent for carrying the sacred things."
6 Then Moses took the carts and oxen
and gave them to the Levites, 7-8 who were
under the leadership of Ithamar son of
Aaron. Moses gave two carts and four oxen
to the Gershonites for their work, and four
carts and eight oxen to the Merarites for
their work. 9 But Moses did not give any to
the Kohathites, because they were in
charge of the sacred objects that had to be
carried on their shoulders.
10 On the day the altar was dedicated,
the twelve leaders brought offerings for its
dedication. 11 The LORD said to Moses,
"Each day one leader is to give his offering
for the dedication."
12-83 So each leader brought the following gifts:
a silver bowl that weighed over three
pounds and a silver sprinkling bowl weighing almost two pounds, both of them filled
with flour and olive oil as grain sacrifices
and weighed according to the official standards;

[m]**6.14** *sacrifice to ask my blessing*: This sacrifice has traditionally been called a "peace offering" or an "offering of well-being." A main purpose of such a sacrifice was to ask the LORD's blessing, and so in the CEV it is often called a "sacrifice to ask the LORD's blessing." [n]**6.20** *lift them up*: See the note at 5.25. [o]**7.2** *the same men . . . the people*: See 1.1-19.

6.13-21 Ac 21.23, 24.

a small gold dish filled with incense;

a young bull, a full-grown ram, and a year-old ram as sacrifices to please the LORD;[p]

a goat[q] as a sacrifice for sin;

and two bulls, five full-grown rams, five goats, and five rams a year old as sacrifices to ask the LORD's blessing.[r]

The tribal leaders brought their gifts and offerings in the following order:

On the first day
Nahshon from Judah,
on the second day
Nethanel from Issachar,
on the third day
Eliab from Zebulun,
on the fourth day
Elizur from Reuben,
on the fifth day
Shelumiel from Simeon,
on the sixth day
Eliasaph from Gad,
on the seventh day
Elishama from Ephraim,
on the eighth day
Gamaliel from Manasseh,
on the ninth day
Abidan from Benjamin,
on the tenth day
Ahiezer from Dan,
on the eleventh day
Pagiel from Asher,
on the twelfth day
Ahira from Naphtali.

84-88 And so when the altar was dedicated to the LORD, these twelve leaders brought the following gifts:

twelve silver bowls and twelve silver sprinkling bowls, weighing a total of about sixty pounds, according to the official standards;

twelve gold dishes filled with incense and weighing about three pounds;

twelve bulls, twelve full-grown rams, and twelve rams a year old as sacrifices to please the LORD, along with the proper grain sacrifices;

twelve goats as sacrifices for sin;

and twenty-four bulls, sixty full-grown rams, sixty goats, and sixty rams a year old as sacrifices to ask the LORD's blessing.

89 Whenever Moses needed to talk with the LORD, he went into the sacred tent, where he heard the LORD's voice coming from between the two winged creatures above the lid of the sacred chest.

Aaron Puts the Gold Lamps in Place

8 The LORD said to Moses, 2 "Tell Aaron to put the seven lamps on the lampstand so they shine toward the front."

3 Aaron obeyed and placed the lamps as he was told. 4 The lampstand was made of hammered gold from its base to the decorative flowers on top, exactly like the pattern the LORD had described to Moses.

Instructions for Ordaining the Levites

5 The LORD said to Moses:

6 The Levites must be acceptable to me before they begin working at the sacred tent. So separate them from the rest of the Israelites 7 and sprinkle them with the water that washes away their sins. Then have them shave their entire bodies and wash their clothes.

8 They are to bring a bull and its proper grain sacrifice of flour mixed with olive oil. And they must bring a second bull as a sacrifice for sin.

9 Then you, Moses, will call together all the people of Israel and have the Levites go to my sacred tent, 10 where the people will place their hands on them. 11 Aaron will present the Levites to me as a gift from the people, so that the Levites will do my work.

12 After this, the Levites are to place their hands on the heads of the bulls. Then one of the bulls will be sacrificed for the forgiveness of sin, and the other to make sure that I am pleased. 13 The Levites will stand at my altar in front of Aaron and his sons, who will then dedicate the Levites to me.

14 This ceremony will show that the Levites are different from the other Israelites and belong to me in a special way. 15 After they have been made acceptable and have been dedicated, they will be

[p]**7.12-83** *sacrifices to please the LORD*: See the note at 6.11. [q]**7.12-83** *goat*: Hebrew "male goat." [r]**7.12-83** *sacrifices to ask the LORD's blessing*: See the note at 6.14.

8.1-4 Ex 25.31-40; 37.17-24.

allowed to work at my sacred tent. 16 They are mine and will take the place of the first-born Israelite sons. 17 When I killed the oldest sons of the Egyptians, I decided that the first-born sons in each Israelite family would be mine, as well as every first-born male from their flocks and herds. 18 But now I have chosen these Levites as substitutes for the first-born sons, 19 and I have given them as gifts to Aaron and his sons to serve at the sacred tent. I will hold them responsible for what happens to anyone who gets too close to the sacred tent.[s]

The Levites Are Dedicated to the LORD

20 Moses, Aaron, and the other Israelites made sure that the Levites did everything the LORD had commanded. 21 The Levites sprinkled themselves with the water of forgiveness and washed their clothes. Then Aaron brought them to the altar and offered sacrifices to forgive their sins and make them acceptable to the LORD. 22 After this, the Levites worked at the sacred tent as assistants to Aaron and his sons, just as the LORD had commanded.

23 The LORD also told Moses, 24-25 "Levites who are between the ages of twenty-five and fifty can work at my sacred tent. But once they turn fifty, they must retire. 26 They may help the other Levites in their duties, but they must no longer be responsible for any work themselves. Remember this when you assign their duties."

Regulations for Celebrating Passover

9 During the first month of Israel's second year in the Sinai Desert,[t] the LORD had told Moses 2 to say to the people, "Celebrate Passover 3 in the evening of the fourteenth day of this month[u] and do it by following all the regulations." 4-5 Moses told the people what the LORD had said, and they celebrated Passover there in the desert in the evening of the fourteenth day of the first month.

6 Some people in Israel's camp had touched a dead body and had become unfit to worship the LORD, and they could not celebrate Passover. But they asked Moses and Aaron, 7 "Even though we have touched a dead body, why can't we celebrate Passover and offer sacrifices to the LORD at the same time as everyone else?"

8 Moses said, "Wait here while I go into the sacred tent and find out what the LORD says about this."

9 The LORD then told Moses 10 to say to the community of Israel:

> If any of you or your descendants touch a dead body and become unfit to worship me, or if you are away on a long journey, you may still celebrate Passover. 11 But it must be done in the second month,[v] in the evening of the fourteenth day. Eat the Passover lamb with thin bread and bitter herbs, 12 and don't leave any of it until morning or break any of the animal's bones. Be sure to follow these regulations.
>
> 13 But if any of you refuse to celebrate Passover when you are not away on a journey, you will no longer belong to my people. You will be punished because you did not offer sacrifices to me at the proper time.
>
> 14 Anyone, including foreigners who live among you, can celebrate Passover, if they follow all the regulations.

The Cloud over the Sacred Tent

(Exodus 40.34-38)

15-16 As soon as the sacred tent was set up,[w] a thick cloud appeared and covered it. The cloud was there each day, and during

[s] **8.19** *I will hold . . . sacred tent*: One possible meaning for the difficult Hebrew text. [t] **9.1** *first month . . . Sinai Desert*: The book of Numbers begins in the second month of the second year (see 1.1), so 9.1-5 refers to a Passover celebration that had already taken place. [u] **9.3** *this month*: Abib (also called Nisan), the first month of the Hebrew calendar, from about mid-March to mid-April. [v] **9.11** *second month*: See the note at 1.1. [w] **9.15,16** *As soon as the sacred tent was set up*: According to Exodus 40.17, this took place "on the first day of the first month of the second year" of the Israelites' stay in the desert.

8.17 Ex 13.2. **9.1-5** Ex 12.1-13. **9.12** Ex 12.46; Jn 19.36.

the night, a fire could be seen in it.
17-19 The LORD used this cloud to tell the Israelites when to move their camp and where to set it up again. As long as the cloud covered the tent, the Israelites did not break camp. But when the cloud moved, they followed it, and wherever it stopped, they camped and stayed there,
20-22 whether it was only one night, a few days, a month, or even a year. As long as the cloud remained over the tent, the Israelites stayed where they were. But when the cloud moved, so did the Israelites.
23 They obeyed the LORD's commands and went wherever he directed Moses.

The Silver Trumpets

10 The LORD told Moses:
2 Have someone make two trumpets out of hammered silver. These will be used to call the people together and to give the signal for moving your camp.
3 If both trumpets are blown, everyone is to meet with you at the entrance to the sacred tent.
4 But if just one is blown, only the twelve tribal leaders need to come together.

5-6 Give a signal on a trumpet when it is time to break camp. The first blast will be the signal for the tribes camped on the east side, and the second blast will be the signal for those on the south.
7 But when you want everyone to come together, sound a different signal on the trumpet.
8 The priests of Aaron's family will be the ones to blow the trumpets, and this law will never change.

9 Whenever you go into battle against an enemy attacking your land, give a warning signal on the trumpets. Then I, the LORD, will hear it and rescue you.
10 During the celebration of the New Moon Festival and other religious festivals, sound the trumpets while you offer sacrifices. This will be a reminder that I am the LORD your God.

The Israelites Begin Their Journey

11 On the twentieth day of the second month[x] of that same year, the cloud over the sacred tent moved on.
12 So the Israelites broke camp and left the Sinai Desert. And some time later, the cloud stopped in the Paran Desert.[y]
13 This was the first time the LORD had told Moses to command the people of Israel to move on.

14 Judah and the tribes that camped alongside it marched out first, carrying their banner. Nahshon son of Amminadab was the leader of the Judah tribe,
15 Nethanel son of Zuar was the leader of the Issachar tribe,
16 and Eliab son of Helon was the leader of the Zebulun tribe.

17 The sacred tent had been taken down, and the Gershonites and the Merarites carried it, marching behind the Judah camp.

18 Reuben and the tribes that camped alongside it marched out second, carrying their banner. Elizur son of Shedeur was the leader of the Reuben tribe,
19 Shelumiel son of Zurishaddai was the leader of the Simeon tribe,
20 and Eliasaph son of Deuel was the leader of the Gad tribe.

21 Next were the Kohathites, carrying the objects for the sacred tent, which was to be set up before they arrived at the new camp.

22 Ephraim and the tribes that camped alongside it marched next, carrying their banner. Elishama son of Ammihud was the leader of the Ephraim tribe,
23 Gamaliel son of Pedahzur was the leader of the Manasseh tribe,
24 and Abidan son of Gideoni was the leader of the Benjamin tribe.

25 Dan and the tribes that camped alongside it were to protect the Israelites against an attack from behind, and so they marched last, carrying their banner. Ahiezer son of Ammishaddai was the leader of the tribe of Dan,
26 Pagiel son of Ochran was the leader of the Asher tribe,
27 and Ahira son of Enan was the leader of the Naphtali tribe.

28 This was the order in which the Israelites marched each time they moved their camp.

[x] **10.11** *second month*: See the note at 1.1. [y] **10.12** *the Paran Desert*: Probably a general name for the northernmost part of the Sinai Desert.

29 Hobab[z] the Midianite, the father-in-law of Moses, was there. And Moses said to him, "We're leaving for the place the LORD has promised us. He has said that all will go well for us. So come along, and we will make sure that all goes well for you."

30 "No, I won't go," Hobab answered. "I'm returning home to be with my own people."

31 "Please go with us!" Moses said. "You can be our guide because you know the places to camp in the desert. 32 Besides that, if you go, we will give you a share of the good things the LORD gives us."

33 The people of Israel began their journey from Mount Sinai.[a] They traveled three days, and the Levites who carried the sacred chest led the way, so the LORD could show them where to camp. 34 And the cloud always stayed with them.

35 Each day as the Israelites began their journey, Moses would pray, "Our LORD, defeat your enemies and make them run!" 36 And when they stopped to set up camp, he would pray, "Our LORD, stay close to Israel's thousands and thousands of people."

The Israelites Complain

11 One day the Israelites started complaining about their troubles. The LORD heard them and became so angry that he destroyed the outer edges of their camp with fire.

2 When the people begged Moses to help, he prayed, and the fire went out. 3 They named the place "Burning,"[b] because in his anger the LORD had set their camp on fire.

The People Grumble about Being Hungry

4 One day some worthless foreigners among the Israelites became greedy for food, and even the Israelites themselves began moaning, "We don't have any meat! 5 In Egypt we could eat all the fish we wanted, and there were cucumbers, melons, onions, and garlic. 6 But we're starving out here, and the only food we have is this manna."

7 The manna was like small whitish seeds 8-9 and tasted like something baked with sweet olive oil. It appeared at night with the dew. In the morning the people would collect the manna, grind or crush it into flour, then boil it and make it into thin wafers.

10 The Israelites stood around their tents complaining. Moses heard them and was upset that they had made the LORD angry. 11 He prayed:

I am your servant, LORD, so why are you doing this to me? What have I done to deserve this? You've made me responsible for all these people, 12 but they're not my children. You told me to nurse them along and to carry them to the land you promised their ancestors. 13 They keep whining for meat, but where can I get meat for them? 14 This job is too much for me. How can I take care of all these people by myself? 15 If this is the way you're going to treat me, just kill me now and end my miserable life!

Seventy Leaders Are Chosen To Help Moses

16 The LORD said to Moses:

Choose seventy of Israel's respected leaders and go with them to the sacred tent. 17 While I am talking with you there, I will give them some of your authority, so they can share responsibility for my people. You will no longer have to care for them by yourself.

18 As for the Israelites, I have heard them complaining about not having meat and about being better off in Egypt. So tell them to make themselves acceptable to me, because tomorrow they will have meat. 19-20 In fact, they will have meat day after day for a whole month—not just a few days, or even ten or twenty. They turned against me and wanted to return to Egypt. Now they will eat meat until they get sick of it.

21 Moses replied, "At least six hundred

[z] **10.29** *Hobab*: Hebrew "Hobab son of Reuel." [a] **10.33** *Mount Sinai*: Hebrew "the LORD's mountain." [b] **11.3** *Burning*: Or "Taberah."

10.35 Ps 68.1. **11.7-9** Ex 16.31. **11.8,9** Ex 16.13-15.

thousand grown men are here with me. How can you say there will be enough meat to feed them and their families for a whole month? 22 Even if we butchered all of our sheep and cattle, or caught every fish in the sea, we wouldn't have enough to feed them."

23 The LORD answered, "I can do anything! Watch and you'll see my words come true."

24 Moses told the people what the LORD had said. Then he chose seventy respected leaders and went with them to the sacred tent. While the leaders stood in a circle around the tent, Moses went inside, 25 and the LORD spoke with him. Then the LORD took some authority[c] from Moses and gave it to the seventy leaders. And when the LORD's Spirit took control of them, they started shouting like prophets. But they did it only this one time.

26 Eldad and Medad were two leaders who had not gone to the tent. But when the Spirit took control of them, they began shouting like prophets right there in camp. 27 A boy ran to Moses and told him about Eldad and Medad.

28 Joshua[d] was there helping Moses, as he had done since he was young. And he said to Moses, "Sir, you must stop them!"

29 But Moses replied, "Are you concerned what this might do to me? I wish the LORD would give his Spirit to all his people so everyone could be a prophet." 30 Then Moses and the seventy leaders went back to camp.

The LORD Sends Quails

31 Some time later the LORD sent a strong wind that blew quails in from the sea until Israel's camp was completely surrounded with birds, piled up about three feet high for miles in every direction. 32 The people picked up quails for two days—each person filled at least fifty bushels. Then they spread them out to dry. 33 But before the meat could be eaten, the LORD became angry and sent a disease through the camp.

34 After they had buried the people who had been so greedy for meat, they called the place "Graves for the Greedy."[e]

35 Israel then broke camp and traveled to Hazeroth.

Miriam and Aaron Are Jealous of Moses

12 1-3 Although Moses was the most humble person in all the world, Miriam and Aaron started complaining, "Moses had no right to marry that woman from Ethiopia![f] Who does he think he is? The LORD has spoken to us, not just to him."

The LORD heard their complaint 4 and told Moses, Aaron, and Miriam to come to the entrance of the sacred tent. 5 There the LORD appeared in a cloud and told Aaron and Miriam to come closer. 6 Then after commanding them to listen carefully, he said:

"I, the LORD, speak to prophets
in visions and dreams.
7 But my servant Moses
is the leader of my people.
8 He sees me face to face,
and everything I say to him
is perfectly clear.
You have no right to criticize
my servant Moses."

9 The LORD became angry at Aaron and Miriam. And after the LORD left 10 and the cloud disappeared from over the sacred tent, Miriam's skin turned white with leprosy.[g] When Aaron saw what had happened to her, 11 he said to Moses, "Sir, please don't punish us for doing such a foolish thing. 12 Don't let Miriam's flesh rot away like a child born dead!"

13 Moses prayed, "LORD God, please heal her."

14 But the LORD replied, "Miriam would be disgraced for seven days if her father

[c] **11.25** *some authority*: Or "some of the Spirit's power." [d] **11.28** *Joshua*: Hebrew "Joshua son of Nun." [e] **11.34** *Graves for the Greedy*: Or "Kibroth-Hattaavah." [f] **12.1-3** *Ethiopia*: The Hebrew text has "Cush," which was a region south of Egypt that included parts of the present countries of Ethiopia and Sudan. [g] **12.10** *leprosy*: See the note at 5.2, 3.

12.1-3 Si 45.4. **12.7** He 3.2. **12.14** Nu 5.2, 3.

had punished her by spitting in her face. So make her stay outside the camp for seven days, before coming back."

15 The people of Israel did not move their camp until Miriam returned seven days later. 16 Then they left Hazeroth and set up camp in the Paran Desert.

Twelve Men Are Sent into Canaan

(Deuteronomy 1.19-33)

13 The LORD said to Moses, 2 "Choose a leader from each tribe and send them into Canaan to explore the land I am giving you."

3 So Moses sent twelve tribal leaders from Israel's camp in the Paran Desert 4-16 with orders to explore the land of Canaan. And here are their names:

Shammua son of Zaccur
from Reuben,
Shaphat son of Hori
from Simeon,
Caleb son of Jephunneh
from Judah,
Igal son of Joseph
from Issachar,
Joshua son of Nun
from Ephraim,[h]
Palti son of Raphu
from Benjamin,
Gaddiel son of Sodi
from Zebulun,
Gaddi son of Susi
from Manasseh,
Ammiel son of Gemalli
from Dan,
Sethur son of Michael
from Asher,
Nahbi son of Vophsi
from Naphtali,
and Geuel son of Machi
from Gad.

17 Before Moses sent them into Canaan, he said:

After you go through the Southern Desert of Canaan, continue north into the hill country 18 and find out what those regions are like. Be sure to remember how many people live there, how strong they are, 19-20 and if they live in open towns or walled cities. See if the land is good for growing crops and find out what kinds of trees grow there. It's time for grapes to ripen, so try to bring back some of the fruit that grows there.

21 The twelve men left to explore Canaan from the Zin Desert in the south all the way to the town of Rehob near Lebo-Hamath in the north. 22 As they went through the Southern Desert, they came to the town of Hebron, which was seven years older than the Egyptian town of Zoan. In Hebron, they saw the three Anakim[i] clans of Ahiman, Sheshai, and Talmai. 23-24 When they got to Bunch Valley,[j] they cut off a branch with such a huge bunch of grapes, that it took two men to carry it on a pole. That's why the place was called Bunch Valley. Along with the grapes, they also took back pomegranates[k] and figs.

The Men Report Back to the People

25 After exploring the land of Canaan forty days, 26 the twelve men returned to Kadesh in the Paran Desert and told Moses, Aaron, and the people what they had seen. They showed them the fruit 27 and said:

Look at this fruit! The land we explored is rich with milk and honey. 28 But the people who live there are strong, and their cities are large and walled. We even saw the three Anakim[l] clans. 29 Besides that, the Amalekites live in the Southern Desert; the Hittites, Jebusites, and Amorites are in the hill country; and the Canaanites[m] live along the Mediterranean Sea and the Jordan River.

30 Caleb calmed down the crowd and

[h] **13.4-16** *Joshua . . . Ephraim*: Hebrew "Hoshea son of Nun from Ephraim; Moses renamed him Joshua." [i] **13.22** *Anakim*: Perhaps a group of very large people (see Deuteronomy 2.10, 11, 20, 21). [j] **13.23,24** *Bunch Valley*: Or "Eshcol Valley." [k] **13.23,24** *pomegranates*: A bright red fruit that looks like an apple. [l] **13.28** *Anakim*: See the note at verse 22. [m] **13.29** *Amalekites . . . Hittites . . . Jebusites . . . Amorites . . . Canaanites*: These people lived in Canaan before the Israelites.

said, "Let's go and take the land. I know we can do it!"

31 But the other men replied, "Those people are much too strong for us." 32 Then they started spreading rumors and saying, "We won't be able to grow anything in that soil. And the people are like giants. 33 In fact, we saw the Nephilim who are the ancestors of the Anakim. They were so big that we felt as small as grasshoppers."

The Israelites Rebel against Moses

14 After the Israelites heard the report from the twelve men who had explored Canaan, the people cried all night 2 and complained to Moses and Aaron, "We wish we had died in Egypt or somewhere out here in the desert! 3 Is the LORD leading us into Canaan, just to have us killed and our women and children captured? We'd be better off in Egypt." 4 Then they said to one another, "Let's choose our own leader and go back."

5 Moses and Aaron bowed down to pray in front of the crowd. 6 Joshua and Caleb tore their clothes in sorrow 7 and said:

We saw the land ourselves, and it's very good. 8 If we obey the LORD, he will surely give us that land rich with milk and honey. 9 So don't rebel. We have no reason to be afraid of the people who live there. The LORD is on our side, and they won't stand a chance against us!

10 The crowd threatened to stone Moses and Aaron to death. But just then, the LORD appeared in a cloud at the sacred tent.

Moses Prays for the People

11 The LORD said to Moses, "I have done great things for these people, and they still reject me by refusing to believe in my power. 12 So they will no longer be my people. I will destroy them, but I will make you the ancestor of a nation even stronger than theirs."

13-16 Moses replied:

With your mighty power you rescued your people from Egypt, so please don't destroy us here in the desert. If you do, the Egyptians will hear about it and tell the people of Canaan. Those Canaanites already know that we are your people, and that we see you face to face. And they have heard how you lead us with a thick cloud during the day and flaming fire at night. But if you kill us, they will claim it was because you weren't powerful enough to lead us into Canaan as you promised.

17 Show us your great power, LORD. You promised 18 that you love to show mercy and kindness. And you said that you are very patient, but that you will punish everyone guilty of doing wrong—not only them but their children and grandchildren as well.

19 You are merciful, and you treat people better than they deserve. So please forgive these people, just as you have forgiven them ever since they left Egypt.

20 Then the LORD said to Moses:

In answer to your prayer, I do forgive them. 21 But as surely as I live and my power has no limit, 22-23 I swear that not one of these Israelites will enter the land I promised to give their ancestors. These people have seen my power in Egypt and in the desert, but they will never see Canaan. They have disobeyed and tested me too many times.

24 But my servant Caleb isn't like the others. So because he has faith in me, I will allow him to cross into Canaan, and his descendants will settle there.

25 Now listen, Moses! The Amalekites and the Canaanites live in the valleys of Canaan.[n] And tomorrow morning, you'll need to turn around and head back into the desert toward the Red Sea.[o]

[n] **14.25** *The Amalekites and the Canaanites . . . valleys of Canaan*: That is, all possible ways into Canaan were blocked. [o] **14.25** *Red Sea*: Hebrew *yam suph*, here referring to the Gulf of Aqaba, since the term is extended to include the northeastern arm of the Red Sea (see also the note at Exodus 13.18).

13.33 Gn 6.4. **14.9** He 3.16. **14.13-19** Ex 32.11-14. **14.18** Ex 20.5, 6; 34.6, 7; Dt 5.9, 10; 7.9, 10. **14.21-23** He 3.18. **14.24** Js 14.9-12.

The Israelites Are Punished for Complaining

26 The LORD told Moses and Aaron 27-28 to give this message to the people of Israel:

You sinful people have complained against me too many times! Now I swear by my own life that I will give you exactly what you wanted.[p] 29 You will die right here in the desert, and your dead bodies will cover the ground. You have insulted me, and none of you men who are over twenty years old 30 will enter the land that I solemnly promised to give you as your own—only Caleb and Joshua[q] will go in.

31 You were worried that your own children would be captured. But I, the LORD, will let them enter the land you have rejected. 32 You will die here in the desert! 33 Your children will wander around in this desert forty years, suffering because of your sins, until all of you are dead. 34 I will cruelly punish you every day for the next forty years—one year for each day that the land was explored. 35 You sinful people who ganged up against me will die here in the desert.

36 Ten of the men sent to explore the land had brought back bad news and had made the people complain against the LORD. 37 So he sent a deadly disease that killed those men, 38 but he let Joshua and Caleb live.

The Israelites Fail To Enter Canaan

(Deuteronomy 1.41-45)

39 The people of Israel were very sad after Moses gave them the LORD's message. 40 So they got up early the next morning and got ready to head toward the hill country of Canaan. They said, "We were wrong to complain about the LORD. Let's go into the land that he promised us."

41 But Moses replied, "You're disobeying the LORD! Your plan won't work, 42-43 so don't even try it. The LORD refuses to help you, because you turned your backs on him. The Amalekites and the Canaanites are your enemies, and they will attack and defeat you."

44 But the Israelites ignored Moses[r] and marched toward the hill country, even though the sacred chest and Moses did not go with them. 45 The Amalekites and the Canaanites came down from the hill country, defeated the Israelites, and chased them as far as the town of Hormah.

Laws about Sacrifices

15 The LORD told Moses 2 to give the Israelites the following laws about offering sacrifices:

3 Bulls or rams or goats[s] are the animals that you may burn on the altar as sacrifices to please me.[t] You may also offer sacrifices voluntarily or because you made a promise, or because they are part of your regular religious ceremonies. The smell of the smoke from these sacrifices is pleasing to me.

4-5 If you sacrifice a young ram or goat, you must also offer two pounds of your finest flour mixed with a quart of olive oil as a grain sacrifice. A quart of wine must also be poured on the altar.

6-7 And if the animal is a full-grown ram, you must offer four pounds of flour mixed with one and a half quarts of olive oil. One and a half quarts of wine must also be poured on the altar. The smell of this smoke is pleasing to me.

8 If a bull is offered as a sacrifice to please me or to ask my blessing,[u] 9 you must offer six pounds of flour mixed with two quarts of olive oil. 10 Two quarts of wine must also be poured on the altar. The smell of this smoke is pleasing to me.

11-13 If you are a native Israelite, you must obey these rules each time you offer a bull, a ram, or a goat as a sacrifice. 14 And

[p] **14.27,28** *wanted*: See verse 2. [q] **14.30** *Caleb and Joshua*: Hebrew "Caleb son of Jephunneh and Joshua son of Nun." [r] **14.44** *ignored Moses*: One possible meaning for the difficult Hebrew text. [s] **15.3** *goats*: See the note at 7.12-83. [t] **15.3** *sacrifices to please me*: See the note at 6.11. [u] **15.8** *to ask my blessing*: See the note at 6.14.

14.29 He 3.17. **14.33** Ac 7.36.

the foreigners who live among you must also follow these rules. 15-16 This law will never change. I am the LORD, and I consider all people the same, whether they are Israelites or foreigners living among you.

17-19 When you eat food in the land that I am giving you, remember to set aside some of it as an offering to me. 20 From the first batch of bread dough that you make after each new grain harvest, make a loaf of bread and offer it to me, just as you offer grain. 21 All your descendants must follow this law and offer part of the first batch of bread dough.

22-23 The LORD also told Moses to tell the people what must be done if they ever disobey his laws:

24 If all of you disobey one of my laws without meaning to, you must offer a bull as a sacrifice to please me, together with a grain sacrifice, a wine offering, and a goat as a sacrifice for sin. 25 Then the priest will pray and ask me to forgive you. And since you did not mean to do wrong, and you offered sacrifices, 26 the sin of everyone—both Israelites and foreigners among you—will be forgiven.

27 But if one of you does wrong without meaning to, you must sacrifice a year-old female goat as a sacrifice for sin. 28 The priest will then ask me to forgive you, and your sin will be forgiven.

29 The law will be the same for anyone who does wrong without meaning to, whether an Israelite or a foreigner living among you.

30-31 But if one of you does wrong on purpose, whether Israelite or foreigner, you have sinned against me by disobeying my laws. You will be sent away and will no longer live among the people of Israel.

A Man Put to Death for Gathering Firewood on the Sabbath

32 Once, while the Israelites were traveling through the desert, a man was caught gathering firewood on the Sabbath.[v] 33 He was taken to Moses, Aaron, and the rest of the community. 34 But no one knew what to do with him, so he was not allowed to leave.

35 Then the LORD said to Moses, "Tell the people to take that man outside the camp and stone him to death!" 36 So he was killed, just as the LORD had commanded Moses.

The Tassels on the People's Clothes

37 The LORD told Moses 38 to say to the people of Israel, "Sew tassels onto the bottom edge of your clothes and tie a purple string to each tassel. 39-40 These will remind you that you must obey my laws and teachings. And when you do, you will be dedicated to me and won't follow your own sinful desires. 41 I am the LORD your God who led you out of Egypt."

Korah, Dathan, and Abiram Lead a Rebellion

16 1-2 Korah son of Izhar was a Levite from the Kohathite clan. One day he called together Dathan, Abiram, and On[w] from the Reuben tribe, and the four of them decided to rebel against Moses. So they asked two hundred fifty respected Israelite leaders for their support, and together they went to Moses 3 and Aaron and said, "Why do you think you're so much better than anyone else? We're part of the LORD's holy people, and he's with all of us. What makes you think you're the only ones in charge?"

4 When Moses heard this, he knelt down to pray.[x] 5 Then he said to Korah and his followers:

Tomorrow morning the LORD will show us the person he has chosen to be his priest, and that man will faithfully serve him.

6-7 Korah, now here is what you and your followers must do: Get some fire pans, fill them with coals and incense,

[v] 15.32 *a man . . . Sabbath*: No work was to be done on the Sabbath (see Exodus 31.12-17).
[w] 16.1,2 *Dathan, Abiram, and On*: Hebrew "Dathan and Abiram the sons of Eliab, and On son of Peleth." [x] 16.4 *he knelt down to pray*: Or "he fell to his knees in sorrow."

15.15,16 Lv 24.22. **15.27,28** Lv 4.27-31. **15.38** Dt 22.12. **16.1-35** Si 45.18-20. **16.1,2** Jd 11.

and place them near the sacred tent.
And the man the LORD chooses will be
his priest.[y] Korah, this time you
Levites have gone too far!
8-9 You know that the God of Israel
has chosen you Levites from all Israel
to serve him by being in charge of the
sacred tent and by helping the community to worship in the proper way.
What more do you want? 10 The LORD
has given you a special responsibility,
and now, Korah, you think you should
also be his priest. 11 You and your followers have rebelled against the LORD,
not against Aaron.
12 Then Moses sent for Dathan and Abiram, but they sent back this message: "We
won't come! 13 It's bad enough that you
took us from our rich farmland in Egypt to
let us die here in the desert. Now you also
want to boss us around! 14 You keep
promising us rich farmlands with fertile
fields and vineyards—but where are they?
Stop trying to trick these people. No, we
won't come to see you."
15 Moses was very angry and said to the
LORD, "Don't listen to these men! I haven't
done anything wrong to them. I haven't
taken as much as a donkey."
16 Then he said to Korah, "Tomorrow
you and your followers must go with Aaron
to the LORD's sacred tent. 17 Each of you
take along your fire pan with incense in it
and offer the incense to the LORD."
18 The next day the men placed incense
and coals in their fire pans and stood with
Moses and Aaron at the entrance to the sacred tent. 19 Meanwhile, Korah had convinced the rest of the Israelites to rebel
against their two leaders.

When that happened, the LORD appeared in all his glory 20 and said to Moses
and Aaron, 21 "Get away from the rest of
the Israelites so I can kill them right now!"
22 But the two men bowed down and
prayed, "Our God, you gave these people
life. Why would you punish everyone here
when only one man has sinned?"
23 The LORD answered Moses, 24 "Tell
the people to stay away from the tents of
Korah, Dathan, and Abiram."
25 Moses walked over to Dathan and
Abiram, and the other leaders of Israel followed. 26 Then Moses warned the people,
"Get away from the tents of these sinful
men! Don't touch anything that belongs to
them or you'll be wiped out." 27 So everyone moved away from those tents, except
Korah, Dathan, Abiram, and their families.
28 Moses said to the crowd, "The LORD
has chosen me and told me to do these
things—it wasn't my idea. And here's how
you will know: 29 If these men die a natural
death, it means the LORD hasn't chosen
me. 30 But suppose the LORD does something that has never been done before. For
example, what if a huge crack appears in
the ground, and these men and their families fall into it and are buried alive, together
with everything they own? Then you will
know they have turned their backs on the
LORD!"
31 As soon as Moses said this, the
ground under the men opened up 32-33 and
swallowed them alive, together with their
families and everything they owned. Then
the ground closed back up, and they were
gone.
34 The rest of the Israelites heard their
screams, so they ran off, shouting, "We
don't want that to happen to us!"
35 Suddenly the LORD sent a fire that
burned up the two hundred fifty men who
had offered incense to him.
36 Then the LORD said to Moses, 37 "Tell
Aaron's son Eleazar to take the fire pans
from the smoldering fire and scatter the
coals. The pans are now sacred, 38 because
they were used for offering incense to me.
Have them hammered into a thin layer of
bronze as a covering for the altar. Those
men died because of their sin, and now
their fire pans will become a warning for
the rest of the community."
39 Eleazar collected the pans and had
them hammered into a thin layer of bronze
as a covering for the altar, 40 just as the
LORD had told Moses. The pans were a

[y] **16.6,7** *Get some fire pans . . . his priest*: Only priests could offer incense at the sacred altar; anyone else who tried would be killed. In this case, the man who lived would be the one the LORD had chosen.

warning to the Israelites that only Aaron's descendants would be allowed to offer incense to the LORD. Anyone else who tried would be punished like Korah and his followers.

The Israelites Rebel and Are Punished

41 The next day the people of Israel again complained against Moses and Aaron, "The two of you killed some of the LORD's people!"

42 As the people crowded around them, Moses and Aaron turned toward the sacred tent, and the LORD appeared in his glory in the cloud covering the tent. 43 So Moses and Aaron walked to the front of the tent, 44 where the LORD said to them, 45 "Stand back! I am going to wipe out these Israelites once and for all."

They immediately bowed down and prayed. 46 Then Moses told Aaron, "Grab your fire pan and fill it with hot coals from the altar. Put incense in it, then quickly take it to where the people are and offer it to the LORD, so they can be forgiven. The LORD is very angry, and people have already started dying!"

47-48 Aaron did exactly what he had been told. He ran over to the crowd of people and stood between the dead bodies and the people who were still alive. He placed the incense on the pan, then offered it to the LORD and asked him to forgive the people's sin. The disease immediately stopped spreading, and no one else died from it. 49 But fourteen thousand seven hundred Israelites were dead, not counting those who had died with Korah and his followers.

50 Aaron walked back and stood with Moses at the sacred tent.

Aaron's Walking Stick Blooms and Produces Almonds

17 The LORD told Moses:

2-3 Call together the twelve tribes of Israel and tell the leader of each tribe to write his name on the walking stick he carries as a symbol of his authority. Make sure Aaron's name is written on the one from the Levi tribe, then collect all the sticks.

4 Place these sticks in the tent right in front of the sacred chest where I appear to you. 5 I will then choose a man to be my priest, and his stick will sprout. After that happens, I won't have to listen to any more complaints about you.

6 Moses told the people what the LORD had commanded, and they gave him the walking sticks from the twelve tribal leaders, including Aaron's from the Levi tribe. 7 Moses took them and placed them in the LORD's sacred tent.

8 The next day when Moses went into the tent, flowers and almonds were already growing on Aaron's stick. 9 Moses brought the twelve sticks out of the tent and showed them to the people. Each of the leaders found his own and took it.

10 But the LORD told Moses, "Put Aaron's stick back! Let it stay near the sacred chest as a warning to anyone who might think about rebelling. If these people don't stop their grumbling about me, I will wipe them out." 11 Moses did what he was told.

12 The Israelites cried out to Moses, "We're done for 13 and doomed if we even get near the sacred tent!"

The Duties of the Priests and Levites

18 The LORD said to Aaron:

You, your sons, and the other Levites of the Kohath clan, are responsible for what happens at the sacred tent.[z] And you and your sons will be responsible for what the priests do. 2 The Levites are your relatives and are here to help you in your service at the tent. 3 You must see that they perform their duties. But if they go near any of the sacred objects or the altar, all of you will die. 4 No one else is allowed to take care of the sacred tent or to do anything connected with it. 5 Follow these instructions, so I won't become angry and punish the Israelites ever again.

[z] **18.1** *are responsible . . . sacred tent*: Or "are to make sure that no one gets near the sacred tent."

16.44-48 Ws 18.20-25. **17.8-10** He 9.4.

[6] I alone chose the Levites from all the other tribes to belong to me, and I have given them to you as your helpers. [7] But only you and your sons can serve as priests at the altar and in the most holy place. Your work as priests is a gift from me, and anyone else who tries to do that work must be put to death.

The Priests' Share of Offerings Given to the LORD

(Deuteronomy 18.1-8)

[8-9] The LORD said to Aaron:

I have put you in charge of the sacred gifts and sacrifices that the Israelites bring to me. And from now on, you, your sons, and your descendants will receive part of the sacrifices for sin, as well as part of the grain sacrifices, and the sacrifices to make things right. Your share of these sacrifices will be the parts not burned on the altar. [10] Since these things are sacred, they must be eaten near the sacred tent, but only men are allowed to eat them.

[11] You will also receive part of the special gifts and offerings that the Israelites bring to me. Any member of your family who is clean and acceptable for worship can eat these things. [12] For example, when the Israelites bring me the first batches of oil, wine, and grain, you can have the best parts of those gifts. [13] And the first part of the crops from their fields and vineyards also belongs to you. The people will offer this to me, then anyone in your family who is clean may have some of it.

[14] Everything in Israel that has been completely dedicated to me[a] will now belong to you.

[15] The first-born son in every Israelite family, as well as the first-born males of their flocks and herds, belong to me. But a first-born son and every first-born donkey[b] must be bought back from me. [16] The price for a first-born son who is at least one month old will be five pieces of silver, weighed according to the official standards. [17] However, all first-born cattle, sheep, and goats belong to me and cannot be bought back. Splatter their blood on the altar and send their fat up in smoke, so I can smell it and be pleased. [18] You are allowed to eat the meat of those animals, just as you can eat the choice ribs and the right hind leg of the special sacrifices.

[19] From now on, the sacred offerings that the Israelites give to me will belong to you, your sons, and your daughters. This is my promise to you and your descendants, and it will never change.

[20] You will not receive any land in Israel as your own. I am the LORD, and I will give you whatever you need.

What the Levites Receive

The LORD said to Aaron:

[21] Ten percent of the Israelites' crops and one out of every ten of their newborn animals belong to me. But I am giving all this to the Levites as their pay for the work they do at the sacred tent. [22-23] They are the only ones allowed to work at the tent, and they must not let anyone else come near it. Those who do must be put to death, and the Levites will also be punished. This law will never change.

Since the Levites won't be given any land in Israel as their own, [24] they will be given the crops and newborn animals that the Israelites offer to me.

What the Levites Must Give

[25] The LORD told Moses [26] to say to the Levites:

When you receive from the people of Israel ten percent of their crops and newborn animals, you must offer a tenth of that to me. [27] Just as the Israelites give me part of their grain and wine, you must set aside part of what you receive [28] as an offering to me. That amount must then be given to Aaron, [29] so the best of what you receive will be mine.

[a] **18.14** *that has been completely dedicated to me*: This translates a Hebrew word that describes property and things that were taken away from humans and given to God forever. Sometimes such things had to be completely destroyed (see Joshua 6.15-19). [b] **18.15** *donkey*: The Hebrew text has "unclean animal," which probably refers to a donkey (see Exodus 13.13; 34.20).

18.14 Lv 27.28. **18.21** Lv 27.30-33; Dt 14.22-29.

30 After you have dedicated the best
parts to me, you can eat the rest, just as the
Israelites eat part of their grain and wine
after offering them to me.[c] 31 Your share
may be eaten anywhere by anyone in your
family, because it is your pay for working at
the sacred tent. 32 You won't be punished
for eating it, as long as you have already offered the best parts to me.

The gifts and sacrifices brought by the
people must remain sacred, and if you eat
any part of them before they are offered to
me, you will be put to death.

The Ceremony To Wash Away Sin

19 1-2 The LORD gave Moses and Aaron
the following law:

The people of Israel must bring Moses a
reddish-brown cow that has nothing wrong
with it and that has never been used for
plowing. 3 Moses will give it to Eleazar the
priest, then it will be led outside the camp
and killed while Eleazar watches. 4 He will
dip his finger into the blood and sprinkle it
seven times in the direction of the sacred
tent. 5 Then the whole cow, including its
skin, meat, blood, and insides must be
burned. 6 A priest[d] is to throw a stick of
cedar wood, a hyssop[e] branch, and a piece
of red yarn into the fire.

7 After the ceremony, the priest is to
take a bath and wash his clothes. Only then
can he go back into the camp, but he remains unclean and unfit for worship until
evening. 8 The man who burned the cow
must also wash his clothes and take a bath,
but he is also unclean until evening.

9 A man who isn't unclean must collect
the ashes of the burnt cow and store them
outside the camp in a clean place. The
people of Israel can mix these ashes
with the water used in the ceremony to
wash away sin. 10 The man who collects
the ashes must wash his clothes, but will
remain unclean until evening. This law
must always be obeyed by the people of
Israel and the foreigners living among
them.

What Must Be Done after Touching a Dead Body

The LORD said:

11 If you touch a dead body, you will be
unclean for seven days. 12 But if you wash
with the water mixed with the cow's ashes
on the third day and again on the seventh
day, you will be clean and acceptable for
worship. You must wash yourself on those
days; if you don't, you will remain unclean.
13 Suppose you touch a dead body, but
refuse to be made clean by washing with
the water mixed with ashes. You will be
guilty of making my sacred tent unclean
and will no longer belong to the people of
Israel.

14 If someone dies in a tent while you
are there, you will be unclean for seven
days. And anyone who later enters the tent
will also be unclean. 15 Any open jar in the
tent is unclean.

16 If you touch the body of someone
who was killed or who died of old age, or if
you touch a human bone or a grave, you
will be unclean for seven days.

17-18 Before you can be made clean,
someone who is clean must take some of
the ashes from the burnt cow and stir them
into a pot of spring water. That same person must dip a hyssop branch in the water
and ashes, then sprinkle it on the tent and
everything in it, including everyone who
was inside. If you have touched a human
bone, a grave, or a dead body, you must be
sprinkled with that water. 19 If this is done
on the third day and on the seventh day,
you will be clean. Then after you take a
bath and wash your clothes, you can worship that evening.

20 If you are unclean and refuse to be
made clean by washing with the water
mixed with ashes, you will be guilty of making my sacred tent unclean, and you will
no longer belong to the people of Israel.
21 These laws will never change.

The man who sprinkled the water and
the ashes on you when you were unclean

[c] **18.30** *just as the Israelites . . . to me*: One possible meaning for the difficult Hebrew text.
[d] **19.6** *A priest*: Or "Eleazar." [e] **19.6** *hyssop*: A plant with small clusters of blue flowers and sweet-smelling leaves.
19.9 He 9.13.

must also wash his clothes. And whoever touches this water is unclean until evening. 22 When you are unclean, everything you touch becomes unclean, and anyone who touches you will be unclean until evening.

Water from a Rock

(Exodus 17.1-7)

20 The people of Israel arrived at the Zin Desert during the first month[f] and set up camp near the town of Kadesh. It was there that Miriam died and was buried.

2 The Israelites had no water, so they went to Moses and Aaron 3 and complained, "Moses, we'd be better off if we had died along with the others in front of the LORD's sacred tent.[g] 4 You brought us into this desert, and now we and our livestock are going to die! 5 Egypt was better than this horrible place. At least there we had grain and figs and grapevines and pomegranates.[h] But now we don't even have any water."

6 Moses and Aaron went to the entrance to the sacred tent, where they bowed down. The LORD appeared to them in all of his glory 7-8 and said, "Moses, get your walking stick.[i] Then you and Aaron call the people together and command that rock to give you water. That's how you will provide water for the people of Israel and their livestock."

9 Moses obeyed and took his stick from the sacred tent. 10 After he and Aaron had gathered the people around the rock, he said, "Look, you rebellious people, and you will see water flow from this rock!" 11 He raised his stick in the air and struck the rock two times. At once, water gushed from the rock, and the people and their livestock had water to drink.

12 But the LORD said to Moses and Aaron, "Because you refused to believe in my power, these people did not respect me. And so, you will not be the ones to lead them into the land I have promised."

13 The Israelites had complained against the LORD, and he had shown them his holy power by giving them water to drink. So they named the place Meribah, which means "Complaining."

Israel Isn't Allowed To Go through Edom

14 Moses sent messengers from Israel's camp near Kadesh with this message for the king of Edom:

> We are Israelites, your own relatives, and we're sure you have heard the terrible things that have happened to us. 15 Our ancestors settled in Egypt and lived there a long time. But later the Egyptians were cruel to us, 16 and when we begged our LORD for help, he answered our prayer and brought us out of that land.
>
> Now we are camped at the border of your territory, near the town of Kadesh. 17 Please let us go through your country. We won't go near your fields and vineyards, and we won't drink any water from your wells. We will stay on the main road[j] until we leave your territory.

18 But the Edomite king answered, "No, I won't let you go through our country! And if you try, we will attack you."

19 Moses sent back this message: "We promise to stay on the main road, and if any of us or our livestock drink your water, we will pay for it. We just want to pass through."

20 But the Edomite king insisted, "You can't go through our land!"

Then Edom sent out its strongest troops 21 to keep Israel from passing through its territory. So the Israelites had to go in another direction.

Aaron Dies

22 After the Israelites had left Kadesh and had gone as far as Mount Hor 23 on the

[f]**20.1** *first month*: See the note at 9.3. [g]**20.3** *if we had died . . . sacred tent*: See 16.41-49. [h]**20.5** *pomegranates*: See the note at 13.23, 24. [i]**20.7,8** *walking stick*: A symbol of his authority. [j]**20.17** *the main road*: The Hebrew text has "the King's Highway," which was an important trade route through what is today the country of Jordan. It connected the city of Damascus in Syria with the Gulf of Aqaba in southern Jordan.

20.2-13 Ex 17.1-7. **20.11** Ws 11.4.

Edomite border, the LORD said, 24 "Aaron,
this is where you will die. You and Moses
disobeyed me at Meribah, and so you will
not enter the land I promised the Israelites. 25 Moses, go with Aaron and his son
Eleazar to the top of the mountain. 26 Then
take Aaron's priestly robe from him
and place it on Eleazar. Aaron will die
there."

27 Moses obeyed, and everyone watched
as he and Aaron and Eleazar walked to the
top of Mount Hor. 28 Moses then took the
priestly robe from Aaron and placed it on
Eleazar. Aaron died there.

When Moses and Eleazar came down,
29 the people knew that Aaron had died,
and they mourned his death for thirty days.

Israel Defeats the Canaanites at Hormah

21 The Canaanite king of Arad lived in
the Southern Desert of Canaan,
and when he heard that the Israelites were
on their way to the village of Atharim, he
attacked and took some of them hostage.

2 The Israelites prayed, "Our LORD, if
you will help us defeat these Canaanites,
we will completely destroy their towns and
everything in them, to show that they belong to you."[k]

3 The LORD answered their prayer and
helped them wipe out the Canaanite army
and completely destroy their towns. That's
why one of the towns is named Hormah,
which means "Destroyed Place."

Moses Makes a Bronze Snake

4 The Israelites had to go around the
territory of Edom, so when they left Mount
Hor, they headed south toward the Red
Sea.[l] But along the way, the people became
so impatient 5 that they complained against
God and said to Moses, "Did you bring us
out of Egypt, just to let us die in the desert?
There's no water out here, and we can't
stand this awful food!"

6 Then the LORD sent poisonous snakes
that bit and killed many of them.

7 Some of the people went to Moses and
admitted, "It was wrong of us to insult you
and the LORD. Now please ask him to make
these snakes go away."

Moses prayed, 8 and the LORD answered,
"Make a snake out of bronze and place it
on top of a pole. Anyone who gets bitten
can look at the snake and won't die."

9 Moses obeyed the LORD. And all of
those who looked at the bronze snake lived,
even though they had been bitten by the
poisonous snakes.

Israel's Journey to Moab

10 As the Israelites continued their journey to Canaan, they camped at Oboth,
11 then at Iye-Abarim in the desert east of
Moab, 12 and then in the Zered Gorge.
13 After that, they crossed the Arnon River
gorge and camped in the Moabite desert
bordering Amorite territory. The Arnon was
the border between the Moabites and the
Amorites. 14 A song in *The Book of the
LORD's Battles*[m] mentions the town of Wa-
heb with its creeks in the territory of
Suphah. It also mentions the Arnon River,
15 with its valleys that lie alongside the
Moabite border and extend to the town
of Ar.

16 From the Arnon, the Israelites went
to the well near the town of Beer, where
the LORD had said to Moses, "Call the people together, and I will give them water to
drink."

17 That's also the same well the Israelites sang about in this song:

Let's celebrate!
    The well has given us water.
18 With their royal scepters,
our leaders pointed out
    where to dig the well.

The Israelites left the desert and
camped near the town of Mattanah, 19 then

[k]**21.2** *completely destroy . . . belong to you*: The complete destruction of a town and everything in it, including its people and animals, showed that the town belonged to the LORD and could no longer be used by humans. [l]**21.4** *Red Sea*: See the note at 14.25. [m]**21.14** *The Book of the LORD's Battles*: This may have been a collection of ancient war songs.

20.28 Ex 29.29, 30; Nu 33.38; Dt 10.6. **21.1** Nu 33.40. **21.4** Dt 2.1. **21.5,6** 1 Co 10.9. **21.9** 2 K 18.4; Jn 3.14.

at Nahaliel, and then at Bamoth. 20 Finally, they reached Moabite territory, where they camped near Mount Pisgah[n] in a valley overlooking the desert north of the Dead Sea.

Israel Defeats King Sihon the Amorite
(Deuteronomy 2.26-37)

21 The Israelites sent this message to King Sihon of the Amorites:

> 22 Please let us pass through your territory. We promise to stay away from your fields and vineyards, and we won't drink any water from your wells. As long as we're in your land, we won't get off the main road.[o]

23 But Sihon refused to let Israel travel through his land. Instead, he called together his entire army and marched into the desert to attack Israel near the town of Jahaz. 24 Israel defeated them and took over the Amorite territory from the Arnon River gorge in the south to the Jabbok River gorge in the north. Beyond the Jabbok was the territory of the Ammonites, who were much stronger than Israel.

25 The Israelites settled in the Amorite towns, including the capital city of Heshbon with its surrounding villages. 26 King Sihon had ruled from Heshbon, after defeating the Moabites and taking over their land north of the Arnon River gorge. 27 That's why the Amorites had written this poem about Heshbon:

Come and rebuild Heshbon,
King Sihon's capital city!
28 His armies marched out
like fiery flames,
burning down the town of Ar
and destroying[p] the hills
along the Arnon River.
29 You Moabites are done for!
Your god Chemosh
deserted your people;
they were captured, taken away
by King Sihon the Amorite.
30 We completely defeated Moab.
The towns of Heshbon and Dibon,
of Nophah and Medeba
are ruined and gone.[q]

31 After the Israelites had settled in the Amorite territory, 32 Moses sent some men to explore the town of Jazer. Later, the Israelites captured the villages surrounding it and forced out the Amorites who lived there.

Israel Defeats King Og of Bashan
(Deuteronomy 3.1-11)

33 The Israelites headed toward the region of Bashan, where King Og ruled, and he led his entire army to Edrei to meet Israel in battle.

34 The LORD said to Moses, "Don't be afraid of Og. I will help you defeat him and his army, just as you did King Sihon who ruled in Heshbon. Og's territory will be yours."

35 So the Israelites wiped out Og, his family, and his entire army—there were no survivors. Then Israel took over the land of Bashan.

22 Israel moved from there to the hills of Moab, where they camped across the Jordan River from the town of Jericho.

King Balak of Moab Hires Balaam To Curse Israel

2-3 When King Balak[r] of Moab and his people heard how many Israelites there were and what they had done to the Amorites, he and the Moabites were terrified and panicked. 4 They said to the Midianite leaders, "That bunch of Israelites will wipe out everything in sight, like a bull eating grass in a field."

So King Balak 5 sent a message to Balaam son of Beor who lived among his relatives in the town of Pethor near the Euphrates River. It said:

> I need your help. A huge group of people has come here from Egypt and settled near my territory. 6 They are too powerful for us to defeat, so would

[n]**21.20** *Mount Pisgah*: This probably refers to the highest peak in the Abarim Mountains in Moab. [o]**21.22** *the main road*: See the note at 20.17. [p]**21.28** *destroying*: One ancient translation; Hebrew "the rulers of." [q]**21.30** *gone*: One possible meaning for the difficult Hebrew text of verse 30. [r]**22.2,3** *Balak*: Hebrew "Balak son of Zippor."

21.28,29 Jr 48.45, 46. **22.5** Nu 31.8; 2 P 2.15, 16; Jd 11.

you come and place a curse on them? Maybe then we can run them off. I know that anyone you bless will be successful, but anyone you curse will fail.

7 The leaders of Moab and Midian left and took along money to pay Balaam for his work. When they got to his house, they gave him Balak's message.

8 "Spend the night here," Balaam replied, "and tomorrow I will tell you the LORD's answer." So the officials stayed at his house.

9 During the night, God asked Balaam, "Who are these people at your house?"

10 "They are messengers from King Balak of Moab," Balaam answered. "He sent them 11 to ask me to go to Moab and place a curse on the people who have come there from Egypt. They have settled everywhere around him, and he wants to run them off."

12 But God replied, "Don't go with Balak's messengers. I have blessed those people who have come from Egypt, so don't curse them."

13 The next morning, Balaam said to Balak's officials, "Go on back home. The LORD says I cannot go with you."

14 The officials left and told Balak that Balaam refused to come.

15 Then Balak sent a larger group of officials, who were even more important than the first ones. 16 They went to Balaam and told him that Balak had said, "Balaam, if you come to Moab, 17 I'll pay you very well and do whatever you ask. Just come and place a curse on these people."

18 Balaam answered, "Even if Balak offered me a palace full of silver or gold, I wouldn't do anything to disobey the LORD my God. 19 You are welcome to spend the night here, just as the others did. I will find out if the LORD has something else to say about this."

20 That night, God said, "Balaam, I'll let you go to Moab with Balak's messengers, but do only what I say."

21 So Balaam got up the next morning and saddled his donkey, then left with the Moabite officials.

Balaam and His Donkey Meet an Angel

22 Balaam was riding his donkey to Moab, and two of his servants were with him. But God was angry that Balaam had gone, so one of the LORD's angels stood in the road to stop him. 23 When Balaam's donkey saw the angel standing there with a sword, it walked off the road and into an open field. Balaam had to beat the donkey to get it back on the road.

24 Then the angel stood between two vineyards, in a narrow path with a stone wall on each side. 25 When the donkey saw the angel, it walked so close to one of the walls that Balaam's foot scraped against the wall. Balaam beat the donkey again.

26 The angel moved once more and stood in a spot so narrow that there was no room for the donkey to go around. 27 So it just lay down. Balaam lost his temper, then picked up a stick and smacked the donkey.

28 When that happened, the LORD told the donkey to speak, and it asked Balaam, "What have I done to you that made you beat me three times?"

29 "You made me look stupid!" Balaam answered. "If I had a sword, I'd kill you here and now!"

30 "But you're my owner," replied the donkey, "and you've ridden me many times. Have I ever done anything like this before?"

"No," Balaam admitted.

31 Just then, the LORD let Balaam see the angel standing in the road, holding a sword, and Balaam bowed down.

32 The angel said, "You had no right to treat your donkey like that! I was the one who blocked your way, because I don't think you should go to Moab.[s] 33 If your donkey had not seen me and stopped those three times, I would have killed you and let the donkey live."

34 Balaam replied, "I was wrong. I didn't know you were trying to stop me. If you don't think I should go, I'll return home right now."

35 "It's all right for you to go," the LORD's angel answered. "But you must say

[s]**22.32** *I don't think you should go to Moab*: One possible meaning for the difficult Hebrew text.

only what I tell you." So Balaam went on
with Balak's officials.

King Balak Meets Balaam

36 When Balak heard that Balaam was
coming, he went to meet him at the town
of Ir, which is on the northern border of
Moab. 37 Balak asked, "Why didn't you
come when I invited you the first time?
Did you think I wasn't going to pay you?"
38 "I'm here now," Balaam answered.
"But I will say only what God tells me
to say."
39 They left and went to the town of
Kiriath-Huzoth, 40 where Balak sacrificed
cattle and sheep and gave some of the
meat to Balaam and the officials who were
with him.
41 The next morning, Balak took Balaam
to the town of Bamoth-Baal. From there,
Balaam could see some of the Israelites.[t]

Balaam's First Message

23 Balaam said to Balak, "Build seven
altars here, then bring seven bulls
and seven rams."
2 After Balak had done this, they sacrificed a bull and a ram on each altar. 3 Then
Balaam said, "Wait here beside your offerings, and I'll go somewhere to be alone.
Maybe the LORD will appear to me. If he
does, I will tell you everything he says."
And he left.
4 When God appeared to him, Balaam
said, "I have built seven altars and have
sacrificed a bull and a ram on each one."
5 The LORD gave Balaam a message,
then sent him back to tell Balak. 6 When
Balaam returned, he found Balak and his
officials standing beside the offerings.
7 Balaam said:

"King Balak of Moab brought me
from the hills of Syria
to curse Israel
and announce its doom.
8 But I can't go against God!
He did not curse
or condemn Israel.
*9 "From the mountain peaks,
I look down and see Israel,
the obedient people of God.
10 They are living alone in peace.
And though they are many,
they don't bother
the other nations.

"I hope to obey God
for as long as I live
and to die in such peace."

11 Balak said, "What are you doing? I
asked you to come and place a curse on my
enemies. But you have blessed them instead!"
12 Balaam answered, "I can say only
what the LORD tells me."

Balaam's Second Message

13 Balak said to Balaam, "Let's go somewhere else. Maybe if you see a smaller part
of the Israelites, you will be able to curse
them for me." 14 So he took Balaam to a
field on top of Mount Pisgah where lookouts were stationed.[u] Then he built seven
altars there and sacrificed a bull and a ram
on each one.
15 "Wait here beside your offerings,"
Balaam said. "The LORD will appear to me
over there."
16 The LORD appeared to Balaam and
gave him another message, then he told
him to go and tell Balak. 17 Balaam went
back and saw him and his officials standing
beside the offerings.
Balak asked, "What did the LORD say?"
18 Balaam answered:

"Pay close attention
to my words—
19 God is no mere human!
He doesn't tell lies
or change his mind.
God always keeps his promises.

20 "My command from God
was to bless these people,

[t]**22.41** *Balaam could see some of the Israelites*: For a curse to work, the people or thing being cursed had to be seen. [u]**23.14** *a field . . . where lookouts were stationed*: Or "Zophim Field on the top of Mount Pisgah."

and there's nothing I can do
to change what he has done.
21 Israel's king is the LORD God.
He lives there with them
and intends them no harm.
22 With the strength of a wild ox,
God led Israel out of Egypt.
23 No magic charms can work
against them—
just look what God has done
for his people.
24 They are like angry lions
ready to attack;
and they won't rest
until their victim
is gobbled down."

25 Balak shouted, "If you're not going
to curse Israel, then at least don't bless
them."
26 "I've already told you," Balaam answered. "I will say only what the LORD
tells me."

Balaam's Third Message

27 Balak said to Balaam, "Come on, let's
try another place. Maybe God will let you
curse Israel from there." 28 So he took Balaam to Mount Peor overlooking the desert
north of the Dead Sea.
29 Balaam said, "Build seven altars here,
then bring me seven bulls and seven
rams."
30 After Balak had done what Balaam
asked, he sacrificed a bull and a ram on
each altar.

24 Balaam was sure that the LORD
would tell him to bless Israel again.
So he did not use any magic to find out
what the LORD wanted him to do, as he had
the first two times. Instead, he looked out
toward the desert 2 and saw the tribes of
Israel camped below. Just then, God's
Spirit took control of him, 3 and Balaam
said:

"I am the son of Beor,
and my words are true,[v]
so listen to my message!
4 It comes from the LORD,
the God All-Powerful.
I bowed down to him
and saw a vision of Israel.

5 "People of Israel,
your camp is lovely.
6 It's like a grove of palm trees[w]
or a garden beside a river.
You are like tall aloe trees
that the LORD has planted,
or like cedars
growing near water.
7 You and your descendants
will prosper like an orchard
beside a stream.
Your king will rule with power
and be a greater king
than Agag the Amalekite.[x]
8 With the strength of a wild ox,
God led you out of Egypt.
You will defeat your enemies,
shooting them with arrows[y]
and crushing their bones.
9 Like a lion you lie down,
resting after an attack.
Who would dare disturb you?

"Anyone who blesses you
will be blessed;
anyone who curses you
will be cursed."

10 When Balak heard this, he was so furious that he pounded his fist against his
hand and said, "I called you here to place a
curse on my enemies, and you've blessed
them three times. 11 Leave now and go
home! I told you I would pay you well, but
since the LORD didn't let you do what I
asked, you won't be paid."
12 Balaam answered, "I told your messengers 13 that even if you offered me a
palace full of silver or gold, I would still
obey the LORD. And I explained that I
would say only what he told me. 14 So I'm
going back home, but I'm leaving you with
a warning about what the Israelites will
someday do to your nation."

[v]**24.3** *my words are true*: One possible meaning for the difficult Hebrew text. [w]**24.6** *grove of palm trees*: Or "green valley." [x]**24.7** *Agag the Amalekite*: The Amalekites were long-time enemies of the Israelites (see Exodus 17.8-16), and Agag was one of their most powerful kings.
[y]**24.8** *shooting them with arrows*: One possible meaning for the difficult Hebrew text.
24.9 **a** Gn 49.9; **b** Gn 12.3.

Balaam's Fourth Message

15 Balaam said:

"I am the son of Beor,
and my words are true,[z]
so listen to my message!
16 My knowledge comes
from God Most High,
the LORD All-Powerful.
I bowed down to him
and saw a vision of Israel.

17 "What I saw in my vision
hasn't happened yet.
But someday, a king of Israel
will appear like a star.
He will wipe out you Moabites[a]
and destroy[b] those tribes
who live in the desert.[c]
18 Israel will conquer Edom
and capture the land
of that enemy nation.
19 The king of Israel will rule
and destroy the survivors
of every town there.[d]

20 "And I saw this vision
about the Amalekites:[e]
Their nation is now great,
but it will someday
disappear forever.[f]

21 "And this is what I saw
about the Kenites:[g]
They think they're safe,
living among the rocks,
22 but they will be wiped out
when Assyria conquers them.[h]

23 "No one can survive
if God plans destruction.[i]
24 Ships will come from Cyprus,
bringing people who will invade
the lands of Assyria and Eber.
But finally, Cyprus itself
will be ruined."

25 After Balaam finished, he started
home, and Balak also left.

The Israelites Worship Baal

25 While the Israelites were camped
at Acacia, some of the men had sex
with Moabite women. 2 These women then
invited the men to ceremonies where sacrifices were offered to their gods. The men
ate the meat from the sacrifices and worshiped the Moabite gods.
3 The LORD was angry with Israel because they had worshiped the god Baal
Peor. 4 So he said to Moses, "Take the Israelite leaders who are responsible for this
and have them killed in front of my sacred
tent where everyone can see. Maybe then I
will stop being angry with the Israelites."
5 Moses told Israel's officials,[j] "Each of
you must put to death any of your men
who worshiped Baal."
6 Later, Moses and the people were at
the sacred tent, crying, when one of the Israelite men brought a Midianite[k] woman to
meet his family. 7 Phinehas, the grandson
of Aaron[l] the priest, saw the couple and left
the crowd. He found a spear 8 and followed
the man into his tent, where he ran the
spear through the man and into the
woman's stomach. The LORD immediately
stopped punishing Israel with a deadly disease, 9 but twenty-four thousand Israelites
had already died.
10 The LORD said to Moses, 11 "In my
anger, I would have wiped out the Israelites

[z] **24.15** *my words are true*: One possible meaning for the difficult Hebrew text. [a] **24.17** *you Moabites*: Or "the territories of Moab." [b] **24.17** *destroy*: The Standard Hebrew Text; the Samaritan Hebrew Text "the skulls of." [c] **24.17** *those tribes . . . desert*: The Hebrew text has "the descendants of Sheth," which probably refers to the people who lived in the desert areas of Canaan before the Israelites. [d] **24.19** *every town there*: Or "Ir in Moab." [e] **24.20** *the Amalekites*: See the note at 24.7. [f] **24.20** *but . . . forever*: One possible meaning for the difficult Hebrew text. [g] **24.21** *the Kenites*: A group of people who lived in the desert south of Israel.
[h] **24.22** *them*: One possible meaning for the difficult Hebrew text of verse 22.
[i] **24.23** *destruction*: One possible meaning for the difficult Hebrew text of verse 23.
[j] **25.5** *officials*: These were special leaders who were probably responsible for an entire tribe or part of a tribe. [k] **25.6** *Midianite*: Used here as a general term for various peoples who lived east of the Jordan River. Some of these people were probably ruled by the Moabite king (see Genesis 36.35).
[l] **25.7** *Phinehas . . . Aaron*: Hebrew "Phinehas, son of Eleazar and grandson of Aaron."

if Phinehas had not been faithful to me. 12-13 But instead of punishing them, I forgave them. So because of the loyalty that Phinehas showed, I solemnly promise that he and his descendants will always be my priests."

14 The Israelite man that was killed was Zimri son of Salu, who was one of the leaders of the Simeon tribe. 15 And the Midianite woman killed with him was Cozbi, the daughter of a Midianite clan leader named Zur.

16 The LORD told Moses, 17-18 "The Midianites are now enemies of Israel, so attack and defeat them! They tricked the people of Israel into worshiping their god at Peor, and they are responsible for the death of Cozbi, the daughter of one of their own leaders."

The Israelites Are Counted a Second Time

26 After the LORD had stopped the deadly disease from killing the Israelites, he said to Moses and Eleazar son of Aaron, 2 "I want you to find out how many Israelites are in each family. And list every man twenty years and older who is able to serve in Israel's army."

3 Israel was now camped in the hills of Moab across the Jordan River from the town of Jericho. Moses and Eleazar told them 4 what the LORD had said about counting the men twenty years and older, just as Moses and their ancestors had done when they left Egypt.[m]

5-7 There were 43,730 men from the tribe of Reuben, the oldest son of Jacob.[n] These men were from the clans of Hanoch, Pallu, Hezron, and Carmi. 8 Pallu was the father of Eliab 9 and the grandfather of Nemuel, Dathan, and Abiram. These are the same Dathan and Abiram who had been chosen by the people, but who followed Korah and rebelled against Moses, Aaron, and the LORD. 10 That's when the LORD made the earth open up and swallow Dathan, Abiram, and Korah. At the same time, fire destroyed two hundred fifty men as a warning to the other Israelites.[o] 11 But the Korahite clan wasn't destroyed.

12-14 There were 22,200 men from the tribe of Simeon; they were from the clans of Nemuel, Jamin, Jachin, Zerah, and Shaul.

15-18 There were 40,500 men from the tribe of Gad; they were from the clans of Zephon, Haggi, Shuni, Ozni, Eri, Arod, and Areli.

19-22 There were 76,500 men from the tribe of Judah; they were from the clans of Shelah, Perez, Zerah, Hezron, and Hamul. Judah's sons Er and Onan had died in Canaan.[p]

23-25 There were 64,300 men from the tribe of Issachar; they were from the clans of Tola, Puvah, Jashub, and Shimron.

26-27 There were 60,500 men from the tribe of Zebulun; they were from the clans of Sered, Elon, and Jahleel.

28-34 There were 52,700 men from the tribe of Manasseh son of Joseph; they were from the clan of Machir, the clan of Gilead his son, and the clans of his six grandsons: Iezer, Helek, Asriel, Shechem, Shemida, and Hepher. Zelophehad son of Hepher had no sons, but he had five daughters: Mahlah, Noah, Hoglah, Milcah, and Tirzah.[q]

35-37 There were 32,500 men from the tribe of Ephraim son of Joseph; they were from the clans of Shuthelah, Becher, Tahan, and Eran the son of Shuthelah.

38-41 There were 45,600 men from the tribe of Benjamin; they were from the clans of Bela, Ashbel, Ahiram, Shephupham, Hupham, as well as from Ard and Naaman, the two sons of Bela.

42-43 There were 64,400 men from the tribe of Dan; they were all from the clan of Shuham.

44-47 There were 53,400 men from the tribe of Asher; they were from the clans of Imnah, Ishvi, and Beriah, and from the two clans of Heber and Malchiel, the sons of Beriah. Asher's daughter was Serah.

[m]**26.4** *just as . . . Egypt*: One possible meaning for the difficult Hebrew text. [n]**26.5-7** *Jacob*: The Hebrew text has "Israel," Jacob's name after God renamed him. [o]**26.10** *Israelites*: See 16.1-35. [p]**26.19-22** *Judah's sons . . . Canaan*: See Genesis 38.1-10.
[q]**26.28-34** *Zelophehad . . . Tirzah*: See also 27.1-11; 36.1-12.
26.1-51 Nu 1.1-46.

48-50 There were 45,400 men from the tribe of Naphtali; they were from the clans of Jahzeel, Guni, Jezer, and Shillem.

51 The total number of Israelite men listed was 601,730.

52 The LORD said to Moses, 53 "Divide the land of Canaan among these tribes, according to the number of people in each one, 54 so the larger tribes have more land than the smaller ones. 55-56 I will show you[r] what land to give each tribe, and they will receive as much land as they need, according to the number of people in it."

57 The tribe of Levi included the clans of the Gershonites, Kohathites, Merarites, 58 as well as the clans of Libni, Hebron, Mahli, Mushi, and Korah. Kohath the Levite was the father of Amram, 59 the husband of Levi's daughter Jochebed, who was born in Egypt. Amram and Jochebed's three children were Aaron, Moses, and Miriam. 60 Aaron was the father of Nadab, Abihu, Eleazar, and Ithamar. 61 But Nadab and Abihu had died when they offered fire that was unacceptable to the LORD.[s]

62 In the tribe of Levi there were 23,000 men and boys at least a month old. They were not listed with the other tribes, because they would not receive any land in Canaan.

63 Moses and Eleazar counted the Israelites while they were camped in the hills of Moab across the Jordan River from Jericho. 64 None of the people that Moses and Aaron had counted in the Sinai Desert were still alive, 65 except Caleb son of Jephunneh and Joshua son of Nun. The LORD had said that everyone else would die there in the desert.[t]

The Daughters of Zelophehad Are Given Land

27 Zelophehad[u] was from the Manasseh tribe, and he had five daughters, whose names were Mahlah, Noah, Hoglah, Milcah, and Tirzah.

2 One day his daughters went to the sacred tent, where they met with Moses, Eleazar, and some other leaders of Israel, as well as a large crowd of Israelites. The young women said:

> 3 You know that our father died in the desert. But it was for something he did wrong, not for joining with Korah in rebelling against the LORD.
>
> Our father left no sons 4 to carry on his family name. But why should his name die out for that reason? Give us some land like the rest of his relatives in our clan, so our father's name can live on.

5 Moses asked the LORD what should be done, 6 and the LORD answered:

> 7 Zelophehad's daughters are right. They should each be given part of the land their father would have received.
>
> 8 Tell the Israelites that when a man dies without a son, his daughter will inherit his land. 9 If he has no daughter, his brothers will inherit the land. 10 But if he has no brothers, his father's brothers will inherit the land. 11 And if his father has no brothers, the land must be given to his nearest relative in the clan. This is my law, and the Israelites must obey it.

Joshua Is Appointed Israel's Leader

(Deuteronomy 31.1-8)

12 The LORD said to Moses, "One day you will go up into the Abarim Mountains, and from there you will see the land I am giving the Israelites. 13 After you have seen it, you will die,[v] just like your brother Aaron, 14 because both of you disobeyed me at Meribah near the town of Kadesh in the Zin Desert. When the Israelites insulted me there, you didn't believe in my holy power."[w]

15 Moses replied, 16 "You are the LORD God, and you know what is in everyone's

[r]**26.55,56** *I will show you*: The Hebrew text has "Cast lots to find out." Pieces of wood or stone (called "lots") were used to find out what the LORD wanted his people to do. [s]**26.61** *Nadab and Abihu . . . the LORD*: See 3.1-4 and Leviticus 10.1, 2. [t]**26.64,65** *None of the people . . . the desert*: See 14.26-30. [u]**27.1** *Zelophehad*: Hebrew "Zelophehad son of Hepher son of Gilead son of Machir son of Manasseh son of Joseph." [v]**27.12,13** *One day . . . you will die*: The story of Moses' death is in Deuteronomy 34.1-8. [w]**27.14** *both of you . . . my holy power*: See 20.1-13.

26.52-56 Nu 34.13; Js 14.1-5. **26.60** Nu 3.2. **26.61** Lv 10.1, 2; Nu 3.4. **26.65** Nu 14.26-35. **27.7** Nu 36.2. **27.12-14** Dt 3.23-27; 32.48-52.

heart. So I ask you to appoint a leader for Israel. 17 Your people need someone to lead them into battle, or else they will be like sheep wandering around without a shepherd."

18 The LORD answered, "Joshua son of Nun can do the job. Place your hands on him to show that he is the one to take your place. 19 Then go with him and have him stand in front of Eleazar the priest and the Israelites. Appoint Joshua as their new leader 20 and tell them they must now obey him, just as they obey you. 21 But Joshua must depend on Eleazar to find out from me[x] what I want him to do as he leads Israel into battle."

22 Moses followed the LORD's instructions and took Joshua to Eleazar and the people, 23 then he placed his hands on Joshua and appointed him Israel's leader.

Regular Daily Sacrifices

(Exodus 29.38-43; Leviticus 6.8-13)

28 The LORD told Moses 2 to say to the people of Israel:

Offer sacrifices to me at the appointed times of worship, so that I will smell the smoke and be pleased.

3 Each day offer two rams a year old as sacrifices to please me.[y] The animals must have nothing wrong with them; 4 one will be sacrificed in the morning, and the other in the evening. 5 Along with each of them, two pounds of your finest flour mixed with a quart of olive oil must be offered as a grain sacrifice. 6 This sacrifice to please me was first offered on Mount Sinai. 7 Finally, along with each of these two sacrifices, a quart of wine must be poured on the altar as a drink offering. 8 The second ram will be sacrificed that evening, along with the other offerings, just like the one sacrificed that morning. The smell of the smoke from these sacrifices will please me.

The Sacrifice on the Sabbath

The LORD said:

9-10 On the Sabbath, in addition to the regular daily sacrifices,[z] you must sacrifice two rams a year old to please me.[a] These rams must have nothing wrong with them, and they will be sacrificed with a drink offering and four pounds of your finest flour mixed with olive oil.

The Sacrifices on the First Day of the Month

The LORD said:

11 On the first day of each month, bring to the altar two bulls, one full-grown ram, and seven rams a year old that have nothing wrong with them. Then offer these as sacrifices to please me.[a] 12 Six pounds of your finest flour mixed with olive oil must be offered with each bull as a grain sacrifice. Four pounds of flour mixed with oil must be offered with the ram, 13 and two pounds of flour mixed with oil must be offered with each of the young rams. The smell of the smoke from these sacrifices will please me.

14-15 Offer two quarts of wine as a drink offering with each bull, one and a half quarts with the ram, and one quart with each of the young rams.

Finally, you must offer a goat[b] as a sacrifice for sin.

These sacrifices are to be offered on the first day of each month, in addition to the regular daily sacrifices.[c]

The Sacrifices during Passover and the Festival of Thin Bread

(Leviticus 23.4-8)

The LORD said:

16 Celebrate Passover in honor of me on the fourteenth day of the first month[d] of each year. 17 The following day will begin

[x]**27.21** *from me*: The Hebrew text has "by the urim," something used by the priests to get answers from the LORD. [y]**28.3** *sacrifices to please me*: See the note at 6.11. [z]**28.9,10** *regular daily sacrifices*: See 28.1-8. [a]**28.9,10,11** *sacrifice . . . to please me*: See the note at 6.11.
[b]**28.14,15** *goat*: See the note at 7.12-83. [c]**28.14,15** *regular daily sacrifices*: See 28.1-8.
[d]**28.16** *first month*: See the note at 9.3.

27.17 1 K 22.17; Ez 34.5; Mt 9.36; Mk 6.34. **27.18** Ex 24.13. **27.21** Ex 28.30; 1 S 14.41; 28.6. **27.23** Dt 31.23. **28.16** Ex 12.1-13; Dt 16.1, 2. **28.17-25** Ex 12.14-20; 23.15; 34.18; Dt 16.3-8.

the Festival of Thin Bread, which will last for a week. During this time you must honor me by eating bread made without yeast.

18 On the first day of this festival, you must rest from your work and come together for worship. 19 Bring to the altar two bulls, one full-grown ram, and seven rams a year old that have nothing wrong with them. And then offer these as sacrifices to please me.[e] 20 Six pounds of your finest flour mixed with olive oil must be offered with each bull as a grain sacrifice. Four pounds of flour mixed with oil must be offered with the ram, 21 and two pounds of flour mixed with oil must be offered with each of the young rams. 22 Also offer a goat[f] as a sacrifice for the sins of the people. 23-24 All of these are to be offered in addition to the regular daily sacrifices,[g] and the smoke from them will please me. 25 Then on the last day of the festival, you must once again rest from work and come together for worship.

The Sacrifices during the Harvest Festival
(Leviticus 23.15-22)

The LORD said:

26 On the first day of the Harvest Festival, you must rest from your work, come together for worship, and bring a sacrifice of new grain. 27 Offer two young bulls, one full-grown ram, and seven rams a year old as sacrifices to please me.[h] 28 Six pounds of your finest flour mixed with olive oil must be offered with each bull as a grain sacrifice. Four pounds of flour mixed with oil must be offered with the ram, 29 and two pounds of flour mixed with oil must be offered with each of the young rams. 30 Also offer a goat[i] as a sacrifice for sin. 31 The animals must have nothing wrong with them and are to be sacrificed along with the regular daily sacrifices.[j]

The Sacrifices at the Festival of Trumpets
(Leviticus 23.23-25)

The LORD said:

29 On the first day of the seventh month,[k] you must rest from your work and come together to celebrate at the sound of the trumpets. 2 Bring to the altar one bull, one full-grown ram, and seven rams a year old that have nothing wrong with them. And then offer these as sacrifices to please me.[l] 3 Six pounds of your finest flour mixed with olive oil must be offered with the bull as a grain sacrifice. Four pounds of flour mixed with oil must be offered with the ram, 4 and two pounds of flour mixed with oil must be offered with each of the young rams. 5 You must also offer a goat[m] as a sacrifice for sin. 6 These sacrifices will be made in addition to the regular daily sacrifices[n] and the sacrifices for the first day of the month.[o] The smoke from these sacrifices will please me.

The Sacrifices on the Great Day of Forgiveness
(Leviticus 23.26-32)

The LORD said:

7 The tenth day of the seventh month[p] is the Great Day of Forgiveness.[q] On that day you must rest from all work and come together for worship. Show sorrow for your sins by going without food, 8 and bring to the altar one young bull, one full-grown ram, and seven rams a year old that have nothing wrong with them. Then offer these as sacrifices to please me.[r] 9 Six pounds of

[e]**28.19** *sacrifices to please me*: See the note at 6.11. [f]**28.22** *goat*: See the note at 7.12-83. [g]**28.23,24** *regular daily sacrifices*: See 28.1-8. [h]**28.27** *sacrifices to please me*: See the note at 6.11. [i]**28.30** *goat*: See the note at 7.12-83. [j]**28.31** *regular daily sacrifices*: See 28.1-8. [k]**29.1** *seventh month*: Tishri (also called Ethanim), the seventh month of the Hebrew calendar, from about mid-September to mid-October. [l]**29.2** *sacrifices to please me*: See the note at 6.11. [m]**29.5** *goat*: Hebrew "male goat." [n]**29.6** *regular daily sacrifices*: See 28.1-8. [o]**29.6** *sacrifices . . . month*: See 28.11-15. [p]**29.7** *seventh month*: See the note at 29.1. [q]**29.7** *Great Day of Forgiveness*: Traditionally known as the Day of Atonement. [r]**29.8** *sacrifices to please me*: See the note at 6.11.

28.26-31 Ex 23.16; 34.22; Dt 16.9-12. **29.7-11** Lv 16.29-34.

your finest flour mixed with olive oil must be offered with the bull as a grain sacrifice. Four pounds of flour mixed with oil must be offered with the ram, [10] and two pounds of flour mixed with oil must be offered with each of the young rams. [11] A goat[s] must also be sacrificed for the sins of the people. You will offer these sacrifices in addition to the sacrifice to ask forgiveness and the regular daily sacrifices.[t]

The Sacrifices during the Festival of Shelters

(Leviticus 23.33-44)

The LORD *said:*

[12] Beginning on the fifteenth day of the seventh month[u] and continuing for seven days, everyone must celebrate the Festival of Shelters in honor of me.

[13] On the first day, you must rest from your work and come together for worship. Bring to the altar thirteen bulls, two full-grown rams, and fourteen rams a year old that have nothing wrong with them. Then offer these as sacrifices to please me.[v] [14] Six pounds of your finest flour mixed with olive oil must be offered with each bull as a grain sacrifice. Four pounds of flour mixed with oil must be offered with each of the rams, [15] and two pounds of flour mixed with oil must be offered with each of the young rams. [16] You must also offer a goat[w] as a sacrifice for sin. These are to be offered in addition to the regular daily sacrifices.[x]

[17-34] For the next six days of the festival, you will sacrifice one less bull than the day before, so that on the seventh day, seven bulls will be sacrificed. The other sacrifices and offerings must remain the same for each of these days.

[35] On the eighth day, you must once again rest from your work and come together for worship. [36] Bring to the altar one bull, one full-grown ram, and seven rams a year old that have nothing wrong with them. Then offer these as sacrifices to please me. [37] You must also offer the proper grain sacrifices and drink offerings of wine with each animal. [38] And offer a goat[y] as the sacrifice to ask forgiveness for the people. These sacrifices are made in addition to the regular daily sacrifices.[z]

[39] You must offer all these sacrifices to me at the appointed times of worship, together with any offerings that are voluntarily given or given because of a promise.

[40] Moses told the people of Israel everything the LORD had told him about the sacrifices.

Making Promises to the LORD

30 The LORD told Moses to say to Israel's tribal leaders:

[2] When one of you men makes a promise to the LORD,[a] you must keep your word.

[3] Suppose a young woman who is still living with her parents makes a promise to the LORD. [4] If her father hears about it and says nothing, she must keep her promise. [5] But if he hears about it and objects, then she no longer has to keep her promise. The LORD will forgive her, because her father did not agree with the promise.

[6-7] Suppose a woman makes a promise to the LORD and then gets married. If her husband later hears about the promise but says nothing, she must do what she said, whether she meant it or not. [8] But if her husband hears about the promise and objects, she no longer has to keep it, and the LORD will forgive her.

[9] Widows and divorced women must keep every promise they make to the LORD.

[10] Suppose a married woman makes a promise to the LORD. [11] If her husband hears about the promise and says nothing, she must do what she said. [12] But if he hears about the promise and does object, she no longer has to keep it. The LORD will

[s] **29.11** *goat*: See the note at 7.12-83. [t] **29.11** *regular daily sacrifices*: See 28.1-8. [u] **29.12** *seventh month*: See the note at 29.1. [v] **29.13** *sacrifices to please me*: See the note at 6.11. [w] **29.16** *goat*: See the note at 7.12-83. [x] **29.16** *regular daily sacrifices*: See 28.1-8. [y] **29.38** *goat*: See the note at 7.12-83. [z] **29.38** *regular daily sacrifices*: See 28.1-8.
[a] **30.2** *a promise to the* LORD: Either the promise of a gift or the promise to do something.
29.12-38 Lv 23.34; Dt 16.13-15. **30.2** Dt 23.21-23; Mt 5.33.

forgive her, because her husband would not allow her to keep the promise. 13 Her husband has the final say about any promises she makes to the LORD. 14 If her husband hears about a promise and says nothing about it for a whole day, she must do what she said—since he did not object, the promise must be kept. 15 But if he waits until the next day to stop her from keeping her promise, he is the one who must be punished.

16 These are the laws that the LORD gave Moses about husbands and wives, and about young daughters who still live at home.

Israel's War against Midian

31 The LORD said to Moses, 2 "Before you die, make sure that the Midianites are punished for what they did to Israel."[b]

3 Then Moses told the people, "The LORD wants to punish the Midianites. So have our men prepare for battle. 4 Each tribe will send a thousand men to fight."

5 Twelve thousand men were picked from the tribes of Israel, and after they were prepared for battle, 6 Moses sent them off to war. Phinehas the son of Eleazar went with them and took along some things from the sacred tent[c] and the trumpets for sounding the battle signal.

7 The Israelites fought against the Midianites, just as the LORD had commanded Moses. They killed all the men, 8 including Balaam son of Beor and the five Midianite kings, Evi, Rekem, Zur, Hur, and Reba. 9 The Israelites captured every woman and child, then led away the Midianites' cattle and sheep, and took everything else that belonged to them. 10 They also burned down the Midianite towns and villages.

11 Israel's soldiers gathered together everything they had taken from the Midianites, including the captives and the animals. 12-13 Then they returned to their own camp in the hills of Moab across the Jordan River from Jericho, where Moses, Eleazar, and the other Israelite leaders met the troops outside camp.

14 Moses became angry with the army commanders 15 and said, "I can't believe you let the women live! 16 They are the ones who followed Balaam's advice and invited our people to worship the god Baal Peor. That's why the LORD punished us by killing so many of our people. 17 You must put to death every boy and all the women who have ever had sex. 18 But do not kill the young women who have never had sex. You may keep them for yourselves."

19 Then Moses said to the soldiers, "If you killed anyone or touched a dead body, you are unclean and have to stay outside the camp for seven days. On the third and seventh days, you must go through a ceremony to make yourselves and your captives clean. 20 Then wash your clothes and anything made from animal skin, goat's hair, or wood."

21-23 Eleazar then explained, "If you need to purify something that won't burn, such as gold, silver, bronze, iron, tin, or lead, you must first place it in a hot fire. After you take it out, sprinkle it with the water that purifies. Everything else should only be sprinkled with the water. Do all of this, just as the LORD commanded Moses. 24 Wash your clothes on the seventh day, and after that, you will be clean and may return to the camp."

Everything Taken from the Midianites Is Divided

25 The LORD told Moses:

> 26-27 Make a list of everything taken from the Midianites, including the captives and the animals. Then divide them between the soldiers and the rest of the people. Eleazar the priest and the family leaders will help you.
>
> 28-29 From the half that belongs to the soldiers, set aside for the LORD one out of every five hundred people or animals and give these to Eleazar.
>
> 30 From the half that belongs to the

[b]**31.2** *Midianites . . . to Israel*: See 25.1-18. [c]**31.6** *Phinehas . . . sacred tent*: Phinehas would serve as the priest during the battle, so he took along the things needed to ask God what he wanted done.

31.16 Nu 25.1-9.

people, set aside one out of every fifty and give these to the Levites in charge of the sacred tent.

31 Moses and Eleazar followed the LORD's instructions 32-35 and listed everything that had been taken from the Midianites. The list included 675,000 sheep and goats, 72,000 cattle, 61,000 donkeys, and 32,000 young women who had never had sex.

36-47 Each half included 337,500 sheep and goats, 36,000 cattle, 30,500 donkeys, and 16,000 young women. From the half that belonged to the soldiers, Moses counted out 675 sheep and goats, 72 cattle, 61 donkeys, and 32 women and gave them to Eleazar to be dedicated to the LORD. Then from the half that belonged to the people, Moses set aside one out of every fifty animals and women, as the LORD had said, and gave them to the Levites.

48 The army commanders went to Moses 49 and said, "Sir, we have counted our troops, and not one soldier is missing. 50 So we want to give the LORD all the gold jewelry we took from the Midianites. It's our gift to him for watching over us and our troops."

51 Moses and Eleazar accepted the jewelry from the commanders, 52 and its total weight was over four hundred pounds. 53 This did not include the things that the soldiers had kept for themselves. 54 So Moses and Eleazar placed the gold in the LORD's sacred tent to remind Israel of what had happened.[d]

Land East of the Jordan River Is Settled

(Deuteronomy 3.12-22)

32 The tribes of Reuben and Gad owned a lot of cattle and sheep, and they saw that the regions of Jazer and Gilead had good pastureland. 2 So they went to Moses, Eleazar, and the other leaders of Israel and said, 3-4 "The LORD has helped us capture the land around the towns of Ataroth, Dibon, Jazer, Nimrah, Heshbon, Elealeh, Sebam, Nebo, and Beon. That's good pastureland, and since we own cattle and sheep, 5 would you let us stay here east of the Jordan River and have this land as our own?"

6 Moses answered:

You mean you'd stay here while the rest of the Israelites go into battle? 7 If you did that, it would discourage the others from crossing over into the land the LORD promised them. 8 This is exactly what happened when I sent your ancestors from Kadesh-Barnea to explore the land. 9 They went as far as Eshcol Valley, then returned and told the people that we should not enter it. 10 The LORD became very angry. 11 And he said that no one who was twenty years or older when they left Egypt would enter the land he had promised to Abraham, Isaac, and Jacob. Not one of those people believed in the LORD's power, 12 except Caleb and Joshua.[e] They remained faithful to the LORD, 13 but he was so angry with the others that he forced them to wander around in the desert forty years. By that time everyone who had sinned against him had died.

14 Now you people of Reuben and Gad are doing the same thing and making the LORD even angrier. 15 If you reject the LORD, he will once again abandon his people and leave them here in the desert. And you will be to blame!

16 The men from Reuben and Gad replied:

Let us build places to keep our sheep and goats, and towns for our wives and children, 17 where they can stay and be safe. Then we'll prepare to fight and lead the other tribes into battle. 18 We will stay with them until they have settled in their own tribal lands. 19 The land on this side of the Jordan River will be ours, so we won't expect to receive any on the other side.

20 Moses said:

You promised that you would be

[d]**31.54** *to remind . . . happened*: Or "so the LORD would continue to help Israel." [e]**32.12** *Caleb and Joshua*: See the note at 14.30.

32.8,9 Nu 13.17-33. **32.10-13** Nu 14.26-35.

ready to fight for the LORD. 21 You also agreed to cross the Jordan and stay with the rest of the Israelites, until the LORD forces our enemies out of the land. If you do these things, 22 then after the LORD helps Israel capture the land, you can return to your own land. You will no longer have to stay with the others. 23 But if you don't keep your promise, you will sin against the LORD and be punished.

24 Go ahead and build towns for your wives and children, and places for your sheep and goats. Just be sure to do what you have promised.

25 The men from Reuben and Gad answered:

Sir, we will do just what you have said. 26 Our wives and children and sheep and cattle will stay here in the towns in Gilead. 27 But those of us who are prepared for battle will cross the Jordan and fight for the LORD.

28 Then Moses said to Eleazar, Joshua, and the family leaders, 29 "Make sure that the tribes of Gad and Reuben prepare for battle and cross the Jordan River with you. If they do, then after the land is in your control, give them the region of Gilead as their tribal land. 30 But if they break their promise, they will receive land on the other side of the Jordan, like the rest of the tribes."

31 The tribes of Gad and Reuben replied, "We are your servants and will do whatever the LORD has commanded. 32 We will cross the Jordan River, ready to fight for the LORD in Canaan. But the land we will inherit as our own will be on this side of the river."

33 So Moses gave the tribes of Gad, Reuben, and half of Manasseh[f] the territory and towns that King Sihon the Amorite had ruled, as well as the territory and towns that King Og of Bashan had ruled.[g]

34 The tribe of Gad rebuilt the towns of Dibon, Ataroth, Aroer, 35 Atroth-Shophan, Jazer, Jogbehah, 36 Beth-Nimrah, and Beth-Haran. They built walls around them and also built places to keep their sheep and goats.

37 The tribe of Reuben rebuilt Heshbon, Elealeh, Kiriathaim, 38 Sibmah, as well as the towns that used to be known as Nebo and Baal-Meon. They renamed all those places.

39 The clan of Machir from the tribe of East Manasseh went to the region of Gilead, captured its towns, and forced out the Amorites. 40 So Moses gave the Machirites the region of Gilead, and they settled there.

41 Jair from the Manasseh tribe captured villages and renamed them "Villages of Jair."[h]

42 Nobah captured the town of Kenath with its villages and renamed it Nobah.

Israel's Journey from Egypt to Moab

33 As Israel traveled from Egypt under the command of Moses and Aaron, 2 Moses kept a list of the places they camped, just as the LORD had instructed. Here is the record of their journey:

3-4 Israel left the Egyptian city of Rameses on the fifteenth day of the first month.[i] This was the day after the LORD had punished Egypt's gods by killing the first-born sons in every Egyptian family. So while the Egyptians were burying the bodies, they watched the Israelites proudly[j] leave their country.

5 After the Israelites left Rameses, they camped at Succoth, 6 and from there, they moved their camp to Etham on the edge of the desert. 7 Then they turned back toward Pi-Hahiroth, east of Baal-Zephon, and camped near Migdol. 8 They left Pi-Hahiroth,[k] crossed the Red Sea,[l] then walked three days into the Etham Desert and camped at Marah. 9 Next, they camped at Elim, where there were twelve springs of

[f]**32.33** *half of Manasseh*: Or "East Manasseh." [g]**32.33** *ruled*: One possible meaning for the difficult Hebrew text of verse 33. [h]**32.41** *Villages of Jair*: Or "Havvoth-Jair." [i]**33.3,4** *first month*: See the note at 9.3. [j]**33.3,4** *proudly*: Or "bravely." [k]**33.8** *Pi-Hahiroth*: Two ancient translations and the Samaritan Hebrew Text; the Standard Hebrew Text "a place near Hahiroth." [l]**33.8** *Red Sea*: Hebrew *hayyam* "the Sea," understood as *yam suph*, "Sea of Reeds" (see also the note at Exodus 13.18).

32.28-32 Js 1.12-15.

water and seventy palm trees. 10 They left Elim and camped near the Red Sea,[m] 11 then turned east and camped along the western edge of the Sinai Desert.[n] 12-14 From there they went to Dophkah, Alush, and Rephidim, where they had no water.[o] 15 They left Rephidim and finally reached the Sinai Desert.

16-36 As Israel traveled from the Sinai Desert to Kadesh in the Zin Desert, they camped at Kibroth-Hattaavah, Hazeroth, Rithmah, Rimmon-Perez, Libnah, Rissah, Kehelathah, Mount Shepher, Haradah, Makheloth, Tahath, Terah, Mithkah, Hashmonah, Moseroth, Bene-Jaakan, Hor-Haggidgad, Jotbathah, Abronah, Ezion-Geber, and finally Kadesh. 37 When they left Kadesh, they came to Mount Hor, on the border of Edom.

38 That's where the LORD commanded Aaron the priest to go to the top of the mountain. Aaron died there on the first day of the fifth month,[p] forty years after the Israelites left Egypt. 39 He was one hundred twenty-three years old at the time.

40 It was then that the Canaanite king of Arad, who lived in the Southern Desert of Canaan, heard that Israel was headed that way.

41-47 The Israelites left Mount Hor and headed toward Moab. Along the way, they camped at Zalmonah, Punon, Oboth, Iye-Abarim in the territory of Moab, Dibon-Gad, Almon-Diblathaim, at a place near Mount Nebo in the Abarim Mountains, 48 and finally in the lowlands of Moab across the Jordan River from Jericho. 49 Their camp stretched from Beth-Jeshimoth to Acacia.

The LORD's Command To Conquer Canaan

50 While Israel was camped in the lowlands of Moab across the Jordan River from Jericho, the LORD told Moses 51 to give the people of Israel this message:

When you cross the Jordan River and enter Canaan, 52 you must force out the people living there. Destroy their idols and tear down their altars. 53 Then settle in the land—I have given it to you as your own.

54 I will show you[q] how to divide the land among the tribes, according to the number of clans in each one, so that the larger tribes will have more land than the smaller ones.

55 If you don't force out all the people there, they will be like pointed sticks in your eyes and thorns in your back. They will always be trouble for you, 56 and I will treat you as cruelly as I planned on treating them.

Israel's Borders

34 The LORD told Moses 2 to tell the people of Israel that their land in Canaan would have the following borders:

3 The southern border will be the Zin Desert and the northwest part of Edom. This border will begin at the south end of the Dead Sea. 4 It will go west from there, but will turn southward to include Scorpion Pass, the village of Zin, and the town of Kadesh-Barnea. From there, the border will continue to Hazar-Addar and on to Azmon. 5 It will run along the Egyptian Gorge and end at the Mediterranean Sea.

6 The western border will be the Mediterranean Sea.

7 The northern border will begin at the Mediterranean, then continue eastward to Mount Hor.[r] 8 After that, it will run to Lebo-Hamath and across to Zedad, which is the northern edge of your land. 9 From Zedad, the border will continue east to Ziphron and end at Hazar-Enan.

10 The eastern border will begin at

[m]**33.10** *Red Sea*: Hebrew *yam suph*, here referring to the Gulf of Suez, since the term is extended to include the northwestern arm of the Red Sea (see also the note at Exodus 13.18). [n]**33.11** *the western edge of the Sinai Desert*: Hebrew "the Sin Desert." [o]**33.12-14** *Rephidim . . . no water*: See Exodus 17.1-7. [p]**33.38** *fifth month*: Ab, the fifth month of the Hebrew calendar, from about mid-July to mid-August. [q]**33.54** *I will show you*: See the note at 26.55, 56. [r]**34.7** *Mount Hor*: Not the same as in 33.37.

33.38 Nu 20.22-28; Dt 10.6; 32.50. **33.40** Nu 21.1. **33.54** Nu 26.54-56.

Hazar-Enan in the north, then run south to Shepham, 11 and on down to Riblah on the east side of Ain. From there, it will go south to the eastern hills of Lake Galilee,[s] 12 then follow the Jordan River down to the north end of the Dead Sea.

The land within those four borders will belong to you.

13 Then Moses told the people, "You will receive the land inside these borders. It will be yours, but the LORD has commanded you to divide it among the nine and a half tribes. 14 The tribes of Reuben, Gad, and East Manasseh have already been given their land 15 across from Jericho, east of the Jordan River."

The Leaders Who Will Divide the Land

16 The LORD said to Moses, 17 "Eleazar the priest and Joshua son of Nun will divide the land for the Israelites. 18 One leader from each tribe will help them, 19-28 and here is the list of their names:

Caleb son of Jephunneh
from Judah,
Shemuel son of Ammihud
from Simeon,
Elidad son of Chislon
from Benjamin,
Bukki son of Jogli
from Dan,
Hanniel son of Ephod
from Manasseh,
Kemuel son of Shiphtan
from Ephraim,
Elizaphan son of Parnach
from Zebulun,
Paltiel son of Azzan
from Issachar,
Ahihud son of Shelomi
from Asher,
and Pedahel son of Ammihud
from Naphtali."

29 These are the men the LORD commanded to help Eleazar and Joshua divide the land for the Israelites.

The Towns for the Levites

35 While the people of Israel were still camped in the lowlands of Moab across the Jordan River from Jericho, the LORD told Moses 2 to say to them:

When you receive your tribal lands, you must give towns and pastures to the Levi tribe. 3 That way, the Levites will have towns to live in and pastures for their animals. 4-5 The pasture around each of these towns must be in the shape of a square, with the town itself in the center. The pasture is to measure three thousand feet on each side, with fifteen hundred feet of land outside each of the town walls. This will be the Levites' pastureland.

6 Six of the towns you give them will be Safe Towns where a person who has accidentally killed someone can run for protection. But you will also give the Levites forty-two other towns, 7 so they will have a total of forty-eight towns with their surrounding pastures.

8 Since the towns for the Levites must come from Israel's own tribal lands, the larger tribes will give more towns than the smaller ones.

The Safe Towns

(Deuteronomy 19.1-13; Joshua 20.1-9)

9 The LORD then told Moses 10 to tell the people of Israel:

After you have crossed the Jordan River and are settled in Canaan, 11 choose Safe Towns, where a person who has accidentally killed someone can run for protection. 12 If the victim's relatives think it was murder, they might try to take revenge.[t] Anyone accused of murder can run to one of these Safe Towns for protection and not be killed before a trial is held.

13 There are to be six of these Safe Towns, 14 three on each side of the Jordan River. 15 They will be places of protection for anyone who lives in Israel and accidentally kills someone.

[s] **34.11** *Lake Galilee*: The Hebrew text has "Lake Chinnereth," an earlier name for Lake Galilee.
[t] **35.12,19** *the victim's relatives . . . revenge*: At this time in Israel's history, the clan would appoint the closest male relative to find and kill a person who had killed a member of their clan.

34.13 Nu 26.52-56. **34.13-15** Js 14.1-5. **35.1-8** Js 21.1-42. **35.9-28** Dt 19.2-4; Js 20.1-9.

Laws about Murder and Accidental Killing

The LORD said:

16-18 Suppose you hit someone with a piece of iron or a large stone or a dangerous wooden tool. If that person dies, then you are a murderer and must be put to death 19 by one of the victim's relatives.[t] He will take revenge for his relative's death as soon as he finds you.

20-21 Or suppose you get angry and kill someone by pushing or hitting or by throwing something. You are a murderer and must be put to death by one of the victim's relatives.

22-24 But if you are not angry and accidentally kill someone in any of these ways, the townspeople must hold a trial and decide if you are guilty. 25 If they decide that you are innocent, you will be protected from the victim's relative and sent to stay in one of the Safe Towns until the high priest dies. 26 But if you ever leave the Safe Town 27 and are killed by the victim's relative, he cannot be punished for killing you. 28 You must stay inside the town until the high priest dies; only then can you go back home.

29 The community of Israel must always obey these laws.

30 Death is the penalty for murder. But no one accused of murder can be put to death unless there are at least two witnesses to the crime. 31 You cannot give someone money to escape the death penalty; you must pay with your own life! 32 And if you have been proven innocent of murder and are living in a Safe Town, you cannot pay to go back home; you must stay there until the high priest dies.

33-34 I, the LORD, live among you people of Israel, so your land must be kept pure. But when a murder takes place, blood pollutes the land, and it becomes unclean. If that happens, the murderer must be put to death, so the land will be clean again. Keep murder out of Israel!

The Laws about Married Women and Land

36 One day the family leaders from the Gilead clan of the Manasseh tribe went to Moses and the other family leaders of Israel 2 and said, "Sir, the LORD has said that he will show[u] what land each tribe will receive as their own. And the LORD has commanded you to give the daughters of our relative Zelophehad the land that he would have received. 3 But if they marry men from other tribes of Israel, the land they receive will become part of that tribe's inheritance and will no longer belong to us. 4 Even when land is returned to its original owner in the Year of Celebration,[v] we will not get back Zelophehad's land—it will belong to the tribe into which his daughters married."

5 So Moses told the people that the LORD had said:

> These men from the Manasseh tribe are right. 6 I will allow Zelophehad's daughters to marry anyone, as long as those men belong to one of the clans of the Manasseh tribe.
>
> 7 Tribal land must not be given to another tribe—it will remain the property of the tribe that received it. 8-9 In the future, any daughter who inherits land must marry someone from her own tribe. Israel's tribal land is never to be passed from one tribe to another.

10-11 Mahlah, Tirzah, Hoglah, Milcah, and Noah the daughters of Zelophehad obeyed the LORD and married their uncles' sons 12 and remained part of the Manasseh tribe. So their land stayed in their father's clan.

13 These are the laws that the LORD gave to Moses and the Israelites while they were camped in the lowlands of Moab across the Jordan River from Jericho.

[t]**35.12,19** *the victim's relatives . . . revenge*: At this time in Israel's history, the clan would appoint the closest male relative to find and kill a person who had killed a member of their clan.

[u]**36.2** *that he will show*: See the note at 26.55, 56.

[v]**36.4** *Year of Celebration*: This was a sacred year for Israel, traditionally called the "Year of Jubilee." During this year, all property had to go back to its original owner. But here, the property was not sold; it became part of the other tribe's land when the daughter who owned it married into that tribe. So the property could not be returned even during this year.

35.30 Dt 17.5-7; 19.15. **36.2** Nu 27.7.

DEUTERONOMY

ABOUT THIS BOOK

It was almost time for the people of Israel to cross the Jordan River and conquer Canaan. But God refused to let Moses lead them into the land. Instead, Moses had been told that he was going to die on the eastern side of the Jordan. So Moses gave several farewell speeches to the people of Israel in which he repeated many of God's laws.

Because Moses was giving these laws to Israel for a second time, the book is now called "Deuteronomy," which comes from a Greek phrase meaning "second law."

Moses also reminded the Israelites about the past forty years. God had rescued them from Egypt and taken care of them in the desert, but they had not always been faithful or obedient to him.

Moses told the Israelites that if they kept their agreement to worship and obey the Lord, they would be a successful and powerful nation. But if they broke their agreement and worshiped idols, the Lord promised to put terrible curses on the people. They would be defeated by their enemies and lose their land and their lives.

Much later, when Jesus was asked which one of God's commands was the most important, he answered by quoting one of the commands from Deuteronomy:

> *"Listen, Israel! The LORD our God is the only true God! So love the LORD your God with all your heart, soul, and strength."*
>
> *(6.4, 5)*

A QUICK LOOK AT THIS BOOK

- The First Speech: Moses Reviews the Past (1.1—4.43)
- The Second Speech:
  Moses Tells What the Lord Requires (4.44—29.1)
- The Third Speech:
  Israel Must Keep Its Agreement with the Lord (29.2—30.20)
- Joshua Is Appointed Leader of Israel (31.1-13)
- Israel Will Reject the Lord (31.14-29)
- The Song of Moses (31.30—32.47)
- Moses Sees the Land and Blesses the Tribes of Israel (32.48—33.29)
- The Death of Moses (34.1-12)

The Final Speeches of Moses

1
1-5 This book contains the speeches that Moses made while Israel was in the land of Moab, camped near the town of Suph in the desert east of the Jordan River. The town of Paran was in one direction from their camp, and the towns of Tophel, Laban, Hazeroth, and Dizahab[a] were in the opposite direction.

Earlier, Moses had defeated the Amorite King Sihon of Heshbon. Moses had also de-

[a] **1.1-5** *Suph . . . Paran . . . Tophel, Laban, Hazeroth, and Dizahab*: The exact location of these towns is not known.

1.1-5 Nu 21.21-35.

feated King Og of Bashan, who used to live
in Ashtaroth for part of the year and in
Edrei for the rest of the year.
Although it takes only eleven days to
walk from Mount Sinai[b] to Kadesh-Barnea
by way of the Mount Seir Road, these
speeches were not made until forty years
after Israel left Egypt.[c]

The First Speech: Moses Reviews the Past

The LORD's Command at Mount Sinai

The LORD had given Moses his laws for
the people of Israel. And on the first day of
the eleventh month,[d] Moses began explaining those laws by saying:
6 People of Israel, when we were in our
camp at Mount Sinai,[e] the LORD our God
told us:

> You have stayed here long enough.
> 7 Leave this place and go into the land
> that belongs to the Amorites and their
> neighbors the Canaanites. This land
> includes the Jordan River valley, the
> hill country, the western foothills, the
> Southern Desert, the Mediterranean
> seacoast, the Lebanon Mountains, and
> all the territory as far as the Euphrates
> River. 8 I give you this land, just as I
> promised your ancestors Abraham,
> Isaac, and Jacob. Now you must go
> and take the land.

Leaders Were Appointed

(Exodus 18.13-27)

Moses said:
9 Right after the LORD commanded us to
leave Mount Sinai,[e] I told you:

> Israel, being your leader is too big a
> job for one person. 10 The LORD our
> God has blessed us, and so now there
> are as many of us as there are stars in
> the sky. 11 God has even promised to
> bless us a thousand times more, and I
> pray that he will. 12 But I cannot take
> care of all your problems and settle all
> your arguments alone. 13 Each tribe
> must choose some experienced men
> who are known for their wisdom and
> understanding, and I will make those
> men the official leaders of their
> tribes.

14 You answered, "That's a good idea!"
15 Then I took these men, who were already wise and respected leaders, and I appointed them as your official leaders. Some
of them became military officers in charge
of groups of a thousand, or a hundred, or
fifty, or ten, 16 and others became judges. I
gave these judges the following instructions:

> When you settle legal cases, your
> decisions must be fair. It doesn't mat-
> ter if the case is between two Is-
> raelites, or between an Israelite and a
> foreigner living in your community.
> 17 And it doesn't matter if one is help-
> less and the other is powerful. Don't be
> afraid of anyone! No matter who
> shows up in your court, God will help
> you make a fair decision.
>
> If any case is too hard for you, bring
> the people to me, and I will make the
> decision.

18 After I gave these instructions to the
judges, I taught you the LORD's commands.

Men Were Sent To Explore the Hill Country

(Numbers 13.1-33)

Moses said to Israel:
19 The LORD had commanded us to
leave Mount Sinai[e] and go to the hill country that belonged to the Amorites, so we
started out into the huge desert. You remember how frightening it was, but soon
we were at Kadesh-Barnea, 20-21 and I told
you, "We have reached the hill country. It
belongs to the Amorites now, but the LORD
our God is giving it to us. He is the same
God our ancestors worshiped, and he has
told us to go in and take this land, so don't
hesitate and be afraid."

[b] **1.1-5** *Mount Sinai*: The Hebrew text has "Horeb," another name for Mount Sinai.
[c] **1.1-5** *Egypt*: The Israelites would soon enter Canaan, but they would have entered the land of Canaan from Kadesh-Barnea forty years earlier if they had not rebelled against God (see verses 6-40).
[d] **1.1-5** *eleventh month*: Shebat, the eleventh month of the Hebrew calendar, from about mid-January to mid-February.
[e] **1.6,9,19** *Mount Sinai*: See the note at 1.1-5.

22 Then all of you came to me and said, "Before we go into the land, let's send some men to explore it. When they come back, they can tell us about the towns we will find and what roads we should take to get there."

23 It seemed like a good idea, so I chose twelve men, one from each tribe. 24 They explored the hill country as far as Bunch Valley[f] 25 and even brought back some of the fruit. They said, "The LORD our God is giving us good land."

Israel Refused To Obey the LORD
(Numbers 14.1-45)

Moses said to Israel:

26 You did not want to go into the land, and you refused to obey the LORD your God. 27 You stayed in your tents and grumbled, "The LORD must hate us—he brought us out of Egypt, just so he could hand us over to the Amorites and get rid of us. 28 We are afraid, because the men who explored the land told us that the cities are large, with walls that reach to the sky. The people who live there are taller and stronger than we are,[g] and some of them are Anakim.[h] We have nowhere to go."

29 Then I said, "Don't worry! 30 The LORD our God will lead the way. He will fight on our side, just as he did when we saw him do all those things to the Egyptians. 31 And you know that the LORD has taken care of us the whole time we've been in the desert, just as you might carry one of your children."

32 But you still would not trust the LORD, 33 even though he had always been with us in the desert. During the daytime, the LORD was in the cloud, leading us in the right direction and showing us where to camp. And at night, he was there in the fire.[i]

34 You had made the LORD angry, and he said:

> 35 You people of this generation are evil, and I refuse to let you go into the good land that I promised your ancestors. 36 Caleb son of Jephunneh is the only one of your generation that I will allow to go in. He obeyed me completely, so I will give him and his descendants the land he explored.

37 The LORD was even angry with me because of you people, and he said, "Moses, I won't let you go into the land either. 38 Instead, I will let Joshua[j] your assistant lead Israel to conquer the land. So encourage him."

39 Then the LORD spoke to you again:

> People of Israel, you said that your innocent young children would be taken prisoner in the battle for the land. But someday I will let them go into the land, and with my help they will conquer it and live there.
>
> 40 Now, turn around and go back into the desert by way of Red Sea[k] Road.

41 Then you told me, "We disobeyed the LORD our God, but now we want to obey him. We will go into the hill country and fight, just as he told us to do." So you picked up your weapons, thinking it would be easy to take over the hill country.

42 But the LORD said, "Moses, warn them not to go into the hill country. I won't help them fight, and their enemies will defeat them."

43 I told you what the LORD had said, but you paid no attention. You disobeyed him and went into the hill country anyway. You thought you were so great! 44 But when the Amorites in the hill country attacked from their towns, you ran from them as you would run from a swarm of bees. The Amorites chased your troops into Seir[l] as

[f] **1.24** *Bunch Valley*: Or "Eshcol Valley," famous for its large bunches of grapes. [g] **1.28** *The people . . . we are*: Most Hebrew manuscripts; a few Hebrew manuscripts and one ancient translation "the people who live there are stronger than we are, and there are more of them than there are of us." [h] **1.28** *Anakim*: Perhaps a group of very tall people that lived in or near Palestine before the Israelites. See also 2.10, 11, 20, 21; Numbers 13.33. [i] **1.33** *the cloud . . . the fire*: See Exodus 40.34-38; Numbers 9.15-23. [j] **1.38** *Joshua*: Hebrew "Joshua son of Nun." [k] **1.40** *Red Sea*: Hebrew *yam suph*, here referring to the Gulf of Aqaba, since the term is extended to include the northeastern arm of the Red Sea (see also the note at 11.4). [l] **1.44** *Seir*: An area of hills and mountains that was part of the territory of Edom.

1.26 Dt 9.23; He 3.16. **1.31** Ac 13.18. **1.32** He 3.19. **1.34,35** He 3.18.

far as Hormah, killing them as they went.
45 Then you came back to the place of worship at Kadesh-Barnea and wept, but the
LORD would not listen to your prayers.

Israel Spent Years in the Desert

Moses said to Israel:

46 After we had been in Kadesh for a
few months, we obeyed the LORD and
headed back into the desert by way of Red
2 Sea[m] Road. 1 We spent many years
wandering around outside the hill
country of Seir,[n] 2 until the LORD said:

Moses, 3 Israel has wandered in
these hills long enough. Turn and go
north. 4 And give the people these orders: "Be very careful, because you will
soon go through the land that belongs
to your relatives, the descendants of
Esau.[o] They are afraid of you, 5 but
don't start a war with them. I have
given them the hill country of Seir, so I
won't give any of it to you, not even
enough to set a foot on. 6 And as you
go through their land, you will have to
buy food and water from them."

7 The LORD has helped us and taken
care of us during the past forty years that
we have been in this huge desert. We've
had everything we needed, and the LORD
has blessed us and made us successful in
whatever we have done.

8 We went past the territory that belonged to our relatives, the descendants of
Esau.[p] We followed Arabah Road that starts
in the south at Elath and Ezion-Geber,
then we turned onto the desert road that
leads to Moab.

9 The LORD told me, "Don't try to start a
war with Moab. Leave them alone, because
I gave the land of Ar[q] to them,[r] and I will
not let you have any of it."

Tribes That Lived near Canaan

10 Before the LORD gave the Moabites
their land, a large and powerful tribe lived
there. They were the Emim, and they were
as tall as the Anakim. 11 The Moabites
called them Emim, though others sometimes used the name Rephaim[s] for both
the Anakim and the Emim.

12 The Horites used to live in Seir, but
the Edomites[t] took over that region. They
killed many of the Horites and forced the
rest of them to leave, just as Israel did to
the people in the land that the LORD gave
them.

Israel Crossed the Zered Gorge

Moses said to Israel:

13 When we came to the Zered Gorge
along the southern border of Moab, the
LORD told us to cross the gorge into Moab,
and we did. 14 This was thirty-eight years
after we left Kadesh-Barnea, and by that
time all the men who had been in the army
at Kadesh-Barnea had died, just as the
LORD had said they would. 15-16 The LORD
kept getting rid of[u] them until finally none
of them were left.

17 Then the LORD told me, 18 "Moses,
now go past the town of Ar and cross
Moab's northern border 19 into Ammon.
But don't start a war with the Ammonites. I
gave them[v] their land, and I won't give any
of it to Israel."

[m] **1.46** *Red Sea*: See the notes at 1.40; 11.4. [n] **2.1** *hill country of Seir*: See the note at 1.44. [o] **2.4** *your relatives, the descendants of Esau*: Esau was the brother of Jacob, the ancestor of the nation of Israel. Esau's descendants were also known as the nation of Edom. [p] **2.8** *We went past . . . Esau*: According to Numbers 20.14-21, the king of Edom did not let the Israelites go through his land. [q] **2.9** *Ar*: One of the main cities of Moab (see Numbers 21.28); sometimes it may have stood for the whole territory of Moab. [r] **2.9** *them*: The Hebrew text has "the descendants of Lot"; the nation of Moab descended from Moab, who was the son of Lot, the nephew of Abraham. [s] **2.10,11** *Emim . . . Anakim . . . Rephaim*: These may refer to a group or groups of very tall people that lived in or near Palestine before the Israelites (see also Numbers 13.33). [t] **2.12** *Edomites*: The Hebrew text has "the descendants of Esau," who became the nation of Edom. [u] **2.15,16** *getting rid of*: Or "sending diseases on." [v] **2.19** *them*: The Hebrew text has "descendants of Lot"; the nation of Ammon descended from Benammi, who was the son of Lot, the nephew of Abraham.

2.1 Nu 21.4. **2.4** Gn 36.8. **2.9** Gn 19.37. **2.14** Nu 14.27-35. **2.19** Gn 19.38.

More Nations That Lived near Canaan

[20] Before the Ammonites conquered the land that the LORD had given them, some of the Rephaim used to live there, although the Ammonites called them Zamzummim. [21] The Zamzummim were a large and powerful tribe and were as tall as the Anakim.[w] But the LORD helped the Ammonites, and they killed many of the Zamzummim and forced the rest to leave. Then the Ammonites settled there. [22] The LORD helped them as he had helped the Edomites,[x] who killed many of the Horites in Seir and forced the rest to leave before settling there themselves.

[23] A group called the Avvim used to live in villages as far south as Gaza, but the Philistines[y] killed them and settled on their land.

Israel Crossed the Arnon Gorge

Moses said:

[24] After we went through Ammon, the LORD told us:

Israel, pack up your possessions, take down your tents, and cross the Arnon River gorge.[z] The territory of the Amorite King Sihon of Heshbon lies on the other side of the river, but I now give you his land. So attack and take it! [25] Today I will start making all other nations afraid of you. They will tremble with fear when anyone mentions you, and they will be terrified when you show up.

The Defeat of King Sihon of Heshbon

(*Numbers 21.21-30*)

Moses said to Israel:

[26] After we had crossed the Arnon and had set up camp in the Kedemoth Desert, I sent messengers to King Sihon of Heshbon, telling him that his nation and ours could be at peace. I said:

[27] Please let Israel go across your country. We will walk straight through, without turning off the road. [28-29] You can even sell us food and water, and we will pay with silver. We need to reach the Jordan River and cross it, because the LORD our God is giving us the land on the west side. The Edomites and Moabites[a] have already let us cross their land. Please let us cross your land as well.

[30-31] But Sihon refused to let us go across his country, because the LORD made him stubborn and eager to fight us. The LORD told me, "I am going to help you defeat Sihon and take his land, so attack him!"

[32] We met Sihon and his army in battle at Jahaz, [33] and the LORD our God helped us defeat them. We killed Sihon, his sons, and everyone else in his army. [34] Then we captured and destroyed every town in Sihon's kingdom, killing everyone, [35] but keeping the livestock and everything else of value. [36] The LORD helped us capture every town from the Arnon River gorge north to the boundary of Gilead, including the town of Aroer on the edge of the gorge and the town in the middle of the gorge.

[37] However, we stayed away from all the Ammonite towns, both in the hill country and near the Jabbok River, just as the LORD had commanded.

The Defeat of King Og of Bashan

(*Numbers 21.31-35*)

Moses said to Israel:

3 When we turned onto the road that leads to Bashan, King Og of Bashan led out his whole army to fight us at Edrei. [2] But the LORD told me, "Moses, don't be afraid of King Og. I am going to help you defeat him and his army and take over his land. Destroy him and his people, just as you did with the Amorite King Sihon of Heshbon."

[3-6] The LORD our God helped us destroy Og and his army and conquer his entire kingdom of Bashan, including the Argob region. His kingdom had lots of villages and

[w]**2.21** *Anakim*: See the note at 2.10, 11. [x]**2.22** *Edomites*: See the note at 2.12.
[y]**2.23** *Philistines*: The Hebrew text has "the Caphtorim from Caphtor," probably referring to the Philistines who originally came from Crete. [z]**2.24** *Arnon River gorge*: The northern boundary of Moab's territory and the southern boundary of Sihon's kingdom. [a]**2.28,29** *Edomites and Moabites*: Hebrew "descendants of Esau, who live in Seir and Moabites who live in Ar."

Sarah laughs when she hears that she will have a baby.

Genesis 18.1-15

Joseph and his brothers *Genesis 37.3-4*

sixty towns with high walls and gates that locked with bars. We completely destroyed[b] them all, killing everyone, 7 but keeping the livestock and everything else of value.

8 Sihon and Og had ruled Amorite kingdoms east of the Jordan River. Their land stretched from the Arnon River gorge in the south to Mount Hermon in the north, and we captured it all. 9 Mount Hermon is called Mount Sirion by the people of Sidon, and it is called Mount Senir by the Amorites. 10 We captured all the towns in the highlands, all of Gilead, and all of Bashan as far as Salecah and Edrei, two of the towns that Og had ruled.

Og's Coffin

11 King Og was the last of the Rephaim,[c] and his coffin[d] is in the town of Rabbah in Ammon. It is made of hard black rock[e] and is thirteen and a half feet long and six feet wide.

The Land East of the Jordan River Is Divided

(Numbers 32.1-42)

Moses said to Israel:

12-17 I gave some of the land and towns we captured to the tribes of Reuben and Gad. Their share started at the Arnon River gorge in the south, took in the town of Aroer on the edge of the gorge, and went far enough north to include the southern half of the Gilead region. The northern part of their land went as far east as the upper Jabbok River gorge, which formed their border with the Ammonites.[f] I also gave them the eastern side of the Jordan River valley, from Lake Galilee[g] south to the Dead Sea[h] below the slopes of Mount Pisgah.

I gave the northern half of Gilead and all of the Bashan region to half the tribe of Manasseh.[i] Bashan had belonged to King Og, and the Argob region in Bashan used to be called the Land of the Rephaim. Jair from the Manasseh tribe conquered the Argob region as far west as the kingdoms of Geshur and Maacah. The Israelites even started calling Bashan by the name "Villages of Jair,"[j] and that is still its name. I gave the northern half of Gilead to the Machir clan.[k]

18-19 At that time I told the men of Reuben, Gad, and East Manasseh:

> The LORD our God told me to give you this land with its towns, and that's what I have done. Now your wives and children can stay here with your large flocks of sheep and goats and your large herds of cattle. But all of you men that can serve in our army must cross the Jordan River and help the other tribes, because they are your relatives. 20 The LORD will let them defeat the enemy nations on the west side of the Jordan and take their land. Afterwards, you can come back here to the land I gave you.

21-22 Then I told Joshua, "You saw how the LORD our God helped us destroy King Sihon and King Og. So don't be afraid! Wherever you go, the LORD will fight on your side and help you destroy your enemies."

God Refused To Let Moses Enter Canaan

Moses said to Israel:

23 At that time I prayed and begged, 24 "Our LORD, it seems that you have just begun to show me your great power. No other god in the sky or on earth is

[b]**3.3-6** *completely destroyed*: The Hebrew word means that the town was given completely to the LORD, and since it could not be used for normal purposes any more, it had to be destroyed. Every person was killed and sometimes all the animals as well. [c]**3.11** *Rephaim*: See the note at 2.10, 11. [d]**3.11** *coffin*: Or "bed." [e]**3.11** *hard black rock*: The Hebrew text has "iron," which probably refers to basalt, a hard black rock. [f]**3.12-17** *The northern part . . . border with the Ammonites*: The Jabbok River flowed from south to north, then it turned west and formed the northern border of the land belonging to the Reuben and Gad tribes. [g]**3.12-17** *Lake Galilee*: The Hebrew text has "Lake Chinnereth," an earlier name. [h]**3.12-17** *the Dead Sea*: Hebrew "the Sea of the Arabah, the Salt Sea." [i]**3.12-17** *half the tribe of Manasseh*: Or "East Manasseh." [j]**3.12-17** *Villages of Jair*: Or "Havvoth-Jair." [k]**3.12-17** *Machir clan*: One of the clans of the Manasseh tribe.

3.18-20 Js 1.12-15. **3.23-27** Nu 27.12-14; Dt 32.48-52.

able to do the mighty things that you do. 25 The land west of the Jordan is such good land. Please let me cross the Jordan and see the hills and the Lebanon Mountains."

26 But the LORD was angry with me because of you people,[l] and he refused to listen. "That's enough!" he said. "I don't want to hear any more. 27 Climb to the top of Mount Pisgah and look north, south, east, and west. Take a good look, but you are not going to cross the Jordan River. 28 Joshua will lead Israel across the Jordan to take the land, so help him be strong and brave and tell him what he must do."

29 After this we stayed in the valley at Beth-Peor.

Israel Must Obey God

Moses said:

4 Israel, listen to these laws and teachings! If you obey them, you will live, and you will go in and take the land that the LORD is giving you. He is the God your ancestors worshiped, 2 and now he is your God. I am telling you everything he has commanded, so don't add anything or take anything away.

3 You saw how he killed everyone who worshiped the god Baal Peor.[m] 4 But all of you that were faithful to the LORD your God are still alive today.

5-8 No other nation has laws that are as fair as the ones the Lord my God told me to give you. If you faithfully obey them when you enter the land, you will show other nations how wise you are. In fact, everyone that hears about your laws will say, "That great nation certainly is wise!" And what makes us greater than other nations? We have a God who is close to us and answers our prayers.

9 You must be very careful not to forget the things you have seen God do for you. Keep reminding yourselves, and tell your children and grandchildren as well. 10 Do you remember the day you stood in the LORD's presence at Mount Sinai?[n] The LORD said, "Moses, bring the people of Israel here. I want to speak to them so they will obey me as long as they live, and so they will teach their children to obey me too."

11 Mount Sinai[n] was surrounded by deep dark clouds, and fire went up to the sky. You came to the foot of the mountain, 12 and the LORD spoke to you from the fire. You could hear him and understand what he was saying, but you couldn't see him. 13 The LORD said he was making an agreement with you, and he told you that your part of the agreement is to obey the Ten Commandments. Then the LORD wrote these Commandments on two flat stones.

14 That's when the LORD commanded me to give you the laws and teachings you must obey in the land that you will conquer west of the Jordan River.

Don't Worship Idols

Moses said to Israel:

15 When God spoke to you from the fire, he was invisible. So be careful 16 not to commit the sin of worshiping idols. Don't make idols to be worshiped, whether they are shaped like men, women, 17 animals, birds, 18 reptiles, or fish. 19 And when you see the sun or moon or stars, don't be tempted to bow down and worship them. The LORD put them there for all the other nations to worship. 20 But you are the LORD's people, because he led you through fiery trials and rescued you from Egypt.

21 The LORD was angry at me because of what you said,[o] and he told me that he would not let me cross the Jordan River into the good land that he is giving you.[p] 22 So I must stay here and die on this side of the Jordan, but you will cross the river and take the land.

[l] **3.26** *But the LORD . . . people*: See 1.37. [m] **4.3** *Baal Peor*: See Numbers 25.1-9.
[n] **4.10,11** *Mount Sinai*: See the note at 1.1-5. [o] **4.21** *what you said*: Or "you people."
[p] **4.21** *The LORD was angry . . . giving you*: See 1.37; 3.26.

4.2 Rev 22.18, 19. **4.3** Nu 25.1-9. **4.5-8** 3 Macc 3.5. **4.11,12** Ex 19.16-18; He 12.18, 19. **4.13** Ex 31.18; 34.28; Dt 9.9-11. **4.14** Ex 21.1. **4.16** Ex 20.4; Lv 26.1; Dt 5.8; 27.14-26. **4.17,18** Ro 1.23. **4.20** Ex 19.5; Dt 7.6; 14.2; 26.18; Titus 2.14; 1 P 2.9. **4.21** Nu 20.12.

23 Always remember the agreement that the LORD your God made with you, and don't make an idol in any shape or form. 24 The LORD will be angry if you worship other gods, and he can be like a fire destroying everything in its path.

25-26 Soon you will cross the Jordan River and settle down in the land. Then in the years to come, you will have children, and they will give you grandchildren. After many years, you might lose your sense of right and wrong and make idols, even though the LORD your God hates them. So I am giving you fair warning today, and I call the earth and the sky as witnesses. If you ever make idols, the LORD will be angry, and you won't have long to live, because the LORD will let you be wiped out. 27 Only a few of you will survive, and the LORD will force you to leave the land and will scatter you among the nations. 28 There you will have to worship gods made of wood and stone, and these are nothing but idols that can't see or hear or eat or smell.

29-30 In all of your troubles, you may finally decide that you want to worship only the LORD. And if you turn back to him and obey him completely, he will again be your God. 31 The LORD your God will have mercy—he won't destroy you or desert you. The LORD will remember his promise, and he will keep the agreement he made with your ancestors.

32-34 When the LORD your God brought you out of Egypt, you saw how he fought for you and showed his great power by performing terrifying miracles. You became his people, and at Mount Sinai you heard him talking to you out of fiery flames. And yet you are still alive! Has anything like this ever happened since the time God created humans? No matter where you go or who you ask, you will get the same answer. No one has ever heard of another god even trying to do such things as the LORD your God has done for you.

35-36 The LORD wants you to know he is the only true God, and he wants you to obey him. That's why he let you see his mighty miracles and his fierce fire on earth, and why you heard his voice from that fire and from the sky.

37 The LORD loved your ancestors and decided that you would be his people. So the LORD used his great power to bring you out of Egypt. 38 Now you face other nations more powerful than you are, but the LORD has already started forcing them out of their land and giving it to you.

39 So remember that the LORD is the only true God, whether in the sky above or on the earth below. 40 Today I am explaining his laws and teachings. And if you always obey them, you and your descendants will live long and be successful in the land the LORD is giving you.

Safe Towns

41-43 Moses said, "People of Israel, you must set aside the following three towns east of the Jordan River as Safe Towns: Bezer in the desert highlands belonging to the Reuben tribe; Ramoth in Gilead, belonging to the Gad tribe; and Golan in Bashan, belonging to the Manasseh tribe. If you kill a neighbor without meaning to, and if you had not been angry with that person, you can run to one of these towns and find safety."[q]

THE SECOND SPEECH: MOSES TELLS WHAT THE LORD DEMANDS

Israel at Beth-Peor

44-46 The Israelites had come from Egypt and were camped east of the Jordan River near Beth-Peor, when Moses gave these laws and teachings. The land around their camp had once belonged to King Sihon of Heshbon. But Moses and the Israelites defeated him 47 and King Og of Bashan, and took their lands. These two Amorite kings had ruled the territory east of the Jordan River 48 from the town of Aroer on the edge of the Arnon River gorge,

[q] **4.41-43** *find safety*: From the victim's clan, who might appoint one of their men to track down and put to death the killer (see also 19.1-13).

4.24 He 12.29. **4.27,28** Dt 28.36. **4.29,30** Jr 29.13; 3 Macc 2.10. **4.35,36** Mk 12.32. **4.41-43** Js 20.8, 9.

north to Mount Hermon.[r] 49 Their land included the eastern side of the Jordan River valley, as far south as the Dead Sea[s] below the slopes of Mount Pisgah.

The Ten Commandments
(Exodus 20.1-17)

5 Moses called together the people of Israel and said:

Today I am telling you the laws and teachings that you must follow, so listen carefully. 2 The LORD our God made an agreement with our nation at Mount Sinai.[t] 3 That agreement wasn't only with[u] our ancestors but with us, who are here today. 4 The LORD himself spoke to you out of the fire, 5 but you were afraid of the fire and refused to go up the mountain. So I spoke with the LORD for you, then I told you that he had said:

6 I am the LORD your God, the one who brought you out of Egypt where you were slaves.

7 Do not worship any god except me.

8 Do not make idols that look like anything in the sky or on earth or in the ocean under the earth. 9 Don't bow down and worship idols. I am the LORD your God, and I demand all your love. If you reject me and worship idols, I will punish your families for three or four generations. 10 But if you love me and obey my laws, I will be kind to your families for thousands of generations.

11 Do not misuse my name.[v] I am the LORD your God, and I will punish anyone who misuses my name.

12 Show respect for the Sabbath Day—it belongs to me. 13 You have six days when you can do your work, 14 but the seventh day of the week belongs to me, your God. No one is to work on that day—not you, your children, your oxen or donkeys or any other animal, not even those foreigners who live in your towns. And don't make your slaves do any work. 15 This special day of rest will remind you that I reached out my mighty arm and rescued you from slavery in Egypt.

16 Respect your father and mother, and you will live a long and successful life in the land I am giving you.

17 Do not murder.

18 Be faithful in marriage.

19 Do not steal.

20 Do not tell lies about others.

21 Do not want anything that belongs to someone else. Don't want anyone's wife or husband, house, land, slaves, oxen, donkeys, or anything else.

22 When we were gathered on the mountain, the LORD spoke to us in a loud voice from the dark fiery cloud. The LORD gave us these commands, and only these. Then he wrote them on two flat stones and gave them to me.

The People Were Afraid
(Exodus 20.18-21)

Moses said to Israel:

23 When fire blazed from the mountain, and you heard the voice coming from the darkness, your tribal leaders came to me 24 and said:

Today the LORD our God has shown us how powerful and glorious he is. He spoke to us from the fire, and we

[r] **4.48** *Hermon*: The Hebrew text also includes the name "Sion," probably another form of "Sirion," the name used by the Sidonians. [s] **4.49** *the Dead Sea*: Hebrew "the Sea of the Arabah."
[t] **5.2** *Mount Sinai*: See the note at 1.1-5. [u] **5.3** *wasn't only with*: Hebrew "wasn't with."
[v] **5.11** *misuse my name*: Probably includes breaking promises, telling lies after swearing to tell the truth, using the LORD's name as a curse word or a magic formula, and trying to control the LORD by using his name.

5.8,9 Lv 26.1; Dt 4.15-18; 27.14-26. **5.9,10** Ex 34.6, 7; Nu 14.18; Dt 7.9, 10. **5.11** Lv 19.12. **5.12** Ex 16.23-30; 31.12-15. **5.13,14** Ex 23.12; 31.14, 15; 34.21; 35.2; Lv 23.3. **5.16 a** Dt 27.14-26; Si 3.1-16; Mt 15.4; 19.19; Mk 7.10; 10.19; Lk 18.20; Eph 6.2; **b** Eph 6.3. **5.17** Gn 9.5, 6; Lv 24.17; Mt 5.21; 19.18; Mk 10.19; Lk 18.20; Ro 13.9; Jas 2.11. **5.18** Lv 20.10; Mt 5.27; 19.18; Mk 10.19; Lk 18.20; Ro 13.9; Jas 2.11. **5.19** Lv 19.11; Mt 19.18; Mk 10.19; Lk 18.20; Ro 13.9. **5.20** Ex 23.1; Mt 19.18; Mk 10.19; Lk 18.20. **5.21** Ro 7.7; 13.9. **5.22-27** He 12.18, 19.

learned that people can live, even though God speaks to them. [25] But we don't want to take a chance on being killed by that terrible fire, and if we keep on hearing the LORD's voice, we will die. [26] Has anyone else ever heard the only true God speaking from fire, as we have? And even if they have, would they live to tell about it? [27] Moses, go up close and listen to the LORD. Then come back and tell us, and we will do everything he says.

[28] The LORD heard you and said:

Moses, I heard what the people said to you, and I approve. [29] I wish they would always worship me with fear and trembling and be this willing to obey me! Then they and their children would always enjoy a successful life.

[30] Now, tell them to return to their tents, [31] but you come back here to me. After I tell you my laws and teachings, you will repeat them to the people, so they can obey these laws in the land I am giving them.

Moses said:

[32] Israel, you must carefully obey the LORD's commands. [33] Follow them, because they make a path that will lead to a long successful life in the land the LORD your God is giving you.

The Most Important Commandment

Moses said to Israel:

6 The LORD told me to give you these laws and teachings,[w] so you can obey them in the land he is giving you. Soon you will cross the Jordan River and take that land. [2] And if you and your descendants want to live a long time, you must always worship the LORD and obey his laws. [3] Pay attention, Israel! Our ancestors worshiped the LORD, and he promised to give us this land that is rich with milk and honey. Be careful to obey him, and you will become a successful and powerful nation.

[4] Listen, Israel! The LORD our God is the only true God![x] [5] So love the LORD your God with all your heart, soul, and strength. [6] Memorize his laws [7] and tell them to your children over and over again. Talk about them all the time, whether you're at home or walking along the road or going to bed at night, or getting up in the morning. [8] Write down copies and tie them to your wrists and foreheads to help you obey them. [9] Write these laws on the door frames of your homes and on your town gates.

Worship Only the LORD

Moses said to Israel:

[10] The LORD promised your ancestors Abraham, Isaac, and Jacob that he would give you this land. Now he will take you there and give you large towns, with good buildings that you didn't build, [11] and houses full of good things that you didn't put there. The LORD will give you wells[y] that you didn't have to dig, and vineyards and olive orchards that you didn't have to plant. But when you have eaten so much that you can't eat any more, [12] don't forget it was the LORD who set you free from slavery and brought you out of Egypt. [13] Worship and obey the LORD your God with fear and trembling, and promise that you will be loyal to him.

[14] Don't have anything to do with gods that are worshiped by the nations around you. [15] If you worship other gods, the LORD will be furious and wipe you off the face of the earth. The LORD your God is with you, [16] so don't try to make him prove that he can help you, as you did at Massah.[z] [17] Always obey the laws that the LORD has given you [18-19] and live in a way that pleases him. Then you will be able to go in and take this good land from your enemies, just as he promised your ancestors.

[20] Someday your children will ask, "Why did the LORD give us these laws and teachings?"

[w] **6.1** *these laws and teachings*: Or "the following commandment with its laws and teachings" (see 6.4, 5). [x] **6.4** *The LORD . . . true God*: Or "Only the LORD is our God." [y] **6.11** *wells*: Cisterns cut into the rock to collect rainwater. [z] **6.16** *Massah*: See Exodus 17.1-7; Numbers 20.2-13.

6.4 Mk 12.29. **6.5** Mt 22.37; Mk 12.30; Lk 10.27. **6.6-9** Dt 11.18-20. **6.10** **a** Gn 12.7; **b** Gn 26.3; **c** Gn 28.13. **6.13** Mt 4.10; Lk 4.8. **6.16** **a** Mt 4.7; Lk 4.12; **b** Ex 17.1-7.

21 Then you will answer:
We were slaves of the king of Egypt,
but the LORD used his great power and
set us free. 22 We saw him perform
miracles and make horrible things
happen to the king, his officials, and
everyone else. 23 The LORD rescued us
from Egypt, so he could bring us into
this land, as he had promised our ancestors. 24-25 That's why the LORD our
God demands that we obey his laws
and worship him with fear and trembling. And if we do, he will protect us
and help us be successful.

Force the Other Nations Out of the Land

(Exodus 34.11-16)

Moses said:

7 People of Israel, the LORD your God
will help you take the land of the Hittites, the Girgashites, the Amorites, the
Canaanites, the Perizzites, the Hivites, and
the Jebusites. These seven nations have
more people and are stronger than Israel,
but when you attack them, 2 the LORD will
force them out of the land. Then you must
destroy them without mercy. Don't make
any peace treaties with them, 3 and don't
let your sons and daughters marry any of
them. 4 If you do, those people will lead
your descendants to worship other gods
and to turn their backs on the LORD. That
will make him very angry, and he will
quickly destroy Israel.
5 So when you conquer these nations,
tear down the altars where they worship
their gods. Break up their sacred stones,
cut down the poles that they use in worshiping the goddess Asherah, and throw
their idols in the fire.

The LORD's Chosen People

Moses said:

6 Israel, you are the chosen people of
the LORD your God. There are many nations on this earth, but he chose only Israel
to be his very own. 7 You were the weakest
of all nations, 8 but the LORD chose you because he loves you and because he had
made a promise to your ancestors. Then
with his mighty arm, he rescued you from
the king of Egypt, who had made you his
slaves.
9 You know that the LORD your God is
the only true God. So love him and obey
his commands, and he will faithfully keep
his agreement with you and your descendants for a thousand generations. 10 But
if you turn against the LORD, he will
quickly destroy you. 11 So be sure to obey
his laws and teachings I am giving you
today.

The LORD Will Bless You if You Obey

(Deuteronomy 28.1-14; Leviticus 26.3-13)

Moses said to Israel:

12 If you completely obey these laws, the
LORD your God will be loyal and keep the
agreement he made with you, just as he
promised our ancestors. 13 The LORD will
love you and bless you by giving you many
children and plenty of food, wine, and olive
oil. Your herds of cattle will have many
calves, and your flocks of sheep will have
many lambs. 14 God will bless you more
than any other nation—your families will
grow and your livestock increase. 15 You
will no longer suffer with the same horrible
diseases that you sometimes had in Egypt.
You will be healthy, but the LORD will make
your enemies suffer from those diseases.

Destroy the Nations and Their Gods

Moses said to Israel:

16 When the LORD helps you defeat your
enemies, you must destroy them without
pity! And don't get trapped into worshiping
their gods.
17 You may be thinking, "How can we
destroy these nations? They are more powerful than we are." 18 But stop worrying!
Just remember what the LORD your God
did to Egypt and its king. 19 You saw how
the LORD used his tremendous power to
work great miracles and bring you out of
Egypt. And he will again work miracles for
you when you face these enemies you fear

7.1 Ac 13.19. **7.5** Dt 12.3. **7.6** Ex 19.5; Dt 4.20; 14.2; 26.18; Titus 2.14; 1 P 2.9.
7.9,10 Ex 20.5, 6; 34.6, 7; Nu 14.18; Dt 5.9, 10. **7.12-16** Dt 11.13-17.

so much. [20] Some of them may try to survive by hiding from you, but the LORD will make them panic, and soon they will be dead.[a] [21] So don't be frightened when you meet them in battle. The LORD your God is great and fearsome, and he will fight at your side.

[22] As you attack these nations, the LORD will force them out little by little. He won't let you get rid of them all at once—if he did, there wouldn't be enough people living in the land to keep down the number of wild animals. [23-24] But when you attack your enemies, the LORD will make them panic, and you will easily destroy them. You will defeat them one after another until they are gone, and no one will remember they ever lived.

[25] After you conquer a nation, burn their idols. Don't get trapped into wanting the silver or gold on an idol. Even the metal on an idol is disgusting to the LORD, [26] so destroy it. If you bring it home with you, both you and your house will be destroyed. Stay away from those disgusting idols!

The LORD Takes Care of You

Moses said:

8 Israel, do you want to go into the land the LORD promised your ancestors? Do you want to capture it, live there, and become a powerful nation? Then be sure to obey every command I am giving you.

[2] Don't forget how the LORD your God has led you through the desert for the past forty years. He wanted to find out if you were truly willing to obey him and depend on him, [3] so he made you go hungry. Then he gave you manna,[b] a kind of food that you and your ancestors had never even heard about. The LORD was teaching you that people need more than food to live—they need every word that the LORD has spoken.

[4] Over the past forty years, your clothing hasn't worn out, and your feet haven't swollen. [5] So keep in mind that the LORD has been correcting you, just as parents correct their children. [6] Obey the commands the LORD your God has given you and worship him with fear and trembling.

[7] The LORD your God is bringing you into a good land with streams that flow from springs in the valleys and hills. [8-9] You can dig for copper in those hills, and the stones are made of iron ore. And you won't go hungry. Wheat and barley fields are everywhere, and so are vineyards and orchards full of fig, pomegranate,[c] and olive trees, and there is plenty of honey.

Don't Forget the LORD

Moses said to Israel:

[10] After you eat and are full, give praise to the LORD your God for the good land he gave you. [11] Make sure that you never forget the LORD or disobey his laws and teachings that I am giving you today. If you always obey them, [12] you will have plenty to eat, and you will build good houses to live in. [13] You will get more and more cattle, sheep, silver, gold, and other possessions.

[14] But when all this happens, don't be proud! Don't forget that you were once slaves in Egypt and that it was the LORD who set you free. [15] Remember how he led you in that huge and frightening desert where poisonous snakes and scorpions live. There was no water, but the LORD split open a rock, and water poured out so you could drink. [16] He also gave you manna,[d] a kind of food your ancestors had never even heard about. The LORD was testing you to make you trust him, so that later on he could be good to you.

[17] When you become successful, don't say, "I'm rich, and I've earned it all myself." [18] Instead, remember that the LORD your God gives you the strength to make a living. That's how he keeps the promise he made to your ancestors.

[19-20] But I'm warning you—if you forget the LORD your God and worship other gods, the LORD will destroy you, just as he destroyed the nations you fought.

[a]**7.20** *make them . . . dead*: Or "send hornets to kill them." [b]**8.3** *manna*: See Exodus 16.1-36. [c]**8.8,9** *pomegranate*: A bright red fruit that looks like an apple. [d]**8.16** *manna*: See the note at 8.3.

8.3 Mt 4.4; Lk 4.4. **8.5** Ws 11.8-10. **8.11-16** Ho 13.5, 6.

Why the LORD Will Help Israel

Moses said:

9 Israel, listen to me! You will soon cross the Jordan River and go into the land to force out the nations that live there. They are more powerful than you are, and the walls around their cities reach to the sky. 2 Some of these nations are descendants of the Anakim.[e] You know how tall and strong they are, and you've heard that no one can defeat them in battle. 3 But the LORD your God has promised to go ahead of you, like a raging fire burning everything in its path. So when you attack your enemies, it will be easy for you to destroy them and take their land.

4-6 After the LORD helps you wipe out these nations and conquer their land, don't think he did it because you are such good people. You aren't good—you are stubborn! No, the LORD is going to help you, because the nations that live there are evil, and because he wants to keep the promise he made to your ancestors Abraham, Isaac, and Jacob.

When Israel Made an Idol

(Exodus 32)

Moses said to Israel:

7 Don't ever forget how you kept rebelling and making the LORD angry the whole time you were in the desert. You rebelled from the day you left Egypt until the day you arrived here.

8 At Mount Sinai[f] you made the LORD so angry that he was going to destroy you. 9-11 It happened during those forty days and nights that I was on the mountain, without anything to eat or drink. He had told me to come up there so he could give me the agreement he made with us. And this agreement was actually the same Ten Commandments[g] he had announced to you when he spoke from the fire on the mountain. The LORD had written them on two flat stones with his own hand. But after giving me the two stones, 12 he said:

> Moses, hurry down the mountain to those people you led out of Egypt. They have already disobeyed me and committed the terrible sin of making an idol.
>
> 13 I've been watching the Israelites, and I've seen how stubborn and rebellious they are. 14 So don't try to stop me! I am going to wipe them out, and no one on earth will remember they ever lived. Then I will let your descendants become an even bigger and more powerful nation than Israel.

Moses said:

15 Fire was raging on the mountaintop as I went back down, carrying the two stones with the commandments on them. 16 I saw how quickly you had sinned and disobeyed the LORD your God. There you were, worshiping the metal idol you had made in the shape of a calf. 17 So I threw down the two stones and smashed them before your very eyes.

18-20 I bowed down at the place of worship and prayed to the LORD, without eating or drinking for forty days and nights. You had committed a terrible sin by making that idol, and the LORD hated what you had done. He was angry enough to destroy all of you and Aaron as well. So I prayed for you and Aaron as I had done before, and this time the LORD answered my prayers.[h]

21 It was a sin for you to make that idol, so I threw it into the fire to melt it down. Then I took the lump of gold, ground it into powder, and threw the powder into the stream flowing down the mountain.

22 You also made the LORD angry when you were staying at Taberah,[i] at Massah,[j] and at Kibroth-Hattaavah.[k] 23 Then at Kadesh-Barnea the LORD said, "I am giving you the land, so go ahead and take it!" But since you didn't trust the LORD, you

[e]**9.2** *Anakim*: See the note at 2.10, 11. [f]**9.8** *Mount Sinai*: See the note at 1.1-5. [g]**9.9-11** *Ten Commandments*: Hebrew "commandments." [h]**9.18-20** *as I had done before . . . prayers*: This may refer to Moses' praying for Israel before he came down from the mountain (see Exodus 32.11-14). [i]**9.22** *Taberah*: See Numbers 11.1-3. [j]**9.22** *Massah*: See the note at 6.16. [k]**9.22** *Kibroth-Hattaavah*: See Numbers 11.31-34.

9.9-11 Ex 24.17, 18. **9.22** **a** Nu 11.3; **b** Ex 17.7; **c** Nu 11.34. **9.23** **a** Nu 13.17; **b** Dt 1.20, 21; **c** Nu 13.31; Dt 1.26; He 3.16.

rebelled and disobeyed his command.[l] 24 In fact, you've rebelled against the LORD for as long as he has[m] known you.

25 After you had made the idol in the shape of a calf, the LORD said he was going to destroy you. So I bowed down in front of the sacred tent for forty days and nights, 26 and I prayed:

Our LORD, please don't wipe out your people. You used your great power to rescue them from Egypt and to make them your very own. 27 Israel's ancestors Abraham, Isaac, and Jacob obeyed you faithfully. Think about them, and not about Israel's stubbornness, evil, and sin. 28 If you destroy your people, the Egyptians will say, "The LORD promised to give Israel land, but he wasn't powerful enough to keep his promise. In fact, he hated them so much that he took them into the desert and killed them." 29 But you, our LORD, chose the people of Israel to be your own, and with your mighty power you rescued them from Egypt.

The Second Set of Commandments
(Exodus 34.1-10)

Moses said to the people:

10 The LORD told me to chisel out two flat stones, just like the ones he had given me earlier. He also commanded me to make a wooden chest, then come up the mountain and meet with him. 2 He told me that he would write the same words on the new stones that he had written on the ones I broke, and that I could put these stones in this sacred chest.

3 So I made a chest out of acacia wood, and I chiseled two flat stones like the ones I broke. Then I carried the stones up the mountain, 4 where the LORD wrote the Ten Commandments on them, just as he had done the first time. The commandments were exactly what he had announced from the fire, when you were gathered at the mountain.

After the LORD returned the stones to me, 5 I took them down the mountainside and put them in the chest, just as he had commanded. And they are still there.

Aaron Died
(Numbers 20.22-29)

Moses said to Israel:

6 Later we set up camp at the wells belonging to the descendants of Jaakan.[n] Then we moved on and camped at Moserah, where Aaron died and was buried, and his son Eleazar became the priest. 7 Next, we camped at Gudgodah and then at Jotbathah, where there are flowing streams.

The Levites Were Appointed To Carry the Chest

Moses said to Israel:

8 After I put the two stones in the sacred chest,[o] the LORD chose the tribe of Levi, not only to carry the chest, but also to serve as his priests at the place of worship and to bless the other tribes in his name. And they still do these things. 9 The LORD promised that he would always provide for the tribe of Levi, and that's why he won't give them any land, when he divides it among the other tribes.

The LORD Answered the Prayers of Moses
(Exodus 34.9, 10, 27-29)

Moses said to Israel:

10 When I had taken the second set of stones up the mountain, I spent forty days and nights there, just as I had done before. Once again, the LORD answered my prayer and did not destroy you. 11 Instead, he told me, "Moses, get ready to lead the people into the land that I promised their ancestors."[p]

What the LORD Wants

Moses said:

12 People of Israel, what does the LORD your God want from you? The LORD wants

[l] **9.23** *Kadesh-Barnea . . . you rebelled and disobeyed his command*: See Numbers 13, 14.
[m] **9.24** *he has*: The Samaritan Hebrew Text and one ancient translation; the Standard Hebrew Text "I have." [n] **10.6** *the wells . . . Jaakan*: Or "Beeroth Bene-Jaakan." [o] **10.8** *After . . . chest*: Or "After Israel reached Jotbathah." [p] **10.11** *lead . . . ancestors*: The LORD would later tell Moses that he would not be allowed to enter the land (see 1.37; 3.23-28; Numbers 20.10-12).
10.6 Nu 20.28; 33.38. **10.8** Nu 3.5-8. **10.10** Ex 34.28.

you to respect and follow him, to love and serve him with all your heart and soul, 13 and to obey his laws and teachings that I am giving you today. Do this, and all will go well for you.

14 Everything belongs to the LORD your God, not only the earth and everything on it, but also the sky and the highest heavens. 15 Yet the LORD loved your ancestors and wanted them to belong to him. So he chose them and their descendants rather than any other nation, and today you are still his people.

16 Remember your agreement with the LORD and stop being so stubborn. 17 The LORD your God is more powerful than all other gods and lords, and his tremendous power is to be feared. His decisions are always fair, and you cannot bribe him to change his mind. 18 The LORD defends the rights of orphans and widows. He cares for foreigners and gives them food and clothing. 19 And you should also care for them, because you were foreigners in Egypt.

20 Respect the LORD your God, serve only him, and make promises in his name alone. 21 Offer your praises to him, because you have seen him work such terrifying miracles for you.

22 When your ancestors went to live in Egypt, there were only seventy of them. But the LORD has blessed you, and now there are more of you than there are stars in the sky.

If You Are Loyal to the LORD, He Will Bless You

Moses said to Israel:

11 The LORD is your God, so you must always love him and obey his laws and teachings. 2 Remember, he corrected you and not your children. You are the ones who saw the LORD use his great power 3 when he worked miracles in Egypt, making terrible things happen to the king and all his people. 4 And when the Egyptian army chased you in their chariots, you saw the LORD drown them and their horses in the Red Sea.[q] Egypt still suffers from that defeat!

5 You saw what the LORD did for you while you were in the desert, right up to the time you arrived here. 6 And you saw how the LORD made the ground open up in the middle of our camp underneath the tents of Dathan and Abiram,[r] who were swallowed up along with their families, their animals, and their tents.

7 With your own eyes, you saw the LORD's mighty power do all these things.

8 Soon you will cross the Jordan River, and if you obey the laws and teachings I'm giving you today, you will be strong enough to conquer the land 9 that the LORD promised your ancestors and their descendants. It's rich with milk and honey, and you will live there and enjoy it for a long time. 10 It's better land than you had in Egypt, where you had to struggle just to water your crops.[s] 11 But the hills and valleys in the promised land are watered by rain from heaven,[t] 12 because the LORD your God keeps his eye on this land and takes care of it all year long.

13 The LORD your God commands you to love him and to serve him with all your heart and soul. If you obey him, 14-15 he will send rain at the right seasons,[u] so you will have more than enough food, wine, and olive oil, and there will be plenty of grass for your cattle.

16 But watch out! You will be tempted to turn your backs on the LORD. And if you

[q] **11.4** *Red Sea*: Hebrew *yam suph* "Sea of Reeds," one of the marshes or fresh water lakes near the eastern part of the Nile Delta. This identification is based on Exodus 13.7—14.9, which lists towns on the route of the Israelites before crossing the sea. In the Greek translation of the Scriptures made about 200 B.C., the "Sea of Reeds," was named "Red Sea." [r] **11.6** *Dathan and Abiram*: Hebrew "Dathan and Abiram, the sons of Eliab from the Reuben tribe." [s] **11.10** *where . . . crops*: One possible meaning for the difficult Hebrew text. [t] **11.10,11** *to water your crops . . . rain from heaven*: Egypt was flat and had very little rain. All water for crops had to come from the Nile River. [u] **11.14,15** *rain . . . seasons*: In Palestine, almost all the rain for the year comes during the months from October through April.

10.17 1 Ti 6.15; Rev 17.14; 19.16; Ac 10.34; Ro 2.11; Ga 2.6; Eph 6.9. **10.18** Si 35.12-15. **10.22** **a** Gn 46.27; **b** Gn 15.5; 22.17. **11.3** Ex 7.8—12.13. **11.4** Ex 14.28. **11.6** Nu 16.31-33. **11.13-17** Lv 26.3-5; Dt 7.12-16; 28.1-14.

worship other gods, [17] the LORD will become angry and keep the rain from falling. Nothing will grow in your fields, and you will die and disappear from the good land that the LORD is giving you.

[18] Memorize these laws and think about them. Write down copies and tie them to your wrists and your foreheads to help you obey them. [19] Teach them to your children. Talk about them all the time—whether you're at home or walking along the road or going to bed at night, or getting up in the morning. [20] Write them on the door frames of your homes and on your town gates. [21] Then you and your descendants will live a long time in the land that the LORD promised your ancestors. Your families will live there as long as the sky is above the earth.

[22] Love the LORD your God and obey all the laws and teachings that I'm giving you today. If you live the way the LORD wants, [23] he will help you take the land. And even though the nations there are more powerful than you, the LORD will force them to leave when you attack. [24] You will capture the land everywhere you go, from the Southern Desert to the Lebanon Mountains, and from the Euphrates River west to the Mediterranean Sea. [25] No one will be able to stand up to you. The LORD will make everyone terrified of you, just as he promised.

[26] You have a choice—do you want the LORD to bless you, or do you want him to put a curse on you? [27] Today I am giving you his laws, and if you obey him, he will bless you. [28] But if you disobey him and worship those gods that have never done anything for you, the LORD will put a curse on you.

[29] After the LORD your God helps you take the land, you must have a ceremony where you announce his blessings from Mount Gerizim and his curses from Mount Ebal. [30] You know that these two mountains are west of the Jordan River in land now controlled by the Canaanites living in the Jordan River valley. The mountains are west of the road near the sacred trees of Moreh on the other side of Gilgal.

[31] Soon you will cross the Jordan River to conquer the land that the LORD your God is giving you. And when you have settled there, [32] be careful to obey his laws and teachings that I am giving you today.

Only One Place To Worship the LORD

Moses said to Israel:

12 Now I'll tell you the laws and teachings that you have to obey as long as you live. Your ancestors worshiped the LORD, and he is giving you this land. [2] But the nations that live there worship other gods. So after you capture the land, you must completely destroy their places of worship—on mountains and hills or in the shade of large trees. [3] Wherever these nations worship their gods, you must tear down their altars, break their sacred stones, burn the sacred poles[v] used in worshiping the goddess Asherah, and smash their idols to pieces. Destroy these places of worship so completely that no one will remember they were ever there. [4] Don't worship the LORD your God in the way those nations worship their gods.

[5-19] Soon you will cross the Jordan, and the LORD will help you conquer your enemies and let you live in peace, there in the land he has given you. But after you are settled, life will be different. You must not offer sacrifices just anywhere you want to. Instead, the LORD will choose a place somewhere in Israel where you must go to worship him. All of your sacrifices and offerings must be taken there, including sacrifices to please the LORD[w] and any gift you promise or voluntarily give him. That's where you must also take one tenth of your

[v] **12.3** *sacred poles*: Or "trees," used as symbols of Asherah, the goddess of fertility.

[w] **12.5-19** *sacrifices to please the LORD*: These sacrifices have traditionally been called "whole burnt offerings" because the whole animal was burned on the altar. A main purpose of such sacrifices was to please the LORD with the smell of the sacrifice, and so in the CEV they are often called "sacrifices to please the LORD."

11.18-20 Dt 6.6-9. **11.24,25** Js 1.3-5. **11.29** Dt 27.11-26; Js 8.33-35.
12.3 Dt 7.5. **12.15-19** Gn 9.4; Lv 7.26, 27; 17.10-14; 19.26; Dt 15.23.

grain, wine, and olive oil,[x] as well as the first-born of your cattle, sheep, and goats.[y] You and your family and servants will eat your gifts and sacrifices[z] and celebrate there at the place of worship, because the LORD your God has made you successful in everything you have done. And since Levites will not have any land of their own, you must ask some of them to come along and celebrate with you.

Sometimes you may want to kill an animal for food and not as a sacrifice. If the LORD has blessed you and given you enough cows or sheep or goats, then you can butcher one of them where you live. You can eat it just like the meat from a deer or gazelle that you kill when you go hunting. And even those people who are unclean and unfit for worship can have some of the meat. But you must not eat the blood of any animal—let the blood drain out on the ground.

20-21 The LORD has promised that later on he will give Israel more land, and some of you may not be able to travel all the way from your homes to the place of worship each time you are hungry for meat.[a] But the LORD will give you cattle, sheep, and goats, and you can butcher any of those animals at home and eat as much as you want. 22 It is the same as eating the meat from a deer or a gazelle that you kill when you go hunting. And in this way, anyone who is unclean and unfit for worship can have some of the meat.[b]

23-24 But don't eat the blood. It is the life of the animal, so let it drain out on the ground before you eat the meat. 25 Do you want the LORD to make you successful? Do you want your children to be successful even after you are gone? Then do what pleases the LORD and don't eat blood.

26-27 All sacrifices and offerings to the LORD must be taken to the place where he chooses to be worshiped. If you offer a sacrifice to please the LORD, all of its meat must be burned on the altar. You can eat the meat from certain kinds of sacrifices, but you must always pour out the animal's blood on the altar.

28 If you obey these laws, you will be doing what the LORD your God says is right and good. Then he will help you and your descendants be successful.

Worship the LORD in the Right Way

Moses said:

29 Israel, as you go into the land and attack the nations that are there, the LORD will get rid of them, and you can have their land.

30 But that's when you must be especially careful not to ask, "How did those nations worship their gods? Shouldn't we worship the LORD in the same way?" 31 No, you should not! The LORD hates the disgusting way those nations worship their gods, because they even burn their sons and daughters as sacrifices.

32 Obey all the laws and teachings I am giving you. Don't add any, and don't take any away.

Don't Worship Other Gods

Moses said to Israel:

13 1-2 Someday a prophet[c] may come along who is able to perform miracles or tell what will happen in the future. Then the prophet may say, "Let's start worshiping some new gods—some gods that we know nothing about." 3 If the prophet says this, don't listen! The LORD your God will be watching to find out whether or not you love him with all your heart and soul. 4 You must be completely faithful to the LORD.

[x] **12.5-19** *one tenth of your grain, wine, and olive oil*: The Israelites had to give one tenth of their harvest of these products to the LORD each year (see 14.22-29; 26.12, 13; Leviticus 27.30-33).
[y] **12.5-19** *the first-born of your cattle, sheep, and goats*: The Israelites had to sacrifice these to the LORD (see 15.19-22). [z] **12.5-19** *sacrifices*: Some sacrifices were completely burned on the altar; in other sacrifices, part of the animal was burned and part was given to the priests, but most of the meat was eaten by the worshipers as a sacred meal. [a] **12.20,21** *meat*: Usually eaten only on special occasions, such as during a sacred meal when sacrifices were offered to the LORD.
[b] **12.22** *anyone . . . the meat*: Only those who were properly prepared for worship, or "clean," could eat a sacred meal, but anyone could eat this kind of meat. [c] **13.1,2** *a prophet*: Hebrew adds "or a dreamer of dreams," another name for a prophet.

12.23,24 Lv 17.10-14. **12.32** Dt 4.2; Rev 22.18, 19.

Worship and obey only the LORD and do
this with fear and trembling, 5 because he
rescued you from slavery in Egypt.

If a prophet tells you to disobey the LORD
your God and to stop worshiping him, then
that prophet is evil and must be put to death.
6-10 Someone else may say to you, "Let's
worship other gods." That person may be
your best friend, your brother or sister, your
son or daughter, or your own dear wife or
husband. But you must not listen to people
who say such things. Instead, you must stone
them to death. You must be the first to throw
the stones, then others from the community will finish the job. Don't show any pity.

The gods worshiped by other nations
have never done anything for you or your
ancestors. People who ask you to worship
other gods are trying to get you to stop worshiping the LORD, who rescued you from
slavery in Egypt. So put to death anyone
who asks you to worship another god.
11 And when the rest of Israel hears about
it, they will be afraid, and no one else will
ever do such an evil thing again.

12 After the LORD your God gives you
towns to live in, you may hear a rumor
about one of the towns. 13 You may hear
that some worthless people have talked
everyone there into worshiping other gods,
even though these gods had never done
anything for them. 14 You must carefully
find out if the rumor is true. Then if the
people of that town have actually done
such a disgusting thing in your own country, 15 you must take your swords and kill
every one of them, and their livestock too.
16-17 Gather all the possessions of the people who lived there, and pile them up in
the marketplace, without keeping anything
for yourself. Set the pile and the whole
town on fire, and don't ever rebuild the
town. The whole town will be a sacrifice to
the LORD your God. Then he won't be angry
anymore, and he will have mercy on you
and make you successful, just as he
promised your ancestors. 18 That's why you
must do what the LORD your God says is
right. I am giving you his laws and teachings today, and you must obey them.

Don't Mourn like Other Nations

Moses said:

14 People of Israel, you are the LORD's
children, so when you mourn for
the dead, you must not cut yourselves or
shave your forehead.[d] 2 Out of all the nations on this earth, the LORD your God
chose you to be his own. You belong to the
LORD, so don't behave like those who worship other gods.

Animals That Can Be Eaten

(Leviticus 11.1-47)

3 Don't eat any disgusting animals.
4-5 You may eat the meat of cattle,
sheep, and goats; wild sheep and goats; and
gazelles, antelopes, and all kinds of deer.
6 It is all right to eat meat from any animals
that have divided hoofs and also chew the cud.[e]
7 But don't eat camels, rabbits, and rock
badgers. These animals chew the cud but do
not have divided hoofs. You must treat them
as unclean. 8 And don't eat pork, since pigs
have divided hoofs, but they do not chew
their cud. Don't even touch a dead pig!
9 You can eat any fish that has fins and
scales. But there are other creatures that
live in the water, 10 and if they do not have
fins and scales, you must not eat them.
Treat them as unclean.
11 You can eat any clean bird. 12-18 But
don't eat the meat of any of the following
birds: eagles, vultures, falcons, kites,
ravens, ostriches, owls, sea gulls, hawks,
pelicans, ospreys, cormorants, storks,
herons, and hoopoes.[f] You must not eat
bats. 19 Swarming insects are unclean, so
don't eat them. 20 However, you are allowed
to eat certain kinds of winged insects.[g]

[d] **14.1** *when you mourn . . . forehead*: Or "you must not worship Baal, cutting yourselves and shaving your forehead." [e] **14.6** *chew the cud*: Some animals that eat grass and leaves have more than one stomach, and they chew their food a second time, after it has been partly digested in the first stomach. This partly digested food is called "cud." [f] **14.12-18** *eagles . . . hoopoes*: Some of the birds in this list are difficult to identify. [g] **14.20** *certain kinds of winged insects*: These were locusts, crickets, and grasshoppers; see Leviticus 11.21, 22.

13.6-18 3 Macc 7.10. **14.1** Lv 19.27, 28; 21.5. **14.2** Ex 19.5, 6; Dt 4.20; 7.6; 26.18; Titus 2.14; 1 P 2.9. **14.3-21** 4 Macc 1.34.

21 You belong to the LORD your God, so if you happen to find a dead animal, don't eat its meat. You may give it to foreigners who live in your town or sell it to foreigners who are visiting your town.

Don't boil a young goat in its mother's milk.

Give the LORD Ten Percent of Your Harvest

Moses said:

22 People of Israel, every year you must set aside ten percent of your grain harvest. 23 Also set aside ten percent of your wine and olive oil, and the first-born of every cow, sheep, and goat. Take these to the place where the LORD chooses to be worshiped, and eat them there. This will teach you to always respect the LORD your God.

24 But suppose you can't carry that ten percent of your harvest to the place where the LORD chooses to be worshiped. If you live too far away, or if the LORD gives you a big harvest, 25 then sell this part and take the money there instead. 26 When you and your family arrive, spend the money on food for a big celebration. Buy cattle, sheep, goats, wine, beer, and if there are any other kinds of food that you want, buy those too. 27 And since people of the Levi tribe won't own any land for growing crops, remember to ask the Levites to celebrate with you.

28 Every third year, instead of using the ten percent of your harvest for a big celebration, bring it into town and put it in a community storehouse. 29 The Levites have no land of their own, so you must give them food from the storehouse. You must also give food to the poor who live in your town, including orphans, widows, and foreigners. If they have enough to eat, then the LORD your God will be pleased and make you successful in everything you do.

Loans
(Leviticus 25.1-7)

Moses said:

15 1-2 Every seven years you must announce, "The LORD says loans do not need to be paid back." Then if you have loaned money to another Israelite, you can no longer ask for payment.[h] 3 This law applies only to loans you have made to other Israelites. Foreigners will still have to pay back what you have loaned them.

4-6 No one in Israel should ever be poor. The LORD your God is giving you this land, and he has promised to make you very successful, if you obey his laws and teachings that I'm giving you today. You will lend money to many nations, but you won't have to borrow. You will rule many nations, but they won't rule you.

7 After the LORD your God gives land to each of you, there may be poor Israelites in the town where you live. If there are, then don't be mean and selfish with your money. 8 Instead, be kind and lend them what they need. 9 Be careful! Don't say to yourself, "Soon it will be the seventh year, and then I won't be able to get my money back." It would be horrible for you to think that way and to be so selfish that you refuse to help the poor. They are your relatives, and if you don't help them, they may ask the LORD to decide whether you have done wrong. And he will say that you are guilty. 10 You should be happy to give the poor what they need, because then the LORD will make you successful in everything you do.

11 There will always be some Israelites who are poor and needy. That's why I am commanding you to be generous with them.

Setting Slaves Free
(Exodus 21.1-11)

Moses said to Israel:

12 If any of you buy Israelites as slaves, you must set them free after six years. 13 And don't just tell them they are free to

[h] **15.1,2** *The LORD says . . . no longer ask for payment*: Or " 'The LORD says loans do not need to be paid back this year.' Then if you have loaned money to another Israelite, you cannot ask for payment until the next year."

14.21 Ex 23.19; 34.26. **14.22-29** Lv 27.30-33; Nu 18.21. **15.7,8** Lv 25.35. **15.11** Mt 26.11; Mk 14.7; Jn 12.8. **15.12-18** Lv 25.39-46.

leave—[14] give them sheep and goats and a good supply of grain and wine. The more the LORD has given you, the more you should give them. [15] I am commanding you to obey the LORD as a reminder that you were slaves in Egypt before he set you free. [16] But one of your slaves may say, "I love you and your family, and I would be better off staying with you, so please don't make me leave." [17] Take the slave to the door of your house and push a sharp metal rod through one earlobe and into the door. Such slaves will belong to you for life, whether they are men or women.

[18] Don't complain when you have to set a slave free. After all, you got six years of service at half the cost of hiring someone to do the work.[i]

First-Born Animals

(*Leviticus 27.26, 27; Numbers 18.15-18*)

Moses said to Israel:

[19] If the first-born animal of a cow or sheep or goat is a male, it must be given to the LORD. Don't put first-born cattle to work or cut wool from first-born sheep. [20] Instead, each year you must take the first-born of these animals to the place where the LORD your God chooses to be worshiped. You and your family will sacrifice them to the LORD and then eat them as part of a sacred meal.

[21] But if the animal is lame or blind or has something else wrong with it, you must not sacrifice it to the LORD your God. [22] You can butcher it where you live, and eat it just like the meat of a deer or gazelle that you kill while hunting. Even those people who are unclean and unfit for worship can have some. [23] But you must never eat the blood of an animal—let it drain out on the ground.

Passover

(*Exodus 12.1-20; Leviticus 23.4-8*)

Moses said:

16 People of Israel, you must celebrate Passover in the month of Abib,[j] because one night in that month years ago, the LORD your God rescued you from Egypt. [2] The Passover sacrifice must be a cow, a sheep, or a goat, and you must offer it at the place where the LORD chooses to be worshiped. [3-4] Eat all of the meat of the Passover sacrifice that same night. But don't serve bread made with yeast at the Passover meal. Serve the same kind of thin bread that you ate when you were slaves suffering in Egypt[k] and when you had to leave Egypt quickly. As long as you live, this thin bread will remind you of the day you left Egypt.

For seven days following Passover,[l] don't make any bread with yeast. In fact, there should be no yeast anywhere in Israel.

[5] Don't offer the Passover sacrifice in just any town where you happen to live. [6] It must be offered at the place where the LORD chooses to be worshiped. Kill the sacrifice at sunset, the time of day when you left Egypt.[m] [7] Then cook it and eat it there at the place of worship, returning to your tents the next morning.

[8] Eat thin bread for the next six days. Then on the seventh day, don't do any work. Instead, come together and worship the LORD.

The Harvest Festival

(*Exodus 34.22; Leviticus 23.15-21*)

Moses said to Israel:

[9] Seven weeks after you start your grain harvest, [10-11] go to the place where the LORD chooses to be worshiped and celebrate the Harvest Festival[n] in honor of the

[i] **15.18** *six years . . . work*: Or "six years of service, and it cost you no more than if you had hired someone to do the work"; or "six years of service, for what you would have had to pay a worker for two years." [j] **16.1** *in the month of Abib*: Abib (also called Nisan), the first month of the Hebrew calendar, from about mid-March to mid-April. Passover was celebrated on the evening of the fourteenth of Abib (see Exodus 12.6; Leviticus 23.4, 5). [k] **16.3,4** *the same kind . . . in Egypt*: One possible meaning for the difficult Hebrew text. [l] **16.3,4** *seven days following Passover*: This period was called the Festival of Thin Bread (see also verse 16). [m] **16.6** *sunset, the time of day when you left Egypt*: Or "sunset on the same date as when you left Egypt." [n] **16.10,11** *Harvest Festival*: Traditionally called the "Festival of Weeks," and known in New Testament times as "Pentecost."

15.19 Ex 13.12. **15.23** Gn 9.4; Lv 7.26, 27; 17.10-14; 19.26; Dt 12.5-19, 23, 24.
16.1-8 Ex 12.1-20; Lv 23.4-8; Nu 28.16-25. **16.9-12** Lv 23.15-21; Nu 28.26-31.

LORD your God. Bring him an offering as large as you can afford, depending on how big a harvest he has given you. Be sure to take along your sons and daughters and all your servants. Also invite the poor, including Levites, foreigners, orphans, and widows. 12 Remember that you used to be slaves in Egypt, so obey these laws.

The Festival of Shelters

(Leviticus 23.33-43; Numbers 29.12-38)

Moses said to Israel:

13-15 After you have finished the grain harvest and the grape harvest,[o] take your sons and daughters and all your servants to the place where the LORD chooses to be worshiped. Celebrate the Festival of Shelters for seven days. Also invite the poor, including Levites, foreigners, orphans, and widows.

The LORD will give you big harvests and make you successful in everything you do. You will be completely happy, so celebrate this festival in honor of the LORD your God.

Three Festivals at the Place of Worship

(Exodus 23.14-17)

Moses said:

16 Each year there are three festivals when all Israelite men must go to the place where the LORD chooses to be worshiped. These are the Festival of Thin Bread, the Harvest Festival,[p] and the Festival of Shelters. And don't forget to take along a gift for the LORD. 17 The bigger the harvest the LORD gives you, the bigger your gift should be.

Treat Everyone with Justice

Moses said to Israel:

18-19 After you are settled in the towns that you will receive from the LORD your God, the people in each town must appoint judges and other officers. Those of you that become judges must be completely fair when you make legal decisions, even if someone important is involved. Don't take bribes to give unfair decisions. Bribes keep people who are wise from seeing the truth and turn honest people into liars.[q]

20 People of Israel, if you want to enjoy a long and successful life, make sure that everyone is treated with justice in the land the LORD is giving you.

Don't Set Up Sacred Poles or Stones

Moses said to Israel:

21 When you build the altar for offering sacrifices to the LORD your God, don't set up a sacred pole[r] for the worship of the goddess Asherah. 22 And don't set up a sacred stone! The LORD hates these things.

Sacrifices That Have Something Wrong with Them

Moses said to Israel:

17 If an ox or a sheep has something wrong with it, don't offer it as a sacrifice to the LORD your God—he will be disgusted!

Put To Death People Who Worship Idols

Moses said to Israel:

2-3 The LORD your God is giving you towns to live in. But later, a man or a woman in your town may start worshiping other gods, or even the sun, moon, or stars.[s] I have warned you not to worship other gods, because whoever worships them is disobeying the LORD and breaking the agreement he made with you. 4 So when you hear that someone in your town is committing this disgusting sin, you must carefully find out if that person really is guilty. 5-7 But you will need two or three witnesses—one witness isn't enough to prove a person guilty.

[o] **16.13-15** *After you . . . harvest*: Leviticus 23.34 gives the exact date as the fifteenth day of the seventh month of the Hebrew calendar, which would be early in October. [p] **16.16** *Harvest Festival*: See the note at 16.10, 11. [q] **16.18,19** *turn . . . liars*: Or "keep innocent people from getting justice." [r] **16.21** *sacred pole*: See the note at 12.3. [s] **17.2,3** *sun, moon, or stars*: Some people thought these were gods and worshiped them.

16.13-15 Lv 23.33-36, 39-43; Nu 29.12-38. **16.18,19** Ex 23.6-8; Lv 19.15. **16.21** Ex 34.13. **16.22** Lv 26.1. **17.2,3** Ex 22.20. **17.5-7** **a** Nu 35.30; Dt 19.15; Mt 18.16; 2 Co 13.1; 1 Ti 5.19; He 10.28; **b** 1 Co 5.13.

Get rid of those who are guilty of such evil. Take them outside your town gates and have everyone stone them to death. But the witnesses must be the first to throw stones.

Difficult Cases

Moses said to Israel:

8-12 It may be difficult to find out the truth in some legal cases in your town. You may not be able to decide if someone was killed accidentally or murdered. Or you may not be able to tell whether an injury or some property damage was done by accident or on purpose. If the case is too difficult, take it to the court at the place where the LORD your God chooses to be worshiped.

This court will be made up of one judge and several priests[t] who serve at the LORD's altar. They will explain the law to you and give you their decision about the case. Do exactly what they tell you, or you will be put to death. 13 When other Israelites hear about it, they will be afraid and obey the decisions of the court.

The King

Moses said:

14 People of Israel, after you capture the land the LORD your God is giving you, and after you settle on it, you will say, "We want a king, just like the nations around us."

15 Go ahead and appoint a king, but make sure that he is an Israelite and that he is the one the LORD has chosen.

16 The king should not have many horses, especially those from Egypt. The LORD has said never to go back there again. 17 And the king must not have a lot of wives—they might tempt him to be unfaithful to the LORD.[u] Finally, the king must not try to get huge amounts of silver and gold.

18 The official copy of God's laws[v] will be kept by the priests of the Levi tribe. So, as soon as anyone becomes king, he must go to the priests and write out a copy of these laws while they watch. 19 Each day the king must read and obey these laws, so that he will learn to worship the LORD with fear and trembling 20 and not think that he's better than everyone else.

If the king completely obeys the LORD's commands, he and his descendants will rule Israel for many years.

Special Privileges for Priests and Levites

(*Numbers 18.8-32*)

Moses said to Israel:

18 The people of the Levi tribe, including the priests, will not receive any land. Instead, they will receive part of the sacrifices that are offered to the LORD, 2 because he has promised to provide for them in this way.

3 When you sacrifice a bull or sheep, the priests will be given the shoulder, the jaws, and the stomach.[w] 4 In addition, they will receive the first part of your grain harvest and part of your first batches of wine and olive oil.[x] You must also give them the first wool that is cut from your sheep each year. 5 Give these gifts to the priests, because the LORD has chosen them and their descendants out of all the tribes of Israel to be his special servants at the place of worship.

6 Any Levite can leave his hometown, and go to the place where the LORD chooses to be worshiped, 7 and then be a special servant of the LORD[y] there, just like all the other Levites. 8 Some Levites may

[t] **17.8-12** *several priests*: The Hebrew text has "the priests, the Levites"; priests belonged to the Levi tribe. [u] **17.17** *a lot of wives . . . unfaithful to the LORD*: A king would often marry the daughter of another king that he was making a treaty with. These foreign women would naturally want to worship their own gods, and would want their husband the king to do so as well. [v] **17.18** *God's laws*: Or "God's laws for the king." [w] **18.3** *stomach*: Certain portions of the stomach were considered a delicacy. [x] **18.4** *grain . . . olive oil*: An Israelite was supposed to offer the first part of the harvest as a gift to the LORD (see Leviticus 23.10, 11). [y] **18.7** *a special servant of the LORD*: Or "one of the LORD's priests."

17.14 1 S 8.5. **17.16** 1 K 10.28; 2 Ch 1.16, 17; 9.28. **17.17 a** 1 K 11.1-8; **b** 1 K 10.14-22, 27; 2 Ch 1.15; 9.27. **18.2** Nu 18.20.

have money from selling family possessions, and others may not. But all Levites serving at the place of worship will receive the same amount of food from the sacrifices and gifts brought by the people.

Don't Do Disgusting Things

Moses said to Israel:

9 Soon you will go into the land that the LORD your God is giving you. The nations that live there do things that are disgusting to the LORD, and you must not follow their example. 10-11 Don't sacrifice your son or daughter. And don't try to use any kind of magic or witchcraft to tell fortunes[z] or to cast spells or to talk with spirits of the dead.

12 The LORD is disgusted with anyone who does these things, and that's why he will help you destroy the nations that are in the land. 13 Never be guilty of doing any of these disgusting things!

A Prophet like Moses

Moses said to Israel:

14 You will go in and take the land from nations that practice magic and witchcraft. But the LORD your God won't allow you to do those things. 15 Instead, he will choose one of your own people to be a prophet just like me, and you must do what that prophet says. 16 You were asking for a prophet the day you were gathered at Mount Sinai[a] and said to the LORD, "Please don't let us hear your voice or see this terrible fire again—if we do, we will die!"

17 Then the LORD told me:

Moses, they have said the right thing. 18 So when I want to speak to them, I will choose one of them to be a prophet like you. I will give my message to that prophet, who will tell the people exactly what I have said. 19 Since the message comes from me, anyone who doesn't obey the message will have to answer to me.

20 But if I haven't spoken, and a prophet claims to have a message from me, you must kill that prophet, and you must also kill any prophet who claims to have a message from another god.

Moses said to Israel:

21 You may be asking yourselves, "How can we tell if a prophet's message really comes from the LORD?" 22 You will know, because if the LORD says something will happen, it will happen. And if it doesn't, you will know that the prophet was falsely claiming to speak for the LORD. Don't be afraid of any prophet whose message doesn't come from the LORD.

Safe Towns

(Numbers 35.9-28; Joshua 20.1-9)

Moses said to Israel:

19 Soon you will go into the land and attack the nations. The LORD your God will destroy them and give you their lands, towns, and homes. Then after you are settled, 2-4 you must choose three of your towns to be Safe Towns. Divide the land into three regions with one Safe Town near the middle of each, so that a Safe Town can be easily reached from anywhere in your land.

Then, if one of you accidentally kills someone, you can run to a Safe Town and find protection from being put to death. But you must not have been angry with the person you killed.

5 For example, suppose you and a friend go into the forest to cut wood. You are chopping down a tree with an ax, when the ax head slips off the handle, hits your friend, and kills him. You can run to one of the Safe Towns and save your life. 6 You don't deserve to die, since you did not mean to harm your friend. But he did get killed, and his relatives might be very angry. They might even choose one of the men

[z] **18.10,11** *tell fortunes*: Fortunetellers thought they could learn secrets or learn about the future by watching the flight of birds or looking at the livers of animals or in many other ways.

[a] **18.16** *Mount Sinai*: See the note at 1.1-5.

18.10,11 a Lv 19.26; **b** Ex 22.18; **c** Lv 19.31. **18.13** Mt 5.48. **18.15** Ac 3.22; 7.37. **18.19** Ac 3.23. **19.1-13** Js 20.1-9.

from their family to track you down and kill you. If it is too far to one of the Safe Towns, the victim's relative might be able to catch you and kill you. 7 That's why I said there must be three Safe Towns.

8-9 Israel, the LORD your God has promised that if you obey his laws and teachings I'm giving you, and if you always love him, then he will give you the land he promised your ancestors. When that happens, you must name three more Safe Towns in the new territory. 10 You will need them, so innocent people won't be killed on your land while they are trying to reach a Safe Town that is too far away. You will be guilty of murder, if innocent people lose their lives because you didn't name enough Safe Towns in the land the LORD your God will give you.

11 But what if you really do commit murder? Suppose one of you hates a neighbor. So you wait in a deserted place, kill the neighbor, and run to a Safe Town. 12 If that happens, the leaders of your town must send messengers to bring you back from the Safe Town. They will hand you over to one of the victim's relatives, who will put you to death.

13 Israel, for the good of the whole country, you must kill anyone who murders an innocent person. Never show mercy to a murderer!

Property Lines

Moses said to Israel:

14 In the land the LORD is giving you, there are already stones set up to mark the property lines between fields. So don't move those stones.

Witnesses Must Tell the Truth

Moses said to Israel:

15 Before you are convicted of a crime, at least two witnesses must be able to testify that you did it.

16 If you accuse someone of a crime, but seem to be lying, 17-18 then both you and the accused must be taken to the court at the place where the LORD is worshiped. There the priests and judges will find out if you are lying or telling the truth.

If you are lying and the accused is innocent, 19-21 then you will be punished without mercy. You will receive the same punishment the accused would have received if found guilty, whether it means losing an eye, a tooth, a hand, a foot, or even your life.

Israel, the crime of telling lies in court must be punished. And when people hear what happens to witnesses that lie, everyone else who testifies in court will tell the truth.

Laws for Going to War

Moses said to Israel:

20 If you have to go to war, you may find yourselves facing an enemy army that is bigger than yours and that has horses and chariots. But don't be afraid! The LORD your God rescued you from Egypt, and he will help you fight. 2 Before you march into battle, a priest will go to the front of the army 3 and say, "Soldiers of Israel, listen to me! Today when you go into battle, don't be afraid of the enemy, and when you see them, don't panic. 4 The LORD your God will fight alongside you and help you win the battle."

5 Then the tribal officials will say to the troops:

> If any of you have built a new house, but haven't yet moved in, you may go home. It isn't right for you to die in battle and for somebody else to live in your new house.
>
> 6 If any of you have planted a vineyard but haven't had your first grape harvest, you may go home. It isn't right for you to die in battle and for somebody else to enjoy your grapes.
>
> 7 If any of you are engaged to be married, you may go back home and get married. It isn't right for you to die in battle and for somebody else to marry the woman you are engaged to.
>
> 8 Finally, if any of you are afraid,

19.14 Dt 27.14-26. **19.15** Nu 35.30; Dt 17.5-7; Mt 18.16; Jn 8.17; 2 Co 13.1; 1 Ti 5.19; He 10.28. **19.19-21** Ex 21.23-25; Lv 24.19, 20; Mt 5.38.

you may go home. We don't want you to discourage the other soldiers.

9 When the officials are finished giving these orders, they will appoint officers to be in command of the army.

10-15 Before you attack a town that is far from your land, offer peace to the people who live there. If they surrender and open their town gates, they will become your slaves. But if they reject your offer of peace and try to fight, surround their town and attack. Then, after the LORD helps you capture it, kill all the men. Take the women and children as slaves and keep the livestock and everything else of value.

16 Whenever you capture towns in the land the LORD your God is giving you, be sure to kill all the people and animals. 17 He has commanded you to completely wipe out the Hittites, the Amorites, the Canaanites, the Perizzites, the Hivites, and the Jebusites. 18 If you allow them to live, they will persuade you to worship their disgusting gods, and you will be unfaithful to the LORD.

19 When you are attacking a town, don't chop down its fruit trees, not even if you have had the town surrounded for a long time. Fruit trees aren't your enemies, and they produce food that you can eat, so don't cut them down. 20 You may need wood to make ladders and towers to help you get over the walls and capture the town. But use only trees that you know are not fruit trees.

Unsolved Murder

Moses said to Israel:

21 Suppose the body of a murder victim is found in a field in the land the LORD your God is giving you, and no one knows who the murderer is. 2 The judges and other leaders from the towns around there must find out what town is the closest to where the body was found. 3 The leaders from that town will go to their cattle herds and choose a young cow that has never been put to work.[b] 4-5 They and some of the priests will take this cow to a nearby valley where there is a stream, but no crops. Once they reach the valley, the leaders will break the cow's neck.

The priests must be there, because the LORD your God has chosen them to be his special servants at the place of worship. The LORD has chosen them to bless the people in his name and to be judges in all legal cases, whether property or injury is involved.

6 The town leaders will wash their hands over the body of the dead cow 7 and say, "We had no part in this murder, and we don't know who did it. 8-9 But since an innocent person was murdered, we beg you, our LORD, to accept this sacrifice and forgive Israel. We are your people, and you rescued us. Please don't hold this crime against us."

If you obey the LORD and do these things, he will forgive Israel.

Marrying a Woman Taken Prisoner in War

Moses said to Israel:

10 From time to time, you men will serve as soldiers and go off to war. The LORD your God will help you defeat your enemies, and you will take many prisoners. 11-13 One of these prisoners may be a beautiful woman, and you may want to marry her. But first you must bring her into your home, and have her shave her head, cut her nails, get rid of her foreign clothes, and start wearing Israelite clothes. She will mourn a month for her father and mother, then you can marry her.

14 Later on, if you are not happy with the woman, you can divorce her, and she can go free. But you have slept with her as your wife, so you cannot sell her as a slave or make her into your own slave.

Rights of a First-Born Son

Moses said to Israel:

15-17 Suppose a man has two wives and loves one more than the other. The first son of either wife is the man's first-born son, even if the boy's mother is the wife the man doesn't love. Later, when the man is

[b]**21.3** *young cow . . . work*: Cows and oxen pulled plows and wagons.

near death and is dividing up his property, he must give a double share to his firstborn son, simply because he was the first to be born.

A Son Who Rebels

Moses said to Israel:

18 A father and a mother may have a stubborn and rebellious son who refuses to obey them even after he has been punished. 19 If a son is like that, his parents must drag him to the town gate, where the leaders of the town hold their meetings.
20 The parents will tell the leaders, "This son of ours is stubborn and never obeys. He spends all his time drinking and partying."
21 The men of the town will stone that son to death, because they must get rid of the evil he brought into the community. Everyone in Israel will be afraid when they hear how he was punished.

The Body of a Criminal

Moses said to Israel:

22 If a criminal is put to death, and you
hang the dead body on a tree, 23 you must not let it hang there overnight. Bury it the same day, because the dead body of a criminal will bring God's curse on the land. The LORD your God is giving this land to you, so don't make it unclean by leaving the bodies of executed criminals on display.

Helping Others

Moses said to Israel:

22 If you see a cow or sheep wandering around lost, take the animal
back to its owner. 2 If the owner lives too
far away, or if you don't know who the owner is, take the animal home with you and take care of it. The owner will come looking for the animal, and then you can
give it back. 3 That's what you should do if you find anything that belongs to someone else. Do whatever you can to help, whether you find a cow or sheep or donkey or some clothing.
4 Oxen and donkeys that carry heavy loads can stumble and fall, and be unable to get up by themselves. So as you walk along the road, help anyone who is trying to get an ox or donkey back on its feet.

Don't Pretend To Be the Opposite Sex

Moses said to Israel:

5 Women must not pretend to be men, and men must not pretend to be women.[c] The LORD your God is disgusted with people who do that.

Don't Take a Mother Bird

Moses said to Israel:

6-7 As you walk along the road, you might see a bird's nest in a tree or on the ground. If the mother bird is in the nest with either her eggs or her baby birds, you are allowed to take the baby birds or the eggs, but not the mother bird. Let her go free, and the LORD will bless you with a long and successful life.

Put a Wall around Your Flat Roof

8 If you build a house, make sure to put a low wall around the edge of the flat roof.[d] Then if someone falls off the roof and is killed, it won't be your fault.

Laws against Mixing Different Things

Moses said to Israel:

9 If you plant a vineyard, don't plant any other fruit tree or crop in it. If you do plant something else there, you must bring to the place of worship everything you harvest from the vineyard.
10 Don't hitch an ox and a donkey to your plow at the same time.
11 When you weave cloth for clothing, you can use thread made of flax[e] or wool, but not both together. 12 And when you
make a coat, sew a tassel on each of the four corners.

[c]**22.5** *pretend to be men . . . pretend to be women*: Or "wear men's clothing . . . wear women's clothing." [d]**22.8** *flat roof*: Houses usually had flat roofs. In hot dry weather, it was cooler on the roof than in the house, and so roofs were used for sleeping and living quarters, and for entertaining guests. [e]**22.11** *flax*: The stalks of flax plants were harvested, soaked in water, and dried, then their fibers were separated and spun into thread, which was woven into linen cloth.

21.23 Ga 3.13. **22.1-4** Ex 23.4, 5. **22.9-11** Lv 19.19. **22.12** Nu 15.37-41.

When a Husband Accuses His Wife

Moses said to Israel:

13 Suppose a man starts hating his wife soon after they are married. 14 He might tell ugly lies about her, and say, "I married this woman, but when we slept together, I found out she wasn't a virgin."

15 If this happens, the bride's father and mother must go to the town gate to show the town leaders the proof that the woman was a virgin. 16 Her father will say, "I let my daughter marry this man, but he started hating her 17 and accusing her of not being a virgin. But he is wrong, because here is proof that she was a virgin!" Then the bride's parents will show them the bed sheet from the woman's wedding night.

18 The town leaders will beat the man with a whip 19 because he accused his bride of not being a virgin. He will have to pay her father one hundred pieces of silver and will never be allowed to divorce her.

20 But if the man was right and there is no proof that his bride was a virgin, 21 the men of the town will take the woman to the door of her father's house and stone her to death.

This woman brought evil into your community by sleeping with someone before she got married, and you must get rid of that evil by killing her.

Laws about Illegal Sex

Moses said:

22 People of Israel, if a man is caught having sex with someone else's wife, you must put them both to death. That way, you will get rid of the evil they have done in Israel.

23-24 If a man is caught in town having sex with an engaged woman who isn't screaming for help, they both must be put to death. The man is guilty of having sex with a married woman.[f] And the woman is guilty because she didn't call for help, even though she was inside a town and people were nearby. Take them both to the town gate and stone them to death. You must get rid of the evil they brought into your community.

25 If an engaged woman is raped out in the country, only the man will be put to death. 26 Do not punish the woman at all; she has done nothing wrong, and certainly nothing deserving death. This crime is like murder, 27 because the woman was alone out in the country when the man attacked her. She screamed, but there was no one to help her.

28 Suppose a woman isn't engaged to be married, and a man talks her into sleeping with him. If they are caught, 29 they will be forced to get married. He must give her father fifty pieces of silver as a bride-price and[g] can never divorce her.

30 A man must not marry a woman who was married to his father. This would be a disgrace to his father.

Who Cannot Become One of the LORD's People

Moses said to Israel:

23 If a man's private parts have been crushed or cut off,[h] he cannot fully belong to the LORD's people.

2 No one born outside of a legal marriage, or any of their descendants for ten generations, can fully belong to the LORD's people.

3 No Ammonites or Moabites, or any of their descendants for ten generations, can become part of Israel, the LORD's people. 4 This is because when you came out of Egypt, they refused to provide you with food and water. And besides, they hired Balaam[i] to put a curse on you. 5 But the LORD your God loves you, so he refused to listen to Balaam and turned Balaam's curse into a blessing. 6 Don't even think

[f]**22.23,24** *engaged woman . . . married woman*: An engaged woman was legally married, but had not yet slept with her husband or started living with him. [g]**22.28,29** *talks her into sleeping with him . . . bride-price and*: Or "forces her to have sex. 29Then if they are caught, he will have to marry her. He must give her father fifty pieces of silver as a bride-price and." [h]**23.1** *a man's private parts have been crushed or cut off*: This was sometimes done to show devotion to pagan gods.
[i]**23.4** *Balaam*: Hebrew "Balaam son of Beor from Pethor."

22.25-27 4 Macc 18.8. **22.28,29** Ex 22.16, 17. **22.30** Lv 18.8; 20.11; Dt 27.14-26. **23.3-5** Ne 13.1, 2. **23.4** Nu 22.1-6. **23.5** Nu 23.7—24.9.

of signing a peace treaty with Moab or Ammon.

7 But Edomites are your relatives, and you lived as foreigners in the country of Egypt. Now you must be kind to Edomites and Egyptians 8 and let their great-grandchildren become part of Israel, the LORD's people.

Keep the Army Camp Acceptable

Moses said to Israel:

9 When you men go off to fight your enemies, make sure your camp is acceptable to the LORD.

10 For example, if something happens at night that makes a man unclean and unfit for worship, he[j] must go outside the camp and stay there 11 until late afternoon. Then he must take a bath, and at sunset he can go back into camp.

12 Set up a place outside the camp to be used as a toilet area. 13 And make sure that you have a small shovel in your equipment. When you go out to the toilet area, use the shovel to dig a hole. Then, after you relieve yourself, bury the waste in the hole. 14 You must keep your camp clean of filthy and disgusting things. The LORD is always present in your camp, ready to rescue you and give you victory over your enemies. But if he sees something disgusting in your camp, he may turn around and leave.

Runaway Slaves from Other Countries

Moses said:

15 When runaway slaves from other countries come to Israel and ask for protection, you must not hand them back to their owners. 16 Instead, you must let them choose which one of your towns they want to live in. Don't be cruel to runaway slaves.

Temple Prostitutes

Moses said:

17 People of Israel, don't any of you ever be temple prostitutes.[k] 18 The LORD your God is disgusted with men and women who are prostitutes of any kind, and he will not accept a gift from them, even if it had been promised to him.

Interest on Loans

Moses said:

19 When you lend money, food, or anything else to another Israelite, you are not allowed to charge interest. 20 You can charge a foreigner interest. But if you charge other Israelites interest, the LORD your God will not let you be successful in the land you are about to take.

Sacred Promises to the LORD

Moses said:

21 People of Israel, if you make a sacred promise to give a gift to the LORD, then do it as soon as you can. If the LORD has to come looking for the gift you promised, you will be guilty of breaking that promise. 22 On the other hand, if you never make a sacred promise, you can't be guilty of breaking it. 23 You must keep whatever promises you make to the LORD. After all, you are the one who chose to make the promises.

Eating Someone Else's Produce

24 If you go into a vineyard that belongs to someone else, you are allowed to eat as many grapes as you want while you are there. But don't take any with you when you leave. 25 In the same way, if you are in a grain field that belongs to someone else, you can pick heads of grain and eat the kernels. But don't cut down the stalks of grain and take them with you.

A Law about Divorce

Moses said to Israel:

24 Suppose a woman was divorced by her first husband because he found something disgraceful about her.[l] He wrote out divorce papers, gave them to her, and sent her away. 2 Later she married another

[j]**23.10** *if something . . . worship, he*: Or "if a man has a flow of semen at night, he is unclean and unfit for worship, and he." [k]**23.17** *temple prostitutes*: Some Canaanites worshiped by going to their temples and having sex with prostitutes that represented their gods. [l]**24.1** *something disgraceful about her*: One possible meaning for the difficult Hebrew text.

23.17 Lv 19.29. **23.19,20** Ex 22.25; Lv 25.36, 37; Dt 15.7-11. **23.21** Nu 30.1-16; Mt 5.33. **24.1** Mt 5.31; 19.7; Mk 10.4.

man, [3] who then either divorced her in the same way or died. [4] Since she has slept with her second husband, she cannot marry her first husband again. Their marriage would pollute the land that the LORD your God is giving you, and he would be disgusted.

Newlyweds

Moses said to Israel:

[5] If a man and a woman have been married less than one year, he must not be sent off to war or sent away to do forced labor. He must be allowed to stay home for a year and be happy with his wife.

Loans

Moses said to Israel:

[6] When you lend money to people, you are allowed to keep something of theirs as a guarantee that they will pay back the loan. But don't take one or both of their millstones, or else they may starve. They need these stones for grinding grain into flour to make bread.

Kidnapping

Moses said to Israel:

[7] If you are guilty of kidnapping Israelites and forcing them into slavery, you will be put to death to remove this evil from the community.

Skin Diseases

Moses said to Israel:

[8] I have told the priests[m] what to do if any of you have leprosy,[n] so do exactly what they say. [9] And remember what the LORD your God did to Miriam[o] after you left Egypt.

Loans

Moses said to Israel:

[10] When you lend money to people, you are allowed to keep something of theirs as a guarantee that the money will be paid back. But you must not go into their house to get it. [11] Wait outside, and they will bring out the item you have agreed on.

[12] Suppose someone is so poor that a coat is the only thing that can be offered as a guarantee on a loan. Don't keep the coat overnight. [13] Instead, give it back before sunset, so the owner can keep warm and sleep and ask the LORD to bless you. Then the LORD your God will notice that you have done the right thing.

Poor People's Wages

Moses said:

[14] If you hire poor people to work for you, don't hold back their pay,[p] whether they are Israelites or foreigners who live in your town. [15] Pay them their wages at the end of each day, because they live in poverty and need the money to survive. If you don't pay them on time, they will complain about you to the LORD, and he will punish you.

The Death Penalty

Moses said to Israel:

[16] Parents must not be put to death for crimes committed by their children, and children must not be put to death for crimes committed by their parents. Don't put anyone to death for someone else's crime.

Don't Mistreat the Powerless

Moses said to Israel:

[17] Make sure that orphans and foreigners are treated fairly. And if you lend money to a widow and want to keep something of hers to guarantee that she will pay you back, don't take any of her clothes. [18] You were slaves in Egypt until the LORD your God rescued you. That's why I am giving you these laws.

[m]**24.8** *the priests*: See the note at 17.8-12. [n]**24.8** *leprosy*: The word "leprosy" was used for many different kinds of skin diseases. [o]**24.9** *what the LORD your God did to Miriam*: See Numbers 12.1-16. [p]**24.14** *don't hold back their pay*: The Dead Sea Scrolls; the Standard Hebrew Text "treat them right."

24.7 Ex 21.16. **24.8** Lv 13.1—14.57. **24.9** Nu 12.10. **24.10-13** Ex 22.26, 27. **24.14,15** Lv 19.13. **24.16** 2 K 14.6; 2 Ch 25.4; Ez 18.20. **24.17,18** Ex 23.9; Lv 19.33, 34; Dt 27.14-26.

Leave Some of Your Harvest for the Poor

Moses said to Israel:

19 If you forget to bring in a stack of harvested grain, don't go back in the field to get it. Leave it for the poor, including foreigners, orphans, and widows, and the LORD will make you successful in everything you do.

20 When you harvest your olives, don't try to get them all for yourself, but leave some for the poor. 21 And when you pick your grapes, go over the vines only once, then let the poor have what is left. 22 You lived in poverty as slaves in Egypt until the LORD your God rescued you. That's why I am giving you these laws.

Whipping as Punishment for a Crime

Moses said to Israel:

25 1-2 Suppose you and someone else each accuse the other of doing something wrong, and you go to court, where the judges decide you are guilty. If your punishment is to be beaten with a whip,[q] one of the judges will order you to lie down, and you will receive the number of lashes you deserve. 3 Forty lashes is the most that you can be given, because more than that might make other Israelites think you are worthless.

Don't Muzzle an Ox

Moses said to Israel:

4 Don't muzzle an ox while it is threshing grain.[r]

A Son for a Dead Brother

Moses said to Israel:

5-6 Suppose two brothers are living on the same property, when one of them dies without having a son to carry on his name. If this happens, his widow must not marry anyone outside the family. Instead, she must marry her late husband's brother, and their first son will be the legal son of the dead man.

7 But suppose the brother refuses to marry the widow. She must go to a meeting of the town leaders at the town gate and say, "My husband died without having a son to carry on his name. And my husband's brother refuses to marry me so I can have a son."

8 The leaders will call the living brother to the town gate and try to persuade him to marry the widow. But if he doesn't change his mind and marry her, 9 she must go over to him while the town leaders watch. She will pull off one of his sandals and spit in his face, while saying, "That's what happens to a man who won't help provide descendants for his dead brother." 10 From then on, that man's family will be known as "the family of the man whose sandal was pulled off."

When Two Men Fight

Moses said to Israel:

11 If two men are fighting, and the wife of one man tries to rescue her husband by grabbing the other man's private parts, 12 you must cut off her hand. Don't have any mercy.

Be Honest in Business

Moses said to Israel:

13-14 Don't try to cheat people by having two sets of weights or measures, one to get more when you are buying, and the other to give less when you are selling. 15 If you weigh and measure things honestly, the LORD your God will let you enjoy a long life in the land he is giving you. 16 But the LORD is disgusted with anyone who cheats or is dishonest.

Wipe Out Amalek

Moses said:

17 People of Israel, do you remember what the Amalekites did to you after you

[q]25.1,2 *whip*: Or "rod." [r]25.4 *threshing grain*: Oxen were used at the threshing place to walk on heads of grain, or pull heavy slabs of wood over it, to separate the kernels from the husks.

24.19-21 Lv 19.9, 10; 23.22. **25.3** 2 Co 11.24. **25.4** 1 Co 9.8, 9; 1 Ti 5.18. **25.5,6** Mt 22.24; Mk 12.19; Lk 20.28. **25.7-10** Ru 4.7, 8. **25.13-16** Lv 19.35, 36. **25.17-19** Ex 17.8-14; 1 S 15.2-9.

came out of Egypt? 18 You were tired, and
they followed along behind, attacking those
who could not keep up with the others.
This showed that the Amalekites have no
respect for God.
19 The LORD your God will help you capture the land, and he will give you peace.
But when that day comes, you must wipe
out Amalek so completely that no one will
remember they ever lived.

Give the LORD the First Part of Your Harvest

Moses said to Israel:

26 The LORD is giving you the land,
and soon you will conquer it, settle
down, 2 and plant crops. And when you begin harvesting each of your crops, the very
first things you pick must be put in a basket. Take them to the place where the LORD
your God chooses to be worshiped, 3 and
tell the priest, "Long ago the LORD our God
promised our ancestors that he would give
us this land. And today, I thank him for
keeping his promise and giving me a share
of the land."
4 The priest will take the basket and set
it in front of the LORD's altar. 5 Then,
standing there in front of the place of worship, you must pray:

My ancestor was homeless,
an Aramean who went to live
in Egypt.
There were only a few
in his family then,
but they became great
and powerful,
a nation of many people.

6 The Egyptians were cruel
and had no pity on us.
They mistreated our people
and forced us into slavery.
7 We called out for help
to you, the LORD God
of our ancestors.
You heard our cries;
you knew we were in trouble
and abused.
8 Then you terrified the Egyptians
with your mighty miracles
and rescued us from Egypt.
9 You brought us here
and gave us this land
rich with milk and honey.
10 Now, LORD, I bring to you
the best of the crops
that you have given me.

After you say these things, place the basket in front of the LORD's altar and bow down to worship him.

11 Then you and your family must celebrate by eating a meal at the place of worship to thank the LORD your God for giving
you such a good harvest. And remember to
invite the Levites and the foreigners who
live in your town.

Ten Percent of the Harvest

Moses said to Israel:

12 Every year you are to give ten percent
of your harvest to the LORD.[s] But every
third year,[t] this ten percent must be given
to the poor who live in your town, including Levites, foreigners, orphans, and widows. That way, they will have enough to
eat. 13 Then you must pray:

Our LORD and our God, you have said that ten percent of my harvest is sacred. I have obeyed your command and given this to the poor, including the Levites, foreigners, orphans, and widows.

14 I have not eaten any of this sacred food while I was in mourning; in
fact, I never touched it when I was unclean.[u] And none of it has been offered
as a sacrifice to the spirits of the dead.
I have done everything exactly as you
commanded.

15 Our LORD, look down from your
temple in heaven and bless your people Israel. You promised our ancestors
that you would give us this land rich

[s]**26.12** *Every year . . . LORD*: See 14.22-29. [t]**26.12** *every third year*: Probably the third and sixth years of the seven-year cycle described in 15.1-11 and Leviticus 25.1-7. [u]**26.14** *in mourning . . . unclean*: Touching a dead body made a person unclean and unfit to worship God. Ten percent of the harvest belonged to God, and was not to be touched by an unclean person.

26.2 Ex 23.19. **26.12** Dt 14.28, 29.

with milk and honey, and you have kept your promise.

The LORD Is Your God, and You Are His People

Moses said to Israel:

16 Today the LORD your God has commanded you to obey these laws and teachings with all your heart and soul.

17 In response, you have agreed that the LORD will be your God, that you will obey all his laws and teachings, and that you will listen when he speaks to you.

18 Since you have agreed to obey the LORD, he has agreed that you will be his people and that you will belong to him, just as he promised. 19 The LORD created all nations, but he will make you more famous than any of them, and you will receive more praise and honor. You will belong only to the LORD your God, just as he promised.

Build an Altar on Mount Ebal

27 Moses stood together with the leaders and told the people of Israel:

Obey all the laws and teachings that I am giving you today. 2-4 Soon you will enter the land that the LORD your God is giving to you. He is the God your ancestors worshiped, and he has promised that this land is rich with milk and honey.

After you cross the Jordan River, go to Mount Ebal. Set up large slabs of stone, then cover them with white plaster and write on them a copy of these laws.

5 At this same place, build an altar for offering sacrifices to the LORD your God. But don't use stones that have been cut with iron tools. 6 Look for stones that can be used without being cut. Then offer sacrifices to please the LORD,[v] burning them completely on the altar. 7 Next, offer sacrifices to ask the LORD's blessing,[w] and serve the meat at a sacred meal where you will celebrate in honor of the LORD.

8 Don't forget to write out a copy of these laws on the stone slabs that you are going to set up. Make sure that the writing is easy to read.

Curses on Those Who Disobey

9 Moses stood together with the priests[x] and said, "Israel, be quiet and listen to me! Today you have become the people of the LORD your God.[y] 10 So you must obey his laws and teachings that I am giving you."

11 That same day, Moses gave them the following instructions:

12-13 After you cross the Jordan River, you will go to Mount Gerizim and Mount Ebal.[z] The tribes of Simeon, Levi, Judah, Issachar, Ephraim, Manasseh,[a] and Benjamin will go up on Mount Gerizim, where they will bless the people of Israel. The tribes of Reuben, Gad, Asher, Zebulun, Dan, and Naphtali will go up on Mount Ebal where they will agree to the curses.

14-26 The people of the Levi tribe will speak each curse in a loud voice, then the rest of the people[b] will agree to that curse by saying, "Amen!" Here are the curses:

We ask the LORD to put a curse on anyone who makes an idol or worships idols, even secretly. The LORD is disgusted with idols.

We ask the LORD to put a curse on all who do not show respect for their father and mother.

[v] **27.6** *sacrifices to please the LORD*: See the note at 12.5-19. [w] **27.7** *sacrifices to ask the LORD's blessing*: These sacrifices have traditionally been called "peace offerings" or "offerings of well-being." A main purpose was to ask for the LORD's blessing, and so in the CEV they are sometimes called "sacrifices to ask the LORD's blessing." [x] **27.9** *priests*: See the note at 17.8-12. [y] **27.9** *Today you have become the people of the LORD your God*: As a result of the agreement that the LORD had made with them, recorded in 26.16-19. [z] **27.12,13** *Mount Gerizim and Mount Ebal*: These mountains were separated by a valley. [a] **27.12,13** *Ephraim, Manasseh*: The Hebrew text has "Joseph"; the descendants of Joseph formed the two tribes of Ephraim and Manasseh.
[b] **27.14-26** *the rest of the people*: Or "all the people who are standing on Mount Ebal."

26.18 Ex 19.5; Dt 4.20; 7.6; 14.2; Titus 2.14; 1 P 2.9. **27.2-8** Js 8.30-32. **27.5,6** Ex 20.25. **27.12,13** Dt 11.29; Js 8.33-35. **27.14-26** **a** Ex 20.4; 34.17; Lv 19.3, 4; 26.1; Dt 4.15-18; 5.8; **b** Ex 20.12; Dt 5.16. **c** Dt 19.14; **d** Lv 19.14; **e** Ex 22.21; 23.9; Lv 19.33, 34; Dt 24.17, 18; **f** Lv 18.8; 20.11; Dt 22.30; **g** Ex 22.19; Lv 18.23; 20.15, 16; **h** Lv 18.9; 20.17; **i** Lv 18.17; 20.14; **j** Ga 3.10.

We ask the LORD to put a curse on anyone who moves the rocks that mark property lines.

We ask the LORD to put a curse on anyone who tells blind people to go the wrong way.

We ask the LORD to put a curse on anyone who keeps the poor from getting justice, whether these poor are foreigners, widows, or orphans.

We ask the LORD to put a curse on any man who sleeps with his father's wife; that man has shown no respect for his father's marriage.

We ask the LORD to put a curse on anyone who has sex with an animal.

We ask the LORD to put a curse on any man who sleeps with his sister or his half sister or his mother-in-law.

We ask the LORD to put a curse on anyone who commits murder, even when there are no witnesses to the crime.

We ask the LORD to put a curse on anyone who accepts money to murder an innocent victim.

We ask the LORD to put a curse on anyone who refuses to obey his laws.

And so, to each of these curses, the people will answer, "Amen!"

The LORD Will Bless You if You Obey

Moses said to Israel:

28 [1-2] Today I am giving you the laws and teachings of the LORD your God. Always obey them, and the LORD will make Israel the most famous and important nation on earth, and he will bless you in many ways.

3 The LORD will make your businesses and your farms successful.

4 You will have many children. You will harvest large crops, and your herds of cattle and flocks of sheep and goats will produce many young.

5 You will have plenty of bread[c] to eat.

6 The LORD will make you successful in your daily work.

7 The LORD will help you defeat your enemies and make them scatter in all directions.

8 The LORD your God is giving you the land, and he will make sure you are successful in everything you do. Your harvests will be so large that your storehouses will be full.

9 If you follow and obey the LORD, he will make you his own special people, just as he promised. 10 Then everyone on earth will know that you belong to the LORD, and they will be afraid of you.

11 The LORD will give you a lot of children and make sure that your animals give birth to many young. The LORD promised your ancestors that this land would be yours, and he will make it produce large crops for you.

12 The LORD will open the storehouses of the skies where he keeps the rain, and he will send rain on your land at just the right times. He will make you successful in everything you do. You will have plenty of money to lend to other nations, but you won't need to borrow any yourself.

13 Obey the laws and teachings that I'm giving you today, and the LORD your God will make Israel a leader among the nations, and not a follower. Israel will be wealthy and powerful, not poor and weak. 14 But you must not reject any of his laws and teachings or worship other gods.

The LORD Will Put Curses on You if You Disobey

(*Leviticus 26.14-46*)

Moses said:

15 Israel, today I am giving you the laws and teachings of the LORD your God. And if you don't obey them all, he will put many curses on you.

16 Your businesses and farms will fail.

17 You won't have enough bread[c] to eat.

18 You'll have only a few children, your crops will be small, and your herds of cattle and flocks of sheep and goats won't produce many young.

19 The LORD will make you fail in everything you do.

20 No matter what you try to accomplish, the LORD will confuse you, and you

[c]**28.5,17** *bread*: The main food of the Israelites.
28.1-14 Dt 11.13-17.

will feel his anger. You won't last long, and
you may even meet with disaster, all because you rejected the LORD.
21-23 The LORD will send terrible diseases to attack you, and you will never be
well again. You will suffer with burning
fever and swelling and pain until you die
somewhere in the land that you captured.
The LORD will make the sky overhead
seem like a bronze roof that keeps out the
rain, and the ground under your feet will
become as hard as iron. Your crops will be
scorched by the hot east wind or ruined by
mildew. 24 He will send dust and sand-
storms instead of rain, and you will be
wiped out.
25 The LORD will let you be defeated by
your enemies, and you will scatter in all directions. You will be a horrible sight for the
other nations to see, 26 and no one will disturb the birds and wild animals while they
eat your dead bodies.
27 The LORD will make you suffer with
diseases that will cause oozing sores or
crusty itchy patches on your skin or boils
like the ones that are common in Egypt.
And there will be no cure for you! 28 You
will become insane and go blind. The LORD
will make you so confused, 29 that even in
bright sunshine you will have to feel your
way around like a blind person, who cannot
tell day from night. For the rest of your life,
people will beat and rob you, and no one
will be able to stop them.
30 A man will be engaged to a woman,
but before they can get married, she will be
raped by enemy soldiers. Some of you will
build houses, but never get to live in them.
If you plant a vineyard, you won't be
around long enough to enjoy the first harvest. 31 Your cattle will be killed while you
watch, but you won't get to eat any of the
meat. Your donkeys and sheep will be
stolen from you, and no one will be around
to force your enemies to give them back.
32 Your sons and daughters will be dragged
off to a foreign country, while you stand
there helpless. And even if you watch for
them until you go blind, you will never see
them again.
33 You will work hard on your farms, but
everything you harvest will be eaten by foreigners, who will mistreat you and abuse
you for the rest of your life.
34 What you see will be so horrible that
you will go insane, 35 and the LORD will
punish you from head to toe with boils that
never heal.
36 The LORD will let you and your king
be taken captive to a country that you and
your ancestors have never even heard of,
and there you will have to worship idols[d]
made of wood and stone. 37 People of
nearby countries will shudder when they
see your terrible troubles, but they will still
make fun of you.
38 You will plant a lot of seed, but gather
a small harvest, because locusts[e] will eat
your crops. 39 You will plant vineyards and
work hard at taking care of them, but you
won't gather any grapes, much less get any
wine, and the vines themselves will be
eaten by worms. 40 Even if your olive trees
grow everywhere in your country, the olives
will fall off before they are ready, and there
won't be enough olive oil for combing your
hair.[f]
41 Even your infant sons and daughters
will be taken as prisoners of war.
42 Locusts[g] will eat your crops and strip
your trees of leaves and fruit.
43 Foreigners in your towns will become
wealthy and powerful, while you become
poor and powerless. 44 You will be so short
of money that you will have to borrow from
those foreigners. They will be the leaders
in the community, and you will be the
followers.

More Curses for Disobedience

Moses said:
45 Israel, if you don't obey the laws and
teachings that the LORD your God is giving
you, he will send these curses to chase, attack, and destroy you. 46 Then everyone
will look at you and your descendants and

[d]**28.36** *have to worship idols*: It was sometimes thought that only the gods of a country could be worshiped within the borders of that country. [e]**28.38** *locusts*: A type of grasshopper that comes in swarms and causes great damage to plant life. [f]**28.40** *olive oil . . . hair*: Olive oil was used for combing the hair. [g]**28.42** *Locusts*: See the note at 28.38.

realize that the LORD has placed you under
a curse.
47 If the LORD makes you wealthy, but
you don't joyfully worship and honor him,
48 he will send enemies to attack you and
make you their slaves. Then you will live in
poverty with nothing to eat, drink, or wear,
and your owners will work you to death.
49 Foreigners who speak a strange language will be sent to attack you without
warning, just like an eagle swooping down.
50 They won't show any mercy, and they
will have no respect for old people or pity
for children. 51 They will take your cattle,
sheep, goats, grain, wine, and olive oil,
then leave you to starve.
52 All over the land that the LORD your
God gave you, the enemy army will surround your towns. You may feel safe inside
your town walls, but the enemy will tear
them down, 53 while you wait in horror. Finally, you will get so hungry that you will
eat the sons and daughters that the LORD
gave you. 54-55 Because of hunger, a man
who had been gentle and kind will eat his
own children and refuse to share the meal
with his brother or wife or with his other
children. 56-57 A woman may have grown up
in such luxury that she never had to put a
foot on the ground. But times will be so bad
that she will secretly eat both her newborn
baby and the afterbirth, without sharing
any with her husband or her other children.

Disobedience Brings Destruction

Moses said to Israel:
58 You must obey everything in *The Book
of God's Law*. Because if you don't respect
the LORD, 59 he will punish you and your
descendants with incurable diseases, 60 like
those you were so afraid of in Egypt. 61 Remember! If the LORD decides to destroy
your nation, he can use any disease or disaster, not just the ones written in *The Book
of God's Law*.
62 There are as many of you now as the
stars in the sky, but if you disobey the LORD
your God, only a few of you will be left.
63 The LORD is happy to make you successful and to help your nation grow while you
conquer the land. But if you disobey him,
he will be just as happy to pull you up by
your roots.
64 Those of you that survive will be scattered to every nation on earth, and you will
have to worship stone and wood idols[h] that
never helped you or your ancestors. 65 You
will be restless—always longing for home,
but never able to return. 66 You will live in
constant fear of death. 67 Each morning
you will wake up to such terrible sights that
you will say, "I wish it were night!" But at
night you will be terrified and say, "I wish it
were day!"
68 I told you never to go back to Egypt.
But now the LORD himself will load you on
ships and send you back. Then you will
even try to sell yourselves as slaves, but no
one will be interested.

The Agreement in Moab

29 So Moses finished telling the Israelites what they had to do in order to keep the agreement the LORD was
making with them in Moab, which was in
addition to the one the LORD had made
with them at Mount Sinai.[i]

THE THIRD SPEECH: ISRAEL MUST KEEP ITS AGREEMENT WITH THE LORD

The LORD Is Your God

2-3 Moses called the nation of Israel together and told them:
When you were in Egypt, you saw the
LORD perform great miracles that caused
trouble for the king, his officials, and everyone else in the country. 4-6 He has even
told you, "For forty years I, the LORD, led
you through the desert, but your clothes
and your sandals didn't wear out, and I
gave you special food.[j] I did these things so
you would realize that I am your God."
But the LORD must give you a change of
heart before you truly understand what you
have seen and heard.
7 When we first camped here, King
Sihon of Heshbon and King Og of Bashan

[h]**28.64** *have to worship . . . idols*: See the note at 28.36. [i]**29.1** *Mount Sinai*: See the note at 1.1-5. [j]**29.4-6** *I gave . . . food*: Hebrew "you didn't eat bread or drink any wine or beer."

28.56,57 2 K 6.28, 29; Lm 4.10. **29.7** **a** Nu 21.21-30; **b** Nu 21.31-35.

attacked, but we defeated them. [8] Then we captured their land and divided it among the tribes of Reuben, Gad, and East Manasseh.

Keep the Agreement

Moses said:

[9] Israel, the LORD has made an agreement with you, and if you keep your part, you will be successful in everything you do. [10-12] Today everyone in our nation is standing here in the LORD's presence, including leaders and officials, parents and children, and even those foreigners who cut wood and carry water for us. We are at this place of worship to promise that we will keep our part of the agreement with the LORD our God.

[13-15] In this agreement, the LORD promised that you would be his people and that he would be your God. He first made this promise to your ancestors Abraham, Isaac, and Jacob, and today the LORD is making this same promise to you. But it isn't just for you; it is also for your descendants.

[16-17] When we lived in Egypt, you saw the Egyptians worship disgusting idols of wood, stone, silver, and gold. Then as we traveled through other nations, you saw those people worship other disgusting idols. [18] So make sure that everyone in your tribe remains faithful to the LORD and never starts worshiping gods of other nations.

If even one of you worships idols, you will be like the root of a plant that produces bitter, poisonous fruit. [19] You may be an Israelite and know all about the LORD's agreement with us, but he won't bless you if you rebel against him. You may think you can get away with it, but you will cause the rest of Israel to be punished along with you.[k] [20-21] The LORD will be furious, and instead of forgiving you, he will separate you from the other tribes. Then he will destroy you, by piling on you all the curses in *The Book of God's Law*, and you will be forgotten forever.

[22] The LORD will strike your country with diseases and disasters. Your descendants and foreigners from distant countries will see that your land [23] has become a scorching desert of salt and sulfur, where nothing is planted, nothing sprouts, and nothing grows. It will be as lifeless as the land around the cities of Sodom, Gomorrah, Admah, and Zeboiim, after the LORD became angry and destroyed them.[l]

[24] People from other nations will ask, "Why did the LORD destroy this country? Why was he so furious?"

[25] And they will be given this answer:

> Our ancestors worshiped the LORD, but after he brought them out of Egypt and made an agreement with them, they rejected the agreement [26] and decided to worship gods that had never helped them. The LORD had forbidden Israel to worship these gods, [27-28] and so he became furious and punished the land with all the curses in *The Book of God's Law*. Then he pulled up Israel by the roots and tossed them into a foreign country, where they still are today.

[29] The LORD our God hasn't explained the present or the future, but he has commanded us to obey the laws he gave to us and our descendants.

The LORD Will Bring You Back

Moses said to Israel:

30 I have told you everything the LORD your God will do for you, and I've also told you the curses he will put on you if you reject him. He will scatter you in faraway countries, but when you realize that he is punishing you, [2] return to him with all your heart and soul and start obeying the commands I have given to you today. [3-4] Then he will stop punishing you and treat you with kindness. He may have scattered you to the farthest countries on earth, but he will bring you back [5] to the land that had belonged to your ancestors and make you even more successful and powerful than they ever were.

[k]**29.19** *you will cause the rest of Israel to be punished along with you*: Hebrew "The mud will be swept away as well as the dust." [l]**29.23** *Sodom . . . destroyed them*: See Genesis 18.16-28.

29.8 Nu 32.33. **29.18** He 12.15. **29.23** Gn 19.24, 25; 3 Macc 2.5.
30.1-6 3 Macc 2.10.

6 You and your descendants are stubborn, but the LORD will make you willing to obey him and love him with all your heart and soul, and you will enjoy a long life.

7 Then the LORD your God will remove the curses from you and put them on those enemies who hate and attack you.

8 You will again obey the laws and teachings of the LORD, 9 and he will bless you with many children, large herds and flocks, and abundant crops. The LORD will be happy to do good things for you, just as he did for your ancestors. 10 But you must decide once and for all to worship him with all your heart and soul and to obey everything in *The Book of God's Law*.

Choose Life, Not Death

Moses said to Israel:

11 You know God's laws, and it isn't impossible to obey them. 12 His commands aren't in heaven, so you can't excuse yourselves by saying, "How can we obey the LORD's commands? They are in heaven, and no one can go up to get them, then bring them down and explain them to us." 13 And you can't say, "How can we obey the LORD's commands? They are across the sea, and someone must go across, then bring them back and explain them to us." 14 No, these commands are nearby and you know them by heart. All you have to do is obey!

15 Today I am giving you a choice. You can choose life and success or death and disaster. 16-18 I am commanding you to be loyal to the LORD, to live the way he has told you, and to obey his laws and teachings. You are about to cross the Jordan River and take the land that he is giving you. If you obey him, you will live and become successful and powerful.

On the other hand, you might choose to disobey the LORD and reject him. So I'm warning you that if you bow down and worship other gods, you won't have long to live.

19 Right now I call the sky and the earth to be witnesses that I am offering you this choice. Will you choose for the LORD to make you prosperous and give you a long life? Or will he put you under a curse and kill you? Choose life! 20 Be completely faithful to the LORD your God, love him, and do whatever he tells you. The LORD is the only one who can give life, and he will let you live a long time in the land that he promised to your ancestors Abraham, Isaac, and Jacob.

FINAL SPEECHES AND THE DEATH OF MOSES

Joshua Is Appointed the Leader of Israel

31 Moses again spoke to the whole nation of Israel:

2 I am a hundred twenty years old, and I am no longer able to be your leader. And besides that, the LORD your God has told me that he won't let me cross the Jordan River. 3-5 But he has promised that he and Joshua will lead you across the Jordan to attack the nations that live on the other side. The LORD will destroy those nations just as he destroyed Sihon and Og, those two Amorite kings. Just remember—whenever you capture a place, kill everyone who lives there.

6 Be brave and strong! Don't be afraid of the nations on the other side of the Jordan. The LORD your God will always be at your side, and he will never abandon you.

7 Then Moses called Joshua up in front of the crowd and said:

> Joshua, be brave and strong as you lead these people into their land. The LORD made a promise long ago to Israel's ancestors that this land would someday belong to Israel. That time has now come, and you must divide up the land among the people. 8 The LORD will lead you into the land. He will always be with you and help you, so don't ever be afraid of your enemies.

Read These Laws

9 Moses wrote down all of these laws and teachings and gave them to the priests

30.12-14 Ro 10.6-8. **30.15** Si 15.16, 17. **30.20** **a** Gn 12.7; **b** Gn 26.3; **c** Gn 28.13.
31.2 Nu 20.12. **31.3-5** Nu 21.21-35. **31.8** Js 1.5; He 13.5.

and the leaders of Israel. The priests were from the Levi tribe, and they carried the sacred chest that belonged to the LORD. 10-11 Moses told these priests and leaders:

Each year the Israelites must come together to celebrate the Festival of Shelters at the place where the LORD chooses to be worshiped. You must read these laws and teachings to the people at the festival every seventh year, the year when loans do not need to be repaid.[m] 12-13 Everyone must come—men, women, children, and even the foreigners who live in your towns. And each new generation will listen and learn to worship the LORD their God with fear and trembling and to do exactly what is said in God's Law.

Israel Will Reject the LORD

14 The LORD told Moses, "You will soon die, so bring Joshua to the sacred tent, and I will appoint him the leader of Israel."

Moses and Joshua went to the sacred tent, 15 and the LORD appeared in a thick cloud right over the entrance to the tent. 16 The LORD said:

Moses, you will soon die. But Israel is going into a land where other gods are worshiped, and Israel will reject me and start worshiping these gods. The people will break the agreement I made with them, 17 and I will be so furious that I will abandon them and ignore their prayers. I will send disasters and suffering that will nearly wipe them out. Finally, they will realize that the disasters happened because I abandoned them. 18 They will pray to me, but I will ignore them because they were evil and started worshiping other gods.

19 Moses and Joshua, I am going to give you the words to a new song. Write them down and teach the song to the Israelites. If they learn it, they will know what I want them to do, and so they will have no excuse for not obeying me. 20 I am bringing them into the land that I promised their ancestors. It is a land rich with milk and honey, and the Israelites will have more than enough food to eat. But they will get fat and turn their backs on me and start worshiping other gods. The Israelites will reject me and break the agreement that I made with them.

21 When I punish the Israelites and their descendants with suffering and disasters, I will remind them that they know the words to this song, so they have no excuse for not obeying me.

I will give them the land that I promised, but I know the way they are going to live later on.

22 Moses wrote down the words to the song[n] right away, and he taught it to the Israelites.

23 The LORD told Joshua, "Be brave and strong! I will help you lead the people of Israel into the land that I have promised them."

24 Moses wrote down all these laws and teachings in a book, 25 then he went to the Levites who carried the sacred chest and said:

26 This is *The Book of God's Law*. Keep it beside the sacred chest that holds the agreement the LORD your God made with Israel. This book is proof that you know what the LORD wants you to do. 27 I know how stubborn and rebellious you and the rest of the Israelites are. You have rebelled against the LORD while I have been alive, and it will only get worse after I am gone. 28 So call together the leaders and officials of the tribes of Israel. I will bring this book and read every word of it to you, and I will call the sky and the earth as witnesses that all of you know what you are supposed to do.

29 I am going to die soon, and I know that in the future you will stop caring about what is right and what is wrong, and so you will disobey the LORD and stop living the way I told you

[m] **31.10,11** *every seventh year . . . repaid*: See 15.1, 2 and the note there. [n] **31.22** *the words to the song*: See 32.1-43.

31.10,11 a Dt 15.1, 2; **b** Dt 16.13-15. **31.23** Nu 27.23; Js 1.6-8.

to live. The LORD will be angry, and terrible things will happen to you.

The Song of Moses

30 Moses called a meeting of all the people of Israel, so he could teach them the words to the song that the LORD had given him. And here are the words:

32 Earth and Sky,
listen to what I say!
2 Israel, I will teach you.
My words will be like gentle rain
on tender young plants,
or like dew on the grass.

3 Join with me in praising
the wonderful name
of the LORD our God.
4 The LORD is a mighty rock,[o]
and he never does wrong.
God can always be trusted
to bring justice.
5 But you lie and cheat
and are unfaithful to him.
You have disgraced yourselves
and are no longer worthy
to be his children.[p]
6 Israel, the LORD is your Father,
the one who created you,
but you repaid him
by being foolish.
7 Think about past generations.
Ask your parents
or any of your elders.
They will tell you
8 that God Most High
gave land to every nation.
He assigned a guardian angel
to each of them,[q]
9 but the LORD himself
takes care of Israel.[r]
10 Israel, the LORD discovered you
in a barren desert
filled with howling winds.
God became your fortress,
protecting you as though
you were his own eyes.
11 The LORD was like an eagle
teaching its young to fly,
always ready to swoop down
and catch them on its back.
12 Israel, the LORD led you,
and without the aid
of a foreign god,
13 he helped you
capture the land.
Your fields were rich
with grain.
Olive trees grew
in your stony soil,
and honey was found
among the rocks.
14 Your flocks and herds
produced milk and yogurt,
and you got choice meat
from your sheep and goats
that grazed in Bashan.
Your wheat was the finest,
and you drank the best wine.

15 Israel,[s] you grew fat and rebelled
against God, your Creator;
you rejected the Mighty Rock,[t]
your only place of safety.
16 You made God jealous and angry
by worshiping disgusting idols
and foreign gods.
17 You offered sacrifices
to demons, those useless gods[u]
that never helped you,
new gods that your ancestors
never worshiped.

[o]**32.4** *mighty rock*: The Hebrew text has "rock," which is sometimes used in poetry to compare the LORD to a mountain where his people can run for protection from their enemies. [p]**32.5** *and are unfaithful . . . children*: One possible meaning for the difficult Hebrew text. [q]**32.8** *He assigned . . . them*: The Dead Sea Scrolls and one ancient translation; the Standard Hebrew Text "So there were as many nations as Israel (that is, Jacob) had children." [r]**32.9** *Israel*: The Hebrew text has "Jacob," another name for Israel's ancestor. [s]**32.15** *Israel*: The Standard Hebrew Text has "Jeshurun," a rare name for Israel related to a word meaning "honest." The Samaritan Hebrew Text and one ancient translation also use "Jacob," another name for the ancestor of the nation of Israel. [t]**32.15** *Mighty Rock*: See the note at 32.4. [u]**32.16,17** *disgusting idols . . . foreign gods . . . demons . . . those useless gods*: Different ways of referring to gods of other nations.

32.8 Ac 17.26. **32.17** 1 Co 10.20.

18 You turned away
from God, your Creator;
you forgot the Mighty Rock,[v]
the source of your life.
19 You were the LORD's children,
but you made him angry.
Then he rejected you 20 and said,
"You are unfaithful
and can't be trusted.
So I won't answer your prayers;
I'll just watch and see
what happens to you.
21 You worshiped worthless idols,
and made me jealous
and angry!
Now I will send a cruel[w]
and worthless nation
to make you jealous and angry.

22 "My people, I will breathe out fire
that sends you down
to the world of the dead.
It will scorch your farmlands
and burn deep down
under the mountains.
23 I'll send disaster after disaster
to strike you like arrows.
24 You'll be struck by starvation
and deadly diseases,
by the fangs of wild animals
and poisonous snakes.
25 Young and old alike
will be killed in the streets
and terrified at home.

26 "I wanted to scatter you,
so no one would remember
that you had ever lived.
27 But I dreaded the sound
of your enemies saying,
'We defeated Israel with no help
from the LORD.' "

28 People of Israel,
that's what the LORD
has said to you.
But you don't have good sense,
and you never listen
to advice.
29 If you did, you could see
where you are headed.
30 How could one enemy soldier
chase a thousand
of Israel's troops?
Or how could two of theirs
pursue ten thousand of ours?
It can only happen if the LORD
stops protecting Israel
and lets the enemy win.
31 Even our enemies know
that only our God
is a Mighty Rock.[x]

32 Our enemies are grapevines
rooted in the fields
of Sodom and Gomorrah.[y]
The grapes they produce
are full of bitter poison;
33 their wine is more deadly
than cobra venom.
34 But the LORD has written
a list of their sins
and locked it in his vault.
35 Soon our enemies will get
what they deserve[z]—
suddenly they will slip,
and total disaster
will quickly follow.

36 When only a few
of the LORD's people remain,
when their strength is gone,
and some of them are slaves,
the LORD will feel sorry for them
and give them justice.

37 But first the LORD will say,
"You ran for safety to other gods—
couldn't they help you?
38 You offered them wine
and your best sacrifices.
Can't those gods help you now
or give you protection?

[v]**32.18** *Mighty Rock*: See the note at 32.4. [w]**32.21** *cruel*: One possible meaning for the difficult Hebrew text. [x]**32.31** *Mighty Rock*: See the note at 32.4. [y]**32.32** *Sodom and Gomorrah*: Two cities that the LORD destroyed because their people were so evil (see Genesis 18.16—19.28). [z]**32.35** *our enemies . . . deserve*: The Samaritan Hebrew Text and one ancient translation; the Standard Hebrew Text "I will pay them back."

32.21 **a** 1 Co 10.22; **b** Ro 10.19. **32.35** Ro 12.19; He 10.30. **32.36** **a** Ps 135.14.

39 Don't you understand?
I am the only God;
there are no others.
I am the one who takes life
and gives it again.
I punished you with suffering.
But now I will heal you,
and nothing can stop me!

40 "I make this solemn promise:
Just as I live forever,
41 I will take revenge
on my hateful enemies.
I will sharpen my sword
and let it flash
like lightning.
42 My arrows will get drunk
on enemy blood;
my sword will taste the flesh
and the blood of the enemy.
It will kill prisoners,
and cut off the heads
of their leaders."[a]

43 Tell the heavens to celebrate
and all gods to bow down
to the LORD,[b]
because he will take revenge
on those hateful enemies
who killed his people.
He will forgive the sins of Israel
and purify their land.[c]

44-45 Moses spoke the words of the song
so that all the Israelites could hear, and
Joshua[d] helped him. When Moses had
finished, 46 he said, "Always remember
this song I have taught you today. And let
it be a warning that you must teach
your children to obey everything written
in *The Book of God's Law*. 47 The Law
isn't empty words. It can give you a long
life in the land that you are going to
take."

Moses Will See the Land

48 Later that day the LORD said to
Moses:
49 Go up into the Abarim Mountain
range here in Moab across the Jordan
River valley from Jericho. And when
you reach the top of Mount Nebo, you
will be able to see the land of Canaan,
which I am giving to Israel. 50 Then
you will die and be buried on the
mountaintop, just as your brother
Aaron died and was buried on Mount
Hor. 51 Both of you were unfaithful
to me at Meribah Spring near Kadesh
in the Zin Desert.[e] I am God, but
there in front of the Israelites, you did
not treat me with the honor and
respect I deserve. 52 So I will give the
land to the people of Israel, but
you will only get to see it from a
distance.

Moses Blesses the Tribes of Israel

33 Moses was a prophet, and before he
died, he blessed the tribes of Israel
by saying:

2 The LORD came from Mount Sinai.
From Edom, he gave light
to his people,
and his glory was shining
from Mount Paran.
Thousands of his warriors
were with him, and fire
was at his right hand.[f]
3 The LORD loves the tribes
of Israel,[g]
and he protects his people.
They listen to his words
and worship at his feet.
*4 I called a meeting
of the tribes of Israel[h]
and gave you God's Law.

[a]**32.42** *leaders*: Or "long-haired warriors," who let their hair grow to show that they had made sacred promises to their gods. [b]**32.43** *Tell . . . LORD*: The Dead Sea Scrolls and one ancient translation; the Standard Hebrew Text "Let the nations, his people, celebrate." [c]**32.43** *because he will . . . land*: One possible meaning for the difficult Hebrew text. [d]**32.44,45** *Joshua*: The Hebrew text has "Hoshea," another form of Joshua's name. [e]**32.51** *Both of you were unfaithful . . . the Zin Desert*: See Numbers 20.1-13. [f]**33.2** *Thousands . . . right hand*: One possible meaning for the difficult Hebrew text. [g]**33.3** *the tribes of Israel*: Or "the nations." [h]**33.4** *Israel*: The Hebrew text also uses the name "Jeshurun," a rare name for "Israel."
32.43 Ro 15.10; Rev 19.2. **32.48-52** Nu 27.12-14; Dt 3.23-27. **33.3** 4 Macc 17.19.

5 Then you and your leaders
made the LORD your king.

6 Tribe of Reuben, you will live,
even though your tribe
will always be small.[i]

7 The LORD will listen to you,
tribe of Judah, as you beg
to come safely home.
You fought your enemies alone;[j]
now the LORD will help you.

8 At Massah and Meribah Spring,[k]
the LORD tested you,
tribe of Levi.
You were faithful,[l]
and so the priesthood[m] belongs
to the Levi tribe.
9 Protecting Israel's agreement
with the LORD
was more important to you
than the life of your father
or mother,
or brothers or sisters,
or your own children.[n]

10 You teach God's laws to Israel,[o]
and at the place of worship
you offer sacrifices
and burn incense.
11 I pray that the LORD will bless
everything you do,
and make you strong enough
to crush your enemies.

12 The LORD Most High[p] loves you,
tribe of Benjamin.
He will live among your hills
and protect you.

13 Descendants of Joseph,
the LORD will bless you
with precious water
from deep wells
and with dew from the sky.
14 Month by month, your fruit
will ripen in the sunshine.
15 You will have a rich harvest
from the slopes
of the ancient hills.
16 The LORD who appeared
in the burning bush
wants to give you the best
the land can produce,
and it will be a princely crown
on Joseph's head.

17 The armies of Ephraim
and Manasseh
are majestic and fierce
like a bull or a wild ox.
They will run their spears
through faraway nations.

18 Be happy, Zebulun,
as your boats set sail;
be happy, Issachar,
in your tents.
19 The sea will make you wealthy,
and from the sandy beach
you will get treasure.[q]
So invite the other tribes[r]
to celebrate with you
and offer sacrifices to God.

20 Tribe of Gad,
the LORD will bless you
with more land.
So shout his praises!
Your tribe is like a lion
ripping up its victim.
21 Your leaders met together
and chose the best land
for your tribe,

[i]33.6 *even though . . . small*: One possible meaning for the difficult Hebrew text. [j]33.7 *beg . . . alone*: One possible meaning for the difficult Hebrew text. [k]33.8 *Massah and Meribah Spring*: See Exodus 17.1-7; Numbers 20.1-13. [l]33.8 *the LORD tested you, tribe of Levi. You were faithful*: Or "the LORD tested me. I was faithful" or "the LORD tested Aaron and me. We were faithful." [m]33.8 *priesthood*: The Hebrew text has "your thummim and your urim," objects that were used by priests to get answers from God. [n]33.9 *Protecting Israel's agreement . . . your own children*: See Exodus 32.25-29. [o]33.10 *Israel*: See the note at 32.9. [p]33.12 *Most High*: One possible meaning for the difficult Hebrew text. [q]33.19 *sandy beach . . . treasure*: Possibly a reference to glass made from sand; glass was rare and very valuable. [r]33.19 *other tribes*: Or "nations."

33.8 a Ex 28.30; **b** Ex 17.7; **c** Ex 17.7; Nu 20.13.

but you obeyed the LORD
and helped the other tribes.[s]

22 Tribe of Dan,
you are like a lion cub,
startled by a snake.[t]

23 The LORD is pleased with you,
people of Naphtali.
He will bless you
and give you the land
to the west and the south.[u]

24 The LORD's greatest blessing
is for you, tribe of Asher.
You will be the favorite
of all the other tribes.
You will be rich with olive oil
25 and have strong town gates
with bronze and iron bolts.
Your people will be powerful
for as long as they live.

26 Israel,[v] no other god
is like ours—
the clouds are his chariot
as he rides across the skies
to come and help us.
27 The eternal God
is our hiding place;
he carries us in his arms.
When God tells you
to destroy your enemies,
he will make them run.
28 Israel, you will live in safety;
your enemies will be gone.[w]
The dew will fall from the sky,
and you will have plenty
of grain and wine.
29 The LORD has rescued you
and given you more blessings
than any other nation.
He protects you like a shield
and is your majestic sword.
Your enemies will bow in fear,
and you will trample
on their backs.

The Death of Moses

34 Sometime later, Moses left the lowlands of Moab. He went up Mount
Pisgah to the peak of Mount Nebo,[x] which
is across the Jordan River from Jericho.
The LORD showed him all the land as far
north as Gilead and the town of Dan. 2 He
let Moses see the territories that would
soon belong to the tribes of Naphtali,
Ephraim, Manasseh, and Judah, as far west
as the Mediterranean Sea. 3 The LORD also
showed him the land in the south, from the
valley near the town of Jericho, known as
The City of Palm Trees, down to the town
of Zoar.
4 The LORD said, "Moses, this is the land
I was talking about when I solemnly
promised Abraham, Isaac, and Jacob that I
would give land to their descendants. I
have let you see it, but you will not cross
the Jordan and go in."
5 And so, Moses the LORD's servant died
there in Moab, just as the LORD had said.
6 The LORD buried him in a valley near the
town of Beth-Peor, but even today no one
knows exactly where. 7 Moses was a hundred twenty years old when he died, yet his
eyesight was still good, and his body was
strong.
8 The people of Israel stayed in the lowlands of Moab, where they mourned and
grieved thirty days for Moses, as was their
custom.

Joshua Becomes the Leader of Israel

9 Before Moses died, he had placed his
hands on Joshua, and the LORD had given
Joshua wisdom. The Israelites paid atten-

[s] **33.21** *tribes*: One possible meaning for the difficult Hebrew text of verse 21. The Gad tribe asked for some of the land east of the Jordan River, but promised that their warriors would cross the Jordan and help the other tribes take over the land west of the Jordan (see Numbers 32.1-33; Joshua 4.10-13). [t] **33.22** *startled by a snake*: Or "jumping out from the forest of Bashan." [u] **33.23** *land to the west and the south*: Or "land south as far as Lake Galilee." [v] **33.26** *Israel*: See the note at 33.4. [w] **33.28** *your enemies will be gone*: One possible meaning for the difficult Hebrew text. [x] **34.1** *Mount Pisgah . . . Mount Nebo*: Mount Nebo was probably one peak of the ridge known as Mount Pisgah.

34.4 a Gn 12.7; **b** Gn 26.3; **c** Gn 28.13.

tion to what Joshua said and obeyed the commands that the LORD had given Moses.

Moses Was a Great Prophet

10 There has never again been a prophet in Israel like Moses. The LORD spoke face to face with him 11 and sent him to perform powerful miracles in the presence of the king of Egypt and his entire nation. 12 No one else has ever had the power to do such great things as Moses did for everyone to see.

34.10 Ex 33.9-11; Si 45.1-5.

JOSHUA

ABOUT THIS BOOK

The book of Joshua tells how Israel settled in Canaan, the land God promised to give them. The book gets its name from its main character, Joshua, who had become the leader of Israel following the death of Moses.

The book of Joshua has two parts. In the first part (1–12) the Lord helped Israel capture many of the cities and towns of Canaan. Sometimes this help involved miracles. For example, in the battle at Jericho the Lord made the city walls collapse (6.20). Later, in the battle at Gibeon the Lord made huge hailstones fall from the sky and crush the enemy soldiers. Then he made the sun stand still so the Israelites had a longer period of daylight to catch and kill as many of the enemy soldiers as possible before night came (10.1-15).

But the Lord refused to help Israel if the people broke their agreement to worship only him and to obey his commands. For example, in the battle at Ai, Israel was defeated because one person broke Israel's agreement with the Lord (7.1-12).

The second part of the book (13–24) describes how each tribe received its land. Israel had captured territory east of the Jordan River. This land had already been promised to the tribes of Reuben, Gad, and half of Manasseh, but they had to help the other tribes take over the rest of Canaan. The tribes of Judah, Ephraim, and West Manasseh took over their sections of the land fairly quickly. Then the rest of the land was explored and divided into sections, and the Lord showed Joshua which sections to assign to each of the remaining tribes. But since the Levites were the special servants of the Lord, they did not receive a large area of land like the other tribes. Instead, they were given towns scattered throughout the whole country.

At the end of the book, Joshua made two speeches emphasizing how good the Lord had been to the Israelites. Then Joshua gave them a challenge:

> *"Worship the LORD, obey him, and always be faithful."*
> *(24.14a)*

A QUICK LOOK AT THIS BOOK

- Joshua Becomes the Leader of Israel (1.1-9)
- Israel Crosses the Jordan River and Conquers Jericho (1.10—6.27)
- Achan Disobeys the Lord (7.1-26)
- The Battle at Ai (8.1-35)
- The People of Gibeon Trick the Leaders of Israel (9.1-27)
- Joshua Commands the Sun To Stand Still (10.1-15)
- Israel Takes Over Much of the Land of Canaan (10.16—12.24)
- Land that Israel Did Not Take Over (13.1-7)
- Tribal Lands that Moses Had Assigned East of the Jordan (13.8-33)
- Tribal Lands West of the Jordan (14.1—19.51)
- Towns for Protecting People Accused of Murder (20.1-9)
- Towns for the Levi Tribe (21.1-45)
- The Eastern Tribes Return Home (22.1-34)
- Joshua's Farewell Speeches and Death (23.1—24.33)

Joshua Becomes the Leader of Israel

1 Moses, the LORD's servant, was dead. So the LORD spoke to Joshua son of Nun, who had been the assistant of Moses. The LORD said:

2 My servant Moses is dead. Now you must lead Israel across the Jordan River into the land I'm giving to all of you. 3 Wherever you go, I'll give you that land, as I promised Moses. 4 It will reach from the Southern Desert to the Lebanon Mountains in the north, and to the northeast as far as the great Euphrates River. It will include the land of the Hittites,[a] and the land from here at the Jordan River to the Mediterranean Sea on the west. 5 Joshua, I will always be with you and help you as I helped Moses, and no one will ever be able to defeat you.

6-8 Long ago I promised the ancestors of Israel that I would give this land to their descendants. So be strong and brave! Be careful to do everything my servant Moses taught you. Never stop reading *The Book of the Law*[b] he gave you. Day and night you must think about what it says. If you obey it completely, you and Israel will be able to take this land.

9 I've commanded you to be strong and brave. Don't ever be afraid or discouraged! I am the LORD your God, and I will be there to help you wherever you go.

The Eastern Tribes Promise To Help

10 Joshua ordered the tribal leaders 11 to go through the camp and tell everyone:

In a few days we will cross the Jordan River to take the land that the LORD our God is giving us. So fix as much food as you'll need for the march into the land.

12 Joshua told the men of the tribes of Reuben, Gad, and East Manasseh:[c]

13-14 The LORD's servant Moses said that the LORD our God has given you land here on the east side of the Jordan River, where you could live in peace. Your wives and children and your animals can stay here in the land Moses gave you. But all of you that can serve in our army must pick up your weapons and lead the men of the other tribes across the Jordan River. They are your relatives, so you must help them 15 conquer the land that the LORD is giving them. The LORD will give peace to them as he has given peace to you, and then you can come back and settle here in the land that Moses promised you.

16 The men answered:

We'll cross the Jordan River and help our relatives. We'll fight anywhere you send us. 17-18 If the LORD our God will help you as he helped Moses, and if you are strong and brave, we will obey you as we obeyed Moses. We'll even put to death anyone who rebels against you or refuses to obey you.

Rahab Helps the Israelite Spies

2 Joshua chose two men as spies and sent them from their camp at Acacia with these instructions: "Go across the river and find out as much as you can about the whole region, especially about the town of Jericho."

The two spies left the Israelite camp at Acacia and went to Jericho, where they decided to spend the night at the house of a prostitute[d] named Rahab.

2 But someone found out about them and told the king of Jericho, "Some Israelite men came here tonight, and they are spies." 3-7 So the king sent soldiers to Rahab's house to arrest the spies.

Meanwhile, Rahab had taken the men up to the flat roof of her house and had

[a] **1.4** *the land . . . Hittites*: This refers to the northern part of Syria, which had been the southernmost part of the Hittite empire. [b] **1.6-8** *the Law*: Or "Teachings." [c] **1.12** *East Manasseh*: The half of Manasseh that settled east of the Jordan River. [d] **2.1** *prostitute*: Rahab was possibly an innkeeper.

1.3-5 Dt 11.24, 25. **1.5** Dt 31.6, 8; He 13.5. **1.6-8** Dt 31.6, 7, 23. **1.12-15** Nu 32.28-32; Dt 3.18-20; Js 22.1-9. **2.1** He 11.31; Jas 2.25.

hidden them under some piles of flax
plants[e] that she had put there to dry.
The soldiers came to her door and demanded, "Let us have the men who are
staying at your house. They are spies."
She answered, "Some men did come to
my house, but I didn't know where they
had come from. They left about sunset, just
before it was time to close the town gate.[f] I
don't know where they were going, but if
you hurry, maybe you can catch them."
The guards at the town gate let the soldiers leave Jericho, but they closed the gate
again as soon as the soldiers went through.
Then the soldiers headed toward the Jordan River to look for the spies at the place
where people cross the river.
8 Rahab went back up to her roof.
The spies were still awake, so she told
them:

> 9 I know that the LORD has given Is-
> rael this land. Everyone shakes with
> fear because of you. 10 We heard how
> the LORD dried up the Red Sea[g] so you
> could leave Egypt. And we heard how
> you destroyed Sihon and Og, those two
> Amorite kings east of the Jordan River.
> 11 We know that the LORD your God
> rules heaven and earth, and we've lost
> our courage and our will to fight.
>
> 12 Please promise me in the LORD's
> name that you will be as kind to my
> family as I have been to you. Do some-
> thing to show 13 that you won't let your
> people kill my father and mother and my
> brothers and sisters and their families.

14 "Rahab," the spies answered, "if
you keep quiet about what we're doing,
we promise to be kind to you when the
LORD gives us this land. We pray that the
LORD will kill us if we don't keep our
promise!"[h]
15 Rahab's house was built into the town
wall,[i] and one of the windows in her house
faced outside the wall. She gave the spies a
rope, showed them the window, and said,
"Use this rope to let yourselves down to the
ground outside the wall. 16 Then hide in
the hills. The men who are looking for you
won't be able to find you there. They'll give
up and come back after a few days, and you
can be on your way."
17-20 The spies said:

> You made us promise to let you and
> your family live. We will keep our
> promise, but you can't tell anyone why
> we were here. You must tie this red
> rope on your window when we attack,
> and your father and mother, your
> brothers, and everyone else in your
> family must be here with you. We'll
> take the blame if anyone who stays in
> this house gets hurt. But anyone who
> leaves your house will be killed, and it
> won't be our fault.

21 "I'll do exactly what you said," Rahab
promised. Then she sent them on their way
and tied the red rope to the window.
22 The spies hid in the hills for three
days while the king's soldiers looked for
them along the roads. As soon as the soldiers gave up and returned to Jericho,
23 the two spies went down into the Jordan
valley and crossed the river. They reported
to Joshua and told him everything that had
happened. 24 "We're sure the LORD has
given us the whole country," they said.
"The people there shake with fear every
time they think of us."

Israel Crosses the Jordan River

3 Early the next morning, Joshua and
the Israelites packed up and left Acacia. They went to the Jordan River and

[e]**2.3-7** *flax plants*: The stalks of flax plants were harvested, soaked in water, and dried, then their fibers were separated and spun into thread, which was woven into linen cloth. [f]**2.3-7** *gate*: Many towns and cities had walls with heavy gates that were closed at night for protection. [g]**2.10** *Red Sea*: Hebrew *yam suph* "Sea of Reeds," one of the marshes or fresh water lakes near the eastern part of the Nile Delta. This identification is based on Exodus 13.17—14.9, which lists the towns on the route of the Israelites before crossing the sea. In the Greek translation of the Scriptures made about 200 B.C., the "Sea of Reeds" was named "Red Sea." [h]**2.14** *We pray . . . promise*: Or "If you save our lives, we will save yours!" [i]**2.15** *wall*: In ancient times, cities and larger towns had high walls around them to protect them against attack. Sometimes houses were built against the wall so that the city wall formed one wall of the house. This added strength to the city wall.

2.10 **a** Ex 14.21; **b** Nu 21.21-35.

camped there that night. 2 Two days later[j]
their leaders went through the camp,
3-4 shouting, "When you see some of the
priests[k] carrying the sacred chest, you'll
know it is time to cross to the other side.
You've never been there before, and you
won't know the way, unless you follow the
chest. But don't get too close! Stay about
half a mile back."
5 Joshua told the people, "Make yourselves acceptable[l] to worship the LORD, because he is going to do some amazing
things for us."
6 Then Joshua turned to the priests and
said, "Take the chest and cross the Jordan
River ahead of us." So the priests picked up
the chest by its carrying poles and went on
ahead.
7 The LORD told Joshua, "Beginning today I will show the people that you are
their leader, and they will know that I am
helping you as I helped Moses. 8 Now, tell
the priests who are carrying the chest to go
a little way into the river and stand there."
9 Joshua spoke to the people:
Come here and listen to what the
LORD our God said he will do! 10 The
Canaanites, the Hittites, the Hivites,
the Perizzites, the Girgashites, the
Amorites, and the Jebusites control the
land on the other side of the river. But
the living God will be with you and will
force them out of the land when you
attack. And now, God is going to prove
that he's powerful enough to force
them out. 11-13 Just watch the sacred
chest that belongs to the LORD, the
ruler of the whole earth. As soon as
the priests carrying the chest step into
the Jordan, the water will stop flowing
and pile up as if someone had built a
dam across the river.
The LORD has also said that each of
the twelve tribes should choose one
man to represent it.
14 The Israelites packed up and left
camp. The priests carrying the chest
walked in front, 15 until they came to the
Jordan River. The water in the river had
risen over its banks, as it often does in
springtime.[m] But as soon as the feet of the
priests touched the water, 16-17 the river
stopped flowing, and the water started piling up at the town of Adam near Zarethan.
No water flowed toward the Dead Sea, and
the priests stood in the middle of the dry
riverbed near Jericho while everyone else
crossed over.

The People Set Up a Monument

4 After Israel had crossed the Jordan,
the LORD said to Joshua:
2-3 Tell[n] one man from each of the
twelve tribes to pick up a large rock
from where the priests are standing.
Then have the men set up those rocks
as a monument at the place where you
camp tonight.
4 Joshua chose twelve men; he called
them together, 5 and told them:
Go to the middle of the riverbed
where the sacred chest is, and pick up
a large rock. Carry it on your shoulder
to our camp. There are twelve of you,
so there will be one rock for each tribe.
6-7 Someday your children will ask,
"Why are these rocks here?" Then you
can tell them how the water stopped
flowing when the chest was being carried across the river. These rocks will
always remind our people of what happened here today.
8 The men followed the instructions
that the LORD had given Joshua. They
picked up twelve rocks, one for each tribe,
and carried them to the camp, where they
put them down.
9 Joshua had some other men set up a
monument next to the place where the
priests were standing. This monument was
also made of twelve large rocks, and it is
still there in the middle of the river.

[j] **3.2** *Two days later*: The Hebrew text has "At the end of three days," two days after they had set up camp. [k] **3.3,4** *the priests*: The Hebrew text has "the priests, the Levites"; priests belonged to the tribe of Levi. [l] **3.5** *Make yourselves acceptable*: People had to do certain things to make themselves acceptable to worship the LORD (see Leviticus 7.20, 21; 15.2, 33; 22.4-8; Deuteronomy 23.10, 11). [m] **3.15** *springtime*: Or "harvest time"; the grain harvest was in late spring. [n] **4.1-3** *Joshua . . . Tell*: Or "Joshua, you and the other leaders must tell."

The People of Israel Set Up Camp at Gilgal

10-13 The army got ready for battle and crossed the Jordan. They marched quickly past the sacred chest[o] and into the desert near Jericho. Forty thousand soldiers from the tribes of Reuben, Gad, and East Manasseh[p] led the way, as Moses had ordered.[q]

The priests stayed right where they were until the army had followed the orders that the LORD had given Moses and Joshua. Then the army watched as the priests carried the chest the rest of the way across.

14-18 "Joshua," the LORD said, "have the priests come up from the Jordan and bring the chest with them." So Joshua went over to the priests and told them what the LORD had said. And as soon as the priests carried the chest past the highest place that the floodwaters of the Jordan had reached, the river flooded its banks again.

That's how the LORD showed the Israelites that Joshua was their leader.[r] For the rest of Joshua's life, they respected him as they had respected Moses.

19 It was the tenth day of the first month[s] of the year when Israel crossed the Jordan River. They set up camp at Gilgal, which was east of the land controlled by Jericho. 20 The men who had carried the twelve rocks from the Jordan brought them to Joshua, and they made them into a monument. 21 Then Joshua told the people:

> Years from now your children will ask you why these rocks are here. 22-23 Tell them, "The LORD our God dried up the Jordan River so we could walk across. He did the same thing here for us that he did for our people at the Red Sea,[t] 24 because he wants everyone on earth to know how powerful he is. And he wants us to worship only him."

5 The Amorite kings west of the Jordan River and the Canaanite kings along the Mediterranean Sea lost their courage and their will to fight, when they heard how the LORD had dried up the Jordan River to let Israel go across.

Israel Gets Ready To Celebrate Passover

2 While Israel was camped at Gilgal, the LORD said, "Joshua, make some flint knives[u] and circumcise the rest of the Israelite men and boys."[v]

3 Joshua made the knives, then circumcised those men and boys at Haaraloth Hill.[w] 4-7 This had to be done, because none of Israel's baby boys had been circumcised during the forty years that Israel had wandered through the desert after leaving Egypt.

And why had they wandered for forty years? It was because right after they left Egypt, the men in the army had disobeyed the LORD. And the LORD had said, "None of you men will ever live to see the land that I promised Israel. It is a land rich with milk and honey, and someday your children will live there, but not before you die here in the desert."

8 Everyone who had been circumcised needed time to heal, and they stayed in camp.

9 The LORD told Joshua, "It was a disgrace for my people to be slaves in Egypt, but now I have taken away that disgrace." So the Israelites named the place Gilgal,[x] and it still has that name.

10 Israel continued to camp at Gilgal in

[o] **4.10-13** *the sacred chest*: The Hebrew text has "the LORD." The army was marching past the sacred chest, which was a symbol of God's throne on earth (see 1 Samuel 4.4 and Exodus 25.10-22; 37.1-9). [p] **4.10-13** *Forty thousand soldiers from the tribes of Reuben, Gad, and East Manasseh*: Or "There were forty thousand soldiers altogether, and those from the tribes of Reuben, Gad, and East Manasseh." [q] **4.10-13** *Moses . . . ordered*: See Numbers 32.16-32; Joshua 1.12-16.
[r] **4.14-18** *leader*: See 3.7. [s] **4.19** *first month*: Abib (also called Nisan), the first month of the Hebrew calendar, from about mid-March to mid-April. [t] **4.22,23** *Red Sea*: See the note at 2.10. [u] **5.2** *flint knives*: Flint is a stone that can be chipped until it forms a very sharp edge.
[v] **5.2** *circumcise . . . men and boys*: They could not celebrate Passover unless they were circumcised (see Exodus 12.43-49). [w] **5.3** *Haaraloth Hill*: Or "Foreskin Hill."
[x] **5.9** *Gilgal*: In Hebrew "Gilgal" sounds like "take away."
5.4-7 Nu 14.27-35. **5.10** Ex 12.1-13.

the desert near Jericho, and on the fourteenth day of the same month,[y] they celebrated Passover.

11-12 The next day, God stopped sending the Israelites manna[z] to eat each morning, and they started eating food grown in the land of Canaan. They ate roasted grain[a] and thin bread[b] made of the barley they had gathered from nearby fields.

Israel Captures Jericho

13 One day, Joshua was near Jericho when he saw a man standing some distance in front of him. The man was holding a sword, so Joshua walked up to him and asked, "Are you on our side or on our enemies' side?"

14 "Neither," he answered. "I am here because I am the commander of the LORD's army."

Joshua fell to his knees and bowed down to the ground. "I am your servant," he said. "Tell me what to do."

15 "Take off your sandals," the commander answered. "This is a holy place."

So Joshua took off his sandals.

6 Meanwhile, the people of Jericho had been locking the gates in their town wall because they were afraid of the Israelites. No one could go out or come in.

2-3 The LORD said to Joshua:

With my help, you and your army will defeat the king of Jericho and his army, and you will capture the town. Here is how to do it: March slowly around Jericho once a day for six days.
4 Take along the sacred chest and have seven priests walk in front of it, carrying trumpets.[c]

But on the seventh day, march slowly around the town seven times while the priests blow their trumpets.
5 Then the priests will blast on their trumpets, and everyone else will shout. The wall will fall down, and your soldiers can go straight in from every side.

6 Joshua called the priests together and said, "Take the chest and have seven priests carry trumpets and march ahead of it."

7-10 Next, he gave the army their orders: "March slowly around Jericho. A few of you will go ahead of the chest to guard it, but most of you will follow it. Don't shout the battle cry or yell or even talk until the day I tell you to. Then let out a shout!"

As soon as Joshua finished giving the orders, the army started marching. One group of soldiers led the way, with seven priests marching behind them and blowing trumpets. Then came the priests carrying the chest, followed by the rest of the soldiers.
11 They obeyed Joshua's orders and carried the chest once around the town before returning to camp for the night.

12-14 Early the next morning, Joshua and everyone else started marching around Jericho in the same order as the day before. One group of soldiers was in front, followed by the seven priests with trumpets and the priests who carried the chest. The rest of the army came next. The seven priests blew their trumpets while everyone marched slowly around Jericho and back to camp. They did this once a day for six days.

15 On the seventh day, the army got up at daybreak. They marched slowly around Jericho the same as they had done for the past six days, except on this day they went around seven times.
16 Then the priests blew the trumpets, and Joshua yelled:

Get ready to shout! The LORD will let you capture this town.
17 But you must destroy it and everything in it, to

[y]**5.10** *the same month*: See the note at 4.19. [z]**5.11,12** *manna*: The special food that God provided for the Israelites while they were in the desert for forty years. It was about the size of a small seed, and it appeared on the ground during the night, except on the Sabbath. It was gathered early in the morning, ground up, and then baked or boiled (see Exodus 16.13-35; Numbers 11.4-9).
[a]**5.11,12** *roasted grain*: Roasted grain was made by cooking the grain in a dry pan or on a flat rock, or by holding a bunch of grain stalks over a fire. [b]**5.11,12** *thin bread*: Bread made without yeast. Israelites were not supposed to eat bread made with yeast for the week following Passover. That week is called the Festival of Thin Bread (see Exodus 12.14-20; 13.3-7). [c]**6.4** *trumpets*: These were hollowed-out ram's horns.

5.11,12 Ex 16.35, 36.

show that it now belongs to the LORD.[d]
The woman Rahab helped the spies we
sent,[e] so protect her and the others
who are inside her house. But kill
everyone else in the town. 18-19 The silver and gold and everything made of
bronze and iron belong to the LORD
and must be put in his treasury. Be
careful to follow these instructions, because if you see something you want
and take it, the LORD will destroy Israel. And it will be all your fault.[f]
20 The priests blew their trumpets
again, and the soldiers shouted as loud as
they could. The walls of Jericho fell flat.
Then the soldiers rushed up the hill, went
straight into the town, and captured it.
21-25 They killed everyone, men and
women, young and old, everyone except
Rahab and the others in her house. They
even killed every cow, sheep, and donkey.

Joshua said to the two men who had been spies, "Rahab kept you safe when I sent you to Jericho. We promised to protect her and her family, and we will keep that promise. Now go into her house and bring them out."

The two men went into Rahab's house and brought her out, along with her father and mother, her brothers, and her other relatives. Rahab and her family had to stay in a place just outside the Israelite army camp.[g] But later they were allowed to live among the Israelites, and her descendants still do.

The Israelites took the silver and gold and the things made of bronze and iron and put them with the rest of the treasure that was kept at the LORD's house.[h] Finally,
they set fire to Jericho and everything in it.
26 After Jericho was destroyed, Joshua
warned the people, "Someday a man will rebuild Jericho, but the LORD will put a curse on him, and the man's oldest son will die when he starts to build the town wall. And by the time he finishes the wall and puts gates in it, all his children will be dead."[i]

27 The LORD helped Joshua in every-
thing he did, and Joshua was famous everywhere in Canaan.

Achan Is Punished for Stealing from the LORD

7 The LORD had said that everything in
Jericho belonged to him.[j] But Achan[k] from the Judah tribe took some of the things from Jericho for himself. And so the LORD was angry with the Israelites, because one of them had disobeyed him.[l]
2 While Israel was still camped near
Jericho, Joshua sent some spies with these instructions: "Go to the town of Ai[m] and find out whatever you can about the region around the town."

The spies left and went to Ai, which is
east of Bethel and near Beth-Aven. 3 They
went back to Joshua and reported, "You don't need to send the whole army to attack Ai—two or three thousand troops will be enough. Why bother the whole army for a town that small?"

4-5 Joshua sent about three thousand
soldiers to attack Ai. But the men of Ai fought back and chased the Israelite soldiers away from the town gate and down the hill to the stone quarries.[n] Thirty-six Is-

[d]**6.17** *destroy . . . now belongs to the LORD*: Destroying a city and everything in it, including its people and animals, showed that it belonged to the LORD and could no longer be used by humans.
[e]**6.17** *sent*: See 2.1, 21. [f]**6.18,19** *Be careful . . . fault*: One ancient translation; Hebrew "Don't keep any of it for yourself. If you do, the LORD will destroy both you and Israel." [g]**6.21-25** *camp*: Rahab and her family were Canaanites and were considered unclean. If they stayed in the Israelite army camp, the Lord would not help the Israelite army in battle (see Deuteronomy 23.9-14). However, Rahab and her family later became part of Israel. [h]**6.21-25** *the LORD's house*: A name for the place of worship, which at that time was the sacred tent. [i]**6.26** *by the time . . . dead*: Or "when he puts gates into the town wall, his youngest son will die." [j]**7.1** *belonged to him*: See the note at 6.17. [k]**7.1** *Achan*: The Hebrew text has "Achan, son of Carmi, grandson of Abdi, and great-grandson of Zerah." [l]**7.1** *the LORD was angry . . . disobeyed him*: Even though only one person had disobeyed, it meant that the LORD's instructions to the people of Israel had not been followed, and the whole nation was held responsible. [m]**7.2** *of Ai*: Or "called The Ruins."
[n]**7.4,5** *stone quarries*: Or "Shebarim."
6.20 He 11.30. **6.21-25** He 11.31. **6.26** 1 K 16.34.

raelite soldiers were killed, and the Israelite
army felt discouraged.
6 Joshua and the leaders of Israel tore
their clothes and put dirt on their heads to
show their sorrow. They lay facedown on
the ground in front of the sacred chest until sunset. 7 Then Joshua said:

Our LORD, did you bring us across
the Jordan River just so the Amorites
could destroy us? This wouldn't have
happened if we had agreed to stay on
the other side of the Jordan. 8 I don't
even know what to say to you, since Israel's army has turned and run from
the enemy. 9 Everyone will think you
weren't strong enough to protect your
people. Now the Canaanites and
everyone else who lives in the land will
surround us and wipe us out.

10 The LORD answered:

Stop lying there on the ground! Get
up! 11 I said everything in Jericho belonged to me and had to be destroyed.
But the Israelites have kept some of
the things for themselves. They stole
from me and hid what they took. Then
they lied about it. 12 What they stole
was supposed to be destroyed, and now
Israel itself must be destroyed. I cannot help you anymore until you do exactly what I have said. That's why Israel turns and runs from its enemies
instead of standing up to them.

13 Tell the people of Israel, "Tomorrow you will meet with the LORD your
God, so make yourselves acceptable to
worship him. The LORD says that you
have taken things that should have
been destroyed. You won't be able to
stand up to your enemies until you get
rid of those things.

14 "Tomorrow morning everyone
must gather near the place of worship.
You will come forward tribe by tribe,
and the LORD will show which tribe is
guilty. Next, the clans in that tribe
must come forward, and the LORD will
show which clan is guilty. The families
in that clan must come, and the LORD
will point out the guilty family. Finally,
the men in that family must come,
15 and the LORD will show who stole what
should have been destroyed. That man
must be put to death, his body burned,
and his possessions thrown into the
fire. He has done a terrible thing by
breaking the sacred agreement that the
LORD made with Israel."

16 Joshua got up early the next morning
and brought each tribe to the place of worship, where the LORD showed that the
Judah tribe was guilty. 17 Then Joshua
brought the clans of Judah to the LORD,
and the LORD showed that the Zerah clan
was guilty. One by one he brought the
leader of each family in the Zerah clan to
the LORD, and the LORD showed that
Zabdi's family was guilty. 18 Finally, Joshua
brought each man in Zabdi's family to the
LORD, and the LORD showed that Achan
was the guilty one.

19 "Achan," Joshua said, "the LORD God
of Israel has decided that you are guilty. Is
this true? Tell me what you did, and don't
try to hide anything."

20 "It's true," Achan answered. "I sinned
and disobeyed the LORD God of Israel.
21-22 While we were in Jericho, I saw a
beautiful Babylonian robe, two hundred
pieces of silver, and a gold bar that weighed
the same as fifty pieces of gold. I wanted
them for myself, so I took them. I dug a
hole under my tent and hid the silver, the
gold, and the robe."

Joshua had some people run to Achan's
tent, where they found the silver, the gold,
and the robe. 23 They brought them back
and put them in front of the sacred chest,
so Joshua and the rest of the Israelites
could see them. 24 Then everyone took
Achan and the things he had stolen to
Trouble Valley.[o] They also took along his
sons and daughters, his cattle, donkeys,
and sheep, his tent, and everything else
that belonged to him.

25 Joshua said, "Achan, you caused us a
lot of trouble. Now the LORD is paying you
back with the same kind of trouble."

The people of Israel then stoned to
death Achan and his family. They made a
fire and burned the bodies, together with
what Achan had stolen, and all his posses-

[o] **7.24** *Trouble Valley*: Or "Achor Valley."

sions. [26] They covered the remains with a big pile of rocks, which is still there. Then the LORD stopped being angry with Israel.

That's how the place came to be called Trouble Valley.

Israel Destroys the Town of Ai

8 [1-2] The LORD told Joshua:

Don't be afraid, and don't be discouraged by what happened at the town of Ai. Take the army and attack again. But first, have part of the army set up an ambush on the other side of the town. I will help you defeat the king of Ai and his army, and you will capture the town and the land around it. Destroy Ai and kill its king as you did at Jericho. But you may keep the livestock and everything else you want.

[3-4] Joshua quickly got the army ready to attack Ai. He chose thirty thousand of his best soldiers and gave them these orders:

Tonight, while it is dark, march to Ai and take up a position behind the town. Get as close to the town as you can without being seen, but be ready to attack.

[5-6] The rest of the army will come with me and attack near the gate. When the people of Ai come out to fight, we'll run away and let them chase us. They will think we are running from them just like the first time. But when we've let them chase us far enough away, [7] you come out of hiding. The LORD our God will help you capture the town. [8] Then set it on fire, as the LORD has told us to do. Those are your orders, [9] now go!

The thirty thousand soldiers went to a place on the west side of Ai, between Ai and Bethel, where they could hide and wait to attack.

That night, Joshua stayed in camp with the rest of the army. [10] Early the next morning he got his troops ready to move out, and he and the other leaders of Israel led them to Ai. [11] They set up camp in full view of the town, across the valley to the north. [12] Joshua had already sent five thousand soldiers to the west side of the town to hide and wait to attack. [13] Now all his troops were in place. Part of the army was in the camp to the north of Ai, and the others were hiding to the west, ready to make a surprise attack. That night, Joshua went into the valley.[p]

[14-15] The king of Ai saw Joshua's army, so the king and his troops hurried out early the next morning to fight them. Joshua and his army pretended to be beaten, and they let the men of Ai chase them toward the desert. The king and his army were facing the Jordan valley as Joshua had planned.

The king did not realize that some Israelite soldiers were hiding behind the town. [16-17] So he called out every man in Ai to go after Joshua's troops. They all rushed out to chase the Israelite army, and they left the town gates wide open. Not one man was left in Ai or in Bethel.[q]

Joshua let the men of Ai chase him and his army farther and farther away from Ai. [18] Finally, the LORD told Joshua, "Point your sword[r] at the town of Ai, because now I am going to help you defeat it!"

As soon as Joshua pointed his sword at the town, [19] the soldiers who had been hiding got up and ran into the town. They captured it and set it on fire.

[20-21] When Joshua and his troops saw smoke rising from the town, they knew that the other part of their army had captured it. So they turned and attacked.

The men of Ai looked back and saw smoke rising from their town. But they could not escape, because the soldiers they had been chasing had suddenly turned and started fighting. [22-24] Meanwhile, the other Israelite soldiers had come from the town and attacked the men of Ai from the rear. The Israelites captured the king of Ai and brought him to Joshua. They also chased the rest of the men of Ai into the desert and killed them.[s]

The Israelite army went back to Ai and

[p] **8.13** *valley*: This may refer either to the Jordan River valley or to the valley between the Israelite camp and Ai. [q] **8.16,17** *Ai or in Bethel*: Hebrew; one ancient translation "Ai." [r] **8.18** *sword*: Or "spear." [s] **8.22-24** *Joshua. They also chased . . . them*: Or "Joshua. The men of Ai had chased the Israelites into the desert, but the Israelites killed them there."

killed everyone there. [25-26] Joshua kept his sword pointed at the town of Ai until every last one of Ai's twelve thousand people was dead. [27] But the Israelites took the animals and the other possessions of the people of Ai, because this was what the LORD had told Joshua to do.

[28-29] Joshua made sure every building in Ai was burned to the ground. He told his men to kill the king of Ai and hang his body on a tree. Then at sunset he told the Israelites to take down the body,[t] throw it in the gateway of the town, and cover it with a big pile of rocks. Those rocks are still there, and the town itself has never been rebuilt.

Joshua Reads the Blessings and Curses

(Deuteronomy 27.1-26)

[30-32] One day, Joshua led the people of Israel to Mount Ebal, where he told some of his men, "Build an altar for offering sacrifices to the LORD. And use stones that have never been cut with iron tools,[u] because that is what Moses taught in *The Book of the Law*."[v]

Joshua offered sacrifices to please the LORD[w] and to ask his blessing.[x] Then with the Israelites still watching, he copied parts of *The Book of the Law*[y] of Moses onto stones.

[33-35] Moses had said that everyone in Israel was to go to the valley between Mount Ebal and Mount Gerizim, where they were to be blessed. So everyone went there, including the foreigners, the leaders, officials, and judges. Half of the people stood on one side of the valley, and half on the other side, with the priests from the Levi tribe standing in the middle with the sacred chest. Then in a loud voice, Joshua read the blessings and curses from *The Book of the Law*[y] of Moses.[z]

The People of Gibeon Trick the Leaders of Israel

9 [1-2] The kings west of the Jordan River heard about Joshua's victories, and so they got together and decided to attack Joshua and Israel. These kings were from the hill country and from the foothills to the west, as well as from the Mediterranean seacoast as far north as the Lebanon Mountains. Some of them were Hittites, others were Amorites or Canaanites, and still others were Perizzites, Hivites, or Jebusites.

[3] The people of Gibeon had also heard what Joshua had done to Jericho and Ai. [4] So they decided that some of their men should pretend to be messengers to Israel from a faraway country.[a] The men put worn-out bags on their donkeys and found some old wineskins that had cracked and had been sewn back together. [5] Their sandals were old and patched, and their clothes were worn out. They even took along some dry and crumbly bread. [6] Then they went to the Israelite camp at Gilgal, where they said to Joshua and the men of Israel, "We have come from a country that is far from here. Please make a peace treaty with us."

[7-8] The Israelites replied, "But maybe you really live near us. We can't make a peace treaty with you if you live nearby."[b]

The Gibeonites[c] said, "If you make a peace treaty with us, we will be your servants."

[t]**8.28,29** *take down the body*: See Deuteronomy 21.22, 23. [u]**8.30-32** *use stones . . . iron tools*: See Exodus 20.25. [v]**8.30-32** *taught . . . Law*: Or "commanded . . . Teachings." [w]**8.30-32** *sacrifices to please the LORD*: These sacrifices have been traditionally called "whole burnt offerings" because the whole animal was burned on the altar. A main purpose of such sacrifices was to please the LORD with the smell of the sacrifice, and so in the CEV they are often called "sacrifices to please the LORD." [x]**8.30-32** *to ask his blessing*: These sacrifices have traditionally been called "peace offerings," or "offerings of well-being." A main purpose was to ask for the LORD's blessing, and so in the CEV they are often called "sacrifices to ask the LORD's blessing." [y]**8.30-32,33-35** *Law*: Or "Teachings." [z]**8.33-35** *the blessings . . . Moses*: Or "all of *The Book of the Law of Moses*, including the blessings and the curses." [a]**9.4** *So . . . country*: One possible meaning for the difficult Hebrew text. [b]**9.7,8** *nearby*: See Deuteronomy 20.10-18. [c]**9.7,8** *Gibeonites*: Hebrew "Hivites."

8.30-32 **a** Dt 27.2-8; **b** Ex 20.25 **8.33-35** Dt 11.29; 27.11-26. **9.7,8** Ex 23.32; 34.12; Dt 7.2.

"Who are you?" Joshua asked. "Where do you come from?"

They answered:

> 9 We are your servants, and we live far from here. We came because the LORD your God is so famous. We heard what the LORD did in Egypt 10 and what he did to those two Amorite kings on the other side of the Jordan: King Og of Bashan, who lived in Ashtaroth, and King Sihon of Heshbon.
>
> 11 Our leaders and everyone who lives in our country told us to meet with you and tell you that all of us are your servants. They said to ask you to make a peace treaty with our people. They told us to be sure and take along enough food for our journey. 12 See this dry, crumbly bread of ours? It was hot out of the oven when we packed the food on the day we left our homes. 13 These cracked wineskins were new when we filled them, and our clothes and sandals are worn out because we have traveled so far.

14 The Israelites tried some of the food,[d] but they did not ask the LORD if he wanted them to make a treaty. 15 So Joshua made a peace treaty with the messengers and promised that Israel would not kill their people. Israel's leaders swore that Israel would keep this promise.

16-17 A couple of days later,[e] the Israelites found out that these people actually lived in the nearby towns of Gibeon, Chephirah, Beeroth, and Kiriath-Jearim.[f] So the Israelites left the place where they had camped and arrived at the four towns two days later.[g] 18 But they did not attack the towns, because the Israelite leaders had sworn in the name of the LORD that they would let these people live.

The Israelites complained about their leaders' decision not to attack, 19-21 but the leaders reminded them, "We promised these people in the name of the LORD God of Israel that we would let them live, so we must not harm them. If we break our promise, God will punish us. We'll let them live, but we'll make them cut wood and carry water for our people."

22 Joshua told some of his soldiers, "I want to meet with the Gibeonite leaders. Bring them here."

When the Gibeonites came, Joshua said, "You live close to us. Why did you lie by claiming you lived far away? 23 Now you are under a curse, and your people will have to send workers to cut wood and carry water for the place of worship."[h]

24 The Gibeonites answered, "The LORD your God told his servant Moses that you were to kill everyone who lives here and take their land for yourselves. We were afraid you would kill us, and so we tricked you into making a peace treaty. But we agreed to be your servants, 25 and you are strong enough to do anything to us that you want. We just ask you to do what seems right."

26 Joshua did not let the Israelites kill the Gibeonites, 27 but he did tell the Gibeonites that they would have to be servants of the nation of Israel. They would have to cut firewood and bring it for the priests to use for burning sacrifices on the LORD's altar, wherever the LORD decided the altar would be. The Gibeonites would also have to carry water for the priests. And that is still the work of the Gibeonites.

Joshua Commands the Sun To Stand Still

10 King Adonizedek of Jerusalem[i] heard that Joshua had captured and destroyed the town of Ai, and then killed its king as he had done at Jericho. He

[d]**9.14** *tried . . . food*: Probably to see if it really was old or to show that they wanted peace.
[e]**9.16,17** *A couple . . . later*: The Hebrew text has "At the end of three days," meaning two days after the day the treaty was made. [f]**9.16,17** *Gibeon, Chephirah, Beeroth, and Kiriath-Jearim*: These towns were twenty to thirty miles west of the Israelite camp at Gilgal. [g]**9.16,17** *A couple of days . . . later*: Or "A couple of days later, the Israelites moved their camp to the area near the towns of Gibeon, Chephirah, Beeroth, and Kiriath-Jearim. When they arrived, they realized that they had made a peace treaty with the people of these nearby towns!" [h]**9.23** *the place of worship*: The Hebrew text has "God's house," which at that time was the sacred tent. [i]**10.1** *Jerusalem*: Jerusalem was not an Israelite city at this time.
9.10 Nu 21.21-35.

also learned that the Gibeonites had signed
a peace treaty with Israel. 2 This frightened
Adonizedek and his people. They knew that
Gibeon was a large town, as big as the
towns that had kings, and even bigger than
the town of Ai had been. And all of the
men of Gibeon were warriors. 3 So
Adonizedek sent messages to the kings of
four other towns: King Hoham of Hebron,
King Piram of Jarmuth, King Japhia of
Lachish, and King Debir of Eglon. The
messages said, 4 "The Gibeonites have
signed a peace treaty with Joshua and the
Israelites. Come and help me attack
Gibeon!"
5 When these five Amorite kings called
their armies together and attacked Gibeon,
6 the Gibeonites sent a message to the Israelite camp at Gilgal: "Joshua, please
come and rescue us! The Amorite kings
from the hill country have joined together
and are attacking us. We are your servants,
so don't let us down. Please hurry!"
7 Joshua and his army, including his
best warriors, left Gilgal. 8 "Joshua," the
LORD said, "don't be afraid of the Amorites.
They will run away when you attack, and I
will help you defeat them."
9 Joshua marched all night from Gilgal
to Gibeon and made a surprise attack on
the Amorite camp. 10 The LORD made the
enemy panic, and the Israelites started
killing them right and left. They[j] chased
the Amorite troops up the road to Beth-
Horon and kept on killing them, until they
reached the towns of Azekah and
Makkedah.[k] 11 And while these troops were
going down through Beth-Horon Pass,[l] the
LORD made huge hailstones fall on them all
the way to Azekah. More of the enemy soldiers died from the hail than from the Israelite weapons.
12-13 The LORD was helping the Israelites defeat the Amorites that day. So
about noon, Joshua prayed to the LORD
loud enough for the Israelites to hear:

"Our LORD, make the sun stop
in the sky over Gibeon,
and the moon stand still
over Aijalon Valley."[m]
So the sun and the moon
stopped and stood still
until Israel defeated its enemies.

This poem can be found in *The Book of
Jashar*.[n] The sun stood still and didn't go
down for about a whole day. 14 Never before
and never since has the LORD done anything like that for someone who prayed.
The LORD was really fighting for Israel.
15 After the battle, Joshua and the Israelites went back to their camp at Gilgal.

Joshua Kills the Five Enemy Kings

16 While the enemy soldiers were running from the Israelites, the five enemy
kings ran away and hid in a cave near
Makkedah. 17 Joshua's soldiers told him,
"The five kings have been found in a cave
near Makkedah."
18 Joshua answered, "Roll some big
stones over the mouth of the cave and
leave a few soldiers to guard it. 19 But you
and everyone else must keep after the enemy troops, because they will be safe if they
reach their walled towns. Don't let them
get away! The LORD our God is helping us
get rid of them." 20 So Joshua and the Israelites almost wiped out the enemy soldiers. Only a few safely reached their
walled towns.
21 The Israelite army returned to their
camp at Makkedah, where Joshua was
waiting for them. No one around there
dared say anything bad about the Israelites.
22 Joshua told his soldiers, "Now, move the
rocks from the entrance to the cave and
bring those five kings to me."
23 The soldiers opened the entrance to
the cave and brought out the kings of
Jerusalem, Hebron, Jarmuth, Lachish, and
Eglon. 24 After Joshua had called the army

[j] **10.10** *They*: Or "The LORD." [k] **10.10** *Makkedah*: A total distance of about twenty-five miles. [l] **10.11** *Beth-Horon Pass*: A two-mile long, steeply-sloping valley between the towns of Upper Beth-Horon and Lower Beth-Horon. [m] **10.12,13** *Aijalon Valley*: A valley southwest of Beth-Horon Pass. [n] **10.12,13** *Book of Jashar*: This book may have been a collection of ancient war songs.

10.12,13 2 S 1.18; Si 46.4-6.

together, he forced the five kings to lie down on the ground. Then he called his officers forward and told them, "You fought these kings along with me, so put your feet on their necks." The officers did,
25 and Joshua continued, "Don't ever be afraid or discouraged. Be brave and strong. This is what the LORD will do to all your enemies."

26 Joshua killed the five kings and told his men to hang each body on a tree. Then at sunset
27 he told some of his troops, "Take the bodies down and throw them into the cave where the kings were found. Cover the entrance to the cave with big rocks."

Joshua's troops obeyed his orders, and those rocks are still there.

Joshua Continues the Fighting

28 Later that day, Joshua captured Makkedah and killed its king and everyone else in the town, just as he had done at Jericho.

29 Joshua and his army left Makkedah and attacked the town of Libnah.
30 The LORD let them capture the town and its king, and they killed the king and everyone else, just as they had done at Jericho.

31 Joshua then led his army to Lachish, and they set up camp around the town. They attacked,
32 and the next day the LORD let them capture the town. They killed everyone, as they had done at Libnah.
33 King Horam of Gezer arrived to help Lachish, but Joshua and his troops attacked and destroyed him and his army.

34 From Lachish, Joshua took his troops to Eglon, where they set up camp surrounding the town. They attacked,
35 captured it that same day, then killed everyone, as they had done at Lachish.

36 Joshua and his army left Eglon and attacked Hebron.
37 They captured the town and the nearby villages, then killed everyone, including the king. They destroyed Hebron in the same way they had destroyed Eglon.

38 Joshua and the Israelite army turned and attacked Debir.
39 They captured the town, and its nearby villages. Then they destroyed Debir and killed its king, together with everyone else, just as they had done with Hebron and Libnah.

40 Joshua captured towns everywhere in the land: In the central hill country and the foothills to the west, in the Southern Desert and the region that slopes down toward the Dead Sea. Whenever he captured a town, he would kill the king and everyone else, as the LORD God of Israel had commanded.
41 Joshua wiped out towns from Kadesh-Barnea to Gaza, everywhere in the region of Goshen,[o] and as far north as Gibeon.
42-43 The LORD fought on Israel's side, so Joshua and the Israelite army were able to capture these kings and take their land. They fought one battle after another, then they went back to their camp at Gilgal after capturing all that land.

Joshua Captures Towns in the North

11 King Jabin of Hazor heard about Joshua's victories, so he sent messages to many nearby kings and asked them to join him in fighting Israel. He sent these messages to King Jobab of Madon, the kings of Shimron and Achshaph,
2 the kings in the northern hill country and in the Jordan River valley south of Lake Galilee,[p] and the kings in the foothills and in Naphath-Dor to the west.
3 He sent messages to the Canaanite kings in the east and the west, to the Amorite, Hittite, Perizzite, and Jebusite kings in the hill country, and to the Hivite kings in the region of Mizpah, near the foot of Mount Hermon.[q]

4-5 The kings and their armies went to Merom Pond,[r] where they set up camp, and got ready to fight Israel. It seemed as though there were more soldiers and horses and chariots than there are grains of sand on a beach.

6 The LORD told Joshua:

Don't let them frighten you! I'll

[o] **10.41** *Goshen*: A region between the hill country of Judah and the desert further south. Not the same Goshen as in Genesis 47.4-6. [p] **11.2** *Lake Galilee*: The Hebrew text has "Lake Chinnereth," an earlier name. [q] **11.3** *Mizpah, near the foot of Mount Hermon*: Probably the same region as Mizpeh Valley in verses 8, 9, but different from the two other places named Mizpeh in 15.37-41; 18.25-28, and also different from the Mizpah mentioned in Genesis 31.49 and Judges 10.17. [r] **11.4,5** *Pond*: Or "Gorge."

help you defeat them, and by this time tomorrow they will be dead.

When you attack, the first thing you have to do is to cripple their horses. Then after the battle is over,[s] burn their chariots.

7 Joshua and his army made a surprise attack against the enemy camp at Merom Pond[t] 8-9 and crippled the enemies' horses.[u] Joshua followed the LORD's instructions, and the LORD helped Israel defeat the enemy. The Israelite army even chased enemy soldiers as far as Misrephoth-Maim to the northwest,[v] the city of Sidon to the north, and Mizpeh Valley to the northeast.[w] None of the enemy soldiers escaped alive. The Israelites came back after the battle and burned the enemy's chariots.

10 Up to this time, the king of Hazor had controlled the kingdoms that had joined together to attack Israel, so Joshua led his army back and captured Hazor. They killed its king 11 and everyone else, then they set the town on fire.

12-15 Joshua captured all the towns where the enemy kings had ruled. These towns were built on small hills,[x] and Joshua did not set fire to any of these towns, except Hazor. The Israelites kept the animals and everything of value from these towns, but they killed everyone who lived in them, including their kings. That's what the LORD had told his servant Moses to do, that's what Moses had told Joshua to do, and that's exactly what Joshua did.

16 Joshua and his army took control of the northern and southern hill country, the foothills to the west, the Southern Desert, the whole region of Goshen,[y] and the Jordan River valley. 17-18 They took control of the land from Mount Halak near the country of Edom in the south to Baal-Gad in Lebanon Valley at the foot of Mount Hermon in the north. Joshua and his army were at war with the kings in this region for a long time, but finally they captured and put to death the last king.

19-20 The LORD had told Moses that he wanted the towns in this region destroyed and their people killed without mercy. That's why the LORD made the people in the towns stubborn and determined to fight Israel. The only town that signed a peace treaty with Israel was the Hivite town of Gibeon. The Israelite army captured the rest of the towns in battle.

21 During this same time, Joshua and his army killed the Anakim[z] from the northern and southern hill country. They also destroyed the towns where the Anakim had lived, including Hebron, Debir, and Anab. 22 There were not any Anakim left in the regions where the Israelites lived, although there were still some in Gaza, Gath, and Ashdod.[a]

23 That's how Joshua captured the land, just as the LORD had commanded Moses, and Joshua divided it up among the tribes.

Finally, there was peace in the land.

The Kings Defeated by the Israelites

12 Before Moses died, he and the people of Israel had defeated two kings east of the Jordan River. These kings had ruled the region from the Arnon River gorge in the south to Mount Hermon in the north, including the eastern side of the Jordan River valley.

2 The first king that Moses and the Israelites defeated was an Amorite, King Sihon of Heshbon.[b] The southern border of

[s]**11.6** *When . . . over*: Or "After the battle is over, cripple their horses and burn their chariots."
[t]**11.7** *Pond*: See the note at 11.4, 5. [u]**11.8,9** *and crippled the enemies' horses*: It is also possible that the Israelites crippled the enemies' horses after the battle at the same time they burned the enemies' chariots; see the note at 11.6. [v]**11.8,9** *Misrephoth-Maim . . . northwest*: Or "the town of Misrephoth to the northwest" or "the Misrephoth River." [w]**11.8,9** *northeast*: These three areas were twenty to thirty-five miles north of Merom. [x]**11.12-15** *small hills*: Towns were often built on top of the ruins of a previous town that had been destroyed. When this happened many times at one place, a hill was formed. [y]**11.16** *Goshen*: See the note at 10.41.
[z]**11.21** *Anakim*: Perhaps a group of very large people that lived in Palestine before the Israelites (see Numbers 13.33 and Deuteronomy 2.10, 11, 20, 21). [a]**11.22** *Gaza, Gath, and Ashdod*: Towns in Philistia. [b]**12.2** *King Sihon of Heshbon*: See Numbers 21.21-31.
11.19,20 Dt 7.16. **12.1-5** Nu 21.21-35; Dt 2.26—3.11.

his kingdom ran down the middle of the Arnon River gorge, taking in the town of Aroer on the northern edge of the gorge. The Jabbok River separated Sihon's kingdom from the Ammonites on the east. Then the Jabbok turned west and became his northern border, so his kingdom included the southern half of the region of Gilead. 3 Sihon also controlled the eastern side of the Jordan River valley from Lake Galilee[c] south to Beth-Jeshimoth and the Dead Sea. In addition to these regions, he ruled the town called Slopes of Mount Pisgah[d] and the land south of there at the foot of the hill.

4 Next, Moses and the Israelites defeated King Og of Bashan,[e] who lived in the town of Ashtaroth part of each year and in Edrei the rest of the year. Og was one of the last of the Rephaim.[f] 5 His kingdom stretched north to Mount Hermon, east to the town of Salecah, and included the land of Bashan as far west as the borders of the kingdoms of Geshur and Maacah. He also ruled the northern half of Gilead.

6 Moses, the LORD's servant, had led the people of Israel in defeating Sihon and Og. Then Moses gave their land to the tribes of Reuben, Gad, and East Manasseh.

7-8 Later, Joshua and the Israelites defeated many kings west of the Jordan River, from Baal-Gad in Lebanon Valley in the north to Mount Halak near the country of Edom in the south. This region included the hill country and the foothills, the Jordan River valley and its western slopes, and the Southern Desert. Joshua and the Israelites took this land from the Hittites, the Amorites, the Canaanites, the Perizzites, the Hivites, and the Jebusites. Joshua divided up the land among the tribes of Israel.

The Israelites defeated the kings of the following towns west of the Jordan River:

9-24 Jericho, Ai near Bethel, Jerusalem, Hebron, Jarmuth, Lachish, Eglon, Gezer, Debir, Geder, Hormah, Arad, Libnah, Adullam, Makkedah, Bethel, Tappuah, Hepher, Aphek, Lasharon,[g] Madon, Hazor, Shimron-Meron, Achshaph, Taanach, Megiddo, Kedesh, Jokneam on Mount Carmel, Dor in Naphath-Dor, Goiim in Galilee,[h] and Tirzah.[i]

There were thirty-one of these kings in all.

The Land Israel Had Not Yet Taken

13 Many years later, the LORD told Joshua:

Now you are very old, but there is still a lot of land that Israel has not yet taken. 2-7 First, there is the Canaanite territory that starts at the Shihor River just east of Egypt and goes north to Ekron. The southern part of this region belongs to the Avvites and the Geshurites,[j] and the land around Gaza, Ashdod, Ashkelon, Gath, and Ekron belongs to the five Philistine rulers.

The other Canaanite territory is in the north. Its northern border starts at the town of Arah, which belongs to the Sidonians. From there, it goes to Aphek,[k] then along the Amorite border[l] to Hamath Pass.[m] The eastern border starts at Hamath Pass and goes south to Baal-Gad at the foot of Mount Hermon, and its southern boundary runs west from there to Misrephoth-Maim.[n] This northern region includes the Lebanon Mountains and the land

[c] **12.3** *Lake Galilee*: See the note at 11.2. [d] **12.3** *the town called Slopes of Mount Pisgah*: Or "the slopes of Mount Pisgah." [e] **12.4** *King Og of Bashan*: See Numbers 21.33-35.
[f] **12.4** *Rephaim*: Perhaps a group of very large people that lived in Palestine before the Israelites (see Deuteronomy 2.10, 11, 20, 21). [g] **12.9-24** *Aphek, Lasharon*: Or "Aphek in the Sharon Plain." [h] **12.9-24** *Galilee*: One ancient translation; Hebrew "Gilgal." [i] **12.9-24** *Jericho . . . Tirzah*: There are some differences in this list between the Hebrew and several ancient translations. [j] **13.2-7** *Geshurites*: Not the same Geshur as in 12.5 and 13.11. One ancient translation has "Gezerites." Gezer was a town north of Ekron that the Israelites did not capture (see Judges 1.29). [k] **13.2-7** *Aphek*: Not the same Aphek as in 12.9-24. [l] **13.2-7** *Amorite border*: What had been the southern border of the old Amorite kingdom of Amurru. [m] **13.2-7** *Hamath Pass*: Or "Lebo-Hamath." [n] **13.2-7** *Misrephoth-Maim*: Or "Misrephoth" or "the Misrephoth River."
12.6 Nu 32.33; Dt 3.12-17. **13.2-7** Nu 33.54.

that belongs to the Gebalites[o] and the Sidonians who live in the hill country from the Lebanon Mountains to Misrephoth-Maim.

With my help, Israel will capture these Canaanite territories and force out the people who live there. But you must divide up the land from the Jordan River to the Mediterranean Sea[p] among the nine tribes and the half of Manasseh that don't have any land yet. Then each tribe will have its own land.

The Land East of the Jordan River

8 Moses had already given land east of the Jordan River to the tribes of Reuben, Gad, and half of Manasseh. 9 This region stretched north from the town in the middle of the Arnon River valley, and included the town of Aroer on the northern edge of the valley. It covered the flatlands of Medeba north of Dibon, 10 and took in the towns that had belonged to Sihon, the Amorite king of Heshbon. Some of these towns were as far east as the Ammonite border.

11-12 Geshur and Maacah were part of this region, and so was the whole territory that King Og had ruled, that is, Gilead, Mount Hermon, and all of Bashan as far east as Salecah. Og had lived in Ashtaroth part of each year, and he had lived in Edrei the rest of the year. Og had been one of the last of the Rephaim,[q] but Moses had defeated Sihon and Og and their people[r] and had forced them to leave their land. 13 However, the Israelites did not force the people of Geshur and Maacah to leave, and they still live there among the Israelites.

Moses Did Not Give Land to the Levi Tribe

14 Moses did not give any land to the Levi tribe, because the LORD God of Israel had told them, "Instead of land, you will receive the sacrifices offered at my altar."

Moses Gives Land to the Reuben Tribe

15 Moses gave land to each of the clans in the Reuben tribe. 16 Their land started in the south at the town in the middle of the Arnon River valley, took in the town of Aroer on the northern edge of the valley, and went as far north as the flatlands around Medeba. 17-21 The Amorite King Sihon had lived in Heshbon and had ruled the towns in the flatlands. Now Heshbon belonged to Reuben, and so did the following towns in the flatlands: Dibon, Bamoth-Baal, Beth-Baal-Meon, Jahaz, Kedemoth, Mephaath, Kiriathaim, Sibmah, Zereth-Shahar on the hill in the valley, Beth-Peor, Slopes of Mount Pisgah, and Beth-Jeshimoth.

Moses defeated Sihon and killed him and the Midianite chiefs who ruled parts of his kingdom for him. Their names were Evi, Rekem, Zur, Hur, and Reba. 22 The Israelites also killed Balaam the son of Beor, who had been a fortuneteller.

23 This region with its towns and villages was the land for the Reuben tribe, and the Jordan River was its western border.

Moses Gives Land to the Gad Tribe

24 Moses also gave land to each of the clans in the Gad tribe. 25 It included the town of Jazer, and in the Gilead region their territory took in the land and towns as far east as the town of Aroer[s] just west of Rabbah.[t] This was about half of the land that had once belonged to the Ammonites. 26 The land given to Gad stretched from Heshbon in the south to Ramath-Mizpeh and Betonim in the north, and even further north to Mahanaim and Lidebor.[u] 27 Gad also received the eastern half of the Jordan River valley, which had been ruled by King Sihon of Heshbon. This territory stretched as far north as Lake Galilee,[v] and

[o] **13.2-7** *Gebalites*: Gebal was another name for Byblos. [p] **13.2-7** *from . . . Sea*: One ancient translation; the Hebrew text does not have these words. [q] **13.11,12** *Rephaim*: See the note at 12.4. [r] **13.11,12** *Sihon . . . people*: Or "the Rephaim." [s] **13.25** *Aroer*: Not the same town as the Aroer in verse 16. [t] **13.25** *Rabbah*: The capital city of Ammon. [u] **13.26** *Lidebor*: This may be another name for Lodebar, a town a few miles east of the Jordan River and about ten miles south of Lake Galilee. [v] **13.27** *Lake Galilee*: See the note at 11.2.

13.8 Nu 32.33; Dt 3.12-17. **13.14** Dt 18.1.

included the towns of Beth-Haram, Beth-Nimrah, Succoth, and Zaphon. [28] These regions with their towns and villages were given to the Gad tribe.

Moses Gives Land to Half of the Manasseh Tribe

[29] Moses gave land east of the Jordan River to half of the clans from the Manasseh tribe. [30-31] Their land started at Mahanaim and took in the region that King Og of Bashan had ruled, including Ashtaroth and Edrei, the two towns where he had lived. The villages where the Jair clan settled were part of Manasseh's land, and so was the northern half of the region of Gilead. The clans of this half of Manasseh had sixty towns in all.

The Manasseh tribe is sometimes called the Machir tribe, after Manasseh's son Machir.

[32] That was how Moses divided up the Moab Plains to the east of Jericho on the other side of the Jordan River, so these two and a half tribes would have land of their own. [33] But Moses did not give any land to the Levi tribe, because the LORD had promised that he would always provide for them.

The Land West of the Jordan River

14 [1-5] Nine and a half tribes still did not have any land, although two and a half tribes had already received land east of the Jordan River. Moses had divided that land among them, and he had also said that the Levi tribe would not receive a large region like the other tribes. Instead, the people of Levi would receive towns and the nearby pastures for their sheep, goats, and cattle. And since the descendants of Joseph had become the two tribes of Ephraim and Manasseh, there were still nine and a half tribes that needed land. The LORD had told Moses that he would show those tribes[w] how to divide up the land of Canaan.

When the priest Eleazar, Joshua, and the leaders of the families and tribes of Israel met to divide up the land of Canaan, the LORD showed them how to do it.

Joshua Gives Hebron to Caleb

[6] One day while the Israelites were still camped at Gilgal, Caleb the son of Jephunneh went to talk with Joshua. Caleb belonged to the Kenaz clan, and many other people from the Judah tribe went with Caleb. He told Joshua:

You know that back in Kadesh-Barnea the LORD talked to his prophet Moses about you and me. [7] I was forty years old at the time Moses sent me from Kadesh-Barnea into Canaan as a spy. When I came back and told him about the land, everything I said was true. [8] The other spies said things that made our people afraid, but I completely trusted the LORD God. [9] The same day I came back, Moses told me, "Since you were faithful to the LORD God, I promise that the places where you went as a spy will belong to you and your descendants forever."

[10] Joshua, it was forty-five years ago that the LORD told Moses to make that promise, and now I am eighty-five. Even though Israel has moved from place to place in the desert, the LORD has kept me alive all this time as he said he would. [11] I'm just as strong today as I was then, and I can still fight as well in battle.

[12] So I'm asking you for the hill country that the LORD promised me that day. You were there. You heard the other spies talk about that part of the hill country and the large, walled towns where the Anakim[x] live. But maybe the LORD will help me take their land, just as he promised.

[13] Joshua prayed that God would help Caleb, then he gave Hebron to Caleb and his descendants. [14] And Hebron still be-

[w] **14.1-5** *he would show those tribes*: The Hebrew text has "those tribes must cast lots to find out." Pieces of wood or stone (called "lots") were used to find out what God wanted his people to do.

[x] **14.12** *Anakim*: See the note at 11.21.

13.33 Nu 18.20; Dt 18.2. **14.1-5** **a** Nu 26.52-56; 34.13; **b** Nu 32.33; 34.14, 15; Dt 3.12-17. **14.6** Nu 14.30. **14.7** Nu 13.1-30. **14.9** Nu 14.24.

longs to Caleb's descendants, because he
was faithful to the LORD God of Israel.
15 Hebron used to be called Arba's
Town,[y] because Arba had been one of the
greatest[z] of the Anakim.
There was peace in the land.

Judah's Land

15 The clans of the Judah tribe were
given land that went south along
the border of Edom, and at its farthest
point south it even reached the Zin Desert.
2 Judah's southern border started at the
south end of the Dead Sea. 3 As it went
west from there, it ran south of Scorpion
Pass[a] to Zin, and then came up from the
south to Kadesh-Barnea. It continued past
Hezron up to Addar, turned toward Karka,
4 and ran along to Azmon. After that, it followed the Egyptian Gorge and ended at the
Mediterranean Sea. This was also Israel's
southern border.
5 Judah's eastern border ran the full
length of the Dead Sea.
The northern border started at the
northern end of the Dead Sea.[b] 6 From
there it went west up to Beth-Hoglah, continued north of Beth-Arabah, and went up
to the Monument of Bohan,[c] who belonged
to the Reuben tribe. 7 From there, it went
to Trouble Valley[d] and Debir,[e] then turned
north and went to Gilgal,[f] which is on the
north side of the valley across from Adummim Pass. It continued on to Enshemesh,
Enrogel, 8 and up through Hinnom Valley
on the land sloping south from Jerusalem.
The city of Jerusalem itself belonged to the
Jebusites.
Next, the border went up to the top of
the mountain on the west side of Hinnom
Valley and at the north end of Rephaim Valley. 9 At the top of the mountain it turned
and went to Nephtoah Spring and then to
the ruins[g] on Mount Ephron. From there,
it went to Baalah, which is now called
Kiriath-Jearim.
10 From Baalah the northern border
curved west to Mount Seir and then ran
along the northern ridge of Mount Jearim, where Chesalon is located. Then it
went down to Beth-Shemesh[h] and over to
Timnah. 11 It continued along to the hillside north of Ekron, curved around to
Shikkeron, and then went to Mount
Baalah. After going to Jabneel, the border
finally ended at the Mediterranean Sea,
12 which was Judah's western border.
The clans of Judah lived within these
borders.

Caleb's Land

(Judges 1.12-15)

13 Joshua gave Caleb some land among
the people of Judah, as God had told him
to do. Caleb's share was Hebron, which at
that time was known as Arba's Town,[i] because Arba was the famous ancestor of the
Anakim.[j]
14 Caleb attacked Hebron and forced the
three Anakim clans of[k] Sheshai, Ahiman,
and Talmai to leave. 15 Next, Caleb started
a war with the town of Debir, which at that
time was called Kiriath-Sepher. 16 He told
his men, "The man who captures Kiriath-
Sepher can marry my daughter Achsah."
17 Caleb's nephew Othniel[l] captured
Kiriath-Sepher, and Caleb let him marry
Achsah. 18 Right after the wedding, Achsah
started telling Othniel that he[m] ought to
ask her father for a field. She went to see

[y] **14.15** *Arba's Town*: Or "Kiriath-Arba." [z] **14.15** *Arba's Town, because . . . greatest*: Hebrew; one ancient translation "Arba's Town. It was one of the main towns." [a] **15.3** *Scorpion Pass*: Or "Akrabbim Pass." [b] **15.5** *at . . . Dead Sea*: One possible meaning for the difficult Hebrew text. [c] **15.6** *Monument of Bohan*: Or "Bohan Rock," possibly a natural rock formation. [d] **15.7** *Trouble Valley*: Or "Achor Valley." [e] **15.7** *Debir*: Not the same town as in 10.38, 39. [f] **15.7** *Gilgal*: Not the same "Gilgal" as in 4.19. [g] **15.9** *ruins*: Hebrew; one ancient translation "towns." [h] **15.10** *Beth-Shemesh*: Probably the same town as the Ir-Shemesh of 19.41-46. Two other towns were also named Beth-Shemesh (see 19.17-23 and 19.35-39). [i] **15.13** *Arba's Town*: See the note at 14.15. [j] **15.13** *Anakim*: See the note at 11.21. [k] **15.14** *clans of*: Or "warriors." [l] **15.17** *Caleb's nephew Othniel*: Hebrew "Othniel the son of Caleb's brother Kenaz." [m] **15.18** *Achsah . . . Othniel . . . he*: Hebrew; one manuscript of one ancient translation and two ancient translations of the parallel in Judges 1.14 "Othniel . . . Achsah . . . she."

15.13,14 Jg 1.20.

her father, and while she was getting down from[n] her donkey, Caleb asked her, "What's bothering you?"

19 She answered, "I need your help. The land you gave me is in the Southern Desert, so I really need some spring-fed ponds[o] for a water supply."

Caleb gave her a couple of small ponds, named Higher Pond and Lower Pond.[p]

Towns in Judah's Land

20 The following is a list of the towns in each region given to the Judah clans:

21-32 The first region was located in the Southern Desert along the border with Edom, and it had the following twenty-nine towns with their surrounding villages:

Kabzeel, Eder, Jagur, Kinah, Dimonah, Aradah,[q] Kedesh, Hazor of Ithnan,[r] Ziph, Telem, Bealoth, Hazor-Hadattah, Kerioth-Hezron, which is also called Hazor, Amam, Shema, Moladah, Hazar-Gaddah, Heshmon, Beth-Pelet, Hazar-Shual, Beersheba and its surrounding villages,[s] Baalah, Iim, Ezem, Eltolad, Chesil, Hormah, Ziklag, Madmannah, Sansannah, Lebaoth, Shilhim, and Enrimmon.[t]

33-36 The second region was located in the northern part of the lower foothills, and it had the following fourteen towns with their surrounding villages:

Eshtaol, Zorah, Ashnah, Zanoah, En-Gannim, Tappuah, Enam, Jarmuth, Adullam, Socoh, Azekah, Shaaraim, Adithaim, Gederah, and Gederothaim.

37-41 The third region was located in the southern part of the lower foothills, and it had the following sixteen towns with their surrounding villages:

Zenan, Hadashah, Migdalgad, Dilan, Mizpeh, Joktheel, Lachish, Bozkath, Eglon, Cabbon, Lahmas,[u] Chitlish, Gederoth, Beth-Dagon, Naamah, and Makkedah.

42-44 The fourth region was located in the central part of the lower foothills, and it had the following nine towns with their surrounding villages:

Libnah, Ether, Ashan, Iphtah, Ashnah, Nezib, Keilah, Achzib, and Mareshah.

45-47 The fifth region was located along the Mediterranean seacoast, and it had the following towns with their surrounding settlements and villages:

Ekron and the towns between there and the coast, Ashdod and the larger towns nearby, Gaza, the towns from Gaza to the Egyptian Gorge, and the towns along the coast of the Mediterranean Sea.

48-51 The sixth region was in the southwestern part of the hill country, and it had the following eleven towns with their surrounding villages:

Shamir, Jattir, Socoh, Dannah, Kiriath-Sannah, which is now called Debir, Anab, Eshtemoh,[v] Anim, Goshen, Holon, and Giloh.

52-54 The seventh region was located in the south-central part of Judah's hill country, and it had the following nine towns with their surrounding villages:

Arab, Dumah,[w] Eshan, Janim, Beth-Tappuah, Aphekah, Humtah, Kiriath-Arba, which is now called Hebron, and Zior.

55-57 The eighth region was located in the southeastern part of the hill country, and it had the following ten towns with their surrounding villages:

Maon, Carmel, Ziph, Juttah, Jezreel,[x] Jokdeam,[y] Zanoah, Kain, Gibeah,[z] and Timnah.

[n] **15.18** *getting down from*: One possible meaning for the difficult Hebrew text. [o] **15.19** *spring-fed ponds*: Or "wells." [p] **15.19** *small ponds . . . Pond . . . Pond*: Or "wells . . . Well . . . Well." [q] **15.21-32** *Aradah*: One possible meaning for the difficult Hebrew text. [r] **15.21-32** *Hazor of Ithnan*: One ancient translation; Hebrew "Hazor and Ithnan." [s] **15.21-32** *its . . . villages*: One ancient translation; Hebrew "Biziothiah." [t] **15.21-32** *Enrimmon*: One ancient translation; Hebrew "Ain and Rimmon." [u] **15.37-41** *Lahmas*: Most Hebrew manuscripts; many other Hebrew manuscripts and one manuscript of one ancient translation "Lahmam." [v] **15.48-51** *Eshtemoh*: Another spelling for the name Eshtemoa (see 21.9-19). [w] **15.52-54** *Dumah*: Most Hebrew manuscripts; some Hebrew manuscripts and one ancient translation "Rumah." [x] **15.55-57** *Jezreel*: Not the same Jezreel as in 19.17-23. [y] **15.55-57** *Jokdeam*: Hebrew; one ancient translation "Jorkeam." [z] **15.55-57** *Gibeah*: Not the same Gibeah as in 18.25-28.

58-59 The ninth region was located in the central part of Judah's hill country, and it had the following six towns with their surrounding villages:

Halhul, Beth-Zur, Gedor, Maarath, Beth-Anoth, and Eltekon.

The tenth region was located in the north-central part of Judah's hill country, and it had the following eleven towns with their surrounding villages:

Tekoa, Ephrath, which is also called Bethlehem, Peor, Etam, Culon, Tatam, Shoresh, Kerem, Gallim, Bether, and Manahath.[a]

60 The eleventh region was located in the northern part of Judah's hill country, and it had the following two towns with their surrounding villages:

Rabbah, and Kiriath-Baal, which is also called Kiriath-Jearim.

61-62 The twelfth region was located in the desert along the Dead Sea, and it had the following six towns with their surrounding villages:

Beth-Arabah, Middin, Secacah, Nibshan, Salt Town, and En-Gedi.

The Jebusites

63 The Jebusites lived in Jerusalem, and the people of the Judah tribe could not capture the city and get rid of them. That's why Jebusites still live in Jerusalem along with the people of Judah.[b]

Ephraim's Land

16 1-4 Ephraim and Manasseh are the two tribes descended from Joseph, and the following is a description of the land they received. The southern border of their land started at the Jordan River east of the spring at Jericho. From there it went west through the desert up to the hill country around Bethel. From Bethel it went to Luz and then[c] to the border of the Archites in Ataroth.[d] It continued west down to the land that belonged to the Japhlet clan, then went on to Lower Beth-Horon, Gezer, and the Mediterranean Sea.

5 The following is a description of the land that was divided among the clans of the Ephraim tribe. Their southern border started at Ataroth-Addar and went west to Upper Beth-Horon 6-8 and the Mediterranean Sea. Their northern border started on the east at Janoah, curved a little to the north, then came back south to Michmethath and Tappuah, where it followed the Kanah Gorge west to the Mediterranean Sea.

The eastern border started on the north near Janoah and went between Janoah on the southwest and Taanath-Shiloh on the northeast. Then it went south to Ataroth, Naarah, and on as far as the edge of the land that belonged to Jericho. At that point it turned east and went to the Jordan River. The clans of Ephraim received this region as their tribal land. 9 Ephraim also had some towns and villages that were inside Manasseh's tribal land.

10 Ephraim could not force the Canaanites out of Gezer, so there are still some Canaanites who live there among the Israelites. But now these Canaanites have to work as slaves for the Israelites.

Manasseh's Land West of the Jordan River

17 1-6 Manasseh was Joseph's oldest son, and Machir was Manasseh's oldest son. Machir had a son named Gilead, and some of his descendants had already received the regions of Gilead and Bashan because they were good warriors. The other clans of the Manasseh tribe descended from Gilead's sons Abiezer, Helek, Asriel, Shechem, Hepher, and Shemida. The following is a description of the land they received.

Hepher's son Zelophehad did not have any sons, but he did have five daughters: Mahlah, Noah, Hoglah, Milcah, and Tirzah. One day the clans that were

[a] **15.58,59** *The tenth region . . . Manahath*: One ancient translation; the Hebrew text does not have these words. [b] **15.63** *Jebusites . . . Judah*: Israel captured Jerusalem in King David's time, but even then the Jebusites were not forced to leave. [c] **16.1-4** *it . . . then*: Or "which is also called Luz, it went." [d] **16.1-4** *Ataroth*: This is the same Ataroth as Ataroth-Addar in verse 5, but a different Ataroth from the one in verses 6-8.

15.63 Jg 1.21; 2 S 5.6; 1 Ch 11.4. **16.10** Jg 1.29. **17.1-6** Nu 27.1-7.

descendants of Zelophehad's five daughters went to the priest Eleazar, Joshua, and the leaders of Israel. The people of these clans said, "The LORD told Moses to give us land just as he gave land to our relatives."[e]

Joshua followed the LORD's instructions and gave land to these five clans, as he had given land to the five clans that had descended from Hepher's brothers.[f] So Manasseh's land west of the Jordan River was divided into ten parts.

7 The land of the Manasseh tribe went from its northern border with the Asher tribe south to Michmethath, which is to the east of Shechem. The southern border started there, but curved even farther south to include the people who lived around Tappuah Spring.[g] 8 The town of Tappuah was on Manasseh's border with Ephraim. Although the land around Tappuah belonged to Manasseh, the town itself belonged to Ephraim.

9-10 Then the border went west to the Kanah Gorge and ran along the northern edge of the gorge to the Mediterranean Sea. The land south of the gorge belonged to Ephraim. And even though there were a few towns that belonged to Ephraim north of the gorge, the land north of the gorge belonged to Manasseh.

The western border of Manasseh was the Mediterranean Sea, and the tribe shared a border with the Asher tribe on the northwest and with the Issachar tribe on the northeast.

11 Manasseh was supposed to have the following towns with their surrounding villages inside the borders of Issachar's and Asher's tribal lands:

Beth-Shan, Ibleam, Endor, Taanach, Megiddo, and Dor, which is also called Naphath.[h]

12 But the people of Manasseh could not capture these towns, so the Canaanites kept on living in them. 13 When the Israelites grew stronger, they made the Canaanites in these towns work as their slaves, though they never did force them to leave.

Joseph's Descendants Ask for More Land

14 One day the Joseph tribes[i] came to Joshua and asked, "Why didn't you give us more land? The LORD has always been kind to us, and we have too many people for this small region."

15 Joshua replied, "If you have so many people that you don't have enough room in the hill country of Ephraim, then go into the forest that belonged to the Perizzites and the Rephaim.[j] Clear out the trees and make more room for yourselves there."

16 "Even if we do that," they answered, "there still won't be enough land for us in the hill country. And we can't move down into Jezreel Valley, because the Canaanites who live in Beth-Shan and in other parts of the valley have iron chariots."

17 "Your tribes do have a lot of people," Joshua admitted. "I'll give you more land. Your tribes are powerful, 18 so you can have the rest of the hill country, but it's a forest, and you'll have to cut down the trees and clear the land. You can also have Jezreel Valley. Even though the Canaanites there are strong and have iron chariots, you can force them to leave the valley."

Joshua Gives Out the Rest of the Land

18 After Israel had captured the land, they met at Shiloh and set up the sacred tent.[k] 2 There were still seven tribes without any land, 3-7 so Joshua told the people:

[e] **17.1-6** *The LORD told Moses . . . relatives*: See Numbers 27.1-11; 36.1-12. [f] **17.1-6** *the clans that were descendants of Zelophehad's five daughters . . . Hepher's brothers*: Or "Zelophehad's five daughters went to the priest Eleazar, Joshua, and the leaders of Israel. The five sisters said, 'The LORD told Moses to give us land just as he gave land to our relatives.' Joshua followed the LORD's instructions and gave land to these five sisters, as he had given land to Hepher's brothers."
[g] **17.7** *to include . . . Tappuah Spring*: Hebrew; one ancient translation "to Jassiben-Tappuah" or "and turns toward Tappuah Spring." [h] **17.11** *Dor . . . Naphath*: One possible meaning for the difficult Hebrew text. [i] **17.14** *Joseph tribes*: Ephraim and the half of Manasseh that lived west of the Jordan River. [j] **17.15** *Rephaim*: See the note at 12.4. [k] **18.1** *sacred tent*: Or "meeting tent."

17.12,13 Jg 1.27, 28.

The Judah tribe has already settled in its land in the south, and the Joseph tribes[l] have settled in their land in the north. The tribes of Gad, Reuben, and East Manasseh already have the land that the LORD's servant Moses gave them east of the Jordan River. And the people of Levi won't get a single large region of the land like the other tribes. Instead, they will serve the LORD as priests.

But the rest of you haven't done a thing to take over any land. The LORD God who was worshiped by your ancestors has given you the land, and now it's time to go ahead and settle there.

Seven tribes still don't have any land. Each of these tribes should choose three men, and I'll send them to explore the remaining land. They will divide it into seven regions, write a description of each region, and bring these descriptions back to me. I will find out[m] from the LORD our God what region each tribe should get.

8 Just before the men left camp, Joshua repeated their orders: "Explore the land and write a description of it. Then come back to Shiloh, and I will find out from the LORD how to divide the land."

9 The men left and went across the land, dividing it into seven regions. They wrote down a description of each region, town by town, and returned to Joshua at the camp at Shiloh. 10 Joshua found out from the LORD how to divide the land, and he told the tribes what the LORD had decided.

Benjamin's Land

11 Benjamin was the first tribe chosen to receive land. The region for its clans lay between the Judah tribe on the south and the Joseph tribes[n] on the north. 12 Benjamin's northern border started at the Jordan River and went up the ridge north of Jericho, then on west into the hill country as far as the Beth-Aven Desert. 13-14 From there it went to Luz, which is now called Bethel. The border ran along the ridge south of Luz, then went to Ataroth-Orech[o] and on as far as the mountain south of Lower Beth-Horon. At that point it turned south and became the western border. It went as far south as Kiriath-Baal, a town in Judah now called Kiriath-Jearim.

15 Benjamin's southern border started at the edge of Kiriath-Jearim and went east to the ruins[p] and on to Nephtoah Spring. 16 From there it went to the bottom of the hill at the northern end of Rephaim Valley. The other side of this hill faces Hinnom Valley, which is on the land that slopes south from Jerusalem.[q] The border went down through Hinnom Valley until it reached Enrogel.

17 At Enrogel the border curved north and went to Enshemesh and on east to Geliloth,[r] which is across the valley from Adummim Pass. Then it went down to the Monument of Bohan,[s] who belonged to the Reuben tribe. 18 The border ran along the hillside north of Beth-Arabah,[t] then down into the Jordan River valley. 19 Inside the valley it went south as far as the northern hillside of Beth-Hoglah. The last section of the border went from there to the northern end of the Dead Sea,[u] at the mouth of the Jordan River. 20 The Jordan River itself was Benjamin's eastern border.

These were the borders of Benjamin's tribal land, where the clans of Benjamin lived.

21-24 One region of Benjamin's tribal land had twelve towns with their surrounding villages. Those towns were Jericho, Beth-Hoglah, Emek-Keziz, Beth-Arabah, Zemaraim, Bethel, Avvim, Parah, Ophrah, Chephar-Ammoni, Ophni, and Geba.

[l] **18.3-7** *Joseph tribes*: See the note at 17.14. [m] **18.3-7** *find out*: Hebrew "cast lots to find out" (see the note at 14.1-5). [n] **18.11** *Joseph tribes*: See the note at 17.14. [o] **18.13,14** *Ataroth-Orech*: One ancient translation; Hebrew "Ataroth-Addar." [p] **18.15** *the ruins*: One possible meaning for the difficult Hebrew text. [q] **18.16** *Jerusalem*: Hebrew "the Jebusite town." [r] **18.17** *Geliloth*: Probably another name for Gilgal. [s] **18.17** *Monument of Bohan*: See the note at 15.6. [t] **18.18** *hillside north of Beth-Arabah*: One ancient translation (see also the border description in 15.6); Hebrew "the northern hillside overlooking the Jordan River valley." [u] **18.19** *northern . . . Dead Sea*: One possible meaning for the difficult Hebrew text.

25-28 In the other region there were the following fourteen towns with their surrounding villages: Gibeon, Ramah, Beeroth, Mizpeh, Chephirah, Mozah, Rekem, Irpeel, Taralah, Zelah, Haeleph, Gibeah, Kiriath-Jearim,[v] and Jerusalem, which is also called Jebusite Town.

These regions are the tribal lands of Benjamin.

Simeon's Land

19 Simeon was the second tribe chosen to receive land, and the region for its clans was inside Judah's borders.
2-6 In one region of Simeon's tribal land there were the following thirteen towns with their surrounding villages:

Beersheba, Shema,[w] Moladah, Hazar-Shual, Balah, Ezem, Eltolad, Bethul, Hormah, Ziklag, Beth-Marcaboth, Hazar-Susah, Beth-Lebaoth, and Sharuhen.

7 In another region, Simeon had the following four towns with their surrounding villages:

Enrimmon,[x] Tachan,[y] Ether, and Ashan.

8 Simeon's land also included all the other towns and villages as far south as Baalath-Beer, which is also called Ramah of the South.

9 Simeon's tribal land was actually inside Judah's territory. Judah had received too much land for the number of people in its tribe, so part of Judah's land was given to Simeon.

Zebulun's Land

10-12 Zebulun was the third tribe chosen to receive land. The southern border for its clans started in the west at the edge of the gorge near Jokneam. It went east to the edge of the land that belongs to the town of Dabbesheth, and continued on to Maralah and Sarid. It took in the land that belongs to Chislothtabor, then ended at Daberath.

The eastern border went up to Japhia
13 and continued north to Gath-Hepher, Ethkazin, and Rimmonah,[z] where it curved[a] toward Neah
14 and became the northern border. Then it curved south around Hannathon and went as far west as Iphtahel Valley.

15 Zebulun had twelve towns with their surrounding villages. Some of these were Kattath, Nahalal, Shimron, Jiralah,[b] and Bethlehem.[c]

16 This is the tribal land, and these are the towns and villages of the Zebulun clans.

Issachar's Land

17-23 Issachar was the fourth tribe chosen to receive land. The northern border for its clans went from Mount Tabor east to the Jordan River. Their land included the following sixteen towns with their surrounding villages:

Jezreel, Chesulloth, Shunem, Hapharaim, Shion, Anaharath, Debirath,[d] Kishion, Ebez, Remeth, En-Gannim, Enhaddah, Beth-Pazzez, Tabor,[e] Shahazumah and Beth-Shemesh.[f]

[v] **18.25-28** *Kiriath-Jearim*: One ancient translation; Hebrew "Kiriath." [w] **19.2-6** *Shema*: One ancient translation and some manuscripts of another ancient translation (see also the list at 15.21-32); Hebrew and some manuscripts of one ancient translation "Sheba." The list in 1 Chronicles 4.28 does not have either "Shema" or "Sheba." [x] **19.7** *Enrimmon*: Some Hebrew manuscripts and one ancient translation; most Hebrew manuscripts "Ain, Rimmon."
[y] **19.7** *Tachan*: Some manuscripts of one ancient translation; the Hebrew text does not have this word. [z] **19.13** *Rimmonah*: Or "Rimmon." [a] **19.13** *Rimmonah . . . curved*: One possible meaning for the difficult Hebrew text. [b] **19.15** *Jiralah*: Some Hebrew manuscripts and two ancient translations; most Hebrew manuscripts "Idalah." [c] **19.15** *Bethlehem*: This town is different from the Bethlehem in 15.58, 59. [d] **19.17-23** *Debirath*: One ancient translation; Hebrew "Rabbith." Debirath is probably the same place as Daberath in verse 12.
[e] **19.17-23** *Mount Tabor . . . Tabor*: In Hebrew the name "Tabor" is used only once. It was probably intended as the name of a town located at the foot of Mount Tabor and which formed one point on the northern border of Issachar. [f] **19.17-23** *Beth-Shemesh*: Not the same Beth-Shemesh as in 15.10 or 19.35-39.
19.2-8 1 Ch 4.28-33.

Asher's Land

24-26 Asher was the fifth tribe chosen to receive land, and the region for its clans included the following towns:

Helkath, Hali, Beten, Achshaph, Allammelech, Amad, and Mishal.

Asher's southern border ran from the Mediterranean Sea southeast along the Shihor-Libnath River at the foot of Mount Carmel, 27 then east to Beth-Dagon. On the southeast, Asher shared a border with Zebulun along the Iphtahel Valley. On the eastern side their border ran north to Beth-Emek, went east of Cabul, and then on to Neiel, 28 Abdon,[g] Rehob, Hammon, Kanah, and as far north as the city of Sidon. 29-31 Then it turned west to become the northern border and went to Ramah[h] and the fortress-city of Tyre.[i] Near Tyre it turned toward Hosah and ended at the Mediterranean Sea.

Asher had a total of twenty-two towns with their surrounding villages, including Mahalab,[j] Achzib, Acco,[k] Aphek, and Rehob.

Naphtali's Land

32-34 Naphtali was the sixth tribe chosen to receive land. The southern border for its clans started in the west, where the tribal lands of Asher and Zebulun meet near Hukkok. From that point it ran east and southeast along the border with Zebulun as far as Aznoth-Tabor. From there the border went east to Heleph, Adami-Nekeb, Jabneel,[l] then to the town called Oak in Zaanannim,[m] and Lakkum. The southern border ended at the Jordan River, at the edge of the town named Jehudah.[n] Naphtali shared a border with Asher on the west. 35-39 The Naphtali clans received this region as their tribal land, and it included nineteen towns with their surrounding villages. The following towns had walls around them:

Ziddim, Zer, Hammath, Rakkath, Chinnereth, Adamah, Ramah,[o] Hazor, Kedesh, Edrei,[p] Enhazor, Iron, Migdalel, Horem, Beth-Anath, and Beth-Shemesh.[q]

Dan's Land

40-46 Dan was the seventh tribe chosen to receive land, and the region for its clans included the following towns:

Zorah, Eshtaol, Ir-Shemesh,[r] Shaalabbin, Aijalon, Ithlah, Elon, Timnah, Ekron, Eltekeh, Gibbethon, Baalath, Jehud, Azor,[s] Beneberak, Gath-Rimmon, Mejarkon, and Rakkon.

Dan's tribal land[t] went almost as far as Joppa. 47-48 Its clans received this land and these towns with their surrounding villages.

Later, when enemies[u] forced them to leave their tribal land, they went to the town of Leshem. They attacked the town, captured it, and killed the people who lived there. Then they settled there themselves and renamed the town Dan after their ancestor.

Joshua's Land

49-51 The Israelites were still gathered in Shiloh in front of the sacred tent,[v] when Eleazar the priest, Joshua, and the family

[g] **19.28** *Abdon*: A few Hebrew manuscripts and one ancient translation; most Hebrew manuscripts "Ebron." [h] **19.29-31** *Ramah*: Not the same "Ramah" as in 18.25-28 or 19.35-39.
[i] **19.29-31** *fortress-city of Tyre*: Tyre was a walled city built on an island about half a mile from shore. [j] **19.29-31** *Mahalab*: One possible meaning for the difficult Hebrew text.
[k] **19.29-31** *Acco*: One ancient translation; Hebrew "Ummah." [l] **19.32-34** *Jabneel*: This town is not the same Jabneel as in 15.11. [m] **19.32-34** *the town . . . Zaanannim*: Or "the oak tree in the town of Zaanannim." [n] **19.32-34** *at . . . Jehudah*: One possible meaning for the difficult Hebrew text. [o] **19.35-39** *Ramah*: Not the same "Ramah" as in 18.25-28 or 19.29-31.
[p] **19.35-39** *Edrei*: Not the same Edrei as the town in Bashan east of the Jordan River where King Og had lived (see 12.4; 13.11, 12, 30, 31). [q] **19.35-39** *Beth-Shemesh*: Not the same Beth-Shemesh as in 15.10 or 19.17-23. [r] **19.40-46** *Ir-Shemesh*: Possibly the same town as the Beth-Shemesh of 15.10. [s] **19.40-46** *Azor*: Some manuscripts of one ancient translation; the Hebrew text does not have this word. [t] **19.40-46** *Gath-Rimmon, Mejarkon, and Rakkon. Dan's tribal land*: Or "Gath-Rimmon, and Rakkon. Dan's tribal land also included the Yarkon River and."
[u] **19.47,48** *enemies*: Probably the Philistines. [v] **19.49-51** *sacred tent*: Or "meeting tent."
19.47,48 Jg 18.27-29.

leaders of Israel finished giving out the land to the tribes. The LORD had told the people to give Joshua whatever town he wanted. So Joshua chose Timnath-Serah in the hill country of Ephraim, and the people gave it to him. Joshua went to Timnath-Serah, rebuilt it, and lived there.

The Safe Towns

(Numbers 35.9-15; Deuteronomy 19.1-13)

20 One day the LORD told Joshua:

2 When Moses was still alive, I had him tell the Israelites about the Safe Towns. Now you tell them that it is time to set up these towns. 3-4 If a person accidentally kills someone and the victim's relatives say it was murder, they might try to take revenge.[w] Anyone accused of murder can run to one of the Safe Towns and be safe from the victim's relatives. The one needing protection will stand at the entrance to the town gate and explain to the town leaders what happened. Then the leaders will bring that person in and provide a place to live in their town.

5 One of the victim's relatives might come to the town, looking for revenge. But the town leaders must not simply hand over the person accused of murder. After all, the accused and the victim had been neighbors, not enemies. 6 The citizens of that Safe Town must come together and hold a trial. They may decide that the victim was killed accidentally and that the accused is not guilty of murder.

Everyone found not guilty[x] must still live in the Safe Town until the high priest dies. Then they can go back to their own towns and their homes that they had to leave behind.

7 The Israelites decided that the following three towns west of the Jordan River would be Safe Towns:

Kedesh in Galilee in Naphtali's hill country, Shechem in Ephraim's hill country, and Kiriath-Arba in Judah's hill country. Kiriath-Arba is now called Hebron.

8 The Israelites had already decided on the following three towns east of the Jordan River:

Bezer in the desert flatlands of Reuben, Ramoth in Gilead, which was a town that belonged to Gad, and Golan in Bashan, which belonged to Manasseh.

9 These Safe Towns were set up, so that if Israelites or even foreigners who lived in Israel accidentally killed someone, they could run to one of these towns. There they would be safe until a trial could be held, even if one of the victim's relatives came looking for revenge.

Levi's Towns

21 1-2 While the Israelites were still camped at Shiloh in the land of Canaan, the family leaders of the Levi tribe went to speak to the priest Eleazar, Joshua, and the family leaders of the other Israelite tribes. The leaders of Levi said, "The LORD told Moses that you have to give us towns and provide pastures for our animals."[y]

3 Since the LORD had said this, the leaders of the other Israelite tribes agreed to give some of the towns and pastures from their tribal lands to Levi. 4 The leaders asked the LORD to show them[z] in what order the clans of Levi would be given towns, and which towns each clan would receive.

The Kohath clans were first. The descendants of Aaron, Israel's first priest,[a] were given thirteen towns from the tribes of Judah, Simeon, and Benjamin. 5 The other members of the Kohath clans received ten towns from the tribes of

[w] **20.3,4** *revenge*: At this time in Israel's history, the clan could appoint a close male relative to find and kill a person who had killed a member of their clan. [x] **20.6** *not guilty*: If the person was found to be guilty of murder, the citizens of the Safe Town were to let the victim's relatives kill the murderer (see Deuteronomy 19.11-13). [y] **21.1,2** *The LORD told Moses . . . animals*: See Numbers 35.1-8. [z] **21.4** *asked the LORD to show them*: Hebrew "cast lots to find out." See the note at 14.1-5. [a] **21.4** *The descendants . . . priest*: Hebrew text; three ancient translations "The priests, the descendants of Aaron." The male descendants of Aaron would also be priests.

20.1-9 Nu 35.9-34; Dt 4.41-43; 19.1-13. **21.1,2** Nu 35.1-8.

Ephraim, Dan, and West Manasseh. 6 The clans that were descendants of Gershon were given thirteen towns from the tribes of Issachar, Asher, Naphtali, and East Manasseh. 7 The clans that were descendants of Merari[b] received twelve towns from the tribes of Reuben, Gad, and Zebulun.

8 The LORD had told Moses that he would show the Israelites which towns and pastures to give to the clans of Levi, and he did.

Towns from Judah, Simeon, Benjamin

9-19 The descendants of Aaron from the Kohath clans of Levi were priests, and they were chosen to receive towns first. They were given thirteen towns and the pastureland around them. Nine of these towns were from the tribes of Judah and Simeon and four from Benjamin.

Hebron, Libnah, Jattir, Eshtemoa, Holon, Debir, Ashan,[c] Juttah, and Beth-Shemesh were from Judah and Simeon. Hebron, located in the hill country of Judah, was earlier called Arba's Town.[d] It had been named after Arba, the ancestor of the Anakim.[e] Hebron's pasturelands went along with the town, but its farmlands and the villages around it had been given to Caleb.[f] Hebron was also one of the Safe Towns for people who had accidentally killed someone.

Gibeon, Geba, Anathoth, and Almon were from Benjamin.

Towns from Ephraim, Dan, West Manasseh

20-26 The rest of the Kohath clans of the Levi tribe received ten towns and the pastureland around them. Four of these towns were from the tribe of Ephraim, four from Dan, and two from West Manasseh.

Shechem, Gezer, Kibzaim, and Beth-Horon were from Ephraim. Shechem was located in the hill country, and it was also one of the Safe Towns for people who had accidentally killed someone.

Elteke, Gibbethon, Aijalon, and Gath-Rimmon were from Dan.

Taanach and Jibleam[g] were from West Manasseh.

Towns from East Manasseh, Issachar, Asher, Naphtali

27-33 The clans of Levi that were descendants of Gershon received thirteen towns and the pastureland around them. Two of these towns were from the tribe of East Manasseh, four from Issachar, four from Asher, and three from Naphtali.

Golan in Bashan and Beeshterah were from East Manasseh.

Kishion, Daberath, Jarmuth, and En-Gannim were from Issachar.

Mishal, Abdon, Helkath, and Rehob were from Asher.

Kedesh in Galilee, Hammothdor, and Kartan were from Naphtali. Golan in Bashan and Kedesh in Galilee were also Safe Towns for people who had accidentally killed someone.

Towns from Zebulun, Reuben, Gad

34-40 The rest of the Levi clans were descendants of Merari, and they received twelve towns with the pastureland around them. Four towns were from the tribe of Zebulun, four from Reuben, and four from Gad.

Jokneam, Kartah, Rimmonah,[h] and Nahalal were from Zebulun.

Bezer, Jazah, Kedemoth, and Mephaath were from Reuben. Bezer was located in the desert flatlands east of the Jordan River across from Jericho.[i]

Ramoth in Gilead, Mahanaim, Heshbon, and Jazer were from Gad.

Bezer and Ramoth in Gilead were Safe Towns[j] for people who had accidentally killed someone.

41-42 The people of the Levi tribe had a total of forty-eight towns within Israel, and

[b] **21.4-7** *Kohath . . . Gershon . . . Merari*: Sons of Levi, the ancestor of the tribe of Levi.
[c] **21.9-19** *Ashan*: One ancient translation and the parallel in 1 Chronicles 6.59; Hebrew "Ain."
[d] **21.9-19** *Arba's Town*: See the note at 14.15.
[e] **21.9-19** *Anakim*: See the note at 11.21.
[f] **21.9-19** *Caleb*: See 14.6-14.
[g] **21.20-26** *Jibleam*: One ancient translation and the parallel in 1 Chronicles 6.70; Hebrew "Gath-Rimmon."
[h] **21.34-40** *Rimmonah*: One possible meaning for the difficult Hebrew text.
[i] **21.34-40** *Bezer . . . Jericho*: One possible meaning for the difficult Hebrew text.
[j] **21.34-40** *Bezer and Ramoth in Gilead were Safe Towns*: One ancient translation; Hebrew "Ramoth in Gilead was a Safe Town."

they had pastures around each one of their
towns.

Israel Settles in the Land

43 The LORD gave the Israelites the land
he had promised their ancestors, and they
captured it and settled in it. 44 There still
were enemies around Israel, but the LORD
kept his promise to let his people live in
peace. And whenever the Israelites did
have to go to war, no enemy could defeat
them. The LORD always helped Israel win.
45 The LORD promised to do many good
things for Israel, and he kept his promise
every time.

The Two and a Half Tribes Return Home

22 Joshua had the men of the tribes of
Reuben, Gad, and East Manasseh
come for a meeting, and he told them:

2-3 You have obeyed every command
of the LORD your God and of his servant Moses. And you have done everything I've told you to do. It's taken a
long time, but you have stayed and
helped your relatives. 4 The LORD
promised to give peace to your relatives, and that's what he has done.
Now it's time for you to go back to your
own homes in the land that Moses
gave you east of the Jordan River.

5 Moses taught you to love the LORD
your God, to be faithful to him, and to
worship and obey him with your whole
heart and with all your strength. So be
very careful to do everything Moses
commanded.

6-9 You've become rich from what
you've taken from your enemies. You
have big herds of cattle, lots of silver,
gold, bronze, and iron, and plenty of
clothes. Take everything home with
you and share with the people of your
tribe.

I pray that God will be kind to you.
You are now free to go home.

The tribes of Reuben and Gad started
back to Gilead, their own land. Moses had
given the land of Bashan to the East Manasseh tribe, so they started back along
with Reuben and Gad. God had told Moses
that these two and a half tribes should conquer Gilead and Bashan, and they had
done so.

Joshua had given land west of the Jordan River to the other half of the Manasseh
tribe, so they stayed at Shiloh in the land of
Canaan with the rest of the Israelites.

10-11 The tribes of Reuben, Gad, and
East Manasseh reached the western side of
the Jordan River valley[k] and built a huge
altar there beside the river.

When the rest of the Israelites heard
what these tribes had done,[l] 12 the Israelite
men met at Shiloh to get ready to attack
the two and a half tribes. 13 But first they
sent a priest, Phinehas the son of Eleazar,
to talk with the two and a half tribes.
14 Each of the tribes at Shiloh sent the
leader of one of its families along with
Phinehas.

15 Phinehas and these leaders went to
Gilead and met with the tribes of Reuben,
Gad, and East Manasseh. They said:

16 All of the LORD's people have
gathered together and have sent us to
find out why you are unfaithful to our
God. You have turned your backs
on the LORD by building that altar.
Why are you rebelling against him?
17 Wasn't our people's sin at Peor[m] terrible enough for you? The LORD punished us by sending a horrible sickness
that killed many of us, and we still suffer because of that sin.[n] 18 Now you
are turning your backs on the LORD
again.

If you don't stop rebelling against
the LORD right now, he will be angry at
the whole nation. 19 If you don't think
your land is a fit place to serve God,
then move across the Jordan and live
with us in the LORD's own land, where

[k]**22.10,11** *western . . . valley*: Or "the town of Geliloth, which is in the land of Canaan near the Jordan River." [l]**22.10,11** *built a huge altar . . . tribes had done*: According to Deuteronomy 12.5-14, the LORD wanted the Israelites to have only one altar for offering sacrifices. To build another altar would be to disobey the LORD. [m]**22.17** *our people's sin at Peor*: See Numbers 25.
[n]**22.17** *we still . . . sin*: Or "There are still people in Israel who want to worship other gods."
22.2,3 Nu 32.20-32; Js 1.12-15. **22.16** Dt 12.5-19. **22.17** Nu 25.1-9.

his sacred tent is located. But don't rebel against the LORD our God or against us by building another altar besides the LORD's own altar.[o] 20 Don't you remember what happened when Achan was unfaithful[p] and took some of the things that belonged to God? This made God angry with the entire nation. Achan died because he sinned, but he also caused the death of many others.

21 The tribes of Reuben, Gad, and East Manasseh answered:

22 The LORD is the greatest God! We ask him to be our witness, because he knows whether or not we were rebellious or unfaithful when we built that altar. If we were unfaithful, then we pray that God won't rescue us today. Let us tell you why we built that altar, 23 and we ask the LORD to punish us if we are lying. We didn't build it so we could turn our backs on the LORD. We didn't even build it so we could offer animal or grain sacrifices to please the LORD or ask his blessing.

24-25 We built that altar because we were worried. Someday your descendants might tell our descendants, "The LORD made the Jordan River the boundary between us Israelites and you people of Reuben and Gad. The LORD is Israel's God, but you're not part of Israel, so you can't take part in worshiping the LORD."

Your descendants might say that and try to make our descendants stop worshiping and obeying the LORD. 26 That's why we decided to build the altar. It isn't for offering sacrifices, not even sacrifices to please the LORD.[q] 27-29 To build another altar for offering sacrifices would be the same as turning our backs on the LORD and rebelling against him. We could never do that! No, we built the altar to remind us and you and the generations to come that we will worship the LORD. And so we will keep bringing our sacrifices to the LORD's altar, there in front of his sacred tent. Now your descendants will never be able to say to our descendants, "You can't worship the LORD."

But if they do say this, our descendants can answer back, "Look at this altar our ancestors built! It's like the LORD's altar, but it isn't for offering sacrifices. It's here to remind us and you that we belong to the LORD, just as much as you do."

30-31 Phinehas and the clan leaders were pleased when they heard the tribes of Reuben, Gad, and East Manasseh explain why they had built the altar. Then Phinehas told them, "Today we know that the LORD is helping us. You have not been unfaithful to him, and this means that the LORD will not be angry with us."

32 Phinehas and the clan leaders left Gilead and went back to Canaan to tell the Israelites about their meeting with the Reuben and Gad tribes. 33 The Israelites were happy and praised God. There was no more talk about going to war and wiping out the tribes of Reuben and Gad.

34 The people of Reuben and Gad named the altar "A Reminder to Us All That the LORD Is Our God."[r]

Joshua's Farewell Speech

23 The LORD let Israel live in peace with its neighbors for a long time, and Joshua lived to a ripe old age. 2 One day he called a meeting of the leaders of the tribes of Israel, including the old men, the judges, and the officials. Then he told them:

I am now very old. 3 You have seen how the LORD your God fought for you

[o] **22.19** *or against . . . altar*: Or "by building another altar besides the LORD's own altar. That would even make us into rebels along with you." [p] **22.20** *Achan was unfaithful*: See 7.1, 26.
[q] **22.26** *sacrifices to please the LORD*: See the note at 8.30-32. [r] **22.34** *named . . . God*: Or "gave a name to the altar. They explained, 'This altar is here to remind us all that the LORD is our God' "; most Hebrew manuscripts. A few Hebrew manuscripts and one ancient translation "named the altar 'Reminder.' They explained, 'This altar is here to remind us all that the LORD is our God.' "
22.20 Js 7.1-26.

and helped you defeat the nations who lived in this land. [4-5] There are still some nations left, but the LORD has promised you their land. So when you attack them, he will make them run away. I have already divided their land among your tribes, as I did with the land of the nations I defeated between the Jordan River and the Mediterranean Sea.

[6] Be sure that you carefully obey everything written in *The Book of the Laws*[s] of Moses and do exactly what it says.

[7] Don't have anything to do with the nations that live around you. Don't worship their gods or pray to their idols or make promises in the names of their gods. [8] Be as faithful to the LORD as you have always been.

[9] When you attacked powerful nations, the LORD made them run away, and no one has ever been able to stand up to you. [10] Any one of you can defeat a thousand enemy soldiers, because the LORD God fights for you, just as he promised. [11] Be sure to always love the LORD your God. [12-13] Don't ever turn your backs on him by marrying people from the nations that are left in the land. Don't even make friends with them. I tell you that if you are friendly with those nations, the LORD won't chase them away when you attack. Instead, they'll be like a trap for your feet, a whip on your back, and thorns in your eyes. And finally, none of you will be left in this good land that the LORD has given you.

[14] I will soon die, as everyone must. But deep in your hearts you know that the LORD has kept every promise he ever made to you. Not one of them has been broken. [15-16] Yes, when the LORD makes a promise, he does what he has promised. But when he makes a threat, he will also do what he has threatened. The LORD is our God. He gave us this wonderful land and made an agreement with us that we would worship only him. But if you worship other gods, it will make the LORD furious. He will start getting rid of you, and soon not one of you will be left in this good land that he has given you.

We Will Worship and Obey the LORD

24 Joshua called the tribes of Israel together for a meeting at Shechem.
He had the leaders, including the old men,
the judges, and the officials, come up and
stand near the sacred tent.[t] 2 Then Joshua
told everyone to listen to this message from
the LORD, the God of Israel:

Long ago your ancestors lived on
the other side of the Euphrates River,
and they worshiped other gods. This
continued until the time of your ancestor Terah and his two sons, Abraham and Nahor. 3 But I brought Abra-
ham across the Euphrates River and
led him through the land of Canaan. I
blessed him by giving him Isaac, the
first in a line of many descendants.
4 Then I gave Isaac two sons, Jacob
and Esau. I had Esau live in the hill
country of Mount Seir, but your ancestor Jacob and his children went to live
in Egypt.

5-6 Later I sent Moses and his
brother Aaron to help your people, and
I made all those horrible things happen to the Egyptians. I brought your
ancestors out of Egypt, but the Egyptians got in their chariots and on their
horses and chased your ancestors,
catching up with them at the Red
Sea.[u] 7 Your people cried to me for
help, so I put a dark cloud between
them and the Egyptians. Then I
opened up the sea and let your people
walk across on dry ground. But when

[s]**23.6** *Law*: See the note at 8.30-32. [t]**24.1** *near . . . tent*: Or "in front of the sacred chest"; Hebrew "in the presence of God." [u]**24.5,6** *Red Sea*: See the note at 2.10.

23.10 a Dt 32.30; **b** Dt 3.21, 22. **24.2** Gn 11.26-28. **24.3 a** Gn 12.1-9; **b** Gn 21.1-3. **24.4 a** Gn 25.24-26; **b** Gn 36.8; Dt 2.5; **c** Gn 46.1-7. **24.5-7 a** Ex 3.1—12.42; **b** Ex 14.1-31.

the Egyptians tried to follow, I commanded the sea to swallow them, and they drowned while you watched.

You lived in the desert for a long time, 8 then I brought you into the land east of the Jordan River. The Amorites were living there, and they fought you. But with my help, you defeated them, wiped them out, and took their land. 9 King Balak decided that his nation Moab would go to war against you, so he asked Balaam[v] to come and put a curse on you. 10 But I wouldn't listen to Balaam, and I rescued you by making him bless you instead of curse you.

11 You crossed the Jordan River and came to Jericho. The rulers of Jericho fought you, and so did the Amorites, the Perizzites, the Canaanites, the Hittites, the Girgashites, the Hivites, and the Jebusites. I helped you defeat them all. 12 Your enemies ran from you, but not because you had swords and bows and arrows. I made your enemies panic and run away, as I had done with the two Amorite kings east of the Jordan River.

13 You didn't have to work for this land—I gave it to you. Now you live in towns you didn't build, and you eat grapes and olives from vineyards and trees you didn't plant.

14 Then Joshua told the people:

Worship the LORD, obey him, and always be faithful. Get rid of the idols your ancestors worshiped when they lived on the other side of the Euphrates River and in Egypt. 15 But if you don't want to worship the LORD, then choose right now! Will you worship the same idols your ancestors did? Or since you're living on land that once belonged to the Amorites, maybe you'll worship their gods. I won't. My family and I are going to worship and obey the LORD!

16 The people answered:

We could never worship other gods or stop worshiping the LORD. 17 The LORD is our God. We were slaves in Egypt as our ancestors had been, but we saw the LORD work miracles to set our people free and to bring us out of Egypt. Even though other nations were all around us, the LORD protected us wherever we went. 18 And when we fought the Amorites and the other nations that lived in this land, the LORD made them run away. Yes, we will worship and obey the LORD, because the LORD is our God.

19 Joshua said:

The LORD is fearsome; he is the one true God, and I don't think you are able to worship and obey him in the ways he demands. You would have to be completely faithful, and if you sin or rebel, he won't let you get away with it. 20 If you turn your backs on the LORD and worship the gods of other nations, the LORD will turn against you. He will make terrible things happen to you and wipe you out, even though he had been good to you before.

21 But the people shouted, "We won't worship any other gods. We will worship and obey only the LORD!"

22 Joshua said, "You have heard yourselves say that you will worship and obey the LORD. Isn't that true?"

"Yes, it's true," they answered.

23 Joshua said, "But you still have some idols, like those the other nations worship. Get rid of your idols! You must decide once and for all that you really want to obey the LORD God of Israel."

24 The people said, "The LORD is our God, and we will worship and obey only him."

25 Joshua helped Israel make an agreement with the LORD that day at Shechem. Joshua made laws for Israel 26 and wrote them down in *The Book of the Law*[w] *of God*. Then he set up a large stone under

[v] **24.9** *King Balak . . . Balaam*: The Hebrew text has "King Balak the son of Zippor . . . Balaam the son of Beor." [w] **24.26** *Law*: See the note at 8.30-32.

24.8 Nu 21.21-35. **24.9,10** Nu 22.1—24.25. **24.11** **a** Js 3.14-17; **b** Js 6.1-25.
24.12 Ex 23.28; Dt 7.20. **24.13** Dt 6.10, 11.

the oak tree at the place of worship in Shechem 27 and told the people, "Look at this stone. It has heard everything that the LORD has said to us. Our God can call this stone as a witness if we ever reject him."

28 Joshua sent everyone back to their homes.

Joshua, Joseph, and Eleazar Are Buried

29 Not long afterwards, the LORD's servant Joshua died at the age of one hundred ten. 30 The Israelites buried him in his own land at Timnath-Serah, north of Mount Gaash in the hill country of Ephraim.

31 As long as Joshua lived, Israel worshiped and obeyed the LORD. There were other leaders old enough to remember everything that the LORD had done for Israel. And for as long as these men lived, Israel continued to worship and obey the LORD.

32 When the people of Israel left Egypt, they brought the bones of Joseph along with them. They took the bones to the town of Shechem and buried them in the field that Jacob had bought for one hundred pieces of silver[x] from Hamor, the founder of Shechem. The town and the field both[y] became part of the land belonging to the descendants of Joseph.

33 When Eleazar the priest[z] died, he was buried in the hill country of Ephraim on a hill that belonged to his son Phinehas.

[x]**24.32** *pieces of silver*: One possible meaning for the difficult Hebrew word. [y]**24.32** *town . . . both*: One possible meaning for the difficult Hebrew text. [z]**24.33** *Eleazar the priest*: Hebrew "Eleazar the son of Aaron."

24.30 Js 19.49-51. **24.32** Gn 33.19; 50.24, 25; Ex 13.19; Jn 4.5; Ac 7.16.

JUDGES

ABOUT THIS BOOK

The book of Judges tells how the Israelites kept rejecting the Lord and worshiping idols. Each time they did this, the Lord punished them by letting other nations attack and defeat them. As a result, the Israelites turned back to the Lord and asked for his help, and he sent a special leader called a "judge," who helped them defeat their enemies. A time of peace followed, and the Israelites were faithful to the Lord for as long as the judge lived. But then they again rejected the Lord. All these things happened time after time.

Some judges may have led the entire nation, but usually a judge led a few tribes at the most. Israel at this time was a loosely-bound group of tribes, and the Israelites did not think of themselves as being a single, united country. They did not yet have a king, and so during this time "everyone did what they thought was right" (21.25). But the people had to learn that they were to worship only the Lord, and when they were unfaithful, the Lord punished them.

A QUICK LOOK AT THIS BOOK

- Israel Captures Only Part of the Land (1.1-36)
- The Lord Chooses Judges for Israel (2.1—3.6)
- Othniel, Ehud, and Shamgar (3.7-31)
- Deborah, Barak, and Jael (4.1—5.31)
- Gideon (5.31—8.35)
- Abimelech (9.1-57)
- Tola, Jair, and Jephthah (10.1—12.7)
- Ibzan, Elon, and Abdon (12.8-15)
- Samson (13.1—16.31)
- The Tribe of Dan and Their Place of Worship (17.1—18.31)
- Civil War against the Tribe of Benjamin (19.1—21.25)

The Tribes of Judah and Simeon Fight the Canaanites

1 After the death of Joshua, the Israelites asked the LORD, "Which of our tribes should attack the Canaanites first?"

2 "Judah!" the LORD answered. "I'll help them take the land."

3 The people of Judah went to their relatives, the Simeon tribe, and said, "Canaanites live in the land God gave us. Help us fight them, and we will help you."

Troops from Simeon came to help Judah.
4-5 Together they attacked an army of ten thousand Canaanites and Perizzites at Bezek, and the LORD helped Judah defeat them. During the battle, Judah's army found out where the king of Bezek[a] was, and they attacked there.
6 Bezek tried to escape, but soldiers from Judah caught him. They cut off his thumbs and big toes,
7 and he said, "I've cut off the thumbs and big toes of seventy kings and made those kings crawl around under my table for scraps of food. Now God is paying me back."

The army of Judah took the king of Bezek along with them to Jerusalem, where

[a]1.4,5 *king of Bezek*: Or "Adoni-Bezek."

he died. 8 They attacked Jerusalem,[b] captured it, killed everyone who lived there, and then burned it to the ground.

9 Judah's army fought the Canaanites who lived in the hill country, the Southern Desert, and the foothills to the west. 10 After that, they attacked the Canaanites who lived at Hebron, defeating the three clans called[c] Sheshai, Ahiman, and Talmai. At that time, Hebron was called Kiriath-Arba.

11 From Hebron, Judah's army went to attack Debir, which at that time was called Kiriath-Sepher. 12 Caleb[d] told his troops, "The man who captures Kiriath-Sepher can marry my daughter Achsah."

13 Caleb's nephew Othniel captured Kiriath-Sepher, so Caleb let him marry Achsah. Othniel was the son of Caleb's younger brother Kenaz.[e] 14 Right after the wedding, Achsah started telling Othniel that he[f] ought to ask her father for a field. She went to see her father, and while she was getting down from[g] her donkey, Caleb asked, "What's bothering you?"

15 She answered, "I need your help. The land you gave me is in the Southern Desert, so please give me some spring-fed ponds for a water supply."

Caleb gave her a couple of small ponds named Higher Pond and Lower Pond.[h]

16 The people who belonged to the Kenite clan were the descendants of the father-in-law of Moses. They left Jericho[i] with the people of Judah and settled near Arad in the Southern Desert of Judah not far from the Amalekites.[j]

17 Judah's army helped Simeon's army attack the Canaanites who lived at Zephath. They completely destroyed[k] the town and renamed it Hormah.[l]

18-19 The LORD helped the army of Judah capture Gaza, Ashkelon, Ekron, and the land near those towns. They also took the hill country. But the people who lived in the valleys had iron chariots, so Judah was not able to make them leave or to take their land.

20 The tribe of Judah gave the town of Hebron to Caleb, as Moses had told them to do. Caleb defeated the three Anakim[m] clans[n] and took over the town.

The Benjamin Tribe Does Not Capture Jerusalem

21 The Jebusites were living in Jerusalem, and the Benjamin tribe did not defeat them or capture the town. That's why Jebusites still live in Jerusalem along with the people of Benjamin.

The Ephraim and Manasseh Tribes Capture Bethel

22-23 The Ephraim and Manasseh tribes[o] were getting ready to attack Bethel, which at that time was called Luz. And the LORD helped them when they sent spies to find out as much as they could about Bethel. 24 While the spies were watching the town, a man came out, and they told him, "If you

[b] **1.8** *Jerusalem*: This probably refers to towns and villages belonging to Jerusalem but lying in Judah's territory south of the city wall. Jerusalem itself was just inside Benjamin's territory, but was not captured by Israel at this time (see verse 21; Joshua 15.5-9; 18.15-18). [c] **1.10** *clans called*: Or "warriors." [d] **1.12** *Caleb*: One of the leaders of Judah; see Joshua 14.6-14 and Numbers 13.6, 30; 14.6, 10, 20-24. For verses 12-15, see Joshua 15.13-19. [e] **1.13** *Othniel was the son of . . . Kenaz*: Or "Othniel and Caleb both belonged to the Kenaz clan, but Othniel was younger than Caleb." [f] **1.14** *Achsah . . . Othniel . . . he*: Hebrew; two ancient translations "Othniel . . . Achsah . . . she." [g] **1.14** *getting down from*: One possible meaning for the difficult Hebrew text. [h] **1.15** *spring-fed ponds . . . small ponds . . . Higher Pond and Lower Pond*: Or "wells . . . wells . . . Higher Well and Lower Well." [i] **1.16** *Jericho*: The Hebrew text has "Town of Palm Trees," another name for Jericho. [j] **1.16** *not far . . . Amalekites*: One possible meaning for the difficult Hebrew text. [k] **1.17** *completely destroyed*: The Hebrew word means that the town was given completely to the LORD, and since it could not be used for normal purposes any more, it had to be destroyed. [l] **1.17** *Hormah*: In Hebrew "Hormah" sounds like "completely destroyed."
[m] **1.20** *Anakim*: Perhaps a group of very large people that lived in Palestine before the Israelites (see Numbers 13.33 and Deuteronomy 2.10, 11, 20, 21). [n] **1.20** *clans*: See the note at 1.10.
[o] **1.22,23** *The Ephraim and Manasseh tribes*: The Hebrew text has "The Joseph family," which was divided into these two tribes named after Joseph's sons.

1.20 Js 15.13, 14. **1.21** Js 15.63; 2 S 5.6; 1 Ch 11.4.

show us how our army can get into the town,[p] we will make sure that you aren't harmed." 25 The man showed them, and the two Israelite tribes attacked Bethel, killing everyone except the man and his family. The two tribes made the man and his family leave, 26 so they went to the land of the Hittites,[q] where he built a town. He named the town Luz, and that is still its name.

Israel Does Not Get Rid of All the Canaanites

27-28 Canaanites lived in the towns of Beth-Shan, Taanach, Dor, Ibleam, Megiddo, and all the villages nearby. The Canaanites were determined to stay, and the Manasseh tribe never did get rid of them. But later on, when the Israelites grew more powerful, they made slaves of the Canaanites.

29 The Ephraim tribe did not get rid of the Canaanites who lived in Gezer, so the Canaanites lived there with Israelites all around them.

30 The Zebulun tribe did not get rid of the Canaanites who lived in Kitron and Nahalol, and the Canaanites stayed there with Israelites around them. But the people of Zebulun did force the Canaanites into slave labor.

31-32 The Asher tribe did not get rid of the Canaanites who lived in Acco, Sidon, Ahlab, Achzib, Helbah, Aphik, and Rehob, and the Asher tribe lived with Canaanites all around them.

33 The Naphtali tribe did not get rid of the Canaanites who lived in Beth-Shemesh and Beth-Anath, but they did force the Canaanites into slave labor. The Naphtali tribe lived with Canaanites around them.

34 The Amorites[r] were strong enough to keep the tribe of Dan from settling in the valleys, so Dan had to stay in the hill country.

35 The Amorites on Mount Heres and in Aijalon and Shaalbim were also determined to stay. Later on, as Ephraim and Manasseh grew more powerful, they forced those Amorites into slave labor.

The Amorite-Edomite Border

36 The old Amorite-Edomite border used to go from Sela through Scorpion Pass[s] into the hill country.[t]

The LORD's Angel Speaks to Israel

2 The LORD's angel went from Gilgal to Bochim[u] and gave the Israelites this message from the LORD:

I promised your ancestors that I would give this land to their families, and I brought your people here from Egypt. We made an agreement that I promised never to break, 2 and you promised not to make any peace treaties with the other nations that live in the land. Besides that, you agreed to tear down the altars where they sacrifice to their idols. But you didn't keep your promise.

3 And so, I'll stop helping you defeat your enemies. Instead, they will be there to trap[v] you into worshiping their idols.

4 The Israelites started crying loudly,
5 and they offered sacrifices to the LORD. From then on, they called that place "Crying."[w]

Israel Stops Worshiping the LORD

6-9 Joshua had been faithful to the LORD. And after Joshua sent the Israelites to take the land they had been promised, they remained faithful to the LORD until Joshua died at the age of one hundred ten. He was buried on his land in Timnath-Heres, in

[p] **1.24** *If you . . . town*: Sometimes there were small doors in the town wall that could be opened from the inside even when the main town gates were shut and locked. [q] **1.26** *land of the Hittites*: The Hittites had an empire centered in what is now Turkey. At one time their empire reached south into Syria, north of Israel. [r] **1.34** *Amorites*: Used in the general sense of nations that lived in Canaan before the Israelites. [s] **1.36** *Scorpion Pass*: Or "Akrabbim Pass." [t] **1.36** *country*: One possible meaning for the difficult Hebrew text of verse 36. [u] **2.1** *Bochim*: In Hebrew "Bochim" means "crying" (see verse 5). [v] **2.3** *trap*: One possible meaning for the difficult Hebrew text. [w] **2.5** *Crying*: Or "Bochim."

1.27,28 Js 17.11-13. **1.29** Js 16.10. **2.2** Ex 34.12, 13; Dt 7.2-5. **2.6-9** Js 19.49, 51.

the hill country of Ephraim north of Mount Gaash. Even though Joshua was gone, the Israelites were faithful to the LORD during the lifetime of those men who had been leaders with Joshua and who had seen the wonderful things the LORD had done for Israel.

10 After a while the people of Joshua's generation died, and the next generation did not know the LORD or any of the things he had done for Israel. 11-13 The LORD had brought their ancestors out of Egypt, and they had worshiped him. But now the Israelites stopped worshiping the LORD and worshiped the idols of Baal and Astarte, as well as the idols of other gods from nearby nations.

The LORD was so angry 14-15 at the Israelites that he let other nations raid Israel and steal their crops and other possessions. Enemies were everywhere, and the LORD always let them defeat Israel in battle. The LORD had warned Israel he would do this, and now the Israelites were miserable.

The LORD Chooses Leaders for Israel

16 From time to time, the LORD would choose special leaders known as judges.[x] These judges would lead the Israelites into battle and defeat the enemies that made raids on them. 17 In years gone by, the Israelites had been faithful to the LORD, but now they were quick to be unfaithful and to refuse even to listen to these judges. The Israelites would disobey the LORD, and instead of worshiping him, they would worship other gods.

18 When enemies made life miserable for the Israelites, the LORD would feel sorry for them. He would choose a judge and help that judge rescue Israel from its enemies. The LORD would be kind to Israel as long as that judge lived. 19 But afterwards, the Israelites would become even more sinful than their ancestors had been. The Israelites were stubborn—they simply would not stop worshiping other gods or following the teachings of other religions.

The LORD Lets Enemies Test Israel

20 The LORD was angry with Israel and said:

> The Israelites have broken the agreement I made with their ancestors. They won't obey me, 21 so I'll stop helping them defeat their enemies. Israel still had a lot of enemies when Joshua died, 22 and I'm going to let those enemies stay. I'll use them to test Israel, because then I can find out if Israel will worship and obey me as their ancestors did.

23 That's why the LORD had not let Joshua get rid of all those enemy nations right away.

3 1-2 And the LORD had another reason for letting these enemies stay. The Israelites needed to learn how to fight in war, just as their ancestors had done. Each new generation would have to learn by fighting 3 the Philistines and their five rulers, as well as the Canaanites, the Sidonians, and the Hivites that lived in the Lebanon Mountains from Mount Baal-Hermon to Hamath Pass.[y]

4 Moses had told the Israelites what the LORD had commanded them to do, and now the LORD was using these nations to find out if Israel would obey. 5-6 But they refused. And it was because of the Canaanites, Hittites, Amorites, Perizzites, Hivites, and Jebusites who lived all around them. Some of the Israelites married the people of these nations, and that's how they started worshiping foreign gods.

Othniel

7 The Israelites sinned against the LORD by forgetting him and worshiping idols of Baal and Astarte. 8 This made the LORD angry, so he let Israel be defeated by King Cushan Rishathaim of northern Syria,[z] who ruled Israel eight years and made everyone pay taxes. 9 The Israelites begged the LORD for help, and he chose Othniel to

[x]**2.16** *special leaders known as judges*: The Hebrew text has "judges." In addition to leading Israelites in battle, these special leaders also decided legal cases and sometimes performed religious duties. [y]**3.3** *Hamath Pass*: Or "Lebo-Hamath." [z]**3.8** *northern Syria*: The Hebrew text has "Aram-Naharaim," probably referring to the land around the city of Haran (see Genesis 24.10; 25.20; 28.2, 6; 31.18, 20; 33.18; 35.23-26; 46.8-15; 48.7).

rescue them. Othniel was the son of
Caleb's younger brother Kenaz.[a] 10 The
Spirit of the LORD took control of Othniel,
and he led Israel in a war against Cushan
Rishathaim. The LORD gave Othniel victory,
11 and Israel was at peace until Othniel
died about forty years later.

Ehud

12 Once more the Israelites started disobeying the LORD. So he let them be defeated by King Eglon of Moab, 13 who had
joined forces with the Ammonites and the
Amalekites to attack Israel. Eglon and his
army captured Jericho.[b] 14 Then he ruled
Israel for eighteen years and forced the Israelites to pay heavy taxes.

15-16 The Israelites begged the LORD for
help, and the LORD chose Ehud[c] from the
Benjamin tribe to rescue them. They put
Ehud in charge of taking the taxes to King
Eglon, but before Ehud went, he made a
double-edged dagger. Ehud was left-
handed, so he strapped the dagger to his
right thigh, where it would be hidden under his robes.

17-18 Ehud and some other Israelites
took the taxes to Eglon, who was a very fat
man. As soon as they gave the taxes to
Eglon, Ehud said it was time to go home.

19-20 Ehud went with the other Israelites
as far as the statues[d] at Gilgal.[e] Then he
turned back and went upstairs to the cool
room[f] where Eglon had his throne. Ehud
said, "Your Majesty, I need to talk with you
in private."

Eglon replied, "Don't say anything yet!"
His officials left the room, and Eglon stood
up as Ehud came closer.

"Yes," Ehud said, "I have a message for
you from God!" 21 Ehud pulled out the dagger with his left hand and shoved it so far
into Eglon's stomach 22-23 that even the
handle was buried in his fat. Ehud left the
dagger there. Then after closing and locking the doors to the room, he climbed
through a window onto the porch[g] 24 and
left.

When the king's officials came back and
saw that the doors were locked, they said,
"The king is probably inside relieving himself." 25 They stood there waiting until they
felt foolish, but Eglon never opened the
doors. Finally, they unlocked the doors and
found King Eglon lying dead on the floor.
26 But by that time, Ehud had already escaped past the statues.[h]

Ehud went to the town of Seirah 27-28 in
the hill country of Ephraim and started
blowing a signal on a trumpet. The Israelites came together, and he shouted,
"Follow me! The LORD will help us defeat
the Moabites."

The Israelites followed Ehud down to
the Jordan valley, and they captured the
places where people cross the river on the
way to Moab. They would not let anyone go
across, 29 and before the fighting was over,
they killed about ten thousand Moabite
warriors—not one escaped alive.

30 Moab was so badly defeated that it
was a long time before they were strong
enough to attack Israel again. And Israel
was at peace for eighty years.

Shamgar

31 Shamgar the son of Anath was the
next to rescue Israel. In one battle, he used
a sharp wooden pole[i] to kill six hundred
Philistines.

Deborah and Barak

4 After the death of Ehud, the Israelites
again started disobeying the LORD. 2 So
the LORD let the Canaanite King Jabin of
Hazor conquer Israel. Sisera, the commander of Jabin's army, lived in Harosheth-
Ha-Goiim. 3 Jabin's army had nine hundred

[a]3.9 *Othniel was the son of . . . Kenaz*: See the note at 1.13. [b]3.13 *Jericho*: See the note at 1.16. [c]3.15,16 *Ehud*: Hebrew "Ehud the son of Gera." [d]3.19,20 *statues*: Or "stone idols" or "stone monuments." [e]3.19,20 *Gilgal*: About a mile and a half from Jericho, where Eglon probably was (see verse 13). [f]3.19,20 *upstairs . . . cool room*: Houses usually had flat roofs, and sometimes a room was built on one corner of the roof where it could best catch the breeze and be kept cooler than the rest of the house. [g]3.22,23 *he climbed . . . porch*: One possible meaning for the difficult Hebrew text. [h]3.26 *statues*: See the note at 3.19, 20. [i]3.31 *sharp wooden pole*: The Hebrew text has "cattle-prod," a pole with a sharpened tip or metal point at one end.

iron chariots, and for twenty years he made
life miserable for the Israelites, until finally
they begged the LORD for help.

4 Deborah the wife of Lappidoth was a
prophet and a leader[j] of Israel during those
days. 5 She would sit under Deborah's
Palm Tree between Ramah and Bethel in
the hill country of Ephraim, where Israelites would come and ask her to settle
their legal cases.

6 One day, Barak the son of Abinoam
was in Kedesh in Naphtali, and Deborah
sent word for him to come and talk with
her. When he arrived, she said:

I have a message for you from the
LORD God of Israel! You are to get together an army of ten thousand men
from the Naphtali and Zebulun tribes
and lead them to Mount Tabor. 7 The
LORD will trick Sisera into coming out
to fight you at the Kishon River. Sisera
will be leading King Jabin's army as
usual, and they will have their chariots, but the LORD has promised to help
you defeat them.

8 "I'm not going unless you go!" Barak
told her.

9 "All right, I'll go!" she replied. "But I'm
warning you that the LORD is going to let a
woman defeat Sisera, and no one will
honor you for winning the battle."

Deborah and Barak left for Kedesh,
10 where Barak called together the troops
from Zebulun and Naphtali. Ten thousand
soldiers gathered there, and Barak
led them out from Kedesh. Deborah
went too.

11 At this time, Heber of the Kenite clan
was living near the village of Oak in Zaanannim,[k] not far from Kedesh. The Kenites were descendants of Hobab, the
father-in-law of Moses, but Heber had
moved and had set up his tents away from
the rest of the clan.

12 When Sisera learned that Barak had
led an army to Mount Tabor, 13 he called
his troops together and got all nine hundred iron chariots ready. Then he led his
army away from Harosheth-Ha-Goiim to
the Kishon River.

14 Deborah shouted, "Barak, it's time to
attack Sisera! Because today the LORD is
going to help you defeat him. In fact, the
LORD has already gone on ahead to fight for
you."

Barak led his ten thousand troops down
from Mount Tabor. 15 And during the battle, the LORD confused Sisera, his chariot
drivers, and his whole army. Everyone was
so afraid of Barak and his army, that even
Sisera jumped down from his chariot and
tried to escape. 16 Barak's forces went after
Sisera's chariots and army as far as
Harosheth-Ha-Goiim.

Sisera's entire army was wiped out.
17 Only Sisera escaped. He ran to Heber's
camp, because Heber and his family had a
peace treaty with the king of Hazor. Sisera
went to the tent that belonged to Jael,
Heber's wife. 18 She came out to greet him
and said, "Come in, sir! Please come on in.
Don't be afraid."

After they had gone inside, Sisera lay
down, and Jael covered him with a blanket.
19 "Could I have a little water?" he asked.
"I'm thirsty."

Jael opened a leather bottle and poured
him some milk, then she covered him
back up.

20 "Stand at the entrance to the tent,"
Sisera told her. "If someone comes by and
asks if anyone is inside, tell them 'No.' "

21 Sisera was exhausted and soon fell
fast asleep. Jael took a hammer and drove a
tent-peg through his head into the ground,
and he died.

22 Meanwhile, Barak had been following Sisera, and Jael went out to meet
him. "The man you're looking for is inside," she said. "Come in and I'll show him
to you."

They went inside, and there was Sisera—dead and stretched out with a tent-
peg through his skull.

23 That same day the Israelites defeated
the Canaanite King Jabin, and his army
was no longer powerful enough to attack
the Israelites. 24 Jabin grew weaker while
the Israelites kept growing stronger, and at
last the Israelites destroyed him.

[j] **4.4** *leader*: See 2.16 and the note there.

[k] **4.11** *the village . . . Zaanannim*: Or "the oak tree in the town of Zaanannim."

Deborah and Barak Sing for the LORD

5 After the battle was over that day, Deborah and Barak sang this song:

2 We praise you, LORD!
Our soldiers volunteered,
ready to follow you.
3 Listen, kings and rulers,
while I sing for the LORD,
the God of Israel.

*4 Our LORD, God of Israel,
when you came from Seir,
where the Edomites live,
5 rain poured from the sky,
the earth trembled,
and mountains shook.

6 In the time of Shamgar
son of Anath,
and now again in Jael's time,
roads were too dangerous
for caravans.
Travelers had to take
the back roads,
7 and villagers couldn't work
in their fields.[l]
Then Deborah[m] took command,
protecting Israel as a mother
protects her children.
8 The Israelites worshiped
other gods,
and the gates of their towns
were then attacked.[n]
But they had no shields
or spears to fight with.
9 I praise you, LORD,
and I am grateful
for those leaders and soldiers
who volunteered.
10 Listen, everyone!
Whether you ride a donkey
with a padded saddle
or have to walk.
11 Even those who carry water[o]
to the animals will tell you,
"The LORD has won victories,
and so has Israel."

Then the LORD's people marched
down to the town gates
12 and said, "Deborah, let's go!
Let's sing as we march.
Barak, capture our enemies."

13 The LORD's people who were left
joined with their leaders
and fought at my side.[p]
14 Troops came from Ephraim,
where Amalekites once lived.
Others came from Benjamin;
officers and leaders came
from Machir and Zebulun.
15 The rulers of Issachar
came along with Deborah,
and Issachar followed Barak
into the valley.

But the tribe of Reuben
was no help at all![q]
16 Reuben, why did you stay
among your sheep pens?[r]
Was it to listen to shepherds
whistling for their sheep?
No one could figure out
why Reuben wouldn't come.[s]
17 The people of Gilead stayed
across the Jordan.
Why did the tribe of Dan
remain on their ships
and the tribe of Asher
stay along the coast
near the harbors?

18 But soldiers of Zebulun
and Naphtali
risked their lives
to attack the enemy.[t]
19 Canaanite kings fought us

[l]5.7 *villagers . . . fields*: One possible meaning for the difficult Hebrew text. [m]5.7 *Deborah*: Or "I, Deborah." [n]5.8 *The Israelites . . . attacked*: One possible meaning for the difficult Hebrew text. [o]5.11 *Even . . . water*: One possible meaning for the difficult Hebrew text. [p]5.13 *side*: One possible meaning for the difficult Hebrew text of verse 13. [q]5.15 *But . . . at all*: Or "But the people of Reuben couldn't make up their minds." [r]5.16 *sheep pens*: Or "campfires." [s]5.16 *No . . . come*: Or "The people of Reuben couldn't make up their minds." [t]5.18 *to attack the enemy*: One possible meaning for the difficult Hebrew text.
5.5 Ex 19.18.

at Taanach by the stream
near Megiddo[u]—
but they couldn't rob us
of our silver.[v]
20 From their pathways in the sky
the stars[w] fought Sisera,
21 and his soldiers were swept away
by the ancient Kishon River.

I will march on and be brave.

22 Sisera's horses galloped off,
their hoofs thundering
in retreat.

23 The LORD's angel said,
"Put a curse on Meroz Town!
Its people refused
to help the LORD fight
his powerful enemies."
24 But honor Jael,
the wife of Heber
from the Kenite clan.
Give more honor to her
than to any other woman
who lives in tents.
Yes, give more honor to her
than to any other woman.
25 Sisera asked for water,
but Jael gave him milk—
cream in a fancy cup.
26 She reached for a tent-peg
and held a hammer
in her right hand.
And with a blow to the head,
she crushed his skull.
27 Sisera sank to his knees
and fell dead at her feet.

28 Sisera's mother looked out
through her window.
"Why is he taking so long?"
she asked.
"Why haven't we heard
his chariots coming?"
29 She and her wisest women
gave the same answer:
30 "Sisera and his troops
are finding treasures
to bring back—
a woman, or maybe two,
for each man,
and beautiful dresses
for those women to wear."[x]

31 Our LORD, we pray
that all your enemies
will die like Sisera.
But let everyone who loves you
shine brightly like the sun
at dawn.

Midian Steals Everything from Israel

6 There was peace in Israel for about
forty years. 1 Then once again the Israelites started disobeying the LORD, so he
let the nation of Midian control Israel for
seven years. 2 The Midianites were so cruel
that many Israelites ran to the mountains
and hid in caves.
3 Every time the Israelites would plant
crops, the Midianites invaded Israel together with the Amalekites and other eastern nations. 4-5 They rode in on their
camels, set up their tents, and then let
their livestock eat the crops as far as the
town of Gaza. The Midianites stole food,
sheep, cattle, and donkeys. Like a swarm of
locusts,[y] they could not be counted, and
they ruined the land wherever they went.
6-7 The Midianites took almost everything that belonged to the Israelites, and
the Israelites begged the LORD for help.
8-9 Then the LORD sent a prophet to them
with this message:

I am the LORD God of Israel, so listen to what I say. You were slaves in Egypt, but I set you free and led you out of Egypt into this land. And when nations here made life miserable for you, I rescued you and helped you get

[u]5.19 *stream near Megiddo*: Probably refers to one of the streams that flow into the Kishon River. [v]5.19 *rob us of our silver*: The army that won a battle would take everything of value from the dead enemy soldiers. [w]5.20 *stars*: In ancient times, the stars were sometimes regarded as supernatural beings. [x]5.30 *and beautiful . . . wear*: One possible meaning for the difficult Hebrew text. [y]6.4,5 *locusts*: Insects like grasshoppers that travel in swarms and cause great damage to crops.

rid of them and take their land. 10 I am your God, and I told you not to worship Amorite gods, even though you are living in the land of the Amorites. But you refused to listen.

The LORD Chooses Gideon

11 One day an angel from the LORD went to the town of Ophrah and sat down under the big tree that belonged to Joash, a member of the Abiezer clan. Joash's son Gideon was nearby, threshing grain in a shallow pit, where he could not be seen by the Midianites.

12 The angel appeared and spoke to Gideon, "The LORD is helping you, and you are a strong warrior."

13 Gideon answered, "Please don't take this wrong, but if the LORD is helping us, then why have all of these awful things happened? We've heard how the LORD performed miracles and rescued our ancestors from Egypt. But those things happened long ago. Now the LORD has abandoned us to the Midianites."

14 Then the LORD himself said, "Gideon, you will be strong, because I am giving you the power to rescue Israel from the Midianites."

15 Gideon replied, "But how can I rescue Israel? My clan is the weakest one in Manasseh, and everyone else in my family is more important than I am."

16 "Gideon," the LORD answered, "you can rescue Israel because I am going to help you! Defeating the Midianites will be as easy as beating up one man."

17 Gideon said, "It's hard to believe that I'm actually talking to the LORD. Please do something so I'll know that you really are the LORD. 18 And wait here until I bring you an offering."

"All right, I'll wait," the LORD answered.

19 Gideon went home and killed a young goat, then started boiling the meat. Next, he opened a big sack of flour and made it into thin bread.[z] When the meat was done, he put it in a basket and poured the broth into a clay cooking pot. He took the meat, the broth, and the bread and placed them under the big tree.

20 God's angel said, "Gideon, put the meat and the bread on this rock, and pour the broth over them." Gideon did as he was told. 21 The angel was holding a walking stick, and he touched the meat and the bread with the end of the stick. Flames jumped from the rock and burned up the meat and the bread.

When Gideon looked, the angel was gone. 22 Gideon realized that he had seen one of the LORD's angels. "Oh!" he moaned. "Now I'm going to die."[a]

23 "Calm down!" the LORD told Gideon. "There's nothing to be afraid of. You're not going to die."

24 Gideon built an altar for worshiping the LORD and called it "The LORD Calms Our Fears." It still stands there in Ophrah, a town in the territory of the Abiezer clan.

Gideon Tears Down Baal's Altar

25 That night the LORD spoke to Gideon again:

> Get your father's second-best bull, the one that's seven years old. Use it to pull down the altar where your father worships Baal and cut down the sacred pole[b] next to the altar. 26 Then build an altar for worshiping me on the highest part of the hill where your town is built. Use layers of stones for my altar, not just a pile of rocks. Cut up the wood from the pole, make a fire, kill the bull, and burn it as a sacrifice to me.

27 Gideon chose ten of his servants to help him, and they did everything God had said. But since Gideon was afraid of his family and the other people in town, he did it all at night.

28 When the people of the town got up the next morning, they saw that Baal's altar had been knocked over, and the sacred pole

[z]**6.19** *thin bread*: Bread made without yeast, since there was no time for the dough to rise.
[a]**6.22** *Now I'm going to die*: The Hebrew text has "I have seen an angel of the LORD face to face." Some people believed that if they saw one of the LORD's angels, they would die (see 13.22).
[b]**6.25** *sacred pole*: Or "sacred tree," used as a symbol of Asherah, the Canaanite goddess of fertility.

next to it had been cut down. Then they
noticed the new altar covered with the remains of the sacrificed bull.
29 "Who could have done such a thing?"
they asked. And they kept on asking, until
finally someone told them, "Gideon the son
of Joash did it."
30 The men of the town went to Joash
and said, "Your son Gideon knocked over
Baal's altar and cut down the sacred pole
next to it. Hand him over, so we can kill
him!"
31 The crowd pushed closer and closer,
but Joash replied, "Are you trying to take revenge for Baal? Are you trying to rescue
Baal? If you are, you will be the ones who
are put to death, and it will happen before
another day dawns. If Baal really is a god,
let him take his own revenge on someone
who tears down his altar."
32 That same day, Joash changed
Gideon's name to Jerubbaal, explaining,
"He tore down Baal's altar, so let Baal take
revenge himself."[c]

Gideon Defeats the Midianites

33 All the Midianites, Amalekites, and
other eastern nations got together and
crossed the Jordan River. Then they invaded the land of Israel and set up camp in
Jezreel Valley.
34 The LORD's Spirit took control of
Gideon, and Gideon blew a signal on a
trumpet to tell the men in the Abiezer clan
to follow him. 35 He also sent messengers
to the tribes of Manasseh, Asher, Zebulun,
and Naphtali, telling the men of these
tribes to come and join his army. Then they
set out toward the enemy camp.
36-37 Gideon prayed to God, "I know that
you promised to help me rescue Israel, but
I need proof. Tonight I'll put some wool on
the stone floor of that threshing-place over
there. If you really will help me rescue Israel, then tomorrow morning let there be
dew on the wool, but let the stone floor
be dry."
38 And that's just what happened. Early
the next morning, Gideon got up and
checked the wool. He squeezed out enough
water to fill a bowl. 39 But Gideon prayed to
God again. "Don't be angry at me," Gideon
said. "Let me try this just one more time,
so I'll really be sure you'll help me. Only
this time, let the wool be dry and the stone
floor be wet with dew."
40 That night, God made the stone floor
wet with dew, but he kept the wool dry.
7 Early the next morning, Gideon and
his army got up and moved their camp
to Fear Spring.[d] The Midianite camp was to
the north, in the valley at the foot of Moreh
Hill.[e]
2 The LORD said, "Gideon, your army is
too big. I can't let you win with this many
soldiers. The Israelites would think that
they had won the battle all by themselves
and that I didn't have anything to do with
it. 3 So call your troops together and tell
them that anyone who is really afraid can
leave Mount Gilead[f] and go home."

Twenty-two thousand men returned
home, leaving Gideon with only ten thousand soldiers.
4 "Gideon," the LORD said, "you still
have too many soldiers. Take them down to
the spring and I'll test them. I'll tell you
which ones can go along with you and
which ones must go back home."
5 When Gideon led his army down to
the spring, the LORD told him, "Watch how
each man gets a drink of water. Then divide them into two groups—those who lap
the water like a dog and those who kneel
down to drink."
6 Three hundred men scooped up water
in their hands and lapped it, and the rest
knelt to get a drink. 7 The LORD said,
"Gideon, your army will be made up of
everyone who lapped the water from their
hands. Send the others home. I'm going to
rescue Israel by helping you and your army
of three hundred defeat the Midianites."
8 Then Gideon gave these orders, "You

[c] **6.32** *Jerubbaal . . . take revenge himself*: In Hebrew, "Jerubbaal" means "Let Baal take revenge."
[d] **7.1** *Fear Spring*: Or "Harod Spring." [e] **7.1** *Moreh Hill*: About 5 miles north of Fear Spring.
[f] **7.3** *Mount Gilead*: Usually "Gilead" refers to an area east of the Jordan River, but in this verse it refers to a place near Jezreel Valley west of the Jordan.
7.3 Dt 20.8.

three hundred men stay here. The rest of you may go home, but leave your food and trumpets with us."

Gideon's army camp was on top of a hill overlooking the Midianite camp in the valley.

9 That night, the LORD said to Gideon. "Get up! Attack the Midianite camp. I am going to let you defeat them, 10 but if you're still afraid, you and your servant Purah should sneak down to their camp. 11 When you hear what the Midianites are saying, you'll be brave enough to attack."

Gideon and Purah worked their way to the edge of the enemy camp, where soldiers were on guard duty. 12 The camp was huge. The Midianites, Amalekites, and other eastern nations covered the valley like a swarm of locusts.[g] And it would be easier to count the grains of sand on a beach than to count their camels. 13 Gideon overheard one enemy guard telling another, "I had a dream about a flat[h] loaf of barley bread that came tumbling into our camp. It hit the headquarters tent,[i] and the tent flipped over and fell down."

14 The other soldier answered, "Your dream must have been about Gideon, the Israelite commander. It means God will let him and his army defeat the Midianite army and everyone else in our camp."

15 As soon as Gideon heard about the dream and what it meant, he bowed down to praise God. Then he went back to the Israelite camp and shouted, "Let's go! The LORD is going to let us defeat the Midianite army."

16 Gideon divided his little army into three groups of one hundred men, and he gave each soldier a trumpet and a large clay jar with a burning torch inside. 17-18 Gideon said, "When we get to the enemy camp, spread out and surround it. Then wait for me to blow a signal on my trumpet. As soon as you hear it, blow your trumpets and shout, 'Fight for the LORD! Fight for Gideon!' "

19 Gideon and his group reached the edge of the enemy camp a few hours after dark, just after the new guards had come on duty.[j] Gideon and his soldiers blew their trumpets and smashed the clay jars that were hiding the torches. 20 The rest of Gideon's soldiers blew the trumpets they were holding in their right hands. Then they smashed the jars and held the burning torches in their left hands. Everyone shouted, "Fight with your swords for the LORD and for Gideon!"

21 The enemy soldiers started yelling and tried to run away. Gideon's troops stayed in their positions surrounding the camp 22 and blew their trumpets again. As they did, the LORD made the enemy soldiers pull out their swords and start fighting each other.

The enemy army tried to escape from the camp. They ran to Acacia Tree Town, toward Zeredah,[k] and as far as the edge of the land that belonged to the town of Abel-Meholah near Tabbath.[l]

23 Gideon sent word for more Israelite soldiers to come from the tribes of Naphtali, Asher, and both halves of Manasseh[m] to help fight the Midianites. 24 He also sent messengers to tell all the men who lived in the hill country of Ephraim, "Come and help us fight the Midianites! Put guards at every spring, stream, and well, as far as Beth-Barah before the Midianites can get to them. And guard the Jordan River."

Troops from Ephraim did exactly what Gideon had asked, 25 and they even helped chase the Midianites on the east side of the Jordan River. These troops captured Raven

[g] **7.12** *locusts*: See the note at 6.4, 5. [h] **7.13** *flat*: Or "moldy." [i] **7.13** *the headquarters tent*: Or "a tent." [j] **7.19** *a few hours after dark, just . . . duty*: The Hebrew text has "at the beginning of the second watch, just . . . duty." The night was divided into three periods called "watches," each about four hours long, and different guards would come on duty at the beginning of each watch. The first watch began at sunset, so the beginning of the second watch would have been shortly after 10:00 P.M. [k] **7.22** *Zeredah*: Some Hebrew manuscripts; most Hebrew manuscripts "Zererah"; these may be different names for the town of Zarethan in the Jordan River valley. [l] **7.22** *Acacia Tree Town . . . Zeredah . . . Abel-Meholah near Tabbath*: These were places east of the Jordan River. [m] **7.23** *both halves of Manasseh*: Half of Manasseh lived east of the Jordan River, and the other half lived on the west.

and Wolf,[n] the two Midianite leaders. They
killed Raven at a large rock that has come
to be known as Raven Rock, and they killed
Wolf near a wine-pit that has come to be
called Wolf Wine-Pit.[o]
The men of Ephraim brought the heads
of the two Midianite leaders to Gideon.

8 [1] But the men were really upset with
Gideon and complained, "When you
went to war with Midian, you didn't ask us
to help! Why did you treat us like that?"
[2] Gideon answered:

Don't be upset! Even though you
came later, you were able to do much
more than I did. It's just like the grape
harvest: The grapes your tribe doesn't
even bother to pick are better than the
best grapes my family can grow. [3] Besides, God chose you to capture Raven
and Wolf. I didn't do a thing compared
to you.

By the time Gideon had finished talking,
the men of Ephraim had calmed down and
were no longer angry at him.

Gideon Finishes Destroying the Midianite Army

[4] After Gideon and his three hundred
troops had chased the Midianites as far as
the Jordan River, they were exhausted.
[5] The town of Succoth was nearby, so he
went there and asked, "Please give my
troops some food. They are worn out, but
we have to keep chasing Zebah and Zalmunna, the two Midianite kings."
[6] The town leaders of Succoth answered, "Why should we feed your army?
We don't know if you really will defeat Zebah and Zalmunna."
[7] "Just wait!" Gideon said. "After the
LORD helps me defeat them, I'm coming
back here. I'll make a whip out of thorns
and rip the flesh from your bones."
[8] After leaving Succoth, Gideon went to
Penuel and asked the leaders there for
some food. But he got the same answer as
he had gotten at Succoth. [9] "I'll come back
safe and sound," Gideon said, "but when I
do, I'm going to tear down your tower!"[p]
[10] Zebah and Zalmunna were in Karkor[q]
with an army of fifteen thousand troops.
They were all that was left of the army of
the eastern nations, because one hundred
twenty thousand of their warriors had been
killed in the battle.
[11] Gideon reached the enemy camp by
going east along Nomad[r] Road past Nobah
and Jogbehah. He made a surprise attack,
[12] and the enemy panicked. Zebah and Zalmunna tried to escape, but Gideon chased
and captured them.
[13] After the battle, Gideon set out for
home. As he was going through Heres Pass,
[14] he caught a young man who lived in
Succoth. Gideon asked him who the town
officials of Succoth were, and the young
man wrote down seventy-seven names.
[15] Gideon went to the town officials and
said, "Here are Zebah and Zalmunna. Remember how you made fun of me? You
said, 'We don't know if you really will defeat
those two Midianite kings. So why should
we feed your worn-out army?' "
[16] Gideon made a whip from thorn
plants and used it to beat the town officials.
[17] Afterwards he went to Penuel, where he
tore down the tower and killed all the town
officials[s] there.
[18] Then Gideon said, "Zebah and Zalmunna, tell me about the men you killed at
Tabor."
"They were a lot like you," the two kings
answered. "They were dignified, almost like
royalty."
[19] "They were my very own brothers!"
Gideon said. "I swear by the living LORD
that if you had let them live, I would let
you live."
[20] Gideon turned to Jether, his oldest
son. "Kill them!" Gideon said.
But Jether was young,[t] and he was too
afraid to even pull out his sword.

[n]**7.25** *Raven and Wolf*: Or "Oreb and Zeeb." [o]**7.25** *Raven Rock . . . Wolf Wine-Pit*: Or "Oreb Rock . . . Zeeb Wine-Pit." [p]**8.9** *tower*: Towers were often part of a town wall. [q]**8.10** *Karkor*: A little over 100 miles east of the Dead Sea. [r]**8.11** *Nomad*: A person who lives in a tent and moves from place to place. [s]**8.17** *all . . . officials*: Or "every man in town." [t]**8.20** *young*: Gideon wanted to insult the kings by having a young boy kill them.

8.3-5 Ps 83.11.

21 "What's the matter, Gideon?" Zebah and Zalmunna asked. "Do it yourself, if you're not too much of a coward!"

Gideon jumped up and killed them both. Then he took the fancy gold ornaments from the necks of their camels.

The Israelites Ask Gideon To Be Their King

22 After the battle with the Midianites, the Israelites said, "Gideon, you rescued us! Now we want you to be our king. Then after your death, your son and then your grandson will rule."

23 "No," Gideon replied, "I won't be your king, and my son won't be king either. Only the LORD is your ruler. 24 But I will ask you to do one thing: Give me all the earrings you took from the enemy."

The enemy soldiers had been Ishmaelites,[u] and they wore gold earrings.

25 The Israelite soldiers replied, "Of course we will give you the earrings." Then they spread out a robe on the ground and tossed the earrings on it. 26 The total weight of this gold was over forty pounds. In addition, there was the gold from the camels' ornaments and from the beautiful jewelry worn by the Midianite kings. Gideon also took their purple robes.

27-29 Gideon returned to his home in Ophrah and had the gold made into a statue, which the Israelites soon started worshiping. They became unfaithful to God, and even Gideon and his family were trapped into worshiping the statue.[v]

The Midianites had been defeated so badly that they were no longer strong enough to attack Israel. And so Israel was at peace for the remaining forty years of Gideon's life.

Gideon Dies

30 Gideon had many wives and seventy sons. 31 He even had a wife[w] who lived at Shechem.[x] They had a son, and Gideon named him Abimelech.

32 Gideon lived to be an old man. And when he died, he was buried in the family tomb in his hometown of Ophrah, which belonged to the Abiezer clan.

33 Soon after Gideon's death, the Israelites turned their backs on God again. They set up idols of Baal and worshiped Baal Berith[y] as their god. 34 The Israelites forgot that the LORD was their God, and that he had rescued them from the enemies who lived around them. 35 Besides all that, the Israelites were unkind to Gideon's family, even though Gideon had done so much for Israel.

Abimelech Tries To Be King

9 Abimelech the son of Gideon[z] went to Shechem. While there, he met with his mother's relatives 2 and told them to say to the leaders of Shechem, "Do you think it would be good to have all seventy of Gideon's sons ruling us? Wouldn't you rather have just one man be king? Abimelech would make a good king, and he's related to us."

3 Abimelech's uncles talked it over with the leaders of Shechem who agreed, "Yes, it would be better for one of our relatives to be king." 4 Then they gave Abimelech seventy pieces[a] of silver from the temple of their god Baal Berith.[b]

Abimelech used the silver to hire a gang of rough soldiers who would do anything for money. 5 Abimelech and his soldiers went to his father's home in Ophrah and brought out Gideon's other sons to a large rock, where they murdered all seventy.

[u] **8.24** *Ishmaelites*: According to Genesis 25.1, 2, 12, both Ishmaelites and Midianites were descendants of Abraham. It is possible that in this passage "Ishmaelites" has the meaning "nomadic traders," while "Midianites" (verses 22, 26-29) refers to their ethnic origin. [v] **8.27-29** *statue . . . statue*: Or "sacred priestly vest . . . vest." [w] **8.31** *wife*: This translates a Hebrew word for a woman who was legally bound to a man, but without the full privileges of a wife. [x] **8.31** *who lived at Shechem*: Sometimes marriages were arranged so that the wife lived with her parents, and the husband visited her from time to time. [y] **8.33** *Baal Berith*: Or "Baal of the Agreement" or "the Lord of the Agreement." [z] **9.1** *Gideon*: The Hebrew text has "Jerubbaal," another name for Gideon (see 6.32). [a] **9.4** *seventy pieces*: About 28 ounces. [b] **9.4** *Baal Berith*: See the note at 8.33.

Gideon's youngest son Jotham hid from the soldiers, but he was the only one who escaped.

6 The leaders of Shechem, including the priests and the military officers,[c] met at the tree next to the sacred rock[d] in Shechem to crown Abimelech king. 7 Jotham heard what they were doing. So he climbed to the top of Mount Gerizim and shouted down to the people who were there at the meeting:

Leaders of Shechem,
listen to me,
and maybe God
will listen to you.

8 Once the trees searched
for someone to be king;
they asked the olive tree,
"Will you be our king?"
9 But the olive tree replied,
"My oil brings honor
to people and gods.
I won't stop making oil,
just to have my branches wave
above the other trees."

10 Then they asked the fig tree,
"Will you be our king?"
11 But the fig tree replied,
"I won't stop growing
my delicious fruit,
just to have my branches wave
above the other trees."

12 Next they asked the grape vine,
"Will you be our king?"
13 But the grape vine replied,
"My wine brings cheer
to people and gods.
I won't stop making wine,
just to have my branches wave
above the other trees."

14 Finally, they went
to the thornbush and asked,
"Will you be our king?"
15 The thornbush replied,
"If you really want me
to be your king,
then come into my shade
and I will protect you.
But if you're deceiving me,
I'll start a fire
that will spread out and destroy
the cedars of Lebanon."[e]

After Jotham had finished telling this story, he said:

16-18 My father Gideon risked his life for you when he fought to rescue you from the Midianites. Did you reward Gideon by being kind to his family? No, you did not! You attacked his family and killed all seventy of his sons on that rock.

And was it right to make Abimelech your king? He's merely the son of my father's slave girl.[f] But just because he's your relative, you made him king of Shechem.

19 So, you leaders of Shechem, if you treated Gideon and his family the way you should have, then I hope you and Abimelech will make each other very happy. 20 But if it was wrong to treat Gideon and his family the way you did, then I pray that Abimelech will destroy you with fire, and I pray that you will do the same to him.

21 Jotham ran off and went to live in the town of Beer, where he could be safe from his brother Abimelech.

Abimelech Destroys Shechem

22 Abimelech had been a military commander of Israel for three years, 23-24 when God decided to punish him and the leaders of Shechem for killing Gideon's seventy sons.

So God turned the leaders of Shechem against Abimelech. 25 Then they sent some men to hide on the hilltops and watch for Abimelech and his troops, while they sent others to rob everyone that went by on the

[c]**9.6** *including the priests and the military officers*: The Hebrew text has "and the Millo house," another name for the temple of Baal Berith. It probably also served as a military fortress. [d]**9.6** *tree . . . rock*: One ancient translation; Hebrew "propped-up sacred tree." [e]**9.15** *cedars of Lebanon*: The cedars that grew in the Lebanon mountains were some of the largest trees in that part of the world. [f]**9.16-18** *son of . . . slave girl*: See 8.31.

road. But Abimelech found out what they were doing.

26 One day, Gaal son of Ebed went to live in Shechem. His brothers moved there too, and soon the leaders of Shechem started trusting him.

27 The time came for the grape harvest, and the people of Shechem went into their vineyards and picked the grapes. They put the grapes in their wine-pits and walked on them to squeeze out the juice in order to make wine. Then they went into the temple of their god and threw a big party. There was a lot of eating and drinking, and before long they were cursing Abimelech.

28 Gaal said:

> Hamor was the founder of Shechem, and one of his descendants should be our ruler. But Abimelech's father was Gideon, so Abimelech isn't really one of us. He shouldn't be our king, and we shouldn't have to obey him or Zebul, who rules Shechem for him. 29 If I were the ruler of Shechem, I'd get rid of that Abimelech. I'd tell him, "Get yourself an even bigger army, and we will still defeat you."

30 Zebul was angry when he found out what Gaal had said. 31 And so he sent some messengers to Abimelech. But they had to pretend to be doing something else, or they would not have been allowed to leave Shechem.[g] Zebul told the messengers to say:

> Gaal the son of Ebed has come to Shechem along with his brothers, and they have persuaded the people to let Gaal rule Shechem instead of you. 32 This is what I think you should do. Lead your army here during the night and hide in the fields. 33 Get up the next morning at sunrise and rush out of your hiding places to attack the town. Gaal and his followers will come out to fight you, but you will easily defeat them.

34 So one night, Abimelech led his soldiers to Shechem. He divided them into four groups, and they all hid near the town.

35 The next morning, Gaal went out and stood in the opening of the town gate. Abimelech and his soldiers left their hiding places, 36 and Gaal saw them. Zebul was standing there with Gaal, and Gaal remarked, "Zebul, that looks like a crowd of people coming down from the mountaintops."

"No," Zebul answered, "it's just the shadows of the mountains. It only looks like people moving."

37 "But Zebul, look over there," Gaal said. "There's a crowd coming down from the sacred mountain,[h] and another group is coming along the road from the tree where people talk with the spirits of the dead."

38 Then Zebul replied, "What good is all of your bragging now? You were the one who said Abimelech shouldn't be the ruler of Shechem. Out there is the army that you made fun of. So go out and fight them!"

39 Gaal and the leaders of Shechem went out and fought Abimelech. 40 Soon the people of Shechem turned and ran back into the town. However, Abimelech and his troops were close behind and killed many of them along the way.

41 Abimelech stayed at Arumah,[i] and Zebul forced Gaal and his brothers out of Shechem.

42 The next morning, the people of Shechem were getting ready to work in their fields as usual, but someone told Abimelech about it. 43 Abimelech divided his army into three groups and set up an ambush in the fields near Shechem. When the people came out of the town, he and his army rushed out from their hiding places and attacked. 44 Abimelech and the troops with him ran to the town gate and took control of it, while two other groups attacked and killed the people who were in the fields. 45 He and his troops fought in Shechem all day, until they had killed everyone in town. Then he and his men

[g] **9.31** *But . . . Shechem*: One possible meaning for the difficult Hebrew text. [h] **9.37** *sacred mountain*: The Hebrew text has "the navel of the land," which probably refers to Mount Gerizim as a sacred mountain linking heaven and earth. [i] **9.41** *Arumah*: About five miles from Shechem.

tore down the houses and buildings and scattered salt[j] everywhere.

46 Earlier that day, the leaders of the temple of El Berith[k] at Shechem had heard about the attack. So they went into the temple fortress, 47 but Abimelech found out where they were. 48 He led his troops to Mount Zalmon, where he took an ax and chopped off a tree branch. He lifted the branch onto his shoulder and shouted, "Hurry! Cut off a branch just as I did."

49 When they all had branches, they followed Abimelech back to Shechem. They piled the branches against the fortress and set them on fire, burning down the fortress and killing about one thousand men and women.

50 After destroying Shechem, Abimelech went to Thebez. He surrounded the town and captured it. 51 But there was a tall fortress in the middle of the town, and the town leaders and everyone else went inside. Then they barred the gates and went up to the flat roof.

52 Abimelech and his army rushed to the fortress and tried to force their way inside. Abimelech himself was about to set the heavy wooden doors on fire, 53 when a woman on the roof dropped a large rock[l] on his head and cracked his skull. 54 The soldier who carried his weapons was nearby, and Abimelech told him, "Take out your sword and kill me. I don't want people to say that I was killed by a woman!"

So the soldier ran his sword through Abimelech. 55 And when the Israelite soldiers saw that their leader was dead, they went back home.

56 That's how God punished Abimelech for killing his brothers and bringing shame on his father's family. 57 God also punished the people of Shechem for helping Abimelech.[m] Everything happened just as Jotham's curse said it would.

Tola

10 Tola was the next person to rescue Israel. He belonged to the Issachar tribe, but he lived in Shamir, a town in the hill country of Ephraim. His father was Puah, and his grandfather was Dodo. 2 Tola was a leader[n] of Israel for twenty-three years, then he died and was buried in Shamir.

Jair

3 The next leader[n] of Israel was Jair, who lived in Gilead. He was a leader for twenty-two years. 4 He had thirty sons, and each son had his own mule[o] and was in charge of one town in Gilead. Those thirty towns are still called The Settlements of Jair.[p] 5 When he died, he was buried in the town of Kamon.

Israel Is Unfaithful Again

6 Before long, the Israelites began disobeying the LORD by worshiping Baal, Astarte, and gods from Syria, Sidon, Moab, Ammon, and Philistia.

7 The LORD was angry at Israel and decided to let Philistia and Ammon conquer them. 8 So the same year that Jair died, Israel's army was crushed by these two nations. For eighteen years, Ammon was cruel to the Israelites who lived in Gilead, the region east of the Jordan River that had once belonged to the Amorites. 9 Then the Ammonites began crossing the Jordan and attacking the tribes of Judah, Benjamin, and Ephraim. Life was miserable for the Israelites. 10 They begged the LORD for help and confessed, "We were unfaithful to you, our LORD. We stopped worshiping you and started worshiping idols of Baal."

11-12 The LORD answered:

In the past when you came crying to me for help, I rescued you. At one

[j]**9.45** *scattered salt*: This may have been part of a ceremony to place a curse on the town.
[k]**9.46** *temple of El Berith*: The Hebrew text also calls all or part of this temple the "Fortress of Shechem." El Berith, "the God of the Agreement," was also known as Baal Berith, "the Lord of the Agreement" (see also 8.33; 9.4).
[l]**9.53** *large rock*: One that was used in the grinding of grain.
[m]**9.57** *helping Abimelech*: Hebrew "their evil" (see 9.3, 4).
[n]**10.2,3** *leader*: See 2.16 and the note there.
[o]**10.4** *each son had his own mule*: A sign that the family was wealthy.
[p]**10.4** *The Settlements of Jair*: Or "Havvoth-Jair."
9.53 2 S 11.21.

time or another I've rescued you from the Egyptians, the Amorites, the Ammonites, the Philistines, the Sidonians, the Amalekites, and the Maonites.[q] 13-14 But I'm not going to rescue you any more! You've left me and gone off to worship other gods. If you're in such big trouble, go cry to them for help!

15 "We have been unfaithful," the Israelites admitted. "If we must be punished, do it yourself, but please rescue us from the Ammonites."

16 Then the Israelites got rid of the idols of the foreign gods, and they began worshiping only the LORD. Finally, there came a time when the LORD could no longer stand to see them suffer.

The Ammonites Invade Gilead

17 The rulers of Ammon called their soldiers together and led them to Gilead, where they set up camp.

The Israelites gathered at Mizpah[r] and set up camp there. 18 The leaders of Gilead asked each other, "Who can lead an attack on the Ammonites?" Then they agreed, "If we can find someone who can lead the attack, we'll make him the ruler of Gilead."

Jephthah

11 1-5 The leaders of the Gilead clan decided to ask a brave warrior named Jephthah son of Gilead to lead the attack against the Ammonites.

Even though Jephthah belonged to the Gilead clan, he had earlier been forced to leave the region where they had lived. Jephthah was the son of a prostitute, but his half-brothers were the sons of his father's wife.

One day his half-brothers told him, "You don't really belong to our family, so you can't have any of the family property." Then they forced Jephthah to leave home.

Jephthah went to the country of Tob, where he was joined by a number of men who would do anything for money.

So the leaders of Gilead went to Jephthah and said, 6 "Please come back to Gilead! If you lead our army, we will be able to fight off the Ammonites."

7 "Didn't you hate me?" Jephthah replied. "Weren't you the ones who forced me to leave my family? You're coming to me now, just because you're in trouble."

8 "But we do want you to come back," the leaders said. "And if you lead us in battle against the Ammonites, we will make you the ruler of Gilead."

9 "All right," Jephthah said. "If I go back with you and the LORD lets me defeat the Ammonites, will you really make me your ruler?"

10 "You have our word," the leaders answered. "And the LORD is a witness to what we have said."

11 So Jephthah went back to Mizpah[r] with the leaders of Gilead. The people of Gilead gathered at the place of worship and made Jephthah their ruler. Jephthah also made promises to them.

12 After the ceremony, Jephthah sent messengers to say to the king of Ammon, "Are you trying to start a war? You have invaded my country, and I want to know why!"

13 The king of Ammon replied, "Tell Jephthah that the land really belongs to me, all the way from the Arnon River in the south, to the Jabbok River in the north, and west to the Jordan River. When the Israelites came out of Egypt, they stole it. Tell Jephthah to return it to me, and there won't be any war."

14 Jephthah sent the messengers back to the king of Ammon, 15 and they told him that Jephthah had said:

> Israel hasn't taken any territory from Moab or Ammon. 16 When the Israelites came from Egypt, they traveled in the desert to the Red Sea[s] and then to Kadesh. 17 They sent messengers to

[q] **10.11,12** *Maonites*: Hebrew; one ancient translation "Midianites." [r] **10.17; 11.11** *Mizpah*: In chapters 10–12, Mizpah is the name of a town in Gilead (see 11.29), not the same town as the Mizpah of chapters 20, 21. [s] **11.16** *Red Sea*: Hebrew *yam suph*, here referring to the Gulf of Aqaba, since the term is extended to include the northeastern arm of the Red Sea (see also the note at Exodus 13.18).

11.17 Nu 20.14-21.

the king of Edom and said, "Please, let us go through your country." But the king of Edom refused. They also sent messengers to the king of Moab, but he wouldn't let them cross his country either. And so the Israelites stayed at Kadesh.

18 A little later, the Israelites set out into the desert, going east of Edom and Moab, and camping on the eastern side of the Arnon River gorge. The Arnon is the eastern border of Moab, and since the Israelites didn't cross it, they didn't even set foot in Moab.

19 The Israelites sent messengers to the Amorite King Sihon of Heshbon. "Please," they said, "let our people go through your country to get to our own land."

20 Sihon didn't think the Israelites could be trusted, so he called his army together. They set up camp at Jahaz, then they attacked the Israelite camp.
21 But the LORD God helped Israel defeat Sihon and his army. Israel took over all of the Amorite land where Sihon's people had lived,
22 from the Arnon River in the south to the Jabbok River in the north, and from the desert in the east to the Jordan River in the west.

23 The messengers also told the king of Ammon that Jephthah had said:

The LORD God of Israel helped his nation get rid of the Amorites and take their land. Now do you think you're going to take over that same territory?
24 If Chemosh your god[t] takes over a country and gives it to you, don't you have a right to it? And if the LORD takes over a country and gives it to us, the land is ours!

25 Are you better than Balak the son of Zippor? He was the king of Moab, but he didn't quarrel with Israel or start a war with us.

26 For three hundred years, Israelites have been living in Heshbon and Aroer and the nearby villages, and in the towns along the Arnon River gorge. If the land really belonged to you Ammonites, you wouldn't have waited until now to try to get it back.

27 I haven't done anything to you, but it's certainly wrong of you to start a war. I pray that the LORD will show whether Israel or Ammon is in the right.

28 But the king of Ammon paid no attention to Jephthah's message.

29 Then the LORD's Spirit took control of Jephthah, and Jephthah went through Gilead and Manasseh, raising an army. Finally, he arrived at Mizpah in Gilead, where
30 he promised the LORD, "If you will let me defeat the Ammonites
31 and come home safely, I will sacrifice to you whoever comes out to meet me first."

32 From Mizpah, Jephthah attacked the Ammonites, and the LORD helped him defeat them.

33 Jephthah and his army destroyed the twenty towns between Aroer and Minnith, and others as far as Abel-Keramim. After that, the Ammonites could not invade Israel any more.

Jephthah's Daughter

34 When Jephthah returned to his home in Mizpah, the first one to meet him was his daughter. She was playing a tambourine and dancing to celebrate his victory, and she was his only child.

35 "Oh!" Jephthah cried. Then he tore his clothes in sorrow and said to his daughter, "I made a sacred promise to the LORD, and I must keep it. Your coming out to meet me has broken my heart."

36 "Father," she said, "you made a sacred promise to the LORD, and he let you defeat the Ammonites. Now, you must do what you promised, even if it means I must die.
37 But first, please let me spend two months, wandering in the hill country with my friends. We will cry together, because I can never get married and have children."

[t] **11.24** *Chemosh your god*: Chemosh was actually the national god of Moab, not Ammon. The land that Ammon was trying to take over had belonged to the Moabites before belonging to the Amorites (see Numbers 21.26). So the Ammonites may have thought that Chemosh controlled it.

11.18 Nu 21.4. **11.19-22** Nu 21.21-24. **11.25** Nu 22.1-6. **11.35** Nu 30.2.

[38] "Yes, you may have two months," Jephthah said.

She and some other girls left, and for two months they wandered in the hill country, crying because she could never get married and have children. [39] Then she went back to her father. He did what he had promised, and she never got married.

That's why [40] every year, Israelite girls walk around for four days, weeping for[u] Jephthah's daughter.

The Ephraim Tribe Fights Jephthah's Army

12 The men of the Ephraim tribe got together an army and went across the Jordan River to Zaphon to meet with Jephthah. They said, "Why did you go to war with the Ammonites without asking us to help? Just for that, we're going to burn down your house with you inside!"

[2] "But I did ask for your help," Jephthah answered. "That was back when the people of Gilead and I were having trouble with the Ammonites, and you wouldn't do a thing to help us. [3] So when we realized you weren't coming, we risked our lives and attacked the Ammonites. And the LORD let us defeat them. There's no reason for you to come here today to attack me."

[4] But the men from Ephraim said, "You people of Gilead are nothing more than refugees from Ephraim. You even live on land that belongs to the tribes of Ephraim and Manasseh."[v]

So Jephthah called together the army of Gilead, then they attacked and defeated the army from Ephraim. [5] The army of Gilead also posted guards at all the places where the soldiers from Ephraim could cross the Jordan River to return to their own land.

Whenever one of the men from Ephraim would try to cross the river, the guards would say, "Are you from Ephraim?"

"No," the man would answer, "I'm not from Ephraim."

[6] The guards would then tell them to say "Shiboleth," because they knew that people of Ephraim could say "Sibboleth," but not "Shiboleth."

If the man said "Sibboleth," the guards would grab him and kill him right there. Altogether, forty-two thousand men from Ephraim were killed in the battle and at the Jordan.

[7] Jephthah was a leader[w] of Israel for six years, before he died and was buried in his hometown Mizpah[x] in Gilead.

Ibzan

[8] Ibzan, the next leader[y] of Israel, came from Bethlehem. [9] He had thirty daughters and thirty sons, and he let them all marry outside his clan.

Ibzan was a leader for seven years, [10] before he died and was buried in Bethlehem.

Elon

[11] Elon from the Zebulun tribe was the next leader[y] of Israel. He was a leader for ten years, [12] before he died and was buried in Aijalon that belonged to the Zebulun tribe.

Abdon

[13-15] Abdon the son of Hillel was the next leader[y] of Israel. He had forty sons and thirty grandsons, and each one of them had his own donkey.[z] Abdon was a leader for eight years, before he died and was buried in his hometown of Pirathon, which is located in the part of the hill country of Ephraim where Amalekites used to live.

Samson Is Born

13 Once again the Israelites started disobeying the LORD. So he let the Philistines take control of Israel for forty years.

[2] Manoah from the tribe of Dan lived in the town of Zorah. His wife was not able to

---

[u] **11.40** *weeping for*: Or "remembering." [v] **12.4** *You people of Gilead . . . Ephraim and Manasseh*: One possible meaning for the difficult Hebrew text. [w] **12.7** *leader*: See 2.16 and the note there. [x] **12.7** *his hometown Mizpah*: One possible meaning for the difficult Hebrew text. [y] **12.8,11,13-15** *leader*: See 2.16 and the note there. [z] **12.13-15** *each . . . donkey*: A sign that the family was wealthy.

have children, 3-5 but one day an angel from the LORD appeared to her and said:

You have never been able to have any children, but very soon you will be pregnant and have a son. He will belong to God[a] from the day he is born, so his hair must never be cut. And even before he is born, you must not drink any wine or beer or eat any food forbidden by God's laws.

Your son will begin to set Israel free from the Philistines.

6 She went to Manoah and said, "A prophet who looked like an angel of God came and talked to me. I was so frightened, that I didn't even ask where he was from. He didn't tell me his name, 7 but he did say that I'm going to have a baby boy. I'm not supposed to drink any wine or beer or eat any food forbidden by God's laws. Our son will belong to God for as long as he lives."

8 Then Manoah prayed, "Our LORD, please send that prophet again and let him tell us what to do for the son we are going to have."

9 God answered Manoah's prayer, and the angel went back to Manoah's wife while she was resting in the fields. Manoah wasn't there at the time, 10 so she found him and said, "That same man is here again! He's the one I saw the other day."

11 Manoah went with his wife and asked the man, "Are you the one who spoke to my wife?"

"Yes, I am," he answered.

12 Manoah then asked, "When your promise comes true, what rules must he obey and what will be his work?"

13 "Your wife must be careful to do everything I told her," the LORD's angel answered. 14 "She must not eat or drink anything made from grapes. She must not drink wine or beer or eat anything forbidden by God's laws. I told her exactly what to do."

15 "Please," Manoah said, "stay here with us for just a little while, and we'll fix a young goat for you to eat." 16 Manoah didn't realize that he was really talking to one of the LORD's angels.

The angel answered, "I can stay for a little while, although I won't eat any of your food. But if you would like to offer the goat as a sacrifice to the LORD, that would be fine."

17 Manoah said, "Tell us your name, so we can honor you after our son is born."

18 "No," the angel replied. "You don't need to know my name. And if you did, you couldn't understand it."

19 So Manoah took a young goat over to a large rock he had chosen for an altar, and he built a fire on the rock. Then he killed the goat, and offered it with some grain as a sacrifice to the LORD. But then an amazing thing happened. 20 The fire blazed up toward the sky, and the LORD's angel went up toward heaven in the fire. Manoah and his wife bowed down low when they saw what happened.

21 The angel was gone, but Manoah and his wife realized that he was one of the LORD's angels. 22 Manoah said, "We have seen an angel.[b] Now we're going to die."[c]

23 "The LORD isn't going to kill us," Manoah's wife responded. "The LORD accepted our sacrifice and grain offering, and he let us see something amazing. Besides, he told us that we're going to have a son."

24 Later, Manoah's wife did give birth to a son, and she named him Samson. As the boy grew, the LORD blessed him. 25 Then, while Samson was staying at Dan's Camp[d] between the towns of Zorah and Eshtaol, the Spirit of the LORD took control of him.

Samson Gets Married

14 One day, Samson went to Timnah, where he saw a Philistine woman. 2 When he got back home, he told his parents, "I saw a Philistine woman in Timnah, and I want to marry her. Get her for me!"[e]

[a] **13.3-5** *belong to God*: The Hebrew text has "be a Nazirite of God." Nazirites were dedicated to God and had to follow special rules to stay that way (see Numbers 6.1, 21). [b] **13.22** *angel*: The Hebrew text has "god," which can be used of God or of other supernatural beings. [c] **13.22** *We have seen an angel. Now we're going to die*: Some people believed that if they saw the LORD or one of the LORD's angels, they would die. [d] **13.25** *Dan's Camp*: Or "Mahaneh-Dan." [e] **14.2** *Get her for me*: At that time, parents arranged marriages for their children.

13.5 Nu 6.1-5.

[3] His parents answered, "There are a lot of women in our clan and even more in the rest of Israel. Those Philistines are pagans. Why would you want to marry one of their women?"

"She looks good to me," Samson answered. "Get her for me!"

[4] At that time, the Philistines were in control of Israel, and the LORD wanted to stir up trouble for them. That's why he made Samson desire that woman.

[5] As Samson and his parents reached the vineyards near Timnah, a fierce young lion suddenly roared and attacked Samson. [6] But the LORD's Spirit took control of Samson, and with his bare hands he tore the lion apart, as though it had been a young goat. His parents didn't know what he had done, and he didn't tell them.

[7] When they got to Timnah, Samson talked to the woman, and he was sure that she was the one for him.

[8] Later,[f] Samson returned to Timnah for the wedding. And when he came near the place where the lion had attacked, he left the road to see what was left of the lion. He was surprised to see that bees were living in the lion's skeleton, and that they had made some honey. [9] He scooped up the honey in his hands and ate some of it as he walked along. When he got back to his parents, he gave them some of the honey, and they ate it too. But he didn't tell them he had found the honey in the skeleton of a lion.[g]

[10] While Samson's father went to make the final arrangements with the bride and her family, Samson threw a big party,[h] as grooms[i] usually did. [11] When the Philistines saw what Samson was like, they told thirty of their young men to stay with him at the party.

[12] Samson told the thirty young men, "This party will last for seven days. Let's make a bet: I'll tell you a riddle, and if you can tell me the right answer before the party is over, I'll give each one of you a shirt and a full change of clothing. [13] But if you can't tell me the answer, then each of you will have to give me a shirt and a full change of clothing."

"It's a bet!" the Philistines said. "Tell us the riddle."

[14] Samson said:

Once so strong and mighty—
now so sweet and tasty!

Three days went by, and the Philistine young men had not come up with the right answer. [15] Finally, on the seventh[j] day of the party they went to Samson's bride and said, "You had better trick your husband into telling you the answer to his riddle. Have you invited us here just to rob us? If you don't find out the answer, we will burn you and your family to death."

[16] Samson's bride went to him and started crying in his arms. "You must really hate me," she sobbed. "If you loved me at all, you would have told me the answer to your riddle."

"But I haven't even told my parents the answer!" Samson replied. "Why should I tell you?"

[17] For the entire seven days of the party, she had been whining and trying to get the answer from him. But that seventh day she put so much pressure on Samson that he finally gave in and told her the answer. She went straight to the young men and told them.

[18] Before sunset that day, the men of the town went to Samson with this answer:

A lion is the strongest—
honey is the sweetest!

Samson replied,

This answer you have given me
doubtless came
from my bride-to-be.

[19] Then the LORD's Spirit took control of Samson. He went to Ashkelon,[k] where he killed thirty men and took their clothing.

[f] **14.8** *Later*: Or "The following year." [g] **14.9** *But he didn't tell them . . . skeleton of a lion*: To eat anything that had touched a skeleton was against God's laws (see Leviticus 11.27-40).
[h] **14.10** *party*: The Hebrew term means a party that involved a lot of drinking. [i] **14.10** *grooms*: Or "warriors." [j] **14.15** *Finally, on the seventh*: Hebrew; three ancient translations "on the fourth." [k] **14.19** *Ashkelon*: Another Philistine town.

Samson then gave it to the thirty young
men at Timnah and stormed back home to
his own family.
20 The father of the bride had Samson's
wife marry one of the thirty young men
that had been at Samson's party.[l]

15 Later, during the wheat harvest,
Samson went to visit the young
woman he thought was still his wife.[m] He
brought along a young goat as a gift and
said to her father, "I want to go into my
wife's bedroom."

"You can't do that," he replied. 2 "When
you left the way you did, I thought you
were divorcing[n] her. So I arranged for her
to marry one of the young men who were at
your party. But my younger daughter is
even prettier, and you can have her as your
wife."
3 "This time," Samson answered, "I
have a good reason for really hurting some
Philistines."

Samson Takes Revenge

4 Samson went out and caught three
hundred foxes and tied them together in
pairs with oil-soaked rags around their
tails. 5 Then Samson took the foxes into
the Philistine wheat fields that were ready
to be harvested. He set the rags on fire and
let the foxes go. The wheat fields went up
in flames, and so did the stacks of wheat
that had already been cut. Even the Philistine vineyards and olive orchards burned.
6 Some of the Philistines started asking
around, "Who could have done such a
thing?"

"It was Samson," someone told them.
"He married the daughter of that man in
Timnah, but then the man gave Samson's
wife to one of the men at the wedding."

The Philistine leaders went to Timnah
and burned to death Samson's wife and her
father.[o]
7 When Samson found out what they
had done, he went to them and said, "You
killed them! And I won't rest until I
get even with you." 8 Then Samson
started hacking them to pieces with his
sword.[p]

Samson left Philistia and went to live in
the cave at Etam Rock. 9 But it wasn't long
before the Philistines invaded Judah[q] and
set up a huge army camp at Jawbone.[r]
10 The people of Judah asked, "Why
have you invaded our land?"

The Philistines answered, "We've come
to get Samson. We're going to do the same
things to him that he did to our people."
11 Three thousand men from Judah
went to the cave at Etam Rock and said to
Samson, "Don't you know that the
Philistines rule us, and they will punish us
for what you did?"

"I was only getting even with them,"
Samson replied. "They did the same things
to me first."
12 "We came here to tie you up and turn
you over to them," said the men of Judah.

"I won't put up a fight," Samson answered, "but you have to promise not to
hurt me yourselves."
13-14 "We promise," the men said. "We
will only tie you up and turn you over to
the Philistines. We won't kill you." Then
they tied up his hands and arms with two
brand-new ropes and led him away from
Etam Rock.

When the Philistines saw that Samson
was being brought to their camp at Jawbone, they started shouting and ran toward
him. But the LORD's Spirit took control of
Samson, and Samson broke the ropes, as
though they were pieces of burnt cloth.
15 Samson glanced around and spotted the
jawbone of a donkey. The jawbone had not
yet dried out, so it was still hard and heavy.
Samson grabbed it and started hitting
Philistines—he killed a thousand of them!
16 After the fighting was over, he made up

[l] **14.20** *one . . . at Samson's party*: One possible meaning for the difficult Hebrew text.
[m] **15.1** *Samson went to visit . . . his wife*: See the note at 8.31. [n] **15.2** *divorcing*: It was often very easy for a husband to divorce his wife. [o] **15.6** *and her father*: Most Hebrew manuscripts; many Hebrew manuscripts and two ancient translations "and her family." [p] **15.8** *hacking . . . sword*: One possible meaning for the difficult Hebrew text. [q] **15.9** *Judah*: Samson belonged to the Dan tribe, but his hideout in the cave at Etam Rock was in Judah, a few miles southwest of Bethlehem. [r] **15.9** *Jawbone*: Or "Lehi" (see verse 17).

this poem about what he had done to the Philistines:

I used a donkey's jawbone
to kill a thousand men;
I beat them with this jawbone
over and over again.[s]

17 Samson tossed the jawbone on the ground and decided to call the place Jawbone Hill.[t] It is still called that today.

18 Samson was so thirsty that he prayed, "Our LORD, you helped me win a battle against a whole army. Please don't let me die of thirst now. Those heathen Philistines will carry off my dead body."

19 Samson was tired and weary, but God sent water gushing from a rock.[u] Samson drank some and felt strong again.

Samson named the place Caller Spring,[v] because he had called out to God for help. The spring is still there at Jawbone.

20 Samson was a leader[w] of Israel for twenty years, but the Philistines were still the rulers of Israel.

Samson Carries Off the Gates of Gaza

16 One day while Samson was in Gaza, he saw a prostitute and went to her house to spend the night. 2 The people who lived in Gaza found out he was there, and they decided to kill him at sunrise. So they went to the city gate and waited all night in the guardrooms on each side of the gate.[x]

3 But Samson got up in the middle of the night and went to the town gate. He pulled the gate doors and doorposts out of the wall and put them on his shoulders. Then he carried them all the way to the top of the hill that overlooks Hebron,[y] where he set the doors down, still closed and locked.

Delilah Tricks Samson

4 Some time later, Samson fell in love with a woman named Delilah, who lived in Sorek Valley. 5 The Philistine rulers[z] went to Delilah and said, "Trick Samson into telling you what makes him so strong and what can make him weak. Then we can tie him up so he can't get away. If you find out his secret, we will each give you eleven hundred pieces of silver."[a]

6 The next time Samson was at Delilah's house, she asked, "Samson, what makes you so strong? How can I tie you up so you can't get away? Come on, you can tell me."

7 Samson answered, "If someone ties me up with seven new bowstrings that have never been dried,[b] it will make me just as weak as anyone else."

8-9 The Philistine rulers gave seven new bowstrings to Delilah. They also told some of their soldiers to go to Delilah's house and hide in the room where Samson and Delilah were. If the bowstrings made Samson weak, they would be able to capture him.

Delilah tied up Samson with the bowstrings and shouted, "Samson, the Philistines are attacking!"

Samson snapped the bowstrings, as though they were pieces of scorched string. The Philistines had not found out why Samson was so strong.

10 "You lied and made me look like a fool," Delilah said. "Now tell me. How can I really tie you up?"

11 Samson answered, "Use some new ropes. If I'm tied up with ropes that have never been used, I'll be just as weak as anyone else."

12 Delilah got new ropes and again had some Philistines hide in the room. Then she tied up Samson's arms and

[s] **15.16** *I beat . . . again*: One possible meaning for the difficult Hebrew text. [t] **15.17** *Jawbone Hill*: Or "Ramath-Lehi." [u] **15.19** *God sent . . . a rock*: One possible meaning for the difficult Hebrew text. [v] **15.19** *Caller Spring*: Or "Enhakkore." [w] **15.20** *leader*: See 2.16 and the note there. [x] **16.2** *guardrooms . . . gate*: The gate was often in a part of the town wall that was thicker and taller than the rest of the wall, and that had rooms where guards stayed when they were on duty. [y] **16.3** *Hebron*: About forty miles from Gaza. [z] **16.5** *Philistine rulers*: There were five rulers, each one controlling part of Philistia. [a] **16.5** *silver*: About 140 pounds of silver altogether. [b] **16.7** *new bowstrings . . . dried*: The string for a bow was often made from sinews or internal organs of animals. These strings were made while the animal tissues were still moist, and they became much stronger, once they were dry.

shouted, "Samson, the Philistines are attacking!"

Samson snapped the ropes as if they were threads.

13 "You're still lying and making a fool of me," Delilah said. "Tell me how I can tie you up!"

"My hair is in seven braids," Samson replied. "If you weave my braids into the threads on a loom and nail the loom[c] to a wall, then I will be as weak as anyone else."

14 While Samson was asleep, Delilah wove his braids into the threads on a loom and nailed the loom to a wall.[d] Then she shouted, "Samson, the Philistines are attacking!"

Samson woke up and pulled the loom free from its posts in the ground and from the nails in the wall. Then he pulled his hair free from the woven cloth.

15 "Samson," Delilah said, "you claim to love me, but you don't mean it! You've made me look like a fool three times now, and you still haven't told me why you are so strong." 16 Delilah started nagging and pestering him day after day, until he couldn't stand it any longer.

17 Finally, Samson told her the truth. "I have belonged to God[e] ever since I was born, so my hair has never been cut. If it were ever cut off, my strength would leave me, and I would be as weak as anyone else."

18 Delilah realized that he was telling the truth. So she sent someone to tell the Philistine rulers, "Come to my house one more time. Samson has finally told me the truth."

The Philistine rulers went to Delilah's house, and they brought along the silver they had promised her. 19 Delilah had lulled Samson to sleep with his head resting in her lap. She signaled to one of the Philistine men as she began cutting off Samson's seven braids. And by the time she was finished, Samson's strength was gone. Delilah tied him up 20 and shouted, "Samson, the Philistines are attacking!"

Samson woke up and thought, "I'll break loose and escape, just as I always do." He did not realize that the LORD had stopped helping him.

21 The Philistines grabbed Samson and poked out his eyes. They took him to the prison in Gaza and chained him up. Then they put him to work, turning a millstone to grind grain. 22 But they didn't cut his hair any more, so it started growing back.

23 The Philistine rulers threw a big party and sacrificed a lot of animals to their god Dagon. The rulers said:

Samson was our enemy,
but our god Dagon
helped us capture him!

24-25 Everyone there was having a good time, and they shouted, "Bring out Samson—he's still good for a few more laughs!"

The rulers had Samson brought from the prison, and when the people saw him, this is how they praised their god:

Samson ruined our crops
and killed our people.
He was our enemy,
but our god helped us
capture him.

They made fun of Samson for a while, then they told him to stand near the columns that supported the roof. 26 A young man was leading Samson by the hand, and Samson said to him, "I need to lean against something. Take me over to the columns that hold up the roof."

27 The Philistine rulers were celebrating in a temple packed with people and with three thousand[f] more on the flat roof. They had all been watching Samson and making fun of him.[g]

28 Samson prayed, "Please remember me, LORD God. The Philistines poked out my eyes, but make me strong one last time,

[c]**16.13** *loom*: A large wooden frame on which cloth is woven. [d]**16.13,14** *If you weave . . . to a wall*: Some manuscripts of one ancient translation; Hebrew "Weave my braids into the threads on a loom. She nailed the loom to a wall." [e]**16.17** *belonged to God*: See the note at 13.3-5.
[f]**16.27** *three thousand*: Hebrew; some manuscripts of one ancient translation "seven hundred."
[g]**16.27** *They . . . him*: Samson may have been in a courtyard visible from the roof.

so I can take revenge for at least one of my eyes!"[h]

29 Samson was standing between the two middle columns that held up the roof. He felt around and found one column with his right hand, and the other with his left hand. 30 Then he shouted, "Let me die with the Philistines!" He pushed against the columns as hard as he could, and the temple collapsed with the Philistine rulers and everyone else still inside. Samson killed more Philistines when he died than he had killed during his entire life.

31 His brothers and the rest of his family went to Gaza and took his body back home. They buried him in his father's tomb,[i] which was located between Zorah and Eshtaol.

Samson was a leader[j] of Israel for twenty years.

Micah Makes Idols and Hires a Priest

17 Micah[k] belonged to the Ephraim tribe and lived in the hill country. 2 One day he told his mother, "Do you remember those eleven hundred pieces of silver[l] that were stolen from you? I was there when you put a curse on whoever stole them. Well, I'm the one who did it."

His mother answered, "I pray that the LORD will bless[m] you, my son."

3-4 Micah returned the silver to his mother, and she said, "I give this silver to the LORD, so my son can use it to make an idol." Turning to her son, she said, "Micah, now the silver belongs to you."

But Micah handed it back to his mother. She took two hundred pieces[n] of the silver and gave them to a silver worker, who made them into an idol.[o] They kept the idol in Micah's house. 5 He had a shrine for worshiping God there at his home, and he had made some idols and a sacred priestly vest. Micah chose one of his own sons to be the priest for his shrine.

6 This was before kings ruled Israel, so all the Israelites did whatever they thought was right.

7-8 One day a young Levite came to Micah's house in the hill country of Ephraim. He had been staying with one of the clans of Judah in Bethlehem, but he had left Bethlehem to find a new place to live[p] where he could be a priest.[q]

9 "Where are you from?" Micah asked.

"I am a Levite from Bethlehem in Judah," the man answered, "and I'm on my way to find a new place to live."

10 Micah said, "Why don't you stay here with me? You can be my priest and tell me what God wants me to do. Every year I'll give you ten pieces of silver and one complete set of clothes, and I'll provide all your food."

The young man went for a walk, 11-12 then he agreed to stay with Micah and be his priest. He lived in Micah's house, and Micah treated him like one of his own sons. 13 Micah said, "I have a Levite as my own priest. Now I know that the LORD will be kind to me."

18 These things happened before kings ruled Israel.

The Tribe of Dan Takes Micah's Priest and Idols

About this time, the tribe of Dan was looking for a place to live. The other tribes had land, but the people of Dan did not really have any to call their own. 2 The tribe chose five warriors to represent their clans and told them, "Go and find some land where we can live."

The warriors left the area of Zorah and Eshtaol and went into the hill country of Ephraim. One night they stayed at Micah's house, 3 because they heard the young Levite talking, and they knew from his accent that he was from the south. They

[h] **16.28** *one of my eyes*: Or "my eyes." [i] **16.31** *buried him in his father's tomb*: Several family members were often buried in one tomb. [j] **16.31** *leader*: See 2.16 and the note there. [k] **17.1** *Micah*: The Hebrew also uses the longer form "Micaiah." [l] **17.2** *eleven hundred . . . silver*: About 28 pounds. [m] **17.2** *curse . . . bless*: A curse could not be taken back, but it could be made powerless by a blessing. [n] **17.3,4** *two hundred pieces*: About 5 pounds. [o] **17.3,4** *idol*: Probably carved from wood and covered with the silver. [p] **17.7,8** *place to live*: The people of the Levi tribe did not have a large area of land like the other tribes. [q] **17.7,8** *to find . . . priest*: Or "and was on his way to find a new place to live."

17.6 Jg 21.25.

asked him, "What are you doing here? Who brought you here?"

4 The Levite replied, "Micah hired me as his priest." Then he told them how well Micah had treated him.

5 "Please talk to God for us," the men said. "Ask God if we will be successful in what we are trying to do."

6 "Don't worry," answered the priest. "The LORD is pleased with what you are doing."

7 The five men left and went to the town of Laish, whose people were from Sidon,[r] but Sidon was too far away to protect them. Even though their town had no walls, the people thought they were safe from attack. So they had not asked anyone else[s] for protection, which meant that the tribe of Dan could easily take over Laish.[t]

8 The five men went back to Zorah and Eshtaol, where their relatives asked, "Did you find any land?"

9-10 "Let's go!" the five men said. "We saw some very good land with enough room for all of us, and it has everything we will ever need. What are you waiting for? Let's attack and take it. You'll find that the people think they're safe, but God is giving the land to us."

11 Six hundred men from the tribe of Dan strapped on their weapons and left Zorah and Eshtaol with their families.[u]
12 One night they camped near Kiriath-Jearim in the territory of Judah, and that's why the place just west of Kiriath-Jearim is
still known as Dan's Camp.[v] 13 Then they
went into the hill country of Ephraim.

When they came close to Micah's
house, 14 the five men who had been spies asked the other warriors, "Did you know that someone in this village has several idols and a sacred priestly vest? What do you think we should do about it?"

15-18 The six hundred warriors left the road and went to the house on Micah's property where the young Levite priest lived. They stood at the gate and greeted the priest. Meanwhile, the five men who had been there before went into Micah's house and took the sacred priestly vest and the idols.

"Hey!" the priest shouted. "What do you think you're doing?"

19 "Quiet!" the men said. "Keep your mouth shut and listen. Why don't you come with us and be our priest, so you can tell us what God wants us to do? You could stay here and be a priest for one man's family, but wouldn't you rather be the priest for a clan or even a whole tribe of Israel?"

20 The priest really liked that idea. So he took the vest and the idols and joined the
others 21 from the tribe of Dan. Then they
turned and left, after putting their children, their cattle, and the rest of their other possessions in front.

22 They had traveled for some time, before Micah asked his neighbors to help him get his things back. He and his men caught
up with the people of Dan 23 and shouted
for them to stop.

They turned to face him and asked, "What's wrong? Why did you bring all these men?"

24 Micah answered, "You know what's wrong. You stole the gods[w] I made, and you took my priest. I don't have anything left."

25 "We don't want to hear any more about it," the people of Dan said. "And if you make us angry, you'll only get yourself
and your family killed." 26 After saying this,
they turned and left.

Micah realized there was no way he could win a fight with them, and so he went back home.

The Tribe of Dan Captures Laish

27-28 The tribe of Dan took Micah's priest and the things Micah had made, and headed for Laish, which was located in a valley controlled by the town of Beth-Rehob. Laish was defenseless, because it had no walls and was too far from Sidon for the Sidonians to help defend it. The lead-

[r]18.7 *whose people . . . Sidon*: One possible meaning for the difficult Hebrew text.
[s]18.7 *anyone else*: Hebrew; one ancient translation has "the Arameans," who were a short distance to the north. [t]18.7 *which . . . Laish*: One possible meaning for the difficult Hebrew text.
[u]18.11 *Eshtaol with their families*: Hebrew "Eshtaol" (see verse 21). [v]18.12 *Dan's Camp*: See the note at 13.25. [w]18.24 *gods*: Or "god."

The baby Moses in the reed basket

Exodus 2.1-10

Moses with the Ten Commandments *Exodus 19, 20*

ers of Laish had not even asked nearby towns to help them in case of an attack.

The warriors from Dan made a surprise attack on Laish, killing everyone and burning it down. Then they rebuilt the town and settled there themselves. 29 But they named it Dan, after one of Israel's[x] sons, who was the ancestor of their tribe.

30-31 Even though the place of worship[y] was in Shiloh, the people of Dan set up the idol Micah had made. They worshiped the idol, and the Levite was their priest. His name was Jonathan, and he was a descendant of Gershom the son of Moses.[z] His descendants served as priests for the tribe of Dan, until the people of Israel were taken away as prisoners by their enemies.

A Woman Is Murdered

19 Before kings ruled Israel, a Levite[a] was living deep in the hill country of the Ephraim tribe. He married[b] a woman from Bethlehem in Judah, 2 but she was unfaithful and went back to live with her family in Bethlehem.

Four months later 3 her husband decided to try and talk her into coming back. So he went to Bethlehem, taking along a servant and two donkeys. He talked with his wife, and she invited him into her family's home. Her father was glad to see him 4 and did not want him to leave. So the man stayed three days, eating and drinking with his father-in-law.

5 When everyone got up on the fourth day, the Levite started getting ready to go home. But his father-in-law said, "Don't leave until you have a bite to eat. You'll need strength for your journey."

6 The two men sat down together and ate a big meal. "Come on," the man's father-in-law said. "Stay tonight and have a good time."

7 The Levite tried to leave, but his father-in-law insisted, and he spent one more night. 8 The fifth day, the man got up early to leave, but his wife's father said, "You need to keep up your strength! Why don't you leave right after lunch?" So the two of them started eating.

9 Finally, the Levite got up from the meal, so he and his wife and servant could leave. "Look," his father-in-law said, "it's already late afternoon, and if you leave now, you won't get very far before dark. Stay with us one more night and enjoy yourself. Then you can get up early tomorrow morning and start home."

10 But the Levite decided not to spend the night there again. He had the saddles put on his two donkeys, then he and his wife and servant traveled as far as Jebus, which is now called Jerusalem. 11 It was beginning to get dark, and the man's servant said, "Let's stop and spend the night in this town where the Jebusites live."

12 "No," the Levite answered. "They aren't Israelites, and I refuse to spend the night there. We'll stop for the night at Gibeah, 13 because we can make it to Gibeah or maybe even to Ramah[c] before dark."

14 They walked on and reached Gibeah in the territory of Benjamin just after sunset. 15 They left the road and went into Gibeah. But the Levite couldn't find a house where anyone would let them spend the night, and they sat down in the open area just inside the town gates.

16 Soon an old man came in through the gates on his way home from working in the fields. Most of the people who lived in Gibeah belonged to the tribe of Benjamin, but this man was originally from the hill country of Ephraim. 17 He noticed that the Levite was just in town to spend the night. "Where are you going?" the old man asked. "Where did you come from?"

18 "We've come from Bethlehem in Judah," the Levite answered. "We went there

[x] **18.29** *Israel's*: Israel was another name for Jacob, the father of the twelve ancestors of the tribes of Israel. [y] **18.30,31** *place of worship*: The Hebrew text has "house of God," which at this time was probably the sacred tent. [z] **18.30,31** *Moses*: Some manuscripts of two ancient translations; the Standard Hebrew Text has "Manasseh," but written in a special way that tells the reader "Moses" had been changed to "Manasseh." [a] **19.1** *a Levite*: Someone from the Levi tribe, which had no tribal lands of its own. [b] **19.1** *married*: See the note at 8.31. [c] **19.13** *Gibeah . . . Ramah*: It was about three miles from Jerusalem to Gibeah, and another three miles to Ramah.

on a visit. Now we're going to the place
where the LORD is worshiped, and later we
will return to our home in the hill country
of Ephraim. But no one here will let us
spend the night[d] in their home. 19 We
brought food for our donkeys and bread
and wine for ourselves, so we don't need
anything except a place to sleep."
20 The old man said, "You are welcome
to spend the night in my home and to be
my guest, but don't stay out here!"
21 The old man brought them into his
house and fed their donkeys. Then he and
his guests washed their feet[e] and began
eating and drinking. 22 They were having a
good time, when some worthless men of
that town surrounded the house and
started banging on the door and shouting,
"A man came to your house tonight. Send
him out, so we can have sex with him!"
23 The old man went outside and said,
"My friends, please don't commit such a
horrible crime against a man who is a guest
in my house. 24 Let me send out my daughter instead. She's a virgin. And I'll even
send out the man's wife.[f] You can rape
them or do whatever else you want, but
please don't do such a horrible thing to this
man."
25 The men refused to listen, so the
Levite grabbed his wife and shoved her
outside. The men raped her and abused
her all night long. Finally, they let her go
just before sunrise, 26 and it was almost
daybreak when she went back to the house
where her husband[g] was staying. She collapsed at the door and lay there until sunrise.
27 About that time, her husband woke
up and got ready to leave. He opened the
door and went outside, where he found his
wife lying at the door with her hands on
the doorstep. 28 "Get up!" he said. "It's
time to leave."
But his wife didn't move.[h]
He lifted her body onto his donkey and
left. 29 When he got home, he took a
butcher knife and cut her body into twelve
pieces. Then he told some messengers,
"Take one piece to each tribe of Israel
30 and ask everyone if anything like this has
ever happened since Israel left Egypt. Tell
them to think about it, talk it over, and tell
us what should be done."
Everyone who saw a piece of the body
said, "This is horrible! Nothing like this has
ever happened since the day Israel left
Egypt."[i]

Israel Gets Ready for War

20 1-3 The Israelites called a meeting
of the nation. And since they were
God's people, the meeting was held at the
place of worship in Mizpah. Men who
could serve as soldiers came from everywhere in Israel—from Dan in the north,
Beersheba in the south, and Gilead east of
the Jordan River. Four hundred thousand
of them came to Mizpah, and they each felt
the same about what those men from the
tribe of Benjamin had done.
News about the meeting at Mizpah
reached the tribe of Benjamin.
As soon as the leaders of the tribes of Israel took their places, the Israelites said,
"How could such a horrible thing happen?"
4 The husband of the murdered woman
answered:
My wife[j] and I went into the town
of Gibeah in Benjamin to spend the
night. 5 Later that night, the men of
Gibeah surrounded the house. They
wanted to kill me, but instead they
raped and killed my wife. 6 It was a

[d] **19.18** *spend the night*: People usually considered it a duty to ask travelers to spend the night in their homes, since there were often no other places to stay. [e] **19.21** *washed their feet*: This was a custom, since people wore open sandals and their feet would be dirty after walking on the dirt roads or working in the fields. [f] **19.24** *wife*: See the note at 8.31. [g] **19.26** *husband*: Or "owner"; the Hebrew word may mean that she was his slave and had no legal rights. [h] **19.28** *move*: Hebrew; one ancient translation "move. She was dead." [i] **19.29,30** *he told some messengers . . . since Israel left Egypt*: One ancient translation; Hebrew "he told some messengers, 'Take one piece to each tribe of Israel.' Everyone who saw a piece of the body said, 'This is horrible! Nothing like this has ever happened since Israel left Egypt. Think of it! Let's talk it over and decide what to do.' "
[j] **20.4** *wife*: See the note at 8.31.

19.22-24 Gn 19.5-8. **19.29** 1 S 11.7.

terrible thing for Israelites to do! So I
cut up her body and sent pieces everywhere in Israel.
7 You are the people of Israel, and
you must decide today what to do
about the men of Gibeah.
8 The whole army was in agreement,
and they said, "None of us will go home.
9-10 We'll send one tenth of the men from
each tribe to get food for the army. And
we'll ask God[k] who should attack Gibeah,
because those men[l] deserve to be punished
for committing such a horrible crime in
Israel."
11 Everyone agreed that Gibeah had to
be punished.
12 The tribes of Israel sent messengers
to every town and village in Benjamin. And
wherever the messengers went, they said,
"How could those worthless men in Gibeah
do such a disgusting thing? 13 We can't allow such a terrible crime to go unpunished
in Israel! Hand the men over to us, and we
will put them to death."
But the people of Benjamin refused to
listen to the other Israelites. 14 Men from
towns all over Benjamin's territory went to
Gibeah and got ready to fight Israel. 15 The
Benjamin tribe had twenty-six thousand
soldiers, not counting the seven hundred
who were Gibeah's best warriors. 16 In this
army there were seven hundred left-
handed experts who could sling a rock[m] at
a target the size of a hair and hit it every
time.
17 The other Israelite tribes organized
their army and found they had four hundred thousand experienced soldiers. 18 So
they went to the place of worship at
Bethel[n] and asked God, "Which tribe
should be the first to attack the people of
Benjamin?"
"Judah," the LORD answered.
19 The next morning the Israelite army
moved its camp to a place near Gibeah.
20 Then they left their camp and got into
position to attack the army of Benjamin.

The War Between Israel and Benjamin

21 Benjamin's soldiers came out of
Gibeah and attacked, and when the day
was over, twenty-two thousand Israelite soldiers lay dead on the ground.
22-24 The people of Israel went to the
place of worship and cried until sunset.
Then they asked the LORD, "Should we attack the people of Benjamin again, even
though they are our relatives?"
"Yes," the LORD replied, "attack them
again!"
The Israelite soldiers encouraged each
other to be brave and to fight hard. Then
the next day they went back to Gibeah and
took up the same positions as they had
before.
25 That same day, Benjamin's soldiers
came out of Gibeah and attacked, leaving
another eighteen thousand Israelite soldiers dead on the battlefield.
26-28 The people of Israel went to the
place of worship at Bethel,[n] where the sacred chest was being kept. They sat on the
ground, crying and not eating for the rest of
the day. Then about sunset, they offered
sacrifices to please the LORD and to ask his
blessing.[o] Phinehas[p] the priest then
prayed, "Our LORD, the people of Benjamin
are our relatives. Should we stop fighting or
attack them again?"
"Attack!" the LORD answered. "Tomorrow I will let you defeat them."
29 The Israelites surrounded Gibeah,
but stayed where they could not be seen.
30 Then the next day, they took the same
positions as twice before, 31-41 but this time
they had a different plan. They said,
"When the men of Benjamin attack, we
will run off and let them chase us away

[k]**20.9,10** *ask God*: The Hebrew text has "use lots to decide"; small pieces of wood or stone called "lots" were used to find out what God wanted his people to do. [l]**20.9,10** *those men*: One Hebrew manuscript and one ancient translation; The Standard Hebrew text "the men of Geba."
[m]**20.16** *sling a rock*: By using a sling made from a leather strap. [n]**20.18,26-28** *place . . . Bethel*: The Hebrew text has "beth-el," which means "house of God." This could refer to the town of Bethel, to the place of worship at Mizpah, or to the sacred tent at Shiloh (see 18.30, 31).
[o]**20.26-28** *sacrifices . . . blessing*: See Leviticus 1–3. [p]**20.26-28** *Phinehas*: Hebrew "Phinehas the son of Eleazar the son of Aaron."

from the town and into the country roads."

The soldiers of Benjamin attacked the Israelite army and started pushing it back from the town. They killed about thirty Israelites in the fields and along the road between Gibeah and Bethel. The men of Benjamin were thinking, "We're mowing them down like we did before."

The Israelites were running away, but they headed for Baal-Tamar, where they regrouped. They had set an ambush, and they were sure it would work. Ten thousand of Israel's best soldiers had been hiding west of Gibeah,[q] and as soon as the men of Benjamin chased the Israelites into the countryside, these ten thousand soldiers made a surprise attack on the town gates. They dashed in and captured Gibeah, killing everyone there. Then they set the town on fire, because the smoke would be the signal for the other Israelite soldiers to turn and attack the soldiers of Benjamin.

The fighting had been so heavy around the soldiers of Benjamin, that they did not know the trouble they were in. But then they looked back and saw clouds of smoke rising from the town. They looked in front and saw the soldiers of Israel turning to attack. This terrified them, because they realized that something horrible was happening. And it was horrible—over twenty-five thousand[r] soldiers of Benjamin died that day, and those who were left alive knew that the LORD had given Israel the victory.

42 The men of Benjamin headed down the road toward the desert, trying to escape from the Israelites. But the Israelites stayed right behind them, keeping up their attack. Men even came out of the nearby towns to help kill the men of Benjamin, 43 who were having to fight on all sides. The Israelite soldiers never let up their attack.[s] They chased and killed the warriors of Benjamin as far as a place directly east of Gibeah,[t] 44 until eighteen thousand of these warriors lay dead.

45 Some other warriors of Benjamin turned and ran down the road toward Rimmon Rock in the desert. The Israelites killed five thousand of them on the road, then chased the rest until they had killed[u] two thousand more. 46 Twenty-five thousand soldiers of Benjamin died that day, all of them experienced warriors. 47 Only six hundred of them finally made it into the desert to Rimmon Rock, where they stayed for four months.

48 The Israelites turned back and went to every town in Benjamin's territory, killing all the people and animals, and setting the towns on fire.

Wives for the Men of Benjamin

21 When the Israelites had met at Mizpah before the war with Benjamin,[v] they had made this sacred promise: "None of us will ever let our daughters marry any man from Benjamin."

2 After the war with Benjamin, the Israelites went to the place of worship at Bethel and sat there until sunset. They cried loudly and bitterly 3 and prayed, "Our LORD, you are the God of Israel. Why did you let this happen? Now one of our tribes is almost gone."

4 Early the next morning, the Israelites built an altar and offered sacrifices to please the LORD and to ask his blessing.[w] 5 Then they asked each other, "Did any of the tribes of Israel fail to come to the place of worship? We made a sacred promise that anyone who didn't come to the meeting at Mizpah would be put to death."

6 The Israelites were sad about what had happened to the Benjamin tribe, and they said, "One of our tribes was almost wiped out. 7 Only a few men of Benjamin weren't killed in the war. We need to get wives for them, so the tribe won't completely disappear. But how can we do that, after promising in the LORD's name that we wouldn't let them marry any of our daughters?"

8-9 Again the Israelites asked, "Did any

[q]**20.31-41** *west of Gibeah*: three ancient translations; Hebrew "in a field at Geba."
[r]**20.31-41** *over twenty-five thousand*: Hebrew "twenty-five thousand one hundred."
[s]**20.42,43** *Men even came out . . . their attack*: One possible meaning for the difficult Hebrew text.
[t]**20.43** *Gibeah*: Or "Geba."
[u]**20.45** *until . . . killed*: Or "as far as Gidom, killing."
[v]**21.1** *the Israelites . . . Benjamin*: See 20.1-3.
[w]**21.4** *sacrifices . . . blessing*: See the note at 20.26-28.

of the tribes stay away from the meeting at Mizpah?"

After asking around, they discovered that no one had come from Jabesh in Gilead. 10-11 So they sent twelve thousand warriors with these orders: "Attack Jabesh in Gilead and kill everyone, except the women who have never been married."

12 The warriors attacked Jabesh in Gilead, and returned to their camp in Canaan[x] with four hundred young women.

13 The Israelites met and sent messengers to the men of Benjamin at Rimmon Rock, telling them that the Israelites were willing to make peace with them. 14 So the men of Benjamin came back from Rimmon Rock, and the Israelites let them marry the young women from Jabesh. But there weren't enough women.

15 The Israelites were very sad, because the LORD had almost wiped out one of their tribes. 16 Then their national leaders said:

All the women of the Benjamin tribe were killed. How can we get wives for the men of Benjamin who are left? 17 If they don't have children, one of the Israelite tribes will die out. 18 But we can't let the men of Benjamin marry any of our daughters. We made a sacred promise not to do that, and if we break our promise, we will be under our own curse.

19 Then someone suggested, "What about the LORD's Festival that takes place each year in Shiloh? It's held north of Bethel, south of Lebonah, and just east of the road that goes from Bethel to Shechem."

20 The leaders told the men of Benjamin who still did not have wives:

Go to Shiloh and hide in the vineyards near the festival. 21 Wait there for the young women of Shiloh to come out and perform their dances. Then rush out and grab one of the young women, then take her home as your wife.22 If the fathers or brothers of these women complain about this, we'll say, "Be kind enough to let those men keep your daughter. After all, we couldn't get enough wives for all the men of Benjamin in the battle at Jabesh. And because you didn't give them permission to marry your daughters, you won't be under the curse we earlier agreed on.[y]

23 The men of Benjamin went to Shiloh and hid in the vineyards. The young women soon started dancing, and each man grabbed one of them and carried her off. Then the men of Benjamin went back to their own land and rebuilt their towns and started living in them again.

24 Afterwards, the rest of the Israelites returned to their homes and families.

Israel Was Not Ruled by a King

25 In those days Israel wasn't ruled by a king, and everyone did what they thought was right.

[x]**21.12** *in Canaan*: Jabesh was in Gilead, across the Jordan River from the land of Canaan.
[y]**21.22** *on*: One possible meaning for the difficult Hebrew text of verse 22.
21.25 Jg 17.6.

RUTH

ABOUT THIS BOOK

The book of Ruth gives a glimpse into the life of an Israelite family during the period of the judges. This family later became very important to Israel, because one of Ruth's great-grandchildren was King David.

In addition to Ruth, the other main character in the book is Naomi, who lived in Bethlehem with her husband and two sons. But the crops failed, and the family moved to the country of Moab. Naomi's husband died, and her sons married Moabite women. Ruth was one of those women.

After Naomi's two sons died in Moab, she decided to return to Bethlehem. Naomi told her two daughters-in-law to stay in Moab and find new husbands. But Ruth refused to stay and instead went to Bethlehem with her. The rest of the book tells how Ruth married a rich relative named Boaz.

According to the law, Moabites were not allowed to become Israelites. But this book tells how Ruth became completely loyal and faithful to the Lord and was allowed to join the people of Israel. She told Naomi:

"I will go where you go,
I will live where you live;
your people will be my people,
your God will be my God.
I will die where you die
and be buried beside you.
May the LORD punish me
if we are ever separated,
even by death!"
(1.16b, 17)

A QUICK LOOK AT THIS BOOK

- Ruth Is Loyal to Naomi (1)
- Ruth Meets Boaz (2)
- Naomi Makes Plans for Ruth (3)
- Ruth and Boaz Get Married (4)

Ruth Is Loyal to Naomi

1 1-2 Before Israel was ruled by kings,
Elimelech from the tribe of Ephrath
lived in the town of Bethlehem. His wife
was named Naomi, and their two sons were
Mahlon and Chilion. But when their crops
failed, they moved to the country of Moab.[a]
And while they were there, 3 Elimelech
died, leaving Naomi with only her two sons.
4 Later, Naomi's sons married Moabite
women. One was named Orpah and the
other Ruth. About ten years later, 5 Mahlon
and Chilion also died. Now Naomi had no
husband or sons.
6-7 When Naomi heard that the LORD

[a] **1.1,2** *Moab*: The people of Moab worshiped idols and were usually enemies of the people of Israel.

had given his people a good harvest, she
and her two daughters-in-law got ready to
leave Moab and go to Judah. As they were
on their way there, 8 Naomi said to them,
"Don't you want to go back home to your
own mothers? You were kind to my husband and sons, and you have always been
kind to me. I pray that the LORD will be
just as kind to you. 9 May he give each
of you another husband and a home of
your own."

Naomi kissed them. They cried 10 and
said, "We want to go with you and live
among your people."

11 But she replied, "My daughters, why
don't you return home? What good will
it do you to go with me? Do you think
I could have more sons for you to
marry?[b] 12 You must go back home, because I am too old to marry again. Even if
I got married tonight and later had
more sons, 13 would you wait for them to
become old enough to marry? No, my
daughters! Life is harder for me than it is
for you, because the LORD has turned
against me."[c]

14 They cried again. Orpah kissed her
mother-in-law good-by, but Ruth held on to
her. 15 Naomi then said to Ruth, "Look,
your sister-in-law is going back to her people and to her gods! Why don't you go with
her?"

16 Ruth answered,

"Please don't tell me
to leave you
    and return home!
I will go where you go,
    I will live where you live;
your people will be my people,
    your God will be my God.
17 I will die where you die
    and be buried beside you.
May the LORD punish me
    if we are ever separated,
    even by death!"[d]

18 When Naomi saw that Ruth had
made up her mind to go with her, she
stopped urging her to go back.

19 They reached Bethlehem, and the
whole town was excited to see them. The
women who lived there asked, "Can this really be Naomi?"

20 Then she told them, "Don't call me
Naomi any longer! Call me Mara,[e] because
God has made my life bitter. 21 I had everything when I left, but the LORD has brought
me back with nothing. How can you still
call me Naomi, when God has turned
against me and made my life so hard?"

22 The barley harvest was just beginning
when Naomi and Ruth, her Moabite
daughter-in-law, arrived in Bethlehem.

Ruth Meets Boaz

2 1-3 One day, Ruth said to Naomi, "Let
me see if I can find someone who will
let me pick up the grain left in the fields by
the harvest workers."[f]

Naomi answered, "Go ahead, my daughter." So right away, Ruth went out to pick
up grain in a field owned by Boaz. He was a
relative of Naomi's husband Elimelech, as
well as a rich and important man.

4 When Boaz left Bethlehem and went
out to his field, he said to the harvest workers, "The LORD bless you!"

They replied, "And may the LORD bless you!"

5 Then Boaz asked the man in charge of
the harvest workers, "Who is that young
woman?"

6 The man answered, "She is the one
who came back from Moab with Naomi.
7 She asked if she could pick up grain left
by the harvest workers, and she has been
working all morning without a moment's
rest."[g]

[b] **1.11** *for you to marry*: When a married man died and left no children, it was the custom for one of his brothers to marry his widow. Any children they had would then be thought of as those of the dead man, so that his family name would live on. [c] **1.13** *Life . . . me*: Or "I'm sorry that the LORD has turned against me and made life so hard for you." [d] **1.17** *even by death*: Or "by anything but death." [e] **1.20** *Mara*: In Hebrew "Naomi" means "pleasant," and "Mara" means "bitter." [f] **2.1-3** *grain left . . . workers*: It was the custom at harvest time to leave some grain in the field for the poor to pick up (see Leviticus 19.10; 23.22). [g] **2.7** *she has . . . rest*: One possible meaning for the difficult Hebrew text.

2.1-3 Lv 19.9, 10; Dt 24.19.

8 Boaz went over to Ruth and said, "I
think it would be best for you not to pick up
grain in anyone else's field. Stay here with
the women 9 and follow along behind
them, as they gather up what the men have
cut. I have warned the men not to bother
you, and whenever you are thirsty, you can
drink from the water jars they have filled."
10 Ruth bowed down to the ground and
said, "You know I come from another country. Why are you so good to me?"
11 Boaz answered, "I've heard how
you've helped your mother-in-law ever
since your husband died. You even left your
own father and mother to come and live in
a foreign land among people you don't
know. 12 I pray that the LORD God of Israel
will reward you for what you have done.
And now that you have come to him for
protection, I pray that he will bless you."
13 Ruth replied, "Sir, it's good of you to
speak kindly to me and make me feel so welcome. I'm not even one of your servants."
14 At mealtime Boaz said to Ruth,
"Come, eat with us. Have some bread and
dip it in the sauce." Right away she sat
down with the workers, and Boaz handed
her some roasted grain. Ruth ate all she
wanted and had some left over.
15 When Ruth got up to start picking up
grain, Boaz told his men, "Don't stop her,
even if she picks up grain from where it is
stacked. 16 Be sure to pull out some stalks
of grain from the bundles and leave them
on the ground for her. And don't speak
harshly to her!"
17 Ruth worked in the field until
evening. Then after she had pounded the
grain off the stalks, she had a large basket
full of grain. 18 She took the grain to town
and showed Naomi how much she had
picked up. Ruth also gave her the food left
over from her lunch.
19 Naomi said, "Where did you work today? Whose field was it? God bless the
man who treated you so well!" Then Ruth
told her that she had worked in the field of
a man named Boaz.
20 "The LORD bless Boaz!" Naomi
replied. "He[h] has shown that he is still loyal
to the living and to the dead. Boaz is a
close relative, one of those who is supposed
to look after us."
21 Ruth told her, "Boaz even said I could
stay in the field with his workers until they
had finished gathering all his grain."
22 Naomi replied, "My daughter, it's
good that you can pick up grain alongside
the women who work in his field. Who
knows what might happen to you in someone else's field!" 23 And so, Ruth stayed
close to the women, while picking up grain
in his field.

Ruth worked in the fields until the barley and wheat were harvested. And all this
time she lived with Naomi.

Naomi Makes Plans for Ruth

3 One day, Naomi said to Ruth:
It's time I found you a husband,
who will give you a home and take care
of you.
2 You have been picking up grain
alongside the women who work for
Boaz, and you know he is a relative of
ours. Tonight he will be threshing the
grain. 3 Now take a bath and put on
some perfume, then dress in your best
clothes. Go where he is working, but
don't let him see you until he has finished eating and drinking. 4 Watch
where he goes to spend the night, then
when he is asleep, lift the cover and lie
down at his feet.[i] He will tell you what
to do.
5 Ruth answered, "I'll do whatever you
say." 6 She went out to the place where
Boaz was working and did what Naomi had
told her.
7 After Boaz finished eating and drinking and was feeling happy, he went over
and fell asleep near the pile of grain. Ruth
slipped over quietly. She lifted the cover
and lay down near his feet.
8 In the middle of the night, Boaz suddenly woke up and was shocked to see a
woman lying at his feet. 9 "Who are you?"
he asked.

[h] **2.20** *He*: Or "The LORD." [i] **3.4** *lift the cover . . . feet*: To ask for protection and possibly for marriage.

2.20 Lv 25.25.

"Sir, I am Ruth," she answered, "and you are the relative who is supposed to take care of me. So spread the edge of your cover over me."[j]

10 Boaz replied:

The LORD bless you! This shows how truly loyal you are to your family. You could have looked for a younger man, either rich or poor, but you didn't. 11 Don't worry, I'll do what you have asked. You are respected by everyone in town.

12 It's true that I am one of the relatives who is supposed to take care of you, but there is someone who is an even closer relative. 13 Stay here until morning, then I will find out if he is willing to look after you. If he isn't, I promise by the living God to do it myself. Now go back to sleep until morning.

14 Ruth lay down again, but she got up before daylight, because Boaz did not want anyone to know she had been there. 15 Then he told her to spread out her cape. And he filled it with a lot of grain and placed it on her shoulder.

When Ruth got back to town, 16 Naomi asked her[k] what had happened, and Ruth told her everything. 17 She also said, "Boaz gave me this grain, because he didn't want me to come back without something for you."

18 Naomi replied, "Just be patient and don't worry about what will happen. He won't rest until everything is settled today!"

Ruth and Boaz Get Married

4 In the meanwhile, Boaz had gone to the meeting place at the town gate and was sitting there when the other close relative came by. So Boaz invited him to come over and sit down, and he did. 2 Then Boaz got ten of the town leaders and also asked them to sit down. After they had sat down, 3 he said to the man:

Naomi has come back from Moab and is selling the land that belonged to her husband Elimelech. 4 I am telling you about this, since you are his closest relative and have the right to buy the property. If you want it, you can buy it now. These ten men and the others standing here can be witnesses. But if you don't want the property, let me know, because I am next in line.

The man replied, "I will buy it!"

5 "If you do buy it from Naomi," Boaz told him, "you must also marry Ruth. Then if you have a son by her, the property will stay in the family of Ruth's first husband."

6 The man answered, "If that's the case, I don't want to buy it! That would make problems with the property I already own.[l] You may buy it yourself, because I cannot."

7 To make a sale legal in those days, one person would take off a sandal and give it to the other. 8 So after the man had agreed to let Boaz buy the property, he took off one of his sandals and handed it to Boaz.

9 Boaz told the town leaders and everyone else:

All of you are witnesses that today I have bought from Naomi the property that belonged to Elimelech and his two sons, Chilion and Mahlon. 10 You are also witnesses that I have agreed to marry Mahlon's widow Ruth, the Moabite woman. This will keep the property in his family's name, and he will be remembered in this town.

11 The town leaders and the others standing there said:

We are witnesses to this. And we pray that the LORD will give your wife many children, just as he did Leah and Rachel, the wives of Jacob. May you be a rich man in the tribe of Ephrath and an important man in Bethlehem. 12 May the children you have by this young woman make your family as

[j]**3.9** *So . . . me*: To show that he would protect and take care of her. [k]**3.15,16** *When . . . her*: Some Hebrew manuscripts and two ancient translations; most Hebrew manuscripts "Boaz went back to town. [16]Naomi asked Ruth." [l]**4.6** *property . . . own*: This property would then have to be shared with Ruth and her children as well as with his own family.

3.12 Ru 2.20. **4.7,8** Dt 25.9. **4.10** Dt 25.5, 6. **4.11** Gn 29.31. **4.12** Gn 38.27-30.

famous as the family of Perez,[m] the son of Tamar and Judah.

13 Boaz married Ruth, and the LORD blessed her with a son. 14 After his birth, the women said to Naomi:

Praise the LORD! Today he has given you a grandson to take care of you. We pray that the boy will grow up to be famous everywhere in Israel. 15 He will[n] make you happy and take care of you in your old age, because he is the son of your daughter-in-law. And she loves you more than seven sons of your own would love you.

16 Naomi loved the boy and took good care of him. 17 The neighborhood women named him Obed, but they called him "Naomi's Boy."

When Obed grew up he had a son named Jesse, who later became the father of King David. 18-22 Here is a list of the ancestors of David: Jesse, Obed, Boaz, Salmon, Nahshon, Amminadab, Ram, Hezron, and Perez.

[m]**4.12** *Perez*: One of the sons of Judah; he was an ancestor of Boaz and of many others who lived in Bethlehem. [n]**4.14,15** *We pray that . . . famous . . .* 15 *He will*: Or "We pray that the LORD will be praised everywhere in Israel. 15Your grandson will."

1 SAMUEL

ABOUT THIS BOOK

First Samuel is actually the first half of a single book that was divided into two parts, 1 and 2 Samuel, because together they were too long to fit on one scroll. The books are named for one of the main characters, who was a prophet and also the last judge to lead Israel.

The first part of 1 Samuel (1–7) tells about the life of Samuel and how he helped Israel's army fight against enemies that were making raids in Israel. But when he grew old, the people decided to ask the Lord for a king who could lead the army.

In the second part of this book (8.1—15.35) the Lord told Samuel to appoint Saul son of Kish to be the first king of Israel. Saul and his oldest son Jonathan won several battles against the Ammonites and Philistines, but Saul did not completely obey the Lord.

In the third part of the book (15.35—31.13), the Lord told Samuel to secretly appoint a young man named David to be the next king. The book tells how David soon became a national hero after he killed the giant Philistine warrior, Goliath from Gath. But as David continued to become more popular, Saul became suspicious of David. Saul tried to have him killed, even though David was married to Saul's daughter Michal and was best friends with Saul's son Jonathan. The rest of 1 Samuel tells how David escaped and became the leader of his own small army in the desert. Saul continued to hunt for David, and so David finally had to lead his followers to Philistia to be safe from Saul.

The book concludes with the death of Saul and his sons in a battle with the Philistine army. The Lord was keeping his promise to make David the king of Israel:

> *"I've rejected Saul, and I refuse to let him be king any longer. Stop feeling sad about him. . . . go visit a man named Jesse, who lives in Bethlehem. I've chosen one of his sons to be my king."*
>
> *(16.1)*

A QUICK LOOK AT THIS BOOK

- The Birth and Early Childhood of Samuel (1.1—2.10)
- Samuel at the Sacred Tent (2.11—4.1)
- The Sacred Chest Is Captured and Returned (4.1—7.2)
- Samuel as the Leader of Israel (7.3-17)
- Saul, the First King of Israel (8.1—11.15)
- Samuel's Farewell Speech (12.1-25)
- Saul Disobeys the Lord,
and the Lord Rejects Him as King (13.1—15.35)
- The Lord Chooses David To Be the Next King (15.35—16.13)
- David Plays a Harp For Saul (16.14-23)
- David Kills Goliath (17.1—18.5)
- Saul Tries To Kill David (18.6-30)
- Jonathan, Michal, Samuel, and Ahimelech Help David (19.1—21.9)
- David Runs from Saul (21.10—22.5)
- Saul Kills the Priests of the Lord (22.6-23)

- David Refuses To Kill Saul (23.1—26.25)
- David in Philistia (26.25—27.12)
- Saul Talks with Samuel's Ghost (28.1-25)
- David Rescues the Families of His Troops (29.1—30.31)
- Saul and His Sons Die in Battle against the Philistines (31.1-13)

Hannah Asks the LORD for a Child

1 Elkanah lived in Ramah,[a] a town in
the hill country of Ephraim. His great-
great-grandfather was Zuph, so Elkanah
was a member of the Zuph clan of the
Ephraim tribe. Elkanah's father was Jeroham, his grandfather was Elihu, and his
great-grandfather was Tohu.
2 Elkanah had two wives,[b] Hannah and
Peninnah. Although Peninnah had children, Hannah did not have any.
3 Once a year Elkanah traveled from his
hometown to Shiloh, where he worshiped
the LORD All-Powerful and offered sacrifices. Eli was the LORD's priest there, and
his two sons Hophni and Phinehas served
with him as priests.[c]
4 Whenever Elkanah offered a sacrifice,
he gave some of the meat[d] to Peninnah
and some to each of her sons and daughters. 5 But he gave Hannah even more, because he loved Hannah very much, even
though the LORD had kept her from having
children of her own.
6 Peninnah liked to make Hannah feel
miserable about not having any children,
7 especially when the family went to the
house of the LORD[e] each year.
One day, Elkanah was there offering a
sacrifice, when Hannah began crying and
refused to eat. 8 So Elkanah asked, "Hannah, why are you crying? Why won't you
eat? Why do you feel so bad? Don't I mean
more to you than ten sons?"
9 When the sacrifice had been offered,
and they had eaten the meal, Hannah got
up and went to pray. Eli was sitting in his
chair near the door to the place of worship.
10 Hannah was brokenhearted and was crying as she prayed, 11 "LORD All-Powerful, I
am your servant, but I am so miserable!
Please let me have a son. I will give him to
you for as long as he lives, and his hair will
never be cut."[f]
12-13 Hannah prayed silently to the LORD
for a long time. But her lips were moving,
and Eli thought she was drunk. 14 "How
long are you going to stay drunk?" he
asked. "Sober up!"
15-16 "Sir, please don't think I'm no
good!" Hannah answered. "I'm not drunk,
and I haven't been drinking. But I do feel
miserable and terribly upset. I've been
praying all this time, telling the LORD about
my problems."
17 Eli replied, "You may go home now
and stop worrying. I'm sure the God of Israel will answer your prayer."
18 "Sir, thank you for being so kind to
me," Hannah said. Then she left, and after
eating something, she felt much better.

Samuel Is Born

19 Elkanah and his family got up early
the next morning and worshiped the LORD.
Then they went back home to Ramah.
Later the LORD blessed Elkanah and
Hannah 20 with a son. She named him
Samuel because she had asked the LORD
for him.[g]

[a] **1.1** *Ramah*: The Hebrew has "Ramathaim," a longer form of "Ramah" (see verse 19).
[b] **1.2** *two wives*: Having more than one wife was allowed in those times. [c] **1.3** *Eli . . . priests*: One ancient translation; Hebrew "Hophni and Phinehas, the two sons of Eli, served the LORD as priests." [d] **1.4** *meat*: For some sacrifices, like this one, only part of the meat was burned. Some was given to the priest, and the rest was eaten by the family and guests of the worshiper (see Leviticus 3.1-17; 7.11-18). [e] **1.7** *house of the LORD*: Another name for the place of worship at Shiloh, which still may have been the sacred tent at this time. [f] **1.11** *his hair . . . cut*: Never cutting the child's hair would be a sign that he would belong to the LORD (see Numbers 6.1, 21, especially verse 5). [g] **1.20** *him*: In Hebrew "Samuel" sounds something like "Someone from God" or "The name of God" or "His name is God."
1.11 Nu 6.5.

Hannah Gives Samuel to the LORD

21 The next time Elkanah and his family went to offer their yearly sacrifice, he took along a gift that he had promised to give to the LORD. 22 But Hannah stayed home, because she had told Elkanah, "Samuel and I won't go until he's old enough for me to stop nursing him. Then I'll give him to the LORD, and he can stay there at Shiloh for the rest of his life."

23 "You know what's best," Elkanah said. "Stay here until it's time to stop nursing him. I'm sure the LORD will help you do what you have promised."[h] Hannah did not go to Shiloh until she stopped nursing Samuel.

24-25 When it was the time of year to go to Shiloh again, Hannah and Elkanah[i] took Samuel to the LORD's house. They brought along a three-year-old bull,[j] a twenty-pound sack of flour, and a clay jar full of wine. Hannah and Elkanah offered the bull as a sacrifice, then brought the little boy to Eli.

26 "Sir," Hannah said, "a few years ago I stood here beside you and asked the LORD
27 to give me a child. Here he is! The LORD gave me just what I asked for. 28 Now I am giving him to the LORD, and he will be the LORD's servant for as long as he lives."

Hannah Prays

2 Elkanah[k] worshiped the LORD there at Shiloh, and 1 Hannah prayed:

You make me strong
and happy, LORD.
You rescued me.
Now I can be glad
and laugh at my enemies.
2 No other god[l] is like you.
We're safer with you
than on a high mountain.[m]
3 I can tell those proud people,
"Stop your boasting!
Nothing is hidden from the LORD,
and he judges what we do."

4 Our LORD, you break
the bows of warriors,
but you give strength
to everyone who stumbles.
5 People who once
had plenty to eat
must now hire themselves out
for only a piece of bread.
But you give the hungry more
than enough to eat.
A woman did not have a child,
and you gave her seven,
but a woman who had many
was left with none.
6 You take away life,
and you give life.
You send people down
to the world of the dead
and bring them back again.

7 Our LORD, you are the one
who makes us rich or poor.
You put some in high positions
and bring disgrace on others.
8 You lift the poor and homeless
out of the garbage dump
and give them places of honor
in royal palaces.

You set the world on foundations,
and they belong to you.
9 You protect your loyal people,
but everyone who is evil
will die in darkness.

We cannot win a victory
by our own strength.
10 Our LORD, those who attack you
will be broken in pieces

[h] **1.23** *the LORD . . . promised*: The Dead Sea Scrolls and two ancient translations; the Standard Hebrew Text "the LORD will do what he said." [i] **1.24,25** *When it was the time of year to go to Shiloh again, Hannah and Elkanah*: The Dead Sea Scrolls and one ancient translation; the Standard Hebrew Text "she." [j] **1.24,25** *a three-year-old bull*: The Dead Sea Scrolls and two ancient translations; the Standard Hebrew Text "three bulls." [k] **1.28** *Elkanah*: Or "They" or "Samuel." [l] **2.2** *god*: The Hebrew text has "holy one," a term for supernatural beings or gods. [m] **2.2** *mountain*: One possible meaning for the difficult Hebrew text of verse 2.

2.1-10 Lk 1.46-55. **2.6** Ws 16.13; Tb 13.2.

when you fight back
with thunder from heaven.
You will judge the whole earth
and give power and strength
to your chosen king.

Samuel Stays with Eli

11 Elkanah and Hannah went back
home to Ramah, but the boy Samuel stayed
to help Eli serve the LORD.

Eli's Sons

12-13 Eli's sons were priests, but they
were dishonest and refused to obey the
LORD. So, while people were boiling the
meat from their sacrifices, these priests
would send over a servant with a large,
three-pronged fork. 14 The servant would
stick the fork into the cooking pot, and
whatever meat came out on the fork was
taken back to the priests. That is how these
two priests treated every Israelite who
came to offer sacrifices in Shiloh. 15 Sometimes, when people were offering sacrifices,
the servant would come over, even before
the fat had been cut off and sacrificed to
the LORD.[n]

Then the servant would tell them, "The
priest doesn't want his meat boiled! Give
him some raw meat that he can roast!"

16 Usually the people answered, "Take
what you want. But first, let us sacrifice the
fat to the LORD."

"No," the servant would reply. "If you
don't give it to me now, I'll take it by force."

17 Eli's sons did not show any respect
for the sacrifices that the people offered.
This was a terrible sin, and it made the
LORD very angry.

Hannah Visits Samuel

18 The boy Samuel served the LORD and
wore a special linen garment[o] 19 and the
clothes[p] his mother made for him. She
would bring new clothes every year, when
she and her husband came to offer sacrifices at Shiloh.

20 Eli would always bless Elkanah and
his wife and say, "Samuel was born in answer to your prayers. Now you have given
him to the LORD. I pray that the LORD will
bless you with more children to take his
place." After Eli had blessed them, Elkanah and Hannah would return home.

21 The LORD was kind to Hannah, and
she had three more sons and two daughters. But Samuel grew up at the LORD's
house in Shiloh.

Eli Warns His Sons

22 Eli was now very old, and he heard
what his sons were doing to the people of
Israel.[q] 23-24 "Why are you doing these awful things?" he asked them. "I've been
hearing nothing but complaints about you
from all of the LORD's people. 25 If you
harm another person, God can help make
things right between the two of you. But if
you commit a crime against the LORD, no
one can help you!"

But the LORD had already decided to kill
them. So he kept them from listening to
their father.

A Prophet Speaks to Eli

26 Each day the LORD and his people
liked Samuel more and more.

27 One day a prophet came to Eli and
gave him this message from the LORD:

When your ancestors were slaves of
the king of Egypt, I came and showed
them who I am. 28-29 Out of all the
tribes of Israel, I chose your family to
be my priests. I wanted them to offer
sacrifices and burn incense to me and
to find out from me what I want my
people to do. I commanded everyone
to bring their sacrifices here where I
live, and I allowed you and your family

[n]**2.15** *sacrificed to the LORD*: The fat belonged to the LORD and was supposed to be burned as a sacrifice before the rest of the animal was cooked and eaten (see Leviticus 3.3, 4, 9, 10, 14, 15).
[o]**2.18** *a special linen garment*: Either a loin cloth or a jacket or a vest worn only by priests.
[p]**2.19** *clothes*: The Hebrew word means a sleeveless coat or robe that was worn by priests. Samuel was a small child, but his mother made him clothes just like those worn by priests.
[q]**2.22** *Israel*: The Dead Sea Scrolls and one ancient translation; the Standard Hebrew Text adds "He heard that his sons were even sleeping with the women who worked at the entrance to the sacred tent."
2.26 Si 46.13; Lk 2.52. **2.28,29** **a** Ex 28.1-4; **b** Lv 7.35, 36.

to keep those that were not offered to
me on the altar.
But you honor your sons instead of
me! You don't respect[r] the sacrifices
and offerings that are brought to me,
and you've all gotten fat from eating
the best parts.
30 I am the LORD, the God of Israel.
I promised to always let your family
serve me as priests, but now I tell you
that I cannot do this any longer! I
honor anyone who honors me, but I
put a curse on anyone who hates me.
31 The time will come when I will kill
you and everyone else in your family.
Not one of you will live to an old age.
32 Your family[s] will have a lot of
trouble. I will be kind to Israel,[t] but
everyone in your family will die young.
33 If I let anyone from your family be a
priest, his[u] life will be full of sadness
and sorrow. But most of the men in
your family will die a violent death![v]
34 To prove to you that I will do these
things, your two sons, Hophni and
Phinehas, will die on the same day.
35 I have chosen someone else to be
my priest, someone who will be faithful and obey me. I will always let his
family serve as priests and help my
chosen king. 36 But if anyone is left
from your family, he will come to my
priest and beg for money or a little
bread. He may even say to my priest,
"Please let me be a priest, so I will at
least have something to eat."

The LORD Speaks to Samuel

3 1-2 Samuel served the LORD by helping
Eli the priest, who was by that time almost blind. In those days, the LORD hardly
ever spoke directly to people, and he did
not appear to them in dreams very often.
But one night, Eli was asleep in his room,
3 and Samuel was sleeping on a mat near
the sacred chest in the LORD's house. They
had not been asleep very long[w] 4 when the
LORD called out Samuel's name.
"Here I am!" Samuel answered. 5 Then
he ran to Eli and said, "Here I am. What
do you want?"
"I didn't call you," Eli answered. "Go
back to bed."
Samuel went back.
6 Again the LORD called out Samuel's
name. Samuel got up and went to Eli.
"Here I am," he said. "What do you want?"
Eli told him, "Son, I didn't call you. Go
back to sleep."
7 The LORD had not spoken to Samuel
before, and Samuel did not recognize the
voice. 8 When the LORD called out his name
for the third time, Samuel went to Eli again
and said, "Here I am. What do you want?"
Eli finally realized that it was the LORD
who was speaking to Samuel. 9 So he said,
"Go back and lie down! If someone speaks
to you again, answer, 'I'm listening, LORD.
What do you want me to do?' "
Once again Samuel went back and lay
down.
10 The LORD then stood beside Samuel
and called out as he had done before,
"Samuel! Samuel!"
"I'm listening," Samuel answered.
"What do you want me to do?"
11 The LORD said:
Samuel, I am going to do something
in Israel that will shock everyone who
hears about it! 12 I will punish Eli and
his family, just as I promised. 13 He
knew that his sons refused to respect
me,[x] and he let them get away with it,
even though I said I would punish his
family forever. 14 I warned Eli that sacrifices or offerings could never make
things right! His family has done too
many disgusting things.

[r]**2.28,29** *don't respect*: The Standard Hebrew Text; the Dead Sea Scrolls and one ancient translation "are greedy for." [s]**2.32** *Your family*: Or "My house of worship." [t]**2.31,32** *Not one . . . to Israel*: The Standard Hebrew Text; the Dead Sea Scrolls and one ancient translation do not have these words. [u]**2.33** *his*: The Dead Sea Scrolls and one ancient translation; the Standard Hebrew Text "your." [v]**2.33** *die a violent death*: The Dead Sea Scrolls and one ancient translation; the Standard Hebrew Text "die." [w]**3.3** *They . . . long*: The Hebrew text has "The lamp was still burning." An olive oil lamp would go out after a few hours if the wick was not adjusted. [x]**3.13** *refused . . . me*: Or "were insulting everyone."
2.34 1 S 4.11.

15 The next morning, Samuel got up
and opened the doors to the LORD's house.
He was afraid to tell Eli what the LORD had
said. 16 But Eli told him, "Samuel, my boy,
come here!"

"Here I am," Samuel answered.

17 Eli said, "What did God say to you?
Tell me everything. I pray that God will
punish you terribly if you don't tell me
every word he said!"

18 Samuel told Eli everything. Then Eli
said, "He is the LORD, and he will do what's
right."

The LORD Helps Samuel

19 As Samuel grew up, the LORD helped
him and made everything Samuel said
come true. 20 From the town of Dan in the
north to the town of Beersheba in the
south, everyone in the country knew that
Samuel was truly the LORD's prophet.
21 The LORD often appeared to Samuel at
4 Shiloh and told him what to say. 1 Then
Samuel would speak to the whole nation of Israel.

The Philistines Capture the Sacred Chest

One day the Israelites went out to fight
the Philistines. They set up camp near
Ebenezer, and the Philistines camped at
Aphek. 2 The Philistines made a fierce attack. They defeated the Israelites and killed
about four thousand of them.

3 The Israelite army returned to their
camp, and the leaders said, "Why did the
LORD let us lose to the Philistines today?
Let's get the sacred chest where the LORD's
agreement with Israel is kept. Then the
LORD[y] will help us and rescue us from our
enemies."

4 The army sent some soldiers to bring
back the sacred chest from Shiloh, because
the LORD All-Powerful has his throne on
the winged creatures on top of the chest.

As Eli's two sons, Hophni and Phinehas,
5 brought the chest into camp, the army
cheered so loudly that the ground shook.
6 The Philistines heard the noise and said,
"What are those Hebrews shouting about?"
When the Philistines learned that the
sacred chest had been brought into the
camp, 7 they were scared to death and said:

> The gods have come into their
> camp. Now we're in real trouble!
> Nothing like this has ever happened to
> us before. 8 We're in big trouble! Who
> can save us from these powerful gods?
> They're the same gods who made all
> those horrible things happen to the
> Egyptians in the desert.
>
> 9 Philistines, be brave and fight
> hard! If you don't, those Hebrews will
> rule us, just as we've been ruling
> them. Fight and don't be afraid.

10 The Philistines did fight. They killed
thirty thousand Israelite soldiers, and all
the rest ran off to their homes. 11 Hophni
and Phinehas were killed, and the sacred
chest was captured.

Eli Dies

12 That same day a soldier from the
tribe of Benjamin ran from the battlefront
to Shiloh. He had torn his clothes and put
dirt on his head to show his sorrow. 13 He
went into town and told the news about the
battle, and everyone started crying.

Eli was afraid that something might
happen to the sacred chest. So he was sitting on his chair beside the road, just
waiting. 14-15 He was ninety-eight years
old and blind, but he could hear everyone
crying, and he asked, "What's all that
noise?"

The soldier hurried over and told Eli,
16 "I escaped from the fighting today and
ran here."

"Young man, what happened?" Eli
asked.

17 "Israel ran away from the Philistines,"
the soldier answered. "Many of our people
were killed, including your two sons,
Hophni and Phinehas. But worst of all, the
sacred chest was captured."

18 Eli was still sitting on a chair beside
the wall of the town gate. And when the
man said that the Philistines had taken the
sacred chest, Eli fell backwards. He was a
very heavy old man, and the fall broke his

[y] **4.3** *LORD*: Or "chest."
4.4 Ex 25.22.

neck and killed him. He had been a leader[z]
of Israel for forty years.
19 The wife of Phinehas was about to
give birth. And soon after she heard that
the sacred chest had been captured and
that her husband and his father had died,
her baby came. The birth was very hard,
20 and she was dying. But the women taking care of her said, "Don't be afraid—it's
a boy!"

She didn't pay any attention to them.
21-22 Instead she kept thinking about losing her husband and her father-in-law. So
she said, "My son will be named Ichabod,[a]
because the glory of Israel left our country
when the sacred chest was captured."

God Causes Trouble for the Philistines

5 The Philistines took the sacred chest
from near Ebenezer to the town of
Ashdod. 2 They brought it into the temple
of their god Dagon and put it next to the
statue of Dagon, which they worshiped.
3 When the people of Ashdod got up
early the next morning, they found the
statue lying facedown on the floor in front
of the sacred chest. They put the statue
back where it belonged. 4 But early the next
morning, it had fallen over again and was
lying facedown on the floor in front of the
chest. The body of the statue was still in
one piece, but its head and both hands had
broken off and were lying on the stone floor
in the doorway. 5 This is the reason the
priests and everyone else step over that
part of the doorway when they enter the
temple of Dagon in Ashdod.
6 The LORD caused a lot of trouble for
the people of Ashdod and their neighbors.
He made sores break out all over their bodies,[b] and everyone was in a panic.[c] 7 Finally, they said, "The God of Israel did this.
He is the one who caused all this trouble
for us and our god Dagon. We've got to get
rid of this chest."
8 The people of Ashdod had all the
Philistine rulers come to Ashdod, and they
asked them, "What can we do with the sacred
chest that belongs to the God of Israel?"

"Send it to Gath," the rulers answered.
But after they took it there, 9 the LORD
made sores break out on everyone in town.
The people of Gath were frightened, 10 so
they sent the sacred chest to Ekron. But
before they could take it through the town
gates, the people of Ekron started screaming, "They've brought the sacred chest that
belongs to the God of Israel! It will kill us
and our families too!"

The Philistines Send Back the Sacred Chest

11 The people of Ekron called for another meeting of the Philistine rulers and
told them, "Send this chest back where it
belongs. Then it won't kill us."

Everyone was in a panic, because God
was causing a lot of people to die, 12 and
those who had survived were suffering
from the sores. They all cried to their gods
for help.

6 After the sacred chest had been in
Philistia for seven months,[d] 2 the Philistines called in their priests and fortunetellers, and asked, "What should we do
with this sacred chest? Tell us how to send
it back where it belongs!"
3 "Don't send it back without a gift," the
priests and fortunetellers answered. "Send
along something to Israel's God to make up
for taking the chest in the first place. Then
you will be healed, and you will find out why
the LORD was causing you so much trouble."
4 "What should we send?" the Philistines asked.

The priests and fortunetellers answered:

> There are five Philistine rulers, and
> they all have the same disease that
> you have. 5 So make five gold models
> of the sores and five gold models
> of the rats that are wiping out your
> crops. If you honor the God of Israel
> with this gift, maybe he will stop caus-
> ing trouble for you and your gods

[z]**4.18** *leader*: The Hebrew word means that Eli may have been an army commander, a judge, and a priest. [a]**4.21,22** *Ichabod*: Ichabod means "where is the glory?" or "there is no glory."
[b]**5.6** *sores . . . bodies*: Or "He struck them with bubonic plague." [c]**5.6** *panic*: Two ancient translations add "Rats came from their ships, and people were dying right and left."
[d]**6.1** *months*: One ancient translation adds "and rats were everywhere" or "and rats ate the crops."

and your crops. 6 Don't be like the Egyptians and their king. They were stubborn, but when Israel's God was finished with them, they had to let Israel go.

7 Get a new cart and two cows that have young calves and that have never pulled a cart. Hitch the cows to the cart, but take the calves back to their barn. 8 Then put the chest on the cart. Put the gold rats and soresinto a bag and put it on the cart next to the chest. Then send it on its way.

9 Watch to see if the chest goes on up the road to the Israelite town of Beth-Shemesh. If it goes back to its own country, you will know that it was the LORD who made us suffer so badly. But if the chest doesn't go back to its own country, then the LORD had nothing to do with the disease that hit us—it was simply bad luck.

10 The Philistines followed their advice. They hitched up the two cows to the cart, but they kept their calves in a barn. 11 Then they put the chest on the cart, along with the bag that had the gold rats and sores in it.

12 The cows went straight up the road toward Beth-Shemesh, mooing as they went. The Philistine rulers followed them until they got close to Beth-Shemesh.

13 The people of Beth-Shemesh were harvesting their wheat[e] in the valley. When they looked up and saw the chest, they were so happy that they stopped working and started celebrating.

14-15 The cows left the road and pulled the cart into a field that belonged to Joshua from Beth-Shemesh, and they stopped beside a huge rock. Some men from the tribe of Levi were there. So they took the chest off the cart and placed it on the rock, and then they did the same thing with the bag of gold rats and sores. A few other people chopped up the cart and made a fire. They killed the cows and burned them as sacrifices to the LORD. After that, they offered more sacrifices.

16 When the five rulers of the Philistines saw what had happened, they went back to Ekron that same day.

17 That is how the Philistines sent gifts to the LORD to make up for taking the sacred chest. They sent five gold sores, one each for their towns of Ashdod, Gaza, Ashkelon, Gath, and Ekron. 18 They also sent one gold rat for each walled town and for every village that the five Philistine rulers controlled. The huge stone[f] where the Levites set the chest is still there in Joshua's field as a reminder of what happened.

The Sacred Chest Is Sent to Kiriath-Jearim

19 Some of the men of Beth-Shemesh looked inside the sacred chest, and the LORD God killed seventy[g] of them. This made the people of Beth-Shemesh very sad, 20 and they started saying, "No other God is like the LORD! Who can go near him and still live? We'll have to send the chest away from here. But where can we send it?"

21 They sent messengers to tell the people of Kiriath-Jearim, "The Philistines have sent back the sacred chest. Why don't you take it and keep it there with you?"

7 The people of Kiriath-Jearim got the chest and took it to Abinadab's house, which was on a hill in their town. They chose his son Eleazar to take care of it, 2 and it stayed there for twenty years.

During this time everyone in Israel was very sad and begged the LORD for help.[h]

The People of Israel Turn Back to the LORD

3 One day, Samuel told all the people of Israel, "If you really want to turn back to the LORD, then prove it. Get rid of your foreign idols, including the ones of the goddess Astarte. Turn to the LORD with all your

[e]**6.13** *wheat*: The wheat harvest took place in May and June. [f]**6.18** *stone*: A few Hebrew manuscripts; most Hebrew manuscripts "meadow" or "stream." [g]**6.19** *seventy*: A few Hebrew manuscripts; most Hebrew manuscripts "seventy men, fifty thousand men." [h]**7.2** *Israel . . . help*: Or "Israel turned to the LORD and begged him for help."

7.1 2 S 6.2-4; 1 Ch 13.5-7.

heart and worship only him. Then he will rescue you from the Philistines."

4 The people got rid of their idols of Baal and Astarte and began worshiping only the LORD.

5 Then Samuel said, "Tell everyone in Israel to meet together at Mizpah, and I will pray to the LORD for you."

6 The Israelites met together at Mizpah with Samuel as their leader. They drew water from the well and poured it out as an offering to the LORD. On that same day they went without eating to show their sorrow, and they confessed they had been unfaithful to the LORD.

The Philistines Attack Israel

7 When the Philistine rulers found out about the meeting at Mizpah, they sent an army there to attack the people of Israel.

The Israelites were afraid when they heard that the Philistines were coming. 8 "Don't stop praying!" they told Samuel. "Ask the LORD our God to rescue us."

9-10 Samuel begged the LORD to rescue Israel, then he sacrificed a young lamb to the LORD. Samuel had not even finished offering the sacrifice when the Philistines started to attack. But the LORD answered his prayer and made thunder crash all around them. The Philistines panicked and ran away. 11 The men of Israel left Mizpah and went after them as far as the hillside below Beth-Car, killing every enemy soldier they caught.

12-13 The Philistines were so badly beaten that it was quite a while before they attacked Israel again. After the battle, Samuel set up a monument between Mizpah and the rocky cliffs. He named it "Help Monument"[i] to remind Israel how much the LORD had helped them.

For as long as Samuel lived, the LORD helped Israel fight the Philistines. 14 The Israelites were even able to recapture their towns and territory between Ekron and Gath.

Israel was also at peace with the Amorites.[j]

Samuel Is a Leader in Israel

15 Samuel was a leader[k] in Israel all his life. 16 Every year he would go around to the towns of Bethel, Gilgal, and Mizpah where he served as judge for the people. 17 Then he would go back to his home in Ramah and do the same thing there. He also had an altar built for the LORD at Ramah.

The People of Israel Want a King

8 1-2 Samuel had two sons. The older one was Joel, and the younger one was Abijah. When Samuel was getting old, he let them be leaders[k] at Beersheba. 3 But they were not like their father. They were dishonest and accepted bribes to give unfair decisions.

4 One day the nation's leaders came to Samuel at Ramah 5 and said, "You are an old man. You set a good example for your sons, but they haven't followed it. Now we want a king to be our leader,[k] just like all the other nations. Choose one for us!"

6 Samuel was upset to hear the leaders say they wanted a king, so he prayed about it. 7 The LORD answered:

> Samuel, do everything they want you to do. I am really the one they have rejected as their king. 8 Ever since the day I rescued my people from Egypt, they have turned from me to worship idols. Now they are turning away from you. 9 Do everything they ask, but warn them and tell them how a king will treat them.

10 Samuel told the people who were asking for a king what the LORD had said:

> 11 If you have a king, this is how he will treat you. He will force your sons to join his army. Some of them will ride in his chariots, some will serve in the cavalry, and others will run ahead of his own chariot.[l] 12 Some of them

[i] **7.12,13** *Help Monument*: Or "Ebenezer." [j] **7.14** *Amorites*: In this verse, the non-Israelite peoples of Canaan. [k] **7.15; 8.1,2,5** *leader(s)*: The Hebrew word could mean an army commander, a judge, and a religious leader. [l] **8.11** *others . . . chariot*: These men were probably his bodyguards.

7.9,10 Si 46.16-18. **8.5** Dt 17.14.

will be officers in charge of a thousand soldiers, and others will be in charge of fifty. Still others will have to farm the king's land and harvest his crops, or make weapons and parts for his chariots. 13 Your daughters will have to make perfume or do his cooking and baking.

14 The king will take your best fields, as well as your vineyards, and olive orchards and give them to his own officials. 15 He will also take a tenth of your grain and grapes and give it to his officers and officials.

16 The king will take your slaves and your best young men and your donkeys and make them do his work. 17 He will also take a tenth of your sheep and goats. You will become the king's slaves, 18 and you will finally cry out for the LORD to save you from the king you wanted. But the LORD won't answer your prayers.

19-20 The people would not listen to Samuel. "No!" they said. "We want to be like other nations. We want a king to rule us and lead us in battle."

21 Samuel listened to them and then told the LORD exactly what they had said. 22 "Do what they want," the LORD answered. "Give them a king."

Samuel told the people to go back to their homes.

Saul Meets Samuel

9 Kish was a wealthy man who belonged to the tribe of Benjamin. His father was Abiel, his grandfather was Zeror, his great-grandfather was Becorath, and his great-great-grandfather was Aphiah. 2 Kish had a son named Saul, who was better looking and more than a head taller than anyone else in all Israel.

3 Kish owned some donkeys, but they had run off. So he told Saul, "Take one of the servants and go look for the donkeys."

4 Saul and the servant went through the hill country of Ephraim and the territory of Shalishah, but they could not find the donkeys. Then they went through the territories of Shaalim and Benjamin, but still there was no sign of the donkeys. 5 Finally they came to the territory where the clan of Zuph[m] lived. "Let's go back home," Saul told his servant. "If we don't go back soon, my father will stop worrying about the donkeys and start worrying about us!"

6 "Wait!" the servant answered. "There's a man of God who lives in a town near here. He's amazing! Everything he says comes true. Let's talk to him. Maybe he can tell us where to look."

7 Saul said, "How can we talk to the prophet when I don't have anything to give him? We don't even have any bread left in our sacks. What can we give him?"

8 "I have a small piece of silver," the servant answered. "We can give him that, and then he will tell us where to look for the donkeys."

9-10 "Great!" Saul replied. "Let's go to the man who can see visions!" He said this because in those days God would answer questions by giving visions to prophets.

Saul and his servant went to the town where the prophet lived. 11 As they were going up the hill to the town, they met some young women coming out to get water,[n] and the two men said to them, "We're looking for the man who can see visions. Is he in town?"

12 "Yes, he is," they replied. "He's in town today because there's going to be a sacrifice and a sacred meal at the place of worship. In fact, he's just ahead of you. Hurry 13 and you should find him right inside the town gate. He's on his way out to the place of worship to eat with the invited guests. They can't start eating until he blesses the sacrifice. If you go now, you should find him."

14 They went to the town, and just as they were going through the gate, Samuel was coming out on his way to the place of worship.

15 The day before Saul came, the LORD had told Samuel, 16 "I've seen how my people are suffering, and I've heard their call

[m]9.5 *Zuph*: Samuel's father Elkanah was from the Zuph clan. [n]9.11 *water*: Towns were often built on a hill near a source of water, which would often be down in the valley outside of the town. It was usually the job of women to get water for their family.

for help. About this time tomorrow I'll send you a man from the tribe of Benjamin, who will rescue my people from the Philistines. I want you to pour olive oil[o] on his head to show that he will be their leader."

17 Samuel looked at Saul, and the LORD told Samuel, "This is the man I told you about. He's the one who will rule Israel."

18 Saul went over to Samuel in the gateway and said, "A man who can see visions lives here in town. Could you tell me the way to his house?"

19 "I am the one who sees visions!" Samuel answered. "Go on up to the place of worship. You will eat with me today, and in the morning I'll answer your questions. 20 Don't worry about your donkeys that ran off three days ago. They've already been found. Everything of value in Israel now belongs to you and your family."[p]

21 "Why are you telling me this?" Saul asked. "I'm from Benjamin, the smallest tribe in Israel, and my clan is the least important in the tribe."

Saul Eats with Samuel and Stays at His House

22 Samuel took Saul and his servant into the dining room at the place of worship. About thirty people were there for the dinner, but Samuel gave Saul and his servant the places of honor. 23-24 Then Samuel told the cook, "I gave you the best piece of meat and told you to set it aside. Bring it here now."

The cook brought the meat over and set it down in front of Saul. "This is for you," Samuel told him. "Go ahead and eat it. I had this piece saved especially for you, and I invited these guests to eat with you."

After Saul and Samuel had finished eating, 25 they went down from the place of worship and back into town. A bed was set up for Saul on the flat roof[q] of Samuel's house, 26 and Saul slept there.

About sunrise the next morning,[r] Samuel called up to Saul on the roof, "Time to get up! I'll help you get started on your way."

Saul got up. He and Samuel left together 27 and had almost reached the edge of town when Samuel stopped and said, "Have your servant go on. Stay here with me for a few minutes, and I'll tell you what God has told me."

Samuel Tells Saul He Will Be King

10 After the servant had gone, 1 Samuel took a small jar of olive oil and poured it on Saul's head. Then he kissed[s] Saul and told him:

The LORD has chosen you to be the leader and ruler of his people.[t] 2 When you leave me today, you'll meet two men near Rachel's tomb at Zelzah in the territory of Benjamin. They'll tell you, "The donkeys you've been looking for have been found. Your father has forgotten about them, and now he's worrying about you! He's wondering how he can find you."

3 Go on from there until you reach the big oak tree at Tabor, where you'll meet three men on their way to worship God at Bethel. One of them will be leading three young goats, another will be carrying three round loaves of bread, and the last one will be carrying a clay jar of wine. 4 After they greet you, they'll give you two loaves of bread.

5 Next, go to Gibeah,[u] where the Philistines have an army camp. As you're going into the town, you'll meet

[o] **9.16** *olive oil*: Olive oil was poured on the head of someone who was chosen to be a priest, a prophet, or a king. [p] **9.20** *Everything . . . family*: Or "You and your family are what all Israel wants." [q] **9.25** *roof*: Guests often slept on the flat roof of their host's house, where it was cool and breezy. [r] **9.25,26** *was set . . . morning*: One ancient translation; Hebrew "Samuel spoke with Saul on the flat roof of his house. They got up early the next morning, around sunrise, and . . ."

[s] **10.1** *kissed*: Relatives or close friends often greeted one another with a kiss. But this may have been a ceremonial kiss after Samuel poured oil on Saul's head to show that he was to be the king.

[t] **10.1** *people*: One ancient translation adds "You will rule the LORD's people and save them from their enemies who are all around them. These things will prove that what I say is true."

[u] **10.5** *Gibeah*: The Hebrew text has "Gibeah of God," which may or may not have been the same Gibeah as Saul's hometown.

a group of prophets coming down from
the place of worship. They'll be going
along prophesying while others are
walking in front of them, playing small
harps, small drums, and flutes.
6 The Spirit of the LORD will suddenly take control of you.[v] You'll become a different person and start
prophesying right along with them.
7 After these things happen, do whatever you think is right! God will
help you.
8 Then you should go to Gilgal. I'll
come a little later, so wait for me. It
may even take a week for me to get
there, but when I come, I'll offer sacrifices and offerings to the LORD. I'll also
tell you what to do next.

Saul Goes Back Home

9 As Saul turned around to leave
Samuel, God made Saul feel like a different
person. That same day, everything happened just as Samuel had said. 10 When
Saul arrived at Gibeah, a group of prophets
met him. The Spirit of God suddenly took
control of him,[w] and right there in the middle of the group he began prophesying.
11 Some people who had known Saul for
a long time saw that he was speaking and
behaving like a prophet. They said to each
other, "What's happened? How can Saul be
a prophet?"
12 "Why not?" one of them answered.
"Saul has as much right to be a prophet as
anyone else!"[x] That's why everyone started
saying, "How can Saul be a prophet?"
13 After Saul stopped prophesying, he
went to the place of worship.
14 Later, Saul's uncle asked him,
"Where have you been?"
Saul answered, "Looking for the donkeys. We couldn't find them, so we went to
talk with Samuel."
15 "And what did he tell you?" Saul's uncle asked.
16 Saul answered, "He told us the donkeys had been found." But Saul didn't
mention that Samuel had chosen him to be
king.

The LORD Shows Israel that Saul Will Be King

17 Samuel sent messengers to tell the Israelites to come to Mizpah and meet with
the LORD. 18 When everyone had arrived,
Samuel said:
The LORD God of Israel told me to
remind you that he had rescued you
from the Egyptians and from the other
nations that abused you.
19 God has rescued you from your
troubles and hard times. But you have
rejected your God and have asked for a
king. Now each tribe and clan must
come near the place of worship so the
LORD can choose a king.
20 Samuel brought each tribe, one after
the other, to the altar, and the LORD chose
the Benjamin tribe. 21 Next, Samuel
brought each clan of Benjamin there, and
the LORD chose the Matri clan. Finally,
Saul the son of Kish was chosen. But when
they looked for him, he was nowhere to be
found.
22 The people prayed, "Our LORD, is
Saul here?"
"Yes," the LORD answered, "he is hiding
behind the baggage."
23 The people ran and got Saul and
brought him into the middle of the crowd.
He was more than a head taller than anyone else. 24 "Look closely at the man the
LORD has chosen!" Samuel told the crowd.
"There is no one like him!"
The crowd shouted, "Long live the
king!"
25 Samuel explained the rights and duties of a king and wrote them all in a book.
He put the book in a temple building at
one of the places where the LORD was worshiped. Then Samuel sent everyone home.
26 God had encouraged some young
men to become followers of Saul, and
when he returned to his hometown of
Gibeah, they went with him. 27 But some

[v] **10.6** *take . . . you*: Or "will take control of you in a powerful way." [w] **10.10** *suddenly . . . him*: Or "came over him in a powerful way." [x] **10.12** *Why not . . . anyone else*: Or "Sure he is! He's probably the leader of the prophets!" or "How can he be? Those prophets are nobodies!"
10.12 1 S 19.23, 24.

worthless fools said, "How can someone like Saul rescue us from our enemies?" They did not want Saul to be their king, and so they didn't bring him any gifts. But Saul kept calm.

Saul Rescues the Town of Jabesh in Gilead

11 About this time,[y] King Nahash of Ammon came with his army and surrounded the town of Jabesh in Gilead. The people who lived there told Nahash, "If you will sign a peace treaty with us, you can be our ruler, and we will pay taxes to you."

2 Nahash answered, "Sure, I'll sign a treaty! But not before I insult Israel by poking out the right eye of every man who lives in Jabesh."

3 The town leaders said, "Give us seven days so we can send messengers everywhere in Israel to ask for help. If no one comes here to save us, we will surrender to you."

4 Some of the messengers went to Gibeah, Saul's hometown. They told what was happening at Jabesh, and everyone in Gibeah started crying. 5 Just then, Saul came in from the fields, walking behind his oxen.

"Why is everyone crying?" Saul asked.

They told him what the men from Jabesh had said. 6 Then the Spirit of God suddenly took control of Saul and made him furious. 7 Saul killed two of his oxen, cut them up in pieces, and gave the pieces to the[z] messengers. He told them to show the pieces to everyone in Israel and say, "Saul and Samuel are getting an army together. Come and join them. If you don't, this is what will happen to your oxen!"

The LORD made the people of Israel terribly afraid. So all the men came together 8 at Bezek. Saul had them organized and counted. There were three hundred thousand from Israel and thirty thousand[a] from Judah.

9 Saul and his officers sent the messengers back to Jabesh with this promise: "We will rescue you tomorrow afternoon." The messengers went back to the people at Jabesh and told them that they were going to be rescued.

Everyone was encouraged! 10 So they told the Ammonites, "We will surrender to you tomorrow, and then you can do whatever you want to."

11 The next day, Saul divided his army into three groups and attacked before daylight. They started killing Ammonites and kept it up until afternoon. A few Ammonites managed to escape, but they were scattered far from each other.

12 The Israelite soldiers went to Samuel and demanded, "Where are the men who said they didn't want Saul to be king? Bring them to us, and we will put them to death!"

13 "No you won't!" Saul told them. "The LORD rescued Israel today, and no one will be put to death."

Saul Is Accepted as King

14 "Come on!" Samuel said. "Let's go to Gilgal and make an agreement that Saul will continue to be our king."

15 Everyone went to the place of worship at Gilgal, where they agreed that Saul would be their king. Saul and the people sacrificed animals to ask for the LORD's blessing,[b] and they had a big celebration.

Samuel's Farewell Speech

12 Samuel told the Israelites:

I have given you a king, just as you asked. 2 You have seen how I have led you ever since I was a young man. I'm already old. My hair is gray, and my

[y] **10.27—11.1** *But Saul . . . time*: The Standard Hebrew Text; the Dead Sea Scrolls add "King Nahash of Ammon was making the people of Gad and Reuben miserable. He was poking out everyone's right eye, and no one in Israel could stop him. He had poked out the right eye of every Israelite man who lived east of the Jordan River. Only seven thousand men had escaped from the Ammonites, and they had gone into the town of Jabesh in Gilead. About a month later . . ."
[z] **11.7** *the*: Or "some other." [a] **11.8** *three hundred thousand . . . thirty thousand*: The Dead Sea Scrolls and some ancient translations have different numbers. [b] **11.15** *sacrificed . . . blessing*: This kind of sacrifice is described in Leviticus 3; 7.11-36; 19.5-8. People who offered these sacrifices were allowed to eat most of the meat, and they could invite others to share it with them.

own sons are grown. Now you must
see how well your king will lead you.
3 Let me ask this. Have I ever taken
anyone's ox or donkey or forced you to
give me anything? Have I ever hurt
anyone or taken a bribe to give an unfair decision? Answer me so the LORD
and his chosen king can hear you. And
if I have done any of these things, I
will give it all back.
4 "No," the Israelites answered. "You've
never cheated us in any way!"
5 Samuel said, "The LORD and his chosen
king are witnesses to what you have said."
"That's true," they replied.
6 Then Samuel told them:

The LORD brought your ancestors
out of Egypt and chose Moses and
Aaron to be your leaders. 7 Now the
LORD will be your judge. So stand here
and listen, while I remind you how often the LORD has saved you and your
ancestors from your enemies.

8 After Jacob went to Egypt, your
ancestors cried out to the LORD for
help, and he sent Moses and Aaron.
They led your ancestors out of Egypt
and had them settle in this land. 9 But
your ancestors forgot the LORD, so he
let them be defeated by the Philistines,
the king of Moab, and Sisera, the commander of Hazor's army.

10 Again your ancestors cried out to
the LORD for help. They said, "We have
sinned! We stopped worshiping you,
our LORD, and started worshiping Baal
and Astarte. But now, if you rescue us
from our enemies, we will worship you."

11 The LORD sent Gideon,[c] Bedan,
Jephthah, and Samuel to rescue you
from your enemies, and you didn't
have to worry about being attacked.
12 Then you saw that King Nahash of
Ammon was going to attack you. And
even though the LORD your God is
your king, you told me, "This time it's
different. We want a king to rule us!"

13 You asked for a king, and you
chose one. Now he stands here where
all of you can see him. But it was really
the LORD who made him your king.
14 If you and your king want to be followers of the LORD, you must worship
him[d] and do what he says. Don't be
stubborn! 15 If you're stubborn and
refuse to obey the LORD, he will turn
against you and your king.[e]

16 Just stand here and watch the
LORD show his mighty power. 17 Isn't
this the dry season?[f] I'm going to ask
the LORD to send a thunderstorm.
When you see it, you will realize how
wrong you were to ask for a king.

18 Samuel prayed, and that same day the
LORD sent a thunderstorm. Everyone was
afraid of the LORD and of Samuel. 19 They
told Samuel, "Please, pray to the LORD your
God for us! We don't want to die. We have
sinned many times in the past, and we
were very wrong to ask for a king."
20 Samuel answered:

Even though what you did was
wrong, you don't need to be afraid. But
you must always follow the LORD and
worship him with all your heart.
21 Don't worship idols! They don't have
any power, and they can't help you or
save you when you're in trouble. 22 But
the LORD has chosen you to be his own
people. He will always take care of you
so that everyone will know how great
he is.

23 I would be disobeying the LORD if
I stopped praying for you! I will always
teach you how to live right. 24 You also
must obey the LORD—you must worship him with all your heart and remember the great things he has done
for you. 25 But if you and your king do
evil, the LORD will wipe you out.

[c] **12.11** *Gideon*: The Hebrew text has "Jerubbaal," another name for "Gideon."
[d] **12.14** *If . . . him*: Or "If you and your king want things to go well for you, then you must worship the LORD." [e] **12.15** *and your king*: One ancient translation; Hebrew "and your ancestors" or "as he was against your ancestors." [f] **12.17** *the dry season*: The Hebrew text has "time for wheat harvest," which was usually in the spring, the beginning of the dry season.

12.3 Si 46.19. **12.6** Ex 6.26. **12.8** Ex 2.23. **12.9** **a** Jg 4.2; **b** Jg 13.1; **c** Jg 3.12. **12.10** Jg 10.10-15. **12.10,11** 3 Macc 2.12. **12.11** **a** Jg 7.1; **b** Jg 4.6; **c** Jg 11.29; **d** 1 S 3.20. **12.12** 1 S 8.19.

Saul Disobeys the LORD

13 Saul was a young man[g] when he became king, and he ruled Israel for two years. 2 Then[h] he chose three thousand men from Israel to be full-time soldiers and sent everyone else[i] home. Two thousand of these troops stayed with him in the hills around Michmash and Bethel. The other thousand were stationed with Jonathan[j] at Gibeah[k] in the territory of Benjamin.

3 Jonathan led an attack on the Philistine army camp at Geba.[l] The Philistine camp was destroyed, but[m] the other Philistines heard what had happened. Then Saul told his messengers, "Go to every village in the country. Give a signal with the trumpet, and when the people come together, tell them what has happened."

4 The messengers then said to the people of Israel, "Saul has destroyed the Philistine army camp at Geba.[n] Now the Philistines really hate Israel, so every town and village must send men to join Saul's army at Gilgal."

5 The Philistines called their army together to fight Israel. They had three thousand[o] chariots, six thousand cavalry, and as many foot soldiers as there are grains of sand on the beach. They went to Michmash and set up camp there east of Beth-Aven.[p]

6 The Israelite army realized that they were outnumbered and were going to lose the battle. Some of the Israelite men hid in caves or in clumps of bushes,[q] and some ran to places where they could hide among large rocks. Others hid in tombs[r] or in deep dry pits. 7 Still others[s] went to Gad and Gilead on the other side of the Jordan River.

Saul stayed at Gilgal. His soldiers were shaking with fear, 8 and they were starting to run off and leave him. Saul waited there seven days, just as Samuel had ordered him to do,[t] but Samuel did not come. 9 Finally, Saul commanded, "Bring me some animals, so we can offer sacrifices to please the LORD and ask for his help."

Saul killed one of the animals, 10 and just as he was placing it on the altar, Samuel arrived. Saul went out to welcome him.

11 "What have you done?" Samuel asked.

Saul answered, "My soldiers were leaving in all directions, and you didn't come when you were supposed to. The Philistines were gathering at Michmash, 12 and I was worried that they would attack me here at Gilgal. I hadn't offered a sacrifice to ask for the LORD's help, so I forced myself to offer a sacrifice on the altar fire."

13 "That was stupid!" Samuel said. "You didn't obey the LORD your God. If you had obeyed him, someone from your family would always have been king of Israel. 14 But no, you disobeyed, and so the LORD won't choose anyone else from your family to be king. In fact, he has already chosen the one he wants to be the next leader of his people." 15 Then Samuel left Gilgal.

[g] **13.1** *a young man*: One possible meaning for the difficult Hebrew text; several manuscripts of one ancient translation have "thirty years old." [h] **13.1,2** *for . . . Then*: One possible meaning for the difficult Hebrew text. [i] **13.2** *everyone else*: People who were not full-time soldiers, but fought together with the army when the nation was in danger. [j] **13.2** *Jonathan*: Saul's son (see verse 16). [k] **13.2** *Michmash . . . Bethel . . . Gibeah*: These three towns form a triangle, with Bethel to the north. [l] **13.3** *Geba*: Geba was between Gibeah and Michmash. [m] **13.3** *led an attack . . . destroyed, but*: Or "killed the Philistine military governor who lived at Geba, and . . . " [n] **13.4** *destroyed . . . Geba*: Or "killed the Philistine military governor who lived at Geba." [o] **13.5** *three thousand*: Some ancient translations; Hebrew "thirty thousand." [p] **13.5** *Beth-Aven*: This Beth-Aven was probably located about a mile southwest of Michmash, between Michmash and Geba. [q] **13.6** *in . . . bushes*: Or "in cracks in the rocks." [r] **13.6** *tombs*: The Hebrew word may mean a room cut into solid rock and used as a burial place, or it may mean a cellar. [s] **13.7** *Still others*: This translates a Hebrew word which may be used of wandering groups of people who sometimes became outlaws or hired soldiers (see also 14.21). [t] **13.8** *Samuel . . . to do*: See 10.8.

13.8 1 S 10.8. **13.14** Ac 13.22.

Part of Saul's army had not deserted him,
and he led them to Gibeah in Benjamin to
join his other troops. Then he counted
them[u] and found that he still had six hundred men. 16 Saul, Jonathan, and their
army set up camp at Geba in Benjamin.

Jonathan Attacks the Philistines

The Philistine army was camped at
Michmash. 17 Each day they sent out patrols to attack and rob villages and then destroy them. One patrol would go north
along the road to Ophrah in the region of
Shual. 18 Another patrol would go west
along the road to Beth-Horon. A third patrol would go east toward the desert on
the road to the ridge that overlooks Zeboim
Valley.

19 The Philistines would not allow any
Israelites to learn how to make iron tools.
"If we allowed that," they said, "those
worthless Israelites would make swords and
spears."

20-21 Whenever the Israelites wanted to
get an iron point put on a cattle prod,[v] they
had to go to the Philistines. Even if they
wanted to sharpen plow-blades, picks, axes,
sickles,[w] and pitchforks[x] they still had to go
to them. And the Philistines charged high
prices. 22 So, whenever the Israelite soldiers had to go into battle, none of them
had a sword or a spear except Saul and his
son Jonathan.

23 The Philistines moved their camp to
14 the pass at Michmash, 1-3 and Saul
was in Geba[y] with his six hundred men. Saul's own tent was set up under a fruit tree[z] by the threshing place[a] at
the edge of town. Ahijah was serving as
priest, and one of his jobs was to get answers from the LORD for Saul. Ahijah's
father was Ahitub, and his father's brother
was Ichabod. Ahijah's grandfather was
Phinehas, and his great-grandfather Eli
had been the LORD's priest at Shiloh.

One day, Jonathan told the soldier who
carried his weapons that he wanted to attack the Philistine camp on the other side
of the valley. So they slipped out of the Israelite camp without anyone knowing it.
Jonathan didn't even tell his father he was
leaving.

4-5 Jonathan decided to get to the Philistine camp by going through the pass that
led between Shiny Cliff and Michmash to
the north and Thornbush Cliff[b] and Geba
to the south.

6 Jonathan and the soldier who carried
his weapons talked as they went toward the
Philistine camp. "It's just the two of us
against all those godless men," Jonathan
said. "But the LORD can help a few soldiers
win a battle just as easily as he can help a
whole army. Maybe the LORD will help us
win this battle."

7 "Do whatever you want," the soldier
answered. "I'll be right there with you."

8 "This is what we will do," Jonathan
said. "We will go across and let them see us.
9 If they agree to come down the hill and
fight where we are, then we won't climb up
to their camp. 10 But we will go if they tell
us to come up the hill and fight. That will
mean the LORD is going to help us win."

11-12 Jonathan and the soldier stood at
the bottom of the hill where the Philistines
could see them. The Philistines said,
"Look! Those worthless Israelites have
crawled out of the holes where they've
been hiding." Then they yelled down to
Jonathan and the soldier, "Come up here,
and we will teach you a thing or two!"

Jonathan turned to the soldier and said,
"Follow me! The LORD is going to let
us win."

13 Jonathan crawled up the hillside with
the soldier right behind him. When they
got to the top, Jonathan killed the Phi-

[u] **13.15** *Then Samuel . . . counted them*: Two ancient translations; Hebrew "Then Samuel left Gilgal and went to Gibeah in Benjamin. Saul counted his army." [v] **13.20,21** *cattle prod*: A pole used to poke cattle and make them move. [w] **13.20,21** *sickles*: One ancient translation; Hebrew "plow-blades." [x] **13.20,21** *pitchforks*: One possible meaning for the difficult Hebrew text.
[y] **14.1-3** *Geba*: Or "Gibeah." In 13.16 and 14.5 the name "Geba" is used, while 14.2,16 have "Gibeah." In ancient Hebrew writing there is only one letter different between the two words.
[z] **14.1-3** *fruit tree*: Hebrew "pomegranate tree." A pomegranate is a bright red fruit that looks like an apple. [a] **14.1-3** *threshing place*: Or "in Migron." [b] **14.4,5** *Shiny Cliff . . . Thornbush Cliff*: Or "Bozez Cliff . . . Seneh Cliff."

listines who attacked from the front, and the soldier killed those who attacked from behind.[c] 14 Before they had gone a hundred feet,[d] they had killed about twenty Philistines.

15 The whole Philistine army panicked—those in camp, those on guard duty, those in the fields, and those on raiding patrols. All of them were afraid and confused. Then God sent an earthquake, and the ground began to tremble.[e]

Israel Defeats the Philistines

16 Saul's lookouts at Geba[f] saw that the Philistine army was running in every direction, like melted wax. 17 Saul told his officers, "Call the roll and find out who left our camp." When they had finished, they found out that Jonathan and the soldier who carried his weapons were missing.

18 At that time, Ahijah was serving as priest for the army of Israel, and Saul told him, "Come over here! Let's ask God what we should do."[g] 19 Just as Saul finished saying this, he could see that the Philistine army camp was getting more and more confused, and he said, "Ahijah, never mind!"

20 Saul quickly called his army together, then led them to the Philistine camp. By this time the Philistines were so confused that they were killing each other.

21 There were also some hired soldiers[h] in the Philistine camp, who now switched to Israel's side and fought for Saul and Jonathan.

22 Many Israelites had been hiding in the hill country of Ephraim. And when they heard that the Philistines were running away, they came out of hiding and joined in chasing the Philistines.

23-24 So the LORD helped Israel win the battle that day.

Saul's Curse on Anyone Who Eats

Saul had earlier told his soldiers, "I want to get even with those Philistines by sunset. If any of you eat before then, you will be under a curse!" So he made them swear not to eat.

By the time the fighting moved past Beth-Aven,[i] the Israelite troops were weak from hunger. 25-26 The army and the people who lived nearby had gone into a forest, and they came to a place where honey was dripping on the ground.[j] But no one ate any of it, because they were afraid of being put under the curse.

27 Jonathan did not know about Saul's warning to the soldiers. So he dipped the end of his walking stick in the honey and ate some with his fingers. He felt stronger and more alert. 28 Then a soldier told him, "Your father swore that anyone who ate food today would be put under a curse, and we agreed not to eat. That's why we're so weak."

29 Jonathan said, "My father has caused you a lot of trouble. Look at me! I had only a little of this honey, but already I feel strong and alert. 30 I wish you had eaten some of the food the Philistines left behind. We would have been able to kill a lot more of them."

31 By evening the Israelite army was exhausted from killing Philistines all the way from Michmash to Aijalon.[k] 32 They grabbed the food they had captured from the Philistines and started eating. They even killed sheep and cows and calves right on the ground and ate the meat without draining the blood.[l] 33 Someone told Saul,

[c] **14.13** *Jonathan killed . . . from behind*: Or "Jonathan attacked the Philistines with his sword, and the soldier killed those who fell to the ground wounded." [d] **14.14** *a hundred feet*: One possible meaning for the difficult Hebrew text. [e] **14.15** *Then . . . tremble*: Or "Then the ground began to tremble, and everyone was in a terrible panic." Or "Then the ground began to tremble, and God made them all panic." [f] **14.16** *Geba*: See the note at 14.1-3. [g] **14.18** *At that time . . . should do*: One ancient translation; Hebrew "Saul told Ahijah, 'Bring the sacred chest,' because at that time it was with the army of Israel." [h] **14.21** *hired soldiers*: See the note at 13.7.
[i] **14.23,24** *Beth-Aven*: See the note at 13.5. [j] **14.25,26** *The army . . . ground*: One possible meaning for the difficult Hebrew text. [k] **14.31** *Aijalon*: About 20 miles west of Michmash.
[l] **14.32** *blood*: The Israelites were supposed to drain the blood from a butchered animal before the meat was cooked and eaten (see Genesis 9.4; Leviticus 17.11; Deuteronomy 12.23).
14.33 Gn 9.4; Lv 7.26, 27; 17.10-14; 19.26; Dt 12.5-19, 23, 24; 15.23.

"Look! The army is disobeying the LORD by
eating meat before the blood drains out."
"You're right," Saul answered. "They are
being unfaithful to the LORD! Hurry! Roll a
big rock over here.[m] 34 Then tell everyone
in camp to bring their cattle and lambs to
me. They can kill the animals on this
rock,[n] then eat the meat. That way no one
will disobey the LORD by eating meat with
blood still in it."
That night the soldiers brought their
cattle over to the big rock and killed them
there. 35 It was the first altar Saul had built
for offering sacrifices to the LORD.[o]

The Army Rescues Jonathan

36 Saul said, "Let's attack the Philistines
again while it's still dark. We can fight
them all night. Let's kill them and take
everything they own!"
The people answered, "We will do whatever you want."
"Wait!" Ahijah the priest said. "Let's ask
God what we should do."
37 Saul asked God, "Should I attack the
Philistines? Will you help us win?"
This time God did not answer. 38 Saul
called his army officers together and said,
"We have to find out what sin has kept
God from answering. 39 I swear by the
living LORD that whoever sinned must
die, even if it turns out to be my own son
Jonathan."
No one said a word.
40 Saul told his army, "You stand on that
side of the priest, and Jonathan and I will
stand on the other side."
Everyone agreed.
41 Then Saul prayed, "Our LORD, God of
Israel, why haven't you answered me today? Please show us who sinned. Was it my
son Jonathan and I, or was it your people
Israel?"[p]
The answer came back that Jonathan or
Saul had sinned, not the army. 42 Saul told
Ahijah, "Now ask the LORD to decide between Jonathan and me."
The answer came back that Jonathan
had sinned. 43 "Jonathan," Saul exclaimed,
"tell me what you did!"
"I dipped the end of my walking stick in
some honey and ate a little. Now you say I
have to die!"
44 "Yes, Jonathan. I swear to God that
you must die."
45 "No!" the soldiers shouted. "God
helped Jonathan win the battle for us. We
won't let you kill him. We swear to the
LORD that we won't let you kill him or even
lay a hand on him!" So the army kept Saul
from killing Jonathan.
46 Saul stopped hunting down the
Philistines, and they went home.

Saul Fights His Enemies

47-48 When Saul became king, the
Moabites, the Ammonites, the Edomites,
the kings of Zobah, the Philistines, and the
Amalekites had all been robbing the Israelites. Saul fought back against these enemies and stopped them from robbing Israel. He was a brave commander and
always won his battles.[q]

Saul's Family

49-51 Saul's wife was Ahinoam, the
daughter of Ahimaaz. They had three sons:
Jonathan, Ishvi,[r] and Malchishua. They
also had two daughters: The older one was
Merab, and the younger one was Michal.
Abner, Saul's cousin, was the commander of the army. Saul's father Kish and Abner's father Ner were sons of Abiel.

War with the Philistines

52 Saul was at war with the Philistines
for as long as he lived. Whenever he found
a good warrior or a brave man, Saul made
him join his army.

[m] **14.33** *over here*: One ancient translation; Hebrew "today." [n] **14.34** *kill . . . rock*: That is, up off the ground so the blood could drain out. [o] **14.35** *offering sacrifices to the LORD*: Even when animals were killed for food, it was often done as a sacrifice to the LORD. [p] **14.41** *why . . . Israel*: One ancient translation; Hebrew "give me an answer." [q] **14.47,48** *won his battles*: One ancient translation; Hebrew "hurt them." [r] **14.49-51** *Ishvi*: Also known as Eshbaal (see 1 Chronicles 8.33; 9.39) and Ishbosheth (see 2 Samuel 2.8-13; 3.8-15; 4.5-12).

14.41 Ex 28.30; Nu 27.21; 1 S 28.6.

Saul Disobeys the LORD

15 One day, Samuel told Saul:

The LORD had me choose you to be king of his people, Israel. Now listen to this message from the LORD: 2 "When the Israelites were on their way out of Egypt, the nation of Amalek attacked them. I am the LORD All-Powerful, and now I am going to make Amalek pay!

3 "Go and attack the Amalekites! Destroy them and all their possessions. Don't have any pity. Kill their men, women, children, and even their babies. Slaughter their cattle, sheep, camels, and donkeys."

4 Saul sent messengers who told every town and village to send men to join the army at Telaim. There were two hundred ten thousand troops in all, and ten thousand of these were from Judah. Saul organized them, 5 then led them to a valley near one of the towns in[s] Amalek, where they got ready to make a surprise attack. 6 Some Kenites lived nearby, and Saul told them, "Your people were kind to our nation when we left Egypt, and I don't want you to get killed when I wipe out the Amalekites. Leave here and stay away from them."

The Kenites left, 7 and Saul attacked the Amalekites from Havilah[t] to Shur, which is just east of Egypt. 8 Every Amalekite was killed except King Agag. 9 Saul and his army let Agag live, and they also spared the best sheep and cattle. They didn't want to destroy anything of value, so they only killed the animals that were worthless or weak.[u]

The LORD Rejects Saul

10 The LORD told Samuel, 11 "Saul has stopped obeying me, and I'm sorry that I made him king."

Samuel was angry, and he cried out in prayer to the LORD all night. 12 Early the next morning he went to talk with Saul. Someone told him, "Saul went to Carmel, where he had a monument built so everyone would remember his victory. Then he left for Gilgal."

13 Samuel finally caught up with Saul,[v] and Saul told him, "I hope the LORD will bless you! I have done what the LORD told me."

14 "Then why," Samuel asked, "do I hear sheep and cattle?"

15 "The army took them from the Amalekites," Saul explained. "They kept the best sheep and cattle, so they could sacrifice them to the LORD your God. But we destroyed everything else."

16 "Stop!" Samuel said. "Let me tell you what the LORD told me last night."

"All right," Saul answered.

17 Samuel continued, "You may not think you're very important, but the LORD chose you to be king, and you are in charge of the tribes of Israel. 18 When the LORD sent you on this mission, he told you to wipe out those worthless Amalekites. 19 Why didn't you listen to the LORD? Why did you keep the animals and make him angry?"

20 "But I did listen to the LORD!" Saul answered. "He sent me on a mission, and I went. I captured King Agag and destroyed his nation. 21 All the animals were going to be destroyed[w] anyway. That's why the army brought the best sheep and cattle to Gilgal as sacrifices to the LORD your God."

22 "Tell me," Samuel said. "Does the LORD really want sacrifices and offerings? No! He doesn't want your sacrifices. He wants you to obey him. 23 Rebelling against God or disobeying him because you are proud is just as bad as worshiping idols or asking them for advice. You refused to do what God told you, so God has decided that you can't be king."

24 "I have sinned," Saul admitted. "I disobeyed both you and the LORD. I was

[s] **15.5** *one . . . in*: Or "the town of." [t] **15.7** *from Havilah*: Or "from the valley" (see 15.5). [u] **15.9** *animals . . . weak*: One possible meaning for the difficult Hebrew text. [v] **15.13** *Saul*: One ancient translation adds "Saul had sacrificed to the LORD the best animals they had taken from Amalek, when Samuel came up to him . . ." [w] **15.21** *animals . . . destroyed*: The Hebrew means things that were set aside for God. They could not be used for anything else, so they had to be destroyed.

15.1 1 S 10.1. **15.2** Ex 17.8-14; Dt 25.17-19.

afraid of the army, and I listened to them
instead. 25 Please forgive me and come
back with me so I can worship the LORD."
26 "No!" Samuel replied, "You disobeyed
the LORD, and I won't go back with you.
Now the LORD has said that you can't be
king of Israel any longer."
27 As Samuel turned to go, Saul grabbed
the edge of Samuel's robe. It tore!
28 Samuel said, "The LORD has torn the
kingdom of Israel away from you today, and
he will give it to someone who is better
than you. 29 Besides, the eternal[x] God of Israel isn't a human being. He doesn't tell
lies or change his mind."
30 Saul said, "I did sin, but please honor
me in front of the leaders of the army and
the people of Israel. Come back with me, so
I can worship the LORD your God."
31 Samuel followed Saul back, and Saul
worshiped the LORD. 32 Then Samuel
shouted, "Bring me King Agag of Amalek!"
Agag came in chains,[y] and he was saying to himself, "Surely they won't kill me
now."[z]
33 But Samuel said, "Agag, you have
snatched children from their mothers'
arms and killed them. Now your mother
will be without children." Then Samuel
chopped Agag to pieces at the place of worship in Gilgal.
34 Samuel went home to Ramah, and
Saul returned to his home in Gibeah.
35 Even though Samuel felt sad about Saul,
Samuel never saw him again.

The LORD Chooses David To Be King

16 The LORD was sorry he had made Saul
the king of Israel.1 One day he said,
"Samuel, I've rejected Saul, and I
refuse to let him be king any longer. Stop
feeling sad about him. Put some olive oil[a]
in a small container[b] and go visit a man
named Jesse, who lives in Bethlehem. I've
chosen one of his sons to be my king."
2 Samuel answered, "If I do that, Saul
will find out and have me killed."
"Take a calf with you," the LORD replied.
"Tell everyone that you've come to offer it
as a sacrifice to me, 3 then invite Jesse to
the sacrifice.[c] When I show you which one
of his sons I have chosen, pour the olive oil
on his head."
4 Samuel did what the LORD told him
and went to Bethlehem. The town leaders
went to meet him, but they were terribly
afraid and asked, "Is this a friendly visit?"
5 "Yes, it is!" Samuel answered. "I've
come to offer a sacrifice to the LORD. Get
yourselves ready[d] to take part in the sacrifice and come with me." Samuel also invited Jesse and his sons to come to the sacrifice, and he got them ready to take part.
6 When Jesse and his sons arrived,
Samuel noticed Jesse's oldest son, Eliab.
"He has to be the one the LORD has chosen," Samuel said to himself.
7 But the LORD told him, "Samuel, don't
think Eliab is the one just because he's tall
and handsome. He isn't the one I've chosen. People judge others by what they look
like, but I judge people by what is in their
hearts."
8 Jesse told his son Abinadab to go over
to Samuel, but Samuel said, "No, the LORD
hasn't chosen him."
9 Next, Jesse sent his son Shammah to
him, and Samuel said, "The LORD hasn't
chosen him either."
10 Jesse had all seven of his sons go over
to Samuel. Finally, Samuel said, "Jesse, the
LORD hasn't chosen any of these young
men. 11 Do you have any more sons?"
"Yes," Jesse answered. "My youngest son
David is out taking care of the sheep."
"Send for him!" Samuel said. "We won't
start the ceremony until he gets here."
12 Jesse sent for David. He was a
healthy, good-looking boy with a sparkle in
his eyes. As soon as David came, the LORD

[x] **15.29** *eternal*: Or "glorious." [y] **15.32** *in chains*: One possible meaning for the difficult Hebrew text. [z] **15.32** *Surely . . . now*: Hebrew; one ancient translation "It would have been better to die in battle!" [a] **16.1** *olive oil*: See the note at 9.16. [b] **16.1** *small container*: Hebrew "horn"; animal horns were sometimes hollowed out and used as containers. [c] **16.3** *sacrifice*: A sacrifice often involved a dinner where the meat from the sacrificed animal would be served. [d] **16.5** *Get yourselves ready*: The people of Israel sometimes had to perform certain ceremonies to make themselves acceptable to God.

15.27,28 1 S 28.17; 1 K 11.30, 31. **16.1,13** Ps 151.4. **16.7,10** Ps 151.5. **16.11** Ps 151.1.

told Samuel, "He's the one! Get up and pour the olive oil on his head."[e]

13 Samuel poured the oil on David's head while his brothers watched. At that moment, the Spirit of the LORD took control of David and stayed with him from then on.

Samuel returned home to Ramah.

David Plays the Harp for Saul

14 The Spirit of the LORD had left Saul, and an evil spirit from the LORD was terrifying him. 15 "It's an evil spirit from God that's frightening you," Saul's officials told him. 16 "Your Majesty, let us go and look for someone who is good at playing the harp. He can play for you whenever the evil spirit from God bothers you, and you'll feel better."

17 "All right," Saul answered. "Find me someone who is good at playing the harp and bring him here."

18 "A man named Jesse who lives in Bethlehem has a son who can play the harp," one official said. "He's a brave warrior, he's good-looking, he can speak well, and the LORD is with him."

19 Saul sent a message to Jesse: "Tell your son David to leave your sheep and come here to me."

20 Jesse loaded a donkey with bread and a goatskin full of wine,[f] then he told David to take the donkey and a young goat to Saul. 21 David went to Saul and started working for him. Saul liked him so much that he put David in charge of carrying his weapons. 22 Not long after this, Saul sent another message to Jesse: "I really like David. Please let him stay with me."

23 Whenever the evil spirit from God bothered Saul, David would play his harp. Saul would relax and feel better, and the evil spirit would go away.

Goliath Challenges Israel's Army

17 The Philistines got ready for war and brought their troops together to attack the town of Socoh in Judah. They set up camp at Ephes-Dammim, between Socoh and Azekah.[g] 2-3 King Saul and the Israelite army set up camp on a hill overlooking Elah Valley, and they got ready to fight the Philistine army that was on a hill on the other side of the valley.

4 The Philistine army had a hero named Goliath who was from the town of Gath and was over nine feet[h] tall. 5-6 He wore a bronze helmet and had bronze armor to protect his chest and legs. The chest armor alone weighed about one hundred twenty-five pounds. He carried a bronze sword strapped on his back, 7 and his spear was so big that the iron spearhead alone weighed more than fifteen pounds. A soldier always walked in front of Goliath to carry his shield.

8 Goliath went out and shouted to the army of Israel:

> Why are you lining up for battle? I'm the best soldier in our army, and all of you are in Saul's army. Choose your best soldier to come out and fight me! 9 If he can kill me, our people will be your slaves. But if I kill him, your people will be our slaves. 10 Here and now I challenge Israel's whole army! Choose someone to fight me!

11 Saul and his men heard what Goliath said, but they were so frightened of Goliath that they couldn't do a thing.

David Meets King Saul

12 David's father Jesse was an old man, who belonged to the Ephrath clan and lived in Bethlehem in Judah. Jesse had eight sons: 13-14 the oldest was Eliab, the next was Abinadab, and Shammah was the third. The three of them had gone off to fight in Saul's army.

David was Jesse's youngest son. 15 He took care of his father's sheep, and he went back and forth between Bethlehem and Saul's camp.

16 Goliath came out and gave his challenge every morning and every evening for forty days.

[e] **16.12** *olive oil on his head*: See the note at 9.16. [f] **16.20** *wine*: Wine was sometimes kept in bottles made of goatskin sewn up with the fur on the outside. [g] **17.1** *Socoh and Azekah*: Socoh was controlled by the Israelites, while Azekah was in Philistine hands. [h] **17.4** *over nine feet*: The Standard Hebrew Text; the Dead Sea Scrolls and some manuscripts of one ancient translation have "almost seven feet."

16.23 Ps 151.2. **17.15** Ps 151.1.

17 One day, Jesse told David, "Hurry and
take this sack of roasted grain and these
ten loaves of bread to your brothers at the
army camp. 18 And here are ten large chunks
of cheese to take to their commanding officer. Find out how your brothers are doing
and bring back something that shows that
they're all right. 19 They're with Saul's army,
fighting the Philistines in Elah Valley."

20 David obeyed his father. He got up
early the next morning and left someone
else in charge of the sheep; then he loaded
the supplies and started off. He reached
the army camp just as the soldiers were
taking their places and shouting the battle
cry. 21 The army of Israel and the Philistine
army stood there facing each other.

22 David left his things with the man in
charge of supplies and ran up to the battle
line to ask his brothers if they were well.
23 While David was talking with them, Goliath came out from the line of Philistines and
started boasting as usual. David heard him.

24 When the Israelite soldiers saw Goliath, they were scared and ran off. 25 They
said to each other, "Look how he keeps
coming out to insult us. The king is offering a big reward to the man who kills Goliath. That man will even get to marry the
king's daughter, and no one in his family
will ever have to pay taxes again."

26 David asked some soldiers standing
nearby, "What will a man get for killing this
Philistine and stopping him from insulting our people? Who does that worthless
Philistine think he is? He's making fun of
the army of the living God!"

27 The soldiers told David what the king
would give the man who killed Goliath.

28 David's oldest brother Eliab heard
him talking with the soldiers. Eliab was angry at him and said, "What are you doing
here, anyway? Who's taking care of that little flock of sheep out in the desert? You
spoiled brat! You came here just to watch
the fighting, didn't you?"

29 "Now what have I done?" David answered. "Can't I even ask a question?"
30 Then he turned and asked another soldier the same thing he had asked the others, and he got the same answer.

31 Some soldiers overheard David talking, so they told Saul what David had said.
Saul sent for David, and David came.
32 "Your Majesty," he said, "this Philistine
shouldn't turn us into cowards. I'll go out
and fight him myself!"

33 "You don't have a chance against
him," Saul replied. "You're only a boy, and
he's been a soldier all his life."

34 But David told him:

Your Majesty, I take care of my
father's sheep. And when one of them
is dragged off by a lion or a bear, 35 I go
after it and beat the wild animal until
it lets the sheep go. If the wild animal
turns and attacks me, I grab it by the
throat and kill it.

36 Sir, I have killed lions and bears
that way, and I can kill this worthless
Philistine. He shouldn't have made fun
of the army of the living God! 37 The
LORD has rescued me from the claws
of lions and bears, and he will keep me
safe from the hands of this Philistine.

"All right," Saul answered, "go ahead
and fight him. And I hope the LORD will
help you."

38 Saul had his own military clothes and
armor put on David, and he gave David a
bronze helmet to wear. 39 David strapped
on a sword and tried to walk around, but he
was not used to wearing those things.

"I can't move with all this stuff on,"
David said. "I'm just not used to it."

David took off the armor 40 and picked
up his shepherd's stick. He went out to a
stream and picked up five smooth rocks
and put them in his leather bag. Then with
his sling in his hand, he went straight toward Goliath.

David Kills Goliath

41 Goliath came toward David, walking
behind the soldier who was carrying his
shield. 42 When Goliath saw that David was
just a healthy, good-looking boy, he made
fun of him. 43 "Do you think I'm a dog?"
Goliath asked. "Is that why you've come after me with a stick?" He cursed David in
the name of the Philistine gods 44 and
shouted, "Come on! When I'm finished

17.43 Ps 151.6.

with you, I'll feed you to the birds and wild animals!"

45 David answered:

You've come out to fight me with a sword and a spear and a dagger. But I've come out to fight you in the name of the LORD All-Powerful. He is the God of Israel's army, and you have insulted him too!

46 Today the LORD will help me defeat you. I'll knock you down and cut off your head, and I'll feed the bodies of the other Philistine soldiers to the birds and wild animals. Then the whole world will know that Israel has a real God. 47 Everybody here will see that the LORD doesn't need swords or spears to save his people. The LORD always wins his battles, and he will help us defeat you.

48 When Goliath started forward, David ran toward him. 49 He put a rock in his sling and swung the sling around by its straps. When he let go of one strap, the rock flew out and hit Goliath on the forehead. It cracked his skull, and he fell facedown on the ground. 50 David defeated Goliath with a sling and a rock. He killed him without even using a sword.

51 David ran over and pulled out Goliath's sword. Then he used it to cut off Goliath's head.

When the Philistines saw what had happened to their hero, they started running away. 52 But the soldiers of Israel and Judah let out a battle cry and went after them as far as Gath[i] and Ekron. The bodies of the Philistines were scattered all along the road from Shaaraim to Gath and Ekron.

53 When the Israelite army returned from chasing the Philistines, they took what they wanted from the enemy camp. 54 David took Goliath's head to Jerusalem, but he kept Goliath's weapons in his own tent.

David Becomes One of Saul's Officers

55 After King Saul had watched David go out to fight Goliath, Saul turned to the commander of his army and said, "Abner, who is that young man?"

"Your Majesty," Abner answered, "I swear by your life that I don't know."

56 "Then find out!" Saul told him.

57 When David came back from fighting Goliath, he was still carrying Goliath's head.

Abner took David to Saul, 58 and Saul asked, "Who are you?"

"I am David the son of Jesse, a loyal Israelite from Bethlehem."

18 David and Saul finished talking, and soon David and Jonathan[j] became best friends. Jonathan thought as much of David as he did of himself. 2 From that time on, Saul kept David in his service and would not let David go back to his own family.

3 Jonathan liked David so much that they promised to always be loyal friends. 4 Jonathan took off the robe that he was wearing and gave it to David. He also gave him his military clothes,[k] his sword, his bow and arrows, and his belt.

5 David was a success in everything that Saul sent him to do, and Saul made him a high officer in his army. That pleased everyone, including Saul's other officers.

Saul Becomes David's Enemy

6 David had killed Goliath, the battle was over, and the Israelite army set out for home. As the army went along, women came out of each Israelite town to welcome King Saul. They were singing happy songs and dancing to the music of tambourines and harps. 7 They sang:

Saul has killed
a thousand enemies;
David has killed
ten thousand enemies!

8 This song made Saul very angry, and he thought, "They are saying that David has killed ten times more enemies than I ever did. Next they will want to make him king." 9 Saul never again trusted David.

10 The next day the LORD let an evil

[i] **17.52** *Gath*: One ancient translation; Hebrew "a valley." [j] **18.1** *Jonathan*: Saul's oldest son (see chapter 14). [k] **18.4** *military clothes*: Or "armor."

17.50 2 S 21.19. **17.51** 2 S 21.19; Ps 151.7. **18.7** 1 S 21.11; 29.5.

spirit take control of Saul, and he began
acting like a crazy man inside his house.
David came to play the harp for Saul as
usual, but this time Saul had a spear in his
hand. 11 Saul thought, "I'll pin David to
the wall." He threw the spear at David
twice, but David dodged and got away both
times.

12 Saul was afraid of David, because the
LORD was helping David and was no longer
helping him. 13 Saul put David in charge of
a thousand soldiers and sent him out to
fight. 14 The LORD helped David, and he
and his soldiers always won their battles.
15 This made Saul even more afraid of
David. 16 But everyone else in Judah and
Israel was loyal to[l] David, because he led
the army in battle.

17 One day, Saul told David, "If you'll be
brave and fight the LORD's battles for me,
I'll let you marry my oldest daughter
Merab." But Saul was really thinking, "I
don't want to kill David myself, so I'll let
the Philistines do it for me."

18 David answered, "How could I possibly marry your daughter? I'm not very important, and neither is my family."

19 But when the time came for David to
marry Saul's daughter Merab, Saul told her
to marry Adriel from the town of Meholah.

20 Saul had another daughter. Her name
was Michal, and Saul found out that she
was in love with David. This made Saul
happy, 21 and he thought, "I'll tell David he
can marry Michal, but I'll set it up so that
the Philistines will kill him." He told David,
"I'm going to give you a second chance to
marry one of my daughters."

22-23 Saul ordered his officials to speak
to David in private, so they went to David
and said, "Look, the king likes you, and all
of his officials are loyal to you. Why not ask
the king if you can marry his daughter
Michal?"

"I'm not rich[m] or famous enough to
marry princess Michal!" David answered.

24 The officials went back to Saul and
told him exactly what David had said.
25 Saul was hoping that the Philistines
would kill David, and he told his officials to
tell David, "The king doesn't want any silver or gold. He only wants to get even with
his enemies. All you have to do is to bring
back proof that you have killed a hundred
Philistines!"[n] 26 The officials told David,
and David wanted to marry the princess.

King Saul had set a time limit, and before it ran out, 27 David and his men left
and killed two hundred Philistines. He
brought back the proof and showed it to
Saul, so he could marry Michal. Saul
agreed to let David marry Michal. 28 Saul
knew that she loved David,[o] and he also realized that the LORD was helping David.
29 But knowing those things made Saul
even more afraid of David, and he was
David's enemy for the rest of his life.

30 The Philistine rulers kept coming to
fight Israel, but whenever David fought
them, he won. He was famous because he
won more battles against the Philistines
than any of Saul's other officers.

Saul Tries To Have David Killed

19 One day, Saul told his son Jonathan
and his officers to kill David. But
Jonathan liked David a lot, 2-3 and he
warned David, "My father is trying to have
you killed, so be very careful. Hide in a
field tomorrow morning, and I'll bring him
there. Then I'll talk to him about you, and
if I find out anything, I'll let you know."

4-5 The next morning, Jonathan reminded Saul about the many good things
David had done for him. Then he said,
"Why do you want to kill David? He hasn't
done anything to you. He has served in
your army and has always done what's
best for you. He even risked his life to kill
Goliath. The LORD helped Israel win a
great victory that day, and it made you
happy."

[l] **18.16** *was loyal to*: Or "loved." [m] **18.22,23** *not rich*: It was the custom for a man to give the bride's father some silver or gold in order to marry his daughter, and it would take a large amount to marry the daughter of the king. [n] **18.25** *proof . . . Philistines*: Hebrew "one hundred Philistine foreskins." In ancient times soldiers would sometimes cut off body parts of their dead enemies to prove how many they had killed. [o] **18.28** *she . . . David*: Hebrew; one ancient translation "all Israel was loyal to David."

6 Saul agreed and promised, "I swear by
the living LORD that I won't have David
killed!"
7 Jonathan called to David and told him
what Saul had said. Then he brought David
to Saul, and David served in Saul's army
just as he had done before.
8 The next time there was a war with
the Philistines, David fought hard and
forced them to retreat.

Michal Helps David Escape

9-10 One night, David was in Saul's
home, playing the harp for him. Saul was
sitting there, holding a spear, when an evil
spirit from the LORD took control of him.
Saul tried to pin David to the wall with the
spear, but David dodged, and it stuck in the
wall. David ran out of the house and escaped.
11 Saul sent guards to watch David's
house all night and then to kill him in the
morning.
Michal, David's wife, told him, "If you
don't escape tonight, they'll kill you tomorrow!" 12 She helped David go through a
window and climb down to the ground.[p] As
David ran off, 13 Michal put a statue in his
bed. She put goat hair on its head and
dressed it in some of David's clothes.
14 The next morning, Saul sent guards
to arrest David. But Michal told them,
"David is sick."
15 Saul sent the guards back and told
them, "Get David out of his bed and bring
him to me, so I can have him killed."
16 When the guards went in, all they
found in the bed was the statue with the
goat hair on its head.
17 "Why have you tricked me this way?"
Saul asked Michal. "You helped my enemy
get away!"
She answered, "He said he would kill
me if I didn't help him escape!"

Samuel Helps David Escape

18 Meanwhile, David went to Samuel at
Ramah and told him what Saul had done.
Then Samuel and David went to Prophets
Village[q] and stayed there.
19 Someone told Saul, "David is at
Prophets Village in Ramah."
20 Saul sent a few soldiers to bring
David back. They went to Ramah and
found Samuel in charge of a group of
prophets who were all prophesying. Then
the Spirit of God took control of the soldiers and they started prophesying too.
21 When Saul heard what had happened, he sent another group of soldiers,
but they prophesied the same way. He sent
a third group of soldiers, but the same
thing happened to them. 22 Finally, Saul
left for Ramah himself. He went as far as
the deep pit[r] at the town of Secu, and he
asked, "Where are Samuel and David?"
"At Prophets Village in Ramah," the people answered.
23 Saul left for Ramah. But as he walked
along, the Spirit of God took control of him,
and he started prophesying. Then, when he
reached Prophets Village, 24 he stripped off
his clothes and prophesied in front of
Samuel. He dropped to the ground and lay
there naked all day and night. That's how
the saying started, "Is Saul now a prophet?"

Jonathan Helps David Escape

20 David escaped from Prophets Village. Then he ran to see Jonathan
and asked, "Why does your father Saul
want to kill me? What have I done
wrong?"
2 "My father can't be trying to kill you!
He never does anything without telling me
about it. Why would he hide this from me?
It can't be true!"
3 "Jonathan, I swear it's true! But your
father knows how much you like me, and
he didn't want to break your heart. That's
why he didn't tell you. I swear by the living
LORD and by your own life that I'm only
one step ahead of death."
4 Then Jonathan said, "Tell me what to
do, and I'll do it."
5 David answered:

[p] **19.12** *ground*: The house was probably built into the town wall, allowing David to come down outside the wall. [q] **19.18** *Prophets Village*: Or "Naioth." [r] **19.22** *pit*: A cistern, a large pit dug down into the rock and used for storing rainwater.

19.11 Ps 59 Title. **19.24** 1 S 10.11, 12. **20.5** Nu 28.11.

Tomorrow is the New Moon Festival,[s] and I'm supposed to eat dinner
with your father. But instead, I'll hide
in a field until the evening of the next
day. 6 If Saul wonders where I am, tell
him, "David asked me to let him go to
his hometown of Bethlehem, so he
could take part in a sacrifice his family
makes there every year."
7 If your father says it's all right,
then I'm safe. But if he gets angry,
you'll know he wants to harm me. 8 Be
kind to me. After all, it was your idea
to promise the LORD that we would always be loyal friends. If I've done anything wrong, kill me yourself, but don't
hand me over to your father.
9 "Don't worry," Jonathan said. "If I find
out that my father wants to kill you, I'll certainly let you know."
10 "How will you do that?" David asked.
11 "Let's go out to this field, and I'll tell
you," Jonathan answered.
When they got there, 12 Jonathan said:
I swear by the LORD God of Israel,
that two days from now I'll know what
my father is planning. Of course I'll let
you know if he's friendly toward you.
13 But if he wants to harm you, I
promise to tell you and help you escape. And I ask the LORD to punish me
severely if I don't keep my promise.
I pray that the LORD will bless you,
just as he used to bless my father.
14-15 Someday the LORD will wipe out
all of your enemies. Then if I'm still
alive, please be as kind to me as the
LORD has been. But if I'm dead, be
kind to my family.
16 Jonathan and David made an agreement that even David's descendants would
have to keep.[t] Then Jonathan said, "I
pray that the LORD will take revenge on
your descendants if they break our
promise."[u]
17 Jonathan thought as much of David
as he did of himself, so he asked David to
promise once more that he would be a loyal
friend. 18 After this Jonathan said:
Tomorrow is the New Moon Festival, and people will wonder where you
are, because your place will be empty.
19 By the day after tomorrow, everyone
will think you've been gone a long
time.[v] Then go to the place where you
hid before and stay beside Going-Away
Rock.[w] 20 I'll shoot three arrows at a
target off to the side of the rock, 21 and
send my servant to find the arrows.
You'll know if it's safe to come out
by what I tell him. If it is safe, I swear
by the living LORD that I'll say, "The arrows are on this side of you! Pick them
up!" 22 But if it isn't safe, I'll say to the
boy, "The arrows are farther away!"
This will mean that the LORD wants
you to leave, and you must go. 23 But
he will always watch us to make sure
that we keep the promise we made to
each other.
24 So David hid there in the field.
During the New Moon Festival, Saul sat
down to eat 25 by the wall, just as he always
did. Jonathan sat across from him,[x] and
Abner sat next to him. But David's place
was empty. 26 Saul didn't say anything that
day, because he was thinking, "Something
must have happened to make David unfit
to be at the Festival.[y] Yes, something must
have happened."
27 The day after the New Moon Festival, when David's place was still empty,
Saul asked Jonathan, "Why hasn't that son
of Jesse come to eat with us? He wasn't

[s]**20.5** *New Moon Festival*: The first day of the month, when Israelites offered special sacrifices to the LORD and had special sacred meals. [t]**20.16** *Jonathan . . . keep*: Or, continuing Jonathan's statement to David, "You and your descendants must not kill off my descendants." [u]**20.16** *I pray . . . promise*: Or "I pray that the LORD take revenge on you if you break our promise!" [v]**20.19** *By . . . time*: One possible meaning for the difficult Hebrew text. [w]**20.19** *Going-Away Rock*: Or "Ezel Rock"; one ancient translation "that mound" (see 20.41). [x]**20.25** *sat . . . him*: One ancient translation; Hebrew "stood up." [y]**20.26** *unfit . . . Festival*: During the New Moon Festival a sacred meal was served that could only be eaten by people who were properly prepared. Some of the things that could make a person unfit are listed in Leviticus 7.20, 21; 15.2, 31; 22.4-8; Deuteronomy 23.10, 11.

20.14,15 2 S 9.1.

here yesterday, and he still isn't here today!"
28-29 Jonathan answered, "The reason
David hasn't come to eat with you is that
he begged me to let him go to Bethlehem.
He said, 'Please let me go. My family is offering a sacrifice, and my brother told me I
have to be there. Do me this favor and let
me slip away to see my brothers.' "
30 Saul was furious with Jonathan and
yelled, "You're no son of mine, you traitor!
I know you've chosen to be loyal to that son
of Jesse. You should be ashamed of yourself! And your own mother should be
ashamed that you were ever born. 31 You'll
never be safe, and your kingdom will be in
danger as long as that son of Jesse is alive.
Turn him over to me now! He deserves
to die!"
32 "Why do you want to kill David?"
Jonathan asked. "What has he done?"
33 Saul threw his spear at Jonathan and
tried to kill him. Then Jonathan was sure
that his father really did want to kill David.
34 Jonathan was angry that his father had
insulted David[z] so terribly. He got up, left
the table, and didn't eat anything all
that day.
35 In the morning, Jonathan went out to
the field to meet David. He took a servant
boy along 36 and told him, "When I shoot
the arrows, you run and find them for me."
The boy started running, and Jonathan
shot an arrow so that it would go beyond
him. 37 When the boy got near the place
where the arrow had landed, Jonathan
shouted, "Isn't the arrow on past you?"
38 Jonathan shouted to him again, "Hurry
up! Don't stop!"
The boy picked up the arrows and
brought them back to Jonathan, 39 but he
had no idea about what was going on. Only
Jonathan and David knew. 40 Jonathan gave
his weapons to the boy and told him, "Take
these back into town."
41 After the boy had gone, David got up
from beside the mound[a] and bowed very
low three times. Then he and Jonathan
kissed[b] each other and cried, but David
cried louder. 42 Jonathan said, "Take care of
yourself. And remember, we each have
asked the LORD to watch and make sure
that we and our descendants keep our
promise forever."
David left and Jonathan went back to
town.

Ahimelech Helps David

21 David went to see Ahimelech, a
priest who lived in the town of Nob.
Ahimelech was trembling with fear as he
came out to meet David. "Why are you
alone?" Ahimelech asked. "Why isn't anyone else with you?"
2 "I'm on a mission for King Saul,"
David answered. "He ordered me not to tell
anyone what the mission is all about, so I
had my soldiers stay somewhere else. 3 Do
you have any food you can give me? Could
you spare five loaves of bread?"
4 "The only bread I have is the sacred
bread," the priest told David. "You can have
it if your soldiers didn't sleep with women
last night."[c]
5 "Of course we didn't sleep with
women," David answered. "I never let my
men do that when we're on a mission.
They have to be acceptable to worship God
even when we're on a regular mission, and
today we're on a special mission."
6 The only bread the priest had was the
sacred bread that he had taken from the
place of worship after putting out the fresh
loaves. So he gave it to David.
7 It so happened that one of Saul's officers was there, worshiping the LORD that
day. His name was Doeg the Edomite,[d] and
he was the strongest of[e] Saul's shepherds.
8 David asked Ahimelech, "Do you have
a spear or a sword? I had to leave so
quickly on this mission for the king that I
didn't bring along my sword or any other
weapons."

[z]**20.34** *insulted David*: Or "insulted him" (that is, Jonathan). [a]**20.41** *the mound*: One ancient translation; Hebrew "from the south side." [b]**20.41** *kissed*: A common way of greeting or saying good-by in biblical times (see Mark 14.44). [c]**21.4** *night*: Having sex was one of the things that would make someone temporarily unfit to take part in worship or a sacred meal (see Exodus 19.15; Leviticus 15.18). [d]**21.7** *Edomite*: A person from the country of Edom, to the south of Israel. [e]**21.7** *the strongest of*: Or "in charge of."

21.1-6 Mt 12.3, 4; Mk 2.25, 26; Lk 6.3, 4. **21.6** Lv 24.5-9.

9 The priest answered, "The only sword
here is the one that belonged to Goliath the
Philistine. You were the one who killed him
in Elah Valley, and so you can take his
sword if you want to. It's wrapped in a cloth
behind the statue."

"It's the best sword there is," David said.
"I'll take it!"

David Tries To Find Safety in Gath

10 David kept on running from Saul that
day until he came to Gath,[f] where he met
with King Achish. 11 The officers of King
Achish were also there, and they asked
Achish, "Isn't David a king back in his own
country? Don't the Israelites dance and
sing,

'Saul has killed
  a thousand enemies;
David has killed
  ten thousand enemies'?"

12 David thought about what they were
saying, and it made him afraid of Achish.
13 So right there in front of everyone, he
pretended to be insane. He acted confused
and scratched up the doors of the town
gate, while drooling in his beard.

14 "Look at him!" Achish said to his officers. "You can see he's crazy. Why did you
bring him to me? 15 I have enough crazy
people without your bringing another one
here. Keep him away from my palace!"

People Join David

22 When David escaped from the
town of Gath, he went to Adullam
Cave. His brothers and the rest of his
family found out where he was, and they
followed him there. 2 A lot of other people
joined him too. Some were in trouble,
others were angry or in debt, and David
was soon the leader of four hundred men.

3 David left Adullam Cave and went to
the town of Mizpeh in Moab, where he
talked with the king of Moab. "Please,"
David said, "let my father and mother stay
with you until I find out what God will do
with me." 4 So he brought his parents to
the king of Moab, and they stayed with him
while David was in hiding.

5 One day the prophet Gad told David,
"Don't stay here! Go back to Judah." David
then left and went to Hereth Forest.

Saul Kills the Priests of the LORD

6 Saul was sitting under a small tree on
top of the hill at Gibeah when he heard
that David and his men had been seen.
Saul was holding his spear, and his officers
were standing in front of him. 7 He told
them:

Listen to me! You belong to the
Benjamin tribe,[g] so if that son of Jesse
ever becomes king, he won't give you
fields or vineyards. He won't make you
officers in charge of thousands or hundreds as I have done. 8 But you're all
plotting against me! Not one of you
told me that my own son Jonathan had
made an agreement with him. Not one
of you cared enough to tell me that
Jonathan had helped one of my officers[h] rebel. Now that son of Jesse is
trying to ambush me.

9 Doeg the Edomite was standing with
the other officers and spoke up, "When I
was in the town of Nob, I saw that son of
Jesse. He was visiting the priest Ahimelech
the son of Ahitub. 10 Ahimelech talked to
the LORD for him, then gave him food and
the sword that had belonged to Goliath the
Philistine."

11 Saul sent a message to Ahimelech
and his whole family of priests at Nob, ordering them to come to him. When they
came, 12 Saul told them, "Listen to me, you
son of Ahitub."

"Certainly, Your Majesty," Ahimelech
answered.

13 Saul demanded, "Why did you plot

---

[f] **21.10** *Gath*: One of the five main Philistine towns. [g] **22.7** *You . . . Benjamin tribe*: David was from the Judah tribe and would have given special privileges to the people of his own tribe rather than to those of Benjamin. [h] **22.7,8** *son of Jesse . . . officers*: That is, David. Saul avoids even saying David's name.

21.9 1 S 17.51. **21.11** 1 S 18.7; 29.5. **21.12** Ps 56 Title. **21.13** Ps 34 Title.
22.1 Ps 57 Title; Ps 142 Title. **22.9,10** 1 S 21.7-9; Ps 52 Title.

against me with that son of Jesse? You
helped him rebel against me by giving him
food and a sword, and by talking with God
for him. Now he's trying to ambush me!"
14 "Your Majesty, none of your officers is
more loyal than David!" Ahimelech replied.
"He's your son-in-law and the captain of
your bodyguard. Everyone in your family
respects him. 15 This isn't the first time I've
talked with God for David, and it's never
made you angry before! Please don't accuse
me or my family like this. I have no idea
what's going on!"
16 "Ahimelech," Saul said, "you and your
whole family are going to die."
17 Saul shouted to his bodyguards,
"These priests of the LORD helped David!
They knew he was running away, but they
didn't tell me. Kill them!"

But the king's officers would not attack
the priests of the LORD.
18 Saul turned to Doeg, who was from
Edom, and said, "Kill the priests!"

On that same day, Doeg killed eighty-
five priests. 19 Then he attacked the town
of Nob, where the priests had lived, and he
killed everyone there—men, women, children, and babies. He even killed their cattle, donkeys, and sheep.

Only Abiathar Escapes from Nob

20 Ahimelech's son Abiathar was the
only one who escaped. He ran to David
21 and told him, "Saul has murdered the
priests at Nob!"
22 David answered, "That day when I
saw Doeg, I knew he would tell Saul! Your
family died because of me. 23 Stay here.
Isn't the same person trying to kill both of
us? Don't worry! You'll be safe here with me."

David Rescues the Town of Keilah

23 One day some people told David,
"The Philistines keep attacking the
town of Keilah and stealing grain from the
threshing place."
2 David asked the LORD, "Should I attack these Philistines?"

"Yes," the LORD answered. "Attack them
and rescue Keilah."
3 But David's men said, "Look, even
here in Judah we're afraid of the
Philistines. We will be terrified if we try to
fight them at Keilah!"[i]
4 David asked the LORD about it again.
"Leave right now," the LORD answered. "I
will give you victory over the Philistines at
Keilah."
5 David and his men went there
and fiercely attacked the Philistines. They
killed many of them, then led away
their cattle, and rescued the people of
Keilah.
6-8 Meanwhile, Saul heard that David
was in Keilah. "God has let me catch
David," Saul said. "David is trapped inside
a walled town where the gates can be
locked." Saul decided to go there and surround the town, in order to trap David and
his men. He sent messengers who told the
towns and villages, "Send men to serve in
Saul's army!"

By this time, Abiathar had joined David
in Keilah and had brought along everything he needed to get answers from God.
9 David heard about Saul's plan to capture him, and he told Abiathar, "Let's ask
God what we should do."
10 David prayed, "LORD God of Israel, I
was told that Saul is planning to come
here. What should I do? Suppose he
threatens to destroy the town because of
me. 11 Would the leaders of Keilah turn me
over to Saul? Or is he really coming?
Please tell me, LORD."

"Yes, he will come," the LORD answered.
12 David asked, "Would the leaders of
Keilah hand me and my soldiers over to
Saul?"

"Yes, they would," the LORD answered.
13 David and his six hundred men got
out of there fast and started moving from
place to place. Saul heard that David had
left Keilah, and he decided not to go after him.

Jonathan Says David Will Be King

14 David stayed in hideouts in the hill
country of Ziph Desert. Saul kept searching, but God never let Saul catch him.
15 One time, David was at Horesh in

[i] **23.3** *Keilah*: Keilah was probably not controlled by Israelites at this time.

Ziph Desert. He was afraid because[j] Saul had come to the area to kill him. 16 But Jonathan went to see David, and God helped him encourage David. 17 "Don't be afraid," Jonathan said. "My father Saul will never get his hands on you. In fact, you're going to be the next king of Israel, and I'll be your highest official. Even my father knows it's true."

18 They both promised the LORD that they would always be loyal to each other. Then Jonathan went home, but David stayed at Horesh.

David Escapes from Saul

19 Some people from the town of Ziph went to Saul at Gibeah and said, "Your Majesty, David has a hideout not far from us! It's near Horesh, somewhere on Mount Hachilah south of Jeshimon.[k] 20 If you come, we will help you catch him."

21 Saul told them:

You've done me a big favor, and I pray that the LORD will bless you. 22 Now please do just a little more for me. Find out exactly where David is, as well as where he goes, and who has seen him there. I've been told that he's very tricky. 23 Find out where all his hiding places are and come back when you're sure. Then I'll go with you. If he is still in the area, or anywhere among the clans of Judah, I'll find him.

24 The people from Ziph went back ahead of Saul, and they found out that David and his men were still south of Jeshimon in the Maon Desert. 25 Saul and his army set out to find David. But David heard that Saul was coming, and he went to a place called The Rock, one of his hideouts in Maon Desert.

Saul found out where David was and started closing in on him. 26 Saul was going around a hill on one side, and David and his men were on the other side, trying to get away. Saul and his soldiers were just about to capture David and his men, 27 when a messenger came to Saul and said, "Come quickly! The Philistines are attacking Israel and taking everything."

28 Saul stopped going after David and went back to fight the Philistines. That's why the place is called "Escape Rock."

29 David left and went to live in the hideouts at En-Gedi.

David Lets Saul Live

24 When Saul got back from fighting off the Philistines, he heard that David was in the desert around En-Gedi. 2 Saul led three thousand of Israel's best soldiers out to look for David and his men near Wild Goat Rocks at En-Gedi. 3 There were some sheep pens along the side of the road, and one of them was built around the entrance to a cave. Saul went into the cave to relieve himself.

David and his men were hiding at the back of the cave. 4 They whispered to David, "The LORD told you he was going to let you defeat your enemies and do whatever you want with them. This must be the day the LORD was talking about."

David sneaked over and cut off a small piece[l] of Saul's robe, but Saul didn't notice a thing. 5 Afterwards, David was sorry that he had even done that, 6-7 and he told his men, "Stop talking foolishly. We're not going to attack Saul. He's my king, and I pray that the LORD will keep me from doing anything to harm his chosen king."

Saul left the cave and started down the road. 8 Soon, David also got up and left the cave. "Your Majesty!" he shouted from a distance.

Saul turned around to look. David bowed down very low 9 and said:

Your Majesty, why do you listen to people who say that I'm trying to harm you? 10 You can see for yourself that the LORD gave me the chance to catch you in the cave today. Some of my men wanted to kill you, but I wouldn't let them do it. I told them, "I will not harm the LORD's chosen king!" 11 Your Majesty, look at what I'm holding. You

[j] **23.15** *He . . . because*: Or "He saw that." [k] **23.19** *Jeshimon*: A place in the desert near the southern border of Judah. [l] **24.4** *small piece*: Hebrew "corner" or "lower hem."

23.18 1 S 18.3. **23.19** Ps 54 Title. **24.3** Ps 57 Title; Ps 142 Title. **24.6,7** 1 S 26.11.

can see that it's a piece of your robe. If I could cut off a piece of your robe, I could have killed you. But I let you live, and that should prove I'm not trying to harm you or to rebel. I haven't done anything to you, and yet you keep trying to ambush and kill me.

12 I'll let the LORD decide which one of us has done right. I pray that the LORD will punish you for what you're doing to me, but I won't do anything to you. 13 An old proverb says, "Only evil people do evil things," and so I won't harm you.

14 Why should the king of Israel be out chasing me, anyway? I'm as worthless as a dead dog or a flea. 15 I pray that the LORD will help me escape and show that I am in the right.

16 "David, my son—is that you?" Saul asked. Then he started crying 17 and said:

David, you're a better person than I am. You treated me with kindness, even though I've been cruel to you. 18 You've told me how you were kind enough not to kill me when the LORD gave you the chance. 19 If you really were my enemy, you wouldn't have let me leave here alive. I pray that the LORD will give you a big reward for what you did today.

20 I realize now that you will be the next king, and a powerful king at that. 21 Promise me with the LORD as your witness, that you won't wipe out my descendants. Let them live to keep my family name alive.

22 So David promised, and Saul went home. David and his men returned to their hideout.

Samuel Dies

25 Samuel died, and people from all over Israel gathered to mourn for him when he was buried at his home[m] in Ramah. Meanwhile, David moved his camp to Paran Desert.[n]

Abigail Keeps David from Killing Innocent People

2-3 Nabal was a very rich man who lived in Maon. He owned three thousand sheep and a thousand goats, which he kept at Carmel.[o] His wife Abigail was sensible and beautiful, but he was from the Caleb clan[p] and was rough and mean.

4 One day, Nabal was in Carmel, having his servants cut the wool from his sheep. David was in the desert when he heard about it. 5-6 So he sent ten men to Carmel with this message for Nabal:

I hope that you and your family are healthy and that all is going well for you. 7 I've heard that you are cutting the wool from your sheep.

When your shepherds were with us in Carmel, we didn't harm them, and nothing was ever stolen from them. 8 Ask your shepherds, and they'll tell you the same thing.

My servants are your servants, and you are like a father to me. This is a day for celebrating,[q] so please be kind and share some of your food with us.

9 David's men went to Nabal and gave him David's message, then they waited for Nabal's answer.

10 This is what he said:

Who does this David think he is? That son of Jesse is just one more slave on the run from his master, and there are too many of them these days. 11 What makes you think I would take my bread, my water, and the meat that I've had cooked for my own servants[r] and give it to you? Besides, I'm not sure that David sent you![s]

12 The men returned to their camp and told David everything Nabal had said.

[m]**25.1** *at his home*: Hebrew "in his house." Family tombs were sometimes underneath the house or in the courtyard of the home. [n]**25.1** *Paran Desert*: Hebrew; some manuscripts of one ancient translation "Maon Desert." [o]**25.2,3** *Carmel*: About one mile north of Maon in the Southern Desert of Judah. [p]**25.2,3** *from the Caleb clan*: Or "behaved like a dog." [q]**25.8** *celebrating*: Cutting the wool from the sheep was a time for celebrating as well as for working.
[r]**25.11** *servants*: Hebrew "shearers," the servants who cut the wool from the sheep.
[s]**25.11** *I'm not sure . . . sent you*: Or "I don't know where you come from."
24.14 1 S 26.20.

[13] "Everybody get your swords!" David ordered.

They all strapped on their swords. Two hundred men stayed behind to guard the camp, but the other four hundred followed David.

[14-16] Meanwhile, one of Nabal's servants told Abigail:

David's men were often nearby while we were taking care of the sheep in the fields. They were very good to us, they never hurt us, and nothing was ever stolen from us while they were nearby. With them around day or night, we were as safe as we would have been inside a walled city.

David sent some messengers from the desert to wish our master well, but he shouted insults at them. [17] He's a bully who won't listen to anyone.

Isn't there something you can do? Please think of something! Or else our master and his family and everyone who works for him are all doomed.

[18] Abigail quickly got together two hundred loaves of bread, two large clay jars of wine, the meat from five sheep, a large sack of roasted grain, a hundred handfuls of raisins, and two hundred handfuls of dried figs. She loaded all the food on donkeys [19] and told her servants, "Take this on ahead, and I'll catch up with you." She didn't tell her husband Nabal what she was doing.

[20] Abigail was riding her donkey on the path that led around the hillside, when suddenly she met David and his men heading straight at her.

[21] David had just been saying, "I surely wasted my time guarding Nabal's things in the desert and keeping them from being stolen! I was good to him, and now he pays me back with insults. [22] I swear that by morning, there won't be a man or boy left from his family or his servants' families. I pray that God will punish me[t] if I don't do it!"

[23] Abigail quickly got off her donkey and bowed down in front of David. [24] Then she said:

Sir, please let me explain! [25] Don't pay any attention to that good-for-nothing Nabal. His name means "fool," and it really fits him!

I didn't see the men you sent, [26-27] but please take this gift of food that I've brought and share it with your followers. The LORD has kept you from taking revenge and from killing innocent people. But I hope your enemies and anyone else who wants to harm you will end up like Nabal. I swear this by the living LORD and by your life.

[28] Please forgive me if I say a little more. The LORD will always protect you and your family, because you fight for him. I pray that you won't ever do anything evil as long as you live. [29] The LORD your God will keep you safe when your enemies try to kill you. But he will snatch away their lives quicker than you can throw a rock from a sling.

[30] The LORD has promised to do many good things for you, even to make you the ruler of Israel. The LORD will keep his promises to you, [31] and now your conscience will be clear, because you won't be guilty of taking revenge and killing innocent people.

When the LORD does all those good things for you, please remember me.

[32] David told her:

I praise the LORD God of Israel! He must have sent you to meet me today. [33] And you should also be praised. Your good sense kept me from taking revenge and killing innocent people. [34] If you hadn't come to meet me so quickly, every man and boy in Nabal's family and in his servants' families would have been killed by morning. I swear by the living LORD God of Israel who protected you that this is the truth.

[35] David accepted the food Abigail had brought. "Don't worry," he said. "You can go home now. I'll do what you asked."

[36] Abigail went back home and found Nabal throwing a party fit for a king. He was very drunk and feeling good, so she

[t] **25.22** *me*: One ancient translation; Hebrew "my enemies."

didn't tell him anything that night. 37 But
when he sobered up the next morning, Abigail told him everything that had happened. Nabal had a heart attack, and he lay
in bed as still as a stone. 38 Ten days later,
the LORD took his life.
39-40 David heard that Nabal had died. "I
praise the LORD!" David said. "He has
judged Nabal guilty for insulting me. The
LORD kept me from doing anything wrong,
and he made sure that Nabal hurt only
himself with his own evil."

David and Abigail Are Married

Abigail was still at Carmel. So David
sent messengers to ask her if she would
marry him.
41 She bowed down and said, "I would
willingly be David's slave and wash his servants' feet."
42 Abigail quickly got ready and went
back with David's messengers. She rode on
her donkey, while five of her servant
women walked alongside. She and David
were married as soon as she arrived.
43 David had earlier married Ahinoam
from the town of Jezreel, so both she and
Abigail were now David's wives.[u] 44 Meanwhile, Saul had arranged for Michal[v] to
marry Palti the son of Laish, who came
from the town of Gallim.

David Again Lets Saul Live

26 Once again,[w] some people from
Ziph went to Gibeah to talk with
Saul. "David has a hideout on Mount
Hachilah near Jeshimon out in the desert,"
they told him.
2 Saul took three thousand of Israel's
best soldiers and went to look for David
there in Ziph Desert. 3 Saul set up camp on
Mount Hachilah, which is across the road
from Jeshimon. But David was hiding out
in the desert.
When David heard that Saul was following him, 4 he sent some spies to find out if
it was true. 5 Then he sneaked up to Saul's
camp. He noticed that Saul and his army
commander Abner the son of Ner were
sleeping in the middle of the camp, with
soldiers sleeping all around them. 6 David
asked Ahimelech the Hittite and Joab's
brother Abishai,[x] "Which one of you will go
with me into Saul's camp?"
"I will!" Abishai answered.
7 That same night, David and Abishai
crept into the camp. Saul was sleeping, and
his spear was stuck in the ground not far
from his head. Abner and the soldiers were
sound asleep all around him.
8 Abishai whispered, "This time God has
let you get your hands on your enemy! I'll
pin him to the ground with one thrust of
his own spear."
9 "Don't kill him!" David whispered
back. "The LORD will punish anyone who
kills his chosen king. 10 As surely as the
LORD lives, the LORD will kill Saul, or Saul
will die a natural death or be killed in battle. 11 But I pray that the LORD will keep me
from harming his chosen king. Let's grab
his spear and his water jar and get out of
here!"
12 David took the spear and the water
jar, then left the camp. None of Saul's soldiers knew what had happened or even
woke up—the LORD had made all of them
fall sound asleep. 13 David and Abishai
crossed the valley and went to the top of
the next hill, where they were at a safe distance. 14 "Abner!" David shouted toward
Saul's army. "Can you hear me?"
Abner shouted back. "Who dares disturb
the king?"
15 "Abner, what kind of a man are you?"
David replied. "Aren't you supposed to be
the best soldier in Israel? Then why didn't
you protect your king? Anyone who went
into your camp could have killed him
tonight.[y] 16 You're a complete failure! I
swear by the living LORD that you and your
men deserve to die for not protecting the
LORD's chosen king. Look and see if you

[u]**25.43** *wives*: Having more than one wife was allowed in those times. [v]**25.44** *Michal*: David's first wife (see 18.20—19.17). [w]**26.1** *again*: See 23.19. [x]**26.6** *Abishai*: Hebrew "Abishai the son of Zeruiah." Zeruiah was David's older sister, so Abishai and Joab were David's nephews (see 1 Chronicles 2.12-17; 2 Samuel 17.25 and the note there). [y]**26.15** *Anyone . . . tonight*: Or "Someone went into your camp to kill him tonight."

25.44 2 S 3.14-16. **26.1** Ps 54 Title. **26.11** 1 S 24.6, 7.

can find the king's spear and the water jar that were near his head."

17 Saul could tell it was David's voice, and he called out, "David, my son! Is that you?"

"Yes it is, Your Majesty. 18 Why are you after me? Have I done something wrong, or have I committed a crime? 19 Please listen to what I have to say. If the LORD has turned you against me, maybe a sacrifice will make him change his mind. But if some people have turned you against me, I hope the LORD will punish them! They have forced me to leave the land that belongs to the LORD and have told me to worship foreign gods.[z] 20 Don't let me die in a land far away from the LORD. I'm no more important than a flea! Why should the king of Israel hunt me down as if I were a bird in the mountains?"

21 "David, you had the chance to kill me today. But you didn't. I was very wrong about you. It was a terrible mistake for me to try to kill you. I've acted like a fool, but I'll never try to harm you again. You're like a son to me, so please come back."

22 "Your Majesty, here's your spear! Have one of your soldiers come and get it. 23 The LORD put you in my power today, but you are his chosen king and I wouldn't harm you. The LORD rewards people who are faithful and live right. 24 I saved your life today, and I pray that the LORD will protect me and keep me safe."

25 "David, my son, I pray that the Lord will bless you and make you successful!"

David in Philistia

27 Saul went back home. David also left, 1 but he thought to himself, "One of these days, Saul is going to kill me. The only way to escape from him is to go to Philistia. Then I'll be outside of Israel, and Saul will give up trying to catch me."

2-3 David and his six hundred men went across the border to stay in Gath with King Achish the son of Maoch. His men brought their families with them. David brought his wife Ahinoam whose hometown was Jezreel, and he also brought his wife Abigail who had been married to Nabal from Carmel. 4 When Saul found out that David had run off to Gath, he stopped trying to catch him.

5 One day, David was talking with Achish and said, "If you are happy with me, then let me live in one of the towns in the countryside. I'm not important enough to live here with you in the royal city."

6 Achish gave David the town of Ziklag that same day, and Ziklag has belonged to the kings of Judah ever since.

7 David was in Philistia for a year and four months. 8 The Geshurites, the Girzites, and the Amalekites lived in the area from Telam to Shur[a] and on as far as Egypt, and David often attacked their towns. 9 Whenever David and his men attacked a town, they took the sheep, cattle, donkeys, camels, and the clothing, and killed everyone who lived there.

After he returned from a raid, David always went to see Achish, 10 who would ask, "Where did you attack today?"[b]

David would answer, "Oh, we attacked some desert town that belonged to the Judah tribe." Sometimes David would say, "Oh, we attacked a town in the desert where the Jerahmeel clan lives" or "We attacked a town in the desert where the Kenites[c] live." 11 That's why David killed everyone in the towns he attacked. He thought, "If I let any of them live, they might come to Gath and tell what I've really been doing."

David made these raids all the time he was in Philistia. 12 But Achish trusted David and thought, "David's people must be furious with him. From now on he will have to take orders from me."

[z]**26.19** *gods*: In ancient times it was often believed that gods (even the God of Israel) could only be properly worshiped in their own countries, and only a country's gods should be worshiped in that country. [a]**27.8** *lived . . . Shur*: One ancient translation; Hebrew "had lived for a long time in Shur." [b]**27.10** *Where . . . today*: A few Hebrew manuscripts, the Dead Sea Scrolls, and three ancient translations; most Hebrew manuscripts "Didn't you make a raid today?"
[c]**27.10** *Jerahmeel . . . Kenites*: These were clans of the Judah tribe.

Saul Talks with Samuel's Ghost

28 1-3 Samuel had died some time earlier,[d] and people from all over Israel had attended his funeral in his hometown of Ramah.
Meanwhile, Saul had been trying to get
rid of everyone who spoke with the spirits
of the dead.[e] But one day the Philistines
brought their soldiers together to attack
Israel.
Achish told David, "Of course, you know
that you and your men must fight as part of
our Philistine army."
David answered, "That will give you a
chance to see for yourself just how well we
can fight!"
"In that case," Achish said, "you and
your men will always be my bodyguards."
4 The Philistines went to Shunem and
set up camp. Saul called the army of Israel
together, and they set up their camp in
Gilboa. 5 Saul took one look at the Philistine army and started shaking with fear.
6 So he asked the LORD what to do. But
the LORD would not answer, either in a
dream or by a priest or a prophet. 7 Then
Saul told his officers, "Find me a woman
who can talk to the spirits of the dead.
I'll go to her and find out what's going to
happen."
His servants told him, "There's a
woman at Endor who can talk to spirits of
the dead."
8 That night, Saul put on different
clothing so nobody would recognize him.
Then he and two of his men went to the
woman, and asked, "Will you bring up the
ghost of someone for us?"
9 The woman said, "Why are you trying
to trick me and get me killed? You know
King Saul has gotten rid of everyone who
talks to the spirits of the dead!"
10 Saul replied, "I swear by the living
LORD that nothing will happen to you because of this."
11 "Who do you want me to bring up?"
she asked.
"Bring up the ghost of Samuel," he answered.
12 When the woman saw Samuel, she
screamed. Then she turned to Saul and
said, "You've tricked me! You're the king!"
13 "Don't be afraid," Saul replied. "Just
tell me what you see."
She answered, "I see a spirit rising up
out of the ground."
14 "What does it look like?"
"It looks like an old man wearing a
robe."
Saul knew it was Samuel, so he bowed
down low.
15 "Why are you bothering me by bringing me up like this?" Samuel asked.
"I'm terribly worried," Saul answered.
"The Philistines are about to attack me.
God has turned his back on me and won't
answer any more by prophets or by dreams.
What should I do?"
16 Samuel said:

> If the LORD has turned away from
> you and is now your enemy, don't ask
> me what to do. 17 I've already told you:
> The LORD has sworn to take the king-
> dom from you and give it to David.
> And that's just what he's doing!
> 18 When the LORD was angry with the
> Amalekites, he told you to destroy
> them, but you didn't do it. That's why
> the LORD is doing this to you. 19 To-
> morrow the LORD will let the
> Philistines defeat Israel's army, then
> you and your sons will join me down
> here in the world of the dead.

20 At once, Saul collapsed and lay
stretched out on the floor, terrified at what
Samuel had said. He was weak because
he had not eaten anything since the day
before.
21 The woman came over to Saul, and
when she saw that he was completely terrified, she said, "Your Majesty, I listened to
you and risked my life to do what you
asked. 22 Now please listen to me. Let me
get you a little something to eat. It will give
you strength for your walk back to camp."

[d]**28.1-3** *earlier*: See 25.1. [e]**28.1-3** *dead*: Many people believed that it was possible to talk to spirits of the dead, and that these spirits could tell the future.

28.1-3 a 1 S 25.1; **b** Lv 20.27; Dt 18.10, 11. **28.6** Nu 27.21. **28.11** Si 46.20. **28.17** 1 S 15.28. **28.18** 1 S 15.3-9.

23 "No, I won't eat!"

But his officers and the woman kept on urging Saul, until he finally agreed. He got up off the floor and sat on the bed. 24 Right away the woman killed a calf that she had been fattening up. She cooked part of the meat and baked some thin bread.[f] 25 Then she served the food to Saul and his officers, who ate and left before daylight.

The Philistines Send David Back

29 The Philistines had brought their whole army to Aphek,[g] while Israel's army was camping near Jezreel Spring. 2-3 The Philistine rulers and their troops were marching past the Philistine army commanders in groups of a hundred and a thousand. When David and his men marched by at the end with Achish, the commanders said, "What are these worthless Israelites doing here?"

"They are David's men," Achish answered. "David used to be one of Saul's officers, but he left Saul and joined my army a long time ago. I've never had even one complaint about him."

4 The Philistine army commanders were angry and shouted:

> Send David back to the town you gave him. We won't have him going into the battle with us. He could turn and fight against us! Saul would take David back as an officer if David brought him the heads of our soldiers.
> 5 The Israelites even dance and sing,
>
> "Saul has killed
>   a thousand enemies;
> David has killed
>   ten thousand enemies!"

6 Achish called David over and said:

> I swear by the living LORD that you've been honest with me, and I want you to fight by my side. I don't think you've done anything wrong from the day you joined me until this very moment. But the other Philistine rulers don't want you to come along. 7 Go on back home and try not to upset them.

8 "But what have I done?" David asked. "Do you know of anything I've ever done that would keep me from fighting the enemies of my king?"[h]

9 Achish said:

> I believe that you're as good as an angel of God, but our army commanders have decided that you can't fight in this battle. 10 You and your troops will have to go back to the town I gave you.[i] Get up and leave tomorrow morning as soon as it's light. I am pleased with you, so don't let any of this bother you.[j]

11 David and his men got up early in the morning and headed back toward Philistia, while the Philistines left for Jezreel.

David Rescues His Soldiers' Families

30 It took David and his men three days to reach Ziklag. But while they had been away, the Amalekites had been raiding in the desert around there. They had attacked Ziklag, burned it to the ground, 2 and had taken away the women and children. 3 When David and his men came to Ziklag, they saw the burned-out ruins and learned that their families had been taken captive. 4 They started crying and kept it up until they were too weak to cry any more. 5 David's two wives, Ahinoam and Abigail, had been taken captive with everyone else.

6 David was desperate. His soldiers were so upset over what had happened to their sons and daughters that they were thinking about stoning David to death. But he felt the LORD God giving him strength, 7 and he said to the priest, "Abiathar, let's ask God what to do."

Abiathar brought everything he needed to get answers from God, and he went over

[f]**28.24** *thin bread*: Bread made without yeast, since there was no time for the bread to rise. [g]**29.1** *Aphek*: The events of chapter 29 probably took place as the Philistine army was on its way to Shunem, which they reached in 28.4. [h]**29.8** *my king*: David may be referring to either Saul or Achish. [i]**29.10** *go . . . you*: One ancient translation; these words are not in the Hebrew text. [j]**29.10** *I am . . . bother you*: One ancient translation; these words are not in the Hebrew text.

29.5 1 S 18.7; 21.11. **30.5** 1 S 25.42, 43. **30.7** 1 S 22.20-23.

to David. [8] Then David asked the LORD, "Should I go after the people who raided our town? Can I catch up with them?"

"Go after them," the LORD answered. "You will catch up with them, and you will rescue your families."

[9-10] David led his six hundred men to Besor Gorge, but two hundred of them were too tired to go across. So they stayed behind, while David and the other four hundred men crossed the gorge.

[11] Some of David's men found an Egyptian out in a field and took him to David. They gave the Egyptian some bread, and he ate it. Then they gave him a drink of water, [12] some dried figs, and two handfuls of raisins. This was the first time in three days he had tasted food or water. Now he felt much better.

[13] "Who is your master?" David asked. "And where do you come from?"

"I'm from Egypt," the young man answered. "I'm the servant of an Amalekite, but he left me here three days ago because I was sick. [14] We had attacked some towns in the desert where the Cherethites live, in the area that belongs to Judah, and in the desert where the Caleb clan lives. And we burned down Ziklag."

[15] "Will you take me to those Amalekites?" David asked.

"Yes, I will, if you promise with God as a witness that you won't kill me or hand me over to my master."

[16] He led David to the Amalekites. They were eating and drinking everywhere, celebrating because of what they had taken from Philistia and Judah. [17] David attacked just before sunrise the next day and fought until sunset.[k] Four hundred Amalekites rode away on camels, but they were the only ones who escaped.

[18] David rescued his two wives and everyone else the Amalekites had taken from Ziklag. [19] No one was missing—young or old, sons or daughters. David brought back everything that had been stolen, [20] including their livestock.

David also took the sheep and cattle that the Amalekites had with them, but he kept these separate from the others. Everyone agreed that these would be David's reward.

[21] On the way back, David went to the two hundred men he had left at Besor Gorge, because they had been too tired to keep up with him. They came toward David and the people who were with him. When David was close enough, he greeted the two hundred men and asked how they were doing.

[22] Some of David's men were good-for-nothings, and they said, "Those men didn't go with us to the battle, so they don't get any of the things we took back from the Amalekites. Let them take their wives and children and go!"

[23] But David said:

> My friends, don't be so greedy with what the LORD has given us! The LORD protected us and gave us victory over the people who attacked. [24] Who would pay attention to you, anyway? Soldiers who stay behind to guard the camp get as much as those who go into battle.

[25] David made this a law for Israel, and it has been the same ever since.

[26] David went back to Ziklag with everything they had taken from the Amalekites. He sent some of these things as gifts to his friends who were leaders of Judah, and he told them, "We took these things from the LORD's enemies. Please accept them as a gift."

[27-31] This is a list of the towns where David sent gifts: Bethel,[l] Ramoth in the Southern Desert, Jattir, Aroer, Siphmoth, Eshtemoa, Racal, the towns belonging to the Jerahmeelites and the Kenites, Hormah, Bor-Ashan, Athach, and Hebron. He also sent gifts to the other towns where he and his men had traveled.

Saul and His Sons Die

31 Meanwhile, the Philistines were fighting Israel at Mount Gilboa. Israel's soldiers ran from the Philistines, and many of them were killed. [2] The Philistines closed in on Saul and his sons, and they killed his sons Jonathan, Abinadab, and

[k]**30.17** *just . . . sunset*: Or "at dusk, and fought until sunset on the next day." [l]**30.27-31** *Bethel*: Or "Bethuel" (see Joshua 19.4).

Malchishua. 3 The fighting was fierce around Saul, and he was badly wounded by enemy arrows.

4 Saul told the soldier who carried his weapons, "Kill me with your sword! I don't want those worthless Philistines to torture me and make fun." But the soldier was afraid to kill him.

Saul then took out his own sword; he stuck the blade into his stomach, and fell on it. 5 When the soldier knew that Saul was dead, he killed himself in the same way.

6 Saul was dead, his three sons were dead, and the soldier who carried his weapons was dead. They and all his soldiers died on that same day. 7 The Israelites on the other side of Jezreel Valley[m] and the other side of the Jordan learned that Saul and his sons were dead. They saw that the Israelite army had run away. So they ran away too, and the Philistines moved into the towns the Israelites had left behind.

8 The day after the battle, when the Philistines returned to the battlefield to take the weapons of the dead Israelite soldiers, they found Saul and his three sons lying dead on Mount Gilboa. 9-10 The Philistines cut off Saul's head and pulled off his armor. Then they put his armor in the temple of the goddess Astarte, and they nailed his body to the city wall of Beth-Shan. They also sent messengers everywhere in Philistia to spread the good news in the temples of their idols and among their people.

11 The people who lived in Jabesh in Gilead heard what the Philistines had done to Saul's body. 12 So one night, some brave men from Jabesh went to Beth-Shan. They took down the bodies of Saul and his sons, then brought them back to Jabesh and burned them. 13 They buried the bones under a small tree in Jabesh, and for seven days, they went without eating to show their sorrow.

[m]**31.7** *Jezreel Valley*: Hebrew "valley." Shunem (see 28.4) and Gilboa (see verse 1) were across the Jezreel Valley from each other.

2 SAMUEL

ABOUT THIS BOOK

Second Samuel is actually the second half of a single book that was divided into two parts, 1 and 2 Samuel, because together they were too long to fit on one scroll. Most of 2 Samuel is a history of the rule of King David.

After the death of King Saul, the people of the Judah tribe chose David to be their king. And for the next seven years David was at war with Saul's son, King Ishbosheth of Israel. Then David became king of the entire nation.

David captured Jerusalem from the Jebusites, made it his new capital, and brought the sacred chest there. He wanted to build a temple to honor the Lord and as a place to keep the sacred chest, but the Lord refused to let him do so. Instead, the Lord promised that David would be a powerful ruler and that one of his descendants would always be king.

David conquered the enemies of Israel and became the ruler of a small empire. But he also had an affair with Bathsheba, the wife of an army officer who was away at war. As a result, the Lord allowed David to have serious troubles later on, and many of those troubles came from within his own family. For example, one of David's sons, Amnon, raped David's daughter Tamar. Amnon was then killed by David's son Absalom, who later led a rebellion against David.

David wasn't perfect, but he was loyal to the Lord and worshiped only him. And for as long as Judah continued as a nation, the Lord kept the promise he made to David:

> *"Now I promise that you and your descendants will be kings. I'll choose one of your sons to be king when you reach the end of your life and are buried in the tomb of your ancestors. I'll make him a strong ruler, and no one will be able to take his kingdom away from him. . . . I will be his father, and he will be my son."*
>
> *(7.11b-14)*

A QUICK LOOK AT THIS BOOK

David Finds Out about Saul's Death

1 Saul was dead.
Meanwhile, David had defeated the
Amalekites and returned to Ziklag. 2 Three
days later, a soldier came from Saul's army.
His clothes were torn, and dirt was on his
head.[a] He went to David and knelt down in
front of him.
3 David asked, "Where did you come
from?"
The man answered, "From Israel's army.
I barely escaped with my life."
4 "Who won the battle?" David asked.
The man said, "Our army turned and
ran, but many were wounded and died.
Even King Saul and his son Jonathan are
dead."
5 David asked, "How do you know Saul
and Jonathan are dead?"
6 The young man replied:
I was on Mount Gilboa and saw
King Saul leaning on his spear. The
enemy's war chariots and cavalry were
closing in on him. 7 When he turned
around and saw me, he called me over.
I went and asked what he wanted.
8 Saul asked me, "Who are you?"
"An Amalekite," I answered.
9 Then he said, "Kill me! I'm dying,
and I'm in terrible pain."[b]
10 So I killed him. I knew he was
too badly wounded to live much longer.
Then I took his crown and his arm-
band, and I brought them to you, Your
Majesty. Here they are.
11 Right away, David and his soldiers
tore their clothes in sorrow. 12 They cried
all day long and would not eat anything.
Everyone was sad because Saul, his son
Jonathan, and many of the LORD's people
had been killed in the battle.
13 David asked the young man, "Where
is your home?"
The man replied, "My father is an
Amalekite, but we live in Israel."
14-16 David said to him, "Why weren't
you afraid to kill the LORD's chosen king?
And you even told what you did. It's your
own fault that you're going to die!"
Then David told one of his soldiers,
"Come here and kill this man!"

David Sings in Memory of Saul

17 David sang a song in memory of Saul
and Jonathan, 18 and he ordered his men to
teach the song to everyone in Judah. He
called it "The Song of the Bow," and it can
be found in *The Book of Jashar*.[c] This is the
song:

19 Israel, your famous hero
lies dead on the hills,
and your mighty warriors
have fallen!
20 Don't tell it in Gath
or spread the news
on the streets of Ashkelon.
The godless Philistine women
will be happy
and jump for joy.
21 Don't let dew or rain fall
on the hills of Gilboa.
Don't let its fields
grow offerings for God.
There the warriors' shields
were smeared with mud,
and Saul's own shield
was left unpolished.[d]

22 The arrows of Jonathan struck,
and warriors died.
The sword of Saul cut
the enemy apart.

23 It was easy to love Saul
and Jonathan.
Together in life,
together in death,
they were faster than eagles
and stronger than lions.

24 Women of Israel, cry for Saul.
He brought you fine red cloth
and jewelry made of gold.
25 Our warriors have fallen
in the heat of battle,

[a] **1.2** *His clothes . . . his head*: People tore their clothes and put dirt on their heads to show they were sad because someone had died. [b] **1.9** *in terrible pain*: Or "very weak." [c] **1.18** *The Book of Jashar*: This book may have been a collection of ancient war songs. [d] **1.21** *unpolished*: Some shields were made of leather and were polished with olive oil.

1.6-10 1 S 31.1-6; 1 Ch 10.1-6. **1.18** Js 10.13.

and Jonathan lies dead
on the hills of Gilboa.

26 Jonathan, I miss you most!
I loved you
like a brother.
You were truly loyal to me,
more faithful than a wife
to her husband.[e]

27 Our warriors have fallen,
and their weapons[f]
are destroyed.

David Becomes King of Judah

2 Later, David asked the LORD, "Should
I go back to one of the towns of
Judah?"

The LORD answered, "Yes."

David asked, "Which town should I
go to?"

"Go to Hebron," the LORD replied.

2 David went to Hebron with his two
wives, Ahinoam and Abigail. Ahinoam was
from Jezreel, and Abigail was the widow of
Nabal from Carmel. 3 David also had his
men and their families come and live in
the villages near Hebron.

4 The people of Judah met with David at
Hebron and poured olive oil on his head to
show that he was their new king. Then
they told David, "The people from Jabesh
in Gilead buried Saul."

5 David sent messengers to tell them:

The LORD bless you! You were kind
enough to bury Saul your ruler, 6 and I
pray that the LORD will be kind and
faithful to you. I will be your friend because of what you have done. 7 Saul is
dead, but the tribe of Judah has made
me their king. So be strong and have
courage.

Ishbosheth Becomes King of Israel

8 Abner the son of Ner[g] had been the
general of Saul's army. He took Saul's son
Ishbosheth[h] across the Jordan River to Mahanaim 9 and made him king of Israel,[i] including the areas of Gilead, Asher,[j] Jezreel,
Ephraim, and Benjamin. 10 Ishbosheth was
forty years old at the time, and he ruled for
two years. But the tribe of Judah made
David their king, 11 and he ruled from Hebron for seven and a half years.

The War between David and Ishbosheth

12 One day, Abner and the soldiers of
Ishbosheth[k] left Mahanaim and went to
Gibeon. 13 Meanwhile, Joab the son of
Zeruiah[l] was leading David's soldiers, and
the two groups met at the pool in Gibeon.[m]
Abner and his men sat down on one side of
the pool, while Joab and his men sat on the
other side. 14 Abner yelled to Joab, "Let's
have some of our best soldiers get up and
fight each other!"

Joab agreed, 15 and twelve of Ishbosheth's men from the tribe of Benjamin
got up to fight twelve of David's men.
16 They grabbed each other by the hair and
stabbed each other in the side with their
daggers. They all died right there! That's
why the place in Gibeon is called "Field of
Daggers."[n] 17 Then everyone started fighting. Both sides fought very hard, but

[e] **1.26** *You . . . husband*: Or "You loved me more than a wife could possibly love her husband."
[f] **1.27** *weapons*: This may refer to Saul and Jonathan.
[g] **2.8** *son of Ner*: Abner was Saul's cousin (see 1 Samuel 14.50).
[h] **2.8** *Ishbosheth*: One ancient translation has "Ishbaal" (see also 1 Chronicles 8.33). In Hebrew "baal" means "lord" and was used as the name of a Canaanite god. The people of Israel often changed "baal" to "bosheth" (which means "shame") in personal names. Ishbosheth was probably called Ishvi or Ishyo in 1 Samuel 14.49.
[i] **2.9** *Israel*: Sometimes "Israel" means the northern tribes and does not include the tribes of Judah and Simeon. That is how it is used in this verse.
[j] **2.9** *Asher*: The Hebrew text has "Ashur," which is the Hebrew name for the Assyrians. It may be another spelling for Asher (one of the tribes of Israel) or it may refer to Geshur (a small area between Gilead and Jezreel, east of Lake Galilee).
[k] **2.12** *Ishbosheth*: See the note at 2.8.
[l] **2.13** *the son of Zeruiah*: Zeruiah was David's older sister, so Joab was David's nephew (see 1 Chronicles 2.12-17 and the note at 2 Samuel 17.25).
[m] **2.13** *pool in Gibeon*: This pool was located just inside the city wall and was used for storing water. It was in the shape of a circle and was 36 feet wide and 36 feet deep.
[n] **2.16** *Field of Daggers*: Or "Field of Opponents" or "Battlefield."

2.2 1 S 25.42, 43. **2.4** 1 S 31.11-13.

David's soldiers defeated Abner and the
soldiers of Israel.
18 Zeruiah's three sons were there: Joab,
Abishai, and Asahel. Asahel could run as
fast as a deer in an open field, 19 and he
ran straight after Abner, without looking to
the right or to the left.
20 When Abner turned and saw him, he
said, "Is that you, Asahel?"

Asahel answered, "Yes it is."

21 Abner said, "There are soldiers all
around. Stop chasing me and fight one of
them! Kill him and take his clothes and
weapons for yourself."

But Asahel refused to stop.

22 Abner said, "If you don't turn back,
I'll have to kill you! Then I could never
face your brother Joab again."

23 But Asahel would not turn back, so
Abner struck him in the stomach with the
back end of his spear. The spear went all
the way through and came out of his back.
Asahel fell down and died. Everyone who
saw Asahel lying dead just stopped and
stood still. 24 But Joab and Abishai went after Abner. Finally, about sunset, they came
to the hill of Ammah, not far from Giah on
the road to Gibeon Desert. 25 Abner
brought the men of Benjamin together in
one group on top of a hill, and they got
ready to fight.

26 Abner shouted to Joab, "Aren't we
ever going to stop killing each other? Don't
you know that the longer we keep on doing
this, the worse it's going to be when it's all
over? When are you going to order your
men to stop chasing their own relatives?"

27 Joab shouted back, "I swear by the living God, if you hadn't spoken, my men
would have chased their relatives all
night!" 28 Joab took his trumpet and blew
the signal for his soldiers to stop chasing
the soldiers of Israel. Right away, the fighting stopped.

29 Abner and his troops marched
through the Jordan River valley all that
night. Then they crossed the river and
marched all morning[o] until they arrived
back at Mahanaim.

30 As soon as Joab stopped chasing Abner, he got David's troops together and
counted them. There were nineteen missing besides Asahel. 31 But David's soldiers
had killed 360 of Abner's men from the
tribe of Benjamin. 32 Joab and his troops
carried Asahel's body to Bethlehem and
buried him in the family burial place. Then
they marched all night and reached Hebron before sunrise.

3 This battle was the beginning of a long
war between the followers of Saul and
the followers of David. Saul's power grew
weaker, but David's grew stronger.

David's Sons Born in Hebron

(1 Chronicles 3.1-4)

2-5 Several of David's sons were born
while he was living in Hebron. His oldest
son was Amnon, whose mother was Ahinoam from Jezreel. David's second son was
Chileab, whose mother was Abigail, who
had been married to Nabal from Carmel.
Absalom was the third. His mother was
Maacah, the daughter of King Talmai of
Geshur. The fourth was Adonijah, whose
mother was Haggith. The fifth was Shephatiah, whose mother was Abital. The sixth
was Ithream, whose mother was Eglah, another one of David's wives.

Abner Decides To Help David

6 As the war went on between the families of David and Saul, Abner was gaining
more power than ever in Saul's family. 7 He
had even slept with a wife[p] of Saul by the
name of Rizpah the daughter of Aiah. But
Saul's son Ishbosheth[q] told Abner, "You
shouldn't have slept with one of my father's
wives!"

8 Abner was very angry at what Ishbosheth had said, and he told Ishbosheth:

> Am I some kind of worthless dog
> from Judah? I've always been loyal to
> your father's family and to his relatives
> and friends. I haven't turned you over
> to David. And yet you talk to me as
> if I've committed a crime with this
> woman.

[o] **2.29** *all morning*: One possible meaning for the difficult Hebrew text. [p] **3.7** *wife*: This translates a Hebrew word for a woman who was legally bound to a man, but without the full privileges of a wife. [q] **3.7** *Ishbosheth*: See the note at 2.8.

[9] I ask God to punish me if I don't
help David get what the LORD
promised him! [10] God said that he
wouldn't let anyone in Saul's family
ever be king again and that David
would be king instead. He also said
that David would rule both Israel and
Judah, all the way from Dan in the
north to Beersheba in the south.[r]

[11] Ishbosheth was so afraid of Abner that he could not even answer.

[12] Abner sent some of his men to David with this message: "You should be the ruler of the whole nation.[s] If you make an agreement with me, I will persuade everyone in Israel to make you their king."

[13] David sent this message back: "Good! I'll make an agreement with you. But before I will even talk with you about it, you must get Saul's daughter Michal back for me."

[14] David sent a few of his officials to Ishbosheth to give him this message: "Give me back my wife Michal! I killed a hundred Philistines so I could marry her."[t]

[15] Ishbosheth sent some of his men to take Michal away from her new husband, Paltiel the son of Laish. [16] Paltiel followed Michal and the men all the way to Bahurim, crying as he walked. But he went back home after Abner ordered him to leave.

[17] Abner talked with the leaders of the tribes of Israel and told them, "You've wanted to make David your king for a long time now. [18] So do it! After all, God said he would use his servant David to rescue his people Israel from their enemies, especially from the Philistines."

[19] Finally, Abner talked with the tribe of Benjamin. Then he left for Hebron to tell David everything that the tribe of Benjamin and the rest of the people of Israel wanted to do. [20] Abner took twenty soldiers with him, and when they got to Hebron, David gave a big feast for them.

[21] After the feast, Abner said, "Your Majesty, let me leave now and bring Israel here to make an agreement with you. You'll be king of the whole nation, just as you've been wanting."

David told Abner he could leave, and he left without causing any trouble.

Joab Kills Abner

[22] Soon after Abner had left Hebron, Joab and some of David's soldiers came back, bringing a lot of things they had taken from an enemy village. [23] Right after they arrived, someone told Joab, "Abner visited the king, and the king let him go. Abner even left without causing any trouble."

[24] Joab went to David and said, "What have you done? Abner came to you, and you let him go. Now he's long gone! [25] You know Abner—he came to trick you. He wants to find out how strong your army is and to know everything you're doing."

[26] Joab left David, then he sent some messengers to catch up with Abner. They brought him back from the well at Sirah,[u] but David did not know anything about it. [27] When Abner returned to Hebron, Joab pretended he wanted to talk privately with him. So he took Abner into one of the small rooms that were part of the town gate and stabbed him in the stomach. Joab killed him because Abner had killed Joab's brother Asahel.

Abner's Funeral

[28] David heard how Joab had killed Abner, and he said, "I swear to the LORD that I am completely innocent of Abner's death! [29] Joab and his family are the guilty ones. I pray that Joab's family will always be sick with sores and other skin diseases. May they all be cowards,[v] and may they die in war or starve to death."

[30] Joab and his brother Abishai killed Abner because he had killed their brother Asahel in the battle at Gibeon.

[r]**3.10** *from . . . south*: Hebrew "from Dan to Beersheba." This was one way of describing all of the Israelite land, from north to south. [s]**3.12** *You . . . nation*: Or "I like you." [t]**3.14** *I killed . . . marry her*: See 1 Samuel 18.20-27. [u]**3.26** *well at Sirah*: Or "oasis of Sirah" or "cistern at Sirah." [v]**3.29** *cowards*: One possible meaning for the difficult Hebrew text.

3.10 1 S 15.28. **3.14** 1 S 18.27.

31 David told Joab and everyone with
him, “Show your sorrow by tearing your
clothes and wearing sackcloth![w] Walk in
front of Abner’s body and cry!”

David walked behind the stretcher on
which Abner’s body was being carried.
32 Abner was buried in Hebron, while
David and everyone else stood at the tomb
and cried loudly. 33 Then the king sang a
funeral song about Abner:

Abner, why should you
have died like an outlaw?[x]
34 No one tied your hands
or chained your feet,
yet you died as a victim
of murderers.

Everyone started crying again. 35 Then
they brought some food to David and told
him he would feel better if he had something to eat. It was still daytime, and David
said, “I swear to God that I’ll not take a bite
of bread or anything else until sunset!”

36 Everyone noticed what David did,
and they liked it, just as they always liked
what he did. 37 Now the people of Judah
and Israel were certain that David had
nothing to do with killing Abner.

38 David said to his officials, “Don’t you
realize that today one of Israel’s great leaders has died? 39 I am the chosen king, but
Joab and Abishai have more power than I
do. So God will have to pay them back[y] for
the evil thing they did.”

Ishbosheth Is Killed

4 Ishbosheth[z] felt like giving up after he
heard that Abner had died in Hebron.
Everyone in Israel was terrified.

2 Ishbosheth had put the two brothers
Baanah and Rechab in charge of the soldiers who raided enemy villages. Rimmon
was their father, and they were from the
town of Beeroth, which belonged to the
tribe of Benjamin. 3 The people who used
to live in Beeroth had run away to Gittaim,
and they still live[a] there.

4 Saul’s son Jonathan had a son named
Mephibosheth,[b] who had not been able
to walk since he was five years old. It
happened when someone from Jezreel told
his nurse that Saul and Jonathan
had died.[c] She hurried off with the boy
in her arms, but he fell and injured his
legs.

5 One day about noon, Rechab and
Baanah went to Ishbosheth’s house. It was
a hot day, and he was resting 6-7 in his bedroom. The two brothers went into the
house, pretending to get some flour. But
once they were inside, they stabbed Ishbosheth in the stomach and killed him.
Then they cut off his head and took it with
them.

Rechab and Baanah walked through the
Jordan River valley all night long. 8 Finally
they turned west and went to Hebron.
They went in to see David and told him,
“Your Majesty, here is the head of Ishbosheth, the son of your enemy Saul who
tried to kill you! The LORD has let you get
even with Saul and his family.”

9 David answered:

I swear that only the LORD rescues
me when I’m in trouble! 10 When a
man came to Ziklag and told me that
Saul was dead, he thought he deserved
a reward for bringing good news. But I
grabbed him and killed him.

11 You evil men have done something much worse than he did. You’ve
killed an innocent man in his own
house and on his own bed. I’ll make
you pay for that. I’ll wipe you from the
face of the earth!

12 Then David said to his troops, “Kill
these two brothers! Cut off their hands and
feet and hang their bodies by the pool in
Hebron. But bury Ishbosheth’s head in Abner’s tomb near Hebron.” And they did.

[w]**3.31** *sackcloth*: Sackcloth was a rough, dark-colored cloth made from goat or camel hair and was used to make grain sacks. People wore sackcloth or tore their clothes in times of trouble or sorrow. [x]**3.33** *outlaw*: Or “fool.” [y]**3.39** *God . . . back*: Or “I pray that God will pay them back.” [z]**4.1** *Ishbosheth*: Hebrew “The Son of Saul.” [a]**4.3** *live*: The Hebrew word means that they did not have the full legal rights of citizens. [b]**4.4** *Mephibosheth*: Some manuscripts of one ancient translation have “Mephibaal.” In 1 Chronicles 8.34 and 9.40 he is called “Meribbaal.” See the note on “baal” and “bosheth” at 2.8. [c]**4.4** *Saul . . . died*: See 1 Samuel 31.1-6.

4.4 2 S 9.3. **4.10** 2 S 1.1-16.

David Becomes King of Israel
(1 Chronicles 11.1-3)

5 Israel's leaders met with David at Hebron and said, "We are your relatives.
2 Even when Saul was king, you led our nation in battle. And the LORD promised that
someday you would rule Israel and take
care of us like a shepherd."
3 During the meeting, David made an
agreement with the leaders and asked the
LORD to be their witness. Then the leaders
poured olive oil on David's head to show
that he was now the king of Israel.
4 David was thirty years old when he
became king, and he ruled for forty years.
5 He lived in Hebron for the first seven
and a half years and ruled only Judah.Then
he moved to Jerusalem, where he ruled
both Israel and Judah for thirty-three years.

How David Captured Jerusalem
(1 Chronicles 11.4-9; 14.1, 2)

6 The Jebusites lived in Jerusalem, and
David led his army there to attack them.
The Jebusites did not think he could get in,
so they told him, "You can't get in here! We
could run you off, even if we couldn't see
or walk!"
7-9 David told his troops, "You will have
to go up through the water tunnel to get
those Jebusites. I hate people like them
who can't walk or see."[d]
That's why there is still a rule that says,
"Only people who can walk and see are allowed in the temple."[e]
David captured the fortress on Mount
Zion, then he moved there and named it
David's City. He had the city rebuilt, starting with the landfill to the east. 10 David
became a great and strong ruler, because
the LORD All-Powerful was on his side.
11 King Hiram of Tyre sent some officials
to David. Carpenters and stone workers
came with them, and they brought cedar
logs so they could build David a palace.
12 David knew that the LORD had made
him king of Israel and that he had made
him a powerful ruler for the good of his
people.

David's Sons Born in Jerusalem
(1 Chronicles 14.3-7)

13 After David left Hebron and moved
to Jerusalem, he married many women[f]
from Jerusalem,[g] and he had a lot of children. 14 His sons who were born there
were Shammua, Shobab, Nathan, Solomon, 15 Ibhar, Elishua, Nepheg, Japhia,
16 Elishama, Eliada,[h] and Eliphelet.

David Fights the Philistines
(1 Chronicles 14.8-17)

17 The Philistines heard that David was
now king of Israel, and they came into the
hill country to try and capture him. But
David found out and went into his fortress.[i]
18 So the Philistines camped in Rephaim
Valley.[j]
19 David asked the LORD, "Should I attack the Philistines? Will you let me win?"
The LORD told David, "Attack! I will let
you win."
20 David attacked the Philistines and defeated them. Then he said, "I watched the
LORD break through my enemies like a
mighty flood." So he named the place "The
Lord Broke Through."[k] 21 David and his
troops also carried away the idols that the
Philistines had left behind.
22 Some time later, the Philistines came
back into the hill country and camped in
Rephaim Valley. 23 David asked the LORD
what he should do, and the LORD answered:

Don't attack them from the front.
Circle around behind and attack from
among the balsam[l] trees. 24 Wait until

[d]**5.7-9** *You will . . . or see*: One possible meaning for the difficult Hebrew text. [e]**5.7-9** *temple*: Or "palace." [f]**5.13** *married many women*: Some of these women were second-class wives (see the note at 3.7). [g]**5.13** *from Jerusalem*: Or "in Jerusalem." [h]**5.16** *Eliada*: See 1 Chronicles 3.8. First Chronicles 14.7 has "Baalyada." [i]**5.17** *fortress*: Probably the fortress of Adullam, which was David's former hideout (see 1 Samuel 22.1,4; 24.22). Or it could refer to the older walled city of Jerusalem, called the "fortress on Mount Zion" in verses 7-9. [j]**5.18** *Rephaim Valley*: A few miles southwest of Jerusalem. [k]**5.20** *The Lord Broke Through*: Or "Baal-Perazim." [l]**5.23** *balsam*: One possible meaning for the difficult Hebrew text.

5.4,5 1 K 2.10, 11; 1 Ch 3.1-4; 29.27. **5.6** Js 15.63; Jg 1.21.

you hear a sound like troops marching through the tops of the trees. Then attack quickly! That sound will mean I have marched out ahead of you to fight the Philistine army.

25 David obeyed the LORD and defeated the Philistines. He even chased them all the way from Geba to the entrance to Gezer.

David Brings the Sacred Chest Back to Jerusalem

(1 Chronicles 13.1-14; 15.1—16.3,43)

6 David brought together thirty thousand of Israel's best soldiers and 2 led them to Baalah in Judah, which was also called Kiriath-Jearim. They were going there[m] to get the sacred chest and bring it back to Jerusalem. The throne of the LORD All-Powerful is above the winged creatures[n] on top of this chest, and he is worshiped there.[o]

3 They put the sacred chest on a new ox cart and started bringing it down the hill from Abinadab's house. Abinadab's sons Uzzah and Ahio were guiding the ox cart, 4 with Ahio[p] walking in front of it. 5 Some of the people of Israel were playing music on small harps and other stringed instruments, and on tambourines, castanets, and cymbals. David and the others were happy, and they danced for the LORD with all their might.

6 But when they came to Nacon's threshing-floor, the oxen stumbled, so Uzzah reached out and took hold of the sacred chest. 7 The LORD God was very angry at Uzzah for doing this, and he killed Uzzah right there beside the chest.

8 David got angry at God for killing Uzzah. He named that place "Bursting Out Against Uzzah,"[q] and that's what it's still called.

9 David was afraid of the LORD and thought, "Should I really take the sacred chest to my city?" 10 He decided not to take it there. Instead, he turned off the road and took it to the home of Obed Edom, who was from Gath.[r]

11-12 The chest stayed there for three months, and the LORD greatly blessed Obed Edom, his family, and everything he owned. Then someone told King David, "The LORD has done this because the sacred chest is in Obed Edom's house."

Right away, David went to Obed Edom's house to get the chest and bring it to David's City. Everyone was celebrating. 13 The people carrying the chest walked six steps, then David sacrificed an ox and a choice cow. 14 He was dancing for the LORD with all his might, but he wore only a linen cloth.[s] 15 He and everyone else were celebrating by shouting and blowing horns while the chest was being carried along.

16 Saul's daughter Michal looked out her window and watched the chest being brought into David's City. But when she saw David jumping and dancing for the LORD, she was disgusted.

17 They put the chest inside a tent that David had set up for it. David worshiped the LORD by sacrificing animals and burning them on an altar,[t] 18 then he blessed the people in the name of the LORD All-Powerful. 19 He gave all the men and women in the crowd a small loaf of bread, some meat, and a handful of raisins, and everyone went home.

Michal Talks to David

20 David went home so he could ask the LORD to bless his family. But Saul's daughter Michal went out and started yelling at

[m]**6.2** *to Baalah . . . there*: The Dead Sea Scrolls and 1 Chronicles 13.6; the Standard Hebrew Text "from Baalah in Judah. They had gone there." [n]**6.2** *winged creatures*: Two golden statues of winged creatures were on top of the sacred chest and were symbols of the LORD's throne on earth (see Exodus 25.18). [o]**6.2** *he is worshiped there*: Or "the chest belongs to him." [p]**6.3,4** *Ahio . . . Ahio*: Or "his brother . . . his brother." [q]**6.8** *Bursting . . . Uzzah*: Or "Perez-Uzzah." [r]**6.10** *Gath*: Or perhaps, "Gittaim." [s]**6.14** *only a linen cloth*: The Hebrew word is "ephod," which can mean either a piece of clothing like a skirt that went from the waist to the knee or a garment like a vest or a jacket that only the priests wore. [t]**6.17** *sacrificing . . . altar*: The Hebrew mentions two kinds of sacrifices. In one kind of sacrifice, the whole animal was burned on the altar. In the other kind, only part was burned, and the worshipers ate the rest, as in verse 19 (see Leviticus 1.2-17; 3.1-17).

6.2 Ex 25.22. **6.3** 1 S 7.1, 2. **6.11** 1 Ch 26.4, 5. **6.19,20** 1 Ch 16.43.

him. "You were really great today!" she said. "You acted like a dirty old man, dancing around half-naked in front of your servants' slave-girls."

21 David told her, "The LORD didn't choose your father or anyone else in your family to be the leader of his people. The LORD chose me, and I was celebrating in honor of him. 22 I'll show you just how great I can be! I'll even be disgusting to myself. But those slave-girls you talked about will still honor me!"

23 Michal never had any children.

The LORD's Message to David

(1 Chronicles 17.1-15)

7 King David moved into his new palace, and the LORD let his kingdom be at peace. 2 Then one day, as David was talking with Nathan the prophet, David said, "Look around! I live in a palace made of cedar, but the sacred chest has to stay in a tent."

3 Nathan replied, "The LORD is with you, so do what you want!"

4 That night, the LORD told Nathan 5 to go to David and give him this message:

David, you are my servant, so listen to what I say. Why should you build a temple for me? 6 I didn't live in a temple when I brought my people out of Egypt, and I don't live in one now. A tent has always been my home wherever I have gone with them. 7 I chose leaders and told them to be like shepherds for my people Israel. But did I ever say anything to even one of them about building a cedar temple for me?

8 David, this is what I, the LORD All-Powerful, say to you. I brought you in from the fields where you took care of sheep, and I made you the leader of my people. 9 Wherever you went, I helped you and destroyed your enemies right in front of your eyes. I have made you one of the most famous people in the world.

10 I have given my people Israel a land of their own where they can live in peace, and they won't have to tremble with fear any more. Evil nations won't bother them, as they did 11 when I let judges rule my people. And I have kept your enemies from attacking you.

Now I promise that you and your descendants will be kings. 12 I'll choose one of your sons to be king when you reach the end of your life and are buried in the tomb of your ancestors. I'll make him a strong ruler, 13 and no one will be able to take his kingdom away from him. He will be the one to build a temple for me. 14 I will be his father, and he will be my son.

When he does wrong, I'll see that he is corrected, just as children are corrected by their parents. 15 But I will never put an end to my agreement with him, as I put an end to my agreement with Saul, who was king before you. 16 I will make sure that one of your descendants will always be king.

17 Nathan told David exactly what he had heard in the vision.

David Gives Thanks to the LORD

(1 Chronicles 17.16-27)

18 David went into the tent he had set up for the sacred chest. Then he sat there and prayed:

LORD All-Powerful, my family and I don't deserve what you have already done for us, 19 and yet you have promised to do even more. Is this the way you usually treat people?[u] 20 I am your servant, and you know my thoughts, so there is nothing more that I need to say. 21 You have done this wonderful thing, and you have let me know about it, because you wanted to keep your promise.

22 LORD All-Powerful, you are greater than all others. No one is like you, and you alone are God. Everything we have heard about you is true. 23 And there is no other nation on earth like Israel, the nation you rescued from slavery in Egypt to be your

[u]**7.19** *Is this . . . people*: One possible meaning for the difficult Hebrew text.

7.8 Ps 151.4. **7.12** Ps 89.3, 4; 132.11; Jn 7.42; Ac 2.30. **7.14** Ps 89.26, 27; 2 Co 6.18; He 1.5. **7.16** Ps 89.36, 37. **7.23** Dt 4.32-34.

own. You became famous by using great and wonderful miracles to force other nations and their gods out of your land, so your people could live here.[v] 24 You have chosen Israel to be your people forever, and you have become their God.

25 And now, LORD God, please do what you have promised me and my descendants. 26 Then you will be famous forever, and everyone will say, "The LORD God All-Powerful rules Israel, and David's descendants are his chosen kings." 27 After all, you really are Israel's God, the LORD All-Powerful. You've told me that you will let my descendants be kings. That's why I have the courage to pray to you like this, even though I am only your servant.

28 LORD All-Powerful, you are God. You have promised me some very good things, and you can be trusted to do what you promise. 29 Please bless my descendants and let them always be your chosen kings. You have already promised, and I'm sure that you will bless my family forever.

A List of David's Victories in War
(1 Chronicles 18.1-13)

8 Later, David attacked and badly defeated the Philistines. Israel was now free from their control.[w]

2 David also defeated the Moabites. Then he made their soldiers lie down on the ground, and he measured them off with a rope. He would measure off two lengths of the rope and have those men killed, then he would measure off one length and let those men live. The people of Moab had to accept David as their ruler and pay taxes to him.

3 David set out for the Euphrates River to build a monument[x] there. On his way,[y] he defeated the king of Zobah, whose name was Hadadezer the son of Rehob. 4 In the battle, David captured seventeen hundred cavalry[z] and twenty thousand foot soldiers. He also captured war chariots, but he destroyed all but one hundred of them.[a] 5 When troops from the Aramean kingdom of Damascus came to help Hadadezer, David killed twenty thousand of them. 6 He left some of his soldiers in Damascus, and the Arameans had to accept David as their ruler and pay taxes to him.

Everywhere David went, the LORD helped him win battles.

7 Hadadezer's officers had carried their arrows in gold cases hung over their shoulders, but David took these cases[b] and brought them to Jerusalem. 8 He also took a lot of bronze from the cities of Betah and Berothai, which had belonged to Hadadezer.

9-10 King Toi of Hamath and King Hadadezer had been enemies. So when Toi heard that David had attacked and defeated[c] Hadadezer's whole army, he sent his son Joram to praise and congratulate David. Joram also brought him gifts made of silver, gold, and bronze. 11 David gave these to the LORD, just as he had done with the silver and gold that he had captured from 12 Edom,[d] Moab, Ammon, Philistia, and from King Hadadezer of Zobah.

13 David fought the Edomite[e] army in

[v] **7.23** *You . . . here*: One possible meaning for the difficult Hebrew text. [w] **8.1** *Israel . . . control*: Or "David also took the town of Metheg-Ammah away from them." [x] **8.3** *monument*: Kings sometimes set up monuments in lands they had conquered. [y] **8.3** *David . . . way*: One possible meaning for the difficult Hebrew text. It may have been Hadadezer who was going to the Euphrates River. And he may have gone there either to build a monument or to put down a rebellion.
[z] **8.4** *seventeen hundred cavalry*: Hebrew; one ancient translation and 1 Chronicles 18.4 "a thousand chariots and seven thousand cavalry." [a] **8.4** *He also captured . . . them*: Or "He crippled all but one hundred of the horses." [b] **8.7** *Hadadezer's . . . cases*: Or "Hadadezer's soldiers carried gold shields, but David took these shields." [c] **8.9,10** *defeated*: Or "killed." [d] **8.12** *Edom*: Some Hebrew manuscripts and two ancient translations (see also 1 Chronicles 18.11); most Hebrew manuscripts "Aram." In Hebrew the words for "Edom" and "Aram" look almost alike.
[e] **8.13** *Edomite*: Some Hebrew manuscripts and two ancient translations (see also 1 Chronicles 18.12); most Hebrew manuscripts "Aramean." In Hebrew the words for "Edomite" and "Aramean" look almost alike.
8.13 Ps 60 Title.

Salt Valley and killed eighteen thousand of their soldiers. When he returned, he built a monument.[f] 14 David left soldiers all through Edom, and the people of Edom had to accept him as their ruler.

Wherever David went, the LORD helped him.

A List of David's Officials

(1 Chronicles 18.14-17)

15 David ruled all Israel with fairness and justice.

16 Joab the son of Zeruiah was the commander in chief of the army.

Jehoshaphat the son of Ahilud kept the government records.

17 Zadok the son of Ahitub, and Abiathar the son of Ahimelech,[g] were the priests.

Seraiah was the secretary.

18 Benaiah the son of Jehoiada was the commander of[h] David's bodyguard.[i]

David's sons were priests.

David Is Kind to Mephibosheth

9 One day, David thought, "I wonder if any of Saul's family are still alive. If they are, I will be kind to them, because I made a promise to Jonathan." 2 David called in Ziba, one of the servants of Saul's family. David said, "So you are Ziba."

"Yes, Your Majesty, I am."

3 David asked, "Are any of Saul's family still alive? If there are, I want to be kind to them."

Ziba answered, "One of Jonathan's sons is still alive, but he can't walk."

4 "Where is he?" David asked.

Ziba replied, "He lives in Lo-Debar with Machir the son of Ammiel."

5-6 David sent some servants to bring Jonathan's son from Lo-Debar. His name was Mephibosheth,[j] and he was the grandson of Saul. He came to David and knelt down.

David asked, "Are you Mephibosheth?"

"Yes, I am, Your Majesty."

7 David said, "Don't be afraid. I'll be kind to you because Jonathan was your father. I'm going to give you back the land that belonged to your grandfather Saul. Besides that, you will always eat with me at my table."

8 Mephibosheth knelt down again and said, "Why should you care about me? I'm worth no more than a dead dog."

9 David called in Ziba, Saul's chief servant, and told him, "Since Mephibosheth is Saul's grandson, I've given him back everything that belonged to your master Saul and his family. 10 You and your fifteen sons and twenty servants will work for Mephibosheth. You will farm his land and bring in his crops, so that Saul's family and servants[k] will have food. But Mephibosheth will always eat with me at my table."

11-13 Ziba replied, "Your Majesty, I will do exactly what you tell me to do." So Ziba's family and servants worked for Mephibosheth.

Mephibosheth was lame, but he lived in Jerusalem and ate at David's[l] table, just like one of David's own sons. And he had a young son of his own, named Mica.

Israel Fights Ammon

(1 Chronicles 19.1-19)

10 Some time later, King Nahash of Ammon died, and his son Hanun became king. 2 David said, "Nahash was kind to me, and I will be kind to his son." So he sent some officials to the country of Ammon to tell Hanun how sorry he was that his father had died.

3 But Hanun's officials told him, "Do you really believe David is honoring your father by sending these people to comfort you? He probably sent them to spy on our city, so he can destroy it." 4 Hanun arrested David's officials and had their beards

[f]**8.13** *built a monument*: Or "was famous." [g]**8.17** *Abiathar the son of Ahimelech*: One ancient translation and 1 Samuel 22.11-23; Hebrew "Ahimelech the son of Abiathar." [h]**8.18** *was the commander of*: Not in the Hebrew text of this verse, but see 1 Chronicles 18.17. [i]**8.18** *David's bodyguard*: The Hebrew text has "the Cherethites and the Pelethites," who were foreign soldiers hired by David to be his bodyguard. [j]**9.5,6** *Mephibosheth*: Or "Mephibaal" (see the note at 4.4). [k]**9.10** *Saul's family and servants*: Some manuscripts of one ancient translation; Hebrew "the son of your master." [l]**9.11-13** *David's*: Hebrew "my."

9.1 1 S 20.15-17. **9.3** 2 S 4.4.

shaved off on one side of their faces. He had their robes cut off just below the waist, and then he sent them away. [5] They were terribly ashamed.

When David found out what had happened to his officials, he sent a message and told them, "Stay in Jericho until your beards grow back. Then you can come home."

[6] The Ammonites realized that they had made David very angry, so they hired more foreign soldiers. Twenty thousand of them were foot soldiers from the Aramean cities of Beth-Rehob and Zobah, one thousand were from the king of Maacah, and twelve thousand were from the region of Tob. [7] David heard what they had done, and he sent out Joab with all of his well-trained soldiers.

[8] The Ammonite troops came out and got ready to fight in front of the gate to their city. The Arameans from Zobah and Rehob and the soldiers from Tob and Maacah formed a separate group in the nearby fields.

[9] Joab saw that he had to fight in front and behind at the same time, and he picked some of the best Israelite soldiers to fight the Arameans. [10] He put his brother Abishai in command of the rest of the army and had them fight the Ammonites. [11] Joab told his brother, "If the Arameans are too much for me to handle, you can come and help me. If the Ammonites are too strong for you, I'll come and help you. [12] Be brave and fight hard to protect our people and the cities of our God. I pray that the LORD will do whatever pleases him."

[13] Joab and his soldiers attacked the Arameans, and the Arameans ran from them. [14] When the Ammonite soldiers saw that the Arameans had run away, they ran from Abishai's soldiers and went back into their own city. Joab stopped fighting the Ammonites and returned to Jerusalem.

[15] The Arameans realized they had lost the battle, so they brought all their troops together again. [16] Hadadezer sent messengers to call in the Arameans who were on the other side of the Euphrates River. Then Shobach, the commander of Hadadezer's army, led them to the town of Helam.

[17] David found out what the Arameans were doing, and he brought Israel's whole army together. They crossed the Jordan River and went to Helam, where the Arameans were ready to meet them. [18] The Arameans attacked, but then they ran from Israel. David killed seven hundred chariot drivers and forty thousand cavalry.[m] He also killed Shobach, their commander.

[19] When the kings who had been under Hadadezer's rule saw that Israel had beaten them, they made peace with Israel and accepted David as their ruler. The Arameans were afraid to help Ammon any more.

David and Bathsheba

(1 Chronicles 20.1a)

11 It was now spring, the time when kings go to war.[n] David sent out the whole Israelite army under the command of Joab and his officers. They destroyed the Ammonite army and surrounded the capital city of Rabbah, but David stayed in Jerusalem.

[2-4] Late one afternoon, David got up from a nap and was walking around on the flat roof of his palace. A beautiful young woman was down below in her courtyard, bathing as her religion required.[o] David happened to see her, and he sent one of his servants to find out who she was.

The servant came back and told David, "Her name is Bathsheba. She is the daughter of Eliam, and she is the wife of Uriah the Hittite."

David sent some messengers to bring her to his palace. She came to him, and he slept with her. Then she returned home. [5] But later, when she found out that she was going to have a baby, she sent someone to David with this message: "I'm pregnant!"

[6] David sent a message to Joab: "Send Uriah the Hittite to me."

[m] **10.18** *cavalry*: The Hebrew manuscripts and ancient translations differ as to how many and what kind of soldiers were killed. [n] **11.1** *when . . . war*: Or "when the messengers had gone to Ammon" (see 10.2) or "the time when the kings had gone to war" (see 10.6-8). [o] **11.2-4** *as . . . required*: This bathing was often a requirement for worshiping God.

11.1 1 Ch 20.1.

Joab sent Uriah 7 to David's palace, and David asked him, "Is Joab well? How is the army doing? And how about the war?" 8 Then David told Uriah, "Go home and clean up."[p] Uriah left the king's palace, and David had dinner sent to Uriah's house. 9 But Uriah didn't go home. Instead, he slept outside the entrance to the royal palace, where the king's guards slept.

10 Someone told David that Uriah had not gone home. So the next morning David asked him, "Why didn't you go home? Haven't you been away for a long time?"

11 Uriah answered, "The sacred chest and the armies of Israel and Judah are camping out somewhere in the fields[q] with our commander Joab and his officers and troops. Do you really think I would go home to eat and drink and sleep with my wife? I swear by your life that I would not!"

12 Then David said, "Stay here in Jerusalem today, and I will send you back tomorrow."

Uriah stayed in Jerusalem that day. Then the next day, 13 David invited him for dinner. Uriah ate with David and drank so much that he got drunk, but he still did not go home. He went out and slept on his mat near the palace guards. 14 Early the next morning, David wrote a letter and told Uriah to deliver it to Joab. 15 The letter said: "Put Uriah on the front line where the fighting is the worst. Then pull the troops back from him, so that he will be wounded and die."

16 Joab had been carefully watching the city of Rabbah, and he put Uriah in a place where he knew there were some of the enemy's best soldiers. 17 When the men of the city came out, they fought and killed some of David's soldiers—Uriah the Hittite was one of them.

18 Joab sent a messenger to tell David everything that was happening in the war. 19 He gave the messenger these orders:

> When you finish telling the king everything that has happened, 20 he may get angry and ask, "Why did you go so near the city to fight? Didn't you know they would shoot arrows from the wall? 21 Don't you know how Abimelech the son of Gideon[r] was killed at Thebez? Didn't a woman kill him by dropping a large rock from the top of the city wall? Why did you go so close to the city walls?"
>
> Then you tell him, "One of your soldiers who was killed was Uriah the Hittite."

22 The messenger went to David and reported everything Joab had told him. 23 He added, "The enemy chased us from the wall and out into the open fields. But we pushed them back as far as the city gate. 24 Then they shot arrows at us from the top of the wall. Some of your soldiers were killed, and one of them was Uriah the Hittite."

25 David replied, "Tell Joab to cheer up and not to be upset about what happened. You never know who will be killed in a war. Tell him to strengthen his attack against the city and break through its walls."[s]

26 When Bathsheba heard that her husband was dead, she mourned for him. 27 Then after the time for mourning was over, David sent someone to bring her to the palace. She became David's wife, and they had a son.

The LORD's Message for David

12 The LORD was angry at what David had done, 1 and he sent Nathan the prophet to tell this story to David:

> A rich man and a poor man lived in the same town. 2 The rich man owned a lot of sheep and cattle, 3 but the poor man had only one little lamb that he had bought and raised. The lamb became a pet for him and his children. He even let it eat from his plate and drink from his cup and sleep on his lap. The lamb was like one of his own children.

[p]11.8 *and clean up*: Or "and sleep with your wife." [q]11.11 *somewhere in the fields*: Or "at Succoth." [r]11.21 *Gideon*: The Hebrew text has Jerubbesheth, which stands for "Jerubbaal," another name for Gideon. See Judges 6.32 and the note on "bosheth" at 2.8 ("besheth" means the same as "bosheth"). [s]11.25 *break . . . walls*: Or "destroy it."

11.21 Jg 9.53. **12.1** Ps 51 Title.

4 One day someone came to visit the rich man, but the rich man didn't want to kill any of his own sheep or cattle and serve it to the visitor. So he stole the poor man's little lamb and served it instead.

5 David was furious with the rich man and said to Nathan, "I swear by the living LORD that the man who did this deserves to die! 6 And because he didn't have any pity on the poor man, he will have to pay four times what the lamb was worth."

7 Then Nathan told David:

You are that rich man! Now listen to what the LORD God of Israel says to you: "I chose you to be the king of Israel. I kept you safe from Saul 8 and even gave you his house and his wives. I let you rule Israel and Judah, and if that had not been enough, I would have given you much more. 9 Why did you disobey me and do such a horrible thing? You murdered Uriah the Hittite by having the Ammonites kill him, so you could take his wife.

10 "Because you wouldn't obey me and took Uriah's wife for yourself, your family will never live in peace. 11 Someone from your own family will cause you a lot of trouble, and I will take your wives and give them to another man before your very eyes. He will go to bed with them while everyone looks on. 12 What you did was in secret, but I will do this in the open for everyone in Israel to see."

13-14 David said, "I have disobeyed the LORD."

"Yes, you have!" Nathan answered. "You showed you didn't care what the LORD wanted.[t] He has forgiven you, and you won't die. But your newborn son will."
15 Then Nathan went back home.

David's Young Son Dies

The LORD made David's young son very sick.

16 So David went without eating to show his sorrow, and he begged God to make the boy well. David would not sleep on his bed, but spent each night lying on the floor. 17 His officials stood beside him and tried to talk him into getting up. But he would not get up or eat with them.

18 After the child had been sick for seven days, he died, but the officials were afraid to tell David. They said to each other, "Even when the boy was alive, David wouldn't listen to us. How can we tell him his son is dead? He might do something terrible!"

19 David noticed his servants whispering, and he knew the boy was dead. "Did my son die?" he asked his servants.

"Yes, he did," they answered.

20 David got up off the floor; he took a bath, combed his hair, and dressed. He went into the LORD's tent and worshiped, then he went back home. David asked for something to eat, and when his servants brought him some food, he ate it.

21 His officials said, "What are you doing? You went without eating and cried for your son while he was alive! But now that he's dead, you're up and eating."

22 David answered:

While he was still alive, I went without food and cried because there was still hope. I said to myself, "Who knows? Maybe the LORD will have pity on me and let the child live."
23 But now that he's dead, why should I go without eating? I can't bring him back! Someday I will join him in death, but he can't return to me.

Solomon Is Born

24 David comforted his wife Bathsheba and slept with her. Later on, she gave birth to another son and named him Solomon. The LORD loved Solomon
25 and sent Nathan the prophet to tell David, "The LORD will call him Jedidiah."[u]

[t] **12.13,14** *what . . . wanted*: One manuscript of one ancient translation; one Hebrew manuscript "what the LORD had said"; most Hebrew manuscripts "what the enemies of the LORD would think."
[u] **12.25** *Jedidiah*: In Hebrew this name means "Loved by the LORD."
12.11,12 2 S 16.22.

The End of the War with Ammon
(1 Chronicles 20.1b-3)

26 Meanwhile, Joab had been in the
country of Ammon, attacking the city of
Rabbah. He captured the royal fortress
27 and sent a messenger to tell David:

> I have attacked Rabbah and cap-
> tured the fortress guarding the city wa-
> ter supply. 28 Call the rest of the army
> together. Then surround the city, and
> capture it yourself. If you don't, every-
> one will remember that I captured the
> city.

29 David called the rest of the army together and attacked Rabbah. He captured
the city 30 and took the crown from the
statue of their god Milcom.[v] The crown was
made of seventy-five pounds of gold, and
there was a valuable jewel on it. David put
the jewel on his own crown.[w] He also carried off everything else of value. 31 David
made the people of Rabbah tear down the
city walls[x] with iron picks and axes, and
then he put them to work making bricks.
He did the same thing with all the other
Ammonite cities.

David went back to Jerusalem, and the
people of Israel returned to their homes.

Amnon Disgraces Tamar

13 David had a beautiful daughter
named Tamar, who was the sister of
Absalom. She was also the half sister of
Amnon,[y] who fell in love with her. 2 But
Tamar was a virgin, and Amnon could not
think of a way to be alone with her. He was
so upset about it that he made himself
sick.

3 Amnon had a friend named Jonadab,
who was the son of David's brother
Shimeah. Jonadab always knew how to get
what he wanted, 4 and he said to Amnon,
"What's the matter? You're the king's son!
You shouldn't have to go around feeling
sorry for yourself every morning."

Amnon said, "I'm in love with Tamar,
my brother Absalom's sister."

5 Jonadab told him, "Lie down on your
bed and pretend to be sick. When your
father comes to see you, ask him to send
Tamar, so you can watch her cook something for you. Then she can serve you the
food."

6 So Amnon went to bed and pretended
to be sick. When the king came to see him,
Amnon said, "Please, ask Tamar to come
over. She can make some special bread[z]
while I watch, and then she can serve me
the bread."

7 David told Tamar, "Go over to Amnon's
house and fix him some food." 8 When she
got there, he was lying in bed. She mixed
the dough, made the loaves, and baked
them while he watched. 9 Then she took
the bread out of the pan and put it on his
plate, but he refused to eat it.

Amnon said, "Send the servants out of
the house." After they had gone, 10 he said
to Tamar, "Serve the food in my bedroom."

Tamar picked up the bread that she had
made and brought it into Amnon's bedroom. 11 But as she was taking it over to
him, he grabbed her and said, "Come to
bed with me!"

12 She answered, "No! Please don't
force me! This sort of thing isn't done in Israel. It's too disgusting! 13 Think of me. I'll
be disgraced forever! And think of yourself.
Everyone in Israel will say you're nothing
but trash! Just ask the king, and he will let
you marry me."

14 But Amnon would not listen to what
she said. He was stronger than she was, so
he overpowered her and raped her. 15 Then
Amnon hated her even more than he had
loved her before. So he told her, "Get up
and get out!"

16 She said, "Don't send me away! That
would be worse than what you have already
done."

But Amnon would not listen. 17 He
called in his servant and said, "Throw this
woman out and lock the door!"

18 The servant made her leave, and he
locked the door behind her.

The king's unmarried daughters used to

[v] **12.30** *the statue of their god Milcom*: Or "their king." [w] **12.30** *David . . . crown*: Or "and David wore the crown." [x] **12.31** *tear . . . walls*: One possible meaning for the difficult Hebrew text. [y] **13.1** *Tamar . . . Absalom . . . Amnon*: David was their father, but Amnon had a different mother. [z] **13.6** *special bread*: Or "heart-shaped bread" or "dumplings."

wear long robes with sleeves.[a] 19 Tamar tore the robe she was wearing and put ashes on her head. Then she covered her face with her hands and cried loudly as she walked away.

Absalom Kills Amnon

20 Tamar's brother Absalom said to her, "How could Amnon have done such a terrible thing to you! But since he's your brother, don't tell anyone what happened. Just try not to think about it."

Tamar soon moved into Absalom's house, but she was always sad and lonely. 21 When David heard what had happened to Tamar, he was very angry. But Amnon was his oldest son and also his favorite, and David would not do anything to make Amnon unhappy.[b]

22 Absalom treated Amnon as though nothing had happened, but he hated Amnon for what he had done to his sister Tamar.

23 Two years later, Absalom's servants were cutting wool from his sheep in Baal-Hazor near the town of Ephraim, and Absalom invited all of the king's sons to be there.[c] 24 Then he went to David and said, "My servants are cutting the wool from my sheep. Please come and join us!"

25 David answered, "No, my son, we won't go. It would be too expensive for you." Absalom tried to get him to change his mind, but David did not want to go. He only said that he hoped they would have a good time.

26 Absalom said, "If you won't go, at least let my brother Amnon come with us."

David asked, "Why should he go with you?" 27 But Absalom kept on insisting, and finally David let Amnon and all his other sons go with Absalom.

Absalom prepared a banquet fit for a king.[d] 28 But he told his servants, "Keep an eye on Amnon. When he gets a little drunk from the wine and is feeling good, I'll give the signal. Then kill him! I've commanded you to do it, so don't be afraid. Be strong and brave."

29 Absalom's servants killed Amnon, just as Absalom had told them. The rest of the king's sons quickly rode away on their mules to escape from Absalom.

30 While they were on their way to Jerusalem, someone told David, "Absalom has killed all of your sons! Not even one is left." 31 David got up, and in his sorrow he tore his clothes and lay down on the ground. His servants remained standing, but they tore their clothes too.

32 Then David's nephew[e] Jonadab said, "Your Majesty, not all of your sons were killed! Only Amnon is dead. On the day that Amnon raped Tamar, Absalom decided to kill him. 33 Don't worry about the report that all your sons were killed. Only Amnon is dead, 34 and Absalom has run away."

One of the guards noticed a lot of people coming along the hillside on the road to Horonaim.[f] He went and told the king, "I saw some men coming along Horonaim Road."[g]

35 Jonadab said, "Your Majesty, look! Here come your sons now, just as I told you."

36 No sooner had he said it, than David's sons came in. They were weeping out loud, and David and all his officials cried just as loudly. 37-38 David was sad for a long time because Amnon was dead.

David Lets Absalom Come Home

Absalom had run away to Geshur, where he stayed for three years with King Talmai[h] the son of Ammihud. 39 David still felt so sad over the loss of Amnon that he wanted

[a] **13.18** *long . . . sleeves*: One possible meaning for the difficult Hebrew text. [b] **13.21** *But Amnon . . . unhappy*: The Dead Sea Scrolls and one ancient translation; these words are not in the Standard Hebrew Text. [c] **13.23** *invited . . . there*: Cutting the wool from sheep was a time for celebrating as well as working. [d] **13.27** *Absalom prepared . . . king*: One ancient translation; these words are not in the Hebrew text. [e] **13.32** *David's nephew*: The Hebrew text has "the son of David's brother Shimeah." [f] **13.34** *the road to Horonaim*: Or "the road behind him" or "the road to the west." [g] **13.34** *He . . . Road*: One ancient translation; these words are not in the Hebrew text. [h] **13.37,38** *King Talmai*: Absalom's grandfather (see 3.3).

13.37,38 2 S 3.2-5.

to take his army there and capture Absalom.[i]

14

Joab knew that David couldn't stop
thinking about Absalom, 2-3 and he
sent someone to bring in the wise woman
who lived in Tekoa. Joab told her, "Put on
funeral clothes and don't use any makeup.
Go to the king and pretend you have spent
a long time mourning the death of a loved
one." Then he told her what to say.

4 The woman from Tekoa went to David.
She bowed very low and said, "Your
Majesty, please help me!"

5 David asked, "What's the matter?"

She replied:

My husband is dead, and I'm a
widow. 6 I had two sons, but they got
into a fight out in a field where there
was no one to pull them apart, and
one of them killed the other. 7 Now all
of my relatives have come to me and
said, "Hand over your son! We're going
to put him to death for killing his
brother." But what they really want is
to get rid of him, so they can take over
our land.

Please don't let them put out my
only flame of hope! There won't be
anyone left on this earth to carry on
my husband's name.

8 "Go on home," David told her. "I'll
take care of this matter for you."

9 The woman said, "I hope your decision doesn't cause any problems for you.
But if it does, you can blame me."[j]

10 He said, "If anyone gives you any
trouble, bring them to me, and it won't
happen again!"

11 "Please," she replied, "swear by the
LORD your God that no one will be allowed
to kill my son!"

He said, "I swear by the living LORD that
no one will touch even a hair on his head!"

12 Then she asked, "Your Majesty, may I
say something?"

"Yes," he answered.

13 The woman said:

Haven't you been hurting God's
people? Your own son had to leave the
country. And when you judged in my
favor, it was the same as admitting that
you should have let him come back.
14 We each must die and disappear like
water poured out on the ground. But
God doesn't take our lives.[k] Instead, he
figures out ways of bringing us back
when we run away.

15 Your Majesty, I came here to tell
you about my problem, because I was
afraid of what someone might do to
me. I decided to come to you, because
I thought you could help. 16 In fact, I
knew that you would listen and save
my son and me from those who want
to take the land that God gave us.[l]

17 I can rest easy now that you have
given your decision. You know the difference between right and wrong just
like an angel of God, and I pray that
the LORD your God will be with you.

18 Then David said to the woman, "Now
I'm going to ask you a question, and don't
try to hide the truth!"

The woman replied, "Please go ahead,
Your Majesty."

19 David asked, "Did Joab put you up to
this?"

The woman answered, "Your Majesty, I
swear by your life that no one can hide the
truth from you. Yes, Joab did tell me what
to say, 20 but only to show you the other
side of this problem. You must be as wise as
the angel of God to know everything that
goes on in this country."

21 David turned to Joab and said, "It
seems that I have already given my decision. Go and bring Absalom back."

22 Joab bowed very low and said, "Your
Majesty, I thank you for giving your permission. It shows that you approve of me."

23 Joab went to Geshur to get Absalom.
But when they came back to Jerusalem,
24 David told Joab, "I don't want to see my
son Absalom. Tell him to stay away from

[i] **13.39** *David . . . Absalom*: Or "David was comforted over the loss of Amnon, and he no longer wanted to take his army there to capture Absalom." [j] **14.9** *I hope . . . me*: Or "May I speak some more?" [k] **14.14** *take our lives*: Or "make any exceptions." [l] **14.16** *take . . . us*: Or "make sure we have no part in God's people."

14.17 2 S 19.27.

me." So Absalom went to his own house without seeing his father.

Absalom Was Handsome

25 No one in all Israel was as handsome and well-built as Absalom. 26 He got his hair cut once a year, and when the hair was weighed, it came to about five pounds.

27 Absalom had three sons. He also had a daughter named Tamar, who grew up to be very beautiful.

Absalom Finally Sees David

28 Absalom lived in Jerusalem for two years without seeing his father. 29 He wanted Joab to talk to David for him. So one day he sent a message asking Joab to come over, but Joab refused. Absalom sent another message, but Joab still refused. 30 Finally, Absalom told his servants, "Joab's barley field is right next to mine. Go set it on fire!" And they did.

31 Joab went to Absalom's house and demanded, "Why did your servants set my field on fire?"

32 Absalom answered, "You didn't pay any attention when I sent for you. I want you to ask my father why he told me to come back from Geshur. I was better off there. I want to see my father now! If I'm guilty, let him kill me."

33 Joab went to David and told him what Absalom had said. David sent for Absalom, and Absalom came. He bowed very low, and David leaned over and kissed him.

Absalom Rebels against David

15 Some time later, Absalom got himself a chariot with horses to pull it, and he had fifty men run in front. 2 He would get up early each morning and wait by the side of the road that led to the city gate.[m] Anyone who had a complaint to bring to King David would have to go that way, and Absalom would ask each of them, "Where are you from?"

If they said, "I'm from a tribe in the north," 3 Absalom would say, "You deserve to win your case. It's too bad the king doesn't have anyone to hear complaints like yours. 4 I wish someone would make me the judge around here! I would be fair to everyone."

5 Whenever anyone would come to Absalom and start bowing down, he would reach out and hug and kiss them. 6 That's how he treated everyone from Israel who brought a complaint to the king. Soon everyone in Israel liked Absalom better than they liked David.

7 Four years[n] later, Absalom said to David, "Please, let me go to Hebron. I have to keep a promise that I made to the LORD, 8 when I was living with the Arameans in Geshur. I promised that if the LORD would bring me back to live in Jerusalem, I would worship him in Hebron."[o]

9 David gave his permission, and Absalom went to Hebron. 10-12 He took two hundred men from Jerusalem with him, but they had no idea what he was going to do. Absalom offered sacrifices in Hebron and sent someone to Gilo to tell David's advisor Ahithophel to come.

More and more people were joining Absalom and supporting his plot. Meanwhile, Absalom had secretly sent some messengers to the northern tribes of Israel. The messengers told everyone, "When you hear the sound of the trumpets, you must shout, 'Absalom now rules as king in Hebron!' "

David Has To Leave Jerusalem

13 A messenger came and told David, "Everyone in Israel is on Absalom's side!"

14 David's officials were in Jerusalem with him, and he told them, "Let's get out of here! We'll have to leave soon, or none of us will escape from Absalom. Hurry! If he moves fast, he could catch us while we're still here. Then he will kill us and everyone else in the city."

15 The officials said, "Your Majesty, we'll do whatever you say."

16-17 David left behind ten of his wives[p] to take care of the palace, but the rest of his family and his officials and soldiers went with him.

They stopped at the last house at the edge of the city. 18 Then David stood there

[m] **15.2** *the city gate*: Or "the entrance to the king's palace." [n] **15.7** *Four years*: The Hebrew text has "forty years." [o] **15.8** *in Hebron*: Some manuscripts of one ancient translation; these words are not in the Hebrew text. [p] **15.16,17** *wives*: See the note at 3.7.

and watched while his regular troops and his bodyguards[q] marched past. The last group was the six hundred soldiers who had followed him from Gath.[r] Their commander was Ittai.

19 David spoke to Ittai and said, "You're a foreigner from the town of Gath. You don't have to leave with us. Go back and join the new king! 20 You haven't been with me very long, so why should you have to follow me, when I don't even know where I'm going? Take your soldiers and go back. I pray that the Lord will be[s] kind and faithful to you."

21 Ittai answered, "Your Majesty, just as surely as you and the LORD live, I will go where you go, no matter if it costs me my life."

22 "Then come on!" David said.

So Ittai and all his men and their families walked on past David.

David Sends the Sacred Chest Back to Jerusalem

23 The people of Jerusalem were crying and moaning as David and everyone with him passed by. He led them across Kidron Valley[t] and along the road toward the desert.

24 Zadok and Abiathar the priests were there along with several men from the tribe of Levi who were carrying the sacred chest. They set the chest down, and left it there until David and his followers had gone out of the city.

25 Then David said:

Zadok, take the sacred chest back to Jerusalem. If the LORD is pleased with me, he will bring me back and let me see it and his tent again. 26 But if he says he isn't pleased with me, then let him do what he knows is best.

27 Zadok, you are a good judge of things,[u] so return to the city and don't cause any trouble. Take your son Ahimaaz with you. Abiathar and his son Jonathan will also go back. 28 I'll wait at the river crossing in the desert until I hear from you.

29 Zadok and Abiathar took the sacred chest back into Jerusalem and stayed there. 30 David went on up the slope of the Mount of Olives. He was barefoot and crying, and he covered his head to show his sorrow. Everyone with him was crying, and they covered their heads too.

31 Someone told David, "Ahithophel is helping Absalom plot against you!"

David said, "Please, LORD, keep Ahithophel's plans from working!"

David Sends Hushai Back as a Spy

32 When David reached the top of the Mount of Olives, he met Hushai the Archite[v] at a place of worship. Hushai's robe was torn, and dust was on his head.[w] 33 David told him:

If you come with me, you might slow us down.[x] 34 Go back into the city and tell Absalom, "Your Majesty, I am your servant. I will serve you now, just as I served your father in the past."

Hushai, if you do that, you can help me ruin Ahithophel's plans. 35 Zadok and Abiathar the priests will be there with you, and you can tell them everything you hear in the palace. 36 Then have them send their sons Ahimaaz and Jonathan to tell me what you've heard.

37 David's advisor Hushai slipped back into Jerusalem, just about the same time that Absalom was coming in.

Ziba Gives Food to David

16 David had started down the other side of the Mount of Olives, when he was met by Ziba, the chief servant of Mephibosheth.[y] Ziba had two donkeys that were carrying two hundred loaves of bread,

[q] **15.18** *bodyguards*: See the note at 8.18. [r] **15.18** *the six . . . Gath*: These were Philistine soldiers who were loyal to David. [s] **15.20** *I pray . . . be*: One ancient translation; these words are not in the Hebrew text. [t] **15.23** *Kidron Valley*: This was considered the eastern boundary of Jerusalem. [u] **15.27** *you . . . things*: Or "You are a prophet" or "You are not a prophet."
[v] **15.32** *Archite*: The Archites were part of the tribe of Benjamin (see Joshua 16.2).
[w] **15.32** *Hushai's . . . head*: See the note at 1.2. [x] **15.33** *you might slow us down*: Hushai was probably very old. [y] **16.1** *chief servant of Mephibosheth*: See 9.1-13.
16.1 2 S 9.9, 10.

a hundred handfuls of raisins, a hundred figs,[z] and some wine.

2 "What's all this?" David asked.

Ziba said, "The donkeys are for your family to ride. The bread and fruit are for the people to eat, and the wine is for them to drink in the desert when they are tired out."

3 "And where is Mephibosheth?" David asked.

Ziba answered, "He stayed in Jerusalem, because he thinks the people of Israel want him to rule the kingdom of his grandfather Saul."

4 David then told him, "Everything that used to belong to Mephibosheth is now yours."

Ziba said, "Your Majesty, I am your humble servant, and I hope you will be pleased with me."

Shimei Curses David

5 David was near the town of Bahurim when a man came out and started cursing him. The man was Shimei the son of Gera, and he was one of Saul's distant relatives. 6 He threw stones at David, at his soldiers, and at everyone else, including the bodyguards who walked on each side of David.

7 Shimei was yelling at David, "Get out of here, you murderer! You good-for-nothing, 8 the LORD is paying you back for killing so many in Saul's family. You stole his kingdom, but now the LORD has given it to your son Absalom. You're a murderer, and that's why you're in such big trouble!"

9 Abishai said, "Your Majesty, this man is as useless as a dead dog! He shouldn't be allowed to curse you. Let me go over and chop off his head."

10 David replied, "What will I ever do with you and your brother Joab? If Shimei is cursing me because the LORD has told him to, then who are you to tell him to stop?"

11 Then David said to Abishai and all his soldiers:

My own son is trying to kill me!
Why shouldn't this man from the tribe
of Benjamin want me dead even more?
Let him curse all he wants. Maybe the
LORD did tell him to curse me. 12 But if
the LORD hears these curses and sees
the trouble I'm in, maybe he will have
pity on me instead.

13 David and the others went on down the road. Shimei went along the hillside by the road, cursing and throwing rocks and dirt at them. 14 When David and those with him came to the Jordan River, they were tired out. But after they rested, they[a] felt much better.

Hushai Meets Absalom

15 By this time, Absalom, Ahithophel, and the others had reached Jerusalem. 16 David's friend Hushai came to Absalom and said, "Long live the king! Long live the king!"

17 But Absalom asked Hushai, "Is this how you show loyalty to your friend David? Why didn't you go with him?"

18 Hushai answered, "The LORD and the people of Israel have chosen you to be king. I can't leave. I have to stay and serve the one they've chosen. 19 Besides, it seems right for me to serve you, just as I served your father."

Ahithophel's Advice

20 Absalom turned to Ahithophel and said, "Give us your advice! What should we do?"

21 Ahithophel answered, "Some of your father's wives[b] were left here to take care of the palace. You should have sex with them. Then everyone will find out that you have publicly disgraced your father. This will make you and your followers even more powerful."

22 Absalom had a tent set up on the flat roof of the palace, and everyone watched as he went into the tent with his father's wives.

23 Ahithophel gave such good advice in those days that both Absalom and David thought it came straight from God.

[z] **16.1** *figs*: Or "pomegranates," a bright red fruit that looks like an apple. [a] **16.14** *they*: Hebrew "he." [b] **16.21** *wives*: See the note at 3.7.

16.3 2 S 19.25-27. **16.22** 2 S 12.11, 12.

17 Ahithophel said to Absalom:
Let me choose twelve thousand men and attack David tonight,
2 while he is tired and discouraged. He
will panic, and everyone with him will
run away. I won't kill anyone except
David, 3 since he's the one you want to
get rid of. Then I'll bring the whole nation back to you like a bride coming
home to her husband.[c] This way there
won't be a civil war.

Hushai Fools Absalom

4 Absalom and all the leaders of the
tribes of Israel agreed that Ahithophel had
a good plan. 5 Then Absalom said, "Bring in
Hushai the Archite. Let's hear what he has
to say."
6 Hushai came in, and Absalom told him
what Ahithophel had planned. Then Absalom said, "Should we do what he says? And
if we shouldn't, can you come up with anything better?"
7 Hushai said:
This time Ahithophel's advice isn't
so good. 8 You know that your father
and his followers are real warriors.
Right now they are as fierce as a
mother bear whose cubs have just
been killed. Besides, your father has a
lot of experience in fighting wars, and
he won't be spending the night with
the others. 9 He has probably already
found a hiding place in a cave or
somewhere else.
As soon as anyone hears that some
of your soldiers have been killed,
everyone will think your whole army
has been destroyed. 10 Then even
those who are as brave as a lion will
lose their courage. All Israel knows
what a great warrior your father is and
what brave soldiers he has.
11 My advice is to gather all the
fighting men of Israel from the town of
Dan in the north down to the town of
Beersheba in the south. You will have
more soldiers than there are grains of
sand on the seashore. Absalom, you
should lead them yourself, 12 and we
will all go to fight David wherever he
is. We will fall on him just as dew falls
and covers the ground. He and all his
soldiers will die! 13 If they go into a
walled town, we will put ropes around
that town and drag it into the river. We
won't leave even one small piece of a
stone.
14 Absalom and the others liked
Hushai's plan better than Ahithophel's
plan. This was because the LORD had
decided to keep Ahithophel's plan
from working and to cause trouble for Absalom.

Jonathan and Ahimaaz Tell David the News

15 Right away, Hushai went to Zadok
and Abiathar. He told them what advice
Ahithophel had given to Absalom and to
the leaders of Israel. He also told them
about the advice he had given. 16 Then he
said, "Hurry! Send someone to warn David
not to spend the night on this side of the
river. He must get across the river, so he
and the others won't be wiped out!"
17 Jonathan and Ahimaaz[d] had been
waiting at Rogel Spring[e] because they did
not want to be seen in Jerusalem. A servant
girl went to the spring and gave them the
message for David. 18 But a young man
saw them and went to tell Absalom. So
Jonathan and Ahimaaz left and hurried to
the house of a man who lived in Bahurim.
Then they climbed down into a well in the
courtyard. 19 The man's wife put the cover
on the well and poured grain on top of it,
so the well could not be seen.[f]
20 Absalom's soldiers came to the
woman and demanded, "Where are Ahimaaz and Jonathan?"
The woman answered, "They went
across the stream."
The soldiers went off to look for the two

[c] **17.3** *back to you . . . husband*: One ancient translation; Hebrew "back to you. The man you are chasing is like bringing back the whole nation." [d] **17.17** *Jonathan and Ahimaaz*: See 15.27. [e] **17.17** *Rogel Spring*: South of Jerusalem in Kidron Valley. [f] **17.19** *The man's wife . . . seen*: Everyone would have thought that the woman was drying grain on a mat that she had spread on the ground.

men. But when they did not find the men,
they went back to Jerusalem.
21 After the soldiers had gone, Jonathan
and Ahimaaz climbed out of the well. They
went to David and said, "Hurry! Get ready
to cross the river!" Then they told him
about Ahithophel's plan.
22 David and the others got ready and
started crossing the Jordan River. By sunrise all of them were on the other side.

Ahithophel Kills Himself

23 When Ahithophel saw that Absalom
and the leaders of Israel were not going to
follow his advice, he saddled his donkey
and rode back to his home in Gilo. He told
his family and servants what to do. Then
he hanged himself, and they buried him in
his family's burial place.

Absalom Puts Amasa in Charge of the Army

24 David went to the town of Mahanaim,
and Absalom crossed the Jordan River with
the army of Israel. 25 Absalom put Amasa in
Joab's place as commander of the army.
Amasa's father was Ithra[g] from the family
of Ishmael,[h] and his mother was Abigal,[i]
the daughter of Nahash and the sister of
Joab's mother Zeruiah. 26 The Israelites
under Absalom's command set up camp in
the region of Gilead.

Friends Bring Supplies to David

27 After David came to the town of Mahanaim, Shobi the son of Nahash came
from Rabbah in Ammon,[j] Machir the son
of Ammiel came from Lo-Debar, and
Barzillai the Gileadite came from Rogelim.
28-29 Here is a list of what they brought:
sleeping mats, blankets, bowls, pottery jars,
wheat, barley, flour, roasted grain, beans,
lentils, honey, yogurt, sheep, and cheese.
They brought the food for David and the
others because they knew that everyone
would be hungry, tired, and thirsty from being out in the desert.

David Gets Ready for Battle

18 David divided his soldiers into
groups of a hundred and groups of
a thousand. Then he chose officers to be in
command of each group. 2 He sent out
one-third of his army under the command
of Joab, another third under the command
of Abishai the son of Zeruiah, and the rest
under the command of Ittai from Gath.
He told the soldiers, "I'm going into battle
with you."
3 But the soldiers said, "No, don't go
into battle with us! It won't matter to our
enemies if they make us all run away, or
even if they kill half of us. But you are
worth ten thousand of us. It would be better for you to stay in town and send help if
we need it."
4-6 David said, "All right, if you think I
should."
Then in a voice loud enough for everyone to hear, he said, "Joab! Abishai! Ittai!
For my sake, be sure that Absalom comes
back unharmed."
David stood beside the town gate as his
army marched past in groups of a hundred
and in groups of a thousand.

Joab Kills Absalom

The war with Israel took place in
Ephraim Forest. 7-8 Battles were being
fought all over the forest, and David's soldiers were winning. Twenty thousand soldiers were killed[k] that day, and more of
them died from the dangers of the forest
than from the fighting itself.
9 Absalom was riding his mule under a
huge tree when his head[l] caught in the
branches. The mule ran off and left Absalom hanging in midair. Some of David's sol-

[g] **17.25** *Ithra*: Or "Jether." [h] **17.25** *the family of Ishmael*: Some manuscripts of one ancient translation; other manuscripts of the same translation "the town of Jezreel"; Hebrew "the people of Israel." [i] **17.25** *Amasa . . . Abigal*: Abigal and Zeruiah (Joab's mother) were full sisters, and David was evidently their half brother with the same mother, but a different father. This made Amasa one of David's nephews (see 1 Chronicles 2.12-17). [j] **17.27** *Shobi . . . Ammon*: Shobi was probably the new king of the Ammonites that David had appointed after he captured Rabbah (see 2 Samuel 10.1-3; 12.26-31). [k] **18.7,8** *Twenty . . . killed*: This may refer to the total number or to the number of Absalom's soldiers who were killed. [l] **18.9** *head*: Or "hair."

diers happened by, [10] and one of them went and told Joab, "I saw Absalom hanging in a tree!"

[11] Joab said, "You saw Absalom? Why didn't you kill him? I would have given you ten pieces of silver and a special belt."

[12] The man answered, "Even if you paid me a thousand pieces of silver here and now, I still wouldn't touch the king's son. We all heard King David tell you and Abishai and Ittai not to harm Absalom. [13] He always finds out what's going on. I would have been risking my life to kill Absalom, because you would have let me take the blame."

[14] Joab said, "I'm not going to waste any more time on you!"

Absalom was still alive, so Joab took three spears and stuck them through Absalom's chest. [15] Ten of Joab's bodyguards came over and finished him off. [16] Then Joab blew a trumpet to signal his troops to stop chasing Israel's soldiers. [17] They threw Absalom's body into a deep pit in the forest and put a big pile of rocks over it.

Meanwhile, the people of Israel had all run back to their own homes.

[18] When Absalom was alive, he had set up a stone monument for himself in King's Valley. He explained, "I don't have any sons[m] to keep my name alive." He called it Absalom's Monument, and that is the name it still has today.[n]

Ahimaaz Wants To Tell David

[19] Ahimaaz the son of Zadok said, "Joab, let me run and tell King David that the LORD has rescued him from his enemies."

[20] Joab answered, "You're not the one to tell the king that his son is dead. You can take him a message some other time, but not today."

[21] Someone from Ethiopia[o] was standing there, and Joab told him, "Go and tell the king what you have seen." The man knelt down in front of Joab and then got up and started running.

[22] Ahimaaz spoke to Joab again, "No matter what happens, I still want to run. And besides, the Ethiopian has already left."

Joab said, "Why should you run? You won't get a reward for the news you have!"

[23] "I'll run no matter what!" Ahimaaz insisted.

"All right then, run!" Joab said.

Ahimaaz took the road through the Jordan Valley and outran the Ethiopian.

[24] Meanwhile, David was sitting between the inner and outer gates[p] in the city wall. One of his soldiers was watching from the roof of the gate-tower. He saw a man running toward the town [25] and shouted down to tell David.

David answered, "If he's alone, he must have some news."

The runner was getting closer, [26] when the soldier saw someone else running. He shouted down to the gate, "Look! There's another runner!"

David said, "He must have some news too."

[27] The soldier on the roof shouted, "The first one runs just like Ahimaaz the son of Zadok."

This time David said, "He's a good man. He must have some good news."

[28] Ahimaaz called out, "We won! We won!" Then he bowed low to David and said, "Your Majesty, praise the LORD your God! He has given you victory over your enemies."

[29] "Is my son Absalom all right?" David asked.

Ahimaaz said, "When Joab sent your personal servant and me, I saw a noisy crowd. But I don't know what it was all about."

[30] David told him, "Stand over there and wait."

[m] **18.18** *I don't have any sons*: According to 14.27, Absalom had three sons. But they could have died young or been put to death for Absalom's murder of Amnon. [n] **18.18** *today*: That is, at the time of writing. This monument is not the same as the structure now known as "Absalom's Tomb," which was built at least 600 years later. [o] **18.21** *Ethiopia*: The Hebrew text has "Cush," which was a region south of Egypt that included parts of the present countries of Ethiopia and Sudan.
[p] **18.24** *between . . . gates*: The city gate was often like a tower in the city wall, with one gate on the outside of the wall and another gate on the inside of the wall.

Ahimaaz went over and stood there.
31 The Ethiopian came and said, "Your
Majesty, today I have good news! The LORD
has rescued you from all your enemies!"
32 "Is my son Absalom all right?" David
asked.
The Ethiopian replied, "I wish that all
Your Majesty's enemies and everyone who
tries to harm you would end up like him!"

David Cries for Absalom

33 David started trembling. Then he
went up to the room above the city gate to
cry. As he went, he kept saying, "My son
Absalom! My son, my son Absalom! I wish I
could have died instead of you! Absalom,
my son, my son!"[q]

19 Someone told Joab, "The king is
crying because Absalom is dead."
2 David's army found out he was crying
because his son had died, and their day of
victory suddenly turned into a day of sadness. 3 The troops were sneaking into Mahanaim, just as if they had run away from a
battle and were ashamed.
4 David held his hands over his face and
kept on crying loudly, "My son, Absalom!
Absalom, my son, my son!"
5 Joab went to the house where David
was staying and told him:

> You've made your soldiers
> ashamed! Not only did they save your
> life, they saved your sons and daugh-
> ters and wives as well. 6 You're more
> loyal to your enemies than to your
> friends. What you've done today has
> shown your officers and soldiers that
> they don't mean a thing to you. You
> would be happy if Absalom was still
> alive, even if the rest of us were dead.
> 7 Now get up! Go out there and
> thank them for what they did. If you
> don't, I swear by the LORD that you
> won't even have one man left on your
> side tomorrow morning. You may have
> had a lot of troubles in the past, but
> this will be the worst thing that has
> ever happened to you!

8 David got up and went to the town gate
and sat down. When the people heard that
he was sitting there, they came to see him.

Israel and Judah Want David Back

After Israel's soldiers had all returned
home, 9-10 everyone in Israel started arguing. They were saying to each other, "King
David rescued us from the Philistines and
from our other enemies. But then we chose
Absalom to be our new leader, and David
had to leave the country to get away. Absalom died in battle, so why hasn't something
been done to bring David back?"
11 When David found out what they
were saying, he sent a message to Zadok
and Abiathar the priests. It said:

> Say to the leaders of Judah, "Why
> are you the last tribe to think about
> bringing King David back home? 12 He
> is your brother, your own relative! Why
> haven't you done anything to bring
> him back?"
> 13 And tell Amasa, "You're my
> nephew, and with God as a witness, I
> swear I'll make you commander of my
> army instead of Joab."

14 Soon the tribe of Judah again became
followers of David, and they sent him this
message: "Come back, and bring your soldiers with you."

David Starts Back for Jerusalem

15 David started back and had gone as
far as the Jordan River when he met the
people of Judah. They had gathered at Gilgal and had come to help him cross the
river.
16 Shimei[r] the son of Gera was there
with them. He had hurried from Bahurim
to meet David. Shimei was from the tribe
of Benjamin, and 17 a thousand others from
Benjamin had come with him.
Ziba, the chief servant of Saul's family,
also came to the Jordan River. He and his
fifteen sons and twenty servants waded
across[s] to meet David. 18 Then they
brought David's family and servants back
across the river, and they did everything he
wanted them to do.

[q]**18.33** *son*: In Hebrew, this verse is 19.1. [r]**19.16** *Shimei*: See 16.5-13. [s]**19.17** *waded across*: Or "rushed."

19.16 2 S 16.5-13.

Shimei Meets with David

Shimei crossed the Jordan River and
bowed down in front of David. 19 He said,
"Your Majesty, I beg you not to punish me!
Please, forget what I did when you were
leaving Jerusalem. Don't even think about
it. 20 I know I was wrong. That's why I
wanted to be the first one from the northern tribes to meet you."

21 But Abishai shouted, "You should
be killed for cursing the LORD's chosen
king!"

22 David said, "Abishai, what will I ever
do with you and your brother Joab? Is it
your job to tell me who has done wrong?
I've been made king of all Israel today, and
no one will be put to death!" 23 Then David
promised Shimei that he would not be
killed.

Mephibosheth Meets with David

24 Mephibosheth, the grandson of
Saul, also came to meet David. He had
missed David so much that he had not
taken a bath or trimmed his beard or
washed his clothes the whole time David
was gone.

25 After they had gone back to
Jerusalem, Mephibosheth came to see
David, who asked him, "Why didn't you go
with me?"

26 He answered, "Your Majesty, you
know I can't walk. I told my servant to saddle a donkey for me[t] so I could go with you.
But my servant left without me, and
27 then he lied about me. You're as wise as
an angel of God, so do what you think is
right. 28 After all, you could have killed my
whole family and me. But instead, you let
me eat at your own table. Your Majesty,
what more could I ask?"

29 David answered, "You've said enough!
I've decided to divide the property[u] between you and Ziba."

30 Mephibosheth replied, "He can have
it all! I'm just glad you've come home
safely."

Barzillai Returns Home

31 Barzillai came from Rogelim in Gilead
to meet David at the Jordan River and go
across with him. 32 Barzillai was eighty
years old. He was very rich and had sent
food to David in Mahanaim.

33 David said to him, "Cross the river
and go to Jerusalem with me. I will take
care of you."

34 Barzillai answered:

Your Majesty, why should I go to
Jerusalem? I don't have much longer
to live. 35 I'm already eighty years old,
and my body is almost numb. I can't
taste my food or hear the sound of
singing, and I would be nothing but a
burden. 36 I'll cross the river with you,
but I'll only go a little way on the other
side. You don't have to be so kind to
me. 37 Just let me return to my hometown, where I can someday be buried
near my father and mother. My servant Chimham[v] can go with you, and
you can treat him as your own.

38 David said, "I'll take Chimham with
me, and whatever you ask me to do for
him, I'll do. And if there's anything else you
want, I'll also do that."

39 David's soldiers went on across the
river, while he stayed behind to tell Barzillai good-by and to wish him well. Barzillai
returned home, but 40 Chimham crossed
the river with David.

Israel and Judah Argue

All of Judah's army and half of Israel's
army were there to help David cross the
river. 41 The soldiers from Israel came to
him and said, "Why did our relatives from
Judah sneak you and your family and your
soldiers across the Jordan?"

42 The people of Judah answered, "Why
are you so angry? We are the king's relatives. He didn't give us any food, and we
didn't take anything for ourselves!"

43 Those from Israel said, "King David
belongs to us ten times more than he

[t] **19.26** *I told . . . me*: Two ancient translations; Hebrew, "I said, 'I will saddle a donkey for myself.'"
[u] **19.29** *the property*: The property that had belonged to Saul (see 9.7; 16.4). [v] **19.37** *My servant Chimham*: Or "My son Chimham."

19.24 2 S 9.1-13; 16.1-4. **19.31** 2 S 17.27-29.

belongs to you.[w] Why didn't you think we were good enough to help you? After all, we were the first ones to think of bringing him back!"

The people of Judah spoke more harshly than the people of Israel.

Sheba Rebels against David

20 A troublemaker from the tribe of Benjamin was there. His name was Sheba the son of Bichri, and he blew a trumpet to get everyone's attention. Then he said, "People of Israel, David the son of Jesse doesn't belong to us! Let's go home."

2 So they stopped following David and went off with Sheba. But the people of Judah stayed close to David all the way from the Jordan to Jerusalem.

David's Ten Wives

3 David had left ten of his wives in Jerusalem to take care of his palace. But when he came back, he had them taken to another house, and he placed soldiers there to guard them. He gave them whatever they needed, but he never slept with any of them again.[x] They had to live there for the rest of their lives as if they were widows.

The Army Goes after Sheba

4 David said to Amasa, "Three days from now I want you and all of Judah's army to be here!"

5 Amasa started bringing the army together, but it was taking him more than three days. 6 So David said to Abishai, "Sheba will hurt us more than Absalom ever did. Take my best soldiers and go after him. We don't want him to take over any walled cities and get away from us."[y]

Joab Kills Amasa

7 Abishai left Jerusalem to try and capture Sheba. He took along Joab and his soldiers, as well as David's bodyguard[z] and best troops. 8 They had gone as far as the big rock at Gibeon when Amasa caught up with them. Joab had a dagger strapped around his waist over his military uniform, but it fell out as he started toward Amasa.

9 Joab said, "Amasa, my cousin, how are you?" Then Joab took hold of Amasa's beard with his right hand, so that he could greet him with a kiss. 10 Amasa did not see the dagger in Joab's other hand. Joab stuck it in Amasa's stomach, and his insides spilled out on the ground. Joab only struck him once, but Amasa was dying.

Joab and his brother Abishai went off to chase Sheba. 11 One of Joab's soldiers stood by Amasa and shouted, "If any of you like Joab, and if you are for David, then follow Joab!"

12 Amasa was still rolling in his own blood in the middle of the road. The soldier who had shouted noticed that everyone who passed by would stop, so he dragged Amasa off the road and covered him with a blanket. 13 After this, no one else stopped. They all walked straight past him on their way to help Joab capture Sheba.

Sheba Hides Out in the Town of Abel

14 Sheba had gone through all of the tribes of Israel when he came to the town of Abel Beth-Maacah. All of his best soldiers[a] met him there and followed him into the town.

15 Joab and his troops came and surrounded Abel, so that no one could go in or come out. They made a dirt ramp up to the town wall and then started to use a battering ram to knock the wall down.

A Wise Woman Saves the Town

16 A wise woman shouted from the top of the wall,[b] "Listen to me! Listen to me! I have to talk to Joab! Tell him to come here!" 17 When he came, the woman said, "Are you Joab?"

[w] **19.43** *King David . . . you*: In this verse "Israel" stands for the ten northern tribes and does not include the tribe of Judah in the south. [x] **20.3** *he . . . again*: Because of what Absalom had done (see 16.21,22). [y] **20.6** *get . . . us*: One possible meaning for the difficult Hebrew text. [z] **20.7** *bodyguard*: See the note at 8.18. [a] **20.14** *best soldiers*: One ancient translation; the difficult Hebrew text may mean either "Berites" or "Bichrites," Sheba's relatives. [b] **20.16** *the top of the wall*: Or "the town."

20.1 1 K 12.15-19; 2 Ch 10.15-19. **20.3** 2 S 16.22.

"Yes, I am," he answered.
She said, "Please, listen to what I have
to say."
"All right," he said. "I'll listen."
18 She said, "Long ago people used to
say, 'If you want good advice, go to the town
of Abel to get it.' The answers they got here
were all that was needed to settle any problem. 19 We are Israelites, and we want
peace! You can trust us. Why are you trying
to destroy a town that's like a mother in Israel? Why do you want to wipe out the
LORD's people?"
20 Joab answered, "No, no! I'm not trying to wipe you out or destroy your town!
21 That's not it at all. There's a man in your
town from the hill country of Ephraim. His
name is Sheba, and he is the leader of a rebellion against King David. Turn him over
to me, and we will leave your town alone."
The woman told Joab, "We will throw
his head over the wall."
22 She went to the people of the town
and talked them into doing it. They cut off
Sheba's head and threw it to Joab.
Joab blew a signal on his trumpet, and
the soldiers returned to their homes. Joab
went back to David in Jerusalem.

Another List of David's Officials[c]

23 Joab was the commander of Israel's
entire army.
Benaiah the son of Jehoiada was in
command of David's bodyguard.[d]
24 Adoram[e] was in charge of the slave-
labor force.
Jehoshaphat the son of Ahilud kept
government records.
25 Sheva was the secretary.
Zadok and Abiathar were the priests.
26 Ira from Jair was David's priest.

The Gibeonites Hang Saul's Descendants

21 While David was king, there were
three years in a row when the nation of Israel could not grow enough food.
So David asked the LORD for help, and the
LORD answered, "Saul and his family are
guilty of murder, because he had the
Gibeonites killed."
2 The Gibeonites were not Israelites;
they were descendants of the Amorites.
The people of Israel had promised not to
kill them,[f] but Saul had tried to kill them
because he wanted Israel and Judah to
control all the land.
David had the Gibeonites come, and he
talked with them. 3 He said, "What can I
do to make up for what Saul did, so that
you'll ask the LORD to be kind to his people
again?"[g]
4 The Gibeonites answered, "Silver and
gold from Saul and his family are not
enough. On the other hand, we don't have
the right to put any Israelite to death."
David said, "I'll do whatever you ask."[h]
5 They replied, "Saul tried to kill all our
people so that none of us would be left in
the land of Israel. 6 Give us seven of his descendants. We will hang[i] these men near
the place where the LORD is worshiped in
Gibeah, the hometown of Saul, the LORD's
chosen king."
"I'll give them to you," David said.
7 David had made a promise to
Jonathan with the LORD as his witness, so
he spared Jonathan's son Mephibosheth,
the grandson of Saul. 8 But Saul and Rizpah the daughter of Aiah had two sons
named Armoni and Mephibosheth. Saul's
daughter Merab[j] had five sons whose
father was Adriel the son of Barzillai from

[c] **20.23** *Another List of David's Officials*: See also the list in 8.16,17. [d] **20.23** *David's bodyguard*: See the note at 8.18. [e] **20.24** *Adoram*: One ancient translation "Adoniram" (see 1 Kings 4.6; 5.14). [f] **21.2** *promised . . . them*: See Joshua 9.3-27. [g] **21.3** *ask . . . again*: Saul's guilt had become a curse on Israel that had resulted in famine. For the effects of this curse to be removed, the Gibeonites would have to ask the LORD to be kind to Israel. [h] **21.4** *I'll . . . ask*: Or "What are you asking me to do for you?" [i] **21.6** *hang*: One possible meaning for the difficult Hebrew text. [j] **21.8** *Merab*: Some Hebrew manuscripts and some manuscripts of one ancient translation. Most other manuscripts have "Michal," Saul's daughter who was one of David's wives, but she never had any children (see 2 Samuel 6.23). According to 1 Samuel 18.19, Merab was Saul's daughter, and she married Adriel from Meholah.

21.2 Js 9.3-15. **21.7** 1 S 20.14-17; 2 S 9.1-7. **21.8** 1 S 18.19.

Meholah.[k] David took Rizpah's two sons and Merab's five sons and 9 turned them over to the Gibeonites, who hanged[l] all seven of them on the mountain near the place where the LORD was worshiped. This happened right at the beginning of the barley harvest.[m]

Rizpah Takes Care of the Bodies

10 Rizpah spread out some sackcloth[n] on a nearby rock. She wouldn't let the birds land on the bodies during the day, and she kept the wild animals away at night. She stayed there from the beginning of the harvest until it started to rain.[o]

The Burial of Saul and His Descendants

11-12 Earlier the Philistines had killed Saul and Jonathan on Mount Gilboa and had hung their bodies in the town square at Beth-Shan. The people of Jabesh in Gilead had secretly taken the bodies away, but David found out what Saul's wife[p] Rizpah had done, and he went to the leaders of Jabesh to get the bones of Saul and his son Jonathan. 13-14 David had their bones taken to the land of Benjamin and buried in a side room in Saul's family burial place. Then he gave orders for the bones of the men who had been hanged[q] to be buried there. It was done, and God answered prayers to bless the land.

The Descendants of the Rephaim

(1 Chronicles 20.4-8)

15 One time David got very tired when he and his soldiers were fighting the Philistines. 16 One of the Philistine warriors was Ishbibenob, who was a descendant of the Rephaim,[r] and he tried to kill David. Ishbibenob was armed with a new sword,[s] and his bronze spearhead[t] alone weighed seven and a half pounds. 17 But Abishai[u] came to the rescue and killed the Philistine.

David's soldiers told him, "We can't let you risk your life in battle anymore! You give light to our nation, and we want that flame to keep burning."

18 There was another battle with the Philistines at Gob, where Sibbecai from Hushah killed a descendant of the Rephaim named Saph.

19 There was still another battle with the Philistines at Gob. A soldier named Elhanan killed Goliath[v] from Gath, whose spear shaft was like a weaver's beam.[w] Elhanan's father was Jari[x] from Bethlehem.

20 There was another war, this time in Gath. One of the enemy soldiers was a descendant of the Rephaim. He was as big as a giant and had six fingers on each hand and six toes on each foot. 21 But when he made fun of Israel, David's nephew Jonathan killed him. Jonathan was the son of David's brother Shimei.

22 David and his soldiers killed these four men who were descendants of the Rephaim from Gath.

David Sings to the LORD

(Psalm 18.1-50)

22 David sang a song to the LORD after the LORD had rescued him from his enemies, especially Saul. These are the words to David's song:

[k]**21.8** *Meholah*: Also known as Abel-Meholah. [l]**21.9** *hanged*: One possible meaning for the difficult Hebrew text. [m]**21.9** *This . . . harvest*: This would have been late in April.
[n]**21.10** *sackcloth*: See the note at 3.31. [o]**21.10** *started to rain*: This may have been the beginning of the rainy season in September or October. It usually didn't rain from May to September. Or, it may have been a sign that now there would be enough rain again. [p]**21.11,12** *wife*: See the note at 3.7. [q]**21.13,14** *hanged*: One possible meaning for the difficult Hebrew text.
[r]**21.16** *Rephaim*: This may refer to a group of people that lived in Palestine before the Israelites and who were famous for their large size. [s]**21.16** *new sword*: One possible meaning for the difficult Hebrew text. [t]**21.16** *spearhead*: Or "helmet." [u]**21.17** *Abishai*: David's nephew, the brother of Joab. [v]**21.19** *Goliath*: According to 1 Chronicles 20.5, Elhanan killed the brother of Goliath. [w]**21.19** *weaver's beam*: A large wooden rod used by a weaver when making cloth.
[x]**21.19** *Jari*: Or "Jaare."

21.11,12 1 S 31.8-13. **21.17** 1 K 11.36; Ps 132.17.

2 Our LORD and our God,
you are my mighty rock,[y]
my fortress, my protector.
3 You are the rock
where I am safe.
You are my shield,
my powerful weapon,[z]
and my place of shelter.

You rescue me and keep me
from being hurt.
4 I praise you, our LORD!
I prayed to you,
and you rescued me
from my enemies.
5 Death, like ocean waves,
surrounded me,
and I was almost swallowed
by its flooding waters.

6 Ropes from the world
of the dead
had coiled around me,
and death had set a trap
in my path.
7 I was in terrible trouble
when I called out to you,
but from your temple
you heard me
and answered my prayer.
8 Earth shook and shivered!
The columns supporting the sky[a]
rocked back and forth.
You were angry
9 and breathed out smoke.
Scorching heat and fiery flames
spewed from your mouth.

10 You opened the heavens
like curtains,
and you came down
with storm clouds
under your feet.
11 You rode on the backs
of flying creatures.[b]
You appeared[c]
with the wind as wings.
12 Darkness was your tent!
Thunderclouds filled the sky,
hiding you from sight.
13 Fiery coals lit up the sky
in front of you.

14 LORD Most High, your voice
thundered from the heavens.
15 You scattered your enemies
with arrows of lightning.
16 You roared at the sea,
and its deepest channels
could be seen.
You snorted,
and the earth shook
to its foundations.

17 You reached down from heaven,
and you lifted me
from deep in the ocean.
18 You rescued me from enemies
who were hateful
and too powerful for me.
19 On the day disaster struck,
they came and attacked,
but you defended me.
20 When I was fenced in,
you freed and rescued me
because you love me.
21 You are good to me, LORD,
because I do right,
and you reward me
because I am innocent.
22 I do what you want
and never turn to do evil.
23 I keep your laws in mind
and never turn away
from your teachings.
24 I obey you completely
and guard against sin.
25 You have been good to me
because I do right;
you have rewarded me

[y] **22.2** *mighty rock*: The Hebrew text has "rock," which is sometimes used in poetry to compare the LORD to a mountain where his people can run for protection from their enemies. [z] **22.3** *powerful weapon*: The Hebrew has "the horn," which refers to the horn of a bull, one of the most powerful animals in ancient Palestine. [a] **22.8** *columns . . . sky*: The sky was sometimes described as a dome that was held up by a foundation or pillars. [b] **22.11** *flying creatures*: These were supernatural beings (see the note at 6.2). [c] **22.11** *appeared*: Most Hebrew manuscripts; some Hebrew manuscripts "swooped down" (see Psalm 18.10).

for being innocent
by your standards.

26 You are always loyal
to your loyal people,
and you are faithful
to the faithful.
27 With all who are sincere
you are sincere,
but you treat the unfaithful
as their deeds deserve.
28 You rescue the humble,
but you look for ways
to put down the proud.

29 Our LORD and God,
you are my lamp.
You turn darkness to light.
30 You help me defeat armies
and capture cities.

31 Your way is perfect, LORD,
and your word is correct.
You are a shield for those
who run to you for help.
32 You alone are God!
Only you are a mighty rock.[d]
33 You are my strong fortress,
and you set me free.
34 You make my feet run as fast
as those of a deer,
and you help me stand
on the mountains.

35 You teach my hands to fight
and my arms to use
a bow of bronze.
36 You alone are my shield,
and by coming to help me,
you have made me famous.
37 You clear the way for me,
and now I won't stumble.

38 I kept chasing my enemies
until I caught them
and destroyed them.
39 I destroyed them!
I stuck my sword
through my enemies,
and they were crushed
under my feet.

40 You helped me win victories
and forced my attackers
to fall victim to me.

41 You made my enemies run,
and I killed them.
42 They cried out for help,
but no one saved them;
they called out to you,
but there was no answer.
43 I ground them to dust,
and I squashed them
like mud in the streets.

44 You rescued me
from my stubborn people
and made me the leader
of foreign nations,
who are now my slaves.
45 They obey and come crawling.
46 They have lost all courage
and from their fortresses
they come trembling.

47 You are the living LORD!
I will praise you!
You are a mighty rock.[d]
I will honor you
for keeping me safe.
48 You took revenge for me,
and you put nations
in my power.
49 You protected me
from violent enemies,
and you made me much greater
than all of them.

50 I will praise you, LORD,
and I will honor you
among the nations.
51 You give glorious victories
to your chosen king.
Your faithful love for David
and for his descendants
will never end.

David's Last Words

23 These are the last words
of David the son of Jesse.
The God of Jacob chose David
and made him a great king.

[d]**22.32,47** *mighty rock*: See the note at 22.2.
22.34 Hb 3.19. **22.50** Ro 15.9.

The Mighty God of Israel
loved him.[e]
When God told him to speak,
David said:
2 The Spirit of the LORD
has told me what to say.
3 Our Mighty Rock,[f]
the God of Jacob, told me,
"A ruler who obeys God
and does right
4 is like the sunrise
on a cloudless day,
or like rain that sparkles
on the grass."[g]

5 I have ruled this way,
and God will never break
his promise to me.
God's promise is complete
and unchanging;
he will always help me
and give me what I hope for.
6 But evil people are pulled up
like thornbushes.
They are not dug up by hand,
7 but with a sharp spear
and are burned on the spot.

The Three Warriors
(1 Chronicles 11.10-19)

8 These are the names of David's warriors:
Ishbosheth[h] the son of Hachmon[i] was
the leader of the Three Warriors.[j] In one
battle, he killed eight hundred men with
his spear.[k]
9 The next one of the Three Warriors
was Eleazar the son of Dodo the Ahohite.
One time when the Philistines were at war
with Israel, he and David dared the
Philistines to fight them. Every one of the
Israelite soldiers turned and ran, 10 except
Eleazar. He killed Philistines until his hand
was cramped, and he couldn't let go of his
sword. When Eleazar finished, all the Israelite troops had to do was come back and
take the enemies' weapons and armor. The
LORD gave Israel a great victory that day.
11 Next was Shammah the son of Agee
the Hararite. One time the Philistines
brought their army together to destroy a
crop of peas growing in a field near Lehi.
The rest of Israel's soldiers ran away from
the Philistines, 12 but Shammah stood in
the middle of the field and killed the
Philistines. The crops were saved, and the
LORD gave Israel a great victory.
13 One year at harvest time, the Three
Warriors[l] went to meet David at Adullam
Cave.[m] The Philistine army had set up
camp in Rephaim Valley 14 and had taken
over Bethlehem. David was in his fortress,
15 and he was very thirsty. He said, "I wish I
had a drink from the well by the gate at
Bethlehem."
16 The Three Warriors[n] sneaked into the
Philistine camp and got some water from
the well near Bethlehem's gate. But after
they brought the water back to David, he
refused to drink it. Instead, he poured it
out as a sacrifice 17 and said to the LORD, "I
can't drink this water! It's like the blood of
these men who risked their lives to get it
for me."

The Three Warriors did these brave deeds.

The Thirty Warriors
(1 Chronicles 11.20-47)

18 Joab's brother Abishai was the leader
of the Thirty Warriors,[o] and in one battle

[e]**23.1** *The Mighty . . . him*: Or "He wrote Israel's favorite songs." [f]**23.3** *Mighty Rock*: See the note at 22.2. [g]**23.4** *sparkles . . . grass*: Or "makes the grass grow." [h]**23.8** *Ishbosheth*: Hebrew "Josheb Bashebeth," which seems to be another spelling of Ishbosheth. See the note at 2.8, although this is a different Ishbosheth. [i]**23.8** *the son of Hachmon*: Or "the Tahchemonite" (see 1 Chronicles 11.11). [j]**23.8** *the Three Warriors*: The most honored group of warriors. They may have been part of the Thirty Warriors. "Three" and "thirty" are spelled almost the same in Hebrew, so there is some confusion in the manuscripts as to which group is being talked about in some places in the following lists. [k]**23.8** *with . . . spear*: One possible meaning for the difficult Hebrew text (see 1 Chronicles 11.11). [l]**23.13** *the Three Warriors*: Or "three warriors." Hebrew "three of the thirty most important." [m]**23.13** *Adullam Cave*: This may have happened during the time that David was an outlaw (see 1 Samuel 22.1-6). [n]**23.16** *the Three Warriors*: Or "three warriors." [o]**23.18** *the Thirty Warriors*: The second most honored group of warriors. They may have also been officers in the army (see the note at 23.8).

he killed three hundred men with his spear. He was as famous as the Three Warriors
19 and certainly just as famous as the rest of the Thirty Warriors. He was the commander of the Thirty Warriors, but he still did not become one of the Three Warriors.
20 Benaiah the son of Jehoiada was a brave man from Kabzeel who did some amazing things. He killed two of Moab's best fighters,[p] and on a snowy day he went down into a pit and killed a lion.
21 Another time, he killed an Egyptian, as big as a giant.[q] The Egyptian was armed with a spear, but Benaiah only had a club. Benaiah grabbed the spear from the Egyptian and killed him with it.
22-23 Benaiah did these things. He never became one of the Three Warriors, but he was just as famous as they were and certainly just as famous as the rest of the Thirty Warriors. David made him the leader of his bodyguard.
24-39 Some of the Thirty Warriors were:

Asahel the brother of Joab
Elhanan the son of Dodo from Bethlehem
Shammah from Harod
Elika from Harod
Helez the Paltite
Ira the son of Ikkesh from Tekoa
Abiezer from Anathoth
Mebunnai[r] the Hushathite
Zalmon the Ahohite
Maharai from Netophah
Heleb the son of Baanah from Netophah
Ittai the son of Ribai from Gibeah of the tribe of Benjamin
Benaiah from Pirathon
Hiddai from the streams on Mount Gaash
Abialbon from Beth-Arabah
Azmaveth from Bahurim[s]
Eliahba from Shaalbon
Jashen[t]
Jonathan the son of Shammah the Hararite[u]
Ahiam the son of Sharar the Hararite
Eliphelet the son of Ahasbai from Maacah
Eliam the son of Ahithophel from Gilo
Hezro from Carmel
Paarai the Arbite
Igal the son of Nathan from Zobah
Bani the Gadite
Zelek from Ammon
Naharai from Beeroth, who carried the weapons of Joab the son of Zeruiah
Ira the Ithrite
Gareb the Ithrite
Uriah the Hittite
There were thirty-seven in all.

David Counts the People
(1 Chronicles 21.1-6)

24 The LORD was angry at Israel again, and he made David think it would be a good idea to count the people in Israel and Judah.
2 So David told Joab and the army officers,[v] "Go to every tribe in Israel, from the town of Dan in the north all the way south to Beersheba, and count everyone who can serve in the army. I want to know how many there are."
3 Joab answered, "I hope the LORD your God will give you a hundred times more soldiers than you already have. I hope you will live to see that day! But why do you want to do a thing like this?"
4 But when David refused to change his mind, Joab and the army officers went out and started counting the people.
5 They crossed the Jordan River and began with[w] Aroer and the town in the middle of the river valley. From there they went toward Gad and on as far as Jazer.
6 They went to Gilead and to Kadesh in Syria.[x] Then they went to Dan, Ijon,[y] and on toward Sidon.

[p] **23.20** *Moab's best fighters*: Or "big lions in Moab;" one ancient translation "sons of Ariel from Moab." [q] **23.21** *Egyptian . . . giant*: First Chronicles 11.23; in this verse the Hebrew text has "good-looking Egyptian." [r] **23.24-39** *Mebunnai*: Or "Sibbecai" (see 1 Chronicles 11.26-47). [s] **23.24-39** *Bahurim*: Or "Barhum." [t] **23.24-39** *Jashen*: Hebrew "sons of Jashen." [u] **23.24-39** *Jonathan . . . Hararite*: Some manuscripts of one ancient translation (see 1 Chronicles 26-47). In the Hebrew text Jonathan and Shammah are separate members of the list. [v] **24.2** *Joab . . . officers*: Some manuscripts of one ancient translation (see 24.4); 1 Chronicles 21.2; Hebrew "Joab, the officer of the army." [w] **24.5** *began with*: Some manuscripts of one ancient translation; Hebrew "set up camp in." [x] **24.6** *Kadesh in Syria*: Or "the lower slopes of Mount Hermon." [y] **24.6** *Dan, Ijon*: Or "Danjaan," an unknown place.

7 They came to the fortress of Tyre, then
went through every town of the Hivites and
the Canaanites. Finally, they went to Beersheba in the Southern Desert of Judah.
8 After they had gone through the whole
land, they went back to Jerusalem. It had
taken them nine months and twenty days.
9 Joab came and told David, "In Israel
there are eight hundred thousand who can
serve in the army, and in Judah there are
five hundred thousand."

The LORD Punishes David

(1 Chronicles 21.7-17)

10 After David had everyone counted, he
felt guilty and told the LORD, "What I did
was stupid and terribly wrong. LORD, please
forgive me."
11 Before David even got up the next
morning, the LORD had told David's
prophet Gad 12-13 to take a message to
David. Gad went to David and told him:

> You must choose one of three ways for the LORD to punish you: Will there be seven[z] years when the land won't grow enough food for your people? Or will your enemies chase you and make you run from them for three months? Or will there be three days of horrible disease in your land? Think about it and decide, because I have to give your answer to God, who sent me.

14 David was really frightened and said,
"It's a terrible choice to make! But the
LORD is kind, and I'd rather have him punish us than for anyone else to do it."
15-16 So that morning, the LORD sent an
angel to spread a horrible disease everywhere in Israel, from Dan to Beersheba.
And before it was over, seventy thousand
people had died.

When the angel was about to destroy Jerusalem, the LORD felt sorry for all the suffering he had caused and told the angel, "That's enough! Don't touch them." This happened at the threshing place that belonged to Araunah the Jebusite.

17 David saw the angel killing everyone
and told the LORD, "These people are like
sheep with me as their shepherd.[a] I have
sinned terribly, but they have done nothing
wrong. Please, punish me and my family
instead of them!"

David Buys Araunah's Threshing Place

(1 Chronicles 21.18—22.1)

18-19 That same day the prophet Gad
came and told David, "Go to the threshing
place that belongs to Araunah and build an
altar there for the LORD."

So David went.

20 Araunah looked and saw David and
his soldiers coming up toward him. He
went over to David, bowed down low, 21 and
said, "Your Majesty! Why have you come to
see me?"

David answered, "I've come to buy your threshing place. I have to build the LORD an altar here, so this disease will stop killing the people."

22 Araunah said, "Take whatever you
want and offer your sacrifice. Here are
some oxen for the sacrifice. You can use
the threshing-boards[b] and the wooden
yokes for the fire. 23 Take them—they're
yours! I hope the LORD your God will be
pleased with you."
24 But David answered, "No! I have to
pay you what they're worth. I can't offer the
LORD my God a sacrifice that I got for nothing." So David bought the threshing place
and the oxen for fifty pieces of silver.
25 Then he built an altar for the LORD. He
sacrificed animals and burned them on the
altar.

The LORD answered the prayers of the people, and no one else died from the terrible disease.

[z]**24.12,13** *seven*: Hebrew; some manuscripts of one ancient translation "three" (see 1 Chronicles 21.12). [a]**24.17** *as their shepherd*: The Dead Sea Scrolls, and some manuscripts of two ancient translations (see 1 Chronicles 21.17); these words are not in the Standard Hebrew Text of this verse. [b]**24.22** *threshing-boards*: Heavy boards with bits of rock or metal on the bottom. They were dragged across the grain to separate the husks from the kernels.

1 KINGS

ABOUT THIS BOOK

First Kings is the first half of a single book that was divided into two parts, 1 and 2 Kings, because together they were too long to fit on one scroll. These books continue the history of Israel.

The book of 1 Kings has three parts. The first part (1–2) tells about the last years of King David's life and how his son Solomon became the king of Israel. The second part (3–11) includes events from Solomon's rule and tells how famous and rich he was. Much of this second part tells how Solomon built and dedicated the temple in Jerusalem. The last part of the book (12–22) reports what happened after Solomon's death—the northern tribes rebelled against Rehoboam his son, and the nation of Israel was divided into two separate kingdoms: Judah in the south and Israel in the north. This part of 1 Kings includes stories about the kings of these two kingdoms. The book concludes with the rule of King Jehoshaphat of Judah and King Ahaziah of Israel.

Each king in the book is judged according to his faithfulness to the Lord. If the king was faithful and obeyed God's Law, he was praised as being good; but if he disobeyed and did wrong, he was condemned as being evil. All the kings of Israel were judged to be evil, because they rejected the Lord and worshiped idols. However, most of the kings of Judah were judged to be good, because they followed the example of their ancestor King David and worshiped the Lord.

First Kings also includes the familiar stories about Elijah the prophet, who opposed the evil King Ahab and Queen Jezebel of the northern kingdom. Elijah warned the people of Israel to obey the Lord and not to worship other gods. Elijah wanted to prove that the Lord was the one true God, and so he arranged a contest between the Lord and the pagan god Baal. Elijah and the prophets of Baal would offer a sacrifice to their own God, but the fire on the altars would not be lit. Elijah explained to the people:

> *"How much longer will you try to have things both ways? If the LORD is God, worship him! But if Baal is God, worship him! . . . The prophets of Baal will pray to their god, and I will pray to the LORD. The one who answers by starting the fire is God."*
>
> *(18.21b, 24)*

A QUICK LOOK AT THIS BOOK

- Solomon Becomes King (1.1-53)
- David's Final Words and His Death (2.1-12)
- Solomon Takes Control of the Kingdom (2.13-46)
- Solomon's Wisdom and His Officials (3.1—4.34)
- Building and Dedication of the Jerusalem Temple (5.1—8.66)
- Other Events During Solomon's Rule (9.1—10.29)
- Solomon's Unfaithfulness, Enemies, and Death (11.1-43)
- The Northern Tribes of Israel Rebel against King Rehoboam (12.1-24)
- King Jeroboam of Israel
  Makes Two Gold Statues of Calves (12.25-33)

- Prophets Condemn Jeroboam (13.1—14.20)
- Kings of Judah and Israel (14.21—16.34)
- Elijah the Prophet (17.1—19.21)
- King Ahab and Queen Jezebel (20.1—22.40)
- King Jehoshaphat of Judah and King Ahaziah of Israel (22.41-53)

David in His Old Age

1 King David was now an old man, and
he always felt cold, even under a lot of
blankets. 2 His officials said, "Your Majesty,
we will look for a young woman to take care
of you. She can lie down beside you and
keep you warm." 3-4 They looked everywhere in Israel until they found a very
beautiful young woman named Abishag,
who lived in the town of Shunem.[a] They
brought her to David, and she took care of
him. But David did not have sex with her.

Adonijah Tries To Become King

5-6 Adonijah was the son of David and
Haggith. He was Absalom's younger
brother[b] and was very handsome. One day,
Adonijah started bragging, "I'm going to
make myself king!" So he got some chariots
and horses, and he hired fifty men as bodyguards. David did not want to hurt his feelings, so he never asked Adonijah why he
was doing these things.
7 Adonijah met with Joab the son of
Zeruiah and Abiathar the priest and asked
them if they would help him become king.
Both of them agreed to help. 8 But Zadok
the priest, Benaiah the son of Jehoiada,
Nathan the prophet, Shimei, Rei,[c] and
David's bodyguards all refused.
9 Adonijah invited his brothers and
David's officials from Judah to go with him
to Crawling Rock[d] near Rogel Spring,
where he sacrificed some sheep, cattle, and
fat calves.[e] 10 But he did not invite Nathan,
Benaiah, David's bodyguards, or his own
brother Solomon.
11 When Nathan heard what had happened, he asked Bathsheba, Solomon's
mother:

Have you heard that Adonijah the
son of Haggith has made himself king?
But David doesn't know a thing about
it. 12 You and your son Solomon will be
killed, unless you do what I tell you.
13 Go say to David, "You promised me
that Solomon would be the next king.
So why is Adonijah now king?"
14 While you are still talking to
David, I'll come in and tell him that
everything you said is true.

15 Meanwhile, David was in his bedroom
where Abishag was taking care of him because he was so old. Bathsheba went in
16 and bowed down.
"What can I do for you?" David asked.
17 Bathsheba answered:

Your Majesty, you promised me in
the name of the LORD your God that
my son Solomon would be the next
king. 18 But Adonijah has already been
made king, and you didn't know anything about it. 19 He sacrificed a lot of
cattle, calves, and sheep. And he invited Abiathar the priest, Joab your
army commander, and all your sons to
be there, except Solomon, your loyal
servant.
20 Your Majesty, everyone in Israel
is waiting for you to announce who will
be the next king. 21 If you don't, they
will say that Solomon and I have rebelled. They will treat us like criminals
and kill us as soon as you die.

22 Just then, Nathan the prophet
arrived. 23 Someone told David that he was
there, and Nathan came in. He bowed with
his face to the ground 24 and said:

Your Majesty, did you say that
Adonijah would be king? 25 Earlier today, he sacrificed a lot of cattle, calves,

[a] **1.3,4** *Shunem*: A town in northern Israel, just north of Jezreel Valley. [b] **1.5,6** *brother*: Since Absalom was dead, Adonijah was now David's oldest living son and would be next in line to be king.
[c] **1.8** *Shimei, Rei*: Or "Shimei his advisor." [d] **1.9** *Crawling Rock*: Or "Zoheleth Rock."
[e] **1.9** *sacrificed . . . calves*: This was part of a ceremony where Adonijah was made the new king.
1.5,6 2 S 3.2-5. **1.11** 2 S 12.24.

and sheep. He invited the army commanders, Abiathar, and all your sons to be there. Right now they are eating and drinking and shouting, "Long live King Adonijah!" 26 But he didn't invite me or Zadok the priest or Benaiah or Solomon. 27 Did you say they could do this without telling the rest of us who would be the next king?

Solomon Becomes King

28 David said, "Tell Bathsheba to come here." She came and stood in front of him. 29-30 Then he said, "The living LORD God of Israel has kept me safe. And so today, I will keep the promise I made to you in his name: Solomon will be the next king!"

31 Bathsheba bowed with her face to the ground and said, "Your Majesty, I pray that you will live a long time!"

32 Then David said, "Tell Zadok, Nathan, and Benaiah to come here."

When they arrived, 33 he told them:

Take along some of my officials and have Solomon ride my own mule to Gihon Spring. 34 When you get there, Zadok and Nathan will make Solomon the new king of Israel. Then after the ceremony[f] is over, have someone blow a trumpet and tell everyone to shout, "Long live King Solomon!" 35 Bring him back here, and he will take my place as king. He is the one I have chosen to rule Israel and Judah.

36 Benaiah answered, "We will do it, Your Majesty. I pray that the LORD your God will let it happen. 37 The LORD has always watched over you, and I pray that he will now watch over Solomon. May the LORD help Solomon to be an even greater king than you."

38 Zadok, Nathan, and Benaiah left and took along the two groups of David's special bodyguards.[g] Solomon rode on David's mule as they led him to Gihon Spring. 39 Zadok the priest brought some olive oil from the sacred tent and poured it on Solomon's head to show that he was now king. A trumpet was blown and everyone shouted, "Long live King Solomon!" 40 Then they played flutes and celebrated as they followed Solomon back to Jerusalem. They made so much noise that the ground shook.

41 Adonijah and his guests had almost finished eating when they heard the noise. Joab also heard the trumpet and asked, "What's all that noise about in the city?"

42 Just then, Jonathan son of Abiathar came running up. "Come in," Adonijah said. "An important man like you must have some good news."

43 Jonathan answered:

No, I don't! David has just announced that Solomon will be king. 44-45 Solomon rode David's own mule to Gihon Spring, and Zadok, Nathan, Benaiah, and David's special bodyguards[h] went with him. When they got there, Zadok and Nathan made Solomon king. Then everyone celebrated all the way back to Jerusalem. That's the noise you hear in the city. 46 Solomon is now king.

47 And listen to this! David's officials told him, "We pray that your God will help Solomon to be an even greater king!"

David was in his bed at the time, but he bowed 48 and prayed, "I praise you, LORD God of Israel. You have made my son Solomon king and have let me live to see it."

49 Adonijah's guests shook with fear when they heard this news, and they left as fast as they could. 50 Adonijah himself was afraid of what Solomon might do to him, so he ran to the sacred tent and grabbed hold of the corners of the altar for protection.[i]

51 Someone told Solomon, "Adonijah is afraid of you and is holding onto the corners of the altar. He wants you to promise that you won't kill him."

52 Solomon answered, "If Adonijah

[f] **1.34** *the ceremony*: Part of this ceremony was pouring olive oil on Solomon's head to show that he was now king. [g] **1.38** *the two . . . bodyguards*: The Hebrew text has "the Cherethites and the Pelethites," who were foreign soldiers hired by David to be part of his bodyguard. [h] **1.44,45** *David's special bodyguards*: See the note at 1.38. [i] **1.50** *the corners . . . for protection*: The four corners of some ancient altars looked like animal horns. Since the entire altar was sacred, anyone holding on to its corners was supposed to be safe from being killed.

doesn't cause any trouble, I won't hurt him. But if he does, I'll have him killed." 53 Then he sent someone to the altar to get Adonijah.

After Adonijah came and bowed down, Solomon said, "Adonijah, go home."

David's Instructions to Solomon

2 Not long before David died, he told Solomon:

2 My son, I will soon die, as everyone must. But I want you to be strong and brave. 3 Do what the LORD your God commands and follow his teachings. Obey everything written in the Law of Moses. Then you will be a success, no matter what you do or where you go. 4 You and your descendants must always faithfully obey the LORD. If you do, he will keep the solemn promise he made to me that someone from our family will always be king of Israel.

5 Solomon, don't forget what Joab did to me by killing Abner son of Ner and Amasa son of Jether, the two commanders of Israel's army. He killed them as if they were his enemies in a war, but he did it when there was no war.[j] He is guilty, and now it's up to you to punish him 6 in the way you think best. Whatever you do, don't let him die peacefully in his old age.

7 The sons of Barzillai from Gilead helped me when I was running from your brother Absalom.[k] Be kind to them and let them eat at your table.

8 Be sure to do something about Shimei son of Gera from Bahurim in the territory of Benjamin. He cursed and insulted me the day I went to Mahanaim. But later, when he came to meet me at the Jordan River, I promised that I wouldn't kill him.[l] 9 Now you must punish him. He's an old man, but you're wise enough to know that you must have him killed.

David Dies

10-11 David was king of Israel forty years. He ruled seven years from Hebron and thirty-three years from Jerusalem. Then he died and was buried in Jerusalem.[m] 12 His son Solomon became king and took control of David's kingdom.

Adonijah Is Killed

13 One day, Adonijah went to see Bathsheba, Solomon's mother, and she asked, "Is this a friendly visit?"

"Yes. 14 I just want to talk with you."

"All right," she told him, "go ahead."

15 "You know that I was king for a little while," Adonijah replied. "And everyone in Israel accepted me as their ruler. But the LORD wanted my brother to be king, so now things have changed. 16 Would you do me a favor?"

"What do you want?" Bathsheba asked.

17 "Please ask Solomon to let me marry Abishag. He won't say no to you."

18 "All right," she said. "I'll ask him."

19 When Bathsheba went to see Solomon, he stood up to meet her, then bowed low. He sat back down and had another throne brought in, so his mother could sit at his right side.[n] 20 Bathsheba sat down and then asked, "Would you do me a small favor?"

Solomon replied, "Mother, just tell me what you want, and I will do it."

21 "Allow your brother Adonijah to marry Abishag," she answered.

22 Solomon said:

What? Let my older brother marry Abishag? You may as well ask me to let him rule the kingdom! And why don't you ask such favors for Abiathar and Joab?[o]

23 I swear in the name of the LORD that Adonijah will die because he asked for this! If he doesn't, I pray that

[j]**2.5** *war*: See 2 Samuel 3.22-27 and 20.7-10. [k]**2.7** *Absalom*: See 2 Samuel 17.27-29. [l]**2.8** *him*: See 2 Samuel 16.5-14 and 19.16-23. [m]**2.10,11** *Jerusalem*: Hebrew "the city of David." [n]**2.19** *at his right side*: The place of honor. [o]**2.22** *And why . . . Joab*: One possible meaning for the difficult Hebrew text.

2.5 a 2 S 3.27; **b** 2 S 20.10. **2.7** 2 S 17.27-29. **2.8** 2 S 16.5-13; 19.16-23. **2.10,11** 2 S 5.4, 5; 1 Ch 3.1-4. **2.12** 1 Ch 29.23. **2.17** 1 K 1.3, 4.

God will severely punish me. [24] The LORD made me king in my father's place and promised that the kings of Israel would come from my family. Yes, I swear by the living LORD that Adonijah will die today.

[25] "Benaiah," Solomon shouted, "go kill Adonijah." So Adonijah died.

Abiathar Is Sent Back Home

[26] Solomon sent for Abiathar the priest and said:

Abiathar, go back home to Anathoth! You ought to be killed too, but I won't do it now. When my father David was king, you were in charge of the sacred chest, and you went through a lot of hard times with my father. [27] But I won't let you be a priest of the LORD anymore.

And so the promise that the LORD had made at Shiloh about the family of Eli came true.[p]

Joab Is Killed

[28] Joab had not helped Absalom try to become king, but he had helped Adonijah. So when Joab learned that Adonijah had been killed, he ran to the sacred tent and grabbed hold of the corners of the altar for protection.[q] [29] When Solomon heard about this, he sent someone to ask Joab, "Why did you run to the altar?"

Joab sent back his answer, "I was afraid of you, and I ran to the LORD for protection."[r]

Then Solomon shouted, "Benaiah, go kill Joab!"

[30] Benaiah went to the sacred tent and yelled, "Joab, the king orders you to come out!"

"No!" Joab answered. "Kill me right here."

Benaiah went back and told Solomon what Joab had said.

[31-32] Solomon replied:

Do what Joab said. Kill him and bury him! Then my family and I won't be responsible for what he did to Abner the commander of Israel's army and to Amasa the commander of Judah's army. He killed those innocent men without my father knowing about it. Both of them were better men than Joab. Now the LORD will make him pay for those murders. [33] Joab's family will always suffer because of what he did, but the LORD will always bless David's family and his kingdom with peace.

[34] Benaiah went back and killed Joab. His body was taken away and buried near his home in the desert.

[35] Solomon put Benaiah in Joab's place as army commander, and he put Zadok in Abiathar's place as priest.

Shimei Is Killed

[36] Solomon sent for Shimei and said, "Build a house here in Jerusalem and live in it. But whatever you do, don't leave the city! [37] If you ever cross Kidron Valley and leave Jerusalem, you will be killed. And it will be your own fault."

[38] "That's fair, Your Majesty," Shimei answered. "I'll do that." So Shimei lived in Jerusalem from then on.

[39] About three years later, two of Shimei's servants ran off to King Achish in Gath. When Shimei found out where they were, [40] he saddled his donkey and went after them. He found them and brought them back to Jerusalem.

[41] Someone told Solomon that Shimei had gone to Gath and was back. [42] Solomon sent for him and said:

Shimei, you promised in the name of the LORD that you would never leave Jerusalem. I warned you that you would die if you did. You agreed that this was fair, didn't you? [43] You have disobeyed me and have broken the promise you made to the LORD.

[44] I know you remember all the cruel things you did to my father David. Now the LORD is going to punish you for what you did. [45] But the

[p]**2.27** *the promise . . . came true*: See 1 Samuel 2.27-34. [q]**2.28** *the corners . . . for protection*: See the note at 1.50. [r]**2.29** *he sent someone . . . for protection*: One ancient translation; these words are not in the Hebrew text.

2.26 a 2 S 15.24; **b** 1 S 22.20-23. **2.27** 1 S 2.27-36.

LORD will bless me and make my father's kingdom strong forever.

46 "Benaiah," Solomon shouted, "kill Shimei." So Shimei died.

Solomon was now in complete control of his kingdom.

The LORD Makes Solomon Wise

(2 Chronicles 1.1-13)

3 Solomon signed a treaty with the king of Egypt and married his daughter. She lived in the older part of Jerusalem[s] until the palace, the LORD's temple, and the wall around Jerusalem were completed.

2 At that time, there was no temple for worshiping the LORD, and everyone offered sacrifices at the local shrines.[t] 3 Solomon loved the LORD and followed his father David's instructions, but Solomon also offered sacrifices and burned incense at the shrines.

4 The most important shrine was in Gibeon, and Solomon had offered more than a thousand sacrifices on that altar.

5 One night while Solomon was in Gibeon, the LORD God appeared to him in a dream and said, "Solomon, ask for anything you want, and I will give it to you."

6 Solomon answered:

My father David, your servant, was honest and did what you commanded. You were always loyal to him, and you gave him a son who is now king.

7 LORD God, I'm your servant, and you've made me king in my father's place. But I'm very young and know so little about being a leader. 8 And now I must rule your chosen people, even though there are too many of them to count.

9 Please make me wise and teach me the difference between right and wrong. Then I will know how to rule your people. If you don't, there is no way I could rule this great nation of yours.

10-11 God said:

Solomon, I'm pleased that you asked for this. You could have asked to live a long time or to be rich. Or you could have asked for your enemies to be destroyed. Instead, you asked for wisdom to make right decisions. 12 So I'll make you wiser than anyone who has ever lived or ever will live.

13 I'll also give you what you didn't ask for. You'll be rich and respected as long as you live, and you'll be greater than any other king. 14 If you obey me and follow my commands, as your father David did, I'll let you live a long time.

15 Solomon woke up and realized that God had spoken to him in the dream. He went back to Jerusalem and stood in front of the sacred chest, where he offered sacrifices to please the Lord[u] and sacrifices to ask his blessing.[v] Then Solomon gave a feast for his officials.

Solomon Makes a Difficult Decision

16 One day two women[w] came to King Solomon, 17 and one of them said:

Your Majesty, this woman and I live in the same house. Not long ago my baby was born at home, 18 and three days later her baby was born. Nobody else was there with us.

19 One night while we were all asleep, she rolled over on her baby, and he died. 20 Then while I was still asleep, she got up and took my son out of my bed. She put him in her bed, then she put her dead baby next to me.

21 In the morning when I got up to feed my son, I saw that he was dead. But when I looked at him in the light, I knew he wasn't my son.

22 "No!" the other woman shouted. "He was your son. My baby is alive!"

"The dead baby is yours," the first woman yelled. "Mine is alive!"

They argued back and forth in front of

[s] **3.1** *the older . . . Jerusalem*: Hebrew "the city of David." [t] **3.2** *local shrines*: The Hebrew text has "high places," which were local places to worship God or foreign gods. [u] **3.15** *sacrifices to please the Lord*: See Leviticus 1.1-17. [v] **3.15** *sacrifices to ask his blessing*: See Leviticus 3.1-17. [w] **3.16** *women*: Hebrew "prostitutes."

3.4-9 Ws 9.1-18.

Solomon, 23 until finally he said, "Both of
you say this live baby is yours. 24 Someone
bring me a sword."
A sword was brought, and Solomon ordered, 25 "Cut the baby in half! That way
each of you can have part of him."
26 "Please don't kill my son," the baby's
mother screamed. "Your Majesty, I love him
very much, but give him to her. Just don't
kill him."
The other woman shouted, "Go ahead
and cut him in half. Then neither of us will
have the baby."
27 Solomon said, "Don't kill the baby."
Then he pointed to the first woman, "She
is his real mother. Give the baby to her."
28 Everyone in Israel was amazed when
they heard how Solomon had made his decision. They realized that God had given
him wisdom to judge fairly.

Solomon's Officials

4 1-6 Here is a list of Solomon's highest
officials while he was king of Israel:

Azariah son of Zadok was the priest;
Elihoreph and Ahijah sons of Shisha
were the secretaries;
Jehoshaphat son of Ahilud kept the
government records;
Benaiah son of Jehoiada was the army
commander;
Zadok and Abiathar were priests;
Azariah son of Nathan was in charge of
the regional officers;
Zabud son of Nathan was a priest and
the king's advisor;
Ahishar was the prime minister;
Adoniram son of Abda was in charge of
the forced labor.

7 Solomon chose twelve regional officers, who took turns bringing food for him
and his household. Each officer provided
food from his region for one month of the
year. 8 These were the twelve officers:
The son of Hur was in charge of the hill
country of Ephraim.
9 The son of Deker was in charge of the
towns of Makaz, Shaalbim, Beth-Shemesh,
and Elon-Beth-Hanan.
10 The son of Hesed was in charge of
the towns of Arubboth and Socoh, and the
region of Hepher.
11 The son of Abinadab was in charge
of Naphath-Dor and was married to
Solomon's daughter Taphath.
12 Baana son of Ahilud was in charge
of the towns of Taanach and Megiddo. He
was also in charge of the whole region of
Beth-Shan near the town of Zarethan,
south of Jezreel from Beth-Shan to Abel-
Meholah to the other side of Jokmeam.
13 The son of Geber was in charge of the
town of Ramoth in Gilead and the villages
in Gilead belonging to the family of Jair, a
descendant of Manasseh. He was also in
charge of the region of Argob in Bashan,
which had sixty walled towns with bronze
bars on their gates.
14 Ahinadab son of Iddo was in charge of
the territory of Mahanaim.
15 Ahimaaz was in charge of the territory of Naphtali and was married to Solomon's daughter Basemath.
16 Baana son of Hushai was in charge
of the territory of Asher and the town of
Bealoth.
17 Jehoshaphat son of Paruah was in
charge of the territory of Issachar.
18 Shimei son of Ela was in charge of
the territory of Benjamin.
19 Geber son of Uri was in charge of
Gilead, where King Sihon of the Amorites
and King Og of Bashan had lived.
And one officer was in charge of the territory of Judah.[x]

The Size of Solomon's Kingdom

20 There were so many people living in
Judah and Israel while Solomon was king
that they seemed like grains of sand on a
beach. Everyone had enough to eat and
drink, and they were happy.
21 Solomon ruled every kingdom between the Euphrates River and the land
of the Philistines down to Egypt. These
kingdoms paid him taxes as long as he
lived.
22 Every day, Solomon needed one hundred fifty bushels of fine flour, three hun-

[x]**4.19** *of Judah*: One ancient translation; these words are not in the Hebrew text.
4.21 Gn 15.18; 2 Ch 9.26.

dred bushels of coarsely-ground flour,
23 ten grain-fed cattle, twenty pasture-fed
cattle, one hundred sheep, as well as deer,
gazelles, and geese.

24 Solomon ruled the whole region west
of the Euphrates River, from Tiphsah to
Gaza, and he was at peace with all of the
countries around him. 25 Everyone living in
Israel, from the town of Dan in the north to
Beersheba in the south, was safe as long as
Solomon lived. Each family sat undisturbed
beneath its own grape vines and fig trees.

26 Solomon had forty thousand stalls of
chariot horses and twelve thousand chariot
soldiers.

27 Each of the twelve regional officers
brought food to Solomon and his household for one month of the year. They provided everything he needed, 28 as well as
barley and straw for the horses.

Solomon's Wisdom

29 Solomon was brilliant. God had
blessed him with insight and understanding. 30-31 He was wiser than anyone else in
the world, including the wisest people of
the east and of Egypt. He was even wiser
than Ethan the Ezrahite, and Mahol's
three sons, Heman, Calcol, and Darda.
Solomon became famous in every country
around Judah and Israel. 32 Solomon wrote
three thousand wise sayings and composed
more than one thousand songs. 33 He could
talk about all kinds of plants, from large
trees to small bushes, and he taught about
animals, birds, reptiles, and fish. 34 Kings
all over the world heard about Solomon's
wisdom and sent people to listen to him
teach.

Solomon Asks Hiram To Help Build the Temple

(2 *Chronicles* 2.1-16)

5 King Hiram of Tyre[y] had always been
friends with Solomon's father David.
When Hiram learned that Solomon was
king, he sent some of his officials to meet
with Solomon.

2 Solomon sent a message back to
Hiram:

3 Remember how my father David
wanted to build a temple where the
LORD his God could be worshiped? But
enemies kept attacking my father's
kingdom, and he never had the
chance. 4 Now, thanks to the LORD
God, there is peace in my kingdom and
no trouble or threat of war anywhere.

5 The LORD God promised my
father that when his son became king,
he would build a temple for worshiping the LORD. So I've decided to do
that.

6 I'd like you to have your workers
cut down cedar trees in Lebanon for
me. I will pay them whatever you say
and will even have my workers help
them. We both know that your workers
are more experienced than anyone
else at cutting lumber.

7 Hiram was so happy when he heard
Solomon's request that he said, "I am
grateful that the LORD gave David such a
wise son to be king of that great nation!"
8 Then he sent back his answer:

I received your message and will
give you all the cedar and pine logs
you need. 9 My workers will carry them
down from Lebanon to the Mediterranean Sea. They will tie the logs together and float them along the coast
to wherever you want them. Then they
will untie the logs, and your workers
can take them from there.

To pay for the logs, you can provide
the grain I need for my household.

10 Hiram gave Solomon all the cedar
and pine logs he needed. 11 In return,
Solomon gave Hiram about one hundred
twenty-five thousand bushels of wheat and
about one thousand one hundred gallons of
pure olive oil each year.

12 The LORD kept his promise and made
Solomon wise. Hiram and Solomon signed
a treaty and never went to war against each
other.

[y]**5.1** *Tyre*: The most important city in Phoenicia. It was located on the coast of the Mediterranean Sea north of Israel, in what is today southern Lebanon.

4.26 1 K 10.26; 2 Ch 1.14; 9.25. **4.30,31** Ps 89 Title. **4.32** Pr 1.1; 10.1; 25.1; Sgs 1.1. **5.5** 2 S 7.12, 13; 1 Ch 17.11, 12.

Solomon's Workers

13 Solomon ordered thirty thousand
people from all over Israel to cut logs for
the temple, 14 and he put Adoniram in
charge of these workers. Solomon divided
them into three groups of ten thousand.
Each group worked one month in Lebanon
and had two months off at home.
15 He also had eighty thousand workers
to cut stone in the hill country of Israel,
seventy thousand workers to carry the
stones, 16 and over three thousand assistants to keep track of the work and to supervise the workers. 17 He ordered the
workers to cut and shape large blocks of
good stone for the foundation of the
temple.
18 Solomon's and Hiram's men worked
with men from the city of Gebal,[z] and together they got the stones and logs ready
for the temple.

The Outside of the Temple Is Completed

6 Solomon's workers started building the
temple during Ziv,[a] the second month
of the year. It had been four years since
Solomon became king of Israel, and four
hundred eighty years since the people of Israel left Egypt.
2 The inside of the LORD's temple was
ninety feet long, thirty feet wide, and forty-
five feet high. 3 A fifteen-foot porch went
all the way across the front of the temple.
4 The windows were narrow on the outside
but wide on the inside.
5-6 Along the sides and back of the temple, there were three levels of storage
rooms. The rooms on the bottom level were
seven and a half feet wide, the rooms on
the middle level were nine feet wide, and
those on the top level were ten and a half
feet wide. There were ledges on the outside
of the temple that supported the beams of
the storage rooms, so that nothing was built
into the temple walls.
7 Solomon did not want the noise of
hammers and axes to be heard at the place
where the temple was being built. So he
had the workers shape the blocks of stone
at the quarry.
8 The entrance to the bottom storage
rooms was on the south side of the building, and stairs to the other rooms were also
there. 9 The roof of the temple was made
out of beams and cedar boards.
The workers finished building the outside of the temple. 10 Storage rooms seven
and a half feet high were all around the
temple, and they were attached to the temple by cedar beams.
11 The LORD told Solomon:
12-13 If you obey my commands and
do what I say, I will keep the promise I
made to your father David. I will live
among my people Israel in this temple
you are building, and I will not desert
them.
14 So Solomon's workers finished building the temple.

The Inside of the Temple Is Furnished

(2 Chronicles 3.8-14)

15 The floor of the temple was made out
of pine, and the walls were lined with cedar
from floor to ceiling.[b]
16 The most holy place was in the back
of the temple, and it was thirty feet square.
Cedar boards standing from floor to ceiling[c]
separated it from the rest of the temple.
17 The temple's main room was sixty feet
long, and it was in front of the most holy
place.
18 The inside walls were lined with cedar
to hide the stones, and the cedar was decorated with carvings of gourds and flowers.
19 The sacred chest was kept in the
most holy place. 20-22 This room was thirty
feet long, thirty feet wide, and thirty feet
high, and it was lined with pure gold. There
were also gold chains across the front of
the most holy place. The inside of the temple, as well as the cedar altar in the most
holy place, was covered with gold.
23 Solomon had two statues of winged

[z]**5.18** *Gebal*: Later known as Byblos. [a]**6.1** *Ziv*: The second month of the Hebrew calendar, from about mid-April to mid-May. [b]**6.15** *from floor to ceiling*: One possible meaning for the difficult Hebrew text. [c]**6.16** *standing . . . ceiling*: One possible meaning for the difficult Hebrew text.

5.14 1 K 12.15-19. **6.16** Ex 26.31-34. **6.20-22** Ex 30.1-3. **6.23-28** Ex 25.18-20.

creatures[d] made from olive wood to put in the most holy place. Each creature was fifteen feet tall 24-26 and fifteen feet across. They had two wings, and the wings were seven and a half feet long. 27 Solomon put them next to each other in the most holy place. Their wings were spread out and reached across the room. 28 The creatures were also covered with gold.

29 The walls of the two rooms were decorated with carvings of palm trees, flowers, and winged creatures. 30 Even the floor was covered with gold.

31-32 The two doors to the most holy place were made out of olive wood and were decorated with carvings of palm trees, flowers, and winged creatures. The doors and the carvings were covered with gold. The door frame came to a point at the top.

33-34 The two doors to the main room of the temple were made out of pine, and each one had two sections[e] so they could fold open. The door frame was shaped like a rectangle and was made out of olive wood. 35 The doors were covered with gold and were decorated with carvings of palm trees, flowers, and winged creatures.

36 The inner courtyard of the temple had walls made out of three layers of cut stones with one layer of cedar beams.

37 Work began on the temple during Ziv,[f] the second month of the year, four years after Solomon became king of Israel. 38 Seven years later the workers finished building it during Bul,[g] the eighth month of the year. It was built exactly as it had been planned.

Solomon's Palace Is Built

7 Solomon's palace took thirteen years to build.

2-3 Forest Hall was the largest room in the palace. It was one hundred fifty feet long, seventy-five feet wide, and forty-five feet high, and was lined with cedar from Lebanon. It had four rows of cedar pillars, fifteen in a row, and they held up forty-five cedar beams. The ceiling was covered with cedar. 4 Three rows of windows on each side faced each other, 5 and there were three doors on each side near the front of the hall.

6 Pillar Hall was seventy-five feet long and forty-five feet wide. A covered porch supported by pillars went all the way across the front of the hall.

7 Solomon's throne was in Justice Hall, where he judged cases. This hall was completely lined with cedar.

8 The section of the palace where Solomon lived was behind Justice Hall and looked exactly like it. He had a similar place built for his wife, the daughter of the king of Egypt.

9 From the foundation all the way to the top, these buildings and the courtyard were made out of the best stones[h] carefully cut to size, then smoothed on every side with saws. 10 The foundation stones were huge, good stones—some of them fifteen feet long and others twelve feet long. 11 The cedar beams and other stones that had been cut to size were on top of these foundation stones. 12 The walls around the palace courtyard were made out of three layers of cut stones with one layer of cedar beams, just like the front porch and the inner courtyard of the temple.

Hiram Makes the Bronze Furnishings

(2 Chronicles 3.15-17; 4.1-10)

13-14 Hiram was a skilled bronze worker from the city of Tyre.[i] His father was now dead, but he also had been a bronze worker from Tyre, and his mother was from the tribe of Naphtali.

King Solomon asked Hiram to come to Jerusalem and make the bronze furnishings to use for worship in the LORD's temple, and he agreed to do it.

15 Hiram made two bronze columns twenty-seven feet tall and about six feet

[d] **6.23** *statues of winged creatures*: These were symbols of the LORD's throne on earth (see Exodus 25.18-22). [e] **6.33,34** *two sections*: One possible meaning for the difficult Hebrew text. [f] **6.37** *Ziv*: See the note at 6.1. [g] **6.38** *Bul*: The eighth month of the Hebrew calendar, from about mid-October to mid-November. [h] **7.9** *From . . . best stones*: One possible meaning for the difficult Hebrew text. [i] **7.13,14** *Hiram . . . city of Tyre*: This is not the same person as "King Hiram of Tyre" (see 5.1).

7.8 1 K 3.1.

across. 16 For the top of each column, he
also made a bronze cap seven and a half
feet high. 17 The caps were decorated with
seven rows of designs that looked like
chains,[j] 18 with two rows of designs that
looked like pomegranates.[k]
19 The caps for the columns of the
porch were six feet high and were shaped
like lilies.[l]
20 The chain designs on the caps were
right above the rounded tops of the two
columns, and there were two hundred
pomegranates in rows around each cap.
21 Hiram placed the two columns on each
side of the main door of the temple. The
column on the south side was called
Jachin,[m] and the one on the north was
called Boaz.[n]
22 The lily-shaped caps were on top of
the columns.

This completed the work on the
columns.
23 Hiram also made a large bowl called
the Sea. It was seven and a half feet deep,
about fifteen feet across, and forty-five feet
around. 24 Two rows of bronze gourds were
around the outer edge of the bowl, ten
gourds to every eighteen inches. 25 The
bowl itself sat on top of twelve bronze bulls
with three bulls facing outward in each of
four directions. 26 The sides of the bowl
were four inches thick, and its rim was like
a cup that curved outward like flower
petals. The bowl held about eleven thousand gallons.
27 Hiram made ten movable bronze
stands, each one four and a half feet high,
six feet long, and six feet wide. 28-29 The
sides were made with panels attached to
frames decorated with flower designs. The
panels themselves were decorated with figures of lions, bulls, and winged creatures.
30-31 Each stand had four bronze wheels
and axles and a round frame twenty-seven
inches across, held up by four supports
eighteen inches high. A small bowl rested
in the frame. The supports were decorated
with flower designs, and the frame with
carvings.

The side panels of the stands were
square, 32 and the wheels and axles were
underneath them. The wheels were about
twenty-seven inches high 33 and looked like
chariot wheels. The axles, rims, spokes,
and hubs were made out of bronze.
34-35 Around the top of each stand was
a nine-inch strip, and there were four
braces[o] attached to the corners of each
stand. The panels and the supports were
attached to the stands, 36 and the stands
were decorated with flower designs and figures of lions, palm trees, and winged creatures. 37 Hiram made the ten bronze stands
from the same mold, so they were exactly
the same size and shape.
38 Hiram also made ten small bronze
bowls, one for each stand. The bowls were
six feet across and could hold about two
hundred thirty gallons.
39 He put five stands on the south side
of the temple, five stands on the north side,
and the large bowl at the southeast corner
of the temple.
40 Hiram made pans for hot ashes, and
also shovels and sprinkling bowls.

A List of Everything inside the Temple

(2 Chronicles 4.11—5.1)

This is a list of the bronze items that Hiram made for the LORD's temple: 41 two
columns; two bowl-shaped caps for the tops
of the columns; two chain designs on the
caps; 42 four hundred pomegranates[p] for
the chain designs; 43 ten movable stands;
ten small bowls for the stands; 44 a large
bowl; twelve bulls that held up the bowl;
45 pans for hot ashes, and also shovels and
sprinkling bowls.

Hiram made these bronze things for
Solomon 46 near the Jordan River between
Succoth and Zarethan by pouring melted
bronze into clay molds.

[j] **7.17** *seven rows . . . chains*: One possible meaning for the difficult Hebrew text.
[k] **7.18** *pomegranates*: One possible meaning for the difficult Hebrew text of verse 18. A pomegranate is a bright red fruit that looks like an apple. In ancient times, it was a symbol of life. [l] **7.19** *lilies*: One possible meaning for the difficult Hebrew text of verse 19. [m] **7.21** *Jachin*: Or "He makes secure." [n] **7.21** *Boaz*: Or "He is strong." [o] **7.34,35** *braces*: Or "handles."
[p] **7.42** *pomegranates*: See the note at 7.18.
7.38 Ex 30.17-21.

47 There were so many bronze things
that Solomon never bothered to weigh
them, and no one ever knew how much
bronze was used.
48 Solomon gave orders to make the following temple furnishings out of gold: the
altar; the table that held the sacred loaves
of bread;[q] 49 ten lampstands that went in
front of the most holy place; flower designs;
lamps and tongs; 50 cups, lamp snuffers,
and small sprinkling bowls; dishes for incense; fire pans; and the hinges for the
doors to the most holy place and the main
room of the temple.
51 After the LORD's temple was finished,
Solomon put into its storage rooms everything that his father David had dedicated
to the LORD, including the gold and the silver.

Solomon Brings the Sacred Chest to the Temple

(2 Chronicles 5.2—6.2)

8 1-2 The sacred chest had been kept on
Mount Zion, also known as the city of
David. But Solomon decided to have the
chest moved to the temple while everyone
was in Jerusalem, celebrating the Festival
of Shelters during Ethanim,[r] the seventh
month of the year.
Solomon called together the important
leaders of Israel. 3-4 Then the priests and
the Levites carried to the temple the sacred
chest, the sacred tent, and the objects used
for worship. 5 Solomon and a crowd of people walked in front of the chest, and along
the way they sacrificed more sheep and
cattle than could be counted.
6 The priests carried the chest into the
most holy place and put it under the
winged creatures, 7 whose wings covered
the chest and the poles used for carrying it.
8 The poles were so long that they could be
seen from right outside the most holy
place, but not from anywhere else. And
they stayed there from then on.
9 The only things kept in the chest were
the two flat stones Moses had put there
when the LORD made his agreement with
the people of Israel at Mount Sinai,[s] after
bringing them out of Egypt.
10 Suddenly a cloud filled the temple as
the priests were leaving the most holy
place. 11 The LORD's glory was in the cloud,
and the light from it was so bright that the
priests could not stay inside to do their
work. 12 Then Solomon prayed:

"Our LORD, you said that you
would live in a dark cloud.
13 Now I have built a glorious temple
where you can live forever."

Solomon Speaks to the People

(2 Chronicles 6.3-11)

14 Solomon turned toward the people
standing there. Then he blessed them
15-16 and said:
Praise the LORD God of Israel! Long
ago he brought his people out of Egypt.
He later kept his promise to make my
father David the king of Israel. The LORD
also said that he had not chosen the
city where his temple would be built.
17 So when David wanted to build a
temple for the LORD God of Israel,
18 the LORD said, "It's good that you
want to build a temple where I can be
worshiped. 19 But you're not the one to
do it. Your son will build a temple to
honor me."
20 The LORD has done what he
promised. I am the king of Israel like
my father, and I've built a temple for
the LORD our God. 21 I've also made a
place in the temple for the sacred
chest. And in that chest are the two
flat stones on which is written the
solemn agreement the LORD made
with our ancestors when he led them
out of Egypt.

[q]**7.48** *sacred loaves of bread*: This bread was offered to the LORD and was a symbol of the LORD's presence in the temple. It was put out on a special table, and was replaced with fresh bread each week (see Leviticus 24.5-9). [r]**8.1,2** *Ethanim*: The seventh month of the Hebrew calendar, from about mid-September to mid-October. [s]**8.9** *Sinai*: Hebrew "Horeb."

7.48 a Ex 30.1-3; **b** Ex 25.23-30. **7.49** Ex 25.31-40. **7.51** 2 S 8.11; 1 Ch 18.11. **8.1,2 a** 2 S 6.11-16; 1 Ch 15.25-29; **b** Lv 23.34. **8.9** Dt 10.5. **8.10,11** Ex 40.34, 35. **8.12** Ps 18.11; 97.2. **8.16** 2 S 7.4-11; 1 Ch 17.3-10. **8.17,18** 2 S 7.1-3; 1 Ch 17.1, 2. **8.19** 2 S 7.12, 13; 1 Ch 17.11, 12.

Solomon Prays at the Temple

(2 *Chronicles* 6.12-42)

22 Solomon stood facing the altar with everyone standing behind him. Then he lifted his arms toward heaven 23 and prayed:

LORD God of Israel, no other god in heaven or on earth is like you!

You never forget the agreement you made with your people, and you are loyal to anyone who faithfully obeys your teachings. 24 My father David was your servant, and today you have kept every promise you made to him.

25 LORD God of Israel, you promised my father that someone from his family would always be king of Israel, if they do their best to obey you, just as he did. 26 Please keep this promise you made to your servant David.

27 There's not enough room in all of heaven for you, LORD God. How could you possibly live on earth in this temple I have built? 28 But I ask you to answer my prayer. 29 This is the temple where you have chosen to be worshiped. Please watch over it day and night and listen when I turn toward it and pray. 30 I am your servant, and the people of Israel belong to you. So whenever any of us look toward this temple and pray, answer from your home in heaven and forgive our sins.

31 Suppose someone accuses a person of a crime, and the accused has to stand in front of the altar in your temple and say, "I swear I am innocent!" 32 Listen from heaven and decide who is right. Then punish the guilty person and let the innocent one go free.

33 Suppose your people Israel sin against you, and then an enemy defeats them. If they come to this temple and beg for forgiveness, 34 listen from your home in heaven. Forgive them and bring them back to the land you gave their ancestors.

35 Suppose your people sin against you, and you punish them by holding back the rain. If they turn toward this temple and pray in your name and stop sinning, 36 listen from your home in heaven and forgive them. The people of Israel are your servants, so teach them to live right. And please send rain on the land you promised them forever.

37 Sometimes the crops may dry up or rot or be eaten by locusts[t] or grasshoppers, and your people will be starving. Sometimes enemies may surround their towns, or your people will become sick with deadly diseases. 38 Listen when anyone in Israel truly feels sorry and sincerely prays with arms lifted toward your temple. 39 You know what is in everyone's heart. So from your home in heaven answer their prayers, according to the way they live and what is in their hearts. 40 Then your people will worship and obey you for as long as they live in the land you gave their ancestors.

41-42 Foreigners will hear about you and your mighty power, and some of them will come to live among your people Israel. If any of them pray toward this temple, 43 listen from your home in heaven and answer their prayers. Then everyone on earth will worship you, just like your people Israel, and they will know that I have built this temple to honor you.

44 Our LORD, sometimes you will order your people to attack their enemies. Then your people will turn toward this temple I have built for you in your chosen city, and they will pray to you. 45 Answer their prayers from heaven and give them victory.

46 Everyone sins. But when your people sin against you, suppose you get angry enough to let their enemies drag them away to foreign countries. 47-49 Later, they may feel sorry for what they did and ask your forgiveness. Answer them when they pray toward this temple I have built for you in your chosen city, here in this land you gave their ancestors. From your home in heaven, listen to their sincere prayers

[t] **8.37** *locusts*: A type of grasshopper that comes in swarms and causes great damage to plant life.

8.25 1 K 2.4. **8.27** 2 Ch 2.6; 3 Macc 2.15. **8.29** Dt 12.5-19. **8.33-53** 3 Macc 2.10.

and do what they ask. 50 Forgive your
people no matter how much they have
sinned against you. Make the enemies
who defeated them be kind to them.
51 Remember, they are the people you
chose and rescued from Egypt that was
like a blazing fire to them.

52 I am your servant, and the people of Israel belong to you. So listen
when any of us pray and cry out for
your help. 53 When you brought our
ancestors out of Egypt, you told your
servant Moses to say to them, "From
all people on earth, the LORD God has
chosen you to be his very own."

Solomon Blesses the People

54 When Solomon finished his prayer at
the altar, he was kneeling with his arms
lifted toward heaven. He stood up,
55 turned toward the people, blessed them,
and said loudly:

56 Praise the LORD! He has kept his
promise and given us peace. Every
good thing he promised to his servant
Moses has happened.

57 The LORD our God was with our
ancestors to help them, and I pray that
he will be with us and never abandon
us. 58 May the LORD help us obey him
and follow all the laws and teachings
he gave our ancestors.

59 I pray that the LORD our God will
remember my prayer day and night.
May he help everyone in Israel each
day, in whatever way we need it.
60 Then every nation will know that
the LORD is the only true God.

61 Obey the LORD our God and follow his commands with all your heart,
just as you are doing today.

Solomon Dedicates the Temple

(2 Chronicles 7.4-10)

62-63 Solomon and the people dedicated
the temple to the LORD by offering twenty-
two thousand cattle and one hundred
twenty thousand sheep as sacrifices to ask
the LORD's blessing.[u] 64 On that day, Solomon dedicated the courtyard in front of
the temple and made it acceptable for worship. He offered the sacrifices there because the bronze altar in front of the temple was too small.

65 Solomon and the huge crowd celebrated the Festival of Shelters at the temple
for seven days.[v] There were people from as
far away as the Egyptian Gorge in the south
and Lebo-Hamath in the north. 66 Then on
the eighth day, he sent everyone home. They
said good-by and left, very happy, because
of all the good things the LORD had done
for his servant David and his people Israel.

The LORD Appears to Solomon Again

(2 Chronicles 7.11-22)

9 The LORD's temple and Solomon's
palace were now finished, and
Solomon had built everything he wanted.
2 Some time later the LORD appeared to
him again in a dream, just as he had done
at Gibeon. 3 The LORD said:

I heard your prayer and what you
asked me to do. This temple you have
built is where I will be worshiped forever. It belongs to me, and I will never
stop watching over it.

4 You must obey me, as your father
David did, and be honest and fair.
Obey my laws and teachings, 5 and I
will keep my promise to David that
someone from your family will always
be king of Israel.

6 But if you or any of your descendants disobey my commands or start
worshiping foreign gods, 7 I will no
longer let my people Israel live in this
land I gave them. I will desert this
temple where I said I would be worshiped. Then people everywhere will
think this nation is only a joke and will
make fun of it. 8 This temple will become a pile of rocks![w] Everyone who
walks by will be shocked, and they will
ask, "Why did the LORD do such a

[u] **8.62,63** *sacrifices to ask the LORD's blessing*: See Leviticus 3.1-17. [v] **8.65** *seven days*: One ancient translation; Hebrew "seven days and seven more days, fourteen days in all." [w] **9.8** *a pile of rocks*: Some ancient translations; Hebrew "high."

8.56 Dt 12.5-19; Js 21.44, 45. **9.2** 1 K 3.5; 2 Ch 1.7. **9.3** 3 Macc 2.9. **9.5** 1 K 2.4.
9.8 2 K 25.9; 2 Ch 36.19.

terrible thing to his people and to this temple?" 9 Then they will answer, "We know why the LORD did this. The people of Israel rejected the LORD their God, who rescued their ancestors from Egypt, and they started worshiping other gods."

Other Things Solomon Did

(2 *Chronicles* 8.1-18)

10 It took twenty years for the LORD's temple and Solomon's palace to be built. 11 Later, Solomon gave King Hiram of Tyre twenty towns in the region of Galilee to repay him for the cedar, pine, and gold he had given Solomon.

12 When Hiram went to see the towns, he did not like them. 13 He said, "Solomon, my friend, are these the kind of towns you want to give me?" So Hiram called the region Cabul because he thought it was worthless.[x] 14 He sent Solomon only five tons of gold in return.

15 After Solomon's workers had finished the temple and the palace, he ordered them to fill in the land on the east side of Jerusalem,[y] to build a wall around the city, and to rebuild the towns of Hazor, Megiddo, and Gezer.

16 Earlier, the king of Egypt had captured the town of Gezer; he burned it to the ground and killed the Canaanite people living there. Then he gave it to his daughter as a wedding present when she married Solomon. 17 So Solomon had the town rebuilt.

Solomon had his workers rebuild Lower Beth-Horon, 18 Baalath, and Tamar in the desert of Judah. 19 They also built towns where he could keep his supplies and his chariots and horses. Solomon had them build whatever he wanted in Jerusalem, Lebanon, and anywhere in his kingdom.

20-22 Solomon did not force the Israelites to do his work. They were his soldiers, officials, leaders, commanders, chariot captains, and chariot drivers. But he did make slaves of the Amorites, Hittites, Perizzites, Hivites, and Jebusites who were living in Israel. These were the descendants of those foreigners the Israelites could not destroy, and they remained Israel's slaves.

23 Solomon appointed five hundred fifty officers to be in charge of his workers and to watch over his building projects.

24 Solomon's wife, the daughter of the king of Egypt, moved from the older part of Jerusalem[z] to her new palace. Then Solomon had the land on the east side of Jerusalem filled in.[a]

25 Three times a year, Solomon burned incense and offered sacrifices to the LORD on the altar he had built.

Solomon had now finished building the LORD's temple.

26 He also had a lot of ships at Ezion-Geber, a town in Edom near Eloth on the Red Sea.[b] 27-28 King Hiram let some of his experienced sailors go to the country of Ophir[c] with Solomon's own sailors, and they brought back about sixteen tons of gold for Solomon.

The Queen of Sheba Visits Solomon

(2 *Chronicles* 9.1-12)

10 The Queen of Sheba heard how famous Solomon was, so she went to Jerusalem to test him with difficult questions. 2 She took along several of her officials, and she loaded her camels with gifts of spices, jewels, and gold. When she arrived, she and Solomon talked about everything she could think of. 3 He answered every question, no matter how difficult it was.

4-5 The Queen was amazed at Solomon's wisdom. She was breathless when she saw his palace, the food on his table, his offi-

[x]**9.13** *Cabul . . . worthless*: Cabul sounds like the Hebrew word for "worthless." [y]**9.15** *fill . . . Jerusalem*: The Hebrew text has "build the Millo," which probably refers to a landfill to strengthen and extend the hill where the city was built. [z]**9.24** *the older . . . Jerusalem*: See the note at 3.1. [a]**9.24** *the land . . . filled in*: See the note at 9.15. [b]**9.26** *Red Sea*: Hebrew *yam suph*, here referring to the Gulf of Aqaba, since the term is extended to include the northeastern arm of the Red Sea (see also the note at Exodus 13.11). [c]**9.27,28** *Ophir*: The location of this place is not known.

9.25 Ex 23.17; 34.23; Dt 16.16. **10.1-10** Mt 12.42; Lk 11.31.

Samson destroys the temple *Judges 16.23-31*

Naomi holding her infant grandson Obed *Ruth 4.13-17*

cials, his servants in their uniforms, the people who served his food, and the sacrifices he offered at the LORD's temple. 6 She said:

> Solomon, in my own country I had heard about your wisdom and all you've done. 7 But I didn't believe it until I saw it with my own eyes! And there's so much I didn't hear about. You are wiser and richer than I was told. 8 Your wives[d] and officials are lucky to be here where they can listen to the wise things you say.
>
> 9 I praise the LORD your God. He is pleased with you and has made you king of Israel. The LORD loves Israel, so he has given them a king who will rule fairly and honestly.

10 The Queen of Sheba gave Solomon almost five tons of gold, many jewels, and more spices than anyone had ever brought into Israel.

11-13 In return, Solomon gave her the gifts he would have given any other ruler, but he also gave her everything else she wanted. Then she and her officials went back to their own country.

Solomon's Wealth

(2 Chronicles 9.13-28)

King Hiram's ships brought gold, juniper wood, and jewels from the country of Ophir. Solomon used the wood to make steps[e] for the temple and palace, and harps and other stringed instruments for the musicians. It was the best juniper wood anyone in Israel had ever seen.

14 Solomon received about twenty-five tons of gold a year. 15 The merchants and traders, as well as the kings of Arabia and rulers from Israel, also gave him gold.

16 Solomon made two hundred gold shields and used about seven and a half pounds of gold for each one. 17 He also made three hundred smaller gold shields, using almost four pounds for each one, and he put the shields in his palace in Forest Hall.

18 His throne was made of ivory and covered with pure gold. 19-20 The back of the throne was rounded at the top, and it had armrests on each side. There was a statue of a lion on both sides of the throne, and there was a statue of a lion at both ends of each of the six steps leading up to the throne. No other throne in the world was like Solomon's.

21 Since silver was almost worthless in those days, everything was made of gold, even the cups and dishes used in Forest Hall.

22 Solomon had a lot of seagoing ships.[f] Every three years he sent them out with Hiram's ships to bring back gold, silver, and ivory, as well as monkeys and peacocks.[g]

23 He was the richest and wisest king in the world. 24 People from every nation wanted to hear the wisdom God had given him. 25 Year after year people came and brought gifts of silver and gold, as well as clothes, weapons, spices, horses, or mules.

26 Solomon had one thousand four hundred chariots and twelve thousand horses that he kept in Jerusalem and other towns.

27 While he was king, there was silver everywhere in Jerusalem, and cedar was as common as ordinary sycamore trees in the foothills.

28-29 Solomon's merchants bought his horses and chariots in the regions of Musri and Kue.[h] They paid about fifteen pounds of silver for a chariot and almost four pounds of silver for a horse. They also sold horses and chariots to the Hittite and Syrian kings.

Solomon Disobeys the LORD

11 1-2 The LORD did not want the Israelites to worship foreign gods, so he had warned them not to marry anyone who was not from Israel.

Solomon loved his wife, the daughter of

[d] **10.8** *wives*: Two ancient translations; Hebrew "men." [e] **10.11-13** *steps*: Or "stools" or "railings." [f] **10.22** *seagoing ships*: The Hebrew text has "ships of Tarshish," which may have been a Phoenician city in Spain. "Ships of Tarshish" probably means large, seagoing ships. [g] **10.22** *peacocks*: Or "baboons." [h] **10.28,29** *Musri and Kue*: Hebrew "Egypt and Kue." Musri and Kue were regions located in what is today southeast Turkey.

10.26 1 K 4.26. **10.27** Dt 17.17. **10.28,29** Dt 17.16. **11.1,2** **a** Dt 17.17; **b** Ex 34.16; Dt 7.3, 4.

the king of Egypt. But he also loved some women from Moab, Ammon, and Edom, and others from Sidon and the land of the Hittites. 3-4 Seven hundred of his wives were daughters of kings, but he also married three hundred other women.[i]

As Solomon got older, some of his wives led him to worship their gods. He wasn't like his father David, who had worshiped only the LORD God. 5 Solomon also worshiped Astarte the goddess of Sidon, and Milcom the disgusting god of Ammon. 6 Solomon's father had obeyed the LORD with all his heart, but Solomon disobeyed and did what the LORD hated.

7 Solomon built shrines on a hill east of Jerusalem to worship Chemosh the disgusting god of Moab, and Molech the disgusting god of Ammon. 8 In fact, he built a shrine for each of his foreign wives, so all of them could burn incense and offer sacrifices to their own gods.

9-10 The LORD God of Israel had appeared to Solomon two times and warned him not to worship foreign gods. But Solomon disobeyed and did it anyway. This made the LORD very angry, 11 and he said to Solomon:

> You did what you wanted and not what I told you to do. Now I'm going to take your kingdom from you and give it to one of your officials. 12 But because David was your father, you will remain king as long as you live. I will wait until your son becomes king, then I will take the kingdom from him. 13 When I do, I will still let him rule one tribe, because I have not forgotten that David was my servant and Jerusalem is my city.

Hadad Becomes an Enemy of Solomon

14 Hadad was from the royal family of Edom, and here is how the LORD made him Solomon's enemy:

15-16 Some time earlier, when David conquered the nation of Edom,[j] Joab his army commander went there to bury those who had died in battle. Joab and his soldiers stayed in Edom six months, and during that time they killed every man and boy who lived there.

17-19 Hadad was a boy at the time, but he escaped to Midian with some of his father's officials. At Paran some other men joined them, and they went to the king of Egypt. The king liked Hadad and gave him food, some land, and a house, and even let him marry the sister of Queen Tahpenes. 20 Hadad and his wife had a son named Genubath, and the queen let the boy grow up in the palace with her own children.

21 When Hadad heard that David and Joab were dead, he said to the king, "Your Majesty, please let me go back to my own country."

22 "Why?" asked the king. "Do you want something I haven't given you?"

"No, I just want to go home."

Rezon Becomes an Enemy of Solomon

23 Here is how God made Rezon son of Eliada an enemy of Solomon:

Rezon had run away from his master, King Hadadezer of Zobah. 24-25 He formed his own small army and became its leader after David had defeated Hadadezer's troops.[k] Then Rezon and his army went to Damascus, where he became the ruler of Syria and an enemy of Israel.

Both Hadad and Rezon were enemies of Israel while Solomon was king, and they caused him a lot of trouble.

The LORD Makes a Promise to Jeroboam

26 Jeroboam was from the town of Zeredah in Ephraim. His father Nebat had died, but his mother Zeruah was still alive. Jeroboam was one of Solomon's officials, but even he rebelled against Solomon. 27 Here is how it happened:

While Solomon's workers were filling in the land on the east side of Jerusalem[l] and repairing the city walls, 28 Solomon noticed that Jeroboam was a hard worker. So he put Jeroboam in charge of the work force from Manasseh and Ephraim.

29-30 One day when Jeroboam was leav-

[i] **11.3,4** *other women*: This translates a Hebrew word for a woman who was legally bound to a man, but without the full privileges of a wife.
[j] **11.15,16** *Edom*: See 2 Samuel 8.13, 14.
[k] **11.24,25** *troops*: See 2 Samuel 8.3-6.
[l] **11.27** *filling . . . Jerusalem*: See the note at 9.15.

ing Jerusalem, he met Ahijah, a prophet from Shiloh. No one else was anywhere around. Suddenly, Ahijah took off his new coat and ripped it into twelve pieces.
31 Then he said:

Jeroboam, take ten pieces of this coat and listen to what the LORD God of Israel says to you. "Jeroboam, I am the LORD God, and I am about to take Solomon's kingdom from him and give you ten tribes to rule.
32 But Solomon will still rule one tribe,[m] since he is the son of David my servant, and Jerusalem is my chosen city.

33 "Solomon and the Israelites are not like their ancestor David. They will not listen to me, obey me, or do what is right. They have turned from me to worship Astarte the goddess of Sidon, Chemosh the god of Moab, and Milcom the god of Ammon.

34 "Solomon is David's son, and David was my chosen leader, who did what I commanded. So I will let Solomon be king until he dies.
35 Then I will give you ten tribes to rule,
36 but Solomon's son will still rule one tribe. This way, my servant David will always have a descendant ruling in Jerusalem, the city where I have chosen to be worshiped.

37 "You will be king of Israel and will rule every nation you want.
38 I'll help you if you obey me. And if you do what I say, as my servant David did, I will always let someone from your family rule in Israel, just as someone from David's family will always rule in Judah. The nation of Israel will be yours.

39 "I will punish the descendants of David, but not forever."

40 When Solomon learned what the LORD had told Jeroboam, Solomon tried to kill Jeroboam. But he escaped to King Shishak of Egypt and stayed there until Solomon died.

Solomon Dies
(2 Chronicles 9.29-31)

41 Everything else Solomon did while he was king is written in the book about him and his wisdom.
42 After he had ruled forty years from Jerusalem,
43 he died and was buried there in the city of his father David. His son Rehoboam then became king.

Some of the People Rebel against Rehoboam
(2 Chronicles 10.1-19)

12 Rehoboam went to Shechem where everyone was waiting to crown him king.

2 Jeroboam son of Nebat heard what was happening, and he stayed in Egypt,[n] where he had gone to hide from Solomon.
3 But the people from the northern tribes of Israel sent for him. Then together they went to Rehoboam and said,
4 "Your father Solomon forced us to work very hard. But if you make our work easier, we will serve you and do whatever you ask."

5 "Give me three days to think about it," Rehoboam replied, "then come back for my answer." So the people left.

6 Rehoboam went to some leaders who had been his father's senior officials, and he asked them, "What should I tell these people?"

7 They answered, "If you want them to serve and obey you, then you should do what they ask today. Tell them you will make their work easier."

8 But Rehoboam refused their advice and went to the younger men who had grown up with him and were now his officials.
9 He asked, "What do you think I should say to these people who asked me to make their work easier?"

10 His younger advisors said:

Here's what we think you should say to them: "Compared to me, my father was weak.[o]
11 He made you work hard, but I'll make you work even harder. He punished you with whips,

[m] **11.31,32** *ten tribes . . . one tribe*: By this time the tribe of Simeon had become part of the tribe of Judah. "One tribe" refers to Judah. Instead of "one tribe," one ancient translation has "two tribes." [n] **12.2** *he stayed in Egypt*: Hebrew; two ancient translations "he returned from Egypt" (see also 2 Chronicles 10.2). [o] **12.10** *Compared . . . weak*: Hebrew "My little finger is bigger than my father's waist."

but I'll use whips with pieces of sharp metal!"
12 Three days later, Jeroboam and the others came back. 13 Rehoboam ignored the advice of the older advisors. 14 He spoke bluntly and told them exactly what his own advisors had suggested: "My father made you work hard, but I'll make you work even harder. He punished you with whips, but I'll use whips with pieces of sharp metal!"

15-19 When the people realized that Rehoboam would not listen to them, they shouted: "We don't have to be loyal to David's family. We can do what we want. Come on, people of Israel, let's go home! Rehoboam can rule his own people."

Adoniram[p] was in charge of the forced labor, and Rehoboam sent him to talk to the people. But they stoned him to death. Then Rehoboam ran to his chariot and hurried back to Jerusalem.

So the people from the northern tribes of Israel went home, leaving Rehoboam to rule only the people from the towns in Judah. Ever since that day, the people of Israel have opposed David's family in Judah. All of this happened just as the LORD's prophet Ahijah had told Jeroboam.

20 When the Israelites heard that Jeroboam was back, they called everyone together. Then they sent for Jeroboam and made him king of Israel. Only the people from the tribe of Judah[q] remained loyal to David's family.

Shemaiah Warns Rehoboam

(2 Chronicles 11.1-4)

21 After Rehoboam returned to Jerusalem, he decided to attack Israel and take control of the whole country. So he called together one hundred eighty thousand soldiers from the tribes of Judah and Benjamin.
22 Meanwhile, God told Shemaiah the prophet
23 to give Rehoboam and everyone from Judah and Benjamin this warning:
24 "Don't go to war against the people from Israel—they are your relatives. Go home! I am the LORD, and I made these things happen."

Rehoboam and his army obeyed the LORD and went home.

Jeroboam Makes Religious Changes

25 Jeroboam rebuilt Shechem in Ephraim and made it a stronger town, then he moved there. He also fortified the town of Penuel.

26-27 One day, Jeroboam started thinking, "Everyone in Israel still goes to the temple in Jerusalem to offer sacrifices to the LORD. What if they become loyal to David's family again? They will kill me and accept Rehoboam as their king."

28 Jeroboam asked for advice and then made two gold statues of calves. He showed them to the people and said, "Listen everyone! You won't have to go to Jerusalem to worship anymore. Here are your gods[r] who rescued you from Egypt."
29-30 Then he put one of the gold calves in the town of Bethel. He put the other one in the town of Dan, and the crowd walked out in front as the calf was taken there.[s] What Jeroboam did was a terrible sin.

31 Jeroboam built small places of worship at the shrines[t] and appointed men who were not from the tribe of Levi to serve as priests.
32-33 He also decided to start a new festival for the Israelites on the fifteenth day of the eighth month, just like the one in Judah.[u] On that day, Jeroboam went to Bethel and offered sacrifices on the altar to the gold calf he had put there. Then he assigned the priests their duties.

A Prophet Condemns the Altar at Bethel

13 1-2 One day, Jeroboam was standing at the altar in Bethel, ready to make an offering. Suddenly one of God's

[p] **12.15-19** *Adoniram*: Two ancient translations (see also 4.6 and 5.14); Hebrew "Adoram."
[q] **12.20** *Israelites . . . Israel . . . Judah*: From this time on, "Israel" usually refers to the northern kingdom, and "Israelites" refers to the people who lived there. The southern kingdom is called "Judah."
[r] **12.28** *Here are your gods*: Or "Here is your God."
[s] **12.29,30** *the crowd . . . taken there*: One possible meaning for the difficult Hebrew text.
[t] **12.31** *shrines*: See the note at 3.2.
[u] **12.32,33** *the one in Judah*: This probably refers to the Festival of Shelters.

12.15-19 2 S 20.1. **12.28** Ex 32.4. **12.32,33** Lv 23.33, 34. **13.1,2** 2 K 23.15, 16.

prophets[v] arrived from Judah and shouted:

The LORD sent me with a message about this altar. A child named Josiah will be born into David's family. He will sacrifice on this altar the priests who make offerings here, and human bones will be burned on it.

3 You will know that the LORD has said these things when the altar splits in half, and the ashes on it fall to the ground.

4 Jeroboam pointed at the prophet and shouted, "Grab him!" But right away, Jeroboam's hand became stiff, and he could not move it. 5 The altar split in half, and the ashes fell to the ground, just as the prophet had warned.

6 "Please pray to the LORD your God and ask him to heal my hand," Jeroboam begged.

The prophet prayed, and Jeroboam's hand was healed.

7 "Come home with me and eat something," Jeroboam said. "I want to give you a gift for what you have done."

8 "No, I wouldn't go with you, even if you offered me half of your kingdom. I won't eat or drink here either. 9 The LORD said I can't eat or drink anything and that I can't go home the same way I came."
10 Then he started home down a different road.

An Old Prophet from Bethel

11 At that time an old prophet lived in Bethel, and one of his sons told him what the prophet from Judah had said and done.

12 "Show me which way he went," the old prophet said, and his sons pointed out the road. 13 "Put a saddle on my donkey," he told them. After they did, he got on the donkey 14 and rode off to look for the prophet from Judah.

The old prophet found him sitting under an oak tree and asked, "Are you the prophet from Judah?"

"Yes, I am."

15 "Come home with me," the old prophet said, "and have something to eat."

16 "I can't go back with you," the prophet replied, "and I can't eat or drink anything with you. 17 The LORD warned me not to eat or drink or to go home the same way I came."

18 The old prophet said, "I'm a prophet too. One of the LORD's angels told me to take you to my house and give you something to eat and drink."

The prophet from Judah did not know that the old prophet was lying, 19 so he went home with him and ate and drank.

20 During the meal the LORD gave the old prophet 21 a message for the prophet from Judah:

Listen to the LORD's message. You have disobeyed the LORD your God.
22 He told you not to eat or drink anything here, but you came home and ate with me. And so, when you die, your body won't be buried in your family tomb.

23 After the meal the old prophet got a donkey ready, 24 and the prophet from Judah left. Along the way, a lion attacked and killed him, and the donkey and the lion stood there beside his dead body.

25 Some people walked by and saw the body with the lion standing there. They ran into Bethel, telling everyone what they had seen.

26 When the old prophet heard the news, he said, "That must be the prophet from Judah. The LORD warned him, but he disobeyed. So the LORD sent a lion to kill him."

27 The old prophet told his sons to saddle his donkey, and when it was ready, 28 he
left. He found the body lying on the road, with the donkey and lion standing there. The lion had not eaten the body or attacked the donkey. 29 The old prophet picked up the body, put it on his own donkey, and took it back to Bethel, so he could bury it and mourn for the prophet from Judah.

30 He buried the body in his own family tomb and cried for the prophet. 31 He said to his sons, "When I die, bury my body next to this prophet. 32 I'm sure that everything he said about the altar in Bethel and the shrines in Samaria will happen."

33 But Jeroboam kept on doing evil

[v] **13.1,2** *one of God's prophets*: Hebrew "a man of God."

things. He appointed men to be priests at the local shrines, even if they were not Levites. In fact, anyone who wanted to be a priest could be one. [34] This sinful thing led to the downfall of his kingdom.

Jeroboam's Son Dies

14 About the same time, Abijah son of Jeroboam got sick. [2-3] Jeroboam told his wife:

Disguise yourself so no one will know you're my wife, then go to Shiloh, where the prophet Ahijah lives. Take him ten loaves of bread, some small cakes, and honey, and ask him what will happen to our son. He can tell you, because he's the one who told me I would become king.

[4] She got ready and left for Ahijah's house in Shiloh.

Ahijah was now old and blind, [5] but the LORD told him, "Jeroboam's wife is coming to ask about her son. I will tell you what to say to her."

Jeroboam's wife came to Ahijah's house, pretending to be someone else. [6] But when Ahijah heard her walking up to the door, he said:

Come in! I know you're Jeroboam's wife—why are you pretending to be someone else? I have some bad news for you. [7] Give your husband this message from the LORD God of Israel: "Jeroboam, you know that I, the LORD, chose you over anyone else to be the leader of my people Israel. [8] I even took David's kingdom away from his family and gave it to you. But you are not like my servant David. He always obeyed me and did what was right.

[9] "You have made me very angry by rejecting me and making idols out of gold. Jeroboam, you have done more evil things than any king before you.

[10] "Because of this, I will destroy your family by killing every man and boy in it, whether slave or free. I will wipe out your family, just as fire burns up trash. [11] Dogs will eat the bodies of your relatives who die in town, and vultures will eat the bodies of those who die in the country. I, the LORD, have spoken and will not change my mind!"

[12] That's the LORD's message to your husband. As for you, go back home, and right after you get there, your son will die. [13] Everyone in Israel will mourn at his funeral. But he will be the last one from Jeroboam's family to receive a proper burial, because he's the only one the LORD God of Israel is pleased with.

[14] The LORD will soon choose a new king of Israel, who will destroy Jeroboam's family. And I mean very soon.[w] [15] The people of Israel have made the LORD angry by setting up sacred poles[x] for worshiping the goddess Asherah. So the LORD will punish them until they shake like grass in a stream. He will take them out of the land he gave to their ancestors, then scatter them as far away as the Euphrates River. [16] Jeroboam sinned and caused the Israelites to sin. Now the LORD will desert Israel.

[17] Jeroboam's wife left and went back home to the town of Tirzah. As soon as she set foot in her house, her son died. [18] Everyone in Israel came and mourned at his funeral, just as the LORD's servant Ahijah had said.

Jeroboam Dies

[19] Everything else Jeroboam did while he was king, including the battles he won, is written in *The History of the Kings of Israel.* [20] He was king of Israel for twenty-two years, then he died, and his son Nadab became king.

King Rehoboam of Judah

(*2 Chronicles* 11.5—12.16)

[21] Rehoboam son of Solomon was forty-one years old when he became king of Judah, and he ruled seventeen years from Jerusalem, the city where the LORD had

[w] **14.14** *And I mean very soon*: One possible meaning for the difficult Hebrew text.
[x] **14.15** *sacred poles*: Or "trees," used as symbols of Asherah, the goddess of fertility.
14.10 1 K 15.29.

chosen to be worshiped. His mother
Naamah was from Ammon.
22 The people of Judah disobeyed the
LORD and made him even angrier than
their ancestors had. 23 They also built their
own local shrines[y] and stone images of foreign gods, and they set up sacred poles[z] for
worshiping the goddess Asherah on every
hill and in the shade of large trees. 24 Even
worse, they allowed prostitutes[a] at the
shrines, and followed the disgusting customs of the foreign nations that the LORD
had forced out of Canaan.
25 After Rehoboam had been king for
four years, King Shishak of Egypt attacked
Jerusalem. 26 He took everything of value
from the temple and the palace, including
Solomon's gold shields.
27 Rehoboam had bronze shields made
to replace the gold ones, and he ordered
the guards at the city gates to keep them
safe. 28 Whenever Rehoboam went to the
LORD's temple, the guards carried the
shields. But they always took them back to
the guardroom as soon as he was finished.
29 Everything else Rehoboam did while
he was king is written in *The History of the
Kings of Judah*. 30 He and Jeroboam were
constantly at war. 31 Rehoboam's mother
Naamah was from Ammon, but when Rehoboam died, he was buried beside his ancestors in Jerusalem.[b] His son Abijam then
became king.

King Abijam of Judah

(2 Chronicles 13.1-22)

15 Abijam became king of Judah in
Jeroboam's eighteenth year as king
of Israel, 2 and he ruled from Jerusalem for
three years. His mother was Maacah the
daughter of Abishalom.
3 Abijam did not truly obey the LORD his
God as his ancestor David had done. Instead, he was sinful just like his father Rehoboam. 4-5 David had always obeyed the
LORD's commands by doing right, except in
the case of Uriah.[c] And since Abijam was
David's great-grandson, the LORD kept
Jerusalem safe and let Abijam have a son
who would be the next king.
6-7 The war that had broken out between Rehoboam and Jeroboam continued
during the time that Abijam was king.
Everything else Abijam did while he was
king is written in *The History of the Kings
of Judah*. 8 Abijam died and was buried in
Jerusalem,[d] and his son Asa became king.

King Asa of Judah

(2 Chronicles 15.16—16.6, 11-13)

9 Asa became king of Judah in the twentieth year of Jeroboam's rule in Israel,
10 and he ruled forty-one years from Jerusalem. His grandmother was Maacah the
daughter of Abishalom.
11 Asa obeyed the LORD, as David had
done. 12 He forced the prostitutes[e] at the
shrines to leave the country, and he got rid
of the idols his ancestors had made. 13 His
own grandmother Maacah had made an
idol of Asherah, and Asa took it and burned
it in Kidron Valley. Then he removed
Maacah from her position as queen
mother.[f]
14 As long as Asa lived, he was completely faithful to the LORD, even though he
did not destroy the local shrines. 15 He
placed in the temple all the silver and gold
objects that he and his father had dedicated to the LORD.
16 Asa was always at war with King
Baasha of Israel. 17 One time, Baasha invaded Judah and captured the town of
Ramah. He started making the town

[y] **14.23** *local shrines*: See the note at 3.2. [z] **14.23** *sacred poles*: See the note at 14.15. [a] **14.24** *prostitutes*: Men and women sometimes served at the local shrines as prostitutes in the worship of Canaanite gods, but the LORD had forbidden the people of Israel to worship in this way (see Deuteronomy 23.17, 18). [b] **14.31** *Jerusalem*: See the note at 2.10, 11. [c] **15.4,5** *Uriah*: A Hittite who served in David's army; David had him killed so he could marry his wife Bathsheba (see 2 Samuel 11.1-27). [d] **15.8** *Jerusalem*: See the note at 2.10, 11. [e] **15.12** *prostitutes*: See the note at 14.24. [f] **15.13** *queen mother*: Or "the mother of the king," an important position in biblical times (see 2.19).

14.23 2 K 17.9, 10. **14.24** Dt 23.17. **14.25** 2 Ch 12.2-8. **14.26** 1 K 10.16, 17; 2 Ch 9.15, 16. **15.4,5 a** 2 S 11.1-27; **b** 1 K 11.36. **15.6,7** 2 Ch 13.3-21. **15.12** 2 Ch 15.8-15.

stronger, so he could put troops there to
stop people from going in and out of Judah.
18 When Asa heard about this, he took
the silver and gold from his palace and
from the LORD's temple. He gave it to some
of his officials and sent them to Damascus
with this message for King Benhadad[g] of
Syria: 19 "Our fathers signed a peace treaty.
Why don't we do the same thing? This silver and gold is a present for you. So, would
you please break your treaty with Baasha
and force him to leave my country?"
20 Benhadad did what Asa asked and
sent the Syrian army into Israel. They captured the towns of Ijon, Dan, and Abel-
Bethmaacah, and the territories of Chin-
neroth and Naphtali. 21 When Baasha
heard about it, he left Ramah and went
back to Tirzah.
22 Asa ordered everyone in Judah to
carry away the stones and wood Baasha
had used to strengthen the town of Ramah.
Then he used these same stones and wood
to fortify the town of Geba in the territory
of Benjamin and the town of Mizpah.
23 Everything else Asa did while he was
king, including his victories and the towns
he rebuilt, is written in *The History of the
Kings of Judah*. When he got older, he had
a foot disease. 24 Asa died and was buried
in the tomb of his ancestors in Jerusalem.[h]
His son Jehoshaphat then became king.

King Nadab of Israel

25 Nadab son of Jeroboam became king
of Israel in Asa's second year as king of Judah, and he ruled two years. 26 Nadab disobeyed the LORD by following the evil example of his father, who had caused the
Israelites to sin.
27-28 Baasha son of Ahijah was from the
tribe of Issachar, and he made plans to kill
Nadab. When Nadab and his army went to
attack the town of Gibbethon in Philistia,
Baasha killed Nadab there. So in the third
year of Asa's rule, Baasha became king of
Israel.
29 The LORD's prophet Ahijah had earlier said, "Not one man or boy in Jeroboam's family will be left alive." And, as
soon as Baasha became king, he killed
everyone in Jeroboam's family, 30 because
Jeroboam had made the LORD God of Israel
angry by sinning and causing the Israelites
to sin.
31 Everything else Nadab did while he
was king is written in *The History of the
Kings of Israel*.
32 King Asa of Judah and King Baasha of
Israel were always at war.

King Baasha of Israel

33 Baasha son of Ahijah became king of
Israel in Asa's third year as king of Judah,
and he ruled twenty-four years from
Tirzah. 34 Baasha also disobeyed the LORD
by acting like Jeroboam, who had caused
the Israelites to sin.

16 The LORD sent Jehu son of Hanani
to say to Baasha:
2 Nobody knew who you were until
I, the LORD, chose you[i] to be the
leader of my people Israel. And now
you're acting exactly like Jeroboam by
causing the Israelites to sin. What
you've done has made me so angry
3 that I will destroy you and your family,
just as I did the family of Jeroboam.
4 Dogs will eat the bodies of your relatives
who die in town, and vultures will eat
the bodies of those who die in the
country.

5-7 Baasha made the LORD very angry,
and that's why the LORD gave Jehu this
message for Baasha and his family. Baasha
constantly disobeyed the LORD by following
Jeroboam's sinful example—but even
worse, he killed everyone in Jeroboam's
family!
Everything else Baasha did while he was
king, including his brave deeds, is written
in *The History of the Kings of Israel*.
Baasha died and was buried in Tirzah, and
his son Elah became king.

King Elah of Israel

8 Elah son of Baasha became king of Israel after Asa had been king of Judah for

[g] **15.18** *Benhadad*: Hebrew "Benhadad son of Tabrimmon son of Hezion." [h] **15.24** *Jerusalem*: Hebrew "the city of David his ancestor." [i] **16.2** *Nobody . . . you*: Hebrew "I pulled you up out of the dust."

15.29 1 K 14.10.

twenty-five years, and he ruled from Tirzah for two years.

9 Zimri commanded half of Elah's chariots, and he made plans to kill Elah.

One day, Elah was in Tirzah, getting drunk at the home of Arza, his prime minister, 10 when Zimri went there and killed Elah. So Zimri became king in the twenty-seventh year of Asa's rule in Judah.

11 As soon as Zimri became king, he killed everyone in Baasha's family. Not one man or boy in his family was left alive—even his close friends were killed. 12 Baasha's family was completely wiped out, just as the LORD's prophet Jehu had warned. 13 Baasha and Elah sinned and caused the Israelites to sin, and they made the LORD angry by worshiping idols.

14 Everything else Elah did while he was king is written in *The History of the Kings of Israel*.

King Zimri of Israel

15-16 Zimri became king of Israel in Asa's twenty-seventh year as king of Judah, but he ruled only seven days from Tirzah.

Israel's army was camped near Gibbethon in Philistia under the command of Omri. The soldiers heard that Zimri had killed Elah, and they made Omri their king that same day. 17 At once, Omri and his army marched to Tirzah and attacked. 18 When Zimri saw that the town was captured, he ran into the strongest part of the palace and killed himself by setting it on fire. 19 Zimri had disobeyed the LORD by following the evil example of Jeroboam, who had caused the Israelites to sin.

20 Everything else Zimri did while he was king, including his rebellion against Elah, is written in *The History of the Kings of Israel*.

King Omri of Israel

21 After Zimri died, some of the Israelites wanted Tibni son of Ginath to be king, but others wanted Omri. 22 Omri's followers were stronger than Tibni's, so Tibni was killed, and Omri became king of Israel 23 in the thirty-first year of Asa's rule in Judah.

Omri ruled Israel for twelve years. The first six years he ruled from Tirzah, 24 then he bought the hill of Samaria from Shemer for about one hundred fifty pounds of silver. He built a town there and named it Samaria, after Shemer who had owned the hill.

25 Omri did more evil things than any king before him. 26 He acted just like Jeroboam and made the LORD God of Israel angry by causing the Israelites to sin and to worship idols.

27 Everything else Omri did while he was king, including his brave deeds, is written in *The History of the Kings of Israel*. 28 Omri died and was buried in Samaria, and his son Ahab became king.

King Ahab of Israel

29 Ahab son of Omri became king of Israel in the thirty-eighth year of Asa's rule in Judah, and he ruled twenty-two years from Samaria.

30 Ahab did more things to disobey the LORD than any king before him. 31 He acted just like Jeroboam. Even worse, he married Jezebel the daughter of King Ethbaal of Sidon[j] and started worshiping Baal. 32 Ahab built an altar and temple for Baal in Samaria 33 and set up a sacred pole[k] for worshiping the goddess Asherah. Ahab did more to make the LORD God of Israel angry than any king of Israel before him.

34 While Ahab was king, a man from Bethel named Hiel rebuilt the town of Jericho. But while Hiel was laying the foundation for the town wall, his oldest son Abiram died. And while he was finishing the gates, his youngest son Segub died. This happened just as the LORD had told Joshua to say many years ago.[l]

Elijah Stops the Rain

17 Elijah was a prophet from Tishbe in Gilead.[m] One day he went to King Ahab and said, "I'm a servant of the living

[j]**16.31** *Sidon*: One of the most important cities in Phoenicia. It was located on the coast of the Mediterranean Sea, north of Israel, in what is today southern Lebanon. [k]**16.33** *sacred pole*: See the note at 14.15. [l]**16.34** *a man from Bethel . . . ago*: See Joshua 6.26. [m]**17.1** *from Tishbe in Gilead*: Or "from the settlers in Gilead."

16.34 Js 6.26. **17.1** Jas 5.17.

LORD, the God of Israel. And I swear in his name that it won't rain until I say so. There won't even be any dew on the ground."

2 Later, the LORD said to Elijah, 3 "Leave and go across the Jordan River so you can hide near Cherith Creek. 4 You can drink water from the creek, and eat the food I've told the ravens to bring you."

5 Elijah obeyed the LORD and went to live near Cherith Creek. 6 Ravens brought him bread and meat twice a day, and he drank water from the creek. 7 But after a while, it dried up because there was no rain.

Elijah Helps a Widow in Zarephath

8 The LORD told Elijah, 9 "Go to the town of Zarephath in Sidon and live there. I've told a widow in that town to give you food."

10 When Elijah came near the town gate of Zarephath, he saw a widow gathering sticks for a fire. "Would you please bring me a cup of water?" he asked. 11 As she left to get it, he asked, "Would you also please bring me a piece of bread?"

12 The widow answered, "In the name of the living LORD your God, I swear that I don't have any bread. All I have is a handful of flour and a little olive oil. I'm on my way home now with these few sticks to cook what I have for my son and me. After that, we will starve to death."

13 Elijah said, "Everything will be fine. Do what you said. Go home and fix something for you and your son. But first, please make a small piece of bread and bring it to me. 14 The LORD God of Israel has promised that your jar of flour won't run out and your bottle of oil won't dry up before he sends rain for the crops."

15 The widow went home and did exactly what Elijah had told her. She and Elijah and her family had enough food for a long time. 16 The LORD kept the promise that his prophet Elijah had made, and she did not run out of flour or oil.

Elijah Brings a Boy Back to Life

17 Several days later, the son of the woman who owned the house[n] got sick, and he kept getting worse, until finally he died.

18 The woman shouted at Elijah, "What have I done to you? I thought you were God's prophet. Did you come here to cause the death of my son as a reminder that I've sinned against God?"[o]

19 "Bring me your son," Elijah said. Then he took the boy from her arms and carried him upstairs to the room where he was staying. Elijah laid the boy on his bed 20 and prayed, "LORD God, why did you do such a terrible thing to this woman? She's letting me stay here, and now you've let her son die." 21 Elijah stretched himself out over the boy three times, while praying, "LORD God, bring this boy back to life!"

22 The LORD answered Elijah's prayer, and the boy started breathing again. 23 Elijah picked him up and carried him downstairs. He gave the boy to his mother and said, "Look, your son is alive."

24 "You are God's prophet!" the woman replied. "Now I know that you really do speak for the LORD."

Elijah Proves He Is the LORD's Prophet

18 1-2 For three years no rain fell in Samaria, and there was almost nothing to eat anywhere. The LORD said to Elijah, "Go and meet with King Ahab. I will soon make it rain." So Elijah went to see Ahab.

3-4 At that time Obadiah was in charge of Ahab's palace, but he faithfully worshiped the LORD. In fact, when Jezebel was trying to kill the LORD's prophets, Obadiah hid one hundred of them in two caves and gave them food and water.

Ahab sent for Obadiah 5 and said, "We have to find something for our horses and mules to eat. If we don't, we will have to kill them. Let's look around every creek and spring in the country for some grass.

[n]**17.17** *the woman who owned the house*: This may or may not be the same woman as the widow in verses 8-16. [o]**17.18** *Did you . . . God*: In ancient times people sometimes thought that if they sinned, something terrible would happen to them.

17.9 Lk 4.25, 26. **17.21** 2 K 4.34, 35.

6 You go one way, and I'll go the other." Then they left in separate directions.

7 As Obadiah was walking along, he met Elijah. Obadiah recognized him, bowed down, and asked, "Elijah, is it really you?"

8 "Yes. Go tell Ahab I'm here."

9 Obadiah replied:

King Ahab would kill me if I told him that. And I haven't even done anything wrong. 10 I swear to you in the name of the living LORD your God that the king has looked everywhere for you. He sent people to look in every country, and when they couldn't find you, he made the leader of each country swear that you were not in that country. 11 Do you really want me to tell him you're here?

12 What if the LORD's Spirit takes you away as soon as I leave? When Ahab comes to get you, he won't find you. Then he will surely kill me.

I have worshiped the LORD since I was a boy. 13 I even hid one hundred of the LORD's prophets in caves when Jezebel was trying to kill them. I also gave them food and water. 14 Do you really want me to tell Ahab you're here? He will kill me!

15 Elijah said, "I'm a servant of the living LORD All-Powerful, and I swear in his name that I will meet with Ahab today."

16 Obadiah left and told Ahab where to find Elijah.

Ahab went to meet Elijah, 17 and when he saw him, Ahab shouted, "There you are, the biggest troublemaker in Israel!"

18 Elijah answered:

You're the troublemaker—not me! You and your family have disobeyed the LORD's commands by worshiping Baal.

19 Call together everyone from Israel and have them meet me on Mount Carmel. Be sure to bring along the four hundred fifty prophets of Baal and the four hundred prophets of Asherah who eat at Jezebel's table.

20 Ahab got everyone together, then they went to meet Elijah on Mount Carmel. 21 Elijah stood in front of them and said, "How much longer will you try to have things both ways? If the LORD is God, worship him! But if Baal is God, worship him!"

The people did not say a word.

22 Then Elijah continued:

I am the LORD's only prophet, but Baal has four hundred fifty prophets.

23 Bring us two bulls. Baal's prophets can take one of them, kill it, and cut it into pieces. Then they can put the meat on the wood without lighting the fire. I will do the same thing with the other bull, and I won't light a fire under it either.

24 The prophets of Baal will pray to their god, and I will pray to the LORD. The one who answers by starting the fire is God.

"That's a good idea," everyone agreed.

25 Elijah said to Baal's prophets, "There are more of you, so you go first. Pick out a bull and get it ready, but don't light the fire. Then pray to your god."

26 They chose their bull, then they got it ready and prayed to Baal all morning, asking him to start the fire. They danced around the altar and shouted, "Answer us, Baal!" But there was no answer.

27 At noon, Elijah began making fun of them. "Pray louder!" he said. "Baal must be a god. Maybe he's day-dreaming or using the toilet or traveling somewhere. Or maybe he's asleep, and you have to wake him up."

28 The prophets kept shouting louder and louder, and they cut themselves with swords and knives until they were bleeding. This was the way they worshiped, 29 and they kept it up all afternoon. But there was no answer of any kind.

30 Elijah told everyone to gather around him while he repaired the LORD's altar. 31-32 Then he used twelve stones to build an altar in honor of the LORD. Each stone stood for one of the tribes of Israel, which was the name the LORD had given to their ancestor Jacob. Elijah dug a ditch around the altar, large enough to hold about thirteen quarts. 33 He placed the wood on the altar, then they cut the bull into pieces and laid the meat on the wood.

18.31,32 Gn 32.28; 35.9-11.

He told the people, "Fill four large jars
with water and pour it over the meat and
the wood." After they did this, 34 he told
them to do it two more times. They did
exactly as he said 35 until finally, the water
ran down the altar and filled the ditch.
36 When it was time for the evening sacrifice, Elijah prayed:

> Our LORD, you are the God of Abra-
> ham, Isaac, and Israel. Now, prove that
> you are the God of this nation,[p] and
> that I, your servant, have done this at
> your command. 37 Please answer me,
> so these people will know that you are
> the LORD God, and that you will turn
> their hearts back to you.[q]

38 The LORD immediately sent fire, and
it burned up the sacrifice, the wood, and
the stones. It scorched the ground everywhere around the altar and dried up every
drop of water in the ditch. 39 When the
crowd saw what had happened, they all
bowed down and shouted, "The LORD is
God! The LORD is God!"
40 Just then, Elijah said, "Grab the
prophets of Baal! Don't let any of them get
away."

So the people captured the prophets
and took them to Kishon River, where Elijah killed every one of them.

It Starts To Rain

41 Elijah told Ahab, "Get something to
eat and drink. I hear a heavy rain coming."
42 Ahab left, but Elijah climbed back to
the top of Mount Carmel. Then he stooped
down with his face almost to the ground
43 and said to his servant, "Look toward
the sea."

The servant left. And when he came
back, he said, "I looked, but I didn't see
anything." Elijah told him to look seven
more times.
44 After the seventh time the servant
replied, "I see a small cloud coming this
way. But it's no bigger than a fist."

Elijah told him, "Tell Ahab to get his
chariot ready and start home now. Otherwise, the rain will stop him."
45-46 A few minutes later, it got very
cloudy and windy, and rain started pouring
down. So Elijah wrapped his coat around
himself, and the LORD gave him strength to
run all the way to Jezreel. Ahab followed him.

Elijah Runs Away from Ahab and Jezebel

19 Ahab told his wife Jezebel what Elijah had done and that he had killed
the prophets. 2 She sent a message to Elijah: "You killed my prophets. Now I'm going to kill you! I pray that the gods will
punish me even more severely if I don't do
it by this time tomorrow."
3 Elijah was afraid when he got her message, and he ran to the town of Beersheba
in Judah. He left his servant there, 4 then
walked another whole day into the desert.
Finally, he came to a large bush and sat
down in its shade. He begged the LORD,
"I've had enough. Just let me die! I'm no
better off than my ancestors." 5 Then he
lay down in the shade and fell asleep.

Suddenly an angel woke him up and
said, "Get up and eat." 6 Elijah looked
around, and by his head was a jar of water
and some baked bread. He sat up, ate and
drank, then lay down and went back to
sleep.
7 Soon the LORD's angel woke him again
and said, "Get up and eat, or else you'll get
too tired to travel." 8 So Elijah sat up and
ate and drank.

The food and water made him strong
enough to walk forty more days. At last, he
reached Mount Sinai,[r] the mountain of
God, 9 and he spent the night there in a
cave.

The LORD Appears to Elijah

While Elijah was on Mount Sinai, the
LORD asked, "Elijah, why are you here?"
10 He answered, "LORD God All-
Powerful, I've always done my best to obey
you. But your people have broken their solemn promise to you. They have torn down
your altars and killed all your prophets,

[p] **18.36** *this nation*: Hebrew "Israel." [q] **18.37** *will turn . . . to you*: One possible meaning for the difficult Hebrew text. [r] **19.8** *Sinai*: Hebrew "Horeb."

18.42-46 Jas 5.18. **19.4** Jon 4.3. **19.10,14** Ro 11.3.

except me. And now they are even trying to kill me!"

11 "Go out and stand on the mountain," the LORD replied. "I want you to see me when I pass by."

All at once, a strong wind shook the mountain and shattered the rocks. But the LORD was not in the wind. Next, there was an earthquake, but the LORD was not in the earthquake. 12 Then there was a fire, but the LORD was not in the fire.

Finally, there was a gentle breeze,[s] 13 and when Elijah heard it, he covered his face with his coat. He went out and stood at the entrance to the cave.

The LORD[t] asked, "Elijah, why are you here?"

14 Elijah answered, "LORD God All-Powerful, I've always done my best to obey you. But your people have broken their solemn promise to you. They have torn down your altars and killed all your prophets, except me. And now they are even trying to kill me!"

15 The LORD said:

> Elijah, you can go back to the desert near Damascus. And when you get there, appoint[u] Hazael to be king of Syria. 16 Then appoint Jehu son of Nimshi to be king of Israel, and Elisha son of Shaphat[v] to take your place as my prophet.
>
> 17 Hazael will start killing the people who worship Baal. Jehu will kill those who escape from Hazael, and Elisha will kill those who escape from Jehu.
>
> 18 But seven thousand Israelites have refused to worship Baal, and they will live.

Elisha Becomes Elijah's Assistant

19 Elijah left and found Elisha plowing a field with a pair of oxen. There were eleven other men in front of him, and each one was also plowing with a pair of oxen. Elijah went over and put his own coat on Elisha.[w]

20 Elisha stopped plowing and ran after him. "Let me kiss my parents good-by, then I'll go with you," he said.

"You can go," Elijah said. "But remember what I've done for you."

21 Elisha left and took his oxen with him. He killed them and boiled them over a fire he had made with the wood from his plow. He gave the meat to the people who were with him, and they ate it. Then he left with Elijah and became his assistant.

Syria Attacks Israel

20 King Benhadad of Syria[x] called his army together. He was joined by thirty-two other kings with their horses and chariots, and together they marched to Samaria and attacked. 2 Benhadad sent a messenger to tell King Ahab of Israel, 3 "Ahab, give me your silver and gold, your wives,[y] and your strongest sons!"

4 "Your Majesty," Ahab replied, "everything I have is yours, including me."

5 Later, Benhadad sent another messenger to say to Ahab, "I already told you to give me your silver and gold, your wives, and your children. 6 But tomorrow at this time, I will send my officials into your city to search your palace and the houses of your officials. They will take everything else that you[z] own."

7 Ahab called a meeting with the leaders of Israel and said, "Benhadad is causing real trouble. He told me to give him my wives and children, as well as my silver and gold. And I agreed."

8 "Don't listen to him!" they answered. "You don't have to do what he says."

9 So Ahab sent someone to tell Benhadad, "Your Majesty, I'll give you my silver and gold, and even my wives and children. But I won't let you have anything else."

[s] **19.12** *a gentle breeze*: Or "a soft whisper" or "hardly a sound." [t] **19.13** *The LORD*: Hebrew "A voice." [u] **19.15** *appoint*: This would have included a ceremony in which olive oil would be poured on his head to show that he was now king. [v] **19.16** *Shaphat*: Hebrew "Shaphat from Abel-Meholah." [w] **19.19** *put . . . Elisha*: This was a sign that Elijah wanted Elisha to follow him and become a prophet. [x] **20.1** *King Benhadad of Syria*: This is probably not the same Benhadad mentioned in 15.18-21. [y] **20.3** *wives*: Having more than one wife was allowed in those times. [z] **20.6** *you*: Hebrew; three ancient translations "they."

19.15 2 K 8.7-13. **19.16** 2 K 9.1-6. **19.18** Ro 11.4.

When Benhadad got his answer, 10 he replied, "I'll completely destroy Samaria! There won't even be enough of it left for my soldiers to carry back in their hands. If I don't do it, I pray that the gods will punish me terribly."

11 Ahab then answered, "Benhadad, don't brag before the fighting even begins. Wait and see if you live through it."

12 Meanwhile, Benhadad and the other kings had been drinking in their tents. But when Ahab's reply came, he ordered his soldiers to prepare to attack Samaria, and they all got ready.

13 At that very moment, a prophet ran up to Ahab and said, "You can see that Benhadad's army is very strong. But the LORD has promised to help you defeat them today. Then you will know that the LORD is in control."

14 "Who will fight the battle?" Ahab asked.

The prophet answered, "The young bodyguards who serve the district officials."

"But who will lead them into battle?" Ahab asked.

"You will!" the prophet replied.

15 So Ahab called together the two hundred thirty-two young soldiers and the seven thousand troops in Israel's army, and he got them ready to fight the Syrians.

Israel Defeats the Syrians

16-17 At noon, King Ahab and his Israelite army marched out of Samaria, with the young soldiers in front.

King Benhadad of Syria and the thirty-two kings with him were drunk when the scouts he had sent out ran up to his tent, shouting, "We just now saw soldiers marching out of Samaria!"

18 "Take them alive!" Benhadad ordered. "I don't care if they have come out to fight or to surrender."

19 The young soldiers led Israel's troops into battle, 20 and each of them attacked and killed an enemy soldier. The rest of the Syrian army turned and ran, and the Israelites went after them. Benhadad and some others escaped on horses, 21 but Ahab and his soldiers followed them and captured[a] their horses and chariots.

Ahab and Israel's army crushed the Syrians.

22 Later, the prophet[b] went back and warned Ahab, "Benhadad will attack you again next spring. Build up your troops and make sure you have some good plans."

Syria Attacks Israel Again

23 Meanwhile, Benhadad's officials went to him and explained:

> Israel's gods are mountain gods. We fought Israel's army in the hills, and that's why they defeated us. But if we fight them on flat land, there's no way we can lose.
>
> 24 Here's what you should do. First, get rid of those thirty-two kings and put army commanders in their places. 25 Then get more soldiers, horses, and chariots, so your army will be as strong as it was before. We'll fight Israel's army on flat land and wipe them out.

Benhadad agreed and did what they suggested.

26 In the spring, Benhadad got his army together, and they marched to the town of Aphek to attack Israel. 27 The Israelites also prepared to fight. They marched out to meet the Syrians, and the two armies camped across from each other. The Syrians covered the whole area, but the Israelites looked like two little flocks of goats.

28 The prophet went to Ahab and said, "The Syrians think the LORD is a god of the hills and not of the valleys. So he has promised to help you defeat their powerful army. Then you will know that the LORD is in control."

29 For seven days the two armies stayed in their camps, facing each other. Then on the seventh day the fighting broke out, and before sunset the Israelites had killed one hundred thousand Syrian troops. 30 The rest of the Syrian army ran back to Aphek, but the town wall fell and crushed twenty-seven thousand of them.

Benhadad also escaped to Aphek and hid in the back room of a house. 31 His offi-

[a] **20.21** *captured*: One ancient translation; Hebrew "attacked." [b] **20.22** *the prophet*: See verse 13.

cials said, "Your Majesty, we've heard that Israel's kings keep their agreements. We will wrap sackcloth around our waists, put ropes around our heads, and ask Ahab to let you live."

32 They dressed in sackcloth and put ropes on their heads, then they went to Ahab and said, "Your servant Benhadad asks you to let him live."

"Is he still alive?" Ahab asked. "Benhadad is like a brother to me."

33 Benhadad's officials were trying to figure out what Ahab was thinking, and when he said "brother," they quickly replied, "You're right! You and Benhadad are like brothers."

"Go get him," Ahab said.

When Benhadad came out, Ahab had him climb up into his chariot.

34 Benhadad said, "I'll give back the towns my father took from your father. And you can have shops in Damascus, just as my father had in Samaria."

Ahab replied, "If you do these things, I'll let you go free." Then they signed a peace treaty, and Ahab let Benhadad go.

A Prophet Condemns Ahab

35 About this time the LORD commanded a prophet to say to a friend, "Hit me!" But the friend refused, 36 and the prophet told him, "You disobeyed the LORD, and as soon as you walk away, a lion will kill you." The friend left, and suddenly a lion killed him.

37 The prophet found someone else and said, "Hit me!" So this man beat him up.

38 The prophet left and put a bandage over his face to disguise himself. Then he went and stood beside the road, waiting for Ahab to pass by.

39 When Ahab went by, the prophet shouted, "Your Majesty, right in the heat of battle, someone brought a prisoner to me and told me to guard him. He said if the prisoner got away, I would either be killed or forced to pay seventy-five pounds of silver.
40 But I got busy doing other things, and the prisoner escaped."

Ahab answered, "You will be punished just as you have said."

41 The man quickly tore the bandage off his face, and Ahab saw that he was one of the prophets.
42 The prophet said, "The LORD told you to kill Benhadad, but you let him go. Now you will die in his place, and your people will die in place of his people."

43 Ahab went back to Samaria, angry and depressed.

Jezebel Has Naboth Killed

21 Naboth owned a vineyard in Jezreel near King Ahab's palace.

2 One day, Ahab said, "Naboth, your vineyard is near my palace. Give it to me so I can turn it into a vegetable garden. I'll give you a better vineyard or pay whatever you want for yours."

3 Naboth answered, "This vineyard has always been in my family. I won't let you have it."

4 So Ahab went home, angry and depressed because of what Naboth had told him. He lay on his bed, just staring at the wall and refusing to eat a thing.

5 Jezebel his wife came in and asked, "What's wrong? Why won't you eat?"

6 "I asked Naboth to sell me his vineyard or to let me give him a better one," Ahab replied. "And he told me I couldn't have it."

7 "Aren't you the king of Israel?" Jezebel asked. "Get out of bed and eat something! Don't worry, I'll get Naboth's vineyard for you."

8-10 Jezebel wrote a letter to each of the leaders of the town where Naboth lived. In the letters she said:

> Call everyone together and tell them to go without eating[c] today. When they come together, give Naboth a seat at the front. Have two liars sit across from him and swear that Naboth has cursed God and the king. Then take Naboth outside and stone him to death!

She signed Ahab's name to the letters and sealed them with his seal. Then she sent them to the town leaders.

[c]**21.8-10** *to go without eating*: People sometimes came together to worship and to go without eating to show that they were sorry for their sins.

20.36 1 K 13.24.

11 After receiving her letters, they did exactly what she had asked. 12 They told the people that it was a day to go without eating, and when they all came together, they seated Naboth at the front. 13 The two liars came in and sat across from Naboth. Then they accused him of cursing God and the king, so the people dragged Naboth outside and stoned him to death.

14 The leaders of Jezreel sent a message back to Jezebel that said, "Naboth is dead."

15 As soon as Jezebel got their message, she told Ahab, "Now you can have the vineyard Naboth refused to sell. He's dead." 16 Ahab got up and went to take over the vineyard.

Elijah Condemns Ahab

17 The LORD said to Elijah the prophet, 18 "King Ahab of Israel is in Naboth's vineyard right now, taking it over. 19 Go tell him that I say, 'Ahab, you murdered Naboth and took his property. And so, in the very spot where dogs licked up Naboth's blood, they will lick up your blood.' "

When Elijah found him, 20 Ahab said, "So, my enemy, you found me at last."

Elijah answered:

> Yes, I did! Ahab, you have managed to do everything the LORD hates. 21 Now you will be punished. You and every man and boy in your family will die, whether slave or free. 22 Your whole family will be wiped out, just like the families of King Jeroboam and King Baasha. You've made the LORD very angry by sinning and causing the Israelites to sin.
>
> 23 And as for Jezebel, dogs will eat her body there in Jezreel. 24 Dogs will also eat the bodies of your relatives who die in town, and vultures will eat the bodies of those who die in the country.

25-29 When Ahab heard this, he tore his clothes and wore sackcloth day and night. He was depressed and refused to eat.

Some time later, the LORD said, "Elijah, do you see how sorry Ahab is for what he did? I won't punish his family while he is still alive. I'll wait until his son is king."

No one was more determined than Ahab to disobey the LORD. And Jezebel encouraged him. Worst of all, he had worshiped idols, just as the Amorites[d] had done before the LORD forced them out of the land and gave it to Israel.

Micaiah Warns Ahab about Disaster

(2 Chronicles 18.2-27)

22 For the next three years there was peace between Israel and Syria. 2 During the third year King Jehoshaphat of Judah went to visit King Ahab of Israel.

3 Ahab asked his officials, "Why haven't we tried to get Ramoth in Gilead back from the Syrians? It belongs to us." 4 Then he asked Jehoshaphat, "Would you go to Ramoth with me and attack the Syrians?"

"Just tell me what to do," Jehoshaphat answered. "My army and horses are at your command. 5 But first, let's ask the LORD."

6 Ahab sent for about four hundred prophets and asked, "Should I attack the Syrians at Ramoth?"

"Yes!" the prophets answered. "The Lord will help you defeat them."

7 But Jehoshaphat said, "Just to make sure, is there another of the LORD's prophets we can ask?"

8 "We could ask Micaiah son of Imlah," Ahab said. "But I hate Micaiah. He always has bad news for me."

"Don't say that!" Jehoshaphat replied. 9 Then Ahab sent someone to bring Micaiah as soon as possible.

10 All this time, Ahab and Jehoshaphat were dressed in their royal robes and were seated on their thrones at the threshing place near the gate of Samaria. They were listening to the prophets tell them what the LORD had said.

11 Zedekiah son of Chenaanah was one of the prophets. He had made some horns out of iron and shouted, "Ahab, the LORD says you will attack the Syrians like a bull with iron horns and wipe them out!"

12 All the prophets agreed that Ahab

[d]**21.25-29** *Amorites*: A name sometimes used of the people who lived in Palestine before the Israelites.

21.23 2 K 9.36.

should attack the Syrians at Ramoth, and they promised that the LORD would help him defeat them.

13 Meanwhile, the messenger who went to get Micaiah whispered, "Micaiah, all the prophets have good news for Ahab. Now go and say the same thing."

14 "I'll say whatever the living LORD tells me to say," Micaiah replied.

15 Then Micaiah went to Ahab, and Ahab asked, "Micaiah, should I attack the Syrians at Ramoth?"

"Yes!" Micaiah answered. "The LORD will help you defeat them."

16 "Micaiah, I've told you over and over to tell me the truth!" Ahab shouted. "What does the LORD really say?"

17 He answered, "In a vision[e] I saw Israelite soldiers walking around in the hills like sheep without a shepherd to guide them. The LORD said, 'This army has no leader. They should go home and not fight.' "

18 Ahab turned to Jehoshaphat and said, "I told you he would bring bad news!"

19 Micaiah replied:

> Listen to this! I also saw the LORD seated on his throne with every creature in heaven gathered around him. 20 The LORD asked, "Who can trick Ahab and make him go to Ramoth where he will be killed?"
>
> They talked about it for a while, 21 then finally a spirit came forward and said to the LORD, "I can trick Ahab."
>
> "How?" the LORD asked.
>
> 22 "I'll make Ahab's prophets lie to him."
>
> "Good!" the LORD replied. "Now go and do it."
>
> 23 This is exactly what has happened, Ahab. The LORD made all your prophets lie to you, and he knows you will soon be destroyed.

24 Zedekiah walked up to Micaiah and slapped him on the face. Then he asked, "Do you really think the LORD would speak to you and not to me?"

25 Micaiah answered, "You'll find out on the day you have to hide in the back room of some house."

26 Ahab shouted, "Arrest Micaiah! Take him to Prince Joash and Governor Amon of Samaria. 27 Tell them to put him in prison and to give him nothing but bread and water until I come back safely."

28 Micaiah said, "If you do come back, I was wrong about what the LORD wanted me to say." Then he told the crowd, "Don't forget what I said!"

Ahab Dies at Ramoth

(2 Chronicles 18.28-34)

29 Ahab and Jehoshaphat led their armies to Ramoth in Gilead. 30 Before they went into battle, Ahab said, "Jehoshaphat, I'll disguise myself, but you wear your royal robe." Then Ahab disguised himself and went into battle.

31 The king of Syria had ordered his thirty-two chariot commanders to attack only Ahab. 32 So when they saw Jehoshaphat in his robe, they thought he was Ahab and started to attack him. But when Jehoshaphat shouted out to them, 33 they realized he wasn't Ahab, and they left him alone.

34 However, during the fighting a soldier shot an arrow without even aiming, and it hit Ahab where two pieces of his armor joined. He shouted to his chariot driver, "I've been hit! Get me out of here!"

35 The fighting lasted all day, with Ahab propped up in his chariot so he could see the Syrian troops. He bled so much that the bottom of the chariot was covered with blood, and by evening he was dead.

36 As the sun was going down, someone in Israel's army shouted to the others, "Retreat! Go back home!"

37 Ahab's body was taken to Samaria and buried there. 38 Some workers washed his chariot near a spring in Samaria, and prostitutes washed themselves in his blood.[f] Dogs licked Ahab's blood off the ground, just as the LORD had warned.

39 Everything else Ahab did while he was king, including the towns he strengthened and the palace he built and furnished

[e] **22.17** *vision*: In ancient times, prophets often told about future events from what they had seen in visions or dreams. [f] **22.38** *prostitutes . . . blood*: Or "they cleaned his weapons."

22.17 Nu 27.17; Mt 9.36; Mk 6.34. **22.19** Job 1.6; Is 6.1.

with ivory, is written in *The History of the
Kings of Israel*. 40 Ahab died, and his son
Ahaziah became king.

King Jehoshaphat of Judah
(2 *Chronicles* 20.31—21.1)

41 Jehoshaphat son of Asa became king
of Judah in Ahab's fourth year as king of Israel. 42 Jehoshaphat was thirty-five years
old when he became king, and he ruled
from Jerusalem for twenty-five years. His
mother was Azubah daughter of Shilhi.

43-46 Jehoshaphat obeyed the LORD, just
as his father Asa had done, and during his
rule he was at peace with the king of Israel.

He got rid of the rest of the prostitutes[g] from the local shrines, but he did not destroy the shrines, and they were still used as places for offering sacrifices.

Everything else Jehoshaphat did while he was king, including his brave deeds and military victories, is written in *The History of the Kings of Judah*.

47 The country of Edom had no king at the time, so a lower official ruled the land.

48 Jehoshaphat had seagoing ships[h] built
to sail to Ophir for gold. But they were
wrecked at Ezion-Geber and never sailed.
49 Ahaziah son of Ahab offered to let his
sailors go with Jehoshaphat's sailors, but
Jehoshaphat refused.

50 Jehoshaphat died and was buried beside his ancestors in Jerusalem,[i] and his son Jehoram became king.

King Ahaziah of Israel

51 Ahaziah son of Ahab became king of Israel in the seventeenth year of Jehoshaphat's rule in Judah, and he ruled two years from Samaria.

52 Ahaziah disobeyed the LORD, just as
his father, his mother, and Jeroboam had
done. They all led Israel to sin. 53 Ahaziah
worshiped Baal and made the LORD God of
Israel very angry, just as his father had
done.

[g] **22.43-46** *prostitutes*: See the note at 14.24. [h] **22.48** *seagoing ships*: See the note at 10.22. [i] **22.50** *Jerusalem*: Hebrew "the city of his ancestor David."

2 KINGS

ABOUT THIS BOOK

Second Kings is the second half of a single book that was divided into two parts, 1 and 2 Kings, because together they were too long to fit on one scroll. The book of 2 Kings continues the history of the two separate kingdoms of Judah and Israel.

The book of 2 Kings has two main parts. The first part (1–17) is the history of the two kingdoms until 722 B.C., when the northern kingdom was conquered by the Assyrians. Samaria, the capital city of Israel, was destroyed, and the people of that kingdom were taken as prisoners to Assyria. Only Judah, the southern kingdom, was left.

The second part of the book (18–25) is the history of Judah until 586 B.C., when it was conquered by King Nebuchadnezzar of Babylonia. Jerusalem, the capital city, was completely destroyed, and many of the people of Judah and Jerusalem were led away as prisoners to Babylonia. King Nebuchadnezzar then made Gedaliah ruler of those left in Judah. The book concludes with some hope for Judah's future: King Jehoiachin is released from prison in Babylon and is invited to eat with the Babylonian king every day.

According to the book of 2 Kings, Israel and Judah were destroyed because the people refused to be faithful to the Lord. He had sent prophets over and over to warn the people and their kings to stop worshiping other gods and to turn back to him. Finally, the people were punished. The two kingdoms were destroyed, and the people were forced to live in foreign nations, far from their own land. The fall of Jerusalem is one of the most important events in Israel's history. The book itself explains why this disaster took place:

> *The people of Judah and Jerusalem had made the LORD so angry that he finally turned his back on them. That's why these horrible things were happening.*
>
> *(24.20b)*

A QUICK LOOK AT THIS BOOK

- Elijah the Prophet Condemns King Ahaziah of Israel (1.1-18)
- Elisha the Prophet (2.1—8.15)
- Kings of Judah and Israel (8.16—16.20)
- King Hoshea of Israel and the Defeat of the Northern Kingdom (17.1-41)
- King Hezekiah of Judah and the Assyrian Invasion (18.1—20.21)
- Two Evil Kings of Judah: Manasseh and Amon (21.1-26)
- The Rule of King Josiah and *The Book of God's Law* (22.1—23.30)
- The Last Kings of Judah (23.31—24.20)
- Jerusalem Is Destroyed and the People Are Taken to Babylonia (25.1-21)
- Gedaliah Is Made Ruler and King Jehoiachin Is Released from Prison (25.22-30)

The LORD Condemns Ahaziah

1 1-2 Soon after King Ahab of Israel died,
the country of Moab rebelled against
his son King Ahaziah.[a]
One day, Ahaziah fell through the
wooden slats around the porch on the flat
roof of his palace in Samaria, and he was
badly injured. So he sent some messengers
to the town of Ekron[b] with orders to ask
the god Baalzebub if he would get well.
3 About the same time, an angel from
the LORD sent Elijah the prophet from
Tishbe to say to the king's messengers,
"Ahaziah has rejected Israel's own God by
sending you to ask Baalzebub about his injury. 4 Tell him that because he has done
this, he's on his deathbed!" And Elijah did
what he was told.
5 When the messengers returned to
Ahaziah, he asked, "Why are you back so
soon?"
6 "A man met us along the road with a
message for you from the LORD," they answered. "The LORD wants to know why you
sent us to ask Baalzebub about your injury
and why you don't believe there's a God in
Israel. The man also told us that the LORD
says you're going to die."
7 "What did the man look like?" Ahaziah
asked.
8 "He was hairy[c] and had a leather belt
around his waist," they answered.
"It must be Elijah!" replied Ahaziah.
9 So at once he sent an army officer and
fifty soldiers to meet Elijah.
Elijah was sitting on top of a hill[d] at the
time. The officer went up to him and said,
"Man of God,[e] the king orders you to come
down and talk with him."
10 "If I am a man of God," Elijah answered, "God will send down fire on you
and your fifty soldiers." Fire immediately
came down from heaven and burned up
the officer and his men.
11 Ahaziah sent another officer and fifty
more soldiers to Elijah. The officer said,
"Man of God, the king orders you to come
see him right now."
12 "If I am a man of God," Elijah answered, "fire will destroy you and your fifty
soldiers." And God sent down fire[f] from
heaven on the officer and his men.
13 Ahaziah sent a third army officer and
fifty more soldiers. This officer went up to
Elijah, then he got down on his knees and
begged, "Man of God, please be kind to me
and these fifty servants of yours. Let us
live! 14 Fire has already wiped out the other
officers and their soldiers. Please don't let
it happen to me."
15 The angel from the LORD said to Elijah, "Go with him and don't be afraid." So
Elijah got up and went with the officer.
16 When Elijah arrived, he told Ahaziah,
"The LORD wants to know why you sent
messengers to Ekron to ask Baalzebub
about your injury. Don't you believe there's
a God in Israel? Ahaziah, because you did
that, the LORD says you will die."
17 Ahaziah died, just as the LORD had
said. But since Ahaziah had no sons,
Joram[g] his brother[h] then became king.
This happened in the second year that Jehoram son of Jehoshaphat was king of Judah.[i] 18 Everything else Ahaziah did while
he was king is written in *The History of
the Kings of Israel*.

The LORD Takes Elijah Away

2 Not long before the LORD took Elijah
up into heaven in a strong wind, Elijah
and Elisha were leaving Gilgal. 2 Elijah said
to Elisha, "The LORD wants me to go to
Bethel, but you must stay here."

[a] **1.1,2** *the country . . . King Ahaziah*: The story of Moab's rebellion is in 3.4-27. [b] **1.1,2** *Ekron*: An important Philistine town about forty miles southwest of Samaria. [c] **1.8** *hairy*: Or "wearing a furry coat." [d] **1.9** *a hill*: Probably Mount Carmel. [e] **1.9** *Man of God*: Another name for a prophet of the LORD. [f] **1.12** *God sent down fire*: Or "A mighty fire came down." [g] **1.17** *Joram*: The Hebrew text has "Jehoram," another spelling of the name. [h] **1.17** *his brother*: Some ancient translations (see also 3.1); these words are not in the Hebrew text. [i] **1.17** *This happened . . . Judah*: According to 3.1, this was also the eighteenth year of Jehoshaphat's rule in Judah. In biblical times, a father and son would sometimes rule as kings at the same time. This way, when the father died, the son would already have control of the kingdom (see also 8.16).

1.8 Mt 3.4; Mk 1.6. **1.10,12** Lk 9.54.

Elisha replied, "I swear by the living LORD and by your own life that I will stay with you no matter what!" And he went with Elijah to Bethel.
3 A group of prophets who lived there asked Elisha, "Do you know that today the LORD is going to take away your master?"

"Yes, I do," Elisha answered. "But don't remind me of it."

4 Elijah then said, "Elisha, now the LORD wants me to go to Jericho, but you must stay here."

Elisha replied, "I swear by the living LORD and by your own life, that I will stay with you no matter what!" And he went with Elijah to Jericho.
5 A group of prophets who lived there asked Elisha, "Do you know that today the LORD is going to take away your master?"

"Yes, I do," Elisha answered. "But don't remind me of it."

6 Elijah then said to Elisha, "Now the LORD wants me to go to the Jordan River, but you must stay here."

Elisha replied, "I swear by the living LORD and by your own life that I will never leave you!" So the two of them walked on together.
7 Fifty prophets followed Elijah and Elisha from Jericho, then stood at a distance and watched as the two men walked toward
the river. 8 When they got there, Elijah took off his coat, then he rolled it up and struck the water with it. At once a path opened up through the river, and the two of them walked across on dry ground.
9 After they had reached the other side, Elijah said, "Elisha, the LORD will soon take me away. What can I do for you before that happens?"

Elisha answered, "Please give me twice as much of your power as you give the other prophets, so I can be the one who takes your place as their leader."

10 "It won't be easy," Elijah answered. "It can happen only if you see me as I am being taken away."

11 Elijah and Elisha were walking along and talking, when suddenly there appeared between them a flaming chariot pulled by fiery horses. Right away, a strong wind took
Elijah up into heaven. 12 Elisha saw this
and shouted, "Israel's cavalry and chariots have taken my master away!"[j] After Elijah had gone, Elisha tore his clothes in sorrow.

13 Elijah's coat had fallen off, so Elisha picked it up and walked back to the Jordan
River. 14 He struck the water with the coat and wondered, "Will the LORD perform miracles for me as he did for Elijah?" As soon as Elisha did this, a dry path opened up through the water, and he walked across.

15 When the prophets from Jericho saw what happened, they said to each other, "Elisha now has Elijah's power."

They walked over to him, bowed down,
16 and said, "There are fifty strong men here with us. Please let them go look for your master. Maybe the Spirit of the LORD carried him off to some mountain or valley."

"No," Elisha replied, "they won't find him."

17 They kept begging until he was embarrassed to say no. He finally agreed, and the prophets sent the men out. They looked three days for Elijah but never found
him. 18 They returned to Jericho, and Elisha said, "I told you that you wouldn't find him."

Elisha Makes the Water Pure at Jericho

19 One day the people of Jericho said, "Elisha, you can see that our city is in a good spot. But the water from our spring is so bad that it even keeps our crops from growing."

20 He replied, "Put some salt in a new bowl and bring it to me."

They brought him the bowl of salt,
21 and he carried it to the spring. He threw the salt into the water and said, "The LORD has made this water pure again. From now on you'll be able to grow crops, and no one will starve."

22 The water has been fine ever since, just as Elisha said.

[j]**2.12** *Israel's . . . away*: Or "Master, you were like cavalry and chariots for the people of Israel!"
2.9 Dt 21.15-17. **2.12** 2 K 13.14; Si 48.9, 12.

Some Boys Make Fun of Elisha

23 Elisha left and headed toward Bethel. Along the way some boys started making fun of him by shouting, "Go away, baldy! Get out of here!"

24 Elisha turned around and stared at the boys. Then he cursed them in the name of the LORD. Right away two bears ran out of the woods and ripped to pieces forty-two of the boys.

25 Elisha went up to Mount Carmel, then returned to Samaria.

King Joram of Israel

3 Joram[k] son of Ahab became king of Israel in Jehoshaphat's eighteenth year as king of Judah.[l] Joram ruled twelve years from Samaria 2 and disobeyed the LORD by doing wrong. He tore down the stone image his father had made to honor Baal, and so he wasn't as sinful as his parents. 3 But he kept doing the sinful things that Jeroboam son of Nebat had led Israel to do.[m]

The Country of Moab Rebels against Israel

4 For many years the country of Moab had been controlled by Israel and was forced to pay taxes to the kings of Israel. King Mesha of Moab raised sheep, so he paid the king of Israel one hundred thousand lambs and the wool from one hundred thousand rams. 5 But soon after the death of Ahab, Mesha rebelled against Israel.

6 One day, Joram left Samaria and called together Israel's army. 7 He sent this message to King Jehoshaphat of Judah, "The king of Moab has rebelled. Will you go with me to attack him?"

"Yes, I will," Jehoshaphat answered. "I'm on your side, and my soldiers and horses are at your command. 8 But which way should we go?"

"We will march through Edom Desert," Joram replied.

9 So Joram, Jehoshaphat, and the king of Edom led their troops out. But seven days later, there was no drinking water left for them or their animals. 10 Joram cried out, "This is terrible! The LORD must have led us out here to be captured by Moab's army."

11 Jehoshaphat said, "Which of the LORD's prophets is with us? We can find out from him what the LORD wants us to do."

One of Joram's officers answered, "Elisha son of Shaphat is here. He was one of Elijah's closest followers."

12 Jehoshaphat replied, "He can give us the LORD's message."

The three kings went over to Elisha, 13 and he asked Joram, "Why did you come to me? Go talk to the prophets of the foreign gods your parents worshiped."[n]

"No," Joram answered. "It was the LORD who led us out here, so that Moab's army could capture us."

14 Elisha said to him, "I serve the LORD All-Powerful, and as surely as he lives, I swear I wouldn't even look at you if I didn't respect King Jehoshaphat." 15 Then Elisha said, "Send for someone who can play the harp."

The harpist began playing, and the LORD gave Elisha this message for Joram:

> 16 The LORD says that this dry riverbed will be filled with water.[o] 17 You won't feel any wind or see any rain, but there will be plenty of water for you and your animals.
>
> 18 That simple thing isn't all the LORD is going to do. He will also help you defeat Moab's army. 19 You will capture all their walled cities and important towns. You will chop down every good tree and stop up every spring of water, then ruin their fertile fields by covering them with rocks.

20 The next morning, while the sacrifice was being offered, water suddenly started flowing from the direction of Edom, and it flooded the land.

[k]**3.1** *Joram*: See the note at 1.17. [l]**3.1** *Joram . . . Judah*: See 1.17 and 8.16 and the notes there. [m]**3.3** *the sinful things . . . to do*: When Jeroboam became king of Israel, he made two gold statues of calves and put them in the towns of Bethel and Dan, so the people of Israel could worship them (see 1 Kings 12.26-30). [n]**3.13** *the prophets . . . worshiped*: These were prophets of the Canaanite god Baal and the goddess Asherah (see 1 Kings 16.30-33; 18.19). [o]**3.16** *that . . . water*: Or "to dig holes everywhere in this riverbed."

[21] Meanwhile, the people of Moab had heard that the three kings were coming to attack them. They had called together all of their fighting men, from the youngest to the oldest, and these troops were now standing at their border, ready for battle. [22] When they got up that morning, the sun was shining across the water, making it look red. The Moabite troops took one look [23] and shouted, "Look at that blood! The armies of those kings must have fought and killed each other. Come on, let's go take what's left in their camp."

[24] But when they arrived at Israel's camp, the Israelite soldiers came out and attacked them, until they turned and ran away. Israel's army chased them all the way back to Moab, and even there they kept up the attack.[p] [25] The Israelites destroyed the Moabite towns. They chopped down the good trees and stopped up the springs of water, then covered the fertile fields with rocks.

Finally, the only city left standing was Kir-Hareseth, but soldiers armed with slings surrounded and attacked it. [26] King Mesha of Moab saw that he was about to be defeated. So he took along seven hundred soldiers with swords and tried to break through the front line where the Edomite troops were positioned. But he failed. [27] He then grabbed his oldest son who was to be the next king and sacrificed him as an offering on the city wall. The Israelite troops were so horrified that[q] they left the city and went back home.

Elisha Helps a Poor Widow

4 One day the widow of one of the LORD's prophets said to Elisha, "You know that before my husband died, he was a follower of yours and a worshiper of the LORD. But he owed a man some money, and now that man is on his way to take my two sons as his slaves."

[2] "Maybe there's something I can do to help," Elisha said. "What do you have in your house?"

"Sir, I have nothing but a small bottle of olive oil."

[3] Elisha told her, "Ask your neighbors for their empty jars. And after you've borrowed as many as you can, [4] go home and shut the door behind you and your sons. Then begin filling the jars with oil and set each one aside as you fill it." [5] The woman left.

Later, when she and her sons were back inside their house, the two sons brought her the jars, and she began filling them.

[6] At last, she said to one of her sons, "Bring me another jar."

"We don't have any more," he answered, and the oil stopped flowing from the small bottle.

[7] After she told Elisha what had happened, he said, "Sell the oil and use part of the money to pay what you owe the man. You and your sons can live on what is left."

Elisha Brings a Rich Woman's Son Back to Life

[8] Once, while Elisha was in the town of Shunem,[r] he met a rich woman who invited him to her home for dinner. After that, whenever he was in Shunem, he would have a meal there with her and her husband.

[9] Some time later the woman said to her husband, "I'm sure the man who comes here so often is a prophet of God. [10] Why don't we build him a small room on the flat roof of our house? We can put a bed, a table and chair, and an oil lamp in it. Then whenever he comes, he can stay with us."

[11] The next time Elisha was in Shunem, he stopped at their house and went up to his room to rest. [12-13] He said to his servant Gehazi, "This woman has been very helpful. Have her come up here to the roof for a moment." She came, and Elisha told Gehazi to say to her, "You've gone to a lot of trouble for us, and we want to help you. Is there something we can request the king or army commander to do?"[s]

The woman answered, "With my relatives nearby, I have everything I need."

[p] **3.24** *chased . . . attack*: One possible meaning for the difficult Hebrew text. [q] **3.27** *The Israelite . . . that*: One possible meaning for the difficult Hebrew text. [r] **4.8** *Shunem*: A town in Israel, about twenty-five miles north of Samaria. [s] **4.12,13** *request the king . . . do*: Elisha may have meant that he could ask these leaders to lower her taxes.

14 “Then what can we do for her?” Elisha asked Gehazi.

Gehazi replied, “I do know that her husband is old, and that she doesn’t have a son.”

15 “Ask her to come here again,” Elisha told his servant. He called for her, and she came and stood in the doorway of Elisha’s room. 16 Elisha said to her, “Next year at this time, you’ll be holding your own baby son in your arms.”

“You’re a man of God,” the woman replied. “Please don’t lie to me.”

17 But a few months later, the woman got pregnant. She gave birth to a son, just as Elisha had promised.

18 One day while the boy was still young, he was out in the fields with his father, where the workers were harvesting the crops. 19 Suddenly he shouted, “My head hurts. It hurts a lot!”

“Carry him back to his mother,” the father said to his servant. 20 The servant picked up the boy and carried him to his mother. The boy lay on her lap all morning, and by noon he was dead. 21 She carried him upstairs to Elisha’s room and laid him across the bed. Then she walked out and shut the door behind her.

22 The woman called to her husband, “I need to see the prophet. Let me use one of the donkeys. Send a servant along with me, and let me leave now, so I can get back quickly.”

23 “Why do you need to see him today?” her husband asked. “It’s not the Sabbath or time for the New Moon Festival.”

“That’s all right,” she answered. 24 She saddled the donkey and said to her servant, “Let’s go. And don’t slow down unless I tell you to.” 25 She left at once for Mount Carmel to talk with Elisha.[t]

When Elisha saw her coming, he said, “Gehazi, look! It’s the woman from Shunem. 26 Run and meet her. And ask her if everything is all right with her and her family.”

“Everything is fine,” she answered Gehazi. 27 But as soon as she got to the top of the mountain, she went over and grabbed Elisha by the feet. Gehazi started toward her to push her away, when Elisha said, “Leave her alone! Don’t you see how sad she is? But the LORD hasn’t told me why.”

28 The woman said, “Sir, I begged you not to get my hopes up, and I didn’t even ask you for a son.”

29 “Gehazi, get ready and go to her house,” Elisha said. “Take along my walking stick, and when you get there, lay it on the boy’s face. Don’t stop to talk to anyone, even if they try to talk to you.”

30 But the boy’s mother said to Elisha, “I swear by the living LORD and by your own life that I won’t leave without you.” So Elisha got up and went with them.

31 Gehazi ran on ahead and laid Elisha’s walking stick on the boy’s face, but the boy didn’t move or make a sound. Gehazi ran back to Elisha and said, “The boy didn’t wake up.”

32 Elisha arrived at the woman’s house and went straight to his room, where he saw the boy’s body on his bed. 33 He walked in, shut the door, and prayed to the LORD. 34 Then he got on the bed and stretched out over the dead body, with his mouth on the boy’s mouth, his eyes on his eyes, and his hand on his hands. As he lay there, the boy’s body became warm. 35 Elisha got up and walked back and forth in the room, then he went back and leaned over the boy’s body. The boy sneezed seven times and opened his eyes.

36 Elisha called out to Gehazi, “Have the boy’s mother come here.” Gehazi did, and when she was at the door, Elisha said, “You can take your son.”

37 She came in and bowed down at Elisha’s feet. Then she picked up her son and left.

Elisha Makes Some Stew Taste Better

38 Later, Elisha went back to Gilgal, where there was almost nothing to eat, because the crops had failed.

One day while the prophets who lived there were meeting with Elisha, he said to his servant, “Fix a big pot of stew for these prophets.”

[t] **4.25** *Elisha*: Mount Carmel is about twenty-five miles from Shunem.

4.16 Gn 18.14. **4.34,35** 1 K 17.21.

39 One of them went out into the woods
to gather some herbs. He found a wild vine
and picked as much of its fruit as he could
carry, but he didn't know that the fruit was
very sour. When he got back, he cut up the
fruit and put it in the stew.
40 The stew was served, and when the
prophets started eating it, they shouted,
"Elisha, this stew tastes terrible! We can't
eat it."
41 "Bring me some flour," Elisha said.
He sprinkled the flour in the stew and said,
"Now serve it to them." And the stew
tasted fine.

Elisha Feeds One Hundred People

42 A man from the town of Baal-
Shalishah[u] brought Elisha some freshly cut
grain and twenty loaves of bread made
from the first barley that was harvested.
Elisha said, "Give it to the people so they
can eat."
43 "There's not enough here for a hundred people," his servant said.
"Just give it to them," Elisha replied.
"The LORD has promised there will be more
than enough."
44 So the servant served the bread and
grain to the people. They ate and still had
some left over, just as the LORD had
promised.

Elisha Heals Naaman

5 Naaman was the commander of the
Syrian army. The LORD had helped
him and his troops defeat their enemies, so
the king of Syria respected Naaman very
much. Naaman was a brave soldier, but he
had leprosy.[v]
2 One day while the Syrian troops were
raiding Israel, they captured a girl, and she
became a servant of Naaman's wife. 3 Some
time later the girl said, "If your husband
Naaman would go to the prophet in
Samaria, he would be cured of his leprosy."
4 When Naaman told the king what the
girl had said, 5 the king replied, "Go ahead!
I will give you a letter to take to the king of
Israel."
Naaman left and took along seven hundred fifty pounds of silver, one hundred
fifty pounds of gold, and ten new outfits.
6 He also carried the letter to the king of Israel. It said, "I am sending my servant Naaman to you. Would you cure him of his
leprosy?"
7 When the king of Israel read the letter,
he tore his clothes in fear and shouted,
"That Syrian king believes I can cure this
man of leprosy! Does he think I'm God
with power over life and death? He must
be trying to pick a fight with me."
8 As soon as Elisha the prophet[w] heard
what had happened, he sent the Israelite
king this message: "Why are you so afraid?
Send the man to me, so that he will know
there is a prophet in Israel."
9 Naaman left with his horses and chariots and stopped at the door of Elisha's
house. 10 Elisha sent someone outside to
say to him, "Go wash seven times in the
Jordan River. Then you'll be completely
cured."
11 But Naaman stormed off, grumbling,
"Why couldn't he come out and talk to me?
I thought for sure he would stand in front
of me and pray to the LORD his God, then
wave his hand over my skin and cure me.
12 What about the Abana River[x] or the
Pharpar River? Those rivers in Damascus
are just as good as any river in Israel. I
could have washed in them and been
cured."
13 His servants went over to him and
said, "Sir, if the prophet had told you to do
something difficult, you would have done
it. So why don't you do what he said? Go
wash and be cured."
14 Naaman walked down to the Jordan;
he waded out into the water and stooped
down in it seven times, just as Elisha had
told him. Right away, he was cured, and his
skin became as smooth as a child's.

[u]**4.42** *Baal-Shalishah*: The exact location of this town is not known, but it was probably somewhere near Shechem. [v]**5.1** *leprosy*: The word translated "leprosy" was used for many different kinds of skin diseases. [w]**5.8** *the prophet*: Hebrew "the man of God." [x]**5.12** *Abana River*: Most Hebrew manuscripts; some Hebrew manuscripts and two ancient translations "Amana River."
5.1-14 Lk 4.27.

15 Naaman and his officials went back to Elisha. Naaman stood in front of him and announced, "Now I know that the God of Israel is the only God in the whole world. Sir, would you please accept a gift from me?"

16 "I am a servant of the living LORD," Elisha answered, "and I swear that I will not take anything from you."

Naaman kept begging, but Elisha kept refusing. 17 Finally Naaman said, "If you won't accept a gift, then please let me take home as much soil as two mules can pull in a wagon. Sir, from now on I will offer sacrifices only to the LORD.[y] 18 But I pray that the LORD will forgive me when I go into the temple of the god Rimmon and bow down there with the king of Syria."

19 "Go on home, and don't worry about that," Elisha replied. Then Naaman left.

Elisha Places a Curse on Gehazi

After Naaman had gone only a short distance, 20 Gehazi said to himself, "Elisha let that Syrian off too easy. He should have taken Naaman's gift. I swear by the living LORD that I will talk to Naaman myself and get something from him." 21 So he hurried after Naaman.

When Naaman saw Gehazi running after him, he got out of his chariot to meet him. Naaman asked, "Is everything all right?"

22 "Yes," Gehazi answered. "But my master has sent me to tell you about two young prophets from the hills of Ephraim. They came asking for help, and now Elisha wants to know if you would give them about seventy-five pounds of silver and some new clothes?"

23 "Sure," Naaman replied. "But why don't you take twice that amount of silver?" He convinced Gehazi to take it all, then put the silver in two bags. He handed the bags and the clothes to his two servants, and they carried them for Gehazi.

24 When they reached the hill where Gehazi lived, he took the bags from the servants and placed them in his house, then sent the men away. After they had gone, 25 Gehazi went in and stood in front of Elisha, who asked, "Gehazi, where have you been?"

"Nowhere, sir," Gehazi answered.

26 Elisha asked, "Don't you know that my spirit was there when Naaman got out of his chariot to talk with you? Gehazi, you have no right to accept money or clothes, olive orchards or vineyards, sheep or cattle, or servants. 27 Because of what you've done, Naaman's leprosy[z] will now be on you and your descendants forever!"

Suddenly, Gehazi's skin became white with leprosy, and he left.

Elisha Makes an Ax Head Float

6 One day the prophets said to Elisha, "The place where we meet with you is too small. 2 Why don't we build a new meeting place near the Jordan River? Each of us could get some wood, then we could build it."

"That's a good idea," Elisha replied, "get started."

3 "Aren't you going with us?" one of the prophets asked.

"Yes, I'll go," Elisha answered, 4 and he left with them.

They went to the Jordan River and began chopping down trees. 5 While one of the prophets was working, his ax head fell off and dropped into the water. "Oh!" he shouted. "Sir, I borrowed this ax."

6 "Where did it fall in?" Elisha asked. The prophet pointed to the place, and Elisha cut a stick and threw it into the water at that spot. The ax head floated to the top of the water.

7 "Now get it," Elisha told him. And the prophet reached in and grabbed it.

Elisha Stops an Invasion of the Syrian Army

8 Time after time, when the king of Syria was at war against the Israelites, he met with his officers and announced, "I've decided where we will set up camp."

9 Each time, Elisha[a] would send this warning to the king of Israel: "Don't go

[y] **5.17** *let me take . . . the LORD*: It was believed that the LORD had to be worshiped in Israel or on soil taken from Israel. [z] **5.27** *leprosy*: See the note at 5.1. [a] **6.9** *Elisha*: Hebrew "the man of God."

near there. That's where the Syrian troops
have set up camp."[b] 10 So the king would
warn the Israelite troops in that place to be
on guard.
11 The king of Syria was furious when
he found out what was happening. He
called in his officers and asked, "Which
one of you has been telling the king of Israel our plans?"
12 "None of us, Your Majesty," one of
them answered. "It's an Israelite named
Elisha. He's a prophet, so he can tell his
king everything—even what you say in your
own room."
13 "Find out where he is!" the king ordered. "I'll send soldiers to bring him
here."
They learned that Elisha was in the
town of Dothan[c] and reported it to the
king. 14 He ordered his best troops to go
there with horses and chariots. They
marched out during the night and surrounded the town.
15 When Elisha's servant got up the
next morning, he saw that Syrian troops
had the town surrounded. "Sir, what are we
going to do?" he asked.
16 "Don't be afraid," Elisha answered.
"There are more troops on our side than on
theirs." 17 Then he prayed, "LORD, please
help him to see." And the LORD let the
servant see that the hill[d] was covered with
fiery horses and flaming chariots all around
Elisha.
18 As the Syrian army came closer, Elisha prayed, "LORD, make those soldiers
blind!" And the LORD blinded them with a
bright light.
19 Elisha told the enemy troops, "You've
taken the wrong road and are in the wrong
town. Follow me. I'll lead you to the man
you're looking for." Elisha led them straight
to the capital city of Samaria.
20 When all the soldiers were inside the
city, Elisha prayed, "LORD, now let them
see again." The LORD let them see that they
were standing in the middle of Samaria.
21 The king of Israel saw them and
asked Elisha, "Should I kill them, sir?"
22 "No!" Elisha answered. "You didn't
capture these troops in battle, so you have
no right to kill them. Instead, give them
something to eat and drink and let them
return to their leader."
23 The king ordered a huge meal to be
prepared for Syria's army, and when they
finished eating, he let them go.
For a while, the Syrian troops stopped
invading Israel's territory.

King Benhadad of Syria Attacks Samaria

24 Some time later, King Benhadad of
Syria[e] called his entire army together, then
they marched to Samaria and attacked.
25 They kept up the attack until there was
nothing to eat in the city. In fact, a donkey's head cost about two pounds of silver,
and a small bowl of pigeon droppings[f] cost
about two ounces of silver.
26 One day as the king of Israel[g] was
walking along the top of the city wall, a
woman shouted to him, "Please, Your
Majesty, help me!"
27 "Let the LORD help you!" the king
said. "Do you think I have grain or wine to
give you?" 28 Then he asked, "What's the
matter anyway?"
The woman answered, "Another woman
and I were so hungry that we agreed to eat
our sons. She said if we ate my son one
day, we could eat hers the next day. 29 So
yesterday we cooked my son and ate him.
But today when I went to her house to eat
her son, she had hidden him."
30 The king tore off his clothes in sorrow, and since he was on top of the city
wall, the people saw that he was wearing
sackcloth underneath. 31 He said, "I pray
that God will punish me terribly, if Elisha's

[b]**6.9** *have set up camp*: Or "are going." [c]**6.13** *Dothan*: About ten miles north of Samaria. [d]**6.17** *the hill*: The hill on which the town was built. [e]**6.24** *King Benhadad of Syria*: This may or may not be the same Benhadad mentioned in 1 Kings 20.1. Several of the Syrian kings were named Benhadad. [f]**6.25** *pigeon droppings*: This may have been used for food or to burn for fuel. It also may have been a popular name for roasted beans or the shells of certain seeds. [g]**6.26** *the king of Israel*: Probably either Jehoahaz or Jehoash, but possibly even Joram.
6.29 Dt 28.57; Lm 4.10.

head is still on his shoulders by this time tomorrow." 32 Then he sent a messenger to Elisha.

Elisha was home at the time, and the important leaders of Israel were meeting with him. Even before the king's messenger arrived, Elisha told the leaders, "That murderer[h] is sending someone to cut off my head. When you see him coming, shut the door and don't let him in. I'm sure the king himself will be right behind him."

33 Before Elisha finished talking, the messenger[i] came up and said, "The LORD has made all these terrible things happen to us. Why should I think he will help us now?"

7 Elisha answered, "I have a message for you. The LORD promises that tomorrow here in Samaria, you will be able to buy a large sack of flour or two large sacks of barley for almost nothing."

2 The chief officer there with the king replied, "I don't believe it! Even if the LORD sent a rainstorm, it couldn't produce that much grain by tomorrow."

"You will see it happen, but you won't eat any of the food," Elisha warned him.

The Syrian Army Stops Its Attack

3 About the same time, four men with leprosy[j] were just outside the gate of Samaria. They said to each other, "Why should we sit here, waiting to die? 4 There's nothing to eat in the city, so we would starve if we went inside. But if we stay out here, we will die for sure. Let's sneak over to the Syrian army camp and surrender. They might kill us, but they might not."
5-8 That evening the four men got up and left for the Syrian camp.

As they walked toward the camp, the Lord caused the Syrian troops to hear what sounded like the roar of a huge cavalry. The soldiers said to each other, "Listen! The king of Israel must have hired Hittite and Egyptian troops to attack us. Let's get out of here!" So they ran out of their camp that night, leaving their tents and horses and donkeys.

When the four men with leprosy reached the edge of the Syrian camp, no one was there. They walked into one of the tents, where they ate and drank, before carrying off clothes, as well as silver and gold. They hid all this, then walked into another tent; they took what they wanted and hid it too.

9 They said to each other, "This isn't right. Today is a day to celebrate, and we haven't told anyone else what has happened. If we wait until morning, we will be punished. Let's go to the king's palace right now and tell the good news."

10 They went back to Samaria and shouted up to the guards at the gate, "We've just come from the Syrian army camp, and all the soldiers are gone! The tents are empty, and the horses and donkeys are still tied up. We didn't see or hear anybody."

11 The guards reported the news to the king's palace. 12 The king got out of bed and said to his officers, "I know what those Syrians are doing. They know we're starving, so they're hiding in the fields, hoping we will go out to look for food. When we do, they can capture us and take over our city."

13 One of his officers replied, "We have a few horses left—why don't we let some men take five of them and go to the Syrian camp and see what's happening? We're going to die anyway like those who have already died."[k] 14 They found two chariots, and the king commanded the men to find out what had happened to the Syrian troops.

15 The men rode as far as the Jordan River. All along the way they saw clothes and equipment that the Syrians had thrown away as they escaped. Then they went back to the king and told him what they had seen.

16 At once the people went to the Syrian camp and carried off what was left. They took so much that a large sack of flour and two large sacks of barley sold for almost nothing, just as the LORD had promised.

17 The king of Israel had put his chief

[h]**6.32** *That murderer*: Hebrew "That murderer's son." [i]**6.33** *messenger*: Or "king" (see 7.2,18); the two Hebrew words are very similar. [j]**7.3** *leprosy*: See the note at 5.1. [k]**7.13** *We're going . . . died*: One possible meaning for the difficult Hebrew text.

officer in charge of the gate, but he died when the people trampled him as they rushed out of the city. 18 Earlier, when the king was at Elisha's house, Elisha had told him that flour or barley would sell for almost nothing. 19 But the officer refused to believe that even the LORD could do that. So Elisha warned him that he would see it happen, but would not eat any of the food. 20 And that's exactly what happened—the officer was trampled to death.

The Woman from Shunem Is Given Back Her Land

8 Elisha told the woman whose son he had brought back to life,[l] "The LORD has warned that there will be no food here for seven years. Take your family and go live somewhere else for a while." 2 The woman did exactly what Elisha had said and went to live in Philistine territory.

She and her family lived there seven years. 3 Then she returned to Israel and immediately begged the king to give back her house and property.

4 Meanwhile, the king was asking Gehazi the servant of Elisha about the amazing things Elisha had been doing. 5 While Gehazi was telling him that Elisha had brought a dead boy back to life, the woman and her son arrived.

"Here's the boy, Your Majesty," Gehazi said. "And this is his mother."

6 The king asked the woman to tell her story, and she told him everything that had happened. He then said to one of his officials, "I want you to make sure that this woman gets back everything that belonged to her, including the money her crops have made since the day she left Israel."

Hazael Kills Benhadad

7 Some time later Elisha went to the capital city of Damascus to visit King Benhadad of Syria, who was sick. And when Benhadad was told he was there, 8 he said to Hazael,[m] "Go meet with Elisha the man of God and have him ask the LORD if I will get well. And take along a gift for him."

9 Hazael left with forty camel loads of the best things made in Damascus as a gift for Elisha. He found the prophet and said, "Your servant, King Benhadad, wants to know if he will get well."

10 "Tell him he will," Elisha said to Hazael. "But the LORD has already told me that Benhadad will definitely die." 11 Elisha stared at him until Hazael was embarrassed, then Elisha began crying.[n]

12 "Sir, why are you crying?" Hazael asked.

Elisha answered, "Because I know the terrible things you will do to the people of Israel. You will burn down their walled cities and slaughter their young men. You will even crush the heads of their babies and rip open their pregnant women."

13 "How could I ever do anything like that?" Hazael replied. "I'm only a servant and don't have that kind of power."

"Hazael, the LORD has told me that you will be the next king of Syria."

14 Hazael went back to Benhadad and told him, "Elisha said that you will get well." 15 But the very next day, Hazael got a thick blanket; he soaked it in water and held it over Benhadad's face until he died. Hazael then became king.

King Jehoram of Judah
(*2 Chronicles 21.2-20*)

16 Jehoram son of Jehoshaphat became king of Judah in Joram's fifth year as king of Israel, while Jehoshaphat was still king of Judah.[o] 17 Jehoram was thirty-two years old when he became king, and he ruled eight years from Jerusalem.

18 Jehoram disobeyed the LORD by doing wrong. He married Ahab's daughter and was as sinful as Ahab's family and the kings of Israel. 19 But the LORD refused to destroy Judah, because he had promised his

[l]**8.1** *Elisha . . . life*: See 4.8-37. [m]**8.8** *Hazael*: Probably one of Benhadad's officials. [n]**8.11** *Elisha stared . . . crying*: Or "Hazael stared at him until Elisha was embarrassed and began to cry." [o]**8.16** *while Jehoshaphat . . . Judah*: In biblical times, a father and son would sometimes rule as kings at the same time. That way, when the father died, his son would already have control of the kingdom.

8.1 2 K 4.8-37. **8.13** 1 K 19.15. **8.19** 1 K 11.36.

servant David that someone from his family would always rule in Judah.

20 While Jehoram was king, the people of Edom rebelled and chose their own king.
21 So Jehoram[p] and his cavalry marched to Zair, where the Edomite army surrounded him and his commanders. During the night he attacked the Edomites, but he was defeated, and his troops escaped to their homes.[q]
22 Judah was never able to regain control of Edom. Even the town of Libnah[r] rebelled at that time.

23 Everything else Jehoram did while he was king is written in *The History of the Kings of Judah*.
24 Jehoram died and was buried beside his ancestors in Jerusalem.[s] His son Ahaziah then became king.

King Ahaziah of Judah
(2 Chronicles 22.1-6)

25 Ahaziah son of Jehoram became king of Judah in the twelfth year of Joram's rule in Israel.
26 Ahaziah was twenty-two years old when he became king, and he ruled from Jerusalem for only one year. His mother was Athaliah, a granddaughter of King Omri of Israel.
27 Since Ahaziah was related to Ahab's family,[t] he acted just like them and disobeyed the LORD by doing wrong.

28 Ahaziah went with King Joram of Israel to attack King Hazael and the Syrian troops at Ramoth in Gilead. Joram was wounded in that battle,
29 so he went to the town of Jezreel to recover. Ahaziah went there to visit him.

Jehu Becomes King of Israel

9 One day, Elisha called for one of the other prophets and said:

Take this bottle of olive oil and get ready to go to the town of Ramoth in Gilead.
2 When you get there, find Jehu son of Jehoshaphat and grandson of Nimshi. Take him to a place where the two of you can be alone,
3 then pour olive oil on his head to show that he is the new king. Say to him, "The LORD has chosen you to be king of Israel." Then leave quickly—don't wait around for anything!

4 The young prophet left for Ramoth.
5 When he arrived, the army officers were meeting together. "Sir, I have a message for you," he said.

"For which one of us?" Jehu asked.

"You, sir," the prophet answered.
6 So Jehu got up and went inside.[u] The prophet poured olive oil on Jehu's head and told him:

The LORD God of Israel has this message for you: "I am the LORD, and I have chosen you to be king of my people Israel.
7 I want you to wipe out the family of Ahab, so Jezebel will be punished for killing the prophets and my other servants.
8 Every man and boy in Ahab's family must die, whether slave or free.
9 His whole family must be destroyed, just like the families of Jeroboam son of Nebat and Baasha son of Ahijah.
10 As for Jezebel, her body will be eaten by dogs in the town of Jezreel. There won't be enough left of her to bury."

Then the young prophet opened the door and ran out.

11 Jehu went back to his officers, and one of them asked, "What did that crazy prophet want? Is everything all right?"

"You know him and how he talks," Jehu answered.

12 "No, we don't. What did he say?" they asked.

"He had a message from the LORD," Jehu replied. "He said that the LORD has chosen me to be the next king of Israel."

13 They quickly grabbed their coats and spread them out on the steps where Jehu

[p]**8.21** *Jehoram*: The Hebrew text has "Joram," another spelling of the name. [q]**8.21** *he attacked . . . homes*: One possible meaning for the difficult Hebrew text. [r]**8.22** *Even the town of Libnah*: This was a town on the border between Philistia and Judah, which means that Jehoram was facing rebellion on two sides of his kingdom. [s]**8.24** *Jerusalem*: Hebrew "the city of David." [t]**8.27** *Since . . . family*: Ahaziah's mother was Ahab's daughter (see verse 18). [u]**9.6** *went inside*: The officers were probably meeting outside in an open courtyard of some building.

8.20 Gn 27.40. **9.6** 1 K 19.16. **9.10** 1 K 21.23.

was standing. Someone blew a trumpet, and everyone shouted, "Jehu is king!"

Jehu Kills Joram and Ahaziah

14-16 King Joram[v] of Israel had been badly wounded in the battle at Ramoth, trying to defend it against King Hazael and the Syrian army. Joram was now recovering in Jezreel, and King Ahaziah of Judah was there, visiting him.

Meanwhile, Jehu was in Ramoth, making plans to kill Joram. He said to his officers, "If you want me to be king, then don't let anyone leave this town. They might go to Jezreel and tell Joram." Then Jehu got in his chariot and rode to Jezreel.

17 When the guard in the watchtower at Jezreel saw Jehu and his men riding up, he shouted to the king, "I see a bunch of men coming this way."

Joram ordered, "Send someone out to ask them if this is a friendly visit."

18 One of the soldiers rode out and said to Jehu, "King Joram wants to know if this is a friendly visit."

"What's it to you?" Jehu asked. "Just stay behind me with the rest of my troops!"

About the same time the guard in the watchtower said, "Your Majesty, the rider got there, but he isn't coming back."

19 So Joram sent out another rider, who rode up to Jehu and said, "The king wants to know if this is a friendly visit."

"What's it to you?" Jehu asked. "Just get behind me with the rest of my troops!"

20 The guard in the watchtower said, "Your Majesty, the rider got there, but he isn't coming back either. Wait a minute! That one man is a reckless chariot driver—it must be Jehu!"

21 Joram commanded, "Get my chariot ready." Then he and Ahaziah got in their chariots and rode out to meet Jehu. They all met on the land that had belonged to Naboth.[w]
22 Joram asked, "Jehu, is this a peaceful visit?"

"How can there be peace?" Jehu asked. "Your mother Jezebel has caused everyone to worship idols and practice witchcraft."

23 "Ahaziah, let's get out of here!" Joram yelled. "It's a trap!" As Joram tried to escape,
24 Jehu shot an arrow. It hit Joram between his shoulders, then it went through his heart and came out his chest. He fell over dead in his chariot.

25-26 Jehu commanded his assistant Bidkar, "Get Joram's body and throw it in the field that Naboth once owned. Do you remember when you and I used to ride side by side behind Joram's father Ahab? It was then that the LORD swore to Ahab that he would be punished in the same field where he had killed Naboth and his sons. So throw Joram's body there, just as the LORD said."

27 Ahaziah saw all of this happen and tried to escape to the town of Beth-Haggan, but Jehu caught up with him and shouted, "Kill him too!" So his troops shot Ahaziah with an arrow while he was on the road to Gur near Ibleam. He went as far as Megiddo, where he died.
28 Ahaziah's officers put his body in a chariot and took it back to Jerusalem, where they buried him beside his ancestors.

29 Ahaziah had become king of Judah in the eleventh year of the rule of Ahab's son Joram.

Jehu Kills Jezebel

30 Jehu headed toward Jezreel, and when Jezebel heard he was coming, she put on eye shadow and brushed her hair. Then she stood at the window, waiting for him to arrive.
31 As he walked through the city gate, she shouted down to him, "Why did you come here, you murderer? To kill the king? You're no better than Zimri!"[x]

32 He looked up toward the window and asked, "Is anyone up there on my side?" A few palace workers stuck their heads out of a window,
33 and Jehu shouted, "Throw her out the window!" They threw her down, and her blood splattered on the walls and on the horses that trampled her body.[y]

[v]**9.14-16** *Joram*: The Hebrew text has "Jehoram," another spelling of the name. [w]**9.21** *the land . . . Naboth*: See 1 Kings 21. [x]**9.31** *Zimri*: An Israelite king who killed King Elah and his family so he could become king, but who ruled only seven days (see 1 Kings 16.8-20). [y]**9.33** *horses . . . her body*: Two ancient translations; Hebrew "horses. Then Jehu trampled her body."
9.25,26 1 K 21.19.

34 Jehu left to get something to eat and
drink. Then he told some workers, "Even
though she was evil, she was a king's
daughter,[z] so make sure she has a proper
burial."

35 But when they went out to bury her
body, they found only her skull, her hands,
and her feet. 36 They reported this to Jehu,
and he said, "The LORD told Elijah the
prophet that Jezebel's body would be eaten
by dogs right here in Jezreel. 37 And he
warned that her bones would be spread all
over the ground like manure, so that no
one could tell who it was."

Jehu Kills All of Ahab's Descendants

10 Ahab still had seventy descendants
living in Samaria. So Jehu wrote a
letter to each of the important leaders
and officials of the town,[a] and to those
who supported Ahab. In the letters he
wrote:

> 2 Your town is strong, and you're
> protected by chariots and an armed
> cavalry. And I know that King Ahab's
> descendants live there with you. So as
> soon as you read this letter, 3 choose
> the best person for the job and make
> him the next king. Then be prepared
> to defend Ahab's family.

4 The officials and leaders read the letters and were very frightened. They said to
each other, "Jehu has already killed King
Joram and King Ahaziah! We have to do
what he says." 5 The prime minister, the
mayor of the city, as well as the other leaders and Ahab's supporters, sent this answer
to Jehu, "We are your servants, Your Majesty, and we will do whatever you tell
us. But it's not our place to choose someone to be king. You do what you think is
best."

6 Jehu then wrote another letter which
said, "If you are on my side and will obey
me, then prove it. Bring me the heads of
the descendants of Ahab! And be here in
Jezreel by this time tomorrow."

The seventy descendants of King Ahab
were living with some of the most important people of the city. 7 And when these
people read Jehu's second letter, they
called together all seventy of Ahab's descendants. They killed them, put their
heads in baskets, and sent them to Jezreel.

8 When Jehu was told what had happened, he said, "Put the heads in two piles
at the city gate, and leave them there until
morning."

9 The next morning, Jehu went out and
stood where everyone could hear him, and
he said, "You people are not guilty of anything. I'm the one who plotted against Joram and had him killed. But who killed all
these men? 10 Listen to me. Everything the
LORD's servant Elijah promised about
Ahab's family will come true."[b]

11 Then Jehu killed the rest of Ahab's
relatives living in Jezreel, as well as his
highest officials, his priests, and his closest
friends. No one in Ahab's family was left
alive in Jezreel.

12-13 Jehu left for Samaria, and along
the way, he met some relatives of King
Ahaziah of Judah at a place where shepherds meet.[c] He asked, "Who are you?"

"We are relatives of Ahaziah," they answered. "We're going to visit his family."

14 "Take them alive!" Jehu said to his officers. So they grabbed them and led them
to the well near the shepherds' meeting
place, where they killed all forty-two of
them.

15 As Jehu went on, he saw Jehonadab
son of Rechab[d] coming to meet him. Jehu
greeted him, then said, "Jehonadab, I'm on
your side. Are you on mine?"

"Yes, I am."

"Then give me your hand," Jehu answered. He helped Jehonadab into his
chariot 16 and said, "Come with me and see
how faithful I am to the LORD."

They rode together in Jehu's chariot
17 to Samaria. Jehu killed everyone there
who belonged to Ahab's family, as well as all

[z] **9.34** *she . . . daughter*: Her father was King Ethbaal of Sidon (see 1 Kings 16.31). [a] **10.1** *the town*: Two ancient translations; Hebrew "Jezreel." [b] **10.10** *Everything . . . come true*: See 1 Kings 21.17-24. [c] **10.12,13** *at a place where shepherds meet*: Or "at Betheked of the Shepherds." [d] **10.15** *Jehonadab son of Rechab*: Or "Jehonadab the chariot driver."

9.36 1 K 21.23. **10.11** Ho 1.4.

his officials. Everyone in his family was now dead, just as the LORD had promised Elijah.

Jehu Kills All the Worshipers of Baal

18 Jehu called together the people in Samaria and said:

> King Ahab sometimes worshiped Baal, but I will be completely faithful to Baal. 19 I'm going to offer a huge sacrifice to him. So invite his prophets and priests, and be sure everyone who worships him is there. Anyone who doesn't come will be killed.

But this was a trick—Jehu was really planning to kill the worshipers of Baal. 20 He said, "Announce a day of worship for Baal!" After the day had been announced, 21 Jehu sent an invitation to everyone in Israel. All the worshipers of Baal came, and the temple was filled from one end to the other. 22 Jehu told the official in charge of the sacred robes to make sure that everyone had a robe to wear.

23 Jehu and Jehonadab went into the temple, and Jehu said to the crowd, "Look around and make sure that only the worshipers of Baal are here. No one who worships the LORD is allowed in." 24 Then they began to offer sacrifices to Baal.

Earlier, Jehu had ordered eighty soldiers to wait outside the temple. He had warned them, "I will get all these worshipers here, and if any of you let even one of them escape, you will be killed instead!"

25 As soon as Jehu finished offering the sacrifice, he told the guards and soldiers, "Come in and kill them! Don't let anyone escape." They slaughtered everyone in the crowd and threw the bodies outside. Then they went back into the temple 26 and carried out the image of Baal. They burned it 27 and broke it into pieces, then they completely destroyed Baal's temple. And since that time, it's been nothing but a public toilet.[e]

28 That's how Jehu stopped the worship of Baal in Israel. 29 But he did not stop the worship of the gold statues of calves at Dan and Bethel that Jeroboam had made for the people to worship.[f]

30 Later the LORD said, "Jehu, you have done right by destroying Ahab's entire family, just as I had planned. So I will make sure that the next four kings of Israel will come from your own family."

31 But Jehu did not completely obey the commands of the LORD God of Israel. Instead, he kept doing the sinful things that Jeroboam had caused the Israelites to do.

Jehu Dies

32 In those days the LORD began to reduce the size of Israel's territory. King Hazael of Syria defeated the Israelites and took control 33 of the regions of Gilead and Bashan east of the Jordan River and north of the town of Aroer near the Arnon River. This was the land where the tribes of Gad, Reuben, and Manasseh had once lived.

34 Everything else Jehu did while he was king, including his brave deeds, is written in *The History of the Kings of Israel*. 35 Jehu died and was buried in Samaria, and his son Jehoahaz became king. 36 Jehu had ruled Israel twenty-eight years from Samaria.

Queen Athaliah of Judah

(2 *Chronicles* 22.10-12)

11 As soon as Athaliah heard that her son King Ahaziah was dead, she decided to kill any relative who could possibly become king. She would have done that, 2 but Jehosheba rescued Joash son of Ahaziah just as he was about to be murdered. Jehosheba, who was Jehoram's[g] daughter and Ahaziah's half sister, hid her nephew Joash and his personal servant in a bedroom in the LORD's temple where he was safe from Athaliah. 3 Joash hid in the temple with Jehosheba[h] for six years while Athaliah ruled as queen of Judah.

[e] **10.27** *public toilet*: Or "garbage dump." [f] **10.29** *gold statues . . . to worship*: See 1 Kings 12.26-30. [g] **11.2** *Jehoram's*: The Hebrew text has "Joram's," another spelling of the name. [h] **11.3** *Jehosheba*: Jehosheba was the wife of Jehoiada the priest (see 2 Chronicles 22.11), which is why she could hide Joash in one of the private bedrooms used only by the priests.

10.29 1 K 12.28-30.

Jehoiada Makes Joash King of Judah

(2 Chronicles 23.1-21)

4 Joash son of Ahaziah had hidden in the LORD's temple six years. Then in the seventh year, Jehoiada the priest sent for the commanders of the king's special bodyguards[i] and the commanders of the palace guards. They met him at the temple, and he asked them to make a promise in the name of the LORD. Then he brought out Joash 5 and said to them:

> Here's what I want you to do. Three of your guard units will be on duty on the Sabbath. I want one unit to guard the palace. 6 Another unit will guard Sur Gate, and the third unit will guard the palace gate and relieve the palace guards.
>
> 7 The other two guard units are supposed to be off duty on the Sabbath. But I want both of them to stay here at the temple and protect King Joash. 8 Make sure they follow him wherever he goes, and have them keep their swords ready to kill anyone who tries to get near him.

9 The commanders followed Jehoiada's orders. Each one called together his guards—those coming on duty and those going off duty. 10 Jehoiada brought out the swords and shields that had belonged to King David and gave them to the commanders. 11 Then they gave the weapons to their guards, who took their positions around the temple and the altar to protect Joash on every side.

12 Jehoiada brought Joash outside, where he placed the crown on his head and gave him a copy of instructions for ruling the nation. Olive oil was poured on his head to show that he was now king, while the crowd clapped and shouted, "Long live the king!"

13 Queen Athaliah heard the crowd and went to the temple. 14 There she saw Joash standing by one of the columns, which was the usual place for the king. The singers[j] and the trumpet players were standing next to him, and the people were celebrating and blowing trumpets. Athaliah tore her clothes in anger and shouted, "You betrayed me, you traitors!"

15 Right away, Jehoiada said to the army commanders, "Kill her! But don't do it anywhere near the LORD's temple. Take her out in front of the troops and kill anyone who is with her!" 16 So the commanders dragged her to the gate where horses are led into the palace, and they killed her there.

17 Jehoiada the priest asked King Joash and the people to promise that they would be faithful to each other and to the LORD. 18 Then the crowd went to the temple built to honor Baal and tore it down. They smashed the altars and idols and killed Mattan the priest of Baal right in front of the altars.

After Jehoiada had placed guards around the LORD's temple, 19 he called together all the commanders, the king's special bodyguards,[k] the palace guards, and the people. They led Joash from the temple, through the Guards' Gate, and into the palace. He took his place on the throne and became king of Judah. 20 Everyone celebrated because Athaliah had been killed and Jerusalem was peaceful again. 21 Joash was only seven years old when this happened.

King Joash of Judah

(2 Chronicles 24.1-16)

12 Joash[l] became king of Judah in Jehu's seventh year as king of Israel, and he ruled forty years from Jerusalem. His mother Zibiah was from the town of Beersheba.

2 Jehoiada the priest taught Joash what was right, and so for the rest of his life Joash obeyed the LORD. 3 But even Joash did not destroy the local shrines,[m] and they

[i] **11.4** *the king's special bodyguards*: The Hebrew text has "the Carites," who were probably foreign soldiers hired to serve as royal bodyguards. [j] **11.14** *singers*: Two ancient translations; Hebrew "commanders." [k] **11.19** *the king's special bodyguards*: See the note at verse 4.
[l] **12.1** *Joash*: The Hebrew text has "Jehoash," another spelling of the name. [m] **12.3** *local shrines*: The Hebrew text has "high places," which were local places to worship God or foreign gods.

11.14 2 K 23.3.

were still used as places for offering sacrifices.

4 One day, Joash said to the priests, "Collect all the money that has been given to the LORD's temple, whether from taxes or gifts, 5 and use it to repair the temple. You priests can contribute your own money too."[n]

6 But the priests never started repairing the temple. So in the twenty-third year of his rule, 7 Joash called for Jehoiada and the other priests and said, "Why aren't you using the money to repair the temple? Don't take any more money for yourselves. It is only to be used to pay for the repairs." 8 The priests agreed that they would not collect any more money or be in charge of the temple repairs.

9 Jehoiada found a wooden box; he cut a hole in the top of it and set it on the right side of the altar where people went into the temple. Whenever someone gave money to the temple, the priests guarding the entrance would put it into this box. 10 When the box was full of money, the king's secretary and the chief priest would count the money and put it in bags. 11 Then they would give it to the men supervising the repairs to the temple. Some of the money was used to pay the builders, the woodworkers, 12 the stonecutters, and the men who built the walls. And some was used to buy wood and stone and to pay any other costs for repairing the temple.

13 While the repairs were being made, the money that was given to the temple was not used to make silver bowls, lamp snuffers, small sprinkling bowls, trumpets, or anything gold or silver for the temple. 14 It went only to pay for repairs. 15 The men in charge were honest, so no one had to keep track of the money.

16 The fines that had to be paid along with the sacrifices to make things right and the sacrifices for sin did not go to the temple. This money belonged only to the priests.

17 About the same time, King Hazael of Syria attacked the town of Gath and captured it. Next, he decided to attack Jerusalem. 18 So Joash collected everything he and his ancestors Jehoshaphat, Jehoram, and Ahaziah had dedicated to the LORD, as well as the gold in the storage rooms in the temple and palace. He sent it all to Hazael as a gift, and when Hazael received it, he ordered his troops to leave Jerusalem.

19 Everything else Joash did while he was king is written in *The History of the Kings of Judah*. 20-21 At the end of his rule, some of his officers rebelled against him. Jozabad[o] son of Shimeath and Jehozabad son of Shomer murdered him in a building where the land was filled in on the east side of Jerusalem,[p] near the road to Silla. Joash was buried beside his ancestors in Jerusalem,[q] and his son Amaziah became king.

King Jehoahaz of Israel

13 Jehoahaz son of Jehu became king of Israel in the twenty-third year of Joash's rule in Judah. Jehoahaz ruled seventeen years from Samaria 2 and disobeyed the LORD by doing wrong. He never stopped following the example of Jeroboam, who had caused the Israelites to sin.

3 The LORD was angry at the Israelites, so he let King Hazael of Syria and his son Benhadad rule over them for a long time. 4 Jehoahaz prayed to the LORD for help, and the LORD saw how terribly Hazael was treating the Israelites. He answered Jehoahaz 5 by sending Israel a leader who rescued them from the Syrians,[r] and the Israelites lived in peace as they had before. 6-7 But Hazael had defeated Israel's army so badly that Jehoahaz had only ten chariots, fifty cavalry troops, and ten thousand regular soldiers left in his army.

The Israelites kept sinning and following the example of Jeroboam's family. They did

[n] **12.5** *You priests . . . money too*: One possible meaning for the difficult Hebrew text.
[o] **12.20,21** *Jozabad*: Some manuscripts of the Hebrew text; other manuscripts "Jozacar."
[p] **12.20,21** *where . . . Jerusalem*: The Hebrew text has "on the Millo," which probably refers to a landfill to strengthen and extend the hill where the city was built.
[q] **12.20,21** *Jerusalem*: See the note at 8.24.
[r] **13.5** *by sending . . . the Syrians*: The name of this leader is not given, but it may refer to Elisha the prophet, King Jehoash of Israel, or his son King Jeroboam.

12.4 Ex 30.11-16. **12.15** 2 K 22.7. **12.16** Lv 7.7.

not tear down the sacred poles[s] that had been set up in Samaria for the worship of the goddess Asherah.

8 Everything else Jehoahaz did while he was king, including his brave deeds, is written in *The History of the Kings of Israel*. 9 Jehoahaz died and was buried in Samaria, and his son Jehoash became king.

King Jehoash of Israel

10 Jehoash became king of Israel in the thirty-seventh year of Joash's rule in Judah, and he ruled sixteen years from Samaria. 11 He disobeyed the LORD by doing just like Jeroboam, who had caused the Israelites to sin.

12 Everything else Jehoash did while he was king, including his war against King Amaziah of Judah, is written in *The History of the Kings of Israel*. 13 Jehoash died and was buried in Samaria beside the other Israelite kings. His son Jeroboam then became king.

Elisha the Prophet Dies

14 Some time before the death of King Jehoash, Elisha the prophet was very sick and about to die. Jehoash went in and stood beside him, crying. He said, "Master, what will Israel's chariots and cavalry be able to do without you?"[t]

15-16 "Grab a bow and some arrows," Elisha told him, "and hold them in your hand." Jehoash grabbed the bow and arrows and held them. Elisha placed his hand on the king's hand 17 and said, "Open the window facing east." When it was open, Elisha shouted, "Now shoot!" Jehoash shot an arrow and Elisha said, "That arrow is a sign that the LORD will help you completely defeat the Syrian army at Aphek."

18 Elisha said, "Pick up the arrows and hit the ground with them." Jehoash grabbed the arrows and hit the ground three times, then stopped. 19 Elisha became angry at the king and exclaimed, "If you had struck it five or six times, you would completely wipe out the Syrians. Now you will defeat them only three times."

20 Elisha died and was buried.

Every year in the spring, Moab's leaders sent raiding parties into Israel. 21 Once, while some Israelites were burying a man's body, they saw a group of Moabites. The Israelites quickly threw the body into Elisha's tomb and ran away. As soon as the man's body touched the bones of Elisha, the man came back to life and stood up.

Israel Defeats Syria

22 Israel was under the power of King Hazael of Syria during the entire rule of Jehoahaz. 23 But the LORD was kind to the Israelites and showed them mercy because of his solemn agreement with their ancestors Abraham, Isaac, and Jacob. In fact, he has never turned his back on them or let them be completely destroyed.

24 Hazael died, and his son Benhadad then became king of Syria. 25 King Jehoash of Israel attacked and defeated the Syrian army three times. He took back from Benhadad all the towns Hazael had captured in battle from his father Jehoahaz.

King Amaziah of Judah

(*2 Chronicles* 25.1-24)

14 Amaziah son of Joash became king of Judah in the second year of Jehoash's rule in Israel. 2 Amaziah was twenty-five years old when he became king, and he ruled twenty-nine years from Jerusalem, which was also the hometown of his mother Jehoaddin.

3 Amaziah followed the example of his father Joash by obeying the LORD and doing right. But he was not as faithful as his ancestor David. 4 Amaziah did not destroy the local shrines, and they were still used as places for offering sacrifices.

5 As soon as Amaziah had control of Judah, he arrested and killed the officers who had murdered his father. 6 But the children of those officers were not killed. The LORD had commanded in the Law of Moses that

[s] **13.6,7** *sacred poles*: Or "trees," used as symbols of Asherah, the goddess of fertility.

[t] **13.14** *Master . . . without you*: Or "Master, you were like chariots and cavalry for Israel!"

13.14 2 K 2.12. **14.6** Dt 24.16.

only the people who sinned were to be punished, not their parents or children.[u]

7 While Amaziah was king, he killed ten thousand Edomite soldiers in Salt Valley. He captured the town of Sela and renamed it Joktheel, which is still its name.

8 One day, Amaziah sent a message to King Jehoash of Israel: "Come out and face me in battle!"

9 Jehoash sent back this reply:

> Once upon a time, a small thornbush in Lebanon announced that his son was going to marry the daughter of a large cedar tree. But a wild animal came along and trampled the small bush.
>
> 10 Amaziah, you think you're so powerful because you defeated Edom. Go ahead and celebrate—but stay at home. If you cause any trouble, both you and your kingdom of Judah will be destroyed.

11 But Amaziah refused to listen. So Jehoash and his troops marched to the town of Beth-Shemesh in Judah to attack Amaziah and his troops. 12 During the battle, Judah's army was crushed. Every soldier from Judah ran back home, 13 and Jehoash captured Amaziah.

Jehoash then marched to Jerusalem and broke down the city wall from Ephraim Gate to Corner Gate, a section about six hundred feet long. 14 He took the gold and silver, as well as everything of value from the LORD's temple and the king's treasury. He took hostages, then returned to Samaria.

15 Everything else Jehoash did while he was king, including his brave deeds and how he defeated King Amaziah of Judah, is written in *The History of the Kings of Israel*. 16 Jehoash died and was buried in Samaria beside the other Israelite kings. His son Jeroboam then became king.

17 Fifteen years after Jehoash died, 18-20 some people in Jerusalem plotted against Amaziah. He was able to escape to the town of Lachish, but another group of people caught him and killed him there. His body was taken back to Jerusalem on horseback and buried beside his ancestors.

Everything else Amaziah did while he was king is written in *The History of the Kings of Judah*. 21 After his death the people of Judah made his son Azariah king, even though he was only sixteen at the time. 22 Azariah was the one who later recaptured and rebuilt the town of Elath.

King Jeroboam the Second of Israel

23 Jeroboam son of Jehoash became king of Israel in the fifteenth year of Amaziah's rule in Judah. Jeroboam ruled forty-one years from Samaria. 24 He disobeyed the LORD by following the evil example of Jeroboam son of Nebat, who had caused the Israelites to sin.

25 Jeroboam extended the boundaries of Israel from Lebo-Hamath in the north to the Dead Sea in the south, just as the LORD had promised his servant Jonah son of Amittai, who was a prophet from Gath-Hepher. 26 The LORD helped Jeroboam do this because he had seen how terribly the Israelites were suffering, whether slave or free, and no one was left to help them. 27 And since the LORD had promised that he would not let Israel be completely destroyed, he helped Jeroboam rescue them.

28 Everything else Jeroboam did while he was king, including his brave deeds and how he recaptured the towns of Damascus and Hamath,[v] is written in *The History of the Kings of Israel*. 29 Jeroboam died and was buried, and his son Zechariah became king.

King Azariah of Judah

(2 Chronicles 26.1-23)

15 Azariah son of Amaziah became king of Judah in Jeroboam's twenty-seventh year as king of Israel. 2 He was only sixteen years old when he became king, and he ruled fifty-two years from Jerusalem, which was also the hometown of his mother Jecoliah.

3 Azariah obeyed the LORD by doing right, as his father Amaziah had done.

[u] **14.6** *The LORD had commanded . . . children*: See Deuteronomy 24.16. [v] **14.28** *how he recaptured . . . Hamath*: One possible meaning for the difficult Hebrew text.

14.25 Jon 1.1.

4 But Azariah did not destroy the local
shrines,[w] and they were still used as places
for offering sacrifices.
5 The LORD punished Azariah with leprosy[x] for the rest of his life. He wasn't allowed to live in the royal palace, so his son
Jotham lived there and ruled in his place.
6 Everything else Azariah did while he
was king is written in *The History of the*
Kings of Judah. 7 Azariah died and was
buried beside his ancestors in Jerusalem.
His son Jotham then became king.

King Zechariah of Israel

8 Zechariah son of Jeroboam became
king of Israel in the thirty-eighth year of
Azariah's rule in Judah, but he ruled only
six months from Samaria. 9 Like his ancestors, Zechariah disobeyed the LORD by following the evil ways of Jeroboam son of
Nebat, who had caused the Israelites to sin.
10 Shallum son of Jabesh plotted against
Zechariah and killed him in public.[y] Shallum then became king. 11-12 So the LORD
had kept his promise to Jehu that the next
four kings of Israel would come from his
family.[z]

Everything else Zechariah did while he
was king is written in *The History of the*
Kings of Israel.

King Shallum of Israel

13 Shallum became king of Israel in the
thirty-ninth year of Azariah's[a] rule in Judah. But only one month after Shallum became king, 14-16 Menahem son of Gadi
came to Samaria from Tirzah and killed
him. Menahem then became king. The
town of Tiphsah would not surrender to
him, so he destroyed it and all the surrounding towns as far as Tirzah. He killed
everyone living in Tiphsah, and with his
sword he even ripped open pregnant
women.

Everything else Shallum did while he
was king, including his plot against
Zechariah, is written in *The History of the*
Kings of Israel.

King Menahem of Israel

17 Menahem became king of Israel in
Azariah's thirty-ninth year as king of Judah,
and he ruled Israel ten years from Samaria.
18 He constantly disobeyed the LORD by following the example of Jeroboam son of
Nebat, who had caused the Israelites to sin.
19 During Menahem's rule, King Tiglath
Pileser[b] of Assyria invaded Israel. He
agreed to help Menahem keep control of
his kingdom, if Menahem would pay him
over thirty tons of silver. 20 So Menahem
ordered every rich person in Israel to give
him at least one pound of silver, and he
gave it all to Tiglath Pileser, who stopped
his attack and left Israel.
21 Everything else Menahem did while
he was king is written in *The History of the*
Kings of Israel. 22 Menahem died, and his
son Pekahiah became king.

King Pekahiah of Israel

23 Pekahiah became king of Israel in the
fiftieth year of Azariah's rule in Judah, and
he ruled two years from Samaria. 24 He
disobeyed the LORD and caused the Israelites to sin, just as Jeroboam son of
Nebat had done.
25 Pekah son of Remaliah was Pekahiah's
chief officer, but he made plans to kill the king.
So he and fifty men from Gilead broke into
the strongest part of the palace in Samaria
and murdered Pekahiah, together with Argob and Arieh.[c] Pekah then became king.
26 Everything else Pekahiah did while
he was king is written in *The History of the*
Kings of Israel.

King Pekah of Israel

27 Pekah son of Remaliah became king
of Israel in Azariah's fifty-second year as
king of Judah, and he ruled twenty years
from Samaria. 28 He disobeyed the LORD
and followed the evil example of Jeroboam

[w] **15.4** *local shrines*: See the note at 12.3. [x] **15.5** *leprosy*: See the note at 5.1. [y] **15.10** *in public*: Hebrew; some manuscripts of one ancient translation "in Ibleam." [z] **15.11,12** *So the LORD . . . family*: See 10.28-31. [a] **15.13** *Azariah's*: The Hebrew text has "Uzziah's," another spelling of the name. [b] **15.19** *Tiglath Pileser*: The Hebrew text has "Pul," another name for Tiglath Pileser, who ruled Assyria from 745 to 727 B.C. [c] **15.25** *together with Argob and Arieh*: One possible meaning for the difficult Hebrew text.

15.7 Is 6.1. **15.11,12** 2 K 10.30.

son of Nebat, who had caused the Israelites
to sin.
29 During Pekah's rule, King Tiglath
Pileser of Assyria marched into Israel. He
captured the territories of Gilead and
Galilee, including the towns of Ijon, Abel-
Bethmaacah, Janoah, Kedesh, and Hazor,
as well as the entire territory of Naphtali.
Then he took Israelites from those regions
to Assyria as prisoners.[d]
30 In the twentieth year of Jotham's rule
in Judah, Hoshea son of Elah plotted
against Pekah and murdered him. Hoshea
then became king of Israel.
31 Everything else Pekah did while he
was king is written in *The History of the
Kings of Israel*.

King Jotham of Judah
(2 Chronicles 27.1-9)

32 Jotham son of Azariah[e] became king
of Judah in the second year of Pekah's rule
in Israel. 33 Jotham was twenty-five years
old when he became king, and he ruled
sixteen years from Jerusalem. His mother
Jerusha was the daughter of Zadok.
34 Jotham followed the example of his
father by obeying the LORD and doing right.
35 It was Jotham who rebuilt the Upper
Gate that led into the court around the
LORD's temple. But the local shrines were
not destroyed, and they were still used as
places for offering sacrifices.
36 Everything else Jotham did while he
was king is written in *The History of the
Kings of Judah*. 37 During his rule, the
LORD let King Rezin of Syria and King
Pekah of Israel start attacking Judah.
38 Jotham died and was buried beside his
ancestors in Jerusalem, and his son Ahaz
became king.

King Ahaz of Judah
(2 Chronicles 28.1-27)

16 Ahaz son of Jotham became king of
Judah in the seventeenth year of
Pekah's rule in Israel. 2 He was twenty
years old at the time, and he ruled from
Jerusalem for sixteen years.
Ahaz wasn't like his ancestor David. Instead, he disobeyed the LORD 3 and was even
more sinful than the kings of Israel. He
sacrificed his own son, which was a disgusting custom of the nations that the
LORD had forced out of Israel. 4 Ahaz offered
sacrifices at the local shrines, as well as
on every hill and in the shade of large
trees.
5-6 While Ahaz was ruling Judah, the
king of Edom recaptured the town of Elath
from Judah and forced out the people of
Judah. Edomites[f] then moved into Elath,
and they still live there.
About the same time, King Rezin of
Syria and King Pekah of Israel marched to
Jerusalem and attacked, but they could not
capture it.
7 Ahaz sent a message to King Tiglath
Pileser of Assyria that said, "Your Majesty,
King Rezin and King Pekah are attacking
me, your loyal servant. Please come and
rescue me." 8 Along with the message,
Ahaz sent silver and gold from the LORD's
temple and from the palace treasury as a
gift for the Assyrian king.
9 As soon as Tiglath Pileser received the
message, he and his troops marched to
Syria. He captured the capital city of Damascus, then he took the people living
there to the town of Kir as prisoners and
killed King Rezin.[g]
10 Later, Ahaz went to Damascus to
meet Tiglath Pileser. And while Ahaz was
there, he saw an altar and sent a model of
it back to Uriah the priest, along with the
plans for building one. 11 Uriah followed
the plans and built an altar exactly like the
one in Damascus, finishing it just before
Ahaz came back.
12 When Ahaz returned, he went to see
the altar and to offer sacrifices on it. He
walked up to the altar 13 and poured wine
over it. Then he offered sacrifices to please
the LORD, to give him thanks, and to ask for

[d] **15.29** *prisoners*: The events in this verse probably took place around 733 B.C. [e] **15.32** *Azariah*: See the note at 15.13. [f] **16.5,6** *the king of Edom . . . Edomites*: The Hebrew text has "King Rezin of Syria . . . Syrians"; in Hebrew, there is only one letter difference between "Edom" and "Aram," which is the usual Hebrew name for Syria in the Bible (see also 2 Chronicles 28.17).
[g] **16.9** *King Rezin*: This probably took place around 734 B.C., before the events in 15.29.
16.3 Dt 12.31. **16.5,6** Is 7.1.

his blessings.[h] 14 After that, he had the bronze altar moved aside,[i] so his new altar would be right in front of the LORD's temple. 15 He told Uriah the priest:

From now on, the morning and evening sacrifices as well as all gifts of grain and wine are to be offered on this altar. The sacrifices for the people and for the king must also be offered here. Sprinkle the blood from all the sacrifices on it, but leave the bronze altar for me to use for prayer and finding out what God wants me to do.

16 Uriah did everything Ahaz told him.

17 Ahaz also had the side panels and the small bowls taken off the movable stands in the LORD's temple. He had the large bronze bowl, called the Sea, removed from the bronze bulls on which it rested and had it placed on a stand made of stone. 18 He took down the special tent that was used for worship on the Sabbath[j] and closed up the private entrance that the kings of Judah used for going into the temple. He did all these things to please Tiglath Pileser.

19 Everything else Ahaz did while he was king is written in *The History of the Kings of Judah*. 20 Ahaz died and was buried beside his ancestors in Jerusalem,[k] and his son Hezekiah became king.

King Hoshea of Israel

17 Hoshea son of Elah became king of Israel in the twelfth year of Ahaz's rule in Judah, and he ruled nine years from Samaria. 2 Hoshea disobeyed the LORD and sinned, but not as much as the earlier Israelite kings had done.

3 During Hoshea's rule, King Shalmaneser of Assyria[l] invaded Israel; he took control of the country and made Hoshea pay taxes. 4 But later, Hoshea refused to pay the taxes and asked King So of Egypt to help him rebel. When Shalmaneser found out, he arrested Hoshea and put him in prison.

Samaria Is Destroyed and the Israelites Are Taken to Assyria

5 Shalmaneser invaded Israel and attacked the city of Samaria for three years, 6 before capturing it in the ninth year of Hoshea's rule. The Assyrian king[m] took the Israelites away to Assyria as prisoners. He forced some of them to live in the town of Halah, others to live near the Habor River in the territory of Gozan, and still others to live in towns where the Median people lived.

7 All of this happened because the people of Israel had sinned against the LORD their God, who had rescued them from Egypt, where they had been slaves. They worshiped foreign gods, 8 followed the customs of the nations that the LORD had forced out of Israel, and were just as sinful as the Israelite kings. 9 Even worse, the Israelites tried to hide their sins from the LORD their God. They built their own local shrines everywhere in Israel—from small towns to large, walled cities. 10 They also built stone images of foreign gods and set up sacred poles[n] for the worship of Asherah on every hill and under every shady tree. 11 They offered sacrifices at the shrines,[o] just as the foreign nations had done before the LORD forced them out of Israel. They did sinful things that made the LORD very angry.

12 Even though the LORD had commanded the Israelites not to worship idols,[p] they did it anyway. 13 So the LORD made sure that every prophet warned Israel and Judah with these words: "I, the LORD, command you to stop doing sinful things and

[h] **16.13** *offered . . . blessings*: In traditional translations, these sacrifices are usually called "whole burnt offerings," "grain offerings," and "peace offerings." These are described in Leviticus 1–3. [i] **16.14** *aside*: Hebrew "to the north." [j] **16.18** *the special tent . . . Sabbath*: One possible meaning for the difficult Hebrew text. [k] **16.20** *Jerusalem*: See the note at 8.24. [l] **17.3** *King Shalmaneser of Assyria*: The son of Tiglath Pileser, who ruled Assyria from 727 to 722 B.C.
[m] **17.6** *The Assyrian king*: Probably Sargon, Shalmaneser's successor. Shalmaneser died after the city of Samaria was captured (722 B.C.) but before the people were taken away as prisoners (720 B.C.). Sargon ruled Assyria from 721 to 705 B.C. [n] **17.10** *sacred poles*: See the note at 13.6,7.
[o] **17.11** *shrines*: See the note at 12.3. [p] **17.12** *the LORD . . . idols*: See Exodus 20.4,5.
16.14 Ex 27.1, 2; 2 Ch 4.1. **16.17** 1 K 7.23-39; 2 Ch 4.2-6. **16.20** Is 14.28.
17.10 1 K 14.23.

start obeying my laws and teachings! I gave
them to your ancestors, and I told my servants the prophets to repeat them to you."
14 But the Israelites would not listen;
they were as stubborn as their ancestors
who had refused to worship the LORD their
God. 15 They ignored the LORD's warnings
and commands, and they rejected the solemn
agreement he had made with their ancestors. They worshiped worthless idols and
became worthless themselves. The LORD
had told the Israelites not to do the things
that the foreign nations around them were
doing, but Israel became just like them.
16 The people of Israel disobeyed all the
commands of the LORD their God. They
made two gold statues of calves and set up
a sacred pole for Asherah; they also worshiped the stars and the god Baal. 17 They
used magic and witchcraft and even sacrificed their own children. The Israelites
were determined to do whatever the LORD
hated. 18 The LORD became so furious with
the people of Israel that he allowed them to
be carried away as prisoners.
Only the people living in Judah were
left, 19 but they also disobeyed the LORD's
commands and acted like the Israelites.
20 So the LORD turned his back on everyone
in Israel and Judah[q] and let them be punished and defeated until no one was left.
21 Earlier, when the LORD took the
northern tribes away from David's family,[r]
the people living in northern Israel chose
Jeroboam son of Nebat as their king. Jeroboam caused the Israelites to sin and to
stop worshiping the LORD. 22 The people
kept on sinning like Jeroboam, 23 until the
LORD got rid of them, just as he had
warned his servants the prophets.
That's why the people of Israel were
taken away as prisoners to Assyria, and
that's where they remained.

Foreigners Are Resettled in Israel

24 The king of Assyria took people who
were living in the cities of Babylon,
Cuthah, Avva, Hamath, and Sepharvaim,
and forced them to move to Israel. They
took over the towns where the Israelites
had lived, including the capital city of
Samaria.
25 At first these people did not worship
the LORD, so he sent lions to attack them,
and the lions killed some of them. 26 A
messenger told the king of Assyria, "The
people you moved to Israel don't know how
to worship the god of that country. So he
sent lions that have attacked and killed
some of them."
27 The king replied, "Get one of the Israelite priests we brought here and send
him back to Israel. He can live there and
teach them about the god of that country."
28 One of the Israelite priests was chosen to
go back to Israel. He lived in Bethel and
taught the people how to worship the LORD.
29 But in towns all over Israel, the different groups of people made statues of
their own gods, then they placed these
idols in local Israelite[s] shrines. 30 The people from Babylonia made the god Succoth-
Benoth; those from Cuthah made the god
Nergal; those from Hamath made Ashima;
31 those from Avva made Nibhaz and Tar-
tak; and the people from Sepharvaim sacrificed their children to their own gods
Adrammelech and Anammelech. 32-33 They
worshiped their own gods, just as they had
before they were taken away to Israel. They
also worshiped the LORD, but they chose
their own people to be priests at the
shrines. 34 Everyone followed their old customs. None of them worshiped only the
LORD, and they refused to obey the laws
and commands that the LORD had given to
the descendants of Jacob, the man he
named Israel. 35 At the time when the
LORD had made his solemn agreement with
the people of Israel, he told them:

> Do not worship any other gods! Do
> not bow down to them or offer them a
> sacrifice. 36 Worship only me! I am the
> one who rescued you from Egypt with

[q] **17.20** *Israel and Judah*: Or "Israel," that is, the northern kingdom only. [r] **17.21** *when the LORD . . . family*: See 1 Kings 11.29-39. [s] **17.29** *Israelite*: The Hebrew text has "Samaritan," which is a later word to describe the people who lived in northern Israel at this time.

17.16 1 K 12.28. **17.17** Dt 18.10, 11. **17.34** Gn 32.28; 35.9-11. **17.35** Ex 20.5; Dt 5.9. **17.36** Dt 6.13.

my mighty power. Bow down to me and offer sacrifices. 37 Never worship any other god, always obey my laws and teachings, 38 and remember the solemn agreement between us.

I will say it again: Do not worship any god 39 except me. I am the LORD your God, and I will rescue you from all your enemies.

40 But the people living in Israel ignored that command and kept on following their old customs. 41 They did worship the LORD, but they also worshiped their own idols. Their descendants did the same thing.

King Hezekiah of Judah

(2 Chronicles 29.1, 2; 31.1)

18 Hezekiah son of Ahaz became king of Judah in the third year of Hoshea's rule in Israel. 2 Hezekiah was twenty-five years old when he became king, and he ruled twenty-nine years from Jerusalem. His mother Abi was the daughter of Zechariah.

3 Hezekiah obeyed the LORD, just as his ancestor David had done. 4 He destroyed the local shrines, then tore down the images of foreign gods and cut down the sacred pole for worshiping the goddess Asherah. He also smashed the bronze snake Moses had made. The people had named it Nehushtan[t] and had been offering sacrifices to it.

5 Hezekiah trusted the LORD God of Israel. No other king of Judah was like Hezekiah, either before or after him. 6 He was completely faithful to the LORD and obeyed the laws the LORD had given to Moses for the people. 7 The LORD helped Hezekiah, so he was successful in everything he did. He even rebelled against the king of Assyria, refusing to be his servant. 8 Hezekiah defeated the Philistine towns as far away as Gaza—from the smallest towns to the large, walled cities.

9 During the fourth year of Hezekiah's rule, which was the seventh year of Hoshea's rule in Israel, King Shalmaneser of Assyria led his troops to Samaria, the capital city of Israel. They attacked 10 and captured it three years later,[u] in the sixth year of Hezekiah's rule and the ninth year of Hoshea's rule. 11 The king of Assyria[v] took the Israelites away as prisoners; he forced some of them to live in the town of Halah, others to live near the Habor River in the territory of Gozan, and still others to live in towns where the Median people lived. 12 All of that happened because the people of Israel had not obeyed the LORD their God. They rejected the solemn agreement he had made with them, and they ignored everything that the LORD's servant Moses had told them.

King Sennacherib of Assyria Invades Judah

(2 Chronicles 32.1-19; Isaiah 36.1-22)

13 In the fourteenth year of Hezekiah's rule in Judah, King Sennacherib of Assyria invaded the country and captured every walled city,[w] except Jerusalem. 14 Hezekiah sent this message to Sennacherib, who was in the town of Lachish: "I know I am guilty of rebellion. But I will pay you whatever you want, if you stop your attack."

Sennacherib told Hezekiah to pay about eleven tons of silver and almost a ton of gold. 15 So Hezekiah collected all the silver from the LORD's temple and the royal treasury. 16 He even stripped the gold that he had used to cover the doors and doorposts[x] in the temple. He gave it all to Sennacherib.

17 The king of Assyria ordered his three highest military officers to leave Lachish and take a large army to Jerusalem. When they arrived, the officers stood on the road near the cloth makers' shops along the canal from the upper pool. 18 They called out to Hezekiah, and three of his highest officials came out to meet them. One of

[t] **18.4** *the bronze snake . . . Nehushtan*: See Numbers 21.8,9. "Nehushtan" is a nickname that sounds like the Hebrew words for "snake" and "bronze." [u] **18.10** *three years later*: When the Israelites measured time, part of a year could be counted as a whole year. [v] **18.11** *The king of Assyria*: Probably Sargon, Shalmaneser's successor (see the note at 17.6). [w] **18.13** *King Sennacherib . . . walled city*: Sennacherib ruled Assyria 705-681 B.C., and this event probably took place in 701 B.C. [x] **18.16** *doorposts*: One possible meaning for the difficult Hebrew text.

18.4 Nu 21.9. **18.13** 3 Macc 6.5.

them was Hilkiah's son Eliakim, who was the prime minister. The other two were Shebna, assistant to the prime minister, and Joah son of Asaph, keeper of the government records.

19 One of the Assyrian commanders told them:

I have a message for Hezekiah from the great king of Assyria. Ask Hezekiah why he feels so sure of himself. 20 Does he think he can plan and win a war with nothing but words? Who is going to help him, now that he has turned against the king of Assyria? 21 Is he depending on Egypt and its king? That's the same as leaning on a broken stick, and it will go right through his hand.

22 Is Hezekiah now depending on the LORD your God? Didn't Hezekiah tear down all except one of the LORD's altars and places of worship?[y] Didn't he tell the people of Jerusalem and Judah to worship at that one place?

23 The king of Assyria wants to make a bet with you people. He will give you two thousand horses, if you have enough troops to ride them. 24 How could you even defeat our lowest ranking officer, when you have to depend on Egypt for chariots and cavalry? 25 Don't forget that it was the LORD who sent me here with orders to destroy your nation!

26 Eliakim, Shebna, and Joah said, "Sir, we don't want the people listening from the city wall to understand what you are saying. So please speak to us in Aramaic instead of Hebrew."

27 The Assyrian army commander answered, "My king sent me to speak to everyone, not just to you leaders. These people will soon have to eat their own body waste and drink their own urine! And so will the three of you."

28 Then, in a voice loud enough for everyone to hear, he shouted in Hebrew:

Listen to what the great king of Assyria says! 29 Don't be fooled by Hezekiah. He can't save you. 30 Don't trust him when he tells you that the LORD will protect you from the king of Assyria. 31 Stop listening to Hezekiah! Pay attention to my king. Surrender to him. He will let you keep your own vineyards, fig trees, and cisterns 32 for a while. Then he will come and take you away to a country just like yours, where you can plant vineyards, raise your own grain, and have plenty of olive oil and honey. Believe me, you won't starve there.

Hezekiah claims the LORD will save you. But don't be fooled by him. 33 Were any other gods able to defend their land against the king of Assyria? 34 What happened to the gods of Hamath and Arpad? What about the gods of Sepharvaim, Hena, and Ivvah? Were the gods of Samaria able to protect their land against the Assyrian forces? 35 None of these gods kept their people safe from the king of Assyria. Do you think the LORD your God can do any better?

36-37 Eliakim, Shebna, and Joah had been warned by King Hezekiah not to answer the Assyrian commander. So they tore their clothes in sorrow and reported to Hezekiah everything the commander had said.

Hezekiah Asks Isaiah the Prophet for Advice

(Isaiah 37.1-13)

19 As soon as Hezekiah heard the news, he tore off his clothes in sorrow and put on sackcloth. Then he went into the temple of the LORD. 2 He told Prime Minister Eliakim, Assistant Prime Minister Shebna, and the senior priests to dress in sackcloth and tell the prophet Isaiah:

3 These are difficult and disgraceful times. Our nation is like a woman too weak to give birth, when it's time for her baby to be born. 4 Please pray for

[y] **18.22** *worship*: Hezekiah actually had torn down the places where idols were worshiped, and he had told the people to worship the LORD at the one place of worship in Jerusalem. But the Assyrian leader was confused and thought these were also places where the LORD was supposed to be worshiped.

those of us who are left alive. The king
of Assyria sent his army commander to
insult the living God. Perhaps the
LORD heard what he said and will do
something, if you will pray.
5 When these leaders went to Isaiah,
6 he told them that the LORD had this message for Hezekiah:

I am the LORD. Don't worry about
the insulting things that have been
said about me by these messengers
from the king of Assyria. 7 I will upset
him with rumors about what's happening in his own country. He will go
back, and there I will make him die a
violent death.

8 Meanwhile, the commander of the Assyrian forces heard that his king had left
the town of Lachish and was now attacking
Libnah. So he went there.
9 About this same time the king of Assyria learned that King Tirhakah of
Ethiopia[z] was on his way to attack him.
Then the king of Assyria sent some messengers with this note for Hezekiah:

10 Don't trust your God or be fooled
by his promise to defend Jerusalem
against me. 11 You have heard how we
Assyrian kings have completely wiped
out other nations. What makes you
feel so safe? 12 The Assyrian kings before me destroyed the towns of Gozan,
Haran, Rezeph, and everyone from
Eden who lived in Telassar. What good
did their gods do them? 13 The kings of
Hamath, Arpad, Sepharvaim, Hena,
and Ivvah have all disappeared.

Hezekiah Prays
(Isaiah 37.14-20)

14 After Hezekiah had read the note
from the king of Assyria, he took it to the
temple and spread it out for the LORD to
see. 15 He prayed:

LORD God of Israel, your throne is
above the winged creatures.[a] You created the heavens and the earth, and
you alone rule the kingdoms of this
world. 16 But just look how Sennacherib has insulted you, the living God.
17 It is true, our LORD, that Assyrian
kings have turned nations into deserts.
18 They destroyed the idols of wood
and stone that the people of those nations had made and worshiped. 19 But
you are our LORD and our God! We ask
you to keep us safe from the Assyrian
king. Then everyone in every kingdom
on earth will know that you are the
only God.

The LORD's Answer to Hezekiah
(Isaiah 37.21-35)

20 Isaiah went to Hezekiah and told him
that the LORD God of Israel had said:

Hezekiah, I heard your prayer
about King Sennacherib of Assyria.
21 Now this is what I say to that king:

The people of Jerusalem
hate and make fun of you;
they laugh
behind your back.

22 Sennacherib, you cursed,
shouted, and sneered at me,
the holy God of Israel.
23 You let your officials
insult me, the Lord.
And here is what you
have said about yourself,
"I led my chariots
to the highest heights
of Lebanon's mountains.
I went deep into its forest,
cutting down the best cedar
and cypress trees.
24 I dried up every stream
in the land of Egypt,
and I drank water
from wells I had dug."

25 Sennacherib, now listen
to me, the Lord.
I planned all this long ago.
And you don't even realize
that I alone am the one

[z] **19.9** *Ethiopia*: The Hebrew text has "Cush," which was a region south of Egypt that included parts of the present countries of Ethiopia and Sudan. [a] **19.15** *winged creatures*: Two winged creatures made of gold were on the top of the sacred chest and were symbols of the LORD's throne on earth (see Exodus 25.18; 2 Samuel 6.2).

19.15 Ex 25.22.

who decided that you
would do these things.
I let you make ruins
of fortified cities.
26 Their people became weak,
terribly confused.
They were like wild flowers
or tender young grass
growing on a flat roof,
scorched before it matures.[b]

27 I know all about you,
even how fiercely angry
you are with me.
28 I have seen your pride
and the tremendous hatred
you have for me.
Now I will put a hook
in your nose,
a bit in your mouth,[c]
then I will send you back
to where you came from.

29 Hezekiah, I will tell you what's
going to happen. This year you will eat
crops that grow on their own, and the
next year you will eat whatever springs
up where those crops grew. But the
third year you will plant grain and
vineyards, and you will eat what you
harvest. 30 Those who survive in Judah
will be like a vine that puts down deep
roots and bears fruit. 31 I, the LORD All-
Powerful, will see to it that some who
live in Jerusalem will survive.
32 I promise that the king of Assyria
won't get into Jerusalem, or shoot an
arrow into the city, or even surround it
and prepare to attack. 33 As surely as
I am the LORD, he will return by the
way he came and will never enter
Jerusalem. 34 I will protect it for myself
and for my servant David.

The Death of King Sennacherib

(Isaiah 37.36-38)

35 That same night the LORD sent an angel to the camp of the Assyrians, and he
killed one hundred eighty-five thousand of
them. And so the next morning, the camp
was full of dead bodies. 36 After this King
Sennacherib went back to Assyria and lived
in the city of Nineveh. 37 One day he was
worshiping in the temple of his god Nisroch, when his sons, Adrammelech and
Sharezer, killed him with their swords.
They escaped to the land of Ararat, and his
son Esarhaddon became king.[d]

Hezekiah Gets Sick and Almost Dies

(2 Chronicles 32.24-26; Isaiah 38.1-8, 21, 22)

20 About this time, Hezekiah got sick
and was almost dead. Isaiah the
prophet went in and told him, "The LORD
says you won't ever get well. You are going
to die, so you had better start doing what
needs to be done."
2 Hezekiah turned toward the wall and
prayed, 3 "Don't forget that I have been
faithful to you, LORD. I have obeyed you
with all my heart, and I do whatever you
say is right." After this, he cried hard.
4 Before Isaiah got to the middle court
of the palace, 5 the LORD sent him back to
Hezekiah with this message:

Hezekiah, you are the ruler of my
people, and I am the LORD God, who
was worshiped by your ancestor David.
I heard you pray, and I saw you cry. I
will heal you, so that three days from
now you will be able to worship in my
temple. 6 I will let you live fifteen years
more, while I protect you and your city
from the king of Assyria. I will defend
this city as an honor to me and to my
servant David.

7 Then Isaiah said to the king's servants,
"Bring some mashed figs and place them
on the king's open sore. He will then get
well."
8 Hezekiah asked Isaiah, "Can you prove
that the LORD will heal me, so that I can
worship in his temple in three days?"
9 Isaiah replied, "The LORD will prove to
you that he will keep his promise. Will the

[b] **19.26** *tender young grass . . . matures*: Many of the houses had roofs made of packed earth. Grass would sometimes grow out of the roof, but would die quickly because of the sun and hot winds.
[c] **19.28** *I will put . . . your mouth*: This is how the Assyrians treated their prisoners, and now the LORD will treat Sennacherib the same way. [d] **19.37** *Esarhaddon became king*: Ruled Assyria 681-669 B.C.
19.35-37 3 Macc 6.5.

shadow made by the setting sun on the stairway go forward ten steps or back ten steps?"[e]

10 "It's normal for the sun to go forward," Hezekiah answered. "But how can it go back?"

11 Isaiah prayed, and the LORD made the shadow go back ten steps on the stairway built for King Ahaz.[f]

The LORD Is Still with Hezekiah

(Isaiah 39.1-8)

12 Merodach[g] Baladan, the son of Baladan, was now king of Babylonia.[h] And when he learned that Hezekiah had been sick, he sent messengers with letters and a gift for him. 13 Hezekiah welcomed[i] the messengers and showed them all the silver, the gold, the spices, and the fine oils that were in his storehouse. He even showed them where he kept his weapons. Nothing in his palace or in his entire kingdom was kept hidden from them.

14 Isaiah asked Hezekiah, "Where did these men come from? What did they want?"

"They came all the way from Babylonia," Hezekiah answered.

15 "What did you show them?" Isaiah asked.

Hezekiah answered, "I showed them everything in my kingdom."

16 Then Isaiah told Hezekiah:

> I have a message for you from the LORD. 17 One day everything you and your ancestors have stored up will be taken to Babylonia. The LORD has promised that nothing will be left. 18 Some of your own sons will be taken to Babylonia, where they will be disgraced and made to serve in the king's palace.

19 Hezekiah thought, "At least our nation will be at peace for a while." So he told Isaiah, "The message you brought me from the LORD is good."

Hezekiah Dies

(2 Chronicles 32.32, 33)

20 Everything else Hezekiah did while he was king, including how he made the upper pool and tunnel to bring water into Jerusalem, is written in *The History of the Kings of Judah*. 21 Hezekiah died, and his son Manasseh became king.

King Manasseh of Judah

(2 Chronicles 33.1-20)

21 Manasseh was twelve years old when he became king of Judah, and he ruled fifty-five years from Jerusalem. His mother was Hephzibah. 2 Manasseh disobeyed the LORD by following the disgusting customs of the nations that the LORD had forced out of Israel. 3 He rebuilt the local shrines that his father Hezekiah had torn down. He built altars for the god Baal and set up a sacred pole for worshiping the goddess Asherah, just as King Ahab of Israel had done. And he faithfully worshiped the stars in heaven.

4 In the temple, where only the LORD was supposed to be worshiped, Manasseh built altars for pagan gods 5 and for the stars. He placed these altars in both courts of the temple, 6-7 and even set up the pole for Asherah there. Manasseh practiced magic and witchcraft; he asked fortunetellers for advice and sacrificed his own son. He did many sinful things and made the LORD very angry.

Years ago the LORD had told David and his son Solomon:

> Jerusalem is the place I prefer above all others in Israel. It belongs to me, and there I will be worshiped forever. 8 If my people will faithfully obey all the commands in the Law of my servant Moses, I will never make them leave the land I gave to their ancestors.

9 But the people of Judah disobeyed the LORD. They listened to Manasseh and did

[e]**20.9** *Will . . . steps*: One possible meaning for the difficult Hebrew text. [f]**20.11** *the shadow . . . Ahaz*: One possible meaning for the difficult Hebrew text. [g]**20.12** *Merodach*: The Hebrew text has "Berodach," another spelling of the name. [h]**20.12** *Merodach Baladan . . . Babylonia*: Ruled Babylonia 722-710 and 704-703 B.C. [i]**20.13** *welcomed*: Or "listened to."

20.17 2 K 24.13; 2 Ch 36.10. **20.18** 2 K 24.14, 15; Dn 1.1-7. **21.2** Jr 15.4. **21.4** 2 S 7.13. **21.6-8** 1 K 9.3-5; 2 Ch 7.12-18.

even more sinful things than the nations
the LORD had wiped out.
10 One day the LORD said to some of his
prophets:

> 11 King Manasseh has done more
> disgusting things than the Amorites,[j]
> and he has led my people to sin by
> forcing them to worship his idols.
> 12 Now I, the LORD God of Israel, will
> destroy both Jerusalem and Judah!
> People will hear about it but won't be-
> lieve it. 13 Jerusalem is as sinful as
> Ahab and the people of Samaria were.
> So I will wipe out Jerusalem and be
> done with it, just as someone wipes
> water off a plate and turns it over
> to dry.
>
> 14 I will even get rid of my people
> who survive. They will be defeated and
> robbed by their enemies. 15 My people
> have done what I hate and have not
> stopped making me angry since their
> ancestors left Egypt.

16 Manasseh was guilty of causing the
people of Judah to sin and disobey the
LORD. He also refused to protect innocent
people—he even let so many of them be
killed[k] that their blood filled the streets of
Jerusalem.
17 Everything else Manasseh did while
he was king, including his terrible sins, is
written in *The History of the Kings of Judah*. 18 He died and was buried in Uzza
Garden near his palace, and his son Amon
became king.

King Amon of Judah
(2 Chronicles 33.21-25)

19 Amon was twenty-two years old when
he became king of Judah, and he ruled
from Jerusalem for two years. His mother
Meshullemeth was the daughter of Haruz
from Jotbah. 20 Amon disobeyed the LORD,
just as his father Manasseh had done.
21 Amon worshiped the idols Manasseh
had made and 22 refused to be faithful to
the LORD, the God his ancestors had
worshiped.
23 Some of Amon's officials plotted
against him and killed him in his palace.
24-26 He was buried in Uzza Garden. Soon
after that, the people of Judah killed the
murderers of Amon, then they made his
son Josiah king.

Everything else Amon did while he was
king is written in *The History of the Kings
of Judah*.

King Josiah of Judah
(2 Chronicles 34.1, 2)

22 Josiah was eight years old when he
became king of Judah, and he
ruled thirty-one years from Jerusalem. His
mother Jedidah was the daughter of Adaiah
from Bozkath. 2 Josiah always obeyed the
LORD, just as his ancestor David had done.

Hilkiah Finds *The Book of God's Law*
(2 Chronicles 34.8-28)

3 After Josiah had been king for
eighteen years, he told Shaphan,[l] one of
his highest officials:

> Go to the LORD's temple 4 and ask
> Hilkiah the high priest to collect from
> the guards all the money that the peo-
> ple have donated. 5 Have Hilkiah give
> it to the men supervising the repairs to
> the temple. They can use some of the
> money to pay 6 the workers, and with
> the rest of it they can buy wood and
> stone for the repair work. 7 They are
> honest, so we won't ask them to keep
> track of the money.

8 While Shaphan was at the temple,
Hilkiah handed him a book and said, "Look
what I found here in the temple—*The Book
of God's Law*."

Shaphan read it, 9 then went back to
Josiah and reported, "Your officials collected the money in the temple and gave it
to the men supervising the repairs. 10 But
there's something else, Your Majesty. The
priest Hilkiah gave me this book." Then
Shaphan read it out loud.
11 When Josiah heard what was in *The
Book of God's Law*, he tore his clothes in
sorrow. 12 At once he called together
Hilkiah, Shaphan, Ahikam son of Shaphan,

[j] **21.11** *Amorites*: Here used in the general sense of nations that lived in Canaan before the Israelites. [k] **21.16** *He also refused . . . killed*: Or "He killed so many innocent people."
[l] **22.3** *Shaphan*: Hebrew "Shaphan son of Azaliah son of Meshullam."
22.1 Jr 3.6. **22.7** 2 K 12.15.

Achbor son of Micaiah, and his own servant Asaiah. He said, 13 "The LORD must be furious with me and everyone else in Judah, because our ancestors did not obey the laws written in this book. Go find out what the LORD wants us to do."

14 The five men left right away and went to talk with Huldah the prophet. Her husband was Shallum,[m] who was in charge of the king's clothes. Huldah lived in the northern part of Jerusalem, and when they met in her home, 15 she said:

> You were sent here by King Josiah, and this is what the LORD God of Israel says to him: 16 "Josiah, I am the LORD! And I will see to it that this country and everyone living in it will be destroyed. It will happen just as this book says. 17 The people of Judah have rejected me. They have offered sacrifices to foreign gods and have worshiped their own idols. I cannot stand it any longer. I am furious.
>
> 18 "Josiah, listen to what I am going to do. 19 I noticed how sad you were when you read that this country and its people would be completely wiped out. You even tore your clothes in sorrow, and I heard you cry. 20 So I will let you die in peace, before I destroy this place."

The men left and took Huldah's answer back to Josiah.

Josiah Reads *The Book of God's Law*

(2 *Chronicles* 34.29-33)

23 King Josiah called together the older leaders of Judah and Jerusalem. 2 Then he went to the LORD's temple, together with the people of Judah and Jerusalem, the priests, and the prophets. Finally, when everybody was there, he read aloud *The Book of God's Law*[n] that had been found in the temple.

3 After Josiah had finished reading, he stood by one of the columns. He asked the people to promise in the LORD's name to faithfully obey the LORD and to follow his commands. The people agreed to do everything written in the book.

Josiah Follows the Teachings of God's Law

(2 *Chronicles* 34.3-7)

4 Josiah told Hilkiah the priest, the assistant priests, and the guards at the temple door to go into the temple and bring out the things used to worship Baal, Asherah, and the stars. Josiah had these things burned in Kidron Valley just outside Jerusalem, and he had the ashes carried away to the town of Bethel.

5 Josiah also got rid of the pagan priests at the local shrines in Judah and around Jerusalem. These were the men that the kings of Judah had appointed to offer sacrifices to Baal and to the sun, moon, and stars. 6 Josiah had the sacred pole[o] for Asherah brought out of the temple and taken to Kidron Valley, where it was burned. He then had its ashes ground into dust and scattered over the public cemetery there. 7 He had the buildings torn down where the male prostitutes[p] lived next to the temple, and where the women wove sacred robes[q] for the idol of Asherah.

8 In almost every town in Judah, priests had been offering sacrifices to the LORD at local shrines.[r] Josiah brought these priests to Jerusalem and had their shrines made unfit for worship—every shrine from Geba just north of Jerusalem to Beersheba in the south. He even tore down the shrine at Beersheba that was just to the left of Joshua Gate, which was named after the highest official of the city. 9 Those local priests could not serve at the LORD's altar in Jerusalem, but they were allowed to eat sacred

[m]**22.14** *Shallum*: Hebrew "Shallum son of Tikvah son of Harhas." [n]**23.2** *The Book of God's Law*: The Hebrew text has "The Book of God's Agreement," which is the same as "The Book of God's Law" in 22.8,11. In traditional translations this is called "The Book of the Covenant." [o]**23.6** *sacred pole*: See the note at 13.6,7. [p]**23.7** *male prostitutes*: Young men or boys sometimes served as prostitutes in the worship of Canaanite gods, but the LORD had forbidden the people of Israel and Judah to worship in this way (see Deuteronomy 23.17,18). [q]**23.7** *sacred robes*: Or "coverings." [r]**23.8** *local shrines*: See the note at 12.3.

23.4-6 2 K 21.3; 2 Ch 33.3.

bread,[s] just like the priests from Jerusalem. 10 Josiah sent some men to Hinnom Valley just outside Jerusalem with orders to make the altar there unfit for worship. That way, people could no longer use it for sacrificing their children to the god Molech. 11 He also got rid of the horses that the kings of Judah used in their ceremonies to worship the sun, and he destroyed the chariots along with them. The horses had been kept near the entrance to the LORD's temple, in a courtyard[t] close to where an official named Nathan-Melech lived.

12 Some of the kings of Judah, especially Manasseh, had built altars in the two courts of the temple and in the room that Ahaz had built on the palace roof. Josiah had these altars torn down and smashed to pieces, and he had the pieces thrown into Kidron Valley, just outside Jerusalem. 13 After that, he closed down the shrines that Solomon had built east of Jerusalem and south of Spoil Hill to honor Astarte the disgusting goddess of Sidon, Chemosh the disgusting god of Moab, and Milcom the disgusting god of Ammon.[u] 14 He tore down the stone images of foreign gods and cut down the sacred pole used in the worship of Asherah. Then he had the whole area covered with human bones.[v]

15 But Josiah was not finished yet. At Bethel he destroyed the shrine and the altar that Jeroboam son of Nebat had built and that had caused the Israelites to sin. Josiah had the shrine and the Asherah pole burned and ground into dust. 16 As he looked around, he saw graves on the hillside. He had the bones in them dug up and burned on the altar, so that it could no longer be used. This happened just as God's prophet had said when Jeroboam was standing at the altar, celebrating a festival.[w]

Then Josiah saw the grave of the prophet who had said this would happen 17 and he asked,[x] "Whose grave is that?"

Some people who lived nearby answered, "It belongs to the prophet from Judah who told what would happen to this altar."

18 Josiah replied, "Then leave it alone. Don't dig up his bones." So they did not disturb his bones or the bones of the old prophet from Israel who had also been buried there.[y]

19 Some of the Israelite kings had made the LORD angry by building pagan shrines all over Israel. So Josiah sent troops to destroy these shrines just as he had done to the one in Bethel. 20 He killed the priests who served at them and burned their bones on the altars.

After all that, Josiah went back to Jerusalem.

Josiah and the People of Judah Celebrate Passover

(2 Chronicles 35.1-19)

21 Josiah told the people of Judah, "Celebrate Passover in honor of the LORD your God, just as it says in *The Book of God's Law*."[z]

22 This festival had not been celebrated in this way since kings ruled Israel and Judah. 23 But in Josiah's eighteenth year as king of Judah, everyone came to Jerusalem to celebrate Passover.

The LORD Is Still Angry at the People of Judah

24 Josiah got rid of every disgusting person and thing in Judah and Jerusalem—including magicians, fortunetellers, and idols. He did his best to obey every law written in the book that the priest Hilkiah found in the LORD's temple. 25 No other king before or after Josiah tried as hard as he did to obey the Law of Moses.

[s]**23.9** *sacred bread*: The Hebrew text has "thin bread," which may be either the pieces of thin bread made without yeast to be eaten during the Passover Festival (see verses 21-23) or the baked flour used in sacrifices to give thanks to the LORD (see Leviticus 2.4,5). [t]**23.11** *in a courtyard*: One possible meaning for the difficult Hebrew text. [u]**23.13** *the shrines . . . Ammon*: See 1 Kings 11.5-7. [v]**23.14** *Then he . . . human bones*: This made the whole area unfit for the worship of any god. [w]**23.16** *just . . . festival*: See 1 Kings 13.1,2. [x]**23.16,17** *said when Jeroboam . . . asked*: One ancient translation; Hebrew "said. 17 Then Josiah asked." [y]**23.18** *old prophet . . . there*: See 1 Kings 13.11-32. [z]**23.21** *The Book of God's Law*: See the note at verse 2.

23.10 **a** Jr 7.31; 19.1-6; 32.35; **b** Lv 18.21. **23.12** 2 K 21.5; 2 Ch 33.5. **23.13** 1 K 11.7. **23.15** 1 K 12.32, 33. **23.16** 1 K 13.1, 2. **23.17** 1 K 13.30-32.

26 But the LORD was still furious with
the people of Judah because Manasseh had
done so many things to make him angry.
27 The LORD said, "I will desert the people
of Judah, just as I deserted the people of Israel. I will reject Jerusalem, even though I
chose it to be mine. And I will abandon this
temple built to honor me."

Josiah Dies in Battle
(2 Chronicles 35.20—36.1)

28 Everything else Josiah did while he
was king is written in *The History of the
Kings of Judah*. 29 During Josiah's rule,
King Neco of Egypt led his army north to
the Euphrates River to help the king of Assyria. Josiah led his troops north to fight
Neco, but when they met in battle at
Megiddo, Josiah was killed.[a] 30 A few of
Josiah's servants put his body in a chariot
and took it back to Jerusalem, where they
buried it in his own tomb. Then the people
of Judah found his son Jehoahaz and
poured olive oil on his head to show that he
was their new king.

King Jehoahaz of Judah
(2 Chronicles 36.2-4)

31 Jehoahaz was twenty-three years old
when he became king of Judah, and he
ruled from Jerusalem only three months.
His mother Hamutal was the daughter of
Jeremiah from Libnah. 32 Jehoahaz disobeyed the LORD, just as some of his ancestors had done.
33 King Neco of Egypt had Jehoahaz arrested and put in prison at Riblah[b] near
Hamath. Then he forced the people of Judah to pay him almost four tons of silver
and about seventy-five pounds of gold as
taxes. 34 Neco appointed Josiah's son Eliakim king of Judah, and changed his name
to Jehoiakim. He took Jehoahaz as a prisoner to Egypt, where he died.
35 Jehoiakim forced the people of Judah
to pay higher taxes, so he could give Neco
the silver and gold he demanded.

King Jehoiakim of Judah
(2 Chronicles 36.5-8)

36 Jehoiakim was twenty-five years old
when he was appointed king, and he ruled
eleven years from Jerusalem. His mother
Zebidah was the daughter of Pedaiah from
Rumah. 37 Jehoiakim disobeyed the LORD
by following the example of his ancestors.
24 During Jehoiakim's rule, King Nebuchadnezzar of Babylonia[c] invaded
and took control of Judah. Jehoiakim
obeyed Nebuchadnezzar for three years,
but then he rebelled.
2 At that time, the LORD started sending
troops to rob and destroy towns in Judah.
Some of these troops were from Babylonia,
and others were from Syria, Moab, and
Ammon. The LORD had sent his servants
the prophets to warn Judah about this,
3 and now he was making it happen. The
country of Judah was going to be wiped
out, because Manasseh had sinned 4 and
caused many innocent people to die. The
LORD would not forgive this.
5 Everything else Jehoiakim did while he
was king is written in *The History of the
Kings of Judah*. 6 Jehoiakim died, and his
son Jehoiachin became king.
7 King Nebuchadnezzar defeated King
Neco of Egypt and took control of his land
from the Egyptian Gorge all the way north
to the Euphrates River. So Neco never invaded Judah again.[d]

King Jehoiachin of Judah Is Taken to Babylon
(2 Chronicles 36.9, 10)

8 Jehoiachin was eighteen years old
when he became king of Judah, and he

[a] **23.29** *killed*: At this time, King Neco of Egypt (609-595 B.C.) was fighting on the side of the Assyrians. He marched north to fight the Babylonian army and help Assyria keep control of its land. Since Josiah considered Assyria an enemy, he set out to stop Neco and the Egyptian troops.
[b] **23.33** *Riblah*: An important town in Syria on the Orontes River.
[c] **24.1** *King Nebuchadnezzar of Babylonia*: Ruled Babylonia 605-562 B.C.
[d] **24.7** *again*: Nebuchadnezzar defeated the Egyptian army in 605 B.C. at the town of Carchemish. But a few years later, he was forced to retreat all the way back to Babylonia, which allowed Jehoiakim to rebel (see verse 1).

23.34 Jr 22.11, 12. **23.36** Jr 22.18, 19; 26.1-6; 35.1-19. **24.1** Jr 25.1-38; Dn 1.1, 2.

ruled only three months from Jerusalem. His mother Nehushta was the daughter of Elnathan from Jerusalem. 9 Jehoiachin disobeyed the LORD, just as his father Jehoiakim had done.

10 King Nebuchadnezzar of Babylonia sent troops to attack Jerusalem soon after Jehoiachin became king. 11 During the attack, Nebuchadnezzar himself arrived at the city. 12 Jehoiachin immediately surrendered, together with his mother and his servants, as well as his army officers and officials. Then Nebuchadnezzar had Jehoiachin arrested. These things took place in the eighth year of Nebuchadnezzar's rule in Babylonia.[e]

13 The LORD had warned[f] that someday the treasures would be taken from the royal palace and from the temple, including the gold objects that Solomon had made for the temple. And that's exactly what Nebuchadnezzar ordered his soldiers to do. 14 He also led away as prisoners the Jerusalem officials, the military leaders, and the skilled workers—ten thousand in all. Only the very poorest people were left in Judah.

15 Nebuchadnezzar took Jehoiachin to Babylon, along with his mother, his wives, his officials, and the most important leaders of Judah. 16 He also led away seven thousand soldiers, one thousand skilled workers, and anyone who would be useful in battle.

17 Then Nebuchadnezzar appointed Jehoiachin's uncle Mattaniah king of Judah and changed his name to Zedekiah.

King Zedekiah of Judah

(2 Chronicles 36.11-16; Jeremiah 52.1-3)

18 Zedekiah was twenty-one years old when he was appointed king of Judah, and he ruled from Jerusalem for eleven years. His mother Hamutal was the daughter of Jeremiah from Libnah. 19 Zedekiah disobeyed the LORD, just as Jehoiakim had done. 20 It was Zedekiah who finally rebelled against Nebuchadnezzar.

The people of Judah and Jerusalem had made the LORD so angry that he finally turned his back on them. That's why these horrible things were happening.

Jerusalem Is Captured and Destroyed

(2 Chronicles 36.17-21; Jeremiah 52.3-30)

25 In Zedekiah's ninth year as king, on the tenth day of the tenth month,[g] King Nebuchadnezzar of Babylonia led his entire army to attack Jerusalem. The troops set up camp outside the city and built ramps up to the city walls.

2-3 After a year and a half, all the food in Jerusalem was gone. Then on the ninth day of the fourth[h] month, 4 the Babylonian troops broke through the city wall.[i] That same night, Zedekiah and his soldiers tried to escape through the gate near the royal garden, even though they knew the enemy had the city surrounded. They headed toward the desert, 5 but the Babylonian troops caught up with them near Jericho. They arrested Zedekiah, but his soldiers scattered in every direction.

6 Zedekiah was taken to Riblah, where Nebuchadnezzar put him on trial and found him guilty. 7 Zedekiah's sons were killed right in front of him. His eyes were then poked out, and he was put in chains and dragged off to Babylon.

8 About a month later,[j] in Nebuchadnezzar's nineteenth year as king, Nebuzaradan, who was his official in charge of the guards, arrived in Jerusalem. 9 Nebuzaradan burned down the LORD's temple, the king's palace, and every important building in the city, as well as all the houses. 10 Then he ordered the Babylonian

[e] **24.12** *Babylonia*: These events took place in 597 B.C. [f] **24.13** *warned*: See 20.16-18. [g] **25.1** *tenth month*: Tebeth, the tenth month of the Hebrew calendar, from about mid-December to mid-January. [h] **25.2,3** *fourth*: This word is not in the Hebrew text here, but see the parallel in Jeremiah 52.5,6. [i] **25.4** *wall*: Jerusalem was destroyed in 586 B.C. [j] **25.8** *About a month later*: Hebrew "On the seventh day of the fifth month."

24.12 Jr 22.24-30; 24.1-10; 29.1, 2. **24.15** Ez 17.12. **24.17** Jr 37.1; Ez 17.13. **24.18** Jr 27.1-22; 28.1-17. **24.20** Ez 17.15. **25.1** Jr 21.1-10; 34.1-5; Ez 24.2. **25.4** Ez 33.21. **25.7** Ez 12.13. **25.9** 1 K 9.8.

soldiers to break down the walls around Jerusalem. [11] He led away as prisoners the people left in the city, including those who had become loyal to Nebuchadnezzar. [12] Only some of the poorest people were left behind to work the vineyards and the fields.

[13] The Babylonian soldiers took the two bronze columns that stood in front of the temple, the ten movable bronze stands, and the large bronze bowl called the Sea. They broke them into pieces so they could take the bronze to Babylonia. [14] They carried off the bronze things used for worship at the temple, including the pans for hot ashes, and the shovels, snuffers, and also the dishes for incense, [15] as well as the fire pans and the sprinkling bowls. Nebuzaradan ordered his soldiers to take everything made of gold or silver.

[16] The pile of bronze from the columns, the stands, and the large bowl that Solomon had made for the temple was too large to be weighed. [17] Each column had been twenty-seven feet tall with a bronze cap four and a half feet high. These caps were decorated with bronze designs—some of them like chains and others like pomegranates.[k]

[18] Next, Nebuzaradan arrested Seraiah the chief priest, Zephaniah his assistant, and three temple officials. [19] Then he arrested one of the army commanders, the king's five personal advisors, and the officer in charge of gathering the troops for battle. He also found sixty more soldiers who were still in Jerusalem. [20] Nebuzaradan led them all to Riblah [21] near Hamath, where Nebuchadnezzar had them killed.

The people of Judah no longer lived in their own country.

Gedaliah Is Made Ruler of the People Left in Judah

(Jeremiah 40.7-9; 41.1-3)

[22] King Nebuchadnezzar appointed Gedaliah son of Ahikam[l] to rule the few people still living in Judah. [23] When the army officers and troops heard that Gedaliah was their ruler, the officers met with him at Mizpah. These men were Ishmael son of Nethaniah, Johanan son of Kareah, Seraiah son of Tanhumeth from Netophah, and Jaazaniah from Maacah.

[24] Gedaliah said to them, "Everything will be fine, I promise. We don't need to be afraid of the Babylonian rulers, if we live here peacefully and do what Nebuchadnezzar says."

[25] Ishmael[m] was from the royal family. And about two months after Gedaliah began his rule,[n] Ishmael and ten other men went to Mizpah. They killed Gedaliah and his officials, including those from Judah and those from Babylonia. [26] After that, the army officers and all the people in Mizpah, whether important or not, were afraid of what the Babylonians might do. So they left Judah and went to Egypt.

Jehoiachin Is Set Free

(Jeremiah 52.31-34)

[27] Jehoiachin was a prisoner in Babylon for thirty-seven years. Then Evil-Merodach became king of Babylonia,[o] and in the first year of his rule, on the twenty-seventh day of the twelfth month,[p] he let Jehoiachin out of prison. [28] Evil-Merodach was kind to Jehoiachin and honored him more than any of the other kings held prisoner there. [29] Jehoiachin was even allowed to wear regular clothes, and he ate at the king's table every day. [30] As long as Jehoiachin lived, he was paid a daily allowance to buy whatever he needed.

[k]**25.17** *pomegranates*: A bright red fruit that looks like an apple. [l]**25.22** *Ahikam*: Hebrew "Ahikam son of Shaphan." [m]**25.25** *Ishmael*: Hebrew "Ishmael son of Nethaniah son of Elishama." [n]**25.25** *about two months . . . his rule*: Hebrew "in the seventh month." [o]**25.27** *Evil-Merodach . . . Babylonia*: The son of Nebuchadnezzar, who ruled Babylonia from 562 to 560 B.C. [p]**25.27** *twelfth month*: Adar, the twelfth month of the Hebrew calendar, from about mid-February to mid-March.

25.13 a 1 K 7.15-26; 2 Ch 3.15-17; **b** 1 K 7.23-26; 2 Ch 4.2-5. **25.14** 1 K 7.45; 2 Ch 4.16. **25.22-24** Jr 40.7-9. **25.25** Jr 41.1-3. **25.26** Jr 43.5-7.

1 CHRONICLES

ABOUT THIS BOOK

First Chronicles is the first half of a single book that was divided into two parts, 1 and 2 Chronicles, because together they were too long to fit on one scroll. These two books retell the history of Israel from a slightly different viewpoint than that of Samuel and Kings, although many of the same stories are repeated.

King David is the most important person in the book of 1 Chronicles. He is the one who made Jerusalem the center for the worship of the Lord God, and who made sure the Lord was worshiped in the proper way. David is also honored as the founder of the temple, even though it was his son Solomon who actually built it.

Much of 1 Chronicles is made up of lists that trace the descendants of Adam to the time of King Saul (1–9). After reporting how Saul died (10), the rest of the book (11–29) focuses on King David, and these chapters can be divided into four parts. The first part (11–12) tells how David became king and made Jerusalem his capital city. This part also includes information about David's warriors and military officers. The second part (13–16) describes how David moved the sacred chest to its new home in Jerusalem. The third part (17–20) includes events during his rule, and the final part (21–29) describes his preparations for building the Lord's temple and his instructions to his son Solomon about the proper worship of the Lord.

In 1 Chronicles, David is used as an example of someone who faithfully worships and obeys the Lord. At the end of David's rule, he praises the Lord in front of everyone in Israel and says:

> *"I praise you forever, LORD! You are the God our ancestor Jacob worshiped. Your power is great, and your glory is seen everywhere in heaven and on earth. You are king of the entire world, and you rule with strength and power."*
>
> *(29.10b-12a)*

A QUICK LOOK AT THIS BOOK

The Descendants of Adam

(Genesis 5.1-32; 10.1-32; 11.10-32)

1 1-4 Adam was the father of Seth, and his descendants were Enosh, Kenan, Mahalalel, Jared, Enoch, Methuselah, Lamech, and Noah, who had three sons: Shem, Ham, and Japheth.

5 Japheth was the father of Gomer, Magog, Madai, Javan, Tubal, Meshech, and Tiras, and they were the ancestors of the kingdoms named after them. 6 Gomer was the ancestor of Ashkenaz, Riphath,[a] and Togarmah. 7 Javan was the ancestor of Elishah, Tarshish, Kittim, and Dodanim.[b]

8 Ham was the father of Ethiopia,[c] Egypt, Put, and Canaan, and they were the ancestors of the kingdoms named after them. 9 Ethiopia was the ancestor of Seba, Havilah, Sabta, Raamah, and Sabteca. Raamah was the ancestor of Sheba and Dedan. 10 Ethiopia was also the father of Nimrod, the world's first mighty warrior. 11 Egypt was the ancestor of Ludim, Anamim, Lehabim, Naphtuhim, 12 Pathrusim, Casluhim, and Caphtorim, the ancestor of the Philistines.[d] 13 Canaan's oldest son was Sidon; his other son was Heth. 14-16 Canaan was also the ancestor of the Jebusites, the Amorites, the Girgashites, the Hivites, and Arkites, the Sinites, the Arvadites, the Zemarites, and the Hamathites.

17 Shem was the ancestor of Elam, Asshur, Arpachshad, Lud, Aram, Uz, Hul, Gether, and Meshech;[e] they were the ancestors of the kingdoms named after them. 18 Arpachshad was Shelah's father and Eber's grandfather. 19 Eber named his first son Peleg,[f] because in his time the earth was divided into tribal regions. Eber's second son was Joktan, 20-23 the ancestor of Almodad, Sheleph, Hazarmaveth, Jerah, Hadoram, Uzal, Diklah, Ebal, Abimael, Sheba, Ophir, Havilah, and Jobab.

24-27 Shem's descendants included Arpachshad, Shelah, Eber, Peleg, Reu, Serug, Nahor, Terah, and Abram, later renamed Abraham.

Abraham's Family

(Genesis 25.1-4, 12-16)

28 Abraham was the father of Isaac and Ishmael.

29-31 Ishmael had twelve sons, who were born in the following order: Nebaioth, Kedar, Adbeel, Mibsam, Mishma, Dumah, Massa, Hadad, Tema, Jetur, Naphish, and Kedemah.

32 Abraham and his slave woman Keturah had six sons: Zimran, Jokshan, Medan, Midian, Ishbak, and Shuah. Jokshan was the father of Sheba and Dedan. 33 Midian was the father of Ephah, Epher, Hanoch, Abida, and Eldaah.

Esau's Family

(Genesis 36.1-14)

34 Abraham's son Isaac was the father of Esau and Jacob.[g] 35 Esau was the father of Eliphaz, Reuel, Jeush, Jalam, and Korah. 36 Eliphaz was the father of Teman, Omar, Zephi, Gatam, Kenaz, Timna, and Amalek. 37 Reuel was the father of Nahath, Zerah, Shammah, and Mizzah.

The First Edomites and Their Kings

(Genesis 36.20-43)

38 Seir was the father of Lotan, Shobal, Zibeon, Anah, Dishon, Ezer, and Dishan. 39 Lotan was the father of Hori and Homam; Lotan's sister was Timna. 40 Shobal was the father of Alvan,[h] Mana-

[a] **1.6** *Riphath*: Most Hebrew manuscripts and two ancient translations (see also Genesis 10.2-5); some Hebrew manuscripts "Diphath." In Hebrew the letters "d" and "r" look almost exactly the same. [b] **1.7** *Dodanim*: Most Hebrew manuscripts and one ancient translation (see also Genesis 10.2-5); some Hebrew manuscripts "Rodanim." In Hebrew the letters "d" and "r" look almost exactly the same. [c] **1.8** *Ethiopia*: The Hebrew text has "Cush," which was a region south of Egypt that included parts of the present countries of Ethiopia and Sudan. [d] **1.12** *Casluhim, and Caphtorim, the ancestor of the Philistines*: The Hebrew text has "Casluhim, the ancestor of the Philistines, and Caphtorim"; but see Jeremiah 47.4 and Amos 9.7. [e] **1.17** *Meshech*: Most Hebrew manuscripts; a few Hebrew manuscripts and some manuscripts of one ancient translation "Mash" (see also Genesis 10.21-31). [f] **1.19** *Peleg*: In Hebrew "Peleg" means "divided." [g] **1.34** *Jacob*: The Hebrew text has "Israel," which was Jacob's name after God renamed him. [h] **1.40** *Alvan*: Or "Alian."

hath, Ebal, Shephi, and Onam. Zibeon was
the father of Aiah and Anah.
41 Anah was the father of Dishon and
the grandfather of Hemdan,[i] Eshban,
Ithran, and Cheran. 42 Ezer was the father
of Bilhan, Zaavan, and Jaakan.[j] Dishan[k]
was the father of Uz and Aran.
43 Before kings ruled in Israel, Bela son
of Beor ruled the country of Edom from its
capital of Dinhabah. 44 After Bela's death,
Jobab son of Zerah from Bozrah became
king. 45 After Jobab's death, Husham from
the land of Teman became king. 46 After
Husham's death, Hadad son of Bedad became king and ruled from Avith. Earlier,
Bedad had defeated the Midianites in the
territory of Moab. 47 After Hadad's death,
Samlah from Masrekah became king; 48 after Samlah's death, Shaul from the town of
Rehoboth on the Euphrates River became
king; 49 and after Shaul's death, Baal
Hanan son of Achbor became king. 50 After
Baal Hanan's death, Hadad ruled from Pai.
His wife was Mehetabel, the daughter of
Matred and granddaughter of Mezahab.
51 The Edomite clans[l] were Timna, Al-
vah,[m] Jetheth, 52 Oholibamah, Elah, Pinon,
53 Kenaz, Teman, Mibzar, 54 Magdiel, and
Iram.

The Descendants of Judah

2 1-2 Jacob[n] was the father of twelve
sons: Reuben, Simeon, Levi, Judah,
Issachar, Zebulun, Dan, Joseph, Benjamin,
Naphtali, Gad, and Asher.
3 Judah and his Canaanite wife Bathshua had three sons: Er, Onan, and Shelah.
But the LORD had Er put to death, because
he disobeyed and did what the LORD
hated. 4 Judah and his daughter-in-law Tamar
also had two sons: Perez and Zerah.
5 Perez was the father of Hezron and
Hamul. 6 Zerah was the father of Zimri,
Ethan, Heman, Calcol, and Darda.[o]
7 Achan,[p] who was a descendant of Zerah
and the son of Carmi, caused trouble for
Israel, because he kept for himself things
that belonged only to the LORD.[q] 8 Ethan's
son was Azariah.

The Ancestors of King David

9 Hezron was the father of Jerahmeel,
Ram, and Caleb.[r] 10 Ram was the father of
Amminadab and the grandfather of Nahshon, a tribal leader of Judah. 11 Nahshon's descendants included Salma, Boaz,
12 Obed, and Jesse. 13-15 Jesse had seven
sons, who were born in the following order:
Eliab, Abinadab, Shimea, Nethanel, Rad-
dai, Ozem, and David. 16 Jesse also had two
daughters: Zeruiah and Abigail. Zeruiah
was the mother of Abishai, Joab, and Asahel. 17 Abigail's husband was Jether, who
was a descendant of Ishmael, and their son
was Amasa.

The Descendants of Hezron

18 Hezron's son Caleb married Azubah,
and their daughter was Jerioth,[s] the
mother of Jesher, Shobab, and Ardon. 19 After the death of Azubah, Caleb married
Ephrath. Their son Hur 20 was the father
of Uri and the grandfather of Bezalel.
21 When Hezron was sixty years old, he
married the daughter of Machir, who settled the region of Gilead. Their son Segub
22 was the father of Jair, who ruled twenty-
three villages in the region of Gilead.
23 Some time later the nations of Geshur
and Aram captured sixty towns in that region, including the villages that belonged to
Jair, as well as the town of Kenath and the
nearby villages. Everyone from the region
of Gilead was a descendant of Machir.

[i] **1.41** *Hemdan*: Most Hebrew manuscripts and some manuscripts of one ancient translation (see also Genesis 36.26); other Hebrew manuscripts "Hamran." [j] **1.42** *Jaakan*: Or "Akan" (see Genesis 36.27). [k] **1.42** *Dishan*: The Hebrew text has "Dishon," another spelling of the name (see Genesis 36.28). [l] **1.51** *The Edomite clans*: Or "The leaders of the Edomite clans." [m] **1.51** *Alvah*: Or "Aliah." [n] **2.1,2** *Jacob*: See the note at 1.34. [o] **2.6** *Darda*: Most Hebrew manuscripts and two ancient translations (see also 1 Kings 4.30, 31); some Hebrew manuscripts "Dara." [p] **2.7** *Achan*: The Hebrew text has "Achar," which means "trouble." [q] **2.7** *Achan . . . the LORD*: See Joshua 7.1-26. [r] **2.9** *Caleb*: The Hebrew text has "Chelubai," another form of the name. [s] **2.18** *married Azubah . . . Jerioth*: One possible meaning for the difficult Hebrew text.

2.7 Js 7.1.

24 After the death of Hezron, Caleb married Ephrath, his father's wife. Their son
was Ashhur,[t] who later settled the town of
Tekoa.

The Descendants of Jerahmeel

25 Jerahmeel, Hezron's oldest son, was
the father of Ram, Bunah, Oren, Ozem,
and Ahijah. 26 Jerahmeel had a second
wife, Atarah, who gave birth to Onam.
27 Ram was the father of Maaz, Jamin, and
Eker. 28 Onam was the father of Shammai
and Jada.

Shammai was the father of Nadab and
Abishur. 29 Abishur married Abihail, and
their two sons were Ahban and Molid.
30 Nadab was the father of Seled and Appaim. Seled had no children; 31 Appaim's
son was Ishi, the father of Sheshan and the
grandfather of Ahlai.

32 Jada was the father of Jether and
Jonathan. Jether had no children, 33 but
Jonathan had two sons: Peleth and Zaza.

34-35 Sheshan had no sons, and so he let
one of his daughters marry Jarha, his
Egyptian slave. Their son was Attai, 36 the
father of Nathan and the grandfather of
Zabad. 37-41 Zabad's descendants included
Ephlal, Obed, Jehu, Azariah, Helez,
Eleasah, Sismai, Shallum, Jekamiah, and
Elishama.

The Descendants of Caleb

42 Caleb, Jerahmeel's brother, had the
following descendants: Mesha,[u] Ziph,
Mareshah,[v] Hebron, 43 and Hebron's four
sons, Korah, Tappuah, Rekem, and Shema.
44 Shema was the father of Raham and the
grandfather of Jorkeam. Rekem was the
father of Shammai, 45 the grandfather of
Maon, and the great-grandfather of Bethzur.

46 Ephah was one of Caleb's wives,[w] and
their sons were Haran, Moza, and Gazez.
Haran named his son after his brother
Gazez. 47 Ephah was the daughter of Jah-
dai, who was also the father of Regem,
Jotham, Geshan, Pelet, and Shaaph.[x]

48 Maacah was another of Caleb's
wives,[y] and their sons were Sheber and
Tirhanah. 49 Later, they had two more sons:
Shaaph the father of Madmannah, and
Sheva the father of Machbenah and Gibea.
Caleb's daughter was Achsah. 50-51 All of
these were Caleb's descendants.

Hur, the oldest son of Caleb and
Ephrath, had three sons: Shobal, Salma,
and Hareph, who settled the town of Beth-
Gader. 52 Shobal, who settled the town of
Kiriath-Jearim, was the ancestor of
Haroeh, half of the Menuhoth clan, 53 and
the clans that lived near Kiriath-Jearim;
they were the Ithrites, the Puthites, the
Shumathites, and the Mishraites. The Zo-
rathites and the Eshtaolites were descendants of the Mishraites.

54 Salma settled the town of Bethlehem
and was the ancestor of the Netophathites,
the people of Atroth-Bethjoab, half of the
Manahathite clan, and the Zorites.
55 Salma was also the ancestor of the clans
in Jabez that kept the court and government records; they were the Tirathites, the
Shimeathites, and the Sucathites. These
clans were the descendants of Hammath
the Kenite, who was also the ancestor of
the Rechabites.

The Descendants of King David

3 1-4 King David ruled from Hebron for
seven years and six months, and during that time he had six sons, who were
born in the following order: Amnon,
Daniel, Absalom, Adonijah, Shephatiah,
and Ithream. Ahinoam from Jezreel was
the mother of Amnon; Abigail from Carmel
was the mother of Daniel; Maacah daughter of King Talmai of Geshur was the
mother of Absalom; Haggith was the
mother of Adonijah; Abital was the mother
of Shephatiah; and Eglah was the mother
of Ithream.

David then ruled from Jerusalem for
thirty-three years, 5 and during that time,
he had thirteen more sons. His wife

[t]**2.24** *After the death of Hezron . . . Ashhur*: Two ancient translations; Hebrew "After Hezron died in Caleb-Ephrathah, Abijah his wife gave birth to Ashhur." [u]**2.42** *Mesha*: Hebrew; one ancient translation "Mareshah." [v]**2.42** *following descendants . . . Mareshah*: One possible meaning for the difficult Hebrew text. [w]**2.46** *wives*: See the note at 3.9. [x]**2.47** *Shaaph*: One possible meaning for the difficult Hebrew text of verse 47. [y]**2.48** *wives*: See the note at 3.9.

3.1-4 2 S 5.4, 5; 1 K 2.10, 11; 1 Ch 29.27. **3.5** 2 S 11.2-4.

Bathsheba[z] daughter of Ammiel gave birth
to Shimea, Shobab, Nathan, and Solomon.
6-8 David's other sons included Ibhar, Elishua,[a] Eliphelet, Nogah, Nepheg, Japhia,
Elishama, Eliada, and Eliphelet. 9 David's
other wives[b] also gave birth to sons. Tamar
was his daughter.

The Descendants of King Solomon

10-15 Solomon's descendants included
the following kings: Rehoboam, Abijah, Asa,
Jehoshaphat, Jehoram,[c] Ahaziah, Joash,
Amaziah, Azariah, Jotham, Ahaz, Hezekiah,
Manasseh, Amon, and Josiah and his four
sons, Johanan, Jehoiakim, Zedekiah, and
Jehoahaz.[d] 16 Jehoiakim was the father of
Jehoiachin and Zedekiah.
17 Jehoiachin, who was taken to Bab-
ylon as a prisoner, had seven sons: Sheal-
tiel, 18 Malchiram, Pedaiah, Shenazzar,
Jekamiah, Hoshama, and Nedabiah.
19 Pedaiah had two sons: Zerubbabel and
Shimei. Zerubbabel was the father of
Meshullam, Hananiah, and Shelomith
their sister. 20 He also had five other sons:
Hashubah, Ohel, Berechiah, Hasadiah, and
Jushabhesed. 21 Hananiah's descendants
were Pelatiah, Jeshaiah, Rephaiah, Arnan,
Obadiah, and Shecaniah,[e] 22 the father of
Shemaiah and the grandfather of Hattush,
Igal, Bariah, Neariah, and Shaphat.
23 Neariah was the father of Elioenai,
Hizkiah, and Azrikam. 24 Elioenai was the
father of Hodaviah, Eliashib, Pelaiah,
Akkub, Johanan, Delaiah, and Anani.

The Descendants of Judah

4 Judah was the father of five sons:
Perez, Hezron, Carmi, Hur, and
Shobal. 2 Shobal was the father of Reaiah,
the grandfather of Jahath, and the great-
grandfather of Ahumai and Lahad.
These men all belonged to the Zorathite clan.
3-4 Hur was the oldest son of Caleb and
Ephrath. Some of his descendants settled
the town of Bethlehem. Hur's other descendants included Etam, Penuel, and
Ezer. Etam's sons[f] were Jezreel, Ishma, and
Idbash, and his daughter was Hazzelelponi.
Penuel settled the town of Gedor, and Ezer
settled the town of Hushah.
5 Ashhur, who settled the town of Tekoa,
had two wives: Helah and Naarah. 6 Ashhur and Naarah were the parents of Ahuz-
zam, Hepher, Temeni, and Haahashtari.
7 Ashhur and Helah were the parents of
Zereth, Izhar, and Ethnan.
8 Koz, the father of Anub and Zobebah,
was also the ancestor of the clans of
Aharhel, the son of Harum.
9 Jabez was a man who got his name because of the pain he caused his mother
during birth.[g] But he was still the most respected son in his family. 10 One day he
prayed to Israel's God, "Please bless me
and give me a lot of land. Be with me so I
will be safe from harm."[h] And God did just
what Jabez had asked.
11 Chelub was the brother of Shuhah
and the father of Mehir. Later, Mehir had a
son, Eshton, 12 whose three sons were
Bethrapha, Paseah, and Tehinnah. It was
Tehinnah who settled the town of Nahash.[i]
These men and their families lived in the
town of Recah.
13 Kenaz was the father of Othniel and
Seraiah. Othniel had two sons: Hathath
and Meonothai,[j] 14 who was the father of
Ophrah. Seraiah was the father of Joab,
who settled a place called "Valley of
Crafts"[k] because the people who lived
there were experts in making things.

[z] **3.5** *Bathsheba*: Two ancient translations (see also 2 Samuel 11); Hebrew "Bathshua."
[a] **3.6-8** *Elishua*: Some Hebrew manuscripts and some manuscripts of one ancient translation (see also 2 Samuel 5.14, 15); most Hebrew manuscripts "Elishama." [b] **3.9** *other wives*: This translates a Hebrew word for women who were legally bound to a man, but without the full privileges of a wife. [c] **3.10-15** *Jehoram*: The Hebrew text has "Joram," another spelling of the name.
[d] **3.10-15** *Jehoahaz*: The Hebrew text has "Shallum," probably another name for Jehoahaz (see also 2 Kings 23.30). [e] **3.21** *Shecaniah*: One possible meaning for the difficult Hebrew text of verse 21. [f] **4.3,4** *Etam's sons*: Some manuscripts of one ancient translation; Hebrew "Etam's ancestors." [g] **4.9** *Jabez . . . pain . . . birth*: In Hebrew "Jabez" sounds like "pain." [h] **4.10** *I . . . harm*: Or "keep me from harm, so I won't cause any pain." [i] **4.12** *who settled the town of Nahash*: Or "who was the father of Irnahash." [j] **4.13** *and Meonothai*: Two ancient translations; these words are not in the Hebrew text. [k] **4.14** *Valley of Crafts*: Hebrew "Geharashim."

15 Caleb son of Jephunneh had three
sons: Iru, Elah, and Naam. Elah was the
father of Kenaz.
16 Jehallelel was the father of Ziph,
Ziphah, Tiria, and Asarel.
17-18 Ezrah was the father of Jether,
Mered, Epher, and Jalon. Mered was married to Bithiah the daughter of the king of
Egypt. They had a daughter named Miriam
and two sons: Shammai and Ishbah. It was
Ishbah who settled the town of Eshtemoa.
Mered was also married to a woman from
the tribe of Judah, and their sons were
Jered, Heber, and Jekuthiel. Jered settled the
town of Gedor; Heber settled the town of
Soco; and Jekuthiel settled the town of
Zanoah.
19 A man named Hodiah was married to
the sister of Naham. Hodiah's descendants
included Keilah of the Garmite clan and
Eshtemoa of the Maacathite clan.
20 Shimon was the father of Amnon,
Rinnah, Benhanan, and Tilon.
Ishi was the father of Zoheth and Ben-
zoheth.
21-22 Judah also had a son named Shelah, whose descendants included Jokim
and the people of the town of Cozeba, as
well as Er who settled the town of Lecah
and Laadah who settled the town of
Mareshah. The people who lived in Beth-
Ashbea were also descendants of Shelah,
and they were experts in weaving cloth.
Shelah was the ancestor of Joash and
Saraph, two men who married Moabite
women and then settled near Bethlehem[l]—but these family records are
very old. 23 The members of these clans
were the potters who lived in the towns of
Netaim and Gederah and worked for the
king.

The Descendants of Simeon

24 Simeon had five sons: Nemuel,
Jamin, Jarib, Zerah, and Shaul. 25 The descendants of Shaul included his son Shallum, his grandson Mibsam, and his
great-grandson Mishma. 26 The descendants of Mishma included his son Ham-
muel, his grandson Zaccur, and his great-
grandson Shimei. 27 Shimei had sixteen
sons and six daughters. But his brothers
did not have as many children, so the
Simeon tribe was smaller than the Judah
tribe.
28-31 Before David became king, the people of the Simeon tribe lived in the following towns: Beersheba, Moladah, Hazar-
Shual, Bilhah, Ezem, Tolad, Bethuel,
Hormah, Ziklag, Beth-Marcaboth, Ha-
zarsusim, Bethbiri, and Shaaraim. 32 They
also lived in the five villages of Etam, Ain,
Rimmon, Tochen, and Ashan, 33 as well as
in the nearby villages as far as the town of
Baal. These are the places where Simeon's
descendants had settled, according to their
own family records.
34-38 As their families and clans became
larger, the people of Simeon had the following leaders: Meshobab, Jamlech, Joshah
son of Amaziah, Joel, Jehu,[m] Elioenai,
Jaakobah, Jeshohaiah, Asaiah, Adiel,
Jesimiel, Benaiah, and Ziza.[n] 39 When
the people needed more pastureland for
their flocks and herds, they looked as far
as the eastern side of the valley where
the town of Gerar[o] is located, 40 and they
found a lot of good pastureland that was
quiet and undisturbed. This had once belonged to the Hamites, 41 but when Hezekiah was king of Judah, the descendants of
Simeon attacked and forced the Hamites and
Meunites off the land, then settled there.
42 Some time later, five hundred
men from the Simeon tribe went into
Edom[p] under the command of Pelatiah,
Neariah, Rephaiah, and Uzziel the
sons of Ishi. 43 They killed the last of
the Amalekites and lived there from
then on.

[l] **4.21,22** *who married Moabite women and then settled near Bethlehem*: Or "who ruled in Moab and Jashubi-Lahem" or "who ruled in Moab but then returned to Lahem." [m] **4.34-38** *Jehu*: Hebrew "Jehu son of Joshibiah son of Seraiah son of Asiel." [n] **4.34-38** *Ziza*: Hebrew "Ziza son of Shiphi son of Allon son of Jedaiah son of Shimri son of Shemaiah." [o] **4.39** *Gerar*: One ancient translation; Hebrew "Gedor." [p] **4.42** *Edom*: The Hebrew text has "Mount Seir," a common name for the nation of Edom.

4.28-33 Js 19.2-8.

The Descendants of Reuben

5 Reuben was the oldest son of Jacob,[q]
but he lost his rights as the first-born
son[r] because he slept with one of his
father's wives.[s] The honor of the first-born
son was then given to Joseph, 2 even
though it was the Judah tribe that became
the most powerful and produced a leader.
3 Reuben had four sons: Hanoch, Pallu,
Hezron, and Carmi.
4-6 The descendants of Joel included
Shemaiah, Gog, Shimei, Micah, Reaiah,
Baal, and Beerah, a leader of the Reuben
tribe. Later, King Tiglath Pileser of Assyria
took Beerah away as prisoner.
7-8 The family records also include Jeiel,
who was a clan leader, Zechariah, and Bela
son of Azaz and grandson of Shema of the
Joel clan. They lived in the territory around
the town of Aroer, as far north as Nebo and
Baal-Meon, 9 and as far east as the desert
just west of the Euphrates River. They
needed this much land because they owned
too many cattle to keep them all in Gilead.
10 When Saul was king, the Reuben
tribe attacked and defeated the Hagrites,
then took over their land east of Gilead.

The Descendants of Gad

11 The tribe of Gad lived in the region of
Bashan, north of the Reuben tribe. Gad's
territory extended all the way to the town
of Salecah. 12 Some of the clan leaders
were Joel, Shapham, Janai, and Shaphat.
13 Their relatives included Michael, Meshullam, Sheba, Jorai, Jacan, Zia, and Eber.
14 They were all descendants of Abihail,
whose family line went back through Huri,
Jaroah, Gilead, Michael, Jeshishai, Jahdo,
and Buz. 15 Ahi, the son of Abdiel and the
grandson of Guni, was the leader of their
clan.
16 The people of Gad lived in the towns
in the regions of Bashan and Gilead, as well
as in the pastureland of Sharon. 17 Their
family records were written when Jotham was
king of Judah and Jeroboam was king of
Israel.
18 The tribes of Reuben, Gad, and East
Manasseh had 44,760 soldiers trained to
fight in battle with shields, swords, bows,
and arrows. 19 They fought against the
Hagrites and the tribes of Jetur, Naphish,
and Nodab. 20 Whenever these soldiers
went to war against their enemies, they
prayed to God and trusted him to help.
That's why the tribes of Reuben, Gad, and
East Manasseh defeated the Hagrites and
their allies. 21 These Israelite tribes captured fifty thousand camels, two hundred
fifty thousand sheep, two thousand donkeys, and one hundred thousand people.
22 Many of the Hagrites died in battle, because God was fighting this battle against
them. The tribes of Reuben, Gad, and East
Manasseh lived in that territory until they
were taken as prisoners to Assyria.[t]

The Tribe of East Manasseh

23 East Manasseh was a large tribe, so
its people settled in the northern region of
Bashan, as far north as Baal-Hermon,[u]
Senir, and Mount Hermon. 24 Epher, Ishi,
Eliel, Azriel, Jeremiah, Hodaviah, and
Jahdiel were their clan leaders; they were
well-known leaders and brave soldiers.

The Tribes of Reuben, Gad, and East Manasseh Are Defeated

25 The people of the tribes of Reuben,
Gad, and East Manasseh were unfaithful to
the God their ancestors had worshiped,
and they started worshiping the gods of the
nations that God had forced out of Canaan.
26 So God sent King Tiglath Pileser[v] of Assyria to attack these Israelite tribes. The
king led them away as prisoners to Assyria,
and from then on, he forced them to live
in Halah, Habor, Hara, and near the Gozan
River.

[q] **5.1** *Jacob*: See the note at 1.34. [r] **5.1** *rights as the first-born son*: The first-born son inherited the largest amount of property, as well as the leadership of the family. [s] **5.1** *wives*: See Genesis 35.22; 49.3, 4. [t] **5.22** *they were taken as prisoners to Assyria*: See 2 Kings 15.29; 17.5-23. [u] **5.23** *Baal-Hermon*: The location of this place is unknown. [v] **5.26** *King Tiglath Pileser*: The Hebrew text also includes "King Pul," another name by which he was known.

5.1 Gn 35.22; 49.3, 4. **5.2** Gn 49.8-10. **5.4-6** 2 K 15.29. **5.26** **a** 2 K 15.19; **b** 2 K 15.29; **c** 2 K 17.6.

The Descendants of Levi

6 Levi was the father of Gershon, Kohath, and Merari.

2 Kohath was the father of Amram, Izhar, Hebron, and Uzziel. 3 Amram was the father of Aaron, Moses, and Miriam.

Aaron had four sons: Nadab, Abihu, Eleazar, and Ithamar.

4-14 Eleazar's descendants included Phinehas, Abishua, Bukki, Uzzi, Zerahiah, Meraioth, Amariah, Ahitub, Zadok, Ahimaaz, Azariah, Johanan, Azariah the priest who served in the temple built by King Solomon, Amariah, Ahitub, Zadok, Shallum, Hilkiah, Azariah, Seraiah, and Jehozadak. 15 King Nebuchadnezzar of Babylonia took Jehozadak to Babylon as prisoner when the LORD let the people of Judah and Jerusalem be dragged from their land.[w]

16 Levi's three sons had sons of their own. 17 Gershon was the father of Libni and Shimei. 18 Kohath was the father of Amram, Izhar, Hebron, and Uzziel. 19 Merari was the father of Mahli and Mushi. These descendants of Levi each became leaders of their own clans.

20-21 Gershon's descendants included Libni, Jahath, Zimmah, Joah, Iddo, Zerah, and Jeatherai.

22-24 Kohath's descendants included Amminadab, Korah, Assir, Elkanah, Ebiasaph, Assir, Tahath, Uriel, Uzziah, and Shaul.

25 Elkanah was the father of Amasai and Ahimoth. 26-27 Ahimoth's descendants included Elkanah, Zophai, Nahath, Eliab, Jeroham, and Elkanah.

28 Samuel was the father of Joel[x] and Abijah, born in that order.

29-30 Merari's descendants included Mahli, Libni, Shimei, Uzzah, Shimea, Haggiah, and Asaiah.

The Temple Musicians

31 After King David had the sacred chest moved to Jerusalem, he appointed musicians from the Levi tribe to be in charge of the music at the place of worship. 32 These musicians served at the sacred tent and later at the LORD's temple that King Solomon built.

33-38 Here is a list of these musicians and their family lines:

Heman from the Kohathite clan was the director. His ancestors went all the way back to Jacob and included Joel, Samuel, Elkanah, Jeroham, Eliel, Toah, Zuph, Elkanah, Mahath, Amasai, Elkanah, Joel, Azariah, Zephaniah, Tahath, Assir, Ebiasaph, Korah, Izhar, Kohath, Levi.

39-43 Asaph was Heman's relative and served as his assistant. Asaph's ancestors included Berechiah, Shimea, Michael, Baaseiah, Malchijah, Ethni, Zerah, Adaiah, Ethan, Zimmah, Shimei, Jahath, Gershon, and Levi.

44-47 Ethan was also Heman's relative and served as his assistant. Ethan belonged to the Merari clan, and his ancestors included Kishi, Abdi, Malluch, Hashabiah, Amaziah, Hilkiah, Amzi, Bani, Shemer, Mahli, Mushi, Merari, and Levi.

48 The rest of the Levites were appointed to work at the sacred tent.

The Descendants of Aaron

49 Only Aaron and his descendants were allowed to offer sacrifices and incense on the two altars at the sacred tent.[y] They were in charge of the most holy place and the ceremonies to forgive sins, just as God's servant Moses had commanded.

50-53 Aaron's descendants included his son Eleazar, Phinehas, Abishua, Bukki, Uzzi, Zerahiah, Meraioth, Amariah, Ahitub, Zadok, and Ahimaaz.

The Towns for the Levites

(Joshua 21.1-42)

54 Aaron's descendants belonged to the Levite clan of Kohath, and they were the first group chosen to receive towns to live in. 55 They received the town of Hebron in the territory of Judah and the pastureland around it. 56 But the farmland and villages around Hebron were given to Caleb son of

[w]6.15 *King Nebuchadnezzar . . . dragged from their land*: See 2 Kings 24.8-17; 25.1-21.
[x]6.28 *Joel*: Two ancient translations (see also verse 33 and 1 Samuel 8.1, 2); this name is not in the Hebrew text. [y]6.49 *the two altars at the sacred tent*: The Hebrew text mentions two different altars: A large altar for offering sacrifices, and a smaller altar for offering incense.
6.16-19 Ex 6.16-19.

Jephunneh. 57-59 So Aaron's descendants
received the following Safe Towns[z] and the
pastureland around them: Hebron, Libnah,
Jattir, Eshtemoa, Hilen, Debir, Ashan, and
Beth-Shemesh. 60 From the Benjamin tribe
they were given the towns of Geba,
Alemeth, and Anathoth and the pastureland around them. Thirteen towns were
given to Aaron's descendants.
61 The rest of the Levite clan of Kohath
received ten towns from West Manasseh.
62 The Levite clan of Gershon received
thirteen towns from the tribes of Issachar,
Asher, Naphtali, and East Manasseh in
Bashan.
63 The Levite clan of Merari received
twelve towns from the tribes of Reuben,
Gad, and Zebulun.
64 So the people of Israel gave the
Levites towns to live in and the pastureland
around them. 65 All the towns were chosen
with the LORD's help,[a] including those
towns from the tribes of Judah, Simeon,
and Benjamin.
66 Some of the families of the Kohath
clan received their towns from the tribe of
Ephraim. 67-69 These families received the
following Safe Towns and the pastureland
around them: Shechem in the hill country,
Gezer, Jokmeam, Beth-Horon, Aijalon, and
Gath-Rimmon. 70 And from West Manasseh
they received Aner and Bileam, together
with their pastureland.
71 The Gershonite clan received two
towns from the tribe of East Manasseh:
Golan in Bashan and Ashtaroth, including
the pastureland around them. 72-73 The
Gershonites also received four towns from
the tribe of Issachar: Kedesh, Daberath,
Ramoth, and Anem, including the pastureland around them. 74-75 The Gershonites
received four towns from the tribe of
Asher: Mashal, Abdon, Hukok, and Rehob,
including the pastureland around them.
76 Finally, the Gershonites received three
towns from the tribe of Naphtali: Kedesh in
Galilee, Hammon, and Kiriathaim, including the pastureland around them.
77 The rest of the Merari clan received
the towns of Rimmono and Tabor and their
pastureland from the tribe of Zebulun.
78-79 They also received four towns east of
the Jordan River from the tribe of Reuben:
Bezer in the flatlands, Jahzah, Kedemoth,
and Mephaath, including the pastures
around them. 80-81 And from the tribe of
Gad the Merarites received the towns of
Ramoth in Gilead, Mahanaim, Heshbon,
and Jazer, including the pastureland
around them.

The Descendants of Issachar

7 Issachar was the father of four sons:
Tola, Puah, Jashub, and Shimron.
2 Tola was the father of Uzzi, Rephaiah,
Jeriel, Jahmai, Ibsam, and Shemuel, who
were all brave soldiers and family leaders in
their clan. There were 22,600 people in Tola's
family by the time David became king.
3 Uzzi was the father of Izrahiah and
the grandfather of Michael, Obadiah, Joel,
and Isshiah, who were also family leaders.
4 Their families were so large that they had
36,000 soldiers in their clans. 5 In fact, according to family records, the tribe of Issachar had a total of 87,000 warriors.

The Descendants of Benjamin and Dan

6 Benjamin was the father of three sons:
Bela, Becher, and Jediael.
7 Bela was the father of Ezbon, Uzzi,
Uzziel, Jerimoth, and Iri. They were all
brave soldiers and family leaders in their
father's clan. The number of soldiers in
their clan was 22,034.
8 Becher was the father of Zemirah,
Joash, Eliezer, Elioenai, Omri, Jeremoth,
Abijah, Anathoth, and Alemeth. 9 The official family records listed 20,200 soldiers in
the families of this clan, as well as their
family leaders.
10 Jediael was the father of Bilhan and
the grandfather of Jeush, Benjamin, Ehud,
Chenaanah, Zethan, Tarshish, and Ahisha-
har. 11 They were family leaders in their

[z]**6.57-59** *Safe Towns*: These were special towns set aside where a person who had accidentally killed someone could run for protection from the victim's relatives (see Numbers 35.9-15; Deuteronomy 19.1-13; Joshua 20.1-9). [a]**6.65** *with the LORD's help*: The Hebrew text has "by lot." Pieces of wood or stone (called "lots") were used to find out what God wanted his people to do.

clan, which had 17,200 soldiers prepared
to fight in battle. 12 Ir was the father of
Shuppim and Huppim, who also belonged
to this clan.
Dan[b] was the father of Hushim.

The Descendants of Naphtali

13 Naphtali's mother was Bilhah,[c] and
he was the father of Jahziel, Guni, Jezer,
and Shallum.

The Descendants of Manasseh

14 Manasseh and his Syrian wife[d] were
the parents of Asriel and Machir the father
of Gilead. 15 Machir found a wife for Huppim and one for Shuppim. Machir had a
sister named Maacah.
Zelophehad was also a descendant of
Manasseh, and he had five daughters.[e]
16 Machir and his wife Maacah were the
parents of Peresh and Sheresh. Peresh was
the father of Ulam and Rekem. 17 Ulam
was the father of Bedan. These were all descendants of Gilead, the son of Machir and
the grandson of Manasseh.
18 Gilead's sister Hammolecheth was
the mother of Ishhod, Abiezer, and Mahlah.
19 Shemida, another descendant of
Manasseh, was the father of Ahian, Shechem, Likhi, and Aniam.

The Descendants of Ephraim

20 Ephraim was the father of Shuthelah
and the ancestor of Bered, Tahath, Ele-
adah, Tahath, 21 Zabad, and Shuthelah.
Ephraim had two other sons, Ezer and
Elead. But they were killed when they tried
to steal livestock from the people who lived
in the territory of Gath. 22 Ephraim
mourned for his sons a long time, and his
relatives came to comfort him. 23 Some
time later his wife gave birth to another
son, and Ephraim named him Beriah, because he was born during a time of misery.[f]
24 Ephraim's daughter was Sheerah.
She built the towns of Lower Beth-Horon,
Upper Beth-Horon, and Uzzen-Sheerah.
25 Ephraim also had a son named
Rephah, and his descendants included
Resheph, Telah, Tahan, 26 Ladan, Ammihud, Elishama, 27 Nun, and Joshua.
28 The descendants of Ephraim took
over the territory as far south as Bethel, as
far east as Naaran, and as far west as
Gezer. Their territory included all the villages around these towns, as well as Shechem, Ayyah, and the nearby villages.
29 The descendants of Manasseh settled
in the territory that included Beth-Shan,
Taanach, Megiddo, Dor, and the nearby
villages.
The descendants of Joseph[g] lived in
these towns and villages.

The Descendants of Asher

30 Asher had four sons, Imnah, Ishvah,
Ishvi, and Beriah, and one daughter, Serah.
31 Beriah was the father of Heber and
Malchiel the father of Birzaith. 32 Heber
was the father of three sons, Japhlet,
Shomer, and Hotham, and one daughter,
Shua. 33 Japhlet was the father of Pasach,
Bimhal, and Ashvath. 34 Shomer was the
father of Ahi, Rohgah, Hubbah, and Aram.
35 And Japhlet's brother Hotham[h] was the
father of Zophah, Imna, Shelesh, and
Amal. 36 Zophah was the father of Suah,
Harnepher, Shual, Beri, Imrah, 37 Bezer,
Hod, Shamma, Shilshah, Ithran, and
Beera. 38 Jether was the father of Jephunneh, Pispa, and Ara.
39 Ulla was the father of Arah, Hanniel,
and Rizia.
40 These were the descendants of Asher,
and they were all respected family leaders
and brave soldiers. The tribe of Asher had a
total of 26,000 soldiers.

More Descendants of Benjamin

8 Benjamin had five sons, who were
born in the following order: Bela, Ashbel, Aharah, 2 Nohah, and Rapha. 3 Bela

[b]**7.12** *Dan*: The Hebrew text has "Aher," which can mean "someone else" (see Genesis 46.23-25). [c]**7.13** *Bilhah*: One of Jacob's wives and the mother of Dan and Naphtali (see Genesis 46.23-25). [d]**7.14** *wife*: See the note at 3.9. [e]**7.15** *Zelophehad . . . daughters*: One possible meaning for the difficult Hebrew text (see also Numbers 26.28-33). [f]**7.23** *Beriah . . . misery*: In Hebrew "Beriah" sounds like "in misery." [g]**7.29** *Joseph*: Hebrew "Joseph son of Israel." [h]**7.35** *Hotham*: The Hebrew text has "Helem," another spelling of the name.

was the father of Addar, Gera, Abihud, 4 Abishua, Naaman, Ahoah, 5 Gera, Shephuphan, and Huram.

6-7 Ehud was the father of Naaman, Ahijah, and Gera. They were clan leaders in the town of Geba, but were later forced to move to the town of Manahath, and Gera led the way. He had two sons: Uzza and Ahihud.

8-11 Shaharaim and his wife Hushim had two sons: Abitub and Elpaal. But Shaharaim later divorced her and his other wife, Baara. Then he moved to the country of Moab and married Hodesh, and they had seven sons: Jobab, Zibia, Mesha, Malcam, Jeuz, Sachia, and Mirmah. They were all family leaders in his clan. 12 Elpaal was the father of Eber, Misham, and Shemed, who settled the towns of Ono and Lod, as well as the nearby villages.

13 Beriah and Shema were family leaders in the clan that lived in the town of Aijalon and that forced out the people of Gath. 14-16 Beriah's descendants included Ahio, Shashak, Jeremoth, Zebadiah, Arad, Eder, Michael, Ishpah, and Joha. 17-18 Elpaal's descendants included Zebadiah, Meshullam, Hizki, Heber, Ishmerai, Izliah, and Jobab. 19-21 Shimei's descendants included Jakim, Zichri, Zabdi, Elienai, Zillethai, Eliel, Adaiah, Beraiah, and Shimrath. 22-25 Shashak's descendants included Ishpan, Eber, Eliel, Abdon, Zichri, Hanan, Hananiah, Elam, Anthothijah, Iphdeiah, and Penuel. 26-27 Jeroham's descendants included Shamsherai, Shehariah, Athaliah, Jaareshiah, Elijah, and Zichri. 28 These were the family leaders in their ancestor's clan, and they and their descendants lived in Jerusalem.

29 Jeiel[i] settled the town of Gibeon. He and his wife Maacah lived there 30 along with their sons, who were born in the following order: Abdon, Zur, Kish, Baal, Ner,[j] Nadab, 31 Gedor, Ahio, Zecher, 32 and Mikloth the father of Shimeah. Some of them went to live in Jerusalem near their relatives.

The Descendants of King Saul

33 Ner was the father of Kish and the grandfather of King Saul.

Saul had four sons: Jonathan, Malchishua, Abinadab, and Eshbaal.[k] 34 Jonathan was the father of Meribbaal,[l] the grandfather of Micah, 35 and the great-grandfather of Pithon, Melech, Tarea, and Ahaz. 36 Saul's other descendants were Jehoaddah, Alemeth, Azmaveth, Zimri, Moza, 37 Binea, Raphah, Eleasah, Azel, 38 as well as Azel's six sons: Azrikam, Bocheru, Ishmael, Sheariah, Obadiah, and Hanan. 39 Azel's brother Eshek was the father of Ulam, Jeush, and Eliphelet. 40 Ulam's sons were brave soldiers who were experts at using a bow and arrows. They had a total of one hundred fifty children and grandchildren.

All of these belonged to the tribe of Benjamin.

The People Who Returned from Babylonia and Settled in Jerusalem

9 Everyone in Israel was listed in the official family records that were included in the history of Israel's kings.

The people of Judah were taken to Babylonia as prisoners because they sinned against the LORD. 2 And the first people to return to their towns included priests, Levites, temple workers, and other Israelites. 3 People from the tribes of Judah, Benjamin, Ephraim, and Manasseh settled in Jerusalem.

4-6 There were six hundred ninety people from the Judah tribe who settled in Jerusalem. They were all descendants of Judah's three sons: Perez, Shelah, and Zerah. Their leaders were Uthai, Asaiah, and Jeuel. Uthai was the son of Ammihud and a descendant of Omri, Imri, Bani, and Perez. Asaiah was a descendant of Shelah; Jeuel was a descendant of Zerah.

7-9 There were also nine hundred fifty-six family leaders from the Benjamin tribe

[i] **8.29** *Jeiel*: One ancient translation and 9.35; the Hebrew text does not have this name.
[j] **8.30** *Ner*: One ancient translation and 9.36; the Hebrew text does not have this name.
[k] **8.33** *Eshbaal*: Also called "Ishbosheth" (see 2 Samuel 2.8 and the note there).
[l] **8.34** *Meribbaal*: Also called "Mephibosheth" (see 2 Samuel 4.4 and the note there).
9.2,3 Ezra 2.21-35; Ne 7.73.

who settled in Jerusalem. They included:
Sallu son of Meshullam, grandson of Hodaviah, and great-grandson of Hassenuah;
Ibneiah son of Jeroham; Elah son of Uzzi
and grandson of Michri; Meshullam son of
Shephatiah, grandson of Reuel, and great-
grandson of Ibnijah.

The Priests Who Settled in Jerusalem

10-12 Here is a list of priests who settled
in Jerusalem: Jedaiah; Jehoiarib; Jachin;
Azariah, who was a temple official, and
whose ancestors included Hilkiah, Meshullam, Zadok, Meraioth, and Ahitub; Adaiah
son of Jeroham, whose ancestors included
Pashhur and Malchijah; Maasai son of
Adiel, whose ancestors included Jahzerah,
Meshullam, Meshillemith, and Immer.
13 There was a total of 1,760 priests, all
of them family leaders in their clan and
trained in the work at the temple.

The Levites Who Settled in Jerusalem

14-16 Here is a list of Levites who settled
in Jerusalem: Shemaiah from the Merari
clan, whose ancestors included Hasshub,
Azrikam, and Hashabiah; Bakbakkar;
Heresh; Galal; Mattaniah son of Mica,
whose ancestors included Zichri and
Asaph; Obadiah son of Shemaiah, whose
ancestors included Galal and Jeduthun;
Berechiah son of Asa and grandson of Elkanah, who had lived in the villages near the
town of Netophah.

The Temple Guards Who Settled in Jerusalem

17 Shallum, Akkub, Talmon, Ahiman,
and their relatives were the guards at the
temple gates. Shallum was the leader of
this clan, 18 and for a long time they had
been the guards at the King's Gate on the
east side of the city. Before that, their ancestors guarded the entrance to the Levite
camp.
19 Shallum son of Kore,[m] as well as the
other men in the Korahite clan, guarded
the entrance to the temple, just as their ancestors had guarded the entrance to the sacred tent. 20 Phinehas son of Eleazar had
supervised their work because the LORD
was with him.
21 Zechariah son of Meshelemiah was
also one of the guards at the temple.
22 There was a total of two hundred
twelve guards, all of them listed in the family records in their towns. Their ancestors
had been chosen by King David and by
Samuel the prophet to be responsible for
this work, 23 and now they guarded the
temple gates.
24 There was one full-time guard appointed to each of the four sides of the
temple. 25 Their assistants lived in the villages outside the city, and every seven days
a group of them would come into the city
and take their turn at guard duty. 26 The
four full-time guards were Levites, and
they supervised the other guards and were
responsible for the rooms in the temple
and the supplies kept there. 27 They
guarded the temple day and night and
opened its doors every morning.

The Duties of the Levites

28 Some of the Levites were responsible
for the equipment used in worship at the
temple, and they had to count everything
before and after it was used. 29 Others were
responsible for the temple furnishings and
its sacred objects, as well as the flour, wine,
olive oil, incense, and spices. 30 But only
the priests could mix the spices. 31 Mattithiah, Shallum's oldest son, was a member of the Levite clan of Korah, and he was
in charge of baking the bread used for offerings.[n] 32 The Levites from the Kohath
clan were in charge of baking the sacred
loaves of bread for each Sabbath.[o]
33 The Levite family leaders who were
the musicians also lived at the temple.
They had no other responsibilities, because
they were on duty day and night.
34 All of these men were family leaders
in the Levi tribe and were listed that way
in their family records. They lived in
Jerusalem.

[m] **9.19** *Shallum son of Kore*: Hebrew "Shallum son of Kore, grandson of Ebiasaph, and great-grandson of Korah." [n] **9.31** *the bread used for offerings*: See Leviticus 2.4-7. [o] **9.32** *the sacred loaves of bread for each Sabbath*: See Leviticus 24.5-9.

King Saul's Family
(1 Chronicles 8.29-38)

35 Jeiel had settled the town of Gibeon, where he and his wife Maacah lived. 36 They had ten sons, who were born in the following order: Abdon, Zur, Kish, Baal, Ner, Nadab, 37 Gedor, Ahio, Zechariah, and Mikloth 38 the father of Shimeam. Some of them went to live in Jerusalem near their relatives.

39 Ner was the father of Kish and the grandfather of King Saul.

Saul had four sons: Jonathan, Malchishua, Abinadab, and Eshbaal.[p] 40-41 Jonathan was the father of Meribbaal,[q] the grandfather of Micah, and the great-grandfather of Pithon, Melech, Tahrea, and Ahaz.[r] 42-44 The descendants of Ahaz included Jarah, Alemeth, Azmaveth, Zimri, Moza, Binea, Rephaiah, Eleasah, and Azel and his six sons: Azrikam, Bocheru, Ishmael, Sheariah, Obadiah, and Hanan.

King Saul and His Sons Die
(1 Samuel 31.1-13)

10 The Philistines fought against Israel in a battle at Mount Gilboa. Israel's soldiers ran from the Philistines, and many of them were killed. 2 The Philistines closed in on Saul and his sons and killed three of them: Jonathan, Abinadab, and Malchishua. 3 The fighting was fierce around Saul, and he was badly wounded by enemy arrows.

4 Saul told the soldier who carried his weapons, "Kill me with your sword! I don't want those godless Philistines to torture and make fun of me."

But the soldier was afraid to kill him. Then Saul stuck himself in the stomach with his own sword and fell on the blade. 5 When the soldier realized that Saul was dead, he killed himself in the same way.

6 Saul, three of his sons, and all his male relatives were dead. 7 The Israelites who lived in Jezreel Valley[s] learned that their army had run away and that Saul and his sons were dead. They ran away too, and the Philistines moved into the towns the Israelites left behind.

8 The next day the Philistines came back to the battlefield to carry away the weapons of the dead Israelite soldiers. When they found the bodies of Saul and his sons on Mount Gilboa, 9 they took Saul's weapons, pulled off his armor, and cut off his head. Then they sent messengers everywhere in Philistia to spread the news among their people and to thank the idols of their gods. 10 They put Saul's armor in the temple of their gods and hung his head in the temple of their god Dagon.

11 When the people who lived in Jabesh in Gilead heard what the Philistines had done to Saul, 12 some brave men went to get his body and the bodies of his three sons. The men brought the bodies back to Jabesh, where they buried them under an oak tree. Then for seven days, they went without eating to show their sorrow.

13 Saul died because he was unfaithful and disobeyed the LORD. He even asked advice from a woman who talked to spirits of the dead, 14 instead of asking the LORD. So the LORD had Saul killed and gave his kingdom to David, the son of Jesse.

David Becomes King of Israel
(2 Samuel 5.1-3)

11 Israel's leaders met with David at Hebron and said, "We are your relatives, 2 and we know that you have led our army into battle, even when Saul was still our king. The LORD God has promised that you would rule our country and take care of us like a shepherd. 3 So we have come to crown you king of Israel."

David made an agreement with the leaders and asked the LORD to be their witness. Then the leaders poured olive oil on David's head to show that he was now king of Israel. This happened just as the LORD's prophet Samuel had said.

[p]**9.39** *Eshbaal*: See the note at 8.33. [q]**9.40,41** *Meribbaal*: See the note at 8.34.
[r]**9.40,41** *and Ahaz*: Most ancient translations and 8.35; the Hebrew text does not have this name.
[s]**10.7** *Jezreel Valley*: Hebrew "the valley."
10.13 **a** 1 S 13.8-14; 15.1-24; **b** Lv 19.31; 20.6; 1 S 28.7, 8.

David Captures Jerusalem
(2 Samuel 5.6-10)

4 Jerusalem was called Jebus at the
time, and David led Israel's army to attack
the town. 5 The Jebusites said, "You won't
be able to get in here!" But David captured
the fortress of Mount Zion, which is now
called the City of David.
6 David had told his troops, "The first
soldier to kill a Jebusite will become my army
commander." And since Joab son of Zeruiah
attacked first, he became commander.
7 Later, David moved to the fortress—
that's why it's called the City of David. 8 He
had the city rebuilt, starting at the landfill
on the east side.[t] Meanwhile, Joab supervised the repairs to the rest of the city.
9 David became a great and strong ruler,
because the LORD All-Powerful was on his
side.

The Three Warriors
(2 Samuel 23.8-17)

10 The LORD had promised that David
would become king, and so everyone in Israel gave David their support. Certain warriors also helped keep his kingdom strong.
11 The first of these warriors was
Jashobeam the son of Hachmoni, the
leader of the Three Warriors.[u] In one battle
he killed three hundred men with his
spear.
12 Another one of the Three Warriors
was Eleazar son of Dodo the Ahohite.
13 During a battle against the Philistines
at Pas-Dammim, all the Israelite soldiers
ran away, 14 except Eleazar, who stayed
with David. They took their positions in a
nearby barley field and defeated the
Philistines! The LORD gave Israel a great
victory that day.
15 One time the Three Warriors[v] went to
meet David among the rocks at Adullam
Cave. The Philistine army had set up camp
in Rephaim Valley 16 and had taken over
Bethlehem. David was in a fortress, 17 and
he said, "I'm very thirsty. I wish I had a
drink of water from the well by the gate to
Bethlehem."
18 The Three Warriors sneaked through
the Philistine camp and got some water
from the well near Bethlehem's gate. They
took it back to David, but he refused to
drink it. Instead, he poured out the water
as a sacrifice to the LORD 19 and said,
"Drinking this water would be like drinking
the blood of these men who risked their
lives to get it for me."
The Three Warriors did these brave deeds.

The Thirty Warriors
(2 Samuel 23.18-39)

20 Joab's brother Abishai was the leader
of the Thirty Warriors,[w] and in one battle
he killed three hundred men with his
spear. He was just as famous as the Three
Warriors 21 and was more famous than the
rest of the Thirty Warriors. He was their
commander, but he never became one of
the Three Warriors.[x]
22 Benaiah the son of Jehoiada was a
brave man from Kabzeel who did some
amazing things. One time he killed two of
Moab's best fighters, and one snowy day he
went into a pit and killed a lion. 23 Another
time he killed an Egyptian who was seven
and a half feet tall and was armed with
a spear. Benaiah only had a club, so he
grabbed the spear from the Egyptian and
killed him with it. 24 Benaiah did things
like that; he was just as brave as the Three
Warriors, 25 even though he never became
one of them. And he was certainly as famous as the rest of the Thirty Warriors. So

[t] **11.8** *the landfill on the east side*: The Hebrew text has "the Millo," which probably refers to a landfill to strengthen and extend the hill where the city was built. [u] **11.11** *the Three Warriors*: One ancient translation and 2 Samuel 23.8; Hebrew "the Thirty Warriors." The "Three Warriors" was the most honored group of warriors and may have been part of the "Thirty Warriors." "Three" and "thirty" are spelled almost the same in Hebrew, so there is some confusion in the manuscripts as to which group is being talked about in some places in the following lists. [v] **11.15** *the Three Warriors*: Hebrew "three of the thirty most important warriors." [w] **11.20** *the Thirty Warriors*: One ancient translation; Hebrew "the Three Warriors." The "Thirty Warriors" was the second most honored group of warriors and may have also been officers in the army. [x] **11.20,21** *Warriors*: One possible meaning for the difficult Hebrew text of these verses.

11.4 Js 15.63; Jg 1.21.

David made him the leader of his own bodyguard.

26-47 Here is a list of the other famous warriors:

Asahel the brother of Joab; Elhanan the son of Dodo from Bethlehem; Shammoth from Haror; Helez from Pelon; Ira the son of Ikkesh from Tekoa; Abiezer from Anathoth; Sibbecai the Hushathite; Ilai[y] the Ahohite; Maharai from Netophah; Heled the son of Baanah from Netophah; Ithai the son of Ribai from Gibeah in Benjamin; Benaiah from Pirathon; Hurai[z] from near the streams on Mount Gaash; Abiel from Arbah; Azmaveth from Baharum; Eliahba from Shaalbon; Hashem[a] the Gizonite; Jonathan the son of Shagee from Harar; Ahiam the son of Sachar the Hararite; Eliphal the son of Ur; Hepher from Mecherah; Ahijah from Pelon; Hezro from Carmel; Naarai the son of Ezbai; Joel the brother of Nathan; Mibhar the son of Hagri; Zelek from Ammon; Naharai from Beeroth who carried Joab's weapons; Ira the Ithrite; Gareb the Ithrite; Uriah the Hittite; Zabad the son of Ahlai; Adina the son of Shiza, a leader in the Reuben tribe, and thirty of his soldiers; Hanan the son of Maacah; Joshaphat from Mithan; Uzzia from Ashterah; Shama and Jeiel the sons of Hotham from Aroer; Jediael and Joha the sons of Shimri from Tiz; Eliel from Mahavah; Jeribai and Joshaviah the sons of Elnaam; Ithmah from Moab; Eliel, Obed, and Jaasiel from Mezobah.

David's Men at Ziklag

12 Some time earlier, David had gone to live in the town of Ziklag to escape from King Saul. While David was there, several brave warriors joined him to help fight his battles.[b]

Warriors from the Benjamin tribe

2 Several of these warriors were from King Saul's own tribe of Benjamin. They were experts at using a bow and arrows, and they could shoot an arrow or sling a stone with either hand. 3-7 Their leaders were Ahiezer and Joash, the sons of Shemaah from Gibeah. Here is a list of those men from Benjamin: Jeziel and Pelet the sons of Azmaveth; Beracah and Jehu from Anathoth; Ishmaiah from Gibeon, who was the leader of the Thirty Warriors; Jeremiah, Jahaziel, Johanan, and Jozabad from Gederah; Eluzai, Jerimoth, Bealiah, Shemariah, and Shephatiah from Haruph; Elkanah, Isshiah, Azarel, Joezer, and Jashobeam from the Korah clan; Joelah and Zebadiah the sons of Jeroham from Gedor.

Warriors from the Gad tribe

8 Men from the tribe of Gad also joined David at his fortress in the desert and served as his warriors. They were also brave soldiers—fierce as lions and quick as gazelles. They were always prepared to fight with shields and spears. 9-13 There were eleven of them, ranked in the following order: Ezer the leader, then Obadiah, Eliab, Mishmannah, Jeremiah, Attai, Eliel, Johanan, Elzabad, Jeremiah, and Machbannai.

14 All these men were army officers; some were high-ranking officers over a thousand troops, and others were officers over a hundred troops. 15 Earlier, they had crossed the Jordan River when it flooded, and they chased out the people who lived in the valleys on each side of the river.

Warriors from the Benjamin and Judah tribes

16 One time a group of men from the tribes of Benjamin and Judah went to the fortress where David was staying. 17 David met them outside and said, "If you are coming as friends to fight on my side, then stay and join us. But if you try to turn me over to my enemies, the God our ancestors worshiped will punish you, because I have done nothing wrong."

[y] **11.26-47** *Ilai*: Or "Zalmon" (see 2 Samuel 23.24-39). [z] **11.26-47** *Hurai*: Or "Hiddai" (see 2 Samuel 23.24-39). [a] **11.26-47** *Hashem*: One ancient translation; Hebrew "the sons of Hashem." [b] **12.1** *David had gone . . . battles*: Ziklag was the Philistine town that King Achish of Gath gave David in return for his loyalty (see 1 Samuel 27.6). This happened during the time that David was living as an outlaw, so the events in this chapter actually took place before chapter 11 when David became king of Israel.

18 Amasai, who later became the leader
of the Thirty Warriors, was one of these
men who went to David. God's Spirit took
control of him, and he said, "We will join
you, David son of Jesse! You and your followers will always be successful, because
God fights on your side."

So David agreed to let them stay, and he
even put them in charge of his soldiers who
raided enemy villages.

Warriors from the Manasseh tribe

19 Some of the warriors who joined
David were from the tribe of Manasseh.
They had earlier gone with David when he
agreed to fight on the side of the Philistines
against King Saul. But as soon as the
Philistine rulers realized that David might
turn against them and rejoin Saul, they
sent David away to the town of Ziklag.
20 That's when the following men from
Manasseh joined him: Adnah, Jozabad, Jediael, Michael, Jozabad, Elihu, and Zillethai. They had all been commanders in
Saul's army 21 and brave soldiers, and so
David made them officers in his army.
They fought on his side when enemy troops
attacked.

22 Day after day, new men came to join
David, and soon he had a large, powerful
army.

David's Men at Hebron

23-37 The kingdom of Israel had been
taken away from Saul, and it now belonged
to David. He was ruling from Hebron, and
thousands of well-trained soldiers from
each tribe went there to crown David king
of all Israel, just as the LORD had promised.
These soldiers, who were always prepared
for battle, included: 6,800 from Judah, who
were armed with shields and spears; 7,100
from Simeon; 4,600 from Levi, including
Jehoiada, who was a leader from Aaron's
descendants, and his 3,700 men, as well as
Zadok, who was a brave soldier, and 22 of
his relatives, who were also officers; 3,000
from Benjamin, because this was Saul's
own tribe and most of the men had remained loyal to him; 20,800 from Ephraim,
who were not only brave, but also famous
in their clans; 18,000 from West Manasseh,
who had been chosen to help make David
king; 200 leaders from Issachar, along with
troops under their command—these leaders knew the right time to do what needed
to be done; 50,000 from Zebulun, who
were not only loyal, but also trained to use
any weapon; 1,000 officers from Naphtali
and 37,000 soldiers armed with shields
and spears; 28,600 from Dan; 40,000 from
Asher; and 120,000 from the tribes
of Reuben, Gad, and East Manasseh, who
were armed with all kinds of weapons.

38 All of these soldiers voluntarily came
to Hebron because they wanted David to
become king of Israel. In fact, everyone in
Israel wanted the same thing. 39 The soldiers stayed in Hebron three days, eating
and drinking what their relatives had prepared for them. 40 Other Israelites from
as far away as the territories of Issachar,
Zebulun, and Naphtali brought cattle and
sheep to slaughter for food. They also
brought donkeys, camels, mules, and oxen
that were loaded down with flour, dried
figs, wine, and olive oil.

Everyone in Israel was very happy.

David Moves the Sacred Chest to Jerusalem

(2 Samuel 6.1-12a)

13 Some time later, David talked with
his army commanders, 2-3 and then
announced to the people of Israel:

> While Saul was king, the sacred
> chest was ignored. But now it's time to
> bring the chest to Jerusalem. We will
> invite everyone in Israel to come here,
> including the priests and the Levites
> in the towns surrounded by pasture-
> land. But we will do these things only
> if you agree, and if the LORD our God
> wants us to.

4 The people agreed this was the right
thing to do.

5 David gathered everyone from the Shihor River in Egypt to Lebo-Hamath in the
north. 6 Then he led them to Baalah in Judah, which was also called Kiriath-Jearim.
They went there to get the sacred chest

13.6 a 1 S 7.1, 2; **b** Ex 25.22.

and bring it to Jerusalem, because it belonged to the LORD God, whose throne is above the winged creatures[c] on the lid of the chest.

7 The sacred chest was still at Abinadab's house,[d] and when David and the crowd arrived there, they brought the chest outside and placed it on a new ox cart. Abinadab's sons[e] Uzzah and Ahio guided the cart, 8 while David and the crowd danced and sang praises to the LORD with all their might. They played music on small harps and other stringed instruments, and on tambourines, cymbals, and trumpets.

9 But when they came to Chidon's threshing place, the oxen stumbled, and Uzzah reached out and took hold of the chest to stop it from falling. 10 The LORD God was very angry at Uzzah for doing this, and he killed Uzzah right there beside the chest.

11 David then got angry at God for killing Uzzah. So he named that place "Attack on Uzzah,"[f] and it's been called that ever since.

12 David was afraid what the LORD might do to him, and he asked himself, "Should I really be the one to take care of the sacred chest?" 13 So instead of taking it to Jerusalem, David decided to take it to the home of Obed-Edom, who lived in the town of Gath.

14 The chest stayed there for three months, and the LORD blessed Obed-Edom, his family, and everything he owned.

David's Palace in Jerusalem

(2 *Samuel* 5.11-16)

14 King Hiram of Tyre sent some officials to David. They brought along carpenters and stone workers, and enough cedar logs to build David a palace. 2 David now knew that the LORD had made him a powerful king of Israel for the good of his people.

3 After David moved to Jerusalem, he married more women and had more sons and daughters. 4-7 His children born there were Shammua, Shobab, Nathan, Solomon, Ibhar, Elishua, Elpelet, Nogah, Nepheg, Japhia, Elishama, Beeliada,[g] and Eliphelet.

David Defeats the Philistines

(2 *Samuel* 5.17-25)

8 When the Philistines heard that David had become king of Israel, they came to capture him. But David heard about their plan and marched out to meet them in battle. 9 The Philistines had already camped in Rephaim Valley and were raiding the nearby villages.

10 David asked God, "Should I attack the Philistines? Will you help me win?"

The LORD told David, "Yes, attack them! I will give you victory."

11 David and his army marched to Baal-Perazim, where they attacked and defeated the Philistines. He said, "I defeated my enemies because God broke through them like a mighty flood." So he named the place "The Lord Broke Through."[h] 12 Then David ordered his troops to burn the idols that the Philistines had left behind.

13 Some time later, the Philistines came back into the hill country and camped in Rephaim Valley. 14 David asked God what he should do, and God answered, "Don't attack them from the front. Circle around behind them where the balsam[i] trees are. 15 Wait there until you hear the treetops making the sound of marching troops. That sound will mean I have marched out ahead of you to fight the Philistine army. So you must then attack quickly!"

16 David obeyed God and he defeated the Philistines. He even chased them all the way from Gibeon to the entrance to Gezer.

17 From then on, David became even more famous, and the LORD made all the nations afraid of him.

[c]**13.6** *winged creatures*: Two golden statues of winged creatures were on top of the sacred chest and were symbols of the LORD's throne on earth (see Exodus 25.18). [d]**13.7** *The sacred chest . . . Abinadab's house*: See 1 Samuel 6.19—7.2. [e]**13.7** *Abinadab's sons*: These words are not in the Hebrew text, but see 2 Samuel 6.3. [f]**13.11** *Attack on Uzzah*: Or "Perez-Uzzah." [g]**14.4-7** *Beeliada*: Or "Eliada" (see 3.6-8). [h]**14.11** *The Lord Broke Through*: Or "Baal-Perazim." [i]**14.14** *balsam*: One possible meaning for the difficult Hebrew text.
13.14 1 Ch 26.4, 5.

David Gets Ready To Bring the Sacred Chest to Jerusalem

15 David had several buildings built in Jerusalem, and he had a tent set up where the sacred chest would be kept. 2 He said, "Only Levites will be allowed to carry the chest, because the LORD has chosen them to do that work and to serve him forever."

3 Next, David invited everyone to come to Jerusalem and watch the sacred chest being carried to the place he had set up for it. 4 He also sent for Aaron's descendants and for the Levites. The Levites that came were: 5 Uriel, the leader of the Kohath clan, and one hundred twenty of his relatives; 6 Asaiah, the leader of the Merari clan, and two hundred twenty of his relatives; 7 Joel, the leader of the Gershon clan, and one hundred thirty of his relatives; 8 Shemaiah, the leader of the Elizaphan clan, and two hundred of his relatives; 9 Eliel, the leader of the Hebron clan, and eighty of his relatives; and 10 Amminadab, the leader of the Uzziel clan, with one hundred twelve of his relatives.

11 David called together these six Levites and the two priests, Zadok and Abiathar. 12 He said to them, "You are the leaders of the clans in the Levi tribe. You and your relatives must first go through the ceremony to make yourselves clean and acceptable to the LORD. Then you may carry the sacred chest that belongs to the LORD God of Israel and bring it to the place I have prepared for it. 13 The first time we tried to bring the chest to Jerusalem, we didn't ask the LORD what he wanted us to do. He was angry at us, because you Levites weren't there to carry the chest."

14 The priests and the Levites made themselves clean. They were now ready to carry the sacred chest 15 on poles that rested on their shoulders, just as the LORD had told Moses to do.

16 David then told the leaders to choose some Levites to sing and play music on small harps, other stringed instruments, and cymbals. 17-21 The men chosen to play the cymbals were Heman the son of Joel, his relative Asaph the son of Berechiah, and Ethan the son of Kushaiah from the Merari clan. Some of their assistants played the smaller harps: they were Zechariah, Aziel, Shemiramoth, Jehiel, Unni, Eliab, Maaseiah, and Benaiah. Others played the larger harps: they were Mattithiah, Eliphelehu, Mikneiah, Azaziah, and two of the temple guards, Obed-Edom and Jeiel.

22 Chenaniah was chosen to be the music director, because he was a skilled musician.

23-24 Four Levites were then appointed to guard the sacred chest. They were Berechiah, Elkanah, Obed-Edom, and Jehiah.

Finally, David chose priests to walk in front of the sacred chest and blow trumpets. They were Shebaniah, Joshaphat, Nethanel, Amasai, Zechariah, Benaiah, and Eliezer.

The Sacred Chest Is Brought to Jerusalem

(*2 Samuel* 6.12-22)

25 David, the leaders of Israel, and the army commanders were very happy as they went to Obed-Edom's house to get the sacred chest. 26 God gave the Levites the strength they needed to carry the chest, and so they sacrificed seven bulls and seven rams.

27 David, the Levites, Chenaniah the music director, and all the musicians were wearing linen robes, and David was also wearing a linen cloth.[j] 28 While the sacred chest was being carried into Jerusalem, everyone was celebrating by shouting and playing music on horns, trumpets, cymbals, harps, and other stringed instruments.

29 Saul's daughter Michal[k] looked out her window and watched the chest being brought into David's City. But when she

[j] **15.27** *a linen cloth*: The Hebrew word is "ephod," which can mean either a piece of clothing like a skirt that went from the waist to the knee or a garment like a vest or jacket that only the priests wore. [k] **15.29** *Michal*: One of David's wives.

15.2 Dt 10.8. **15.15** Ex 25.14.

saw David jumping and dancing in honor
of the LORD, she was disgusted.

16 They put the sacred chest inside
the tent that David had set up for
it, then they offered sacrifices to please the
LORD[l] and sacrifices to ask his blessing.[m]
2 After David had finished, he blessed the
people in the name of the LORD 3 and gave
every person in the crowd a small loaf of
bread, some meat, and a handful of raisins.
4 David appointed some of the Levites to
serve at the sacred chest; they were to play
music and sing praises to the LORD God
of Israel. 5 Asaph was their leader, and
Zechariah was his assistant. Jeiel, Shemiramoth, Jehiel, Mattithiah, Eliab, Benaiah,
Obed-Edom, and another man named Jeiel
were appointed to play small harps and
stringed instruments. Asaph himself played
the cymbals, 6 and the two priests Benaiah
and Jahaziel were to blow trumpets every
day in front of the sacred chest.

David's Song of Praise

(Psalms 105.1-15; 96.1-13; 106.1, 47, 48)

7 That same day, David instructed Asaph
and his relatives for the first time to sing
these praises to the LORD:

8 Praise the LORD
and pray in his name!
Tell everyone
what he has done.
9 Sing praises to the LORD!
Tell about his miracles.
10 Celebrate and worship
his holy name
with all your heart.

11 Trust the LORD
and his mighty power.
Worship him always.
12 Remember his miracles
and all his wonders
and his fair decisions.
13 You belong to the family
of Israel, his servant;
you are his chosen ones,
the descendants of Jacob.

14 The LORD is our God,
bringing justice
everywhere on earth.
15 We must never forget
his agreement and his promises,
not in thousands of years.
*16 God made an eternal promise
17 to Abraham, Isaac, and Jacob
18 when he said, "I'll give you
the land of Canaan."

19 At the time there were
only a few of us,
and we were homeless.
20 We wandered from nation
to nation, from one country
to another.
21 God did not let anyone
mistreat our people.
Instead he protected us
by punishing rulers
22 and telling them,
"Don't touch my chosen leaders
or harm my prophets!"

23 Everyone on this earth,
sing praises to the LORD.
Day after day announce,
"The LORD has saved us!"
24 Tell every nation on earth,
"The LORD is wonderful
and does marvelous things!
25 The LORD is great and deserves
our greatest praise!
He is the only God
worthy of our worship.
26 Other nations worship idols,
but the LORD created
the heavens.
27 Give honor and praise
to the LORD,

[l] **16.1** *sacrifices to please the LORD*: These sacrifices have traditionally been called "whole burnt offerings" because the whole animal was burned on the altar. A main purpose of such sacrifices was to please the LORD with the smell of the sacrifice, and so in the CEV they are often called "sacrifices to please the LORD." [m] **16.1** *sacrifices to ask his blessing*: These sacrifices have traditionally been called "peace offerings" or "offerings of well-being." A main purpose was to ask for the LORD's blessing, and so in the CEV they are sometimes called "sacrifices to ask the LORD's blessing."

16.16-18 **a** Gn 12.7; **b** Gn 26.3; **c** Gn 28.13. **16.21,22** Gn 20.3-7.

whose power and beauty
fill his holy temple."

28 Tell everyone of every nation,
"Praise the glorious power
of the LORD.
29 He is wonderful! Praise him
and bring an offering
into his temple.
Worship the LORD,
majestic and holy.
30 Everyone on earth, now tremble!"

The world stands firm,
never to be shaken.
31 Tell the heavens and the earth
to be glad and celebrate!
And announce to the nations,
"The LORD is King!"
32 Command the ocean to roar
with all of its creatures
and the fields to rejoice
with all of their crops.
33 Then every tree in the forest
will sing joyful songs
to the LORD.
He is coming to judge
all people on earth.

34 Praise the LORD
because he is good to us,
and his love never fails.
35 Say to him, "Save us, LORD God!
Bring us back
from among the nations.
Let us celebrate and shout
in praise of your holy name.
36 LORD God of Israel,
you deserve to be praised
forever and ever."

After David finished, the people shouted, "Amen! Praise the LORD!"

David Appoints Worship Leaders at Jerusalem and Gibeon

37 David chose Asaph and the Levites in
his clan to be in charge of the daily worship
at the place where the sacred chest was
kept. 38 Obed-Edom and sixty-eight of his
relatives were their assistants, and Hosah
and Obed-Edom the son of Jeduthun were
the guards.
39 David also chose Zadok the priest and
his relatives who were priests to serve at
the LORD's sacred tent at Gibeon. 40 They
were to offer sacrifices on the altar every
morning and evening, just as the LORD had
commanded in the Law he gave Israel.
41 Heman and Jeduthun were their assistants, as well as the other men who had
been chosen to praise the LORD for his
never-ending love. 42 Heman and Jeduthun
were also responsible for blowing the trumpets, and for playing the cymbals and other
instruments during worship at the tent.
The Levites in Jeduthun's clan were the
guards at Gibeon.
43 After that, everyone went home, and
David went home to his family.

The LORD's Message to David

(2 Samuel 7.1-17)

17 Soon after David moved into his
new palace, he said to Nathan the
prophet, "Look around! I live in a palace
made of cedar, but the sacred chest is kept
in a tent."
2 Nathan replied, "The LORD is with
you—do what you want."
3 That night, the LORD told Nathan 4 to
go to David and tell him:

David, you are my servant, so listen
carefully: You are not the one to build
a temple for me. 5 I didn't live in a
temple when I brought my people out
of Egypt, and I don't live in one now. A
tent has always been my home wherever I have gone with them. 6 I chose
special leaders and told them to be like
shepherds for my people Israel. But
did I ever say anything to even one
of them about building a cedar temple
for me?

7 David, this is what I, the LORD All-
Powerful, say to you. I brought you in
from the fields where you took care of
sheep, and I made you the leader of
my people. 8 Wherever you went, I
helped you and destroyed your ene-

16.34 2 Ch 5.11-13; 7.3; Ezra 3.11; Ps 100.5; 106.1; 107.1; 118.1; 136.1; Jr 33.11.
16.41,42 2 Ch 5.11-13; 3 Macc 6.32. **16.43** 2 S 6.19, 20.

mies right in front of your eyes. I have made you one of the most famous people in the world.

[9] I have given my people Israel a land of their own where they can live in peace. They will no longer have to tremble with fear—evil nations won't bother them, as they did [10] when I let judges rule my people, and I will keep your enemies from attacking you.

Now I promise that like you, your descendants will be kings. [11] I'll choose one of your sons to be king when you reach the end of your life and are buried beside your ancestors. I'll make him a strong ruler, [12] and no one will be able to take his kingdom away from him. He will be the one to build a temple for me. [13] I will be like a father to him, and he will be like a son to me. I will never put an end to my agreement with him, as I put an end to my agreement with Saul, who was king before you. [14] I will make sure that your son and his descendants will rule my people and my kingdom forever.

[15] Nathan told David exactly what the LORD had said.

David Gives Thanks to the LORD

(*2 Samuel 7.18-29*)

[16] David went into the tent he had set up for the sacred chest. He sat there and prayed:

LORD God, my family and I don't deserve what you have already done for us, [17] and yet you have promised to do even more for my descendants. You are treating me as if I am a very important person.[n] [18] I am your servant, and you know my thoughts. What else can I say, except that you have honored me? [19] It was your choice to do these wonderful things for me and to make these promises.

[20] No other god is like you, LORD—you alone are God. Everything we have heard about you is true. [21] And there is no other nation on earth like Israel, the nation you rescued from slavery in Egypt to be your own. You became famous by using great and wonderful miracles to force other nations and their gods out of your land, so that your people could live here. [22] You have chosen Israel to be your people forever, and you have become their God.

[23] LORD God, please do what you promised me and my descendants. [24] Then you will be famous forever, and everyone will say, "The LORD All-Powerful rules Israel and is their God."

My kingdom will be strong, [25] because you are my God, and you have promised that my descendants will be kings. That's why I have the courage to pray to you like this, even though I am only your servant.

[26] You are the LORD God, and you have made this good promise to me. [27] Now please bless my descendants forever, and let them always be your chosen kings. You have already blessed my family, and I know you will bless us forever.

A List of David's Victories in War

(*2 Samuel 8.1-14*)

18 Later, David attacked and defeated the Philistines. He captured their town of Gath and the nearby villages.

[2] David also defeated the Moabites, and so they had to accept him as their ruler and pay taxes to him.

[3] While King Hadadezer of Zobah was trying to gain control of the territory near the Euphrates River, David met him in battle at Hamath and defeated him. [4] David captured one thousand chariots, seven thousand chariot drivers, and twenty thousand soldiers. And he crippled all but one hundred of the horses.

[5] When troops from the Syrian kingdom of Damascus came to help Hadadezer, David killed twenty-two thousand of them. [6] Then David stationed some of his troops in Damascus, and the people there had to

[n] **17.17** *You are treating me . . . person*: One possible meaning for the difficult Hebrew text.
17.13 2 Co 6.18; He 1.5.

accept David as their ruler and pay taxes to him.

Everywhere David went, the LORD helped him win battles.

7 Hadadezer's officers had carried gold shields, but David took these shields and brought them back to Jerusalem. 8 He also took a lot of bronze from the cities of Tibhath and Cun, which had belonged to Hadadezer. Later, Solomon used this bronze to make the large bowl called the Sea, and to make the pillars and other furnishings for the temple.

9-10 King Tou of Hamath and King Hadadezer had been enemies. So when Tou heard that David had defeated Hadadezer's whole army, he sent his son Hadoram to congratulate David on his victory. Hadoram also brought him gifts made of gold, silver, and bronze. 11 David gave these gifts to the LORD, just as he had done with the silver and gold he had captured from Edom, Moab, Ammon, Philistia, and Amalek.

12 Abishai the son of Zeruiah defeated the Edomite army in Salt Valley and killed eighteen thousand of their troops. 13 Then he stationed troops in Edom, and the people there had to accept David as their ruler.

Everywhere David went, the LORD gave him victory in war.

A List of David's Officials

(*2 Samuel 8.15-18*)

14 David ruled all Israel with fairness and justice.

15 Joab the son of Zeruiah was the commander in chief of the army.

Jehoshaphat the son of Ahilud kept the government records.

16 Zadok the son of Ahitub and Ahimelech the son of Abiathar were the priests.

Shavsha was the secretary.

17 Benaiah the son of Jehoiada was the commander of David's bodyguard.[o]

David's sons were his highest-ranking officials.

Israel Fights Ammon and Syria

(*2 Samuel 10.1-19*)

19 Some time later, King Nahash of Ammon died, and his son Hanun became king. 2 David said, "Nahash was kind to me, so I will be kind to his son." He sent some officials to Ammon to tell Hanun how sorry he was that his father had died.

But when David's officials arrived at Ammon, 3 the Ammonite leaders said to Hanun, "Do you really believe King David is honoring your father by sending these men to comfort you? He probably sent them to spy on our country, so he can come and destroy it."

4 Hanun arrested David's officials and had their beards shaved off and their robes cut off just below the waist, and then he sent them away. 5 They were terribly ashamed.

When David found out what had happened to his officials, he sent a message that told them, "Stay in Jericho until your beards grow back. Then you can come home."

6 The Ammonites realized they had made David furious. So they paid over thirty tons of silver to hire chariot troops from Mesopotamia and from the Syrian kingdoms of Maacah and Zobah. 7 Thirty-two thousand troops, as well as the king of Maacah and his army, came and camped near Medeba. The Ammonite troops also left their towns and came to prepare for battle.

8 David heard what was happening, and he sent out Joab with his army. 9 The Ammonite troops marched to the entrance of the city[p] and prepared for battle, while the Syrian troops took their positions in the open fields.

10 Joab saw that the enemy troops were lined up on both sides of him. So he picked some of the best Israelite soldiers to fight the Syrians. 11 Then he put his brother Abishai in command of the rest of the army and told them to fight against the Am-

[o] **18.17** *David's bodyguard*: The Hebrew text has "the Cherethites and the Pelethites," who were foreign soldiers hired by David to be his bodyguard. [p] **19.9** *the city*: Probably Rabbah, the capital city of Ammon.

18.8 1 K 7.40-47; 2 Ch 4.11-18.

monites. 12 Joab told his brother, "If the Syrians are too much for me to handle, come and help me. And if the Ammonites are too strong for you, I'll come and help you. 13 Be brave and fight hard to protect our people and the towns of our LORD God. I pray he will do whatever pleases him."

14 Joab and his soldiers attacked the Syrians, and the Syrians ran from them. 15 When the Ammonite troops saw that the Syrians had run away, they ran from Abishai's soldiers and went back into their own city. Joab then returned to Jerusalem.

16 As soon as the Syrians realized they had been defeated, they sent for their troops that were stationed on the other side of the Euphrates River. Shophach, the commander of Hadadezer's army, led these troops to Ammon.

17 David found out what the Syrians were doing, and he brought Israel's entire army together. They crossed the Jordan River, and he commanded them to take their positions facing the Syrian troops.

Soon after the fighting began, 18 the Syrians ran from Israel. David killed seven thousand chariot troops and forty thousand regular soldiers. He also killed Shophach, their commander.

19 When the kings who had been under Hadadezer's rule saw that Israel had defeated them, they made peace with David and accepted him as their new ruler. The Syrians never helped the Ammonites again.

The End of the War with Ammon
(2 Samuel 11.1; 12.26-31)

20 The next spring, the time when kings go to war, Joab marched out in command of the Israelite army and destroyed towns all over the country of Ammon. He attacked the capital city of Rabbah and left it in ruins. But David stayed in Jerusalem.

2 Later, David himself went to Rabbah, where he took the crown from the statue of their god Milcom.[q] The crown was made of seventy-five pounds of gold, and there was a valuable jewel on it. David put the jewel on his crown,[r] then carried off everything else of value. 3 He forced the people of Rabbah to work with saws, iron picks, and axes. He also did the same thing with the people in all the other Ammonite towns.

David then led Israel's army back to Jerusalem.

The Descendants of the Rephaim
(2 Samuel 21.15-22)

4 Some time later, Israel fought a battle against the Philistines at Gezer. During this battle, Sibbecai from Hushah killed Sippai, a descendant of the Rephaim,[s] and the Philistines were defeated.

5 In another battle against the Philistines, Elhanan the son of Jair killed Lahmi the brother of Goliath from Gath, whose spear shaft was like a weaver's beam.[t]

6 Another one of the Philistine soldiers who was a descendant of the Rephaim was as big as a giant and had six fingers on each hand and six toes on each foot. During a battle at Gath, 7 he made fun of Israel, so David's nephew Jonathan[u] killed him.

8 David and his soldiers killed these three men from Gath who were descendants of the Rephaim.

David Counts the People
(2 Samuel 24.1-9)

21 Satan decided to cause trouble for Israel by making David think it was a good idea to find out how many people there were in Israel and Judah. 2 David told Joab and the army commanders, "Count everyone in Israel, from the town of Beersheba in the south all the way north to Dan. Then I will know how many people can serve in my army."

[q]**20.2** *the statue of their god Milcom*: Or "their king." [r]**20.2** *David put the jewel on his crown*: Or "David put the crown on his head." [s]**20.4** *Rephaim*: This may refer to a group of people that lived in Palestine before the Israelites and who were famous for their large size. [t]**20.5** *weaver's beam*: When a weaver made cloth, one set of threads was tied onto a large wooden rod that was known as a weaver's beam. [u]**20.7** *David's nephew Jonathan*: Hebrew "Jonathan son of Shimea, David's brother."

18.12 Ps 60 Title. **20.1** 2 S 11.1. **20.5** 1 S 17.4-7.

3 Joab answered, "Your Majesty, even if
the LORD made your kingdom a hundred
times larger, you would still rule everyone
in it. Why do you need to know how many
soldiers there are? Don't you think that
would make the whole nation angry?"
4 But David would not change his mind.
And so Joab went everywhere in Israel and
Judah and counted the people. He returned to Jerusalem 5 and told David that
the total number of men who could serve
in the army was one million one hundred
thousand in Israel and four hundred seventy thousand in Judah. 6 Joab refused to
include anyone from the tribes of Levi and
Benjamin, because he still disagreed with
David's orders.

God Punishes Israel
(2 Samuel 24.10-17)

7 David's order to count the people
made God angry, and he punished Israel.
8 David prayed, "I am your servant. But
what I did was stupid and terribly wrong.
Please forgive me."
9 The LORD said to Gad, one of David's
prophets, 10 "Tell David that I will punish
him in one of three ways. But he will have
to choose which one it will be."
11 Gad went to David and told him:

> You must choose how the LORD will
> punish you: 12 Will there be three
> years when the land won't grow
> enough food for its people? Or will
> your enemies constantly defeat you for
> three months? Or will the LORD send a
> horrible disease to strike your land for
> three days? Think about it and decide,
> because I have to give your answer to
> God who sent me.

13 David was miserable and said, "It's a
terrible choice to make! But the LORD is
kind, and I'd rather have him punish me
than for anyone else to do it."
14 So the LORD sent a horrible disease
on Israel, and seventy thousand Israelites
died. 15 Then he sent an angel to destroy
the city of Jerusalem. But just as the angel
was about to do that, the LORD felt sorry for
all the suffering he had caused the people,
and he told the angel, "Stop! They have
suffered enough." This happened at the
threshing place that belonged to Araunah[v]
the Jebusite.
16 David saw the LORD's angel in the air,
holding a sword over Jerusalem. He and
the leaders of Israel, who were all wearing
sackcloth,[w] bowed with their faces to the
ground, 17 and David prayed, "It's my fault!
I sinned by ordering the people to be
counted. They have done nothing wrong—
they are innocent sheep. LORD God, please
punish me and my family. Don't let the disease wipe out your people."

David Buys Araunah's Threshing Place
(2 Samuel 24.18-25)

18 The LORD's angel told the prophet
Gad to tell David that he must go to Araunah's threshing place and build an altar in
honor of the LORD. 19 David followed the
LORD's instructions.
20 Araunah and his four sons were
threshing wheat at the time, and when
they saw the angel, the four sons ran to
hide. 21 Just then, David arrived, and when
Araunah saw him, he stopped his work and
bowed down.
22 David said, "Would you sell me your
threshing place, so I can build an altar on it
to the LORD? Then this disease will stop
killing the people. I'm willing to pay whatever you say it's worth."
23 Araunah answered, "Take it, Your
Majesty, and do whatever you want with it.
I'll even give you the oxen for the sacrifice
and the wheat for the grain sacrifice. And
you can use the threshing-boards[x] for the
fire. It's all yours!"
24 But David replied, "No! I want to pay
you what they're worth. I can't just take
something from you and then offer the
LORD a sacrifice that cost me nothing."
25 So David paid Araunah six hundred
gold coins for his threshing place. 26 David
built an altar and offered sacrifices to

[v] **21.15** *Araunah*: The Hebrew text has "Ornan," another spelling of Araunah (see 2 Samuel 24.16). [w] **21.16** *sackcloth*: A rough, dark-colored cloth made from goat or camel hair and used to make grain sacks. It was worn in times of trouble or sorrow. [x] **21.23** *threshing-boards*: Heavy boards with bits of rock or metal on the bottom. They were dragged across the grain to separate the husks from the kernels.

please the LORD[y] and sacrifices to ask his blessing.[z] David prayed, and the LORD answered him by sending fire down on the altar. 27 Then the LORD commanded the angel to put the sword away.[a]

28 When David saw that the LORD had answered his prayer, he offered more sacrifices there at the threshing place, 29-30 because he was afraid of the angel's sword and did not want to go all the way to Gibeon. That's where the sacred tent that Moses had made in the desert was kept, as well as the altar where sacrifices were offered to the LORD.

22 David said, "The temple of the LORD God must be built right here at this threshing place. And the altar for offering sacrifices will also be here."

David Prepares To Build the Temple

2 David ordered the foreigners living in Israel to come to Jerusalem. Then he assigned some to cut blocks of stone for building the temple. 3 He got a large supply of iron to make into nails and hinges for the doors, and he provided so much bronze that it could not be weighed. 4 He also had cedar logs brought in from the cities of Sidon and Tyre.

5 He said, "The temple for the LORD must be great, so that everyone in the world will know about it. But since my son Solomon is young and has no experience, I will make sure that everything is ready for the temple to be built."

That's why David did all these things before he died.

David Instructs Solomon To Build the Temple

6 David sent for his son Solomon and told him to build a temple for the LORD God of Israel. 7 He said:

My son, I wanted to build a temple where the LORD my God would be worshiped. 8 But some time ago, he told me, "David, you have killed too many people and have fought too many battles. That's why you are not the one to build my temple. 9 But when your son becomes king, I will give him peace throughout his kingdom. His name will be Solomon, because during his rule I will keep Israel safe and peaceful.[b] 10 Solomon will build my temple. He will be like a son to me, and I will be like a father to him. In fact, one of his descendants will always rule in Israel."

11 Solomon, my son, I now pray that the LORD your God will be with you and keep his promise to help you build a temple for him. 12 May he give you wisdom and knowledge, so that you can rule Israel according to his Law. 13 If you obey the laws and teachings that the LORD gave Moses, you will be successful. Be strong and brave and don't get discouraged or be afraid of anything.

14 I have all the supplies you'll need to build the temple: You have four thousand tons of gold and forty thousand tons of silver. There's also plenty of wood, stone, and more bronze and iron than I could weigh. Ask for anything else you need. 15 I have also assigned men who will cut and lay the stone. And there are carpenters and people who are experts in working with 16 gold, silver, bronze, and iron. You have plenty of workers to do the job. Now get started, and I pray that the LORD will be with you in your work.

17 David then gave orders for the leaders of Israel to help Solomon. 18 David said:

The LORD our God has helped me defeat all the people who lived here before us, and he has given you peace from all your enemies. Now this land belongs to the LORD and his people. 19 Obey the LORD your God with your heart and soul. Begin work on the temple to honor him, so that the sacred chest and the things used for worship can be kept there.

[y]**21.26** *sacrifices to please the LORD*: See the note at 16.1. [z]**21.26** *sacrifices to ask his blessing*: See the note at 16.1. [a]**21.27** *the LORD commanded the angel to put the sword away*: See verse 16. [b]**22.9** *Solomon . . . safe and peaceful*: In Hebrew "Solomon" sounds like "peace."

22.7-10 2 S 7.1-16; 1 Ch 17.1-14. **22.13** Js 1.6-9.

David Assigns the Levites Their Duties

23 David was old when he chose his
son Solomon to be king of Israel.
2 Some time later, David called together all
of Israel's leaders, priests, and Levites.
3 He then counted the Levite men who
were at least thirty years old, and the total
was thirty-eight thousand. 4 He said,
"Twenty-four thousand of the Levites will
be in charge of the temple, six thousand
will be temple officials and judges, 5 four
thousand will be guards at the temple, and
four thousand will praise the LORD by playing
the musical instruments I have given them."
6 David then divided the Levites into
three groups according to the clans of
Levi's sons, Gershon, Kohath, and Merari.
7 Gershon had two sons: Ladan and
Shimei. 8 Ladan was the father of Jehiel,
Zetham, and Joel. 9 They were all family
leaders among their father's descendants.
Shimei was the father of Shelomoth,
Haziel, and Haran. 10-11 Later, Shimei had
four more sons, in the following order: Jahath, Zina, Jeush, and Beriah. But Jeush
and Beriah didn't have many children, so
their descendants were counted as one
family.
12 Kohath had four sons: Amram, Izhar,
Hebron, and Uzziel. 13 Amram was the
father of Aaron and Moses. Aaron and his
descendants were chosen to be in charge of
all the sacred things. They served the LORD
by offering sacrifices to him and by blessing
the people in his name. 14-15 Moses, the
man of God, was the father of Gershom
and Eliezer, and their descendants were
considered Levites. 16 Gershom's oldest son
was Shebuel. 17 Rehabiah, who was
Eliezer's only son, had many children.
18 The second son born to Kohath was
Izhar, and his oldest son was Shelomith.
19 Hebron, the third son of Kohath, was the
father of Jeriah, Amariah, Jahaziel, and
Jekameam. 20 Kohath's youngest son,
Uzziel, was the father of Micah and
Isshiah.
21 Merari had two sons: Mahli and
Mushi. Mahli was the father of Eleazar and
Kish. 22 Eleazar had no sons, only daughters, and they married their uncle's sons.
23 Mushi the second son of Merari, was the
father of Mahli, Eder, and Jeremoth.
24 These were the clans and families of
the tribe of Levi. Those who were twenty
years and older were assigned to work at
the LORD's temple.
25 David said:

The LORD God of Israel has given
his people peace, and he will live in
Jerusalem forever. 26 And so, the
Levites won't need to move the sacred
tent and the things used for worship
from place to place. 27 From now on,
all Levites at least twenty years old
28 will serve the LORD by helping
Aaron's descendants do their work at
the temple, by keeping the courtyards
and rooms of the temple clean, and by
making sure that everything used in
worship stays pure. 29 They will also be
in charge of the sacred loaves of bread,
the flour for the grain sacrifices, the
thin wafers, any offerings to be baked,
and the flour mixed with olive oil.
These Levites will weigh and measure
these offerings.

30 Every morning and evening, the
Levites are to give thanks to the LORD
and sing praises to him. 31 They must
also give thanks and sing praises when
sacrifices are offered on each Sabbath,
as well as during New Moon Festivals
and other religious feasts. There must
always be enough Levites on duty at
the temple to do everything that needs
to be done. 32 They were once in
charge of taking care of the sacred
tent; now they are responsible for the
temple and for helping Aaron's descendants.

David Assigns the Priests Their Duties

24 Aaron's descendants were then divided into work groups. Aaron had
four sons: Nadab, Abihu, Eleazar, and
Ithamar. 2 But Nadab and Abihu died long
before their father, without having any
sons. That's why Eleazar and Ithamar
served as priests.

23.1 1 K 1.1-40. **23.13** Ex 28.1. **23.26** Dt 10.8. **23.28-32** Nu 3.5-9. **24.2** Lv 10.1, 2.

[3] David divided Aaron's descendants into groups, according to their assigned work. Zadok, one of Eleazar's descendants, and Ahimelech, one of Ithamar's descendants, helped David.

[4] Eleazar's descendants were divided into sixteen groups, and Ithamar's were divided into eight groups, because Eleazar's family included more family leaders. [5] However, both families included temple officials and priests, and so to make sure the work was divided fairly, David asked God what to do.[c]

[6] As each group was assigned their duties, Shemaiah the son of Nethanel the Levite wrote down the name of the family leader in charge of that group. The witnesses were David and his officials, as well as Zadok the priest, Ahimelech the son of Abiathar, and the family leaders from the clans of the priests and the Levites.

[7-18] Each group of priests went by the name of its family leader, and they were assigned their duties in the following order: Jehoiarib, Jedaiah, Harim, Seorim, Malchijah, Mijamin, Hakkoz, Abijah, Jeshua, Shecaniah, Eliashib, Jakim, Huppah, Jeshebeab, Bilgah, Immer, Hezir, Happizzez, Pethahiah, Jehezkel, Jachin, Gamul, Delaiah, Maaziah. [19] These men were assigned their duties at the temple, just as the LORD God of Israel had commanded their ancestor Aaron.

The Rest of the Levites Are Assigned Their Duties

[20] Here is a list of the other descendants of Levi:

Amram was the ancestor of Shubael and Jehdeiah.
[21] Rehabiah was the ancestor of Isshiah, the oldest son in his family.
[22] Izhar was the father of Shelomoth and the grandfather of Jahath.
[23] Hebron had four sons, in the following order: Jeriah, Amariah, Jahaziel, and Jekameam.
[24] Uzziel was the father of Micah and the grandfather of Shamir.
[25] Isshiah, Micah's brother, was the father of Zechariah.
[26] Merari was the father of Mahli, Mushi, and Jaaziah.

[27] Jaaziah had three sons: Shoham, Zaccur, and Ibri.[d] [28-29] Mahli was the father of Eleazar and Kish. Eleazar had no sons, but Kish was the father of Jerahmeel. [30] Mushi had three sons: Mahli, Eder, and Jerimoth.

These were the descendants of Levi, according to their clans. [31] Each one was assigned his duties in the same way that their relatives the priests had been assigned their duties. David, Zadok, Ahimelech, and the family leaders of the priests and Levites were the witnesses.

David Assigns the Temple Musicians Their Duties

25 David and the temple officials chose the descendants of Asaph, Heman, and Jeduthun to be in charge of music. They were to praise the LORD by playing cymbals, harps and other stringed instruments. Here is a list of the musicians and their duties:

[2] Asaph's four sons, Zaccur, Joseph, Nethaniah, and Asarelah, were under the direction of their father and played music whenever the king told them to.

[3] Jeduthun's six sons, Gedaliah, Zeri, Jeshaiah, Shimei,[e] Hashabiah, and Mattithiah, were under the direction of their father and played harps and sang praises to the LORD.

[4] Heman had fourteen sons: Bukkiah, Mattaniah, Uzziel, Shebuel, Jerimoth, Hananiah, Hanani, Eliathah, Giddalti, Romamtiezer, Joshbekashah, Mallothi, Hothir, Mahazioth. [5] Heman was one of the king's prophets, and God honored Heman by giving him fourteen sons and three daughters. [6] His sons were under his direction and played cymbals, harps, and other stringed instruments during times of worship at the temple.

[c]**24.5** *asked God what to do*: The Hebrew text has "cast lots" (see the note at 6.65).
[d]**24.26,27** *Ibri*: One possible meaning for the difficult Hebrew text of verses 26, 27.
[e]**25.3** *Shimei*: One Hebrew manuscript and two ancient translations; other Hebrew manuscripts do not have this name.

Asaph, Jeduthun, and Heman took their orders directly from the king.

7 There were two hundred eighty-eight of these men, and all of them were skilled musicians. 8 David assigned them their duties by asking the LORD what he wanted.[f] Everyone was responsible for something, whether young or old, teacher or student.

9-31 The musicians were divided into twenty-four groups of twelve, and each group went by the name of their family leader. They were assigned their duties in the following order: Joseph, Gedaliah, Zaccur, Zeri, Nethaniah, Bukkiah, Asarelah, Jeshaiah, Mattaniah, Shimei, Uzziel, Hashabiah, Shebuel, Mattithiah, Jerimoth, Hananiah, Joshbekashah, Hanani, Mallothi, Eliathah, Hothir, Giddalti, Mahazioth, and Romamtiezer.

The Temple Guards Are Assigned Their Duties

26 The temple guards were also divided into groups according to clans.

Meshelemiah son of Kore was from the Korah clan and was a descendant of Asaph. 2 He had seven sons, who were born in the following order: Zechariah, Jediael, Zebadiah, Jathniel, 3 Elam, Jehohanan, and Eliehoenai.

4-5 Obed-Edom had been blessed with eight sons: Shemaiah, Jehozabad, Joah, Sachar, Nethanel, Ammiel, Issachar, and Peullethai.

6-7 Shemaiah was the father of Othni, Rephael, Obed, Elzabad, Elihu, and Semachiah. They were all respected leaders in their clan. 8 There were sixty-two descendants of Obed-Edom who were strong enough to be guards at the temple.

9 Eighteen descendants of Meshelemiah were chosen for this work.

10-11 Hosah, from the Merari clan, was the father of Shimri, Hilkiah, Tebaliah, and Zechariah. Hosah had made Shimri the family leader, even though he was not the oldest son. Thirteen men from Hosah's family were chosen to be temple guards.

12 The guards were divided into groups, according to their family leaders, and they were assigned duties at the temple, just like the other Levites. 13 Each group, no matter how large or small, was assigned a gate to guard, and they let the LORD show them what he wanted done.[g]

14 Shelemiah[h] was chosen to guard the East Gate. Zechariah his son was a wise man and was chosen to guard the North Gate. 15 Obed-Edom was then chosen to guard the South Gate, and his sons were chosen to guard the storerooms. 16 Shuppim and Hosah were chosen to guard the West Gate and the Shallecheth Gate on the upper road.

The guards were assigned the following work schedule: 17 Each day six guards were on duty on the east side of the temple, four were on duty on the north side, and four were on duty on the south side. Two guards were stationed at each of the two storerooms, 18 four were stationed along the road leading to the west courtyard,[i] and two guards stayed in the court itself.

19 These were the guard duties assigned to the men from the clans of Korah and Merari.

Guards Are Assigned to the Treasury

20 The Levites who were relatives of the Korahites and the Merarites were[j] in charge of guarding the temple treasury and the gifts that had been dedicated to God.

21 Ladan was from the Gershon clan and was the father of Jehieli. Many of his other descendants were family leaders in the clan.[k] 22 Jehieli was the father of

[f] **25.8** *asking the LORD what he wanted*: The Hebrew text has "casting lots" (see the note at 6.65). [g] **26.13** *they let the LORD show them what he wanted done*: The Hebrew text has "they cast lots to find out what the LORD wanted done" (see the note at 6.65). [h] **26.14** *Shelemiah*: Another spelling for Meshelemiah. [i] **26.18** *courtyard*: One possible meaning for the difficult Hebrew text. [j] **26.20** *The Levites . . . were*: One ancient translation; Hebrew "Ahijah the Levite was." [k] **26.21** *Many of his other . . . clan*: One possible meaning for the difficult Hebrew text.

26.4,5 2 S 6.11, 12; 1 Ch 13.14.

Zetham and Joel, and they were responsible for guarding the treasury.
23 Other guards at the treasury were from the Kohathite clans of Amram, Izhar, Hebron, and Uzziel.
24 Shebuel was a descendant of Gershom the son of Moses. He was the chief official in charge of the temple treasury.
25 The descendants of Gershom's brother Eliezer included Rehabiah, Jeshaiah, Joram, Zichri, and Shelomoth.
26 Shelomoth and his relatives were in charge of all the gifts that were dedicated to the LORD. These included the gifts that King David had dedicated, as well as those dedicated by the family leaders, army officers, and army commanders.
27 And whenever valuable things were captured in battle, these men brought some of them to the temple.
28 Shelomoth and his relatives were responsible for any gifts that had been given to the temple, including those from Samuel the prophet, King Saul the son of Kish, Abner the son of Ner,[l] and Joab the son of Zeruiah.

Other Officers Are Assigned Their Duties

29 Chenaniah from the Izhar clan and his sons were government officials and judges. They did not work at the temple.
30 Hashabiah from the Hebron clan and one thousand seven hundred of his skilled relatives were the officials in charge of all religious and government business in the Israelite territories west of the Jordan River.
31-32 Jerijah was the leader of the Hebron clan. David assigned him and two thousand seven hundred of his relatives, who were all respected family leaders, to be the officials in charge of all religious and government business in the tribes of Reuben, Gad, and East Manasseh. David found out about these men during the fortieth year of his rule, when he had a list made of all the families in the Hebron clan. They were from the town of Jazer in the territory of Gilead.

David Assigns Army Commanders

27 Each month a group of twenty-four thousand men served as soldiers in Israel's army. These men, which included the family leaders, army commanders, and officials of the king, were under the command of the following men, arranged by the month of their service:
2 In the first month, Jashobeam the son of Zabdiel,
3 a descendant of Perez;
4 in the second month, Dodai the Ahohite, whose assistant was Mikloth;[m]
5 in the third month, Benaiah the son of Jehoiada the priest,
6 who was the leader of the Thirty Warriors, and whose son Ammizabad was also an army commander;[n]
7 in the fourth month, Asahel the brother of Joab, whose son Zebadiah took over command after him;
8 in the fifth month, Shamhuth from the Izrah clan;
9 in the sixth month, Ira the son of Ikkesh from Tekoa;
10 in the seventh month, Helez from Pelon in the territory of Ephraim;
11 in the eighth month, Sibbecai from Hushah of the Zerah clan;
12 in the ninth month, Abiezer from Anathoth in the territory of Benjamin;
13 in the tenth month, Maharai from Netophah of the Zerah clan;
14 in the eleventh month, Benaiah from Pirathon in the territory of Ephraim;
15 in the twelfth month, Heldai from Netophah, who was a descendant of Othniel.

David Assigns Tribal Leaders

16-22 Here is a list of the leaders of each tribe in Israel:

Eliezer son of Zichri was over Reuben: Shephatiah son of Maacah was over Simeon; Hashabiah son of Kemuel was over the Levites, and Zadok the priest was over the descendants of Aaron; Elihu the brother of David was over Judah; Omri son of Michael was over Issachar; Ishmaiah son of Obadiah was over Zebulun; Jerimoth

[l]**26.28** *Abner the son of Ner*: Abner was King Saul's uncle (see 9.39). [m]**27.4** *whose . . . Mikloth*: One possible meaning for the difficult Hebrew text. [n]**27.6** *whose son Ammizabad . . . army commander*: One possible meaning for the difficult Hebrew text.

son of Azriel was over Naphtali; Hoshea son of Azaziah was over Ephraim; Joel son of Pedaiah was over West Manasseh; Iddo son of Zechariah was over East Manasseh; Jaasiel son of Abner was over Benjamin; Azarel son of Jeroham was over Dan.

23 When David decided to count the people of Israel, he gave orders not to count anyone under twenty years of age, because the LORD had promised long ago that Israel would have as many people as there are stars in the sky. 24 Joab the son of Zeruiah had begun to count the people, but he stopped when the LORD began punishing Israel. So the total number was never included in David's official records.

Officials in Charge of the King's Property

25 Azmaveth the son of Adiel was in charge of the king's personal storage rooms. Jonathan the son of Uzziah was in charge of the king's other storerooms that were in the towns, the villages, and the defense towers in Israel.

26 Ezri the son of Chelub was in charge of the workers who farmed the king's land.

27 Shimei from Ramah was in charge of the vineyards, and Zabdi from Shepham was in charge of storing the wine.

28 Baal Hanan from Geder was in charge of the olive and sycamore trees in the western foothills, and Joash was in charge of storing the olive oil.

29 Shitrai from Sharon was responsible for the cattle that were kept in Sharon Plain, and Shaphat son of Adlai was responsible for those kept in the valleys.

30 Obil the Ishmaelite was in charge of the camels, Jehdeiah from Meronoth was in charge of the donkeys, and Jaziz the Hagrite was in charge of the sheep and goats.

31 These were the men in charge of David's royal property.

David's Personal Advisors

32 David's uncle Jonathan was a wise and intelligent advisor. He and Jehiel the son of Hachmoni taught David's sons. 33 Ahithophel and Hushai the Archite were two of David's advisors. 34 Jehoiada the son of Benaiah was the king's advisor after Ahithophel, and later, Abiathar was his advisor.

Joab was commander of Israel's army.

David Gives Solomon the Plans for the Temple

28 David called a meeting in Jerusalem for all of Israel's leaders, including the tribal leaders, the government officials, the army commanders, the officials in charge of the royal property and livestock, the palace officials, and the brave warriors.

2 After everyone was there, David stood up and said:

Listen to me, my people. I wanted to build a place where the sacred chest would be kept, so we could go there and worship the LORD our God. I have prepared all the supplies for building a temple, 3 but the LORD has refused to let me build it, because he said I have killed too many people in battle.

4 The LORD God chose Judah to be the leading tribe in Israel. Then from Judah, he chose my father's family, and from that family, he chose me to be the king of Israel, and he promised that my descendants will also rule as kings. 5 The LORD has blessed me with many sons, but he chose my son Solomon to be the next king of Israel. 6 The LORD said to me, "Your son Solomon will build my temple, and it will honor me. Solomon will be like a son to me, and I will be like a father to him. 7 If he continues to obey my laws and commands, his kingdom will never end."

8 My friends, you are the LORD's people. And now, with God as your witness, I want you to promise that you will do your best to obey everything the LORD God has commanded us. Then this land will always belong to you and your descendants.

9 Solomon, my son, worship God

27.23 Gn 15.5; 22.17; 26.4. **27.24** 2 S 24.15; 1 Ch 21.1-14. **28.2-7** 2 S 7.1-16; 1 Ch 17.1-14.

and obey him with all your heart and
mind, just as I have done. He knows
all your thoughts and your reasons for
doing things, and so if you turn to him,
he will hear your prayers. But if you ignore him, he will reject you forever.
10 The LORD has chosen you to build a
temple for worshiping him. Be confident and do the work you have been
assigned.

11 After David finished speaking, he
gave Solomon the plans for building the
main rooms of the temple, including the
porch, the storerooms, the rooms upstairs
and downstairs, as well as the most holy
place. 12 He gave Solomon his plans for the
courtyards and the open areas around the
temple, and for the rooms to store the temple treasures and gifts that had been dedicated to God.

13 David also gave Solomon his plans for
dividing the priests and the Levites into
groups, as well as for the work that needed
to be done at the temple and for taking
care of the objects used for worship. 14 He
told Solomon how much gold and silver
was to be used in making the sacred objects, 15 including the lampstands and
lamps, 16 the gold table which held the sacred loaves of bread, the tables made of
silver, 17 the meat forks, the bowls and
cups, 18 the gold incense altar, and the
gold statue of a chariot for the winged creatures which were on the lid of the sacred
chest.

19 David then said to Solomon:

The LORD showed me how his temple is to be built. 20 But you must see
that everything is done according to
these plans. Be confident, and never
be afraid of anything or get discouraged. The LORD my God will help you
do everything needed to finish the
temple, so it can be used for worshiping him. 21 The priests and Levites
have been assigned their duties, and
all the skilled workers are prepared to
do their work. The people and their
leaders will do anything you tell
them.

Gifts for Building the Temple

29 David told the crowd:

God chose my son Solomon to
build the temple, but Solomon is
young and has no experience. This is
not just any building—this is the temple for the LORD God! 2 That's why I
have done my best to get everything
Solomon will need to build it—gold,
silver, bronze, iron, wood, onyx,
turquoise, colored gems, all kinds of
precious stones, and marble.

3 Besides doing all that, I have
promised to give part of my own gold
and silver as a way of showing my love
for God's temple. 4 Almost one hundred twenty tons of my finest gold and
over two hundred fifty tons of my silver
will be used to decorate its walls 5 and
to make the gold and silver objects.
Now, who else will show their dedication to the LORD by giving gifts for
building his temple?

6 After David finished speaking, the
family leaders, the tribal leaders, the army
commanders, and the government officials voluntarily gave gifts 7 for the temple. These gifts included almost two hundred tons of gold, three hundred eighty
tons of silver, almost seven hundred tons
of bronze, and three thousand seven hundred fifty tons of iron. 8 Everyone who
owned precious stones also donated them
to the temple treasury, where Jehiel
from the Levite clan of Gershon guarded
them.

9 David and the people were very happy
that so much had been given to the LORD,
and they all celebrated.

David Praises the LORD

10 Then, in front of everyone, David
sang praises to the LORD:

I praise you forever, LORD! You are
the God our ancestor Jacob[o] worshiped. 11 Your power is great, and
your glory is seen everywhere in
heaven and on earth. You are king of
the entire world, 12 and you rule with

[o] **29.10** *Jacob*: See the note at 1.34.

29.1,2 1 Ch 22.5. **29.11** Mt 6.13.

strength and power. You make people rich and powerful and famous. 13 We thank you, our God, and praise you.

14 But why should we be happy that we have given you these gifts? They belong to you, and we have only given back what is already yours. 15 We are only foreigners living here on earth for a while, just as our ancestors were. And we will soon be gone, like a shadow that suddenly disappears.

16 Our LORD God, we have brought all these things for building a temple to honor you. They belong to you, and you gave them to us. 17 But we are happy, because everyone has voluntarily given you these things. You know what is in everyone's heart, and you are pleased when people are honest. 18 Always make us eager to give, and help us be faithful to you, just as our ancestors Abraham, Isaac, and Jacob faithfully worshiped you. 19 And give Solomon the desire to completely obey your laws and teachings, and the desire to build the temple for which I have provided these gifts.

20 David then said to the people, "Now it's your turn to praise the LORD, the God your ancestors worshiped!" So everyone praised the LORD, and they bowed down to honor him and David their king.

Solomon Is Crowned King

21 The next day, the Israelites slaughtered a thousand bulls, a thousand rams, and a thousand lambs, and they offered them as sacrifices to please the LORD,[p] along with offerings of wine. 22 The people were very happy, and they ate and drank there at the LORD's altar.

That same day, Solomon was crowned king. The people celebrated and poured olive oil on Solomon's head to show that he would be their next king. They also poured oil on Zadok's head to show that he was their priest.

23 So Solomon became king after David his father. Solomon was successful, and everyone in Israel obeyed him. 24 Every official and every soldier, as well as all of David's other sons, were loyal to him. 25 The LORD made Solomon a great king, and the whole nation was amazed at how famous he was. In fact, no other king of Israel was as great as Solomon.

David Dies

26 David the son of Jesse was king of Israel 27 for forty years. He ruled from Hebron for seven years and from Jerusalem for thirty-three years. 28 David was rich and respected and lived to be an old man. Then he died, and his son Solomon became king.

29 Everything David did while he was king is included in the history written by the prophets Samuel, Nathan, and Gad. 30 They wrote about his powerful rule and about the things that happened not only to him, but also to Israel and the other nations.

[p] **29.21** *sacrifices to please the LORD*: See the note at 16.1.

29.23 1 K 2.12. **29.27** 2 S 5.4, 5; 1 Ch 3.1-4.

2 CHRONICLES

ABOUT THIS BOOK

Second Chronicles continues the history of Israel that was begun in 1 Chronicles. This book repeats information and many stories that are in 1 and 2 Kings, but from a slightly different viewpoint.

The book of 2 Chronicles begins with the rule of King Solomon, then tells the history of the two separate kingdoms of Judah and Israel down to the fall of Jerusalem in 586 B.C.

King Solomon is honored as the ideal king of Israel. The first part of 2 Chronicles (1–9) includes events from his rule, especially the building and dedication of the temple in Jerusalem and the beginning of worship there.

The second part of the book (10–36) begins with the rebellion of the northern tribes of Israel and the division of the country into two separate kingdoms, Judah in the south and Israel in the north. This part of 2 Chronicles is the history of Judah down to the time of Jerusalem's fall and destruction. Unlike 2 Kings, the book of 2 Chronicles includes very little information about the northern kingdom. According to 2 Chronicles, the people of Israel were sinful and turned their backs on the Lord, and so their history did not deserve to be told.

Second Chronicles, like 1 Chronicles, is very concerned that the Lord be worshiped in the proper way. Hezekiah and Josiah are two of the most respected kings of Judah, because they were always faithful to the Lord and did many things to see that he was properly worshiped and that his Law was obeyed.

This book tells how Jerusalem was destroyed and the people of Judah were led away as prisoners to Babylonia. But the book concludes with hope for the Jews. King Cyrus of Persia lets them return to Judah, and he promises:

> *"The LORD God will watch over any of his people who want to go back to Judah."*
>
> *(36.23b)*

A QUICK LOOK AT THIS BOOK

- Solomon's Wisdom and Wealth (1.1-17)
- Building and Dedication of the Jerusalem Temple (2.1—7.22)
- Other Events During Solomon's Rule (8.1—9.28)
- The Death of Solomon (9.29-31)
- The Northern Tribes of Israel Rebel against King Rehoboam (10.1-19)
- Kings of Judah (11.1—28.27)
- King Hezekiah and the Assyrian Invasion (29.1—32.33)
- King Manasseh and King Amon (33.1-25)
- King Josiah and *The Book of God's Law* (34.1—35.27)
- The Last Kings of Judah (36.1-16)
- Jerusalem Is Destroyed and the People Are Taken to Babylonia (36.17-21)
- King Cyrus of Persia Lets the Jews Return to Judah (36.22, 23)

The LORD Makes Solomon Wise

(1 Kings 3.1-15)

1 King Solomon, the son of David, was
now in complete control of his kingdom, because the LORD God had blessed
him and made him a powerful king.
2-5 At that time, the sacred tent that
Moses the servant of the LORD had made in
the desert was still kept at Gibeon, and in
front of the tent was the bronze altar that
Bezalel[a] had made.

One day, Solomon told the people of Israel, the army commanders, the officials,
and the family leaders, to go with him to
the place of worship at Gibeon, even
though his father King David had already
moved the sacred chest from Kiriath-
Jearim to the tent that he had set up for it
in Jerusalem. Solomon and the others went
to Gibeon to worship the LORD, 6 and there
at the bronze altar, Solomon offered a thousand animals as sacrifices to please the
LORD.[b]
7 God appeared to Solomon that night in
a dream and said, "Solomon, ask for anything you want, and I will give it to you."
8 Solomon answered:

LORD God, you were always loyal to
my father David, and now you have
made me king of Israel. 9 I am supposed to rule these people, but there
are as many of them as there are
specks of dust on the ground. So keep
the promise you made to my father
10 and make me wise. Give me the
knowledge I'll need to be the king of
this great nation of yours.

11 God replied:

Solomon, you could have asked me
to make you rich or famous or to let
you live a long time. Or you could have
asked for your enemies to be destroyed. Instead, you asked for wisdom
and knowledge to rule my people.
12 So I will make you wise and intelligent. But I will also make you richer
and more famous than any king before
or after you.

13 Solomon then left Gibeon and returned to Jerusalem, the capital city of Israel.

Solomon's Wealth

(1 Kings 10.26-29)

14 Solomon had a force of one thousand
four hundred chariots and twelve thousand
horses that he kept in Jerusalem and other
towns.
15 While Solomon was king of Israel,
there was silver and gold everywhere in
Jerusalem, and cedar was as common as
ordinary sycamore trees in the foothills.
16-17 Solomon's merchants bought his
horses and chariots in the regions of Musri
and Kue.[c] They paid about fifteen pounds
of silver for a chariot and almost four
pounds of silver for a horse. They also sold
horses and chariots to the Hittite and Syrian kings.

Solomon Asks Hiram To Help Build the Temple

(1 Kings 5.1-12)

2 Solomon decided to build a temple
where the LORD would be worshiped,
and also to build a palace for himself. 2 He
assigned seventy thousand men to carry
building supplies and eighty thousand to
cut stone from the hills. And he chose
three thousand six hundred men to supervise these workers.
3 Solomon sent the following message to
King Hiram of Tyre:

Years ago, when my father David
was building his palace, you supplied
him with cedar logs. Now will you send
me supplies? 4 I am building a temple
where the LORD my God will be worshiped. Sweet-smelling incense will be

[a] **1.2-5** *Bezalel*: Hebrew "Bezalel son of Uri son of Hur." [b] **1.6** *sacrifices to please the LORD*: These sacrifices have traditionally been called "whole burnt offerings," because the whole animal was burned on the altar. A main purpose of such sacrifices was to please the LORD with the smell of the sacrifice, and so in the CEV they are often called "sacrifices to please the LORD."

[c] **1.16,17** *Musri and Kue*: Hebrew "Egypt and Kue." Musri and Kue were regions located in what is today southeast Turkey.

1.2-5 a 2 S 6.1-17; 1 Ch 13.5-14; 15.25—16.1; **b** Ex 38.1-7. **1.9** Gn 13.16; 28.14.
1.14 1 K 4.26. **1.16,17** Dt 17.16.

burned there, and sacred bread will be offered to him. Worshipers will offer sacrifices to the LORD every morning and evening, every Sabbath, and on the first day of each month, as well as during all our religious festivals. These things will be done for all time, just as the LORD has commanded.

5 This will be a great temple, because our God is greater than all other gods. 6 No one can ever build a temple large enough for God—even the heavens are too small a place for him to live in! All I can do is build a place where we can offer sacrifices to him.

7 Send me a worker who can not only carve, but who can work with gold, silver, bronze, and iron, as well as make brightly colored cloth. The person you send will work here in Judah and Jerusalem with the skilled workers that my father has already hired.

8 I know that you have workers who are experts at cutting lumber in Lebanon. So would you please send me some cedar, pine, and juniper logs? My workers will be there to help them, 9 because I'll need a lot of lumber to build such a large and glorious temple. 10 I will pay your woodcutters one hundred twenty-five thousand bushels of wheat, the same amount of barley, one hundred fifteen thousand gallons of wine, and that same amount of olive oil.

11 Hiram sent his answer back to Solomon:

I know that the LORD must love his people, because he has chosen you to be their king. 12 Praise the LORD God of Israel who made heaven and earth! He has given David a son who isn't only wise and smart, but who has the knowledge to build a temple for the LORD and a palace for himself.

13 I am sending Huram Abi to you. He is very bright. 14 His mother was from the Israelite tribe of Dan, and his father was from Tyre. Not only is Huram an expert at working with gold, silver, bronze, iron, stone, and wood, but he can also make colored cloth and fine linen. And he can carve anything if you give him a pattern to follow. He can help your workers and those hired by your father King David.

15 Go ahead and send the wheat, barley, olive oil, and wine you promised to pay my workers. 16 I will tell them to start cutting down trees in Lebanon. They will cut as many as you need, then tie them together into rafts, and float them down along the coast to Joppa. Your workers can take them to Jerusalem from there.

Solomon's Work Force

17 Solomon counted all the foreigners who were living in Israel, just as his father David had done when he was king, and the total was 153,600. 18 He assigned 70,000 of them to carry building supplies and 80,000 of them to cut stone from the hills. He chose 3,600 others to supervise the workers and to make sure the work was completed.

The Temple Is Built

(1 Kings 6.1-38)

3 1-2 Solomon's workers began building the temple in Jerusalem on the second day of the second month,[d] four years after Solomon had become king of Israel. It was built on Mount Moriah where the LORD had appeared to David at the threshing place that had belonged to Araunah[e] from Jebus.

3 The inside of the temple was ninety feet long and thirty feet wide, according to the older standards.[f] 4 Across the front of the temple was a porch thirty feet wide and thirty feet[g] high. The inside walls of the porch were covered with pure gold.

[d]**3.1,2** *second month*: Ziv, the second month of the Hebrew calendar, from about mid-April to mid-May. [e]**3.1,2** *Araunah*: The Hebrew text has "Ornan," another spelling of the name (see 2 Samuel 24.18-25; 1 Chronicles 21.18—22.1). [f]**3.3** *according to the older standards*: There were possibly two different standards of measurement during Israel's history. [g]**3.4** *thirty feet*: Some manuscripts of two ancient translations; Hebrew "one hundred eighty feet."

2.6 1 K 8.27; 2 Ch 6.18. **3.1,2** Gn 22.2.

5 Solomon had the inside walls of the
temple's main room paneled first with pine
and then with a layer of gold, and he had
them decorated with carvings of palm trees
and designs that looked like chains. 6 He
used precious stones to decorate the temple, and he used gold imported from Parvaim[h] 7 to decorate the ceiling beams, the
doors, the door frames, and the walls.
Solomon also had the workers carve designs of winged creatures into the walls.

8 The most holy place was thirty feet
square, and its walls were covered with almost twenty-five tons of fine gold. 9 More
than a pound of gold was used to cover the
heads of the nails. The walls of the small
storage rooms were also covered with gold.[i]

10 Solomon had two statues of winged
creatures[j] made to put in the most holy
place, and he covered them with gold.
11-13 Each creature had two wings and was
fifteen feet from the tip of one wing to the
tip of the other wing. Solomon set them
next to each other in the most holy place,
facing the doorway. Their wings were
spread out and reached all the way across
the thirty foot room.

14 A curtain[k] was made of fine linen woven with blue, purple, and red wool, and
embroidered with designs of winged creatures.

The Two Columns
(1 Kings 7.15-22)

15 Two columns were made for the entrance to the temple. Each one was fifty-
two feet tall and had a cap on top that was
seven and a half feet high. 16 The top of
each column was decorated with designs
that looked like chains[l] and with a hundred
carvings of pomegranates.[m] 17 Solomon
had one of the columns placed on the
south side of the temple's entrance; it was
called Jachin.[n] The other one was placed
on the north side of the entrance; it was
called Boaz.[o]

The Furnishings for the Temple
(1 Kings 7.23-51)

4 Solomon had a bronze altar made that
was thirty feet square and fifteen feet
high. 2 He also gave orders to make a large
metal bowl called the Sea. It was fifteen
feet across, about seven and a half feet
deep, and forty-five feet around. 3 Its outer
edge was decorated with two rows of carvings of bulls, ten bulls to every eighteen
inches, all made from the same piece of
metal as the bowl. 4 The bowl itself sat on
top of twelve bronze bulls, with three bulls
facing outward in each of four directions.
5 The sides of the bowl were four inches
thick, and its rim was in the shape of a cup
that curved outward like flower petals. The
bowl held about fifteen thousand gallons.

6 He also made ten small bowls and put
five on each side of the large bowl. The
small bowls were used to wash the animals
that were burned on the altar as sacrifices,
and the priests used the water in the large
bowl to wash their hands.

7 Ten gold lampstands were also made
according to the plans. Solomon placed
these lampstands inside the temple, five on
each side of the main room. 8 He also
made ten tables and placed them in the
main room, five on each side. And he made
a hundred small gold sprinkling bowls.

9 Solomon gave orders to build two
courtyards: a smaller one that only priests
could use and a larger one. The doors to
these courtyards were covered with bronze.
10 The large bowl called the Sea was placed
near the southeast corner of the temple.

11 Huram made shovels, sprinkling
bowls, and pans for hot ashes. Here is a list
of the other furnishings he made for God's
temple: 12 two columns, two bowl-shaped

[h] **3.6** *Parvaim*: An unknown place. [i] **3.9** *The walls . . . gold*: One possible meaning for the difficult Hebrew text. [j] **3.10** *statues of winged creatures*: These were symbols of the LORD's throne on earth (see Exodus 25.18-22). [k] **3.14** *A curtain*: To separate the most holy place from the main room of the temple. [l] **3.16** *designs that looked like chains*: One possible meaning for the difficult Hebrew text. [m] **3.16** *pomegranates*: A pomegranate is a small red fruit that looks like an apple. In ancient times, it was a symbol of life. [n] **3.17** *Jachin*: Or "He (God) makes secure." [o] **3.17** *Boaz*: Or "He (God) is strong."

3.8 Ex 26.31-34. **3.10-13** Ex 25.18-20. **3.14** Ex 26.31-33. **4.1** Ex 27.1, 2. **4.6** Ex 30.17-21. **4.7** Ex 25.31-40. **4.8** Ex 25.23-30.

caps for the tops of these columns, two chain designs on the caps, 13 four hundred pomegranates[p] for the chain designs, 14 the stands and the small bowls, 15 the large bowl and the twelve bulls that held it up, 16 pans for hot ashes, as well as shovels and meat forks.

Huram made all these things out of polished bronze 17 by pouring melted bronze into the clay molds he had set up near the Jordan River, between Succoth and Zeredah.

18 There were so many bronze furnishings that no one ever knew how much bronze it took to make them.

19 Solomon also gave orders to make the following temple furnishings out of gold: the altar, the tables that held the sacred loaves of bread,[q] 20 the lampstands and the lamps that burned in front of the most holy place, 21 flower designs, lamps and tongs, 22 lamp snuffers, small sprinkling bowls, ladles, fire pans, and the doors to the most holy place and the main room of the temple.

5 After the LORD's temple was finished, Solomon put in its storage rooms everything that his father David had dedicated to the LORD, including the gold and silver, and the objects used in worship.

Solomon Brings the Sacred Chest to the Temple

(1 Kings 8.1-13)

2-3 The sacred chest had been kept on Mount Zion, also known as the city of David. But Solomon decided to have the chest moved to the temple while everyone was in Jerusalem to celebrate the Festival of Shelters during the seventh month.[r]

Solomon called together all the important leaders of Israel. 4-5 Then the priests and the Levites picked up the sacred chest, the sacred tent, and the objects used for worship, and they carried them to the temple. 6 Solomon and a crowd of people walked in front of the chest, and along the way they sacrificed more sheep and cattle than could be counted.

7 The priests carried the chest into the most holy place and put it under the winged creatures, 8 whose wings covered the chest and the poles used for carrying it. 9 The poles were so long that they could be seen from just outside the most holy place, but not from anywhere else. And they stayed there from then on.

10 The only things kept in the chest were the two flat stones Moses had put there when the LORD made his agreement with the people of Israel at Mount Sinai,[s] after bringing them out of Egypt.

11-13 The priests of every group had gone through the ceremony to make themselves clean and acceptable to the LORD. The Levite musicians, including Asaph, Heman, Jeduthun, and their sons and relatives, were wearing robes of fine linen. They were standing on the east side of the altar, playing cymbals, small harps, and other stringed instruments. One hundred twenty priests were with these musicians, and they were blowing trumpets.

They were praising the LORD by playing music and singing:

"The LORD is good,
and his love never ends."

Suddenly a cloud filled the temple as the priests were leaving the holy place. 14 The LORD's glory was in that cloud, and the light from it was so bright that the priests could not stay inside to do their work.

6 Solomon prayed:

"Our LORD, you said that you
would live in a dark cloud.
2 Now I've built a glorious temple
where you can live forever."

[p]**4.13** *pomegranates*: See the note at 3.16. [q]**4.19** *sacred loaves of bread*: This bread was offered to the LORD and was a symbol of the LORD's presence in the temple. It was put out on special tables, and was replaced with fresh bread every week (see Leviticus 24.5-9). [r]**5.2,3** *seventh month*: Tishri (also called Ethanim), the seventh month of the Hebrew calendar, from about mid-September to mid-October. [s]**5.10** *Sinai*: Hebrew "Horeb."

5.1 2 S 8.11; 1 Ch 18.11. **5.2,3** 2 S 6.11-15; 1 Ch 15.25-28. **5.10** Dt 10.5. **5.11-13,14 a** 1 Ch 16.41, 42; 3 Macc 6.32; **b** 1 Ch 16.34; 2 Ch 7.3; Ezra 3.11; Ps 100.5; 106.1; 107.1; 118.1; 136.1; Jr 33.11; **c** Ex 40.34, 35.

Solomon Speaks to the People
(1 Kings 8.14-21)

3 Solomon turned toward the people
standing there. Then he blessed them
4-6 and said:

Praise the LORD God of Israel! He
brought his people out of Egypt long
ago and later kept his promise to make
my father David the king of Israel. The
LORD also promised him that Jerusalem would be the city where his temple will be built, and now that promise
has come true.

7 When my father wanted to build a
temple for the LORD God of Israel,
8 the LORD said, "It's good that you
want to build a temple where I can be
worshiped. 9 But you're not the one to
do it. Your son will build the temple to
honor me."

10 The LORD has done what he
promised. I am now the king of Israel,
and I've built a temple for the LORD
our God. 11 I've also put the sacred
chest in the temple. And in that chest
are the two flat stones on which is
written the solemn agreement the
LORD made with our ancestors when
he rescued them from Egypt.

Solomon Prays at the Temple
(1 Kings 8.22-53)

12-13 Earlier, Solomon had a bronze platform made that was about eight feet square
and five feet high, and he put it in the center of the outer courtyard near the altar.
Solomon stood on the platform facing the
altar with everyone standing behind him.
Then he lifted his arms toward heaven; he
knelt down 14 and prayed:

LORD God of Israel, no other god in
heaven or on earth is like you!

You never forget the agreement you
made with your people, and you are
loyal to anyone who faithfully obeys
your teachings. 15 My father David was
your servant, and today you have kept
every promise you made to him.

16 You promised that someone from
his family would always be king of Israel, if they do their best to obey you,
just as he did. 17 Please keep this
promise you made to your servant
David. 18 There's not enough room in
all of heaven for you, LORD God. How
could you possibly live on earth in this
temple I have built? 19 But I ask you to
answer my prayer. 20 This is the temple where you have chosen to be worshiped. Please watch over it day and
night and listen when I turn toward it
and pray. 21 I am your servant, and the
people of Israel belong to you, and so
whenever any of us look toward this
temple and pray, answer from your
home in heaven and forgive our sins.

22 Suppose someone accuses a person of a crime, and the accused has to
stand in front of the altar in your temple and say, "I swear I am innocent!"
23 Listen from heaven and decide who
is right. Then punish the guilty person
and let the innocent one go free.

24 Suppose your people Israel sin
against you, and then an enemy defeats them. If they come to this temple
and beg for forgiveness, 25 listen from
your home in heaven. Forgive them
and bring them back to the land you
gave their ancestors.

26 Suppose your people sin against
you, and you punish them by holding
back the rain. If they stop sinning and
turn toward this temple to pray in your
name, 27 listen from your home in
heaven and forgive them. The people
of Israel are your servants, so teach
them to live right. And send rain on
the land you promised them forever.

28 Sometimes the crops may dry up
or rot or be eaten by locusts[t] or grasshoppers, and your people will be starving. Sometimes enemies may surround their towns, or your people will
become sick with deadly diseases.
29 Please listen when anyone in Israel
truly feels sorry and sincerely prays
with arms lifted toward your temple.
30 You know what is in everyone's
heart. So from your home in heaven

[t]**6.28** *locusts*: A type of grasshopper that comes in swarms and causes great damage to crops.

6.4-9 2 S 7.1-13; 1 Ch 17.1-12. **6.16** 1 K 2.4. **6.18** 2 Ch 2.6. **6.20** Dt 12.5-19.

answer their prayers, according to
what they do and what is in their
hearts. 31 Then your people will worship you and obey you for as long as
they live in the land you gave their
ancestors.

32 Foreigners will hear about you
and your mighty power, and some of
them will come to live among your
people Israel. If any of them pray toward this temple, 33 listen from your
home in heaven and answer their
prayers. Then everyone on earth will
worship you, just as your own people
Israel do, and they will know that I
have built this temple in your honor.

34 Sometimes you will order your
people to attack their enemies. Then
your people will turn toward this temple I have built for you in your chosen
city, and they will pray to you. 35 Answer their prayers from heaven and
give them victory.

36 Everyone sins. But when your
people sin against you, suppose you
get angry enough to let their enemies
drag them away to foreign countries.
37-39 Later, they may feel sorry for what
they did and ask your forgiveness. Answer them when they pray toward this
temple I have built for you in your
chosen city, here in this land you gave
their ancestors. From your home in
heaven, listen to their sincere prayers
and forgive your people who have
sinned against you.

40 LORD God, hear us when we pray
in this temple. 41 Come to your new
home, where we have already placed
the sacred chest, which is the symbol
of your strength. I pray that when the
priests announce your power to save
people, those who are faithful to you
will celebrate what you've done for
them. 42 Always remember the love you
had for your servant David,[u] so that
you will not reject your chosen kings.

Solomon Dedicates the Temple

(1 Kings 8.62-66)

7 As soon as Solomon finished praying,
fire came down from heaven and
burned up the offerings. The LORD's dazzling glory then filled the temple, 2 and the
priests could not go in.

3 When the crowd of people saw the fire
and the LORD's glory, they knelt down and
worshiped the LORD. They prayed:

"The LORD is good,
and his love never ends."

4-5 Solomon and the people dedicated
the temple to the LORD by sacrificing
twenty-two thousand cattle and one hundred twenty thousand sheep. 6 Everybody
stood up during the ceremony. The priests
were in their assigned places, blowing their
trumpets. And the Levites faced them,
playing the musical instruments that David
had made for them to use when they
praised the LORD for his never-ending love.

7 On that same day, Solomon dedicated
the courtyard in front of the temple and got
it ready to be used for worship. The bronze
altar he had made was too small, so he
used the courtyard to offer sacrifices to
please the LORD[v] and grain sacrifices, and
also to send up in smoke the fat from the
other offerings.

8 For seven days, Solomon and the
crowd celebrated the Festival of Shelters,
and people came from as far away as the
Egyptian Gorge in the south and Lebo-
Hamath in the north. 9 Then on the next
day, everyone came together for worship.
They had celebrated a total of fourteen
days, seven days for the dedication of the
altar and seven more days for the festival.
10 Then on the twenty-third day of the seventh month,[w] Solomon sent everyone
home. They left very happy because of all
the good things the LORD had done for
David and Solomon, and for his people
Israel.

[u]**6.42** *the love you had for your servant David*: Or "how loyal your servant David was to you."
[v]**7.7** *sacrifices to please the LORD*: See the note at 1.6. [w]**7.10** *seventh month*: See the note at 5.2, 3.

6.41,42 Ps 132.8-10. **7.1** Lv 9.23, 24. **7.3** 1 Ch 16.34; 2 Ch 5.11-13; Ezra 3.11; Ps 100.5; 106.1; 107.1; 118.1; 136.1; Jr 33.11.

The LORD Appears to Solomon Again

(1 Kings 9.1-9)

11 The LORD's temple and Solomon's palace were now finished. In fact, everything Solomon had planned to do was completed.

12 Some time later, the LORD appeared to Solomon in a dream and said:

I heard your prayer, and I have chosen this temple as the place where sacrifices will be offered to me.

13 Suppose I hold back the rain or send locusts[x] to eat the crops or make my people suffer with deadly diseases. 14 If my own people will humbly pray and turn back to me and stop sinning, then I will answer them from heaven. I will forgive them and make their land fertile once again. 15 I will hear the prayers made in this temple, 16 because it belongs to me, and this is where I will be worshiped forever. I will never stop watching over it.

17 Your father David obeyed me, and now, Solomon, you must do the same. Obey my laws and teachings, 18 and I will keep my solemn promise to him that someone from your family will always be king of Israel.

19 But if you or any of the people of Israel disobey my laws or start worshiping foreign gods, 20 I will pull you out of this land I gave you. I will desert this temple where I said I would be worshiped, so that people everywhere will think it is only a joke and will make fun of it. 21 This temple is now magnificent. But when these things happen, everyone who walks by it will be shocked and will ask, "Why did the LORD do such a terrible thing to his people and to this temple?" 22 Then they will answer, "It was because the people of Israel rejected the LORD their God, who rescued their ancestors from Egypt, and they started worshiping other gods."

Other Things Solomon Did

(1 Kings 9.10-28)

8 It took twenty years for the LORD's temple and Solomon's palace to be built. 2 After that, Solomon had his workers rebuild the towns that Hiram had given him. Then Solomon sent Israelites to live in those towns.

3 Solomon attacked and captured the town of Hamath-Zobah. 4 He had his workers build the town of Tadmor in the desert and some towns in Hamath where he could keep his supplies. 5 He strengthened Upper Beth-Horon and Lower Beth-Horon by adding walls and gates that could be locked. 6 He did the same thing to the town of Baalath and to the cities where he kept supplies, chariots, and horses. Solomon had his workers build whatever he wanted in Jerusalem, Lebanon, and anywhere else in his kingdom.

7-9 Solomon did not force the Israelites to do his work. Instead, they were his soldiers, officers, army commanders, and cavalry troops. But he did make slaves of the Hittites, Amorites, Perizzites, Hivites, and Jebusites who were living in Israel. These were the descendants of those foreigners the Israelites did not destroy, and they remained Israel's slaves.

10 Solomon appointed two hundred fifty officers to be in charge of his workers.

11 Solomon's wife, the daughter of the king of Egypt, moved from the part of Jerusalem called David's City to her new palace that Solomon had built. The sacred chest had been kept in David's City, which made his palace sacred, and so Solomon's wife could no longer live there.

12 Solomon offered sacrifices to the LORD on the altar he had built in front of the temple. 13 He followed the requirements that Moses had given for sacrifices offered on the Sabbath, on the first day of each month, the Festival of Thin Bread, the Harvest Festival, and the Festival of Shelters.

14 Solomon then assigned the priests

[x]**7.13** *locusts*: See the note at 6.28.
7.18 1 K 2.4. **8.13** **a** Nu 28.9, 10; **b** Nu 28.11-15; **c** Ex 23.14-17; 34.22, 23; Nu 28.16—29.39; Dt 16.16.

and the Levites their duties at the temple, and he followed the instructions that his father David had given him. Some of the Levites were to lead music and help the priests in their duties, and others were to guard the temple gates 15 and the storage rooms. The priests and Levites followed these instructions exactly.

16 Everything Solomon had planned to do was now finished—from the laying of the temple's foundation to its completion.

17 Solomon went to Ezion-Geber and Eloth, two Edomite towns on the Red Sea.[y] 18 Hiram sent him ships and some of his experienced sailors. They went with Solomon's own sailors to the country of Ophir[z] and brought back about seventeen tons of gold for Solomon.

The Queen of Sheba Visits Solomon

(1 Kings 10.1-13)

9 The Queen of Sheba heard how famous Solomon was, so she went to Jerusalem to test him with difficult questions. She took along several of her officials, and she loaded her camels with gifts of spices, jewels, and gold. When she arrived, she and Solomon talked about everything she could think of. 2 He answered every question, no matter how difficult it was.

3-4 The Queen was amazed at Solomon's wisdom. She was breathless when she saw his palace,[a] the food on his table, his officials, all his servants in their uniforms, and the sacrifices he offered at the LORD's temple. 5 She said:

> Solomon, in my own country I had heard about your wisdom and all you've done. 6 But I didn't believe it until I saw it with my own eyes! And there's so much I didn't hear about. You are greater than I was told. 7 Your people and officials are lucky to be here where they can listen to the wise things you say.
>
> 8 I praise the LORD your God. He is pleased with you and has made you king of Israel. God loves the people of this country and will never desert them, so he has given them a king who will rule fairly and honestly.

9 The Queen of Sheba gave Solomon almost five tons of gold, a large amount of jewels, and the best spices anyone had ever seen.

10-12 In return, Solomon gave her everything she wanted—even more than she had given him. Then she and her officials went back to their own country.

Solomon's Wealth

(1 Kings 10.14-29)

Hiram's and Solomon's sailors brought gold, juniper wood, and jewels from the country of Ophir. Solomon used the wood to make steps[b] for the temple and palace, and harps and other stringed instruments for the musicians. Nothing like these had ever been made in Judah.

13 Solomon received about twenty-five tons of gold each year, 14 not counting what the merchants and traders brought him. The kings of Arabia and the leaders of Israel also gave him gold and silver.

15 Solomon made two hundred gold shields that weighed about seven and a half pounds each. 16 He also made three hundred smaller gold shields that weighed almost four pounds, and he put these shields in his palace in Forest Hall.

17 His throne was made of ivory and covered with pure gold. 18 It had a gold footstool attached to it and armrests on each side. There was a statue of a lion on each side of the throne, 19 and there were two lion statues on each of the six steps leading up to the throne. No other throne in the world was like Solomon's.

20 Solomon's cups and dishes in Forest Hall were made of pure gold, because silver was almost worthless in those days.

21 Solomon had a lot of seagoing ships.[c]

[y] **8.17** *Red Sea*: Hebrew *yam suph*, here referring to the Gulf of Aqaba, since the term is extended to include the northeastern arm of the Red Sea (see also the note at Exodus 13.18). [z] **8.18** *Ophir*: The location of this place is not known. [a] **9.3,4** *his palace*: Or "the temple." [b] **9.10-12** *steps*: Or "stools" or "railings." [c] **9.21** *seagoing ships*: The Hebrew text has "ships of Tarshish," which may have been a Phoenician city in Spain. "Ships of Tarshish" probably means large, seagoing ships.

9.1-9 Mt 12.42; Lk 11.31.

Every three years he sent them out with Hiram's ships to bring back gold, silver, and ivory, as well as monkeys and peacocks.[d]

22 Solomon was the richest and wisest king in the world. 23-24 Year after year, other kings came to hear the wisdom God had given him. And they brought gifts of silver and gold, as well as clothes, weapons, spices, horses, and mules.

25 Solomon had four thousand stalls for his horses and chariots, and he owned twelve thousand horses that he kept in Jerusalem and other towns.

26 He ruled all the nations from the Euphrates River in the north to the land of Philistia in the south, as far as the border of Egypt.

27 While Solomon was king, there was silver everywhere in Jerusalem, and cedar was as common as the sycamore trees in the western foothills. 28 Solomon's horses were brought in from other countries, including Musri.[e]

Solomon Dies

(1 Kings 11.41-43)

29 Everything else Solomon did while he was king is written in the records of Nathan the prophet, Ahijah the prophet from Shiloh, and Iddo the prophet who wrote about Jeroboam son of Nebat. 30 After Solomon had ruled forty years from Jerusalem, 31 he died and was buried in the city of his father David. His son Rehoboam then became king.

Some of the People Rebel against Rehoboam

(1 Kings 12.1-20)

10 Rehoboam went to Shechem where everyone was waiting to crown him king.

2 Jeroboam son of Nebat heard what was happening, and he returned from Egypt, where he had gone to hide from Solomon. 3 The people from the northern tribes of Israel sent for him. Then together they went to Rehoboam and said, 4 "Your father Solomon forced us to work very hard. But if you make our work easier, we will serve you and do whatever you ask."

5 Rehoboam replied, "Come back in three days for my answer." So the people left.

6 Rehoboam went to some leaders who had been his father's senior officials, and he asked them, "What should I tell these people?"

7 They answered, "If you want them to serve and obey you, then you should be kind and promise to make their work easier."

8 But Rehoboam refused their advice and went to the younger men who had grown up with him and were now his officials. 9 He asked, "What do you think I should say to these people who asked me to make their work easier?"

10 His younger advisors said:

> Here's what we think you should say to them: "Compared to me, my father was weak.[f] 11 He made you work hard, but I'll make you work even harder. He punished you with whips, but I'll use whips with pieces of sharp metal!"

12 Three days later, Jeroboam and the others came back. 13 Rehoboam ignored the advice of the older advisors. He spoke bluntly 14 and told them exactly what his own advisors had suggested. He said: "My father made you work hard, but I'll make you work even harder. He punished you with whips, but I'll use whips with pieces of sharp metal!"

15-19 When the people realized that Rehoboam would not listen to them, they shouted: "We don't have to be loyal to David's family. We can do what we want. Come on, people of Israel, let's go home! Rehoboam can rule his own people."

Adoniram[g] was in charge of the work force, and Rehoboam sent him to talk to the people. But they stoned him to death. Then Rehoboam ran to his chariot and hurried back to Jerusalem.

Everyone from Israel's northern tribes

[d]**9.21** *peacocks*: Or "baboons." [e]**9.28** *Musri*: See the note at 1.16, 17. [f]**10.10** *Compared . . . weak*: Hebrew "My little finger is bigger than my father's waist." [g]**10.15-19** *Adoniram*: The Hebrew text has "Hadoram," another spelling of the name.

9.25 1 K 4.26. **9.26** Gn 15.18; 1 K 4.21. **9.28** Dt 17.16. **10.15-19** 2 S 20.1.

went home, leaving Rehoboam to rule only the people from Judah. And since that day, the people of Israel have been opposed to David's descendants in Judah.[h] All of this happened just as Ahijah the LORD's prophet from Shiloh had told Jeroboam.

Shemaiah the Prophet Warns Rehoboam

(1 Kings 12.21-24)

11 After Rehoboam returned to Jerusalem, he decided to attack Israel and regain control of the whole country. So he called together one hundred eighty thousand soldiers from the tribes of Judah and Benjamin.

2 Meanwhile, the LORD had told Shemaiah the prophet 3 to tell Rehoboam and everyone from Judah and Benjamin, 4 "The LORD warns you not to go to war against the people from the northern tribes—they are your relatives. Go home! The LORD is the one who made these things happen."

Rehoboam and his army obeyed the LORD's message and did not attack Jeroboam and his troops.

Rehoboam Fortifies Cities in Judah

5 Rehoboam ruled from Jerusalem, and he had several cities in Judah turned into fortresses so he could use them to defend his country. These cities included 6 Bethlehem, Etam, Tekoa, 7 Beth-Zur, Soco, Adullam, 8 Gath, Mareshah, Ziph, 9 Adoraim, Lachish, Azekah, 10 Zorah, Aijalon, and Hebron. After he had fortified these cities in the territories of Judah and Benjamin, 11 he assigned an army commander to each of them and stocked them with supplies of food, olive oil, and wine, 12 as well as with shields and spears. He used these fortified cities to keep control of Judah and Benjamin.

The Priests and the Levites Support Rehoboam

13 The priests and Levites from the northern tribes of Israel gave their support to King Rehoboam. 14 And since Jeroboam and the kings of Israel that followed him would not allow any Levites to serve as priests, most Levites left their towns and pasturelands in Israel and moved to Jerusalem and other towns in Judah. 15 Jeroboam chose his own priests to serve at the local shrines[i] in Israel and at the places of worship where he had set up statues of goat-demons and of calves.

16 But some of the people from Israel wanted to worship the LORD God, just as their ancestors had done. So they followed the priests and Levites to Jerusalem, where they could offer sacrifices to the LORD. 17 For the next three years, they lived in Judah and were loyal to Rehoboam and his kingdom, just as they had been loyal to David and Solomon.

Rehoboam's Family

18 Rehoboam married Mahalath, whose father was Jerimoth son of David, and whose mother was Abihail the daughter of Eliab and granddaughter of Jesse. 19 Rehoboam and Mahalath had three sons: Jeush, Shemariah, and Zaham. 20 Then Rehoboam married Maacah the daughter of Absalom. Their sons were Abijah, Attai, Ziza, and Shelomith.

21 Rehoboam had eighteen wives, but he also married sixty other women,[j] and he was the father of twenty-eight sons and sixty daughters. Rehoboam loved his wife Maacah the most, 22 so he chose their oldest son Abijah to be the next king. 23 Rehoboam was wise enough to put one of his sons in charge of each fortified city in his kingdom. He gave them all the supplies they needed and found wives for every one of them.

King Shishak of Egypt Invades Judah

(1 Kings 14.25-28)

12 Soon after Rehoboam had control of his kingdom, he and everyone in Judah stopped obeying the LORD. 2 So in

[h] **10.15-19** *the people of Israel have been opposed . . . Judah*: From this time on, "Israel" usually refers only to the northern kingdom. The southern kingdom is called "Judah." [i] **11.15** *local shrines*: The Hebrew text has "high places," which were local places to worship foreign gods.

[j] **11.21** *other women*: This translates a Hebrew word for women who were legally bound to a man, but without the full privileges of a wife.

11.15 1 K 12.31.

the fifth year of Rehoboam's rule, the LORD punished them for their unfaithfulness and allowed King Shishak of Egypt to invade Judah. 3 Shishak attacked with his army of one thousand two hundred chariots and sixty thousand cavalry troops, as well as Egyptian soldiers from Libya, Sukkoth, and Ethiopia.[k] 4 He captured every one of the fortified cities in Judah and then marched to Jerusalem.

5 Rehoboam and the leaders of Judah had gone to Jerusalem to escape Shishak's invasion. And while they were there, Shemaiah the prophet told them, "The LORD says that because you have disobeyed him, he has now abandoned you. The LORD will not help you against Shishak!"

6 Rehoboam and the leaders were sorry for what they had done and admitted, "The LORD is right. We have deserted him."

7 When the LORD heard this, he told Shemaiah:

> The people of Judah are truly sorry for their sins, and so I won't let Shishak completely destroy them. But because I am still angry, 8 he will conquer and rule them.
>
> Then my people will know what it's like to serve a foreign king instead of serving me.

9 Shishak attacked Jerusalem and took all the valuable things from the temple and from the palace, including Solomon's gold shields.

10 Rehoboam had bronze shields made to replace the gold ones, and he ordered the guards at the city gates to keep them safe. 11 Whenever Rehoboam went to the LORD's temple, the guards carried the shields. But they always took them back to the guardroom as soon as he had finished worshiping.

12 Rehoboam turned back to the LORD, and so the LORD did not let Judah be completely destroyed, and Judah was prosperous again.

Rehoboam's Rule in Judah

(1 Kings 14.21, 29-31)

13 Rehoboam was forty-one years old when he became king, and he ruled seventeen years from Jerusalem, the city where the LORD had chosen to be worshiped. His mother Naamah was from Ammon. Rehoboam was a powerful king, 14 but he still did wrong and refused to obey the LORD.

15 Everything else Rehoboam did while he was king, including a history of his family, is written in the records of the two prophets, Shemaiah and Iddo. During Rehoboam's rule, he and King Jeroboam of Israel were constantly at war. 16 When Rehoboam died, he was buried beside his ancestors in Jerusalem, and his son Abijah became king.

King Abijah of Judah

(1 Kings 15.1-8)

13 Abijah[l] became king of Judah in Jeroboam's eighteenth year as king of Israel, 2 and he ruled from Jerusalem for three years. His mother was Micaiah the daughter of Uriel from Gibeah.

Some time later, Abijah and King Jeroboam of Israel went to war against each other. 3 Abijah's army had four hundred thousand troops, and Jeroboam met him in battle with eight hundred thousand troops.

4 Abijah went to the top of Mount Zemaraim[m] in the hills of Ephraim and shouted:

> Listen, Jeroboam and all you Israelites! 5 The LORD God of Israel has made a solemn promise that every king of Israel will be from David's family. 6 But Jeroboam, you were King Solomon's official, and you rebelled. 7 Then right after Rehoboam became king, you and your bunch of worthless followers challenged Rehoboam, who was too young to know how to stop you.

[k] **12.3** *Ethiopia*: The Hebrew text has "Cush," which was a region south of Egypt that included parts of the present countries of Ethiopia and Sudan. [l] **13.1** *Abijah*: In 1 Kings 15.1-8 his name is spelled "Abijam." [m] **13.4** *Mount Zemaraim*: Probably located on the northern border of the territory of Benjamin.

12.9 1 K 10.16, 17; 2 Ch 9.15, 16.

The LORD speaks to Samuel *1 Samuel 3.1-18*

David and Goliath

1 Samuel 17.1-51

8 Now you and your powerful army think you can stand up to the kingdom that the LORD has given to David's descendants. The only gods you have are those gold statues of calves that Jeroboam made for you. 9 You don't even have descendants of Aaron on your side, because you forced out the LORD's priests and Levites. In their place, you appoint ordinary people to be priests, just as the foreign nations do. In fact, anyone who brings a bull and seven rams to the altar can become a priest of your so-called gods.

10 But we have not turned our backs on the LORD God! Aaron's own descendants serve as our priests, and the Levites are their assistants. 11 Two times every day they offer sacrifices and burn incense to the LORD. They set out the sacred loaves of bread on a table that has been purified, and they light the lamps in the gold lampstand every day at sunset. We follow the commands of the LORD our God—you have rejected him! 12 That's why God is on our side and will lead us into battle when the priests sound the signal on the trumpets. It's no use, Israelites. You might as well give up. There's no way you can defeat the LORD, the God your ancestors worshiped.

13 But while Abijah was talking, Jeroboam had sent some of his troops to attack Judah's army from behind, while the rest attacked from the front. 14 Judah's army realized they were trapped, and so they prayed to the LORD. The priests blew the signal on the trumpet, 15 and the troops let out a battle cry. Then with Abijah leading them into battle, God defeated Jeroboam and Israel's army. 16 The Israelites ran away, and God helped Judah's soldiers slaughter 17 five hundred thousand enemy troops. 18 Judah's army won because they had trusted the LORD God of their ancestors.

19 Abijah kept up his attack on Jeroboam's army and captured the Israelite towns of Bethel, Jeshanah, and Ephron, as well as the villages around them.

20 Jeroboam never regained his power during the rest of Abijah's rule. The LORD punished Jeroboam, and he died, but Abijah became more powerful.

21 Abijah had a total of fourteen wives, twenty-two sons, and sixteen daughters. 22 Everything Abijah said and did while he was king is written in the records of Iddo the prophet.

King Asa of Judah

14 Abijah died and was buried in Jerusalem. Then his son Asa became king, and Judah had ten years of peace.

2 Asa obeyed the LORD his God and did right. 3 He destroyed the local shrines[n] and the altars to foreign gods. He smashed the stone images of gods and cut down the sacred poles[o] used in worshiping the goddess Asherah. 4 Then he told everyone in Judah to worship the LORD God, just as their ancestors had done, and to obey his laws and teachings. 5 He destroyed every local shrine and incense altar in Judah.

6 The LORD blessed Judah with peace while Asa was king, and so during that time, Asa fortified many of the towns. 7 He said to the people, "Let's build walls and defense towers for these towns, and put in gates that can be locked with bars. This land still belongs to us, because we have obeyed the LORD our God. He has given us peace from all our enemies." The people did everything Asa had suggested.

8 Asa had a large army of brave soldiers: Three hundred thousand of them were from the tribe of Judah and were armed with shields and spears; two hundred eighty thousand were from Benjamin and were armed with bows and arrows.

Judah Defeats Ethiopia's Army

9 Zerah from Ethiopia[p] led an army of a million soldiers and three hundred chariots to the town of Mareshah[q] in Judah. 10 Asa

[n]**14.3** *local shrines*: See the note at 11.15. [o]**14.3** *sacred poles*: Or "trees," used as symbols of Asherah, the goddess of fertility. [p]**14.9** *Ethiopia*: See the note at 12.3. [q]**14.9** *Mareshah*: About twenty-five miles southwest of Jerusalem.

met him there, and the two armies prepared for battle in Zephathah Valley.

11 Asa prayed:

LORD God, only you can help a powerless army defeat a stronger one. So we depend on you to help us. We will fight against this powerful army to honor your name, and we know that you won't be defeated. You are the LORD our God.

12 The LORD helped Asa and his army defeat the Ethiopians. The enemy soldiers
ran away, 13 but Asa and his troops chased them as far as Gerar. It was a total defeat—the Ethiopians could not even fight back![r]

The soldiers from Judah took everything
that had belonged to the Ethiopians. 14 The
people who lived in the villages around Gerar learned what had happened and were afraid of the LORD. So Judah's army easily defeated them and carried off everything of value that they wanted from these
towns. 15 They also attacked the camps where the shepherds lived and took a lot of sheep, goats, and camels. Then they went back to Jerusalem.

Asa Destroys the Idols in Judah

15 Some time later, God spoke to Azariah son of Oded. 2 At once,
Azariah went to Asa and said:

Listen to me, King Asa and you people of Judah and Benjamin. The LORD will be with you and help you, as long as you obey and worship him. But if you disobey him, he will desert you.

3 For a long time, the people of Israel did not worship the true God or listen to priests who could teach them about God. They refused to obey God's
Law. 4 But whenever trouble came, Israel turned back to the LORD their God and worshiped him.

5 There was so much confusion in those days that it wasn't safe to go any-
where in Israel. 6 Nations were destroying each other, and cities were wiping out other cities, because God was causing trouble and unrest everywhere.

7 So you must be brave. Don't give up! God will honor you for obeying him.

8 As soon as Asa heard what Azariah the prophet said, he gave orders for all the idols in Judah and Benjamin to be destroyed, including those in the towns he had captured in the territory of Ephraim. He also repaired the LORD's altar that was in front of the temple porch.

9 Asa called together the people from Judah and Benjamin, as well as the people from the territories of Ephraim, West Manasseh, and Simeon who were living in Judah. Many of these people were now loyal to Asa, because they had seen that the LORD was with him.

10 In the third month of the fifteenth year of Asa's rule, they all met in Jeru-
salem. 11 That same day, they took seven hundred bulls and seven thousand sheep and goats from what they had brought back from Gerar and sacrificed them
as offerings to the LORD. 12 They made a solemn promise to faithfully worship the LORD God their ancestors had wor-
shiped, 13 and to put to death anyone who
refused to obey him. 14 The crowd solemnly agreed to keep their promise to the LORD, then they celebrated by shouting and
blowing trumpets and horns. 15 Everyone was happy because they had made this solemn promise, and in return, the LORD blessed them with peace from all their enemies.

16 Asa's grandmother Maacah had made a disgusting idol of the goddess Asherah, so he cut it down, crushed it, and burned it in Kidron Valley. Then he removed Maacah
from her position as queen mother.[s] 17 As
long as Asa lived, he was faithful to the LORD, even though he did not destroy
the local shrines[t] in Israel. 18 He placed in the temple all the silver and gold objects that he and his father had dedicated to God.

19 There was peace in Judah until the thirty-fifth year of Asa's rule.

[r] **14.13** *the Ethiopians could not even fight back*: Or "not one of the Ethiopians survived!"
[s] **15.16** *queen mother*: Or "the mother of the king," which was an important position in biblical times (see 1 Kings 2.19). [t] **15.17** *local shrines*: See the note at 11.15.

King Baasha of Israel Invades Judah
(1 Kings 15.16-22)

16 In the thirty-sixth year of Asa's rule, King Baasha of Israel invaded Judah and captured the town of Ramah. He started making the town stronger, and he put troops there to stop people from going in and out of Judah.

2 When Asa heard about this, he took the silver and gold from his palace and from the LORD's temple. Then he sent it to Damascus with this message for King Benhadad of Syria: 3 "I think we should sign a peace treaty, just as our fathers did. This silver and gold is a present for you. Would you please break your treaty with King Baasha of Israel and force him to leave my country?"

4 Benhadad did what Asa asked and sent the Syrian army into Israel. They captured the towns of Ijon, Dan, Abel-Maim,[u] and all the towns in Naphtali where supplies were kept. 5 When Baasha heard about it, he stopped his work on the town of Ramah.

6 Asa ordered everyone in Judah to carry away the stones and wood Baasha had used to fortify Ramah. Then he fortified the towns of Geba and Mizpah with these same stones and wood.

Hanani the Prophet Condemns Asa

7 Soon after that happened, Hanani the prophet went to Asa and said:

> You depended on the king of Syria instead of depending on the LORD your God. And so, you will never defeat the Syrian army. 8 Remember how powerful the Ethiopian[v] and Libyan army was, with all their chariots and cavalry troops! You trusted the LORD to help you then, and you defeated them. 9 The LORD is constantly watching everyone, and he gives strength to those who faithfully obey him. But you have done a foolish thing, and your kingdom will never be at peace again.

10 When Asa heard this, he was so angry that he put Hanani in prison. Asa was also cruel to some of his people.[w]

Asa Dies
(1 Kings 15.23, 24)

11 Everything Asa did while he was king is written in *The History of the Kings of Judah and Israel*. 12 In the thirty-ninth year of his rule, he got a very bad foot disease, but he relied on doctors and refused to ask the LORD for help. 13 He died two years later.

14 Earlier, Asa had his own tomb cut out of a rock hill in Jerusalem. So he was buried there, and the tomb was filled with spices and sweet-smelling oils. Then the people built a bonfire in his honor.

King Jehoshaphat of Judah

17 Jehoshaphat son of Asa became king and strengthened his defenses against Israel. 2 He assigned troops to the fortified cities in Judah, as well as to other towns in Judah and to those towns in Ephraim that his father Asa had captured.

3-4 When Jehoshaphat's father had first become king of Judah, he was faithful to the LORD and refused to worship the god Baal as the kings of Israel did. Jehoshaphat followed his father's example and obeyed and worshiped the LORD. And so the LORD blessed Jehoshaphat 5 and helped him keep firm control of his kingdom. The people of Judah brought gifts to Jehoshaphat, but even after he became very rich and respected, 6 he remained completely faithful to the LORD. He destroyed all the local shrines[x] in Judah, including the places where the goddess Asherah was worshiped.

7 In the third year of Jehoshaphat's rule, he chose five officials and gave them orders to teach the LORD's Law in every city and town in Judah. They were Benhail, Obadiah, Zechariah, Nethanel, and Micaiah. 8 Their assistants were the following nine Levites: Shemaiah, Nethaniah, Zebadiah, Asahel, Shemiramoth, Jehonathan, Adonijah, Tobijah, and Tob-Adonijah. Two priests, Elishama and Jehoram, also went along. 9 They carried with them a copy of the LORD's Law wherever they went and taught the people from it.

[u] **16.4** *Abel-Maim*: Also called "Abel-Bethmaacah" (see 1 Kings 15.20). [v] **16.8** *Ethiopian*: See the note at 12.3. [w] **16.10** *Asa was also cruel . . . people*: Or "Asa also started being cruel to some of his people." [x] **17.6** *local shrines*: See the note at 11.15.

10 The nations around Judah were afraid of the LORD's power, so none of them attacked Jehoshaphat. 11 Philistines brought him silver and other gifts to keep peace. Some of the Arab people brought him seventy-seven hundred rams and the same number of goats.

12 As Jehoshaphat became more powerful, he built fortresses and cities 13 where he stored supplies. He also kept in Jerusalem some experienced soldiers 14 from the Judah and Benjamin tribes. These soldiers were grouped according to their clans.

Adnah was the commander of the troops from Judah, and he had three hundred thousand soldiers under his command. 15 Jehohanan was second in command, with two hundred eighty thousand soldiers under him. 16 Amasiah son of Zichri, who had volunteered to serve the LORD, was third in command, with two hundred thousand soldiers under him.

17 Eliada was a brave warrior who commanded the troops from Benjamin. He had two hundred thousand soldiers under his command, all of them armed with bows and shields. 18 Jehozabad was second in command, with one hundred eighty thousand soldiers under him. 19 These were the troops who protected the king in Jerusalem, not counting those he had assigned to the fortified cities throughout the country.

Micaiah Warns King Ahab of Israel

(1 Kings 22.1-28)

18 Jehoshaphat was now very rich and famous. He signed a treaty with King Ahab of Israel by arranging the marriage of his son and Ahab's daughter.

2 One day, Jehoshaphat went to visit Ahab in his capital city of Samaria. Ahab slaughtered sheep and cattle and prepared a big feast to honor Jehoshaphat and the officials with him. Ahab talked about attacking the city of Ramoth in Gilead,[y] 3 and finally asked, "Jehoshaphat, would you go with me to attack Ramoth?"

"Yes," Jehoshaphat answered. "My army is at your command. 4 But first let's ask the LORD what to do."

5 Ahab sent for four hundred prophets and asked, "Should I attack the city of Ramoth?"

"Yes!" the prophets answered. "God will help you capture the city."

6 But Jehoshaphat said, "Just to make sure, is there another of the LORD's prophets we can ask?"

7 "We could ask Micaiah son of Imlah," Ahab said. "But I hate Micaiah. He always has bad news for me."

"Don't say that!" Jehoshaphat replied. 8 Then Ahab sent someone to bring Micaiah as soon as possible.

9 All this time, Ahab and Jehoshaphat were dressed in their royal robes and were seated on their thrones at the threshing place near the gate of Samaria, listening to the prophets tell them what the LORD had said.

10 Zedekiah son of Chenaanah was one of the prophets. He had made some horns out of iron and shouted, "Ahab, the LORD says you will attack the Syrians like a bull with iron horns and wipe them out!"

11 All the prophets agreed that Ahab should attack the Syrians at Ramoth and promised that the LORD would help him defeat them.

12 Meanwhile, the messenger who went to get Micaiah whispered, "Micaiah, all the prophets have good news for Ahab. Now go and say the same thing."

13 "I'll say whatever the living LORD my God tells me to say," Micaiah replied.

14 Then Micaiah went up to Ahab, who asked, "Micaiah, should we attack Ramoth?"

"Yes!" Micaiah answered. "The LORD will help you capture the city."

15 Ahab shouted, "Micaiah, I've told you over and over to tell me the truth! What does the LORD really say?"

16 Micaiah answered, "In a vision[z] I saw Israelite soldiers wandering around, lost in

[y] **18.2** *attacking the city of Ramoth in Gilead*: The Syrians had taken control of Ramoth (see 1 Kings 22.3, 4). [z] **18.16** *vision*: In ancient times, prophets often told about future events from what they had seen in visions or dreams.

18.16 Nu 27.17; Ez 34.5; Mt 9.36; Mk 6.34.

the hills like sheep without a shepherd. The LORD said, 'These troops have no leader. They should go home and not fight.' "

17 Ahab turned to Jehoshaphat and said, "I told you he would bring me bad news!"

18 Micaiah replied:

> I then saw the LORD seated on his throne with every creature in heaven gathered around him. 19 The LORD asked, "Who can trick Ahab and make him go to Ramoth where he will be killed?"
>
> They talked about it for a while, 20 then finally a spirit came forward and said to the LORD, "I can trick Ahab."
>
> "How?" the LORD asked.
>
> 21 "I'll make Ahab's prophets lie to him."
>
> "Good!" the LORD replied. "Now go and do it. You will be successful."
>
> 22 Ahab, this is exactly what has happened. The LORD made all your prophets lie to you, and he knows you will soon be destroyed.

23 Zedekiah walked over and slapped Micaiah on the face. Then he asked, "Do you really think the LORD would speak to you and not to me?"

24 Micaiah answered, "You'll find out on the day you have to hide in the back room of some house."

25 Ahab shouted, "Arrest Micaiah! Take him to Prince Joash and Governor Amon of Samaria. 26 Tell them to put him in prison and to give him nothing but bread and water until I come back safely."

27 Micaiah said, "If you do come back, I was wrong about what the LORD wanted me to say." Then he told the crowd, "Don't forget what I said!"

Ahab Dies at Ramoth

(1 Kings 22.29-35)

28 Ahab and Jehoshaphat led their armies to Ramoth in Gilead. 29 Before they went into battle, Ahab said, "Jehoshaphat, I'll disguise myself, but you wear your royal robe." Ahab disguised himself and went into battle.

30 The king of Syria had ordered his chariot commanders to attack only Ahab. 31 So when they saw Jehoshaphat in his robe, they thought he was Ahab and started to attack him. But Jehoshaphat prayed, and the LORD made the Syrian soldiers stop. 32 And when they realized he wasn't Ahab, they left him alone.

33 However, during the fighting a soldier shot an arrow without even aiming, and it hit Ahab between two pieces of his armor. He shouted to his chariot driver, "I've been hit! Get me out of here!"

34 The fighting lasted all day, with Ahab propped up in his chariot so he could see the Syrian troops. He stayed there until evening, and by sundown he was dead.

19 Jehoshaphat returned safely to his palace in Jerusalem. 2 But the prophet Jehu son of Hanani met him and said:

> By helping that wicked Ahab, you have made friends with someone who hates the LORD. Now the LORD God is angry at you! 3 But not everything about you is bad. You destroyed the sacred poles[a] used in worshiping the goddess Asherah—that shows you have tried to obey the LORD.

Jehoshaphat Appoints Judges To Settle Cases

4 Jehoshaphat lived in Jerusalem, but he often traveled through his kingdom, from Beersheba in the south to the edge of the hill country of Ephraim in the north. He talked with the people and convinced them to turn back to the LORD God and worship him, just as their ancestors had done.

5 He assigned judges to each of the fortified cities in Judah 6 and told them:

> Be careful when you make your decisions in court, because these are the LORD's people, and he will know what you decide. 7 So do your work in honor of him and know that he won't allow you to be unfair to anyone or to take bribes.

8 Jehoshaphat also chose some Levites, some priests, and some of the family

[a] **19.3** *sacred poles*: See the note at 14.3.

leaders, and he appointed them to serve as
judges in Jerusalem. 9 He told them:

Faithfully serve the LORD! 10 The
people of Judah will bring you legal cases that involve every type of crime, including murder. You must settle these cases and warn the people to stop sinning against the LORD, so that he won't get angry and punish Judah. Remember, if you follow these instructions, you won't be held responsible for anything that happens.

11 Amariah the high priest will have the final say in any religious case. And Zebadiah, the leader[b] of the Judah tribe, will have the final say in all other cases. The rest of the Levites will serve as your assistants. Be brave, and I pray that the LORD will help you do right.

Moab and Ammon Are Defeated

20 Some time later, the armies of Moab and Ammon, together with the Meunites,[c] went to war against Jehoshaphat.
2 Messengers told Jehoshaphat, "A large army from Edom[d] east of the Dead Sea has invaded our country. They have already reached En-Gedi."[e]

3 Jehoshaphat was afraid, so he asked the LORD what to do. He then told the people of Judah to go without eating to show their sorrow.
4 They immediately left for Jerusalem to ask for the LORD's help.
5 After everyone from Judah and Jerusalem had come together at the LORD's temple, Jehoshaphat stood in front of the new courtyard
6 and prayed:

You, LORD, are the God our ancestors worshiped, and from heaven you rule every nation in the world. You are so powerful that no one can defeat you.
7 Our God, you forced out the nations who lived in this land before your people Israel came here, and you gave it to the descendants of your friend Abraham forever.
8 Our ancestors lived in this land and built a temple to honor you.
9 They believed that whenever this land is struck by war or disease or famine, your people can pray to you at the temple, and you will hear their prayer and save them.

10 You can see that the armies of Ammon, Moab, and Edom are attacking us! Those are the nations you would not let our ancestors invade on their way from Egypt, so these nations were not destroyed.
11 Now they are coming to take back the land you gave us.
12 Aren't you going to punish them? We won't stand a chance when this army attacks. We don't know what to do—we are begging for your help.

13 While every man, woman, and child of Judah was standing there at the temple,
14 the LORD's Spirit suddenly spoke to Jahaziel, a Levite from the Asaph clan.[f]
15 Then Jahaziel said:

Your Majesty and everyone from Judah and Jerusalem, the LORD says that you don't need to be afraid or let this powerful army discourage you. God will fight on your side!
16 So here's what you must do. Tomorrow the enemy armies will march through the desert around the town of Jeruel. March down and meet them at the town of Ziz as they come up the valley.
17 You won't even have to fight. Just take your positions and watch the LORD rescue you from your enemy. Don't be afraid. Just do as you're told. And as you march out tomorrow, the LORD will be there with you.

18 Jehoshaphat bowed low to the ground and everyone worshiped the LORD.
19 Then

[b]**19.11** *Zebadiah, the leader*: Hebrew "Zebadiah son of Ishmael, who is the leader."
[c]**20.1** *Meunites*: One ancient translation (see also 26.7); Hebrew "Ammonites." [d]**20.2** *Edom*: The Hebrew text has "Syria"; in Hebrew there is only one letter difference between "Edom" and "Aram," which is the usual Hebrew name for Syria in the Bible. [e]**20.2** *En-Gedi*: The Hebrew text has "Hazazon-Tamar, also known as En-Gedi," a city on the west shore of the Dead Sea, about twenty-five miles southeast of Jerusalem. [f]**20.14** *Jahaziel, a Levite from the Asaph clan*: Hebrew "Jahaziel son of Zechariah son of Benaiah son of Jeiel son of Mattaniah, who was a Levite from the Asaph clan."

20.7 Is 41.8; Jas 2.23. **20.10** Dt 2.4-19. **20.15-17** Dt 20.1-4. **20.17** Ex 14.13, 14.

some Levites from the Kohath and Korah clans stood up and shouted praises to the LORD God of Israel.

20 Early the next morning, as everyone got ready to leave for the desert near Tekoa, Jehoshaphat stood up and said, "Listen my friends, if we trust the LORD God and believe what these prophets have told us, the LORD will help us, and we will be successful." 21 Then he explained his plan and appointed men to march in front of the army and praise the LORD for his holy power by singing:[g]

"Praise the LORD!
His love never ends."

22 As soon as they began singing, the LORD confused the enemy camp, 23 so that the Ammonite and Moabite troops attacked and completely destroyed those from Edom. Then they turned against each other and fought until the entire camp was wiped out!

24 When Judah's army reached the tower that overlooked the desert, they saw that every soldier in the enemy's army was lying dead on the ground. 25 So Jehoshaphat and his troops went into the camp to carry away everything of value. They found a large herd of livestock,[h] a lot of equipment, clothes,[i] and other valuable things. It took them three days to carry it all away, and there was still some left over.

26 Then on the fourth day, everyone came together in Beracah Valley and sang praises to the LORD. That's why that place was called Praise Valley.[j]

27-28 Jehoshaphat led the crowd back to Jerusalem. And as they marched, they played harps and blew trumpets. They were very happy because the LORD had given them victory over their enemies, so when they reached the city, they went straight to the temple.

29 When the other nations heard how the LORD had fought against Judah's enemies, they were too afraid 30 to invade Judah. The LORD let Jehoshaphat's kingdom be at peace.

Jehoshaphat Dies
(1 Kings 22.41-50)

31 Jehoshaphat was thirty-five years old when he became king of Judah, and he ruled from Jerusalem for twenty-five years. His mother was Azubah daughter of Shilhi. 32 Jehoshaphat obeyed the LORD, just as his father Asa had done, 33 but he did not destroy the local shrines.[k] So the people still worshiped foreign gods, instead of faithfully serving the God their ancestors had worshiped.

34 Everything else Jehoshaphat did while he was king is written in the records of Jehu son of Hanani that are included in *The History of the Kings of Israel*.

35 While Jehoshaphat was king, he signed a peace treaty with Ahaziah the wicked king of Israel. 36 They agreed to build several seagoing ships[l] at Ezion-Geber. 37 But the prophet Eliezer[m] warned Jehoshaphat, "The LORD will destroy these ships because you have supported Ahaziah." The ships were wrecked and never sailed.

21 Jehoshaphat died and was buried beside his ancestors in Jerusalem, and his son Jehoram became king.

King Jehoram of Judah
(2 Kings 8.16-24)

2 King Jehoshaphat had seven sons: Jehoram, Azariah, Jehiel, Zechariah, Azariah, Michael, and Shephatiah. 3 Jehoshaphat gave each of them silver and gold, as well as other valuable gifts. He also put them in charge of the fortified cities in Judah, but he had chosen his oldest son Jehoram to succeed him as king.

4 After Jehoram had taken control of Judah, he had his brothers killed, as well as some of the nation's leaders. 5 He was

[g] **20.21** *to march in front . . . singing*: Or "to put on their sacred robes, lead the army into battle, and praise the LORD by singing." [h] **20.25** *a large herd of livestock*: One ancient translation; Hebrew "among the bodies a large herd of." [i] **20.25** *clothes*: One ancient translation; Hebrew "dead bodies." [j] **20.26** *Beracah Valley . . . sang praises . . . Praise Valley*: In Hebrew the name "Beracah" means "praise." [k] **20.33** *local shrines*: See the note at 11.15. [l] **20.36** *seagoing ships*: See the note at 9.21. [m] **20.37** *Eliezer*: Hebrew "Eliezer son of Dodavahu from Mareshah."

thirty-two years old when he became king,
and he ruled eight years from Jerusalem.
6 Jehoram married Ahab's daughter and
followed the sinful example of Ahab's family and the other kings of Israel. He disobeyed the LORD by doing wrong, 7 but because the LORD had made a solemn
promise to King David that someone from
his family would always rule in Judah, he
refused to wipe out David's descendants.
8 While Jehoram was king, the people of
Edom rebelled and chose their own king.
9 Jehoram, his officers, and his cavalry
marched to Edom, where the Edomite
army surrounded them. He escaped during
the night, 10 but Judah was never able to
regain control of Edom. Even the town of
Libnah[n] rebelled at that time.
Those things happened because Jehoram had turned away from the LORD, the
God his ancestors had worshiped. 11 Jehoram even built local shrines[o] in the hills of
Judah and let the people sin against the
LORD by worshiping foreign gods.
12 One day, Jehoram received a letter
from Elijah the prophet that said:

I have a message for you from the
LORD God your ancestor David worshiped. He knows that you have not
followed the example of Jehoshaphat
your father or Asa your grandfather.
13 Instead you have acted like those
sinful kings of Israel and have encouraged the people of Judah to stop worshiping the LORD, just as Ahab and his
descendants did. You even murdered
your own brothers, who were better
men than you.
14 Because you have done these terrible things, the LORD will severely
punish the people in your kingdom, including your own family, and he will
destroy everything you own. 15 You will
be struck with a painful stomach disease and suffer until you die.

16 The LORD later caused the Philistines
and the Arabs who lived near the Ethiopians[p] to become angry at Jehoram. 17 They
invaded Judah and stole the royal property
from the palace, and they led Jehoram's
wives and sons away as prisoners. The only
one left behind was Ahaziah,[q] his youngest son.
18 After this happened, the LORD struck
Jehoram with an incurable stomach disease. 19 About two years later, Jehoram died
in terrible pain. No bonfire was built to
honor him, even though the people had
done this for his ancestors.
20 Jehoram was thirty-two years old
when he became king, and he ruled eight
years from Jerusalem. He died, and no one
even felt sad. He was buried in Jerusalem,
but not in the royal tombs.

King Ahaziah of Judah

(2 Kings 8.25-29; 9.21, 27, 28)

22 Earlier, when the Arabs led a raid
against Judah, they killed all of Jehoram's sons, except Ahaziah, the youngest
one. So the people of Jerusalem crowned
him their king. 2 He was twenty-two[r] years
old at the time, and he ruled only one year
from Jerusalem.
Ahaziah's mother was Athaliah, a granddaughter of King Omri of Israel, 3 and she
encouraged her son to sin against the
LORD. He followed the evil example of King
Ahab and his descendants. 4 In fact, after
his father's death, Ahaziah sinned against
the LORD by appointing some of Ahab's relatives to be his advisors.
Their advice led to his downfall. 5 He
listened to them and went with King Joram
of Israel to attack King Hazael and the Syrian troops at Ramoth in Gilead. Joram was
wounded in that battle, 6 and he went to
the town of Jezreel to recover. And Ahaziah
later went there to visit him. 7 It was during
that visit that God had Ahaziah put to
death.
When Ahaziah arrived at Jezreel, he and

[n] **21.10** *Even the town of Libnah*: This was a town on the border between Philistia and Judah, which means that Jehoram was facing rebellion on both sides of his kingdom. [o] **21.11** *local shrines*: See the note at 11.15. [p] **21.16** *Ethiopians*: See the note at 12.3. [q] **21.17** *Ahaziah*: The Hebrew text has "Jehoahaz," another spelling of the name. [r] **22.2** *twenty-two*: One ancient translation (see also 2 Kings 8.26); Hebrew "forty-two."

21.7 1 K 11.36. **21.8** Gn 27.40.

Joram went to meet with Jehu grandson of Nimshi. The LORD had already told Jehu to kill every male in Ahab's family, 8 and while Jehu was doing that, he saw some of Judah's leaders and Ahaziah's nephews who had come with Ahaziah. Jehu killed them on the spot, 9 then gave orders to find Ahaziah. Jehu's officers found him hiding in Samaria. They brought Ahaziah to Jehu, who immediately put him to death. They buried Ahaziah only because they respected Jehoshaphat his grandfather, who had done his best to obey the LORD.

There was no one from Ahaziah's family left to become king of Judah.

Queen Athaliah of Judah

(2 Kings 11.1-3)

10 As soon as Athaliah heard that her son King Ahaziah was dead, she decided to kill any relative who could possibly become king. She would have done just that, 11 but Jehosheba[s] rescued Joash son of Ahaziah just as the others were about to be murdered. Jehosheba, who was Jehoram's daughter and Ahaziah's half sister, was married to Jehoiada the priest. So she was able to hide her nephew Joash and his personal servant in a bedroom in the LORD's temple where he was safe from Athaliah. 12 Joash hid in the temple with them for six years while Athaliah ruled as queen of Judah.

Jehoiada Makes Joash King of Judah

(2 Kings 11.4-21)

23 After Ahaziah's son Joash had hidden in the temple for six years, Jehoiada the priest knew that something had to be done. So he made sure he had the support of several army officers. They were Azariah son of Jeroham, Ishmael son of Jehohanan, Azariah son of Obed, Maaseiah son of Adaiah, and Elishaphat son of Zichri. 2 These five men went to the towns in Judah and called together the Levites and the clan leaders. They all came to Jerusalem 3 and gathered at the temple, where they agreed to help Joash.

Jehoiada said to them:

Joash will be our next king, because long ago the LORD promised that one of David's descendants would always be king. 4 Here is what we will do. Three groups of priests and Levites will be on guard duty on the Sabbath—one group will guard the gates of the temple, 5 one will guard the palace, and the other will guard Foundation Gate. The rest of you will stand guard in the temple courtyards. 6 Only the priests and Levites who are on duty will be able to enter the temple, because they will be the only ones who have gone through the ceremony to make themselves clean and acceptable. The others must stay outside in the courtyards, just as the LORD has commanded. 7 You Levites must protect King Joash. Don't let him out of your sight! And keep your swords ready to kill anyone who comes into the temple.

8 The Levites and the people of Judah followed Jehoiada's orders. The guards going off duty were not allowed to go home, and so each commander had all his guards available—those going off duty as well as those coming on duty. 9 Jehoiada went into the temple and brought out the swords and shields that had belonged to King David, and he gave them to the commanders. 10 They gave the weapons to the guards, and Jehoiada then made sure that the guards took their positions around the temple and the altar to protect the king on every side.

11 Jehoiada and his sons brought Joash outside, where they placed the crown on his head and gave him a copy of the instructions for ruling the nation. Olive oil was poured on his head to show that he was now king, and the crowd cheered and shouted, "Long live the king!"

12 As soon as Queen Athaliah heard the crowd cheering for Joash, she went to the temple. 13 There she saw Joash standing by one of the columns near the entrance, which was the usual place for the king. The commanders and the trumpet players were

[s]**22.11** *Jehosheba*: The Hebrew text has "Jehoshabeath," another spelling of the name.
23.3 2 S 7.12.

standing next to him, and the musicians
were playing instruments and leading the
people as they celebrated and blew trumpets. Athaliah tore her clothes in anger and
shouted, "You betrayed me, you traitors!"
14 Right away, Jehoiada said to the army
commanders, "Don't kill her near the
LORD's temple. Take her out in front of the
troops, and be sure to kill all of her followers!" 15 She tried to escape, but the commanders caught and killed her near the
gate where horses are led into the palace.
16 Jehoiada asked King Joash and the
people to join with him in being faithful to
the LORD. They agreed, 17 then rushed to
the temple of the god Baal and tore it
down. They smashed the altars and the
idols and killed Mattan the priest of Baal in
front of the altars.
18 Jehoiada assigned the priests and
Levites their duties at the temple, just as
David had done. They were in charge of offering sacrifices to the LORD according to
the Law of Moses, and they were responsible for leading the celebrations with
singing. 19 Jehoiada ordered the guards at
the temple gates to keep out anyone who
was unclean.
20 Finally, Jehoiada called together the
army commanders, the most important citizens of Judah, and the government officials. The crowd of people followed them as
they led Joash from the temple, through
the Upper Gate, and into the palace, where
he took his place as king of Judah.
21 Everyone celebrated because Athaliah
had been killed and Jerusalem was peaceful again.

King Joash of Judah

(2 Kings 12.1-16)

24 Joash was only seven years old
when he became king of Judah,
and he ruled forty years from Jerusalem.
His mother Zibiah was from the town of
Beersheba.
2 While Jehoiada the priest was alive,
Joash obeyed the LORD by doing right. 3 Jehoiada even chose two women for Joash to
marry so he could have a family.
4 Some time later, Joash decided it was
time to repair the temple. 5 He called together the priests and Levites and said, "Go
everywhere in Judah and collect the an-
nual tax from the people. I want this done
right away—we need that money to repair
the temple."
But the Levites were in no hurry to follow the king's orders. 6 So he sent for Jehoiada the high priest and asked, "Why
didn't you send the Levites to collect the
taxes? The LORD's servant Moses and the
people agreed long ago that this tax would
be collected and used to pay for the upkeep
of the sacred tent. 7 And now we need it to
repair the temple because the sons of that
evil woman Athaliah came in and wrecked
it. They even used some of the sacred objects to worship the god Baal."
8 Joash gave orders for a wooden box to
be made and had it placed outside, near
the gate of the temple. 9 He then sent letters everywhere in Judah and Jerusalem,
asking everyone to bring their taxes to the
temple, just as Moses had required their
ancestors to do.
10 The people and their leaders agreed,
and they brought their money to Jerusalem
and placed it in the box. 11 Each day, after
the Levites took the box into the temple,
the king's secretary and the high priest's
assistant would dump out the money and
count it. Then the empty box would be
taken back outside.
This happened day after day, and soon
a large amount of money was collected.
12 Joash and Jehoiada turned the money
over to the men who were supervising the
repairs to the temple. They used the money
to hire stonecutters, carpenters, and experts in working with iron and bronze.
13 These workers went right to work repairing the temple, and when they were
finished, it looked as good as new. 14 They
did not use all the tax money for the repairs, so the rest of it was handed over to
Joash and Jehoiada, who then used it to
make dishes and other gold and silver objects for the temple.
Sacrifices to please the LORD[t] were of-

[t]**24.14** *Sacrifices to please the LORD*: See the note at 1.6.
24.6 Ex 30.11-16.

fered regularly in the temple for as long as Jehoiada lived. 15 He died at the ripe old age of one hundred thirty years, 16 and he was buried in the royal tombs in Jerusalem, because he had done so much good for the people of Israel, for God, and for the temple.

Joash Turns Away from the LORD

17 After the death of Jehoiada the priest, the leaders of Judah went to Joash and talked him into doing what they wanted. 18 Right away, the people of Judah stopped worshiping in the temple of the LORD God, and they started worshiping idols and the symbols of the goddess Asherah. These sinful things made the LORD God angry at the people of Judah and Jerusalem, 19 but he still sent prophets who warned them to turn back to him. The people refused to listen.

20 God's Spirit spoke to Zechariah son of Jehoiada the priest, and Zechariah told everyone that God was saying: "Why are you disobeying me and my laws? This will only bring punishment! You have deserted me, so now I will desert you."

21-22 King Joash forgot that Zechariah's father had always been a loyal friend. So when the people of Judah plotted to kill Zechariah, Joash joined them and gave orders for them to stone him to death in the courtyard of the temple. As Zechariah was dying, he said, "I pray that the LORD will see this and punish all of you."

Joash Is Killed

23 In the spring of the following year, the Syrian army invaded Judah and Jerusalem, killing all of the nation's leaders. They collected everything of value that belonged to the people and took it back to their king in Damascus. 24 The Syrian army was very small, but the LORD let them defeat Judah's large army, because he was punishing Joash and the people of Judah for turning away from him.

25-26 Joash was severely wounded during the battle, and as soon as the Syrians left Judah, two of his officials, Zabad and Jehozabad,[u] decided to revenge the death of Zechariah. They plotted and killed Joash while he was in bed, recovering from his wounds. Joash was buried in Jerusalem, but not in the royal tombs. 27 *The History of the Kings* also tells more about the sons of Joash, what the prophets said about him, and how he repaired the temple. Amaziah son of Joash became king after his father's death.

King Amaziah of Judah

(2 Kings 14.1-6)

25 Amaziah was twenty-five years old when he became king, and he ruled twenty-nine years from Jerusalem, the hometown of his mother Jehoaddin.[v]

2 Even though Amaziah obeyed the LORD by doing right, he refused to be completely faithful. 3 For example, as soon as he had control of Judah, he arrested and killed the officers who had murdered his father. 4 But the children of those officers were not killed; the LORD had commanded in the Law of Moses that only the people who sinned were to be punished.[w]

Edom Is Defeated

(2 Kings 14.7)

5 Amaziah sent a message to the tribes of Judah and Benjamin and called together all the men who were twenty years old and older. Three hundred thousand men went to Jerusalem, all of them ready for battle and able to fight with spears and shields. Amaziah grouped these soldiers according to their clans and put them under the command of his army officers. 6 Amaziah also paid almost four tons of silver to hire one hundred thousand soldiers from Israel.

7 One of God's prophets said, "Your Majesty, don't let these Israelite soldiers march into battle with you. The LORD has refused to help anyone from the northern kingdom of Israel, 8 and so he will let your enemies defeat you, even if you fight hard. He is the one who brings both victory and defeat."

9 Amaziah replied, "What am I supposed to do about all the silver I paid those troops?"

[u]**24.25,26** *Zabad and Jehozabad*: Hebrew "Zabad son of Shimeath from Ammon and Jehozabad son of Shimrith from Moab." [v]**25.1** *Jehoaddin*: The Hebrew text has "Jehoaddan," another spelling of the name. [w]**25.4** *the LORD had commanded . . . punished*: See Deuteronomy 24.16.

24.20,21 Mt 23.35; Lk 11.51. **25.4** Dt 24.16.

"The LORD will give you back even more than you paid," the prophet answered.

10 Amaziah ordered the troops from Israel to go home, but when they left, they were furious with the people of Judah.

11 After Amaziah got his courage back, he led his troops to Salt Valley, where he killed ten thousand Edomite soldiers in battle. 12 He captured ten thousand more soldiers and dragged them to the top of a high cliff. Then he pushed them over the side, and they all were killed on the rocks below.

13 Meanwhile, the Israelite troops that Amaziah had sent home, raided the towns in Judah between Samaria and Beth-Horon. They killed three thousand people and carried off their possessions.

14 After Amaziah had defeated the Edomite army, he returned to Jerusalem. He took with him the idols of the Edomite gods and set them up. Then he bowed down and offered them sacrifices. 15 This made the LORD very angry, and he sent a prophet to ask Amaziah, "Why would you worship these foreign gods that couldn't even save their own people from your attack?"

16 But before the prophet finished speaking, Amaziah interrupted and said, "You're not one of my advisors! Don't say another word, or I'll have you killed."

The prophet stopped. But then he added, "First you sinned and now you've ignored my warning. It's clear that God has decided to punish you!"

Israel Defeats Judah

(2 Kings 14.8-14)

17 King Amaziah of Judah talked with his officials, then sent a message to King Jehoash[x] of Israel: "Come out and face me in battle!"

18 Jehoash sent back a reply that said:

> Once upon a time, a small thornbush in Lebanon arranged the marriage between his son and the daughter of a large cedar tree. But a wild animal came along and trampled the small bush.
>
> 19 Amaziah, you think you're so powerful because you defeated Edom. But stay at home and do your celebrating. If you cause any trouble, both you and your kingdom of Judah will be destroyed.

20 God made Amaziah stubborn because he was planning to punish him for worshiping the Edomite gods. Amaziah refused to listen to Jehoash's warning, 21 so Jehoash led his army to the town of Beth-Shemesh in Judah to attack Amaziah and his troops. 22 During the battle, Judah's army was crushed. Every soldier from Judah ran back home, 23 and Jehoash captured Amaziah.

Jehoash took Amaziah with him when he went to attack Jerusalem. Jehoash broke down the city wall from Ephraim Gate to Corner Gate, a section about six hundred feet long. 24 He carried away the gold, the silver, and all the valuable furnishings from God's temple where the descendants of Obed-Edom stood guard. He robbed the king's treasury, took hostages, then returned to Samaria.

Amaziah Is Killed

(2 Kings 14.15-20)

25 Amaziah lived fifteen years after Jehoash died. 26 Everything else Amaziah did while he was king is written in *The History of the Kings of Judah and Israel*.

27 As soon as Amaziah started disobeying the LORD, some people in Jerusalem plotted against Amaziah. He was able to escape to the town of Lachish, but another group of people caught him and killed him there. 28 His body was taken to Jerusalem on horseback and buried beside his ancestors.

King Uzziah of Judah

(2 Kings 14.21, 22; 15.1-7)

26 1-3 After the death of King Amaziah, the people of Judah crowned his son Uzziah[y] king, even though he was only sixteen at the time. Uzziah ruled fifty-

[x] **25.17** *King Jehoash*: The Hebrew text has "King Joash son of Jehoahaz son of Jehu"; Jehoash is another spelling for the name Joash. [y] **26.1-3** *Uzziah*: In the parallel passages in 2 Kings, he is called "Azariah" (see also 1 Chronicles 3.10-15). He is also called "Uzziah" in 2 Kings 15.13; Isaiah 1.1; Hosea 1.1; and Amos 1.1. One of these names was probably his birth name, while the other was his name after he became king.

two years from Jerusalem, the hometown
of his mother Jecoliah. During his rule,
he recaptured and rebuilt the town of
Elath.
4 He obeyed the LORD by doing right, as
his father Amaziah had done. 5 Zechariah
was Uzziah's advisor and taught him to
obey God. And so, as long as Zechariah was
alive, Uzziah was faithful to God, and God
made him successful.
6 While Uzziah was king, he started a
war against the Philistines. He smashed
the walls of the cities of Gath, Jabneh, and
Ashdod, then rebuilt towns around Ashdod
and in other parts of Philistia. 7 God helped
him defeat the Philistines, the Arabs living
in Gur-Baal, and the Meunites. 8 Even the
Ammonites paid taxes to Uzziah. He became very powerful, and people who lived
as far away as Egypt heard about him.
9 In Jerusalem, Uzziah built fortified
towers at the Corner Gate, the Valley Gate,
and the place where the city wall turned
inward.[z] 10 He also built defense towers out
in the desert.

He owned such a large herd of livestock
in the western foothills and in the flatlands, that he had cisterns dug there to
catch the rainwater. He loved farming, so
he had crops and vineyards planted in the
hill country wherever there was fertile
soil, and he hired farmers to take care of
them.
11 Uzziah's army was always ready for
battle. Jeiel and Maaseiah were the officers
who kept track of the number of soldiers,
and these two men were under the command of Hananiah, one of Uzziah's officials. 12-13 There were 307,500 trained soldiers, all under the command of 2,600 clan
leaders. These powerful troops protected
the king against any enemy. 14 Uzziah supplied his army with shields, spears, helmets, armor, bows, and stones used for
slinging. 15 Some of his skilled workers invented machines that could shoot arrows
and sling large stones. Uzziah set these up
in Jerusalem at his defense towers and at
the corners of the city wall.

God helped Uzziah become more and
more powerful, and he was famous all over
the world.

Uzziah Becomes Too Proud

16 Uzziah became proud of his power,
and this led to his downfall.

One day, Uzziah disobeyed the LORD his
God by going into the temple and burning
incense as an offering to him.[a] 17 Azariah
the priest and eighty other brave priests followed Uzziah into the temple 18 and said,
"Your Majesty, this isn't right! You are not
allowed to burn incense to the LORD. That
must be done only by priests who are descendants of Aaron. You will have to leave!
You have sinned against the LORD, and so
he will no longer bless you."
19 Uzziah, who was standing next to the
incense altar at the time, was holding the
incense burner, ready to offer incense to
the LORD. He became very angry when he
heard Azariah's warning, and leprosy[b] suddenly appeared on his forehead! 20 Azariah
and the other priests saw it and immediately told him to leave the temple. Uzziah
realized that the LORD had punished him,
so he hurried to get outside.
21 Uzziah had leprosy the rest of his life.
He was no longer allowed in the temple or
in his own palace. That's why his son
Jotham lived there and ruled in his place.
22 Everything else Uzziah did while he
was king is in the records written by the
prophet Isaiah son of Amoz. 23 Since
Uzziah had leprosy, he could not be buried
in the royal tombs. Instead, he was buried
in a nearby cemetery that the kings owned.
His son Jotham then became king.

King Jotham of Judah

(2 Kings 15.32-38)

27 Jotham was twenty-five years old
when he became king of Judah,
and he ruled from Jerusalem for sixteen

[z]**26.9** *the place where the city wall turned inward*: One possible meaning for the difficult Hebrew text. [a]**26.16** *going into the temple and burning incense as an offering to him*: This was to be done only by priests (see Exodus 30.1-10; Numbers 16.39, 40). [b]**26.19** *leprosy*: The word translated "leprosy" was used for many different kinds of skin diseases.

26.18 Ex 30.7, 8; Nu 3.10. **26.23** Is 6.1.

years. Jerushah his mother was the daughter of Zadok.
2 Jotham obeyed the LORD and did right.
He followed the example of his father
Uzziah, except he never burned incense in
the temple as his father had done. But the
people of Judah kept sinning against the
LORD.
3 Jotham rebuilt the Upper Gate of the
temple and did a lot of work to repair the
wall near Mount Ophel. 4 He built towns in
the mountains of Judah and built fortresses
and defense towers in the forests.
5 During his rule he attacked and defeated the Ammonites. Then every year for
the next three years, he forced them to pay
four tons of silver, sixty thousand bushels
of wheat, and sixty thousand bushels of
barley.
6 Jotham remained faithful to the LORD
his God and became a very powerful king.
7 Everything else Jotham did while he
was king, including the wars he fought, is
written in *The History of the Kings of Israel
and Judah*. 8 After he had ruled Judah sixteen years, he died at the age of forty-one.
9 He was buried in Jerusalem, and his son
Ahaz became king.

King Ahaz of Judah

(*2 Kings 16.1-4*)

28 Ahaz was twenty years old when he
became king of Judah, and he
ruled from Jerusalem for sixteen years.
Ahaz was nothing like his ancestor
David. Ahaz disobeyed the LORD 2 and was
as sinful as the kings of Israel. He made
idols of the god Baal, 3 and he offered sacrifices in Hinnom Valley. Worst of all, Ahaz
sacrificed his own sons, which was a disgusting custom of the nations that the
LORD had forced out of Israel. 4 Ahaz offered sacrifices at the local shrines,[c] as well
as on every hill and in the shade of large
trees.

Syria and Israel Attack Judah

(*2 Kings 16.5, 6*)

5-6 Ahaz and the people of Judah sinned
and turned away from the LORD, the God
their ancestors had worshiped. So the
LORD punished them by letting their enemies defeat them.
The king of Syria attacked Judah and
took many of its people to Damascus as
prisoners. King Pekah[d] of Israel later defeated Judah and killed one hundred
twenty thousand of its bravest soldiers in
one day. 7 During that battle, an Israelite
soldier named Zichri killed three men from
Judah: Maaseiah the king's son; Azrikam,
the official in charge of the palace; and
Elkanah, the king's second in command.
8 The Israelite troops captured two hundred thousand women and children and
took them back to their capital city of
Samaria, along with a large amount of their
possessions. They did these things even
though the people of Judah were their own
relatives.

Oded the Prophet Condemns Israel

9 Oded lived in Samaria and was one of
the LORD's prophets. He met Israel's army
on their way back from Judah and said to
them:

> The LORD God of your ancestors let
> you defeat Judah's army only because
> he was angry with them. But you
> should not have been so cruel! 10 If
> you make slaves of the people of Judah
> and Jerusalem, you will be as guilty as
> they are of sinning against the LORD.
> 11 Send these prisoners back
> home—they are your own relatives. If
> you don't, the LORD will punish you in
> his anger.

12 About the same time, four of Israel's
leaders arrived. They were Azariah son of
Johanan, Berechiah son of Meshillemoth,
Jehizkiah son of Shallum, and Amasa son
of Hadlai. They agreed with Oded that the
Israelite troops were wrong, 13 and they
said:

> If you bring these prisoners into
> Samaria, that will be one more thing
> we've done to sin against the LORD.
> And he is already angry enough at us.

14 So in front of the leaders and the
crowd, the troops handed over their prison-

[c]**28.4** *local shrines*: See the note at 11.15.
28.5,6 2 K 16.5, 6; Is 7.1.
[d]**28.5,6** *Pekah*: Hebrew "Pekah son of Remaliah."

ers and the property they had taken from Judah. 15 The four leaders took some of the stolen clothes and gave them to the prisoners who needed something to wear. They later gave them all a new change of clothes and shoes, then fixed them something to eat and drink, and cleaned their wounds with olive oil. They gave donkeys to those who were too weak to walk, and led all of them back to Jericho, the city known for its palm trees. The leaders then returned to Samaria.

Ahaz Asks the King of Assyria for Help

(2 Kings 16.7-9)

16-18 Some time later, the Edomites attacked the eastern part of Judah again and carried away prisoners. And at the same time, the Philistines raided towns in the western foothills and in the Southern Desert. They conquered the towns of Beth-Shemesh, Aijalon, Gederoth, Soco, Timnah, and Gimzo, including the villages around them. Then some of the Philistines went to live in these places.

Ahaz sent a message to King Tiglath Pileser of Assyria and begged for help. 19 But God was punishing Judah with these disasters, because Ahaz had disobeyed him and refused to stop Judah from sinning. 20 So Tiglath Pileser came to Judah, but instead of helping, he made things worse. 21 Ahaz gave him gifts from the LORD's temple and the king's palace, as well as from the homes of Israel's other leaders. The Assyrian king still refused to help Ahaz.

The Final Sin of Ahaz and His Death

22 Even after all these terrible things happened to Ahaz, he sinned against the LORD even worse than before. 23 He said to himself, "The Syrian gods must have helped their kings defeat me. Maybe if I offer sacrifices to those gods, they will help me." That was the sin that finally led to the downfall of Ahaz, as well as to the destruction of Judah.

24 Ahaz collected all the furnishings of the temple and smashed them to pieces. Then he locked the doors to the temple and set up altars to foreign gods on every street corner in Jerusalem. 25 In every city and town in Judah he built local shrines[e] to worship foreign gods. All of this made the LORD God of his ancestors very angry.

26 Everything else Ahaz did while he was king is written in *The History of the Kings of Judah and Israel*. 27 Ahaz died and was buried in Jerusalem, but not in the royal tombs. His son Hezekiah then became king.

King Hezekiah of Judah

(2 Kings 18.1-3)

29 Hezekiah was twenty-five years old when he became king of Judah, and he ruled twenty-nine years from Jerusalem. His mother was Abijah daughter of Zechariah. 2 Hezekiah obeyed the LORD by doing right, just as his ancestor David had done.

The Temple Is Purified

3 In the first month[f] of the first year of Hezekiah's rule, he unlocked the doors to the LORD's temple and had them repaired.[g] 4 Then he called the priests and Levites to the east courtyard of the temple 5 and said:

> It's time to purify the temple of the LORD God of our ancestors. You Levites must first go through the ceremony to make yourselves clean, then go into the temple and bring out everything that is unclean and unacceptable to the LORD. 6 Some of our ancestors were unfaithful and disobeyed the LORD our God. Not only did they turn their backs on the LORD, but they also completely ignored his temple. 7 They locked the doors, then let the lamps go out and stopped burning incense and offering sacrifices to him. 8 The LORD became terribly angry at the people of

[e]**28.25** *local shrines*: See the note at 11.15. [f]**29.3** *first month*: Abib (also called Nisan), the first month of the Hebrew calendar, from about mid-March to mid-April. [g]**29.3** *he unlocked the doors . . . repaired*: King Ahaz had locked the doors and stopped everyone from worshiping the LORD (see 28.24, 25).

28.27 Is 14.28.

Judah and Jerusalem, and everyone was shocked and horrified at what he did to punish them. Not only were [9] our ancestors killed in battle, but our own children and wives were taken captive.

[10] So I have decided to renew our agreement with the LORD God of Israel. Maybe then he will stop being so angry at us. [11] Let's not waste any time, my friends. You are the ones who were chosen to be the LORD's priests and to offer him sacrifices.

[12-14] When Hezekiah finished talking, the following Levite leaders went to work: Mahath son of Amasai and Joel son of Azariah from the Kohath clan; Kish son of Abdi and Azariah son of Jehallelel from the Merari clan; Joah son of Zimmah and Eden son of Joah from the Gershon clan; Shimri and Jeuel from the Elizaphan clan; Zechariah and Mattaniah from the Asaph clan; Jehuel and Shimei from the Heman clan; Shemaiah and Uzziel from the Jeduthun clan.

[15] These leaders gathered together the rest of the Levites, and they all went through the ceremony to make themselves clean. Then they began to purify the temple according to the Law of the LORD, just as Hezekiah had commanded.

[16] The priests went into the temple and carried out everything that was unclean. They put these things in the courtyard, and from there, the Levites carried them outside the city to Kidron Valley.

[17] The priests and Levites began their work on the first day of the first month.[h] It took them one week to purify the courtyards of the temple and another week to purify the temple. So on the sixteenth day of that same month [18] they went back to Hezekiah and said:

Your Majesty, we have finished our work. The entire temple is now pure again, and so is the altar and its utensils, as well as the table for the sacred loaves of bread and its utensils. [19] And we have brought back all the things that King Ahaz took from the temple during the time he was unfaithful to God. We purified them and put them back in front of the altar.

Worship in the Temple

[20] Right away, Hezekiah called together the officials of Jerusalem, and they went to the temple. [21] They brought with them seven bulls, seven rams, seven lambs, and seven goats[i] as sacrifices to take away the sins of Hezekiah's family and of the people of Judah, as well as to purify the temple. Hezekiah told the priests, who were descendants of Aaron, to sacrifice these animals on the altar.

[22] The priests killed the bulls, the rams, and the lambs, then splattered the blood on the altar. [23] They took the goats to Hezekiah and the worshipers, and they laid their hands on the animals. [24] The priests then killed the goats and splattered the blood on the altar as a sacrifice to take away the sins of everyone in Israel, because Hezekiah had commanded that these sacrifices be made for all the people of Israel.

[25] Next, Hezekiah assigned the Levites to their places in the temple. He gave them cymbals, harps, and other stringed instruments, according to the instructions that the LORD had given King David and the two prophets, Gad and Nathan. [26] The Levites were ready to play the instruments that had belonged to David; the priests were ready to blow the trumpets.

[27] As soon as Hezekiah gave the signal for the sacrifices to be burned on the altar, the musicians began singing praises to the LORD and playing their instruments, [28] and everyone worshiped the LORD. This continued until the last animal was sacrificed.

[29] After that, Hezekiah and the crowd of worshipers knelt down and worshiped the LORD. [30] Then Hezekiah and his officials ordered the Levites to sing the songs of praise that David and Asaph the prophet had written. And so they bowed down and joyfully sang praises to the LORD.

[31] Hezekiah said to the crowd, "Now that you are once again acceptable to the LORD, bring sacrifices and offerings to give him thanks."

[h] **29.17** *first month*: See the note at 29.3.
29.26 Ps 151.2.

[i] **29.21** *goats*: Hebrew "male goats."

The people did this, and some of them voluntarily brought animals to be offered as sacrifices. 32 Seventy bulls, one hundred rams, and two hundred lambs were brought as sacrifices to please the LORD;[j] 33 six hundred bulls and three thousand sheep were brought as sacrifices to ask the LORD's blessing.[k] 34 There were not enough priests to skin all these animals, because many of the priests had not taken the time to go through the ceremony to make themselves clean. However, since all the Levites had made themselves clean, they helped the priests until the last animal was skinned. 35 Besides all the sacrifices that were burned on the altar, the fat from the other animal sacrifices was burned, and the offerings of wine were poured over the altar.

So the temple was once again used for worshiping the LORD. 36 Hezekiah and the people of Judah celebrated, because God had helped them make this happen so quickly.

Hezekiah Prepares To Celebrate Passover

30 1-4 Passover wasn't celebrated in the first month,[l] which was the usual time, because many of the priests were still unclean and unacceptable to serve, and because not everyone in Judah had come to Jerusalem for the festival. So Hezekiah, his officials, and the people agreed to celebrate Passover in the second month.[m]

Hezekiah sent a message to everyone in Israel and Judah, including those in the territories of Ephraim and West Manasseh, inviting them to the temple in Jerusalem for the celebration of Passover in honor of the LORD God of Israel. 5 Everyone from Beersheba in the south to Dan in the north was invited. This was the largest crowd of people that had ever celebrated Passover, according to the official records.

6 Hezekiah's messengers went everywhere in Israel and Judah with the following letter:

People of Israel, now that you have survived the invasion of the Assyrian kings,[n] it's time for you to turn back to the LORD God our ancestors Abraham, Isaac, and Jacob worshiped. If you do this, he will stop being angry. 7 Don't follow the example of your ancestors and your Israelite relatives in the north. They were unfaithful to the LORD, and he punished them horribly. 8 Don't be stubborn like your ancestors. Decide now to obey the LORD our God! Come to Jerusalem and worship him in the temple that will belong to him forever. Then he will stop being angry, 9 and the enemies that have captured your families will show pity and send them back home. The LORD God is kind and merciful, and if you turn back to him, he will no longer turn his back on you.

10 The messengers went to every town in Ephraim and West Manasseh as far north as the territory of Zebulun, but everyone laughed and insulted them. 11 Only a few people from the tribes of Asher, West Manasseh, and Zebulun were humble and went to Jerusalem. 12 God also made everyone in Judah eager to do what Hezekiah and his officials had commanded.

Passover Is Celebrated

13 In the second month,[o] a large crowd of people gathered in Jerusalem to celebrate the Festival of Thin Bread.[p] 14 They took all the foreign altars and incense altars in Jerusalem and threw them into Kidron Valley.

15-17 Then, on the fourteenth day of that same month, the Levites began killing the

[j]**29.32** *sacrifices to please the LORD*: See the note at 1.6. [k]**29.33** *sacrifices to ask the LORD's blessing*: These sacrifices have traditionally been called "peace offerings" or "offerings of well-being." A main purpose was to ask for the LORD's blessing, and so in the CEV they are sometimes called "sacrifices to ask the LORD's blessing." [l]**30.1-4** *first month*: See the note at 29.3. [m]**30.1-4** *second month*: See the note at 3.1, 2. [n]**30.6** *the invasion of the Assyrian kings*: See 2 Kings 17.1-22. [o]**30.13** *second month*: See the note at 3.1, 2. [p]**30.13** *the Festival of Thin Bread*: The celebration of this Festival began one day after Passover. And so these two festivals were often referred to as one.

30.1-4 Nu 9.9-11.

lambs for Passover, because many of the worshipers were unclean and were not allowed to kill their own lambs. Meanwhile, some of the priests and Levites felt ashamed because they had not gone through the ceremony to make themselves clean. They immediately went through that ceremony and went to the temple, where they offered sacrifices to please the LORD.[q] Then the priests and Levites took their positions, according to the Law of Moses, the servant of God.

As the Levites killed the lambs, they handed some of the blood to the priests, who splattered it on the altar.

18-19 Most of the people that came from Ephraim, West Manasseh, Issachar, and Zebulun had not made themselves clean, but they ignored God's Law and ate the Passover lambs anyway. Hezekiah found out what they had done and prayed, "LORD God, these people are unclean according to the laws of holiness. But they are worshiping you, just as their ancestors did. So, please be kind and forgive them." 20 The LORD answered Hezekiah's prayer and did not punish them.

21 The worshipers in Jerusalem were very happy and celebrated the Festival for seven days. The Levites and priests sang praises to the LORD every day and played their instruments. 22 Hezekiah thanked the Levites for doing such a good job, leading the celebration.

The worshipers celebrated for seven days by offering sacrifices, by eating the sacred meals, and by praising the LORD God of their ancestors. 23 Everyone was so excited that they agreed to celebrate seven more days.

24 So Hezekiah gave the people one thousand bulls and seven thousand sheep to be offered as sacrifices and to be used as food for the sacred meals. His officials gave one thousand bulls and ten thousand sheep, and many more priests agreed to go through the ceremony to make themselves clean. 25 Everyone was very happy, including those from Judah and Israel, the priests and Levites, and the foreigners living in Judah and Israel. 26 It was the biggest celebration in Jerusalem since the days of King Solomon, the son of David. 27 The priests and Levites asked God to bless the people, and from his home in heaven, he did.

The People Destroy the Local Shrines
(2 Kings 18.4)

31 After the Festival, the people went to every town in Judah and smashed the stone images of foreign gods and cut down the sacred poles[r] for worshiping the goddess Asherah. They destroyed all the local shrines[s] and foreign altars in Judah, as well as those in the territories of Benjamin, Ephraim, and West Manasseh. Then everyone went home.

Offerings for the Priests and Levites

2 Hezekiah divided the priests and Levites into groups, according to their duties. Then he assigned them the responsibilities of offering sacrifices to please the LORD[t] and sacrifices to ask his blessing.[u] He also appointed people to serve at the temple and to sing praises at the temple gates. 3 Hezekiah provided animals from his own herds and flocks to use for the morning and evening sacrifices, as well as for the sacrifices during the Sabbath celebrations, the New Moon Festivals, and the other religious feasts required by the Law of the LORD.

4 He told the people of Jerusalem to bring the offerings that were to be given to the priests and Levites, so that they would have time to serve the LORD with their work. 5 As soon as the people heard what the king wanted, they brought a tenth of everything they owned, including their best grain, wine, olive oil, honey, and other crops. 6 The people from the other towns of Judah brought a tenth of their herds and flocks, as well as a tenth of anything they had dedicated to the LORD. 7 The people

[q] **30.15-17** *sacrifices to please the LORD*: See the note at 1.6. [r] **31.1** *sacred poles*: See the note at 14.3. [s] **31.1** *local shrines*: See the note at 11.15. [t] **31.2** *sacrifices to please the LORD*: See the note at 1.6. [u] **31.2** *sacrifices to ask his blessing*: See the note at 29.33.

31.3 Nu 28.1—29.39. **31.4,5** Nu 18.12, 13, 21.

started bringing their offerings to Jerusalem in the third month,[v] and the last ones arrived four months later. 8 When Hezekiah and his officials saw these offerings, they thanked the LORD and the people.

9 Hezekiah asked the priests and Levites about the large amount of offerings. 10 The high priest at the time was Azariah, a descendant of Zadok, and he replied, "Ever since the people have been bringing us their offerings, we have had more than enough food and supplies. The LORD has certainly blessed his people. Look at how much is left over!"

11 So the king gave orders for storerooms to be built in the temple, and when they were completed, 12-13 all the extra offerings were taken there. Hezekiah and Azariah then appointed Conaniah the Levite to be in charge of these storerooms. His brother Shimei was his assistant, and the following Levites worked with them: Jehiel, Azaziah, Nahath, Asahel, Jerimoth, Jozabad, Eliel, Ismachiah, Mahath, and Benaiah. 14 Kore son of Imnah was assigned to guard the East Gate, and he was put in charge of receiving the offerings voluntarily given to God and of dividing them among the priests and Levites. 15-16 He had six assistants who were responsible for seeing that all the priests in the other towns of Judah also got their share of these offerings. They were Eden, Miniamin, Jeshua, Shemaiah, Amariah, and Shecaniah.

Every priest and every Levite over thirty[w] years old who worked daily in the temple received part of these offerings, according to their duties. 17 The priests were listed in the official records by clans, and the Levites twenty years old and older were listed by their duties. 18 The official records also included their wives and children, because they had also been faithful in keeping themselves clean and acceptable to serve the LORD.

19 Hezekiah also appointed other men to take food and supplies to the priests and Levites whose homes were in the pastureland around the towns of Judah. But the priests had to be descendants of Aaron, and the Levites had to be listed in the official records.

20-21 Everything Hezekiah did while he was king of Judah, including what he did for the temple in Jerusalem, was right and good. He was a successful king, because he obeyed the LORD God with all his heart.

King Sennacherib of Assyria Invades Judah

(2 Kings 18.13-37; Isaiah 36.1-22)

32 After King Hezekiah had faithfully obeyed the LORD's instructions by doing these things, King Sennacherib of Assyria invaded Judah. He attacked the fortified cities and thought he would capture every one of them.

2 As soon as Hezekiah learned that Sennacherib was planning to attack Jerusalem, 3-4 he and his officials worked out a plan to cut off the supply of water outside the city, so that the Assyrians would have no water when they came to attack. The officials got together a large work force that stopped up the springs and streams near Jerusalem.

5 Hezekiah also had workers repair the broken sections of the city wall. Then they built defense towers and an outer wall to help protect the one already there. The landfill on the east side of David's City was also strengthened.

He gave orders to make a large supply of weapons and shields, 6 and he appointed army commanders over the troops. Then he gathered the troops together in the open area in front of the city gate and said to them:

> 7 Be brave and confident! There's no reason to be afraid of King Sennacherib and his powerful army. We are much more powerful, 8 because the LORD our God fights on our side. The Assyrians must rely on human power alone.

These words encouraged the army of Judah.

9 When Sennacherib and his troops

[v]**31.7** *third month*: Sivan, the third month of the Hebrew calendar, from about mid-May to mid-June. [w]**31.15,16** *thirty*: The Hebrew text has "three" instead of "thirty"; in Hebrew, these two words look almost exactly the same (see also Numbers 4.3; 1 Chronicles 23.3).

were camped at the town of Lachish, he
sent a message to Hezekiah and the people
in Jerusalem. It said:
10 I am King Sennacherib of Assyria, and I have Jerusalem surrounded. Do you think you can survive
my attack? 11 Hezekiah your king is
telling you that the LORD your God
will save you from me. But he is lying,
and you'll die of hunger and thirst.
12 Didn't Hezekiah tear down all except one of the LORD's altars and
places of worship?[x] And didn't he tell
you people of Jerusalem and Judah to
worship at that one place?
13 You've heard what my ancestors
and I have done to other nations. Were
the gods of those nations able to defend their land against us? 14 None of
those gods kept their people safe from
the kings of Assyria. Do you really
think your God can do any better?
15 Don't be fooled by Hezekiah! No god
of any nation has ever been able to
stand up to Assyria. Believe me, your
God cannot keep you safe!
16 The Assyrian officials said terrible
things about the LORD God and his servant
Hezekiah. 17 Sennacherib's letter even
made fun of the LORD. It said, "The gods of
other nations could not save their people
from Assyria's army, and neither will the
God that Hezekiah worships." 18 The officials said all these things in Hebrew, so that
everyone listening from the city wall would
understand and be terrified and surrender.
19 The officials talked about the LORD God
as if he were nothing but an ordinary god
or an idol that someone had made.

The Death of King Sennacherib

(2 Kings 19.14-19, 35-37; Isaiah 37.14-20; 37.36-38)

20 Hezekiah and the prophet Isaiah son
of Amoz asked the LORD for help, 21 and he
sent an angel that killed every soldier and
commander in the Assyrian camp.
Sennacherib returned to Assyria, completely disgraced. Then one day he went
into the temple of his god where some of
his sons killed him.
22 The LORD rescued Hezekiah and the
people of Jerusalem from Sennacherib and
also protected them from other enemies.
23 People brought offerings to Jerusalem for
the LORD and expensive gifts for Hezekiah,
and from that day on, every nation on earth
respected Hezekiah.

Hezekiah Gets Sick and Almost Dies

(2 Kings 20.1-11; Isaiah 38.1-8)

24 About this same time, Hezekiah got
sick and was almost dead. He prayed, and
the LORD gave him a sign that he would recover. 25 But Hezekiah was so proud that
he refused to thank the LORD for everything
he had done for him. This made the LORD
angry, and he punished Hezekiah and the
people of Judah and Jerusalem. 26 Hezekiah and the people later felt sorry and
asked the LORD to forgive them. So the
LORD did not punish them as long as
Hezekiah was king.

Hezekiah's Wealth

(2 Kings 20.12-19; Isaiah 39.1-8)

27 Hezekiah was very rich, and everyone
respected him. He built special rooms to
store the silver, the gold, the precious
stones and spices, the shields, and the
other valuable possessions. 28 Storehouses
were also built for his supply of grain, wine,
and olive oil; barns were built for his cattle,
and pens were put up for his sheep. 29 God
made Hezekiah extremely rich, so he
bought even more sheep, goats, and cattle.
And he built towns where he could keep all
these animals.
30 It was Hezekiah who built a tunnel
that carried the water from Gihon Spring
into the city of Jerusalem. In fact, everything he did was successful! 31 Even when
the leaders of Babylonia sent messengers to
ask Hezekiah about the sign God had given
him, God let Hezekiah give his own answer

[x]**32.12** *worship*: Hezekiah actually had torn down the places where idols were worshiped, and he had told the people to worship the LORD at the one place of worship in Jerusalem. But the Assyrian leader was confused and thought these were also places where the LORD was supposed to be worshiped.

to test him and to see if he would remain
faithful.

Hezekiah Dies
(2 Kings 20.20, 21)

32 Everything else Hezekiah did while
he was king, including how faithful he was
to the LORD, is included in the records kept
by Isaiah the prophet. These are written in
*The History of the Kings of Judah and Is-
rael.* 33 When Hezekiah died, he was
buried in the section of the royal tombs
that was reserved for the most respected
kings,[y] and everyone in Judah and
Jerusalem honored him. His son Manasseh
then became king.

King Manasseh of Judah
(2 Kings 21.1-9, 17, 18)

33 Manasseh was twelve years old
when he became king of Judah,
and he ruled fifty-five years from Jerusalem. 2 Manasseh disobeyed the LORD by following the disgusting customs of the nations that the LORD had forced out of
Israel. 3 He rebuilt the local shrines[z] that
his father Hezekiah had torn down. He
built altars for the god Baal and set up sacred poles[a] for worshiping the goddess
Asherah. And he faithfully worshiped the
stars in the sky.
4 In the temple, where only the LORD
was supposed to be worshiped, Manasseh
built altars for pagan gods 5 and for the stars.
He placed these altars in both courtyards of
the temple 6-7 and even set up a stone image
of a foreign god. Manasseh practiced magic
and witchcraft; he asked fortunetellers for
advice and sacrificed his own sons in Hinnom Valley. He did many other sinful
things and made the LORD very angry.
Years ago, God had told David and
Solomon:

> Jerusalem is the place I prefer
> above all others in Israel. It belongs to
> me, and there in the temple I will be
> worshiped forever. 8 If my people will
> faithfully obey all the laws and teach-
> ing I gave to my servant Moses, I will
> never again force them to leave the
> land I gave to their ancestors.

9 But the people of Judah and Jerusalem
listened to Manasseh and did even more
sinful things than the nations the LORD had
wiped out.
10 The LORD tried to warn Manasseh
and the people about their sins, but they ignored the warning. 11 So he let Assyrian
army commanders invade Judah and capture Manasseh. They put a hook in his nose
and tied him up in chains, and they took
him to Babylon. 12 While Manasseh was held
captive there, he asked the LORD God to
forgive him and to help him. 13 The LORD
listened to Manasseh's prayer and saw how
sorry he was, and so he let him go back to
Jerusalem and rule as king. Manasseh
knew from then on that the LORD was God.
14 Later, Manasseh rebuilt the eastern
section of Jerusalem's outer wall and made
it taller. This section went from Gihon Valley north to Fish Gate and around the part
of the city called Mount Ophel. He also assigned army officers to each of the fortified
cities in Judah.[b]
15 Manasseh also removed the idols and
the stone image of the foreign god from the
temple, and he gathered the altars he had
built near the temple and in other parts of
Jerusalem. He threw all these things outside the city. 16 Then he repaired the
LORD's altar and offered sacrifices to thank
him and sacrifices to ask his blessing.[c] He
gave orders that everyone in Judah must
worship the LORD God of Israel. 17 The people obeyed Manasseh, but they worshiped
the LORD at their own shrines.
18 Everything else Manasseh did while
he was king, including his prayer to the
LORD God and the warnings from his
prophets, is written in *The History of the
Kings of Israel.* 19 Hozai[d] wrote a lot about

[y]**32.33** *in the section . . . reserved for the most respected kings*: One possible meaning for the difficult Hebrew text. [z]**33.3** *local shrines*: See the note at 11.15. [a]**33.3** *sacred poles*: See the note at 14.3. [b]**33.14** *fortified cities in Judah*: At this time, Judah was under the control of Assyria. The fortifications mentioned in this verse may have been done under orders from Assyrian officials, hoping to strengthen their southern border against the rising power of Egypt. [c]**33.16** *sacrifices to ask his blessing*: See the note at 29.33. [d]**33.19** *Hozai*: Or "The prophets."
33.2 Jr 15.4. **33.6-8** 1 K 9.3-5; 2 Ch 7.12-18.

Manasseh, including his prayer and God's answer. But Hozai also recorded the evil things Manasseh did before turning back to God, as well as a list of places where Manasseh set up idols, and where he built local shrines and places to worship Asherah. 20 Manasseh died and was buried near the palace, and his son Amon became king.

King Amon of Judah

(2 Kings 21.19-26)

21 Amon was twenty-two years old when he became king of Judah, and he ruled from Jerusalem for two years. 22 Amon disobeyed the LORD, just as his father Manasseh had done, and he worshiped and offered sacrifices to the idols his father had made. 23 Manasseh had turned back to the LORD, but Amon refused to do that. Instead, he sinned even more than his father.

24 Some of Amon's officials plotted against him and killed him in his palace. 25 But the people of Judah killed the murderers of Amon and made his son Josiah king.

King Josiah of Judah

(2 Kings 22.1, 2)

34 Josiah was eight years old when he became king of Judah, and he ruled thirty-one years from Jerusalem. 2 He followed the example of his ancestor David and always obeyed the LORD.

Josiah Stops the Worship of Foreign Gods

(2 Kings 23.4-20)

3 When Josiah was only sixteen years old he began worshiping God, just as his ancestor David had done. Then, four years later, he decided to destroy the local shrines[e] in Judah and Jerusalem, as well as the sacred poles[f] for worshiping the goddess Asherah and the idols of foreign gods. 4 He watched as the altars for the worship of the god Baal were torn down, and as the nearby incense altars were smashed. The Asherah poles, the idols, and the stone images were also smashed, and the pieces were scattered over the graves of their worshipers. 5 Josiah then had the bones of the pagan priests burned on the altars.[g]

And so Josiah got rid of the worship of foreign gods in Judah and Jerusalem. 6 He did the same things in the towns and ruined villages[h] in the territories of West Manasseh, Ephraim, and Simeon, as far as the border of Naphtali. 7 Everywhere in the northern kingdom of Israel, Josiah tore down pagan altars and Asherah poles; he crushed idols to dust and smashed incense altars.

Then Josiah went back to Jerusalem.

Hilkiah Finds *The Book of God's Law*

(2 Kings 22.3-20)

8 In the eighteenth year of Josiah's rule in Judah, after he had gotten rid of all the sinful things from the land and from the LORD's temple, he sent three of his officials to repair the temple. They were Shaphan son of Azaliah, Governor Maaseiah of Jerusalem, and Joah son of Joahaz, who kept the government records.

9 These three men went to Hilkiah the high priest. They gave him the money that the Levite guards had collected from the people of West Manasseh, Ephraim, and the rest of Israel, as well as those living in Judah, Benjamin, and Jerusalem. 10 Then the money was turned over to the men who supervised the repairs to the temple. They used some of it to pay the workers, 11 and they gave the rest of it to the carpenters and builders, who used it to buy the stone and wood they needed to repair the other buildings that Judah's kings had not taken care of.

12 The workers were honest, and their supervisors were Jahath and Obadiah from the Levite clan of Merari, and Zechariah and Meshullam from the Levite clan of Kohath. Other Levites, who were all skilled musicians, 13 were in charge of carrying

[e]**34.3** *local shrines*: See the note at 11.15. [f]**34.3** *sacred poles*: See the note at 14.3.
[g]**34.5** *the bones of the pagan priests burned on the altars*: This made the altars unclean, so that they could not be used in worshiping any god. [h]**34.6** *ruined villages*: One possible meaning for the difficult Hebrew text.

34.1 Jr 3.6. **34.4** 2 K 21.3; 2 Ch 33.3. **34.5** 1 K 13.2.

supplies and supervising the workers. Other Levites were appointed to stand guard around the temple.

14 While the money was being given to these supervisors, Hilkiah found the book that contained the laws that the LORD had given to Moses. 15 Hilkiah handed the book to Shaphan the official and said, "Look what I found here in the temple—*The Book of God's Law*."

16 Shaphan took the book to Josiah and reported, "Your officials are doing everything you wanted. 17 They have collected the money from the temple and have given it to the men supervising the repairs. 18 But there's something else, Your Majesty. The priest Hilkiah gave me this book." Then Shaphan read it aloud.

19 When Josiah heard what was in *The Book of God's Law*, he tore his clothes in sorrow. 20 At once he called together Hilkiah, Shaphan, Ahikam son of Shaphan, Abdon son of Micah,[i] and his own servant Asaiah. He said, 21 "The LORD must be furious with me and everyone else in Israel and Judah, because our ancestors did not obey the laws written in this book. Go find out what the LORD wants us to do."

22 Hilkiah and the four other men left right away and went to talk with Huldah the prophet. Her husband was Shallum,[j] who was in charge of the king's clothes. Huldah lived in the northern part of Jerusalem, and when they met in her home, 23 she said:

> You were sent here by King Josiah, and this is what the LORD God of Israel says to him: 24 "Josiah, I am the LORD! And I intend to punish this country and everyone in it, just as this book says. 25 The people of Judah and Israel have rejected me. They have offered sacrifices to foreign gods and have worshiped their own idols. I can't stand it any longer. I am furious.
>
> 26-27 "Josiah, listen to what I am going to do. I noticed how sad you were when you heard that this country and its people would be completely wiped out. You even tore your clothes in sorrow, and I heard you cry. 28 So before I destroy this place, I will let you die in peace."

The men left and reported to Josiah what Huldah had said.

Josiah Reads *The Book of God's Law*
(*2 Kings* 23.1-3)

29 King Josiah called together the leaders of Judah and Jerusalem. 30 Then he went to the LORD's temple, together with all the people of Judah and Jerusalem, the priests, and the Levites.

Finally, when everybody was there, he read aloud *The Book of God's Law*[k] that had been found in the temple.

31 After Josiah had finished reading, he stood in the place reserved for the king. He promised in the LORD's name to faithfully obey the LORD and to follow his laws and teachings that were written in the book. 32 Then he asked the people of Jerusalem and Benjamin to make that same promise and to obey the God their ancestors had worshiped.

33 Josiah destroyed all the idols in the territories of Israel, and he commanded everyone in Israel to worship only the LORD God. The people did not turn away from the LORD God of their ancestors for the rest of Josiah's rule as king.

Passover Is Celebrated
(*2 Kings* 23.21-23)

35 Josiah commanded that Passover be celebrated in Jerusalem to honor the LORD. So, on the fourteenth day of the first month,[l] the lambs were killed for the Passover celebration.

2 On that day, Josiah made sure the priests knew what duties they were to do in the temple. 3 He called together the Levites who served the LORD and who taught the people his laws, and he said:

[i]**34.20** *Abdon son of Micah*: Also called "Achbor son of Micaiah" (see 2 Kings 22.12).
[j]**34.22** *Shallum*: Hebrew "Shallum son of Tokhath son of Hasrah." [k]**34.30** *The Book of God's Law*: The Hebrew text has "The Book of God's Agreement," which is the same as "The Book of God's Law" in verses 15 and 19. In traditional translations this is called "The Book of the Covenant."
[l]**35.1** *first month*: See the note at 29.3.

No longer will you have to carry the
sacred chest from place to place. It
will stay in the temple built by King
Solomon son of David, where you will
serve the LORD and his people Israel.
4 Get ready to do the work that David
and Solomon assigned to you, according to your clans. 5 Divide yourselves
into groups, then arrange yourselves
throughout the temple so that each
family of worshipers will be able to get
help from one of you.[m] 6 When the
people bring you their Passover lamb,
you must kill it and prepare it to be
sacrificed to the LORD. Make sure the
people celebrate according to the instructions that the LORD gave Moses,
and don't do anything to make yourselves unclean and unacceptable.

7 Josiah donated thirty thousand sheep
and goats, and three thousand bulls from
his own flocks and herds for the people to
offer as sacrifices. 8 Josiah's officials also
voluntarily gave some of their animals to
the people, the priests, and the Levites as
sacrifices. Hilkiah, Zechariah, and Jehiel,
who were the officials in charge of the temple, gave the priests twenty-six hundred
sheep and lambs and three hundred bulls
to sacrifice during the Passover celebration.
9 Conaniah, his two brothers Shemaiah
and Nethanel, as well as Hashabiah, Jeiel,
and Jozabad were leaders of the Levites,
and they gave the other Levites five thousand sheep and goats, and five hundred
bulls to offer as sacrifices.

10 When everything was ready to celebrate Passover, the priests and the Levites
stood where Josiah had told them. 11 Then
the Levites killed and skinned the Passover
lambs, and they handed some of the blood
to the priests, who splattered it on the altar.
12 The Levites set aside the parts of the animal that the worshipers needed for their
sacrifices to please the LORD,[n] just as the
Law of Moses required. They also did the
same thing with the bulls. 13 They sacrificed the Passover animals on the altar and
boiled the meat for the other offerings in
pots, kettles, and pans. Then they quickly
handed the meat to the people so they
could eat it.

14 All day long, the priests were busy offering sacrifices and burning the animals'
fat on the altar. And when everyone had
finished, the Levites prepared Passover animals for themselves and for the priests.

15 During the celebration some of the
Levites prepared Passover animals for
the musicians and the guards, so that the
Levite musicians would not have to leave
their places, which had been assigned to
them according to the instructions of
David, Asaph, Heman, and Jeduthun the
king's prophet. Even the guards at the temple gates did not have to leave their posts.

16 So on that day, Passover was celebrated to honor the LORD, and sacrifices
were offered on the altar to him, just as
Josiah had commanded. 17 The worshipers
then celebrated the Festival of Thin Bread
for the next seven days.

18 People from Jerusalem and from
towns all over Judah and Israel were there.
Passover had not been observed like this
since the days of Samuel the prophet. In
fact, this was the greatest Passover celebration in Israel's history! 19 All these things
happened in the eighteenth year of Josiah's
rule in Judah.

Josiah Dies in Battle

(*2 Kings* 23.28-30)

20 Some time later, King Neco of Egypt
led his army to the city of Carchemish on
the Euphrates River. And Josiah led his
troops north to meet the Egyptians in
battle.[o]

21 Neco sent the following message to
Josiah:

I'm not attacking you, king of Judah! We're not even at war. But God

[m] **35.5** *each family of worshipers . . . you*: One possible meaning for the difficult Hebrew text.
[n] **35.12** *sacrifices to please the LORD*: See the note at 1.6. [o] **35.20** *battle*: At this time, King Neco of Egypt (609-595 B.C.) was fighting on the side of the Assyrians. He marched north to fight the Babylonian army and help Assyria keep control of its land. Since Josiah considered Assyria an enemy, he set out to stop Neco and the Egyptian troops.

35.4 2 Ch 8.14. **35.13** Ex 12.8, 9. **35.15** 1 Ch 25.1. **35.17** Ex 12.1-20.

has told me to quickly attack my enemy. God is on my side, so if you try to
stop me, he will punish you.
22 But Josiah ignored Neco's warning,
even though it came from God! Instead, he
disguised himself and marched into battle
against Neco in the valley near Megiddo.
23 During the battle an Egyptian soldier
shot Josiah with an arrow. Josiah told his
servants, "Get me out of here! I've been
hit." 24 They carried Josiah out of his chariot, then put him in the other chariot he
had there and took him back to Jerusalem,
where he soon died. He was buried beside
his ancestors, and everyone in Judah and
Jerusalem mourned his death.
25 Jeremiah the prophet wrote a funeral
song in honor of Josiah. And since then,
anyone in Judah who mourns the death of
Josiah sings that song. It is included in the
collection of funeral songs.
26 Everything else Josiah did while he
was king, including how he faithfully
obeyed the LORD, 27 is written in *The History of the Kings of Israel and Judah*.

King Jehoahaz of Judah
(*2 Kings* 23.30-35)

36 After the death of Josiah, the people of Judah crowned his son Jehoahaz their new king. 2 He was twenty-
three years old at the time, and he ruled
only three months from Jerusalem. 3 King
Neco of Egypt captured Jehoahaz and
forced Judah to pay almost four tons of silver and seventy-five pounds of gold as
taxes. 4 Then Neco appointed Jehoahaz's
brother Eliakim king of Judah and changed
his name to Jehoiakim. He led Jehoahaz
away to Egypt as his prisoner.

King Jehoiakim of Judah
(*2 Kings* 23.36—24.7)

5 Jehoiakim was twenty-five years old
when he was appointed king, and he ruled
eleven years from Jerusalem. Jehoiakim
disobeyed the LORD his God by doing evil.
6 During Jehoiakim's rule, King Nebuchadnezzar of Babylonia invaded Judah.
He arrested Jehoiakim and put him in
chains, and he sent him to the capital city
of Babylon. 7 Nebuchadnezzar also carried
off many of the valuable things in the
LORD's temple, and he put them in his
palace in Babylon.
8 Everything else Jehoiakim did while he
was king, including all the disgusting and
evil things, is written in *The History of the
Kings of Israel and Judah*. His son Jehoiachin then became king.

King Jehoiachin of Judah
(*2 Kings* 24.8-17)

9 Jehoiachin was eighteen[p] years old
when he became king of Judah, and he
ruled only three months and ten days from
Jerusalem. Jehoiachin also disobeyed the
LORD by doing evil. 10 In the spring of the
year, King Nebuchadnezzar of Babylonia
had Jehoiachin arrested and taken to Babylon, along with more of the valuable items
in the temple. Then Nebuchadnezzar appointed Zedekiah king of Judah.

King Zedekiah of Judah
(*2 Kings* 24.18-20; *Jeremiah* 52.1-3)

11 Zedekiah was twenty-one years old
when he was appointed king of Judah, and
he ruled from Jerusalem for eleven years.
12 He disobeyed the LORD his God and
refused to change his ways, even after
a warning from Jeremiah, the LORD's
prophet.
13 King Nebuchadnezzar of Babylonia
had forced Zedekiah to promise in God's
name that he would be loyal. Zedekiah was
stubborn and refused to turn back to the
LORD God of Israel, so he rebelled against
Nebuchadnezzar. 14 The people of Judah
and even the priests who were their leaders
became more unfaithful. They followed the
disgusting example of the nations around
them and made the LORD's holy temple unfit for worship. 15 But the LORD God felt

[p]36.9 *eighteen*: Some manuscripts of one ancient translation (see also 2 Kings 24.8); Hebrew "eight."

36.4 Jr 22.11, 12. **36.5** Jr 22.18, 19; 26.1-6; 35.1-19. **36.6** Jr 25.1-38; 36.1-32; 45.1-5; Dn 1.1, 2. **36.10** **a** Jr 22.24-30; 24.1-10; 29.1, 2; Ez 17.12; **b** Jr 37.1; Ez 17.13. **36.11** Jr 27.1-22; 28.1-17. **36.13** Ez 17.15.

sorry for his people, and instead of destroying the temple, he sent prophets who warned the people over and over about their sins. 16 But the people only laughed and insulted these prophets. They ignored what the LORD God was trying to tell them, until he finally became so angry that nothing could stop him from punishing Judah and Jerusalem.

Jerusalem Is Destroyed

(2 Kings 25.1-21; Jeremiah 52.3-30)

17 The LORD sent King Nebuchadnezzar of Babylonia to attack Jerusalem. Nebuchadnezzar killed the young men who were in the temple, and he showed no mercy to anyone, whether man or woman, young or old. God let him kill everyone in the city. 18 Nebuchadnezzar carried off everything that was left in the temple; he robbed the treasury and the personal storerooms of the king and his officials. He took everything back to Babylon.

19 Nebuchadnezzar's troops burned down the temple and destroyed every important building in the city. Then they broke down the city wall. 20 The survivors were taken to Babylonia as prisoners, where they were slaves of the king and his sons, until Persia became a powerful nation.

21 Judah was an empty desert, and it stayed that way for seventy years, to make up for all the years it was not allowed to rest.[q] These things happened just as Jeremiah the LORD's prophet had said.[r]

Cyrus Lets the Jews Return Home

(Ezra 1.1-4)

22 In the first year that Cyrus was king of Persia,[s] the LORD had Cyrus send a message to all parts of his kingdom. This happened just as Jeremiah the LORD's prophet had promised. 23 The message said:

I am King Cyrus of Persia.

The LORD God of heaven has made me the ruler of every nation on earth. He has also chosen me to build a temple for him in Jerusalem, which is in Judah. The LORD God will watch over any of his people who want to go back to Judah.

[q]**36.21** *rest*: According to Leviticus 25.1-7, the land was supposed to rest every seventh year.
[r]**36.21** *Jeremiah . . . said*: Jeremiah 25.11, 12; 29.10. According to the Law, the people had to allow the land to rest one out of every seven years (see Leviticus 25.1-7).
[s]**36.22** *the first year that Cyrus was king of Persia*: Probably 538 B.C., when Cyrus captured Babylonia. He had actually ruled Persia since 549 B.C.

36.17 Jr 21.1-10; 34.1-5. **36.19** 1 K 9.8. **36.21** Jr 25.11; 29.10. **36.23** Is 44.28.

EZRA

ABOUT THIS BOOK

This book is named after the main character of its second part.

The book of 2 Chronicles ended with an official message that King Cyrus of Persia sent in 538 B.C., which allowed the Jews to return to their land and to rebuild the Lord's temple. The first part of the book of Ezra (1–6) begins with that same message and then tells how many of the Jews returned to Jerusalem and began work on the temple. But the people in nearby areas caused a lot of trouble for them, and so the work went slowly and even stopped for several years. But the temple was finally finished in 515 B.C.

The first part of the book also tells about problems at a later time, when the Jews had to stop rebuilding the city walls during the rule of Artaxerxes (4.6-23).

The second part of the book (7–10) begins with Ezra arriving in Jerusalem to teach God's laws to the people of Judah. Ezra was horrified to learn that the people of Israel were committing the same sins as other nations. Israel was in serious danger of being punished or even destroyed by the Lord. So Ezra prayed and confessed Israel's sins, and the people agreed to begin obeying God's laws. The book of Nehemiah reports other things that Ezra did.

God's people were no longer an independent nation, but Ezra realized that God was in control, no matter what empire ruled over them. And so Ezra said:

"Praise the LORD God of our ancestors! He made sure that the king honored the LORD's temple in Jerusalem. God has told the king, his advisors, and his powerful officials to treat me with kindness. The LORD God has helped me, and I have been able to bring many Jewish leaders back to Jerusalem."

(7.27b, 28)

A QUICK LOOK AT THIS BOOK

- The Jews Return Home from Exile (1.1—2.70)
- The Altar Is Rebuilt, and Work on the Temple Begins (3.1—4.5)
- Later Trouble Rebuilding Jerusalem (4.6-23)
- The Temple Is Rebuilt (4.24—6.22)
- Ezra Leads Many Jews back to Jerusalem (7.1—8.36)
- Ezra Forces Men To Divorce Their Gentile Wives (9.1—10.44)

Cyrus Lets the Jews Return Home

1 Years ago the LORD sent Jeremiah with a message about a promise[a] for the people of Israel. Then in the first year that Cyrus was king of Persia,[b] the LORD kept his promise by having Cyrus send this official message to all parts of his kingdom:

2-3 I am King Cyrus of Persia.

The LORD God of heaven, who is also the God of Israel, has made me the ruler of all nations on earth. And

[a]1.1 *a promise*: That the people of Israel would be set free from Babylonia after seventy years (see Jeremiah 25.11; 29.10). [b]1.1 *the first year that Cyrus was king of Persia*: Probably 539 B.C., when Cyrus captured Babylonia. He had actually ruled Persia since 549 B.C.

1.1 Jr 25.11; 29.10. **1.2,3** Is 44.28.

he has chosen me to build a temple for him in Jerusalem, which is in Judah. The LORD God will watch over and encourage any of his people who want to go back to Jerusalem and help build the temple.
4 Everyone else must provide what is needed. They must give money, supplies, and animals, as well as gifts for rebuilding God's temple.
5 Many people felt that the LORD God wanted them to help rebuild his temple, and they made plans to go to Jerusalem. Among them were priests, Levites, and leaders of the tribes of Judah and Benjamin.
6 The others helped by giving silver articles, gold, personal possessions, cattle, and other valuable gifts, as well as offerings for the temple.
7 King Cyrus gave back the things that Nebuchadnezzar[c] had taken from the LORD's temple in Jerusalem and had put in the temple of his own gods.
8 Cyrus placed Mithredath, his chief treasurer, in charge of these things. Mithredath counted them and gave a list to Sheshbazzar, the governor of Judah.
9-10 Included among them were: 30 large gold dishes; 1,000 large silver dishes; 29 other dishes;[d] 30 gold bowls; 410 silver bowls; and 1,000 other articles.
11 Altogether, there were 5,400 gold and silver dishes, bowls, and other articles. Sheshbazzar took them with him when he and the others returned to Jerusalem from Babylonia.

A List of People Who Returned from Exile

(Nehemiah 7.4-73)

2 King Nebuchadnezzar[e] of Babylonia had captured many of the people of Judah and had taken them as prisoners to Babylonia. Now they were on their way back to Jerusalem and to their own towns everywhere in Judah.
2-20 Zerubbabel, Joshua,[f] Nehemiah, Seraiah, Reelaiah, Mordecai, Bilshan, Mispar, Bigvai, Rehum, and Baanah were in charge of the ones who were coming back. And here is a list of how many returned from each family group: 2,172 from the family of Parosh; 372 from the family of Shephatiah; 775 from the family of Arah; 2,812 descendants of Jeshua and Joab[g] from the family of Pahath Moab; 1,254 from the family of Elam; 945 from the family of Zattu; 760 from the family of Zaccai; 642 from the family of Bani; 623 from the family of Bebai; 1,222 from the family of Azgad; 666 from the family of Adonikam; 2,056 from the family of Bigvai; 454 from the family of Adin; 98 from the family of Ater, also known as Hezekiah; 323 from the family of Bezai; 112 from the family of Jorah; 223 from the family of Hashum; and 95 from the family of Gibbar.
21-35 Here is how many people returned whose ancestors had come from the following towns: 123 from Bethlehem; 56 from Netophah; 128 from Anathoth; 42 from Azmaveth; 743 from Kiriatharim, Chephirah, and Beeroth; 621 from Ramah and Geba; 122 from Michmas; 223 from Bethel and Ai; 52 from Nebo; 156 from Magbish; 1,254 from the other Elam; 320 from Harim; 725 from Lod, Hadid, and Ono; 345 from Jericho; and 3,630 from Senaah.
36-39 Here is a list of how many returned from each family of priests: 973 descendants of Jeshua from the family of Jedaiah; 1,052 from the family of Immer; 1,247 from the family of Pashhur; and 1,017 from the family of Harim.
40-42 And here is a list of how many returned from the families of Levites: 74 descendants of Hodaviah from the families of Jeshua and Kadmiel; 128 descendants of Asaph from the temple musicians; and 139 descendants of Shallum, Ater, Talmon, Akkub, Hatita, and Shobai from the temple guards.
43-54 Here is a list of the families of tem-

[c] **1.7** *Nebuchadnezzar*: Known as Nebuchadnezzar II, who ruled Babylonia from 605 to 562 B.C. In 586 B.C. he destroyed Jerusalem and took many of its people to Babylonia. [d] **1.9,10** *other dishes*: One possible meaning for the difficult Hebrew text. [e] **2.1** *Nebuchadnezzar*: See the note at 1.7. [f] **2.2-20** *Joshua*: Hebrew "Jeshua." In this translation the name "Joshua" is used of the descendant of Jozadak, the last chief priest before the exile; this same Joshua is often mentioned together with Zerubbabel (2.2-20; 3.2, 8, 9; 4.3; 5.2; 10.18, 19). In other places the name "Jeshua" is used (2.2-20, 36-39, 40-42; 8.33). [g] **2.2-20** *Jeshua and Joab*: Hebrew "Jeshua Joab."

ple workers whose descendants returned: Ziha, Hasupha, Tabbaoth, Keros, Siaha, Padon, Lebanah, Hagabah, Akkub, Hagab, Shamlai, Hanan, Giddel, Gahar, Reaiah, Rezin, Nekoda, Gazzam, Uzza, Paseah, Besai, Asnah, Meunim, Nephisim, Bakbuk, Hakupha, Harhur, Bazluth, Mehida, Harsha, Barkos, Sisera, Temah, Neziah, and Hatipha.

55-57 Here is a list of Solomon's servants whose descendants returned: Sotai, Hassophereth, Peruda, Jaalah, Darkon, Giddel, Shephatiah, Hattil, Pochereth Hazzebaim, and Ami.

58 A total of 392 descendants of temple workers and of Solomon's servants returned.

59-60 There were 652 who returned from the families of Delaiah, Tobiah, and Nekoda, though they could not prove that they were Israelites. They had lived in the Babylonian towns of Tel-Melah, Tel-Harsha, Cherub, Addan, and Immer.

61-62 The families of Habaiah, Hakkoz, and Barzillai could not prove that they were priests. The ancestor of the family of Barzillai had married the daughter of Barzillai from Gilead and had taken his wife's family name. But the records of these three families could not be found, and none of them were allowed to serve as priests. 63 In fact, the governor[h] told them, "You cannot eat the food offered to God until we find out if you really are priests."

64-67 There were 42,360 who returned, in addition to 7,337 servants and 200 musicians, both women and men. They brought with them 736 horses, 245 mules, 435 camels, and 6,720 donkeys.

68 When the people came to where the LORD's temple had been in Jerusalem, some of the family leaders gave gifts so it could be rebuilt in the same place. 69 They gave all they could, and it came to a total of 1,030 pounds of gold, 5,740 pounds of silver, and 100 robes for the priests.

70 Everyone returned to the towns from which their families had come, including the priests, the Levites, the musicians, the temple guards, and the workers.[i]

The First Offering on the New Altar

3 During the seventh month[j] of the year, the Israelites who had settled in their
towns went to Jerusalem. 2 The priest
Joshua son of Jozadak, together with the other priests, and Zerubbabel son of Shealtiel and his relatives rebuilt the altar of Israel's God. Then they were able to offer sacrifices there by following the instructions God had given to Moses. 3 And they
built the altar where it had stood before,[k] even though they were afraid of the people who were already living around there. Then every morning and evening they burned sacrifices and offerings to the LORD.

4 The people followed the rules for celebrating the Festival of Shelters and offered the proper sacrifices each day. 5 They offered sacrifices to please the LORD,[l] sacrifices at each New Moon Festival, and sacrifices at the rest of the LORD's festivals. Every offering the people had brought was presented to the LORD.

6 Although work on the temple itself had not yet begun, the people started offering sacrifices on the LORD's altar on the first day of the seventh month of that year.

The Rebuilding of the Temple Begins

7 King Cyrus of Persia had said the Israelites could have cedar trees brought from Lebanon to Joppa by sea. So they sent grain, wine, and olive oil to the cities of Tyre and Sidon as payment for these trees, and they gave money to the stoneworkers and carpenters.

[h]**2.63** *governor*: In Nehemiah 8.9; 10.1, this same title is used of Nehemiah, though it is doubtful if he is the one referred to here. [i]**2.70** *workers*: One possible meaning for the difficult Hebrew text of verse 70. [j]**3.1** *seventh month*: Tishri (also called Ethanim), the seventh month of the Hebrew calendar, from about mid-September to mid-October. [k]**3.3** *where it had stood before*: One possible meaning for the difficult Hebrew text. [l]**3.5** *sacrifices to please the LORD*: In traditional translations these sacrifices are usually called "whole burnt offerings" (see Leviticus 1.1-16).

2.63 Nu 27.21. **2.70** 1 Ch 9.2; Ne 11.3. **3.2** Ex 27.1. **3.3** Nu 28.1-8. **3.4** Nu 29.12-38. **3.5** Nu 28.11—29.39.

8 During the second month[m] of the second year after the people had returned from Babylonia, they started rebuilding the LORD's temple. Zerubbabel son of Shealtiel, Joshua son of Jozadak, the priests, the Levites, and everyone else who had returned started working. Every Levite over twenty years of age was put in charge of some part of the work. 9 The Levites in charge of the whole project were Joshua and his sons and relatives and Kadmiel and his sons from the family of Hodaviah.[n] The family of Henadad worked along with them.

10 When the builders had finished laying the foundation of the temple, the priests put on their robes and blew trumpets in honor of the LORD, while the Levites from the family of Asaph praised God with cymbals. All of them followed the instructions given years before by King David.[o] 11 They praised the LORD and gave thanks as they took turns singing:

"The LORD is good!
His faithful love for Israel
will last forever."

Everyone started shouting and praising the LORD because work on the foundation of the temple had begun. 12 Many of the older priests and Levites and the heads of families cried aloud because they remembered seeing the first temple years before. But others were so happy that they celebrated with joyful shouts. 13 Their shouting and crying were so noisy that it all sounded alike and could be heard a long way off.

Foreigners[p] Want To Help Rebuild the Temple

4 The enemies of the tribes of Judah and Benjamin heard that the people had come back to rebuild the temple of the LORD God of Israel. 2 So they went to Zerubbabel and to the family leaders and said, "Let us help! Ever since King Esarhaddon of Assyria[q] brought us here, we have worshiped your God and offered sacrifices to him."

3 But Zerubbabel, Joshua, and the family leaders answered, "You cannot take part in building a temple for the LORD our God! We will build it ourselves, just as King Cyrus of Persia commanded us."

4 Then the neighboring people began to do everything possible to frighten the Jews[r] and to make them stop building. 5 During the time that Cyrus was king and even until Darius[s] became king, they kept bribing government officials to slow down the work.

Trouble Rebuilding Jerusalem[t]

6 In the first year that Xerxes was king,[u] the neighboring people brought written charges against the people of Judah and Jerusalem.

7 Later, Bishlam, Mithredath, Tabeel, and their advisors got together and wrote a letter to Artaxerxes when he was king of Persia.[v] It was written in Aramaic and had to be translated.[w]

8-10 A letter was also written to Artaxerxes about Jerusalem by Governor Re-

[m] **3.8** *second month*: Ziv, the second month of the Hebrew calendar, from about mid-April to mid-May. [n] **3.9** *Hodaviah*: Or "Yehudah" or "Hodiah." [o] **3.10** *King David*: Ruled from about 1010 to 970 B.C. [p] **4.1** *Foreigners*: People from foreign countries who had been captured by Assyrian and Babylonian kings and forced to settle in Palestine. [q] **4.2** *King Esarhaddon of Assyria*: Ruled from 681 to 669 B.C. These people may have been brought to Palestine in 677 or 676 B.C., when Esarhaddon invaded Syria. [r] **4.4** *Jews*: This was the name given to those Israelites who settled in Judah after returning from Babylonia. [s] **4.5** *Cyrus . . . Darius*: Cyrus ruled 539-530 B.C. (see the note at 1.1); Darius I, known as Darius the Great, ruled 522-486 B.C. [t] **4.6** *Jerusalem*: Verses 6-23, which tell about the events of a later period, are placed here because they are also concerned with the problem of stopping or slowing down work on the temple. [u] **4.6** *first year that Xerxes was king*: Either the end of 486 or the beginning of 485 B.C. The Hebrew has the king's Persian name "Ahasuerus," but he is better known as "Xerxes," the Greek form of the name. [v] **4.7** *Artaxerxes . . . Persia*: Artaxerxes I (465-425 B.C.). [w] **4.7** *It was . . . translated*: One possible meaning for the difficult Hebrew text. Ezra 4.8—6.18 is written in Aramaic, instead of in Hebrew like most of the Old Testament.

3.10 1 Ch 25.1. **3.11** 1 Ch 16.34; 2 Ch 5.11-13; 7.3; Ps 100.5; 106.1; 107.1; 118.1; 136.1; Jr 33.11; 3 Macc 6.32. **3.12** Tb 14.5. **4.2** 2 K 17.24-41. **4.6** Es 1.1, 2.

hum, Secretary Shimshai, and their advisors, including the judges, the governors, the officials, and the local leaders. They were joined in writing this letter by people from Erech and Babylonia, the Elamites from Susa,[x] and people from other foreign nations that the great and famous Ashurbanipal[y] had forced to settle in Samaria and other parts of Western Province.[z]

11 This letter said:

Your Majesty King Artaxerxes, we are your servants from everywhere in Western Province, and we send you our greetings.

12 You should know that the Jews who left your country have moved back to Jerusalem and are now rebuilding that terrible city. In fact, they have almost finished rebuilding the walls and repairing the foundations. 13 You should also know that if the walls are completed and the city is rebuilt, the Jews won't pay any kind of taxes, and there will be less money in your treasury.

14 We are telling you this, because you have done so much for us, and we want everyone to respect you. 15 If you look up the official records of your ancestors, you will find that Jerusalem has constantly rebelled and has led others to rebel against kings and provinces. That's why the city was destroyed in the first place. 16 If Jerusalem is rebuilt and its walls completed, you will no longer have control over Western Province.

17 King Artaxerxes answered:

Greetings to Governor Rehum, Secretary Shimshai, and to your advisors in Samaria and other parts of Western Province.

18 After your letter was translated and read to me, 19 I had the old records checked. It is true that for years Jerusalem has rebelled and caused trouble for other kings and nations. 20 And powerful kings have ruled Western Province from Jerusalem and have collected all kinds of taxes.

21 I want you to command the people to stop rebuilding the city until I give further notice. 22 Do this right now, so that no harm will come to the kingdom.

23 As soon as this letter was read, Governor Rehum, Secretary Shimshai, and their advisors went to Jerusalem and forced everyone to stop rebuilding the city.

Work on the Temple Starts Again

24 The Jews were forced to stop work on the temple and were not able to do any more building until the year after Darius became king of Persia.[a]

5 1 Then the LORD God of Israel told the prophets Haggai and Zechariah[b] to speak in his name to the people of Judah and Jerusalem. And they did. 2 So Zerubbabel the governor and Joshua the priest urged the people to start working on the temple again, and God's prophets encouraged them.

3 Governor Tattenai of Western Province and his assistant Shethar Bozenai got together with some of their officials. Then they went to Jerusalem and said to the people, "Who told you to rebuild this temple? 4 Give us the names of the workers!"

5 But God was looking after the Jewish leaders. So the governor and his group decided not to make the people stop working on the temple until they could report to Darius and get his advice.

6 Governor Tattenai, Shethar Bozenai, and their advisors sent a report to Darius, 7 which said:

King Darius, we wish you the best!

8 We went to Judah, where the temple of the great God is being built with huge stones and wooden beams set in

[x]**4.8-10** *the judges . . . Susa*: One possible translation for the names and titles. [y]**4.8-10** *Ashurbanipal*: King of Assyria 669-633 (or possibly 627) B.C. In Aramaic the king's name is "Osnapper," but he is better known as Ashurbanipal. [z]**4.8-10** *Western Province*: The land from the Euphrates River west to the Mediterranean Sea. [a]**4.24** *year after . . . king of Persia*: 520 B.C. [b]**5.1** *Zechariah*: Aramaic "Zechariah son of Iddo."

4.24 Hg 1.1; Zec 1.1. **5.1** Hg 1.1; Zec 1.1. **5.2** Hg 1.12; Zec 4.6-9.

the walls. Everyone is working hard,
and the building is going up fast.
9 We asked those in charge to tell
us who gave them permission to rebuild the temple. 10 We also asked for
the names of their leaders, so that we
could write them down for you.
11 They claimed to be servants of
the God who rules heaven and earth.
And they said they were rebuilding the
temple that was built many years ago
by one of Israel's greatest kings.[c]
12 We were told that their people
had made God angry, and he let them
be captured by Nebuchadnezzar,[d] the
Babylonian king[e] who took them away
as captives to Babylonia. Nebuchadnezzar tore down their temple,
13-15 took its gold and silver articles,
and put them in the temple of his own
god in Babylon.

They also said that during the first
year Cyrus was king of Babylonia,[f] he
gave orders for God's temple to be rebuilt in Jerusalem where it had stood
before. So Cyrus appointed Sheshbazzar governor of Judah and sent these
gold and silver articles for him to put
in the temple. 16 Sheshbazzar then
went to Jerusalem and laid the foundation for the temple, and the work is
still going on.
17 Your Majesty, please have someone look up the old records in Babylonia and find out if King Cyrus really
did give orders to rebuild God's temple
in Jerusalem. We will do whatever you
think we should.

King Cyrus' Order Is Rediscovered

6 King Darius ordered someone to go
through the old records kept in Babylonia. 2 Finally, a scroll[g] was found in Ecbatana, the capital of Media Province, and
it said:

This official record will show 3 that
in the first year Cyrus was king, he
gave orders to rebuild God's temple in
Jerusalem, so that sacrifices and offerings could be presented there.[h] It is to
be built ninety feet high and ninety
feet wide, 4 with one[i] row of wooden
beams for each three rows of large
stones. The royal treasury will pay for
everything. 5 Then return to their
proper places the gold and silver things
that Nebuchadnezzar took from the
temple and brought to Babylonia.

King Darius Orders the Work To Continue

6 King Darius sent this message:

Governor Tattenai of Western
Province and Shethar Bozenai, you
and your advisors must stay away from
the temple. 7 Let the Jewish governor
and leaders rebuild it where it stood
before. And stop slowing them down!
8 Starting right now, I am ordering
you to help the leaders by paying their
expenses from the tax money collected
in Western Province. 9 And don't fail to
let the priests in Jerusalem have whatever they need each day so they can
offer sacrifices to the God of heaven.
Give them young bulls, rams, sheep, as
well as wheat, salt, wine, and olive oil.
10 I want them to be able to offer pleasing sacrifices to God and to pray for
me and my family.
11 If any of you don't obey this order, a wooden beam will be taken from
your house and sharpened on one end.
Then it will be driven through your
body,[j] and your house will be torn
down and turned into a garbage dump.

[c]**5.11** *one of Israel's greatest kings*: Solomon (ruled from about 970 to 931 B.C.). [d]**5.12** *Nebuchadnezzar*: See the note at 1.7. [e]**5.12** *the Babylonian king*: Aramaic "the Babylonian king from Chaldea," but Chaldea is another name for Babylonia. [f]**5.13-15** *Cyrus was king of Babylonia*: King Cyrus of Persia became king of Babylonia when the Persians conquered the city of Babylon in 539 B.C. [g]**6.2** *scroll*: A roll of paper or special leather used for writing on. [h]**6.3** *so that . . . there*: One possible meaning for the difficult Aramaic text. [i]**6.4** *one*: One possible meaning for the difficult Aramaic text. [j]**6.11** *driven through your body*: A well-known punishment in the ancient Near East.

5.12 2 K 25.8-12; 2 Ch 36.17-20; Jr 52.12-15. **5.13-15** Ezra 1.2-11.

[12] I ask the God who is worshiped in Jerusalem to destroy any king or nation who tries either to change what I have said or to tear down his temple. I, Darius, give these orders, and I expect them to be followed carefully.

The Temple Is Dedicated

[13] Governor Tattenai, Shethar Bozenai, and their advisors carefully obeyed King Darius. [14] With great success the Jewish leaders continued working on the temple, while Haggai and Zechariah encouraged them by their preaching. And so, the temple was completed at the command of the God of Israel and by the orders of kings Cyrus, Darius, and Artaxerxes of Persia.[k] [15] On the third day of the month of Adar[l] in the sixth year of the rule of Darius,[m] the temple was finished.

[16] The people of Israel, the priests, the Levites, and everyone else who had returned from exile were happy and celebrated as they dedicated God's temple. [17] One hundred bulls, two hundred rams, and four hundred lambs were offered as sacrifices at the dedication. Also twelve goats were sacrificed as sin offerings for the twelve tribes of Israel. [18] Then the priests and Levites were assigned their duties in God's temple in Jerusalem, according to the instructions Moses had written.

The Passover

[19] Everyone who had returned from exile celebrated Passover on the fourteenth day of the first month.[n] [20] The priests and Levites had gone through a ceremony to make themselves acceptable to lead in worship. Then some of them killed Passover lambs for those who had returned, including the other priests and themselves.

[21] The sacrifices were eaten by the Israelites who had returned and by the neighboring people who had given up the sinful customs of other nations in order to worship the LORD God of Israel. [22] For seven days they celebrated the Festival of Thin Bread. Everyone was happy because the LORD God of Israel had made sure that the king of Assyria[o] would be kind to them and help them build the temple.

Ezra Comes to Jerusalem

7 [1-6] Much later, when Artaxerxes[p] was king of Persia, Ezra came to Jerusalem from Babylonia. Ezra was the son of Seraiah and the grandson of Azariah. His other ancestors were Hilkiah, Shallum, Zadok, Ahitub, Amariah, Azariah, Meraioth, Zerahiah, Uzzi, Bukki, Abishua, Phinehas, Eleazar, and Aaron, the high priest.

Ezra was an expert in the Law that the LORD God of Israel had given to Moses, and the LORD made sure that the king gave Ezra everything he asked for.

[7] Other Jews, including priests, Levites, musicians, the temple guards, and servants, came to Jerusalem with Ezra. This happened during the seventh year that Artaxerxes[q] was king.

[8-9] God helped Ezra, and he arrived in Jerusalem on the first day of the fifth month[r] of that seventh year, after leaving Babylonia on the first day of the first month.[s] [10] Ezra had spent his entire life studying and obeying the Law of the LORD and teaching it to others.

Artaxerxes Gives a Letter to Ezra

[11] Ezra was a priest and an expert in the laws and commands that the LORD had given to Israel. One day King Artaxerxes gave Ezra a letter which said:

[12] Greetings from the great King Artaxerxes to Ezra the priest and expert

[k] **6.14** *Artaxerxes of Persia*: See the note at 4.7. [l] **6.15** *Adar*: The twelfth month of the Hebrew calendar, from about mid-February to about mid-March. [m] **6.15** *sixth year . . . Darius*: 515 B.C. [n] **6.19** *the first month*: Nisan, the first month of the Hebrew calendar, from about mid-March to mid-April. [o] **6.22** *king of Assyria*: Meaning the king of Persia, because Assyria was now part of the Persian Empire. [p] **7.1-6** *Artaxerxes*: Either Artaxerxes I (ruled from 465 to 425 B.C.) or Artaxerxes II (ruled from 405-358 B.C.). [q] **7.7** *seventh year . . . Artaxerxes*: 458 B.C. if this is Artaxerxes I; 398 B.C., if this is Artaxerxes II (see the note at 7.1-6). [r] **7.8,9** *fifth month*: Ab, the fifth month of the Hebrew calendar, from about mid-July to mid-August. [s] **7.8,9** *first month*: See the note at 6.19.

6.14 a Hg 1.1; **b** Zec 1.1. **6.19** Ex 12.1-20.

in the teachings of the God of heaven.
13-14 Any of the people of Israel or
their priests or Levites in my kingdom
may go with you to Jerusalem if they
want to. My seven advisors and I agree
that you may go to Jerusalem and Judah to find out if[t] the laws of your God
are being obeyed.
15 When you go, take the silver and
gold that I and my advisors are freely
giving to the God of Israel, whose temple is in Jerusalem. 16 Take the silver
and gold that you collect from everywhere in Babylonia. Also take the gifts
that your own people and priests have
so willingly contributed for the temple
of your God in Jerusalem.
17 Use the money carefully to buy
the best bulls, rams, lambs, grain, and
wine. Then sacrifice them on the altar
at God's temple in Jerusalem. 18 If any
silver or gold is left, you and your people may use it for whatever pleases
your God. 19 Give your God the other
articles that have been contributed for
use in his temple. 20 If you need to get
anything else for the temple, you may
have the money you need from the
royal treasury.
21 Ezra, you are a priest and an expert in the laws of the God of heaven,
and I order all treasurers in Western
Province to do their very best to help
you. 22 They will be allowed to give as
much as 7,500 pounds of silver, 500
bushels of wheat, 550 gallons of wine,
550 gallons of olive oil, and all the salt
you need.
23 They must provide whatever the
God of heaven demands for his temple, so that he won't be angry with me
and with the kings who rule after me.
24 We want you to know that no
priests, Levites, musicians, guards,
temple servants, or any other temple
workers will have to pay any kind of
taxes.
25 Ezra, use the wisdom God has
given you and choose officials and
leaders to govern the people of Western Province. These leaders should
know God's laws and have them taught
to anyone who doesn't know them.
26 Everyone who fails to obey God's
Law or the king's law will be punished
without pity. They will either be executed or put in prison or forced to
leave their country, or have all they
own taken away.

Ezra Praises God

27 Because King Artaxerxes was so kind,
Ezra said:

Praise the LORD God of our ancestors! He made sure that the king honored the LORD's temple in Jerusalem.
28 God has told the king, his advisors,
and his powerful officials to treat me
with kindness. The LORD God has
helped me, and I have been able to
bring many Jewish leaders back to
Jerusalem.

The Families Who Came Back with Ezra

8 Artaxerxes was king of Persia when I[u]
led the following chiefs of the family
groups from Babylonia to Jerusalem:

2-14 Gershom of the Phinehas family;
Daniel of the Ithamar family;
Hattush son of Shecaniah of the David family;
Zechariah and 150 other men of the Parosh family, who had family records;
Eliehoenai son of Zerahiah with 200 men of the Pahath Moab family;
Shecaniah son of Jahaziel with 300 men of the Zattu family;[v]
Ebed son of Jonathan with 50 men of the Adin family;
Jeshaiah son of Athaliah with 70 men of the Elam family;
Zebadiah son of Michael with 80 men of the Shephatiah family;
Obadiah son of Jehiel with 218 men of the Joab family;

[t]**7.13,14** *find out if*: Or "make sure that." [u]**8.1** *I*: Ezra. [v]**8.2-14** *of the Zattu family*: One ancient translation; these words are not in the Hebrew text, but see 2.2-20, where Zattu is mentioned.

Shelomith son of Josiphiah with 160 men of the Bani family;[w]
Zechariah son of Bebai with 28 men of the Bebai family;
Johanan son of Hakkatan with 110 men of the Azgad family;
Eliphelet, Jeuel, and Shemaiah who returned sometime later with 60 men of the Adonikam family;
Uthai and Zaccur with 70 men of the Bigvai family.

Ezra Finds Levites for the Temple

15 I[x] brought everyone together by the river[y] that flows to the town of Ahava[z] where we camped for three days. Not one Levite could be found among the people and priests. 16 So I sent for the leaders Eliezer, Ariel, Shemaiah, Elnathan, Jarib, Elnathan, Nathan, Zechariah, and Meshullam. I also sent for Joiarib and Elnathan, who were very wise. 17 Then I sent them to Iddo, the leader at Casiphia,[a] and I told them to ask him and his temple workers to send people to serve in God's temple.

18 God was kind to us and had them send a skillful man named Sherebiah, who was a Levite from the family of Mahli. Eighteen of his relatives came with him. 19 We were also sent Hashabiah and Jeshaiah from the family of Merari along with twenty of their relatives. 20 In addition, 220 others came to help the Levites in the temple. The ancestors of these workers had been chosen years ago by King David[b] and his officials, and they were all listed by name.

Ezra Asks the People To Go without Eating and To Pray

21 Beside the Ahava River,[c] I[d] asked the people to go without eating[e] and to pray. We humbled ourselves and asked God to bring us and our children safely to Jerusalem with all of our possessions. 22 I was ashamed to ask the king to send soldiers and cavalry to protect us against enemies along the way. After all, we had told the king that our God takes care of everyone who truly worships him, but that he gets very angry and punishes anyone who refuses to obey. 23 So we went without food and asked God himself to protect us, and he answered our prayers.

The Gifts for the Temple

24 I[f] chose twelve of the leading priests—Sherebiah, Hashabiah and ten of their relatives. 25-27 Then I weighed the gifts that had been given for God's temple, and I divided them among the twelve priests I had chosen. There were gifts of silver and gold, as well as the articles that the king, his advisors and officials, and the people of Israel had contributed. In all there were: 25 tons of silver; 100 silver articles weighing 150 pounds; 7,500 pounds of gold; 20 gold bowls weighing 270 ounces; and 2 polished bronze articles as valuable as gold.

28 I said to the priests:

> You belong to the LORD, the God of your ancestors, and these things also belong to him. The silver and gold were willingly given as gifts to the LORD. 29 Be sure to guard them and keep them safe until you reach Jerusalem. Then weigh them inside God's temple in the presence of the chief priests, the Levites, and the heads of the Israelite families.

30 The priests and Levites then took charge of the gifts that had been weighed, so they could take them to the temple of our God in Jerusalem.

The Return to Jerusalem

31 On the twelfth day of the first month,[g] we left the Ahava River[h] and started for Jerusalem. Our God watched

[w] **8.2-14** *of the Bani family*: One ancient translation; these words are not in the Hebrew text, but see 2.2-20. [x] **8.15** *I*: See the note at 8.1. [y] **8.15** *river*: Or "canal." [z] **8.15** *town of Ahava*: A town (or place) in Babylonia, but the exact location is unknown. [a] **8.17** *Casiphia*: The location is not known. [b] **8.20** *King David*: See the note at 3.10. [c] **8.21** *River*: See the note at 8.15. [d] **8.21** *I*: See the note at 8.1. [e] **8.21** *to go without eating*: The Jews often went without eating as a way of worshiping God. This is sometimes called "fasting." [f] **8.24** *I*: See the note at 8.1. [g] **8.31** *first month*: See the note at 6.19. [h] **8.31** *River*: See the note at 8.15.

over us, and as we traveled along, he kept our enemies from ambushing us.

32 After arriving in Jerusalem, we rested for three days. 33 Then on the fourth day we went to God's temple, where the silver, the gold, and the other things were weighed and given to the priest Meremoth son of Uriah. With him were Eleazar son of Phinehas and the two Levites, Jozabad son of Jeshua and Noadiah son of Binnui. 34 Everything was counted, weighed, and recorded.

35 Those who had returned from exile offered sacrifices on the altar to the God of Israel. Twelve bulls were offered for all Israel. Ninety-six rams and seventy-seven[i] lambs were offered on the altar. And twelve goats were sacrificed for the sins of the people. 36 Some of those who had returned took the king's orders to the governors and officials in Western Province. Then the officials did what they could for the people and for the temple of God.

Ezra Condemns Mixed Marriages

9 Later the Jewish leaders came to me[j] and said:

> Many Israelites, including priests and Levites, are living just like the people around them. They are even guilty of some of the horrible sins of the Canaanites, the Hittites, the Perizzites, the Jebusites, the Ammonites, the Moabites, the Egyptians, and the Amorites.
>
> 2 Some Israelite men have married foreign women and have let their sons do the same thing. Our own officials and leaders were the first to commit this disgusting sin, and now God's holy people are mixed with foreigners.

3 This news made me so angry that I ripped my clothes and tore hair from my head and beard. Then I just sat in shock 4 until time for the evening sacrifice. Many of our people were greatly concerned and gathered around me, because the God of Israel had warned us to stay away from foreigners.

Ezra's Prayer

5 At the time of the evening sacrifice, I was still sitting there in sorrow with my clothes all torn. So I got down on my knees, then lifted my arms, 6 and prayed:

> I am much too ashamed to face you, LORD God. Our sins and our guilt have swept over us like a flood that reaches up to the heavens. 7 Since the time of our ancestors, all of us have sinned. That's why we, our kings, and our priests have often been defeated by other kings. They have killed some of us and made slaves of others; they have taken our possessions and made us ashamed, just as we are today.
>
> 8 But for now, LORD God, you have shown great kindness to us. You made us truly happy by letting some of us settle in this sacred place and by helping us in our time of slavery. 9 We are slaves, but you have never turned your back on us. You love us, and because of you, the kings of Persia have helped us. It's as though you have given us new life! You let us rebuild your temple and live safely in Judah and Jerusalem.
>
> 10 Our God, what can we say now? Even after all this, we have disobeyed the commands 11 that were given to us by your servants the prophets. They said the land you are giving us is full of sinful and wicked people, who never stop doing disgusting things.[k] 12 And we were warned not to let our daughters and sons marry their sons and daughters.
>
> Your prophets also told us never to help those foreigners or even let them live in peace. You wanted us to become strong and to enjoy the good things in the land, then someday to leave it to our children forever.
>
> 13 You punished us because of our terrible sins. But you did not punish us nearly as much as we deserve, and you have brought some of us back home. 14 Why should we disobey your com-

[i] **8.35** *seventy-seven*: Or "seventy-two." [j] **9.1** *me*: Ezra. [k] **9.11** *doing disgusting things*: Probably worshiping idols.

9.12 Ex 34.11-16; Dt 7.1-5.

mands again by letting our sons and daughters marry these foreigners who do such disgusting things? That would make you angry enough to destroy us all! 15 LORD God of Israel, you have been more than fair by letting a few of us survive. But once again, our sins have made us ashamed to face you.

The Plan for Ending Mixed Marriages

10 While Ezra was down on his knees in front of God's temple, praying with tears in his eyes, and confessing the sins of the people of Israel, a large number of men, women, and children gathered around him and cried bitterly.

2 Shecaniah son of Jehiel from the family of Elam said:

Ezra, we have disobeyed God by marrying these foreign women. But there is still hope for the people of Israel, 3 if we follow your advice and the advice of others who truly respect the laws of God. We must promise God that we will divorce our foreign wives and send them away, together with their children.

4 Ezra, it's up to you to do something! We will support whatever you do. So be brave!

5 Ezra stood up and made the chief priests, the Levites, and everyone else in Israel swear that they would follow the advice of Shecaniah. 6 Then Ezra left God's temple and went to spend the night in the living quarters of Jehohanan son of Eliashib. He felt sorry for what the people had done, and he did not eat or drink a thing.

7-8 The officials and leaders sent a message to all who had returned from Babylonia and were now living in Jerusalem and Judah. It told them to meet in Jerusalem within three days, or else they would lose everything they owned and would no longer be considered part of the people that had returned from Babylonia.

9 Three days later, on the twentieth day of the ninth month,[l] everyone from Judah and Benjamin came to Jerusalem and sat in the temple courtyard. It was a serious meeting, and they sat there, trembling in the rain.

10 Ezra the priest stood up and said:

You have broken God's Law by marrying foreign women, and you have made the whole nation guilty! 11 Now you must confess your sins to the LORD God of your ancestors and obey him. Divorce your foreign wives and don't have anything to do with the rest of the foreigners who live around here.

12 Everyone in the crowd shouted:

You're right! We will do what you say. 13 But there are so many of us, and we can't just stay out here in this downpour. A lot of us have sinned by marrying foreign women, and the matter can't be settled in only a day or two.

14 Why can't our officials stay on in Jerusalem and take care of this for us? Let everyone who has sinned in this way meet here at a certain time with leaders and judges from their own towns. If we take care of this problem, God will surely stop being so terribly angry with us.

15 Jonathan son of Asahel and Jahzeiah son of Tikvah were the only ones who objected, except for the two Levites, Meshullam and Shabbethai.

16 Everyone else who had returned from exile agreed with the plan. So Ezra the priest chose men[m] who were heads of the families, and he listed their names. They started looking into the matter on the first day of the tenth month,[n] 17 and they did not finish until the first day of the first month[o] of the next year.

The Men Who Had Foreign Wives

18-19 Here is a list of the priests who had agreed to divorce their foreign wives and to sacrifice a ram as a sin offering:

Maaseiah, Eliezer, Jarib, and Gedaliah from the family of Joshua son of Jozadak

[l] **10.9** *ninth month*: Chislev, the ninth month of the Hebrew calendar, from about mid-November to mid-December. [m] **10.16** *So . . . men*: One possible meaning for the difficult Hebrew text.
[n] **10.16** *tenth month*: Tebeth, the tenth month of the Hebrew calendar, from about mid-December to mid-January. [o] **10.17** *first month*: See the note at 6.19.

and his brothers; 20 Hanani and Zebadiah
from the family of Immer; 21 Maaseiah, Elijah, Shemaiah, Jehiel, and Uzziah from the
family of Harim; 22 Elioenai, Maaseiah,
Ishmael, Nethanel, Jozabad, and Elasah
from the family of Pashhur.

23 Those Levites who had foreign wives were: Jozabad, Shimei, Kelaiah (also known as Kelita), Pethahiah, Judah, and Eliezer.

24 Eliashib, the musician, had a foreign wife.

These temple guards had foreign wives: Shallum, Telem, and Uri.

25 Here is a list of the others from Israel who had foreign wives:

Ramiah, Izziah, Malchijah, Mijamin, Eleazar, Hashabiah,[p] and Benaiah from the family of Parosh;

26 Mattaniah, Zechariah, Jehiel, Abdi, Jeremoth, and Elijah from the family of Elam;

27 Elioenai, Eliashib, Mattaniah, Jeremoth, Zabad, and Aziza from the family of Zattu;

28 Jehohanan, Hananiah, Zabbai, and Athlai from the family of Bebai;

29 Meshullam, Malluch, Adaiah, Jashub, Sheal, and Jeremoth from the family of Bani;

30 Adna, Chelal, Benaiah, Maaseiah, Mattaniah, Bezalel, Binnui, and Manasseh from the family of Pahath Moab;

31-32 Eliezer, Isshijah, Malchijah, Shemaiah, Shimeon, Benjamin, Malluch, and Shemariah from the family of Harim;

33 Mattenai, Mattattah, Zabad, Eliphelet, Jeremai, Manasseh, and Shimei from the family of Hashum;

34-37 Maadai, Amram, Uel, Benaiah, Bedeiah, Cheluhi, Vaniah, Meremoth, Eliashib, Mattaniah, Mattenai, and Jaasu from the family of Bani;

38-42 Shimei, Shelemiah, Nathan, Adaiah, Machnadebai, Shashai, Sharai, Azarel, Shelemiah, Shemariah, Shallum, Amariah, and Joseph from the family of Binnui;[q]

43 Jeiel, Mattithiah, Zabad, Zebina, Jaddai, Joel, and Benaiah from the family of Nebo.

44 These men divorced their foreign wives, then sent them and their children away.[r]

[p] **10.25** *Hashabiah*: One ancient translation; Hebrew "Malchijah." [q] **10.38-42** *from the family of Binnui*: One possible meaning for the difficult Hebrew text. [r] **10.44** *away*: One possible meaning for the difficult Hebrew text of verse 44.

NEHEMIAH

ABOUT THIS BOOK

Twelve years after the last events of the book of Ezra, a Jew named Nehemiah received bad news about Jerusalem: The walls of the city were still broken down, and the burned gates had never been replaced.

Nehemiah lived in the Persian city of Susa and was a personal servant to King Artaxerxes. So Nehemiah prayed and asked God to have Artaxerxes send him to Jerusalem to rebuild the city. Artaxerxes did send Nehemiah, and he even provided the materials for the repairs.

After Nehemiah had arrived in Jerusalem and the repair work had begun, the officials from neighboring areas insulted the Jews and accused them of wanting to rebel against Persia. These enemies even planned attacks against Jerusalem and tried to have Nehemiah killed. Finally, the walls and gates were finished and dedicated to God, and they became a sign that God had blessed his people.

But Nehemiah realized that God would continue to bless his people only if they obeyed him. As Nehemiah said in one of his prayers:

> *"LORD God of heaven, you are great and fearsome. And you faithfully keep your promises to everyone who loves you and obeys your commands."*
>
> *(1.5)*

A QUICK LOOK AT THIS BOOK

- King Artaxerxes Sends Nehemiah to Jerusalem (1.1—2.10)
- Rebuilding the Walls of Jerusalem (2.11—4.22)
- Nehemiah's Concern for the Poor (5.1-19)
- The Wall Is Finished, in Spite of Enemy Plots (6.1—7.3)
- Exiles Who Returned (7.4-73)
- Ezra Reads God's Law to the People, and They Celebrate the Festival of Shelters (8.1-18)
- The People Confess Their Sins (9.1-37)
- The People Sign an Agreement To Obey the Lord (9.38—10.39)
- The People Who Settled in Jerusalem and Judah (11.1-36)
- Priests and Levites Who Returned from Exile (12.1-26)
- Nehemiah Dedicates the City Wall (12.27-47)
- Changes Nehemiah Made (13.1-31)

Nehemiah's Prayer

1 I am Nehemiah son of Hacaliah, and in this book I tell what I have done.
During the month of Chislev[a] in the
twentieth year that Artaxerxes[b] ruled Persia, I was in his fortress city of Susa,[c]
2 when my brother Hanani came with some
men from Judah. So I asked them about
the Jews who had escaped[d] from being

---

[a]1.1 *Chislev*: The ninth month of the Hebrew calendar, from about mid-November to mid-December.
[b]1.1 *Artaxerxes*: Probably Artaxerxes I, who ruled Persia 465-425 B.C. [c]1.1 *Susa*: Capital of Elam Province, the winter home of Persian kings. [d]1.2 *escaped*: Or "returned."

captives in Babylonia. I also asked them about the city of Jerusalem.

3 They told me, "Those captives who have come back are having all kinds of troubles. They are terribly disgraced, Jerusalem's walls are broken down, and its gates have been burned."

4 When I heard this, I sat down and cried. Then for several days, I mourned; I went without eating to show my sorrow, and I prayed:

> 5 LORD God of heaven, you are great and fearsome. And you faithfully keep your promises to everyone who loves you and obeys your commands. 6 I am your servant, so please have mercy on me and answer the prayer that I make day and night for these people of Israel who serve you. I, my family, and the rest of your people have sinned 7 by choosing to disobey you and the laws and teachings you gave to your servant Moses.
>
> 8 Please remember the promise you made to Moses. You told him that if we were unfaithful, you would scatter us among foreign nations. 9 But you also said that no matter how far away we were, we could turn to you and start obeying your laws. Then you would bring us back to the place where you have chosen to be worshiped.
>
> 10 Our LORD, I am praying for your servants—those you rescued by your great strength and mighty power. 11 Please answer my prayer and the prayer of your other servants who gladly honor your name. When I serve the king his wine today, make him pleased with me and have him do what I ask.

Nehemiah Goes to Jerusalem

2 During the month of Nisan[e] in the twentieth year that Artaxerxes was king, I served him his wine, as I had done before. But this was the first time I had ever looked depressed. 2 So the king said, "Why do you look so sad? You're not sick. Something must be bothering you."

Even though I was frightened, 3 I answered, "Your Majesty, I hope you live forever! I feel sad because the city where my ancestors are buried is in ruins, and its gates have been burned down."

4 The king asked, "What do you want me to do?"

I prayed to the God who rules from heaven. 5 Then I told the king, "Sir, if it's all right with you, please send me back to Judah, so that I can rebuild the city where my ancestors are buried."

6 The queen was sitting beside the king when he asked me, "How long will it take, and when will you be back?" The king agreed to let me go, and I told him when I would return.

7 Then I asked, "Your Majesty, would you be willing to give me letters to the governors of the provinces west of the Euphrates River, so that I can travel safely to Judah? 8 I will need timber to rebuild the gates of the fortress near the temple and more timber to construct the city wall and to build a place for me to live. And so, I would appreciate a letter to Asaph, who is in charge of the royal forest." God was good to me, and the king did everything I asked.

9 The king sent some army officers and cavalry troops along with me, and as I traveled through the Western Provinces, I gave the letters to the governors. 10 But when Sanballat from Horon[f] and Tobiah the Ammonite official heard about what had happened, they became very angry, because they didn't want anyone to help the people of Israel.

Nehemiah Inspects the Wall of Jerusalem

11 Three days after arriving in Jerusalem, 12 I got up during the night and left my house. I took some men with me, without telling anyone what I thought God

[e] **2.1** *Nisan*: Or Abib, the first month of the Hebrew calendar, from about mid-March to mid-April.

[f] **2.10** *Horon*: Possibly meaning that Sanballat was the official in charge of Beth-Horon, an important town on the road from Jerusalem to Lydda and the Mediterranean Sea.

1.8 Lv 26.33. **1.9** Dt 30.1-5. **2.3** 2 K 25.8-10; 2 Ch 36.19; Jr 52.12-14.

wanted me to do for the city. The only animal I took was the donkey I rode on. 13 I
went through Valley Gate on the west,
then south past Dragon Spring, before
coming to Garbage Gate. As I rode along, I
took a good look at the crumbled walls
of the city and the gates that had been
torn down and burned. 14 On the east
side of the city, I headed north to Fountain Gate and King's Pool, but then the
trail became too narrow for my donkey.
15 So I went down to Kidron Valley and
looked at the wall from there. Then before
daylight I returned to the city through
Valley Gate.

16 None of the city officials knew what
I had in mind. And I had not even told
any of the Jews—not the priests, the leaders, the officials, or any other Jews who
would be helping in the work. 17 But when
I got back, I said to them, "Jerusalem is truly in a mess! The gates have
been torn down and burned, and everything is in ruins. We must rebuild the
city wall so that we can again take pride in
our city."

18 Then I told them how kind God had
been and what the king had said.

Immediately, they replied, "Let's start
building now!" So they got everything
ready.

19 When Sanballat, Tobiah, and Geshem
the Arab heard about our plans, they
started insulting us and saying, "Just
look at you! Do you plan to rebuild the
walls of the city and rebel against the
king?"

20 I answered, "We are servants of the
God who rules from heaven, and he will
make our work succeed. So we will start rebuilding Jerusalem, but you have no right
to any of its property, because you have had
no part in its history."

Rebuilding the Wall of Jerusalem

3 These are the people who helped
rebuild the wall and gates of Jerusalem:

The high priest Eliashib and the
other priests rebuilt Sheep Gate and
hung its doors. Then they dedicated
Sheep Gate and the section of the wall
as far as Hundred Tower and Hananel
Tower.

2 The people of Jericho rebuilt the
next section of the wall, and Zaccur
son of Imri rebuilt the section after
that.

3 The family of Hassenaah built
Fish Gate. They put the beams in
place and hung the doors, then they
added metal bolts and wooden beams
as locks.

4 Meremoth, son of Uriah and
grandson of Hakkoz, completed the
next section of the wall.

Meshullam, son of Berechiah and
grandson of Meshezabel, rebuilt the
next section, and Zadok son of Baana
rebuilt the section beside that.

5 The next section was to be repaired by the men of Tekoa, but their
town leaders refused to do the hard
work they were assigned.[g]

6 Joiada son of Paseah and Meshullam son of Besodeiah restored Ancient
Gate. They put the beams in place,
hung the doors, and added metal bolts
and wooden beams as locks. 7 Melatiah
from Gibeon, Jadon from Meronoth,
and the men from Gibeon and Mizpah rebuilt the next section of the
wall. This section reached as far as
the house of the governor of West Euphrates Province.[h]

8 Uzziel son of Harhaiah the goldsmith rebuilt the next section.

Hananiah the perfume maker rebuilt the section next after that, and it
went as far as Broad Wall.

9 Rephaiah son of Hur ruled half of
the Jerusalem District, and he rebuilt
the next section of the wall.

10 The section after that was close
to the home of Jedaiah son of Ha-
rumaph, and he rebuilt it.

Hattush son of Hashabneiah
constructed the next section of the
wall.

11 Malchijah son of Harim and

[g] 3.5 *refused . . . assigned*: One possible meaning for the difficult Hebrew text. [h] 3.7 *as far as . . . Province*: One possible meaning for the difficult Hebrew text.

Hasshub son of Pahath Moab rebuilt the section after that, and they also built Oven Tower.

12 Shallum son of Hallohesh ruled the other half of the Jerusalem District, and he rebuilt the next section of the wall. Shallum's daughters also worked with him.

13 Hanun and the people who lived in the town of Zanoah rebuilt Valley Gate. They hung the doors and added metal bolts and wooden beams as locks. They also rebuilt the wall for fifteen hundred feet, all the way to Garbage Gate.

14 Malchijah son of Rechab ruled the district of Beth-Haccherem, and he rebuilt Garbage Gate. He hung the doors and added metal bolts and wooden beams as locks.

15 Shallum[i] son of Colhozeh ruled the district of Mizpah, and he rebuilt Fountain Gate. He put a cover over the gateway, then hung the doors and added metal bolts and wooden beams as locks. He also rebuilt the wall at Shelah Pool. This section was next to the king's garden and went as far as the stairs leading down from David's City.

16 Nehemiah son of Azbuk ruled half of the district of Beth-Zur, and he rebuilt the next section of the wall. It went as far as the royal cemetery,[j] the artificial pool, and the army barracks.

Levites Who Worked on the Wall

17 The Levites who worked on the next sections of the wall were Rehum son of Bani; Hashabiah, who ruled half of the district of Keilah and did this work for his district; 18 Binnui[k] son of Henadad, who ruled the other half of the district of Keilah; 19 Ezer son of Jeshua, who ruled Mizpah, rebuilt the section of the wall that was in front of the armory and reached to the corner of the wall; 20 Baruch son of Zabbai eagerly rebuilt the section of the wall that went all the way to the door of the house of Eliashib the high priest; 21 Meremoth, son of Uriah and grandson of Hakkoz, built up to the far end of Eliashib's house.

Priests Who Worked on the Wall

22 Here is a list of the priests who worked on the wall:

Priests from the region around Jerusalem rebuilt the next section of the wall.

23 Benjamin and Hasshub rebuilt the wall in front of their own houses.

Azariah, who was the son of Maaseiah and the grandson of Ananiah, rebuilt the section in front of his house.

24 Binnui son of Henadad rebuilt the section of the wall from Azariah's house to the corner of the wall.

25 Palal son of Uzai rebuilt the next section, which began at the corner of the wall and the tower of the upper palace near the court of the guard.

Pedaiah son of Parosh rebuilt the next section of the wall. 26 He stopped at a place near the Water Gate on the east and the tower guarding the temple. This was close to a section in the city called Ophel, where the temple workers lived.[l]

Other Builders Who Worked on the Wall

27 The men from Tekoa rebuilt the next section of the wall, and it was their second section.[m] It started at a place across from the large tower that guarded the Temple, and it went all the way to the wall near Ophel.

28 Some priests rebuilt the next section of the wall. They began working north of Horse Gate, and each one

[i] **3.15** *Shallum*: A few Hebrew manuscripts and one ancient translation; most Hebrew manuscripts "Shallun"; one ancient translation "Solomon." [j] **3.16** *royal cemetery*: Hebrew "David's tombs." [k] **3.18** *Binnui*: Two ancient translations; Hebrew "Bavvai." [l] **3.26** *This . . . lived*: One possible meaning for the difficult Hebrew text. [m] **3.27** *second section*: See verse 5.

worked on a section in front of his own house.

29 Zadok son of Immer rebuilt the wall in front of his house.

Shemaiah son of Shecaniah, who looked after the East Gate, rebuilt the section after that.

30 Hananiah and Hanun[n] rebuilt the next section, which was the second section[o] for them.

Meshullam son of Berechiah rebuilt the next section, which happened to be in front of his house.

31 Malchijah, a goldsmith, rebuilt the next section, as far as the house used by the temple workers and merchants. This area was across from Gathering Gate, near the room on top of the wall at the northeast corner.

32 The goldsmiths and merchants rebuilt the last section of the wall, which went from the corner room all the way to Sheep Gate.

Nehemiah's Enemies

4 When Sanballat, the governor of Samaria, heard that we were rebuilding the walls of Jerusalem, he became angry and started insulting our people. 2 In front of his friends and the Samaritan army he said, "What is this feeble bunch of Jews trying to do? Are they going to rebuild the wall and offer sacrifices all in one day? Do they think they can make something out of this pile of scorched stones?"

3 Tobiah from Ammon was standing beside Sanballat and said, "Look at the wall they are building! Why, even a fox could knock over this pile of stones."

4 But I prayed, "Our God, these people hate us and have wished horrible things for us. Please answer our prayers and make their insults fall on them! Let them be the ones to be dragged away as prisoners of war. 5 Don't forgive the mean and evil way they have insulted the builders."

6 The people worked hard, and we built the walls of Jerusalem halfway up again. 7 But Sanballat, Tobiah, the Arabs, the Ammonites, and the people from the city of Ashdod saw the walls going up and the holes being repaired. So they became angry 8 and decided to stir up trouble, and to fight against the people of Jerusalem. 9 But we kept on praying to our God, and we also stationed guards day and night.

10 Meanwhile, the people of Judah were singing a sorrowful song:

"So much rubble for us to haul!
Worn out and weary,
will we ever finish this wall?"

11 Our enemies were saying, "Before those Jews know what has happened, we will sneak up and kill them and put an end to their work."

12 On at least ten different occasions, the Jews living near our enemies warned us against attacks from every side,[p] 13 and so I sent people to guard the wall at its lowest places and where there were still holes in it. I placed them according to families, and they stood guard with swords and spears and with bows and arrows. 14 Then I looked things over and told the leaders, the officials, and the rest of the people, "Don't be afraid of your enemies! The Lord is great and fearsome. So think of him and fight for your relatives and children, your wives and homes!"

15 Our enemies found out that we knew about their plot against us, but God kept them from doing what they had planned. So we went back to work on the wall.

16 From then on, I let half of the young men work while the other half stood guard. They wore armor and had spears and shields, as well as bows and arrows. The leaders helped the workers 17 who were rebuilding the wall. Everyone who hauled building materials kept one hand free to carry a weapon. 18 Even the workers who were rebuilding the wall strapped on a sword. The worker who

[n]**3.30** *Hananiah and Hanun*: Hebrew "Hananiah son of Shelemiah and Hanun, Zalaph's sixth son." [o]**3.30** *second section*: See verses 8, 13. [p]**4.12** *against . . . side*: One possible meaning for the difficult Hebrew text.

was to blow the signal trumpet stayed with me.

[19] I told the people and their officials and leaders, "Our work is so spread out, that we are a long way from one another.
[20] If you hear the sound of the trumpet, come quickly and gather around me. Our God will help us fight."

[21] Every day from dawn to dark, half of the workers rebuilt the walls, while the rest stood guard with their spears.

[22] I asked the men in charge and their workers to stay inside Jerusalem and stand guard at night. So they guarded the city at night and worked during the day. [23] I even slept in my work clothes at night; my children, the workers, and the guards slept in theirs as well. And we always kept our weapons close by.[q]

Nehemiah's Concern for the Poor

5 Some of the men and their wives complained about the Jews in power [2] and said, "We have large families, and it takes a lot of grain merely to keep them alive."

[3] Others said, "During the famine we even had to mortgage our fields, vineyards, and homes to them in order to buy grain."

[4] Then others said, "We had to borrow money from those in power to pay the government tax on our fields and vineyards.
[5] We are Jews just as they are, and our children are as good as theirs. But we still have to sell our children as slaves, and some of our daughters have already been raped. We are completely helpless; our fields and vineyards have even been taken from us."

[6] When I heard their complaints and their charges, I became very angry. [7] So I thought it over and said to the leaders and officials, "How can you charge your own people interest?"

Then I called a public meeting and accused the leaders [8] by saying, "We have tried to buy back all of our people who were sold into exile. But here you are, selling more of them for us to buy back!" The officials and leaders did not say a word, because they knew this was true.

[9] I continued, "What you have done is wrong! We must honor our God by the way we live, so the Gentiles can't find fault with us. [10] My relatives, my friends, and I are also lending money and grain, but we must no longer demand payment in return. [11] Now give back the fields, vineyards, olive orchards, and houses you have taken and also the interest you have been paid."

[12] The leaders answered, "We will do whatever you say and return their property, without asking to be repaid."

So I made the leaders promise in front of the priests to give back the property.
[13] Then I emptied my pockets and said, "If you don't keep your promise, that's what God will do to you. He will empty out everything you own, even taking away your houses."

The people answered, "We will keep our promise." Then they praised the LORD and did as they had promised.

Nehemiah Is Generous

[14] I was governor of Judah from the twentieth year that Artaxerxes[r] was king until the thirty-second year. And during these entire twelve years, my relatives and I refused to accept the food that I was allowed. [15] Each governor before me had been a burden to the people by making them pay for his food and wine and by demanding forty silver coins a day. Even their officials had been a burden to the people. But I respected God, and I didn't think it was right to be so hard on them. [16] I spent all my time getting the wall rebuilt and did not buy any property. Everyone working for me did the same thing. [17] I usually fed a hundred fifty of our own Jewish people and their leaders, as well as foreign visitors from surrounding lands. [18] Each day one ox, six of the best sheep, and lots of chickens were prepared. Then every ten days, a large supply of wine was brought in. I knew what a heavy burden this would have been

[q]**4.23** *And . . . by*: One possible meaning for the difficult Hebrew text. [r]**5.14** *Artaxerxes*: See the note at 1.1.
5.7 Ex 22.25; Lv 25.35-37; Dt 23.19, 20.

for the people, and so I did not ask for my
food allowance as governor.
19 I pray that God will bless me for
everything I have done for my people.

Plots against Nehemiah

6 Sanballat, Tobiah, Geshem, and our
other enemies learned that I had completely rebuilt the wall. All I lacked was
hanging the doors in the gates. 2 Then Sanballat and Geshem sent a message, asking
me to meet with them in one of the villages
in Ono Valley. I knew they were planning to
harm me in some way. 3 So I sent messengers to tell them, "My work is too important
to stop now and go there. I can't afford to
slow down the work just to visit with you."
4 They invited me four times, but each
time I refused to go.
5 Finally, Sanballat sent an official to me
with an unsealed letter, 6 which said:

> A rumor is going around among the
> nations that you and the other Jews
> are rebuilding the wall and planning to
> rebel, because you want to be their
> king. And Geshem[s] says it's true! 7 You
> even have prophets in Jerusalem,
> claiming you are now the king of Ju-
> dah. You know the Persian king will
> hear about this, so let's get together
> and talk it over.

8 I sent a message back to Sanballat,
saying, "None of this is true! You are making it all up."
9 Our enemies were trying to frighten us
and to keep us from our work. But I asked
God to give me strength.
10 One day I went to visit Shemaiah.[t]
He was looking very worried, and[u] he said,
"Let's hurry to the holy place of the temple
and hide there.[v] We will lock the temple
doors, because your enemies are planning
to kill you tonight."
11 I answered, "Why should someone
like me have to run and hide in the temple
to save my life? I won't go!"
12 Suddenly I realized that God had not
given Shemaiah this message. But Tobiah
and Sanballat had paid him to trick me
13 and to frighten me into doing something
wrong, because they wanted to ruin my
good name.
14 Then I asked God to punish Tobiah
and Sanballat for what they had done. I
prayed that God would punish the prophet
Noadiah and the other prophets who, together with her, had tried to frighten me.

The Work Is Finished

15 On the twenty-fifth day of the month
Elul,[w] the wall was completely rebuilt. It
had taken fifty-two days. 16 When our enemies in the surrounding nations learned
that the work was finished, they felt helpless, because they knew that our God had
helped us rebuild the wall.
17 All this time the Jewish leaders and
Tobiah had been writing letters back and
forth. 18 Many people in Judah were loyal
to Tobiah for two reasons: Shecaniah son of
Arah was his father-in-law, and Tobiah's
son Jehohanan had married the daughter
of Meshullam son of Berechiah.[x] 19 The
people would always tell me about the good
things Tobiah had done, and then they
would tell Tobiah everything I had said.
So Tobiah kept sending letters, trying to
frighten me.

7 After the wall had been rebuilt and the
gates hung, then the temple guards,
the singers, and the other Levites were assigned their work. 2 I put my brother
Hanani in charge of Jerusalem, along with
Hananiah, the commander of the fortress, because Hananiah could be trusted,
and he respected God more than most
people did. 3 I said to them, "Don't let the
gates to the city be opened until the
sun has been up for a while. And make
sure that they are closed and barred before the guards go off duty at sunset.

[s] **6.6** *Geshem*: Hebrew "Gashmu" (see verse 1 and 2.19). [t] **6.10** *Shemaiah*: Hebrew "Shemaiah son of Delaiah son of Mehetabel." [u] **6.10** *was . . . worried, and*: Or "wasn't supposed to leave his house, but." [v] **6.10** *holy place . . . hide there*: Only priests were allowed to enter the holy place; anyone else could be put to death. [w] **6.15** *Elul*: The sixth month of the Hebrew calendar, from about mid-August to mid-September. [x] **6.18** *Shecaniah . . . Berechiah*: Jews who had helped rebuild the Jerusalem wall (see 3.4, 29, 30).

Choose people from Jerusalem to stand guard at different places around the wall and others to stand guard near their own houses."

A List of Exiles Who Returned

(Ezra 2.1-70)

4 Although Jerusalem covered a large area, not many people lived there, and no new houses had been built. 5-6 So God gave me the idea to bring together the people, their leaders, and officials and to check the family records of those who had returned from captivity in Babylonia, after having been taken there by King Nebuchadnezzar.[y] About this same time, I found records of those who had been the first to return to Jerusalem from Babylon Province.[z] By reading these records, I learned that they settled in their own hometowns, 7 and that they had come with Zerubbabel, Joshua, Nehemiah, Azariah, Raamiah, Nahamani, Mordecai, Bilshan, Mispereth, Bigvai, Nehum, and Baanah.

8-25 Here is how many had returned from each family group: 2,172 from Parosh; 372 from Shephatiah; 652 from Arah; 2,818 from Pahath Moab, who were all descendants of Jeshua and Joab; 1,254 from Elam; 845 from Zattu; 760 from Zaccai; 648 from Binnui; 628 from Bebai; 2,322 from Azgad; 667 from Adonikam; 2,067 from Bigvai; 655 from Adin; 98 from Ater, also known as Hezekiah; 328 from Hashum; 324 from Bezai; 112 from Hariph; and 95 from Gibeon.

26-38 Here is how many people returned whose ancestors had come from the following towns: 188 from Bethlehem and Netophah; 128 from Anathoth; 42 from Beth-Azmaveth; 743 from Kiriath-Jearim, Chephirah, and Beeroth; 621 from Ramah and Geba; 122 from Michmas; 123 from Bethel and Ai; 52 from Nebo;[a] 1,254 from Elam;[b] 320 from Harim; 345 from Jericho; 721 from Lod, Hadid, and Ono; and 3,930 from Senaah.

39-42 Here is how many returned from each family of priests: 973 descendants of Jeshua from Jedaiah; 1,052 from Immer; 1,247 from Pashhur; and 1,017 from Harim.

43-45 Here is how many returned from the families of Levites: 74 descendants of Hodevah from the families of Jeshua and Kadmiel; 148 descendants of Asaph from the temple musicians; and 138 descendants of Shallum, Ater, Talmon, Akkub, Hatita, and Shobai from the temple guards.

46-56 Here are the names of the families of temple workers whose descendants returned: Ziha, Hasupha, Tabbaoth, Keros, Sia, Padon, Lebana, Hagaba, Shalmai, Hanan, Giddel, Gahar, Reaiah, Rezin, Nekoda, Gazzam, Uzza, Paseah, Besai, Meunim, Nephushesim, Bakbuk, Hakupha, Harhur, Bazlith, Mehida, Harsha, Barkos, Sisera, Temah, Neziah, and Hatipha.

57-59 Here are the names of Solomon's servants whose descendants returned: Sotai, Sophereth, Perida, Jaala, Darkon, Giddel, Shephatiah, Hattil, Pochereth Hazzebaim, and Amon.

60 A total of 392 descendants of temple workers and of Solomon's servants returned.

61-62 There were 642 who returned from the families of Delaiah, Tobiah, and Nekoda, though they could not prove they were Israelites. They had lived in the Babylonian towns of Tel-Melah, Tel-Harsha, Cherub, Addon, and Immer.

63-64 The families of Hobaiah, Hakkoz, and Barzillai could not prove they were priests. The ancestor of the family of Barzillai had married the daughter of Barzillai from Gilead and had taken his wife's family name. But the records of these three families could not be found, and none of them were allowed to serve as priests. 65 In fact, the governor told them, "You cannot eat the food offered to God

[y]**7.5,6** *Nebuchadnezzar*: Known as Nebuchadnezzar II, who ruled Babylonia from 605 to 562 B.C. In 586 B.C. he destroyed Jerusalem and took many of its people to Babylonia. [z]**7.5,6** *first to return . . . Province*: Probably 539 B.C., when Cyrus, the ruler of Persia, captured the city of Babylon.
[a]**7.26-38** *Nebo*: Hebrew "the other Nebo." [b]**7.26-38** *Elam*: Hebrew "the other Elam."
7.65 Ex 28.30; Dt 33.8.

until he lets us know if you really are priests."[c]

66-69 There were 42,360 who returned, in addition to 7,337 servants, and 245 musicians. Altogether, they brought with them 736 horses, 245 mules,[d] 435 camels, and 6,720 donkeys.

70-72 Many people gave gifts to help pay for the materials to rebuild the temple. The governor himself gave 17 pounds of gold, 50 bowls to be used in the temple, and 530 robes for the priests. Family leaders gave 337 pounds of gold and 3,215 pounds of silver. The rest of the people gave 337 pounds of gold, 2,923 pounds of silver, and 67 robes for the priests.

73 And so, by the seventh month,[e] priests, Levites, temple guards, musicians, workers, and many of the ordinary people had settled in the towns of Judah.

Ezra Reads God's Law to the People

8 1-2 On the first day of the seventh month,[e] the people came together in the open area in front of the Water Gate. Then they asked Ezra, who was a teacher of the Law of Moses, to read to them from this Law that the LORD had given his people. Ezra the priest came with the Law and stood before the crowd of men, women, and the children who were old enough to understand. 3 From early morning till noon, he read the Law of Moses to them, and they listened carefully. 4 Ezra stood on a high wooden platform that had been built for this occasion. Mattithiah, Shema, Anaiah, Uriah, Hilkiah, and Maaseiah were standing to his right, while Pedaiah, Mishael, Malchijah, Hashum, Hash Baddanah, Zechariah, and Meshullam were standing to his left.

5 Ezra was up on the high platform, where he could be seen by everyone, and when he opened the book, they all stood up. 6 Ezra praised the great LORD God, and the people shouted, "Amen! Amen!" Then they bowed with their faces to the ground and worshiped the LORD.

7-8 After this, the Levites Jeshua, Bani, Sherebiah, Jamin, Akkub, Shabbethai, Hodiah, Maaseiah, Kelita, Azariah, Jozabad, Hanan, and Pelaiah went among the people, explaining the meaning of what Ezra had read.

9 The people started crying when God's Law was read to them. Then Nehemiah the governor, Ezra the priest and teacher, and the Levites who had been teaching the people all said, "This is a special day for the LORD your God. So don't be sad and don't cry!"

10 Nehemiah told the people, "Enjoy your good food and wine and share some with those who didn't have anything to bring. Don't be sad! This is a special day for the LORD, and he will make you happy and strong."

11 The Levites encouraged the people by saying, "This is a sacred day, so don't worry or mourn!" 12 When the people returned to their homes, they celebrated by eating and drinking and by sharing their food with those in need, because they had understood what had been read to them.

Celebrating the Festival of Shelters

13 On the second day of the seventh month,[f] the leaders of all the family groups came together with the priests and the Levites, so Ezra could teach them the Law 14 that the LORD had given to Moses. They learned from the Law that the people of Israel were to live in shelters when they celebrated the festival in the seventh month of the year. 15 They also learned that they

[c] **7.65** *until . . . priests*: The Hebrew text has "until a priest comes with the urim and thummim," sacred objects which were used in some way to receive answers from God. [d] **7.66-69** *736 horses, 245 mules*: A few Hebrew manuscripts; this is not found in most Hebrew manuscripts of verse 68. [e] **7.73; 8.1,2** *seventh month*: Tishri (also called Ethanim), the seventh month of the Hebrew calendar, from about mid-September to mid-October. [f] **8.13; 9.1** *seventh month*: Hebrew "same month."

7.73 1 Ch 9.2; Ne 11.3. **8.14,15** Lv 23.33-36, 39-43; Dt 16.13-15.

were to go into the woods and gather
branches of leafy trees such as olives,
myrtles, and palms for making these
shelters.
16 So the people gathered branches and
made shelters on the flat roofs of their
houses, in their yards, in the courtyard of
the temple, and in the open areas around
the Water Gate and Ephraim Gate.
17 Everyone who had returned from Babylonia built shelters. They lived in them and
joyfully celebrated the Festival of Shelters
for the first time since the days of Joshua
son of Nun. 18 On each of the first seven
days of the festival, Ezra read to the people
from God's Law. Then on the eighth day,
everyone gathered for worship, just as the
Law had said they must.

The People Confess Their Sins

9 On the twenty-fourth day of the seventh month,[f] the people of Israel went
without eating, and they dressed in sackcloth and threw dirt on their heads to show
their sorrow. 2 They refused to let foreigners join them, as they met to confess their
sins and the sins of their ancestors. 3 For
three hours they stood and listened to the
Law of the LORD their God, and then for
the next three hours they confessed their
sins and worshiped the LORD.
4 Jeshua, Bani, Kadmiel, Shebaniah,
Bunni, Sherebiah, Bani, and Chenani
stood on the special platform for the
Levites and prayed aloud to the LORD their
God. 5 Then the Levites Jeshua, Kadmiel,
Bani, Hashabneiah, Sherebiah, Hodiah,
Shebaniah, and Pethahiah said:

"Stand and shout praises
to your LORD,
the eternal God![g]
Praise his wonderful name,
though he is greater
than words can express."

The People Pray

6 You alone are the LORD,
Creator of the heavens
and all the stars,
Creator of the earth
and those who live on it,
Creator of the ocean
and all its creatures.
You are the source of life,
praised by the stars
that fill the heavens.
7 You are the LORD our God,
the one who chose Abram—
you brought him from Ur
in Babylonia
and named him Abraham.
8 Because he was faithful,
you made an agreement
to give his descendants
the land of the Canaanites
and Hittites,
of the Amorites and Perizzites,
and of the Jebusites
and Girgashites.
Now you have kept your promise,
just as you always do.

9 When our ancestors
were in Egypt,
you saw their suffering;
when they were at the Red Sea,[h]
you heard their cry for help.
10 You knew that the King of Egypt
and his officials and his nation
had mistreated your people.
So you worked fearsome miracles
against the Egyptians
and earned a reputation
that still remains.

[f]**8.13; 9.1** *seventh month*: Hebrew "same month." [g]**9.5** *shout . . . God*: Or "shout eternal praises to the LORD your God." [h]**9.9** *Red Sea*: Hebrew *yam suph* "Sea of Reeds," one of the marshes of fresh water lakes near the eastern part of the Nile Delta. This identification is based on Exodus 13.17—14.9, which lists the towns on the route of the Israelites before crossing the sea. In the Greek translation of the Scriptures made about 200 B.C., the "Sea of Reeds" was named "Red Sea."

9.7 a Gn 11.31; 12.1; **b** Gn 17.4, 5. **9.8** Gn 15.18-21. **9.9 a** Ex 3.7; **b** Ex 14.10-12. **9.10** Ex 7.8, 9—12.32.

11 You divided the deep sea,
and your people walked through
on dry land.
But you tossed their enemies in,
and they sank down
like a heavy stone.
12 Each day you led your people
with a thick cloud,
and at night you showed the way
with a flaming fire.
13 At Sinai you came down
from heaven,
and you gave your people
good laws and teachings
that are fair and honest.
14 You commanded them to respect
your holy Sabbath,
and you instructed
your servant Moses
to teach them your laws.
15 When they were hungry,
you sent bread from heaven,
and when they were thirsty,
you let water flow
from a rock.
Then you commanded them
to capture the land
that you had solemnly promised.

*16 Our stubborn ancestors
refused to obey—
they forgot about the miracles
you had worked for them,
and they were determined
to return to Egypt
and become slaves again.
17 But, our God, you are merciful
and quick to forgive;
you are loving, kind,
and very patient.
So you never turned away
from them—
18 not even when they made
an idol shaped like a calf
and insulted you by claiming,
"This is the god who rescued us
from Egypt."

19 Because of your great mercy,
you never abandoned them
in the desert.
And you always guided them
with a cloud by day
and a fire at night.
20 Your gentle Spirit
instructed them,[i]
and you gave them manna[j] to eat
and water to drink.
21 You took good care of them,
and for forty years
they never lacked a thing.
Their shoes didn't wear out,
and their feet were never swollen.

22 You let them conquer kings
and take their land,
including King Sihon of Heshbon
and King Og of Bashan.[k]
23 You brought them into the land
that you had promised
their ancestors,
and you blessed their nation
with people that outnumbered
the stars in the sky.

24 Then their descendants
conquered the land.
You helped them defeat
the kings and nations
and treat their enemies
however they wished.
25 They captured strong cities
and rich farmland;
they took furnished houses,
as well as cisterns,[l]
vineyards, olive orchards,
and numerous fruit trees.
They ate till they were satisfied,
and they celebrated
your abundant blessings.

[i]**9.20** *Your gentle Spirit instructed them*: Or "You gently instructed them." [j]**9.20** *manna*: This was something like a thin wafer (see Exodus 16.1-36). [k]**9.22** *Bashan*: One possible meaning for the difficult Hebrew text of verse 22. [l]**9.25** *cisterns*: Pits dug into the ground to hold water.

9.11 a Ex 14.21-29; **b** Ex 15.4, 5. **9.12** Ex 13.21, 22. **9.13,14** Ex 19.18—23.33. **9.15 a** Ex 16.4-15; **b** Ex 17.1-7; **c** Dt 1.20, 21. **9.16,17** Nu 14.1-4; Dt 1.26-33. **9.17** Ex 34.6; Nu 14.18. **9.18** Ex 32.1-4. **9.19-21** Dt 8.2-4. **9.22** Nu 21.21-35. **9.23 a** Js 3.14-17; **b** Gn 15.5; 22.17. **9.24** Js 11.23. **9.25** Dt 6.10, 11.

26 In spite of this, they rebelled
and disobeyed your laws.
They killed your prophets,
who warned them
to turn back to you,
and they cursed your name.
27 So you handed them over
to their enemies,
who treated them terribly.
But in their sufferings,
they begged you to help.
From heaven you listened
to their prayers
and because of your great mercy,
you sent leaders to rescue them.

28 But when they were at peace,
they would turn against you,
and you would hand them over
to their enemies.
Then they would beg for help,
and because you are merciful,
you rescued them
over and over again.
29 You warned them to turn back
and discover true life
by obeying your laws.
But they stubbornly refused
and continued to sin.
30 For years, you were patient,
and your Spirit[m] warned them
with messages spoken
by your prophets.
Still they refused to listen,
and you handed them over
to their enemies.
31 But you are merciful and kind,
and so you never forgot them
or let them be destroyed.

32 Our God, you are powerful,
fearsome, and faithful,
always true to your word.
So please keep in mind
the terrible sufferings
of our people, kings, leaders,
priests, and prophets,
from the time Assyria ruled
until this very day.
33 You have always been fair
when you punished us
for our sins.
34 Our kings, leaders, and priests
have never obeyed your commands
or heeded your warnings.
35 You blessed them with a kingdom
and with an abundance
of rich, fertile land,
but they refused to worship you
or turn from their evil.
36 Now we are slaves
in this fruitful land
you gave to our ancestors.
37 Its plentiful harvest is taken
by kings you placed over us
because of our sins.
Our suffering is unbearable,
because they do as they wish
to us and our livestock.

The People Make an Agreement

38 And so, a firm agreement was made
that had the official approval of the leaders,
10 the Levites, and priests. 1 As governor, I[n] signed the agreement together with Zedekiah and the following
priests: 2-8 Seraiah, Azariah, Jeremiah,
Pashhur, Amariah, Malchijah, Hattush,
Shebaniah, Malluch, Harim, Meremoth,
Obadiah, Daniel, Ginnethon, Baruch,
Meshullam, Abijah, Mijamin, Maaziah, Bil-
gai, and Shemaiah.
9 The Levites who signed were: Jeshua
son of Azaniah, Binnui from the clan of
Henadad, Kadmiel, 10 Shebaniah, Hodiah,
Kelita, Pelaiah, Hanan, 11 Mica, Rehob,
Hashabiah, 12 Zaccur, Sherebiah, Sheba-
niah, 13 Hodiah, Bani, and Beninu.
14 The leaders who signed were: Parosh,
Pahath Moab, Elam, Zattu, Bani, 15 Bunni,
Azgad, Bebai, 16 Adonijah, Bigvai, Adin,
17 Ater, Hezekiah, Azzur, 18 Hodiah,
Hashum, Bezai, 19 Hariph, Anathoth,
Nebai, 20 Magpiash, Meshullam, Hezir,
21 Meshezabel, Zadok, Jaddua, 22 Pelatiah,
Hanan, Anaiah, 23 Hoshea, Hananiah, Has-

[m] **9.30** *your Spirit*: Or "you." [n] **10.1** *I*: Hebrew "Nehemiah son of Hacaliah."

9.26-28 Jg 2.11-16. **9.26** Ws 2.10-20. **9.28** 3 Macc 2.12. **9.29** Lv 18.5. **9.30** 2 K 17.13-18; 2 Ch 36.15, 16. **9.32** 2 K 15.19, 29; 17.3-6; Ezra 4.2, 8-10.

shub, 24 Hallohesh, Pilha, Shobek, 25 Rehum, Hashabnah, Maaseiah, 26 Ahiah, Hanan, Anan, 27 Malluch, Harim, and Baanah.

The Agreement

28-29 All of us, including priests, Levites, temple guards, singers, temple workers and leaders, together with our wives and children, have separated ourselves from the foreigners in this land and now enter into an agreement with a complete understanding of what we are doing. And so, we now place ourselves under the curse of the LORD our God, if we fail to obey his laws and teachings that were given to us by his servant Moses.

30 We won't let our sons and daughters marry foreigners.

31 We won't buy goods or grain on the Sabbath or on any other sacred day, not even from foreigners.

Every seven years we will let our fields rest, and we will cancel all debts.

32 Once a year we will each donate a small amount of silver to the temple of our God. 33 This is to pay for the sacred bread, as well as for the daily sacrifices and special sacrifices such as those offered on the Sabbath and during the New Moon Festival and the other festivals. It will also pay for the sacrifices to forgive our sins and for all expenses connected with the worship of God in the temple.

34 We have decided that the families[o] of priests, Levites, and ordinary people will supply firewood for the temple each year, so that sacrifices can be offered on the altar, just as the LORD our God has commanded.

35 Each year we will bring to the temple the first part of our harvest of grain and fruit.

36 We will bring our first-born sons and the first-born males of our herds and flocks and offer them to the priests who serve in the temple, because this is what is written in God's Law.[p]

37 To the priests in the temple of our God, we will bring the bread dough from the first harvest, together with our best fruit, and an offering of new wine and olive oil.

We will bring ten percent of our grain harvest to those Levites who are responsible for collecting it in our towns. 38 A priest from the family of Aaron must be there when we give this to the Levites. Then the Levites will put one tenth of this part in the temple storeroom, 39 which is also the place for the sacred objects used by the priests, the temple guards, and the singers.

Levites and everyone else must bring their gifts of grain, wine, and olive oil to this room.

We will not neglect the temple of our God.

People Who Settled in Jerusalem

11 The nation's leaders and their families settled in Jerusalem. But there was room for only one out of every ten of the remaining families, and so they asked God to show them[q] who would live there. 2 Then everyone else asked God to bless those who were willing to live in Jerusalem.

3 Some of the people of Israel, the priests, the Levites, the temple workers, and the descendants of Solomon's servants lived on their own property in the towns of Judah. But the leaders of the province lived in Jerusalem with their families.

[o] **10.34** *that the families*: Or "which families." [p] **10.36** *first-born sons . . . God's Law*: See Exodus 13.2, 12-15; 34.19, 20. [q] **11.1** *asked God to show them*: The Hebrew text has "cast lots." These were made of wood or stone and were thrown on the ground by a priest or official to find out how and when to do something.

10.30 Ex 34.16; Dt 7.3. **10.31** **a** Ex 23.10, 11; Lv 25.1-7; **b** Dt 15.1, 2. **10.32** Ex 30.11-16. **10.35** Ex 23.19; 34.26; Dt 26.2. **10.36** Ex 13.2. **10.37** Nu 18.21. **10.38** Nu 18.26. **11.3-6** Ne 7.73.

The Judah Tribe

4-6 From the Judah tribe, two leaders
settled in Jerusalem with their relatives.
One of them was Athaiah son of Uzziah.
His ancestors were Zechariah, Amariah,
Shephatiah, Mahalalel, and Perez, the son
of Judah. From the descendants of Perez,
four hundred sixty-eight of the best men
lived in Jerusalem.

The other leader from Judah was Maaseiah the son of Baruch. His ancestors
were Colhozeh, Hazaiah, Adaiah, Joiarib,
Zechariah, and Shelah, the son of Judah.

The Benjamin Tribe

7-8 From the Benjamin tribe, three leaders settled in Jerusalem. The first was Sallu
son of Meshullam, and the others were
Gabbai and Sallai. Sallu's ancestors were
Joed, Pedaiah, Kolaiah, Maaseiah, Ithiel,
and Jeshaiah. Altogether, there were
nine hundred twenty-eight men of the
Benjamin tribe living in Jerusalem.
9 Joel son of Zichri was their leader, and
Judah son of Hassenuah was second in
command.

Priests

10 Four priests settled in Jerusalem. The
first was Jedaiah; he was the son of Joiarib
and the uncle of Jachin.[r]

11 The second priest to settle there was
Seraiah son of Hilkiah. His ancestors were
Meshullam, Zadok, Meraioth, and Ahitub,
who had been a high priest. 12 Altogether,
there were eight hundred twenty-two from
his clan who served in the temple.

The third priest to settle there was Adaiah son of Jeroham. His ancestors were
Pelaliah, Amzi, Zechariah, Pashhur, and
Malchijah. 13 Altogether, there were two
hundred forty-two clan leaders among his
relatives.

The fourth priest to settle there was
Amashsai son of Azarel. His ancestors were
Ahzai, Meshillemoth, and Immer. 14 Altogether, there were one hundred twenty-
eight brave warriors from their clans, and
their leader was Zabdiel son of Hagge-
dolim.

Levites

15 Several Levites settled in Jerusalem.
First, there was Shemaiah son of Hasshub.
His ancestors were Azrikam, Hashabiah,
and Bunni.

16 Next, there were Shabbethai and Jozabad, who were in charge of the work outside the temple.

17 Then there was Mattaniah son of
Mica. His ancestors were Zabdi and
Asaph. Mattaniah led the temple choir
in the prayer of praise. Bakbukiah,
who also settled in Jerusalem, was his
assistant.

Finally, there was Abda son of Shammua; his grandfather was Galal, and his
great-grandfather was Jeduthun.

18 Altogether, two hundred eighty-four
Levites settled in the holy city.

Temple Guards and Others

19 One hundred seventy-two temple
guards settled in Jerusalem; their leaders
were Akkub and Talmon.

20 The rest of the Israelites, including
priests and Levites, lived on their own
property in the other towns of Judah.
21 But the temple workers lived in the section of Jerusalem known as Ophel, and the
two men in charge of them were Ziha and
Gishpa.

22 Uzzi son of Bani was the leader of the
Levites in Jerusalem. His grandfather was
Hashabiah, his great-grandfather was Mattaniah, and his great-great-grandfather was
Mica. He belonged to the Asaph clan that
was in charge of the music for the temple
services, 23 though the daily choice of music and musicians was decided by royal de-
cree of the Persian king.

24 The people of Israel were represented
at the Persian court by Pethahiah son of
Meshezabel from the Zerah clan of the Judah tribe.

[r] **11.10** *son of Joiarib and the uncle of Jachin*: See 1 Chronicles 9.10; the Hebrew text has "son of Joiarib, Jachin."

The People in the Other Towns and Villages

25 Some of the people of Judah lived in the following towns near their farms: Kiriath-Arba, Dibon, Jekabzeel, 26 Jeshua, Moladah, Beth-Pelet, 27 Hazar-Shual, Beersheba, 28 Ziklag, Meconah, 29 Enrimmon, Zorah, Jarmuth, 30 Zanoah, Adullam, Lachish, and Azekah. In fact, they settled the towns from Beersheba in the south to Hinnom Valley in the north.

31 The people of Benjamin lived in the towns of Geba, Michmash, Aija, Bethel with its nearby villages, 32 Anathoth, Nob, Ananiah, 33 Hazor, Ramah, Gittaim, 34 Hadid, Zeboim, Neballat, 35 Lod, and Ono, as well as in Craft Valley. 36 Several groups of Levites from the territory of Judah were sent to live among the people of Benjamin.

A List of Priests and Levites

12 Many priests and Levites had returned from Babylonia with Zerubbabel[s] and Joshua as their leaders. Those priests were Seraiah, Jeremiah, Ezra, 2 Amariah, Malluch, Hattush, 3 Shecaniah, Rehum, Meremoth, 4 Iddo, Ginnethoi, Abijah, 5 Mijamin, Maadiah, Bilgah, 6 Shemaiah, Joiarib, Jedaiah, 7 Sallu, Amok, Hilkiah, and another Jedaiah. These were the leading priests and their assistants during the time of Joshua.[t]

8 The Levites who returned were Jeshua, Binnui, Kadmiel, Sherebiah, Judah, and Mattaniah. They and their assistants were responsible for the songs of praise, 9 while Bakbukiah and Unno, together with their assistants, were responsible for the choral responses.

Descendants of Joshua the High Priest

10 Joshua was the father of Joiakim, the grandfather of Eliashib, and the great-grandfather of Joiada. 11 Joiada was the father of Jonathan and the grandfather of Jaddua.

Leaders of the Priestly Clans

12 When Joiakim was high priest, the following priests were leaders of their clans: Meraiah of the Seraiah clan, Hananiah of Jeremiah, 13 Meshullam of Ezra, Jehohanan of Amariah, 14 Jonathan of Malluchi, Joseph of Shebaniah, 15 Adna of Harim, Helkai of Meraioth, 16 Zechariah of Iddo, Meshullam of Ginnethon, 17 Zichri of Abijah,[u] Piltai of Moadiah, 18 Shammua of Bilgah, Jehonathan of Shemaiah, 19 Mattenai of Joiarib, Uzzi of Jedaiah, 20 Kallai of Sallai, Eber of Amok, 21 Hashabiah of Hilkiah, and Nethanel of Jedaiah.

The Priestly and Levite Families

22 During the time of the high priests Eliashib, Joiada, Johanan, and Jaddua, and including the time that Darius was king of Persia, a record was kept of the heads of the Levite and priestly families. 23 However, no official record was kept of the heads of the Levite clans after the death of Johanan,[v] the grandson of Eliashib.

24 Hashabiah, Sherebiah, Jeshua son of Kadmiel,[w] and their assistants organized two choirs of Levites to offer praises to God, just as King David, the man of God, had commanded.

25 Mattaniah, Bakbukiah, Obadiah, Meshullam, Talmon, and Akkub were responsible for guarding the storerooms near the temple gates.

26 All of these men lived during the time of Joiakim[x] and during the time that I was governor and Ezra, a teacher of the Law of Moses, was priest.

Nehemiah Dedicates the City Wall

27 When the city wall was dedicated, Levites from everywhere in Judah were invited to join in the celebration with songs of praise and with the music of cymbals, small harps, and other stringed instruments. 28-29 The Levite singers lived in villages around Jerusalem, and so they came

[s] **12.1** *Zerubbabel*: Hebrew "Zerubbabel son of Shealtiel." [t] **12.7** *Joshua*: Joshua the high priest and friend of Zerubbabel (see verse 1 and Haggai 1.1; 2.2). [u] **12.17** *of Abijah*: The Hebrew text adds ". . . of Miniamin." [v] **12.23** *death of Johanan*: Probably between 408 and 405 B.C., when Darius II died. [w] **12.24** *son of Kadmiel*: Or possibly "Binnui, Kadmiel" (see 10.9; 12.8). [x] **12.26** *Joiakim*: Hebrew "Joiakim son of Joshua son of Jozadak."

from there, as well as from the villages
around Netophah, Beth-Gilgal, Geba, and
Azmaveth. 30 The priests and Levites held
special ceremonies to make themselves
holy, and then they did the same for the
rest of the people and for the gates and
walls of the city.
31 I brought the leaders of Judah to the
top of the city wall and put them in charge
of the two groups that were to march
around on top of the wall, singing praises to
God. One group marched to the right in
the direction of Garbage Gate. 32 Hoshaiah
and half of the leaders followed them.
33 Then came the priests Azariah, Ezra,
Meshullam, 34 Judah, Benjamin, Shemaiah, and Jeremiah, 35 all of them blowing
trumpets. Next, there was Zechariah of the
Asaph clan[y] 36 and his relatives, Shemaiah,
Azarel, Milalai, Gilalai, Maai, Nethanel, Judah, and Hanani. They played musical instruments like those that had been played
by David, the man of God. And they
marched behind Ezra, the teacher of the
Law. 37 When they reached Fountain Gate,
they climbed the steps to David's City and
went past his palace, before stopping at the
Water Gate near the eastern wall of the city.
38 The second group of singers marched
along the wall in the opposite direction,
and I followed them, together with the
other half of the leaders of Judah. We went
past Oven Tower, Broad Wall, 39 Ephraim
Gate, Old Gate, Fish Gate, Hananel Tower,
Hundred Tower, and on to Sheep Gate. Finally, we stopped at Gate of the Guard,
40 where we stood in front of the temple
with the other group, praising God. In the
group with me were half of the leaders,
41 as well as the priests Eliakim, Maaseiah,
Miniamin, Micaiah, Elioenai, Zechariah,
and Hananiah, who were blowing trumpets. 42 Maaseiah, Shemaiah, Eleazar, Uzzi,
Jehohanan, Malchijah, Elam, and Ezer also
stood there, as Jezrahiah led the singers.
43 God had made the people very happy,
and so on that day they celebrated and
offered many sacrifices. The women and
children joined in the festivities, and joyful
shouts could be heard far from the city of
Jerusalem.

Preparation for Worship

44 On that same day, some leaders were
appointed to be responsible for the safekeeping of gifts for the temple and to be in
charge of receiving the first part of the harvest and the ten percent of the crops and
livestock that was offered to God. These
same leaders also collected the part of
crops that the Law of Moses taught was to
be given to the Levites.
Everyone was pleased with the work of
the priests and Levites, 45 when they performed the ceremonies to make people acceptable to worship God. And the singers
and the temple guards did their jobs according to the instructions given by David
and his son Solomon. 46 In fact, ever since
the days of David and Asaph, there had
been song leaders and songs of praise and
worship. 47 During the time that Zerubbabel and I were in charge, everyone in Israel
gave what they were supposed to give for
the daily needs of the singers and temple
guards from the Levi tribe. Then the Levites would give the priests their share from
what they had received.

Foreigners Are Sent Away

13 On that day when the Law of
Moses was read aloud to everyone,
it was discovered that Ammonites and
Moabites were forbidden to belong to the
people of God. 2 This was because they had
refused to give food and water to Israel and
had hired Balaam[z] to call down a curse on
them. However, our God turned the curse
into a blessing. 3 Following the reading of
the Law of Moses, the people of Israel
started sending away anyone who had any
foreign ancestors.

Nehemiah Makes Other Changes

4 The priest Eliashib was a relative of
Tobiah and had earlier been put in charge
of the temple storerooms. 5 So he let Tobiah live in one of these rooms, where all

[y] **12.35** *Zechariah of the Asaph clan*: Hebrew "Zechariah son of Jonathan son of Shemaiah son of Mattaniah son of Micaiah son of Zaccur son of Asaph." [z] **13.2** *Balaam*: See Numbers 22.1-6.

12.45 **a** 1 Ch 25.1-8; **b** 1 Ch 26.12. **13.1,2** Dt 23.3-5. **13.2** Nu 22.1-6.

kinds of things had been stored—the grain offerings, incense, utensils for the temple, as well as the tenth of the grain, wine, and olive oil that had been given for the use of the Levites, singers, and temple guards, and the gifts for the priests.

6 This happened in the thirty-second year that Artaxerxes[a] ruled Babylonia. I was away from Jerusalem at the time, because I was visiting him. Later I received permission from the king 7 to return to Jerusalem. Only then did I find out that Eliashib had done this terrible thing of letting Tobiah have a room in the temple. 8 It upset me so much that I threw out every bit of Tobiah's furniture. 9 Then I ordered the room to be cleaned and the temple utensils, the grain offerings, and the incense to be brought back into the room.

10 I also found out that the temple singers and several other Levites had returned to work on their farms, because they had not been given their share of the harvest. 11 I called the leaders together and angrily asked them, "Why is the temple neglected?" Then I told them to start doing their jobs. 12 After this, everyone in Judah brought a tenth of their grain, wine, and olive oil to the temple storeroom. 13 Finally, I appointed three men with good reputations to be in charge of what was brought there and to distribute it to the others. They were Shelemiah the priest, Zadok the teacher of the Law, and Pedaiah the Levite. Their assistant was Hanan, the son of Zaccur and the grandson of Mattaniah.

14 I pray that my God will remember these good things that I have done for his temple and for those who worship there.

The Sabbath

15 I also noticed what the people of Judah were doing on the Sabbath. Not only were they trampling grapes to make wine, but they were harvesting their grain, grapes, figs, and other crops, and then loading these on donkeys to sell in Jerusalem. So I warned them not to sell food on the Sabbath. 16 People who had moved to Jerusalem from the city of Tyre were bringing in fish and other things to sell there on the Sabbath. 17 I got angry and said to the leaders of Judah, "This evil you are doing is an insult to the Sabbath! 18 Didn't God punish us and this city because our ancestors did these very same things? And here you are, about to make God furious again by disgracing the Sabbath!"

19 I ordered the gates of Jerusalem to be closed on the eve of the Sabbath[b] and not to be opened until after the Sabbath had ended. Then I put some of my own men in charge of the gates to make certain that nothing was brought in on the Sabbath. 20 Once or twice some merchants spent the night outside Jerusalem with their goods. 21 But I warned them, "If you do this again, I'll have you arrested." From then on, they did not come on the Sabbath. 22 I ordered the Levites to make themselves holy and to guard the gates on the Sabbath, so that it would be kept holy.

God is truly merciful, and I pray that he will treat me with kindness and bless me for doing this.

Mixed Marriages

23 I discovered that some Jewish men had married women from Ashdod, Ammon, and Moab. 24 About half of their children could not speak Hebrew—they spoke only the language of Ashdod or some other foreign language. 25 So in my anger, I called down curses on those men. I had them beaten and even pulled out the hair of some of them. Then I made them promise:

> In the name of God we solemnly promise not to let our sons and daughters marry foreigners. 26 God dearly loved King Solomon of Israel and made him the greatest king on earth, but Solomon's foreign wives led him into sin. 27 So we will obey you and not

[a] **13.6** *Artaxerxes*: See the note at 1.1.
[b] **13.19** *eve of the Sabbath*: The Jewish day began at sunset.

13.10 Dt 12.5-19. **13.12** Ml 3.10. **13.15** Ex 20.8-10; Dt 5.12-14; Jr 17.21-24.
13.23-25 Ex 34.11-16; Dt 7.1-5. **13.26** **a** 2 S 12.24, 25; **b** 1 K 11.1-8.

rebel against our God by marrying foreign women.

28 Jehoiada, the son of the high priest Eliashib, had a son who had married a daughter of Sanballat from Horon,[c] and I forced his son to leave.

29 I pray that God will punish them for breaking their priestly vows and disgracing the Levi tribe.

30 Then I made sure that the people were free from every foreign influence, and I assigned duties for the priests and Levites. 31 I also arranged for the people to bring firewood to the altar each day and for them to bring the first part of their harvest to the temple.

I pray that God will bless me for the good I have done.

[c] **13.28** *Horon*: See the note at 2.10.

13.28 Ne 4.1.

ESTHER

ABOUT THIS BOOK

The story of Esther takes place in the city of Susa, in the winter palace of the Persian king. After King Xerxes divorced his queen, he chose a young Jewish woman named Esther as his new queen. She was an orphan but had been adopted and cared for by her cousin, Mordecai, who was given a job as a palace official. Mordecai warned her not to tell anyone that she was a Jew, and she obeyed.

The king's highest official was a man named Haman. He hated the Jews, and he tricked the king into giving permission to have them all killed. The rest of the book tells how Esther risked her own life to save the lives of her people.

Afterward, Mordecai and Esther wrote a letter telling all Jews to celebrate the festival of Purim every year to remember how the nation was saved.

The Hebrew text of the book of Esther doesn't mention God, but the whole plot shows that God was protecting his people by making Esther queen, and as Mordecai put it:

"It could be that you were made queen for a time like this!"
(4.14b)

A QUICK LOOK AT THIS BOOK

- Esther Becomes Queen (1.1—2.23)
- Haman Plans To Destroy the Jews (3.1-15)
- Mordecai Asks for Esther's Help (4.1-17)
- Mordecai Is Honored, Not Killed (5.1—6.14)
- Haman Is Put To Death (7.1-10)
- The Jews Defend Themselves and Kill Their Enemies (8.1—9.19)
- The Festival of Purim (9.20-32)
- The Greatness of Xerxes and Mordecai (10.1-3)

Queen Vashti Disobeys King Xerxes

1 1-2 King Xerxes[a] of Persia lived in his
capital city of Susa[b] and ruled one
hundred twenty-seven provinces from India to Ethiopia.[c] 3 During the third year of
his rule, Xerxes gave a big dinner for all his
officials and officers. The governors and
leaders of the provinces were also invited,
and even the commanders of the Persian
and Median armies came. 4 For one hundred eighty days he showed off his wealth
and spent a lot of money to impress his
guests with the greatness of his kingdom.
5 King Xerxes soon gave another dinner
and invited everyone in the city of Susa, no
matter who they were. The eating and
drinking lasted seven days in the beautiful

[a] **1.1,2** *Xerxes*: The Hebrew text has "Ahasuerus," who was better known as King Xerxes I (485-465 B.C.). [b] **1.1,2** *in his capital city of Susa*: Or "in his royal fortress in the city of Susa." Susa was a city east of Babylon and a winter home for Persian kings. [c] **1.1,2** *Ethiopia*: The Hebrew text has "Cush," which was a region south of Egypt that included parts of the present countries of Ethiopia and Sudan.

1.1,2 Ezra 4.6.

palace gardens. 6 The area was decorated with blue and white cotton curtains tied back with purple linen cords that ran through silver rings fastened to marble columns. Couches of gold and silver rested on pavement that had all kinds of designs made from costly bright-colored stones and marble and mother-of-pearl.

7 The guests drank from gold cups, and each cup had a different design. The king was generous 8 and said to them, "Drink all you want!" Then he told his servants, "Keep their cups full."

9 While the men were enjoying themselves, Queen Vashti gave the women a big dinner inside the royal palace.

10 By the seventh day, King Xerxes was feeling happy because of so much wine. And he asked his seven personal servants, Mehuman, Biztha, Harbona, Bigtha, Abagtha, Zethar, and Carkas, 11 to bring Queen Vashti to him. The king wanted her to wear her crown and let his people and his officials see how beautiful she was.
12 The king's servants told Queen Vashti what he had said, but she refused to go to him, and this made him terribly angry.

13-14 The king called in the seven highest officials of Persia and Media. They were Carshena, Shethar, Admatha, Tarshish, Meres, Marsena, and Memucan. These men were very wise and understood all the laws and customs of the country, and the king always asked them what they thought about such matters.

15 The king said to them, "Queen Vashti refused to come to me when I sent my servants for her. What does the law say I should do about that?"

16 Then Memucan told the king and the officials:

Your Majesty, Queen Vashti has not only embarrassed you, but she has insulted your officials and everyone else in all the provinces.

17 The women in the kingdom will hear about this, and they will refuse to respect their husbands. They will say, "If Queen Vashti doesn't obey her husband, why should we?" 18 Before this day is over, the wives of the officials of Persia and Media will find out what Queen Vashti has done, and they will refuse to obey their husbands. They won't respect their husbands, and their husbands will be angry with them.

19 Your Majesty, if you agree, you should write for the Medes and Persians a law that can never be changed. This law would keep Queen Vashti from ever seeing you again. Then you could let someone who respects you be queen in her place.

20 When the women in your great kingdom hear about this new law, they will respect their husbands, no matter if they are rich or poor.

21 King Xerxes and his officials liked what Memucan had said, 22 and he sent letters to all of his provinces. Each letter was written in the language of the province to which it was sent, and it said that husbands should have complete control over their wives and children.

Esther Becomes Queen

2 After a while, King Xerxes got over being angry. But he kept thinking about what Vashti had done and the law that he had written because of her. 2 Then the king's personal servants said:

Your Majesty, a search must be made to find you some beautiful young women. 3 You can select officers in every province to bring them to the place where you keep your wives in the capital city of Susa. Put your servant Hegai in charge of them since that is his job. He can see to it that they are given the proper beauty treatments.
4 Then let the young woman who pleases you most take Vashti's place as queen.

King Xerxes liked these suggestions, and he followed them.

5 At this time a Jew named Mordecai was living in Susa. His father was Jair, and his grandfather Shimei was the son of Kish from the tribe of Benjamin. 6 Kish[d] was one of the people that Nebuchadnezzar had

[d]**2.6** *Kish*: Or "Mordecai." The Hebrew text has "He."
2.6 2 K 24.10-16; 2 Ch 36.10.

taken from Jerusalem, when he took King Jeconiah of Judah to Babylonia.

7 Mordecai had a very beautiful cousin named Esther, whose Hebrew name was Hadassah. He had raised her as his own daughter, after her father and mother died. 8 When the king ordered the search for beautiful women, many were taken to the king's palace in Susa, and Esther was one of them.

Hegai was put in charge of all the women, 9 and from the first day, Esther was his favorite. He began her beauty treatments at once. He also gave her plenty of food and seven special maids from the king's palace, and they had the best rooms.

10 Mordecai had warned Esther not to tell anyone that she was a Jew, and she obeyed him. 11 He was anxious to see how Esther was getting along and to learn what had happened to her. So each day he would walk back and forth in front of the court where the women lived.

12 The young women were given beauty treatments for one whole year. The first six months their skin was rubbed with olive oil and myrrh, and the last six months it was treated with perfumes and cosmetics. Then each of them spent the night alone with King Xerxes. 13 When a young woman went to the king, she could wear whatever clothes or jewelry she chose from the women's living quarters. 14 In the evening she would go to the king, and the following morning she would go to the place where his wives stayed after being with him. There a man named Shaashgaz was in charge of the king's wives.[e] Only the ones the king wanted and asked for by name could go back to the king.

15-16 Xerxes had been king for seven years when Esther's turn came to go to him during Tebeth,[f] the tenth month of the year. Everyone liked Esther. The king's personal servant Hegai was in charge of the women, and Esther trusted Hegai and asked him what she ought to take with her.[g]

17 Xerxes liked Esther more than he did any of the other young women. None of them pleased him as much as she did, and right away he fell in love with her and crowned her queen in place of Vashti. 18 In honor of Esther he gave a big dinner for his leaders and officials. Then he declared a holiday everywhere in his kingdom and gave expensive gifts.

Mordecai Saves the King's Life

19 When the young women were brought together again, Esther's cousin Mordecai had become a palace official. 20 He had told Esther never to tell anyone that she was a Jew, and she obeyed him, just as she had always done.

21 Bigthana and Teresh were the two men who guarded King Xerxes' rooms, but they got angry with the king and decided to kill him. 22 Mordecai found out about their plans and asked Queen Esther to tell the king what he had found out. 23 King Xerxes learned that Mordecai's report was true, and he had the two men hanged. Then the king had all of this written down in his record book as he watched.

Haman Plans To Destroy the Jews

3 Later, King Xerxes promoted Haman the son of Hammedatha to the highest position in his kingdom. Haman was a descendant of Agag,[h] 2 and the king had given orders for his officials at the royal gate to honor Haman by kneeling down to him. All of them obeyed except Mordecai. 3 When the other officials asked Mordecai why he disobeyed the king's command, 4 he said, "Because I am a Jew." They spoke to him for several days about kneeling down, but he still refused to obey. Finally, they reported this to Haman, to find out if he would let Mordecai get away with it.

5 Haman was furious to learn that

[e] **2.14** *wives*: This translates a Hebrew word for women who were legally bound to a man, but without the full privileges of a wife. [f] **2.15,16** *Tebeth*: The tenth month of the Hebrew calendar, from about mid-December to mid-January. [g] **2.15,16** *her*: The Hebrew text adds, "Esther was the daughter of Abihail and was the cousin of Mordecai, who had adopted her after her parents died" (see verse 7). [h] **3.1** *Agag*: Agag was a king who had fought against the Jews long before the time of Esther (see 1 Samuel 15.1-33).

Mordecai refused to kneel down and honor him. 6 And when he found out that Mordecai was a Jew, he knew that killing only Mordecai was not enough. Every Jew in the whole kingdom had to be killed.

7 It was now the twelfth year of the rule of King Xerxes. During Nisan,[i] the first month of the year, Haman said, "Find out the best time for me to do this."[j] The time chosen was Adar,[k] the twelfth month.

8 Then Haman went to the king and said:

> Your Majesty, there are some people who live all over your kingdom and won't have a thing to do with anyone else. They have customs that are different from everyone else's, and they refuse to obey your laws. We would be better off to get rid of them! 9 Why not give orders for all of them to be killed? I can promise that you will get tons of silver for your treasury.

10 The king handed his official ring to Haman, who hated the Jews, and the king told him, 11 "Do what you want with those people! You can keep their money."

12 On the thirteenth day of Nisan, Haman called in the king's secretaries and ordered them to write letters in every language used in the kingdom. The letters were written in the name of the king and sealed by using the king's own ring.[l] At once they were sent to the king's highest officials, the governors of each province, and the leaders of the different nations in the kingdom of Xerxes.

13 The letters were taken by messengers to every part of the kingdom, and this is what was said in the letters:

> On the thirteenth day of Adar, the twelfth month, all Jewish men, women, and children are to be killed. And their property is to be taken.

14-15 King Xerxes gave orders for these letters to be posted where they could be seen by everyone all over the kingdom. The king's command was obeyed, and one of the letters was read aloud to the people in the walled city of Susa. Then the king and Haman sat down to drink together, but no one in the city[m] could figure out what was going on.

Mordecai Asks for Esther's Help

4 When Mordecai heard about the letter, he tore his clothes in sorrow and put on sackcloth. Then he covered his head with ashes and went through the city, crying and weeping. 2 But he could go only as far as the palace gate, because no one wearing sackcloth was allowed inside the palace. 3 In every province where the king's orders were read, the Jews cried and mourned, and they went without eating.[n] Many of them even put on sackcloth and sat in ashes.

4 When Esther's servant girls and her other servants told her what Mordecai was doing, she became very upset and sent Mordecai some clothes to wear in place of the sackcloth. But he refused to take them. 5 Esther had a servant named Hathach, who had been given to her by the king. So she called him in and said, "Find out what's wrong with Mordecai and why he's acting this way."

6 Hathach went to Mordecai in the city square in front of the palace gate, 7 and Mordecai told him everything that had happened. He also told him how much money Haman had promised to add to the king's treasury, if all the Jews were killed.

8 Mordecai gave Hathach a copy of the orders for the murder of the Jews and told him that these had been read in Susa. He said, "Show this to Esther and explain

[i] **3.7** *Nisan*: The first month of the Hebrew calendar, from about mid-March to mid-April.
[j] **3.7** *Find out . . . do this*: The Hebrew text has "cast lots," which were pieces of wood or stone used to find out how and when to do something. For "lots" the Hebrew text uses the Babylonian word "purim." [k] **3.7** *Adar*: The twelfth month of the Hebrew calendar, from about mid-February to mid-March. [l] **3.12** *king's own ring*: Melted wax was used to seal a letter, and while the wax was still soft, the king's ring was pressed in the wax to show that the letter was official.
[m] **3.14,15** *walled city . . . city*: Or "royal fortress . . . rest of the city." [n] **4.3** *went without eating*: The Israelites would sometimes go without eating (also called "fasting") in times of great sorrow or danger.

3.8 Ws 2.14, 15; 3 Macc 3.2, 7. **4.3** 3 Macc 4.2.

what it means. Ask her to go to the king and beg him to have pity on her people, the Jews!"

9 Hathach went back to Esther and told her what Mordecai had said. 10 She answered, "Tell Mordecai 11 there is a law about going in to see the king, and all his officials and his people know about this law. Anyone who goes in to see the king without being invited by him will be put to death. The only way that anyone can be saved is for the king to hold out the gold scepter to that person. And it's been thirty days since he has asked for me."

12 When Mordecai was told what Esther had said, 13 he sent back this reply, "Don't think that you will escape being killed with the rest of the Jews, just because you live in the king's palace. 14 If you don't speak up now, we will somehow get help, but you and your family will be killed. It could be that you were made queen for a time like this!"

15 Esther sent a message to Mordecai, saying, 16 "Bring together all the Jews in Susa and tell them to go without eating for my sake! Don't eat or drink for three days and nights. My servant girls and I will do the same. Then I will go in to see the king, even if it means I must die."

17 Mordecai did everything Esther told him to do.

Esther Invites the King and Haman to a Dinner

5 Three days later, Esther dressed in her royal robes and went to the inner court of the palace in front of the throne. The king was sitting there, facing the open doorway. 2 He was happy to see Esther, and he held out the gold scepter to her.

When Esther came up and touched the tip of the scepter, 3 the king said, "Esther, what brings you here? Just ask, and I will give you as much as half of my kingdom."

4 Esther answered, "Your Majesty, please come with Haman to a dinner I will prepare for you later today."

5 The king said to his servants, "Hurry and get Haman, so we can accept Esther's invitation."

The king and Haman went to Esther's dinner, 6 and while they were drinking wine, the king asked her, "What can I do for you? Just ask, and I will give you as much as half of my kingdom."

7-8 Esther replied, "Your Majesty, if you really care for me and are willing to do what I want, please come again tomorrow with Haman to the dinner I will prepare for you. At that time I will answer Your Majesty's question."

Haman Plans To Kill Mordecai

9 Haman was feeling great as he left. But when he saw Mordecai at the palace gate, he noticed that Mordecai did not stand up or show him any respect. This made Haman really angry, 10 but he did not say a thing.

When Haman got home, he called together his friends and his wife Zeresh 11 and started bragging about his great wealth and all his sons. He told them the many ways that the king had honored him and how all the other officials and leaders had to respect him. 12 Haman added, "That's not all! Besides the king himself, I'm the only person Queen Esther invited for dinner. She has also invited the king and me to dinner tomorrow. 13 But none of this makes me happy, as long as I see that Jew Mordecai sitting at the palace gate."

14 Haman's wife and friends said to him, "Have a tower built about seventy-five feet high, and tomorrow morning ask the king to hang Mordecai there. Then later, you can have dinner with the king and enjoy yourself."

This seemed like a good idea to Haman, and he had the tower built.

The King Honors Mordecai

6 That night the king could not sleep, and he had a servant read him the records of what had happened since he had been king. 2 When the servant read how Mordecai had kept Bigthana and Teresh from killing the king, 3 the king asked, "What has been done to reward Mordecai for this?"

6.2 Es 2.21, 22.

"Nothing, Your Majesty!" the king's servants replied.
4 About this time, Haman came in to
ask the king to have Mordecai hanged on
the tower he had built. The king saw him
and asked, "Who is that man waiting in
front of the throne room?"
5 The king's servants answered, "Your
Majesty, it is Haman."
"Have him come in," the king commanded.
6 When Haman entered the room, the
king asked him, "What should I do for a
man I want to honor?"
Haman was sure that he was the one
the king wanted to honor. 7 So he replied,
"Your Majesty, if you wish to honor a man,
8 have someone bring him one of your own
robes and one of your own horses with a
fancy headdress. 9 Have one of your highest officials place your robe on this man
and lead him through the streets on your
horse, while someone shouts, 'This is how
the king honors a man!' "
10 The king replied, "Hurry and do just
what you have said! Don't forget a thing.
Get the robe and the horse for Mordecai
the Jew, who is on duty at the palace gate!"
11 Haman got the king's robe and put it
on Mordecai. He led him through the city
on the horse and shouted as he went, "This
is how the king honors a man!"
12 Afterwards, Mordecai returned to his
duties at the palace gate, and Haman hurried home, hiding his face in shame.
13 Haman told his wife and friends what
had happened. Then his wife and his advisors said, "If Mordecai is a Jew, this is just
the beginning of your troubles! You will end
up a ruined man." 14 They were still talking, when the king's servants came and
quickly took Haman to the dinner that
Esther had prepared.

Haman Is Punished

7 The king and Haman were dining with
Esther 2 and drinking wine during the
second dinner, when the king again said,
"Esther, what can I do for you? Just ask,
and I will give you as much as half of my
kingdom!"
3 Esther answered, "Your Majesty, if you
really care for me and are willing to help,
you can save me and my people. That's
what I really want, 4 because a reward has
been promised to anyone who kills my people. Your Majesty, if we were merely going to be sold as slaves, I would not have
bothered you."[o]
5 "Who would dare to do such a thing?"
the king asked.
6 Esther replied, "That evil Haman is
the one out to get us!"
Haman was terrified, as he looked at the
king and the queen.
7 The king was so angry that he got up,
left his wine, and went out into the palace
garden.
Haman realized that the king had already decided what to do with him, and
he stayed and begged Esther to save his
life.
8 Just as the king came back into the
room, Haman got down on his knees beside
Esther, who was lying on the couch. The
king shouted, "Now you're even trying to
rape my queen here in my own palace!"
As soon as the king said this, his servants covered Haman's head. 9 Then Harbona, one of the king's personal servants,
said, "Your Majesty, Haman built a tower
seventy-five feet high beside his house, so
he could hang Mordecai on it. And Mordecai is the very one who spoke up and saved
your life."
"Hang Haman from his own tower!" the
king commanded. 10 Right away, Haman
was hanged on the tower he had built to
hang Mordecai, and the king calmed down.

A Happy Ending for the Jews

8 Before the end of the day, King Xerxes
gave Esther everything that had belonged to Haman, the enemy of the Jews.
Esther told the king that Mordecai was her
cousin. So the king made Mordecai one of
his highest officials 2 and gave him the
royal ring that Haman had worn. Then Esther put Mordecai in charge of Haman's
property.
3 Once again Esther went to speak to
the king. This time she fell down at his

[o] **7.4** *I would . . . bothered you*: One possible meaning for the difficult Hebrew text.

feet, crying and begging, "Please stop
Haman's evil plan to have the Jews killed!"
4 King Xerxes held out the golden scepter
to Esther, 5 and she got up and said, "Your
Majesty, I know that you will do the right
thing and that you really love me. Please
stop what Haman has planned. He has already sent letters demanding that the Jews
in all your provinces be killed, 6 and I can't
bear to see my people and my own relatives
destroyed."

7 King Xerxes then said to Esther and
Mordecai, "I have already ordered Haman
to be hanged and his house given to Esther,
because of his evil plans to kill the Jews. 8 I
now give you permission to make a law that
will save the lives of your people. You may
use my ring to seal the law, so that it can
never be changed."

9 On the twenty-third day of Sivan,[p] the
third month, the king's secretaries wrote
the law. They obeyed Mordecai and wrote
to the Jews, the rulers, the governors, and
the officials of all one hundred twenty-
seven provinces from India to Ethiopia.[q]
The letters were written in every language
used in the kingdom, including the Jewish
language. 10 They were written in the name
of King Xerxes and sealed with his ring.
Then they were taken by messengers who
rode the king's finest and fastest horses.

11-13 In these letters the king said:

> On the thirteenth day of Adar,[r] the twelfth month, the Jews in every city and province will be allowed to get together and defend themselves. They may destroy any army that attacks them, and they may kill all of their enemies, including women and children. They may also take everything that belongs to their enemies.

A copy of this law is to be posted in
every province and read by everyone.

14-15 Then the king ordered his messengers to take their fastest horses and deliver
the law as quickly as possible to every
province. When Mordecai left, he was
wearing clothes fit for a king. He wore blue
and white robes, a large gold crown, and a
cape made of fine linen and purple cloth.

After the law was announced in Susa,
everyone shouted and cheered, 16 and the
Jews were no longer afraid. In fact, they
were very happy and felt that they had won
a victory.

17 In every province and city where the
law was sent, the Jews had parties and celebrated. Many of the people in the
provinces accepted the Jewish religion,
because they were now afraid of the Jews.

The Jews Destroy Their Enemies

9 The first law that the king had made
was to be followed on the thirteenth
day of Adar,[r] the twelfth month. This was
the very day that the enemies of the Jews
had hoped to do away with them. But the
Jews turned things around, 2 and in the
cities of every province they came together
to attack their enemies. Everyone was
afraid of the Jews, and no one could do
anything to oppose them.

3 The leaders of the provinces, the
rulers, the governors, and the court officials were afraid of Mordecai and took sides
with the Jews. 4 Everyone in the provinces
knew that the king had promoted him and
had given him a lot of power.

5 The Jews took their swords and did
away with their enemies, without showing
any mercy. 6-10 They killed five hundred
people in Susa,[s] but they did not take anything that belonged to the ones they killed.
Haman had been one of the worst enemies
of the Jews, and ten of his sons were
among those who were killed. Their names
were Parshandatha, Dalphon, Aspatha, Po-
ratha, Adalia, Aridatha, Parmashta, Arisai,
Aridai, and Vaizatha.

11 Later that day, someone told the king
how many people had been killed in Susa.[s]
12 Then he told Esther, "Five hundred people, including Haman's ten sons, have been
killed in Susa alone. If that many were
killed here, what must have happened in
the provinces? Is there anything else you

[p] **8.9** *Sivan*: The third month of the Hebrew calendar, from about mid-May to mid-June.
[q] **8.9** *Ethiopia*: See the note at 1.1, 2. [r] **8.11-13; 9.1** *Adar*: See the note at 3.7.
[s] **9.6-10,11** *in Susa*: Or "in the royal fortress in Susa."
8.8-10 3 Macc 7.10.

want done? Just tell me, and it will be done."

13 Esther answered, "Your Majesty, please let the Jews in Susa fight to defend themselves tomorrow, just as they did today. And order the bodies of Haman's ten sons to be hanged in public."

14 King Xerxes did what Esther had requested, and the bodies of Haman's sons were hung in Susa. 15 Then on the fourteenth day of Adar the Jews of the city got together and killed three hundred more people. But they still did not take anything that belonged to their enemies.

16-17 On the thirteenth day of Adar, the Jews in the provinces had come together to defend themselves. They killed seventy-five thousand of their enemies, but the Jews did not take anything that belonged to the ones they killed. Then on the fourteenth day of the month the Jews celebrated with a feast.

18 On the fifteenth day of the month the Jews in Susa held a holiday and celebrated, after killing their enemies on the thirteenth and the fourteenth. 19 This is why the Jews in the villages now celebrate on the fourteenth day of the month. It is a joyful holiday that they celebrate by feasting and sending gifts of food to each other.

The Festival of Purim

20 Mordecai wrote down everything that had happened. Then he sent letters to the Jews everywhere in the provinces 21 and told them:

> Each year you must celebrate on both the fourteenth and the fifteenth of Adar, 22 the days when we Jews defeated our enemies. Remember this month as a time when our sorrow was turned to joy, and celebration took the place of crying. Celebrate by having parties and by giving to the poor and by sharing gifts of food with each other.

23 They followed Mordecai's instructions and set aside these two days every year as a time of celebration.

The Reason for the Festival of Purim

24 Haman was the son of Hammedatha and a descendant of Agag. He hated the Jews so much that he planned to destroy them, but he wanted to find out the best time to do it. So he cast lots.[t]

25 Esther went to King Xerxes and asked him to save her people. Then the king gave written orders for Haman and his sons to be punished in the same terrible way that Haman had in mind for the Jews. So they were hanged. 26 Mordecai's letter had said that the Jews must celebrate for two days because of what had happened to them. This time of celebration is called Purim,[u] which is the Hebrew word for the lots that were cast. 27 Now every year the Jews set aside these two days for having parties and celebrating, just as they were told to do. 28 From now on, all Jewish families must remember to celebrate Purim on these two days each year.

29 Queen Esther, daughter of Abihail, wanted to give full authority to Mordecai's letter about the Festival of Purim, and with his help she wrote a letter about the feast. 30 Copies of this letter were sent to Jews in the one hundred twenty-seven provinces of King Xerxes. In the letter they said:

> We pray that all of you will live in peace and safety.
>
> 31 You and your descendants must always remember to celebrate Purim at the time and in the way that we have said. You must also follow the instructions that we have given you about mourning and going without eating.[v]
>
> 32 These laws about Purim are written by the authority of Queen Esther.

The Greatness of Xerxes and Mordecai

10 King Xerxes made everyone in his kingdom pay taxes, even those in lands across the sea. 2 All the great and fa-

[t] **9.24** *cast lots*: See the note at 3.7. [u] **9.26** *Purim*: The Jewish festival of Purim got its name from "purim," which is the Babylonian name for the lots that Haman used. Purim is celebrated each year on the 14th and 15th of Adar, which is about the first of March. [v] **9.31** *going without eating*: See the note at 4.3.

9.18 3 Macc 6.35. **9.24** Es 3.7.

mous things that King Xerxes did are written in the record books of the kings of Media and Persia. These records also tell
about the honors that the king gave to
Mordecai. 3 Next to the king himself,
Mordecai was the highest official in the
kingdom. He was a popular leader of the
Jews, because he helped them in many
ways and would even speak to the king for
them.

JOB

ABOUT THIS BOOK

Job was a very rich man, and although he did not belong to the people of Israel, he worshiped the Lord and was a truly good person. But Satan talked to God and accused Job of serving God only because God was blessing him. God agreed to let Satan take away Job's wealth, his children, and finally, his health, to see whether Job would stay faithful to God. Job did remain faithful.

Then three of Job's friends came to comfort him. They believed that health and prosperity were signs of God's blessing. And because Job had lost both his health and his prosperity, the three friends insisted that God must be punishing Job for some sin. Job answered that he was innocent, and this meant that they were wrong. Job and the friends argued back and forth, with neither side really proving the other wrong, although at the end of the argument, the friends gave up.

Job was suffering deeply, and several times during the argument he asked God to appear and explain the reason for his suffering. Then, after the friends stopped speaking, Job decided that human beings cannot find the kind of wisdom that gives answers to the deep questions of life. Only God has that wisdom. Job ended his speeches by swearing that he was innocent of doing wrong.

At this point, a young bystander named Elihu began talking. He repeated some of what had already been said, but he also criticized both sides of the argument. Elihu finished with a poem praising God's care for nature.

God finally did appear to Job, but he did not explain Job's suffering. Instead, God showed that the many things he does cannot be understood by humans; humans cannot do what God does. God criticized Job for talking so much when he knew so little, but he also said that Job had remained his faithful servant. And so, at the very end, the book tells how God blessed Job and made him twice as wealthy as he had been before.

Job never did understand why he had suffered; he felt bitter, but he never rejected God or turned away from him. Job was convinced that someday, God would rescue him:

"I know that my Savior lives,
and at the end
he will stand on this earth.
My flesh may be destroyed,
yet from this body
I will see God.
Yes, I will see him for myself,
and I long for that moment."
(19.25-27)

A QUICK LOOK AT THIS BOOK

- Job Loses His Wealth, Family, and Health (1.10—2.13)
- Job Curses the Day of His Birth (3.1-26)
- The First Round of the Debate (4.1—14.22)
- The Second Round of the Debate (15.1—21.34)

- The Third Round of the Debate (22.1—26.14)
- Job's Closing Statements (27.1—30.31)
- Job Swears that He Is Innocent (31.1-40)
- Elihu's Speeches (32.1—37.24)
- God's First Speech (38.1—39.30)
- God's Second Speech and Job's Responses (40.1—42.6)
- The Lord Again Blesses Job with Health, Wealth, and Family (42.7-17)

Job and His Family

1 Many years ago, a man named Job lived in the land of Uz.[a] He was a truly good person, who respected God and refused to do evil.

2 Job had seven sons and three daughters. 3 He owned seven thousand sheep, three thousand camels, five hundred pair of oxen, five hundred donkeys, and a large number of servants. He was the richest person in the East.

4 Job's sons took turns having feasts in their homes, and they always invited their three sisters to join in the eating and drinking. 5 After each feast, Job would send for his children and perform a ceremony, as a way of asking God to forgive them of any wrongs they may have done. He would get up early the next morning and offer a sacrifice for each of them, just in case they had sinned or silently cursed God.

Angels, the LORD, and Satan

6 One day, when the angels[b] had gathered around the LORD, and Satan[c] was there with them, 7 the LORD asked, "Satan, where have you been?"

Satan replied, "I have been going all over the earth."

8 Then the LORD asked, "What do you think of my servant Job? No one on earth is like him—he is a truly good person, who respects me and refuses to do evil."

9 "Why shouldn't he respect you?" Satan remarked. 10 "You are like a wall protecting not only him, but his entire family and all his property. You make him successful in whatever he does, and his flocks and herds are everywhere. 11 Try taking away everything he owns, and he will curse you to your face."

12 The LORD replied, "All right, Satan, do what you want with anything that belongs to him, but don't harm Job."

Then Satan left.

Job Loses Everything

13 Job's sons and daughters were having a feast in the home of his oldest son, 14 when someone rushed up to Job and said, "While your servants were plowing with your oxen, and your donkeys were nearby eating grass, 15 a gang of Sabeans[d] attacked and stole the oxen and donkeys! Your other servants were killed, and I was the only one who escaped to tell you."

16 That servant was still speaking, when a second one came running up and saying, "God sent down a fire that killed your sheep and your servants. I am the only one who escaped to tell you."

17 Before that servant finished speaking, a third one raced up and said, "Three gangs of Chaldeans[e] attacked and stole your camels! All of your other servants were killed, and I am the only one who escaped to tell you."

18 That servant was still speaking, when a fourth one dashed up and said, "Your children were having a feast and drinking wine at the home of your oldest son, 19 when suddenly a windstorm from the desert blew the house down, crushing all of your children. I am the only one who escaped to tell you."

20 When Job heard this, he tore his clothes and shaved his head because of his

[a] **1.1** *Uz*: The exact location of this place is unknown, though it was possibly somewhere in northwest Arabia. [b] **1.6** *angels*: See the note at 15.8. [c] **1.6** *Satan*: Hebrew "the accuser."
[d] **1.15** *Sabeans*: Perhaps the people of Sheba in what is now southwest Arabia (see Isaiah 60.6).
[e] **1.17** *Chaldeans*: People from the region of Babylonia, northeast of Palestine.
1.6 Gn 6.1, 2. **1.9-11** Rev 12.10.

great sorrow. He knelt on the ground, then
worshiped God 21 and said:

"We bring nothing at birth;
we take nothing
with us at death.
The LORD alone gives and takes.
Praise the name of the LORD!"

22 In spite of everything, Job did not sin
or accuse God of doing wrong.

Job Loses His Health

2 When the angels[f] gathered around the
LORD again, Satan[g] was there with
them, 2 and the LORD asked, "Satan, where
have you been?"

Satan replied, "I have been going all
over the earth."

3 Then the LORD asked, "What do you
think of my servant Job? No one on earth is
like him—he is a truly good person, who
respects me and refuses to do evil. And
he hasn't changed, even though you
persuaded me to destroy him for no
reason."

4 Satan answered, "There's no pain like
your own.[h] People will do anything to stay
alive. 5 Try striking Job's own body with
pain, and he will curse you to your face."

6 "All right!" the LORD replied. "Make
Job suffer as much as you want, but just
don't kill him." 7 Satan left and caused
painful sores to break out all over Job's
body—from head to toe.

8 Then Job sat on the ash-heap to
show his sorrow. And while he was scraping
his sores with a broken piece of pottery,
9 his wife asked, "Why do you still trust
God? Why don't you curse him and die?"

10 Job replied, "Don't talk like a fool!
If we accept blessings from God, we must
accept trouble as well." In all that happened, Job never once said anything
against God.

Job's Three Friends

11 Eliphaz from Teman, Bildad from
Shuah, and Zophar from Naamah[i] were
three of Job's friends, and they heard about
his troubles. So they agreed to visit Job and
comfort him. 12 When they came near
enough to see Job, they could hardly recognize him. And in their great sorrow, they
tore their clothes, then sprinkled dust on
their heads and cried bitterly. 13 For seven
days and nights, they sat silently on the
ground beside him, because they realized
what terrible pain he was in.

Job's First Speech

Blot Out the Day of My Birth

3 Finally, Job cursed the day
of his birth
2 by saying to God:
3 Blot out the day of my birth
and the night when my parents
created a son.
4 Forget about that day,
cover it with darkness,
5 and send thick, gloomy shadows
to fill it with dread.
6 Erase that night from the calendar
and conceal it with darkness.
7 Don't let children be created
or joyful shouts be heard
ever again in that night.
8 Let those with magic powers[j]
place a curse on that day.
9 Darken its morning stars
and remove all hope of light,
10 because it let me be born
into a world of trouble.

[f]**2.1** *angels*: See the note at 15.8. [g]**2.1** *Satan*: See the note at 1.6. [h]**2.4** *There's no pain like your own*: The Hebrew text has "Skin for skin," which was probably a popular saying.
[i]**2.11** *Teman . . . Shuah . . . Naamah*: Teman was a place in northern Edom; Shuah may have been a town on the Euphrates River or else further south, near the towns of Dedan and Sheba; Naamah may have been located on the road between Beirut and Damascus, though its exact location is unknown. [j]**3.8** *those with magic powers*: The Hebrew text has "those who can place a curse on the day and rouse up Leviathan," which was some kind of sea monster. God's victory over this monster sometimes stood for God's power over all creation and sometimes for his defeat of his enemies (see Isaiah 27.1). In Job 41.1, Leviathan is either a sea monster or a crocodile with almost supernatural powers.

1.21 Si 40.1; 11.14. **3.1-19** Jr 20.14-18; Si 23.14.

Why Didn't I Die at Birth?

11 Why didn't I die at birth?
12 Why was I accepted[k]
and allowed to nurse
at my mother's breast?
13 Now I would be at peace
in the silent world below
14 with kings and their advisors
whose palaces lie in ruins,
15 and with rulers once rich
with silver and gold.
16 I wish I had been born dead
and then buried, never to see
the light of day.
17 In the world of the dead,
the wicked and the weary rest
without a worry.
*18 Everyone is there—
19 where captives and slaves
are free at last.

Why Does God Let Me Live?

20 Why does God let me live
when life is miserable
and so bitter?
21 I keep longing for death
more than I would seek
a valuable treasure.
22 Nothing could make me happier
than to be in the grave.
23 Why do I go on living
when God has me surrounded,
and I can't see the road?
24 Moaning and groaning
are my food and drink,
25 and my worst fears
have all come true.
26 I have no peace or rest—
only troubles and worries.

Eliphaz's First Speech

Please Be Patient and Listen

4 Eliphaz from Teman[l] said:
2 Please be patient and listen
to what I have to say.
*3 Remember how your words
4 have guided and encouraged
many in need.
5 But now you feel discouraged
when struck by trouble.
6 You respect God and live right,
so don't lose hope!
7 No truly innocent person
has ever died young.
8 In my experience, only those
who plant seeds of evil
harvest trouble,
9 and then they are swept away
by the angry breath of God.
10 They may roar and growl
like powerful lions.
But when God breaks their teeth,
11 they starve, and their children
are scattered.

A Secret Was Told to Me

12 A secret was told to me
in a faint whisper—
13 I was overcome by sleep,
but disturbed by dreams;
14 I trembled with fear,
15 and my hair stood on end,
as a wind blew past my face.
16 It stopped and stood still.
Then a form appeared—
a shapeless form.
And from the silence,
I heard a voice say,
17 "No humans are innocent
in the eyes of God
their Creator.
18 He finds fault with his servants
and even with his angels.
19 Humans are formed from clay
and are fragile as moths,
so what chance do you have?
20 Born after daybreak,
you die before nightfall
and disappear forever.
21 Your tent pegs are pulled up,
and you leave this life,
having gained no wisdom."

[k]**3.12** *Why was I accepted*: The Hebrew text has "Why were there knees to receive me," which may refer either to Job's mother or to his father, who would have placed Job on his knees to show that he had accepted him as his child. [l]**4.1** *Teman*: See the note at 2.11.

3.21 Rev 9.6. **4.13** Job 33.15.

Eliphaz Continues

Call Out for Help

5 Job, call out for help
and see if an angel comes!
2 Envy and jealousy
will kill a stupid fool.
3 I have seen fools take root.
But God sends a curse,
suddenly uprooting them
4 and leaving their children
helpless in court.
5 Then hungry and greedy people
gobble down their crops
and grab up their wealth.[m]
6 Our suffering isn't caused
by the failure of crops;
7 it's all part of life,
like sparks shooting skyward.

8 Job, if I were you,
I would ask God for help.
9 His miracles are marvelous,
more than we can count.
10 God sends showers on earth
and waters the fields.
11 He protects the sorrowful
and lifts up those
who have been disgraced.
*12 God swiftly traps the wicked
13 in their own evil schemes,
and their wisdom fails.
14 Darkness is their only companion,
hiding their path at noon.
15 God rescues the needy
from the words of the wicked
and the fist of the mighty.
16 The poor are filled with hope,
and injustice is silenced.

Consider Yourself Fortunate

17 Consider yourself fortunate
if God All-Powerful
chooses to correct you.
18 He may cause injury and pain,
but he will bandage and heal
your cuts and bruises.
19 God will protect you from harm,
no matter how often
trouble may strike.
20 In times of war and famine,
God will keep you safe.
21 You will be sheltered,
without fear of hurtful words
or any other weapon.
22 You will laugh at the threat
of destruction and famine.
And you won't be afraid
of wild animals—
23 they will no longer be fierce,
and your rocky fields
will become friendly.
24 Your home will be secure,
and your sheep will be safe.
25 You will have more descendants
than there are blades of grass
on the face of the earth.
26 You will live a long life,
and your body will be strong
until the day you die.
27 Our experience has proven
these things to be true,
so listen and learn.

Job's Reply to Eliphaz

It's Impossible

6 Job said:
2 It's impossible to weigh
my misery and grief!
3 They outweigh the sand
along the beach,
and that's why I have spoken
without thinking first.
4 The fearsome arrows
of God All-Powerful
have filled my soul
with their poison.
5 Do oxen and wild donkeys
cry out in distress
unless they are hungry?
6 What is food without salt?
What is more tasteless
than the white of an egg?[n]
7 That's how my food tastes,
and my appetite is gone.

[m]**5.5** *wealth*: One possible meaning for the difficult Hebrew text of verse 5. [n]**6.6** *What is more tasteless . . . egg*: One possible meaning for the difficult Hebrew text.

5.9 Si 43.32. **5.13** 1 Co 3.19. **5.17** Pr 3.11, 12; He 12.5, 6. **5.18** Ho 6.1.

*8 How I wish that God
would answer my prayer
9 and do away with me.
10 Then I would be comforted,
knowing that in all of my pain
I have never disobeyed God.
11 Why should I patiently hope
when my strength is gone?
12 I am not strong as stone
or bronze,
13 and I have finally reached
the end of my rope.

My Friends, I Am Desperate

14 My friends, I am desperate,
and you should help me,
even if I no longer respect
God All-Powerful.[o]
*15 But you are treacherous
16 as streams that swell
with melting snow,
17 then suddenly disappear
in the summer heat.
18 I am like a caravan,
lost in the desert
while searching for water.
19 Caravans from Tema and Sheba[p]
20 thought they would find water.
But they were disappointed,
21 just as I am with you.[q]
Only one look at my suffering,
and you run away scared.

What Have I Done Wrong?

22 Have I ever asked any of you
to give me a gift
23 or to purchase my freedom
from brutal enemies?
24 What have I done wrong?
Show me,
and I will keep quiet.
25 The truth is always painful,
but your arguments
prove nothing.
26 Here I am desperate,
and you consider my words
as worthless as wind.
27 Why, you would sell an orphan
or your own neighbor!
28 Look me straight in the eye;
I won't lie to you.
29 Stop accusing me falsely;
my reputation is at stake.
30 I know right from wrong,
and I am not telling lies.

Job Continues

Why Is Life So Hard?

7 Why is life so hard?
Why do we suffer?
2 We are slaves in search of shade;
we are laborers longing
for our wages.
3 God has made my days drag on
and my nights miserable.
4 I pray for night to end,
but it stretches out
while I toss and turn.
5 My parched skin is covered
with worms, dirt, and sores,
6 and my days are running out
quicker than the thread
of a fast-moving needle.

Don't Forget!

7 I beg you, God, don't forget!
My life is just a breath,
and trouble lies ahead.
8 I will vanish from sight,
and no one, including you,
will ever see me again.
9 I will disappear in the grave
or vanish from sight
like a passing cloud.
10 Never will I return home;
soon I will be forgotten.

11 And so, I cry out to you
in agony and distress.

[o]**6.14** *and you should help me . . . God All-Powerful*: Or "and if you don't help me, you no longer respect God All-Powerful." [p]**6.19** *Tema and Sheba*: Tema was a region in northwest Arabia, and Sheba was probably a region in southwest Arabia. [q]**6.21** *just . . . you*: One possible meaning for the difficult Hebrew text.
7.9,10 Ws 2.1-4.

12 Am I the sea or a sea monster?
Is that why you imprison me?[r]
13 I go to bed, hoping for rest,
14 but you torture me
with terrible dreams.
*15 I'd rather choke to death
than live in this body.
16 Leave me alone and let me die;
my life has no meaning.
17 What makes you so concerned
about us humans?
18 Why do you test us
from sunrise to sunset?
19 Won't you look away
just long enough
for me to swallow?
20 Why do you watch us so closely?
What's it to you, if I sin?
Why am I your target
and such a heavy burden?
21 Why do you refuse to forgive?
Soon you won't find me,
because I'll be dead.

Bildad's First Speech

How Long Will You Talk?

8 Bildad from Shuah[s] said:
2 How long will you talk
and keep saying nothing?
3 Does God All-Powerful
stand in the way of justice?
4 He made your children pay
for their sins.
5 So why don't you turn to him
6 and start living right?
Then he will decide
to rescue and restore you
to your place of honor.
7 Your future will be brighter
by far than your past.

Our Ancestors Were Wise

8 Our ancestors were wise,
so learn from them.
9 Our own time has been short,
like a fading shadow,
and we know very little.
10 But they will instruct you
with great understanding.

11 Papyrus reeds grow healthy
only in a swamp,
12 and if the water dries up,
they die sooner than grass.
13 Such is the hopeless future
of all who turn from God
14 and trust in something as frail
as a spider's web—
15 they take hold and fall
because it's so flimsy.
16 Sinful people are like plants
with spreading roots and plenty
of sun and water.
17 They wrap their roots tightly
around rocks.[t]
18 But once they are pulled up,
they have no more place;
19 their life slips away,[u]
and other plants grow there.

20 We know God doesn't reject
an innocent person
or help a sinner.
21 And so, he will make you happy
and give you something
to smile about.
22 But your evil enemies
will be put to shame
and disappear forever.

Job's Reply to Bildad

What You Say Is True

9 Job said:
2 What you say is true.
No human is innocent
in the sight of God.
3 Not once in a thousand times
could we win our case
if we took him to court.
4 God is wise and powerful—
who could possibly
oppose him and win?

[r]**7.12** *sea monster . . . imprison me*: "Sea monster" translates the Hebrew word "Tannin," which was possibly a sea monster similar to Leviathan (3.8), Rahab (9.13), and Behemoth (40.15). According to 38.8-11, God makes the sea his prisoner by setting its boundaries. [s]**8.1** *Shuah*: See the note at 2.11. [t]**8.17** *rocks*: One possible meaning for the difficult Hebrew text of verse 17.
[u]**8.19** *their . . . away*: One possible meaning for the difficult Hebrew text.
7.17 Ps 8.4; 144.3. **8.8** Si 8.9. **9.2** Job 4.17.

5 When God becomes angry,
he can move mountains
before they even know it.
6 God can shake the earth loose
from its foundations
7 or command the sun and stars
to hold back their light.
8 God alone stretched out the sky,
stepped on the sea,[v]
9 and set the stars in place—
the Big Dipper and Orion,
the Pleiades and the stars
in the southern sky.
10 Of all the miracles God works,
we cannot understand a one.
11 God walks right past me,
without making a sound.
12 And if he grabs something,
who can stop him
or raise a question?

13 When God showed his anger,
the servants of the sea monster[w]
fell at his feet.
14 How, then, could I possibly
argue my case with God?

Though I Am Innocent

15 Even though I am innocent,
I can only beg for mercy.
16 And if God came into court
when I called him,
he would not hear my case.
17 He would strike me with a storm[x]
and increase my injuries
for no reason at all.
18 Before I could get my breath,
my miseries would multiply.
19 God is much stronger than I am,
and who would call me into court
to give me justice?

20 Even if I were innocent,
God would prove me wrong.[y]
21 I am not guilty,
but I no longer care
what happens to me.
22 What difference does it make?
God destroys the innocent
along with the guilty.
23 When a good person dies
a sudden death,
God sits back and laughs.
24 And who else but God
blindfolds the judges,
then lets the wicked
take over the earth?

My Life Is Speeding By

25 My life is speeding by,
without a hope of happiness.
26 Each day passes swifter
than a sailing ship
or an eagle swooping down.
27 Sometimes I try to be cheerful
and to stop complaining,
28 but my sufferings frighten me,
because I know that God
still considers me guilty.
29 So what's the use of trying
to prove my innocence?
30 Even if I washed myself
with the strongest soap,
31 God would throw me into a pit
of stinking slime, leaving me
disgusting to my clothes.

32 God isn't a mere human like me.
I can't put him on trial.
33 Who could possibly judge
between the two of us?
34 Can someone snatch away
the stick God carries
to frighten me?
35 Then I could speak up
without fear of him,
but for now, I cannot speak.[z]

Job Complains to God

I Am Sick of Life!

10 I am sick of life!
And from my deep despair,
I complain to you, my God.

[v]**9.8** *sea*: Or "sea monster" (see verse 13 and the note there). [w]**9.13** *the sea monster*: The Hebrew text has "Rahab," which was some kind of sea monster with supernatural powers (see the notes at 3.8 and 26.12). [x]**9.17** *strike . . . storm*: One possible meaning for the difficult Hebrew text. [y]**9.20** *God . . . wrong*: Or "my own words would prove me wrong." [z]**9.35** *but . . . speak*: One possible meaning for the difficult Hebrew text.

9.7,8 Ba 3.34, 35. **9.9** Job 38.31; Am 5.8.

2 Don't just condemn me!
Point out my sin.
3 Why do you take such delight
in destroying those you created
and in smiling on sinners?
4 Do you look at things
the way we humans do?
5 Is your life as short as ours?
6 Is that why you are so quick
to find fault with me?
7 You know I am innocent,
but who can defend me
against you?
8 Will you now destroy
someone you created?
9 Remember that you molded me
like a piece of clay.
So don't turn me back
into dust once again.
10 As cheese is made from milk,
you created my body
from a tiny drop.
11 Then you tied my bones together
with muscles and covered them
with flesh and skin.
12 You, the source of my life,
showered me with kindness
and watched over me.

You Have Not Explained

13 You have not explained
all of your mysteries,
14 but you catch and punish me
each time I sin.
15 Guilty or innocent,
I am condemned and ashamed
because of my troubles.
16 No matter how hard I try,
you keep hunting me down
like a powerful lion.[a]
17 You never stop accusing me;
you become furious and attack
over and over again.

18 Why did you let me be born?
I would rather have died
before birth
19 and been carried to the grave
without ever breathing.
20 I have only a few days left.
Why don't you leave me alone?[b]
Let me find some relief,
*21 before I travel to the land
22 of darkness and despair,
the place of no return.

Zophar's First Speech

So Much Foolish Talk

11 Zophar from Naamah[c] said:
2 So much foolish talk
cannot go unanswered.
3 Your words have silenced others
and made them ashamed;
now it is only right for you
to be put to shame.
4 You claim to be innocent
and argue that your beliefs
are acceptable to God.
5 But I wish he would speak
6 and let you know that wisdom
has many different sides.
You would then discover
that God has punished you
less than you deserve.

7 Can you understand the mysteries
surrounding God All-Powerful?
8 They are higher than the heavens
and deeper than the grave.
So what can you do
when you know so little,
9 and these mysteries outreach
the earth and the ocean?

10 If God puts you in prison
or drags you to court,
what can you do?
11 God has the wisdom to know
when someone is worthless
and sinful,
12 but it's easier to tame
a wild donkey
than to make a fool wise.[d]

[a] **10.16** *lion*: One possible meaning for the difficult Hebrew text of verse 16.
[b] **10.20** *I have only . . . alone*: One possible meaning for the difficult Hebrew text.
[c] **11.1** *Naamah*: See the note at 2.11. [d] **11.12** *it's . . . wise*: One possible meaning for the difficult Hebrew text.
10.7 Ws 16.15. **10.10** Ws 7.1, 2.

Surrender Your Heart to God

13 Surrender your heart to God,
turn to him in prayer,
14 and give up your sins—
even those you do in secret.
15 Then you won't be ashamed;
you will be confident
and fearless.
16 Your troubles will go away
like water beneath a bridge,
17 and your darkest night
will be brighter than noon.
18 You will rest safe and secure,
filled with hope
and emptied of worry.
19 You will sleep without fear
and be greatly respected.
20 But those who are evil
will go blind and lose their way.
Their only escape is death!

Job's Reply to Zophar

You Think You Are So Great

12 *1 Job said to his friends:
2 You think you are so great,
with all the answers.
3 But I know as much as you do,
and so does everyone else.
4 I have always lived right,
and God answered my prayers;
now friends make fun of me.
5 It's easy to condemn
those who are suffering,
when you have no troubles.
6 Robbers and other godless people
live safely at home and say,
"God is in our hands!"[e]

If You Want To Learn

7 If you want to learn,
then go and ask
the wild animals and the birds,
8 the flowers and the fish.
9 Any of them can tell you
what the LORD has done.[f]
10 Every living creature
is in the hands of God.
11 We hear with our ears,
taste with our tongues,
12 and gain some wisdom from those
who have lived a long time.
13 But God is the real source
of wisdom and strength.
14 No one can rebuild
what he destroys, or release
those he has imprisoned.
15 God can hold back the rain
or send a flood,
16 just as he rules over liars
and those they lie to.

17 God destroys counselors,
turns judges into fools,
18 and makes slaves of kings.
19 God removes priests and others
who have great power—
20 he confuses wise,
experienced advisors,
21 puts mighty kings to shame,
and takes away their power.
22 God turns darkness to light;
23 he makes nations strong,
then shatters their strength.
24 God strikes their rulers senseless,
then leaves them to roam
through barren deserts,
25 lost in the dark, staggering
like someone drunk.

Job Continues

I Know and Understand

13 I know and understand
every bit of this.
2 None of you are smarter
than I am;
there's nothing you know
that I don't.
3 But I prefer to argue my case
with God All-Powerful—
4 you are merely useless doctors,
who treat me with lies.
5 The wisest thing you can do
is to keep quiet 6 and listen
to my argument.
7 Are you telling lies for God

[e] **12.6** *God is in our hands*: One possible meaning for the difficult Hebrew text. [f] **12.9** *Any . . . done*: One possible meaning for the difficult Hebrew text.

8 and not telling the whole truth
when you argue his case?
9 If he took you to court,
could you fool him,
just as you fool others?
10 If you were secretly unfair,
he would correct you,
11 and his glorious splendor
would make you terrified.
12 Your wisdom and arguments
are as delicate as dust.

Be Quiet While I Speak

13 Be quiet while I speak,
then say what you will.
14 I will be responsible
for what happens to me.
15 God may kill me, but still
I will trust him[g]
and offer my defense.
16 This may be what saves me,
because no guilty person
would come to his court.
17 Listen carefully to my words!
18 I have prepared my case well,
and I am certain to win.
19 If you can prove me guilty,
I will give up and die.

Job Prays

I Ask Only Two Things

20 I ask only two things
of you, my God,
and I will no longer
hide from you—
21 stop punishing
and terrifying me!

22 Then speak, and I will reply;
or else let me speak,
and you reply.
23 Please point out my sins,
so I will know them.
24 Why have you turned your back
and count me your enemy?
25 Do you really enjoy
frightening a fallen leaf?
26 Why do you accuse me
of horrible crimes
and make me pay for sins
I did in my youth?
27 You have tied my feet down
and keep me surrounded;
28 I am rotting away like cloth
eaten by worms.

Job Continues his Prayer

Life Is Short and Sorrowful

14 Life is short and sorrowful
for every living soul.
2 We are flowers that fade
and shadows that vanish.
3 And so, I ask you, God,
why pick on me?
4 There's no way a human
can be completely pure.
5 Our time on earth is brief;
the number of our days
is already decided by you.
6 Why don't you leave us alone
and let us find some happiness
while we toil and labor?

When a Tree Is Chopped Down

7 When a tree is chopped down,
there is always the hope
that it will sprout again.
8 Its roots and stump may rot,
9 but at the touch of water,
fresh twigs shoot up.
10 Humans are different—
we die, and that's the end.
11 We are like streams and lakes
after the water has gone;
12 we fall into the sleep of death,
never to rise again,
until the sky disappears.
13 Please hide me, God,
deep in the ground—
and when you are angry no more,
remember to rescue me.

Will We Humans Live Again?

14 Will we humans live again?
I would gladly suffer
and wait for my time.
15 My Creator, you would want me;
you would call out,
and I would answer.

[g] **13.15** *God . . . trust him*: Or "God will surely kill me; I have lost all hope."
13.27 Job 33.11. **14.1,2** Ws 2.1; Si 40.1-11; 41.1-4.

16 You would take care of me,
but not count my sins—
17 you would put them in a bag,
tie it tight,
and toss them away.
18 But in the real world,
mountains tumble,
and rocks crumble;
19 streams wear away stones
and wash away soil.
And you destroy our hopes!
20 You change the way we look,
then send us away,
wiped out forever.
21 We never live to know
if our children are praised
or disgraced.
22 We feel no pain but our own,
and when we mourn,
it's only for ourselves.

Eliphaz's Second Speech

If You Had Any Sense

15 Eliphaz from Teman[h] said:
*2 Job, if you had any sense,
3 you would stop spreading
all of this hot air.
4 Your words are enough
to make others turn from God
and lead them to doubt.
5 And your sinful, scheming mind
is the source of all you say.
6 I am not here as your judge;
your own words are witnesses
against you.

7 Were you the first human?
Are you older than the hills?
8 Have you ever been present
when God's council[i] meets?
Do you alone have wisdom?
9 Do you know and understand
something we don't?
10 We have the benefit of wisdom
older than your father.
11 And you have been offered
comforting words from God.
Isn't this enough?
12 Your emotions are out of control,
making you look fierce;
13 that's why you attack God
with everything you say.
14 No human is pure and innocent,
15 and neither are angels—
not in the sight of God.
If God doesn't trust his angels,
16 what chance do humans have?
We are so terribly evil
that we thirst for sin.

Just Listen to What I Know

17 Just listen to what I know,
and you will learn
18 wisdom known by others
since ancient times.
19 Those who gained such insights
also gained the land,
and they were not influenced
by foreign teachings.
20 But suffering is in store
each day for those who sin.
21 Even in times of success,
they constantly hear
the threat of doom.
22 Darkness, despair, and death
are their destiny.
23 They scrounge around for food,
all the while dreading
the approaching darkness.
24 They are overcome with despair,
like a terrified king
about to go into battle.
25 This is because they rebelled
against God All-Powerful
26 and have attacked him
with their weapons.

27 They may be rich and fat,
28 but they will live in the ruins
of deserted towns.
29 Their property and wealth
will shrink and disappear.
30 They won't escape the darkness,
and the blazing breath of God
will set their future aflame.
*31 They have put their trust
in something worthless;

[h]**15.1** *Teman*: See the note at 2.11. [i]**15.8** *God's council*: The angels and others who gather to discuss matters with God (see 1.6; 2.1).
15.14-16 Job 25.4-6.

now they will become worthless
32 like a date palm tree
without a leaf.[j]
33 Or like vineyards or orchards
whose blossoms and unripe fruit
drop to the ground.
34 Yes, the godless and the greedy
will have nothing but flames
feasting on their homes,
35 because they are the parents
of trouble and vicious lies.

Job's Reply to Eliphaz

I Have Often Heard This

16 Job said:
2 I have often heard this,
and it offers no comfort.
3 So why don't you keep quiet?
What's bothering you?
4 If I were in your place,
it would be easy to criticize
or to give advice.
5 But I would offer hope
and comfort instead.

6 If I speak, or if I don't,
I hurt all the same.
My torment continues.
7 God has worn me down
and destroyed my family;
8 my shriveled up skin proves
that I am his prisoner.
9 God is my hateful enemy,
glaring at me and attacking
with his sharp teeth.
10 Everyone is against me;
they sneer and slap my face.
11 And God is the one
who handed me over
to this merciless mob.

Everything Was Going Well

12 Everything was going well,
until God grabbed my neck
and shook me to pieces.
God set me up as the target
13 for his arrows,
and without showing mercy,
he slashed my stomach open,
spilling out my insides.
14 God never stops attacking,
15 and so, in my sorrow
I dress in sackcloth[k]
and sit in the dust.
16 My face is red with tears,
and dark shadows
circle my eyes,
17 though I am not violent,
and my prayers are sincere.

18 If I should die,
I beg the earth not to cover
my cry for justice.
19 Even now, God in heaven
is both my witness
and my protector.
20 My friends have rejected me,
but God is the one I beg[l]
21 to show that I am right,
just as a friend should.
22 Because in only a few years,
I will be dead and gone.

Job Complains to God

My Hopes Have Died

17 My hopes have died,
my time is up,
and the grave is ready.
2 All I can see are angry crowds,
making fun of me.
3 If you, LORD, don't help,
who will pay the price
for my release?
4 My friends won't really listen,
all because of you,
and so you must be the one
to prove them wrong.
5 They have condemned me,
just to benefit themselves;
now blind their children.

6 You, God, are the reason
I am insulted and spit on.
7 I am almost blind with grief;
my body is a mere shadow.

[j] **15.32** *leaf*: One possible meaning for the difficult Hebrew text of verse 32.
[k] **16.15** *sackcloth*: A rough, dark-colored cloth made from goat hair and used to make grain sacks. It was worn in times of trouble or sorrow. [l] **16.20** *My friends . . . beg*: Or "God is my friend, and he is the one I beg."
16.19 Job 19.25.

8 People who are truly good
would feel so alarmed,
that they would become angry
at my worthless friends.
9 They would do the right thing
and because they did,
they would grow stronger.[m]
10 But none of my friends
show any sense.

11 My life is drawing to an end;
hope has disappeared.
12 But all my friends can do
is offer empty hopes.[n]
13 I could tell the world below
to prepare me a bed.
14 Then I could greet the grave
as my father
and say to the worms,
"Hello, mother and sisters!"

15 But what kind of hope is that?
16 Will it keep me company
in the world of the dead?

Bildad's Second Speech

How Long Will You Talk?

18 Bildad from Shuah[o] said:
2 How long will you talk?
Be sensible! Let us speak.
3 Or do you think that we
are dumb animals?
4 You cut yourself in anger.
Will that shake the earth
or even move the rocks?

*5 The lamps of sinful people
soon are snuffed out,
6 leaving their tents dark.
7 Their powerful legs become weak,
and they stumble on schemes
of their own doing.
*8 Before they know it,
9 they are trapped in a net,
10 hidden along the path.
11 Terror strikes and pursues
from every side.
12 Starving, they run,
only to meet disaster,
13 then afterwards to be eaten alive
by death itself.

14 Those sinners are dragged
from the safety of their tents
to die a gruesome death.
15 Then their tents and possessions
are burned to ashes,
16 and they are left like trees,
dried up from the roots.
17 They are gone and forgotten,
18 thrown far from the light
into a world of darkness,
19 without any children
to carry on their name.
20 Everyone, from east to west,
is overwhelmed with horror.
21 Such is the fate of sinners
and their families
who don't know God.

Job's Reply to Bildad

How Long Will You Torture Me?

19 Job said:
2 How long will you torture me
with your words?
3 Isn't ten times enough
for you to accuse me?
Aren't you ashamed?
4 Even if I have sinned,
you haven't been harmed.
5 You boast of your goodness,
claiming I am suffering
because I am guilty.
6 But God is the one at fault
for finding fault with me.

7 Though I pray to be rescued
from this torment,
no whisper of justice
answers me.
8 God has me trapped

[m] **17.9** *stronger*: One possible meaning for the difficult Hebrew text of verses 8, 9.
[n] **17.12** *hopes*: One possible meaning for the difficult Hebrew text of verse 12. [o] **18.1** *Shuah*: See the note at 2.11.
18.5,6 Job 21.17.

with a wall of darkness
9 and stripped of respect.
10 God rips me apart,
uproots my hopes,
11 and attacks with fierce anger,
as though I were his enemy.
12 His entire army advances,
then surrounds my tent.

I Am Forgotten

*13 God has turned relatives
and friends against me,
14 and I am forgotten.
15 My guests and my servants
consider me a stranger,
16 and when I call my servants,
they pay no attention.
17 My breath disgusts my wife;
everyone in my family
turns away.
18 Young children can't stand me,
and when I come near,
they make fun.
19 My best friends and loved ones
have turned from me.
20 I am skin and bones—
just barely alive.
21 My friends, I beg you for pity!
God has made me his target.
22 Hasn't he already done enough?
Why do you join the attack?

23 I wish that my words
could be written down
24 or chiseled into rock.
25 I know that my Savior[p] lives,
and at the end
he will stand on this earth.
26 My flesh may be destroyed,
yet from this body
I will see God.[q]
27 Yes, I will see him for myself,
and I long for that moment.

28 My friends, you think up ways
to blame and torment me, saying
I brought it on myself.
29 But watch out for the judgment,
when God will punish you!

Zophar's Second Speech

Your Words Are Disturbing

20 Zophar from Naamah[r] said:
2 Your words are disturbing;
now I must speak.
3 You have accused
and insulted me,
and reason requires a reply.
4 Since the time of creation,
everyone has known
5 that sinful people are happy
for only a while.
6 Though their pride and power
may reach to the sky,
7 they will disappear like dust,
and those who knew them
will wonder what happened.
8 They will be forgotten
like a dream
9 and vanish from the sight
of family and friends.
10 Their children will have to repay
what the parents took
from the poor.
11 Indeed, the wicked will die
and go to their graves
in the prime of life.

Sinners Love the Taste of Sin

12 Sinners love the taste of sin;
they relish every bite
13 and swallow it slowly.
14 But their food will turn sour
and poison their stomachs.
15 Then God will make them lose
the wealth they gobbled down.
16 They will die from the fangs
of poisonous snakes
17 and never enjoy rivers flowing
with milk and honey.
18 Their hard work will result
in nothing gained,
19 because they cheated the poor
and took their homes.

20 Greedy people want everything
and are never satisfied.[s]

[p] **19.25** *Savior*: Or "Defender." [q] **19.26** *God*: One possible meaning for the difficult Hebrew text of verses 25, 26. [r] **20.1** *Naamah*: See the note at 2.11. [s] **20.20** *are never satisfied*: One possible meaning for the difficult Hebrew text.

19.19 Si 6.8. **20.8** Ws 5.14.

21 But when nothing remains
for them to grab,
they will be nothing.
22 Once they have everything,
distress and despair
will strike them down,
23 and God will make them swallow
his blazing anger.[t]

24 While running from iron spears,
they will be killed
by arrows of bronze,
25 whose shining tips go straight
through their bodies.
They will be trapped by terror,
26 and what they treasure most
will be lost in the dark.
God will send flames
to destroy them in their tents
with all their property.
27 The heavens and the earth
will testify against them,
28 and all their possessions
will be dragged off
when God becomes angry.
29 This is what God has decided
for those who are evil.

Job's Reply to Zophar

If You Want To Offer Comfort

21 Job said:
2 If you want to offer comfort,
then listen to me.
3 And when I have finished,
you can start your insults
all over again.
4 My complaint is against God;
that's why I am impatient.
5 Just looking at me is enough
to make you sick,
6 and the very thought of myself
fills me with disgust.

7 Why do evil people live so long
and gain such power?
8 Why are they allowed to see
their children grow up?[u]
9 They have no worries at home,
and God never punishes them.
10 Their cattle have lots of calves
without ever losing one;
11 their children play and dance
safely by themselves.
12 These people sing and celebrate
to the sound of tambourines,
small harps, and flutes,
13 and they are successful,
without a worry,
until the day they die.

Leave Us Alone!

14 Those who are evil say
to God All-Powerful,
"Leave us alone! Don't bother us
with your teachings.
15 What do we gain from praying
and worshiping you?
16 We succeeded all on our own."
And so, I keep away from them
and their evil schemes.

17 How often does God become angry
and send disaster and darkness
to punish sinners?
18 How often does he strike them
like a windstorm
that scatters straw?

19 You say, "God will punish
those sinners' children
in place of those sinners."
But I say, "Let him punish
those sinners themselves
until they really feel it.
20 Let God All-Powerful force them
to drink their own destruction
from the cup of his anger.
21 Because after they are dead,
they won't care what happens
to their children."

Who Can Tell God What To Do?

22 Who can tell God what to do?
He judges powerful rulers.
*23 Some of us die prosperous,
24 enjoying good health,

[t]**20.23** *anger*: One possible meaning for the difficult Hebrew text of verse 23. [u]**21.8** *up*: One possible meaning for the difficult Hebrew text of verse 8.
20.24 Ws 5.17-23.

25 while others die in poverty,
having known only pain.
26 But we all end up dead,
beneath a blanket of worms.

27 My friends, I know that you
are plotting against me.
28 You ask, "Where is the home
of that important person
who does so much evil?"

29 Everyone, near and far, agrees
30 that those who do wrong
never suffer disaster,
when God becomes angry.
31 No one points out their sin
or punishes them.
32 Then at their funerals,
they are highly praised;
33 the earth welcomes them home,
while crowds mourn.

34 But empty, meaningless words
are the comfort you offer me.

Eliphaz's Third Speech

What Use Are We Humans to God?

22 Eliphaz from Teman[v] said:
2 What use are we humans
to God,
even the wisest of us?
3 If you were completely sinless,
that would still mean nothing
to God All-Powerful.
4 Is he correcting you
for worshiping him?
5 No! It's because
of your terrible sins.
6 To guarantee payment of a debt,
you have taken clothes
from the poor.
7 And you refused bread and water
to the hungry and thirsty,
8 although you were rich,
respected, and powerful.
9 You have turned away widows
and have broken the arms
of orphans.
10 That's why you were suddenly
trapped by terror,
11 blinded by darkness,
and drowned in a flood.

God Lives in the Heavens

12 God lives in the heavens
above the highest stars,
where he sees everything.
13 Do you think the deep darkness
hides you from God?
14 Do thick clouds cover his eyes,
as he walks around heaven's dome
high above the earth?
15 Give up those ancient ideas
believed by sinners,
16 who were swept away
without warning.
17 They rejected God All-Powerful,
feeling he was helpless,
18 although he had been kind
to their families.
The beliefs of these sinners
are truly disgusting.
19 When God's people see
the godless swept away,
they celebrate, 20 saying,
"Our enemies are gone,
and fire has destroyed
their possessions."

Surrender to God All-Powerful

21 Surrender to God All-Powerful!
You will find peace
and prosperity.
22 Listen to his teachings
and take them to heart.
23 If you return to God
and turn from sin,
all will go well for you.
24 So get rid of your finest gold,
as though it were sand.
25 Let God All-Powerful
be your silver and gold,
26 and you will find happiness
by worshiping him.
27 God will answer your prayers,
and you will keep the promises
you made to him.
28 He will do whatever you ask,
and life will be bright.

[v]**22.1** *Teman*: See the note at 2.11.
22.2,3 Job 35.6-8.

29 When others are disgraced,
God will clear their names
in answer to your prayers.
30 Even those who are guilty
will be forgiven,
because you obey God.[w]

Job's Reply to Eliphaz

Today I Complain Bitterly

23 Job said:
2 Today I complain bitterly,
because God has been cruel
and made me suffer.
3 If I knew where to find God,
I would go there
4 and argue my case.
5 Then I would discover
what he wanted to say.
6 Would he overwhelm me
with his greatness?
No! He would listen
7 because I am innocent,
and he would say,
"I now set you free!"

8 I cannot find God anywhere—
in front or back of me,
9 to my left or my right.
God is always at work,
though I never see him.
10 But he knows what I am doing,
and when he tests me,
I will be pure as gold.
*11 I have never refused to follow
any of his commands,
12 and I have always treasured
his teachings.[x]
13 But he alone is God,
and who can oppose him?
God does as he pleases,
14 and he will do exactly
what he intends with me.
*15 Merely the thought
of God All-Powerful
16 makes me tremble with fear.
17 God has covered me
with darkness,
but I refuse to be silent.[y]

Job Continues

Why Doesn't God Set a Time?

24 Why doesn't God
set a time for court?
Why don't his people know
where he can be found?
2 Sinners remove boundary markers
and take care of sheep
they have stolen.
3 They cheat orphans and widows
by taking their donkeys
and oxen.
4 The poor are trampled
and forced to hide
5 in the desert,
where they and their children
must live like wild donkeys
and search for food.
6 If they want grain or grapes,[z]
they must go to the property
of these sinners.
7 They sleep naked in the cold,
because they have no cover,
8 and during a storm
their only shelters are caves
among the rocky cliffs.

9 Children whose fathers have died
are taken from their mothers
as payment for a debt.
10 Then they are forced to work
naked in the grain fields
because they have no clothes,
and they go hungry.
11 They crush olives to make oil
and grapes to make wine—
but still they go thirsty.
12 And along the city streets,
the wounded and dying cry out,
yet God does nothing.

Some Reject the Light

13 Some rebel and refuse
to follow the light.
14 Soon after sunset they murder
the poor and the needy,
and at night they steal.

[w]**22.30** *God*: One possible meaning for the difficult Hebrew text of verses 29, 30.
[x]**23.12** *treasured his teachings*: One possible meaning for the difficult Hebrew text.
[y]**23.17** *silent*: One possible meaning for the difficult Hebrew text of verse 17. [z]**24.6** *If they want grain or grapes*: Poor people were allowed to gather what was left in the fields and vineyards after the harvest.

15 Others wait for the dark,
thinking they won't be seen
if they sleep with the wife
or husband of someone else.
16 Robbers hide during the day,
then break in after dark
because they reject the light.
17 They prefer night to day,
since the terrors of the night
are their friends.

Sinners Are Filthy Foam

18 Those sinners are filthy foam
on the surface of the water.
And so, their fields and vineyards
will fall under a curse
and won't produce.
19 Just as the heat of summer
swallows the snow,
the world of the dead
swallows those who sin.
20 Forgotten here on earth,
and with their power broken,
they taste sweet to worms.

21 Sinners take advantage of widows
and other helpless women.[a]
22 But God's mighty strength
destroys those in power.
Even if they seem successful,
they are doomed to fail.
23 God may let them feel secure,
but they are never
out of his sight.
24 Great for a while; gone forever!
Sinners are mowed down
like weeds,
then they wither and die.
25 If I haven't spoken the truth,
then prove me wrong.

Bildad's Third Speech

God Is the One To Fear

25 Bildad from Shuah[b] said:
2 God is the one to fear,
because God is in control
and rules the heavens.
3 Who can count his army of stars?
Isn't God the source of light?
4 How can anyone be innocent
in the sight of God?
5 To him, not even the light
of the moon and stars
can ever be pure.
6 So how can we humans,
when we are merely worms?

Job's Reply to Bildad

You Have Really Been Helpful

26 Job said:
2 You have really been helpful
to someone weak and weary.
3 You have given great advice
and wonderful wisdom
to someone truly in need.
4 How can anyone possibly speak
with such understanding?

5 Remember the terrible trembling
of those in the world of the dead
below the mighty ocean.
6 Nothing in that land
of death and destruction
is hidden from God,
7 who hung the northern sky
and suspended the earth
on empty space.
8 God stores water in clouds,
but they don't burst,
9 and he wraps them around
the face of the moon.
10 On the surface of the ocean,
God has drawn a boundary line
between light and darkness.
11 And columns supporting the sky
tremble at his command.

12 By his power and wisdom,
God conquered the force
of the mighty ocean.[c]
13 The heavens became bright
when he breathed,
and the escaping sea monster[d]
died at the hands of God.

[a]**24.21** *women*: One possible meaning for the difficult Hebrew text of verse 21. [b]**25.1** *Shuah*: See the note at 2.11. [c]**26.12** *the force of the mighty ocean*: The Hebrew text has "the ocean . . . Rahab." In this passage the sea monster Rahab stands for the fearsome power of the ocean (see the notes at 3.8 and 9.13). [d]**26.13** *sea monster*: The Hebrew text has "snake," which probably stands for some kind of fearsome sea monster, such as Leviathan (see Isaiah 27.1).

14 These things are merely a whisper
of God's power at work.
How little we would understand
if this whisper
ever turned into thunder!

Job Continues

I Am Desperate

27 Job said:
2 I am desperate because
God All-Powerful refuses
to do what is right.
As surely as God lives,
3 and while he gives me breath,
4 I will tell only the truth.
5 Until the day I die,
I will refuse to do wrong
by saying you are right,
6 because each day my conscience
agrees that I am innocent.

7 I pray that my enemies
will suffer no less
than the wicked.
8 Such people are hopeless,
and God All-Powerful
will cut them down,
9 without listening
when they beg for mercy.
10 And that is what God should do,
because they don't like him
or ever pray.
11 Now I will explain in detail
what God All-Powerful does.
12 All of you have seen these things
for yourselves.
So you have no excuse.

How God Treats the Wicked

13 Here is how God All-Powerful
treats those who are wicked
and brutal.
14 They may have many children,
but most of them will go hungry
or suffer a violent death.
15 Others will die of disease,
and their widows
won't be able to weep.
16 The wicked may collect riches
and clothes in abundance
as easily as clay.
17 But God's people will wear
clothes taken from them
and divide up their riches.
18 No homes built by the wicked
will outlast a cocoon
or a shack.
19 Those sinners may go to bed rich,
but they will wake up poor.[e]
20 Terror will strike at night
like a flood or a storm.
21 Then a scorching wind
will sweep them away
22 without showing mercy,
as they try to escape.
23 At last, the wind will celebrate
because they are gone.

Job Continues

Gold and Silver Are Mined

28 Gold and silver are mined,
then purified;
2 the same is done
with iron and copper.
3 Miners carry lanterns
deep into the darkness
to search for these metals.
4 They dig tunnels
in distant, unknown places,
where they dangle by ropes.
5 Far beneath the grain fields,
fires are built
to break loose those rocks
6 that have jewels or gold.[f]

7 Miners go to places unseen
by the eyes of hawks;
8 they walk on soil unknown
to the proudest lions.
9 With their own hands
they remove sharp rocks
and uproot mountains.
10 They dig through the rocks
in search of jewels
and precious metals.
11 They also uncover
the sources of[g] rivers
and discover secret places.

[e]**27.19** *poor*: Or "dead." [f]**28.6** *gold*: One possible meaning for the difficult Hebrew text of verses 5, 6. [g]**28.11** *uncover the sources of*: Two ancient translations; Hebrew "dam up."

Where Is Wisdom Found?

12 But where is wisdom found?
13 No human knows the way.[h]
14 Nor can it be discovered
in the deepest sea.
*15 It is worth much more
than silver or pure gold
16 or precious stones.
17 Nothing is its equal—
not gold or costly glass.[i]
18 Wisdom is worth much more than
coral, jasper,[j] or rubies.
19 All the topaz[k] of Ethiopia[l]
and the finest gold
cannot compare with it.
20 Where then is wisdom?
21 It is hidden from human eyes
and even from birds.
22 Death and destruction
have merely heard rumors
about where it is found.
23 God is the only one who knows
the way to wisdom,
24 because he sees everything
beneath the heavens.
25 When God divided out
the wind and the water,
26 and when he decided the path
for rain and lightning,
27 he also determined the truth
and defined wisdom.
28 God told us, "Wisdom means
that you respect me, the Lord,
and turn from sin."

Job Continues

I Long for the Past

29 Job said:
2 I long for the past,
when God took care of me,
3 and the light from his lamp
showed me the way
through the dark.
4 I was in the prime of life,
God All-Powerful
was my closest friend,
5 and all of my children
were nearby.
6 My herds gave enough milk
to bathe my feet,
and from my olive harvest
flowed rivers of oil.
*7 When I sat down at the meeting
of the city council,
8 the young leaders stepped aside,
*9 while the older ones stood
10 and remained silent.

Everyone Was Pleased

11 Everyone was pleased
with what I said and did.
12 When poor people or orphans
cried out for help,
I came to their rescue.
13 And I was highly praised
for my generosity to widows
and others in poverty.
14 Kindness and justice
were my coat and hat;
15 I was good to the blind
and to the lame.
16 I was a father to the needy,
and I defended them in court,
even if they were strangers.
17 When criminals attacked,
I broke their teeth
and set their victims free.

18 I felt certain that I would live
a long and happy life,
then die in my own bed.
19 In those days I was strong
like a tree with deep roots
and with plenty of water,
20 or like an archer's new bow.
21 Everyone listened in silence
to my welcome advice,
22 and when I finished speaking,
nothing needed to be said.

[h]**28.13** *the way*: Or "its worth." [i]**28.17** *costly glass*: In the ancient world, objects made of glass were costly. [j]**28.18** *jasper*: A valuable stone, usually green or clear. [k]**28.19** *topaz*: A valuable, yellow stone. [l]**28.19** *Ethiopia*: The Hebrew text has "Cush," which was a region south of Egypt that included parts of the present countries of Ethiopia and Sudan.

28.12 Si 1.6; Ba 3.15. **28.13** Ba 3.29-31. **28.23** Ba 3.35-37. **28.27** Si 1.9, 19. **28.28** Ps 111.10; Pr 1.7; 9.10.

23 My words were eagerly accepted
like the showers of spring,
24 and the smile on my face
renewed everyone's hopes.
25 My advice was followed
as though I were a king
leading my troops,
or someone comforting
those in sorrow.

Job Continues

Young People Now Insult Me

30 Young people now insult me,
although their fathers
would have been a disgrace
to my sheep dogs.
2 And those who insult me
are helpless themselves.
3 They must claw the desert sand
in the dark for something
to satisfy their hunger.[m]
4 They gather tasteless shrubs
for food and firewood,
5 and they are run out of towns,
as though they were thieves.
6 Their only homes are ditches
or holes between rocks,
7 where they bray like donkeys
gathering around shrubs.
8 And like senseless donkeys
they are chased away.

Those Worthless Nobodies

9 Those worthless nobodies
make up jokes and songs
to disgrace me.
10 They are hateful
and keep their distance,
even while spitting
in my direction.
11 God has destroyed me,
and so they don't care
what they do.[n]
12 Their attacks never stop,
though I am defenseless,
and my feet are trapped.[o]
13 Without any help,
they prevent my escape,
destroying me completely[p]
14 and leaving me crushed.
15 Terror has me surrounded;
my reputation and my riches
have vanished like a cloud.

I Am Sick at Heart

16 I am sick at heart!
Pain has taken its toll.
17 Night chews on my bones,
causing endless torment,
18 and God has shrunk my skin,
choking me to death.
19 I have been thrown in the dirt
and now am dirt myself.
20 I beg God for help,
but there is no answer;
and when I stand up,
he simply stares.
21 God has turned brutal,
22 stirring up a windstorm
to toss me about.
23 Soon he will send me home
to the world of the dead,
where we all must go.

24 No one refuses help to others,
when disaster strikes.[q]
25 I mourned for the poor
and those who suffered.
26 But when I beg for relief
and light,
all I receive are disaster
and darkness.
27 My stomach is tied in knots;
pain is my daily companion.
28 Suffering has scorched my skin,
and in the city council
I stand and cry out,
29 making mournful sounds
like jackals[r] and owls.
30 My skin is so parched,
that it peels right off,
and my bones are burning.

[m] **30.3** *hunger*: One possible meaning for the difficult Hebrew text of verse 3. [n] **30.11** *God . . . do*: Or "They have destroyed me, and so they don't care what else they do." [o] **30.12** *trapped*: One possible meaning for the difficult Hebrew text of verse 12. [p] **30.13** *destroying . . . completely*: One possible meaning for the difficult Hebrew text. [q] **30.24** *strikes*: One possible meaning for the difficult Hebrew text of verse 24. [r] **30.29** *jackals*: Desert animals related to wolves, but smaller.

31 My only songs are sorrow
and sadness.

Job Continues

I Promised Myself

31 I promised myself
never to stare with desire
at a young woman.
2 God All-Powerful punishes
men who do that.
3 In fact, God sends disaster
on all who sin,
4 and he keeps a close watch
on everything I do.

5 I am not dishonest or deceitful,
6 and I beg God to prove
my innocence.
7 If I have disobeyed him
or even wanted to,
8 then others can eat my harvest
and uproot my crops.
9 If I have desired someone's wife
and chased after her,
10 then let some stranger
steal my wife from me.
11 If I took someone's wife,
it would be a horrible crime,
12 sending me to destruction
and my crops to the flames.[s]

13 When my servants
complained against me,
I was fair to them.
14 Otherwise, what answer
would I give to God
when he judges me?
15 After all, God is the one
who gave life to each of us
before we were born.

I Have Never Cheated Anyone

16 I have never cheated widows
or others in need,
17 and I have always shared
my food with orphans.
18 Since the time I was young,
I have cared for orphans
and helped widows.[t]
19 I provided clothes for the poor,
20 and I was praised
for supplying woolen garments
to keep them warm.
21 If I have ever raised my arm
to threaten an orphan
when the power was mine,
22 I hope that arm will fall
from its socket.
23 I could not have been abusive;
I was terrified at the thought
that God might punish me.
24 I have never trusted
the power of wealth,
25 or taken pride in owning
many possessions.
*26 I have never openly or secretly
27 worshiped the sun or moon.
28 Such horrible sins
would have deserved
punishment from God.
29 I have never laughed
when my enemies
were struck by disaster.
30 Neither have I sinned
by asking God
to send down on them
the curse of death.
31 No one ever went hungry[u]
at my house,
32 and travelers
were always welcome.
33 Many have attempted to hide
their sins from others—
but I refused.
34 And the fear of public disgrace
never forced me to keep silent
about what I had done.

Why Doesn't God Listen?

35 Why doesn't God All-Powerful
listen and answer?
If God has something against me,
let him speak up
or put it in writing!
36 Then I would wear his charges
on my clothes and forehead.
37 And with my head held high,

[s] **31.12** *flames*: One possible meaning for the difficult Hebrew text of verse 12. [t] **31.18** *widows*: One possible meaning for the difficult Hebrew text of verse 18. [u] **31.31** *ever went hungry*: Or "was ever sexually abused" (see Genesis 19.1-11; Judges 17.22-30). In ancient Israel, the lives of one's guests were sacred and had to be protected at any cost.

31.16-18 Tb 4.7-11, 16. **31.24** Si 31.5-10.

I would tell him everything
I have ever done.

38 I have never mistreated
the land I farmed
and made it mourn.[v]
39 Nor have I cheated
my workers
and caused them pain.[w]
40 If I had, I would pray
for weeds instead of wheat
to grow in my fields.
After saying these things,
Job was silent.

Elihu Is Upset with Job's Friends

32 Finally, these three men stopped arguing with Job, because he refused to admit that he was guilty.
2 Elihu from Buz[x] was there, and he had become upset with Job for blaming God instead of himself. 3 He was also angry with Job's three friends for not being able to prove that Job was wrong. 4 Elihu was younger than these three, and he let them speak first. 5 But he became irritated when they could not answer Job, 6 and he said to them:

I am much younger than you,
so I have shown respect
by keeping silent.
7 I once believed age
was the source of wisdom;
8 now I truly realize
wisdom comes from God.
9 Age is no guarantee of wisdom
and understanding.
10 That's why I ask you
to listen to me.

I Eagerly Listened

*11 I eagerly listened
to each of your arguments,
12 but not one of you proved
Job to be wrong.
13 You shouldn't say,
"We know what's right!
Let God punish him."
14 Job hasn't spoken against me,
and so I won't answer him
with your arguments.

15 All of you are shocked;
you don't know what to say.
16 But am I to remain silent,
just because you
have stopped speaking?
17 No! I will give my opinion,
18 because I have so much to say,
that I can't keep quiet.
19 I am like a swollen wineskin,
and I will burst[y]
20 if I don't speak.
*21 I don't know how to be unfair
or to flatter anyone—
22 if I did, my Creator
would quickly destroy me!

Elihu Speaks

Job, Listen to Me!

33 Job, listen to me!
Pay close attention.
*2 Everything I will say
3 is true and sincere,
4 just as surely as the Spirit
of God All-Powerful[z]
gave me the breath of life.
5 Now line up your arguments
and prepare to face me.
6 We each were made from clay,
and God has no favorites,
7 so don't be afraid of me
or what I might do.

I Have Heard You Argue

8 I have heard you argue
9 that you are innocent,
guilty of nothing.

[v]**31.38** *mourn*: In biblical times there were strict regulations for proper use of the land, and land that was abused was said to "mourn" and become no longer productive. [w]**31.39** *pain*: One possible meaning for the difficult Hebrew text of verse 39. [x]**32.2** *Elihu from Buz*: The Hebrew text has "Elihu son of Barachel from Buz of the family of Ram." Buz may have been somewhere in the territory of Edom; in Jeremiah 25.23 it is mentioned along with Dedan and Tema (see 6.19). [y]**32.19** *swollen wineskin . . . burst*: While the juice from grapes was becoming wine, it would swell and stretch the skins in which it had been stored; sometimes the swelling would burst the wineskins. [z]**33.4** *the Spirit of God All-Powerful*: Or "God All-Powerful."

10 You claim that God
has made you his enemy,
11 that he has bound your feet
and blocked your path.
12 But, Job, you're wrong—
God is greater
than any human.
13 So why do you challenge God
to answer you?[a]
14 God speaks in different ways,
and we don't always
recognize his voice.
*15 Sometimes in the night,
he uses terrifying dreams
16 to give us warnings.
17 God does this to make us turn
from sin and pride
18 and to protect us
from being swept away
to the world of the dead.

19 Sometimes we are punished
with a serious illness
and aching joints.
20 Merely the thought
of our favorite food
makes our stomachs sick,
21 and we become so skinny
that our bones stick out.
22 We feel death and the grave
taking us in their grip.

23 One of a thousand angels
then comes to our rescue
by saying we are innocent.
24 The angel shows kindness,
commanding death to release us,
because the price was paid.
25 Our health is restored,
we feel young again,
26 and we ask God to accept us.
Then we joyfully worship God,
and we are rewarded
because we are innocent.
27 When that happens,
we tell everyone,
"I sinned and did wrong,
but God forgave me
28 and rescued me from death!
Now I will see the light."
29 God gives each of us
chance after chance
30 to be saved from death
and brought into the light
that gives life.
31 So, Job, pay attention
and don't interrupt,
32 though I would gladly listen
to anything you say
that proves you are right.
33 Otherwise, listen in silence
to my wisdom.

Elihu Continues

You Men Think You Are Wise

34 Elihu said:
2 You men think you are wise,
but just listen to me!
3 Think about my words,
as you would taste food.
4 Then we can decide the case
and give a just verdict.
5 Job claims he is innocent
and God is guilty
of mistreating him.
6 Job also argues that God
considers him a liar
and that he is suffering severely
in spite of his innocence.
7 But to tell the truth,
Job is shameless!
8 He spends his time with sinners,
9 because he has said,
"It doesn't pay to please God."

If Any of You Are Smart

10 If any of you are smart,
you will listen and learn
that God All-Powerful
does what is right.
11 God always treats everyone
the way they deserve,
12 and he is never unfair.
13 From the very beginning,
God has been in control
of all the world.

14 If God took back the breath
that he breathed into us,

[a]**33.13** *answer you*: One possible meaning for the difficult Hebrew text of verse 13.
33.11 Job 13.27. **33.15** Job 4.13. **34.11** Ps 62.12.

15 we humans would die
and return to the soil.
16 So be smart and listen!
17 The mighty God is the one
who brings about justice,
and you are condemning him.
18 Indeed, God is the one
who condemns unfair rulers.
19 And God created us all;
he has no favorites,
whether rich or poor.
20 Even powerful rulers die
in the darkness of night
when they least expect it,
just like the rest of us.

God Watches Everything We Do

21 God watches everything we do.
22 No evil person can hide
in the deepest darkness.
23 And so, God doesn't need
to set a time for judgment.
24 Without asking for advice,
God removes mighty leaders
and puts others in their place.
25 He knows what they are like,
and he wipes them out
in the middle of the night.
26 And while others look on,
he punishes them
because they were evil
27 and refused to obey him.
28 The persons they mistreated
had prayed for help,
until God answered
their prayers.
29 When God does nothing,
can any person or nation
find fault with him?
30 But still, he punishes rulers
who abuse their people.[b]

31 Job, you should tell God
that you are guilty
and promise to do better.
32 Then ask him to point out
what you did wrong,
so you won't do it again.
33 Do you make the rules,
or does God?
You have to decide—
I can't do it for you;
now make up your mind.
34 Job, anyone with good sense
can easily see
35 that you are speaking nonsense
and lack good judgment.
36 So I pray for you to suffer
as much as possible
for talking like a sinner.
37 You have rebelled against God,
time after time,
and have even insulted us.

Elihu Continues

Are You Really Innocent?

35 Elihu said:
2 Job, are you really innocent
in the sight of God?[c]
3 Don't you honestly believe
it pays to obey him?
4 I will give the answers
to you and your friends.
*5 Look up to the heavens
6 and think!
Do your sins hurt God?
7 Is any good you may have done
at all helpful to him?
8 The evil or good you do
only affects other humans.

9 In times of trouble,
everyone begs the mighty God
to have mercy.
10 But after their Creator
helps them through hard times,
they forget about him,
11 though he makes us wiser
than animals or birds.
12 God won't listen to the prayers
of proud and evil people.
13 If God All-Powerful refuses
to answer their empty prayers,
14 he will surely deny
your impatient request
to face him in court.

[b]**34.30** *people*: One possible meaning for the difficult Hebrew text of verses 29, 30.
[c]**35.2** *are . . . God*: Or "is it right for you to accuse God?"
35.6-8 Job 22.2, 3.

15 Job, you were wrong to say
God doesn't punish sin.
16 Everything you have said
adds up to nonsense.

Elihu Continues

Be Patient a While Longer

36 Elihu said:
2 Be patient a while longer;
I have something else to say
in God's defense.
3 God always does right—
and this knowledge
comes straight from God.[d]
4 You can rest assured
that what I say is true.
5 Although God is mighty,
he cares about everyone
and makes fair decisions.

6 The wicked are cut down,
and those who are wronged
receive justice.
7 God watches over good people
and places them in positions
of power and honor forever.
8 But when people are prisoners
of suffering and pain,
*9 God points out their sin
and their pride,
10 then he warns them
to turn back to him.
11 And if they obey,
they will be successful
and happy from then on.
12 But if they foolishly refuse,
they will be rewarded
with a violent death.

Godless People Are Too Angry

13 Godless people are too angry
to ask God for help
when he punishes them.
14 So they die young
in shameful disgrace.
15 Hard times and trouble
are God's way
of getting our attention!
16 And at this very moment,
God deeply desires
to lead you from trouble
and to spread your table
with your favorite food.

17 Now that the judgment
for your sins
has fallen upon you,
18 don't let your anger
and the pain you endured
make you sneer at God.
19 Your reputation and riches
cannot protect you
from distress,
20 nor can you find safety
in the dark world below.[e]
21 Be on guard! Don't turn to evil
as a way of escape.
22 God's power is unlimited.
He needs no teachers
23 to guide or correct him.

Others Have Praised God

24 Others have praised God
for what he has done,
so join with them.
25 From down here on earth,
everyone has looked up and seen
26 how great God is—
God is more than we imagine;
no one can count the years
he has lived.
*27 God gathers moisture
into the clouds
28 and supplies us with rain.
29 Who can understand
how God scatters the clouds
and speaks from his home
in the thunderstorm?
30 And when God sends lightning,
it can be seen
at the bottom of the sea.
31 By producing such rainstorms,
God rules the world
and provides us with food.
32 Each flash of lightning
is one of his arrows
striking its target,

[d]36.3 *comes straight from God*: The Hebrew text has "comes from a distant place," which refers to the place where God lives; Elihu is claiming that he learned this from God. [e]36.20 *below*: One possible meaning for the difficult Hebrew text of verses 18-20.

33 and the thunder tells
of his anger against sin.[f]

Elihu Continues

I Am Frightened

37 I am frightened
and tremble all over,
2 when I hear the roaring voice
of God in the thunder,
3 and when I see his lightning
flash across the sky.
4 God's majestic voice
thunders his commands,[g]
5 creating miracles too marvelous
for us to understand.
6 Snow and heavy rainstorms
7 make us stop and think
about God's power,
8 and they force animals
to seek shelter.
9 The windstorms of winter strike,
10 and the breath of God
freezes streams and rivers.
11 Rain clouds filled with lightning
appear at God's command,
12 traveling across the sky
13 to release their cargo—
sometimes as punishment for sin,
sometimes as kindness.

Consider Carefully

14 Job, consider carefully
the many wonders of God.
15 Can you explain why lightning
flashes at the orders
16 of God who knows all things?
Or how he hangs the clouds
in empty space?
17 You almost melt in the heat
of fierce desert winds
when the sky is like brass.
18 God can spread out the clouds
to get relief from the heat,
but can you?

19 Tell us what to say to God!
Our minds are in the dark,
and we don't know how
to argue our case.
20 Should I risk my life
by telling God
that I want to speak?
21 No one can stare at the sun
after a breeze has blown
the clouds from the sky.
22 Yet the glorious splendor
of God All-Powerful
is brighter by far.
23 God cannot be seen—
but his power is great,
and he is always fair.
24 And so we humans fear God,
because he shows no respect
for those who are proud
and think they know so much.

The LORD Speaks

From Out of a Storm

38 From out of a storm,
the LORD said to Job:
2 Why do you talk so much
when you know so little?
3 Now get ready to face me!
Can you answer
the questions I ask?
4 How did I lay the foundation
for the earth?
Were you there?
5 Doubtless you know who decided
its length and width.
6 What supports the foundation?
Who placed the cornerstone,
7 while morning stars sang,
and angels rejoiced?

8 When the ocean was born,
I set its boundaries
9 and wrapped it in blankets
of thickest fog.
10 Then I built a wall around it,
locked the gates, 11 and said,
"Your powerful waves stop here!
They can go no farther."

Did You Ever Tell the Sun To Rise?

12 Did you ever tell the sun to rise?
And did it obey?

[f]**36.33** *sin*: One possible meaning for the difficult Hebrew text of verse 33. [g]**37.4** *commands*: One possible meaning for the difficult Hebrew text of verse 4.
38.7 Ba 3.34. **38.8-11** Jr 5.22.

13 Did it take hold of the earth
and shake out the wicked
like dust from a rug?
14 Early dawn outlines the hills
like stitches on clothing
or sketches on clay.
15 But its light is too much
for those who are evil,
and their power is broken.

16 Job, have you ever walked
on the ocean floor?
17 Have you seen the gate
to the world of the dead?
18 And how large is the earth?
Tell me, if you know!

19 Where is the home of light,
and where does darkness live?
20 Can you lead them home?
21 I'm certain you must be able to,
since you were already born
when I created everything.

22 Have you been to the places
where I keep snow and hail,
23 until I use them to punish
and conquer nations?
24 From where does lightning leap,
or the east wind blow?
25 Who carves out a path
for thunderstorms?
Who sends torrents of rain
26 on empty deserts
where no one lives?
27 Rain that changes barren land
to meadows green with grass.
28 Who is the father of the dew
and of the rain?
29 Who gives birth to the sleet
and the frost
30 that fall in winter,
when streams and lakes
freeze solid as a rock?

Can You Arrange Stars?

31 Can you arrange stars in groups
such as Orion
and the Pleiades?
32 Do you control the stars
or set in place the Big Dipper
and the Little Dipper?
33 Do you know the laws
that govern the heavens,
and can you make them rule
the earth?
34 Can you order the clouds
to send a downpour,
35 or will lightning flash
at your command?
36 Did you teach birds to know
that rain or floods
are on their way?[h]
37 Can you count the clouds
or pour out their water
38 on the dry, lumpy soil?

39 When lions are hungry,
do you help them hunt?
40 Do you send an animal
into their den?
41 And when starving young ravens
cry out to me for food,
do you satisfy their hunger?

The LORD Continues

When Do Mountain Goats Give Birth?

39 When do mountain goats
and deer give birth?
Have you been there
when their young are born?
*2 How long are they pregnant
3 before they deliver?
4 Soon their young grow strong
and then leave
to be on their own.

5 Who set wild donkeys free?
6 I alone help them survive
in salty desert sand.
7 They stay far from crowded cities
and refuse to be tamed.
8 Instead, they roam the hills,
searching for pastureland.

9 Would a wild ox agree
to live in your barn
and labor for you?

[h]**38.36** *way*: One possible meaning for the difficult Hebrew text of verse 36.
38.31 Job 9.9; Am 5.8.

10 Could you force him to plow
or to drag a heavy log
to smooth out the soil?
11 Can you depend on him
to use his great strength
and do your heavy work?
12 Can you trust him
to harvest your grain
or take it to your barn
from the threshing place?

An Ostrich Proudly Flaps Her Wings

13 An ostrich proudly
flaps her wings,
but not because
she loves her young.
14 She abandons her eggs
and lets the dusty ground
keep them warm.
15 And she doesn't seem to worry
that the feet of an animal
could crush them all.
16 She treats her eggs as though
they were not her own,
unconcerned that her work
might be for nothing.
17 I myself made her foolish
and without common sense.
18 But once she starts running,[i]
she laughs at a rider
on the fastest horse.

Did You Give Horses Their Strength?

19 Did you give horses their strength
and the flowing hair
along their necks?
20 Did you make them able
to jump like grasshoppers
or to frighten people
with their snorting?

21 Before horses are ridden
into battle,
they paw at the ground,
proud of their strength.
22 Laughing at fear, they rush
toward the fighting,
23 while the weapons of their riders
rattle and flash in the sun.
24 Unable to stand still,
they gallop eagerly into battle
when trumpets blast.
25 Stirred by the distant smells
and sounds of war, they snort
in reply to the trumpet.

26 Did you teach hawks to fly south
for the winter?
*27 Did you train eagles[j] to build
28 their nests on rocky cliffs,
29 where they can look down
to spot their next meal?
30 Then their young gather to feast
wherever the victim lies.

The LORD Continues

I Am the LORD All-Powerful

40 *1 I am the LORD All-Powerful,
2 but you have argued
that I am wrong.
Now you must answer me.

3 Job said to the LORD:
4 Who am I to answer you?
5 I did speak once or twice,
but never again.

6 Then out of the storm
the LORD said to Job:
7 Face me and answer
the questions I ask!
8 Are you trying to prove
that you are innocent
by accusing me of injustice?
9 Do you have a powerful arm
and a thundering voice
that compare with mine?
10 If so, then surround yourself
with glory and majesty.
*11 Show your furious anger!
Throw down and crush
12 all who are proud and evil.
13 Wrap them in grave clothes
and bury them together
in the dusty soil.
14 Do this, and I will agree
that you have won
this argument.

[i]**39.18** *starts running*: One possible meaning for the difficult Hebrew text. [j]**39.27** *eagles*: Or "vultures."
39.30 Mt 24.28; Lk 17.37.

I Created You

15 I created both you
and the hippopotamus.[k]
It eats only grass like an ox,
16 but look at the mighty muscles
in its body 17 and legs.
Its tail is like a cedar tree,
and its thighs are thick.
18 The bones in its legs
are like bronze or iron.

19 I made it more powerful
than any other creature,
yet I am stronger still.
20 Undisturbed, it eats grass
while the other animals
play nearby.[l]
*21 It rests in the shade of trees
along the riverbank
22 or hides among reeds
in the swamp.
23 It remains calm and unafraid
with the Jordan River rushing
and splashing in its face.
24 There is no way to capture
a hippopotamus—
not even by hooking its nose
or blinding its eyes.

The LORD Continues

Can You Catch a Sea Monster?

41 Can you catch a sea monster[m]
by using a fishhook?
Can you tie its mouth shut
with a rope?
2 Can it be led around
by a ring in its nose
or a hook in its jaw?
3 Will it beg for mercy?
4 Will it surrender
as a slave for life?
5 Can it be tied by the leg
like a pet bird
for little girls?
6 Is it ever chopped up
and its pieces bargained for
in the fish-market?
7 Can it be killed
with harpoons or spears?
8 Wrestle it just once—
that will be the end.
9 Merely a glimpse of this monster
makes all courage melt.
10 And if it is too fierce
for anyone to attack,
who would dare oppose me?
11 I am in command of the world
and in debt to no one.

12 What powerful legs,
what a stout body
this monster possesses!
13 Who could strip off its armor
or bring it under control
with a harness?
14 Who would try to open its jaws,
full of fearsome teeth?
*15 Its back[n] is covered
with shield after shield,
16 firmly bound and closer together
17 than breath to breath.

When This Monster Sneezes

18 When this monster sneezes,
lightning flashes, and its eyes
glow like the dawn.
19 Sparks and fiery flames
explode from its mouth.
20 And smoke spews from its nose
like steam
from a boiling pot,
21 while its blazing breath
scorches everything in sight.

22 Its neck is so tremendous
that everyone trembles,
23 the weakest parts of its body
are harder than iron,
24 and its heart is stone.

[k] **40.15** *the hippopotamus*: The Hebrew text has "Behemoth," which was sometimes understood to be a sea monster like Rahab (9.13; 26.12), Leviathan (3.8; 41.1), and Tannin (7.12).
[l] **40.20** *nearby*: One possible meaning for the difficult Hebrew text of verse 20. [m] **41.1** *sea monster*: The Hebrew text has "Leviathan," which may refer to a sea monster or possibly to a crocodile in this verse (see the note at 3.8). [n] **41.15** *back*: Two ancient translations; Hebrew "pride."
41.1 Ps 74.14; 104.26; Is 27.1.

The Israelite servant girl with Naaman's wife

2 Kings 5.1 - 16

Esther and King Xerxes *Esther 5.1-2*

25 When this noisy monster appears,
even the most powerful[o]
turn and run in fear.
26 No sword or spear can harm it,
27 and weapons of bronze or iron
are as useless as straw
or rotten wood.
28 Rocks thrown from a sling
cause it no more harm
than husks of grain.
This monster fears no arrows,
29 it simply smiles at spears,
and striking it with a stick
is like slapping it with straw.

30 As it crawls through the mud,
its sharp and spiny hide
tears the ground apart.
31 And when it swims down deep,
the sea starts churning
like boiling oil,
32 and it leaves behind a trail
of shining white foam.
33 No other creature on earth
is so fearless.
34 It is king of all proud creatures,
and it looks upon the others
as nothing.

Job's Reply to the LORD

No One Can Oppose You

42 Job said:
2 No one can oppose you,
because you have the power
to do what you want.
3 You asked why I talk so much
when I know so little.
I have talked about things
that are far beyond
my understanding.
4 You told me to listen
and answer your questions.[p]
5 I heard about you from others;
now I have seen you
with my own eyes.
6 That's why I hate myself
and sit here in dust and ashes
to show my sorrow.

The LORD Corrects Job's Friends

7 The LORD said to Eliphaz:
What my servant Job has said about
me is true, but I am angry at you and
your two friends for not telling the
truth. 8 So I want you to go over to Job
and offer seven bulls and seven goats
on an altar as a sacrifice to please me.[q]
After this, Job will pray, and I will
agree not to punish you for your foolishness.
9 Eliphaz, Bildad, and Zophar obeyed
the LORD, and he answered Job's prayer.

A Happy Ending

10 After Job had prayed for his three
friends, the LORD made Job twice as rich as
he had been before. 11 Then Job gave a
feast for his brothers and sisters and for his
old friends. They expressed their sorrow for
the suffering the LORD had brought on him,
and they each gave Job some silver and a
gold ring.
12 The LORD now blessed Job more than
ever; he gave him fourteen thousand
sheep, six thousand camels, a thousand
pair of oxen, and a thousand donkeys.
13 In addition to seven sons, Job had
three daughters, 14 whose names were
Jemimah, Keziah, and Keren Happuch.
15 They were the most beautiful women in
that part of the world, and Job gave them
shares of his property, along with their
brothers.
16 Job lived for another one hundred
forty years—long enough to see his great-
grandchildren have children of their own—
17 and when he finally died, he was very old.

[o]**41.25** *most powerful*: Or "gods." [p]**42.4** *questions*: One possible meaning for the difficult Hebrew text of verse 4. [q]**42.8** *sacrifice to please me*: These sacrifices have traditionally been called "whole burnt offerings" because the whole animal was burned on the altar. A main purpose of such sacrifices was to please the LORD with the smell of the sacrifice, and so in the CEV they are often called "sacrifices to please the LORD."

42.3 Job 38.2. **42.4** Job 38.3. **42.10** Job 1.1-3.

PSALMS

ABOUT THIS BOOK

The book of Psalms is the longest book in the Bible. Psalms are poems that can either be sung as songs or spoken as prayers by individuals or groups. There are 150 psalms in this book, and many of them list King David as their author. They were collected over a long period of time and became a very important part of the worship of the people of Israel.

Some of the psalms tell the music leader what instruments should be used and what tunes should be followed. For example, look at Psalm 4 and Psalm 45.

Many of the Bible's main ideas are echoed in the Psalms: praise, thankfulness, faith, hope, sorrow for sin, God's loyalty and help. And at the heart of all the psalms there is a deep trust in God. The writers of the psalms always express their true feelings, whether they are praising God for his blessings or complaining in times of trouble.

In ancient Israel the psalms were used in several different ways: (1) to praise God, as in Psalm 105; (2) to express sorrow, as in Psalm 13; (3) to teach, as in Psalm 1; (4) to honor Israel's king and pray for fairness in his rule, as in Psalm 72; (5) to tell of God's power over all creation, as in Psalm 47; (6) to show love for Jerusalem, as in Psalm 122; and (7) to celebrate festivals, as in Psalm 126. Of course, many of the psalms could be used for more than one purpose.

Jesus used the psalms when he preached and taught, and they were often quoted by the writers of the New Testament. The earliest Christians also used the psalms in worship, teaching, and telling others the good news about what God has done through Jesus Christ. A verse from Psalm 118, for example, is directly referred to six times in the New Testament:

The stone that the builders
tossed aside
has now become
the most important stone.
(118.22)

A QUICK LOOK AT THIS BOOK

The book of Psalms is divided into five sections or "books." Most of the psalms in Books I and II were written by David, while many in Book III were written by either Asaph or the people of Korah. Psalms 120–134 are all "celebration psalms." The five sections of the book of Psalms are:

- Book I (1–41)
- Book II (42–72)
- Book III (73–89)
- Book IV (90–106)
- Book V (107–150)

BOOK I
(Psalms 1–41)

Psalm 1

The Way to Happiness

1 God blesses those people
who refuse evil advice
and won't follow sinners
or join in sneering at God.
2 Instead, the Law of the LORD
makes them happy,
and they think about it
day and night.

3 They are like trees
growing beside a stream,
trees that produce
fruit in season
and always have leaves.
Those people succeed
in everything they do.

4 That isn't true of those
who are evil,
because they are like straw
blown by the wind.
5 Sinners won't have an excuse
on the day of judgment,
and they won't have a place
with the people of God.
6 The LORD protects everyone
who follows him,
but the wicked follow a road
that leads to ruin.

Psalm 2

The LORD's Chosen King

1 Why do the nations plot,[a]
and why do their people
make useless plans?[b]
2 The kings of this earth
have all joined together
to turn against the LORD
and his chosen one.
3 They say, "Let's cut the ropes
and set ourselves free!"
4 In heaven the LORD laughs
as he sits on his throne,
making fun of the nations.
5 The LORD becomes furious
and threatens them.
His anger terrifies them
as he says,
6 "I've put my king on Zion,
my sacred hill."

7 I will tell the promise
that the LORD made to me:
"You are my son, because today
I have become your father.
8 Ask me for the nations,
and every nation on earth
will belong to you.
9 You will smash them
with an iron rod
and shatter them
like dishes of clay."

10 Be smart, all you rulers,
and pay close attention.
11 Serve and honor the LORD;
be glad and tremble.
12 Show respect to his son
because if you don't,
the LORD might become furious
and suddenly destroy you.[c]
But he blesses and protects
everyone who runs to him.

Psalm 3

[*Written by David when he was running from his son Absalom.*]

An Early Morning Prayer

1 I have a lot of enemies, LORD.
Many fight against 2 me and say,
"God won't rescue you!"

3 But you are my shield,
and you give me victory
and great honor.
4 I pray to you, and you answer
from your sacred hill.

[a]**2.1** *Why . . . plot*: Or "Why are the nations restless?" [b]**2.1** *make useless plans*: Or "grumble uselessly." [c]**2.11,12** *Serve . . . you*: One possible meaning for the difficult Hebrew text of verses 11, 12.

1.3 Jr 17.8. **2.1,2** Ac 4.25, 26. **2.7** Ac 13.33; He 1.5; 5.5. **2.9** Rev 2.26-28; 12.5; 19.15. **3 Title** 2 S 15.13—17.22.

5 I sleep and wake up refreshed
because you, LORD,
protect me.
6 Ten thousand enemies attack
from every side,
but I am not afraid.

7 Come and save me, LORD God!
Break my enemies' jaws
and shatter their teeth,
8 because you protect
and bless your people.

Psalm 4

[*A psalm by David for the music leader. Use stringed instruments.*]

An Evening Prayer

1 You are my God and protector.
Please answer my prayer.
I was in terrible distress,
but you set me free.
Now have pity and listen
as I pray.

2 How long will you people
refuse to respect me?[d]
You love foolish things,
and you run after
what is worthless.[e]

3 The LORD has chosen
everyone who is faithful
to be his very own,[f]
and he answers my prayers.
4 But each of you
had better tremble
and turn from your sins.
Silently search your heart
as you lie in bed.
5 Offer the proper sacrifices
and trust the LORD.

6 There are some who ask,
"Who will be good to us?"
Let your kindness, LORD,
shine brightly on us.
7 You brought me more happiness
than a rich harvest
of grain and grapes.
8 I can lie down
and sleep soundly
because you, LORD,
will keep me safe.

Psalm 5

[*A psalm by David for the music leader. Use flutes.*]

A Prayer for Help

1 Listen, LORD, as I pray!
Pay attention when I groan.[g]
2 You are my King and my God.
Answer my cry for help
because I pray to you.
3 Each morning you listen
to my prayer,
as I bring my requests[h] to you
and wait for your reply.

4 You are not the kind of God
who is pleased with evil.
Sinners can't stay with you.
5 No one who boasts can stand
in your presence, LORD,
and you hate evil people.
6 You destroy every liar,
and you despise violence
and deceit.

7 Because of your great mercy,
I come to your house, LORD,
and I am filled with wonder
as I bow down to worship
at your holy temple.
8 You do what is right,
and I ask you to guide me.
Make your teaching clear
because of my enemies.

9 Nothing they say is true!
They just want to destroy.
Their words are deceitful
like a hidden pit,
and their tongues are good
only for telling lies.

[d]**4.2** *me*: Or "my God." [e]**4.2** *foolish . . . worthless*: This may refer to idols and false gods. [f]**4.3** *has chosen . . . very own*: Some Hebrew manuscripts have "work miracles for his faithful people." [g]**5.1** *when I groan*: Or "to my thoughts" or "to my words." [h]**5.3** *requests*: Or "sacrifices."

4.4 Eph 4.26. **5.9** Ro 3.13.

10 Punish them, God,
and let their own plans
bring their downfall.
Get rid of them!
They keep committing crimes
and turning against you.

11 Let all who run to you
for protection
always sing joyful songs.
Provide shelter for those
who truly love you
and let them rejoice.
12 Our LORD, you bless those
who live right,
and you shield them
with your kindness.

Psalm 6

[A psalm by David for the music leader. Use stringed instruments.[i]*]*

A Prayer in Time of Trouble

1 Don't punish me, LORD,
or even correct me
when you are angry!
2 Have pity on me and heal
my feeble body.
My bones tremble with fear,
3 and I am in deep distress.
How long will it be?

4 Turn and come to my rescue.
Show your wonderful love
and save me, LORD.
5 If I die, I cannot praise you
or even remember you.
6 My groaning has worn me out.
At night my bed and pillow
are soaked with tears.
7 Sorrow has made my eyes dim,
and my sight has failed
because of my enemies.

8 You, LORD, heard my crying,
and those hateful people
had better leave me alone.
9 You have answered my prayer
and my plea for mercy.
10 My enemies will be ashamed
and terrified,
as they quickly run away
in complete disgrace.

Psalm 7

[Written by David.[j] *He sang this to the LORD because of Cush from the tribe of Benjamin.]*

The LORD Always Does Right

1 You, LORD God,
are my protector.
Rescue me and keep me safe
from all who chase me.
2 Or else they will rip me apart
like lions attacking a victim,
and no one will save me.

3 I am innocent, LORD God!
4 I have not betrayed a friend
or had pity on an enemy[k]
who attacks for no reason.
5 If I have done any of this,
then let my enemies
chase and capture me.
Let them stomp me to death
and leave me in the dirt.

6 Get angry, LORD God!
Do something!
Attack my furious enemies.
See that justice is done.
7 Make the nations come to you,
as you sit on your throne[l]
above them all.

8 Our LORD, judge the nations!
Judge me and show that I
am honest and innocent.
9 You know every heart and mind,
and you always do right.
Now make violent people stop,
but protect all of us
who obey you.

10 You, God, are my shield,
the protector of everyone
whose heart is right.

[i]**Psalm 6** *instruments*: The Hebrew text adds "according to the sheminith," which may refer to a musical instrument with eight strings. [j]**Psalm 7** *Written by David*: The Hebrew text has "a shiggaion by David," which may refer to a psalm of mourning. [k]**7.4** *had pity on an enemy*: Or "failed to have pity on an enemy." [l]**7.7** *sit . . . throne*: Or "return to your place."

6.1 Ps 38.1. **6.8** Mt 7.23; Lk 13.27. **7.9** Rev 2.23.

11 You see that justice is done,
and each day
you take revenge.
12 Whenever your enemies refuse
to change their ways,
you sharpen your sword
and string your bow.
13 Your deadly arrows are ready
with flaming tips.

14 An evil person is like a woman
about to give birth
to a hateful, deceitful,
and rebellious child.
15 Such people dig a deep hole,
then fall in it themselves.
16 The trouble they cause
comes back on them,
and their heads are crushed
by their own evil deeds.

17 I will praise you, LORD!
You always do right.
I will sing about you,
the LORD Most High.

Psalm 8

[*A psalm by David for the music leader.* [m]]

The Wonderful Name of the LORD

1 Our LORD and Ruler,
your name is wonderful
everywhere on earth!
You let your glory be seen[n]
in the heavens above.
2 With praises from children
and from tiny infants,
you have built a fortress.
It makes your enemies silent,
and all who turn against you
are left speechless.

3 I often think of the heavens
your hands have made,
and of the moon and stars
you put in place.
4 Then I ask, "Why do you care
about us humans?
Why are you concerned
for us weaklings?"
5 You made us a little lower
than you yourself,[o]
and you have crowned us
with glory and honor.

6 You let us rule everything
your hands have made.
And you put all of it
under our power—
7 the sheep and the cattle,
and every wild animal,
8 the birds in the sky,
the fish in the sea,
and all ocean creatures.

9 Our LORD and Ruler,
your name is wonderful
everywhere on earth!

Psalm 9

[*A psalm by David for the music leader. To the tune "The Death of the Son."*]

Sing Praises to the LORD

1 I will praise you, LORD,
with all my heart
and tell about the wonders
you have worked.
2 God Most High, I will rejoice;
I will celebrate and sing
because of you.

3 When my enemies face you,
they run away and stumble
and are destroyed.
4 You take your seat as judge,
and your fair decisions prove
that I was in the right.
5 You warn the nations
and destroy evil people;
you wipe out their names
forever and ever.
6 Our enemies are destroyed
completely for all time.
Their cities are torn down,
and they will never
be remembered again.

[m]**Psalm 8** *leader*: The Hebrew text adds "according to the gittith," which may refer to either a musical instrument or a tune. [n]**8.1** *You . . . seen*: Or "I will worship your glory." [o]**8.5** *you yourself*: Or "the angels" or "the beings in heaven."

7.15,16 3 Macc 6.21. **8.2** Mt 21.16. **8.4** Job 7.17, 18; Ps 144.3; He 2.6-8. **8.5** Ws 2.23; Si 17.1-4. **8.6** 1 Co 15.27; Eph 1.22; He 2.8.

7 You rule forever, LORD,
and you are on your throne,
ready for judgment.
8 You judge the world fairly
and treat all nations
with justice.
9 The poor can run to you
because you are a fortress
in times of trouble.
10 Everyone who honors your name
can trust you,
because you are faithful
to all who depend on you.

11 You rule from Zion, LORD,
and we sing about you
to let the nations know
everything you have done.
12 You did not forget
to punish the guilty
or listen to the cries
of those in need.

13 Please have mercy, LORD!
My enemies mistreat me.
Keep me from the gates
that lead to death,
14 and I will sing about you
at the gate to Zion.
I will be happy there
because you rescued me.

15 Our LORD, the nations fell
into their own pits,
and their feet were caught
in their own traps.
16 You showed what you are like,
and you made certain
that justice is done,
but evil people are trapped
by their own evil deeds.
17 The wicked will go down
to the world of the dead
to be with those nations
that forgot about you.

18 The poor and the homeless
won't always be forgotten
and without hope.

19 Do something, LORD!
Don't let the nations win.
Make them stand trial
in your court of law.
20 Make the nations afraid
and let them all discover
just how weak they are.

Psalm 10

A Prayer for Help

1 Why are you far away, LORD?
Why do you hide yourself
when I am in trouble?
2 Proud and brutal people
hunt down the poor.
But let them get caught
by their own evil plans!

3 The wicked brag about
their deepest desires.
Those greedy people hate
and curse you, LORD.
4 The wicked are too proud
to turn to you
or even think about you.
5 They are always successful,
though they can't understand
your teachings,
and they keep sneering
at their enemies.

6 In their hearts they say,
"Nothing can hurt us!
We'll always be happy
and free from trouble."
7 They curse and tell lies,
and all they talk about
is how to be cruel
or how to do wrong.

8 They hide outside villages,
waiting to strike and murder
some innocent victim.
9 They are hungry lions
hiding in the bushes,
hoping to catch
some helpless passerby.
They trap the poor in nets
and drag them away.
10 They crouch down and wait
to grab a victim.

9.13 Ws 16.13. **9.15,16** 3 Macc 6.21. **10.7** Ro 3.14.

11 They say, "God can't see!
He's got on a blindfold."

12 Do something, LORD God,
and use your powerful arm
to help those in need.
13 The wicked don't respect you.
In their hearts they say,
"God won't punish us!"

14 But you see the trouble
and the distress,
and you will do something.
The poor can count on you,
and so can orphans.
15 Now break the arms
of all merciless people.
Punish them for doing wrong
and make them stop.

16 Our LORD, you will always rule,
but nations will vanish
from the earth.
17 You listen to the longings
of those who suffer.
You offer them hope,
and you pay attention
to their cries for help.
18 You defend orphans
and everyone else in need,
so that no one on earth
can terrify others again.

Psalm 11

[*A psalm by David for the music leader.*]

Trusting the LORD

1 The LORD is my fortress!
Don't say to me,
"Escape like a bird
to the mountains!"
2 You tell me, "Watch out!
Those evil people have put
their arrows on their bows,
and they are standing
in the shadows,
aiming at good people.
3 What can an honest person do
when everything crumbles?"

4 The LORD is sitting
in his sacred temple
on his throne in heaven.
He knows everything we do
because he sees us all.
5 The LORD tests honest people,
but despises those
who are cruel
and love violence.
6 He will send fiery coals[p]
and flaming sulfur
down on the wicked,
and they will drink nothing
but a scorching wind.

7 The LORD always does right
and wants justice done.
Everyone who does right
will see his face.

Psalm 12

[*A psalm by David for the music leader.*[q]]

A Prayer for Help

1 Please help me, LORD!
All who were faithful
and all who were loyal
have disappeared.
2 Everyone tells lies,
and no one is sincere.
3 Won't you chop off
all flattering tongues
that brag so loudly?
4 They say to themselves,
"We are great speakers.
No one else has a chance."

5 But you, LORD, tell them,
"I will do something!
The poor are mistreated
and helpless people moan.
I'll rescue all who suffer."

6 Our LORD, you are true
to your promises,
and your word is like silver
heated seven times
in a fiery furnace.[r]

[p] **11.6** *fiery coals*: Or "trouble, fire." [q] **Psalm 12** *leader*: The Hebrew text adds "according to the sheminith," which may be a musical instrument with eight strings. [r] **12.6** *in a fiery furnace*: The Hebrew text has "in a furnace to the ground," which may describe part of a process for refining silver in Old Testament times.

7 You will protect us
and always keep us safe
from those people.
8 But all who are wicked
will keep on strutting,
while everyone praises
their shameless deeds.[s]

Psalm 13

[*A psalm by David for the music leader.*]

A Prayer for the LORD's Help

1 How much longer, LORD,
will you forget about me?
Will it be forever?
How long will you hide?
2 How long must I be confused
and miserable all day?
How long will my enemies
keep beating me down?

3 Please listen, LORD God,
and answer my prayers.
Make my eyes sparkle again,
or else I will fall
into the sleep of death.
4 My enemies will say,
"Now we've won!"
They will be greatly pleased
when I am defeated.

5 I trust your love,
and I feel like celebrating
because you rescued me.
6 You have been good to me, LORD,
and I will sing about you.

Psalm 14

[*A psalm by David for the music leader.*]

No One Can Ignore the LORD

1 Only a fool would say,
"There is no God!"
People like that are worthless;
they are heartless and cruel
and never do right.

2 From heaven the LORD
looks down to see
if anyone is wise enough
to search for him.
3 But all of them are corrupt;
no one does right.

4 Won't you evil people learn?
You refuse to pray,
and you gobble down
the LORD's people.
5 But you will be frightened,
because God is on the side
of every good person.
6 You may spoil the plans
of the poor,
but the LORD protects them.

7 I long for someone from Zion
to come and save Israel!
Our LORD, when you bless
your people again,
Jacob's family will be glad,
and Israel will celebrate.

Psalm 15

[*A psalm by David.*]

Who May Worship the LORD?

1 Who may stay in God's temple
or live on the holy mountain
of the LORD?

2 Only those who obey God
and do as they should.
They speak the truth
3 and don't spread gossip;
they treat others fairly
and don't say cruel things.

4 They hate worthless people,
but show respect for all
who worship the LORD.
And they keep their promises,
no matter what the cost.
5 They lend their money
without charging interest,
and they don't take bribes
to hurt the innocent.

[s]**12.8** *while . . . deeds*: One possible meaning for the difficult Hebrew text.
14.1-3 Ro 3.10-12.

Those who do these things
will always stand firm.

Psalm 16

[*A special psalm by David.*]

The Best Choice

1 Protect me, LORD God!
I run to you for safety,
2 and I have said,
"Only you are my Lord!
Every good thing I have
is a gift from you."

3 Your people are wonderful,
and they make me happy,[t]
4 but worshipers of other gods
will have much sorrow.[u]
I refuse to offer sacrifices
of blood to those gods
or worship in their name.

5 You, LORD, are all I want!
You are my choice,
and you keep me safe.
6 You make my life pleasant,
and my future is bright.

7 I praise you, LORD,
for being my guide.
Even in the darkest night,
your teachings fill my mind.
8 I will always look to you,
as you stand beside me
and protect me from fear.
9 With all my heart,
I will celebrate,
and I can safely rest.

10 I am your chosen one.
You won't leave me in the grave
or let my body decay.
11 You have shown me
the path to life,
and you make me glad
by being near to me.
Sitting at your right side,[v]
I will always be joyful.

Psalm 17

[*A prayer by David.*]

The Prayer of an Innocent Person

1 I am innocent, LORD!
Won't you listen as I pray
and beg for help?
I am honest!
Please hear my prayer.
2 Only you can say
that I am innocent,
because only your eyes
can see the truth.

3 You know my heart,
and even during the night
you have tested me
and found me innocent.
I have made up my mind
never to tell a lie.
4 I don't do like others.
I obey your teachings
and am not cruel.
5 I have followed you,
without ever stumbling.

6 I pray to you, God,
because you will help me.
Listen and answer my prayer!
7 Show your wonderful love.
Your mighty arm protects those
who run to you for safety
from their enemies.
8 Protect me as you would
your very own eyes;
hide me in the shadow
of your wings.

9 Don't let my brutal enemies
attack from all sides
and kill me.
10 They refuse to show mercy,
and they keep bragging.

11 They have caught up with me!
My enemies are everywhere,
eagerly hoping to smear me
in the dirt.

[t] **16.3** *Your people . . . happy*: Or "I was happy worshiping gods I thought were powerful."
[u] **16.4** *but . . . sorrow*: One possible meaning for the difficult Hebrew text. [v] **16.11** *right side*: The place of power and honor.
16.10 Ac 13.35. **16.8-11** Ac 2.25-28.

12 They are like hungry lions
hunting for food,
or like young lions
hiding in ambush.

13 Do something, LORD!
Attack and defeat them.
Take your sword and save me
from those evil people.
14 Use your powerful arm
and rescue me
from the hands of mere humans
whose world won't last.[w]

You provide food
for those you love.
Their children have plenty,
and their grandchildren
will have more than enough.

15 I am innocent, LORD,
and I will see your face!
When I awake, all I want
is to see you as you are.

Psalm 18

[*For the music leader. A psalm by David, the LORD's servant. David sang this to the LORD after the LORD had rescued him from his enemies, but especially from Saul.*]

David's Song of Thanks

1 I love you, LORD God,
and you make me strong.
2 You are my mighty rock,[x]
my fortress, my protector,
the rock where I am safe,
my shield, my powerful weapon,[y]
and my place of shelter.

3 I praise you, LORD!
I prayed, and you rescued me
from my enemies.
4 Death had wrapped
its ropes around me,
and I was almost swallowed
by its flooding waters.
5 Ropes from the world
of the dead
had coiled around me,
and death had set a trap
in my path.
6 I was in terrible trouble
when I called out to you,
but from your temple
you heard me
and answered my prayer.
7 The earth shook and shivered,
and the mountains trembled
down to their roots.
You were angry
8 and breathed out smoke.
Scorching heat and fiery flames
spewed from your mouth.

9 You opened the heavens
like curtains,
and you came down
with storm clouds
under your feet.
10 You rode on the backs
of flying creatures
and swooped down
with the wind as wings.
11 Darkness was your robe;
thunderclouds filled the sky,
hiding you from sight.
12 Hailstones and fiery coals
lit up the sky
in front of you.

13 LORD Most High, your voice
thundered from the heavens,
as hailstones and fiery coals
poured down like rain.
14 You scattered your enemies
with arrows of lightning.
15 You roared at the sea,
and its deepest channels
could be seen.
You snorted,
and the earth shook
to its foundations.

[w] **17.14** *last*: One possible meaning for the difficult Hebrew text of verse 14. [x] **18.2** *mighty rock*: The Hebrew text has "rock," which is sometimes used in poetry to compare the Lord to a mountain where his people can run for protection from their enemies. [y] **18.2** *my powerful weapon*: The Hebrew text has "the horn," which refers to the horn of a bull, one of the most powerful animals in ancient Palestine.

16 You reached down from heaven,
and you lifted me
from deep in the ocean.
17 You rescued me from enemies,
who were hateful
and too powerful for me.
18 On the day disaster struck,
they came and attacked,
but you defended me.
19 When I was fenced in,
you freed and rescued me
because you love me.

20 You are good to me, LORD,
because I do right,
and you reward me
because I am innocent.
21 I do what you want
and never turn to do evil.
22 I keep your laws in mind
and never look away
from your teachings.
23 I obey you completely
and guard against sin.
24 You have been good to me
because I do right;
you have rewarded me
for being innocent
by your standards.

25 You are always loyal
to your loyal people,
and you are faithful
to the faithful.
26 With all who are sincere,
you are sincere,
but you treat the unfaithful
as their deeds deserve.
27 You rescue the humble,
but you put down all
who are proud.

28 You, the LORD God,
keep my lamp burning
and turn darkness to light.
29 You help me defeat armies
and capture cities.

30 Your way is perfect, LORD,
and your word is correct.
You are a shield for those
who run to you for help.
31 You alone are God!
Only you are a mighty rock.[z]
32 You give me strength
and guide me right.
33 You make my feet run as fast
as those of a deer,
and you help me stand
on the mountains.

34 You teach my hands to fight
and my arms to use
a bow of bronze.
35 You alone are my shield.
Your right hand supports me,
and by coming to help me,
you have made me famous.
36 You clear the way for me,
and now I won't stumble.

37 I kept chasing my enemies,
until I caught them
and destroyed them.
38 I stuck my sword
through my enemies,
and they were crushed
under my feet.
39 You helped me win victories,
and you forced my attackers
to fall victim to me.

40 You made my enemies run,
and I killed them.
41 They cried out for help,
but no one saved them;
they called out to you,
but there was no answer.
42 I ground them to dust
blown by the wind,
and I poured them out
like mud in the streets.

43 You rescued me
from stubborn people,
and you made me the leader
of foreign nations,
who are now my slaves.
44 They obey and come crawling.
45 They have lost all courage,

[z] **18.31,46; 19.14** *mighty rock*: See the note at 18.2.
18.33 Hb 3.19.

and from their fortresses,
they come trembling.

46 You are the living LORD!
I will praise you.
You are a mighty rock.[z]
I will honor you
for keeping me safe.
47 You took revenge for me,
and you put nations
in my power.
48 You protected me
from violent enemies
and made me much greater
than all of them.

49 I will praise you, LORD,
and I will honor you
among the nations.
50 You give glorious victories
to your chosen king.
Your faithful love for David
and for his descendants
will never end.

Psalm 19

[*A psalm by David for the music leader.*]

The Wonders of God and the Goodness of His Law

1 The heavens keep telling
the wonders of God,
and the skies declare
what he has done.
2 Each day informs
the following day;
each night announces
to the next.
3 They don't speak a word,
and there is never
the sound of a voice.
4 Yet their message reaches
all the earth,
and it travels
around the world.

In the heavens a tent
is set up for the sun.
5 It rises like a bridegroom
and gets ready like a hero
eager to run a race.
6 It travels all the way
across the sky.
Nothing hides from its heat.

7 The Law of the LORD is perfect;
it gives us new life.
His teachings last forever,
and they give wisdom
to ordinary people.
8 The LORD's instruction is right;
it makes our hearts glad.
His commands shine brightly,
and they give us light.

9 Worshiping the LORD is sacred;
he will always be worshiped.
All of his decisions
are correct and fair.
10 They are worth more
than the finest gold
and are sweeter than honey
from a honeycomb.

11 By your teachings, Lord,
I am warned;
by obeying them,
I am greatly rewarded.
12 None of us know our faults.
Forgive me when I sin
without knowing it.
13 Don't let me do wrong
on purpose, Lord,
or let sin have control
over my life.
Then I will be innocent,
and not guilty
of some terrible fault.

14 Let my words and my thoughts
be pleasing to you, LORD,
because you are my mighty rock[z]
and my protector.

Psalm 20

[*A psalm by David for the music leader.*]

A Prayer for Victory

1 I pray that the LORD
will listen when you
are in trouble,

[z]**18.31,46; 19.14** *mighty rock*: See the note at 18.2.
18.49 Ro 15.9. **19.4** Ro 10.18. **19.7** Pr 9.10; 4 Macc 1.17.

and that the God of Jacob
will keep you safe.
2 May the LORD send help
from his temple
and come to your rescue
from Mount Zion.
3 May he remember your gifts
and be pleased
with what you bring.

4 May God do what you want most
and let all go well for you.
5 Then you will win victories,
and we will celebrate,
while raising our banners
in the name of our God.
May the LORD answer
all of your prayers!

6 I am certain, LORD,
that you will help
your chosen king.
You will answer my prayers
from your holy place
in heaven,
and you will save me
with your mighty arm.

7 Some people trust the power
of chariots or horses,
but we trust you, LORD God.
8 Others will stumble and fall,
but we will be strong
and stand firm.

9 Give the king victory, LORD,
and answer our prayers.[a]

Psalm 21

[*A psalm by David for the music leader.*]

Thanking the LORD for Victory

1 Our LORD, your mighty power
makes the king glad,
and he celebrates victories
that you have given him.
2 You did what he wanted most
and never told him "No."
3 You truly blessed the king,
and you placed on him
a crown of finest gold.
4 He asked to live a long time,
and you promised him life
that never ends.

5 The king is highly honored.
You have let him win victories
that have made him famous.
6 You have given him blessings
that will last forever,
and you have made him glad
by being so near to him.
7 LORD Most High,
the king trusts you,
and your kindness
keeps him from defeat.

8 With your mighty arm, LORD,
you will strike down all
of your hateful enemies.
9 They will be destroyed by fire
once you are here,
and because of your anger,
flames will swallow them.
10 You will wipe their families
from the earth,
and they will disappear.
11 All their plans to harm you
will come to nothing.
12 You will make them run away
by shooting your arrows
at their faces.

13 Show your strength, LORD,
so that we may sing
and praise your power.

Psalm 22

[*A psalm by David for the music leader. To the tune "A Deer at Dawn."*]

Suffering and Praise

1 My God, my God, why have you
deserted me?
Why are you so far away?
Won't you listen to my groans
and come to my rescue?
2 I cry out day and night,

[a]**20.9** *victory . . . prayers*: Or "victory. He (God or the king) answers us."
22.1 Mt 27.46; Mk 15.34.

but you don't answer,
and I can never rest.

3 Yet you are the holy God,
ruling from your throne
and praised by Israel.
4 Our ancestors trusted you,
and you rescued them.
5 When they cried out for help,
you saved them,
and you did not let them down
when they depended on you.

6 But I am merely a worm,
far less than human,
and I am hated and rejected
by people everywhere.
7 Everyone who sees me
makes fun and sneers.
They shake their heads,
8 and say, "Trust the LORD!
If you are his favorite,
let him protect you
and keep you safe."

9 You, LORD, brought me
safely through birth,
and you protected me
when I was a baby
at my mother's breast.
10 From the day I was born,
I have been in your care,
and from the time of my birth,
you have been my God.

11 Don't stay far off
when I am in trouble
with no one to help me.
12 Enemies are all around
like a herd of wild bulls.
Powerful bulls from Bashan[b]
are everywhere.
13 My enemies are like lions
roaring and attacking
with jaws open wide.

14 I have no more strength
than a few drops of water.
All my bones are out of joint;
my heart is like melted wax.
15 My strength has dried up
like a broken clay pot,
and my tongue sticks
to the roof of my mouth.
You, God, have left me
to die in the dirt.

16 Brutal enemies attack me
like a pack of dogs,
tearing at[c] my hands
and my feet.
17 I can count all my bones,
and my enemies just stare
and sneer at me.
18 They took my clothes
and gambled for them.

19 Don't stay far away, LORD!
My strength comes from you,
so hurry and help.
20 Rescue me from enemy swords
and save me from those dogs.
21 Don't let lions eat me.

You rescued me from the horns
of wild bulls,
22 and when your people meet,
I will praise you, LORD.

23 All who worship the LORD,
now praise him!
You belong to Jacob's family
and to the people of Israel,
so fear and honor the LORD!
24 The LORD doesn't hate
or despise the helpless
in all of their troubles.
When I cried out, he listened
and did not turn away.

25 When your people meet,
you will fill my heart
with your praises, LORD,
and everyone will see me
keep my promises to you.

[b]**22.12** *Bashan*: A land east of the Jordan River, where there were pastures suitable for raising fine cattle. [c]**22.16** *tearing at*: One possible meaning for the difficult Hebrew text.

22.4,5 3 Macc 2.12. **22.7** Mt 27.39; Mk 15.29; Lk 23.34, 35. **22.8** 3 Macc 6.11; Mt 27.43. **22.18** Mt 27.35; Mk 15.24; Lk 23.34, 35; Jn 19.24. **22.22** He 2.12.

26 The poor will eat and be full,
and all who worship you
will be thankful
and live in hope.

27 Everyone on this earth
will remember you, LORD.
People all over the world
will turn and worship you,
28 because you are in control,
the ruler of all nations.

29 All who are rich
and have more than enough
will bow down to you, Lord.
Even those who are dying
and almost in the grave
will come and bow down.
30 In the future, everyone
will worship and learn
about you, our Lord.
31 People not yet born
will be told,
"The Lord has saved us!"

Psalm 23

[*A psalm by David.*]

The Good Shepherd

1 You, LORD, are my shepherd.
I will never be in need.
2 You let me rest in fields
of green grass.
You lead me to streams
of peaceful water,
3 and you refresh my life.

You are true to your name,
and you lead me
along the right paths.
4 I may walk through valleys
as dark as death,
but I won't be afraid.
You are with me,
and your shepherd's rod[d]
makes me feel safe.

5 You treat me to a feast,
while my enemies watch.
You honor me as your guest,
and you fill my cup
until it overflows.
6 Your kindness and love
will always be with me
each day of my life,
and I will live forever
in your house, LORD.

Psalm 24

[*A psalm by David.*]

Who Can Enter the LORD's Temple?

1 The earth and everything on it
belong to the LORD.
The world and its people
belong to him.
2 The LORD placed it all
on the oceans and rivers.

3 Who may climb the LORD's hill[e]
or stand in his holy temple?
4 Only those who do right
for the right reasons,
and don't worship idols
or tell lies under oath.
5 The LORD God, who saves them,
will bless and reward them,
6 because they worship and serve
the God of Jacob.[f]
7 Open the ancient gates,
so that the glorious king
may come in.

8 Who is this glorious king?
He is our LORD, a strong
and mighty warrior.

9 Open the ancient gates,
so that the glorious king
may come in.

10 Who is this glorious king?
He is our LORD,
the All-Powerful!

[d]**23.4** *shepherd's rod*: The Hebrew text mentions two objects carried by the shepherd: a club to defend against wild animals and a long pole to guide and control the sheep. [e]**24.3** *the LORD's hill*: The hill in Jerusalem where the temple was built. [f]**24.6** *worship . . . Jacob*: Two ancient translations; Hebrew "worship God and serve the descendants of Jacob."

23.2 Rev 7.17. **24.1** 1 Co 10.26. **24.4** Mt 5.8.

Psalm 25

[*By David.*]

A Prayer for Guidance and Help

1 I offer you my heart, LORD God,
2 and I trust you.
Don't make me ashamed
or let enemies defeat me.
3 Don't disappoint any
of your worshipers,
but disappoint all
deceitful liars.
4 Show me your paths
and teach me to follow;
5 guide me by your truth
and instruct me.
You keep me safe,
and I always trust you.

6 Please, LORD, remember,
you have always
been patient and kind.
7 Forget each wrong I did
when I was young.
Show how truly kind you are
and remember me.
8 You are honest and merciful,
and you teach sinners
how to follow your path.

9 You lead humble people
to do what is right
and to stay on your path.
10 In everything you do,
you are kind and faithful
to everyone who keeps
our agreement with you.

11 Be true to your name, LORD,
by forgiving each one
of my terrible sins.
12 You will show the right path
to all who worship you.
13 They will have plenty,
and then their children
will receive the land.

14 Our LORD, you are the friend
of your worshipers,
and you make an agreement
with all of us.
15 I always look to you,
because you rescue me
from every trap.
16 I am lonely and troubled.
Show that you care
and have pity on me.
17 My awful worries keep growing.
Rescue me from sadness.
18 See my troubles and misery
and forgive my sins.

19 Look at all my enemies!
See how much they hate me.
20 I come to you for shelter.
Protect me, keep me safe,
and don't disappoint me.
21 I obey you with all my heart,
and I trust you, knowing
that you will save me.

22 Our God, please save Israel
from all of its troubles.

Psalm 26

[*By David.*]

The Prayer of an Innocent Person

1 Show that I am right, LORD!
I stay true to myself,
and I have trusted you
without doubting.
2 Test my thoughts and find out
what I am like.
3 I never forget your kindness,
and I am always faithful
to you.[g]
4 I don't spend my time
with worthless liars
5 or go with evil crowds.

6 I wash my hands, LORD,
to show my innocence,
and I worship at your altar,
7 while gratefully singing
about your wonders.
8 I love the temple
where you live, and where
your glory shines.
9 Don't sweep me away,
as you do sinners.
Don't punish me with death

[g] **26.3** *I am . . . to you*: Or "I trust your faithfulness."

as you do those people
who are brutal
10 or full of meanness
or who bribe others.
11 I stay true to myself.
Be kind and rescue me.

12 Now I stand on solid ground!
And when your people meet,
I will praise you, LORD.

Psalm 27
[*By David.*]

A Prayer of Praise

1 You, LORD, are the light
that keeps me safe.
I am not afraid of anyone.
You protect me,
and I have no fears.
2 Brutal people may attack
and try to kill me,
but they will stumble.
Fierce enemies may attack,
but they will fall.
3 Armies may surround me,
but I won't be afraid;
war may break out,
but I will trust you.

4 I ask only one thing, LORD:
Let me live in your house
every day of my life
to see how wonderful you are
and to pray in your temple.

5 In times of trouble,
you will protect me.
You will hide me in your tent
and keep me safe
on top of a mighty rock.[h]
6 You will let me defeat
all of my enemies.
Then I will celebrate,
as I enter your tent
with animal sacrifices
and songs of praise.

7 Please listen when I pray!
Have pity. Answer my prayer.
8 My heart tells me to pray.
I am eager to see your face,
9 so don't hide from me.
I am your servant,
and you have helped me.
Don't turn from me in anger.
You alone keep me safe.
Don't reject or desert me.
10 Even if my father and mother
should desert me,
you will take care of me.

11 Teach me to follow, LORD,
and lead me on the right path
because of my enemies.
12 Don't let them do to me
what they want.
People tell lies about me
and make terrible threats,
13 but I know I will live
to see how kind you are.

14 Trust the LORD!
Be brave and strong
and trust the LORD.

Psalm 28
[*By David.*]

A Prayer for Help

1 Only you, LORD,
are a mighty rock![h]
Don't refuse to help me
when I pray.
If you don't answer me,
I will soon be dead.
2 Please listen to my prayer
and my cry for help,
as I lift my hands
toward your holy temple.

3 Don't drag me away, LORD,
with those cruel people,
who speak kind words,
while planning trouble.
4 Treat them as they deserve!
Punish them for their sins.
5 They don't pay any attention
to your wonderful deeds.
Now you will destroy them
and leave them in ruin.

[h]**27.5; 28.1** *mighty rock*: See the note at 18.2.
28.4 Rev 22.12.

6 I praise you, LORD,
for answering my prayers.
7 You are my strong shield,
and I trust you completely.
You have helped me,
and I will celebrate
and thank you in song.

8 You give strength
to your people, LORD,
and you save and protect
your chosen ones.
9 Come save us and bless us.
Be our shepherd and always
carry us in your arms.

Psalm 29

[*A psalm by David.*]

The Voice of the LORD in a Storm

1 All of you angels[i] in heaven,
honor the glory and power
of the LORD!
2 Honor the wonderful name
of the LORD,
and worship the LORD
most holy and glorious.[j]

3 The voice of the LORD
echoes over the oceans.
The glorious LORD God
thunders above the roar
of the raging sea,
4 and his voice is mighty
and marvelous.
5 The voice of the LORD
destroys the cedar trees;
the LORD shatters cedars
on Mount Lebanon.
6 God makes Mount Lebanon
skip like a calf
and Mount Hermon
jump like a wild ox.

7 The voice of the LORD
makes lightning flash
8 and the desert tremble.
And because of the LORD,
the desert near Kadesh
shivers and shakes.

9 The voice of the LORD
makes deer give birth
before their time.[k]
Forests are stripped of leaves,
and the temple is filled
with shouts of praise.

10 The LORD rules on his throne,
king of the flood[l] forever.
11 Pray that our LORD
will make us strong
and give us peace.

Psalm 30

[*A psalm by David for the dedication of the temple.*]

A Prayer of Thanks

1 I will praise you, LORD!
You saved me from the grave
and kept my enemies
from celebrating my death.
2 I prayed to you, LORD God,
and you healed me,
3 saving me from death
and the grave.

4 Your faithful people, LORD,
will praise you with songs
and honor your holy name.
5 Your anger lasts a little while,
but your kindness lasts
for a lifetime.
At night we may cry,
but when morning comes
we will celebrate.

6 I was carefree and thought,
"I'll never be shaken!"
7 You, LORD, were my friend,
and you made me strong
as a mighty mountain.
But when you hid your face,
I was crushed.

[i] **29.1** *angels*: Or "supernatural beings" or "gods." [j] **29.2** *most . . . glorious*: Or "in his holy place" or "and wear your glorious clothes." [k] **29.9** *makes . . . time*: Or "twists the oak trees around." [l] **29.10** *king of the flood*: In ancient times the people of Israel believed that a mighty ocean surrounded all of creation, and that God could release the water to flood the earth.
29.1,2 Ps 96.7-9.

8 I prayed to you, LORD,
and in my prayer I said,
9 "What good will it do you
if I am in the grave?
Once I have turned to dust,
how can I praise you
or tell how loyal you are?
10 Have pity, LORD! Help!"

11 You have turned my sorrow
into joyful dancing.
No longer am I sad
and wearing sackcloth.[m]
12 I thank you from my heart,
and I will never stop
singing your praises,
my LORD and my God.

Psalm 31

[*A psalm by David for the music leader.*]

A Prayer for Protection

1 I come to you, LORD,
for protection.
Don't let me be ashamed.
Do as you have promised
and rescue me.
2 Listen to my prayer
and hurry to save me.
Be my mighty rock[n]
and the fortress
where I am safe.

3 You, LORD God,
are my mighty rock
and my fortress.
Lead me and guide me,
so that your name
will be honored.
4 Protect me from hidden traps
and keep me safe.
5 You are faithful,
and I trust you
because you rescued me.

6 I hate the worshipers
of worthless idols,
but I trust you, LORD.
7 I celebrate and shout
because you are kind.
You saw all my suffering,
and you cared for me.
8 You kept me from the hands
of my enemies,
and you set me free.

9 Have pity, LORD!
I am hurting and almost blind.
My whole body aches.
10 I have known only sorrow
all my life long, and I suffer
year after year.
I am weak from sin,
and my bones are limp.

11 My enemies insult me.
Neighbors are even worse,
and I disgust my friends.
People meet me on the street,
and they turn and run.
12 I am completely forgotten
like someone dead.
I am merely a broken dish.
13 I hear the crowds whisper,
"Everyone is afraid!"
They are plotting and scheming
to murder me.

14 But I trust you, LORD,
and I claim you as my God.
15 My life is in your hands.
Save me from enemies
who hunt me down.
16 Smile on me, your servant.
Have pity and rescue me.

17 I pray only to you.
Don't disappoint me.
Disappoint my cruel enemies
until they lie silent
in their graves.
18 Silence those proud liars!
Make them stop bragging
and insulting your people.

19 You are wonderful,
and while everyone watches,

[m] **30.11** *sackcloth*: A rough, dark-colored cloth made from goat or camel hair and used to make grain sacks. It was worn in times of trouble or sorrow. [n] **31.2** *mighty rock*: See the note at 18.2.
31.5 Lk 23.46.

you store up blessings for all
who honor and trust you.
20 You are their shelter
from harmful plots,
and you are their protection
from vicious gossip.

21 I will praise you, LORD,
for showing great kindness
when I was like a city
under attack.
22 I was terrified and thought,
"They've chased me
far away from you!"
But you answered my prayer
when I shouted for help.

23 All who belong to the LORD,
show how you love him.
The LORD protects the faithful,
but he severely punishes
everyone who is proud.
24 All who trust the LORD,
be cheerful and strong.

Psalm 32

[*A special psalm by David.*]

The Joy of Forgiveness

1 Our God, you bless everyone
whose sins you forgive
and wipe away.
2 You bless them by saying,
"You told me your sins,
without trying to hide them,
and now I forgive you."

3 Before I confessed my sins,
my bones felt limp,
and I groaned all day long.
4 Night and day your hand
weighed heavily on me,
and my strength was gone
as in the summer heat.

5 So I confessed my sins
and told them all to you.
I said, "I'll tell the LORD
each one of my sins."
Then you forgave me
and took away my guilt.

6 We worship you, Lord,
and we should always pray
whenever we find out
that we have sinned.[o]
Then we won't be swept away
by a raging flood.
7 You are my hiding place!
You protect me from trouble,
and you put songs in my heart
because you have saved me.

8 You said to me,
"I will point out the road
that you should follow.
I will be your teacher
and watch over you.
9 Don't be stupid
like horses and mules
that must be led with ropes
to make them obey."

10 All kinds of troubles
will strike the wicked,
but your kindness shields those
who trust you, LORD.
11 And so your good people
should celebrate and shout.

Psalm 33

Sing Praises to the LORD

1 You are the LORD's people.
Obey him and celebrate!
He deserves your praise.
2 Praise the LORD with harps!
Use harps with ten strings
to make music for him.
3 Sing a new song. Shout!
Play beautiful music.

4 The LORD is truthful;
he can be trusted.
5 He loves justice and fairness,
and he is kind to everyone
everywhere on earth.

[o]**32.6** *whenever . . . sinned*: Hebrew "at a time of finding only."
31.23 3 Macc 2.3. **32.1,2** Ro 4.7, 8.

6 The LORD made the heavens
and everything in them
by his word.
7 He scooped up the ocean
and stored the water.
8 Everyone in this world
should worship and honor
the LORD!
9 As soon as he spoke
the world was created;
at his command,
the earth was formed.

10 The LORD destroys the plans
and spoils the schemes
of the nations.
11 But what the LORD has planned
will stand forever.
His thoughts never change.
12 The LORD blesses each nation
that worships only him.
He blesses his chosen ones.
13 The LORD looks at the world
14 from his throne in heaven,
and he watches us all.
15 The LORD gave us each a mind,
and nothing we do
can be hidden from him.

16 Mighty armies alone
cannot win wars for a king;
great strength by itself
cannot keep a soldier safe.
17 In war the strength of a horse
cannot be trusted
to take you to safety.
18 But the LORD watches over
all who honor him
and trust his kindness.
19 He protects them from death
and starvation.

20 We depend on you, LORD,
to help and protect us.
21 You make our hearts glad
because we trust you,
the only God.
22 Be kind and bless us!
We depend on you.

Psalm 34

[Written by David when he pretended to be crazy in front of Abimelech, so that Abimelech would send him away, and David could leave.]

Honor the LORD

1 I will always praise the LORD.
2 With all my heart,
I will praise the LORD.
Let all who are helpless,
listen and be glad.
3 Honor the LORD with me!
Celebrate his great name.

4 I asked the LORD for help,
and he saved me
from all my fears.
5 Keep your eyes on the LORD!
You will shine like the sun
and never blush with shame.
6 I was a nobody, but I prayed,
and the LORD saved me
from all my troubles.

7 If you honor the LORD,
his angel will protect you.
8 Discover for yourself
that the LORD is kind.
Come to him for protection,
and you will be glad.

9 Honor the LORD!
You are his special people.
No one who honors the LORD
will ever be in need.
10 Young lions[p] may go hungry
or even starve,
but if you trust the LORD,
you will never miss out
on anything good.

11 Come, my children, listen
as I teach you
to respect the LORD.
12 Do you want to live
and enjoy a long life?
13 Then don't say cruel things
and don't tell lies.
14 Do good instead of evil
and try to live at peace.

[p] **34.10** *Young lions*: In the Psalms wild animals often stand for God's enemies.

33.16 Jdt 9.7; 1 Macc 3.19. **34 Title** 1 S 21.13-15. **34.8** 1 P 2.3. **34.12-16** 1 P 3.10-12.

15 If you obey the LORD,
he will watch over you
and answer your prayers.
16 But God despises evil people,
and he will wipe them all
from the earth,
till they are forgotten.
17 When his people pray for help,
he listens and rescues them
from their troubles.
18 The LORD is there to rescue
all who are discouraged
and have given up hope.

19 The LORD's people
may suffer a lot,
but he will always
bring them safely through.
20 Not one of their bones
will ever be broken.

21 Wicked people are killed
by their own evil deeds,
and if you hate God's people
you will be punished.
22 The LORD saves the lives
of his servants.
Run to him for protection,
and you won't be punished.

Psalm 35

[*A psalm by David.*]

A Prayer for Protection from Enemies

1 Fight my enemies, LORD!
Attack my attackers!
2 Shield me and help me.
3 Aim your spear at everyone
who hunts me down,
but promise to save me.

4 Let all who want to kill me
be disappointed
and disgraced.
Chase away and confuse
all who plan to harm me.
5 Send your angel after them
and let them be like straw
in the wind.
6 Make them run in the dark
on a slippery road,
as your angel chases them.
7 I did them no harm,
but they hid a net
to trap me,
and they dug a deep pit
to catch and kill me.
8 Surprise them with disaster!
Trap them in their own nets
and let them fall and rot
in the pits they have dug.

9 I will celebrate and be joyful
because you, LORD,
have saved me.
10 Every bone in my body
will shout:
"No one is like the LORD!"
You protect the helpless
from those in power;
you save the poor and needy
from those who hurt them.

11 Liars accuse me of crimes
I know nothing about.
12 They repay evil for good,
and I feel all alone.
13 When they were sick,
I wore sackcloth[q]
and went without food.[r]
I truly prayed for them,[s]
14 as I would for a friend
or a relative.
I was in sorrow and mourned,
as I would for my mother.

15 I have stumbled,
and worthless liars
I don't even know
surround me and sneer.
16 Worthless people make fun[t]
and never stop laughing.
17 But all you do is watch!
When will you do something?
Save me from the attack
of those vicious lions.
18 And when your people meet,
I will praise you

[q]**35.13** *sackcloth*: See the note at 30.11. [r]**35.13** *went without food*: People sometimes went without food (called "fasting") to show sorrow. [s]**35.13** *I . . . them*: Or "My prayer wasn't answered, but I prayed." [t]**35.16** *Worthless . . . fun*: One possible meaning for the difficult Hebrew text.

34.20 Jn 19.36. **35.8** 3 Macc 6.21.

and thank you, Lord,
in front of them all.

19 Don't let my brutal enemies
be glad because of me.
They hate me for no reason.
Don't let them wink
behind my back.
20 They say hurtful things,
and they lie to people
who want to live in peace.
21 They are quick to accuse me.
They say, "You did it!
We saw you ourselves."

22 You see everything, LORD!
Please don't keep silent
or stay so far away.
23 Fight to defend me, Lord God,
24 and prove that I am right
by your standards.
Don't let them laugh at me
25 or say to each other,
"Now we've got what we want!
We'll gobble him down!"

26 Disappoint and confuse
all who are glad
to see me in trouble,
but disgrace and embarrass
my proud enemies who say to me,
"You are nothing!"

27 Let all who want me to win
be happy and joyful.
From now on let them say,
"The LORD is wonderful!
God is glad when all goes well
for his servant."
28 Then I will shout all day,
"Praise the LORD God!
He did what was right."

Psalm 36

[For the music leader by David, the LORD's servant.]

Human Sin and God's Goodness

1 Sinners don't respect God;
sin is all they think about.
2 They like themselves too much
to hate their own sins
or even to see them.
3 They tell deceitful lies,
and they don't have the sense
to live right.
4 Those people stay awake,
thinking up mischief,
and they follow the wrong road,
refusing to turn from sin.

5 Your love is faithful, LORD,
and even the clouds in the sky
can depend on you.
6 Your decisions are always fair.
They are firm like mountains,
deep like the sea,
and all people and animals
are under your care.

7 Your love is a treasure,
and everyone finds shelter
in the shadow of your wings.
8 You give your guests a feast
in your house,
and you serve a tasty drink
that flows like a river.
9 The life-giving fountain
belongs to you,
and your light gives light
to each of us.

10 Our LORD, keep showing love
to everyone who knows you,
and use your power to save all
whose thoughts please you.
11 Don't let those proud
and merciless people
kick me around
or chase me away.

12 Look at those wicked people!
They are knocked down,
never to get up again.

Psalm 37

[By David.]

Trust the LORD

1 Don't be annoyed by anyone
who does wrong,
and don't envy them.

35.19 Ps 69.4; Jn 15.25. **36.1** Ro 3.18.

2 They will soon disappear
like grass without rain.

3 Trust the LORD and live right!
The land will be yours,
and you will be safe.
4 Do what the LORD wants,
and he will give you
your heart's desire.

5 Let the LORD lead you
and trust him to help.
6 Then it will be as clear
as the noonday sun
that you were right.

7 Be patient and trust the LORD.
Don't let it bother you
when all goes well for those
who do sinful things.
8 Don't be angry or furious.
Anger can lead to sin.
9 All sinners will disappear,
but if you trust the LORD,
the land will be yours.

10 Sinners will soon disappear,
never to be found,
11 but the poor will take the land
and enjoy a big harvest.

12 Merciless people make plots
against good people
and snarl like animals,
13 but the Lord laughs and knows
their time is coming soon.
14 The wicked kill with swords
and shoot arrows to murder
the poor and the needy
and all who do right.
15 But they will be killed
by their own swords,
and their arrows
will be broken.

16 It is better to live right
and be poor
than to be sinful and rich.
17 The wicked will lose all
of their power,
but the LORD gives strength
to everyone who is good.

18 Those who obey the LORD
are daily in his care,
and what he has given them
will be theirs forever.
19 They won't be in trouble
when times are bad,
and they will have plenty
when food is scarce.

20 Wicked people are enemies
of the LORD
and will vanish like smoke
from a field on fire.

21 An evil person borrows
and never pays back;
a good person is generous
and never stops giving.
22 Everyone the LORD blesses
will receive the land;
everyone the LORD curses
will be destroyed.

23 If you do what the LORD wants,
he will make certain
each step you take is sure.
24 The LORD will hold your hand,
and if you stumble,
you still won't fall.

25 As long as I can remember,
good people have never
been left helpless,
and their children have never
gone begging for food.
26 They gladly give and lend,
and their children
turn out good.

27 If you stop sinning
and start doing right,
you will keep living
and be secure forever.
28 The LORD loves justice,
and he won't ever desert
his faithful people.
He always protects them,
but destroys the children
of the wicked.
29 God's people will own the land
and live here forever.

37.11 Mt 5.5.

30 Words of wisdom come
when good people speak
for justice.
31 They remember God's teachings,
and they never take
a wrong step.

32 The wicked try to trap
and kill good people,
33 but the LORD is on their side,
and he will defend them
when they are on trial.

34 Trust the LORD and follow him.
He will give you the land,
and you will see
the wicked destroyed.

35 I have seen brutal people
abuse others and grow strong
like trees in rich soil.[u]
36 Suddenly they disappeared!
I looked, but they were gone
and no longer there.

37 Think of the bright future
waiting for all the families
of honest and innocent
and peace-loving people.
38 But not a trace will be left
of the wicked
or their families.

39 The LORD protects his people,
and they can come to him
in times of trouble.
40 The LORD helps them
and saves them from the wicked
because they run to him.

Psalm 38

[*A psalm by David to be used when an offering is made.*]

A Prayer in Times of Trouble

1 When you are angry, LORD,
please don't punish me
or even correct me.
2 You shot me with your arrows,
and you struck me
with your hand.
3 My body hurts all over
because of your anger.
Even my bones are in pain,
and my sins 4 are so heavy
that I am crushed.

5 Because of my foolishness,
I am covered with sores
that stink and spread.
6 My body is twisted and bent,
and I groan all day long.
7 Fever has my back in flames,
and I hurt all over.
8 I am worn out and weak,
moaning and in distress.

9 You, Lord, know every one
of my deepest desires,
and my noisy groans
are no secret to you.
10 My heart is beating fast.
I feel weak all over,
and my eyes are red.

11 Because of my sickness,
no friends or neighbors
will come near me.
12 All who want me dead
set traps to catch me,
and those who want
to harm and destroy me
plan and plot all day.

13 I am not able to hear
or speak a word;
14 I am completely deaf
and can't make a sound.

15 I trust you, LORD God,
and you will do something.
16 I said, "Don't let them laugh
or brag because I slip."

17 I am about to collapse
from constant pain.
18 I told you my sins,
and I am sorry for them.
19 Many deadly and powerful
enemies hate me,
20 and they repay evil for good
because I try to do right.

[u]**37.35** *like . . . soil*: One possible meaning for the difficult Hebrew text.

21 You are the LORD God!
Stay nearby
and don't desert me.
22 You are the one who saves me.
Please hurry and help.

Psalm 39

[A psalm by David for Jeduthun, the music leader.]

A Prayer for Forgiveness

1 I told myself, "I'll be careful
not to sin by what I say,
and I'll muzzle my mouth
when evil people are near."
2 I kept completely silent,
but it did no good,[v]
and I hurt even worse.

3 I felt a fire burning inside,
and the more I thought,
the more it burned,
until at last I said:
4 "Please, LORD,
show me my future.
Will I soon be gone?
5 You made my life short,
so brief that the time
means nothing to you.

"Human life is but a breath,
6 and it disappears
like a shadow.
Our struggles are senseless;
we store up more and more,
without ever knowing
who will get it all.

7 "What am I waiting for?
I depend on you, Lord!
8 Save me from my sins.
Don't let fools sneer at me.
9 You treated me like this,
and I kept silent,
not saying a word.

10 "Won't you stop punishing me?
You have worn me down.
11 You punish us severely
because of our sins.
Like a moth, you destroy
what we treasure most.
We are as frail as a breath.

12 "Listen, LORD, to my prayer!
My eyes are flooded with tears,
as I pray to you.
I am merely a stranger
visiting in your home
as my ancestors did.
13 Stop being angry with me
and let me smile again
before I am dead and gone."

Psalm 40

[A psalm by David for the music leader.]

A Prayer for Help

1 I patiently waited, LORD,
for you to hear my prayer.
You listened 2 and pulled me
from a lonely pit
full of mud and mire.
You let me stand on a rock
with my feet firm,
3 and you gave me a new song,
a song of praise to you.
Many will see this,
and they will honor and trust
you, the LORD God.

4 You bless all of those
who trust you, LORD,
and refuse to worship idols
or follow false gods.
5 You, LORD God, have done
many wonderful things,
and you have planned
marvelous things for us.
No one is like you!
I would never be able to tell
all you have done.

6 Sacrifices and offerings
are not what please you;
gifts and payment for sin
are not what you demand.
But you made me willing
to listen and obey.

[v]39.2 *but . . . good*: One possible meaning for the difficult Hebrew text.
40.6-8 He 10.5-7.

7 And so, I said, "I am here
to do what is written
about me in the book,
where it says,
8 'I enjoy pleasing you.
Your Law is in my heart.' "

9 When your people worshiped,
you know I told them,
"Our LORD always helps!"
10 When all your people met,
I did not keep silent.
I said, "Our LORD is kind.
He is faithful and caring,
and he saves us."

11 You, LORD, never fail
to have pity on me;
your love and faithfulness
always keep me secure.

12 I have more troubles
than I can count.
My sins are all around me,
and I can't find my way.
My sins outnumber
the hairs on my head,
and I feel weak.
13 Please show that you care
and come to my rescue.
Hurry and help me!

14 Disappoint and confuse
all who want me dead;
turn away and disgrace
all who want to hurt me.
15 Embarrass and shame
all of those who say,
"Just look at you now!"
16 Our LORD, let your worshipers
rejoice and be glad.
They love you for saving them,
so let them always say,
"The LORD is wonderful!"

17 I am poor and needy,
but, LORD God,
you care about me,
and you come to my rescue.
Please hurry and help.

Psalm 41

[*A psalm by David for the music leader.*]

A Prayer in Time of Sickness

1 You, LORD God, bless everyone
who cares for the poor,
and you rescue those people
in times of trouble.
2 You protect them
and keep them alive.
You make them happy here
in this land,
and you don't hand them over
to their enemies.
3 You always heal them
and restore their strength
when they are sick.
4 I prayed, "Have pity, LORD!
Heal me, though I have sinned
against you."

5 My vicious enemies ask me,
"When will you die
and be forgotten?"
6 When visitors come,
all they ever bring
are worthless words,
and when they leave,
they spread gossip.

7 My enemies whisper about me.
They think the worst,
8 and they say,
"You have some fatal disease!
You'll never get well."
9 My most trusted friend
has turned against me,
though he ate at my table.

10 Have pity, LORD! Heal me,
so I can pay them back.
11 Then my enemies
won't defeat me,
and I will know
that you really care.
12 You have helped me
because I am innocent,
and you will always
be close to my side.

41.9 Mt 26.23; Mk 14.17, 18; Lk 22.21; Jn 13.18.

13 You, the LORD God of Israel,
will be praised forever!
Amen and amen.

BOOK II
(Psalms 42–72)

Psalm 42

[*A special psalm for the people of Korah and for the music leader.*]

Longing for God

1 As a deer gets thirsty
for streams of water,
I truly am thirsty
for you, my God.
2 In my heart, I am thirsty
for you, the living God.
When will I see your face?
3 Day and night my tears
are my only food,
as everyone keeps asking,
"Where is your God?"

4 Sorrow floods my heart,
when I remember
leading the worshipers
to your house.[w]
I can still hear them shout
their joyful praises.
5 Why am I discouraged?
Why am I restless?
I trust you!
And I will praise you again
because you help me,
6 and you are my God.

I am deeply discouraged
as I think about you
from where the Jordan begins
at Mount Hermon
and from Mount Mizar.[x]
7 Your vicious waves
have swept over me
like an angry ocean
or a roaring waterfall.

8 Every day, you are kind,
and at night
you give me a song
as my prayer to you,
the living LORD God.

9 You are my mighty rock.[y]
Why have you forgotten me?
Why must enemies mistreat me
and make me sad?
10 Even my bones are in pain,
while all day long
my enemies sneer and ask,
"Where is your God?"

11 Why am I discouraged?
Why am I restless?
I trust you!
And I will praise you again
because you help me,
and you are my God.

Psalm 43

A Prayer in Times of Trouble

1 Show that I am right, God!
Defend me against everyone
who doesn't know you;
rescue me from each
of those deceitful liars.
2 I run to you
for protection.
Why have you turned me away?
Why must enemies mistreat me
and make me sad?

3 Send your light and your truth
to guide me.
Let them lead me to your house
on your sacred mountain.
4 Then I will worship
at your altar because you
make me joyful.
You are my God,
and I will praise you.
Yes, I will praise you
as I play my harp.

5 Why am I discouraged?
Why am I restless?
I trust you!

[w] **42.4** *leading . . . house*: One possible meaning for the difficult Hebrew text. [x] **42.6** *Mount Mizar*: The location is not known. [y] **42.9** *mighty rock*: See the note at 18.2.
41.13 Ps 106.48.

And I will praise you again
because you help me,
and you are my God.

Psalm 44

[*A special psalm for the people of Korah and for the music leader.*]

A Prayer for Help

1 Our God, our ancestors told us
what wonders you worked
and we listened carefully.
2 You chased off the nations
by causing them trouble
with your powerful arm.
Then you let our ancestors
take over their land.
3 Their strength and weapons
were not what won the land
and gave them victory!
You loved them and fought
with your powerful arm
and your shining glory.

4 You are my God and King,
and you give victory[z]
to the people of Jacob.
5 By your great power,
we knocked our enemies down
and stomped on them.
6 I don't depend on my arrows
or my sword to save me.
7 But you saved us
from our hateful enemies,
and you put them to shame.
8 We boast about you, our God,
and we are always grateful.

9 But now you have rejected us;
you don't lead us into battle,
and we look foolish.
10 You made us retreat,
and our enemies have taken
everything we own.
11 You let us be slaughtered
like sheep,
and you scattered us
among the nations.
12 You sold your people
for little or nothing,
and you earned no profit.

13 You made us look foolish
to our neighbors,
and people who live nearby
insult us and sneer.
14 Foreigners joke about us
and shake their heads.
15 I am embarrassed every day,
and I blush with shame.
16 But others mock and sneer,
as they watch my enemies
take revenge on me.

17 All of this has happened to us,
though we didn't forget you
or break our agreement.
18 We always kept you in mind
and followed your teaching.
19 But you crushed us,
and you covered us
with deepest darkness
where wild animals live.

20 We did not forget you
or lift our hands in prayer
to foreign gods.
21 You would have known it
because you discover
every secret thought.
22 We face death all day for you.
We are like sheep on their way
to be slaughtered.

23 Wake up! Do something, Lord!
Why are you sleeping?
Don't desert us forever.
24 Why do you keep looking away?
Don't forget our sufferings
and all of our troubles.
25 We are flat on the ground,
holding on to the dust.
26 Do something! Help us!
Show how kind you are
and come to our rescue.

[z] **44.4** *and . . . victory*: One ancient translation; Hebrew "please give victory."
44.22 Ro 8.36.

Psalm 45

[*A special psalm for the people of Korah and for the music leader. To the tune "Lilies." A love song.*]

For a Royal Wedding

1 My thoughts are filled
with beautiful words
for the king,
and I will use my voice
as a writer would use
pen and ink.

2 No one is as handsome as you!
Your words are always kind.
That is why God
will always bless you.
3 Mighty king, glorious ruler,
strap on your sword
4 and ride out in splendor!
Win victories for truth
and mercy and justice.
Do fearsome things
with your powerful arm.
5 Send your sharp arrows
through enemy hearts
and make all nations fall
at your feet.

6 You are God, and you will rule
forever as king.[a]
Your royal power
brings about justice.
7 You love justice and hate evil.
And so, your God chose you
and made you happier
than any of your friends.
8 The sweet aroma of the spices
myrrh, aloes, and cassia,
covers your royal robes.
You enjoy the music of harps
in palaces decorated
with ivory.
9 Daughters of kings are here,
and your bride stands
at your right side,
wearing a wedding gown
trimmed with pure gold.[b]
10 Bride of the king,
listen carefully to me.
Forget your own people
and your father's family.
11 The king is your husband,
so do what he desires.
12 All of the richest people
from the city of Tyre
will try to influence you
13 with precious treasures.

Your bride, my king,
has inward beauty,[c]
and her wedding gown is woven
with threads of gold.
14 Wearing the finest garments,
she is brought to you,
followed by her young friends,
the bridesmaids.
15 Everyone is excited,
as they follow you
to the royal palace.

16 Your sons and your grandsons
will also be kings
as your ancestors were.
You will make them the rulers
everywhere on earth.

17 I will make your name famous
from now on,
and you will be praised
forever and ever.

Psalm 46

[*A special song for the people of Korah and for the music leader.*]

God Is Our Mighty Fortress

1 God is our mighty fortress,
always ready to help
in times of trouble.
2 And so, we won't be afraid!
Let the earth tremble
and the mountains tumble
into the deepest sea.
3 Let the ocean roar and foam,
and its raging waves
shake the mountains.

[a]**45.6** *You . . . king*: Or "God has made you king, and you will rule forever." [b]**45.9** *trimmed with pure gold*: Hebrew has "with gold from Ophir," which may have been in Africa or India. Gold from there was considered the very best. [c]**45.13** *has inward beauty*: Or "is dressed in her room."
45.6,7 He 1.8, 9.

4 A river and its streams
bring joy to the city,
which is the sacred home
of God Most High.
5 God is in that city,
and it won't be shaken.
He will help it at dawn.

6 Nations rage! Kingdoms fall!
But at the voice of God
the earth itself melts.
7 The LORD All-Powerful
is with us.
The God of Jacob
is our fortress.

8 Come! See the fearsome things
the LORD has done on earth.
9 God brings wars to an end
all over the world.
He breaks the arrows,
shatters the spears,
and burns the shields.[d]
10 Our God says, "Calm down,
and learn that I am God!
All nations on earth
will honor me."

11 The LORD All-Powerful
is with us.
The God of Jacob
is our fortress.

Psalm 47

[*A psalm for the people of Korah and for the music leader.*]

God Rules the Nations

1 All of you nations,
clap your hands and shout
joyful praises to God.
2 The LORD Most High is fearsome,
the ruler of all the earth.
3 God has put every nation
under our power,
4 and he chose for us the land
that was the pride of Jacob,
his favorite.

5 God goes up to his throne,
as people shout
and trumpets blast.
6 Sing praises to God our King,
7 the ruler of all the earth!
Praise God with songs.

8 God rules the nations
from his sacred throne.
9 Their leaders come together
and are now the people
of Abraham's God.
All rulers on earth
surrender their weapons,
and God is greatly praised!

Psalm 48

[*A song and a psalm for the people of Korah.*]

The City of God

1 The LORD God is wonderful!
He deserves all praise
in the city where he lives.
His holy mountain,
2 beautiful and majestic,
brings joy to all on earth.
Mount Zion, truly sacred,
is home for the Great King.
3 God is there to defend it
and has proved to be
its protector.

4 Kings joined forces
to attack the city,
5 but when they saw it,
they were terrified
and ran away.
6 They trembled all over
like women giving birth
7 or like seagoing ships[e]
wrecked by eastern winds.
8 We had heard about it,
and now we have seen it
in the city of our God,
the LORD All-Powerful.
This is the city that God
will let stand forever.

[d] **46.9** *shields*: Or "chariots." [e] **48.7** *seagoing ships*: The Hebrew text has "ships of Tarshish," which probably means large, seagoing ships.
48.2 Mt 5.35.

9 Our God, here in your temple
we think about your love.
10 You are famous and praised
everywhere on earth,
as you win victories
with your powerful arm.
11 Mount Zion will celebrate,
and all Judah will be glad,
because you bring justice.

12 Let's walk around Zion
and count its towers.
13 We will see its strong walls
and visit each fortress.
Then you can say
to future generations,
14 "Our God is like this forever
and will always[f] guide us."

Psalm 49

[*A psalm for the people of Korah and for the music leader.*]

Don't Depend on Wealth

1 Everyone on this earth,
now listen to what I say!
2 Listen, no matter who you are,
rich or poor.
3 I speak words of wisdom,
and my thoughts make sense.
4 I have in mind a mystery
that I will explain
while playing my harp.

5 Why should I be afraid
in times of trouble,
when I am surrounded
by vicious enemies?
6 They trust in their riches
and brag about
all of their wealth.
7 You cannot buy back your life
or pay off God!
8 It costs far too much
to buy back your life.
You can never pay God enough
9 to stay alive forever
and safe from death.

10 We see that wise people die,
and so do stupid fools.
Then their money is left
for someone else.
11 The grave[g] will be their home
forever and ever,
although they once had land
of their own.
12 Our human glory disappears,
and, like animals, we die.

13 Here is what happens to fools
and to those who trust
the words of fools:
14 They are like sheep
with death as their shepherd,
leading them to the grave.[h]
In the morning God's people
will walk all over them,
as their bodies lie rotting
in their home, the grave.
15 But God will rescue me
from the power of death.

16 Don't let it bother you
when others get rich
and live in luxury.
17 Soon they will die
and all of their wealth
will be left behind.

18 We humans are praised
when we do well,
and all of us are glad
to be alive.
19 But we each will go down
to our ancestors,
never again to see
the light of day.
20 Our human glory disappears,
and, like animals, we die.

Psalm 50

[*A psalm by Asaph.*]

What Pleases God

1 From east to west,
the powerful LORD God

[f] **48.14** *always*: One possible meaning for the difficult Hebrew text. [g] **49.11** *The grave*: Some ancient translations; Hebrew "Their inward thoughts." [h] **49.14** *as their . . . grave*: One possible meaning for the difficult Hebrew text.
49.10 Si 11.19.

has been calling together
everyone on earth.
2 God shines brightly from Zion,
the most beautiful city.

3 Our God approaches,
but not silently;
a flaming fire comes first,
and a storm surrounds him.
4 God comes to judge his people.
He shouts to the heavens
and to the earth,
5 "Call my followers together!
They offered me a sacrifice,
and we made an agreement."

6 The heavens announce,
"God is the judge,
and he is always honest."

7 My people, I am God!
Israel, I am your God.
Listen to my charges
against you.
8 Although you offer sacrifices
and always bring gifts,
9 I won't accept your offerings
of bulls and goats.

10 Every animal in the forest
belongs to me,
and so do the cattle
on a thousand hills.
11 I know all the birds
in the mountains,
and every wild creature
is in my care.

12 If I were hungry,
I wouldn't tell you,
because I own the world
and everything in it.
13 I don't eat the meat of bulls
or drink the blood of goats.
14 I am God Most High!
The only sacrifice I want
is for you to be thankful
and to keep your word.
15 Pray to me in time of trouble.
I will rescue you,
and you will honor me.

16 But to the wicked I say:
"You don't have the right
to mention my laws or claim
to keep our agreement!
17 You refused correction
and rejected my commands.
18 You made friends
with every crook you met,
and you liked people who break
their wedding vows.
19 You talked only about violence
and told nothing but lies;
20 you sat around gossiping,
ruining the reputation
of your own relatives."

21 When you did all of this,
I didn't say a word,
and you thought,
"God is just like us!"
But now I will accuse you.
22 You have ignored me!
So pay close attention
or I will tear you apart,
and no one can help you.

23 The sacrifice that honors me
is a thankful heart.
Obey me,[i] and I, your God,
will show my power to save.

Psalm 51

[For the music leader. A psalm by David when the prophet Nathan came to him after David had been with Bathsheba.]

A Prayer for Forgiveness

1 You are kind, God!
Please have pity on me.
You are always merciful!
Please wipe away my sins.
2 Wash me clean from all
of my sin and guilt.
3 I know about my sins,
and I cannot forget
my terrible guilt.
4 You are really the one
I have sinned against;
I have disobeyed you
and have done wrong.

[i]50.23 *Obey me*: One possible meaning for the difficult Hebrew text.
51 Title 2 S 12.1-15. **51.4** Ro 3.4.

So it is right and fair for you
to correct and punish me.

5 I have sinned and done wrong
since the day I was born.
6 But you want complete honesty,
so teach me true wisdom.
7 Wash me with hyssop[j]
until I am clean
and whiter than snow.
8 Let me be happy and joyful!
You crushed my bones,
now let them celebrate.
9 Turn your eyes from my sin
and cover my guilt.
10 Create pure thoughts in me
and make me faithful again.
11 Don't chase me away from you
or take your Holy Spirit
away from me.

12 Make me as happy as you did
when you saved me;
make me want to obey!
13 I will teach sinners your Law,
and they will return to you.
14 Keep me from any deadly sin.
Only you can save me!
Then I will shout and sing
about your power to save.

15 Help me to speak,
and I will praise you, Lord.
16 Offerings and sacrifices
are not what you want.
17 The way to please you
is to feel sorrow
deep in our hearts.
This is the kind of sacrifice
you won't refuse.

18 Please be willing, Lord,
to help the city of Zion
and to rebuild its walls.
19 Then you will be pleased
with the proper sacrifices,
and we will offer bulls
on your altar once again.

Psalm 52

[A special psalm by David for the music leader. He wrote this when Doeg from Edom went to Saul and said, "David has gone to Ahimelech's house."]

God Is in Control

1 You people may be strong
and brag about your sins,
but God can be trusted
day after day.
2 You plan brutal crimes,
and your lying words cut
like a sharp razor.
3 You would rather do evil
than good, and tell lies
than speak the truth.
4 You love to say cruel things,
and your words are a trap.

5 God will destroy you forever!
He will grab you and drag you
from your homes.
You will be uprooted
and left to die.
6 When good people see
this fearsome sight,
they will laugh and say,
7 "Just look at them now!
Instead of trusting God,
they trusted their wealth
and their cruelty."

8 But I am like an olive tree
growing in God's house,
and I can count on his love
forever and ever.
9 I will always thank God
for what he has done;
I will praise his good name
when his people meet.

Psalm 53

[A special psalm by David for the music leader. To the tune "Mahalath."[k]]

No One Can Ignore God

1 Only a fool would say,
"There is no God!"
People like that are worthless!

[j]**51.7** *hyssop*: A small bush with bunches of small, white flowers. It was sometimes used as a symbol for making a person clean from sin. [k]**Psalm 53** *Mahalath*: Or "For flutes," one possible meaning for the difficult Hebrew text.

52 Title 1 S 22.9, 10. **53.1-3** Ro 3.10-12.

They are heartless and cruel
and never do right.
2 From heaven God
looks down to see
if anyone is wise enough
to search for him.
3 But all of them
are crooked and corrupt.
Not one of them does right.

4 Won't you lawbreakers learn?
You refuse to pray,
and you gobble down
the people of God.
5 But you will be terrified
worse than ever before.
God will scatter the bones
of his enemies,
and you will be ashamed
when God rejects you.

6 I long for someone from Zion
to come and save Israel!
Our God, when you bless
your people again,
Jacob's family will be glad,
and Israel will celebrate.

Psalm 54

[*For the music leader. Use with stringed instruments. A special psalm that David wrote when the people of Ziph went to Saul and said, "David is hiding here with us."*]

Trusting God in Times of Trouble

1 Save me, God, by your power
and prove that I am right.
2 Listen to my prayer
and hear what I say.
3 Cruel strangers have attacked
and want me dead.
Not one of them cares
about you.

4 You will help me, Lord God,
and keep me from falling;
5 you will punish my enemies
for their evil deeds.
Be my faithful friend
and destroy them.

6 I will bring a gift
and offer a sacrifice
to you, LORD.
I will praise your name
because you are good.
7 You have rescued me
from all of my troubles,
and my own eyes have seen
my enemies fall.

Psalm 55

[*A special psalm by David for the music leader. Use with stringed instruments.*]

Betrayed by a Friend

1 Listen, God, to my prayer!
Don't reject my request.
2 Please listen and help me.
My thoughts are troubled,
and I keep groaning
3 because my loud enemies
shout and attack.
They treat me terribly
and hold angry grudges.
4 My heart is racing fast,
and I am afraid of dying.
5 I am trembling with fear,
completely terrified.

6 I wish I had wings
like a dove,
so I could fly far away
and be at peace.
7 I would go and live
in some distant desert.
8 I would quickly find shelter
from howling winds
and raging storms.

9 Confuse my enemies, Lord!
Upset their plans.
Cruelty and violence
are all I see in the city,
10 and they are like guards
on patrol day and night.
The city is full of trouble,
evil, 11 and corruption.
Troublemakers and liars
freely roam the streets.

54 Title 1 S 23.19; 26.1.

12 My enemies are not the ones
who sneer and make fun.
I could put up with that
or even hide from them.
13 But it was my closest friend,
the one I trusted most.
14 We enjoyed being together,
and we went with others
to your house, our God.

15 All who hate me are controlled
by the power of evil.
Sentence them to death
and send them down alive
to the world of the dead.

16 I ask for your help, LORD God,
and you will keep me safe.
17 Morning, noon, and night
you hear my concerns
and my complaints.
18 I am attacked from all sides,
but you will rescue me
unharmed by the battle.
19 You have always ruled,
and you will hear me.
You will defeat my enemies
because they won't turn
and worship you.

20 My friend turned against me
and broke his promise.
21 His words were smoother
than butter, and softer
than olive oil.
But hatred filled his heart,
and he was ready to attack
with a sword.

22 Our LORD, we belong to you.
We tell you what worries us,
and you won't let us fall.
23 But what about those people
who are cruel and brutal?
You will throw them down
into the deepest pit
long before their time.
I trust you, LORD!

Psalm 56

[For the music leader. To the tune "A Silent Dove in the Distance."[l] *A special psalm by David when the Philistines captured him in Gath.]*

A Prayer of Trust in God

1 Have pity, God Most High!
My enemies chase me all day.
2 Many of them are pursuing
and attacking me,
3 but even when I am afraid,
I keep on trusting you.
4 I praise your promises!
I trust you and am not afraid.
No one can harm me.

5 Enemies spend the whole day
finding fault with me;
all they think about
is how to do me harm.
6 They attack from ambush,
watching my every step
and hoping to kill me.
7 They won't get away[m]
with these crimes, God,
because when you get angry,
you destroy people.

8 You have kept record
of my days of wandering.
You have stored my tears
in your bottle
and counted each of them.

9 When I pray, LORD God,
my enemies will retreat,
because I know for certain
that you are with me.
10 I praise your promises!
11 I trust you and am not afraid.
No one can harm me.

12 I will keep my promises
to you, my God,
and bring you gifts.
13 You protected me from death
and kept me from stumbling,
so that I would please you

[l]**Psalm 56** *A Silent . . . Distance*: One possible meaning for the difficult Hebrew text.
[m]**56.7** *They . . . away*: One possible meaning for the difficult Hebrew text.
56 Title 1 S 21.13-15.

and follow the light
that leads to life.

Psalm 57

[*For the music leader. To the tune "Don't Destroy."*[n] *A special psalm by David when he was in the cave while running from Saul.*]

Praise and Trust in Times of Trouble

1 God Most High, have pity on me!
Have mercy. I run to you
for safety.
In the shadow of your wings,
I seek protection
till danger dies down.
2 I pray to you, my protector.
3 You will send help from heaven
and save me,
but you will bring trouble
on my attackers.
You are faithful,
and you can be trusted.

4 I live among lions,
who gobble down people!
They have spears and arrows
instead of teeth,
and they have sharp swords
instead of tongues.

5 May you, my God, be honored
above the heavens;
may your glory be seen
everywhere on earth.

6 Enemies set traps for my feet
and struck me down.
They dug a pit in my path,
but fell in it themselves.
7 I am faithful to you,
and you can trust me.
I will sing and play music
for you, my God.
8 I feel wide awake!
I will wake up my harp
and wake up the sun.
9 I will praise you, Lord,
for everyone to hear,
and I will sing hymns to you
in every nation.
10 Your love reaches higher
than the heavens;
your loyalty extends
beyond the clouds.

11 May you, my God, be honored
above the heavens;
may your glory be seen
everywhere on earth.

Psalm 58

[*A special psalm by David for the music leader. To the tune "Don't Destroy."*[n]]

A Prayer When All Goes Wrong

1 Do you mighty people[o] talk
only to oppose justice?[p]
Don't you ever judge fairly?
2 You are always planning evil,
and you are brutal.
3 You have done wrong and lied
from the day you were born.
4 Your words spread poison
like the bite of a cobra
5 that refuses to listen
to the snake charmer.

6 My enemies are fierce
as lions, LORD God!
Shatter their teeth.
Snatch out their fangs.
7 Make them disappear
like leaking water,
and make their arrows miss.
8 Let them dry up like snails
or be like a child that dies
before seeing the sun.
9 Wipe them out quicker
than a pot can be heated
by setting thorns on fire.[q]

10 Good people will be glad
when they see the wicked
getting what they deserve,
and they will wash their feet
in their enemies' blood.

[n]**Psalms 57; 58** *Don't Destroy*: One possible meaning for the difficult Hebrew text.
[o]**58.1** *mighty people*: Or "mighty rulers" or "mighty gods." [p]**58.1** *Do . . . justice*: One possible meaning for the difficult Hebrew text. [q]**58.9** *Wipe . . . fire*: One possible meaning for the difficult Hebrew text.
57 Title 1 S 22.1; 24.3. **57.6** 3 Macc 6.21.

11 Everyone will say, "It's true!
Good people are rewarded.
God does rule the earth
with justice."

Psalm 59

[For the music leader. To the tune "Don't Destroy."[r] A special psalm by David when Saul had David's house watched so that he could kill him.]

A Prayer for Protection

1 Save me, God! Protect me
from enemy attacks!
2 Keep me safe from brutal people
who want to kill me.

3 Merciless enemies, LORD,
are hiding and plotting,
hoping to kill me.
I have not hurt them
in any way at all.
4 But they are ready to attack.
Do something! Help me!
Look at what's happening.
5 LORD God All-Powerful,
you are the God of Israel.
Punish the other nations
and don't pity those terrible
and rebellious people.

6 My enemies return at evening,
growling like dogs
roaming the city.
7 They curse and their words
cut like swords,
as they say to themselves,
"No one can hear us!"

8 You, LORD, laugh at them
and sneer at the nations.
9 You are my mighty fortress,
and I depend on you.
10 You love me and will let me
see my enemies defeated.
11 Don't kill them,
or everyone may forget!
Just use your mighty power
to make them tremble
and fall.

You are a shield
for your people.
12 My enemies are liars!
So let them be trapped
by their boastful lies.
13 Get angry and destroy them.
Leave them in ruin.
Then all the nations will know
that you rule in Israel.

14 Those liars return at evening,
growling like dogs
roaming the city.
15 They search for scraps of food,
and they snarl
until they are stuffed.

16 But I will sing about
your strength, my God,
and I will celebrate
because of your love.
You are my fortress,
my place of protection
in times of trouble.
17 I will sing your praises!
You are my mighty fortress,
and you love me.

Psalm 60

[For the music leader. To the tune "Lily of the Promise." A special psalm by David for teaching. He wrote it during his wars with the Arameans of northern Syria,[s] when Joab came back and killed twelve thousand Edomites[t] in Salt Valley.]

You Can Depend on God

1 You, God, are angry with us!
We are rejected and crushed.
Make us strong again!
2 You made the earth shake
and split wide open;
now heal its wounds
and stop its trembling.
3 You brought hard times
on your people,

[r]**Psalm 59** *Don't Destroy*: See the note at Psalms 57; 58. [s]**Psalm 60** *wars . . . Syria*: See 2 Samuel 8.3-8; 10.16-18; 1 Chronicles 18.3-11; 19.6-19. [t]**Psalm 60** *killed . . . Edomites*: See 2 Samuel 8.13; 1 Chronicles 18.12.

59 Title 1 S 19.11. **60 Title** 2 S 8.13; 1 Ch 18.12.

and you gave us wine
that made us stagger.

4 You gave a signal to those
who worship you,
so they could escape
from enemy arrows.[u]
5 Answer our prayers!
Use your powerful arm
and give us victory.
Then the people you love
will be safe.

6 Our God, you solemnly promised,
"I would gladly divide up
the city of Shechem
and give away Succoth Valley
piece by piece.
7 The lands of Gilead
and Manasseh are mine.
Ephraim is my war helmet,
and Judah is the symbol
of my royal power.
8 Moab is merely my washbasin.
Edom belongs to me,
and I shout in triumph
over the Philistines."

9 Our God, who will bring me
to the fortress,
or lead me to Edom?
10 Have you rejected us
and deserted our armies?
11 Help us defeat our enemies!
No one else can rescue us.
12 You will give us victory
and crush our enemies.

Psalm 61

[*A psalm by David for the music leader. Use with stringed instruments.*]

Under the Protection of God

1 Please listen, God,
and answer my prayer!
2 I feel hopeless,
and I cry out to you
from a faraway land.
Lead me to the mighty rock[v]
high above me.
3 You are a strong tower,
where I am safe
from my enemies.

4 Let me live with you forever
and find protection
under your wings, my God.
5 You heard my promises,
and you have blessed me,
just as you bless everyone
who worships you.

6 Let the king have a long
and healthy life.
7 May he always rule
with you, God, at his side;
may your love and loyalty
watch over him.

8 I will sing your praises
forever and will always
keep my promises.

Psalm 62

[*A psalm by David for Jeduthun, the music leader.*]

God Is Powerful and Kind

1 Only God can save me,
and I calmly wait for[w] him.
2 God alone is the mighty rock[x]
that keeps me safe
and the fortress
where I am secure.

3 I feel like a shaky fence
or a sagging wall.
How long will all of you
attack and assault me?
4 You want to bring me down
from my place of honor.
You love to tell lies,
and when your words are kind,
hatred hides in your heart.
5 Only God gives inward peace,
and I depend on him.

[u]**60.4** *so . . . arrows*: Some ancient translations and one possible meaning for the difficult Hebrew text. [v]**61.2** *mighty rock*: See the note at 18.2. [w]**62.1** *calmly wait for*: Or "am at peace with." [x]**62.2** *mighty rock*: See the note at 18.2.

6 God alone is the mighty rock
that keeps me safe,
and he is the fortress
where I feel secure.
7 God saves me and honors me.
He is that mighty rock
where I find safety.

8 Trust God, my friends,
and always tell him
each one of your concerns.
God is our place of safety.

9 We humans are only a breath;
none of us are truly great.
All of us together weigh less
than a puff of air.
10 Don't trust in violence
or depend on dishonesty
or rely on great wealth.

11 I heard God say two things:
"I am powerful,
12 and I am very kind."
The Lord rewards each of us
according to what we do.

Psalm 63

[*A psalm by David when he was in the desert of Judah.*]

God's Love Means More than Life

1 You are my God. I worship you.
In my heart, I long for you,
as I would long for a stream
in a scorching desert.

2 I have seen your power
and your glory
in the place of worship.
3 Your love means more
than life to me,
and I praise you.
4 As long as I live,
I will pray to you.
5 I will sing joyful praises
and be filled with excitement
like a guest at a banquet.

6 I think about you
before I go to sleep,
and my thoughts turn to you
during the night.
7 You have helped me,
and I sing happy songs
in the shadow of your wings.
8 I stay close to you,
and your powerful arm
supports me.

9 All who want to kill me
will end up in the ground.
10 Swords will run them through,
and wild dogs will eat them.

11 Because of you, our God,
the king will celebrate
with your faithful followers,
but liars will be silent.

Psalm 64

[*A psalm by David for the music leader.*]

Celebrate because of the LORD

1 Listen to my concerns, God,
and protect me
from my terrible enemies.
2 Keep me safe from secret plots
of corrupt and evil gangs.
3 Their words cut like swords,
and their cruel remarks
sting like sharp arrows.
4 They fearlessly ambush
and shoot innocent people.

5 They are determined to do evil,
and they tell themselves,
"Let's set traps!
No one can see us."[y]
6 They make evil plans and say,
"We'll commit a perfect crime.
No one knows our thoughts."[z]

7 But God will shoot his arrows
and quickly wound them.
8 They will be destroyed
by their own words,

[y]**64.5** *us*: One ancient translation; Hebrew "them."

[z]**64.6** *thoughts*: One possible meaning for the difficult Hebrew text of verse 6.

62.12 Job 34.11; Jr 17.10; Mt 16.27; Ro 2.6; Rev 2.23.

63 Title 1 S 23.14.

and everyone who sees them
will tremble with fear.[a]
9 They will be afraid and say,
"Look at what God has done
and keep it all in mind."

10 May the LORD bless his people
with peace and happiness
and let them celebrate.

Psalm 65

[*A psalm by David and a song for the music leader.*]

God Answers Prayer

1 Our God, you deserve[b] praise
in Zion, where we keep
our promises to you.
2 Everyone will come to you
because you answer prayer.
3 Our terrible sins get us down,
but you forgive us.
4 You bless your chosen ones,
and you invite them
to live near you
in your temple.
We will enjoy your house,
the sacred temple.

5 Our God, you save us,
and your fearsome deeds answer
our prayers for justice!
You give hope to people
everywhere on earth,
even those across the sea.
6 You are strong,
and your mighty power
put the mountains in place.
7 You silence the roaring waves
and the noisy shouts
of the nations.
8 People far away marvel
at your fearsome deeds,
and all who live under the sun
celebrate and sing
because of you.

9 You take care of the earth
and send rain to help the soil
grow all kinds of crops.
Your rivers never run dry,
and you prepare the earth
to produce much grain.
10 You water all of its fields
and level the lumpy ground.
You send showers of rain
to soften the soil
and help the plants sprout.
11 Wherever your footsteps
touch the earth,
a rich harvest is gathered.
12 Desert pastures blossom,
and mountains celebrate.
13 Meadows are filled
with sheep and goats;
valleys overflow with grain
and echo with joyful songs.

Psalm 66

[*A song and a psalm for the music leader.*]

Shout Praises to God

1 Tell everyone on this earth
to shout praises to God!
2 Sing about his glorious name.
Honor him with praises.
3 Say to God, "Everything you do
is fearsome,
and your mighty power makes
your enemies come crawling.
4 You are worshiped by everyone!
We all sing praises to you."

5 Come and see the fearsome things
our God has done!
6 When God made the sea dry up,
our people walked across,
and because of him,
we celebrated there.
7 His mighty power rules forever,
and nothing the nations do
can be hidden from him.
So don't turn against God.

8 All of you people,
come praise our God!
Let his praises be heard.
9 God protects us from death
and keeps us steady.

[a]**64.8** *tremble with fear*: Or "turn and run."
[b]**65.1** *deserve*: One possible meaning for the difficult Hebrew text.
66.6 **a** Ex 14.21; **b** Js 3.14-17.

10 Our God, you tested us,
just as silver is tested.
11 You trapped us in a net
and gave us heavy burdens.
12 You sent war chariots
to crush our skulls.
We traveled through fire
and through floods,
but you brought us
to a land of plenty.

13 I will bring sacrifices
into your house, my God,
and I will do what I promised
14 when I was in trouble.
15 I will sacrifice my best sheep
and offer bulls and goats
on your altar.

16 All who worship God,
come here and listen;
I will tell you everything
God has done for me.
17 I prayed to the Lord,
and I praised him.
18 If my thoughts had been sinful,
he would have refused
to hear me.
19 But God did listen
and answered my prayer.
20 Let's praise God!
He listened when I prayed,
and he is always kind.

Psalm 67

[*A psalm and a song for the music leader. Use with stringed instruments.*]

Tell the Nations To Praise God

1 Our God, be kind and bless us!
Be pleased and smile.
2 Then everyone on earth
will learn to follow you,
and all nations will see
your power to save us.

3 Make everyone praise you
and shout your praises.
4 Let the nations celebrate
with joyful songs,
because you judge fairly
and guide all nations.
5 Make everyone praise you
and shout your praises.

6 Our God has blessed the earth
with a wonderful harvest!
7 Pray for his blessings
to continue
and for everyone on earth
to worship our God.

Psalm 68

[*A psalm and a song by David for the music leader.*]

God Will Win the Battle

1 Do something, God!
Scatter your hateful enemies.
Make them turn and run.
2 Scatter them like smoke!
When you come near,
make them melt
like wax in a fire.
3 But let your people be happy
and celebrate because of you.

4 Our God, you are the one
who rides on the clouds,
and we praise you.
Your name is the LORD,
and we celebrate
as we worship you.

5 Our God, from your sacred home
you take care of orphans
and protect widows.
6 You find families
for those who are lonely.
You set prisoners free
and let them prosper,[c]
but all who rebel will live
in a scorching desert.

7 You set your people free,
and you led them
through the desert.
8 God of Israel,
the earth trembled,
and rain poured down.
You alone are the God
who rules from Mount Sinai.
9 When your land was thirsty,

[c]**68.6** *and let them prosper*: Or "and give them a song."
68.8 Ex 19.18.

you sent showers
to refresh it.
10 Your people settled there,
and you were generous
to everyone in need.

11 You gave the command,
and a chorus of women told
what had happened:
12 "Kings and their armies
retreated and ran,
and everything they left
is now being divided.
13 And for those who stayed back
to guard the sheep,
there are metal doves
with silver-coated wings
and shiny gold feathers."

14 God All-Powerful, you scattered
the kings like snow falling
on Mount Zalmon.[d]

15 Our LORD and our God,
Bashan is a mighty mountain
covered with peaks.
16 Why is it jealous of Zion,
the mountain you chose
as your home forever?

17 When you, LORD God, appeared
to your people[e] at Sinai,
you came with thousands
of mighty chariots.
18 When you climbed
the high mountain,
you took prisoners with you
and were given gifts.
Your enemies didn't want you
to live there,
but they gave you gifts.

19 We praise you, Lord God!
You treat us with kindness
day after day,
and you rescue us.

20 You always protect us
and save us from death.

21 Our Lord and our God,
your terrible enemies
are ready for war,[f]
but you will crush
their skulls.
22 You promised to bring them
from Bashan
and from the deepest sea.
23 Then we could stomp
on their blood,
and our dogs could chew
on their bones.

24 We have seen crowds marching
to your place of worship,
our God and King.
25 The singers come first,
and then the musicians,
surrounded by young women
playing tambourines.
26 They come shouting,
"People of Israel,
praise the LORD God!"
27 The small tribe of Benjamin
leads the way,
followed by the leaders
from Judah.
Then come the leaders
from Zebulun and Naphtali.

28 Our God, show your strength!
Show us once again.
29 Then kings will bring gifts
to your temple
in Jerusalem.[g]

30 Punish that animal
that lives in the swamp![h]
Punish that nation
whose leaders and people
are like wild bulls.
Make them come crawling
with gifts of silver.

[d]**68.14** *Mount Zalmon*: The location of this mountain is not known. [e]**68.17** *to your people*: Or "in all your holiness" or "in your holy place." [f]**68.21** *are ready for war*: The Hebrew text has "have long hair," which probably refers to the ancient custom of wearing long hair on special occasions, such as a "holy war." [g]**68.28,29** *Our God . . . Jerusalem*: One possible meaning for the difficult Hebrew text of verses 28, 29. [h]**68.30** *animal . . . swamp*: Probably Egypt.
68.18 Eph 4.8.

Scatter those nations
that enjoy making war.[i]
31 Force the Egyptians to bring
gifts of bronze;
make the Ethiopians[j] hurry
to offer presents.[k]

32 Now sing praises to God!
Every kingdom on earth,
sing to the Lord!
33 Praise the one who rides
across the ancient skies;
listen as he speaks
with a mighty voice.

34 Tell about God's power!
He is honored in Israel,
and he rules the skies.
35 The God of Israel is fearsome
in his temple,
and he makes us strong.
Let's praise our God!

Psalm 69

[By David for the music leader. To the tune "Lilies."]

God Can Be Trusted

1 Save me, God!
I am about to drown.
2 I am sinking deep in the mud,
and my feet are slipping.
I am about to be swept under
by a mighty flood.
3 I am worn out from crying,
and my throat is dry.
I have waited for you
till my eyes are blurred.

4 There are more people
who hate me for no reason
than there are hairs
on my head.
Many terrible enemies
want to destroy me, God.
Am I supposed to give back
something I didn't steal?

5 You know my foolish sins.
Not one is hidden from you.

6 LORD God All-Powerful,
ruler of Israel,
don't let me embarrass anyone
who trusts and worships you.
7 It is for your sake alone
that I am insulted
and blush with shame.
8 I am like a stranger
to my relatives
and like a foreigner
to my own family.

9 My love for your house
burns in me like a fire,
and when others insulted you,
they insulted me as well.
10 I cried and went without food,[l]
but they still insulted me.
11 They sneered at me
for wearing sackcloth[m]
to show my sorrow.
12 Rulers and judges gossip
about me,
and drunkards make up songs
to mock me.

13 But I pray to you, LORD.
So when the time is right,
answer me and help me
with your wonderful love.
14 Don't let me sink in the mud,
but save me from my enemies
and from the deep water.
15 Don't let me be
swept away by a flood
or drowned in the ocean
or swallowed by death.

16 Answer me, LORD!
You are kind and good.
Pay attention to me!
You are truly merciful.
17 Don't turn away from me.
I am your servant,
and I am in trouble.
Please hurry and help!

[i] **68.30** *war*: One possible meaning for the difficult Hebrew text of verse 30. [j] **68.31** *the Ethiopians*: The Hebrew text has "the people of Cush," which was a region south of Egypt that included parts of the present countries of Ethiopia and Sudan. [k] **68.31** *presents*: One possible meaning for the difficult Hebrew text of verse 31. [l] **69.10** *went without food*: See the note at 35.13. [m] **69.11** *sackcloth*: See the note at 30.11.

69.4 Ps 35.19; Jn 15.25. **69.9** **a** Jn 2.17; **b** Ro 15.3.

18 Come and save me
from my enemies.

19 You know how I am insulted,
mocked, and disgraced;
you know every one
of my enemies.
20 I am crushed by insults,
and I feel sick.
I had hoped for mercy and pity,
but there was none.
21 Enemies poisoned my food,
and when I was thirsty,
they gave me vinegar.

22 Make their table a trap
for them and their friends.
23 Blind them with darkness
and make them tremble.
24 Show them how angry you are!
Be furious and catch them.
25 Destroy their camp
and don't let anyone live
in their tents.

26 They cause trouble for people
you have already punished;
their gossip hurts those
you have wounded.
27 Make them guiltier than ever
and don't forgive them.
28 Wipe their names from the book
of the living;
remove them from the list
of the innocent.
29 I am mistreated and in pain.
Protect me, God,
and keep me safe!

30 I will praise the LORD God
with a song
and a thankful heart.
31 This will please the LORD
better than offering an ox
or a full-grown bull.
32 When those in need see this,
they will be happy,
and the LORD's worshipers
will be encouraged.
33 The LORD will listen
when the homeless cry out,
and he will never forget
his people in prison.

34 Heaven and earth
will praise our God,
and so will the oceans
and everything in them.
35 God will rescue Jerusalem,
and he will rebuild
the towns of Judah.
His people will live there
on their own land,
36 and when the time comes,
their children will inherit
the land.
Then everyone who loves God
will also settle there.

Psalm 70

[By David for the music leader. To be used when an offering is made.]

God Is Wonderful

1 Save me, LORD God!
Hurry and help.
2 Disappoint and confuse
all who want to kill me.
Turn away and disgrace
all who want to hurt me.
3 Embarrass and shame those
who say, "We told you so!"

4 Let your worshipers celebrate
and be glad because of you.
They love your saving power,
so let them always say,
"God is wonderful!"
5 I am poor and needy,
but you, the LORD God,
care about me.

You are the one who saves me.
Please hurry and help!

Psalm 71

A Prayer for God's Protection

1 I run to you, LORD,
for protection.
Don't disappoint me.

69.21 Mt 27.48; Mk 15.36; Lk 23.36; Jn 19.28, 29. **69.22,23** Ro 11.9, 10. **69.25** Ac 1.20.
69.28 Ex 32.32; Rev 3.5; 13.8; 17.8.

2 You do what is right,
so come to my rescue.
Listen to my prayer
and keep me safe.
3 Be my mighty rock,[n] the place
where I can always run
for protection.
Save me by your command!
You are my mighty rock
and my fortress.

4 Come and save me, LORD God,
from vicious and cruel
and brutal enemies!
5 I depend on you,
and I have trusted you
since I was young.
6 I have relied on you[o]
from the day I was born.
You brought me safely
through birth,
and I always praise you.

7 Many people think of me
as something evil.
But you are my mighty protector,
8 and I praise and honor you
all day long.
9 Don't throw me aside
when I am old;
don't desert me
when my strength is gone.
10 My enemies are plotting
because they want me dead.
11 They say, "Now we'll catch you!
God has deserted you,
and no one can save you."
12 Come closer, God!
Please hurry and help.
13 Embarrass and destroy
all who want me dead;
disgrace and confuse
all who want to hurt me.
14 I will never give up hope
or stop praising you.
15 All day long I will tell
the wonderful things you do
to save your people.
But you have done much more
than I could possibly know.

16 I will praise you, LORD God,
for your mighty deeds
and your power to save.

17 You have taught me
since I was a child,
and I never stop telling about
your marvelous deeds.
18 Don't leave me when I am old
and my hair turns gray.
Let me tell future generations
about your mighty power.
19 Your deeds of kindness
are known in the heavens.
No one is like you!

20 You made me suffer a lot,
but you will bring me
back from this deep pit
and give me new life.
21 You will make me truly great
and take my sorrow away.

22 I will praise you, God,
the Holy One of Israel.
You are faithful.
I will play the harp
and sing your praises.
23 You have rescued me!
I will celebrate and shout,
singing praises to you
with all my heart.
24 All day long I will announce
your power to save.
I will tell how you disgraced
and disappointed those
who wanted to hurt me.

Psalm 72

[*By Solomon.*]

A Prayer for God To Guide and Help the King

1 Please help the king
to be honest and fair
just like you, our God.
2 Let him be honest and fair
with all your people,
especially the poor.
3 Let peace and justice rule
every mountain and hill.

[n]**71.3** *mighty rock*: See the note at 18.2. [o]**71.6** *I . . . you*: One possible meaning for the difficult Hebrew text.

4 Let the king defend the poor,
rescue the homeless, and crush
everyone who hurts them.
5 Let the king live[p] forever
like the sun and the moon.
6 Let him be as helpful as rain
that refreshes the meadows
and the ground.
7 Let the king be fair
with everyone,
and let there be peace
until the moon
falls from the sky.

8 Let his kingdom reach
from sea to sea,
from the Euphrates River
across all the earth.
9 Force the desert tribes
to accept his rule,
and make his enemies
crawl in the dirt.
10 Force the rulers of Tarshish[q]
and of the islands
to pay taxes to him.
Make the kings of Sheba
and of Seba[r] bring gifts.
11 Make other rulers bow down
and all nations serve him.

12 Do this because the king
rescues the homeless
when they cry out,
and he helps everyone
who is poor and in need.
13 The king has pity
on the weak and the helpless
and protects those in need.
14 He cares when they hurt,
and he saves them from cruel
and violent deaths.

15 Long live the king!
Give him gold from Sheba.
Always pray for the king
and praise him each day.
16 Let cities overflow with food
and hills be covered with grain,
just like Mount Lebanon.
Let the people in the cities
prosper like wild flowers.
17 May the glory of the king
shine brightly forever
like the sun in the sky.
Let him make nations prosper
and learn to praise him.

18 LORD God of Israel,
we praise you.
Only you can work miracles.
19 We will always praise
your glorious name.
Let your glory be seen
everywhere on earth.
Amen and amen.

20 This ends the prayers
of David, the son of Jesse.

BOOK III
(Psalms 73–89)

Psalm 73
[*A psalm by Asaph.*]

God Is Good

1 God is truly good to Israel,[s]
especially to everyone
with a pure heart.
2 But I almost stumbled and fell,
3 because it made me jealous
to see proud and evil people
and to watch them prosper.
4 They never have to suffer,[t]
they stay healthy,
5 and they don't have troubles
like everyone else.

6 Their pride is like a necklace,
and they commit sin more often
than they dress themselves.
7 Their eyes poke out with fat,
and their minds are flooded
with foolish thoughts.

[p]**72.5** *Let the king live*: One ancient translation; Hebrew "Let them worship you."
[q]**72.10** *Tarshish*: Possibly a city in Spain. [r]**72.10** *Sheba . . . Seba*: Sheba may have been a place in what is now southwest Arabia, and Seba may have been in southern Arabia. [s]**73.1** *to Israel*: Or "to those who do right." [t]**73.4** *They . . . suffer*: Or "They die a painless death."
72.8 Zec 9.10; Si 44.21.

8 They sneer and say cruel things,
and because of their pride,
they make violent threats.
9 They dare to speak against God
and to order others around.

10 God will bring his people back,
and they will drink the water
he so freely gives.[u]

11 Only evil people would say,
"God Most High cannot
know everything!"
12 Yet all goes well for them,
and they live in peace.
13 What good did it do me
to keep my thoughts pure
and refuse to do wrong?
14 I am sick all day,
and I am punished
each morning.
15 If I had said evil things,
I would not have been loyal
to your people.

16 It was hard for me
to understand all this!
17 Then I went to your temple,
and there I understood
what will happen
to my enemies.
18 You will make them stumble,
never to get up again.
19 They will be terrified,
suddenly swept away
and no longer there.
20 They will disappear, Lord,
despised like a bad dream
the morning after.

21 Once I was bitter
and brokenhearted.
22 I was stupid and ignorant,
and I treated you
as a wild animal would.
23 But I never really left you,
and you hold my right hand.
24 Your advice has been my guide,
and later you will welcome me
in glory.[v]

25 In heaven I have only you,
and on this earth
you are all I want.
26 My body and mind may fail,
but you are my strength
and my choice forever.

27 Powerful LORD God,
all who stay far from you
will be lost,
and you will destroy those
who are unfaithful.
28 It is good for me
to be near you.
I choose you as my protector,
and I will tell about
your wonderful deeds.

Psalm 74

[A special psalm by Asaph.]

A Prayer for the Nation in Times of Trouble

1 Our God, why have you
completely rejected us?
Why are you so angry
with the ones you care for?
2 Remember the people
you rescued long ago,
the tribe you chose
to be your very own.
Think of Mount Zion,
your home;
3 walk over to the temple
left in ruins forever
by those who hate us.

4 Your enemies roared like lions
in your holy temple,
and they have placed
their banners there.
5 It looks like a forest
chopped to pieces.[w]
6 They used axes and hatchets
to smash the carvings.
7 They burned down your temple
and badly disgraced it.
8 They said to themselves,
"We'll crush them!"

[u]**73.10** *gives*: One possible meaning for the difficult Hebrew text of verse 10. [v]**73.24** *in glory*: Or "with honor." [w]**74.5** *pieces*: One meaning for the difficult Hebrew text of verse 5.

Then they burned every one
of your meeting places
all over the country.
9 There are no more miracles
and no more prophets.
Who knows how long
it will be like this?

10 Our God, how much longer
will our enemies sneer?
Won't they ever stop
insulting you?
11 Why don't you punish them?
Why are you holding back?

12 Our God and King,
you have ruled
since ancient times;
you have won victories
everywhere on this earth.
13 By your power you made a path
through the sea,
and you smashed the heads
of sea monsters.
14 You crushed the heads
of the monster Leviathan,[x]
then fed him to wild creatures
in the desert.
15 You opened the ground
for streams and springs
and dried up mighty rivers.
16 You rule the day and the night,
and you put the moon
and the sun in place.
17 You made summer and winter
and gave them to the earth.[y]

18 Remember your enemies, LORD!
They foolishly sneer
and won't respect you.
19 You treat us like pet doves,
but they mistreat us.
Don't keep forgetting us
and letting us be fed
to those wild animals.
20 Remember the agreement
you made with us.
Violent enemies are hiding
in every dark corner
of the earth.
21 Don't disappoint those in need
or make them turn from you,
but help the poor and homeless
to shout your praises.
22 Do something, God!
Defend yourself.
Remember how those fools
sneer at you all day long.
23 Don't forget the loud shouts
of your enemies.

Psalm 75

[A psalm and a song by Asaph for the music leader. To the tune "Don't Destroy."[z]]

Praise God for All He Has Done

1 Our God, we thank you
for being so near to us!
Everyone celebrates
your wonderful deeds.

2 You have set a time
to judge with fairness.
3 The earth trembles,
and its people shake;
you alone keep
its foundations firm.
4 You tell every bragger,
"Stop bragging!"
And to the wicked you say,
"Don't boast of your power!
5 Stop bragging! Quit telling me
how great you are."

6 Our LORD and our God,
victory doesn't come
from the east or the west
or from the desert.
7 You are the one who judges.
You can take away power
and give it to others.
8 You hold in your hand
a cup filled with wine,[a]
strong and foaming.
You will pour out some
for every sinful person
on this earth,

[x]**74.14** *Leviathan*: God's victory over this monster sometimes stands for his power over all creation and sometimes for his defeat of Egypt. [y]**74.17** *gave . . . earth*: Or "made boundaries for the earth." [z]**Psalm 75** *Don't Destroy*: See the note at Psalms 57; 58. [a]**75.8** *a cup . . . wine*: In the Old Testament "a cup filled with wine" sometimes stands for God's anger.

74.13 Ex 14.21. **74.14** Job 41.1; Ps 104.26; Is 27.1.

and they will have to drink
until it is gone.
9 But I will always tell about
you, the God of Jacob,
and I will sing your praise.

10 Our Lord, you will destroy
the power of evil people,
but you will give strength
to those who are good.

Psalm 76

[A song and a psalm for the music leader. Use stringed instruments.]

God Always Wins

1 You, our God,
are famous in Judah
and honored in Israel.
2 Your home is on Mount Zion
in the city of peace.
3 There you destroyed
fiery arrows, shields, swords,
and all the other weapons.

4 You are more glorious than
the eternal mountains.[b]
5 Brave warriors were robbed
of what they had taken,
and now they lie dead,
unable to lift an arm.
6 God of Jacob, when you roar,
enemy chariots and horses
drop dead in their tracks.

7 Our God, you are fearsome,
and no one can oppose you
when you are angry.
8 From heaven you announced
your decisions as judge!
And all who live on this earth
were terrified and silent
9 when you took over as judge,
ready to rescue
everyone in need.
10 Even the most angry people
will praise you
when you are furious.[c]
11 Everyone, make your promises
to the LORD your God
and do what you promise.
The LORD is fearsome,
and all of his servants
should bring him gifts.
12 God destroys the courage
of rulers and kings
and makes cowards of them.

Psalm 77

[A psalm by Asaph for Jeduthun, the music leader.]

In Times of Trouble God Is with His People

1 I pray to you, Lord God,
and I beg you to listen.
2 In days filled with trouble,
I search for you.
And at night I tirelessly
lift my hands in prayer,
refusing comfort.
3 When I think of you,
I feel restless and weak.

4 Because of you, Lord God,
I can't sleep.
I am restless
and can't even talk.
5 I think of times gone by,
of those years long ago.
6 Each night my mind
is flooded with questions:[d]
7 "Have you rejected me forever?
Won't you be kind again?
8 Is this the end of your love
and your promises?
9 Have you forgotten
how to have pity?
Do you refuse to show mercy
because of your anger?"
10 Then I said, "God Most High,
what hurts me most
is that you no longer help us
with your mighty arm."

11 Our LORD, I will remember
the things you have done,
your miracles of long ago.

[b]**76.4** *the eternal mountains*: One ancient translation; Hebrew "the mountains of victims (of wild animals)." [c]**76.10** *furious*: One possible meaning for the difficult Hebrew text of verse 10.
[d]**77.6** *my mind . . . questions*: One ancient translation; Hebrew "I remember my music."

12 I will think about each one
of your mighty deeds.
13 Everything you do is right,
and no other god
compares with you.
14 You alone work miracles,
and you have let nations
see your mighty power.
15 With your own arm you rescued
your people, the descendants
of Jacob and Joseph.

16 The ocean looked at you, God,
and it trembled deep down
with fear.
17 Water flowed from the clouds.
Thunder was heard above
as your arrows of lightning
flashed about.
18 Your thunder roared
like chariot wheels.
The world was made bright
by lightning,
and all the earth trembled.

19 You walked through the water
of the mighty sea,
but your footprints
were never seen.
20 You guided your people
like a flock of sheep,
and you chose Moses and Aaron
to be their leaders.

Psalm 78

[*A special psalm by Asaph.*]

What God Has Done for His People

1 My friends, I beg you
to listen as I teach.
2 I will give instruction
and explain the mystery
of what happened long ago.
3 These are things we learned
from our ancestors,
4 and we will tell them
to the next generation.
We won't keep secret
the glorious deeds
and the mighty miracles
of the LORD.

5 God gave his Law
to Jacob's descendants,
the people of Israel.
And he told our ancestors
to teach their children,
6 so that each new generation
would know his Law
and tell it to the next.
7 Then they would trust God
and obey his teachings,
without forgetting anything
God had done.
8 They would be different
from their ancestors,
who were stubborn, rebellious,
and unfaithful to God.

9 The warriors from Ephraim
were armed with arrows,
but they ran away
when the battle began.
10 They broke their agreement
with God,
and they turned their backs
on his teaching.
11 They forgot all he had done,
even the mighty miracles
12 he did for their ancestors
near Zoan[e] in Egypt.

13 God made a path in the sea
and piled up the water
as he led them across.
14 He guided them during the day
with a cloud,
and each night he led them
with a flaming fire.
15 God made water flow
from rocks he split open
in the desert,
and his people drank freely,
as though from a lake.
16 He made streams gush out
like rivers from rocks.

17 But in the desert,
the people of God Most High
kept sinning and rebelling.

[e]**78.12** *Zoan*: A city in the eastern part of the Nile Delta.
78.2 Mt 13.35. **78.12** Ex 7.8—12.32. **78.13** Ex 14.21, 22. **78.14** Ex 13.21, 22. **78.12-16** Ws 16.1—19.22. **78.15,16** Ex 17.1-7; Nu 20.2-13.

18 They stubbornly tested God
and demanded from him
what they wanted to eat.
19 They challenged God by saying,
"Can God provide food
out here in the desert?
20 It's true God struck the rock
and water gushed out
like a river,
but can he give his people
bread and meat?"

21 When the LORD heard this,
he was angry and furious
with Jacob's descendants,
the people of Israel.
22 They had refused to trust him,
and they had doubted
his saving power.

23 But God gave a command
to the clouds,
and he opened the doors
in the skies.
24 From heaven he sent grain
that they called manna.[f]
25 He gave them more than enough,
and each one of them ate
this special food.

26 God's mighty power
brought a strong wind
from the southeast,
27 and it brought birds
that covered the ground,
like sand on the beach.
28 Then God made the birds fall
in the camp of his people
near their tents.

29 God gave his people
all they wanted,
and each of them ate
until they were full.
30 But before they had swallowed
the last bite,
31 God became angry and killed
the strongest and best
from the families of Israel.

32 But the rest kept on sinning
and would not trust
God's miracles.
33 So he cut their lives short
and made them terrified.
34 After he killed some of them,
the others turned to him
with all their hearts.
35 They remembered God Most High,
the mighty rock[g]
that kept them safe.
36 But they tried to flatter God,
and they told him lies;
37 they were unfaithful
and broke their promises.

38 Yet God was kind.
He kept forgiving their sins
and didn't destroy them.
He often became angry,
but never lost his temper.
39 God remembered that they
were made of flesh
and were like a wind
that blows once
and then dies down.

40 While they were in the desert,
they often rebelled
and made God sad.
41 They kept testing him
and caused terrible pain
for the Holy One of Israel.
42 They forgot about his power
and how he had rescued them
from their enemies.
43 God showed them all kinds
of wonderful miracles
near Zoan[h] in Egypt.
44 He turned the rivers of Egypt
into blood,
and no one could drink
from the streams.

[f]**78.24** *manna*: When the people of Israel were wandering through the desert, the Lord gave them a special kind of food to eat. It tasted like a wafer and was called "manna," which in Hebrew means, "What is this?" [g]**78.35** *mighty rock*: See the note at 18.2. [h]**78.43** *Zoan*: See the note at 78.12.

78.18-31 Ex 16.2-15; Nu 11.4-23, 31-35. **78.24** Ws 16.20-29; Jn 6.31. **78.37** Ac 8.21. **78.44** Ex 7.17-21.

45 He sent swarms of flies
to pester the Egyptians,
and he sent frogs
to cause them trouble.

46 God let worms and grasshoppers
eat their crops.
47 He destroyed their grapevines
and their fig trees
with hail and floods.[i]
48 Then he killed their cattle
with hail
and their other animals
with lightning.

49 God was so angry and furious
that he went into a rage
and caused them great trouble
by sending swarms
of destroying angels.
50 God gave in to his anger
and slaughtered them
in a terrible way.
51 He killed the first-born son
of each Egyptian family.

52 Then God led his people
out of Egypt
and guided them in the desert
like a flock of sheep.
53 He led them safely along,
and they were not afraid,
but their enemies drowned
in the sea.

54 God brought his people
to the sacred mountain
that he had taken
by his own power.
55 He made nations run
from the tribes of Israel,
and he let the tribes
take over their land.

56 But the people tested
God Most High,
and they refused
to obey his laws.
57 They were as unfaithful
as their ancestors,
and they were as crooked
as a twisted arrow.
58 God demanded all their love,
but they made him angry
by worshiping idols.

59 So God became furious
and completely rejected
the people of Israel.
60 Then he deserted his home
at Shiloh, where he lived
here on earth.
61 He let enemies capture
the sacred chest[j]
and let them dishonor him.

62 God took out his anger
on his chosen ones
and let them be killed
by enemy swords.
63 Fire destroyed the young men,
and the young women were left
with no one to marry.
64 Priests died violent deaths,
but their widows
were not allowed to mourn.

65 Finally the Lord woke up,
and he shouted
like a drunken soldier.
66 God scattered his enemies
and made them ashamed
forever.

67 Then the Lord decided
not to make his home
with Joseph's descendants
in Ephraim.[k]

[i]**78.47** *floods*: Or "frost." [j]**78.61** *sacred chest*: The Hebrew text has "his power," which refers to the sacred chest. In Psalm 132.8 it is called "powerful." [k]**78.67** *with . . . Ephraim*: Ephraim was Joseph's youngest son. One of the twelve tribes was named after him, and sometimes the northern kingdom of Israel was also known as Ephraim. The town of Shiloh was in the territory of Ephraim, but the place where God was worshiped was moved from there to Zion (Jerusalem) in the territory of Judah.

78.45 **a** Ex 8.20-24; **b** Ex 8.1-6. **78.46** Ex 10.12-15. **78.47,48** Ex 9.22-25. **78.51** Ex 12.29. **78.52** Ex 13.17-22. **78.53** Ex 14.26-28. **78.54** Ex 15.17; Js 3.14-17. **78.55** Js 11.16-23. **78.56** Jg 2.11-15. **78.60** Js 18.1; Jr 7.12-14; 26.6. **78.61** 1 S 4.4-22.

68 Instead he chose the tribe
of Judah,
and he chose Mount Zion,
the place he loves.
69 There he built his temple
as lofty as the mountains
and as solid as the earth
that he had made
to last forever.

70 The Lord God chose David
to be his servant and took him
from tending sheep
71 and from caring for lambs.
Then God made him the leader
of Israel, his own nation.
72 David treated the people fairly
and guided them with wisdom.

Psalm 79

[*A psalm by Asaph.*]

Have Pity on Jerusalem

1 Our God, foreign nations
have taken your land,
disgraced your temple,
and left Jerusalem in ruins.
2 They have fed the bodies
of your servants
to flesh-eating birds;
your loyal people are food
for savage animals.
3 All Jerusalem is covered
with their blood,
and there is no one left
to bury them.
4 Every nation around us
sneers and makes fun.

5 Our LORD, will you keep on
being angry?
Will your angry feelings
keep flaming up like fire?
6 Get angry with those nations
that don't know you
and won't worship you!
7 They have gobbled down
Jacob's descendants
and left the land in ruins.
8 Don't make us pay for the sins
of our ancestors.
Have pity and come quickly!
We are completely helpless.
9 Our God, you keep us safe.
Now help us! Rescue us.
Forgive our sins
and bring honor to yourself.

10 Why should nations ask us,
"Where is your God?"
Let us and the other nations
see you take revenge
for your servants who died
a violent death.

11 Listen to the prisoners groan!
Let your mighty power save all
who are sentenced to die.
12 Each of those nations sneered
at you, our Lord.
Now let others sneer at them,
seven times as much.
13 Then we, your people,
will always thank you.
We are like sheep
with you as our shepherd,
and all generations
will hear us praise you.

Psalm 80

[*A psalm by Asaph for the music leader. To the tune "Lilies of the Agreement."*]

Help Our Nation

1 Shepherd of Israel, you lead
the descendants of Joseph,
and you sit on your throne
above the winged creatures.[l]
Listen to our prayer
and let your light shine
2 for the tribes of Ephraim,
Benjamin, and Manasseh.
Save us by your power.

3 Our God, make us strong again!
Smile on us and save us.

[l]**80.1** *winged creatures*: Two winged creatures made of gold were on the top of the sacred chest and were symbols of the LORD's throne on earth (see Exodus 25.18).

78.70,71 1 S 16.11, 12; 2 S 7.8; 1 Ch 17.7; Ps 151.4. **79.1** 2 K 25.8-10; 2 Ch 36.17-19; Jr 52.12-14. **79.8,13** 3 Macc 2.20. **80.1** Ex 25.22.

4 LORD God All-Powerful,
how much longer
will the prayers of your people
make you angry?
5 You gave us tears for food,
and you made us drink them
by the bowlful.
6 Because of you,
our enemies who live nearby
laugh and joke about us.
7 But if you smile on us,
we will be saved.

8 We were like a grapevine
you brought out of Egypt.
You chased other nations away
and planted us here.
9 Then you cleared the ground,
and we put our roots deep,
spreading over the land.
10 Shade from this vine covered
the mountains.
Its branches climbed
the mighty cedars
11 and stretched to the sea;
its new growth reached
to the river.[m]

12 Our Lord, why have you
torn down the wall
from around the vineyard?
You let everyone who walks by
pick the grapes.
13 Now the vine is gobbled down
by pigs from the forest
and other wild animals.

14 God All-Powerful,
please do something!
Look down from heaven
and see what's happening
to this vine.
15 With your own hands
you planted its roots,
and you raised it
as your very own.
16 Enemies chopped the vine down
and set it on fire.
Now show your anger
and destroy them.
17 But help the one who sits
at your right side,[n]
the one you raised
to be your own.
18 Then we will never turn away.
Put new life into us,
and we will worship you.

19 LORD God All-Powerful,
make us strong again!
Smile on us and save us.

Psalm 81

[*By Asaph for the music leader.*[o]]

God Makes Us Strong

1 Be happy and shout to God
who makes us strong!
Shout praises to the God
of Jacob.
2 Sing as you play tambourines
and the lovely sounding
stringed instruments.
3 Sound the trumpets and start
the New Moon Festival.[p]
We must also celebrate
when the moon is full.
4 This is the law in Israel,
and it was given to us
by the God of Jacob.
5 The descendants of Joseph
were told to obey it,
when God led them out
from the land of Egypt.

In a language unknown to me,
I heard someone say:
6 "I lifted the burden
from your shoulder
and took the heavy basket
from your hands.

[m] **80.11** *the sea . . . the river*: The Mediterranean Sea and the Euphrates River were part of the ideal boundaries for Israel. [n] **80.17** *right side*: See the note at 16.11. [o] **Psalm 81** *leader*: See the note at Psalm 8. [p] **81.3** *New Moon Festival*: Celebrated on the first day of each new moon, which was the beginning of the month. But this may refer to either the New Year celebration or the Harvest Festival. "The moon is full" suggests a festival in the middle of the month.

81.3 Nu 10.10.

7 When you were in trouble,
I rescued you,
and from the thunderclouds,
I answered your prayers.
Later I tested you
at Meribah Spring.[q]

8 "Listen, my people,
while I, the Lord,
correct you!
Israel, if you would only
pay attention to me!
9 Don't worship foreign gods
or bow down to gods
you know nothing about.
10 I am the LORD your God.
I rescued you from Egypt.
Just ask, and I will give you
whatever you need.

11 "But, my people, Israel,
you refused to listen,
and you would have nothing
to do with me!
12 So I let you be stubborn
and keep on following
your own advice.

13 "My people, Israel,
if only you would listen
and do as I say!
14 I, the LORD, would quickly
defeat your enemies
with my mighty power.
15 Everyone who hates me
would come crawling,
and that would be the end
of them.
16 But I would feed you
with the finest bread
and with the best honey[r]
until you were full."

Psalm 82
[*A psalm by Asaph.*]

Please Do Something, God!

1 When all of the other gods[s]
have come together,
the Lord God judges them
and says:
2 "How long will you
keep judging unfairly
and favoring evil people?
3 Be fair to the poor
and to orphans.
Defend the helpless
and everyone in need.
4 Rescue the weak and homeless
from the powerful hands
of heartless people.

5 "None of you know
or understand a thing.
You live in darkness,
while the foundations
of the earth tremble.[t]

6 "I, the Most High God, say
that all of you are gods[u]
and also my own children.
7 But you will die,
just like everyone else,
including powerful rulers."

8 Do something, God!
Judge the nations of the earth;
they belong to you.

Psalm 83
[*A song and a psalm by Asaph.*]

God Rules All the Earth

1 Our God, don't just sit there,
silently doing nothing!
2 Your hateful enemies

[q]**81.7** *Meribah Spring*: When the people of Israel complained to Moses about the need for water, God commanded Moses to strike a rock with his walking stick, and water came out. The place was then named Massah ("test") and Meribah ("complaining"). [r]**81.16** *the best honey*: The Hebrew text has "honey from rocks," referring to honey taken from beehives in holes or cracks in large rocks. [s]**82.1** *the other gods*: This probably refers to the gods of the nations that God defeated, but it could refer to God's servants (angels) in heaven or even to human rulers.
[t]**82.5** *foundations . . . tremble*: In ancient times it was believed that the earth was flat and supported by columns. [u]**82.6** *all of you are gods*: See the note at 82.1.
81.7 Ex 17.7; Nu 20.13. **81.9** Ex 20.2, 3; Dt 5.6, 7. **82.6** Jn 10.34.

are turning against you
and rebelling.
3 They are sly, and they plot
against those you treasure.
4 They say, "Let's wipe out
the nation of Israel
and make sure that no one
remembers its name!"

5 All of them fully agree
in their plans against you,
and among them are
6 Edom and the Ishmaelites;
Moab and the Hagrites;
7 Gebal, Ammon, and Amalek;
Philistia and Phoenicia.[v]
8 Even Assyria has joined forces
with Moab and Ammon.[w]

9 Our Lord, punish all of them
as you punished Midian.
Destroy them, as you destroyed
Sisera and Jabin
at Kishon Creek 10 near Endor,
and let their bodies rot.
11 Treat their leaders as you did
Oreb and Zeeb,
Zebah and Zalmunna.
12 All of them said, "We'll take
God's valuable land!"

13 Our God, scatter them around
like dust in a whirlwind.
14 Just as flames destroy forests
on the mountains,
15 pursue and terrify them
with storms of your own.
16 Make them blush with shame,
until they turn and worship
you, our LORD.
17 Let them be forever ashamed
and confused.
Let them die in disgrace.
18 Make them realize that you
are the LORD Most High,
the only ruler of earth!

Psalm 84

[*For the music leader.*[x] *A psalm for the people of Korah.*]

The Joy of Worship

1 LORD God All-Powerful,
your temple is so lovely!
2 Deep in my heart I long
for your temple,
and with all that I am
I sing joyful songs to you.

3 LORD God All-Powerful,
my King and my God,
sparrows find a home
near your altars;
swallows build nests there
to raise their young.

4 You bless everyone
who lives in your house,
and they sing your praises.
5 You bless all who depend
on you for their strength
and all who deeply desire
to visit your temple.
6 When they reach Dry Valley,[y]
springs start flowing,
and the autumn rain fills it
with pools of water.[z]
7 Your people grow stronger,
and you, the God of gods,
will be seen in Zion.

8 LORD God All-Powerful,
the God of Jacob,
please answer my prayer!
9 You are the shield
that protects your people,
and I am your chosen one.
Won't you smile on me?

10 One day in your temple
is better than a thousand
anywhere else.

[v] **83.7** *Phoenicia*: The Hebrew text has "Tyre," the main city in Phoenicia. [w] **83.8** *Moab and Ammon*: The Hebrew text has "the descendants of Lot," whose older daughter was the mother of the Moabites and whose younger daughter was the mother of the Ammonites (see Genesis 19.30-38). [x] **Psalm 84** *leader*: See the note at Psalm 8. [y] **84.6** *Dry Valley*: Or "Balsam Tree Valley." The exact location is not known. [z] **84.6** *and . . . water*: One possible meaning for the difficult Hebrew text.

83.9 a Jg 7.1-23; **b** Jg 4.6-22. **83.11 a** Jg 7.25; **b** Jg 8.12.

I would rather serve
in your house,
than live in the homes
of the wicked.

11 Our LORD and our God,
you are like the sun
and also like a shield.
You treat us with kindness
and with honor,
never denying any good thing
to those who live right.

12 LORD God All-Powerful,
you bless everyone
who trusts you.

Psalm 85

[*A psalm by the people of Korah for the music leader.*]

A Prayer for Peace

1 Our LORD, you have blessed
your land
and made all go well
for Jacob's descendants.
2 You have forgiven the sin
and taken away the guilt
of your people.
3 Your fierce anger is no longer
aimed at us.

4 Our LORD and our God,
you save us!
Please bring us back home
and don't be angry.
5 Will you always be angry
with us and our families?
6 Won't you give us fresh life
and let your people be glad
because of you?
7 Show us your love
and save us!

8 I will listen to you, LORD God,
because you promise peace
to those who are faithful
and no longer foolish.
9 You are ready to rescue
everyone who worships you,
so that you will live with us
in all of your glory.

10 Love and loyalty
will come together;
goodness and peace
will unite.
11 Loyalty will sprout
from the ground;
justice will look down
from the sky above.

12 Our LORD, you will bless us;
our land will produce
wonderful crops.
13 Justice will march in front,
making a path
for you to follow.

Psalm 86

[*A prayer by David.*]

A Prayer for Help

1 Please listen, LORD,
and answer my prayer!
I am poor and helpless.
2 Protect me and save me
because you are my God.
I am your faithful servant,
and I trust you.
3 Be kind to me!
I pray to you all day.
4 Make my heart glad!
I serve you,
and my prayer is sincere.
5 You willingly forgive,
and your love is always there
for those who pray to you.
6 Please listen, LORD!
Answer my prayer for help.
7 When I am in trouble, I pray,
knowing you will listen.

8 No other gods are like you;
only you work miracles.
9 You created each nation,
and they will all bow down
to worship and honor you.
10 You perform great wonders
because you alone are God.

86.9 Rev 15.4.

11 Teach me to follow you,
and I will obey your truth.
Always keep me faithful.
12 With all my heart I thank you.
I praise you, LORD God.
13 Your love for me is so great
that you protected me
from death and the grave.

14 Proud and violent enemies,
who don't care about you,
have ganged up to attack
and kill me.
15 But you, the Lord God,
are kind and merciful.
You don't easily get angry,
and your love
can always be trusted.
16 I serve you, LORD,
and I am the child
of one of your servants.
Look on me with kindness.
Make me strong and save me.
17 Show that you approve of me!
Then my hateful enemies
will feel like fools,
because you have helped
and comforted me.

Psalm 87

[*A psalm and a song by the people of Korah.*]

The Glory of Mount Zion

1 Zion was built by the LORD
on the holy mountain,
2 and he loves that city
more than any other place
in all of Israel.
3 Zion, you are the city of God,
and wonderful things
are told about you.

4 Egypt,[a] Babylonia, Philistia,
Phoenicia,[b] and Ethiopia[c]
are some of those nations
that know you,
and their people all say,
"I was born in Zion."
5 God Most High will strengthen
the city of Zion.
Then everyone will say,
"We were born here too."
6 The LORD will make a list
of his people,
and all who were born here
will be included.

7 All who sing or dance will say,
"I too am from Zion."

Psalm 88

[*A song and a psalm by the people of Korah for the music leader. To the tune "Mahalath Leannoth."*[d] *A special psalm by Heman the Ezrahite.*]

A Prayer When You Can't Find the Way

1 You keep me safe, LORD God.
So when I pray at night,
2 please listen carefully
to each of my concerns.

3 I am deeply troubled
and close to death;
4 I am as good as dead
and completely helpless.
5 I am no better off
than those in the grave,
those you have forgotten
and no longer help.

6 You have put me in the deepest
and darkest grave;
7 your anger rolls over me
like ocean waves.
8 You have made my friends turn
in horror from me.
I am a prisoner
who cannot escape,
9 and I am almost blind
because of my sorrow.

Each day I lift my hands
in prayer to you, LORD.
10 Do you work miracles
for the dead?

[a]**87.4** *Egypt*: The Hebrew text has "Rahab," the name of a monster that stands for Egypt (see Isaiah 30.7). [b]**87.4** *Phoenicia*: See the note at 83.7. [c]**87.4** *Ethiopia*: See the note at 68.31. [d]**Psalm 88** *To . . . Leannoth*: Or "For the flutes," one possible meaning for the difficult Hebrew text.

Do they stand up
and praise you?
11 Are your love and loyalty
announced in the world
of the dead?
12 Do they know of your miracles
or your saving power
in the dark world below
where all is forgotten?

13 Each morning I pray
to you, LORD.
14 Why do you reject me?
Why do you turn from me?
15 Ever since I was a child,
I have been sick
and close to death.
You have terrified me
and made me helpless.[e]

16 Your anger is like a flood!
And I am shattered
by your furious attacks
17 that strike each day
and from every side.
18 My friends and neighbors
have turned against me
because of you,
and now darkness
is my only companion.

Psalm 89

[*A special psalm by Ethan the Ezrahite.*]

The LORD's Agreement with David

1 Our LORD, I will sing
of your love forever.
Everyone yet to be born
will hear me praise
your faithfulness.
2 I will tell them, "God's love
can always be trusted,
and his faithfulness lasts
as long as the heavens."

3 You said, "David, my servant,
is my chosen one,
and this is the agreement
I made with him:
4 David, one of your descendants
will always be king."

5 Our LORD, let the heavens
now praise your miracles,
and let all of your angels
praise your faithfulness.

6 None who live in the heavens
can compare with you.
7 You are the most fearsome
of all who live in heaven;
all the others fear
and greatly honor you.
8 You are LORD God All-Powerful!
No one is as loving
and faithful as you are.
9 You rule the roaring sea
and calm its waves.
10 You crushed the monster Rahab,[f]
and with your powerful arm
you scattered your enemies.
11 The heavens and the earth
belong to you.
And so does the world
with all its people
because you created them
12 and everything else.[g]

Mount Tabor and Mount Hermon
gladly praise you.
13 You are strong and mighty!
14 Your kingdom is ruled
by justice and fairness
with love and faithfulness
leading the way.

15 Our LORD, you bless those
who join in the festival
and walk in the brightness
of your presence.
16 We are happy all day
because of you,
and your saving power
brings honor to us.

[e] **88.15** *and made me helpless*: One possible meaning for the difficult Hebrew text.
[f] **89.10** *Rahab*: Many people in the ancient world thought that the world was controlled by this sea monster that the Lord destroyed at the time of creation (see Isaiah 51.9).
[g] **89.12** *and everything else*: The Hebrew text has "Zaphon and Yamin," which may either be the names of mountains or refer to the directions "north and south," with the meaning "everything from north to south."

89 Title 1 K 4.30, 31. **89.4** 2 S 7.12-16; 1 Ch 17.11-14; Ps 132.11; Ac 2.30.

17 Your own glorious power
makes us strong,
and because of your kindness,
our strength increases.
18 Our LORD and our King,
the Holy One of Israel,
you are truly our shield.

19 In a vision, you once said
to your faithful followers:
"I have helped a mighty hero.
I chose him from my people
and made him famous.
20 David, my servant, is the one
I chose to be king,
21 and I will always be there
to help and strengthen him.

22 "No enemy will outsmart David,
and he won't be defeated
by any hateful people.
23 I will strike down and crush
his troublesome enemies.
24 He will always be able
to depend on my love,
and I will make him strong
with my own power.
25 I will let him rule the lands
across the rivers and seas.
26 He will say to me,
'You are my Father
and my God,
as well as the mighty rock[h]
where I am safe.'

27 "I have chosen David
as my first-born son,
and he will be the ruler
of all kings on earth.
28 My love for him will last,
and my agreement with him
will never be broken.

29 "One of David's descendants
will always be king,
and his family will rule
until the sky disappears.
30 Suppose some of his children
should reject my Law
and refuse my instructions.
31 Or suppose they should disobey
all of my teachings.
32 Then I will correct
and punish them
because of their sins.
33 But I will always love David
and faithfully keep all
of my promises to him.

34 "I won't break my agreement
or go back on my word.
35 I have sworn once and for all
by my own holy name,
and I won't lie to David.
36 His family will always rule.
I will let his kingdom last
as long as the sun 37 and moon
appear in the sky."

38 You are now angry, God,
and you have turned your back
on your chosen king.
39 You broke off your agreement
with your servant, the king,
and you completely destroyed
his kingdom.
40 The walls of his city
have been broken through,
and every fortress
now lies in ruin.
41 All who pass by
take what they want,
and nations everywhere
joke about the king.

42 You made his enemies powerful
and let them celebrate.
43 But you forced him to retreat
because you did not fight
on his side.
44 You took his crown[i]
and threw his throne
in the dirt.
45 You made an old man of him
and put him to shame.

46 How much longer, LORD?
Will you hide forever?

[h]**89.26** *mighty rock*: See the note at 18.2.

[i]**89.44** *You took . . . crown*: One possible meaning for the difficult Hebrew text.

89.20 a 1 S 13.14; Ac 13.22; **b** 1 S 16.12. **89.27** Rev 1.5.

How long will your anger
keep burning like fire?
47 Remember, life is short![j]
Why did you empty our lives
of all meaning?
48 No one can escape the power
of death and the grave.

49 Our Lord, where is the love
you have always shown
and that you promised
so faithfully to David?
50 Remember your servant, Lord!
People make jokes about me,
and I suffer many insults.
51 I am your chosen one,
but your enemies chase
and make fun of me.

52 Our LORD, we praise you
forever. Amen and amen.

BOOK IV
(Psalms 90–106)

Psalm 90

[*A prayer by Moses, the man of God.*]

God Is Eternal

1 Our Lord, in all generations
you have been our home.
2 You have always been God—
long before the birth
of the mountains,
even before you created
the earth and the world.

3 At your command we die
and turn back to dust,
4 but a thousand years
mean nothing to you!
They are merely a day gone by
or a few hours in the night.

5 You bring our lives to an end
just like a dream.
We are merely tender grass
6 that sprouts and grows
in the morning,
but dries up by evening.
7 Your furious anger frightens
and destroys us,
8 and you know all of our sins,
even those we do in secret.

9 Your anger is a burden
each day we live,
then life ends like a sigh.
10 We can expect seventy years,
or maybe eighty,
if we are healthy,
but even our best years
bring trouble and sorrow.
Suddenly our time is up,
and we disappear.
11 No one knows the full power
of your furious anger,
but it is as great as the fear
that we owe to you.
12 Teach us to use wisely
all the time we have.

13 Help us, LORD! Don't wait!
Pity your servants.
14 When morning comes,
let your love satisfy
all our needs.
Then we can celebrate
and be glad for what time
we have left.
15 Make us happy for as long
as you caused us trouble
and sorrow.
16 Do wonderful things for us,
your servants,
and show your mighty power
to our children.
17 Our Lord and our God,
treat us with kindness
and let all go well for us.
Please let all go well!

Psalm 91

The LORD Is My Fortress

1 Live under the protection
of God Most High
and stay in the shadow
of God All-Powerful.
2 Then you will say to the LORD,

[j] **89.47** *Remember . . . short*: One possible meaning for the difficult Hebrew text.
90.4 2 P 3.8. **90.10** Si 18.8, 9.

"You are my fortress,
my place of safety;
you are my God,
and I trust you."

3 The Lord will keep you safe
from secret traps
and deadly diseases.
4 He will spread his wings
over you
and keep you secure.
His faithfulness is like
a shield or a city wall.[k]

5 You won't need to worry
about dangers at night
or arrows during the day.
6 And you won't fear diseases
that strike in the dark
or sudden disaster at noon.

7 You will not be harmed,
though thousands fall
all around you.
8 And with your own eyes
you will see the punishment
of the wicked.
9 The LORD Most High
is your fortress.
Run to him for safety,
10 and no terrible disasters
will strike you
or your home.

11 God will command his angels
to protect you
wherever you go.
12 They will carry you
in their arms,
and you won't hurt your feet
on the stones.
13 You will overpower
the strongest lions
and the most deadly snakes.

14 The Lord says, "If you love me
and truly know who I am,
I will rescue you
and keep you safe.
15 When you are in trouble,
call out to me.
I will answer and be there
to protect and honor you.
16 You will live a long life
and see my saving power."

Psalm 92

[*A psalm and a song for the Sabbath.*]

Sing Praises to the LORD

1 It is wonderful to be grateful
and to sing your praises,
LORD Most High!
2 It is wonderful each morning
to tell about your love
and at night to announce
how faithful you are.
3 I enjoy praising your name
to the music of harps,
4 because everything you do
makes me happy,
and I sing joyful songs.

5 You do great things, LORD.
Your thoughts are too deep
6 for an ignorant fool
to know or understand.
7 Though the wicked sprout
and spread like grass,
they will be pulled up
by their roots.
8 But you will rule
over all of us forever,
9 and your hateful enemies
will be scattered
and then destroyed.

10 You have given me
the strength of a wild ox,
and you have chosen me
to be your very own.
11 My eyes have seen,
and my ears have heard
the doom and destruction
of my terrible enemies.

[k]**91.4** *city wall*: One possible meaning for a difficult Hebrew word; it may possibly mean some kind of shield or weapon.

91.11 Mt 4.6; Lk 4.10, 11. **91.12** Mt 4.6; Lk 4.10, 11. **91.13** Lk 10.19. **92.6** Ws 13.1.

12 Good people will prosper
like palm trees,
and they will grow strong
like the cedars of Lebanon.
13 They will take root
in your house, LORD God,
and they will do well.
14 They will be like trees
that stay healthy and fruitful,
even when they are old.
15 And they will say about you,
"The LORD always does right!
God is our mighty rock."[l]

Psalm 93

The LORD Is King

1 Our LORD, you are King!
Majesty and power
are your royal robes.
You put the world in place,
and it will never be moved.
2 You have always ruled,
and you are eternal.

3 The ocean is roaring, LORD!
The sea is pounding hard.
4 Its mighty waves are majestic,
but you are more majestic,
and you rule over all.
5 Your decisions are firm,
and your temple will always
be beautiful and holy.

Psalm 94

The LORD Punishes the Guilty

1 LORD God, you punish
the guilty.
Show what you are like
and punish them now.
2 You judge the earth.
Come and help us!
Pay back those proud people
for what they have done.
3 How long will the wicked
celebrate and be glad?

4 All of those cruel people
strut and boast,
5 and they crush and wound
your chosen nation, LORD.
6 They murder widows,
foreigners, and orphans.
7 Then they say,
"The LORD God of Jacob
doesn't see or know."

8 Can't you fools see?
Won't you ever learn?
9 God gave us ears and eyes!
Can't he hear and see?
10 God instructs the nations
and gives knowledge to us all.
Won't he also correct us?
11 The LORD knows how useless
our plans really are.

12 Our LORD, you bless everyone
that you instruct and teach
by using your Law.
13 You give them rest
from their troubles,
until a pit can be dug
for the wicked.
14 You won't turn your back
on your chosen nation.
15 Justice and fairness
will go hand in hand,
and all who do right
will follow along.

16 Who will stand up for me
against those cruel people?
17 If you had not helped me, LORD,
I would soon have gone
to the land of silence.[m]
18 When I felt my feet slipping,
you came with your love
and kept me steady.
19 And when I was burdened
with worries,
you comforted me
and made me feel secure.
20 But you are opposed
to dishonest lawmakers
21 who gang up to murder
innocent victims.

[l]**92.15** *mighty rock*: See the note at 18.2.

[m]**94.17** *land of silence*: The grave or the world of the dead.

94.11 1 Co 3.20.

22 You, LORD God, are my fortress,
that mighty rock[n]
where I am safe.
23 You will pay back my enemies,
and you will wipe them out
for the evil they did.

Psalm 95

Worship and Obey the LORD

1 Sing joyful songs to the LORD!
Praise the mighty rock[n]
where we are safe.
2 Come to worship him
with thankful hearts
and songs of praise.

3 The LORD is the greatest God,
king over all other gods.
4 He holds the deepest part
of the earth in his hands,
and the mountain peaks
belong to him.
5 The ocean is the Lord's
because he made it,
and with his own hands
he formed the dry land.

6 Bow down and worship
the LORD our Creator!
7 The LORD is our God,
and we are his people,
the sheep he takes care of
in his own pasture.

Listen to God's voice today!
8 Don't be stubborn and rebel
as your ancestors did
at Meribah and Massah[o]
out in the desert.
9 For forty years
they tested God and saw
the things he did.
10 Then God got tired of them
and said,
"You never show good sense,
and you don't understand
what I want you to do."
11 In his anger, God told them,
"You people will never enter
my place of rest."

Psalm 96

Sing a New Song to the LORD

1 Sing a new song to the LORD!
Everyone on this earth,
sing praises to the LORD,
2 sing and praise his name.

Day after day announce,
"The LORD has saved us!"
3 Tell every nation on earth,
"The LORD is wonderful
and does marvelous things!
4 The LORD is great and deserves
our greatest praise!
He is the only God
worthy of our worship.
5 Other nations worship idols,
but the LORD created
the heavens.
6 Give honor and praise
to the LORD,
whose power and beauty
fill his holy temple."

7 Tell everyone of every nation,
"Praise the glorious power
of the LORD.
8 He is wonderful! Praise him
and bring an offering
into his temple.
9 Everyone on earth, now tremble
and worship the LORD,
majestic and holy."

10 Announce to the nations,
"The LORD is King!
The world stands firm,
never to be shaken,
and he will judge its people
with fairness."

11 Tell the heavens and the earth
to be glad and celebrate!

[n]**94.22; 95.1** *mighty rock*: See the note at 18.2. [o]**95.8** *Meribah and Massah*: See the note at 81.7.

95.7-11 He 3.7-11. **95.7,8** He 3.15; 4.7. **95.8,9** Ex 17.1-7; Nu 20.2-13. **95.11** Nu 14.20-23; Dt 1.34-36; He 4.3, 5. **96.7-9** Ps 29.1, 2.

Command the ocean to roar
with all of its creatures
12 and the fields to rejoice
with all of their crops.
Then every tree in the forest
will sing joyful songs
13 to the LORD.
He is coming to judge
all people on earth
with fairness and truth.

Psalm 97

The LORD Brings Justice

1 The LORD is King!
Tell the earth to celebrate
and all islands to shout.
2 Dark clouds surround him,
and his throne is supported
by justice and fairness.
3 Fire leaps from his throne,
destroying his enemies,
4 and his lightning is so bright
that the earth sees it
and trembles.
5 Mountains melt away like wax
in the presence of the LORD
of all the earth.

6 The heavens announce,
"The LORD brings justice!"
Everyone sees God's glory.
7 Those who brag about
the useless idols they worship
are terribly ashamed,
and all the false gods
bow down to the LORD.

8 When the people of Zion
and of the towns of Judah
hear that God brings justice,
they will celebrate.
9 The LORD rules the whole earth,
and he is more glorious
than all the false gods.

10 Love the LORD
and hate evil!
God protects his loyal people
and rescues them
from violence.
11 If you obey and do right,
a light will show you the way
and fill you with happiness.
12 You are the LORD's people!
So celebrate and praise
the only God.

Psalm 98

The LORD Works Miracles

1 Sing a new song to the LORD!
He has worked miracles,
and with his own powerful arm,
he has won the victory.
2 The LORD has shown the nations
that he has the power to save
and to bring justice.
3 God has been faithful
in his love for Israel,
and his saving power is seen
everywhere on earth.

4 Tell everyone on this earth
to sing happy songs
in praise of the LORD.
5 Make music for him on harps.
Play beautiful melodies!
6 Sound the trumpets and horns
and celebrate with joyful songs
for our LORD and King!

7 Command the ocean to roar
with all of its creatures,
and the earth to shout
with all of its people.
8 Order the rivers
to clap their hands,
and all of the hills
to sing together.
9 Let them worship the LORD!
He is coming to judge
everyone on the earth,
and he will be honest
and fair.

Psalm 99

Our LORD Is King

1 Our LORD, you are King!
You rule from your throne
above the winged creatures,[p]

[p]**99.1** *winged creatures*: See the note at 80.1.
99.1 Ex 25.22.

as people tremble
and the earth shakes.
2 You are praised in Zion,
and you control all nations.
3 Only you are God!
And your power alone,
so great and fearsome,
is worthy of praise.
4 You are our mighty King,[q]
a lover of fairness,
who sees that justice is done
everywhere in Israel.
5 Our LORD and our God,
we praise you
and kneel down to worship you,
the God of holiness!

6 Moses and Aaron were two
of your priests.
Samuel was also one of those
who prayed in your name,
and you, our LORD,
answered their prayers.
7 You spoke to them
from a thick cloud,
and they obeyed your laws.

8 Our LORD and our God,
you answered their prayers
and forgave their sins,
but when they did wrong,
you punished them.
9 We praise you, LORD God,
and we worship you
at your sacred mountain.
Only you are God!

Psalm 100

[*A psalm of praise.*]

The LORD Is God

1 Shout praises to the LORD,
everyone on this earth.
2 Be joyful and sing
as you come in
to worship the LORD!

3 You know the LORD is God!
He created us,
and we belong to him;
we are his people,
the sheep in his pasture.

4 Be thankful and praise the LORD
as you enter his temple.
5 The LORD is good!
His love and faithfulness
will last forever.

Psalm 101

[*A psalm by David.*]

A King and His Promises

1 I will sing to you, LORD!
I will celebrate your kindness
and your justice.
2 Please help me learn
to do the right thing,
and I will be honest and fair
in my own kingdom.
3 I refuse to be corrupt
or to take part
in anything crooked,
4 and I won't be dishonest
or deceitful.

5 Anyone who spreads gossip
will be silenced,
and no one who is conceited
will be my friend.

6 I will find trustworthy people
to serve as my advisors,
and only an honest person
will serve as an official.

7 No one who cheats or lies
will have a position
in my royal court.
8 Each morning I will silence
any lawbreakers I find
in the countryside
or in the city of the LORD.

Psalm 102

[*A prayer for someone who hurts and needs to ask the LORD for help.*]

A Prayer in Time of Trouble

1 I pray to you, LORD!
Please listen.

[q] **99.4** *You . . . King*: One possible meaning for the difficult Hebrew text.
99.7 Ex 33.9-11. **100.5** 1 Ch 16.34; 2 Ch 5.11-13; 7.3; Ezra 3.11; Ps 106.1; 107.1; 118.1; 136.1; Jr 33.11.

2 Don't hide from me
in my time of trouble.
Pay attention to my prayer
and quickly give an answer.

3 My days disappear like smoke,
and my bones are burning
as though in a furnace.
4 I am wasting away like grass,
and my appetite is gone.
5 My groaning never stops,
and my bones can be seen
through my skin.
6 I am like a lonely owl
in the desert
7 or a restless sparrow
alone on a roof.

8 My enemies insult me all day,
and they use my name
for a curse word.
9 Instead of food,
I have ashes to eat
and tears to drink,
10 because you are furious
and have thrown me aside.
11 My life fades like a shadow
at the end of day
and withers like grass.

12 Our LORD, you are King forever
and will always be famous.
13 You will show pity to Zion
because the time has come.
14 We, your servants,
love each stone in the city,
and we are sad to see them
lying in the dirt.

15 Our LORD, the nations
will honor you,
and all kings on earth
will praise your glory.
16 You will rebuild
the city of Zion.
Your glory will be seen,
17 and the prayers of the homeless
will be answered.

18 Future generations must also
praise the LORD,
so write this for them:
19 "From his holy temple,
the LORD looked down
at the earth.
20 He listened to the groans
of prisoners,
and he rescued everyone
who was doomed to die."

21 All Jerusalem should praise
you, our LORD,
22 when people from every nation
meet to worship you.

23 I should still be strong,
but you, LORD, have made
an old person of me.
24 You will live forever!
Years mean nothing to you.
Don't cut my life in half!

25 In the beginning, LORD,
you laid the earth's foundation
and created the heavens.
26 They will all disappear
and wear out like clothes.
You change them,
as you would a coat,
but you last forever.
27 You are always the same.
Years cannot change you.
28 Every generation of those
who serve you
will live in your presence.

Psalm 103

[*By David.*]

The LORD's Wonderful Love

1 With all my heart
I praise the LORD,
and with all that I am
I praise his holy name!
2 With all my heart
I praise the LORD!
I will never forget
how kind he has been.

3 The LORD forgives our sins,
heals us when we are sick,
4 and protects us from death.

102.25-27 He 1.10-12.

His kindness and love
are a crown on our heads.
5 Each day that we live,[r]
he provides for our needs
and gives us the strength
of a young eagle.

6 For all who are mistreated,
the LORD brings justice.
7 He taught his Law to Moses
and showed all Israel
what he could do.

8 The LORD is merciful!
He is kind and patient,
and his love never fails.
9 The LORD won't always be angry
and point out our sins;
10 he doesn't punish us
as our sins deserve.

11 How great is God's love for all
who worship him?
Greater than the distance
between heaven and earth!
12 How far has the LORD taken
our sins from us?
Farther than the distance
from east to west!

13 Just as parents are kind
to their children,
the LORD is kind
to all who worship him,
14 because he knows
we are made of dust.
15 We humans are like grass
or wild flowers
that quickly bloom.
16 But a scorching wind blows,
and they quickly wither
to be forever forgotten.

17 The LORD is always kind
to those who worship him,
and he keeps his promises
to their descendants
18 who faithfully obey him.

19 God has set up his kingdom
in heaven, and he rules
the whole creation.
20 All of you mighty angels,
who obey God's commands,
come and praise your LORD!
21 All of you thousands
who serve and obey God,
come and praise your LORD!
22 All of God's creation
and all that he rules,
come and praise your LORD!
With all my heart
I praise the LORD!

Psalm 104

The LORD Takes Care of His Creation

1 I praise you, LORD God,
with all my heart.
You are glorious and majestic,
dressed in royal robes
2 and surrounded by light.
You spread out the sky
like a tent,
3 and you built your home
over the mighty ocean.
The clouds are your chariot
with the wind as its wings.
4 The winds are your messengers,
and flames of fire
are your servants.

5 You built foundations
for the earth, and it
will never be shaken.
6 You covered the earth
with the ocean that rose
above the mountains.
7 Then your voice thundered!
And the water flowed
8 down the mountains
and through the valleys
to the place you prepared.
9 Now you have set boundaries,
so that the water will never
flood the earth again.

10 You provide streams of water
in the hills and valleys,

[r] **103.5** *Each . . . live*: One possible meaning for the difficult Hebrew text.
103.8 Jas 5.11. **104.4** He 1.7.

11 so that the donkeys
and other wild animals
can satisfy their thirst.
12 Birds build their nests nearby
and sing in the trees.
13 From your home above
you send rain on the hills
and water the earth.
14 You let the earth produce
grass for cattle,
plants for our food,
15 wine to cheer us up,
olive oil for our skin,
and grain for our health.

16 Our LORD, your trees
always have water,
and so do the cedars
you planted in Lebanon.
17 Birds nest in those trees,
and storks make their home
in the fir trees.
18 Wild goats find a home
in the tall mountains,
and small animals can hide
between the rocks.

19 You created the moon
to tell us the seasons.
The sun knows when to set,
20 and you made the darkness,
so the animals in the forest
could come out at night.
21 Lions roar as they hunt
for the food you provide.
22 But when morning comes,
they return to their dens,
23 then we go out to work
until the end of day.

24 Our LORD, by your wisdom
you made so many things;
the whole earth is covered
with your living creatures.
25 But what about the ocean
so big and wide?
It is alive with creatures,
large and small.
26 And there are the ships,
as well as Leviathan,[s]
the monster you created
to splash in the sea.

27 All of these depend on you
to provide them with food,
28 and you feed each one
with your own hand,
until they are full.
29 But when you turn away,
they are terrified;
when you end their life,
they die and rot.
30 You created all of them
by your Spirit,
and you give new life
to the earth.

31 Our LORD, we pray
that your glory
will last forever
and that you will be pleased
with what you have done.
32 You look at the earth,
and it trembles.
You touch the mountains,
and smoke goes up.
33 As long as I live,
I will sing and praise you,
the LORD God.
34 I hope my thoughts
will please you,
because you are the one
who makes me glad.

35 Destroy all wicked sinners
from the earth
once and for all.
With all my heart
I praise you, LORD!
I praise you!

Psalm 105

The LORD Can Be Trusted

1 Praise the LORD
and pray in his name!
Tell everyone
what he has done.
2 Sing praises to the LORD!
Tell about his miracles.

[s] **104.26** *Leviathan*: See the note at 74.14.
104.26 Job 41.1; Ps 74.14; Is 27.1. **105.1-45** 3 Macc 2.1.

3 Celebrate and worship
his holy name
with all your heart.

4 Trust the LORD
and his mighty power.
5 Remember his miracles
and all his wonders
and his fair decisions.
6 You belong to the family
of Abraham, his servant;
you are his chosen ones,
the descendants of Jacob.

7 The LORD is our God,
bringing justice
everywhere on earth.
8 He will never forget
his agreement or his promises,
not in thousands of years.
*9 God made an eternal promise
10 to Abraham, Isaac, and Jacob,
11 when he said, "I'll give you
the land of Canaan."

12 At the time there were
only a few of us,
and we were homeless.
13 We wandered from nation
to nation, from one country
to another.
14 God did not let anyone
mistreat our people.
Instead he protected us
by punishing rulers
15 and telling them,
"Don't touch my chosen leaders
or harm my prophets!"

16 God kept crops from growing
until food was scarce
everywhere in the land.
17 But he had already sent Joseph,
sold as a slave into Egypt,
18 with chains of iron
around his legs and neck.

19 Joseph remained a slave
until his own words
had come true,
and the LORD had finished
testing him.
20 Then the king of Egypt
set Joseph free
21 and put him in charge
of everything he owned.
22 Joseph was in command
of the officials,
and he taught the leaders
how to use wisdom.

23 Jacob and his family
came and settled in Egypt
as foreigners.
24 They were the LORD's people,
so he let them grow stronger
than their enemies.
25 They served the LORD,
and he made the Egyptians plan
hateful things against them.
26 God sent his servant Moses.
He also chose and sent Aaron
27 to his people in Egypt,
and they worked miracles
and wonders there.
28 Moses and Aaron obeyed God,
and he sent darkness
to cover Egypt.
29 God turned their rivers
into streams of blood,
and the fish all died.
30 Frogs were everywhere,
even in the royal palace.
31 When God gave the command,
flies and gnats
swarmed all around.

32 In place of rain,
God sent hailstones
and flashes of lightning.
33 He destroyed their grapevines
and their fig trees,
and he made splinters
of all the other trees.

105.9 **a** Gn 12.7; 17.8; **b** Gn 26.3. **105.10,11** Gn 28.13. **105.14,15** Gn 20.3-7. **105.16** Gn 41.53-57. **105.17** Gn 37.28; 45.5. **105.18,19** Gn 39.20—40.23. **105.20** Gn 41.14. **105.21** Gn 41.39-41. **105.23** **a** Gn 46.5-7; **b** Gn 47.11. **105.24,25** Ex 1.7-14. **105.26** Ex 3.1—4.17. **105.28** Ex 10.21-23. **105.29** Ex 7.17-21. **105.30** Ex 8.1-6. **105.31** **a** Ex 8.20-24; **b** Ex 8.16, 17. **105.32,33** Ex 9.22-25.

34 God gave the command,
and more grasshoppers came
than could be counted.
35 They ate every green plant
and all the crops that grew
in the land of Egypt.
36 Then God took the life
of every first-born son.

37 When God led Israel from Egypt,
they took silver and gold,
and no one was left behind.
38 The Egyptians were afraid
and gladly let them go.
39 God hid them under a cloud
and guided them by fire
during the night.

40 When they asked for food,
he sent more birds
than they could eat.
41 God even split open a rock,
and streams of water
gushed into the desert.
42 God never forgot
his sacred promise
to his servant Abraham.

43 When the Lord rescued
his chosen people from Egypt,
they celebrated with songs.
44 The Lord gave them the land
and everything else
the nations had worked for.
45 He did this so that his people
would obey all of his laws.
Shout praises to the LORD!

Psalm 106

A Nation Asks for Forgiveness

1 We will celebrate
and praise you, LORD!
You are good to us,
and your love never fails.
2 No one can praise you enough
for all of the mighty things
you have done.
3 You bless those people
who are honest and fair
in everything they do.

4 Remember me, LORD,
when you show kindness
by saving your people.
5 Let me prosper with the rest
of your chosen ones,
as they celebrate with pride
because they belong to you.

6 We and our ancestors
have sinned terribly.
7 When they were in Egypt,
they paid no attention
to your marvelous deeds
or your wonderful love.
And they turned against you
at the Red Sea.[t]

8 But you were true to your name,
and you rescued them to prove
how mighty you are.
9 You said to the Red Sea,[t]
"Dry up!"
Then you led your people across
on land as dry as a desert.
10 You saved all of them
11 and drowned every one
of their enemies.
12 Then your people trusted you
and sang your praises.

13 But they soon forgot
what you had done
and rejected your advice.
14 They became greedy for food
and tested you there
in the desert.
15 So you gave them
what they wanted,

[t] **106.7,9,22** *Red Sea*: Hebrew *yam suph* "Sea of Reeds," one of the marshes or fresh water lakes near the eastern part of the Nile Delta. This identification is based on Exodus 13.17—14.9, which lists the towns on the route of the Israelites before crossing the sea. In the Greek translation of the Scriptures made about 200 B.C., the "Sea of Reeds" was named "Red Sea."

105.34,35 Ex 10.12-15. **105.36** Ex 12.29. **105.37,38** Ex 12.33-36. **105.39** Ex 13.21, 22. **105.40** Ex 16.2-15. **105.41** Ex 17.1-7; Nu 20.2-13. **105.44** Js 11.16-23. **106.1** 1 Ch 16.34; 2 Ch 5.11-13; 7.3; Ezra 3.11; Ps 100.5; 107.1; 118.1; 136.1; Jr 33.11. **106.7** Ex 14.10-12. **106.9-12** Ex 14.21-31. **106.12** Ex 15.1-21. **106.14,15** Nu 11.4-34.

but later you destroyed them
with a horrible disease.

16 Everyone in camp was jealous
of Moses and of Aaron,
your chosen priest.
17 Dathan and Abiram rebelled,
and the earth opened up
and swallowed them.
18 Then fire broke out
and destroyed all
of their followers.

19 At Horeb your people
made and worshiped the statue
20 of a bull, instead of you,
their glorious God.
21 You worked powerful miracles
to save them from Egypt,
but they forgot about you
22 and the fearsome things
you did at the Red Sea.[t]
23 You were angry and started
to destroy them,
but Moses, your chosen leader,
begged you not to do it.

24 They would not trust
you, LORD,
and they did not like
the promised land.
25 They would not obey you,
and they grumbled
in their tents.
26 So you threatened them
by saying, "I'll kill you
out here in the desert!
27 I'll scatter your children
everywhere in the world."

28 Your people became followers
of a god named Baal Peor,
and they ate sacrifices
offered to the dead.[u]
29 They did such terrible things
that you punished them
with a deadly disease.
30 But Phinehas[v] helped them,
and the sickness stopped.
31 Now he will always
be highly honored.

32 At Meribah Spring[w]
they turned against you
and made you furious.
33 Then Moses got into trouble
for speaking in anger.

34 Our LORD, they disobeyed you
by refusing to destroy
the nations.
35 Instead they were friendly
with those foreigners
and followed their customs.
36 Then they fell into the trap
of worshiping idols.
37 They sacrificed their sons
and their daughters to demons
38 and to the gods of Canaan.
Then they poured out the blood
of these innocent children
and made the land filthy.
39 By doing such gruesome things,
they also became filthy.

40 Finally, LORD, you were angry
and terribly disgusted
with your people.
41 So you put them in the power
of nations that hated them.
42 They were mistreated and abused
by their enemies,
43 but you saved them
time after time.

[t] **106.7,9,22** *Red Sea*: Hebrew *yam suph* "Sea of Reeds," one of the marshes or fresh water lakes near the eastern part of the Nile Delta. This identification is based on Exodus 13.17—14.9, which lists the towns on the route of the Israelites before crossing the sea. In the Greek translation of the Scriptures made about 200 B.C., the "Sea of Reeds" was named "Red Sea." [u] **106.28** *the dead*: Or "lifeless idols." [v] **106.30** *Phinehas*: The grandson of Aaron, who put two people to death and kept the Lord from being angry with the rest of his people (see Numbers 25.1-13).
[w] **106.32** *Meribah Spring*: See the note at 81.7.

106.16-18 Nu 16.1-35. **106.19-23** Ex 32.1-14. **106.24-26** Nu 14.1-35. **106.27** Lv 26.33. **106.28-31** Nu 25.1-13. **106.32,33** Nu 20.2-13. **106.34-36** Jg 2.1-3; 3.5, 6. **106.37** 2 K 17.17. **106.38** Nu 35.33, 34. **106.40-46** Jg 2.14-18.

They were determined to rebel,
and their sins caused
their downfall.

44 You answered their prayers
when they were in trouble.
45 You kept your agreement
and were so merciful
46 that their enemies
had pity on them.

47 Save us, LORD God!
Bring us back
from among the nations.
Let us celebrate and shout
in praise of your holy name.

48 LORD God of Israel,
you deserve to be praised
forever and ever.
Let everyone say, "Amen!
Shout praises to the LORD!"

BOOK V
(Psalms 107–150)

Psalm 107

The LORD Is Good to His People

1 Shout praises to the LORD!
He is good to us,
and his love never fails.
2 Everyone the LORD has rescued
from trouble
should praise him,
3 everyone he has brought
from the east and the west,
the north and the south.[x]

4 Some of you were lost
in the scorching desert,
far from a town.
5 You were hungry and thirsty
and about to give up.
6 You were in serious trouble,
but you prayed to the LORD,
and he rescued you.
7 Right away he brought you
to a town.
8 You should praise the LORD
for his love
and for the wonderful things
he does for all of us.
9 To everyone who is thirsty,
he gives something to drink;
to everyone who is hungry,
he gives good things to eat.

10 Some of you were prisoners
suffering in deepest darkness
and bound by chains,
11 because you had rebelled
against God Most High
and refused his advice.
12 You were worn out
from working like slaves,
and no one came to help.
13 You were in serious trouble,
but you prayed to the LORD,
and he rescued you.
14 He brought you out
of the deepest darkness
and broke your chains.

15 You should praise the LORD
for his love
and for the wonderful things
he does for all of us.
16 He breaks down bronze gates
and shatters iron locks.

17 Some of you had foolishly
committed a lot of sins
and were in terrible pain.
18 The very thought of food
was disgusting to you,
and you were almost dead.
19 You were in serious trouble,
but you prayed to the LORD,
and he rescued you.
20 By the power of his own word,
he healed you and saved you
from destruction.

21 You should praise the LORD
for his love
and for the wonderful things
he does for all of us.

[x] **107.3** *south*: The Hebrew text has "sea," probably referring to the Mediterranean Sea.
106.47,48 1 Ch 16.35, 36. **107.1** 1 Ch 16.34; 2 Ch 5.11-13; 7.3; Ezra 3.11; Ps 100.5; 106.1; 118.1; 136.1; Jr 33.11.

22 You should celebrate
by offering sacrifices
and singing joyful songs
to tell what he has done.

23 Some of you made a living
by sailing the mighty sea,
24 and you saw the miracles
the LORD performed there.
25 At his command a storm arose,
and waves covered the sea.
26 You were tossed to the sky
and to the ocean depths,
until things looked so bad
that you lost your courage.
27 You staggered like drunkards
and gave up all hope.
28 You were in serious trouble,
but you prayed to the LORD,
and he rescued you.
29 He made the storm stop
and the sea be quiet.
30 You were happy because of this,
and he brought you to the port
where you wanted to go.

31 You should praise the LORD
for his love
and for the wonderful things
he does for all of us.
32 Honor the LORD
when you and your leaders
meet to worship.

33 If you start doing wrong,
the LORD will turn rivers
into deserts,
34 flowing streams
into scorched land,
and fruitful fields
into beds of salt.

35 But the LORD can also turn
deserts into lakes
and scorched land
into flowing streams.
36 If you are hungry,
you can settle there
and build a town.
37 You can plant fields
and vineyards that produce
a good harvest.
38 The LORD will bless you
with many children
and with herds of cattle.

39 Sometimes you may be crushed
by troubles and sorrows,
until only a few of you
are left to survive.
40 But the LORD will take revenge
on those who conquer you,
and he will make them wander
across desert sands.
41 When you are suffering
and in need,
he will come to your rescue,
and your families will grow
as fast as a herd of sheep.
42 You will see this because
you obey the LORD,
but everyone who is wicked
will be silenced.

43 Be wise! Remember this
and think about the kindness
of the LORD.

Psalm 108

[*A song and a psalm by David.*]

With God on Our Side

1 Our God, I am faithful to you
with all my heart,
and you can trust me.
I will sing
and play music for you
with all that I am.
2 I will start playing my harps
before the sun rises.
3 I will praise you, LORD,
for everyone to hear;
I will sing hymns to you
in every nation.
4 Your love reaches higher
than the heavens,
and your loyalty extends
beyond the clouds.

5 Our God, may you be honored
above the heavens;
may your glory be seen
everywhere on earth.

107.34 Si 39.23.

6 Answer my prayers
and use your powerful arm
to give us victory.
Then the people you love
will be safe.

7 Our God, from your holy place
you made this promise:
"I will gladly divide up
the city of Shechem
and give away Succoth Valley
piece by piece.
8 The lands of Gilead
and Manasseh are mine.
Ephraim is my war helmet,
and Judah is my symbol
of royal power.
9 Moab is merely my washbasin,
and Edom belongs to me.
I shout with victory
over the Philistines."

10 Our God, who will bring me
to the fortress
or lead me to Edom?
11 Have you rejected us?
You don't lead our armies.
12 Help us defeat our enemies!
No one else can rescue us.
13 You are the one
who gives us victory
and crushes our enemies.

Psalm 109

[*A psalm by David for the music leader.*]

A Prayer for the LORD's Help

1 I praise you, God!
Don't keep silent.
2 Destructive and deceitful lies
are told about me,
3 and hateful things are said
for no reason.
4 I had pity and prayed[y]
for my enemies,
but their words to me
were harsh and cruel.
5 For being friendly and kind,
they paid me back
with meanness and hatred.
6 My enemies said,
"Find some worthless fools
to accuse him of a crime.
7 Try him and find him guilty!
Consider his prayers a lie.
8 Cut his life short
and let someone else
have his job.
9 Make orphans of his children
and a widow of his wife;
10 make his children beg for food
and live in the slums.

11 "Let the people he owes
take everything he owns.
Give it all to strangers.
12 Don't let anyone be kind to him
or have pity on the children
he leaves behind.
13 Bring an end to his family,
and from now on let him be
a forgotten man.

14 "Don't let the LORD forgive
the sins of his parents
and his ancestors.
15 Don't let the LORD forget
the sins of his family,
or let anyone remember
his family ever lived.
16 He was so cruel to the poor,
homeless, and discouraged
that they died young.

17 "He cursed others.
Now place a curse on him!
He never wished others well.
Wish only trouble for him!
18 He cursed others more often
than he dressed himself.
Let his curses strike him deep,
just as water and olive oil
soak through to our bones.
19 Let his curses surround him,
just like the clothes
he wears each day."

20 Those are the cruel things
my enemies wish for me.
Let it all happen to them!

[y] **109.4** *and prayed*: One possible meaning for the difficult Hebrew text.
109.8 Ac 1.20.

21 Be true to your name, LORD God!
Show your great kindness
and rescue me.

22 I am poor and helpless,
and I have lost all hope.
23 I am fading away
like an evening shadow;
I am tossed aside
like a crawling insect.
24 I have gone without eating,[z]
until my knees are weak,
and my body is bony.
25 When my enemies see me,
they say cruel things
and shake their heads.

26 Please help me, LORD God!
Come and save me
because of your love.
27 Let others know that you alone
have saved me.
28 I don't care if they curse me,
as long as you bless me.
You will make my enemies fail
when they attack,
and you will make me glad
to be your servant.
29 You will cover them with shame,
just as their bodies
are covered with clothes.

30 I will sing your praises
and thank you, LORD,
when your people meet.
31 You help everyone in need,
and you defend them
when they are on trial.

Psalm 110

[*A psalm by David.*]

The LORD Gives Victory

1 The LORD said to my Lord,
"Sit at my right side,[a]
until I make your enemies
into a footstool for you."
2 The LORD will let your power
reach out from Zion,
and you will rule
over your enemies.
3 Your glorious power
will be seen on the day
you begin to rule.
You will wear the sacred robes
and shine like the morning sun
in all of your strength.[b]
4 The LORD has made a promise
that will never be broken:
"You will be a priest forever,
just like Melchizedek."

5 My Lord is at your right side,
and when he gets angry
he will crush
the other kings.
6 He will judge the nations
and crack their skulls,
leaving piles of dead bodies
all over the earth.
7 He will drink from any stream
that he chooses, while winning
victory after victory.[c]

Psalm 111

Praise the LORD for All He Has Done

1 Shout praises to the LORD!
With all my heart
I will thank the LORD
when his people meet.
2 The LORD has done
many wonderful things!
Everyone who is pleased
with God's marvelous deeds
will keep them in mind.
3 Everything the LORD does
is glorious and majestic,
and his power to bring justice
will never end.

4 The LORD God is famous
for his wonderful deeds,
and he is kind and merciful.

[z] **109.24** *without eating*: See the note at 35.13. [a] **110.1** *right side*: See the note at 16.11. [b] **110.3** *You will . . . strength*: One possible meaning for the difficult Hebrew text. [c] **110.7** *while . . . victory*: Or "God will give him victory after victory."

109.25 Mt 27.39; Mk 15.29. **110.1** Mt 22.44; Mk 12.36; Lk 20.42, 43; Ac 2.34, 35; 1 Co 15.25; Eph 1.20-22; Col 3.1; He 1.13; 8.1; 10.12, 13. **110.4** He 5.6; 6.20; 7.17, 21.

5 He gives food to his worshipers
and always keeps his agreement
with them.
6 He has shown his mighty power
to his people
and has given them the lands
of other nations.

7 God is always honest and fair,
and his laws can be trusted.
8 They are true and right
and will stand forever.
9 God rescued his people,
and he will never break
his agreement with them.
He is fearsome and holy.

10 Respect and obey the LORD!
This is the first step
to wisdom and good sense.[d]
God will always be respected.

Psalm 112

God Blesses His Worshipers

1 Shout praises to the LORD!
The LORD blesses everyone
who worships him and gladly
obeys his teachings.
2 Their descendants will have
great power in the land,
because the LORD blesses
all who do right.
3 They will get rich and prosper
and will always be remembered
for their fairness.
4 They will be so kind
and merciful and good,
that they will be a light
in the dark for others
who do the right thing.

5 Life will go well for those
who freely lend
and are honest in business.
6 They won't ever be troubled,
and the kind things they do
will never be forgotten.
7 Bad news won't bother them;
they have decided
to trust the LORD.
8 They are dependable
and not afraid,
and they will live to see
their enemies defeated.
9 They will always be remembered
and greatly praised,
because they were kind
and freely gave to the poor.
10 When evil people see this,
they angrily bite their tongues
and disappear.
They will never get
what they really want.

Psalm 113

The LORD Helps People in Need

1 Shout praises to the LORD!
Everyone who serves him,
come and praise his name.

2 Let the name of the LORD
be praised now and forever.
3 From dawn until sunset
the name of the LORD
deserves to be praised.
4 The LORD is far above
all of the nations;
he is more glorious
than the heavens.

5 No one can compare
with the LORD our God.
His throne is high above,
6 and he looks down to see
the heavens and the earth.
7 God lifts the poor and needy
from dust and ashes,
8 and he lets them take part
in ruling his people.
9 When a wife has no children,
he blesses her with some,
and she is happy.
Shout praises to the LORD!

Psalm 114

The LORD Works Wonders

1 God brought his people
out of Egypt, that land
with a strange language.

[d]**111.10** *This . . . sense*: Or "This is what wisdom and good sense are all about."
111.10 Job 28.28; Pr 1.7; 9.10. **112.9** 2 Co 9.9. **114.1** Ex 12.51.

2 He made Judah his holy place
and ruled over Israel.

3 When the sea looked at God,
it ran away,
and the Jordan River
flowed upstream.
4 The mountains and the hills
skipped around like goats.

5 Ask the sea why it ran away
or ask the Jordan
why it flowed upstream.
6 Ask the mountains and the hills
why they skipped like goats!

7 Earth, you will tremble,
when the Lord God of Jacob
comes near,
8 because he turns solid rock
into flowing streams
and pools of water.

Psalm 115

The LORD Deserves To Be Praised

1 We don't deserve praise!
The LORD alone deserves
all of the praise,
because of his love
and faithfulness.
2 Why should the nations ask,
"Where is your God?"

3 Our God is in the heavens,
doing as he chooses.
4 The idols of the nations
are made of silver and gold.
5 They have a mouth and eyes,
but they can't speak or see.
6 Their ears can't hear,
and their noses can't smell.
7 Their hands have no feeling,
their legs don't move,
and they can't make a sound.
8 Everyone who made the idols
and all who trust them
are just as helpless
as those useless gods.

9 People of Israel,
you must trust the LORD
to help and protect you.
10 Family of Aaron the priest,
you must trust the LORD
to help and protect you.
11 All of you worship the LORD,
so you must trust him
to help and protect you.

12 The LORD will not forget
to give us his blessing;
he will bless all of Israel
and the family of Aaron.
13 All who worship the LORD,
no matter who they are,
will receive his blessing.

14 I pray that the LORD
will let your family
and your descendants
always grow strong.
15 May the LORD who created
the heavens and the earth
give you his blessing.

16 The LORD has kept the heavens
for himself,
but he has given the earth
to us humans.
17 The dead are silent
and cannot praise the LORD,
18 but we will praise him
now and forevermore.
Shout praises to the LORD!

Psalm 116

When the LORD Saves You from Death

1 I love you, LORD!
You answered my prayers.
2 You paid attention to me,
and so I will pray to you
as long as I live.
3 Death attacked from all sides,
and I was captured
by its painful chains.
But when I was really hurting,
4 I prayed and said, "LORD,
please don't let me die!"

114.3 a Ex 14.21; **b** Js 3.16, 17. **114.8** Ex 17.1-7; Nu 20.2-13. **115.2** 3 Macc 6.11. **115.4-8** Ps 135.15-18; Let Jer 4-73; Rev 9.20. **115.13** Rev 11.18; 19.5.

5 You are kind, LORD,
so good and merciful.
6 You protect ordinary people,
and when I was helpless,
you saved me
7 and treated me so kindly
that I don't need
to worry anymore.

8 You, LORD, have saved
my life from death,
my eyes from tears,
my feet from stumbling.
9 Now I will walk at your side
in this land of the living.
10 I was faithful to you
when I was suffering,
11 though in my confusion I said,
"I can't trust anyone!"

12 What must I give you, LORD,
for being so good to me?
13 I will pour out an offering
of wine to you,
and I will pray in your name
because you
have saved me.
14 I will keep my promise to you
when your people meet.
15 You are deeply concerned
when one of your loyal people
faces death.

16 I worship you, LORD,
just as my mother did,
and you have rescued me
from the chains of death.
17 I will offer you a sacrifice
to show how grateful I am,
and I will pray.
18 I will keep my promise to you
when your people
19 gather at your temple
in Jerusalem.
Shout praises to the LORD!

Psalm 117

Come Praise the LORD

1 All of you nations,
come praise the LORD!
Let everyone praise him.
2 His love for us is wonderful;
his faithfulness never ends.
Shout praises to the LORD!

Psalm 118

The LORD Is Always Merciful

1 Tell the LORD
how thankful you are,
because he is kind
and always merciful.

2 Let Israel shout,
"God is always merciful!"
3 Let the family of Aaron
the priest shout,
"God is always merciful!"
4 Let every true worshiper
of the LORD shout,
"God is always merciful!"

5 When I was really hurting,
I prayed to the LORD.
He answered my prayer,
and took my worries away.
6 The LORD is on my side,
and I am not afraid
of what others can do to me.
7 With the LORD on my side,
I will defeat all
of my hateful enemies.
8 It is better to trust the LORD
for protection
than to trust anyone else,
9 including strong leaders.
10 Nations surrounded me,
but I got rid of them
by the power of the LORD.
11 They attacked from all sides,
but I got rid of them
by the power of the LORD.
12 They swarmed around like bees,
but by the power of the LORD,
I got rid of them
and their fiery sting.
13 Their attacks were so fierce
that I nearly fell,
but the LORD helped me.
14 My power and my strength

116.10 2 Co 4.13. **117.1** Ro 15.11. **118.1** 1 Ch 16.34; 2 Ch 5.11-13; 7.3; Ezra 3.11; Ps 100.5; 106.1; 107.1; 136.1; Jr 33.11. **118.6** He 13.6. **118.14** Ex 15.2; Is 12.2.

come from the LORD,
and he has saved me.

15 From the tents of God's people
come shouts of victory:
"The LORD is powerful!
16 With his mighty arm
the LORD wins victories!
The LORD is powerful!"

17 And so my life is safe,
and I will live to tell
what the LORD has done.
18 He punished me terribly,
but he did not let death
lay its hands on me.
19 Open the gates of justice!
I will enter and tell the LORD
how thankful I am.

20 Here is the gate of the LORD!
Everyone who does right
may enter this gate.

21 I praise the LORD
for answering my prayers
and saving me.
22 The stone that the builders
tossed aside
has now become
the most important stone.

23 The LORD has done this,
and it is amazing to us.
24 This day belongs to the LORD!
Let's celebrate
and be glad today.
25 We'll ask the LORD to save us!
We'll sincerely ask the LORD
to let us win.

26 God bless the one who comes
in the name of the LORD!
We praise you from here
in the house of the LORD.

27 The LORD is our God,
and he has given us light!
Start the celebration!
March with palm branches
all the way to the altar.[e]

28 The LORD is my God!
I will praise him and tell him
how thankful I am.

29 Tell the LORD
how thankful you are,
because he is kind
and always merciful.

Psalm 119

In Praise of the Law of the LORD

1 Our LORD, you bless everyone
who lives right
and obeys your Law.
2 You bless all of those
who follow your commands
from deep in their hearts
3 and who never do wrong
or turn from you.
4 You have ordered us always
to obey your teachings;
5 I don't ever want to stray
from your laws.
6 Thinking about your commands
will keep me from doing
some foolish thing.
7 I will do right and praise you
by learning to respect
your perfect laws.
8 I will obey all of them!
Don't turn your back on me.

9 Young people can live
a clean life
by obeying your word.
10 I worship you
with all my heart.
Don't let me walk away
from your commands.
11 I treasure your word
above all else;

[e] **118.27** *Start . . . altar*: One possible meaning for the difficult Hebrew text.
118.22 Lk 20.17; Ac 4.11; 1 P 2.7. **118.22,23** Mt 21.42; Mk 12.10, 11. **118.25** Mt 21.9; Mk 11.9; Jn 12.13. **118.26** Mt 21.9; 23.39; Mk 11.9; Lk 13.35; 19.38; Jn 12.13.

it keeps me from sinning
against you.
12 I praise you, LORD!
Teach me your laws.
13 With my own mouth,
I tell others the laws
that you have spoken.
14 Obeying your instructions
brings as much happiness
as being rich.
15 I will study your teachings
and follow your footsteps.
16 I will take pleasure
in your laws
and remember your words.

17 Treat me with kindness, LORD,
so that I may live
and do what you say.
18 Open my mind
and let me discover
the wonders of your Law.
19 I live here as a stranger.
Don't keep me from knowing
your commands.
20 What I want most of all
and at all times
is to honor your laws.
21 You punish those boastful,
worthless nobodies who turn
from your commands.
22 Don't let them sneer
and insult me
for following you.
23 I keep thinking about
your teachings, LORD,
even if rulers plot
against me.
24 Your laws are my greatest joy!
I follow their advice.

25 I am at the point of death.
Let your teachings
breathe new life into me.
26 When I told you my troubles,
you answered my prayers.
Now teach me your laws.
27 Help me to understand
your teachings,
and I will think about
your marvelous deeds.
28 I am overcome with sorrow.
Encourage me,
as you have promised to do.
29 Keep me from being deceitful,
and be kind enough
to teach me your Law.
30 I am determined to be faithful
and to respect your laws.
31 I follow your rules, LORD.
Don't let me be ashamed.
32 I am eager to learn all
that you want me to do;
help me to understand
more and more.

33 Point out your rules to me,
and I won't disobey
even one of them.
34 Help me to understand your Law;
I promise to obey it
with all my heart.
35 Direct me by your commands!
I love to do what you say.
36 Make me want to obey you,
rather than to be rich.
37 Take away my foolish desires,
and let me find life
by walking with you.
38 I am your servant!
Do for me what you promised
to those who worship you.
39 Your wonderful teachings
protect me from the insults
that I hate so much.
40 I long for your teachings.
Be true to yourself
and let me live.

41 Show me your love
and save me, LORD,
as you have promised.
42 Then I will have an answer
for everyone who insults me
for trusting your word.
43 I rely on your laws!
Don't take away my chance
to speak your truth.
44 I will keep obeying your Law
forever and ever.
45 I have gained perfect freedom
by following your teachings,
46 and I trust them so much
that I tell them to kings.
47 I love your commands!

They bring me happiness.
48 I love and respect them
and will keep them in mind.

49 Don't forget your promise
to me, your servant.
I depend on it.
50 When I am hurting,
I find comfort in your promise
that leads to life.
51 Conceited people sneer at me,
but I obey your Law.
52 I find true comfort, LORD,
because your laws have stood
the test of time.
53 I get furious when evil people
turn against your Law.
54 No matter where I am,
your teachings
fill me with songs.
55 Even in the night
I think about you, LORD,
and I obey your Law.
56 You have blessed me
because I have always followed
your teachings.

57 You, LORD, are my choice,
and I will obey you.
58 With all my heart
I beg you to be kind to me,
just as you have promised.
59 I pay careful attention
as you lead me,
and I follow closely.
60 As soon as you command,
I do what you say.
61 Evil people may set a trap,
but I obey your Law.
62 Your laws are so fair
that I wake up and praise you
in the middle of the night.
63 I choose as my friends
everyone who worships you
and follows your teachings.
64 Our LORD, your love is seen
all over the world.
Teach me your laws.

65 I am your servant, LORD,
and you have kept your promise
to treat me with kindness.
66 Give me wisdom and good sense.
I trust your commands.
67 Once you corrected me
for not obeying you,
but now I obey.
68 You are kindhearted,
and you do good things,
so teach me your laws.
69 My reputation is being ruined
by conceited liars,
but with all my heart
I follow your teachings.
70 Those liars have no sense,
but I find happiness
in your Law.
71 When you corrected me,
it did me good
because it taught me
to study your laws.
72 I would rather obey you
than to have a thousand pieces
of silver and gold.

73 You created me
and put me together.
Make me wise enough to learn
what you have commanded.
74 Your worshipers will see me,
and they will be glad
that I trust your word.
75 Your decisions are correct,
and you were right
to punish me.
76 I serve you, LORD.
Comfort me with your love,
just as you have promised.
77 I love to obey your Law!
Have mercy and let me live.
78 Put down those proud people
who hurt me with their lies,
because I have chosen
to study your teachings.
79 Let your worshipers come to me,
so they will learn
to obey your rules.
80 Let me truly respect your laws,
so I won't be ashamed.

81 I long for you to rescue me!
Your word is my only hope.
82 I am worn out from waiting
for you to keep your word.
When will you have mercy?
83 My life is wasting away

like a dried-up wineskin,[f]
but I have not forgotten
your teachings.
84 I am your servant!
How long must I suffer?
When will you punish
those troublemakers?
85 Those proud people reject
your teachings,
and they dig pits
for me to fall in.
86 Your laws can be trusted!
Protect me from cruel liars.
87 They have almost killed me,
but I have been faithful
to your teachings.
88 Show that you love me
and let me live,
so that I may obey all
of your commands.

89 Our LORD, you are eternal!
Your word will last as long
as the heavens.[g]
90 You remain faithful
in every generation,
and the earth you created
will keep standing firm.
91 All things are your servants,
and the laws you made
are still in effect today.
92 If I had not found happiness
in obeying your Law,
I would have died in misery.
93 I won't ever forget
your teachings,
because you give me new life
by following them.
94 I belong to you,
and I have respected your laws,
so keep me safe.
95 Brutal enemies are waiting
to ambush and destroy me,
but I obey your rules.
96 Nothing is completely perfect,
except your teachings.

97 I deeply love your Law!
I think about it all day.
98 Your laws never leave my mind,
and they make me much wiser
than my enemies.
99 Thinking about your teachings
gives me better understanding
than my teachers,
100 and obeying your laws
makes me wiser than those
who have lived a long time.
101 I obey your word
instead of following a way
that leads to trouble.
102 You have been my teacher,
and I won't reject
your instructions.
103 Your teachings are sweeter
than honey.
104 They give me understanding
and make me hate all lies.

105 Your word is a lamp
that gives light
wherever I walk.
106 Your laws are fair,
and I have given my word
to respect them all.
107 I am in terrible pain!
Save me, LORD,
as you said you would.
108 Accept my offerings of praise
and teach me your laws.
109 I never forget your teachings,
although my life is always
in danger.
110 Some merciless people
are trying to trap me,
but I never turn my back
on your teachings.
111 They will always be
my most prized possession
and my source of joy.
112 I have made up my mind
to obey your laws forever,
no matter what.

113 I hate anyone
whose loyalty is divided,
but I love your Law.

[f]**119.83** *a dried-up wineskin*: The Hebrew text has "a wineskin in the smoke." In ancient times bags were made from animal skins to hold wine, but when the bags dried up they cracked and could no longer be used. [g]**119.89** *Our . . . heavens*: Or "Our LORD, your word is eternal. It will last as long as the heavens."

114 You are my place of safety
and my shield.
Your word is my only hope.

115 All of you worthless people,
get away from me!
I am determined to obey
the commands of my God.

116 Be true to your word, LORD.
Keep me alive and strong;
don't let me be ashamed
because of my hope.
117 Keep me safe and secure,
so that I will always
respect your laws.
118 You reject all deceitful liars
because they refuse
your teachings.
119 As far as you are concerned,
all evil people are[h] garbage,
and so I follow your rules.
120 I tremble all over
when I think of you
and the way you judge.

121 I did what was fair and right!
Don't hand me over to those
who want to mistreat me.
122 Take good care of me,
your servant,
and don't let me be harmed
by those conceited people.
123 My eyes are weary from waiting
to see you keep your promise
to come and save me.
124 Show your love for me,
your servant,
and teach me your laws.
125 I serve you,
so let me understand
your teachings.
126 Do something, LORD!
They have broken your Law.
127 Your laws mean more to me
than the finest gold.
128 I follow all of your commands,[i]
but I hate anyone
who leads me astray.

129 Your teachings are wonderful,
and I respect them all.
130 Understanding your word
brings light to the minds
of ordinary people.
131 I honestly want to know
everything you teach.
132 Think about me and be kind,
just as you are to everyone
who loves your name.
133 Keep your promise
and don't let me stumble
or let sin control my life.
134 Protect me from abuse,
so I can obey your laws.
135 Smile on me, your servant,
and teach me your laws.
136 When anyone disobeys you,
my eyes overflow with tears.

137 Our LORD, you always do right,
and your decisions are fair.
138 All of your teachings are true
and trustworthy.
139 It upsets me greatly
when my enemies neglect
your teachings.
140 Your word to me, your servant,
is like pure gold;
I treasure what you say.
141 Everyone calls me a nobody,
but I remember your laws.
142 You will always do right,
and your teachings are true.
143 I am in deep distress,
but I love your teachings.
144 Your rules are always fair.
Help me to understand them
and live.

145 I pray to you, LORD!
Please answer me.
I promise to obey your laws.
146 I beg you to save me,
so I can follow your rules.
147 Even before sunrise,
I pray for your help,
and I put my hope
in what you have said.

[h] **119.119** *As far as . . . are*: A few Hebrew manuscripts and ancient translations. Most Hebrew manuscripts have "You get rid of evil people as if they were." [i] **119.128** *I . . . commands*: One possible meaning for the difficult Hebrew text.

148 I lie awake at night,
thinking of your promises.
149 Show that you love me, LORD,
and answer my prayer.
Please do the right thing
and save my life.
150 People who disobey your Law
have made evil plans
and want to hurt me,
151 but you are with me,
and all of your commands
can be trusted.
152 From studying your laws,
I found out long ago
that you made them
to last forever.

153 I have not forgotten your Law!
Look at the trouble I am in,
and rescue me.
154 Be my defender and protector!
Keep your promise
and save my life.
155 Evil people won't obey you,
and so they have no hope
of being saved.
156 You are merciful, LORD!
Please do the right thing
and save my life.
157 I have a lot of brutal enemies,
but still I never turn
from your laws.
158 All of those unfaithful people
who refuse to obey you
are disgusting to me.
159 Remember how I love your laws,
and show your love for me
by keeping me safe.
160 All you say can be trusted;
your teachings are true
and will last forever.

161 Rulers are cruel to me
for no reason.
But with all my heart
I respect your words,
162 because they bring happiness
like treasures taken in war.
163 I can't stand liars,
but I love your Law.
164 I praise you seven times a day
because your laws are fair.
165 You give peace of mind
to all who love your Law.
Nothing can make them fall.
166 You are my only hope
for being saved, LORD,
and I do all you command.
167 I love and obey your laws
with all my heart.
168 You know everything I do.
You know I respect every law
you have given.

169 Please, LORD, hear my prayer
and give me the understanding
that comes from your word.
170 Listen to my concerns
and keep me safe,
just as you have promised.
171 If you will teach me your laws,
I will praise you 172 and sing
about your promise,
because all of your teachings
are what they ought to be.
173 Be ready to protect me
because I have chosen
to obey your laws.
174 I am waiting for you
to save me, LORD.
Your Law makes me happy.
175 Keep me alive,
so I can praise you,
and let me find help
in your teachings.
176 I am your servant,
but I have wandered away
like a lost sheep.
Please come after me,
because I have not forgotten
your teachings.

Psalm 120

[*A song for worship.*]

A Prayer for the LORD's Help

1 When I am in trouble, I pray,
2 "Come and save me, LORD,
from deceitful liars!"

3 What punishment is fitting
for you deceitful liars?
4 Your reward should be
sharp and flaming arrows!

5 But I must live as a foreigner
among the people of Meshech
and in the tents of Kedar.[j]
6 I have spent too much time
living among people
who hate peace.
7 I am in favor of peace,
but when I speak of it,
all they want is war.

Psalm 121

[*A song for worship.*]

The LORD Will Protect His People

1 I look to the hills!
Where will I find help?
2 It will come from the LORD,
who created the heavens
and the earth.

3 The LORD is your protector,
and he won't go to sleep
or let you stumble.
4 The protector of Israel
doesn't doze
or ever get drowsy.

5 The LORD is your protector,
there at your right side
to shade you from the sun.
6 You won't be harmed
by the sun during the day
or by the moon[k] at night.

7 The LORD will protect you
and keep you safe
from all dangers.
8 The LORD will protect you
now and always
wherever you go.

Psalm 122

[*A song by David for worship.*]

A Song of Praise

1 It made me glad
to hear them say,
"Let's go to the house
of the LORD!"
2 Jerusalem, we are standing
inside your gates.

3 Jerusalem, what a strong
and beautiful city you are!
4 Every tribe of the LORD
obeys him and comes to you
to praise his name.
5 David's royal throne is here
where justice rules.

6 Jerusalem, we pray
that you will have peace,
and that all will go well
for those who love you.
7 May there be peace
inside your city walls
and in your palaces.
8 Because of my friends
and my relatives,
I will pray for peace.
9 And because of the house
of the LORD our God,
I will work for your good.

Psalm 123

[*A song for worship.*]

A Prayer for Mercy

1 Our LORD and our God,
I turn my eyes to you,
on your throne in heaven.
2 Servants look to their master,
but we will look to you,
until you have mercy on us.

3 Please have mercy, LORD!
We have been insulted
more than we can stand,
4 and we can't take more abuse
from those proud,
conceited people.

Psalm 124

[*A song by David for worship.*]

Thanking the LORD for Victory

1 The LORD was on our side!
Let everyone in Israel say:

[j] **120.5** *Meshech . . . Kedar*: Meshech was a country near the Black Sea, and Kedar was a tribe of the Syrian desert. [k] **121.6** *harmed . . . sun . . . moon*: In ancient times people saw the harmful effects of the rays of the sun, and they thought that certain illnesses (especially mental disorders) were also caused by the rays of the moon.

2 "The LORD was on our side!
Otherwise, the enemy attack
3 would have killed us all,
because it was furious.
4 We would have been swept away
in a violent flood
5 of high and roaring waves."

6 Let's praise the LORD!
He protected us from enemies
who were like wild animals,
7 and we escaped like birds
from a hunter's torn net.

8 The LORD made heaven and earth,
and he is the one
who sends us help.

Psalm 125

[*A song for worship.*]

The LORD's People Are Safe

1 Everyone who trusts the LORD
is like Mount Zion
that cannot be shaken
and will stand forever.
2 Just as Jerusalem is protected
by mountains on every side,
the LORD protects his people
by holding them in his arms
now and forever.
3 He won't let the wicked
rule his people
or lead them to do wrong.
4 Let's ask the LORD to be kind
to everyone who is good
and completely obeys him.

5 When the LORD punishes
the wicked,
he will punish everyone else
who lives a crooked life.
Pray for peace in Israel!

Psalm 126

[*A song for worship.*]

Celebrating the Harvest

1 It seemed like a dream
when the LORD brought us back
to the city of Zion.[l]
2 We celebrated with laughter
and joyful songs.
In foreign nations it was said,
"The LORD has worked miracles
for his people."
3 And so we celebrated
because the LORD had indeed
worked miracles for us.

4 Our LORD, we ask you to bless
our people again,
and let us be like streams
in the Southern Desert.
5 We cried as we went out
to plant our seeds.
Now let us celebrate
as we bring in the crops.
6 We cried on the way
to plant our seeds,
but we will celebrate and shout
as we bring in the crops.

Psalm 127

[*A song by Solomon for worship.*]

Only the LORD Can Bless a Home

1 Without the help of the LORD
it is useless to build a home
or to guard a city.
2 It is useless to get up early
and stay up late
in order to earn a living.
God takes care of his own,
even while they sleep.[m]

3 Children are a blessing
and a gift from the LORD.
4 Having a lot of children
to take care of you
in your old age
is like a warrior
with a lot of arrows.
5 The more you have,
the better off you will be,
because they will protect you
when your enemies attack
with arguments.

[l] **126.1** *brought . . . Zion*: Or "made the city of Zion prosperous again." [m] **127.2** *God . . . sleep*: One possible meaning for the difficult Hebrew text.

Psalm 128

[*A song for worship.*]

The LORD Rewards His Faithful People

1 The LORD will bless you
if you respect him
and obey his laws.
2 Your fields will produce,
and you will be happy
and all will go well.
3 Your wife will be as fruitful
as a grapevine,
and just as an olive tree
is rich with olives,
your home will be rich
with healthy children.
4 That is how the LORD will bless
everyone who respects him.

5 I pray that the LORD
will bless you from Zion
and let Jerusalem prosper
as long as you live.
6 May you live long enough
to see your grandchildren.
Let's pray for peace in Israel!

Psalm 129

[*A song for worship.*]

A Prayer for Protection

1 Since the time I was young,
enemies have often attacked!
Let everyone in Israel say:
2 "Since the time I was young,
enemies have often attacked!
But they have not defeated me,
3 though my back is like a field
that has just been plowed."

4 The LORD always does right,
and he has set me free
from the ropes
of those cruel people.
5 I pray that all who hate
the city of Zion
will be made ashamed
and forced to turn and run.
6 May they be like grass
on the flat roof of a house,
grass that dries up
as soon as it sprouts.
7 Don't let them be like wheat
gathered in bundles.
8 And don't let anyone
who passes by say to them,
"The LORD bless you!
I give you my blessing
in the name of the LORD."

Psalm 130

[*A song for worship.*]

Trusting the LORD in Times of Trouble

1 From a sea of troubles
I call out to you, LORD.
2 Won't you please listen
as I beg for mercy?

3 If you kept record of our sins,
no one could last long.
4 But you forgive us,
and so we will worship you.

5 With all my heart,
I am waiting, LORD, for you!
I trust your promises.
6 I wait for you more eagerly
than a soldier on guard duty
waits for the dawn.
Yes, I wait more eagerly
than a soldier on guard duty
waits for the dawn.

7 Israel, trust the LORD!
He is always merciful,
and he has the power
to save you.
8 Israel, the LORD will save you
from all of your sins.

Psalm 131

[*A song by David for worship.*]

Trust the LORD!

1 I am not conceited, LORD,
and I don't waste my time
on impossible schemes.
2 But I have learned to feel safe
and satisfied,
just like a young child
on its mother's lap.

130.8 Mt 1.21; Titus 2.14.

3 People of Israel,
you must trust the LORD
now and forever.

Psalm 132

[*A song for worship.*]

The LORD Is Always with His People

1 Our LORD, don't forget David
and how he suffered.
2 Mighty God of Jacob,
remember how he promised:
3 "I won't go home
or crawl into bed
4 or close my eyelids,
5 until I find a home for you,
the mighty LORD God of Jacob."

6 When we were in Ephrath,
we heard that the sacred chest
was somewhere near Jaar.
7 Then we said, "Let's go
to the throne of the LORD
and worship at his feet."

8 Come to your new home, LORD,
you and the sacred chest
with all of its power.
9 Let victory be like robes
for the priests;
let your faithful people
celebrate and shout.
10 David is your chosen one,
so don't reject him.
11 You made a solemn promise
to David, when you said,
"I, the LORD, promise
that someone in your family
will always be king.
12 If they keep our agreement
and follow my teachings,
then someone in your family
will rule forever."

13 You have gladly chosen Zion
as your home, our LORD.
14 You said, "This is my home!
I will live here forever.
15 I will bless Zion with food,
and even the poor will eat
until they are full.
16 Victory will be like robes
for the priests,
and its faithful people
will celebrate and shout.
17 I will give mighty power
to the kingdom of David.
Each one of my chosen kings
will shine like a lamp
18 and wear a sparkling crown.
But I will disgrace
their enemies."

Psalm 133

[*A song for worship.*]

Living Together in Peace

1 It is truly wonderful
when relatives live together
in peace.
2 It is as beautiful as olive oil
poured on Aaron's head[n]
and running down his beard
and the collar of his robe.
3 It is like the dew
from Mount Hermon,
falling on Zion's mountains,
where the LORD has promised
to bless his people
with life forevermore.

Psalm 134

[*A song for worship.*]

Praising the LORD at Night

1 Everyone who serves the LORD,
come and offer praises.
Everyone who has gathered
in his temple tonight,
2 lift your hands in prayer
toward his holy place
and praise the LORD.

3 The LORD is the Creator
of heaven and earth,
and I pray that the LORD
will bless you from Zion.

[n] **133.2** *head*: Olive oil was poured on Aaron's head to show that God had chosen him to be the high priest.

132.6-10 2 Ch 6.41, 42. **132.11** 2 S 7.12-16; 1 Ch 17.11-14; Ps 89.3, 4; Ac 2.30.
132.17 1 K 11.36; Ps 18.28.

Psalm 135

In Praise of the LORD's Kindness

1 Shout praises to the LORD!
You are his servants,
so praise his name.
2 All who serve in the temple
of the LORD our God,
3 come and shout praises.
Praise the name of the LORD!
He is kind and good.
4 He chose the family of Jacob
and the people of Israel
for his very own.

5 The LORD is much greater
than any other god.
6 He does as he chooses
in heaven and on earth
and deep in the sea.
7 The LORD makes the clouds rise
from far across the earth,
and he makes lightning
to go with the rain.
Then from his secret place
he sends out the wind.

8 The LORD killed the first-born
of people and animals
in the land of Egypt.
9 God used miracles and wonders
to fight the king of Egypt
and all of his officials.
10 He destroyed many nations
and killed powerful kings,
11 including King Sihon
of the Amorites
and King Og of Bashan.
He conquered every kingdom
in the land of Canaan
12 and gave their property
to his people Israel.

13 The name of the LORD
will be remembered forever,
and he will be famous
for all time to come.
14 The LORD will bring justice
and show mercy to all
who serve him.

15 Idols of silver and gold
are made and worshiped
in other nations.
16 They have a mouth and eyes,
but they can't speak or see.
17 They are completely deaf,
and they can't breathe.
18 Everyone who makes idols
and all who trust them
will end up as helpless
as their idols.

19 Everyone in Israel,
come praise the LORD!
All the family of Aaron
20 and all the tribe of Levi,[o]
come praise the LORD!
All of his worshipers,
come praise the LORD.
21 Praise the LORD from Zion!
He lives here in Jerusalem.
Shout praises to the LORD!

Psalm 136

God's Love Never Fails

1 Praise the LORD! He is good.
God's love never fails.
2 Praise the God of all gods.
God's love never fails.
3 Praise the Lord of lords.
God's love never fails.

4 Only God works great miracles.[p]
God's love never fails.
5 With wisdom he made the sky.
God's love never fails.
6 The Lord stretched the earth
over the ocean.
God's love never fails.
7 He made the bright lights
in the sky.
God's love never fails.

[o] **135.19,20** *Aaron . . . Levi*: Aaron was from the tribe of Levi, and all priests were from his family. The temple helpers, singers, and musicians were also from the tribe of Levi. [p] **136.4** *great miracles*: One Hebrew manuscript and one ancient translation have "miracles."

135.15-18 Ps 115.4-8; Rev 9.20. **136.1** 1 Ch 16.34; 2 Ch 5.11-13; 7.3; Ezra 3.11; Ps 100.5; 106.1; 107.1; 118.1; Jr 33.11; 3 Macc 6.32. **136.5** Gn 1.1. **136.6** Gn 1.2. **136.7-9** Gn 1.16.

8 He lets the sun rule each day.
God's love never fails.
9 He lets the moon and the stars
rule each night.
God's love never fails.

10 God struck down the first-born
in every Egyptian family.
God's love never fails.
11 He rescued Israel from Egypt.
God's love never fails.
12 God used his great strength
and his powerful arm.
God's love never fails.
13 He split the Red Sea[q] apart.
God's love never fails.

14 The Lord brought Israel safely
through the sea.
God's love never fails.
15 He destroyed the Egyptian king
and his army there.
God's love never fails.
16 The Lord led his people
through the desert.
God's love never fails.

17 Our God defeated mighty kings.
God's love never fails.
18 And he killed famous kings.
God's love never fails.
19 One of them was Sihon,
king of the Amorites.
God's love never fails.
20 Another was King Og of Bashan.
God's love never fails.
21 God took away their land.
God's love never fails.
22 He gave their land to Israel,
the people who serve him.
God's love never fails.

23 God saw the trouble we were in.
God's love never fails.
24 He rescued us from our enemies.
God's love never fails.
25 He gives food to all who live.
God's love never fails.
26 Praise God in heaven!
God's love never fails.

Psalm 137

A Prayer for Revenge

1 Beside the rivers of Babylon
we thought about Jerusalem,
and we sat down and cried.
2 We hung our small harps
on the willow[r] trees.
3 Our enemies had brought us here
as their prisoners,
and now they wanted us to sing
and entertain them.
They insulted us and shouted,
"Sing about Zion!"

4 Here in a foreign land,
how can we sing
about the LORD?
5 Jerusalem, if I forget you,
let my right hand go limp.
6 Let my tongue stick
to the roof of my mouth,
if I don't think about you
above all else.

7 Our LORD, punish the Edomites!
Because the day Jerusalem fell,
they shouted,
"Completely destroy the city!
Tear down every building!"

8 Babylon, you are doomed!
I pray the Lord's blessings
on anyone who punishes you
for what you did to us.
9 May the Lord bless everyone
who beats your children
against the rocks!

Psalm 138

[*By David.*]

Praise the LORD with All Your Heart

1 With all my heart
I praise you, LORD.

[q]**136.13** *Red Sea*: See the note at 106.7, 9, 22. [r]**137.2** *willow*: Or "poplar."
136.10 Ex 12.29. **136.11** Ex 12.51. **136.13-15** Ex 14.21-29. **136.19** Nu 21.21-30.
136.20 Nu 21.31-35. **137.8** Rev 18.6.

In the presence of angels[s]
I sing your praises.
2 I worship at your holy temple
and praise you for your love
and your faithfulness.
You were true to your word
and made yourself more famous
than ever before.[t]
3 When I asked for your help,
you answered my prayer
and gave me courage.[u]

4 All kings on this earth
have heard your promises, LORD,
and they will praise you.
5 You are so famous
that they will sing about
the things you have done.
6 Though you are above us all,
you care for humble people,
and you keep a close watch
on everyone who is proud.

7 I am surrounded by trouble,
but you protect me
against my angry enemies.
With your own powerful arm
you keep me safe.

8 You, LORD, will always
treat me with kindness.
Your love never fails.
You have made us what we are.
Don't give up on us now![v]

Psalm 139

[*A psalm by David for the music leader.*]

The LORD Is Always Near

1 You have looked deep
into my heart, LORD,
and you know all about me.
2 You know when I am resting
or when I am working,
and from heaven
you discover my thoughts.

3 You notice everything I do
and everywhere I go.
4 Before I even speak a word,
you know what I will say,
5 and with your powerful arm
you protect me
from every side.
6 I can't understand all of this!
Such wonderful knowledge
is far above me.

7 Where could I go to escape
from your Spirit
or from your sight?
8 If I were to climb up
to the highest heavens,
you would be there.
If I were to dig down
to the world of the dead
you would also be there.

9 Suppose I had wings
like the dawning day
and flew across the ocean.
10 Even then your powerful arm
would guide and protect me.
11 Or suppose I said, "I'll hide
in the dark until night comes
to cover me over."
12 But you see in the dark
because daylight and dark
are all the same to you.

13 You are the one
who put me together
inside my mother's body,
14 and I praise you because of
the wonderful way
you created me.
Everything you do is marvelous!
Of this I have no doubt.

15 Nothing about me
is hidden from you!
I was secretly woven together
deep in the earth below,
16 but with your own eyes you saw
my body being formed.
Even before I was born,
you had written in your book
everything I would do.

[s] **138.1** *angels*: Or "gods" or "supernatural beings" who worship and serve God in heaven or "rulers" or "leaders." [t] **138.2** *You were . . . before*: One possible meaning for the difficult Hebrew text. [u] **138.3** *and gave me courage*: One possible meaning for the difficult Hebrew text.
[v] **138.8** *You have . . . now*: Or "Please don't desert your people."

17 Your thoughts are far beyond
my understanding,
much more than I
could ever imagine.
18 I try to count your thoughts,
but they outnumber the grains
of sand on the beach.
And when I awake,
I will find you nearby.

19 How I wish that you would kill
all cruel and heartless people
and protect me from them!
20 They are always rebelling
and speaking evil of you.[w]
21 You know I hate anyone
who hates you, LORD,
and refuses to obey.
22 They are my enemies too,
and I truly hate them.

23 Look deep into my heart, God,
and find out everything
I am thinking.
24 Don't let me follow evil ways,
but lead me in the way
that time has proven true.

Psalm 140

[*A psalm by David for the music leader.*]

A Prayer for the LORD's Help

1 Rescue me from cruel
and violent enemies, LORD!
2 They think up evil plans
and always cause trouble.
3 Their words bite deep
like the poisonous fangs
of a snake.

4 Protect me, LORD, from cruel
and brutal enemies,
who want to destroy me.
5 Those proud people have hidden
traps and nets
to catch me as I walk.

6 You, LORD, are my God!
Please listen to my prayer.
7 You have the power to save me,
and you keep me safe
in every battle.

8 Don't let the wicked succeed
in doing what they want,
or else they might never
stop planning evil.
9 They have me surrounded,
but make them the victims
of their own vicious lies.[x]
10 Dump flaming coals on them
and throw them into pits
where they can't climb out.
11 Chase those cruel liars away!
Let trouble hunt them down.

12 Our LORD, I know that you
defend the homeless
and see that the poor
are given justice.
13 Your people will praise you
and will live with you
because they do right.

Psalm 141

[*A psalm by David.*]

A Prayer for the LORD's Protection

1 I pray to you, LORD!
Please listen when I pray
and hurry to help me.
2 Think of my prayer
as sweet-smelling incense,
and think of my lifted hands
as an evening sacrifice.

3 Help me to guard my words
whenever I say something.
4 Don't let me want to do evil
or waste my time doing wrong
with wicked people.
Don't let me even taste
the good things they offer.

5 Let your faithful people
correct and punish me.
My prayers condemn the deeds
of those who do wrong,

[w] **139.20** *you*: One possible meaning for the difficult Hebrew text of verse 20. [x] **140.8,9** *or else . . . lies*: One possible meaning for the difficult Hebrew text.

139.17 Si 18.5-7. **140.3** Ro 3.13. **141.2** Rev 5.8.

so don't let me be friends
with any of them.
6 Everyone will admit
that I was right
when their rulers are thrown
down a rocky cliff,
7 and their bones lie scattered
like broken rocks
on top of a grave.[y]

8 You are my LORD and God,
and I look to you for safety.
Don't let me be harmed.
9 Protect me from the traps
of those violent people,
10 and make them fall
into their own traps
while you help me escape.

Psalm 142

[A special psalm and a prayer by David when he was in the cave.]

A Prayer for Help

1 I pray to you, LORD.
I beg for mercy.
2 I tell you all of my worries
and my troubles,
3 and whenever I feel low,
you are there to guide me.

A trap has been hidden
along my pathway.
4 Even if you look,
you won't see anyone
who cares enough
to walk beside me.
There is no place to hide,
and no one who really cares.

5 I pray to you, LORD!
You are my place of safety,
and you are my choice
in the land of the living.
Please answer my prayer.
I am completely helpless.

6 Help! They are chasing me,
and they are too strong.
7 Rescue me from this prison,
so I can praise your name.
And when your people notice
your wonderful kindness to me,
they will rush to my side.

Psalm 143

[A psalm by David.]

A Prayer in Time of Danger

1 Listen, LORD, as I pray!
You are faithful and honest
and will answer my prayer.
2 I am your servant.
Don't try me in your court,
because no one is innocent
by your standards.
3 My enemies are chasing me,
crushing me in the ground.
I am in total darkness,
like someone long dead.
4 I have given up all hope,
and I feel numb all over.

5 I remember to think about
the many things you did
in years gone by.
6 Then I lift my hands in prayer,
because my soul is a desert,
thirsty for water from you.

7 Please hurry, LORD,
and answer my prayer.
I feel hopeless.
Don't turn away
and leave me here to die.
8 Each morning let me learn
more about your love
because I trust you.
I come to you in prayer,
asking for your guidance.

9 Please rescue me
from my enemies, LORD!
I come to you for safety.[z]
10 You are my God. Show me
what you want me to do,
and let your gentle Spirit
lead me in the right path.

11 Be true to your name, LORD,
and keep my life safe.

[y] **141.5-7** *Let . . . grave*: One possible meaning for the difficult Hebrew text of verses 5-7.
[z] **143.9** *I . . . safety*: Or "You are my hiding place."
142 Title 1 S 22.1; 24.3. **143.2** Ro 3.20; Ga 2.16.

"You, LORD, are my shepherd . . ." *Psalm 23.1*

The Peaceful Kingdom

Isaiah 11.6-7

Use your saving power
to protect me from trouble.
12 I am your servant.
Show how much you love me
by destroying my enemies.

Psalm 144

[*By David.*]

A Prayer for the Nation

1 I praise you, LORD!
You are my mighty rock,[a]
and you teach me
how to fight my battles.
2 You are my friend,
and you are my fortress
where I am safe.
You are my shield,
and you made me the ruler
of our people.[b]

3 Why do we humans mean anything
to you, our LORD?
Why do you care about us?
4 We disappear like a breath;
we last no longer
than a faint shadow.

5 Open the heavens like a curtain
and come down, LORD.
Touch the mountains
and make them send up smoke.
6 Use your lightning as arrows
to scatter my enemies
and make them run away.
7 Reach down from heaven
and set me free.
Save me from the mighty flood
8 of those lying foreigners
who can't tell the truth.

9 In praise of you, our God,
I will sing a new song,
while playing my harp.
10 By your power, kings win wars,
and your servant David is saved
from deadly swords.
11 Won't you keep me safe
from those lying foreigners
who can't tell the truth?

12 Let's pray that our young sons
will grow like strong plants
and that our daughters
will be as lovely as columns
in the corner of a palace.
13 May our barns be filled
with all kinds of crops.
May our fields be covered
with sheep by the thousands,
14 and every cow have calves.[c]
Don't let our city be captured
or any of us be taken away,
and don't let cries of sorrow
be heard in our streets.

15 Our LORD and our God,
you give these blessings
to all who worship you.

Psalm 145

[*By David for praise.*]

The LORD Is Kind and Merciful

1 I will praise you,
my God and King,
and always honor your name.
2 I will praise you each day
and always honor your name.
3 You are wonderful, LORD,
and you deserve all praise,
because you are much greater
than anyone can understand.

4 Each generation will announce
to the next your wonderful
and powerful deeds.
5 I will keep thinking about
your marvelous glory
and your mighty miracles.[d]
6 Everyone will talk about
your fearsome deeds,
and I will tell all nations
how great you are.
7 They will celebrate and sing

[a] **144.1** *mighty rock*: See the note at 18.2.
[b] **144.2** *of our people*: Some Hebrew manuscripts and ancient translations have "of the nations."
[c] **144.14** *have calves*: Or "grow fat."
[d] **145.5** *and . . . miracles*: One Hebrew manuscript and two ancient translations have "as others tell about your mighty miracles."
144.3 Job 7.17, 18; Ps 8.4.

about your matchless mercy
and your power to save.

8 You are merciful, LORD!
You are kind and patient
and always loving.
9 You are good to everyone,
and you take care
of all your creation.

10 All creation will thank you,
and your loyal people
will praise you.
11 They will tell about
your marvelous kingdom
and your power.
12 Then everyone will know about
the mighty things you do
and your glorious kingdom.
13 Your kingdom will never end,
and you will rule forever.

Our LORD, you keep your word
and do everything you say.[e]
14 When someone stumbles or falls,
you give a helping hand.
15 Everyone depends on you,
and when the time is right,
you provide them with food.
16 By your own hand you satisfy
the desires of all who live.

17 Our LORD, everything you do
is kind and thoughtful,
18 and you are near to everyone
whose prayers are sincere.
19 You satisfy the desires
of all your worshipers,
and you come to save them
when they ask for help.
20 You take care of everyone
who loves you,
but you destroy the wicked.

21 I will praise you, LORD,
and everyone will respect
your holy name forever.

Psalm 146

Shout Praises to the LORD

1 Shout praises to the LORD!
With all that I am,
I will shout his praises.
2 I will sing and praise
the LORD God
for as long as I live.

3 You can't depend on anyone,
not even a great leader.
4 Once they die and are buried,
that will be the end
of all their plans.

5 The LORD God of Jacob blesses
everyone who trusts him
and depends on him.
6 God made heaven and earth;
he created the sea
and everything else.
God always keeps his word.
7 He gives justice to the poor
and food to the hungry.

The LORD sets prisoners free
8 and heals blind eyes.
He gives a helping hand
to everyone who falls.
The LORD loves good people
9 and looks after strangers.
He defends the rights
of orphans and widows,
but destroys the wicked.

10 The LORD God of Zion
will rule forever!
Shout praises to the LORD!

Psalm 147

Sing and Praise the LORD

1 Shout praises to the LORD!
Our God is kind,
and it is right and good
to sing praises to him.
2 The LORD rebuilds Jerusalem

[e] **145.13** *Our . . . say*: These words are found in one Hebrew manuscript and two ancient translations.
146.6 Ac 4.24; 14.15.

and brings the people of Israel
back home again.
3 He renews our hopes
and heals our bodies.
4 He decided how many stars
there would be in the sky
and gave each one a name.
5 Our LORD is great and powerful!
He understands everything.
6 The LORD helps the poor,
but he smears the wicked
in the dirt.

7 Celebrate and sing!
Play your harps
for the LORD our God.
8 He fills the sky with clouds
and sends rain to the earth,
so that the hills
will be green with grass.
9 He provides food for cattle
and for the young ravens,
when they cry out.
10 The LORD doesn't care about
the strength of horses
or powerful armies.
11 The LORD is pleased only
with those who worship him
and trust his love.

12 Everyone in Jerusalem,
come and praise
the LORD your God!
13 He makes your city gates strong
and blesses your people
by giving them children.
14 God lets you live in peace,
and he gives you
the very best wheat.
15 As soon as God speaks,
the earth obeys.
16 He covers the ground with snow
like a blanket of wool,
and he scatters frost
like ashes on the ground.
17 God sends down hailstones
like chips of rocks.
Who can stand the cold?
18 At his command the ice melts,
the wind blows,
and streams begin to flow.

19 God gave his laws and teachings
to the descendants of Jacob,
the nation of Israel.
20 But he has not given his laws
to any other nation.
Shout praises to the LORD!

Psalm 148

Come Praise the LORD

1 Shout praises to the LORD!
Shout the LORD's praises
in the highest heavens.
2 All of you angels,
and all who serve him above,
come and offer praise.

3 Sun and moon,
and all of you bright stars,
come and offer praise.
4 Highest heavens, and the water
above the highest heavens,[f]
come and offer praise.

5 Let all things praise
the name of the LORD,
because they were created
at his command.
6 He made them to last forever,
and nothing can change
what he has done.[g]

7 All creatures on earth,
you obey his commands,
so come praise the LORD!

8 Sea monsters and the deep sea,
fire and hail, snow and frost,
and every stormy wind,
come praise the LORD!

9 All mountains and hills,
fruit trees and cedars,
10 every wild and tame animal,
all reptiles and birds,
come praise the LORD!

[f] **148.4** *the water . . . heavens*: It was believed that the earth and the heavens were surrounded by water. [g] **148.6** *nothing . . . done*: Or "his laws will never change."

11 Every king and every ruler,
all nations on earth,
12 every man and every woman,
young people and old,
come praise the LORD!

13 All creation, come praise
the name of the LORD.
Praise his name alone.
The glory of God is greater
than heaven and earth.

14 Like a bull with mighty horns,
the LORD protects
his faithful nation Israel,
because they belong to him.
Shout praises to the LORD!

Psalm 149

A New Song of Praise

1 Shout praises to the LORD!
Sing him a new song of praise
when his loyal people meet.
2 People of Israel, rejoice
because of your Creator.
People of Zion, celebrate
because of your King.
3 Praise his name by dancing
and playing music on harps
and tambourines.
4 The LORD is pleased
with his people,
and he gives victory
to those who are humble.
5 All of you faithful people,
praise our glorious Lord!
Celebrate and worship.
6 Praise God with songs
on your lips
and a sword in your hand.
7 Take revenge and punish
the nations.
8 Put chains of iron
on their kings and rulers.
9 Punish them as they deserve;
this is the privilege
of God's faithful people.
Shout praises to the LORD!

Psalm 150

The LORD Is Good to His People

1 Shout praises to the LORD!
Praise God in his temple.
Praise him in heaven,
his mighty fortress.
2 Praise our God!
His deeds are wonderful,
too marvelous to describe.

3 Praise God with trumpets
and all kinds of harps.
4 Praise him with tambourines
and dancing,
with stringed instruments
and woodwinds.
5 Praise God with cymbals,
with clashing cymbals.
6 Let every living creature
praise the LORD.
Shout praises to the LORD!

149.6 2 Macc 15.27.

PROVERBS

ABOUT THIS BOOK

The book of Proverbs is a collection of sayings that were used in ancient Israel to teach God's people how to live right. For the most part, these sayings go back to Solomon, but others are traced back to Agur (30.1) and King Lemuel (31.1).

Like the psalms, all the proverbs are written in poetic form. A typical proverb takes the form of a short verse in which the first half states the theme and the second half echoes it. What makes the Bible's proverbs so popular is that they make such powerful statements with very few words. This makes them easy to memorize and apply to daily life.

One of the main teachings in Proverbs is that all wisdom is a gift from God. This wisdom supplies practical advice for everyday living, in the home, in society, in politics, at school and at work. The book of Proverbs also teaches the importance of fairness, humility, loyalty and concern for the poor and needy.

Because most proverbs are so brief, and make their point in one verse, many are often not connected to those around them. In some parts of the book, however, a common theme can be found. How not to be a fool is the theme of chapter 26.1-12, for example. In chapters 8–9, Wisdom is pictured as a woman who advises people to turn from their foolish ways and to live wisely.

A QUICK LOOK AT THIS BOOK

How Proverbs Can Be Used

1 These are the proverbs
of King Solomon of Israel,
the son of David.
2 Proverbs will teach you
wisdom and self-control
and how to understand
sayings with deep meanings.
3 You will learn what is right
and honest and fair.
4 From these, an ordinary person
can learn to be smart,
and young people can gain
knowledge and good sense.
5 If you are already wise,
you will become even wiser.
And if you are smart,
6 you will learn to understand
proverbs and sayings,

1.1 1 K 4.32.

as well as words of wisdom
and all kinds of riddles.
7 Respect and obey the LORD!
This is the beginning
of knowledge.[a]
Only a fool rejects wisdom
and good advice.

Warnings against Bad Friends

8 My child, obey the teachings
of your parents,
9 and wear their teachings
as you would a lovely hat
or a pretty necklace.
10 Don't be tempted by sinners
or listen 11 when they say,
"Come on! Let's gang up
and kill somebody,
just for the fun of it!
12 They're well and healthy now,
but we'll finish them off
once and for all.
13 We'll take their valuables
and fill our homes
with stolen goods.
14 If you join our gang,
you'll get your share."

15 Don't follow anyone like that
or do what they do.
16 They are in a big hurry
to commit some crime,
perhaps even murder.
17 They are like a bird
that sees the bait,
but ignores the trap.[b]
18 They gang up to murder someone,
but they are the victims.
19 The wealth you get from crime
robs you of your life.

Wisdom Speaks

20 Wisdom[c] shouts in the streets
wherever crowds gather.
21 She shouts in the marketplaces
and near the city gates
as she says to the people,
22 "How much longer
will you enjoy
being stupid fools?
Won't you ever stop sneering
and laughing at knowledge?
23 Listen as I correct you
and tell you what I think.
24 You completely ignored me
and refused to listen;
25 you rejected my advice
and paid no attention
when I warned you.

26 "So when you are struck
by some terrible disaster,
27 or when trouble and distress
surround you like a whirlwind,
I will laugh and make fun.
28 You will ask for my help,
but I won't listen;
you will search,
but you won't find me.
29 No, you would not learn,
and you refused
to respect the LORD.
30 You rejected my advice
and paid no attention
when I warned you.

31 "Now you will eat the fruit
of what you have done,
until you are stuffed full
with your own schemes.
32 Sin and self-satisfaction
bring destruction and death
to stupid fools.
33 But if you listen to me,
you will be safe and secure
without fear of disaster."

Wisdom and Bad Friends

2 My child, you must follow
and treasure my teachings
and my instructions.
2 Keep in tune with wisdom
and think what it means
to have common sense.
3 Beg as loud as you can
for good common sense.

[a] **1.7** *the beginning of knowledge*: Or "what knowledge is all about." [b] **1.17** *They are . . . trap*: Or "Be like a bird that won't go for the bait, if it sees the trap." [c] **1.20** *Wisdom*: In the book of Proverbs the word "wisdom" is sometimes used as though wisdom were a supernatural being who was with God at the time of creation.

1.7 Job 28.28; Ps 111.10; Pr 9.10; Si 1.14. **1.20,21** Pr 8.1-3.

4 Search for wisdom
as you would search for silver
or hidden treasure.
5 Then you will understand
what it means to respect
and to know the LORD God.

6 All wisdom comes from the LORD,
and so do common sense
and understanding.
7 God gives helpful advice[d]
to everyone who obeys him
and protects all of those
who live as they should.
8 God sees that justice is done,
and he watches over everyone
who is faithful to him.
9 With wisdom you will learn
what is right
and honest and fair.

10 Wisdom will control your mind,
and you will be pleased
with knowledge.
11 Sound judgment and good sense
will watch over you.
12 Wisdom will protect you
from evil schemes
and from those liars
13 who turned from doing good
to live in the darkness.
14 Most of all they enjoy
being mean and deceitful.
15 They are dishonest themselves,
and all they do is crooked.

Wisdom and Sexual Purity

16 Wisdom will protect you
from the smooth talk
of a sinful woman,
17 who breaks her wedding vows
and leaves the man she married
when she was young.
18 The road to her house leads
down to the dark world
of the dead.
19 Visit her, and you will never
find the road to life again.
20 Follow the example
of good people
and live an honest life.
21 If you are honest and innocent,
you will keep your land;
22 if you do wrong
and can never be trusted,
you will be rooted out.

Trust God

3 My child, remember
my teachings and instructions
and obey them completely.
2 They will help you live
a long and prosperous life.
3 Let love and loyalty
always show like a necklace,
and write them in your mind.
4 God and people will like you
and consider you a success.

5 With all your heart
you must trust the LORD
and not your own judgment.
6 Always let him lead you,
and he will clear the road
for you to follow.
7 Don't ever think that you
are wise enough,
but respect the LORD
and stay away from evil.
8 This will make you healthy,
and you will feel strong.
9 Honor the LORD by giving him
your money and the first part
of all your crops.
10 Then you will have
more grain and grapes
than you will ever need.

11 My child, don't turn away
or become bitter
when the LORD corrects you.
12 The LORD corrects
everyone he loves,
just as parents correct
their favorite child.

[d]**2.7** *helpful advice*: Or "wisdom."
2.6 Ws 9.10; Si 1.1. **3.4** Lk 2.52. **3.7** Ro 12.16. **3.11** Job 5.17. **3.11,12** He 12.5, 6.
3.12 Rev 3.19.

The Value of Wisdom

13 God blesses everyone
who has wisdom
and common sense.
14 Wisdom is worth more
than silver;
it makes you much richer
than gold.
15 Wisdom is more valuable
than precious jewels;
nothing you want
compares with her.

16 In her right hand
Wisdom holds a long life,
and in her left hand
are wealth and honor.
17 Wisdom makes life pleasant
and leads us safely along.
18 Wisdom is a life-giving tree,
the source of happiness
for all who hold on to her.

19 By his wisdom and knowledge
the LORD created
heaven and earth.
20 By his understanding
he let the ocean break loose
and clouds release the rain.
21 My child, use common sense
and sound judgment!
Always keep them in mind.
22 They will help you to live
a long and beautiful life.
23 You will walk safely
and never stumble;
24 you will rest without a worry
and sleep soundly.
25 So don't be afraid
of sudden disasters
or storms that strike
those who are evil.
26 You can be sure that the LORD
will protect you from harm.

27 Do all you can for everyone
who deserves your help.
28 Don't tell your neighbor
to come back tomorrow,
if you can help today.
29 Don't try to be mean
to neighbors who trust you.
30 Don't argue just to be arguing,
when you haven't been hurt.
31 Don't be jealous
of cruel people
or follow their example.

32 The LORD doesn't like
anyone who is dishonest,
but he lets good people
be his friends.
33 He places a curse on the home
of everyone who is evil,
but he blesses the home
of every good person.
34 The LORD sneers at those
who sneer at him,
but he is kind to everyone
who is humble.
35 You will be praised
if you are wise,
but you will be disgraced
if you are a stubborn fool.

Advice to Young People

4 My child, listen closely
to my teachings
and learn common sense.
2 My advice is useful,
so don't turn away.
3 When I was still very young
and my mother's favorite child,
my father 4 said to me:
"If you follow my teachings
and keep them in mind,
you will live.
5 Be wise and learn good sense;
remember my teachings
and do what I say.

6 If you love Wisdom
and don't reject her,
she will watch over you.
7 The best thing about Wisdom
is Wisdom herself;
good sense is more important
than anything else.
8 If you value Wisdom
and hold tightly to her,
great honors will be yours.

3.27,28 Si 4.3. **3.34** Jas 4.6; 1 P 5.5.

9 It will be like wearing
a glorious crown
of beautiful flowers.

The Right Way and the Wrong Way

10 My child, if you listen
and obey my teachings,
you will live a long time.
11 I have shown you the way
that makes sense;
I have guided you
along the right path.
12 Your road won't be blocked,
and you won't stumble
when you run.
13 Hold firmly to my teaching
and never let go.
It will mean life for you.
14 Don't follow the bad example
of cruel and evil people.
15 Turn aside and keep going.
Stay away from them.
16 They can't sleep or rest
until they do wrong or harm
some innocent victim.
17 Their food and drink
are violence and cruelty.

18 The lifestyle of good people
is like sunlight at dawn
that keeps getting brighter
until broad daylight.
19 The lifestyle of the wicked
is like total darkness,
and they will never know
what makes them stumble.

20 My child, listen carefully
to everything I say.
21 Don't forget a single word,
but think about it all.
22 Knowing these teachings
will mean true life
and good health for you.
23 Carefully guard your thoughts
because they are the source
of true life.
24 Never tell lies or be deceitful
in what you say.
25 Keep looking straight ahead,
without turning aside.
26 Know where you are headed,
and you will stay
on solid ground.
27 Don't make a mistake by turning
to the right or the left.

Be Faithful to Your Wife

5 My son, if you listen closely
to my wisdom and good sense,
2 you will have sound judgment,
and you will always know
the right thing to say.
3 The words of an immoral woman
may be as sweet as honey
and as smooth as olive oil.
4 But all that you really get
from being with her
is bitter poison and pain.
5 If you follow her,
she will lead you down
to the world of the dead.
6 She has missed the path
that leads to life
and doesn't even know it.

7 My son, listen to me
and do everything I say.
8 Stay away from a bad woman!
Don't even go near the door
of her house.
9 You will lose your self-respect
and end up in debt
to some cruel person
for the rest of your life.
10 Strangers will get your money
and everything else
you have worked for.
11 When it's all over,
your body will waste away,
as you groan 12 and shout,
"I hated advice and correction!
13 I paid no attention
to my teachers,
14 and now I am disgraced
in front of everyone."

15 You should be faithful
to your wife,
just as you take water
from your own well.[e]

[e]**5.15** *own well*: In biblical times water was scarce and wells were carefully guarded.
4.26 He 12.13.

16 And don't be like a stream
from which just any woman
may take a drink.
17 Save yourself for your wife
and don't have sex
with other women.
18 Be happy with the wife
you married
when you were young.
19 She is beautiful and graceful,
just like a deer;
you should be attracted to her
and stay deeply in love.

20 Don't go crazy over a woman
who is unfaithful
to her own husband!
21 The LORD sees everything,
and he watches us closely.
22 Sinners are trapped and caught
by their own evil deeds.
23 They get lost and die
because of their foolishness
and lack of self-control.

Don't Be Foolish

6 My child, suppose you agree
to pay the debt of someone,
who cannot repay a loan.
2 Then you are trapped
by your own words,
3 and you are now in the power
of someone else.
Here is what you should do:
Go and beg for permission
to call off the agreement.
4 Do this before you fall asleep
or even get sleepy.
5 Save yourself, just as a deer
or a bird tries to escape
from a hunter.

6 You lazy people can learn
by watching an anthill.
7 Ants don't have leaders,
8 but they store up food
during harvest season.
9 How long will you lie there
doing nothing at all?
When are you going to get up
and stop sleeping?
10 Sleep a little. Doze a little.
Fold your hands
and twiddle your thumbs.
11 Suddenly, everything is gone,
as though it had been taken
by an armed robber.

12 Worthless liars go around
13 winking and giving signals
to deceive others.
14 They are always thinking up
something cruel and evil,
and they stir up trouble.
15 But they will be struck
by sudden disaster
and left without a hope.

16 There are six or seven
kinds of people
the LORD doesn't like:
17 Those who are too proud
or tell lies or murder,
18 those who make evil plans
or are quick to do wrong,
19 those who tell lies in court
or stir up trouble
in a family.

20 Obey the teaching
of your parents—
21 always keep it in mind
and never forget it.
22 Their teaching will guide you
when you walk,
protect you when you sleep,
and talk to you
when you are awake.

23 The Law of the Lord is a lamp,
and its teachings
shine brightly.
Correction and self-control
will lead you through life.
24 They will protect you
from the flattering words
of someone else's wife.[f]
25 Don't let yourself be attracted

[f] **6.24** *someone else's wife*: Or "an evil woman."

6.1-5 Si 29.14-20. **6.10,11** Pr 24.33, 34. **6.13,14** Si 27.22.

by the charm and lovely eyes
of someone like that.
26 A woman who sells her love
can be bought for as little
as the price of a meal.
But making love
to another man's wife
will cost you everything.
27 If you carry burning coals,
you burn your clothes;
28 if you step on hot coals,
you burn your feet.
29 And if you go to bed
with another man's wife,
you pay the price.

30 We don't put up with thieves,
not even[g] with one who steals
for something to eat.
31 And thieves who get caught
must pay back
seven times what was stolen
and lose everything.
32 But if you go to bed
with another man's wife,
you will destroy yourself
by your own stupidity.
33 You will be beaten
and forever disgraced,
34 because a jealous husband
can be furious and merciless
when he takes revenge.
35 He won't let you pay him off,
no matter what you offer.

The Foolishness of Unfaithfulness

7 My son, pay close attention
and don't forget
what I tell you to do.
2 Obey me, and you will live!
Let my instructions be
your greatest treasure.
3 Keep them at your fingertips
and write them
in your mind.
4 Let wisdom be your sister
and make common sense
your closest friend.
5 They will protect you
from the flattering words
of someone else's wife.

6 From the window of my house,
I once happened to see
7 some foolish young men.
8 It was late in the evening,
sometime after dark.
9 One of these young men
turned the corner
and was walking by the house
of an unfaithful wife.
10 She was dressed fancy
like a woman of the street
with only one thing in mind.
11 She was one of those women
who are loud and restless
and never stay at home,
12 who walk street after street,
waiting to trap a man.

13 She grabbed him and kissed him,
and with no sense of shame,
she said:
14 "I had to offer a sacrifice,
and there is enough meat
left over for a feast.
15 So I came looking for you,
and here you are!
16 The sheets on my bed
are bright-colored cloth
from Egypt.
17 And I have covered it
with perfume made of myrrh,
aloes, and cinnamon.

18 "Let's go there
and make love all night.
19 My husband is traveling,
and he's far away.
20 He took a lot of money along,
and he won't be back home
before the middle
of the month."

21 And so, she tricked him
with all of her sweet talk
and her flattery.
22 Right away he followed her
like an ox on the way
to be slaughtered,
or like a fool on the way
to be punished[h]
23 and killed with arrows.

[g]**6.30** *not even*: Or "except." [h]**7.22** *a fool . . . punished*: One possible meaning for the difficult Hebrew text.

He was no more than a bird
rushing into a trap,
without knowing
it would cost him his life.

24 My son, pay close attention
to what I have said.
25 Don't even think about
that kind of woman
or let yourself be misled
by someone like her.
26 Such a woman has caused
the downfall and destruction
of a lot of men.
27 Her house is a one-way street
leading straight down
to the world of the dead.

In Praise of Wisdom

8 With great understanding,
Wisdom[i] is calling out
2 as she stands at the crossroads
and on every hill.
3 She stands by the city gate
where everyone enters the city,
and she shouts:
4 "I am calling out
to each one of you!
5 Good sense and sound judgment
can be yours.
6 Listen, because what I say
is worthwhile and right.
7 I always speak the truth
and refuse to tell a lie.
8 Every word I speak is honest,
not one is misleading
or deceptive.

9 "If you have understanding,
you will see that my words
are just what you need.
10 Let instruction and knowledge
mean more to you than silver
or the finest gold.
11 Wisdom is worth much more
than precious jewels
or anything else you desire."

Wisdom Speaks

12 I am Wisdom[i]—Common Sense
is my closest friend;
I possess knowledge
and sound judgment.
13 If you respect the LORD,
you will hate evil.
I hate pride and conceit
and deceitful lies.
14 I am strong, and I offer
sensible advice
and sound judgment.
15 By my power kings govern,
and rulers make laws
that are fair.
16 Every honest leader rules
with help from me.

17 I love everyone who loves me,
and I will be found by all
who honestly search.
18 I can make you rich and famous,
important and successful.
19 What you receive from me
is more valuable
than even the finest gold
or the purest silver.
20 I always do what is right,
21 and I give great riches
to everyone who loves me.

22 From the beginning,
I was with the LORD.[j]
I was there before he began
23 to create the earth.
At the very first,
the LORD gave life to[k] me.
24 When I was born,
there were no oceans
or springs of water.
25 My birth was before
mountains were formed
or hills were put in place.
26 It happened long before God
had made the earth
or any of its fields
or even the dust.

27 I was there when the LORD
put the heavens in place
and stretched the sky
over the surface of the sea.

[i] **8.1,12** *Wisdom*: See the note at 1.20. [j] **8.22** *From the beginning . . . with the LORD*: Or "In the very beginning, the LORD created me." [k] **8.23** *gave life to*: Or "formed."

8.1-3 Pr 1.20, 21. **8.11-21** Si 24.1-22. **8.22** Si 1.4, 9; Rev 3.14. **8.27-31** Ws 9.9; Si 24.3-6.

28 I was with him when he placed
the clouds in the sky
and created the springs
that fill the ocean.
29 I was there when he set
boundaries for the sea
to make it obey him,
and when he laid foundations
to support the earth.

30 I was right beside the LORD,
helping him plan and build.[l]
I made him happy each day,
and I was happy at his side.
31 I was pleased with his world
and pleased with its people.

32 Pay attention, my children!
Follow my advice,
and you will be happy.
33 Listen carefully
to my instructions,
and you will be wise.

34 Come to my home each day
and listen to me.
You will find happiness.
35 By finding me, you find life,
and the LORD will be pleased
with you.
36 But if you don't find me,
you hurt only yourself,
and if you hate me,
you are in love with death.

Wisdom Gives a Feast

9 Wisdom has built her house
with its seven columns.
2 She has prepared the meat
and set out the wine.
Her feast is ready.

3 She has sent her servant women
to announce her invitation
from the highest hills:
4 "Everyone who is ignorant
or foolish is invited!
5 All of you are welcome
to my meat and wine.
6 If you want to live,
give up your foolishness
and let understanding
guide your steps."

True Wisdom

7 Correct a worthless bragger,
and all you will get
are insults and injuries.
8 Any bragger you correct
will only hate you.
But if you correct someone
who has common sense,
you will be loved.
9 If you have good sense,
instruction will help you
to have even better sense.
And if you live right,
education will help you
to know even more.

10 Respect and obey the LORD!
This is the beginning
of wisdom.[m]
To have understanding,
you must know the Holy God.
11 I am Wisdom. If you follow me,
you will live a long time.
12 Good sense is good for you,
but if you brag,
you hurt yourself.

A Foolish Invitation

13 Stupidity[n] is reckless,
senseless, and foolish.
14 She sits in front of her house
and on the highest hills
in the town.
15 She shouts to everyone
who passes by,
16 "If you are stupid,
come on inside!"
And to every fool she says,
17 "Stolen water tastes best,
and the food you eat in secret
tastes best of all."
18 None who listen to Stupidity
understand that her guests
are as good as dead.

[l]**8.30** *helping . . . build*: Or "like his own child." [m]**9.10** *the beginning of wisdom*: Or "what wisdom is all about." [n]**9.13** *Stupidity*: Or "A foolish woman."

8.32 Si 14.20-27. **9.10** Job 28.28; Ps 111.10; Pr 1.7; 4 Macc 1.17.

Solomon's Wise Sayings

10 Here are some proverbs
of Solomon:
Children with good sense
make their parents happy,
but foolish children
make them sad.
2 What you gain by doing evil
won't help you at all,
but being good[o]
can save you from death.

3 If you obey the LORD,
you won't go hungry;
if you are wicked,
God won't let you have
what you want.
4 Laziness leads to poverty;
hard work makes you rich.
5 At harvest season
it's smart to work hard,
but stupid to sleep.

6 Everyone praises good people,
but evil hides behind
the words of the wicked.
7 Good people are remembered
long after they are gone,
but the wicked
are soon forgotten.

8 If you have good sense,
you will listen and obey;
if all you do is talk,
you will destroy yourself.
9 You will be safe,
if you always do right,
but you will get caught,
if you are dishonest.
10 Deceit causes trouble,
and foolish talk
will bring you to ruin.[p]
11 The words of good people
are a source of life,
but evil hides behind
the words of the wicked.
12 Hatred stirs up trouble;
love overlooks the wrongs
that others do.
13 If you have good sense,
it will show when you speak.
But if you are stupid,
you will be beaten
with a stick.
14 If you have good sense,
you will learn all you can,
but foolish talk
will soon destroy you.

15 Great wealth can be a fortress,
but poverty
is no protection at all.
16 If you live right,
the reward is a good life;
if you are evil,
all you have is sin.

17 Accept correction,
and you will find life;
reject correction,
and you will miss the road.
18 You can hide your hatred
by telling lies,
but you are a fool
to spread lies.
19 You will say the wrong thing
if you talk too much—
so be sensible and watch
what you say.
20 The words of a good person
are like pure silver,
but the thoughts
of an evil person
are almost worthless.
21 Many are helped
by useful instruction,
but fools are killed
by their own stupidity.

22 When the LORD blesses you
with riches,
you have nothing to regret.[q]
23 Fools enjoy doing wrong,

[o] **10.2** *good*: Or "generous." [p] **10.10** *and foolish . . . ruin*: One ancient translation "but you can help people by correcting them." [q] **10.22** *When . . . regret*: Or "No matter how hard you work, your riches really come from the LORD."
10.12 Jas 5.20; 1 P 4.8.

but anyone with good sense
enjoys acting wisely.
24 What evil people dread most
will happen to them,
but good people will get
what they want most.
25 Those crooks will disappear
when a storm strikes,
but God will keep safe
all who obey him.
26 Having a lazy person on the job
is like a mouth full of vinegar
or smoke in your eyes.

27 If you respect the LORD,
you will live longer;
if you keep doing wrong,
your life will be cut short.
28 If you obey the Lord,
you will be happy,
but there is no future
for the wicked.
29 The LORD protects everyone
who lives right,
but he destroys anyone
who does wrong.
30 Good people will stand firm,
but the wicked
will lose their land.
31 Honest people speak sensibly,
but deceitful liars
will be silenced.
32 If you obey the Lord,
you will always know
the right thing to say.
But no one will trust you
if you tell lies.

Watch What You Say and Do

11 The LORD hates anyone
who cheats,
but he likes everyone
who is honest.
2 Too much pride
can put you to shame.
It's wiser to be humble.
3 If you do the right thing,
honesty will be your guide.
But if you are crooked,
you will be trapped
by your own dishonesty.
4 When God is angry,
money won't help you.
Obeying God is the only way
to be saved from death.
5 If you are truly good,
you will do right;
if you are wicked,
you will be destroyed
by your own sin.
6 Honesty can keep you safe,
but if you can't be trusted,
you trap yourself.
7 When the wicked die,
their hopes die with them.
8 Trouble goes right past
the LORD's people
and strikes the wicked.

9 Dishonest people use gossip
to destroy their neighbors;
good people are protected
by their own good sense.
10 When honest people prosper
and the wicked disappear,
the whole city celebrates.
11 When God blesses his people,
their city prospers,
but deceitful liars
can destroy a city.

12 It's stupid to say bad things
about your neighbors.
If you are sensible,
you will keep quiet.
13 A gossip tells everything,
but a true friend
will keep a secret.
14 A city without wise leaders
will end up in ruin;
a city with many wise leaders
will be kept safe.

15 It's a dangerous thing
to guarantee payment
for someone's debts.
Don't do it!
16 A gracious woman
will be respected,
but a man must work hard
to get rich.[r]

[r]11.16 *but . . . rich*: Or "a ruthless man will only get rich."
11.14 Ws 6.24.

17 Kindness is rewarded—
but if you are cruel,
you hurt yourself.
18 Meanness gets you nowhere,
but goodness is rewarded.
19 Always do the right thing,
and you will live;
keep on doing wrong,
and you will die.

20 The LORD hates sneaky people,
but he likes everyone
who lives right.
21 You can be sure of this:
All crooks will be punished,
but God's people won't.
22 A beautiful woman
who acts foolishly
is like a gold ring
on the snout of a pig.
23 Good people want what is best,
but troublemakers
hope to stir up trouble.[s]

24 Sometimes you can become rich
by being generous
or poor by being greedy.
25 Generosity will be rewarded:
Give a cup of water,
and you will receive
a cup of water in return.
26 Charge too much for grain,
and you will be cursed;
sell it at a fair price,
and you will be praised.
27 Try hard to do right,
and you will win friends;
go looking for trouble,
and you will find it.
28 Trust in your wealth,
and you will be a failure,
but God's people will prosper
like healthy plants.

29 Fools who cause trouble
in the family
won't inherit a thing.
They will end up as slaves
of someone with good sense.
30 Live right, and you will eat
from the life-giving tree.
And if you act wisely,
others will follow.[t]
31 If good people are rewarded[u]
here on this earth,
all who are cruel and mean
will surely be punished.

You Can't Hide behind Evil

12 To accept correction is wise,
to reject it is stupid.
2 The LORD likes everyone
who lives right,
but he punishes everyone
who makes evil plans.
3 Sin cannot offer security!
But if you live right,
you will be as secure
as a tree with deep roots.
4 A helpful wife is a jewel
for her husband,
but a shameless wife
will make his bones rot.

5 Good people have kind thoughts,
but you should never trust
the advice of someone evil.
6 Bad advice is a deadly trap,
but good advice
is like a shield.
7 Once the wicked are defeated,
they are gone forever,
but no one who obeys God
will ever be thrown down.
8 Good sense is worthy of praise,
but stupidity is a curse.
9 It's better to be ordinary
and have only one servant[v]
than to think you are somebody
and starve to death.
10 Good people are kind
to their animals,
but a mean person is cruel.

[s] **11.23** *Good people . . . trouble*: Or "Good people do what is best, but troublemakers just stir up trouble." [t] **11.30** *act . . . follow*: Hebrew; one ancient translation "but violence leads to death." [u] **11.31** *rewarded*: Or "punished." [v] **12.9** *It's . . . servant*: Or "It is better just to have an ordinary job."

11.31 1 P 4.18. **12.1** Si 21.6.

11 Hard working farmers have more
than enough food;
daydreamers are nothing more
than stupid fools.
12 An evil person tries to hide
behind evil;[w]
good people are like trees
with deep roots.
13 We trap ourselves
by telling lies,
but we stay out of trouble
by living right.
14 We are rewarded or punished
for what we say and do.
15 Fools think they know
what is best,
but a sensible person
listens to advice.

16 Losing your temper is foolish;
ignoring an insult is smart.
17 An honest person
tells the truth in court,
but a dishonest person
tells nothing but lies.
18 Sharp words cut like a sword,
but words of wisdom heal.
19 Truth will last forever;
lies are soon found out.
20 An evil mind is deceitful,
but gentle thoughts
bring happiness.
21 Good people never have trouble,
but troublemakers
have more than enough.
22 The LORD hates every liar,
but he is the friend of all
who can be trusted.
23 Be sensible and don't tell
everything you know—
only fools spread
foolishness everywhere.

24 Work hard, and you
will be a leader;
be lazy, and you
will end up a slave.
25 Worry is a heavy burden,
but a kind word
always brings cheer.
26 You are better off to do right,
than to lose your way
by doing wrong.[x]
27 Anyone too lazy to cook
will starve,
but a hard worker
is a valuable treasure.[y]
28 Follow the road to life,
and you won't be bothered
by death.

Wise Friends Make You Wise

13 Children with good sense
accept correction
from their parents,
but stubborn children
ignore it completely.
2 You will be well rewarded
for saying something kind,
but all some people think about
is how to be cruel and mean.
3 Keep what you know to yourself,
and you will be safe;
talk too much,
and you are done for.
4 No matter how much you want,
laziness won't help a bit,
but hard work will reward you
with more than enough.
5 A good person hates deceit,
but those who are evil
cause shame and disgrace.
6 Live right, and you are safe!
But sin will destroy you.

7 Some who have nothing
may pretend to be rich,
and some who have everything
may pretend to be poor.
8 The rich may have
to pay a ransom,
but the poor don't have
that problem.
9 The lamp of a good person
keeps on shining;

[w] **12.12** *An evil . . . evil*: Or "Evil people love what they get from being evil." [x] **12.26** *wrong*: One possible meaning for the difficult Hebrew text of verse 26. [y] **12.27** *but . . . treasure*: One possible meaning for the difficult Hebrew text.
13.3 Si 28.25, 26.

the lamp of an evil person
soon goes out.
10 Too much pride causes trouble.
Be sensible and take advice.

11 Money wrongly gotten
will disappear bit by bit;
money earned little by little
will grow and grow.
12 Not getting what you want
can make you feel sick,
but a wish that comes true
is a life-giving tree.
13 If you reject God's teaching,
you will pay the price;
if you obey his commands,
you will be rewarded.

14 Sensible instruction
is a life-giving fountain
that helps you escape
all deadly traps.
15 Sound judgment is praised,
but people without good sense
are on the way to disaster.[z]
16 If you have good sense,
you will act sensibly,
but fools act like fools.
17 Whoever delivers your message
can make things better
or worse for you.

18 All who refuse correction
will be poor and disgraced;
all who accept correction
will be praised.
19 It's a good feeling
to get what you want,
but only a stupid fool
hates to turn from evil.
20 Wise friends make you wise,
but you hurt yourself
by going around with fools.
21 You are in for trouble
if you sin,
but you will be rewarded
if you live right.
22 If you obey God,
you will have something
to leave your grandchildren.
If you don't obey God,
those who live right
will get what you leave.

23 Even when the land of the poor
produces good crops,
they get cheated
out of what they grow.[a]
24 If you love your children,
you will correct them;
if you don't love them,
you won't correct them.
25 If you live right,
you will have plenty to eat;
if you don't live right,
you will go away empty.

Wisdom Makes Good Sense

14 A woman's family
is held together
by her wisdom,
but it can be destroyed
by her foolishness.
2 By living right, you show
that you respect the LORD;
by being deceitful, you show
that you despise him.
3 Proud fools are punished
for their stupid talk,
but sensible talk
can save your life.
4 Without the help of an ox
there can be no crop,
but with a strong ox
a big crop is possible.
5 An honest witness
tells the truth;
a dishonest witness
tells nothing but lies.

6 Make fun of wisdom,
and you will never find it.
But if you have understanding,
knowledge comes easily.
7 Stay away from fools,
or you won't learn a thing.

[z] **13.15** *people . . . disaster*: One possible meaning for the difficult Hebrew text. [a] **13.23** *grow*: One possible meaning for the difficult Hebrew text of verse 23.
13.20 Si 6.33, 34.

8 Wise people have enough sense
to find their way,
but stupid fools get lost.
9 Fools don't care
if they are wrong,[b]
but God is pleased
when people do right.

10 No one else can really know
how sad or happy you are.
11 The tent of a good person
stands longer than the house
of someone evil.
12 You may think you are
on the right road
and still end up dead.
13 Sorrow may hide
behind laughter,
and happiness may end
in sorrow.
14 You harvest what you plant,
whether good or bad.

15 Don't be stupid
and believe all you hear;
be smart and know
where you are headed.
16 Only a stupid fool
is never cautious—
so be extra careful
and stay out of trouble.
17 Fools have quick tempers,
and no one likes you
if you can't be trusted.
18 Stupidity leads to foolishness;
be smart and learn.

19 The wicked will come crawling
to those who obey God.
20 You have no friends
if you are poor,
but you have lots of friends
if you are rich.
21 It's wrong to hate others,
but God blesses everyone
who is kind to the poor.
22 It's a mistake
to make evil plans,
but you will have loyal friends
if you want to do right.
23 Hard work is worthwhile,
but empty talk
will make you poor.
24 Wisdom can make you rich,
but foolishness leads
to more foolishness.
25 An honest witness
can save your life,
but liars can't be trusted.

26 If you respect the LORD,
you and your children
have a strong fortress
27 and a life-giving fountain
that keeps you safe
from deadly traps.

28 Rulers of powerful nations
are held in honor;
rulers of weak nations
are nothing at all.
29 It's smart to be patient,
but it's stupid
to lose your temper.
30 It's healthy to be content,
but envy can eat you up.
31 If you mistreat the poor,
you insult your Creator;
if you are kind to them,
you show him respect.
32 In times of trouble
the wicked are destroyed,
but even at death
the innocent have faith.[c]

33 Wisdom is found in the minds
of people with good sense,
but fools don't know it.[d]
34 Doing right brings honor
to a nation,
but sin brings disgrace.
35 Kings reward servants
who act wisely,
but they punish those
who act foolishly.

[b]**14.9** *Fools . . . wrong*: One possible meaning for the difficult Hebrew text. [c]**14.32** *but even . . . faith*: One possible meaning for the difficult Hebrew text. Some ancient translations "but good people trust their innocence." [d]**14.33** *but . . . it*: One possible meaning for the difficult Hebrew text; some ancient translations "but not in the mind of a fool."

14.12 Pr 16.25.

The LORD Sees Everything

15 A kind answer
soothes angry feelings,
but harsh words
stir them up.
2 Words of wisdom
come from the wise,
but fools speak foolishness.

3 The LORD sees everything,
whether good or bad.
4 Kind words are good medicine,
but deceitful words
can really hurt.
5 Don't be a fool
and disobey your parents.
Be smart! Accept correction.
6 Good people become wealthy,
but those who are evil
will lose what they have.
7 Words of wisdom
make good sense;
the thoughts of a fool
make no sense at all.

8 The LORD is disgusted
by gifts from the wicked,
but it makes him happy
when his people pray.
9 The LORD is disgusted
with all who do wrong,
but he loves everyone
who does right.
10 If you turn from the right way,
you will be punished;
if you refuse correction,
you will die.

11 If the LORD can see everything
in the world of the dead,
he can see in our hearts.
12 Those who sneer at others
don't like to be corrected,
and they won't ask help
from someone with sense.
13 Happiness makes you smile;
sorrow can crush you.
14 Anyone with good sense
is eager to learn more,
but fools are hungry
for foolishness.

15 The poor have a hard life,
but being content is as good
as an endless feast.
16 It's better to obey the LORD
and have only a little,
than to be very rich
and terribly confused.
17 A simple meal with love
is better than a feast
where there is hatred.

18 Losing your temper
causes a lot of trouble,
but staying calm
settles arguments.
19 Being lazy is like walking
in a thorn patch,
but everyone who does right
walks on a smooth road.
20 Children with good sense
make their parents happy,
but foolish children
are hateful to them.
21 Stupidity brings happiness
to senseless fools,
but everyone with good sense
follows the straight path.

22 Without good advice
everything goes wrong—
it takes careful planning
for things to go right.
23 Giving the right answer
at the right time
makes everyone happy.
24 All who are wise follow a road
that leads upward to life
and away from death.

25 The LORD destroys the homes
of those who are proud,
but he protects the property
of widows.
26 The LORD hates evil thoughts,
but kind words please him.
27 Being greedy causes trouble
for your family,
but you protect yourself
by refusing bribes.
28 Good people think
before they answer,
but the wicked speak evil
without ever thinking.

29 The LORD never even hears
the prayers of the wicked,
but he answers the prayers
of all who obey him.
30 A friendly smile
makes you happy,
and good news
makes you feel strong.
31 Healthy correction is good,
and if you accept it,
you will be wise.
32 You hurt only yourself
by rejecting instruction,
but it makes good sense
to accept it.
33 Showing respect to the LORD
will make you wise,
and being humble
will bring honor to you.

The LORD Has the Final Word

16 We humans make plans,
but the LORD
has the final word.
2 We may think we know
what is right,
but the LORD is the judge
of our motives.
3 Share your plans with the LORD,
and you will succeed.

4 The LORD has a reason
for everything he does,
and he lets evil people live
only to be punished.
5 The LORD doesn't like
anyone who is conceited—
you can be sure
they will be punished.
6 If we truly love God,
our sins will be forgiven;
if we show him respect,
we will keep away from sin.
7 When we please the LORD,
even our enemies
make friends with us.
8 It's better to be honest
and poor
than to be dishonest
and rich.
9 We make our own plans,
but the LORD decides
where we will go.
10 Rulers speak with authority
and are never wrong.
11 The LORD doesn't like it
when we cheat in business.
12 Justice makes rulers powerful.
They should hate evil
13 and like honesty and truth.
14 An angry ruler
can put you to death.
So be wise!
Don't make one angry.
15 When a ruler is happy
and pleased with you,
it's like refreshing rain,
and you will live.

16 It's much better to be wise
and sensible
than to be rich.
17 God's people avoid evil ways,
and they protect themselves
by watching where they go.
18 Too much pride
will destroy you.
19 You are better off
to be humble and poor
than to get rich
from what you take by force.
20 If you know what you're doing,[e]
you will prosper.
God blesses everyone
who trusts him.
21 Good judgment proves
that you are wise,
and if you speak kindly,
you can teach others.
22 Good sense is a fountain
that gives life,
but fools are punished
by their foolishness.
23 You can persuade others
if you are wise
and speak sensibly.

24 Kind words are like honey—
they cheer you up
and make you feel strong.

[e] **16.20** *know what . . . doing*: Or "do what you're taught."
16.6 Tb 12.9. **16.8** Tb 12.8.

25 Sometimes what seems right
is really a road to death.
26 The hungrier you are,
the harder you work.
27 Worthless people plan trouble.
Even their words burn
like a flaming fire.
28 Gossip is no good!
It causes hard feelings
and comes between friends.

29 Don't trust violent people.
They will mislead you
to do the wrong thing.
30 When someone winks
or grins behind your back,
trouble is on the way.
31 Gray hair is a glorious crown
worn by those
who have lived right.
32 Controlling your temper
is better than being a hero
who captures a city.
33 We make our own decisions,
but the LORD alone
determines what happens.

Our Thoughts Are Tested by the LORD

17 A dry crust of bread eaten
in peace and quiet
is better than a feast eaten
where everyone argues.
2 A hard-working slave
will be placed in charge
of a no-good child,
and that slave will be given
the same inheritance
that each child receives.
3 Silver and gold are tested
by flames of fire;
our thoughts are tested
by the LORD.
4 Troublemakers listen
to troublemakers,
and liars listen to liars.
5 By insulting the poor,
you insult your Creator.
You will be punished
if you make fun
of someone in trouble.
6 Grandparents are proud
of their grandchildren,
and children should be proud
of their parents.

7 It sounds strange for a fool
to talk sensibly,
but it's even worse
for a ruler to tell lies.
8 A bribe works miracles
like a magic charm
that brings good luck.
9 You will keep your friends
if you forgive them,
but you will lose your friends
if you keep talking about
what they did wrong.
10 A sensible person
accepts correction,
but you can't beat sense
into a fool.

11 Cruel people want to rebel,
and so vicious attackers
will be sent against them.
12 A bear robbed of her cubs
is far less dangerous
than a stubborn fool.
13 You will always have trouble
if you are mean to those
who are good to you.
14 The start of an argument
is like a water leak—
so stop it before
real trouble breaks out.
15 The LORD doesn't like those
who defend the guilty
or condemn the innocent.
16 Why should fools have money
for an education
when they refuse to learn?

17 A friend is always a friend,
and relatives are born
to share our troubles.
18 It's stupid to guarantee
someone else's loan.
19 The wicked and the proud
love trouble and keep begging
to be hurt.

16.25 Pr 14.12. **16.28** Si 28.13-26. **17.17** Si 6.7-10.

20 Dishonesty does you no good,
and telling lies
will get you in trouble.
21 It's never pleasant
to be the parent of a fool
and have nothing but pain.
22 If you are cheerful,
you feel good;
if you are sad,
you hurt all over.

23 Crooks accept secret bribes
to keep justice
from being done.
24 Anyone with wisdom knows
what makes good sense,
but fools can never
make up their minds.
25 Foolish children bring sorrow
to their father
and pain to their mother.
26 It isn't fair
to punish the innocent
and those who do right.
27 It makes a lot of sense
to be a person of few words
and to stay calm.
28 Even fools seem smart
when they are quiet.

It's Wrong to Favor the Guilty

18 It's selfish and stupid
to think only of yourself
and to sneer at people
who have sense.[f]
2 Fools have no desire to learn;
they would much rather
give their own opinion.
3 Wrongdoing leads to shame
and disgrace.
4 Words of wisdom
are a stream that flows
from a deep fountain.
5 It's wrong to favor the guilty
and keep the innocent
from getting justice.

6 Foolish talk will get you
into a lot of trouble.
7 Saying foolish things
is like setting a trap
to destroy yourself.
8 There's nothing so delicious
as the taste of gossip!
It melts in your mouth.
9 Being lazy is no different
from being a troublemaker.

10 The LORD is a mighty tower
where his people can run
for safety—
11 the rich think their money
is a wall of protection.

12 Pride leads to destruction;
humility leads to honor.
13 It's stupid and embarrassing
to give an answer
before you listen.
14 Being cheerful helps
when we are sick,
but nothing helps
when we give up.
15 Everyone with good sense
wants to learn.
16 A gift will get you in
to see anyone.
17 You may think you have won
your case in court,
until your opponent speaks.
18 Drawing straws is one way
to settle a difficult case.
19 Making up with a friend
you have offended[g]
is harder than breaking
through a city wall.

20 Make your words good—
you will be glad you did.
21 Words can bring death or life!
Talk too much, and you will eat
everything you say.
22 A man's greatest treasure
is his wife—
she is a gift from the LORD.
23 The poor must beg for help,
but the rich can give
a harsh reply.

[f] **18.1** *sense*: One possible meaning for the difficult Hebrew text of verse 1. [g] **18.19** *Making . . . offended*: One possible meaning for the difficult Hebrew text.
17.28 Si 20.5. **18.13** Si 11.8. **18.22** Si 26.1-4.

24 Some friends don't help,[h]
but a true friend is closer
than your own family.

It's Wise To Be Patient

19 It's better to be poor
and live right
than to be a stupid liar.
2 Willingness and stupidity
don't go well together.
If you are too eager,
you will miss the road.
3 We are ruined
by our own stupidity,
though we blame the LORD.

4 The rich have many friends;
the poor have none.
5 Dishonest witnesses and liars
won't escape punishment.
6 Everyone tries to be friends
of those who can help them.
7 If you are poor,
your own relatives reject you,
and your friends are worse.
When you really need them,
they are not there.[i]

8 Do yourself a favor
by having good sense—
you will be glad you did.
9 Dishonest witnesses and liars
will be destroyed.
10 It isn't right for a fool
to live in luxury
or for a slave to rule
in place of a king.
11 It's wise to be patient
and show what you are like
by forgiving others.
12 An angry king roars
like a lion,
but when a king is pleased,
it's like dew on the crops.

13 A foolish son brings disgrace
to his father.
A nagging wife goes on and on
like the drip, drip, drip
of the rain.
14 You may inherit all you own
from your parents,
but a sensible wife
is a gift from the LORD.
15 If you are lazy
and sleep your time away,
you will starve.

16 Obey the Lord's teachings
and you will live—
disobey and you will die.
17 Caring for the poor
is lending to the LORD,
and you will be well repaid.
18 Correct your children
before it's too late;
if you don't punish them,
you are destroying them.
19 People with bad tempers
are always in trouble,
and they need help
over and over again.[j]
20 Pay attention to advice
and accept correction,
so you can live sensibly.

21 We may make a lot of plans,
but the LORD will do
what he has decided.
22 What matters most is loyalty.
It's better to be poor
than to be a liar.
23 Showing respect to the LORD
brings true life—
if you do it, you can relax
without fear of danger.

24 Some people are too lazy
to lift a hand
to feed themselves.
25 Stupid fools learn good sense
by seeing others punished;
a sensible person learns
by being corrected.
26 Children who bring disgrace
rob their father
and chase their mother away.
27 If you stop learning,
you will forget
what you already know.

[h] **18.24** *Some . . . help*: One possible meaning for the difficult Hebrew text. [i] **19.7** *When . . . there*: One possible meaning for the difficult Hebrew text. [j] **19.19** *and they . . . again*: One possible meaning for the difficult Hebrew text.

28 A lying witness makes fun
of the court system,
and criminals think crime
is really delicious.
29 Every stupid fool
is just waiting
to be punished.

Words of Wisdom Are Better than Gold

20 It isn't smart to get drunk!
Drinking makes a fool of you
and leads to fights.
2 An angry ruler
is like a roaring lion—
make either one angry,
and you are dead.
3 It makes you look good
when you avoid a fight—
only fools love to quarrel.
4 If you are too lazy to plow,
don't expect a harvest.
5 Someone's thoughts may be
as deep as the ocean,
but if you are smart,
you will discover them.

6 There are many who say,
"You can trust me!"
But can they be trusted?
7 Good people live right,
and God blesses the children
who follow their example.
8 When rulers decide cases,
they weigh the evidence.
9 Can any of us really say,
"My thoughts are pure,
and my sins are gone"?

10 Two things the LORD hates
are dishonest scales
and dishonest measures.
11 The good or bad
that children do
shows what they are like.
12 Hearing and seeing
are gifts from the LORD.
13 If you sleep all the time,
you will starve;
if you get up and work,
you will have enough food.

14 Everyone likes to brag
about getting a bargain.
15 Sensible words are better
than gold or jewels.

16 You deserve to lose your coat
if you loan it to someone
to guarantee payment
for the debt of a stranger.
17 The food you get by cheating
may taste delicious,
but it turns to gravel.
18 Be sure you have sound advice
before making plans
or starting a war.
19 Stay away from gossips—
they tell everything.
20 Children who curse their parents
will go to the land of darkness
long before their time.
21 Getting rich quick[k]
may turn out to be a curse.
22 Don't try to get even.
Trust the LORD,
and he will help you.

23 The LORD hates dishonest scales
and dishonest weights.
So don't cheat!
24 How can we know
what will happen to us
when the LORD alone decides?
25 Don't fall into the trap
of making promises to God
before you think!
26 A wise ruler severely punishes
every criminal.
27 Our inner thoughts are a lamp
from the LORD,
and they search our hearts.
28 Rulers are protected
by God's mercy and loyalty,
but[l] they must be merciful
for their kingdoms to last.
29 Young people take pride
in their strength,
but the gray hairs of wisdom
are even more beautiful.
30 A severe beating can knock all
of the evil out of you!

[k] **20.21** *quick*: Or "the wrong way."

[l] **20.28** *by God's mercy . . . but*: Or "by their mercy . . . and."

The LORD Is In Charge

21 The LORD controls rulers,
just as he determines
the course of rivers.
2 We may think we are doing
the right thing,
but the LORD always knows
what is in our hearts.
3 Doing what is right and fair
pleases the LORD
more than an offering.
4 Evil people are proud
and arrogant,
but sin is the only crop
they produce.[m]
5 If you plan and work hard,
you will have plenty;
if you get in a hurry,
you will end up poor.

6 Cheating to get rich
is a foolish dream
and no less than suicide.[n]
7 You destroy yourself
by being cruel and violent
and refusing to live right.
8 All crooks are liars,
but anyone who is innocent
will do right.
9 It's better to stay outside
on the roof of your house
than to live inside
with a nagging wife.
10 Evil people want to do wrong,
even to their friends.
11 An ignorant fool learns
by seeing others punished;
a sensible person learns
by being instructed.

12 God is always fair!
He knows what the wicked do
and will punish them.
13 If you won't help the poor,
don't expect to be heard
when you cry out for help.
14 A secret bribe will save you
from someone's fierce anger.
15 When justice is done,
good citizens are glad
and crooks are terrified.
16 If you stop using good sense,
you will find yourself
in the grave.
17 Heavy drinkers and others
who live only for pleasure
will lose all they have.

18 God's people will escape,
but all who are wicked
will pay the price.
19 It's better out in the desert
than at home with a nagging,
complaining wife.
20 Be sensible and store up
precious treasures—
don't waste them
like a fool.
21 If you try to be kind and good,
you will be blessed with life
and goodness and honor.
22 One wise person can defeat
a city full of soldiers
and capture their fortress.
23 Watching what you say
can save you
a lot of trouble.
24 If you are proud and conceited,
everyone will say,
"You're a snob!"

25 If you want too much
and are too lazy to work,
it could be fatal.
26 But people who obey God
are always generous.

27 The Lord despises the offerings
of wicked people
with evil motives.
28 If you tell lies in court,
you are done for;
only a reliable witness
can do the job.
29 Wicked people bluff their way,
but God's people think
before they take a step.

[m] **21.4** *but sin . . . produce*: Or "but sin is the only light they ever follow." [n] **21.6** *and . . . suicide*: One possible meaning for the difficult Hebrew text.

21.1 3 Macc 5.28. **21.9** Si 25.16. **21.27** Si 7.9.

30 No matter how much you know
or what plans you make,
you can't defeat the LORD.
31 Even if your army has horses
ready for battle,
the LORD will always win.

The Value of a Good Reputation

22 A good reputation and respect
are worth much more
than silver and gold.
2 The rich and the poor
are all created
by the LORD.
3 When you see trouble coming,
don't be stupid
and walk right into it—
be smart and hide.

4 Respect and serve the LORD!
Your reward will be wealth,
a long life, and honor.
5 Crooks walk down a road
full of thorny traps.
Stay away from there!
6 Teach your children
right from wrong,
and when they are grown
they will still do right.
7 The poor are ruled by the rich,
and those who borrow
are slaves of moneylenders.
8 Troublemakers get in trouble,
and their terrible anger
will get them nowhere.

9 The LORD blesses everyone
who freely gives food
to the poor.
10 Arguments and fights
will come to an end,
if you chase away those
who insult others.
11 The king is the friend of all
who are sincere
and speak with kindness.

12 The LORD watches over everyone
who shows good sense,
but he frustrates the plans
of deceitful liars.
13 Don't be so lazy that you say,
"If I go to work,
a lion will eat me!"
14 The words of a bad woman
are like a deep pit;
if you make the LORD angry,
you will fall right in.
15 All children are foolish,
but firm correction
will make them change.
16 Cheat the poor to make profit
or give gifts to the rich—
either way you lose.

Thirty Wise Sayings

17 Here are some sayings
of people with wisdom,
so listen carefully
as I teach.
18 You will be glad
that you know these sayings
and can recite them.
19 I am teaching them today,
so that you
may trust the LORD.
20 I have written thirty sayings
filled with sound advice.
21 You can trust them completely
to give you the right words
for those in charge of you.

–1–

22 Don't take advantage
of the poor
or cheat them in court.
23 The LORD is their defender,
and what you do to them,
he will do to you.

–2–

24 Don't make friends with anyone
who has a bad temper.
25 You might turn out like them
and get caught in a trap.

–3–

26 Don't guarantee to pay
someone else's debt.
27 If you don't have the money,
you might lose your bed.

22.6 Si 6.18.

–4–

28 Don't move a boundary marker [o]
set up by your ancestors.

–5–

29 If you do your job well,
you will work for a ruler
and never be a slave.

–6–

23 When you are invited
to eat with a king,
use your best manners.
2 Don't go and stuff yourself!
That would be just the same
as cutting your throat.
3 Don't be greedy for all
of that fancy food!
It may not be so tasty.

–7–

4 Give up trying so hard
to get rich.
5 Your money flies away
before you know it,
just like an eagle
suddenly taking off.

–8–

6 Don't accept an invitation
to eat a selfish person's food,
no matter how good it is.
7 People like that take note
of how much you eat.[p]
They say, "Take all you want!"
But they don't mean it.
8 Each bite will come back up,
and all your kind words
will be wasted.

–9–

9 Don't talk to fools—
they will just make fun.

–10–

10 Don't move a boundary marker [q]
or take the land
that belongs to orphans.
11 God All-Powerful is there
to defend them against you.

–11–

12 Listen to instruction
and do your best to learn.

–12–

13 Don't fail to correct
your children.
You won't kill them
by being firm,
14 and it may even
save their lives.

–13–

15 My children,
if you show good sense,
I will be happy,
16 and if you are truthful,
I will really be glad.

–14–

17 Don't be jealous of sinners,
but always honor the LORD.
18 Then you will truly have hope
for the future.

–15–

19 Listen to me, my children!
Be wise and have enough sense
to follow the right path.
20 Don't be a heavy drinker
or stuff yourself with food.
21 It will make you feel drowsy,
and you will end up poor
with only rags to wear.

–16–

22 Pay attention to your father,
and don't neglect your mother
when she grows old.
23 Invest in truth and wisdom,
discipline and good sense,
and don't part with them.
24 Make your father truly happy
by living right and showing
sound judgment.

[o] **22.28** *marker*: In ancient Israel boundary lines were sacred because all property was a gift from the Lord (see Deuteronomy 19.14). [p] **23.7** *People . . . eat*: One possible meaning for the difficult Hebrew text. [q] **23.10** *marker*: See the note at 22.28.

25 Make your parents proud,
especially your mother.

–17–

26 My son, pay close attention,
and gladly follow
my example.
27 Bad women and unfaithful wives
are like a deep pit—
28 they are waiting to attack you
like a gang of robbers
with victim after victim.

–18–

29 Who is always in trouble?
Who argues and fights?
Who has cuts and bruises?
Whose eyes are red?
30 Everyone who stays up late,
having just one more drink.
31 Don't even look
at that colorful stuff
bubbling up in the glass!
It goes down so easily,
32 but later it bites
like a poisonous snake.
33 You will see weird things,
and your mind
will play tricks on you.
34 You will feel tossed about
like someone trying to sleep
on a ship in a storm.
35 You will be bruised all over,
without even remembering
how it all happened.
And you will lie awake asking,
"When will morning come,
so I can drink some more?"

–19–

24 Don't be jealous of crooks
or want to be their friends.
2 All they think about
and talk about
is violence and cruelty.

–20–

3 Use wisdom and understanding
to establish your home;
4 let good sense fill the rooms
with priceless treasures.

–21–

5 Wisdom brings strength,
and knowledge gives power.
6 Battles are won
by listening to advice
and making a lot of plans.

–22–

7 Wisdom is too much for fools!
Their advice is no good.

–23–

8 No one but troublemakers
think up trouble.
9 Everyone hates senseless fools
who think up ways to sin.

–24–

10 Don't give up and be helpless
in times of trouble.

–25–

11 Don't fail to rescue those
who are doomed to die.
12 Don't say, "I didn't know it!"
God can read your mind.
He watches each of us
and knows our thoughts.
And God will pay us back
for what we do.

–26–

13 Honey is good for you,
my children,
and it tastes sweet.
14 Wisdom is like honey
for your life—
if you find it,
your future is bright.

–27–

15 Don't be a cruel person
who attacks good people
and hurts their families.
16 Even if good people
fall seven times,
they will get back up.
But when trouble strikes
the wicked,
that's the end of them.

–28–

17 Don't be happy
to see your enemies trip
and fall down.
18 The LORD will find out
and be unhappy.
Then he will stop
being angry with them.

–29–

19 Don't let evil people
worry you
or make you jealous.
20 They will soon be gone
like the flame of a lamp
that burns out.

–30–

21 My children, you must respect
the LORD and the king,
and you must not make friends
with anyone who rebels
against either of them.
22 Who knows what sudden disaster
the LORD or a ruler
might bring?

More Sayings That Make Good Sense

23 Here are some more sayings
that make good sense:
When you judge,
you must be fair.
24 If you let the guilty
go free,
people of all nations
will hate and curse you.
25 But if you punish the guilty,
things will go well for you,
and you will prosper.
26 Giving an honest answer
is a sign
of true friendship.
27 Get your fields ready
and plant your crops
before starting a home.
28 Don't accuse anyone
who isn't guilty.
Don't ever tell a lie
29 or say to someone,
"I'll get even with you!"
30 I once walked by the field
and the vineyard
of a lazy fool.
31 Thorns and weeds
were everywhere,
and the stone wall
had fallen down.
32 When I saw this,
it taught me a lesson:
33 Sleep a little. Doze a little.
Fold your hands
and twiddle your thumbs.
34 Suddenly poverty hits you
and everything is gone!

More of Solomon's Wise Sayings

25 Here are more
of Solomon's proverbs.
They were copied by the officials
of King Hezekiah of Judah.
2 God is praised
for being mysterious;
rulers are praised
for explaining mysteries.
3 Who can fully understand
the thoughts of a ruler?
They reach beyond the sky
and go deep in the earth.

4 Silver must be purified
before it can be used
to make something of value.
5 Evil people must be removed
before anyone can rule
with justice.

6 Don't try to seem important
in the court of a ruler.
7 It's better for the ruler
to give you a high position
than for you to be embarrassed
in front of royal officials.
Be sure you are right
8 before you sue someone,
or you might lose your case
and be embarrassed.

9 When you and someone else
can't get along,
don't gossip about it.[r]

[r]**25.9** *When . . . it*: Or "Settle a problem privately between you and your neighbor and don't involve others."
24.33,34 Pr 6.10, 11. **25.6,7** Lk 14.8-10.

10 Others will find out,
and your reputation
will then be ruined.

11 The right word
at the right time
is like precious gold
set in silver.
12 Listening to good advice
is worth much more
than jewelry made of gold.
13 A messenger you can trust
is just as refreshing
as cool water in summer.
14 Broken promises
are worse than rain clouds
that don't bring rain.
15 Patience and gentle talk
can convince a ruler
and overcome any problem.

16 Eating too much honey
can make you sick.
17 Don't visit friends too often,
or they will get tired of it
and start hating you.
18 Telling lies about friends
is like attacking them
with clubs and swords
and sharp arrows.
19 A friend you can't trust
in times of trouble
is like having a toothache
or a sore foot.
20 Singing to someone
in deep sorrow
is like pouring vinegar
in an open cut.[s]

21 If your enemies are hungry,
give them something to eat.
And if they are thirsty,
give them something
to drink.
22 This will be the same
as piling burning coals
on their heads.
And the LORD
will reward you.
23 As surely as rain blows in
from the north,
anger is caused
by cruel words.
24 It's better to stay outside
on the roof of your house
than to live inside
with a nagging wife.

25 Good news from far away
refreshes like cold water
when you are thirsty.
26 When a good person gives in
to the wicked,
it's like dumping garbage
in a stream of clear water.
27 Don't eat too much honey
or always want praise.[t]
28 Losing self-control
leaves you as helpless
as a city without a wall.

Don't Be a Fool

26 Expecting snow in summer
and rain in the dry season
makes more sense
than honoring a fool.
2 A curse you don't deserve
will take wings and fly away
like a sparrow or a swallow.
3 Horses and donkeys
must be beaten and bridled—
and so must fools.
4 Don't make a fool of yourself
by answering a fool.
5 But if you answer any fools,
show how foolish they are,
so they won't feel smart.

6 Sending a message by a fool
is like chopping off your foot
and drinking poison.
7 A fool with words of wisdom
is like an athlete
with legs that can't move.[u]

[s]**25.20** *cut*: One possible meaning for the difficult Hebrew text of verse 20. [t]**25.27** *or . . . praise*: One possible meaning for the difficult Hebrew text. [u]**26.7** *with . . . move*: One possible meaning for the difficult Hebrew text.
25.21,22 Ro 12.20.

8 Are you going to honor a fool?
Why not shoot a slingshot
with the rock tied tight?
9 A thornbush waved around
in the hand of a drunkard
is no worse than a proverb
in the mouth of a fool.

10 It's no smarter to shoot arrows
at every passerby
than it is to hire a bunch
of worthless nobodies.[v]
11 Dogs return to eat their vomit,
just as fools repeat
their foolishness.
12 There is more hope for a fool
than for someone who says,
"I'm really smart!"

13 Don't be lazy and keep saying,
"There's a lion outside!"
14 A door turns on its hinges,
but a lazy person
just turns over in bed.
15 Some of us are so lazy
that we won't lift a hand
to feed ourselves.
16 A lazy person says,
"I am smarter
than everyone else."

17 It's better to take hold
of a mad dog by the ears
than to take part
in someone else's argument.
18 It's no crazier to shoot
sharp and flaming arrows
19 than to cheat someone and say,
"I was only fooling!"

20 Where there is no fuel
a fire goes out;
where there is no gossip
arguments come to an end.
21 Troublemakers start trouble,
just as sparks and fuel
start a fire.
22 There is nothing so delicious
as the taste of gossip!
It melts in your mouth.

23 Hiding hateful thoughts
behind smooth[w] talk
is like coating a clay pot
with a cheap glaze.
24 The pleasant talk
of an enemy
hides more evil plans
25 than can be counted—
so don't believe a word!
26 Everyone will see through
those evil plans.
27 If you dig a pit,
you will fall in;
if you start a stone rolling,
it will roll back on you.
28 Watch out for anyone
who tells lies and flatters—
they are out to get you.

Don't Brag about Tomorrow

27 Don't brag about tomorrow!
Each day brings
its own surprises.
2 Don't brag about yourself—
let others praise you.
3 Stones and sand are heavy,
but trouble caused by a fool
is a much heavier load.
4 An angry person is dangerous,
but a jealous person
is even worse.

5 A truly good friend
will openly correct you.
6 You can trust a friend
who corrects you,
but kisses from an enemy
are nothing but lies.
7 If you have had enough to eat,
honey doesn't taste good,
but if you are really hungry,
you will eat anything.

8 When you are far from home,
you feel like a bird
without a nest.

[v]**26.10** *nobodies*: One possible meaning for the difficult Hebrew text of verse 10.
[w]**26.23** *smooth*: One ancient translation; Hebrew "hateful."
26.11 2 P 2.22. **26.27** Si 27.25-27. **27.1** Jas 4.13-16.

9 The sweet smell of incense
can make you feel good,
but true friendship
is better still.[x]
10 Don't desert an old friend
of your family
or visit your relatives
when you are in trouble.
A friend nearby is better
than relatives far away.

11 My child, show good sense!
Then I will be happy
and able to answer anyone
who criticizes me.
12 Be cautious and hide
when you see danger—
don't be stupid and walk
right into trouble.
13 Don't loan money to a stranger
unless you are given something
to guarantee payment.
14 A loud greeting
early in the morning
is the same as a curse.
15 The steady dripping of rain
and the nagging of a wife
are one and the same.
16 It's easier to catch the wind
or hold olive oil in your hand
than to stop a nagging wife.

17 Just as iron sharpens iron,
friends sharpen the minds
of each other.
18 Take care of a tree,
and you will eat its fruit;
look after your master,
and you will be praised.
19 You see your face in a mirror
and your thoughts
in the minds of others.
20 Death and the grave
are never satisfied,
and neither are we.
21 Gold and silver are tested
in a red-hot furnace,
but we are tested by praise.
22 No matter how hard
you beat a fool,
you can't pound out
the foolishness.

23 You should take good care
of your sheep and goats,
24 because wealth and honor
don't last forever.
25 After the hay is cut
and the new growth appears
and the harvest is over,
26 you can sell lambs and goats
to buy clothes and land.
27 From the milk of the goats,
you can make enough cheese
to feed your family
and all your servants.

The Law of God Makes Sense

28 Wicked people run away
when no one chases them,
but those who live right
are as brave as lions.
2 In time of civil war
there are many leaders,
but a sensible leader
restores law and order.[y]
3 When someone poor takes over
and mistreats the poor,
it's like a heavy rain
destroying the crops.

4 Lawbreakers praise criminals,
but law-abiding citizens
always oppose them.
5 Criminals don't know
what justice means,
but all who respect the LORD
understand it completely.
6 It's better to be poor
and live right,
than to be rich
and dishonest.

7 It makes good sense
to obey the Law of God,
but you disgrace your parents
if you make friends
with worthless nobodies.
8 If you make money by charging
high interest rates,

[x]**27.9** *still*: One possible meaning for the difficult Hebrew text of verse 9. [y]**28.2** *but . . . order*: One possible meaning for the difficult Hebrew text.

you will lose it all to someone
who cares for the poor.
9 God cannot stand the prayers
of anyone who disobeys
his Law.
10 By leading good people to sin,
you dig a pit for yourself,
but all who live right
will have a bright future.

11 The rich think highly
of themselves,
but anyone poor and sensible
sees right through them.
12 When an honest person wins,
it's time to celebrate;
when crooks are in control,
it's best to hide.
13 If you don't confess your sins,
you will be a failure.
But God will be merciful
if you confess your sins
and give them up.
14 The LORD blesses everyone
who is afraid to do evil,
but if you are cruel,
you will end up in trouble.

15 A ruler who mistreats the poor
is like a roaring lion
or a bear hunting for food.
16 A heartless leader is a fool,
but anyone who refuses
to get rich by cheating others
will live a long time.
17 Don't give help to murderers!
Make them stay on the run
for as long as they live.[z]

18 Honesty will keep you safe,
but everyone who is crooked
will suddenly fall.
19 Work hard, and you will have
a lot of food;
waste time, and you will have
a lot of trouble.

20 God blesses his loyal people,
but punishes all who want
to get rich quick.
21 It isn't right to be unfair,
but some people can be bribed
with only a piece of bread.
22 Don't be selfish
and eager to get rich—
you will end up worse off
than you can imagine.

23 Honest correction
is appreciated
more than flattery.
24 If you cheat your parents
and don't think it's wrong,
you are a common thief.
25 Selfish people cause trouble,
but you will live a full life
if you trust the LORD.
26 Only fools would trust
what they alone think,
but if you live by wisdom,
you will do all right.

27 Giving to the poor
will keep you from poverty,
but if you close your eyes
to their needs,
everyone will curse you.
28 When crooks are in control,
everyone tries to hide,
but when they lose power,
good people are everywhere.

Use Good Sense

29 If you keep being stubborn
after many warnings,
you will suddenly discover
you have gone too far.
2 When justice rules a nation,
everyone is glad;
when injustice rules,
everyone groans.
3 If you love wisdom
your parents will be glad,
but chasing after bad women
will cost you everything.
4 An honest ruler
makes the nation strong;
a ruler who takes bribes
will bring it to ruin.

5 Flattery is nothing less
than setting a trap.

[z]**28.17** *live*: One possible meaning for the difficult Hebrew text of verse 17.

6 Your sins will catch you,
but everyone who lives right
will sing and celebrate.
7 The wicked don't care
about the rights of the poor,
but good people do.
8 Sneering at others is a spark
that sets a city on fire;
using good sense can put out
the flames of anger.

9 Be wise and don't sue a fool.
You won't get satisfaction,
because all the fool will do
is sneer and shout.
10 A murderer hates everyone
who is honest
and lives right.[a]
11 Don't be a fool
and quickly lose your temper—
be sensible and patient.

12 A ruler who listens to lies
will have corrupt officials.
13 The poor and all who abuse them
must each depend on God
for light.
14 Kings who are fair to the poor
will rule forever.

15 Correct your children,
and they will be wise;
children out of control
disgrace their mothers.
16 Crime increases
when crooks are in power,
but law-abiding citizens
will see them fall.
17 If you correct your children,
they will bring you peace
and happiness.

18 Without guidance from God
law and order disappear,
but God blesses everyone
who obeys his Law.
19 Even when servants are smart,
it takes more than words
to make them obey.
20 There is more hope for a fool
than for someone who speaks
without thinking.
21 Slaves that you treat kindly
from their childhood
will cause you sorrow.[b]
22 A person with a quick temper
stirs up arguments
and commits a lot of sins.

23 Too much pride brings disgrace;
humility leads to honor.
24 If you take part in a crime
you are your worst enemy,
because even under oath
you can't tell the truth.
25 Don't fall into the trap
of being a coward—
trust the LORD,
and you will be safe.
26 Many try to make friends
with a ruler,
but justice comes
from the LORD.
27 Good people and criminals
can't stand each other.

The Sayings of Agur

30 These are the sayings
and the message
of Agur son of Jakeh.
Someone cries out to God,
"I am completely worn out!
How can I last?[c]
2 I am far too stupid
to be considered human.
3 I never was wise,
and I don't understand
what God is like."

4 Has anyone gone up to heaven
and come back down?
Has anyone grabbed hold
of the wind?
Has anyone wrapped up the sea
or marked out boundaries
for the earth?

[a]**29.10** *and lives right*: Or "and those who live right are friends of honest people." [b]**29.21** *will . . . sorrow*: One possible meaning for the difficult Hebrew text. [c]**30.1** *last*: One possible meaning for the difficult Hebrew text of verse 1.
29.19 Si 33.25-30. **30.4** 3 Macc 2.15.

If you know of any
who have done such things,
then tell me their names
and their children's names.

5 Everything God says is true—
and it's a shield for all
who come to him for safety.
6 Don't change what God has said!
He will correct you and show
that you are a liar.

7 There are two things, Lord,
I want you to do for me
before I die:
8 Make me absolutely honest
and don't let me be too poor
or too rich.
Give me just what I need.
9 If I have too much to eat,
I might forget about you;
if I don't have enough,
I might steal
and disgrace your name.

10 Don't tell a slave owner
something bad about one
of the slaves.
That slave will curse you,
and you will be in trouble.

11 Some people curse their father
and even their mother;
12 others think they are perfect,
but they are stained by sin.
13 Some people are stuck-up
and act like snobs;
14 others are so greedy
that they gobble down
the poor and homeless.

15 Greed[d] has twins,
each named "Give me!"
There are three or four things
that are never satisfied:
16 The world of the dead
and a childless wife,
the thirsty earth
and a flaming fire.

17 Don't make fun of your father
or disobey your mother—
crows will peck out your eyes,
and buzzards will eat
the rest of you.

18 There are three or four things
I cannot understand:
19 How eagles fly so high
or snakes crawl on rocks,
how ships sail the ocean
or people fall in love.

20 An unfaithful wife says,
"Sleeping with another man
is as natural as eating."

21 There are three or four things
that make the earth tremble
and are unbearable:
22 A slave who becomes king,
a fool who eats too much,
23 a hateful woman
who finds a husband,
and a slave who takes the place
of the woman who owns her.

24 On this earth four things
are small but very wise:
25 Ants, who seem to be feeble,
but store up food
all summer long;
26 badgers, who seem to be weak,
but live among the rocks;
27 locusts, who have no king,
but march like an army;
28 lizards,[e] which can be caught
in your hand,
but sneak into palaces.

29 Three or four creatures
really strut around:
30 Those fearless lions
who rule the jungle,
31 those proud roosters,
those mountain goats,
and those rulers
who have no enemies.[f]

[d]**30.15** *Greed*: Or "A leech." [e]**30.28** *lizards*: Or "spiders." [f]**30.31** *enemies*: One possible meaning for the difficult Hebrew text of verse 31.
30.19 Ws 5.10-12.

32 If you are foolishly bragging
or planning something evil,
then stop it now!
33 If you churn milk
you get butter;
if you pound on your nose,
you get blood—
and if you stay angry,
you get in trouble.

What King Lemuel's Mother Taught Him

31 These are the sayings
that King Lemuel of Massa
was taught by his mother.
2 My son Lemuel, you were born
in answer to my prayers,
so listen carefully.
3 Don't waste your life
chasing after women!
This has ruined many kings.

4 Kings and leaders
should not get drunk
or even want to drink.
5 Drinking makes you forget
your responsibilities,
and you mistreat the poor.
6 Beer and wine are only
for the dying or for those
who have lost all hope.
7 Let them drink and forget
how poor and miserable
they feel.
8 But you must defend
those who are helpless
and have no hope.
9 Be fair and give justice
to the poor and homeless.

In Praise of a Good Wife

10 A truly good wife
is the most precious treasure
a man can find!
11 Her husband depends on her,
and she never
lets him down.
12 She is good to him
every day of her life,
13 and with her own hands
she gladly makes clothes.
14 She is like a sailing ship
that brings food
from across the sea.
15 She gets up before daylight
to prepare food for her family
and for her servants.[g]
16 She knows how to buy land
and how to plant a vineyard,
17 and she always works hard.
18 She knows when to buy or sell,
and she stays busy
until late at night.
19 She spins her own cloth,
20 and she helps the poor
and the needy.
21 Her family has warm clothing,
and so she doesn't worry
when it snows.
22 She does her own sewing,
and everything she wears
is beautiful.

23 Her husband is a well-known
and respected leader
in the city.
24 She makes clothes to sell
to the shop owners.
25 She is strong and graceful,[h]
as well as cheerful
about the future.
26 Her words are sensible,
and her advice
is thoughtful.
27 She takes good care
of her family
and is never lazy.
28 Her children praise her,
and with great pride
her husband says,
29 "There are many good women,
but you are the best!"

30 Charm can be deceiving,
and beauty fades away,
but a woman
who honors the LORD
deserves to be praised.
31 Show her respect—
praise her in public
for what she has done.

[g]**31.15** *and . . . servants*: Or "and to tell her servants what to do." [h]**31.25** *She . . . graceful*: Or "The clothes she makes are attractive and of good quality."

ECCLESIASTES

ABOUT THIS BOOK

This book is a search for meaning in life. What can humans do to find satisfaction and happiness? What is worthwhile in life? The search begins with a gloomy outlook—life is boring and as senseless as chasing the wind.

Ecclesiastes looks at one area of life after another, to see whether meaning and purpose for living can be found. The book decides that humans cannot understand the meaning of life, and that life is too short and unfair. This may seem depressing, but Ecclesiastes also shows that some things in life are better than others. For example, it is better to be wise than to be foolish. And God does intend for people to enjoy his gifts of work, food, drink, friendship, and marriage. And most important of all:

Respect and obey God!
This is what life
is all about.
God will judge
everything we do,
even what is done in secret,
whether good or bad.
(12.13, 14)

A QUICK LOOK AT THIS BOOK

- The Search for Meaning in Life (1.1—2.26)
- Everything Has Its Time (3.1-8)
- Life Isn't Always Fair, So Live Wisely (3.9—6.12)
- No One Knows What the Future Will Bring (9.1—11.6)
- Respect and Obey God (11.7—12.14)

Nothing Makes Sense

1 When the son of David was king in Jerusalem, he was known to be very wise,[a] and he said:

2 Nothing makes sense!
Everything is nonsense.
I have seen it all—
nothing makes sense!
3 What is there to show
for all of our hard work
here on this earth?
4 People come, and people go,
but still the world
never changes.

5 The sun comes up,
the sun goes down;
it hurries right back
to where it started from.
6 The wind blows south,
the wind blows north;
round and round it blows
over and over again.

[a] **1.1** *known to be very wise*: This stands for the Hebrew word often translated "preacher" or "teacher." The word may refer to someone who was a very wise leader or to someone who had become wise from collecting sayings about wisdom.
1.4 Si 14.18.

7 All rivers empty into the sea,
but it never spills over;
one by one the rivers return
to their source.[b]

8 All of life is far more boring
than words could ever say.
Our eyes and our ears
are never satisfied
with what we see and hear.
9 Everything that happens
has happened before;
nothing is new,
nothing under the sun.
10 Someone might say,
"Here is something new!"
But it happened before,
long before we were born.
11 No one who lived in the past
is remembered anymore,
and everyone yet to be born
will be forgotten too.

It Is Senseless To Be Wise

12 I said these things when I lived in
Jerusalem as king of Israel. 13 With all my
wisdom I tried to understand everything
that happens here on earth. And God has
made this so hard for us humans to do. 14 I
have seen it all, and everything is just as
senseless as chasing the wind.[c]

15 If something is crooked,
it can't be made straight;
if something isn't there,
it can't be counted.

16 I said to myself, "You are by far the
wisest person who has ever lived in
Jerusalem. You are eager to learn, and you
have learned a lot." 17 Then I decided to
find out all I could about wisdom and foolishness. Soon I realized that this too was as
senseless as chasing the wind.[c]

18 The more you know,
the more you hurt;
the more you understand,
the more you suffer.

It Is Senseless To Be Selfish

2 I said to myself, "Have fun and enjoy
yourself!" But this didn't make sense.
2 Laughing and having fun is crazy. What
good does it do? 3 I wanted to find out what
was best for us during the short time we
have on this earth. So I decided to make
myself happy with wine and find out what
it means to be foolish, without really being
foolish myself.

4 I did some great things. I built houses
and planted vineyards. 5 I had flower gardens and orchards full of fruit trees. 6 And I
had pools where I could get water for the
trees. 7 I owned slaves, and their sons and
daughters became my slaves. I had more
sheep and goats than anyone who had ever
lived in Jerusalem. 8 Foreign rulers brought
me silver, gold, and precious treasures.
Men and women sang for me, and I had
many wives[d] who gave me great pleasure.

9 I was the most famous person who had
ever lived in Jerusalem, and I was very
wise. 10 I got whatever I wanted and did
whatever made me happy. But most of all, I
enjoyed my work. 11 Then I thought about
everything I had done, including the hard
work, and it was simply chasing the wind.[e]
Nothing on earth is worth the trouble.

Wisdom Makes Sense

12 I asked myself, "What can the next
king do that I haven't done?" Then I decided to compare wisdom with foolishness
and stupidity. 13 And I discovered that wisdom is better than foolishness, just as light
is better than darkness. 14 Wisdom is like
having two good eyes; foolishness leaves
you in the dark. But wise or foolish, we all
end up the same.

15 Finally, I said to myself, "Being wise
got me nowhere! The same thing will happen to me that happens to fools. Nothing
makes sense. 16 Wise or foolish, we all die
and are soon forgotten." 17 This made me
hate life. Everything we do is painful; it's
just as senseless as chasing the wind.[e]

[b]**1.7** *return to their source*: Or "flow into the sea." [c]**1.14,17** *chasing the wind*: Or "eating the wind." [d]**2.8** *many wives*: One possible meaning for the difficult Hebrew text. [e]**2.11,17** *chasing the wind*: See the note at 1.14, 17.

1.16 1 K 4.29-31; Si 47.14-18. **2.4-8** 1 K 10.23-27; 2 Ch 9.22-27. **2.7** 1 K 4.23. **2.8** 1 K 10.10, 14-22. **2.9** 1 Ch 29.25.

18 Suddenly I realized that others would someday get everything I had worked for so hard, then I started hating it all. 19 Who knows if those people will be sensible or stupid? Either way, they will own everything I have earned by hard work and wisdom. It doesn't make sense.

20 I thought about all my hard work, and I felt depressed. 21 When we use our wisdom, knowledge, and skill to get what we own, why do we have to leave it to someone who didn't work for it? This is senseless and wrong. 22 What do we really gain from all of our hard work? 23 Our bodies ache during the day, and work is torture. Then at night our thoughts are troubled. It just doesn't make sense.

24 The best thing we can do is to enjoy eating, drinking, and working.[f] I believe these are God's gifts to us, 25 and no one enjoys eating and living more than I do. 26 If we please God, he will make us wise, understanding, and happy. But if we sin, God will make us struggle for a living, then he will give all we own to someone who pleases him. This makes no more sense than chasing the wind.[g]

Everything Has Its Time

3 Everything on earth
has its own time
and its own season.
2 There is a time
for birth and death,
planting and reaping,
3 for killing and healing,
destroying and building,
4 for crying and laughing,
weeping and dancing,
5 for throwing stones
and gathering stones,
embracing and parting.
6 There is a time
for finding and losing,
keeping and giving,
7 for tearing and sewing,
listening and speaking.
8 There is also a time
for love and hate,
for war and peace.

What God Has Given Us To Do

9 What do we gain by all of our hard work? 10 I have seen what difficult things God demands of us. 11 God makes everything happen at the right time. Yet none of us can ever fully understand all he has done, and he puts questions in our minds about the past and the future. 12 I know the best thing we can do is to always enjoy life, 13 because God's gift to us is the happiness we get from our food and drink and from the work we do. 14 Everything God has done will last forever; nothing he does can ever be changed. God has done all this, so that we will worship him.

15 Everything that happens
has happened before,
and all that will be
has already been—
God does everything
over and over again.[h]

The Future Is Known Only to God

16 Everywhere on earth I saw violence and injustice instead of fairness and justice. 17 So I told myself that God has set a time and a place for everything. He will judge everyone, both the wicked and the good. 18 I know that God is testing us to show us that we are merely animals. 19 Like animals we breathe and die, and we are no better off than they are. It just doesn't make sense. 20 All living creatures go to the same place. We are made from earth, and we return to the earth. 21 Who really knows if our spirits go up and the spirits of animals go down into the earth? 22 We were meant to enjoy our work, and that's the best thing we can do. We can never know the future.

4 I looked again and saw people being mistreated everywhere on earth. They were crying, but no one was there to offer

[f]**2.24** *The best . . . working*: One possible meaning for the difficult Hebrew text. [g]**2.26** *chasing the wind*: See the note at 1.14, 17. [h]**3.15** *God does . . . again*: One possible meaning for the difficult Hebrew text.

2.23 Job 5.6, 7; 7.1-3; 14.1. **2.24** Ec 3.13; 5.18; 9.7; Is 56.12; Lk 12.19; 1 Co 15.32.
2.26 Job 32.8; Pr 2.6.

comfort, and those who mistreated them were powerful. 2 I said to myself, "The dead are better off than the living. 3 But those who have never been born are better off than anyone else, because they have never seen the terrible things that happen on this earth."

4 Then I realized that we work and do wonderful things just because we are jealous of others. This makes no more sense than chasing the wind.[i]

5 Fools will fold their hands
and starve to death.
6 Yet a very little food
eaten in peace
is better than twice as much
earned from overwork
and chasing the wind.[i]

7 Once again I saw that nothing on earth makes sense. 8 For example, some people don't have friends or family. But they are never satisfied with what they own, and they never stop working to get more. They should ask themselves, "Why am I always working to have more? Who will get what I leave behind?" What a senseless and miserable life!

It Is Better To Have a Friend

9 You are better off to have a friend than to be all alone, because then you will get more enjoyment out of what you earn. 10 If you fall, your friend can help you up. But if you fall without having a friend nearby, you are really in trouble. 11 If you sleep alone, you won't have anyone to keep you warm on a cold night. 12 Someone might be able to beat up one of you, but not both of you. As the saying goes, "A rope made from three strands of cord is hard to break."

13 You may be poor and young. But if you are wise, you are better off than a foolish old king who won't listen to advice. 14 Even if you were not born into the royal family and have been a prisoner and poor, you can still be king. 15 I once saw everyone in the world follow a young leader who came to power after the king was gone. 16 His followers could not even be counted. But years from now, no one will praise him—this makes no more sense than chasing the wind.[i]

Be Careful How You Worship

5 Be careful what you do when you enter the house of God. Some fools go there to offer sacrifices, even though they haven't sinned.[j] But it's best just to listen when you go to worship. 2 Don't talk before you think or make promises to God without thinking them through. God is in heaven, and you are on earth, so don't talk too much. 3 If you keep thinking about something, you will dream about it. If you talk too much, you will say the wrong thing.

4 God doesn't like fools. So don't be slow to keep your promises to God. 5 It's better not to make a promise at all than to make one and not keep it. 6 Don't let your mouth get you in trouble! And don't say to the worship leader,[k] "I didn't mean what I said." God can destroy everything you have worked for, so don't say something that makes God angry.

7 Respect and obey God! Daydreaming leads to a lot of senseless talk.[l]

8 Don't be surprised if the poor of your country are abused, and injustice takes the place of justice. After all, the lower officials must do what the higher ones order them to do. 9 And since the king is the highest official, he benefits most from the taxes paid on the land.[m]

10 If you love money and wealth, you will never be satisfied with what you have. This doesn't make sense either. 11 The more you have, the more everyone expects from you. Your money won't do you any good—others will just spend it for you. 12 If you have to work hard for a living, you can rest well at night, even if you don't have much to eat. But if you are rich, you can't even sleep.

13 I have seen something terribly unfair. People get rich, but it does them no good.

[i] **4.4,6,16** *chasing the wind*: See the note at 1.14, 17. [j] **5.1** *even . . . sinned*: One possible meaning for the difficult Hebrew text. [k] **5.6** *worship leader*: Or "messenger."
[l] **5.7** *Daydreaming . . . talk*: One possible meaning for the difficult Hebrew text. [m] **5.9** *land*: One possible meaning for the difficult Hebrew text of verse 9.
5.4 Ps 66.13, 14.

14 Suddenly they lose everything in a bad
business deal, then have nothing to leave
for their children. 15 They came into this
world naked, and when they die, they will
be just as naked. They can't take anything
with them, and they won't have anything to
show for all their work. 16 That's terribly
unfair. They leave the world just as they
came into it. They gained nothing from
running after the wind. 17 Besides all this,
they are always gloomy at mealtime, and
they are troubled, sick, and bitter.[n]

18 What is the best thing to do in the
short life that God has given us? I think we
should enjoy eating, drinking, and working
hard. This is what God intends for us to do.
19 Suppose you are very rich and able to
enjoy everything you own. Then go ahead
and enjoy working hard—this is God's gift
to you. 20 God will keep you so happy
that you won't have time to worry about
each day.

Don't Depend on Wealth

6 There is something else terribly unfair,
and it troubles everyone on earth.
2 God may give you everything you want—
money, property, and wealth. Then God
doesn't let you enjoy it, and someone you
don't even know gets it all. That's senseless
and terribly unfair!

3 You may live a long time and have a
hundred children. But a child born dead is
better off than you, unless you enjoy life
and have a decent burial. 4-5 That child will
never live to see the sun or to have a name,
and it will go straight to the world of darkness. But it will still find more rest than
you, 6 even if you live two thousand years
and don't enjoy life. As you know, we all
end up in the same place.

7 We struggle just to have enough to eat,
but we are never satisfied. 8 We may be
sensible, yet we are no better off than a
fool. And if we are poor, it still doesn't do us
any good to try to live right. 9 It's better to
enjoy what we have than to always want
something else, because that makes no
more sense than chasing the wind.[o]

10 Everything that happens was decided
long ago. We humans know what we are
like, and we can't argue with God, because
he is[p] too strong for us. 11 The more we
talk, the less sense we make, so what good
does it do to talk? 12 Life is short and
meaningless, and it fades away like a
shadow. Who knows what is best for us? Who
knows what will happen after we are gone?

The Best in Life

7 A good reputation
at the time of death
is better than loving care
at the time of birth.[q]
2 It's better to go to a funeral
than to attend a feast;
funerals remind us
that we all must die.
3 Choose sorrow over laughter
because a sad face
may hide a happy heart.
4 A sensible person mourns,
but fools always laugh.
5 Harsh correction is better
than the songs of a fool.
6 Foolish laughter is stupid.
It sounds like thorns
crackling in a fire.
7 Corruption[r] makes fools
of sensible people,
and bribes can ruin you.
8 Something completed is better
than something just begun;
patience is better
than too much pride.
9 Only fools get angry quickly
and hold a grudge.
10 It isn't wise to ask,
"Why is everything worse
than it used to be?"
11 Having wisdom is better
than an inheritance.
12 Wisdom will protect you
just like money;

[n]**5.17** *bitter*: One possible meaning for the difficult Hebrew text of verse 17. [o]**6.9** *chasing the wind*: See the note at 1.14, 17. [p]**6.10** *with God, because he is*: Or "with anyone who is." [q]**7.1** *birth*: One possible meaning for the difficult Hebrew text of verse 1. [r]**7.7** *Corruption*: Or "Oppression."

5.15 Job 1.21; Ps 49.17; 1 Ti 6.7. **7.1** Pr 22.1. **7.9** Jas 1.19.

knowledge with good sense
will lead you to life.
13 Think of what God has done!
If God makes something crooked,
can you make it straight?

14 When times are good,
you should be cheerful;
when times are bad,
think what it means.
God makes them both
to keep us from knowing
what will happen next.

Some of Life's Questions

15 I have seen everything during this
senseless life of mine. I have seen good citizens die for doing the right thing, and I
have seen criminals live to a ripe old age.
16 So don't destroy yourself by being too
good or acting too smart! 17 Don't die before your time by being too evil or acting like a fool. 18 Keep to the middle of
the road. You can do this if you truly respect God.

19 Wisdom will make you stronger than
the ten most powerful leaders in your city.

20 No one in this world always does
right.

21 Don't listen to everything that everyone says, or you might hear your servant
cursing you. 22 Haven't you cursed many
others?

23 I told myself that I would be smart
and try to understand all of this, but it was
too much for me. 24 The truth is beyond
us. It's far too deep. 25 So I decided to learn
everything I could and become wise
enough to discover what life is all about. At
the same time, I wanted to understand why
it's stupid and senseless to be an evil fool.

26 Here is what I discovered: A bad
woman is worse than death. She is a trap,
reaching out with body and soul to catch
you. But if you obey God, you can escape. If
you don't obey, you are done for. 27 With all
my wisdom I have tried to find out how
everything fits together, 28 but so far I have
not been able to. I do know there is one
good man in a thousand, but never have I
found a good woman. 29 I did learn one
thing: We were completely honest when
God created us, but now we have twisted
minds.

8 Who is smart enough
to explain everything?
Wisdom makes you cheerful
and gives you a smile.

Obey the King

2 If you promised God that you would be
loyal to the king, I advise you to keep that
promise. 3 Don't quickly oppose the king or
argue when he has already made up his
mind. 4 The king's word is law. No one can
ask him, "Why are you doing this?" 5 If you
obey the king, you will stay out of trouble.
So be smart and learn what to do and when
to do it. 6 Life is hard, but there is a time
and a place for everything, 7 though no one
can tell the future. 8 We cannot control the
wind[s] or determine the day of our death.
There is no escape in time of war, and no
one can hide behind evil. 9 I noticed all this
and thought seriously about what goes on
in the world. Why does one person have
the power to hurt another?

Who Can Understand the Ways of God?

10 I saw the wicked buried with honor,
but God's people had to leave the holy city
and were forgotten.[t] None of this makes
sense. 11 When we see criminals commit
crime after crime without being punished,
it makes us want to start a life of crime.
12 They commit hundreds of crimes and
live to a ripe old age, in spite of the saying:

Everyone who lives right
and respects God
will prosper,
13 but no one who sins
and rejects God
will prosper or live very long.

14 There is something else that doesn't
make sense to me. Good citizens are
treated as criminals, while criminals are
honored as though they were good citizens.
15 So I think we should get as much out of

[s] **8.8** *control the wind*: Or "escape from death."

[t] **8.10** *but . . . forgotten*: One possible meaning for the difficult Hebrew text.

life as we possibly can. There is nothing
better than to enjoy our food and drink and
to have a good time. Then we can make it
through this troublesome life that God has
given us here on earth.
16 Day and night I went without sleep,
trying to understand what goes on in this
world. 17 I saw everything God does, and I
realized that no one can really understand
what happens. We may be very wise, but
no matter how much we try or how much
we claim to know, we cannot understand
it all.

One Day at a Time

9 I thought about these things. Then I
understood that God has power over
everyone, even those of us who are wise
and live right. Anything can happen to any
of us, and so we never know if life will be
good or bad.[u] 2 But exactly[v] the same thing
will finally happen to all of us, whether we
live right and respect God or sin and don't
respect God. Yes, the same thing will happen if we offer sacrifices to God or if we don't,
if we keep our promises or break them.
3 It's terribly unfair for the same thing
to happen to each of us. We are mean and
foolish while we live, and then we die. 4 As
long as we are alive, we still have hope, just
as a live dog is better off than a dead lion.
5 We know that we will die, but the dead
don't know a thing. Nothing good will happen to them—they are gone and forgotten.
6 Their loves, their hates, and their jealous
feelings have all disappeared with them.
They will never again take part in anything
that happens on this earth.
7 Be happy and enjoy eating and drinking! God decided long ago that this is what
you should do. 8 Dress up, comb your hair,
and look your best. 9 Life is short, and you
love your wife, so enjoy being with her. This
is what you are supposed to do as you
struggle through life on this earth. 10 Work
hard at whatever you do. You will soon go
to the world of the dead, where no one
works or thinks or reasons or knows anything.
11 Here is something else I have learned:

The fastest runners
and the greatest heroes
don't always win races
and battles.
Wisdom, intelligence, and skill
don't always make you healthy,
rich, or popular.
We each have our share
of bad luck.

12 None of us know when we might fall
victim to a sudden disaster and find ourselves like fish in a net or birds in a trap.

Better To Be Wise than Foolish

13 Once I saw what people really think
of wisdom. 14 It happened when a powerful
ruler surrounded and attacked a small city
where only a few people lived. The enemy
army was getting ready to break through
the city walls. 15 But the city was saved by
the wisdom of a poor person who was soon
forgotten. 16 So I decided that wisdom is
better than strength. Yet if you are poor, no
one pays any attention to you, no matter
how smart you are.

17 Words of wisdom spoken softly
make much more sense
than the shouts of a ruler
to a crowd of fools.
18 Wisdom is more powerful
than weapons,
yet one mistake can destroy
all the good you have done.

10 A few dead flies in perfume
make all of it stink,
and a little foolishness
outweighs a lot of wisdom.
2 Sensible thoughts lead you
to do right;
foolish thoughts lead you
to do wrong.
3 Fools show their stupidity
by the way they live;
it's easy to see
they have no sense.
4 Don't give up your job
when your boss gets angry.
If you stay calm,
you'll be forgiven.

[u] **9.1** *or bad*: Three ancient translations; the Hebrew text does not have these words.
[v] **9.2** *exactly*: One possible meaning for the difficult Hebrew text.

5 Some things rulers do are terribly unfair: 6 They honor fools, but dishonor the
rich; 7 they let slaves ride on horses, but
force slave owners to walk.

8 If you dig a pit,
you might fall in;
if you break down a wall,
a snake might bite you.[w]
9 You could even get hurt
by chiseling a stone
or chopping a log.
10 If you don't sharpen your ax,
it will be harder to use;
if you are smart,
you'll know what to do.[x]
11 The power to charm a snake
does you no good
if it bites you anyway.

12 If you talk sensibly,
you will have friends;
if you talk foolishly,
you will destroy yourself.
13 Fools begin with nonsense,
and their stupid chatter
ends with disaster.
14 They never tire of talking,
but none of us really know
what the future will bring.
15 Fools wear themselves out—
they don't know enough
to find their way home.[y]

16 A country is in for trouble
when its ruler is childish,
and its leaders
party all day long.
17 But a nation will prosper
when its ruler is mature,
and its leaders
don't party too much.
18 Some people are too lazy
to fix a leaky roof—
then the house falls in.
19 Eating and drinking
make you feel happy,
and bribes can buy
everything you need.
20 Don't even think
about cursing the king;
don't curse the rich,
not even in secret.
A little bird might hear
and tell everything.

It Pays To Work Hard

11 Be generous, and someday
you will be rewarded.[z]
2 Share what you have
with seven or eight others,
because you never know
when disaster may strike.
3 Rain clouds always bring rain;
trees always stay
wherever they fall.
4 If you worry about the weather
and don't plant seeds,
you won't harvest a crop.

5 No one can explain how a baby
breathes before it is born.[a] So how can anyone explain what God does? After all, he
created everything.
6 Plant your seeds early in the morning
and keep working in the field until dark.
Who knows? Your work might pay off, and
your seeds might produce.

Youth and Old Age

7 Nothing on earth is more beautiful
than the morning sun. 8 Even if you live to
a ripe old age, you should try to enjoy each
day, because darkness will come and will
last a long time. Nothing makes sense.[b]
9 Be cheerful and enjoy life while you
are young! Do what you want and find
pleasure in what you see. But don't forget
that God will judge you for everything
you do.

[w] **10.8** *a snake might bite you*: Walls of houses were often made of stones with mud to fill in the cracks between them. If some of the mud washed out, a snake could be living inside the wall.
[x] **10.10** *do*: One possible meaning for the difficult Hebrew text of verse 10.
[y] **10.15** *home*: One possible meaning for the difficult Hebrew text of verse 15.
[z] **11.1** *Be generous . . . rewarded*: Or "Don't be afraid to invest. Someday it will pay off."
[a] **11.5** *how . . . born*: Or "what makes the wind blow or how a baby grows inside its mother."
[b] **11.8** *Nothing makes sense*: Or "There's nothing to look forward to!"

10.8 Ps 7.15; Pr 26.27; Si 27.26, 27.

10 Rid yourself of all worry and pain, because the wonderful moments of youth quickly disappear.

12 Keep your Creator in mind while you are young! In years to come, you will be burdened down with troubles and say, "I don't enjoy life anymore."

2 Someday the light of the sun
and the moon and the stars
will all seem dim to you.
Rain clouds will remain
over your head.
3 Your body will grow feeble,
your teeth will decay,
and your eyesight fail.
4 The noisy grinding of grain
will be shut out
by your deaf ears,
but even the song of a bird
will keep you awake.

5 You will be afraid
to climb up a hill
or walk down a road.
Your hair will turn as white
as almond blossoms.
You will feel lifeless
and drag along
like an old grasshopper.

We each go to our eternal home,
and the streets are filled
with those who mourn.
6 The silver cord snaps,
the golden bowl breaks;
the water pitcher is smashed,
and the pulley at the well
is shattered.
7 So our bodies return
to the earth,
and the life-giving breath[c]
returns to God.
8 Nothing makes sense.
I have seen it all—
nothing makes sense.

Respect and Obey God

9 I was a wise teacher with much understanding, and I collected a number of
proverbs that I had carefully studied.
10 Then I tried to explain these things in
the best and most accurate way.
11 Words of wisdom are like the stick a
farmer uses to make animals move. These
sayings come from God, our only shepherd,
and they are like nails that fasten things together.[d] 12 My child, I warn you to stay
away from any teachings except these.

There is no end to books,
and too much study
will wear you out.

13 Everything you were taught can be
put into a few words:

Respect and obey God!
This is what life
is all about.
14 God will judge
everything we do,
even what is done in secret,
whether good or bad.

[c] **12.7** *life-giving breath*: Or "spirit."

[d] **12.11** *These sayings . . . together*: One possible meaning for the difficult Hebrew text.

SONG OF SONGS

ABOUT THIS BOOK

The title of this book means "the most beautiful of songs"; in some translations, it is called "The Song of Solomon" (see 1.1).

This book is a collection of songs, or poems, in which a woman and a man tell about their love for each other. Sometimes they speak to themselves, sometimes to each other or to friends, and in some of the poems they seem to be remembering earlier times in their relationship.

The poems have been interpreted in different ways. Some have thought that the man was King Solomon himself. Others read the book as a drama: The woman was taken to the court of Solomon, but she was still in love with a man back in her hometown, and finally the two are reunited. Some interpreters believe that the man and woman stand for God and his people or Christ and the Church.

But it is also possible to take the book as a collection of poems expressing the deep and powerful love that a woman and a man can have for each other. In fact, they may have been part of marriage celebrations in ancient Israel. As one of the poems says:

The passion of love
bursting into flame
is more powerful than death,
stronger than the grave.
Love cannot be drowned
by oceans or floods;
it cannot be bought,
no matter what is offered.
(8.6b, 7)

A QUICK LOOK AT THIS BOOK

- Love Is Better than Wine (1.1-17)
- Love Makes Everything Beautiful (2.1—3.5)
- The Wedding (3.6—5.1)
- Why Is the One You Love More Special than Others? (5.2—7.13)
- If Only You and I . . . (8.1-14)

Love Is Better than Wine

1 This is Solomon's
most beautiful song.

She Speaks:
2 Kiss me tenderly!
Your love is better than wine,
3 and you smell so sweet.
All the young women adore you;
the very mention of your name
is like spreading perfume.
*4 Hurry, my king! Let's hurry.
5 Take me to your home.

The Young Women Speak:
We are happy for you!
And we praise your love
even more than wine.

1.1 1 K 4.32.

She Speaks:
Young women of Jerusalem,
it is only right
that you should adore him.
My skin is dark and beautiful,
like a tent in the desert
or like Solomon's curtains.
6 Don't stare at me
just because the sun
has darkened my skin.
My brothers were angry with me;
they made me work in the vineyard,
and so I neglected
my complexion.

Don't let the other shepherds
think badly of me.[a]
7 I'm not one of those women
who shamelessly follow
after shepherds.[b]
My darling, I love you!
Where do you feed your sheep
and let them rest at noon?

He Speaks:
8 My dearest, if you don't know,
just follow the path
of the sheep.
Then feed your young goats
near the shepherds' tents.
9 You move as gracefully
as the pony that leads
the chariot of the king.
10 Earrings add to your beauty,
and you wear a necklace
of precious stones.
11 Let's make you some jewelry
of gold, woven with silver.

She Speaks:
12 My king, while you
were on your couch,
my love was a magic charm.[c]
13 My darling, you are perfume
between my breasts;
14 you are flower blossoms
from the gardens of En-Gedi.[d]

He Speaks:
15 My darling, you are lovely,
so very lovely—
your eyes are those of a dove.

She Speaks:
16 My love, you are handsome,
truly handsome—
the fresh green grass
will be our wedding bed
17 in the shade of cedar
and cypress trees.

Love Makes Everything Beautiful

She Speaks:
2 I am merely a rose[e]
from the land of Sharon,
a lily from the valley.

He Speaks:
2 My darling, when compared
with other young women,
you are a lily among thorns.

She Speaks:
3 And you, my love,
are an apple tree
among trees of the forest.
Your shade brought me pleasure;
your fruit was sweet.
4 You led me to your banquet room
and showered me with love.
5 Refresh and strengthen me
with raisins and apples.
I am hungry for love!
6 Put your left hand under my head
and embrace me
with your right arm.

7 Young women of Jerusalem,
promise me by the power
of deer and gazelles[f]

[a] **1.6** *Don't . . . me*: One possible meaning for the difficult Hebrew text. [b] **1.7** *I'm . . . shepherds*: One possible meaning for the difficult Hebrew text. [c] **1.12** *magic charm*: The Hebrew text has "spikenard" (or "nard"), a sweet-smelling ointment made from a plant that comes from India. The ointment was sometimes used as a love charm. [d] **1.14** *En-Gedi*: An oasis west of the Dead Sea. [e] **2.1** *rose*: The traditional translation. The exact variety of the flower is not known, though it may have been a crocus. [f] **2.7** *deer and gazelles*: Deer and gazelles were sacred animals in some religions of Old Testament times, and they were thought to have special powers.

never to awaken love
before it is ready.

Winter Is Past

She Speaks:
8 I hear the voice
of the one I love,
as he comes leaping
over mountains and hills
9 like a deer or a gazelle.
Now he stands outside our wall,
looking through the window
10 and speaking to me.

He Speaks:
My darling, I love you!
Let's go away together.
11 Winter is past,
the rain has stopped;
12 flowers cover the earth,
it's time to sing.[g]
The cooing of doves
is heard in our land.
13 Fig trees are bearing fruit,
while blossoms on grapevines
fill the air with perfume.
My darling, I love you!
Let's go away together.
14 You are my dove
hiding among the rocks
on the side of a cliff.
Let me see how lovely you are!
Let me hear the sound
of your melodious voice.
15 Our vineyards are in blossom;
we must catch the little foxes
that destroy the vineyards.[h]

She Speaks:
16 My darling, I am yours,
and you are mine,
as you feed your sheep
among the lilies.
17 Pretend to be a young deer
dancing on mountain slopes[i]
until daylight comes
and shadows fade away.

Beautiful Dreams

She Speaks:
3 While in bed at night,
I reached for the one I love
with heart and soul.
I looked for him,
but he wasn't there.
2 So I searched through the town
for the one I love.
I looked on every street,
but he wasn't there.
3 I even asked the guards
patrolling the town,
"Have you seen the one
I love so much?"
4 Right after that, I found him.
I held him and would not let go
until I had taken him
to the home of my mother.
5 Young women of Jerusalem,
promise me by the power
of deer and gazelles,[j]
never to awaken love
before it is ready.

The Groom and the Wedding Party

Their Friends Speak:
6 What do we see approaching
from the desert
like a cloud of smoke?
With it comes the sweet smell
of spices, including myrrh
and frankincense.
7 It is King Solomon
carried on a throne,
surrounded by sixty
of Israel's best soldiers.
8 Each of them wears a sword.
They are experts at fighting,
even in the dark.
9 The throne is made of trees
from Lebanon.
10 Its posts are silver,
the back is gold,
and the seat is covered
with purple cloth.
You women of Jerusalem

[g] **2.12** *sing*: Or "trim the vines." [h] **2.15** *vineyards*: One possible meaning for the difficult Hebrew text of verse 15. [i] **2.17** *mountain slopes*: One possible meaning for the difficult Hebrew text. [j] **3.5** *deer and gazelles*: See the note at 2.7.

have taken great care
to furnish the inside.[k]
11 Now come and see the crown
given to Solomon by his mother
on his happy wedding day.

What a Beautiful Bride

He Speaks:

4 My darling, you are lovely,
so very lovely—
as you look through your veil,
your eyes are those of a dove.
Your hair tosses about
as gracefully as goats
coming down from Gilead.
2 Your teeth are whiter
than sheep freshly washed;
they match perfectly,
not one is missing.
3 Your lips are crimson cords,
your mouth is shapely;
behind your veil are hidden
beautiful rosy cheeks.[l]
4 Your neck is more graceful
than the tower of David,
decorated with thousands
of warriors' shields.

5 Your breasts are perfect;
they are twin deer
feeding among lilies.
6 I will hasten to those hills
sprinkled with sweet perfume
and stay there till sunrise.
7 My darling, you are lovely
in every way.
8 My bride, together
we will leave Lebanon!
We will say good-by
to the peaks of Mount Amana,
Senir, and Hermon,
where lions and leopards
live in the caves.
9 My bride, my very own,
you have stolen my heart!
With one glance from your eyes
and the glow of your necklace,
you have stolen my heart.
10 Your love is sweeter than wine;
the smell of your perfume
is more fragrant than spices.
11 Your lips are a honeycomb;
milk and honey
flow from your tongue.
Your dress has the aroma
of cedar trees from Lebanon.

12 My bride, my very own,
you are a garden, a fountain
closed off to all others.
13 Your arms[m] are vines,
covered with delicious fruits
and all sorts of spices—
henna, nard, 14 saffron,
calamus, cinnamon,
frankincense, myrrh, and aloes
—all the finest spices.
15 You are a spring in the garden,
a fountain of pure water,
and a refreshing stream
from Mount Lebanon.

She Speaks:

16 Let the north wind blow,
the south wind too!
Let them spread the aroma
of my garden,
so the one I love
may enter and taste
its delicious fruits.

He Speaks:

5 My bride, my very own,
I come to my garden
and enjoy its spices.
I eat my honeycomb and honey;
I drink my wine and milk.

Their Friends Speak:

Eat and drink until
you are drunk with love.

Another Dream

She Speaks:

2 I was asleep, but dreaming:
The one I love was at the door,
knocking and saying,
"My darling, my very own,

[k] **3.10** *inside*: One possible meaning for the difficult Hebrew text. [l] **4.3** *beautiful rosy cheeks*: One possible meaning for the difficult Hebrew text. [m] **4.13** *Your arms*: One possible meaning for the difficult Hebrew text.

my flawless dove,
open the door for me!
My head is drenched
with evening dew."

3 But I had already undressed
and bathed my feet.
Should I dress again
and get my feet dirty?
4 Then my darling's hand
reached to open the latch,
and my heart stood still.
5 When I rose to open the door,
my hands and my fingers
dripped with perfume.

6 My heart stood still
while he spoke to me,
but when I opened the door,
my darling had disappeared.
I searched and shouted,
but I could not find him—
there was no answer.
7 Then I was found by the guards
patrolling the town
and guarding the wall.
They beat me up
and stripped off my robe.

8 Young women of Jerusalem,
if you find the one I love,
please say to him,
"She is weak with desire."

Their Friends Speak:

9 Most beautiful of women,
why is the one you love
more special than others?
Why do you ask us
to tell him how you feel?

She Speaks:

10 He is handsome and healthy,
the most outstanding
among ten thousand.
11 His head is purest gold;
his hair is wavy,
black as a raven.
12 His eyes are a pair of doves
bathing in a stream
flowing with milk.[n]
13 His face is a garden
of sweet-smelling spices;
his lips are lilies
dripping with perfume.

14 His arms are branches of gold
covered with jewels;
his body is ivory[o]
decorated with sapphires.
15 His legs are columns of marble
on feet of gold.
He stands there majestic
like Mount Lebanon
and its choice cedar trees.
16 His kisses are sweet.
I desire him so much!
Young women of Jerusalem,
he is my lover and friend.

Their Friends Speak:

6 Most beautiful of women,
tell us where he has gone.
Let us help you find him.

She Speaks:

2 My darling has gone down
to his garden of spices,
where he will feed his sheep
and gather lilies.
3 I am his, and he is mine,
as he feeds his sheep
among the lilies.

He Speaks:

4 My dearest, the cities of Tirzah
and Jerusalem
are not as lovely as you.
Your charms are more powerful
than all of the stars
in the heavens.[p]
5 Turn away your eyes—
they make me melt.
Your hair tosses about
as gracefully as goats
coming down from Gilead.
6 Your teeth are whiter
than sheep freshly washed;

[n]**5.12** *milk*: One possible meaning for the difficult Hebrew text of verse 12. [o]**5.14** *his . . . ivory*: One possible meaning for the difficult Hebrew text. [p]**6.4** *all . . . heavens*: Or "a mighty army ready for war."

they match perfectly,
not one is missing.
7 Behind your veil are hidden
beautiful rosy cheeks.[q]

8 What if I could have
sixty queens, eighty wives,
and thousands of others!
9 You would be my only choice,
my flawless dove,
the favorite child
of your mother.
The young women, the queens,
and all the others
tell how excited you are
as they sing your praises:
10 "You are as majestic
as the morning sky—
glorious as the moon—
blinding as the sun!
Your charms are more powerful
than all the stars above."[r]

She Speaks:
11 I went down to see if blossoms
were on the walnut trees,
grapevines, and fruit trees.
12 But in my imagination
I was suddenly riding
on a glorious chariot.[s]

Their Friends Speak:
13 Dance! Dance!
Beautiful woman from Shulam,
let us see you dance!

She Speaks:
Why do you want to see
this woman from Shulam
dancing with the others?[t]

The Wedding Dance

He Speaks:
7 You are a princess,
and your feet are graceful
in their sandals.
Your thighs are works of art,
each one a jewel;
2 your navel is a wine glass
filled to overflowing.
Your body is full and slender
like a bundle of wheat
bound together by lilies.
3 Your breasts are like twins
of a deer.
4 Your neck is like ivory,
and your eyes sparkle
like the pools of Heshbon
by the gate of Bath-Rabbim.
Your nose is beautiful
like Mount Lebanon
above the city of Damascus.
5 Your head is held high
like Mount Carmel;
your hair is so lovely
it holds a king prisoner.[u]

6 You are beautiful,
so very desirable!
7 You are tall and slender
like a palm tree,
and your breasts are full.
8 I will climb that tree
and cling to its branches.
I will discover that your breasts
are clusters of grapes,
and that your breath
is the aroma of apples.
9 Kissing you is more delicious
than drinking the finest wine.
How wonderful and tasty![v]

She Speaks:
10 My darling, I am yours,
and you desire me.
11 Let's stroll through the fields
and sleep in the villages.
12 At dawn let's slip out and see
if grapevines and fruit trees
are covered with blossoms.
When we are there,
I will give you my love.
13 Perfume from the magic flower[w]
fills the air, my darling.
Right at our doorstep

[q]**6.7** *cheeks*: One possible meaning for the difficult Hebrew text of verse 7. [r]**6.10** *all . . . above*: Or "a mighty army ready for war." [s]**6.12** *chariot*: One possible meaning for the difficult Hebrew text of verse 12. [t]**6.13** *dancing . . . others*: One possible meaning for the difficult Hebrew text. [u]**7.5** *it . . . prisoner*: One possible meaning for the difficult Hebrew text. [v]**7.9** *How . . . tasty*: One possible meaning for the difficult Hebrew text. [w]**7.13** *magic flower*: The Hebrew text has "mandrake," a plant that was thought to give sexual powers.

I have stored up for you
all kinds of tasty fruits.

If Only You and I . . .

She Speaks:

8 If you were my brother,
I could kiss you
whenever we happen to meet,
and no one would say
I did wrong.
2 I could take you to the home
of my mother,
who taught me all I know.[x]
I would give you delicious wine
and fruit juice as well.
3 Put your left hand under my head
and embrace me
with your right arm.

4 Young women of Jerusalem,
promise me by the power
of deer and gazelles[y]
never to awaken love
before it is ready.

Their Friends Speak:

5 Who is this young woman
coming in from the desert
and leaning on the shoulder
of the one she loves?

She Speaks:

I stirred up your passions
under the apple tree
where you were born.
6 Always keep me in your heart
and wear this bracelet
to remember me by.
The passion of love
bursting into flame
is more powerful than death,
stronger than the grave.
7 Love cannot be drowned
by oceans or floods;
it cannot be bought,
no matter what is offered.

Their Friends Speak:

8 We have a little sister
whose breasts
are not yet formed.
If someone asks to marry her,
what should we do?
9 She isn't a wall
that we can defend
behind a silver shield.
Neither is she a room
that we can protect
behind a wooden door.

She Speaks:

10 I am a wall around a city,
my breasts are towers,
and just looking at me
brings him great pleasure.
11 Solomon has a vineyard
at Baal-Hamon,
which he rents to others
for a thousand pieces
of silver each.
12 My vineyard is mine alone!
Solomon can keep his silver
and the others can keep
their share of the profits.

He Speaks:

13 You are in the garden
with friends all around.
Let me hear your voice!

She Speaks:

14 Hurry to me, my darling!
Run faster than a deer
to mountains of spices.

[x] **8.2** *who . . . know*: One possible meaning for the difficult Hebrew text. [y] **8.4** *deer and gazelles*: See the note at 2.7.

ISAIAH

ABOUT THIS BOOK

Isaiah spoke for the Lord to the people of Judah during the reigns of four kings of Judah. Over this period of about forty years, the Assyrian Empire was expanding. Nations joined together to fight Assyria, but Assyria finally conquered Israel and most other nearby countries. Thousands of people were led away as prisoners. And although the kingdom of Judah wasn't completely conquered, it had to pay heavy taxes.

The messages in this book can be divided into three parts. The first part (1–39) is especially concerned about the Lord's holiness and his power as king of the whole earth. As a holy king, the Lord was angry about evil in Judah. Government officials were corrupt; violence and injustice were everywhere. The Lord said he was going to have Assyria and Babylonia punish the people of Judah and other nations. But the Lord offered his people hope for the future, if they turned back to him and trusted him to protect their nation.

In the second part (40–55) the Lord spoke to people who had been punished (40.1, 2). They were discouraged, and he offered them hope. But the Lord wanted them to understand that idols have no power, and that he alone is the true God. If the people of Israel turned back to him, then he would rescue them from Babylonia and the other nations where they had been scattered. They would return to their own land, and he would bless them and make them prosperous. The Lord was able to make this tremendous promise to his people because he created and rules the entire earth.

In the third part (56–66) the Lord promises an especially bright future for those who are faithful to him. And in this section, people from all nations are included, not just the people of Judah. These promises are like windows that allow a glimpse into a future time when the Lord will create a new world full of joy and free from suffering:

"I am creating new heavens
and a new earth;
everything of the past
will be forgotten.
Celebrate and be glad forever!
I am creating a Jerusalem,
full of happy people.
I will celebrate with Jerusalem
and all of its people;
there will be no more crying
or sorrow in that city."
(65.17-19)

A QUICK LOOK AT THIS BOOK

- Introduction (1.1-31)
- Messages about Judah and Israel (2.1—5.30)
- Events from Isaiah's Ministry (6.1—9.7)
- More Messages about Judah and Israel (9.8—12.6)
- God Will Punish Other Nations (13.1—23.18)

- Messages of Hope for the Lord's People Who Are Suffering (24.1—27.13)
- The Lord Will Punish His Rebellious People (28.1—31.9)
- The Lord Will Punish Edom and Bless Jerusalem (32.1—35.10)
- Assyria, Babylonia, King Hezekiah, and Isaiah (36.1—39.8)
- The Lord Will Rescue His People (40.1—48.22)
- The Lord's Servant (49.1—53.12)
- The Lord Will Keep All His Promises (54.1—55.13)
- All Nations Will Be Part of God's People (56.1-8)
- Leaders Unfaithful to God Will Be Punished (56.9—59.21)
- The Future Glory of Jerusalem (60.1—62.12)
- God's Wonderful New Creation (63.1—66.24)

---

1 I am Isaiah, the son of Amoz.
And this is the message[a] that I was given about Judah and Jerusalem when Uzziah, Jotham, Ahaz, and Hezekiah were the kings of Judah:[b]

A Guilty Nation

2 The LORD has said,
"Listen, heaven and earth!
The children I raised
have turned against me.
3 Oxen and donkeys know
who owns and feeds them,
but my people won't ever learn."

4 Israel, you are a sinful nation
loaded down with guilt.
You are wicked and corrupt
and have turned from the LORD,
the holy God of Israel.
5 Why be punished more?
Why not give up your sin?
Your head is badly bruised,
and you are weak all over.
6 From your head to your toes
there isn't a healthy spot.
Bruises, cuts, and open sores
go without care
or oil to ease the pain.

A Country in Ruins

7 Your country lies in ruins;
your towns are in ashes.
Foreigners and strangers
take and destroy your land
while you watch.
8 Enemies surround Jerusalem,
alone like a hut in a vineyard[c]
or in a cucumber field.
9 Zion would have disappeared
like Sodom and Gomorrah,[d]
if the LORD All-Powerful
had not let a few
of its people survive.

Justice, Not Sacrifices

10 You are no better
than the leaders and people
of Sodom and Gomorrah!
So listen to the LORD God:
11 "Your sacrifices
mean nothing to me.
I am sick of your offerings
of rams and choice cattle;
I don't like the blood
of bulls or lambs or goats.

12 "Who asked you to bring all this
when you come to worship me?
Stay out of my temple!
13 Your sacrifices are worthless,
and incense is disgusting.
I can't stand the evil you do
on your New Moon Festivals
or on your Sabbaths
and other times of worship.

[a] **1.1** *message*: Or "vision." [b] **1.1** *kings of Judah*: Uzziah (783-742 B.C.); Jotham (742-735 B.C.); Ahaz (735-715 B.C.); Hezekiah (715-687 B.C.). [c] **1.8** *a hut in a vineyard*: When it was almost time for grapes to ripen, farmers would put up a temporary shelter or hut in the field or vineyard and stay there to keep thieves and wild animals away. [d] **1.9** *Sodom and Gomorrah*: Two ancient cities of Palestine that God destroyed because the people were so wicked (see Genesis 19.1-29).

1.1 a 2 K 15.1-7; 2 Ch 26.1-23; **b** 2 K 15.32-38; 2 Ch 27.1-9; **c** 2 K 16.1-20; 2 Ch 28.1-27; **d** 2 K 18.1—20.21; 2 Ch 29.1—32.33. **1.9** Gn 19.24; Ro 9.29. **1.11-14** Am 5.21, 22.

14 I hate your New Moon Festivals
and all others as well.
They are a heavy burden
I am tired of carrying.

15 "No matter how much you pray,
I won't listen.
You are too violent.
16 Wash yourselves clean!
I am disgusted
with your filthy deeds.
Stop doing wrong
17 and learn to live right.
See that justice is done.
Defend widows and orphans
and help those in need."[e]

An Invitation from the LORD

18 I, the LORD, invite you
to come and talk it over.
Your sins are scarlet red,
but they will be whiter
than snow or wool.
19 If you willingly obey me,
the best crops in the land
will be yours.
20 But if you turn against me,
your enemies will kill you.
I, the LORD, have spoken.

The LORD Condemns Jerusalem

21 Jerusalem, you are like
an unfaithful wife.
Once your judges were honest
and your people lived right;
now you are a city
full of murderers.
22 Your silver is fake,
and your wine
is watered down.
23 Your leaders have rejected me
to become friends of crooks;
your rulers are looking
for gifts and bribes.
Widows and orphans
never get a fair trial.

24 I am the LORD All-Powerful,
the mighty ruler of Israel,
and I make you a promise:
You are now my enemy,
and I will show my anger
by taking revenge on you.
25 I will punish you terribly
and burn away everything
that makes you unfit
to worship me.
26 Jerusalem, I will choose
judges and advisors
like those you had before.
Your new name will be
"Justice and Faithfulness."

The LORD Will Save Jerusalem

27 Jerusalem, you will be saved
by showing justice;[f]
Zion's people who turn to me
will be saved
by doing right.
28 But those rebellious sinners
who turn against me, the LORD,
will all disappear.

29 You will be made ashamed
of those groves of trees
where you worshiped idols.
30 You will be like a grove of trees
dying in a drought.
31 Your strongest leaders
will be like dry wood
set on fire by their idols.[g]
No one will be able to help,
as they all go up in flames.

Peace That Lasts Forever

2 This is the message[h] that I was given about Judah and Jerusalem:

2 In the future, the mountain
with the LORD's temple
will be the highest of all.
It will reach above the hills;
every nation will rush to it.
3 Many people will come and say,
"Let's go to the mountain
of the LORD God of Jacob
and worship in his temple."

The LORD will teach us his Law
from Jerusalem,
and we will obey him.

[e] **1.17** *and help those in need*: Or "and punish cruel people." [f] **1.27** *by showing justice*: Or "by my saving power." [g] **1.31** *Your . . . idols*: Or "Your wealth will be like dry wood, set on fire by its owners." [h] **2.1** *message*: See the note at 1.1.

4 He will settle arguments
between nations.
They will pound their swords
and their spears
into rakes and shovels;
they will never make war
or attack one another.
5 People of Israel, let's live
by the light of the LORD.

Following Sinful Customs

6 Our LORD, you have deserted
your people, Israel,
because they follow customs
of nations from the east.
They worship Philistine gods
and are close friends
of foreigners.[i]
7 They have endless treasures
of silver and gold;
they have countless horses
and war chariots.
8 Everywhere in the country
they worship the idols
they have made.
9 And so, all of them
will be ashamed and disgraced.
Don't help them!

A Day of Judgment

10 Every one of you,
go hide among the rocks
and in the ground,
because the LORD is fearsome,
marvelous, and glorious.
11 When the LORD comes,
everyone who is proud
will be made humble,
and the LORD alone
will be honored.
12 The LORD All-Powerful
has chosen a day
when those who are proud
and conceited
will be put down.

13 The tall and towering
cedars of Lebanon
will be destroyed.
So will the oak trees of Bashan,
14 all high mountains and hills,
15 every strong fortress,
16 all the seagoing ships,[j]
and every beautiful boat.
17 When that day comes,
everyone who is proud
will be put down.
Only the LORD will be honored.
18 Idols will be gone for good.

19 You had better hide
in caves and holes—
the LORD will be fearsome,
marvelous, and glorious
when he comes to terrify
people on earth.

20 On that day everyone will throw
to the rats and bats
their idols of silver and gold
they made to worship.
21 The LORD will be fearsome,
marvelous, and glorious
when he comes to terrify
people on earth—
they will hide in caves
and in the hills.

22 Stop trusting the power
of humans.
They are all going to die,
so how can they help?

Judgment on Jerusalem and Judah

3 The mighty LORD All-Powerful
is going to take away
from Jerusalem and Judah
everything you need—
your bread and water,
*2 soldiers and heroes,
judges and prophets,
leaders and army officers,
3 officials and advisors,
fortunetellers and others
who tell the future.
4 He will let children and babies[k]
become your rulers.

[i]**2.6** *because . . . foreigners*: One possible meaning for the difficult Hebrew text. [j]**2.16** *seagoing ships*: The Hebrew text has "ships of Tarshish," which may have been a Phoenician city in Spain. "Ships of Tarshish" probably means large, seagoing ships. [k]**3.4** *babies*: Or "worthless nobodies."

2.4 Jl 3.10; Mic 4.3. **2.10** Rev 6.15; 2 Th 1.9.

5 You will each be cruel
to friends and neighbors.
Young people will insult
their elders;
no one will show respect
to those who deserve it.

6 Some of you will grab hold
of a relative and say,
"You still have a coat.
Be our leader and rule
this pile of ruins."
7 But the answer will be,
"I can't do you any good.
Don't make me your leader.
There's no food or clothing
left in my house."

8 Jerusalem and Judah,
you rebelled against
your glorious LORD—
your words and your actions,
made you stumble and fall.
9 The look on your faces shows
that you are sinful as Sodom,
and you don't try to hide it.
You are in for trouble,
and you have brought it all
on yourselves.

The Wrong Kind of Leaders

10 Tell those who obey God,
"You're very fortunate—
you will be rewarded
for what you have done."
11 Tell those who disobey,
"You're in big trouble—
what you did to others
will come back to you."
12 Though you are God's people,
you are ruled and abused
by women and children.
You are confused by leaders
who guide you
down the wrong path.

13 The LORD is ready to accuse
and judge all nations.
14 He will even judge
you rulers and leaders
of his own nation.
You destroyed his vineyard[l]
and filled your houses
by robbing the poor.
15 The LORD All-Powerful says,
"You have crushed my people
and rubbed in the dirt
the faces of the poor."

The Women of Jerusalem

16 The LORD says:
The women of Jerusalem
are proud and strut around,
winking shamelessly.
They wear anklets that jingle
and call attention
to the way they walk.
17 But I, the LORD, will cover
their heads with sores,
and I will uncover
their private parts.

18-23 When that day comes, I will take
away from those women all the fine jewelry
they wear on their ankles, heads, necks,
ears, arms, noses, fingers, and on their
clothes. I will remove their veils, their belts,
their perfume, their magic charms, their
royal robes, and all their fancy dresses,
hats, and purses.

24 In place of perfume,
there will be a stink;
in place of belts,
there will be ropes;
in place of fancy hairdos,
they will have bald heads.
Instead of expensive clothes,
they will wear sackcloth;
instead of beauty,
they will have ugly scars.
25 The fighting men of Jerusalem
will be killed in battle.
26 The city will mourn
and sit in the dirt,
emptied of its people.

4 When this happens, seven women will grab the same man, and each of them will say, "I'll buy my own food and clothes! Just marry me and take away my disgrace."[m]

[l] **3.14** *his vineyard*: The nation Israel (see 5.1-7). [m] **4.1** *take away my disgrace*: If a woman did not have a husband or children, it was thought that God was punishing her.

The LORD Will Bless His People Who Survive

2 The time is coming when the LORD
will make his land fruitful and glorious
again, and the people of Israel who survive
will take great pride in what the land produces. 3 Everyone who is left alive in
Jerusalem will be called special, 4 after the
LORD sends a fiery judgment to clean the
city and its people of their violent deeds.
5 Then the LORD will cover the whole
city and its meeting places with a thick
cloud each day and with a flaming fire[n]
each night. God's own glory will be like a
huge tent that covers everything. 6 It will
provide shade from the heat of the sun and
a place of shelter and protection from
storms and rain.

A Song about a Vineyard

The LORD said:

5 I will sing a song
about my friend's vineyard
that was on the side
of a fertile hill.
2 My friend dug the ground,
removed the stones,
and planted the best vines.
He built a watchtower
and dug a pit in rocky ground
for pressing the grapes.
He hoped they would be sweet,
but bitter grapes
were all it produced.

3 Listen, people of Jerusalem
and of Judah!
You be the judge of me
and my vineyard.
4 What more could I have done
for my vineyard?
I hoped for sweet grapes,
but bitter grapes
were all that grew.

5 Now I will let you know
what I am going to do.
I will cut down the hedge
and tear down the wall.
My vineyard will be trampled
and left in ruins.
6 It will turn into a desert,
neither pruned nor hoed;
it will be covered
with thorns and briars.
I will command the clouds
not to send rain.

7 I am the LORD All-Powerful!
Israel is the vineyard,
and Judah is the garden
I tended with care.
I had hoped for honesty
and for justice,
but dishonesty
and cries for mercy
were all I found.

Isaiah Condemns Social Injustice

8 You are in for trouble! You take over
house after house and field after field, until
there is no room left for anyone else in all
the land. 9 But the LORD All-Powerful has
made this promise to me:

Those large and beautiful homes
will be left empty, with no one to take
care of them. 10 Ten acres of grapevines will produce only six gallons
of juice, and five bushels of seed will
produce merely a half-bushel of grain.

11 You are in for trouble! You get up
early to start drinking, and you keep it up
late into the night. 12 At your drinking parties you have the music of stringed instruments, tambourines, and flutes. But you
never even think about all the LORD has
done, 13 and so his people know nothing
about him. That's why many of you will be
dragged off to foreign lands. Your leaders
will starve to death, and everyone else will
suffer from thirst.
14 The world of the dead has opened its
mouth wide and is eagerly waiting for the
leaders of Jerusalem and for its noisy
crowds, especially for those who take pride
in that city. 15 Its citizens have been put
down, and its proud people have been
brought to shame. 16 But the holy LORD

[n]**4.5** *thick . . . fire*: This is how the LORD led the people of Israel during the forty years they were in the desert (see Exodus 13.20-22; 40.36-38).

4.5 Ex 13.21, 22; 24.16. **5.1,2** Mt 21.33; Mk 12.1; Lk 20.9. **5.11** Ws 2.7-9.

God All-Powerful is praised, because he has
shown who he is by bringing justice. 17 His
people will be like sheep grazing in their
own pasture, and they will take off what
was left by others.[o]
18 You are in for trouble! The lies you
tell are like ropes by which you drag along
sin and evil. 19 And you say, "Let the holy
God of Israel hurry up and do what he has
promised, so we can see it for ourselves."
20 You are headed for trouble! You say
wrong is right, darkness is light, and bitter
is sweet.
21 You think you are clever and smart.
22 And you are great at drinking and mixing
drinks. But you are in for trouble. 23 You
accept bribes to let the guilty go free, and
you cheat the innocent out of a fair trial.
24 You will go up in flames like straw
and hay! You have rejected the teaching of
the holy LORD God All-Powerful of Israel.
Now your roots will rot, and your blossoms
will turn to dust.
25 You are the LORD's people, but you
made him terribly angry, and he struck you
with his mighty arm. Mountains shook, and
dead bodies covered the streets like
garbage. The LORD is still angry, and he is
ready to strike you again.[p]

Foreign Nations Will Attack

26 The LORD has signaled for the foreign
nations to come and attack you. He has already whistled, and they are coming as fast
as they can. 27 None of them are tired.
They don't sleep or get drowsy, and they
run without stumbling. Their belts don't
come loose; their sandal straps don't break.
28 Their arrows are sharp, and their bows
are ready. The hoofs of their horses are
hard as flint; the wheels of their war chariots turn as fast as a whirlwind.
29 They roar and growl like fierce young
lions as they grab their victims and drag
them off where no one can rescue them.
30 On the day they attack, they will roar like
the ocean. And across the land you will see
nothing but darkness and trouble, because
the light of day will be covered by thick
clouds.

A Vision of the LORD in the Temple

6 In the year that King Uzziah died,[q] I
had a vision of the LORD. He was on
his throne high above, and his robe filled
the temple. 2 Flaming creatures with six
wings each were flying over him. They covered their faces with two of their wings and
their bodies with two more. They used
the other two wings for flying, 3 as they
shouted,

"Holy, holy, holy,
LORD All-Powerful!
The earth is filled
with your glory."

4 As they shouted, the doorposts of the
temple shook, and the temple was filled
with smoke. 5 Then I cried out, "I'm
doomed! Everything I say is sinful, and
so are the words of everyone around
me. Yet I have seen the King, the LORD
All-Powerful."
6 One of the flaming creatures flew over
to me with a burning coal that it had taken
from the altar with a pair of metal tongs.
7 It touched my lips with the hot coal and
said, "This has touched your lips. Your sins
are forgiven, and you are no longer guilty."
8 After this, I heard the LORD ask, "Is
there anyone I can send? Will someone go
for us?"
"I'll go," I answered. "Send me!"
9 Then the LORD told me to go and
speak this message to the people:

"You will listen and listen,
but never understand.
You will look and look,
but never see."

The LORD also said,

10 "Make these people stubborn!
Make them stop up
their ears,

[o]5.17 *and they . . . others*: One possible meaning for the difficult Hebrew text. [p]5.25 *is ready . . . again*: Or "hasn't given up on you yet." [q]6.1 *the year that King Uzziah died*: Probably 742 B.C.

6.1 2 K 15.7; 2 Ch 26.23. **6.3** Rev 4.8. **6.4** Rev 15.8. **6.9,10** Mt 13.14, 15; Mk 4.12; Lk 8.10; Jn 12.40; Ac 28.26, 27.

cover their eyes,
and fail to understand.
Don't let them turn to me
and be healed."
11 Then I asked the LORD, "How long
will this last?"
The LORD answered:
Until their towns are destroyed and
their houses are deserted, until their
fields are empty, 12 and I have sent
them far away, leaving their land in ruins. 13 If only a tenth of the people are
left, even they will be destroyed. But
just as stumps remain after trees have
been cut down,[r] some of my chosen
ones will be left.

Isaiah Offers Hope to King Ahaz

7 Ahaz, the son of Jotham and the
grandson of Uzziah, was king of Judah
when King Rezin of Syria and King Pekah
son of Remaliah of Israel went to attack
Jerusalem. But they were not able to do
what they had planned.[s] 2 When news
reached the royal palace that Syria had
joined forces with Israel, King Ahaz and
everyone in Judah were so terrified that
they shook like trees in a windstorm.
3 Then the LORD said to me:
Take your son Shearjashub[t] and go
see King Ahaz. You will find him on
the road near the cloth makers' shops
at the end of the canal that brings water from the upper pool. 4 Tell Ahaz to
stop worrying. There's no need for him
to be afraid of King Rezin and King
Pekah. They are very angry, but they
are nothing more than a dying fire.
Ahaz doesn't need to fear 5 their evil
threats 6 to invade and defeat Judah
and Jerusalem and to let the son of
Tabeel be king in his place.
7 I, the LORD, promise that this will
never happen. 8-9 Damascus is just the
capital of Syria, and King Rezin rules
only in Damascus. Samaria is just the
capital of Israel, and King Pekah rules
only in Samaria. But in less than sixty-
five years, Israel will be destroyed. And
if Ahaz and his officials don't trust me,
they will be defeated.

A Son Named Immanuel

10 Once again the LORD God spoke to
King Ahaz. This time he said, 11 "Ask me
for proof that my promise will come true.
Ask for something to happen deep in the
world of the dead or high in the heavens
above."
12 "No, LORD," Ahaz answered. "I won't
test you!"
13 Then I said:
Listen, every one of you in the royal
family of David. You have already tried
my patience. Now you are trying God's
patience by refusing to ask for proof.
14 But the LORD will still give you proof.
A virgin[u] is pregnant; she will have
a son and will name him Immanuel.[v]
15-16 Even before the boy is old enough
to know how to choose between right
and wrong, he will eat yogurt and
honey,[w] and the countries of the two
kings you fear will be destroyed. 17 But
the LORD will make more trouble for
your people and your kingdom than
any of you have known since Israel
broke away from Judah. He will even
bring the king of Assyria to attack you.

The Threat of an Invasion

18 When that time comes, the LORD
will whistle, and armies will come
from Egypt like flies and from Assyria

[r]**6.13** *But just . . . down*: One possible meaning for the difficult Hebrew text. [s]**7.1** *went . . . had planned*: Or "attacked Jerusalem, but could not capture it." [t]**7.3** *Shearjashub*: In Hebrew "Shearjashub" means "a few will return." [u]**7.14** *virgin*: Or "young woman." In this context the difficult Hebrew word did not imply a virgin birth. However, in the Greek translation made about 200 B.C. and used by the early Christians, the word *parthenos* had a double meaning. While the translator took it to mean "young woman," Matthew understood it to mean "virgin" and quoted the passage (Matthew 1.23) because it was the appropriate description of Mary, the mother of Jesus.
[v]**7.14** *Immanuel*: In Hebrew "Immanuel" means "God is with us." [w]**7.15,16** *yogurt and honey*: This may refer either to expensive foods eaten in a time of plenty or to a limited diet eaten in times of a food shortage.

7.1 2 K 16.5, 6; 2 Ch 28.5, 6. **7.14** Mt 1.23.

like bees. 19 They will settle everywhere—in the deep valleys and between the rocks, on every bush and all over the pastureland.

20 The Lord will pay the king of Assyria to bring a razor from across the Euphrates River and shave your head and every hair on your body, including your beard.[x]

21 No one will have more than one young cow and two sheep, 22 but those who do will have enough milk to make yogurt. In fact, everyone left in the land will eat yogurt and honey.[y]

23 Vineyards that had a thousand vines and were worth a thousand pieces of silver will turn into thorn patches. 24 You will go there to hunt with your bow and arrows, because the whole country will be covered with thornbushes. 25 The hills where you once planted crops will be overgrown with thorns and thistles. You will be afraid to go there, and your cattle, sheep, and goats will be turned loose on those hills.

A Warning and a Hope

8 The LORD said, "Isaiah, get something to write on. Then write in big clear letters[z] the name, MAHER-SHALAL-HASH-BAZ.[a] 2 I will have Uriah the priest and Zechariah son of Jeberechiah serve as witnesses to this."

3 Sometime later, my wife and I had a son, and the LORD said, "Name him Maher-Shalal-Hash-Baz. 4 Because before he can say 'Mommy' or 'Daddy', the king of Assyria will attack and take everything of value from Damascus and Samaria."

5 The LORD spoke to me again and said:

6 These people have refused the gentle waters of Shiloah[b] and have gladly gone over to the side of King Rezin and King Pekah. 7 Now I will send the king of Assyria against them with his powerful army, which will attack like the mighty Euphrates River overflowing its banks. 8 Enemy soldiers will cover Judah like a flood reaching up to your neck.

But God is with us.[c]
He will spread his wings
and protect our land.[d]
9 All of you foreign nations,
go ahead and prepare for war,
but you will be crushed.
10 Get together and make plans,
but you will fail
because God is with us.

11 The LORD took hold of me with his powerful hand and said:

I'm warning you! Don't act like these people. 12 Don't call something a rebellious plot, just because they do, and don't be afraid of something, just because they are. 13 I am the one you should fear and respect. I am the holy God, the LORD All-Powerful! 14-15 Run to me for protection. I am a rock that will make both Judah and Israel stumble and break their bones. I am a trap that will catch the people of Jerusalem—they will be captured and dragged away.

Isaiah and His Followers

16 My message and my teachings are to be sealed and given to my followers. 17 Meanwhile, I patiently trust the LORD, even though he is no longer pleased with Israel. 18 My children and I are warning signs to Israel from the LORD All-Powerful, who lives on Mount Zion.

19 Someone may say to you, "Go to the fortunetellers who make soft chirping sounds or ask the spirits of the dead. After all, a nation ought to be able to ask its own gods 20 what it should do."

[x]**7.20** *shave . . . head . . . body . . . beard*: This would have been a terrible insult. [y]**7.22** *yogurt and honey*: See the note at 7.15, 16. [z]**8.1** *in big clear letters*: One possible meaning for the difficult Hebrew text. [a]**8.1** *MAHER-SHALAL-HASH-BAZ*: In Hebrew "Maher-Shalal-Hash-Baz" means "suddenly attacked, quickly taken." [b]**8.6** *Shiloah*: The canal that brought water from Gihon Spring to Jerusalem. [c]**8.8** *God is with us*: Here and in verse 10 this translates the Hebrew word "Immanuel" (see 7.14). [d]**8.8** *But . . . land*: One possible meaning for the difficult Hebrew text.

8.12,13 1 P 3.14, 15. **8.14,15** 1 P 2.8. **8.17** He 2.13. **8.18** He 2.13.

None of those who talk like that will live to see the light of day! 21 They will go around in great pain and will become so hungry that they will angrily curse their king and their gods. And when they try to find help in heaven 22 and on earth, they will find only trouble and darkness, terrible trouble and deepest darkness.

9 But those who have suffered will no longer be in pain.[e] The territories of Zebulun and Naphtali in Galilee were once hated. But this land of the Gentiles across the Jordan River and along the Mediterranean Sea will be greatly respected.

War Is Over

2 Those who walked in the dark
have seen a bright light.
And it shines upon everyone
who lives in the land
of darkest shadows.
3 Our LORD, you have made
your nation stronger.[f]
Because of you, its people
are glad and celebrate
like workers at harvest time
or like soldiers dividing up
what they have taken.

4 You have broken the power
of those who abused
and enslaved your people.
You have rescued them
just as you saved your people
from Midian.[g]
5 The boots of marching warriors
and the blood-stained uniforms
have been fed to flames
and eaten by fire.

A Child Has Been Born

6 A child has been born for us.
We have been given a son
who will be our ruler.
His names will be
Wonderful Advisor
and Mighty God,
Eternal Father
and Prince of Peace.
7 His power will never end;
peace will last forever.
He will rule David's kingdom
and make it grow strong.
He will always rule
with honesty and justice.
The LORD All-Powerful
will make certain
that all of this is done.

God Will Punish Israel

8 The Lord had warned the people of Israel, 9 and all of them knew it, including everyone in the capital city of Samaria. But they were proud and stubborn and said,

10 "Houses of brick and sycamore
have fallen to the ground,
but we will build houses
with stones and cedar."

11 The LORD made their enemies[h] attack them. 12 He sent the Arameans from the east and the Philistines from the west, and they swallowed up Israel. But even this did not stop him from being angry, so he kept on punishing them.[i] 13 The people of Israel still did not turn back to the LORD All-Powerful and worship him.

14 In one day he cut off their head and tail, their leaves and branches. 15 Their rulers and leaders were the head, and the lying prophets were the tail. 16 They had led the nation down the wrong path, and the people were confused. 17 The Lord was angry with his people and kept punishing them, because they had turned against him.[j] They were evil and spoke foolishly. That's why he did not have pity on their young people or on their widows and orphans.

18 Evil had spread like a raging forest fire sending thornbushes up in smoke.

[e] **9.1** *will . . . pain*: One possible meaning for the difficult Hebrew text. [f] **9.3** *stronger*: Or "happy" or "larger." [g] **9.4** *rescued . . . from Midian*: The time when Gideon defeated the people of Midian in Jezreel Valley (see Judges 6–8). [h] **9.11** *their enemies*: Hebrew "the enemies of Rezin." [i] **9.12** *so . . . them*: Or "but he hasn't given up on them yet." [j] **9.17** *and kept . . . against him*: Or "but even though they had turned against him, he still had not given up on them."

9.1 Mt 4.15. **9.2** Mt 4.16; Lk 1.79. **9.7** Lk 1.32, 33.

19 The LORD All-Powerful was angry and
used the people as fuel for a fire that
scorched the land. They turned against
each other 20 like wild animals attacking
and eating everyone around them, even
their own relatives.[k] But still they were not
satisfied. 21 The tribes of Ephraim and
Manasseh turned against each other, then
joined forces to attack Judah. But the LORD
was still angry and ready to punish the nation even more.

10 You people are in for trouble! You
have made cruel and unfair laws
2 that let you cheat the poor and needy and
rob widows and orphans. 3 But what will
you do when you are fiercely attacked and
punished by foreigners? Where will you
run for help? Where will you hide your
valuables? 4 How will you escape being captured[l] or killed? The Lord is still angry, and
he isn't through with you yet![m]

The Lord's Purpose and the King of Assyria

5 The Lord says:
I am furious! And I will use the
king of Assyria[n] as a club 6 to beat
down you godless people. I am angry
with you, and I will send him to attack
you. He will take what he wants and
walk on you like mud in the streets.
7 He has even bigger plans in mind,
because he wants to destroy many
nations.
8 The king of Assyria says:
My army commanders are kings!
9 They have already captured[o] the
cities of Calno, Carchemish, Hamath,
Arpad, Samaria, and Damascus.
10-11 The gods of Jerusalem and
Samaria are weaker than the gods of
those powerful nations. And I will destroy Jerusalem, together with its gods
and idols, just as I did Samaria.

12 The Lord will do what he has planned
against Jerusalem and Mount Zion. Then
he will punish the proud and boastful king
of Assyria, 13 who says:
I did these things by my own power
because I am smart and clever. I attacked kings like a wild bull, and I took
the land and the treasures of their nations. 14 I have conquered the whole
world! And it was easier than taking
eggs from an unguarded nest. No one
even flapped a wing or made a peep.
15 King of Assyria, can an ax or a saw
overpower the one who uses it? Can a
wooden pole lift whoever holds it? 16 The
mighty LORD All-Powerful will send a terrible disease to strike down your army, and
you will burn with fever under your royal
robes. 17 The holy God, who is the light of
Israel, will turn into a fire, and in one day
you will go up in flames, just like a thornbush. 18 The Lord will make your beautiful
forests and fertile fields slowly rot. 19 There
will be so few trees that even a young child
can count them.

Only a Few Will Come Back

20 A time is coming when the survivors
from Israel and Judah will completely depend on the holy LORD of Israel, instead of
the nation[p] that defeated them. 21-22 There
were as many people as there are grains of
sand along the seashore, but only a few will
survive to come back to Israel's mighty
God. This is because he has threatened to
destroy their nation, just as they deserve.
23 The LORD All-Powerful has promised that
everyone on this earth[q] will be punished.
24 Now the LORD God All-Powerful says
to his people in Jerusalem:
The Assyrians will beat you with
sticks and abuse you, just as the Egyptians did. But don't be afraid of them.
25 Soon I will stop being angry with

[k] **9.20** *their own relatives*: One possible meaning for the difficult Hebrew text. [l] **10.4** *escape being captured*: One possible meaning for the difficult Hebrew text. [m] **10.4** *and he . . . yet*: Or "but he hasn't given up on you yet!" [n] **10.5** *king of Assyria*: Probably King Sennacherib who invaded Israel in 701 B.C. [o] **10.9** *already captured*: Calno (in northern Syria), Carchemish (on the Euphrates River), Hamath (on the Orontes River), Arpad (near Aleppo in northern Syria), Samaria, and Damascus had already been captured by Assyrian kings (738-717 B.C.).
[p] **10.20** *nation*: That is, Assyria. [q] **10.23** *on this earth*: Or "in this land."

10.5-34 Is 14.24-27; Nh 1.1—3.19; Zep 2.13-15. **10.10,11** 3 Macc 2.18. **10.22,23** Ro 9.27.

you, and I will punish them for their
crimes.[r] 26 I will beat the Assyrians
with a whip, as I did the people of
Midian near the rock at Oreb. And I
will show the same mighty power that
I used when I made a path through
the sea in Egypt. 27 Then they will no
longer rule your nation. All will go well
for you,[s] and your burden will be lifted.
28 Enemy troops have reached the town
of Aiath.[t] They have gone through Migron,
and they stored their supplies at Michmash, 29 before crossing the valley and
spending the night at Geba.[u] The people of
Ramah are terrified; everyone in Gibeah,
the hometown of Saul, has run away.
30 Loud crying can be heard in the towns of
Gallim, Laishah, and sorrowful Anathoth.
31 No one is left in Madmenah or Gebim.
32 Today the enemy will camp at Nob[v] and
shake a threatening fist at Mount Zion in
Jerusalem.

33 But the LORD All-Powerful
will use his fearsome might
to bring down the tallest trees
and chop off every branch.
34 With an ax, the glorious Lord
will destroy every tree
in the forests of Lebanon.[w]

Peace at Last

11 Like a branch that sprouts
from a stump,
someone from David's family[x]
will someday be king.
2 The Spirit of the LORD
will be with him
to give him understanding,
wisdom, and insight.
He will be powerful,
and he will know
and honor the LORD.
3 His greatest joy will be
to obey the LORD.

This king won't judge
by appearances
or listen to rumors.
4 The poor and the needy
will be treated with fairness
and with justice.
His word will be law
everywhere in the land,
and criminals
will be put to death.
5 Honesty and fairness
will be his royal robes.

6 Leopards will lie down
with young goats,
and wolves will rest
with lambs.
Calves and lions
will eat together
and be cared for
by little children.
7 Cows and bears will share
the same pasture;
their young will rest
side by side.
Lions and oxen
will both eat straw.

8 Little children will play
near snake holes.
They will stick their hands
into dens of poisonous snakes
and never be hurt.

9 Nothing harmful will take place
on the LORD's holy mountain.
Just as water fills the sea,
the land will be filled
with people who know
and honor the LORD.

God's People Will Come Back Home

10 The time is coming when one of
David's descendants[y] will be the signal for
the people of all nations to come together.

[r] **10.25** *punish . . . crimes*: Or "completely destroy them." [s] **10.27** *All . . . you*: One possible meaning for the difficult Hebrew text. [t] **10.28** *Aiath*: Probably Ai (Joshua 7.2). [u] **10.29** *Geba*: Only six miles from Jerusalem. [v] **10.32** *Nob*: Perhaps within two miles of Jerusalem. [w] **10.34** *Lebanon*: One possible meaning for the difficult Hebrew text of verse 34. [x] **11.1** *David's family*: Hebrew "Jesse's family." Jesse was the father of King David. [y] **11.10** *David's descendants*: Hebrew "Jesse's descendants" (see the note at 11.1).

11.1 Rev 5.5; 22.16. **11.5** Eph 6.14. **11.6-9** Is 65.25. **11.9** Hb 2.14. **11.10** Ro 15.12.

They will follow his advice, and his own nation will become famous.
11 When that day comes, the Lord will
again reach out his mighty arm and bring
home his people who have survived in Assyria, Egypt, Pathros, Ethiopia,[z] Elam, Shinar, Hamath, and the land along the coast.[a]
12 He will give a signal to the nations, and
he will bring together the refugees from Judah and Israel, who have been scattered all
over the earth. 13 Israel will stop being jealous of Judah, and Judah will no longer be
the enemy of Israel. 14 Instead, they will get
together and attack the Philistines in the west. Then they will defeat the Edomites, the Moabites, and the Ammonites in the east. They will rule those people and take from them whatever they want.
15 The Lord will dry up the arm of the
Red Sea near Egypt,[b] and he will send a scorching wind to divide the Euphrates River into seven streams that anyone can
step across. 16 Then for his people who survive, there will be a good road from Assyria, just as there was a good road for their ancestors when they left Egypt.

A Song of Praise

12 At that time you will say,
"I thank you, LORD!
You were angry with me,
but you stopped being angry
and gave me comfort.
2 I trust you to save me,
LORD God,
and I won't be afraid.
My power and my strength[c]
come from you,
and you have saved me."

3 With great joy, you people
will get water
from the well of victory.
4 At that time you will say,
"Our LORD, we are thankful,
and we worship only you.
We will tell the nations
how glorious you are
and what you have done.
5 Because of your wonderful deeds
we will sing your praises
everywhere on earth."

6 Sing, people of Zion!
Celebrate the greatness
of the holy LORD of Israel.
God is here to help you.

Babylon Will Be Punished

13 This is the message[d] that I was given about Babylon:

2 From high on a barren hill
give a signal, shout the orders,
and point the way
to enter the gates
of Babylon's proud rulers.
3 The LORD has commanded
his very best warriors
and his proud heroes
to show how angry he is.

4 Listen to the noisy crowds
on the mountains!
Kingdoms and nations
are joining forces.
The LORD All-Powerful
is bringing together
an army for battle.
5 From a distant land
the LORD is coming
fierce and furious—
he brings his weapons
to destroy the earth.

6 Cry and weep!
The day is coming
when the mighty LORD
will bring destruction.
*7 All people will be terrified.
Hands will grow limp;
courage will melt away.
8 Everyone will tremble with pain
like a woman giving birth;

[z] **11.11** *Ethiopia*: The Hebrew text has "Cush," which was a region south of Egypt that included parts of the present countries of Ethiopia and Sudan. [a] **11.11** *land along the coast*: Or "islands." [b] **11.15** *arm of the Red Sea near Egypt*: Gulf of Suez. [c] **12.2** *strength*: Or "song." [d] **13.1** *message*: See the note at 1.1.
11.15 Rev 16.12. **12.2** Ex 15.2; Ps 118.14. **13.1—14.23** Is 47.1-15; Jr 50.1—51.64.
13.6 Jl 1.15.

they will stare at each other
with horror on their faces.

There Will Be No Mercy

9 I, the LORD,
will show no mercy or pity
when that time comes.
In my anger I will destroy
the earth and every sinner
who lives on it.
10 Light will disappear
from the stars in the sky;
the dawning sun will turn dark,
and the moon
will lose its glow.

11 I will punish this evil world
and its people
because of their sins.
I will crush the horrible pride
of those who are cruel.
12 Survivors will be harder to find
than the purest gold.
13 I, the LORD All-Powerful,
am terribly angry—
I will make the sky tremble
and the earth shake loose.

14 Everyone will run
to their homelands,
just as hunted deer run,
and sheep scatter
when they have no shepherd.
15 Those who are captured
will be killed by a sword.
16 They will see their children
beaten against rocks,
their homes robbed,
and their wives abused.

17 The Medes[e] can't be bought off
with silver or gold,
and I'm sending them
to attack Babylonia.
18 Their arrows will slaughter
the young men;
no pity will be shown
to babies and children.

The LORD Will Destroy Babylon

19 The city of Babylon
is glorious and powerful,
the pride of the nation.
But it will be like the cities
of Sodom and Gomorrah
after I, the Lord,
destroyed them.
20 No one will live in Babylon.
Even nomads won't camp nearby,
and shepherds won't let
their sheep rest there.
21 Only desert creatures,
hoot owls, and ostriches
will live in its ruins,
and goats[f] will leap about.
22 Hyenas and wolves will howl
from Babylon's fortresses
and beautiful palaces.
Its time is almost up!

The LORD's People Will Come Home

14 The LORD will have mercy on Israel
and will let them be his chosen
people once again. He will bring them back
to their own land, and foreigners will join
them as part of Israel. 2 Other nations will
lead them home, and Israel will make
slaves of them in the land that belongs to
the Lord. Israel will rule over those who
once governed and mistreated them.

Death to the King of Babylonia!

3 The LORD will set you free from your
sorrow, suffering, and slavery. 4 Then you
will make fun of the King of Babylonia by
singing this song:

That cruel monster is done for!
He won't attack us again.[g]
5 The LORD has crushed the power
of those evil kings,
6 who were furious
and never stopped abusing
the people of other nations.

7 Now all the world is at peace;
its people are celebrating
with joyful songs.

[e] **13.17** *Medes*: People of a nation northeast of Babylonia, which became part of the Persian Empire. [f] **13.21** *goats*: Or "demons." [g] **14.4** *He . . . again*: One possible meaning for the difficult Hebrew text.

13.10 Ez 32.7; Mt 24.29; Mk 13.24, 25; Lk 21.25; Rev 6.12, 13; 8.12. **13.19** Gn 19.24.
13.21 Is 34.14; Zep 2.14; Rev 18.2.

8 King of Babylonia,
even the cypress trees
and the cedars of Lebanon
celebrate and say,
"Since you were put down,
no one comes along
to chop us down."

9 The world of the dead
eagerly waits for you.
With great excitement,
the spirits of ancient rulers
hear about your coming.
10 Each one of them will say,
"Now you are just as weak
as any of us!
11 Your pride and your music
have ended here
in the world of the dead.
Worms are your blanket,
maggots are your bed."

12 You, the bright morning star,
have fallen from the sky!
You brought down other nations;
now you are brought down.
13 You said to yourself,
"I'll climb to heaven
and place my throne
above the highest stars.
I'll sit there with the gods
far away in the north.
14 I'll be above the clouds,
just like God Most High."
15 But now you are deep
in the world of the dead.
16 Those who see you will stare
and wonder, "Is this the man
who made the world tremble
and shook up kingdoms?
17 Did he capture every city
and make earth a desert?
Is he the one who refused
to let prisoners go home?"

18 When kings die, they are buried
in glorious tombs.
19 But you will be left unburied,
just another dead body
lying underfoot
like a broken branch.
You will be one of many
killed in battle and gone down
to the deep rocky pit.[h]
20 You won't be buried with kings;
you ruined your country
and murdered your people.

You evil monster!
We hope that your family
will be forgotten forever.
21 We will slaughter your sons
to make them pay for the crimes
of their ancestors.
They won't take over the world
or build cities
anywhere on this earth.

22 The LORD All-Powerful has promised
to attack Babylonia and destroy everyone
there, so that none of them will ever be remembered again. 23 The LORD will sweep
out the people, and the land will become a
swamp for wild animals.

Assyria Will Be Punished

24 The LORD All-Powerful
has made this promise:
Everything I have planned
will happen just as I said.
25 I will wipe out every Assyrian
in my country,
and I will crush those
on my mountains.
I will free my people
from slavery
to the Assyrians.
26 I have planned this
for the whole world,
and my mighty arm
controls every nation.
27 I, the LORD All-Powerful,
have made these plans.
No one can stop me now!

The Philistines Will Be Punished

28 This message came from the LORD
in the year King Ahaz died:[i]

[h] **14.19** *deep rocky pit*: The world of the dead. [i] **14.28** *King Ahaz died*: 715 B.C.
14.12 Rev 8.10; 9.1. **14.13-15** Mt 11.23; Lk 10.15. **14.24-27** Is 10.5-34; Nh 1.1—3.19; Zep 2.13-15. **14.28** 2 K 16.20; 2 Ch 28.27.

29 Philistines, don't be happy
just because the rod
that punished you
is broken.
That rod will become
a poisonous snake, and then
a flying fiery dragon.

30 The poor and needy will find
pastures for their sheep
and will live in safety.
But I will starve some of you,
and others will be killed.

31 Cry and weep in the gates
of your towns,
you Philistines!
Smoke blows in from the north,[j]
and every soldier is ready.
32 If a messenger comes
from a distant nation,
you must say:
"The LORD built Zion.
Even the poorest of his people
will find safety there."

Moab Will Be Punished

15 This is a message
about Moab:
The towns of Ar and Kir
were destroyed in a night.
Moab is left in ruins!
2 Everyone in Dibon has gone up
to the temple[k] and the shrines
to cry and weep.
All of Moab is crying.
Heads and beards are shaved[l]
because of what happened
at Nebo and Medeba.
3 In the towns and at home,
everyone wears sackcloth
and cries loud and long.
4 From Heshbon and Elealeh,
weeping is heard in Jahaz;
Moab's warriors scream
while trembling with fear.

Pity Moab

5 I pity Moab!
Its people are running to Zoar
and to Eglath-Shelishiyah.
They cry on their way up
to the town of Luhith;
on the road to Horonaim
they tell of disasters.
6 The streams of Nimrim
and the grasslands
have dried up.
Every plant is parched.

7 The people of Moab are leaving,
crossing over Willow Creek,
taking everything they own
and have worked for.
8 In the towns of Eglaim
and of Beerelim
and everywhere else in Moab
mournful cries are heard.
9 The streams near Dimon
are flowing with blood.
But the Lord will bring
even worse trouble to Dimon,[m]
because all in Moab who escape
will be attacked by lions.

More Troubles for Moab

16 Send lambs[n] as gifts
to the ruler of the land.
Send them across the desert
from Sela[o] to Mount Zion.
2 The women of Moab
crossing the Arnon River
are like a flock of birds
scattered from their nests.
3 Moab's messengers say
to the people of Judah,
"Be kind and help us!
Shade us from the heat
of the noonday sun.
Hide our refugees!
Don't turn them away.
4 Let our people live

[j] **14.31** *north*: The Assyrian and Babylonian attacks came from the north. [k] **15.2** *Everyone . . . temple*: One possible meaning for the difficult Hebrew text. [l] **15.2** *Heads . . . shaved*: As a sign of sorrow and mourning. [m] **15.9** *Dimon . . . Dimon*: The Standard Hebrew Text; the Dead Sea Scrolls and one ancient translation have *Dibon . . . Dibon*. [n] **16.1** *lambs*: The main product of Moab. [o] **16.1** *Sela*: A town in Edom.

14.29-31 Jr 47.1-7; Ez 25.15-17; Jl 3.4-8; Am 1.6-8; Zep 2.4-7; Zec 9.5-7.
15.1—16.14 Is 25.10-12; Jr 48.1-47; Ez 25.8-11; Am 2.1-3; Zep 2.8-11.

in your country
and find safety here."

Moab, your cruel enemies
will disappear;
they will no longer attack
and destroy your land.
5 Then a kingdom of love
will be set up,
and someone from David's family
will rule with fairness.
He will do what is right
and quickly bring justice.

Moab's Pride Is Destroyed

6 We have heard of Moab's pride.
Its people strut and boast,
but without reason.
7 Tell everyone in Moab
to mourn for their nation.
Tell them to cry and weep
for those fancy raisins[p]
of Kir-Hareseth.

8 Vineyards near Heshbon
and Sibmah
have turned brown.
The rulers of nations
used to get drunk
on wine from those vineyards[q]
that spread to Jazer,
then across the desert
and beyond the sea.

9 Now I mourn like Jazer
for the vineyards
of Sibmah.
I shed tears for Heshbon
and for Elealeh.
There will be no more
harvest celebrations
10 or joyful and happy times,
while bringing in the crops.
Singing and shouting are gone
from the vineyards.
There are no joyful shouts
where grapes were pressed.
God has silenced them all.

11 Deep in my heart I hurt
for Moab and Kir-Heres.
12 It's useless for Moab's people
to wear themselves out
by going to their altars
to worship and pray.

13 The LORD has already said all of this
about Moab. 14 Now he says, "The contract
of a hired worker is good for three years,
but Moab's glory and greatness won't last
any longer than that. Only a few of its
people will survive, and they will be left
helpless."

Damascus Will Be Punished

17 This is a message
about Damascus:
Damascus is doomed!
It will end up in ruins.
2 The villages around Aroer[r]
will be deserted,
with only sheep living there
and no one to bother them.
3 Israel[s] will lose its fortresses.
The kingdom of Damascus
will be destroyed;
its survivors will suffer
the same fate as Israel.
The LORD All-Powerful
has promised this.

Sin and Suffering

4 When that time comes,
the glorious nation of Israel
will be brought down;
its prosperous people
will be skin and bones.
5 Israel will be like wheat fields
in Rephaim Valley
picked clean of grain.
6 It will be like an olive tree
beaten with a stick,

[p] **16.7** *fancy raisins*: The Hebrew text has "raisin-cakes," which could mean either the rich produce or the prosperous farmers. [q] **16.8** *The rulers . . . vineyards*: Or "The rulers of nations have destroyed those vineyards." [r] **17.2** *Aroer*: Either a city near Damascus with the same name as the Moabite city or the Moabite city itself, here used as an example of what will happen to Damascus. [s] **17.3** *Israel*: The Hebrew text has "Ephraim," another name for the northern kingdom.

17.1-3 Jr 49.23-27; Am 1.3-5; Zec 9.1.

leaving two or three olives
or maybe four or five
on the highest
or most fruitful branches.
The LORD God of Israel
has promised this.

7 At that time the people will turn and trust their Creator, the holy God of Israel. 8 They have built altars and places for burning incense to their goddess Asherah, and they have set up sacred poles[t] for her. But they will stop worshiping at these places.

9 Israel captured powerful cities and chased out the people who lived there. But these cities will lie in ruins, covered over with weeds and underbrush.[u]

10 Israel, you have forgotten
the God who saves you,
the one who is the mighty rock[v]
where you find protection.
You plant the finest flowers
to honor a foreign god.
11 The plants may sprout
and blossom
that very same morning,
but it will do you no good,
because you will suffer
endless agony.

God Defends His People

12 The nations are a noisy,
thunderous sea.
13 But even if they roar
like a fearsome flood,
God will give the command
to turn them back.
They will be like dust,
or like a tumbleweed
blowing across the hills
in a windstorm.
14 In the evening
their attack is fierce,
but by morning
they are destroyed.
This is what happens to those
who raid and rob us.

Ethiopia Will Be Punished

18 Downstream from Ethiopia[w]
lies the country of Egypt,
swarming with insects.[x]
2 Egypt sends messengers
up the Nile River
on ships made of reeds.[y]
Send them fast to Ethiopia,
whose people are tall
and have smooth skin.
Their land is divided by rivers;
they are strong and brutal,
feared all over the world.[z]

3 Everyone on this earth,
listen with care!
A signal will be given
on the mountains,
and you will hear a trumpet.
4 The LORD said to me,
"I will calmly look down
from my home above—
as calmly as the sun at noon
or clouds in the heat
of harvest season."

5 Before the blossoms
can turn into grapes,
God will cut off the sprouts
and hack off the branches.
6 Ethiopians will be food
for mountain buzzards
during the summer
and for wild animals
during the winter.

7 Those Ethiopians are tall and their skin is smooth. They are feared all over the world, because they are strong and brutal. But at that time they will come from their

[t] **17.8** *sacred poles*: Or "trees," used as symbols of Asherah, the goddess of fertility.
[u] **17.9** *covered . . . underbrush*: Hebrew; one ancient translation "like the cities of the Hivites and the Amorites." [v] **17.10** *mighty rock*: The Hebrew text has "rock," which is sometimes used in poetry to compare the Lord to a mountain where his people can run for protection from their enemies.
[w] **18.1** *Ethiopia*: See the note at 11.11. [x] **18.1** *insects*: Or "sailing ships." [y] **18.2** *reeds*: Ancient Egypt was famous for the papyrus reeds that grew in the Nile Delta. [z] **18.2** *world*: One possible meaning for the difficult Hebrew text of verse 2.
18.1-7 Zep 2.12.

land divided by rivers, and they will bring gifts to the LORD All-Powerful, who is worshiped on Mount Zion.

Egypt Will Be Punished

19 This is a message
about Egypt:
The LORD comes to Egypt,
riding swiftly on a cloud.
The people are weak from fear.
Their idols tremble
as he approaches and says,
2 "I will punish Egypt
with civil war—
neighbors, cities, and kingdoms
will fight each other.

3 "Egypt will be discouraged
when I confuse their plans.
They will try to get advice
from their idols,
from the spirits of the dead,
and from fortunetellers.
4 I will put the Egyptians
under the power of a cruel,
heartless king.
I, the LORD All-Powerful,
have promised this."

Trouble along the Nile

5 The Nile River will dry up
and become parched land.
6 Its streams will stink,
Egypt will have no water,
and the reeds and tall grass
will dry up.
7 Fields along the Nile
will be completely barren;
every plant will disappear.

8 Those who fish in the Nile
will be discouraged
and mourn.
9 None of the cloth makers[a]
will know what to do,
and they will turn pale.[b]
10 Weavers will be confused;
paid workers will cry and mourn.

Egypt's Helpless Leaders

11 The king's officials in Zoan[c]
are foolish themselves
and give stupid advice.
How can they say to him,
"We are very wise,
and our families go back
to kings of long ago?"
12 Where are those wise men now?
If they can, let them say
what the LORD All-Powerful
intends for Egypt.

13 The royal officials in Zoan
and in Memphis
are foolish and deceived.
The leaders in every state
have given bad advice
to the nation.
14 The LORD has confused Egypt;
its leaders have made it stagger
and vomit like a drunkard.
15 No one in Egypt can do a thing,
no matter who they are.

16 When the LORD All-Powerful punishes Egypt with his mighty arm, the Egyptians will become terribly weak and will tremble with fear. 17 They will be so terrified of Judah that they will be frightened by the very mention of its name. This will happen because of what the LORD All-Powerful is planning against Egypt.

The LORD Will Bless Egypt, Assyria, and Israel

18 The time is coming when Hebrew will be spoken in five Egyptian cities, and their people will become followers of the LORD. One of these cities will be called City of the Sun.[d]

19 In the heart of Egypt an altar will be set up for the LORD; at its border a shrine

[a] **19.9** *cloth makers*: Cloth was made from several kinds of plants that grew in the fields along the Nile. [b] **19.9** *turn pale*: One possible meaning for the difficult Hebrew text. [c] **19.11** *Zoan*: The city of Tanis in the Nile delta. [d] **19.18** *City of the Sun*: Some manuscripts of the Standard Hebrew Text, the Dead Sea Scrolls, and one ancient translation; most manuscripts of the Standard Hebrew Text have "City of Destruction." This probably refers to Heliopolis which means "City of the Sun" (see Jeremiah 43.13).
19.1-25 Jr 46.2-26; Ez 29.1—32.32.

will be built to honor him. 20 These
will remind the Egyptians that the LORD
All-Powerful is with them. And when they
are in trouble and ask for help, he will send
someone to rescue them from their enemies. 21 The LORD will show the Egyptians
who he is, and they will know and worship
the LORD. They will bring him sacrifices
and offerings, and they will keep their
promises to him. 22 After the LORD has
punished Egypt, the people will turn to
him. Then he will answer their prayers,
and the Egyptians will be healed.

23 At that time a good road will run from
Egypt to Assyria. The Egyptians and the Assyrians will travel back and forth from
Egypt to Assyria, and they will worship together. 24 Israel will join with these two
countries. They will be a blessing to everyone on earth, 25 then the LORD All-Powerful
will bless them by saying,

"The Egyptians are my people.
I created the Assyrians
and chose the Israelites."

Isaiah Acts Out the Defeat of Egypt and Ethiopia

20 King Sargon of Assyria gave orders
for his army commander to capture
the city of Ashdod.[e] 2 About this same time
the LORD had told me, "Isaiah, take off
everything, including your sandals!" I did
this and went around naked and barefoot
3 for three years.

Then the LORD said:

What Isaiah has done is a warning
to Egypt and Ethiopia.[f] 4 Everyone in
these two countries will be led away
naked and barefoot by the king of Assyria. Young or old, they will be taken
prisoner, and Egypt will be disgraced.
5 They will be confused and frustrated,
because they depended on Ethiopia
and bragged about Egypt. 6 When this
happens, the people who live along the
coast[g] will say, "Look what happened
to them! We ran to them for safety,
hoping they would protect us from the
king of Assyria. But now, there is no escape for us."

The Fall of Babylonia[h]

21 This is a message about
a desert beside the sea:[i]
Enemies from a hostile nation
attack like a whirlwind
from the Southern Desert.
2 What a horrible vision
was shown to me—
a vision of betrayal
and destruction.
Tell Elam and Media[j]
to surround and attack
the Babylonians.
The LORD has sworn to end
the suffering they caused.

3 I'm in terrible pain
like a woman giving birth.
I'm shocked and hurt so much
that I can't hear or see.
4 My head spins; I'm horrified!
Early evening, my favorite time,
has become a nightmare.

5 In Babylon the high officials
were having a feast.
They were eating and drinking,
when someone shouted,
"Officers, take your places!
Grab your shields."

6 The LORD said to me,
"Send guards to find out
what's going on.
7 When they see cavalry troops
and columns of soldiers

[e]**20.1** *Ashdod*: King Sargon II of Assyria captured this Philistine city in 711 B.C. [f]**20.3** *Ethiopia*: See the note at 11.11. [g]**20.6** *people . . . coast*: Probably the Philistines. [h]**21.1** *Babylonia*: King Cyrus and his army of Medes and Persians captured the city of Babylon in 539 B.C. [i]**21.1** *This . . . sea*: One possible meaning for the difficult Hebrew text. The prophet may be speaking of Babylonia as a desert, because of the terrible punishment God will bring on it. The southern part of Babylonia on the Persian Gulf was sometimes called "the land beside the sea." [j]**21.2** *Elam and Media*: People from the Iranian highlands; the capital of Elam was Susa, in the hill country east of Babylon.

on donkeys and camels,
tell them to be ready!"

8 Then a guard[k] said,
"I have stood day and night
on this watchtower, Lord.
9 Now I see column after column
of cavalry troops."

Right away someone shouted,
"Babylon has fallen!
Every idol in the city
lies broken on the ground."

10 Then I said, "My people,
you have suffered terribly,
but I have a message for you
from the LORD All-Powerful,
the God of Israel."

How Much Longer?

11 This is a message about Dumah:
From the country of Seir,[l]
someone shouts to me,
"Guard, how much longer
before daylight?"

12 From my guard post, I answered,
"Morning will soon be here,
but night will return.
If you want to know more,
come back later."

13 This is a message for Arabs
who live in the barren desert
in the region of Dedan:[m]
You must order your caravans
14 to bring water for those
who are thirsty.
You people of Tema[n]
must bring food
for the hungry refugees.
15 They are worn out and weary
from being chased by enemies
with swords and arrows.

16 The Lord said to me:
A year from now the glory of the
people of Kedar[o] will all come to an
end, just as a worker's contract ends
after a year. 17 Only a few of their warriors will be left with bows and arrows.
This is a promise that I, the LORD God
of Israel, have made.

Trouble in Vision Valley

22 This is a message
about Vision Valley:[p]
Why are you celebrating
on the flat roofs[q]
of your houses?
2 Your city is filled
with noisy shouts.
Those who lie drunk
in your streets
were not killed in battle.
3 Your leaders ran away,
but they were captured
without a fight.
No matter how far they ran,
they were found and caught.[r]

4 Then I said, "Leave me alone!
Let me cry bitter tears.
My people have been destroyed,
so don't try to comfort me."

5 The LORD All-Powerful
had chosen a time
for noisy shouts and confusion
to fill Vision Valley,
and for everyone to beg
the mountains for help.[s]
6 The people of Elam and Kir[t]

[k]**21.8** *guard*: The Dead Sea Scrolls and one ancient translation; the Standard Hebrew Text has "lion." [l]**21.11** *Dumah . . . Seir*: Dumah was an oasis in the Arabian desert. One ancient translation has "Edom," which may be what is meant. Seir is a mountainous region of Edom southwest of the Dead Sea. [m]**21.13** *Dedan*: A region in northwest Arabia. [n]**21.14** *Tema*: A region in north Arabia. [o]**21.16** *Kedar*: A region in the Arabian desert. [p]**22.1** *Vision Valley*: The exact location is not known. In Hebrew the name sounds something like "Hinnom Valley," where the people of Jerusalem sometimes offered human sacrifices to the gods of Canaan. [q]**22.1** *flat roofs*: In Palestine the houses usually had a flat roof. Stairs on the outside led up to the roof, which was made of beams and boards covered with packed earth. [r]**22.3** *No matter . . . caught*: One possible meaning for the difficult Hebrew text. [s]**22.5** *and for . . . help*: One possible meaning for the difficult Hebrew text. [t]**22.6** *Elam and Kir*: Regions in the Iranian highlands.
21.9 Rev 14.8; 18.2.

attacked with chariots[u]
and carried shields.
7 Your most beautiful valleys
were covered with chariots;
your cities were surrounded
by cavalry troops.
8 Judah was left defenseless.

At that time you trusted in the weapons
you had stored in Forest Palace.[v] 9 You saw
the holes in the outer wall of Jerusalem,
and you brought water from the lower
pool.[w] 10 You counted the houses in Jerusalem and tore down some of them, so you
could get stones to repair the city wall.
11 Then you built a large tank between the
walls[x] to store the water. But you refused to
trust the God who planned this long ago
and made it happen.

A Time To Weep

12 When all of this happened,
the LORD All-Powerful told you
to weep and mourn,
to shave your heads,
and wear sackcloth.
13 But instead, you celebrated
by feasting on beef and lamb
and by drinking wine,
because you said,
"Let's eat and drink!
Tomorrow we may die."

14 The LORD All-Powerful
has spoken to me
this solemn promise:
"I won't forgive them for this,
not as long as they live."

Selfish Officials Are Doomed

15 The LORD All-Powerful is sending you
with this message for Shebna, the prime
minister:

16 Shebna, what gives you the right
to have a tomb carved out of rock in
this burial place of royalty? None of
your relatives are buried here. 17 You
may be powerful, but the LORD is about
to snatch you up and throw you away.
18 He will roll you into a ball and throw
you into a wide open country, where
you will die and your chariots will be
destroyed. You're a disgrace to those
you serve.

19 The LORD is going to take away
your job! 20-21 He will give your official
robes and your authority to his servant
Eliakim son of Hilkiah.

Eliakim will be like a father to the
people of Jerusalem and to the royal
family of Judah. 22 The LORD will put
him in charge of the key that belongs
to King David's family. No one will be
able to unlock what he locks, and no
one will be able to lock what he un-
locks. 23 The LORD will make him as
firm in his position as a tent peg hammered in the ground, and Eliakim will
bring honor to his family.

24 His children and relatives will be
supported by him, like pans hanging
from a peg on the wall. 25 That peg is
fastened firmly now, but someday it
will be shaken loose and fall down.
Then everything that was hanging on
it will be destroyed. This is what the
LORD All-Powerful has promised.

The City of Tyre Will Be Punished

23 This is a message
from distant islands
about the city of Tyre:[y]
Cry, you seagoing ships![z]
Tyre and its houses
lie in ruins.[a]

[u]22.6 *chariots*: One possible meaning for the difficult Hebrew text. [v]22.8 *Forest Palace*: Built by Solomon (1 Kings 7.2) and used as a place for storing weapons. [w]22.9 *the lower pool*: Mentioned only here; probably in the southern part of the Central Valley (Tyropoean Valley) of Jerusalem. [x]22.11 *between the walls*: Some cities had two walls with a space between them. If the enemy broke through the outer wall, the city was still protected by the inner wall. The houses that were torn down to repair the outer wall were probably squatters' huts that had been built between the two walls. [y]23.1 *Tyre*: A fortress city built on an island in the Mediterranean Sea off the coast of what is now Lebanon. [z]23.1 *seagoing ships*: See the note at 2.16.
[a]23.1 *Tyre . . . ruins*: One possible meaning for the difficult Hebrew text.
22.13 1 Co 15.32. **22.22** Rev 3.7. **23.1-18** Ez 26.1—28.19; Jl 3.4-8; Am 1.9, 10; Zec 9.1-4; Mt 11.21, 22; Lk 10.13, 14.

2 Mourn in silence,
you shop owners of Sidon,[b]
you people on the coast.
Your sailors crossed oceans,
making your city rich.
3 Your merchants sailed the seas,
making you wealthy by trading
with nation after nation.
They brought back grain
that grew along the Nile.[c]
4 Sidon, you are a mighty fortress
built along the sea.
But you will be disgraced
like a married woman
who never had children.[d]

5 When Egypt hears about Tyre,
it will tremble.
6 All of you along the coast
had better cry and sail
far across the ocean.[e]
7 Can this be the happy city
that has stood for centuries?
Its people have spread
to distant lands;
8 its merchants were kings
honored all over the world.
Who planned to destroy Tyre?
9 The LORD All-Powerful planned it
to bring shame and disgrace
to those who are honored
by everyone on earth.
10 People of Tyre,[f]
your harbor is destroyed!
You will have to become farmers
just like the Egyptians.[g]

Tyre Will Be Forgotten

11 The LORD's hand has reached
across the sea,
upsetting the nations.
He has given a command
to destroy fortresses
in the land of Canaan.
12 The LORD has said
to the people of Sidon,
"Your celebrating is over—
you are crushed.
Even if you escape to Cyprus,
you won't find peace."

13 Look what the Assyrians have done to Babylonia! They have attacked, destroying every palace in the land. Now wild animals live among the ruins.[h] 14 Not a fortress will be left standing, so tell all the seagoing ships[i] to mourn.

15 The city of Tyre will be forgotten for seventy years, which is the lifetime of a king. Then Tyre will be like that evil woman in the song:

16 You're gone and forgotten,
you evil woman!
So strut through the town,
singing and playing
your favorite tune
to be remembered again.

17 At the end of those seventy years, the LORD will let Tyre get back into business. The city will be like a woman who sells her body to everyone of every nation on earth,
18 but none of what is earned will be kept in the city. That money will belong to the LORD, and it will be used to buy more than enough food and good clothes for those who worship the LORD.

The Earth Will Be Punished

24 The LORD is going to twist the earth out of shape and turn it into a desert. Everyone will be scattered,
2 including ordinary people and priests, slaves and slave owners, buyers and sellers, lenders and borrowers, the rich and the poor.
3 The earth will be stripped bare and left that way. This is what the LORD has promised.

[b]**23.2** *Sidon*: A coastal city just north of Tyre. [c]**23.3** *along the Nile*: The Hebrew text has "grain of Shihor, the harvest of the Nile," but Shihor is probably a name for a region near the lower part of the Nile. [d]**23.4** *children*: One possible meaning for the difficult Hebrew text. [e]**23.6** *far across the ocean*: The Hebrew text has "to Tarshish," probably meaning a long distance.
[f]**23.10** *People of Tyre*: The Hebrew text has "the people of Tarshish," which stands for the colonies of Tyre. [g]**23.10** *Egyptians*: One possible meaning for the difficult Hebrew text of verse 10.
[h]**23.13** *ruins*: One possible meaning for the difficult Hebrew text of verse 13. [i]**23.14** *seagoing ships*: See the note at 2.16.

4 The earth wilts away;
its mighty leaders melt
to nothing.[j]
5 The earth is polluted
because its people
disobeyed the laws of God,
breaking their agreement
that was to last forever.

6 The earth is under a curse;
its people are dying out
because of their sins.
7 Grapevines have dried up;
wine is almost gone—
mournful sounds are heard
instead of joyful shouts.

8 No one plays tambourines
or stringed instruments;
all noisy celebrating
has come to an end.
9 They no longer sing
as they drink their wine,
and it tastes sour.

10 Towns are crushed and in chaos;
houses are locked tight.
11 Happy times have disappeared
from the earth,
and people shout in the streets,
"We're out of wine!"
12 Cities are destroyed;
their gates are torn down.
13 Nations will be stripped bare,
like olive trees or vineyards
after the harvest season.

Praise the God of Justice

14 People in the west shout;
they joyfully praise
the majesty of the LORD.
15 And so, everyone in the east
and those on the islands
should praise the LORD,
the God of Israel.
16 From all over the world
songs of praise are heard
for the God of justice.[k]
But I feel awful,
terribly miserable.
Can anyone be trusted?
So many are treacherous!

There's No Escape

17 Terror, traps, and pits
are waiting for everyone.
18 If you are terrified and run,
you will fall into a pit;
if you crawl out of the pit,
you will get caught in a trap.

The sky has split apart
like a window thrown open.
The foundations of the earth
have been shaken;
19 the earth is shattered,
ripped to pieces.
20 It staggers and shakes
like a drunkard
or a hut in a windstorm.
It is burdened down with sin;
the earth will fall,
never again to get up.

21 On that day the LORD
will punish the powers
in the heavens[l]
and the kings of the earth.
22 He will put them in a pit
and keep them prisoner.
Then later on,
he will punish them.
23 The moon and sun will both
be embarrassed and ashamed.
The LORD All-Powerful will rule
on Mount Zion in Jerusalem,
where he will show its rulers
his wonderful glory.

A Prayer of Thanks to God

25 You, LORD, are my God!
I will praise you
for doing the wonderful things
you had planned and promised
since ancient times.
2 You have destroyed the fortress

[j]**24.4** *its . . . to nothing*: One possible meaning for the difficult Hebrew text. [k]**24.16** *God of justice*: Or "people who do right." [l]**24.21** *the powers in the heavens*: In ancient times the stars were thought of as powerful spiritual beings, and sometimes they stood for pagan gods.

of our enemies,
leaving their city in ruins.
Nothing in that foreign city
will ever be rebuilt.
3 Now strong and cruel nations
will fear and honor you.

4 You have been a place of safety
for the poor and needy
in times of trouble.
Brutal enemies pounded us
like a heavy rain
or the heat of the sun at noon,
but you were our shelter.
5 Those wild foreigners struck
like scorching desert heat.
But you were like a cloud,
protecting us from the sun.
You kept our enemies from singing
songs of victory.

The LORD Has Saved Us

6 On this mountain
the LORD All-Powerful
will prepare for all nations
a feast of the finest foods.
Choice wines and the best meats
will be served.
7 Here the LORD will strip away
the burial clothes
that cover the nations.
8 The LORD All-Powerful
will destroy the power of death
and wipe away all tears.
No longer will his people
be insulted everywhere.
The LORD has spoken!

9 At that time, people will say,
"The LORD has saved us!
Let's celebrate.
We waited and hoped—
now our God is here."
10 The powerful arm of the LORD
will protect this mountain.

The Moabites will be put down
and trampled on like straw
in a pit of manure.
11 They will struggle to get out,
but God will humiliate them
no matter how hard they try.[m]
12 The walls of their fortresses
will be knocked down
and scattered in the dirt.

A Song of Victory

26 The time is coming
when the people of Judah
will sing this song:
"Our city[n] is protected.
The LORD is our fortress,
and he gives us victory.
2 Open the city gates
for a law-abiding nation
that is faithful to God.
3 The LORD gives perfect peace
to those whose faith is firm.
4 So always trust the LORD
because he is forever
our mighty rock.[o]
5 God has put down our enemies
in their mountain city[p]
and rubbed it in the dirt.
6 Now the poor and abused
stomp all over that city."

The LORD Can Be Trusted

7 Our LORD, you always do right,
and you make the path smooth
for those who obey you.
8 You are the one we trust
to bring about justice;
above all else we want
your name to be honored.
9 Throughout the night,
my heart searches for you,
because your decisions
show everyone on this earth
how to live right.

10 Even when the wicked
are treated with mercy
in this land of justice,
they do wrong and are blind
to your glory, our LORD.

[m]**25.11** *no matter . . . try*: One possible meaning for the difficult Hebrew text. [n]**26.1** *city*: Probably Jerusalem. [o]**26.4** *mighty rock*: See the note at 17.10. [p]**26.5** *our enemies . . . city*: One possible meaning for the difficult Hebrew text.

25.8 a 1 Co 15.54; **b** Rev 7.17; 21.4. **25.10-12** Is 15.1—16.14; Jr 48.1-47; Ez 25.8-11; Am 2.1-3; Zep 2.8-11.

11 Your hand is raised and ready
to punish them,
but they don't see it.
Put them to shame!
Show how much you care for us
and throw them into the fire
intended for your enemies.

12 You will give us peace, LORD,
because everything we have done
was by your power.
13 Others have ruled over us
besides you, our LORD God,
but we obey only you.
14 Those enemies are now dead
and can never live again.
You have punished them—
they are destroyed,
completely forgotten.
15 Our nation has grown
because of you, our LORD.
We have more land than before,
and you are honored.

The LORD Gives Life to the Dead

16 When you punished our people,
they turned and prayed
to you, our LORD.[q]
17 Because of what you did to us,
we suffered like a woman
about to give birth.
18 But instead of having a child,
our terrible pain
produced only wind.
We have won no victories,
and we have no descendants
to take over the earth.

19 Your people will rise to life!
Tell them to leave their graves
and celebrate with shouts.
You refresh the earth
like morning dew;
you give life to the dead.

20 Go inside and lock the doors,
my people.
Hide there for a little while,
until the LORD
is no longer angry.

The Earth and the Sea Will Be Punished

21 The LORD will come out
to punish everyone on earth
for their sins.
And when he does,
those who did violent crimes
will be known and punished.

27 On that day, Leviathan,[r]
the sea monster,
will squirm and try to escape,
but the LORD will kill him
with a cruel, sharp sword.

Protection and Forgiveness

The LORD said:
2 At that time you must sing
about a fruitful[s] vineyard.
3 I, the LORD, will protect it
and always keep it watered.
I will guard it day and night
to keep it from harm.
4 I am no longer angry.
But if it produces thorns,
I will go to war against it
and burn it to the ground.
5 Yet if the vineyard depends
on me for protection,
it will become my friend
and be at peace with me.

6 Someday Israel will take root
like a vine.
It will blossom and bear fruit
that covers the earth.

7 I, the LORD, didn't punish and kill
the people of Israel
as fiercely as I punished
and killed their enemies.
8 I carefully measured out
Israel's punishment[t]
and sent the scorching heat
to chase them far away.

[q]**26.16** *LORD*: One possible meaning for the difficult Hebrew text of verse 16. [r]**27.1** *Leviathan*: God's victory over this monster sometimes stands for God's power over all creation and sometimes for his defeat of his enemies, especially Egypt. [s]**27.2** *fruitful*: Some Hebrew manuscripts have "lovely." [t]**27.8** *I . . . punishment*: One possible meaning for the difficult Hebrew text.
26.11 He 10.27. **27.1** Job 41.1; Ps 74.14; 104.26.

9 There's only one way
that Israel's sin and guilt
can be completely forgiven:
They must crush the stones
of every pagan altar
and place of worship.

The LORD Will Bring His People Together

10 Fortress cities are left
like a desert
where no one lives.
Cattle walk through the ruins,
stripping the trees bare.
11 When broken branches
fall to the ground,
women pick them up
to feed the fire.
But these people are so stupid
that the God who created them
will show them no mercy.

12 The time is coming when the LORD
will shake the land between the Euphrates
River and the border of Egypt, and one by
one he will bring all of his people together.
13 A loud trumpet will be heard. Then the
people of Israel who were dragged away to
Assyria and Egypt will return to worship
the LORD on his holy mountain in Jerusalem.

Samaria Will Be Punished

28 The city of Samaria
above a fertile valley
is in for trouble!
Its leaders are drunkards,
who stuff themselves
with food and wine.
But they will be like flowers
that dry up and wilt.
2 Only the Lord is strong
and powerful!
His mighty hand
will strike them down
with the force of a hailstorm
or a mighty whirlwind
or an overwhelming flood.
3 Every drunkard in Ephraim[u]
takes pride in Samaria,
but it will be crushed.
4 Samaria above a fertile valley
will quickly lose its glory.
It will be gobbled down
like the first ripe fig
at harvest season.

5 When this time comes,
the LORD All-Powerful
will be a glorious crown
for his people who survive.
6 He will see that justice rules
and that his people are able
to defend their cities.

Corrupt Leaders Will Be Punished

7 Priests and prophets stumble
because they are drunk.
Their minds are too confused
to receive God's messages
or give honest decisions.
8 Their tables are covered,
completely covered,
with their stinking vomit.

9 You drunken leaders
are like babies!
How can you possibly understand
or teach the LORD's message?
10 You don't even listen—
all you hear is senseless sound
after senseless sound.[v]

11 So, the Lord will speak
to his people
in strange sounds
and foreign languages.[w]
12 He promised you
perfect peace and rest,
but you refused to listen.
13 Now his message to you
will be senseless sound
after senseless sound.[x]
Then you will fall backwards,
injured and trapped.

[u] **28.3** *Ephraim*: The northern kingdom of Israel; Samaria was its capital. [v] **28.10** *sound*: One possible meaning for the difficult Hebrew text of verses 9, 10. [w] **28.11** *in . . . foreign languages*: This probably refers to the language of the Assyrians. [x] **28.13** *Now . . . sound*: One possible meaning for the difficult Hebrew text.
28.11,12 1 Co 14.21.

False Security Is Fatal

14 You rulers of Jerusalem
do nothing but sneer;
now you must listen
to what the LORD says.
15 Do you think you have
an agreement with death
and the world of the dead?
Why do you trust in your lies
to keep you safe from danger
and the mighty flood?

16 And so the LORD says,
"I'm laying a firm foundation
for the city of Zion.
It's a valuable cornerstone
proven to be trustworthy;
no one who trusts it
will ever be disappointed.
17 Justice and fairness
will be the measuring lines
that help me build."

Hailstones and floods
will destroy and wash away
your shelter of lies.
18 Your agreement with death
and the world of the dead
will be broken.
Then angry, roaring waves
will sweep over you.
19 Morning, noon, and night
an overwhelming flood
will wash you away.
The terrible things that happen
will teach you this lesson:
20 Your bed is too short,
your blanket too skimpy.[y]

21 The LORD will fiercely attack
as he did at Mount Perazim[z]
and in Gibeon Valley.[a]
But this time the LORD
will do something surprising,
not what you expect.
22 So you had better stop sneering
or you will be in worse shape
than ever before.
I heard the LORD All-Powerful
threaten the whole country
with destruction.

All Wisdom Comes from the LORD

23 Pay close attention
to what I am saying.
24 Farmers don't just plow
and break up the ground.
25 When a field is ready,
they scatter the seeds
of dill and cumin;
they plant the seeds
of wheat and barley
in the proper places.
26 They learn this from their God.

27 After dill and cumin
have been harvested,
the stalks are pounded,
not run over with a wagon.
28 Wheat and barley are pounded,
but not beaten to pulp;
they are run over with a wagon,
but not ground to dust.
29 This wonderful knowledge comes
from the LORD All-Powerful,
who has such great wisdom.

Jerusalem Will Suffer

The LORD said:

29 Jerusalem, city of David,
the place of my altar,[b]
you are in for trouble!
Celebrate your festivals
year after year.
2 I will still make you suffer,
and your people will cry
when I make an altar of you.[c]

[y]**28.20** *Your bed . . . skimpy*: Isaiah quotes a popular saying to teach that the treaty made with Egypt (verse 18) cannot give the nation security from its enemies. [z]**28.21** *Mount Perazim*: This may refer to David's defeat of the Philistines at Baal Perazim (2 Samuel 5.17-21). [a]**28.21** *Gibeon Valley*: This refers to Joshua's victory at Gibeon (Joshua 10.1-11). [b]**29.1** *the place of my altar*: One possible meaning for "ariel, ariel" of the Hebrew text. In Hebrew "ariel" can mean "God's hero" or "God's lion" or "God's altar." [c]**29.2** *when . . . you*: One possible meaning for the difficult Hebrew text.

28.15 Ws 1.16; Si 14.12. **28.16** Ps 118.22, 23; Ro 9.33; 10.11; 1 P 2.6. **28.21** **a** 2 S 5.20; 1 Ch 14.11; **b** Js 10.10-13.

3 I will surround you and prepare
to attack from all sides.[d]
4 From deep in the earth,
you will call out for help
with only a faint whisper.

5 Then your cruel enemies
will suddenly be swept away
like dust in a windstorm.
6 I, the LORD All-Powerful,
will come to your rescue
with a thundering earthquake
and a fiery whirlwind.

7 Every brutal nation
that attacks Jerusalem
and makes it suffer
will disappear like a dream
when night is over.
8 Those nations that attack
Mount Zion
will suffer from hunger
and thirst.
They will dream of food and drink
but wake up weary and hungry
and thirsty as ever.

Prophets Who Fool Themselves

9 Be shocked and stunned,
you prophets!
Refuse to see.
Get drunk and stagger,
but not from wine.
10 The LORD has made you drowsy;
he put you into a deep sleep
and covered your head.

11 Now his message is like a sealed letter
to you. Some of you say, "We can't read it,
because it's sealed." 12 Others say, "We
can't read it, because we don't know how to
read."
13 The Lord has said:

"These people praise me
with their words,
but they never really
think about me.
They worship me by repeating
rules made up by humans.
14 So once again I will do things
that shock and amaze them,
and I will destroy the wisdom
of those who claim to know
and understand."

15 You are in for trouble,
if you try to hide your plans
from the LORD!
Or if you think what you do
in the dark can't be seen.
16 You have it all backwards.
A clay dish doesn't say
to the potter,
"You didn't make me.
You don't even know how."

Hope for the Future

17 Soon the forest of Lebanon
will become a field with crops,
thick as a forest.[e]
18 The deaf will be able to hear
whatever is read to them;
the blind will be freed
from a life of darkness.
19 The poor and the needy
will celebrate and shout
because of the LORD,
the holy God of Israel.

20 All who are cruel and arrogant
will be gone forever.
Those who live by crime
will disappear,
21 together with everyone
who tells lies in court
and keeps innocent people
from getting a fair trial.

22 The LORD who rescued Abraham
has this to say
about Jacob's descendants:
"They will no longer
be ashamed and disgraced.
23 When they see how great
I have made their nation,
they will praise and honor me,
the holy God of Israel.

[d]**29.3** *from all sides*: One possible meaning for the difficult Hebrew text. One ancient translation has "like David." [e]**29.17** *with . . . forest*: Or "and Mount Carmel will be covered with forests."
29.10 Ro 11.8. **29.13** Mt 15.8, 9; Mk 7.6, 7. **29.14** 1 Co 1.19. **29.16** Is 45.9; Si 33.13; Ro 9.20.

24 Everyone who is confused
will understand,
and all who have complained
will obey my teaching."

Don't Expect Help from Egypt

30 This is the LORD's message
for his rebellious people:
"You follow your own plans
instead of mine;
you make treaties
without asking me,
and you keep on sinning.
2 You trust Egypt for protection.
So you refuse my advice
and send messengers to Egypt
to beg their king for help.

3 You will be disappointed,
completely disgraced
for trusting Egypt.
4 The king's power reaches
from the city of Zoan
as far south as Hanes.[f]
5 But Egypt can't protect you,
and to trust that nation
is useless and foolish.

6 This is a message
about the animals
of the Southern Desert:
You people carry treasures
on donkeys and camels.
You travel to a feeble nation
through a troublesome desert
filled with lions
and flying fiery dragons.
7 Egypt can't help you!
That's why I call that nation
a helpless monster.[g]

Israel Refuses To Listen

8 The LORD told me to write down his
message for his people, so that it would be
there forever. 9 They have turned against
the LORD and can't be trusted. They have
refused his teaching 10 and have said to his
messengers and prophets:
Don't tell us what God has shown
you and don't preach the truth. Just
say what we want to hear, even if it's
false. 11 Stop telling us what God has
said! We don't want to hear any more
about the holy God of Israel.

12 Now this is the answer
of the holy God of Israel:
"You rejected my message,
and you trust in violence
and lies.
13 This sin is like a crack
that makes a high wall
quickly crumble 14 and shatter
like a crushed bowl.
There's not a piece left
big enough to carry hot coals
or to dip out water."

Trust the LORD

15 The holy LORD God of Israel
had told all of you,
"I will keep you safe
if you turn back to me
and calm down.
I will make you strong
if you quietly trust me."

Then you stubbornly 16 said,
"No! We will safely escape
on speedy horses."

But those who chase you
will be even faster.
17 As few as five of them,
or even one, will be enough
to chase a thousand of you.
Finally, all that will be left
will be a few survivors
as lonely as a flag pole
on a barren hill.

The LORD Will Show Mercy

18 The LORD God is waiting
to show how kind he is
and to have pity on you.
The LORD always does right;
he blesses those who trust him.

19 People of Jerusalem, you don't need
to cry anymore. The Lord is kind, and as

[f] **30.4** *Zoan . . . Hanes*: Or "Your messengers have reached the city of Zoan and gone as far as Hanes." Zoan was in northeast Egypt; Hanes was to the south. [g] **30.7** *a helpless monster*: One possible meaning for the difficult Hebrew text.

soon as he hears your cries for help, he will
come. 20 The Lord has given you trouble
and sorrow as your food and drink. But
now you will again see the Lord, your
teacher, and he will guide you. 21 Whether
you turn to the right or to the left, you will
hear a voice saying, "This is the road! Now
follow it." 22 Then you will treat your idols
of silver and gold like garbage; you will
throw them away like filthy rags.

23 The Lord will send rain to water the
seeds you have planted—your fields will
produce more crops than you need, and
your cattle will graze in open pastures.
24 Even the oxen and donkeys that plow
your fields will be fed the finest grain.[h]

25 On that day people will be slaughtered and towers destroyed, but streams
of water will flow from high hills and towering mountains. 26 Then the LORD will bandage his people's injuries and heal the
wounds he has caused. The moon will
shine as bright as the sun, and the sun will
shine seven times brighter than usual. It
will be like the light of seven days all at
once.

Assyria Will Be Punished

27 The LORD is coming
from far away
with his fiery anger
and thick clouds of smoke.[i]
His angry words flame up
like a destructive fire;
28 he breathes out a flood
that comes up to the neck.
He sifts the nations
and destroys them.
Then he puts a bridle
in every foreigner's mouth
and leads them to doom.

29 The LORD's people will sing as they do
when they celebrate a religious festival[j] at
night. The LORD is Israel's mighty rock,[k]
and his people will be as happy as they are
when they follow the sound of flutes to the
mountain where he is worshiped.

30 The LORD will get furious. His fearsome voice will be heard, his arm will be
seen ready to strike, and his anger will be
like a destructive fire, followed by thunderstorms and hailstones. 31 When the Assyrians hear the LORD's voice and see him
striking with his iron rod, they will be terrified. 32 He will attack them in battle, and
each time he strikes them, it will be to the
music of tambourines and harps.

33 Long ago the LORD got a place ready
for burning the body of the dead king.[l] The
place for the fire is deep and wide, the
wood is piled high, and the LORD will start
the fire by breathing out flaming sulfur.

Don't Trust the Power of Egypt

31 You are in for trouble
if you go to Egypt for help,
or if you depend on
an army of chariots
or a powerful cavalry.
Instead you should depend on
and trust the holy LORD God
of Israel.
2 The LORD isn't stupid!
He does what he promises,
and he can bring doom.
If you are cruel yourself,
or help those who are evil,
you will be destroyed.

3 The Egyptians are mere humans.
They aren't God.
Their horses are made of flesh;
they can't live forever.
When the LORD shows his power,
he will destroy the Egyptians
and all who depend on them.
Together they will fall.

4 The LORD All-Powerful
said to me,
"I will roar and attack
like a fearless lion
not frightened by the shouts
of shepherds trying to protect
their sheep.

[h]**30.24** *the finest grain*: The Hebrew text refers to grain with the husks removed. [i]**30.27** *with . . . smoke*: One possible meaning for the difficult Hebrew text. [j]**30.29** *a religious festival*: Probably Passover. [k]**30.29** *mighty rock*: See the note at 17.10. [l]**30.33** *burning . . . king*: Or "sacrificing the king" or "sacrificing to Molech." Human sacrifices were sometimes offered to Molech, a god whose name sounds like the Hebrew word for "king" (see 2 Kings 23.10; Jeremiah 32.35).

That's how I will come down
and fight on Mount Zion.
5 I, the LORD All-Powerful,
will protect Jerusalem
like a mother bird circling
over her nest."

Come Back to the LORD

6 People of Israel, come back!
You have completely turned
from the LORD.
7 The time is coming
when you will throw away
your idols of silver and gold,
made by your sinful hands.

8 The Assyrians will be killed,
but not by the swords
of humans.
Their young men will try
to escape,
but they will be captured
and forced into slavery.
9 Their fortress[m] will fall
when terror strikes;
their army officers
will be frightened
and run from the battle.
This is what the LORD has said,
the LORD whose fiery furnace
is built on Mount Zion.

Justice Will Rule

32 A king and his leaders
will rule with justice.
2 They will be a place of safety
from stormy winds,
a stream in the desert,
and a rock that gives shade
from the heat of the sun.
3 Then everyone who has eyes
will open them and see,
and those who have ears
will pay attention.
4 All who are impatient
will take time to think;
everyone who stutters
will talk clearly.
5 Fools will no longer
be highly respected,
and crooks won't be given
positions of honor.
6 Fools talk foolishness.
They always make plans
to do sinful things,
to lie about the LORD,
to let the hungry starve,
and to keep water from those
who are thirsty.
7 Cruel people tell lies—
they do evil things,
and make cruel plans
to destroy the poor and needy,
even when they beg
for justice.
8 But helpful people
can always be trusted
to make helpful plans.

Punishment for the Women of Jerusalem

9 Listen to what I say,
you women who are carefree
and careless!
10 You may not have worries now,
but in about a year,
the grape harvest will fail,
and you will tremble.

11 Shake and shudder,
you women without a care!
Strip off your clothes—
put on sackcloth.
12 Slap your breasts in sorrow
because of what happened
to the fruitful fields
and vineyards,
13 and to the happy homes
in Jerusalem.
The land of my people
is covered with thorns.

14 The palace will be deserted,
the crowded city empty.
Fortresses and towers
will forever become
playgrounds for wild donkeys
and pastures for sheep.

[m] **31.9** *fortress*: The Hebrew text has "rock," which may refer to the Assyrian god or king, or to their army.

God's Spirit Makes the Difference

15 When the Spirit is given to us
from heaven,
deserts will become orchards
thick as fertile forests.
16 Honesty and justice
will prosper there,
17 and justice will produce
lasting peace and security.

18 You, the LORD's people,
will live in peace,
calm and secure,
19 even if hailstones flatten
forests and cities.
20 You will have God's blessing,
as you plant your crops
beside streams,
while your donkeys and cattle
roam freely about.

Jerusalem Will Be Safe

33 You defeated my people.
Now you're in for trouble!
You've never been destroyed,
but you will be destroyed;
you've never been betrayed,
but you will be betrayed.
When you have finished
destroying and betraying,
you will be destroyed
and betrayed in return.

2 Please, LORD, be kind to us!
We depend on you.
Make us strong each morning,
and come to save us
when we are in trouble.
3 Nations scatter when you roar
and show your greatness.[n]
4 We attack our enemies
like swarms of locusts;[o]
we take everything
that belongs to them.[p]

5 You, LORD, are above all others,
and you live in the heavens.
You have brought justice
and fairness to Jerusalem;
6 you are the foundation
on which we stand today.
You always save us and give
true wisdom and knowledge.
Nothing means more to us[q]
than obeying you.

The LORD Will Do Something

7 Listen! Our bravest soldiers
are running through the streets,
screaming for help.[r]
Our messengers hoped for peace,
but came home crying.
8 No one travels anymore;
every road is empty.
Treaties are broken,
and no respect is shown
to any who keep promises.[s]
9 Fields are dry and barren;
Mount Lebanon wilts
with shame.
Sharon Valley is a desert;
the forests of Bashan and Carmel
have lost their leaves.

10 But the LORD says,
"Now I will do something
and be greatly praised.
11 Your deeds are straw
that will be set on fire
by your very own breath.
12 You will be burned to ashes
like thorns in a fire.
13 Everyone, both far and near,
come look at what I have done.
See my mighty power!"

Punishment and Rewards

14 Those terrible sinners
on Mount Zion tremble
as they ask in fear,
"How can we possibly live
where a raging fire
never stops burning?"

[n]**33.3** *greatness*: One possible meaning for the difficult Hebrew text of verse 3. [o]**33.4** *locusts*: Insects like grasshoppers that travel in swarms and cause great damage to crops. [p]**33.4** *them*: One possible meaning for the difficult Hebrew text of verse 4. [q]**33.6** *Nothing . . . us*: One possible meaning for the difficult Hebrew text. [r]**33.7** *Listen . . . help*: Or "The LORD heard our shouts and will come to help us." [s]**33.8** *to any . . . promises*: The Dead Sea Scrolls; the Standard Hebrew Text "to those in the cities."

15 But there will be rewards
for those who live right
and tell the truth,
for those who refuse
to take money by force
or accept bribes,
for all who hate murder
and violent crimes.
16 They will live in a fortress
high on a rocky cliff,
where they will have food
and plenty of water.

The LORD Is Our King

17 With your own eyes
you will see the glorious King;
you will see his kingdom
reaching far and wide.
18 Then you will ask yourself,
"Where are those officials
who terrified us and forced us
to pay such heavy taxes?"
19 You will never again have to see
the proud people who spoke
a strange and foreign language
you could not understand.

20 Look to Mount Zion
where we celebrate
our religious festivals.
You will see Jerusalem,
secure as a tent with pegs
that cannot be pulled up
and fastened with ropes
that can never be broken.
21 Our wonderful LORD
will be with us!
There will be deep rivers
and wide streams
safe from enemy ships.[t]

The LORD Is Our Judge

22 The LORD is our judge
and our ruler;
the LORD is our king
and will keep us safe.
23 But your nation[u] is a ship
with its rigging loose,
its mast shaky,
and its sail not spread.

Someday even you that are lame
will take everything you want
from your enemies.
24 The LORD will forgive your sins,
and none of you will say,
"I feel sick."

The Nations Will Be Judged

34 Everyone of every nation,
the entire earth,
and all of its creatures,
come here and listen!
2 The LORD is terribly angry
with the nations;
he has condemned them
to be slaughtered.
3 Their dead bodies will be left
to rot and stink;
their blood will flow
down the mountains.
4 Each star[v] will disappear—
the sky will roll up
like a scroll.[w]
Everything in the sky
will dry up and wilt
like leaves on a vine
or fruit on a tree.

Trouble for Edom

5 After the sword of the LORD
has done what it wants
to the skies above,[x]
it will come down on Edom,
the nation that the LORD
has doomed for destruction.

6 The sword of the LORD
is covered with blood
from lambs and goats,
together with fat
from kidneys of rams.

[t]**33.21** *safe . . . ships*: This probably means that Jerusalem will have a lot of water, without the danger of attacks from enemy ships. [u]**33.23** *your nation*: Possibly Judah or Assyria.
[v]**34.4** *star*: Stars were worshiped as gods. [w]**34.4** *scroll*: A roll of paper or specially prepared leather used for writing on. [x]**34.5** *has done . . . above*: The Standard Hebrew Text; the Dead Sea Scrolls "appears in the skies above."

34.4 Mt 24.29; Mk 13.25; Lk 21.26; Rev 6.13, 14. **34.5-17** Is 63.1-6; Jr 49.7-22; Ez 25.12-14; 35.1-15; Am 1.11, 12; Ob 1-14; Ml 1.2-5.

This is because the LORD
will slaughter many people
and make a sacrifice of them
in the city of Bozrah
and everywhere else
in Edom.
7 Edom's leaders are wild oxen.
They are powerful bulls,
but they will die
with the others.
Their country will be soaked
with their blood,
and its soil made fertile
with their fat.

8 The LORD has chosen
the year and the day,
when he will take revenge
and come to Zion's defense.
9 Edom's streams will turn into tar
and its soil into sulfur—
then the whole country
will go up in flames.
10 It will burn night and day
and never stop smoking.
Edom will be a desert,
generation after generation;
no one will ever travel
through that land.
11 Owls, hawks, and wild animals[y]
will make it their home.
God will leave it in ruins,
merely a pile of rocks.

The End of Edom

12 Edom will be called
"Kingdom of Nothing."
Its rulers will also be nothing.
13 Its palaces and fortresses
will be covered with thorns;
only wolves and ostriches
will make their home there.
14 Wildcats and hyenas
will hunt together,
demons will scream to demons,
and creatures of the night
will live among the ruins.
15 Owls will nest there
to raise their young
among its shadows,[z]
while families of buzzards
circle around.

16 In *The Book of the LORD*[a]
you can search and find
where it is written,
"The LORD brought together
all of his creatures
by the power of his Spirit.
Not one is missing."
17 The LORD has decided
where they each should live;
they will be there forever,
generation after generation.

God's Splendor Will Be Seen

35 Thirsty deserts will be glad;
barren lands will celebrate
and blossom with flowers.
2 Deserts will bloom everywhere
and sing joyful songs.
They will be as majestic
as Mount Lebanon,
as glorious as Mount Carmel
or Sharon Valley.
Everyone will see
the wonderful splendor
of the LORD our God.

God Changes Everything

*3 Here is a message for all
who are weak, trembling,
and worried:
4 "Cheer up! Don't be afraid.
Your God is coming
to punish your enemies.
God will take revenge on them
and rescue you."

5 The blind will see,
and the ears of the deaf
will be healed.
6 Those who were lame
will leap around like deer;
tongues once silent
will begin to shout.

[y]**34.11** *Owls . . . animals*: One possible meaning for the difficult Hebrew text. [z]**34.15** *Owls . . . shadows*: One possible meaning for the difficult Hebrew text. [a]**34.16** *The Book of the LORD*: The book that Isaiah refers to is unknown.

34.10 Rev 14.11; 19.3. **35.3** He 12.12. **35.5,6** Mt 11.5; Lk 7.22. **35.6** 4 Macc 10.21.

Water will rush
through the desert.
7 Scorching sand
will turn into a lake,
and thirsty ground
will flow with fountains.
Grass will grow in wetlands,
where packs of wild dogs
once made their home.[b]

God's Sacred Highway

8 A good road will be there,
and it will be named
"God's Sacred Highway."
It will be for God's people;
no one unfit to worship God
will walk on that road.
And no fools can travel
on that highway.[c]
9 No lions or other wild animals
will come near that road;
only those the LORD has saved
will travel there.

10 The people the LORD has rescued
will come back singing
as they enter Zion.
Happiness will be a crown
they will always wear.
They will celebrate and shout
because all sorrows and worries
will be gone far away.

The Assyrians Surround Jerusalem
(2 Kings 18.13-27; 2 Chronicles 32.1-19)

36 Hezekiah had been king of Judah
for fourteen years when King Sennacherib of Assyria invaded the country
and captured every walled city 2 except
Jerusalem. The Assyrian king ordered his
army commander to leave the city of Lachish and to take a large army to Jerusalem.
The commander went there and stood
on the road near the cloth makers' shops
along the canal from the upper pool.
3 Three of the king's highest officials came
out of Jerusalem to meet him. One of them
was Hilkiah's son Eliakim, who was the
prime minister. The other two were
Shebna, assistant to the prime minister,
and Joah son of Asaph, keeper of the government records.
4 The Assyrian commander told them:
I have a message for Hezekiah from
the great king of Assyria. Ask Hezekiah
why he feels so sure of himself. 5 Does
he think he can plan and win a war
with nothing but words? Who is going
to help him, now that he has turned
against the king of Assyria? 6 Is he depending on Egypt and its king? That's
the same as leaning on a broken stick,
and it will go right through his hand.
7 Is Hezekiah now depending on
the LORD, your God? Didn't Hezekiah
tear down all except one of the LORD's
altars and places of worship?[d] Didn't
he tell the people of Jerusalem and Judah to worship at that one place?
8 The king of Assyria wants to make
a bet with you people! He will give you
two thousand horses, if you have
enough troops to ride them. 9 How
could you even defeat our lowest ranking officer, when you have to depend
on Egypt for chariots and cavalry?
10 Don't forget that it was the LORD
who sent me here with orders to destroy your nation!
11 Eliakim, Shebna, and Joah said, "Sir,
we don't want the people listening from the
city wall to understand what you are saying.
So please speak to us in Aramaic instead of
Hebrew."
12 The Assyrian army commander answered, "My king sent me to speak to
everyone, not just to you leaders. These
people will soon have to eat their own body
waste and drink their own urine! And so
will the three of you!"
13 Then, in a voice loud enough for
everyone to hear, he shouted out in
Hebrew:
Listen to what the great king of

[b]**35.7** *where . . . home*: One possible meaning for the difficult Hebrew text. [c]**35.8** *And . . . highway*: Or "And not even a fool can miss that highway." [d]**36.7** *worship*: Hezekiah actually had torn down the places where idols were worshiped, and he had told the people to worship the LORD at the one place of worship in Jerusalem. But the Assyrian leader was confused and thought these were also places where the LORD was supposed to be worshiped.

36.6 Ez 29.6, 7.

Assyria says! 14 Don't be fooled by Hezekiah. He can't save you. 15 Don't trust him when he tells you that the LORD will protect you from the king of Assyria. 16 Stop listening to Hezekiah. Pay attention to my king. Surrender to him. He will let you keep your own vineyards, fig trees, and cisterns 17 for a while. Then he will come and take you away to a country just like yours, where you can plant vineyards and raise your own grain.

18 Hezekiah claims the LORD will save you. But don't be fooled by him. Were any other gods able to defend their land against the king of Assyria? 19 What happened to the gods of Hamath, Arpad, and Sepharvaim? Were the gods of Samaria able to protect their land against the Assyrian forces? 20 None of these gods kept their people safe from the king of Assyria. Do you think the LORD, your God, can do any better?

21-22 Eliakim, Shebna, and Joah had been warned by King Hezekiah not to answer the Assyrian commander. So they tore their clothes in sorrow and reported to Hezekiah everything the commander had said.

Hezekiah Asks Isaiah for Advice

(2 Kings 19.1-13)

37 As soon as Hezekiah heard the news, he tore off his clothes in sorrow and put on sackcloth. Then he went into the temple of the LORD. 2 He told Prime Minister Eliakim, Assistant Prime Minister Shebna, and the senior priests to dress in sackcloth and tell me:

3 Isaiah, these are difficult and disgraceful times. Our nation is like a woman too weak to give birth, when it's time for her baby to be born. 4 Please pray for those of us who are left alive. The king of Assyria sent his army commander to insult the living God. Perhaps the LORD heard what he said and will do something, if you will pray.

5 When these leaders came to me, 6 I told them that the LORD had this message for Hezekiah:

I am the LORD. Don't worry about the insulting things that have been said about me by these messengers from the king of Assyria. 7 I will upset him with rumors about what's happening in his own country. He will go back, and there I will make him die a violent death.

8 Meanwhile the commander of the Assyrian forces heard that his king had left the town of Lachish and was now attacking Libnah. So he went there.

9 About this same time, the king of Assyria learned that King Tirhakah of Ethiopia[e] was on his way to attack him. Then the king of Assyria sent some messengers with this note for Hezekiah:

10 Don't trust your God or be fooled by his promise to defend Jerusalem against me. 11 You have heard how we Assyrian kings have completely wiped out other nations. What makes you feel so safe? 12 The Assyrian kings before me destroyed the towns of Gozan, Haran, Rezeph, and everyone from Eden who lived in Telassar. What good did their gods do them? 13 The kings of Hamath, Arpad, Sepharvaim, Hena, and Ivvah have all disappeared.

Hezekiah Prays

(2 Kings 19.14-19)

14 After Hezekiah had read the note from the king of Assyria, he took it to the temple and spread it out for the LORD to see. 15 Then he prayed:

16 LORD God All-Powerful of Israel, your throne is above the winged creatures.[f] You created the heavens and the earth, and you alone rule the kingdoms of this world. 17 Just look and see how Sennacherib has insulted you, the living God.

[e] **37.9** *Ethiopia*: See the note at 11.11. [f] **37.16** *winged creatures*: Two winged creatures made of gold were on the top of the sacred chest and were symbols of the LORD's throne on earth (see Exodus 25.18; 2 Samuel 6.2).

37.16 Ex 25.22.

18 It is true, our LORD, that Assyrian
kings have turned nations into deserts.
19 They destroyed the idols of wood
and stone that the people of those nations had made and worshiped. 20 But
you are our LORD and our God! We ask
you to keep us safe from the Assyrian
king. Then everyone in every kingdom
on earth will know that you are the
only LORD.

Isaiah Gives the LORD's Answer to Hezekiah

(2 Kings 19.20-34)

21-22 I went to Hezekiah and told him
that the LORD God of Israel had said:
Hezekiah, you prayed to me about
King Sennacherib of Assyria.[g] Now this
is what I say to that king:

The people of Jerusalem
hate and make fun of you;
they laugh behind your back.

23 Sennacherib, you cursed,
shouted, and sneered at me,
the holy God of Israel.
24 You let your officials
insult me, the Lord.
And here is what you
have said about yourself,
"I led my chariots
to the highest heights
of Lebanon's mountains.
I went deep into its forest,
cutting down the best cedar
and cypress trees.
25 I dried up every stream
in the land of Egypt,
and I drank water
from wells I had dug."

26 Sennacherib, now listen
to me, the LORD.
I planned all of this long ago.
And you don't even know
that I alone am the one
who decided that you
would do these things.
I let you make ruins
of fortified cities.
27 Their people became weak,
terribly confused.
They were like wild flowers
or like tender young grass
growing on a flat roof
or like a field of grain
before it matures.[h]

28 I know all about you,
even how fiercely angry
you are with me.
29 I have seen your pride
and the tremendous hatred
you have for me.
Now I will put a hook
in your nose,
a bit in your mouth,[i]
then I will send you back
to where you came from.

30 Hezekiah, I will tell you what's
going to happen. This year you will eat
crops that grow on their own, and the
next year you will eat whatever springs
up where those crops grew. But the
third year, you will plant grain
and vineyards, and you will eat what
you harvest. 31 Those who survive in
Judah will be like a vine that puts
down deep roots and bears fruit. 32 I,
the LORD All-Powerful, will see to it
that some who live in Jerusalem will
survive.

33 I promise that the king of Assyria
won't get into Jerusalem, or shoot an
arrow into the city, or even surround it
and prepare to attack. 34 As surely as I
am the LORD, he will return by the way
he came and will never enter Jerusalem. 35 I will protect it for the
sake of my own honor and because of
the promise I made to my servant
David.

[g]**37.21,22** *Hezekiah, you prayed . . . Assyria*: One possible meaning for the difficult Hebrew text. [h]**37.27** *tender young grass . . . matures*: The Standard Hebrew Text; the Dead Sea Scrolls and some Hebrew manuscripts "tender young grass, growing on a flat roof and scorched by the heat." Many of the houses had roofs made of packed earth. Grass would sometimes grow on the roof, but would die quickly because of the sun and hot winds. [i]**37.29** *I will put . . . your mouth*: This is how the Assyrians treated their prisoners, and now the LORD will treat Sennacherib the same way.

The Death of King Sennacherib
(2 Kings 19.35-37)

36 The LORD sent an angel to the camp
of the Assyrians, and he killed one hundred
eighty-five thousand of them all in one
night. The next morning, the camp was full
of dead bodies. 37 After this, King Sennacherib went back to Assyria and lived in
the city of Nineveh. 38 One day he was worshiping in the temple of his god Nisroch,
when his sons, Adrammelech and Sharezer, killed him with their swords. They escaped to the land of Ararat, and his son
Esarhaddon became king.[j]

Hezekiah Gets Sick and Almost Dies
(2 Kings 20.1-11; 2 Chronicles 32.24-26)

38 About this time, Hezekiah got sick and was almost dead. So I went in and told him, "The LORD says you won't ever get well. You are going to die, and so you had better start doing what needs to be done."

2 Hezekiah turned toward the wall and
prayed, 3 "Don't forget that I have been
faithful to you, LORD. I have obeyed you
with all my heart, and I do whatever you
say is right." After this, he cried hard.
4 Then the LORD sent me 5 with this
message for Hezekiah:

I am the LORD God, who was worshiped by your ancestor David. I heard
you pray, and I saw you cry. I will let
you live fifteen years more, 6 while I
protect you and your city from the king
of Assyria.

7 Now I will prove to you that I will
keep my promise. 8 Do you see the
shadow made by the setting sun on the
stairway built for King Ahaz? I will
make the shadow go back ten steps.

Then the shadow went back ten steps.[k]

King Hezekiah's Song of Praise

9 This is what Hezekiah wrote after he got well:

10 I thought I would die
during my best years
and stay as a prisoner forever
in the world of the dead.
11 I thought I would never again
see you, my LORD,
or any of the people
who live on this earth.
12 My life was taken from me
like the tent that a shepherd
pulls up and moves.
You cut me off like thread
from a weaver's loom;
you make a wreck of me
day and night.

13 Until morning came, I thought
you would crush my bones
just like a hungry lion;
both night and day
you make a wreck of me.[l]
14 I cry like a swallow;
I mourn like a dove.
My eyes are red
from looking to you, LORD.
I am terribly abused.
Please come and help me.[m]
15 There's nothing I can say
in answer to you,
since you are the one
who has done this to me.[n]
My life has turned sour;
I will limp until I die.

16 Your words and your deeds
bring life to everyone,
including me.[o]
Please make me healthy
and strong again.
17 It was for my own good
that I had such hard times.
But your love protected me
from doom in the deep pit,[p]
and you turned your eyes
away from my sins.

[j] **37.38** *Esarhaddon became king*: He ruled Assyria 681-669 B.C. [k] **38.8** *steps*: One possible meaning for the difficult Hebrew text of verse 8. [l] **38.13** *of me*: One possible meaning for the difficult Hebrew text of verse 13. [m] **38.14** *help me*: One possible meaning for the difficult Hebrew text of verse 14. [n] **38.15** *There's . . . me*: One possible meaning for the difficult Hebrew text. [o] **38.16** *Your . . . me*: One possible meaning for the difficult Hebrew text. [p] **38.17** *deep pit*: The world of the dead, as in verse 18.

18 No one in the world of the dead
can thank you or praise you;
none of those in the deep pit
can hope for you to show them
how faithful you are.
19 Only the living can thank you,
as I am doing today.
Each generation tells the next
about your faithfulness.[q]

20 You, LORD, will save me,
and every day that we live
we will sing in your temple
to the music
of stringed instruments.

Isaiah's Advice to Hezekiah

21 I had told King Hezekiah's servants
to put some mashed figs on the king's
open sore, and he would get well.
22 Then Hezekiah asked for proof that he
would again worship in the LORD's temple.

Isaiah Speaks the LORD's Message to Hezekiah

(2 Kings 20.12-19)

39 Merodach Baladan, the son of Baladan, was now king of Babylonia.
And when he learned that Hezekiah was
well, he sent messengers with letters and a
gift for him. 2 Hezekiah welcomed the messengers and showed them all the silver, the
gold, the spices, and the fine oils that were
in his storehouse. He even showed them
where he kept his weapons. Nothing in his
palace or in his entire kingdom was kept
hidden from them.
3 I asked Hezekiah, "Where did these
men come from? What did they want?"

"They came all the way from Babylonia," Hezekiah answered.
4 "What did you show them?" I asked.

Hezekiah answered, "I showed them
everything in my kingdom."
5 Then I told Hezekiah:

I have a message for you from the
LORD All-Powerful. 6 One day everything you and your ancestors have
stored up will be taken to Babylonia.
The LORD has promised that nothing will be left. 7 Some of your own sons
will be taken to Babylonia, where they
will be disgraced and made to serve in
the king's palace.
8 Hezekiah thought, "At least our nation
will be at peace for a while." So he told me,
"The message you brought from the LORD
is good."

Encourage God's People

40 Our God has said:
"Encourage my people!
Give them comfort.
2 Speak kindly to Jerusalem
and announce:
Your slavery is past;
your punishment is over.
I, the LORD, made you pay
double for your sins."

3 Someone is shouting:
"Clear a path in the desert!
Make a straight road
for the LORD our God.
4 Fill in the valleys;
flatten every hill
and mountain.
Level the rough
and rugged ground.
5 Then the glory of the LORD
will appear for all to see.
The LORD has promised this!"

6 Someone told me to shout,
and I asked,
"What should I shout?"
We humans are merely grass,
and we last no longer
than wild flowers.
7 At the LORD's command,
flowers and grass disappear,
and so do we.
8 Flowers and grass fade away,
but what our God has said
will never change.

[q] **38.19** *about your faithfulness*: One possible meaning for the difficult Hebrew text.

38.18 Si 17.27; Ba 2.17. **39.7** Dn 1.1-7; 2 K 24.10-16; 2 Ch 36.10. **40.3** Si 48.10; Ba 5.7; Mt 3.3; Mk 1.3; Jn 1.23. **40.3-5** Lk 3.4-6. **40.6-8** Jas 1.10, 11; 1 P 1.24, 25.

Your God Is Here!

9 There is good news
for the city of Zion.
Shout it as loud as you can[r]
from the highest mountain.
Don't be afraid to shout
to the towns of Judah,
"Your God is here!"
10 Look! The powerful LORD God
is coming to rule
with his mighty arm.
He brings with him
what he has taken in war,
and he rewards his people.
11 The LORD cares for his nation,
just as shepherds care
for their flocks.
He carries the lambs
in his arms,
while gently leading
the mother sheep.

Who Compares with God?

12 Did any of you measure
the ocean by yourself
or stretch out the sky
with your own hands?
Did you put the soil
of the earth in a bucket
or weigh the hills and mountains
on balance scales?

13 Has anyone told the LORD[s]
what he must do
or given him advice?
14 Did the LORD ask anyone
to teach him wisdom
and justice?
Who gave him knowledge
and understanding?
15 To the LORD, all nations
are merely a drop in a bucket
or dust on balance scales;
all of the islands
are but a handful of sand.
16 The cattle
on Lebanon's mountains
would not be enough to offer
as a sacrifice to God,
and the trees would not
be enough for the fire.
17 God thinks of the nations
as far less than nothing.

18 Who compares with God?
Is anything like him?
19 Is an idol at all like God?
It is made of bronze
with a thin layer of gold,
and decorated with silver.
20 Or special wood may be chosen[t]
because it doesn't rot—
then skilled hands
take care to make an idol
that won't fall on its face.

God Rules the Whole Earth

21 Don't you know?
Haven't you heard?
Isn't it clear that God
created the world?[u]
22 God is the one who rules
the whole earth,
and we that live here
are merely insects.
He spread out the heavens
like a curtain or an open tent.

23 God brings down rulers
and turns them into nothing.
24 They are like flowers
freshly sprung up
and starting to grow.
But when God blows on them,
they wilt and are carried off
like straw in a storm.

25 The holy God asks,
"Who compares with me?
Is anyone my equal?"

[r] **40.9** *There . . . can*: Or "City of Jerusalem, you have good news. Shout it as loud as you can."
[s] **40.13** *the LORD*: Or "the LORD's Spirit." [t] **40.20** *Or . . . chosen*: One possible meaning for the difficult Hebrew text. Two kinds of idols seem to be described: bronze idols covered with gold (verse 19) and wooden idols (verse 20). [u] **40.21** *Isn't . . . world*: Or "Hasn't it been clear since the time of creation?"

40.10 Is 62.11; Rev 22.12. **40.11** Ez 34.15; Jn 10.11. **40.13** Ro 11.34; 1 Co 2.16. **40.15** Ws 11.22; Si 10.16, 17. **40.18,19** Ac 17.29. **40.20** Ws 13.11-19; Let Jer 8-40.

26 Look at the evening sky!
Who created the stars?
Who gave them each a name?
Who leads them like an army?
The LORD is so powerful
that none of the stars
are ever missing.

The LORD Gives Strength

27 You people of Israel, say,
"God pays no attention to us!
He doesn't care if we
are treated unjustly."

But how can you say that?
28 Don't you know?
Haven't you heard?
The LORD is the eternal God,
Creator of the earth.
He never gets weary or tired;
his wisdom cannot be measured.

29 The LORD gives strength
to those who are weary.
30 Even young people get tired,
then stumble and fall.
31 But those who trust the LORD
will find new strength.
They will be strong like eagles
soaring upward on wings;
they will walk and run
without getting tired.

The LORD Controls Human Events

41 Be silent and listen,
every island in the sea.
Have courage and come near,
every one of you nations.
Let's settle this matter!
2 Who appointed this ruler
from the east?[v]
Who puts nations and kings
in his power?[w]
His sword and his arrows
turn them to dust
blown by the wind.

3 He goes after them so quickly
that his feet
barely touch the ground—
he doesn't even get hurt.

4 Who makes these things happen?
Who controls human events?
I do! I am the LORD.
I was there at the beginning;
I will be there at the end.
5 Islands and foreign nations
saw what I did and trembled
as they came near.

What Can Idols Do?

6 Worshipers of idols
comfort each other,
saying, "Don't worry!"
7 Woodcarvers, goldsmiths,
and other workers[x]
encourage one another and say,
"We've done a great job!"
Then they nail the idol down,
so it won't fall over.

The LORD's Chosen Servant

8 Israel, you are my servant.
I chose you, the family
of my friend Abraham.
9 From far across the earth
I brought you here and said,
"You are my chosen servant.
I haven't forgotten you."

10 Don't be afraid. I am with you.
Don't tremble with fear.
I am your God.
I will make you strong,
as I protect you with my arm
and give you victories.
11 Everyone who hates you
will be terribly disgraced;
those who attack
will vanish into thin air.
12 You will look around
for those brutal enemies,
but you won't find them
because they will be gone.

[v] **41.2** *ruler from the east*: Probably Cyrus (see 44.28; 45.1; 48.14). [w] **41.2** *Who puts . . . power*: One possible meaning for the difficult Hebrew text. [x] **41.7** *and other workers*: One possible meaning for the difficult Hebrew text.

40.26 Ba 3.34, 35. **41.8** 2 Ch 20.7; Jas 2.23.

13 I am the LORD your God.
I am holding your hand,
so don't be afraid.
I am here to help you.

14 People of Israel, don't worry,
though others may say,
"Israel is only a worm!"
I am the holy God of Israel,
who saves and protects you.
15 I will let you be like a log
covered with sharp spikes.[y]
You will grind and crush
every mountain and hill[z]
until they turn to dust.
16 A strong wind will scatter them
in all directions.
Then you will celebrate
and praise me, your LORD,
the holy God of Israel.

The LORD Helps the Poor

17 When the poor and needy
are dying of thirst
and cannot find water,
I, the LORD God of Israel,
will come to their rescue.
I won't forget them.
18 I will make rivers flow
on mountain peaks.
I will send streams
to fill the valleys.
Dry and barren land
will flow with springs
and become a lake.
19 I will fill the desert
with all kinds of trees—
cedars, acacias, and myrtles;
olive and cypress trees;
fir trees and pines.
20 Everyone will see this
and know that I,
the holy LORD God of Israel,
created it all.

Idols Are Useless

21 I am the LORD,
the King of Israel!
Come argue your case with me.
Present your evidence.
22 Come near me, you idols.[a]
Tell us about the past,
and we will think about it.
Tell us about the future,
so we will know
what is going to happen.
23 Prove that you are gods
by making your predictions
come true.
Do something good or evil,
so we can be amazed
and terrified.[b]
24 You idols are nothing,
and you are powerless.[c]
To worship you
would be disgusting.

25 I, the LORD, appointed a ruler
in the north;
now he comes from the east
to honor my name.
He tramples[d] kings like mud,
as potters trample clay.[e]
26 Did any of you idols predict
what would happen?
Did any of you get it right?
None of you told about this
or even spoke a word.
27 I was the first to tell
the people of Jerusalem,
"Look, it's happening!"[f]
I was the one who announced
this good news to Zion.

28 None of these idols
are able to give advice
or answer questions.
29 They are nothing,[g]
and they can do nothing—

[y] **41.15** *I will let . . . sharp spikes*: In ancient times a heavy object was sometimes dragged over wheat or barley to separate the grain from the husk. This was called threshing. [z] **41.15** *mountain and hill*: These stand for the power and pride of Israel's enemies. [a] **41.22** *Come near . . . idols*: One possible meaning for the difficult Hebrew text. [b] **41.23** *and terrified*: Or "when we see it." [c] **41.24** *powerless*: One possible meaning for the difficult Hebrew text. [d] **41.25** *tramples*: One possible meaning for the difficult Hebrew text. [e] **41.25** *trample clay*: This was done to soften the clay and make it easier to shape. [f] **41.27** *Look . . . happening*: One possible meaning for the difficult Hebrew text. [g] **41.29** *nothing*: One possible meaning for the difficult Hebrew text.

they are less
than a passing breeze.

The LORD's Servant

42 Here is my servant!
I have made him strong.
He is my chosen one;
I am pleased with him.
I have given him my Spirit,
and he will bring justice
to the nations.
2 He won't shout or yell
or call out in the streets.
3 He won't break off a bent reed
or put out a dying flame,
but he will make sure
that justice is done.
4 He won't quit or give up
until he brings justice
everywhere on earth,
and people in foreign nations
long for his teaching.

5 I am the LORD God.
I created the heavens
like an open tent above.
I made the earth and everything
that grows on it.
I am the source of life
for all who live on this earth,
so listen to what I say.
6 I chose you to bring justice,
and I am here at your side.
I selected and sent you[h]
to bring light
and my promise of hope
to the nations.
7 You will give sight
to the blind;
you will set prisoners free
from dark dungeons.

8 My name is the LORD!
I won't let idols or humans
share my glory and praise.
9 Everything has happened
just as I said it would;
now I will announce
what will happen next.

Sing Praises to the LORD

10 Tell the whole world to sing
a new song to the LORD!
Tell those who sail the ocean
and those who live far away
to join in the praise.
11 Tell the tribes of the desert
and everyone in the mountains[i]
to celebrate and sing.
12 Let them announce
his praises everywhere.
13 The LORD is marching out
like an angry soldier,
shouting with all his might
while attacking his enemies.

The LORD Will Help His People

14 For a long time, I, the LORD,
have held my temper;
now I will scream and groan
like a woman giving birth.
15 I will destroy the mountains
and what grows on them;
I will dry up rivers and ponds.

16 I will lead the blind on roads
they have never known;
I will guide them on paths
they have never traveled.
Their road is dark and rough,
but I will give light
to keep them from stumbling.
This is my solemn promise.

17 Everyone who worships idols
as though they were gods
will be terribly ashamed.

God's People Won't Obey

18 You people are deaf and blind,
but the LORD commands you
to listen and to see.
19 No one is as blind or deaf

[h]42.6 *I selected . . . you*: One possible meaning for the difficult Hebrew text. [i]42.11 *desert . . . mountains*: The Hebrew text includes the place names of Kedar in the desert and Sela in the mountains.

42.1 Mt 3.17; 17.5; Mk 1.11; Lk 3.22; 9.35. **42.1-4** Mt 12.18-21. **42.5** Ac 17.24, 25. **42.6** Is 49.6; Lk 2.32; Ac 13.47; 26.23.

as his messenger,
his chosen servant,
20 who sees and hears so much,
but pays no attention.

21 The LORD always does right,
and so he wanted his Law
to be greatly praised.[j]
22 But his people were trapped
and imprisoned in holes
with no one to rescue them.
All they owned had been taken,
and no one was willing
to give it back.
23 Why won't his people
ever learn to listen?

24 Israel sinned and refused
to obey the LORD
or follow his instructions.
So the LORD let them be robbed
of everything they owned.
25 He was furious with them
and punished their nation
with the fires of war.
Still they paid no attention.
They didn't even care
when they were surrounded
and scorched by flames.

The LORD Has Rescued His People

43 Descendants of Jacob,
I, the LORD, created you
and formed your nation.
Israel, don't be afraid.
I have rescued you.
I have called you by name;
now you belong to me.
2 When you cross deep rivers,
I will be with you,
and you won't drown.
When you walk through fire,
you won't be burned
or scorched by the flames.

3 I am the LORD, your God,
the Holy One of Israel,
the God who saves you.
I gave up Egypt, Ethiopia,[k]
and the region of Seba[l]
in exchange for you.
4 To me, you are very dear,
and I love you.
That's why I gave up nations
and people to rescue you.

5 Don't be afraid! I am with you.
From both east and west
I will bring you together.
6 I will say to the north
and to the south,
"Free my sons and daughters!
Let them return
from distant lands.
7 They are my people—
I created each of them
to bring honor to me."

The LORD Alone Is God

The LORD said:
8 Bring my people together.
They have eyes and ears,
but they can't see or hear.
9 Tell everyone of every nation
to gather around.
None of them can honestly say,
"We told you so!"
If someone heard them say this,
then tell us about it now.

10 My people, you are my witnesses
and my chosen servant.
I want you to know me,
to trust me, and understand
that I alone am God.
I have always been God;
there can be no others.

11 I alone am the LORD;
only I can rescue you.
12 I promised to save you,
and I kept my promise.
You are my witnesses
that no other god did this.
I, the LORD, have spoken.
13 I am God now and forever.

[j]**42.21** *greatly praised*: One possible meaning for the difficult Hebrew text of verse 21.
[k]**43.3** *Ethiopia*: See the note at 11.11. [l]**43.3** *Seba*: A region in southwest Arabia. Egypt, Ethiopia, and Seba probably stood for all that was known of Africa in biblical times.

No one can snatch you from me
or stand in my way.

The LORD Will Prepare the Way

14 I, the LORD, will rescue you!
I am Israel's holy God,
and this is my promise:
For your sake, I will send
an army against Babylon
to drag its people away,
crying as they go.[m]

15 I am the LORD, your holy God,
Israel's Creator and King.
16 I am the one who cut a path
through the mighty ocean.
17 I sent an army to chase you
with chariots and horses;
now they lie dead,
unable to move.
They are like an oil lamp
with the flame snuffed out.

Forget the Past

The LORD said:
18 Forget what happened long ago!
Don't think about the past.
19 I am creating something new.
There it is! Do you see it?
I have put roads in deserts,
streams[n] in thirsty lands.
20 Every wild animal honors me,
even jackals[o] and owls.
I provide water in deserts—
streams in thirsty lands
for my chosen people.
21 I made them my own nation,
so they would praise me.

22 I, the LORD, said to Israel:
You have become weary,
but not from worshiping me.
23 You have not honored me
by sacrificing sheep
or other animals.
And I have not burdened you
with demands for sacrifices
or sweet-smelling incense.

24 You have not brought
delicious spices for me
or given me the best part
of your sacrificed animals.
Instead, you burden me down
with your terrible sins.
25 But I wipe away your sins
because of who I am.
And so, I will forget
the wrongs you have done.

26 Meet me in court!
State your case and prove
that you are right.
27 Your earliest ancestor[p]
and all of your leaders[q]
rebelled against me.
28 That's why I don't allow
your priests to serve me;
I let Israel be destroyed
and your people disgraced.

The LORD's Promise to Israel

44 People of Israel,
I have chosen you
as my servant.
2 I am your Creator.
You were in my care
even before you were born.
Israel, don't be terrified!
You are my chosen servant,
my very favorite.[r]

3 I will bless the thirsty land
by sending streams of water;
I will bless your descendants
by giving them my Spirit.
4 They will spring up like grass[s]
or like willow trees
near flowing streams.
5 They will worship me
and become my people.
They will write my name
on the back of their hands.[t]

[m]43.14 *crying as they go*: Or "in their glorious ships." [n]43.19 *streams*: The Standard Hebrew Text; the Dead Sea Scrolls "paths." [o]43.20 *jackals*: Desert animals related to wolves, but smaller. [p]43.27 *earliest ancestor*: Jacob, also known as Israel. [q]43.27 *leaders*: Probably prophets, but perhaps also priests and kings. [r]44.2 *my very favorite*: Or "Jeshurun." [s]44.4 *like grass*: One possible meaning for the difficult Hebrew text. [t]44.5 *write . . . hands*: To show that they belong to the LORD and to Israel.

6 I am the LORD All-Powerful,
the first and the last,
the one and only God.
Israel, I have rescued you!
I am your King.
7 Can anyone compare with me?
If so, let them speak up
and tell me now.
Let them say what has happened
since I made my nation
long ago,
and let them tell
what is going to happen.[u]
8 Don't tremble with fear!
Didn't I tell you long ago?
Didn't you hear me?
I alone am God—
no one else is a mighty rock.[v]

Idols Can't Do a Thing

The LORD said:
9 Those people who make idols
are nothing themselves,
and the idols they treasure
are just as worthless.
Worshipers of idols are blind,
stupid, and foolish.
10 Why make an idol or an image
that can't do a thing?
11 Everyone who makes idols
and all who worship them
are mere humans,
who will end up
sadly disappointed.
Let them face me in court
and be terrified.

Idols and Firewood

12 A metalworker shapes an idol
by using a hammer[w]
and heat from the fire.
In his powerful hand
he holds a hammer,
as he pounds the metal
into the proper shape.
But he gets hungry and thirsty
and loses his strength.
13 Some woodcarver measures
a piece of wood,
then draws an outline.
The idol is carefully carved
with each detail exact.
At last it looks like a person
and is placed in a temple.
14 Either cedar, cypress, oak,
or any tree from the forest
may be chosen.
Or even a pine tree planted
by the woodcarver
and watered by the rain.

15 Some of the wood is used
to make a fire for heating
or for cooking.
One piece is made into an idol,
then the woodcarver bows down
and worships it.
16 He enjoys the warm fire
and the meat that was roasted
over the burning coals.
17 Afterwards, he bows down
to worship the wooden idol.
"Protect me!" he says.
"You are my god."

18 Those who worship idols are stupid
and blind! **19** They don't have enough sense
to say to themselves, "I made a fire with
half of the wood and cooked my bread and
meat on it. Then I made something worthless with the other half. Why worship a
block of wood?"
20 How can anyone be stupid enough to
trust something that can be burned to
ashes?[x] No one can save themselves like
that. Don't they realize that the idols they
hold in their hands are not really gods?

The LORD Won't Forget His People

21 People of Israel,
you are my servant,
so remember all of this.
Israel, I created you,
and you are my servant.
I won't forget you.[y]

[u]**44.7** *Let them say . . . happen*: One possible meaning for the difficult Hebrew text.
[v]**44.8** *mighty rock*: See the note at 17.10. [w]**44.12** *by using a hammer*: One possible meaning for the difficult Hebrew text. [x]**44.20** *How . . . ashes*: One possible meaning for the difficult Hebrew text. [y]**44.21** *I won't forget you*: One possible meaning for the difficult Hebrew text.
44.6 Is 48.12; Rev 1.17; 2.8; 22.13. **44.15** Ws 13.11-19.

22 Turn back to me!
I have rescued you
and swept away your sins
as though they were clouds.

Sing Praises to the LORD

23 Tell the heavens and the earth
to start singing!
Tell the mountains
and every tree in the forest
to join in the song!
The LORD has rescued his people;
now they will worship him.

The LORD Created Everything

24 Israel, I am your LORD.
I am your source of life,
and I have rescued you.
I created everything
from the sky above
to the earth below.

25 I make liars of false prophets
and fools of fortunetellers.
I take human wisdom
and turn it into nonsense.
26 I will make the message
of my prophets come true.
They are saying, "Jerusalem
will be filled with people,
and the LORD will rebuild
the towns of Judah."

27 I am the one who commands
the sea and its streams
to run dry.
28 I am also the one who says,
"Cyrus will lead my people
and obey my orders.
Jerusalem and the temple
will be rebuilt."

Cyrus Obeys the LORD's Commands

45 The LORD said to Cyrus,
his chosen one:
I have taken hold
of your right hand
to help you capture nations
and remove kings from power.
City gates will open for you;
not one will stay closed.
2 As I lead you,
I will level mountains[z]
and break the iron bars
on bronze gates of cities.

3 I will give you treasures
hidden in dark
and secret places.
Then you will know that I,
the LORD God of Israel,
have called you by name.
4 Cyrus, you don't even know me!
But I have called you by name
and highly honored you[a]
because of Israel,
my chosen servant.

5 Only I am the LORD!
There are no other gods.
I have made you strong,
though you don't know me.
6 Now everyone from east to west
will learn that I am the LORD.
No other gods are real.
7 I create light and darkness,
happiness and sorrow.
I, the LORD, do all of this.

8 Tell the heavens
to send down justice
like showers of rain.
Prepare the earth
for my saving power
to sprout and produce justice
that I, the LORD, create.[b]

The LORD's Mighty Power

The LORD said:
9 Israel, you have no right
to argue with your Creator.
You are merely a clay pot
shaped by a potter.
The clay doesn't ask,
"Why did you make me this way?
Where are the handles?"
10 Children don't have the right
to demand of their parents,

[z] **45.2** *mountains*: The Dead Sea Scrolls and one ancient translation; the Standard Hebrew Text "rising waves." [a] **45.4** *But . . . you*: One possible meaning for the difficult Hebrew text.
[b] **45.8** *Prepare . . . create*: One possible meaning for the difficult Hebrew text.
44.25 1 Co 1.20. **44.28** 2 Ch 36.23; Ezra 1.2, 3. **45.9** Is 29.16; Ro 9.20.

"What have you done
to make us what we are?"

11 I am the LORD, the Creator,
the holy God of Israel.
Do you dare question me
about my own nation
or about what I have done?
12 I created the world
and covered it with people;
I stretched out the sky
and filled it with stars.
13 I have done the right thing
by placing Cyrus in power,
and I will make the roads easy
for him to follow.
I am the LORD All-Powerful!
Cyrus will rebuild my city
and set my people free
without being paid a thing.
I, the LORD, have spoken.

The LORD Alone Can Save

14 My people, I, the LORD, promise
that the riches of Egypt
and the treasures of Ethiopia[c]
will belong to you.
You will force into slavery
those tall people of Seba.[d]

They will bow down and say,
"The only true God is with you;
there are no other gods."
15 People of Israel,
your God is a mystery,
though he alone can save.
16 Anyone who makes idols
will be confused
and terribly disgraced.
17 But Israel, I, the LORD,
will always keep you safe
and free from shame.

Everyone Is Invited

18 The LORD alone is God!
He created the heavens
and made a world
where people can live,
instead of creating
an empty desert.
The LORD alone is God;
there are no others.
19 The LORD did not speak
in a dark secret place
or command Jacob's descendants
to search for him in vain.

The LORD speaks the truth,
and this is what he says
20 to every survivor
from every nation:
"Gather around me!
Learn how senseless it is
to worship wooden idols
or pray to helpless gods.

21 "Why don't you get together
and meet me in court?
Didn't I tell you long ago
what would happen?
I am the only God!
There are no others.
I bring about justice,
and have the power to save.

22 "I invite the whole world
to turn to me and be saved.
I alone am God!
No others are real.
23 I have made a solemn promise,
one that won't be broken:
Everyone will bow down
and worship me.
24 They will admit that I alone
can bring about justice.
Everyone who is angry with me
will be terribly ashamed
and will turn to me.
25 I, the LORD, will give
victory and great honor
to the people of Israel."

Babylonia's Gods Are Helpless

The LORD said:

46 The gods Bel and Nebo[e]
are down on their knees,
as wooden images of them

[c]**45.14** *Ethiopia*: See the note at 11.11. [d]**45.14** *Seba*: See the note at 43.3. [e]**46.1** *Bel and Nebo*: Bel was another name for Marduk, the chief god of the Babylonians. Nebo was the son of Marduk and also an important god.

45.23 Ro 14.11; Phil 2.10, 11.

are carried away
on weary animals.[f]
2 They are down on their knees
to rescue the heavy load,
but the images are still taken
to a foreign country.

3 You survivors in Israel,
listen to me, the LORD.
Since the day you were born,
I have carried you along.
4 I will still be the same
when you are old and gray,
and I will take care of you.
I created you. I will carry you
and always keep you safe.

5 Can anyone compare with me?
Is anyone my equal?
6 Some people hire a goldsmith
and give silver and gold
to be formed into an idol
for them to worship.
7 They carry the idol
on their shoulders,
then put it on a stand,
but it cannot move.

They call out to the idol
when they are in trouble,
but it doesn't answer,
and it cannot help.
8 Now keep this in mind,[g]
you sinful people.
And don't ever forget it.

The LORD Alone Is God

9 I alone am God!
There are no other gods;
no one is like me.
Think about what happened
many years ago.
10 From the very beginning,
I told what would happen
long before it took place.

I kept my word 11 and brought
someone from a distant land
to do what I wanted.
He attacked from the east,
like a hawk swooping down.
Now I will keep my promise
and do what I planned.

12 You people are stubborn
and far from being safe,
so listen to me.
13 I will soon come to save you.
I am not far away
and will waste no time;
I take pride in Israel
and will save Jerusalem.

Babylon Will Fall

The LORD said:
47 City of Babylon,
You are delicate
and untouched,
but that will change.
Surrender your royal power
and sit in the dirt.
2 Start grinding grain!
Take off your veil.
Strip off your fancy clothes
and cross over rivers.[h]
3 You will suffer the shame
of going naked,
because I will take revenge,
and no one can escape.[i]
4 I am the LORD All-Powerful,
the holy God of Israel.
I am their Savior.

5 Babylon, be silent!
Sit in the dark.
No longer will nations
accept you as their queen.
6 I was angry with my people.
So I let you take their land
and bring disgrace on them.
You showed them no mercy,
but were especially cruel
to those who were old.
7 You thought that you
would be queen forever.
You didn't care what you did;

[f]**46.1** *as . . . animals*: One possible meaning for the difficult Hebrew text. [g]**46.8** *Now . . . mind*: One possible meaning for the difficult Hebrew text. [h]**47.2** *Strip . . . rivers*: This may be a command to get ready for work that requires wading in the river, or it may be a warning that they are going to be taken away as slaves. [i]**47.3** *escape*: Or "oppose me."
47.1-15 Is 13.1—14.23; Jr 50.1—51.64.

it never entered your mind
that you might get caught.
8 You think that you alone
are all-powerful,
that you won't be a widow
or lose your children.
All you care about is pleasure,
but listen to what I say.
9 Your magic powers and charms
will suddenly fail,
then you will be a widow
and lose your children.

10 You hid behind evil
like a shield and said,
"No one can see me!"
You were fooled by your wisdom
and your knowledge;
you felt sure that you alone
were in full control.
11 But without warning,
disaster will strike—
and your magic charms
won't help at all.

12 Keep using your magic powers
and your charms
as you have always done.
Maybe—just maybe—
you will frighten somebody!
13 You have worn yourself out,
asking for advice
from those who study the stars
and tell the future
month after month.
Go ask them how to be saved
from what will happen.
14 People who trust the stars
are as helpless as straw
in a flaming fire.
No one can even keep warm,[j]
sitting by a fire
that feeds only on straw.
15 These are the fortunetellers
you have done business with
all of your life.
But they don't know
where they are going,
and they can't save you.

The LORD Corrects His People

48 People of Israel,
you come from Jacob's family
and the tribe[k] of Judah.
You claim to worship me,
the LORD God of Israel,
but you are lying.
2 You call Jerusalem your home
and say you depend on me,
the LORD All-Powerful,
the God of Israel.

3 Long ago I announced
what was going to be,
then without warning,
I made it happen.
4 I knew you were stubborn
and hardheaded.
5 And I told you these things,
so that when they happened
you would not say,
"The idols we worship did this."

6 You heard what I said,
and you have seen it happen.
Now admit that it's true!
I will show you secrets
you have never known.
7 Today I am doing something new,
something you cannot say
you have heard before.
8 You have never been willing
to listen to what I say;
from the moment of your birth,
I knew you would rebel.

The LORD Warns Israel

9 I, the LORD, am true to myself;
I will be praised for not punishing
and destroying you.
10 I tested you in hard times
just as silver is refined
in a heated furnace.[l]
11 I did this because of who I am.
I refuse to be dishonored[m]
or share my praise
with any other god.

[j]**47.14** *keep warm*: Or "cook food." [k]**48.1** *tribe*: Hebrew "waters." [l]**48.10** *furnace*: One possible meaning for the difficult Hebrew text of verse 10. [m]**48.11** *I refuse to be dishonored*: One possible meaning for the difficult Hebrew text.
47.8,9 Rev 18.7, 8.

12 Israel, my chosen people,
listen to me.
I alone am the LORD,
the first and the last.
13 With my own hand
I created the earth
and stretched out the sky.
They obey my every command.

The LORD Speaks to the Nations

14 Gather around me, all of you!
Listen to what I say.
Did any of your idols
predict this would happen?
Did they say that my friend[n]
would do what I want done
to Babylonia?[o]
15 I was the one who chose him.
I have brought him this far,
and he will be successful.
16 Come closer and listen!
I have never kept secret
the things I have said,
and I was here
before time began.

It Is Best To Obey the LORD

By the power of his Spirit
the LORD God has sent me
17 with this message:
People of Israel,
I am the holy LORD God,
the one who rescues you.
For your own good,
I teach you, and I lead you
along the right path.
18 How I wish that you
had obeyed my commands!
Your success and good fortune
would then have overflowed
like a flooding river.
19 Your nation would be blessed
with more people
than there are grains of sand
along the seashore.
And I would never have let
your country be destroyed.

20 Now leave Babylon!
Celebrate as you go.
Be happy and shout
for everyone to hear,
"The LORD has rescued
his servant Israel!
21 He led us through the desert
and made water flow from a rock
to satisfy our thirst.
22 But the LORD has promised
that none who are evil
will live in peace."

The Work of the LORD's Servant

49 Everyone, listen,
even you foreign nations
across the sea.
The LORD chose me
and gave me a name
before I was born.
2 He made my words pierce
like a sharp sword
or a pointed arrow;
he kept me safely hidden
in the palm of his hand.
3 The LORD said to me,
"Israel, you are my servant;
and because of you
I will be highly honored."

4 I said to myself,
"I'm completely worn out;
my time has been wasted.
But I did it for the LORD God,
and he will reward me."

5 Even before I was born,
the LORD God chose me
to serve him and to lead back
the people of Israel.
So the LORD has honored me
and made me strong.

6 Now the LORD says to me,
"It isn't enough for you
to be merely my servant.
You must do more than lead back

[n]**48.14** *my friend*: Probably Cyrus (see 44.28; 45.1). [o]**48.14** *Babylonia*: One possible meaning for the difficult Hebrew text of verse 14.

48.12 Is 44.6; Rev 1.17; 22.13. **48.20** Rev 18.4. **48.22** Is 57.21. **49.1** Jr 1.5. **49.2** He 4.12; Rev 1.16. **49.6** **a** Is 42.6; Lk 2.32; Ac 26.23; **b** Ac 13.47.

survivors from the tribes
of Israel.
I have placed you here as a light
for other nations;
you must take my saving power
to everyone on earth."

The LORD Will Rescue His People

7 Israel, I am the holy LORD God,
the one who rescues you.
You are slaves of rulers
and of a nation
who despises you.[p]
Now this is what I promise:
Kings and rulers will honor you
by kneeling at your feet.
You can trust me! I am your LORD,
the holy God of Israel,
and you are my chosen ones.

The LORD Will Lead His People Home

8 This is what the LORD says:
I will answer your prayers
because I have set a time
when I will help
by coming to save you.
I have chosen you
to take my promise of hope
to other nations.[q]
You will rebuild the country
from its ruins,
then people will come
and settle there.
9 You will set prisoners free
from dark dungeons
to see the light of day.

On their way home,
they will find plenty to eat,
even on barren hills.
10 They won't go hungry
or get thirsty;
they won't be bothered
by the scorching sun
or hot desert winds.
I will be merciful
while leading them along
to streams of water.
11 I will level the mountains
and make roads.
12 Then my people will return
from distant lands
in the north and the west
and from the city of Syene.[r]

The LORD's Mercy

13 Tell the heavens and the earth
to celebrate and sing;
command every mountain
to join in the song.
The LORD's people have suffered,
but he has shown mercy
and given them comfort.

14 The people of Zion said,
"The LORD has turned away
and forgotten us."

15 The LORD answered,
"Could a mother forget a child
who nurses at her breast?
Could she fail to love an infant
who came from her own body?
Even if a mother could forget,
I will never forget you.
16 A picture of your city
is drawn on my hand.
You are always in my thoughts!

17 "Your city will be built faster
than it was destroyed[s]—
those who attacked it
will retreat and leave.
18 Look around! You will see
your people coming home.
As surely as I live,
I, the LORD, promise
that your city with its people
will be as lovely as a bride
wearing her jewelry."

Jerusalem's Bright Future

19 Jerusalem is now in ruins!
Nothing is left of the city.

[p] **49.7** *You . . . you*: One possible meaning for the difficult Hebrew text. [q] **49.8** *my . . . nations*: One possible meaning for the difficult Hebrew text. [r] **49.12** *Syene*: The Dead Sea Scrolls; the Standard Hebrew Text "Sinim." The reference may be to modern Aswan, a city in southern Egypt. [s] **49.17** *Your city . . . destroyed*: One possible meaning for the difficult Hebrew text.

49.8 2 Co 6.2. **49.10** Rev 7.16, 17.

But it will be rebuilt
and soon overcrowded;
its cruel enemies
will be gone far away.

20 Jerusalem is a woman
whose children were born
while she was in deep sorrow[t]
over the loss of her husband.
Now those children
will come and seek room
in the crowded city,
21 and Jerusalem will ask,
"Am I really their mother?
How could I have given birth
when I was still mourning
in a foreign land?
Who raised these children?
Where have they come from?"

22 The LORD God says:
"I will soon give a signal
for the nations
to return your sons
and your daughters
to the arms of Jerusalem.
23 The kings and queens
of those nations
where they were raised
will come and bow down.
They will take care of you
just like a slave
taking care of a child.
Then you will know
that I am the LORD.
You won't be disappointed
if you trust me."

The LORD Is on Our Side

24 Is it possible to rescue victims
from someone strong
and cruel?[u]
25 But the LORD has promised
to fight on our side
and to rescue our children
from those strong
and violent enemies.
26 He will make those cruel people
dine on their own flesh
and get drunk from drinking
their own blood.
Then everyone will know
that the LORD is our Savior;
the powerful God of Israel
has rescued his people.

The LORD's Power To Punish

50 The LORD says, "Children,
I didn't divorce your mother
or sell you to pay debts;
I divorced her and sold you
because of your sins.
2 I came and called out,
but you didn't answer.
Have I lost my power
to rescue and save?
At my command oceans and rivers
turn into deserts;
fish rot and stink
for lack of water.
3 I make the sky turn dark
like the sackcloth
you wear at funerals."

God's Servant Must Suffer

4 The LORD God gives me
the right words
to encourage the weary.
Each morning he awakens me
eager to learn his teaching;
5 he made me willing to listen
and not rebel or run away.

6 I let them beat my back
and pull out my beard.
I didn't turn aside
when they insulted me
and spit in my face.
7 But the LORD God keeps me
from being disgraced.
So I refuse to give up,
because I know
God will never let me down.

[t]**49.20** *whose children . . . sorrow*: These "children" are Jews who were born in foreign countries during the time that Jerusalem was in ruins. Jerusalem probably stands for all the cities in Judah that were destroyed by the Babylonians. [u]**49.24** *cruel*: The Dead Sea Scrolls and two ancient translations; the Standard Hebrew Text "good."

49.22 Ba 5.6. **50.1** Ba 4.6. **50.6** Mt 26.67; Mk 14.65.

8 My protector is nearby;
no one can stand here
to accuse me of wrong.
9 The LORD God will help me
and prove I am innocent.
My accusers will wear out
like moth-eaten clothes.

10 None of you respect the LORD
or obey his servant.
You walk in the dark
instead of the light;
you don't trust the name
of the LORD your God.[v]
11 Go ahead and walk in the light
of the fires you have set.[w]
But with his own hand,
the LORD will punish you
and make you suffer.

The LORD Will Bring Comfort

51 If you want to do right
and obey the LORD,
follow Abraham's example.
He was the rock from which
you were chipped.
2 God chose Abraham and Sarah
to be your ancestors.
The LORD blessed Abraham,
and from that one man
came many descendants.

3 Though Zion is in ruins,
the LORD will bring comfort,
and the city will be as lovely
as the garden of Eden
that he provided.
Then Zion will celebrate;
it will be thankful
and sing joyful songs.

The LORD's Victory Will Last

4 The LORD says:
You are my people and nation!
So pay attention to me.
My teaching will cause justice
to shine like a light
for every nation.
5 Those who live across the sea
are eagerly waiting
for me to rescue them.
I am strong and ready;
soon I will come to save
and to rule all nations.

6 Look closely at the sky!
Stare at the earth.
The sky will vanish like smoke;
the earth will wear out
like clothes.
Everyone on this earth
will die like flies.
But my victory will last;
my saving power never ends.

7 If you want to do right
and to obey my teaching
with all your heart,
then pay close attention.
Don't be discouraged
when others insult you
and say hurtful things.
8 They will be eaten away
like a moth-eaten coat.
But my victory will last;
my saving power
will never end.

A Prayer for the LORD's Help

9 Wake up! Do something, LORD.
Be strong and ready.
Wake up! Do what you did
for our people long ago.
Didn't you chop up
Rahab[x] the monster?
10 Didn't you dry up the deep sea
and make a road for your people
to follow safely across?
11 Now those you have rescued
will return to Jerusalem,
singing on their way.
They will be crowned
with great happiness,
never again to be burdened
with sadness and sorrow.

[v]**50.10** *God*: One possible meaning for the difficult Hebrew text of verse 10. [w]**50.11** *Go . . . set*: One possible meaning for the difficult Hebrew text. [x]**51.9** *Rahab*: This may refer to Egypt at the time of the exodus.

50.8,9 Ro 8.33, 34. **51.1** 4 Macc 13.12.

The LORD Gives Hope

12 I am the LORD, the one
who encourages you.
Why are you afraid
of mere humans?
They dry up and die like grass.

13 I spread out the heavens
and laid foundations
for the earth.
But you have forgotten me,
your LORD and Creator.
All day long you were afraid
of those who were angry
and hoped to abuse you.
Where are they now?

14 Everyone crying out in pain
will be quickly set free;
they will be rescued
from the power of death
and never go hungry.
15 I will help them
because I am your God,
the LORD All-Powerful,
who makes the ocean roar.

16 I have told you what to say,
and I will keep you safe
in the palm of my hand.
I spread out the heavens
and laid foundations
for the earth.
Now I say, "Jerusalem,
your people are mine."

A Warning to Jerusalem

17 Jerusalem, wake up! Stand up!
You've drunk too much
from the cup filled
with the LORD's anger.
You have swallowed every drop,
and you can't walk straight.
18 Not one of your many children
is there to guide you
or to offer a helping hand.
19 You have been destroyed
by war and by famine;
I cannot comfort you.[y]
20 The LORD your God is angry,
and on every street corner
your children lie helpless,
like deer trapped in nets.

21 You are in trouble and drunk,
but not from wine.
So pay close attention
22 to the LORD your God,
who defends you and says,
"I have taken from your hands
the cup filled with my anger
that made you drunk.
You will never be forced
to drink it again.
23 Instead I will give it
to your brutal enemies,
who treated you like dirt
and walked all over you."

Jerusalem Can Celebrate

52 Jerusalem, wake up!
Stand up and be strong.
Holy city of Zion,
dress in your best clothes.
Those foreigners who ruined
your sacred city
won't bother you again.
2 Zion, rise from the dirt!
Free yourself from the rope
around your neck.

Suffering Will End

3 The LORD says:
My people, you were sold,
but not for money;
now you will be set free,
but not for a payment.
4 Long ago you went to Egypt
where you lived
as foreigners.
Then Assyria was cruel to you,
5 and now another nation[z]
has taken you prisoner
for no reason at all.
Your leaders groan with pain,[a]
and day after day
my own name is cursed.
6 My people, you will learn

[y]**51.19** *I . . . you*: One possible meaning for the difficult Hebrew text. [z]**52.5** *another nation*: Babylonia. [a]**52.5** *groan with pain*: One possible meaning for the difficult Hebrew text.

51.17 Rev 14.10; 16.19. **52.1** Rev 21.2, 27. **52.5** Ro 2.24.

who I am and who is speaking
because I am here.

A Message of Hope for Jerusalem

7 What a beautiful sight!
On the mountains a messenger
announces to Jerusalem,
"Good news! You're saved.
There will be peace.
Your God is now King."
8 Everyone on guard duty,
sing and celebrate!
Look! You can see the LORD
returning to Zion.
9 Jerusalem, rise from the ruins!
Join in the singing.
The LORD has given comfort
to his people;
he comes to your rescue.
10 The LORD has shown all nations
his mighty strength;
now everyone will see
the saving power of our God.

A Command To Leave Babylon

11 Leave the city of Babylon!
Don't touch anything filthy.
Wash yourselves. Be ready
to carry back everything sacred
that belongs to the LORD.
12 You won't need to run.
No one is chasing you.
The LORD God of Israel
will lead and protect you
from enemy attacks.

The Suffering Servant

13 The LORD says:
My servant will succeed!
He will be given great praise
and the highest honors.
14 Many were horrified
at what happened to him.[b]
But everyone who saw him
was even more horrified
because he suffered until
he no longer looked human.[c]
15 My servant will make
nations worthy to worship me;[d]
kings will be silent
as they bow in wonder.[e]
They will see and think about
things they have never seen
or thought about before.

What God's Servant Did for Us

53 Has anyone believed us
or seen the mighty power
of the LORD in action?
2 Like a young plant or a root
that sprouts in dry ground,
the servant grew up
obeying the LORD.
He wasn't some handsome king.
Nothing about the way he looked
made him attractive to us.
3 He was hated and rejected;
his life was filled with sorrow
and terrible suffering.
No one wanted to look at him.
We despised him and said,
"He is a nobody!"

4 He suffered and endured
great pain for us,
but we thought his suffering
was punishment from God.
5 He was wounded and crushed
because of our sins;
by taking our punishment,
he made us completely well.
6 All of us were like sheep
that had wandered off.
We had each gone our own way,
but the LORD gave him
the punishment we deserved.

7 He was painfully abused,
but he did not complain.
He was silent like a lamb
being led to the butcher,

[b]**52.14** *him*: One ancient translation; Hebrew "you." [c]**52.14** *human*: One possible meaning for the difficult Hebrew text of verse 14. [d]**52.15** *My . . . me*: Hebrew; one ancient translation "The nations will be amazed at him." [e]**52.15** *kings . . . wonder*: One possible meaning for the difficult Hebrew text.

52.7 Nh 1.15; Ro 10.15; Eph 6.15. **52.11** 2 Co 6.17. **52.15** Ro 15.21. **53.1** Ro 10.16; Jn 12.38. **53.5** Mt 8.17; 1 P 2.24. **53.5-12** 4 Macc 6.29. **53.6** 1 P 2.25. **53.7** Rev 5.6. **53.7,8** Ac 8.32, 33. **53.7-12** 4 Macc 10.18.

as quiet as a sheep
having its wool cut off.

8 He was condemned to death
without a fair trial.
Who could have imagined
what would happen to him?
His life was taken away
because of the sinful things
my people[f] had done.
9 He wasn't dishonest or violent,
but he was buried in a tomb
of cruel and rich people.[g]

10 The LORD decided his servant
would suffer as a sacrifice
to take away the sin
and guilt of others.
Now the servant will live
to see his own descendants.[h]
He did everything
the LORD had planned.

11 By suffering, the servant
will learn the true meaning
of obeying the LORD.
Although he is innocent,
he will take the punishment
for the sins of others,
so that many of them
will no longer be guilty.
12 The LORD will reward him
with honor and power
for sacrificing his life.
Others thought he was a sinner,
but he suffered for our sins
and asked God to forgive us.

A Promise of the LORD's Protection

54 Sing and shout,
even though you have never
had children!
The LORD has promised that you
will have more children
than someone married
for a long time.
2 Make your tents larger!
Spread out the tent pegs;
fasten them firmly.
3 You and your descendants
will take over the land
of other nations.
You will settle in towns
that are now in ruins.

4 Don't be afraid or ashamed
and don't be discouraged.
You won't be disappointed.
Forget how sinful you were
when you were young;
stop feeling ashamed
for being left a widow.
5 The LORD All-Powerful,
the Holy God of Israel,
rules all the earth.
He is your Creator and husband,
and he will rescue you.

6 You were like a young wife,
brokenhearted and crying
because her husband
had divorced her.
But the LORD your God says,
"I am taking you back!
7 I rejected you for a while,
but with love and tenderness
I will embrace you again.
8 For a while, I turned away
in furious anger.
Now I will have mercy
and love you forever!
I, your protector and LORD,
make this promise."

The LORD Promises Lasting Peace

9 I once promised Noah that I
would never again destroy
the earth by a flood.
Now I have promised that I
will never again get angry
and punish you.
10 Every mountain and hill
may disappear.
But I will always be kind
and merciful to you;

[f] **53.8** *my people*: Or "his people." [g] **53.9** *but he . . . people*: One possible meaning for the difficult Hebrew text. [h] **53.10** *The LORD . . . descendants*: One possible meaning for the difficult Hebrew text.

53.9 1 P 2.22. **53.12** Mk 15.27, 28; Lk 22.37. **54.1** Ga 4.27. **54.9** Gn 9.8-17. **54.10** Jdt 16.15.

I won't break my agreement
to give your nation peace.

The New Jerusalem

11 Jerusalem, you are sad
and discouraged,
tossed around in a storm.
But I, the LORD,
will rebuild your city
with precious stones;[i]
for your foundation
I will use blue sapphires.
12 Your fortresses[j]
will be built of rubies,
your gates of jewels,
and your walls of gems.
13 I will teach your children
and make them successful.

14 You will be built on fairness
with no fears of injustice;
every one of your worries
will be taken far from you.
15 I will never send anyone
to attack your city,
and you will make prisoners
of those who do attack.
16 Don't forget that I created
metalworkers who make weapons
over burning coals.
I also created armies
that can bring destruction.
17 Weapons made to attack you
won't be successful;
words spoken against you
won't hurt at all.

My servants, Jerusalem is yours!
I, the LORD, promise
to bless you with victory.

The LORD's Invitation

55 If you are thirsty,
come and drink water!
If you don't have any money,
come, eat what you want!
Drink wine and milk
without paying a cent.
2 Why waste your money
on what really isn't food?
Why work hard for something
that doesn't satisfy?
Listen carefully to me,
and you will enjoy
the very best foods.

3 Pay close attention!
Come to me and live.
I will promise you
the eternal love and loyalty
that I promised David.
4 I made him the leader and ruler
of the nations;
he was my witness to them.
5 You will call out to nations
you have never known.
And they have never known you,
but they will come running
because I am the LORD,
the holy God of Israel,
and I have honored you.

God's Words Are Powerful

6 Turn to the LORD!
He can still be found.
Call out to God! He is near.
7 Give up your crooked ways
and your evil thoughts.
Return to the LORD our God.
He will be merciful
and forgive your sins.

8 The LORD says:
"My thoughts and my ways
are not like yours.
9 Just as the heavens
are higher than the earth,
my thoughts and my ways
are higher than yours.

10 "Rain and snow fall from the sky.
But they don't return
without watering the earth

[i] **54.11** *with precious stones*: One possible meaning for the difficult Hebrew text.
[j] **54.12** *fortresses*: One possible meaning for the difficult Hebrew text.
54.11,12 Rev 21.18-21. **54.11** Tb 13.16, 17. **54.13** Jn 6.45. **55.1** Rev 21.6; 22.17. **55.2** Si 24.19-22. **55.3** Ac 13.34. **55.10** 2 Co 9.10.

that produces seeds to plant
and grain to eat.
11 That's how it is with my words.
They don't return to me
without doing everything
I send them to do."

God's People Will Celebrate

12 When you are set free,
you will celebrate
and travel home in peace.
Mountains and hills will sing
as you pass by,
and trees will clap.
13 Cypress and myrtle trees
will grow in fields
once covered by thorns.
And then those trees will stand
as a lasting witness
to the glory of the LORD.

All Nations Will Be Part of God's People

56 The LORD said:
Be honest and fair!
Soon I will come to save you;
my saving power will be seen
everywhere on earth.

2 I will bless everyone
who respects the Sabbath
and refuses to do wrong.

3 Foreigners who worship me
must not say,
"The LORD won't let us
be part of his people."
Men who are unable
to become fathers
must no longer say,
"We are dried-up trees."

4 To them, I, the LORD, say:
Respect the Sabbath,
obey me completely,
and keep our agreement.
5 Then I will set up monuments
in my temple with your names
written on them.
This will be much better
than having children,
because these monuments
will stand there forever.
6 Foreigners will follow me.
They will love me and worship
in my name;
they will respect the Sabbath
and keep our agreement.
7 I will bring them
to my holy mountain,
where they will celebrate
in my house of worship.
Their sacrifices and offerings
will always be welcome
on my altar.
Then my house will be known
as a house of worship
for all nations.
8 I, the LORD, promise
to bring together my people
who were taken away,
and let them join the others.

God Promises To Punish Israel's Leaders

9 Come from the forest,
you wild animals!
Attack and gobble down
your victims.
10 You leaders of Israel
should be watchdogs,
protecting my people.
But you can't see a thing,
and you never warn them.
Dozing and daydreaming
are all you ever do.
11 You stupid leaders are a pack
of hungry and greedy dogs
that never get enough.
You are shepherds
who mistreat your own sheep
for selfish gain.
12 You say to each other,
"Let's drink till we're drunk!
Tomorrow we'll do it again.
We'll really enjoy ourselves."

God's Faithful People Suffer

57 God's faithful people
are dragged off and killed,
and no one even cares.

56.4,5 Ws 3.14, 15. **56.7** Mt 21.13; Mk 11.17; Lk 19.46.

Evil sweeps them away,
2 but in death they find peace
for obeying God.[k]

The LORD Condemns Idolatry

3 You people are unfaithful!
You go to fortunetellers,
and you worship idols.
Now pay close attention!
4 Who are you making fun of?
Who are you sneering at?
Look how your sins
have made fools of you.

5 All you think about is sex
under those green trees
where idols are worshiped.
You sacrifice your children
on altars built in valleys
under rocky slopes.
6 You have chosen to worship
idols made of stone;[l]
you have given them offerings
of wine and grain.
Should I be pleased?

7 You have spread out your beds
on the tops of high mountains,
where you sacrifice to idols.
8 Even in your homes
you have placed pagan symbols
all around your huge beds.
Yes, you have rejected me,
sold yourselves to your lovers,
and gone to bed with them.[m]

9 You smear on olive oil
and all kinds of perfume
to worship the god Molech.[n]
You even seek advice
from spirits of the dead.
10 Though you tired yourself out
by running after idols,
you refused to stop.
Your desires were so strong
that they kept you going.

11 Did you forget about me
and become unfaithful
because you were more afraid
of someone else?
Have I been silent so long[o]
that you no longer fear me?
12 You think you're so good,
but I'll point out the truth.
13 Ask your idols to save you
when you are in trouble.
Be careful though—
it takes only a faint breath
to blow them over.
But if you come to me
for protection,
this land and my holy mountain
will always belong to you.

The LORD Helps the Helpless

14 The LORD says,
"Clear the road!
Get it ready for my people."

15 Our holy God lives forever
in the highest heavens,
and this is what he says:
Though I live high above
in the holy place,
I am here to help those
who are humble
and depend only on me.

16 My people, I won't stay angry
and keep on accusing you.
After all, I am your Creator.
I don't want you to give up
in complete despair.
17 Your greed made me furious.
That's why I punished you
and refused to be found,
while you kept returning
to your old sinful ways.

18 I know what you are like!
But I will heal you, lead you,
and give you comfort,

[k] **57.1,2** *Evil . . . God*: One possible meaning for the difficult Hebrew text. [l] **57.6** *You have . . . stone*: One possible meaning for the difficult Hebrew text. [m] **57.8** *them*: One possible meaning for the difficult Hebrew text of verse 8. [n] **57.9** *the god Molech*: Or "the king." In Hebrew "Molech" and "king" sound alike. [o] **57.11** *so long*: One possible meaning for the difficult Hebrew text.

57.15 3 Macc 2.2; 2.15.

until those who are mourning
19 start singing my praises.[p]
No matter where you are,
I, the LORD, will heal you[q]
and give you peace.

20 The wicked are a restless sea
tossing up mud.
21 But I, the LORD, have promised
that none who are evil
will live in peace.

True Religion

58 Shout the message!
Don't hold back.
Say to my people Israel:
You've sinned! You've turned
against the LORD.
2 Day after day, you worship him
and seem eager to learn
his teachings.
You act like a nation
that wants to do right
by obeying his laws.
You ask him about justice,
and say you enjoy
worshiping the LORD.

3 You wonder why the LORD
pays no attention
when you go without eating
and act humble.
But on those same days
that you give up eating,
you think only of yourselves[r]
and abuse your workers.
4 You even get angry
and ready to fight.
No wonder God won't listen
to your prayers!

5 Do you think the LORD
wants you to give up eating
and to act as humble
as a bent-over bush?
Or to dress in sackcloth
and sit in ashes?
Is this really what he wants
on a day of worship?

6 I'll tell you
what it really means
to worship the LORD.
Remove the chains of prisoners
who are chained unjustly.
Free those who are abused!
7 Share your food with everyone
who is hungry;
share your home
with the poor and homeless.
Give clothes to those in need;
don't turn away your relatives.

8 Then your light will shine
like the dawning sun, and you
will quickly be healed.
Your honesty[s] will protect you
as you advance,
and the glory of the LORD
will defend you from behind.
9 When you beg the LORD for help,
he will answer, "Here I am!"

Don't mistreat others
or falsely accuse them
or say something cruel.
10 Give your food to the hungry
and care for the homeless.
Then your light will shine
in the dark;
your darkest hour will be
like the noonday sun.

11 The LORD will always guide you
and provide good things to eat
when you are in the desert.
He will make you healthy.
You will be like a garden
that has plenty of water
or like a stream
that never runs dry.
12 You will rebuild those houses
left in ruins for years;
you will be known
as a builder and repairer
of city walls and streets.

[p]**57.18,19** *until . . . praises*: One possible meaning for the difficult Hebrew text. [q]**57.19** *heal you*: One possible meaning for the difficult Hebrew text. [r]**58.3** *you think . . . yourselves*: One possible meaning for the difficult Hebrew text. [s]**58.8** *honesty*: Or "honest leader."

57.19 Eph 2.17. **57.21** Is 48.22. **58.7** Mt 25.34.

13 But first, you must start
respecting the Sabbath
as a joyful day of worship.
You must stop doing and saying
whatever you please
on this special day.
14 Then you will truly enjoy
knowing the LORD.
He will let you rule
from the highest mountains
and bless you with the land
of your ancestor Jacob.
The LORD has spoken!

Social Injustice Is Condemned

59 The LORD hasn't lost
his powerful strength;
he can still hear
and answer prayers.
2 Your sins are the roadblock
between you and your God.
That's why he doesn't answer
your prayers
or let you see his face.

3 Your talk is filled with lies
and plans for violence;
every finger on your hands
is covered with blood.
4 You falsely accuse others
and tell lies in court;
sin and trouble are the names
of your children.
5 You eat the deadly eggs
of poisonous snakes,
and more snakes crawl out
from the eggs left to hatch.
You weave spider webs,
6 but you can't make clothes
with those webs
or hide behind them.

You're sinful and brutal.
7 You hurry off to do wrong
or murder innocent victims.
All you think about is sin;
you leave ruin and destruction
wherever you go.
8 You don't know how
to live in peace
or to be fair with others.
The roads you make are crooked;
your followers cannot find peace.

The People Confess Their Sins

9 No one has come to defend us
or to bring about justice.
We hoped for a day of sunshine,
but all we found
was a dark, gloomy night.
10 We feel our way along,
as if we were blind;
we stumble at noon,
as if it were night.
We can see no better
than someone dead.[t]

11 We growl like bears
and mourn like doves.
We hope for justice and victory,
but they escape us.
12 How often have we sinned
and turned against you,
the LORD God?
Our sins condemn us!
We have done wrong.
13 We have rebelled and refused
to follow you.
Our hearts were deceitful,
and so we lied;
we planned to abuse others
and turn our backs on you.

14 Injustice is everywhere;
justice seems far away.
Truth is chased out of court;
honesty is shoved aside.
15 Everyone tells lies;
those who turn from crime
end up ruined.

The LORD Will Rescue His People

When the LORD noticed
that justice had disappeared,
he became very displeased.
16 It disgusted him even more
to learn that no one
would do a thing about it.

[t]59.10 *We can . . . dead:* One possible meaning for the difficult Hebrew text.
59.7,8 Ro 3.15-17. **59.16** Is 63.5.

So with his own powerful arm,
he won victories for truth.
17 Justice was the LORD's armor;
saving power was his helmet;
anger and revenge
were his clothes.

18 Now the LORD will get furious
and do to his enemies,
both near and far,
what they did to his people.
19 He will attack like a flood
in a mighty windstorm.
Nations in the west and the east
will then honor and praise
his wonderful name.
20 The LORD has promised to rescue
the city of Zion
and Jacob's descendants
who turn from sin.

21 The LORD says: "My people,
I promise to give you my Spirit
and my message.
These will be my gifts to you
and your families forever.
I, the LORD, have spoken."

A New Day for Jerusalem

60 Jerusalem, stand up! Shine!
Your new day is dawning.
The glory of the LORD
shines brightly on you.
2 The earth and its people
are covered with darkness,
but the glory of the LORD
is shining upon you.
3 Nations and kings
will come to the light
of your dawning day.

Crowds Are Coming to Jerusalem

The LORD said:
4 Open your eyes! Look around!
Crowds are coming.
Your sons are on their way
from distant lands;
your daughters are being carried
like little children.
5 When you see this,
your faces will glow;
your hearts will pound
and swell with pride.[u]
Treasures from across the sea
and the wealth of nations
will be brought to you.
6 Your country will be covered
with caravans of young camels
from Midian and Ephah.[v]
The people of Sheba[w]
will bring gold and spices
in praise of me, the LORD.
7 Every sheep of Kedar
will come to you;
rams from Nebaioth[x]
will be yours as well.
I will accept them as offerings
and bring honor to my temple.

8 What is that sailing by
like clouds
or like doves flying home?
9 On those distant islands
your people are waiting
for me, the LORD.[y]
Seagoing ships[z] lead the way
to bring them home
with their silver and gold.
I, the holy LORD God of Israel,
do this to honor your people,
so they will honor me.

Jerusalem Will Be Rebuilt

The LORD said:
10 Jerusalem, your city walls
will be rebuilt by foreigners;
their rulers will become
your slaves.
I punished you in my anger;

[u]**60.5** *swell with pride*: One possible meaning for the difficult Hebrew text. [v]**60.6** *Midian . . . Ephah*: Midian was the ancestor of a nomadic tribe of the Arabian desert, east of the Gulf of Aqaba. Ephah was a clan within the tribe of Midian. [w]**60.6** *Sheba*: Perhaps a place in what is now southwest Arabia. The Queen of Sheba brought gifts to Solomon (1 Kings 10.1-13). [x]**60.7** *Kedar . . . Nebaioth*: Regions in northern Arabia. [y]**60.9** *On . . . LORD*: One possible meaning for the difficult Hebrew text. [z]**60.9** *Seagoing ships*: See the note at 2.16.

59.17 Ws 5.17-23; Eph 6.14, 17; 1 Th 5.8. **59.20** Ro 11.26. **60.4** Ba 5.5, 6.

now I will be kind
and treat you with mercy.

11 Your gates will be open
day and night
to let the rulers of nations
lead their people to you
with all their treasures.
12 Any nation or kingdom
that refuses to serve you
will be wiped out.
13 Wood from Lebanon's best trees
will be brought to you—
the pines, the firs,
and the cypress trees.
It will be used in my temple
to make beautiful the place
where I rest my feet.

14 The descendants of enemies
who hated and mistreated you
will kneel at your feet.
They will say, "You are Zion,
the city of the LORD,
the holy God of Israel."

15 You were hated and deserted,
rejected by everyone.
But I will make you beautiful,
a city to be proud of
for all time to come.
16 You will drain the wealth
of kings and foreign nations.
You will know that I,
the mighty LORD God of Israel,
have saved and rescued you.

17 I will bring bronze and iron
in place of wood and stone;
in place of bronze and iron,
I will bring gold and silver.
I will appoint peace and justice
as your rulers and leaders.
18 Violence, destruction, and ruin
will never again be heard of
within your borders.
"Victory" will be the name
you give to your walls;
"Praise" will be the name
you give to your gates.

19 You won't need the light
of the sun or the moon.
I, the LORD your God,
will be your eternal light
and bring you honor.
20 Your sun will never set
or your moon go down.
I, the LORD, will be
your everlasting light,
and your days of sorrow
will come to an end.
21 Your people will live right
and always own the land;
they are the trees I planted
to bring praise to me.
22 Even the smallest family
will be a powerful nation.
I am the LORD,
and when the time comes,
I will quickly do all this.

The Good News of Victory

61 The Spirit of the LORD God
has taken control of me!
The LORD has chosen and sent me
to tell the oppressed
the good news,
to heal the brokenhearted,
and to announce freedom
for prisoners and captives.
2 This is the year
when the LORD God
will show kindness to us
and punish our enemies.

The LORD has sent me
to comfort those who mourn,
3 especially in Jerusalem.
He sent me to give them flowers
in place of their sorrow,
olive oil in place of tears,
and joyous praise
in place of broken hearts.
They will be called
"Trees of Justice,"
planted by the LORD
to honor his name.
4 Then they will rebuild cities
that have been in ruins
for many generations.

60.11 Rev 21.25, 26. **60.14** Rev 3.9. **60.19** Rev 21.23; 22.5. **61.1** Mt 11.5; Lk 7.22. **61.1,2** Lk 4.18, 19. **61.2** Mt 5.4.

5 They will hire foreigners
to take care of their sheep
and their vineyards.
6 But they themselves will be
priests and servants
of the LORD our God.
The treasures of the nations
will belong to them,
and they will be famous.[a]
7 They were terribly insulted
and horribly mistreated;
now they will be greatly blessed
and joyful forever.

The LORD Loves Justice

8 I, the LORD, love justice!
But I hate robbery
and injustice.[b]
My people, I solemnly promise
to reward you
with an eternal agreement.
9 Your descendants will be known
in every nation.
All who see them will realize
that they have been blessed,
by me, the LORD.

Celebrate and Shout

10 I celebrate and shout
because of my LORD God.
His saving power and justice
are the very clothes I wear.
They are more beautiful
than the jewelry worn
by a bride or a groom.
11 The LORD will bring about
justice and praise
in every nation on earth,
like flowers blooming
in a garden.

Jerusalem Will Be Saved

62 Jerusalem, I will speak up
for your good.
I will never be silent
till you are safe and secure,
sparkling like a flame.
2 Your great victory will be seen
by every nation and king;
the LORD will even give you
a new name.
3 You will be a glorious crown,
a royal headband,
for the LORD your God.

4 Your name will no longer be
"Deserted and Childless,"
but "Happily Married."
You will please the LORD;
your country
will be his bride.
5 Your people will take the land,[c]
just as a young man
takes a bride.
The LORD will be pleased
because of you,
just as a husband is pleased
with his bride.

6 Jerusalem, on your walls
I have stationed guards,
whose duty it is
to speak out day and night,
without resting.
They must remind the LORD
7 and not let him rest
till he makes Jerusalem strong
and famous everywhere.

8 The LORD has given his word
and made this promise:
"Never again will I give
to your enemies
the grain and grapes
for which you struggled.
9 As surely as you harvest
your grain and grapes,
you will eat your bread
with thankful hearts,
and you will drink your wine
in my temple."

10 People of Jerusalem,
open your gates!

[a]**61.6** *and . . . famous*: One possible meaning for the difficult Hebrew text. [b]**61.8** *But . . . injustice*: One possible meaning for the difficult Hebrew text. [c]**62.5** *Your . . . land*: One possible meaning for the difficult Hebrew text.
61.10 Rev 21.2.

Repair the road to the city
and clear it of stones;
raise a banner to help
the nations find their way.
11 Here is what the LORD has said
for all the earth to hear:
"Soon I will come to save
the city of Zion,
and to reward you.
12 Then you will be called,
'The LORD's Own People,
The Ones He Rescued!'
Your city will be known
as a good place to live
and a city full of people."

The LORD's Victory over the Nations

63 Who is this coming
from Bozrah[d] in Edom
with clothes stained red?
Who is this hero marching
in his glorious uniform?

"It's me, the LORD!
I have won the battle,
and I can save you!"

2 What are those red spots?
Your clothes look stained
from stomping on grapes.[e]

3 "I alone stomped the grapes!
None of the nations helped.
I stomped nations in my anger
and stained my clothes
with their blood.
4 I did this because I wanted
to take revenge—
the time had come
to rescue my people.
5 No one was there to help me
or to give support;
my mighty arm won the battle,
strengthened by my anger.
6 In my fury I stomped on nations
and made them drunk;
their blood poured out
everywhere on earth."

The LORD's Goodness to His People

7 I will tell about the kind deeds
the LORD has done.
They deserve praise!
The LORD has shown mercy
to the people of Israel;
he has been kind and good.

8 The LORD rescued his people,
and said, "They are mine.
They won't betray me."
9 It troubled the LORD
to see them in trouble,
and his angel saved them.[f]
The LORD was truly merciful,
so he rescued his people.
He took them in his arms
and carried them all those years.

10 Then the LORD's people
turned against him and made
his Holy Spirit sad.
So he became their enemy
and attacked them.
11 But his people remembered
what had happened
during the time of Moses.[g]
Didn't the LORD[h] bring them
and their leaders
safely through the sea?
Didn't he[i] give them
his Holy Spirit?
12 The glorious power of the LORD
marched beside Moses.
The LORD will be praised forever
for dividing the sea.
13 He led his people across
like horses running wild
without stumbling.
14 His Spirit gave them rest,
just as cattle find rest
when led into a valley.[j]

[d]**63.1** *Bozrah*: The main city of Edom. [e]**63.2** *stomping on grapes*: This is one way that grapes were crushed to make them into juice. [f]**63.9** *It . . . them*: One possible meaning for the difficult Hebrew text. [g]**63.11** *But . . . Moses*: One possible meaning for the difficult Hebrew text. [h]**63.11** *the LORD*: Or "Moses." [i]**63.11** *he*: Or "Moses." [j]**63.14** *His . . . valley*: One possible meaning for the difficult Hebrew text.

62.11 Is 40.10; Rev 22.12. **63.1-6** Is 34.5-17; Jr 49.7-22; Ez 25.12-14; 35.1-15; Am 1.11, 12; Ob 1-14; Ml 1.2-5. **63.3** **a** Rev 14.20; 19.15; **b** Rev 19.13. **63.5** Is 59.16. **63.12** Ex 14.21.

The name of the LORD was praised
for doing these things.

A Prayer for Mercy and Help

15 Please, LORD, look down
from your holy and glorious
home in the heavens
and see what's going on.
Have you lost interest?
Where is your power?
Show that you care about us[k]
and have mercy!
16 Our ancestors Abraham and Jacob
have both rejected us.
But you are still our Father;
you have been our protector
since ancient times.

17 Why did you make us turn away
from you, our LORD?
Why did you make us want
to disobey you?
Please change your mind!
We are your servants,
your very own people.
18 For a little while,
your temple belonged to us;[l]
and now our enemies
have torn it down.
19 We act as though you
had never ruled us
or called us your people.

64 Rip the heavens apart!
Come down, LORD;
make the mountains tremble.
2 Be a spark that starts a fire
causing water to boil.[m]
Then your enemies will know
who you are;
all nations will tremble
because you are nearby.

3 Your fearsome deeds
have completely amazed us;
even the mountains shake
when you come down.

4 You are the only God
ever seen or heard of
who works miracles
for his followers.

5 You help all who gladly obey
and do what you want,
but sin makes you angry.
Only by your help
can we ever be saved.[n]
6 We are unfit to worship you;
each of our good deeds
is merely a filthy rag.
We dry up like leaves;
our sins are storm winds
sweeping us away.
7 No one worships in your name
or remains faithful.
You have turned your back on us
and let our sins melt us away.[o]

8 You, LORD, are our Father.
We are nothing but clay,
but you are the potter
who molded us.
9 Don't be so furious
or keep our sins
in your thoughts forever!
Remember that all of us
are your people.
10 Every one of your towns
has turned into a desert,
especially Jerusalem.
11 Zion's glorious and holy temple
where our ancestors praised you
has been destroyed by fire.
Our beautiful buildings
are now a pile of ruins.
12 When you see these things,
how can you just sit there
and make us suffer more?

The LORD Will Punish the Guilty

65 I, the LORD, was ready
to answer even those
who were not asking

[k]**63.15** *us*: Hebrew "me." [l]**63.18** *For . . . us*: One possible meaning for the difficult Hebrew text. [m]**64.2** *Be . . . boil*: One possible meaning for the difficult Hebrew text. [n]**64.5** *saved*: One possible meaning for the difficult Hebrew text of verse 5. [o]**64.7** *and let . . . away*: One possible meaning for the difficult Hebrew text.

63.16 3 Macc 2.21, 22. **64.4** 1 Co 2.9. **65.1** Ro 10.20.

and to be found by those
who were not searching.
To a nation that refused
to worship me,[p]
I said, "Here I am!"

2 All day long I have reached out
to stubborn and sinful people
going their own way.
3 They keep making me angry
by sneering at me,
while offering sacrifices
to idols in gardens
and burning incense
to them on bricks.
4 They spend their nights
hiding in burial caves;
they eat the meat of pigs,[q]
cooked in sauces
made of stuff unfit to eat.
5 And then they say to others,
"Don't come near us!
We're dedicated to God."
Such people are like smoke,
irritating my nose all day.
6 I have written this down;
I won't keep silent.
I'll pay them back
just as their sins deserve.
7 I, the LORD, will make them pay
for their sins and for those
of their ancestors—
they have disgraced me
by burning incense
on mountains.

8 Here is what the LORD says:
A cluster of grapes
that produces wine
is worth keeping!
So, because of my servants,
I won't destroy everyone.
9 I have chosen the people
of Israel and Judah,
and I will bless them
with many descendants.
They will settle here
in this land of mountains,
and it will be theirs.
10 My people will worship me.
Then the coastlands of Sharon
and the land as far
as Achor Valley[r]
will turn into pastureland
where cattle and sheep
will feed and rest.

11 What will I, the LORD, do
if any of you reject me
and my holy mountain?
What will happen to you
for offering food and wine
to the gods you call
"Good Luck" and "Fate"?
12 Your luck will end!
I will see to it that you
are slaughtered with swords.
You refused to answer
when I called out;
you paid no attention
to my instructions.
Instead, you did what I hated,
knowing it was wrong.

13 I, the LORD God, will give
food and drink to my servants,
and they will celebrate.
But all of you sinners
will go hungry and thirsty,
overcome with disgrace.
14 My servants will laugh and sing,
but you will be sad
and cry out in pain.
15 I, the LORD God, promise
to see that you are killed
and that my chosen servants use
your names as curse words.
But I will give new names[s]
to my servants.[t]
16 I am God! I can be trusted.
Your past troubles are gone;
I no longer think of them.

[p]**65.1** *refused . . . me*: One possible meaning for the difficult Hebrew text. [q]**65.4** *burial . . . pigs*: Coming in contact with the dead or eating the meat of pigs made a person unacceptable to God. [r]**65.10** *coastlands of Sharon . . . Achor Valley*: Sharon is the coastal plain on the west, and Achor Valley is in the east near Jericho. These two places stand for the whole country. [s]**65.15** *new names*: The giving of a new name suggests the beginning of a new life. [t]**65.15** *But I . . . servants*: One possible meaning for the difficult Hebrew text.

65.2 Ro 10.21. **65.10** Js 7.24-26.

When you pray for someone
to receive a blessing,
or when you make a promise,
you must do it in my name.
I alone am the God
who can be trusted.

The LORD's New Creation

17 I am creating new heavens
and a new earth;
everything of the past
will be forgotten.
18 Celebrate and be glad forever!
I am creating a Jerusalem,
full of happy people.
19 I will celebrate with Jerusalem
and all of its people;
there will be no more crying
or sorrow in that city.

20 No child will die in infancy;
everyone will live
to a ripe old age.
Anyone a hundred years old
will be considered young,
and to die younger than that
will be considered a curse.

21 My people will live
in the houses they build;
they will enjoy grapes
from their own vineyards.
22 No one will take away
their homes or vineyards.
My chosen people will live
to be as old as trees,
and they will enjoy
what they have earned.
23 Their work won't be wasted,
and their children won't die
of dreadful diseases.[u]
I will bless their children
and their grandchildren.
24 I will answer their prayers
before they finish praying.
25 Wolves and lambs
will graze together;
lions and oxen
will feed on straw.
Snakes will eat only dirt!
They won't bite or harm anyone
on my holy mountain.
I, the LORD, have spoken!

True Worship

66 The LORD said:
Heaven is my throne;
the earth is my footstool.
What kind of house
could you build for me?
In what place will I rest?
2 I have made everything;
that's how it all came to be.[v]
I, the LORD, have spoken.

The people I treasure most
are the humble—
they depend only on me
and tremble when I speak.

3 You sacrifice oxen to me,
and you commit murder;
you sacrifice lambs to me
and dogs to other gods;
you offer grain to me
and pigs' blood to idols;
you burn incense to me
and praise your idols.[w]
You have made your own choice
to do these disgusting things
that you enjoy so much.
4 You refused to answer
when I called out;
you paid no attention
to my instructions.
Instead, you did what I hated,
knowing it was wrong.
Now I will punish[x] you
in a way you dread the most.

[u]**65.23** *their children . . . diseases*: One possible meaning for the difficult Hebrew text.
[v]**66.2** *that's . . . be*: One possible meaning for the difficult Hebrew text. [w]**66.3** *You sacrifice oxen . . . idols*: Or "Sacrificing oxen to me is the same as murder; sacrificing lambs to me is the same as sacrificing dogs to other gods; offering grain to me is the same as offering pigs' blood to idols; and burning incense to me is the same as praising idols." [x]**66.4** *punish*: One possible meaning for the difficult Hebrew text.

65.17 Is 66.22; 2 P 3.13; Rev 21.1. **65.19** Rev 21.4. **65.25** Is 11.6-9. **66.1** **a** 3 Macc 2.15; Mt 5.34; 23.22; **b** Mt 5.35. **66.1,2** **a** Ac 7.49, 50.

The LORD Will Help Jerusalem

5 If you tremble
when the LORD speaks,
listen to what he says:
"Some of your own people hate
and reject you because of me.
They make fun and say,
'Let the LORD show his power!
Let us see him
make you truly happy.'[y]
But those who say these things
will be terribly ashamed."

6 Do you hear that noise
in the city and those shouts
coming from the temple?
It is the LORD shouting
as he punishes his enemies.

7 Have you ever heard of a woman
who gave birth to a child
before having labor pains?
8 Who ever heard of such a thing
or imagined it could happen?
Can a nation be born in a day
or come to life in a second?
Jerusalem is like a mother
who gave birth to her children
as soon as she was in labor.
9 The LORD is the one
who makes birth possible.
And he will see that Zion
has many more children.
The LORD has spoken.

10 If you love Jerusalem,
celebrate and shout!
If you were in sorrow
because of the city,
you can now be glad.
11 She will nurse and comfort you,
just like your own mother,
until you are satisfied.
You will fully enjoy
her wonderful glory.

12 The LORD has promised:
"I will flood Jerusalem
with the wealth of nations
and make the city prosper.
Zion will nurse you at her breast,
carry you in her arms,
and hold you in her lap.
13 I will comfort you there
like a mother
comforting her child."

14 When you see this happen,
you will celebrate;
your strength will return
faster than grass can sprout.
Then everyone will know
that the LORD is present
with his servants,
but he is angry
with his enemies.
15 The LORD will come down
like a whirlwind
with his flaming chariots.
He will be terribly furious
and punish his enemies
with fire.
16 The LORD's fiery sword
will bring justice
everywhere on this earth
and execute many people.

A Threat and a Promise

17 Some of you get yourselves ready and
go to a garden to worship a foreign goddess.[z]
You eat the meat of pigs, lizards, and mice.
But I, the LORD, will destroy you for this.
18 I know everything you do and think!
The time has now come[a] to bring together
the people of every language and nation
and to show them my glory 19 by proving
what I can do.[b] I will send the survivors
to Tarshish, Pul,[c] Lud, Meshech,[d] Tubal,

[y]**66.5** *Some . . . happy*: One possible meaning for the difficult Hebrew text. [z]**66.17** *Some . . . goddess*: One possible meaning for the difficult Hebrew text. [a]**66.18** *I . . . come*: One possible meaning for the difficult Hebrew text. [b]**66.19** *by . . . do*: One possible meaning for the difficult Hebrew text. [c]**66.19** *Pul*: Hebrew; one ancient translation "Put," a country in Africa, but neither the location of Pul or Put is known for certain. [d]**66.19** *Meshech*: One ancient translation; Hebrew "those who use bows and arrows."
66.7 Rev 12.5.

Javan,[e] and to the distant islands. I will
send them to announce my wonderful glory
to nations that have never heard about me.
20 They will bring your relatives from
the nations as an offering to me, the LORD.
They will come on horses, chariots, wagons, mules, and camels[f] to Jerusalem, my
holy mountain. It will be like the people of
Israel bringing the right offering to my temple. 21 I promise that some of them will be
priests and others will be helpers in my
temple. I, the LORD, have spoken.

22 I also promise that you will always
have descendants and will never be forgotten, just as the new heavens and the new
earth that I create will last forever. 23 On
the first day of each month and on each
Sabbath, everyone will worship me. I, the
LORD, have spoken.

24 My people will go out and look at the
dead bodies of those who turned against
me. The worms there never die, the fire
never stops burning, and the sight of those
bodies will be disgusting to everyone.

[e]**66.19** *Tarshish . . . Javan*: Tarshish may have been a Phoenician city in Spain; Put (see note on Pul) and Lud were African people; Meshech and Tubal were regions south or southeast of the Black Sea; the Javan were people of Asia Minor and the Greek islands. [f]**66.20** *camels*: One possible meaning for the difficult Hebrew text.

66.22 Is 65.17; 2 P 3.13; Rev 21.1. **66.24** Jdt 16.17; Mk 9.48.

JEREMIAH

ABOUT THIS BOOK

The world of Jeremiah's time was full of wars as new empires conquered the old ones. The tiny kingdom of Judah was caught in the middle, and during Jeremiah's lifetime, Babylonia conquered Judah and ended its freedom as a nation.

Jeremiah began bringing the Lord's message to the people of Judah when he was young, possibly less than 20 years old. He continued until 586 B.C., when the Babylonians captured Jerusalem. Some of the people of Judah soon forced him to go with them to Egypt, where he continued to speak to them for the Lord.

Many of Jeremiah's messages include the date when they were originally spoken. But when his friend Baruch helped him put the messages into writing, they did not arrange the messages by these dates. Usually the messages are grouped together because they are about similar subjects.

Jeremiah acted out many of his messages, so that the people would know exactly what the Lord was saying (see 13.1-11; 19.1-11; 27.1—28.17; 32.1-44; 43.7-13).

Time after time, Jeremiah said God was going to punish Judah. But because he also said the people of Judah should surrender to the Babylonians, his enemies accused him of being a traitor. They had him thrown in prison and even tried to have him killed. Jeremiah complained to God about his problems, and these complaints are now known as his "Confessions" (see 11.18-23; 12.1-6; 15.10, 11, 15-21; 17.14-18; 18.19-23; 20.7-18).

Jeremiah often reminded the people of Judah that they had broken their agreement to worship only the Lord. And so the Lord was going to punish them by letting the Babylonians take them away to Babylonia. But the Lord had also promised to bring his people back to their land someday, and at that time the Lord would make a new agreement with them:

"I will write my laws
on their hearts and minds.
I will be their God,
and they will be my people.

"No longer will they have to teach one another to obey me. I, the LORD, promise that all of them will obey me, ordinary people and rulers alike. I will forgive their sins and forget the evil things they have done."

(31.33b, 34)

A QUICK LOOK AT THIS BOOK

- God Chooses Jeremiah To Speak for Him (1)
- God Will Punish the People of Judah and Jerusalem (2–26)
- Jeremiah against the Lying Prophets (27–29)
- God Will Someday Bring His People back to their Land (30–33)
- Scenes from Jeremiah's Ministry (34–38)
- The Fall of Jerusalem and Later Events in Judah (39–42)
- Jeremiah in Egypt (43–44)
- A Message for Baruch (45)
- The Lord Speaks about the Nations (46–51)
- Another Account of the Fall of Jerusalem (52)

1 My name is Jeremiah. I am a priest,
and my father Hilkiah and everyone
else in my family are from Anathoth in the
territory of the Benjamin tribe. This book
contains the things that the LORD told me
to say. 2 The LORD first spoke to me in the
thirteenth year that Josiah[a] was king of Judah, 3 and he continued to speak to me
during the rule of Josiah's son Jehoiakim.[b]
The last time the LORD spoke to me was in
the fifth month[c] of the eleventh year that
Josiah's son Zedekiah[d] was king. That was
also when the people of Jerusalem were
taken away as prisoners.

The LORD Chooses Jeremiah

4 The LORD said:

5 "Jeremiah, I am your Creator,
and before you were born,
I chose you to speak for me
to the nations."

6 I replied, "I'm not a good speaker,
LORD, and I'm too young."
7 "Don't say you're too young," the LORD
answered. "If I tell you to go and speak to
someone, then go! And when I tell you
what to say, don't leave out a word! 8 I
promise to be with you and keep you safe,
so don't be afraid."
9 The LORD reached out his hand, then
he touched my mouth and said, "I am giving you the words to say, 10 and I am sending you with authority to speak to the nations for me. You will tell them of doom
and destruction, and of rising and rebuilding again."
11 The LORD showed me something in a
vision. Then he asked, "What do you see,
Jeremiah?"
I answered, "A branch of almonds that
ripen early."
12 "That's right," the LORD replied, "and
I always rise early[e] to keep a promise."
13 Then the LORD showed me something
else and asked, "What do you see now?"
I answered, "I see a pot of boiling water
in the north, and it's about to spill out toward us."
14 The LORD said:

I will pour out destruction
all over the land.
15 Just watch while I send
for the kings of the north.
They will attack and capture
Jerusalem and other towns,
then set up their thrones
at the gates of Jerusalem.

16 I will punish my people,
because they are guilty
of turning from me
to worship idols.

17 Jeremiah, get ready!
Go and tell the people
what I command you to say.
Don't be frightened by them,
or I will make you terrified
while they watch.

18 My power will make you strong
like a fortress
or a column of iron
or a wall of bronze.
You will oppose all of Judah,
including its kings and leaders,
its priests and people.
19 They will fight back,
but they won't win.
I, the LORD, give my word—
I won't let them harm you.

Israel's Unfaithfulness

2 The LORD told me 2 to go to Jerusalem
and tell everyone that he had said:

When you were my young bride,
you loved me and followed me
through the barren desert.
3 You belonged to me alone,
like the first part of the harvest,
and I severely punished
those who mistreated you.

[a] **1.2** *Josiah*: Ruled 640-609 B.C. [b] **1.3** *Jehoiakim*: Ruled 609-598 B.C. [c] **1.3** *fifth month*: Ab, the fifth month of the Hebrew calendar, from about mid-July to mid-August. [d] **1.3** *Zedekiah*: Ruled 598-586 B.C. [e] **1.11,12** *almonds . . . rise early*: In Hebrew "almonds that ripen early" sounds like "always rise early."

1.2 2 K 22.3—23.27; 2 Ch 34.8—35.19. **1.3** **a** 2 K 23.36—24.7; 2 Ch 36.5-8; **b** 2 K 24.18—25.21; 2 Ch 36.11-21.

4 Listen, people of Israel,[f]
5 and I, the LORD, will speak.
I was never unfair
to your ancestors,
but they left me
and became worthless
by following worthless idols.
6 Your ancestors refused
to ask for my help,
though I had rescued them
from Egypt
and led them through
a treacherous, barren desert,
where no one lives
or dares to travel.

7 I brought you here to my land,
where food is abundant,
but you made my land filthy
with your sins.
8 The priests who teach my laws
don't care to know me.
Your leaders rebel against me;
your prophets
give messages from Baal
and worship false gods.

The LORD Accuses His People

9 I will take you to court
and accuse you
and your descendants
*10 of a crime that no nation
has ever committed before.
Just ask anyone, anywhere,
from the eastern deserts
to the islands in the west.
11 You will find that no nation
has ever abandoned its gods
even though they were false.
I am the true and glorious God,
but you have rejected me
to worship idols.
12 Tell the heavens
to tremble with fear!
13 You, my people, have sinned
in two ways—
you have rejected me, the source
of life-giving water,
and you've tried to collect water
in cracked and leaking pits
dug in the ground.

14 People of Israel,
you weren't born slaves;
you were captured in war.
15 Enemies roared like lions
and destroyed your land;
towns lie burned and empty.
16 Soldiers from the Egyptian towns
of Memphis and Tahpanhes
have cracked your skulls.
17 It's all your own fault!
You stopped following me,
the LORD your God,
18 and you trusted the power
of Egypt and Assyria.[g]
19 Your own sins will punish you,
because it was a bitter mistake
for you to reject me
without fear of punishment.
I, the LORD All-Powerful,
have spoken.

20 Long ago you left me
and broke all ties between us,
refusing to be my servant.
Now you worship other gods
by having sex
on hilltops or in the shade
of large trees.[h]
21 You were a choice grapevine,
but now you produce nothing
but small, rotten grapes.

Israel Is Stained with Guilt

22 The LORD said:
People of Israel,
you are stained with guilt,
and no soap or bleach
can wash it away.
23 You deny your sins

[f]**2.4** *Israel*: After the nation was divided, the northern kingdom was called "Israel," and the southern kingdom was called "Judah" (see 1 Kings 12.1-20). In 722 B.C. the Assyrians conquered the northern kingdom, and Judah was all that was left. And so in the book of Jeremiah the name "Israel" is most often used of the southern kingdom. [g]**2.18** *trusted . . . Assyria*: Hebrew "went to Egypt and drank from the Shihor River, and you went to Assyria and drank from the Euphrates River." [h]**2.20** *having sex . . . trees*: In some Canaanite religions, worshipers had sex with temple prostitutes, who represented their gods; many of the Canaanite places of worship were on hilltops or under large trees.

and say, "We aren't unclean.
We haven't worshiped Baal."[i]
But think about what you do
in Hinnom Valley.[j]
And you run back and forth
like young camels,
as you rush to worship one idol
after another.
24 You are a female donkey
sniffing the desert air,
wanting to mate
with just anyone.
You are an easy catch!
25 Your shoes are worn out,
and your throat is parched
from running here and there
to worship foreign gods.
"Stop!" I shouted,
but you replied, "No!
I love those gods too much."

26 You and your leaders
are more disgraceful
than thieves—
you and your kings,
your priests and prophets
27 worship stone idols
and sacred poles
as if they had created you
and had given you life.
You have rejected me,
but when you're in trouble,
you cry to me for help.
28 Go cry to the gods you made!
There should be enough of them
to save you,
because Judah has as many gods
as it has towns.

Israel Rebels against the LORD

29 The LORD said to Israel:

You accuse me of not saving you,
but I say you have rebelled.
30 I tried punishing you,
but you refused
to come back to me,
and like fierce lions
you killed my prophets.

31 Now listen to what I say!
Did I abandon you in the desert
or surround you with darkness?
You are my people,
yet you have told me,
"We'll do what we want,
and we refuse
to worship you!"
32 A bride could not forget
to wear her jewelry
to her wedding,
but you have forgotten me
day after day.
33 You are so clever
at finding lovers
that you could give lessons
to a prostitute.
34 You killed innocent people
for no reason at all.
And even though their blood
can be seen on your clothes,
35 you claim to be innocent,
and you want me to stop
being angry with you.
So I'll take you to court,
and we'll see who is right.

36 When Assyria let you down,
you ran to Egypt,
but you'll find no help there,
37 and you will leave
in great sadness.[k]
I won't let you find help
from those you trust.

Sin and Shame

3 The LORD said to the people of Israel:
If a divorced woman marries,
can her first husband
ever marry her again?
No, because this
would pollute the land.
But you have more gods
than a prostitute has lovers.
Why should I take you back?
2 Just try to find one hilltop
where you haven't gone

[i] **2.23** *Baal*: The Hebrew text has "the Baals," probably because the god Baal was believed to be present in different forms at different places of worship. [j] **2.23** *Hinnom Valley*: Hebrew "the valley" (see 7.31,32; 19.1-6). [k] **2.37** *in great sadness*: Or "as prisoners."

to worship other gods
by having sex.[l]
You sat beside the road
like a robber in ambush,
except you offered yourself
to every passerby.
Your sins of unfaithfulness
have polluted the land.
3 So I, the LORD, refused
to let the spring rains fall.
But just like a prostitute,
you still have no shame
for what you have done.
4 You call me your father
or your long-lost friend;
5 you beg me to stop being angry,
but you won't stop sinning.

The LORD Asks Israel To Come Back to Him

6 When Josiah[m] was king, the LORD
said:
Jeremiah, the kingdom of Israel[n] was
like an unfaithful wife who became a prostitute on the hilltops and in the shade of
large trees.[o] 7-8 I knew that the kingdom of
Israel had been unfaithful and committed many sins, yet I still hoped she might come back to me. But she didn't, so I divorced her and sent her away.

Her sister, the kingdom of Judah, saw what happened, but she wasn't worried in the least, and I watched her become unfaithful like her sister. 9 The kingdom of Ju-
dah wasn't sorry for being a prostitute, and she didn't care that she had made both herself and the land unclean by worshiping
idols of stone and wood. 10 And worst of all,
the people of Judah pretended to come
back to me. 11 Even the people of Israel
were honest enough not to pretend.
12 Jeremiah, shout toward the north:

Israel, I am your LORD—
come back to me!
You were unfaithful
and made me furious,
but I am merciful,
and so I will forgive you.
13 Just admit that you rebelled
and worshiped foreign gods
under large trees everywhere.
14 You are unfaithful children,
but you belong to me.
Come home!
I'll take one or two of you
from each town and clan
and bring you to Zion.
15 Then I'll appoint wise rulers
who will obey me,
and they will care for you
like shepherds.

16 You will increase in numbers,
and there will be no need
to remember the sacred chest
or to make a new one.[p]
17 The whole city of Jerusalem
will be my throne.[q]
All nations will come here
to worship me,
and they will no longer follow
their stubborn, evil hearts.
18 Then, in countries to the north,
you people of Judah and Israel
will be reunited,
and you will return to the land
I gave your ancestors.
19 I have always wanted
to treat you as my children
and give you the best land,
the most beautiful on earth.
I wanted you to call me "Father"
and not turn from me.
20 But instead, you are like a wife
who broke her wedding vows.
You have been unfaithful to me.
I, the LORD, have spoken.

The People Confess Their Sins

The LORD said:
21 Listen to the noise
on the hilltops!

[l]**3.2** *hilltop . . . sex*: See the note at 2.20. [m]**3.6** *Josiah*: Ruled 640-609 B.C. [n]**3.6** *Israel*: The northern kingdom (see the note at 2.4). [o]**3.6** *prostitute . . . trees*: See the note at 2.20. [p]**3.16** *make a new one*: The sacred chest was probably destroyed or taken away by the Babylonians when they captured Jerusalem in 586 B.C. [q]**3.16,17** *sacred chest . . . throne*: The sacred chest was thought to be God's throne on earth.
3.6 2 K 22.1—23.30; 2 Ch 34.1—35.27.

It's the people of Israel,
weeping and begging me
to answer their prayers.
They forgot about me
and chose the wrong path.
22 I will tell them, "Come back,
and I will cure you
of your unfaithfulness."

They will answer,
"We will come back, because you
are the LORD our God.
23 On hilltops, we worshiped idols
and made loud noises,
but it was all for nothing—
only you can save us.
24 Since the days of our ancestors
when our nation was young,
that shameful god Baal[r] has taken
our crops and livestock,
our sons and daughters.
25 We have rebelled against you
just like our ancestors,
and we are ashamed of our sins."

How Israel Can Return to the LORD

4 The LORD said:

Israel, if you really want
to come back to me, get rid
of those disgusting idols.
2 Make promises only in my name,
and do what you promise!
Then all nations will praise me,
and I will bless them.
3 People of Jerusalem and Judah,
don't be so stubborn!
Your hearts have become hard,
like unplowed ground
where thornbushes grow.
4 With all your hearts,
keep the agreement
I made with you.
But if you are stubborn
and keep on sinning,
my anger will burn like a fire
that cannot be put out.

Disaster Is Coming

The LORD said:
*5 "Sound the trumpets, my people.
Warn the people of Judah,[s]
'Run for your lives!
6 Head for Jerusalem
or another walled town!'

"Jeremiah, tell them I'm sending
disaster from the north.
7 An army will come out,
like a lion from its den.
It will destroy nations
and leave your towns empty
and in ruins."

8 Then I said
to the people of Israel,
"Put on sackcloth![t]
Mourn and cry out,
'The LORD is still angry
with us.'"

9 The LORD said,

"When all this happens,
the king and his officials,
the prophets and the priests
will be shocked and terrified."

10 I said, "You are the LORD God. So why have you fooled everyone, especially the people of Jerusalem? Why did you promise peace, when a knife is at our throats?"

The Coming Disaster

11-12 When disaster comes, the LORD will tell you people of Jerusalem,

"I am sending a windstorm
from the desert—
not a welcome breeze.[u]

[r]**3.24** *that shameful god Baal*: The Hebrew text has "The Shame," which was sometimes used as a way of making fun of the Canaanite god Baal. [s]**4.5** *Judah*: Hebrew "Judah and Jerusalem." [t]**4.8** *sackcloth*: A rough, dark-colored cloth made from goat or camel hair and used to make grain sacks. It was worn in times of trouble or sorrow. [u]**4.11,12** *a welcome breeze*: Hebrew "a wind to blow away the husks." Farmers used a special shovel to pitch grain and husks into the air. Wind would blow away the light husks, and the grain would fall back to the ground, where it could be gathered up.
4.3 Ho 10.12.

And it will sweep you away
as punishment for your sins.
13 Look! The enemy army
swoops down like an eagle;
their cavalry and chariots
race faster than storm clouds
blown by the wind."

Then you will answer,
"We are doomed!"

14 But Jerusalem, there is still time
for you to be saved.
Wash the evil from your hearts
and stop making sinful plans,
15 before a message of disaster
arrives from the hills of Ephraim
and the town of Dan.[v]

16-17 The LORD said,

"Tell the nations that my people
have rebelled against me.
And so an army will come
from far away
to surround Jerusalem
and the towns of Judah.
I, the LORD, have spoken.

18 "People of Judah,
your hearts will be in pain,
but it's your own fault
that you will be punished."

Jeremiah's Vision of the Coming Punishment

19 I can't stand the pain!
My heart pounds,
as I twist and turn in agony.
I hear the signal trumpet
and the battle cry of the enemy,
and I cannot be silent.
20 I see the enemy defeating us
time after time,
leaving everything in ruins.
Even my own home
is destroyed in a moment.
21 How long will I see enemy flags
and hear their trumpets?

22 I heard the LORD say,
"My people ignore me.
They are foolish children
who do not understand
that they will be punished.
All they know is how to sin."

23 After this, I looked around.
The earth was barren,
with no form of life.
The sun, moon, and stars
had disappeared.
24 The mountains were shaking;
25 no people could be seen,
and all the birds
had flown away.
26 Farmland had become a desert,
and towns were in ruins.
The LORD's fierce anger
had done all of this.

The Death of Jerusalem

27-28 The LORD said:

I have made my decision,
and I won't change my mind.
This land will be destroyed,
although not completely.
The sky will turn dark,
and the earth will mourn.

29 Enemy cavalry and archers
shout their battle cry.
People run for their lives
and try to find safety
among trees and rocks.
Every town is empty.

30 Jerusalem, your land
has been wiped out.
But you act like a prostitute
and try to win back your lovers,
who now hate you.
You can put on a red dress,
gold jewelry, and eye shadow,
but it's no use—
your lovers are out to kill you!

31 I heard groaning and crying.
Was it a woman giving birth
to her first child?
No, it was Jerusalem.

[v] **4.15** *Ephraim . . . Dan*: The hills of Ephraim were to the north of Jerusalem, and Dan was even farther north. They would be reached by the invading army first.

She was gasping for breath
and begging for help.
"I'm dying!" she said.
"They have murdered me."

Is Anyone Honest and Faithful?

The LORD said to me:
5 "Search Jerusalem
for honest people
who try to be faithful.
If you can find even one,
I'll forgive the whole city.
2 Everyone breaks promises
made in my name."

3 I answered, "I know
that you look for truth.
You punished your people
for their lies,
but in spite of the pain,
they became more stubborn
and refused to turn back
to you."
4 Then I thought to myself,
"These common people
act like fools,
and they have never learned
what the LORD their God
demands of them.
5 I'll go and talk to the leaders.
They know what God demands."
But even they had decided
not to obey the LORD.

6 The people have rebelled
and rejected the LORD
too many times.
So enemies will attack
like lions from the forest
or wolves from the desert.
Those enemies will watch
the towns of Judah,
and like leopards
they will tear to pieces
whoever goes outside.

Enemies Will Punish Judah

The LORD said:
7 People of Judah,
how can I forgive you?
I gave you everything,
but you abandoned me
and worshiped idols.
You men go to prostitutes
and are unfaithful
to your wives.
8 You are no better than animals,
and you always want sex
with someone else's wife.

9 Why shouldn't I punish
the people of Judah?
10 I will tell their enemies,
"Go through my vineyard.
Don't destroy the vines,
but cut off the branches,
because they are the people
who don't belong to me."

11 In every way, Judah and Israel
have been unfaithful to me.
*12 Their prophets lie and say,
"The LORD won't punish us.
We will have peace
and plenty of food."
13 They tell these lies in my name,
so now they will be killed in war
or starve to death.

14 I am the LORD God All-Powerful.
Jeremiah, I will tell you
exactly what to say.
Your words will be a fire;
Israel and Judah
will be the fuel.

15 People of Israel,
I have made my decision.
An army from a distant country
will attack you.
I've chosen an ancient nation,
and you won't understand
their language.
16 All of them are warriors,
and their arrows bring death.
17 This nation will eat your crops
and livestock;
they will leave no fruit
on your vines or trees.
And although you feel safe
behind thick walls,
your towns will be destroyed
and your children killed.

Israel Refused To Worship the LORD

18 The LORD said:
Jeremiah, the enemy army won't kill
everyone in Judah. 19 And the people who
survive will ask, "Why did the LORD our
God do such terrible things to us?" Then
tell them:

I am the LORD,
but you abandoned me
and worshiped other gods
in your own land.
Now you will be slaves
in a foreign country.
20 Tell these things to each other,
you people of Judah,
you descendants of Jacob.

21 You fools! Why don't you listen
when I speak?
Why can't you understand
22 that you should worship me
with fear and trembling?
I'm the one who made the shore
to hold back the ocean.
Waves may crash on the beach,
but they can come no farther.
23 You stubborn people have rebelled
and turned your backs on me.
24 You refuse to say,
"Let's worship the LORD!
He's the one who sends rain
in spring and autumn
and gives us a good harvest."
25 That's why I cannot bless you!

*26 A hunter traps birds
and puts them in a cage,
but some of you trap humans
and make them your slaves.
27 You are evil, and you lie and cheat
to make yourselves rich.
You are powerful
28 and prosperous,
but you refuse to help[w] the poor
get the justice they deserve.
29 You need to be punished,
and so I will take revenge.
30 Look at the terrible things
going on in this country.
I am shocked!
31 Prophets give their messages
in the name of a false god,[x]
my priests don't want
to serve me,[y]
and you—my own people—
like it this way!
But on the day of disaster,
where will you turn for help?

A Warning for the People of Jerusalem

The LORD said:

6 Run for your lives,
people of Benjamin.
Get out of Jerusalem.
Sound a trumpet in Tekoa
and light a signal fire
in Beth-Haccherem.
Soon you will be struck
by disaster from the north.
*2 Jerusalem is a lovely pasture,
but shepherds will surround it
and divide it up,
3 then let their flocks
eat all the grass.[z]
4 Kings will tell their troops,
"If we reach Jerusalem
in the morning,
we'll attack at noon.
But if we arrive later,
5 we'll attack after dark
and destroy its fortresses."

6 I am the LORD All-Powerful,
and I will command these armies
to chop down trees
and build a ramp up to the walls
of Jerusalem.

People of Jerusalem,
I must punish you
for your injustice.
7 Evil pours from your city
like water from a spring.
Sounds of violent crimes
echo within your walls;

[w] **5.28** *refuse to help*: One possible meaning for the difficult Hebrew text. [x] **5.31** *give . . . god*: Or "tell lies." [y] **5.31** *don't . . . me*: Or "don't care what I want." [z] **6.2,3** *Jerusalem . . . grass*: One possible meaning for the difficult Hebrew text.

5.21 Is 6.9, 10; Ez 12.2; Mk 8.18. **5.22** Job 38.8-11.

victims are everywhere,
wounded and dying.

8 Listen to me,
you people of Jerusalem
and Judah.
I will abandon you,
and your land will become
an empty desert.
9 I will tell your enemies
to leave your nation bare
like a vine stripped of grapes.
I, the LORD All-Powerful,
have spoken.

Jeremiah's Anger

10 I have told the people
that you, LORD,
will punish them,
but they just laugh
and refuse to listen.
11 Your anger against Judah
flames up inside me,
and I can't hold it in
much longer.

The LORD's Anger Will Sweep Everyone Away

The LORD answered:
Don't hold back my anger!
Let it sweep away everyone—
the children at play
and all adults,
young and old alike.
12 I'll punish the people of Judah
and give to others
their houses and fields,
as well as their wives.
I, the LORD, have spoken.

13 Everyone is greedy and dishonest,
whether poor or rich.
Even the prophets and priests
cannot be trusted.
14 All they ever offer
to my deeply wounded people
are empty hopes for peace.
15 They should be ashamed
of their disgusting sins,
but they don't even blush.
And so, when I punish Judah,
they will end up on the ground,
dead like everyone else.
I, the LORD, have spoken.

The People of Judah Rejected God's Way of Life

16 The LORD said:
My people, when you stood
at the crossroads,
I told you, "Follow the road
your ancestors took,
and you will find peace."
But you refused.
17 I also sent prophets
to warn you of danger,
but when they sounded the alarm,
you paid no attention.
*18 So I tell all nations on earth,
"Watch what I will do!
19 My people ignored me
and rejected my laws.
They planned to do evil,
and now the evil they planned
will happen to them."

20 People of Judah,
you bring me incense from Sheba
and spices from distant lands.
You offer sacrifices of all kinds.
But why bother?
I hate these gifts of yours!
21 So I will put stumbling blocks
in your path,
and everyone will die,
including parents and children,
neighbors and friends.

An Army from the North

22 The LORD said,
"Look toward the north,
where a powerful nation
has prepared for war.
23 Its well-armed troops are cruel
and never show mercy.
Their galloping horses sound
like ocean waves
pounding on the shore.
This army will attack you,
lovely Jerusalem."

6.14 Ez 13.10. **6.12-15** Jr 8.10-12.

24 Then the people said,

"Just hearing about them
makes us tremble with fear,
and we twist and turn in pain
like a woman giving birth."

25 The LORD said,

"Don't work in your fields
or walk along the roads.
It's too dangerous.
The enemy is well armed
26 and attacks without warning.
So mourn, my people, as though
your only child had died.
Wear clothes made of sackcloth[a]
and roll in the ash pile."

The LORD's People Must Be Tested

The LORD said:

27 Jeremiah, test my people
as though they were metal.
28 And you'll find they are hard
like bronze and iron.
They are stubborn rebels,
always spreading lies.
*29 Silver can be purified
in a fiery furnace,
30 but my people are too wicked
to be made pure,
and so I have rejected them.

Jeremiah Speaks in the Temple

(Jeremiah 26.1-6)

7 1-3 The LORD told me to stand by the
gate of the temple[b] and to tell the
people who were going in that the LORD
All-Powerful, the God of Israel, had said:

Pay attention, people of Judah! Change
your ways and start living right, then I will
let you keep on living in your own country.[c]
4 Don't fool yourselves! My temple is here
in Jerusalem, but that doesn't mean I will
protect you. 5 I will keep you safe only if
you change your ways. Be fair and honest
with each other. 6 Stop taking advantage of
foreigners, orphans, and widows. Don't
kill innocent people. And stop worshiping
other gods. 7 Then I will let you enjoy
a long life in this land I gave your
ancestors.

8 But just look at what is happening! You
put your trust in worthless lies. 9 You steal
and murder; you lie in court and are unfaithful in marriage. You worship idols and
offer incense to Baal, when these gods have
never done anything for you. 10 And then
you come into my temple and worship me!
Do you think I will protect you so that you
can go on sinning? 11 You are thieves, and
you have made my temple your hideout.
But I've seen everything you have done.

12 Go to Shiloh, where my sacred tent
once stood. Take a look at what I did there.
My people Israel sinned, and so I destroyed
Shiloh!

13 While you have been sinning, I have
been trying to talk to you, but you refuse to
listen. 14 Don't think this temple will protect you. Long ago I told your ancestors to
build it and worship me here, but now I
have decided to tear it down, just as I destroyed Shiloh. 15 And as for you, people of
Judah, I'm going to send you away from
my land, just as I sent away the people of
Ephraim and the other northern tribes.

Punishment for Worshiping Other Gods

16 Jeremiah, don't pray for these people!
I, the LORD, would refuse to listen. 17 Do
you see what the people of Judah are doing
in their towns and in the streets of
Jerusalem? 18 Children gather firewood,
their fathers build fires, and their mothers
mix dough to bake bread for the goddess
they call the Queen of Heaven.[d] They even
offer wine sacrifices to other gods, just to
insult me. 19 But they are not only insulting
me; they are also insulting themselves by
doing these shameful things.

20 And now, I, the LORD All-Powerful,
will flood Judah with my fiery anger until
nothing is left—no people or animals, no
trees or crops.

[a]**6.26** *sackcloth*: See the note at 4.8. [b]**7.1-3** *temple*: The Hebrew text has "house of the LORD," another name for the temple. [c]**7.1-3** *let you . . . own country*: Or "live here with you."
[d]**7.18** *Queen of Heaven*: Probably another name for the goddess Astarte.

7.11 Mt 21.13; Mk 11.17; Lk 19.46. **7.12-14** Js 18.1; Ps 78.60; Jr 26.6. **7.18** Jr 44.17-19.

It Is Useless To Offer Sacrifices

21 The LORD told me to say to the people
of Judah:
I am the LORD All-Powerful, the God of
Israel, but I won't accept sacrifices from
you. So don't even bother bringing them to
me. You might as well just cook the meat
for yourselves.
22 At the time I brought your ancestors
out of Egypt, I didn't command them to offer sacrifices to me. 23 Instead, I told them,
"If you listen to me and do what I tell you, I
will be your God, you will be my people,
and all will go well for you." 24 But your ancestors refused to listen. They were stubborn, and whenever I wanted them to go
one way, they always went the other.
25 Ever since your ancestors left Egypt, I
have been sending my servants the
prophets to speak for me. 26 But you have
ignored me and become even more stubborn and sinful than your ancestors ever
were!

Slaughter Valley

The LORD said:
27 Jeremiah, no matter what you do, the
people won't listen. 28 So you must say to
them:
People of Judah, I am the LORD your
God, but you have refused to obey me, and
you didn't change when I punished you.
And now, you no longer even pretend to be
faithful to me.

29 Shave your head bald
    and throw away the hair.
Sing a funeral song
    on top of a barren hill.
You people have made me angry,
    and I have abandoned you.

30 You have disobeyed me by putting
your disgusting idols in my temple, and
now the temple itself is disgusting to me.
31 At Topheth in Hinnom Valley you have
built altars where you kill your children and
burn them as sacrifices to other gods. I
would never think of telling you to do this.
32 So watch out! Someday that place will
no longer be called Topheth or Hinnom
Valley. It will be called Slaughter Valley, because you will bury your dead there until
you run out of room, 33 and then bodies
will lie scattered on the ground. Birds and
wild animals will come and eat, and no one
will be around to scare them off. 34 When I
am finished with your land, there will be
deathly silence in the empty ruins of
Jerusalem and the towns of Judah—no
happy voices, no sounds of parties or wedding celebrations.

8 Then the bones of the dead kings of
Judah and their officials will be dug
up, along with the bones of the priests, the
prophets, and everyone else in Jerusalem
2 who loved and worshiped the sun, moon,
and stars. These bones will be scattered
and left lying on the ground like trash,
where the sun and moon and stars can
shine on them.
3 Some of you people of Judah will be
left alive, but I will force you to go to foreign
countries, and you will wish you were dead.
I, the LORD God All-Powerful, have spoken.

The People Took the Wrong Road

4 The LORD said:

People of Jerusalem,
when you stumble and fall,
    you get back up,
and if you take a wrong road,
    you turn around and go back.[e]
5 So why do you refuse
    to come back to me?
Why do you hold so tightly
    to your false gods?

6 I listen carefully,
but none of you admit
    that you've done wrong.
Without a second thought,
you run down the wrong road[f]
    like cavalry troops
    charging into battle.

7 Storks, doves, swallows,
and thrushes
    all know when it's time

[e] **8.4** *if you take . . . go back*: One possible meaning for the difficult Hebrew text. [f] **8.6** *you run down the wrong road*: One possible meaning for the difficult Hebrew text.

7.31 **a** 2 K 23.10; Jr 32.35; **b** Lv 18.21. **7.34** Jr 16.9; 25.10; Ba 2.23; Rev 18.23.

to fly away for the winter
and when to come back.
But you, my people,
don't know what I demand.
8 You say, "We are wise
because we have the teachings
and laws of the LORD."
But I say that your teachers
have turned my words
into lies!
9 Your wise men
have rejected what I say,
and so they have no wisdom.
Now they will be trapped
and put to shame;
they won't know what to do.
10 I'll give their wives and fields
to strangers.

Everyone is greedy and dishonest,
whether poor or rich.
Even the prophets and priests
cannot be trusted.
11 All they ever offer
to my deeply wounded people
are empty hopes for peace.
12 They should be ashamed
of their disgusting sins,
but they don't even blush.
And so, when I punish Judah,
they will end up on the ground,
dead like everyone else.
13 I will wipe them out.[g]
They are vines without grapes;
fig trees without figs or leaves.
They have not done a thing
that I told them![h]
I, the LORD, have spoken.

The People and Their Punishment

14 The people of Judah
say to each other,
"What are we waiting for?
Let's run to a town with walls
and die there.
We rebelled against the LORD,
and we were sentenced to die
by drinking poison.
15 We had hoped for peace
and a time of healing,
but all we got was terror.
16 Our enemies have reached
the town of Dan in the north,
and the snorting of their horses
makes us tremble with fear.
The enemy will destroy Jerusalem
and our entire nation.
No one will survive."

17 "Watch out!" the LORD says.
"I'm sending poisonous snakes
to attack you,
and no one can stop them."

Jeremiah Mourns for His People

18 I'm burdened with sorrow
and feel like giving up.
19 In a foreign land
my people are crying.
Listen! You'll hear them say,
"Has the LORD deserted Zion?
Is he no longer its king?"

I hear the LORD reply,
"Why did you make me angry
by worshiping useless idols?"

20 The people complain,
"Spring and summer
have come and gone,
but still the LORD
hasn't rescued us."

21 My people are crushed,
and so is my heart.
I am horrified and mourn.
22 If medicine and doctors
may be found in Gilead,
why aren't my people healed?

9 I wish that my eyes
were fountains of tears,
so I could cry day and night
for my people
who were killed.
2 I wish I could go into the desert
and find a hiding place
from all who are treacherous
and unfaithful to God.

[g]8.13 *I will wipe them out*: One possible meaning for the difficult Hebrew text. [h]8.13 *They have not . . . them*: One possible meaning for the difficult Hebrew text.

8.11 Ez 13.10. **8.10-12** Jr 6.12-15.

The LORD Answers Jeremiah

3 The LORD replied:

Lies come from the mouths
of my people,
like arrows from a bow.
With each dishonest deed
their power increases,
and not one of them will admit
that I am God.

4 Jeremiah, all your friends
and relatives
tell lies about you,
so don't trust them.
5 They wear themselves out,
always looking for a new way
to cheat their friends.
6 Everyone takes advantage
of everyone else,
and no one will admit
that I am God.

7 And so I will purify
the hearts of my people
just as gold is purified
in a furnace.
I have no other choice.
8 They say they want peace,
but this lie is deadly,
like an arrow that strikes
when you least expect it.
9 Give me one good reason
not to punish them
as they deserve.
I, the LORD All-Powerful,
have spoken.

Jeremiah Weeps for His People

10 I weep for the pastureland
in the hill country.
It's so barren and scorched
that no one travels there.
No cattle can be found there,
and birds and wild animals
have all disappeared.

11 I heard the LORD reply,
"When I am finished,
Jerusalem and the towns of Judah
will be piles of ruins
where only jackals[i] live."

Why the Land Was Destroyed

12 I said to the LORD, "None of us can understand why the land has become like an uncrossable desert. Won't you explain why?"

13 The LORD said:

I destroyed the land because the
people disobeyed me and rejected my
laws and teachings. 14 They were stubborn and worshiped Baal,[j] just as their
ancestors did. 15 So I, the LORD All-
Powerful, the God of Israel, promise
them poison to eat and drink.[k] 16 I'll
scatter them in foreign countries that
they and their ancestors have never
even heard of. Finally, I will send enemy soldiers to kill every last one of
them.

The Women Who Are Paid To Weep

17 The LORD All-Powerful said,
"Send for the women
who are paid to weep
at funerals,[l]
especially the women
who can cry the loudest."

18 The people answered,
"Let them come quickly
and cry for us,
until our own eyes
are flooded with tears.
19 Now those of us on Zion cry,
'We are ruined!
We can't stand the shame.
Our homes have been destroyed,
and we must leave our land.'

20 "We ask you women
to pay attention
to what the LORD says.

[i]**9.11** *jackals*: Desert animals related to wolves, but smaller. [j]**9.14** *Baal*: See the note at 2.23. [k]**9.15** *poison to eat and drink*: Or "bitter disappointment to eat, and tears to drink." [l]**9.17** *women . . . weep at funerals*: Or "the women who weep for Baal"; the god Baal was believed to have died and come back to life, and some women would go to places of worship and weep over the death of Baal.

We will teach you a funeral song
that you can teach
your daughters and friends:
21 'We were in our fortress,
but death sneaked in
through our windows.
It even struck down
children at play
and our strongest young men.'

22 "The LORD has told us
the ground will be covered
with dead bodies,
like stalks of ungathered grain
or like manure."

What the LORD Likes Best

23 The LORD says:

Don't brag about your wisdom
or strength or wealth.
24 If you feel you must brag,
then have enough sense
to brag about worshiping me,
the LORD.
What I like best
is showing kindness,
justice, and mercy
to everyone on earth.

25-26 Someday I will punish the nations of Egypt, Edom, Ammon, and Moab, and the tribes of the desert.[m] The men of these nations are circumcised, but they don't worship me. And it's the same with you people of Judah. Your bodies are circumcised, but your hearts are unchanged.

The LORD Talks about Idols

10 *1 The LORD said:

Listen to me,
you people of Israel.
2 Don't follow the customs
of those nations
who become frightened
when they see something strange
happen in the sky.
3 Their religion is worthless!
They chop down a tree,
carve the wood into an idol,
4 cover it with silver and gold,
and then nail it down
so it won't fall over.

5 An idol is no better
than a scarecrow.
It can't speak,
and it has to be carried,
because it can't walk.
Why worship an idol
that can't help or harm you?

Jeremiah Praises the LORD

6 Our LORD, great and powerful,
you alone are God.
7 You are King of the nations.
Everyone should worship you.
No human anywhere on earth
is wiser than you.
8 Idols are worthless,
and anyone who worships them
is a fool!
9 Idols are made by humans.
A carver shapes the wood.
A metalworker hammers out
a covering of gold from Uphaz
or of silver from Tarshish.
Then the idol is dressed
in blue and purple clothes.

10 You, LORD, are the only true
and living God.
You will rule for all time.
When you are angry
the earth shakes,
and nations are destroyed.

11 You told me to say
that idols did not create
the heavens and the earth,
and that you, the LORD,
will destroy every idol.

12 With your wisdom and power
you created the earth
and spread out the heavens.
13 The waters in the heavens roar
at your command.
You make clouds appear—
you send the winds
from your storehouse

[m]**9.25,26** *the tribes of the desert*: One possible meaning for the difficult Hebrew text.
9.24 1 Co 1.31; 2 Co 10.17. **10.7** Rev 15.4.

and make lightning flash
in the rain.

14 People who make idols
are so stupid!
They will be disappointed,
because their false gods
are not alive.
15 Idols are merely a joke,
and when the time is right,
they will be destroyed.

16 But you, Israel's God,
created all things,
and you chose Israel
to be your very own.
Your name is the LORD
All-Powerful.

Judah Will Be Thrown from Its Land

17 I said to the people of Judah,
"Gather your things;
you are surrounded.
18 The LORD said these troubles
will lead to your capture,
and he will throw you
from this land
like a rock from a sling."[n]

19 The people answered,
"We are wounded
and doomed to die.
Why did we say
we could stand the pain?
20 Our homes are destroyed;
our children are dead.
No one is left
to help us find shelter."

21 But I told them,
"Our leaders were stupid failures,
because they refused
to listen to the LORD.
And so we've been scattered
like sheep.

22 "Sounds of destruction
rumble from the north
like distant thunder.
Soon our towns will be ruins
where jackals[o] live."

Jeremiah Prays

23 I know, LORD, that we humans
are not in control
of our own lives.
24 Correct me, as I deserve,
but not in your anger,
or I will be dead.
25 Our enemies refuse
to admit that you are God
or to worship you.
They have wiped out our people
and left our nation
lying in ruins.
So get angry
and sweep them away!

Judah Has Broken the LORD's Agreement

11 1-3 The LORD God told me to say to
the people of Judah and Jerusalem:
I, the LORD, am warning you that I
will put a curse on anyone who doesn't
keep the agreement I made with Israel. So pay attention to what it says.
4 My commands haven't changed since
I brought your ancestors out of Egypt,
a nation that seemed like a blazing furnace where iron ore is melted. I told
your ancestors that if they obeyed my
commands, I would be their God, and
they would be my people. 5 Then I did
what I had promised and gave them
this wonderful land, where you now
live.

"Yes, LORD," I replied, "that's true."
6 Then the LORD told me to say to everyone on the streets of Jerusalem and in the
towns of Judah:

Pay attention to the commands in
my agreement with you. 7 Ever since I
brought your ancestors out of Egypt, I
have been telling your people to obey
me. But you and your ancestors 8 have
always been stubborn. You have refused to listen, and instead you have
done whatever your sinful hearts have
desired.

You have not kept the agreement we made, so I will make you suffer every curse that goes with it.

[n] **10.18** *like a rock from a sling*: One possible meaning for the difficult Hebrew text.
[o] **10.22** *jackals*: See the note at 9.11.

9 The LORD said to me:

Jeremiah, the people of Judah and
Jerusalem are plotting against me.
10 They have sinned in the same way
their ancestors did, by turning from me and worshiping other gods. The northern kingdom of Israel broke the agreement I made with your ancestors, and now the southern kingdom of Judah[p] has done the same.
11 Here is what I've decided to do. I
will bring suffering on the people of Judah and Jerusalem, and no one will escape. They will beg me to help, but I
won't listen to their prayers. 12-13 Then
they will offer sacrifices to their other gods and ask them for help. After all, the people of Judah have more gods than towns, and more altars for Baal than there are streets in Jerusalem. But those gods won't be able to rescue the people of Judah from disaster.
14 Jeremiah, don't pray for these
people or beg me to rescue them. If you do, I won't listen, and I certainly won't listen if they pray!
15 Then the LORD told me to say to the
people of Judah:

You are my chosen people,
but you have no right
to be here in my temple,
doing such terrible things.
The sacrifices you offer me
won't protect you from disaster,
so stop celebrating.[q]
16 Once you were like an olive tree
covered with fruit.
But soon I will send a noisy mob
to break off your branches
and set you on fire.

17 I am the LORD All-Powerful. You people of Judah were like a tree that I had planted, but you have made me angry by offering sacrifices to Baal, just as the northern kingdom did. And now I'm going to pull you up by the roots.

The Plot To Kill Jeremiah

*18 Some people plotted to kill me.
And like a lamb
being led to the butcher,
I knew nothing
about their plans.
19 But then the LORD told me
that they had planned
to chop me down like a tree—
fruit and all—
so that no one would ever
remember me again.
20 I prayed, "LORD All-Powerful,
you always do what is right,
and you know every thought.
So I trust you to help me
and to take revenge."

21 Then the LORD said:

Jeremiah, some men from Anathoth[r] say they will kill you, if you keep
on speaking for me. 22 But I will punish them. Their young men will die in battle, and their children will starve to
death. 23 And when I am finished, no
one from their families will be left alive.

Jeremiah Complains to the LORD

12 Whenever I complain
to you, LORD,
you are always fair.
But now I have questions
about your justice.
Why is life easy for sinners?
Why are they successful?
2 You plant them like trees;
you let them prosper
and produce fruit.
Yet even when they praise you,
they don't mean it.

3 But you know, LORD,
how faithful I've always been,
even in my thoughts.
So drag my enemies away
and butcher them like sheep!

4 How long will the ground be dry
and the pasturelands parched?

[p]**11.10** *Israel . . . Judah*: See the note at 2.4. [q]**11.15** *celebrating*: One possible meaning for the difficult Hebrew text of verse 15. [r]**11.21** *Anathoth*: Jeremiah's hometown (see 1.1).
11.20 Ws 1.6-9.

The birds and animals
are dead and gone.
And all of this happened because
the people are so sinful.
They even brag, "God can't see
the sins we commit."[s]

The LORD Answers Jeremiah

5 Jeremiah, if you get tired
in a race against people,
how can you possibly run
against horses?
If you fall in open fields,
what will happen in the forest
along the Jordan River?
6 Even your own family
has turned against you.
They act friendly,
but don't trust them.
They're out to get you,
and so is everyone else.

The LORD Is Furious with His People

7 I loved my people and chose them
as my very own.
But now I will reject them
and hand them over
to their enemies.
8 My people have turned against me
and roar at me like lions.
That's why I hate them.

9 My people are like a hawk
surrounded and attacked
by other hawks.[t]
Tell the wild animals
to come and eat their fill.
10 My beautiful land is ruined
like a field or a vineyard
trampled by shepherds
and stripped bare
by their flocks.
11 Every field I see lies barren,
and no one cares.

12 A destroying army
marches along desert roads
and attacks everywhere.
They are my deadly sword;
no one is safe from them.

13 My people, you planted wheat,
but because I was furious,
I let only weeds grow.
You wore yourselves out
for nothing!

The LORD Will Have Pity on Other Nations

14 The LORD said:
I gave this land to my people Israel, but
enemies around it have attacked and
robbed it. So I will uproot them from their
own countries just as I will uproot Judah
from its land. 15 But later, I will have pity
on these nations and bring them back to
their own lands. 16 They once taught my
people to worship Baal. But if they admit I
am the only true God, and if they let my
people teach them how to worship me,
these nations will also become my people.
17 However, if they don't listen to me, I will
uproot them from their lands and completely destroy them. I, the LORD, have
spoken.

Jeremiah's Linen Shorts

13 The LORD told me, "Go and buy a
pair of linen shorts. Wear them for
a while, but don't wash them." 2 So I
bought a pair of shorts and put them on.
3 Then the LORD said, 4 "Take off the
shorts. Go to Parah[u] and hide the shorts in
a crack between some large rocks." 5 And
that's what I did.
6 Some time later the LORD said, "Go
back and get the shorts." 7 I went back and
dug the shorts out of their hiding place, but
the cloth had rotted, and the shorts were
ruined.
8 Then the LORD said:
9 Jeremiah, I will use Babylonia to[v]
destroy the pride of the people of
Judah and Jerusalem. 10 The people
of Judah are evil and stubborn. So
instead of listening to me, they do

[s] **12.4** *God can't see the sins we commit*: Or "Jeremiah won't live to see what happens to us."
[t] **12.9** *My people . . . other hawks*: Or "My land has become a hyena's den with vultures circling above."
[u] **13.4** *Parah*: Or "the Euphrates River." Parah was a village about five and a half miles northeast of Jerusalem.
[v] **13.9** *I will use Babylonia to*: Or "that's how I'm going to."

whatever they want and even worship
other gods. When I am finished with
these people, they will be good for
nothing, just like this pair of shorts.
11 These shorts were tight around your
waist, and that's how tightly I held
onto the kingdoms of Israel and Judah.
I wanted them to be my people. I
wanted to make them famous, so that
other nations would praise and honor
me, but they refused to obey me.

Wine Jars

The LORD said:
12 Jeremiah, tell the people of Judah,
"The LORD God of Israel orders you to fill
your wine jars with wine."
They will answer, "Of course we fill our
wine jars with wine! Why are you telling us
something we already know?"
13 Then say to them:
I am the LORD, and what I'm going
to do will make everyone in Judah and
Jerusalem appear to be full of wine.
And the worst ones will be the kings of
David's family and the priests and the
prophets. 14 Then I will smash them
against each other like jars. I will have
no pity on the young or the old, and
they will all be destroyed. I, the LORD,
have spoken.

The People of Judah Will Be Taken Away

15 People of Judah,
don't be too proud to listen
to what the LORD has said.
16 You hope for light,
but God is sending darkness.
Evening shadows already deepen
in the hills.
So return to God
and confess your sins to him
before you trip and fall.
17 If you are too proud to listen,
I will weep alone.
Tears will stream from my eyes
when the LORD's people
are taken away as prisoners.

18 The LORD told me to tell you
that your king and his mother[w]
must surrender their thrones
and remove their crowns.[x]
19 The cities in the Southern Desert
are surrounded;
no one can get in or out.
Everyone in Judah
will be taken away.
20 Jerusalem, you were so proud
of ruling the people of Judah.
But where are they now?

Look north, and you will see
your enemies approaching.
21 You once trusted them to help,
but now I'll let them rule you.[y]
What do you say about that?
You will be in pain
like a woman giving birth.

22 Do you know why
your clothes were torn off
and you were abused?
It was because
of your terrible sins.
23 Can you ever change
and do what's right?
Can people change the color
of their skin,
or can a leopard
remove its spots?
If so, then maybe you can change
and learn to do right.

24 I will scatter you,
just as the desert wind
blows husks from grain
tossed in the air.
25 I won't change my mind.
I, the LORD, have spoken.

You rejected me
and worshiped false gods.
*26 You were married to me,
but you were unfaithful.
You even became a prostitute[z]
by worshiping disgusting gods
on hilltops and in fields.

[w] **13.18** *mother*: The king's mother usually had an important position in the royal court.
[x] **13.18** *and remove their crowns*: One possible meaning for the difficult Hebrew text.
[y] **13.21** *You once . . . rule you*: One possible meaning for the difficult Hebrew text.
[z] **13.26** *prostitute*: See the note at 2.20.

27 So I'll rip off your clothes
and leave you naked and ashamed
for everyone to see.
You are doomed!
Will you ever be worthy
to worship me again?

The Land Dries Up

14 When there had been no rain for a long time, the LORD told me to say to the people:

2 Judah and Jerusalem weep
as the land dries up.
3 Rulers send their servants
to the storage pits for water.[a]
But there's none to be found;
they return in despair
with their jars still empty.

4 There has been no rain,
and farmers feel sick
as they watch cracks appear
in the dry ground.[b]

5 A deer gives birth in a field,
then abandons her newborn fawn
and leaves in search of grass.
6 Wild donkeys go blind
from starvation.
So they stand on barren hilltops
and sniff the air,[c]
hoping to smell green grass.

The LORD's People Pray

7 Our terrible sins may demand
that we be punished.
But if you rescue us, LORD,
everyone will see
how great you are.
8 You're our only hope;
you alone can save us now.
You help us one day,
but you're gone the next.
9 Did this disaster
take you by surprise?
Are you a warrior
with your hands tied?
You have chosen us,
and your temple is here.
Don't abandon us!

The LORD's Answer

10 My people,
you love to wander away;
you don't even try
to stay close to me.
So now I will reject you
and punish you for your sins.
I, the LORD, have spoken.

Lying Prophets

11 The LORD said, "Jeremiah, don't ask
me to help these people. 12 They may even
go without eating[d] and offer sacrifices to
please me[e] and to give thanks.[f] But when
they cry out for my help, I won't listen, and
I won't accept their sacrifices. Instead, I'll
send war, starvation, and disease to wipe
them out."
13 I replied, "The other prophets keep
telling everyone that you won't send starvation or war, and that you're going to give us peace."
14 The LORD answered:
They claim to speak for me, but they're lying! I didn't even speak to them, much less choose them to be my prophets. Their messages come from worthless dreams, useless fortune-telling, and their own imaginations.
15 Those lying prophets say there

[a] **14.3** *storage pits for water*: Since water was scarce, pits were dug into solid rock for collecting and storing rainwater. These pits were called "cisterns." [b] **14.4** *cracks . . . ground*: One possible meaning for the difficult Hebrew text. [c] **14.6** *sniff the air*: The Hebrew text has "sniff the air, like jackals" (see the note at 9.11). [d] **14.12** *go without eating*: The people of Israel sometimes went without eating to show sorrow for their sins. [e] **14.12** *sacrifices to please me*: These sacrifices have traditionally been called "whole burnt offerings" because the whole animal was burned on the altar. A main purpose of such sacrifices was to please the LORD with the smell of the sacrifice, and so in the CEV they are sometimes called "sacrifices to please the LORD."
[f] **14.12** *sacrifices . . . to give thanks*: These sacrifices have traditionally been called "grain offerings." A main purpose of such sacrifices was to thank the LORD with a gift of grain, and so in the CEV they are sometimes called "sacrifices to give thanks to the LORD."

will be peace and plenty of food. But I say that those same prophets will die from war and hunger. 16 And everyone who listens to them will be killed, just as they deserve. Their dead bodies will be thrown out into the streets of Jerusalem, because their families will also be dead, and no one will be left to bury them.[g]

17 Jeremiah, go and tell the people how you feel about all this.
So I told them:

"Tears will flood my eyes
both day and night,
because my nation suffers
from a deadly wound.
18 In the fields I see the bodies
of those killed in battle.
And in the towns I see crowds
dying of hunger.
But the prophets and priests
go about their business,
without understanding
what has happened."[h]

Jeremiah Prays to the LORD

19 Have you rejected Judah, LORD?
Do you hate Jerusalem?
Why did you strike down Judah
with a fatal wound?
We had hoped for peace
and a time of healing,
but all we got was terror.
20 We and our ancestors are guilty
of rebelling against you.
21 If you save us, it will show
how great you are.
Don't let our enemies
disgrace your temple,
your beautiful throne.
Don't forget that you promised
to rescue us.
22 Idols can't send rain,
and showers don't fall
by themselves.
Only you control the rain,
so we put our trust in you,
the LORD our God.

The People of Judah Will Die

15 The LORD said to me:
Even if Moses and Samuel were
here, praying with you, I wouldn't change
my mind. So send the people of Judah
away. 2 And when they ask where they are
going, tell them that I, the LORD, have said:

Some of you are going to die
of horrible diseases.
Others are going to die in war
or from starvation.
The rest will be led away
to a foreign country.
3 I will punish you
in four different ways:
You will be killed in war
and your bodies dragged off
by dogs,
your flesh will be eaten by birds,
and your bones will be chewed on
by wild animals.
4 This punishment will happen
because of the horrible things[i]
your King Manasseh[j] did.
And you will be disgusting
to all nations on earth.
5 People of Jerusalem,
who will feel sorry for you?
Will anyone bother
to ask if you are well?
6 My people, you abandoned me
and walked away.
I am tired of showing mercy;
that's why I'll destroy you
7 by scattering you like straw
blown by the wind.
I will punish you with sorrow
and death,
because you refuse
to change your ways.
8 There will be more widows
in Judah
than grains of sand on a beach.

[g] **14.16** *dead bodies . . . bury them*: A proper burial was considered very important. [h] **14.18** *go about . . . has happened*: One possible meaning for the difficult Hebrew text. [i] **15.4** *the horrible things*: See 2 Kings 21.1-16. [j] **15.4** *Manasseh*: Hebrew "Manasseh son of Hezekiah"; he ruled 687-642 B.C.

15.1 **a** Ex 32.11-14; Nu 14.13-19; **b** 1 S 7.5-10. **15.2** Rev 13.10. **15.4** 2 K 21.1-16; 2 Ch 33.1-9.

A surprise attack at noon!
And the mothers in Jerusalem
mourn for their children.
9 A mother is in deep despair
and struggles for breath.
Her daylight has turned
to darkness—
she has suffered the loss
of her seven sons.

I will kill anyone who survives.
I, the LORD, have spoken.

Jeremiah Complains

10 I wish I had never been born!
I'm always in trouble
with everyone in Judah.
I never lend or borrow money,
but everyone curses me
just the same.

11 Then the LORD replied,
"I promise to protect you,
and when disaster comes,
even your enemies
will beg you for help."[k]

The Enemy Cannot Be Defeated

The LORD told me to say:
12 People of Judah,
just as you can't break iron
mixed with bronze,
you can't defeat the enemies
that will attack
from the north.
13 I will give them
everything you own,
because you have sinned
everywhere in your country.
14 My anger is a fire
that cannot be put out,[l]
so I will make you slaves
of your enemies
in a foreign land.[m]

Jeremiah Complains Again

15 You can see how I suffer
insult after insult,
all because of you, LORD.
Don't be so patient
with my enemies;
take revenge on them
before they kill me.

16 When you spoke to me,
I was glad to obey,
because I belong to you,
the LORD All-Powerful.
17 I don't go to parties
and have a good time.
Instead, I keep to myself,
because you have filled me
with your anger.

18 I am badly injured
and in constant pain.
Are you going to disappoint me,
like a stream that goes dry
in the heat of summer?

The LORD Replies

19 Then the LORD told me:
Stop talking like a fool!
If you turn back to me
and speak my message,
I will let you be my prophet
once again.
I hope the people of Judah
will accept what you say.
But you can ignore their threats,
*20 because I am making you strong,
like a bronze wall.
They are evil and violent,
but when they attack,
21 I will be there to rescue you.
I, the LORD, have spoken.

Jeremiah Must Live His Message

16 The LORD said to me:
2 Jeremiah, don't get married
and have children—Judah is no place to
raise a family. 3 I'll tell you what's going to
happen to children and their parents here.
4 They will die of horrible diseases and of war
and starvation. No one will give them a funeral or bury them, and their bodies will be
food for the birds and wild animals. And

[k]**15.11** *help*: One possible meaning for the difficult Hebrew text of verse 11. [l]**15.14** *that cannot be put out*: Some Hebrew manuscripts; most Hebrew manuscripts "against you." [m]**15.14** *I will make . . . land*: Many Hebrew manuscripts; most Hebrew manuscripts "I will make your enemies go through to a land you don't know about."

what's left will lie on the ground like manure.
5 When someone dies, don't visit the
family or show any sorrow. I will no longer
love or bless or have any pity on the people
of Judah. 6 Rich and poor alike will die and
be left unburied. No one will mourn and
show their sorrow by cutting themselves or
shaving their heads.[n] 7 No one will bring
food and wine to help comfort those who are
mourning the death of their father or mother.
8 Don't even set foot in a house where
there is eating and drinking and celebrating. 9 Warn the people of Judah that I, the
LORD All-Powerful, will put an end to all
their parties and wedding celebrations.
10 They will ask, "Why has the LORD our
God threatened us with so many disasters?
Have we done something wrong or sinned
against him?"
11 Then tell them I have said:

People of Judah, your ancestors
turned away from me; they rejected
my laws and teachings and started
worshiping other gods. 12 And you
have done even worse! You are stubborn, and instead of obeying me, you
do whatever evil comes to your mind.
13 So I will throw you into a land that
you and your ancestors know nothing
about, a place where you will have to
worship other gods both day and night.
And I won't feel the least bit sorry
for you.
14 A time will come when you will
again worship me. But you will no
longer call me the Living God who rescued Israel from Egypt. 15 Instead, you
will call me the Living God who rescued you from that country in the
north and from the other countries
where I had forced you to go.

Someday I will bring you back to
this land that I gave your ancestors.
16 But for now, I am sending enemies
who will catch you like fish and hunt
you down like wild animals in the hills
and the caves.
17 I can see everything you are doing, even if you try to hide your sins
from me. 18 I will punish you double
for your sins, because you have made
my own land disgusting. You have
filled it with lifeless idols that remind
me of dead bodies.

The LORD Gives Strength

I prayed to the LORD:

19 Our LORD, you are the one
who gives me strength
and protects me like a fortress
when I am in trouble.
People will come to you
from distant nations and say,
"Our ancestors worshiped
false and useless gods,
20 worthless idols
made by human hands."

21 Then the LORD replied,
"That's why I will teach them
about my power,
and they will know
that I am the true God."

The LORD Will Punish Judah

The LORD said:

17 People of Judah,
your sins cannot be erased.
They are written on your hearts
like words chiseled in stone
or carved on the corners
of your altars.[o]
*2 One generation after another
has set up pagan altars
and worshiped the goddess Asherah
everywhere in your country—
on hills and mountains,
and under large trees.
3 So I'll take everything you own,
including your altars,
and give it all
to your enemies.[p]

[n] **16.6** *mourn and show their sorrow by cutting themselves or shaving their heads*: A custom in some Canaanite religions. [o] **17.1** *carved on the corners of your altars*: When sacrifices were offered to the LORD to ask him to forgive sins, some of the blood was smeared on the corners of the altar (see Leviticus 4.7, 18-20, 25, 26, 30, 31, 34, 35; 16.18). But now the LORD refuses to accept these sacrifices. [p] **17.3** *enemies*: One possible meaning for the difficult Hebrew text of verses 2, 3.
16.9 Jr 7.34; 25.10; Rev 18.23.

4 You will lose[q] the land
that I gave you,
and I will make you slaves
in a foreign country,
because you have made my anger
blaze up like a fire
that won't stop burning.

Trust the LORD

5 I, the LORD, have put a curse
on those who turn from me
and trust in human strength.
6 They will dry up like a bush
in salty desert soil,
where nothing can grow.

7 But I will bless those
who trust me.
8 They will be like trees
growing beside a stream—
trees with roots that reach
down to the water,
and with leaves
that are always green.
They bear fruit every year
and are never worried
by a lack of rain.

9 You people of Judah
are so deceitful
that you even fool yourselves,
and you can't change.
10 But I know your deeds
and your thoughts,
and I will make sure
you get what you deserve.
11 You cheated others,
but everything you gained
will fly away, like birds
hatched from stolen eggs.
Then you will discover
what fools you are.

Jeremiah Prays to the LORD

12 Our LORD, your temple
is a glorious throne
that has stood on a mountain
from the beginning.
13 You are a spring of water
giving Israel life and hope.
But if the people reject
what you have told me,
they will be swept away
like words written in dust.[r]

14 You, LORD, are the one I praise.
So heal me and rescue me!
Then I will be completely well
and perfectly safe.

15 The people of Judah say to me,
"Jeremiah, you claimed to tell us
what the LORD has said.
So why hasn't it come true?"

16 Our LORD, you chose me
to care for your people,
and that's what I have done.
You know everything I have said,
and I have never once
asked you to punish them.[s]
17 I trust you for protection
in times of trouble,
so don't frighten me.
18 Keep me from failure
and disgrace,
but make my enemies fail
and be disgraced.
Send destruction to make
their worst fears come true.

Resting on the Sabbath

19-20 The LORD said:
Jeremiah, stand at each city gate in
Jerusalem, including the one the king uses,
and speak to him and everyone else. Tell
them I have said:
I am the LORD, so pay attention.
21-24 If you value your lives, don't do any
work on the Sabbath. Don't carry anything through the city gates or through
the door of your house, or anywhere
else. Keep the Sabbath day sacred!
I gave this command to your ancestors, but they were stubborn and refused to obey or to be corrected. But if

[q] **17.4** *You will lose*: One possible meaning for the difficult Hebrew text. [r] **17.13** *reject . . . dust*: One possible meaning for the difficult Hebrew text. [s] **17.16** *you chose . . . punish them*: One possible meaning for the difficult Hebrew text.

17.8 Ps 1.3. **17.10** **a** Rev 2.23; **b** Ps 62.12. **17.21-24** **a** Ex 20.8-10; Dt 5.12-14; **b** Ne 13.15-22.

you obey, 25 then Judah and Jerusalem
will always be ruled by kings from
David's family. The king and his officials will ride through these gates on
horses or in chariots, and the people of
Judah and Jerusalem will be with
them. There will always be people living in Jerusalem, 26 and others will
come here from the nearby villages,
from the towns of Judah and Benjamin,[t] from the hill country and the
foothills to the west, and from the
Southern Desert. They will bring sacrifices to please me and to give me
thanks,[u] as well as offerings of grain
and incense.
27 But if you keep on carrying
things through the city gates on the
Sabbath and keep treating it as any
other day, I will set fire to these gates
and burn down the whole city, including the fortresses.

Jeremiah Goes to the Pottery Shop

18 The LORD told me, 2 "Go to the pottery shop, and when you get there,
I will tell you what to say to the people."
3 I went there and saw the potter making clay pots on his pottery wheel. 4 And
whenever the clay would not take the
shape he wanted, he would change his
mind and form it into some other shape.
5 Then the LORD told me to say:
6 People of Israel, I, the LORD, have
power over you, just as a potter has power
over clay. 7 If I threaten to uproot and shatter an evil nation 8 and that nation turns
from its evil, I will change my mind.
9 If I promise to make a nation strong,
10 but its people start disobeying me and
doing evil, then I will change my mind and
not help them at all.
11 So listen to me, people of Judah and
Jerusalem! I have decided to strike you
with disaster, and I won't change my mind
unless you stop sinning and start living
right.
12 But I know you won't listen. You
might as well answer, "We don't care what
you say. We have made plans to sin, and we
are going to be stubborn and do what we
want!"
13 So I, the LORD, command you to ask
the nations, and find out if they have ever
heard of such a horrible sin as what you
have done.

14 The snow
on Lebanon's mountains
never melts away,
and the streams there
never run dry.[v]
15 But you, my people,
have turned from me
to burn incense
to worthless idols.
You have left the ancient road
to follow an unknown path
where you stumble over idols.

16 Your land will be ruined,
and every passerby
will look at it with horror
and make insulting remarks.
17 When your enemies attack,
I will scatter you like dust
blown by an eastern wind.
Then, on that day of disaster,
I will turn my back on you.

The Plot against Jeremiah

18 Some of the people said, "Let's get rid
of Jeremiah! We will always have priests to
teach us God's laws, as well as wise people
to give us advice, and prophets to speak the
LORD's messages. So, instead of listening to
Jeremiah any longer, let's accuse him of a
crime."

Jeremiah Prays about His Enemies

19 Please, LORD, answer my prayer.
Make my enemies stop
accusing me of evil.
20 I tried to help them,
but they are paying me back
by digging a pit to trap me.
I even begged you
not to punish them.

[t] **17.26** *Judah and Benjamin*: These two tribes made up the southern kingdom of Judah.
[u] **17.26** *sacrifices to please me and to give me thanks*: See the notes at 14.12. [v] **18.14** *dry*: One possible meaning for the difficult Hebrew text of verse 14.

21 But now I am asking you
to let their children starve
or be killed in war.
Let women lose
their husbands and sons
to disease and violence.
22 These people have dug pits
and set traps for me, LORD.
Make them scream in fear
when you send enemy troops
to attack their homes.
23 You know they plan to kill me.
So get angry and punish them!
Don't ever forgive
their terrible crimes.

Jeremiah and the Clay Jar

19 The LORD said:
Jeremiah, go to the pottery shop
and buy a clay jar. Then take along some of
the city officials and leading priests 2 and
go to Hinnom Valley, just outside Potsherd[w]
Gate. Tell the people that I have said:
3 I am the LORD All-Powerful, the
God of Israel, and you kings of Judah
and you people of Jerusalem had better pay attention. I am going to bring
so much trouble on this valley that
everyone who hears about it will be
shocked. 4-5 The people of Judah
stopped worshiping me and made this
valley into a place of worship for Baal
and other gods that have never helped
them or their ancestors or their kings.
And they have committed murder
here, burning their young, innocent
children as sacrifices to Baal. I have
never even thought of telling you to do
that. 6 So watch out! Someday this
place will no longer be called Topheth
or Hinnom Valley. It will be called
Slaughter Valley!
7 You people of Judah and Jerusalem may have big plans, but here
in this valley I'll ruin[x] those plans.
I'll let your enemies kill you, and I'll
tell the birds and wild animals to eat
your dead bodies. 8 I will turn Jerusalem into a pile of rubble, and every
passerby will be shocked and horrified and will make insulting remarks.
9 And while your enemies are trying to
break through your city walls to kill
you, the food supply will run out. You
will become so hungry that you will eat
the flesh of your friends and even of
your own children.
10 Jeremiah, as soon as you have said
this, smash the jar while the people are
watching. 11 Then tell them that I have also
said:
I am the LORD All-Powerful, and I
warn you that I will shatter Judah and
Jerusalem just like this jar that is broken beyond repair. You will bury your
dead here in Topheth, but so many of
you will die that there won't be enough
room.
12-13 I will make Jerusalem as unclean as Topheth, by filling the city
with your dead bodies. I will do this
because you and your kings have gone
up to the roofs of your houses and
burned incense to the stars in the sky, as
though they were gods. And you have
given sacrifices of wine to foreign gods.

Jeremiah Speaks in the Temple Courtyard

14 I went to Topheth, where I told the
people what the LORD had said. Then I
went to the temple courtyard and shouted
to the people, 15 "Listen, everyone! Some
time ago, the LORD All-Powerful, the God of
Israel, warned you that he would bring disaster on Jerusalem and all nearby villages.
But you were stubborn and refused to listen. Now the LORD is going to bring the disaster he promised."

Pashhur Arrests Jeremiah

20 Pashhur son of Immer was a priest
and the chief of temple security. He
heard what I had said, 2 and so he hit me.[y]
Then he had me arrested and put in
chains[z] at the Benjamin Gate in the LORD's

[w] **19.2** *Potsherd*: A piece of broken pottery. [x] **19.7** *ruin*: In Hebrew "ruin" sounds like "jar" (see verse 1). [y] **20.2** *hit me*: Or "beat me up" or "had me beaten up." [z] **20.2** *in chains*: Or "in the stocks" (a wooden frame with holes for the hands, neck, or feet of a prisoner) or "in a prison cell."

19.2 2 K 23.10; Jr 7.30-32; 32.34, 35. **19.4,5** Lv 18.21.

temple.[a] 3 The next day, when Pashhur let
me go free, I told him that the LORD had
said:

No longer will I call you Pashhur. Instead, I will call you Afraid-of-
Everything.[b] 4 You will be afraid, and
you will bring fear to your friends as
well. You will see enemies kill them in
battle. Then I will have the king of
Babylonia take everyone in Judah prisoner, killing some and dragging the
rest away to Babylonia. 5 He will clean
out the royal treasury and take everything else of value from Jerusalem.

6 Pashhur, you are guilty of telling
lies and claiming they were messages
from me. That's why I will have the
Babylonians take you, your family, and
your friends as prisoners to Babylonia,
where you will all die and be buried.

Jeremiah Complains to the LORD

7 You tricked me, LORD,
and I was really fooled.
You are stronger than I am,
and you have defeated me.
People never stop sneering
and insulting me.
8 You have let me announce
only destruction and death.
Your message has brought me
nothing but insults
and trouble.
9 Sometimes I tell myself
not to think about you, LORD,
or even mention your name.
But your message burns
in my heart and bones,
and I cannot keep silent.

10 I heard the crowds whisper,
"Everyone is afraid.
Now's our chance
to accuse Jeremiah!"
All of my so-called friends
are just waiting
for me to make a mistake.
They say, "Maybe Jeremiah
can be tricked.
Then we can overpower him
and get even at last."

11 But you, LORD,
are a mighty soldier,
standing at my side.
Those troublemakers
will fall down and fail—
terribly embarrassed,
forever ashamed.

12 LORD All-Powerful,
you test those who do right,
and you know every heart
and mind.
I have told you my complaints,
so let me watch you
take revenge on my enemies.
13 I sing praises to you, LORD.
You rescue the oppressed
from the wicked.

14 Put a curse on the day I was born!
Don't bless my mother.
15 Put a curse on the man
who told my father, "Good news!
You have a son."
16 May that man be like the towns
you destroyed without pity.
Let him hear shouts of alarm
in the morning
and battle cries at noon.
17 He deserves to die
for not killing me
before I was born.
Then my mother's body
would have been my grave.
18 Why did I have to be born?
Was it just to suffer
and die in shame?

The LORD Will Fight against Jerusalem

21 King Zedekiah[c] of Judah sent for
Pashhur son of Malchiah and for a
priest named Zephaniah son of Maaseiah.
Then he told them, "Talk with Jeremiah
for me."

So they came to me and said, 2 "King

[a]**20.2** *the Benjamin Gate in the LORD's temple*: The Hebrew text has "the upper Benjamin Gate in the temple"; the lower Benjamin Gate may have been the city gate of that name.
[b]**20.3** *Afraid-of-Everything*: Hebrew "Magor-Missabib." [c]**21.1** *Zedekiah*: See the note at 1.3.
20.14-18 Job 3.1-19. **21.2** 2 K 25.1-11; 2 Ch 36.17-21.

Nebuchadnezzar[d] of Babylonia has attacked Judah. Please ask the LORD to work miracles for our people, as he has done in the past, so that Nebuchadnezzar will leave us alone."

3-7 I told them that the LORD God of Israel had told me to say to King Zedekiah:

The Babylonians have surrounded Jerusalem and want to kill you and your people. You are asking me to save you, but you have made me furious. So I will stretch out my mighty arm and fight against you myself. Your army is using spears and swords to fight the Babylonians, but I will make your own weapons turn and attack you. I will send a horrible disease to kill many of the people and animals in Jerusalem, and there will be nothing left to eat. Finally, I will let King Nebuchadnezzar and his army fight their way to the center of Jerusalem and capture everyone who is left alive, including you and your officials. But Nebuchadnezzar won't be kind or show any mercy—he will have you killed! I, the LORD, have spoken.

8 Then I told them that the LORD had said:

People of Jerusalem, I, the LORD, give you the choice of life or death.
9 The Babylonian army has surrounded Jerusalem, so if you want to live, you must go out and surrender to them. But if you want to die because of hunger, disease, or war, then stay
here in the city. 10 I have decided not to rescue Jerusalem. Instead, I am going to let the king of Babylonia burn it to the ground. I, the LORD, have spoken.

The LORD Warns the King of Judah

*11 Pay attention, you that belong
to the royal family.
12 Each new day, make sure
that justice is done,
and rescue those
who are being robbed.
Or else my anger will flame up
like a fire that never goes out.

13 Jerusalem,
from your mountaintop
you look out over the valleys[e]
and think you are safe.
But I, the LORD, am angry,
14 and I will punish you
as you deserve.
I'll set your palace[f] on fire,
and everything around you
will go up in smoke.

The LORD Will Punish the King of Judah

22 1-3 The LORD sent me to the palace of the king of Judah to speak to the king, his officials, and everyone else who was there. The LORD told me to say:

I am the LORD, so pay attention! You have been allowing people to cheat, rob, and take advantage of widows, orphans, and foreigners who live here. Innocent people have become victims of violence, and some of them have even been killed. But now I command you to do what is right and see that justice is done. Rescue everyone who has suffered from injustice.

4 If you obey me, the kings from David's family will continue to rule Judah from this palace. They and their officials will ride in and out on their horses or in their chariots.
5 But if you ignore me, I promise in my own name that this palace will lie in ruins.
6 Listen to what I think about it:

The palace of Judah's king
is as glorious as Gilead
or Lebanon's highest peaks.
But it will be as empty
as a ghost-town
when I'm through with it.
7 I'll send troops to tear it apart,
and its beautiful cedar beams
will be used for firewood.

8 People from different nations will pass by and ask, "Why did the LORD do this to

[d]**21.2** *Nebuchadnezzar*: Ruled 605-562 B.C. [e]**21.13** *Jerusalem . . . valleys*: One possible meaning for the difficult Hebrew text. [f]**21.14** *your palace*: The Hebrew text has "the forest"; the largest room in the king's palace was known as Forest Hall (see 1 Kings 7.2,3).

21.8 4 Macc 15.2. **22.5** Mt 23.28; Lk 13.35.

such a great city as Jerusalem?" 9 Others will answer, "It's because the people worshiped foreign gods and broke the agreement that the LORD their God had made with them."

King Jehoahaz

The LORD said:

10 King Josiah is dead,
so don't cry for him.[g]
Instead, cry for his son
King Jehoahaz,[h]
dragged off to another country,
never to return.

11-12 Jehoahaz[i] became king of Judah after his father King Josiah died. But Jehoahaz was taken as a prisoner to a foreign country. Now I, the LORD, promise that he will die there without ever seeing his own land again.

King Jehoiakim

The LORD told me to say:

*13 King Jehoiakim,[j] you are doomed!
You built a palace
with large rooms upstairs.
14 You put in big windows
and used cedar paneling
and red paint.
But you were unfair
and forced the builders to work
without pay.

*15 More cedar in your palace
doesn't make you a better king
than your father Josiah.
He always did right—
he gave justice to the poor
and was honest.
16 That's what it means
to truly know me.
So he lived a comfortable life
and always had enough
to eat and drink.

17 But all you think about
is how to cheat
or abuse or murder
some innocent victim.
18 Jehoiakim, no one will cry
at your funeral.
They won't turn to each other
and ask,
"Why did our great king
have to die?"
19 You will be given a burial
fit for a donkey;
your body will be dragged
outside the city gates
and tossed in the dirt.
I, the LORD, have spoken.

King Jehoiachin and the People of Jerusalem

The LORD told me to say:

20 People of Jerusalem,
the nations[k] you trusted
have been crushed.
Go to Lebanon and weep;
cry in the land of Bashan
and in Moab.
21 When times were good,
I warned you.
But you ignored me,
just as you have done
since Israel was young.
22 Now you will be disgraced
because of your sins.
Your leaders will be swept away
by the wind,
and the nations you trusted
will be captured and dragged
to a foreign country.
23 Those who live in the palace
paneled with cedar[l]

[g]**22.10** *King Josiah . . . him*: The Hebrew text has "don't cry for the dead one," meaning King Josiah, who ruled 640-609 B.C. [h]**22.10** *his son, King Jehoahaz . . . country*: The Hebrew text has "the one who was dragged off to another country," meaning King Jehoahaz, who ruled for three months in 609 B.C. [i]**22.11,12** *Jehoahaz*: The Hebrew text has "Shallum," another name for Jehoahaz. [j]**22.13** *Jehoiakim*: See the note at 1.3. [k]**22.20** *nations*: Or "gods." [l]**22.23** *who live in the palace paneled with cedar*: The Hebrew text has "who live in Lebanon and who nest among the cedars," which probably means Forest Hall in the royal palace at Jerusalem, which was paneled with cedar and had cedar columns and a cedar ceiling, all from Lebanon (see 1 Kings 7.2, 3).
22.11,12 2 K 23.31-34; 2 Ch 36.1-4. **22.18** 2 K 23.36—24.6; 2 Ch 36.5-7.

will groan with pain
like women giving birth.

24 King Jehoiachin,[m] son of Jehoiakim,[n]
even if you were the ring I wear as the sign
of my royal power, I would still pull you
from my finger. 25 I would hand you over to
the enemy you fear, to King Nebuchadnezzar[o] and his army, who want to kill you.
26 You and your mother[p] were born in Judah, but I will throw both of you into a foreign country, where you will die, 27 longing
to return home.

28 Jehoiachin, you are unwanted
like a broken clay pot.
So you and your children
will be thrown into a country
you know nothing about.

29 Land of Judah, I am the LORD.
Now listen to what I say!
30 Erase the names
of Jehoiachin's children
from the royal records.
He is a complete failure,
and so none of them
will ever be king.
I, the LORD, have spoken.

A Message of Hope

The LORD said:

23 You leaders of my people are like
shepherds that kill and scatter the
sheep. 2 You were supposed to take care of
my people, but instead you chased them
away. So now I'll really take care of you, and
believe me, you will pay for your crimes!
3 I will bring the rest of my people home
from the lands where I have scattered
them, and they will grow into a mighty nation. 4 I promise to choose leaders who will
care for them like real shepherds. All of my
people will be there, and they will never
again be frightened.

5 Someday I will appoint
an honest king
from the family of David,
a king who will be wise
and rule with justice.
6 As long as he is king,
Israel will have peace,
and Judah will be safe.
The name of this king will be
"The LORD Gives Justice."

7 A time will come when you will again
worship me. But you will no longer call me
the Living God who rescued Israel from
Egypt. 8 Instead, you will call me the Living
God who rescued you from the land in the
north and from all the other countries
where I had forced you to go. And you will
once again live in your own land.

Jeremiah Thinks about Unfaithful Prophets

9 When I think of the prophets,
I am shocked, and I tremble[q]
like someone drunk,
because of the LORD
and his sacred words.
10 Those unfaithful prophets
misuse their power
all over the country.
So God turned the pasturelands
into scorching deserts.[r]

The LORD Will Punish Unfaithful Prophets

11 The LORD told me to say:

You prophets and priests
think so little of me, the LORD,
that you even sin
in my own temple!
12 Now I will punish you
with disaster,
and you will slip and fall
in the darkness.
I, the LORD, have spoken.

13 The prophets in Samaria
were disgusting to me,
because they preached
in the name of Baal
and led my people astray.

[m]**22.24** *Jehoiachin*: The Hebrew text has "Coniah," another form of Jehoiachin's name; he ruled for three months in 598 B.C. [n]**22.24** *Jehoiakim*: See the note at 1.3. [o]**22.25** *Nebuchadnezzar*: See the note at 21.2. [p]**22.26** *mother*: See the note at 13.18. [q]**23.9** *tremble*: Or "become weak." [r]**23.10** *deserts*: One possible meaning for the difficult Hebrew text of verse 10.
22.24 2 K 24.8-15; 2 Ch 36.9, 10. **23.5,6** Jr 33.14-16.

14 And you prophets in Jerusalem
are even worse.
You're unfaithful in marriage[s]
and never tell the truth.[t]
You even lead others to sin
instead of helping them
turn back to me.
You and the people of Jerusalem
are evil like Sodom
and Gomorrah.[u]
15 You prophets in Jerusalem
have spread evil everywhere.
That's why I, the LORD, promise
to give you bitter poison
to eat and drink.

The LORD Gives a Warning

The LORD said:
16 Don't listen to the lies
of these false prophets,
you people of Judah!
The message they preach
is something they imagined;
it did not come from me,
the LORD All-Powerful.
17 These prophets go to people
who refuse to respect me
and who are stubborn
and do whatever they want.
The prophets tell them,
"The LORD has promised
everything will be fine."

18 But I, the LORD, tell you
that these prophets
have never attended a meeting
of my council in heaven[v]
or heard me speak.
19 They are evil! So in my anger
I will strike them
like a violent storm.
20 I won't calm down,
until I have finished
what I have decided to do.
Someday you will understand
exactly what I mean.

21 I did not send these prophets
or speak to them,
but they ran to find you
and to preach their message.
22 If they had been in a meeting
of my council in heaven,
they would have told
you people of Judah
to give up your sins
and come back to me.

23 I am everywhere—
both near and far,
24 in heaven and on earth.
There are no secret places
where you can hide from me.

25 These unfaithful prophets claim that
I have given them a dream or a vision, and
then they tell lies in my name. 26 But
everything they say comes from their own
twisted minds. How long can this go on?
27 They tell each other their dreams and try
to get my people to reject me, just as their
ancestors left me and worshiped Baal.
28 Their dreams and my truth are as different as straw and wheat. But when prophets
speak for me, they must say only what
I have told them. 29 My words are a powerful fire; they are a hammer that shatters
rocks.

30-32 These unfaithful prophets claim I
give them their dreams, but it isn't true. I
didn't choose them to be my prophets, and
yet they babble on and on, speaking in my
name, while stealing words from each
other. And when my people hear these
liars, they are led astray instead of being
helped. So I warn you that I am now the
enemy of these prophets. I, the LORD, have
spoken.

News and Nuisance

The LORD said to me:

33 Jeremiah, when a prophet or a priest
or anyone else comes to you and asks,
"Does the LORD have news for us?" tell

[s]**23.14** *in marriage*: Or "to me." [t]**23.14** *never tell the truth*: Or "worship other gods."
[u]**23.14** *Sodom and Gomorrah*: Two cities that the LORD destroyed because their people were so evil (see Genesis 18.16—19.29). [v]**23.18** *a meeting of my council in heaven*: Sometimes, prophets had visions of the LORD meeting with his angels (see 1 Kings 22.19-23).
23.14 Gn 18.20; Ez 16.49. **23.24** Ws 1.7; Si 16.17.

them, "You people are a nuisance[w] to the LORD, and he[x] will get rid of you."

34 If any of you say, "Here is news from the LORD," I will punish you and your families, even if you are a prophet or a priest. 35 Instead, you must ask your friends and relatives, "What answer did the LORD give?" or "What has the LORD said?" 36 It seems that you each have your own news! So if you say, "Here is news from the LORD," you are twisting my words into a lie. Remember that I am your God, the LORD All-Powerful.

37 If you go to a prophet, it's all right to ask, "What answer did the LORD give to my question?" or "What has the LORD said?" 38 But if you disobey me and say, "Here is news from the LORD," 39 I will pick you up[y] and throw you far away. And I will abandon this city of Jerusalem that I gave to your ancestors. 40 You will never be free from your shame and disgrace.

Jeremiah Has a Vision of Two Baskets of Figs

24 The LORD spoke to me in a vision after King Nebuchadnezzar[z] of Babylonia had come to Judah and taken King Jehoiachin,[a] his officials, and all the skilled workers back to Babylonia. In this vision I saw two baskets of figs in front of the LORD's temple. 2 One basket was full of very good figs that ripened early, and the other was full of rotten figs that were not fit to eat.

3 "Jeremiah," the LORD asked, "what do you see?"

"Figs," I said. "Some are very good, but the others are too rotten to eat."

4 Then the LORD told me to say:

> 5 People of Judah, the good figs stand for those of you I sent away as exiles to Babylonia, 6 where I am watching over them. Then someday I will bring them back to this land. I will plant them, instead of uprooting them, and I will build them up, rather than tearing them down. 7 I will give them a desire to know me and to be my people. They will want me to be their God, and they will turn back to me with all their heart.
>
> 8 The rotten figs stand for King Zedekiah[b] of Judah, his officials, and all the others who were not taken away to Babylonia, whether they stayed here in Judah or went to live in Egypt. 9 I will punish them with a terrible disaster, and everyone on earth will tremble when they hear about it. I will force the people of Judah to go to foreign countries, where they will be cursed and insulted. 10 War and hunger and disease will strike them, until they finally disappear from the land that I gave them and their ancestors.

Seventy Years of Exile

25 1-2 In the fourth year that Jehoiakim was king of Judah,[c] which was the first year that Nebuchadnezzar[d] was king of Babylonia, the LORD told me to speak to the people of Judah and Jerusalem. So I told them:

3 For twenty-three years now, ever since the thirteenth year that Josiah[e] was king, I have been telling you what the LORD has told me. But you have not listened.

4 The LORD has sent prophets to you time after time, but you refused to listen. 5 They told you that the LORD had said:

> Change your ways! If you stop doing evil, I will let you stay forever in this land that I gave your ancestors. 6 I don't want to harm you. So don't make

[w] **23.33** *news . . . nuisance*: The Hebrew word for "news" in verses 33-38 is the same as "nuisance" and is related to "pick up" in verse 39. [x] **23.33** *You people are a nuisance to the LORD, and he*: Two ancient translations; Hebrew "Does the LORD have news for us? He." [y] **23.39** *pick you up*: A few Hebrew manuscripts and three ancient translations; most Hebrew manuscripts "forget you completely." [z] **24.1** *Nebuchadnezzar*: See the note at 21.2. [a] **24.1** *Jehoiachin*: The Hebrew text has "Jeconiah," another form of Jehoiachin's name; he ruled for three months in 598 B.C. [b] **24.8** *Zedekiah*: Ruled 598-586 B.C. [c] **25.1,2** *Jehoiakim . . . Judah*: See the note at 1.3. [d] **25.1,2** *Nebuchadnezzar*: See the note at 21.2. [e] **25.3** *Josiah*: Hebrew "Josiah son of Amon"; Josiah ruled 640-609 B.C.

24.1 2 K 24.12-16; 2 Ch 36.10. **25.1,2** 2 K 24.1; 2 Ch 36.5-7; Dn 1.1, 2.

me angry by worshiping idols and
other gods.
7 But you refused to listen to my
prophets. So I, the LORD, say that you
have made me angry by worshiping
idols, and you are the ones who were
hurt by what you did. 8 You refused to
listen to me, 9 and now I will let you be
attacked by nations from the north,
and especially by my servant, King
Nebuchadnezzar of Babylonia. You and
other nearby nations will be destroyed
and left in ruins forever. Everyone who
sees what has happened will be
shocked, but they will still make fun of
you. 10 I will put an end to your parties
and wedding celebrations; no one will
grind grain or be here to light the
lamps at night. 11 This country will be
as empty as a desert, because I will
make all of you the slaves of the king
of Babylonia for seventy years.
12 When that time is up, I will punish the king of Babylonia and his
people for everything they have done
wrong, and I will turn that country
into a wasteland forever. 13 My servant
Jeremiah has told you what I said I will
do to Babylonia and to the other nations, and he wrote it all down in this
book. I will do everything I threatened.
14 I will pay back the Babylonians for
every wrong they have done. Great
kings from many other nations will
conquer the Babylonians and force
them to be slaves.

The Cup Full of God's Anger

15 The LORD God of Israel showed me a
vision in which he said, "Jeremiah, here is
a cup filled with the wine of my anger. Take
it and make every nation drink some.
16 They will vomit and act crazy, because of
the war this cup of anger will bring to them."
17 I took the cup from the LORD's hand,
and I went to the kings of the nations and
made each of them drink some. 18 I started
with Jerusalem and the towns of Judah,
and the king and his officials were removed
from power in disgrace. Everyone still
makes insulting jokes about them and uses
their names as curse words. 19 The second
place I went was Egypt, where everyone
had to drink from the cup, including the
king and his officials, the other government
workers, the rest of the Egyptians, 20 and
all the foreigners who lived in the country.
Next I went to the king of Uz, and then
to the four kings of Philistia, who ruled
from Ashkelon, Gaza, Ekron, and what was
left of Ashdod.[f] 21 Then I went to the kings
of Edom, Moab, Ammon, 22 and to the
kings of Tyre, Sidon, and their colonies
across the sea. 23-24 After this, I went to the
kings of Dedan, Tema, Buz, the tribes of
the Arabian Desert,[g] 25 Zimri, Elam, Media, 26 and the countries in the north, both
near and far.
I went to all the countries on earth, one
after another, and finally to Babylonia.[h]
27 The LORD had said to tell each king,
"The LORD All-Powerful, the God of Israel,
commands you to drink from this cup that
is full of the wine of his anger. It will make
you so drunk that you will vomit. And when
the LORD sends war against the nations,
you will be completely defeated."
28 The LORD told me that if any of them
refused to drink from the cup, I must tell
them that he had said, "I, the LORD All-
Powerful, command you to drink. 29 Starting with my own city of Jerusalem, everyone on earth will suffer from war. So there
is no way I will let you escape unharmed."
30 The LORD told me to say:

From my sacred temple
  I will roar like thunder,
while I trample my people
and everyone else
  as though they were grapes.
31 My voice will be heard
  everywhere on earth,
accusing nations of their crimes
and sentencing the guilty
  to death.

[f]**25.20** *what was left of Ashdod*: It was defeated by the king of Egypt after being surrounded for twenty-nine years. [g]**25.23,24** *the tribes of the Arabian Desert*: One possible meaning for the difficult Hebrew text. [h]**25.26** *Babylonia*: The Hebrew text has "Sheshach," a secret way of writing "Babylonia."

25.10 **a** Jr 7.34; 16.9; **b** Rev 18.22, 23. **25.11** 2 Ch 36.21; Jr 29.10; Dn 9.2.

Disaster Is Coming

32 The LORD All-Powerful says:
You can see disaster spreading
from far across the earth,
from nation to nation
like a horrible storm.

33 When it strikes, I will kill so many people that their bodies will cover the ground like manure. No one will be left to bury them or to mourn.

The Leaders of Judah Will Be Punished

34 The LORD's people are his flock,
and you leaders
were the shepherds.
But now it's your turn
to be butchered like sheep.
You'll shatter like fine pottery
dropped on the floor.[i]
So roll on the ground,
crying and mourning.
35 You have nowhere to run,
nowhere to hide.

*36 Listen to the cries
of the shepherds,
37 as the LORD's burning anger
turns[j] peaceful meadows
into barren deserts.
38 The LORD has abandoned
his people[k]
like a lion leaving its den.

Jeremiah's Message in the Temple

(Jeremiah 7.1-15)

26 Soon after Jehoiakim[l] became king of Judah, the LORD said:
2 Jeremiah, I have a message for every-
one who comes from the towns of Judah to
worship in my temple. Go to the temple
courtyard and speak every word that I tell
you. 3 Maybe the people will listen this
time. And if they stop doing wrong, I will
change my mind and not punish them for
their sins. 4 Tell them that I have said:
You have refused to listen to me
and to obey my laws and teachings.
5 Again and again I have sent my servants the prophets to preach to you, but
you ignored them as well. Now I am
warning you that if you don't start
obeying me right away, 6 I will destroy
this temple, just as I destroyed the
town of Shiloh.[m] Then everyone on
earth will use the name "Jerusalem" as
a curse word.

Jeremiah on Trial

7 The prophets, the priests, and everyone else in the temple heard what I said,
8-9 and as soon as I finished, they all
crowded around me and started shouting, "Why did you preach that the LORD will destroy this temple, just as he destroyed Shiloh? Why did you say that Jerusalem will be empty and lie in ruins? You ought to be put to death for saying such things in the LORD's name!" Then they had me arrested.
10 The royal officers heard what had
happened, and they came from the palace to the new gate of the temple to be the
judges at my trial.[n] 11 While they listened,
the priests and the prophets said to the crowd, "All of you have heard Jeremiah prophesy that Jerusalem will be destroyed. He deserves the death penalty."
12-13 Then I told the judges and every-
one else:
The LORD himself sent me to tell you about the terrible things he will do to you, to Jerusalem, and to the temple. But if you change your ways and start obeying the LORD, he will change his mind.
14 You must decide what to do with
me. Just do whatever you think is
right. 15 But if you put me to death,
you and everyone else in Jerusalem

[i]**25.34** *You'll shatter . . . floor*: One possible meaning for the difficult Hebrew text.
[j]**25.37** *anger turns*: Or "anger and enemy armies turn." [k]**25.38** *The LORD has . . . people*: Or "And his people leave their homes." [l]**26.1** *Jehoiakim*: See the note at 1.3. [m]**26.6** *Shiloh*: The sacred tent had once stood at Shiloh. [n]**26.10** *new gate . . . trial*: Public trials were often held in an open area at a gate of a city, palace, or temple.
26.1 2 K 23.36—24.6; 2 Ch 36.5-7. **26.6** Js 18.1; Ps 78.60; Jr 7.12-14.

will be guilty of murdering an innocent man, because everything I preached came from the LORD.

16 The judges and the other people told the priests and prophets, "Since Jeremiah only told us what the LORD our God had said, we don't think he deserves to die."

17 Then some of the leaders from other towns stepped forward. They told the crowd that 18 years ago when Hezekiah[o] was king of Judah, a prophet named Micah from the town of Moresheth had said:

"I, the LORD All-Powerful, say
Jerusalem will be plowed under
and left in ruins.
Thorns will cover the mountain
where the temple
now stands."[p]

19 Then the leaders continued:

No one put Micah to death for saying that. Instead, King Hezekiah prayed to the LORD with fear and trembling and asked him to have mercy. Then the LORD decided not to destroy Jerusalem, even though he had already said he would.

People of Judah, if Jeremiah is killed, we will bring a terrible disaster on ourselves.

20-24 After these leaders finished speaking, an important man named Ahikam son of Shaphan spoke up for me as well. And so, I wasn't handed over to the crowd to be killed.

Uriah the Prophet

While Jehoiakim[q] was still king of Judah, a man named Uriah son of Shemaiah left his hometown of Kiriath-Jearim and came to Jerusalem. Uriah was one of the LORD's prophets, and he was saying the same things about Judah and Jerusalem that I had been saying. And when Jehoiakim and his officials and military officers heard what Uriah said, they tried to arrest him, but he escaped to Egypt. So Jehoiakim sent Elnathan son of Achbor and some other men after Uriah, and they brought him back. Then Jehoiakim had Uriah killed and his body dumped in a common burial pit.

Slaves of Nebuchadnezzar

27 1-2 Not long after Zedekiah became king of Judah,[r] the LORD told me:

Jeremiah, make a wooden yoke[s] with leather straps, and place it on your neck.
3 Then send a message to the kings of Edom, Moab, Ammon, Tyre, and Sidon. Some officials from these countries are in Jerusalem, meeting with Zedekiah. 4 So have them tell their kings that I have said:

I am the All-Powerful LORD God of Israel, 5 and with my power I created the earth, its people, and all animals. I decide who will rule the earth, 6-7 and I have chosen my servant King Nebuchadnezzar[t] of Babylonia to rule all nations, including yours. I will even let him rule the wild animals. All nations will be slaves of Nebuchadnezzar, his son, and his grandson. Then many nations will join together, and their kings will be powerful enough to make slaves of the Babylonians.

8 This yoke stands for the power of King Nebuchadnezzar, and I will destroy any nation that refuses to obey him. Nebuchadnezzar will attack, and many will die in battle or from hunger and disease. 9 You might have people in your kingdom who claim they can tell the future by magic or by talking with the dead or by dreams or messages from a god. But don't pay attention if any of them tell you not to obey Nebuchadnezzar. 10 If you listen to such lies, I will have you dragged far from your country and killed. 11 But if you and your nation are willing to obey

[o]**26.18** *Hezekiah*: Ruled 716-687 B.C. [p]**26.18** *Jerusalem . . . stands*: See Micah 3.12. [q]**26.20-24** *Jehoiakim*: See the note at 1.3. [r]**27.1,2** *Not long after Zedekiah became king of Judah*: A few manuscripts and one ancient translation; most Hebrew manuscripts "Not long after Jehoiakim became king of Judah"; most manuscripts of another ancient translation do not have these words. Jehoiakim ruled 609-598 B.C., and Zedekiah ruled 598-586 B.C. [s]**27.1,2** *yoke*: A wooden collar that fits around the neck of an ox, so the ox can be made to pull a plow or a cart.
[t]**27.6,7** *Nebuchadnezzar*: See the note at 21.2.

26.18 Mic 3.12. **27.1,2** 2 K 24.18-20; 2 Ch 36.11-13. **27.6,7** Ba 3.16, 17.

Nebuchadnezzar, I will let you stay in your country, and your people will continue to live and work on their farms.

12 After I had spoken to the officials from the nearby kingdoms, I went to King Zedekiah and told him the same thing. Then I said:

Zedekiah, if you and the people of Judah want to stay alive, you must obey Nebuchadnezzar and the Babylonians. 13 But if you refuse, then you and your people will die from war, hunger, and disease, just as the LORD has warned. 14 Your prophets have told you that you don't need to obey Nebuchadnezzar, but don't listen to their lies. 15 Those prophets claim to be speaking for the LORD, but he didn't send them. They are lying! If you do what they say, he will have both you and them dragged off to another country and killed. The LORD has spoken.

16 When I finished talking to the king, I went to the priests and told them that the LORD had said:

Don't listen to the prophets when they say that very soon the Babylonians will return the things they took from my temple. Those prophets are lying! 17 If you choose to obey the king of Babylonia, you will live. But if you listen to those prophets, this whole city will be nothing but a pile of rubble.

18 If I really had spoken to those prophets, they would know what I am going to do. Then they would be begging me not to let everything else be taken from the temple and the king's palace and the rest of Jerusalem. 19-21 After all, when Nebuchadnezzar took King Jehoiachin[u] to Babylonia as a prisoner, he didn't take everything of value from Jerusalem. He left the bronze pillars, the huge bronze bowl called the Sea, and the movable bronze stands in the temple, and he left a lot of other valuable things in the palace and in the rest of Jerusalem.

But now I, the LORD All-Powerful, the God of Israel, say that all these things 22 will be taken to Babylonia, where they will remain until I decide to bring them back to Jerusalem. I, the LORD, have spoken.

Jeremiah Accuses Hananiah of Being a False Prophet

28 Later that same year, in the fifth month of the fourth year that Zedekiah[v] was king,[w] the prophet Hananiah son of Azzur from Gibeon came up to me in the temple. And while the priests and others in the temple were listening, 2 he told me that the LORD had said:

I am the LORD All-Powerful, the God of Israel, and I will smash the yoke[x] that Nebuchadnezzar[y] put on the necks of the nations to make them his slaves. 3 And within two years, I will bring back to Jerusalem everything that he took from my temple and carried off to Babylonia. 4 King Jehoiachin[z] and the other people who were taken from Judah to Babylonia will be allowed to come back here as well. All this will happen because I will smash the power of the king of Babylonia!

5 The priests and the others were still standing there, so I said:

6 Hananiah, I hope the LORD will do exactly what you said. I hope he does bring back everything the Babylonians took from the temple, and that our people who were taken to Babylonia will be allowed to return home. 7 But let me remind you and everyone else 8 that long before we were born, prophets were saying powerful kingdoms would be struck by war, disaster, and disease. 9 Now you are saying we will have peace. We will just have to wait and see if that is really what the LORD has said.[a]

[u]**27.19-21** *Jehoiachin*: Hebrew "Jeconiah" (see the note at 24.1). [v]**28.1** *Zedekiah*: See the note at 1.3. [w]**28.1** *Later . . . king*: One possible meaning for the difficult Hebrew text.
[x]**28.2** *yoke*: See the note at 27.1, 2. [y]**28.2** *Nebuchadnezzar*: See the note at 21.2.
[z]**28.4** *Jehoiachin*: Hebrew "Jeconiah" (see the note at 24.1). [a]**28.9** *We will . . . said*: See Deuteronomy 18.21, 22.
28.1 2 K 24.18-20; 2 Ch 36.11-13.

10 Hananiah grabbed the wooden yoke from my neck and smashed it. 11 Then he said, "The LORD says this is the way he will smash the power Nebuchadnezzar has over the nations, and it will happen in less than two years."

I left the temple, 12 and a little while later, the LORD told me 13-14 to go back and say to Hananiah:

> I am the LORD All-Powerful, the God of Israel. You smashed a wooden yoke, but I will replace it with one made of iron. I will put iron yokes on all the nations, and they will have to do what King Nebuchadnezzar commands. I will even let him rule the wild animals.
>
> 15-16 Hananiah, I have never sent you to speak for me. And yet you have talked my people into believing your lies and rebelling against me. So now I will send you—I'll send you right off the face of the earth! You will die before this year is over.

17 Two months later, Hananiah died.

Jeremiah's Letter to the People of Judah in Babylonia

29 1-2 I had been left in Jerusalem when King Nebuchadnezzar[b] took many of the people of Jerusalem and Judah to Babylonia as prisoners, including King Jehoiachin,[c] his mother, his officials, and the metal workers and others in Jerusalem who were skilled in making things. So I wrote a letter to the prophets, the priests, the leaders, and the rest of our people in Babylonia. 3 I gave the letter to Elasah and Gemariah,[d] two men that King Zedekiah[e] of Judah was sending to Babylon to talk with Nebuchadnezzar. In the letter, I wrote 4 that the LORD All-Powerful, the God of Israel, had said:

> I had you taken from Jerusalem to Babylonia. Now I tell you 5 to settle there and build houses. Plant gardens and eat what you grow in them. 6 Get married and have children, then help your sons find wives and help your daughters find husbands, so they can have children as well. I want your numbers to grow, not to get smaller.
>
> 7 Pray for peace in Babylonia and work hard to make it prosperous. The more successful that nation is, the better off you will be.
>
> 8-9 Some of your people there in Babylonia are fortunetellers, and you have asked them to tell you what will happen in the future. But they will only lead you astray. And don't let the prophets fool you, either. They speak in my name, but they are liars. I have not spoken to them.
>
> 10 After Babylonia has been the strongest nation for seventy years, I will be kind and bring you back to Jerusalem, just as I have promised. 11 I will bless you with a future filled with hope—a future of success, not of suffering. 12 You will turn back to me and ask for help, and I will answer your prayers. 13 You will worship me with all your heart, and I will be with you 14 and accept your worship. Then I will gather you from all the nations where I scattered you, and you will return to Jerusalem.
>
> 15 You feel secure, because you think I have sent prophets to speak for me in Babylonia.
>
> 16-19 But I have been sending prophets to the people of Judah for a long time, and the king from David's family and the people who are left in Jerusalem and Judah still don't obey me. So I, the LORD All-Powerful, will keep attacking them with war and hunger and disease, until they are as useless as rotten figs. I will force them to leave the land, and all nations will be disgusted and shocked at what happens to them. The nations will sneer and make fun of them and use the

[b]**29.1,2** *Nebuchadnezzar*: See the note at 21.2. [c]**29.1,2** *Jehoiachin*: Hebrew "Jeconiah" (see the note at 24.1). [d]**29.3** *Elasah and Gemariah*: Hebrew "Elasah son of Shaphan and Gemariah son of Hilkiah." [e]**29.3** *Zedekiah*: See the note at 1.3.

29.1,2 2 K 24.12-16; 2 Ch 36.10. **29.10** 2 Ch 36.21; Jr 25.11; Dn 9.1, 2. **29.13** Dt 4.29, 30; Ws 6.12, 13.

names "Judah" and "Jerusalem" as curse words.

And you have not obeyed me, even though 20 I had you taken from Jerusalem to Babylonia. But you had better listen to me now. 21-23 You think Ahab son of Kolaiah and Zedekiah son of Maaseiah are prophets because they claim to speak for me. But they are lying! I haven't told them anything. They are also committing other horrible sins in your community, such as sleeping with the wives of their friends. So I will hand them over to King Nebuchadnezzar, who will put them to death while the rest of you watch. And in the future, when you want to put a curse on someone, you will say, "I pray that the LORD will kill you in the same way the king of Babylonia burned Zedekiah and Ahab to death!"

A Message for Shemaiah

24-25 The LORD All-Powerful, the God of Israel, told me what would happen to Shemaiah,[f] who was one of our people in Babylonia. After my letter reached Babylonia, Shemaiah wrote letters to the people of Jerusalem, including the priest Zephaniah son of Maaseiah, and the other priests. The letter to Zephaniah said:

26 After the death of Jehoiada the priest, the LORD chose you to be the priest in charge of the temple security force. You know that anyone who acts crazy and pretends to be a prophet should be arrested and put in chains[g] and iron collars. 27 Jeremiah from the town of Anathoth is pretending to be a prophet there in Jerusalem, so why haven't you punished him? 28 He even wrote a letter to the people here in Babylonia, saying we would be here a long time. He told us to build homes and to plant gardens and grow our own food.

29 When Zephaniah received Shemaiah's letter, he read it to me. 30 Then the LORD told me what to write in a second letter 31 to the people of Judah who had been taken to Babylonia. In this letter, I wrote that the LORD had said:

I, the LORD, have not chosen Shemaiah to be one of my prophets, and he has misled you by telling lies in my name. 32 He has even talked you into disobeying me. So I will punish Shemaiah. He and his descendants won't live to see the good things I will do for my people. I, the LORD, have spoken.

The LORD Will Rescue Israel and Judah

30 1-2 The LORD God of Israel said, "Jeremiah, get a scroll[h] and write down everything I have told you. 3 Someday I will let my people from both Israel[i] and Judah return to the land I gave their ancestors."

4-5 Then the LORD told me to say to Israel and Judah:

I, the LORD, hear screams
of terror,
and there is no peace.
6 Can men give birth?
Then why do I see them
looking so pale
and clutching their stomachs
like women in labor?
7 My people, soon you will suffer
worse than ever before,
but I will save you.

8 Now you are slaves
of other nations,
but I will break the chains
and smash the yokes[j]
that keep you in slavery.
9 Then you will be my servants,
and I will choose a king for you
from the family of David.

*10 Israel,[k] you belong to me,
so don't be afraid.

[f]**29.24,25** *Shemaiah*: Hebrew "Shemaiah, who came from the town of Nehelam." [g]**29.26** *in chains*: See the note at 20.2. [h]**30.1,2** *scroll*: A roll of paper or special leather used for writing on. [i]**30.3** *Israel*: The northern kingdom. [j]**30.8** *yokes*: See the note at 27.1, 2.
[k]**30.10** *Israel*: The people of the northern and southern kingdoms.
30.10,11 Jr 46.27, 28.

You deserved to be punished;
that's why I scattered you
in distant nations.
But I am with you,
and someday I will destroy
those nations.
11 Then I will bring you
and your descendants
back to your land,
where I will protect you
and give you peace.
Then your fears will be gone.
I, the LORD, have spoken.

The LORD Will Heal Israel and Judah

12 The LORD said:

My people, you are wounded
and near death.
13 You are accused of a crime
with no one to defend you,
and you are covered with sores
that no medicine can cure.
*14 Your friends have forgotten you;
they don't care anymore.
Even I have acted like an enemy.
And because your sins
are horrible and countless,
I will be cruel
as I punish you.
15 So don't bother to cry out
for relief from your pain.

16 But if your enemies try to rob
or destroy you,
I will rob and destroy them,
and they will be led as captives
to foreign lands.
17 No one wants you as a friend
or cares what happens to you.
But I will heal your injuries,
and you will get well.

The LORD Will Rescue Israel and Judah

18 The LORD said:

Israel, I will be kind to you
and let you come home.
Jerusalem now lies in ruins,
but you will rebuild it,
complete with a new palace.[l]
19 Other nations will respect
and honor you.
Your homes will be filled
with children,
and you will celebrate,
singing praises to me.

20 It will be just like old times.
Your nation will worship me,
and I will punish anyone
who abuses you.
21 One of your own people
will become your ruler.
And when I invite him
to come near me
at the place of worship,
he will do so.
No one would dare to come near
without being invited.

22 You will be my people,
and I will be your God.
I, the LORD, have spoken.

23 I am furious!
And like a violent storm
I will strike those
who do wrong.
24 I won't calm down
until I have finished
what I have decided to do.
Someday, you will understand
what I mean.

Israel Will Return to God

31 The LORD said:

Israel, I promise
that someday all your tribes
will again be my people,
and I will be your God.
2 In the desert I was kind
to those who escaped death.
I gave them peace,
and when the time is right,
I'll do the same for you.[m]
I, the LORD, have spoken.

[l]30.18 *Jerusalem . . . palace*: Or "Your towns lie in ruins, but you will rebuild them, and your homes will be where they were before." [m]31.2 *In the desert . . . same for you*: One possible meaning for the difficult Hebrew text.

The LORD Will Rebuild Israel

3 Some time ago, the LORD appeared to me[n] and told me to say:

Israel, I will always love you;
that's why I've been so patient
and kind.
4 You are precious to me,
and so I will rebuild
your nation.
Once again you will dance for joy
and play your tambourines.
5 You will plant vineyards
on the hills of Samaria
and enjoy the grapes.
6 Someday those who guard
the hill country of Ephraim
will shout, "Let's go to Zion
and worship the LORD our God."

Israel Will Return to Its Own Land

7 The LORD says:

Celebrate and sing for Israel,
the greatest of nations.
Offer praises and shout,
"Come and rescue
your people, LORD!
Save what's left of Israel."

8 I, the LORD, will bring
my people back from Babylonia[o]
and everywhere else on earth.
The blind and the lame
will be there.
Expectant mothers
and women about to give birth
will come and be part
of that great crowd.
9 They will weep and pray
as I bring them home.
I will lead them
to streams of water.
They will walk on a level[p] road
and not stumble.
I am a father to Israel,[q]
my favorite children.

10 Listen to me, you nations
nearby or across the sea.
I scattered the people of Israel,
but I will gather them again.
I will protect them like a shepherd
guarding a flock;
11 I will rescue them from enemies
who could overpower them.
12 My people will come
to Mount Zion
and celebrate;
their faces will glow
because of my blessings.
I'll give them grain, grapes,
and olive oil,
as well as sheep and cattle.
Israel will be prosperous
and grow like a garden
with plenty of water.
13 Young women and young men,
together with the elderly,
will celebrate and dance,
because I will comfort them
and turn their sorrow
into happiness.
14 I will bless my people
with more food
than they need,
and the priests will enjoy
the choice cuts of meat.
I, the LORD, have spoken.

The LORD Offers Hope

15 In Ramah[r] a voice is heard,
crying and weeping loudly.
Rachel mourns for her children[s]
and refuses to be comforted,
because they are dead.
*16 But I, the LORD, say
to dry your tears.
Someday your children

[n]**31.3** *Some time . . . me*: Or "The LORD appeared to me from far away." [o]**31.8** *Babylonia*: The Hebrew text has "that country in the north," referring to Babylonia. [p]**31.9** *level*: Or "straight." [q]**31.9** *Israel*: The Hebrew text also has "Ephraim," the leading tribe of the northern kingdom of Israel, which sometimes stands for the whole northern kingdom. [r]**31.15** *In Ramah*: Or "In the hills." [s]**31.15** *Rachel . . . children*: Rachel was one of the wives of Jacob, the ancestor of the nation of Israel. She was the mother of Joseph and Benjamin. Joseph's two sons Ephraim and Manasseh were the ancestors of the leading tribes of the northern kingdom of Israel.

31.15 **a** Gn 35.16-19; **b** Mt 2.18.

will come home
from the enemy's land.
Then all you have done for them
will be greatly rewarded.
17 So don't lose hope.
I, the LORD, have spoken.

18 The people of Israel[t] moan
and say to me,
"We were like wild bulls,
but you, LORD, broke us,
and we learned to obey.
You are our God—
please let us come home.
19 When we were young,
we strayed and sinned,
but then we realized
what we had done.
We are ashamed and disgraced
and want to return to you."

20 People of Israel,
you are my own dear children.
Don't I love you best of all?
Though I often make threats,
I want you to be near me,
so I will have mercy on you.
I, the LORD, have spoken.

21 With rock piles and signposts,
mark the way home,
my dear people.
It is the same road
by which you left.
22 Will you ever decide
to be faithful?
I will make sure that someday
things will be different,
as different as a woman
protecting a man.[u]

The LORD Will Bring Judah Home

23 The LORD All-Powerful, the God of Israel, said:
I promise to set the people of Judah free
and to lead them back to their hometowns.
And when I do, they will once again say,

"We pray that the LORD
will bless his home,
the sacred hill in Jerusalem
where his temple stands."

24 The people will live in Jerusalem and
in the towns of Judah. Some will be farmers, and others will be shepherds. 25 Those
who feel tired and worn out will find new
life and energy, 26 and when they sleep,
they will wake up refreshed.[v]
27 Someday, Israel and Judah will be my
field where my people and their livestock
will grow. 28 In the past, I took care to uproot them, to tear them down, and to destroy
them. But when that day comes, I will take
care to plant them and help them grow.
29 No longer will anyone go around saying,

"Sour grapes eaten by parents
leave a sour taste in the mouths
of their children."

30 When that day comes, only those who
eat sour grapes will get the sour taste, and
only those who sin will be put to death.

The New Agreement with Israel and Judah

31 The LORD said:
The time will surely come when I will
make a new agreement with the people of
Israel and Judah. 32 It will be different from
the agreement I made with their ancestors
when I led them out of Egypt. Although I
was their God, they broke that agreement.
33 Here is the new agreement that I, the
LORD, will make with the people of Israel:

"I will write my laws
on their hearts and minds.
I will be their God,
and they will be my people.

34 "No longer will they have to teach
one another to obey me. I, the LORD, promise that all of them will obey me, ordinary
people and rulers alike. I will forgive their
sins and forget the evil things they have
done."

[t]**31.18** *Israel*: Hebrew "Ephraim" (see the note at 31.9). [u]**31.22** *I will make sure . . . a woman protecting a man*: One possible meaning for the difficult Hebrew text. [v]**31.26** *and when they sleep . . . refreshed*: One possible meaning for the difficult Hebrew text.

31.29 Ez 18.2. **31.31** Mt 26.28; Mk 14.24; Lk 22.20; 1 Co 11.25; 2 Co 3.6. **31.31-34** He 8.8-12. **31.33** He 10.16. **31.34** He 10.17.

35 I am the LORD All-Powerful.
I command the sun
to give light each day,
the moon and stars
to shine at night,
and ocean waves to roar.
36 I will never forget
to give those commands,
and I will never let Israel
stop being a nation.
I, the LORD, have spoken.

37 Can you measure the heavens?
Can you explore
the depths of the earth?
That's how hard it would be
for me to reject Israel forever,
even though they have sinned.
I, the LORD, have spoken.

Jerusalem Will Be Rebuilt

38 The LORD said:
Someday, Jerusalem will truly belong to
me. It will be rebuilt with a boundary line
running from Hananel Tower to Corner
Gate. 39 From there, the boundary will go in
a straight line to Gareb Hill, then turn toward Goah. 40 Even that disgusting Hinnom Valley[w] will be sacred to me, and so
will the eastern slopes that go down from
Horse Gate into Kidron Valley. Jerusalem
will never again be destroyed.

Jeremiah Buys a Field

32 The LORD spoke to me in the tenth
year that Zedekiah[x] was king of Judah, which was the eighteenth year that
Nebuchadnezzar[y] was king of Babylonia.
2 At that time, the Babylonian army had
surrounded Jerusalem, and I was in the
prison at the courtyard of the palace
guards. 3 Zedekiah had ordered me to be
held there because I told everyone that the
LORD had said:

I am the LORD, and I am about to
let the king of Babylonia conquer Jerusalem. 4 King Zedekiah will be captured and taken to King Nebuchadnezzar, who will speak with him face to
face. 5 Then Zedekiah will be led away
to Babylonia, where he will stay until I
am finished with him. So, if you people of Judah fight against the Babylonians, you will lose. I, the LORD, have
spoken.

6 Later, when I was in prison, the LORD
said:

7 Jeremiah, your cousin Hanamel,
the son of your uncle Shallum, will
visit you. He must sell his field near
the town of Anathoth, and because you
are his nearest relative, you have the
right and the responsibility to buy it
and keep it in the family.[z]

8 Hanamel came, just as the LORD had
promised. And he said, "Please buy my
field near Anathoth in the territory of the
Benjamin tribe. You have the right to buy
it, and if you do, it will stay in our family."
The LORD had told me to buy it 9 from
Hanamel, and so I did. The price was seventeen pieces of silver, and I weighed out
the full amount on a scale. 10-11 I had two
copies of the bill of sale written out, each
containing all the details of our agreement.
Some witnesses and I signed the official
copy, which was folded and tied, before being sealed shut with hot wax.[a] Then I gave
Hanamel the silver. 12 And while he, the
witnesses, and all the other Jews sitting in
the courtyard were still watching, I gave
both copies to Baruch son of Neriah.[b]

13-14 I told Baruch that the LORD had
said:

Take both copies of this bill of sale,
one sealed shut and the other open,
and put them in a clay jar so they
will last a long time. 15 I am the LORD

[w] **31.40** *that disgusting Hinnom Valley*: The Hebrew text has "the whole valley of the dead bodies and of the fatty ashes," which probably refers to Hinnom Valley, just southwest of Jerusalem, where human sacrifices had been offered to foreign gods. [x] **32.1** *Zedekiah*: See the note at 1.3. [y] **32.1** *Nebuchadnezzar*: See the note at 21.2. [z] **32.7** *you have the right . . . in the family*: See Leviticus 25.25-32. [a] **32.10,11** *signed the official copy, which was folded and tied, before being sealed shut with hot wax*: The signing was actually done by pressing a carved clay stamp (called a "seal") into the hot wax, leaving the design in the wax. [b] **32.12** *Baruch son of Neriah*: Hebrew "Baruch son of Neriah and grandson of Mahseiah."

32.1 2 K 25.1-7.

All-Powerful, the God of Israel, and I promise you that people will once again buy and sell houses, farms, and vineyards in this country.

Jeremiah Questions the LORD

16 Then I prayed:

17 LORD God, you stretched out your mighty arm and made the sky and the earth. You can do anything. 18 You show kindness for a thousand generations,[c] but you also punish people for the sins of their parents. You are the LORD All-Powerful. 19 With great wisdom you make plans, and with your great power you do all the mighty things you planned. Nothing we do is hidden from your eyes, and you reward or punish us as we deserve.

20 You are famous because you worked miracles in Egypt, and you are still working them in Israel and in the rest of the world as well. 21 You terrified the Egyptians with your miracles, and you reached out your mighty arm and rescued your people Israel from Egypt. 22 Then you gave Israel this land rich with milk and honey, just as you had promised our ancestors.

23 But when our ancestors took over the land, they did not obey you. And now you have punished Israel with disaster. 24 Jerusalem is under attack, and we suffer from hunger and disease. The Babylonians have already built dirt ramps up to the city walls, and you can see that Jerusalem will be captured just as you said.

25 So why did you tell me to get some witnesses and buy a field with my silver, when Jerusalem is about to be captured by the Babylonians?

The LORD Explains about the Field

26 The LORD explained:

27 Jeremiah, I am the LORD God. I rule the world, and I can do anything!

28 It is true that I am going to let King Nebuchadnezzar[d] of Babylonia capture Jerusalem. 29 The Babylonian army is already attacking, and they will capture the city and set it on fire. The people of Jerusalem have made me angry by going up to the flat roofs of their houses and burning incense to Baal and offering wine sacrifices to other gods. Now these houses will be burned to the ground!

30-33 The kings and the officials, the priests and the prophets, and everyone else in Israel and Judah have turned from me and made me angry by worshiping idols. Again and again I have tried to teach my people to obey me, but they refuse to be corrected.

I am going to get rid of Jerusalem, because its people have done nothing but evil. 34 They have set up disgusting idols in my temple, and now it isn't a fit place to worship me. 35 And they led Judah into sin by building places to worship Baal in Hinnom Valley, where they also sacrificed their sons and daughters to the god Molech. I have never even thought of telling them to commit such disgusting sins.

36 Jeremiah, what you said is true. The people of Jerusalem are suffering from hunger and disease, and so the king of Babylonia will be able to capture Jerusalem.

37 I am angry at the people of Jerusalem, and I will scatter them in foreign countries. But someday I will bring them back here and let them live in safety. 38 They will be my people, and I will be their God. 39-41 I will make their thoughts and desires pure. Then they will realize that, for their own good and the good of their children, they must worship only me. They will even be afraid to turn away from me. I will make an agreement with them that will never end, and I won't ever stop doing good things for them. With all my heart I promise that they will be planted in this land once again. 42 Even though I have brought disaster on the people, I will someday do all these good things for them.

43 Jeremiah, when you bought the field, you showed that fields will someday be bought and sold again. You say that this

[c]**32.18** *for a thousand generations*: Or "to thousands of people." [d]**32.28** *Nebuchadnezzar*: See the note at 21.2.

32.28 2 K 25.1-11; 2 Ch 36.17-21. **32.34** 2 K 23.10; Jr 7.30, 31; 19.1-6. **32.35** **a** 2 K 23.10; Jr 7.31; **b** Lv 18.21.

land has been conquered by the Babylonians and has become a desert, emptied of people and animals. 44 But someday, people will again spend their silver to buy fields everywhere—in the territory of Benjamin, the region around Jerusalem and the towns of Judah, and in the hill country, the foothills to the west, and the Southern Desert. Buyers and sellers and witnesses will sign and seal the bills of sale for the fields. It will happen, because I will give this land back to my people. I, the LORD, have spoken.

The LORD Promises To Give the Land Back to His People

33 1-2 I was still being held prisoner in the courtyard of the palace guards when the LORD told me:

I am the LORD, and I created the whole world.[e] 3 Ask me, and I will tell you things that you don't know and can't find out.

4-5 Many of the houses in Jerusalem and some of the buildings at the royal palace have been torn down to be used in repairing the walls to keep out the Babylonian attackers.[f] Now there are empty spaces where the buildings once stood. But I am furious, and these spaces will be filled with the bodies of the people I kill. The people of Jerusalem will cry out to me for help, but they are evil, and I will ignore their prayers.

6 Then someday, I will heal this place and my people as well, and let them enjoy unending peace.[g] 7 I will give this land to Israel and Judah once again, and I will make them as strong as they were before. 8 They sinned and rebelled against me, but I will forgive them and take away their guilt. 9 When that happens, all nations on earth will see the good things I have done for Jerusalem, and how I have given it complete peace. The nations will celebrate and praise and honor me, but they will also tremble with fear.

10 Jeremiah, you say that this land is a desert without people or animals, and for now, you are right. The towns of Judah and the streets of Jerusalem are deserted, and people and animals are nowhere to be seen. But someday you will hear 11 happy voices and the sounds of parties and wedding celebrations. And when people come to my temple to offer sacrifices to thank me, you will hear them say:

"We praise you,
  LORD All-Powerful!
You are good to us,
  and your love never fails."

The land will once again be productive. 12-13 Now it is empty, without people or animals. But when that time comes, shepherds will take care of their flocks in pastures near every town in the hill country, in the foothills to the west, in the Southern Desert, in the land of the Benjamin tribe, and around Jerusalem and the towns of Judah.

I, the LORD, have spoken.

The LORD's Wonderful Promise

14 The LORD said:

I made a wonderful promise to Israel and Judah,[h] and the days are coming when I will keep it.

15 I promise that the time will come
when I will appoint a king
  from the family of David,
a king who will be honest
  and rule with justice.
16 In those days,
  Judah will be safe;
Jerusalem will have peace
and will be named,
  "The LORD Gives Justice."

17 The king of Israel will be one of David's descendants, 18 and there will always be priests from the Levi tribe serving at my altar and offering sacrifices to please me and to give thanks.[i]

[e]33.1,2 *the whole world*: One ancient translation; Hebrew "it." [f]33.4,5 *have been torn down . . . Babylonian attackers*: One possible meaning for the difficult Hebrew text. [g]33.6 *let them enjoy unending peace*: One possible meaning for the difficult Hebrew text. [h]33.14 *Israel and Judah*: See the note at 2.4. [i]33.18 *sacrifices to please me and to give thanks*: See the notes at 14.12.

33.11 1 Ch 16.34; 2 Ch 5.11-13; 7.3; Ezra 3.11; Ps 100.5; 106.1; 107.1; 118.1; 136.1.
33.14-16 Jr 23.5, 6. **33.17** 2 S 7.12-16; 1 K 2.4; 1 Ch 17.11-14. **33.18** Nu 3.5-10.

[19] Then the LORD told me:

[20] I, the LORD, have an agreement with day and night, so they always come at the right time. You can't break the agreement I made with them, [21] and you can't break the agreements I have made with David's family and with the priests from the Levi tribe who serve at my altar. A descendant of David will always rule as king of Israel, [22] and there will be more descendants of David and of the priests from the Levi tribe than stars in the sky or grains of sand on the beach.

[23] The LORD also said:

[24] You've heard foreigners insult my people by saying, "The LORD chose Israel and Judah, but now he has rejected them, and they are no longer a nation."

[25] Jeremiah, I will never break my agreement with the day and the night or let the sky and the earth stop obeying my commands. [26] In the same way, I will never reject the descendants of Abraham, Isaac, and Jacob or break my promise that they will always have a descendant of David as their king. I will be kind to my people Israel, and they will be successful again.

Jeremiah Warns Zedekiah

34 King Nebuchadnezzar[j] had a large army made up of people from every kingdom in his empire. He and his army were attacking Jerusalem and all the nearby towns, when the LORD told me [2] to say to King Zedekiah:[k]

I am the LORD, and I am going to let Nebuchadnezzar capture this city and burn it down. [3] You will be taken prisoner and brought to Nebuchadnezzar, and he will speak with you face to face. Then you will be led away to Babylonia.

[4] Zedekiah, I promise that you won't die in battle. [5] You will die a peaceful death. People will mourn when you die, and they will light bonfires in your honor, just as they did for your ancestors, the kings who ruled before you.

[6] I went to Zedekiah and told him what the LORD had said. [7] Meanwhile, the king of Babylonia was trying to break through the walls of Lachish, Azekah, and Jerusalem, the only three towns of Judah that had not been captured.

The People Break a Promise

[8-10] King Zedekiah,[k] his officials, and everyone else in Jerusalem made an agreement to free all Hebrew[l] men and women who were slaves. No Jew would keep another as a slave. And so, all the Jewish slaves were given their freedom.

[11] But those slave owners changed their minds and forced their former slaves back into slavery. [12] That's when the LORD told me to say to the people:

[13] I am the LORD God of Israel, and I made an agreement with your ancestors when I brought them out of Egypt, where they had been slaves. [14] As part of this agreement, you must let a Hebrew slave go free after six years of service.

Your ancestors did not obey me, [15-16] but you decided to obey me and do the right thing by setting your Hebrew slaves completely free. You even went to my temple, and in my name you made an agreement to set them free. But you have abused my name, because you broke your agreement and forced your former slaves back into slavery.

[17] You have disobeyed me by not giving your slaves their freedom. So I will give you freedom—the freedom to die in battle or from disease or hunger. I will make you disgusting to all other nations on earth.

[18] You asked me to be a witness when you made the agreement to set your slaves free. And as part of the ceremony you cut a calf into two parts, then walked between the parts. But you people of Jerusalem have broken that agreement as well as my agreement with Israel. So I will do to you what you did to that calf. [19-20] I will let your enemies take all of you prisoner, including the leaders of Judah and Jerusalem, the

[j] **34.1** *Nebuchadnezzar*: See the note at 21.2. [k] **34.2,8-10** *Zedekiah*: See the note at 1.3.
[l] **34.8-10** *Hebrew*: An earlier term for Israelite and Jewish.
34.1 2 K 25.1-11; 2 Ch 36.17-21. **34.14** Ex 21.2; Dt 15.12.

royal officials, the priests, and everyone
else who walked between the two parts of
the calf. These enemies will kill you and
leave your bodies lying on the ground as
food for birds and wild animals.
21-22 These enemies are King Nebuchadnezzar[m] of Babylonia and his army.
They have stopped attacking Jerusalem,
but they want to kill King Zedekiah and his
high officials. So I will command them to
return and attack again. This time they will
conquer the city and burn it down, and
they will capture Zedekiah and his officials.
I will also let them destroy the towns of
Judah, so that no one can live there any
longer.

Learn a Lesson from the Rechabites

35 When Jehoiakim[n] was king of Judah,
the LORD told me, 2 "Go to the Rechabite clan and invite them to meet you in
one of the side rooms[o] of the temple. When
they arrive, offer them a drink of wine."
3 So I went to Jaazaniah,[p] the leader
of the clan, and I invited him and all the
men of his clan. 4 I brought them into
the temple courtyard and took them upstairs to a room belonging to the prophets
who were followers of Hanan son of Ig-
daliah. It was next to a room belonging to
some of the officials, and that room was
over the one belonging to Maaseiah, a
priest who was one of the high officials in
the temple.[q]
5 I set out some large bowls full of wine
together with some cups, and then I said to
the Rechabites, "Have some wine!"
6 But they answered:
No! The ancestor of our clan, Jonadab son of Rechab,[r] made a rule that
we must obey. He said, "Don't ever
drink wine 7 or build houses or plant
crops and vineyards. Instead, you
must always live in tents and move
from place to place. If you obey
this command, you will live a long
time."
8-10 Our clan has always obeyed
Jonadab's command. To this very day,
we and our wives and sons and daughters don't drink wine or build houses
or plant vineyards or crops. And we
have lived in tents, 11 except now we
have to live inside Jerusalem because
Nebuchadnezzar[s] has taken over the
countryside with his army from Babylonia and Syria.
12-13 Then the LORD told me to say to
the people of Judah and Jerusalem:
I, the LORD All-Powerful, the God
of Israel, want you to learn a lesson
14 from the Rechabite clan. Their ancestor Jonadab told his descendants
never to drink wine, and to this very
day they have obeyed him. But I have
spoken to you over and over, and you
haven't obeyed me! 15 You refused to
listen to my prophets, who kept telling
you, "Stop doing evil and worshiping
other gods! Start obeying the LORD,
and he will let you live in this land he
gave your ancestors."
16 The Rechabites have obeyed the
command of their ancestor Jonadab,
but you have not obeyed me, 17 your
God. I am the LORD All-Powerful, and I
warned you about the terrible things
that would happen to you if you did
not listen to me. You have ignored me,
so now disaster will strike you. I, the
LORD, have spoken.

The LORD Makes a Promise to the Rechabites

18 Then the LORD told me to say to the
Rechabite clan:
I am the LORD All-Powerful, the God of
Israel. You have obeyed your ancestor Jon-
adab, 19 so I promise that your clan will be
my servants and will never die out.

[m]**34.21,22** *Nebuchadnezzar*: See the note at 21.2. [n]**35.1** *Jehoiakim*: See the note at 1.3. [o]**35.2** *side rooms*: Probably a room with walls on three sides, and open to the courtyard on the fourth side. [p]**35.3** *Jaazaniah*: The Hebrew text has "Jaazaniah son of Jeremiah son of Habazziniah"; this is a different Jeremiah than the author of the book. [q]**35.4** *Maaseiah . . . temple*: Hebrew "Maaseiah son of Shallum, the keeper of the temple door." [r]**35.6** *Jonadab son of Rechab*: See 2 Kings 10.15-23. In the Hebrew of this chapter, "Jonadab" is sometimes spelled "Jehonadab." [s]**35.11** *Nebuchadnezzar*: See the note at 21.2.

35.1 2 K 23.36—24.6; 2 Ch 36.5-7.

King Jehoiakim Burns Jeremiah's First Scroll

36 During the fourth year that Jehoiakim[t] son of Josiah[u] was king of
Judah, the LORD said to me, "Jeremiah,
2 since the time Josiah was king, I have
been speaking to you about Israel, Judah,
and the other nations. Now, get a scroll[v]
and write down everything I have told you,
3 then read it to the people of Judah. Maybe
they will stop sinning when they hear what
terrible things I plan for them. And if they
turn to me, I will forgive them."

4 I sent for Baruch son of Neriah and
asked him to help me. I repeated everything the LORD had told me, and Baruch
wrote it all down on a scroll. 5 Then I said,

> Baruch, the officials refuse to let
> me go into the LORD's temple, 6 so you
> must go instead. Wait for the next holy
> day when the people of Judah come to
> the temple to pray and to go without
> eating.[w] Then take this scroll to the
> temple and read it aloud. 7 The LORD
> is furious, and if the people hear how
> he is going to punish them, maybe
> they will ask to be forgiven.

8-10 In the ninth month[x] of the fifth year
that Jehoiakim was king, the leaders set a
day when everyone who lived in Jerusalem
or who was visiting here had to pray and go
without eating. So Baruch took the scroll to
the upper courtyard of the temple. He went
over to the side of the courtyard and stood
in a covered area near New Gate, where he
read the scroll aloud.

This covered area belonged to Gemariah,[y] one of the king's highest officials.
11 Gemariah's son Micaiah was there and
heard Baruch read what the LORD had said.
12 When Baruch finished reading, Micaiah
went down to the palace. His father
Gemariah was in the officials' room, meeting with the rest of the king's officials, including Elishama, Delaiah, Elnathan, and
Zedekiah.[z] 13 Micaiah told them what he
had heard Baruch reading to the people.
14 Then the officials sent Jehudi and
Shelemiah[a] to tell Baruch, "Bring us that
scroll."

When Baruch arrived with the scroll,
15 the officials said, "Please sit down and
read it to us," which he did. 16 After they
heard what was written on the scroll, they
were worried and said to each other, "The
king needs to hear this!" Turning to
Baruch, they asked, 17 "Did someone tell
you what to write on this scroll?"

18 "Yes, Jeremiah did," Baruch replied.
"I wrote down just what he told me."

19 The officials said, "You and Jeremiah
must go into hiding, and don't tell anyone
where you are."

20-22 The officials put the scroll in
Elishama's room and went to see the king,
who was in one of the rooms where he
lived and worked during the winter. It was
the ninth month[b] of the year, so there was
a fire burning in the fireplace,[c] and the
king was sitting nearby. After the officials
told the king about the scroll, he sent Jehudi to get it. Then Jehudi started reading
the scroll to the king and his officials.
23-25 But every time Jehudi finished reading
three or four columns, the king would tell
him to cut them off with his penknife and
throw them in the fire. Elnathan, Delaiah,
and Gemariah begged the king not to burn
the scroll, but he ignored them, and soon
there was nothing left of it.

The king and his servants listened to
what was written on the scroll, but they

[t]**36.1** *Jehoiakim*: See the note at 1.3. [u]**36.1** *Josiah*: See the note at 3.6. [v]**36.2** *scroll*: See the note at 30.1, 2. [w]**36.6** *to go without eating*: As a way of asking for God's help. [x]**36.8-10** *ninth month*: Chislev, the ninth month of the Hebrew calendar, from about mid-November to mid-December. [y]**36.8-10** *Gemariah*: Hebrew "Gemariah son of Shaphan"; Gemariah's brother Ahikam had earlier protected Jeremiah (see 26.20-24). [z]**36.12** *Delaiah, Elnathan, and Zedekiah*: Hebrew "Delaiah son of Shemaiah, Elnathan son of Achbor, and Zedekiah son of Hananiah." [a]**36.14** *Jehudi and Shelemiah*: Hebrew "Jehudi son of Nethaniah and Shelemiah son of Cushi." [b]**36.20-22** *ninth month*: See the note at 36.8-10. [c]**36.20-22** *fireplace*: Probably a large metal or clay pot on a movable stand, with the fire burning inside.

36.1 2 K 24.1; 2 Ch 36.5-7; Dn 1.1, 2.

were not afraid, and they did not tear their clothes in sorrow.[d]

26 The king told his son Jerahmeel to take Seraiah and Shelemiah[e] and to go arrest Baruch and me.[f] But the LORD kept them from finding us.

Jeremiah's Second Scroll

27 I had told Baruch what to write on that first scroll,[g] but King Jehoiakim[h] had burned it. So the LORD told me 28 to get another scroll and write down everything that had been on the first one. 29 Then he told me to say to King Jehoiakim:

> Not only did you burn Jeremiah's scroll, you had the nerve to ask why he had written that the king of Babylonia would attack and ruin the land, killing all the people and even the animals. 30 So I, the LORD, promise that you will be killed and your body thrown out on the ground. The sun will beat down on it during the day, and the frost will settle on it at night. And none of your descendants will ever be king of Judah. 31 You, your children, and your servants are evil, and I will punish all of you. I warned you and the people of Judah and Jerusalem that I would bring disaster, but none of you have listened. So now you are doomed!

32 After the LORD finished speaking to me, I got another scroll and gave it to Baruch. Then I told him what to write, so this second scroll would contain even more than was on the scroll Jehoiakim had burned.

King Zedekiah Asks Jeremiah To Pray

37 King Nebuchadnezzar[i] of Babylonia had removed Jehoiachin[j] son of Jehoiakim[k] from being the king of Judah and had made Josiah's[l] son Zedekiah[m] king instead.[n] 2 But Zedekiah, his officials, and everyone else in Judah ignored everything the LORD had told me.

3-5 Later, the Babylonian army attacked Jerusalem, but they left after learning that the Egyptian army[o] was headed in this direction.

One day, Zedekiah sent Jehucal and the priest Zephaniah[p] to talk with me. At that time, I was free to go wherever I wanted, because I had not yet been put in prison. Jehucal and Zephaniah said, "Jeremiah, please pray to the LORD our God for us."

6-7 Then the LORD told me to send them back to Zedekiah with this message:

> Zedekiah, you wanted Jeremiah to ask me, the LORD God of Israel, what is going to happen. So I will tell you. The king of Egypt and his army came to your rescue, but soon they will go back to Egypt. 8 Then the Babylonians will return and attack Jerusalem, and this time they will capture the city and set it on fire. 9 Don't fool yourselves into thinking that the Babylonians will leave as they did before. 10 Even if you could defeat their entire army, their wounded survivors would still be able to leave their tents and set Jerusalem on fire.

Jeremiah Is Put in Prison

11 The Babylonian army had left because the Egyptian army was on its way to help us. 12 So I decided to leave Jerusalem and go to the territory of the Benjamin tribe to claim my share of my family's land. 13 I was leaving Jerusalem through Benjamin Gate, when I was stopped by Irijah,[q] the officer in charge of the soldiers at the gate. He said, "Jeremiah, you're under arrest for trying to join the Babylonians."

14 "I'm not trying to join them!" I

[d]**36.23-25** *they did not tear their clothes in sorrow*: Such actions would have shown that they were sorry for disobeying the LORD and were turning back to him. [e]**36.26** *Seraiah and Shelemiah*: Hebrew "Seraiah son of Azriel and Shelemiah son of Abdeel." [f]**36.26** *me*: Jeremiah. [g]**36.27** *scroll*: See the note at 30.1,2. [h]**36.27** *Jehoiakim*: See the note at 1.3. [i]**37.1** *Nebuchadnezzar*: See the note at 21.2. [j]**37.1** *Jehoiachin*: Hebrew "Coniah" (see the note at 22.24). [k]**37.1** *Jehoiakim*: See the note at 1.3. [l]**37.1** *Josiah's*: Josiah was the father of both Jehoiakim and Zedekiah. Josiah ruled 640-609 B.C. [m]**37.1** *Zedekiah*: See the note at 1.3. [n]**37.1** *King Nebuchadnezzar . . . instead*: See 2 Kings 24.10-17. [o]**37.3-5** *Egyptian army*: Led by King Apries, also known as Hophra. [p]**37.3-5** *Jehucal and the priest Zephaniah*: Hebrew "Jehucal son of Shelemiah, and the priest Zephaniah son of Maaseiah." [q]**37.13** *Irijah*: Hebrew "Irijah son of Shelemiah and grandson of Hananiah."

37.1 2 K 24.17; 2 Ch 36.10.

answered. But Irijah wouldn't listen, and he took me to the king's officials. 15-16 They were angry and ordered the soldiers to beat me. Then I was taken to the house that belonged to Jonathan, one of the king's officials. It had been turned into a prison, and I was kept in a basement room.

After I had spent a long time there,
17 King Zedekiah secretly had me brought to his palace, where he asked, "Is there any message for us from the LORD?"

"Yes, there is, Your Majesty," I replied. "The LORD is going to let the king of Babylonia capture you."

18 Then I continued, "Your Majesty, why have you put me in prison? Have I committed a crime against you or your officials or
the nation? 19 Have you locked up the prophets who lied to you and said that the king of Babylonia would never attack
Jerusalem? 20 Please, don't send me back to that prison at Jonathan's house. If you do, I will die."

21 King Zedekiah had me taken to the prison cells in the courtyard of the palace guards. He told the soldiers to give me a loaf of bread[r] from one of the bakeries every day until the city ran out of grain.

Jeremiah Is Held Prisoner in a Dry Well

38 One day, Shephatiah, Gedaliah, Jehucal,[s] and Pashhur[t] heard me tell
the people of Judah 2-3 that the LORD had said, "If you stay here in Jerusalem, you will die in battle or from disease or hunger, and the Babylonian army will capture the city anyway. But if you surrender to the Babylonians, they will let you live."

4 So the four of them went to the king and said, "You should put Jeremiah to death, because he is making the soldiers and everyone else lose hope. He isn't trying to help our people; he's trying to harm them."

5 Zedekiah replied, "Do what you want with him. I can't stop you."

6 Then they took me back to the courtyard of the palace guards and let me down with ropes into the well that belonged to Malchiah, the king's son. There was no water in the well, and I sank down in the mud.

7-8 Ebedmelech from Ethiopia[u] was an official at the palace, and he heard what they had done to me. So he went to speak with King Zedekiah, who was holding court
at Benjamin Gate. 9 Ebedmelech said, "Your Majesty, Jeremiah is a prophet, and those men were wrong to throw him into a well. And when Jerusalem runs out of food, Jeremiah will starve to death down there."

10 Zedekiah answered, "Take thirty[v] of my soldiers and pull Jeremiah out before he dies."

11 Ebedmelech and the soldiers went to the palace and got some rags from the room under the treasury. He used ropes to
lower them into the well. 12 Then he said, "Put these rags under your arms so the
ropes won't hurt you." After I did, 13 the
men pulled me out. And from then on, I was kept in the courtyard of the palace guards.

King Zedekiah Questions Jeremiah

14 King Zedekiah[w] had me brought to his private entrance[x] to the temple, and he said, "I'm going to ask you something, and I want to know the truth."

15 "Why?" I replied. "You won't listen, and you might even have me killed!"

16 He said, "I swear in the name of the living LORD our Creator that I won't have you killed. No one else can hear what we say, and I won't let anyone kill you."

17 Then I told him that the LORD had said: "Zedekiah, I am the LORD God All-Powerful, the God of Israel. I promise that if you surrender to King Nebuchadnezzar's[y] officers, you and your family won't

[r]**37.21** *a loaf of bread*: Bread was the main food of the Israelites. During this time of emergency in Jerusalem, everyone probably received the same amount each day. [s]**38.1** *Jehucal*: The Hebrew text has "Jucal," another form of the name. [t]**38.1** *Shephatiah, Gedaliah, Jehucal, and Pashhur*: Hebrew "Shephatiah son of Mattan, Gedaliah son of Pashhur, Jucal son of Shelemiah, and Pashhur son of Malchiah." [u]**38.7,8** *Ethiopia*: The Hebrew text has "Cush," a region south of Egypt that included parts of the present countries of Ethiopia and Sudan. [v]**38.10** *thirty*: Most Hebrew manuscripts; one Hebrew manuscript "three." [w]**38.14** *Zedekiah*: See the note at 1.3.
[x]**38.14** *his private entrance*: One possible meaning for the difficult Hebrew text.
[y]**38.17** *Nebuchadnezzar's*: See the note at 21.2.

be killed, and Jerusalem won't be burned down. 18 But if you don't surrender, I will let the Babylonian army capture Jerusalem and burn it down, and you will be taken prisoner."

19 Zedekiah answered, "I can't surrender to the Babylonians. I'm too afraid of the Jews that have already joined them. The Babylonians might hand me over to those Jews, and they would torture me."

20 I said, "If you will just obey the LORD, the Babylonians won't hand you over to those Jews. You will be allowed to live, and all will go well for you. 21 But the LORD has shown me that if you refuse to obey, 22 then the women of your palace will be taken prisoner by Nebuchadnezzar's officials. And those women will say to you:

Friends you trusted led you astray.
Now you're trapped in mud,
and those friends you trusted
have all turned away.

23 The Babylonian army will take your wives and children captive, you will be taken as a prisoner to the King of Babylonia, and Jerusalem will be burned down."[z]

24 Zedekiah said, "Jeremiah, if you tell anyone what we have talked about, you might lose your life. 25 And I'm sure that if my officials hear about our meeting, they will ask you what we said to each other. They might even threaten to kill you if you don't tell them. 26 So if they question you, tell them you were begging me not to send you back to the prison at Jonathan's house, because going back there would kill you."

27 The officials did come and question me about my meeting with the king, and I told them exactly what he had ordered me to say. They never spoke to me about the meeting again, since no one had heard us talking.

28 I was held in the courtyard of the palace guards until the day Jerusalem was captured.

Jerusalem Is Captured by the Babylonians

(Jeremiah 52.4-16; 2 Kings 25.1-12)

39 1-3 In the tenth month[a] of the ninth year that Zedekiah[b] was king of Judah, King Nebuchadnezzar[c] and the Babylonian army began their attack on Jerusalem. They kept the city surrounded for a year and a half. Then, on the ninth day of the fourth month[d] of the eleventh year that Zedekiah was king, they broke through the city walls.

After Jerusalem was captured,[e] Nebuchadnezzar's highest officials,[f] including Nebo Sarsechim[g] and Nergal Sharezer from Simmagir,[h] took their places at Middle Gate to show they were in control of the city.[i]

4 When King Zedekiah and his troops saw that Jerusalem had been captured, they tried to escape from the city that same night. They went to the king's garden, where they slipped through the gate between the two city walls[j] and headed toward the Jordan River valley. 5 But the Babylonian troops caught up with them near Jericho. They arrested Zedekiah and took him to the town of Riblah in the land

[z] **38.23** *Jerusalem will be burned down*: A few Hebrew manuscripts and three ancient translations; most Hebrew manuscripts "you will burn Jerusalem down"; one ancient translation "he will burn Jerusalem down." [a] **39.1-3** *the tenth month*: Tebeth, the tenth month of the Hebrew calendar, from about mid-December to mid-January. [b] **39.1-3** *Zedekiah*: See the note at 1.3. [c] **39.1-3** *Nebuchadnezzar*: See the note at 21.2. [d] **39.1-3** *fourth month*: Tammuz, the fourth month of the Hebrew calendar, from about mid-June to mid-July. [e] **39.1-3** *After Jerusalem was captured*: This phrase is from 38.28. [f] **39.1-3** *highest officials*: The Hebrew text gives Nergal Sharezer's title as "the Rabmag," and Nebo Sarsechim's title as "the Rabsaris," but the exact meaning of the titles and the duties of these offices are not known. [g] **39.1-3** *Nebo Sarsechim*: Probably another form of the name Nebushazban (see verse 13). [h] **39.1-3** *Nergal Sharezer from Simmagir*: One possible meaning for the difficult Hebrew text. Probably Nebuchadnezzar's son-in-law, who was king of Babylonia 560-556 B.C. It is also possible that the Hebrew text mentions a second official named Nergal Sharezer. [i] **39.1-3** *took their places . . . control of the city*: The rulers and leaders often sat in the broad open area at the gate of a city to take care of official business and hold trials. [j] **39.4** *the gate between the two city walls*: The construction of the city walls at this point is not known.

38.28 Ez 33.21.

of Hamath, where Nebuchadnezzar put him on trial, then found him guilty 6 and gave orders for him to be punished. Zedekiah's sons were killed there in front of him, and so were the leaders of Judah's ruling families. 7 His eyes were poked out, and he was put in chains, so he could be dragged off to Babylonia.

8 Meanwhile, the Babylonian army had burned the houses in Jerusalem, including[k] the royal palace, and they had broken down the city walls. 9 Nebuzaradan, the Babylonian officer in charge of the guards, led away everyone from the city as prisoners, even those who had deserted to Nebuchadnezzar. 10 Only the poorest people who owned no land were left behind in Judah, and Nebuzaradan gave them fields and vineyards.

11 Nebuchadnezzar had given the following orders to Nebuzaradan: 12 "Find Jeremiah and keep him safe. Take good care of him and do whatever he asks."

13 Nebuzaradan, Nebushazban, Nergal Sharezer, and the other officers of King Nebuchadnezzar 14 sent some of their troops to bring me from the courtyard of the royal palace guards. They put me in the care of Gedaliah son of Ahikam[l] and told him to take me to my home. And so I was allowed to stay with the people who remained in Judah.

The LORD Promises To Protect Ebedmelech

15 While I was a prisoner in the courtyard of the palace guard, the LORD told me to say 16 to Ebedmelech from Ethiopia:[m]

I am the LORD All-Powerful, the God of Israel. I warned everyone that I would bring disaster, not prosperity, to this city. Now very soon I will do what I said, and you will see it happen. 17-18 But because you trusted me,[n] I will protect you from the officials of Judah, and when Judah is struck by disaster, I will rescue you and keep you alive. I, the LORD, have spoken.

Jeremiah Is Set Free

40 I was led away in chains along with the people of Judah and Jerusalem who were being taken to Babylonia. Nebuzaradan was the officer in charge of the guard, and while we were stopped at Ramah, the LORD had him set me free. 2 Nebuzaradan said:

Jeremiah, the LORD your God warned your people that he would bring disaster on this land. 3 But they continued to rebel against him, and now he has punished them just as he threatened.

4 Today I am taking the chains off your wrists and setting you free! If you want to, you can come with me to Babylonia, and I will see that you are taken care of. Or if you decide to stay here, you can go wherever you wish. 5 King Nebuchadnezzar[o] has chosen Gedaliah to rule Judah. You can live near Gedaliah, and he will provide for you, or you can live anywhere else you want.

Nebuzaradan gave me a supply of food, then let me leave. 6 I decided to stay with the people of Judah, and I went to live near Gedaliah in Mizpah.

The Harvest Is Brought In

7-8 Ishmael the son of Nethaniah, together with Johanan and Jonathan, the two sons of Kareah, had been officers in Judah's army. And so had Seraiah the son of Tanhumeth, the sons of Ephai the Netophathite, and Jezaniah from Maacah. They and their troops had been stationed outside Jerusalem and had not been captured. They heard that Gedaliah had been chosen to rule Judah, and that the poorest men, women, and children had not been taken away to Babylonia. So they went to Mizpah and met with their new ruler.

9 Gedaliah told them, "There's no need to be afraid of the Babylonians. Everything will be fine, if we live peacefully and obey

[k] **39.8** *the houses in Jerusalem, including*: Or "the temple and." [l] **39.14** *son of Ahikam*: Hebrew "son of Ahikam and grandson of Shaphan." [m] **39.16** *Ethiopia*: See the note at 38.7, 8.
[n] **39.17,18** *you trusted me*: See 38.7-13, where Ebedmelech helped Jeremiah.
[o] **40.5,9** *Nebuchadnezzar*: See the note at 21.2.
40.7-9 2 K 25.22-24.

King Nebuchadnezzar.[o] 10 I will stay here at Mizpah and meet with the Babylonian officials on each of their visits. But you must go back to your towns and bring in the harvest, then store the wine, olive oil, and dried fruit."

11-12 Earlier, when the Babylonians had invaded Judah, many of the Jews escaped to Moab, Ammon, Edom, and several other countries. But these Jews heard that the king of Babylonia had appointed Gedaliah as ruler of Judah, and that only a few people were left there. So the Jews in these other countries came back to Judah and helped with the grape and fruit harvest, which was especially large that year.

Gedaliah Is Murdered

13 One day, Johanan got together with some of the other men who had been army officers, and they came to Mizpah and met with Gedaliah. 14 They said, "Gedaliah, we came to warn you that King Baalis of Ammon hired Ishmael to murder you!"

Gedaliah refused to believe them, 15 so Johanan went to Gedaliah privately and said, "Let me kill Ishmael. No one will find out who did it. There are only a few people left in Judah, but they are depending on you. And if you are murdered, they will be scattered or killed."

16 Gedaliah answered, "Don't kill Ishmael! What you've said about him can't be true."

41 But in the seventh month,[p] Ishmael[q] came to Mizpah with ten of his soldiers. He had been one of the king's officials and was a member of the royal family. Ishmael and his men were invited to eat with Gedaliah. 2 During the meal, Ishmael and his soldiers killed Gedaliah, the man chosen as ruler of Judah by the king of Babylonia. 3 Then they killed the Jews who were with Gedaliah, and they also killed the Babylonian soldiers who were there.

4 The next day, the murders had still not been discovered, 5 when eighty men came down the road toward Mizpah from the towns of Shechem, Shiloh, and Samaria. They were on their way to the temple to offer gifts of grain and incense to the LORD. They had shaved off their beards, torn their clothes, and cut themselves, because they were mourning.

6 Ishmael went out the town gate to meet them. He pretended to be weeping, and he asked them to come into Mizpah to meet with Gedaliah, the ruler of Judah. 7 But after they were inside the town, Ishmael had his soldiers kill them and throw their bodies into a well. 8 He let ten of the men live, because they offered to give him supplies of wheat, barley, olive oil, and honey they had hidden in a field. 9 The well that he filled with bodies had been dug by King Asa[r] of Judah to store rainwater, because he was afraid that King Baasha[s] of Israel might surround Mizpah and keep the people from getting to their water supply.

10 Nebuzaradan, King Nebuchadnezzar's[t] officer in charge of the guard, had left King Zedekiah's[u] daughters and many other people at Mizpah, and he had put Gedaliah in charge of them. But now Ishmael took them all prisoner and led them toward Ammon, on the other side of the Jordan River.

11 Johanan and the other army officers heard what Ishmael had done. 12 So they and their troops chased Ishmael and caught up with him at the large pit at Gibeon. 13 When Ishmael's prisoners saw Johanan and the officers, they were happy 14 and turned around and ran toward Johanan. 15 But Ishmael and eight of his men escaped and went to Ammon.

Johanan Decides To Take the People to Egypt

16 Johanan and the officers had rescued the women, children, and royal officials that Ishmael had taken prisoner after

[o]**40.5,9** *Nebuchadnezzar*: See the note at 21.2. [p]**41.1** *seventh month*: Tishri, also called Ethanim, the seventh month of the Hebrew calendar, from about mid-September to mid-October. [q]**41.1** *Ishmael*: Hebrew "Ishmael son of Nethaniah and grandson of Elishama."
[r]**41.9** *Asa*: Ruled 911-870 B.C. [s]**41.9** *Baasha*: Ruled 909-886 B.C.
[t]**41.10** *Nebuchadnezzar's*: See the note at 21.2. [u]**41.10** *Zedekiah's*: See the note at 1.3.
41.1-3 2 K 25.25.

killing Gedaliah. Johanan led the people from Gibeon 17-18 toward Egypt. They wanted to go there, because they were afraid of what the Babylonians would do when they found out that Ishmael had killed Gedaliah, the ruler appointed by King Nebuchadnezzar.[v]

The People Ask Jeremiah To Pray for Them

On the way to Egypt, we[w] stopped at the town of Geruth Chimham near Bethle-
42 hem. 1 Johanan, Jezaniah,[x] the other army officers, and everyone else in the group, came to me 2 and said, "Please pray to the LORD your God for us. Judah used to have many people, but as you can see, only a few of us are left. 3 Ask the LORD to tell us where he wants us to go and what he wants us to do."

4 "All right," I answered, "I will pray to the LORD your God, and I will tell you everything he says."

5 They answered, "The LORD himself will be our witness that we promise to do whatever he says, 6 even if it isn't what we want to do. We will obey the LORD so that all will go well for us."

7 Ten days later, the LORD gave me an answer for 8 Johanan, the officers, and the other people. So I called them together 9 and told them that the LORD God of Israel had said:

You asked Jeremiah to pray and find out what you should do. 10 I am sorry that I had to punish you, and so I now tell you to stay here in Judah, where I will plant you and build you up, instead of tearing you down and uprooting you. 11 Don't be afraid of the King of Babylonia. I will protect you from him, 12 and I will even force him to have mercy on you and give back your farms.

13 But you might keep on saying, "We won't stay here in Judah, and we won't obey the LORD our God. 14 We are going to Egypt, where there is plenty of food and no danger of war."

15 People of Judah, you survived when the Babylonian army attacked. Now you are planning to move to Egypt, and if you do go, this is what will happen. 16-17 You are afraid of war, starvation, and disease here in Judah, but they will follow you to Egypt and kill you there. None of you will survive the disasters I will send.

18 I, the LORD, was angry with the people of Jerusalem and punished them. And if you go to Egypt, I will be angry and punish you the same way. You will never again see your homeland. People will be horrified at what I do to you, and they will use the name of your city as a curse word.

Jeremiah Gives a Warning

19 I told the people:

You escaped the disaster that struck Judah, but now the LORD warns you to stay away from Egypt. 20 You asked me to pray and find out what the LORD our God wants you to do, and you promised to obey him. But that was a terrible mistake, 21 because now that I have given you the LORD's answer, you refuse to obey him. 22 And so, you will die in Egypt from war, hunger, and disease.

The People Go to Egypt

43 I told the people everything the LORD had told me. 2 But Azariah, Johanan[y] and some other arrogant men said to me, "You're lying! The LORD didn't tell you to say that we shouldn't go to Egypt. 3 Baruch son of Neriah must have told you to say that. He wants the Babylonians to capture us, so they can take us away to Babylonia or even kill us."

4 Johanan, the other army officers, and everyone else refused to stay in Judah in spite of the LORD's command. 5 So Johanan

[v] **41.17,18** *Nebuchadnezzar*: See the note at 21.2. [w] **41.17,18** *we*: The group of people included Jeremiah, since he had been staying with Gedaliah near Mizpah (see 40.6).
[x] **42.1** *Jezaniah*: Hebrew "Jezaniah son of Hoshaiah"; one ancient translation "Azariah son of Hoshaiah" (see also 43.2 and the note there). [y] **43.2** *Azariah, Johanan*: Hebrew "Azariah son of Hoshaiah, Johanan son of Kareah."
43.5-7 2 K 25.26.

and the officers led us away toward Egypt. The group that left Judah included those who had been scattered in other countries and who had then come back to live in Judah. 6 Baruch and I and others in the group had been staying with Gedaliah, because Nebuzaradan, the Babylonian officer in charge of the guard, had ordered him to take care of the king's daughters and quite a few men, women, and children.

7 The people disobeyed the LORD and went to Egypt. The group had settled in Tahpanhes, 8 when the LORD told me:

9 Jeremiah, carry some large stones to the entrance of the government building in Tahpanhes. Bury the stones underneath the brick pavement[z] and be sure the Jews are watching.

10 Then tell them that I, the LORD All-Powerful, the God of Israel, have sent for my servant, Nebuchadnezzar[a] of Babylonia. I will bring him here and have him set up his throne and his royal tent over these stones that I told you to bury. 11 He will attack Egypt and kill many of its people; others will die of disease or be dragged away as prisoners. 12-13 I will have him set Egypt's temples on fire, and he will either burn or carry off their idols. He will destroy the sacred monuments at the temple of the sun-god.[b] Then Nebuchadnezzar will pick the land clean, just like a shepherd picking the lice off his clothes. And he will return safely home.

The LORD Will Destroy the People of Judah

44 The LORD told me to speak with the Jews who were living in the towns of Migdol, Tahpanhes, and Memphis in northern Egypt, and also to those living in southern Egypt. He told me to tell them:

2 I am the LORD All-Powerful, the God of Israel. You saw how I destroyed Jerusalem and the towns of Judah. They lie empty and in ruins today, 3 because the people of Judah made me angry by worshiping gods that had never helped them or their ancestors.

4 Time after time I sent my servants the prophets to tell the people of Judah how much I hated their disgusting sins. The prophets warned them to stop sinning, 5 but they refused to listen and would not stop worshiping other gods. 6 Finally, my anger struck like a raging flood, and today Jerusalem and the towns of Judah are nothing but empty ruins.

7 Why do you now insist on heading for another disaster? A disaster that will destroy not only you, but also your children and babies. 8 You have made me angry by worshiping idols and burning incense to other gods after you came here to Egypt. You will die such a disgusting death, that other nations will use the name of Judah as a curse word. 9 When you were living in Jerusalem and Judah, you followed the example of your ancestors in doing evil things, just like your kings and queens. 10 Even now, your pride keeps you from respecting me and obeying the laws and teachings I gave you and your ancestors.

11 I, the LORD All-Powerful, have decided to wipe you out with disasters. 12 There were only a few of you left in Judah, and you decided to go to Egypt. But you will die such horrible deaths in war or from starvation, that people of other countries will use the name of Judah as a curse word. 13 I punished Jerusalem with war, hunger, and disease, and that's how I will punish you. 14 None of you will survive. You may hope to return to Judah someday, but only a very few of you will escape death and be able to go back.

The People Refuse To Worship the LORD

15 A large number of Jews from both northern and southern Egypt listened to me as I told them what the LORD had said.

[z]**43.9** *underneath the brick pavement*: One possible meaning for the difficult Hebrew text.
[a]**43.10** *Nebuchadnezzar*: See the note at 21.2. [b]**43.12,13** *at the temple of the sun-god*: Or "in the city of Heliopolis."

Most of the men in the crowd knew that their wives often burned incense to other gods. So they and their wives shouted:

16 Jeremiah, what do we care if you speak in the LORD's name? We refuse to listen! 17 We have promised to worship the goddess Astarte, the Queen of Heaven,[c] and that is exactly what we are going to do. We will burn incense and offer sacrifices of wine to her, just as we, our ancestors, our kings, and our leaders did when we lived in Jerusalem and the other towns of Judah. We had plenty of food back then. We were well off, and nothing bad ever happened to us. 18 But since the time we stopped burning incense and offering wine sacrifices to her, we have been dying from war and hunger.

19 Then the women said, "When we lived in Judah, we worshiped the Queen of Heaven and offered sacrifices of wine and special loaves of bread shaped like her. Our husbands knew what we were doing, and they approved of it."

20 Then I told the crowd:

21 Don't you think the LORD knew that you and your ancestors, your leaders and kings, and the rest of the people were burning incense to other gods in Jerusalem and everywhere else in Judah? 22 And when he could no longer put up with your disgusting sins, he placed a curse on your land and turned it into a desert, as it is today. 23 This disaster happened because you worshiped other gods and rebelled against the LORD by refusing to obey him or follow his laws and teachings.

24-25 Then I told the men and their wives, that the LORD All-Powerful, the God of Israel, had said:

Here in Egypt you still keep your promises to burn incense and offer sacrifices of wine to the so-called Queen of Heaven. 26 Keep these promises! But let me tell you what will happen. As surely as I am the LORD God, I swear that I will never again accept any promises you make in my name. 27 Instead of watching over you, I will watch for chances to harm you. Some of you will die in war, and others will starve to death. 28 Only a few will escape and return to Judah. Then everyone who went to live in Egypt will know that when I say something will happen, it will—no matter what you say.

29 And here is how you will know that I will keep my threats to punish you in Egypt. 30 I will hand over King Hophra of Egypt to those who want to kill him,[d] just as I handed Zedekiah[e] over to Nebuchadnezzar,[f] who wanted to kill him.

The LORD Will Not Let Baruch Be Killed

45 In the fourth year that Jehoiakim[g] was king of Judah, Baruch wrote down everything I had told him.[h] 2 Then later, the LORD God of Israel told me to say to Baruch:

3 You are moaning and blaming me, the LORD, for your troubles and sorrow, and for being so tired that you can't even rest. 4 But all over the earth I am tearing down what I built and pulling up what I planted. 5 I am bringing disaster everywhere, so don't even think about making any big plans for yourself. However, I promise that wherever you go, I will at least protect you from death. I, the LORD, have spoken.

The LORD Speaks about the Nations

46 The LORD often told me what to say about the different nations of the world.

[c] **44.17** *the goddess Astarte, the Queen of Heaven*: The Hebrew text has "the queen of heaven," which probably refers to the goddess Astarte. [d] **44.30** *King Hophra . . . kill him*: Hophra, also known as Apries, ruled Egypt from 589 to 570 B.C., when he was killed by Ahmosis II, who then became king of Egypt and ruled until 526 B.C. [e] **44.30** *Zedekiah*: See the note at 1.3. [f] **44.30** *Nebuchadnezzar*: See the note at 21.2. [g] **45.1** *Jehoiakim*: See the note at 1.3. [h] **45.1** *Baruch wrote down everything I had told him*: See 36.1-32.

44.30 2 K 25.1-7. **45.1** 2 K 24.1; 2 Ch 36.5-7; Dn 1.1, 2.

What the LORD Says about Egypt

2 In the fourth year that Jehoiakim[i] was
king of Judah, King Nebuchadnezzar[j] of
Babylonia defeated King Neco of Egypt[k] in
a battle at the city of Carchemish near the
Euphrates River. And here is what the
LORD told me to say about the Egyptian
army:

3 It's time to go into battle!
So grab your shields,
4 saddle your horses,
and polish your spears.
Put on your helmets and armor,
then take your positions.

5 I can see the battle now—
you are defeated
and running away,
never once looking back.
Terror is all around.
6 You are strong and run fast,
but you can't escape.
You fall in battle
near the Euphrates River.

7 What nation is this,
that rises like the Nile River
overflowing its banks?
8 It is Egypt, rising with a roar
like a raging river
and saying,
"I'll flood the earth,
destroying cities, and killing
everyone in them."

9 Go ahead, Egypt.
Tell your chariots and cavalry
to attack and fight hard.
Order your troops to march out,
with Ethiopians[l] and Libyans
carrying shields,
and the Lydians[m] armed with bows
and arrows.

10 But the LORD All-Powerful
will win this battle
and take revenge
on his enemies.
His sword will eat them
and drink their blood
until it is full.
They will be killed in the north
near the Euphrates River,
as a sacrifice to the LORD.

11 Egypt, no medicine can heal you,
not even the soothing lotion
from Gilead.
12 All nations have heard you weep;
you are disgraced,
and they know it.
Your troops fall to the ground,
stumbling over each other.

A Warning for Egypt

13-14 When King Nebuchadnezzar[n] of
Babylonia was on his way to attack Egypt,
the LORD sent me with a warning for every
Egyptian town, but especially for Migdol,
Memphis, and Tahpanhes. He said to tell
them:

Prepare to defend yourselves!
Everywhere in your nation,
people are dying in war.
15 I have struck down
your mighty god Apis[o]
and chased him away.[p]
16 Your soldiers stumble
over each other
and say, "Get up!
The enemy will kill us,
unless we can escape
to our own land."

17 Give the king of Egypt
this new name,
"Talks-Big-Does-Nothing."

[i]**46.2** *Jehoiakim*: See the note at 1.3. [j]**46.2** *King Nebuchadnezzar*: Ruled 605-562 B.C. At the time of the battle in 605 B.C., he was crown prince, but his father died a few months later, and he became king. [k]**46.2** *King Neco of Egypt*: Neco II, ruled 609-594 B.C. [l]**46.9** *Ethiopians*: See the note at 38.7, 8. [m]**46.9** *Lydians*: Probably hired soldiers from Lydia, an area in west-central Asia minor. [n]**46.13,14** *Nebuchadnezzar*: See the note at 21.2. [o]**46.15** *Apis*: A sacred bull, kept in a temple at Memphis, Egypt, and worshiped as a god. [p]**46.15** *I have . . . him away*: One possible meaning for the difficult Hebrew text.

46.2-26 Is 19.1-25; Ez 29.1—32.32. **46.13,14** Jr 43.10-13.

18 Egypt, I am the true king,
the LORD All-Powerful,
and as surely as I live,
those enemies who attack
will tower over you
like Mount Tabor among the hills
or Mount Carmel by the sea.
19 You will be led away captive,
so pack a few things
to bring with you.
Your capital, Memphis,
will lie empty and in ruins.

20 An enemy from the north
will attack you, beautiful Egypt,
like a fly biting a cow.
21 The foreign soldiers you hired
will turn and run.
But they are doomed,
like well-fed calves
being led to the butcher.

*22 The enemy army will go forward
like a swarm of locusts.[q]
Your troops will feel helpless,
like a snake in a forest
23 when men with axes
start chopping down trees.
It can only hiss
and try to escape.
24 Your people will be disgraced
and captured by the enemy
from the north.

25 I am the LORD All-Powerful, the God
of Israel. Soon I will punish the god Amon
of Thebes[r] and the other Egyptian gods,
the Egyptian kings, the people of Egypt,
and everyone who trusts in the Egyptian
power. 26 I will hand them over to King
Nebuchadnezzar and his army. But I also
promise that Egypt will someday have people living here again, just as it had before. I,
the LORD, have spoken.

The LORD Will Bring Israel Home

The LORD said:
27 Israel,[s] don't be afraid.
Someday I will bring you home
from foreign lands.
You and your descendants
will live in peace and safety,
with nothing to fear.
28 So don't be afraid,
even though now
you deserve to be punished
and have been scattered
among other nations.
But when I destroy them,
I will protect you.
I, the LORD, have spoken.

What the LORD Says about the Philistines

47 Before the king of Egypt attacked the town of Gaza,[t] the LORD told me to say to the Philistines:

2 I, the LORD, tell you
that your land will be flooded
with an army from the north.
It will destroy your towns
and sweep you away,
moaning and screaming.
3 When you hear the thunder
of horses and chariots,
your courage will vanish,
and parents will abandon
their own children.
4 You refugees from Crete,[u]
your time has now come,
and I will destroy you.
None of you will be left
to help the cities
of Tyre and Sidon.
*5 The Anakim who survive[v]
in Gaza and Ashkelon
will mourn for you

[q]**46.22** *locusts*: A type of grasshopper that comes in swarms and causes great damage to plant life. [r]**46.25** *the god Amon of Thebes*: Amon was the king of the Egyptian gods and was the special god of the Egyptian kings. [s]**46.27** *Israel*: See the note at 30.10, 11. [t]**47.1** *attacked the town of Gaza*: One of the major Philistine towns; nothing is known about this attack. [u]**47.4** *Crete*: Hebrew "Caphtor," another name for Crete, the original homeland of the ancestor of the Philistines. [v]**47.5** *Anakim who survive*: One ancient translation; Hebrew "people in the valley who survive." The Anakim may have been a group of very large people that lived in Palestine before the Israelites (see Numbers 13.33; Deuteronomy 2.10, 11, 20, 21; and Joshua 11.21, 22).

46.27,28 Jr 30.10, 11. **47.1-7** Is 14.29-31; Ez 25.15-17; Jl 3.4-8; Am 1.6-8; Zep 2.4-7; Zec 9.5-7.

by shaving their heads
and sitting in silence.
6 You ask how long will I continue
to attack you with my sword,
then you tell me to put it away
and leave you alone.
7 But how can my sword rest,
when I have commanded it
to attack Ashkelon
and the seacoast?

What the LORD Says about Moab

48 The LORD All-Powerful, the God of Israel, told me to say to the nation of Moab:

The town of Nebo is doomed;
Kiriathaim will be captured
and disgraced,
and even its fortress
will be left in ruins.
2 No one honors you, Moab.
In Heshbon, enemies make plans
to end your life.
My sword will leave only silence
in your town named "Quiet."[w]
3 The people of Horonaim
will cry for help,
as their town is attacked
and destroyed.

4 Moab will be shattered!
Your children will sob
5 and cry on their way up
to the town of Luhith;
on the road to Horonaim
they will tell of disasters.

6 Run for your lives!
Head into the desert
like a wild donkey.[x]
7 You thought you could be saved
by your power and wealth,
but you will be captured
along with your god Chemosh,
his priests, and officials.
8 Not one of your towns
will escape destruction.

I have told your enemies,
"Wipe out the valley
and the flatlands of Moab.
9 Spread salt on the ground
to kill the crops.[y]
Leave its towns in ruins,
with no one living there.
10 I want you to kill the Moabites,
and if you let them escape,
I will put a curse on you."

11 Moab, you are like wine
left to settle undisturbed,
never poured from jar to jar.
And so, your nation continues
to prosper and improve.[z]
12 But now, I will send enemies
to pour out the wine
and smash the jars!
13 Then you will be ashamed,
because your god Chemosh
cannot save you,
just as Bethel[a] could not help
the Israelites.

14 You claim that your soldiers
are strong and brave.
15 But I am the LORD,
the all-powerful King,
and I promise that enemies
will overpower your towns.
Even your best warriors
will die in the battle.
16 It won't be long now—
disaster will hit Moab!

17 I will order the nearby nations
to mourn for you and say,
"Isn't it sad? Moab ruled others,
but now its glorious power
has been shattered."

[w] **48.2** *silence . . . Quiet*: In Hebrew the name of the town was "Madmen," which sounds like the word for "silence." [x] **48.6** *like a wild donkey*: One ancient translation; Hebrew "like (the town of) Aroer" (see verse 19). [y] **48.9** *Spread salt . . . crops*: One possible meaning for the difficult Hebrew text. [z] **48.11** *continues . . . improve*: Or "remains as evil as ever." [a] **48.13** *Bethel*: It may refer to the Phoenician or Canaanite god of that name; or it may refer to the town where people of the northern kingdom worshiped at a local shrine (see 1 Kings 12.26-30).

48.1-47 Is 15.1—16.14; 25.10-12; Ez 25.8-11; Am 2.1-3; Zep 2.8-11.

18 People in the town of Dibon,[b]
you will be honored no more,
so have a seat in the dust.
Your walls will be torn down
when the enemies attack.

19 You people of Aroer,[c]
go wait beside the road,
and when refugees run by,
ask them, "What happened?"
20 They will answer,
"Moab has been defeated!
Weep with us in shame.
Tell everyone at the Arnon River
that Moab is destroyed."

*21 I will punish every town
that belongs to Moab,
but especially Holon,
Jahzah, Mephaath,
22 Dibon, Nebo,
Beth-Diblathaim, 23 Kiriathaim,
Beth-Gamul, Beth-Meon,
24 Kerioth, and Bozrah.[d]
25 My decision is final—
your army will be crushed,
and your power broken.

26 People of Moab, you claim
to be stronger than I am.
Now I will tell other nations
to make you drunk
and to laugh while you collapse
in your own vomit.
27 You made fun of my people
and treated them like criminals
caught in the act.
28 Now you must leave your towns
and live like doves
in the shelter of cliffs
and canyons.

29 I know about your pride,
and how you strut and boast.
30 But I also know bragging
will never save you.
31 So I will cry and mourn
for Moab
and its town of Kir-Heres.

32 People of Sibmah,
you were like a vineyard
heavy with grapes,
and with branches reaching
north to the town of Jazer
and west to the Dead Sea.[e]
But you have been destroyed,
and so I will weep for you,
as the people of Jazer weep
for the vineyards.

33 Harvest celebrations are gone
from the orchards and farms
of Moab.
There are no happy shouts
from people making wine.
34 Weeping from Heshbon
can be heard as far
as Elealeh and Jahaz;
cries from Zoar are heard
in Horonaim
and Eglath-Shelishiyah.
And Nimrim Creek has run dry.

35 I will get rid of anyone
who burns incense
to the gods of Moab
or offers sacrifices
at their shrines.
I, the LORD, have spoken.

36 In my heart I moan for Moab,
like a funeral song
played on a flute.
I mourn for the people
of the town of Kir-Heres,
because their wealth is gone.

*37 The people of Moab
mourn on the rooftops
and in the streets.
Men cut off their beards,
people shave their heads;
they make cuts on their hands
and wear sackcloth.[f]
38 And it's all because I, the LORD,
have shattered Moab like a jar
that no one wants.

[b]**48.18** *Dibon*: The capital city of Moab. [c]**48.19** *Aroer*: A Moabite town located just north of the Arnon River. [d]**48.24** *Bozrah*: Not the same Bozrah as in 49.13. [e]**48.32** *reaching north . . . Dead Sea*: One possible meaning for the difficult Hebrew text. [f]**48.37** *sackcloth*: See the note at 4.8.

39 Moab lies broken!
Listen to its people cry
as they turn away in shame.
Other nations are horrified
at what happened,
but still they laugh.

40 Moab, an enemy swoops down
like an eagle spreading its wings
over your land.
41 Your cities[g] and fortresses
will be captured,
and your warriors
gripped by fear.[h]
42 You are finished as a nation,
because you dared oppose me,
the LORD.
43 Terror, pits, and traps
are waiting for you.
44 If you are terrified and run,
you will fall into a pit;
and if you crawl out of the pit,
you'll get caught in a trap.
The time has come
for you to be punished.

45 Near the city of Heshbon,
where Sihon once ruled,
tired refugees stand in shadows
cast by the flames
of their burning city.
Soon, the towns on other hilltops,
where those warlike people live,
will also go up in smoke.

46 People of Moab, you worshiped
Chemosh, your god,
but now you are done for,
and your children are prisoners
in a foreign country.
47 Yet someday, I will bring
your people back home.
I, the LORD, have spoken.

What the LORD Says about Ammon

49 The LORD has this to say about the nation of Ammon:

The people of Israel
have plenty of children
to inherit their lands.
So why have you worshipers
of the god Milcom[i]
taken over towns and land
belonging to the Gad tribe?
2 Someday I will send an army
to attack you in Rabbah,
your capital city.
It will be left in ruins,
and the surrounding villages
will lie in ashes.
You took some of Israel's land,
but on that day
Israel will take yours!

3 Cry, people of Heshbon;[j]
your town will become
a pile of rubble.[k]
You will turn here and there,
but your path will be blocked.[l]

Put on sackcloth[m] and mourn,
you citizens of Rabbah,
because the idol you worship[n]
will be taken
to a foreign country,
along with its priests
and temple officials.
4 You rebellious Ammonites
trust your wealth and ask,
"Who could attack us?"
But I warn you not to boast
when your strength is fading.[o]
5 I, the LORD All-Powerful,
will send neighboring nations
to strike you with terror.
You will be scattered,

[g] **48.41** *Your cities*: Or "Kerioth." [h] **48.41** *gripped by fear*: One possible meaning for the difficult Hebrew text. [i] **49.1** *Milcom*: The national god of Ammon, probably the same as the god Molech in 32.35. [j] **49.3** *Heshbon*: See also 48.45; since Heshbon was near the border of Moab and Ammon, it was probably ruled by the country that was stronger at the time. [k] **49.3** *your town will become a pile of rubble*: Or "because the town of Ai has been destroyed"; referring to an Ammonite town named Ai, not the town of that name near Bethel in the land of Israel. [l] **49.3** *You will turn . . . blocked*: One possible meaning for the difficult Hebrew text. [m] **49.3** *sackcloth*: See the note at 4.8. [n] **49.3** *the idol you worship*: Hebrew "Milcom" (see verse 1 and the note there). [o] **49.4** *when . . . fading*: One possible meaning for the difficult Hebrew text.
49.1-6 Ez 21.28-32; 25.1-7; Am 1.13-15; Zep 2.8-11.

with no one to care
for your refugees.
6 Yet someday, I will bring
your people back home.
I, the LORD, have spoken.

What the LORD Says about Edom

7-8 The LORD All-Powerful says about Edom:

Wisdom and common sense
have vanished from Teman.[p]
I will send disaster to punish
you descendants of Esau,[q]
so anyone from Dedan[r]
had better turn around
and run back home.[s]
9 People who harvest grapes
leave some for the poor.
Thieves who break in at night
take only what they want.
10 But I will take everything
that belongs to you,
people of Edom,
and I will uncover every place
where you try to hide.
Then you will die,
and so will your children,
relatives, and neighbors.
11 But I can be trusted
to care for your orphans
and widows.

12 Even those nations that don't deserve
to be punished will have to drink from
the cup of my anger. So how can you possibly hope to escape? 13 I, the LORD, swear in
my own name that your city of Bozrah[t] and
all your towns will suffer a horrible fate.
They will lie in ruins forever, and people
will use the name "Bozrah" as a curse
word.

14 I have sent a messenger
to command the nations
to prepare for war
against you people of Edom.
15 Your nation will be small,
yet hated by other nations.
16 Pride tricks you into thinking
that other nations
look at you with fear.[u]
You live along the cliffs
and high in the mountains
like the eagles,
but I am the LORD,
and I will bring you down.
17 People passing by your country
will be shocked and horrified
to see a disaster
18 as bad as the destruction
of Sodom and Gomorrah
and towns nearby.
The towns of Edom will be empty.

19 I will attack you
like a lion from the forest,
attacking sheep in a meadow
along the Jordan.
In a moment the flock runs,
and the land is empty.
Who will I choose to attack you?
I will do it myself!
No one can force me to fight
or chase me away.
20 Listen to my plans for you,
people of Edom.[v]
Your children will be dragged off
and your country destroyed.
21 The sounds of your destruction
will reach the Red Sea[w]
and cause the earth to shake.
22 An enemy will swoop down
to attack you,
like an eagle spreading its wings
and circling over Bozrah.

[p] **49.7,8** *Teman*: The name of a town in Edom, sometimes used as the name of the northern half of the nation of Edom; here it probably stands for the whole nation. [q] **49.7,8** *Esau*: The ancestor of the nation of Edom. [r] **49.7,8** *Dedan*: The name of a town in northwest Arabia, also used of the northwest region of Arabia along the Red Sea. [s] **49.7,8** *anyone . . . home*: One possible meaning for the difficult Hebrew text. [t] **49.13** *Bozrah*: The main city and capital of Edom.
[u] **49.16** *Pride . . . fear*: One possible meaning for the difficult Hebrew text. [v] **49.20** *Edom*: The Hebrew text also uses the name "Teman" (see the note at verses 7,8). [w] **49.21** *Red Sea*: Hebrew *yam suph*, here referring to the Gulf of Aqaba, since the term is extended to include the northeastern arm of the Red Sea (see also the note at Exodus 13.18).

49.7-22 Is 34.5-17; 63.1-6; Ez 25.12-14; 35.1-15; Am 1.11, 12; Ob 1-14; Ml 1.2-5.
49.7,8 Ba 3.22, 23. **49.18** Gn 19.24, 25. **49.19** Ws 12.12.

Your warriors will be gripped
by fear.[x]

What the LORD Says about Damascus

23 The LORD says about Damascus:

The towns of Hamath and Arpad[y]
have heard your bad news.
They have lost hope,
and worries roll over them
like ocean waves.[z]
24 You people of Damascus
have lost your courage,
and in panic you turn to run,
gripped by fear and pain.[a]

25 I once was pleased
with your famous city.
But now I warn you, "Escape
while you still can!"[b]
26 Soon, even your best soldiers
will lie dead in your streets.
I, the LORD All-Powerful,
have spoken.

27 I will set fire to your city walls
and burn down the fortresses
King Benhadad built.

Nebuchadnezzar and the People of the Desert

28 Here is what the LORD says about the
Kedar tribe and the desert villages[c] that
were conquered by King Nebuchadnezzar[d]
of Babylonia:

Listen, you people of Kedar
and the other tribes
of the eastern desert.
I have told Nebuchadnezzar
to attack and destroy you.
29 His fearsome army
will surround you,
taking your tents and possessions,
your sheep and camels.

30 Run and hide,
you people of the desert
who live in villages![e]
Nebuchadnezzar has big plans
for you.
31 You have no city walls
and no neighbors to help,
yet you think you're safe—
so I told him to attack.
32 Then your camels
and large herds
will be yours no longer.

People of the Arabian Desert,[f]
disaster will strike you
from every side,
and you will be scattered
everywhere on earth.
33 Only jackals[g] will live
where your villages[h] once stood.
I, the LORD, have spoken.

What the LORD Says about Elam

34-35 Not long after Zedekiah[i] became
king of Judah, the LORD told me to say:

People of Elam,[j]
I, the LORD All-Powerful,
will kill the archers
who make your army strong.
36 Enemies will attack
from all directions,
and you will be led captive
to every nation on earth.
37 Their armies will crush
and kill you,

[x] **49.22** *will be gripped by fear*: One possible meaning for the difficult Hebrew text.
[y] **49.23** *Hamath and Arpad*: Two towns in Syria that had been the capitals of small kingdoms allied with the more powerful kingdom whose capital was Damascus. [z] **49.23** *worries . . . waves*: One possible meaning for the difficult Hebrew text. [a] **49.24** *gripped by fear and pain*: One possible meaning for the difficult Hebrew text. [b] **49.25** *can*: One possible meaning for the difficult Hebrew text of verse 25. [c] **49.28** *desert villages*: The Hebrew text has "kingdoms of Hazor," which probably refers to several kingdoms of desert peoples who were not nomads, but who lived in small villages. [d] **49.28** *Nebuchadnezzar*: See the note at 21.2. [e] **49.30** *villages*: See the note at 49.28. [f] **49.32** *People of the Arabian Desert*: One possible meaning for the difficult Hebrew text. [g] **49.33** *jackals*: See the note at 9.11. [h] **49.33** *villages*: See the note at 49.28.
[i] **49.34,35** *Zedekiah*: See the note at 1.3. [j] **49.34,35** *Elam*: A nation east of Babylonia, attacked by Nebuchadnezzar about 596 B.C.
49.23-27 Is 17.1-3; Am 1.3-5; Zec 9.1.

and you will face the disaster
that my anger brings.
38 Your king and his officials
will die, and I will rule
in their place.
I, the LORD, have spoken.

39 But I promise that someday
I will bring your people
back to their land.

Babylon Will Be Captured

50 *1 The LORD told me to say:

Announce what will happen
and don't leave anything out.
2 Raise the signal flags;
shout so all nations can hear—
Babylon will be captured!

Marduk,[k] Babylon's god,
will be ashamed and terrified,
and his idols broken.
3 The attack on the Babylonians
will come from the north;
they and their animals will run,
leaving the land empty.

Israel and Judah Will Return to Their Land

4 The LORD said:

People of Israel and Judah,
when these things happen
you will weep, and together
you will return to your land
and worship me,
the LORD your God.
5 You will ask the way to Zion
and then come and join with me
in making an agreement
you won't break or forget.

6 My people, you are lost sheep
abandoned by their shepherds
in the mountains.
You don't even remember
your resting place.
7 I am your true pastureland,
the one who gave hope
to your ancestors.
But you abandoned me,
so when your enemies found you,
they felt no guilt
as they gobbled you down.

8 Escape from Babylonia,
my people.
Get out of that country!
Don't wait for anyone else.
9 In the north I am bringing
great nations together.
They will attack Babylon
and capture it.
The arrows they shoot
are like the best soldiers,[l]
always finding their target.
10 Babylonia will be conquered,
and its enemies will carry off
everything they want.

Babylon Will Be Disgraced

The LORD said:
11 People of Babylonia,
you were glad
to rob my people.
You had a good time,
making more noise
than horses
and jumping around
like calves threshing grain.[m]
12 The city of Babylon
was like a mother to you.
But it will be disgraced
and become nothing
but a barren desert.
13 My anger will destroy Babylon,
and no one will live there.
Everyone who passes by
will be shocked to see
what has happened.

14 Babylon has rebelled against me.
Archers, take your places.
Shoot all your arrows at Babylon.
15 Attack from every side!

[k]**50.2** *Marduk*: The Hebrew text has "Bel" and "Marduk," two names for the same god.
[l]**50.9** *the best soldiers*: Some Hebrew manuscripts and two ancient translations; most Hebrew manuscripts "soldiers that kill children." [m]**50.11** *threshing grain*: Hebrew; two ancient translations "in a pasture."

50.1—51.64 Is 13.1—14.23; 47.1-15. **50.8** Rev 18.4.

Babylon surrenders!
The enemy tears down
its walls and towers.
I am taking my revenge
by doing to Babylon what it did
to other cities.
16 There is no one in Babylonia
to plant or harvest crops.
Even foreigners who lived there
have left for their homelands,
afraid of the enemy armies.

17 Israel is a flock of sheep
scattered by hungry lions.
The king of Assyria[n]
first gobbled Israel down.
Then Nebuchadnezzar,[o]
king of Babylonia,
crunched on Israel's bones.
18 I, the LORD All-Powerful,
the God of Israel,
punished the king of Assyria,
and I will also punish
the king of Babylonia.
19 But I will bring Israel
back to its own land.
The people will be like sheep
eating their fill
on Mount Carmel
and in Bashan,
in the hill country of Ephraim
and in Gilead.
20 I will rescue a few people
from Israel and Judah.
I will forgive them so completely
that their sin and guilt
will disappear,
never to be found.

The LORD's Commands to the Enemies of Babylonia

21 The LORD said:

I have told
the enemies of Babylonia,
"Attack the people of Merathaim
and Pekod.[p]
Kill them all!
Destroy their possessions!"

22 Sounds of war
and the noise of destruction
can be heard.
23 Babylonia was a hammer
pounding every country,
but now it lies broken.
What a shock to the nations
of the world!

24 Babylonia challenged me,
the LORD God All-Powerful,
but that nation doesn't know
it is caught in a trap
that I set.
25 I've brought out my weapons,
and with them I will put a curse
on Babylonia.

26 Come from far away,
you enemies of Babylon!
Pile up the grain
from its storehouses,
and destroy it completely,
along with everything else.
27 Kill the soldiers of Babylonia,
because the time has come
for them to be punished.

28 The Babylonian army
destroyed my temple,
but soon I will take revenge.
Then refugees from Babylon
will tell about it in Zion.

29 Attack Babylon, enemy archers;
set up camp around the city,
and don't let anyone escape.
It challenged me, the holy God,
so do to it
what it did to other cities.

[n]**50.17** *king of Assyria*: Either Shalmaneser V, who ruled 726-722 B.C., conquered most of the northern kingdom, and surrounded its capital city Samaria; or Sargon II, who ruled 721-705 B.C. and took thousands of prisoners back to Assyria. [o]**50.17** *Nebuchadnezzar*: See the note at 21.2.
[p]**50.21** *Merathaim . . . Pekod*: Hebrew forms of two Babylonian names that refer to the land of Babylonia. Merathaim probably referred to lagoons near the mouth of the Tigris and Euphrates rivers or to the Persian Gulf, but in Hebrew it means "Twice as Rebellious." Pekod referred to a tribe of southeastern Babylonia, but in Hebrew it means "Punishment."
50.29 Rev 18.6.

Proud Babylon Will Fall

30 People of Babylon,
I, the LORD, promise
that even your best soldiers
will lie dead in the streets.

31 Babylon, you should be named,
"The Proud One."
But the time has come when I,
the LORD All-Powerful,
will punish you.
32 You are proud,
but you will stumble and fall,
and no one will help you up.
I will set your villages on fire,
and everything around you
will go up in flames.

33 You Babylonians were cruel
to Israel and Judah.
You took them captive, and now
you refuse to let them go.
34 But I, the LORD All-Powerful,
will rescue and protect them.
I will bring peace to their land
and trouble to yours.
35 I have declared war on you,
your officials, and advisors.
36 This war will prove
that your prophets
are liars and fools.
And it will frighten
your warriors.
37 Then your chariot horses
and the foreigners in your army
will refuse to go into battle,
and the enemy will carry away
everything you treasure.
38 Your rivers and canals
will dry up.

All of this will happen,
because your land
is full of idols,
and they have made fools
of you.
39 Never again will people live
in your land—
only desert animals, jackals,[q]
and unclean birds.
40 I destroyed Sodom and Gomorrah
and the nearby towns,
and I will destroy Babylon
just as completely.
No one will live there again.

Babylonia Is Invaded

The LORD said:
41 Far to the north,
a nation and its allies
have been awakened.
They are powerful
and ready for war.
42 Bows and arrows and swords
are in their hands.
The soldiers are cruel
and show no pity.
The hoofbeats of their horses
echo like ocean waves
crashing against the shore.
The army has lined up for battle
and is coming to attack you,
people of Babylonia!

43 Ever since your king heard
about this army,
he has been weak with fear;
he twists and turns in pain
like a woman giving birth.
44 Babylonia, I will attack you
like a lion from the forest,
attacking sheep in a meadow
along the Jordan.
In a moment the flock runs,
and the land is empty.
Who will I choose to attack you?
I will do it myself!
No one can force me to fight
or chase me away.
45 Listen to my plans for you,
people of Babylonia.
Your children will be dragged off,
and your country destroyed.
46 The sounds of your destruction
will be heard among the nations,
and the earth will shake.

[q]**50.39** *jackals*: See the note at 9.11.
50.39 Rev 18.2. **50.40** Gn 19.24, 25.

Babylon Will Be Destroyed

51 I, the LORD, am sending
a wind[r] to destroy
the people of Babylonia[s]
and Babylon, its capital.
2 Foreign soldiers will come
from every direction,
and when the disaster is over,
Babylonia will be empty
and worthless.
3 I will tell these soldiers,
"Attack quickly,
before the Babylonians
can string their bows
or put on their armor.[t]
Kill their best soldiers
and destroy their army!"
4 Their troops will fall wounded
in the streets of Babylon.

5 Everyone in Israel and Judah
is guilty.
But I, the LORD All-Powerful,
their holy God,
have not abandoned them.

6 Get out of Babylon!
Run for your lives!
If you stay, you will be killed
when I take revenge on the city
and punish it for its sins.

7 Babylon was my golden cup,
filled with the wine
of my anger.
The nations of the world
got drunk on this wine
and went insane.
8 But suddenly, Babylon will fall
and be destroyed.

I, the LORD, told the foreigners[u]
who lived there,
"Weep for the city!
Get medicine for its wounds;
maybe they will heal."

9 The foreigners answered,
"We have already tried
to treat Babylon's wounds,
but they would not heal.
Come on, let's all go home
to our own countries.
Nothing is left in Babylonia;
everything is destroyed."

10 The people of Israel said,
"Tell everyone in Zion!
The LORD has taken revenge
for what Babylon did to us."

The LORD Wants Babylon Destroyed

11 I, the LORD,
want Babylon destroyed,
because its army
destroyed my temple.
So, you kings of Media,[v]
sharpen your arrows
and pick up your shields.
12 Raise the signal flag
and attack the city walls.
Post more guards.
Have soldiers watch the city
and set up ambushes.
I have made plans
to destroy Babylon,
and nothing will stop me.

13 People of Babylon, you live
along the Euphrates River
and are surrounded by canals.
You are rich,
but now the time has come
for you to die.[w]
14 I, the LORD All-Powerful,
swear by my own life
that enemy soldiers
will fill your streets
like a swarm of locusts.[x]

[r]**51.1** *wind*: Or "spirit." [s]**51.1** *Babylonia*: The Hebrew text has "Leb-Qamai," a secret way of writing "Babylonia." [t]**51.3** *I will tell . . . armor*: Or "Attack quickly! String your bows and put on your armor." [u]**51.8** *the foreigners*: Or "my people." [v]**51.11** *kings of Media*: Probably kings of smaller kingdoms that were part of the Median Empire (see also verse 27 and the note there). [w]**51.13** *for you to die*: One possible meaning for the difficult Hebrew text. [x]**51.14** *locusts*: See the note at 46.22.

51.7 Rev 17.2-4; 18.3. **51.13** Rev 17.1.

They will shout
and celebrate their victory.

A Hymn of Praise
(Jeremiah 10.12-16)

15 God used his wisdom and power
to create the earth
and spread out the heavens.
16 The waters in the heavens roar
at his command.
He makes clouds appear;
he sends the wind
from his storehouse
and makes lightning flash
in the rain.

17 People who make idols
are stupid!
They will be disappointed,
because their false gods
cannot breathe.
18 Idols are merely a joke,
and when the time is right,
they will be destroyed.
19 But the LORD, Israel's God,
is all-powerful.
He created everything,
and he chose Israel
to be his very own.

God's Hammer

The LORD said:
20 Babylonia, you were my hammer;
I used you to pound nations
and break kingdoms,
21 to shatter cavalry and chariots,
22 as well as men and women,
young and old,
23 shepherds and their flocks,
farmers and their oxen,
and governors and leaders.

24 But now, my people will watch,
while I repay you
for what you did to Zion.

25 You destroyed the nations
and seem strong as a mountain,
but I am your enemy.
I might even grab you
and roll you off a cliff.
When I am finished,
you'll only be a pile
of scorched bricks.
26 Your stone blocks won't be reused
for cornerstones
or foundations,
and I promise that forever
you will be a desert.
I, the LORD, have spoken.

The Nations Will Attack Babylon

The LORD said:
27 Signal the nations
to get ready to attack.
Raise a flag and blow a trumpet.
Send for the armies of Ararat,
Minni, and Ashkenaz.[y]
Choose a commander;
let the cavalry attack
like a swarm of locusts.
28 Tell the kings and governors,
the leaders and the people
of the kingdoms of the Medes
to prepare for war!

29 The earth twists and turns
in torment,
because I have decided
to make Babylonia a desert
where no one can live,
and I won't change my mind.

30 The Babylonian soldiers
have lost their strength
and courage.[z]
They stay in their fortresses,
unable to fight,
while the enemy breaks through
the city gates,
then sets their homes on fire.
31 One messenger after another
announces to the king,
"Babylon has been captured!
32 The enemy now controls
the river crossings!

[y]**51.27** *Ararat, Minni, and Ashkenaz*: Kingdoms to the north of Babylonia that were part of the Median Empire (see also verse 28). [z]**51.30** *have lost their strength and courage*: Hebrew "have lost their strength and have become like women."

Daniel in a pit of lions *Daniel 6.1-23*

The story of Jonah *Jonah 1 – 4*

The marshes[a] are on fire!
Your army has panicked!"

33 I am the LORD All-Powerful,
the God of Israel,
and I make this promise—
"Soon Babylon will be leveled
and packed down
like a threshing place
at harvest time."[b]

Babylonia Will Pay!

34 The people of Jerusalem say,
"King Nebuchadnezzar[c]
made us panic.
That monster stuffed himself
with us and our treasures,
leaving us empty—
he gobbled down
what he wanted
and spit out the rest.
35 The people of Babylonia
harmed some of us[d]
and killed others.
Now, LORD, make them pay!"

The LORD Will Take Revenge on Babylon

36 My people, I am on your side,
and I will take revenge
on Babylon.
I will cut off its water supply,
and its stream[e] will dry up.
37 Babylon will be a pile of rubble
where only jackals[f] live.
People will laugh,
but they will be afraid
to walk among the ruins.
38 The Babylonians roar and growl
like young lions.
39 And since they are hungry,
I will give them a banquet.
They will celebrate, get drunk,
then fall asleep,
never to wake up!
40 I will lead them away to die,
like sheep, lambs, and goats
being led to the butcher.
41 All nations now praise Babylon,[g]
but when it is captured,
those same nations
will be horrified.
42 Babylon's enemies will rise
like ocean waves
and flood the city.
43 Horrible destruction will strike
the nearby towns.
The land will become
a barren desert,
where no one can live
or even travel.
44 I will punish Marduk,[h]
the god of Babylon,
and make him vomit up
everything he gobbled down.
Then nations will no longer
bring him gifts,
and Babylon's walls will crumble.

The LORD Offers Hope to His People

45 Get out of Babylon, my people,
and run for your lives,
before I strike the city
in my anger!
46 Don't be afraid or lose hope,
though year after year
there are rumors
of leaders fighting for control
in the city of Babylon.
47 The time will come
when I will punish
Babylon's false gods.
Everyone there will die,
and the whole nation
will be disgraced,
48 when an army attacks
from the north
and brings destruction.
Then the earth and the heavens

[a]**51.32** *marshes*: The tall grass in the marshes could have provided hiding places for people trying to escape from Babylon. [b]**51.33** *leveled . . . harvest time*: A threshing place with a dirt surface had to be leveled and packed down before it could be used. [c]**51.34** *Nebuchadnezzar*: See the note at 21.2. [d]**51.35** *harmed some of us*: One possible meaning for the difficult Hebrew text.
[e]**51.36** *stream*: Probably the Euphrates River. [f]**51.37** *jackals*: See the note at 9.11.
[g]**51.41** *Babylon*: The Hebrew text has "Sheshach," a secret way of writing the name "Babylon."
[h]**51.44** *Marduk*: Hebrew "Bel" (see the note at 50.2).
51.48 Rev 18.20.

and everything in them
will celebrate.
49 Babylon must be overthrown,
because it slaughtered
the people of Israel
and of many other nations.

50 My people, you escaped death
when Jerusalem fell.
Now you live far from home,
but you should trust me
and think about Jerusalem.
Leave Babylon! Don't stay!

51 You feel ashamed and disgraced,
because foreigners have entered
my sacred temple.
52 Soon I will send a war
to punish Babylon's idols
and leave its wounded people
moaning everywhere.
53 Although Babylon's walls
reach to the sky,
the army I send
will destroy that city.
I, the LORD, have spoken.

Babylon Will Be Destroyed

The LORD said:
54 Listen to the cries for help
coming from Babylon.
Everywhere in the country
the sounds of destruction
can be heard.
55 The shouts of the enemy,
like crashing ocean waves,
will drown out Babylon's cries
as I level the city.

56 An enemy will attack
and destroy Babylon.
Its soldiers will be captured
and their weapons broken,
because I am a God
who takes revenge against nations
for what they do.
57 I, the LORD All-Powerful,
the true King, promise
that the officials and advisors,
the governors and leaders
and the soldiers of Babylon
will get drunk, fall asleep,
and never wake up.
58 The thick walls of that city
will be torn down,
and its huge gates burned.
Everything that nation
worked so hard to gain
will go up in smoke.

Jeremiah Gives Seraiah a Scroll

59 During Zedekiah's[i] fourth year as
king of Judah, he went to Babylon. And
Baruch's brother Seraiah[j] went along as
the officer in charge of arranging for places
to stay overnight.[k]
60 Before they left, I wrote on a scroll[l] all
the terrible things that would happen to
Babylon. 61 I gave the scroll to Seraiah and
said:

When you get to Babylon, read this
scroll aloud, 62 then pray, "Our LORD,
you promised to destroy this place and
make it into a desert where no people
or animals will ever live."
63 When you finish praying, tie the
scroll to a rock and throw it in the Euphrates River. Then say, 64 "This is
how Babylon will sink when the LORD
destroys it. Everyone in the city will
die, and it won't have the strength to
rise again."

The End of Jeremiah's Writing

Jeremiah's writing ends here.

Jerusalem Is Captured

(2 *Kings 24.18—25.30;*
2 *Chronicles 36.11-21)*

52 Zedekiah was twenty-one years old
when he was appointed king of Judah,[m] and he ruled from Jerusalem for

[i]**51.59** *Zedekiah's*: See the note at 1.3. [j]**51.59** *Baruch's brother Seraiah*: Hebrew "Seraiah son of Neriah and grandson of Mahseiah"; Baruch helped Jeremiah write down his messages (see 32.12; 36.4-10). [k]**51.59** *arranging for places to stay overnight*: Hebrew and one ancient translation; two ancient translations, "the tax money." [l]**51.60** *scroll*: See the note at 30.1, 2.
[m]**52.1** *appointed king of Judah*: By Nebuchadnezzar (see 37.1).
51.49 Rev 18.24. **51.63,64** Rev 18.21.

eleven years.[n] His mother Hamutal was the daughter of Jeremiah from the town of Libnah.[o] 2 Zedekiah disobeyed the LORD, just as Jehoiakim had done, 3 and it was Zedekiah who finally rebelled against Nebuchadnezzar.[p]

The people of Judah and Jerusalem had made the LORD so angry that he finally turned his back on them. That's why horrible things were happening.

4 In Zedekiah's ninth year as king, on the tenth day of the tenth month,[q] King Nebuchadnezzar of Babylonia led his entire army to attack Jerusalem. The troops set up camp outside the city and built ramps up to the city walls.

5-6 After a year and a half,[r] all the food in Jerusalem was gone. Then on the ninth day of the fourth month,[s] 7 the Babylonian troops broke through the city wall. That same night, Zedekiah and his soldiers tried to escape through the gate near the royal garden, even though they knew the enemy had the city surrounded. They headed toward the Jordan River valley, 8 but the Babylonian troops caught up with them near Jericho. The Babylonians arrested Zedekiah, but his soldiers scattered in every direction. 9 Zedekiah was taken to Riblah in the land of Hamath, where Nebuchadnezzar put him on trial and found him guilty. 10 Zedekiah's sons and the officials of Judah were killed while he watched, 11 then his eyes were poked out. He was put in chains, then dragged off to Babylon and kept in prison until he died.

12 Jerusalem was captured during Nebuchadnezzar's nineteenth year as king of Babylonia.

About a month later,[t] Nebuchadnezzar's officer in charge of the guards arrived in Jerusalem. His name was Nebuzaradan, 13 and he burned down the LORD's temple, the king's palace, and every important building in the city, as well as all the houses. 14 Then he ordered the Babylonian soldiers to break down the walls around Jerusalem. 15 He led away the people left in the city, including everyone who had become loyal to Nebuchadnezzar, the rest of the skilled workers,[u] and even some of the poor people of Judah. 16 Only the very poorest were left behind to work the vineyards and the fields.

17-20 Nebuzaradan ordered his soldiers to go to the temple and take everything made of gold or silver, including bowls, fire pans, sprinkling bowls, pans, lampstands, dishes for incense, and the cups for wine offerings. The Babylonian soldiers took all the bronze things used for worship at the temple, including the pans for hot ashes, and the shovels, lamp snuffers, sprinkling bowls, and dishes for incense. The soldiers also took everything else made of bronze, including the two columns that stood in front of the temple, the large bowl called the Sea, the twelve bulls that held it up, and the movable stands.[v] The soldiers broke these things into pieces so they could take them to Babylonia. There was so much bronze that it could not be weighed. 21 For example, the columns were about twenty-seven feet high and eighteen feet around. They were hollow, but the bronze was about three inches thick. 22 Each column had a bronze cap over seven feet high that was decorated with bronze designs. Some of these designs were like chains and others were like pomegranates.[w] 23 There were ninety-six pomegranates evenly spaced[x] around each column, and a total of

[n]**52.1** *he ruled . . . years*: Ruled 598-586 B.C. [o]**52.1** *Jeremiah from the town of Libnah*: Not the same Jeremiah as the author of this book (see 1.1). [p]**52.3** *Nebuchadnezzar*: See the note at 21.2. [q]**52.4** *tenth month*: See the note at 39.1-3. [r]**52.5,6** *After a year and a half*: Jerusalem was captured in 586 B.C. [s]**52.5,6** *fourth month*: See the note at 39.1-3. [t]**52.12** *About a month later*: Hebrew "On the seventh day of the fifth month." [u]**52.15** *the rest of the skilled workers*: Nebuchadnezzar had taken away some of the skilled workers eleven years before (see 2 Kings 24.14-16). [v]**52.17-20** *the large bowl called the Sea, the twelve bulls that held it up, and the movable stands*: One ancient translation; Hebrew "the large bowl called the Sea, and the twelve bulls under the movable stands." [w]**52.22** *pomegranates*: A small red fruit that looks like an apple. [x]**52.23** *evenly spaced*: One possible meaning for the difficult Hebrew text.

52.4 Ez 24.2. **52.7** Ez 33.21. **52.11** Ez 12.13. **52.13** 1 K 9.8. **52.17-23** 1 K 7.15-47.

one hundred pomegranates were located above the chains.

24 Next, Nebuzaradan arrested Seraiah the chief priest, Zephaniah his assistant, and three temple officials. 25 Then he arrested one of the army commanders, seven of King Zedekiah's personal advisors, and the officer in charge of gathering the troops for battle. He also found sixty more soldiers who were still in Jerusalem. 26-27 Nebuzaradan led them to Riblah in the land of Hamath, where Nebuchadnezzar had them killed.

The people of Judah no longer lived in their own country.

People of Judah Taken Prisoner

28-30 Here is a list of the number of the people of Judah that Nebuchadnezzar[y] took to Babylonia as prisoners:

In his seventh year as king, he took
3,023 people.
In his eighteenth year as king, he took
832 from Jerusalem.
In his twenty-third year as king, his
officer Nebuzaradan took 745 people.

So, Nebuchadnezzar took a total of 4,600 people from Judah to Babylonia.

Jehoiachin Is Set Free
(2 *Kings* 25.27-30)

31 Jehoiachin was a prisoner in Babylon for thirty-seven years. Then Evil Merodach[z] became king of Babylonia, and in the first year of his rule, on the twenty-fifth day of the twelfth month,[a] he let Jehoiachin out of prison. 32 Evil Merodach was kind to Jehoiachin and honored him more than any of the other kings held prisoner there. 33 Jehoiachin was allowed to wear regular clothes instead of a prison uniform, and he even ate at the king's table every day. 34 As long as Jehoiachin lived, he was paid a daily allowance to buy whatever he needed.

[y]**52.28-30** *Nebuchadnezzar*: See the note at 21.2. [z]**52.31** *Evil Merodach*: The son of Nebuchadnezzar who ruled Babylonia from 562-560 B.C. [a]**52.31** *twelfth month*: Adar, the twelfth month of the Hebrew calendar, from about mid-February to mid-March.

LAMENTATIONS

ABOUT THIS BOOK

This book is a collection of five poems expressing deep sorrow about the destruction of Jerusalem. The poems, sometimes called laments, are presented as being spoken by the city of Jerusalem and by the writer, who is called "the prophet" in the CEV.

The prophet realized that Jerusalem was being punished because its people had sinned, but the suffering seemed greater than what their sins deserved. Still, there was hope. Someday, God would be merciful again if the people would give up their sins and turn back to him.

"Then I remember something
that fills me with hope.
The LORD's kindness never fails!
If he had not been merciful,
we would have been destroyed.
The LORD can always be trusted
to show mercy each morning.
Deep in my heart I say,
'The LORD is all I need;
I can depend on him!'"

(3.21-24)

A QUICK LOOK AT THIS BOOK

- First Lament: Lonely Jerusalem (1)
- Second Lament: The Lord Was Like an Enemy (2)
- Third Lament: There Is Still Hope (3)
- Fourth Lament: The Punishment of Jerusalem (4)
- Fifth Lament: A Prayer for Mercy (5)

Lonely Jerusalem

The Prophet Speaks:

1 Jerusalem, once so crowded,
lies deserted and lonely.
This city that was known
all over the world
is now like a widow.
This queen of the nations
has been made a slave.

2 Each night, bitter tears
flood her cheeks.
None of her former lovers
are there to offer comfort;
her friends[a] have betrayed her
and are now her enemies.

3 The people of Judah are slaves,
suffering in a foreign land,
with no rest from sorrow.
Their enemies captured them
and were terribly cruel.[b]

[a]**1.2** *lovers . . . friends*: Israel's former allies. [b]**1.3** *Their . . . cruel*: One possible meaning for the difficult Hebrew text.
1.1 Ba 4.12.

4 The roads to Zion mourn
because no one travels there
to celebrate the festivals.
The city gates are deserted;
priests are weeping.
Young women are raped;[c]
Zion is in sorrow!
5 Enemies now rule the city
and live as they please.
The LORD has punished Jerusalem
because of her awful sins;
he has let her people
be dragged away.

6 Zion's glory has disappeared.
Her leaders are like deer
that cannot find pasture;
they are hunted down
till their strength is gone.
7 Her people recall the good life
that once was theirs;
now they suffer
and are scattered.
No one was there to protect them
from their enemies who sneered
when their city was taken.

8 Jerusalem's horrible sins
have made the city a joke.
Those who once admired her
now hate her instead—
she has been disgraced;
she groans and turns away.

9 Her sins had made her filthy,
but she wasn't worried
about what could happen.
And when Jerusalem fell,
it was so tragic.
No one gave her comfort
when she cried out,
"Help! I'm in trouble, LORD!
The enemy has won."

10 Zion's treasures were stolen.
Jerusalem saw foreigners
enter her place of worship,
though the LORD
had forbidden them
to belong to his people.[d]
11 Everyone in the city groans
while searching for food;
they trade their valuables
for barely enough scraps
to stay alive.

Jerusalem Speaks:
Jerusalem shouts to the LORD,
"Please look and see
how miserable I am!"
12 No passerby even cares.[e]
Why doesn't someone notice
my terrible sufferings?
You were fiercely angry, LORD,
and you punished me
worst of all.
13 From heaven you sent a fire
that burned in my bones;
you set a trap for my feet
and made me turn back.
All day long you leave me
in shock from constant pain.
14 You have tied my sins
around my neck,[f]
and they weigh so heavily
that my strength is gone.
You have put me in the power
of enemies too strong for me.

15 You, LORD, have turned back
my warriors and crushed
my young heroes.
Judah was a woman untouched,
but you let her be trampled
like grapes in a wine pit.
16 Because of this, I mourn,
and tears flood my eyes.
No one is here to comfort
or to encourage me;
we have lost the war—
my people are suffering.

The Prophet Speaks:
17 Zion reaches out her hands,
but no one offers comfort.
The LORD has turned

[c] **1.4** *raped*: One possible meaning for the difficult Hebrew text. [d] **1.10** *to . . . people*: Or "to enter his temple." [e] **1.12** *No . . . cares*: One possible meaning for the difficult Hebrew text. [f] **1.14** *You . . . neck*: One possible meaning for the difficult Hebrew text.

the neighboring nations
against Jacob's descendants.
Jerusalem is merely a filthy rag
to her neighbors.

Jerusalem Speaks:
18 The LORD was right,
but I refused to obey him.
Now I ask all of you to look
at my sufferings—
even my young people
have been dragged away.
19 I called out to my lovers,
but they betrayed me.
My priests and my leaders died
while searching the city
for scraps of food.

20 Won't you look and see
how upset I am, our LORD?
My stomach is in knots,
and my heart is broken
because I betrayed you.
In the streets and at home,
my people are slaughtered.

21 Everyone heard my groaning,
but no one offered comfort.
My enemies know of the trouble
that you have brought on me,
and it makes them glad.
Hurry and punish them,
as you have promised.
22 Don't let their evil deeds
escape your sight.
Punish them as much
as you have punished me
because of my sins.
I never stop groaning—
I've lost all hope!

The LORD Was Like an Enemy

The Prophet Speaks:
2 The Lord was angry!
So he disgraced[g] Zion
though it was Israel's pride
and his own place of rest.
In his anger he threw Zion down
from heaven to earth.
2 The LORD had no mercy!
He destroyed the homes
of Jacob's descendants.
In his anger he tore down
every walled city in Judah;
he toppled the nation
together with its leaders,
leaving them in shame.

3 The Lord was so furiously angry
that he wiped out
the whole army[h] of Israel
by not supporting them
when the enemy attacked.
He was like a raging fire
that swallowed up
the descendants of Jacob.
4 He attacked like an enemy
with a bow and arrows,
killing our loved ones.
He has burned to the ground
the homes on Mount Zion.[i]

5 The Lord was like an enemy!
He left Israel in ruins
with its palaces
and fortresses destroyed,
and with everyone in Judah
moaning and weeping.
6 He shattered his temple
like a hut in a garden;[j]
he completely wiped out
his meeting place,
and did away with festivals
and Sabbaths
in the city of Zion.
In his fierce anger he rejected
our king and priests.

7 The Lord abandoned his altar
and his temple;
he let Zion's enemies
capture her fortresses.
Noisy shouts were heard
from the temple,
as if it were a time
of celebration.

[g] **2.1** *disgraced*: One possible meaning for the difficult Hebrew text. [h] **2.3** *army*: The Hebrew text has "horn," which refers to the horn of a bull, one of the most powerful animals in ancient Palestine. [i] **2.4** *the homes on Mount Zion*: Or "the temple on Mount Zion." [j] **2.6** *He . . . garden*: Or "He shattered the temple walls, as if they were the walls of a garden."

8 The LORD had decided
to tear down the walls of Zion
stone by stone.
So he started destroying
and did not stop
until walls and fortresses
mourned and trembled.
9 Zion's gates have fallen
facedown on the ground;
the bars that locked the gates
are smashed to pieces.
Her king and royal family
are prisoners
in foreign lands.
Her priests don't teach,
and her prophets don't have
a message from the LORD.

10 Zion's leaders are silent.
They just sit on the ground,
tossing dirt on their heads
and wearing sackcloth.
Her young women can do nothing
but stare at the ground.

11 My eyes are red from crying,
my stomach is in knots,
and I feel sick all over.
My people are being wiped out,
and children lie helpless
in the streets of the city.
12 A child begs its mother
for food and drink,
then blacks out
like a wounded soldier
lying in the street.
The child slowly dies
in its mother's arms.

13 Zion, how can I comfort you?
How great is your pain?[k]
Lovely city of Jerusalem,
how can I heal your wounds,
gaping as wide as the sea?
14 Your prophets deceived you
with false visions
and lying messages—
they should have warned you
to leave your sins
and be saved from disaster.
15 Those who pass by
shake their heads and sneer
as they make fun and shout,
"What a lovely city you were,
the happiest on earth,
but look at you now!"

16 Zion, your enemies curse you
and snarl like wild animals,
while shouting,
"This is the day
we've waited for!
At last, we've got you!"

17 The LORD has done everything
that he had planned
and threatened long ago.
He destroyed you without mercy
and let your enemies boast about
their powerful forces.[l]

18 Zion, deep in your heart
you cried out to the Lord.
Now let your tears overflow
your walls day and night.
Don't ever lose hope
or let your tears stop.
19 Get up and pray for help
all through the night.
Pour out your feelings
to the Lord,
as you would pour water
out of a jug.
Beg him to save your people,
who are starving to death
at every street crossing.

Jerusalem Speaks:
20 Think about it, LORD!
Have you ever been this cruel
to anyone before?
Is it right for mothers
to eat their children,
or for priests and prophets
to be killed in your temple?
21 My people, both young and old,
lie dead in the streets.

[k]**2.13** *How great . . . pain*: Or "What are you really like?" or "What can I say about you?"
[l]**2.17** *powerful forces*: The Hebrew text has "horn," which refers to the horn of a bull, one of the most powerful animals in ancient Palestine.

Because you were angry,
my young men and women
were brutally slaughtered.
22 When you were angry, LORD,
you invited my enemies
like guests for a party.
No one survived that day;
enemies killed my children,
my own little ones.

There Is Still Hope

The Prophet Speaks:

3 I have suffered much
because God was angry.
2 He chased me into a dark place,
where no light could enter.
3 I am the only one he punishes
over and over again,
without ever stopping.
4 God caused my skin and flesh
to waste away,
and he crushed my bones.
5 He attacked and surrounded me
with hardships and trouble;
6 he forced me to sit in the dark
like someone long dead.

7 God built a fence around me
that I cannot climb over,
and he chained me down.
8 Even when I shouted
and prayed for help,
he refused to listen.
9 God put big rocks in my way
and made me follow
a crooked path.
10 God was like a bear or a lion
waiting in ambush for me;
11 he dragged me from the road,
then tore me to shreds.[m]
12 God took careful aim
and shot his arrows
13 straight through my heart.

14 I am a joke to everyone—
no one ever stops
making fun of me.
15 God has turned my life sour.
16 He made me eat gravel
and rubbed me in the dirt.
17 I cannot find peace
or remember happiness.

18 I tell myself, "I am finished!
I can't count on the LORD
to do anything for me."
19 Just thinking of my troubles
and my lonely wandering
makes me miserable.
20 That's all I ever think about,
and I am depressed.[n]
21 Then I remember something
that fills me with hope.
22 The LORD's kindness never fails!
If he had not been merciful,
we would have been destroyed.[o]
23 The LORD can always be trusted
to show mercy each morning.
24 Deep in my heart I say,
"The LORD is all I need;
I can depend on him!"

25 The LORD is kind to everyone
who trusts and obeys him.
26 It is good to wait patiently
for the LORD to save us.
27 When we are young,
it is good to struggle hard
28 and to sit silently alone,
if this is what
the LORD intends.
29 Being rubbed in the dirt
can teach us a lesson;[p]
30 we can also learn from insults
and hard knocks.

31 The Lord won't always reject us!
32 He causes a lot of suffering,
but he also has pity
because of his great love.
33 The Lord doesn't enjoy
sending grief or pain.

34 Don't trample prisoners
under your feet

[m]**3.11** *shreds*: One possible meaning for the difficult Hebrew text of verse 11. [n]**3.20** *I am depressed*: One possible meaning for the difficult Hebrew text. [o]**3.22** *destroyed*: One possible meaning for the difficult Hebrew text of verse 22. [p]**3.29** *lesson*: One possible meaning for the difficult Hebrew text of verse 29.

35 or cheat anyone out of
what is rightfully theirs.
God Most High sees everything,
36 and he knows when you refuse
to give someone a fair trial.
37 No one can do anything
without the Lord's approval.
38 Good and bad each happen
at the command
of God Most High.
39 We're still alive!
We shouldn't complain
when we are being punished
for our sins.
40 Instead, we should think
about the way we are living,
and turn back to the LORD.

41 When we lift our hands
in prayer to God in heaven,
we should offer him our hearts
and say, 42 "We've sinned!
We've rebelled against you,
and you haven't forgiven us!
43 Anger is written all over you,
as you pursue and slaughter us
without showing pity.
44 You are behind a wall of clouds
that blocks out our prayers.
45 You allowed nations
to treat us like garbage;
46 our enemies curse us.
47 We are terrified and trapped,
caught and crushed."

48 My people are destroyed!
Tears flood my eyes,
49 and they won't stop
50 until the LORD looks down
from heaven and helps.
51 I am horrified when I see
what enemies have done
to the young women of our city.

52 No one had reason to hate me,
but I was hunted down
like a bird.
53 Then they tried to kill me
by tossing me into a pit
and throwing stones at me.
54 Water covered my head—
I thought I was gone.

55 From the bottom of the pit,
I prayed to you, LORD.
56 I begged you to listen.
"Help!" I shouted. "Save me!"
You answered my prayer
57 and came when I was in need.
You told me, "Don't worry!"
58 You rescued me
and saved my life.
59 You saw them abuse me, LORD,
so make things right.
60 You know every plot
they have made against me.
61 Yes, you know their insults
and their evil plans.
62 All day long they attack
with words and whispers.
63 No matter what they are doing,
they keep on mocking me.

64 Pay them back for everything
they have done, LORD!
65 Put your curse on them
and make them suffer.[q]
66 Get angry and go after them
until not a trace is left
under the heavens.

The Punishment of Jerusalem

The Prophet Speaks:

4 The purest gold is ruined
and has lost its shine;
jewels from the temple
lie scattered in the streets.
2 These are Zion's people,
worth more than purest gold;
yet they are counted worthless
like dishes of clay.

3 Even jackals[r] nurse their young,
but my people are like ostriches
that abandon their own.

[q]**3.65** *make them suffer*: One possible meaning for the difficult Hebrew text. [r]**4.3** *jackals*: Desert animals related to wolves, but smaller.

4 Babies are so thirsty
that their tongues are stuck
to the roof of the mouth.
Children go begging for food,
but no one gives them any.
5 All who ate expensive foods
lie starving in the streets;
those who grew up in luxury
now sit on trash heaps.

6 My nation was punished worse
than the people of Sodom,
whose city was destroyed
in a flash without the help
of human hands.[s]
7 The leaders of Jerusalem
were purer than snow
and whiter than milk;
their bodies were healthy
and glowed like jewels.[t]
8 Now they are blacker than tar,
and no one recognizes them;
their skin clings to their bones
and is drier than firewood.
9 Being killed with a sword
is better than slowly
starving to death.
10 Life in the city is so bad
that loving mothers have boiled
and eaten their own children.

11 The LORD was so fiercely angry
that he burned the city of Zion
to the ground.
12 Not a king on this earth
or the people of any nation
believed enemies could break
through her gates.

13 Jerusalem was punished because
her prophets and her priests
had sinned and caused the death
of innocent victims.
14 Yes, her prophets and priests
were covered with blood;
no one would come near them,
as they wandered
from street to street.
15 Instead, everyone shouted,
"Go away! Don't touch us!
You're filthy and unfit
to belong to God's people!"

So they had to leave
and become refugees.
But foreign nations told them,
"You can't stay here!"[u]
16 The LORD is the one
who sent them scattering,
and he has forgotten them.
No respect or kindness
will be shown
to the priests or leaders.
17 Our eyes became weary,
hopelessly looking
for help from a nation[v]
that could not save us.
18 Enemies hunted us down
on every public street.
Our time was up;
our doom was near.
19 They swooped down faster
than eagles from the sky.
They hunted for us in the hills
and set traps to catch us
out in the desert.
20 The LORD's chosen leader[w]
was our hope for survival!
We thought he would keep us safe
somewhere among the nations,
but even he was caught
in one of their traps.

21 You people of Edom
can celebrate now!
But your time will come
to suffer and stagger
around naked.
22 The people of Zion
have paid for their sins,
and the Lord will soon
let them return home.
But, people of Edom,

[s] **4.6** *hands*: One possible meaning for the difficult Hebrew text of verse 6. [t] **4.7** *jewels*: One possible meaning for the difficult Hebrew text of verse 7. [u] **4.15** *here*: One possible meaning for the difficult Hebrew text of verse 15. [v] **4.17** *nation*: Egypt, a former ally of Judah. [w] **4.20** *chosen leader*: Probably Zedekiah, the last king of Judah, taken away to Babylonia in 586 B.C.
4.6 Gn 19.24. **4.10** Dt 28.56, 57; Ez 5.10.

you will be punished,
and your sins exposed.

A Prayer for Mercy

The People of Jerusalem Pray:[x]

5 Our LORD, don't forget
how we have suffered
and been disgraced.
2 Foreigners and strangers
have taken our land
and our homes.
3 We are like children
whose mothers are widows.
4 The water we drink
and the wood we burn
cost far too much.
5 We are terribly mistreated;[y]
we are worn out
and can find no rest.
6 We had to surrender
to[z] Egypt and Assyria
because we were hungry.

7 Our ancestors sinned,
but they are dead,
and we are left to pay
for their sins.
8 Slaves are now our rulers,
and there is no one
to set us free.
9 We are in danger
from brutal desert tribes;
we must risk our lives
just to bring in our crops.[a]
10 Our skin is scorched
from fever and hunger.
11 On Zion and everywhere in Judah
our wives and daughters
are being raped.
12 Our rulers are strung up
by their arms,
and our nation's advisors
are treated shamefully.
13 Young men are forced
to do the work of slaves;
boys must carry
heavy loads of wood.
14 Our leaders are not allowed
to decide cases in court,
and young people
no longer play music.

15 Our hearts are sad;
instead of dancing,
we mourn.
16 Zion's glory has disappeared!
And we are doomed
because of our sins.
17 We feel sick all over
and can't even see straight;
18 our city is in ruins,
overrun by wild dogs.

19 You will rule forever, LORD!
You are King for all time.
20 Why have you forgotten us
for so long?
21 Bring us back to you!
Give us a fresh start.
22 Or do you despise us so much
that you don't want us?

[x]**5.1** *The People of Jerusalem Pray*: Or "The Prophet Prays." [y]**5.5** *We . . . mistreated*: One possible meaning for the difficult Hebrew text. [z]**5.6** *surrender to*: Or "make treaties with." [a]**5.9** *crops*: One possible meaning for the difficult Hebrew text of verse 9.

EZEKIEL

ABOUT THIS BOOK

Ezekiel was a priest and a prophet. He had been taken away as a prisoner to Babylonia, where he lived among the other exiles from Judah. The Lord chose Ezekiel to be his prophet and to preach his message, not only to the exiles in Babylonia, but also to the people still living in Jerusalem. Ezekiel's ministry probably began around 593 B.C., during the last years of the kingdom of Judah, and it ended sometime around 570 B.C., several years after the fall of Jerusalem (586 B.C.). Ezekiel preached before and after this horrible disaster, and so some of his messages threatened judgment and others offered hope.

The book of Ezekiel can be divided into five main parts. The first part (1–3) describes Ezekiel's vision of the Lord's glory and tells how the Lord appointed Ezekiel to be his prophet. The second part (4–24) includes several messages warning the people of Judah that they will soon be punished for turning away from the Lord. Ezekiel acted out many of these warnings. And the third part of the book (25–32) includes the Lord's judgments on nearby nations.

The fourth part of the book (33–39) is made up of Ezekiel's messages after he heard that Jerusalem had been captured. These are messages of hope. The Lord promises he will forgive his people and bring them back to Judah and Jerusalem. Finally, the fifth part of the book (40–48) is Ezekiel's vision of the new temple in Jerusalem, its regulations for proper worship, and how the restored land of Israel will be divided among the tribes.

When the Lord speaks to Ezekiel, he calls him "son of man." Although this expression shows that Ezekiel is a mere human, it also shows that he has been appointed to preach the Lord's message to the people of Judah and Jerusalem.

One of the most familiar passages in the book is Ezekiel's vision of the valley full of dried-out bones. Ezekiel watches the Lord's Spirit blow life into the dead bodies, and he sees them come back to life. The Lord then tells Ezekiel:

> *"The people of Israel are like dead bones. They complain that they are dried up and that they have no hope for the future. So tell them, 'I, the LORD God, promise to open your graves and set you free. I will bring you back to Israel. . . . My Spirit will give you breath, and you will live again.' "*
>
> *(37.11, 12, 14a)*

A QUICK LOOK AT THIS BOOK

- Ezekiel Sees the Lord's Glory and
  Is Chosen To Be His Prophet (1.1—3.27)
- Ezekiel Acts Out
  the Coming Destruction of Judah and Jerusalem (4.1—5.17)
- Disaster Is Near (6.1—7.27)
- The Lord's Glory Leaves Sinful Jerusalem (8.1—11.25)
- Messages of Doom for Judah and Jerusalem (12.1—24.27)
- Judgment on Foreign Nations (25.1—32.32)
- Ezekiel Must Warn the People
  To Turn from Their Sinful Ways (33.1-20)

- The News of Jerusalem's Fall (33.21, 22)
- The Lord Promises To Bring the People Home and To Restore Judah (34.1—37.28)
- Gog Will Be Defeated and Israel Will Be Restored (38.1—39.29)
- Ezekiel Sees the Future Temple in Jerusalem (40.1—46.24)
- The Stream Flowing from the Temple (47.1-12)
- The Borders of the Restored Land and Its Division Among the Tribes (47.13—48.35)

Ezekiel Sees the LORD's Glory

1 1-3 I am Ezekiel—a priest and the son of Buzi.[a]

Five years after King Jehoiachin of Judah had been led away as a prisoner to Babylonia, I was living near the Chebar River among those who had been taken there with him. Then on the fifth day of the fourth month[b] of the thirtieth year,[c] the heavens suddenly opened. The LORD placed his hand upon me[d] and showed me some visions.

4 I saw a windstorm blowing in from the north. Lightning flashed from a huge cloud and lit up the whole sky with a dazzling brightness. The fiery center of the cloud was as shiny as polished metal, 5 and in that center I saw what looked like four living creatures. They were somewhat like humans, 6 except that each one had four faces and four wings. 7 Their legs were straight, but their feet looked like the hoofs of calves and sparkled like bronze. 8 Under each of their wings, these creatures had a human hand. 9 The four creatures were standing back to back with the tips of their wings touching. They moved together in every direction, without turning their bodies.

10 Each creature had the face of a human in front, the face of a lion on the right side, the face of a bull on the left, and the face of an eagle in back. 11 Two wings[e] of each creature were spread out and touched the wings of the creatures on either side. The other two wings of each creature were folded against its body.

12 Wherever the four living creatures went, they moved together without turning their bodies, because each creature faced straight ahead. 13 The creatures were glowing like hot coals, and I saw something like a flaming torch moving back and forth among them. Lightning flashed from the torch every time its flame blazed up.[f] 14 The creatures themselves moved as quickly as sparks jumping from a fire.[g]

15 I then noticed that on the ground beside each of the four living creatures was a wheel,[h] 16 shining like chrysolite.[i] Each wheel was exactly the same and had a second wheel that cut through the middle of it,[j] 17 so that they could move in any direction without turning. 18 The rims of the wheels were large and had eyes all the way around them.[k] 19-21 The creatures controlled when and where the wheels moved—the wheels went wherever the four creatures went and stopped whenever they stopped. Even when the creatures flew in the air, the wheels were beside them.

22-23 Above the living creatures, I saw something that was sparkling like ice, and

[a] **1.1-3** *a priest and the son of Buzi*: Or "the son of Buzi the priest." [b] **1.1-3** *Five years . . . prisoner . . . fourth month*: Probably July of 593 B.C. [c] **1.1-3** *thirtieth year*: The event from which this date is figured is unknown. [d] **1.1-3** *The LORD placed his hand upon me*: This was a sign that the LORD had chosen Ezekiel to be his prophet. [e] **1.11** *Two wings*: One possible meaning for the difficult Hebrew text. [f] **1.13** *up*: One possible meaning for the difficult Hebrew text of verse 13. [g] **1.14** *as sparks jumping from a fire*: Or "as flashes of lightning." [h] **1.15** *wheel*: One possible meaning for the difficult Hebrew text of verse 15. [i] **1.16** *chrysolite*: A precious stone that has an olive green color. [j] **1.16** *a second wheel that cut through the middle of it*: Or "a smaller wheel inside it." [k] **1.18** *them*: One possible meaning for the difficult Hebrew text of verse 18.

1.1-3 **a** 2 K 24.10-16; 2 Ch 36.9, 10; **b** Rev 19.11. **1.5** Rev 4.6. **1.10** Ez 10.14; Rev 4.7. **1.13** Rev 4.5. **1.15-21** Ez 10.9-13. **1.18** Rev 4.8. **1.22,23** Rev 4.6.

it reminded me of a dome. Each creature had two of its wings stretched out toward the creatures on either side, with the other two wings folded against its body. 24 Whenever the creatures flew, their wings roared like an ocean or a large army or even the voice of God All-Powerful. And whenever the creatures stopped, they folded their wings against their bodies.

25 When the creatures stopped flapping their wings, I heard a sound coming from above the dome. 26 I then saw what looked like a throne made of sapphire,[l] and sitting on the throne was a figure in the shape of a human. 27 From the waist up, it was glowing like metal in a hot furnace, and from the waist down it looked like the flames of a fire. The figure was surrounded by a bright light, 28 as colorful as a rainbow that appears after a storm.

I realized I was seeing the brightness of the LORD's glory! So I bowed with my face to the ground, and just then I heard a voice speaking to me.

The LORD Chooses Ezekiel

2 The LORD[m] said, "Ezekiel, son of man,[n] I want you to stand up and listen." 2 After he said this, his Spirit took control of me and lifted me to my feet. Then the LORD said:

3 Ezekiel, I am sending you to the people of Israel. They are just like their ancestors who rebelled against me and refused to stop. 4 They are stubborn and hardheaded. But I, the LORD God, have chosen you to tell them what I say. 5 Those rebels may not even listen, but at least they will know that a prophet has come to them.

6 Don't be afraid of them or of anything they say. You may think you're in the middle of a thorn patch or a bunch of scorpions. But be brave 7 and preach my message to them, whether they choose to listen or not. 8 Ezekiel, don't rebel against me, as they have done. Instead, listen to everything I tell you.

And now, Ezekiel, open your mouth and eat what I am going to give you.

9 Just then, I saw a hand stretched out toward me. And in it was a scroll.[o] 10 The hand opened the scroll, and both sides of it were filled with words of sadness, mourning, and grief.

3 The LORD said, "Ezekiel, son of man, after you eat this scroll, go speak to the people of Israel."

2-3 He handed me the scroll and said, "Eat this and fill up on it." So I ate the scroll, and it tasted sweet as honey.

4 The LORD said:

Ezekiel, I am sending you to your own people. 5-6 They are Israelites, not some strangers who speak a foreign language you can't understand. If I were to send you to foreign nations, they would listen to you. 7 But the people of Israel will refuse to listen, because they have refused to listen to me. All of them are stubborn and hardheaded, 8 so I will make you as stubborn as they are. 9 You will be so determined to speak my message that nothing will stop you. I will make you hard like a diamond, and you'll have no reason to be afraid of those arrogant rebels.

10 Listen carefully to everything I say and then think about it. 11 Then go to the people who were brought here to Babylonia with you and tell them you have a message from me, the LORD God. Do this, whether they listen to you or not.

12 The Spirit[p] lifted me up, and as the glory of the LORD started to leave,[q] I heard

[l] **1.26** *sapphire*: A precious stone that has a blue color. [m] **2.1** *The LORD*: Hebrew "The voice." [n] **2.1** *Ezekiel, son of man*: The Hebrew text has "Son of man," which is often used in this book when the LORD speaks directly to Ezekiel. It means that Ezekiel is a mere human, yet he is the one the LORD has chosen to be his prophet who speaks for him to the people of Israel.
[o] **2.9** *scroll*: A roll of paper or special leather used for writing on. [p] **3.12** *The Spirit*: Or "A wind." [q] **3.12** *as the glory of the LORD started to leave*: One possible meaning for the difficult Hebrew text.

1.24 Rev 1.15; 19.6. **1.26** Ez 10.1; Rev 4.2, 3. **1.27** Ez 8.2. **2.9,10** Rev 5.1.
3.1-3 Rev 10.9, 10.

a loud, thundering noise behind me. 13 It was the sound made by the creatures' wings as they brushed against each other, and by the rumble of the wheels beside them. 14 Then the Spirit carried me away.

The LORD's power had taken complete control of me, and I was both annoyed and angry.

15 When I was back with the others living at Abib Hill near the Chebar River, I sat among them for seven days, shocked at what had happened to me.

The LORD Appoints Ezekiel To Stand Watch

(Ezekiel 33.1-9)

16 Seven days after I had seen the brightness of the LORD's glory, the LORD said:

17 Ezekiel, son of man, I have appointed you to stand watch for the people of Israel. So listen to what I say, then warn them for me. 18 When I tell wicked people they will die because of their sins, you must warn them to turn from their sinful ways so they won't be punished. If you refuse, you are responsible for their death. 19 However, if you do warn them, and they keep on sinning, they will die because of their sins, and you will be innocent.

20 Now suppose faithful people start sinning, and I decide to put stumbling blocks in their paths to make them fall. They deserve to die because of their sins. So if you refuse to warn them, I will forget about the times they were faithful, and I will hold you responsible for their death. 21 But if you do warn them, and they listen to you and stop sinning, I will let them live. And you will be innocent.

Ezekiel Cannot Talk

22 The LORD took control of me and said, "Stand up! Go into the valley, and I will talk with you there."

23 I immediately went to the valley, where I saw the brightness of the LORD's glory, just as I had seen near the Chebar River, and I bowed with my face to the ground. 24 His Spirit took control of me and lifted me to my feet. Then the LORD said:

Go back and lock yourself in your house! 25 You will be tied up to keep you inside, 26 and I will make you unable to talk or to warn those who have rebelled against me. 27 But the time will come, when I will tell you what to say, and you will again be able to speak my message.[r] Some of them will listen; others will be stubborn and refuse to listen.

Ezekiel Acts Out an Attack on Jerusalem

The LORD said:

4 Ezekiel, son of man, find a brick and sketch a picture of Jerusalem on it. 2 Then prepare to attack the brick as if it were a real city. Build a dirt mound and a ramp up to the top and surround the brick with enemy camps. On every side put large wooden poles as though you were going to break down the gate to the city. 3 Set up an iron pan like a wall between you and the brick. All this will be a warning for the people of Israel.

4-5 After that, lie down on your left side and stay there for three hundred ninety days as a sign of Israel's punishment[s]—one day for each year of its suffering. 6 Then turn over and lie on your right side forty more days. That will be a sign of Judah's punishment—one day for each year of its suffering.

7 The brick stands for Jerusalem, so attack it! Stare at it and shout angry warnings. 8 I will tie you up, so you can't leave until your attack has ended.

9 Get a large bowl. Then mix together wheat, barley, beans, lentils, and millet, and make some bread. This is what you will eat for the three hundred ninety days you are lying down. 10 Eat only a small loaf of bread each day 11 and drink only two large cups of water. 12 Use dried human waste to start a fire, then bake the bread on the

[r]**3.27** *again . . . speak my message*: See 33.21,22. [s]**4.4,5** *Israel's punishment*: Israel here refers to the northern kingdom that was destroyed in 722 B.C.

coals where everyone can watch you.
13 When I scatter the people of Israel among the nations, they will also have to eat food that is unclean, just as you must do.[t]

14 I said, "LORD God, please don't make me do that! Never in my life have I eaten food that would make me unacceptable to you. I've never eaten anything that died a natural death or was killed by a wild animal or that you said was unclean."

15 The LORD replied, "Instead of human waste, I will let you bake your bread on a fire made from cow manure. 16 Ezekiel, the people of Jerusalem will starve. They will have so little food and water that they will be afraid and hopeless. 17 Everyone will be shocked at what is happening, and, because of their sins, they will die a slow death."

Jerusalem's Coming Destruction

The LORD said:

5 Ezekiel, son of man, get a sharp sword and use it to cut off your hair and beard. Weigh the hair and divide it into three equal piles. 2 After you attack the brick that stands for Jerusalem, burn one pile of your hair on the brick. Chop up the second pile and let the small pieces of hair fall around the brick. Throw the third pile into the wind, and I will strike it with my own sword.

3 Keep a few of the hairs and wrap them in the hem of your clothes. 4 Then pull out a few of those hairs and throw them in the fire, so they will also burn. This fire will spread, destroying everyone in Israel.

5 I am the LORD God, and I have made Jerusalem the most important place in the world, and all other nations admire it. 6 But the people of Jerusalem rebelled and refuse to obey me. They ignored my laws and have become even more sinful than the nations around them.

7 So tell the people of Jerusalem:

I am the LORD God! You have refused to obey my laws and teachings, and instead you have obeyed the laws of the surrounding nations. You have become more rebellious than any of them! 8 Now all those nations will watch as I turn against you and punish you 9 for your sins. Your punishment will be more horrible than anything I've ever done or will ever do again. 10 Parents will be so desperate for food that they will eat their own children, and children will eat their parents. Those who survive this horror will be scattered in every direction.

11 Your disgusting sins have made my temple unfit as a place to worship me. So I swear by my own life that I will turn my back on you and show you no pity. 12 A third of you will die here in Jerusalem from disease or starvation. Another third will be killed in war. And I will scatter the last third of you in every direction, then track you down and kill you.

13 You will feel my fierce anger until I have finished taking revenge. Then you will know that I, the LORD, was furious because of your disobedience. 14 Every passerby will laugh at your destruction. Foreign nations 15 will insult you and make fun of you, but they will also be shocked and terrified at what I did in my anger. 16 I will destroy your crops until you starve to death, and disasters will strike you like arrows. 17 Starvation and wild animals will kill your children. I'll punish you with horrible diseases, and your enemies will strike you down with their swords. I, the LORD, have spoken.

Israel Is Doomed

6 The LORD God said:

2 Ezekiel, son of man, face the hills of Israel and tell them:

3 Listen, you mountains and hills, and every valley and gorge! I, the

[t]**4.13** *have to eat food that is unclean, just as you must do*: The LORD had forbidden the people of Israel to mix certain things (see Deuteronomy 22.9-11), and so the people would not have been allowed to eat this bread under normal conditions. It is used here to show that when a city is under attack, people eat whatever food is left, even if the LORD had said it was unclean.

5.10 Lm 4.10. **5.17** Rev 6.8.

LORD, am about to turn against you
and crush all the places where foreign
gods are worshiped. 4 Every altar will
be smashed, and in front of the idols I
will put to death the people who worship them. 5 Dead bodies and bones
will be lying around the idols and the
altars. 6 Every town in Israel will be
destroyed to make sure that each
shrine, idol, and altar is smashed—
everything the Israelites made will be a
pile of ruins. 7 All over the country,
your people will die. And those who
survive will know that I, the LORD, did
these things. 8 I will let some of the
people live through this punishment,
but I will scatter them among the nations, 9 where they will be prisoners.
And when they think of me, they will
realize that they disgraced me by rebelling and by worshiping idols. They
will hate themselves for the evil things
they did, 10 and they will know that I
am the LORD and that my warnings
must be taken seriously.

11 The LORD God then said:

Ezekiel, beat your fists together and
stomp your feet in despair! Moan in
sorrow, because the people of Israel
have done disgusting things and now
will be killed by enemy troops, or they
will die from starvation and disease.
12 Those who live far away will be
struck with deadly diseases. Those
who live nearby will be killed in war.
And the ones who are left will starve to
death. I will let loose my anger on
them! 13 These people used to offer incense to idols at altars built on hills
and mountaintops and in the shade of
large oak trees. But when they see
dead bodies lying around those altars,
they will know that I am the LORD. 14 I
will make their country a barren
wasteland, from the Southern Desert
to the town of Diblah in the north.
Then they will know that I, the LORD,
have done these things.

Disaster Is Near

7 The LORD God said:
2 Ezekiel, son of man, tell the people of Israel that I am saying:

Israel will soon come to an end!
Your whole country is about to be destroyed 3 as punishment for your
disgusting sins. I, the LORD, am so angry 4 that I will show no pity. I will
punish you for the evil you've done,
and you will know that I am the
LORD.

5 There's never been anything like
the coming disaster.[u] 6 And when it
comes, your life will be over. 7 You people of Israel are doomed! Soon there
will be panic on the mountaintops instead of celebration.[v] 8 I will let loose
my anger and punish you for the evil
things you've done. You'll get what you
deserve. 9 Your sins are so terrible, that
you'll get no mercy from me. Then you
will know that I, the LORD, have punished you.

10 Disaster is near! Injustice and
arrogance are everywhere, 11 and violent criminals run free. None of you
will survive the disaster, and everything you own and value will be shattered.[w] 12 The time is coming when
everyone will be ruined. Buying and
selling will stop, 13 and people who
sell property will never get it back, because all of you must be punished for
your sins. And I won't change my
mind![x]

14 A signal has been blown on the
trumpet, and weapons are prepared for
battle. But no one goes to war, because
in my anger I will strike down everyone in Israel.

Israel Is Surrounded

The LORD said to the people of Israel:

15 War, disease, and starvation are
everywhere! People who live in the countryside will be killed in battle, and those

[u] **7.5** *disaster*: One possible meaning for the difficult Hebrew text of verse 5. [v] **7.7** *celebration*: One possible meaning for the difficult Hebrew text of verse 7. [w] **7.11** *shattered*: One possible meaning for the difficult Hebrew text of verses 10,11. [x] **7.13** *mind*: One possible meaning for the difficult Hebrew text of verse 13.

who live in towns will die from starvation or deadly diseases. 16 Anyone who survives will escape into the hills, like doves who leave the valleys to find safety.

All of you will moan[y] because of your sins. 17 Your hands will tremble, and your knees will go limp. 18 You will put on sackcloth[z] to show your sorrow, but terror will overpower you. Shame will be written all over your faces, and you will shave your heads in despair. 19 Your silver and gold will be thrown into the streets like garbage, because those are the two things that led you into sin, and now they cannot save you from my anger. They are not even worth enough to buy food. 20 You took great pride in using your beautiful jewelry to make disgusting idols of foreign gods. So I will make your jewelry worthless.

21 Wicked foreigners will rob and disgrace you. 22 They will break into my temple[a] and leave it unfit as a place to worship me, but I will look away and let it happen.

23 Your whole country is in confusion![b] Murder and violence are everywhere in Israel, 24 so I will tell the most wicked nations to come and take over your homes. They will put an end to the pride you have in your strong army, and they will make your places of worship unfit to use. 25 You will be terrified and will desperately look for peace—but there will be no peace. 26 One tragedy will follow another, and you'll hear only bad news. People will beg prophets to give them a message from me. Priests will stop teaching my Law, and wise leaders won't be able to give advice. 27 Even your king and his officials will lose hope and cry in despair. Your hands will tremble with fear.

I will punish you for your sins and treat you the same way you have treated others. Then you will know that I am the LORD.

Ezekiel Sees the Terrible Sins of Jerusalem

8 Six years after King Jehoiachin and the rest of us had been led away as prisoners to Babylonia, the leaders of Judah were meeting with me in my house. On the fifth day of the sixth month,[c] the LORD God suddenly took control of me, 2 and I saw something in the shape of a human.[d] This figure was like fire from the waist down, and it was bright as polished metal from the waist up. 3 It reached out what seemed to be a hand and grabbed my hair. Then in my vision the LORD's Spirit lifted me into the sky and carried me to Jerusalem.

The Spirit took me to the north gate of the temple's inner courtyard, where there was an idol that disgusted the LORD and made him furious. 4 Then I saw the brightness of the glory of the God of Israel, just as I had seen it near the Chebar River.

5 God said to me, "Ezekiel, son of man, look north." And when I did, I saw that disgusting idol by the altar near the gate.

6 God then said, "Do you see the terrible sins of the people of Israel? Their sins are making my holy temple unfit as a place to worship me. Yet you will see even worse things than this."

7 Next, I was taken to the entrance of the courtyard, where I saw a hole in the wall.

8 God said, "Make this hole bigger." And when I did, I realized it was a doorway. 9 "Go in," God said, "and see what horrible and evil things the people are doing."

10 Inside, I saw that the walls were covered with pictures of reptiles and disgusting, unclean animals,[e] as well as with idols that the Israelites were worshiping. 11 Seventy Israelite leaders were standing there, including Jaazaniah son of Shaphan. Each of these leaders was holding an incense

[y]**7.16** *will moan*: Hebrew; two ancient translations "will die." [z]**7.18** *sackcloth*: A rough, dark-colored cloth made from goat or camel hair and used to make grain sacks. It was worn in times of trouble or sorrow. [a]**7.22** *my temple*: The Hebrew text has "my treasure," which may refer to the temple, to Jerusalem, or to Israel itself. [b]**7.23** *Your whole country is in confusion*: One ancient translation; Hebrew "Get chains ready to drag away the dead bodies of your people." [c]**8.1** *Six years . . . sixth month*: Probably September of 592 B.C. [d]**8.2** *a human*: One ancient translation; Hebrew "a fiery figure." [e]**8.10** *disgusting, unclean animals*: See, for example, Leviticus 11.9-19.

8.2 Ez 1.27. **8.4** Ez 1.28.

burner, and the smell of incense filled the
room.
12 God said, "Ezekiel, do you see what
horrible things Israel's leaders are doing in
secret? They have filled their rooms with
idols. And they say I can't see them, because they think I have already deserted Israel. 13 But I will show you something even
worse than this."
14 He took me to the north gate of the
temple, where I saw women mourning for
the god Tammuz.[f] 15 God asked me, "Can
you believe what these women are doing?
But now I want to show you something
worse."
16 I was then led into the temple's inner
courtyard, where I saw about twenty-five
men standing near the entrance, between
the porch and the altar. Their backs were
to the LORD's temple, and they were bowing
down to the rising sun.
17 God said, "Ezekiel, it's bad enough
that the people of Judah are doing these
disgusting things. But they have also spread
violence and injustice everywhere in Israel
and have made me very angry. They have
disgraced and insulted me in the worst possible way.[g] 18 So in my fierce anger, I will
punish them without mercy and refuse to
help them when they cry out to me."

The LORD Gives the Command To Punish Jerusalem

9 After that, I heard the LORD shout,
"Come to Jerusalem, you men chosen
to destroy the city. And bring your
weapons!"
2 I saw six men come through the north
gate of the temple, each one holding a
deadly weapon. A seventh man dressed in a
linen robe was with them, and he was carrying things to write with. The men went
into the temple and stood by the bronze
altar.
3 The brightness of God's glory then left
its place above the statues of the winged
creatures[h] inside the temple and moved to
the entrance. The LORD said to the man in
the linen robe, 4 "Walk through the city of
Jerusalem and mark the forehead of anyone who is truly upset and sad about the
disgusting things that are being done here."
5-6 He turned to the other six men and
said, "Follow him and put to death everyone who doesn't have a mark on their forehead. Show no mercy or pity! Kill men and
women, parents and children. Begin here
at my temple and be sure not to harm
those who are marked."
The men immediately killed the leaders
who were standing there.
7 Then the LORD said, "Pollute the temple by piling the dead bodies in the courtyards. Now get busy!" They left and started
killing the people of Jerusalem.
8 I was then alone, so I bowed down and
cried out to the LORD, "Why are you doing
this? Are you so angry at the people of
Jerusalem that everyone must die?"
9 The LORD answered, "The people of Israel and Judah have done horrible things.
Their country is filled with murderers, and
Jerusalem itself is filled with violence. They
think that I have deserted them, and that I
can't see what they are doing. 10 And so I
will not have pity on them or forgive them.
They will be punished for what they have
done."
11 Just then, the man in the linen robe
returned and said, "I have done what you
commanded."

The LORD's Glory Leaves the Temple

10 I saw the dome that was above the
four winged creatures,[i] and on it
was the sapphire[j] throne.[k] 2 The LORD said
to the man in the linen robe, "Walk among
the four wheels beside the creatures and
pick up as many hot coals as you can carry.
Then scatter them over the city of Jeru-

[f] **8.14** *the god Tammuz*: A god of vegetation who was thought to die in the dry season. During the Hebrew month of Tammuz (from about mid-June to mid-July), women mourned the death of this god, hoping to bring him back to life. [g] **8.17** *disgraced and insulted me . . . way*: One possible meaning for the difficult Hebrew text. [h] **9.3** *the statues of the winged creatures*: These were symbols of the LORD's throne on earth (see Exodus 25.18-22; 1 Kings 6.23-28). [i] **10.1** *winged creatures*: See the note at 9.3. [j] **10.1** *sapphire*: See the note at 1.26. [k] **10.1** *dome . . . creatures . . . throne*: See 1.22-26.

9.4 Rev 7.3; 9.4; 14.1. **10.1** Ez 1.26; Rev 4.2. **10.2** Rev 8.5.

salem." I watched him as he followed the
LORD's instructions.
3 The winged creatures were standing
south of the temple when the man walked
among them. A cloud filled the inner
courtyard, 4 and the brightness of the
LORD's glory moved from above the creatures and stopped at the entrance of
the temple. The entire temple was filled
with his glory, and the courtyard was dazzling bright. 5 The sound of the creatures'
wings was as loud as the voice of God All-
Powerful and could even be heard in the
outer courtyard.
6 The man in the robe was now standing
beside a wheel. 7 One of the four creatures
reached its hand into the fire among them
and gave him some of the hot coals. The
man took the coals and left.
8 I noticed again that each of the four
winged creatures had what looked like human hands under their wings, 9 and I saw
the four wheels near the creatures. These
wheels were shining like chrysolite.[l]
10 Each wheel was exactly the same and
had a second wheel that cut through the
middle of it,[m] 11 so that they could move in
any direction without turning. The wheels
moved together whenever the creatures
moved. 12 I also noticed that the wheels
and the creatures' bodies, including their
backs, their hands, and their wings, were
covered with eyes. 13 And I heard a voice
calling these "the wheels that spin."
14 Each of the winged creatures had
four faces: the face of a bull,[n] the face of a
human, the face of a lion, and the face of
an eagle. 15-17 These were the same creatures I had seen near the Chebar River.
They controlled when and where the
wheels moved—the wheels went wherever
the creatures went and stopped whenever
they stopped. Even when the creatures flew
in the air, the wheels stayed beside them.
18 Then I watched the brightness of the
LORD's glory move from the entrance of the
temple and stop above the winged creatures. 19 They spread their wings and flew
into the air with the wheels at their side.
They stopped at the east gate of the temple, and the LORD's glory was above them.
20 I knew for sure that these were the
same creatures I had seen beneath the
LORD's glory near the Chebar River.
21-22 They had four wings with hands beneath them, and they had the same four
faces as those near the River. Each creature moved straight ahead without turning.

Ezekiel Condemns Jerusalem's Wicked Leaders

11 The LORD's Spirit[o] lifted me up and
took me to the east gate of the temple, where I saw twenty-five men, including
the two leaders, Jaazaniah son of Azzur
and Pelatiah son of Benaiah. 2 The LORD
said, "Ezekiel, son of man, these men are
making evil plans and giving dangerous advice to the people of Jerusalem. 3 They say
things like, 'Let's build more houses.[p] This
city is like a cooking pot over a fire, and we
are the meat, but at least the pot keeps us
from being burned in the fire.'[q] 4 So,
Ezekiel, condemn them!"
5 The LORD's Spirit took control of me
and told me to tell these leaders:

> I, the LORD God, know what you
> leaders are saying. 6 You have mur-
> dered so many people that the city is
> filled with dead bodies! 7 This city is
> indeed a cooking pot, but the bodies of
> those you killed are the meat. And so I
> will force you to leave Jerusalem, 8 and
> I'll send armies to attack you, just as
> you fear. 9 Then you will be captured
> and punished by foreign enemies.[r]
> 10 You will be killed in your own coun-
> try, but not before you realize that I,
> the LORD, have done these things.
> 11 You leaders claim to be meat in
> a cooking pot, but you won't be pro-
> tected by this city. No, you will die at

[l]**10.9** *chrysolite*: See the note at 1.16. [m]**10.10** *a second wheel that cut through the middle of it*: See the note at 1.16. [n]**10.14** *a bull*: The Hebrew text has "a winged creature," but see 1.10. [o]**11.1** *The LORD's Spirit*: Or "A wind." [p]**11.3** *Let's . . . houses*: One possible meaning for the difficult Hebrew text. [q]**11.3** *the pot keeps us from being burned in the fire*: These leaders were trying to convince the people of Jerusalem that they were secure, and that their future was bright. [r]**11.9** *foreign enemies*: That is, the Babylonians.

10.9-13 Ez 1.15-21. **10.12** Rev 4.8. **10.14** Ez 1.10; Rev 4.7.

the border of Israel. 12 You will realize that while you were following the laws of nearby nations, you were disobeying my laws and teachings. And I am the LORD!

13 Before I finished speaking, Pelatiah dropped dead. I bowed down and cried out, "Please, LORD God, don't kill everyone left in Israel."

A Promise of Hope

14 The LORD replied:

15 Ezekiel, son of man, the people living in Jerusalem claim that you and the other Israelites who were taken to Babylonia are too far away to worship me. They also claim that the land of Israel now belongs only to them. 16 But here is what I want you to tell the Israelites in Babylonia:

It's true that I, the LORD God, have forced you out of your own country and made you live among foreign nations. But for now, I will be with you wherever you are, so that you can worship me. 17 And someday, I will gather you from the nations where you are scattered and let you live in Israel again. 18 When that happens, I want you to clear the land of all disgusting idols. 19 Then I will take away your stubbornness and make you eager to be completely faithful to me. You will want to obey me 20 and all my laws and teachings. You will be my people, and I will be your God. 21 But those who worship idols will be punished and get what they deserve. I, the LORD God, have spoken.

The LORD's Glory Leaves Jerusalem

22 After the LORD had finished speaking, the winged creatures spread their wings and flew into the air, and the wheels were beside them. The brightness of the LORD's glory above them 23 left Jerusalem and stopped at a hill east of the city.

24 Then in my vision, the LORD's Spirit[s] lifted me up and carried me back to the other exiles in Babylonia. The vision faded away, 25 and I told them everything the LORD had shown me.

Ezekiel Acts Out Israel's Captivity

12 The LORD said:

2 Ezekiel, son of man, you are living among rebellious people. They have eyes, but refuse to see; they have ears, but refuse to listen. 3 So before it gets dark, here is what I want you to do. Pack a few things as though you were going to be taken away as a prisoner. Then go outside where everyone can see you and walk around from place to place. Maybe as they watch, they will realize what rebels they are. 4 After you have done this, return to your house.

Later that evening leave your house as if you were going into exile. 5 Dig through the wall of your house[t] and crawl out, carrying the bag with you. Make sure everyone is watching. 6 Lift the bag to your shoulders, and with your face covered, take it into the darkness, so that you cannot see the land you are leaving. All of this will be a warning for the people of Israel.

7 I did everything the LORD had said. I packed a few things. Then as the sun was going down, and while everyone was watching, I dug a hole through one of the walls of my house. I pulled out my bag, then lifted it to my shoulders and left in the darkness.

8 The next morning, the LORD 9 reminded me that those rebellious people didn't even ask what I was doing. 10 So he sent me back to tell them:

The LORD God has a message for the leader of Jerusalem and everyone living there!

11 I have done these things to show them what will happen when they are taken away as prisoners.

12 The leader of Jerusalem will lift his own bag to his shoulders at sunset

[s] **11.24** *the LORD's Spirit*: See the note at 11.1. [t] **12.5** *Dig through the wall of your house*: The walls of most houses in Babylonia were made of mud bricks that had been dried in the sun. A hole could easily have been dug through these bricks.

11.19,20 Ez 36.26-28. **11.22,23** Ez 43.2-5. **12.2** Is 6.9, 10; Jr 5.21; Mk 8.18.

and leave through a hole that the others have dug in the wall of his house. He will cover his face, so he can't see the land he is leaving. 13 The LORD will spread out a net and trap him as he leaves Jerusalem. He will then be led away to the city of Babylon, but will never see that place,[u] even though he will die there. 14 His own officials and troops will scatter in every direction, and the LORD will track them down and put them to death.

15 The LORD will force the rest of the people in Jerusalem to live in foreign nations, where they will realize that he has done all these things. 16 Some of them will survive the war, the starvation, and the deadly diseases. That way, they will be able to tell foreigners how disgusting their sins were, and that it was the LORD who punished them in this way.

A Sign of Fear

17 The LORD said:

18 Ezekiel, son of man, shake with fear when you eat, and tremble when you drink. 19 Tell the people of Israel that I, the LORD, say that someday everyone in Jerusalem will shake when they eat and tremble when they drink. Their country will be destroyed and left empty, because they have been cruel and violent. 20 Every town will lie in ruins, and the land will be a barren desert. Then they will know that I am the LORD.

The Words of the LORD Will Come True

21 The LORD said:

22 Ezekiel, son of man, you've heard people in Israel use the saying, "Time passes, and prophets are proved wrong." 23 Now tell the people that I, the LORD, am going to prove that saying wrong. No one will ever be able to use it again in Israel, because very soon everything I have said will come true! 24 The people will hear no more useless warnings and false messages. 25 I will give them my message, and what I say will certainly happen. Warn those rebels that the time has come for them to be punished. I, the LORD, make this promise.

26-27 Ezekiel, the people of Israel are also saying that your visions and messages are only about things in the future. 28 So tell them that my words will soon come true, just as I have warned. I, the LORD, have spoken.

Lying Prophets

13 The LORD said:

2 Ezekiel, son of man, condemn the prophets of Israel who say they speak in my name, but who preach messages that come from their own imagination. Tell them it's time to hear my message.

3 I, the LORD God, say those lying prophets are doomed! They don't see visions—they make up their own messages! 4 Israel's prophets are no better than jackals[v] that hunt for food among the ruins of a city. 5 They don't warn the people about coming trouble or tell them how dangerous it is to sin against me. 6 Those prophets lie by claiming they speak for me, but I have not even chosen them to be my prophets. And they still think their words will come true. 7 They say they're preaching my messages, but they are full of lies—I did not speak to them!

8 So I am going to punish those lying prophets for deceiving the people of Israel with false messages. 9 I will turn against them and no longer let them belong to my people. They will not be allowed to call themselves Israelites or even to set foot in Israel. Then they will realize that I am the LORD God.

10 Those prophets refuse to be honest. They tell my people there will be peace, even though there's no peace to be found. They are like workers who think they can fix a shaky wall by covering it with paint. 11 But when I send rainstorms, hailstones, and strong winds, the wall will surely

[u] **12.13** *He will then be led away . . . that place*: According to 2 Kings 25.6,7, King Zedekiah of Judah was blinded before he was taken to Babylon. [v] **13.4** *jackals*: Desert animals related to wolves, but smaller.

12.13 2 K 25.7; Jr 52.11. **13.10** Jr 6.14; 8.11.

collapse. 12 People will then ask the workers why the paint didn't hold it up.
13 That wall is the city of Jerusalem.
And I, the LORD God, am so angry that I
will send strong winds, rainstorms, and
hailstones to destroy it. 14 The lying
prophets have tried to cover up the evil in
Jerusalem, but I will tear down the city, all
the way to its foundations. And when it col-
lapses, those prophets will be killed, and
everyone will know that I have done these
things.
15 The city of Jerusalem and its lying
prophets will feel my fierce anger. Then I
will announce that the city has fallen and
that the lying prophets are dead, 16 because
they promised my people peace, when
there was no peace. I, the LORD God, have
spoken.

Women Who Wear Magic Charms

The LORD said:

17 Ezekiel, son of man, now condemn
the women of Israel who preach messages
that come from their own imagination.
18 Tell them they're doomed! They wear
magic charms on their wrists and scarves
on their heads, then trick others into believing they can predict the future.[w] They
won't get away with telling those lies.
19 They charge my people a few handfuls of
barley and a couple pieces of bread, and
then give messages that are insulting to
me. They use lies to sentence the innocent
to death and to help the guilty go free. And
my people believe them!
20 I hate the magic charms they use to
trick people into believing their lies. I will
rip those charms from their wrists and set
free the people they have trapped like
birds.[x] 21 I will tear the scarves from their
heads and rescue my people from their
power once and for all. Then they will
know that I am the LORD God.
22 They do things I would never do.
They lie to good people and encourage
them to do wrong, and they convince the
wicked to keep sinning and ruin their lives.
23 I will no longer let these women give
false messages and use magic, and I will
free my people from their control. Then
they will know that I, the LORD, have done
these things.

Ezekiel Encourages the People To Turn Back to the LORD

14 One day, some of Israel's leaders
came to me and asked for a message from the LORD. 2 While they were
there, the LORD said:
3 Ezekiel, son of man, these men have
started worshiping idols, though they know
it will cause them to sin even more. So I
refuse to give them a message!
4 Tell the people of Israel that if they sin
by worshiping idols and then go to a
prophet to find out what I say, I will give
them the answer their sins deserve.
5 When they hear my message, maybe they
will see that they need to turn back to me
and stop worshiping those idols.
6 Now, Ezekiel, tell everyone in Israel:

I am the LORD God. Stop worshiping your disgusting idols and come
back to me.

7 Suppose one of you Israelites or a
foreigner living in Israel rejects me and
starts worshiping idols. If you then go
to a prophet to find out what I say, I
will answer 8 by turning against you. I
will make you a warning to anyone
who might think of doing the same
thing, and you will no longer belong to
my people. Then you will know that I
am the LORD and that you have sinned
against me.
9 If a prophet gives a false message,
I am the one who caused that prophet
to lie. But I will still reject him and cut
him off from my people, 10 and anyone
who goes to that prophet for a message
will be punished in the same way. 11 I
will do this, so that you will come back
to me and stop destroying yourselves
with these disgusting sins. So turn
back to me! Then I will be your God,
and you will be my people. I, the LORD
God, make this promise.

[w] **13.18** *They wear . . . the future*: One possible meaning for the difficult Hebrew text.
[x] **13.20** *like birds*: One possible meaning for the difficult Hebrew text.

Judgment on a Sinful Nation

12 The LORD God said:
13 Ezekiel, son of man, suppose an entire nation sins against me, and I punish it
by destroying the crops and letting its people and livestock starve to death. 14 Even if
Noah, Daniel,[y] and Job were living in that
nation, their faithfulness would not save
anyone but themselves.
15 Or suppose I punish a nation by sending wild animals to eat people and scare
away every passerby, so that the land becomes a barren desert. 16 As surely as I live,
I promise that even if these three men
lived in that nation, their own children
would not be spared. The three men would
live, but the land would be an empty desert.
17 Or suppose I send an enemy to attack
a sinful nation and kill its people and livestock. 18 If these three men were in that
nation when I punished it, not even their
children would be spared. Only the three
men would live.
19 And suppose I am so angry that
I send a deadly disease to wipe out the
people and livestock of a sinful nation.
20 Again, even if Noah, Daniel, and Job were
living there, I, the LORD, promise that the
children of these faithful men would also
die. Only the three of them would be spared.
21 I am the LORD God, and I promise to
punish Jerusalem severely. I will send war,
starvation, wild animals, and deadly disease
to slaughter its people and livestock. 22 And
those who survive will be taken from their
country and led here to Babylonia. Ezekiel,
when you see how sinful they are, you will
know why I did all these things to
Jerusalem. 23 You will be convinced that I,
the LORD God, was right in doing what I did.

Jerusalem Is a Useless Vine

15 Some time later, the LORD said:
2 Ezekiel, son of man, what happens to the wood of a grapevine after the
grapes have been picked? It isn't like other
trees in the forest, 3 because the wood of a
grapevine can't be used to make anything,
not even a small peg to hang things on. 4 It
can only be used as firewood. But after its
ends are burnt and its middle is charred, it
can't be used for anything. 5 The wood is
useless before it is burned, and afterwards,
it is completely worthless.
6 I, the LORD God, promise that just
as the wood of a grapevine is burned as
firewood, 7 I will punish the people of
Jerusalem with fire. Some of them have
escaped one destruction, but soon they
will be completely burned. And when that
happens, you, Ezekiel, will know that I am the
LORD. 8 I will make their country an empty
wasteland, because they have not been
loyal to me. I, the LORD God, have spoken.

Jerusalem Is Unfaithful

16 The LORD said:
2 Ezekiel, son of man, remind
the people of Jerusalem of their disgusting
sins 3 and tell them that I, the LORD God,
am saying:
Jerusalem, you were born in the country
where Canaanites lived. Your father was an
Amorite, and your mother was a Hittite.[z]
4 When you were born, no one cut you
loose from your mother or washed your
body. No one rubbed your skin with salt
and olive oil,[a] and wrapped you in warm
blankets. 5 Not one person loved you
enough to do any of these things, and no
one even felt sorry for you. You were despised, thrown into a field, and forgotten.
6 I saw you lying there, rolling around in
your own blood, and I couldn't let you die.
7 I took care of you, like someone caring for
a tender, young plant. You grew up to be a
beautiful young woman with perfect breasts
and long hair, but you were still naked.
8 When I saw you again, you were old
enough to have sex. So I covered your
naked body with my own robe.[b] Then I
solemnly promised that you would belong

[y] **14.14** *Daniel*: Or "Danel," possibly a well-known hero or wise man. [z] **16.3** *Amorite . . . Hittite*: People who lived in Canaan before the Israelites and who worshiped idols. [a] **16.4** *rubbed your skin with salt and olive oil*: People believed this toughened the skin of the babies. [b] **16.8** *I covered your naked body with my own robe*: To show that he would protect and take care of her.
14.21 Rev 6.8.

to me and that I, the LORD God, would take care of you.

9 I washed the blood off you and rubbed your skin with olive oil. 10 I gave you the finest clothes and the most expensive robes,[c] as well as sandals made from the best leather. 11 I gave you bracelets, a necklace, 12 a ring for your nose, some earrings, and a beautiful crown. 13 Your jewelry was gold and silver, and your clothes were made of only the finest material and embroidered linen. Your bread was baked from fine flour, and you ate honey and olive oil. You were as beautiful as a queen, 14 and everyone on earth knew it. I, the LORD God, had helped you become a lovely young woman.

15 You learned that you were attractive enough to have any man you wanted, so you offered yourself to every passerby.[d] 16 You made shrines for yourself and decorated them with some of your clothes. That's where you took your visitors to have sex with them. These things should never have happened![e] 17 You made idols out of the gold and silver jewelry I gave you, then you sinned by worshiping those idols. 18 You dressed them in the clothes you got from me, and you offered them the olive oil and incense I gave you. 19 I supplied you with fine flour, olive oil, and honey, but you sacrificed it all as offerings to please those idols. I, the LORD God, watched this happen.

20 But you did something even worse than that—you sacrificed your own children to those idols! 21 You slaughtered my children, so you could offer them as sacrifices. 22 You were so busy sinning and being a prostitute that you refused to think about the days when you were young and were rolling around naked in your own blood.

23 Now I, the LORD God, say you are doomed! Not only did you do these evil things, 24 but you also built places on every street corner 25 where you disgraced yourself by having sex with anyone who walked by. And you did that more and more every day! 26 To make me angry, you even offered yourself to Egyptians, who were always ready to sleep with you.

27 So I punished you by letting those greedy Philistine enemies take over some of your territory. But even they were offended by your disgusting behavior.

28 You couldn't get enough sex, so you chased after Assyrians and slept with them. You still weren't satisfied, 29 so you went after Babylonians. But those merchants could not satisfy you either.

30 I, the LORD God, say that you were so disgusting that you would have done anything to get what you wanted.[f] 31 You had sex on every street corner, and when you finished, you refused to accept money. That's worse than being a prostitute! 32 You are nothing but an unfaithful wife who would rather have sex with strangers than with your own husband. 33 Prostitutes accept money for having sex, but you bribe men from everywhere to have sex with you. 34 You're not like other prostitutes. Men don't ask you for sex—you offer to pay them!

Jerusalem Must Be Punished

The LORD said:

35 Jerusalem, you prostitute, listen to me. 36 You chased after lovers, then took off your clothes and had sex. You even worshiped disgusting idols and sacrificed your own children as offerings to them. 37 So I, the LORD God, will gather every one of your lovers, those you liked and those you hated. They will stand around you, and I will rip off your clothes and let all of those lovers stare at your nakedness. 38 I will find you guilty of being an unfaithful wife and a murderer, and in my fierce anger I will sentence you to death! 39 Then I will hand you over to your lovers, who will tear down the places where you had sex. They will take your clothes and jewelry, leaving you naked and empty-handed.

40 Your lovers and an angry mob will

[c] **16.10** *most expensive robes*: One possible meaning for the difficult Hebrew text. [d] **16.15** *so you offered yourself to every passerby*: One possible meaning for the difficult Hebrew text.
[e] **16.16** *These things should never have happened*: One possible meaning for the difficult Hebrew text. [f] **16.30** *wanted*: One possible meaning for the difficult Hebrew text of verse 30.

stone you to death; they will cut your dead body into pieces [41] and burn down your houses. Other women will watch these terrible things happen to you. I promise to stop you from being a prostitute and paying your lovers for sex.

[42] Only then will I calm down and stop being angry and jealous. [43] You made me furious by doing all these disgusting things and by forgetting how I took care of you when you were young. Then you made things worse by acting like a prostitute. You must be punished! I, the LORD God, have spoken.

Jerusalem's Two Sisters

The LORD said:

[44] People will use this saying about you, Jerusalem: "If the mother is bad, so is her daughter." [45] You are just like your mother, who hated her husband and her own children. You are also like your sisters, who hated their husbands and children. Your father was an Amorite, and your mother was a Hittite.[g] [46] Your older sister was Samaria, that city to your north with her nearby villages. Your younger sister was Sodom, that city to your south with her nearby villages. [47] You followed their way of life and their wicked customs, and soon you were more disgusting than they were.

[48] As surely as I am the living LORD God, the people of Sodom and its nearby villages were never as sinful as you. [49] They were arrogant and spoiled; they had everything they needed and still refused to help the poor and needy. [50] They thought they were better than everyone else, and they did things I hate. And so I destroyed them.

[51] You people of Jerusalem have sinned twice as much as the people of Samaria. In fact, your evil ways have made both Sodom and Samaria look innocent. [52] So their punishment will seem light compared to yours. You will be disgraced and put to shame because of your disgusting sins.

Jerusalem Will Be Ashamed

The LORD said to Jerusalem:

[53] Someday I will bless Sodom and Samaria and their nearby villages. I will also bless you, Jerusalem. [54] Then you will be ashamed of how you've acted, and Sodom and Samaria will be relieved that they weren't as sinful as you. [55] When that day comes, you and Sodom and Samaria will once again be well-off, and all nearby villages will be restored.

[56] Jerusalem, you were so arrogant that you sneered at Sodom. [57] But now everyone has learned how wicked you really are. The countries of Syria and Philistia, as well as your other neighbors, hate you and make insulting remarks. [58] You must pay for all the vulgar and disgusting things you have done. I, the LORD, have spoken.

The LORD Makes a Promise to Jerusalem

The LORD said:

[59] Jerusalem, you deserve to be punished, because you broke your promises and ignored our agreement. [60] But I remember the agreement I made with you when you were young,[h] and so I will make you a promise that will last forever. [61] When you think about how you acted, you will be ashamed, especially when I return your sisters[i] to you as daughters, even though this was not part of our agreement.[j] [62] I will keep this solemn promise, and you will know that I am the LORD. [63] I will forgive you, but you will think about your sins and be too ashamed to say a word. I, the LORD God, have spoken.

A Story about Two Eagles and a Vine

17 The LORD said:

[2] Ezekiel, son of man, tell the people of Israel the following story, [3] so they will understand what I am saying to them:

A large eagle with strong wings and beautiful feathers once flew to Lebanon. It broke the top branch off a cedar tree, [4] then carried it to a nation of merchants

[g] **16.45** *Amorite . . . Hittite*: See the note at 16.3. [h] **16.60** *the agreement . . . when you were young*: See verse 8. [i] **16.61** *sisters*: Sodom and Samaria (see verses 44-52). [j] **16.61** *even though this was not part of our agreement*: One possible meaning for the difficult Hebrew text.

and left it in one of their cities. 5 The eagle
also took seed from Israel and planted it in
a fertile field with plenty of water, like a
willow tree beside a stream.[k] 6 The seed
sprouted and grew into a grapevine that
spread over the ground. It had lots of leaves
and strong, deep roots, and its branches
grew upward toward the eagle.

7 There was another eagle with strong
wings and thick feathers. The roots and
branches of the grapevine soon turned toward this eagle, hoping it would bring water for the soil. 8 But the vine was already
growing in fertile soil, where there was
plenty of water to produce healthy leaves
and large grapes.

9 Now tell me, Ezekiel, do you think this
grapevine will live? Or will the first eagle pull
it up by its roots and pluck off the grapes
and let its new leaves die? The eagle could
easily kill it without the help of a large and
powerful army. 10 The grapevine is strong
and healthy, but as soon as the scorching
desert wind blows, it will quickly wither.

The LORD Explains the Story

11 The LORD said:

12 Ezekiel, ask the rebellious people of
Israel if they know what this story means.
Tell them that the king of Babylonia
came to Jerusalem, then he captured the
king of Judah[l] and his officials, and took
them back to Babylon as prisoners. 13 He
chose someone from the family of Judah's
king[m] and signed a treaty with him, then
made him swear to be loyal. He also led
away other important citizens, 14 so that
the rest of the people of Judah would obey
only him and never gain control of their
own country again.

15 But this new king of Judah later rebelled against Babylonia and sent officials
to Egypt to get horses and troops. Will this
king be successful in breaking the treaty
with Babylonia? Or will he be punished for
what he's done?

16 As surely as I am the living LORD God,
I swear that the king of Judah will die in
Babylon, because he broke the treaty with
the king of Babylonia, who appointed him
king. 17 Even the king of Egypt and his
powerful army will be useless to Judah
when the Babylonians attack and build dirt
ramps to invade the cities of Judah and kill
its people. 18 The king of Judah broke his
own promises and ignored the treaty with
Babylonia. And so he will be punished!

19 He made a promise in my name and
swore to honor the treaty. And now that he
has broken that promise, my name is disgraced. He must pay for what he's done.
20 I will spread out a net to trap him. Then
I will drag him to Babylon and see that he
is punished for his unfaithfulness to me.
21 His best troops[n] will be killed in battle,
and the survivors will be scattered in every
direction. I, the LORD, have spoken.

*22 Someday, I, the LORD,
will cut a tender twig
from the top of a cedar tree,
then plant it on the peak
of Israel's tallest mountain,
where it will grow
strong branches
and produce large fruit.
23 All kinds of birds will find
shelter under the tree,
and they will rest in the shade
of its branches.
24 Every tree in the forest
will know that I, the LORD,
can bring down tall trees
and help short ones grow.
I dry up green trees
and make dry ones green.
I, the LORD, have spoken,
and I will keep my word.

Those Who Sin Will Die

18 The LORD said:
2 Ezekiel, I hear the people of Israel using the old saying,

"Sour grapes eaten by parents
leave a sour taste in the mouths
of their children."

[k] **17.5** *like a willow tree beside a stream*: One possible meaning for the difficult Hebrew text.
[l] **17.12** *king of Judah*: Probably King Jehoiachin (see 2 Kings 24.10-12,15,16). [m] **17.13** *someone from the family of Judah's king*: Probably King Zedekiah (see 2 Kings 24.17). [n] **17.21** *best troops*: Two ancient translations; Hebrew "troops that ran away."
17.12-15 2 K 24.15-20; 2 Ch 36.10-13. **18.2** Jr 31.29.

3 Now tell them that I am the LORD God, and as surely as I live, that saying will no longer be used in Israel. 4 The lives of all people belong to me—parents as well as children. Only those who sin will be put to death.

5 Suppose there is a truly good man who always does what is fair and right. 6 He refuses to eat meat sacrificed to foreign gods at local shrines or to worship Israel's idols. He doesn't have sex with someone else's wife or with a woman having her monthly period. 7 He never cheats or robs anyone and always returns anything taken as security for a loan; he gives food and clothes to the poor 8 and doesn't charge interest when lending money. He refuses to do anything evil; he is fair to everyone 9 and faithfully obeys my laws and teachings. This man is good, and I promise he will live.

10 But suppose this good man has an evil son who is violent and commits sins 11 his father never did. He eats meat at local shrines, has sex with someone else's wife, 12 cheats the poor, and robs people. He keeps what is given to him as security for a loan. He worships idols, does disgusting things, 13 and charges high interest when lending money. An evil man like that will certainly not live. He is the one who has done these horrible sins, so it's his own fault that he will be put to death.

14 But suppose this evil man has a son who sees his father do these things and refuses to act like him. 15 He doesn't eat meat at local shrines or worship Israel's idols, and he doesn't have sex with someone else's wife. 16 He never cheats or robs anyone and doesn't even demand security for a loan. He gives food and clothes to the poor 17 and refuses to do anything evil[o] or to charge interest. And he obeys all my laws and teachings. Such a man will live. His own father sinned, but this good man will not be put to death for the sins of his father. 18 It is his father who will die for cheating and robbing and doing evil.

19 You may wonder why a son isn't punished for the sins of his father. It is because the son does what is right and obeys my laws. 20 Only those who sin will be put to death. Children won't suffer for the sins of their parents, and parents won't suffer for the sins of their children. Good people will be rewarded for what they do, and evil people will be punished for what they do.

21 Suppose wicked people stop sinning and start obeying my laws and doing right. They won't be put to death. 22 All their sins will be forgiven, and they will live because they did right. 23 I, the LORD God, don't like to see wicked people die. I enjoy seeing them turn from their sins and live.

24 But when good people start sinning and doing disgusting things, will they live? No! All their good deeds will be forgotten, and they will be put to death because of their sins.

25 You people of Israel accuse me of being unfair! But listen—I'm not unfair; you are! 26 If good people start doing evil, they must be put to death, because they have sinned. 27 And if wicked people start doing right, they will save themselves from punishment. 28 They will think about what they've done and stop sinning, and so they won't be put to death. 29 But you still say that I am unfair. You are the ones who have done wrong and are unfair!

30 I will judge each of you for what you've done. So stop sinning, or else you will certainly be punished. 31 Give up your evil ways and start thinking pure thoughts. And be faithful to me! Do you really want to be put to death for your sins? 32 I, the LORD God, don't want to see that happen to anyone. So stop sinning and live!

A Funeral Song for Israel's Leaders

The LORD said:

19 Ezekiel, sing a funeral song for two of Israel's leaders:[p]

2 Your mother was a brave lioness
who raised her cubs
among lions.

[o] **18.17** *evil*: One ancient translation; Hebrew "for the poor." [p] **19.1** *two of Israel's leaders*: Probably Jehoahaz (ruled three months in 609 B.C.) and Jehoiachin (ruled three months in 598 B.C.) or Zedekiah (598-586 B.C.).

18.9 Lv 18.5. **18.20** Dt 24.16. **18.32** Ws 1.13.

3 She taught one of them to hunt,
and he learned to eat people.
4 When the nations heard of him,
they trapped him in a pit,
then they used hooks
to drag him to Egypt.

5 His mother waited
for him to return.
But soon she lost all hope
and raised another cub,
who also became fierce.
6 He hunted with other lions
and learned to eat people.
7 He destroyed fortresses[q]
and ruined towns;
his mighty roar
terrified everyone.
8 Nations plotted to kill him,
and people came from all over
to spread out a net
and catch him in a trap.
9 They put him in a cage
and took him to Babylonia.
The lion was locked away,
so that his mighty roar
would never again be heard
on Israel's hills.

10 Your mother was a vine[r]
growing near a stream.
There was plenty of water,
so she was filled with branches
and with lots of fruit.
11 Her strong branches
became symbols of authority,
and she was taller
than all other trees—
everyone could see how strong
and healthy she was.
12 But in anger, I pulled her up
by the roots
and threw her to the ground,
where the scorching desert wind
dried out her fruit.
Her strong branches wilted
and burned up.
13 Then she was planted
in a hot, dry desert,
14 where her stem caught fire,
and flames burned
her branches and fruit.
Not one strong branch is left;
she is stripped bare.

This funeral song must be sung with sorrow.

Israel Keeps On Rebelling

20 Seven years after King Jehoiachin
and the rest of us had been led
away as prisoners to Babylonia, some of Israel's leaders came to me on the tenth day
of the fifth month.[s] They sat down and
asked for a message from the LORD. 2 Just
then, the LORD God said:
3 Ezekiel, son of man, these leaders
have come to find out what I want them to
do. As surely as I live, I will not give them
an answer of any kind.
4 Are you willing to warn them, Ezekiel?
Then remind them of the disgusting sins of
their ancestors.
5 Tell them that long ago I, the LORD
God, chose Israel to be my own. I appeared
to their ancestors in Egypt and made a
solemn promise that I would be their God
and the God of their descendants. 6 I swore
that I would rescue them from Egypt and
lead them to a land I had already chosen.
This land was rich with milk and honey
and was the most splendid land of all. 7 I
told them to get rid of their disgusting idols
and not to sin by worshiping the gods of
Egypt. I reminded them that I was the
LORD their God, 8 but they still rebelled
against me. They refused to listen and kept
on worshiping their idols and foreign
gods.
In my anger, I decided to punish the Israelites in Egypt. 9 But that would have
made me look like a liar, because I had already promised in front of everyone that
I would lead them out of Egypt. 10 So I
brought them out and led them into the
desert. 11 I gave them my laws and teachings, so they would know how to live right.

[q] **19.7** *He destroyed fortresses*: One possible meaning for the difficult Hebrew text. [r] **19.10** *Your mother was a vine*: One possible meaning for the difficult Hebrew text. [s] **20.1** *Seven years . . . fifth month*: Probably August of 591 B.C.

20.5,6 Ex 6.2-8. **20.11,13** Lv 18.5.

12 And I commanded them to respect the
Sabbath as a way of showing that they were
holy and belonged to me. 13 But the Israelites rebelled against me in the desert.
They refused to obey my laws and teachings, and they treated the Sabbath like any
other day.

Then in my anger, I decided to destroy
the Israelites in the desert once and for all.
14 But that would have disgraced me, because many other nations had seen me
bring the Israelites out of Egypt. 15 Instead,
I told them in the desert that I would not
lead them into the beautiful, fertile land I
had promised. 16 I said this because they
had not only ignored my laws and teachings, but had disgraced my Sabbath and
worshiped idols.

17 Yet, I felt sorry for them and could
not let them die in the desert. 18 So I
warned the children not to act like their
parents or follow their evil ways or worship
their idols. 19 I reminded them that I was
the LORD their God and that they should
obey my laws and teachings. 20 I told them
to respect my Sabbath to show that they
were my people and that I was the LORD
their God. 21 But the children also rebelled
against me. They refused to obey my laws
and teachings, and they treated the Sabbath as any other day.

I became angry and decided to punish
them in the desert. 22 But I did not. That
would have disgraced me in front of the
nations that had seen me bring the Israelites out of Egypt. 23 So I solemnly swore
that I would scatter the people of Israel
across the nations, 24 because they had disobeyed my laws and ignored my teachings;
they had disgraced my Sabbath and worshiped the idols their ancestors had made.
25 I gave them laws that bring punishment
instead of life, 26 and I let them offer me
unacceptable sacrifices, including their
first-born sons. I did this to horrify them
and to let them know that I, the LORD, was
punishing them.

27 Ezekiel, tell the people of Israel that
their ancestors also rejected and insulted
me 28 by offering sacrifices, incense, and
wine to gods on every hill and under every
large tree. I was very angry, because they
did these things in the land I had given
them! 29 I asked them where they went to
worship those gods, and they answered, "At
the local shrines."[t] And those places of
worship are still called shrines.

30 Then ask the Israelites why they are
following the example of their wicked ancestors 31 by worshiping idols and by sacrificing their own children as offerings. They
commit these sins and still think they can
ask me for a message. As surely as I am the
living LORD God, I will give them no answer. 32 They may think they can be like
other nations and get away with worshiping
idols made of wood and stone. But that will
never happen!

The LORD Promises To Restore Israel

The LORD said to the people of Israel:

33 As surely as I am the living LORD God,
I will rule over you with my powerful arm.
You will feel my fierce anger 34 and my
power, when I gather you from the places
where you are scattered 35 and lead you
into a desert surrounded by nations. I will
meet you there face to face. Then I will
pass judgment on you 36 and punish you,
just as I punished your ancestors in the
desert near Egypt.[u] 37 I will force each of
you to obey the regulations of our solemn
agreement. 38 I will separate the sinful
rebels from the rest of you, and even
though I will bring them from the nations
where they live in exile, they won't be allowed to return to Israel. Then you will
know that I am the LORD.

39 Go ahead and worship your idols for
now, you Israelites, because soon I will no
longer let you dishonor me by offering gifts
to them. You will have no choice but to
obey me![v] 40 When that day comes, everyone in Israel will worship me on Mount

[t]**20.29** *where they went to worship those gods . . . local shrines*: In Hebrew "where they went" sounds like "local shrines." These were places to worship foreign gods. [u]**20.36** *the desert near Egypt*: The Sinai Desert. [v]**20.39** *me*: One possible meaning for the difficult Hebrew text of verse 39.

20.12 Ex 31.13-17. **20.15** Nu 14.26-35. **20.23** Lv 26.33.

Zion, my holy mountain in Jerusalem. I
will once again call you my own, and I will
accept your sacred offerings and sacrifices.
41 When I bring you home from the places
where you are now scattered, I will be
pleased with you, just as I am pleased with
the smell of the smoke from your sacrifices.
Every nation on earth will see that I am
holy, 42 and you will know that I, the LORD,
am the one who brought you back to Israel,
the land I promised your ancestors.
43 Then you will remember your wicked
sins, and you will hate yourselves for doing
such horrible things. They have made you
unacceptable to me, 44 so you deserve to be
punished. But I will treat you in a way that
will bring honor to my name, and you will
know that I am the LORD God.

Fire from the South

45 The LORD said, 46 "Ezekiel, son of
man, turn toward the south and warn the
forests 47 that I, the LORD God, will start a
fire that will burn up every tree, whether
green or dry. Nothing will be able to put out
the blaze of that fire as it spreads to the
north and burns everything in its path.
48 Everyone will know that I started it, and
that it cannot be stopped."

49 But I complained, "LORD God, I don't
want to do that! People already say I confuse them with my messages."

The LORD Will Punish Jerusalem

21 The LORD said:
2 Ezekiel, son of man, condemn
the places in Jerusalem where people worship. Warn everyone in Israel 3 that I am
about to punish them. I will pull out my
sword and have it ready to kill everyone,
whether good or evil. 4 From south to
north, people will die, 5 knowing that my
sword will never be put away.

6 Ezekiel, groan in sorrow and despair
so that everyone can hear you. 7 When they
ask why you are groaning, tell them you
have terrifying news that will make them
faint and tremble in fear and lose all
courage. These things will happen soon. I,
the LORD God, make this promise!

A Sword Is Ready To Attack Israel

8 The LORD said:
9-10 Ezekiel, son of man, tell the people
of Jerusalem:

I have sharpened my sword
to slaughter you;
it is shiny and will flash
like lightning!
Don't celebrate—
punishment is coming,
because everyone has ignored
my warnings.[w]
11 My sword has been polished;
it's sharp and ready to kill.

12 Groan in sorrow, Ezekiel;
the sword is drawn against
my people and their leaders.
They will die!
So give up all hope.
13 I am testing my people,
and they can do nothing
to stop me.[x]
I, the LORD, have spoken.

14 Ezekiel, warn my people,
then celebrate my victory
by clapping your hands.
My vicious sword will attack
again and again,
killing my people
with every stroke.
15 They will lose all courage
and stumble with fear.
My slaughtering sword
is waiting at every gate,
flashing and ready to kill.[y]
16 It will slash right and left,
wherever the blade is pointed.
17 Then I will stop being angry,
and I will clap my hands
in victory.
I, the LORD, have spoken.

The King of Babylonia and His Sword

18 The LORD said:

19 Ezekiel, son of man, mark two roads
for the king of Babylonia to follow when he

[w]21.9,10 *Don't celebrate . . . my warnings*: One possible meaning for the difficult Hebrew text.
[x]21.13 *I am testing . . . me*: One possible meaning for the difficult Hebrew text. [y]21.15 *My slaughtering sword . . . ready to kill*: One possible meaning for the difficult Hebrew text.

comes with his sword. The roads will begin at the same place, but be sure to put up a signpost where the two roads separate and go in different directions. 20 Clearly mark where the two roads lead. One goes to Rabbah, the capital of Ammon, and the other goes to Jerusalem, the fortified capital of Judah. 21 When the Babylonian king stands at that signpost, he will decide which way to go by shaking his arrows, by asking his idols, and by carefully looking at the liver of a sacrificed animal.[z] 22 His right hand will pull out the arrow marked "Jerusalem." Then he will immediately give the signal to shout the battle cry, to build dirt ramps to the top of the city walls, to break down its walls and gates with large wooden poles, and to kill the people. 23 Everyone in Jerusalem had promised to be loyal to Babylonia, and so none of them will believe that this could happen to them. But Babylonia's king will remind them of their sinful ways and warn them of their coming captivity.

24 Ezekiel, tell the people of Jerusalem and their ruler that I, the LORD God, am saying:

Everything you do is wicked and shows how sinful you are. You are guilty and will be taken away as prisoners.

25 And now, you evil and wicked ruler of Israel, your day of final punishment is almost here. 26 I, the LORD God, command you to take off your royal turban and your crown, because everything will be different. Those who had no power will be put in charge, and those who now rule will become nobodies. 27 I will leave Jerusalem in ruins when my chosen one comes to punish this city.

Judgment against Ammon

28 The LORD God said:

Ezekiel, son of man, the Ammonites have insulted Israel, so condemn them and tell them I am saying:

A sword is drawn,
ready to slaughter;
it is polished and prepared
to kill as fast as lightning.

29 You wicked Ammonites see false visions and believe untrue messages. But your day of punishment is coming soon, and my sword will slaughter you!

30 Your days to punish others are over, so put your swords away.[a] You will be punished in the land of your birth. 31 My furious anger will scorch you like fire, and I will hand you over to cruel men who are experts in killing. 32 You will be burned and will die in your own land. Then you will be forgotten forever. I, the LORD, have spoken.

Jerusalem Is Condemned

22 Some time later, the LORD said:
2 Ezekiel, son of man, are you ready to condemn Jerusalem? That city is filled with murderers, so remind the people of their sins 3 and tell them I am saying:

Jerusalem, you have murdered many of your own people and have worshiped idols. You will soon be punished! 4 Those crimes have made you guilty, and the idols have made you unacceptable to me. So your final punishment is near. Other nations will laugh at you and make insulting remarks, 5 and people far and near will make fun of your misery.

6 Your own leaders use their power to murder. 7 None of you honor your parents, and you cheat foreigners, orphans, and widows. 8 You show no respect for my sacred places and treat the Sabbath just like any other day. 9 Some of your own people tell lies, so that others will be put to death. Some of you eat meat sacrificed to idols at local shrines, and others never stop doing vulgar things. 10 Men have sex with their father's wife or with women who are having their monthly period 11 or with someone else's wife. Some men even sleep with their

[z]**21.21** *shaking . . . animal*: These were ways the Babylonians found out what their gods wanted them to do. [a]**21.30** *Your days . . . put your swords away*: One possible meaning for the difficult Hebrew text.

21.28-32 Jr 49.1-6; Ez 25.1-7; Am 1.3-15; Zep 2.8-11. **22.7** **a** Ex 20.12; Dt 5.16; **b** Ex 22.21, 22; Dt 24.17. **22.8** Lv 19.30; 26.2. **22.10,11** Lv 18.7-20.

own daughter-in-law or half sister. [12] Others of you accept money to murder someone. Your own people charge high interest when making a loan to other Israelites, and they get rich by cheating. Worst of all, you have forgotten me, the LORD God.

[13] I will shake my fist in anger at your violent crimes. [14] When I'm finished with you, your courage will disappear, and you will be so weak that you won't be able to lift your hands. I, the LORD, have spoken and will not change my mind. [15] I will scatter you throughout every nation on earth and put a stop to your sinful ways. [16] You[b] will be humiliated in the eyes of other nations. Then you will know that I, the LORD God, have done these things.

Jerusalem Must Be Purified

[17] The LORD said:

[18] Ezekiel, son of man, I consider the people of Israel as worthless as the leftover metal in a furnace after silver has been purified. [19] So I am going to bring them together in Jerusalem. [20-21] I will be like a metalworker who collects that metal from the furnace and melts it down. I will collect the Israelites and blow on them with my fiery anger. They will melt inside the city of Jerusalem [22] like silver in a furnace. Then they will know that I, the LORD, have punished them in my anger.

Everyone in Jerusalem Is Guilty

[23] The LORD said:

[24] Ezekiel, son of man, tell the people of Israel that their country is full of sin, and that I, the LORD, am furious! [25] Their leaders are like[c] roaring lions, tearing apart their victims. They put people to death, then steal everything of value. Husbands are killed, and many women are left as widows.

[26] The priests of Israel ignore my Law! Not only do they refuse to respect any of my sacred things, but they don't even teach the difference between what is sacred and what is ordinary, or between what is clean and what is unclean. They treat my Sabbath like any other day, and so my own people no longer honor me.

[27] Israel's officials are like ferocious wolves, ripping their victims apart. They make a dishonest living by injuring and killing people.

[28] And then the prophets in Israel cover up these sins by giving false visions. I have never spoken to them, but they lie and say they have a message from me. [29] The people themselves cheat and rob; they abuse the poor and take advantage of foreigners.

[30] I looked for someone to defend the city and to protect it from my anger, as well as to stop me from destroying it. But I found no one. [31] So in my fierce anger, I will punish the Israelites for what they have done, and they will know that I am furious. I, the LORD, have spoken.

Two Sinful Sisters

23 The LORD said:

[2] Ezekiel, son of man, listen to this story about two sisters. [3] While they were young and living in Egypt, they became prostitutes. [4] The older one was named Oholah, which stands for Samaria; the younger one was Oholibah, which stands for Jerusalem.[d] They became my wives and gave birth to my children.

[5] Even though Oholah was my wife, she continued to be a prostitute and chased after Assyrian lovers. [6] She offered herself to soldiers in purple uniforms, to every handsome, high-ranking officer, and to cavalry troops. [7] She had sex with all the important Assyrian officials and even worshiped their disgusting idols. [8] Once she started doing these things in Egypt, she never stopped. Men slept with her, and she was always ready for sex.

[9] So I gave Oholah to the Assyrian lovers she wanted so badly. [10] They ripped off her

[b]**22.16** *You*: Hebrew; two ancient translations "Because of you, I." [c]**22.25** *Their leaders are like*: One ancient translation; Hebrew "Their prophets are like herds of." [d]**23.4** *Samaria . . . Jerusalem*: After the nation of Israel was divided, the northern kingdom was called "Israel," and the southern kingdom was called "Judah." Samaria was the capital of the northern kingdom, and Jerusalem was the capital of the southern kingdom.

22.12 Ex 23.8; Dt 16.18, 19; Ex 22.25; Lv 25.36, 37; Dt 23.19. **22.26** Lv 10.10.

clothes, then captured her children and killed her. Women everywhere talked about what had happened to Oholah.

[11] Oholibah saw all this, but she was more sinful and wanted sex more than her sister Oholah ever did. [12] Oholibah also chased after good-looking Assyrian officers, uniformed soldiers, and cavalry troops. [13] Just like her sister, she did vulgar things.

[14] But Oholibah behaved worse than her sister. Oholibah saw images of Babylonian men carved into walls and painted red. [15] They had belts around their waists and large turbans on their heads, and they reminded her of Babylonian cavalry officers. [16] As soon as she looked at them, she wanted to have sex with them. And so, she sent messengers to bring them to her. [17] Men from Babylonia came and had sex with her so many times that she got disgusted with them. [18] She let everyone see her naked body and didn't care if they knew she was a prostitute. That's why I turned my back on her, just as I had done with her older sister.

[19] Oholibah didn't stop there, but became even more immoral and acted as she had back in Egypt. [20] She eagerly wanted to go to bed with Egyptian men, who were famous for their sexual powers. [21] And she longed for the days when she was a young prostitute, when men enjoyed having sex with her.

The LORD Will Punish Oholibah

[22] The LORD God said:

Oholibah,[e] though you no longer want to be around your lovers, they will surround you like enemies, when I turn them against you. [23] I will gather all the handsome young officials and the high-ranking cavalry officers from Babylonia and Assyria, as well as from the Chaldean tribes of Pekod, Shoa, and Koa. [24] Their large armies will come from the north[f] with chariots and wagons carrying weapons. They will wear shields and helmets and will surround you, and I will let them judge and sentence you according to their own laws. [25] I am angry with you, so I will let them be very cruel. They will cut off your nose and ears; they will kill your children and put to death anyone in your family who is still alive. [26] Your clothes and jewelry will be torn off. [27] I will stop your wickedness and the prostitution you started back in Egypt. You will never want to think about those days again.

[28] I, the LORD God, am ready to hand you over to those hateful enemies that you find so disgusting. [29] They will cruelly take away everything you have worked for and strip you naked. Then everyone will see you for the prostitute you really are. Your own vulgar sins [30] have led to this. You were the one determined to have sex with men from other nations and to worship their idols. [31] You have turned out no better than your older sister, and now you must drink from the cup filled with my anger.

[32] I, the LORD God, gave your sister a large, deep cup filled with my anger. And when you drink from that cup, you will be mocked and insulted. [33] You will end up drunk and devastated, because that cup is filled with horror and ruin. [34] But you must drink every drop! Then smash the cup to pieces and use them to cut your breasts in sorrow. I, the LORD God, have spoken.

[35] You have completely rejected me, and so I promise that you will be punished for the disgusting things you did as a prostitute.

The Two Sisters Are Condemned

[36] The LORD said:

Ezekiel, son of man, it's time for you to tell Oholah and Oholibah[g] that they are guilty. Remind them of their evil ways! [37] They have been unfaithful by worshiping idols, and they have committed murder by sacrificing my own children as offerings to idols. [38-39] They came into my temple that same day, and that made it unfit as a place to worship me. They have even stopped respecting the Sabbath.

[40] They sent messengers to attract men from far away. When those men arrived,

[e]**23.22** *Oholibah*: That is, Jerusalem (see verse 4). [f]**23.24** *from the north*: One ancient translation; Hebrew "with weapons." [g]**23.36** *Oholah and Oholibah*: That is, Samaria and Jerusalem (see verse 4).

the two sisters took baths and put on eye shadow and jewelry. 41 They sat on a fancy couch, and in front of them was a table for the olive oil and incense that had belonged to me. 42 Their room was always filled with a noisy crowd of drunkards brought in from the desert. These men gave the women bracelets and beautiful crowns, 43 and I noticed that the men were eager to have sex with these women, though they were exhausted from being prostitutes.[h] 44 In fact, the men had sex over and over with Oholah and Oholibah, the two sinful sisters. 45 But good men will someday accuse those two of murder and of being unfaithful, because they are certainly guilty.

46 So I, the LORD God, now say to these sisters:

I will call together an angry mob that will abuse and rob you. 47 They will stone you to death and cut you to pieces; they will kill your children and burn down your houses. 48 I will get rid of sinful prostitution in this country, so that women everywhere will be warned not to act as you have. 49 You will be punished for becoming prostitutes and for worshiping idols, and you will know that I am the LORD God.

A Cooking Pot

24 Nine years after King Jehoiachin and the rest of us had been led away as prisoners to Babylonia, the LORD spoke to me on the tenth day of the tenth month.[i] He said:

2 Ezekiel, son of man, write down today's date, because the king of Babylonia has just begun attacking the city of Jerusalem. 3 Then tell my rebellious people:

"Pour water in a cooking pot
and set it over a fire.
*4 Throw in the legs and shoulders
of your finest sheep
and put in the juicy bones.
5 "Pile wood[j] underneath the pot,
and let the meat and bones
boil until they are done."

6 These words mean that Jerusalem is doomed! The city is filled with murderers and is like an old, rusty pot. The meat is taken out piece by piece, and no one cares what happens to it.[k] 7 The people of Jerusalem murdered innocent people in the city and didn't even try to cover up the blood that flowed out on the hard ground. 8 But I have seen that blood, and it cries out for me to take revenge.

9 I, the LORD God, will punish that city of violence! I will make a huge pile of firewood, 10 so bring more wood and light it. Cook the meat and boil away the broth[l] to let the bones scorch. 11 Then set the empty pot over the hot coals until it is red-hot. That will clean the pot and burn off the rust. 12 I've tried everything else. Now the rust must be burned away.[m]

13 Jerusalem is so full of sin and evil that I can't get it clean, even though I have tried. It will stay filthy until I let loose my fierce anger against it. 14 That time will certainly come! And when it does, I won't show the people of Jerusalem any pity or change my mind. They must be punished for the evil they have done. I, the LORD God, have spoken.

Ezekiel's Wife Dies

15 The LORD said, 16 "Ezekiel, son of man, I will suddenly take the life of the person you love most. But I don't want you to complain or cry. 17 Mourn in silence and don't show that you are grieving. Don't remove your turban or take off your sandals; don't cover your face to show your sorrow, or eat the food that mourners eat."[n]

18 One morning, I was talking with the

[h] **23.43** *prostitutes*: One possible meaning for the difficult Hebrew text of verse 43. [i] **24.1** *Nine years . . . tenth month*: Probably January of 588 B.C. [j] **24.5** *Pile wood*: Or "Stack the bones." [k] **24.6** *and no one cares what happens to it*: One possible meaning for the difficult Hebrew text. [l] **24.10** *boil away the broth*: One ancient translation; Hebrew "mix the spices." [m] **24.12** *away*: One possible meaning for the difficult Hebrew text of verse 12. [n] **24.17** *Don't remove your turban . . . take off your sandals . . . cover your face . . . eat the food that mourners eat*: The usual way people mourned was to remove anything worn on the head, to go barefoot, to cover their faces, and to eat special food to show they were grieving.

24.2 2 K 25.1; Jr 52.4.

people as usual, and by sunset my wife was dead. The next day I did what the LORD told me, [19] and when people saw me, they asked, "Why aren't you mourning for your wife?"

[20] I answered:

The LORD God says [21] he is ready to destroy the temple in which you take such pride and which makes you feel so safe. Your children who now live in Jerusalem will be killed. [22] Then you will do the same things I have done. You will leave your face uncovered and refuse to eat the food that mourners usually eat. [23] You won't take off your turbans and your sandals.[o] You won't cry or mourn, but all day long you will go around groaning because of your sins.

[24] I am a warning sign—everything I have done, you will also do. And then you will know the LORD God has made these things happen.

[25] The LORD said, "Ezekiel, I will soon destroy the temple that makes everyone feel proud and safe, and I will take away their children as well. [26] On that same day, someone will escape from the city and come to tell you what has happened. [27] Then you will be able to speak again,[p] and the two of you will talk. You will be a warning sign to the people, and they will know that I am the LORD."

Judgment on Ammon

25 The LORD God said:

[2] Ezekiel, son of man, condemn the people of Ammon [3] and tell them:

You celebrated when my temple was destroyed, when Israel was defeated, and when my people were taken away as prisoners. [4] Now I am going to let you be conquered by tribes from the eastern desert. They will set up their camps in your land and eat your fruit and drink your milk. [5] Your capital city of Rabbah will be nothing but pastureland for camels, and the rest of the country will be pastures for sheep. Then you will know that I am the LORD God.

[6] You hated Israel so much that you clapped and shouted and celebrated. [7] And so I will hand you over to enemies who will rob you. I will completely destroy you. There won't be enough of your people left to be a nation ever again, and you will know that I, the LORD, have done these things.

Judgment on Moab

[8] The LORD God said, "The people of Moab[q] thought Judah was no different from any other nation. [9] So I will let Moab's fortress towns along its border be attacked, including Beth-Jeshimoth, Baal-Meon, and Kiriathaim. [10] The same eastern desert tribes that invade Ammon will invade Moab, and just as Ammon will be forgotten forever, [11] Moab will be punished. Then the people there will know that I am the LORD."

Judgment on Edom

[12] The LORD God then said, "The people of Edom are guilty of taking revenge on Judah. [13] So I will punish Edom by killing all its people and livestock. It will be an empty wasteland all the way from Teman to Dedan. [14] I will send my own people to take revenge on the Edomites by making them feel my fierce anger. And when I punish them, they will know that I am the LORD God."

Judgment on Philistia

[15] The LORD God said, "The cruel Philistines have taken revenge on their enemies over and over and have tried to destroy them. [16] Now it's my turn to treat the Philistines as my enemies and to kill

[o]**24.22,23** *You will leave your face uncovered . . . refuse to eat the food . . . won't take off your turbans and your sandals*: See the note at 24.17. [p]**24.27** *you will be able to speak again*: See 3.25-27; 33.21,22. [q]**25.8** *Moab*: One ancient translation; Hebrew "Moab and Edom."

25.1-7 Jr 49.1-6; Ez 21.28-32; Am 1.13-15; Zep 2.8-11. **25.8-11** Is 15.1—16.14; 25.10-12; Jr 48.1-47; Am 2.1-3; Zep 2.8-11. **25.12-14** Is 34.5-17; 63.1-6; Jr 49.7-22; Ez 35.1-15; Am 1.11, 12; Ob 1-14; Ml 1.2-5. **25.15-17** Is 14.29-31; Jr 47.1-7; Jl 3.4-8; Am 1.6-8; Zep 2.4-7; Zec 9.5-7.

everyone[r] living in their towns along the
seacoast. 17 In my fierce anger, I will take
revenge on them. And when I punish
them, they will know that I am the LORD."

Judgment on the City of Tyre

26 Eleven years[s] after King Jehoiachin
and the rest of us had been led
away as prisoners to Babylonia, the LORD
spoke to me on the first day of the month.
He said:
2 Ezekiel, son of man, the people of the
city of Tyre[t] have celebrated Jerusalem's
defeat by singing,

"Jerusalem has fallen!
It used to be powerful,
a center of trade.
Now the city is shattered,
and we will take its place."

3 Because the people of Tyre have sung
that song, I have the following warning for
them: I am the LORD God, and I am now
your enemy! I will send nations to attack
you, like waves crashing against the shore.
4 They will tear down your city walls and
defense towers. I will sweep away the ruins
until all that's left of you is a bare rock,
5 where fishermen can dry their nets along
the coast. I promise that you will be robbed
6 and that the people who live in your
towns along the coast will be killed. Then
you will know that I am the LORD.
7 King Nebuchadnezzar of Babylonia is
the world's most powerful king, and I will
send him to attack you. He will march from
the north with a powerful army, including
horses and chariots and cavalry troops.
8 First, he will attack your towns along the
coast and kill the people who live there.
Then he will build dirt ramps up to the top
of your city walls and set up rows of shields
around you. 9 He will command some of
his troops to use large wooden poles to beat
down your walls, while others use iron rods
to knock down your watchtowers. 10 He will
have so many horses that the dust they stir
up will seem like a thick fog. And as his
chariots and cavalry approach, even the
walls will shake, especially when he proudly
enters your ruined city. 11 His troops will
ride through your streets, killing people left
and right, and your strong columns will
crumble to the ground. 12 The troops
will steal your valuable possessions; they will
break down your walls, and crush your expensive houses. Then the stones and wood
and all the remains will be dumped into
the sea. 13 You will have no reason to sing
or play music on harps, 14 because I will
turn you into a bare rock where fishermen
can dry their nets. And you will never rebuild your city. I, the LORD God, make this
promise.
15 The people of the nations up and
down the coast will shudder when they
hear your screams and moans of death.
16 The kings will step down from their
thrones, then take off their royal robes and
fancy clothes, and sit on the ground, trembling. They will be so shocked at the news
of your defeat that they will shake in fear
17 and sing this funeral song:

"The great city beside the sea
is destroyed![u]
Its people once ruled the coast
and terrified everyone there.
18 But now Tyre is in ruins,
and the people on the coast
stare at it in horror
and tremble in fear."

19 I, the LORD God, will turn you into a
ghost-town. The ocean depths will rise over
you 20 and carry you down to the world of
the dead, where you will join people of ancient times and towns ruined long ago. You
will stay there and never again be a city
filled with people.[v] 21 You will die a horrible

[r] **25.16** *kill everyone*: The Hebrew text also has the name "Cherethites," which was a group of people that lived just southeast of Philistia, and was often identified with the Philistines. [s] **26.1** *Eleven years*: Probably late in 587 B.C. [t] **26.2** *Tyre*: One of the two major cities of Phoenicia; Sidon was the other. [u] **26.17** *The great city . . . is destroyed*: One possible meaning for the difficult Hebrew text. [v] **26.20** *You will stay there . . . with people*: One possible meaning for the difficult Hebrew text.

26.1—28.19 Is 23.1-18; Jl 3.4-8; Am 1.9, 10; Zec 9.1-4; Mt 11.21, 22; Lk 10.13, 14. **26.13** Rev 18.22. **26.16-18** Rev 18.9, 10. **26.21** Rev 18.21.

death! People will come looking for your city, but it will never be found. I, the LORD, have spoken.

A Funeral Song for Tyre

27 The LORD said:
2 Ezekiel, son of man, sing a fu-
neral song for Tyre,[w] 3 the city that is built
along the sea and that trades with nations
along the coast. Tell the people of Tyre that
the following message is from me:

Tyre, you brag about
your perfect beauty,
4 and your control of the sea.[x]

You are a ship
built to perfection.
5 Builders used cypress trees
from Mount Hermon
to make your planks
and a cedar tree from Lebanon
for your tall mast.
6 Oak trees from Bashan
were shaped into oars;
pine trees from Cyprus[y]
were cut for your deck,
which was then decorated
with strips of ivory.
7 The builders used fancy linen
from Egypt for your sails,
so everyone could see you.
Blue and purple cloth
from Cyprus was used
to shade your deck.
8 Men from Sidon and Arvad
did the rowing,
and your own skilled workers
were the captains.
9 Experienced men from Byblos
repaired any damages.
Sailors from all over
shopped at the stores
in your port.
10 Brave soldiers from Persia,
Lydia, and Libya
served in your navy,
protecting you with shields
and helmets,
and making you famous.
11 Your guards came from
Arvad and Cilicia,
and men from Gamad
stood watch in your towers.
With their weapons
hung on your walls,
your beauty was complete.

12 Merchants from southern Spain[z]
traded silver, iron, tin, and lead for your
products. 13 The people of Greece, Tubal,
and Meshech traded slaves and things
made of bronze, 14 and those from Beth-
Togarmah traded work horses, war horses,
and mules. 15 You also did business with
people from Rhodes,[a] and people from
nations along the coast gave you ivory
and ebony[b] in exchange for your goods.
16 Edom[c] traded emeralds, purple cloth,
embroidery, fine linen, coral, and rubies.
17 Judah and Israel gave you their finest
wheat, fancy figs,[d] honey, olive oil, and
spices in exchange for your merchandise.
18 The people of Damascus saw what you
had to offer and brought you wine from
Helbon and wool from Zahar. 19 Vedan and
Javan near Uzal[e] traded you iron and
spices. 20 The people of Dedan supplied
you with saddle blankets, 21 while people
from Arabia and the rulers of Kedar traded
lambs, sheep, and goats. 22 Merchants from
Sheba and Raamah gave you excellent
spices, precious stones, and gold in exchange for your products. 23 You also did
business with merchants from the cities of
Haran, Canneh, Eden, Sheba, Asshur, and
Chilmad, 24 and they gave you expensive
clothing, purple and embroidered cloth,
brightly colored rugs, and strong rope.

[w]**27.2** *Tyre*: See the note at 26.2. [x]**27.4** *and your control of the sea*: One possible meaning for the difficult Hebrew text. [y]**27.6** *pine trees from Cyprus*: One possible meaning for the difficult Hebrew text. [z]**27.12** *southern Spain*: The Hebrew text has "Tarshish," which may have been a Phoenician city in southern Spain. [a]**27.15** *Rhodes*: One ancient translation; Hebrew "Dedan." [b]**27.15** *ebony*: A valuable black wood. [c]**27.16** *Edom*: Some Hebrew manuscripts and one ancient translation; most Hebrew manuscripts "Syria." [d]**27.17** *their finest wheat, fancy figs*: One possible meaning for the difficult Hebrew text. [e]**27.19** *Vedan and Javan near Uzal*: One possible meaning for the difficult Hebrew text.

25 Large, seagoing ships[f] carried your goods wherever they needed to go.

You were like a ship
loaded with heavy cargo
26 and sailing across the sea,
but you were wrecked
by strong eastern winds.
27 Everything on board was lost—
your valuable cargo,
your sailors and carpenters,
merchants and soldiers.
28 The shouts of your drowning crew
were heard on the shore.

29 Every ship is deserted;
rowers and sailors and captains
all stand on shore,
30 mourning for you.
They show their sorrow
by putting dust on their heads
and rolling in ashes;
31 they shave their heads
and dress in sackcloth[g]
as they cry in despair.
32 In their grief they sing
a funeral song for you:
"Tyre, you were greater
than all other cities.
But now you lie in silence
at the bottom of the sea.[h]

33 "Nations that received
your merchandise
were always pleased;
kings everywhere got rich
from your costly goods.
34 But now you are wrecked
in the deep sea,
with your cargo and crew
scattered everywhere.
35 People living along the coast
are shocked at the news.
Their rulers are horrified,
and terror is written
across their faces.
36 The merchants of the world
can't believe what happened.
Your death was gruesome,
and you are gone forever."

Judgment on the King of Tyre

28 The LORD God said:
2 Ezekiel, son of man, tell the
king of Tyre[i] that I am saying:

You are so arrogant that you think you're a god and that the city of Tyre is your throne. You may claim to be a god, though you're nothing but a mere human.
3 You think you're wiser than Daniel[j] and know everything.[k]

4 Your wisdom has certainly made you rich, because you have storehouses filled with gold and silver.
5 You're a clever businessman and are extremely wealthy, but your wealth has led to arrogance!

6 You compared yourself to a god, so
now I, the LORD God, 7 will make you the victim of cruel enemies. They will destroy all the possessions you've worked so hard to get.
8 Your enemies will brutally kill you, and the sea will be your only grave.

9 When you face your enemies, will you still claim to be a god? They will attack, and you will suffer like any other human.
10 Foreigners will kill you, and you will die the death of those who don't worship me. I, the LORD, have spoken.

A Funeral Song for the King of Tyre

11 The LORD said:
12 Ezekiel, son of man, sing a funeral song for the king of Tyre[l] and tell him I am saying:

At one time, you were perfect,[m] intelligent, and good-looking.
13 You lived in the garden of Eden and wore jewelry made of brightly colored gems and

[f]**27.25** *Large, seagoing ships*: The Hebrew text has "Ships of Tarshish," which may have been a Phoenician city in Spain. "Ships of Tarshish" probably means large, seagoing ships.
[g]**27.31** *sackcloth*: See the note at 7.18. [h]**27.32** *Tyre, you were greater . . . the bottom of the sea*: One possible meaning for the difficult Hebrew text. [i]**28.2** *Tyre*: See the note at 26.2.
[j]**28.3** *Daniel*: See the note at 14.14. [k]**28.3** *and know everything*: One possible meaning for the difficult Hebrew text. [l]**28.12** *Tyre*: See the note at 26.2. [m]**28.12** *you were perfect*: One possible meaning for the difficult Hebrew text.
27.25-36 Rev 18.11-19.

precious stones. They were all set in
gold[n] and were ready for you on the
day you were born. 14 I appointed a
winged creature to guard your home[o] on
my holy mountain, where you walked
among gems that dazzled like fire.
15 You were truly good from the
time of your birth, but later you started
doing wicked things. 16 You traded
with other nations and became more
and more cruel and evil. So I forced
you to leave my mountain, and the
creature that had been your protector
now chased you away from the gems.
17 It was your good looks that made
you arrogant, and you were so famous
that you started acting like a fool.
That's why I threw you to the ground
and let other kings sneer at you. 18 You
have cheated so many other merchants that your places of worship are
corrupt. So I set your city on fire and
burned it down. Now everyone sees
only ashes where your city once stood,
19 and the people of other nations are
shocked. Your punishment was horrible, and you are gone forever.

Judgment on Sidon and Peace for Israel

20 The LORD said:
21 Ezekiel, son of man, condemn the
city of Sidon[p] 22 and tell its people:
I, the LORD God, am your enemy!
People will praise me when I punish
you, and they will see that I am holy.
23 I will send deadly diseases to wipe
you out, and I will send enemies to invade and surround you. Your people
will be killed, and you will know that I
am the LORD.
24 When that happens, the people
of Israel will no longer have cruel
neighbors that abuse them and make
them feel as though they are in a field
of thorns and briers. And the Israelites
will know that I, the LORD God, have
done these things.

A Blessing for Israel

25 The LORD God said:
Someday I will gather the people of
Israel from the nations where they are
now scattered, and every nation will
see that I am holy. The Israelites will
once again live in the land I gave to my
servant Jacob. 26 They will be safe and
will build houses and plant vineyards.
They will no longer be in danger, because I will punish their hateful neighbors. Israel will know that I am the
LORD their God.

Judgment on the King of Egypt

29 Ten years after King Jehoiachin
and the rest of us had been led
away as prisoners to Babylonia, the LORD
spoke to me on the twelfth day of the tenth
month.[q] He said:
2 Ezekiel, son of man, condemn the
king of Egypt. Tell him and his people
3 that I am saying:
King of Egypt, you were like a giant
crocodile lying in a river. You acted as
though you owned the Nile and made
it for yourself. But now I, the LORD
God, am your enemy! 4 I will put a
hook in your jaw and pull you out of
the water, and all the fish in your river
will stick to your scaly body.[r] 5 I'll
throw you and the fish into the desert,
and your body will fall on the hard
ground. You will be left unburied,[s] and
wild animals and birds will eat your
flesh. 6 Then everyone in Egypt will
know that I am the LORD.
You and your nation refused to help
the people of Israel and were nothing

[n]**28.13** *They were all set in gold*: One possible meaning for the difficult Hebrew text. [o]**28.14** *I appointed a winged creature to guard your home*: One possible meaning for the difficult Hebrew text. [p]**28.21** *Sidon*: See the note at 26.2. [q]**29.1** *Ten years . . . tenth month*: Probably January of 587 B.C. [r]**29.4** *all the fish in your river will stick to your scaly body*: All the king's officials will be removed from power and destroyed along with the king himself. [s]**29.5** *You will be left unburied*: A proper burial in a royal tomb was extremely important to Egyptian kings, because they often thought of themselves as gods.

28.20-26 Jl 3.4-8; Zec 9.1, 2; Mt 11.21, 22; Lk 10.13, 14. **29.1—32.32** Is 19.1-25; Jr 46.2-26. **29.6** Is 36.6.

more than a broken stick. 7 When they
reached out to you for support, you
broke in half, cutting their arms and
making them fall.[t]
8 So I, the LORD God, will send
troops to attack you, king of Egypt.
They will kill your people and livestock, 9 until your land is a barren
desert. Then you will know that I have
done these things.

You claimed that you made the Nile
River and control it. 10 Now I am turning against you and your river. Your nation will be nothing but an empty
wasteland all the way from the town
of Migdol in the north to Aswan in the
south, and as far as the border of Ethiopia.[u] 11 No human or animal will even
dare travel through Egypt, because
no sign of life will be found there for
forty years. 12 It will be the most barren place on earth. Every city in Egypt
will lie in ruins during those forty
years, and I will scatter your people
throughout the nations of the world.
13 Then after those forty years have
passed, I will bring your people back
from the places where I scattered
them. 14 They will once again live in
their homeland in southern Egypt. But
they will be a weak kingdom 15 and
won't ever be strong enough to rule
nations, as they did in the past. 16 My
own people Israel will never again depend on your nation. In fact, when the
Israelites remember what happened to
you Egyptians, they will realize how
wrong they were to turn to you for
help. Then the Israelites will know
that I, the LORD God, did these things.

King Nebuchadnezzar of Babylonia Will Conquer Egypt

17 Twenty-seven years after King Jehoiachin and the rest of us had been led
away as prisoners to Babylonia, the LORD
spoke to me on the first day of the first
month.[v] He said:
18 King Nebuchadnezzar of Babylonia has attacked the city of Tyre. He
forced his soldiers to carry so many
heavy loads that their heads were
rubbed bald, and their shoulders were
red and sore. Nebuchadnezzar and his
army still could not capture the city.
19 So now I will hand over the nation
of Egypt to him. He will take Egypt's
valuable treasures and give them to his
own troops. 20 Egypt will be his reward,
because he and his army have been
following my orders. I, the LORD God,
have spoken.
21 Ezekiel, when Egypt is defeated,
I will make the people of Israel strong,
and I will give you the power to speak
to them. Then they will know that I,
the LORD, have done these things.

Egypt Will Be a Barren Desert

30 The LORD said:
2 Ezekiel, son of man, tell the
people of Egypt that I am saying:

Cry out in despair,
3 because you will soon
be punished!
That will be a time
of darkness and doom
for all nations.
4 Your own nation of Egypt
will be attacked,
and Ethiopia[w] will suffer.
You will be killed in battle,
and your land will be robbed
and left in ruins.

5 Soldiers hired from Ethiopia, Libya,
Lydia, Arabia, Kub, as well as from Israel,[x]
will die in that battle. 6 All of your allies will
be killed, and your proud strength will
crumble. People will die from Migdol in the
north to Aswan in the south. I, the LORD,
have spoken.
7 Your nation of Egypt will be the most
deserted place on earth, and its cities will
lie in complete ruin. 8 I will set fire to your
land, and anyone who defended your na-

[t] **29.7** *making them fall*: One possible meaning for the difficult Hebrew text. [u] **29.10** *Ethiopia*: The Hebrew text has "Cush," which was a region south of Egypt that included parts of the present countries of Ethiopia and Sudan. [v] **29.17** *Twenty-seven . . . first month*: Probably March of 571 B.C. [w] **30.4** *Ethiopia*: See the note at 29.10. [x] **30.5** *as well as from Israel*: One possible meaning for the difficult Hebrew text.

tion will die. Then you will know that I am
the LORD.
[9] On the same day I destroy Egypt, I will
send messengers to the Ethiopians to announce their coming destruction. They think
they are safe, but they will be terrified.
[10] Your Egyptian army is very strong, but
I will send King Nebuchadnezzar of Babylonia to completely defeat that army. [11] He
and his cruel troops will invade and destroy
your land and leave your dead bodies piled
everywhere.
[12] I will dry up the Nile River, then sell
the land to evil buyers. I will send foreigners to turn your entire nation into a barren
desert. I, the LORD, have spoken.

Egypt's Proud Cities Will Lie in Ruins

The LORD said to the people of Egypt:
[13] All the idols and images you Egyptians worship in the city of Memphis[y] will
be smashed. No one will be left to rule your
nation, and terror will fill the land. [14] The
city of Pathros will be left in ruins, and
Zoan will be burned to the ground.
Thebes,[z] your capital city, will also be destroyed! [15] The fortress city of Pelusium
will feel my fierce anger, and all the troops
stationed at Thebes will be slaughtered.
[16] I will set fire to your nation of Egypt!
The city of Pelusium will be in anguish.
Thebes will fall, and the people of Memphis will live in constant fear.[a] [17] The
young soldiers in the cities of Heliopolis
and Bubastis[b] will die in battle, and the rest
of the people will be taken prisoner. [18] You
were so proud of your nation's power, but
when I crush that power and kill that
pride, darkness will fall over the city of
Tahpanhes. A dark, gloomy cloud will cover
the land as you are being led away into
captivity. [19] When I'm through punishing
Egypt, you will know that I am the LORD.

Egypt's King Is Powerless

[20] Eleven years after King Jehoiachin
and the rest of us had been led away as
prisoners to Babylonia, the LORD spoke to
me on the seventh day of the first month.[c]
He said:
[21] Ezekiel, son of man, I, the LORD, have
defeated the king of Egypt! I broke his arm,
and no one has wrapped it or put it in a
sling, so that it could heal and get strong
enough to hold a sword. [22] So tell him that
I am now his worst enemy. I will break both
his arms—the good one and the broken
one! His sword will drop from his hand forever, [23] and I will scatter the Egyptians all
over the world.
[24-25] I will strengthen the power of Babylonia's king and give him my sword to use
against Egypt. I will also make the
wounded king of Egypt powerless, and he
will moan in pain and die in front of the
Babylonian king. Then everyone on earth
will know that I am the LORD. [26] I will force
the Egyptians to live as prisoners in foreign
nations, and they will know that I, the
LORD, have punished them.

Egypt's King Will Be Chopped Down like a Cedar Tree

31 Eleven years after King Jehoiachin
and the rest of us had been led
away as prisoners to Babylonia, the LORD
spoke to me on the first day of the third
month.[d] He said:
[2] Ezekiel, son of man, tell the king of
Egypt and his people that I am saying:

You are more powerful
than anyone on earth.
Now listen to this.
[3] There was once a cedar tree
in Lebanon
with large, strong branches
reaching to the sky.[e]
[4] This tree had plenty of water
to help it grow tall,
and nearby streams watered
the other trees
in the forest.
[5] But this tree towered over
those other trees,

[y]**30.13** *Memphis*: Hebrew "Noph." [z]**30.14** *Thebes*: Hebrew "No." [a]**30.16** *the people of Memphis . . . constant fear*: One possible meaning for the difficult Hebrew text.
[b]**30.17** *Heliopolis and Bubastis*: Hebrew "On and Pi-Beseth." [c]**30.20** *Eleven years . . . first month*: Probably March of 587 B.C. [d]**31.1** *Eleven years . . . third month*: Probably May of 587 B.C. [e]**31.3** *sky*: One possible meaning for the difficult Hebrew text of verse 3.

and its branches
grew long and thick.
6 Birds built nests
in its branches,
and animals were born
beneath it.
People from all nations
lived in the shade
of this strong tree.
7 It had beautiful,
long branches,
and its roots found water
deep in the soil.
8 None of the cedar trees
in my garden of Eden
were as beautiful
as this tree;
no tree of any kind
had such long branches.
9 I, the LORD, gave this tree
its beauty,
and I helped the branches
grow strong.
All other trees in Eden
wanted to be just like it.

10 King of Egypt, now listen to what I,
the LORD God, am saying about that tree:
The tree grew so tall that it reached
the sky[f] and became very proud and
arrogant. 11 So I, the LORD God, will
reject the tree and hand it over to a
foreign ruler, who will punish it for its
wickedness. 12 Cruel foreigners will
chop it down and leave it wherever it
falls. Branches and broken limbs will
be scattered over the mountains and
in the valleys. The people living in the
shade of those branches will go somewhere else. 13 Birds will then nest on
the stump of the fallen tree, and wild
animals will trample its branches.
14 Never again will any tree dare to
grow as tall as this tree, no matter how
much water it has. Every tree must
die, just as humans die and go down to
the world of the dead.
15 On the day this tree dies and
goes to the world below, I, the LORD
God, will command rivers and streams
to mourn its death. Every under-
ground spring of water and every river
will stop flowing.[g] The mountains
in Lebanon will be covered with darkness as a sign of their sorrow, and all
the trees in the forest will wither.
16 This tree will crash to the ground,
and I will send it to the world below.
Then the nations of the earth will
tremble.
The trees from Eden and the
choice trees from Lebanon are now
in the world of the dead, and they will
be comforted when this tree falls.
17 Those people who found protection
in its shade will also be sent to the
world below, where they will join the
dead.[h]
18 King of Egypt, all these things
will happen to you and your people!
You were like this tree at one time—
taller and stronger than anyone on
earth. But now you will be chopped
down, just as every tree in the garden
of Eden must die. You will be sent
down to the world of the dead, where
you will join the godless and the other
victims of violent death. I, the LORD
God, have spoken.

A Funeral Song for the King of Egypt

32 Twelve years after King Jehoiachin
and the rest of us had been led
away as prisoners to Babylonia, the LORD
spoke to me on the first day of the twelfth
month.[i] He said:
2 Ezekiel, son of man, condemn the
king of Egypt and tell him I am saying:

You act like a lion
roaming the earth;
but you are nothing more than
a crocodile in a river,
churning up muddy water
with your feet.

[f]**31.10** *the sky*: One ancient translation; Hebrew "over the thick branches." [g]**31.15** *rivers and streams . . . stop flowing*: One possible meaning for the difficult Hebrew text. [h]**31.17** *dead*: One possible meaning for the difficult Hebrew text of verse 17. [i]**32.1** *Twelve years . . . twelfth month*: Probably February of 585 B.C.
31.8 Gn 2.9.

3 King of Egypt, listen to me. I, the LORD
God, will catch you in my net and let a
crowd of foreigners drag you to shore. 4 I
will throw you into an open field, where
birds and animals will come to feed on your
body. 5 I will spread your rotting flesh[j] over
the mountains and in the valleys, 6 and
your blood will flow throughout the land
and fill up the streams. 7 I will cover the
whole sky and every star with thick clouds,
so that the sun and moon will stop shining.
8 The heavens will become black, leaving
your country in total darkness. I, the LORD,
have spoken.

9 Foreign nations you have never heard
of will be shocked when I tell them how I
destroyed you.[k] 10 They will be horrified,
and when I flash my sword in victory on
the day of your death, their kings will tremble in the fear of what could happen to
them.

11 The king of Babylonia is coming to attack you, king of Egypt! 12 Your soldiers will
be killed by the cruelest army in the world,
and everything you take pride in will be
crushed. 13 I will slaughter your cattle that
graze by the river,[l] and no people or livestock will be left to muddy its water. 14 The
water will be clear, and streams will be
calm. I, the LORD God, have spoken.

15 Egypt will become a barren wasteland, and no living thing will ever survive
there. Then you and your people will know
that I am the LORD.

16 This is your warning, and it will be
used as a funeral song by foreign women to
mourn the death of your people. I, the
LORD God, have spoken.

A Sad Ending for Egypt

17 On the fifteenth day of that same
month,[m] the LORD said:

18 Ezekiel, son of man, mourn for the
Egyptians and condemn them to the world
of the dead, where they will be buried
alongside the people of other powerful nations.[n] 19 Say to them:

You may be more beautiful
than the people
of other nations,
but you will also die
and join the godless
in the world below.

20 You cannot escape! The enemy's
sword is ready to slaughter every one of
you.[o] 21 Brave military leaders killed in battle will gladly welcome you and your allies
into the world of the dead.

22-23 The graves of soldiers from Assyria
are there. They once terrified people, but
they were killed in battle and now lie deep
in the world of the dead.[p]

24-25 The graves of soldiers from Elam
are there. The very sight of those godless
soldiers once terrified their enemies and
made them panic. But now they are disgraced and ashamed as they lie in the
world of the dead, alongside others who
were killed in battle.

26 The graves of soldiers from Meshech
and Tubal are there. These godless soldiers
who terrified people were all killed in battle. 27 They were not given a proper burial
like the heroes of long ago,[q] who were
buried with their swords under their heads
and with their shields[r] over their bodies.
These were the heroes who made their enemies panic.

28 You Egyptians will be cruelly defeated, and you will be buried alongside
these other godless soldiers who died in
battle.

29 The graves of kings and leaders from
Edom are there. They were powerful at one
time. Now they are buried in the world of
the dead with other godless soldiers killed
in battle.

[j] **32.5** *rotting flesh*: One possible meaning for the difficult Hebrew text. [k] **32.9** *when I tell them how I destroyed you*: Hebrew; one ancient translation "when I scatter you like prisoners among them." [l] **32.13** *the river*: This possibly refers to the Nile River. [m] **32.17** *that same month*: See verse 1. [n] **32.18** *where they will be buried . . . powerful nations*: One possible meaning for the difficult Hebrew text. [o] **32.20** *The enemy's sword . . . you*: One possible meaning for the difficult Hebrew text. [p] **32.22,23** *deep in the world of the dead*: The place of greatest dishonor. [q] **32.27** *heroes of long ago*: One ancient translation; Hebrew "godless heroes." [r] **32.27** *shields*: One possible meaning for the difficult Hebrew text.

32.7 Is 13.10; Mt 24.29; Mk 13.24, 25; Lk 21.25; Rev 6.12, 13; 8.12.

30 The graves of the rulers of the north[s] are there, as well as those of the Sidonians. Their powerful armies once terrified enemies. Now they lie buried in the world of the dead, where they are disgraced like other soldiers killed in battle.

31 The LORD God says:

When your king of Egypt sees all of these graves, he and his soldiers will be glad they are not the only ones suffering. 32 I sent him to terrify people all over the earth. But he and his army will be killed and buried alongside other godless soldiers in the world of the dead. I, the LORD God, have spoken.

The LORD Appoints Ezekiel To Stand Watch

(Ezekiel 3.16-21)

33 The LORD said:

2 Ezekiel, son of man, warn your people by saying:

Someday, I, the LORD, may send an enemy to invade a country. And suppose its people choose someone to stand watch 3 and to sound a warning signal when the enemy is seen coming. 4-5 If any of these people hear the signal and ignore it, they will be killed in battle. But it will be their own fault, because they could have escaped if they had paid attention.

6 But suppose the person watching fails to sound the warning signal. The enemy will attack and kill some of the sinful people in that country, and I, the LORD, will hold that person responsible for their death.

7 Ezekiel, I have appointed you to stand watch for the people of Israel. So listen to what I say, then warn them for me. 8 When I tell wicked people they will die because of their sins, you must warn them to turn from their sinful ways. But if you refuse to warn them, you are responsible for their death. 9 If you do warn them, and they keep sinning, they will die because of their sins, and you will be innocent.

The LORD Is Always Fair

(Ezekiel 18.21-30)

10 The LORD said:

Ezekiel, son of man, the people of Israel are complaining that the punishment for their sins is more than they can stand. They have lost all hope for survival, and they blame me. 11 Tell them that as surely as I am the living LORD God, I don't like to see wicked people die. I enjoy seeing them turn from their sins and live. So if the Israelites want to live, they must stop sinning and turn back to me.

12 Tell them that when good people start sinning, all the good they did in the past cannot save them from being punished. And remind them that when wicked people stop sinning, their past sins will be completely forgiven, and they won't be punished.

13 Suppose I promise good people that they will live, then later they start sinning and believe they will be saved by the good they did in the past. These people will certainly be put to death because of their sins. Their good deeds will be forgotten.

14 Suppose I warn wicked people that they will die because of their sins, and they stop sinning and start doing right. 15 For example, they need to return anything they have taken as security for a loan and anything they have stolen. Then if they stop doing evil and start obeying my Law, they will live. 16 Their past sins will be forgiven, and they will live because they have done right.

17 Ezekiel, your people accuse me of being unfair. But they are the ones who are unfair. 18 If good people start doing evil, they will be put to death, because they have sinned. 19 And if wicked people stop sinning and start doing right, they will save themselves from punishment. 20 But the Israelites still think I am unfair. So warn them that they will be punished for what they have done.

The News of Jerusalem's Fall

21 Twelve years after King Jehoiachin and the rest of us had been led away as

[s]**32.30** *the rulers of the north*: Probably the Phoenicians.
33.21 2 K 25.2-10; Jr 39.1-8; 52.4-14.

prisoners to Babylonia, a refugee who had
escaped from Jerusalem came to me on the
fifth day of the tenth month.[t] He told me
that the city had fallen.
22 The evening before this man arrived
at my house, the LORD had taken control of
me. So when the man came to me the next
morning, I could once again speak.[u]

What Will Happen to Those Left in Israel?

23 Then the LORD said:
24 Ezekiel, son of man, the people living
in the ruined cities of Israel are saying,
"Abraham was just one man, and the LORD
gave him this whole land of Israel. There
are many of us, and so this land must be ours."
25 So, Ezekiel, tell them I am saying:

How can you think the land is still
yours? You eat meat with blood in it
and worship idols. You commit murder
26 and spread violence throughout the
land. Everything you do is wicked; you
are even unfaithful in marriage. And
you claim the land is yours!

27 As surely as I am the living LORD
God, you people in the ruined cities
will be killed in battle. Those of you
living in the countryside will be eaten
by wild animals, and those hiding in
caves and on rocky cliffs will die from
deadly diseases. 28 I will make the
whole country an empty wasteland and
crush the power in which you take
such pride. Even the mountains will
be bare, and no one will try to cross
them. 29 I will punish you because of
your sins, and I will turn your nation
into a barren desert. Then you will
know that I am the LORD.

The People Listen, but Don't Change

The LORD said:

30 Ezekiel, son of man, the people with
you in Babylonia talk about you when they
meet by the city walls or in the doorways of
their houses. They say, "Let's ask Ezekiel
what the LORD has said today." 31 So they
all come and listen to you, but they refuse
to do what you tell them. They claim to be
faithful, but they are forever trying to cheat
others out of their money. 32 They treat you
as though you were merely singing love
songs or playing music. They listen, but
don't do anything you say.
33 Soon they will be punished, just as
you warned, and they will know that a
prophet has been among them.

Israel's Leaders Are Worthless Shepherds

34 The LORD God said:
2 Ezekiel, son of man, Israel's
leaders are like shepherds taking care of my
sheep, the people of Israel. But I want you
to condemn these leaders and tell them:

I, the LORD God, say you shepherds
of Israel are doomed! You take care of
yourselves while ignoring my sheep.
3 You drink their milk and use their
wool to make your clothes. Then you
butcher the best ones for food. But you
don't take care of the flock! 4 You have
never protected the weak ones or
healed the sick ones or bandaged
those that get hurt. You let them wander off and never look for those that
get lost. You are cruel and mean to my
sheep. 5 They strayed in every direction, and because there was no shepherd to watch them, they were attacked and eaten by wild animals. 6 So
my sheep were scattered across the
earth. They roamed on hills and
mountains, without anyone even bothering to look for them.

7-8 Now listen to what I, the living
LORD God, am saying to you shepherds. My sheep have been attacked
and eaten by wild animals, because
you refused to watch them. You never
went looking for the lost ones, and you
fed yourselves without feeding my
sheep. 9-10 So I, the LORD, will punish
you! I will rescue my sheep from you
and never let you be their shepherd
again or butcher them for food. I, the
LORD, have spoken.

[t] **33.21** *Twelve years . . . tenth month*: Probably December of 586 B.C. [u] **33.22** *I could once again speak*: See 3.27.
34.5 Nu 27.17; 1 K 22.17; Mt 9.36; Mk 6.34.

The LORD Is the Good Shepherd

11 The LORD God then said:

I will look for my sheep and take care of them myself, 12 just as a shepherd looks for lost sheep. My sheep have been lost since that dark and miserable day when they were scattered throughout the nations.[v] But I will rescue them 13 and bring them back from the foreign nations where they now live. I will be their shepherd and will let them graze on Israel's mountains and in the valleys and fertile fields. 14 They will be safe as they feed on grassy meadows and green hills. 15 I promise to take care of them and keep them safe, 16 to look for those that are lost and bring back the ones that wander off, to bandage those that are hurt and protect the ones that are weak. I will also slaughter[w] those that are fat and strong, because I always do right.

Judgment on the Strong Sheep

17 The LORD God said to his sheep, the people of Israel:

I will carefully watch each one of you to decide which ones are the strong sheep and which ones are weak. 18 Some of you eat the greenest grass, then trample down what's left when you finish. Others drink clean water, then step in the water to make the rest of it muddy. 19 That means my other sheep have nothing fit to eat or drink.

20 So I, the LORD God, will separate you strong sheep from the weak. 21 You strong ones have used your powerful horns to chase off those that are weak, 22 but I will rescue them and no longer let them be mistreated. I will separate the good from the bad.

23 After that, I will give you a shepherd from the family of my servant King David. All of you, both strong and weak, will have the same shepherd, and he will take good care of you. 24 He will be your leader, and I will be your God. I, the LORD, have spoken.

A Bright Future for the LORD's Sheep

The LORD God said:

25 The people of Israel are my sheep, and I solemnly promise that they will live in peace. I will chase away every wild animal from the desert and the forest, so my sheep will not be afraid. 26 They will live around my holy mountain,[x] and I will bless them by sending more than enough rain 27 to make their trees produce fruit and their crops to grow. I will set them free from slavery and let them live safely in their own land. Then they will know that I am the LORD. 28 Foreign nations will never again rob them, and wild animals will no longer kill and eat them. They will have nothing to fear. 29 I will make their fields produce large amounts of crops, so they will never again go hungry or be laughed at by foreigners. 30 Then everyone will know that I protect my people Israel. I, the LORD, make this promise. 31 They are my sheep; I am their God, and I take care of them.

Edom Will Be a Wasteland

35 The LORD said:

2 Ezekiel, son of man, condemn the people of Edom[y] 3 and say to them:

I, the LORD God,
am now your enemy!
And I will turn your nation
into an empty wasteland,
4 leaving your towns in ruins.
Your land will be a desert,
and then you will know
that I am the LORD.

5 People of Edom, not only have you been Israel's longtime enemy, you simply watched when disaster wiped out its people as punishment for their sins. 6 And so, as surely as I am the living LORD God, you are guilty of murder and must be put to death. 7 I will destroy your nation and kill anyone who travels through it. 8 Dead bodies will cover your mountains and fill up your val-

[v] **34.12** *dark and miserable day . . . nations*: That is, the day the Babylonians defeated Jerusalem and led its people away as prisoners. [w] **34.16** *slaughter*: Hebrew; three ancient translations "take care of." [x] **34.26** *my holy mountain*: That is, Mount Zion in Jerusalem. [y] **35.2** *Edom*: The Hebrew text has "Mount Seir," another name for Edom.

34.23 Rev 7.17. **34.24** Ez 37.24, 25. **35.1-15** Is 34.5-17; 63.1-6; Jr 49.7-22; Ez 25.12-14; Am 1.11, 12; Ob 1-14; Ml 1.2-5.

leys, 9 and your land will lie in ruins forever. No one will live in your towns ever again. You will know that I am the LORD.

10 You thought the nations of Judah and Israel belonged to you, and that you could take over their territory. But I am their God, 11 and as surely as I live, I will punish you for treating my people with anger and hatred. Then they will know that I, the LORD, am punishing you! 12 And you will finally realize that I heard you laugh at their destruction and say their land was yours to take. 13 You even insulted me, but I heard it all.

14 Everyone on earth will celebrate when I destroy you, 15 just as you celebrated when Israel was destroyed. Your nation of Edom will be nothing but a wasteland. Then everyone will know that I am the LORD.

A Message for Israel's Mountains

36 The LORD said:

Ezekiel, son of man, tell the mountains of Israel 2 that I, the LORD God, am saying:

Your enemies sneered and said that you mountains belonged to them. 3 They ruined and crushed you from every side, and foreign nations captured and made fun of you. 4 So all you mountains and hills, streams and valleys, listen to what I will do. Your towns may now lie in ruins, and nations may laugh and insult you. 5 But in my fierce anger, I will turn against those nations, and especially the Edomites, because they laughed at you the loudest and took over your pasturelands. 6 You have suffered long enough, and, I, the LORD God, am very angry! Nations have insulted you, 7 so I will now insult and disgrace them. That is my solemn promise.

8 Trees will grow on you mountains of Israel and produce fruit for my people, because they will soon come home. 9 I will take care of you by plowing your soil and planting crops on your fertile slopes. 10 The people of Israel will return and rebuild your ruined towns and live in them. 11 Children will be born, and animals will give birth to their young. You will no longer be deserted as you are now, but you will be covered with people and treated better than ever. Then you will know that I am the LORD.

12 I will bring my people Israel home, and they will live on you mountains, because you belong to them, and your fertile slopes will never again let them starve. 13 It's true that you have been accused of not producing enough food and of letting your people starve. 14-15 But I, the LORD, promise that you won't hear other nations laugh and sneer at you ever again. From now on, you will always produce plenty of food for your people. I, the LORD God, have spoken.

The LORD Will Be Honored

16 The LORD said:

17 Ezekiel, son of man, when the people of Israel were living in their own country, they made the land unclean by the way they behaved, just as a woman's monthly period makes her unclean. 18 They committed murders and worshiped idols, which made the land even worse. So in my anger, I punished my people 19 and scattered them throughout the nations, just as they deserved. 20 Wherever they went, my name was disgraced, because foreigners insulted my people by saying I had forced them out of their own land.

21 I care what those foreigners think of me, 22 so tell the Israelites that I am saying:

You have disgraced my holy name among the nations where you now live. So you don't deserve what I'm going to do for you. I will lead you home to bring honor to my name 23 and to show foreign nations that I am holy. Then they will know that I am the LORD God. I have spoken.

24 I will gather you from the foreign nations and bring you home. 25 I will sprinkle you with clean water, and you will be clean and acceptable to me. I will wash away everything that makes you unclean, and I will remove your disgusting idols. 26 I will take away your stubborn heart and give you a new heart and a desire to be faithful. You will have only pure thoughts, 27 because I will put my Spirit in you and make you eager to obey my laws

36.26-28 Ez 11.19, 20.

and teachings. 28 You will once again
live in the land I gave your ancestors;
you will be my people, and I will be
your God.
29 I will protect you from anything
that makes you unclean. Your fields
will overflow with grain, and no one
will starve. 30 Your trees will be filled
with fruit, and crops will grow in your
fields, so that you will never again feel
ashamed for not having enough food.
31 You will remember your evil ways
and hate yourselves for what you've
done. 32 People of Israel, I'm not doing
these things for your sake. You sinned
against me, and you must suffer
shame and disgrace for what you have
done. I, the LORD God, have spoken.
33 After I have made you clean, I
will let you rebuild your ruined towns
and let you live in them. 34 Your land
will be plowed again, and nobody will
be able to see that it was once barren.
35 Instead, they will say that it looks as
beautiful as the garden of Eden. They
won't see towns lying in ruins, but they
will see your strong cities filled with
people. 36 Then the nearby nations
that survive will know that I am the
one who rebuilt the ruined places and
replanted the barren fields. I, the
LORD, make this promise.
37 I will once again answer your
prayers, and I will let your nation grow
until you are like a large flock of sheep.
38 The towns that now lie in ruins will
be filled with people, just as Jerusalem
was once filled with sheep to be offered as sacrifices during a festival.
Then you will know that I am the LORD.

Dry Bones Live Again

37 Some time later, I felt the LORD's
power take control of me, and his
Spirit carried me to a valley full of bones.
2 The LORD showed me all around, and
everywhere I looked I saw bones that were
dried out. 3 He said, "Ezekiel, son of man,
can these bones come back to life?"
I replied, "LORD God, only you can answer that."
4 He then told me to say:
Dry bones, listen to what the LORD
is saying to you, 5 "I, the LORD God,
will put breath in you, and once again
you will live. 6 I will wrap you with
muscles and skin and breathe life into
you. Then you will know that I am the
LORD."
7 I did what the LORD said, but before I
finished speaking, I heard a rattling noise.
The bones were coming together! 8 I saw
muscles and skin cover the bones, but they
had no life in them.
9 The LORD said:
Ezekiel, now say to the wind,[z] "The
LORD God commands you to blow from
every direction and to breathe life into
these dead bodies, so they can live
again."
10 As soon as I said this, the wind blew
among the bodies, and they came back to
life! They all stood up, and there were
enough to make a large army.
11 The LORD said:
Ezekiel, the people of Israel are like
dead bones. They complain that they
are dried up and that they have no
hope for the future. 12 So tell them, "I,
the LORD God, promise to open your
graves and set you free. I will bring you
back to Israel, 13 and when that happens, you will realize that I am the LORD.
14 My Spirit will give you breath, and you
will live again. I will bring you home,
and you will know that I have kept my
promise. I, the LORD, have spoken."

Judah and Israel Together Again

15 The LORD said:
16 Ezekiel, son of man, get a stick and
write on it, "The kingdom of Judah." Then
get another stick and write on it, "The
kingdom of Israel."[a] 17 Hold these two
sticks end to end, so they look like one
stick. 18 And when your people ask you
what this means, 19 tell them that I, the
LORD, will join together the stick of Israel

[z]**37.9** *wind*: Or "breath." The Hebrew word may mean either. [a]**37.16** *Israel*: The Hebrew text has "Joseph, that is, Ephraim," the leading tribe in the northern kingdom.
37.10 Rev 11.11.

and the stick of Judah. I will hold them in my hand, and they will become one.

20 Hold these two sticks where they can be seen by everyone 21 and then say:

I, the LORD God, will gather the people of Israel and bring them home from the foreign nations where they now live. 22 I will make them into one nation and let them once again live in the land of Israel. Only one king will rule them, and they will never again be divided into two nations. 23 They will no longer worship idols and do things that make them unacceptable to me. I will wash away their sin and make them clean, and I will protect them from everything that makes them unclean. They will be my people, and I will be their God.

24-25 Their king will always come from the family of my servant King David and will care for them like a shepherd. The people of Israel will faithfully obey my laws. They and their descendants will live in the land I gave my servant Jacob, just as their ancestors did. 26 I solemnly promise to bless the people of Israel with unending peace. I will protect them and let them become a powerful nation. My temple will stand in Israel for all time, 27 and I will live among my people and be their God. 28 Every nation on earth will know that my temple is in Israel and that I have chosen the Israelites to be my people.

Gog Invades Israel

38 The LORD said:

2 Ezekiel, son of man, condemn Gog, that wicked ruler of the kingdoms of Meshech and Tubal in the land of Magog. Tell him:

3 I, the LORD God, am your enemy, 4 and I will make you powerless! I will put a hook in your jaw and drag away both you and your large army. You command cavalry troops that wear heavy armor and carry shields and swords. 5 Your army includes soldiers from Persia, Ethiopia,[b] and Libya, 6 as well as from Gomer and Beth-Togarmah in the north. Your army is enormous! 7 So keep your troops prepared to fight, 8 because in a few years, I will command you to invade Israel, a country that was ruined by war. It was deserted for a long time, but its people have returned from the foreign nations where they once lived. The Israelites now live in peace in the mountains of their own land. 9 But you and your army will attack them like a fierce thunderstorm and surround them like a cloud.

10 When that day comes, I know that you will have an evil plan 11 to take advantage of Israel, that weak and peaceful country where people live safely inside towns that have no walls or gates or locks. 12 You will rob the people in towns that were once a pile of rubble. These people lived as prisoners in foreign nations, but they have returned to Israel, the most important place in the world, and they own livestock and property. 13 The people of Sheba and Dedan, along with merchants from villages in[c] southern Spain,[d] will be your allies. They will want some of the silver and gold, as well as the livestock and property that your army takes from Israel.

14 I, the LORD God, know that when you see[e] my people Israel living in peace, 15 you will lead your powerful cavalry from your kingdom in the north. 16 You will attack my people like a storm-cloud that covers their land. I will let you invade my country Israel, so that every nation on earth will know that I, the LORD, am holy.

Judgment on Gog

17 The LORD said to Gog:

Long ago, I had my prophets warn the

[b]**38.5** *Ethiopia*: See the note at 29.10. [c]**38.13** *from villages in*: One ancient translation; Hebrew "and soldiers from." [d]**38.13** *southern Spain*: See the note at 27.12. [e]**38.14** *when you see*: One possible meaning for the difficult Hebrew text.

37.24,25 Ez 34.24. **37.27** 2 Co 6.16; Rev 21.3. **38.2** Rev 20.8.

people of Israel that someday I would send an enemy to attack them. You, Gog, are that enemy, and that day is coming. 18 When you invade Israel, I will become furious, 19 and in my anger I will send a terrible earthquake to shake Israel. 20 Every living thing on earth will tremble in fear of me—every fish and bird, every wild animal and reptile, and every human. Mountains will crumble, cliffs will fall, and cities will collapse. 21 I, the LORD, will make the mountains of Israel turn against you.[f] Your troops will be so terrified that they will attack each other. 22 I will strike you with diseases and punish you with death. You and your army will be pounded with rainstorms, hailstones, and burning sulfur. 23 I will do these things to show the world that I, the LORD, am holy.

Gog Is Defeated

The LORD said:

39 Ezekiel, son of man, condemn Gog and tell him:

You are the ruler of Meshech and Tubal, but I, the LORD, am your enemy! 2 I will turn you around and drag you from the north until you reach the mountains of Israel. 3 I will knock the bow out of your left hand and the arrows out of your right hand, 4 and you and your army will die on those mountains. Then birds and wild animals will eat the flesh 5 of your dead bodies left lying in open fields. I, the LORD, have spoken.

6 I will set fire to the land of Magog and to those nations along the seacoast that think they are so secure, and they will know that I am the LORD.

7 My people Israel will know me, and they will no longer disgrace my holy name. Everyone on earth will know that I am the holy LORD God of Israel. 8 The day is coming when these things will happen, just as I have promised.

9 When that day comes, the people in the towns of Israel will collect the weapons of their dead enemies. They will use these shields, bows and arrows, spears, and clubs as firewood, and there will be enough to last for seven years. 10 They will burn these weapons instead of gathering sticks or chopping down trees. That's how the Israelites will take revenge on those who robbed and abused them. I, the LORD, have spoken.

The Burial of Gog

The LORD said:

11 After Gog has been destroyed, I will bury him and his army in Israel, in Travelers'[g] Valley, east of the Dead Sea. That graveyard will be so large that it will block the way of anyone who tries to walk through the valley,[h] which will then be known as "The Valley of Gog's Army."[i] 12 The Israelites will spend seven months burying dead bodies and cleaning up their land. 13 Everyone will help with the burial, and they will be honored for this on the day the brightness of my glory is seen. 14 After those seven months, the people will appoint a group of men to look for any dead bodies left unburied. This must be done for seven months to make sure that the land is no longer unclean. 15 Whenever they find a human bone, they will set up a marker next to it. Then the gravediggers will bury it in "The Valley of Gog's Army" 16 near the town of "Gog's Army." After that, the land will be pure again.

17 Ezekiel, son of man, I am going to hold a feast on Israel's mountains and offer sacrifices there. So invite all the birds and wild animals to come from every direction and eat the meat of sacrifices and drink the blood. The birds and animals 18 will feast on the bodies of warriors and foreign rulers that I will sacrifice like sheep, goats, and bulls. 19 I want the birds and animals to eat until they are full and drink until they are drunk. 20 They will come to my table and stuff themselves with the flesh of horses and warriors of every kind. I, the LORD God, have spoken.

[f] **38.21** *I, the LORD . . . against you*: One possible meaning for the difficult Hebrew text.
[g] **39.11** *Travelers'*: Hebrew "Abarim." [h] **39.11** *That graveyard . . . the valley*: One possible meaning for the difficult Hebrew text. [i] **39.11** *Gog's Army*: Hebrew "Hamon-Gog."
39.4 3 Macc 6.34. **39.17-20** Rev 19.17, 18.

Israel Will Be Restored

The LORD said:

21 When I punish the nations of the earth, they will see the brightness of my glory. 22 The people of Israel will know from then on that I am the LORD their God. 23 Foreign nations will realize that the Israelites were forced to leave their own land because they sinned against me. I turned my back on my people and let enemies attack and kill them. 24 Their lives were wicked and corrupt, and they deserved to be punished.

25 Now I will show mercy to the people of Israel and bring them back from the nations where they are living. They are Jacob's descendants, so I will bless them and show that I am holy. 26 They will live safely in their own land, but will be ashamed when they remember their evil ways and how they disgraced me.[j] 27 Foreign nations will watch as I take the Israelites from enemy lands and bring them back home, and those nations will see that I am holy.

28 My people will realize that I, the LORD their God, sent them away as prisoners and now will bring them back to their own land. 29 Never again will I turn my back on the people of Israel, and my Spirit will live in them. I, the LORD, have spoken.

Ezekiel Sees the Future Temple in Jerusalem

40 1-2 Twenty-five years after King Jehoiachin and the rest of us had been led away as prisoners to Babylonia, and fourteen years after the Babylonians had captured Jerusalem, the LORD's power took control of me on the tenth day of the first month.[k] The LORD showed me some visions in which I was carried to the top of a high mountain in Jerusalem. I looked to the south and saw what looked like a city full of buildings. 3 In my vision the LORD took me closer, and I saw a man who was sparkling like polished bronze. He was standing near one of the gates and was holding a tape measure in one hand and a measuring stick in the other. 4 The man said, "Ezekiel, son of man, pay close attention to everything I'm going to show you—that's why you've been brought here. Listen carefully, because you must tell the people of Israel what you see."

The East Gate

5 The first thing I saw was an outer wall that completely surrounded the temple area. The man took his measuring stick, which was ten feet long, and measured the wall; it was ten feet high and ten feet thick. 6-7 Then he went to the east gate, where he walked up steps that led to a long passageway. On each side of this passageway were three guardrooms, which were ten feet square, and they were separated by walls over eight feet thick. The man measured the distance between the opening of the gate and the first guardroom, and it was ten feet, the thickness of the outer wall.

At the far end of this passageway, I saw an entrance room that faced the courtyard of the temple itself. There was also a distance of ten feet between the last guardroom and the entrance room 8-9 at the end of the passageway. The man measured this room: It was thirteen feet from the doorway to the opposite wall, and the distance from the doorway to the wall on either side was three feet. 10 The three guardrooms on each side of the passageway were the same size, and the walls that separated them were the same thickness.

11 Next, the man measured the width of the passageway, and it was twenty-two feet, but the two doors of the gate were only sixteen feet wide.[l] 12 In front of the guardrooms, which were ten feet square, was a railing about twenty inches high and twenty inches thick. 13 The man measured the distance from the back wall[m] of one of these rooms to the same spot in the room

[j] **39.26** *me*: One possible meaning for the difficult Hebrew text of verse 26. [k] **40.1,2** *Twenty-five years . . . first month*: Probably March of 573 B.C. [l] **40.11** *the width of the passageway . . . twenty-two feet . . . the two doors of the gate . . . sixteen feet wide*: The doors themselves probably were hung on stone sockets, which could explain the six-foot difference in width between the passageway and the doors. [m] **40.13** *back wall*: One ancient translation; Hebrew "roof."

40.1,2 Rev 21.10. **40.3** Rev 11.1; 21.15. **40.5—42.20** 1 K 6.1-38; 2 Ch 3.1-9.

directly across the passageway, and it was
forty-two feet. 14 He measured the entrance room at the far end of the passageway, and it was thirty-four feet wide.[n] 15 Finally, he measured the total length of the
passageway, from the outer wall to the entrance room, and it was eighty-five feet.
16 The three walls in the guardrooms had
small windows in them, just like the ones
in the entrance room.[o] The walls along the
passageway were decorated with carvings of
palm trees.

The Outer Courtyard

17 The man then led me through the
passageway and into the outer courtyard of
the temple, where I saw thirty rooms built
around the outside of the courtyard.[p]
These side rooms were built against the
outer wall, and in front of them was a sidewalk that circled the courtyard. 18 This was
known as the lower sidewalk, and it was
eighty-five feet wide.

19 I saw the gates that led to the inner
courtyard of the temple and noticed that
they were higher than those leading to the
outer courtyard. The man measured the
distance between the outer and inner
gates, and it was one hundred seventy
feet.[q]

The North Gate

20 Next, the man measured the north
gate that led to the outer courtyard. 21 This
gate also had three guardrooms on each
side of a passageway. The measurements of
these rooms, the walls between them, and
the entrance room at the far end of the
passageway were exactly the same as those
of the east gate. The north gate was also
eighty-five feet long and forty-two feet
wide, 22 and the windows, the entrance
room, and the carvings of palm trees were
just like those in the east gate. The entrance room also faced the courtyard of the
temple and had seven steps leading up to
it. 23 Directly across the outer courtyard
was a gate that led to the inner courtyard,
just as there was for the east gate. The man
measured the distance between the outer
and inner gate, and it was one hundred
seventy feet.

The South Gate

24 The man then took me to the south
gate. He measured the walls and the entrance room of this gate, and the measurements were exactly the same as those of
the other two gates. 25 There were windows
in the guardrooms of this gate and in the
entrance room, just like the others, and
this gate was also eighty-five feet long and
forty-two feet wide. 26 Seven steps led up to
the gate; the entrance room was at the far
end of the passageway and faced the courtyard of the temple. Carvings of palm trees
decorated the walls along the passageway.
27 And directly across the outer courtyard
was a gate on the south side of the inner
courtyard. The man measured the distance
between the outer and inner gate, and it
was also one hundred seventy feet.

The Gates Leading to the Inner Courtyard

28 We then went into the inner courtyard, through the gate on the south side of
the temple. The man measured the gate,
and it was the same size as the gates in the
outer wall. 29-30 In fact, everything along
the passageway was also the same size, including the guardrooms, the walls separating them, the entrance room at the far end,
and the windows. This gate, like the others,
was eighty-five feet long and forty-two feet
wide. 31 The entrance room of this gate
faced the outer courtyard, and carvings of
palm trees decorated the walls of the passageway. Eight steps led up to this gate.

32 Next, we went through the east gate
to the inner courtyard. The man measured
this gate, and it was the same size as the
others. 33 The guardrooms, the walls separating them, and its entrance room had the

[n]**40.14** *wide*: One possible meaning for the difficult Hebrew text of verse 14. [o]**40.16** *just like the ones in the entrance room*: One possible meaning for the difficult Hebrew text.
[p]**40.17** *thirty rooms built around the outside of the courtyard*: These were probably used by worshipers as places to meet and share sacrificial meals (see, for example, Jeremiah 35.2).
[q]**40.19** *feet*: The Hebrew text adds "the east and the north."

same measurements as the other gates. The guardrooms and the entrance room had windows, and the gate was eighty-five feet long and forty-two feet wide. 34 The entrance room faced the outer courtyard, and the walls in the passageway were decorated with carvings of palm trees. Eight steps also led up to this gate.

35 Then the man took me to the north gate. He measured it, and it was the same size as the others, 36 including the guardrooms, the walls separating them, and the entrance room. There were also windows in this gate. It was eighty-five feet long and forty-two feet wide, 37 and like the other inner gates, its entrance room faced the outer courtyard, and its walls were decorated with carvings of palm trees. Eight steps also led up to this gate.

The Rooms for Sacrificing Animals

38-39 Inside the entrance room of the north gate, I saw four tables, two on each side of the room, where the animals to be sacrificed were killed. Just outside[r] this room was a small building used for washing the animals before they were offered as sacrifices to please the LORD[s] or sacrifices for sin[t] or sacrifices to make things right.[u] 40 Four more tables were in the outer courtyard, two on each side of the steps leading into the entrance room. 41 So there was a total of eight tables, four inside and four outside, where the animals were killed, 42-43 and where the meat was placed until it was sacrificed on the altar.[v]

Next to the tables in the entrance room were four stone tables twenty inches high and thirty inches square; the equipment used for killing the animals was kept on top of these tables. All around the walls of this room was a three inch shelf.[w]

The Rooms Belonging to the Priests

44 The man then took me to the inner courtyard, where I saw two buildings, one beside the inner gate on the north and the other beside the inner gate on the south.[x]
45 He said, "The building beside the north gate belongs to the priests who serve in the temple, 46 and the building beside the south gate belongs to those who serve at the altar. All of them are descendants of Zadok and are the only Levites allowed to serve as the LORD's priests."

The Inner Courtyard and the Temple

47 Now the man measured the inner courtyard; it was one hundred seventy feet square. I also saw an altar in front of the temple.

48 We walked to the porch of the temple, and the man measured the doorway of the porch: It was twenty-four feet long,[y] eight feet wide, and the distance from the doorway to the wall on either side was five feet.
49 The porch itself was thirty-four feet by twenty[z] feet, with steps[a] leading up to it. There was a column on each side of these steps.

41 Next we went into the main room of the temple. The man measured the doorway of this room: It was ten feet wide,[b] 2 seventeen feet long, and the distance from the doorway to the wall on either side was eight feet. The main room itself was sixty-eight feet by thirty-four feet.
3-4 Then the man walked to the far end of the temple's main room and said, "Beyond this doorway is the most holy place." He first measured the doorway: It was three feet wide, ten feet long, and the distance from the doorway to the wall on either side was twelve feet. Then he

[r]**40.38,39** *Just outside*: Or "Inside." [s]**40.38,39** *sacrifices to please the LORD*: These sacrifices have traditionally been called "whole burnt offerings" because the whole animal was burned on the altar. A main purpose of such sacrifices was to please the LORD with the smell of the sacrifice, and so in the CEV they are often called "sacrifices to please the LORD." [t]**40.38,39** *sacrifices for sin*: See Leviticus 4.1,2; 6.24-30. [u]**40.38,39** *sacrifices to make things right*: See Leviticus 5.14-19; 7.1-10. [v]**40.42,43** *where the meat . . . altar*: One possible meaning for the difficult Hebrew text. [w]**40.42,43** *was a three inch shelf*: Or "were three inch pegs." [x]**40.44** *south*: One possible meaning for the difficult Hebrew text of verse 44. [y]**40.48** *twenty-four feet long*: One ancient translation; these words are not in the Hebrew text of this verse. [z]**40.49** *twenty*: One ancient translation; Hebrew "eighteen." [a]**40.49** *steps*: Hebrew; one ancient translation "ten steps." [b]**41.1** *It was ten feet wide*: One possible meaning for the difficult Hebrew text.

measured the most holy place, and it was thirty-four feet square.

The Storage Rooms of the Temple

5 The man measured the wall of the temple, and it was ten feet thick. Storage rooms seven feet wide were built against the outside of the wall. 6 There were three levels of rooms, with thirty rooms on each level, and they rested on ledges that were attached to the temple walls, so that nothing was built into the walls. 7 The walls of the temple were thicker at the bottom than at the top, which meant that the storage rooms on the top level were wider than those on the bottom level.[c] Steps led from the bottom level, through the middle level, and into the top level.

8 The temple rested on a stone base ten feet high, which also served as the foundation for the storage rooms. 9 The outside walls of the storage rooms were eight feet thick; there was nothing between these walls 10 and the nearest buildings thirty-four feet away. 11 One door led into the storage rooms on the north side of the temple, and another door led to those on the south side. The stone base extended eight feet beyond the outside wall of the storage rooms.

The West Building and the Measurements of the Temple

12 I noticed another building: It faced the west end of the temple and was one hundred seventeen feet wide, one hundred fifty feet long, and had walls over eight feet thick.

13 The man measured the length of the temple, and it was one hundred seventy feet. He then measured from the back wall of the temple, across the open space behind the temple, to the back wall of the west building; it was one hundred seventy feet. 14 The distance across the front of the temple, including the open space on either side, was also one hundred seventy feet.

15 Finally, the man measured the length of the west building, including the side rooms on each end, and it was also one hundred seventy feet.

The Inside of the Temple

The inside walls of the temple's porch and main room[d] 16 were paneled with wood all the way from the floor to the windows, while the doorways, the small windows, and the three side rooms were trimmed in wood.[e] 17 The paneling stopped just above the doorway. These walls were decorated[f] 18-20 with carvings of winged creatures and had a carving of a palm tree between the creatures. Each winged creature had two faces: A human face looking at the palm tree on one side, and a lion's face looking at the palm tree on the other side. These designs were carved into the paneling all the way around the two rooms.

21 The doorframe to the temple's main room was in the shape of a rectangle.

The Wooden Altar

In front of the doorway to the most holy place was something that looked like 22 a wooden altar. It was five feet high and four feet square,[g] and its corners, its base,[h] and its sides were made of wood. The man said, "This is a reminder that the LORD is constantly watching over his temple."

The Doors in the Temple

23 Both the doorway to the main room of the temple and the doorway to the most holy place had two doors, 24 and each door had two sections that could fold open. 25 The doors to the main room were decorated with carvings of winged creatures and palm trees just like those on the walls, and there was a wooden covering over the porch just outside these doors. 26 The walls on each side of this porch had small windows and were also decorated with carvings of palm trees.

[c] **41.7** *which meant that . . . on the bottom level*: One possible meaning for the difficult Hebrew text. [d] **41.15** *The inside walls of the temple's porch and main room*: One possible meaning for the difficult Hebrew text. [e] **41.16** *were trimmed in wood*: One possible meaning for the difficult Hebrew text. [f] **41.17** *decorated*: One possible meaning for the difficult Hebrew text of verse 17. [g] **41.22** *four feet square*: One ancient translation; Hebrew "four feet wide." [h] **41.22** *base*: One ancient translation; Hebrew "length."

The Sacred Rooms for the Priests

42 [1-2] After the man and I left the temple and walked back to the outer courtyard, he showed me a set of rooms on the north side of the west building.[i] This set of rooms was one hundred seventy feet long and eighty-five feet wide. [3] On one side of them was the thirty-four feet of open space that ran alongside the temple,[j] and on the other side was the sidewalk that circled the outer courtyard.[k] The rooms were arranged in three levels [4] with doors that opened toward the north, and in front of them was a walkway seventeen feet wide and one hundred seventy feet long.[l] [5] The rooms on the top level were narrower than those on the middle level, and the rooms on the middle level were narrower than those on the bottom level. [6] The rooms on the bottom level supported those on the two upper levels, and so these rooms did not have columns like other buildings in the courtyard. [7-8] To the north was a privacy wall eighty-five feet long,[m] [9-10] and at the east end of this wall was the door leading from the courtyard to these rooms.

There was also a set of rooms on the south[n] side of the west building. [11] These rooms were exactly like those on the north side, and they also had a walkway in front of them. [12] The door to these rooms was at the east end of the wall that stood in front of them.

[13] The man then said to me:

These rooms on the north and south sides of the temple are the sacred rooms where the LORD's priests will eat the most holy offerings. These offerings include the grain sacrifices, the sacrifices for sin, and the sacrifices to make things right. [14] When the priests are ready to leave the temple, they must go through these rooms before they return to the outer courtyard. They must leave their sacred clothes in these rooms and put on regular clothes before going anywhere near other people.

The Size of the Temple Area

[15] After the man had finished measuring the buildings inside the temple area, he took me back through the east gate and measured the wall around this area. [16] He used his measuring stick to measure the east side of this wall; it was eight hundred forty feet long. [17-19] Then he measured the north side, the south side, and the west side of the wall, and they were each eight hundred forty feet long, [20] and so the temple area was a perfect square. The wall around this area separated what was sacred from what was ordinary.

The LORD's Glory Returns to the Temple

43 The man took me back to the east gate of the temple, [2] where I saw the brightness of the glory of Israel's God coming from the east. The sound I heard was as loud as ocean waves, and everything around was shining with the dazzling brightness of his glory. [3] This vision was like the one I had seen when God came to destroy Jerusalem and like the one I had seen near the Chebar River.

I immediately bowed with my face to the ground, [4] and the LORD's glory came through the east gate and into the temple.[o] [5] The LORD's Spirit lifted me to my feet and carried me to the inner courtyard, where I saw that the LORD's glory had filled the temple.

[6] The man was standing beside me, and I heard the LORD[p] say from inside the temple:

[7] Ezekiel, son of man, this temple is

[i] **42.1,2** *he showed me . . . the west building*: One possible meaning for the difficult Hebrew text. [j] **42.3** *the thirty-four feet of open space . . . the temple*: See 41.10. [k] **42.3** *the sidewalk that circled the outer courtyard*: See 40.17. [l] **42.4** *one hundred seventy feet long*: Two ancient translations; Hebrew "twenty inches long." [m] **42.7,8** *long*: One possible meaning for the difficult Hebrew text of verses 5-8. [n] **42.9,10** *south*: One ancient translation; Hebrew "east."
[o] **43.4** *the LORD's glory . . . temple*: This was the same gate the LORD's glory went through when it left Jerusalem (see 10.19 and 11.22,23). [p] **43.6** *the LORD*: Hebrew "a voice."
43.2 Ez 10.3, 4, 18, 19; 11.22, 23; Rev 1.15.

my throne on earth. I will live here among the people of Israel forever. They and their kings will never again disgrace me by worshiping idols at local shrines or by setting up memorials to their dead kings.[q] 8 Israel's kings built their palaces so close to my holy temple that only a wall separated them from me. Then these kings disgraced me with their evil ways, and in my fierce anger I destroyed them. 9 But if the people and their kings stop worshiping other gods and tear down those memorials, I will live among them forever.

10 The people of Israel must suffer shame for sinning against me, so tell them about my holy temple. Let them think about it, 11 then if they are truly sorry, describe for them the design and shape of the temple, the gates, the measurements, and how the buildings are arranged. Explain the regulations about worshiping there, then write down these things, so they can study and obey them.

12 The temple area on my holy mountain must be kept sacred! This is the most important law about the temple.

The Altar

13 According to the official standards, the altar in the temple had the following measurements: Around the bottom of the altar was a gutter twenty inches wide and twenty inches deep, with a ten inch ledge on the outer rim. 14-17 The altar rested on a base and had three sections, each one of them square. The bottom section was twenty-seven feet on each side and three feet high. The middle section was twenty-four feet on each side and seven feet high, and it had a ten inch rim around its outer edge. The top section, which was twenty feet on each side and seven feet high, was the place where sacrifices were burned, and the four corners of the top section looked like the horns of a bull. The steps leading up to the altar were on the east side.

The Dedication of the Altar

18 The LORD God said:

Ezekiel, son of man, after the altar is built, it must be dedicated by offering sacrifices on it and by splattering it with blood. Here is what you must do: 19 The priests of the Levi tribe from the family of Zadok the priest are the only ones who may serve in my temple—this is my law. So give them a young bull to slaughter as a sacrifice for sin. 20 Take some of the animal's blood and smear it on the four corners of the altar, some on the corners of the middle section, and some more on the rim around its edge. That will purify the altar and make it fit for offering sacrifices to me. 21 Then take the body of the bull outside the temple area and burn it at the special place.

22 The next day, a goat[r] that has nothing wrong with it must be offered as a sacrifice for sin. Purify the altar with its blood, just as you did with the blood of the bull. 23 Then choose a young bull and a young ram that have nothing wrong with them, 24 and bring them to my temple. The priests will sprinkle salt on them[s] and offer them as sacrifices to please me.[t]

25 Each day for the next seven days, you must offer a goat and a bull and a ram as sacrifices for sin. These animals must have nothing wrong with them. 26 The priests will purify the altar during those days, so that it will be acceptable to me and ready to use. 27 From then on, the priests will use this altar to offer sacrifices to please me and sacrifices to ask my blessing.[u] Then I will be pleased with the people of Israel. I, the LORD God, have spoken.

The East Gate Must Remain Closed

44 The man took me back to the outer courtyard, near the east gate of the

[q]**43.7** *by setting up memorials to their dead kings*: One possible meaning for the difficult Hebrew text. [r]**43.22** *goat*: Hebrew "male goat." [s]**43.24** *The priests will sprinkle salt on them*: See Leviticus 2.13. [t]**43.24** *sacrifices to please me*: See the note at 40.38,39. [u]**43.27** *sacrifices to ask my blessing*: These sacrifices have traditionally been called "peace offerings" or "offerings of well-being." A main purpose was to ask for the LORD's blessing, and so in the CEV they are sometimes called "sacrifices to ask the LORD's blessing."

43.13-17 Ex 27.1, 2; 2 Ch 4.1. **43.18-27** Ex 29.35-37; 1 Macc 4.52-56.

temple area. I saw that the doors to this gate were closed. [2] The LORD said:

I, the LORD God of Israel, came through this gate, so it must remain closed forever! No one must ever use it. [3] The ruler of Israel may come here to eat a sacrificial meal that has been offered to me, but he must use only the entrance room of this gate.

People Who Are Not Allowed in the Temple

[4] Then the man took me through the north gate to the front of the temple. I saw that the brightness of the LORD's glory had filled the temple, and I immediately bowed with my face to the ground.

[5] The LORD said:

Ezekiel, son of man, I am going to give you the laws for my temple. So pay attention and listen carefully to what kind of people are allowed to come in the temple, and what kind are not. [6] Tell those rebellious people of Israel:

I, the LORD God, command you to stop your evil ways! [7] My temple has been disgraced, because you have let godless, stubborn foreigners come here when sacrifices are being offered to me. You have sinned and have broken our solemn agreement. [8] Instead of following the proper ways to worship me, you have put foreigners in charge of worship at my temple.

[9] And so I, the LORD God, say that no godless foreigner who disobeys me will be allowed in my temple. This includes any foreigner living in Israel.

The Levites Are Punished

The LORD said:

[10] Some of the Levites turned their backs on me and joined the other people of Israel in worshiping idols. So these Levites must be punished! [11] They will still be allowed to serve me as temple workers by guarding the gates and by killing the animals to be sacrificed and by helping the worshipers. [12] But because these Levites served the people of Israel when they worshiped idols, I, the LORD God, promise that the Levites will be punished. They did not stop the Israelites from sinning, [13] and now I will no longer let the Levites serve as my priests or come near anything sacred to me. They must suffer shame and disgrace for their disgusting sins. [14] They will be responsible for all the hard work that must be done in the temple.

Rules for Priests

The LORD said:

[15] The priests of the Levi tribe who are descendants of Zadok the priest were faithful to me, even when the rest of the Israelites turned away. And so, these priests will continue to serve as my priests and to offer the fat and the blood of sacrifices. [16] They will come into my temple, where they will offer sacrifices at my altar and lead others in worship.

[17] When they come to the inner courtyard, they must wear their linen priestly clothes. My priests must never wear anything made of wool when they are on duty in this courtyard or in the temple. [18] Even their turbans and underwear must be made of linen to keep my priests from sweating when they work. [19] And before they leave to join the other people in the outer courtyard, they must take off their priestly clothes, then place them in the sacred rooms and put on their regular clothes.[v] That way, no one will touch their sacred clothes and be harmed.[w]

[20] Priests must never shave their heads when they are mourning. But they must keep their hair properly trimmed and not let it grow too long. [21] They must not drink wine before going to the inner courtyard.

[22] A priest must not marry a divorced woman; he can marry only a virgin from Israel or the widow of another priest.

[23] Priests must teach my people the

[v] **44.19** *take off their priestly clothes . . . put on their regular clothes*: See 42.14. [w] **44.19** *no one will touch . . . and be harmed*: Ordinary people were forbidden to touch anything that was sacred. If they did, it was believed they would somehow be harmed.

44.17,18 Ex 28.39-43; Lv 16.4. **44.19** Lv 16.23, 24. **44.20** Lv 21.5. **44.21** Lv 10.9. **44.22** Lv 21.7, 13, 14. **44.23** Lv 10.10.

difference between what is sacred and what is ordinary, and between what is clean and what is unclean. 24 They will make decisions in difficult legal cases, according to my own laws. They must also observe the religious festivals my Law requires and must always respect the Sabbath.

25 Touching a dead body will make a person unclean. So a priest must not go near a dead body, unless it is one of his parents or children, or his brother or unmarried sister. 26 If a priest touches a dead body, he is unclean and must go through a ceremony to make himself clean. Then seven days later, 27 he must go to the inner courtyard of the temple and offer a sacrifice for sin. After that, he may once again serve as my priest. I, the LORD God, have spoken.

28 I myself will provide for my priests, and so they won't receive any land of their own. 29 Instead, they will receive part of the grain sacrifices, as well as part of the sacrifices for sin and sacrifices to make things right. They will also be given everything in Israel that has been completely dedicated to me.[x] 30 The first part of every harvest will belong to the priests. They will also receive part of all special gifts and offerings the Israelites bring to me. And whenever any of my people bake bread, they will give their first loaf as an offering to the priests, and I will bless the homes of the people when they do this.

31 Priests must not eat any bird or animal that dies a natural death or that has been killed by a wild animal.

The LORD's Sacred Land

The LORD said:

45 When the land of Israel is divided among the twelve tribes, you must set aside an area that will belong to me. This sacred area will be eight miles long and six[y] miles wide. 2 The temple will be on a piece of land eight hundred forty feet square, and the temple will be completely surrounded by an open space eighty-four feet wide.

3-4 I will give half of my sacred land, a section eight miles long and three miles wide, to the priests who serve in the temple. Their houses will be in this half, as well as my temple, which is the most sacred place of all.

5 I will give the other half of my land to the Levites who work in my temple, and the towns[z] where they will live will be there.

6 Next to my sacred land will be an area eight miles long and two miles wide. This will belong to the people of Israel and will include the city of Jerusalem.

Land for Israel's Ruler

The LORD said:

7-8 The regions west and east of my sacred land and the city of Jerusalem will belong to the ruler of Israel. He will be given the region between the western edge of my land and the Mediterranean Sea, and between the eastern edge of my land and the Jordan River. This will mean that the length of his property will be the same as the sections of land given to the tribes.

This property will belong to every ruler of Israel, so they will always be fair to my people and will let them live peacefully in the land given to their tribes.

Israel's Rulers Must Be Honest

9 The LORD God said:

You leaders of Israel have robbed and cheated my people long enough! I want you to stop sinning and start doing what is right and fair. You must never again force my people off their own land. I, the LORD, have spoken.

10 So from now on, you must use honest weights and measures. 11 The *ephah* will be the standard dry measure, and the *bath* will be the standard liquid measure. Their

[x]**44.29** *that has been completely dedicated to me*: This translates a Hebrew word that describes property and things that were taken away from humans and given to God. In the early history of Israel, such things often had to be destroyed (see Joshua 6.15-19). [y]**45.1** *six*: One ancient translation; Hebrew "three." [z]**45.5** *the towns*: One ancient translation; Hebrew "the twenty rooms."

44.25 Lv 21.1-4. **44.28** Nu 18.20. **44.29,30** Nu 18.8-19. **44.31** Lv 22.8.
45.10 Lv 19.35, 36.

size will be based on the *homer*, which will equal ten *ephahs* or ten *baths*.[a]

12 The standard unit of weight will be the *shekel*.[b] One *shekel* will equal twenty *gerahs*, and sixty *shekels* will equal one *mina*.

13 Leaders of Israel, the people must bring you one sixtieth of their grain harvests as offerings to me. 14 They will also bring one percent of their olive oil. These things will be measured according to the *bath*, and ten *baths* is the same as one *homer* or one *cor*. 15 Finally, they must bring one sheep out of every two hundred from their flocks.

These offerings will be used as grain sacrifices, as well as sacrifices to please me[c] and those to ask my blessing.[d] I, the LORD, will be pleased with these sacrifices and will forgive the sins of my people.

16 The people of Israel will bring you these offerings. 17 But during New Moon Festivals, Sabbath celebrations, and other religious feasts, you leaders will be responsible for providing animals for the sacrifices, as well as the grain and wine. All these will be used for the sacrifices for sin, the grain sacrifices, the sacrifices to please me, and those to ask my blessing. I will be pleased and will forgive the sins of my people.

The Festivals

(Exodus 12.1-20; Leviticus 23.33-43)

18 The LORD God said:

On the first day of the first month,[e] a young bull that has nothing wrong with it must be offered as a sacrifice to purify the temple. 19 The priest will take some blood from this sacrifice and smear it on the doorposts of the temple, as well as on the four corners of the altar and on the doorposts of the gates that lead into the inner courtyard.

20 The same ceremony must also be done on the seventh day of the month, so that anyone who sins accidentally or without knowing it will be forgiven, and so that my temple will remain holy.

21 Beginning on the fourteenth day of the first month, and continuing for seven days, everyone will celebrate Passover and eat bread made without yeast. 22 On the first day, the ruler will bring a bull to offer as a sacrifice for his sins and for the sins of the people. 23 Each day of the festival he is to bring seven bulls and seven rams as sacrifices to please me,[f] and he must bring a goat[g] as a sacrifice for sin. These animals must have nothing wrong with them. 24 He will also provide twenty pounds of grain and four quarts of olive oil to be offered with each bull and each ram.

25 The Festival of Shelters will begin on the fifteenth day of the seventh month[h] and will continue for seven days. On each day of this festival, the ruler will provide the same number of animals that he did each day during Passover, as well as the same amount of grain and olive oil for the sacrifices.

Various Laws for the Ruler and the People

46 The LORD said:

The east gate of the inner courtyard must remain closed during the six working days of each week. But on the Sabbath and on the first day of the month, this gate will be opened. 2 Israel's ruler will go from the outer courtyard into the entrance room of this gate and stand in the doorway while the priest offers sacrifices to ask my

[a]**45.11** *the homer . . . ten ephahs . . . ten baths*: A *homer* was either a dry or a liquid measure and equaled about five bushels or fifty-five gallons; an *ephah* would be about a half bushel, and a *bath* would be about five and a half gallons. [b]**45.12** *the shekel*: The *shekel* was about four-tenths of an ounce. [c]**45.15** *sacrifices to please me*: See the note at 40.38,39. [d]**45.15** *sacrifices . . . to ask my blessing*: See the note at 43.27. [e]**45.18** *the first month*: Abib (also called Nisan), the first month of the Hebrew calendar, from about mid-March to mid-April. [f]**45.23** *sacrifices to please me*: See the note at 40.38,39. [g]**45.23** *goat*: See the note at 43.22. [h]**45.25** *seventh month*: Tishri (also called Ethanim), the seventh month of the Hebrew calendar, from about mid-September to mid-October.

45.21 Ex 12.1-20; Nu 28.16-25. **45.25** Lv 23.33-36; Nu 29.12-38.

blessing[i] and sacrifices to please me.[j] The
ruler will bow with his face to the ground
to show that he has worshiped me. Then
he will leave, and the gate will remain open
until evening.
3 Each Sabbath and on the first day of
each month, the people of Israel must also
come to the east gate and worship me.
4 On the Sabbath, the ruler will bring six
lambs and one ram to be offered as sacrifices to please me. There must be nothing
wrong with any of these animals. 5 With
the ram, he is to offer twenty pounds of
grain, and with each of the lambs, he can
offer as much as he wants. He must also
offer four quarts of olive oil with every
twenty pounds of grain.
6 The ruler is to bring six lambs, a bull,
and a ram to be offered as sacrifices at the
New Moon Festival. There must be nothing wrong with any of these animals.
7 With the bull and the ram, he is to offer
twenty pounds of grain, and with each
of the lambs, he can offer as much as he
wants. He must also offer four quarts of
olive oil with every twenty pounds of
grain. 8 The ruler must come through the
entrance room of the east gate and leave
the same way.
9 When my people come to worship me
during any festival, they must always leave
by the opposite gate from which they came:
Those who come in the north gate must
leave by the south gate, and those who
come in the south gate must leave by the
north gate. 10 Their ruler will come in at
the same time they do and leave at the
same time they leave.
11 At all other festivals and celebrations,
twenty pounds of grain will be offered with
a bull, and twenty pounds will be offered
with a ram. The worshipers can offer as
much grain as they want with each lamb.
Four quarts of olive oil must be offered with
every twenty pounds of grain.
12 If the ruler voluntarily offers a sacrifice to please me or to ask my blessing, the
east gate of the inner courtyard will be
opened for him. He will offer his sacrifices
just as he does on each Sabbath; then he
will leave, and the gate will be closed.
13 Each morning a year-old lamb that
has nothing wrong with it must be offered
as a sacrifice to please me. 14 Along with it,
three pounds of fine flour mixed with a
quart of olive oil must be offered as a grain
sacrifice. This law will never change—
15 the lamb, the flour, and the olive oil will
be offered to me every morning for all time.

Laws about the Ruler's Land

16 The LORD God said:
If the ruler of Israel gives some of his
land to one of his children, it will belong to
the ruler's child as part of the family property. 17 But if the ruler gives some of his
land to one of his servants, the land will belong to the servant until the Year of Celebration, when it will be returned to the
ruler.[k] Only the ruler's children can keep
what is given to them.
18 The ruler must never abuse my people
by taking land from them. Any land he gives
his children must already belong to him.

The Sacred Kitchens

19 The man who was showing me the
temple[l] then took me back to the inner
courtyard. We walked to the south side of
the courtyard and stopped at the door to
the sacred rooms that belonged to the
priests. He showed me more rooms at the
western edge of the courtyard 20 and said,
"These are the kitchens where the priests
must boil the meat to be offered as sacrifices to make things right[m] and as sacrifices
for sin.[n] They will also bake the grain for
sacrifices in these kitchens. That way,
these sacred offerings won't have to be carried through the outer courtyard, where
someone could accidentally touch them
and be harmed."[o]

[i] **46.2** *sacrifices to ask my blessing*: See the note at 43.27. [j] **46.2** *sacrifices to please me*: See the note at 40.38,39. [k] **46.17** *the Year of Celebration . . . to the ruler*: This was a sacred year for Israel, traditionally called the "Year of Jubilee." During this year, all property had to go back to its original owner (see Leviticus 25.8-34). [l] **46.19** *The man . . . temple*: See 40.3.
[m] **46.20** *sacrifices to make things right*: See the note at 40.38,39. [n] **46.20** *sacrifices for sin*: See the note at 40.38,39. [o] **46.20** *someone . . . touch them and be harmed*: See the note at 44.19.
46.17 Lv 25.10.

[21] We went back to the outer courtyard and walked past the four corners. [22] At each corner I saw a smaller courtyard, sixty-eight feet long and fifty feet wide. [23] Around the inside of these smaller courtyards was a low wall of stones, and against the wall were places to build fires.[p] [24] The man said, "These are the kitchens where the temple workers will boil the meat that worshipers offer as sacrifices."

The Stream Flowing from the Temple

47 The man took me back to the temple, where I saw a stream flowing from under the entrance. It began in the south part of the temple, where it ran past the altar and continued east through the courtyard.

[2] We walked out of the temple area through the north gate and went around to the east gate. I saw the small stream of water flowing east from the south side of the gate.

[3] The man walked east, then took out his measuring stick and measured five hundred sixty yards downstream. He told me to wade through the stream there, and the water came up to my ankles. [4] Then he measured another five hundred sixty yards downstream, and told me to wade through it there. The water came up to my knees. Another five hundred sixty yards downstream the water came up to my waist. [5] Another five hundred sixty yards downstream, the stream had become a river that could be crossed only by swimming. [6] The man said, "Ezekiel, son of man, pay attention to what you've seen."

We walked to the riverbank, [7] where I saw dozens of trees on each side. [8] The man said:

> This water flows eastward to the Jordan River valley and empties into the Dead Sea, where it turns the salt water into fresh water. [9] Wherever this water flows, there will be all kinds of animals and fish, because it will bring life and fresh water to the Dead Sea. [10] From En-Gedi to Eneglaim, people will fish in the sea and dry their nets along the coast. There will be as many kinds of fish in the Dead Sea as there are in the Mediterranean Sea. [11] But the marshes along the shore will remain salty, so that people can use the salt from them.
>
> [12] Fruit trees will grow all along this river and produce fresh fruit every month. The leaves will never dry out, because they will always have water from the stream that flows from the temple, and they will be used for healing people.

The Borders of the Land

[13-14] The LORD God said to the people of Israel:

> When the land is divided among the twelve tribes of Israel, the Joseph tribe[q] will receive two shares. Divide the land equally, because I promised your ancestors that this land would someday belong to their descendants. These are the borders of the land:
>
> [15] The northern border will begin at the Mediterranean Sea, then continue eastward to Hethlon, to Lebo-Hamath, then across to Zedad, [16] Berothah,[r] and Sibraim, which is on the border between the two kingdoms of Damascus and Hamath. The border will end at Hazer-Hatticon, which is on the border of Hauran. [17] So the northern border will run between the Mediterranean Sea and Hazar-Enon, which is on the border between Damascus and Hamath.[s]
>
> [18] The eastern border will begin on the border between the two kingdoms of Hauran and Damascus. It will run south along the Jordan River, which separates the territories of Gilead and Israel, and it will end at the Dead Sea near the town of Tamar.[t]

[p]46.23 *fires*: One possible meaning for the difficult Hebrew text of verse 23. [q]**47.13,14** *the Joseph tribe*: That is, the two tribes of Manasseh and Ephraim, Joseph's sons. [r]**47.15,16** *to Lebo-Hamath, then across to Zedad,* [16] *Berothah*: One ancient translation; Hebrew "to Lebo-Zedad, [16] then across to Hamath, Berothah." [s]**47.17** *which is on the border between Damascus and Hamath*: One possible meaning for the difficult Hebrew text. [t]**47.18** *near the town of Tamar*: One possible meaning for the difficult Hebrew text.

47.1 Zec 14.8; Jn 7.38; Rev 22.1. **47.12** Rev 22.2.

19 The southern border will begin at Tamar, then run southwest to the springs near Meribath-Kadesh. It will continue along the Egyptian Gorge and will end at the Mediterranean Sea.

20 The western border will run north along the Mediterranean Sea to a point just west of Lebo-Hamath.

21 That is the land to be divided among the tribes of Israel. 22 It will belong to the Israelites and to any foreigners living among them whose children were born in Israel. These foreigners must be treated like any other Israelite citizen, and they will receive 23 a share of the land given to the tribe where they live. I, the LORD God, have spoken.

The Division of Land among Tribes in the North

The LORD said:

48 1-7 Each tribe will receive a section of land that runs from the eastern border of Israel west to the Mediterranean Sea. The northern border of Israel will run along the towns of Hethlon and Lebo-Hamath, and will end at Hazar-Enon, which is on the border between the kingdoms of Damascus and Hamath. The tribes will receive their share of land in the following order, from north to south: Dan, Asher, Naphtali, Manasseh, Ephraim, Reuben, and Judah.

The Special Section of Land

The LORD said:

8 South of Judah's territory will be a special section of land. Its length will be eight miles, and its width will run from the eastern border of Israel west to the Mediterranean Sea. My temple will be located in this section of land.

9 An area in the center of this land will belong to me. It will be eight miles long and six[u] miles wide.

10 I, the LORD, will give half of my sacred land to the priests. Their share will be eight miles long and three miles wide, and my temple will be right in the middle. 11 Only priests who are descendants of Zadok will receive a share of this sacred land, because they remained faithful to me when the Levites and the rest of the Israelites started sinning. 12 The land belonging to the priests will be the most sacred area and will lie south of the area that belongs to the Levites.

13 I will give the other half of my sacred land to the Levites. Their share will also be eight miles long and three miles wide, 14 and they must never sell or trade any of this land—it is the best land and belongs to me.

15 South of my sacred land will be a section eight miles long and two miles wide. It will not be sacred, but will belong to the people of Israel and will include the city of Jerusalem, together with its houses and pastureland. 16 The city will be a square: Each side will be a mile and a half long, 17 and an open area four hundred twenty feet wide will surround the city. 18 The land on the east and west sides of the city limits will be farmland for the people of Jerusalem; both sections will be three miles long and two miles wide. 19 People from the city will farm the land, no matter which tribe they belong to.

20 And so the center of this special section of land will be for my sacred land, as well as for the city and its property. The land will be a square, eight miles on each side.

21 The regions east and west of this square of land will belong to the ruler of Israel. His property will run east to the Jordan River and west to the Mediterranean Sea. In the very center of his property will be my sacred land, as well as the temple, 22 together with the share belonging to the Levites and the city of Jerusalem. The northern border of the ruler's property will be the land that belongs to Judah, and the southern border will be the land that belongs to Benjamin.

The Division of Land among Tribes in the South

The LORD God said:

23-27 South of this special section will be the land that belongs to the rest of Israel's

[u]**48.9** *six*: The Hebrew text has "three" (but see 45.1 and the note there).

tribes. Each tribe will receive a section of land that runs from the eastern border of Israel west to the Mediterranean Sea. The tribes will receive their share of land in the following order, from north to south: Benjamin, Simeon, Issachar, Zebulun, and Gad.

28 Gad's southern border is also the southern border of Israel. It will begin at the town of Tamar, then run southwest to the springs near Meribath-Kadesh. It will continue along the Egyptian Gorge and end at the Mediterranean Sea.

29 That's how the land of Israel will be divided among the twelve tribes. I, the LORD God, have spoken.

The Gates of Jerusalem

The LORD said:

30-34 The city of Jerusalem will have twelve gates, three on each of the four sides of the city wall. These gates will be named after the twelve tribes of Israel. The gates of Reuben, Judah, and Levi will be in the north; Joseph, Benjamin, and Dan will be in the east; Simeon, Issachar, and Zebulun will be in the south; Gad, Asher, and Naphtali will be in the west. Each side of the city wall will be a mile and a half long,
35 and so the total length of the wall will be six miles. The new name of the city will be "The-LORD-Is-Here!"

48.30-34 Rev 21.12, 13.

DANIEL

ABOUT THIS BOOK

As a young man, Daniel had been taken prisoner by the Babylonian army when Jerusalem was captured. The first half of this book (1–6) tells how he and three of his friends from Judah became important officials in the government at Babylon. They remained completely faithful to the Lord, even when it meant risking their lives. This half of the book concludes with Daniel serving in the government of the Medo-Persian Empire after it had conquered Babylonia.

In the second half of the book (7–12) Daniel reports several visions that he had and how the meanings of those visions were explained to him by angels.

This book shows that God is in control of human events. He guides empires into power, but later he lets them be conquered by other empires. God also cares for individuals who are faithful to him, and someday he will finally bring justice to the world and provide victory for his people. Here is how Daniel spoke about this future time of victory:

"I saw what looked like
a son of man
coming with the clouds of heaven,
and he was presented
to the Eternal God.
He was crowned king
and given power and glory,
so that all people
of every nation and race
would serve him.
He will rule forever,
and his kingdom is eternal,
never to be destroyed."
(7.13b, 14)

A QUICK LOOK AT THIS BOOK

- Daniel and His Three Friends (1.1-21)
- King Nebuchadnezzar's Dream (2.1-49)
- God Rescues Shadrach, Meshach, and Abednego (3.1-30)
- Nebuchadnezzar Loses His Kingdom for Seven Years (4.1-37)
- King Belshazzar and the Writing on the Wall (5.1-31)
- God Rescues Daniel from the Pit of Lions (6.1-28)
- Daniel's Vision of Four Beasts (7.1-28)
- Daniel's Vision of a Ram and a Goat (8.1-27)
- Daniel Prays for His People (9.1-27)
- Daniel Has a Vision beside the Tigris River (10.1—12.13)

Daniel and His Friends

1 In the third year that Jehoiakim was king of Judah,[a] King Nebuchadnezzar of Babylonia attacked Jerusalem. 2 The Lord let Nebuchadnezzar capture Jehoiakim and take away some of the things used in God's temple. And when the king returned to Babylonia,[b] he put these things in the temple of his own god.

3 One day the king ordered Ashpenaz, his highest palace official, to choose some young men from the royal family of Judah and from other leading Jewish families. 4 The king said, "They must be healthy, handsome, smart, wise, educated, and fit to serve in the royal palace. Teach them how to speak and write our language 5 and give them the same food and wine that I am served. Train them for three years, and then they can become court officials."

6 Four of the young Jews chosen were Daniel, Hananiah, Mishael, and Azariah, all from the tribe of Judah. 7 But the king's chief official gave them Babylonian names: Daniel became Belteshazzar, Hananiah became Shadrach, Mishael became Meshach, and Azariah became Abednego.

8 Daniel made up his mind to eat and drink only what God had approved for his people to eat. And he asked the king's chief official for permission not to eat the food and wine served in the royal palace. 9 God had made the official friendly and kind to Daniel. 10 But the man still told him, "The king has decided what you must eat and drink. And I am afraid he will kill me, if you eat something else and end up looking worse than the other young men."

11 The king's official had put a guard in charge of Daniel and his three friends. So Daniel said to the guard, 12 "For the next ten days, let us have only vegetables and water at mealtime. 13 When the ten days are up, compare how we look with the other young men, and decide what to do with us." 14 The guard agreed to do what Daniel had asked.

15 Ten days later, Daniel and his friends looked healthier and better than the young men who had been served food from the royal palace. 16 After this, the guard let them eat vegetables instead of the rich food and wine.

17 God made the four young men smart and wise. They read a lot of books and became well educated. Daniel could also tell the meaning of dreams and visions.

18 At the end of the three-year period set by King Nebuchadnezzar, his chief palace official brought all the young men to him. 19 The king interviewed them and discovered that none of the others were as outstanding as Daniel, Hananiah, Mishael, and Azariah. So they were given positions in the royal court. 20 From then on, whenever the king asked for advice, he found their wisdom was ten times better than that of any of his other advisors and magicians. 21 Daniel served there until the first year of King Cyrus.[c]

Nebuchadnezzar's Dream

2 During the second year that Nebuchadnezzar was king, he had such horrible nightmares that he could not sleep. 2 So he called in his counselors, advisors, magicians, and wise men, 3 and said, "I am disturbed by a dream that I don't understand, and I want you to explain it."

4 They answered in Aramaic,[d] "Your Majesty, we hope you live forever! We are your servants. Please tell us your dream, and we will explain what it means."

5 But the king replied, "No! I have made up my mind. If you don't tell me both the dream and its meaning, you will be chopped to pieces and your houses will be torn down. 6 However, if you do tell me both the dream and its meaning, you will be greatly rewarded and highly honored. Now tell me the dream and explain what it means."

7 "Your Majesty," they said, "if you will only tell us your dream, we will interpret it for you."

[a] **1.1** *Jehoiakim . . . king of Judah*: Ruled 609-598 B.C. [b] **1.2** *Babylonia*: The Hebrew text has "Shinar," another name for Babylonia. [c] **1.21** *first year of King Cyrus*: 539 B.C.
[d] **2.4** *Aramaic*: Chapter 2.4—7.28 is written in Aramaic, a language closely related to Hebrew.
1.1 2 K 24.1; 2 Ch 36.5-7. **1.2-4** 2 K 20.17, 18; 24.10-16; 2 Ch 36.10; Is 39.7, 8.

[8] The king replied, "You're just stalling for time, [9] because you know what's going to happen if you don't come up with the answer. You've decided to make up a bunch of lies, hoping I might change my mind. Now tell me the dream, and that will prove that you can interpret it."

[10] His advisors explained, "Your Majesty, you are demanding the impossible! No king, not even the most famous and powerful, has ever ordered his advisors, magicians, or wise men to do such a thing. [11] It can't be done, except by the gods, and they don't live here on earth."

[12-13] This made the king so angry that he gave orders for every wise man in Babylonia to be put to death, including Daniel and his three friends.

God Tells Nebuchadnezzar's Dream to Daniel

[14] Arioch was the king's official in charge of putting the wise men to death. He was on his way to have it done, when Daniel very wisely went to him [15] and asked, "Why did the king give such cruel[e] orders?" After Arioch explained what had happened, [16] Daniel rushed off and said to the king, "If you will just give me some time, I'll explain your dream."

[17] Daniel returned home and told his three friends. [18] Then he said, "Pray that the God who rules from heaven will be merciful and explain this mystery, so that we and the others won't be put to death." [19] In a vision one night, Daniel was shown the dream and its meaning. Then he praised the God who rules from heaven:

[20] "Our God, your name
will be praised
forever and forever.
You are all-powerful,
and you know everything.
[21] You control human events—
you give rulers their power
and take it away,
and you are the source
of wisdom and knowledge.
[22] "You explain deep mysteries,
because even the dark
is light to you.
[23] You are the God
who was worshiped
by my ancestors.
Now I thank you and praise you
for making me wise
and telling me the king's dream,
together with its meaning."

Daniel Interprets the Dream

[24] Daniel went back to Arioch, the official in charge of executing the wise men. Daniel said, "Don't kill those men! Take me to the king, and I will explain the meaning of his dream."

[25] Arioch rushed Daniel to the king and announced, "Your Majesty, I have found out that one of the men brought here from Judah can explain your dream."

[26] The king asked Daniel,[f] "Can you tell me my dream and what it means?"

[27] Daniel answered:

Your Majesty, not even the smartest person in all the world can do what you are demanding. [28-29] But the God who rules from heaven can explain mysteries. And while you were sleeping, he showed you what will happen in the future. [30] However, you must realize that these mysteries weren't explained to me because I am smarter than everyone else. Instead, it was done so that you would understand what you have seen.

[31] Your Majesty, what you saw standing in front of you was a huge and terrifying statue, shining brightly. [32] Its head was made of gold, its chest and arms were silver, and from its waist down to its knees, it was bronze. [33] From there to its ankles it was iron, and its feet were a mixture of iron and clay.

[34] As you watched, a stone was cut from a mountain—but not by human hands. The stone struck the feet, completely shattering the iron and clay. [35] Then the iron, the clay, the bronze,

[e]**2.15** *cruel*: Or "urgent." [f]**2.26** *Daniel*: Aramaic "Daniel whose name was Belteshazzar" (see 1.7).

the silver, and the gold were crushed
and blown away without a trace, like
husks of wheat at threshing time. But
the stone became a tremendous mountain that covered the entire earth.
36 That was the dream, and now I'll
tell you what it means. 37 Your Majesty,
you are the greatest of kings, and God
has highly honored you with power
38 over all humans, animals, and birds.
You are the head of gold. 39 After you
are gone, another kingdom will rule,
but it won't be as strong. Then it will
be followed by a kingdom of bronze
that will rule the whole world. 40 Next,
a kingdom of iron will come to power,
crushing and shattering everything.[g]
41-42 This fourth kingdom will be divided—it will be both strong and brit-
tle, just as you saw that the feet and
toes were a mixture of iron and clay.
43 This kingdom will be the result of a
marriage between kingdoms, but it will
crumble, just as iron and clay don't
stick together.
44-45 During the time of those kings,
the God who rules from heaven will set
up an eternal kingdom that will never
fall. It will be like the stone that was
cut from the mountain, but not by human hands—the stone that crushed
the iron, bronze, clay, silver, and gold.
Your Majesty, in your dream the great
God has told you what is going to happen, and you can trust this interpretation.

Daniel Is Promoted

46 King Nebuchadnezzar bowed low to
the ground and worshiped Daniel. Then he
gave orders for incense to be burned and a
sacrifice of grain to be offered in honor of
Daniel. 47 The king said, "Now I know that
your God is above all other gods and kings,
because he gave you the power to explain
this mystery." 48 The king then presented
Daniel with a lot of gifts; he promoted him
to governor of Babylon Province and put
him in charge of the other wise men. 49 At
Daniel's request, the king appointed
Shadrach, Meshach, and Abednego to high
positions in Babylon Province, and he let
Daniel stay on as a palace official.

King Nebuchadnezzar's Gold Statue

3 King Nebuchadnezzar ordered a gold
statue to be built ninety feet high and
nine feet wide. He had it set up in Dura
Valley near the city of Babylon, 2 and he
commanded his governors, advisors, treasurers, judges, and his other officials to
come from everywhere in his kingdom to
the dedication of the statue. 3 So all of
them came and stood in front of it.
4 Then an official stood up and announced:

People of every nation and race,
now listen to the king's command!
5 Trumpets, flutes, harps, and all other
kinds of musical instruments will soon
start playing. When you hear the music, you must bow down and worship
the statue that King Nebuchadnezzar has set up. 6 Anyone who refuses
will at once be thrown into a flaming
furnace.

7 As soon as the people heard the music,
they bowed down and worshiped the gold
statue that the king had set up.
8 Some Babylonians used this as a
chance to accuse the Jews to King Nebuchadnezzar. 9 They said, "Your Majesty, we
hope you live forever! 10 You commanded
everyone to bow down and worship the
gold statue when the music played. 11 And
you said that anyone who did not bow
down and worship it would be thrown into
a flaming furnace. 12 Sir, you appointed
three men to high positions in Babylon
Province, but they have disobeyed you.
Those Jews, Shadrach, Meshach, and
Abednego, refuse to worship your gods and
the statue you have set up."
13 King Nebuchadnezzar was furious. So
he sent for the three young men and said,
14 "I hear that you refuse to worship my
gods and the gold statue I have set up.
15 Now I am going to give you one more

[g] **2.40** *crushing . . . everything*: Three ancient translations; Aramaic adds "and like iron crushing."

3.1-30 4 Macc 13.9.

chance. If you bow down and worship the
statue when you hear the music, everything will be all right. But if you don't, you
will at once be thrown into a flaming furnace. No god can save you from me."
16 The three men replied, "Your Majesty,
we don't need to defend ourselves. 17 The
God we worship can save us from you and
your flaming furnace. 18 But even if he
doesn't, we still won't worship your gods
and the gold statue you have set up."
19 Nebuchadnezzar's face twisted with
anger at the three men. And he ordered the
furnace to be heated seven times hotter
than usual. 20 Next, he commanded some
of his strongest soldiers to tie up the men
and throw them into the flaming furnace.
21-23 The king wanted it done at that very
moment. So the soldiers tied up Shadrach,
Meshach, and Abednego and threw them
into the flaming furnace with all of their
clothes still on, including their turbans.
The fire was so hot that flames leaped out
and killed the soldiers.
24 Suddenly the king jumped up and
shouted, "Weren't only three men tied up
and thrown into the fire?"

"Yes, Your Majesty," the people answered.
25 "But I see four men walking around
in the fire," the king replied. "None of
them is tied up or harmed, and the fourth
one looks like a god."[h]
26 Nebuchadnezzar went closer to the
flaming furnace and said to the three
young men, "You servants of the Most High
God, come out at once!"

They came out, 27 and the king's high
officials, governors, and advisors all
crowded around them. The men were not
burned, their hair wasn't scorched, and
their clothes didn't even smell like smoke.
28 King Nebuchadnezzar said:

Praise their God for sending an angel to rescue his servants! They
trusted their God and refused to obey
my commands. Yes, they chose to die
rather than to worship or serve any
god except their own. 29 And I won't allow people of any nation or race to say
anything against their God. Anyone
who does will be chopped up and their
houses will be torn down, because no
other god has such great power
to save.

30 After this happened, the king appointed Shadrach, Meshach, and Abednego
to even higher positions in Babylon
Province.

King Nebuchadnezzar's Letter about His Second Dream

4 King Nebuchadnezzar sent the following letter to the people of all nations
and races on the earth:

Greetings to all of you!
2 I am glad to tell about
the wonderful miracles
God Most High
has done for me.
3 His miracles are mighty
and marvelous.
He will rule forever,
and his kingdom
will never end.

4 I was enjoying a time of peace and
prosperity, 5 when suddenly I had some
horrifying dreams and visions. 6 Then I
commanded every wise man in Babylonia
to appear in my court, so they could explain the meaning of my dream. 7 After
they arrived, I told them my dream, but
they were not able to say what it meant.
8 Finally, a young man named Daniel came
in, and I told him the dream. The holy gods
had given him special powers, and I had renamed him Belteshazzar after my own god.
9 I said, "Belteshazzar, not only are you
the wisest of all advisors and counselors,
but the holy gods have given you special
powers to solve the most difficult mysteries. So listen to what I dreamed and tell me
what it means:

10 In my sleep I saw
a very tall tree
in the center of the world.
11 It grew stronger and higher,
until it reached to heaven

[h] **3.25** *a god*: Aramaic, "a son of the gods."
3.21-23 Az/S of 3 H 1-68; 3 Macc 6.6.

and could be seen
from anywhere on earth.
12 It was covered with leaves
and heavy with fruit—
enough for all nations.
Wild animals enjoyed its shade,
birds nested in its branches,
and all creatures on earth
lived on its fruit.

13 "While I was in bed, having this vision, a holy angel[i] came down from heaven
14 and shouted:

'Chop down the tree
and cut off its branches;
strip off its leaves
and scatter its fruit.
Make the animals leave its shade
and send the birds flying
from its branches.
15 But leave its stump and roots
in the ground,
surrounded by grass
and held by chains
of iron and bronze.

'Make sure that this ruler
lives like the animals
out in the open fields,
unprotected from the dew.
16 Give him the mind
of a wild animal
for seven long years.[j]
17 This punishment is given
at the command
of the holy angels.[k]
It will show to all who live
that God Most High
controls all kingdoms
and chooses for their rulers
persons of humble birth.'

18 "Daniel,[l] that was the dream that none of the wise men in my kingdom were able to understand. But I am sure that you will understand what it means, because the holy gods have given you some special powers."

19 For a while, Daniel[l] was terribly confused and worried by what he was thinking. But I said, "Don't be bothered either by the dream or by what it means."

Daniel replied:

Your Majesty, I wish the dream had been against your enemies.
20 You saw a tree that grew so big and strong that it reached up to heaven and could be seen from anywhere on earth.
21 Its leaves were beautiful, and it produced enough fruit for all living creatures; animals lived in its shade, and birds nested in its branches.
22 Your Majesty, that tree is you. Your glorious reputation has reached heaven, and your kingdom covers the earth.

23 Then you saw a holy angel[m] come down from heaven and say, "Chop down the tree and destroy it! But leave its stump and roots in the ground, fastened there by a chain of iron and bronze. Let it stay for seven years[n] out in the field with the wild animals, unprotected from the dew."

24 Your Majesty, God Most High has sent you this message, and it means
25 that you will be forced to live with the wild animals, far away from humans. You will eat grass like a wild animal and live outdoors for seven years,[n] until you learn that God Most High controls all earthly kingdoms and chooses their rulers.
26 But he gave orders not to disturb the stump and roots. This is to show that you will be king once again, after you learn that the God who rules from heaven is in control.
27 Your Majesty, please be willing to do what I say. Turn from your sins and start living right; have mercy on those who are mistreated. Then all will go well with you for a long time.

The Rest of Nebuchadnezzar's Letter about His Second Dream

28-30 About twelve months later, I was walking on the flat roof of my royal palace

[i]**4.13** *angel*: The Aramaic text has "watcher," which may be some special class of angel.
[j]**4.16** *long years*: Aramaic "times."
[k]**4.17** *angels*: See the note at 4.13.
[l]**4.18,19** *Daniel*: See the note at 2.26.
[m]**4.23** *angel*: See the note at 4.13.
[n]**4.23,25,32** *years*: Aramaic "times."
4.27 Tb 12.9; Si 3.30.

and admiring the beautiful city of Babylon,
when these things started happening to
me. I was saying to myself, "Just look at this
wonderful capital city that I have built by
my own power and for my own glory!"
31 But before I could finish speaking, a
voice from heaven interrupted:

King Nebuchadnezzar, this kingdom
is no longer yours. 32 You will be forced
to live with the wild animals, away
from people. For seven years[n] you will
eat grass, as though you were an ox,
until you learn that God Most High is
in control of all earthly kingdoms and
that he is the one who chooses their
rulers.

33 This was no sooner said than done—I
was forced to live like a wild animal; I ate
grass and was unprotected from the dew.
As time went by, my hair grew longer than
eagle feathers, and my fingernails looked
like the claws of a bird.
34 Finally, I prayed to God in heaven,
and my mind was healed. Then I said:

"I praise and honor
God Most High.
He lives forever,
and his kingdom
will never end.
35 To him the nations
are far less than nothing;
God controls the stars in the sky
and everyone on this earth.
When God does something,
we cannot change it
or even ask why."

36 At that time my mind was healed, and
once again I became the ruler of my glorious kingdom. My advisors and officials returned to me, and I had greater power than
ever before. 37 That's why I say:

"Praise and honor the King
who rules from heaven!
Everything he does
is honest and fair,
and he can shatter the power
of those who are proud."

King Belshazzar's Banquet

5 One evening, King Belshazzar gave a
great banquet for a thousand of his
highest officials, and he drank wine with
them. 2 He got drunk and ordered his servants to bring in the gold and silver cups his
father Nebuchadnezzar[o] had taken from
the temple in Jerusalem. Belshazzar
wanted the cups, so that he and all his
wives and officials could drink from them.
3-4 When the gold cups were brought in,
everyone at the banquet drank from them
and praised their idols made of gold, silver,
bronze, iron, wood, and stone.
5 Suddenly a human hand was seen
writing on the plaster wall of the palace.
The hand was just behind the lampstand,
and the king could see it writing. 6 He was
so frightened that his face turned pale, his
knees started shaking, and his legs became
weak.
7 The king called in his advisors, who
claimed they could talk with the spirits of
the dead and understand the meanings
found in the stars. He told them, "The man
who can read this writing and tell me what
it means will become the third most powerful man in my kingdom. He will wear robes
of royal purple and a gold chain around his
neck."
8 All of King Belshazzar's highest officials came in, but not one of them could
read the writing or tell what it meant, 9 and
they were completely puzzled. Now the
king was more afraid than ever before, and
his face turned white as a ghost.
10 When the queen heard the king and
his officials talking, she came in and said:

Your Majesty, I hope you live forever! Don't be afraid or look so pale.
11 In your kingdom there is a man who
has been given special powers by the
holy gods. When your father Nebuchadnezzar was king, this man was
known to be as smart, intelligent, and
wise as the gods themselves. Your
father put him in charge of all who
claimed they could talk with the spirits

[n]**4.23,25,32** *years*: Aramaic "times." [o]**5.2** *his father Nebuchadnezzar*: Belshazzar was actually the son of King Nabonidus, who was from another family. But in ancient times, it was possible to refer to a previous king as the "father" of the present king.

4.34 Si 18.1. **5.3,4** 3 Macc 4.16.

or understand the meanings in the stars or tell about the future. 12 He also changed the man's name from Daniel to Belteshazzar. Not only is he wise and intelligent, but he can explain dreams and riddles and solve difficult problems. Send for Daniel, and he will tell you what the writing means.

13 When Daniel was brought in, the king said:

So you are Daniel, one of the captives my father brought back from Judah! 14 I was told that the gods have given you special powers and that you are intelligent and very wise. 15 Neither my advisors nor the men who talk with the spirits of the dead could read this writing or tell me what it means. 16 But I have been told that you understand everything and that you can solve difficult problems. Now then, if you can read this writing and tell me what it means, you will become the third most powerful man in my kingdom. You will wear royal purple robes and have a gold chain around your neck.

17 Daniel answered:

Your Majesty, I will read the writing and tell you what it means. But you may keep your gifts or give them to someone else. 18 Sir, the Most High God made your father a great and powerful man and brought him much honor and glory. 19 God did such great things for him that people of all nations and races shook with fear.

Your father had the power of life or death over everyone, and he could honor or ruin anyone he chose. 20 But when he became proud and stubborn, his glorious kingdom was taken from him. 21 His mind became like that of an animal, and he was forced to stay away from people and live with wild donkeys. Your father ate grass like an ox, and he slept outside where his body was soaked with dew. He was forced to do this until he learned that the Most High God rules all kingdoms on earth and chooses their kings.

22 King Belshazzar, you knew all of this, but you still refused to honor the Lord who rules from heaven. 23 Instead, you turned against him and ordered the cups from his temple to be brought here, so that you and your wives and officials could drink wine from them. You praised idols made of silver, gold, bronze, iron, wood, and stone, even though they cannot see or hear or think. You refused to worship the God who gives you breath and controls everything you do. 24 That's why he sent the hand to write this message on the wall.

25-28 The words written there are *mene*, which means "numbered," *tekel*, which means "weighed," and *parsin*,[p] which means "divided." God has numbered the days of your kingdom and has brought it to an end. He has weighed you on his balance scales, and you fall short of what it takes to be king. So God has divided your kingdom between the Medes and the Persians.

29 Belshazzar gave a command for Daniel to be made the third most powerful man in his kingdom and to be given a purple robe and a gold chain.

30 That same night, the king was killed.

31 Then Darius the Mede, who was sixty-two years old, took over his kingdom.

Daniel in a Pit of Lions

6 Darius divided his kingdom into a hundred and twenty states and placed a governor in charge of each one. 2 In order to make sure that his government was run properly, Darius put three other officials in charge of the governors. One of these officials was Daniel. 3 And he did his work so much better than the other governors and officials that the king decided to let him govern the whole kingdom.

4 The other men tried to find something wrong with the way Daniel did his work for the king. But they could not accuse him of

[p]**5.25-28** *mene . . . tekel . . . parsin*: In the Aramaic text of verse 25, the words "mene, tekel, parsin," are used, and in verses 26-28 the words "mene, tekel, peres" (the singular of "parsin") are used. "Parsin" means "divided," but "peres" can mean either "divided" or "Persia."

anything wrong, because he was honest
and faithful and did everything he was supposed to do. 5 Finally, they said to one another, "We will never be able to bring any
charge against Daniel, unless it has to do
with his religion."
6 They all went to the king and said:
Your Majesty, we hope you live forever! 7 All of your officials, leaders, advisors, and governors agree that you
should make a law forbidding anyone
to pray to any god or human except
you for the next thirty days. Everyone
who disobeys this law must be thrown
into a pit of lions. 8 Order this to be
written and then sign it, so it cannot
be changed, just as no written law of
the Medes and Persians can be
changed."
9 So King Darius made the law and had
it written down.
10 Daniel heard about the law, but when
he returned home, he went upstairs and
prayed in front of the window that faced
Jerusalem. In the same way that he had always done, he knelt down in prayer three
times a day, giving thanks to God.
11 The men who had spoken to the king
watched Daniel and saw him praying to his
God for help. 12 They went back to the king
and said, "Didn't you make a law that forbids anyone to pray to any god or human
except you for the next thirty days? And
doesn't the law say that everyone who
disobeys it will be thrown into a pit of
lions?"
"Yes, that's the law I made," the king
agreed. "And just like all written laws of the
Medes and Persians, it cannot be changed."
13 The men then told the king, "That
Jew named Daniel, who was brought here
as a captive, refuses to obey you or the law
that you ordered to be written. And he still
prays to his god three times a day." 14 The
king was really upset to hear about this,
and for the rest of the day he tried to think
how he could save Daniel.
15 At sunset the men returned and said,
"Your Majesty, remember that no written
law of the Medes and Persians can be
changed, not even by the king."
16 So Darius ordered Daniel to be
brought out and thrown into a pit of lions.
But he said to Daniel, "You have been
faithful to your God, and I pray that he will
rescue you."
17 A stone was rolled over the pit, and it
was sealed. Then Darius and his officials
stamped the seal to show that no one
should let Daniel out. 18 All night long the
king could not sleep. He did not eat anything, and he would not let anyone come in
to entertain him.
19 At daybreak the king got up and ran
to the pit. 20 He was anxious and shouted,
"Daniel, you were faithful and served your
God. Was he able to save you from the
lions?"
21 Daniel answered, "Your Majesty, I
hope you live forever! 22 My God knew that
I was innocent, and he sent an angel to
keep the lions from eating me. Your
Majesty, I have never done anything to
hurt you."
23 The king was relieved to hear
Daniel's voice, and he gave orders for him
to be taken out of the pit. Daniel's faith in
his God had kept him from being harmed.
24 And the king ordered the men who had
brought charges against Daniel to be
thrown into the pit, together with their
wives and children. But before they even
reached the bottom, the lions ripped them
to pieces.
25 King Darius then sent this message to
all people of every nation and race in the
world:

"Greetings to all of you!
26 I command everyone
in my kingdom
to worship and honor
the God of Daniel.
He is the living God,
the one who lives forever.
His power and his kingdom
will never end.
27 He rescues people
and sets them free
by working great miracles.
Daniel's God has rescued him
from the power of the lions."

6.7,24 3 Macc 6.7. **6.16** Bel 31-42. **6.22** Tb 4.17; 12.14, 15.

[28] All went well for Daniel while Darius
was king, and even when Cyrus the Persian
ruled.[q]

Daniel's Vision of the Four Beasts

7 [1-2] Daniel wrote:
In the first year of King Belshazzar[r]
of Babylonia, I had some dreams and visions while I was asleep one night, and I
wrote them down.

The four winds were stirring up the
mighty sea, [3] when suddenly four powerful
beasts came out of the sea. Each beast was
different. [4] The first was like a lion with the
wings of an eagle. As I watched, its wings
were pulled off. Then it was lifted to an up-
right position and made to stand on two
feet, just like a human, and it was given a
human mind.

[5] The second beast looked like a bear
standing on its hind legs.[s] It held three ribs
in its teeth, and it was told, "Attack! Eat all
the flesh you want."

[6] The third beast was like a leopard—except that it had four wings and four heads.
It was given authority to rule.

[7] The fourth beast was stronger and more
terrifying than the others. Its huge teeth
were made of iron, and what it didn't grind
with its teeth, it smashed with its feet. It
was different from the others, and it had
horns on its head—ten of them. [8] Just as I
was thinking about these horns, a smaller
horn appeared, and three of the other horns
were pulled up by the roots to make room
for it. This horn had the eyes of a human
and a mouth that spoke with great pride.

Judgment

Daniel wrote:

[9] Thrones were set up
while I was watching,
and the Eternal God[t]
took his place.
His clothing and his hair
were white as snow.
His throne was a blazing fire
with fiery wheels,
[10] and flames were dashing out
from all around him.
Countless thousands
were standing there
to serve him.
The time of judgment began,
and the books[u] were opened.

[11] I watched closely to see what would
happen to this smaller horn because of the
arrogant things it was saying. Then before
my very eyes, the fourth beast was killed
and its body destroyed by fire. [12] The other
three beasts had their authority taken from
them, but they were allowed to live a while
longer.[v] [13] As I continued to watch the
vision that night,

I saw what looked like
a son of man[w]
coming with the clouds of heaven,
and he was presented
to the Eternal God.[x]
[14] He was crowned king
and given power and glory,
so that all people
of every nation and race
would serve him.
He will rule forever,
and his kingdom is eternal,
never to be destroyed.

The Meaning of Daniel's Vision

[15] Daniel wrote:

I was terrified by these visions, and I
didn't know what to think. [16] So I asked
one of those standing there,[y] and he

[q]**6.28** *Cyrus the Persian ruled*: 539-530 B.C. [r]**7.1,2** *first year of King Belshazzar*: 554 B.C. [s]**7.5** *standing on its hind legs*: Or "higher on one side than the other" or "with a paw lifted up." [t]**7.9** *Eternal God*: Aramaic "Ancient of Days." [u]**7.10** *books*: Containing the record of the good and evil that each person has done. [v]**7.12** *a while longer*: Aramaic "for a time and a season." [w]**7.13** *son of man*: Or "human." In Aramaic "son of man" may mean a human or even "oneself" ("I" or "me"). Jesus often used the phrase "the Son of Man" when referring to himself. [x]**7.13** *Eternal God*: See the note at 7.9. [y]**7.16** *one of those standing there*: Possibly an angel sent to interpret the visions or one of those thousands mentioned in verse 10.

7.3 Rev 13.1; 17.8. **7.4-6** Rev 13.2. **7.7** Rev 12.3; 13.1. **7.8** Rev 13.5, 6. **7.9** **a** Rev 20.4; **b** Rev 1.14. **7.10** **a** Rev 5.11; **b** Rev 20.12. **7.13** Mt 24.30; 26.64; Mk 13.26; 14.62; Lk 21.27; Rev 1.7, 13; 14.14. **7.14** Rev 11.15.

explained, 17 "The four beasts are four
earthly kingdoms. 18 But God Most High
will give his kingdom to his chosen ones,
and it will be theirs forever and ever."

19 I wanted to know more about the
fourth beast,[z] because it was so different
and much more terrifying than the others.
What was the meaning of its iron teeth and
bronze claws and of its feet that smashed
what the teeth and claws had not ground
and crushed? 20 I also wanted to know
more about all ten of those horns on its
head. I especially wanted to know more
about the one that took the place of three
of the others—the horn that had eyes and
spoke with arrogance and seemed greater
than the others. 21 While I was looking, this
horn attacked God's chosen ones and was
winning the battle. 22 Then God Most High,
the Eternal God,[a] came and judged in favor
of his chosen ones, because the time had
arrived for them to be given the kingdom.

23 Then I was told
by the one standing there:
"The fourth beast
will be a fourth kingdom
to appear on earth.
It will be different
from all the others—
it will trample the earth
and crush it to pieces.
24 All ten of those horns are kings
who will come from this kingdom,
and one more will follow.
This horn will be different
from the others,
and it will conquer
three other kings.

25 "This king will speak evil
of God Most High,
and he will be cruel
to God's chosen ones.
He will try to change God's Law
and the sacred seasons.
And he will be able to do this
for a time, two times,
and half a time.[b]
26 But he will finally be judged,
and his kingdom
completely destroyed.

27 "Then the greatest kingdom of all
will be given to the chosen ones
of God Most High.
His kingdom will be eternal,
and all others will serve
and obey him."

28 That was what I saw and heard.
I turned pale with fear and kept it all to
myself.

Vision of a Ram and a Goat

8 Daniel wrote:
In the third year of King Belshazzar
of Babylonia,[c] I had a second vision 2 in
which I was in Susa, the chief city of Babylonia's Elam Province. I was beside the
Ulai River,[d] 3 when I looked up and saw a
ram standing there with two horns on its
head—both of them were long, but the second one was longer than the first. 4 The
ram went charging toward the west, the
north, and the south. No other animals
were strong enough to oppose him, and
nothing could save them from his power.
So he did as he pleased and became even
more powerful.

5 I kept on watching and saw a goat
come from the west and charge across the
entire earth, without even touching the
ground. Between his eyes was a powerful
horn,[e] 6 and with tremendous anger the
goat started toward the ram that I had seen
beside the river.[f] 7 The goat was so fierce
that its attack broke both horns of the ram,
leaving him powerless. Then the goat
stomped on the ram, and no one could do
anything to help. 8 After this, the goat became even more powerful. But at the peak
of his power, his mighty horn was broken,
and four other mighty horns took its

[z]**7.19** *fourth beast*: See verses 7, 8. [a]**7.22** *Eternal God*: See the note at 7.9. [b]**7.25** *for . . . time*: Or "for a year, two years, and half a year." [c]**8.1** *third year . . . Babylonia*: 552 B.C., two years after the first vision (see 7.1, 2). [d]**8.2** *River*: Or "Gate." [e]**8.5** *powerful horn*: Hebrew "horn of vision." [f]**8.6** *river*: See the note at 8.2.

7.18 Rev 22.5. **7.21** Rev 13.7. **7.22** Rev 20.4. **7.24** Rev 17.12. **7.25** Rev 12.14; 13.5, 6. **7.27** **a** Rev 20.4; **b** Rev 22.5.

place—one pointing to the north and one to the east, one to the south and one to the west.

9 A little horn came from one of these, and its power reached to the south, the east, and even to the holy land.[g] 10 It became so strong that it attacked the stars in the sky, which were heaven's army.[h] Then it threw some of them down to the earth and stomped on them. 11-12 It humiliated heaven's army and dishonored its leader[i] by keeping him from offering the daily sacrifices. In fact, it was so terrible that it even disgraced the temple and wiped out true worship. It also did everything else it wanted to do.

13 Then one of the holy angels asked another, "When will the daily sacrifices be offered again? What about this horrible rebellion? When will the temple and heaven's army no longer be trampled in the dust?"

14 The other answered, "It will be two thousand three hundred evenings and mornings before the temple is dedicated and in use again."

Gabriel Interprets the Vision

15 Daniel wrote:

I was trying to figure out the meaning of the vision, when someone suddenly appeared there beside me. 16 And from beside the Ulai River,[j] a voice like that of a human said, "Gabriel, help him understand the vision."

17 Gabriel came over, and I fell to the ground in fear. Then he said, "You are merely a human, but you need to understand that this vision is about the end of time."

18 While he was speaking, I fell facedown in a deep sleep. But he lifted me to my feet 19 and said:

Listen, and I will tell you what will happen at the end of time, when God has chosen to show his anger. 20 The two horns of the ram are the kings of Media and Persia, 21 the goat is the kingdom of Greece, and the powerful horn between his eyes is the first of its kings. 22 After this horn is broken, four other kingdoms will appear, but they won't be as strong.

23 When these rulers have become as evil as possible, their power will end, and then a king who is dangerous and cannot be trusted will appear. 24 He will gain strength, but not on his own, and he will cause terrible destruction. He will wipe out powerful leaders and God's people as well. 25 His deceitful lies will make him so successful, that he will think he is really great. Suddenly he will kill many people, and he will even attack God, the Supreme Ruler. But God will crush him!

26 This vision about the evenings and mornings is true, but these things won't happen for a long time, so don't tell it to others.

27 After this, I was so worn out and weak that it was several days before I could get out of bed and go about my duties for the king. I was disturbed by this vision that made no sense to me.

Daniel Prays for the People

9 1-2 Daniel wrote:

Some years later, Darius the Mede,[k] who was the son of Xerxes,[l] had become king of Babylonia. And during his first year as king, I found out from studying the writings of the prophets that the LORD had said to Jeremiah, "Jerusalem will lie in ruins for seventy years."[m] 3-4 Then, to show my sorrow, I went without eating and dressed in sackcloth[n] and sat in ashes. I confessed my sins and earnestly prayed to the LORD my God:

Our Lord, you are a great and fearsome God, and you faithfully keep your

[g]**8.9** *holy land*: Hebrew "the lovely land." [h]**8.10** *heaven's army*: In verses 10-13 the Hebrew word translated "heaven's army" may also mean "God's people." [i]**8.11,12** *leader*: Hebrew "prince." [j]**8.16** *River*: See the note at 8.2. [k]**9.1,2** *Darius the Mede*: See 5.31. [l]**9.1,2** *Xerxes*: Hebrew "Ahasuerus." [m]**9.1,2** *seventy years*: See Jeremiah 25.11-13; 29.10. [n]**9.3,4** *sackcloth*: A rough, dark-colored cloth made from goat or camel hair and used to make grain sacks. It was worn in times of trouble or sorrow.

8.10 Rev 12.4. **8.16** Lk 1.19, 26. **9.1,2** Jr 25.11; 29.10.

agreement with those who love and
obey you. 5 But we have sinned terribly
by rebelling against you and rejecting
your laws and teachings. 6 We have
ignored the message your servants
the prophets spoke to our kings, our
leaders, our ancestors, and everyone
else.
7 Everything you do is right, our
Lord. But still we suffer public disgrace because we have been unfaithful
and have sinned against you. This includes all of us, both far and near—the
people of Judah, Jerusalem, and Israel,
as well as those you dragged away to
foreign lands, 8 and even our kings,
our officials, and our ancestors. 9 LORD
God, you are merciful and forgiving,
even though we have rebelled against
you 10 and rejected your teachings that
came to us from your servants the
prophets.
11 Everyone in Israel has stubbornly
refused to obey your laws, and so those
curses written by your servant Moses
have fallen upon us. 12 You warned us
and our leaders that Jerusalem would
suffer the worst disaster in human history, and you did exactly as you had
threatened. 13 We have not escaped
any of the terrible curses written by
Moses, and yet we have refused to beg
you for mercy and to remind ourselves
of how faithful you have always been.
14 And when you finally punished us
with this horrible disaster, that was
also the right thing to do, because we
deserved it so much.
15 Our Lord God, with your own
mighty arm you rescued us from Egypt
and made yourself famous to this very
day, but we have sinned terribly. 16 In
the past, you treated us with such
kindness, that we now beg you to stop
being so terribly angry with Jerusalem.
After all, it is your chosen city built on
your holy mountain, even though it
has suffered public disgrace because of
our sins and those of our ancestors.
17 I am your servant, Lord God, and
I beg you to answer my prayers and
bring honor to yourself by having pity
on your temple that lies in ruins.
18 Please show mercy to your chosen
city, not because we deserve it, but because of your great kindness. 19 Forgive
us! Hurry and do something, not only
for your city and your chosen people,
but to bring honor to yourself.

The Seventy Weeks

Daniel wrote:
20 I was still confessing my sins and
those of all Israel to the LORD my God, and
I was praying for the good of his holy
mountain,[o] 21 when Gabriel suddenly came
flying in at the time of the evening sacrifice. This was the same Gabriel I had seen
in my vision, 22 and he explained:

Daniel, I am here to help you understand the vision. 23 God thinks
highly of you, and at the very moment
you started praying, I was sent to give
you the answer. 24 God has decided
that for seventy weeks,[p] your people
and your holy city must suffer as the
price of their sins. Then evil will disappear, and justice will rule forever; the
visions and words of the prophets will
come true, and a most holy place will
be dedicated.[q]
25 You need to realize that from the
command to rebuild Jerusalem until
the coming of the Chosen Leader,[r] it
will be seven weeks and another sixty-
two weeks.[s] Streets will be built in
Jerusalem, and a trench will be dug
around the city for protection, but

[o] **9.20** *holy mountain*: Jerusalem (see verse 16) or the temple. [p] **9.24** *seventy weeks*: Or "seventy times seven years." [q] **9.24** *a most holy place will be dedicated*: Or "God's Holy One will appear." [r] **9.25** *the Chosen Leader*: Or "a chosen leader." In Hebrew the word "chosen" means "to pour oil (on someone's head)." In Old Testament times it was the custom to pour oil on a person's head when that person was chosen to be a priest or a king. [s] **9.25** *seven weeks and another sixty-two weeks*: Or "seven times seven years and another sixty-two times seven years."

9.7 Ba 1.15-17. **9.11** Ba 1.19-22. **9.15** Ba 2.11-13. **9.17** Ba 2.14. **9.18** Ba 2.19. **9.21** Lk 1.19, 26.

these will be difficult times.[t] 26 At the end of the sixty-two weeks,[u] the Chosen Leader[v] will be killed and left with nothing.[w]

A foreign ruler and his army will sweep down like a mighty flood, leaving both the city and the temple in ruins, and war and destruction will continue until the end, just as God has decided. 27 For one week[x] this foreigner[y] will make a firm agreement with many people, and halfway through this week,[z] he will end all sacrifices and offerings. Then the "Horrible Thing" that causes destruction will be put there. And it will stay there until the time God has decided to destroy this one who destroys.

Daniel's Vision beside the Tigris River

10 In the third year[a] of Cyrus the king of Persia, a message came to Daniel[b] from God, and it was explained in a vision. The message was about a horrible war, and it was true. 2 Daniel wrote:

For three weeks I was in sorrow. 3 I ate no fancy food or meat, I drank no wine, and I put no olive oil on my face or hair.[c] 4 Then, on the twenty-fourth day of the first month,[d] I was standing on the banks of the great Tigris River, 5 when I looked up and saw someone dressed in linen and wearing a solid gold belt.[e] 6 His body was like a precious stone,[f] his face like lightning, his eyes like flaming fires, his arms and legs like polished bronze, and his voice like the roar of a crowd. 7 Although the people who were with me did not see the vision, they became so frightened that they scattered and hid. 8 Only I saw this great vision. I became weak and pale, 9 and at the sound of his voice, I fell facedown in a deep sleep.

10 He raised me to my hands and knees 11 and then said, "Daniel, your God thinks highly of you, and he has sent me. So stand up and pay close attention." I stood trembling, while the angel said:

> 12 Daniel, don't be afraid! God has listened to your prayers since the first day you humbly asked for understanding, and he has sent me here. 13 But the guardian angel[g] of Persia opposed me for twenty-one days. Then Michael, who is one of the strongest guardian angels,[h] came to rescue me from the kings of Persia.[i] 14 Now I have come here to give you another vision about what will happen to your people in the future.

15 While this angel was speaking to me, I stared at the ground, speechless. 16 Then he appeared in human form and touched my lips. I said, "Sir, this vision has brought me great pain and has drained my strength. 17 I am merely your servant. How can I possibly speak with someone so powerful, when I am almost too weak to get my breath?"

18-19 The angel touched me a second time and said, "Don't be frightened! God thinks highly of you, and he intends this for your good, so be brave and strong."

At this, I regained my strength and replied, "Please speak! You have already made me feel much better."

[t]**9.25** *it will be seven . . . difficult times*: Or "it will be seven weeks. Then streets will be built in Jerusalem, and a trench will be dug around the city for protection. But Jerusalem will have difficult times for sixty-two weeks." [u]**9.26** *sixty-two weeks*: Or "sixty-two times seven years." [v]**9.26** *the Chosen Leader*: See the note at 9.25. [w]**9.26** *left with nothing*: Or "no one will take his place." [x]**9.27** *one week*: Or "seven years." [y]**9.27** *this foreigner*: Or "the Chosen Leader." [z]**9.27** *halfway through this week*: Or "for half of this week of seven years." [a]**10.1** *third year*: 536 B.C. [b]**10.1** *Daniel*: See the note at 2.26. [c]**10.3** *olive oil . . . hair*: On special occasions, it was the custom to put olive oil on one's face and hair. [d]**10.4** *first month*: Nisan (also known as Abib), the first month of the Hebrew calendar, from about mid-March to mid-April. [e]**10.5** *solid gold belt*: Hebrew "belt of gold from Uphaz." [f]**10.6** *a precious stone*: The Hebrew text has "beryl," which is green or bluish-green. [g]**10.13** *guardian angel*: Hebrew "prince." [h]**10.13** *one of the strongest guardian angels*: Hebrew "chief prince." [i]**10.13** *came . . . Persia*: One possible meaning for the difficult Hebrew text.

9.27 Dn 11.31; 12.11; 1 Macc 1.44-50, 54; Mt 24.15; Mk 13.14. **10.5,6** Rev 1.13-15; 2.18; 19.12. **10.7** 3 Macc 6.18; Ac 9.7; 22.6-9. **10.13,21** Rev 12.7.

20 Then the angel said:

Now do you understand why I have come? Soon I must leave to fight against the guardian angel of Persia. Then after I have defeated him, the guardian angel of Greece will attack me. 21 I will tell you what is written in *The Book of Truth*. But first, you must realize that no one except Michael, the guardian angel of Israel, is on my side.

11 1 You also need to know that I protected and helped Darius the Mede[j] in his first year as king.

The Angel's Message to Daniel

Part One: The Four Kings and their Successors

2 What I am going to tell you is certain to happen. Four kings will rule Persia, one after the other, but the fourth one will become much richer than the others. In fact, his wealth will make him so powerful that he will turn everyone against the kingdom of Greece. 3 Then a mighty king will come to power and will be able to do whatever he pleases. 4 But suddenly his kingdom will be crushed and scattered to the four corners of the earth, where four more kingdoms will rise. But these won't be ruled by his descendants or be as powerful as his kingdom.

5 The king of the south will grow powerful. Then one of his generals will rebel and take over most of the kingdom. 6 Years later the southern kingdom and the northern kingdom will make a treaty, and the daughter of the king of the south will marry the king of the north. But she will lose her power. Then she, her husband, their child,[k] and the servants who came with her will all be killed.

After this, 7 one of her relatives will become the ruler of the southern kingdom. He will attack the army of the northern kingdom and capture its fortresses. 8 Then he will carry their idols to Egypt, together with their precious treasures of silver and gold, but it will be a long time before he attacks the northern kingdom again. Some years later 9 the king of the north will invade the southern kingdom, but he will be forced back to his own country.

10 The sons of the king of the north will gather a huge army that will sweep down like a roaring flood, reaching all the way to the fortress of the southern kingdom. 11 But this will make the king of the south angry, and he will defeat this large army from the north. 12 The king of the south will feel proud because of the many thousands he has killed. But his victories won't last long, 13 because the king of the north will gather a larger and more powerful army than ever before. Then in a few years, he will start invading other countries.

14 At this time many of your own people will try to make this vision come true by rebelling against the king of the south, but their rebellion will fail. 15 Then the army from the north will surround and capture a fortress in the south, and not even the most experienced troops of the southern kingdom will be able to make them retreat. 16 The king who invaded from the north will do as he pleases, and he will even capture and destroy the holy land.[l] 17 In fact, he will decide to invade the south with his entire army. Then he will attempt to make peace by giving the king of the south a bride from the northern kingdom, but this won't be successful.

18 Afterwards, this proud king of the north will invade and conquer many of the nations along the coast, but a military leader will defeat him and make him lose his pride. 19 He will retreat to his fortresses in his own country, but on the way he will be defeated and never again be seen.

20 The next king of the north will try to collect taxes for the glory of his kingdom. However, he will come to a sudden end in some mysterious way, instead of in battle or because of someone's anger.

Part Two: The Evil King from the North

21 The successor of this king of the north will be a worthless nobody, who doesn't come from a royal family. He will

[j] **11.1** *Darius the Mede*: See 5.30. [k] **11.6** *their child*: One Hebrew manuscript and two ancient translations; most Hebrew manuscripts "her father." [l] **11.16** *the holy land*: See the note at 8.9.

11.11 3 Macc 1.1.

suddenly appear and gain control of the kingdom by treachery. 22 Then he will destroy armies and remove God's chosen high priest. 23 He will make a treaty, but he will be deceitful and break it, even though he has only a few followers. 24 Without warning, he will successfully invade a wealthy province, which is something his ancestors never did. Then he will divide among his followers all of its treasures and property. But none of this will last very long.

25 He will gather a large and powerful army, and with great courage he will attack the king of the south. The king of the south will meet him with a much stronger army, but he will lose the battle, because he will be betrayed 26 by members of the royal court. He will be ruined, and most of his army will be slaughtered.

27 The two kings will meet around a table and tell evil lies to each other. But their plans will fail, because God has already decided what will happen. 28 Then the king of the north will return to his country with great treasures. But on the way, he will attack the religion of God's people and do whatever else he pleases.

29 At the time God has decided, the king of the north will invade the southern kingdom again, but this time, things will be different. 30 Ships from the west will come to attack him, and he will be discouraged. Then he will start back to his own country and take out his anger on the religion of God's faithful people, while showing kindness to those who are unfaithful. 31 He will send troops to pollute the temple and the fortress, and he will stop the daily sacrifices. Then he will set up that "Horrible Thing" that causes destruction. 32 The king will use deceit to win followers from those who are unfaithful to God, but those who remain faithful will do everything possible to oppose him.

33 Wise leaders will instruct many of the people. But for a while, some of these leaders will either be killed with swords or burned alive, or else robbed of their possessions and thrown into prison. 34 They will receive only a little help in their time of trouble, and many of their followers will be treacherous. 35 Some of those who are wise will suffer, so that God will make them pure and acceptable until the end, which will still come at the time he has decided.

36 This king will do as he pleases. He will proudly claim to be greater than any god and will insult the only true God. Indeed, he will be successful until God is no longer angry with his people. 37 This king will reject the gods his ancestors worshiped and the god preferred by women.[m] In fact, he will put himself above all gods 38 and worship only the so-called god of fortresses, who was unknown to his ancestors. And he will honor it with gold, silver, precious stones, and other costly gifts. 39 With the help of this foreign god, he will capture the strongest fortresses. Everyone who worships this god will be put in a position of power and rewarded with wealth and land.

Part Three: The Time of the End

40 At the time of the end, the king of the south will attack the kingdom of the north. But its king will rush out like a storm with war chariots, cavalry, and many ships. Indeed, his forces will flood one country after another, 41 and when they reach the holy land,[n] tens of thousands will be killed. But the countries of Edom and Moab and the ruler of Ammon[o] will escape.

42 The king of the north will invade many countries, including Egypt, 43 and he will take its rich treasures of gold and silver. He will also conquer Libya and Ethiopia.[p] 44 But he will be alarmed by news from the east and the north, and he will become furious and cause great destruction. 45 After this, he will set up camp between the Mediterranean Sea and Mount Zion. Then he will be destroyed, and no one will be able to save him.

[m] **11.37** *god preferred by women*: Perhaps Tammuz or Adonis, which were popular among the women of that time. [n] **11.41** *the holy land*: See the note at 8.9. [o] **11.41** *the ruler of Ammon*: Or "what is left of Ammon." [p] **11.43** *Ethiopia*: The Hebrew text has "Cush," which was a region south of Egypt that included parts of the present countries of Ethiopia and Sudan.

11.30 2 Macc 5.11. **11.31** Dn 9.27; 12.11; Mt 24.15; Mk 13.14. **11.36** **a** 2 Th 2.3, 4; **b** Rev 13.5, 6.

Part Four: The Dead Will Rise to Life

12 Michael, the chief of the angels, is
the protector of your people, and
he will come at a time of terrible suffering,
the worst in all of history. And your people
who have their names written in *The Book*[q]
will be protected. 2 Many of those who lie
dead in the ground will rise from death.
Some of them will be given eternal life, and
others will receive nothing but eternal
shame and disgrace. 3 Everyone who has
been wise will shine as bright as the sky
above, and everyone who has led others to
please God will shine like the stars.
4 Daniel, I now command you to keep
the message of this book secret until the
end of time, even though many people will
go everywhere, searching for the knowledge
to be found in it.[r]

The End of Time

5 Daniel wrote:
I looked around and saw two other
people—one on this side of the river
and one on the other side. 6 The angel
who had spoken to me was dressed in
linen and was standing upstream from
them.[s] So one of the two beside the
river asked him, "How long before
these amazing things happen?"
7 The angel then raised both hands
toward heaven and said, "In the name
of the God who lives forever, I solemnly promise that it will be a time,
two times, and half a time.[t] Everything
will be over, when the suffering of
God's holy people comes to an end."
8 I heard what the angel said, but I
didn't understand. So I asked, "Sir,
how will it all end?"
The angel in my vision then replied:
9 Daniel, go about your business,
because the meaning of this message
will remain secret until the end of time.
10 Many people will have their hearts
and lives made pure and clean, but
those who are evil will keep on being
evil and never understand. Only the
wise will understand. 11 There will be
one thousand two hundred ninety days
from the time that the daily sacrifices
are stopped, until someone sets up the
"Horrible Thing" that causes destruction. 12 God will bless everyone who
patiently waits until one thousand three
hundred thirty-five days have gone by.
13 So, Daniel, be faithful until the
end! You will rest, and at the end of
time, you will rise from death to
receive your reward.

[q] **12.1** *The Book*: Either the book with the names of God's people in it or the book with the record of the good and evil that people have done. [r] **12.4** *even though . . . in it*: One possible meaning for the difficult Hebrew text. [s] **12.6** *angel . . . upstream from them*: See 10.4-6. [t] **12.7** *a time, two times, and half a time*: Or "a year, two years, and half a year," that is, about 1260 days.

12.1 a Rev 12.7; **b** Mt 24.21; Mk 13.19; Rev 7.14. **12.2** Is 26.19; 2 Macc 7.9-11, 14; Mt 25.46; Jn 5.29. **12.3** 2 Esd 7.97. **12.4** Rev 22.10. **12.7 a** Rev 10.5; **b** Rev 12.14. **12.10** Rev 22.11. **12.11** Dn 9.27; 11.31; Mt 24.15; Mk 13.14.

HOSEA

ABOUT THIS BOOK

Hosea was a prophet in the northern kingdom during its final years as a nation. In the first three chapters of this book, Hosea's family life became a living picture of the message he preached to his country. The Lord told Hosea to marry a prostitute, as a way of showing how unfaithful Israel had been. Then the Lord told Hosea what to name his children, and these names were reminders that Israel was going to be punished. But Hosea was told to love his unfaithful wife, and his love was to be a picture of the Lord's continuing love for unfaithful Israel.

The rest of the book emphasizes the agreement that the Lord had made with Israel. This agreement demanded that Israel and the Lord be loyal and faithful to each other. The Lord had always lived up to the agreement, but the people had broken it time after time. They had trusted their own military strength and the power of foreign countries, rather than depending on the Lord to protect their nation. And the people had worshiped other gods and trusted them to provide good crops and large herds of livestock.

In this book the Lord put Israel and Judah on trial and charged them with breaking their agreement with him. They were guilty and would be punished.

But the Lord still loved his people in spite of everything they had done. And so he promised to forgive them and bless them again after they learned to be faithful to him:

"Israel, you have rejected me,
but my anger is gone;
I will heal you and love you
without limit."
(14.4)

A QUICK LOOK AT THIS BOOK

- Hosea's Family Is a Picture of the Lord's Unfaithful People (1.1—3.5)
- The Lord Accuses Israel, Judah, and Their Leaders (4.1—5.15)
- The People Pretend To Turn to the Lord (6.1—7.10)
- Israel Refused To Trust the Lord (7.11—8.14)
- Israel Will Get the Punishment It Deserves (9.1-16)
- Warnings for Israel (10.1-15)
- God's Love for His People (11.1-11)
- Israel and Judah Are Doomed (11.12—13.16)
- Future Forgiveness and Blessings (14.1-9)

---

1 I am Hosea son of Beeri. When Uzziah, Jotham, Ahaz, and Hezekiah were the kings of Judah, and when Jeroboam son of Jehoash[a] was king of Israel,[b] the LORD spoke this message to me.

[a]**1.1** *Jehoash*: The Hebrew text has "Joash," another spelling of the name. [b]**1.1** *kings of Judah . . . king of Israel*: Uzziah (781-740 B.C.), Jotham (740-736), Ahaz (736-716), Hezekiah (716-687), and Jeroboam II (783-743).

1.1 **a** 2 K 15.1-7; 2 Ch 26.1-23; **b** 2 K 15.32-38; 2 Ch 27.1-8; **c** 2 K 16.1-20; 2 Ch 28.1-27; **d** 2 K 18.1—20.21; 2 Ch 29.1—32.33; **e** 2 K 14.23-29.

Hosea's Family

2 The LORD said, "Hosea, Israel has betrayed me like an unfaithful wife.[c] Marry
such a woman and have children by her."
3 So I married Gomer the daughter of Dib-
laim, and we had a son.
4 Then the LORD said, "Hosea, name
your son Jezreel,[d] because I will soon punish the descendants of King Jehu of Israel
for the murders he committed in Jezreel
Valley.[e] I will destroy his kingdom, 5 and in
Jezreel Valley I will break the power of Israel."
6 Later, Gomer had a daughter, and the
LORD said, "Name her Lo-Ruhamah,[f] because I will no longer have mercy and forgive Israel. 7 But I am the LORD God of Judah, and I will have mercy and save Judah
by my own power—not by wars and arrows
or swords and cavalry."
8 After Gomer had stopped nursing Lo-
Ruhamah, she had another son. 9 Then the
LORD said, "Name him Lo-Ammi,[g] because
these people are not mine, and I am not
their God."

Hope for Israel

10 Someday it will be impossible to
count the people of Israel, because there
will be as many of them as there are grains
of sand along the seashore. They are now
called "Not My People," but in the future
they will be called "Children of the Living
God." 11 Israel and Judah will unite and
choose one leader. Then they will take back
their land, and this will be a great day for
2 Jezreel.[h] 1 So let your brothers be
called "My People" and your sisters be
called "Shown Mercy."[i]

The LORD Promises To Punish Israel

2 Accuse! Accuse your mother!
She is no longer my wife,
and now I, the LORD,
am not her husband.
Beg her to give up prostitution
and stop being unfaithful,[j]
3 or I will strip her naked
like the day she was born.
I will make her barren
like a desert,
and she will die of thirst.
4 You children are the result
of her unfaithfulness,
and I'll show you no pity.
5 Your mother was unfaithful.
She was disgraceful and said,
"I'll run after my lovers.
Everything comes from them—
my food and drink,
my linen and wool,
my olive oil and wine."

6 I, the LORD, will build
a fence of thorns
to block her path.
7 She will run after her lovers,
but not catch them;
she will search,
but not find them.
Then she will say, "I'll return
to my first husband.
Life was better then."
8 She didn't know that her grain,
wine, and olive oil
were gifts from me,
as were the gold and silver
she used in worshiping Baal.[k]

[c]**1.2** *unfaithful wife*: In some Canaanite religions of Old Testament times, young women were expected to have sex with the worshipers of their god before marriage. Such women were called "temple prostitutes." Many of the Israelite women did this same thing, and Hosea is told to marry one of them to show that the nation has turned from the LORD to worship idols. [d]**1.4** *Jezreel*: In Hebrew "Jezreel" means "God scatters (seed)." Here the name is used as a threat (meaning the LORD will punish Israel by scattering its people), while in verse 11 it is used as a promise (meaning the LORD will bless Israel by giving their nation many people, just as a big harvest comes when many seeds are scattered in a field). [e]**1.4** *murders . . . Valley*: Jehu murdered the wife and relatives of King Ahab (see 2 Kings 9.15—10.14). [f]**1.6** *Lo-Ruhamah*: In Hebrew "Lo-Ruhamah" means "No Mercy." [g]**1.9** *Lo-Ammi*: In Hebrew "Lo-Ammi" means "Not My People." [h]**1.11** *Jezreel*: See the note at verse 4. [i]**2.1** *My People . . . Shown Mercy*: In Hebrew "My People" is "Ammi" and "Shown Mercy" is "Ruhamah" (see Lo-Ruhamah in 1.6 and Lo-Ammi in 1.9). [j]**2.2** *prostitution . . . unfaithful*: See the note at 1.2. [k]**2.8** *Baal*: A Canaanite god of fertility.

1.4 2 K 10.11. **1.10** Ro 9.26.

9 So I'll hold back the harvest
of grain and grapes.
I'll take back
my wool and my linen
that cover her body.
10 Then I'll strip her naked
in the sight of her lovers.[l]
No one can rescue her.

11 I'll stop Israel's celebrations—
no more New Moon Festivals,
Sabbaths, or other feasts.
12 She said, "My lovers gave me
vineyards and fig trees
as payment[m] for sex."

Now I, the LORD, will ruin
her vineyards and fig trees;
they will become clumps of weeds
eaten by wild animals.

13 I'll punish her for the days
she worshiped Baal
and burned incense to him.
I'll punish her for the times
she forgot about me
and wore jewelry and rings
to attract her lovers.
I, the LORD, have spoken!

The LORD Will Help Israel

14 Israel, I, the LORD,
will lure you into the desert
and speak gently to you.
15 I will return your vineyards,
and then Trouble Valley[n]
will become Hopeful Valley.
You will say "Yes" to me
as you did in your youth,
when leaving Egypt.

16 I promise that from that day on, you
will call me your husband instead of your
master.[o] 17 I will no longer even let you
mention the names of those pagan gods
that you called "Master." 18 And I will agree
to let you live in peace—you will no longer
be attacked by wild animals and birds or by
weapons of war. 19 I will accept you as my
wife forever, and instead of a bride price[p] I
will give you justice, fairness, love, kindness, 20 and faithfulness. Then you will
truly know who I am.
21 I will command the sky to send rain
on the earth, 22 and it will produce grain,
grapes, and olives in Jezreel Valley. 23 I will
scatter the seeds and show mercy to Lo-
Ruhamah.[q] I will say to Lo-Ammi,[r] "You
are my people," and they will answer, "You
are our God."

God's Love Offers Hope

3 Once again the LORD spoke to me. And
this time he said, "Hosea, fall in love
with an unfaithful woman[s] who has a lover.
Do this to show that I love the people of Israel, even though they worship idols
and enjoy the offering cakes made with
fruit."
2 So I paid fifteen pieces of silver and
about ten bushels of grain for such a
woman. 3 Then I said, "Now you are mine!
You will have to remain faithful to me,
though it will be a long time before we
sleep together."
4 It will also be a long time before Israel
has a king or before sacrifices are offered at
the temple or before there is any way to get
guidance from God. 5 But later, Israel will
turn back to the LORD their God and to
David their king. At that time they will

[l]**2.10** *I'll strip . . . lovers*: Or "I'll show her lovers how disgusting she is." [m]**2.12** *fig trees . . . payment*: Hosea uses an unusual word for "fig tree," which is spelled something like the word for "payment." [n]**2.15** *Trouble Valley*: Or "Achor Valley." The exact location of the valley is unknown, but in Hebrew "Achor" sounds like "Achan," who brought trouble on Israel by disobeying the Lord (see Joshua 7.24-26). [o]**2.16** *husband . . . master*: In Hebrew the word "master" is the same as the name of the god Baal. But the LORD promises that his people will have a deep personal relationship with him (like a devoted wife and husband) rather than merely a legal tie (like a wife and her "master"). [p]**2.19** *bride price*: It was the custom for the husband to pay his wife's parents a bride price. Instead of money, the LORD will give much better benefits to Israel. [q]**2.23** *Lo-Ruhamah*: See the note at 1.6. [r]**2.23** *Lo-Ammi*: See the note at 1.9. [s]**3.1** *unfaithful woman*: This may refer to Gomer, the woman Hosea married (see 1.3), or it may refer to another woman.

2.15 Js 7.24-26. **2.23** Ro 9.25; 1 P 2.10.

come to the LORD with fear and trembling,
and he will be good to them.

Israel Is Unfaithful

4 Israel, listen
as the LORD accuses
everyone in the land!
No one is faithful or loyal
or truly cares about God.
2 Cursing, dishonesty, murder,
robbery, unfaithfulness—
these happen all the time.
Violence is everywhere.
3 And so your land is a desert.
Every living creature is dying—
people and wild animals,
birds and fish.

The LORD Warns the Priests

4 Don't accuse just anyone!
Not everyone is at fault.
My case is against you,
the priests.[t]
5 You and the prophets
will stumble day and night;
I'll silence your mothers.
6 You priests have rejected me,
and my people are destroyed
by refusing to obey.
Now I'll reject you and forget
your children, because you
have forgotten my Law.

7 By adding more of you priests,
you multiply the number
of people who sin.
Now I'll change your pride
into shame.
8 You encourage others to sin,
so you can stuff yourselves
on their sin offerings.

9 That's why I will punish
the people for their deeds,
just as I will punish
you priests.
10 Their food won't satisfy,
and having sex at pagan shrines
won't produce children.
My people have rebelled
11 and have been unfaithful
to me, their LORD.

God Condemns Israel's Idolatry

My people, you are foolish
because of too much pleasure
and too much wine.
12 You expect wooden idols
and other objects of wood
to give you advice.
Lusting for sex at pagan shrines
has made you unfaithful
to me, your God.
13 You offer sacrifices
on mountaintops and hills,
under oak trees, and wherever
good shade is found.

Your own daughters
and daughters-in-law
sell themselves for sex.
14 But I won't punish them.
You men are to blame,
because you go to prostitutes
and offer sacrifices with them
at pagan shrines.
Your own foolishness
will lead to your ruin.
15 Israel, you are unfaithful,
but don't lead Judah to sin.
Stop worshiping at Gilgal
or at sinful Bethel.[u]
And quit making promises
in my name— the name
of the living LORD.
16 You are nothing more
than a stubborn cow—
so stubborn that I, the LORD,
cannot feed you like lambs
in an open pasture.

17 You people of Israel[v]
are charmed by[w] idols.
Leave them alone!

[t] **4.4** *priests*: One possible meaning for the difficult Hebrew text of verse 4. Hosea may have had in mind only one priest, possibly the chief priest. [u] **4.15** *sinful Bethel*: The Hebrew text has "Beth-Aven," which means "house of sin" or "house of nothing," referring to "Bethel," which means "house of God." [v] **4.17** *Israel*: The Hebrew text has "Ephraim," the leading tribe of the northern kingdom of Israel, which sometimes stands for the whole kingdom. [w] **4.17** *charmed by*: Or "joined to."

18 You get drunk, then sleep
with prostitutes;
you would rather be vulgar
than lead a decent life.[x]
19 And so you will be swept away
in a whirlwind
for sacrificing to idols.

Israel and Judah Will Be Judged

The LORD *said:*

5 Listen, you priests!
Pay attention, Israel![y]
Listen, you members
of the royal family.
Justice was your duty.
But[z] at Mizpah and Mount Tabor
you trapped the people.
2 At the place of worship
you were a treacherous pit,[a]
and I will punish you.

3 Israel, I know all about you,
and because of your unfaithfulness,
I find you unacceptable.
4 Your evil deeds are the reason
you won't return to me,
your LORD God.
And your constant craving for sex
keeps you from knowing me.

5 Israel, your pride
testifies to your guilt;
it makes you stumble,
and Judah stumbles too.
6 You offer sheep and cattle
as sacrifices to me,
but I have turned away
and refuse to be found.
7 You have been unfaithful
to me, your LORD;
you have had children
by prostitutes.[b]
So at the New Moon Festival,
you and your crops
will be destroyed.[c]

The LORD Warns Israel and Judah

8 Give a warning on the trumpet!
Let it be heard in Gibeah,
Ramah, and sinful Bethel.[d]
Benjamin, watch out![e]
9 I, the LORD, will punish
and wipe out Israel.
This is my solemn promise
to every tribe of Israel.
10 Judah's leaders are like crooks
who move boundary markers;
that's why I will flood them
with my anger.

11 Israel was brutally crushed.
They got what they deserved
for worshiping useless idols.[f]
12 Now I, the LORD,
will fill Israel with maggots
and make Judah rot.
13 When Israel and Judah saw
their sickness and wounds,
Israel asked help from Assyria
and its mighty king.[g]

But the king cannot cure them
or heal their wounds.
14 So I'll become a fierce lion
attacking Israel and Judah.
I'll snatch and carry off
what I want,
and no one can stop me.
15 Then I'll return to my temple
until they confess their guilt
and worship me,
until they are desperate
and beg for my help.

[x]**4.18** *life*: One possible meaning for the difficult Hebrew text of verse 18. [y]**5.1** *Israel*: Probably meaning the tribal leaders of Israel. [z]**5.1** *Justice . . . duty. But*: Or "You are doomed, because." [a]**5.2** *At . . . pit*: One possible meaning for the difficult Hebrew text.
[b]**5.7** *prostitutes*: See 4.14, and the note at 1.2. [c]**5.7** *So . . . destroyed*: One possible meaning for the difficult Hebrew text. [d]**5.8** *sinful Bethel*: See the note at 4.15. Gibeah is three miles north of Jerusalem, Ramah is five miles north, and Bethel is eleven miles north. The attack comes from the south, and all the land of Benjamin (belonging to Israel) is in danger. [e]**5.8** *watch out*: Or "lead the way." [f]**5.11** *for . . . idols*: One possible meaning for the difficult Hebrew text.
[g]**5.13** *and . . . king*: One possible meaning for the difficult Hebrew text.

The LORD's People Speak

6 Let's return to the LORD.
He has torn us to shreds,
but he will bandage our wounds
and make us well.
2 In two or three days
he will heal us
and restore our strength
that we may live with him.
3 Let's do our best
to know the LORD.
His coming is as certain
as the morning sun;
he will refresh us like rain
renewing the earth
in the springtime.

The LORD Speaks to Israel and Judah

4 People of Israel and Judah,
what can I do with you?
Your love for me disappears
more quickly than mist
or dew at sunrise.
5 That's why I slaughtered you
with the words
of my prophets.
That's why my judgments blazed
like the dawning sun.[h]
6 I'd rather for you to be faithful
and to know me
than to offer sacrifices.

7 At a place named Adam,
you[i] betrayed me
by breaking our agreement.
8 Everyone in Gilead is evil;
your hands are stained
with the blood of victims.[j]
9 You priests are like a gang
of robbers in ambush.[k]
On the road to Shechem[l]
you murder and commit
other horrible crimes.
10 I have seen a terrible thing
in Israel—
you are unfaithful
and unfit to worship me.
11 People of Judah,
your time is coming too.

The LORD Wants To Help Israel

I, the LORD, would like to make
my nation prosper again
7 1 and to heal its wounds.
But then I see the crimes
in Israel[m] and Samaria.
Everyone is deceitful;
robbers roam the streets.
2 No one realizes
that I have seen their sins
surround them like a flood.

3 The king and his officials
take great pleasure
in their sin and deceit.
4 Everyone burns with desire—
they are like coals in an oven,
ready to burst into flames.
5 On the day their king
was crowned,
his officials got him drunk,
and he joined
in their foolishness.[n]

6 Their anger is a fire
that smolders all night,
then flares up at dawn.
7 They are flames
destroying their leaders.
And their kings are powerless;
none of them trust me.

8 The people of Israel[o]
have mixed with foreigners;
they are a thin piece of bread
scorched on one side.

[h] **6.5** *That's why my . . . sun*: One possible meaning for the difficult Hebrew text. [i] **6.7** *At . . . you*: Or "Like Adam, you" or "Each one of you." [j] **6.8** *your hands . . . victims*: This may refer to child sacrifice. [k] **6.9** *You . . . ambush*: One possible meaning for the difficult Hebrew text. [l] **6.9** *Shechem*: This was one of the towns where people could run for safety, if they had accidentally killed someone (see Joshua 20.1-9). [m] **7.1** *Israel*: See the note at 4.17. Samaria was the capital city of Israel. [n] **7.5** *foolishness*: One possible meaning for the difficult Hebrew text of verse 5. [o] **7.8,11** *Israel*: Hebrew "Ephraim" (see the note at 4.17).
6.6 Mt 9.13; 12.7.

9 They don't seem to realize
how weak and feeble they are;
their hair has turned gray,
while foreigners rule.
10 I am the LORD, their God,
but in all of their troubles
their pride keeps them
from returning to me.

No Help from Foreign Nations

The LORD said:

11 Israel[o] is a senseless bird,
fluttering back and forth
between Egypt and Assyria.
12 But I will catch them in a net
as hunters trap birds;
I threatened to punish them,
and indeed I will.[p]
13 Trouble and destruction
will be their reward
for rejecting me.
I would have rescued them,
but they told me lies.

14 They don't really pray to me;
they just howl in their beds.
They have rejected me for Baal
and slashed themselves,[q]
in the hope that Baal
will bless their crops.
15 I taught them what they know,
and I made them strong.
Now they plot against me
16 and refuse to obey.[r]
They are more useless
than a crooked arrow.
Their leaders will die in war
for saying foolish things.
Egyptians will laugh at them.

Israel Rejects the LORD

The LORD said:

8 Sound a warning!
Israel, you broke our agreement
and ignored my teaching.
Now an eagle is swooping down
to attack my land.
2 Israel, you say, "We claim you,
the LORD, as our God."
3 But your enemies
will chase you for rejecting
our good agreement.[s]

4 You chose kings and leaders
without consulting me;
you made silver and gold idols
that led to your downfall.
5 City of Samaria, I'm angry
because of your idol
in the shape of a calf.
When will you ever
be innocent again?
6 Someone from Israel built
that idol for you,
but only I am God.
And so it will be smashed
to pieces.[t]

7 If you scatter wind
instead of wheat,
you will harvest a whirlwind
and have no wheat.
Even if you harvest grain,
enemies will steal it all.

8 Israel, you are ruined,
and now the nations
consider you worthless.
9 You are like a wild donkey
that goes its own way.
You've run off to Assyria
and hired them as allies.
10 You can bargain with nations,
but I'll catch you anyway.
Soon you will suffer abuse
by kings and rulers.

11 Israel, you have built
many altars where you offer
sacrifices for sin.

[o]**7.8,11** *Israel*: Hebrew "Ephraim" (see the note at 4.17). [p]**7.12** *I threatened . . . will*: One possible meaning for the difficult Hebrew text. [q]**7.14** *slashed themselves*: One ancient translation and some Hebrew manuscripts; other Hebrew manuscripts "gather together." Slashing themselves was one way of worshiping Baal (see 1 Kings 18.28). [r]**7.16** *and . . . obey*: One possible meaning for the difficult Hebrew text. [s]**8.3** *our good agreement*: Or "me, the Good One" (referring to God). [t]**8.6** *smashed to pieces*: Or "destroyed by fire."

But these altars have become
places for sin.
12 My instructions for sacrifices
were written in detail,
but you ignored them.
13 You sacrifice your best animals
and eat the sacrificial meals,[u]
but I, the LORD,
refuse your offerings.
I will remember your sins
and punish you.
Then you will return to Egypt.[v]

14 Israel, I created you,
but you forgot me.
You and Judah built palaces
and many strong cities.[w]
Now I will send fire to destroy
your towns and fortresses.

Israel Will Be Punished

9 Israel, don't celebrate
or make noisy shouts[x]
like other nations.
You have been unfaithful
to your God.
Wherever grain is threshed,
you behave like prostitutes
because you enjoy
the money you receive.[y]
2 But you will run short
of grain and wine,
3 and you will have to leave
the land of the LORD.
Some of you will go to Egypt;
others will go to Assyria
and eat unclean food.
4 You won't be able to offer
sacrifices of wine
to the LORD.
None of your sacrifices
will please him—
they will be unclean
like food offered to the dead.
Your food will only be used
to satisfy your hunger;
none of it will be brought
to the LORD's temple.
5 You will no longer be able
to celebrate the festival
of the LORD.[z]
6 Even if you escape alive,
you will end up in Egypt
and be buried in Memphis.[a]
Your silver treasures
will be lost among weeds;[b]
thorns will sprout in your tents.

7 Israel, the time has come.
You will get what you deserve,
and you will know it.
"Prophets are fools," you say.
"And God's messengers
are crazy."
Your terrible guilt
has filled you with hatred.

8 Israel, the LORD sent me
to look after you.[c]
But you trap his prophets
and flood his temple
with your hatred.
9 You are brutal and corrupt,
as were the men of Gibeah.[d]
But God remembers your sin,
and you will be punished.

[u] **8.13** *sacrifice . . . sacrificial meals*: One possible meaning for the difficult Hebrew text. Two kinds of sacrifices are referred to: Those in which the whole animal is burned on the altar ("whole burnt offerings" in traditional translations) and those in which part is eaten by the worshipers ("fellowship offerings" in traditional translations). [v] **8.13** *return to Egypt*: Either as slaves or to find help against Assyria. [w] **8.14** *built palaces . . . cities*: They did this because they no longer trusted the LORD to protect them. "Palaces" may also mean "temples." [x] **9.1** *or . . . shouts*: One possible meaning for the difficult Hebrew text. [y] **9.1** *Wherever . . . receive*: Grain was threshed on hills or other places where the wind could blow away the husks. People also met at these places to worship Baal, the god they thought had given them the grain harvest. [z] **9.5** *festival of the LORD*: Probably the Festival of Shelters. [a] **9.6** *Memphis*: An Egyptian city with a famous cemetery. [b] **9.6** *Your silver . . . weeds*: One possible meaning for the difficult Hebrew text. [c] **9.8** *Israel . . . you*: One possible meaning for the difficult Hebrew text. [d] **9.9** *the men of Gibeah*: They raped and murdered a woman (see Judges 19).

9.7 Lk 21.22. **9.9** Jg 19.1-30.

Sin's Terrible Results

10 Israel, when I, the LORD,
found you long ago
it was like finding
grapes in a barren desert
or tender young figs.
Then you worshiped Baal Peor,
that disgusting idol,
and you became as disgusting
as the idol you loved.

11 And so, Israel, your glory
will fly away like birds—
your women will no longer
be able to give birth.
12 Even if you do have children,
I will take them all
and leave you to mourn.
I will turn away,
and you will sink down
in deep trouble.
13 Israel, when I first met you,
I thought of you as palm trees
growing in fertile ground.[e]
Now you lead your people out,
only to be slaughtered.

Hosea's Advice

14 Our LORD, do just one thing
for your people—
make their women unable
to have children
or to nurse their babies.

The LORD's Judgment on Israel

15 Israel, I first began
to hate you because
you did evil at Gilgal.[f]
Now I will chase you
out of my house.
No longer will I love you;
your leaders betrayed me.
16 Israel, you are a vine
with dried-up roots
and fruitless branches.
Even if you had more children
and loved them dearly,
I would slaughter them all.

Hosea Warns Israel

17 Israel, you disobeyed my God.
Now he will force you to roam
from nation to nation.

10 You were a healthy vine
covered with grapes.
But the more grapes you grew,
the more altars you built;
the better off you became,
the better shrines you set up
for pagan gods.
2 You are deceitful and disloyal.
So you will pay
for your sins,
because the LORD will destroy
your altars and images.

3 "We don't have a king,"
you will say.
"We don't fear the LORD.
And what good are kings?"
4 Israel, you break treaties
and don't keep promises;
you turn justice
into poisonous weeds
where healthy plants should grow.[g]

5 All who live in Samaria tremble
with concern for the idols[h]
at sinful Bethel.[i]
The idol there was the pride
of the priests,
but it has been put to shame;
now everyone will cry.
6 It will be taken to Assyria
and given to the great king.
Then Israel will be disgraced
for worshiping that idol.

7 Like a twig in a stream,
the king of Samaria
will be swept away.
8 The altars at sinful Bethel
will be destroyed
for causing Israel to sin;
they will be grown over
with thorns and thistles.

[e]**9.13** *Israel, when . . . ground*: One possible meaning for the difficult Hebrew text.
[f]**9.15** *Gilgal*: See 4.15. [g]**10.4** *you turn . . . grow*: One possible meaning for the difficult Hebrew text. [h]**10.5** *idols*: The Hebrew text has "calves," referring to the idols made in the shape of calves. [i]**10.5** *sinful Bethel*: See the note at 4.15.
9.10 Nu 25.1-5. **10.8** Lk 23.30; Rev 6.16.

Then everyone will beg
the mountains and hills
to cover and protect them.

The LORD Promises To Punish Israel

9 Israel, you have never
stopped sinning[j]
since that time at Gibeah.[k]
That's why you
will be attacked at Gibeah.[l]
10 Your sins have doubled,
and you are rebellious.
Now I have decided
to send nations to attack
and put you in chains.

11 Once you were obedient
like a calf
that loved to thresh grain.
But I will put a harness
on your powerful neck;
you and Judah must plow
and cultivate the ground.
12 Plow your fields,
scatter seeds of justice,
and harvest faithfulness.
Worship me, the LORD,
and I will send my saving power
down like rain.
13 You have planted evil,
harvested injustice, and eaten
the fruit of your lies.
You trusted your own strength
and your powerful forces.
14 So war will break out,
and your fortresses
will be destroyed.
Your enemies will do to you
what Shalman[m] did to the people
of Beth-Arbel—
mothers and their children
will be beaten to death
against rocks.
15 Bethel, this will be your fate
because of your evil.
Israel, at dawn your king
will be killed.

God's Love for His People

11 When Israel was a child,
I loved him, and I called
my son out of Egypt.
2 But as the saying goes,
"The more they were called,
the more they rebelled."[n]
They never stopped offering
incense and sacrifices
to the idols of Baal.

3 I took Israel by the arm
and taught them to walk.
But they would not admit
that I was the one
who had healed them.
4 I led them with kindness
and with love,
not with ropes.
I held them close to me;[o]
I bent down to feed them.

5 But they trusted Egypt
instead of returning to me;
now Assyria will rule them.
6 War will visit their cities,
and their plans will fail.[p]
7 My people are determined
to reject me for a god
they think is stronger,
but he can't help.[q]

8 Israel, I can't let you go.
I can't give you up.
How could I possibly destroy you
as I did the towns of Admah
and Zeboiim?[r]
I just can't do it.

[j] **10.9** *never stopped sinning*: One possible meaning for the difficult Hebrew text. [k] **10.9** *Gibeah*: See the note at 9.9. [l] **10.9** *That's why . . . Gibeah*: One possible meaning for the difficult Hebrew text. [m] **10.14** *Shalman*: Perhaps a Moabite king, also known as Salamanu.
[n] **11.2** *But . . . rebelled*: One possible meaning for the difficult Hebrew text. [o] **11.4** *I held . . . to me*: One possible meaning for the difficult Hebrew text. [p] **11.6** *fail*: One possible meaning for the difficult Hebrew text of verse 6. [q] **11.7** *help*: One possible meaning for the difficult Hebrew text of verse 7. [r] **11.8** *Admah and Zeboiim*: When the LORD destroyed Sodom and Gomorrah, he also destroyed these two towns (see Deuteronomy 29.23).
10.9 Jg 19.1-30. **10.12** Jr 4.3. **11.1** Ex 4.22; Mt 2.15. **11.8** Dt 29.23.

My feelings for you
are much too strong.
9 Israel, I won't lose my temper
and destroy you again.
I am the Holy God—
not merely some human,
and I won't stay angry.

10 I, the LORD, will roar like a lion,
and my children will return,
trembling from the west.
11 They will come back,
fluttering like birds from Egypt
or like doves from Assyria.
Then I will bring them
back to their homes.
I, the LORD, have spoken!

Israel and Judah Compared

12 Israel is deceitful to me,
their loyal and holy God;
they surround me with lies,
and Judah worships
other gods.[s]

12 All day long Israel chases
wind from the desert;
deceit and violence
are found everywhere.
Treaties are made with Assyria;
olive oil is taken to Egypt.

Israel and Judah Condemned

2 The LORD also brings charges
against the people of Judah,
the descendants of Jacob.
He will punish them
for what they have done.
3 Even before Jacob was born,
he cheated his brother,[t]
and when he grew up,
he fought against God.[u]
4 At Bethel, Jacob wrestled
with an angel and won;
then with tears in his eyes,
he asked for a blessing,
and God spoke to us[v] there.
5 God's name is the LORD,
the LORD God All-Powerful.
6 So return to your God.
Patiently trust him,
and show love and justice.

7 Israel, you enjoy cheating
and taking advantage
of others.
8 You say to yourself, "I'm rich!
I earned it all on my own,
without committing a sin."[w]

The LORD Is Still the God of Israel

9 Israel, I, the LORD,
am still your God,
just as I have been
since the time
you were in Egypt.
Now I will force you
to live in tents once again,
as you did in the desert.[x]
10 I spoke to the prophets—
often I spoke in visions.
And so, I will send my prophets
with messages of doom.
11 Gilead is terribly sinful
and will end up ruined.
Bulls are sacrificed in Gilgal
on altars made of stones,
but those stones will be scattered
in every field.
12 Jacob[y] escaped to Syria[z]

[s] **11.12** *and Judah worships other gods*: Or "but Judah remains faithful." [t] **12.3** *Jacob . . . cheated . . . brother*: In Hebrew "Jacob" sounds like "cheat" and also like "heel." Jacob grabbed his twin brother Esau by the heel at the time of their birth (see Genesis 25.26). Later he cheated him out of his rights and blessings as the first-born son (see Genesis 25.29-34; 27.1-40).
[u] **12.3** *fought against God*: See Genesis 32.22-32. [v] **12.4** *us*: Hebrew; two ancient translations "him." [w] **12.8** *without . . . sin*: One possible meaning for the difficult Hebrew text.
[x] **12.9** *as . . . desert*: One possible meaning for the difficult Hebrew text. This probably refers to the forty years of wandering through the desert after leaving Egypt, though it could refer to the "tents" (or "shelters") in which the Israelites lived during the Festival of Shelters (see 9.5, 6).
[y] **12.12** *Jacob*: His name was later changed to Israel (see Genesis 32.28), and he became the ancestor of the nation by that name. [z] **12.12** *Syria*: The Hebrew text has "Aram," probably referring to northern Syria in the region of Haran.

12.3 Gn 25.26. **12.3,4** Gn 32.24-26. **12.4** Gn 28.10-22. **12.9** Lv 23.42, 43. **12.12** Gn 29.1-20.

where he tended sheep
to earn himself a wife.
13 I sent the prophet Moses
to lead Israel from Egypt
and to keep them safe.
14 Israel, I will make you pay
for your terrible sins
and for insulting me.

Israel Is Doomed

The LORD said:
13 When your leaders[a] spoke,
everyone in Israel trembled
and showed great respect.
But you sinned by worshiping Baal,
and you were destroyed.
2 Now you continue to sin
by designing and making
idols of silver
in the shape of calves.
You are told to sacrifice
to these idols[b]—
yes, even to kiss them.
3 And so, all of you will vanish
like the mist or the dew
of early morning,
or husks of grain in the wind
or smoke from a chimney.

4 I, the LORD, have been your God
since the time
you were in Egypt.
I am the only God you know,
the only one who can save.
5 I took care of you
in a thirsty desert.[c]
6 I fed you till you were satisfied,
then you became proud
and forgot about me.
7 Now I will attack like a lion,
ambush you like a leopard,
8 and rip you apart like a bear
robbed of her cubs.
I will gnaw on your bones,
as though I were a lion
or some other wild animal.
9 Israel, you are done for.
Don't expect help from me.[d]
10 You wanted a king and rulers.
Where is your king now?
What cities have rulers?
11 In my anger, I gave you a king;
in my fury, I took him away.

Israel's Terrible Fate

The LORD said:
12 Israel, your terrible sins
are written down
and stored away.
13 You are like a senseless child
who refuses to be born
at the proper time.
14 Should I, the LORD, rescue you
from death and the grave?
No! I call death and the grave
to strike you like a plague.
I refuse to show mercy.

15 No matter how much you prosper
more than the other tribes,[e]
I, the LORD, will wipe you out,
just as a scorching desert wind
dries up streams of water.
I will take away
your precious treasures.
16 Samaria[f] will be punished
for turning against me.
It will be destroyed in war—
children will be beaten
against rocks,
and pregnant women
will be ripped open.

Turn Back to the LORD

14 Israel, return! Come back
to the LORD, your God.
Sin has made you fall.
2 Return to the LORD and say,
"Please forgive our sins.

[a] **13.1** *your leaders*: The Hebrew text has "Ephraim," here meaning Mount Ephraim, where the royal palace of Samaria (capital of the northern kingdom of Israel) was located. [b] **13.2** *You are told . . . idols*: One possible meaning for the difficult Hebrew text. [c] **13.5** *thirsty desert*: The forty years that Israel wandered through the desert, after leaving Egypt. [d] **13.9** *Don't . . . me*: Or "You are against me, the one who helps you." [e] **13.15** *more . . . tribes*: One possible meaning for the difficult Hebrew text. [f] **13.16** *Samaria*: The capital of the northern kingdom of Israel.

12.13 Ex 12.50, 51. **13.5,6** Dt 8.11-17. **13.10** 1 S 8.5, 6. **13.11 a** 1 S 10.17-24; **b** 1 S 15.26. **13.14** 1 Co 15.55.

Accept our good sacrifices
of praise instead of bulls.[g]
3 Assyria can't save us,
and chariots can't help.
So we will no longer worship
the idols we have made.
Our LORD, you show mercy
to orphans."

The LORD Promises To Forgive

4 Israel, you have rejected me,
but my anger is gone;
I will heal you and love you
without limit.
5 I will be like the dew—
then you will blossom like lilies
and have roots like a tree.[h]
6 Your branches will spread
with the beauty
of an olive tree
and with the aroma
of Lebanon Forest.
7 You will rest in my shade,
and your grain will grow.
You will blossom
like a vineyard
and be famous as the wine
from Lebanon.

8 Israel, give up your idols!
I will answer your prayers
and take care of you.[i]
I am that glorious tree,
the source of your fruit.[j]

9 If you are wise, you will know
and understand what I mean.
I am the LORD, and I lead you
along the right path.
If you obey me,
we will walk together,
but if you are wicked,
you will stumble.

[g] **14.2** *Accept . . . bulls*: One possible meaning for the difficult Hebrew text.
[h] **14.5** *like a tree*: The Hebrew text has "like Lebanon," probably referring to the famous cedar trees on Mount Lebanon. [i] **14.8** *Israel . . . you*: One possible meaning for the difficult Hebrew text. [j] **14.8** *I am . . . fruit*: This is the only place in the Old Testament where the LORD is compared to a tree. Hosea reminds the people that it is the LORD who is the source of life, rather than the Canaanite gods and goddesses that are worshiped under trees at the local shrines.

JOEL

ABOUT THIS BOOK

Joel was a prophet who had watched swarm after swarm of locusts cover the land of Israel and wipe out the crops. He described these locusts as though they were an enemy army destroying everything in sight, and he said that the Lord had sent the locusts as punishment for the sins of Israel. Joel also used the locusts as a way of talking about a real army that was going to attack Israel. But the Lord promised that if the people would turn back to him, he would forgive them and bless them once again.

The locusts caused horrible destruction, but it was only a small taste of what will happen on the judgment day of the Lord. At that time the Lord will put all nations on trial for what they have done to his people, and those who are guilty will be punished.

Crowds fill Decision Valley.
The judgment day of the LORD
will soon be here—
no light from the sun or moon,
and stars no longer shine.
From the heart of Jerusalem
the LORD roars like a lion,
shaking the earth and sky.
But the LORD is a fortress,
a place of safety
for his people Israel.
(3.14-16)

A QUICK LOOK AT THIS BOOK

- Locusts and an Enemy Army (1.1—2.17)
- The Lord Will Bless His People (2.18-32)
- The Lord Will Punish the Nations (3.1-21)

---

1 I am Joel the son of Pethuel.
And this is the message
the LORD gave to me.

Locusts Cover the Land

2 Listen, you leaders
and everyone else
in the land.
Has anything like this
ever happened before?
3 Tell our children!
Let it be told
to our grandchildren
and their children too.

4 Swarm after swarm of locusts[a]
has attacked our crops,
eating everything in sight.
5 Sober up, you drunkards!

[a]**1.4** *Swarm . . . locusts*: The Hebrew text lists either four kinds of locusts or locusts in four stages of their development. Locusts are a type of grasshopper that comes in swarms and causes great damage to plant life.

Cry long and loud;
your wine supply is gone.
6 A powerful nation[b]
with countless troops
has invaded our land.
They have the teeth and jaws
of powerful lions.
7 Our grapevines and fig trees
are stripped bare;
only naked branches remain.

8 Grieve like a young woman
mourning for the man
she was to marry.
9 Offerings of grain and wine
are no longer brought
to the LORD's temple.
His servants, the priests,
are deep in sorrow.
10 Barren fields mourn;
grain, grapes, and olives
are scorched and shriveled.

11 Mourn for our farms
and our vineyards!
There's no wheat or barley
growing in our fields.
12 Grapevines have dried up
and so has every tree—
figs and pomegranates,[c]
date palms and apples.
All happiness has faded away.

Return to God

13 Mourn, you priests who serve
at the altar of my God.
Spend your days and nights
wearing sackcloth.[d]
Offerings of grain and wine
are no longer brought
to the LORD's temple.

14 Tell the leaders and people
to come together
at the temple.
Order them to go without eating[e]
and to pray sincerely.

15 We are in for trouble!
Soon the LORD All-Powerful
will bring disaster.
16 Our food is already gone;
there's no more celebrating
at the temple of our God.

17 Seeds dry up in the ground;[f]
no harvest is possible.
Our barns are in bad shape,
with no grain
to store in them.
18 Our cattle wander aimlessly,
moaning for lack of pasture,
and sheep are suffering.[g]
19 I cry out to you, LORD.
Grasslands and forests are eaten
by the scorching heat.
20 Wild animals have no water
because of you;
rivers and streams are dry,
and pastures are parched.

Locusts and an Enemy Army

2 Sound the trumpet on Zion,
the LORD's sacred hill.
Warn everyone to tremble!
The judgment day of the LORD
is coming soon.
2 It will be dark and gloomy
with storm clouds overhead.
Troops will cover the mountains
like thunderclouds.
No army this powerful
has ever been gathered before
or will ever be again.
3 Fiery flames surround them;
no one escapes.
Before they invaded,
the land was like Eden;
now only a desert remains.

4 They look like horses
and charge like cavalry.
5 They roar over mountains
like noisy chariots,

[b]**1.6** *A powerful nation*: The swarms of locusts. [c]**1.12** *pomegranates*: A bright red fruit that looks like an apple. [d]**1.13** *sackcloth*: A rough, dark-colored cloth made from goat or camel hair and used to make grain sacks. It was worn in times of trouble or sorrow. [e]**1.14** *go without eating*: As a way of showing sorrow for their sins. [f]**1.17** *Seeds . . . ground*: One possible meaning for the difficult Hebrew text. [g]**1.18** *sheep are suffering*: One possible meaning for the difficult Hebrew text.

1.6 Rev 9.8. **1.15** Is 13.6. **2.4,5** Rev 9.7-9.

or a mighty army
ready for battle.
They are a forest fire
that feasts on straw.
6 The very sight of them
is frightening.[h]
7 They climb over walls
like warriors;
they march in columns
and never turn aside.
8 They charge straight ahead,
without pushing each other;
even arrows and spears
cannot make them retreat.
9 They swarm over city walls
and enter our homes;
they crawl in through windows,
just like thieves.

10 They make the earth tremble
and the heavens shake;
the sun and moon turn dark,
and stars stop shining.
11 The LORD God leads this army
of countless troops,
and they obey his commands.
The day of his judgment
is so terrible
that no one can stand it.

The LORD's Invitation

12 The LORD said:

It isn't too late.
You can still return to me
with all your heart.
Start crying and mourning!
Go without eating.
13 Don't rip your clothes
to show your sorrow.
Instead, turn back to me
with broken hearts.
I am merciful, kind, and caring.
I don't easily lose my temper,
and I don't like to punish.

14 I am the LORD your God.
Perhaps I will change my mind
and treat you with mercy.
Then you will be blessed
with enough grain and wine
for offering sacrifices to me.

15 Sound the trumpet on Zion!
Call the people together.
Show your sorrow
by going without food.
16 Make sure that everyone
is fit to worship me.[i]
Bring adults, children, babies,
and even bring newlyweds
from their festivities.

17 Tell my servants, the priests,
to cry inside the temple
and to offer this prayer
near the altar:[j]
"Save your people, LORD God!
Don't let foreign nations
make jokes about us.
Don't let them laugh and ask,
'Where is your God?' "

The LORD Will Bless the Land

18 The LORD was deeply concerned
about his land
and had pity on his people.
19 In answer to their prayers
he said,
"I will give you enough grain,
wine, and olive oil
to satisfy your needs.
No longer will I let you
be insulted by the nations.
20 An army attacked from the north,
but I will chase it
into a scorching desert.
There it will rot and stink
from the Dead Sea
to the Mediterranean."

The LORD works wonders
21 and does great things.
So tell the soil to celebrate
22 and wild animals
to stop being afraid.
Grasslands are green again;

[h]**2.6** *The very . . . frightening*: One possible meaning for the difficult Hebrew text. [i]**2.16** *fit to worship me*: This required going through certain kinds of ceremonies. [j]**2.17** *inside . . . altar*: The Hebrew text has "between the porch and the altar," which is the place where the priests usually prayed for the people.

2.10 Rev 8.12. **2.11** Rev 6.17. **2.16** 3 Macc 1.19. **2.17** 1 Macc 7.36-38.

fruit trees and fig trees
are loaded with fruit.
Grapevines are covered
with grapes.

23 People of Zion,[k]
celebrate in honor
of the LORD your God!
He is generous and has sent
the autumn and spring rains
in the proper seasons.[l]
24 Grain will cover
your threshing places;
jars will overflow
with wine and olive oil.

The LORD Will Rescue His People

25 I, the LORD your God,
will make up for the losses
caused by those swarms
and swarms of locusts[m]
I sent to attack you.
26 My people, you will eat
until you are satisfied.
Then you will praise me
for the wonderful things
I have done.
Never again will you
be put to shame.

27 Israel, you will know
that I stand at your side.
I am the LORD your God—
there are no other gods.
Never again will you
be put to shame.

The LORD Will Work Wonders

The LORD said:
28 Later, I will give my Spirit
to everyone.
Your sons and daughters
will prophesy.
Your old men
will have dreams,
and your young men
will see visions.
29 In those days I will even give
my Spirit to my servants,
both men and women.

30 I will work wonders
in the sky above
and on the earth below.
There will be blood and fire
and clouds of smoke.
31 The sun will turn dark,
and the moon
will be as red as blood
before that great
and terrible day
when I appear.

32 Then the LORD will save everyone
who faithfully worships him. He has
promised there will be survivors on Mount
Zion and in Jerusalem, and among them
will be his chosen ones.

The LORD Will Judge the Nations

3 At that time I, the LORD, will make Judah and Jerusalem prosperous again.
2 Then in Judgment Valley[n] I will bring
together the nations that scattered my people Israel everywhere in the world, and I
will bring charges against those nations.
They divided up my land 3 and gambled to
see who would get my people; they sold
boys and girls to pay for prostitutes and
wine.
4 You people of Tyre and Sidon[o] and you
Philistines, why are you doing this? Are you
trying to get even with me? I'll strike back
before you know what's happened. 5 You've
taken my prized possessions, including my
silver and gold, and carried them off to
your temples.[p] 6 You have dragged the people of Judah and Jerusalem from their land
and sold them to the Greeks.
7 But I'll make the people of Judah

[k]**2.23** *Zion*: Jerusalem. [l]**2.23** *in . . . seasons*: Or "as he used to do." [m]**2.25** *swarms . . . locusts*: See the note at 1.4. [n]**3.2** *Judgment Valley*: The Hebrew text has "Jehoshaphat Valley," which means "Valley of the LORD's Judgment." This valley is mentioned here and in verse 12, but nowhere else in the Bible. [o]**3.4** *Tyre and Sidon*: Two Phoenician coastal cities.
[p]**3.5** *temples*: Or "palaces."
2.31 Mt 24.29; Mk 13.24, 25; Lk 21.25; Rev 6.12, 13. **2.28-32** Ac 2.17-21.
2.32 Ro 10.13. **3.4-8** **a** Is 23.1-18; Ez 26.1—28.26; Am 1.9, 10; Zec 9.1-4; Mt 11.21, 22; Lk 10.13, 14; **b** Is 14.29-31; Jr 47.1-7; Ez 25.15-17; Am 1.6-8; Zep 2.4-7; Zec 9.5-7.

determined to come home, and what happened to them will happen to you. 8 I'll
hand over your sons and daughters to the
people of Judah, and they will sell them to
the Sabeans,[q] who live far away. I, the
LORD, have spoken!

Judgment in Judgment Valley

9 Say to the nations:

"Get ready for war!
Be eager to fight.
Line up for battle
and prepare to attack.
10 Make swords out of plows
and spears out of garden tools.
Strengthen every weakling."

11 Hurry, all you nations!
Come quickly.
Ask the LORD to bring
his warriors along.[r]
12 You must come now
to Judgment Valley,[s]
where the LORD will judge
the surrounding nations.

13 They are a field of ripe crops.
Bring in the harvest!
They are grapes piled high.
Start trampling them now![t]
If our enemy's sins were wine,
every jar would overflow.
14 Crowds fill Decision Valley.
The judgment day of the LORD
will soon be here—
15 no light from the sun or moon,
and stars no longer shine.
16 From the heart of Jerusalem
the LORD roars like a lion,
shaking the earth and sky.
But the LORD is a fortress,
a place of safety
for his people Israel.

God Will Bless His People

17 I am the LORD your God.
And you will know I live on Zion,
my sacred hill,
because Jerusalem will be sacred,
untouched by foreign troops.
18 On that day, fruitful vineyards
will cover the mountains.
And your cattle and goats
that graze on the hills
will produce a lot of milk.
Streams in Judah
will never run dry;
a stream from my house
will flow in Acacia Valley.[u]

19 Egypt and Edom were cruel
and brutal to Judah,
without a reason.
Now their countries will become
a barren desert,
20 but Judah and Jerusalem
will always have people.
21 I, the LORD, live on Mount Zion.
I will punish the guilty
and defend the innocent.[v]

[q]**3.8** *Sabeans*: The people of Seba, a region in southwest Arabia. [r]**3.11** *Ask . . . along*: One possible meaning for the difficult Hebrew text. [s]**3.12** *Judgment Valley*: See the note at 3.2. [t]**3.13** *grapes . . . now*: People trampled grapes with their bare feet to squeeze out the juice. [u]**3.18** *Acacia Valley*: In the plains of Moab, northeast of the Dead Sea. [v]**3.21** *I will . . . innocent*: One possible meaning for the difficult Hebrew text.

3.10 Is 2.4; Mic 4.3. **3.13 a** Rev 14.14-16; **b** Rev 14.19, 20; 19.15. **3.16** Am 1.2.

AMOS

ABOUT THIS BOOK

Amos wasn't a professional prophet and had never been trained to be a prophet (7.14). But when the Lord gave him messages for the people in the northern kingdom, Amos left his hometown of Tekoa in Judah and went to preach in the town of Bethel in Israel, probably at the famous place of worship.

In this book, Amos first condemns many of the nearby nations, and then he condemns the people of Israel, especially the rich who lived in luxury. They had great power and used it to rob the poor and to make slaves of them. And even though most of the people were worshiping other gods besides the Lord, they still expected the Lord to protect them. But Amos warned the people that they would be punished, and he said:

"Choose good instead of evil!
See that justice is done.
Maybe I, the LORD God All-Powerful,
will be kind to what's left
of your people."

(5.15)

A QUICK LOOK AT THIS BOOK

- Crimes of the Nations Will Be Punished (1.1—3.2)
- Israel and Samaria Will Be Destroyed (3.3—6.14)
- Five Visions of Israel's Punishment (7.1—9.10)
- Israel's Bright Future (9.11-15)

---

1 I am Amos. And I raised sheep near
the town of Tekoa[a] when Uzziah was
king of Judah and Jeroboam[b] son of Jehoash[c] was king of Israel.
Two years before the earthquake,[d] the
LORD gave me several messages[e] about Israel, 2 and I said:

When the LORD roars
from Jerusalem,
pasturelands and Mount Carmel
dry up and turn brown.

Judgment on Syria

3 The LORD said:

I will punish Syria[f]
for countless crimes,
and I won't change my mind.
They dragged logs with spikes[g]
over the people of Gilead.
4 Now I will burn down the palaces
and fortresses of King Hazael
and of King Benhadad.[h]

[a] **1.1** *Tekoa*: In the hill country of Judah about five miles south of Bethlehem. [b] **1.1** *Uzziah . . . Jeroboam*: Uzziah was king of Judah 781-740 B.C., and Jeroboam II was king of Israel 783-743 B.C. [c] **1.1** *Jehoash*: The Hebrew text has "Joash," another spelling of the name. [d] **1.1** *Two years . . . earthquake*: Possibly the earthquake of 760 B.C., which seems to have been especially violent. [e] **1.1** *messages*: Or "visions." [f] **1.3** *Syria*: The Hebrew text has "Damascus," the leading city of Syria. [g] **1.3** *logs with spikes*: These were dragged over grain to thresh it. [h] **1.4** *Hazael . . . Benhadad*: Two Syrian kings.

1.1 **a** 2 K 15.1-7; 2 Ch 26.1-23; **b** 2 K 14.23-29. **1.2** Jl 3.16. **1.3-5** Is 17.1-3; Jr 49.23-27; Zec 9.1.

5 I will break through
the gates of Damascus.
I will destroy the people[i]
of Wicked Valley[j]
and the ruler of Beth-Eden.[k]
Then the Syrians will be dragged
as prisoners to Kir.[l]
I, the LORD, have spoken!

Judgment on Philistia

6 The LORD said:

I will punish Philistia[m]
for countless crimes,
and I won't change my mind.
They dragged off my people[n]
from town after town
to sell them as slaves
to the Edomites.

7 That's why I will burn down
the walls and fortresses
of the city of Gaza.
8 I will destroy the king[o] of Ashdod
and the ruler of Ashkelon.
I will strike down Ekron,[p]
and that will be the end
of the Philistines.
I, the LORD, have spoken!

Judgment on Phoenicia

9 The LORD said:

I will punish Phoenicia[q]
for countless crimes,
and I won't change my mind.
They broke their treaty
and dragged off my people[r]
from town after town
to sell them as slaves
to the Edomites.
10 That's why I will send flames
to burn down the city of Tyre
along with its fortresses.

Judgment on Edom

11 The LORD said:

I will punish Edom
for countless crimes,
and I won't change my mind.
They killed their own relatives[s]
and were so terribly furious
that they showed no mercy.
12 Now I will send fire to wipe out
the fortresses of Teman
and Bozrah.[t]

Judgment on Ammon

13 The LORD said:

I will punish Ammon
for countless crimes,
and I won't change my mind.
In Gilead they ripped open
pregnant women,
just to take the land.

14 Now I will send fire to destroy
the walls and fortresses
of Rabbah.[u]
Enemies will shout and attack
like a whirlwind.

[i] **1.5** *people*: Or "king." [j] **1.5** *Wicked Valley*: The Hebrew text has "Aven Valley," probably the fertile valley between the Lebanon and the anti-Lebanon mountains. [k] **1.5** *I will . . . Beth-Eden*: Or "I will destroy the people of Wicked Valley and the king who rules from Beth-Eden." Beth-Eden was a city-state on the banks of the Euphrates River. [l] **1.5** *Kir*: The exact location of this country is not known; in 9.7 Amos refers to Kir as the original home of the Syrians, and so the verse probably means that the Syrians will lose everything they have gained as a people. [m] **1.6** *Philistia*: The Hebrew text has "Gaza," one of the main Philistine cities. [n] **1.6** *my people*: The people of Israel. [o] **1.8** *king*: Or "people." [p] **1.8** *Ashdod . . . Ashkelon . . . Ekron*: Philistine cities. [q] **1.9** *Phoenicia*: The Hebrew text has "Tyre," which was one of the two Phoenician cities; the other was Sidon, which is not mentioned by Amos. [r] **1.9** *my people*: See the note at 1.6. [s] **1.11** *their own relatives*: The Edomites were descendants of Esau, the brother of Jacob, the ancestor of the Israelites. [t] **1.12** *Teman and Bozrah*: These stand for all of Edom; Teman may have been a city or a district. Bozrah, the chief city of northern Edom, was thirty miles southeast of the Dead Sea. [u] **1.14** *Rabbah*: The capital city of Ammon.

1.6-8 Is 14.29-31; Jr 47.1-7; Ez 25.15-17; Jl 3.4-8; Zep 2.4-7; Zec 9.5-7. **1.9,10** Is 23.1-18; Ez 26.1—28.19; Jl 3.4-8; Zec 9.1-4; Mt 11.21, 22; Lk 10.13, 14. **1.11,12** Is 34.5-17; 63.1-6; Jr 49.7-22; Ez 25.12-14; 35.1-15; Ob 1-14; Ml 1.2-5. **1.13-15** Jr 49.1-6; Ez 21.28-32; 25.1-7; Zep 2.8-11.

15 Ammon's king and leaders
will be dragged away.
I, the LORD, have spoken!

Judgment on Moab

2 The LORD said:

I will punish Moab
for countless crimes,
and I won't change my mind.
They made lime from the bones[v]
of the king of Edom.
2 Now I will send fire to destroy
the fortresses of Kerioth.[w]
Battle shouts and trumpet blasts
will be heard as I destroy Moab
3 with its king and leaders.
I, the LORD, have spoken!

Judgment on Judah

4 The LORD said:

I will punish Judah
for countless crimes,
and I won't change my mind.
They have rejected my teachings
and refused to obey me.
They were led astray
by the same false gods
their ancestors worshiped.
5 Now I will send fire on Judah
and destroy the fortresses
of Jerusalem.

Judgment on Israel

6 The LORD said:

I will punish Israel
for countless crimes,
and I won't change my mind.
They sell honest people for money,
and the needy are sold
for the price of sandals.
7 They smear the poor in the dirt
and push aside
those who are helpless.
My holy name is dishonored,
because fathers and sons sleep
with the same young women.
8 They lie down beside altars
on clothes taken
as security for loans.
And they drink wine in my temple,
wine bought with the money
they received from fines.

9 Israel, the Amorites[x] were there
when you entered Canaan.
They were tall as cedars
and strong as oaks.
But I wiped them out—
I destroyed their branches
and their roots.
10 I had rescued you from Egypt,
and for forty years I had led you
through the desert.
Then I gave you the land
of the Amorites.

11 I chose some of you
to be prophets
and others to be Nazirites.[y]
People of Israel,
you know this is true.
I, the LORD, have spoken!
12 But you commanded the prophets
not to speak their message,
and you pressured the Nazirites
into drinking wine.

13 And so I will crush you,
just as a wagon full of grain
crushes the ground.[z]
14 No matter how fast you run,
you won't escape.
No matter how strong you are,
you will lose your strength
and your life.
15 Even if you are an expert
with a bow and arrow,
you will retreat.

[v]**2.1** *They . . . bones*: They dug up the bodies of kings and made lime out of them to use as whitewash on their houses and walls. [w]**2.2** *Kerioth*: A leading city of Moab and a center for the worship of Chemosh, the chief god of Moab. [x]**2.9** *Amorites*: This word is used for all the people who lived in Canaan at the time Israel took over the land. [y]**2.11** *Nazirites*: People who promised the LORD that they would never drink wine or cut their hair or come in contact with a dead body. [z]**2.13** *ground*: One possible meaning for the difficult Hebrew text of verse 13.
2.1-3 Is 15.1—16.14; 25.10-12; Jr 48.1-47; Ez 25.8-11; Zep 2.8-11. **2.9** Dt 3.8-11.
2.11 Nu 6.1-8.

And you won't get away alive,
not even if you run fast
or ride a horse.
16 You may be brave and strong,
but you will run away,
stripped naked.
I, the LORD, have spoken!

3 People of Israel,
I rescued you from Egypt.
Now listen to my judgment
against you.
2 Of all nations on earth,
you are the only one
I have chosen.
That's why I will punish you
because of your sins.

The Work of a Prophet

3 Can two people walk together
without agreeing to meet?
4 Does a lion roar in the forest
unless it has caught
a victim?
Does it growl in its den
unless it is eating?
5 How can anyone catch a bird
without using a net?
Does a trap spring shut
unless something is caught?

6 Isn't the whole city frightened
when the trumpet
signals an attack?
Isn't it the LORD who brings
disaster on a city?
7 Whatever the LORD God
plans to do,
he tells his servants,
the prophets.
8 Everyone is terrified
when a lion roars—
and ordinary people
become prophets
when the LORD God speaks.

Samaria Is Doomed

9 Here is a message
for the leaders
of Philistia[a] and Egypt—
tell everyone to come together
on the hills of Samaria.
Let them see the injustice
and the lawlessness
in that city.
10 The LORD has said
that they don't even know how
to do right.
They have become rich
from violence and robbery.
11 And so the LORD God has sworn
that they will be surrounded.
Enemies will break through
their defenses
and steal their treasures.

12 The LORD has promised
that only a few from Samaria
will escape with their lives
and with some broken pieces
of their beds and couches.[b]
It will be like when a shepherd
rescues two leg bones
and part of a sheep's ear
from the jaws of a lion.[c]

The Altars at Bethel

13 The LORD God All-Powerful
told me to speak this message
against Jacob's descendants:
14 When I, the LORD, punish Israel
for their sins,
I will destroy the altars
at Bethel.
Even the corners of the altar[d]
will be left in the dirt.
15 I will tear down winter homes
and summer homes.
Houses decorated with ivory

[a]**3.9** *Philistia*: The Hebrew text has "Ashdod," one of the leading cities of Philistia. [b]**3.12** *some . . . couches*: One possible meaning for the difficult Hebrew text. [c]**3.12** *lion*: When a wild animal attacked and killed a sheep, the shepherd had to rescue part of the sheep and take it to the owner as proof that it had been killed by an animal. Otherwise, the shepherd had to pay the owner the cost of the sheep. [d]**3.14** *altar*: Altars were places of worship but also places of protection. People whose lives were in danger could grab hold of the corners of an altar, and no one was allowed to kill them.

3.14 2 K 23.15.

and all other mansions
will be gone forever.
I, the LORD, have spoken!

The Women of Samaria

The LORD said:

4 You women of Samaria
are fat cows![e]
You mistreat and abuse
the poor and needy,
then you say to your husbands,
"Bring us more drinks!"
2 I, the LORD God, have sworn
by my own name
that your time is coming.
Not one of you will be left—
you will be taken away
by sharp hooks.[f]
3 You will be dragged through holes
in your city walls,
and you will be thrown
toward Harmon.[g]
I, the LORD, have spoken!

Israel Refuses To Obey

The LORD said:

4 Come to Bethel and Gilgal.[h]
Sin all you want!
Offer sacrifices the next morning
and bring a tenth of your crops
on the third day.[i]
5 Bring offerings to show me
how thankful you are.
Gladly bring more offerings
than I have demanded.
You really love to do this.
I, the LORD God, have spoken!

How the LORD Warned Israel

6 I, the LORD, took away the food
from every town and village,
but still you rejected me.
7 Three months before harvest,
I kept back the rain.
Sometimes I would let it fall
on one town or field
but not on another,
and pastures dried up.
8 People from two or three towns
would go to a town
that still had water,
but it wasn't enough.
Even then you rejected me.
I, the LORD, have spoken!

9 I dried up your grain fields;
your gardens and vineyards
turned brown.
Locusts[j] ate your fig trees
and olive orchards,
but even then you rejected me.
I, the LORD, have spoken!

10 I did terrible things to you,
just as I did to Egypt—
I killed your young men in war;
I let your horses be stolen,
and I made your camp stink
with dead bodies.
Even then you rejected me.
I, the LORD, have spoken!

11 I destroyed many of you,
just as I did the cities
of Sodom and Gomorrah.
You were a burning stick
I rescued from the fire.
Even then you rejected me.
I, the LORD, have spoken!

12 Now, Israel, I myself
will deal with you.
Get ready to face your God!

13 I created the mountains
and the wind.

[e]**4.1** *fat cows*: The Hebrew text has "cows of Bashan," a fertile plain famous for its rich pastures and well-fed cattle. [f]**4.2** *taken . . . hooks*: One possible meaning for the difficult Hebrew text.
[g]**4.3** *Harmon*: Hebrew; some manuscripts of one ancient translation "Mount Hermon," a mountain in the north of Palestine, on the way to Assyria. [h]**4.4** *Bethel and Gilgal*: These were two of the most important centers of worship in northern Israel. Amos mentions these together again in 5.5. [i]**4.4** *Offer . . . day*: Or "Offer sacrifices each morning and bring a tenth of your crops every three days." In verses 4, 5 God is condemning the people for meaningless acts of worship.
[j]**4.9** *Locusts*: A type of grasshopper that comes in swarms and causes great damage to plant life.
4.6 Ws 12.2, 10. **4.11** Gn 19.24.

I let humans know
what I am thinking.[k]
I bring darkness at dawn
and step over hills.
I am the LORD God All-Powerful!

Turn Back to the LORD

5 Listen, nation of Israel,
to my mournful message:
2 You, dearest Israel, have fallen,
never to rise again—
you lie deserted in your own land,
with no one to help you up.

3 The LORD God has warned,
"From every ten soldiers
only one will be left;
from a thousand troops,
only a hundred will survive."

4 The LORD keeps saying,
"Israel, turn back to me
and you will live!
5 Don't go to Gilgal or Bethel
or even to Beersheba.[l]
Gilgal will be dragged away,
and Bethel will end up
as nothing."[m]

6 Turn back to the LORD,
you descendants of Joseph,[n]
and you will live.
If you don't, the LORD
will attack like fire.
Bethel will burn to the ground,
and no one can save it.
7 You people are doomed!
You twist the truth
and stomp on justice.

8 But the LORD created the stars
and put them in place.[o]
He turns darkness to dawn
and daylight to darkness;
he scoops up the ocean
and empties it on the earth.
9 God destroys mighty soldiers
and strong fortresses.

Choose Good Instead of Evil!

The LORD said:
10 You people hate judges
and honest witnesses;
11 you abuse the poor and demand
heavy taxes from them.
You have built expensive homes,
but you won't enjoy them;
you have planted vineyards,
but you will get no wine.
12 I am the LORD, and I know
your terrible sins.
You cheat honest people
and take bribes;
you rob the poor of justice.
13 Times are so evil
that anyone with good sense
will keep quiet.

14 If you really want to live,
you must stop doing wrong
and start doing right.
I, the LORD God All-Powerful,
will then be on your side,
just as you claim I am.
15 Choose good instead of evil!
See that justice is done.
Maybe I, the LORD All-Powerful,
will be kind to what's left
of your people.[p]

[k]**4.13** *I let . . . thinking*: Or "No one's secret thoughts are hidden from me." [l]**5.5** *Gilgal . . . Bethel . . . Beersheba*: These were ancient places of worship, but the LORD had warned his people to stay away from them. [m]**5.5** *Gilgal . . . nothing*: In Hebrew "Gilgal" and "dragged away" sound something alike. Bethel (meaning "house of God") is sometimes called "house of nothing" or "house of sin" by the prophets (see Hosea 4.15; 5.8; 10.5-8). [n]**5.6** *descendants of Joseph*: Another name for the people of the northern kingdom of Israel. [o]**5.8** *the stars . . . place*: The Hebrew text mentions two groups of stars, Pleiades and Orion. Since the LORD is the Creator of the stars, he controls the seasons that are signaled by the different positions of the stars. Moreover, the stars are created objects and should not be worshiped. [p]**5.15** *your people*: Hebrew "Joseph's descendants" (see the note at verse 6).
5.8 Job 9.9; 38.31.

Judgment Is Coming

16 This is what the LORD has sworn:

Noisy crying will be heard
in every town and street.
Even farmers will be told
to mourn for the dead,
together with those
who are paid to mourn.[q]
17 Your vineyards will be filled
with crying and weeping,[r]
because I will punish you.
I, the LORD, have spoken!

When the LORD Judges

18 You look forward to the day
when the LORD comes to judge.
But you are in for trouble!
It won't be a time of sunshine;
all will be darkness.
19 You will run from a lion,
only to meet a bear.
You will escape to your house,
rest your hand on the wall,
and be bitten by a snake.
20 The day when the LORD judges
will be dark, very dark,
without a ray of light.

What the LORD Demands

21 I, the LORD, hate and despise
your religious celebrations
and your times of worship.
22 I won't accept your offerings
or animal sacrifices—
not even your very best.
23 No more of your noisy songs!
I won't listen
when you play your harps.
24 But let justice and fairness
flow like a river
that never runs dry.
25 Israel, for forty years
you wandered in the desert,
without bringing offerings
or sacrifices to me.
26 Now you will have to carry
the two idols you made—
Sakkuth, the one you call king,
and Kaiwan, the one you built
in the shape of a star.[s]
27 I will force you to march
as captives beyond Damascus.
I, the LORD God All-Powerful,
have spoken![t]

Israel Will Be Punished

6 Do you rulers in Jerusalem
and in the city of Samaria
feel safe and at ease?
Everyone bows down to you,
and you think you are better
than any other nation.
But you are in for trouble!
2 Look what happened
to the cities of Calneh,
powerful Hamath,
and Gath[u] in Philistia.
Are you greater than any
of those kingdoms?
3 You are cruel, and you forget
the coming day of judgment.

4 You rich people lounge around
on beds with ivory posts,
while dining on the meat
of your lambs and calves.
5 You sing foolish songs
to the music of harps,
and you make up new tunes,
just as David used to do.
6 You drink all the wine you want
and wear expensive perfume,
but you don't care about
the ruin of your nation.[v]

[q] **5.16** *paid to mourn*: In ancient times some people were paid to mourn and make loud cries at funerals. [r] **5.17** *Your vineyards . . . weeping*: Instead of happy celebrations that were often held in vineyards after the harvest. [s] **5.26** *star*: One possible meaning for the difficult Hebrew text of verse 26. [t] **5.27** *I, the LORD . . . spoken*: Israel did not offer sacrifices and gifts to the LORD during the time they wandered through the desert. But now they have made idols to carry during their ceremonies. So the LORD warns that he will make them "march" away as captives beyond Damascus, where Israel had extended its borders by victories in war (see 2 Kings 14.28). [u] **6.2** *Calneh . . . Hamath . . . Gath*: City-states captured by the Assyrians: Calneh in 738 B.C., Hamath in 720, and Gath in 711. [v] **6.6** *your nation*: Hebrew "Joseph's descendants" (see the note at 5.6).

5.21,22 Is 1.11-14. **5.25-27** Ac 7.42, 43.

7 So you will be the first
to be dragged off as captives;
your good times will end.

8 The LORD God All-Powerful
has sworn by his own name:
"You descendants of Jacob
make me angry by your pride,
and I hate your fortresses.
And so I will surrender your city
and possessions
to your enemies."

9 If only ten of you survive
by hiding in a house
you will still die.
10 As you carry out a corpse
to prepare it for burial,[w]
your relative in the house
will ask, "Are there others?"
You will answer, "No!"
Then your relative will reply,
"Be quiet! Don't dare mention
the name of the LORD."[x]
11 At the LORD's command,
houses great and small
will be smashed to pieces.

12 Horses can't gallop on rocks;
oceans[y] can't be plowed.
But you have turned justice
and fairness
into bitter poison.
13 You celebrate the defeat
of Lo-Debar and Karnaim,[z]
and you boast by saying,
"We did it on our own."

14 But the LORD God All-Powerful
will send a nation to attack
you people of Israel.
They will capture Lebo-Hamath
in the north,
Arabah Creek[a] in the south,
and everything in between.

A Vision of Locusts

7 The LORD God showed me that he is
going to send locusts[b] to attack your
crops. It will happen after the king has already been given his share of the grain and
before the rest of the grain has been harvested.[c] 2 In my vision the locusts ate every
crop in the land, and I said to the LORD,
"Forgive me for asking, but how can the nation survive? It's so weak."
3 Then the LORD felt sorry and answered, "I won't let it be destroyed."

A Vision of Fire

4 The LORD showed me that he is going
to send a ball of fire to burn up everything
on earth, including the ocean. 5 Then I
said, "Won't you please stop? How can our
weak nation survive?"
6 Again the LORD felt sorry and answered, "I won't let it be destroyed."

A Vision of a Measuring Line

7 The LORD showed me a vision of himself standing beside a wall and holding a
string with a weight tied to the end of it.
The string and weight had been used to
measure the straightness of the wall.
8 Then he asked, "Amos, what do you see?"
"A measuring line," I answered.
The LORD said, "I'm using this measuring line to show that my people Israel don't
measure up, and I won't forgive them any
more. 9 Their sacred places will be destroyed, and I will send war against the nation of King Jeroboam."[d]

[w]**6.10** *prepare . . . burial*: Or "burn it" or "burn incense for it." [x]**6.10** *the name of the LORD*: Two relatives seem to be carrying out corpses for burial. One of them warns the other to be careful not even to say "Thank the LORD!" for fear that the mention of his name may cause something worse to happen. [y]**6.12** *oceans*: Or "rocks." [z]**6.13** *Lo-Debar and Karnaim*: Two cities east of the Jordan River that were captured by Jeroboam II (see 2 Kings 14.25). In Hebrew "Lo-Debar" can mean "nothing," and "Karnaim" means "two horns (of a bull)." Horns were symbols of strength, and so the people are bragging about their military power (defeat of "two horns"), which Amos says is "nothing" (Lo-Debar). [a]**6.14** *Lebo-Hamath . . . Arabah Creek*: The northern and southern boundaries of the northern kingdom. [b]**7.1** *locusts*: See the note at 4.9. [c]**7.1** *harvested*: This would have been an especially bad time for a locust attack. The non-grain crops such as vegetables and onions were just beginning to sprout, and the grain crops were almost ready to be harvested. [d]**7.9** *Jeroboam*: Jeroboam II, who ruled Israel 783-743 B.C.

Amos and Amaziah

10 Amaziah the priest at Bethel sent this
message to King Jeroboam of Israel, "Amos is
plotting against you in the very heart of Israel.
Our nation cannot put up with his message
for very long. 11 Here is what he is saying:

'Jeroboam will be put to death,
and the people will be taken
to a foreign country.' "

12 Then Amaziah told me, "Amos, take
your visions and get out! Go back to Judah
and earn your living there as a prophet.
13 Don't do any more preaching at Bethel.
The king worships here at our national
temple."

14 I answered:

I'm not a prophet! And I wasn't
trained to be a prophet. I am a shepherd, and I take care of fig trees. 15 But
the LORD told me to leave my herds
and preach to the people of Israel.
16 And here you are, telling me not to
preach! 17 Now, listen to what the
LORD says about you:

Your wife will become
a prostitute in the city,
your sons and daughters
will be killed in war,
and your land will be divided
among others.
You will die in a country
of foreigners,
and the people of Israel
will be dragged
from their homeland.

A Basket of Fruit

8 The LORD God showed me a basket of
ripe fruit 2 and asked, "Amos, what do
you see?"

"A basket of ripe fruit," I replied.

Then he said,

"This is the end[e]
for my people Israel.
I won't forgive them again.
3 Instead of singing
in the temple,
they will cry and weep.
Dead bodies will be everywhere.
So keep silent!
I, the LORD, have spoken!"

Israel Is Doomed

The LORD said:

4 You people crush those in need
and wipe out the poor.
5 You say to yourselves,
"How much longer before the end
of the New Moon Festival?
When will the Sabbath[f] be over?
Our wheat is ready,
and we want to sell it now.
We can't wait to cheat
and charge high prices
for the grain we sell.
We will use dishonest scales
6 and mix dust in the grain.
Those who are needy and poor
don't have any money.
We will make them our slaves
for the price
of a pair of sandals."

7 I, the LORD, won't forget
any of this,
though you take great pride
in your ancestor Jacob.[g]
8 Your country will tremble,
and you will mourn.
It will be like the Nile River
that rises and overflows,
then sinks back down.

9 On that day, I, the LORD God,
will make the sun
go down at noon,
and I will turn daylight
into darkness.
10 Your festivals and joyful singing
will turn into sorrow.
You will wear sackcloth[h]
and shave your heads,

[e]**8.2** *end*: In Hebrew "ripe fruit" and "end" sound alike. [f]**8.5** *New Moon Festival . . . Sabbath*: Selling grain at these times was forbidden by the Law of Moses. [g]**8.7** *though . . . Jacob*: Or "though I am the God that Jacob proudly worshiped." [h]**8.10** *sackcloth*: A rough, dark-colored cloth made from goat or camel hair and used to make grain sacks. It was worn in times of trouble or sorrow.

as you would at the death
of your only son.
It will be a horrible day.

11 I, the LORD, also promise you
a terrible shortage,
but not of food and water.
You will hunger and thirst
to hear my message.
12 You will search everywhere—
from north to south,
from east to west.
You will go all over the earth,
seeking a message
from me, the LORD.
But you won't find one.

13 Your beautiful young women
and your young men
will faint from thirst.
14 You made promises
in the name of Ashimah,
the goddess of Samaria.
And you made vows in my name
at the shrines
of Dan and Beersheba.[i]
But you will fall
and never get up.

Judgment on Israel

9 I saw a vision of the LORD
standing by the temple altar,[j]
and he said,
"Shake the columns
until the tops fall loose,
and the doorposts crumble.
Then make the pieces fall
on the people below.
I will take a sword and kill
anyone who escapes.

2 "If they dig deep into the earth
or climb to the sky,
I'll reach out and get them.
3 If they escape to the peaks
of Mount Carmel,
I'll search and find them.
And if they hide from me
at the bottom of the ocean,
I'll command a sea monster
to bite them.
4 I'll send a sword to kill them,
wherever their enemies
drag them off as captives.
I'm determined to hurt them,
not to help them."

His Name Is the LORD

5 When the LORD God All-Powerful
touches the earth, it melts,
and its people mourn.
God makes the earth rise
and then fall,
just like the Nile River.
6 He built his palace in the heavens
and let its foundations
rest on the earth.[k]
He scoops up the ocean
and empties it on the earth.
His name is the LORD.

The LORD Is God

7 Israel, I am the LORD God,
and the Ethiopians[l]
are no less important to me
than you are.
I brought you out of Egypt,
but I also brought
the Philistines from Crete[m]
and the Arameans from Kir.[n]
8 My eyes have seen
what a sinful nation you are,
and I'll wipe you out.
But I will leave a few
of Jacob's descendants.
I, the LORD, have spoken!

9 At my command, all of you
will be sifted like grain.
Israelites who remain faithful

[i]**8.14** *You made . . . Beersheba*: Or "You made promises to the goddess Ashimah at Samaria, and you made vows in the names of other gods at the shrines of Dan and Beersheba." [j]**9.1** *the temple altar*: The one at Bethel. [k]**9.6** *He built . . . earth*: One possible meaning for the difficult Hebrew text. [l]**9.7** *Ethiopians*: The Hebrew text has "people of Cush," which was a region south of Egypt that included parts of the present countries of Ethiopia and Sudan. [m]**9.7** *Crete*: Hebrew "Caphtor." [n]**9.7** *Philistines . . . Arameans from Kir*: The Philistines were Israel's enemies to the west, and the Arameans were enemies to the northeast. For Kir, see the note at 1.5.

will be scattered
among the nations.
And the others will be trapped
like trash in a sifter.
10 Some of you are evil,
and you deny
that you will ever get caught.
But you will be killed.

The LORD's Promise to Israel

11 In the future, I will rebuild
David's fallen kingdom.
I will build it from its ruins
and set it up again,
just as it used to be.
12 Then you will capture Edom
and the other nations
that are mine.
I, the LORD, have spoken,
and my words will come true.

13 You will have such a harvest
that you won't be able
to bring in all of your wheat
before plowing time.
You will have grapes left over
from season to season;
your fruitful vineyards
will cover the mountains.

14 I'll make Israel prosper again.
You will rebuild your towns
and live in them.
You will drink wine
from your own vineyards
and eat the fruit you grow.
15 I'll plant your roots deep
in the land I have given you,
and you won't ever
be uprooted again.
I, the LORD God, have spoken!

9.11,12 Ac 15.16-18.

OBADIAH

ABOUT THIS BOOK

Obadiah was a prophet, but nothing else is known about him. His name, meaning "worshiper of the Lord," was fairly common in ancient Israel.

Obadiah wrote about the nation of Edom, which was south of the Dead Sea. The Edomites had been cruel to the Lord's people Israel, and so the Lord was going to punish them and give their land to Israel.

The book of Obadiah is so short that it wasn't divided into chapters.

A QUICK LOOK AT THIS BOOK

- Edom's Pride and Punishment (1-9)
- Edom's Cruelty (10-14)
- Victory for Israel (15-21)

Edom's Pride and Punishment

The LORD God gave Obadiah
a message[a] about Edom,
and this is what we heard:
"I, the LORD, have sent
a messenger
with orders for the nations
to attack Edom."

2 The LORD said to Edom:
I will make you the weakest
and most despised nation.
3 You live in a mountain fortress,[b]
because your pride
makes you feel safe from attack,
but you are mistaken.
4 I will still bring you down,
even if you fly higher
than an eagle
or nest among the stars.
I, the LORD, have spoken!

5 If thieves break in at night,
they steal
only what they want.
And people who harvest grapes
always leave some unpicked.
But, Edom, you are doomed!
6 Everything you treasure most
will be taken from you.
7 Your allies can't be trusted.
They will force you out
of your own country.
Your best friends
will trick and trap you,
even before you know it.

8 Edom, when this happens,
I, the LORD, will destroy
all your marvelous wisdom.
9 Warriors from the city of Teman[c]
will be terrified,
and you descendants of Esau[d]
will be wiped out.

---

[a] **1** *message*: Or "vision." [b] **3** *mountain fortress*: The Hebrew text has "rocky cliff," which sounds like "Sela," the capital of Edom, a fortress city built on a mountain. [c] **9** *Teman*: A famous city in Edom. [d] **9** *descendants of Esau*: The people of Edom were descendants of Esau, the brother of Jacob (Israel).

1-14 Is 34.5-17; 63.1-6; Jr 49.7-22; Ez 25.12-14; 35.1-15; Am 1.11, 12; Ml 1.2-5.

The LORD Condemns Edom's Cruelty

10 You were cruel to your relatives,
the descendants of Jacob.[e]
Now you will be destroyed,
disgraced forever.
11 You stood there and watched
as foreigners entered Jerusalem
and took what they wanted.
In fact, you were no better
than those foreigners.
12 Why did you celebrate
when such a dreadful disaster
struck your relatives?
Why were you so pleased
when everyone in Judah
was suffering?
13 They are my people,
and you were cruel to them.
You went through their towns,
sneering and stealing
whatever was left.
14 In their time of torment,
you ambushed refugees
and handed them over
to their attackers.

The LORD Will Judge the Nations

15 The day is coming
when I, the LORD,
will judge the nations.
And, Edom, you will pay in full
for what you have done.

16 I forced the people of Judah[f]
to drink the wine of my anger
on my sacred mountain.
Soon the neighboring nations
must drink their fill—
then vanish without a trace.

Victory for Israel

17 The LORD's people who escape
will go to Mount Zion,
and it will be holy.
Then Jacob's descendants
will capture the land of those
who took their land.
18 Israel[g] will be a fire,
and Edom will be straw
going up in flames.
The LORD has spoken!

19 The people of Israel
who live in the Southern Desert
will take the land of Edom.
Those who live in the hills
will capture Philistia,
Ephraim, and Samaria.
And the tribe of Benjamin
will conquer Gilead.

20 Those who return from captivity
will control Phoenicia
as far as Zarephath.[h]
Captives from Jerusalem
who were taken to Sepharad[i]
will capture the towns
of the Southern Desert.
21 Those the LORD has saved
will live on Mount Zion
and rule over Edom.[j]
Then the kingdom will belong
to the LORD.

[e] **10** *descendants of Jacob*: Jacob and Esau were brothers (see the note on Esau at verse 9). [f] **16** *I forced . . . Judah*: Or "I will force the people of Edom." [g] **18** *Israel*: Hebrew "The descendants of Jacob and of Joseph." [h] **20** *Those who return . . . Zarephath*: One possible meaning for the difficult Hebrew text. [i] **20** *Sepharad*: Possibly the city of Sardis, the capital of Lydia, a country north and west of Media. This would refer to those captives from Judah who had been taken beyond the kingdom of Babylonia. [j] **21** *Those the LORD . . . Edom*: Or "Leaders on (from) Mount Zion will save the people and rule over Edom."

JONAH

ABOUT THIS BOOK

The book of Jonah is different from the other prophetic books, because it gives only one sentence of what the prophet Jonah preached. Instead, this book tells how Jonah disobeyed the Lord and refused to warn Nineveh that it was going to be destroyed. Jonah even wanted the city to be destroyed, because it was the capital city of Assyria, a hated enemy of Israel. But the Lord corrected Jonah; then Jonah went to Nineveh and preached the Lord's message.

When many people think about the book of Jonah, they think only of Jonah being swallowed by a huge fish. However, the message of this book is that the Lord wants to have mercy on everyone; as Jonah says to him:

> *"You are a kind and merciful God, and you are very patient. You always show love, and you don't like to punish anyone, not even foreigners."*
>
> *(4.2b)*

A QUICK LOOK AT THIS BOOK

- Jonah Runs from the Lord (1)
- Jonah Prays to the Lord (2)
- Jonah Goes to Nineveh, and Its People Believe God's Message (3)
- Jonah Is Angry Because the Lord Showed Mercy (4)

Jonah Runs from the Lord

1 One day the Lord told Jonah, the son
of Amittai, 2 to go to the great city of
Nineveh[a] and say to the people, "The Lord
has seen your terrible sins. You are
doomed!"
3 Instead, Jonah ran from the Lord. He
went to the seaport of Joppa and bought a
ticket on a ship that was going to Spain.
Then he got on the ship and sailed away to
escape.
4 But the Lord made a strong wind
blow, and such a bad storm came up that
the ship was about to be broken to pieces.
5 The sailors were frightened, and they all
started praying to their gods. They even
threw the ship's cargo overboard to make
the ship lighter.
All this time, Jonah was down below
deck, sound asleep. 6 The ship's captain
went to him and said, "How can you sleep
at a time like this? Get up and pray to your
God! Maybe he will have pity on us and
keep us from drowning."
7 Finally, the sailors got together and said,
"Let's ask our gods to show us[b] who caused
all this trouble." It turned out to be Jonah.
8 They started asking him, "Are you the
one who brought all this trouble on us?
What business are you in? Where do you
come from? What is your country? Who
are your people?"

[a]**1.2** *Nineveh*: Capital city of Assyria, a hated enemy of Israel. [b]**1.7** *ask . . . show us*: The Hebrew text has "cast lots," which were pieces of wood or stone used to find out how and when to do something. In this case, the lots would show who was the guilty person.
1.1 2 K 14.25.

9 Jonah answered, "I'm a Hebrew, and I worship the LORD God of heaven, who made the sea and the dry land."
10 When the sailors heard this, they were frightened, because Jonah had already told them he was running from the LORD. Then they said, "Do you know what you have done?"
11 The storm kept getting worse, until finally the sailors asked him, "What should we do with you to make the sea calm down?"
12 Jonah told them, "Throw me into the sea, and it will calm down. I'm the cause of this terrible storm."
13 The sailors tried their best to row to the shore. But they could not do it, and the storm kept getting worse every minute.
14 So they prayed to the LORD, "Please don't let us drown for taking this man's life. Don't hold us guilty for killing an innocent man. All of this happened because you
wanted it to." 15 Then they threw Jonah overboard, and the sea calmed down.
16 The sailors were so terrified that they offered a sacrifice to the LORD and made all kinds of promises.
17 The LORD sent a big fish to swallow Jonah, and Jonah was inside the fish for three days and three nights.

Jonah's Prayer

2 From inside the fish, Jonah prayed to the LORD his God:

2 When I was in trouble, LORD,
I prayed to you,
and you listened to me.
From deep in the world
of the dead,
I begged for your help,
and you answered my prayer.

3 You threw me down
to the bottom of the sea.
The water was churning
all around;
I was completely covered
by your mighty waves.
4 I thought I was swept away
from your sight,
never again to see
your holy temple.

5 I was almost drowned
by the swirling waters
that surrounded me.
Seaweed had wrapped
around my head.
6 I had sunk down below
the underwater mountains;
I knew that forever,
I would be a prisoner there.

But, you, LORD God,
rescued me from that pit.
7 When my life was slipping away,
I remembered you—
and in your holy temple
you heard my prayer.

8 All who worship worthless idols
turn from the God
who offers them mercy.
9 But with shouts of praise,
I will offer a sacrifice
to you, my LORD.
I will keep my promise,
because you are the one
with power to save.

10 The LORD commanded the fish to vomit up Jonah on the shore. And it did.

Jonah Goes to Nineveh

3 Once again the LORD told Jonah 2 to go to that great city of Nineveh and preach his message of doom.
3 Jonah obeyed the LORD and went to Nineveh. The city was so big that it took
three days just to walk through it. 4 After walking for a day, Jonah warned the people, "Forty days from now, Nineveh will be destroyed!"
5 They believed God's message and set a time when they would go without eating to show their sorrow. Then everyone in the city, no matter who they were, dressed in sackcloth.

1.17 Mt 12.40. **2.10** 3 Macc 6.8. **3.4,5** Mt 12.41; Lk 11.32.

[6] When the king of Nineveh heard what was happening, he also dressed in sackcloth; he left the royal palace and sat in dust.[c] [7-9] Then he and his officials sent out an order for everyone in the city to obey. It said:

None of you or your animals may eat or drink a thing. Each of you must wear sackcloth, and you must even put sackcloth on your animals.

You must also pray to the LORD God with all your heart and stop being sinful and cruel. Maybe God will change his mind and have mercy on us, so we won't be destroyed.

[10] When God saw that the people had stopped doing evil things, he had pity and did not destroy them as he had planned.

Jonah Gets Angry at the LORD

4 Jonah was really upset and angry. [2] So he prayed:

Our LORD, I knew from the very beginning that you wouldn't destroy Nineveh. That's why I left my own country and headed for Spain. You are a kind and merciful God, and you are very patient. You always show love, and you don't like to punish anyone, not even foreigners.

[3] Now let me die! I'd be better off dead.

[4] The LORD replied, "What right do you have to be angry?"

[5] Jonah then left through the east gate of the city and made a shelter to protect himself from the sun. He sat under the shelter, waiting to see what would happen to Nineveh.

[6] The LORD made a vine grow up to shade Jonah's head and protect him from the sun. Jonah was very happy to have the vine, [7] but early the next morning the LORD sent a worm to chew on the vine, and the vine dried up. [8] During the day the LORD sent a scorching wind, and the sun beat down on Jonah's head, making him feel faint. Jonah was ready to die, and he shouted, "I wish I were dead!"

[9] But the LORD asked, "Jonah, do you have the right to be angry about the vine?"

"Yes, I do," he answered, "and I'm angry enough to die."

[10] But the LORD said:

You are concerned about a vine that you did not plant or take care of, a vine that grew up in one night and died the next. [11] In that city of Nineveh there are more than a hundred twenty thousand people who cannot tell right from wrong, and many cattle are also there. Don't you think I should be concerned about that big city?

[c] **3.5,6** *dressed in sackcloth . . . sat in dust*: Sackcloth was a rough, dark-colored cloth made from goat or camel hair and used to make grain sacks. Sometimes people wore sackcloth and sat in dust to show how sorry they were for their sins.

4.2 Ex 34.6. **4.3** 1 K 19.4.

MICAH

ABOUT THIS BOOK

The messages in this book were especially for Samaria, the capital of Israel, and for Jerusalem, the capital of Judah. Instead of leading their nations to worship and obey the Lord, the officials and people of these capital cities had led their nations to worship other gods and to cheat and rob the poor. And so the Lord was going to punish Israel and Judah.

But the Lord had also promised that in the future the people of Israel and Judah would return to him. Then he and his chosen king would take care of the people, just as shepherds take care of sheep, and there would be peace everywhere:

He will settle arguments
between distant
and powerful nations.
They will pound their swords
and their spears
into rakes and shovels;
they will never again make war
or attack one another.
Everyone will find rest
beneath their own fig trees
or grape vines,
and they will live in peace.
(4.3, 4)

A QUICK LOOK AT THIS BOOK

- The Lord Will Punish His People (1.1—2.11)
- A Promise of Hope (2.12, 13)
- The Lord Will Punish Evil Rulers and Lying Prophets (3.1-12)
- A New Temple in a New Israel (4.1—5.15)
- Israel Is Declared Guilty (6.1—7.7)
- The Nation Turns to God (7.8-20)

---

1 I am Micah from Moresheth.[a] And this
is the message about Samaria and
Jerusalem[b] that the LORD gave to me when
Jotham, Ahaz, and Hezekiah[c] were the
kings of Judah.

[a]**1.1** *Moresheth*: A town in southern Judah not far from Gath. In verse 14 it is called Moresheth-Gath. [b]**1.1** *Samaria and Jerusalem*: Samaria was the capital of the northern kingdom (Israel), and Jerusalem was the capital of the southern kingdom (Judah). [c]**1.1** *Jotham, Ahaz, and Hezekiah*: Jotham, the son of Uzziah, ruled Judah 740-736 B.C.; Ahaz, the son of Jotham, ruled 736-716 B.C.; Hezekiah, the son of Ahaz, ruled 716-687 B.C.

1.1 **a** 2 K 15.32-38; 2 Ch 27.1-7; **b** 2 K 16.1-20; 2 Ch 28.1-27; **c** 2 K 18.1—20.21; 2 Ch 29.1—32.33.

Judgment on Samaria

2 Listen, all of you!
Earth and everything on it,
pay close attention.
The LORD God accuses you
from his holy temple.[d]
3 And he will come down
to crush underfoot
every pagan altar.
4 Mountains will melt
beneath his feet
like wax beside a fire.
Valleys will vanish like water
rushing down a ravine.
5 This will happen because of
the terrible sins of Israel,
the descendants of Jacob.
Samaria has led Israel to sin,
and pagan altars at Jerusalem
have made Judah sin.

6 So the LORD will leave Samaria
in ruins—
merely an empty field
where vineyards are planted.
He will scatter its stones
and destroy its foundations.
7 Samaria's idols will be smashed,
and the wages
of temple prostitutes[e]
will be destroyed by fire.
Silver and gold from those idols
will then be used by foreigners
as payment for prostitutes.

Judah Is Doomed

8 Because of this tragedy,[f]
I go barefoot and naked.
My crying and weeping
sound like howling wolves
or ostriches.
9 The nation is fatally wounded.
Judah is doomed.
Jerusalem will fall.

10 Don't tell it in Gath!
Don't even cry.
Instead, roll in the dust
at Beth-Leaphrah.[g]
11 Depart naked and ashamed,
you people of Shaphir.[h]
The town of Bethezel[i] mourns
because no one from Zaanan[j]
went out to help.[k]
12 Everyone in Maroth[l]
hoped for the best,
but the LORD sent disaster
down on Jerusalem.

13 Get the war chariots ready,
you people of Lachish.[m]
You led Jerusalem into sin,
just as Israel did.[n]
14 Now you will have to give
a going-away gift[o]
to Moresheth.[p]

[d]**1.2** *holy temple*: Possibly the one in heaven, though it may be the Jerusalem temple.
[e]**1.7** *wages of temple prostitutes*: At pagan temples, people had sex with prostitutes as a way of worshiping the idols, and the money earned in this way was used to support the pagan religion.
[f]**1.8** *this tragedy*: Either the destruction of Samaria (verses 6,7) or the coming destruction of Judah and Jerusalem. [g]**1.10** *Gath . . . Beth-Leaphrah*: Gath was a Philistine city; Beth-Leaphrah is unknown, but in Hebrew it sounds like "House of Dust." [h]**1.11** *Shaphir*: Mentioned only here in the Old Testament; in Hebrew "Shaphir" means "beautiful." [i]**1.11** *Bethezel*: Mentioned only here in the Old Testament; in Hebrew "Bethezel" means "house next door." [j]**1.11** *Zaanan*: Mentioned only here in the Old Testament; in Hebrew "Zaanan" means "one who goes out."
[k]**1.11** *The town . . . help*: Or "No one from Zaanan refused to desert their town, and Bethezel mourns because it is left undefended." [l]**1.12** *Maroth*: Mentioned only here in the Old Testament; in Hebrew "Maroth" means "bitter." [m]**1.13** *Lachish*: The chief city of southwest Judah, about thirty miles from Jerusalem. [n]**1.13** *led . . . sin . . . did*: Or "You led Jerusalem and Israel into sin." In Hebrew "Lachish" sounds like "a team of horses (that pulls a war chariot)." And the sin may be that Lachish led the nation to trust the power of war chariots instead of the LORD. But the sin could be idolatry or some false teachings that were brought in from Egypt by way of Lachish. [o]**1.14** *going-away gift*: The gift (dowry) that a bride's father gave her when she left the home of her parents to live with the family of her husband. In Hebrew the word for "bride" or "fiancee" sounds like "Moresheth." [p]**1.14** *Moresheth*: Hebrew "Moresheth-Gath"; the home of Micah (see verse 1).

Israel's kings will discover
that they cannot trust
the town of Achzib.[q]

15 People of Mareshah,[r]
the LORD will send someone
to capture your town.
Then Israel's glorious king
will be forced to hide
in Adullam Cave.[s]
16 Judah, shave your head
as bald as a buzzard
and start mourning.
Your precious children[t]
will be dragged off
to a foreign country.

Punishment for Those Who Abuse Their Power

2 Doomed! You're doomed!
At night you lie in bed,
making evil plans.
And when morning comes,
you do what you've planned
because you have the power.
2 You grab any field or house
that you want;
you cheat families
out of homes and land.

3 But here is what the LORD says:
"I am planning trouble for you.
Your necks will be caught
in a noose,
and you will be disgraced
in this time of disaster."

4 When that happens,
this sorrowful song
will be sung about you:
"Ruined! Completely ruined!
The LORD has taken our land
and given it to traitors."[u]
5 And so you will never again
own property
among the LORD's people.

6 "Enough of your preaching!"
That's what you tell me.
"We won't be disgraced,
so stop preaching!"

7 Descendants of Jacob,
is it right for you to claim
that the LORD did what he did
because he was angry?
Doesn't he always bless
those who do right?
8 My people, you have even stolen
clothes right off the backs
of your unsuspecting soldiers
returning home from battle.
9 You take over lovely homes
that belong to the women
of my nation.
Then you cheat their children
out of the inheritance
that comes from the LORD.[v]

10 Get out of here, you crooks!
You'll find no rest here.
You're not fit to belong
to the LORD's people,
and you will be destroyed.[w]
11 The only prophet you want
is a liar who will say,
"Drink and get drunk!"

A Promise of Hope

12 I, the LORD, promise
to bring together
the people of Israel
who have survived.

[q]**1.14** *Achzib*: Meaning "lie" or "deception" was near Adullam Cave (verse 15), where David hid from King Saul (see 1 Samuel 22.1, 2). Micah probably means that the people of Israel (including their king) will have to run for their lives, but will find that all hope for escape is merely a "lie" (see verse 15). [r]**1.15** *Mareshah*: Sounds something like the Hebrew word for "conqueror" and was only a few miles northeast of Lachish. [s]**1.15** *Adullam Cave*: See the note at 1.14. [t]**1.16** *precious children*: The towns mentioned in verses 10-15. [u]**2.4** *The LORD . . . traitors*: One possible meaning for the difficult Hebrew text. [v]**2.9** *inheritance . . . LORD*: The Hebrew text has "my glory," which refers to the inheritance of land that the LORD had promised his people. [w]**2.10** *destroyed*: One possible meaning for the difficult Hebrew text.

I will gather them,
just as a shepherd
brings sheep together,
and there will be many.
13 I will break down the gate
and lead them out—
then I will be their king.

Evil Rulers and Lying Prophets

3 Listen to me,
you rulers of Israel!
You know right from wrong,
2 but you prefer to do evil
instead of what is right.
You skin my people alive.
You strip off their flesh,
3 break their bones,
cook it all in a pot,
and gulp it down.

4 Someday you will beg the LORD
to help you,
but he will turn away
because of your sins.

5 You lying prophets promise
security for anyone
who gives you food,
but disaster for anyone
who refuses to feed you.
Here is what the LORD says
to you prophets:
6 "You will live in the dark,
far from the sight of the sun,
with no message from me.
7 You prophets and fortunetellers
will all be disgraced,
with no message from me."

8 But the LORD has filled me
with power and his Spirit.
I have been given the courage
to speak about justice
and to tell you people of Israel
that you have sinned.
9 So listen to my message,
you rulers of Israel!
You hate justice
and twist the truth.
10 You make cruelty and murder
a way of life in Jerusalem.
11 You leaders accept bribes
for dishonest decisions.
You priests and prophets
teach and preach,
but only for money.

Then you say,
"The LORD is on our side.
No harm will come to us."
12 And so, because of you,
Jerusalem will be plowed under
and left in ruins.
Thorns will cover the mountain
where the temple now stands.

Peace and Prosperity

4 In the future, the mountain
with the LORD's temple
will be the highest of all.
It will reach above the hills,
and every nation
will rush to it.
2 People of many nations
will come and say,
"Let's go up to the mountain
of the LORD God of Jacob
and worship in his temple."

The LORD will teach us his Law
from Jerusalem,
and we will obey him.
3 He will settle arguments
between distant
and powerful nations.
They will pound their swords
and their spears
into rakes and shovels;
they will never again make war
or attack one another.
4 Everyone will find rest
beneath their own fig trees
or grape vines,
and they will live in peace.
This is a solemn promise
of the LORD All-Powerful.

5 Others may follow their gods,
but we will always follow
the LORD our God.

3.12 Jr 26.18. **4.3** Is 2.4; Jl 3.10. **4.4** Zec 3.10.

The LORD Will Lead His People Home

6 The LORD said:
At that time
I will gather my people—
the lame and the outcasts,
and all into whose lives
I have brought sorrow.
7 Then the lame and the outcasts
will belong to my people
and become a strong nation.
I, the LORD, will rule them
from Mount Zion forever.
8 Mount Zion in Jerusalem,
guardian of my people,
you will rule again.

9 Jerusalem, why are you crying?
Don't you have a king?
Have your advisors gone?
Are you suffering
like a woman in childbirth?
10 Keep on groaning with pain,
you people of Jerusalem!
If you escape from your city
to the countryside,
you will still be taken
as prisoners to Babylonia.
But later I will rescue you
from your enemies.

11 Zion, because of your sins
you are surrounded
by many nations who say,
"We can hardly wait
to see you disgraced."[x]
12 But they don't know
that I, the LORD,
have gathered them here
to grind them like grain.
13 Smash them to pieces, Zion!
I'll let you be like a bull
with iron horns
and bronze hoofs.
Crush those nations
and bring their wealth to me,
the LORD of the earth.

A Promised Ruler

5 Jerusalem, enemy troops
have surrounded you;[y]
they have struck Israel's ruler
in the face with a stick.

2 Bethlehem Ephrath,
you are one of the smallest towns
in the nation of Judah.
But the LORD will choose
one of your people
to rule the nation—
someone whose family
goes back to ancient times.[z]
3 The LORD will abandon Israel
only until this ruler is born,
and the rest of his family
returns to Israel.
4 Like a shepherd
taking care of his sheep,
this ruler will lead
and care for his people
by the power and glorious name
of the LORD his God.
His people will live securely,
and the whole earth will know
his true greatness,
5 because he will bring peace.

Assyria Will Be Defeated

Let Assyria attack our country
and our palaces.
We will counterattack,
led by a number of rulers
6 whose strong army will defeat
the nation of Assyria.[a]
Yes, our leaders will rescue us,
if those Assyrians
dare to invade our land.

The Survivors Will Be Safe

7 A few of Jacob's descendants
survived and are scattered
among the nations.
But the LORD will let them
cover the earth like dew and rain
that refreshes the soil.

[x] **4.11** *We . . . disgraced*: Or "We'll pull up your skirt and expose your nakedness!"
[y] **5.1** *Jerusalem . . . you*: Or "Jerusalem, you are slashing yourself in sorrow, because of the enemy troops." [z] **5.2** *family . . . times*: Or "kingdom is eternal." [a] **5.6** *the nation of Assyria*: The Hebrew text uses both "land of Assyria" and "land of Nimrod," which was a poetic name for Assyria.
5.2 Mt 2.6; Jn 7.42. **5.6** Gn 10.6-20.

8 At present they are scattered,
but later they will attack,
as though they were fierce lions
pouncing on sheep.
Their enemies will be torn
to shreds,
with no one to save them;
9 they will be helpless,
completely destroyed.

Idols Will Be Destroyed in Israel

10 The LORD said:
At that time I will wipe out
your cavalry and chariots,
11 as well as your cities
and your fortresses.
12 I will stop you
from telling fortunes
and practicing witchcraft.
13 You will no longer worship
the idols or stone images
you have made—
I will destroy them,
14 together with the sacred poles[b]
and even your towns.
15 I will become furious
and take revenge on the nations
that refuse to obey me.

The LORD's Challenge to His People

6 The LORD said to his people:
Come and present your case
to the hills and mountains.
2 Israel, I am bringing charges
against you—
I call upon the mountains
and the earth's firm foundation
to be my witnesses.

3 My people, have I wronged you
in any way at all?
Please tell me.
4 I rescued you from Egypt,
where you were slaves.
I sent Moses, Aaron, and Miriam
to be your leaders.
5 Don't forget the evil plans
of King Balak of Moab
or what Balaam son of Beor[c]
said to him.
Remember how I, the LORD,
saved you many times
on your way from Acacia
to Gilgal.[d]

True Obedience

6 What offering should I bring
when I bow down to worship
the LORD God Most High?
Should I try to please him[e]
by sacrificing
calves a year old?
7 Will thousands of sheep
or rivers of olive oil
make God satisfied with me?
Should I sacrifice to the LORD
my first-born child as payment
for my terrible sins?
8 The LORD God has told us
what is right
and what he demands:
"See that justice is done,
let mercy be your first concern,
and humbly obey your God."

Cheating and Violence

9 I am the LORD,
and it makes sense to respect
my power to punish.
So listen to my message
for the city of Jerusalem:[f]
10 You store up stolen treasures
and use dishonest scales.[g]
11 But I, the LORD, will punish you
for cheating with weights
and with measures.
12 You rich people are violent,
and everyone tells lies.

[b]**5.14** *sacred poles*: Used in the worship of Asherah, the fertility goddess. [c]**6.5** *Balak . . . Beor*: See Numbers 22–24. [d]**6.5** *Acacia to Gilgal*: Acacia was where the Israelites camped after the experience with Balaam (see Numbers 25.1; Joshua 2.1; 3.1); Gilgal was where they camped while waiting to attack Jericho (see Joshua 4.19—5.12). [e]**6.6** *try to please him*: This refers to what are traditionally called "burnt sacrifices," which were offered as a way of pleasing the LORD. [f]**6.9** *Jerusalem*: One possible meaning for the difficult Hebrew text of verse 9. [g]**6.10** *scales*: One possible meaning for the difficult Hebrew text of verse 10.

6.4 a Ex 12.50, 51; **b** Ex 4.10-16; **c** Ex 15.20. **6.5 a** Nu 22.2—24.25; **b** Js 3.1—4.19.

13 Because of your sins,
I will wound you and leave you
ruined and defenseless.
14 You will eat,
but still be hungry;
you will store up goods,
but lose everything—
I, the LORD, will let it all
be captured in war.
15 You won't harvest what you plant
or use the oil
from your olive trees
or drink the wine
from grapes you grow.

16 Jerusalem, this will happen
because you followed
the sinful example
of kings Omri and Ahab.[h]
Now I will destroy you
and your property.
Then the people of every nation
will make fun and insult you.

Israel Is Corrupt

7 I feel so empty inside—
like someone starving
for grapes or figs,
after the vines and trees
have all been picked clean.
2 No one is loyal to God;
no one does right.
Everyone is brutal
and eager to deceive
everyone else.
3 People cooperate to commit crime.
Judges and leaders demand bribes,
and rulers cheat in court.[i]
4 The most honest of them
is worse than a thorn patch.

Your doom has come!
Lookouts sound the warning,
and everyone panics.
5 Don't trust anyone,
not even your best friend,
and be careful what you say
to the one you love.

6 Sons refuse to respect
their own fathers,
daughters rebel against
their own mothers,
and daughters-in-law despise
their mothers-in-law.
Your family is now your enemy.
7 But I trust the LORD God
to save me,
and I will wait for him
to answer my prayer.

The Nation Turns to God

8 My enemies, don't be glad
because of my troubles!
I may have fallen,
but I will get up;
I may be sitting in the dark,
but the LORD is my light.
9 I have sinned against the LORD.
And so I must endure his anger,
until he comes to my defense.
But I know that I will see him
making things right for me
and leading me to the light.

10 You, my enemies, said,
"The LORD God is helpless."
Now each of you
will be disgraced
and put to shame.
I will see you trampled
like mud in the street.

A Bright Future

11 Towns of Judah, the day is coming
when your walls will be rebuilt,
and your boundaries enlarged.
12 People will flock to you
from Assyria and Egypt,
from Babylonia[j]
and everywhere else.

[h]**6.16** *Omri and Ahab*: King Ahab was the son of Omri and the husband of the evil Jezebel. Almost two centuries before Micah, the prophet Elijah had spoken against the idolatry and the other sinful practices that Ahab had encouraged in Israel (see 1 Kings 16.21-34; 18.1-18; 21.1-26).
[i]**7.3** *court*: One possible meaning for the difficult Hebrew text of verse 3. [j]**7.12** *Babylonia*: The Hebrew text has "the river," meaning the Euphrates River, which stood for Babylonia.
6.16 a 1 K 16.23-28; **b** 1 K 16.29-34; 21.25-29. **7.6** Mt 10.35, 36; Lk 12.53.

13 Those nations will suffer disaster
because of what they did.

Micah's Prayer and the LORD's Answer

14 Lead your people, LORD!
Come and be our shepherd.
Grasslands surround us,
but we live in a forest.
So lead us to Bashan and Gilead,[k]
and let us find pasture
as we did long ago.

15 I, the LORD, will work miracles
just as I did when I led you
out of Egypt.
16 Nations will see this
and be ashamed because
of their helpless armies.
They will be in shock,
unable to speak or hear,
17 because of their fear of me,
your LORD and God.
Then they will come trembling,
crawling out of their fortresses
like insects or snakes,
lapping up the dust.

No One Is Like God

The people said:
18 Our God, no one is like you.
We are all that is left
of your chosen people,
and you freely forgive
our sin and guilt.
You don't stay angry forever;
you're glad to have pity
19 and pleased to be merciful.
You will trample on our sins
and throw them in the sea.
20 You will keep your word
and be faithful to Jacob
and to Abraham,
as you promised our ancestors
many years ago.

[k]**7.14** *Bashan and Gilead*: Two regions east of the Jordan River, known for their fertile pasturelands.

NAHUM

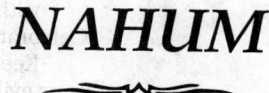

ABOUT THIS BOOK

In this book, the prophet Nahum said the Lord was going to bring justice and punish Assyria, because it had been so cruel to other nations. Many Old Testament books also talk about the Lord's mercy when they discuss the Lord's justice. But in this book the Lord is merciful and good only to those who turn to him (1.7). Nahum also hinted that one way God has mercy on his people is to punish enemies like Assyria and give his people freedom from their power (1.13-15). And the Lord can do this because he rules the earth:

The LORD God demands loyalty.
In his anger, he takes revenge
on his enemies.
The LORD is powerful,
yet patient;
he makes sure that the guilty
are always punished.
He can be seen in storms
and in whirlwinds;
clouds are the dust from his feet.
(1.2, 3)

A QUICK LOOK AT THIS BOOK

- The Fierce Anger of the Lord (1.1-6)
- Assyria's Doom Brings Hope for the Lord's People (1.7-15)
- Nineveh, the Capital of Assyria, Will Be Destroyed (2.1—3.19)

---

1 I am Nahum from Elkosh.[a] And this is the message[b] that I wrote down about Nineveh.[c]

The Fierce Anger of the LORD

2 The LORD God demands loyalty.
In his anger, he takes revenge
on his enemies.
3 The LORD is powerful,
yet patient;
he makes sure that the guilty
are always punished.
He can be seen in storms
and in whirlwinds;
clouds are the dust from his feet.

4 At the LORD's command,
oceans and rivers dry up.
Bashan, Mount Carmel,
and Lebanon[d] wither,
and their flowers fade.
5 At the sight of the LORD,
mountains and hills
tremble and melt;

[a]**1.1** *Elkosh*: The location of Elkosh is not known. [b]**1.1** *message*: Or "vision." [c]**1.1** *Nineveh*: The capital of Assyria, the hated enemy of Israel. [d]**1.4** *Bashan, Mount Carmel, and Lebanon*: Three regions noted for their trees and flowers.
1.1—3.19 Is 10.5-34; 14.24-27; Zep 2.13-15.

the earth and its people
shudder and shake.
6 Who can stand the heat
of his furious anger?
It flashes out like fire
and shatters stones.

The Power of Assyria Will Be Broken

7 The LORD is good.
He protects those who trust him
in times of trouble.
8 But like a roaring flood,
the LORD chases his enemies
into dark places
and destroys them.
9 So don't plot against the LORD!
He wipes out his enemies,
and they never revive.
10 They are like drunkards
overcome by wine,
or like dry thornbushes
burning in a fire.[e]
11 Assyria, one of your rulers
has made evil plans
against the LORD.

12 But the LORD says, "Assyria,
no matter how strong you are,
you are doomed!
My people Judah,
I have troubled you before,
but I won't do it again.
13 I'll snap your chains
and set you free
from the Assyrians."

14 Assyria, this is what else
the LORD says to you:
"Your name will be forgotten.
I will destroy every idol
in your temple,
and I will send you to the grave,
because you are worthless."

15 Look toward the mountains,
people of Judah!
Here comes a messenger
with good news of peace.
Celebrate your festivals.
Keep your promises to God.
Your evil enemies are destroyed
and will never again
invade your country.

Nineveh Will Fall

2 Nineveh, someone is coming
to attack and scatter you.
Guard your fortresses!
Watch the road! Be brave!
Prepare for battle!
2 Judah and Israel are like trees
with branches broken
by their enemies.
But the LORD is going to restore
their power and glory.

*3 Nineveh, on this day of attack,
your enemies' shields are red;
their uniforms are crimson.
4 Their horses[f] prance,
and their armored[g] chariots
dart around like lightning
or flaming torches.
5 An officer gives a command.
But his soldiers stumble,
as they hasten to build
a shelter to protect themselves
against rocks thrown down
from the city wall.

6 The river gates[h] fly open,
and panic floods the palace.
7 Nineveh is disgraced.
The queen is dragged off.
Her servant women mourn;
they sound like doves,
and they beat their breasts
in sorrow.[i]
8 Nineveh is like a pond
with leaking water.
Shouts of "Stop! Don't go!"
can be heard everywhere.
But everyone is leaving.

[e] **1.10** *fire*: One possible meaning for the difficult Hebrew text of verse 10. [f] **2.4** *horses*: Two ancient translations; Hebrew "spears." [g] **2.4** *armored*: One possible meaning for the difficult Hebrew text. [h] **2.6** *river gates*: Nineveh was protected by a moat filled with water from the nearby Tigris River. [i] **2.7** *sorrow*: One possible meaning for the difficult Hebrew text of verse 7.
1.15 Is 52.7.

9 Enemy soldiers shout,
"The city is full of treasure
and all kinds of wealth.
Steal her silver! Grab her gold!"

10 Nineveh is doomed! Destroyed!
Her people tremble with fear;
their faces turn pale.[j]
11 What happened to this city?
They were safer there
than powerful lions in a den,
with no one to disturb them.
12 These are the same lions
that ferociously attacked
their victims,
then dragged away the flesh
to feed their young.

13 The LORD All-Powerful
is against you, Nineveh.
God will burn your chariots
and send an army to kill
those young lions of yours.
You will never again
make victims of others
or send messengers to threaten
everyone on this earth.

Punishment for Nineveh

The LORD said:

3 Doom to the crime capital!
Nineveh, city of murder
and treachery,
2 here is your fate—
cracking whips,
churning wheels;
galloping horses,
roaring chariots;
3 cavalry attacking,
swords and spears flashing;
soldiers stumbling
over piles of dead bodies.
4 You were nothing more
than a prostitute
using your magical charms
and witchcraft
to attract and trap nations.
5 But I, the LORD All-Powerful,
am now your enemy.
I will pull up your skirt
and let nations and kingdoms
stare at your nakedness.
6 I will cover you with garbage,
treat you like trash,
and rub you in the dirt.
7 Everyone who sees you
will turn away and shout,
"Nineveh is done for!
Is anyone willing to mourn
or to give her comfort?"

Nineveh's Fate Is Sealed

8 Nineveh, do you feel safer
than the city of Thebes?[k]
The Nile River
was its wall of defense.[l]
9 Thebes trusted the mighty power
of Ethiopia[m] and Egypt;
the nations of Put[n] and Libya
were her allies.
10 But she was captured and taken
to a foreign country.
Her children were murdered
at every street corner.
The members of her royal family
were auctioned off,
and her high officials
were bound in chains.

11 Nineveh, now it's your turn!
You will get drunk and try to hide
from your enemy.
12 Your fortresses are fig trees
with ripe figs.
Merely shake the trees,
and fruit will fall
into every open mouth.
13 Your army is weak.
Fire has destroyed the crossbars
on your city gates;
now they stand wide open
to your enemy.

[j] **2.10** *faces turn pale*: Or "ashes cover their faces." [k] **3.8** *Thebes*: In 663 B.C., the Assyrian King Ashurbanipal captured this Egyptian city, which seems to have been built with protection similar to that of Nineveh. [l] **3.8** *was its . . . defense*: One possible meaning for the difficult Hebrew text. [m] **3.9** *Ethiopia*: The Hebrew text has "Cush," which was a region south of Egypt that included parts of the present countries of Ethiopia and Sudan. [n] **3.9** *Put*: A region in Africa, possibly part of the present country of Libya.

14 Your city is under attack.
Haul in extra water!
Strengthen your defenses!
Start making bricks!
Stir the mortar!
15 You will still go up in flames
and be cut down by swords
that will wipe you out like wheat
attacked by grasshoppers.
So, go ahead and increase
like a swarm of locusts![o]

16 More merchants are in your city
than there are stars
in the sky—
but they are like locusts
that eat everything,
then fly away.
17 Your guards and your officials
are swarms of locusts.
On a chilly day
they settle on a fence,
but when the sun comes out,
they take off
to who-knows-where.

18 King of Assyria,
your officials and leaders
sleep the eternal sleep,
while your people are scattered
in the mountains.
Yes, your people are sheep
without a shepherd.
19 You're fatally wounded.
There's no hope for you.
But everyone claps
when they hear this news,
because your constant cruelty
has caused them pain.

[o]**3.15** *locusts*: A type of grasshopper that comes in swarms and causes great damage to plant life.

HABAKKUK

ABOUT THIS BOOK

The first two chapters of this book report a conversation between Habakkuk and the Lord. Habakkuk complained that Judah was full of injustice and crime. The Lord answered that he was going to have the Babylonians punish the people of Judah. But then Habakkuk complained that this would be unfair, because the Babylonians were even worse sinners than the people of Judah! The Lord answered that Babylonia would be punished later.

The last chapter of the book is a prayer in which Habakkuk praises the Lord's power and glory.

A QUICK LOOK AT THIS BOOK

- Habakkuk Complains, and the Lord Answers (1–2)
- Habakkuk Gives Praise to the Lord (3)

---

1 I am Habakkuk the prophet. And this
is the message[a] that the LORD gave me.

Habakkuk Complains to the LORD

2 Our LORD, how long must I beg
for your help
before you listen?
How long before you save us
from all this violence?
3 Why do you make me watch
such terrible injustice?
Why do you allow violence,
lawlessness, crime, and cruelty
to spread everywhere?
4 Laws cannot be enforced;
justice is always the loser;
criminals crowd out honest people
and twist the laws around.

The LORD Answers Habakkuk

5 Look and be amazed
at what's happening
among the nations!
Even if you were told,
you would never believe
what's taking place now.
6 I am sending the Babylonians.
They are fierce and cruel—
marching across the land,
conquering cities and towns.

7 How fearsome and frightening.
Their only laws and rules
are the ones they make up.
8 Their cavalry troops are faster
than leopards,
more ferocious than wolves
hunting at sunset,
and swifter than hungry eagles
suddenly swooping down.

9 They are eager to destroy,[b]
and they gather captives
like handfuls of sand.
10 They make fun of rulers
and laugh at fortresses,
while building dirt mounds
so they can capture cities.[c]

[a]**1.1** *message*: Or "vision." [b]**1.9** *eager to destroy*: One possible meaning for the difficult Hebrew text. [c]**1.10** *dirt mounds . . . cities*: Attacking armies often build dirt mounds against city walls to make it easier for them to climb the wall and capture the city.

1.5 Ac 13.41. **1.6** 2 K 24.2.

11 Then suddenly they disappear
like a gust of wind—
those sinful people who worship
their own strength.

Habakkuk Complains Again

12 Holy LORD God, mighty rock,[d]
you are eternal,
and we[e] are safe from death.
You are using those Babylonians
to judge and punish others.[f]
13 But you can't stand sin or wrong.
So don't sit by in silence
while they gobble down people
who are better than they are.

14 The people you put on this earth
are like fish or reptiles
without a leader.
15 Then an enemy comes along
and takes them captive
with hooks and nets.
It makes him so happy
16 that he offers sacrifices
to his fishing nets,
because they make him rich
and provide choice foods.
17 Will he keep hauling in his nets
and destroying nations
without showing mercy?

The LORD Answers Habakkuk Again

2 While standing guard
on the watchtower,
I waited for the LORD's answer,
before explaining the reason
for my complaint.[g]
2 Then the LORD told me:
"I will give you my message
in the form of a vision.
Write it clearly enough
to be read at a glance.
3 At the time I have decided,
my words will come true.
You can trust what I say
about the future.
It may take a long time,
but keep on waiting—
it will happen!

4 "I, the LORD, refuse to accept
anyone who is proud.
Only those who live by faith
are acceptable to me."[h]

Trouble for Evil People

5 Wine[i] is treacherous,
and arrogant people
are never satisfied.
They are no less greedy
than death itself—
they open their mouths as wide
as the world of the dead
and swallow everyone.

6 But they will be mocked
with these words:
You're doomed!
You stored up stolen goods
and cheated others
of what belonged to them.
7 But without warning,
those you owe
will demand payment.
Then you will become
a frightened victim.
8 You robbed cities and nations
everywhere on earth
and murdered their people.
Now those who survived
will be as cruel to you.

9 You're doomed!
You made your family rich
at the expense of others.
You even said to yourself,
"I'm above the law."
10 But you will bring shame
on your family
and ruin to yourself
for what you did to others.
11 The very stones and wood

[d]**1.12** *mighty rock*: The Hebrew text has "rock," which is sometimes used in poetry to compare the LORD to a mountain where his people can run for protection from their enemies. [e]**1.12** *we*: Hebrew; one ancient Jewish tradition "you." [f]**1.12** *You . . . others*: Or "You will judge and punish those Babylonians." [g]**2.1** *I . . . complaint*: One possible meaning for the difficult Hebrew text. [h]**2.4** *Only . . . me*: Or "But those who are acceptable to me will live because of their faithfulness." [i]**2.5** *Wine*: The Standard Hebrew Text; the Dead Sea Scrolls "Wealth."
2.3 He 10.37. **2.4** Ro 1.17; Ga 3.11; He 10.38.

in your home
will testify against you.

12 You're doomed! You built a city
on crime and violence.
13 But the LORD All-Powerful
sends up in flames
what nations and people
work so hard to gain.

14 Just as water fills the sea,
the land will be filled
with people who know
and honor the LORD.

15 You're doomed!
You get your friends drunk,
just to see them naked.
16 Now you will be disgraced
instead of praised.
The LORD will make you drunk,
and when others see you naked,
you will lose their respect.
17 You destroyed trees and animals
on Mount Lebanon;
you were ruthless to towns
and people everywhere.
Now you will be terrorized.

Idolatry Is Foolish

18 What is an idol worth?
It's merely a false god.
Why trust a speechless image
made from wood or metal
by human hands?
19 What can you learn from idols
covered with silver or gold?
They can't even breathe.
Pity anyone who says to an idol
of wood or stone,
"Get up and do something!"

20 Let all the world be silent—
the LORD is present
in his holy temple.

Habakkuk's Prayer

3 This is my prayer:[j]
2 I know your reputation, LORD,
and I am amazed
at what you have done.
Please turn from your anger
and be merciful;
do for us what you did
for our ancestors.

3 You are the same Holy God
who came from Teman
and Paran[k] to help us.
The brightness of your glory
covered the heavens,
and your praises were heard
everywhere on earth.
4 Your glory shone like the sun,
and light flashed from your hands,
hiding your mighty power.
5 Dreadful diseases and plagues
marched in front
and followed behind.
6 When you stopped,
the earth shook;
when you stared,
nations trembled;
when you walked
along your ancient paths,
eternal mountains and hills
crumbled and collapsed.
7 The tents of desert tribes
in Cushan and Midian[l]
were ripped apart.

8 Our LORD, were you angry
with the monsters
of the deep?[m]

[j]**3.1** *prayer*: The Hebrew text adds "according to the shigionoth," which may mean a prayer of request or a prayer to be accompanied by a special musical instrument. [k]**3.3** *Teman . . . Paran*: Teman is a district in Edom, but the name is sometimes used of the whole country of Edom; Paran is the hill country along the western border of the Gulf of Aqaba. In Judges 5.4, the LORD is said to have marched from Edom to help his people; in Deuteronomy 33.2, Paran is mentioned in connection with the LORD's appearance at Sinai. [l]**3.7** *Cushan and Midian*: Tribes of the Arabian desert who were enemies of Israel. [m]**3.8** *monsters of the deep*: The Hebrew text has "rivers and oceans," which may stand for the powerful monsters that were thought to have lived there before the LORD defeated them.

2.13 Si 14.19. **2.14** Is 11.9.

You attacked in your chariot
and wiped them out.
9 Your arrows were ready
and obeyed your commands.[n]

You split the earth apart
with rivers and streams;
10 mountains trembled
at the sight of you;
rain poured from the clouds;
ocean waves roared and rose.
11 The sun and moon stood still,
while your arrows and spears
flashed like lightning.

12 In your furious anger,
you trampled on nations
13 to rescue your people
and save your chosen one.[o]
You crushed a nation's ruler
and stripped his evil kingdom
of its power.[p]
14 His troops had come like a storm,
hoping to scatter us
and glad to gobble us down.
To them we were refugees
in hiding—
but you smashed their heads
with their own weapons.[q]
15 Then your chariots churned
the waters of the sea.

Habakkuk's Response to God's Message

16 When I heard this message,[r]
I felt weak from fear,
and my lips quivered.
My bones seemed to melt,
and I stumbled around.
But I will patiently wait.
Someday those vicious enemies
will be struck by disaster.[s]

Trust in a Time of Trouble

17 Fig trees may no longer bloom,
or vineyards produce grapes;
olive trees may be fruitless,
and harvest time a failure;
sheep pens may be empty,
and cattle stalls vacant—
18 but I will still celebrate
because the LORD God
saves me.
19 The LORD gives me strength.
He makes my feet as sure
as those of a deer,
and he helps me stand
on the mountains.[t]

To the music director:
Use stringed instruments.

[n]**3.9** *obeyed your commands*: One possible meaning for the difficult Hebrew text. [o]**3.13** *chosen one*: Or "chosen ones." [p]**3.13** *You crushed . . . power*: One possible meaning for the difficult Hebrew text. [q]**3.14** *but you . . . weapons*: One possible meaning for the difficult Hebrew text. [r]**3.16** *heard this message*: Or "saw this vision." [s]**3.16** *I will . . . disaster*: One possible meaning for the difficult Hebrew text. [t]**3.19** *stand on the mountains*: One possible meaning for the difficult Hebrew text.
3.19 2 S. 22.34; Ps 18.33.

ZEPHANIAH

ABOUT THIS BOOK

The people of Judah had thought that at a certain time in the future, the Lord was going to make them powerful and would wipe out their enemies. This future time of justice, victory, and celebration was called "the day of the Lord." But Zephaniah told the people that when the day of the Lord did come, the Lord would punish everyone who had not obeyed him. And this included Judah, as well as other nations. The only way that Judah could avoid being swept away by the Lord's anger was to obey the Lord and worship only him:

If you humbly obey the LORD,
then come and worship him.
If you do right and are humble,
perhaps you will be safe
on that day when the LORD
turns loose his anger.

(2.3)

A QUICK LOOK AT THIS BOOK

- Judah and Jerusalem Will Be Punished on the Day of the Lord (1.1-18)
- Turn to the Lord (2.1-3)
- The Nations Will Be Punished (2.4-15)
- Judah and Other Nations Will Turn to the Lord (3.1-20)

---

1 I am Zephaniah, the son of Cushi, the grandson of Gedaliah, the great-grandson of Amariah, and the great-great-grandson of Hezekiah.[a]

When Josiah son of Amon was king of Judah,[b] the LORD gave me this message.

Judgment on Judah

2 I, the LORD, now promise
to destroy everything
on this earth—
3 people and animals,
birds and fish.
Everyone who is evil
will crash to the ground,[c]
and I will wipe out
the entire human race.
4 I will reach out to punish
Judah and Jerusalem—
nothing will remain
of the god Baal;[d]
nothing will be remembered
of his pagan priests.
5 Not a trace will be found
of those who worship stars
from their rooftops,
or bow down to the god Milcom,[e]
while claiming loyalty
to me, the LORD.
6 Nothing will remain of anyone

[a] **1.1** *Hezekiah*: Ruled 716-687 B.C. [b] **1.1** *Josiah . . . king of Judah*: Ruled 640-609 B.C. [c] **1.3** *Everyone . . . ground*: One possible meaning for the difficult Hebrew text. [d] **1.4** *Baal*: A Caananite fertility god. [e] **1.5** *Milcom*: An Ammonite fertility god.

1.1 2 K 22.1—23.30; 2 Ch 34.1—35.27.

who has turned away
and rejected me.

7 Be silent! I am the LORD God,
and the time is near.
I am preparing
to sacrifice my people
and to invite my guests.
8 On that day I will punish
national leaders
and sons of the king,
along with all who follow
foreign customs.[f]
9 I will punish worshipers
of pagan gods[g]
and cruel palace officials
who abuse their power.

10 I, the LORD, promise
that on that day
noisy crying will be heard
from Fish Gate, New Town,
and Upper Hills.
11 Everyone in Lower Hollow[h]
will mourn loudly,
because merchants
and money changers
will be wiped out.
12 I'll search Jerusalem with lamps
and punish those people
who sit there unworried
while thinking,
"The LORD won't do anything,
good or bad."
13 Their possessions will be taken,
their homes left in ruins.
They won't get to live
in the houses they build,
or drink wine from the grapes
in their own vineyards.

A Terrible Day

14 The great day of the LORD
is coming soon, very soon.
On that terrible day,
fearsome shouts of warriors
will be heard everywhere.
15 It will be a time of anger—
of trouble and torment,
of disaster and destruction,
of darkness and despair,
of storm clouds and shadows,
16 of trumpet calls
and battle cries
against fortified cities
and mighty fortresses.

17 The LORD warns everyone
who has sinned against him,
"I'll strike you blind!
Then your blood and your insides
will gush out like vomit.
18 Not even your silver or gold
can save you on that day
when I, the LORD, am angry.
My anger will flare up
like a furious fire
scorching the earth
and everyone on it."

Turn to the LORD

2 You disgraceful nation,
gather around,
2 before it's too late.
The LORD has set a time
when his fierce anger
will strike like a storm
and sweep you away.
3 If you humbly obey the LORD,
then come and worship him.
If you do right and are humble,
perhaps you will be safe
on that day when the LORD
turns loose his anger.

Judgment on Philistia

4 Gaza and Ashkelon
will be deserted
and left in ruins.
Ashdod will be emptied

[f]**1.8** *follow foreign customs*: Hebrew "wear foreign clothes." [g]**1.9** *worshipers . . . gods*: The Hebrew text has "all who jump over the threshold," which was a Philistine religious practice (see 1 Samuel 5.5). [h]**1.10,11** *Fish Gate, New Town, and Upper Hills . . . Lower Hollow*: Names for different sections of Jerusalem: Fish Gate was probably the main gate on the north side of the city; New Town was a newer section; Upper Hills may have been a suburb north of the city; Lower Hollow was probably on the southern edge of town.

2.4-7 Is 14.29-31; Jr 47.1-7; Ez 25.15-17; Jl 3.4-8; Am 1.6-8; Zec 9.5-7.

in broad daylight,
and Ekron[i] uprooted.
5 To you people of Philistia[j]
who live along the coast,
the LORD has this to say:
"I am now your enemy,
and I'll wipe you out!"

6 Your seacoast will be changed
into pastureland
and sheep pens.[k]
7 The LORD God hasn't forgotten
those survivors in Judah,
and he will help them—
his people will take your land
to use for pasture.
And when evening comes,
they will rest
in houses at Ashkelon.[l]

Judgment on Moab and Ammon

*8 The LORD All-Powerful,
the God of Israel, said:
I've heard Moab and Ammon
insult my people
and threaten their nation.[m]
9 And so, I swear by my very life
that Moab and Ammon will end up
like Sodom and Gomorrah—
covered with thornbushes
and salt pits forever.
Then my people who survive
will take their land.
10 This is how Moab and Ammon
will at last be repaid
for their pride—
and for sneering at the nation
that belongs to me,
the LORD All-Powerful.
11 I will fiercely attack.
Then every god on this earth
will shrink to nothing,
and everyone of every nation
will bow down to me,
right where they are.

Judgment on Ethiopia

12 People of Ethiopia,[n]
the sword of the LORD
will slaughter you!

Judgment on Assyria

13 The LORD will reach to the north
to crush Assyria
and overthrow Nineveh.[o]
14 Herds of wild animals
will live in its rubble;
all kinds of desert owls
will perch on its stones
and hoot in the windows.
Noisy ravens will be heard
inside its buildings,
stripped bare of cedar.[p]
15 This is the glorious city
that felt secure and said,
"I am the only one!"
Now it's merely ruins,
a home for wild animals.
Every passerby simply sneers
and makes vulgar signs.

Sinful Jerusalem

3 Too bad for that disgusting,
corrupt, and lawless city!
2 Forever rebellious
and rejecting correction,
Jerusalem refuses to trust
or obey the LORD God.
3 Its officials are roaring lions,
its judges are wolves;
in the evening they attack,
by morning nothing is left.
4 Jerusalem's prophets are proud
and not to be trusted.

[i]2.4 *Gaza . . . Ekron*: Gaza, Ashkelon, Ashdod, Ekron, and Gath (not mentioned because it was already destroyed) were the five major Philistine towns. [j]2.5 *people of Philistia*: The Hebrew text also mentions "Canaan" and "Cherethites," which are other ways of referring to the Philistines. [k]2.6 *pens*: One possible meaning for the difficult Hebrew text of verse 6. [l]2.7 *Ashkelon*: A Philistine town; see the note at 2.4. [m]2.8 *threaten their nation*: Or "boast about their own nation." [n]2.12 *Ethiopia*: The Hebrew text has "Cush," which was a region south of Egypt that included parts of the present countries of Ethiopia and Sudan. [o]2.13 *Nineveh*: The capital of Assyria; Nineveh was protected by a moat filled with water from the nearby Tigris River. [p]2.14 *stripped . . . cedar*: One possible meaning for the difficult Hebrew text.

2.8-11 a Is 15.1—16.14; 25.10-12; Jr 48.1-47; Ez 25.8-11; Am 1.13-15; **b** Jr 49.1-6; Ez 21.28-32; 25.1-7; Am 1.13-15. **2.9** Gn 19.24. **2.12** Is 18.1-7. **2.13-15** Is 10.5-34; 14.24-27; Nh 1.1—3.19.

The priests have disgraced
the place of worship
and abused God's Law.
5 All who do evil are shameless,
but the LORD does right
and is always fair.
With the dawn of each day,
God brings about justice.

6 The LORD wiped out nations
and left fortresses
crumbling in the dirt.
Their streets and towns
were reduced to ruins
and emptied of people.
7 God felt certain that Jerusalem
would learn to respect
and obey him.
Then he would hold back
from punishing the city
and not wipe it out.
But everyone there was eager
to start sinning again.

Nations Will Turn to the LORD

8 The LORD said:
Just wait for the day
when I accuse you nations.
I have decided on a day,
when I will bring together
every nation and kingdom
and punish them all
in my fiery anger.
I will become furious
and destroy the earth.

9 I will purify each language
and make those languages
acceptable for praising me.[q]
Then, with hearts united,
everyone will serve
only me, the LORD.
10 From across the rivers
of Ethiopia,[r]
my scattered people,
my true worshipers,
will bring offerings to me.

11 When that time comes,
you won't rebel against me
and be put to shame.
I'll do away with those
who are proud and arrogant.
Never will any of them
strut around
on my holy mountain.
12 But I, the LORD, won't destroy
any of your people
who are truly humble
and turn to me for safety.
13 The people of Israel who survive
will live right
and refuse to tell lies.
They will eat and rest
with nothing to fear.

A Song of Celebration

14 Everyone in Jerusalem and Judah,
celebrate and shout
with all your heart!
15 Zion, your punishment is over.
The LORD has forced your enemies
to turn and retreat.
Your LORD is King of Israel
and stands at your side;
you don't have to worry
about any more troubles.

16 Jerusalem, the time is coming,
when it will be said to you:
"Don't be discouraged
or grow weak from fear!
17 The LORD your God
wins victory after victory
and is always with you.
He celebrates and sings
because of you,
and he will refresh your life
with his love."[s]

The LORD's Promise to His People

18 The LORD has promised:
Your sorrow has ended,
and you can celebrate.[t]

[q] **3.9** *I will . . . praising me*: Or "I will change the hearts of all people and make them fit for praising me." [r] **3.10** *Ethiopia*: See the note at 2.12. [s] **3.17** *refresh . . . love*: Two ancient translations; Hebrew "silently show you his love." [t] **3.18** *celebrate*: One possible meaning for the difficult Hebrew text of verse 18.
3.13 Rev 14.5.

19 I will punish those
who mistreat you.
I will bring together the lame
and the outcasts,
then they will be praised,
instead of despised,
in every country on earth.

20 I will lead you home,
and with your own eyes
you will see me bless you
with all you once owned.
Then you will be famous
everywhere on this earth.
I, the LORD, have spoken!

HAGGAI

ABOUT THIS BOOK

By 520 B.C., many of the Jews had returned to Judah from the exile in Babylonia. The leaders were fairly well off, but most of the people were struggling just to survive. The Lord told Haggai that the reason the people had to struggle was because the temple still had not been rebuilt. Their lack of respect for the Lord's temple showed that they did not respect the Lord himself, and so he refused to bless them.

The people began work on the temple, and then the Lord promised to bless them and make them prosperous.

A QUICK LOOK AT THIS BOOK

- The Lord Says to Rebuild the Temple (1.1-15)
- The Lord Promises To Bless His People (2.1-19)
- The Lord Promises To Be with Zerubbabel (2.20-23)

Rebuild the Temple

1 On the first day of the sixth month
of the second year that Darius was
king of Persia,[a] the LORD told Haggai the
prophet to speak his message to the governor of Judah and to the high priest.

So Haggai told Governor Zerubbabel
and High Priest Joshua[b] 2-5 that the LORD
All-Powerful had said to them and to the
people:

You say this isn't the right time to
build a temple for me. But is it right
for you to live in expensive houses,[c]
while my temple is a pile of ruins? Just
look at what's happening. 6 You harvest
less than you plant, you never have
enough to eat or drink, your clothes
don't keep you warm, and your wages
are stored in bags full of holes.

7 Think about what I have said!
8 But first, go to the hills and get wood
for my temple, so I can take pride in it
and be worshiped there. 9 You expected much, but received only a little.
And when you brought it home, I
made that little disappear. Why have I
done this? It's because you hurry off to
build your own houses, while my temple is still in ruins. 10 That's also why
the dew doesn't fall and your harvest
fails. 11 And so, at my command everything will become barren—your farmland and pastures, your vineyards and
olive trees, your animals and you yourselves. All your hard work will be for
nothing.

12 Zerubbabel and Joshua, together with
the others who had returned from exile in
Babylonia, obeyed the LORD's message spoken by his prophet Haggai, and they started
showing proper respect for the LORD.
13 Haggai then told them that the LORD had

---

[a] **1.1** *sixth month . . . king of Persia*: Elul, the sixth month of the Hebrew calendar, from about mid-August to mid-September; the second year of the rule of Darius was 520 B.C. [b] **1.1** *Governor . . . Joshua*: Hebrew "Governor Zerubbabel son of Shealtiel and High Priest Joshua son of Jehozadak." [c] **1.2-5** *expensive houses*: Either houses with paneled interiors or with roofs; the temple was not yet completely rebuilt at this time.

1.1 Ezra 4.24—5.2; 6.14.

promised to be with them. 14 So the LORD God All-Powerful made everyone eager to work on his temple, especially Zerubbabel and Joshua. 15 And the work began on the twenty-fourth day of that same month.

The Glorious New Temple

2 1-2 On the twenty-first day of the next month,[d] the LORD told Haggai the prophet to speak this message to Governor Zerubbabel, High Priest Joshua, and everyone else:

3 Does anyone remember how glorious this temple used to be? Now it looks like nothing. 4 But cheer up! Because I, the LORD All-Powerful, will be here to help you with the work, 5 just as I promised your ancestors when I brought them out of Egypt. Don't worry. My Spirit is[e] right here with you.

6 Soon I will again shake the heavens and the earth, the sea and the dry land. 7 I will shake the nations, and their treasures[f] will be brought here. Then the brightness of my glory will fill this temple. 8 All silver and gold belong to me, 9 and I promise that this new temple will be more glorious than the first one. I will also bless this city[g] with peace.

The Past and the Future

10 On the twenty-fourth day of the ninth month,[h] the LORD God All-Powerful told the prophet Haggai 11 to ask the priests for their opinion on the following matter:

12 Suppose meat ready to be sacrificed to God is being carried in the folds of someone's clothing, and the clothing rubs against some bread or stew or wine or olive oil or any other food. Would those foods that were touched then become acceptable for sacrifice?

"Of course not," the priests answered.

13 Then Haggai said, "Suppose someone has touched a dead body and is considered unacceptable to worship God. If that person touches these foods, would they become unclean?"

"Of course they would," the priests answered.

14 So the LORD told Haggai to say:

That's how it is with this entire nation. Everything you do and every sacrifice you offer is unacceptable to me. 15 But from now on, things will get better. Before you started laying the foundation for the temple, 16 you recalled what life was like in the past.[i] When you wanted twenty bushels of wheat, there were only ten, and when you wanted fifty jars of wine, there were only twenty. 17 I made all of your hard work useless by sending mildew, mold, and hail—but you still did not return to me, your LORD.

18 Today you have completed the foundation for my temple, so listen to what your future will be like. 19 Although you have not yet harvested any grain, grapes, figs, pomegranates,[j] or olives, I will richly bless you in the days ahead.

God's Promise to Zerubbabel

20 That same day the LORD spoke to Haggai again and said:

21 Tell Governor Zerubbabel of Judah that I am going to shake the heavens and the earth 22 and wipe out kings and their kingdoms. I will overturn war chariots, and then cavalry troops will start slaughtering each other. 23 But tell my servant Zerubbabel that I, the LORD All-Powerful, have chosen him, and he will rule in my name.[k]

[d]**2.1,2** *the next month*: Tishri (also called Ethanim), the seventh month of the Hebrew calendar, from about mid-September to mid-October (see the note at 1.1). [e]**2.5** *My Spirit is*: Or "I am." [f]**2.7** *their treasures*: Hebrew "what they most desire." [g]**2.9** *city*: Or "temple." [h]**2.10** *ninth month*: Chislev, the ninth month of the Hebrew calendar, from about mid-November to mid-December. [i]**2.16** *you recalled . . . past*: One possible meaning for the difficult Hebrew text. [j]**2.19** *pomegranates*: A bright red fruit that looks like an apple. [k]**2.23** *rule in my name*: The Hebrew text has "be my signet ring," which signified authority.

2.3 Ezra 3.12. **2.5** Ex 29.45, 46. **2.6** He 12.26. **2.13** Nu 19.11-22.

ZECHARIAH

ABOUT THIS BOOK

The people of Jerusalem had problems. They had begun to rebuild the temple, but the new temple could never be as great as the original one. There was no king from David's family, and Judah was only a small part of the Medo-Persian Empire.

In the first part of this book (1–8) Zechariah tells how the Lord gave him eight meaningful visions to help the people overcome these problems. Someday, the Lord's chosen king would again rule in Jerusalem, and all the nations would turn to the Lord and become his people. But for now, the Lord had chosen Zerubbabel to be the governor and Joshua to be the high priest, and they were to be in charge of the Lord's people.

In the second part of this book (9–11) the Lord promised he would punish many of the nearby nations and also the leaders of Judah who had been unfaithful.

In the third part (12–14) the Lord gave Zechariah messages about a time even farther in the future, when Jerusalem and Judah will be attacked by all nations. Many of the people of Judah will be killed, but the Lord himself will appear and rescue his people. They will turn back to him, and he will forgive them. Then mountains around Jerusalem will be flattened, but Jerusalem will remain on the mountain towering high above the land around it. Life-giving streams will flow from Jerusalem, and all people on earth will worship the Lord.

The Lord promised that someday he would again choose a king for his people. In the New Testament both Matthew and John quote part of this verse from the book of Zechariah, to show that God had chosen Jesus to be that king:

Everyone in Jerusalem,
celebrate and shout!
Your king has won a victory,
and he is coming to you.
He is humble
and rides on a donkey;
he comes on the colt
of a donkey.
(9.9)

A QUICK LOOK AT THIS BOOK

- First Vision: Horses and Riders (1.1-17)
- Second Vision: Animal Horns (1.18-21)
- Third Vision: A Measuring Line (2.1-13)
- Fourth Vision: Joshua and Satan (3.1-10)
- Fifth Vision: A Lampstand and Olive Trees (4.1-14)
- Sixth Vision: A Flying Scroll (5.1-4)
- Seventh Vision: A Woman in a Basket (5.5-11)
- Eighth Vision: Four Chariots (6.1-8)
- Mourning and Celebrating (6.9—8.23)

- The Lord Will Rescue His People and Punish Their Enemies (9.1—11.3)
- Israel's Leaders Are Worthless Shepherds (11.4-17)
- Victory for Jerusalem (12.1-9)
- The People Will Mourn and Return to the Lord (12.10—13.9)
- The Final War and the Lord's Victory (14.1-21)

Turn to the LORD

1 I am the prophet Zechariah, the son of
Berechiah and the grandson of Iddo.
In the eighth month of the second year
that Darius was king of Persia,[a] the LORD
told me to say:

2-3 Israel, I, the LORD All-Powerful,
was very angry with your ancestors.
But if you people will return to me, I
will turn and help you. 4 Don't be stubborn like your ancestors. They were
warned by the earlier prophets[b] to give
up their evil and turn back to me, but
they paid no attention.

5 Where are your ancestors now?
Not even prophets live forever. 6 But
my warnings and my words spoken by
the prophets caught up with your ancestors. So they turned back to me and
said, "LORD All-Powerful, you have
punished us for our sins, just as you
had planned."

First Vision: Horses and Riders

7-8 On the twenty-fourth day of Shebat,[c]
which was the eleventh month of that
same year,[d] the LORD spoke to me in a vision during the night: In a valley among
myrtle trees,[e] I saw someone on a red
horse, with riders on red, brown, and white
horses behind him. 9 An angel was there to
explain things to me, and I asked, "Sir, who
are these riders?"

"I'll tell you," the angel answered.

10 Right away, the man standing among
the myrtle trees said, "These are the ones
the LORD has sent to find out what's happening on earth."

11 Then the riders spoke to the LORD's
angel, who was standing among the myrtle
trees, and they said, "We have gone everywhere and have discovered that the whole
world is at peace."

12 At this, the angel said, "LORD All-
Powerful, for seventy years you have been
angry with Jerusalem and the towns of Judah. When are you ever going to have
mercy on them?"

13 The LORD's answer was kind and
comforting. 14 So the angel told me to announce:

I, the LORD All-Powerful, am very
protective of Jerusalem. 15 For a while
I was angry at the nations, but now I
am furious, because they have made
things worse for Jerusalem and are not
the least bit concerned. 16 And so, I
will have pity on Jerusalem. The city
will be completely rebuilt, and my temple will stand again. 17 I also promise
that my towns will prosper—Jerusalem
will once again be my chosen city, and
I will comfort the people of Zion.

Second Vision: Animal Horns

18 Next, I saw four animal horns.[f]
19-21 The angel who was sent to explain was
there, and so I asked, "What do these
mean?"

His answer was, "These horns are the
nations that scattered the people of Judah,
Israel, and Jerusalem, and took away their
freedom."

[a] **1.1** *eighth month . . . second year . . . king of Persia*: Bul, the eighth month of the Hebrew calender, from about mid-October to mid-November; the second year of the rule of Darius was 520 B.C.
[b] **1.4** *the earlier prophets*: Those who preached before the fall of Jerusalem in either 587 or 586 B.C. [c] **1.7,8** *Shebat*: The eleventh month of the Hebrew calendar, from about mid-January to mid-February. [d] **1.7,8** *that same year*: See verse 1 and the note there. [e] **1.7,8** *myrtle trees*: Evergreen shrubs, which in ancient times were symbols of fertility and renewal.
[f] **1.18** *animal horns*: Horns, especially those of a bull, were symbols of power in ancient times. The number "four" would signal completeness, one representing each of the four directions.
1.1 Ezra 4.24—5.1; 6.14. **1.7,8** **a** Rev 6.4; **b** Rev 6.2.

Then the LORD showed me four blacksmiths, and I asked, "What are they going to do?"

He replied, "They are going to terrify and crush those horns."

Third Vision: A Measuring Line

2 This time I saw someone holding a measuring line, 2 and I asked, "Where are you going?"

"To measure Jerusalem," was the answer. "To find out how wide and long it is."

3 The angel who had spoken to me was leaving, when another angel came up to him 4 and said, "Hurry! Tell that man with the measuring line that Jerusalem won't have any boundaries. It will be too full of people and animals even to have a wall. 5 The LORD himself has promised to be a protective wall of fire surrounding Jerusalem, and he will be its shining glory in the heart of the city."

A Call to Action

6 The LORD says to his people, "Run! Escape from the land in the north, where I scattered you to the four winds. 7 Leave Babylonia and hurry back to Zion."

8 Then the glorious LORD All-Powerful ordered me to say to the nations that had raided and robbed Zion:

Zion is as precious to the LORD as
are his eyes. Whatever you do to Zion,
you do to him. 9 And so, he will put
you in the power of your slaves, and
they will raid and rob you. Then you
will know that I am a prophet of the
LORD All-Powerful.

10 City of Zion, sing and celebrate!
The LORD has promised to come and
live with you. 11 When he does, many
nations will turn to him and become
his people. At that time you will know
that I am a prophet of the LORD All-
Powerful. 12 Then Judah will be his
part of the holy land, and Jerusalem
will again be his chosen city.

13 Everyone, be silent!
The LORD is present
and moving about
in his holy place.

Fourth Vision: Joshua and Satan

3 I was given another vision. This time Joshua the high priest was standing in front of the LORD's angel. And there was Satan, standing at Joshua's right side, ready to accuse him. 2 But the LORD said, "Satan, you are wrong. Jerusalem is my chosen city, and this man was rescued like a stick from a flaming fire."

3 Joshua's clothes were filthy. 4 So the angel told some of the people to remove Joshua's filthy clothes. Then he said to Joshua, "This means you are forgiven. Now I will dress you in priestly clothes."

5 I spoke up and said, "Also put a clean priestly turban on his head." Then they dressed him in priestly clothes and put the turban on him, while the LORD's angel stood there watching.

6 After this, the angel encouraged Joshua by telling him that the LORD All-Powerful had promised:

7 If you truly obey me, I will put you
in charge of my temple, including the
courtyard around it, and you will be allowed to speak at any time with the
angels standing beside me.[g] 8 Listen
carefully, High Priest Joshua and all of
you other priests. You are a sign of
things to come, because I am going to
bring back my servant, the Chosen
King.[h]

9 Joshua, I have placed in front of
you a stone with seven sides. I will engrave something on that stone, and in
a single day I will forgive this guilty
country. 10 Then each of you will live
at peace and entertain your friends in
your own vineyard and under your
own fig trees.

[g]**3.7** *with the angels . . . me*: Or "with me." The angels are members of God's Council, who stand beside the throne of God in heaven and are allowed to speak with him and for him. [h]**3.8** *Chosen King*: The Hebrew text has "Sprout" or "Branch," a term used of royalty (see Isaiah 11.1).

3.1 **a** Ezra 5.2; **b** Rev 12.10. **3.2** Jd 9. **3.8** Jr 23.5; 33.15; Zec 6.12, 13.
3.10 Mic 4.4.

Fifth Vision: A Lampstand and Olive Trees

4 The angel who explained the visions
woke me from what seemed like sleep.
2 Then he asked, "What do you see?"
"A solid gold lampstand with an oil container above it," I answered. "On the stand
are seven lamps, each with seven flames.
3 One olive tree is on the right side and another on the left of the oil container. 4 But,
sir, what do these mean?"
5 Then he asked, "Don't you know?"
"No sir," I replied.
6 So the angel explained that it was the
following message of the LORD to Zerubbabel:[i]

I am the LORD All-Powerful. So don't
depend on your own power or strength,
but on my Spirit. 7 Zerubbabel, that
mountain in front of you will be leveled to the ground. Then you will bring
out the temple's most important stone
and shout, "God has been very kind."[j]

8 The LORD spoke to me again and said:

9 Zerubbabel laid the foundation
for the temple, and he will complete
it. Then everyone will know that
you were sent by me, the LORD All-
Powerful. 10 Those who have made
fun of this day of small beginnings will
celebrate when they see Zerubbabel
holding this important stone.[k]

Those seven lamps represent my
eyes—the eyes of the LORD—and they
see everything on this earth.

11 Then I asked the angel, "What about
the olive trees on each side of the lampstand? What do they represent? 12 And
what is the meaning of the two branches
from which golden olive oil[l] flows through
the two gold pipes?"
13 "Don't you know?" he asked.
"No sir, I don't," was my answer.
14 Then he told me, "These branches
are the two chosen leaders[m] who stand beside the Lord of all the earth."

Sixth Vision: A Flying Scroll

5 When I looked the next time, I saw a
flying scroll,[n] 2 and the angel asked,
"What do you see?"
"A flying scroll," I answered. "About
thirty feet long and fifteen feet wide."
3 Then he told me:

This scroll puts a curse on everyone
in the land who steals or tells lies. The
writing on one side tells about the destruction of those who steal, while the
writing on the other side tells about
the destruction of those who lie.

4 The LORD All-Powerful has said, "I
am sending this scroll into the house
of everyone who is a robber or tells lies
in my name, and it will remain there
until every piece of wood and stone in
that house crumbles."

Seventh Vision: A Woman in a Basket

5 Now the angel who was there to explain the visions came over and said, "Look
up and tell me what you see coming."
6 "I don't know what it is," was my reply.
"It's a big basket," he said. "And it shows
what everyone in the land has in mind."[o]
7 The lead cover of the basket was opened,
and in the basket was a woman. 8 "This
woman represents evil," the angel explained.
Then he threw her back into the basket
and slammed the heavy cover down tight.
9 Right after this I saw two women coming through the sky like storks with wings
outstretched in the wind. Suddenly they
lifted the basket into the air, 10 and I asked
the angel, "Where are they taking the
basket?"
11 "To Babylonia,"[p] he answered, "where

[i] **4.6** *Zerubbabel*: Governor of Judah (see Haggai 1.1). [j] **4.7** *God . . . kind*: Or "What a beautiful stone." [k] **4.10** *important stone*: Or "measuring line (with a stone attached to the end)." [l] **4.12** *golden olive oil*: The Hebrew text has "gold," which possibly refers to the color of the olive oil as it flows through the gold pipe. [m] **4.14** *chosen leaders*: The Hebrew text has "people of oil." In ancient times prophets, priests, and kings had olive oil poured over their heads to show that they had been chosen (see 1 Samuel 10.1; 16.13). [n] **5.1** *scroll*: A roll of paper or special leather used for writing on. [o] **5.6** *what . . . mind*: Hebrew; one ancient translation "the sin of everyone in the land." [p] **5.11** *Babylonia*: The Hebrew text has "Shinar," an ancient name for Babylonia.

4.3 Rev 11.4. **4.6** Ezra 5.2. **4.10** Rev 5.6. **4.11** Rev 11.4.

they will build a house for the basket and
set it down inside."

Eighth Vision: Four Chariots

6 Finally, I looked up and saw four chariots coming from between two bronze
mountains. 2 The first chariot was pulled
by red horses, and the second by black
horses; 3 the third chariot was pulled by white
horses, and the fourth by spotted gray horses.
4 "Sir," I asked the angel. "What do
these stand for?"
5 Then he explained, "These are the
four winds[q] of heaven, and now they are
going out, after presenting themselves to
the Lord of all the earth. 6 The chariot with
black horses goes toward the north, the
chariot with white horses goes toward the
west,[r] and the one with spotted horses goes
toward the south."
7 The horses came out eager to patrol
the earth, and the angel told them, "Start
patrolling the earth."

When they had gone on their way, 8 he
shouted to me, "Those that have gone to
the country in the north will do what the
LORD's Spirit[s] wants them to do there."

The Chosen Leader

9 The LORD said to me:
10-11 Heldai, Tobijah, and Jedaiah
have returned from Babylonia. Collect
enough silver and gold from them to
make a crown.[t] Then go with them to
the house of Josiah son of Zephaniah
and put the crown on the head of the
high priest Joshua son of Jehozadak.[u]
12-13 Tell him that I, the LORD All-
Powerful, say, "Someone will reach out
from here like a branch and build a
temple for me. I will name him
'Branch,' and he will rule with royal
honors. A priest will stand beside his
throne,[v] and the two of them will be
good friends. 14 This crown will be kept
in my temple as a reminder and will be
taken care of by Heldai,[w] Tobijah,
Jedaiah, and Josiah."[x]
15 When people from distant lands come
and help build the temple of the LORD All-
Powerful, you will know that the LORD is
the one who sent me. And this will happen,
if you truly obey the LORD your God.

A Question about Going without Eating

7 On the fourth day of Chislev, the ninth
month of the fourth year that Darius
was king of Persia,[y] the LORD again spoke
to me. 2-3 It happened after the people of
Bethel had sent Sharezer with Regem-
Melech and his men to ask the priests in
the LORD's temple and the prophets to pray
for them. So they prayed, "Should we
mourn and go without eating during the
fifth month,[z] as we have done for many
years?"
4-5 It was then that the LORD All-
Powerful told me to say to everyone in the
country, including the priests:
For seventy years you have gone
without eating during the fifth and
seventh months of the year. But did
you really do it for me? 6 And when
you eat and drink, isn't it for your own
enjoyment? 7 My message today is the
same one I commanded the earlier
prophets[a] to speak to Jerusalem and
its villages when they were prosperous,

[q]**6.5** *winds*: Or "spirits." The Hebrew word may mean either. [r]**6.6** *goes toward the west*: Or "follows behind." [s]**6.8** *LORD's Spirit*: Or "LORD." [t]**6.10,11** *a crown*: Two ancient translations; Hebrew "some crowns." [u]**6.10,11** *Heldai . . . Jehozadak*: Or "Go to the house of Josiah son of Zephaniah, where you will find Heldai, Tobijah, and Jedaiah, who have returned from Babylonia. Collect enough silver and gold from them to make a crown. Then put it on the head of the high priest Joshua son of Jehozadak." [v]**6.12,13** *stand beside his throne*: Or "sit on a throne." [w]**6.14** *Heldai*: One ancient translation; Hebrew "Helem." [x]**6.14** *Josiah*: One ancient translation; Hebrew "Hen." [y]**7.1** *Chislev . . . fourth year . . . king of Persia*: Chislev, the ninth month of the Hebrew calendar, from about mid-November to mid-December; the fourth year of the rule of Darius was 518 B.C. [z]**7.2,3** *fifth month*: Ab, the fifth month of the Hebrew calendar, from about mid-July to mid-August. The temple was destroyed by the Babylonians in the year 587 or 586 B.C. [a]**7.7** *the earlier prophets*: See the note at 1.4.

6.2 **a** Rev 6.4; **b** Rev 6.5. **6.3** Rev 6.2. **6.5** Rev 7.1, 2. **6.12** Jr 23.5; 33.15; Zec 3.8.

and when all of Judah, including the
Southern Desert and the hill country,
was filled with people.
8-9 So once again, I, the LORD All-
Powerful, tell you, "See that justice is
done and be kind and merciful to one
another! 10 Don't mistreat widows or
orphans or foreigners or anyone who is
poor, and stop making plans to hurt
each other."
11-12 But everyone who heard those
prophets, stubbornly refused to obey.
Instead, they turned their backs on
everything my Spirit[b] had commanded
the earlier prophets to preach. So I,
the LORD, became angry 13 and said,
"You people paid no attention when I
called out to you, and now I'll pay no
attention when you call out to me."
14 That's why I came with a whirlwind and scattered them among foreign nations, leaving their lovely country empty of people and in ruins.

The LORD's Promises to Zion

8 The LORD All-Powerful said to me:
2 I love Zion so much that her
enemies make me angry. 3 I will return
to Jerusalem and live there on Mount
Zion. Then Jerusalem will be known as
my faithful city, and Zion will be
known as my holy mountain.
4 Very old people with walking
sticks will once again sit around in
Jerusalem, 5 while boys and girls play
in the streets. 6 This may seem impossible for my people who are left, but it
isn't impossible for me, the LORD All-
Powerful. 7 I will save those who were
taken to lands in the east and the west,
8 and I will bring them to live in
Jerusalem. They will be my people,
and I will be their God, faithful to
bring about justice.
9 I am the LORD All-Powerful! So
don't give up. Think about the message
my prophets spoke when the foundation of my temple was laid. 10 Before
that time, neither people nor animals
were rewarded for their work, and no
one was safe anywhere, because I had
turned them against each other.
11 My people, only a few of you are
left, and I promise not to punish you
as I did before. 12 Instead, I will make
sure that your crops are planted in
peace and your vineyards are fruitful,
that your fields are fertile and the dew
falls from the sky. 13 People of Judah
and Israel, you have been a curse to
the nations, but I will save you and
make you a blessing to them. So don't
be afraid or lose courage.
14 When your ancestors made me
angry, I decided to punish you with
disasters, and I didn't hold back.
15 Now you no longer need to be
afraid. I have decided to treat Jerusalem and Judah with kindness. 16 But
you must be truthful with each other,
and in court you must give fair decisions that lead to peace. 17 Don't ever
plan evil things against others or tell
lies under oath. I, the LORD, hate such
things.

A Time of Celebration

18 The LORD All-Powerful told me to say:
19 People of Judah, I, the LORD, demand that whenever you go without
food as a way of worshiping me, it
should become a time of celebration.
No matter if it's the fourth month, the
fifth month, the seventh month, or the
tenth month, you should have a joyful
festival. So love truth and live at
peace.
20 I tell you that people will come
here from cities everywhere. 21 Those
of one town will go to another and
say, "We're going to ask the LORD All-
Powerful to treat us with kindness.
Come and join us."
22 Many people from strong nations
will come to Jerusalem to worship me
and to ask me to treat them with kindness. 23 When this happens, ten people from nations with different languages will grab a Jew by his clothes
and say, "Let us go with you. We've

[b]**7.11,12** *my Spirit*: Or "I."
8.16 Eph 4.25.

heard that God is on your side." I, the
LORD All-Powerful, have spoken!

Israel's Enemies Will Be Punished

9 This is a message
from the LORD:
His eyes are on everyone,
especially the tribes
of Israel.[c]
So he pronounces judgment
against the cities
of Hadrach and Damascus.[d]
2 Judgment will also fall
on the nearby city
of Hamath,
as well as on Tyre and Sidon,[e]
whose people are clever.
3 Tyre has built a fortress
and piled up silver and gold,
as though they were dust
or mud from the streets.
4 Now the Lord will punish Tyre
with poverty;
he will sink its ships
and send it up in flames.

5 Both Ashkelon and Gaza
will tremble with fear;
Ekron will lose all hope.
Gaza's king will be killed,
and Ashkelon emptied
of its people.
6 A mob of half-breeds
will settle in Ashdod,[f]
and the Lord himself
will rob Philistia of pride.

7 No longer will the Philistines
eat meat with blood in it
or any unclean food.[g]
They will become part
of the people of our God
from the tribe of Judah.
And God will accept
the people of Ekron,
as he did the Jebusites.[h]

8 God says, "I will stand guard
to protect my temple from those
who come to attack.
I know what's happening,
and no one will mistreat
my people ever again."

The LORD Tells about the Coming King

9 Everyone in Jerusalem,
celebrate and shout!
Your king has won a victory,
and he is coming to you.
He is humble
and rides on a donkey;
he comes on the colt
of a donkey.
10 I, the LORD, will take away
war chariots and horses
from Israel[i] and Jerusalem.
Bows that were made for battle
will be broken.
I will bring peace to nations,
and your king will rule
from sea to sea.
His kingdom will reach
from the Euphrates River
across the earth.

The LORD Promises To Rescue Captives

11 When I made a sacred agreement
with you, my people,
we sealed it with blood.[j]

[c]**9.1** *His . . . Israel*: One possible meaning for the difficult Hebrew text. [d]**9.1** *Hadrach and Damascus*: Hadrach was north of both Damascus (the main city of Syria) and Hamath (verse 2). [e]**9.2** *Tyre and Sidon*: Phoenician cities. [f]**9.5,6** *Ashkelon and Gaza . . . Ekron . . . Ashdod*: Philistine cities. [g]**9.7** *eat . . . food*: The Philistines will become part of Judah and no longer eat meat with blood in it (see Genesis 9.4) or any other forbidden foods (see Leviticus 11.1-23; Deuteronomy 14.3-21). [h]**9.7** *Jebusites*: The original people of Canaan, who lived in Jerusalem before it was captured by David (see 2 Samuel 5.6-10) and were later accepted as part of Israel. [i]**9.10** *Israel*: The Hebrew text has "Ephraim," the leading tribe of the northern kingdom of Israel, which sometimes stands for the whole kingdom. [j]**9.11** *an agreement . . . blood*: The agreement at Mount Sinai (see Exodus 24.7, 8).

9.1 Is 17.1-3; Jr 49.23-27; Am 1.3-5. **9.1-4** Is 23.1-18; Ez 26.1—28.26; Jl 3.4-8; Am 1.9, 10; Mt 11.21, 22; Lk 10.13, 14. **9.5-7** Is 14.29-31; Jr 47.1-7; Ez 25.15-17; Jl 3.4-8; Am 1.6-8; Zep 2.4-7. **9.9** Mt 21.5; Jn 12.15. **9.10** Ps 72.8. **9.11** Ex 24.8.

Now some of you are captives
in waterless pits,
but I will come to your rescue
12 and offer you hope.
Return to your fortress,
because today I will reward you
with twice what you had.
13 I will use Judah as my bow
and Israel[k] as my arrow.
I will take the people of Zion
as my sword
and attack the Greeks.

The LORD Will Protect His People

14 Like a cloud, the LORD God
will appear over his people,
and his arrows will flash
like lightning.
God will sound his trumpet
and attack in a whirlwind
from the south.
15 The LORD All-Powerful
will protect his people,
and they will trample down
the sharpshooters
and their slingshots.
They will drink and get rowdy;
they will be as full as a bowl
at the time of sacrifice.

16 The LORD God will save them
on that day,
because they are his people,
and they will shine on his land
like jewels in a crown.
17 How lovely they will be.
Young people will grow there
like grain in a field
or grapes in a vineyard.

A Bright Future for Judah and Israel

10 I, the LORD, am the one
who sends storm clouds
and showers of rain
to make fields produce.
So when the crops need rain,
you should pray to me.
2 You can't believe idols
and fortunetellers,
or depend on the hope
you receive from witchcraft
and interpreters of dreams.
But you have tried all of these,
and now you are like sheep
without a shepherd.

3 I, the LORD All-Powerful,
am fiercely angry
with you leaders,
and I will punish you.
I care for my people,
the nation of Judah,
and I will change
this flock of sheep
into charging war horses.

4 From this flock will come leaders
who will be strong
like cornerstones and tent pegs
and weapons of war.
5 They will join in the fighting,
and together they will trample
their enemies like mud.
They will fight,
because I, the LORD,
will be on their side.
And they will crush
the enemy cavalry.

6 I will strengthen
the kingdoms of Judah
and Israel.[l]
And I will show mercy
because I am the LORD,
their God.
I will answer their prayers
and bring them home.
Then it will seem as though
I had never rejected them.
7 Israel[m] will be like
a tribe of warriors
celebrating with wine.
When their children see this,

[k]**9.13** *Israel*: Hebrew "Ephraim" (see the note at 9.10). [l]**10.6** *Israel*: The Hebrew text has "family of Joseph," the ancestor of Ephraim and Manasseh, the leading tribes of the northern kingdom (Israel). [m]**10.7** *Israel*: Hebrew "Ephraim" (see the note at 9.10).
10.2 Mt 9.36; Mk 6.34.

they will also be happy
because of me, the LORD.

8 I will give a signal
for them to come together
because I have rescued them.
And there will be as many
as ever before.
9 Although I scattered my people
in distant countries,
they won't forget me.
Once their children are raised,[n]
they will return—
10 I will bring them home
from Egypt and Assyria,
then let them settle
as far as Gilead and Lebanon,
until the land overflows
with them.
11 My people will go through
an ocean of troubles,
but I will overcome the waves
and dry up the deepest part
of the Nile.
Assyria's great pride
will be put down,
and the power of Egypt
will disappear.
12 I'll strengthen my people
because of who I am,
and they will follow me.
I, the LORD, have spoken!

Trouble for Israel's Enemies

11 Lebanon, open your gates!
Let the fire come in
to destroy your cedar trees.
2 Cry, you cyprus trees!
The glorious cedars have fallen
and are rotting.
Cry, you oak trees of Bashan!
The dense forest
has been chopped down.
3 Listen! Shepherds are crying.
Their glorious pastures
have been ruined.
Listen! Lions are roaring.
The forests of the Jordan Valley
are no more to be found.

Worthless Shepherds

4 The LORD my God said to me:
Tend those sheep doomed for
slaughter! 5 The people who buy and
butcher them go unpunished, while
everyone who sells them says, "Praise
the LORD! I'm rich." Not even their
shepherds have pity on them.
6 Tend those sheep because I, the
LORD, will no longer have pity on the
people of this earth. I'll turn neighbor
against neighbor and make them
slaves of a king. They will bring disaster on the earth, and I'll do nothing to
rescue any of them.
7 So I became a shepherd of those sheep
doomed to be slaughtered by the sheep
dealers.[o] And I gave names to the two
sticks I used for tending the sheep: One of
them was named "Mercy" and the other
"Unity." 8 In less than a month, I became
impatient with three shepherds who didn't
like me, and I got rid of them. 9 Then I
said, "I refuse to be your shepherd. Let the
sheep that are going to die, go on and die,
and those that are going to be destroyed, go
on and be destroyed. Then let the others
eat one another alive."
10 On that same day, I broke the stick
named "Mercy" to show that the LORD had
canceled his agreement with all people.
11 The sheep dealers who saw me knew
right away that this was a message from the
LORD. 12-13 I told them, "Pay me my wages,
if you think you should; otherwise, forget
it." So they handed me my wages, a measly
thirty pieces of silver.
Then the LORD said, "Throw the money
into the treasury."[p] So I threw the money into
the treasury at the LORD's temple. 14 Then I
broke the stick named "Unity" and canceled the ties between Judah and Israel.
15 Next, the LORD said to me, "Act like a
shepherd again—this time a worthless
shepherd. 16 Once more I am going to let a
worthless nobody rule the land—one who
won't care for the strays or search for the
young or heal the sick or feed the healthy.

[n] **10.9** *Once . . . raised*: One possible meaning for the difficult Hebrew text. [o] **11.7** *by the sheep dealers*: One ancient translation; Hebrew "especially the weak ones." [p] **11.12,13** *Throw . . . treasury*: Hebrew "Throw the money to the potter."

10.9,10 Ba 2.20-32. **11.12,13** Mt. 26.15; Mt 27.9, 10.

He will just dine on the fattest sheep, leaving nothing but a few bones."

17 You worthless shepherd,
deserting the sheep!
I hope a sword
will cripple your arm
and blind your right eye.

Victory for Jerusalem

12 This is a message from the LORD
about Israel:
I am the LORD! I stretched out the
heavens; I put the earth on its foundations and gave breath to humans. 2 I
have decided that Jerusalem will become a bowl of wine that makes the
neighboring nations drunk. And when
Jerusalem is attacked, Judah will also
be attacked.[q] 3 But I will turn Jerusalem into a heavy stone that crushes
anyone who tries to lift it.
When all nations on earth surround
Jerusalem, 4 I will make every horse
panic and every rider confused. But at
the same time, I will watch over Judah. 5 Then every clan in Judah will
realize that I, the LORD All-Powerful,
am their God, and that I am the
source of their strength.
6 At that time I will let the clans of
Judah be like a ball of fire in a wood
pile or a fiery torch in a hay stack. Then
Judah will send the surrounding nations
up in smoke. And once again the city of
Jerusalem will be filled with people.
7 But I will first give victory to Judah, so the kingdom of David and the
city of Jerusalem in all of their glory
won't be thought of more highly than
Judah itself. 8 I, the LORD God, will
protect Jerusalem. Even the weakest
person there will be as strong as David,
and David's kingdom will rule as
though my very own angel were its
leader. 9 I am determined to wipe out
every nation that attacks Jerusalem.

Mourning for the One Pierced with a Spear

10 I, the LORD, will make the descendants of David and the people of Jerusalem
feel deep sorrow and pray when they see
the one they pierced with a spear. They will
mourn and weep for him, as parents weep
over the death of their only child or their
first-born. 11 On that day the people of
Jerusalem will mourn as much as everyone
did for Hadad Rimmon[r] on the flatlands
near Megiddo. 12 Everyone of each family
in the land will mourn, and the men will
mourn separately from the women. This
includes those from the family of David,
and the families of Nathan, 13 Levi,
Shimei,[s] 14 and all other families as well.

Getting Rid of Idols and False Prophets

13 In the future there will be a fountain, where David's descendants
and the people of Jerusalem can wash away
their sin and guilt.
2 The LORD All-Powerful says:
When that time comes, I will get rid
of every idol in the country, and they
will be forgotten forever. I will also do
away with their prophets and those evil
spirits that control them. 3 If any such
prophets ever appear again, their own
parents must warn them that they will
die for telling lies in my name—the
name of the LORD. If those prophets
don't stop speaking, their parents must
then kill them with a sword.
4 Those prophets will be ashamed
of their so-called visions, and they
won't deceive anyone by dressing like a
true prophet. 5 Instead, they will say,
"I'm no prophet. I've been a farmer all
my life."[t]
6 And if any of them are asked why
they are wounded,[u] they will answer,
"It happened at the house of some
friends."

[q] **12.2** *Judah . . . attacked*: One possible meaning for the difficult Hebrew text. [r] **12.11** *Hadad Rimmon*: Not mentioned elsewhere in the Old Testament. [s] **12.13** *Shimei*: A descendant of Gershon son of Levi (see Numbers 3.18). [t] **13.5** *I've . . . my life*: One possible meaning for the difficult Hebrew text. [u] **13.6** *wounded*: Probably from slashing themselves in the worship of a false god (see 1 Kings 18.28).
12.10 Jn 19.34, 37; Rev 1.7.

A Wounded Shepherd and Scattered Sheep

7 The LORD All-Powerful said:

My sword, wake up! Attack
my shepherd and friend.
Strike down the shepherd!
Scatter the little sheep,
and I will destroy them.
8 Nowhere in the land
will more than a third of them
be left alive.
9 Then I will purify them
and put them to the test,
just as gold and silver
are purified and tested.
They will pray in my name,
and I will answer them.
I will say, "You are my people,"
and they will reply,
"You, LORD, are our God!"

War and Victory

14 The LORD will have his day. And
when it comes, everything that was
ever taken from Jerusalem will be returned
and divided among its people. 2 But first,
he will bring many nations to attack
Jerusalem—homes will be robbed, women
raped, and half of the population dragged
off, though the others will be allowed to
remain.

3 The LORD will attack those nations like
a warrior fighting in battle. 4 He will take
his stand on the Mount of Olives east of
Jerusalem, and the mountain will split in
half, forming a wide valley that runs from
east to west. 5 Then you people will escape
from the LORD's mountain, through this
valley, which reaches to Azal.[v] You will run
in all directions, just as everyone did when
the earthquake struck[w] in the time of King
Uzziah of Judah. Afterwards, the LORD my
God will appear with his holy angels.

6 It will be a bright day that won't turn
cloudy.[x] 7 And the LORD has decided when
it will happen—this time of unending day.

8 In both summer and winter, life-giving
streams will flow from Jerusalem, half
of them to the Dead Sea in the east and
half to the Mediterranean Sea in the west.
9 Then there will be only one LORD who
rules as King and whose name is worshiped
everywhere on earth.

10-11 From Geba down to Rimmon[y]
south of Jerusalem, the entire country will
be turned into flatlands, with Jerusalem
still towering above. Then the city will be
full of people, from Benjamin Gate, Old
Gate Place, and Hananel Tower in the
northeast part of the city over to Corner
Gate in the northwest and down to King's
Wine Press in the south. Jerusalem will always be secure and will never again be
destroyed.

12 Here is what the LORD will do to those
who attack Jerusalem: While they are
standing there, he will make their flesh rot
and their eyes fall from their sockets and
their tongues drop out. 13 The LORD will
make them go into a frenzy and start
attacking each other, 14-15 until even the
people of Judah turn against those in
Jerusalem.[z] This same terrible disaster will
also strike every animal nearby, including
horses, mules, camels, and donkeys. Finally, everything of value in the surrounding nations will be collected and brought
to Jerusalem—gold, silver, and piles of
clothing.

16 Afterwards, the survivors from those
nations that attacked Jerusalem will go
there each year to worship the King, the
LORD All-Powerful, and to celebrate the
Festival of Shelters. 17 No rain will fall on
the land of anyone in any country who
refuses to go to Jerusalem to worship
the King, the LORD All-Powerful. 18-19 This

[v] **14.5** *to Azal*: One possible meaning for the difficult Hebrew text. The location of Azal is unknown. [w] **14.5** *earthquake struck*: See Amos 1.1. [x] **14.6** *a bright . . . cloudy*: One possible meaning for the difficult Hebrew text. [y] **14.10,11** *From Geba down to Rimmon*: Approximately the northern and southern borders of Judah before the exile (see 2 Kings 23.8); Geba is about ten miles north of Jerusalem, and Rimmon is about ten miles north of Beersheba.
[z] **14.13-15** *each other . . . Jerusalem*: Or "each other. 14-15 But the people of Judah will fight on the side of Jerusalem."

13.7 Mt 26.31; Mk 14.27. **14.8** Ez 47.1; Jn 7.38; Rev 22.1. **14.10,11** Rev 22.3. **14.16** Lv 23.39-43.

horrible disaster will strike the Egyptians and everyone else who refuses to go there for the celebration.

20-21 At that time the words "Dedicated to the LORD" will be engraved on the bells worn by horses. In fact, every ordinary cooking pot in Jerusalem will be just as sacred to the LORD All-Powerful as the bowls used at the altar. Any one of them will be acceptable for boiling the meat of sacrificed animals, and there will no longer be a need to sell special pots and bowls.[a]

[a] **14.20,21** *special pots and bowls*: Since all pots and bowls will be considered acceptable for use in the temple, there will be no more need for merchants to sell special ones to those people who come to offer sacrifices.

MALACHI

ABOUT THIS BOOK

The book of Malachi comes from a time after many people of Judah had returned from Babylonia, but just before Ezra and Nehemiah returned. The temple had been rebuilt, and the priests were again offering the people's sacrifices to the Lord. But times were hard, and the people had lost most of their hope for a bright new future in Judah. The people and the priests were no longer showing the proper respect for the Lord or for his temple. They were also making wrong sacrifices and disobeying the laws of God. They were mistreating the poor and powerless, and men were divorcing their wives.

Malachi challenged the people and especially the priests to be faithful to the agreement the Lord had made with Israel. They were to honor the Lord by offering the right kind of sacrifices and by giving ten percent of their harvest to him. Then the Lord would bless them.

A QUICK LOOK AT THIS BOOK

- The Lord's Love for Israel (1.1-5)
- Against the Priests (1.6—2.9)
- Broken Agreements (2.10-17)
- The Lord Will Come (3.1-4)
- Don't Cheat God (3.5-15)
- The Lord Will Reward Faithful People and Punish Those Who Are Evil (3.16—4.6)

---

1 I am Malachi. And this is the message that the LORD gave me for Israel.

The LORD's Love for Israel

2 Israel, I, the LORD, have loved you.
And yet you ask in what way have I loved
you. Don't forget that Esau was the brother
of your ancestor Jacob, but I chose Jacob
3 instead of Esau. And I turned Esau's hill
country into a barren desert where jackals[a]
roam. 4 Esau's descendants may say, "Although our nation Edom is in ruins, we will
rebuild."

But I, the LORD All-Powerful, promise to tear down whatever they build. Then everyone will know that I will never stop being angry with them as long as they are so sinful.

5 Israel, when you see this, you will shout, "The LORD's great reputation reaches beyond our borders."

Judgment against Priests

6 I, the LORD All-Powerful, have something to say to you priests. Children respect their fathers, and servants respect their masters. I am your father and your master, so why don't you respect me? You priests have insulted me, and now you ask, "How did we insult you?"

7 You embarrass me by offering worthless food on my altar. Then you ask, "How have we embarrassed you?" You have done it by saying, "What's so great about the LORD's altar?"

[a]**1.3** *jackals*: Desert animals related to wolves, but smaller.
1.2,3 Ro 9.13. **1.2-5** Is 34.5-17; 63.1-6; Jr 49.7-22; Ez 25.12-14; 35.1-15; Am 1.11, 12; Ob 1-14.

8 But isn't it wrong to offer animals that
are blind, crippled, or sick? Just try giving
those animals to your governor. That certainly wouldn't please him or make him
want to help you. 9 I am the LORD God All-
Powerful, and you had better try to please
me. You have sinned. Now see if I will have
mercy on any of you.
10 I wish someone would lock the doors
of my temple, so you would stop wasting
time building fires on my altar. I am not
pleased with you priests, and I refuse to accept any more of your offerings. 11 From
dawn until dusk my name is praised by
every nation on this earth, as they burn incense and offer the proper sacrifices to me.
12 But even you priests insult me by saying,
"There's nothing special about the LORD's
altar, and these sacrifices are worthless."
13 You get so disgusted that you even
make vulgar signs at me.[b] And for an offering, you bring stolen[c] animals or those that
are crippled or sick. Should I accept these?
14 Instead of offering the acceptable animals you have promised, you bring me
those that are unhealthy. I will punish you
for this, because I am the great King, the
LORD All-Powerful, and I am worshiped by
nations everywhere.

True and False Priests

2 I, the LORD All-Powerful, have something else to say to you priests. 2 You
had better take seriously the need to honor
my name. Otherwise, when you give a
blessing, I will turn it into a curse. In fact, I
have already done this, because you haven't
taken to heart your duties as priests. 3 I will
punish your descendants and rub your
faces in the manure from your animal sacrifices, and then be done with you.[d]
4 I am telling you this, so I can continue
to keep my agreement with your ancestor
Levi. 5 I blessed him with a full life, as I
had promised, and he kept his part of the
agreement by honoring me and respecting
my name. 6 He taught the truth and never
told lies, and he led a lot of people to turn
from sin, because he obeyed me and lived
right.
7 You priests should be eager to spread
knowledge, and everyone should come to
you for instruction, because you speak for
me, the LORD All-Powerful. 8 But you have
turned your backs on me. Your teachings
have led others to do sinful things, and you
have broken the agreement I made with
your ancestor Levi. 9 So I caused everyone
to hate and despise you, because you disobeyed me and failed to treat all people
alike.

A Broken Agreement

10 Don't you know that we all have God
as our Father? Didn't the one God create
each of us? Then why do you cheat each
other by breaking the agreement God made
with your ancestors? 11 You people in Judah and Jerusalem have been unfaithful to
the LORD. You have disgraced the temple
that he loves, and you have committed the
disgusting sin of worshiping other gods.[e]
12 I pray that the LORD will no longer let
those who are guilty belong to his people,
even if they eagerly decide to offer the
LORD a gift.[f]
13 And what else are you doing? You cry
noisily and flood the LORD's altar with your
tears, because he isn't pleased with your offerings and refuses to accept them. 14 And
why isn't God pleased? It's because he
knows that each of you men has been unfaithful to the wife you married when you
were young. You promised that she would
be your partner, but now you have broken
that promise. 15 Didn't God create you to
become like one person with your wife?[g]
And why did he do this? It was so you
would have children, and then lead them
to become God's people. Don't ever be unfaithful to your wife. 16 The LORD God All-
Powerful of Israel hates anyone who is
cruel enough to divorce his wife. So take
care never to be unfaithful!

[b] **1.13** *me*: Or "the altar." [c] **1.13** *stolen*: Or "injured." [d] **2.3** *and then be done with you*: One possible meaning for the difficult Hebrew text. [e] **2.11** *worshiping other gods*: Or "marrying the worshipers of other gods." [f] **2.12** *even if . . . gift*: One possible meaning for the difficult Hebrew text. [g] **2.15** *Didn't . . . wife*: One possible meaning for the difficult Hebrew text.
1.8 Dt 15.21. **2.4** Nu 3.11-13. **2.5** Nu 25.12, 13.

17 You have worn out the LORD with
your words. And yet, you ask, "How did we
do that?"

You did it by saying, "The LORD is
pleased with evil and doesn't care about
justice."

The Promised Messenger

3 1 I, the LORD All-Powerful,
will send my messenger
to prepare the way for me.
Then suddenly the Lord
you are looking for
will appear in his temple.
The messenger you desire
is coming with my promise,
and he is on his way.

A Day of Change

2 On the day the Lord comes, he will be
like a furnace that purifies silver or like
strong soap in a washbasin. No one will be
able to stand up to him. 3 The LORD will
purify the descendants of Levi,[h] as though
they were gold or silver. Then they will
bring the proper offerings to the LORD,
4 and the offerings of the people of Judah
and Jerusalem will please him, just as they
did in the past.

Don't Cheat God

5 The LORD All-Powerful said:

I'm now on my way to judge you.
And I will quickly condemn all who
practice witchcraft or cheat in marriage or tell lies in court or rob workers
of their pay or mistreat widows and orphans or steal the property of foreigners or refuse to respect me.

6 Descendants of Jacob, I am the
LORD All-Powerful, and I never
change. That's why you haven't been
wiped out, 7 even though you have ignored and disobeyed my laws ever
since the time of your ancestors. But if
you return to me, I will return to you.

And yet you ask, "How can we return?"

8 You people are robbing me, your
God. And, here you are, asking, "How
are we robbing you?"

You are robbing me of the offerings
and of the ten percent that belongs to
me.[i] 9 That's why your whole nation is
under a curse. 10 I am the LORD All-
Powerful, and I challenge you to put
me to the test. Bring the entire ten
percent into the storehouse, so there
will be food in my house. Then I will
open the windows of heaven and flood
you with blessing after blessing.[j] 11 I
will also stop locusts[k] from destroying
your crops and keeping your vineyards
from producing. 12 Everyone of every
nation will talk about how I have
blessed you and about your wonderful
land. I, the LORD All-Powerful, have
spoken!

13 You have said horrible things
about me, and yet you ask, "What have
we said?"

14 Here is what you have said: "It's
foolish to serve the LORD God All-
Powerful. What do we get for obeying
him and from going around looking
sad? 15 See how happy those arrogant
people are. Everyone who does wrong
is successful, and when they put God
to the test, they always get away with
it."

Faithfulness Is Rewarded

16 All those who truly respected the
LORD and honored his name started dis-
cussing these things, and when God saw
what was happening, he had their names[l]
written as a reminder in his book.

17 Then the LORD All-Powerful said:

You people are precious to me, and

[h]**3.3** *descendants of Levi*: The priests. [i]**3.8** *the ten percent . . . to me*: The people of Israel were supposed to give a tenth of their harvests and of their flocks and herds to the LORD (see Leviticus 27.30-33; Deuteronomy 14.22-29). [j]**3.10** *open the windows . . . blessing*: This may refer to rain, since there seems to have been a terrible drought at this time. [k]**3.11** *locusts*: A kind of grasshopper that comes in swarms and causes great damage to plant life. [l]**3.16** *names*: Or "deeds."

3.1 Mt 11.10; Mk 1.2; Lk 1.76; 7.27. **3.2** Jl 2.11; Rev 6.17. **3.6** Si 48.10. **3.10** Lv 27.30; Nu 18.21-24; Dt 12.5-19; 14.22-29; Ne 13.12.

when I come to bring justice, I will
protect you, just as parents protect an
obedient child. 18 Then everyone will
once again see the difference between
those who obey me by doing right and
those who reject me by doing wrong.

The Day of Judgment

The LORD said:

4 The day of judgment is certain to
come. And it will be like a red-hot furnace with flames that burn up proud and
sinful people, as though they were straw.
Not a branch or a root will be left. I, the
LORD All-Powerful, have spoken! 2 But for
you that honor my name, victory will shine
like the sun with healing in its rays, and
you will jump around like calves at play.
3 When I come to bring justice, you will
trample those who are evil, as though they
were ashes under your feet. I, the LORD All-
Powerful, have spoken!

4 Don't ever forget the laws and teachings I gave my servant Moses on Mount
Sinai.[m]

5 I, the LORD, promise to send the
prophet Elijah before that great and terrible
day comes. 6 He will lead children and parents to love each other more, so that when
I come, I won't bring doom to the land.

[m]**4.4** *Sinai*: Hebrew "Horeb."
4.5 Mt 11.14; 17.10-13; Mk 9.11-13; Lk 1.17; Jn 1.21.

DEUTEROCANONICALS/ APOCRYPHA

This group of books is known by two names. Catholics call them "Deuterocanonicals," a Greek term which means "second list". The name refers to the list of books that were included in the ancient Greek translation of the Old Testament but that were not found in the Hebrew Old Testament. Protestants more often use the term "Apocrypha," which originally meant "secret" or "to be read only in private." But as applied to these books, "Apocrypha" came to mean "not on the list" of the books of the Hebrew Old Testament.

The Council of Trent in A.D. 1546 stated that these books belong in the sacred Scriptures, and so Catholics accept them as part of the Old Testament. The Eastern churches also accept some or all of the books. Protestants do not accept them as part of the Old Testament, but they do believe that the books are special and are good for Christians to read, because they tell about God's people, the Jews, just before the time of Christ.

The writings included in the Deuterocanonicals are:

Tobith
Judith
Esther (Greek Version)
Wisdom of Solomon
Sirach
Baruch
Letter of Jeremiah
The Additions to Daniel:
The Prayer of Azariah and the Song of the Three Hebrews
Susanna
Bel and the Dragon
1 Maccabees
2 Maccabees

TOBIT

ABOUT THIS BOOK

The book of Tobit is named after one of the characters in the story, who was always faithful to God, even though others in his tribe in the northern kingdom of Israel were unfaithful and worshiped idols. Tobit was taken prisoner by the Assyrian army and led away to Nineveh, the Assyrian capital city. Tobit became rich, but then he lost his wealth and eyesight. Being blind kept him from going to a faraway town in the country of Media where he had left a lot of his money for safekeeping. Tobit was suffering so much that he prayed God would let him die, but then he quickly decided he should send his son Tobias to get the money before God answered his prayer.

Meanwhile, a relative named Sarah was in deep despair and asked God to let her die. Sarah was a beautiful young woman who lived in Media. She had been married seven times, but after each wedding and before she could sleep with her new husband, a demon had always killed him.

Tobit hired a man as a guide so Tobias could go to Media and bring back the money. But the man was actually the angel Raphael in disguise, and on the way to Media, he helped Tobias catch a fish whose insides had special powers to get rid of demons and to cure blindness. The rest of the story tells how Sarah and Tobias were married, the demon was chased away, Tobit was healed, and the family became wealthy again.

The book of Tobit teaches that just as God rescued and helped his faithful people Tobit and Sarah, someday he will once again rescue and help Jerusalem and the entire nation of Israel:

> *"God will punish your holy city*
> *because you have sinned,*
> *but if you obey him,*
> *he will again be kind to you."*
> *(13.9)*

A QUICK LOOK AT THIS BOOK

- Tobit and His Blindness (1.1—2.14)
- Tobit and Sarah Pray (3.1-16)
- Tobias and Raphael Go to Media (4.1—6.18)
- Sarah and Tobias Are Married (7.1—9.6)
- The Trip Back to Nineveh (10.1—11.5)
- Tobit Is Healed and Raphael Explains (11.6—12.22)
- Tobit Praises God (13.1—14.1)
- Tobit's Last Words (14.1-11)
- Tobias and Sarah Move to Media (14.12-15)

The CEV translation of the book of Tobit is based on the version of the book contained in the ancient biblical manuscript called "Codex Sinaiticus." In the CEV footnotes, this manuscript is referred to as "the primary manuscript." But it does not have two brief sections, 4.7-19 and 13.6-10. For these two passages, other ancient Greek manuscripts were used.

Tobit Obeyed God in Israel

1 My name is Tobit, and this book tells my story. I belong to the Asiel clan of the tribe of Naphtali, and my ancestors include my father Tobiel, my grandfather Hananiel, and then Aduel, Gabael, and Raphael. 2-3 My hometown is Thisbe in Galilee. Thisbe is south of the town of Kedesh in Naphtali, and it is northwest of Hazor and north of Phogor. But when Shalmaneser[a] was king of Assyria, I was one of many Jews who were captured by the Assyrian army and taken to Nineveh in Assyria.

All my life, I have been honest and done what is right. And even after we were brought here to Nineveh, I still gave help to my relatives and other Jews, whenever they were in need.

4 When I was a young man in Israel, my tribe had already rejected the descendants of David[b] as their kings. In fact, the people of Naphtali never went to Jerusalem to worship, even though that is where God's sacred temple had been built. The temple will be God's home forever, and so God said that the tribes of Israel must go there to offer sacrifices to him. 5 But my relatives and everyone else in my tribe went to the town of Dan and offered sacrifices to the idol that King Jeroboam[c] had made in the shape of a calf.[d] They also worshiped on hilltops all over Galilee.

6 I was the only one who went to Jerusalem for the festivals, just as God's unchanging command says to do.[e] I would hurry to Jerusalem with my sacrifices and offerings, whether they were the first part of the harvest, the firstborn of a sheep, the tenth of my livestock,[f] or the first wool from my sheep. 7 I would always take these offerings to the temple and give them to the priests at the altar. And I would always bring to Jerusalem the tenth of my grain, wine, olive oil, pomegranates,[g] figs, and other kinds of fruit, and I would give this tenth to the Levites who served in the temple. Also, for six years out of seven,[h] I would sell a second tenth of my harvest and take the money to Jerusalem and spend it there on a celebration.[i]

8 When I was young, my father died and left me as an orphan. So it was my grandmother[j] Deborah who told me to be careful and obey what the Law of Moses commanded about taking care of orphans and widows and of those who had come from other countries to become part of Israel. That's why every third year, I would set aside a third tenth[k] of my harvest and use part of it to hold a festival for them. Then I would give them the rest.

9 When I was old enough, I married a woman from my own tribe,[l] and we had a son. I named him Tobias.

Tobit Obeys God in Assyria

10 Later, after we were led away to Assyria as prisoners, we went to live in the city of Nineveh.[m] All my brothers and other relatives ate the same food as everyone else in Assyria. 11 But I decided to eat only what was allowed by the Law of Moses. 12 Obeying God was the most important thing in my life. 13 That's why God Most High made King Shalmaneser so pleased with me. Shalmaneser even put me in charge of buying all the supplies for his palace, 14 and I held that position for the rest of his life. I used to travel to Media[n] on business trips,

[a]**1.2,3** *Shalmaneser*: Shalmaneser V, ruled 727-722 B.C. [b]**1.4** *David*: Ruled about 1010-970 B.C. [c]**1.5** *King Jeroboam*: Jeroboam I, the first king of the northern kingdom, ruled 931-910 B.C. [d]**1.5** *the idol . . . calf*: See 1 Kings 12.26-33. [e]**1.6** *went to Jerusalem . . . command says to do*: See Deuteronomy 16.16. [f]**1.6** *livestock*: Or "newborn livestock." [g]**1.7** *pomegranates*: A reddish fruit with a hard rind. [h]**1.7** *six years out of seven*: The seventh year, the Israelites were not supposed to plant or harvest crops, but were supposed to let the land rest (see Leviticus 25.1-7). [i]**1.7** *take the money . . . celebration*: See Deuteronomy 14.22-27. [j]**1.8** *grandmother*: One possible meaning for the difficult Greek text. [k]**1.8** *a third tenth*: Some Greek manuscripts and one ancient translation; other Greek manuscripts have "the second tenth." [l]**1.9** *a woman from my own tribe*: Other Greek manuscripts and some ancient translations have "Anna, a woman from my own tribe" (see also 1.20). [m]**1.10** *Nineveh*: The capital city of Assyria. [n]**1.14** *Media*: A mountainous country east of Assyria and north of Persia, in what is today northwest Iran.

1.2 2 K 17.3; 18.9. **1.5** 1 K 12.28-30. **1.6** Dt 16.16.

and on one of those trips, I put one hundred twenty thousand of my own silver
coins[o] in bags, then left them for safekeeping with Gabael the brother of Gabri.
15 Later, after Shalmaneser died and his son
Sennacherib[p] took his place as king, Media
was no longer a safe place to travel. And so,
I never went back for my silver coins.

16 While Shalmanesser was king, I often
helped my relatives and other Jews when
they were in need. 17 I gave them food
when they were hungry and clothes when
they had none. And whenever I saw the
dead body of an Israelite tossed outside
Nineveh's city wall,[q] I always buried the
body. 18 King Sennacherib had invaded Judah and insulted God, the King of Heaven.
So God punished him and his army, forcing
him to run for his life. Sennacherib was
angry, and he killed many Israelites when
he got back to Assyria. But I secretly took
the bodies away and buried them, and
when Sennacherib looked for them, they
were gone.

19 Someone in Nineveh went to the king
and told him that I had secretly buried the
bodies. And when I found out that the king
knew what I had done and wanted me
hunted down and killed, I was afraid and
ran away. 20 Then the king seized everything I owned—all I had left were my wife
Anna and my son Tobias.

21 About forty days later, Sennacherib
was murdered by two of his sons. They ran
away to the Ararat mountains, and Sennacherib's other son Esarhaddon[r] became
king. Esarhaddon appointed Ahikar, the
son of my brother Hanael, to be in charge
of both the royal accounting department
and the treasury.[s] 22 My nephew Ahikar
had been in charge of the accounting department and the treasury under Sennacherib, and he had also been responsible
for Sennacherib's official ring[t] and his
wine. Ahikar talked Esarhaddon into letting
me come back to Nineveh.

Tobit Becomes Blind

2 I returned to my home while Esarhaddon[u] was king, and my wife Anna and
my son Tobias were allowed to come back
to me.

That year at the Harvest Festival,[v]
which is also called the Festival of Weeks,[w]
a wonderful dinner was prepared for me,
and I sat down to eat. 2 But so much food
was put on the table that I said to Tobias,
"Son, many other Israelites were brought to
Nineveh as captives. Go out and find someone who is poor and very loyal to God.
Bring him here to share this meal with us.
We will wait until you get back."

3 Tobias went out to look for some Israelites who were poor. But he returned
alone and said, "Father!"

"What's the matter?" I asked.

"An Israelite has been murdered!" Tobias answered. "He was strangled, then his
body was thrown down and left lying in the
street."[x]

4 We had not started eating, and so I
jumped up from the table and went to the
street where the body was. I brought it back
to my own home and left it in one of the
rooms, because I could not bury it until after dark.[y] 5 Then I washed myself and ate

[o]**1.14** *one hundred twenty thousand . . . silver coins*: The Greek text gives the total weight of the coins as 750 pounds, which would be one hundred twenty thousand of the silver coins mentioned in 5.15. [p]**1.15** *Sennacherib*: Ruled Assyria 705-681 B.C. Sennacherib's father was Sargon II (ruled 722-705 B.C.), who may have been the brother of Shalmaneser; but a previous king could be called the "father" of the current king. [q]**1.17** *the dead body . . . city wall*: Probably Israelites who had been put to death by the king. [r]**1.21** *Esarhaddon*: Ruled Assyria 681-669 B.C. [s]**1.21** *and the treasury*: Or "and so he had a lot of authority in every area of the king's government."
[t]**1.22** *Sennacherib's official ring*: The king would use this ring to put his special mark on documents to make them official. [u]**2.1** *Esarhaddon*: See the note at 1.21. [v]**2.1** *the Harvest Festival*: Greek "Pentecost"; at this festival, Israelites celebrated the wheat harvest. "Pentecost" means "fifty," and this festival was held in mid-spring, fifty days after Passover. [w]**2.1** *also called the Festival of Weeks*: Because it was held seven weeks and one day after Passover. [x]**2.3** *street*: The Greek text has "marketplace," usually a public square or wide street where people would buy and sell food and other items. [y]**2.4** *I could not . . . dark*: Probably because the Harvest Festival would end at sunset.
1.17 Job 31.16-20. **2.1** Ex 23.16. **2.5** Nu 19.11-13.

the festival meal, but I was very sad. [6] I remembered that the prophet Amos had said, "Your festivals and joyful singing will turn into sorrow,"[z] and [7] I began crying.

Later, after the sun had set, I went out and dug a grave and buried the body. [8] My neighbors made fun of me and said to each other, "Tobit had to go into hiding once, when the king tried to have him arrested and put to death for burying people like this one. You would think Tobit would be afraid to do the same thing again."

[9] That night after I washed, I went into my courtyard and lay down next to the wall. The night was so hot that I wanted to sleep under the open sky. [10] I didn't know that some sparrows were perched on the wall above me. Their fresh droppings fell right into my eyes, and a film of white spots started covering the clear part of my eyes.

I went to doctors and looked for a cure, but the more medicine they smeared on my eyes, the worse the white spots became, until at last I could not see a thing and was completely blind for four years. All my relatives felt sorry for me, and for two of those years, Ahikar gave me money to live on, but then he had to move to Elymais.

[11-12] After Ahikar left Nineveh, my wife worked at home. She would weave a piece of cloth, and when it was finished, she would send it to the owners of the weaving business, and they would pay her. Then, on the seventh day of the month of Dystrus,[a] my wife finished a piece of cloth and sent it to the owners. They gave her the regular payment, and they also gave her a young goat, so we could have a feast.

[13] When she came back, the goat was going, "baa, baa." So I yelled at her and said, "Where did you get that goat? You must have stolen it! Take it back to its owner. We shouldn't eat something that is stolen—it just wouldn't be right."

[14] She replied, "That goat was given to me as a gift along with the usual payment for my work!"

But I didn't believe her, and my face was red with anger as I told her to return the goat to its owners.

She answered, "Tobit, why have you changed so much? You used to be so kind, and, as everyone knows, you always did the right thing!"

Tobit Prays

3 My heart was filled with sorrow, and as I groaned and wept, I began praying:

[2] You, Lord, rule the world
with honesty, justice,
and mercy.
[3] Please be kind and forgive me,
especially for those sins
I didn't mean to commit.
And don't make me suffer
for the sins of my ancestors.
[4] They disobeyed your commands,
and so you let us be robbed,
or killed,
or laughed at and insulted,
while being led away as captives
all over the world.

[5] We didn't obey your commands;
we weren't faithful to you.
And so, you were right
to punish me many times.

[6] Do whatever you want with me!
Take away my life.
Send my body to the grave,
and set me free
from life on earth.
I would rather die
than to live in such suffering
and great sorrow,
listening to insults
I don't deserve.
Set me free; take me away
to my eternal place.
But please, Lord,
don't turn your back on me.

A Woman Named Sarah

[7] That same day, in the city of Ecbatana in Media,[b] a woman named Sarah, the

[z]**2.6** *Amos . . . sorrow*: See Amos 8.10. [a]**2.11,12** *Dystrus*: The month in the Macedonian calendar that is about the same as March. [b]**3.7** *Media*: See the note at 1.14.

2.6 Am 8.10.

daughter of Raguel, was being insulted by one of her father's servant women. 8 Sarah had gone through seven wedding ceremonies with seven different husbands, but each time, before she and her new husband had gone to bed on their wedding night, he was killed by the demon Asmodeus. That's why the servant had told her, "You've already been married seven times, and each of those times you have killed your husband before he could give you a son.[c] 9 So why do you strike at us because your husbands have died? Just go where they are! We hope you never have any children!"

10 Sarah's heart was heavy with sorrow, and she was crying as she went to an upstairs room in her father's house, where she planned to hang herself. But after thinking about it, she decided:

No, I won't kill myself. Everyone would talk about my father behind his back. They would tell each other how he had only one child and that he loved her very much, and yet she had so many troubles that she hanged herself. My father would never get over his sorrow if I committed suicide. But I can't stand to listen to these insults any longer, so I will ask the Lord to take my life.

Sarah Prays

11 Sarah stretched out her arms toward a window and prayed:

I praise you, Lord,
for your mercy.
I pray that all your creation
will honor your name forever.
12 Now in prayer I look to you
13 and ask you to release me
from this life
and free me from these insults.

*14 You know I haven't disgraced
my father's name, or mine,
by committing the sin
of sleeping with a man
who wasn't my husband.
15 I have married seven men,
but all of them died.
I am an only child,
living far from my homeland.
There are no relatives here
who could marry me,
so we could have a child
to carry on the family line.

I have no reason to live, Lord.
But if you won't take my life,
at least stop people
from insulting me.

God Hears the Prayers of Tobit and Sarah

Tobit speaks:

16 Sarah and I were praying to God at exactly the same time, and he decided 17 to send the angel Raphael to heal both of us. God told Raphael to get rid of the white covering from my eyes, so I could see again. And he told Raphael to free Sarah from the demon Asmodeus and arrange for her to marry Tobias, my son. And of course, Tobias had the right to marry her, since he was Sarah's closest relative.

As I was leaving my courtyard and going back inside my house, Sarah was coming down from the upstairs room.

Tobit Gives Instructions to Tobias

4 Later that day, I remembered the silver coins I had left with Gabael in the town of Rages in Media. 2 I said to myself, "Since I have prayed that I will die soon, I had better call in my son Tobias and explain to him about the silver coins." 3 So I called for Tobias and said:

My son, when I die, make sure that I have a proper burial. Always respect your mother and do whatever she asks. Don't ever neglect her or cause her any sorrow. 4 Remember, she risked her life to give birth to you! And when she dies, bury her next to me.

5 Honor the Lord and follow his teachings as long as you live. Always do what is right and refuse to do wrong.

[c]**3.8** *before he could give you a son*: Or "before you could sleep with him and make the marriage official"; other Greek manuscripts "before he could do you any good."

3.17 Nu 36.6-9; Tb 6.10-12.

6 People who are honest are always successful. And if people do what is right 7 but[d] are poor, give them some money to help them out. And be cheerful when you give, because if you help others with their needs, God will help you with yours. 8 If you are rich, give generously to the poor. On the other hand, if you don't have much money, don't be afraid to give them at least a little. 9 If you help the poor, then later, when you are in need, others will help you. 10 Giving to the poor will keep you from going down into the dark world of the dead. 11 Helping the poor is one of the best offerings you can give to God Most High.

12 My son, don't sleep with any woman except your wife and don't marry a foreigner. Some of our ancestors were prophets, so keep our family line pure and choose a woman from our own tribe. Remember that our ancestors Noah, Abraham, Isaac, and Jacob all married their own relatives. God blessed their families with children and gave the land of Israel to their descendants. 13 Have love in your heart for the people of your own nation. Don't be proud and think you are too good to marry an Israelite woman. Pride like that will confuse and destroy you, just as laziness will make you poor and starving.

14 Don't ever fail to pay your hired workers at the end of the day. Serve God, and you will be rewarded. Have self-control in everything you do. 15 Don't treat others in ways that you would not want to be treated. Don't be a heavy drinker or ever get drunk. 16 Provide food and clothes for the poor. Give your extra money to those in need, and do it cheerfully! 17 Honor the memory of good people, but not of the wicked. 18 Show respect for the wise and never reject good advice. 19 Always praise the Lord God and pray for his guidance, so you will be successful in whatever you do. No other nations have understanding, but the Lord can either make them wise or bring them to ruin.

My son, be sure to keep in mind everything I have told you to do.

20 Now I need to tell you that I once left one hundred twenty thousand silver coins[e] for safekeeping with Gabael son of Gabrias, who lives in the town of Rages in Media. 21 We have become poor, but don't be afraid. You will be rich if you show the proper respect for the Lord our God. So obey him and run from sin.

5 Tobias replied, "Father, I will do everything you have told me. 2 But how can I possibly get the money? I don't know Gabael, and he doesn't know me! What can I do to prove I am your son, so he will let me have the money? And I don't even know the way to Media."

3 I answered, "Twenty years ago Gabael and I signed an agreement that we cut in half. I kept one half and left the other with the coins. Find someone you can trust, and we will hire him to travel there and back with you. But be sure to get that money!"

4 Tobias left to look for someone who knew the way and would go there with him. Suddenly God's angel Raphael was standing in front of him, but Tobias did not know he was an angel. 5 Tobias asked, "Who are you?"

He answered, "I am an Israelite, just like you, and I have come here, looking for work."

Tobias asked, "Do you know the way to the country of Media?"

6 "Of course!" he replied. "I've been there many times, and I know all the roads. I always stay with our relative Gabael in Rages, which is in the mountains. It takes about two days to get there from Ecbatana in the valley."

7 Tobias said, "I want to hire you to go to

[d]**4.7** *but*: Verses 7-18 and part of verse 19 are not in the primary manuscript. [e]**4.20** *one hundred twenty thousand silver coins*: See the note at 1.14.

4.7 Dt 15.7, 8; Pr 19.17; Si 3.30—4.6; 1 Jn 3.17. **4.15** Mt 7.12; Lk 6.31. **4.21** 1 Ti 6.6-8. **5.4** He 13.2.

Media with me. Please wait here until I tell
my father."
8 "All right," he answered. "I'll wait, but
don't take too long."
9 When Tobias returned home, he said
to me, "Father, I have found an Israelite,
and he is one of our relatives!"
"Ask him to come here," I replied. "I
want to know something about his family
and tribe, so I can decide if he can be
trusted to go with you to Rages."
10 Tobias invited the young man to come
in and meet me, and I immediately greeted
him. The young man replied, "Sir, I hope
all goes well for you."
"How can anything go well for me?" I
answered. "I am as blind as a dead man in
the dark! In fact, I may as well be dead, because I hear people, but I can't see them."
The young man told me, "Cheer up!
God will soon heal you."
Then I said, "My son Tobias wants to go
to Media. And I will pay you, if you can go
along and show him the way."
He replied, "Yes, I can. I've been there
many times, and I know all the roads
through the valleys and across the mountains."
11 Then I said, "Tell me, my friend, what
family and tribe are you from?"
12 "Why do you want to know?" the
young man asked.
I answered, "I just want to know for certain who your father is and what your
name is."
13 The young man said, "My name is
Azariah, and I am the son of Hananiah, a
great man who was[f] one of your relatives."
14 I replied:

> Then you are welcome here, my
> brother, and I pray that God will pro-
> tect you. Please don't be upset with
> me; I had to find out for certain what
> family you are from. You really are one
> of our relatives, and you come from a
> good family. I knew Hananiah and his
> brother Nathan, the sons of Sheme-
> liah. Hananiah was a great man! He
> and Nathan used to go to Jerusalem
> with me to worship, and they never
> worshiped other gods. Yes, you come
> from a very good family, and you are
> most welcome in our home! 15 Now
> then, if you will go to Media with my
> son, I will pay you one silver coin for
> each day, as well as all your expenses
> and those of my son. 16 Plus, I will give
> you a bonus.

The young man answered, "Don't worry,
I'll go! And when we return, we will be just
as healthy as we are now, because the roads
aren't dangerous."
17 I replied, "I pray for God to bless you,
my brother!"
Then I turned to my son and said, "Get
whatever supplies you will need, then start
on the journey with your friend. I pray that
God in heaven will watch over you until
you return, and that his angel will travel
with the two of you and keep you safe."
Before Tobias left, he kissed his mother
and me good-by, and I said, "Have a safe
trip." 18 But his mother started crying and
said to me, "Tobit, why are you sending my
son away like this? He is the only person
we can depend on, and he is always here to
help us. 19 I don't care about the money!
Forget it, then our son won't have to risk
his life. 20 The Lord has blessed us with
life, and that should be enough for us."
21-22 I replied, "Don't be afraid, dear.
You'll see—our son Tobias will come home
just as healthy as he is now. Stop worrying!
A good angel will go along, and Tobias will
come home safely and bring the money
with him."
6 So she stopped crying.

Tobias and His Friend Travel to Rages

Tobias and the angel left for Rages,
2 with Tobias's dog[g] following along. That
night they camped beside the Tigris River,
3 and Tobias went down to wash his feet.
Suddenly a big fish jumped out of the water
and tried to swallow one of his feet. Tobias let out a scream, 4 but the angel said,
"Quick—grab the fish!" So Tobias grabbed
it and dragged it up on the river bank.
5 The angel said, "Cut it open and take

[f] **5.13** *was*: Or "is."
[g] **6.2** *Tobias's dog*: Greek "the dog."
5.16 Gn 24.7, 40.

out its heart, liver, and gall bladder, because these can be used for medicine. But throw the rest of its insides away."
6 Tobias obeyed the angel. Then he cooked and ate some of the fish and salted the rest to keep it from spoiling. And the next morning, the two of them again set out on their journey.

When they were getting near Media,
7 Tobias asked the angel, "Azariah, how can these parts from that fish be used as medicine?"

8 The angel said, "If a demon is causing sickness or trouble for a man or a woman, take the heart and liver and burn them nearby. The smoke will stop the demon from bothering that person ever again.
9 And if someone has white spots covering their eyes and cannot see, you can rub the gall bladder on their eyes and blow on the white spots, and that person will be able to see again."

Raphael's Instructions to Tobias

10 Tobias and Raphael had reached Media and were on their way to Ecbatana,
11 when Raphael said, "Tobias, listen to me."

"I'm listening," Tobias answered.

Then Raphael said:

Tonight we will stay in the home of your relative Raguel. He has a daughter named Sarah,
12 and she is his only child. You are her closest relative, and so you have the right to marry her and to inherit whatever her father leaves. He is a good man, and she is sensible, courageous, and very beautiful.
13 Now listen carefully. Raguel knows that you have the right to marry his daughter and that the Law of Moses teaches that he must be put to death, if he lets any other man marry her. So tonight I will make the wedding arrangements with him, and you can take Sarah home as your bride when we return from Rages.

14 Tobias answered:

I have heard that she has already been married seven times, but each of the men died before going to bed with her. The rumor is that a demon killed them.
15 It doesn't harm her; it just kills anyone who tries to marry her. I am an only child, and if I were killed by that demon, my parents would have great sorrow and be left with no one to bury them.[h]

16 Raphael then said:

Don't you remember that your father told you to marry someone from his side of the family? So agree to marry Sarah, because I know that tonight she can be your bride. You don't have to worry about the demon if you pay close attention to my instructions.
17 Before you enter the bedroom with Sarah, put some of the liver and heart of the fish on the burning incense. It will give off such a bad odor
18 that the demon will leave and never return.

Then, before the two of you go to bed, you must stand up and pray that the Lord of Heaven will be merciful and watch over you. Don't worry! Even before the time of creation, God had already chosen Sarah to be your wife. You will save her from disgrace, and she will return to your home with you. I promise that the two of you will have sons, and you will love them very much. So don't argue with me!

As soon as Tobias learned that Sarah was related to him on his father's side of the family, he fell deeply in love with her.

At the Home of Raguel

7 When they entered the city of Ecbatana, Tobias said, "Azariah, take me straight to Raguel's home." He did, and they found Raguel sitting beside the gate that led into his yard. They greeted him, and he answered, "I hope you are happy and healthy. Welcome to my home; please come in."

2 Raguel turned to his wife Edna and said, "Doesn't this young man remind you of my relative Tobit?"

3 Edna asked Tobias and Raphael, "So, our new friends, where do you come from?"

They answered, "We are from the tribe

[h]6.15 *no one to bury them*: A proper burial was considered very important.

of Naphtali, and we live in exile in Nineveh."
4 "Do you know our relative Tobit?"
Edna asked.

"Yes, we do," they answered.

"Is he well?" she asked.

5 "He is alive and well," they replied.
Then Tobias added, "And he is my father!"
6 Raguel jumped up and kissed Tobias
and started weeping. 7 Raguel said, "I pray
that God will bless you. Your father Tobit is
a generous and honest man. It's a terrible
shame that someone so good has become
blind." Then Raguel hugged Tobias and
cried some more. 8 Raguel's wife Edna and
his daughter Sarah were also crying for Tobit. 9 Then Raguel killed one of his sheep,
so its meat could be prepared for dinner,
and he made Tobias and Raphael feel welcome in his home.

After they had bathed and were eating dinner, Tobias whispered to Raphael, "Ask him to let me marry Sarah!"

10 Raguel overheard Tobias and said,
"Eat and drink and have a good time. No
one except you has the right to marry my
daughter Sarah. You are my closest relative,
and so I would not be allowed to let anyone
else marry her. However, there are a few
things I must tell you. 11 I have already let
Sarah marry seven of my relatives, and
each one of them died when he went into
the bedroom to sleep with her. So now,
Tobias, eat and drink, and the Lord will
help you."

But Tobias replied, "I won't eat or drink anything until you make this marriage official."

"Then I will make it official right now!" Raguel said. "Tobias, I give my daughter Sarah to you as your wife according to the laws in the Book of Moses. God himself wanted you to marry her, and from this moment you will forever be husband and wife. I pray that the Lord of Heaven will bless the two of you tonight, and that he will be merciful and give you peace."

12 Raguel sent for his daughter, and
when she came, he took her by the hand
and led her over to Tobias. Then he said,
"Tobias, Sarah is now your wife in keeping
with the laws and teachings of the Book of
Moses. Make sure that she arrives unharmed at your father's home, and I will
pray that the God of Heaven will keep you
safe as you travel."

13 Raguel asked his wife Edna to bring
him something to write on, and he wrote
out a contract stating that Sarah was married to Tobias according to the Law of
Moses. 14 Then they all ate and drank.
15 Afterwards, Raguel said, "Edna,
please get the other bedroom ready and
take Sarah there." 16 So Edna made the
bed and brought Sarah to the room. Edna
wept for her daughter, then she wiped away
the tears and said, "Don't worry, Sarah! Cheer
up, because the God of Heaven will soon
turn your sorrow into joy." Then Edna left.

Tobias Chases Off the Demon

8 When everyone had finished eating
and drinking, they decided it was time
to go to bed, and they brought Tobias to the
bedroom. 2 Then Tobias remembered what
Raphael had told him about the liver and
the heart of the fish. So he took them out
of the bag where he had kept them, and he
put them on the burning incense. 3 The
terrible odor made the demon go all the
way to Egypt, where Raphael captured him
and immediately tied him up so tightly that
he couldn't move.

Tobias Prays

4 After Sarah's parents had left and the
bedroom door was shut, Tobias stood up
and said, "Sarah, my darling, please get up.
Let's pray that the Lord will be merciful
and watch over us." 5 So she got up, and
they begged the Lord to keep them safe.
Tobias began by praying:

"God of our ancestors,
    we praise your name;
all future generations
    will praise you as well.
Heaven and the rest of creation
    should always praise you.

6 "You made Adam and said,
'It isn't good for the man
    to live alone.

7.6 Gn 33.4; 45.14; Lk 15.20. **8.3** Mt 12.43. **8.5** Az/S of 3 H 3. **8.6** Gn 2.18.

So we will make
a suitable partner for him,
someone like himself.'
Then you gave him Eve—
the perfect companion—
and they were the source
of the whole human race.

7 "I have married
this relative of mine—
not because of lust,
but because of love.
Please be kind and bless us
with a long life together."

8 Tobias and Sarah both said, "Amen!"
9 and then went to sleep for the night.

Raguel Digs a Grave for Tobias

Later that night, Raguel woke up his
servants and took them outside, where they
dug a grave. 10 He told them, "If Tobias dies
and our neighbors find out, they will make
fun of us and insult us." 11 When they had
finished digging the grave, Raguel went
into the house. He woke up his wife 12 and
told her, "Send one of the young servant
women into the room to see if Tobias is still
alive. If he is dead, then we can bury him
now and no one will know about it."
13 Edna lit a lamp and gave it to a
servant, then she opened the door and sent
her inside. Tobias and Sarah were both
sound asleep. 14 The servant came back out
and told Raguel and Edna that Tobias was
still alive, and that nothing bad had happened to him. 15 They praised the God of
Heaven, and Raguel[i] said,

"Our God, you are worthy
to be praised for all time[j]
with words that come
from hearts that are pure.
16 I offer my praise, because you
have given me happiness—
I expected a tragedy,
but it did not happen.
You had mercy on us
17 and on Sarah and Tobias,
the only children
of their parents.
Be merciful to these young people!
Keep them safe and bless them
with happiness."

18 Then Raguel told his servants to fill
in the grave before sunrise.

The Wedding Celebration

19 Raguel went to his wife and told her
to bake a lot of bread. Then he went out to
his herd of livestock and brought back two
bulls and four rams, and he gave orders for
his servants to slaughter them. And so,
everyone began preparing for a big celebration.
20 Raguel called in Tobias and told him:
Please stay[k] here at least two weeks.
You can eat and drink with me, and
you can cheer up my daughter, who
has gone through some horrible suffering. 21 When you leave, you can take
half of everything I own and return
safely to your father. Then, whenever
my wife Edna and I die, you can have
the other half as well. Don't worry
about a thing, Tobias. From now on,
you will be a son to us, and we will
care for you as much as we do for our
daughter Sarah, your wife.

9 Tobias went to Raphael and said:
2-4 Azariah, my friend, you know
that my father has been counting the
days it should take us to go to Rages
and back, and if we are even one day
late, he will be worried sick. You heard
how Raguel has made a solemn
promise that I must stay,[l] and I don't
want to make him break his promise.
So take four servants and two camels
and go to the town of Rages and find
Gabael. Give him my father's half of
the agreement,[m] then get the silver
coins, and bring Gabael back with you
to the wedding celebration.

[i]**8.15** *Raguel*: Greek "they." [j]**8.15** *time*: Some Greek manuscripts add "by your angels, your chosen people, and all your creatures." [k]**8.20** *Please stay*: Many Greek manuscripts; a few Greek manuscripts and one ancient translation, "I have made a solemn promise to God that you must stay." [l]**9.2-4** *Raguel has made a solemn promise that I must stay*: See the note at 8.20. [m]**9.2-4** *my father's half of the agreement*: Greek "the agreement"; see 5.1-3.
8.20 Gn 24.55.

5 Raphael took four servants and two camels to the town of Rages in Media, where he stayed with Gabael. Raphael gave him the agreement and told him how Tobit's son Tobias had gotten married and had invited him to the wedding celebration. Gabael went and got the bags of silver coins and counted them as he gave them to Raphael. All the bags were there, and none of them had been opened. Raphael and Gabael loaded the bags onto the camels,[n] 6 and early the next morning, the two men got up and went to the wedding celebration at Raguel's home in Ecbatana. Tobias was eating[o] when they arrived, but he jumped up and greeted Gabael.

Gabael started weeping and said, "You are honest and good, just like your father Tobit. And he was such a generous man! Now I pray that God will bless you from heaven, and also that he will bless your wife and her parents. I praise God, Tobias, because you are just like your father."

Tobit and Anna Are Worried

Tobit speaks:

10 I knew how long it should take Tobias to travel to the town of Rages and back, and I counted each day. But when the time had gone by, 2-3 I became so worried, that at last I wondered out loud, "What could be keeping Tobias? Maybe Gabael is dead, and there is no one else to give him the money."

4 Anna replied, "I'm sure it's my son who is dead!" Then she started weeping and cried out, 5 "I've never known such sorrow! My son made my eyes sparkle. Why did I ever let him go?"

6 But I kept trying to encourage her by saying, "Now my darling, don't cry. There's no need to worry—I'm sure Tobias is all right. After all, the man who went with him is a relative of ours, and he can be trusted. Something unexpected must have delayed them. Tobias will be home soon, so you don't need to worry or even talk about it anymore."

7 "You're the one who should stop talking!" she answered. "Don't try to hide the truth from me. I know my son is dead."

Each morning Anna hurried out and started watching the road, hoping to see our son, and no one could change her mind. Then at sunset, she would come back inside and weep bitterly all night long, without getting a wink of sleep.

Tobias and Sarah Start Home

Raguel had promised his daughter a wedding celebration of fourteen days. And at the end of those two weeks, Tobias went to him and said, "Soon after I arrived here, I told you my father was in bad health. I am sure that by now, both he and my mother must think I am dead and that they will never see me again. So please let me return home."

8 But Raguel replied, "Stay with us, my son, and I will send someone to tell your father the news about you."

9 "Sir, I beg you," Tobias answered, "please let me return home!"

10 So Raguel immediately agreed to let Tobias leave with Sarah, and he gave Tobias half of everything he owned, including his slaves, his oxen and sheep, his donkeys and camels, and his clothing, money, and household things. 11 Then, before sending the two of them away with his blessing, he hugged Tobias and said, "Good-by, my son. I hope you don't have any trouble along the way. And I now ask the Lord to make you and your wife successful and to bless you with children. I pray that I will see them before I die."

12 After this, Raguel kissed Sarah and said, "My daughter, you must now go to live with[p] your father-in-law and mother-in-law, because they are now as much your parents as your mother and I. You go with my blessing, but make sure that I always hear good things about you. Good-by, my dear."

[n]**9.5** *loaded the bags onto the camels*: Some ancient translations; the primary Greek manuscript has "placed the bags together." [o]**9.6** *eating*: The Greek text has "lying down"; in ancient times at a dinner, people lay on the floor around a low table. They would prop themselves up on one elbow, which would leave one hand free to eat with. [p]**10.12** *you must now go to live with*: The primary Greek manuscript; other manuscripts "show proper respect to."

Then Raguel's wife Edna said, "Tobias, my son, I pray that the Lord will let you and Sarah return here before I die, so I may see my grandchildren. And, with God as my witness, I place my daughter Sarah in your care. Please don't ever cause her any sorrow. My son, I am your mother, and Sarah is your dear wife. I pray that God will always bless our family. Now I wish you a safe journey." Then she kissed them both and said good-by.

13 As Tobias was leaving, he was so happy that he shouted:

"I praise the Lord
of heaven and earth,
the King of all creation,
who made my trip successful.
Raguel and Edna,
I will show you proper respect
for as long as I live."[q]

Then he told them good-by.

Going Home

11 When Tobias and the angel Raphael came near the town of Kaserin, not far from Nineveh, Raphael said, 2 "Tobias, you know the condition your father was in when we left. 3 So why don't you and I run on ahead of your wife Sarah and get things ready at the house?" 4 Then as the two of them ran along, followed by Tobias's dog,[r] Raphael said, "Have the gall bladder of the fish ready."

5 Meanwhile, Anna was sitting beside the road, just staring. 6 When she saw Tobias coming, she called out to her husband, "Our son is coming down the road! And that man is with him."

Tobit's Eyes Are Healed

7 Before they got there, Raphael said to Tobias, "Your father's eyes will be healed. 8 Just smear the gall bladder of the fish on his eyes, and the film-like stuff that is covering them will shrink and peel off. Then your father will be able to see again."

9 Anna ran to Tobias and hugged him. Then she said, "Now that I have seen you, my son, I can die in peace." And she began crying.

Tobit speaks:

10 I jumped up and went stumbling through the gate leading out to the road. Tobias hurried toward me, 11-12 carrying the gall bladder. He breathed on my eyes and said, "Don't worry!" He immediately steadied me and started rubbing the gall bladder on my eyes. 13 Then, with both hands, he began at the corners of my eyes and peeled away the stuff that had made me blind.

I hugged Tobias 14 and started crying, then I said, "I can see you, my son! Now life is worth living again."[s] Then I continued:

"Praise God and his great name!
Praise his holy angels!
I pray for God to be with us!
Praise his angels forever.
15 He caused me great suffering,
but now I see my son Tobias!"

I kept on celebrating and praising God as loud as I could.

After a while, Tobias told me how successful his travels had been—not only had he recovered the money, but he had married Sarah, who was near the gate of Nineveh at that very moment.

16 I started walking toward the city gate, still celebrating and praising God. But those who saw me hurrying along were amazed that no one was leading me. 17 So I told everyone that God had been merciful and had healed my eyes. And when I saw Sarah, I gave her my blessing and said, "My daughter, we welcome you into our family! I praise God for bringing you to us, and I ask him to bless your parents and my son and you. Our home is your home, and I pray God will bless you with health and happiness in this place. Welcome!"

On that same day, every Jew in Nineveh joined in the celebration, 18 and my nephews Ahikar[t] and Nadab also came to celebrate with us.[u]

[q]**10.13** *I will show . . . I live*: One possible meaning for the difficult Greek text. [r]**11.4** *Tobias's dog*: See the note at 6.2. [s]**11.14** *Now life is worth living again*: Greek "You are the light of my eyes." [t]**11.18** *Ahikar*: See 1.21, 22; 2.10-12. [u]**11.18** *us*: Some Greek manuscripts add "and for seven days we all held a wedding celebration for Tobias."

11.11-13 Ac 9.18.

The Angel Raphael's Advice

Tobit speaks:

12 After the wedding celebration, I
called in Tobias and said, "My son,
it's time to pay the man who went with
you, and he deserves a bonus."
2 Tobias anwered, "How much should I
give him? We could give him half of what I
brought back, and we would still have
plenty for ourselves. 3 After all, he got me
back home safely, he healed my wife, he
brought back the silver coins to you, and he
healed you. So how much should I give
him as a bonus?"
4 "My son," I replied, "he deserves to get
half of everything he brought back."
5 Tobias called in Raphael and said,
"You have earned half of everything you
brought back. And now it's time for us to
say good-by."
6 Then Raphael spoke to Tobias and me
in private and said:
Be sure to praise and honor God by
telling everyone the good things he has
done for you. Celebrate God's name
with praises and with songs, and don't
ever hesitate to tell others about him.
7 Don't tell anyone the secrets of a
king, but honor God by letting others
know what he has done for you.
If you do what is right, nothing bad
will happen to you. 8 It is good to pray
sincerely. And it is better to be honest
and generous to the poor than to be
wealthy, but dishonest. You are better
off giving to the poor than getting lots
of gold, 9 because giving to the poor
saves you from death and washes away
every sin. People who are generous to
the poor will have a full life, 10 but
people who sin and are dishonest are
actually harming themselves.

Raphael Tells Tobit and Tobias Who He Is

11 Raphael said to Tobias and me:
Now I will tell you the whole truth
about everything that has happened.
In fact, I have already hinted at it
when I said, "Don't tell anyone the secrets of a king, but honor God by letting others know what he has done for
you." 12 Tobit, when you and Sarah
prayed, I was the one who presented
your prayers to the glorious God, and
when you buried the dead, I told God
what you had done. 13 When you left
the banquet to bury that man who had
been murdered, 14 God sent me to test
you, and he also sent me to heal you
and to help your daughter-in-law
Sarah. 15 I am Raphael, one of the
seven angels who stand in the presence of the glorious God.
16 Tobias and I were so terribly frightened
that we fell face down. 17 But Raphael said:
Don't worry! Just remember to always praise God. 18 Don't give me the
credit; it was God who did all of this.
That's why you must sing praises to
God every day. 19 When you thought
you saw me eating and drinking, it
only seemed that way. 20 So praise God
and thank him for as long as you live.
Now I will return to the one who sent
me, and I command you to write down
everything that has happened to you.
Then Raphael went up into heaven.
21 Tobias and I stood up, but we could
no longer see Raphael. 22 Then we began
singing praises to God because of the great
things he had done, especially for sending
the angel to us.

Tobit Praises God

13 I said:

I will praise the eternal God,
who rules forever.
2 God punishes and shows mercy;
he can send people down
to the world of the dead,
or rescue them
from great destruction.
No one can escape his power.

3 People of Israel,
God scattered you
among the nations,
so tell them about him.

12.8 Si 29.8-13. **12.9** Pr 11.4; Dn 4.27; Si 3.30. **12.12** Job 33.23, 24; Ac 10.4; Rev 8.3, 4.
12.15 Zec 4.10; Lk 1.19; Rev 8.2.

4 He has shown you his greatness.
And while everyone listens,
you should praise him,
because he will forever be
our Lord and God and Father.
5 He will punish you if you sin,
but then he will have mercy
and gather you[v] from the nations
where you are scattered.
6 If you turn to God
with all your heart
and are faithful to him,
he will turn to you once again;
no longer will he refuse
to help you.
Shout praises to him,
because he has been so kind
and faithful to you,
and he will rule as king forever!

I must live far from my country,
but I will still praise God
and tell this nation of sinners
how great and powerful he is.
I will say, Turn from your sins,
and obey God.
Who knows?
Maybe God will be kind
and have mercy on you.

7 I will praise my God,
the King of Heaven,
and celebrate his greatness.
8 Praise him, people of Jerusalem.
9 God will punish your holy city
because you have sinned,
but if you obey him,
he will again be kind to you.
10 The Lord is good, so praise him
and honor his kingdom;[w]
then he will again allow you
to set up his sacred tent
and celebrate there.
He will cheer up your exiles
and always show his love
to those who are suffering.
11 Jerusalem, you will give light
to the whole world,
and people will come to you
from faraway nations,
bringing gifts for your holy God,
the King of Heaven.
One generation after another
will celebrate in you,
the city God has chosen.

12 God will put a curse
on those who insult you,
and on those who capture you
and tear down your walls,
destroy your towers,
and burn your homes.
But he will bless anyone
who shows respect for you.
13 Celebrate, because the Lord
will gather together those
who are faithful to him,
and he will bless them
for all time.
14 He will bless those
who love you, Jerusalem—
those who are happy
when you have peace,
and who are sad
when you have trouble.
They will celebrate with you
and see your joy forever.

15 I praise the Lord,
the Great King,
16 because, Jerusalem,
you will be rebuilt,
and you will be his home
for all time.
I will be glad
if one of my descendants
can see your glory
and praise the King of Heaven.
Your gates will be made
of sapphires and emeralds,
and your walls will be covered
with other jewels.
Your towers will be of gold
all the way to the top.
The streets within you
will be paved with rubies
and jewels from Ophir.

[v]**13.5** *and gather you*: These words are not in the primary manuscript and one ancient translation.
[w]**13.6-10** *I must live far from my country . . . honor his kingdom*: Verses 6-9 and the first part of verse 10 are not in the primary manuscript.

13.4 Is 63.16; Jr 3.4; Ws 14.3; Si 23.1, 4; 3 Macc 7.6; Mt 6.9. **13.9-18** Is 60.1-22; Rev 21.9—22.5.

[17] Your gates will sing with joy,
and your houses will shout,
"Praise the Lord!
Praise the God of Israel!"
And God's people will praise
his holy name forever.

14 That is how I ended my song of praise.

Tobit's Last Words

Tobit died peacefully at the age of one hundred twelve and was honored at his burial in Nineveh. [2] He was sixty-two when he became blind, and after his sight was restored, he was once again wealthy and generous to the poor. He was always praising God and telling others about God's power.

[3] Just before Tobit died, he called in his son and said:

Tobias, take your children [4] and go to Media! I believe what God said when he told the prophet Nahum what will happen to Nineveh and Assyria. And time after time, God gave messages to other prophets in Israel, telling them what will happen. Every message they spoke will come true at the right time. You will be safe in Media, but not here in Assyria or in Babylonia.

Our relatives, the people of Israel, will be taken from that good land and scattered in other countries. The whole land of Israel, including the cities of Samaria and Jerusalem, will be deserted. Even God's temple will suffer and lie in ashes for a while.
[5] Then God will have mercy on Israel again, and he will return them to their own land. They will rebuild the temple, but it won't be as glorious a building, until the time that all of God's promises come true. And when that happens, God will bring Israel back from their exile, and they will rebuild Jerusalem into a truly glorious city. God's temple will also be rebuilt there, just as the prophets have said.

[6] All the Gentiles on earth will stop worshiping idols, because idols only deceive people and lead them away from the truth. The Gentiles will then turn to God and worship only him.
[7] They will praise and obey the eternal God.

God will protect those Israelites who are truly loyal to him, and at that time, he will gather them together and bring them back to Jerusalem. God will give them the land he once gave to Abraham, and they will live in safety there forever.

[8-9] Now, my son and my grandchildren, I give you these commands: Worship and obey the Lord. Be faithful and do what pleases him. Tell your own children to do right and to be generous to the poor. Always think about God, and don't just pretend to praise God—praise him with all your strength.

My son, you must leave Nineveh
[10] on the same day your mother dies and you bury her beside me. Don't even spend that night here. Nineveh is a very evil place, and its people aren't even ashamed that they are so dishonest. Just look at what Nadab did—he tried to kill Ahikar,[x] who had raised him. Ahikar had to hide in a tomb to escape the deadly trap Nadab had set. Ahikar lived to see the light of day, because he had given so generously to poor people. But God punished Nadab for his treachery! Nadab was killed in his own trap and went down into the
place of eternal darkness. [11] So, my
children, you can see that God will protect you if you give to the poor; but when you do what is evil, you will be killed. And now, my life is slipping away.

They helped Tobit lie down on his bed, and when he died, they buried him with honor.

Tobias Moves to Media

[12] Some time later, Tobias's mother Anna died, and he buried her beside his

[x]**14.10** *Nadab . . . Ahikar*: See 1.21, 22; 2.10, 11; 11.18.
14.4 Nh 1.2—3.19.

father. Then Tobias and his wife Sarah moved to the city of Ecbatana in Media, where he lived with his father-in-law Raguel and his mother-in-law Edna.
13 He treated them with great respect and took care of them until they died; then he buried them. Tobias inherited all of Raguel's property, in addition to what had belonged to his own father Tobit.

Everyone respected Tobias,
14 and he died at the age of one hundred seventeen.
15 But he lived long enough to hear that Nineveh had been destroyed, and to see its people being led as prisoners into Media by Cyaxares,[y] the king of Media. And from that time until the day Tobias died, he offered joyful praises to God for what he had done to Nineveh and Assyria.

[y]**14.15** *Cyaxares*: One possible meaning for the difficult Greek text.
14.15 3 Macc 7.23.

JUDITH

ABOUT THIS BOOK

This book tells how a beautiful Israelite woman named Judith rescued Israel from the attack of Holofernes, a powerful general of the Assyrian army. Judith was a widow who faithfully worshiped God and completely obeyed the Law of Moses.

Judith lived in Bethulia, a town guarding a mountain pass on the road to Jerusalem. Holofernes had cut off Bethulia from its water supply so he could capture the town and move his army through the pass. But Judith prayed for God's help, then tricked Holofernes and killed him. The next day, the people of Israel attacked and defeated the Assyrian army.

Judith saved Israel because she had courage and obeyed God. The high priest and the leaders of Israel praised Judith after their victory:

> *"Judith, you are the pride of Jerusalem and the hero of our nation Israel. You alone won this victory for Israel. The Lord God All-Powerful is certainly pleased with you, and we pray that he will bless you forever."*
>
> *(15.9, 10)*

A QUICK LOOK AT THIS BOOK

- The Assyrians Conquer the Nations (1.1—3.10)
- The Israelites Prepare To Defend Themselves (4.1-15)
- The Advice of Achior the Ammonite (5.1—6.21)
- The Assyrian Army Attacks Bethulia (7.1-32)
- Judith Meets with the Leaders of Bethulia (8.1-36)
- Judith Prays for God's Help (9.1-14)
- Judith Tricks and Kills Holofernes (10.1—13.20)
- The Israelites Defeat the Assyrian Army (14.1—15.14)
- Judith Praises God (16.1-25)

Nebuchadnezzar Defeats Arphaxad

1 During the years that King Nebuchadnezzar ruled Assyria from the capital city of Nineveh,[a] King Arphaxad ruled over Media Province from his capital city of Ecbatana.[b]

In the twelfth year of Nebuchadnezzar's
rule, 2 Arphaxad began fortifying Ecbatana
by building a wall around it that was over one hundred feet high and seventy-five feet thick. The wall was made out of cut stones, each one of them four and a half
feet wide and nine feet long. 3 Beside each
gate into the city, he built a tower one hundred fifty feet tall with a base that was
ninety feet wide. 4 Each gate had an opening one hundred five feet high and sixty

[a]**1.1** *King Nebuchadnezzar . . . Assyria . . . Nineveh*: Nebuchadnezzar was king of Babylonia (605-562 B.C.), not Assyria, and he never ruled from Nineveh, which had been destroyed in 612 B.C. by his father Nabopolassar. It is possible that in this book Nebuchadnezzar is a symbol for every powerful ruler who was an enemy of Israel, while Nineveh is a symbol for every large, enemy city.

[b]**1.1** *King Arphaxad . . . Media Province . . . Ecbatana*: Although nothing is known about a King Arphaxad, the city of Ecbatana was the capital of Media, an important province of the Persian empire. Ecbatana was about 300 miles northeast of Babylonia and 325 miles southeast of Nineveh.

feet wide—big enough for his powerful army to march out in rows on its way into battle.

5 In that same year, Nebuchadnezzar went to war against Arphaxad in the large valley near the city of Ragau.[c] 6 Many other nations sent their armies to help Nebuchadnezzar fight Arphaxad, including those from the mountains south of Ecbatana, those living along the Euphrates, the Tigris, and the Hydaspes Rivers,[d] as well as those from the valley ruled by King Arioch of Elam.[e] This large and powerful army went with Nebuchadnezzar into battle against Arphaxad.

7 Nebuchadnezzar sent messengers to ask the people of nearby regions and cities to join him in this battle. His messengers went to the Persians and to regions west of Assyria, including Cilicia, Damascus, Lebanon, and Anti-Lebanon. They also went to the people who lived along the coast of the Mediterranean Sea 8 and to those living in the regions of Carmel, Gilead, northern Galilee, and Jezreel Valley. 9 Nebuchadnezzar even asked the people from the city of Samaria and its nearby towns, as well as those from Jerusalem, Bethany, Chelous, Kadesh, and those living as far west as the Nile River. His messengers went all the way to the Egyptian region of Goshen, including the cities of Tahpanhes, Raamses, 10 Tanis, and Memphis, until they reached the border of Ethiopia.

11 But all of these people ignored Nebuchadnezzar's message and refused to be his allies in his battle against Arphaxad. None of them thought Nebuchadnezzar was someone to fear, and so they sent his messengers back, empty-handed and embarrassed.

12 Nebuchadnezzar was so angry that he swore he would give up his entire kingdom, if he did not kill everyone who had refused to help him—all the people of Cilicia, Damascus, Syria, Moab, Ammon, Judea, and Egypt, as far as the coasts of the two seas.[f]

13 In the seventeenth year of his rule, Nebuchadnezzar led his army into battle against Arphaxad. It was a complete victory for Nebuchadnezzar! He defeated all of Arphaxad's troops, including his entire cavalry and all his chariots. 14 After Nebuchadnezzar had captured every town in Media, he attacked the capital city of Ecbatana. He destroyed its guard towers, then stole everything of value from the marketplace and turned the proud city into a pile of ruins. 15 He also captured Arphaxad in the mountains near Ragau and killed him with spears.

16 After that, Nebuchadnezzar and his large army returned to Nineveh with everything they had taken. Then they rested and celebrated for four months.

Nebuchadnezzar Plans His Attack on the Nations of the West

2 In the eighteenth year of Nebuchadnezzar's rule, on the twenty-second day of the first month,[g] he and his officials decided to keep his promise and take revenge on the nations that had refused to help him fight Arphaxad.[h] 2 Nebuchadnezzar called together his highest officials and respected leaders, then explained that some nations had refused to be his allies.[i] He told how he planned to destroy these rebellious nations, 3 and every one of his officials agreed that it must be done.

4 After that meeting, King Nebuchadnezzar of Assyria[j] called for Holofernes, the general of his army, who ranked second only to the king himself. Nebuchadnezzar said to Holofernes:

> 5 I am Nebuchadnezzar, the great king, the ruler of the earth! I want you to choose one hundred twenty thousand foot soldiers and twelve thousand

[c]**1.5** *Ragau*: An important Median city about two hundred miles northeast of Ecbatana.
[d]**1.6** *Euphrates . . . Tigris . . . Hydaspes Rivers*: Three of the most important rivers in ancient Mesopotamia. [e]**1.6** *as well as those . . . King Arioch of Elam*: One possible meaning for the difficult Greek text. Nothing is known about King Arioch, though Elam was possibly a province of the Persian empire. [f]**1.12** *the two seas*: Probably the Red Sea and the Mediterranean Sea.
[g]**2.1** *first month*: Abib (also called Nisan), the first month of the Hebrew calendar, from about mid-March to mid-April. [h]**2.1** *he and his officials . . . take revenge . . . Arphaxad*: See 1.12.
[i]**2.2** *that some nations had refused to be his allies*: One possible meaning for the difficult Greek text.
[j]**2.4** *King Nebuchadnezzar of Assyria*: See the note at 1.1.

cavalry troops—all of them brave and
experienced in war. 6 Then attack the
nations of the west,[k] because they refused to help me fight King Arphaxad.
7 Tell those nations that I am prepared to attack, and so they have no
choice but to surrender.[l] I will command my troops to invade every inch
of their land and take everything of
value. 8 The valleys and gorges will be
filled with wounded people, and the
land will be flooded, because dead
bodies will block every stream and
river. 9 Then I will capture everyone
left alive and scatter them all over the
earth.
10 Holofernes, I want you to go
ahead of me and take over their land.
Keep control of the nations that surrender to you, and when I arrive, I will
punish them myself. 11 But destroy
those nations that refuse to surrender.
Show them no mercy and command
your troops to take their possessions.
12 As surely as I rule this powerful
kingdom, I will keep my solemn promise to punish those nations. 13 I am
your king, so don't disobey any of my
commands. Go and follow every order
I have given you.

Holofernes Attacks the Nations

14 Holofernes left and called together all
the commanders and officers of the Assyrian army. 15 Just as Nebuchadnezzar had
ordered, he chose one hundred twenty
thousand of the best foot soldiers and
twelve thousand cavalry troops who were
experts with bows and arrows. 16 Holofernes prepared this army for war. 17 He
took enough camels, donkeys, and mules to
carry all the equipment, and he also took a
large number of sheep, oxen, and goats for
food. 18 Each soldier was given plenty of
food and water and was paid a huge
amount of gold and silver from the royal
treasury.
19 Holofernes and his army marched out
with chariots, cavalry, and foot soldiers to
invade the western nations, while King
Nebuchadnezzar stayed in Nineveh.
20 Holofernes had more troops than could
be counted; they were like a swarm of locusts or like grains of sand on the seashore.
21 They left Nineveh, and after they had
marched three days, they reached the valley around the city of Bectileth, where they
set up camp across from the city, near the
mountains north of Cilicia. 22 From there,
Holofernes led his entire army of soldiers
and chariots into the foothills. 23 He completely destroyed the nations of Libya and
Lydia, then took everything from the Ras-
sisites and the Ishmaelites living on the
edge of the desert south of Chellean.[m]
24 Holofernes and his army crossed[n] the
Euphrates River and marched through
Mesopotamia, destroying every walled city
along the Abron River, as far as the Mediterranean Sea. 25 He took over the territory
of Cilicia, killing everyone who tried to resist him. Then he went as far as the southern border of Japheth, near Arabia. 26 After
his army had surrounded the Midianites,
he burned down their tents and slaughtered their sheep. 27 Next, he led his army
into the valley around Damascus. It was
during the wheat harvest, and so he first
burned all the wheat fields, then he slaughtered the sheep and goats. He raided the
towns and tore up the countryside, killing
all the young men.

The Nations of the West Surrender to Nebuchadnezzar

28 Everyone living along the Mediterranean Sea was terrified of Holofernes, including those in the cities of Tyre, Sidon,
Sur, Ocina, Jamnia, Azotus, and Ascalon.
3 So they sent messengers to Holofernes
to say: 2 "We are servants of the great
King Nebuchadnezzar. We surrender to
you, General Holofernes. Do to us whatever you want. 3 Our buildings, our land,

[k]**2.6** *the nations of the west*: Syria and Egypt, including the nations and regions they controlled.
[l]**2.7** *they have no choice but to surrender*: Greek "to prepare offerings of earth and water"; this was a Persian custom that showed complete surrender and submission to a powerful enemy.
[m]**2.23** *Chellean*: This place is unknown. [n]**2.24** *crossed*: Or "followed."
2.20 Jg 7.12; Jl 2.2-11.

our wheat fields, our livestock, and our
tents are yours. 4 Every town belongs to
you. Treat us as you please, because we are
your slaves."

5 After Holofernes had listened to their
message, 6 he led his army to the Mediterranean coast, where he stationed guards in
every walled city and took the best men
from these cities as soldiers.

7 The people in these cities and in the
surrounding countryside welcomed Holofernes by wearing flowers around their
necks and playing tambourines and dancing. 8 But when Holofernes arrived, he tore
down all their places of worship[o] and cut
down their sacred poles.[p] He did this because he had been ordered to get rid of
their idols, so that every nation and tribe
would worship only Nebuchadnezzar and
pray to him as if he were a god.

9 Holofernes then marched into Jezreel
Valley, not far from the city of Dothan,
which is in sight of the hills in Judea. 10 He
set up camp between the cities of Geba and
Scythopolis, and stayed there a month
while he gathered the supplies his army
needed.

The Israelites Plan To Defend Themselves

4 The Israelites living in Judea heard
that General Holofernes of the Assyrian army had destroyed the places of worship in the surrounding nations and that
he had stolen everything of value. 2 They
were terrified because he was coming to do
the same thing to Jerusalem and to the
temple of the Lord their God. 3 The people
had just returned from Babylonia, where
they had lived as captives. And they had
only recently rededicated the temple, the
altar, and the sacred utensils, after they had
been made unfit for worshiping the Lord.

4 So the Israelites warned the people living in the territory of Samaria, including the
towns of Kona, Beth-Horon, Belmain, Jericho, Choba, and Aesora, and those living in
the valley near Salem.[q] 5 Since their fields
had already been harvested, they immediately began preparing for war by setting up
defenses in the hill country, by fortifying
the towns there, and by storing up food.

6 Joakim the high priest was in Jerusalem at the time. He wrote to the people
living in Bethulia and Betomesthaim,[r] two
towns that face Jezreel Valley not far from
Dothan. 7 Joakim wrote, "Set up defenses
right away in the mountain passes that lead
into Judea. They are wide enough for only
two people to use at a time, so you'll easily
stop enemy troops from invading."

8 The Israelites obeyed Joakim and the
other leaders of Israel who were meeting
together in Jerusalem.

The Israelites Pray for Mercy

9 All the men of Israel prayed sincerely
and went without eating to show their sorrow. 10 Then everyone in the country
wrapped sackcloth[s] around their waists—
men, women, and children, as well as foreigners and slaves and hired workers. They
even put sackcloth on their livestock!
11 Every man, woman, and child in Jerusalem went to the temple and bowed low to
the ground. They put ashes on their heads
and spread out sackcloth in front of the
temple 12 and covered the altar with it.
Then the men prayed aloud to the Lord
their God, asking him not to let their wives
and children be captured and taken away
or to let their towns be destroyed. They
begged him not to give foreigners the pleasure of taking over the temple and polluting
the place of worship. 13 The Lord heard
their prayers and saw how much they were
suffering.

For several days, the people of Judea

[o] **3.8** *places of worship*: One ancient translation; Greek "borders." [p] **3.8** *sacred poles*: Or "trees," used as symbols of a god or goddess. [q] **4.4** *Kona . . . Belmain . . . Choba, and Aesora . . . the valley near Salem*: These places cannot be identified, although they were probably located within the territory of Samaria. [r] **4.6** *Bethulia and Betomesthaim*: The identification of these two towns is not known, though they may be used to refer to Shechem and Samaria. Bethulia is the place where most of the events of this book take place and may mean "house of God." [s] **4.10** *sackcloth*: A rough, dark-colored cloth made from goat or camel hair and used to make grain sacks. It was worn in times of trouble or sorrow.

3.8 Ex 34.13; 2 Ch 17.6. **4.10-12** Jon 3.7-9; Es 4.1-3. **4.13** Es 4.16.

and Jerusalem stayed there at the temple of the Lord All-Powerful and went without eating. 14 Joakim the high priest and the priests who served in the temple wore sackcloth as they offered the daily sacrifices to please the Lord,[t] as well as the sacrifices offered to keep a promise and the offerings voluntarily given to him. 15 They also sprinkled ashes on their turbans and prayed aloud, asking the Lord to have mercy on the entire nation of Israel.

Achior the Ammonite Tells Holofernes about the Israelites

5 General Holofernes of the Assyrian army heard that the Israelites had prepared for war by setting up defenses in the mountain passes, by fortifying the hills, and by blocking paths through the valleys. 2 He was furious! So he called together the leaders of the Moabites, the army commanders of the Ammonites, and the rulers of the nations along the Mediterranean coast. 3 He said to them:

I want to know about these people who have settled in the hills of Canaan. You also live in Canaan, so tell me what cities they control, how large their army is, and what makes them powerful. Tell me who their king is and who commands their army. 4 And find out why they're the only nation in the west that refuses to surrender to me!

5 Achior the Ammonite leader answered:

Sir, I am your loyal servant. Please listen as I tell you about the people who live up in the hill country near your army camp. I will be completely honest.

6 These Israelites are really descendants of the Babylonians.[u] 7-8 But the Israelites refused to follow the customs of their ancestors or to worship the Babylonian gods. Instead, they started worshiping another God, the God of Heaven. The Babylonians immediately forced the Israelites to leave their country, and they settled in Mesopotamia and lived there a long time. 9 Later, their God told them to leave Mesopotamia and settle in Canaan, where they became very rich and owned a lot of gold and silver and livestock.[v]

10 Some years later, a terrible famine forced the Israelites to leave Canaan and go to Egypt, where there was plenty of food.[w] And it wasn't long before they became a nation with too many people to count. 11 The king of Egypt disgraced them by making them his slaves and by mistreating them and forcing them to make bricks. 12 But the Israelites prayed to their God, and he severely punished the whole nation of Egypt. So the Egyptians made the Israelites leave.[x] 13 The God of the Israelites then caused the Red Sea[y] to open up, and the people walked safely through on dry land.[z] 14 He later led them to Mount Sinai and Kadesh-Barnea.

Along the way, the Israelites forced out everyone who was living in the desert,[a] 15 and they settled in the land belonging to the Amorites. They also wiped out the people in the region of Heshbon before crossing the Jordan River and taking control of the entire

[t]**4.14** *sacrifices to please the Lord*: These sacrifices have traditionally been called "burnt offerings" because the whole animal was burned on the altar. A main purpose of such sacrifices was to please the Lord with the smell of the sacrifice, and so in the CEV they are often called "sacrifices to please the Lord." [u]**5.6** *descendants of the Babylonians*: Abraham was born in Ur, a city in Babylonia (see Genesis 11.26-31). [v]**5.9** *where . . . very rich . . . livestock*: See Genesis 13.2. [w]**5.10** *a terrible famine . . . plenty of food*: See Genesis 42.1-5; 46.1-7. [x]**5.12** *the Israelites prayed to their God . . . punished . . . leave*: See Exodus 6.28—12.42. [y]**5.13** *Red Sea*: This refers to the body of water that the Israelites crossed and was one of the marshes or fresh water lakes near the eastern part of the Nile Delta, where they lived and where the towns of Exodus 13.17—14.9 were located. [z]**5.13** *God . . . dry land*: See Exodus 14.1-31. [a]**5.14** *desert*: Probably the desert in the southern part of Canaan.

4.14 Jl 2.17. **5.9** Gn 11.31—12.5. **5.10** Gn 42.1-5; Ex 1.7. **5.11** Ex 1.8-14. **5.12** Ex 7.1—12.46. **5.13** Ex 14.21, 22.

hill country of Canaan. 16 There they
forced out the Canaanites, the Perizzites, the Jebusites, the Shechemites,
and the Gergesites. The Israelites have
lived in Canaan ever since.

17 Their God hates any wrongdoing,
so as long as they obeyed him, they
were successful. 18 But as soon as they
ignored his teachings, he let them be
defeated by enemy after enemy, until
finally they were taken away as captives to a foreign nation. The temple of
their God was destroyed, and their
cities were taken over by enemies.

19 But now the Israelites have
started worshiping their God again,
and they have returned home from the
places where they were scattered. The
Israelites are living in Jerusalem,
where their temple again stands, and
in the hill country where no other people have settled.

20 Sir, if we find out that these Israelites have started disobeying their
God again, we can attack and defeat
them, even if they have accidentally
sinned against him. 21 But if they are
innocent, you should leave them
alone. Their God will defend them,
and every nation in the world would
laugh at us.

22 When Achior finished speaking, the
people standing around the tent started
complaining. The commanders of Holofernes' army, together with the Moabites
and the people from the Mediterranean
coast, demanded that Achior be beaten to
death. 23 They said, "We aren't afraid of
those weak Israelites! They don't have the
strength to fight. 24 Let's attack them, General Holofernes! Your powerful army will
easily defeat them."

Holofernes Rejects Achior's Advice

6 The noise from the crowd of people
died down. Then General Holofernes
of the Assyrian army said to Achior[b] in
front of all the foreigners there:

2 Achior, who do you think you are,
coming here with your hired soldiers
from Ephraim?[c] You must think you're
some kind of prophet! You warned us
not to fight against the Israelites because their God will defend them. But
King Nebuchadnezzar is the only god!
He will send enough troops to completely wipe them out, and the God of
those Israelites won't be able to help
them. 3 We are Nebuchadnezzar's servants, and we will defeat them as if
their entire army were only one soldier.
They won't stand a chance against our
powerful cavalry. 4 We will destroy
them completely. The hills of Israel
will be covered with their blood, and
the valleys will be filled with their dead
bodies. The Israelites will disappear
from the earth, and not a trace of
them will be left. This is the command
of King Nebuchadnezzar, the ruler of
the whole earth, and everything he
said will happen.

5 Achior, you're nothing but a hired
soldier from Ammon, and you have insulted the nation of Assyria. You will
not see me again until I return from
taking revenge on those people who escaped from Egypt. 6 Then my troops
will put you to death, and you will die
like one of the Israelites.

7 Or better yet, my men will take
you into their hill country and leave
you in one of their towns, 8 where you
will die with them. 9 Don't look so upset, Achior. After all, you're the one
who believes the Israelites can't be defeated. Just remember that I will do
everything I have said!

Achior Is Taken to Bethulia

10 The servants who waited on General
Holofernes were there in his tent. So he ordered them to take Achior to the Israelite
town of Bethulia and hand him over to its
people. 11 The servants obeyed and led
Achior from the Assyrian camp, through

[b]6.1 *Achior*: Some Greek manuscripts; other Greek manuscripts "Achior and the Moabites."
[c]6.2 *Ephraim*: Some Greek manuscripts; other Greek manuscripts "Ammon." Since Ephraim was an Israelite tribe, Holofernes may have meant this as an insult.
5.17 Dt 28.1-68.

the valley, and into the hill country, until
they got to the springs of water just below
Bethulia.
12 When the men of Bethulia saw the
Assyrians coming with Achior, they grabbed
their weapons and ran to the top of the hill
where the town was built. They were able
to stop the Assyrians from getting any
closer by using slings to throw stones at
them. 13 The Assyrians had to hide among
the foothills around Bethulia, and so they
tied up Achior and left him at the bottom of
the hill. Then they returned to their camp.
14 Some time later, the Israelites came
down the hill and untied Achior, then led
him back to Bethulia. They took him to the
town officials, 15 who at the time were
Uzziah, Chabris, and Charmis.[d] 16 They
called together the other leaders of Bethulia, while all the young men and women
ran to join them. Achior was then brought
in, and Uzziah asked him exactly what had
happened.
17 Achior said that he had been at the
meeting between Holofernes and the commanders of the Assyrian army, and he repeated everything he had heard. Then he
told the crowd what Holofernes himself
had promised to do to the Israelites.
18 When the people of Bethulia heard
this, they got on their knees and prayed,
19 "Our Lord God of heaven, these arrogant
enemies have completely insulted us. Have
pity and be kind to us, because we are your
people."
20 Then they encouraged Achior for
what he had done and praised him very
much. 21 Uzziah took him to his own
house, where he held a feast for all the
town leaders. They prayed to the God of Israel all night long and asked him to help
them.

Holofernes Attacks Bethulia

7 The next day, Holofernes commanded
his entire army, together with his allies, to march toward the town of Bethulia
and take control of the mountain passes
leading there, then to attack the Israelites.
2 His army was very large—one hundred
seventy thousand foot soldiers and twelve
thousand cavalry troops, not counting the
soldiers who carried the supplies. So they
marched out 3 and set up camp by the
spring in the valley near Bethulia. The
camp covered an area that stretched from
Dothan to Balbaim, and from Bethulia to
Cyamon, a town facing Jezreel Valley.
4 When the Israelites saw how many Assyrians were ready to attack, they were terrified and said to one another, "That army
will wipe out everything in sight, including
the mountains and the valleys." 5 Although
the Israelites were afraid, they immediately
grabbed their weapons and lit the signal
fires in the watchtowers, ready to stand
guard all night long.
6 The next day, Holofernes led his cavalry troops to a place where the Israelites in
Bethulia could see them. 7 He inspected
every road into the town and found the
sources of its water supply. He posted soldiers to guard these springs, then returned
to camp.
8 All the commanders of the Edomite
and Moabite armies, together with the
commanders of the troops from the
Mediterranean coast, came to Holofernes
and said:

9 Sir, listen to our advice, and we
promise that your troops will not be
defeated. 10 These Israelites count on
the mountains and hills around them
to keep them safe, even more than
they count on their weapons. That's
because the mountains are very steep
and difficult to climb. 11 So, General
Holofernes, if you attack Bethulia as
you would usually attack a town, many
of your soldiers will be killed. 12 Instead, order your troops to stay in
camp. And command the soldiers you
posted at the springs to guard them
carefully, 13 because that's the only
place the people of Bethulia can go for
water. They will soon be so thirsty that
they will have to surrender.
Meanwhile, we will lead our armies

[d]**6.15** *Uzziah, Chabris, and Charmis*: Greek "Uzziah son of Micah from the tribe of Simeon, Chabris son of Gothoniel, and Charmis son of Melchiel.

7.5 1 Macc 12.28, 29.

to the tops of the nearby foothills and set up camp. We will make sure that no one leaves Bethulia. [14] Every man, woman, and child in the town will starve to death, and the streets will be filled with dead bodies, even before your army attacks. [15] That's how you can pay them back for rebelling and refusing to surrender peacefully.

[16] Holofernes and his officials liked what the commanders said, and so he gave orders to carry out their plan at once. [17] Part of the Ammonite[e] army and five thousand Assyrian soldiers marched into the valley and took control of the springs that supplied Bethulia with water. [18] The Edomite army and the rest of the Ammonite troops marched into the hills and set up camp opposite the town of Dothan. They also sent some men southeast toward Egrebeh, which is near Chusi, a town on the Mochmur Creek. The rest of the Assyrian army set up camp in the valley. Their army was so large that tents and supplies covered the entire countryside.

The Israelites Cry Out to the Lord

[19] The Israelites lost all hope, when they realized they were surrounded and had no way to escape. So they cried out to the Lord their God for help.

[20] The entire Assyrian army, including the foot soldiers, the cavalry, and the soldiers in chariots, had surrounded Bethulia. And after thirty-four days, the town's water supply was almost gone—[21] every well and cistern was drying up. So each day, drinking water was carefully measured out to make sure everyone had some water to drink. Finally, there was not enough left to go around. [22] The children were getting weak, and all over town young men and women were fainting from thirst. No one had enough strength to survive much longer.

[23] Then every person in Bethulia, both young and old, gathered around Uzziah and the other town leaders and shouted:

> [24] This is all your fault! You decided not to surrender peacefully to the Assyrians. We pray that God will punish you for the trouble you've caused. [25] We are completely helpless, because God has let their powerful army surround us. And now we are exhausted and dying of thirst.
>
> [26] Tell the Assyrians that you have decided to surrender. Let Holofernes and his troops have our town and take everything we own. [27] We would rather be taken captives and become slaves than to die here. At least then we wouldn't have to watch our children and wives die slow and painful deaths. [28] We are begging you to surrender today.[f] Heaven and earth are our witnesses, and so is the Lord God our ancestors worshiped. He is punishing us because they sinned against him and because we have done the same thing.

[29] Everyone then began crying loudly and praying to the Lord God. [30] But Uzziah said to them, "Be brave, my friends! Let's wait five more days to see if the Lord our God will have pity on us. I'm sure he won't let us die. [31] If he doesn't help us in five days, I will do what you have said."

[32] Uzziah then ordered the men to go back to their guard posts on the town walls and in the watchtowers, and he told the women and children to return home. Everyone in Bethulia was still very upset and hopeless.

Judith the Widow

8 [1-2] A widow named Judith lived in Bethulia and knew everything that was happening. She was the daughter of Merari and the granddaughter of Ox. Her ancestors included Joseph, Oziel, Elkiah, Ananias, Gideon, Raphain, Ahitub, Elijah, Hilkiah, Eliab, Nathanael, Salamiel, Sarasadai, and Israel.

Judith and her husband Manasseh had belonged to the same tribe and clan, and he had died during a barley harvest. [3] He had stood a long time in the hot sun, supervising his workers, and he became so hot that he went to bed, where he later died. Manasseh was buried in his family burial place in a field between the towns of

[e]**7.17** *Ammonite*: Greek; one ancient translation "Moabite." [f]**7.28** *We are begging . . . today*: One possible meaning for the difficult Greek text.

Dothan and Balamon, near his hometown of Bethulia.

4 Judith had now been a widow for three years and four months, 5 and she had moved into a small shelter she had made on the roof of her house. She wore widow's clothes and wrapped pieces of sackcloth[g] around her waist. 6 To show her sorrow, Judith went without eating, although she did eat on those days when it was commanded by God's Law: on each Sabbath and the day before it, on each New Moon Festival and the day before it, as well as on every joyous festival the Israelites celebrated.

7 Judith was very beautiful. And she was also very rich, because her husband had left her a lot of gold and silver, as well as male and female slaves, property, and livestock. 8 Judith faithfully worshiped God, and no one ever said anything bad about her.

Judith Meets with the Leaders of Bethulia

9 Judith heard that the people of Bethulia were weak from a shortage of water and that they had blamed Uzziah[h] for their misery. She also learned that Uzziah had promised to surrender to the Assyrians in five days. 10 So at once Judith sent her most trusted servant woman[i] to invite the three town leaders Uzziah, Chabris, and Charmis to her home.

11 When they arrived, she said:

I realize that you are the leaders of Bethulia, but please listen to me. What you said to the people today was wrong. You should not have promised them that you would surrender to the Assyrians, if the Lord God doesn't help us within the next few days. This promise was even made in God's name. 12 You have no right to test God like that, and you certainly have no business trying to control the lives of people. God is in control of that. 13 You are testing the Lord All-Powerful! You can never 14 know what goes on in a person's heart or learn what someone else is thinking. How do you expect to know what God is thinking or what he is planning? The only thing you're doing is making him angry. 15 Even if God does refuse to help us within the next five days, he still has the power to rescue us anytime he chooses. Or he may decide to let our enemies defeat us. 16 Don't put limits on what the Lord our God can do. God is not a mere human. He cannot be threatened or forced into doing something. 17 All we can do is pray for his help and wait for him to rescue us from our enemies. It is up to God to answer us when he chooses.

18 It's true that many of our ancestors worshiped gods made by human hands. Yet none of us alive today has ever sinned like that. 19 Enemies violently abused and killed our ancestors because they worshiped these gods. 20 But since we worship only the Lord God, I pray that he will not reject us or any of our people.

21 If our town is captured, then before long all of Judea will fall and our temple in Jerusalem will be in ruins. And if the temple becomes an unfit place for worship, God will make us pay with our lives. 22 He will punish us for the slaughter of our people and for the destruction and capture of the land he gave us as our own. We will be slaves to other nations, and they will insult and make fun of us. 23 They will never honor us if we are their slaves. We will only be disgraced—the Lord our God will certainly see to that.

24 Our people are depending on us. In fact, the future of the altar and the temple is in our hands. And so, my friends, let's show them that we haven't given up hope. 25 Even though things are difficult, we should thank the Lord our God. He is testing us to see how faithful we are, just as he tested our ancestors long ago. 26 Do

[g] **8.5** *sackcloth*: See the note at 4.10. [h] **8.9** *they had blamed Uzziah*: See 7.23-28. [i] **8.10** *her most trusted servant woman*: Greek "the servant woman who took care of all her property."

8.5 Jg 3.19, 20; 2 K 4.10. **8.12** Dt 6.16. **8.14** Ro 11.33, 34; 1 Co 2.11. **8.26** Gn 22.1-18; 29.1—31.55.

you remember how the Lord tested
Abraham and Isaac or what happened
to Jacob while he was taking care of
his uncle Laban's sheep in Mesopotamia? 27 The Lord isn't testing our
faithfulness to him as severely as he
tested the faith of our ancestors, and
he isn't taking revenge on us. These
hard times were sent as a warning.
28 Uzziah replied:
Judith, everything you have said is
true, and no one would disagree.
29 And this is certainly not the first time
you have spoken so wisely. Even as a
child, you showed good sense, and the
people of Bethulia have always known
how wise and fair your decisions are.
30 But everyone in town is dying of
thirst, and they begged us until we finally made them a solemn promise
that we can't break. 31 You faithfully
worship the Lord God, so pray for us all
and ask him to send enough rain to fill
our wells. Once we have drinking water, our strength will return.
32 Judith said to the three town leaders:
I'm going to do something—something that will never be forgotten.
33 The Lord will use me to rescue the
people of Israel before the day you
agreed to surrender to the Assyrians.
I want the three of you to stand
guard at the town gate tonight, so that
my servant woman and I can leave
safely. 34 Don't try to figure out what
I'm doing. I will tell you everything after I have finished.
35 Uzziah and the others replied, "This
sounds good to us! We pray that the Lord
God will help you take revenge on our
enemies."
36 The three men left Judith's rooftop
shelter and took their positions at the gate.

Judith Prays for God's Help

9 Judith put ashes on her head and removed her robe, uncovering the pieces
of sackcloth[j] she was wearing under her
widow's clothes. She then bowed with her
face to the ground. The time was early
evening, exactly when the incense was being offered on the altar in the Jerusalem
temple. Judith prayed in a loud voice:
2 Our Lord God, my ancestor
Simeon worshiped you, and so you
helped him take revenge on the evil
foreigners who violently abused and
disgraced Dinah. They ripped off her
clothes and raped an innocent virgin,
though you had said that sort of thing
should never be done. 3 That's why
you let their rulers be killed in the very
bed where they raped Dinah.[k] All the
officials of those foreigners were destroyed, and even their servants.
4 Their wives were raped, and their
children were carried off to become
slaves. Dinah's relatives were furious
and were eager to take revenge on the
foreigners who had disgraced their
family, and so they called on you for
help. That's why you let the Israelites
carry off the wealth of those foreigners.
Lord God, I am a widow. Please listen to my prayer. 5 I know that you
caused all of these things to happen,
and everything else as well. You control what is happening now and what
will take place in the future, 6 because
everything happens according to your
plan. You always know ahead of time
what you will do and what decisions
you will make.
7 The Assyrian troops that are now
attacking us are more powerful than
ever. They are constantly bragging
about their strong cavalry and mighty
soldiers who trust in swords, shields,
bows, and slings to win their wars.
They don't realize that you are the
Lord, a warrior who always wins. 8 So,
in your anger, use your strength to
completely destroy their army. Those
Assyrians plan to disgrace the temple
where you are worshiped and to chop
off the corners of your altar with their
swords.
9 You've seen how arrogant those

[j] **9.1** *sackcloth*: See the note at 4.10. [k] **9.3** *their rulers . . . Dinah*: One possible meaning for the difficult Greek text.

9.2 Gn 34.1-31. **9.8** 3 Macc 2.14.

Assyrians are. Destroy them in your
anger, and give me, a widow, the
strength to do what I have planned.
10 Use my deceit to slaughter the Assyrian rulers and their slaves, and let
my strength crush their pride. 11 Your
power doesn't depend on mighty
armies. You are a God who cares for
and protects the weak and helpless,
and you rescue those who have given
up hope. 12 You are the ruler of everything in heaven and on earth, and you
created all rivers and oceans. And you
are the God my ancestors worshiped, so
please hear my sincere prayer. 13 Help
me carry out my deceitful plan to
wound and kill our enemies, who have
plotted evil against your agreement
with us and your holy temple, and
against Mount Zion and the land you
have given your people. 14 Let every
tribe in your nation of Israel know for
certain that you are God All-Powerful
and that you alone protect Israel.

Judith Leaves Bethulia

10 After Judith finished praying to the
God of Israel, 2 she got up and
called for her servant woman. Then Judith
left her rooftop shelter and went down into
her house, where she stayed on Sabbath
days and during religious festivals. 3 After
taking off her widow's clothes and the
pieces of sackcloth, she took a bath. She
put on expensive perfume, then brushed
her hair and put on a fancy headband. Judith dressed in the beautiful clothes she
had worn for celebrations when her husband Manasseh was alive. 4 She put on
sandals and all kinds of jewelry, including
rings and earrings, as well as bracelets for
her ankles and wrists. Judith made sure
that she was beautiful enough to get the attention of every man who saw her.

5 Judith gave her servant a leather bottle
of wine and a small jar of olive oil, then
filled a bag with roasted grain, dried figs,
and her best bread.[l] Finally, she carefully
wrapped up her dishes and gave them to
the servant.

6 Together the two women left the
house and walked to the gate of Bethulia,
where they found Uzziah, the town leader,
with Chabris and Charmis, the other two
leaders. 7 When these men saw Judith
dressed this way and wearing make-up,
they were amazed at her beauty, and said,
8 "We will be praying that the God of our
ancestors will help you carry out your
plans, so that the people of Israel will be
blessed and the city of Jerusalem will be
honored."

Judith bowed in prayer, 9 then replied,
"Tell someone to open the town gate, so
that I can do all these things."

They told some young men to open the
gate, 10 and Judith and her servant walked
down the hill and into the valley. The
young men watched them until they were
out of sight.

Judith Is Taken to the Assyrian Camp

11 As Judith and her servant woman
were walking through the valley near
Bethulia, they were seen by a group of Assyrian soldiers patrolling the area. 12 The
soldiers arrested Judith and asked, "What
nationality are you? Tell us where you're
coming from and where you're going."

She said, "I am a Hebrew from Bethulia.
But I am running away, because your army
is about to completely wipe out my hometown! 13 I'm on my way to tell General
Holofernes how to invade the hill country
of Israel and capture every town, without
having any of his soldiers captured or
killed."

14 The men noticed that Judith was very
beautiful. So after she finished talking, they
said, 15 "You have saved your life by being
eager to talk to General Holofernes. Some
of us will take you to his tent and arrange
for you to see him. 16 When you meet him,
don't be afraid. Tell him exactly what you
told us, and he will be kind to you."

17 One hundred men were assigned to
take Judith and her servant to the tent of
Holofernes. 18 Soon everyone in the Assyrian camp wanted to see Judith. Soldiers
gathered around her as she stood outside

[l] **10.5** *bread*: Greek; other ancients translations "bread and cheese."
9.13 Gk Est 14.13, 14.

the tent, waiting to see Holofernes. 19 She
was so beautiful that they stared at her and
said to each other, "If every Israelite
woman is this lovely, no one would want to
destroy their nation. We need to be sure to
kill all the Israelite men, so that they won't
be able to use their beautiful women to
trick and defeat the whole world."

Judith Meets with Holofernes

20 The bodyguards and servants that
were with General Holofernes came out of
his tent and led Judith inside. 21 Holofernes was lying on his bed under a mosquito net made of purple thread and decorated with gold and emeralds and other
precious stones.
22 When Holofernes was told that Judith
was there, he walked out to the front part
of his tent, with servants carrying silver
lamps in front of him. 23 As Judith came
forward to meet Holofernes, he and his
servants could hardly believe that she was
so beautiful. Judith bowed low to the
ground to honor him, but his servants
helped her to her feet.

11 Holofernes said to Judith:
Don't be afraid! You have
nothing to worry about. I have never
harmed anyone who chooses to serve
Nebuchadnezzar, the ruler of the
whole earth. 2 I wouldn't even be attacking your people in the hill country
if they had surrendered to me. They
insulted me by resisting, and so all this
violence is their own fault. 3 Now that
you're safe, tell me why you left them
and came to our side. It doesn't really
matter, though—we will protect you
for as long as you want to stay. So don't
be afraid! Your life won't be in danger
tonight or at any other time. 4 No one
will ever try to harm you, and you will
be treated very well, just as if you were
one of King Nebuchadnezzar's own
personal servants.
5 Judith answered:
Sir, I am your servant. Please listen
to what I have to say. It will be the
truth, 6 and if you follow my advice,
God will use you to carry out the great
plans he has in mind. 7 I swear to you
by the life of King Nebuchadnezzar
himself, the ruler of the earth, that you
have brought every living creature under his control. People of all nations
serve him because of what you've
done, and wild animals and livestock
and birds will live under the control of
Nebuchadnezzar and his family forever.[m] 8 My people have heard how
wise and talented you are. In fact, the
whole world realizes that you are the
bravest and most clever army commander in the Assyrian kingdom.
9 The people of Bethulia kept
Achior alive, and he told us everything
he said at the meeting with you. 10 Sir,
you should take seriously what he told
you, because everything he said is
true. No enemy can conquer or defeat
our nation of Israel, unless we are
guilty of sinning against our God.
11 But you can defeat the Israelites,
just as you have planned, because they
are about to make our God furious by
sinning against him. And when that
happens, they will certainly die.
12 They are almost out of food and water, so they have decided to slaughter
their livestock and eat foods that God
has forbidden them to eat. 13 They're
going to eat the offerings that have
been dedicated to God and have been
set aside for the priests who serve him
in the Jerusalem temple. These offerings include the first harvests of wheat
and ten percent of their wine and olive
oil. Only the priests are supposed to
touch these things, 14 but even the
people of Jerusalem have already broken that law. So my own people in
Bethulia have sent messengers to ask
the religious leaders in Jerusalem if
the same thing could be done here.
15 On the same day that these messengers return with the news, the people
in Bethulia will begin eating these
foods. That's when you will be able to
defeat them.

[m]**11.7** *People . . . forever*: One possible meaning for the difficult Greek text.

11.7 Jr 27.6, 7; Dn 2.37, 38. **11.13** Ex 23.19; Lv 27.30.

16 As soon as I realized what was
happening, I hurried away from
Bethulia. God has sent me here to help
you do things that will shock everyone
in the world. I am your servant, 17 but
I am still a faithful worshiper of the
God of Heaven. I will stay here in this
camp, and each night I will go into the
valley to pray to God, and he will tell
me when the Israelites have sinned.
18 Then I will immediately tell you, so
that you can lead your army into battle. The Israelites won't have a chance
to defend themselves. 19 After that victory, I will lead you through Judea until
we reach Jerusalem, where I will
crown you king in front of everyone.
You will rule them as if they were
sheep without a shepherd. Not even a
dog will growl and oppose you.

God has told me these things will
happen, and he sent me to tell you as
well.

20 Holofernes and his servants liked
what Judith had said. They were so amazed
at her wisdom that they said to each other,
21 "She must be the wisest and most beautiful woman in all the world!"

22 Holofernes told Judith, "God was
right in sending you to tell us these things,
so that we can defeat the people who have
dishonored King Nebuchadnezzar. 23 Not
only are you beautiful, you also speak
wisely. So I promise that if you do everything you have said here today, I will worship your God as my own. And you will live
in King Nebuchadnezzar's palace and be
famous throughout the world."

Holofernes Offers Food to Judith

12 Holofernes commanded his servants to lead Judith to the table that
had been set with his silver dinnerware and
to serve her some of his own special food
and wine. 2 But Judith said, "God's Law
will not allow me to eat your food, so I
brought enough of my own."

3 Holofernes replied, "But what if you
run out of your food supply? There aren't
any of your people in this camp, and we
won't be able to get you more food."

4 Judith answered, "Sir, as surely as you
live, I have plenty of food to last until the
Lord has finished using me to do what he
has planned."

5 After that, Holofernes' servants took
Judith to her tent, where she went to sleep.
Then just before dawn, she got up 6 and
sent a message to Holofernes, asking if
she could go into the valley to pray. 7 Holofernes ordered his guards to let Judith leave
the camp.

The same thing happened for the next
three days: Judith went into the valley near
Bethulia each night and washed herself in
the spring water. 8 After bathing, she
prayed to the Lord God of Israel and asked
him to show her the best way to rescue the
Israelites. 9 Judith then returned to her
tent, completely clean, and stayed there
until it was time for her evening meal.

Holofernes' Banquet

10 On Judith's fourth day in the Assyrian
camp, Holofernes held a banquet for only
his personal servants—none of his military
officers were invited. 11 Bagoas was the
servant in charge of his personal business,
and Holofernes said to him, "Since you are
the one taking care of the Hebrew woman,
I want you to talk her into coming to the
banquet, so she can eat and drink with us.
12 It would be a shame not to sleep with
such a beautiful woman. I'm sure she
would laugh at us, if I didn't at least try to
talk her into it."

13 Bagoas left and went to see Judith.
He said, "You are such a beautiful woman
that General Holofernes has invited you to
his tent to drink wine with him. You will be
his honored guest and will be treated like
the Assyrian women who serve in King
Nebuchadnezzar's palace."

14 Judith answered, "It would be foolish
to refuse such an invitation. I will gladly go
to his tent, and I will remember this night
for as long as I live."

15 At once, Judith put on her finest
clothes. Her servant woman then went to
Holofernes' tent and placed at his feet the
piece of lambskin that Bagoas had given
Judith to sit on while she ate.

12.2 Dn 1.8; Gk Est 14.17.

16 Judith then entered the tent and sat
down on the lambskin. Holofernes was very
excited to be with Judith and wanted to
sleep with her right away. In fact, he had
been waiting for this opportunity since he
first saw her. 17 He said, "Have some wine,
Judith. Enjoy yourself!"

18 She replied, "I'd love to, sir. This is
the happiest day of my life." 19 But Judith
ate and drank only what her own servant
had brought for her. 20 Holofernes was enjoying being with Judith so much, that he
drank more wine at one meal than he ever
had in any one day of his whole life.

Judith Kills Holofernes

13 When it was late in the evening,
the servants hurried out. Then
Bagoas left and closed Holofernes' tent
from the outside and ordered the servants
to stay out. The meal had lasted such a
long time that all the servants were exhausted and went straight to bed.

2 Judith was alone with Holofernes in
his tent, but he was so drunk that he was
sound asleep on his bed.

3 Judith's servant woman was standing
outside the tent, because Judith had asked
her to wait there until it was time for Judith to pray. Judith had also told Bagoas
that she would be leaving camp, just as she
had done the past three nights.

4 Now that all the servants and guests
had gone home, Judith walked over and
stood by the bed and whispered, "Lord God
All-Powerful, help me with what I'm about
to do, so that Jerusalem will be honored.
5 It is now the time for you to rescue your
people Israel and carry out my plan to defeat the enemies who are attacking us."

6 She walked to the bedpost nearest
Holofernes' head and took down his sword
that was hanging there. 7 She moved closer
to him and grabbed him by his hair, while
praying, "Lord God of Israel, give me the
strength to do this!" 8 Then she struck him
two times in the neck with the sword as
hard as she could and cut off his head.
9 She rolled his body off the bed and ripped
down the mosquito net from the bedposts.
Judith then left the tent and handed the
head to her servant, 10 who put it in the
bag used for carrying food.

Judith Returns to Bethulia

Judith and her servant woman left the
Assyrian camp, just as they always did
when they went to pray. They walked
across the valley and up the hill to the town
of Bethulia.

As they got closer, 11 Judith called out to
the guards on duty, "Open the gate! Open the
gate! Our powerful God of Israel has shown
his strength today by defeating our enemies."

12 Some of the men of Bethulia recognized Judith's voice, and they ran to the
gate and called the town leaders. 13 Then
all the people of Bethulia, both young and
old, hurried to the gate—no one could believe that Judith had returned safely. They
opened the gate and greeted Judith and her
servant woman. Someone started a bonfire,
and everyone gathered around the two
women.

14 Judith said, "Shout praises to God for
showing mercy to the people of Israel! He
helped me destroy our enemies this very
night."

15 She then reached into the bag and
pulled out the head and shouted:

> This is the head of General Holo-
> fernes of the Assyrian army, and here
> is the mosquito net that covered his
> bed. The Lord used a woman to kill
> Holofernes while he lay there drunk.
> 16 My beauty tricked him and led to his
> death, but as surely as the Lord lives,
> Holofernes never touched me. I was
> not disgraced, because the Lord pro-
> tected me at all times.

17 Everyone was truly amazed. They
bowed down and worshiped God by saying,
"We praise you, our God. You have disgraced our enemies today."

18 Uzziah said to Judith:

> God Most High deserves our praise,
> because he has blessed you more than
> any other woman on earth. The same
> God who created heaven and earth has
> helped you cut off the head of our en-
> emy's leader. 19 When people tell what
> mighty things God has done today, they

13.18 Jg 5.24; Lk 1.28, 42.

will remember how you trusted him.
20 I pray that God will honor you for
what you have done. May he bless you
forever, because you were faithful to
him and risked your own life to save
our nation from ruin.

All the people agreed with Uzziah and
replied, "Amen."

Judith's Plan To Defeat the Assyrians

14 Judith said:

Listen to this plan, my friends.
Take the head of Holofernes and hang
it from the top of the town wall.
2 Then as soon as the sun comes up
tomorrow morning, all of you strong
men choose a leader for yourselves.
Take your weapons and march out of
town, as if you were going into the valley to attack the Assyrian guards on
duty there. 3 When they see you, they
will grab their weapons and run back
to their camp and wake up their officers, who will rush to the tent of General Holofernes. They will panic when
they find his dead body, and the entire
Assyrian army will run from you in terror. 4 Then you and everyone else in
Israel will kill them as they run away.

5 But before you do any of this,
bring Achior the Ammonite here. I
want him to see the head of the man
who insulted the nation of Israel and
who sent him to Bethulia to be killed
along with the rest of us.

6 Achior was brought from Uzziah's
house, and when he saw the head of
Holofernes in the hands of one of the men,
he fainted and collapsed on the ground.
7 Achior was helped to his feet, and at once
he bowed down to show his respect for Judith. He said, "Every family in Judea
thanks you, and I pray that all nations will
shake with fear when your name is mentioned. 8 Please tell me how you did it."

Judith told Achior and the crowd everything that had happened from the day she
left Bethulia until she returned. 9 As soon
as she finished her story, the people of the
town celebrated with shouts of joy.

10 After Achior had listened to what the
God of Israel had done, he completely put
his faith in God. Then he was circumcised
and became an Israelite. And from that day
on, he and his descendants worshiped God.

The Assyrians Panic

11 Early the next morning, the Israelites
hung the head of Holofernes on the town
wall. The men armed themselves with
weapons, then went out in groups and
stood on the hills around Bethulia.

12 As soon as the Assyrian guards saw
what was happening, they reported it to
their commanders, who made sure every
Assyrian officer was alerted. 13 The highest-
ranking officers went to Holofernes' tent
and said to Bagoas, "You need to wake
General Holofernes and tell him those Israelites had the nerve to march out of
Bethulia to attack us. They may think we
can be defeated, but we will wipe out every
one of them."

14 So Bagoas went inside and shook the
curtain that separated Holofernes' bedroom from the rest of the tent. Bagoas
waited, because he thought Judith was still
with Holofernes. 15 No one answered, and
so Bagoas opened the curtain and walked
in. He saw the headless body of Holofernes
lying on the floor, 16 and he began moaning
and crying and tearing his clothes in sorrow. 17 Bagoas ran quickly to Judith's tent
and saw that it was empty. Then he ran
back out and shouted to the officers,
18 "We've been tricked. King Nebuchadnezzar's entire kingdom has been disgraced by
one woman. Look! There's Holofernes lying dead on the ground—and his head is
gone!"

19 As soon as the Assyrian officers
learned what had happened, they tore their
uniforms in sorrow. Loud crying and moaning was heard everywhere in camp.

The Israelites Defeat the Assyrians

15 When the Assyrian soldiers heard
their officers crying, they were terrified 2 and started trembling with fear.
They ran out of camp in every direction,
not waiting for anyone, and tried to escape
in the valley and the nearby mountains.
3 The soldiers who had camped in the hills
around Bethulia also ran away in fear.

Just then, the Israelite troops attacked.

4 At the same time, Uzziah sent messengers to the towns of Betomasthaim, Choba,
Kola, and other towns in Israel to tell
everyone what was happening and to ask
them to join in the attack. 5 When the people in these towns received the message,
they came and helped attack the Assyrians.
The Israelites chased their enemies as far
as Choba, and along the way they killed
many of them. The people of Jerusalem
and southern Judea also heard the news
and joined in the attack.

Meanwhile, the people living in the regions of Gilead and Galilee blocked the retreating Assyrians, killing many of them
and chasing the others into the region of
Damascus.

6 The rest of the people of Bethulia entered the Assyrian camp and carried off
most of the valuable possessions. 7 When
the Israelite soldiers returned from battle,
they took everything else. The amount of
things taken from the Assyrians was so
large that the people shared the wealth
with their neighbors in the surrounding
towns and villages.

The Israelites Celebrate Their Victory

8 Joakim the high priest and the other
leaders of Israel came from Jerusalem to
see what wonderful things the Lord had
done for Israel. They also wanted to meet
and congratulate Judith. 9 When they arrived in Bethulia, they said, "Judith, you
are the pride of Jerusalem and the hero of
our nation Israel. 10 You alone won this victory for Israel. The Lord God All-Powerful
is certainly pleased with you, and we pray
that he will bless you forever."

All the people agreed and said, "Amen."

11 For thirty days, the Israelites carried
off the wealth of the Assyrian camp. They
gave Judith the tent of Holofernes and
everything in it, including his silver dinnerware, his bowls, his couches, and the rest
of his furniture. She loaded down her mule
and filled her carts with these things.

12 All the women of Israel came to meet
and sing praises to Judith; many of them
also danced in her honor. Judith took leaf-
covered branches and gave one to every
woman who was there with her, 13 and they
all wore wreaths of olive leaves on their
heads. Judith led the women in joyful
dancing, with the men following behind,
waving their weapons in the air and wearing strings of flowers and singing songs of
praise.

14 Judith began singing a song of praise
to God, and the crowd joined in the singing.

Judith's Song of Praise

16 Judith sang:

Shout praises to my Lord God;
play tambourines and cymbals.
Sing a new song of praise
and pray for his help.
2 The Lord God is a warrior
who rescued me from my enemy.
God wins every battle
and camps among his people.

3 The Assyrians marched down
from the mountains in the north.
Thousands of soldiers blocked
the rivers and streams;
cavalry troops covered
the mountain like a blanket.
4 They threatened to burn our land
and slaughter our young men,
to kill our babies
to capture our children,
and to carry off
all of our young women.

5 But the Lord All-Powerful
fooled the Assyrians
and used a woman
to wipe them out.
6 The mighty Assyrian leader
wasn't killed by young men
or cruel warriors[n] or giants.
I, Judith the daughter of Merari,
used my charm
to strike him dead.

7 I put aside my widow's clothes
and won a victory
for troubled Israel.

[n] **16.6** *cruel warriors*: Greek "the sons of the Titans." In Greek mythology, the Titans were powerful warriors who ruled the world for a time.

ESTHER
GREEK VERSION

ABOUT THIS BOOK

The Greek version of the book of Esther is a longer form of the story than the Hebrew original and contains blocks of extra material called "additions." The Latin Vulgate translation, made in the late 4th century A.D., included the additions to the book, but they were gathered together at the end. When the Vulgate was later given chapter and verse numbers, the additions at the end were numbered 10.4—16.24. In the *CEV,* the entire Greek version of Esther is translated with all the additions returned to their proper places, so the reader can more easily see how they fit in with the rest of the book. But this means that the texts from chapters 11 through 16 are in various places in the book.

The Greek version of the book of Esther emphasizes that it was God who saved Queen Esther and her people from being destroyed. Esther has a more important part in the action of the story than she had in the Hebrew version, and the Greek is often anti-Gentile.

A QUICK LOOK AT THIS BOOK

- Mordecai's Dream (11.2—12.6)
- Esther Becomes Queen (1.1—2.23)
- Haman Plans To Destroy the Jews (3.1-13)
- The Letter Commanding Everyone To Kill the Jews (13.1-7)
- Mordecai Asks for Esther's Help (3.14—4.17)
- Mordecai's Prayer (13.8-18)
- Esther's Prayer (14.1-19)
- Esther Invites the King and Haman to Dinner (15.1-16)
- Mordecai Is Honored, Not Killed (5.3—6.14)
- Haman Is Put To Death (7.1-10)
- The King Allows the Jews To Defend Themselves (8.1-12)
- A Copy of the King's Letter (16.1-24; 8.13)
- The Letters Are Sent Out (8.14-17)
- The Jews Destroy Their Enemies (9.1-19)
- The Festival of Purim (9.20-32)
- The Greatness of Artaxerxes and Mordecai (10.1-3)
- Mordecai Remembers His Dream (10.4-13)
- A Note about the Festival of Purim (11.1)

I put on perfume 8 and placed
a fancy headband in my hair,
and I dressed in linen
to attract and fool him.
9 He liked my sandals
and thought I was lovely;
then I took his own sword
and cut off his head.
10 My courage shocked the Persians
and stunned the Medes.

11 Our weak and abused people
let out shouts of victory,
while the Assyrians
trembled in fear and ran.[o]
12 Though our ancestors were slaves,
we, the Lord's mighty army,
attacked and killed
enemy troops.

13 I will sing a new song of praise
to the Lord our God;
he is glorious and all-powerful,
and his strength never fails.
14 Let all living creatures
worship the Lord.
By his word, he gave them life;
his breath created them.
Nothing can oppose
the Lord's command.

15 Mountains and oceans
shake with fear,
and rocks melt like wax,
when the Lord approaches.
But he shows mercy to all
who are faithful to him.

16 It is much better
to obey the Lord
than to offer
sweet-smelling sacrifices
or the fat of choice meat.

17 All nations that oppose Israel
will fall into ruin;
the Lord All-Powerful
will punish them
on the day of judgment.
Fire and worms
will destroy their bodies,
and they will always
groan in pain.

The People Celebrate in Jerusalem

18 When the crowd reached Jerusalem,
they immediately got ready to worship God
by going through the ceremonies to make
themselves clean. Then they offered the required sacrifices to please God,[p] including
the voluntary offering and other sacrifices
and gifts.
19 Judith brought along all of Holofernes' possessions that the people had
given her, and she dedicated them to God.
She also gave the mosquito net from the
bed of Holofernes as a special offering to
keep a promise.
20 Judith stayed in Jerusalem for three
months, while she and the people celebrated at the temple.

The Rest of Judith's Life

21 After the victory celebration, everyone went back home, and Judith returned
to her place in Bethulia. She was famous
everywhere in Israel for as long as she
lived. 22 Although a lot of men asked to
marry her, she always refused and never re-
married after her husband Manasseh died.
23-24 Judith became more famous as time
went by, and she continued to live in the
house Manasseh had left her.

Some time before Judith died, she divided her possessions and property among her own closest relatives, as well as those of her husband, and she allowed her servant woman to go free.

Judith died in Bethulia at the age of one hundred five. She was buried beside her husband in their family tomb, and everyone in Israel mourned her death for seven days.
25 As long as Judith was alive, and for
many years after her death, no enemy nation terrorized the people of Israel.

[o]**16.11** *ran*: One possible meaning for the difficult Greek text of verse 11. [p]**16.18** *sacrifices to please God*: See the note at 4.14.

16.13 Ps 144.9. **16.16** 1 S 15.22; Ps 51.16, 17; Ho 6.6.

ADDITION A[a]

Mordecai's Dream

11 [2-4] Mordecai son of Jair[b] was a Jew from the Benjamin tribe, and he lived in the city of Susa in Persia. Mordecai had been taken away from Jerusalem as a prisoner, when King Nebuchadnezzar of Babylonia[c] had captured King Jehoiachin.[d] Mordecai had become an important official in the court of Artaxerxes the Great,[e] the king of Persia. And on the first day of the month of Nisan[f] in the second year that Artaxerxes was king, Mordecai had a dream.

In Mordecai's dream, [5] there was confusion and unrest all over the world. He heard crashing thunder, and the earth shook with an earthquake [6] as two huge dragons went toward each other, ready to fight. They roared, [7] and every nation on earth prepared to go to war against God's people. [8] It was a dark and hopeless time; the world was full of suffering and hardship and conflict.

[9] God's people were afraid of the disaster that was about to strike them, and they were sure they were going to be killed. [10] But when they cried out to God for help, a tiny stream suddenly became a mighty river, [11] and the sun rose and shone brightly. God's people were given power, and they destroyed those who had oppressed them.

[12] Mordecai woke up, but he knew that in his dream he had seen what God was planning to do. And so, Mordecai thought about his dream all day, trying to understand exactly what it meant.

Mordecai Saves the King's Life

12 That night,[g] Mordecai was in the palace courtyard. He was resting not far from Gabatha and Tharra, the two officers who were on guard duty. [2] Mordecai overheard them talking, and as he listened carefully, he realized they were planning to murder King Artaxerxes.

Mordecai warned Artaxerxes about the plot to kill him. [3] The two officers confessed when Artaxerxes questioned them, and so he gave orders for them to be put to death. [4] He also ordered that a report of these events be written in his records, and Mordecai also wrote down what had happened. [5] Artaxerxes appointed Mordecai to a position[h] in the royal court and gave him a reward.

[6] Haman son of Hammedatha[i] was one of the king's most honored officials, and he became angry because the two officers had been put to death. So he decided to find a way to harm Mordecai and all the Jewish people.

END OF ADDITION A

Queen Vashti Disobeys King Artaxerxes

1 [1-3] King Artaxerxes[j] lived in his capital city of Susa[k] and ruled one hundred twenty-seven provinces from India to Ethiopia.

During the third year of his rule, King Artaxerxes paid for a festival and asked a special group known as the Friends of the King to come. He also invited a large number of people from his own empire and

[a]**11.2-4** The verses 11.2—12.6 are sometimes numbered as A.1-17 or 1.1a-1s.
[b]**11.2-4** *Mordecai son of Jair*: Greek "Mordecai the son of Jair, the son of Shimei, the son of Kish."
[c]**11.2-4** *King Nebuchadnezzar of Babylonia*: Ruled 605-562 B.C. [d]**11.2-4** *Jehoiachin*: Ruled Judah for three months in 598 B.C. [e]**11.2-4** *Artaxerxes the Great*: Probably Artaxerxes I (ruled 465-425 B.C.) but may refer to Artaxerxes II (ruled 405-358 B.C.). In the Hebrew version of Esther, the king is identified as Ahaseurus, better known as Xerxes I (ruled 485-465 B.C.). [f]**11.2-4** *Nisan*: Also called Abib, the first month of the Hebrew calendar, from about mid-March to mid-April.
[g]**12.1** *That night*: Or "One night." [h]**12.5** *position*: Or "a higher position." [i]**12.6** *Haman son of Hammedatha*: The Greek text adds "a Bougean." However, the meaning of this term is not known. [j]**1.1-3** *King Artaxerxes*: Probably Artaxerxes I (ruled 465-425 B.C.), but may refer to Artaxerxes II (ruled 405-358 B.C.). In the Hebrew version of Esther, the king is identified as Ahaseurus, better known as Xerxes I (ruled 485-465 B.C.). [k]**1.1-3** *Susa*: A city east of Babylon and a winter home for Persian kings.

11.2-4 2 K 24.10-16. **1.1,2** Ezra 4.6.

from other nations. The rulers of the Persian provinces came, and so did many important people from the province of Media.
4 For one hundred eighty days Artaxerxes showed off his wealth and spent a lot of money to impress his guests with the celebrations.

5 After this festival,[l] Artaxerxes invited all the men in the city of Susa to a drinking party in the courtyard of his palace. The party went on for six days.

6 The palace had been decorated with cotton and linen curtains tied back with purple linen cords. These cords were attached to gold and silver square pegs on columns, which were made of marble and other stones. Couches of gold and silver were arranged on pavement that had all kinds of designs made from emeralds, mother-of-pearl, and marble. These couches were covered with see-through cloth woven with designs of different colors, and around each couch were roses.

7 The wine cups were made of gold and silver, and the king had put on display one small cup that was decorated with rubies worth over sixteen hundred tons of silver.
There was plenty of the king's favorite sweet wine, 8 and he had told everyone, "Drink all you want!" Then he told his servants, "Keep our cups full."

9 Meanwhile, in another part of the palace, Queen Vashti[m] was giving a drinking party for the women of Susa.

10 By the seventh day of the party, King Artaxerxes was really feeling happy, and he told his seven personal servants Haman,[n] Bazan, Tharra, Boraze, Zatholtha, Abataza, and Tharaba 11 to bring Vashti to him.
Artaxerxes wanted to place the crown on her head again, to show everyone she was the queen. He also wanted to show his governors and the people from different countries just how beautiful she really was.

12 But Vashti did not go back with the servants—she refused to obey the king! Artaxerxes was furious because she had embarrassed him, 13 and he said to his friends,[o] "Vashti has refused to obey me! Tell me what the law says about a case like this."

14 Arkesaeus, Sarsathaeus, and Malesear went up to the king. They were his highest officials as well as being governors of the Persians and Medes, and they were always given the seats closest to the king.
15 They said, "You sent your servants with a command for Queen Vashti. But since she refused to obey you, the law says she must be punished."

16-17 Then Muchaeus, another official, told the king and the governors:

> King Artaxerxes has told us what Queen Vashti said and how she refused to obey him. She humiliated the king, and soon all his governors and officials will be humiliated too.
> 18 We are governors of the Persians and Medes, but when our wives hear what the queen said to the king, our wives will dare to insult us in the same way.
>
> 19 Your Majesty, if you agree, you should make a law that Vashti is never to be with you again. Put it in writing, according to the laws of the Medes and Persians, so that it cannot be changed. And find some other woman who is more suited to be queen than Vashti.
>
> 20 Finally, make sure everyone in your kingdom is told what you have decided to do. Then each wife will honor her husband, whether he is rich or poor.

21 Artaxerxes and his officials liked what Muchaeus had said, 22 and Artaxerxes sent a copy of the law to all of his provinces. Each copy was written in the language of the province to which it was sent, and it said that every husband must be respected by his family.

Esther Is Made Queen

2 After a while, King Artaxerxes got over being angry. He stopped being lonely for Vashti, and he forgot about all the

[l]**1.5** *festival*: Most Greek manuscripts "wedding party"; some Greek manuscripts "drinking party." [m]**1.9** *Vashti*: The Hebrew form of the name; Greek "Astin." [n]**1.10** *Haman*: This was probably a different Haman than Haman son of Hammedatha mentioned elsewhere in the book.
[o]**1.13** *friends*: Probably refers to an important group known as "The Friends of the King," the king's most honored and close advisors.

things he had said about her when he divorced her. 2 Then his personal servants said:

Your Majesty, a search must be made to find you some beautiful young women who have good reputations 3 and are virgins. You can select officers in every province to bring them to the place where you keep your wives here in the capital city of Susa. Your servant who is in charge of your wives can be in charge of the young women and make sure they are given beauty creams and whatever else they need. 4 Choose the woman who pleases you the most and make her your queen instead of Vashti.

Artaxerxes liked these suggestions, and he followed them.

5 At this time a Jew named Mordecai[p] was living in Susa, the capital of Persia. His father was named Jair, and his grandfather Shimei was the son of Kish from the tribe of Benjamin. 6 Mordecai[q] was one of the people that King Nebuchadnezzar of Babylonia[r] had taken prisoner from Jerusalem.

7 Mordecai's uncle Aminadab had a daughter named Esther. But Aminadab and his wife had died, and so Mordecai had raised his cousin Esther as his own daughter. She had grown into a beautiful young woman, 8 and when the king's command was sent out, she was taken to the palace along with the many young women who had been brought to Susa. She and the others were placed in the care of Gai, who was in charge of all the king's wives. 9 Esther was Gai's favorite, and he began her beauty treatments at once. He also gave her plenty of food and seven maids from the king's palace. Esther and her servants were treated better than the other women.

10 Mordecai had warned Esther not to tell anyone she was a Jew, and she obeyed him. 11 He was anxious to find out what would happen to her. So each day he would walk back and forth in front of the courtyard at the building where the women lived.

12 Each of the young women was given beauty treatments for a whole year before going to King Artaxerxes. The first six months her skin was rubbed with olive oil and myrrh, and the last six months it was treated with beauty cream mixed with spices. 13 Then she spent one night alone with Artaxerxes. He sent a servant to bring her to the palace 14 in the evening. The next morning she went to the place where the king's wives stayed after being with him. There the king's servant Gai was in charge of them, and only the ones that the king asked for by name could go back to him.

15-16 Esther's turn[s] to go to King Artaxerxes came in the month of Adar, the twelfth month,[t] in the seventh year that he was king. Esther did everything Gai told her to do. Everyone liked her, 17 and even Artaxerxes liked her better than any of the other young women he had seen. In fact, he fell in love with her and placed the queen's crown on her head. 18 Then he gave a seven-day drinking party to celebrate his marriage to Esther, and he made a law that for a certain length of time, no one in his kingdom would have to pay any taxes.

Mordecai Saves the King's Life

19 At this time, Mordecai was serving as one of the king's officials. 20 He had warned Esther not to tell anyone that she was a Jew, but he had also told her to continue worshiping God and obeying his commands, just as she had done when she was living in Mordecai's home. Esther obeyed Mordecai and did not change her way of life.

21 The king's two chief bodyguards were angry that Mordecai had been promoted, and they decided to murder the king.

[p]**2.5** *Mordecai*: See 11.2—12.5. [q]**2.6** *Mordecai*: Or "Kish"; Greek "He." [r]**2.6** *King Nebuchadnezzar of Babylonia*: Ruled 605-562 B.C. [s]**2.15,16** *Esther's turn*: Greek "the turn of Esther, the daughter of Aminadab the brother of Mordecai's father" (see also 2.7). [t]**2.15,16** *the month of Adar, the twelfth month*: From about mid-February to mid-March.
2.6 2 K 24.10-16; 2 Ch 36.10.

22 But when Mordecai found out about their plot, he warned Esther, and she told the king.

23 King Artaxerxes questioned the two men to make sure they were guilty, then he had them hanged. He also had someone write up a report praising Mordecai for the kindness he had shown, and the report was placed in the royal library.

Haman Plans To Destroy the Jews

3 Later, King Artaxerxes promoted Haman the son of Hammedatha[u] to the highest position in his kingdom. 2 The king ordered all of his officials to bow down to Haman, and all of them obeyed except Mordecai. 3 The other officials went to Mordecai and asked, "Why are you ignoring what the king said?" 4 They spoke to Mordecai like this for several days, but he told them he was a Jew and would not bow down to Haman. The other officials went to Haman and told him that Mordecai was Jewish and refused to do what the king said.

5 Haman was furious when he learned that Mordecai refused to bow down to him, 6 and he started planning how to get rid of all the Jews in the kingdom. 7 It was now the twelfth year that Artaxerxes was king, and Haman decided[v] to find out what would be the best month and day to kill Mordecai and the rest of the Jews. He found that the best date was Adar[w] fourteenth.

8 Then Haman went to King Artaxerxes and said, "Your Majesty, the people from a certain nation are scattered throughout your kingdom. Their customs are different from ours, and they refuse to obey your laws. You would be better off to get rid of them. 9 If you give orders for all of them to be killed, I will pay over five hundred tons of silver to your treasury."[x]

10 Artaxerxes handed his royal ring to Haman, so the law against the Jews could be made official.[y] 11 Then the king said, "Do what you want with those people! And you can keep their money."

12 On the thirteenth day of the first month,[z] Haman called in the king's secretaries and ordered them to write a letter and make copies in every language used in the kingdom. The letter was to be written in the name of King Artaxerxes and sent to the generals of his army and to the governors of his one hundred twenty-seven provinces from India to Ethiopia. 13 Then messengers would deliver the copies of the letter, which said that on a certain day in Adar, the twelfth month, the people were to get rid of all the Jews and take their property.

ADDITION B[a]

A Copy of the Letter

13 This is a copy of the letter:

From Artaxerxes, the Great King, to the governors and officials of my one hundred twenty-seven provinces from India to Ethiopia.

2 I rule many nations, and I am the most powerful king in the world. But I have never used my power in a proud or arrogant way. Instead, I have always been reasonable and kind to the people in my kingdom. I know they want peace, and so I have decided to make every part of my kingdom peaceful and safe for travel.

3-4 When I asked my advisors to tell me the best way to bring about peace and safety, Haman had an answer. He is the

[u]3.1 *Haman the son of Hammedatha*: The Greek text adds "a Bougean." However, the meaning of this term is not known. [v]3.7 *decided*: The Greek text has "cast lots," which were small pieces of wood or bone that were often used to get an answer from a god. They were tossed on the ground, and the way they landed showed what the answer was. [w]3.7 *Adar*: See the note at 2.15, 16.
[x]3.9 *I will pay . . . to your treasury*: Possibly from the possessions of the Jews that would be killed. [y]3.10 *ring . . . official*: Melted wax was used to seal a document, and while the wax was still soft, the king's ring was pressed into it. The special design left in the wax showed that the document was official. [z]3.12 *the first month*: Nisan (also called Abib), the first month of the Hebrew calendar, from about mid-March to mid-April. [a]13.1 The verses 13.1-7 are sometimes numbered as B.1-7 or as 3.13a-13g.

13.3-5 3 Macc 3.7.

wisest man in my kingdom and is always loyal and kind, which is why I made him my highest official. He told us that the people from a certain nation are scattered throughout all the other nations of the world. These people are always causing trouble, and they have laws that make them disobey those of the nations where they live. And when I make laws in the hope of uniting the people in my kingdom, the people of this nation refuse to obey. 5 In fact, they seem to be the only people who always go against everyone else and insist on following their own strange customs. They don't like the way I rule, and they commit every horrible crime they can to keep my kingdom from being peaceful.

6 Haman, my highest and most honored official, has written letters telling what these people are like. So I have made a law that all of them—even the women and children—must be put to death without mercy on the fourteenth day of the month of Adar[b] of this year. 7 They have worked against us for a long time, and so on this one day, we will use violence to send them down to the world of the dead. Then our kingdom will be peaceful and free from trouble forever.

END OF ADDITION B

The Letters Are Displayed

3 14 Copies of this letter were displayed publicly in each province, so that every nation would be ready for that day. 15 Copies were quickly posted in Susa, but no one in the city could figure out what was going on. Meanwhile, Artaxerxes and Haman got drunk together.

Mordecai Asks for Esther's Help

4 Mordecai learned what had happened, and he tore his clothes in sorrow and put on clothes made of sackcloth.[c] Then he sprinkled himself with ashes[d] and ran through the city streets, shouting at the top of his voice, "An innocent nation is going to be destroyed!" 2 But he could go only as far as the palace gate, because no one wearing sackcloth or sprinkled with ashes was allowed inside the palace courtyard.

3 In every province, wherever the king's orders had been read, the Jews cried bitterly and mourned; they put on sackcloth and sprinkled themselves with ashes.

4 When Esther's servant girls and her other servants told her what Mordecai was doing, she was terribly upset and sent Mordecai some clothes to wear instead of the sackcloth. But he refused. 5-6 Then Esther called in her personal servant Hachratheus and sent him to find out exactly what was the matter with Mordecai.[e]

7 Mordecai told Hachratheus everything that had happened, and especially how Haman had promised to put over five hundred tons of silver into the king's treasury if all the Jews were killed. 8 Mordecai handed Hachratheus a copy of the orders posted in Susa for the murder of the Jews, then he said:

> Hachratheus, after you show these orders to Esther and explain what they mean, ask her to go to the king and beg him to have pity on her people, the Jews! Then give her this message from me: "Esther, remember that I raised you and that you were once an ordinary person just as we are. And now Haman, the king's highest official, has lied about us, and we have been condemned to die. Beg the Lord for help, then speak to the king for us and save us from death."

9 Hachratheus went back to Esther and told her what Mordecai had said. 10 Esther answered, "Tell Mordecai 11 that there is a law about going into the inner courtyard to see the king. Everyone in the kingdom knows that if you go in without being invited by him, the penalty is death. The only thing that can save you is for him to hold

[b]**13.6** *Adar*: See the note at 2.15, 16. [c]**4.1** *sackcloth*: A rough, dark-colored cloth made from goat or camel hair and used to make grain sacks. It was worn in times of trouble or sorrow. [d]**4.1** *sprinkled . . . ashes*: A way of showing sorrow. [e]**4.5,6** *Mordecai*: Some manuscripts add "Hachratheus went to Mordecai, who was in the street across from the city gate."

out his golden scepter[f] to you. And it's been
thirty days since he has asked for me."
12 When Hachratheus told Mordecai
everything Esther had said, 13 Mordecai
told him to go back to Esther and say, "Esther, if all the Jews are going to be killed,
don't think that you will escape. 14 If you
refuse to help us, we will find help and protection from someone else, but you and
your family will be wiped out. It could be
that you were made queen just for a time
like this!"
15 Esther sent Hachratheus[g] back to
Mordecai to tell him, 16 "Hurry and bring
together all the Jews in Susa. Tell them to
go without eating for my sake. Don't eat or
drink for three days and nights, and my
servant girls and I will do the same. Then I
will break the law and go in to see the king,
even if it means I must die!"
17 Mordecai left and did everything Esther had told him to do.

ADDITION C[h]

Mordecai's Prayer

13 8 Mordecai prayed and begged the
Lord to save his people, and he
thanked the Lord for the times he had
helped them in the past. 9 Mordecai said:

> Our Lord, you are King and Ruler
> of the whole earth, and so no one can
> stop you when you decide to save Is-
> rael. 10 You are the Creator of heaven
> and earth and of all the amazing
> things on earth as well. 11 Everything
> obeys your commands, and no one can
> stand against you.
> 12 Since you know everything, you
> know that I wasn't being proud or arro-
> gant or vain when I have refused to
> bow down to that arrogant Haman. 13 I
> would even kiss the soles of his feet if
> that would save Israel. 14 But you are
> my God, and that's why I refused to
> honor a human the way I honor you. I
> don't want to sound arrogant, but I
> won't bow down to anyone except you.
> 15-16 Long ago, our ancestor Abra-
> ham worshiped you, Lord. You are our
> God and king, and we are your people.
> We have always belonged to you, ever
> since you set us free from Egypt. Don't
> abandon us now; save us from our en-
> emies, who want to destroy us. 17 An-
> swer my prayer and have mercy on us.
> Turn our sadness into celebration. Let
> us live, and we will sing praises to your
> name; we honor you, so please don't
> let death silence our voices.

18 All the Israelites wept bitterly,
because they could see they were going
to die.

Esther's Prayer

14 Queen Esther was worried and upset, and she realized that only the
Lord could save her people from being
killed. 2 So she took off her beautiful royal
robes and put on clothes that showed it
was a time of suffering and death. She put
ashes and dirt[i] all over her head, rather
than using any of her expensive lotions.[j]
And instead of doing everything she could
to look beautiful and dignified, Esther just
let her long hair hang down in tangles.
3 Then she prayed to the Lord God of Israel:

> You, Lord, are the only King we
> have. And no one except you can help
> me now, because I'm all alone, 4 and
> I've decided to risk my life.
> 5 Ever since I was born, those who
> belong to my family's tribe have told
> me that long ago you chose our ances-
> tors to become Israel, your own special
> people. You have always kept your
> promises to us. 6 But we sinned
> against you, Lord, and you let our ene-
> mies conquer us 7 because we had
> worshiped their gods. You were right to
> punish us this way.
> 8 But our enemies weren't satisfied
> just to keep us in bitter slavery. Now

[f]**4.11** *scepter*: A decorated rod, often made of gold, that a king held in his hand as a sign of his royal power. [g]**4.15** *Hachratheus*: Greek "the man who came." [h]**13.8** The verses 13.8—14.19 are sometimes numbered as C.1-30 or 4.17a-17z. [i]**14.2** *dirt*: Or "manure." [j]**14.2** *lotions*: Or "perfumes."

13.13,14 Jdt 9.13. **13.15,16** Ex 3.6.

they have made an agreement with
their idols 9 to kill all of us, your special people. And if they get rid of us,
your promises to us will be meaningless. We will no longer be able to praise
you, and we won't be able to worship
you and offer sacrifices in your temple.
10 Then the nations will praise their
idols and forever give honor to a mere
earthly king.
11 Please, Lord, don't hand over
your royal power[k] to gods that are
nothing. We have fallen down, but
don't let our enemies laugh at us. They
have made plans to kill us, but turn
their own plans against them. And
make an example of the one who is behind those plans. 12 You are king of the
gods and are above every other ruler,
so show your power and rescue us in
this time of great danger. Give me
courage 13 and the right words to say
to the king,[l] so that he will change his
mind and hate the man who is attacking us. I pray that the king will get rid
of him and those who support his plot.
14 Reach down and save us, Lord. I'm
all alone—no one but you can help
me now.
15-16 You know all things—you know
how much I hate being the queen of this
evil country. I hate the honor that the
people give me, and wearing my crown
when I go out in public is like having a
blood-soaked rag placed around my
head. That's why I refuse to wear it in
my own living quarters. And you also
know that I even hate to sleep with my
husband the king, because he isn't one
of your people and isn't circumcised.
17 I am your servant, Lord, and I have
never eaten at the same table as
Haman, and I have never attended the
king's banquets or drunk wine that
had been offered to other gods.
18 You are the Lord God that Abraham worshiped, and only you have given
me any joy since I was brought here.
19 We have little hope left. But you,
Lord, have power over everything, so
please hear our prayers and rescue us
from those who are evil. And help me
not to be afraid.

END OF ADDITION C

ADDITION D[m]

Esther Invites the King and Haman to a Dinner

15 Esther prayed for three days,[n] then
she changed her clothes and put
on her royal robes once again.[o] 2 When Esther finished getting ready, she was beautiful. She prayed once more to God, the
Savior who watches over all things, and she
left with her two favorite servant girls.
3 One of them helped her walk, 4 and the
other followed right behind and kept her
long robes from dragging on the floor. 5 Esther's beauty was perfect. Her face was
glowing with happiness, as though she
knew the king loved her. However, in her
heart she felt paralyzed by fear.
6 Finally Esther passed through the last
doorway and into the throne room, where
she stopped in front of King Artaxerxes. He
was seated there, wearing majestic royal
robes that were covered with jewels and
gold—a terrifying sight.
7 The king looked up, and his face was
burning with royal anger. Queen Esther
went pale! She fainted and fell right on top
of her servant,[p] who was just in front of her.
8 Then God changed the king's anger into
concern for Esther, and the king jumped
up and ran over to her. He took Esther in
his arms, holding her until she came to.
Then he comforted her and gently said,
9 "Esther, what's wrong? Don't be afraid!

[k]**14.11** *power*: Greek "scepter," a decorated rod, often made of gold, that a king held in his hand as a sign of his royal power. [l]**14.13** *king*: Greek "lion." [m]**15.1** The verses 15.1-16 are sometimes numbered as D.1-16 or 5.1a-1f, 2, 2a, 2b, 15.4-19. Addition D replaces 5.1, 2 of the Hebrew text. [n]**15.1** *three days*: See 4.16. [o]**15.1** *once again*: See 14.2. [p]**15.7** *right on top of her servant*: One possible meaning for the difficult Greek text.

14.17 Dn 1.8; Jdt 12.2.

I'm your husband,[q] 10 so that law about being put to death doesn't apply to you; it
only applies to our people.[r] Please get up."
11-12 Still holding her in his arms, the
king touched Esther's neck with his golden
scepter[s] and said, "Esther, speak to me. Say
something."
13 Esther replied, "Your Majesty, when I
saw you, it was like seeing one of God's angels. I was struck with fear of your royal
splendor. 14 My king, your power is amazing, but your face is full of kindness."
15 Then Esther fainted and fell again.
16 The king was worried and upset, and
all his servants came and helped Esther.

END OF ADDITION D

Mordecai Is Honored, Not Killed

5 3 A little while later, the king said, "Esther, what brings you here? Just ask,
and I will give you as much as half my
kingdom."
4 Esther answered, "Your Majesty, today
is special to me. Please come with Haman to
a dinner I will prepare for you later today."
5 The king said to his servants, "Hurry
and get Haman, so we can accept Esther's
invitation."
The king and Haman went to the dinner
that Esther had spoken about, 6 and while
they were drinking wine, the king asked,
"What can I do for you, Queen Esther? I
will do whatever you ask."
7-8 Esther replied, "Your Majesty, if you
really care for me, please bring Haman
again tomorrow, and I will prepare another
dinner just like this one."

Haman Plans To Kill Mordecai

9 Haman was feeling great as he left the
king, but when he saw Mordecai the Jew
in the palace courtyard, Haman became
furious.
10 When Haman got home, he called together his friends and his wife Zosara
11 and started bragging about his great
wealth. Then he told them the many ways
the king had honored him and how the
king had promoted him so that he was now
the highest royal official. 12 Finally, Haman
said, "And today, I was the only person, besides the king himself, that the queen invited to dinner. I have even been invited
back for dinner again tomorrow. 13 But none
of this makes me happy, as long as I see
that Jew Mordecai in the palace courtyard."
14 Then Haman's wife Zosara and his
friends said, "Build a tower about seventy-
five feet high, and tomorrow morning ask
the king to hang Mordecai there! Then
later, you can have dinner with the king
and enjoy yourself."
This seemed like a good idea to Haman,
and he gave orders for the tower to be built.

The King Honors Mordecai

6 That night, the Lord did not let King
Artaxerxes get any sleep. So he called
in his secretary[t] and said, "Bring the daily
reports of the decisions I have made, and
read them to me."
2 They came across the report of how
Mordecai had saved the king's life by telling
him about the two guards who planned to
kill him. 3-4 Artaxerxes asked his servants,
"What did we do to reward Mordecai for
his kindness?"
"Your Majesty," they answered, "you
haven't done anything for him."
Just then, Haman came into the palace
courtyard to ask the king to have Mordecai
hanged on the tower he had built. The king
saw him and said, "Who is that man waiting in front of the throne room?"
5 The king's servants answered, "Your
Majesty, it is Haman."
"Tell him to come in," the king commanded.
6 "Tell me, Haman," the king said, "what
should I do for a man I want to honor?"
Haman thought, "The king must be asking how I want to be honored!" 7 So he
replied, "Your Majesty, if you wish to honor

[q]**15.9** *husband*: The Greek text has "brother," which was sometimes used by a wife as a loving term for her husband. [r]**15.10** *it . . . people*: One possible meaning for the difficult Greek text. [s]**15.11,12** *scepter*: See the note at 4.11. [t]**6.1** *secretary*: Greek "teacher."
5.3 Mk 6.23.

a man, 8 order your servants to bring out one of your own fine linen robes and one of your own horses. 9 Have one of your most honored friends put the robe on this man you like so well. Then the man will ride your horse and be led through the city streets, while someone shouts, 'This is how the king honors a man!' "

10 "That's a great idea!" the king exclaimed. "I want to honor Mordecai the Jew, who is on duty in the palace courtyard. Do just what you have said, and don't forget a thing."

11 Haman got the king's robe. He put it on Mordecai and helped him get on the king's horse. Then, as he led Mordecai through the city streets, Haman shouted, "This is how the king honors a man."

12 Afterwards, Mordecai went back to the palace courtyard, and Haman turned around and went home, hiding his face in shame. 13 He told his wife Zosara and his friends what had happened, and they replied, "Since Mordecai is a Jew, this is only the beginning of your troubles! You are doomed, and there's nothing you can do about it, because the living God is helping him."

14 They were still talking when the king's servants came and quickly took Haman to the dinner that Esther had prepared.

Haman Is Punished

7 King Artaxerxes and Haman dined with Queen Esther 2 on that second day. And while they were drinking wine, Artaxerxes said, "Esther, my queen, what can I do for you? Just ask, and I will give you as much as half of my kingdom!"

3 Esther answered, "Your Majesty, if you really care for me, you can save me and my people. 4 I have learned that all of us, even our children, have been sold, so that we can be robbed and made slaves or killed. We have an enemy in your court who is not worthy to serve you."

5 "Who would dare to do such a thing?" the king asked.

6 Esther replied, "That evil Haman is the one out to get us!"

Haman was terrified as he sat there in front of the king and the queen.

7 The king got up from the table and went into the palace garden.

Haman started begging Queen Esther for mercy, because he knew he was in trouble. 8 He even threw himself on her couch to plead with her. Just then the king came in from the garden and shouted, "He's even trying to rape my wife in my own house!"

Haman knew he was doomed.

9 Then Bugathan, one of the king's personal servants, said, "Your Majesty, Haman built a tower seventy-five feet high beside his house, so he could hang Mordecai on it. And Mordecai is the one who spoke up and saved your life."

"Hang Haman from his own tower!" the king said. 10 And immediately, Haman was hanged on the tower he had built to hang Mordecai. Afterward, the king calmed down.

A Happy Ending for the Jews

8 Before the end of the day, King Artaxerxes gave Esther everything that had belonged to Haman, the enemy of the Jews. Esther told the king that Mordecai was related to her, and the king had Mordecai brought in. 2 The king gave Mordecai the royal ring that Haman had worn, and Esther put Mordecai in charge of Haman's property.

3 Once again, Esther went to speak to the king. This time she fell down at his feet and begged him to do something about the horrible things that Haman had planned for the Jews. 4 The king held out his golden scepter[u] to her, and she got up and stood next to him. 5 Then she said, "Your Majesty, Haman sent letters demanding that all the Jews in your kingdom be killed. Please send out a command that Haman's letters are not to be obeyed. 6 I can't bear to see my own people destroyed, and if everyone from my nation is killed, I will be too."

7 The king replied, "Esther, Haman attacked the Jews, and so I gave orders for Haman to be hanged from his own wooden tower, and I have given you his property. Tell me what more you want me to do.

[u]**8.4** *scepter*: See the note at 4.11.

8 Better yet, I give you and Mordecai permission to send out letters in my name.
Write whatever you think is best. Be sure to
use my ring to seal the letters, because once
my commands are written down and sealed
with my ring, they cannot be changed."
9 That same year, on the twenty-third
day of Nisan,[v] the first month, the king's
secretaries were called in and were told to
write letters containing the king's commands about the Jews. These letters were
to be sent to the governors and officials of all
one hundred twenty-seven provinces from
India to Ethiopia. Each letter was written
in the language of the province where it
was sent. 10 The letters were written at the
king's command and were sealed with his
ring, then they were delivered by messengers. 11-12 In the letters, King Artaxerxes
commanded the Jews of every city in his
kingdom to obey their own laws. And on
the thirteenth day of Adar,[w] the twelfth
month, they were to defend themselves
and to do anything they wanted to their
enemies.

Addition E[x]

A Copy of the Letter Sent by King Artaxerxes

16 This is a copy of the letter:
From Artaxerxes, the Great
King, to the governors of my one hundred
twenty-seven provinces from India to
Ethiopia, and to everyone who is loyal to
me. I send you my greetings.
2 People often become proud when I
show kindness and honor them. 3 Their
success makes them arrogant, and they try
to harm other people in my kingdom. And
as if that wasn't bad enough, they plot
against me, although I have always been
good to them. 4 They refuse to be grateful,
and they believe all the flattering things
they are told by those who hate what is
good. These people think that God won't
punish them, even though he hates evil
and can see everything they do.
5-6 A king who wants to be good to his
people will often let his friends be officials
in his government, because he trusts them to
give good advice and to do right. But when
they are evil, they tell lies and persuade the
king to kill innocent people or to do other
horrible things that can never be made
right. 7 When we look at historical records
passed down to us, we see how much evil
can be done when high officials are unworthy of their positions and use their power
in a destructive way. But we can see this
even more clearly by looking at what has
just happened here in our own kingdom.
8 From now on, I am going to concen-
trate on making my kingdom a place where
everyone can find safety and peace. 9 I will
change the way I rule, and when I make
decisions, I will be fair to everyone.
10-11 As for Haman son of Hammedatha,
he wasn't even a Persian—he was from
Macedonia![y] I have always tried to be kind
to people from every nation, and I was especially kind to Haman. He was welcomed
as a guest in my kingdom, and he became
my highest official. Everyone bowed down to
him, and I trusted him like my own father.
But Haman was never kind to anyone.
12 He was full of pride, and so he plotted to
kill me and take over my kingdom. 13 His
evil plans included tricking me into having
all the Jews killed, including Mordecai, who
saved my life and who is always doing good
things for me. Queen Esther is also Jewish,
which means that Haman would have killed
her too, even though she shares my royal
rule and has never done anything wrong.
14 Haman thought that if he could have all
the Jews killed, I would have no one to support me, and then he could take over the Persian empire and give it to the Macedonians.
15 The Jews were sentenced to death by
this man who deserved to be under a
curse. But I have found that Jews are not
criminals at all. Instead, they live their lives

[v]**8.9** *twenty-third day of Nisan*: Ten days after Haman had sent out his letters (see 3.12). Nisan, also called Abib, was from about mid-March to mid-April. [w]**8.11,12** *Adar*: See the note at 2.15, 16. [x]**16.1** The verses 16.1-24 are sometimes numbered as E.1-24 or 8.12a-12x.
[y]**16.10,11** *Macedonia*: A nation in northern Greece that was an enemy of Persia.
8.8 Dn 6.8.

according to laws that are fair to everyone.
16 And the Jews are the children of the
highest and greatest God, the living God,
who has guided my ancestors and me in
ruling Persia the best way possible.

17 So, it is best for you to ignore the letters sent by Haman, 18 since he and his
whole family have now been hanged at the
city gate of Susa. God rules the world and
was quick to punish Haman as he deserved.

19 A copy of this letter is to be put on
public display in every town.

You must allow the Jews to live by their
own laws. 20 And since the thirteenth day
of the month of Adar[z] will bring trouble for
them, you must give them support, so that
they will be able to defend themselves
when they are attacked.

21 God rules all things, and he has decided to make the thirteenth of Adar a day
when his chosen people will celebrate, instead of being killed.

22 Place this special day on the list of
festivals to be celebrated in your province.
23 This day will always remind us and all
other loyal Persians how we were saved. It
will also remind everyone that those who
plot against us will be destroyed.

24 I will be furious with any city or
province that disobeys my instructions, and
I will send my army to destroy it with fire.
No one will be able to travel there, and
even the wild animals and birds will hate to
be anywhere near it.

End of Addition E

---

8 13 Copies of this letter are to be put on
public display everywhere in the kingdom, so that all the Jews will be prepared to
fight their enemies on the thirteenth of
Adar.

The Letters Are Sent Out

14 The king ordered his messengers to
take their horses and deliver the letters as
quickly as possible to every province, and
he also had copies of the letter put on display in Susa.

15 Mordecai left the palace wearing one
of the king's robes, as well as a strip of purple linen cloth around his turban, and a
gold crown. The people of Susa started
cheering when they saw him.

16 The Jews no longer felt doomed; instead, they were full of joy. 17 Copies of the
letter were displayed in public in every city
and province, and Jews all over the kingdom held parties to celebrate. Many Gentiles accepted the Jewish religion and were
circumcised, because they were afraid of
the Jews.

The Jews Destroy Their Enemies

9 1-2 In his letter, the king had given
commands about the thirteenth day of
Adar,[z] the twelfth month. And when that
day arrived, the Jews completely destroyed
their enemies, because those enemies were
too afraid to fight back. 3 The rulers, the
royal officials, and the governors of the
provinces were afraid of Mordecai and
showed respect for all the Jews. 4-5 Mordecai
was well known throughout the kingdom
because of the letters the king had sent.

6-10 The Jews killed five hundred men[a]
in the city of Susa and took[b] what had belonged to the ones they killed. Haman the
son of Hammedatha[c] had been one of the
worst enemies of the Jews; his ten sons
were among those who were killed. Their
names were Pharsannestain, Delphon,
Phasga, Pharadatha, Barea, Sarbacha,
Marmasima, Aruphaeus, Arsaeus, and
Zabutheus.

11 That same day, someone reported to
the king how many people the Jews had
killed in Susa. 12 The king said to Esther,
"The Jews have killed five hundred men[d]
in the city of Susa alone. If that many were
killed here, what must have happened out
in the provinces? Is there anything else
you want? Just tell me, and it will be
done."

[z]**16.20; 9.1,2** *Adar*: See the note at 2.15, 16. [a]**9.6-10** *men*: Or "people." [b]**9.6-10** *and took*: Greek; other ancient translations and the Hebrew text "but did not take" (see also 9.15-17).
[c]**9.6-10** *Haman the son of Hammedatha*: The Greek text adds "a Bougean," but the meaning of this term is not known. [d]**9.12,15** *men*: See the note at 9.6-10.
16.24 3 Macc 3.30. **9.1,2** 1 Macc 7.48, 49; 2 Macc 15.36.

13 Esther answered, "Please let the Jews do the same tomorrow as they have done today, and let them hang the bodies of Haman's ten sons."

14 The king gave the orders to allow the Jews to fight a second day, and he had the bodies of Haman's sons handed over to the Jews of Susa, so they could hang them. 15 Then on the next day, Adar fourteenth, the Jews of the city got together and killed three hundred more men,[d] but on this day they did not take anything that had belonged to the ones they killed. 16-17 On Adar thirteenth the Jews in the provinces had come together to defend themselves. They killed fifteen thousand of their enemies but took nothing that belonged to the ones they killed. Then on Adar fourteenth these Jews rested and celebrated their victory.

18 On the fourteenth, the Jews in Susa were still defending themselves, and so they celebrated on the fifteenth. 19 That's why the Jews who live in small villages or on farms now observe this holiday on Adar fourteenth, while the Jews that live in the large cities observe it on the fifteenth. It is a joyful holiday that they celebrate by sending gifts of food to each other.

The Festival of Purim

20 Mordecai wrote a book reporting everything that had happened, and he sent copies of it to the Jews everywhere in the kingdom of Artaxerxes. 21 He also sent a letter that said:

> Celebrate on both the fourteenth and fifteenth of Adar,[e] 22 the days when we Jews defeated our enemies. Remember this month as a time when our sorrow was turned to joy, a time when celebration took the place of grief. Celebrate during the whole month of Adar by having weddings and parties and sending gifts of food to your neighbors and to the poor.

23 The Jews welcomed Mordecai's report 24 of how Haman son of Hammedatha, the Macedonian, had fought against them. Mordecai also told how Haman had used small pieces of wood or bone, called lots,[f] to find the best time to destroy them. 25 Then he went to the king to ask him to hang Mordecai. But Haman became the victim of his own plot, and he and his sons were all hanged instead. 26-28 Mordecai's letter said that the Jews must celebrate for two days because of what had happened to them. And so the Jews made an agreement that they, their descendants, and everyone who accepted their religion in the future would always celebrate these two days to remind themselves of everything that had happened. They would celebrate, no matter what family they belonged to or where they lived.

This time of celebration came to be known as "Purim," which is the name in Hebrew for the lots that Haman had used.

29-30 Esther[g] wanted to give her full authority as queen to Mordecai's letter about the Festival of Purim, and she had Mordecai help her write down everything they had done. 31 Mordecai and Queen Esther used their own authority to make Purim an official Jewish festival. Then they promised that for as long as they had health and strength, they would both do their best to make sure every Jew celebrated Purim.[h] 32 Esther even had a law made, so that the Jews would never forget to celebrate it.

The Greatness of Artaxerxes and Mordecai

10 King Artaxerxes made everyone in his kingdom pay taxes, even those in lands across the sea. 2 The record books of the kings of Persia and Media tell how strong and brave he was, and they also describe the wealth and glory of his kingdom. 3 Next to the king himself, Mordecai was the highest official in the kingdom. The Jews all loved and honored him because he helped them in many ways.

[d]**9.12,15** *men*: See the note at 9.6-10. [e]**9.21** *Adar*: See the note at 2.15, 16. [f]**9.24** *lots*: These were often used to get an answer from a god. They were tossed on the ground, and the way they landed showed what the answer was. [g]**9.29,30** *Esther*: Greek "Esther, the daughter of Aminadab." [h]**9.31** *they promised . . . celebrated Purim*: One possible meaning for the difficult Greek text.
9.24-28 Es 3.7.

ADDITION F[i]

Mordecai Remembers His Dream

10 [4-5] Mordecai said:
I remember that I had a
dream[j] about these things, and God has
made everything in it come true. [6] In the
dream I had, I saw a tiny stream become a
mighty river, then I watched the sun rise
and give its light. The river stood for Esther, because the king married her and
crowned her queen. [7] Haman and I were
the two dragons. [8] And just as I dreamed,
the other nations came together to destroy
the Jews. [9] Our people cried out to the
Lord God for help, and he performed miracles and saved us from all the evil things
that were going to happen. No one had
ever seen such powerful miracles before.
[10] Long ago God chose us to be his people, but he rejected the other nations.
[11] Then, when those nations were against
us, God had to decide between us and
them. [12] God remembered that we were his
people, and he decided that we were in the
right. [13] And so from now on, we Jews must
observe the fourteenth and fifteenth days
of the month of Adar[k] by coming together
to worship him and to celebrate.

A Note about the Letter Concerning Purim

11 [1] In the fourth year that Ptolemy and Cleopatra ruled Egypt,[l] Dositheus and his son Ptolemy brought the letter about the Festival of Purim to Egypt. Dositheus claimed to be a priest from the Levi tribe, and he said that the letter was true and had been translated into Greek by Lysimachus son of Ptolemy,[m] who lived in Jerusalem.

END OF ADDITION F

[i]**10.4,5** The verses 10.4—11.1 are sometimes numbered as F.1-10 or 10.3a-3l. [j]**10.4,5** *I had a dream*: See 11.2-11. [k]**10.13** *Adar*: See the note at 2.15, 16. [l]**11.1** *the fourth year . . . ruled Egypt*: There were three kings named Ptolemy whose queen was named Cleopatra, so the year referred to might be 114 B.C., 77 B.C., or 44 B.C. [m]**11.1** *Ptolemy . . . Ptolemy . . . Ptolemy*: These refer to three different men named Ptolemy.

WISDOM OF SOLOMON

ABOUT THIS BOOK

Although this book is written as though Solomon was the author, it was probably written in the first century B.C. in Alexandria, Egypt, to encourage the Jews living there to be faithful to God. Some had abandoned the Jewish faith and adopted Greek religions, and the author wanted to show the Jews that the teachings and wisdom found in the Scriptures were better than those of Greek religion and philosophy. To do this, the author also had to deal with the old problem of why evil people are often successful, while good people are suffering. The author states that God will bring about justice when he judges all people after death. The wicked will be punished, but those who were faithful to God will live with him forever:

The Lord Most High
takes care of his people;
he will reward them,
and they will live forever.
(5.15)

A QUICK LOOK AT THIS BOOK

- God Created People To Live (1.1-15)
- Evil Thoughts of Evil People Lead to Death (1.16—2.24)
- The Lord's Faithful People Will Live Forever (3.1—5.23)
- Search for Wisdom and the Gifts She Brings (6.1—10.14)
- The Lord—and Wisdom—Rescued Israel from Egypt (10.15—12.27)
- It Is Foolish To Worship Nature and Idols (13.1—15.13)
- God Blessed and Protected Israel and Punished the Egyptians (15.14—19.17)
- The Harmony of the Universe (19.17-22)

Trust the Lord

1 You rulers of this earth
should love justice;
you should do what is right
and keep the Lord in mind.
2 The Lord will answer your prayers,
if you trust and don't doubt.
3 Our deceitful thoughts
separate us from God,
and by putting God to the test,
we make fools of ourselves,
4 because Wisdom[a] won't live
with deceitful slaves of sin.
5 A pure mind and self-control
won't let you be deceitful;
you will reject foolish thoughts
and hate injustice.[b]

Our Words and Thoughts Are Known to God

6 Although Wisdom is friendly,
she will still hold you guilty
if you speak evil of God.

[a]**1.4** *Wisdom*: In this book, the word "wisdom" is sometimes used as though wisdom were a supernatural being who was with God at the time of creation. [b]**1.5** *injustice*: One possible meaning for the difficult Greek text of verse 5.

1.1 Ws 6.1-11.

Even words spoken in secret
and our most private thoughts
are known to God,
7 because the Spirit of the Lord
is everywhere in this world.
His Spirit holds it all together
and hears every word.
8 And so liars will be judged
and then punished—
9 their evil plans and deeds
will be discovered,
then reported to the Lord,
and they will be sentenced.
10 Nothing can escape being heard,
not even a faint grumble.
11 So stop all useless complaining
and fault-finding.
Even a faint whisper
can cause a problem,
and lies are deadly.

God Created Us To Live

12 Don't invite death
and destruction
by living like a fool.
13 God did not create us for death,
and when we die,
it doesn't make him glad.
14 God created all creatures
with life that continues.
All living beings
should keep on living
untouched by deadly poison,
because the Kingdom of Death
doesn't rule this world,
15 and justice lives forever.

Evil Thoughts of Evil People

16 The words and deeds
of evil people
are an invitation to death.
They think of death
as friendly and desirable—
they are partners with death,
just as they deserve.

2 Their foolish minds lead them
to say to each other:
"Life is short and sad—
the end is certain to come,
and no one escapes the grave.
2 Only by chance were we born,
and after we are gone,
everything will be
as though we had never been.
Our breath is merely smoke,
and reason is a spark
from the beat of our hearts.
3 When that beating ends,
our bodies turn to dust,
and our spirits vanish
into thin air.
4 In time we will be forgotten
and so will our deeds.
Life disappears like a cloud;
it melts away like mist
in the heat of the sun.
5 Time fades away like a shadow,
and no one returns from death.

6 "So make the most of life,
especially while you're young.
7 Drink the very best wine,
wear expensive perfume,
and enjoy the spring flowers.
8 Decorate your head with rosebuds
before they wilt.
9 Do your share of celebrating!
Party always and everywhere—
that's what life is all about.
10 Abuse the poor and the honest!
And do the same to widows
and old people.
11 After all, might is right,
and weakness is useless.

12 "Destroy law-abiding people!
Get them out of the way.
All they do is condemn you
for breaking the law and doing
what we know is wrong.
13 They claim to know the Lord God
and to be his children.
14 That's why they criticize
your very thoughts.

15 "Just looking at good people
is a heavy burden—
their lifestyle is so different;
in fact, it's strange.
16 They think you're trash,

1.13 Ez 18.32; 33.11; 2 Esd 3.7; 2 P 3.9. **1.16** Pr 8.36; Is 28.15; Si 14.12. **2.6** Is 22.13; 1 Co 15.32. **2.12-20** 3 Macc 6.11.

and they won't have anything
to do with you.
They claim God is their Father
and that he will reward them.

17 "So test what they say
by watching them die.
18 If those so-called good people
really are God's children,
he will look after them.
19 We will insult and torture them
to find out how gentle
and patient they are.
20 We will sentence them
to a shameful death—
after all, they have said
that they will be protected."

Evil People Are Foolish

21 That's the reasoning of those
who are evil, and they are
both blind and foolish.
22 They don't understand
what God has in mind,
and they don't know the reward
for living right.
23 God created us to live forever,
just as he himself does.
24 But death entered the world
because the devil was jealous,
and so all his followers die.

The Future of Those Who Please God

3 The souls of those
who have pleased God
are safe in his hands
and protected from pain.
2 Only in the minds of the foolish
are those people dead
and their death considered
a disaster 3 or a destruction.
In fact, they are at peace
4 and destined never to die,
though others may have thought
they were being punished.
5 They will be richly rewarded,
because God tested them
for a while
and found them worthy
of being his children.
6 God tested them like gold
in a fiery furnace,
and he accepted them
like a pleasing sacrifice.

7 When God shows them mercy,
they will be like shining sparks
setting weeds on fire.
8 The Lord will rule them forever
and let them rule over nations.
9 All of God's faithful people
will understand truth
and live with him in love,
because God is kind and merciful
to those he chooses
to be his holy people.[c]

Punishment for the Wicked

10 The wicked will be punished,
as their evil thoughts deserve.
They rebelled against the Lord
and abused his people.
11 They are terribly miserable,
because they reject wisdom
and sound advice.
Their future is hopeless,
and everything they do
is completely useless.
12 Their wives are foolish;
their children are evil
13 and under God's curse.

God Blesses the Needy

A wife who remains faithful
will be given children
at a time that God decides.
14 Men who remain faithful to God
and do good deeds
will receive special blessings
and be given honored positions
in the temple of the Lord,
even though they may be unable
to have children.
15 Remember that good deeds
are easily recognized—
they are like fruit on a vine
that has wisdom as its roots.

16 But children born to persons
who have committed

[c]**3.9** *to those . . . people*: One possible meaning for the difficult Greek text.
2.23 Gn 1.26, 27. **3.2** Ws 4.17. **3.5,6** Ro 8.18; 2 Co 4.17.

some terrible sexual sin[d]
will die before they grow up.
17 Even if they live a long time,
they won't be respected.
18 And if they die in their youth,
they will be without hope
on the day of judgment,
19 because misery is the reward
for doing evil.

4 Living right is better
than having children—
both God and people
will always remember you
and the good you have done.
2 People imitate[e] goodness,
and they miss it
when it is gone.
Goodness always triumphs;
it receives the highest honors
because it is unselfish.[f]

3 But all of the many children
born to sinners
will be useless and helpless
like trees without roots.
4 They may blossom for a while,
but they will be swept away
in a gust of wind.
5 Their branches will be broken
before they mature,
and the fruit they produce
will be worthless.
6 When God judges the world,
these children will be witnesses
against their sinful parents.

7 Good people may die early,
but they will be at rest.
8 True respect isn't gained
merely by growing old—
9 people are honored because of
their wisdom and goodness.

10 Enoch, a person God loved
and who pleased him,
was living among sinners.
But God took him away[g]
11 to protect his mind and soul
from the influence of evil.
12 Even the most innocent person
can be deceived and destroyed
by sinful thoughts.

13 But Enoch loved the Lord;
he became mature in a few years
14 and pleased the Lord.
So he quickly took Enoch away
to protect him from evil.
15 Others failed to understand
that this is how
God shows kindness and mercy
and protects his holy people.

Good People Will Triumph

16 Good people may die young,
but they shame those sinners
who live a long time.
17 Sinners fail to understand
why God gives them a long life
and lets the wise die young.
18 When they see this happen,
they simply sneer.
But God will laugh at them
because their dead bodies
will be forever disgusting
to the rest of the dead.
19 God will throw them speechless
to the ground, and they will be
like buildings that crumble.
They will suffer and rot,
then be forgotten.

The Final Judgment

20 Sinners will be horrified
when they are condemned
by their evil deeds.

5 But all who have pleased God
will stand with confidence
in the presence of those
who abused them and made fun
of the good they did.
2 When those evil ones see
how God has saved his people,
they will tremble with fear
and be completely amazed.

[d]**3.16** *some terrible sexual sin*: This probably refers to the laws about the wrong kind of marriages that are forbidden in Leviticus 18.6-18, though it would possibly include unfaithfulness in marriage as well. [e]**4.2** *imitate*: Some manuscripts "honor." [f]**4.2** *because it is unselfish*: One possible meaning for the difficult Greek text. [g]**4.10** *took him away*: See Genesis 5.21-24; Hebrews 11.5.
4.1 Si 16.3. **4.10-14** Gn 5.21-24; Si 44.16; He 11.5.

3 They will groan and say
to each other,
"We should have turned from sin!
4 We were fools to sneer
at those people,
but we thought they were fools
who had died in disgrace.
5 Why are they God's children?
Why are they his holy people?

6 "So we were the ones
who turned from truth
and rejected the light
from those good people.
7 We refused to follow the Lord!
Instead we were lawless
and followed a desert road
that led us to destruction.
8 All of our pride and wealth
has proved to be useless.

9 "Everything that we treasured
has vanished like a shadow
or a hastily spoken word,
*10 or like the wake of a ship
on ocean waves,
11 or like the flight of a bird
through the air,
12 or like the unknown path
of an arrow on its way
to the target.
13 As soon as we were born,
we began to disappear
because we followed only evil
and left behind no traces
of anything good."

14 Sinners have no more hope
than dust in the wind,
or frost in the heat of the sun,
or smoke in a breeze.
They are remembered no longer
than an overnight guest.

The Lord's People Will Be Rewarded

15 The Lord Most High
takes care of his people;
he will reward them,
and they will live forever.
16 The Lord will protect them
with his powerful right arm,
and he will bless them
with a glorious crown.
17 Eagerness will be like armor
for the Lord, and he will equip
all creation to fight
and punish his enemies.

18 The Lord will protect his chest
with deeds of fairness,
and for a helmet he will wear
equal justice for all.
19 Holiness will be his strong shield,
20 and fierce anger will be
his sharp sword.
All creation will join with him
in fighting his crazy enemies.
21 Arrows of lightning will leap
from behind the clouds
and never miss their target.
22 Fearsome hailstones will strike
the Lord's enemies,
while ocean waves and rivers
roll over them like a flood.
23 Then a mighty windstorm
will sweep them away—
because lawlessness and evil
bring ruin to the whole earth
and to every kingdom.

Rulers Should Desire Wisdom

6 Now listen and learn,
you kings and judges!
2 Listen, all of you rulers,
who control many nations.
3 You received your authority
from the Lord Most High,
and he will judge your deeds
and your thoughts.
4 Although you were his servants,
you disobeyed him
and ruled unjustly.
5 So now the Lord will punish you
both quickly and harshly
because you are in power.
6 God forgives ordinary people,
but severely punishes
the high and the mighty.

7 The Lord created everyone—
the powerful and the weak.

5.17-23 Eph 6.11-17. **6.3** Ro 13.1.

God has no favorites;
he isn't afraid of anyone,
8 and he requires rulers
to answer for what they do.
9 I am speaking to you rulers,
so that you will have wisdom
and not sin against God.
10 If you want to belong
to the Lord's holy people
and to defend yourself
on the day of judgment,
11 then eagerly desire to learn
all that I am teaching.

What Wisdom Is Like

12 Wisdom[h] shines brightly
and never fades.
She is easily recognized
by those who love her
and look for her.
13 Wisdom wants to be known
by those who desire her.
14 If you get up early
to look for wisdom
you find her at your door.
15 Just thinking about Wisdom
leads to full understanding,
and caring about Wisdom
will soon set you free
from all other cares.
16 Wisdom searches eagerly
for those who are seeking,
and she lets them find her
in all of their thoughts.

17 If you really want Wisdom,
then fall in love with her
and desire to learn.
18 If you truly love Wisdom,
you will obey her laws;
then you will be sure
of life after death.
19 And just as life after death
will bring you near to God,
20 the desire for Wisdom
will protect your kingdom.
21 So if you want to rule
for a long time,
you must respect Wisdom.
22 I will now tell you clearly
the full truth about her
from the very beginning.
23 I won't be jealous or conceal
anything I know—
that isn't the way of Wisdom.
24 The only hope for the world
is for many of us to be wise;
indeed, a wise ruler
gives security to a nation.
25 So be guided by my teachings,
and you will be successful.

Solomon Speaks about Death

7 Like everyone else,
I am destined to die.
I too am a descendant
of that man who was made
from the soil of the earth.
And my body took shape
inside my mother's womb.
2 For ten months I was there,
growing in her blood
from seed left by my father[i]
as they were making love.
3 And when I was born,
I breathed the same air as others
and touched the same earth.
Like all other children,
my first sound was a cry.
4 I was nursed with love
and dressed in baby clothes.
5 No rulers have their beginning
any differently—
6 all enter life in the same way
and leave in the same way.

Solomon Praises Wisdom

7 I asked God for Wisdom
and for understanding,
and my prayer was answered.
8 Nothing compares with Wisdom!
And so I chose her
over power and wealth.

[h]**6.12** *Wisdom*: Here, as in Proverbs 1.20—2.22; 8.1—9.6, Wisdom is spoken of as a supernatural being. [i]**7.2** *her blood . . . seed left by my father*: It was believed that a child's body was made from a combination of the mother's blood and sperm from the father.
7.1-6 4 Macc 12.13. **7.7** 1 K 3.6-9; Ws 9.1-18.

9 In comparison with Wisdom,
precious gems are nothing;
gold is merely sand,
and silver is simply clay.

10 I preferred Wisdom more than
a healthy and handsome body;
the brightest light grows dim
when compared with her.
11 Wisdom brought me wealth
and everything good.
12 I was pleased with all
that she brought me,
though I failed to realize
that Wisdom was the source.
13 I sincerely studied,
then freely shared the riches
I learned from Wisdom.
14 Wisdom's treasures never end.
God approves of her,
and those who gain Wisdom
are friends of God.

Solomon Prays for Wisdom

15 I pray that God will help me
to say the right thing
and to have thoughts
worthy of his gifts to me.
God shows Wisdom the way
and instructs wise people.
16 Our lives and our words,
our understanding and skills
are all in the hands of God.

17 From God came my knowledge
about the universe
and how its parts work;
18 about the way a calendar
is determined;
about the movement of the sun
and the changing seasons;
19 about the way the years
come and go on schedule;
about the groups of stars
20 and the way animals behave,
both tame and wild;
about the motion of the wind
and the thoughts of humans;
about all kinds of plants
and the value of roots.
21 I learned hidden mysteries
and things known to all,
22 because I was taught by Wisdom,
who made everything.

Wisdom is both intelligent
and holy.
Though one of a kind,
she appears in many forms
and is a spiritual being
that moves freely about.
Wisdom is clear and pure,
spotless and innocent,
and she loves goodness.
Wisdom is sharp and victorious,
23 generous, helpful, dependable,
and she never worries.
Wisdom is all-powerful;
she sees everything
and is ever present
with those who are intelligent,
pure, and truly spiritual.

24 Wisdom moves more easily
than anything else
and is so pure that she is
everywhere at once.
25 Wisdom is the breath
of God's power,
the true reflection of the glory
of God All-Powerful,
and so she cannot be touched
by anything impure.

26 Wisdom is like a mirror
reflecting the eternal light
of God's deeds and goodness.
27 Though Wisdom is and remains
only one being,
she can do anything
and she renews all things.
In each generation she enters
the souls of the faithful,
making them into prophets
and friends of God,
28 since God's favorite people
are those who live with her.

29 Wisdom is more beautiful than
the sun and the stars.
She is far superior to daylight,
30 because it turns to darkness,
but she cannot be changed
by the power of evil.

8 Wisdom rules the universe
and keeps it in order.

Solomon's Love for Wisdom

2 Since the time I was young,
I have loved and searched
for Wisdom.
I was charmed by her beauty
and wanted her for my bride.
3 The Lord God of all loves her,
and her glorious origin
becomes even more glorious,
because she lives with God.
4 She understands God's mysteries
and works together with him.

5 Wisdom is more desirable
than wealth—she makes
everything run smoothly.
6 Wisdom is more useful
than knowledge—she designed
everything that is.
7 If you truly love what is right,
learn from her,
the source of all goodness:
of justice and courage,
understanding and self-control;
all the important things
that help us live our lives.

8 Do you desire wide experience?
Wisdom knows what has happened
and predicts the future;
she knows the meaning of words
and the answers to riddles.
Wisdom knows in advance
the miracles God will work
and all that will take place.

Rulers Need Wisdom

9 So I decided to bring Wisdom
home to live with me—
she will offer good advice,
as well as comfort in times
of suffering and grief.
10 She will bring me great honor
from advisors and many others,
even though I am young.
11 I will have sound judgment
and be admired by rulers.
12 They will wait for my opinion,
then listen when I speak,
and they will be amazed
at my marvelous speeches.

13 Because of Wisdom,
my name will live on forever.
14 I will rule many nations
15 and be a hero in battle;
oppressive rulers will tremble
at the mention of my name.
16 With Wisdom as my friend,
I will live happily and at peace,
with no bitter regrets.

17 I thought deeply about Wisdom
and all that she offered—
unending life 18 and perfect joy
because of her friendship;
wealth and understanding
because of her companionship;
and fame because of her words.
So I searched for Wisdom.

19 I was an intelligent child,
born with a good soul—
20 rather, since my soul was good,
it entered a perfect body.
21 I had the insight to realize
Wisdom is the gift of God,
and so with all my heart
I prayed for Wisdom.

Solomon's Prayer for Wisdom

9 Merciful Lord God
of my ancestors,
you created everything
by your word.
2 And by your Wisdom,
you let us humans rule
all other creatures.
3 We are to be honest and fair
in every decision,
4 so share with me the Wisdom
that sits beside your throne,
and let me be a child of yours.
5 My mother was your servant,
and so am I—a mere human
whose life is short.

8.2 Si 15.2. **8.4** Pr 8.27-30. **8.7** 4 Macc 1.18. **9.1-18** 1 K 3.6-9; Ws 7.7.

I understand only a little
about laws and judgments,
6 because even a perfect human
is really nothing
without Wisdom from you.

7 You have chosen me to rule
and judge your people.
8 and here, on your holy mountain
in the city where you live,
you have commanded me to build
an altar and a temple,
just like that sacred temple
you made at the beginning.[j]

9 Wisdom has always been with you.
She knows your mighty deeds,
and she was there
when you created the world.
Wisdom knows what pleases you,
and she knows what is right
according to your commands.
10 So from your glorious and holy
throne in the heavens,
please send Wisdom
to work beside me and teach me
what is pleasing to you.

11 Wisdom will guide me
in all that I do,
and her glory will guard me,
because she knows everything.
12 Then you will approve my actions,
and I will rule your people
with fairness,
which will show that I am worthy
to succeed my father as king.

13 No one can know what you,
the Lord God,
demand of us humans—
14 our reasoning is faulty,
and our schemes often fail,
15 because our mortal bodies
are merely earthly tents
that burden down our souls
and our anxious minds.

16 We struggle and know so little
about things here on earth.
How could we possibly learn
about things in heaven?
17 Who has known your thoughts
before you gave them Wisdom
and your Holy Spirit?
18 Then they found the right path;
they learned what pleased you
and were saved by Wisdom.

Wisdom in the Time of Moses

Solomon continues praying:

10 Wisdom protected Adam, the
father of the human race. When he
was alone on earth, she kept him from sin
2 and gave him the power to rule everything.
3 But Adam's son Cain was evil, and he
rejected Wisdom. Then in his anger, he destroyed himself by killing his brother.
4 When Cain's sin caused a flood, Wisdom came to the rescue, by guiding the
good man Noah in that flimsy wooden boat.
5 When nations were frustrated by their
own evil plans, Wisdom noticed that Abraham was a good man. So she gave him
strength to obey God, though Abraham
dearly loved his son Isaac.[k]
6 Wisdom rescued the good man Lot,
when the ungodly people of those five cities
died in the flames. 7 The evidence of their
evil can still be seen—the smoke that keeps
rising from the desert, those trees with fruit
that never ripens, and the pillar of salt that
stands as a witness to Lot's wife, who refused to believe. 8 By rejecting Wisdom,
these people became blind to what was
right, and so they left a permanent witness
to their foolishness. 9 But she protected
those who were obedient to her.
10 Wisdom guided that good man Jacob
along the right paths when he was running
from his angry brother. She showed him
your kingdom and helped him understand
sacred things. She also made him successful in everything he did. 11 Wisdom even

[j] **9.8** *temple . . . beginning*: Either a reference to Exodus 25.9, 40, where God commands Moses to build the temple according to the plan that he had given Moses, or to the Jewish teaching that the temple was present before the world was created. [k] **10.5** *Abraham . . . his son Isaac*: Abraham was willing to offer Isaac as a sacrifice to the Lord (see Genesis 22.1-19).

10.1,2 Gn 1.26-28. **10.3** Gn 4.8-13. **10.4** Gn 7.1—8.22. **10.5** Gn 11.1-9; 12.1-3; 22.1-19; 4 Macc 13.12. **10.6-9** Gn 19.1-29. **10.10-12** Gn 27.43; 28.10-22; 32.24-30.

stood by him and made him rich when he was being mistreated by people who were jealous of him. 12 She protected him from enemies who were waiting to attack, and when he wrestled with an angel, she let him learn that obeying you, our God, is what makes a person really powerful.

13 When that good man Joseph was sold as a slave, Wisdom kept him from committing a terrible sin. She even went down into the dungeon 14 where he was a prisoner, and she stayed with him until he was given authority over those who had been in charge of him. Wisdom proved that his accusers were wrong and brought him honor that will last forever.

Wisdom Led Israel out of Egypt

Solomon continues praying:

15 Wisdom rescued the holy and faultless nation of Israel from those who were oppressing them. 16 She did this by entering the soul of your servant Moses and opposing cruel kings with her amazing miracles. 17 Wisdom rewarded those holy people for their hardships and guided them in a wonderful way, providing shade for them during the day and starlight at night. 18 She brought them safely through the Red Sea,[l] 19 but she drowned their enemies and washed their bodies up on the shore. 20 So your obedient people took the possessions of those ungodly people. Then they sang praises to your holy name and praised you for protecting them, 21 because Wisdom healed those who could not talk and helped infants to speak clearly.

Wisdom Led Israel through the Desert

Solomon continues praying:

11 Wisdom made the people of Israel successful by sending them the holy prophet Moses. 2 They went through a desert where no one lived and camped in places where no one had ever been. 3 They defeated their enemies, 4 and when they were thirsty and prayed for your help, you made water flow from a solid rock.

The Egyptians Were Punished

Solomon continues praying:

5 Our Lord, your people were helped by the same disasters that were used to punish their enemies. 6 You turned the ever-flowing Nile River into filthy blood 7 to punish the Egyptians for ordering the Hebrew children to be killed, then you surprised everyone by providing your people with more than enough water to satisfy their thirst. 8-9 You mercifully let your people go thirsty for a while to show how severely you would punish their ungodly enemies in your anger. 10 You corrected your people like parents correcting their children as a warning, but you punished the others like a harsh king condemning a criminal.

11 All the Egyptians suffered—those who lived near your people and those who lived far away. 12 In fact, they suffered at the time of these disasters and again whenever they remembered what had happened. 13 And when the Egyptians learned that your people had benefited from these troubles, they realized that you, Lord, had done it all. 14 Earlier they had made fun of Moses, who had been placed outside to die when he was a baby, but now they were amazed at him, because they suffered from thirst much more severely than your people.

More Punishment for the Egyptians

Solomon continues praying:

15 The Egyptians were so foolish and evil that they worshiped mindless snakes and worthless animals, and so you sent swarms of senseless creatures to punish them 16 and to teach them that sin brings its own punishment. 17 With your own mighty arm, you made the world out of something that had no form, and so you

[l] **10.18** *Red Sea*: This refers to the body of water that the Israelites crossed and was one of the marshes or fresh water lakes near the eastern part of the Nile Delta, where they lived and where the towns of Exodus 13.17—14.9 were located.

10.13,14 Gn 37.12-36; 39.1-23; 41.37-44. **10.15-21** Ex 1.1—15.21. **11.1-5** Ex 15.22—17.16. **11.10** 3 Macc 7.6. **11.15,16** Ex 8.1-24; 10.12-15.

could have sent a lot of bears or ferocious lions. [18] Or you could have created savage beasts just to punish them—beasts that breathe out fire and smoke and shoot sparks from their eyes, [19] killing people not only by the injuries they cause but by their very appearance. [20] In fact, you could have wiped out the Egyptians with a single breath, while you were scattering them with your power and treating them as they deserved. But you do everything fairly and according to the laws of nature that you created.

God Is Powerful and Merciful

Solomon continues praying:

[21] You always have the strength to do what you want, and no one can oppose you. [22] In your sight, the universe is merely a grain of sand that tips a balance scale or a drop of dew in the early morning. [23] You can do anything, and yet you patiently show mercy to everyone, so that they will turn from their sins. [24] In all creation there is nothing you don't love; otherwise, you would not have created everything. [25] Nothing would have lasted, unless you had wanted it to. [26] All living creatures belong to you, and you love them all,

12 [1] because your eternal spirit is in each of them. [2] That's why you correct us for our sins a little at a time, as a reminder and a warning for us to turn from sin and have faith in you, our Lord.

The Sins of the People of Canaan

Solomon continues praying:

[3] And what about those who lived in your holy land before your people settled there? [4] You hated them because of their horrible deeds—they practiced magic and did vulgar things when they worshiped their gods; [5] they mercilessly sacrificed children and ate human flesh and blood. They were members of pagan cults [6] and murdered their own helpless children. That's why you decided to let our ancestors destroy them, [7] so that your most precious land would accept a group of people worthy to be your servants.

[8] But since these people were merely human, you spared many of them and sent hornets ahead of your army to destroy them a little at a time. [9] You did this, even though you could have let your own people destroy that evil nation, or you could have wiped them out all at once with fierce animals or with one harsh word. [10] Although you knew that they were sinful by nature and that they would never give up their evil thoughts, you still punished them little by little, giving them time to turn back to you. [11] They were under your curse from the beginning, and though you were not afraid of anyone, you let them go unpunished.

God Rules All People

Solomon continues praying:

[12] All of us are merely human, and we cannot question what you have done, nor can we refuse to let you punish us. No one would dare to blame you for destroying those nations you created or dare to defend the guilty in your court of law. [13] You alone are God, and you care for all creation.[m] So you don't have to prove to any other gods that you do what is right, [14] and no kings or rulers can accuse you of wrongly punishing anyone. [15] You are always perfectly fair, and you would never punish innocent people. [16] You do what is right because you have the strength to do so, and your great power makes you merciful to everyone.

[17] When anyone doubts your strength, you show how strong you are, and you correct anyone who understands and still doubts. [18] Although you have power to do all things, you are gentle when you judge us, and you rule us with great patience.

Lessons God Taught His People

Solomon continues:

[19] Our God, by the things you have done, you have given your people a wonderful hope and have taught them to live right and be kind because you have let them turn from evil. [20] The enemies of your people deserved death, but you patiently gave them time to give up their sins, before punishing them. [21] You did severely

[m]**12.13** *creation*: Or "people."

12.3-7 Dt 12.31; 18.9-13. **12.8** Ex 23.28. **12.10** 2 Esd 9.11.

punish your people, even though you had
made wonderful promises and agreements
with them. 22 Yes, we were punished! But
our enemies were punished ten thousand
times worse, so that when we judge others,
we will remember your kindness, and when
we are being judged, we can expect mercy.

God Punished the Egyptians

Solomon continues praying:

23 The Egyptians foolishly lived a sinful
life, but you punished them by using those
disgusting creatures they worshiped. 24 In
fact, they had gone so far from the truth
that they were like senseless children, worshiping the most worthless animals. 25 And
so you made them look like stupid children,
when you punished them. 26 Those who
failed to take this warning seriously then
received from you the punishment they deserved. 27 While they were being punished
because of the creatures they had worshiped, they became angry at those creatures and finally realized that you are the
only true God, even though they had always refused to worship you. All this explains why they were punished so terribly.

It Is Foolish To Worship Nature

Solomon continues praying:

13 You are the living God. And only
those who are fools by birth could
look at your creation and not learn about
you. But instead, some people worshiped
the things you created, 2 such as fire and
wind, and storms and stars, and rivers and
planets. Those fools believed these things
were the gods that ruled the world, 3 because they were so beautiful.

But you are the Lord, as well as the
source of all beauty, so let those fools know
how much more beautiful you are than any
of these things. 4 And if anyone is amazed
at the mighty power of nature, then they
should realize that the Creator is even
more powerful. 5 Indeed, the power and
beauty of nature should convince us that
their Creator is even more powerful and
beautiful.

6 On the other hand, these people are
not entirely to blame for taking the wrong
path in their desire to know and to find
you. 7 It is to be expected that while
searching, they would learn to trust the
beautiful things they were seeing. 8 However, this is no excuse, 9 because if they
possessed the ability to examine the universe, why did it take them so long to find
you, the Lord of the universe?

Idolatry Is Foolish

Solomon continues praying:

10 Some people are miserable because
they have set their hopes either on lifeless
idols crafted in the shape of animals from
gold and silver, or else on some old pieces
of worthless stone. 11 A woodcutter may
saw down a small tree, then peel off the
bark and skillfully make something worthwhile from the wood. 12 Some of the leftover wood may be used for a cooking fire,
13 while a crooked and knotty piece may be
carefully carved into the shape of a human
14 or of some useless animal, before being
painted red to cover all its flaws.

15 A special shelf is made on the wall,
and the idol is fastened to the shelf with
metal nails 16 to keep it from falling, because the one who made it realizes that it
is merely a helpless idol. 17 Then—without
shame—its maker prays to this lifeless idol
for help with finances, marriage, or family.
18 Its maker asks for good health from
something weak, for life from something
dead, for guidance from something without
experience, for a safe journey from something that cannot walk, 19 and for wealth
and success from something that cannot
move its hands.

Praying to an Idol Is Foolish

Solomon continues praying:

14 Sailors preparing to travel across
dangerous waters will pray for
safety to a flimsy piece of wood, less sturdy
than their ship. 2 Shipmakers use their
own wisdom to build a ship that will make
them rich. 3 But, our Father, you are the
one who guides it safely through the sea
4 to show that you alone can protect inexperienced travelers from danger. 5 By your
wisdom you created the laws of nature, and

13.10—14.31 Is 44.9-20; Jr 10.1-16; Let Jer 8-73.

so people trust even the smallest splinter of
wood to bring them safely to land. 6-7 When
this world was still young, you sent a flood
to destroy giants, while at the same time
you gave hope for a generation of good
people by letting their ancestors find safety
in a boat made of wood[n] that God had
blessed.
8 Idols are under your curse because
those perishable things are called gods, and
their makers are under your curse for having made them. 9 In fact, you hate evil people
as much as you hate the evil they produce,
10 and you will equally punish evildoers together with their deeds. 11 You will destroy
those horrible pagan idols, because they
were made from part of your creation and
have become a trap for foolish people.

Idolatry and Evil

Solomon continues praying:
12 Our God, the idea of making an idol
was itself the first step toward being unfaithful to you. 13 Idols were not here in the
beginning, and they won't be around forever. 14 They resulted from human pride,
and so you have plans for them to end quickly.
15 For example, a father made an idol to
look like his child who had suddenly died,
and the dead child then became an object
of worship by later generations, who followed mysterious and secret ceremonies.
16 Over the years, such godless ceremonies
became customs and then laws, as rulers
commanded idols of themselves to be
carved and worshiped. 17 And when people
lived far from their rulers, they tried to
make idols that looked like their rulers, so
that they could honor and flatter those
rulers as if they were there with them.
18-19 In fact, some people who did not
know what their rulers looked like were led
to worship them, because of the skill and
the tireless efforts of those who made beautiful idols to please their rulers. 20 Finally,
many people started worshiping their
earthly rulers as gods. 21 As a result, idolatry became a hidden trap for those who
were suffering or were under the authority
of rulers, and they called these idols gods,
although you alone are God.
22 Not only are such people ignorant
about you, but this ignorance makes them
terrible enemies of each other, even while
they think they are living at peace. 23 They
kill their children as sacrifices and conduct
secret ceremonies, they follow strange customs and act like wild people, 24 they are
immoral and cause great pain by being unfaithful in marriage, and they are deceitful
murderers. 25 Violence, murder, robbery,
deceit, corruption, dishonesty, riots, and lying are everywhere. 26 No one knows right
from wrong or shows gratitude or cares
about anyone else; all of them are sexual
perverts or share weird marriage unions or
are otherwise completely disgusting.
27 The worship of worthless[o] idols is the
cause and result of all kinds of evil. 28 Their
worshipers act crazy, or give false messages
in the name of God, or live sinful lives.
They never speak the truth, and they tell
lies in court 29 because they trust in these
lifeless idols and don't expect to be punished. 30 But they will be punished for worshiping idols instead of you, the Holy God,
and for disgracing you with their deceitful
lies. 31 Sinners don't receive help from the
idols they worship, but the penalty for their
sins follows them in hot pursuit.

It Pays To Worship God

Solomon continues praying:

15 You, our God,
are gentle and trustworthy,
patiently ruling the universe
with mercy.
2 We know your mighty power,
and so we remain your people,
even if we sin.
But knowing we are yours
will keep us from sin.
3 Nothing is more fitting
than knowing you
and realizing that your power
is the way to endless life.
4 We have not been misled
by wicked artists,

[n]**14.6,7** *their ancestors find safety in a boat made of wood*: Noah and his family (see Genesis 6.1-22). [o]**14.27** *worthless*: Or "unmentionable."

14.6,7 a 3 Macc 2.4; **b** 4 Macc 15.31.

who made bright-colored idols
5 to encourage fools to worship
those lifeless images.
6 Those who make or worship
idols as objects of hope
will get what they deserve
for loving such evil things.

It Is Foolish To Worship Clay Idols

Solomon continues praying:

7 Potters form ordinary dishes and special dishes from the same lump of clay, and
only the potters decide which ones will be
ordinary or special. 8 Then—wasting their
energy—these potters form a useless idol
from the same clay. And not long ago, these
potters themselves were made from the soil
and will soon turn back into soil, just like
all other humans, when it is time to return
our borrowed souls.

9 But these potters don't care that we all
must die or that life is short. They consider
it a wonderful thing to mold false gods, and
all they care about is competing with others, who make idols out of gold or silver or
copper. 10 The heart of such workers is
made of ashes, their hope is worth no more
than dirt, and their lives are of less value
than clay, 11 because they don't know you,
the God who formed their bodies, then
filled them with a lively soul and breathed
into them a living spirit. 12 They think of
life as a meaningless game or as a festival
for making money, because they believe
that we should try to get rich in every way
possible, even by dishonesty. 13 More than
anyone else, these people realize that they
are sinning when they make dishes and
idols from the same clay.

The Egyptians

Solomon continues praying:

14 Our God, those Egyptians who
abused your people were the most foolish
of all and were more pitiful than infants.
15 This is because they believed that their
pagan idols really were gods—those images
that could neither see nor breathe nor hear
nor use their hands or feet. 16 They were
made by some human whose soul was borrowed, and none of us can make a god that
is our equal. 17 In fact, we humans are
mortal ourselves, and any idol we make
with our own evil hands is less than we are
and is completely lifeless.

18 Those Egyptians worshiped snakes,
the lowest form of animal life, 19 a form of
life so ugly that you did not even give it
16 your blessing. 1 You were right to
punish the Egyptians by sending
snakes to attack those worshipers of
snakes. 2 But you did not punish your own
people. Instead, you treated them with
kindness and sent tasty quails for them to
eat and enjoy. 3 You did these things, so
that when those Egyptians were hungry,
they would feel sick and lose their ap-
petites, because they would have to eat the
horrible meat of snakes. However, after suffering for a while, your own people enjoyed
the best of foods. 4 In this way, those who
had been oppressed could watch their op-
pressors suffer cruel punishment.

5 When you were angry with your people
and were destroying them with poisonous
snakes, you stopped before all of them died,
6 because you did this merely as a warning.
Then you told them to make a metal snake,
so that they would be rescued and remember to obey your Law. 7 Everyone who
looked at the metal snake was saved, not
because of the snake itself, but because of
you, the Savior of all people.

8 By doing this, you proved to our enemies that you alone can protect people
from harm, 9 because many of them got
what they deserved, when they died from
the bites of locusts and flies. 10 But you
were merciful to your children and healed
them from poisonous snake bites, 11 so that
they would remember your teachings and
never forget your kindness.[p] 12 Medicine
isn't what healed them. Only your word can
heal, 13 because you rule both life and
death and possess the power to give life or
to take it away. 14 It's easy enough for us
humans to kill another in anger, but we
don't have the power to bring back a

[p] **16.11** *never forget your kindness*: One possible meaning for the difficult Greek text.
16.2 Ex 16.11-13; Nu 11.31, 32. **16.5-7** Nu 21.6-9.

departed spirit or to set a soul free from the
world of the dead.

Egypt Is Struck by Storms

Solomon continues praying:

15 No one can escape from you, our
God. 16 And when those evil Egyptians rejected you and tried to escape, you punished them with your mighty arm and
wiped them out with rainstorms, hailstones, and fiery lightning. 17 Although water is used to put out a fire, an amazing
thing happened—the water made the fire
even more destructive, because nature itself protects good people.

18 One time you kept the fire under control, so that it would not destroy the frogs
and flies that were sent to punish those pagans and to let them know that you were
the one doing all of this. 19 But at another
time, you let it burn out of control—even in
water—to wipe out the crops in that evil
country.

God Provides Manna for His People

Solomon continues praying:

20 You blessed your people with manna,[q]
that food of angels, the bread you sent
down from heaven. It satisfied their hunger
and tasted delicious. 21 Your care for your
people was as sweet as this bread that
everyone enjoyed so much. 22 And though
the bread was frail as snowflakes, it did not
melt in the fiery flames that your enemies
saw destroying their crops during the hailstorm. 23 Contrary to nature, the fire did
not spread to the crops of your people.

24 All of creation serves you, its Creator,
and uses its power to punish those who are
evil and to show kindness to those who
trust in you. 25 And so on that occasion, the
forces of the universe changed the way
they work, in order to serve your purpose
by answering the prayers 26 of your
precious children. This was also your
way of teaching them not to depend upon
their crops, but rather to depend upon
your word, since it takes care of those
who trust you. 27 Even the manna that
survived the fire then melted in the
warmth of the sun. 28 This shows that we
must rise before dawn to pray to you, 29 because if we are ungrateful, our hope will
melt like frost and flow away like dirty
water.

The Egyptians Are Struck by Terror

Solomon continues praying:

17 Your decisions are difficult to explain, and people who have not
been taught have followed the wrong path.
2 For example, those lawless Egyptians
thought that your chosen people were under their power. But they themselves became prisoners in their very own homes for
a long, dark night, because they were not
under the protection of your eternal care.
3-4 They thought that you had forgotten and
that their secret sins were hidden behind a
curtain of darkness, when gruesome creatures seemed to appear. Nowhere in their
homes were they safe from the fear of terrifying noises and the frightening faces of
gloomy ghosts. 5 On that miserable night,
the darkness was so thick that neither
flaming lamps nor bright stars could be
seen. 6 And when lightning flashed, the
fearsome sight was worse than the darkness.[r]

7 The Egyptians had depended on their
magical powers and had boasted about
their great wisdom, but all of this proved
useless. 8 There were some who said they
could cure the fears and worries of sick
minds, but they themselves became sick
with foolish fear. 9 Even if nothing else
frightened them, they were terrified by the
sounds of wild animals outside and by hiss-
ing snakes. 10 They were so frightened that
they refused to open their eyes. But keeping them closed did not relieve their fears,
11 because evil people are cowards condemned by their own consciences, and
whatever they fear becomes even more
frightening.[s]

[q] **16.20** *manna*: It was something like a thin wafer made of honey (see Exodus 16.1-36).
[r] **17.6** *darkness*: One possible meaning for the difficult Greek text of verse 6. [s] **17.11** *evil people . . . frightening*: One possible meaning for the difficult Greek text.
16.20-29 Ex 16.1-36. **17.3,15** Ws 18.14-19; 2 Macc 3.25-29; 3 Macc 6.18.

12 Fear takes over when people stop reasoning. 13 They no longer think straight,
and their only hope is to deny the real
source of their problems. 14 Night itself is
powerless, since it comes from the powerless world of the dead. And yet the Egyptians slept restlessly on that night, 15 because of the horrible and unexpected
nightmares brought on by the surrender of
their souls to the forces of evil. 16-17 Every
one of the Egyptians—including farmers
and shepherds—fell prisoner to the fear of
a darkness that was more difficult to escape
than iron chains. 18-19 The slightest noise
made them paralyzed with fear—the songs
of birds in the trees, the rhythm of rushing
water, the surprising crash of a rock, the
hoofbeats of animals jumping about, the
roar of lions, or even an echo in the mountains.
20 Everywhere else in the world, everyone went about their own business in broad
daylight, 21 while these Egyptians were covered with a heavy blanket of darkness like
the darkness of death that would soon capture them. But the trouble they brought
upon themselves was an even heavier burden than the darkness.

God Sends Light To Guide His People

Solomon continues praying:

18 A bright light was shining on your
chosen people. And although the
Egyptians could not see your people, they
could hear them and considered them
lucky, because they were not suffering.
2 The Egyptians were thankful that the
people they had abused were not abusing
them in return, and so they begged your
chosen people for forgiveness.[t] 3 Then,
with a flaming fire at night and with the
warmth of the sun during the day, you
guided your people through places they
had never traveled before. 4 Their enemies
deserved to be prisoners of absolute darkness, because they had imprisoned your
children, who would bring the light of your
Law to the world.

Death of the First-Born Sons of the Egyptians

Solomon continues praying:

5 The Egyptians wanted to kill the newborn sons of your chosen people, but Moses
was rescued and survived. Then you decided to punish the Egyptians by killing
their first-born sons and by drowning their
army in the sea. 6 However, the night before our ancestors left Egypt, you warned
them of what would happen. So they were
able to celebrate, knowing that you would
keep your promise 7 to rescue your obedient people and to destroy their enemies,
just as they knew you would.
8 By these same events you punished
your enemies and rewarded us, your chosen people. 9 At this time also, the wonderful ancestors of our holy nation secretly offered sacrifices to you, and all of them
agreed to obey your Law, so that together
they would share in the same blessings and
dangers. Already they were singing hymns
of praise to you,[u] 10 while their enemies
cried bitter tears and made mournful
sounds over the death of their children.
11 Every family suffered the same punishment, whether they were slaves or slave
owners, ordinary people or royalty. 12 In
one brief moment, the dearest child in
each family died, leaving not even enough
people to bury the dead. 13 The Egyptians
had been deceived by displays of magic.
However, after the death of their first-born
sons, they realized that we were the children of God.
14 In the middle of the night—when all
was peaceful and quiet—15 your mighty
word came down from your royal throne in
heaven to attack a doomed land. Your word
was like a fierce warrior 16 carrying a sharp
sword and ready to obey your every command by killing people everywhere. When
he stood on the earth, his head touched
the sky. 17-19 Many of the Egyptians died a
dreadful death that night, but not before
nightmares and terrifying dreams showed
them why they were being punished.

[t] **18.2** *The Egyptians . . . forgiveness*: One possible meaning for the difficult Greek text.
[u] **18.9** *hymns of praise to you*: Another Greek manuscript "hymns of praise to their ancestors."
18.1-4 Ex 13.17-22. **18.13** 3 Macc 6.28. **18.14-19** Ws 17.3, 15; 2 Macc 3.25-29; 3 Macc 6.18.

God's People in the Desert

Solomon continues praying:
20 For a while, you were angry with your
people in the desert and killed many of
them with a terrible disease. 21 Then a
good man by the name of Aaron came to
their rescue by using prayer and incense as
a shield to protect your people from punishment for their sins, because he was a
priest. So he stood up against your anger
and ended the disaster. 22 He did not convince the crowd and end their suffering by
his own strength or by weapons—he did it
by reminding them of the wonderful agreements you had made with our ancestors.[v]
23 Piles of dead bodies were everywhere
when Aaron succeeded in turning away
your anger, and in keeping others from being struck down. 24 And his long robe sym-
bolized the entire universe, while the four
rows of precious stones on his breastpiece[w]
stood for our glorious ancestors, and his
turban[x] represented you, our majestic God.
25 At the sight of these, the death angel retreated in fear. A little of your anger was
enough.

The Egyptians Drown in the Red Sea

Solomon continues praying:
19 You remained angry with those
worthless Egyptians and kept punishing them without mercy, because you already knew 2 how they would change their
minds and chase your people, after hur-
riedly setting them free. 3 As a matter of
fact, they made this foolish decision even
before they had finished mourning for their
dead. Then they started pursuing those
very people they had begged and even
forced to leave. 4 They were urged on by
the destruction they deserved, and it made
them forget what had already happened, so
that they would be fully punished 5 by dying an unusual death and so that your people would have an amazing journey.

God Protects His People and Punishes the Egyptians

Solomon continues praying:
6 At your command the laws of nature
were changed[y] to protect your children
from harm. 7 A cloud guided them, and dry
land appeared like a field of grass in the
middle of the Red Sea,[z] 8 so that your people could see wonderful miracles and pass
safely through under your protection.
9 They were like horses on an open range
or like lambs leaping around, as they
praised you for saving them. 10 And they
still remembered what had happened in
Egypt—the land was covered with gnats instead of animals, and the rivers were filled
with frogs instead of fish. 11 Later, when
they were starving in the desert and begged
for something delicious to eat, you provided them with a special kind of bird, 12 by
sending quails from the direction of the
Mediterranean Sea.
13 Those sinful Egyptians had a terrible
hatred for strangers, and so you punished
them horribly, but not without first warning them with violent thunderstorms.
14-16 Years earlier, the people of Sodom had
refused to welcome strangers,[a] and they
were punished for what they did. But these
Egyptians did much worse. They first welcomed our ancestors with a glorious celebration, and then after we had helped their
nation, they made slaves of us, even
though we were citizens like everyone else.
17 Those people of Sodom were struck
blind, just as they reached the door of the
home of that good man Lot, and they had
to feel their way back through the darkness
to their own homes. In the same way, these
Egyptians were covered with deep darkness.[b]

[v]**18.22** *He did not . . . ancestors*: Or possibly, "He overcame this time of distress, not by his own strength or by weapons, but by reminding the death angel of your faithful promises to our ancestors." [w]**18.24** *four rows . . . breastpiece*: See Exodus 28.15-21. [x]**18.24** *turban*: Fastened to Aaron's turban was a narrow strip of pure gold with the words "Dedicated to the LORD" engraved on it (see Exodus 28.36). [y]**19.6** *the laws of nature were changed*: This refers to the crossing of the Red Sea (see Exodus 14.1-31). [z]**19.7** *Red Sea*: See the note at 10.18. [a]**19.14-16** *people of Sodom . . . strangers*: See Genesis 19.1-21. [b]**19.17** *darkness*: One possible meaning for the difficult Greek text of verse 17.

18.20-25 Nu 16.41-50; 4 Macc 7.11.

Harmony of the Universe

Solomon continues praying:

18 Different tunes can be played on the
same harp, though the strings remain the
same. And this is similar to what happened
in those days, as can be seen from the following examples. 19 Land animals became
sea creatures, and sea creatures became
land animals; 20 fire kept burning, even
when it was covered with water, 21 and yet
its flames did not destroy the flesh of humans or melt that delicate and dainty food
called manna[c] that came down from heaven.

22 Our Lord, you have always
greatly honored your people.
You have never failed
to help them at any time
or in any place.

[c]**19.21** *manna*: See the note at 16.20.

SIRACH
THE WISDOM OF JESUS, SON OF SIRACH

ABOUT THIS BOOK

The author of this book was Jesus or Joshua, son of Eleazar son of Sirach (see 50.27). He is often referred to as Jesus son of Sirach, but usually just as Sirach, which was actually the Greek form of *Sira'*, his grandfather's Hebrew name. Sirach traveled a lot, but he lived in Jerusalem, where he seems to have been a teacher of the Law of Moses. His book, also known by the title Ecclesiasticus, was published there around 180 B.C., probably not long before his death. The book was translated by his grandson into Greek in Alexandria, Egypt, and published shortly after 117 B.C.

Sirach lived his whole life under the rule of the Greek kings of Egypt and Syria. These kings tried to influence everyone in their kingdoms to live like Greeks, and many of the Jewish people were attracted to the teachings of Greek religion and philosophy. One of the main reasons Sirach wrote his book was to show the Jews that continuing to fear the Lord would bring them the best wisdom as well as success and happiness:

The person who finds wisdom
finds great happiness,
but happiest of all is the one
who fears the Lord,
because fearing him
is more important
than anything else.
(25.10, 11)

A QUICK LOOK AT THIS BOOK

- Preface by the Author's Grandson
- Wisdom and the Fear of the Lord (1.1—4.10)
- Study Wisdom and Obey the Lord (4.11—6.17)
- Finding Wisdom, Wealth, and Happiness (6.18—15.10)
- Wise People, Sinners, and Fools (15.11—23.27)
- Wisdom, Family, and Friends (24.1—33.33)
- Wisdom and Worshiping the Lord (34.1—38.23)
- Wisdom and Blessings Come from God, the Creator (38.24—43.33)
- A Song Praising Israel's Ancestors (44.1—50.21)
- Read This Book and Learn Wisdom (50.22-29)
- A Prayer To Give Thanks (51.1-12)
- Search for Wisdom (51.13-30)

Preface by the Author's Grandson

Many great and wise teachings have been handed down to us in the Scriptures, that is, in the Law, the Prophets, and the other writings.[a] We should praise earlier generations of Israel for writing and saving these books. And if you really love to study the Scriptures, it is very important for you to be able to explain them to others, whether by talking or by writing.

That's why my grandfather Jesus studied the Scriptures until he became an expert, then wrote this book to help others learn about wisdom. So if you love to learn, you should study this book, and you will come closer and closer to living as the Law requires.

But I ask you to read with a good attitude and not to be critical of my translation. I worked hard at it, so be understanding in those places where it isn't perfect. The meaning of any Hebrew book changes a little when it is translated, whether it is from the Law or the Prophets or is one of the other books in the Scriptures.

I came to Egypt in the thirty-eighth year of King Euergetes, and I stayed there for as long as he was king.[b] While I was there, I studied copies of many books, and that's when I realized I should translate this one. Translating carefully takes a lot of hard work, and I spent many sleepless nights before my translation was completed. And now that it is finished, those who live outside of Judea can read this book to learn how best to obey God's Law in their own lives.

Only the Lord Can Give Wisdom

1 Only the Lord can give Wisdom,
and his Wisdom lasts forever.
2 And who but the Lord
can count the raindrops
or the days in eternity
or the sand on the seashore?
3 And who else can measure
the height of heaven
or the width of the earth
or the depth of the sea?
4 The Lord created Wisdom
long before anything else.
5 The Wisdom in God's commands
flows from his word in heaven
like streams from a spring.[c]

6 Who can understand
the deep thoughts of Wisdom
or how clever she[d] is?
7 Can anyone be taught
all of her knowledge?
Can anyone understand
how much she has learned?[e]
8 Only the Lord is that wise;
he is fearsome and majestic
as he rules from his throne.
9 The Lord created Wisdom
and watched her grow,
then he gave her
to his creation—
10 to every living thing—
but especially to those people
who love him.[f]
11 If you fear the Lord,
you will be proud
of the honors you receive,
and you will wear happiness
like a crown.
12 And if you fear him,
your life will be long
and filled with joy.[g]
13 You will die happy,
blessed by the Lord
on the day of your death.

14 Respect and obey the Lord—
that's where Wisdom begins,
and she will stay
with faithful people
from the day of their birth.

[a]*Law . . . Prophets . . . writings*: The Jewish way of categorizing the books of the Old Testament.
[b]*thirty-eighth year . . . he was king*: King Ptolemy VIII Euergetes II (Physkon) was co-ruler with his brother and sister 170-164 B.C., and he was the only ruler 146-117 B.C. He counted the years of his rule from 170 B.C., and so his thirty-eighth year was 132 B.C.
[c]**1.5** *spring*: Verse 5 is not in some manuscripts.
[d]**1.6** *she*: In this book, Wisdom is often pictured as a wise woman.
[e]**1.7** *learned*: Verse 7 is not in some manuscripts.
[f]**1.10** *him*: Some manuscripts add, "It is wise to love the Lord, and he gives us wisdom so we can know him."
[g]**1.12** *joy*: Some manuscripts add, "Being able to fear the Lord is a gift from him, and his love will keep you from stumbling."
1.1 Pr 2.6. **1.9** Pr 8.22-31; Si 24.9.

15 She has lived among us humans
since the beginning of time,
and she will never desert
our descendants.
16 Respect and obey the Lord—
this is complete Wisdom.
Be drunk on the wine
of Wisdom,
17 and let her fill your house
and your barns
with the harvest she brings.
18 Wisdom will give you
respect for the Lord,
to be worn like a crown
woven from the flowers
of peace and good health.[h]
19 Hold on to Wisdom,
and she will honor you
by sending knowledge
and complete understanding
like showers of rain.
20 Wisdom is like a tree—
at its root is respect
for the Lord,
and its branches represent
a long lifetime.

21 Fear of the Lord
forces sin and anger
out of your life.[i]
22 It is never right to be angry
without a good reason,
because anger will start you
down the path to disaster.
23 Just be patient and stay calm
until your anger fades.
24 Then when the time is right
you can speak,
and others will tell
of your good sense.

Be Faithful to the Lord

25 Wisdom collects wise sayings,
but faithfulness to God
is disgusting to a sinner.
26 If you want lots of Wisdom
from the Lord,
then obey his commands.
27 Respect and obey the Lord,
and you will learn Wisdom;
be faithful and humble,
and he will be pleased.
28 Faithfully obey the Lord
and worship him
with all your heart.
29 Others are watching you,
so be careful—
don't say one thing
and then do something else.
30 If you boast and then fail,
you will be disgraced.
And if you only pretend
to worship the Lord,
he will bring you down
and show everyone
that you are a fake.

Be Faithful When Tested

2 Students, if you decide
to worship and obey the Lord,
be ready to face problems.
2 Have firm self-control
and don't act too quickly
if trouble strikes.
3 Don't turn from the Lord,
but be faithful;
that's the way to succeed.
4 Accept everything that happens.
Be patient if others
humiliate you—
5 humiliation tests people
as a furnace tests gold.[j]
6 The Lord will give his help,
if you depend only on him
and do right.
7 If you fear the Lord
and are patient,
he will show you mercy.
But if you turn away,
you will fall.
8 Put your trust in him,
and he will reward you.
9 Don't give up hoping
for good things, like mercy
and a life full of joy.
10 Look at past generations—

[h] **1.18** *health*: Some manuscripts add, "The Lord will give them to you along with honor if you love him." [i] **1.21** *life*: Verse 21 is not in some manuscripts. [j] **2.5** *gold*: Some manuscripts add, "Trust the Lord if you become sick or poor."

1.17 Ws 7.11. **1.20** Pr 3.16; 4.10. **2.5** Ws 3.5, 6; 1 P 1.7.

did the Lord desert those people
who trusted and feared him?
Or did he fail to answer those
who asked him for help?
11 The Lord is kind
and shows mercy
by forgiving our sins
and rescuing us from trouble.

12 But the Lord will send trouble
if you don't have the courage
to be faithful
and to stay away from sin.
13 If you are too afraid
to put your trust in him,
he will not protect you
when problems come.
14 And if you give up,
you will be in for trouble
when the Lord decides
to judge your life.

*15 If you love the Lord
and respect him,
you will obey his commands.
16 You will try to please him
and to be completely faithful
to his Law.
17 If you fear the Lord,
you will prepare yourself
to worship him
with humility.

18 We pray, Lord, that you
will decide our future.
You are as merciful
as you are majestic,[k]
so don't leave our fate
in human hands.

Respect for Parents

3 Students, I have been
like a father to you,
and you will be safe
if you do what I say.
2 The Lord has told children
to honor and obey
their parents.
3 If you honor your father,
your sins will be forgiven;
4 show respect to your mother,
and you will be truly rich.
5 Honor your father—
then your own children
will make you happy,
and God will hear them
when they pray.
6 If you want to live a long time,
then you must obey the Lord
by respecting your parents;
7 serve them as if you
were their slave.
8 If you speak to your father
with respect
and do what he asks,
he will bless you,
9 and your own family
will have success.
But if your mother
places a curse on you,
your family will face ruin.
10 You cannot get respect
by disgracing your parents.
11 What brings honor to them
also brings honor to you.

12 Help your father
as he grows old;
try not to upset him.
13 And when you are strong,
but his mind is fading,
don't make fun—
instead, be patient.
14 God sees your kindness,
and right away,
some of your sins
will be forgiven.
15 And if you later have troubles
because of your sins,
they will all melt away
in the warmth of your kindness,
like frost in the sunshine.
16 But abandoning your father
or making your mother angry
is as bad as cursing the Lord,
and so he will curse you.

17 Students, be humble
in your work,

[k]**2.18** *majestic*: One ancient translation adds, "and you live up to your reputation."
2.15,16 Ws 6.18; Jn 14.15, 21, 23. **3.8** Ex 20.12.

and you will be loved
by God's people.
18 The more powerful you are,
the more humble you must be
if you want the Lord
to be kind to you.
19 Many people are important
and famous,
but God gives his secrets
only to the humble.[l]
20 God is extremely powerful,
and he will accept praise only
from those who are not proud.

21 Don't try to learn things
you cannot understand.
22 Instead, think about God's Law
and don't worry about secrets
God keeps to himself.
23 He has already shown you
matters beyond understanding,
and anything more
is none of your business.
24 Proud thoughts have led many
to turn from following God,
and evil ideas have ruined
the way they think.

25 Without eyes, you cannot see,
and without gaining knowledge
you can never get wisdom.
26 If you are stubborn,
you will end up in trouble,
and if you love danger,
it will kill you someday.
27 Those who are stubborn
are burdened with suffering,
and sinners carry
a heavy load of sins.
28 Evil has taken root
inside the arrogant,
and so when disaster strikes,
they cannot be rescued.
29 The wise always try to listen,
and they will pay attention
to a wise saying.

30 Money given to the poor
brings forgiveness for sins,
just as water
puts out a fire.
31 If you think that in the future
you might ever need help,
then repay other people now
when they do favors for you.

4 Students, if the poor
work for you,
don't cheat on their wages,
but pay them right away.
2 Don't disappoint the hungry
or upset the needy.
3 And if they are upset already,
don't make things worse
by being slow in giving them
what they need.
4 When people ask for help,
don't turn them down;
and if others are in need,
don't turn away.
5 If you pretend not to notice,
they will have good reason
to curse you.
6 And if their curses flow
from hearts you made bitter,
God, the Creator, will hear them
and do what they ask.

7 Be friendly to everyone
in the community
and show proper respect
to the town leaders.
8 When the poor greet you,
be polite and greet them
in return.
9 Rescue everyone
who suffers from injustice;
have the courage
to make the right decisions;
10 provide for orphans and widows,
as if they were your own
children or wife.
Then you will be a true child
of God Most High,
and he will love you more
than your own mother does.

11 If you study Wisdom,
you will become her child,

[l]**3.19** *humble*: Verse 19 is not in some manuscripts.
3.18 Phil 2.3. **3.22** Dt 29.29.

and she will help you
be successful.
12 If you love life
and want to find happiness,
love Wisdom enough
to get up early and study.
13 Hold tightly to her—
you will receive glory,
and the Lord will bless
everyone around you.
14 To obey her is to worship
the Holy Lord God,
and if you love Wisdom,
the Lord will love you.
15 Pay attention and obey Wisdom;
you will live in safety
and even rule nations.
16 Remain faithful to her,
and she will belong to you
and your descendants.
17 At first, Wisdom will test you
with her commands,
and you will walk in fear
along twisting pathways.
Her discipline
will bring suffering
until you are truly faithful.
18 But then she will return
straight to you,
bringing happiness
and telling her secrets.
19 But if you wander away,
she will let you go off
to your doom.

20 Be on your guard against evil,
but use every opportunity
for doing good.
And don't be ashamed
of who you are.
21 To be ashamed of your sins
leads to forgiveness
and honor,
but some other kinds of shame
are sins themselves.
22 If you play favorites
or let bullies push you around,
you will get hurt.
23 If you can make things right
by speaking up, then do so.
Don't let the opinions of others
make you hide your wisdom.[m]
24 If your wisdom and knowledge
are to make any difference,
you will have to speak.
25 Don't ever try
to make the truth seem false,
but always be humble
about things you don't know.
26 Don't try to hide your sins
from God—
it would be easier
to stop a river from flowing.
27 Never promise to obey a fool,
and don't play favorites
while a ruler is watching.
28 And even if you risk your life
fighting for truth,
the Lord God will be there,
fighting by your side.

29 Don't be arrogant
in what you say,
or slow and weak
in what you do.
30 When you are at home,
don't be fierce as a lion
or suspicious of servants.
31 Don't hold out your hand
when it's time to receive,
then close your fist
when its time to give.

5 Don't trust your wealth
and say,
"I don't need anyone's help.
2 I'm strong and smart enough
to get anything I want,
3 and no one has the power
to make me obey."
Talk like that,
and God will punish you!

4 And don't reply, "I sinned,
but God didn't punish me."
God was being patient.

[m]**4.23** *Don't let . . . your wisdom*: Some Greek manuscripts; Hebrew and two ancient translations "Don't hide your wisdom"; most Greek manuscripts do not have these words.
4.31 Ac 20.35. **5.4** Ec 8.11.

5 Never be so sure
of his forgiveness
that you keep on sinning
6 and say, "God is very kind,
and he will forgive me
even though I sin a lot."
Yes, God is kind,
but he also gets angry
and punishes sinners.
7 Turn back to the Lord now—
don't wait until tomorrow.
If he gets angry,
he will quickly punish you
with death.
8 And wealth gotten by cheating
won't save you from disaster.

9 Not every wind is good
for blowing away husks
from threshed grain.
And not every path leads
where you want to go.
But sinners will say anything
to get what they want.[n]
10 Stand up for what you believe,
and don't change what you say
from one time to the next.
11 Be willing to listen to anyone,
but think before you answer.
12 Then speak up, if you know
what to say;
and if not, just keep quiet.
13 Your words can bring you honor,
but they can also cause
your ruin and disgrace.
14 When you speak,
don't tear others down
or try to make them say
something wrong.
You would receive
severe punishment,
far worse than the shame
felt by thieves.
15 So don't make big mistakes,
or even little ones,

6 that turn you into an enemy
instead of a friend.
A reputation for being dishonest
will bring you nothing
but shame and insults.
2 Don't fall under the power
of evil desires.
They are burning flames
that will destroy you,[o]
3 and you will be left to wither,
like a tree with burned leaves
and scorched fruit.
4 Evil desires will destroy you,
and your enemies will laugh.

5 If you speak pleasantly
and politely,
you will make friends
and be welcome anywhere.
6 Be friendly with everyone,
but only listen to advice
from those few you can trust.
7 Make sure they are true friends
before you trust them,
8 because some will be friendly
when everything is fine,
but they won't help
when you have trouble.
9 If you argue with other friends,
they will become enemies
and tell about the argument
so you will look bad.
10 Still others will come to dinner
but not to help
if you have trouble.
11 In good times,
they will be so close,
that your servants
will have to obey them.
12 But if you lose your wealth,
they will disappear.

13 Keep your distance
from enemies
and don't be fooled
by false friends.
*14 Loyal friends will protect you
with all their strength
15 and are worth more
than any other treasure.
*16 They are even like medicine
that can save your life.
And here's how you can have
such loyal friends:
17 obey the Lord and choose friends
who also obey him.

[n]**5.9** *But sinners . . . want*: Greek; these words are not in the Hebrew text. [o]**6.2** *you*: One possible meaning for the difficult text of verse 2.

18 Students, be disciplined
and learn Wisdom
when you are young,
and as your hair turns gray,
she will never desert you.
19 Learning Wisdom isn't so hard.
It's like plowing a little
and planting a few seeds—
then a short time later
eating food from the harvest.
20 But to those who are fools
or have no discipline,
the job will seem too great,
and they will give up.
21 When Wisdom tests them,
they will toss her aside,
as if she were a stone
too heavy to carry.
22 Wisdom is hidden
from most people,
just as her name suggests.[p]

23 Pay attention, students—
don't reject my advice.
24 Become a slave to Wisdom,
with her chains fastened
around your neck and feet.
25 Carry her on your shoulders
and don't let those chains
make you angry.
26 Make up your mind to follow
and stay close to Wisdom
wherever she goes.
27 Search, and you will find her;
once she is yours,
hold her tightly.
28 Then she will give you
a peaceful and happy life.
29 Her chains on your feet
will become your protection,
and those on your neck
will turn into a royal robe,
30 decorated with gold jewelry
and tied with a purple cord.
31 You will wear Wisdom
like a beautiful robe
or like a crown
at a victory celebration.
32 Students, you are able
to discipline yourself
and learn Wisdom—
just put your mind to it!
33 Do you love to listen?
That's all it really takes
to gain Wisdom.
34 Spend time with older people
and stay close to those
who are wise.
35 When godly people speak,
pay attention, and memorize
every wise saying you hear.
36 If you know smart people,
visit them whenever you can,
until their welcome mat
wears thin from your feet.
37 Never stop considering
God's laws and commands,
and he will strengthen your mind
with the Wisdom you want.

7 If you don't do evil,
then evil cannot harm you.
2 Always be fair with others,
and injustice will stay
away from you.
3 But those who farm
the fields of injustice,
will harvest seven times more
than they plant.

4 Don't ask the Lord
to make you a leader,
and don't ask the king
to give you honor.
5 Don't try to impress the Lord
with your goodness,
or to show off your wisdom
in front of the king.
6 Don't seek to be a judge
unless you have the strength
to do away with injustice.
And if you don't have courage
to stand up to the powerful,
you will ruin your good name.

7 Don't disgrace yourself
by sinning
against your community.

[p]**6.22** *just as her name suggests*: In Hebrew one word for wisdom sounds like a word meaning "withdrawn" or "hidden."

6.19 Jas 5.7, 8. **6.37** Js 1.6-8; Ps 1.2.

8 You won't escape punishment
if you commit a sin even once,
much less twice.
9 And do not think
that God Most High
will pardon you,
just because you have offered
a lot of sacrifices.

10 Don't let anything
discourage you from praying
or giving to the poor.
11 God can take away your success
as easily as he gave it,
so do not make fun of anyone
who is bitter from suffering.
12 Do not tell lies to a relative
or a friend 13 or anyone else.
No good ever comes
from telling lies.
14 In a town council meeting,
don't talk too much.
And in your prayers,
don't repeat the same things
over and over again.
15 Enjoy all kinds of hard work,
especially farming, because
God Most High created it.

16 Do not join others in sinning—
just think of how quickly
God can punish.
17 So be as humble as you can,
because those who are ungodly
will be eaten by worms
and burned by fire.
18 Don't betray a friend for money
or a relative for pure gold.[q]

19 If your wife is wise and good
and gracious,
she is more valuable than gold,
so do not divorce her.
20 If your workers or slaves
work hard and well,
don't mistreat them.
21 If you have wise slaves,
love them as much
as you love yourself
and set them free
when you are supposed to.[r]
22 If you have cattle,
give them good care
and keep them as long
as they bring you a profit.

23 While your children are young,
teach them to obey you.
24 Do not let a daughter
always have her own way,
but protect her from men.
25 Finding a husband for her
is important, but be certain
to find one who is wise.
26 Don't divorce your wife
if she pleases you,
but if you can't stand her,
then don't trust her.

27 Honor your father
with all your heart
and remember that your birth
gave your mother great pain.
28 How can you ever repay them
for the gift of life?

29 Fear the Lord
with all that you are,
and respect his priests.
30 Put all your strength
into loving your Creator
and be sure that his servants
make a good living.
31 Fear the Lord
and honor his priests
with what he has commanded.
Bring them the first part
of your harvest
and the sacrifice
to make things right.
Give them the shoulders
from other sacrifices
and all offerings and holy food
dedicated to the Lord.

32 The Lord will give you
complete success,
if you give to the poor.

[q]**7.18** *pure gold*: Greek has "gold from Ophir," which may have been in Africa or India. Gold from there was considered the very best. [r]**7.21** *set them free . . . supposed to*: Jewish slave-owners were supposed to set a Jewish slave free after six years of service (see Exodus 21.2; Deuteronomy 15.12).

7.21 Ex 21.2; Dt 15.12-15. **7.27,28** Ex 20.12.

33 So be generous to everyone,
especially to those
whose loved ones have died.[s]
34 Go to see them
and weep as they mourn.
35 If you visit the sick,
everyone will love you.
36 You can keep from sinning
by always reminding yourself
that you will someday die.

8 Don't fight those in power
if you have no chance to win.
2 Don't argue with those
who have plenty of gold—
they will drag you down
by bribing others
or by persuading the king
to see things their way.
3 And arguing with those
who talk too much
is like piling more wood
on a fire.
4 Don't laugh at those
who are crude,
unless you want to hear them
insult your ancestors.
5 If people are trying
to stop committing sins,
don't make them feel guilty;
remember that we all deserve
to be punished for our sins.
6 Don't dishonor old people—
the rest of us
are getting older too.
7 Never be happy
when someone dies.
Remember, all of us
must die someday.
8 When wise people speak,
pay attention, then study
what they have said.
You will learn discipline
and how to serve
those in power.
9 Listen when old people tell you
what they learned
from their ancestors.
Then you will understand
how to give the best answer
when one is needed.
10 Don't encourage sinners to sin;
they might blaze up like a fire
and you would get burned.
11 Don't argue with the arrogant—
they will try to turn
your own words against you.
12 Never lend to someone
who is stronger than you;
if you make such a loan,
don't count on being repaid.
13 Don't ever guarantee a loan
for more than you can afford,
and don't be surprised
if you have to repay
a loan you guaranteed.
14 Never sue judges—
their influence is so great
that they will always win.

15 Don't travel with those
who like danger.
They will do what they please
and cause you problems,
and their foolishness
might get you killed.
16 Don't start a fight
with hot-tempered people.
They don't care who they kill,
so don't travel with them
along deserted roads,
where you would be helpless
if they attacked.

17 Fools can't keep a secret,
so don't ask them for advice.
18 And when strangers are around
don't do anything
that you want kept secret—
you never know
who they might tell.
19 Do not discuss with just anyone
what you really think,
and don't let others
do favors for you.

Advice for Men

9 Love your wife,
but don't act jealous—
that will only invite her
to hurt you.

[s]**7.33** *especially . . . have died*: Or "and provide a proper burial for those who have died."
9.1 Nu 5.12-15.

2 If you let yourself fall
under the spell of a woman,
she will walk all over you.
3 You had best stay away
from an immoral woman,
or you will be caught
in her traps.
4 Do not spend too much time
with a woman who sings
to entertain men—
she can use many tricks
to take control of you.
5 Do not gaze too long
at a virgin—
if you talk her into having sex,
you will have to pay a fine
and marry her.[t]
6 Don't let yourself be controlled
by a desire for prostitutes,
or you will lose everything
that you inherited.
7 So don't look for them;
stay off the lonely streets
where they are found.

8 Don't stare at a married woman
with a beautiful figure.
A woman's beauty
can set men on fire
and has led many astray.
9 Never have dinner or drinks
with someone else's wife.
To fall in love with her
is to fall to your death.

Looking for Happiness

10 Don't desert old friends—
like bottles of aged wine,
they bring cheer
more than new ones.

11 Don't be jealous of sinners
who receive praise;
you never can tell
how their life will end.
12 Don't look for happiness
where ungodly people do.
You know they won't always
get away with their sins.
13 Stay away from those
who are able to kill you,
and you won't live in fear
of death.
To be near them is to walk
through a field full of traps
or across a ledge
high on the city walls—
make one false step
and your life is over.

14 Do your best to know
your close neighbors,
but only ask the wise ones
for advice.
15 Speak with the wise
about the Law
of God Most High.
16 Ask godly people over for dinner
and be proud
that you fear the Lord.

Leaders

17 Craftsmen receive praise
if their work shows skill,
and the leaders of a nation
will be honored
for wise words.
18 But loud, reckless leaders
are hated and feared.

10 A wise judge teaches the laws
to the people,
and a smart ruler
gets things organized.
2 The people of a town
and its lower officials
usually follow the example
set by the judges and rulers.
3 A stupid king
destroys his nation,
but a city grows
if its leaders can rule well.

4 The Lord controls
all authorities on earth,
and he appoints the best rulers
for each situation and time.
5 God alone gives the success
that brings honor to those
who write the laws.

Why Are We Humans So Proud?

6 When neighbors harm you,
don't be angry or proud.

[t]**9.5** *a virgin . . . marry her*: See Deuteronomy 22.28, 29; Exodus 22.16, 17.

7 The Lord and all people
hate pride and become angry
at injustice.
8 A wealthy and arrogant nation
that fails to show justice
will soon be conquered.

9 Why are we humans so proud?
We are only dust and ashes,
and we easily lose
our health and strength.[u]
10 A long illness mocks the skill
of physicians,[v]
and even a king
can die without warning.
11 Then after our death,
our bodies are eaten
by wild animals and maggots
and worms.

12 We humans start to be arrogant
when our hearts turn away
from the Lord our Creator.
13 Sins are the source of pride,
and if we hold on to it,
our lives will be flooded
with more disgusting sins.
So the Lord destroys[w] the proud
by punishing them with disasters
they never dreamed possible.
14 He removes powerful rulers,
replacing them with
the humble.
15 When God decides to give land
to a humble nation,
he pulls up others by the roots
16 and plows through their fields
until nothing remains.
17 The Lord destroys some of them
so completely, that no one
remembers they ever lived.

18 When the Lord created humans,
he did not intend for us
to be proud and angry.
19 We deserve honor
only when we fear the Lord,
but we should not be honored
if we break his laws.
20 A family should give honor
to its leader,
but God honors all
who fear him.
21 He accepts them,
but he rejects those
who are proud and stubborn.[x]
22 Fearing the Lord is something
to be proud of—
whether you are poor,
or rich and famous,
a Jew, or a Gentile.
23 Don't look down on those
who are wise but poor,
and don't honor sinners.

24 Honor always comes to judges
and people in power,
but anyone who fears the Lord
is even more deserving.
25 So if you are smart,
you will understand
when you see a master
serving a wise servant.

26 Don't spend your time thinking
of ways to avoid work,
and don't pretend to be well off
if you are short of money.
27 It's better to work
and have more than enough
than to boast and go hungry.
28 Students, be humble
but remember to have
proper self-esteem.
29 Who will think you are innocent
if you call yourself guilty?
And who will give you honor
if you refuse
to respect yourself?

30 The poor receive honor
if they are educated,
while the wealthy are praised
because they have money.
31 So when the poor become rich
they will be praised more,
but the disgrace of the wealthy

[u] **10.9** *and we . . . strength*: One possible meaning for the difficult Greek text. [v] **10.10** *A long illness . . . physicians*: One possible meaning for the difficult Greek text. [w] **10.13** *destroys*: Or "destroyed." [x] **10.21** *stubborn*: Some manuscripts and ancient translations do not have verse 21.
10.14 1 S 2.8; Lk 1.52.

will become much worse
if they lose their money.

11 Those in power
always make room
for someone wise and humble.
2 Do not praise or despise anyone
on the basis of their looks.
3 The honeybee is very small,
but it makes
the sweetest food.
4 Don't boast about your clothes
or act important
when you are honored.
Only the Lord does things
truly worthy of praise,
but he keeps them hidden
from our sight.
5 Kings often lose their power
to those who had seemed
to be nobodies,
6 while honored rulers
are captured and disgraced.

All Things Come from the Lord

7 Find out the truth
before you criticize.
8 Don't interrupt others—
hear them out,
then give your answer.
9 If it's none of your business,
then don't argue with them,
and stay away from sinners
when they discuss what to do.

10 Students, don't let yourself
become too busy.
If you do, you will sin
and not find success
or escape trouble.
11 Some people work all day long
as hard as they can,
but they keep getting poorer.
12 Others are poor and weak;
they work slowly
and always need help.
But the Lord shows kindness
13 and to everyone's surprise,
he lifts them from poverty
and gives them honor.
14 All things, whether good or bad,
come from the Lord.
He gives life and riches
or takes them away.
15 The Lord gives wisdom
by teaching us
to understand his Law.
He helps us love each other
and do right.
16 Sinners are dishonest
and live in darkness,
proud of their evil
from the day they are born,
and so evil will stay with them
until the day they die.[y]
17 But the Lord gives success
to his faithful people
and blesses them with gifts
that last forever.
18 You can become rich,
if you work hard
and never spend any money.
But then what?
19 When you finally retire
to enjoy what you own,
you soon may die,
and then your wealth
will belong to others.
20 When you agree to do work,
stay busy and don't quit.
21 Don't be surprised
at what sinners do;
trust the Lord and keep working,
because he can make you rich
in a moment's time.
22 Suddenly, he will reward you
and bless you with prosperity,
if you are faithful to him.
*23 So don't say, "I already have
everything I need—
what more could the Lord
do for me?
24 Nothing can harm me now!"

25 When people are well off,
they never mention
how needy they once were,
and when they have trouble,
the good times are forgotten.

[y]**11.15,16** *The Lord gives wisdom . . . until the day they die*: Verses 15, 16 are not in some manuscripts.
11.18,19 Ps 49.10; Lk 12.16-21.

26 But at the end of life,
the Lord will pay us back
for what we have done.
27 Pleasant memories fade
after an hour of pain,
but the way that you lived
is made clear by how you die
28 and by what kind of children
you leave behind.
So don't praise anyone
until they are dead.

Be Careful

29 Don't let just anyone
come to your house.
Dishonest people will trick you,
30 as bird hunters use decoys
to trap quails.
They watch you like spies,
waiting for some mistake
31 or for a chance
to make your good deeds
seem evil.

32 One spark can start a fire,
and one sinner's evil plan
can end in murder.
33 Watch out for the schemes
of those who do evil,
or they may ruin
your good name.
34 And if you let foreigners
come to live in your home,
they will cause trouble
and persuade you to accept
their customs and gods.[z]

Do Good to Those Who Deserve It

12 Do good to those
who deserve it,
and they will thank you.
2 Be kind to the godly,
and they—or God Most High—
will reward you.
3 But you will have no success
if you keep doing evil
and refuse to give
to the poor.
*4 Help those who are humble
and faithful to God,
5 but don't help the ungodly.
If you give food to sinners,
they will become strong
and overpower you.
Do a good deed for them,
and they will reward you
by wronging you twice.
6 But God Most High
hates ungodly sinners
and will punish them.
7 Yes, give to good people,
not to sinners.

True Friends

8 In hard times you will discover
your true friends
and your real enemies.
9 Even your enemies act friendly
when you are well off,
but only true friends stay
when trouble strikes.

10 Never trust your enemies—
their evil will attack you
like rust 11 eating away
at an unpolished mirror.[a]
So be on guard against them,
even if they bow down
and act humble.
12 Don't make them your partners,
or they will push you aside
and take over.
Then you will know I was right,
and you will feel the sting
of my words.

13 If you try to charm snakes
or to tame wild animals,
who will take pity
when you get bitten?
14 In the same way,
no one will take pity
if you are friendly with sinners
and start sinning yourself.

15 Enemies act loyal for a while,
but they won't stand by you
when you need help.
16 They tell you how much
they want to be your friends,

[z]**11.34** *persuade . . . gods*: Greek "make you a foreigner to your own family." [a]**12.10,11** *rust . . . mirror*: Mirrors were made of metal, and would rust if not kept clean, dry, and polished.
12.1 Mt 7.6.

all the while plotting
to put you in your grave.
They weep when you are sad,
but they will try to kill you
the first chance they get.
17 If you are struck by disaster,
they pretend to help
but pull you down instead.
18 Then they laugh and sneer,
making vulgar hand signs,
showing what kind of friends
they really are.

Staying Humble

13 Can you stay humble
if your friends are proud?
Only if you can handle tar
and stay clean!
2 And watch out if your friends
are rich and powerful.
You cannot match their strength,
and you might be crushed,
just like a clay jar
struck by an iron pan.
3 The rich oppress
and insult the poor,
then demand an apology!
4 The rich will try to use you,
but if you need help,
don't bother to ask.
5 When they come to visit you,
they will soak up
what little you have.
6 If they need your help,
they smile and act kind
and even ask how they
can be of service.
But don't be fooled—
it's all lies!
7 They will invite you to dinner,
but in the long run you'll pay
three times what it cost.
And when you have nothing left,
they will laugh and sneer
and keep their distance.
8 So be smart and careful,
not deceived and humiliated.

9 Important people
will want you around,
if you don't try too hard
to be their friend.
10 Push yourself on them,
and you will face rejection;
act cold, and they will forget
that you are alive.
11 Don't try to be their equal
or trust them when they
have long talks with you.
They are smiling,
but you are being tested.

12 Those who tell secrets are cruel
and would just as soon hurt you
or send you to prison.
13 Be careful! Don't risk disaster
by sharing your secrets.
14 Wake up and pay attention!
Every day of your life,
love the Lord and pray
that he will protect you.[b]

*15 Animals and people
16 love their own kind.
17 Wolves and lambs
have about as much in common
as sinners and God's people.
18 Hyenas and dogs
are natural enemies,
just like the poor
and the rich.
19 Desert lions will always feast
on wild donkeys,
and the rich will gobble down
the needy.
20 The rich and proud
consider the poor and humble
to be disgusting.

The Rich and the Poor

21 When the rich start to stumble
their friends lend a hand,
but let the poor fall down,
and their friends pretend
not to know them.
22 When the rich are in trouble,
many will offer to help
and will even make excuses
when the rich insult them.
But let the poor get in trouble,
and all they get is criticism,
even if they speak wisely.
23 When the rich speak,

[b]**13.14** *you*: Some manuscripts do not have verse 14.

everyone listens
with great respect.
But if the poor speak,
everyone asks, "Just who
do they think they are?"
And if the poor start to trip,
people give them a push.
24 It's good to have wealth
if you got it honestly,
but don't be ungodly and claim
that being poor is evil.

Be Good to Yourself

25 With one look at your face
anyone can see
if you are happy or sad.
26 A smile shows you are happy,
and a tired look may mean
you have been trying too hard
to think up a proverb.

14 You will be happiest
if you keep from sinning
and saying stupid things,
2 and if you have no reason
to feel guilty
and have not given up hope.

*3 What's the use of being rich
if you don't enjoy
spending money on yourself?
4 Are you just saving it
so others can live in luxury
after you are dead and gone?

5 Those who refuse to enjoy
a few things money can buy,
probably won't give much
to someone in need.
6 They spend nothing,
and punish themselves
with the greatest misery.

*7 If they do a good deed,
it is only by accident,
and the end of their life
shows how evil they were:
8 they pretended not to notice
others in need;
9 they were never happy
with their own fair share;
and by taking
what belonged to others,
their souls shriveled away.
10 They wouldn't even give
their families enough to eat!

11 Be good to yourself
according to what you have
and be generous in your giving
to the Lord.
12 You cannot know the time
for you to die,
and when it arrives,
death will not wait,
13 so now is the time
to help your friends
with generous gifts.
14 Every day, you should enjoy
the good things you want,
15 because after you are gone,
others will divide up everything
you worked so hard to get.
16 Give and accept gifts,
and treat yourself well,
because there is nothing good
in the world of the dead.
17 Every living creature wears out
like old clothes
and obeys the ancient law
that says, "You will die."
18 Generations pass away,
and others are born
to take their place,
just as new leaves
on a tall tree
replace those that fall.
19 Everything you ever made
will someday turn to dust,
then even the memory of you
will disappear.

Search for Wisdom

20 Wisdom always blesses those
who learn how to reason
by thinking about her.
21 They consider
what Wisdom has done
and the secrets she knows.
22 They wait for her
like hunters along a path,
then they follow her 23 home,

14.20-25 Pr 8.32-35.

where they peek
through the windows
and listen at the door.
*24 They set up camp
so close to her house,
that their tent pegs
are hammered into its walls.
25 There is no better place to live
than in her home—
26 like a shade tree, she protects
the children of her followers
27 from the heat,
and they live in a place
of great beauty.

15 If you fear the Lord
and obey his Law,
you will find Wisdom
when you search.
2 She will care for you
like your own mother
and welcome you, as a bride
welcomes her husband.
3 And instead of something
to eat and drink,
she will give you wisdom
and understanding.
4 You can depend on her
to keep you from disgrace.
5 She will tell you what to say,
and you will be honored
because of your wise speeches
in town meetings.
6 Your life will be happy,
and you will be remembered
for all time.

7 But fools and sinners
will never find Wisdom.
8 She won't come near the proud
or enter the mind of a liar.
9 That's why the Lord
refuses to accept praise
from sinners.
10 Only the wise can offer
acceptable praise.

Choosing How To Live

11 The Lord hates it when you say
that he forced you to sin.
12 And he doesn't like sinners,
so don't claim he tempted you
to become one.
13 The Lord and all who fear him
hate disgusting sins.
14 The Lord created us humans,
and from the very beginning,
he gave us the ability
to choose how we will live.
15 You are able to obey his Law
if you really want to,
and you can please him
by being faithful.
*16 Life and death are as different
as fire and water,
17 and the Lord will give you
whichever you choose.

18 The Lord is extremely wise
and tremendously powerful.
He can see all things—
19 every deed that we do—
and if we fear him,
he will watch over us.
20 He has neither commanded
nor given permission for anyone
to be evil or to sin.

Children

16 Ungodly children are worthless
and are nothing to desire
or to celebrate.
2 You can have lots of children,
but they will bring joy
only if they fear the Lord.
3 Having lots of ungodly children
won't help you in old age—
you will outlive them all.
One good child,
or even no children at all,
is better than a thousand
who are ungodly.
4 A family that disobeys the law
can make a city a ghost town,
but one smart person can fill
an empty city with people.

Mercy and Punishment

5 Here are but a few
of the important things
I have seen and heard:

15.11-20 Si 17.1-12.

6 If a small group of sinners
sets the Lord's anger ablaze,
then it will be worse by far
if a whole nation is sinful.
7 Long ago, the Lord refused
to forgive the mighty giants
who rebelled against him.
8 And he so hated the arrogance
of the people of Sodom,[c]
that he destroyed them.
9 They were doomed
because of their sins,
and the Lord showed no mercy
as he swept them away.
10 Nor did he have pity
on six hundred thousand
stubborn Assyrian soldiers
who attacked his people.
11 Even if only one person
refused to obey the Lord,
I would be surprised if he
did not punish that one.
The Lord loves to show mercy
and to use his mighty power
to forgive his people,
but when his anger overflows
against sinners,
12 he uses that same power
to punish them.
Everyone will receive
either mercy or punishment
as each deserves.
13 The Lord refuses to let sinners
profit from their crimes,
and he will reward his people
if they patiently wait.
14 He remembers every good deed
and gives everyone
what they deserve.

15 The Lord wanted everyone
to know his mighty power,
so he put a stubborn heart
in the king of Egypt.
16 But the Lord also wants everyone
to know about his mercy,
so he separated those
who have his light
from those who remain
in darkness.[d]

Foolish Thoughts

17 Never say to yourself,
"The Lord cannot see me.
He doesn't even know my name.
There are just too many people
for him to keep me in mind.
18 One glance from him
causes quaking and shaking
in the earth and the sky,
in the highest heaven
and the deepest sea,
19 in the mountains
and the foundations
of the earth.
20 But no human can understand
how his mighty power works.
21 Most of what God does
cannot be seen,
just like the wind
in a violent storm.
22 So who will tell him
when I do what is right?
And who has the patience
to wait for him
to keep his promises?"
23 That is how fools speak—
they cannot think straight
and have no understanding.

The Lord Created the World

24 Listen, students;
pay attention,
and you will learn.
25 I will train you and tell you
exactly what I know.

26 In the beginning, when the Lord
created the world,
he gave each thing
its proper place.
27 He designed the forces of nature
to last for all time—
they never tire or get hungry
or stop working.
28 They don't get in the way
of each other,
and they will never
disobey him.

[c]**16.8** *the people of Sodom*: Greek "the neighbors of Lot," Abraham's nephew, who lived in the city of Sodom (see Genesis 19.1-29). [d]**16.15,16** *darkness*: Verses 15, 16 are not in some manuscripts.
16.7 Gn 6.4; Ws 14.6, 7; 3 Macc 2.4.

29 After God created the earth,
he looked it over
and filled it with creatures
that were good;
30 animals of all kinds
covered the ground,
and when they die,
they return to it.

17 The Lord created us humans
from the soil,
and he makes us return there
when we die.
2 Our lives are short,
but the Lord has given us
power to rule the earth.
3 We were made to be like him
and were given power
much like his own.
4 He let us rule all animals
and made them afraid of us.
5 We were given the five senses
of sight and hearing,
taste, touch, and smell;
and we were also given
the ability to think
and to interpret
what our senses tell us.[e]
6 He gave us tongues for speaking,
eyes for seeing,
and minds for thinking
and for making choices.
7 Our minds are filled
with knowledge and Wisdom
that come from the Lord,
and we understand the difference
between right and wrong.
8 The Lord made us fear him
so that we would know
his mighty power.
9 Now we will tell others
about his powerful deeds
10 and praise his holy name.[f]
*11 The Lord gave to our ancestors
laws that bring knowledge
and life,
12 and his agreement with them
will last forever.
13 Our ancestors saw
the glorious power of the Lord
and heard his mighty voice
14 warning them about injustice
and commanding them how
to treat each other.

The Lord Is Watching

15 The Lord watches us and knows
our every deed.
16 Most people do wrong
from an early age
and have a cruel heart
that they cannot change.[g]
17 The Lord placed rulers
over all the nations,
but he himself rules Israel.
18 He raised our people Israel
as his own first-born child,
with loving care,
but also with discipline.
19 He can see our actions
as easily as we see the sun.
20 That's the reason
we can't hide our sins—
he can see them all.
21 But he knows what we are like,
and so he shows mercy
and never deserts us.[h]
22 The Lord values
our gifts to the poor
as much as we value fine jewelry
or a most prized possession.
23 Later, he will punish the wicked
as they deserve,
24 but he accepts all those
who turn from sinning,
and he encourages everyone
whose hope is slipping away.

Return to the Lord

25 Stop sinning and return
to the Lord;
your punishment will be less
if you pray to him.
26 So turn back to the Lord
and hate what he hates.

[e] **17.5** *us*: Verse 5 is not in some manuscripts. [f] **17.10** *name*: Most Greek manuscripts place verse 10 before verse 9. [g] **17.16** *change*: Verse 16 is not in some manuscripts. [h] **17.21** *us*: Verse 21 is not in some manuscripts.

17.1-3 Gn 1.26-28; 2.7. **17.7** Gn 2.17. **17.25,26** Jr 3.12.

27 Only the living
can thank the Lord—
no one in the world of the dead
can praise him;
28 they no longer exist
and cannot offer thanks.
But those who are alive
and healthy
can still sing praises to him.
29 The Lord will show great mercy
and forgive all of your sins
if you turn back to him.
30 But we cannot live forever;
we are human and find it hard
to turn to God.
31 If a thick dark cloud can hide
the bright rays of the sun,
then evil can just as easily
darken our minds.
32 We are merely dust and ashes,
but God commands the armies
of the highest heaven.

We Cannot Understand God's Power

18 The Lord, who lives forever,
created all things,
2 and he alone
is always faithful.
He is the only true God;
3 one signal from his hand
and the universe obeys.
The Lord, its mighty King,
decides what we
are allowed to use,
and what he will keep
for himself alone.[i]
4 We cannot understand
or tell other people
what God's power has done,
5 because we cannot measure it
or count the times
he has shown us mercy.
6 Nor can we make that number
larger or smaller.
We just stand in amazement
at the things he has done,
7 and at the end of a lifetime
of studying them,
we are still confused.
8 As for us humans, what are we?
Do we have any purpose?
What is good for us
and what is bad?
9 Few of us live a hundred years,
10 which is a very short time
when compared to forever,
like a drop of ocean water
or a grain of sand
along a beach.
11 That's why the Lord
patiently shows us mercy,
time after time.
12 He is eager to forgive,
because he knows that we
are condemned to die.
13 We show mercy to our friends,
but the Lord has mercy
on everyone.
He corrects and disciplines
and teaches us,
and leads us back to him
like a shepherd
leading a flock of sheep.
14 If we pay attention
when he corrects us,
and if we study his laws,
he will be merciful.

Don't Ruin a Gift

15 Students, be careful
not to ruin a gift
by criticizing the person
you give it to.
16 Like a refreshing dew
in the heat of summer,
saying the right thing
can mean more than giving
17 even a generous gift.
But a truly gracious person
will be ready with both.
18 So don't be a fool.
People's eyes will sparkle,
if your generosity is sincere
and you speak with kindness.

Now Is the Time

19 Know what you're talking about
before you start speaking

[i]**18.2,3** *He is the only true God . . . for himself alone*: These words are not in some manuscripts.
17.27,28 Ps 6.5; Is 38.18; Ba 2.17, 18.

and look after your health
before it fails.
20 If you turn from sin now—
before you are judged—
you will find forgiveness.
21 Be humble and show that you
have turned from sin,
and you won't be punished
with illness.

22 If you promise the Lord a gift,
give it now.
Don't wait until you are dying
to keep your promise,
23 and don't make promises to him
unless you are ready
to keep them.
Don't test the Lord's patience.
24 When your time comes to die
and face him as judge,
if he is angry, he will refuse
to even look at you.

25 If you have grown wealthy
and have plenty of food,
remember when you yourself
were poor and hungry.
26 Between sunrise and sunset
is plenty of time for the Lord
to turn everything around.

27 The wise are always careful,
and they make sure to do right
when others are sinning.
28 Smart people recognize Wisdom,
and they praise everyone
who finds her.
29 If you study the writings
of the wise,
you will learn enough Wisdom
to share with others.

Self-Control[j]

30 Control your desires;
don't let them control you.
31 If you allow yourself to enjoy
everything you want,
you will look like a fool,
and your enemies will laugh.
32 Do not live in luxury
that you cannot afford,
or you will become poor.
33 If you have nothing,
don't borrow money
to give a banquet.

19 A worker who is always drunk
will never get rich,
and people who are careless
with small things
will gradually slip
into poverty.
2 Even a wise man can be deceived
by wine and women,
and men who visit prostitutes
are taking terrible risks.
3 Death will come suddenly,
then their bodies will rot
and be eaten by worms.

4 If you trust people too quickly,
you aren't very smart.
If you sin, you harm yourself.
5 And if you are happy about evil,
you will be judged guilty.

Rumors and Gossip

6 Trouble doesn't stay
where gossip is hated.
7 It doesn't cost you a thing
to forget a rumor.
8 So don't tell it to your enemies
or even your friends,
unless you would be doing wrong
by not speaking up.
9 People may be listening
and watching,
and if you repeat gossip,
they might start hating you.
10 Treat rumors as secrets
to be kept until you die;
they can even make you feel
as though you might explode,
but be brave—you won't.
11 It's harder for a fool
not to repeat gossip,
than for a woman in labor
not to give birth
12 or a soldier to ignore an arrow
sticking out of his leg.

[j]**18.30** *Self-Control*: Most Greek and Latin manuscripts include this title.

*13 Talk to friends or neighbors
if you hear that they
have wronged you
or said something to harm
your reputation.
14 If they didn't do it,
you will find out,
and if they did,
they won't do it again.
15 Talk to them and get the truth,
because you should not believe
everything you hear.
16 We are all guilty
of saying things
that we didn't really mean.
17 So don't threaten your friends
before you talk with them,
and always obey the Law
of God Most High.

Fear the Lord

18 If you fear the Lord,
he will accept you,
and if you are wise,
he will give you his love.
19 If you learn and follow
the Lord's commands,
you will please him,
and he will allow you to eat
fruit from the tree
that lets you live forever.[k]

20 Fearing the Lord
and obeying his Law
are really the same
as having wisdom.
21 If slaves refuse to do
what they are told,
their master will be angry
even if they later obey.
22 Sin isn't the source of Wisdom,
and so sinners cannot give
good advice.
23 Some people are clever
in doing disgusting things;
others are fools only because
they never learned wisdom.

24 It is better to fear the Lord
and not be so intelligent,
than to be very smart
and to break his Law.
25 Some people are highly skilled
at being unfair
and can even twist your kindness
to help them win
their case in court.

26 Some dishonest people
act like they are mourning,
27 hiding their faces from you
and pretending not to listen.
But they will use your words
to take advantage of you
when no one is looking.
28 They may not be able
to do so now,
but they will wrong you
the first chance they get.

29 Merely by looking at people
you know what they are like.
And the first time you meet,
you can tell if someone
has good sense
30 by what they wear
and how they walk or laugh.

20 If you are smart,
you will know
when to keep quiet
and when to criticize.
2 It is better to speak up
than to let anger
eat away at you.
3 When you are wrong, admit it,
and you will save yourself
a lot of trouble.
4 If a man is unable to have sex,
he can't be forced to do so;
but it seems harder to force
some people to do right.

Things Might Not Be As They Seem

5 People who talk too much
are not well liked,
but people who keep quiet
are often considered wise.
6 Their silence may just mean
they have nothing to say.
Or it may mean they are waiting

[k]**19.18,19** *tree . . . forever*: See Genesis 2.9; 3.22-24. Verses 18,19 are not in some manuscripts.

for the right time to speak,
7 and that is true wisdom.
But fools who always talk
about themselves
are never quiet.
8 They are disgusting,
and others who grab for power
also earn our hatred.

9 Sometimes our troubles
end up helping us,
and other times, good luck
turns out to be bad.
10 Often a gift
isn't really helpful,
and when some people give,
they expect to be repaid
twice what the gift is worth.

11 If you search for glory
you may lose what you have,
but success can come to those
who had humble beginnings.
12 What seems to be a bargain
may cost you seven times
what it is worth.
13 People love to hear
wise people speak.
But fools, though polite,
are still fools,
14 and you would be better off
without gifts from them,
because they will expect you
to give even more in return.
15 A small gift, they think,
gives them the right
to criticize—loudly.
Today, they make a loan;
tomorrow, they ask
for their money back.
I cannot stand people like this!

16 Fools think they have no friends
and that no one appreciates
their good deeds.
They invite you over for a meal
but believe that you will later
say bad things about them.
17 They deserve to be mocked,
and few people
will pass up the chance.

18 It is better to slip and fall
than to suffer a slip
of the tongue.
And something that small
can bring sudden disaster
to those who are evil.
19 A rude person is disgusting,
just like the dirty stories
ignorant people tell.
20 Everyone ignores a proverb
repeated by a fool,
because fools never choose
the right one.

21 You may be too poor
to commit some sins,
but you can sleep at night
with a clear conscience.
22 Have a little self-respect
and don't act like a fool,
or you may risk disaster.

23 Broken promises turn friends
into enemies,
so do not make promises
that you cannot keep.
24 The ignorant are always lying,
not knowing that telling a lie
leaves an ugly scar.
25 Liars are worse than thieves,
but both are on the road
to destruction.
26 Telling lies brings disgrace
and shame that never ends.

Some Proverbs[l]

27 If you are wise
and want to succeed,
you will try to please
those in power.
28 If you plow and plant,
you will harvest a crop,
and if you please the powerful,
they will overlook
your mistakes.
29 Favors and gifts keep the wise
from seeing the truth
and muzzle the mouths of those
who criticize.
*30 Wisdom kept secret

[l]**20.27** *Some Proverbs*: Most Greek manuscripts include this title.

and wealth never used
do not help anybody,
31 but a fool does best
to keep foolishness hidden.

21 Students, if you
are sinning, stop.
Ask God to forgive you.
2 Sin is a deadly snake
with lion's fangs.
Stay away! If you come close
you will be bitten.
3 Lawlessness kills
like a sword with two edges
swung this way and that.
4 If you are too shy
or proud and arrogant,
you can lose your wealth
and even your home.
5 The prayers of the poor
go straight to God's ear,
and he quickly answers.
6 If you hate correction,
you will become a sinner,
but if you take it to heart,
you will obey the Lord.
7 Good speakers can be famous,
but people with common sense
will catch every mistake.
8 Borrowing to build your house
is like gathering stones
to mark your own grave.
9 A meeting of evil people
is a bundle of straw,
where a small flame
ends in a blazing fire.
10 For a sinner, the road of life
is smooth, but it slopes down
to the world of the dead.

Fear the Lord and Become Wise

11 Fear the Lord in every way,
and you will become wise;
Control your thoughts,
and you can obey his Law.
12 You have to be smart to learn,
but some kinds of smartness
only make other people bitter.
13 The knowledge of the wise
is an overflowing river,
and their advice
is a life-giving spring.
14 The mind of a fool
is a leaking jar
that holds nothing for long.
15 When the wise hear a proverb,
they give it praise
and add more to it;
but fools merely laugh
and forget it.
16 Listening to a fool is tiring,
like carrying a heavy backpack
on a journey,
but listening to someone smart
is refreshing.
17 In a town meeting, people look
for some common sense,
and when they hear it,
they will think about
what was said.

18 Knowledge means nothing
to ignorant fools,
and wisdom is useless
as a burned-down house.
19 Fools think learning puts chains
on their hands and feet,
20 and they laugh at it loudly.
But smart people just smile,
21 because they know that learning
is a golden bracelet.

22 Fools will push past you
into your home,
but the wise will wait
at your door.
*23 They are polite and will not try
to see inside
or to hear what is going on,
24 because that would be rude
and shameful.

25 Some people won't stop talking
about things that are none
of their business.
But sensible people
weigh each word
before it is spoken.
26 In a fool, the mind thinks
only after the mouth speaks,
but in a wise person,
the mind controls the mouth.
27 The ungodly fall under any curse

21.5 Si 35.17-19.

that they try to place
on their enemies.
28 If you spread gossip,
your character will be ruined
and your neighbors
will hate you.

22 Lazy people
are like stones
that everyone spits on,
2 or a pile of manure
that you have to walk around.
If you touch them,
you want to wash your hands.

Children's Behavior

3 A father is ashamed if his son
isn't well behaved,
and a disobedient daughter
is even worse.
4 If a daughter is sensible
she will get a good husband,
but a shameless girl
only brings her father pain.
5 If a woman insults her father
and her husband,
they will be disgraced
and in return
will humiliate her.
6 Picking the wrong time
to criticize your children
is like playing happy music
at a funeral,
but punishment and correction
are always wise.
7 Bring up your children well
and no one will guess
you were poor as a child.
8 But rude and arrogant children
are a disgrace
to a good family.[m]

Trying To Teach Fools

9 Just try to wake someone
from deep sleep,
to fix shattered pottery,
or to teach fools!
10 Tell them a story,
and they will doze off;
and afterwards, they will ask,
"So what's your point?"

11 Mourn for the dead,
who rest in darkness,
but weep even more for fools,
doomed to live
in the darkness of stupidity.
12 After a death,
you mourn seven days,
but you mourn for ungodly fools
until the day they die.
13 To avoid lots of problems
and have a peaceful life,
stay away from stupid people
and do not talk to them.
When a wet dog shakes itself,
water flies everywhere,
but humans who have no sense
splatter everyone nearby
with troubles.
14 A fool is a heavier burden
than a load of lead,
15 or a bag of sand or salt,
or a lump of iron ore.

A Mind That Thinks and Reasons Well

16 An earthquake cannot loosen
a wooden beam set firmly
in the walls of a building,
and no crisis can shake you up
if you have prepared your mind
and decided what you must do.
17 A mind that thinks
and reasons well
is like a smooth wall
decorated with carvings.[n]
18 But foolish cowards
will not stand firm
when fearsome disaster hits,
just as small rocks are blown
from the top of a vineyard wall[o]
by the wind.

[m]**22.7,8** *Bring up . . . good family*: Verses 7, 8 are not in some manuscripts; some translations number these verses as 9, 10. [n]**22.17** *carvings*: One ancient translation; Greek "plaster." [o]**22.18** *small rocks . . . top of a vineyard wall*: When a jackal or other small animal climbed over the wall to eat the ripening grapes, the sound of these rocks falling on the ground would alert a person guarding the vineyard. Some manuscripts have "posts supporting grapevines on top of a hill are blown over."

22.12 Gn 50.10; Jdt 16.23, 24.

Friends and Neighbors

19 Poke someone in the eye
and they will shed tears;
but wound their heart
and they will show deep pain.
20 You can throw stones
to frighten birds away,
and you can end a friendship
by tossing insults.
21 Threaten a friend with a sword,
and you can still hope
the friendship will heal.
22 And you can argue with friends
and later, win them back.
But if you are arrogant
and insult them,
if you tell their secrets
or harm them
when they trusted you,
they will be gone for good.

23 Earn the trust of your neighbors
when they are poor,
and if they become wealthy
you can celebrate with them.
Be a true friend
when they have troubles,
and later they will share
their inheritance with you.

24 When you smell smoke
you will soon see flames,
and when you hear insults,
you will soon see murder.

25 I will never be ashamed
to protect my friends,
and I will always be there
when I am needed.
26 But if they turn and harm me,
all who find out
will be on their guard
against them.

A Prayer

27 Our Lord, help me to be careful
in everything I say,
so that my mouth
will not be my downfall.

23 You are my Father
and rule my life—
don't let my mouth
control my destiny
and bring me down.
2 Please send wisdom
to whip my thoughts
and train my mind,
to tell me when I have sinned,
and to correct me
when I am wrong.
3 Otherwise, I will sin more often
and make more mistakes,
allowing my enemies
to destroy me and celebrate.

4 Our Lord, you are God;
you gave me life.
Don't let me look with arrogance
at other people.
5 Help me not to want things
that are not rightfully mine.
6 And don't let me be controlled
by shameless desires
for food or sex
or anything else.

Controlling What You Say[p]

7 Students, if you listen to me
and control what you say,
your words cannot trap you.
8 Sinners are caught
when they talk too much,
and the arrogant are tripped up
because they insult others.
9 Don't get in the habit
of using God's name
when you make promises.
10 Every time you do this,
God starts watching you closely
as a master watches a slave,
and he will notice all your sins
and punish you for them.
11 The wicked make promises
with God as their witness,
but when a promise is broken,
they just explain
that it was made by mistake.
Or they forget it on purpose,

[p]**23.7** *Controlling What You Say*: Most Greek and Latin manuscripts include this or a similar title.
23.9 Mt 5.34; Jas 5.12.

which means that they
are twice as guilty.
And if they lied in God's name,
they will not be forgiven
and their family is doomed.

*12 Vulgar talk is sinful
and deadly.
Godly people do not enjoy sin,
so they don't use evil words,
and I pray that none
will ever be heard in Israel.
13 Avoid sin
by training your mouth
not to use bad language,
14 and always remember
your parents will be honored
if you behave properly.
Then when you meet
with important people,
you won't get excited
and start talking like a fool
and end up wishing
you had never been born.
15 As long as you are in the habit
of insulting others,
you will always be a fool.

Three Kinds of Sinners

16 Three kinds of sinners
bring down God's anger:
first are those who always burn
with desire for sex.
Their desire is a flame
that must burn itself out.
Next are those
who won't stop having sex
with a near relative.
God will send fire
to destroy them!
17 Last are those who have sex
with anyone they can
and will do so
until they die.

Unfaithfulness in Marriage

18 A man unfaithful to his wife
says to himself,
"It's dark outside,
and no one can see me here
inside the house.
Why worry, anyway?
God will forgive me."

19 People like that are only afraid
of being seen by others
and forget that God's eyes shine
ten thousand times brighter
than the sun.
He can see every hidden place
in our lives.
20 He knew all things
before he created them,
just as he knows them now.
21 So unfaithful husbands
will be caught
when they suspect nothing
and will be punished
in the city streets.

22 If an unfaithful wife
has a child by another man,
she will be punished.
23 She has broken God's Law
and sinned against her husband
by having sex with another man
and giving birth to his child.
24 She will be put on trial
in a town meeting,
and she will be punished.
Even her children will suffer,
25 because they will be rejected
by the people of the town.
26 Her shame will never be erased,
and people will curse
when they remember her.
27 But they will be reminded
that it is always best
to fear the Lord
and obey his commands.

A Poem Praising Wisdom

24 *1 Wisdom sings her own praise
and tells her greatness
2 to those who worship the Lord
and to the Lord's armies
in heaven.
3 And this is what she says:
I came from the mouth
of God Most High
and like a mist I moved
over the earth.[q]

[q]24.3 *like a . . . earth*: Wisdom is comparing herself with the Spirit of God in Genesis 1.2.

4 Highest heaven was my home,
and my throne was a cloud.
5 Only I could travel
around the horizon
and walk in ocean depths.
6 I ruled every nation,
the land, and the sea.
7 But where could I find
a place to settle down?
In what nation should I live?

8 Then the Creator of the world
gave me a command
telling me to set up my tent
among the descendants of Jacob,
the people of Israel.
9 He created me ages ago,
before time began,
and I will never die.
10 I served in his sacred tent,
and later in the temple
in Zion.[r]
11 He gave me a resting place
in Jerusalem, the city he loves,
and this is where I rule.
12 Here, I put down roots
among the glorious people
who belong to the Lord.

13 I grew tall, like a cedar tree
in Lebanon
or a cypress on Mount Hermon;
14 like a palm tree at En-gedi,
or the roses in Jericho;
like a beautiful olive tree
in a field,
or like an evergreen.

15 My perfume smelled sweet
like the spices cinnamon and cane
mixed with fine myrrh,[s]
or like smoke in the sacred tent
from the incense of galbanum,
onycha, and stacte.[t]
16 I spread out my branches,
beautiful and graceful,
like a giant oak,
17 and like a grapevine,
they grew buds and blossoms,
and finally clusters of rich,
sweet fruit.
18 Beautiful love is my child,
and so are fear and knowledge
and hope that trusts God,
and he gives me and my children
to his own people.[u]

19 So come, if you want,
and enjoy my fruit
until you are full.
20 I am sweeter than honey
straight from the honeycomb,
and the sweet taste will remain
even when you have finished.
21 But the more of me
that you eat and drink,
the more you will want.
22 Obey me and let me work
in your life,
and you will never sin
or be disgraced.

Wisdom Is God's Law

23 The wisdom of God Most High
is the Book of the Law
of Moses,
the agreement God made
with our ancestors
and gives to each new generation
as an inheritance.

24 Always stay close
to the Lord All-Powerful, and he
will give you strength.
The Lord is the only true God—
he alone can rescue.[v]

*25 God's wisdom and understanding
overflow from his Law
just as in early springtime,[w]
the Tigris and Pishon Rivers,

[r]**24.10** *Zion*: A hill in Jerusalem, on which the temple and palace were built. [s]**24.15** *the spices cinnamon . . . myrrh*: With cassia and olive oil, the ingredients of the sacred oil for dedicating the sacred tent and its equipment (see Exodus 30.23-33). [t]**24.15** *galbanum . . . stacte*: Mixed with frankincense, these were ingredients for the holy incense that was used in the sacred tent (see Exodus 30.34-38). [u]**24.18** *people*: Verse 18 is not in some manuscripts. [v]**24.24** *rescue*: Verse 24 is not in some manuscripts. [w]**24.25** *in early springtime*: Greek "at the time of the first part of the harvest"; the grain harvest was in the spring.
24.4 Ex 33.9-11.

26 the Euphrates and the Jordan,
overflow their banks.
27 God's teachings flood the land[x]
like the Nile River[y]
in early fall.[z]

28 The first human did not know
Wisdom very well,
nor will the last one,
29 because her thoughts
are wider than the ocean,
and her advice is deeper
than the sea.

30 I thought of myself
as a small canal
from the river of God's Wisdom
to my garden,
31 bringing water for my flowers
and fruit trees.
But soon this canal
became wide as a river
and then as the sea.

32 And so, I will teach wisdom
and make it shine like sunrise,
clearly seen from far away.
33 My words flow quickly,
and like a prophet
I will leave them
for generations not yet born.
34 You see, my work hasn't been
for myself alone,
but for everyone who desires
to find Wisdom.

Three Things Make Me Happy

25 Three things
make me happy
and are beautiful to the Lord
and to humans:
a family that agrees,
neighbors who are friends,
and a happy marriage.
2 But I hate three kinds of people
and the way they live:
the poor that brag,
the rich that tell lies,
and the old that are foolish
and unfaithful in marriage.

3 If you don't start learning
when you are young,
you will have no wisdom
when you grow old.
4 Good sense and sound advice
are beautiful in those
whose hair is now gray.
5 Wisdom and understanding
are just right for the old
and honorable.
6 They have seen so many things,
but they only boast
that they fear the Lord.

7 Ten kinds of people
can be called truly happy:
those who enjoy their children,
and those who live long enough
to see their enemies fall;
8 men who have sensible wives,
farmers that do not hitch
a donkey and an ox
to one plow,[a]
people who don't sin
by what they say,
and servants whose masters
have as much ability
as the servants do;
9 people with common sense,
and those who speak to others
who are really listening.
*10 The person who finds wisdom
finds great happiness,
but happiest of all is the one
who fears the Lord,
11 because fearing him
is more important
than anything else.
12 And it is the first step
in loving him,
just as having faith
is the first step in becoming
one of his followers.[b]

[x]**24.27** *God's teachings flood the land*: One ancient translation; Greek "It makes God's teaching shine like light." [y]**24.27** *Nile River*: The Greek also uses the name, "Gihon River," which was sometimes used as another name for the Nile. [z]**24.27** *in early fall*: Greek "at the time of the grape harvest." [a]**25.8** *farmers . . . plow*: One ancient translation; the Greek text does not have these words. [b]**25.12** *followers*: Verse 12 is not in some manuscripts.

Advice about Women

13 The breaking of your heart
by an evil woman
is the most painful
of all injuries.
14 No suffering seems worse
than when an enemy hates you
and takes revenge,
15 but a woman's anger is strongest,
just as snakes have
the strongest poison.

16 I would be happier to live
with a lion and a dragon
than to be married
to an evil woman.
17 An evil woman's face is changed
into something dark,
like the face of a bear.
18 Her husband is depressed,
sighing bitterly
even among his friends.
19 The sins of men are small
compared to those of women,
and I pray that women who sin
will be severely punished.

20 It is easier for an old person
to climb a hill of sand
than for a quiet man to live
with a chattering wife.
21 Do not be taken captive
by the beauty of a woman,
and don't desire her wealth.[c]
22 When the wife's possessions
support the family,
their home will be filled
with anger, insults,
and shame.

23 An evil wife brings no happiness
to her husband;
instead, she makes him sad
and depressed;
she breaks his heart,
and he is afraid
to make any decisions.
24 Sin began with the first woman,
and because of her
we all must die.
25 Do not let water leak
from your storage jars,
and if your wife is evil,
don't let her talk in public.
26 If she will not obey you,
then get a divorce.

26 A man who is married
to a good woman
is happy, and he will live
twice as long.
2 If a wife has courage,
her husband will find happiness
and live a peaceful life.
3 A good wife is the best gift
given by the Lord
to those men who fear him,
4 and whether such a man
is rich or poor,
the smile on his face
comes from a happy heart.

5 I am always extra careful
when I hear ugly gossip
being repeated in the city,
or when a mob comes together,
or when the innocent
are falsely accused.
I would rather die than be part
of those three things.
But a fourth is even worse:
6 to have two wives,
with one of them being jealous
of the other.
She can only bring heartache
and sorrow,
as her words cut the family
to pieces.

7 To marry an evil woman
is to hold a scorpion
in your hand,
or to wear an ox-yoke[d]
that rubs your shoulders raw.
8 When a wife gets drunk
she can be unfaithful,
and then her husband's anger
will explode.
9 You know a wife is unfaithful
if her eyes have a look
of invitation.

[c]**25.21** *her wealth*: Hebrew; Greek "a woman."
[d]**26.7** *ox-yoke*: A wooden collar that fits around the neck of an ox, so the ox can be made to pull a plow or a cart.

*10 If your daughter is rebellious
and wants her own way,
watch her closely
11 and don't be surprised
if she sins against you
the first chance she gets.
12 She will try to have sex
with every man she sees,
just as thirsty travelers
will drink any water
they can find.

13 A gracious wife is pleasing
to her husband,
and her cooking skills
keep him fat.[e]
14 Her silence is a gift
from the Lord,
and her self-control
is without price.
15 Her modesty is the crown
on all her graces;
her faithfulness to her husband
has value beyond measure.
16 She has organized her home,
and her beauty there
is like the sun as it rises
in the Lord's heaven.
17 A lovely face on a good figure
shines like the lamps
on the sacred lampstand,
18 and shapely legs with firm feet
are like golden columns
resting on silver bases.
19 Students, when you come of age,
stay away from immoral women
and stay healthy.[f]
20 To find a good wife
is to find a good field
where you can plant
your own seed,
knowing that it will produce
a good harvest.
21 And as your children grow,
they will have confidence
in your family line
and will become successful.

22 A prostitute is worth
less than spit,
and affairs with married women
are deadly.
23 Reject God's Law,
and he will give you
a godless wife.
But if you fear the Lord,
your wife will be
faithful to him.
24 A shameless wife is vulgar
in public,
but a good woman is modest,
even alone with her husband.
25 If a wife does what she pleases,
she is no better than a dog,
but if she is ashamed
to do wrong,
she will fear the Lord.
26 Everyone can tell
that a wife is wise
if she honors her husband,
but if she is proud and refuses,
they will see she is ungodly.
Yes, a man who is married
to a good woman
is happy, and he will live
twice as long.
27 But the constant talking
of a loud wife
is a trumpet signal
for a battle to begin,
and her family will live
in the chaos of war.[g]

Doing Right

28 It makes me terribly sad
when the rich become poor
or the wise are insulted.
But I get angry
if those who do right
start doing wrong.
The Lord will punish them
with a violent death.

29 It is almost impossible
to succeed in business
and still be honest.
27 People sin
when they try to get rich,
and they convince themselves
they are not being dishonest.

[e]**26.13** *fat*: This was considered a sign of prosperity and God's blessing. [f]**26.19** *healthy*: Verses 19-27 are not in some manuscripts. [g]**26.27** *war*: See the note at verse 19.

2 But sin is stuck tightly
between buying and selling,
just like a wooden peg
hammered between two stones
in a wall.
3 And if you disobey the Lord,
your home[h]
will soon be destroyed.

4 Impurities can easily be seen
after flour is sifted
and after someone speaks.
5 The quality of a clay dish
is seen in the heat
of the pottery furnace,
just as our true character
is seen in what we say.
6 Fruit shows how much care
a tree has received,
and our words show the care
we have given to our minds.
7 So don't start praising people,
until you hear what they say.

8 Make fairness your goal;
you will reach it
and receive great honor.
9 Just as birds of the same kind
come together in a flock,
people will be honest with you,
if you are honest with them.
10 But sin is watching like a lion
and is ready to gobble you up
if you do evil.

11 Good people always speak wisely,
but you never can tell
what a fool will say next.
12 Don't waste your time
listening to stupid people;
spend it with those
who know how to think.
13 It is disgusting to listen to fools
laughing about their sins.
*14 Their cursing and arguing
makes your hair stand on end
and your ears ache.
15 But fools are too proud
to stop sinning,
until someone gets hurt.
16 Your friends won't trust you
or like you anymore
if you can't keep a secret.
17 If you don't tell their secrets,
your friends will know
that you really like them.
But if you tell their secrets,
they won't want you around,
18 and your friendship is as dead
as a soldier
killed by the enemy.
19 It is gone for good,
like a captive bird
that has been set free
20 or a deer that has escaped
from a trap.
So don't bother trying
to get back that friendship.
21 Wounds can be bandaged
and insults forgiven,
but nothing can heal the harm
of telling someone's secret.

22 Stay away from those who wink
and plan to deceive others.
23 They tell you how great you are
and how well you speak,
but later, they twist your words
to make you look bad.
24 I hate people like them
more than anything else,
and even the Lord hates them.
25 Striking a friend is the same
as throwing a stone
straight up in the air—
you will be the one
who gets hurt.
26 And you will get caught
in traps that you set
to cheat others.
27 No one seems to realize
that evil always returns
to the one who does it.
28 Proud people insult others,
but revenge will follow them
like a lion stalking a victim.
29 When God's people
are in trouble,
those who make fun of them
will die in terrible pain,
like an animal in a trap.

[h]**27.3** *home*: Or "family."
27.6 Mt 7.17; 12.33; Lk 6.44. **27.16-21** Pr 20.19; 25.9.

Anger, Revenge, and Forgiveness

30 Taking revenge in anger
is disgusting—yet sinners
just won't give it up.

28 The Lord keeps a record
of those who take revenge
and he will punish them
for their sins.
2 So forgive those who harm you,
and when you pray,
God will forgive you.
3 But don't expect
the Lord to forgive you
if you hold a grudge
4 or refuse to show mercy.
5 God won't accept sacrifices
for your sins
if you stay angry at others.
6 Life is too short
to waste it by being angry,
so obey God
and forgive your enemies.
7 Remember his commands
and his agreement with us.
Don't let the faults of others
make you angry at them.

Arguments

8 If you control your temper,
you won't start arguments
or sin as much.
9 And remember, it is sinful
to start an argument
that destroys a friendship.
10 Stubbornness heats up
an argument,
just as adding wood
heats up a fire.
If you are rich and powerful,
you can afford
to lose your temper.
11 A quick temper can blaze up
and lead to murder.
12 Blow on a spark
and it bursts into flames;
spit on a spark
and it dies out.
In the same way, your words
can either heat up an argument
or make it cool down.

Gossip, Lies, and Cruel Words

13 Those who gossip and tell lies
are under God's curse,
because they have brought ruin
to innocent people
14 and forced many others
to leave home and country.
Such talk has been the downfall
of strong cities
and powerful leaders.
15 Because of lies others told,
faithful, hard-working wives
have been divorced
and have lost everything[i]
16 So if you want peace of mind,
don't listen to gossip!

17 Whips leave painful stripes
on the skin,
but cruel words break bones
deep down inside
18 and can be more deadly
than a sword.
*19 You should be happy
if you have never been attacked
with lies and gossip,
or felt them wrap around you
20 like heavy bronze chains
or a collar[j] made of iron.

21 Cruel words cause suffering[k]
worse than death itself.
22 Although they are fiery flames,
they cannot harm
God's faithful people,
23 but those who reject him
will be burned to ashes.
And these cruel words
are like lions and leopards,
hunting down their victims
and tearing them apart.

24 You protect your land
with a hedge of thornbushes

[i]**28.15** *have been . . . everything*: Often, only husbands had the right to divorce, and the wife usually had no claim on the family's property, possessions, or money. [j]**28.20** *collar*: Greek "yoke," a collar that fits around the neck of an ox, so the ox can be made to pull a plow or a cart.
[k]**28.21** *suffering*: Greek "evil death."
28.2 Mt 6.14; Mk 11.25, 26. **28.13-26** Si 51.2-6; Jas 3.5-12.

and you keep your money
locked away safely.
25 Be just as careful
to guard what you say.
Always think before you speak,
and know when to be silent,
26 so that others cannot attack you
for what you have said.

Loans

29 [*1] Obey God's Law
about helping
your neighbors;
have mercy and lend them money
when they truly need it.
2 If others lend you money,
pay them back,
and don't be late!
3 If you keep your promises
to pay what you owe,
others will be glad
to lend you what you need.

4 Many think what they borrow
is theirs to keep,
and this causes trouble
when others try to help them.
5 Those who lend money
are treated with great respect
until the time comes
for loans to be repaid.
Then all they get are excuses
and stories of hard times.
6 Sometimes they feel lucky
to get back half
of the money they lent.
And instead of respect,
a lender often gets nothing
but curses and angry words
from a borrower
who is robbing the lender
by not paying back the loan.

7 That's why many refuse to lend;
they do care about others,
but they have no desire
to be cheated.

Give Generously to the Poor

8 However, give to the poor;
be quick and generous.
9 Obey the Lord's command—
don't refuse to help
when people are in need.
10 Give away your silver
to a brother or a friend;
don't hide it under a rock,
where it will rust.
11 Give your gold to the needy
as God Most High commands,
and you will be better off
than if you had kept it.
12 Your gifts to the poor
are a treasure
that will rescue you
when trouble comes,
13 and they give better protection
than the strongest shields
and spears.

Guaranteeing a Loan for a Friend

14 When a friend needs a loan,
a good person will guarantee
that the loan will be repaid.
To refuse to help this friend
would be a disgrace.

15 And remember—if friends
have helped you this way,
they have risked all they own
to be kind [*]16 and rescue you.
So if they are forced to repay
what you borrowed,
17 you are not only ungrateful,
you are a sinner.
18 People of wealth and power
have often become poor
and homeless,
drifting from place to place
in foreign countries,
their wealth taken in payment
for loans they guaranteed.

19 Sinners want to make big profits
from guaranteed loans,
but they may get only trouble
and lawsuits in court.

20 Be careful! There is danger
when you guarantee a loan,
but you have to help a friend
as much as you can.

29.1-7 Ex 22.25; Lv 25.35-38.

Your Own Home Is Best

21 Life's most important things
are water, food, clothing,
and a home that gives you
some privacy.
22 It is better to be poor
in your own home,
than to live with others
and be treated to banquets.
23 Be content with what you have,
because you will be insulted
if you live off others.[l]
24 You will always be miserable
and will not dare say a word,
if you have to depend on others
for food and a place to sleep.
25 You will become their servant,
and instead of thanking you,
they will say,
26 "Stranger, set the table!"
Or, "I'm still hungry—
give me your food."
27 Finally they will tell you to leave
so they can give your room
to a relative
or some important guest.
28 Such comments are insulting
to a sensitive person,
just like those of a lender
demanding payment of a loan.

Raising Children

30 Parents show love
for their children
by spanking them
whenever they do wrong.
Later those parents will be glad
to see their children
grow into fine adults.
2 If parents correct a child,
they will someday boast
about how much help
that child has been to them.
3 Parents who give their children
an education
make their enemies jealous
and can boast to friends.
*4 These parents have no regrets
when they die,
and they live on
in their children,
5 who brought them such joy.
6 Then it is up to the children
to take revenge
on their parents' enemies,
and to be kind
to their parents' friends.

7 If you spoil your children,
you will have to put bandages
on the wounds they will get,
and you will shake with fear
every time you hear shouting.
8 That's why you
must correct them,
so they will not be as stubborn
as unbroken horses.
*9 If you give children
everything they desire
and laugh when they sin,
10 they will end up giving you
sadness, terror, and pain.
11 Don't let them do
just anything they want,
but correct their mistakes.
12 Break their stubbornness
by whipping them
while they are young,
or else they will disobey you
and bring you deep sorrow.
13 Take care to discipline them,
so they will not disgrace you
when they are older.

Health Is Better than Wealth

14 I would rather be poor,
yet healthy and strong,
than to be rich and sickly.
15 To have your health
and a good attitude[m]
is better than gold
and infinite riches.
16 No amount of money
can compare with health
or bring happiness
deep inside your heart.
17 Death is better
than a life of constant pain
and sickness.
18 If a fine dinner is served,

[l]29.23 *you will . . . others*: One possible meaning for the difficult text. [m]30.15 *good attitude*: Hebrew; Greek "strong body."

but the guests
are too sick to eat,
the dinner will go to waste,
like food placed on a grave[n]
19 or like a sacrifice to an idol,
which cannot eat or smell.
If the Lord punishes people
by making them sick,
20 they can only stare at food
and groan like a young man
unable to have sex
who holds a virgin
in his arms.

Enjoy Life and Forget Sorrow

21 Don't stay sad for too long
or look for reasons
to be upset.
22 Joy and happiness will help you
to live longer.
23 So enjoy life and forget sorrow,
because sorrow never helps,
and it has destroyed many.
24 Jealousy and anger
will cut your life short,
and worrying makes you old
before your time.
25 If you are cheerful at meals,
the food you eat
will do you more good.

Money Problems

31 The rich lie awake at night
worrying about their money,
and they waste away
from lack of rest.
2 It is hard to fall asleep
when you are very sick
or worried about money.

3 The rich work hard
and get richer,
then they rest in luxury.
4 But the poor work hard
and barely earn a living,
and if they rest,
they become even poorer.
5 Some people love gold
and aim to make big profits,
and they will be led to do wrong
instead of right.
6 Because of gold,
many lives have been ruined
or have ended in destruction.
7 Money controls those fools
who worship it.

8 God will bless those rich people
who do only what is right
and don't try to get richer.
9 If you ever find such people,
you should honor them
for doing the impossible.
10 When tested by money,
who can always do right?
When people could cheat
to get more money
but instead are honest,
they have something
to boast about.
11 The community will honor them
for the kind things they do,
and their wealth will grow.

Advice to Dinner Guests

12 When you go to a banquet,
don't stuff yourself
just because so much food
is on the table.
13 Some people's eyes
want everything they see.
Is anything more evil?
Such eyes will have plenty
of tears.
14 Don't reach out and grab
the food you want
or push others aside.
15 Be thoughtful of others—
they have feelings too.
16 Eat what is served,
but you won't be welcome
if you gobble it down
like an animal.
17 Show good manners;
stop eating before others do.
If you keep on eating,
they will be offended.
18 And in a large group of people,
don't be the first one
to reach for the serving dish.

[n]**30.18** *food placed on a grave*: Probably as an offering to the spirits of the dead.
30.21-25 Ec 11.9, 10.

19 Train yourself to be satisfied
with a little food,
and later, in bed,
you will not be in pain
when you try to breathe.
20 You will sleep well
and wake up early,
feeling good.
But overeating causes cramps,
as well as an upset stomach
and sleepless nights.
21 If your host makes you overeat,
leave the table and vomit—
you will feel much better.
22 Listen to me! Pay attention,
and later on,
you will thank me.
Don't try to eat[o] too much,[p]
and you will stay healthy.

23 It is right to honor those
who are generous with food
at their dinner parties.
24 But the whole town is right
to complain about a host
who gives only a snack.

25 Wine has destroyed many lives,
and heavy drinking is no way
to prove you are strong.
26 The strength of iron is seen
when it is heated,
then dipped in water.
And people show their arrogance
when they argue
after drinking wine.

27 A little wine is refreshing,
and to live without wine
is hardly living at all.
God created wine
to make us happy.
28 A little wine at the right time
helps us celebrate.
29 But drinking too much wine
leads us to hate others
and to take revenge.[q]

30 When fools are drunk,
they become angry and fight,
but their strength is gone,
and so they get hurt.

31 Don't scold your friends
or be disgusted
when they drink and celebrate
at a party.
And don't make them feel bad
or upset them with a reminder
that they owe you money.

32 *1 If you are placed in charge
of a dinner party,
don't try to act important.
Just make sure all the guests
have what they need
2 before you are seated.
Then enjoy the dinner
with everyone else,
and they will honor you
for a job well done.

3 If you are an older guest,
it is right for you to talk.
But be sure what you say is true,
and don't talk during the music
4 or other entertainment.
That is not the right time
for clever remarks.
*5 Good wine and good music
at a banquet
6 are like rubies and emeralds
in settings of gold.

7 If you are a younger guest,
don't talk unless someone
asks you a question.
Don't speak more than twice,
8 and say as much as you can
in as few words as possible.
This will show your knowledge
and also your self-control.
9 Treat important people
with proper respect,
and don't chatter on and on
if someone older is talking.

[o]**31.22** *eat*: Or "do." [p]**31.22** *Don't . . . much*: Hebrew and one ancient translation; the Greek text has "try to do as much as you can." [q]**31.29** *But drinking too much wine . . . revenge*: Greek; the Hebrew has "But drinking wine when you are angry will bring you hatred, headaches, and disgrace."

10 Lightning goes ahead of thunder,
and if you are humble,
you will be liked and accepted
before you even arrive.
11 Then later, at the proper time,
just say good-by and go home.
Don't wait around
to be the last to leave.
12 At home, you can have fun
doing whatever you want—
but be careful not to sin
by speaking with arrogance.
13 And give thanks to your Creator,
who lets you enjoy
all the good things he made.

Obey the Lord

14 If you obey the Lord,
expect him to correct you,
but do your best,
and you will be accepted.
15 Sincerely studying God's Law
will bring contentment,
but if you are not sincere
that Law will condemn you.
16 If you obey the Lord,
you will be well known
for justice and fairness.
17 But sinners refuse
to be corrected,
and they twist the Law
so they can do
whatever they please.

18 A wise person can take a hint,
but even fear of great danger
won't stop an arrogant fool.[r]
19 Give plenty of thought
to what you will do,
and afterwards, don't worry
about how well you did.
20 Don't look for trouble,
but learn from your mistakes.[s]
21 It's easy to be careless
on a smooth road,
22 so always pay attention
to the path ahead.[t]
23 Think your actions through,[u]
and you will be able
to obey the Lord's commands.

24 If you believe in God's Law,
then do what it says.
Trust the Lord,
and you will have success.
33 If you obey him,
you will be protected
and rescued from danger.
2 You are wise to love God's Law,
but if you are not sincere,
you will be tossed around
like a boat in a storm.
3 Be sensible and trust
what God has said in his Law.

4 If you want others to listen,
then think about what you know
and how to say it best.
5 Fools talk in circles
like a wheel going around.
6 To make fun of a friend
is to act like a horse
that snorts at anyone
who tries to ride.

Differences between People

7 Each day of the year
depends on the sun for light,
so why are some days
more important than others?
8 The Lord used his wisdom
and made them different.
Some have a special meaning,
others are festivals,
9 and some are sacred days—
but most are ordinary.

10 We humans were made
from the soil,[v]
11 and the Lord used great wisdom
to make each of us different,
with different destinies.
12 He blessed our ancestors
and made them great,

[r]**32.18** *but even . . . arrogant fool*: One possible meaning for the difficult Greek text. [s]**32.20** *but learn from your mistakes*: Hebrew; Greek "and don't choose a path full of rocks." [t]**32.22** *so always pay attention to the path ahead*: Hebrew; Greek "and don't trust your children."
[u]**32.23** *Think your actions through*: Hebrew; Greek "Trust yourself." [v]**33.10** *We humans were made from the soil*: See Genesis 2.7; 3.19.
33.3 Ex 28.30; Si 45.10, 11.

and he even let some
be his holy priests.
But he put a curse
on the nations of Canaan—
they were defeated
and forced to leave the land.

13 Humans become
what the Creator chooses,
just as clay is shaped
by the hands of the potter.
14 There are many opposites—
good and evil, life and death,
sinners and God's people.
15 You can see that God Most High
made everything the opposite
of something else.

The Last of the Teachers of Wisdom

16 I am the last in the line
of the teachers of wisdom,
like a poor man picking grapes
after the main harvest.[w]
17 But the Lord blessed me,
and I gathered enough grapes
to fill a wine-pit.
18 I wasn't working
just for my own good,
but to help all those
who want to learn wisdom.
19 So pay attention to what I say,
all you officials and leaders.

Freedom

20 Never give anyone else power
to make decisions for you—
not your husband or wife,[x]
and not your children,
relatives, or friends.
And don't give away property—
if you later want it returned,
you will have to beg for it.
21 As long as you are alive,
don't let others run your life.
22 It is better that your children
ask you for money
than for you to ask them.
23 Be the best at whatever you do,
and do only what brings honor
and not shame.
24 Wait until you are about to die
before giving your children
their inheritance.

How To Treat Slaves

25 If you feed your donkeys
and beat them with a stick,
they will carry their loads.
Slaves are like that—
feed and discipline them,
and they will do their work.
26 If you don't want trouble,
keep your slaves busy;
otherwise, they will have time
to think about becoming free.
27 Use collars and leather straps
to keep slaves at their work,
and punish the rebellious ones
by torturing them.
*28 Keep your slaves busy
or they will have time to think
29 of ways to cause trouble.
30 Slaves are supposed to work,
so give them something to do,
and if they refuse to obey,
put them in chains.
But always be fair,
not arrogant.

31 If one slave is all you have,
treat him like a family member
or even as you treat yourself.
You worked a long time
to buy that slave,
and you need his help
to survive.
32 If you are mean,
and that slave runs away,
33 where will you look for him?

Dreams

34 Empty hopes deceive
ignorant people,
and dreams lead fools
to be even more foolish.
2 Believing in dreams
is like holding on to shadows
or chasing the wind.
3 Just as a mirror
reflects your face,

[w]**33.16** *a poor man . . . main harvest*: The poor were allowed to pick the grapes left after the main grape harvest (see Deuteronomy 24.21). [x]**33.20** *husband or wife*: Greek "wife."
34.1-8 Dt 13.1-5.

your dreams reflect
your concerns.
4 Something clean cannot come
from something dirty,
and truth cannot come
from a lie.
5 Dreams are meaningless,
like something said
by a fortuneteller,[y]
because they can mean anything
you want them to.[z]
6 So unless a dream has been sent
by God Most High,
ignore it.
7 Dreams have fooled many—
first giving them hope,
then disappointing them.
8 You can obey God's Law
and learn from wise people,
without paying attention
to deceitful dreams.

Learning by Traveling

9 A person who has traveled
has learned many things,
and knows about them
from experience.
10 If you have few experiences,
you won't learn much,
11 but the more you travel,
the smarter you will become.
12 I saw many things
when I traveled,
and I learned more
than I can tell you.
13 My life was often in danger,
but what I had learned
always helped me escape.

Fear the Lord

*14 If you fear the Lord
and put your trust in him,
15 he will keep you safe,
16 and so you can be brave
and face any danger.
17 The Lord will bless you
if you fear him
18 and ask for his help.
19 And if you love the Lord,
he will give you strength
and keep you from falling.
He will be your shield,
protecting you and giving shade
from the burning heat
of the summer sun at noon.
20 Your eyes will sparkle
with the happiness he gives,
and he will bless you
with health and a long life.

Sacrifices

21 A stolen animal isn't fit
as a sacrifice for the Lord,
22 and he won't accept gifts
from those who reject his Law.
23 Sinners cannot please
God Most High,
and he will not forgive them,
even if they offer
sacrifice after sacrifice.

24 Stealing food from the poor
to offer as a sacrifice
is like murdering children
while their parents watch.
25 The poor have so little food,
that taking it is the same
as committing murder.
26 Stealing what someone needs
to earn a living
is the same as murder,
27 and refusing to pay the wages
of someone who works for you
is just as evil.

28 So, if you steal possessions
that others worked for,[a]
you will cause trouble
for yourself and for them.
29 When they are asking God
to put a curse on you,
will he listen to your prayer?
30 If you are unclean
from touching a dead body,
what's the point of washing[b]
if you touch the body again?

[y]**34.5** *fortuneteller*: Fortunetellers thought they could learn secrets or learn about the future by watching the flight of birds or by looking at the livers of animals or in many other ways.
[z]**34.5** *because . . . want them to*: One possible meaning for the difficult Greek text.
[a]**34.28** *if you steal possessions that others worked for*: Greek "if you tear down what someone else has built."
[b]**34.30** *unclean . . . washing*: See Numbers 19.11, 12.

31 Suppose you go without eating
to show sorrow for your sins
and then commit
the same sins again.
Will God forgive you?
No, it was all for nothing.

35 Obeying the Law
of the Lord
is the same
as bringing him many gifts,
2 and obeying his commands
is like offering a sacrifice
to ask his blessing.[c]
3 Showing kindness to someone
who has been kind to you
is like offering a sacrifice
to give thanks to the Lord.[d]
4 And giving to the poor
is offering a sacrifice
that gives the Lord praise.
5 So please the Lord
and seek his forgiveness,
by staying away from evil.

6 However, do not come
to worship the Lord
without bringing him a gift
7 as his Law commands.
8 When one of God's people
burns the fat of a sacrifice,
God Most High is pleased
with the smell of the smoke
rising from the altar.
9 Such sacrifices
are acceptable to God
and will not be forgotten.

10 When you offer to the Lord
the first part of the harvest
or a sacrifice to give thanks,
be generous—not stingy.
11 Be happy and cheerful
when you give him a gift
or a tenth of your harvest.
12 Be as generous with the Lord
as he has been with you.
13 Remember! The Lord is the one
who repays seven times more
than you give him.

14 You cannot bribe the Lord
by offering a sacrifice,
15 and he won't accept as a gift
what you get by cheating.
The Lord is a judge
who doesn't take sides,
16 especially against the poor,
but he answers the prayers
of all who suffer injustice.
17 God listens when an orphan
begs for his help.
He hears the complaints
of a mistreated widow
as she cries out
18 with tears in her eyes
19 and tells him about the one
who has abused her.

20 If you obey the Lord,
he will accept you
and answer when you pray.
21 Be humble, and your prayers
will go up beyond the clouds
and be heard
by God Most High.
22 He will quickly punish those
who have wronged his people
and completely crush those
who have shown no mercy.
23 God will take revenge
on evil, arrogant Gentiles,[e]
breaking their power
and destroying them.
24 And someday, all humans
will be repaid, as their thoughts
and deeds deserve.
25 Then God will judge
in favor of his people,
and they will celebrate
because he showed mercy.

[c]**35.2** *sacrifice to ask his blessing*: These sacrifices have traditionally been called "peace offerings" or "offerings of well-being." A main purpose was to ask for the Lord's blessing, and so in the CEV they are sometimes called "sacrifices to ask the Lord's blessing." [d]**35.3** *sacrifice to give thanks to the Lord*: These sacrifices have traditionally been called "grain offerings." A main purpose of such sacrifices was to thank the Lord with a gift of grain, and so in the CEV they are sometimes called "sacrifices to give thanks to the Lord." [e]**35.23** *Gentiles*: Or "nations."
35.9 2 Co 9.7.

26 We welcome God's mercy
when we are in trouble,
just as we welcome rain
in hot, dry weather.

A Prayer

36 Our God, you rule all things;
have mercy on us
2 and show all nations
that they should fear you.
3 Let them see your power
as you attack them.
4 They have seen that you are holy
in the way you treat us.
Now show us that you are great
as you deal with them!
5 Teach them, our Lord,
as you taught us,
that you alone are God.
6 Perform new miracles,
7 so that everyone will know
how powerful you are.
8 Get really angry
9 and destroy our enemies.
10 You have set a time to do this—
please let it come quickly,
then everyone will be talking
about your mighty power.
11 And if any survive of those
who had harmed your people,
destroy those enemies
with your fiery anger.
12 Crush the heads of their rulers
who say, "All that matters
is what we want to do."
13 Gather together
the tribes of Israel,[f]
16 and[g] once again give them
control of their land.
17 Have pity on us, our Lord.
We are known as your nation,
your first-born child.
18 Show mercy to Jerusalem,
your holy city, your home.
19 Then everyone in Zion
will celebrate as they tell
of your mighty deeds.
20 Prove that you chose us
as your people.
You told your prophets
to make promises to us;
now keep these promises
21 so your prophets
will not have lied.
Please reward us
for waiting patiently.
22 Our Lord, we are your servants.
If you are pleased with us,
answer our prayer,
and then the whole world
will know that you
are the Eternal Lord God.

Recognizing Lies

23 There are many different foods,
but you like some
better than others.
24 And just as your taste tells you
what you are eating,
a smart mind will know
when it hears a lie.
25 People with twisted minds
cause a lot of trouble,
but if you learn from experience
you can send the trouble
back on them.

Choosing a Wife

26 A woman cannot choose
the man she will marry,
but a man can choose his wife,
and some women
make better wives than others.
27 Beauty is important to men,
and most men would be happy
to marry a beautiful woman.
28 But a man is really lucky
if his wife speaks
with humility and kindness.
29 The most important thing
a man can have
is a wife who helps him
and is a suitable partner.
30 Without a fence around a home,
robbers can steal
whatever they want.
And without a wife,
a man wanders aimlessly,

[f]36.13 *Israel*: Greek "Jacob," an earlier name of Israel's ancestor. [g]36.16 *and*: Due to a problem with the numbering in Greek manuscripts, there are no verses numbered 14 or 15, but no verses have been left out.

31 homeless, spending the night
wherever he can,
trusted no more than a thief
who is always on the run.

Deceitful Friends

37 Someone who claims
to be your friend
may not be telling the truth.
2 The sorrow when a close friend
becomes an enemy
is almost like mourning
for a friend who has died.

3 Why do people's thoughts
lead them to do wrong
and spread deceit everywhere?

4 Some friends are happy for you
when everything is fine,
but when you have trouble
they turn against you.
5 Another friend seems to help
only for a free meal,
but when you both go off to war,
he gives you protection.[h]
6 Never forget your friends,
and if you are successful,
share your wealth with them.

7 When people claim to offer
advice that is good for you,
it may really be good
for them.
8 Before you do what they say,
see if they are looking out
for themselves
and putting you at risk
9 with their advice,
while they can safely watch
what happens to you.

10 If someone is jealous
or suspicious of you,
don't ask them for advice
or tell them your plans.
11 If a man has two wives,
don't ask one about the other.
Take care who you ask
for advice.
A coward can't tell you
how to fight in battle,
and a store owner won't tell
how much something
is really worth.

Can someone with a grudge
show you how to be grateful,
or someone mean
tell you how to be kind?
Don't bother asking
a lazy person
if work needs to be done.
And don't ask someone
who gets paid by the hour
how long a job should take.

12 If you need advice, ask someone
who obeys God's commands
and thinks like you—
someone who will be sad
if you fail.
13 And trust your own judgment—
you care more about yourself
than anyone else does.
14 Thinking for yourself
will often tell you more
than if you had seven lookouts
in a high tower.
15 But the most important thing
is to pray that God Most High
will show you what to do.

16 Before you begin a project,
talk with others
and get their advice.
17 Everything starts as an idea,[i]
18 whether it helps or harms,
or brings life or death,
and how people talk
determines what they do.

19 Some people can give
excellent advice to others
but show no wisdom
in their own lives.
20 And some who can speak well
will be hated and starve,
21 because they speak

[h]**37.5** *gives you protection*: Greek "carries your shield." [i]**37.17** *Everything starts as an idea*: Hebrew; Greek "What people do shows what they have been thinking."

without wisdom from the Lord,
and they offend others.
22 If you see that certain people
make wise choices themselves,
you can depend on the advice
they give to you.[j]
23 The wise teach their wisdom
to God's people
so their wisdom will live on.
24 The wise are admired and praised
by everyone they meet.
25 Life is short for each of us,
but Israel will last forever,
26 honoring the memory of those
who shared their wisdom.

Eating

27 Take notice, students,
what foods make you feel sick,
and stay away from them.
28 After all, no one likes
every kind of food.
29 Control any desire to overeat
or to have lots of fancy food
at every meal.
30 You will get sick
if you eat too much.
31 Be careful!
Many have died young
from overeating.

Medicine

38 The Lord chose some people
to be doctors, so honor them
for helping others get well.
2 God Most High gave them
the ability to heal,
and they are rewarded
by the king.
3 Their skills
make them important,
and they are admired
by powerful people.

4 Medicines are part
of the Lord's creation,
and if you are sensible,
you will use them.
5 One time even a piece of wood
made water fit to drink,[k]
and this showed God's power.
6 He gives knowledge to humans
so that we will praise him
for his amazing creations.
*7 Doctors relieve pain
and bring healing
by mixing medicines
from things that God created.
8 God will always be at work
bringing health
to everyone on earth.

9 Students, if you get sick,
quickly pray to the Lord,
and you will be healed.
10 Give up all your sins
and decide to do right.
11 Offer a sacrifice of fine flour
and as much olive oil
as you can afford,[l]
and the smell of the smoke
will be pleasing to God.
12 But God also created doctors,
and you need their help,
so don't reject them.
13 Someday your life
will be in their hands,
14 and they will ask the Lord
how to make you well
and relieve your pain.

15 Those who sin against God,
their Creator,
will also reject doctors.[m]

Mourning

16 When someone dies,
you should mourn and weep
as though you were in pain.
Prepare the body to be buried,
and attend the funeral.
17 Weep bitterly to show respect
for the dead.
If you don't grieve at all,
you will be criticized,

[j]**37.22** *you can depend . . . give to you*: One possible meaning for the difficult text. [k]**38.5** *a piece of wood made water fit to drink*: See Exodus 15.22-25. [l]**38.11** *as much olive oil as you can afford*: One possible meaning for the difficult text. [m]**38.15** *will also reject doctors*: Hebrew; Greek "will have doctors as their only hope."

38.5 Ex 15.23-25. **38.16-23** Si 22.11, 12.

but don't mourn for longer
than a day or two.
18 If you don't stop grieving,
you will grow weak
and die.
19 After a funeral, sorrow remains,
but don't let it drag you down
into poverty.[n]
20 Put away your grief
and enjoy what is left
of your own life.
21 You cannot bring back
those who have died.
Grieving won't help them,
and it can harm you.
22 Just remember that in the past,
death caught up with them,
and in the future,
it will catch up with you.
23 The dead are at rest,
so be strong
and stop thinking about them
all the time.

Teachers of Wisdom

24 If teachers are to become wise,
they need lots of time to study
and freedom from other work.

*25 Who has time to study wisdom?
Not farmers!
All day long they guide oxen
to plow 26 in straight lines.
Then they work at night
feeding their livestock.
Farmers talk about cattle,
not wisdom.

27 Who has time to study wisdom?
Not artists who carve designs
on rings and other jewelry.
These artists work with care
night and day, making sure
each design is different
and leaves a perfect pattern
when pressed in soft wax.[o]

28 Who has time to study wisdom?
Not the blacksmith,
soaked in sweat from the heat
of the furnace,
going deaf from the noise
as he hammers the red-hot iron,
shaping it on his anvil.
He wants to finish this piece,
and will work late to see
all its decorations completed.

29 Who has time to study wisdom?
A potter doesn't.
His feet must always move
to spin the pottery wheel.
He keeps his mind on his work—
so many pieces to make,
30 and so much to do.
He works the clay with his feet
to make it soft,
then shapes it with his hands
before baking it.
And then at night,
he cleans out the furnace.

31 All these are skilled people
who work with their hands.
32 Without them in a town,
no one would live there
or even visit.
But they are not asked to serve
on public committees,
33 and they don't become leaders
in the town council.
They are not judges
and cannot explain
the decisions of the court.
They cannot even tell stories
that teach lessons.
34 But they do pray
about their work,
and they keep life going
for everyone else.

Teachers who study the Law
of God Most High
are different.
39 In their search for wisdom,
they study the old writings,
especially those
of the prophets.[p]

[n]**38.19** *After a funeral . . . poverty*: One possible meaning for the difficult text. [o]**38.27** *carve designs . . . soft wax*: Instead of signing agreements and other documents, a person would drip hot wax onto it and then press their own special ring into the soft wax. [p]**38.34—39.1** *Law . . . writings . . . prophets*: May refer to the three divisions of the Hebrew Bible, which were called by these names.

[2] These teachers learn the sayings
of famous people
and understand the meaning
of stories, [3] even those parts
that are difficult.
And they look for the meaning
hidden in a proverb.
[4] They give advice to leaders,
and they travel
in other countries
to see the good and the bad
done there.
[5] These teachers get up early
to pray to the Lord Most High,
their Creator—
they tell him what they need
and ask that their sins
be forgiven.

[6] The great Lord may choose
to give special understanding
to a teacher's mind.
Such teachers will pray
and thank the Lord
for the wise advice
that they now can give.
[7] They will study those things
the Lord has kept secret.
He will help them learn
and tell them what to say,
[8] and they will teach
what they have learned.
They will be proud
of the Lord's Law
and agreement with Israel.
[9] Their understanding
will be praised by many,
and their names remembered
for all time.
[10] Israel will honor them,
and other nations will admire
their wisdom.
[11] If they live to old age,
they will be famous,
and if not, they will be content
to be at rest.[q]

A Song of Praise

[12] I have hardly begun to tell you
all the things I want to say.
[13] You, my students,
are faithful to God,
so listen, and you will blossom
like rose bushes
planted beside a stream.
[14] You will grow faster than lilies,
and your songs praising the Lord
for what he has done
will be a pleasant smell,
spreading like incense.
[15] So play your harps
and sing praises to the Lord.
Give honor to him
with this song:

[16] "Everything the Lord does
is very good,
and his commands
will be obeyed
at the right moment.
[17] For now, we must not question
what God has done,
but he has set a time
to explain everything.
He created places
for all the water,
and when he commanded the sea,
it piled up like a wall.[r]
[18] When he gives an order,
it is obeyed,
and no one can stop him
when he decides to rescue.

[19] "We can't hide from God;
he has watched everything
that each human has done.
[20] He sees the past and the future;
there is nothing
he cannot do.
[21] So don't question
what God has done;
he had a purpose in mind
for each thing he created.

[22] "God will bless us greatly,
like a river that overflows
and soaks the dry ground.
[23] But the Gentiles
will feel his anger,

[q] **39.11** *if not . . . rest*: One possible meaning for the difficult text. [r] **39.17** *sea . . . like a wall*: See Exodus 14.22; 15.8.

as he makes their fresh water
too salty to drink.
24 God lets his people walk
on a straight pathway,
but those who reject his laws
will find that their path
is lined with hidden traps.
25 From the very beginning
God prepared good things
for good people,
and horrible things for sinners.

26 "What do we need for daily life?
Iron tools, water, and fire;
flour, milk, and honey,
wine, olive oil, and salt;
and, of course, clothing.
27 All of these are good
for God's loyal people
but become evil in the hands
of sinners.

28 "The Lord created furious winds
to take revenge for him.
And on the day of judgment,
they will punish his enemies,
then his anger will be calmed.
*29 God also created other things
to take revenge for him—
fire and hail, along with famine
and deadly diseases,
30 wild animals and scorpions,
and poisonous snakes,
not to mention war.
31 They are ready to serve him,
and at his command,
they gladly and quickly obey."

32 I have believed all these things
since my childhood,
but I thought deeply about them
before I wrote them down
in that song.
33 The Lord made only good things,
and at the right time
he will give us what we need.
34 Everything he created
has its own purpose,
and so, you cannot say,
"This is better than that."
35 Sing praises to the Lord
with all your heart,
and give him thanks!

Human Misery and Evil

40 God plans for us humans
to work hard
from the day of our birth
until we are buried in the soil
from which we were made.[s]
2 We don't understand life,
so we worry and dread the day
that it will end.
*3 And each of us is bothered
by troubling feelings—
from the king,
seated on his glorious throne
and wearing his crown
and royal robes,
*4 to the homeless in the street,
sitting in dirt and grime
and wearing worn-out clothes.
5 We are angry, jealous,
or hateful;
or maybe we feel guilty
or are afraid of death.
Sometimes we are confused
by a dream,
6 or lie awake
worrying about our work,
and so we get little rest.[t]
We see ourselves
running for our lives,
7 and almost reaching safety,
then we wake up, amazed—
it was all a dream.

8 The troubles that sinners have
will be seven times worse
than those of other people.
Any living creature
9 can suffer a violent death
when there is war or fighting,
or they can die from disaster,
horrible disease, or famine.
10 But God created these troubles
to punish those who do wrong,
as when he sent the flood.[u]
11 Animals and humans

[s]**40.1** *we are buried . . . made*: One possible meaning for the difficult text; see also Genesis 2.7.
[t]**40.6** *or lie awake . . . rest*: One possible meaning for the difficult text. [u]**40.10** *flood*: See Genesis 6.5—7.23.

were created from the soil,
and will return to it,[v]
just as water
returns to the sea.

12 What you gain by being honest
will last forever,
but wealth you get
by bribery and cheating
will disappear.
13 It will dry up like a stream
in the summer heat,
or quickly fade, like thunder
from a passing storm.
14 And while generous people
can celebrate success,
those who disobey God
will be failures.
15 Their children will be like trees
growing out of a rocky cliff
and having rotten roots
and few branches.
16 They are like the tall grass
that grows beside a stream—
when the stream runs dry,
the grass quickly withers.
17 But those who show kindness,
especially to the poor,
are gardens that always bloom
with blessing after blessing.

What Is Good for People

18 It is good to have a job
and earn your own money,
but it is even better
to discover hidden treasure.
19 Having wisdom is better
than giving your name
to your children or to a city
that you have built.
Cattle and fruit trees
can bring you wealth,[w]
but a happy marriage[x]
is better than riches.
20 Wine and music bring happiness,
but if you love wisdom,
you will be even happier.
21 A pleasant voice is sweeter
than the music
of flutes and harps.
22 Our eyes like beauty
and graceful movement,
but most of all, we want to see
our fields becoming green
with sprouting wheat.
23 Having friends and neighbors
is important,
but being married
is even better.
24 Relatives and friends can help
when you are in trouble,
but the best help comes
from giving to the poor.
25 Gold and silver
may give security,
but they don't compare
with good advice.
26 Many trust wealth and power,
but if you obey the Lord,
he will give you
whatever you need
if you will just ask.
27 If you obey the Lord,
he will protect you
and make your life a garden
where blessings grow.

Don't Be a Beggar

28 You would be better off dead
than to be a beggar.
29 If you have to beg for food,
your life isn't your own,
and you won't have
any respect for yourself.
If you are smart
and have learned anything,
you won't beg.
30 No matter what beggars say,
they really are ashamed
of what they do.

Thoughts about Dying

41 Death is a bitter thought
for those who are prosperous
and without a worry.
They have everything

[v]**40.11** *Animals and humans . . . return to it*: See Genesis 1.24; 2.7; 3.19. [w]**40.19** *to your children . . . wealth*: Hebrew; the Greek does not have these words. [x]**40.19** *a happy marriage*: Hebrew text; the Greek text has "a wife who has no faults."

and are healthy enough
to enjoy good food.
2 But others would rather die
because they are poor and sick,
old and worn out.
They are grumpy and impatient,
always finding something
to worry about.

3 When it's your time to die,
don't be afraid—
you are merely following those
who have gone on before.
And everyone else
will soon follow you,
4 because the Lord has commanded
that life ends with death,
and we all must obey.
No one in the world of the dead
will ask how long you lived,
whether it was ten, a hundred,
or a thousand years.

5 The children of sinners
are disgusting,
because they are raised
in godless homes.
6 They will lose everything
they inherited,
and their own children
will live in disgrace.

7 If parents reject God,
their children are disgraced
and blame them.
8 The godless are in for trouble,
because they refuse to obey
the Law of God Most High.
9 They will groan as disaster
strikes their children,[y]
and at the death of the godless,
God's people will celebrate[z]
and will curse them.
10 All living creatures
will return to the soil
from which they were made,
but sinners are under a curse
and will be destroyed.

11 When someone dies,
we usually mourn,
but everyone tries to forget
those who were evil.
12 So be careful! Your reputation
won't die with you—
it will outlast the gold
in a thousand treasure chests.
13 Every one of us must die,
but our reputations won't.

When To Be Ashamed

14 Students, you have learned well.
So don't worry; just do
what you have been taught.
Your wisdom is a treasure—
bring it out and use it,
don't bury it!
15 Fools who hide their stupidity
will be better off than you,
if you hide your wisdom.

16 Certain deeds are shameful,
although not everyone agrees
what these are.
So listen carefully,
and I will tell you.
17 You should be ashamed
if you are immoral
and your parents find out;
if a leader discovers
that you have lied;
18 if you commit a crime
and everyone in town
comes to watch your trial;
if you cheat your friends
19 or steal from neighbors;
if you break promises
that you made in God's name;
if you have bad manners
when eating dinner,
or when giving a gift
or receiving one;
20 if you don't reply
when someone greets you;
if you men look at a prostitute
*21 or if you desire the wife
of another man

[y]**41.9** *They will groan . . . children*: Hebrew text; the Greek text does not have these words.
[z]**41.9** *and at . . . celebrate*: Hebrew text; the Greek text has "If they are born, they will be born for a curse."

or if you try to have sex
with one of his slave girls;
if you refuse to help a relative
or if you take what was given
to someone else;
22 if you insult your friends,
even though you have given
a gift to them;
42 if you repeat rumors
or tell someone's secret.
If someone catches you
doing any of these things,
show how ashamed you are,
then others will forgive you.

When Not To Be Ashamed

Don't ever be ashamed
to do what is right,
even if others don't approve.
2 For example, don't be ashamed
if you obey the Law
of God Most High;
or if a godless person
is on trial,
and you vote "innocent"
because you believe it's true;
3 if you pay your fair share
of the expenses for business
or travel;
if you divide up an inheritance
among all those
who deserve a share;
4 if you have accurate scales
for weighing what you buy
and sell;
if you buy much or little,
5 or if you make a profit
on what you sell;
if you punish your children
when they need it;
if your slaves do wrong,
and you whip them
until they bleed.

Some Good Advice

6 Husbands, if your wife
cannot be trusted,
or if a lot of visitors
will be in your home,
lock up everything of value.
7 If you leave valuable items
with someone for safekeeping,
be sure to get a receipt,
and keep records of everything
you give or receive.
8 Do not be embarrassed
to correct stupid fools
or even an older person
who is being immoral.

If you follow my advice,
others will honor you
for the lessons of wisdom
you have learned.

Advice to Fathers about Daughters

9 I know that secretly you fathers
worry about your daughters
and lose sleep, while questions
trouble your minds.
Will she find a husband?
Will he love her, 10 and will she
be faithful to him?
Will she get pregnant
before she gets married
and leaves your home?
Or will she be able
to have children?

11 If your daughter
always wants her own way,
watch her closely,
or she may embarrass you.
Your enemies will laugh,
and everyone in town
will talk about it.
Don't let her bedroom window
look down on the front door,
and a room without a window
is even better.[a]
12 Don't let men see her beauty,
and keep her away
from married women,
13 because evil comes from women
as fast as moths that fly
from wool clothing.
14 Women are the cause
of so much disgrace,
that the wrong things men do
are better than the good
done by women.

[a]**42.11** *Don't let her bedroom . . . better*: Hebrew; the Greek text does not have these words.
42.9-11 Si 7.24, 25; 26.10-12.

The Lord's Creation

15 Now let me tell you
what the Lord has done;
this is what I have seen.
When he gives a command,
things begin to happen,
and his creatures obey.[b]
16 When the sun starts shining,
God's glory can be seen
in all the earth.
17 Even his angels cannot explain
everything he has done,
because he wants all creation
to show how great he is.
18 God knows everything—
from the unseen world
of the ocean floor,
to the secret thoughts
deep in our hearts,
to those things that change
from one age to the next.
19 God explains the past to us
and tells what lies ahead;
he even shows us clues
to the mysteries of creation.
20 Each thought and word
are known to him.
21 The laws of nature
show his great wisdom.
God has never changed
and never will;
he has no need of advice.
22 Look at his creation—
it sparkles with beauty,
23 and year after year, each part
fulfills its purpose.
24 Every part has an opposite,
and together,
they make creation complete,
25 each one contributing
something good to the other.
Who could ever see enough
of such majestic beauty?

43 Nothing can compare
with the glorious sight
of the clear, blue sky.
2 And you can almost hear
the rising sun say,
"I am a wonderful creation
of the Most High God."
3 By noon its fiery heat
has dried out the soil.
It forces people into the shade,
4 and scorches mountain slopes.
The sun's blinding light
is three times hotter
than any fire we can build.
5 Our great Lord created the sun,
and when he commands,
it hurries to obey.

6 The moon also has its turn
in the sky
serving as a sign
of the changing months,
7 and setting the times
for sacred festivals.
When its light has become dark,
a new month begins—
8 the word "month"
even comes from "moon"—
then we watch in amazement,
as the moon gradually grows
until it is full,
giving light to God's armies
in the heavens above.

9 Heaven, the Lord's home,
is decorated at night
with beautiful, twinkling stars.
10 They never rest but stand guard
where he has placed them.

11 Look at the rainbow,
bright and beautiful,
and praise its Creator,
12 who bent it with his hands
and placed it around the sky.

13 At the Lord's command,
snow begins to fall,
and lightning quickly obeys.
14 And like birds, the clouds fly
from his storehouse.
15 He gives them his great power,
and he crushes hailstones.
*16 His voice thunders at the earth,
and at the sight of him,
mountains tremble.
17 The whirlwind obeys him,

[b]**42.15** *and his creatures obey*: Hebrew; the Greek text does not have these words.

as do winds from the south
and storms from the north.
God sends the snow,
and it settles on the ground
like a flock of birds
or a swarm of locusts.
18 We watch amazed
as it floats down,
white and lovely.
19 He sprinkles frost
as though it were salt,
and icicles form.
20 A freezing north wind
makes the surface of every pond
hard as armor.

21 God sends the fiery heat,
and deserted mountain pastures
are scorched and withered.
22 But soon the early morning mist
and the refreshing dew
will heal the damage.

23 The Lord calmed the oceans
and placed the islands,
all according to his plan.
24 And when sailors tell stories
of danger at sea,
we are amazed.
25 The oceans are home
to strange creatures
and huge monsters.

26 God tells each of these things
what to do,
and because of his power,
they never fail.
All creation is held together
by his command.

27 We could never finish telling
what God has done,
so we should say,
"The Lord can be seen
in all his creation."[c]
28 But he is far greater
than what he created,
so where can we look
for strength to praise him?
29 The Lord is fearsome
and powerful,
30 so always praise him
with all your strength.
Don't let yourself grow tired—
he deserves more praise
than you can give.
31 Since no one has seen the Lord
and described him to us,
we really don't know
how to praise him.
32 We have seen so little
of God's creation,
and we do not understand
so many things.
33 Still, the Lord created it all,
and he has given wisdom
to those who worship him.

A Song Praising Israel's Ancestors

44 Sing the praises of our ancestors,
those famous men
who lived long ago.
2 The Lord gave them honor
and showed them his power
from the very first.
3 Some of them were kings
or were famous
for their courage.
Some gave wise advice
or spoke messages from God.
4 There were leaders
who made good decisions,
who learned the wisdom
passed down by our people,
and who taught it to others.
5 Some of our ancestors
wrote poetry or music;
6 others were rich and powerful,
but lived in peace.
7 All these men
were highly honored
in their own time;
8 their reputations live on,
and even today
they still are praised.

9 Others of our people
are best[d] forgotten,

[c]**43.27** *The Lord . . . creation*: One possible meaning for the difficult text. [d]**44.9** *are best*: Or "have been."

as if they and their descendants
had never been born.
10 But the ancestors we praise
were faithful to God,
and so we will remember
their good deeds.
11 Their good name
has been handed down,
generation by generation,[e]
12 to those who follow them
in being faithful
to their agreement with God.
*13 Their families will live on,
and each new generation
will honor these ancestors,
14 even though their bodies
were long ago laid to rest.
15 Israel praises them,
and other nations still tell
about their wisdom.

Enoch

16 Enoch turned to the Lord
and became an example
for all time,
and the Lord was so pleased
that he took Enoch to heaven.

Noah

17 Noah was perfectly loyal to God.
And so when God in his anger
sent the flood
to sweep humans from the earth,
he spared Noah's life.
18 And God made an agreement
with him—
never again will such a flood
destroy all living creatures.

Abraham

19 No one is more famous
than Abraham, the great ancestor
of many nations.
20 He obeyed the Law
of God Most High
and made an agreement with God
that left a mark on his body.
And when tested by the Lord,
Abraham remained faithful.
21 And so, the Lord promised
that Abraham's descendants
would be more numerous
than the stars in the sky
or specks of dust on earth.
All nations would be blessed
by his descendants,
and they would be given land
from sea to sea,
and from the Euphrates River
to the end of the earth.

Isaac

*22 God later made the same promise
to Isaac, the son of Abraham.

Jacob

God's agreement and promise
then came to Jacob—
all people would be blessed
by his descendants,
23 and God would bless him
and give him land to be divided
among the twelve tribes.[f]

Moses

One of Jacob's descendants
was faithful to the Lord
and pleasing to everyone;
45 he was well loved
by Israel and God.
The man was Moses,
and we still give thanks
whenever we think of him.
2 The Lord gave Moses glory
equal to the angels
and power that terrified
his enemies.
*3 When Moses spoke,
miracles happened,
and even the king of Egypt
was forced to honor him.
The Lord chose Moses
to see his glory
and to receive the Law
4 because Moses was faithful
and humble.

[e]**44.11** *generation*: One possible meaning for the difficult text of verse 11. [f]**44.23** *the twelve tribes*: Israel, the descendants of Jacob.

44.16 Gn 5.23, 24; He 11.5; Jd 14. **44.17,18** Gn 6.9—9.18. **44.19-21** Gn 15.1—17.27; 22.1-18. **44.22,23** Gn 17.19; 26.3-5; 27.28; 28.14. **45.1-5** Ex 6.28—11.10; 20.1-21.

5 He heard the Lord's voice
and saw him face to face,
when the Lord told him
to teach Israel the commands
that give knowledge and life.

Aaron the Priest

6 Aaron the brother of Moses
was a holy man
from the tribe of Levi,
and the Lord chose him
*7 and his descendants
to be Israel's priests
for all time.
The Lord told him to wear
glorious clothing
8 with beautiful decorations
and jewelry.
Three things truly showed
Aaron's priestly power—
the linen shorts, the robe,
and the sacred vest.
9 Pomegranates[q] were embroidered
along the hem of the robe,
and gold bells were sewn there,
so others could hear the ringing
as he walked in the temple.
*10 The vest was embroidered
with blue and purple yarn
and decorated with gold.
11 The breastpiece was decorated
with red yarn,
and it held the sacred items
used in getting answers
from God.
On it were precious stones,
set in finely worked gold
and engraved with the names
of Israel's twelve tribes.
12 On Aaron's turban
was a beautiful strip of gold
made by an expert
and engraved with the words,
"Dedicated to the Lord."
13 All these things were made
for Aaron the priest,
and since his time,
only his descendants
have ever worn them.
14 Twice each day,
these priests offer sacrifices
to please the Lord.

15 Moses ordained Aaron as priest
by pouring sacred olive oil
on his head.
And the Lord promised Aaron
that his descendants would serve
as his priests forever
and bless the people of Israel
in his name.
16 The Lord chose only him
to burn sacrifices and incense
with a pleasing smell,
reminding the Lord of his people
and asking him
to forgive their sins.
17 Aaron was made a judge
and was given the Law
with instructions to teach it
to Israel.
18 When Israel was in the desert,
some men who were not priests
became jealous of Aaron,
and they rebelled, led by Dathan,
Abiram, and Korah.
19 But the Lord wasn't pleased,
and to show he was furious,
he sent down fire
to destroy them.

20 The Lord honored Aaron
even more
by giving to him
the offerings of the first part
of the harvest.
And so these offerings
are the priests' inheritance,
21 along with other sacrifices
the Lord gave to them.
22 Their inheritance is the Lord,
not a piece of ground
among the rest of Israel.

Phinehas the Priest

23 Phinehas son of Eleazar
is almost as famous
as Moses and Aaron.

[q]**45.9** *Pomegranates*: A red fruit that looks something like an apple.

45.6 Ex 4.14. **45.7-13** Ex 28.1-43. **45.15** Lv 8.1-36. **45.18,19** Nu 16.1-35. **45.22** Nu 18.20; Dt 12.5-19. **45.23-26** Nu 25.7-13.

Phinehas was brave
and eager to obey the Lord,
when the other Israelites
were unfaithful.
And so, because of what he did,
God spared Israel
24 and promised to Phinehas
and his descendants
the honor of forever being
leaders of the nation
and priests in the temple.
25 According to this promise
made by the Lord,
only a descendant of Aaron
can be a priest,
just as Israel's king must be
from the family of David.

A Short Prayer for the Priests

26 Give thanks to the Lord
who has given glory
to you priests.[h]
I pray he will give you wisdom
so you will make fair decisions
when you judge his people.
Then they will be successful
and famous forever.

Joshua

46 Joshua the son of Nun
was a mighty warrior
and the next prophet
after Moses.
His name means,
"The Lord rescues,"
and Joshua did rescue Israel
by defeating their enemies,
as he led Israel into the land
God had promised them.
2 Joshua was glorious
as he raised his sword
and gave the signal
to attack a city.
3 He had more courage
than any warrior before him,
because he was fighting
at the Lord's command.
4 Joshua even kept the sun
from moving across the sky,
so that one day lasted
as long as two.
5 His enemies attacked all around,
but he prayed
to our Mighty God,
and the Lord, the Most High,
made deadly hailstones fall
on the enemy army.
6 As the battle moved down
the mountain slopes
Joshua defeated and destroyed
the enemy army,
so that everyone would know
he fought under the command
of the Mighty Lord of Israel,
and that the Lord himself
fought on their side.

Caleb

7 Earlier, Caleb son of Jephunneh,
along with Joshua,
proved he was loyal to God
by standing up to the people
who rebelled against Moses.
These two held back the people
from sinning
and put an end
to their complaints.
8 Six hundred thousand men died,
but Caleb and Joshua
were spared
and led Israel into the land
rich with milk and honey.
9 The Lord kept Caleb strong,
and although Caleb was old,
he captured the hill country.
Then he handed down his land
to his descendants
10 to remind Israel of the benefits
of being faithful to the Lord.

The Judges

11 Some of Israel's special leaders
were the famous judges[i]
who never turned from the Lord
to worship idols.
And we still honor them
because they were faithful.
12 Though they are now dead,

[h] **45.26** *Give thanks . . . you priests*: Hebrew; the Greek text does not have these words.
[i] **46.11** *judges*: These led the Israelites in battle, decided legal cases, and sometimes performed religious duties.

46.1-6 Js 1.1—11.23. **46.7-10** Nu 14.6-10; Js 14.6-11. **46.11** Jg 1.1—16.31.

we pray their good names
will be honored by the way
their descendants live.

The Prophet Samuel

13 The Lord loved Samuel,
the prophet who appointed
the first kings of Israel
and other rulers.
14 Samuel judged the nation
according to the Lord's Law,
and so the Lord
watched over Israel.[j]
15 The people knew that Samuel
spoke for the Lord,
because Samuel was faithful,
and his words came true.

16 One time, Israel's enemies
attacked from every side,
but Samuel prayed
to the Mighty Lord
and sacrificed a lamb.
17 Then the Lord thundered
his answer from heaven
18 and defeated the leaders
of Tyre and[k] Philistia.

19 Before Samuel died,
he asked the Lord and the king
to be his witnesses
so that no one could accuse him
of ever taking anything
that wasn't rightfully his—
not even a pair of sandals.
20 And then, after he had died,
he spoke from the grave
and predicted King Saul's death,
which brought to an end
Saul's disobedience.

The Prophet Nathan

47 The next prophet was Nathan,
and while David was king,
Nathan spoke God's message.

King David

2 The Lord set David apart
from Israel, his people,
just as the fat
is taken from sacrifices
and is given to the Lord.
3 David played with lions and bears
as if they were young goats
or lambs from his flock.

4 When David was a boy,
he put a stone in his sling
and swung it around.
Then he let the stone fly,
and it brought down Goliath,
the giant whose boasting
had put Israel to shame.
5 David had prayed
to the Lord Most High,
and the Lord gave David strength
to defeat this mighty soldier
and give victory to Israel.
6 Israel praised David
for killing enemies
by the thousands
and for being blessed
by the Lord.
And when he became king,
7 he conquered his enemies
on every side,
especially the Philistines,
who have never recovered.

8 Whenever David won a victory,
he thanked the Holy God
and sang songs of praise
with all his heart,
expressing love for his Creator,
the Lord Most High.
9 David also commanded singers
to stand in front of the altar
and sing beautiful songs.
10 And so, all day long,
at every festival,
Israel hears songs of praise
in the temple courtyard.

11 The Lord forgave David's sins
and made him a glorious king,
and he also promised
that the kings of Israel

[j]**46.14** *Israel*: The Greek text has "Jacob," an earlier name for the ancestor of the nation.
[k]**46.18** *Tyre and*: Greek; the Hebrew text does not have these words.
46.13-20 1 S 3.19, 20; 7.9-11; 10.1; 12.3; 16.13; 28.18, 19. **47.1** 2 S 7.2, 3; 12.1.
47.2-11 1 S 17.34—18.7; 2 S 5.7-9; 8.1; 12.13, 14.

would be David's descendants
for all time.

King Solomon

*12 Solomon, the wise son of David,
became the next king,
and for David's sake,
13 the Lord kept enemies
from attacking Israel.
And so, Solomon ruled
in a time of peace,
because he had been chosen
to build the Lord a temple
that would last forever.
14 When Solomon was young,
his wisdom overflowed
like a river
15 and spread across the land,
filling it with proverbs
and riddles.
16 He was famous in faraway islands;
he brought peace,
and so he was loved.
17 His songs, proverbs, stories,
and answers
amazed many nations.
18 Solomon ruled in the name
of the Lord God of Israel
and gathered silver and gold
as if they were tin or lead.
19 But he married lots of wives,
and they used his desire for sex
to gain control over him.
20 Solomon ruined his reputation
and that of his descendants.
The Lord punished them
for Solomon's sins,
and they mourned,
21 because the northern kingdom[l]
broke away, dividing Israel.
22 But the Lord will continue
to have mercy;
he will never abandon
those he has chosen
and who love him.
And so, the Lord has kept alive
a few of David's descendants
for the sake of Israel.[m]

King Rehoboam and King Jeroboam

23 Solomon died, and the next king
was his son Rehoboam,
the nation's worst fool,
and his senseless decisions
caused the people to rebel.
Then Jeroboam[n] son of Nebat
led the northern kingdom
into sin.
*24 Israel sinned so much
and in so many ways,
that the Lord
finally punished them,
25 and they were led as prisoners
from their land.

The Prophet Elijah

48 Earlier, God had sent
the prophet Elijah
to speak messages
that burned like fire.
2 At Elijah's command,
a famine hit Israel,
and many of the people died.
3 Elijah performed miracles
by God's power—
he held back rain from Israel
and three times commanded fire
to fall from heaven.
4 He is worthy of honor,
because who else could do
such amazing miracles?
5 By the power of God Most High
he brought back life
into a dead body.
6 But he also destroyed kings
and told famous people
they would die of disease.

7 God corrected Elijah
at Mount Sinai[o]
and told him to announce

[l]**47.21** *the northern kingdom*: Greek "Ephraim," the name of the most powerful tribe in the northern kingdom. [m]**47.22** *Israel*: Greek "Jacob," an earlier name for the great ancestor of the nation of Israel. [n]**47.23** *Jeroboam*: Jeroboam I, the first king of the northern kingdom, ruled 931-910 B.C. [o]**48.7** *Mount Sinai*: The Greek text also uses the name "Mount Horeb."

47.13-17 1 K 4.21-32. **47.18** 1 K 10.21, 27. **47.19** 1 K 11.1, 2. **47.21** 1 K 12.15-20. **47.22** 2 S 7.15. **47.23-25** 1 K 11.43; 12.10-30; 2 K 17.6, 18. **48.1-11** 1 K 17.1-24; 18.38; 19.15, 16; 2 K 1.10-16; 2.11; Ml 4.5, 6.

that God's enemies
would be punished.
8 So Elijah appointed kings
to punish these enemies,
and he appointed prophets
to carry on his own work.
9 Then God took him to heaven
in a fiery whirlwind—
a chariot and horses
made of fire.

10 It is written that Elijah
will come at the right time,
to calm God's anger
before it overflows,
and help parents
love their children.
Then Israel will be successful
once again.
11 Those who live until he comes
will be blessed by the Lord,
and God's people who have died
will live again.[p]

The Prophet Elisha

12 When Elijah disappeared
in the whirlwind,
God gave Elisha the same power
he had given to Elijah.
Elisha wasn't afraid of kings
and could not be forced
to do what they wanted.
*13 No problem was too hard for him,
and he did marvelous things.
14 Even after his death,
his body caused a miracle.

15 But the northern kingdom
still did not give up sinning
and they did not turn to God.
And so, they were captured
and led away
to foreign countries.

The kingdom of Judah
had few people,
but at least they had a king
from David's family.
16 Sometimes they did right,
but often they sinned
worse than ever.

King Hezekiah and the Prophet Isaiah

17 Hezekiah fortified Jerusalem,
and using iron tools
he cut a tunnel through rock
to bring water in,
and dug cisterns to store it.
18 During Hezekiah's rule,
Sennacherib attacked Judah,
and before he left,
he sent his highest officer
to Jerusalem.

This arrogant officer boasted,
making threats against Zion.
19 The people of Jerusalem
trembled with fear,
and they suffered
like a woman giving birth.
20 But they lifted up their hands
and prayed to the Lord,
the merciful and holy God.
He heard their prayers
and sent the prophet Isaiah
to rescue them.
21 Then the Lord sent an angel,
who killed all the Assyrians
in their own army camp.
22 Jerusalem was saved
because Hezekiah obeyed Isaiah
and pleased the Lord
by following the example
of his ancestor King David.

When this great prophet
had a vision, it came true.
23 One time, Isaiah caused the sun
to move backward,
and he gave a longer life
to the king.
24 God's Spirit gave him power
to see the future,
and he comforted those in Zion
who were in sorrow,
25 by telling them the secrets
hidden in the future
as far as the end of time.

[p]**48.11** *again*: One possible meaning for the difficult text of verse 11.
48.12 2 K 2.9, 13. **48.13,14** 2 K 13.20, 21. **48.15** 2 K 18.11, 12. **48.17** 2 K 20.20.
48.18 2 K 18.13-17. **48.20,21** 2 K 19.15-20, 35. **48.23** 2 K 20.10, 11.

King Josiah

49 The memory of Josiah
is pleasant,
like skillfully mixed incense
or the taste of honey,
or like music at a banquet
where wine is served.
2 He did right and led the nation
to get rid of its idols
and turn back to God.
3 Many had rejected God's Law,
but Josiah was faithful
and encouraged others
to obey God.

The Prophet Jeremiah and the Evil Kings of Judah

4 David, Hezekiah, and Josiah
were good kings,
but the other kings of Judah
sinned terribly
and rejected the Law
of God Most High.
So he took away their kingdom
5 and gave their glorious power
to foreigners
6 who burned down Jerusalem,
the city God had chosen
for his temple.
The city streets lay empty,
just as Jeremiah had said.
7 He had been chosen as a prophet
before his birth
and was later told to speak
of doom and destruction,
of rising and rebuilding.
But the evil kings of Judah
mistreated him.

The Prophet Ezekiel

8 Ezekiel saw a vision
of the Lord's glory
above the living creatures
that were his chariot.

Job

9 God said that Job
always did what was right.

The Twelve Prophets

10 I pray that the twelve prophets
will live on
in their descendants
because they helped Israel
stand firm during hard times
by giving them hope.

Zerubbabel

11 What is the best way
to praise Zerubbabel?
He was like a valuable ring
on the Lord's right hand,
12 as was Joshua son of Jozadak.
They built a holy temple
for the Lord,
and it will always be famous.

Nehemiah

13 We should honor Nehemiah
because he rebuilt
the homes in Jerusalem;
he repaired the city walls
and put in strong new gates.

Other Great Ancestors

14 No one like Enoch
has ever been born—
he was taken up
from earth to heaven.
15 And no one like Joseph
has ever been born—
he kept Israel from starving
and ruled his brothers;
then after his death,
the people of Israel
watched over his bones.
16 Shem and Seth are also honored,
but of all God's creatures,
Adam was the greatest.

Simon the Priest

50 High Priest Simon
the son of Onias
repaired and fortified
the temple,
2 and he laid the foundations
for the high double walls
that went around it.[q]

[q] **50.2** *it*: One possible meaning for the difficult text of verse 2.

49.1-3 2 K 22.1; 22.11-13; 23.3, 25. **49.6,7** Jr 1.4-10; 39.8. **49.8,9** Ez 1.3-15; 14.14-20. **49.11** Ezra 3.2; Hg 2.23. **49.12** Hg 1.1, 12. **49.13** Ne 6.15.

3 Simon also dug a cistern[r]
as big as the large bronze bowl
called "the Sea."[s]
4 He fortified Jerusalem
and drew up plans
in case it was ever attacked
or surrounded.
5 When he came out
from the Most Holy Place
and walked among the people,
he looked glorious,
6 like the morning star
between the clouds
or a full moon
during a festival,
7 or like sunshine on the temple
of God Most High,
or a brilliant rainbow
set against beautiful clouds.
8 Seeing him was as pleasant
as the first roses of spring
or lilies beside a stream,
or green grass on a hot day
in the Lebanon mountains.
9 He was majestic, like the smoke
from burning incense,
or a golden bowl set with jewels
of every kind,
10 or like an olive tree
heavy with olives,
or a cypress tree
reaching toward the clouds.
11 The whole temple courtyard
reflected his glory
when he wore his special robes
and went up to the sacred altar.

12 Then he stood beside the altar,
and other priests gave him
the sacrifices to be burned.
These priests stood around him
like palm trees near a cedar
in the Lebanon mountains.
13 They wore beautiful robes
and held the sacrifices
in their hands.
All Israel watched
14 while Simon placed each offering
on the altar fires.
15 Then he was handed a cup
of blood-red wine,
which he poured out
at the foot of the altar
as a pleasant-smelling offering
to God Most High,
the King of all creation.
16 After this, the priests shouted
and blew silver trumpets,
making a loud noise
as a prayer
to the Most High God.

17 Immediately, everyone bowed
with their face to the ground
to worship the all-powerful
Lord God Most High.
18 The temple choir began singing,
and sweet songs of praise
echoed through the courtyard.
19 Meanwhile, the people prayed
to their God,
the merciful Lord Most High,
until the ceremonies of worship
were finished.
20 Then Simon came down
from the altar
and raised his hands
to praise the Lord
and to bless the people
in his name.
21 They bowed down again
to receive Simon's blessing
and to worship God Most High.

Praise God

22 Praise the God of all creation,
because he works miracles
everywhere on earth.
He watches over us as we grow,
and shows mercy to us.
23 Now we pray for happiness
and peace in Israel,
as it used to be.
24 May he be merciful
and rescue us before we die.

[r]**50.3** *dug a cistern*: Hebrew; Greek "made a cistern smaller." [s]**50.3** *the large bronze . . . "the Sea:"* This huge bowl had stood in the temple courtyard, and was about fifteen feet across (see 1 Kings 7.23-26).
50.20 Nu 6.24-27.

Nations Hated by Sirach

*25 Two nations I hate are Edom[t]
and Philistia,
26 and I also hate
the people of Shechem—
those fools are unworthy
to even be called a nation.

The Wisdom in This Book

27 My name is Jesus son of Eleazar
son of Sirach,[u]
and I wrote this book
to help you learn and understand
the wisdom that overflows
from my heart.
28 If you read and pay attention
to the wisdom in this book,
you will be happy and wise.
29 The Lord's wisdom gives light
to the pathway of life.
Follow wisdom,
and you will never fail.

A Prayer To Give Thanks

51 I praise you, Lord God,
because you are my king,
and you rescued me.
I give you thanks
2 for protection and help
when I was in danger
from enemies
who tried to destroy me
with cruel lies.
3 My enemies wanted me dead
and were about
to gobble me down,
but you had pity and rescued me
from the trouble they caused.

4 I was surrounded by fires
they had set,
and I could not breathe
for the smoke.
*5 Death was ready to swallow me,
because their filthy lies
6 had reached the king.
I was standing at the edge
of an open grave.
7 Enemies surrounded me,
and I called for help—
but no one came.

8 Then, Lord, I remembered
your mercy and kindness
and how you have always saved
those who trusted you
when they were attacked
by evil people.
9 So I prayed and cried out,
"Don't let me die!
10 I am in trouble,
facing arrogant enemies
with no one to help me.
But you are my Lord and Father,
so please don't let me down.
Rescue me,
11 and I will honor you forever
with songs of praise."

I know you heard my prayer,
12 because you saved me from death
and rescued me from danger.
That's why I thank you
and give you honor and praise.

Sirach Looked for Wisdom

*13 When I was young
and before I had traveled,
14 I prayed in the temple courtyard
and openly asked for Wisdom.
And I will look for her[v]
every day of my life.
15 Now I am old,
but ever since I was a child,
I have loved Wisdom
and always followed her
on the path where she walked.
16 When I listened even a little
to what she said,
I learned many things.
17 So I continued to study,
and I praise God,
who gives me Wisdom.

18 I chose to live by Wisdom
and always do right,
and I have never had a reason
to be ashamed.

[t]**50.25** *Edom*: Hebrew; Greek "Samaria." [u]**50.27** *Eleazar son of Sirach*: Hebrew; Greek "Sirach Eleazar." [v]**51.14** *her*: Wisdom is here pictured as a woman.

19 Whenever I had to struggle
to follow her completely,
I would lift my hands in prayer
and tell God I was sorry
I knew so little of Wisdom.
20 But I was set on finding her,
and I did, by removing sin
from my heart.
Now, I grow wiser and wiser,
and she will never leave me.

21 I made the effort to find Wisdom
because I really wanted her,
and she is worth it all.
22 The Lord also rewarded me
with a gift for using words,
and so I will use that gift
to offer him praise.

23 If Wisdom is a subject
you have never studied,
then come to my school.
24 If your desire for her
is like a great thirst,
why haven't you quenched it?
25 Here is my advice—
you cannot buy Wisdom,
26 and you need not travel far.
You just have to be willing
to do what she says.
27 Studying wisdom has filled
my life with peace,
and you can see it is worth
any effort I have made.
28 And even if learning Wisdom
costs you a lot of silver,
she will bring you
even more in gold.

Celebrate the Mercy of God!

29 Celebrate the mercy of God!
Don't be ashamed to tell others
how great he is.
30 Work when it is time to work,
and God will reward you
when the time is right.

BARUCH

ABOUT THIS BOOK

Baruch was a friend of Jeremiah, the prophet, and helped Jeremiah write down everything the Lord told him to say (Jeremiah 36.4; 45.1). This book is written as though Baruch was its author, writing it while Israel was in exile in Babylonia. However, the book is actually much later, and was put together from Old Testament words and phrases.

The book of Baruch gives advice to the people of Jerusalem and Judah, sometimes directly, and sometimes as though they were still living in exile in Babylonia. They should admit that they have sinned and should ask the Lord to forgive them. Then they should study God's laws and teachings to find wisdom so that they can live in ways that please him. If they do these things, God will lead them home and be with them:

> *God has commanded every forest and every sweet-smelling tree to shade the Israelites as he leads them home, and they will celebrate and shout for joy on their way. The brightness of God's own glory will guide them, and his mercy and justice will go with them.*
>
> *(5.8, 9)*

A QUICK LOOK AT THIS BOOK

- Baruch Returns to Jerusalem from Babylon (1.1-14)
- A Prayer Confessing Sins and Asking for Forgiveness (1.15—3.8)
- Wisdom Is Praised (3.9—4.4)
- Words of Hope and Promise (4.5—5.9)

Baruch Reads His Book to the Jews in Babylon

1 I am Baruch son of Neriah and grandson of Mahseiah, and my ancestors include Zedekiah, Hasadiah, and Hilkiah. I
wrote this book in the city of Babylon 2 on
the seventh day of the month of Ab,[a] exactly five years after the Babylonians had
captured and burned down Jerusalem.[b]
3 I read the book to King Jehoiachin[c] of
Judah, son of Jehoiakim, and to everyone
who came to listen: 4 the government officials and the religious leaders, together
with all the people of Israel, both young
and old, who lived in Babylon near the Sud
River.[d]
5 After they had listened to me read the
book, everyone cried and prayed to the
Lord, then went without eating to show
their sorrow. 6 They collected as much
money as they could 7 and sent it to
Jerusalem for Priest Jehoiakim[e] and the
other priests, as well as for the people living there.
8 On the tenth day of the month of

[a] **1.2** *the month of Ab*: Greek "the month"; probably Ab, the fifth month of the Hebrew calendar, from about mid-July to mid-August. This was the anniversary of Jerusalem's capture and destruction (see 2 Kings 25.1-12), and the people of Judah, whether living there or in Babylonia, remembered it by praying and by going without eating to show their sorrow (see Zechariah 7.3). [b] **1.2** *five years after . . . Jerusalem*: Probably 581 B.C. [c] **1.3** *Jehoiachin*: The Greek text has "Jeconiah," another form of Jehoiachin's name (ruled 598 B.C.). [d] **1.4** *Sud River*: Nothing is known about this river. [e] **1.7** *Priest Jehoiakim*: Greek "Priest Jehoiakim son of Hilkiah and grandson of Shallum."

1.1 Jr 36.4. **1.3,4** 2 K 24.8-17.

Sivan,[f] I got together all the sacred things that had been taken from the Lord's temple in Jerusalem and took them back to Judah. These included the silver things that King Zedekiah of Judah[g] had made 9 and that King Nebuchadnezzar of Babylonia[h] had taken from Jerusalem. He brought these to Babylon, along with King Jehoiachin, the important leaders of Judah, the prisoners, and most of the people.

A Letter to the Jews in Jerusalem

10 The Jews living in Babylon wrote the following letter for Baruch to take with him to Judah:

> Please use the money we are sending to buy animals for sacrifices to please the Lord[i] and sacrifices for sin, as well as to buy incense and to prepare grain offerings. These sacrifices and offerings must be offered on the altar built to honor the Lord our God.
>
> 11 Pray that King Nebuchadnezzar of Babylonia and his son Belshazzar will live forever, like the heavens above. 12 And pray that the Lord will keep our people strong and show us how to be faithful. Then King Nebuchadnezzar and King Belshazzar will be pleased with us and protect us, and in return we will be loyal to them. 13 Finally, pray for us—we have sinned against the Lord our God, and he is still angry. 14 When you go to the temple during festivals and other religious celebrations to confess your sins to the Lord, be sure to have this book read aloud.

A Prayer To Confess Sins to the Lord

The people also wrote:

15 Pray the following prayer when you confess your sins to the Lord:

The Lord our God always does right, but we are deeply ashamed of what we have done. We are the people of Judah and Jerusalem, but all of us, 16 including our kings and rulers, our priests and prophets, are guilty. Even our ancestors did what was wrong! 17 We have all sinned against the Lord our God. 18 We have disobeyed him and have refused to follow the laws he has given. 19 In fact, ever since the Lord brought our ancestors out of Egypt, we have been unfaithful and have ignored him. 20 The Lord rescued our ancestors from Egypt, so that he could give them a land that is rich with milk and honey. He also warned his servant Moses that terrible things would happen, if our ancestors refused to obey the Lord. And so, because they disobeyed him, we are suffering from those curses. 21 Even when the Lord's prophets came and told us how the Lord our God wanted us to live, we refused to listen. 22 Instead, we did what we wanted and followed our own evil ways—we worshiped other gods and did what the Lord hated.

2 That's why the Lord did everything he threatened. He punished our judges, our kings, and our leaders, as well as the people of Israel and Judah.[j] 2 The Lord severely punished the city of Jerusalem, just as he had warned in the Law of Moses. Nothing on earth has ever been as horrible as that destruction. 3 There was so little food that some of us ate our own children. 4 The Lord scattered our people all over the world, where foreign nations ruled over us and insulted and made fun of us. 5 Our country was defeated and humiliated in every way, because we had disobeyed the Lord our God and sinned against him.

A Prayer To Ask the Lord's Forgiveness

The people wrote this prayer:

6 Our Lord God, we are filled with shame, just as our ancestors were in the

[f]**1.8** *Sivan*: The third month of the Hebrew calendar, from about mid-May to mid-June.
[g]**1.8** *King Zedekiah of Judah*: Greek "King Zedekiah of Judah, the son of Josiah." [h]**1.9** *King Nebuchadnezzar of Babylonia*: Ruled 605-562 B.C. [i]**1.10** *sacrifices to please the Lord*: These sacrifices have traditionally been called "burnt offerings" because the whole animal was burned on the altar. A main purpose of such sacrifices was to please the Lord with the smell of the sacrifice, and so in the CEV they are often called "sacrifices to please the Lord." [j]**2.1** *Israel and Judah*: Israel here stands for the northern kingdom that was destroyed in 722 B.C., and Judah stands for the southern kingdom that was destroyed in 586 B.C.
1.20 Dt 28.15-68.

past. You were right 7 to punish us terribly, just as you had warned us. 8 Even then we refused to stop our evil ways and turn back to you. 9-10 All your commands are completely fair, yet we were unfaithful and rejected the Law you had given us. That's why you punished us in all these painful ways that you had kept ready for us.

11 Lord God of Israel, you brought your people out of Egypt and worked miracles to show your mighty power. You made a great name for yourself, and you are still famous.

12 But we have sinned against you, our Lord God. We have been unfaithful and have disobeyed all your commands. 13 There are only a few of us left here in the nations where you scattered us. Please stop being angry! 14 Listen to our sincere prayer and rescue us, so that you will bring honor to your name. Let those who led us away as captives have pity on us. 15 Then everyone in the world will know that you, the Lord God, have chosen the people of Israel to be your very own.

16 Look down from your home in heaven, Lord, and think about us. Listen when we call out to you. 17 Open your eyes and see how we are suffering. Those who are in the world of the dead have no life and cannot praise you or tell others how fair and just you are. 18 But even though we are in terrible pain, and we can hardly see or walk, we are alive. And so we can praise you and tell others how good you are.

19 Our Lord God, we pray for your mercy, even though our ancestors and our kings refused to do what was right. 20 You have punished us in your anger, just as your servants the prophets warned. 21 Long ago, your prophets gave us your message and told us that if we would obey the king of Babylonia and serve him, we would not be carried away from our homeland. 22 They told us that if we refused to obey you and serve the king, 23 you would make Judah and Jerusalem places of sadness where no joyful sounds are heard, even at wedding feasts. You threatened to make our country an empty wasteland.

24 We did not obey your command to serve the king of Babylonia. So you have done everything you threatened to do, just as your prophets warned. The bones of our kings and our ancestors were dug up 25 and now lie scattered all over, scorched by the sun during the day and covered with frost at night. Our ancestors died horrible deaths from starvation, war, and disease. 26 And because the people of Israel and Judah did evil, you destroyed the temple that was built in your honor, and it lies in ruins even today.

27 But you, Lord God, have shown us mercy. You are always patient and kind, 28 just as you told your servant Moses on the day you commanded him to write down your Law while our ancestors watched. Then you said:

> 29 If you refuse to obey me, I will scatter you among the nations, and this mighty nation of yours will be nothing but a handful of people. 30 Yet I know you will disobey me, because you people are stubborn! Someday, after you have been taken captive and forced to live in foreign nations, you will realize what you have done. 31 Then you will know that I am the Lord your God. I will give you a new heart, and you will be faithful and will listen to what I say. 32 There in the nation where you are living, you will praise me and turn back to me. 33 You will remember what happened to your ancestors when they sinned against me, and you will stop being stubborn and wicked. 34 Then I will let you return to the land that I promised to your ancestors Abraham, Isaac, and Jacob. You will once again rule there and increase in numbers. Never again will you be a small, powerless country. 35 I will make a solemn agreement with you, and it will last forever—I will be your God, and you will be my people. I will promise never again to take you out of the land that I have given you as your own.

3 Lord All-Powerful, God of Israel, we are worn out with trouble and distress, and we pray to you for help. 2 Though we

2.21-23 Jr 7.34; 27.10-12. **2.23** 3 Macc 1.19. **2.24** Jr 8.1, 2. **2.28,29** Dt 28.58, 62. **2.35** Jr 32.38-41.

have sinned against you, won't you answer our prayer and have mercy on us. 3 You rule as king forever, but when we die, we are gone forever. 4 So when we cry out to you, please listen. We are almost dead, because we are being punished for the sins of our ancestors. 5 Forget their sins, and think only of your own power and glory. 6 You are the Lord our God, and we will praise you. 7 You have made us fear you, so that we would pray to you. We are here as captives, yet we will praise you and turn from the sinful ways of our ancestors. 8 They sinned against you, and you have punished us by scattering us here among the nations, where we have been insulted and cursed.

Wisdom Comes from God

9 Listen carefully, people of Israel, so you can learn about wisdom and the commands that lead to life. 10 You have lived in this enemy land so long that you are now much older. You are unfit to worship the Lord and are unclean, like a dead body.[k] 11 In fact, you are almost dead yourselves! Don't you know why these things are happening to you? 12 It's because you have turned away from the only source of wisdom. 13 If you had followed the ways of God, you would have lived in peace forever. 14 Learn where wisdom, strength, and knowledge come from. Then you will know how to have a long and peaceful life, and you will find light to guide you.

15 No one knows where Wisdom[l] lives or where she keeps her treasures. 16 People have tried hard to find her, including rulers of nations, people who tamed wild animals 17 and raised birds, greedy people who did anything to get more of the silver and gold they believed would protect them, 18 and selfish people who worried about not having enough money and thought of ways to make more. But all of these people have disappeared—they died 19 and went to the world below, and others have taken their place.

20-21 Neither could any of their descendants find the way to knowledge. They couldn't find out how to gain Wisdom or even how to look for her.

22 The Canaanites and the Edomites never heard of Wisdom. 23 The Ishmaelites[m] think they have knowledge, but they haven't found Wisdom. They are just like the merchants of Merran and Teman[n] or the story-tellers or those who desire intelligence—none of them has learned the way to true Wisdom.

24 People of Israel, the universe that God has created is very large! He lives here and controls the entire world. 25 There is no end to the universe, and no one can measure its width or height. 26 Long ago, the famous giants were born here. They were powerful and skilled warriors, 27 yet God did not choose them to be his own or tell them the way to knowledge. 28 So they all died because they were fools and lacked Wisdom.

29 No one has gone up into heaven and brought Wisdom down to earth. 30 No one has sailed across the ocean and found her or bought her with pure gold. 31 There's no one who knows how to gain Wisdom or how to find the path that leads to her.

32 God alone knows Wisdom, because he knows everything. In fact, he discovered Wisdom with his own knowledge. God created the earth to last forever, and then filled it with all kinds of animals. 33 When he commanded light to shine, it trembled and obeyed, and now goes wherever he sends it. 34 Even the stars obeyed his voice, and they are happy to shine wherever and whenever he commands. 35 He is our God, and nothing is as great as he is. 36 God found the complete way to knowledge, then

[k]**3.10** *unclean, like a dead body*: One possible meaning for the difficult Greek text.
[l]**3.15** *Wisdom*: In chapters 3 and 4 the word "wisdom" is used of a supernatural being who was with God at the time of creation.
[m]**3.23** *Ishmaelites*: Greek "The descendants of Hagar" (Genesis 16.15, 16); the Ishmaelites were merchants who lived in the desert east of Israel (see Genesis 37.25).
[n]**3.23** *Merran and Teman*: Nothing is known about Merran; Teman was a town in Edom, sometimes used as the name of the northern half of the entire nation of Edom.

3.9 Pr 4.20-22. **3.15** Job 28.12, 20. **3.24,25** 3 Macc 2.9. **3.26** Gn 6.4; Ws 14.6, 7; 3 Macc 2.4.

gave it to his servant Israel, the one he
loved. 37 Since then, Wisdom has lived on
earth among human beings.

4 Wisdom is found in the book of God's
laws and teachings, and they will last
forever. Everyone who follows Wisdom will
live, but those who ignore her will die.
2 People of Israel,[o] you must turn to Wisdom and keep her with you always. Her
light shines brightly, so walk toward it.
3 Don't give away to any other nation the
glorious Wisdom that rightfully belongs to
you. 4 We should celebrate, because we are
the people of Israel, the only ones who
know what pleases God.

God Will Save Israel

5 Be brave, my people. Keep Israel's
name alive! 6 You were not sold to enemy
nations to be destroyed. Instead, those nations dragged you away as captives because
you did things that God hated. 7 God is
your Creator, yet you made him angry by
offering sacrifices to demons instead of to
him. 8 You rejected the eternal God who
gave you life. And you caused much sadness for Jerusalem, the city that was a
mother to you. 9 When she saw God punish
you in anger, she said:

Listen to me, you nearby towns.
God has made me very sad, 10 because
I have watched my children Israel being dragged away to foreign nations.
The eternal God has done this to punish them! 11 I was very happy raising
my children, but now I cry and mourn
while they are taken from me.
12 Please don't be happy about my sadness. I am a widow and a deserted
city—all of my children have been
forced to leave because they rejected
God's Law. 13 They ignored and
refused to obey his teachings. His
laws would have helped them live
right, yet my children simply refused
to obey.

14 Come and see how the eternal
God has punished my children by leading them away as captives! 15 God
brought a cruel and foreign nation
here, and it had no pity on anyone,
whether young or old. 16 That nation
stole my sons and daughters, and now
I am a lonely widow.

17 As for you, my children Israel, I
can do nothing to help you. 18 God
punished you in these terrible ways,
and now only God can rescue you from
your enemies. 19 Go on with your life,
my children—I am alone. 20 I have
taken off the clothes I wore during my
time of peace, and I have put on the
clothes that show I am in mourning. I
will cry out to the eternal God until
the day I die.

21 Be brave, my children, and beg
God to help you! He is the one who
will rescue you from your powerful enemy. 22 I know without a doubt that
the Holy and eternal God will save
you. In fact, it makes me happy to
think that he will soon show you
mercy. 23 I cried and moaned as I
watched you leave, but God will bring
you back to me, and I will celebrate
and shout forever. 24 The neighboring
cities also watched while you were
taken captive. And soon they will see
your eternal God save you with his
mighty and glorious power.

25 For now, my children, be patient.
God has punished you in anger, and
your enemies rule over you. Yet soon
they will be destroyed, and you will
have power over them. 26 My dear children, you are suffering now in a foreign nation, like sheep that have been
dragged off by an enemy.

27 Be brave and cry out to God for
help. He has not forgotten you, even
though he has done all these things to
punish you. 28 Just as you were determined to turn away from God in the
past, you should be ten times more
determined to obey him now. 29 The
same God who punished you with
these disasters will save you and give
you never-ending happiness.

[o] **4.2** *Israel*: The Greek text has "Jacob," which was the name of the nation's ancestor before God renamed him.

4.1 Si 24.23. **4.19** 2 Esd 2.2.

God Will Comfort Jerusalem

30 City of Jerusalem, be brave! Your God
chose you long ago as his own, and he will
soon comfort you. 31 Disaster will come to
those nations who mistreated you and celebrated your destruction. 32 The cities that
made your children their slaves will one
day be miserable, and the city of Babylon,
where your people now live, will suffer
pain. 33 Babylon was glad when you fell and
were destroyed; now she will moan at her
own destruction. 34 God will turn her pride
into mourning, and she will no longer be
proud of her great people. 35 The eternal
God will send down fire, and she will burn
for days and days, until nothing can live
there except demons.

36-37 Jerusalem, look toward the east
and be glad, because God is bringing your
children home! They were once dragged
away as captives, yet at his command they
are now gathered together from the east
and the west and are praising God's glorious power.

5 Jerusalem, take off the clothes that
show you are sad and mourning. Put
on the beautiful clothes of God's bright
glory and never take them off! 2 Wear the
robe of God's justice and the crown of his
eternal power. 3 God will let every nation
on earth see your brightness, 4 and he will
give you this new name forever: "Right-
Living-Brings-Peace and Faith-in-God-
Brings-Honor."

5 So stand on top of the mountain and
look east. Our Holy God has gathered your
children from the east and the west, and
they are celebrating because he hasn't forgotten them. 6 Their enemies forced them
to leave on foot, and now God will bring
them back to you with great honor, as if
they were kings being carried on beautiful
thrones. 7 He has commanded every high
mountain and ancient hill to be made low,
and every valley to be filled up, so that the
people of Israel can return home safely on
level ground. They will show God's glory to
the world. 8 God has commanded every forest and every sweet-smelling tree to shade
the Israelites 9 as he leads them home, and
they will celebrate and shout for joy on
their way. The brightness of God's own
glory will guide them, and his mercy and
justice will go with them.

5.1,2 Is 52.1; 61.3, 10; Rev 21.2. **5.6-9** 3 Macc 7.16.

LETTER OF JEREMIAH

ABOUT THIS BOOK

The Letter of Jeremiah is written as though the prophet Jeremiah was its author. It is addressed to the people of Judah and Jerusalem, just as they were taken away as captives to Babylonia. There they would see the Babylonians worshiping many idols. But this book encourages the Israelites to worship only the Lord, because idols are not gods; they can do nothing, and so there is no reason to fear them. The Letter of Jeremiah is sometimes considered to be chapter 6 of the book of Baruch.

A QUICK LOOK AT THIS BOOK

- Worship Only the Lord (1-7)
- Idols Cannot Protect Themselves (8-29)
- Idols Cannot Help Anyone (30-44)
- Idols Are Powerless (45-73)

This is a copy of the letter that Jeremiah the prophet sent to the people of Judah and Jerusalem, just before the king of Babylonia took them as captives to the city of Babylon. The letter contains the message that God sent Jeremiah to tell them.

Worship Only the Lord

2 You have sinned against God! That's
why King Nebuchadnezzar of Babylonia[a] is
taking you as captives to Babylon. 3 You will
be forced to live there a very long time—as
long as seven generations. Then God will
lead you home in peace.
4 While you are in Babylon, you will see
people carrying around idols made of silver
and gold and wood. The people worship
these so-called gods out of fear that something terrible might happen if they refuse.
5 Don't act like these heathens or be frightened into worshiping their idols. 6 When
you see crowds worshiping idols, tell yourselves to worship only the Lord, 7 and
God's angel will help you.

Idols Are Not Gods

8 Idols are not really gods—they can't
even talk! They are covered with gold and
silver, and their tongues were carved out of
wood. 9 People make gold crowns like the
ones young women love to wear, and they
put these crowns on their idols. 10 Sometimes the priests steal the gold and silver
from these idols and spend it on themselves 11 or give it to temple prostitutes.[b]
People dress up their idols as if they
were human, even though they are nothing
but chunks of silver or gold or wood.
12 They cannot even protect themselves
from rust and decay.[c] They are decorated
with purple robes, 13 but someone needs to
wipe off their faces when dust from the
temple settles on them. 14 These idols hold
a scepter[d] in their hands, just like human
judges, yet these idols have no power to

[a]**2** *King Nebuchadnezzar of Babylonia*: Ruled 605-562 B.C. [b]**11** *prostitutes*: Young women sometimes served as prostitutes in the worship of foreign gods, but the Lord had forbidden the people of Israel and Judah to worship in this way (see Deuteronomy 23.17, 18). [c]**12** *decay*: One possible meaning for the difficult Greek text. [d]**14** *scepter*: A symbol of a ruler's power.

1 Jr 29.1, 2.

punish any criminal. 15 Some of them even hold small swords or axes, but they cannot defend themselves from being destroyed in war or stolen. 16 All of this proves that idols are not gods. So don't fear them!

Idols Cannot Protect Themselves

17 A broken dish is useless! 18 And so are the idols in the temples. They can't see, because their eyes are covered with the dust that people stir up when they walk. These idols are locked up in their temples like prisoners about to be put to death for committing a crime against the king. They can't protect the temples, so the priests must close the heavy doors and lock them with bolts to keep robbers out. 19 The priests light more lamps in honor of the idols than they do for themselves, yet the idols can't see even one of them. 20 These idols are nothing but wood, just like the beams in the temple, and their insides and their clothes are eaten by worms and insects. They don't even know 21 when the smoke in the temple makes their faces black. 22 Bats, swallows, and other birds perch on their heads and bodies, and cats sleep on them. 23 All this proves that idols are not gods. So don't fear them!

Idols Are Not Alive

24-25 No matter how much money it took to make these idols, there is no life in them. They didn't feel a thing when they were being made out of melted gold poured into molds—even the gold used to make them beautiful must be polished before it shines.[e] 26 They are so helpless that they must be carried around—they can't walk on their own.

People who worship idols are put to shame, 27 because whenever an idol falls, someone has to pick it up. And after someone sets it back up, the idol cannot move itself anywhere. Even if an idol starts to lean, it cannot straighten itself up.

Offering gifts to an idol is no better than giving gifts to a dead body.[f] 28 The priests sell the sacrifices that have been offered to these idols and spend the money on themselves. And their wives use salt to preserve the meat that is left over from the sacrifices, then save it for their own use, instead of giving it to the poor. 29 Women who are having their monthly periods or who have just given birth are even allowed to touch the sacrifices offered to these idols.[g] Such things prove that idols are not gods. So don't fear them!

Idols Cannot Help Anyone

30 How could these idols of silver and gold and wood ever be gods, when women are allowed to make offerings to them?[h] 31 The priests shave their beards and hair when they mourn, then they go to the temples in torn clothes, where they sit with their heads uncovered. 32 They moan and shout in the temples of these idols, just as some people do at a funeral. 33 They even take some of the idols' clothes and give them to their own wives and children. 34 You see, it doesn't matter how anyone treats these idols—they cannot reward or punish in return.

Idols aren't able to help anyone become king or take away a king's power. 35 They can't make people rich or force them to pay for not keeping a promise. 36 These idols cannot keep anyone from dying or protect the weak from the strong. 37 They can't give sight to a blind person or rescue someone from danger 38 or show mercy to widows and orphans. 39 These idols are nothing but chunks of wood covered with gold and silver. They are no more powerful than stones dug from a mountain, and all who worship them will be put to shame. 40 Only a fool would think that these idols should be called gods!

The Babylonians Are Foolish Enough To Worship Idols

The Babylonians dishonor their own gods by deserting them when they are unable to help. For example, when the Babylonians see a person who cannot talk, they ask the god Bel to heal that person, as if

[e]**24,25** *even the gold . . . shines*: One possible meaning for the difficult Greek text. [f]**27** *Offering gifts . . . dead body*: Or "People offer gifts to these idols just as they do to people who have died."
[g]**29** *Women . . . idols*: This was forbidden by the Law of Moses (see Leviticus 12.1-8).
[h]**30** *women . . . them*: Only men were allowed to make offerings in the Lord's temple.

Bel can really hear and understand. 41 But when the Babylonians realize these gods have no sense, they just leave them.[i]

42 Some Babylonian women wrap cords around their heads as a decoration,[j] then they sit along the roads, burning incense and offering themselves as prostitutes.[k] 43 And after one of them returns from sleeping with a stranger, that prostitute makes fun of the one sitting next to her for not being pretty enough to be chosen.

44 Everything the Babylonians do to serve their idols is useless. How could anyone ever believe that idols are gods?

Idols Are Made by Humans

45 Idols are made by woodworkers and metalworkers, and so the idols always turn out to be exactly what the workers want. 46 These workers are humans and die like everyone else. 47 How could they ever make a god? The only thing they can leave for future generations is deceit and disgrace.

48 When war or trouble comes, priests must decide where they will go to escape and hide with their so-called gods. 49 The idols cannot save themselves from war or trouble because they aren't gods.

50 Idols are nothing more than wood covered with gold and silver. Someday people will finally realize that they are fake. 51 People from every nation, including kings, will know that these powerless idols were made by human hands. 52 Everyone will realize that they are not gods.[l]

Idols Are Powerless

53 Idols don't have the power to make someone king or to send rain. 54 They can't make their own decisions or free a person who has been wronged. They are powerless 55 and as useless as crows flying through the air.

If a temple catches on fire, the priests will run to safety. But since the idols are merely wood covered with gold or silver, they will burn like logs.

56 Since idols cannot oppose an enemy or a king, it's foolish to believe they are gods.

57 These wooden idols covered with silver and gold cannot even protect themselves from thieves, 58 who strip off the silver and gold, as well as the clothes. All of it can be easily carried off by robbers because these false gods can do nothing to stop them.

59 Anything is better than an idol, including a brave king, a household pot, a door that protects things in a house, or a wooden column in a palace. All these are more useful than false gods.

60-61 The sun, moon, and stars, as well as the lightning and the wind, all do what they are supposed to do. 62-63 And when God tells clouds to cover the earth or commands fire to burn forests, they also obey. But idols cannot do a thing! 64 No one should ever believe that idols are gods. They can't help anyone or make decisions about justice. 65 You know they are not gods, so why fear them?

66 Idols cannot punish or bless kings, 67 and they can't make strange things happen in the sky. They don't shine like the sun or the moon. 68 Even wild animals are better off than idols—at least they can run to protect themselves from danger. 69 Nothing shows that these idols are gods. So don't fear them!

70 The Babylonian gods are pieces of wood covered with gold and silver, and they are as helpless as a scarecrow guarding a cucumber patch. 71 They are like a thornbush that birds use as a place to perch or like a dead body thrown out into the darkness. 72 The purple linen[m] robes they wear will rot—this also proves they are not really gods. Someday the idols themselves will waste away to nothing, and they will be a disgrace to their worshipers.

73 People who do right have no use at all for idols. And these people are better off, because they will never be put to shame.

[i]**41** *them*: One possible meaning for the difficult Greek text of verse 41. [j]**42** *Babylonian women . . . decoration*: One possible meaning for the difficult Greek text. [k]**42** *prostitutes*: See the note at verse 11. [l]**52** *gods*: One possible meaning for the difficult Greek text of verse 52. [m]**72** *linen*: One possible meaning for the difficult Greek text.

41 Is 46.1.

PRAYER OF AZARIAH and SONG OF THE THREE HEBREWS

ABOUT THIS BOOK

The ancient Greek translation of Daniel includes three additions that are not in the Hebrew text. The first of these is called the Prayer of Azariah and the Song of the Three Hebrews, and it is found in between 3.23 and 3.24 of the Hebrew version. The second addition is Susanna, and the third is Bel and the Dragon. The *CEV* translates these additions from the Greek version known as Theodotion, since that was the version of Daniel used most often by the early church.

This first addition begins just after Hananiah, Mishael, and Azariah were thrown into the flaming furnace. Azariah confessed that the entire nation of Israel had sinned, and he admitted that God was right to punish them. But he also prayed that God would help Israel and crush those who had harmed them.

Although Azariah doesn't directly ask God to rescue him and his two friends, God sent an angel to cool the furnace so the flames would not harm them. Then the three Hebrews together sang praises to God and called on every part of creation to join with them:

So praise the Lord
for his goodness,
and praise him for his mercy,
because it will never end.
(67)

A QUICK LOOK AT THIS BOOK

- The Prayer of Azariah (1-27)
- The Song of the Three Hebrews (28-68)

The Prayer of Azariah

1 Hananiah, Mishael, and Azariah[a]
walked around in the flames, singing
praises to the Lord God. 2 Then Azariah
stood still and prayed out loud:

3 You, Lord God of our ancestors,
are worthy to be praised,
and your name
should be honored forever.
4 Everything you do is right;
your decisions bring justice.

5 You were right to punish us
and to destroy holy Jerusalem,
the city of our ancestors.

---

[a]1 *Hananiah, Mishael, and Azariah*: Their Hebrew names; they were also known by the Babylonian names Shadrach, Meshach, and Abednego (see Daniel 1.6, 7).

1 Dn 3.23.

Our people have sinned;
6 we have broken all your laws
and turned away from you.
7 We have disobeyed,
even though your commands
were for our own good.

8 You were right to punish us
9 and to let us be conquered
by our hateful enemies.
They refuse to obey your Law,
and the most evil king on earth
is their ruler.
10 They insult us, your servants.
We are a disgrace
and have no excuse.

But we worship and obey you.
11 Please, Lord, for the sake
of your reputation,
keep your agreement with us,
and someday set us free.
12 You loved Abraham;
Isaac obeyed you,
and you chose Jacob.[b]
For their sakes, don't take
your mercy from us.
13 You promised to give them
more descendants
than there are stars in the sky
or grains of sand on a beach.

14 But we sinned,
and so we have become
the smallest nation.
We are ashamed
15 because we have no rulers,
no prophets, no leaders.
We have no incense, no altar,
and no sacrifices to please you
or to ask for your mercy.
16 But if we are humble
and truly sorry for our sins,
17 you will accept us
as if we had offered
a thousand rams and bulls
and ten thousand fat lambs.

You never disappoint those
who trust you, Lord.
We want to be your followers,[c]
so please answer our prayer.
18 We promise with all our hearts
to worship and obey you
and to continue praying.
19 So please be patient with us
and show us your mercy.
20 Work a miracle and rescue us,
so that you, Lord,
will be honored.
21 We, your servants, pray
that those who have harmed us
will be disgraced;
crush their mighty power
so they will fail.
22 Show them that you alone
are the glorious Lord God,
the Ruler of all the earth.

An Angel Comes into the Fire

23 After the king's servants threw Hananiah, Mishael, and Azariah into the furnace, the servants kept tossing in oil, tar,
dried flax plants, and small pieces of firewood. 24 The flames blazed up seventy-five
feet above the furnace, 25 and they also
shot out from the furnace and burned the
Babylonians who were standing nearby.
26 But one of the Lord's angels came down
into the furnace to protect Azariah and his
two friends. The angel forced the flames
out of the furnace, 27 so that the inside of
the furnace felt as if a cool breeze were
blowing. The fire didn't touch the three
men at all, and it caused them no pain or
trouble.

The Song of the Three Hebrews

28 Then Hananiah, Mishael, and
Azariah praised God together in the furnace, and they sang:

29 You, Lord God of our ancestors,
are always worthy
to be praised.
30 Your glorious and holy name
will always deserve
the greatest honor.
31 So let songs of praise
be sung in your holy temple

[b]**12** *Jacob*: The Greek text has "Israel," another name for Jacob, the third great ancestor of the nation of Israel. [c]**17** *We want to be your followers*: One possible meaning for the difficult Greek text.
23-27 3 Macc 6.6. **26** Tb 5.4.

for all time.
*32 There, from your throne
above the winged creatures,
33 you watch everything on earth
and rule the world
with glory and majesty.
We pray that your praises
will be sung forever.
34 And age after age
in the starry skies,
songs will be sung
to honor you.

Sing Praises to the Lord

Hananiah, Mishael, and Azariah continued to sing:

35 All of creation
should sing praises
to the Lord forever.

*36 Everything in the heavens
and the water above the sky[d]
*37 should sing praises
to the Lord forever.
*38 The angels and the rulers
in the heavens
39 should sing praises
to the Lord forever.
*40 The sun, the moon,
41 and the stars
should sing praises
to the Lord forever.
*42 The wind and the rain
43 and the dew,
*44 as well as the freezing snow,
*45 and the fiery heat
46 should sing praises
to the Lord forever.
*47 The dark of night
and the light of day
48 should sing praises
to the Lord forever.
*49 The frost and snow,
*50 the icy cold,
51 and the thunderstorms
should sing praises
to the Lord forever.[e]
52 Everything on this earth
should sing praises
to the Lord forever.
*53 The mountains and hills
54 and all trees and plants
should sing praises
to the Lord forever.
*55 The springs and rivers,
*56 together with the oceans
57 and every sea creature,
whether large or small,
should sing praises
to the Lord forever.
*58 Each bird in the sky,
59 and every animal,
wild or tame,
should sing praises
to the Lord forever.

60 Every human should sing praises
to the Lord forever,
*61 especially his priests
62 and his chosen people.
*63 We humans should be humble
*64 and obey the Lord
65 with all our heart and soul,
and we should sing praises
to him forever.

66 The three of us—
Hananiah, Azariah,
and Mishael—
should sing praises
to the Lord forever,
because if he hadn't rescued us,
we would have died
in a flaming furnace
and gone down
to the world of the dead.
67 So praise the Lord
for his goodness,
and praise him for his mercy,
because it will never end.

68 Everyone who worships the Lord,
the Supreme God,
should sing his praises
and thank him for his mercy,
because it will never end.

[d]**36-39** *water above the sky*: See Genesis 1.6-8. [e]**42-51** *forever*: Some Greek manuscripts and ancient translations put these verses in different orders.

SUSANNA

ABOUT THIS BOOK

This story is chapter 13 in the ancient Greek translation of the book of Daniel, but it isn't found in the Hebrew original. See also "About This Book" for the Prayer of Azariah and the Song of the Three Hebrews.

Susanna was a Jewish woman who lived in Babylon. She was very beautiful, and two judges tried to force her to have sex with them. She refused, and they falsely accused her of being unfaithful to her husband. Susanna was put on trial and condemned to die, but Daniel stepped in and showed that she was innocent. Susanna was rescued, because she obeyed God and trusted him. As she told the two judges when they tried to force her to disobey God's law:

> *. . . it is better to refuse and to suffer what you can do to me, than to sin against God.*
>
> *(23)*

A QUICK LOOK AT THIS BOOK

- Susanna Introduced (1-5)
- Two Judges Try To Force Susanna To Have Sex (6-27)
- Susanna's Trial (28-41)
- Daniel Rescues Susanna (42-64)

Daniel Rescues Susanna

1 A man named Joakim lived in the city of Babylon 2 and was married to a very beautiful woman, Susanna the daughter of Hilkiah. Susanna faithfully worshiped the Lord 3 and obeyed the Law of Moses, just as she had been taught by her parents, who were very religious.

4 Joakim was very rich and had a large walled garden[a] next to his house. He was the most highly honored Jewish man in Babylon, and all the other Jews would come and talk with him.

5 One year, two of the older Jewish leaders were appointed to be judges for their community in Babylon. The Lord had said he would punish older leaders who refused to obey his laws and rule the people wisely.[b] And that is exactly what these leaders did.

6 The two judges spent so much time at Joakim's house that people went there to have their cases judged. 7 Each day, the people left the house at noon, then Susanna would go for a walk in her husband's garden. 8 The two men watched her every day as she walked in the garden, and soon all they could think about was sleeping with her. 9 They even stopped praying to God and forgot that they were supposed to be fair when they judged legal cases. 10-11 Each of them was so ashamed of his desire for her, that they didn't tell the other how they felt. 12 Day after day they would wait around, hoping to get a look at her.

13 One day at noon, they said, "It's

[a]4 *large walled garden*: It seems to have contained a pool of water where Susanna could bathe on warm days (see verses 15-17), several varieties of trees (see verses 53-58), and probably bushes and other plants. [b]5 *older leaders . . . wisely*: This may be a reference to Jeremiah 29.20-23.

lunchtime—let's go home." They left in different directions, [14] but before long they both turned around and went back to Joakim's house. They saw one another, and each started asking the other why he had come back. Finally, they both admitted that they wanted to sleep with Susanna, and they agreed to find a time when they could catch her alone.

[15] The two men watched for their chance, and one hot day, Susanna went into the garden to take a bath. Two of her servant girls were there with her, [16] though no one else was in the garden, except the two men, who were watching her from their hiding place. [17] Susanna told her servants, "Bring me some soap and lotion, then close the gates to the garden so I can bathe."[c]

[18] The servants did what she said. They shut the main gates to the garden, then they went into the house through the side gate and brought her some soap and lotion. But they did not see the two men.

[19] As soon as the servants had gone, the men left their hiding places. They ran over to Susanna [20] and said, "Look, the gates are shut, and no one can see us here in the garden. We both want you, and so you had better agree to what we want! [21] If you refuse, we will testify in court that we saw you send your servant girls away so you could make love with a young man."

[22] "I'm trapped, and there's no way out," Susanna moaned. "If I give in to you, I could be put to death.[d] If I refuse, you will have me killed. [23] But it is better to refuse and to suffer what you can do to me, than to sin against God."

[24] Susanna screamed for help,[e] and the two leaders began shouting at her. [25] One of them ran to the main gates of the garden and opened them. [26] The household servants heard the noise, and they all rushed in through the side gate to see what had happened to Susanna. [27] But when they heard the two men accusing her, the servants were ashamed. No one had ever said such things about Susanna before.

[28] The next day, the Jewish people in Babylon came together at Joakim's house. The two men also arrived, ready to go ahead with their terrible plans to have Susanna put to death. [29] They went to the front of the crowd and said, "Someone bring in Joakim's wife Susanna, the daughter of Hilkiah."

[30] Susanna came in, along with her parents, her children, and all her relatives. [31] Susanna was a beautiful woman with a very good figure. [32] When she came in, her face was covered with a veil. But the two evil men wanted to get one last good look at her, so they ordered her to take off her veil. [33] Susanna's family was crying, and so was everyone else.

[34] The two men stood in the middle of the group and put their hands on Susanna's head, so they could officially accuse her.[f] [35] But Susanna trusted the Lord to rescue her, and as she cried, she looked up toward heaven. [36] Then the two men said:

> While we were walking in the garden, Susanna came in with two servant girls. She shut the gates and told them to leave. [37] Then a young man came out of hiding and went over to her, and they lay down and started making love. [38] We were over in the corner of the garden, and we realized they were disobeying God's Law, so we ran over to them. [39] We saw them making love, but we weren't able to catch the young man, because he was stronger than we were. He opened the gates and ran off.
>
> [40] We grabbed Susanna and asked her who the young man was, [41] but she refused to tell us. We swear that we are telling the truth.

Both men were leaders and judges, and

[c] **17** *close the gates . . . bathe*: The garden was probably surrounded by high stone walls with solid wood gates, so Susanna thought she would have privacy. [d] **22** *put to death*: If a woman was unfaithful to her husband, she could be put to death (see Deuteronomy 22.22). [e] **24** *screamed for help*: Susanna could not be considered innocent if she did not scream for help (see Deuteronomy 22.23, 24). [f] **34** *put their hands . . . accuse her*: It was a custom for the accusers in a trial to place their hands on the head of the accused (see Leviticus 24.14).

22 Lv 20.10; Dt 22.22.

so everyone believed them and agreed that
Susanna should be put to death.
42 Susanna cried out, "Eternal God, you
know all secrets and everything that will
happen in the future. 43 You know that these
two men have told evil lies against me in
court today. Now I am going to be killed, even
though I haven't done anything wrong."
44 The Lord heard Susanna's prayer,
45 and as she was being led away to be
executed, he chose a young man named
Daniel to help her. Daniel was upset 46 and
shouted, "I will not take part in murdering
this woman!"
47 The crowd turned to him and asked,
"What do you mean?"
48 Daniel went to the center of the
crowd and said, "People of Israel, are you
fools? You have condemned one of your
own women to death, and you haven't even
tried to find out what really happened.
49 Go back to court, and I will prove that
the two men who accused Susanna were
lying."
50 Everyone rushed back to the place
where the trial was held, and the group of
leaders told Daniel, "So God has chosen
you to be a leader, too! Sit down and tell us
what you mean."
51 Daniel said, "Separate the two men
who accused Susanna, and take them far
enough away that they can't hear us. Then
I will call them over one at a time and
question them."
52 When the two had been taken to different places, Daniel called the first one
over and said:

You are an evil old man, and it's
clear that you've been sinning for a
long time. 53 You've been giving unfair
decisions in court. You have set the
guilty free and condemned innocent
people, even though the Lord said not
to put an innocent person to death.
54 Now, you have testified that Susanna was making love with a young
man under a tree. So tell us, what kind
of a tree was it?

"It was a small gum tree," the man answered.
55 "Is that so?" Daniel replied. "You will
pay for that lie with your head! God has already sent his angel to cut you in half."[g]
56 Daniel ordered the people to take the
first man aside and to bring over the second one. Daniel told him:

You're not a Jew; you're a filthy
Canaanite! You were under the spell of
Susanna's beauty, and your desire for
her made you do wrong instead of
right. 57 You two men have been frightening women from Israel into sleeping
with you. But this faithful Jewish
woman wouldn't stand for your evil
ways. 58 Now tell me, when Susanna
and this young man were making love,
what tree were they under?

"They were under a big oak tree," the
man answered.
59 "Is that so?" Daniel replied. "You will
pay for that lie with your head! The Lord's
angel is waiting to chop you in half,[h] and
then both of you leaders will be dead."
60 The crowd shouted praises to God,
because he rescues those who trust him.
61-62 Then they condemned the two leaders, since their answers to Daniel's questions proved that they had lied in court to
have Susanna killed. The Law of Moses
says that anyone who does this should be
put to death,[i] and that is what quickly happened to the two men. And so an innocent
woman's life was saved.
63 Susanna's father and mother praised
God, and so did her husband Joakim and
all her relatives, because she had been
found innocent of a shameful crime.
64 And from then on, Daniel was famous.

[g] **54,55** *small gum tree . . . cut you in half*: In Greek, the word for "small gum tree" sounds like the word for "cut in half." [h] **58,59** *big oak tree . . . chop you in half*: In Greek, the word for "big oak tree" sounds like the word for "chop in half." [i] **61,62** *Law of Moses . . . put to death*: See Deuteronomy 19.16-21.

53 Ex 23.7. **61,62** Dt 19.16-21.

BEL AND THE DRAGON

ABOUT THIS BOOK

This brief book is actually chapter 14 in the ancient Greek translation of Daniel, but it isn't found in the Hebrew original. See also "About This Book" for the Prayer of Azariah and the Song of the Three Hebrews.

Daniel is the hero of the two short stories in the book, and both of the stories make fun of worshiping false gods. In the first story, Daniel outsmarts the priests of Bel, the chief god of Babylonia. Every day, the Babylonians brought a large amount of food to the idol. The food was always eaten by the next morning, but Daniel proves that it was being eaten by the priests and their families, not the idol. The priests were killed, and the idol was destroyed.

In the second story, Daniel kills a creature worshiped by the Babylonians, proving to the king that the creature wasn't a god. The creature is called a dragon, which may refer to a huge snake.

The Babylonians were furious that two of their gods had been destroyed, and they forced the king to throw Daniel into a pit where lions were kept. God protected and rescued Daniel, then the king admitted:

You, the Lord God of Daniel, are powerful! You alone are the true God!
(41)

A QUICK LOOK AT THIS BOOK

- Bel (1-22)
- The Dragon (23-27)
- Daniel Is Rescued from the Pit of Lions (28-42)

Daniel Defeats the Priests of Bel

1 When King Astyages was buried in the tomb with his ancestors, Cyrus the Persian took his place as king.[a] 2 Daniel was a friend and advisor of King Cyrus, and the king honored him more than anyone else.

3 Every day, the Babylonians took food to the idol of their god Bel.[b] They brought six hundred pounds of the best wheat flour, fifty gallons of wine, and the meat from forty sheep.

4 King Cyrus believed that Bel was a powerful god, and he worshiped the idol every day, but Daniel worshiped only his own God. One day, Cyrus asked Daniel, "Why don't you worship Bel?"

5 Daniel answered, "I refuse to worship idols—they are made by humans. Instead, I worship the living God, because he created heaven and earth, and he rules everyone who lives."

6 "But, Daniel," the king replied, "isn't Bel a living god? Haven't you seen how much he eats and drinks each day?"

[a]**1** *King Astyages . . . king*: Astyages was the last king of Media. He was defeated in battle in 550 B.C. by his grandson Cyrus the Great, the king of Persia, who then became king of the Medes and the Persians and ruled until 530 B.C. [b]**3** *Bel*: Another name for Marduk, the chief god of Babylonia. Bel means "lord."

3 Is 46.1; Jr 51.44.

7 Daniel laughed and said, "Don't be fooled, Your Majesty. That idol is merely clay on the inside and bronze on the outside! It never ate or drank anything."

8 This made the king angry. So he called in his priests and told them, "Prove to me that Bel[c] is eating all this food! If you can't, then you will die. 9 But if you can prove that Bel really is eating the food, then Daniel will die, because he has insulted the god Bel."

Daniel said, "Your Majesty, that sounds fair enough to me."

10 Now there were seventy priests of Bel, and they and their wives had lots of children.

The king went with Daniel into the temple of Bel, 11 and the priests said, "Your Majesty, we will go outside now. Please set out the food and the wine yourself, then shut the door. Drip some hot wax along the edge of the door and press your ring into the wax to leave your special mark. This will show that only you are allowed to open the door.[d] 12 When you come back in the morning, if you find that Bel hasn't eaten everything, then you can put us to death. But if the food is gone, this will prove Daniel has been lying, and you can put him to death."

13 The priests were not worried at all. They had a secret trap door under the table, and that was how they sneaked into the temple every night to eat the food.

14 The priests left, and the king arranged Bel's food on the table. Then Daniel told his servants to scatter ashes over the temple floor. The king was the only other person who saw them do this. They shut the door as they went outside, and the king placed his special mark on some hot wax along the edge of the door so that they could tell if the door had been opened. Then they all left.

15 Later that night, the priests and their wives and children went to the temple as they always did, and they ate and drank everything.

16 Early the next morning, the king brought Daniel to the temple 17 and asked him, "Daniel, has the wax been broken? Has the door been opened?"

"No, Your Majesty," Daniel answered.

18 As soon as the door was opened,[e] the king looked at the empty table and shouted, "Bel, you are a great god, and you always tell the truth!"

19 Daniel just laughed. He kept the king from entering the temple and said, "Look at the floor—I wonder who left all those footprints?"

20 The king said, "I can see the footprints of men, women, and children!" 21 He was furious and told his guards to arrest the priests along with their wives and children. Then the priests showed him the secret door that they used when they sneaked into the temple to eat the food that was on Bel's table.

22 The king told his guards to kill the priests and their families. Then he gave the temple and the idol of Bel to Daniel, who had them destroyed.

Daniel Kills the Dragon

23 The Babylonians also worshiped a huge dragon[f] as a god, 24 and the king of Babylonia said to Daniel, "You can't say this god isn't alive! So you ought to worship it."

25 Daniel answered, "I worship the Lord, because he is the living God. 26 Your Majesty, if you will give me permission, I will kill this dragon, without striking it with a sword or a club."

"I give you permission to try," the king replied.

27 Daniel put some tar and animal fat and hair in a pot and boiled them together. Then he shaped the mixture into cakes that looked something like loaves of barley bread and fed them to the dragon. It swelled up and burst open, and Daniel

[c] **8** *Prove to me that Bel*: Greek "Tell me who." [d] **11** *Drip some hot wax . . . open the door*: The king's ring had a special design on it, and he pressed the ring into the soft, hot wax. Then, after the wax cooled, the door could not be opened without breaking the wax. [e] **18** *door was opened*: Greek "doors were opened." [f] **23** *dragon*: Or "snake"; the Greek word can refer either to a snake or to an imaginary snake-like monster. The snake may have represented the Babylonian goddess Tiamat.

said, "Take a look at what you Babylonians
worship."
28 But when the Babylonians heard
what had happened, they were so upset
with the king that they began plotting
against him. "Has the king become a Jew?"
they asked each other. "First he destroyed
our idol Bel and killed its priests. And now
he has killed our dragon-god."
29 The Babylonians went to the king and
said, "Hand Daniel over to us. If you don't,
we will kill you and everyone in your family!"
30 The king saw that he really had no
choice, and so he was forced to let them
have Daniel.
31-32 The Babylonians kept seven lions
in a large pit and fed them two people and
two sheep each day. Daniel was thrown into
this pit, and for the next six days the lions
were given no other food. The Babylonians
wanted to make sure that the lions would
eat Daniel.
33 Meanwhile, far away in Judea, the
prophet Habakkuk had made a pot of stew
and put some pieces of bread into a bowl.
He was about to take it to the workers
who were harvesting wheat in the fields,
34 when an angel told him, "Take this meal
to the lion pit in Babylon, and give it to
Daniel."
35 Habakkuk replied, "But, sir, I've never
been to Babylon, and I don't know where
the lion pit is."
36 The angel lifted up Habakkuk by his
hair and carried him to Babylon as fast as
the wind. He set Habakkuk down at the
edge of the lion pit, 37 and Habakkuk
shouted, "Daniel, take this food that God
has sent you."
38 Daniel prayed, "Thank you, God, for
remembering me. You always take care of
those who love you."
39 Daniel got up and ate the food, while
God's angel quickly returned Habakkuk to
his home.
40 Seven days later, the king came to the
lion pit to mourn for Daniel. But when he
looked into the pit, he saw Daniel sitting
there, alive. 41 Then the king shouted out
this prayer: "You, the Lord God of Daniel,
are powerful! You alone are the true God!"
42 The king had Daniel pulled up out of
the pit, then he arrested the men who had
tried to have Daniel killed. The king had
them thrown into the pit, and he watched
the lions gobble them down.

31,32 Dn 6.16-24. **36** Ez 8.3.

1 MACCABEES

ABOUT THIS BOOK

First Maccabees covers the period 175-134 B.C. and tells the story of the Jewish revolt against the Greek kings that had ruled Palestine since the death of Alexander the Great in 323 B.C. At first, Palestine had been under the rule of the kings of Egypt, but in 201 B.C., the kings of Syria had taken control of the area.

According to this book, the revolt was begun in 167 B.C. by an old priest named Mattathias and was continued by his sons, who one after the other gave their lives for the freedom of Israel. The first of the brothers was Judas, whose nickname "the Maccabee" has been applied to all the brothers, and so it has become the title by which this book is known. The nickname could possibly mean "the hammer," but more probably it means "chosen by the Lord."

After the brothers and their army had captured and rededicated the temple to the Lord and had established their military control over parts of Palestine, they also used political methods to help increase their power. For example, they became friends and allies of Rome and Sparta, and when more than one man claimed to be the rightful king of Syria, the brothers would support one or the other in return for more power or more freedoms for the Jews.

The later part of the rule of Simon, the last of the brothers, was remembered as a time of peace and prosperity:

Life was peaceful on the farms;
the earth produced grain,
and fruit grew on the trees.
In towns the old folks
talked about the good things
that had happened,
while young soldiers strolled by
in their fancy uniforms.
(14.8, 9)

A QUICK LOOK AT THIS BOOK

- The Jews Suffer under the Greek Kings of Syria (1.1-64)
- Mattathias Leads a Rebellion (2.1-70)
- Judas Becomes the Leader of the Jews (3.1—4.35)
- The Temple Is Rededicated to the Lord (4.36-61)
- Judas and His Brothers Continue the War (5.1—7.50)
- Judas Makes an Agreement with Rome (8.1-32)
- The Death of Judas (9.1-22)
- Jonathan Leads the Jews (9.23—11.74)
- Jonathan Makes Treaties with Rome and Sparta (12.1-23)
- Jonathan Is Captured (12.24-53)
- Jonathan Dies, and Simon Becomes Leader of the Jews (13.1—14.3)
- Simon Is Honored (14.4-49)
- Quarrels with Syria Continue (15.1-41)
- Simon Dies, and His Son John Becomes Leader (16.1-24)

Alexander the Great

1 Alexander the Great[a] led his army
from Macedonia to attack Darius, the
king of Persia and Media. He conquered
Darius and became the first Greek to rule
that part of the world.[b] 2 Alexander fought
a lot of wars; he captured strong fortresses
and put kings to death. 3 In fact, he went
across the whole earth and took the treasures of many countries.

Every nation on earth surrendered to
Alexander, and he became very famous, but
also very arrogant. 4 He got together a powerful army and conquered lands, nations,
and rulers, forcing them all to pay taxes
to him.

5-7 Alexander had ruled for twelve years,
when he became sick and knew he was going to die. So he called together some of
the men who had grown up with him. They
were now his most famous generals, and he
gave each one a part of his kingdom.

8 The generals each took control of their
countries. 9 Then after Alexander's death,
they crowned themselves kings. Their descendants also ruled as kings[c] for many
years and caused trouble all over the world.

Antiochus Epiphanes and the Jewish Nation

(2 Maccabees 4.7-17)

10 Antiochus Epiphanes,[d] the evil son of
King Antiochus the Third[e] of Syria, was a
descendant of one of these generals and
had been a hostage in Rome.[f] Then in the
year 137[g] of the Syrian Kingdom, he became its ruler.

11 About this time, some worthless Jews
rejected God's Law and talked many others
into following them by saying, "Let's make
an agreement with the Gentiles around
here. We've had nothing but trouble ever
since we stopped cooperating with them."

12 Many of the people thought this was a
good idea, 13 and with great enthusiasm
they went to King Antiochus, who gave
them permission to live like Gentiles.

14 So these Jews built a place in
Jerusalem just like those in Gentile cities
where young men exercise in the nude.
15 Some of them even had surgery to keep
anyone from knowing that they had ever
been circumcised. And so, they broke their
agreement with God by cooperating with
Gentiles and doing other evil things.

Antiochus Attacks Egypt

16 When Antiochus had everything under control, he decided to attack Egypt and
make it part of his kingdom. 17 So he got
together a powerful army, including chariots and elephants, and he also gathered a
large navy. Then he invaded Egypt 18 and
attacked the army of King Ptolemy the
Sixth,[h] who turned and ran, losing many of
his troops. 19 Antiochus captured the
Egyptian towns and fortresses and took
everything of value.

Antiochus Robs the Temple in Jerusalem

20 In the year 143[i] of the Syrian Kingdom, as Antiochus was leading his powerful army home, he attacked Jerusalem.
21 He walked arrogantly right into the
Jerusalem temple and took the gold altar,
the lampstand, and everything that went
with it. 22 He took the table for the sacred

[a]**1.1** *Alexander the Great*: Greek "Alexander the son of Philip of Macedonia"; he ruled 356-323 B.C. [b]**1.1** *and became . . . that part of the world*: One possible meaning for the difficult Greek text. [c]**1.9** *Their descendants also ruled as kings*: 1 Maccabees speaks of many "kings" and "rulers," especially of Syria. Quite often one of them ruled only part of the Syrian Kingdom, while another ruled a different part, yet each would still call himself a "king" or "ruler." [d]**1.10** *Antiochus Epiphanes*: Also known as Antiochus IV (ruled 175-164 B.C.). The name Epiphanes means "god in person." Antiochus chose it to impress others and force them to obey him. [e]**1.10** *Antiochus the Third*: Ruled 223-187 B.C. [f]**1.10** *hostage in Rome*: In 190 or 189 B.C. the Roman army soundly defeated Antiochus the Third at the battle of Magnesia (northeast of Smyrna), and Antiochus the Fourth was taken as a hostage to Rome, where he stayed for twelve or thirteen years. [g]**1.10** *year 137*: That is, 175 B.C. In 1 Maccabees the dates are based on the beginning of the Syrian Kingdom in 312 B.C. [h]**1.18** *Ptolemy the Sixth*: Ruled Egypt 180-145 B.C. [i]**1.20** *year 143*: That is, 169 B.C.

1.10 2 Macc 4.7. **1.15** 1 Co 7.18. **1.16-19** 4 Macc 4.22. **1.20-63** 4 Macc 4.15.

loaves of bread as well as the special bowls,
the cups for wine offerings, the curtain, the
crowns, and the gold pots for burning incense. Antiochus even stripped off every
piece of the gold decoration from the front
of the temple. 23 He also took the silver, the
gold, the fine dishes, and the other treasures that he found hidden in the temple.
24 Then he returned to his own country
with the things he had stolen.

Antiochus had murdered many people and boasted about what he had done.

*25 And so, all of Israel's leaders
and everyone else
cried and moaned.
26 Young people became sick,
and women
lost their beauty.
27 Newlyweds sang about death
and mourned
on their wedding day.
28 The land itself felt sorrow,
and everyone in Israel
was terribly ashamed.

Antiochus Punishes the Jews

29 Two years later, Antiochus sent an officer to collect taxes from the towns in
Judea. The officer led a strong army to
Jerusalem, 30 and he lied to the people by
promising peace. They believed him, but
suddenly he attacked Jerusalem, damaging
the city and killing many of its people.
31 After taking everything he wanted, he set
fire to the city, destroying its houses and
walls. 32 His soldiers even dragged away
women, children, and livestock.
33 Antiochus had his army build a
fortress in Jerusalem[j] and put up high,
thick walls and strong towers. 34 There they
stationed some Jewish troops who had rejected God's Law. 35 They stored in the fortress the weapons, the food, and everything
they had stolen from Jerusalem. And they
became a great threat.

36 The soldiers in the fortress
attacked the temple
and never stopped doing
horrible things to Israel.
37 They killed innocent people
all around the temple,
and they made it unfit
as a place of worship.

38 Everyone ran from Jerusalem.
Their own city became
a foreign country to them,
and strangers moved in.
39 The temple was barren
just like a desert,
and its festivals and Sabbaths
became times of sorrow
and of shame.
Jerusalem had lost all respect.
40 Shame and sorrow replaced
its former glory and pride.

Antiochus Attacks the Jewish Religion

41-42 Antiochus wanted everyone in his
kingdom to follow the same customs. So he
made a law that said, "You must give up
the traditions of your ancestors."
43 The Gentiles obeyed the king, and
many Jews gladly accepted his religion.
They offered sacrifices to idols and broke
the laws of the Sabbath.
44 Messengers from Antiochus brought
letters, telling everyone in Jerusalem and
in all the towns of Judea about this law.
They said:

You must obey the king's law and
accept these new customs. 45 Don't
offer sacrifices in the temple or celebrate the Sabbath and your other festivals. 46 Make the temple and everything in it unfit for the worship of your
God. 47 Build altars and other special
places for worshiping our gods and for
sacrificing pigs and other animals that
your laws forbid.
48 Don't circumcise your sons. Forget about what your religion teaches is
right or wrong. 49 Change your laws
and forget about those teachings.
50 Anyone who doesn't obey the
king will be put to death.

[j] **1.33** *Jerusalem*: The Greek text has "City of David," which covered the large western hill of Jerusalem. The fortress would have been a threat to the temple, which was on a lower hill to the east.
1.26,27 3 Macc 4.6.

51 After Antiochus had sent this law to
everyone in his kingdom, his officials went
to every town of Judea and tried to make
sure that the Jews offered sacrifices to foreign gods. 52 Many of the people obeyed the
king and gave up God's Law. They did evil
things everywhere 53 and forced the faithful
Jews to go into hiding.

The Horrible Thing

54 On the fifteenth day of the month of
Chislev[k] in the year 145[l] of the Syrian
Kingdom, Antiochus set up a "Horrible
Thing"[m] on the temple altar. His followers
built altars in towns all around Judea,
55 and they burned incense in front of their
houses and in the streets.
56 Antiochus' soldiers tore up and
burned any copies of the Jewish Scriptures
that they found. 57 They obeyed Antiochus
and murdered everyone they caught obeying God's Law. These troops also killed any
Jew who owned a copy of the Scriptures.
58 Month after month and in town after
town, his soldiers tortured every faithful
Jew they captured.
59 On the twenty-fifth day of each
month, the king's followers offered sacrifices on the altar they had put on top of the
temple altar. 60 They followed orders and
murdered any Jewish mother who let her
son be circumcised. 61 Antiochus even told
these troops, "Hang the baby around his
mother's neck, and kill the whole family, as
well as the man who circumcised the baby."

Many Jews Stay Faithful to Their Religion

62 Many Jews firmly made up their
minds never to eat what their religion said
was unclean. 63 They chose to die rather
than to eat forbidden food and break the
agreement God had made with them. Many
of them died, 64 and the nation suffered
terribly.

The Family of Mattathias

2 About this time, Mattathias,[n] a priest
from the family of Joarib, moved from
Jerusalem to Modein.
2-5 Mattathias had five sons, whose
names were John, Simon, Judas, Eleazar,
and Jonathan. Each son had a nickname.
John was called Gaddi, Simon was known
as Thassi, and Judas was called Maccabeus.[o] Eleazar was nicknamed Avaran,
and Jonathan was known as Apphus.

Mattathias Is Sad

6 When Mattathias found out that the
people of Judea and Jerusalem were rejecting God's Law, 7 he said:

Why have I lived to see
enemies crushing my people
    and the holy city?
Foreigners now occupy Jerusalem;
they have taken over the temple,
8   making it a place of shame.
9 All of its sacred objects
    have been dragged away.
Young people are slaughtered
    by enemy swords,
and our streets are covered
    with the bodies of children.
10 Is there any nation
that hasn't robbed us
    and stolen our treasures?
11 Jerusalem—once glorious—
has lost its beauty
    and is now a slave.

12 The holy temple was our pride
    and our joy,
until foreigners ruined it
    with their filthy idols.
13 We'd be better off dead!

14 Mattathias and his five sons cried bitterly; they tore their clothes and put on
sackcloth[p] to show their sorrow.

[k]**1.54** *Chislev*: The ninth month of the Hebrew calendar, from about mid-November to mid-December. [l]**1.54** *year 145*: That is, 167 B.C. [m]**1.54** *"Horrible Thing"*: Possibly an altar to the Greek god Zeus, though it could have been an image or images of other pagan gods or goddesses, such as the "Queen of Heaven" or Dionysus, the son of Zeus. [n]**2.1** *Mattathias*: Greek "Mattathias the son of John and the grandson of Simeon." [o]**2.2-5** *Maccabeus*: Means "hammer," or more likely "chosen by the Lord." [p]**2.14** *sackcloth*: A rough, dark-colored cloth made from goat or camel hair and used to make grain sacks. It was worn in times of trouble or sorrow.

1.54 Dn 9.27; 11.31; 12.11; 1 Macc 6.7; Mt 24.15; Mk 13.14. **1.60** 2 Macc 6.10.

Mattathias Starts a War

15 The king's officials were trying to force everyone to break the Law of Moses by offering pagan sacrifices. And one day the officials went to the town of Modein, 16 where many of the people came out to meet them, including Mattathias and his sons. 17 The officials said to Mattathias:

> You're an important and honored leader in this town, and your relatives will follow your example. 18 So why don't you obey the king and accept his religion, just as every Gentile and Jew in Judea and Jerusalem has already done? Then you and your family will be known as "Trusted Friends of the King,"[q] and you will be rewarded with gold and silver and other gifts.

19 Mattathias answered in a loud voice:

> What do I care if everyone in the king's entire kingdom turns from their own religion and starts obeying his laws? 20 My family and I will always keep the promises our ancestors made to God. 21-22 We will never give up our faith or disobey even one of God's laws. We will not obey Antiochus!

23 When Mattathias finished speaking, everyone watched as a Jew from Modein stepped forward to obey the king by offering a sacrifice on the altar. 24 Mattathias was furious, and he was so eager to see justice done that he rushed over to the altar and killed the man. 25 Then he destroyed the altar and killed the official who ordered the sacrifice. 26 Indeed, Mattathias showed that he loved God's Law as much as Phinehas,[r] who had killed Zimri the son of Salu many years ago.

27 Mattathias shouted to everyone in Modein, "Follow me, if you truly love the Law of Moses and want to keep our agreement with God!" 28 Then Mattathias and his sons ran to the hills, leaving behind everything they owned.

One Thousand Jews Are Killed

29-30 Many of the Jews were now in serious trouble for trying to obey God and live right. So they took their families and livestock and moved to the desert. 31 But the king's officers and soldiers in the fortress at Jerusalem found out what these Jews had done. 32 So a large number of the troops went after them and camped nearby. Then on the Sabbath 33 they said to the Jews, "This is your last chance! Come out and obey the king's orders, or you will die."

34 The Jews answered, "We're not coming out! And we refuse to break the laws of the Sabbath by obeying the king's orders!"

35 At once the enemy forces attacked. 36 But the Jews did not try to defend themselves; not one of them threw a rock or even tried to pile up rocks in front of the caves. 37 They just said, "We've done nothing deserving death! Everyone in heaven and on earth knows that you are wrong to kill us."

38 On that Sabbath one thousand Jewish men, women, and children were slaughtered, together with their sheep and goats.

Mattathias Takes Charge

39 When Mattathias and his followers heard what had happened, they mourned a long time. 40 Then they said to each other, "We can't let that happen to us! We've got to defend ourselves and our way of life, even on the Sabbath. If we don't, the Gentiles will soon wipe us out." 41 On that very day they made up their minds not to die like their relatives in the caves, and they decided to fight anyone who attacked them on the Sabbath.

42 About this time a very devout group of Jews[s] joined Mattathias; they were some of the nation's best fighters and were willing to die for God's Law. 43 In fact, many others had found themselves in trouble with the Gentiles, and they also went to Mat-

[q] **2.18** *"Trusted Friends of the King"*: This was a title that Greek kings gave to special advisors and officials. These friends received gifts, honors, and other privileges. [r] **2.26** *Phinehas*: According to Numbers 25.6-15, Phinehas killed a man and his wife who disobeyed God's Law. [s] **2.42** *devout group of Jews*: The Greek text has "Hasideans," which translates the Hebrew word "hasidim," meaning "devout," and referred to Jews who were especially faithful to their religion.

2.26 Nu 25.6-15. **2.32-38** 2 Macc 6.11. **2.39-41** 3 Macc 1.22.

tathias, who soon had a large force. 44 Then
those angry troops violently attacked the
unfaithful Jews, forcing those who escaped
to run to the Gentiles for protection.
45 Mattathias and his followers tore
down every altar they found. 46 They had
the young boys in Israel circumcised,
47 and they terrorized their arrogant enemies. Everything went well for Mattathias
and his troops, 48 because they defended
their laws against the Gentiles and Antiochus. No evil person stood a chance.

The Death of Mattathias

49 Right before Mattathias died, he said
to his sons:
The Gentiles are proud and violent,
and we're going to have a horrible
time. 50 But you, my sons, should be
faithful to God's Law and be willing to
die for the agreement that our ancestors made with God.
51 Keep in mind their brave deeds,
and you will be famous forever.
52 Abraham was faithful when God
tested him, and so God accepted him.
53 Joseph obeyed God in a time of trouble, and he became ruler of Egypt.
54 Because our ancestor Phinehas
obeyed everything in God's Law, the
men of our family have become priests
forever.
55 Joshua followed God's orders and
became a leader of Israel. 56 Caleb told
the people of Israel the truth, and God
gave him some of the land. 57 David's
family will rule as kings forever because David had mercy on others.
58 Elijah obeyed God's Law and was
taken to heaven. 59 Hananiah, Azariah,
and Mishael trusted God, so he saved
them from the flames. 60 Daniel was
rescued from the hungry lions because
of his loyalty to God.
61 Think about these past heroes.
They trusted God and were strong.
62 Don't let the threats of that brutal
Antiochus frighten you! He may be famous, but he's nothing but food for
worms. 63 He talks big now, but soon
you won't hear that loud mouth anymore. Dust is all that will remain of
him and his plans.
64 My sons, you must find courage
and strength in God's Law; then everyone will honor you.
65 Your brother Simon is wise. So
always obey him, just as you would
obey me. 66 Judas Maccabeus has been
a brave fighter all his life. Now he will
command your army and lead you in
battle.
67 Find soldiers who love God's Law
and then lead them to punish everyone who has mistreated your people,
68 including the Gentiles. Always follow
God's teaching.
69-70 Mattathias blessed his sons, and
then he died. His family buried him in
their tomb near the town of Modein. This
happened in the year 146[t] of the Syrian
Kingdom, and everyone in Israel mourned
for a long time.

Judas Maccabeus Wins Many Victories

3 Judas Maccabeus took his father's
place as leader. 2 His four brothers and
his father's soldiers eagerly helped him
fight for Israel.

3 Judas was a mighty warrior
and made Israel more glorious
than ever.
When he put on his armor
and took up his sword,
he marched into battle
and protected his troops.
4 He roared and attacked
like a hungry lion.
5 He went after those Jews
who disobeyed God's Law,
and he burned to death those
who abused his people.

6 Judas confused and terrified
everyone who broke God's Law,
but he kept his people safe.
7 Kings were furious

[t]**2.69,70** *year 146*: That is, 166 B.C.

2.52 Gn 15.6; 22.15-18. **2.53** Gn 39.1—45.28. **2.55,56** Nu 13.1—14.12. **2.57** 2 S 7.16. **2.58** 2 K 2.9-12. **2.59** Dn 3.1-30. **2.60** Dn 6.1-24; Bel 31-42.

because of his victories,
but Israel rejoiced.
Judas will be remembered
and praised forever.

8 After Judas had killed
the unfaithful Jews
in the towns of Judea,
God was no longer angry.
9 Now the whole world knew
that Judas had rescued those
who were to be slaughtered.

Apollonius Is Defeated

10 A man by the name of Apollonius[u] decided to invade Israel. So he got together an army of Gentiles and many Samaritans.
11 When Judas learned about this, he attacked, killing Apollonius and a large number of his soldiers. The others ran for their
lives. 12 Then everyone took what they wanted from the dead soldiers. Judas himself took Apollonius' sword and used it from then on.

The Battle of Beth-Horon

13 Seron, the commander of the Syrian forces, heard about Judas and the many loyal troops who were always ready to fight
for him. 14 Seron thought, "Judas and his soldiers are rebels. So I'll destroy them and make a name for myself everywhere in the
kingdom!" 15 Then Seron led his soldiers and a large number of unfaithful Jews out of his camp to attack them.
16 While Seron and his army were going through the hills toward the town of Beth-Horon,[v] Judas and a small force went out
to attack. 17 But when they saw the enemy closing in, they said, "There are only a few of us. How can we fight against such a strong army? And besides, we feel weak, because we haven't had anything to eat all day long."
18 Judas said to his soldiers:
God doesn't care how many soldiers
Seron has or how few we have. Our
small army can easily destroy his
forces. 19 It isn't the size of the army, it
is the power of God that wins battles.
20 Seron and his troops are arrogant
sinners who want to kill us and our
families, so they can steal everything
we own. 21 But we're fighting for our
faith as much as for ourselves. 22 God
will let us wipe out Seron's army. So
don't be afraid!
23 Judas and his soldiers struck quickly.
They defeated Seron and his army 24 and
chased them to the valley below the hills of Beth-Horon. Eight hundred enemy soldiers were killed, and the rest ran away to the country of the Philistines.

King Antiochus Makes War Plans

25 The Gentiles in this whole region were now terrified of Judas and his brothers.
26 In fact, everyone talked about his victories so much that even King Antiochus[w] finally heard about Judas.
27 Antiochus was furious and brought his troops together from everywhere in his kingdom to build up a powerful army.
28 He took money from his treasury and gave each soldier a year's pay. Then he told them, "Be ready to fight at a moment's notice!"
29 Soon Antiochus ran out of money, and it became difficult to collect taxes, because of the hard feelings and trouble he had caused by doing away with the ancient customs of the land.
30 Once again Antiochus started worrying about how he would pay his bills and outdo the other kings before him who gave
expensive gifts. 31 He was so upset that he decided to take his army and collect all the taxes he could from Persia and the other countries nearby.

Antiochus Puts Lysias in Charge

32 A man by the name of Lysias was a respected member of the royal family[x] and King Antiochus put him in charge of the land from the Euphrates River to the border of Egypt.
33 Then Antiochus told him:

[u]3.10 *Apollonius*: Possibly the governor of Samaria, since his troops were from Samaria.
[v]3.16 *Beth-Horon*: On the border between Judea and Samaria. [w]3.26 *King Antiochus*: Antiochus IV, also known as Epiphanes (see 1.10 and the note there). [x]3.32 *member . . . family*: This is a title that Greek kings gave to their most important officials.

Look after my son[y] until I get back.
34 I am placing half of my army and all
of my elephants under your command.
Obey my orders, especially concerning
the people of Judea and Jerusalem.
35 Destroy the army of Judas and kill
anyone you find in Jerusalem. Make
the whole world forget that those Jews
ever lived 36 and give their land to
Gentiles.

37 In the year 147[z] of the Syrian Kingdom, Antiochus and the rest of his army set
out from the capital city of Antioch. They
crossed the Euphrates River and started
through Mesopotamia.

Judas and His Brothers
(2 Maccabees 8.8-29, 34-36)

38 Nicanor, Gorgias, and Ptolemy the
son of Dorymenes were three important
and trusted friends[a] of Antiochus. So
Lysias chose them as army commanders.
39 He told them what the king had commanded and gave them forty thousand soldiers and seven thousand cavalry troops to
invade and destroy the land of Judea.
40 Nicanor, Gorgias, and Ptolemy then led
the whole army to Judea and set up camp
in the valley near the town of Emmaus.
41 Local slave traders heard about these
three commanders and went to their camp,
taking with them chains[b] and plenty of silver and gold to buy Israelite prisoners as
slaves. Armies from Syria and the land of
the Philistines[c] also came.
42 Judas and his brothers realized that
things were worse now than ever, because
their enemies had invaded Judea with orders from the king to wipe out the Jewish
people. 43 But Judas and his brothers were
determined to make their nation strong
again and to defend their people and temple. 44 So Judas organized an army, and
when his troops were ready, they prayed for
God's mercy and kindness.

45 Jerusalem was a barren desert
that no one could enter
or leave.
The temple was trampled down,
and foreign troops
took over the fortress.
Everyone in Israel was sad;
their flutes and harps
were silent.

46 Judas led his army a short distance
from Jerusalem to the town of Mizpah,
which had been a place of worship. 47 That
day Judas and his troops went without eating; they put on sackcloth,[d] then rubbed
ashes on their heads and tore their clothes.
48 Instead of praying to idols, as the
Gentiles do, they read in their Jewish Law
to find what God wanted them to do.
49 They also brought together a tenth of
their crops and the best part of their harvest, as well as the clothes of the priests.
Judas also called together those who
had completed their time of special service
to God[e] and now had to offer sacrifices.
50 Then everyone prayed out loud:

Where can we take these people
to offer their sacrifices?
51 Your temple has been disgraced
and made unfit for worship;
the priests are humiliated
and brokenhearted.
52 Our God, you know these Gentiles
are here to destroy us,
53 and there is nothing we can do
without your help.

54 Then trumpets were blown, and
everyone shouted. 55 Judas divided his
army into groups of a thousand, groups of a
hundred, groups of fifty, and groups of ten,
and he put an officer in charge of each
group. 56 He obeyed the Law of Moses[f] by
sending home any soldier who was either
building a house or engaged to get married

[y]**3.33** *son*: Antiochus V. [z]**3.37** *year 147*: That is, 165 B.C. [a]**3.38** *trusted friends*: See the note at 2.18. [b]**3.41** *chains*: Or "slaves." [c]**3.41** *land of the Philistines*: Greek "land of strangers." [d]**3.47** *sackcloth*: See the note at 2.14. [e]**3.49** *those who . . . special service to God*: The Greek text has Nazirites, which refers to persons who had promised to serve God in a special way for a limited time. When this time of service was over, they had to offer sacrifices in the temple (see Numbers 6.1-21). [f]**3.56** *Law of Moses*: See Deuteronomy 20.5-8.
3.56 Dt 20.5-8; Jg 7.3.

or who was planting a vineyard or was simply afraid to fight.
57 Judas and his troops left Mizpah and
set up camp south of the town of Emmaus,
58 where he said to them:

Our enemies have come together to
destroy us and our temple. So get your
weapons ready and be brave! We'll attack early tomorrow morning. 59 It's
better to die in battle than to watch our
country and temple crumble.60 But
God will do whatever he has decided.

Judas Defeats Gorgias at Emmaus

4 During the night, Gorgias[g] took five
thousand soldiers and a thousand of
his best cavalry and left Emmaus 2 to make
a surprise attack on Judas. He was led
there by some men from the fortress in
Jerusalem.
3-4 But Judas found out what Gorgias
was planning. So he and his soldiers left
their camp to attack the troops that Gorgias
had left behind at Emmaus.
5 Late that night, when Gorgias arrived
at the camp of Judas, no one was there. He
thought Judas and the others were hiding
in the hills, and so he led his troops after
them. 6 Meanwhile, Judas and his three
thousand soldiers came to the valley near
Emmaus about dawn. They did not have
enough swords or armor for the battle,
7 and they saw expert cavalry patrolling
every side of the well-guarded camp.
8 Judas told his troops:

The enemy army is strong, but don't
be afraid when they attack. 9 Years ago
our ancestors were attacked at the Red
Sea[h] by the king of Egypt and his army,
but God rescued them.

10 Let's ask God to be kind and
keep the agreement he made with our
ancestors. If God helps us defeat Gorgias today, 11 then every Gentile will
know that our God saves and rescues
his people.

12 The Jewish troops started toward the
Gentiles, who saw them coming 13 and
went out to fight. Then Judas shouted,
"Blow the trumpets 14 and attack!" The
Jews crushed the Gentiles and chased their
soldiers to the valley, 15 killing everyone
they caught.
Some of the enemy troops ran as far as
the towns of Gazara, Azotus, and Jamnia.
Others reached the valley near Idumea. Judas went after them, and that day three
thousand Gentiles died.
16 After Judas and his men had stopped
chasing the enemy, 17 he said to everyone:

Don't be eager to take anything
from the bodies of the dead now. We
will still have to fight 18 Gorgias and
his troops when they come out of the
nearby hills. Then you can take anything you want.

19 About this time, an enemy patrol
came out of the hills. 20 They saw smoke
and knew that their army and their camp
had been wiped out. 21 Then they looked
over at the valley and saw the Jewish army
lined up for battle. They were terrified
22 and ran to the land of the Philistines.[i]
23 Judas now went back and let his soldiers take whatever they wanted from the
enemy camp. They found bags of gold and
silver, as well as some blue and purple
cloth, and many other valuable things.
24-25 Then on the way home, they sang
hymns of praise to God who had given
them a great victory that day. They sang:
"Our God, your mercy lasts forever!"

Judas Defeats Lysias
(2 *Maccabees* 11.1-12)

26 Some enemy soldiers escaped and
told Lysias everything that had happened.
27 Lysias was confused and completely disappointed, because he had failed to wipe
out the Jews, as King Antiochus had ordered him to do.
28 The next year, Lysias got together
sixty thousand of his best soldiers and five
thousand cavalry to crush the Jews. 29 He
then led this army to Idumea, where he set
up camp near the town of Beth-Zur.

[g]**4.1** *Gorgias*: See 3.38,40. [h]**4.9** *Red Sea*: This refers to the body of water that the Israelites crossed and was one of the marshes or fresh water lakes near the eastern part of the Nile Delta, where they lived and where the towns of Exodus 13.17—14.9 were located. [i]**4.22** *land of the Philistines*: Greek "land of strangers."

Judas and ten thousand soldiers marched out to fight Lysias. 30 When Judas realized how powerful the enemy force was, he prayed:

> Our God, we praise you for always rescuing us. When Saul was king, you let your servant David kill a Philistine giant.[j] You also let Saul's son Jonathan and one other soldier capture an entire Philistine camp. 31 Now help us destroy this enemy camp and make fools of their soldiers and cavalry. 32 Turn them into cowards who are too weak to fight, and make them tremble while we destroy them.
>
> 33 Our God, we love you. Please let us slaughter our enemies. Then all of your worshipers will praise you with songs.

34 The two armies moved forward, and in the battle, Lysias lost five thousand soldiers.[k] 35 As he watched his army falling apart, he said to himself, "Those Jews are brave fighters, who live and die with honor."

Lysias returned to the city of Antioch and hired some foreign soldiers, so he could invade Judea with an even stronger army.

Judas Dedicates the Temple

(2 Maccabees 10.1-8)

36 Judas and his brothers said, "Now that we've defeated our enemies, let's make the temple an acceptable place for worship and dedicate it to the Lord once again."

37 So the entire army went to Mount Zion.[l] 38 They saw the deserted temple and the unclean altar, where the Gentiles had sacrificed unfit animals. The temple's doors had been burned, and the priests' rooms were damaged. Tall bushes and weeds were growing in the temple courtyard, making it look like a forest or a mountain.

39 Judas and his soldiers grieved terribly. They tore their clothes, then threw ashes on their heads 40 and lay face down on the ground. A trumpet was blown, and they began praying out loud to their God.

41 Judas ordered some of his soldiers to keep the enemy fortress under attack, so that others could clean up the temple. 42 He chose honest and faithful priests 43 and put them in charge of cleaning out the temple.

The priests hauled away the unclean stones to a garbage heap. 44-45 And they wondered what to do about the altar for offering sacrifices, because it had been polluted by the Gentiles who had sacrificed unclean animals on it. Finally, they decided to remove this disgrace by tearing down the altar and hauling away the stones. 46 They piled them in a special place on the temple hill, believing that God would someday send a prophet who would know what to do with them.

47 The priests did just as the Law of Moses commands.[m] They found stones that had never been cut, and they set up a new altar exactly like the old one. 48 The priests also rebuilt the inside and the outside of the temple, and they cleaned the temple courtyard, making it a proper place for worship once again.

49 The priests made some new bowls to be used in worship, and they took into the temple the lampstand, the incense altar, and the table for the sacred bread. 50 They burned incense on the altar and lit the lamps on the stand, filling the temple with light. 51 Then they set the sacred bread on the table and hung up the temple curtains. Finally, everything was done.

52-53 It was now the twenty-fifth day of Chislev,[n] the ninth month, in the year 148[o] of the Syrian Kingdom. On this day the priests got up early to sacrifice an animal on the new altar, just as the Law of Moses commands.[p]

54 Exactly three years earlier, the Gentiles had offered sacrifices to their idols on

[j] **4.30** *David . . . giant*: See 1 Samuel 17.41-54. [k] **4.34** *soldiers*: Or ". . . soldiers, and some of the Jewish troops were also killed." [l] **4.37** *Mount Zion*: Jerusalem, especially the part where the temple was built. [m] **4.47** *the Law of Moses commands*: See Exodus 20.25; Deuteronomy 27.5,6. [n] **4.52,53** *Chislev*: See the note at 1.54. [o] **4.52,53** *year 148*: That is, 164 B.C. [p] **4.52,53** *the Law of Moses commands*: See Exodus 29.38-42.

4.30 1 S 17.41-54; 14.1-24. **4.47** Ex 20.25; Dt 27.5, 6. **4.52-54** 1 Macc 1.54.

the altar and had made it unfit for worship.
But now the priests were worshiping God at
the altar again, while the rest of the people
sang and played harps, cymbals, and small
stringed instruments. 55 Then everyone lay
face down on the ground to honor and
praise the Lord who had given them victory. 56 For eight days they celebrated the
dedication of the new altar and offered gifts
and sacrifices to thank the Lord and to ask
his blessing.

57 The people decorated the front of the
temple with gold crowns and small shields,
and they repaired the rooms where the
priests lived, hanging new doors in them,
as well as new gates for the temple.
58 Everyone was happy because the disgrace that the Gentiles had brought on the
temple had been removed.

59 Judas and his brothers, together with
everyone else, decided to celebrate the
dedication of the altar[q] each year at this
same time. This joyous festival would begin
on the twenty-fifth day of the month of
Chislev[r] and last eight days.

60 Then they built strong walls and high
towers around Mount Zion to protect the
temple from being destroyed by Gentiles
again, 61 and Judas stationed soldiers there.
He also built a fortress in the town of Beth-
Zur to keep Israel safe from attack by the
Idumeans.

The Wars of Judas

(2 Maccabees 10.14-33; 12.10-45)

5 When the neighboring nations heard
that the altar and the temple were
again ready to be used in worship, they became furious 2 and were determined to kill
every Jew who lived among them. So they
started killing the Jewish people.

3 Judas fought back by attacking the
Idumeans,[s] who had often ambushed the
people of Israel. Finally, in the region of
Akrabattene,[t] he wiped out most of them
and took everything of value.

4-5 Then Judas promised God, "Now I'll
destroy the Baeanites, that gang of robbers
and murderers who set traps for Jewish
travelers." So he ordered his troops to surround the towers where they were hiding
and to burn down the towers with everyone
inside.

6 Judas also invaded the country of Ammon, where someone by the name of Timothy ruled a large number of people. Timothy's army was strong, 7 and Judas had to
attack many times before completely destroying it. 8 Judas captured the town of
Jazer and its villages, then he went back to
Judea.

Simon and Judas Win More Victories

9 Some of the Israelites in Gilead took
shelter in the fortress at Dathema, because
an army of Gentiles in that region planned
to attack. 10 Then they sent a letter to Judas and his brothers. It said:

> An army of Gentiles is about to sur-
> round us at Dathema, 11 and their
> leader is Timothy.[u]
>
> 12 Please send help right away.
> These Gentiles have not only killed
> many of us, 13 but they've robbed and
> murdered just about every Jew in Tob[v]
> and captured their families. Almost a
> thousand have already died.

14 Before Judas finished reading this letter, messengers arrived from Galilee. They
had torn their clothes to show their sorrow,
15 and they said, "An army is ready to destroy us. It is made up of Gentiles from all
over Galilee and of troops from the cities of
Ptolemais, Tyre, and Sidon."

16 Judas and his troops listened to these
reports. Then they called together a large
group to decide what should be done to
help those who were in danger and under
attack. 17 Judas said to his brother Simon,
"Take some soldiers to Galilee and rescue
our people. Our brother Jonathan and I
will lead an army to Gilead."

18-19 Judas left two officials, Azariah and

[q]**4.59** *celebrate the dedication of the altar*: The Jewish people still celebrate this festival, which they call Hanukkah. [r]**4.59** *Chislev*: See the note at 1.54. [s]**5.3** *Idumeans*: Greek "descendants of Esau in Idumea"; they were earlier known as Edomites. [t]**5.3** *Akrabattene*: Southwest of the Dead Sea. [u]**5.11** *Timothy*: Probably a different Timothy from the one mentioned in verse 6. [v]**5.13** *Jew . . . Tob*: Or "Jew in Tobias' army."

4.56 3 Macc 6.36.

Joseph,[w] in command of his troops in Judea, and he told them, "You're in charge. But don't attack the Gentiles until we return."

20 Simon led three thousand soldiers to Galilee, and Judas took eight thousand to Gilead. 21 In Galilee, Simon had to attack the Gentiles many times before completely destroying them. 22 He and his soldiers pushed them back to the city of Ptolemais, where they killed about three thousand Gentiles and took everything they wanted.

23 Simon brought the Jews of Galilee and Arbatta,[x] along with their families and their possessions, to Judea. When they arrived, everyone was shouting and celebrating.

Judas and Jonathan in Gilead

24 Meanwhile, Judas Maccabeus and his brother Jonathan crossed the Jordan River and traveled through the desert for three days. 25 Some friendly Nabateans[y] told them everything Timothy[z] had done to the Jews in Gilead. 26-27 They said:

> Your people are being kept prisoner in the large, walled towns of Gilead, including Bozrah, Bosor, Alema, Chaspho, Maked, and Carnaim.
>
> Besides this, the Gentiles are going to attack your fortresses tomorrow, and in one day they can overpower your troops there and kill everyone.

28 Judas and his army saw that the attack had already begun, so they hurried along the desert road to Bozrah. They captured the town and killed every man and boy in it. Then they took everything of value and set the town on fire.

29 That night, Judas and his army left Bozrah and went straight to the fortress of Dathema, 30 where they arrived early the next morning. More Gentiles than could be counted were attacking the fortress with ladders and weapons to break through the walls.

31 Judas knew that the battle had begun, because shouts to God and trumpet blasts were coming from the fortress. 32 So he told his army, "Today you must fight for your people!"

33 Judas divided his army into three groups. Then a signal was blown on the trumpet, and the troops shouted prayers as they attacked the enemy from behind. 34 When Timothy and his army realized that Judas Maccabeus was leading the attack, they tried to escape. But he attacked them fiercely, and about eight thousand of them were slaughtered that day.

35 Judas led his army to the town of Maapha,[a] which they attacked and captured. Then after killing the men and boys and taking everything of value, they burned the town. 36 Judas also captured the other towns in Gilead, including Chaspho, Maked, and Bosor.

37 Timothy then got together another army and camped on the other side of the stream near the town of Raphon. 38 Meanwhile, Judas had sent out spies who came back and told him, "Timothy has a large army of Gentiles from all around here, 39 and he has even hired some Arabs to join him. He's camped on the other side of the stream, eager to fight with you."

Judas led his army to meet them, 40 and they took up their positions near the stream.

When Timothy saw them, he said to his officers:

> If Judas crosses the stream to attack, we won't have a chance, and he will destroy us. 41 But if he stops and sets up camp on the other side of the stream, that means he's afraid of us. Then we will cross over and destroy him.

42 Judas ordered his troops to move close to the stream, then he told his officers, "Stand here beside the stream and make sure that no one stays behind to set up camp. Everyone must join in the attack." 43 Afterwards, Judas led all the troops across and wiped out Timothy's army.

The enemies threw down their weapons

[w]**5.18,19** *Joseph*: Greek "Joseph son of Zechariah." [x]**5.23** *Arbatta*: A region between Ptolemais and Jerusalem. [y]**5.25** *Nabateans*: A desert tribe who lived in this region. [z]**5.25** *Timothy*: See the note at verse 11. [a]**5.35** *Maapha*: Some manuscripts have "Alema."

and ran for safety to a temple[b] in the town of Carnaim. 44 But the Jewish troops captured Carnaim and burned the temple down with everyone inside. Carnaim was left in ruins, and the Gentiles in Gilead stopped bothering Judas.

Judas Returns to Judea

45-46 Judas brought together the Jews of Gilead, no matter how rich or poor they were. Then they set out for Judea with their families and all of their possessions. On the way, this large crowd came to the walled town of Ephron.[c] They had to go through the town, because it was impossible for them to take their families and possessions around it. 47 But the people of Ephron piled up stones in front of the town gates and refused to let them pass through.

48 Judas sent a friendly message to the town, saying, "Please let us pass through. We're on our way to Judea, and we won't make any trouble." But the people of Ephron still refused to let them in.

49 So Judas ordered his troops to set up camp there, 50 and they attacked Ephron all day and night. When they broke through the walls, 51 they killed the men and boys and took everything of value. Then they destroyed Ephron and walked right over the dead bodies on their way through the town.

52 Judas crossed the Jordan River and came to the great valley near the town of Beth-Shan. 53 From there, he led the people to Judea, encouraging and helping everyone, especially those who were dragging behind. 54 After they had arrived safely in Jerusalem, they went to the temple and offered sacrifices.

Azariah and Joseph Are Defeated

55-56 Joseph[d] and Azariah were in command of the Jewish forces in Judea, when they heard about the victories of Judas and Jonathan in Gilead and about Simon's success in attacking the town of Ptolemais in Galilee. 57 And they said, "Let's attack the Gentiles around here and make ourselves famous!"

58 So Azariah and Joseph ordered their troops to attack the fortress of Jamnia, 59 where Gorgias[e] and his army were stationed. The enemy came out of the fortress to fight, 60 and defeated Joseph and Azariah, chasing their troops all the way to Judea and killing about two thousand of them.

61 This battle was lost because Azariah and Joseph disobeyed Judas and his brothers by trying to win a victory for themselves. 62 God had chosen the family of Judas to rescue Israel, and Azariah and Joseph were not from that family.

63 Judas and his brothers became even more famous among both Jews and Gentiles, 64 and people traveled to Jerusalem to honor them.

Judas Fights More Wars

65 Judas and his brothers left Jerusalem with an army to invade the land south of them where the Idumeans[f] lived. Their army surrounded the town of Hebron and its villages; then they destroyed its fortresses and burned its towers.

66 On their way to invade the land of the Philistines, Judas and his brothers came to the town of Marisa.[g] 67 That same day, some priests foolishly started a battle because they wanted to become heroes. But instead they died in the fighting.

68 Judas and his troops turned aside into the territory of Azotus,[h] where they tore down the altars and burned the wooden idols. Then they attacked and robbed some nearby towns before returning to Judea.

The Death of King Antiochus the Fourth

(2 Maccabees 1.11-17; 9.1-29; 10.9-11)

6 One day, as King Antiochus the Fourth[i] was leading his army through Mesopotamia, he heard about the Persian

[b]**5.43** *temple*: In ancient times people were supposed to be safe if they were in a temple.
[c]**5.45,46** *Ephron*: East of the Jordan River, about twelve miles southwest of the Sea of Galilee.
[d]**5.55,56** *Joseph*: Greek "Joseph son of Zechariah." [e]**5.59** *Gorgias*: See 3.38,40; 4.1.
[f]**5.65** *Idumeans*: See the note at 5.3. [g]**5.66** *Marisa*: Some manuscripts have "Samaria."
[h]**5.68** *territory of Azotus*: The Greek text has "Azotus in the land of the Philistines," referring to territory where the Philistines had lived years before the time of the Maccabees. [i]**6.1** *Antiochus the Fourth*: Also known as Antiochus Epiphanes (see 1.10 and the note there).

city of Elymais, which was famous for its treasures of silver and gold. 2 The temple in Elymais was especially rich because of the gold shields, armor, and weapons that had been left there by Alexander the Great,[j] the first king to rule the Greeks.

3-4 Antiochus tried to capture the city of Elymais and take its treasures. But his attack failed because the people found out about his plans and fought hard against him.

Antiochus was terribly frustrated and started back toward Babylonia. 5 But while he was still in Persia, a messenger came and said:

> The Jews have crushed the armies you sent to Judea, 6 including the huge army Lysias[k] led there. They are now a powerful force because they have taken a lot of weapons, supplies, and other things from the armies they defeated.
>
> 7 The Jews have always despised the "Horrible Thing"[l] you placed on their altar in Jerusalem. Now they have torn it down and once again built high walls around their temple and turned your town of Beth-Zur into a fortress.

8 Antiochus was so shocked and discouraged by this report that he got sick and had to stay in bed 9 for many days. He never got over the shock, and just before he died, 10 he called together his trusted friends[m] and said:

> I can't close my eyes at night. I'm sick from worry 11 and keep saying to myself, "How did you ever get into such a mess? Why are you up to your neck in troubles? After all, you're a kind ruler, and everyone likes you."
>
> 12 My friends, I can't forget about the crimes I committed in Jerusalem. I robbed the city of its silver and gold, and I sent soldiers to murder the innocent people of Judea. 13 These crimes are the reason I'm dying of sorrow here in a foreign land.

14-15 Antiochus told his friend Philip to come near his bed. He put Philip in command of the whole kingdom and gave him his crown, his robe, and his ring.[n] Then he said, "Raise my son, so that he will be ready to rule the kingdom." 16 Antiochus died in the year 149[o] of the Syrian Kingdom.

Antiochus the Fifth Becomes King

17 The young son of Antiochus the Fourth had been brought up by Lysias, and when Lysias heard that Antiochus was dead, he crowned the boy Antiochus the Fifth[p] and named him Eupator.[q]

Antiochus the Fifth and Judas

(2 Maccabees 13.1-26; 11.22-26)

18 Meanwhile, some enemies were still in the Jerusalem fortress, where they were trying to keep control of the temple and help the Gentiles by causing trouble for the Jews.

19 Judas decided to attack the fortress and get rid of those troublemakers. 20 So he and his troops set up movable towers and other weapons of war and attacked in the year 150[r] of the Syrian Kingdom.

21 Some of the troops in the fortress escaped and were joined by a group of unfaithful Jews. 22 Together they went to Antiochus the Fifth and said:

> Aren't you ever going to get even with those Jews for what they did to our group? 23 We gladly obeyed your father's laws, and we liked working for him. 24 That's why those Jews hate us and are attacking the fortress.[s]
>
> King Antiochus, they have captured and killed some of our people. They've stolen our property 25 and attacked all the countries near Judea as well.

[j]**6.2** *Alexander the Great*: See 1.1 and the note there. [k]**6.6** *Lysias*: See 3.32-36; 4.26-35. [l]**6.7** *"Horrible Thing"*: See 1.54 and the note there. [m]**6.10** *trusted friends*: See the note at 2.18. [n]**6.14,15** *crown . . . robe . . . ring*: This would give Philip more authority than Lysias (3.32), who was defeated by Judas (4.26-35). [o]**6.16** *year 149*: That is, 163 B.C. [p]**6.17** *Antiochus the Fifth*: Ruled 164-162 B.C. [q]**6.17** *Eupator*: It was the custom for the king to take a new name when he was crowned. [r]**6.20** *year 150*: That is, 162 B.C. [s]**6.24** *are attacking the fortress*: One possible meaning for the difficult Greek text.

6.7 1 Macc 1.54; 3 Macc 2.18.

26 Their temple and the town of
Beth-Zur are powerful fortresses, and
right now those Jews are attacking the
fortress in Jerusalem. 27 Do something
fast! Soon there will be no way to stop
them.

28 When Antiochus heard this, he became furious. So he, together with his
trusted friends[t] and army officers, decided
on a plan of attack. 29 He hired soldiers
from other kingdoms and from the Greek
islands, 30 until he had a hundred thousand soldiers and twenty thousand cavalry.
He also had thirty-two elephants trained
for war.

31 He led his army through Idumea, and
for a long time, he attacked the town of
Beth-Zur with weapons to break through
the wall. But the people fought back
bravely. They even rushed out of the town
and set fire to the weapons of war.

Judas Fights the Gentiles at Beth-Zechariah

32 Judas called off his attack on the
Jerusalem fortress and led his army to
the town of Beth-Zechariah,[u] where he
camped not far from the army of Antiochus
the Fifth.

33 Early the next morning, Antiochus
moved his army toward them at Beth-
Zechariah. Then he ordered his troops to
line up for battle and to blow their war
trumpets.

34 Some of the soldiers gave the elephants grape juice and mulberry juice to
make them eager to fight. 35 Others then
led the elephants to their places among the
troops. Five hundred expert cavalry and a
thousand troops with bronze helmets and
metal armor worked with each animal.
36 These men were commanded not to
leave the elephants until the battle was
over.

37 A strong wooden platform with four
sides and a top was strapped on the back of
each elephant. Then four[v] well-armed soldiers and someone from India to guide the
elephant were stationed on the platform.

38 Antiochus placed the rest of his cavalry to the right and to the left of the army,
because he wanted the cavalry troops to
stay close to his army for protection and to
attack the Jewish forces whenever they
could. 39-40 His huge army covered the hills
and the valleys. And when the columns of
soldiers marched forward, their gold and
brass shields caught the rays of the sun and
made the hillsides blaze with light.

41 The loud and clanging sound of this
powerful army brought terror to the hearts
of all who heard them coming. 42 But Judas
and his troops still attacked, and they killed
six hundred of the enemy troops.

The Death of Eleazar

43 Eleazar[w] noticed that the largest elephant was dressed in the royal armor. So
he said to himself, "I'm certain Antiochus
must be up there!"

44-46 Eleazar killed every enemy soldier
around him, and others ran away as he
bravely fought his way toward the huge elephant. Then he ran under it and stabbed
it to death. But the heavy elephant sank
down and crushed him. Eleazar gave up
his life to save his people, and he will never
be forgotten.

47 Suddenly the Jews realized how helpless they were against the fierce attack of
the king's army, and they started running
away.

Antiochus the Fifth Attacks the Temple

48-49 Antiochus the Fifth surrounded
Jerusalem with part of his army, while the
rest of his troops set up camp everywhere
in Judea. All of this happened during the
Seventh Year,[x] when the Jews do not plant
crops.

Antiochus attacked the town of Beth-Zur. Its people soon ran out of food and had to stop fighting, so they surrendered

[t]**6.28** *trusted friends*: See the note at 2.18. [u]**6.32** *Beth-Zechariah*: Southwest of Jerusalem. [v]**6.37** *four*: Some manuscripts have "three," "thirty," or "thirty-two." [w]**6.43** *Eleazar*: Greek "Eleazar known as Avaran" (see 2.2-5). [x]**6.48,49** *Seventh Year*: Every seventh year, the Jews let the ground rest, and they did not plant crops (see Exodus 23.10,11; Leviticus 25.1-7).

and left their town. 50 Then Antiochus stationed his own soldiers there. 51 Mean-
while, his army was still attacking the troops stationed in the temple. They built movable towers and weapons that hurled fire, stones, arrows, and other deadly objects.

52 The Jews then built the same kinds of weapons and fought back for several days.
53 But it was the year when they had let the fields rest, and they ran out of supplies, because they had given what little food they had stored in the temple to those who had run away from the Gentiles and had come
to Judea. 54 Most of the people went home, because they were starving. Only a small group was left in the temple.

Lysias Wants Peace

55-56 Before Antiochus the Fourth died, he had made his friend Philip promise that the younger Antiochus[y] would take his place as king.[z] Philip wanted control of the kingdom, and so he brought back the part of the army that had been in Persia and Media.

When Lysias[a] found out what Philip was
doing, 57 he said to the young Antiochus the Fifth and to the officers and the soldiers:

> You must leave Jerusalem at once! Things are getting worse every day. We're short of food, and the enemy fortress is powerful. Besides, we have other problems to solve.
>
> 58 Let's sign a treaty with these
> Jews and the rest of their nation 59 to
> let them follow their own customs again. After all, they got angry and did all these things, because we ordered them to give up the traditions of their ancestors.

60-61 Antiochus and his officers liked what Lysias had suggested. So he promised to let the Jews live in peace, and then they left the fortress.

62 But when Antiochus came to Mount Zion and saw what a powerful fortress it was, he broke his promise and ordered his soldiers to tear down the fortress walls.
63 Then he rushed off to the city of Antioch where he found Philip in command. He attacked him and recaptured the city.

Bacchides and Alcimus
(2 *Maccabees* 7.1-25)

7 In the year 151[b] of the Syrian Kingdom, Demetrius,[c] the son of Seleucus,[d] sailed with a few soldiers from Rome to the coastal city of Tripolis,[e] where he appointed himself king.

2 From there, Demetrius went to his ancestors' palace in Antioch,[f] and he arrived just as some soldiers were arresting Antiochus and Lysias. The soldiers wanted to
hand them over to Demetrius. 3 But he
said, "I don't even want to look at them!"
4 The soldiers put them to death, and he took command of the whole kingdom.

5 Alcimus, leader of the unfaithful Jews, wanted Demetrius to appoint him high priest. So one day, he and his followers
went to Demetrius 6 and brought charges against the other Jews. They said:

> Judas and his brothers have killed all of your trusted friends[g] and forced
> us out of our country. 7 Please send an
> officer you can rely on and let him see the damage they have done to our property and to your kingdom. Then punish them and their followers.

8 Demetrius did as they requested and sent his trusted friend[g] Bacchides to Judea. Bacchides was a powerful and loyal official, who was governor of the region between
Egypt and the Euphrates River.[h] 9 But
Demetrius also appointed that worthless Alcimus to be high priest and sent him

[y]**6.55,56** *the younger Antiochus*: Antiochus V (see verse 17). [z]**6.55,56** *Philip promise . . . as king*: See verses 14,15. [a]**6.55,56** *Lysias*: See 3.32-36; 4.26-35. [b]**7.1** *year 151*: That is, 161 B.C. [c]**7.1** *Demetrius*: Demetrius the First (ruled Syria 162-150 B.C.). [d]**7.1** *Seleucus*: Seleucus was the brother of Antiochus IV (see 1.10). [e]**7.1** *Tripolis*: Greek "a city" (see 2 Maccabees 14.1); located on the Phoenician coast. [f]**7.2** *ancestors' palace in Antioch*: Greek "the royal palace of his ancestors." Antioch was about 170 miles from Tripolis. [g]**7.6,8** *trusted friends*: See the note at 2.18. [h]**7.8** *region . . . River*: That is, the land between the Nile and the Euphrates River.

along with instructions to punish the people of Judea.

10 Bacchides and Alcimus led a powerful army to Judea. Then they sent Judas and his brothers some messengers who lied and promised peace. 11 But no one believed them, because Bacchides and Alcimus had brought such a large army.

Some Jewish Leaders Visit Alcimus and Bacchides

12-13 Some very devout Jews wanted to make peace with the Gentiles. So they sent some of their experts in the Law of Moses to ask Bacchides and Alcimus to treat their people fairly. 14 These experts had said to themselves, "Alcimus has come with the army, but he is a priest from the family of Aaron, and he will surely treat us with kindness."

15 Alcimus promised to let these devout Jews live in peace, 16 and they believed him. But he later arrested sixty of them and put them all to death in one day. This is what the Scriptures[i] said would happen:

17 The blood-stained bodies
of God's faithful people
now lie scattered
everywhere in Jerusalem.
And there's no one left
to bury the dead.

18 Everyone started trembling with fear and said, "Alcimus and Bacchides are deceitful liars who never keep their word."

19 Bacchides moved his army out of Jerusalem and set up camp near Beth-Zaith. From there he sent soldiers to arrest some of the Jews and those troops who had deserted his army.[j] Then the soldiers murdered them all and dumped their bodies into a deep well.

20 Bacchides returned to Demetrius and left Alcimus with a large group of troops to control Judea. 21 Alcimus had a hard time keeping his position as high priest. 22 But a lot of troublemakers helped him, and together they took control of the nation and did horrible things to the people.

Judas Takes Action

23 When Judas found out that Alcimus and his followers were causing so much trouble, he said, "They're worse than the Gentiles." 24 Then Judas and his soldiers went to the nearby towns of Judea, punishing the unfaithful Jews, without letting any of them escape.

25 Alcimus realized that he could not oppose Judas and his powerful army. So he returned to King Demetrius and accused them of terrible crimes.

Nicanor Fights Judas

(2 Maccabees 15.1-36)

26 King Demetrius had an outstanding officer by the name of Nicanor, who hated the Jews. And the king ordered him to destroy them all. 27 When Nicanor and his large army arrived in Jerusalem, he sent messengers with false promises of peace to Judas and his brothers. 28 The messengers said, "Let's not get into a fight! A few of my bodyguards and I just want to have a friendly talk with you here in your camp."

29 Nicanor gave orders for his bodyguards to kidnap Judas. So Nicanor went with them to the camp, where Nicanor greeted him like a friend. 30 But Judas found out what Nicanor had in mind, and he was frightened and refused to meet with him.

31 When Nicanor realized that he could not trick Judas, he attacked him near the town of Caphar-Salama.[k] 32 Nicanor lost about five hundred soldiers in the battle, before the rest of his army retreated to the fortress in Jerusalem.

Nicanor Disgraces the Temple

33 Sometime later, Nicanor went up to Mount Zion, where he was met by some priests and leaders outside the temple. They welcomed him peacefully and showed him how they offered sacrifices as a way of asking God to bless King Demetrius.

34 Nicanor laughed and made fun of the priests and leaders. He even spit on them

[i]**7.16** *Scriptures*: See Psalm 79.1-3. [j]**7.19** *some . . . army*: Or "some Jews who had joined his army." [k]**7.31** *Caphar-Salama*: The exact location is unknown, though it was somewhere near Jerusalem.

7.17 Ps 79.2, 3.

and made them unfit to serve God. He was
so arrogant 35 and angry that he said, "If
Judas and his soldiers aren't handed over
to me immediately, I'll return here and destroy your temple just as soon as I defeat
him." Nicanor was furious when he left.
36 The priests returned to the temple
courtyard, where they stared at the temple
and the altar. Then with tears in their eyes,
they prayed:

37 "You have chosen this temple
as the place where your people
must worship in your name.
38 Defeat Nicanor and his army!
Destroy them in battle.
Don't ever forget
how they insulted you,
and don't let them live!"

39 Nicanor led his troops out of Jerusalem, and they camped near the town of
Beth-Horon, where they were joined by a
force of Syrian soldiers.
40 After Judas and his army of three
thousand soldiers set up camp near the
town of Adasa,[l] Judas prayed:
41 Our God, a long time ago the
king of Assyria sent messengers to insult you. But your angel slaughtered a
hundred eighty-five thousand of his
soldiers.[m]
42 Destroy Nicanor's army today,
and it will show our enemies that
Nicanor cannot get away with disgracing your temple.

God Punishes Nicanor

43 The battle took place on the thirteenth day of the month of Adar,[n] and
Nicanor's army was wiped out. He himself
was the first to be killed, 44 and when his
troops saw what had happened, they threw
down their weapons and ran for their lives.
45 For the rest of the day, Judas and his
soldiers chased the enemy troops from
Adasa as far as Gazara. They blew trumpets
as they went along, 46 and their friends
rushed out from nearby villages of Judea.
They attacked the enemy from the side
and forced them to turn back toward Judas
and his army. Not one of Nicanor's troops
survived.
47 The Jews took everything of value
from the dead enemy soldiers. Then they
chopped off Nicanor's head and the right
hand he had used to disgrace the temple
and took them to Jerusalem, where they
displayed them outside the city.
48-49 The Jews held a joyful victory celebration and decided to celebrate on the
thirteenth day of Adar each year.
50 And so, there was peace in Judea for
a while.

What Judas Heard about the Romans

8 This is what Judas heard about the
Romans:
The Romans are a famous and
mighty nation. But they are kind and
friendly to their allies and to other
countries that ask them for help.
2 Powerful Roman armies have already won great victories in Gaul.[o] Not
only have they defeated that country,
but they have forced it to pay taxes.
3 The Romans have also captured the
gold and silver mines in Spain. 4 In
fact, by patient and careful planning,
they have conquered all of Spain, even
though it is a great distance from
Rome.
The Romans have crushed the
kings of every nation that attacked
them, and they have forced the kings
who survived to pay taxes to them
each year. 5 The Roman armies have
also destroyed other enemies, including kings Perseus and Philip of Macedonia 6 and King Antiochus the Great
of Asia.[p]
The Romans even crushed the
forces of King Antiochus when he

[l]**7.40** *Adasa*: North of Jerusalem. [m]**7.41** *soldiers*: See 2 Kings 18.13-25; 19.20-37.
[n]**7.43** *Adar*: The twelfth month of the Hebrew calendar, from about mid-February to mid-March. [o]**8.2** *Gaul*: The area between the Alps, the Rhine River, the Atlantic Ocean, and the Pyrenees Mountains. Modern-day France covers much of this territory. [p]**8.6** *King Antiochus the Great of Asia*: The grandfather of Antiochus Epiphanes (see 1.10 and the note there).

7.41 2 K 19.35. **7.48,49** 3 Macc 6.36.

attacked with chariots, cavalry, one hundred twenty elephants, and a huge army. 7 They took him alive and ordered him and his descendants to give them a lot of money and many hostages. Antiochus also had to hand over to them 8 the countries of India, Media, and Lydia, as well as some of the best areas he controlled. Then the Romans gave all this territory to King Eumenes.

9-10 When the Romans found out that the Greeks were plotting against them, they sent a general to attack the Greeks. His army killed and wounded many of them and then captured their families and took everything of value. After the Romans had conquered Greece, they tore down its fortresses, and they still rule that country today.

11 The Romans destroyed the rest of the kingdoms and islands that opposed them, and they put Roman rulers in charge. 12-13 But they are kind to their allies and to other nations who ask for help.

If the Romans want to make someone a king, they do it. If they want to get rid of a king, they do that too. The way the Romans treat kings all over the world makes everyone terrified of them.

Although Rome is a mighty nation, 14 its rulers don't show off by wearing crowns or purple robes. 15 Instead, they have built a meeting house where three hundred twenty[q] senators meet each day to pass good laws for ruling their nation. 16 Every year, the Romans elect one man to govern them and the countries under their control. Everyone obeys this ruler, and no one is ever jealous of him.

Judas Makes an Agreement with Rome

17-18 Judas realized that he needed to make an agreement with the Romans in order to rescue his people from King Demetrius, who wanted to make them his slaves. So Judas sent Eupolemus and Jason[r] to work out an agreement with them.

19 After making the long trip to Rome, they met with the Roman senators and said, 20 "Judas Maccabeus and his brothers, together with all our people, have sent us, because they want you to make a peace treaty with us Jews and let us be your allies."

21 The Romans liked what Eupolemus and Jason said, 22 and they replied by writing a letter on sheets of bronze. They sent the letter to Jerusalem, to serve as a reminder that Rome was a friend and ally. The letter said:

> 23 We pray that all will go well with the Romans and Jews, both on land and sea, and that we will never have any wars or enemies.
>
> 24-25 You Jewish people must be ready and willing to do all you can, if enemies attack Rome or any of the nations under our rule. 26 As it was decided in Rome, you must not send food, weapons, money, or ships to these enemies. So keep your part of this agreement and don't expect anything in return.
>
> 27 In this same way, we Romans will gladly do all we can if you are attacked. 28 We won't supply your enemies with food, weapons, money, or ships, and we will keep our word, without any tricks.
>
> 29 This is the agreement that we Romans have now made with you Jews, 30 but it can be changed, if later we both agree to do so. And any changes will be just as binding.

31 The Romans also told the Jewish messengers:

> We've written to King Demetrius about the trouble he is causing you, and we told him:
>
> "King Demetrius, the Jews are friends and allies of Rome. Why are

[q]**8.15** *three hundred twenty*: Some manuscripts have "three hundred." [r]**8.17,18** *Eupolemus and Jason*: Greek "Eupolemus, the son of John and the grandson of Accos, and Jason the son of Eleazar."

8.17,18 2 Macc 4.11. **8.22** 1 Macc 14.18.

you so cruel to them? 32 If we hear of
any more trouble, we will defend their
rights and attack you with our army
and navy."

Bacchides Returns to Judea

9 King Demetrius found out that
Nicanor and all his soldiers had been
killed. So he sent Bacchides and Alcimus[s]
the high priest back to Judea with half of
his army.

2 On the way to Gilgal in Judea, Bacchides and Alcimus captured the town of
Mesaloth in Arbela,[t] and they killed many
of the people. 3 They reached Jerusalem
early in the year 152[u] of the Syrian Kingdom and set up camp outside the city.
4 Then they stationed twenty thousand soldiers and two thousand cavalry in the town
of Berea.

5 Three thousand of the Jews' best soldiers were camped at Elasa under the command of Judas. 6 But when they saw the
size of the enemy army, they were terrified
and ran. Only about eight hundred soldiers
stayed in camp.

7 When the fighting was about to start,
Judas suddenly realized that most of his
troops had deserted, and he was terribly
discouraged because there was no time to
bring them back. 8 Judas felt like giving up,
but he said to his remaining troops, "Get
ready to attack! We've got a good chance
to win."

9 But they argued with Judas and said,
"We will all be killed if we attack with such
a small force. Let's wait and come back
with a larger army."

10 Judas answered, "We will never back
down from a fight with the enemy! If it's
our time to die for the honor of our nation,
then let's die like heroes."

11-12 Bacchides led his army out of camp
and placed half of his cavalry to the left of
his soldiers and half to the right. His best
troops led the way, followed by men who
were experts with bows and arrows or rocks
and slings. Bacchides himself was on the
right side of his army.

Both armies gave the signal to attack,
and the battle began. 13 The fighting lasted
from daylight until dark, and the ground
trembled because of the noise.

14 At one point in the battle, Judas
looked over at the right side of the enemy
army and saw Bacchides and many of his
best soldiers there. So Judas and his
bravest troops attacked 15 and destroyed
most of that part of the enemy army. The
few who escaped were chased as far as
Mount Azotus.[v]

16 When the soldiers on the left side of
Bacchides' army learned that the rest of
their army had been wiped out, they swung
around and attacked from behind. 17 The
fighting was fierce, and many from both
armies were either killed or wounded.
18 Judas himself died in the battle, and the
rest of the Jews ran away.

19 Jonathan and Simon took the body of
their brother Judas back to Modein and
buried him in the family tomb. 20 They
cried bitterly, and everyone in Israel
mourned for a long time. They said:

21 "Judas was a mighty warrior
who saved our nation.
Why did he have to die?"

22 Indeed, Judas was a brave warrior
and a great hero, and he did many other
important things that are not included in
this book.

Jonathan Leads the Jews

23 After the death of Judas, some troublemakers and their worthless friends
showed up again everywhere in Judea.
24 The crops had failed that year, and
everyone in the whole country joined
these troublemakers.

25 Bacchides appointed some godless
people to rule the country, 26 and they
searched carefully for any followers of

[s]**9.1** *Bacchides and Alcimus*: See 7.5-11. [t]**9.2** *Mesaloth in Arbela*: Arbela was west of Lake Galilee. In Hebrew "Mesaloth" means "paths," probably referring to those that led to the numerous caves in this region that were used as hiding places. [u]**9.3** *year 152*: That is, 160 B.C.
[v]**9.15** *Mount Azotus*: Azotus is the Greek name for Ashdod (a Philistine town), but it is likely that another town of the same name is being referred to.

Judas. Then they brought them to Bacchides, who laughed as he punished them.
27 The troubles in Israel were worse now than they had been since the time God had stopped sending prophets.
28 The followers of Judas got together and said to Jonathan:
29 Ever since your brother Judas died, we haven't had anyone like him to lead us into battle against enemies like Bacchides or against our own people who hate us.
30 So today we have chosen you to take the place of Judas. Be our ruler and lead us in battle.
31 Jonathan agreed.

The Wars of Jonathan

32 Bacchides plotted to kill Jonathan as soon as he found out that Jonathan was the new leader.
33 But his plan failed, because Jonathan and his brother Simon were warned and escaped with their followers to a camp near the water hole at Asphar in the desert around Tekoa.
34 On a Sabbath, Bacchides learned where the camp was, and he led his army across the Jordan River.[w]
35 Jonathan's brother John was also one of the Jewish leaders. One day, on orders from Jonathan, he asked some friendly Nabateans[x] to guard their huge stock of supplies.
36 But some people of the Jambri tribe from Medeba captured John and the supplies, then rode away.
37 Later, Jonathan and his brother Simon were told:

> The Jambri tribe is holding a big wedding celebration, and the bride is being brought here from the town of Nadabath. Many soldiers are guarding her because she's the daughter of a very important man from Canaan.

38 Meanwhile, Jonathan and Simon had learned that this tribe had murdered their brother John. So they left camp and set an ambush on a hillside overlooking the road.
39 Soon they saw a noisy group of travelers with a lot of baggage. It was the bride, with her family and friends. The groom and his friends were coming to meet them, playing drums and musical instruments, and all of them were armed.
40 The Jews attacked from their hiding places, killing and wounding many in the wedding party. Then they took everything of value from the dead, and the others ran off into the hills.

41 A wedding was turned
    into a funeral,
and wedding music
    into funeral songs.

42 After Jonathan and Simon had punished the tribe of Jambri, they returned to their camp in the marshes along the Jordan River.
43 But Bacchides found out where they were camped, and on the Sabbath he led a large army to the edge of the river.
44 Jonathan warned his soldiers:

> Get ready to fight for your lives! We've never been in this much danger before,
> 45 and there is no way out. The enemy army is both in front of us and behind us, and the river is on one side, and the marshes covered with thornbushes are on the other.
> 46 So pray for God to rescue us.

47 As soon as the battle began, Jonathan tried to kill Bacchides; however, he escaped to the rear of his army.
48 Jonathan and his soldiers then jumped into the river and started swimming toward the other side, but the enemy troops did not go after them.
49 That day Bacchides lost about a thousand men.

Bacchides Builds Fortresses in Judea

50 Bacchides returned to Jerusalem and started building high walls and strong gates for some of the towns of Judea, including Emmaus, Beth-Horon, Bethel, Timnath, Pharathon, and Tephon, and the fortress at Jericho.
51 He stationed soldiers in these towns, and they caused trouble for the Jews.
52 Bacchides also strengthened the fortress in Jerusalem and the towns of Beth-Zur and Gazara. He put soldiers and food supplies in these strongholds.
53 Then he took the sons of the Jewish leaders as

[w]**9.34** This verse seems to be in the wrong place and may belong with verse 43.
[x]**9.35** *Nabateans*: See the note at 5.25.

hostages and locked them up in the Jerusalem fortress.

Alcimus the High Priest Dies

54 In the second month of the year 153[y]
of the Syrian Kingdom, Alcimus the high
priest ordered his followers to destroy the
wall in the temple courtyard that prophets
of earlier times had said should be built.
55 But no sooner had the work begun, than
Alcimus got sick and everything stopped.
He couldn't move or even give instructions
for making out his will. 56 He died a very
painful death.
57 After Bacchides learned that Alcimus
had died, he returned to King Demetrius,
and Judea had peace for two years.

Bacchides Attacks Jonathan

58 Once again the troublemakers started
plotting against Jonathan and his followers by saying, "They feel safe and aren't
suspecting a thing, so let's send for Bacchides. He could easily capture them in
one night."
59 The troublemakers met with Bacchides and planned an attack. 60 Then Bacchides set out for Judea with a large army.
On the way, he sent secret orders for his
followers there to capture Jonathan and his
troops.
But they could not do this, because
Jonathan and his followers learned of Bacchides' plan, 61 and so they arrested about
fifty leaders of the plot and put them to
death.
62 Jonathan and Simon led their forces
to the desert town of Beth-Basi.[z] Part of the
town had been destroyed, but they repaired
it and built high walls with strong gates.
63 When Bacchides found out about
this, he got together his whole army and
sent orders to his followers in Judea.
64 Then he led his army to Beth-Basi and
surrounded the town. His soldiers set up
weapons to break through the walls, and
they attacked that town for a long time.
65 At one point in the battle, Jonathan
put his brother Simon in command of the
town. Then he led a small group into the
country, 66 where he defeated Odomera
and his tribe. He also wiped out another
tribe called the Phasirites. 67 Those who
were left joined his army and helped him
fight against Bacchides.[a]
Meanwhile, Simon and his soldiers
rushed out of Beth-Basi and set fire to the
weapons that had been set up for breaking
through the walls. 68 In fact, they destroyed
the entire army of Bacchides and ruined all
of his plans for war.
69 Bacchides was so furious at the troublemakers who had told him to invade
Judea that he put many of them to death.
Then he got ready to return to his own
country.
70 When Jonathan found out that Bacchides was about to leave Judea, he sent
him some messengers who said, "Let's
make peace and set our prisoners free."
71-72 Bacchides agreed. He released the
Jews he had captured in Judea and
promised not to bother Judas again. Then
he went back to his own country and never
returned to Judea.
73 Now there was peace in Israel.
Jonathan ruled from the town of Michmash[b] and started destroying godless people everywhere in the nation.

Demetrius Makes Friends with Jonathan

10 Alexander Epiphanes[c] was the son
of King Antiochus the Fourth.[d] He
landed on the Phoenician coast and captured the city of Ptolemais in the year 160[e]
of the Syrian Kingdom. The people welcomed Alexander as their king.
2 When King Demetrius[f] found out that
Alexander was in Ptolemais, he got together a mighty army and set out to attack
him. 3 Demetrius sent Jonathan a friendly

[y] **9.54** *second month . . . year 153*: That is, 159 B.C. The second month of the Hebrew calendar was Iyyar or Ziv, from about mid-April to mid-May. [z] **9.62** *Beth-Basi*: Southeast of Jerusalem.
[a] **9.67** *Those . . . Bacchides*: Or "Then Jonathan and his soldiers set out for another attack."
[b] **9.73** *Michmash*: North of Jerusalem. [c] **10.1** *Alexander Epiphanes*: Better known as Alexander Balas (ruled Syria 150-145 B.C.). [d] **10.1** *Antiochus the Fourth*: See 1.10 and the note there.
[e] **10.1** *year 160*: That is, 152 B.C. [f] **10.2** *King Demetrius*: See 7.1; 8.31; 9.1.

letter that flattered him. 4-5 He was thinking, "Jonathan could not have forgotten the
terrible things I did to him and his brothers
and his nation. If I don't hurry and make
peace with him, he will join forces with
Alexander and attack."
6 In the letter Demetrius said:
Jonathan, you have my permission
to build a strong army and to be my
ally. And I have told my soldiers to
release to you the hostages that I'm
keeping in the fortress at Jerusalem.
7 Jonathan took this letter to Jerusalem
and read it to everyone, including those in
the fortress. 8 His enemies were terrified by
the letter, because it allowed him to build
up an army. 9 The soldiers in the fortress
immediately released the hostages to
Jonathan, and he let them go home to their
parents.
10 Jonathan moved to Jerusalem and began repairing and rebuilding the city. 11 He
ordered the workers to cut square blocks of
stone and to build strong walls around
Jerusalem and Mount Zion. The workers
followed his orders.
12-13 Bacchides had left foreign soldiers
in the fortresses he had built, but they
quickly returned home. 14 Only a few Jews
who were unfaithful to the Law stayed in
Beth-Zur for their own safety.

Jonathan Becomes High Priest

15 Someone told King Alexander,[g]
"Jonathan and his brothers are brave fighters who have fought many wars and who
know what it means to suffer. And Demetrius has promised them many things if
they will join him."
16 Alexander replied, "I'd better make
Jonathan my friend and ally. I'll never find
anyone else like him."
17 Alexander then sent Jonathan a letter, in which he said:
18 King Alexander sends greetings
to his dear friend Jonathan!
19 I've been told that you are a powerful soldier and the kind of man who
deserves to be one of my trusted
friends.[h] 20 So I appoint you high
priest for your nation and a friend of
the king. This means that you must be
a very loyal follower. I'm also sending
you a purple robe and a gold crown.
21 During the Festival of Shelters, in the
seventh month of the year 160[i] of the Syrian Kingdom, Jonathan became high priest;
he also built up a strong army.

King Demetrius Writes to Jonathan Again

22 When King Demetrius heard the
news about Alexander and Jonathan, he
was deeply distressed and said, 23 "What
have we done? Alexander's agreement with
the Jews has made him very powerful.
24 Now I must write a friendly letter to the
Jews and promise them better gifts and
more honors. Then they'll come over to my
side."
25 And so, Demetrius wrote:
King Demetrius sends greetings to
the Jewish nation.
26 I was very pleased to learn that
you have kept your promises. This
means you are still my friends and
allies.
27 If you remain loyal to me, I will
reward you for everything you do. 28 I
will give you valuable gifts and not
make you pay heavy taxes.
29 My Jewish friends, you are ex-
cused from paying taxes on salt, as
well as the other usual taxes, including
the special royal tax. 30 And from now
on, you no longer have to give me a
share of your grain and fruit.[j]
I will never again take anything you
grow in Judea or in the three districts
added to Judea from Samaria and
Galilee. 31 And I consider Jerusalem
and the land that belongs to it so holy
that I won't tax the money you receive
from these places.
32 The high priest will take over
from me the control of the Jerusalem

[g]**10.15** *King Alexander*: See verse 1. [h]**10.19** *trusted friends*: See the note at 2.18.
[i]**10.21** *year 160*: That is, 152 B.C. [j]**10.30** *a share . . . fruit*: Greek "one-third of the grain and one-half of the fruit from the trees."
10.30 1 Macc 11.34.

fortress, and his own soldiers can guard it. 33 I will free every Jew who has been taken prisoner anywhere in my kingdom. You won't have to pay anything for them, and they won't have to pay taxes, not even on their livestock.[k]

34 On special days such as festivals, Sabbaths, or the first day of a month, my officials will not collect taxes or fees from any Jew in the kingdom. And on the three days before and after festivals, my officials will not collect taxes or fees. 35 No one will collect taxes from you or bother you for any reason on those special days.

36 I will let as many as thirty thousand Jewish soldiers join my army, and they will be paid the same as the other soldiers. 37 Some of them will help guard my main fortresses, and others will be given important jobs in the kingdom. I'll let them live by their own laws and choose their own leaders and officers. In fact, this is how things already are in Judea.

38 The three districts of Judea that belonged to Samaria will become a permanent part of Judea. The high priest will be the only ruler for Judea and these three districts, and everyone must obey him.

39 I have given the city of Ptolemais and the land around it as a gift to the temple in Jerusalem, in order to supply money to help pay for running the temple.

40 Every year, I'll send you fifteen thousand pieces of silver from the treasuries in places under my control.

41 For the past few years my officials have failed to send you the extra money that they should have sent. Now they will start sending it again to meet the needs of the temple.[l]

42 In the past, you had to pay me five thousand pieces of silver every year as a tax on the money the temple earned. Now this tax money will go to the priests who serve in the temple.

43 If anyone is hiding in or around the Jerusalem temple because they owe money to me or someone else, they are free to leave. And any property they own in my kingdom will be returned to them.

44-45 I will pay for repairing and rebuilding the temple. I will also pay for fixing the walls and towers in the towns in Judea, including Jerusalem.

The Death of King Demetrius

46 Jonathan and the others remembered how cruel King Demetrius had been to them, and they did not believe a word he had written. 47 Instead, they sided with King Alexander, because he had come with the best offer of peace, and they remained his allies until he died.

48 Alexander built up a mighty army and led it into battle against the army of Demetrius.

49-50 The fighting was fierce and lasted until dark. Finally, the soldiers of Demetrius ran away, but Alexander and his army went after them and killed many, including Demetrius himself.[m]

Alexander and Ptolemy Become Allies

51 King Alexander sent a message to King Ptolemy the Sixth[n] of Egypt. It said:

52 I've returned to rule the kingdom of my ancestors. But before I could take control, I had to do away with Demetrius. 53 So I destroyed him and his army, and now I am king.

54 Ptolemy, I would like for us to become allies. Let me marry your daughter and be your son-in-law. Then I will give each of you gifts that are worthy of a king and his daughter.

55 Ptolemy wrote back:

Alexander, it was a happy day when you came back to rule the kingdom of your ancestors. 56 I'll let you marry my daughter, just as you asked in your

[k]**10.33** *and they . . . livestock*: One possible meaning for the difficult Greek text. [l]**10.41** *to meet the needs of the temple*: Or "for worship services in the temple." [m]**10.49,50** *Finally . . . himself*: Some manuscripts add "At one point, Alexander's troops ran away and the army of Demetrius went after them. Demetrius died in the fighting." [n]**10.51** *Ptolemy the Sixth*: Ruled 180-145 B.C.

letter. But first, meet me in the city of Ptolemais, so we can get to know each other.

57 In the year 162[o] of the Syrian Kingdom, Ptolemy and his daughter Cleopatra[p] left Egypt and went to the city of Ptolemais. 58 The two kings met each other, and Ptolemy let Alexander marry Cleopatra. They had a very fancy wedding, just as kings always do.

59 Meanwhile, Jonathan the high priest received a letter from Alexander, inviting him to come to Ptolemais for a visit with him and Ptolemy. 60 Jonathan accepted the invitation and won their friendship by giving both kings and their trusted friends[q] some silver and gold, as well as many other gifts.

61 One day, a group of troublemakers and rebels came from Judea and brought charges against Jonathan. But Alexander would not listen to them. 62 Instead, he let Jonathan wear the purple robes of royalty 63 and sit next to him. The king told his officers, "Take Jonathan to the center of the city and order everyone to stop bothering him with all these charges."

64 The troublemakers listened to the officers telling everyone to leave Jonathan alone. And when they saw Jonathan standing there in his purple robes, they realized how important he was. So they all ran away.

65 Alexander gave Jonathan even more honors. He included him among his most trusted friends and made him governor of Judea and a general in the Syrian army. 66 After this, Jonathan returned to Jerusalem, safe and sound.

Jonathan and Apollonius

67 Demetrius the Second was the son of Demetrius, and in the year 165[r] of the Syrian Kingdom, he sailed from Crete to the land of his ancestors. 68 When Alexander heard about this, he became worried and returned to the city of Antioch.

69 Demetrius appointed Apollonius ruler of Southwest Syria Province.[s] So Apollonius built up a large army and set up camp near the town of Jamnia. Then he sent the following letter to Jonathan the high priest:

> 70 Jonathan, you are the only one who is still fighting against us, and you are making others laugh and sneer at me. Why do you keep rebelling against us there in the hill country?
>
> 71 If you're so proud of your army, come down out of the hills and fight. You will find out that the people in the towns are on our side. 72 Just ask anyone, and they will tell you who I am and who my followers are. You don't stand a chance against us.
>
> Your own ancestors were defeated twice right here in their own land. 73 What makes you think you can win a battle in the valley against my army and cavalry? There are no rocks or stones to crawl behind, and there is no place where you can run away.

74 Jonathan was furious when he read this letter. He chose ten thousand soldiers, then left Jerusalem to meet his brother Simon, who was coming to help him.

75 The two brothers surrounded the town of Joppa, because Apollonius had soldiers there. No one would let them in at first. 76 But they attacked and frightened the people into opening the gates; then they took command of the town.

77 When Apollonius found out that they had taken Joppa, he brought three thousand cavalry and a large force of soldiers to the town of Azotus. He wanted the Jews to think he was only passing through the town. So he led his troops out to the nearby valley, where he was sure his cavalry could protect the soldiers.

78 Jonathan followed Apollonius to Azotus, and a battle broke out 79 when a thousand of Apollonius' cavalry suddenly left their hiding places and attacked from behind. 80 The cavalry surrounded Jonathan's

[o]**10.57** *year 162*: That is, 150 B.C. [p]**10.57** *Cleopatra*: Cleopatra Thea III, not the more famous Cleopatra VII (69-30 B.C.). [q]**10.60** *trusted friends*: See the note at 2.18. [r]**10.67** *year 165*: That is, 147 B.C. [s]**10.69** *Southwest Syria Province*: "Coele-Syria" in traditional translations; it originally referred to the land between the Lebanon and the Anti-Lebanon mountains, but at this time it included all Palestine and Phoenicia as well.

troops and shot arrows at them from early morning until late afternoon. 81 But Jonathan's forces held their ground, and he told them to keep fighting until the enemy cavalry wore themselves out.

82 Then Simon led some of his soldiers into the battle and overpowered the enemy army. The enemy foot soldiers ran for their lives, 83 and the cavalry scattered over the valleys.

Some of the enemy soldiers ran back to Azotus and hid in the temple of their god Dagon, thinking they would be safe. 84 But Jonathan destroyed Azotus and the nearby towns and took everything of value. Then he burned down the temple with everyone inside. 85 Eight thousand enemy soldiers died in the battle and the fire.

86 Jonathan left Azotus and ordered his army to set up camp near the town of Askalon, where the people came out to honor him. 87 Then Jonathan and his soldiers, loaded down with everything they had taken, returned to Jerusalem.

88 When Alexander heard about Jonathan's victories, he gave him even more honors. 89 He sent a gold buckle that only the most respected members of the king's family[t] were allowed to wear. Alexander also gave Jonathan the town of Ekron and the land around it.

A Battle between Ptolemy and Alexander

11 King Ptolemy the Sixth[u] of Egypt got together more ships and soldiers than anyone could count. Then he made a secret plan to take over the kingdom of his son-in-law Alexander.

2 Ptolemy led his forces toward Syria and told each town he came to that he was on a friendly visit. Everyone believed Ptolemy and welcomed him, just as his son-in-law Alexander had ordered them to do. 3 But he stationed soldiers in their towns.

4 The people of Azotus met Ptolemy and showed him all that was left of their town, of the nearby villages, and of the temple of Dagon that had been destroyed by fire. They also showed him the piles of dead and burned bodies they had heaped up beside the road after the battle with Jonathan. 5 Everyone blamed Jonathan for all the damage, but Ptolemy said nothing.

6 Jonathan met Ptolemy at the town of Joppa, and Jonathan honored him. The two men spent the night there, 7 then the next day Jonathan rode with him to the Eleutherus River[v] before heading back for Jerusalem.

8 Soon Ptolemy had command of the towns on the coast as far as Seleucia. He kept plotting against Alexander, 9 and one day he sent a message to Demetrius the king, which said:

> Let's make an agreement. I will arrange for you to marry my daughter Cleopatra,[w] the wife of Alexander. Then you can rule your father's kingdom. 10 It was a big mistake to let Alexander marry her. He even tried to have me murdered!

11 Ptolemy said other insulting things about Alexander because he wanted his kingdom. 12 Then he ordered Cleopatra to leave Alexander, and he told Demetrius to marry her. Now Ptolemy and Alexander hated each other, and everyone knew it. 13 Ptolemy went to the city of Antioch, where he crowned himself king—both of Syria and of Egypt.

Alexander and Ptolemy Die

14 Meanwhile, Alexander had gone to the country of Cilicia because some towns there had rebelled against him. 15 When Alexander heard what Ptolemy had done, he attacked him, but Ptolemy's large army defeated Alexander and forced him to retreat.

16 After Ptolemy won this important victory, Alexander found a hiding place in Arabia, 17 but Zabdiel the Arab chopped off Alexander's head and sent it to Ptolemy. 18 Three days later, Ptolemy himself died,

[t] **10.89** *members of the king's family*: This is one of the highest titles that Greek kings gave to their advisors and officials (see 3.32). [u] **11.1** *King Ptolemy the Sixth*: Ruled 180-145 B.C. (see 1.18). [v] **11.7** *Eleutherus River*: In Syria about twenty miles from Tripolis (see 7.1). [w] **11.9** *Cleopatra*: See the note at 10.57.

and the people in his fortresses killed the soldiers he had stationed there.

19 In the year 167[x] of the Syrian Kingdom, Demetrius the Second[y] became king.

Jonathan and King Demetrius the Second

20 A little later, Jonathan gathered an army in Judea. He built a lot of weapons to break through city walls and then attacked the fortress in Jerusalem.

21 King Demetrius the Second found out about the attack from some Jews who really hated the other Jews. 22 Demetrius became furious, and right away he went to the city of Ptolemais. From there he wrote a letter to Jonathan and said, "Stop attacking the fortress in Jerusalem! Come to Ptolemais as soon as you can. We need to talk."

23 After Jonathan read the letter, he ordered his soldiers to keep up the attack. Then he risked his own life by taking some of the priests and leaders 24 to Ptolemais. He brought silver, gold, some clothing, and many other gifts for Demetrius, which made Demetrius friendly toward him.

25 Some Jews who were unfaithful to their Law kept bringing charges against Jonathan. 26 But Demetrius treated him well, just as the rulers before him had done. And one day, when all the trusted friends[z] of Demetrius were there, he gave Jonathan an even higher honor 27 by making him one of his most trusted friends. Demetrius also let Jonathan continue as high priest and keep all the honors he had already been given.

28 Jonathan asked Demetrius to stop collecting taxes from Judea and the three districts of Samaria,[a] and, in return, he promised to give him three hundred thousand pieces of silver. 29 Demetrius agreed, then wrote the following letter:

30 King Demetrius sends greetings to his good friend Jonathan and to the Jewish nation.

31 I am sending you a copy of the letter I wrote about you to my friend Lasthenes, and here is what I said:

32 "King Demetrius sends greetings to his dear friend Lasthenes.

33 "The Jews are our friends, and I have decided to do them a big favor since they are loyal to us and can be trusted to keep their promises. 34 The three regions of Aphairema, Lydda, and Ramathaim,[b] together with the land around them, used to belong to Samaria. Now they belong to Judea and are an official possession of the Jews.

"Those Jews who offer sacrifices in Jerusalem don't have to pay me my share of their grain and fruit each year.[c] 35 And they don't have to pay me a tenth of their crops, the fee on salt, the special royal tax, or any other taxes.

36 "Lasthenes, no one may ever change even one of these orders. 37 Make a copy of this letter and send it to Jonathan. He will put it on God's holy mountain where it can be seen by everyone."

Trypho Plots against Demetrius the Second

38 No one opposed King Demetrius the Second, and his kingdom was at peace. So he sent his own soldiers back home and kept only the foreign troops he had hired from the Greek islands. But this made his own soldiers turn against him, because they had fought for many years, first in his father's army and then in his.

39 Trypho had been a follower of Alexander Epiphanes,[d] and when he found out how angry all of Demetrius' troops were, he went to Imalkue the Arab, who was taking

[x]**11.19** *year 167*: That is, 145 B.C. (Demetrius II ruled 145-139 B.C.). [y]**11.19** *Demetrius the Second*: The son of Demetrius I [z]**11.26** *trusted friends*: See the note at 2.18. [a]**11.28** *the three districts of Samaria*: Greek "the three districts and Samaria." [b]**11.34** *Ramathaim*: Other Greek manuscripts have "Rathamin" (that is, Arimathea). [c]**11.34** *Those Jews . . . each year*: Or "These places were given to the Jews to help everyone who offers sacrifices in Jerusalem. Now they don't have to pay me my share." [d]**11.39** *Alexander Epiphanes*: See 10.1 and the note there.

11.34 1 Macc 10.30.

care of Antiochus the Sixth,[e] the young son of King Alexander.

40 Trypho stayed with Imalkue a long time and kept begging him to hand over the young boy. He said, "Antiochus should take his father's place as king, because Demetrius has let all of his own soldiers go, and they hate him for it."

41 Meanwhile, Jonathan sent the following message to Demetrius:

> Please take your soldiers out of the fortresses around here, especially the one in Jerusalem. They keep attacking us.

42 Demetrius wrote back:

> Jonathan, of course I will do what you and your people have asked. And I will show great honors to you and your people as soon as I can.
>
> 43 For now, please do me a favor and send some troops to help me, because my own soldiers have rebelled.

44 Jonathan sent a heavily armed force of three thousand soldiers to the city of Antioch, and Demetrius was very glad to see them.

45 Not long after this, a mob of about a hundred twenty thousand people tried to kill Demetrius. 46 They took over the streets and started rioting. So Demetrius ran away to his palace 47 and ordered the Jewish soldiers to protect him.

They came and made sure Demetrius was safe. Then they went through the entire city, killing almost a hundred thousand people. 48 They not only rescued Demetrius that day, but they also set the city on fire and took everything of value.

49 When the people of Antioch saw that the Jews had taken over their city, they were terrified and begged Demetrius for help. They shouted, 50 "Please make peace with us! Order the Jews to stop attacking us and our city."

51 Demetrius made peace with the people as soon as they had put down their weapons. The Jewish soldiers had earned the respect of everyone in his kingdom, and they returned to Jerusalem with all the things they had captured.

52 Demetrius was now in complete control of his kingdom again, and there was no more trouble. 53 Before long, he forgot how much Jonathan had helped him, and he broke his promises to Jonathan by treating him like an enemy and causing him a lot of trouble.

Jonathan and Antiochus Become Friends

54 When Trypho came back from his visit to Imalkue the Arab, he brought young Antiochus the Sixth[e] with him, and the boy began to rule as king.

55 The soldiers that King Demetrius the Second had sent home now sided with Antiochus and Trypho. They attacked Demetrius, forcing him to run for his life. 56 Trypho captured Demetrius' elephants[f] as well as the city of Antioch.

57 Young King Antiochus wrote a letter to Jonathan, in which he said:

> I will let you continue as high priest. I have also made you one of my trusted friends[g] and the ruler of the four regions.[h]
>
> 58 I am sending you some gold plates and dishes, and I am giving you permission to drink from a gold cup and to wear royal robes and a gold buckle.[i]
>
> 59 Your brother Simon is now the ruler of the land from Phoenicia to the Egyptian border.

The Wars of Jonathan and Simon

60 Jonathan left Judea and led his army across the Jordan River. They were going from town to town, when the entire Syrian army arrived and offered to help them fight. So Jonathan took his forces to the town of Askalon, where the people welcomed and honored them.

61 He led his troops to the town of Gaza, but its people refused to let them

[e]**11.39,54** *Antiochus the Sixth*: Ruled 145-142 B.C. [f]**11.56** *elephants*: Or "wild animals." [g]**11.57** *trusted friends*: See the note at 2.18. [h]**11.57** *four regions*: See 11.34. [i]**11.58** *gold plates . . . buckle*: Only the most important friends of the king could use such dishes and wear such clothes and jewelry.

enter. Then they surrounded the town and
took everything of value from the villages
nearby.
When Jonathan's forces burned down
these villages, 62 the people of Gaza begged
him not to destroy their town. He agreed,
but he sent the sons of Gaza's rulers as
hostages to Jerusalem. After this, Jonathan
led his army as far as Damascus.
63 Someone told Jonathan:

> King Demetrius the Second has sent a large force under the command of royal officers to the town of Kadesh in Galilee. The officers have orders to make you give up your position as high priest.

64 Simon stayed behind in Judea while
his brother Jonathan set out to attack the
army of Demetrius. 65 Simon attacked the
town of Beth-Zur and kept it surrounded
for a long time 66 before it surrendered to
him. He took command of Beth-Zur and
told its people to leave. Then he stationed
his own troops there.
67 Meanwhile, Jonathan and his soldiers
had set up camp near Lake Galilee. And
early one morning, he led them to Hazor
Valley.
68 Demetrius' army of foreign troops was
waiting for them in the valleys. Some of
them attacked immediately, while others
waited behind some hills, ready to make a
surprise attack.
69 When the enemy soldiers came out of
their hiding places and attacked, 70 almost
all the Jewish troops ran away, except two
officers by the names of Mattathias and
Judas.[j]
71 Jonathan ripped his clothes and put
dirt on his head to show his sorrow. Then
he prayed 72 and returned to the battle. His
army defeated their enemies and made
them run for their lives.
73 When the Jewish troops that had deserted saw their enemies trying to escape,
they returned and helped chase them as
far as the enemy camp at Kadesh. The
Jews set up camp there, 74 and Jonathan
went back to Jerusalem. About three thousand foreign soldiers were killed that day.

Jonathan Makes Treaties with Rome and Sparta

12 Jonathan realized that this was a
good time to make sure the Romans remained on friendly terms with the
Jews. So he sent some messengers to
Rome. 2 He also wrote letters to the city
of Sparta and other places for the same
reason.
3 When the messengers arrived in
Rome, they met with the Roman senators
and said, "Jonathan the high priest and the
Jewish people have sent us here to renew
our friendship with Rome and to make sure
that we remain allies."
4 After the meeting, the Romans wrote
letters to the other nations where the messengers were going. In these letters they
said, "Help these men return safely to
Judea."
5 Jonathan himself wrote a letter to the
people of Sparta in which he said:

> 6 Jonathan the high priest, the
> other priests, the Jewish council, and
> the rest of our people send greetings to
> our dear friends in Sparta.
> 7 Some time ago, your king, Arius,
> sent a letter to Onias, our high priest.
> Arius said that Jews and Spartans are
> related, as you can see from the copy
> of the king's letter we have sent along
> with this letter.
> 8 When Onias read this, he wel-
> comed your messenger with honors,
> because your letter clearly stated that
> Jews and Spartans should become
> friends and allies.
> 9 We Jews don't really need friends
> and allies, since our Scriptures give us
> hope and strength. 10 But we decided
> to write you anyway to renew our
> friendship and to make sure that we
> are still on good terms. After all, it has
> been a long time since you wrote us,
> and we don't want to become like
> strangers to each other.
> 11 It is our custom and duty to re-
> member relatives. So during our festi-
> vals and other special days, we always
> think of you as we pray and offer sacri-

[j]11.70 *Mattathias and Judas*: Greek "Mattathias the son of Absalom and Judas the son of Chalphi."

fices. 12 We are very pleased that you have become so famous.

13 We have had plenty of troubles and wars of our own. Even the nearby kings have attacked us. 14 However, there was no reason to bother you or other friends and allies with our problems. 15 God always helps us, and we defeated our enemies and were rescued from them.

16 We have sent Numenius and Antipater[k] as messengers to Rome to make sure that we and the Romans remain on good terms. 17 They also have orders to bring this letter to you with our greetings, because we want to be certain that you still consider us your relatives.

18 Please send a reply.

19 Here is a copy of the letter that King Arius wrote to Onias some time ago:

20 "King Arius of Sparta sends greetings to Onias the high priest.

21 "We have found a document that says Spartans and Jews are relatives because both nations descended from Abraham. 22 Now that I know this, I want you to write and tell me how you are doing. 23 I am writing to tell you that your livestock together with everything else you own belongs to us. And our livestock together with everything else we own belongs to you.

"My messengers have orders to tell you about this."

Other Wars of Jonathan and Simon

24 Jonathan found out that the officers of King Demetrius the Second[l] were now ready to invade his country with a more powerful army than before.

25 Jonathan did not want the king's army to invade Jerusalem, so he led his troops to the region around Hamath,[m] where he saw the enemy camp. 26 Jonathan sent out spies, who came back and reported, "The king's army is getting ready to attack us tonight."

27 At sunset, Jonathan stationed some of his troops on lookout duty around the camp, and he told the others, "Stay awake and be ready to fight at any time."

28 But the king's troops lost their nerve and were frightened when someone informed them that the Jews were ready for their attack. So they lit campfires and ran away.[n]

29 The campfires burned all night, and the Jews did not find out until morning that the enemy had left. 30 Jonathan sent troops after them, but the king's army had already crossed the Eleutherus River.

31 There was a tribe of Arabs named the Zabadeans, and Jonathan ordered his troops to destroy them. The troops took everything of value, 32 then Jonathan led them all the way to Damascus.

33-34 Meanwhile, Simon took his soldiers as far as Askalon and the nearby fortresses. Someone told him, "The town of Joppa is about to join Demetrius." Simon made a surprise attack on Joppa; he captured the town and stationed some of his troops there to guard it.

Jerusalem Is Made Stronger

35 Jonathan returned to Jerusalem and met with the Jewish leaders. They decided to build fortresses in Judea 36 and to make Jerusalem's walls even higher. They also agreed to construct a strong, high wall between the enemy fortress and the rest of the city, in order to separate the fortress from the city and to keep enemy soldiers from going in and out for supplies.

37 Everyone worked together to rebuild Jerusalem; they repaired part of the collapsed eastern wall and the section of the city[o] called Chaphenatha.

38 Meanwhile, Simon and his workers rebuilt the town of Adida at the edge of the hill country, and they put a wall around it with strong gates.

[k] **12.16** *Numenius and Antipater*: Greek "Numenius the son of Antiochus and Antipater the son of Jason." [l] **12.24** *Demetrius the Second*: See 11.19 and the note there. [m] **12.25** *Hamath*: A town in the country of Syria. [n] **12.28** *and ran away*: These words are not in some manuscripts. [o] **12.37** *city*: Or "wall."

Trypho Captures Jonathan

39 Trypho wanted to be king of Asia, and he began plotting against King Antiochus the Sixth. 40 But Trypho was afraid Jonathan would go to war to protect Antiochus. So he decided to do away with Jonathan, and he led his army to the town of Beth-Shan.

41 Jonathan and forty thousand of his best soldiers left Jerusalem to attack Trypho at Beth-Shan.

42 When Trypho saw the large army, he was too frightened to fight. 43 Instead, he brought Jonathan to his camp and gave him honors and gifts. Trypho bragged about Jonathan to all his trusted friends[p] and troops and said, "Obey Jonathan's orders, just as you obey mine."

44 Trypho told Jonathan:

> We're not at war! Why have you caused these people so much trouble? 45 I've come here to give you the city of Ptolemais and the other fortresses and to put you in charge of all the officers and troops. After I've done this, I'll go home. Choose a few troops to go with you and me to Ptolemais, then send the others back to Judea.

46-47 Jonathan believed Trypho and sent all but three thousand of his soldiers back to Judea. Two thousand of them stayed behind in Galilee, while a thousand went with Jonathan to Ptolemais. 48 But as soon as he entered the city, its gates were closed. Then he was captured, and his soldiers were killed.

49 Trypho's troops and cavalry went to the Great Valley in Galilee[q] to kill the rest of Jonathan's soldiers. 50 However, when Jonathan's troops heard what had happened to him and the others, they encouraged each other and marched away, ready to fight. 51 Trypho's soldiers and cavalry caught up with them, but they turned back when they realized that the Jews would fight for their lives.

52 After the Jewish soldiers from Galilee returned safely to Judea, the whole nation mourned for Jonathan and his troops. Everyone was terrified 53 because the Gentiles around there were saying, "The Jews have no ruler or general. Let's destroy them and make the world forget they ever lived."

Simon Is Chosen Leader

13 1-2 Trypho got together a large army to invade Judea and destroy it. The Jews were terrified when they heard what he was up to. But Simon went to Jerusalem, where he called the people together 3 and encouraged everyone by saying:

> You know the wonderful things my family has done for the Law of Moses and our temple. You've heard how my brothers and I suffered in the wars 4 and how they died fighting for our people.
>
> I'm the only one in my family left alive. 5 But in these troubled times I'm ready to die for our people, just as my brothers did. 6 I want to get even with the other nations. They hate us and have come together to destroy our people, our temple, and our families.

7 Simon's speech encouraged everyone, 8 and they shouted, "Be our leader, just like your brothers Judas and Jonathan. 9 Take command of our army, and we will obey your orders."

10 Simon called the troops together, and they worked quickly to finish the walls and towers that protected Jerusalem on every side. 11 Simon ordered Jonathan the son of Absalom to take a large force of soldiers to the town of Joppa. Jonathan forced the people to leave, and he took over Joppa.

Trypho Tricks Simon

12 Trypho was still holding Simon's brother Jonathan as a hostage, and he brought Jonathan along when he led his large army out of Ptolemais to invade Judea.

13-14 Someone told Trypho, "Simon is now leader of the Jews, and he's ready to attack." Then Trypho sent a message to Simon, whose camp was at Adida overlooking the valleys.[r] The message said:

[p] **12.43** *trusted friends*: See the note at 2.18. [q] **12.49** *Great Valley in Galilee*: Probably the Valley of Jezreel. [r] **13.13,14** *Adida . . . valleys*: Adida was a town at the western edge of the hill country (see 12.38).

[15] Your brother Jonathan was a royal official, but he owed money to the king, and so I arrested him. [16] I'll set him free as soon as you send me one hundred thousand pieces of silver and two of his sons as hostages. That way he won't rebel against me anymore.

[17] Simon knew the messengers were lying, but he sent for the money and Jonathan's sons. He knew if he did not, the Jewish people would hate him and say, [18] "If Simon had given Trypho what he wanted, Jonathan would still be alive!" [19] Simon sent Jonathan's sons and the money to Trypho. However, Trypho broke his promise and did not release Jonathan.

[20] Trypho and his soldiers now set out to invade and destroy the country. They marched south and came up on the road from Adora. But each time Trypho tried to cross the border, he was blocked by Simon and his forces.

[21] Meanwhile, the enemy troops in the fortress at Jerusalem kept sending messages to Trypho, begging him to go around by way of the desert and bring them food. [22] Finally, Trypho ordered his cavalry to get ready to leave for Jerusalem.

But that night, Trypho was stopped by a heavy snowstorm, and he took his army to the country of Gilead. [23] When he reached the town of Baskama, he had Jonathan killed and buried. [24] Then he returned to his own country.

A Burial Place for the Maccabees

[25] Simon had the body of his brother Jonathan taken back to Modein, the town of his ancestors. He buried him there, [26] and everyone in Israel cried and mourned for a long time.

[27] Simon had a tall stone monument built over his family grave. It was shiny on the front and back, and could be seen a long way off. [28] He also built a row of seven pyramids to honor his father, his mother, and his four brothers.

[29-30] He set up tall stone columns around the pyramids. Then he hung suits of armor on these columns, so that everyone would remember what his family had done. Next to the suits of armor he put carved figures of ships that could be seen by anyone passing by on the sea. This family burial place is a work of art, and even today it can be seen in Modein.

Simon and Demetrius the Second Make Peace

[31] Antiochus the Sixth was still a young boy[s] when Trypho had him murdered. [32] Now Trypho was ruler and made everyone miserable.

[33] During this time, Simon ordered the Jews to build thick walls, high towers, and strong gates for the fortresses in Judea and to supply them with plenty of food. [34] Simon sent messengers to King Demetrius the Second, and they begged him, "Please make things easier for our country. Trypho is robbing us of everything."

Demetrius the Second Makes Judea a Free Country

[35] Demetrius the Second did what Simon wanted and wrote him the following letter:

[36] King Demetrius sends greetings to the Jewish people and their leaders, including Simon, who is high priest and a trusted friend[t] of the king.

[37] Thank you for the gold crown and the gold palm branch you sent me. I am ready to make a lasting peace by ordering my officials to stop collecting taxes from you. [38] I will give you everything I have promised in our treaties. Besides that, you can keep the fortresses you have just built.

[39] I forgive everything you have done wrong in the past. And from now on, I won't collect the special royal tax or any of the other taxes I used to receive from Jerusalem.

[40] I will hire any of your people who are prepared to help me in my kingdom.[u] Let's give peace a chance!

[s] **13.31** *a young boy*: Probably about seven years old. [t] **13.36** *trusted friend*: See the note at 2.18. [u] **13.40** *to help me in my kingdom*: Or "to work as my bodyguards" or "to serve as advisors."

41 So in the year 170[v] of the Syrian Kingdom, the Jews won their freedom from the Gentiles. 42 And on their documents and contracts they wrote, "The first year of Simon, the great high priest and the commander and ruler of the Jews."

Simon Captures the Town of Gazara

43 About this time, Simon and the Jewish forces surrounded the town of Gazara[w] and set up a large weapon to break through the wall. They pushed it up to the town wall, where they broke through and captured one of the towers. 44 Then the soldiers who were operating the weapon rushed into Gazara, causing a terrible uproar.

45 Everyone in Gazara tore their clothes to show their sorrow. They climbed to the top of the town wall where they shouted to Simon and begged him for peace, 46 saying, "We've done wrong and deserve to be punished. But please have mercy on us."

47 Simon agreed to stop the fighting. But he ordered everyone to leave the town, and he took the idols out of the houses where they were kept. Then he and his troops entered Gazara, singing hymns of praise.

48 Simon removed everything that made the town unclean according to their religion, and he made the fortresses of Gazara stronger. He built a house for himself and let faithful Jews live in the town.

Simon Captures the Fortress in Jerusalem

49 The enemy troops in the Jerusalem fortress still could not go into the country to buy food, and many of them starved to death. 50 Finally, the survivors begged Simon for peace. He agreed, then ordered them to leave the fortress, so he could remove everything that made it unclean according to their religion.

51 On the twenty-third day of the second month in the year 171[x] of the Syrian Kingdom, Simon led his soldiers into the fortress. They carried palm branches and praised God with all kinds of songs and musical instruments. God had completely crushed their powerful enemy! 52 Simon decided that a joyous festival should be held on this same day every year. He strengthened the wall on the side of the temple hill that faced the fortress. Then he and his troops made the fortress their headquarters.

53 John the son of Simon was now a grown man. So Simon put him in command of the whole army, and John lived in the town of Gazara.

Demetrius the Second Is Taken Prisoner

14 In the year 172[y] of the Syrian Kingdom, King Demetrius the Second[z] led an army to the country of Media, where he hoped to hire soldiers to help him fight Trypho.

2 When King Arsaces of Persia and Media learned that Demetrius had invaded his country, he sent one of his generals 3 to capture him alive. This general defeated the army of Demetrius and took Demetrius to King Arsaces, who put him in prison.

In Praise of Simon

4 The country was at peace
while Simon ruled,
because he worked
for the good of the nation.
Everyone was glad that he ruled,
and they honored him
for as long as he lived.

5 Simon became a true hero
by capturing
the seaport of Joppa.
Now ships can sail
to faraway islands.
6 Simon made the country larger
and ruled the entire region.
7 He took many prisoners
and also captured the towns
of Gazara and Beth-Zur.

[v]**13.41** *year 170*: That is, 142 B.C. [w]**13.43** *Gazara*: Greek "Gaza" (in verses 43-48).
[x]**13.51** *second month . . . year 171*: That is, 141 B.C. The second month of the Hebrew calendar was Iyyar or Ziv, from about mid-April to mid-May. [y]**14.1** *year 172*: That is, 140 B.C.
[z]**14.1** *Demetrius the Second*: See 11.19 and the note there.
13.43 2 Macc 10.32-38. **13.52** 3 Macc 6.36.

And when he took control
of the Jerusalem fortress,
he removed all the idols
that had made it unclean.
No one could oppose him!

8 Life was peaceful on the farms;
the earth produced grain,
and fruit grew on the trees.
9 In towns the old folks
talked about the good things
that had happened,
while young soldiers strolled by
in their fancy uniforms.

10 Simon supplied the towns
with food and protection
and was famous everywhere.
11 He brought peace
and great joy to Israel.
12 Everyone rested unafraid
beneath their own grapevines
and fig trees;
13 troublemakers and enemy kings
had been crushed.
14 Simon helped the poor
and obeyed the Law of God
by destroying outlaws
and rebellious people.
15 He gave gifts to the temple
and made it more glorious.

Simon Makes a Treaty with Rome and Sparta

16 Cities as far away as Rome and Sparta mourned at the news of Jonathan's death.
17 But they were pleased that Jonathan's brother Simon had taken his place as high priest and ruler of Judea.

18 The Romans and Spartans wanted Simon to be their friend and ally, just as his brothers had been, so they wrote him letters on sheets of bronze.

19 The Jews then read these letters during a meeting in Jerusalem.
20 The letter from the Spartans said:

The city of Sparta and its leaders send greetings to Simon the high priest, to the other leaders and priests, and to our relatives, the Jews.
21 Your messengers made us very happy when they told us how famous you are.
22 The details of their visit are in our record books, which say:

"The Jews sent Numenius and Antipater[a] to us as messengers to make sure that we were on friendly terms.
23 We Spartans gladly welcomed these men and honored them. Moreover, we placed a copy of their message in the public building where all our record books are kept. We have also sent a copy to Simon the high priest, telling what we have done."

24 After the Jews had finished their meeting, Simon sent Numenius to Rome to make certain that the Romans were still their allies. Numenius took them a heavy gold shield that weighed almost a thousand pounds.[b]

25 When the people found out what Simon was doing, they said, "How can we repay Simon and his descendants?
26 He and his brothers and the rest of his father's family have been strong; they have defeated our enemies and set us free."

The people wrote on sheets of bronze the things Simon had done, then they fastened the sheets to stone columns on Mount Zion.
27-28 This is what they wrote:

After Simon the great high priest had ruled for three years in Asaramel,[c] our priests, rulers, and leaders held an important meeting on the eighteenth day of the month of Elul[d] in the year 172[e] of the Syrian Kingdom. This is what we were told:

29 "Simon the son of Mattathias was a priest from Joarib's family.[f] He and his brothers risked their lives and fought back whenever our enemies attacked us. They protected our temple

[a]**14.22** *Numenius and Antipater*: See the note at 12.16. [b]**14.24** *After the Jews . . . pounds*: See 15.15-24. [c]**14.27,28** *in Asaramel*: Or "in the council of the people of God" or "as prince of the people of God." [d]**14.27,28** *Elul*: The sixth month of the Hebrew calendar, from about mid-August to mid-September. [e]**14.27,28** *year 172*: That is, 140 B.C. [f]**14.29** *Mattathias was a priest from Joarib's family*: One possible meaning for the difficult Greek text.

14.18 1 Macc 8.22.

and the Law of Moses, and they made
us famous.

30 "Simon's brother Jonathan
united our people, and we chose him
to be our high priest. But after he died,
31 our enemies prepared to invade
Judea, because they wanted to attack
our temple and destroy the country.[g]

32 "Simon took command of our
army. He spent a lot of his own money
to pay our soldiers and to buy weapons
and armor for us. 33 He put up strong
walls and towers in the towns of Judea,
as well as in the border town of Beth-
Zur, where the enemy used to store
weapons. Then he stationed Jewish
soldiers at Beth-Zur.

34 "Simon built a fortress in the
coastal town of Joppa as well as in the
town of Gazara, because it was close to
Azotus, which had been a stronghold
for our enemies. Simon settled Jews in
Gazara, and he gave everyone in these
towns whatever they needed to make
the towns fit to live in.

35 "Simon was a dependable man
who had high hopes for our country
and did all he could to make our nation glorious. So we chose him to be
our ruler and high priest.

36 "The Gentiles had built a fortress
in Jerusalem and had stationed some
soldiers there, who then attacked the
rest of us and made the temple and
everything else unclean. But Simon
successfully forced the Gentiles out
of Judea; he got rid of the troops in
the fortress and was in full control of
everything.

37 "Simon strengthened the walls of
the Jerusalem fortress and stationed
soldiers there to guard the country and
city. He also made the walls around
Jerusalem higher.

38 "Simon did everything well, so
King Demetrius accepted him as our
high priest. 39 Demetrius called Simon
his trusted friend[h] and gave him many
other honors. 40 He did this because
he knew that the Romans had welcomed Simon's messengers and considered Jews their friends, allies, and
relatives.

41 "Our people and priests gladly
chose Simon and his descendants[i] to
be our rulers and high priests forever,
or until God sends a true prophet.

42 "Simon will rule over us and care
for our temple, our country, our weapons, and our fortresses. 43 Everyone
must obey his orders and write his
name on all official documents in
Judea. Simon has permission to wear
purple clothes and gold jewelry, just
like a king.

44 "Our people and our priests must
never change any of these orders.
They must obey Simon and never hold
meetings in the country without first
asking him. And none of them may
wear purple clothes and a gold buckle,
as though they were kings. 45 Anyone
who disobeys or rejects these orders
will be punished."

46-47 The people agreed with these decisions that Simon should be high priest,
commander, and ruler of the nation and its
priests. Simon was glad to do all this, and
he promised to protect them.

48 The agreement was written on sheets
of bronze, then put in the temple for everyone to see. 49 Copies were also stored in the
treasury for Simon and his family.

Antiochus Writes to Simon

15 Antiochus the Seventh,[j] the son of
Demetrius the Second,[k] sent a letter from the Greek islands to the Jews and
to Simon the high priest and ruler. 2 It said:

> King Antiochus sends greetings to
> the Jewish people and to Simon their
> high priest and ruler.
>
> 3 Some rebels have taken control of
> my ancestors' kingdom. I want it back
> so I can make it a great kingdom again.
> I have hired a large army and navy,

[g] **14.31** *destroy the country*: These words are not in some manuscripts. [h] **14.39** *trusted friend*: See the note at 2.18. [i] **14.41** *Simon and his descendants*: The Greek has "Simon." See 14.25 where the Jews ask how they can honor Simon and his descendants. [j] **15.1** *Antiochus the Seventh*: Ruled 138-129 B.C. [k] **15.1** *Demetrius the Second*: See 11.19 and the note there.

4 and I am ready to land on the coast. I
am going to punish everyone who has
destroyed my country and ruined so
many of its towns.
5 I will follow the example of other
kings and excuse you from paying
some taxes and fees. 6 I will let you
make your own coins 7 and allow you
to keep all of the weapons and fortresses you have built. As of today, I
will remove all soldiers from Jerusalem
and its temple, 8 and you won't be required to repay money you owe the
king.
9 As soon as I get my kingdom back,
I will make you and your temple prosperous and famous. Then the whole
world will know how outstanding
you are.

Antiochus the Seventh Attacks Trypho

10 In the year 174[l] of the Syrian Kingdom, Antiochus the Seventh invaded the
land of his ancestors. Soon most of Trypho's soldiers deserted and joined the army
of Antiochus, leaving Trypho with only a
few soldiers. 11 He retreated to the town of
Dor on the coast, and Antiochus got ready
to attack him there. 12 Trypho was in real
trouble now, because he did not have
enough troops to fight back.
13 Antiochus led a hundred twenty thousand soldiers and eight thousand cavalry to
Dor 14 and surrounded the town. At the
same time, his ships attacked from the sea,
and the people of Dor were trapped.

A Letter to Ptolemy the Eighth

15 Meanwhile, Numenius[m] and the other
messengers returned to Jerusalem from
Rome with letters to different countries
and rulers. One of the letters said:
16 Lucius, a Roman official, sends
greetings to King Ptolemy[n] of Egypt.
17 Simon the high priest and the
Jewish people have sent messengers to
Rome to make sure that Jews and
Romans are still friends and allies.
18 These messengers brought us a gold
shield that weighs almost a thousand[o]
pounds.
19-20 We are keeping this gift and
writing letters to countries and kings,
warning them not to cause any trouble
for the Jews.
Please don't attack the towns or
country of the Jews or help any enemies who do. 21 If troublemakers escape from their country and come to
you, they must be sent back to Simon
the high priest, who will punish them
according to the Law of Moses.

A Letter to Other Rulers

22 Lucius sent the same letter to King
Demetrius and to Attalus, Ariarathes, and
Arsaces. 23 It went to every country, includ-
ing Sampsames[p] and Sparta. And it went to
Caria, Pamphylia, and Lycia, as well as to
the islands of Delos, Samos, Rhodes, Cos,
Aradus, and Cyprus and to the cities of
Myndos, Sicyon, Halicarnassus, Cnidus,
Gortyna, Cyrene, Phaselis, and Side.
24 Simon the high priest also received a
copy of the letter.

Antiochus the Seventh Quarrels with Simon

25 Antiochus the Seventh made a second attack against the town of Dor. His soldiers set up weapons for breaking through
the wall; they fought long and hard and
kept Trypho from leaving.
26 Simon wanted to help Antiochus. So
he sent him two thousand of his best soldiers, together with silver and gold and
many supplies. 27 Antiochus not only refused Simon's help, but he turned against
him and broke every promise he had ever
made.
28 Antiochus told his trusted friend[q]
Athenobius to meet with Simon and tell
him:
The towns of Joppa and Gazara and

[l]**15.10** *year 174*: That is, 138 B.C. [m]**15.15** *Numenius*: See 12.16; 14.22. [n]**15.16** *Ptolemy*: Ptolemy VIII (ruled 145-116 B.C.). [o]**15.18** *a thousand*: Some manuscripts have "five thousand." [p]**15.23** *Sampsames*: The location is not known. [q]**15.28** *trusted friend*: See the note at 2.18.

15.15 1 Macc 12.16.

the fortress in Jerusalem are now under your control. But these places,
29 along with others you have taken,
belong to me, the king.

You have ruined the land around
these towns and done a lot of other
damage to my kingdom.

30 Simon, give back these towns
and return the tax money from the
places you captured outside of Judea.
31 If you don't want to do this, then pay
five hundred thousand pieces of silver
for damaging the towns you captured.
And turn over to me five hundred
thousand more to make up for the tax
money you took from the towns.

If you don't do this, it's war!

32 When Athenobius arrived in Jerusalem, he could not take his eyes off Simon's great wealth. Simon had a table with
dishes made of gold and silver, and he
owned many other valuable things.[r] Then
Athenobius told Simon what the king had
said.

33 Simon answered:

Our ancestors gave us this land and
property. Later our enemies stole it
from us. So how can you say we have
taken things that belong to others?
34 We intend to keep our land and
property now that we have them back
once again.

35-36 The towns of Joppa and Gazara that you want have been a constant bother to us, and we will pay you
a hundred thousand pieces of silver for
them.

Athenobius was so furious that he could
not speak. He returned to Antiochus and
told him what Simon had said. He also let
him know about Simon's great wealth and
everything else he had seen. This report
made Antiochus very angry.

King Antiochus Appoints Cendebeus

37 Meanwhile, Trypho had escaped by
ship from Dor and sailed to the town of Or-
thosia. 38-39 Antiochus went after him, but
left Cendebeus in command of the coast-
land. He gave him soldiers and cavalry and
said, "Get ready to invade Judea and attack
the Jews. Make the fortress at Kedron even
stronger."

40 Cendebeus led his army to Jamnia
and started causing trouble in the town. He
invaded Judea and killed everyone he captured. 41 After he made the fortress at Kedron stronger, he stationed some soldiers
and cavalry there. Then he told them, "The
king has ordered us to patrol the roads in
Judea."

John Attacks Cendebeus

16 Simon's son John went from
Gazara at the time and told his
father what Cendebeus had done. 2 Then
Simon met with John and Judas, his two
oldest sons, and said to them:

My brothers and I, and everyone
else in my father's family, have fought
for our people ever since we were
young. God blessed us when we
fought, and we rescued Israel many
times.

3 I am an old man now. But God
has shown kindness by letting you become mature enough to lead our people in battle, just as my brothers and I
have done. I pray that God will be with
you as you fight!

4 John immediately left to attack Cendebeus with twenty thousand foot soldiers
and cavalry from Judea. That night, the
troops made camp at Modein. 5 Then early
the next morning, they went out to the valley and stopped beside a flooding stream.
On the other side of it, a large number of
soldiers and cavalry were moving toward
them.

6 John lined up his troops for battle. He
waded into the stream first, because he
knew his soldiers were afraid of the water.
They watched John, then followed him
across.

7 John noticed that Cendebeus had a lot
of cavalry. So John divided his men into
groups and ordered them to take up positions around their own cavalry. 8 Then they
blew war trumpets and attacked Cendebeus. His forces ran away, and many of his
troops died in the battle. Those who escaped ran back into their fortress.

[r]**15.32** *he owned . . . things*: One possible meaning for the difficult Greek text.

9 During the battle, John's brother Judas was wounded. But John and his troops chased the enemy soldiers. Some of them ran as far as Kedron, the town that Cendebeus had rebuilt. 10 Others reached the towers in the open country near the town of Azotus. But John burned the town and killed about two thousand enemy troops. After this, he led his army safely back to Judea.

The Death of Simon

11 Ptolemy the son of Abubus was in command of the valley near Jericho. He was a rich man 12 and was married to the daughter of Simon the high priest. 13 But Ptolemy was very proud and thought he deserved to be the ruler. So he began plotting to kill Simon and his sons.

14 In the year 177[s] of the Syrian Kingdom, Simon was going from town to town in Judea, trying to help the people. Later that year during the month of Shebat,[t] he and his sons Mattathias and Judas arrived in Jericho.

15 Ptolemy pretended he was glad to see Simon and his sons. Then he invited them to a banquet in their honor at a small fortress that he had built and named Dok.

Some of Ptolemy's soldiers were hiding near the dining room. 16 As soon as Simon and his sons were drunk, the soldiers rushed out of their hiding places with swords in their hands. They attacked Simon, his two sons, and some of their servants, killing them all.

17 So Ptolemy betrayed a friend and proved that he could not be trusted.

John Becomes the Leader of Israel

18 Ptolemy wrote and told King Antiochus that he had killed Simon. He asked the king to give him soldiers and to put him in command of Judea and its towns. 19-20 Ptolemy also wrote letters to the Jewish army commanders, promising them silver and gold and other gifts if they would help him.

Some of Ptolemy's troops set out to take over Jerusalem and the temple hill, while others went to murder John in Gazara. 21 But someone warned John, "Ptolemy has already murdered your father and brothers. And now he has sent soldiers to kill you!" 22 John was shocked by this news. He found out which soldiers had come to kill him, and he had them arrested and put to death.

23-24 Everything else that John the high priest did is found in his priestly record books that tell about his wars, his victories, and how he rebuilt the walls of Jerusalem. John began keeping records as soon as he had taken his father's place as high priest.

[s]**16.14** *year 177*: That is, 135 B.C. [t]**16.14** *Shebat*: The eleventh month of the Hebrew calendar, from about mid-January to mid-February.

2 MACCABEES

ABOUT THIS BOOK

Second Maccabees is a "condensed book"—the author took a five-volume history by Jason of Cyrene and shortened it into one volume. This material begins in chapter 3, and like 1 Maccabees, it tells the story of how the Jews rebelled against the Greek kings that had ruled Palestine since the time of Alexander the Great (see 1 Maccabees, "About This Book"). However, 2 Maccabees begins the story about ten years earlier than 1 Maccabees and ends it before the death of Judas Maccabeus in 160 B.C.

Second Maccabees teaches that God punishes those who do evil, including his own people. But if they turn back to him, he will rescue them and give them victory. The book also shows the importance of worshiping the Lord in the proper way at the Jerusalem temple, and that the Lord's people could depend on him to protect his temple. As the priests prayed after the temple had been threatened,

> *"Our holy Lord God, you have everything, and yet you were pleased to let us build a temple, so that you could live here with us. We have only recently dedicated this temple again. Please keep it holy forever and ever."*
>
> *(14.35, 36)*

A QUICK LOOK AT THIS BOOK

- A Letter to the Jews in Egypt (1.1-9)
- An Earlier Letter to the Jews in Egypt (1.10—2.18)
- Preface to the Shortened History of the Maccabees (2.19-32)
- Heliodorus Tries To Rob the Temple (3.1-40)
- High Priests Onias, Jason, and Menelaus (4.1—5.16)
- King Antiochus Tries To Destroy the Jewish Way of Life (5.17—7.42)
- Judas Maccabeus Leads a Rebellion against Antiochus (8.1—9.29)
- The Temple Is Rededicated to the Lord (10.1-8)
- Judas Continues To Fight (10.9—11.15)
- Copies of Letters (11.16-38)
- Judas Wins More Battles (12.1—15.37)
- Some Final Thoughts (15.38, 39)

A Letter to the Jews in Egypt

1 The Jews of Jerusalem and Judea
wrote a letter to their Jewish relatives
in Egypt. It said:

Greetings and lasting peace!

2 We pray that God will be kind to
you and remember the promise that he
made to his faithful servants, Abraham, Isaac, and Jacob. 3 May God make
you willing and eager to worship and
obey him with all your heart. 4 May
he bless you with peace and with
an understanding of his Law and its
commands. 5 We ask him to answer
your prayers and forgive your sins
and never turn from you in times of
trouble.

6 All of us here are now praying
for you.

7 In the year 169[a] of the Syrian kingdom, when Demetrius[b] was our ruler, we wrote you a letter in which we said:

We have had terrible troubles ever since Jason the high priest[c] and his troops rebelled against our country and its leaders. 8 They destroyed the temple gate and killed innocent people. But we begged the Lord for help, and when he answered our prayers, we brought sacrifices and offerings of grain into the temple. We lit the lamps and put the sacred loaves of bread on the table.

9 And so, we now urge you to celebrate in the month of Chislev a festival like the Festival of Shelters.[d]

We are writing to you in the year 188[e] of the Greek Kingdom.

Another Letter to the Jews in Egypt

10 The Jews of Jerusalem and Judea had also written an earlier letter. It said:

The Jews of Jerusalem and Judea, together with Judas and the council, send greetings to Aristobulus and the rest of our Jewish friends in Egypt.

Aristobulus belongs to the family of chosen priests, and he is King Ptolemy's[f] teacher. We wish Aristobulus and all the rest of you good health!

11 We thank God because he has rescued us from King Antiochus,[g] who put us in dreadful danger.[h] 12 The king's troops attacked our holy city of Jerusalem, but God forced him to retreat.

13-14 Antiochus then invaded Persia with an army that seemed too powerful for anyone to defeat. He and his trusted friends[i] went into the temple of the goddess Nanea, where Antiochus lied and said he planned to marry her.[j] But all he really wanted were the temple treasures that he would receive as wedding gifts.

The priests of the temple made a clever plan to kill Antiochus. 15 They set out the treasures, and when Antiochus and a few of his friends entered the temple, the priests immediately locked the doors behind him. 16 Then they killed him and his friends by dropping heavy stones on them from a trap door in the roof. Afterwards, the priests chopped the dead bodies into pieces and tossed the heads to the people outside.

17 Let's always praise our God for punishing these wicked enemies!

Nehemiah Gets Fire for a Sacrifice

The Letter Continues:

18 On the twenty-fifth day of the month of Chislev,[k] we will celebrate the Temple Festival.[l] We think you need to know this, so you can celebrate it just as you celebrate the Festival of Shelters and the Festival of Fire.[m]

This Festival of Fire goes back to Nehemiah,[n] who rebuilt the temple and its

[a]**1.7** *year 169*: That is, 143 B.C. [b]**1.7** *Demetrius*: Demetrius II (ruled 145-140 B.C.).
[c]**1.7** *Jason the high priest*: He had become high priest by bribery and held this position 174-171 B.C.
[d]**1.9** *Festival of Shelters*: This festival was normally celebrated in the month of Tishri, the seventh month of the Hebrew calendar, from about mid-September to mid-October. Chislev was the ninth month of the Hebrew calendar, from about mid-November to mid-December. [e]**1.9** *year 188*: That is, 124 B.C. [f]**1.10** *King Ptolemy's*: Also known as Ptolemy VI (ruled 181-145 B.C.).
[g]**1.11** *Antiochus*: Also known as Antiochus IV or Antiochus Epiphanes (ruled 175-164 B.C.).
[h]**1.11** *We thank . . . danger*: One possible meaning for the difficult Greek text. [i]**1.13,14** *trusted friends*: This was a title that Greek kings gave to special advisors and officials. These friends received many gifts, honors, and other privileges. [j]**1.13,14** *the goddess Nanea . . . to marry her*: Nanea was a goddess of fertility. In the ancient world the ceremonial marriage of the king with the goddess of fertility was intended to guarantee good crops for the coming year, but Antiochus had other reasons for marrying her. [k]**1.18** *Chislev*: See the note at 1.9. [l]**1.18** *Temple Festival*: This is the same festival referred to in 1 Maccabees 4.56. [m]**1.18** *the Festival of Fire*: This festival is not mentioned anywhere else in the Bible, though fire played an important part in the Temple Festival, which is sometimes called the Festival of Lights (see 1 Maccabees 4.50). [n]**1.18** *Nehemiah*: Nehemiah was an important official in the court of King Artaxerxes I of Persia. In 445 B.C. Artaxerxes made Nehemiah governor of Judea and sent him back to Jerusalem to rebuild the city walls.
1.13-16 1 Macc 6.1-4; 2 Macc 9.1-10.

altar, then offered sacrifices. 19 All this happened long ago, when our ancestors were
dragged away to Persia,[o] and some faithful
priests took fire from the altar. They secretly hid the fire at the bottom of a dry cistern, and they hid it so well that no one
ever found it.
20 Many years later, when it pleased
God, the Persian king sent Nehemiah back
to Jerusalem. Nehemiah then told some
descendants of those priests to find the
hidden fire. But after returning, they told
us, "There is nothing in the cistern except
an oily liquid."
Nehemiah told them to dip out some of
the liquid and bring it to him. 21 Then, after the sacrifice was ready, Nehemiah ordered the priests to sprinkle the liquid over
the offerings and the firewood, 22 and they
did. A little while later, the sun came out
from behind the clouds. Then the firewood
and offerings suddenly burst into flames, as
everyone stared in amazement.

Jonathan Prays

The Letter Continues:
23 While the offerings were being
burned, a priest named Jonathan[p] began
praying. Nehemiah, the other priests, and
the rest of the people also joined in the
prayer 24 that went something like this:

> Our Lord and our God, you created
> everything. You are powerful and fear-
> some, but faithful and merciful. You
> alone are kind, and only you are king.
> 25 No one else is fair and gives us
> everything we need; no one else is all-
> powerful and lives forever.
>
> Long ago, you chose our ancestors
> to be your holy people, and since then
> you have rescued our nation from
> every danger.
>
> 26 Please accept our sacrifice that
> we are offering for everyone in Israel,
> your chosen nation. Protect us from
> danger and make us holy.
>
> 27 Bring home our scattered people
> and free those Jews who are slaves in
> foreign nations. We are hated and mis-
> treated. So have pity on us and show
> Gentiles that you are the God of Israel.
>
> 28 Take revenge against our arro-
> gant enemies, who attack and insult
> us. 29 Then give your nation a lasting
> home in your holy land, just as Moses
> said you would.[q]

The King of Persia Learns about the Fire

The Letter Continues:
30 When everyone had finished praying,
the priests started singing hymns. 31 Soon
the fire burned up the offerings. Then Nehemiah ordered the rest of the liquid to be
poured over some large rocks. 32 As soon as
this was done, the rocks started burning,
but flames from the altar put out the fire.
33 People everywhere heard what had
happened. Even the Persian king learned
that an oily liquid had been discovered in
the place where the priests had hidden the
altar fire just before they were dragged
away to Persia. The king was also told that
Nehemiah and his followers had offered a
sacrifice, using the liquid to start their fire.
34 After the king had carefully checked on
this story, he surrounded the cistern with a
high wall and built a shrine there.
35 Then the king exchanged gifts with
the people he liked. 36 Nehemiah and his
followers called the oil "nephthar," which
means "cleaning." But everyone else calls it
"naphtha."[r]

A Story about Jeremiah

The Letter Continues:
2 One of our writings[s] says that it was
Jeremiah the prophet who ordered our
people to hide some of the altar fire before
we were forced to go to Persia,[t] just as I
have already told you.
2 We also know from this writing that
Jeremiah taught these Jews the Law of the
Lord. He warned them never to forget the

[o]**1.19** *Persia*: The author is thinking of 587 B.C. when the Jewish people were taken away as prisoners to Babylonia, which later became part of the Persian Empire. [p]**1.23** *Jonathan*: Probably Johanan of Nehemiah 12.22, 23. [q]**1.29** *just . . . would*: See Exodus 15.17. [r]**1.36** *naphtha*: This sounds like a Persian word that means "crude oil." [s]**2.1** *One of our writings*: Probably the Letter of Jeremiah. [t]**2.1** *Persia*: See the note at 1.19.

Lord's commands after they arrived in Persia, and he also begged our people not to be tricked into worshiping idols, even the ones decorated with gold and silver. 3 He said many similar things, while urging them to always think about the teachings of the Law.

4 This same writing tells us that Jeremiah had a vision, in which he was ordered to take the sacred tent and the sacred chest to the mountain that Moses had climbed to look at the land God had promised us.[u]

5 After Jeremiah came to the mountain, he found a big cave, where he hid the tent, the chest, and the altar for burning incense. Then he blocked the entrance to the cave. 6 Meanwhile, a few of our people had followed Jeremiah, hoping to mark the path to the cave, but they could not. 7 Jeremiah got angry with them when he discovered what they had tried to do, and he said:

> No one can know about the cave until the Lord God has pity on us again and brings our people back home. 8 At that time, he will show where these things are hidden. A cloud will appear, blazing with God's own dazzling light, just as it did when he came to Moses.[v] This is also how the Lord came to King Solomon,[w] when Solomon asked him to make the holy temple glorious and acceptable as a place for worship.

Solomon and Moses

The Letter Continues:

9 We also know that Solomon was wise and built our temple, then offered a sacrifice to make it completely acceptable. 10 When Solomon prayed, some fire came down from heaven and burned up his sacrifices.[x] This is the same thing that happened[y] when Moses prayed, 11 "I am offering a sacrifice for sin. So it must be completely burned, and none of it eaten."[z]

12 Solomon's festival lasted for eight days.

Nehemiah Builds a Library

The Letter Continues:

13 You will find all this information in our record books as well as in the writings of Nehemiah, who built a library and filled it with the writings about prophets and kings. The books of King David and the letters that the kings wrote about offerings are also in his library.

14 Judas Maccabeus collected all the books that we had lost track of during the war,[a] and we still have them here. 15 Send someone after these books if you ever need them.

Celebrating a Festival

The Letter Concludes:

16 We are ready to celebrate the Temple Festival, and so we are writing to say that you should celebrate it as well.

17 God has rescued his nation and returned our sacred land that we inherited from our ancestors. God has also given us back our kingdom, our priests, and our sacred way of life,[b] 18 just as he promised in the Law of Moses.[c] He has saved us from dreadful danger and made our temple holy again. Because of this, we will always trust in the kindness of God, who will bring us back home from every nation on earth and lead us to his holy temple.

The Five Books of Jason

19-23 Jason of Cyrene[d] wrote five books about Judas Maccabeus and his brothers in which he told how they made our great temple an acceptable place of worship once again and how they dedicated its altar. He also told us about the wars they fought against Antiochus Epiphanes and his son Eupator.[e]

[u]**2.4** *the mountain . . . us*: See Deuteronomy 34.1. [v]**2.8** *Moses*: See Exodus 40.34. [w]**2.8** *Solomon*: See 1 Kings 8.8, 10, 11. [x]**2.10** *sacrifices*: See 2 Chronicles 7.1. [y]**2.10** *happened*: See Leviticus 9.23, 24. [z]**2.11** *eaten*: One possible meaning for the difficult Greek text of verse 11. [a]**2.14** *we had lost . . . war*: See 1 Maccabees 1.56. [b]**2.17** *our sacred way of life*: Or "our temple services." [c]**2.18** *just as . . . Moses*: See Exodus 19.5, 6.
[d]**2.19-23** *Jason of Cyrene*: An unknown Jewish author whose writings are lost.
[e]**2.19-23** *Antiochus . . . Eupator*: Antiochus Epiphanes is also known as Antiochus IV (ruled 175-164 B.C.). His son Eupator is also known as Antiochus V (ruled 164-162 B.C.).
2.8 Ex 16.10; 24.16; 1 K 8.10, 11. **2.16** 1 Macc 4.59.

Jason described some visions these brave warriors were given from heaven as they defended our Jewish way of life.[f] He also explained how our small army made raids across the whole country, forcing the cruel barbarians to run for their lives. And because of the Lord's kindness and mercy, our troops recaptured our world-famous temple. They also freed Jerusalem and put back into effect the laws that those barbarians had hoped to wipe out.

I will now try to summarize Jason's books in one volume. 24 They are so full of facts and details that they discourage readers who want to learn about these events. 25 My shorter version will please everyone—people who read for pleasure will enjoy it, and those who like to memorize things will find it easy to remember.

26-27 Writing a short version of a long book is like trying to prepare a banquet for a crowd of people with different tastes. So I worked night and day and lost a lot of sleep. But that's all right, because I am glad to work hard in order to satisfy my readers.

28 My story is merely a summary of the main events included in Jason's account. 29 He was like a builder who had to know every detail about the new house he was constructing. I am simply a decorator whose only job is to make things look beautiful.

30 Historians learn as much as possible about their subjects, then present every side of a story, without leaving out a thing. 31 But writers who summarize books are allowed to be brief and to leave out many of the details.

32 Enough said is enough said! Now is the time to begin the story itself. How foolish it would be to write such a long introduction that I would have to leave out part of the history.

Heliodorus in Jerusalem

3 When Onias[g] was high priest of the nation, the holy city of Jerusalem always had peace. Onias hated evil and loved God, which made everyone careful to obey the Law. 2 Many kings showed great respect for the temple in those days and even brought it expensive gifts. 3 For example, King Seleucus[h] of Asia used to pay for the daily sacrifices[i] with money from the taxes he collected.

4 While Onias was still high priest, a man named Simon from the Benjamin[j] tribe was a high official in the temple. And one day he started arguing with Onias about how to run the Jerusalem marketplace. 5 Simon lost the argument and went to Apollonius,[k] the governor of Southwest Syria Province,[l] 6 and said, "There is more money in the temple treasury than can be counted. And since the money is not used to pay for sacrifices,[m] it may as well be placed under the authority of the king."

7 Apollonius told King Seleucus about the money in the temple, and the king ordered Heliodorus, his highest official, to bring it to him. 8 So Heliodorus left at once for Jerusalem. But he told everyone that he was on his way to inspect the towns of Southwest Syria Province.

9 Onias the high priest warmly welcomed Heliodorus to Jerusalem. Then Heliodorus explained, "I came to the city because someone told me there is a lot of money in your temple treasury. Is this true?"

[f]**2.19-23** *Jewish way of life*: The Greek has "Judaism," a term referring to the complete teachings and way of life of the Jews. [g]**3.1** *Onias*: Also known as Onias III. He belonged to the family of priests that descended from Zadok. Members of Zadok's family served as priests and high priests for almost eight hundred years from the time of David (2 Samuel 20.25) and Solomon (1 Kings 1.39-45) down to 171 B.C. [h]**3.3** *King Seleucus*: Seleucus IV (ruled 187-175 B.C.). [i]**3.3** *daily sacrifices*: See Leviticus 6.8-12; Numbers 28.1-8. [j]**3.4** *Benjamin*: Some manuscripts have "Bilgah," one of the families of priests listed in 1 Chronicles 24.14; Nehemiah 12.5, 18. [k]**3.5** *Apollonius*: Greek "Apollonius son of Tharseas" (probably the same Apollonius mentioned in 4.4, 21 and referred to as "Apollonius son of Menestheus"). [l]**3.5** *Southwest Syria Province*: "Coele-Syria" in traditional translations; it originally referred to the land between the Lebanon and the Anti-Lebanon mountains, but at this time it included all Palestine and Phoenicia as well. [m]**3.6** *pay for sacrifices*: According to Greek custom, money that was set aside for sacrifices could never be taken from a temple.

3.5 4 Macc 4.3.

10 Onias answered:

There is money in the treasury, but some of it is for widows and orphans, 11 and some of it belongs to Hyrcanus,[n] a very important man. At the most, you will find only four hundred thousand silver coins and two hundred thousand pieces of gold. That devil Simon lied to you. 12 Anyway, I can't possibly let you rob our people of their silver and gold. They trust this sacred temple and think their money is safe. After all, everyone in the world respects this holy place.

13 Heliodorus answered, "King Seleucus has ordered me to collect the money for the royal treasury, and I'm going to do just that."

Heliodorus Causes an Uproar in Jerusalem

14 After Heliodorus had set a day to collect the money, he went into the temple to take charge of the workers who were counting the silver and gold.

Meanwhile, everyone in Jerusalem was in terrible agony. 15 The priests in their sacred robes were lying face down on the ground in front of the altar and praying, "Our God, please protect this silver and gold! You yourself made the law that keeps our money safe while it is stored in the temple."

16 It was heartbreaking just to look at Onias the high priest. His face was pale because of his suffering, 17 and his trembling body showed that he was terrified and tormented.

18 Heliodorus was about to disgrace the temple, and so families ran out of their houses and huddled together in the streets to pray. 19 Grown women put on sackcloth[o] skirts. Young women who had never been allowed outdoors ran to the city gates or to the city wall, or just stared out of their windows. 20 Everyone raised their hands toward heaven, begging God for help.

21 It was a dreadful sight to see the high priest in such anguish and agony and the people lying face down on the ground.

God Punishes Heliodorus

22 Everyone kept begging the Lord All-Powerful to protect the money that had been left in the temple. 23-24 Meanwhile, Heliodorus and his guards walked right into the treasury, just as they had planned. But God is more powerful than all spirits and authorities, and he sent such a horrible vision that it terrified Heliodorus and his arrogant followers, leaving them weak from fear. 25 In the vision, they saw a gruesome rider with gold weapons and gold armor. The rider's horse wore a fancy harness and charged furiously at Heliodorus, kicking at him with its hoofs.

26 Two very strong and handsome young men in fine clothes suddenly appeared. One stood on each side of Heliodorus and beat him severely with whips, 27 until he fainted and fell to the ground. Then his guards picked him up and placed him on a mat.

28 Only a short time before this happened, Heliodorus had led a crowd of followers and guards into the treasury. Now they had to carry this helpless man away, and everyone clearly saw the power of God.

29 After Heliodorus had seen and felt God's mighty strength, he lay speechless and near death. 30 But everyone else praised the Lord God All-Powerful because of the miracle that had kept the temple safe. A little while earlier, the temple was filled with fear and confusion, but now there was joy and happiness because the Lord had appeared.

Heliodorus Tells Everyone about God

31 Heliodorus was at the point of death, and a few of his friends quickly begged Onias to ask God Most High to let him live. 32 Onias did not want King Seleucus to think that the Jews had plotted to kill Heliodorus. And so he offered a sacrifice and asked God to make Heliodorus well.

[n]**3.11** *Hyrcanus*: Greek "Hyrcanus son of Tobias." Tobias was the governor of the region Ammanitis.
[o]**3.19** *sackcloth*: A rough, dark-colored cloth made from goat or camel hair and used to make grain sacks. It was worn in times of trouble and sorrow.

3.22-28 3 Macc 2.21, 22. **3.25-29** Ws 17.3, 15; 18.14-19; 3 Macc 6.18.

33 While Onias was offering the sacrifice, the two young men appeared to Heliodorus again. They were still dressed in
their fine clothes, and they said, "Heliodorus, you should be grateful for Onias!
It was because of him that the Lord did not
take your life. 34 God in heaven was the one
who punished you. Now you must tell
everyone how powerful God is." After saying this, the young men disappeared.
35 Heliodorus offered his own sacrifice,
then made a lot of promises to the Lord who
had saved his life. He said good-by to Onias
and led his soldiers back to King Seleucus.
36 He told everyone, "With my own eyes, I
have seen God Most High work miracles."
37 One day, Seleucus asked Heliodorus, "Who should I send to Jerusalem this
time?"
Heliodorus answered, 38 "Send someone
you don't like or an enemy of your government! Whoever you send will be killed or
badly beaten, because God's power surrounds the Jerusalem temple. 39 This God
lives in heaven, but he guards that place
and kills everyone who tries to harm it."
40 So God kept Heliodorus from robbing
the temple treasury.

Simon Plots against Onias

4 I have already told you that Simon
caused a lot of trouble for our country
by telling Apollonius about the money in
the temple. Then later, Simon lied and
blamed Onias for the attack on Heliodorus
and for all the terrible things that happened.
2 Simon even dared to claim that Onias
was plotting against the government, although everyone knew that Onias had been
generous to Jerusalem and that he had protected our nation and had been in favor of
its laws. 3 Simon hated Onias so much that
he had even hired some men to commit
murders.
4 Apollonius,[p] the governor of Southwest Syria Province,[q] started encouraging
Simon with his evil plans. Finally, Onias
understood that his life was in danger,
5 and he asked King Seleucus for help.
Onias did not want to bring charges against
other Jews. He only hoped to find ways of
privately and publicly doing good for the
entire nation. 6 But he knew that he
needed the king's help to bring peace to
the country and to bring Simon to his
senses.

Jason Becomes High Priest

7 After the death of King Seleucus,[r] Antiochus Epiphanes[s] became ruler. Shortly
afterwards, Jason, the brother of Onias, became high priest by bribery. 8 Jason went to
the king[t] and promised him three hundred
sixty thousand silver coins from one of his
accounts and eighty thousand from another. 9 He also agreed to pay one hundred
fifty thousand silver coins for permission to
do two things. He wanted to make the Jews
in Jerusalem citizens of Antioch,[u] and he
wanted to build a place where young Jewish men could exercise and have organized
sports.[v]

Jason Forces the Jews To Live Like Greeks

10 King Antiochus gave Jason everything
he wanted. But no sooner had Jason become high priest than he began forcing
Jews to live like Greeks. 11 He did away
with our rights that John, the father of Eupolemus, had received from former kings.
Eupolemus was the messenger who later
went to the Romans and made them our
friends and allies.[w]

[p]**4.4** *Apollonius*: See the note at 3.5. [q]**4.4** *Southwest Syria Province*: See the note at 3.5. [r]**4.7** *King Seleucus*: Seleucus IV (ruled 187-175 B.C.). [s]**4.7** *Antiochus Epiphanes*: Antiochus IV (ruled 175-164 B.C.); he was the brother of Seleucus IV. [t]**4.8** *went to the king*: Or "wrote the king a letter." [u]**4.9** *to make . . . Antioch*: Or "to make a list of the Jews in Jerusalem who were citizens of Antioch." Jason wanted the king's permission to turn Jerusalem into a Greek city whose citizens would have the same rights and privileges as citizens of Antioch, the most important city in the eastern Mediterranean. [v]**4.9** *build . . . sports*: These were not only places for exercise, but centers for military training and promoting the Greek way of life, and one was built in every major Greek city. The men trained naked, which was against the Jewish religion. [w]**4.11** *friends and allies*: See 1 Maccabees 8.17.

3.36 3 Macc 1.9. **4.7** 1 Macc 1.10; 4 Macc 4.16. **4.11** 1 Macc 8.17.

Jason put an end to our Jewish way of life and taught new customs that went against our laws. 12 He eagerly built the place for exercise and sports near the temple. Then he ordered our finest young men to take part in activities there.[x]

13 Jason was so terribly evil that he did not deserve to be high priest. In fact, it was his fault that our people began to adopt the foreign customs that came with the Greek way of life. 14 Even our priests gave up worshiping at the altar. They cared nothing about the temple, and they neglected offering sacrifices. And when the signal was given, they hurried off to take part in games that were against our teachings. 15 They sneered at the values our ancestors had prized, and their only goal in life was to receive Greek honors.

16 This love of the Greek way of life caused the downfall of our country, when these foreign rulers became our enemies and punished our nation. They did this, even though many Jews liked and tried to follow their way of life. 17 When people disobey God's Law, they are taking a big risk, as the following events will show.

Jason and the Greeks

18 King Antiochus attended a sports festival that was held once every four[y] years in the city of Tyre. While he was there, 19 that evil Jason sent some messengers from Jerusalem to Tyre with three hundred silver coins for a sacrifice to the god Hercules.[z]

Although these messengers were honorary citizens of Antioch,[a] they knew it was wrong to pay for a sacrifice to Hercules with the silver. So they decided instead 20 to give the money for building warships.

21 About this same time, Antiochus sent Apollonius[b] to Egypt, so that Apollonius could attend the crowning[c] of King Philometor.[d] When Antiochus learned that Philometor had become his enemy, he took actions to protect his kingdom. Then Antiochus left for Jerusalem, passing through the town of Joppa on the way. 22 In Jerusalem, Jason and a cheering crowd with torches gave him a glorious welcome. From Jerusalem, Antiochus led his army to Phoenicia.

Menelaus Becomes High Priest

23 Three years later, Jason sent a man by the name of Menelaus to King Antiochus with money in order to do some important business. Menelaus was the brother of the Simon who was mentioned earlier.[e] 24 Menelaus was introduced to the king and tried to impress him by acting like a powerful official. Then he bought the position of high priest by offering the king three hundred thousand silver coins more than Jason had offered.

25 When Menelaus returned to Jerusalem, he carried papers from the king, saying he was the new high priest. But he was completely unfit for the job—he was cruel and had a violent temper worse than any wild animal.

26 Jason had earlier cheated his brother Onias out of the position of high priest. And now someone was cheating him out of being high priest, and he had to run to the Ammonites for his own safety.

27 Menelaus continued as high priest, though he never paid any of the money he had promised Antiochus. 28 He was asked many times for it by an official named Sostratus, who commanded the enemy fortress in Jerusalem, and whose duty it was to collect the king's money.

Finally, the king ordered both men to come to him and discuss the matter. 29 Menelaus let his brother Lysimachus act as high priest while he was away. Sostratus assigned his responsibilities to Crates, the commander of the soldiers from Cyprus.

[x]**4.12** *to take part in activities there*: The Greek has "to wear a sun hat." The Greek god Hermes was the hero of athletes and was thought of as wearing a broad-brimmed hat. Greek athletes wore similar hats to show their devotion to Hermes and to protect their heads from the sun. [y]**4.18** *four*: Or "five." [z]**4.19** *Hercules*: One of the most popular Greek gods during this period.
[a]**4.19** *honorary . . . Antioch*: See the note at 4.9. [b]**4.21** *Apollonius*: See the note at 3.5.
[c]**4.21** *the crowning*: One possible meaning for the difficult Greek text. [d]**4.21** *Philometor*: Ptolemy VI (ruled 180-145 B.C.); he was fourteen at the time. [e]**4.23** *Simon . . . earlier*: See 3.4-6; 4.1-3.
4.12 4 Macc 4.20.

Onias Is Murdered

30 About this time, King Antiochus gave the cities of Tarsus and Mallus to his lover Antiochis. But the cities rebelled, 31 and the king hurried off to put down the revolt, leaving a senior official named Andronicus in charge of the kingdom.

32 Menelaus now saw his chance to steal some gold dishes from the temple, and he did it. Then he gave the dishes to Andronicus. Earlier, he had also taken gold dishes from the temple and sold them to the people of Tyre and of other nearby cities. 33 Onias found out what had happened and ran for safety to a temple[f] at Daphne, not far from the city of Antioch. There he started publicly accusing Menelaus.

34 Shortly after this, Menelaus met privately with Andronicus and persuaded him to kill Onias. So Andronicus went to the temple and warmly greeted Onias. Then he lied to Onias by shaking his right hand[g] and promising to treat him with kindness. Onias didn't really trust Andronicus, but Andronicus talked him into leaving his place of safety in the temple. Then without any regard for the Law, Andronicus murdered him on the spot.

The King Punishes Andronicus

35 Our people were shocked and outraged by this violent murder, and so were many from other nations. 36 When King Antiochus returned from Cilicia, the Jews in Antioch[h] asked him to do something about this senseless crime. Many Greeks also told the king how much they despised this brutal murder.

37 The king cried and grieved terribly as he thought about Onias, a man of common sense and self-control. 38 Then he became furious and tore off Andronicus' clothes, including his royal robe. He made Andronicus walk naked through the whole city until they reached the place where Andronicus had murdered Onias. Right then and there, the king had this butcher put to death.

This was how the Lord gave Andronicus the punishment he deserved.

Lysimachus Is Killed

39 In the meantime, Menelaus had been helping his brother Lysimachus rob the Jerusalem temple of its gold dishes and other sacred objects. News of these crimes spread, and a crowd got together to complain about Lysimachus. 40 But since this crowd was turning into an angry mob, Lysimachus handed out swords to about three thousand followers. He put a foolish old man named Auranus in command of this force, then ordered a brutal attack.

41 Our people saw Lysimachus and his troops running toward them. So they immediately picked up rocks, as well as handfuls of ashes[i] and chunks of wood. They threw them wildly at the attackers, 42 wounding many and killing a few, while the rest ran away. The temple robber Lysimachus was killed not far from the temple treasury.

Menelaus Is Set Free

43 Because of what had happened, Menelaus was charged with serious crimes 44 and put on trial in the city of Tyre when King Antiochus arrived there. The Jerusalem council sent three messengers, who testified against him.

45 When Menelaus realized that he was going to be punished, he offered a huge bribe to the king's friend Ptolemy,[j] because he wanted Ptolemy to influence the king to say he was innocent. 46 So Ptolemy took Antiochus out on a porch, saying they needed a breath of fresh air. He convinced Antiochus to change his mind 47 and to drop the charges against Menelaus, the cause of the trouble.

Afterwards, Antiochus sentenced the three messengers to death. Even the

[f] **4.33** *ran . . . temple*: In ancient times temples were thought of as places where people could run for safety from their enemies. [g] **4.34** *shaking his right hand*: A public sign of friendship and support. [h] **4.36** *in Antioch*: Or "in each city." [i] **4.41** *ashes*: The fighting took place in the temple courtyard where priests scattered ashes from the sacrifices. [j] **4.45** *Ptolemy*: Greek "Ptolemy the son of Dorymenes."

4.34 Dn 9.26. **4.47** 3 Macc 7-5; 4 Macc 10.7.

cruelest judge[k] would have freed those
men, 48 but Antiochus had them quickly
and wrongfully killed. He did this because
they had spoken in behalf of Jerusalem, its
people,[l] and the sacred dishes that had
been stolen.

49 The citizens of Tyre were so disgusted
by the murder of these three men that they
honored them with elaborate funerals.
50 But because our rulers were greedy,
Menelaus was allowed to continue as high
priest. He grew so cruel that we considered
him our worst enemy.

Visions in Jerusalem

5 About this time, King Antiochus began
a second invasion of Egypt. 2 And for
more than forty days, the people of Jerusalem saw visions of cavalry in gold armor,
galloping through the air. The cavalry rode
in companies, and the riders were holding
spears and swords. 3 They lined up like
armies facing one another, then they attacked and counterattacked. Gold ornaments and all kinds of armor glittered and
sparkled in the sunlight. Shields flashed,
and spears and arrows filled the sky. 4 Everyone prayed that these visions meant something good.

The Death of Jason

5 Soon a rumor spread around that King
Antiochus was dead. Right away, Jason got
together a force of over one thousand
soldiers and made a surprise attack on
Jerusalem, defeating the troops that
Menelaus had stationed on the city walls.
After this, they captured the city and forced
Menelaus to retreat to the fortress overlooking the temple. 6 But Jason kept on
killing more Jews, without realizing that a
victory which destroys your own people is
the worst possible defeat. He seemed to
think he had won a battle against enemies
rather than against other Jews.

7 But Jason wasn't able to take control of
the government. In fact, he was so disgraced by what he had done that he had to
run for his life once again to the country of
the Ammonites. 8 Afterwards, he died a
miserable death.

Accused before the court
of Aretas, the Arab ruler,[m]
Jason was forced to hide
in town after town.
He was hunted and hated
by everyone,
because he had rebelled
against the Law of God
and had sentenced to death
many Jews in Israel.

9 Jason lived in Egypt for a while,
then sailed to Sparta,[n]
so he could beg protection
from distant relatives.
This man who had forced Jews
to live in foreign countries
died in that foreign city.

10 Because he didn't even bury
the Jews he killed,
no one grieved when he died,
or gave him a funeral,
or made a place for his body
in the family grave.

Antiochus Attacks Jerusalem

(1 Maccabees 1.20-63)

11 When King Antiochus heard about
the fighting in Jerusalem, he thought that
Judea had rebelled against him. So in his
fury, he led his army from Egypt and captured Jerusalem. 12 Then he ordered his
soldiers to kill everyone they found, even
those hiding in their own homes.

13-14 Forty thousand men, women, children, and babies were killed in this slaughter 14 that lasted for three days. Forty thousand more were sold as slaves.

15 As though that were not enough,

[k]**4.47** *cruelest judge*: The Greek text has "Scythians," people who were known for their cruelty.
[l]**4.48** *its people*: Some ancient manuscripts have "the nearby towns." [m]**5.8** *Accused . . . ruler*: One possible meaning for the difficult Greek text. [n]**5.9** *Sparta*: The Greek has "Lacedaemonians," the people who lived in Sparta. According to one Jewish tradition, Jews and Spartans were related (see 1 Maccabees 12.1-23).

5.2 3 Macc 4.15. **5.11—6.11** 4 Macc 4.15.

Antiochus walked straight into the world's
most sacred temple and was shown around
by Menelaus, who had betrayed our laws
and our nation. 16 Then, with his own filthy
hands, Antiochus took away sacred dishes
and helped himself to the treasures given
by other kings to the honor and glory of the
temple.

Why God Punished the People

17 Antiochus was really proud of himself.
But he did not understand that the Lord
was punishing the people of Jerusalem, because they had sinned and made him angry
for a while. And this was the reason the
Lord had let Antiochus disgrace the temple. 18 If the people had not sinned so terribly, the Lord would have beaten him with
whips and stopped him from doing such a
foolish thing, just as he did to Heliodorus,
when Seleucus sent him to examine the
treasury.[o]
19 But the Lord did not choose the nation for the good of the temple. He chose
the temple for the good of the nation.
20 That's why the temple and our people
suffered together and were later blessed together. So when God All-Powerful got angry
with us, he deserted our temple. But after
God had made peace with us, he gave the
temple back its glory.

Antiochus Torments the People

21 After King Antiochus had stolen a
million eight hundred thousand silver coins
from the temple, he rushed back to Antioch, arrogant and drunk with power. He
believed he could walk on water and sail on
dry land!
22 Antiochus picked cruel rulers to govern the people. He appointed Philip from
Phrygia[p] to be governor of Jerusalem, and
this man was more of a savage than the
king himself. 23 Then Antiochus put Andronicus in charge of Mount Gerizim. Even
Menelaus was made a ruler, and although
he was a Jew himself, he was more abusive
than any of the other governors.
King Antiochus hated the Jews so much,
24 that he sent[q] a Mysian officer[r] named
Apollonius to Jerusalem with twenty-two
thousand soldiers. Apollonius had orders to
kill every man in the city and to sell their
families as slaves.
25 When Apollonius arrived in Jerusalem, he lied and said he wanted peace. But
on the Sabbath, which is our sacred day of
rest, he ordered his soldiers to take their
weapons and parade outside the city.
26 Some of the people came out to watch,
and Apollonius ordered his troops to
slaughter them all. After this, he and his
soldiers ran into the city where they killed
many others.
27 Judas Maccabeus and about nine of
his followers escaped to the rugged hill
country, where they survived like wild animals by eating only things that grew wild.
The men did this, so they could keep themselves fit to worship God.

Antiochus Wants To Destroy the Jewish Way of Life

6 It was not long before King Antiochus
sent Geron of Athens[s] to our nation
with the following orders:

> Force the Jews to give up the Law
> of their God and their ancient cus-
> toms. 2 Make the temple in Jerusalem
> unfit as a place to worship their God
> by turning it into a temple for Zeus of
> Olympus.[t] Then name the temple on
> Mount Gerizim, "The Temple for Zeus
> Who Welcomes Strangers,"[u] since that
> is what it was earlier called by the peo-
> ple who live there.

3 After this, those foreigners abused our
people so cruelly that we almost lost hope.
4 They held wild parties and did other disgusting things in the temple, such as hav-

[o]**5.18** *treasury*: See 3.1-30. [p]**5.22** *Phrygia*: Phrygia was located in the southwest corner of Asia Minor (modern-day Turkey). [q]**5.23,24** *more abusive . . . he sent*: Or "more abusive than the others, because he hated the Jews so much. King Antiochus sent . . . " [r]**5.24** *Mysian officer*: Mysia was a region in northwestern Asia Minor. [s]**6.1** *Geron of Athens*: Or "an old man named Athenaeus," or "a senator from Athens," or "an old man from Athens." Some ancient manuscripts have "a senator from Antioch." [t]**6.2** *Zeus of Olympus*: Zeus was one of the most important Greek gods. Greeks believed he lived on Mount Olympus. [u]**6.2** *Zeus . . . Strangers*: Greek gods and goddesses often had several names.

ing sex with prostitutes and setting up vulgar idols.[v] 5 Even our altar was piled high
with unclean sacrifices that were forbidden
by our Law. 6 It became a crime to worship
on the Sabbath, or to celebrate our ancient
festivals, or even to admit that you were
a Jew.

7 Each month, the foreigners celebrated
the king's birthday. And during the ceremony
they cruelly forced our people to eat the insides of sacrificed animals.[w] Besides this,
they made us wear sprigs of ivy in our hair
and walk in parades whenever they celebrated a festival to honor the god Dionysus.[x]
8 About this time, the citizens of Ptolemais[y] suggested that the same law be made
for some nearby Greek towns, and it was
done. The law required these towns to
force Jews to eat the meat of sacrifices.
9 Death would be the penalty for refusing
to live like a Greek.

Our people now realized that a time of
dreadful suffering had arrived. 10 For example, some soldiers arrested two Jewish
mothers whose baby boys had been circumcised. They hung each child from its
mother's breasts, then led the women in
broad daylight through the town, before
throwing them from the city wall.

11 One Sabbath a group of Jews gathered secretly to worship in caves not far
from Jerusalem. But someone informed
Philip[z] the governor, who then had everyone burned alive. These Jews respected
this most holy day so much, that they did
not even try to defend themselves.

Why God Punishes the Jews

12 My dear readers, please don't be depressed by these sad stories. Remember
that these sufferings were not to destroy us,
but to instruct us.

13 In fact, God shows his kindness by
punishing sinners as soon as they disobey him, rather than waiting until later.
14 When God deals with other nations, he
waits patiently for them to sin terribly before he punishes them. But God treats us
differently. 15 He punishes us right away—
before our sins are too great.

16 Our God never stops being kind to us,
his chosen people. He lets our sufferings
teach us to do right, but he never deserts
us. 17 I have said these things to remind
you of God's way of dealing with us. Now
back to my story.

The Death of Eleazar

18 Eleazar was an elderly gentleman and
a highly respected teacher of the Law. One
day some men forced his mouth open and
tried to make him eat the meat of a pig.[a]
19 Eleazar chose to die with honor rather
than to live with shame. So he willingly
walked to the place of torture, spitting out
the meat as he went. 20 This is a fine example of courage for everyone who is willing to
refuse unclean food, even if it means death.
21 The men in charge of the lawless sacrifice had known Eleazar for a long time.
So they took him aside and said to him in
private:

> Get some meat that your religion
> says can be eaten. Then pretend you
> are eating meat from the pig that the
> king ordered us to sacrifice. 22 Do this,
> and you won't be killed. We have been
> friends for a long time, so let us do this
> favor for you.

23 But Eleazar did the only honorable
thing that a man of his age and reputation
could do. He firmly made up his mind
to obey God's Law, just as he had always
done. And so he immediately said:

[v]**6.4** *setting . . . idols*: The Greek has "brought in things that were against our Law." [w]**6.7** *the insides of sacrificed animals*: The Jews were not supposed to eat insides of sacrificed animals. These had to be completely burned on the altar (Leviticus 1.9) or at some other place (Leviticus 4.11, 12); the fat around them could not be eaten, because it belonged to God (Leviticus 3.3, 4, 8-10). However, in pagan sacrifices, the heart, lungs, liver, and kidneys were eaten at the beginning of the sacrifice by the worshipers. [x]**6.7** *Dionysus*: The Greek god of wine (see 14.33). [y]**6.8** *the citizens of Ptolemais*: One possible meaning for the difficult Greek text. [z]**6.11** *Philip*: Ruler of Jerusalem (see 5.22). [a]**6.18** *the meat of a pig*: The Law of Moses did not allow Jews to eat pigs (see Leviticus 11.7; Deuteronomy 14.8).

6.7 3 Macc 2.29. **6.10** 1 Macc 1.60, 61. **6.11** 1 Macc 2.32-38. **6.18** Lv 11.4-8; 3 Macc 6.1. **6.18-31** 4 Macc 5.1. **6.21** 4 Macc 6.15.

Kill me here and now! 24 It would
be disgraceful for someone my age
to pretend to eat unlawful food. Our
young people would think that I had
given up my Jewish faith after ninety
years. 25 I might live a little longer, but
I would cause our young people to
deny their faith, and I would end up a
shameful, disgusting old man.

26 I might escape torture at the
hands of humans for now, but even
when I am dead, I cannot escape from
God All-Powerful!

27 By dying bravely I can prove that
I was worthy of the long life that God
has given me. 28 And my death will set
a good example for our young people—
it will show them that we should not
be afraid to die for our sacred laws.

When Eleazar had finished speaking, he
walked straight[b] to the place of torture.
29 But the same men who had earlier been
kind to him now sneered, because they
thought he was talking nonsense.

30 When Eleazar had been beaten almost to the point of death, he groaned and
shouted, "The Lord God knows everything!
He knows that I could have escaped this
terrible torture and death, but I have gladly
suffered for him, because I honor him with
all my heart and soul."

31 Eleazar's brave and honorable death
set an example for our whole nation, and
especially for our young people.

A Brave Mother

7 King Antiochus once arrested seven
Jewish brothers and their mother. He
had them beaten with heavy whips and
tried to make them eat the meat of pigs,
which is against our laws. 2 But one of the
brothers spoke up and said, "Why are you
torturing us like this? We will die before we
disobey the laws of our ancestors!"

3 This made the king so angry that he
ordered his men to heat up big pots and pans,
4 and they quickly did this. Meanwhile, the
king forced the boy's family to watch him
being tortured. Some soldiers cut out his
tongue, then scalped him and chopped off
his hands and feet, 5 making him completely helpless. While the boy was still
alive, the king told his soldiers, "Carry him to
one of the big pans on the fire and fry him."

When smoke from the pan started
spreading everywhere, the brothers and
their mother each said, "Let's die bravely!
6 The Lord God will have pity on us, because he always takes care of his servants,
just as Moses said in the song he wrote to
correct our rebellious ancestors."[c]

7 When the first brother was dead, the
soldiers grabbed the second brother. They
made fun of him and scalped him. Then
they asked, "Wouldn't you rather eat some
meat from a pig than to be slowly tortured
to death?"

8 In his native language[d] the boy replied,
"No!" Then the soldiers tortured him, just
as they had done to the first brother.

9 When the second brother was almost
dead, he said to the king, "How can you be
so cruel? Even if you kill us, the King of
this world will raise us to life. And then we
will live forever, because we died, rather
than deny our faith."

10 When he died, they started torturing
the third brother and shouted, "Stick out
your tongue!"

He immediately obeyed and bravely
stretched out his arms as well. 11 He had a
lot of courage and said, "God in heaven
gave these to me. But I will give them up to
obey his laws, because I know God will give
them back."

12 The king and his troops were amazed
at the young man's courage. Here was someone willing to suffer.

13 After he was dead, the king's troops
beat and tortured the fourth brother in the
same way. 14 But just before he died, he
told them, "God has promised to raise us to
life! And so we are willing to die, but you
have no hope for life after death."

15 As the fifth brother was being tortured, 16 he looked straight at the king and
said, "You order people around and make
them obey you. But someday you will die.

[b]**6.28** *walked straight*: Some manuscripts have "was dragged." [c]**7.6** *ancestors*: See Deuteronomy 32.36. [d]**7.8** *In . . . language*: Either Hebrew or Aramaic.

7.1-42 4 Macc 8–13; He 11.35, 36. **7.6** Dt 32.36.

Don't think God has turned his back on our
nation. 17 Just wait! God will use his mighty
power to make you and your family suffer."
18 Next, they tortured the sixth brother.
He was almost dead when he told the men,
"Don't fool yourselves! We're suffering all
these terrible things because we have
disobeyed our God. 19 Now you're fighting
against God, so don't think that you won't
be punished too."
20 The mother of these young men was
a wonderful woman, and she deserves to be
remembered with praise. She saw all seven
of her sons die on the same day, but she
was brave and never stopped trusting the
Lord. 21 She was a very special person, and
with the feelings of a woman and the
courage of a man, she encouraged each of
her sons by telling them in their native
language:[e]

> 22 My son, I don't understand how
> you grew inside me. I am not the one
> who gave you life and breath or shaped
> your bodies. 23 You are sacrificing your
> life to obey the laws of the God who
> created this world and all of its people.
> But God will be merciful and give life
> and breath back to you.

24 From the way the mother was talking,
King Antiochus could tell that she was
insulting him and sneering at him. The
youngest son was still alive. So Antiochus
made all kinds of promises to the boy and
tried to make him change his mind. He
said, "If you will forget about the teachings
of your ancestors, I will make you rich and
respected. You will be one of my trusted
friends[f] and a government official."
25-26 When the boy refused to listen, the
king turned to the mother, urging her to
make the boy change his mind. Finally, she
agreed 27 and leaned toward her son. She
spoke in her native language and mocked
the cruel king:

> My son, have pity on me! Even be-
> fore you were born, you grew inside my
> body for nine months. Then I nursed
> you at my breast for three years. And
> until this very day, I have looked after
> you and taken care of you.
> 28 Now, I beg you to look at the
> heavens and the earth and think about
> what you see. God made all of this out
> of nothing, and he made us humans in
> the same way.
> 29 Don't be afraid of this butcher!
> Die willingly and show that you are
> just like your brothers. Then God will
> have pity and give you back to me on
> the day he gives me your brothers.

30 While the mother was still speaking,
the boy said to the king:

> What are you waiting for? I'm not
> going to obey your orders! I only obey
> God's teachings that Moses gave to our
> ancestors.
> 31 You have caused terrible troubles
> for our people, but you won't escape
> the punishment God will send on you.
> 32-33 We have disobeyed God and made
> him angry with us. So for a little while
> the living Lord is letting us suffer be-
> cause he wants to correct us and teach
> us to do right. But we are still his serv-
> ants, and he will soon forgive us.
> 34 King Antiochus, you're the most
> disgusting and godless creature that
> ever lived. Stop acting so high and
> mighty, and stop making foolish prom-
> ises to yourself as you torture God's
> people. 35 You will never escape God
> All-Powerful! He sees everything and
> will punish you.
> 36 My brothers stayed faithful to our
> sacred agreement with God. So for a lit-
> tle while they had to suffer. Now, how-
> ever, they have drunk the water that
> gives eternal life.[g] But because of your
> pride, God will judge you and punish you
> as you deserve. 37 I am willing to die
> along with my brothers for the laws of
> our ancestors. Meanwhile, I pray that
> God will soon forgive our people and
> show us mercy. I also pray that he will
> punish you so severely that you will fi-
> nally confess that the Lord alone is God.

[e] **7.21** *native language*: See the note at verse 8. [f] **7.24** *trusted friends*: See the note at 1.13, 14.
[g] **7.36** *My brothers . . . eternal life*: Or "My brothers suffered for a little while, then God let them drink the water that gives the eternal life he promised in our agreement with him."
7.36 4 Macc 17.11, 12.

38 God All-Powerful was right to be angry with our whole nation. But I pray that his anger will end with the sufferings that my brothers and I are going through.

39 When Antiochus realized that the boy was mocking him, he became more furious than ever and tortured him worse than the others. 40 So the boy died, completely trusting the Lord and still faithful to his beliefs.

41 Last of all, the king put their mother to death.

42 Enough said about eating sacrifices and being tortured.

Judas Maccabeus Fights for the Jews
(1 Maccabees 3.1-26)

8 Meanwhile, Judas Maccabeus and his followers were going secretly through our towns and villages, gathering a force of about six thousand faithful Jews. 2 Afterwards, they prayed:

> Our Lord, we've been horribly abused by everyone! Please have pity on us and on your temple that these godless foreigners have made unfit for worship. 3 Rescue Jerusalem from those enemies who have left it in ruins.
>
> Take revenge on those murderers! 4 Punish them for slaughtering innocent children and insulting you. Show how much you hate evil.

5 After Judas and his troops were ready for battle, the Lord's anger toward his people turned to mercy, and the foreigners did not stand a chance. 6 Judas burned towns and villages without warning; he captured fortresses and forced their troops to run for their lives. 7 He liked to make these attacks after dark, and soon everyone was talking about this brave warrior.

Nicanor Attacks Judas
(1 Maccabees 3.38-41)

8 When Philip,[h] the governor, found out that Judas was winning more and more victories and slowly taking over the country, he wrote a letter to Ptolemy, the royal governor of Southwest Syria Province.[i] The letter said, "Send someone to help me protect the government of King Antiochus."

9 Right away, Ptolemy chose Nicanor,[j] one of the king's most trusted friends.[k] He also picked Gorgias, who was a high-ranking official and an expert in war. Then Ptolemy ordered them to take an army of more than twenty thousand foreign soldiers to Judea and destroy our nation.

10 Antiochus owed two million silver coins to the Romans,[l] and Nicanor planned to raise the money by selling captured Jews as slaves. 11 So he decided to charge about ten silver coins for each slave, then he sent news of the sale to the coastal towns.

Nicanor did not expect it, but God All-Powerful was about to punish him.

Judas Attacks Nicanor
(1 Maccabees 3.42-54)

12 When Judas found out that Nicanor had invaded Judea, he told his army what had happened. 13 Some of his troops were cowards, and others did not believe that God would punish the foreigners. And so all of them ran away. 14 Others sold their property[m] and prayed:

> Our Lord, please rescue your troops from that godless Nicanor. He has already started selling us as slaves, before the battle has even begun.
>
> 15 If you don't want to help us for our sake alone, then do it because of the promises you made to our ancestors. After all, you are the holy and glorious God who chose them.

16 After Judas had gotten together his army of six thousand soldiers, he encouraged them by saying:

> Don't be afraid and panic when you see the huge army of foreigners! They were wrong to invade our country, so fight them bravely. 17 Don't ever forget

[h]**8.8** *Philip*: Ruler of Jerusalem (see 5.22; 6.11). [i]**8.8** *Southwest Syria Province*: See the note at 3.5. [j]**8.9** *Nicanor*: Greek "Nicanor the son of Patroclus." [k]**8.9** *trusted friends*: See the note at 1.13, 14. [l]**8.10** *Romans*: The Romans defeated Antiochus III in 188 B.C. and made him promise to pay them a huge sum of money. His sons Seleucus IV and Antiochus IV had to help pay off the debt. [m]**8.14** *sold their property*: Since Nicanor would have taken it anyway.

7.41 4 Macc 17.1. **8.1** 3 Macc 1.22.

how they disgraced our holy temple, or how they brought terrible troubles to Jerusalem and refused to let us follow the customs of our ancestors.

18 They depend on their weapons and on heroic deeds to win battles. But we depend on God All-Powerful, who can wipe out these enemies and the whole world by simply shaking his head.

19 I can recall many times when God came to the rescue of our ancestors. For example, when ·King Sennacherib of Assyria attacked Jerusalem, he lost one hundred eighty-five thousand soldiers.[n]

20 On another occasion, eight thousand Jews were fighting on the side of four thousand Macedonians who were losing a battle against the Galatians in Babylonia. God helped our troops, and they killed one hundred twenty thousand enemy soldiers, then took everything of value that they wanted.

21 These stories encouraged the troops and made them willing to die for their faith and their nation.

Judas now divided his army into four groups 22 of fifteen hundred soldiers each. He and his brothers Simon, Joseph, and Jonathan each took command of one group. 23 Then he told Eleazar to read[o] the Scriptures to the troops, and Judas ordered them to go into battle shouting, "God will help us!" Judas himself led the first group into the battle against Nicanor.

24 God All-Powerful helped our forces kill more than nine thousand of Nicanor's soldiers. They wounded many more and forced the rest of them to run for their lives. 25 When the fighting was over, they took the money from those who had come to buy them as slaves. Then they chased after the rest of Nicanor's army for a long way. But when evening came, they had to return, 26 because it was almost time to celebrate the Sabbath.[p]

27 After the troops had collected the valuables from the dead enemy soldiers, they celebrated the Sabbath, and they praised and thanked the Lord for keeping them safe while they fought. This victory meant that God was being kind to our nation once again.

28 After the Sabbath, Judas and his army shared some of their valuables with the widows, the orphans, and the torture victims. They gave the rest to their own families. 29 Then everyone prayed together, begging our merciful Lord to be friendly to us.

Judas Fights Timothy and Bacchides

30 Judas and his soldiers fought against the armies of Timothy and Bacchides, killing more than twenty thousand enemy troops and capturing some strong hill fortresses. The soldiers gave equal shares of everything they had captured to their families, the widows, the orphans, the elderly, and the victims of torture. 31 The enemy's weapons were gathered up and carefully stored where they would be ready for use, and everything else taken from the enemy was carried back to Jerusalem.

32 The commander of Timothy's army was cruel and had mistreated our people, and so he was put to death.

33 Then we celebrated our victory in Jerusalem, the city of our ancestors, and found Callisthenes and some other enemies hiding in a small house. They had earlier set the gates of our holy temple on fire, so we burned them alive, just as they deserved.

Nicanor Praises God

34 Nicanor was a horrible man who had asked a thousand slave traders to buy captured Jews. 35 But with the Lord's help, Nicanor was defeated by the very people he most despised. In fact, Nicanor ended up throwing away his fancy uniform and sneaking away by himself like a slave on the run, until he reached the city of Antioch. He had succeeded only in destroying his own army.

[n]**8.19** *soldiers*: See 2 Kings 19.1-35. [o]**8.23** *Eleazar to read*: One possible meaning of the difficult Greek text. [p]**8.26** *celebrate the Sabbath*: The Sabbath begins at sunset on Friday and ends at sunset on Saturday.

8.23 1 Macc 3.48.

36 Nicanor had planned to capture the
Jews of Jerusalem and sell them as slaves,
so the king could pay his debt to Rome. But
now Nicanor told everyone, "God defends
and protects the Jews! They obey his laws,
and he will never let them be defeated."

King Antiochus Is Punished
(1 Maccabees 6.1-13)

9 1-2 Meanwhile, King Antiochus and his
army had invaded Persia, where they
attempted to capture the city of Persepolis
and to rob its temples. But the citizens of
Persepolis fought back, until Antiochus and
his army were forced to retreat in shame
and confusion.
3 When Antiochus reached the city of
Ecbatana,[q] he was told what Judas had done
to the armies of Nicanor and Timothy.
4 This made him furious, and he decided to
take revenge on our people for the defeat
he had just suffered at Persepolis. So he told
his chariot driver to take him straight to
Jerusalem. In his arrogance he thought, "I'll
turn Jerusalem into a pile of Jewish bones!"

Antiochus did not realize that the Lord
God of Israel was about to punish him. 5 And
at that very moment the Lord who sees
everything struck him with a mysterious
and deadly disease that made him double
up with endless pain. 6 This was the perfect punishment for someone who had tortured others so often and with such cruelty.
7-8 But the pain just made Antiochus
more arrogant than ever. He shouted terrible curses against our people and ordered
his chariot driver to go even faster.

Not long before this, he had felt so
proud and powerful that he had said to
himself, "Ocean waves obey me, and
mountains move at my command!" But as
his chariot was speeding along, he suddenly fell to the ground with such a thud
that every part of his body ached. Then he
was carried away on a stretcher, and everyone saw the power of God.
9 This godless Antiochus was still alive,
but his body was tormented by throbbing
pain. His skin began rotting, and worms
started crawling out of his eyes.[r] He was
stinking so badly that his entire army felt
like vomiting, 10 and so no one was willing
to carry this man who once thought he could
reach up and touch the stars.
11 God punished King Antiochus with
unending pain and depression, until the
king began to lose his pride and started
thinking clearly. 12 And when he could no
longer stand his own smell, he said, "We
humans are nothing compared to the Lord
God, and we should obey him."[s]

Antiochus Makes a Promise to God

13 The Lord refused to be merciful to
Antiochus any longer, even though this disgusting man made the following promises
to the Lord:

> 14 Recently, I planned to trample
> down the holy city of Jerusalem and to
> turn it into a pile of Jewish bones. But
> now I give you my word that Jerusalem
> will be a free city. 15 I also intended to
> let the birds and the wild animals eat
> the bodies of the Jews and their chil-
> dren that I had thrown outside. After
> all, I did not consider them worth bury-
> ing. But instead I'll give them the same
> legal rights as the people of Athens.[t]
> 16 Some time ago, I robbed the holy
> temple in Jerusalem of its sacred dishes.
> But now I'm going to fill the temple
> with expensive gifts and return those
> sacred dishes, so there will be more of
> them than ever before. And I'll pay for
> all the sacrifices with my own money.
> 17 Finally, I'll become a Jew and
> travel to every village, town, and city,
> telling people about the power of God.

Antiochus Writes to the Jews

18 God was punishing Antiochus just as
he deserved, and so none of these promises
relieved his suffering. Then Antiochus
wrote the following letter to our people:

[q]**9.3** *Ecbatana*: About five hundred miles northwest of Persepolis. [r]**9.9** *eyes*: Some manuscripts have "body." [s]**9.12** *We . . . him*: Or "We cannot think thoughts that only God is allowed to have." [t]**9.15** *Athens*: Athens was one of the most famous cities in the ancient world, and kings treated its people with great respect.

9.4-10 3 Macc 2.21, 22. **9.15** 3 Macc 6.34.

19 King Antiochus, commander of the army, sends greetings to the Jews. You are some of my most important citizens, and I wish all of you good health and success.

20 I pray that you and your families are healthy and that all is going well for you. I have now placed my hope in God, 21 and I have pleasant memories of how you treated me with kindness and respect.

On my way home from the country of Persia, I suddenly became very sick and started making plans to protect everyone in my kingdom. 22 I think I will get well, and so I am not depressed about being sick. 23 But I know that my father always named someone to take his place as king whenever he was at war in the northern part of the kingdom. 24 That way, if something unexpected happened, or if some bad news came, everyone in the kingdom remained calm, knowing that the government was in good hands.

25 Moreover, in the countries along our borders, certain rulers are watching and waiting for a chance to take over our kingdom.

For these reasons, I have appointed my son Antiochus[u] the next king. I have already told you about him, and some of you even looked after him when I had to hurry off to the northern part of my kingdom.

I have sent Antiochus a copy of this letter. 26 Please remember the favors I did for you, both publicly and privately, and keep on being good to me and my son. 27 I am sure he will follow my example and treat you kindly and fairly.

The Death of King Antiochus
(1 Maccabees 6.14-16)

28 King Antiochus murdered people and insulted God. So after he had suffered the same horrible pains that he had caused others, he died a pitiful death in the mountains of a foreign country. 29 Philip, who had been brought up with him, took the king's body home. But Philip did not trust the son of Antiochus, and so he went over to King Ptolemy Philometor[v] of Egypt.

Judas Dedicates the Jerusalem Temple
(1 Maccabees 4.36-61)

10 The Lord led Judas Maccabeus and our troops into battle, and they recaptured the temple and the city of Jerusalem. 2 Then they destroyed the places where the foreigners had worshiped, including the altars they had built in the public market.

3 Judas and his followers made the temple an acceptable place of worship once again. They built a new altar for sacrifices and started a fire on it by rubbing flint rocks together.[w] After this, they offered sacrifices for the first time in two years. They burned incense, then lit the lamps and brought out the sacred loaves of bread.

4 When all of this was done, the troops lay face down on the ground and prayed, "Our Lord, please don't let us suffer such terrible troubles again. If we should ever turn from you, don't correct us so harshly. And please, never again hand us over to these foreign savages, who insult you."

5 The dedication of the temple took place on the twenty-fifth day of the month of Chislev[x]—the same day of the same month that the foreigners had made the temple unfit for worship. 6 We celebrated a joyful festival for eight days, and it was just like the Festival of Shelters. In fact, while our people celebrated, they kept remembering the recent Festival of Shelters, when they were forced to roam the hills and live in caves like wild animals. 7 But now they walked around carrying sticks decorated with twisted ivy and holding up branches, including some from palm trees. They sang hymns and thanked the Lord for making our holy temple clean again. 8 Afterwards,

[u]**9.25** *Antiochus*: Antiochus V (ruled 164-162 B.C.). [v]**9.29** *Ptolemy Philometor*: See 4.21 and the note there. [w]**10.3** *flint rocks together*: According to Jewish custom, the fire for the altar in the temple had to be a new fire. People who used an old fire risked being punished like Nadab and Abihu (see Leviticus 10.1, 2). [x]**10.5** *Chislev*: See the note at 1.9.

10.6 3 Macc 6.36.

everyone decided to make this a yearly festival for our whole nation.

Antiochus Eupator Becomes King

9 Antiochus Epiphanes was dead, and
10 Antiochus Eupator,[y] the son of that godless man, became king. I will now give a
brief summary of the horrible wars and
other things that happened during his rule.
11 After Antiochus Eupator became
king, he put Lysias in charge of his kingdom. Antiochus also made him[z] the governor of Southwest Syria Province[a] in place
of 12 Ptolemy Macron.

Ptolemy knew how much we Jews had
suffered, and he did all he could to treat us
fairly and to live in peace with us. 13 Because of this, some friends[b] of King Eupator brought charges against Ptolemy. They
told the king:

> When King Philometor of Egypt
> made Ptolemy the ruler of Cyprus Is-
> land, Ptolemy ran away from that
> place and sided with King Antiochus
> Epiphanes. Now everyone says Ptol-
> emy is a traitor.

Ptolemy felt that no one respected him
as governor any more,[c] so he committed suicide by swallowing some poison.

Judas Attacks the Idumeans
(1 Maccabees 5.1-8)

14 When Gorgias became governor of
Idumea,[d] he hired an army of professional
soldiers and attacked our people whenever
he could. 15 Even the Idumeans themselves
attacked us, hoping to turn the whole
country into a battleground.[e] They controlled strong fortresses and welcomed all
the troublemakers who had been run out of
Jerusalem.
16 Because of these attacks, Judas and
his troops begged God for help. Then they
quickly set out for the Idumean fortresses.
17 They made violent attacks on them and
forced the enemy soldiers to retreat from
their positions on the walls. Then after
they had captured these places, they killed
everyone they could. At least twenty thousand of their enemies died.
18 About nine thousand enemy troops
took cover in two strong towers that had
everything they needed to fight off attackers. 19 So Judas ordered his brothers Simon
and Joseph, along with an officer named
Zacchaeus and his troops, to surround
these towers. And since they had enough
soldiers to capture the towers, Judas left for
other parts of the country that needed his
help even more.
20 But a few of Simon's troops became
greedy. They took a bribe of twelve thousand silver coins from some enemy forces
in the towers, then let them sneak away.
21 When Judas found out what had happened, he called together his officers and
brought charges against these soldiers. He
said, "They have sold out their friends, and
now the enemy troops who escaped will return and attack us."
22 Judas had the guilty soldiers put to
death. Then he and his troops immediately
captured the two towers 23 and killed more
than twenty thousand enemy soldiers.
Judas was successful in every battle he
fought.

Judas Attacks Timothy

24 Someone named Timothy got together a powerful force of foreign soldiers,
as well as a large number of cavalry from
Asia. He then set out to invade Judea, even
though he had already been defeated once
before[f] by the Jewish troops.
25 As Timothy's army came nearer, Judas and our troops prayed sincerely. They
smeared dirt on their heads and put on
clothes made of sackcloth.[g] 26 Then they

[y] **10.10** *Antiochus Eupator*: Also known as Antiochus V (ruled 164-162 B.C.). [z] **10.11** *him*: Or "a man named Protarchos." [a] **10.11** *Southwest Syria Province*: See the note at 3.5. [b] **10.13** *friends*: See the note at 1.13, 14. [c] **10.13** *Ptolemy felt . . . more*: One possible meaning for the difficult Greek text. [d] **10.14** *Idumea*: The Greek has "the region." According to 12.32 the region is Idumea, an area just south of Judea and the home of the Herod family mentioned frequently in the New Testament. [e] **10.15** *hoping to turn . . . battleground*: Or "hoping to make the war last as long as possible." [f] **10.24** *even though . . . before*: Or "even though another commander named Timothy had already been defeated." [g] **10.25** *sackcloth*: See the note at 3.19.

10.10 1 Macc 6.17.

lay face down on the steps leading to the
altar and prayed, "Please be kind to us and
wipe out our enemies, just as our sacred
Scriptures promise."[h]
27 After Judas and his troops had
finished praying, they picked up their
weapons and set out from Jerusalem on a
long march. They camped not far from the
enemy army, 28 and at dawn the next day
the battle began. Our troops were brave
and they trusted the Lord, which was a
sure path to victory. But Timothy's soldiers
fought only because they were angry.
29 In the heat of battle, the enemy saw
five handsome riders on horses with gold
bridles suddenly appear from heaven
and take command of our troops. 30 They
formed a circle around Judas and protected
him with their shields and weapons, while
sending a flood of arrows and lightning
bolts at Timothy's army.

Blinded and confused, the enemy troops
scattered in every direction and were cut
down. 31 Twenty thousand five hundred of
their soldiers and six hundred of their cavalry died that day. 32 Timothy himself
escaped to the fortress at Gazara, where
his brother Chaereas[i] commanded a large
force.
33 Judas and his troops eagerly attacked
Gazara for four days. 34 But the enemy soldiers inside the fortress kept cursing God
and shouting horrible insults, because they
felt safe behind the strong walls of their
fortress.
35 Finally these insults made twenty of
our brave young soldiers furious. So at
dawn of the fifth day, they fought their way
over the fortress wall, killing everyone they
met. 36 At the same time, others fought
their way over another section of the wall
and attacked. They set fire to the whole
fortress, including its towers, and burned
alive those troops who had cursed God.
Then some of our soldiers beat down the
gates, allowing the rest of our army to capture the town.
37 Timothy was found hiding in a cistern, and so our troops killed him, together
with his brother Chaereas and a soldier
named Apollophanes. 38 When the battle
was over, Judas and our army sang hymns
of praise to the Lord, because he is very
kind to Israel and gives us victory.

Lysias Attacks the Jews

(1 Maccabees 4.26-35)

11 Lysias was a relative and the
guardian of young King Antiochus
Eupator.[j] He was also running the government for the king.

Soon afterwards, when Lysias learned
what had happened to Timothy, he became
furious 2 and got together his cavalry and
almost eighty thousand soldiers to attack
our people. He planned to turn Jerusalem
into a Greek city 3 and to tax the temple, as
he had done to the temples in other nations. He also wanted to sell the position of
high priest to the highest bidder each year.
4 Lysias took great pride in his army that
had tens of thousands of soldiers, as well as
thousands of cavalry troops and eighty elephants. But he completely forgot about
the power of God. 5 Lysias led this army
into Judea, where he fiercely attacked the
fortress at Beth-Zur, about twenty miles
from Jerusalem.
6 Meanwhile, Judas and his soldiers
found out that Lysias was attacking the fortresses. So they and everyone else cried
and begged God to send a good angel to
rescue Israel. 7 When they had finished
praying, Judas was the first to reach for his
weapons. Then he urged his troops to do
the same. "Let's save our people, no matter
what the cost!" he said.

They eagerly set out for the enemy
camp. 8 But no sooner had they left Jerusalem, than they noticed someone on
horseback leading them. He was dressed in
white and carrying weapons of gold. 9 Together they thanked God for having pity on
them and sending an angel. They felt brave
enough to attack humans, or the most savage animals, or even fortresses of solid iron.
10 Our troops marched in battle formation, led by the angel that their merciful

[h] **10.26** *sacred Scriptures promise*: See Exodus 23.22. [i] **10.32** *his brother Chaereas*: See 10.37.
[j] **11.1** *young King Antiochus Eupator*: Also known as Antiochus V (164-162 B.C.). He was only about nine years old when he became king.

Lord had sent. 11 They attacked the enemy army like lions, killing eleven thousand soldiers and sixteen hundred cavalry. The rest of the enemy soldiers ran for their lives,
12 since most of them were wounded and without weapons. Lysias himself ran away like a coward.

Lysias and the Jews Make Peace
(1 Maccabees 6.56-61)

13 Lysias was a smart man, and he kept thinking about the defeat he had just suffered. Finally, he realized that he could never destroy the Jewish people. After all, God All-Powerful fought on our side. So he
wrote a letter 14 urging our people to sign a peace treaty that would be fair. Lysias also promised that he would persuade King Antiochus to be kind to our nation.[k]

15 Judas wanted to do what was best for everyone, so he agreed to do what Lysias had asked, since the king had always agreed to every request that he had made in writing to Lysias.[l]

A Letter from Lysias to the Jews

16 This is a copy of the letter that Lysias wrote:

Lysias sends greetings to the Jewish people.

17 You sent your messengers John and Absalom to me with your official list of demands, and we have gone over them in detail.

18 Some of the items on the list needed to be discussed with the king. So I did this, and he has agreed to do
all he possibly can. 19 Meanwhile, remain faithful to our government, and from now on I'll do everything I can to
make your nation prosper. 20 I have ordered John and Absalom, together with my own messengers, to discuss the details of this matter with you.

21 Good-by. The date of this letter is the twenty-fourth day of the month of Dioscorinthius[m] in the year 148[n] of the Syrian Kingdom.

A Letter from King Antiochus to Lysias

22 This is a copy of the letter that Antiochus wrote to Lysias:

King Antiochus sends greetings to his good friend[o] Lysias.

23 Now that my father is dead, I am letting everyone in my kingdom take charge of their own lives, without being bothered by anyone. 24 I know that the Jews refused to obey my father, who wanted them to live like Greeks. But they have their own customs and have asked permission to live according to their laws.

25 I have decided that the Jews are free to live the way they want, just like any other nation in my kingdom. So give them back their temple and let them follow the traditions of their ancestors.

26 Send messengers to inform the Jews of my decision and to guarantee them that we are now on good terms. They will be glad to know that they can live in peace and do as they wish.

A Letter from the King to the Jews

27 This is a copy of the letter from Antiochus to our nation:

King Antiochus sends greetings to the Jews and their council.

28 I am in good health, and I hope you are too.

29 Menelaus the high priest[p] told me that you want to return home and
live according to your traditions. 30 I will let you do that, but you must leave by the thirtieth day of the month Xanthicus[q] if you want to stay on good
terms with me. 31 I also give you permission to continue your food laws and other customs. None of you will be punished for what you have done in ignorance.

32 I have sent Menelaus to encourage you.

[k] **11.14** *Lysias . . . nation*: One possible meaning for the difficult Greek text. [l] **11.15** *since . . . Lysias*: One possible meaning for the difficult Greek text. [m] **11.21** *Dioscorinthius*: The month of March. [n] **11.21** *year 148*: That is, 164 B.C. [o] **11.22** *good friend*: See the note at 1.13, 14. [p] **11.29** *Menelaus the high priest*: See 4.23-29, 43-50; 5.15-23. [q] **11.30** *Xanthicus*: A month from the Macedonian calendar; possibly Nisan or Adar of the Jewish calendar.

33 Good-by. The date of this letter is
the fifteenth day of the month of Xanthicus in the year 148[r] of the Syrian
Kingdom.

A Letter from the Romans to the Jews

34 This is a copy of the letter the Romans sent to the Jews:

Quintus Memmius and Titus Ma-
nius, messengers from Rome, send
greetings to the Jews.
35 Rome approves the terms of the
peace treaty that you were given by
Lysias, the relative of King Antiochus.
36 We are now on the way to the
city of Antioch, and we want you to
study carefully the matters that Lysias
discussed with the king. Then quickly
send a messenger to us, and we will
inform the king what is in your best
interests.
37 Do not delay. Send the messengers as soon as you can, because we
need to know how you feel about these
matters.
38 Good-by. The date of this letter is
the fifteenth day of the month of Xanthicus[s] in the year 148[t] of the Syrian
Kingdom.

Troubles in Joppa and Jamnia

12 After the agreememt was signed,
Lysias went back to King Antiochus, and our people started farming
again. 2 But some of the local officials, especially Timothy, Apollonius,[u] Hieronymus,
and Demophon, kept causing trouble, and
so did Nicanor, who was an official in
Cyprus.
3 The people of Joppa also committed a
terrible crime against their Jewish neighbors. They pretended to be on good terms
with them and said, "We want you and
your families to go sailing with us. We'll
provide the ships."
4 They accepted this invitation since the
whole town of Joppa had voted to invite
them. Besides, they wanted to be on good
terms with the Gentiles and didn't suspect
a plot. But when the ships reached the
open sea, the people of Joppa drowned
about two hundred of the Jews.
5 When Judas heard that such cruel
things had been done to his own people,
he told his troops what had to be done.[v]
6 Everyone prayed to God, who always
judges fairly. Then after dark, Judas and his
troops attacked the murderers and set the
harbor on fire. They destroyed its ships and
killed everyone they caught hiding there.
7 But when Judas found the gates to Joppa
closed, he led his troops away, planning to
wipe out the town another time.
8 Judas was then told that the citizens
of Jamnia also planned to kill their Jewish
neighbors. 9 So one night, he and his
troops attacked the town and set fire to the
harbor and its ships. The light from the
fire could be seen thirty miles away in
Jerusalem.

The Wars of Judas in Gilead
(1 Maccabees 5.9-54)

10 Judas and his troops left Jamnia to go
after Timothy.[w] But about a mile from
town, they were attacked by a force of almost five thousand Arabs and five hundred
cavalry. 11 The fighting was fierce. But God
helped Judas defeat these desert tribes,
and they begged Judas for peace and offered him cattle and promised other help
as well. 12 Judas knew that they could be
useful in many ways, and so he agreed to
make peace. The Arabs accepted his terms
and went back to their camp.
13 Then Judas surrounded the fortress
at Caspin, a town protected by huge
mounds of earth[x] and high walls. Foreigners from many places lived there, 14 and
they had a large supply of food. In fact,
they felt so secure behind their walls that
they shouted insults against Judas and his
troops, and they cursed God.
15 Judas and his troops prayed, "Lord
God All-Powerful, you rule the world. And
long ago, when Joshua was our leader, you

[r]**11.33** *year 148*: That is, 164 B.C. [s]**11.38** *Xanthicus*: See the note at verse 30. [t]**11.38** *year 148*: That is, 164 B.C. [u]**12.2** *Apollonius*: Greek "Apollonius the son of Gennaeus." [v]**12.5** *he told . . . to be done*: Or "he got his soldiers together." [w]**12.10** *Timothy*: See 12.2.
[x]**12.13** *huge mounds of earth*: One possible meaning for the difficult Greek text.

helped our people destroy the town of
Jericho,[y] without using anything to knock
down the gates or climb over the walls."
Then our troops fiercely attacked Caspin, 16 because God wanted them to capture it. They killed countless enemies—so
many that a nearby lake, which was a
fourth of a mile wide, seemed to be filled
with blood.

Timothy's Army Is Defeated

(1 Maccabees 5.37-44)

17 From Caspin, Judas led his troops
ninety-five miles to the Jewish town of
Charax, not far from the city of Tob. 18 Timothy had been there and gone. He had not
done any damage, but he had stationed a
very strong force in a nearby fortress. 19 So
Judas gave orders for Dositheus and Sosipater to take some of the Jewish troops
and attack the fortress. They were successful and killed more than ten thousand of
the soldiers left there by Timothy.
20 Judas now divided up his soldiers into
two groups, placing one under the command of Dositheus and the other under
the command of Sosipater. Then they all
hurried after Timothy, who had a hundred
twenty thousand soldiers and two thousand
five hundred cavalry.
21 But Timothy learned that Judas' army
was coming after him. So he ordered the
families of his soldiers to go to the town of
Carnaim and take all their baggage with
them. This town was a hard place to attack
or even to reach because of the narrow
passes leading to it.
22 When the first group of our soldiers
reached Timothy's camp, the God who sees
everything terrified the enemy troops and
sent them scattering in all directions, injuring themselves and others with their own
swords. 23 Our troops eagerly chased Timothy's wicked army and slaughtered almost
thirty thousand of them.
24 The soldiers under the command of
Dositheus and Sosipater caught up with
Timothy himself, who very cleverly said,
"Many of your parents and brothers and
other relatives are my prisoners, and if you
kill me, they will be shown no mercy."
25 So after Timothy had solemnly promised to release his prisoners unharmed, he
was set free.

Judas Fights More Battles

(1 Maccabees 5.45-54)

26 Judas and his troops attacked the
town of Carnaim and the temple of the
goddess Atargatis, where they killed twenty-
five thousand people 27 and destroyed both
the temple and the town. Then they surrounded the fortress at Ephron because
Lysias and people from many different nations lived there.[z] But the people of Ephron
had stationed strong young soldiers just
outside the town wall, who fiercely defended it. And inside the town they had
stored a lot of military supplies and
weapons.
28 Our troops prayed for help from our
mighty Lord, who crushes powerful enemies. Then we captured Ephron and killed
almost twenty-five thousand people.
29 From Ephron, our army hurried to
Scythopolis, a town about seventy-five
miles from Jerusalem. 30 The Jews who
lived there told our troops that the people
of the town were always kind and helpful,
especially in times of trouble. 31 So our soldiers thanked those people and urged them
to always stay on good terms with the Jews.
Then Judas and our troops returned to
Jerusalem, just before the Harvest Festival,
which is also known as Pentecost.

Judas' Victory over Gorgias

32 Following the Harvest Festival, Judas
and his troops quickly left Jerusalem and
attacked Gorgias, the governor of Idumea,[a]
33 whose army of three thousand soldiers
and four hundred cavalry fought back
34 and killed a few of our troops.
35 Dositheus, a very strong man, belonged to the group of our cavalry led by
Bacenor, and he did something very heroic.

[y] **12.15** *town of Jericho*: See Joshua 6.1-20. [z] **12.27** *because Lysias and . . . lived there*: Some ancient manuscripts have "because all kinds of people lived there." [a] **12.32** *governor of Idumea*: See 10.14.

12.32 Ex 23.16.

He wanted to capture Gorgias alive, so he grabbed that evil man by his coat and started dragging him away. However, a Thracian horseman suddenly rode by Dositheus and chopped off his right arm. Then Gorgias escaped to the town of Marisa.

36 After our troops under the command of Esdris had been fighting a long time and were worn out, Judas prayed, "Our Lord, please be our leader and help us win this battle."

37 In his native language,[b] Judas sang some hymns and then shouted the battle cry, as he led his troops in a surprise attack that forced Gorgias and his army to retreat.

Judas Prays for the Dead

38 Judas brought his troops together and led them to the town of Adullam. It was now the day before the Sabbath, so they went through the traditional ceremonies to prepare themselves for that holy day. Then they celebrated the Sabbath.

39 The next day, Judas and his troops had to collect the bodies of those who had been killed in battle and to bring them home for burial in their family graves.
40 But under the shirt of each dead soldier they found good luck charms in the shape of those idols in the temple at Jamnia. Since our Jewish Law[c] doesn't allow us to wear such things, everyone knew why these soldiers had died in the fighting.

41 Our troops praised the Lord, who judges fairly and makes all secrets known.
42 They also begged the Lord to forgive this terrible sin. Judas, that wonderful man, said, "You have seen for yourselves how God punished those who disobeyed him. So I warn you not to sin!"

43 Then Judas collected from his troops two thousand silver coins, which he sent to Jerusalem as payment for a sacrifice to forgive this sin. Judas did this generous and honorable thing because he firmly believed God raises the dead to life.
44 Otherwise, it would have been useless and foolish of him to have spent this money on prayers for the dead.
45 But he was a man of deep faith, who was convinced that God's faithful servants would receive a wonderful reward after death. So he paid for a special sacrifice to take away the sin of those dead soldiers.

King Antiochus Invades Judea

13 In the year 149[d] of the Greek Kingdom, someone told Judas and our troops:

King Antiochus Eupator[e] is on his way to invade Judea,
2 and he is bringing his guardian Lysias, who runs the government for him.

They[f] are leading a huge Greek army with a hundred ten thousand soldiers, five thousand three hundred cavalry, and twenty-two elephants. Besides this, they have three hundred chariots with sharp blades sticking out from the sides of their wheels.

King Antiochus Puts Menelaus to Death

3 Menelaus the high priest tried to deceive King Antiochus and Lysias by encouraging them to attack us. He did not do this for the benefit of the country, but to regain his position as high priest.
4 Meanwhile, Lysias told Antiochus that Menelaus was to blame for all of the country's problems. Then our God, the King of kings, turned Antiochus against Menelaus. And right away, Antiochus sentenced this troublemaker to be killed in the town of Beroea, where they had a special way of executing prisoners.
5 In Beroea there was a seventy-five foot tower full of ashes, and the inside wall of the tower sloped down into the ash pile.
6 Criminals who were guilty of dishonoring a temple or of some other horrible crime were thrown down inside the tower to die.
7 So that was how the lawbreaker Menelaus died—and without even a proper burial afterwards.
8 Such a death was a perfect punishment for someone who had so often

[b]**12.37** *his native language*: Either Hebrew or Aramaic. [c]**12.40** *Law*: See Deuteronomy 7.25, 26. [d]**13.1** *year 149*: That is, 163 B.C. [e]**13.1** *Antiochus Eupator*: Also known as Antiochus V (164-162 B.C.). [f]**13.2** *They*: Or "They each."
12.40 Dt 7.25.

disgraced the temple altar, together with its holy ashes and fire.

The Battle of Modein

9 Antiochus was an arrogant and savage king, who wanted to punish the people of Judea more severely than his father had ever done. He was on his way to invade the country, 10 when Judas found out what was happening. So Judas told the people to pray day and night, and they prayed, "Our Lord, we need you now more than ever before! Please don't let our Law and our nation and our holy temple be destroyed. 11 You have just given your people a fresh start. Don't let those godless Gentiles rule us again."

12 For three days, they lay face down on the ground, crying and refusing to eat, while begging the Lord to have pity and send help. After this, Judas encouraged everyone, then ordered his troops to prepare for battle.

13 Judas met privately with the nation's leaders, and together they decided that with God's help Judas could attack and defeat Antiochus before he invaded Judea and captured Jerusalem. 14 So Judas left everything in the hands of God, the Creator of the world, and urged his soldiers to be willing to die for the Law, the temple, Jerusalem, the country, and our Jewish way of life.

Judas camped with his army near the town of Modein, 15 and he told them, "When you go into battle, shout, 'God gives victory!' " Then later that night, he and a chosen group of brave young troops attacked the enemy camp near the king's tent. They killed almost two thousand foreigners, as well as the soldier who was leading the elephants.[g]

16 Our troops terrified and confused the enemy soldiers, then left victoriously 17 at dawn, because the Lord had been helping Judas.

Antiochus and Judas Make an Agreement

(1 Maccabees 6.48-63)

18 King Antiochus had seen how bravely our Jewish soldiers fought. So he decided on a plan to destroy the places where they had stationed their troops. 19 His troops surrounded and attacked their strong fortress at Beth-Zur, but they were turned back and defeated.

20 Meanwhile, Judas had been sending supplies to the soldiers in Beth-Zur. 21 At the same time, a Jewish soldier named Rhodocus was passing secrets to the king, but he was finally captured and put in prison.

22 Sometime later, Antiochus decided to try a second time to make peace with the people of Beth-Zur. He did so and then attacked Judas. However, he lost this battle as well.

23 Antiochus had left an official named Philip to run the government for him in Antioch, but Philip rebelled. Antiochus did not know what else to do, and so he worked out an agreement with our people, giving us everything we wanted and promising to treat us fairly. He also offered a sacrifice, then he honored the temple in Jerusalem with gifts, 24 and he had a friendly meeting with Judas.

Finally, Antiochus appointed Hegemonides governor of the territory between the towns of Ptolemais and Gerar. 25 Then he went to Ptolemais, where the Gentiles were furious with him for making an agreement with us. In fact, they were so angry that they urged him to cancel the treaty. 26 But Lysias made a speech in which he thoroughly explained the agreement. Everyone was fully convinced and pleased by what he said, and then he left for Antioch.

So the invasion by Antiochus turned into a retreat.

Alcimus Causes Trouble for Judas

(1 Maccabees 7.1-21)

14 Three years later, Judas and his army learned that Demetrius, the son of King Seleucus,[h] had sailed into the port city of Tripolis with a powerful army and navy. 2 They also found out that Demetrius had put to death both King Antiochus and Lysias his guardian and was now ruling the country.

3 A man named Alcimus had earlier

[g] **13.15** *as well as . . . elephants*: One possible meaning for the difficult Greek text.
[h] **14.1** *Demetrius . . . Seleucus*: Demetrius I ruled 161-150 B.C., and Seleucus IV ruled 187-175 B.C.

been appointed high priest,[i] but when our nation was at war,[j] he eagerly adopted the Greek way of life. Because of this, Alcimus knew that he was in danger from our people and would never be high priest again.

4 So in about the year 151[k] of the Syrian Kingdom, Alcimus went to King Demetrius and presented him with a gold crown and a palm branch. He also handed him some olive branches from the temple area, as was the custom. However, Alcimus did not mention his desire to be high priest.

5 Some time later, Demetrius invited Alcimus to a meeting of the royal council and asked him to explain what the Jewish people were planning. Alcimus immediately took this chance to express his own crazy ideas, and he said:

> 6 King Demetrius, there is a devout group of Jews,[l] who are led by Judas Maccabeus. They are nothing but rebels, and they will never stop causing trouble in your kingdom. 7 And so, I have given up the honorable position of high priest that has always been in my family.
>
> I have come here, 8 not only because I am truly concerned about your interests as ruler, but because I am eager to help my people. That foolish group of Jews has brought terrible suffering on our nation.
>
> 9 Now you know the truth, so please be kind and generous, just as you always are, and help our oppressed people. 10 As long as Judas is alive, your kingdom will never have any peace.

11 After Alcimus had finished talking, the other advisors told how much they hated Judas. Then Demetrius became so furious 12 that he immediately appointed Nicanor to be the new governor of Judea. This was the same Nicanor who had been the commander of his war elephants. Then Demetrius sent him to Judea 13 with orders to kill Judas and scatter his army and afterwards to make Alcimus high priest of the glorious temple.

14 Many foreigners in Judea had been attacked by Judas at one time or another, and so they rushed to join Nicanor's army, hoping to profit from any trouble they could cause our people.

Nicanor Treats the Jews with Kindness

15 When our people found out that Nicanor was coming to attack with all of these Gentiles, they smeared dirt on their heads to show their sorrow. Then they prayed to God, who had chosen them to be his people forever and had always used his power to rescue them.

16 Judas ordered his troops to march at once to the village of Dessau,[m] where they attacked Nicanor. 17 Judas' brother Simon also ordered his troops into the battle, but for the moment they were retreating because of a surprise move on the part of Nicanor's army.

18 Meanwhile, someone told Nicanor just how fearless Judas and his soldiers were, and how fiercely they defended their nation. So Nicanor changed his mind about trying to defeat them in battle, 19 and instead he sent Posidonius, Theodotus, and Mattathias to make peace with them.

20 After the details of a peace treaty had been decided, Nicanor[n] informed his troops, and they made an agreement. 21 Then Judas and Nicanor chose a day to meet privately. And when that day arrived, a chariot came out of each camp, and fancy chairs were set up. 22 Judas had placed armed guards at key positions around the meeting place, just in case the

[i]**14.3** *high priest*: Antiochus Eupator (ruled 164-162 B.C.) had made Alcimus the high priest, replacing Menelaus. [j]**14.3** *at war*: Some ancient manuscripts have "at peace."
[k]**14.4** *year 151*: That is, 161 B.C. [l]**14.6** *devout group of Jews*: The Greek text has "Hasideans," which translates the Hebrew word "hasidim," meaning "devout" and refers to Jews who were especially faithful to their religion (see 1 Maccabees 2.42). [m]**14.16** *Dessau*: Possibly the same site as Adasa (see 1 Maccabees 7.40, 45). [n]**14.20** *Nicanor*: The Greek has "the leader," which could also be "Judas."
14.15-25 1 Macc 7.27, 28.

enemy had set a trap. But the meeting was very friendly.

23 Nicanor stayed in Jerusalem for a time, but he did not cause any trouble, and he sent home many people who had sided with him. 24 He and Judas became close friends and spent a lot of time together. 25 Judas even followed Nicanor's advice to get married and start a family like everyone else.

Nicanor and Judas Become Enemies Again

26 When Alcimus the high priest discovered that Nicanor and Judas were friends, he took a copy of their agreement to King Demetrius[o] and said, "Nicanor has betrayed your government. He's going to let that rebel Judas take his place as governor."

27 Demetrius became so irritated and angry as he listened to that worthless Alcimus make these charges that he wrote and told Nicanor, "I do not like the agreement that you made with Judas, and I order you to arrest him and send him to Antioch at once!"

28 Nicanor was upset and saddened by the orders to cancel an agreement with this innocent man. 29 Still, he could not disobey the king, so he started looking for an opportunity to take Judas by surprise. 30 Judas noticed that Nicanor was no longer treating him like a friend, and he guessed that trouble was on the way. So he and a number of his followers went into hiding.

31 When Nicanor found out that he had been outsmarted, he went to the famous and holy Jerusalem temple at the time of sacrifice and demanded that the priests hand Judas over to him. 32 But the priests swore that they did not know where to find Judas.

33 Nicanor shook his right fist at the temple and said, "Find Judas, or else I swear that I'll destroy this temple and the altar of your God! Then I'll build a glorious temple for the god Dionysus[p] on this very spot." 34 After this, he left.

The priests immediately stretched their arms toward heaven and prayed to God, the Defender of our nation. They said, 35 "Our holy Lord God, you have everything, and yet you were pleased to let us build a temple, so that you could live here with us. 36 We have only recently dedicated this temple again. Please keep it holy forever and ever."

Razis Gives His Life for the Nation

37-38 Razis was one of the most highly respected leaders in Jerusalem, and during the war for freedom, he had risked his life for his faith. In fact, he was so generous that he was known as the father of our country.

Someone brought charges against him to Nicanor, 39-40 who took this as an opportunity to show his hatred for our people by doing us some real harm. So he sent more than five hundred troops to arrest Razis, 41 who was in a tower surrounded by a walled-in courtyard. But the soldiers started beating down the gate to the courtyard, while shouting orders to set the doors of the tower on fire. Razis knew he was trapped, and he threw himself on his sword, 42 because he was from an important family and wanted to die with honor, rather than at the hands of godless men.

43 In all the confusion, Razis only wounded himself with the sword. Meanwhile, crowds of people were forcing their way into the tower. And so, with great courage, Razis climbed to the top of the tower and jumped. 44 Everyone on the ground quickly moved back, making room for him to land on the ground.

45 Alive but angry, Razis stood up and ran through the crowd to the top of a steep rock, with blood gushing from his terrible wounds. 46 He had lost most of his blood, when he tore out his insides with both hands and threw them down at the people, while praying aloud, "Lord of life and breath, I trust you to give these back to me." Then he died.

[o]**14.26** *Demetrius*: Demetrius I (ruled 161-150 B.C.) (see 6.7).

[p]**14.33** *Dionysus*: The Greek god of wine

14.31 1 Macc 7.29, 30. **14.35,36** 3 Macc 2.9.

Nicanor's Cruel Plan

15 Nicanor was told that Judas had led our army to the region of Samaria. So Nicanor planned to attack on the Sabbath, when we would not fight back.[q]

2 Nicanor had forced some of our people to join his army, and they said, "The God who sees everything has appointed the Sabbath to be the most holy day, and it would be vicious and cruel to attack Jews on that day."

3 But that horrible Nicanor replied, "Did some great ruler in heaven really command you Jews to honor the Sabbath?"

4 "Yes!" they answered. "And that Ruler is the living Lord and King of Heaven."

5 Then Nicanor remarked, "Well, I'm your ruler here on earth, and I order you to get your weapons and finish the job the king gave you to do."

But Nicanor was unable to carry out his cruel plan.

Judas Encourages His Troops

6 With great pride, Nicanor boasted that he would build a public monument in honor of his victory over Judas and his army. 7 But Judas was certain that the Lord would come to their rescue, 8 and he encouraged his troops by saying, "Don't be afraid when the enemy attacks. Remember God All-Powerful will send help from heaven today, just as he has done in the past."

9 Judas encouraged his troops by reading to them from their sacred Scriptures and by reminding them of the battles they had already won. 10 The troops were now excited and eager to fight. So Judas gave them their orders and pointed out that Gentiles never kept their promises. 11 His words offered them more hope and encouragement than their shields and spears.

Judas Has a Dream

Judas gave his troops further encouragement by telling them what he had seen in a dream—one[r] that he knew they could trust. He said:

> 12 I saw Onias the high priest.[s] He was both gentle and kind, as well as humble and honest. He also had a gift for speaking and had been brought up well. In my dream, Onias was praying for the whole nation, with his arms outstretched.
>
> 13 Next I saw a dignified and very important looking man with gray hair. 14 Onias said to me, "This man is God's prophet Jeremiah. He loves our nation and our holy city of Jerusalem so much that he never stops praying for us."
>
> 15 Then with his right hand, Jeremiah handed me a gold sword and said, 16 "This sacred sword is a gift from God. Take it and cut your enemies to pieces."

17 Everyone, young and old, was encouraged by what Judas had said. They felt so brave and strong that they decided to rush out of camp[t] and fight Nicanor's troops in hand-to-hand combat, in order to protect the city, the holy things, and the temple. 18 In fact, they went into battle so concerned about the sacred temple, that they gave no thought to their own families. 19 Meanwhile, the people of Jerusalem were anxious and worried about those who had left to fight in the countryside.

Judas Defeats Nicanor's Army

20 Everyone was waiting to see who would win the battle. The enemy troops had lined up and were moving forward, protected on both sides by cavalry. They also had elephants stationed in places where they could help the most.

21 As Judas watched this huge enemy army advance, he looked carefully at the different kinds of weapons and the savage elephants. Then he stretched his arms toward heaven and prayed to the Lord who works miracles, because he knew that the Lord gives victory to those who deserve it,

[q] **15.1** *Sabbath . . . not fight back*: Many Jews refused to fight on the Sabbath (see 6.11).
[r] **15.11** *seen . . . one*: One possible meaning for the difficult Greek text. [s] **15.12** *Onias the high priest*: Menelaus had him murdered around 170 B.C. (see 4.34). [t] **15.17** *to rush out of camp*: One possible meaning for the difficult Greek text.

and not to those who have a lot of swords and armor. 22 This is what he prayed:

Lord of Heaven, when Hezekiah was king of Judea, you sent an angel who killed a hundred eighty-five thousand troops that belonged to King Sennacherib.[u]

23 Now please send a good angel to make our enemies tremble with fear. 24 Then use your mighty arm to destroy those who have cursed you and attacked your holy people.

25 Nicanor's soldiers blew trumpets and chanted war songs as they attacked. 26 But our troops begged God for help and fought back 27 with swords in their hands and prayers in their hearts. They killed at least thirty-five thousand enemy troops that day, and they celebrated because God had shown them his power.

28 After the battle, Judas and his soldiers were happily on their way home when they found Nicanor lying dead on the ground, but still wearing his armor. 29 So they all shouted and jumped about, praising the Lord All-Powerful in their native language.[v]

30 Judas had always been a faithful defender of his country, and he was just as patriotic now as he was when he was young. So he ordered his troops to chop off Nicanor's head and right arm and take them to Jerusalem.

31 When they reached the city, Judas called everyone together. He told the priests to stand in front of the altar, and he sent for the enemy soldiers in the fortress. 32 Judas showed them the head of that godless Nicanor. Then he let them see the arm of this arrogant and disgusting man, who had shaken his fist at the holy temple of God All-Powerful.

33 Finally, he cut out the tongue of this worthless man and said, "I am going to feed it piece by piece to the birds. Then I am going to nail his head and arm on the wall of the fortress opposite the temple, as proof of his foolishness."

34 Everyone looked toward heaven and prayed, "Our Lord, we praise you for protecting your sacred temple and for showing us your wonderful power."

35 Judas nailed Nicanor's head to the wall of the fortress, as evidence that the Lord had helped his people. 36 Then everyone decided to remember this day forever by celebrating a festival on the thirteenth day of the twelfth month, which is called Adar in Aramaic.[w] The Festival of Mordecai[x] is celebrated the day before.

37 This was how Nicanor died. And now that our people have ruled Jerusalem since his death, it is time to bring my story to an end.

Some Final Thoughts

38 I have tried to write a brief, but interesting book. If it is boring and poorly written, I can only say that I have done my best. 39 To drink wine by itself can be harmful to your health, and the same can be said of drinking water by itself. But if they are mixed together, they make an enjoyable drink. And so, I have mixed a variety of styles, to make my book interesting both for those who read it aloud and for those who hear it read.

The end.

[u] **15.22** *when . . . Sennacherib*: See 2 Kings 18.13—19.35. [v] **15.29** *native language*: See the note at 12.37. [w] **15.36** *Aramaic*: The Greek has "Syriac," a later form of Aramaic. [x] **15.36** *Festival of Mordecai*: This is the Festival of Purim that honors Queen Esther and Mordecai for rescuing Jews living in Persia (see Esther 9.20-32).

15.22 2 K 19.35. **15.25-35** 1 Macc 7.43-50. **15.36** 1 Macc 7.48, 49; 3 Macc 6.36.

SOME ADDITIONAL BOOKS

The books of 1 Esdras, 2 Esdras, and the Prayer of Manasseh are accepted by some Protestants as belonging to the Apocrypha (see the introduction to the "Deuterocanonicals/Apocrypha"). Also in this section of the *CEV* are Psalm 151, 3 Maccabees, and 4 Maccabees, which are part of the Greek and Slavonic Bibles.

1 ESDRAS

ABOUT THIS BOOK

Esdras is another form of the name Ezra, one of the main characters of this book. It was probably written in Hebrew, but only the Greek and other later translations are now available. The book of 1 Esdras was adapted from passages in 2 Chronicles, Ezra, and Nehemiah, as the following chart shows:

1 Esdras	*Adapted From*
1.1-58	2 Chronicles 35.1—36.21
2.1-15	2 Chronicles 36.22,23; Ezra 1.1-11
2.16-30	Ezra 4.7-24
3.1—5.6	(not found elsewhere)
5.7-73	Ezra 2.1—4.5
6.1—9.36	Ezra 5.1—10.44
9.37-55	Nehemiah 7.73—8.13

The book of 1 Esdras emphasizes the importance of King David's descendants and of rebuilding the temple, and the book also explains why the Lord allowed King Josiah of Judah to die so young, even though Josiah had been faithful to God.

A QUICK LOOK AT THIS BOOK

- The Last Kings of Judah (1.1-58)
- Work on Rebuilding Jerusalem Is Stopped (2.1-30)
- Zerubbabel Wins a Contest at the Royal Palace in Persia (3.1—4.40)
- Many of the Jews Return to Jerusalem and Rebuild the Temple (4.41—7.15)
- Ezra Leads More Jews To Return to Jerusalem (8.1-67)
- Ezra Forces Jewish Men To Divorce Their Gentile Wives (8.68—9.36)
- Ezra Reads God's Law to the People (9.37-55)

Passover Is Celebrated

(2 Chronicles 35.1-19; 2 Kings 23.21-23)

1 Josiah[a] commanded that Passover be celebrated in Jerusalem to honor the Lord, and on the fourteenth day of the first month,[b] the lambs were killed for the Passover celebration.

2 Josiah first made sure that each priest was wearing the proper priestly clothes and had been assigned to one of the priestly groups. Then he gave orders for the priests to take their places in the Lord's temple.
3-4 And he told the Levites who helped the priests in the temple:

> No longer will you have to carry the sacred chest from place to place. It will stay in the temple built by King Solomon son of David. Now, be the servants of the Lord your God and his people Israel. Prepare yourselves, so that each Levite family and clan will

[a]**1.1** *Josiah*: Ruled 640-609 B.C. [b]**1.1** *first month*: Abib (also called Nisan), the first month of the Hebrew calendar, from about mid-March to mid-April.

be holy and worthy to serve in the
Lord's temple.
5 King Solomon built this wonderful
temple, and you Levites who serve in it
must follow the directions that his
father King David gave for worship
here. Each of your families and clans
must stand together. 6 When someone
brings you a Passover lamb, you must
kill it and prepare it to be sacrificed to
the Lord. Make sure the people celebrate according to the commands that
the Lord gave to Moses.
7 Josiah donated thirty thousand young
sheep and goats and three thousand calves
from his own flocks and herds, so that the
people who had come to celebrate Passover
could offer them as sacrifices. Josiah did
this to keep a promise he had made to the
people, the priests, and the Levites. 8 In
addition, Hilkiah, Zechariah, and Jehiel,
the officials in charge of the temple, gave
the priests two thousand six hundred sheep
and three hundred calves, so that the
priests could celebrate Passover. 9 Finally,
Jeconiah, Shemaiah and his brother
Nethanel, together with Hashabiah,
Ochiel, and Joram, also donated animals.
These men were army commanders in
charge of a thousand troops each, and together they gave the Levites a total of
five thousand sheep and seven hundred
calves.
10-11 On the morning of the Passover
Festival, the priests and the Levites dressed
in their special robes and brought the thin
bread[c] into the temple. They took their assigned places in groups of families and
clans in front of the people. Then they began offering the Passover sacrifices to the
Lord, as the Law of Moses commands.
12 The Passover lambs were roasted over
fires, just as the Law said, and the meat
from the other sacrifices was boiled in large
bronze pots. The cooking meat smelled
wonderful! 13-14 All day long, the priests
were busy offering sacrifices and burning
the animals' fat on the altar. And when the
Passover animals had been prepared for all
the people, the Levites then prepared animals for themselves and for their relatives,
the priests. 15-16 During the celebration,
some of the Levites prepared Passover animals for those Levites of the Asaph clan
who were temple musicians, and also for
those Levites who were guards at the temple gates. They did this so that the musicians did not have to leave the places they
had been assigned by King David and his
official representatives, Asaph, Zechariah,
and Eddinus, and so that the temple
guards did not have to leave their posts.
17-18 On that day, the people honored
the Lord by celebrating Passover, and on
the altar they offered sacrifices to him, just
as King Josiah had commanded. 19 The
people who had come for Passover then
celebrated the Festival of Thin Bread for
the next seven days.
20 Passover had not been observed like
this since the time of Samuel the prophet.
21 No king before Josiah had ever held a
better celebration of Passover. It was celebrated by priests and Levites and by people
who came into Jerusalem from towns all
over Judah, together with the people of
Jerusalem and even with people from
northern Israel who were living in
Jerusalem. 22 This Passover was in the
eighteenth year of Josiah's rule[d] in Judah.

Josiah Dies in Battle

(2 Chronicles 35.20-27; 2 Kings 23.28-30)

23 King Josiah[e] wanted to be a faithful
follower of the Lord, so everything he did
was pleasing to the Lord. 24 But the old historical records show that some of the people of Judah sinned worse and were more
evil than any other nation. They were so
disappointing to the Lord, that he had to
punish the whole nation as he had threatened to do.
25 Several years after Josiah had done
these things, the king of Egypt led his army
to attack the city of Carchemish on the Euphrates River. And Josiah led his troops

[c]**1.10,11** *thin bread*: Only thin bread was to be eaten during the Passover Festival and the seven-day Festival of Thin Bread that followed (see Exodus 12.8, 15-20). [d]**1.22** *the eighteenth year of Josiah's rule*: 622 B.C. [e]**1.23** *King Josiah*: Ruled 640-609 B.C.

1.5 2 Ch 8.14. **1.12** Ex 12.8, 9. **1.19** Ex 12.1-20.

north to meet the Egyptians in battle.[f]
26 The king of Egypt sent the following
message to Josiah:

King of Judah, I'm not attacking
you. 27 The Lord God did not send me
to fight you. My enemies are at the Euphrates River, and the Lord will help
me win. He wants me to get there
quickly, so get out of my way! Don't try
to stop the Lord!

28 Even the prophet Jeremiah told
Josiah that the Lord wanted him to get in
his chariot and go back home, but instead,
Josiah decided to stay and fight. 29 He attacked the Egyptian army in the broad valley near Megiddo, but the Egyptian commanders counterattacked near him. 30 He
told his servants, "Get me out of here! I'm
badly wounded." His servants quickly took
him away from the fighting. 31 Josiah got
into his spare chariot and was taken back
to Jerusalem, where he died. He was
buried in the family tomb.

32 Everyone in Judah mourned for Josiah. Jeremiah the prophet wrote a funeral
song in honor of him, and it is still a custom in Israel for important men and their
wives to sing sad songs about Josiah as they
mourn his death.

33 All these things are recorded in *The
History of the Kings of Judah*. Josiah did
many great things. He received many honors, and he understood the Law of the Lord
very well. All these and other things that he
did can be found in *The Book of the Kings
of Israel and Judah*.

King Jeconiah

(2 Chronicles 36.1-4; 2 Kings 23.30-35)

34 After the death of Josiah, the people
of Judah crowned his son Jeconiah[g] their
new king. He was twenty-three years old at
the time. 35 After he had ruled Judah from
Jerusalem for only three months, the king
of Egypt[h] removed him from being king
36 and made the nation of Judah pay a fine
of seven thousand five hundred pounds of
silver and seventy-five pounds of gold.
37 Then the king of Egypt appointed Jeconiah's brother Jehoiakim as king of Judah
and Jerusalem.

King Jehoiakim

(2 Chronicles 36.5-8; 2 Kings 23.36—24.7)

38 King Jehoiakim[i] put many of Judah's
most important men in prison,[j] and he had
his brother Zarius arrested in Egypt and
brought back to Jerusalem. 39 Jehoiakim
was twenty-five years old when he was appointed king in Judah and Jerusalem, and
he disobeyed the Lord by doing evil.

40 During Jehoiakim's rule, King Nebuchadnezzar of Babylonia[k] invaded Judah.
He arrested Jehoiakim and put him in
bronze chains, then sent him to the capital
city of Babylon. 41 Nebuchadnezzar also
carried off to Babylon many of the sacred
things in the Lord's temple, and he put
them in the temple of his own god. 42 The
stories about Jehoiakim, including all the
disgusting and evil things he did, are found
in *The Book of the Records of the Kings*.
43 His son Jehoiachin[l] then became king.

King Jehoiachin

(2 Kings 24.8-17; 2 Chronicles 36.9, 10)

Jehoiachin was eighteen years old when
he became king of Judah,[m] 44 but he ruled
from Jerusalem for only three months and
ten days. Jehoiachin also disobeyed the
Lord by doing evil. 45 At the beginning of

[f] **1.25** *battle*: This took place in 609 B.C., and the king of Egypt was Neco, who ruled 609-595 B.C. He was fighting on the side of the Assyrians against the Medes and Babylonians, and he marched north to help Assyria keep control of its land. Since Josiah considered Assyria an enemy, he set out to stop Neco and the Egyptian troops. [g] **1.34** *Jeconiah*: A few Greek manuscripts; most Greek manuscripts "Jehoahaz" (see also 2 Kings 23.30 and 2 Chronicles 36.1); "Jeconiah" is probably another name for Jehoahaz, who ruled for three months in 609 B.C. [h] **1.35** *king of Egypt*: King Neco (ruled 609-595 B.C.). [i] **1.38** *Jehoiakim*: Ruled 609-598 B.C. [j] **1.38** *important men in prison*: Probably those who had supported Jehoahaz as king. [k] **1.40** *King Nebuchadnezzar of Babylonia*: Ruled 605-562 B.C. [l] **1.43** *Jehoiachin*: The Greek text has "Jehoiakim," but see 2 Kings 24.6; 2 Chronicles 36.8. [m] **1.43** *when he became king of Judah*: In 598 B.C.

1.37 Jr 22.11, 12. **1.39** Jr 22.18, 19; 26.1. **1.40** Dn 1.1, 2. **1.45** Jr 22.24-30; 24.1; 29.1, 2; Ez 17.12.

the year, King Nebuchadnezzar of Babylonia[n] arrested Jehoiachin and gave orders
for him to be taken to Babylon, along with
more of the sacred things from the temple.
46 Then Nebuchadnezzar appointed Zedekiah[o] king of Judah and Jerusalem.

King Zedekiah

(2 Kings 24.18-20; 2 Chronicles 36.11-16; Jeremiah 52.1-3)

Zedekiah was twenty-one years old
when he was appointed king[p] of Judah, and
he ruled for eleven years. 47 He disobeyed
the Lord, and refused to listen when Jeremiah gave him warnings from the Lord.
48 King Nebuchadnezzar of Babylonia[q] had
forced Zedekiah to make a sacred promise
in the Lord's name that he would be loyal.
But Zedekiah was stubborn. He broke the
laws of the Lord God of Israel, and he rebelled against Nebuchadnezzar.

49 The priests and the other leaders of
the people also refused to obey the laws of
the Lord, and time after time they insulted
him by their actions. They did even more
disgusting things than the nations around
them. God had made his temple holy, but
they made it unclean and unfit for worship.

50-51 The ancestors of the people of Judah had worshiped the Lord, and he did
not want to destroy his people and his temple. So he sent prophets as messengers to
tell his people, "Turn back to the Lord!"
But the people only laughed and insulted
them.

Jerusalem Is Destroyed

(2 Kings 25.1-21; 2 Chronicles 36.17-21; Jeremiah 52.3-30)

52 Finally, the Lord was so angry at the
people of Judah, that he gave orders for the
kings of Babylonia to attack Jerusalem.
53 The Babylonians killed the young men
who were around the temple, and they
showed no mercy to anyone in the city,
whether man or woman, young or old.
54 The Babylonians took all the sacred
things from the temple, and they carried
off the temple treasure chests, as well as
everything from the personal storerooms of
the king. All of this was sent back to Babylonia.

55 The Babylonians burned down the
temple and the towers in the city walls, and
then they broke down those walls. 56 Beautiful Jerusalem lay in ruins.

The survivors were taken to Babylonia
as prisoners, 57 where they were servants of
the king and his sons until Persia conquered Babylonia. It was just as the Lord
had told Jeremiah the prophet, 58 "The
land will be deserted for seventy years, to
make up for all the years it was not allowed
to rest."[r]

Cyrus Lets the Jews Return Home

(2 Chronicles 36.22, 23; Ezra 1.1-11)

2 1-2 In the first year that Cyrus was king
of Persia,[s] the Lord had Cyrus send an
official message in writing to all parts of his
kingdom. This happened just as Jeremiah
the Lord's prophet had promised. 3 The
message said:

> I am King Cyrus of Persia.
>
> The Most High God, the Lord of Is-
> rael, has made me the ruler of the
> world. 4 And he has chosen me to
> build a temple for him in Jerusalem,
> which is in Judah. 5 The Lord will
> watch over and encourage any of his
> people who want to go back to
> Jerusalem and help build the temple.
>
> 6 Everyone else must provide what
> is needed. They must give gold and sil-
> ver, 7 as well as supplies, horses, cattle,
> and gifts for building the Lord's temple
> in Jerusalem.

8 Many people felt that the Lord wanted
them to help rebuild his temple, and they
decided to go to Jerusalem. Among them
were priests and Levites and leaders of the
tribes of Judah and Benjamin. 9 The others

[n] **1.45** *King Nebuchadnezzar of Babylonia*: See the note at 1.40. [o] **1.46** *Zedekiah*: Ruled 598-587 B.C. [p] **1.46** *when he was appointed king*: 598 B.C. [q] **1.48** *King Nebuchadnezzar of Babylonia*: See the note at 1.40. [r] **1.58** *The land will be deserted . . . allowed to rest*: Jeremiah 25.11-13; 29.10. According to Leviticus 25.1-7, the people were supposed to allow the land to rest one out of every seven years. [s] **2.1,2** *the first year . . . Persia*: Probably refers to 539 B.C., when Cyrus captured Babylon. He actually ruled Persia 549-529 B.C.

1.48 Ez 17.15. **1.58** Jr 25.11; 29.10. **2.3** Is 44.28.

felt that the Lord wanted them to help with
everything, so they gave gifts that included
silver and gold, as well as horses and cattle
and a very large number of offerings for the
temple.
10 King Cyrus gave back the things that
Nebuchadnezzar had taken from the Lord's
temple in Jerusalem and had put in the
temple of his idols. 11 Cyrus placed Mithridates, his treasurer, in charge of these
things, 12 and Mithridates turned them
over to Sheshbazzar, the governor of Judah.
13 Included among them were one thousand gold cups, one thousand silver cups,
twenty-nine silver holders for burning incense, thirty gold bowls, two thousand four
hundred ten silver bowls, and one thousand other gold and silver items. 14 Altogether, there were five thousand four hundred sixty-nine of these gold and silver
cups, bowls, and other items 15 that Sheshbazzar took with him, when he and the
others returned to Jerusalem from Babylonia.

Trouble Rebuilding Jerusalem

(Ezra 4.7-24)

16 Later, when Artaxerxes[t] had become
king of Persia, a group of important men
got together and wrote a letter to him,
complaining about the people of Judah and
Jerusalem. This group included Bishlam,
Mithridates,[u] Tabeel, Rehum, Beltethmus,
Secretary Shimshai, as well as their advisors and friends who lived in Samaria
and elsewhere. 17 This letter said:

Your Majesty King Artaxerxes, the
group sending you this letter includes
Rehum, who is one of your officials,
and Secretary Shimshai, as well as the
members of their council and several
judges in Southwest Syria Province.[v]
18 We want you to know that the
Jews who left your country have
moved back to Jerusalem and are now
rebuilding that terrible city. They have
been working on repairing the marketplaces and city walls, and they have
laid the foundations for a temple.
19 You should also know that if the
walls are completed and the city is rebuilt, the Jews will rebel against you
and refuse to pay any taxes. 20 Since
they are working on the temple right
now, we thought that it was too important a matter to ignore, 21 and we decided to tell you about it. Please look in
the official records of your ancestors.
22 You will find that Jerusalem has rebelled against other kings and other
cities, 23 and troops from Jerusalem
have often attacked other cities. That's
why it was destroyed in the first place.
24 So, Your Majesty, if Jerusalem is
rebuilt and its walls are completed, you
will no longer be able even to visit
Southwest Syria Province.

25 The king sent a letter back to Rehum,
Beltethmus, Shimshai, and the others.
This letter said:

26 I read the letter you sent me, and
I had the records checked. It is true
that for years Jerusalem fought against
kings, 27 and its people were always rebelling and fighting wars. Strong, cruel
kings ruled the city and forced other
cities in Southwest Syria Province to
pay taxes.
28 For these reasons, I am now
commanding the people of Jerusalem
to stop rebuilding their city. 29 I don't
want them to cause me any trouble!

30 As soon as Rehum, Shimshai, and the
others read the king's letter, they led cavalry troops and a large number of foot soldiers to Jerusalem, where they forced
everyone to stop rebuilding the city. And so
the Jews were not able to do any more work
on the temple until the year after Darius
became king of Persia.[w]

[t]**2.16** *Artaxerxes*: Artaxerxes I (ruled 465-425 B.C.). [u]**2.16** *Mithridates*: Not the same Mithridates as was mentioned in verses 11, 12. [v]**2.17** *Southwest Syria Province*: "Coele-Syria" in traditional translations; it originally referred to the land between the Lebanon and the Anti-Lebanon mountains, but at this time it included all Palestine and Phoenicia as well. [w]**2.30** *And so . . . king of Persia*: Darius ruled 522-486 B.C., before Artaxerxes. In the parallel in Ezra, this verse refers to troubles the Jews had during the rule of King Cyrus (538-529 B.C.) or King Cambyses (529-522 B.C.).

A Contest

3 King Darius[x] held a banquet and invited his family, the palace officials, the leaders of Media and Persia, 2 and the governors, generals, and officials in his one hundred twenty-seven provinces from India to Ethiopia. 3 Everyone ate and drank as much as they wanted, and after they left the banquet hall, Darius went to bed. He fell asleep, but soon he woke up.

4 Then the three young men who were the king's bodyguards said to each other:

5 Let's have a contest. Each of us will write down our answer to the question, "What is the strongest thing in the world?" Then King Darius will decide the winner and give him expensive prizes and gifts. 6 The winner will get to wear purple robes, a turban made of fine linen, and a necklace. He will also get to drink from gold cups, as well as sleep in a gold bed and ride in a chariot pulled by horses with gold bridles. 7 And because the wisest man will win the contest, he will be the king's closest advisor and will receive the title, "Relative of the King."[y]

8 Each of the men wrote down their answer, then they sealed the papers shut with hot wax and put them under the king's pillow. 9 They said, "As soon as King Darius wakes up, he will be given the papers, and he and his officials will decide who gave the wisest answer and wins the contest." 10 The first man had written, "Wine is the strongest." 11 The second man's answer was, "The king is the strongest." 12 And the third wrote, "Women are the strongest; however, truth can conquer anything."

13 When the king got up in the morning, his servants gave him the three answers. He read the answers 14 and sent for everyone who had come to his banquet the night before. 15 After going to his throne room and taking his seat, he read the three answers to everyone who had gathered there. 16 Then he said, "Bring in the young men, and they will explain their answers to us." 17 They were brought in, and the king said to them, "Explain these answers you have written."

Wine Is the Strongest

The first young man had answered that wine was the strongest, and he said:

18 Men of Media and Persia, is wine the strongest thing in the world? I believe it is, because when people drink wine, they can't think straight. 19 Wine makes everybody's mind the same, whether the person is a king or an orphan, slave or free, poor or rich. 20 When people drink wine, all they can think about is eating and having fun—wine makes their sadness disappear, and they forget that they owe a lot of money. 21 They feel wealthy, and it's easy for them to talk about money as if they were very rich. And sometimes, wine even makes people forget that they have to obey the king and his governors.

22 When people drink wine, they forget to be kind to family and friends, and before long, they are threatening each other with swords. 23 But later, after they sober up, they can't remember what they did. 24 Men of Media and Persia, if wine can affect people this way, isn't it the strongest thing in the world?

Then the first young man stopped talking.

The King Is the Strongest

4 The second young man had answered that the king was the strongest, and he said:

2 Men of Media and Persia, I say that men are the strongest force in the world, because together men rule the land and the sea and everything that lives in them. 3 But the king is really the strongest, because he is the ruler of all men, and whenever he tells them to do something, they obey. 4 If he orders them to attack each other, they do. And if the king tells them to march

[x]**3.1** *King Darius*: Ruled 522-486 B.C. [y]**3.7** *Relative of the King*: Receiving this title was one of the highest possible honors a king could give to a special advisor or high officials, and those with this title received many gifts and privileges.

out to fight an enemy, they go, and they climb mountains and break through walls and pull down towers to do it. 5 They kill the enemy, and they would rather be killed themselves than disobey their king's orders. And if they win the battle, they take all the enemy's possessions back to the king.

6 It's the same with farmers, who plant and harvest crops instead of fighting in the army. They take part of their harvest to the king, and they even force each other to pay taxes to him.

7 The king is only one man, but at his command, his people kill their enemies. Or if he orders them to release their prisoners, they do so. 8-9 If he says to attack and destroy, they attack and destroy. And if he tells them to build or to cut something down or to plant crops, they obey him. 10 All of his people and his armies do whatever he says. And whenever he sits down for a meal or goes to bed, 11 his guards watch over him. They don't leave to take care of personal business, and they never disobey him.

12 Men of Media and Persia, if the king can make people do these things, isn't he the strongest in the world?

Then the second young man stopped talking.

Truth Is the Strongest

13 The third young man, Zerubbabel, had answered that women and truth were the strongest, and he said:

14 Men of Media and Persia, I agree that the king is great, that there are lots of men, and that wine is strong. But who rules them all? Women, that's who! 15-16 Women give birth to kings and to all those who rule the land and sea. And women raise the little boys who become men and plant the vineyards that produce wine. 17 Women make the clothes men wear, and they tell men how great they are. Men could not live without women.

18 A man might have a lot of gold and silver and other valuable things. But if he sees a beautiful woman, 19 he will leave his wealth and stare at her. He would rather have her than silver or gold! 20 A man will abandon the father who raised him and even leave his own country, just to be with his wife. 21 He will spend the rest of his life with her, without ever thinking of his father or mother or country.

22 Don't you men realize that you are controlled by women? You work long and hard, then what do you do with your wages? You give them to women. 23 A man takes his sword and goes out on the roads, the rivers, and the seas, robbing and stealing. 24 He is in danger from wild animals, and he has to travel at night. But everything he takes, he brings home to the woman he loves.

25 A man loves his wife more than he loves his father and mother. 26 Lots of men have gone crazy because of women, and many others have become slaves 27 or criminals, their lives ruined or even destroyed, all because of women. 28 It is the truth, isn't it?

Look at his majesty, King Darius.[z] He is so powerful that no one from any country would dare to touch him. 29 But I have seen him with his wife[a] Apame, the daughter of that great man, Bartacus. One day Apame was sitting at the king's right side, 30 when she took the crown off his head and put it on her own. And she kept slapping his face with her left hand. 31 But all the king did was to stare at her with his mouth hanging open.

If Apame smiles at the king, he is happy. If Apame is angry with him, he tells her how wonderful and beautiful she is until she isn't angry anymore.

32 Men of Media and Persia, if women can do all these things, I say that they are very strong!

33 The king and his officials just stared at each other. Then Zerubbabel began to speak again—this time about truth:

[z]**4.28** *King Darius*: See the note at 3.1. [a]**4.29** *wife*: This translates a Greek word for a woman who was legally bound to a man, but without the full privileges of a wife.

34 Men of Media and Persia, women
are strong, the earth is huge, and the
heavens are high above it. The sun
moves quickly and finishes its path in
the heavens in one day, then returns to
its starting point again. 35 God must be
extremely strong to have created these
things. But truth is the strongest of
everything he created. 36 Everyone on
earth asks for truth, and it has the
blessing of God in heaven.[b]

Truth makes all creation tremble,
because there is no injustice in truth.[c]
37 Many things do cause injustice, for
example, wine, kings, and women. As
a matter of fact, we humans are dishonest and deceitful and cause injustice in everything we do, and so we will
die. 38 But truth will live and last and
be strong forever. 39 Truth always does
what is fair and right, never what is
evil. Everyone likes truth 40 because its
decisions are always fair. Truth will
rule as a powerful and glorious king
forever. Praise God, the source of all
truth!

Darius Allows Jerusalem and the Temple To Be Rebuilt

41 When Zerubbabel finished speaking,
everyone shouted, "Truth is great! Truth is
the strongest of all!"

42 King Darius[d] said, "Zerubbabel, you
are the wisest, and I will give you whatever
you ask for, even more than I promised.
You will sit next to me, and you will receive
the title, 'Relative of the King.' "[e]

43 Zerubbabel replied, "Your Majesty, the
day you became king, you made a solemn
promise to rebuild Jerusalem. 44 You also
promised to give back all the sacred things
from the Jerusalem temple. King Cyrus[f]
saved them when he started to tear down
Babylon, and he promised to send them
back to Jerusalem. 45 And you promised to
rebuild the temple in Jerusalem—the temple that was burned down by the Edomites
after Judah was crushed by the Babylonians. 46 Your Majesty, all I ask is that you
show how great you are by keeping these
promises you made to God, the King of
Heaven."

47 King Darius got up and kissed him,
then he wrote letters to the governors, generals, and officials in the provinces of Persia. The letters said:

You must protect Zerubbabel and
those with him when they go through
your provinces on their way to rebuild
Jerusalem.

48 The governors in Southwest
Syria Province[g] must bring cedar logs
from Lebanon to Jerusalem. These
governors will also provide workers to
help rebuild the city.

49 No governor, official, or tax collector is allowed to stop the work on
Jerusalem, or to enter the Jews' homes
to force them to pay taxes. 50 In fact,
those Jews who are returning to Judah
will not have to pay any taxes on their
land.

Moreover, the Edomites must give
back the towns they took from the
Jews.

51 Every year until the Jerusalem
temple is finished, my treasurer will
give the Jews one thousand five hundred pounds of silver to help with the
cost of building. 52 He will also give
them another seven hundred fifty
pounds of silver a year, to buy animals
for the seventeen sacrifices that must
be offered each day to please God.[h]

53 The priests and other Jews
who returned to rebuild Jerusalem are
to be set free, together with their children.

[b]**4.36** *Everyone on earth . . . in heaven*: Or "The whole earth asks for truth, and the sky blesses it."
[c]**4.36** *truth*: Or "God." [d]**4.42** *King Darius*: See the note at 3.1. [e]**4.42** *Relative of the King*: See 3.7 and the note there. [f]**4.44** *King Cyrus*: Ruled Persia 549-529 B.C. [g]**4.48** *Southwest Syria Province*: See the note at 2.17. [h]**4.52** *sacrifices . . . to please God*: Traditionally called "whole burnt offerings" because the whole animal was burned on the altar. While these sacrifices did involve forgiveness for sin, a main purpose was to please the Lord with the smell of the smoke from the sacrifice, and so in the CEV they are often called "sacrifices to please God" (see Leviticus 1).
4.45 Ob 10-14.

54-55 Until the temple is finished
and Jerusalem is rebuilt, my treasurer
will give the priests and Levites money
to live on. Furthermore, each priest is
to be given one of the special robes
that he must wear to serve in the
temple.
56 Those men who guard the city
must be given a piece of land, and they
must be paid wages.
57 King Cyrus had kept many of the
sacred things that came from the
Jerusalem temple. These must now be
returned to Jerusalem, along with anything else Cyrus promised to return.
58 After Zerubbabel left the palace, he
faced Jerusalem and looked up toward
heaven. Then he praised the King of
Heaven and prayed, 59 "Our Lord, you are
the one who gives victory and wisdom. So
you should receive all the honor for what
has happened here today. I am only your
servant, 60 just as our ancestors were. I
thank you and praise you for giving me
wisdom."
61 Zerubbabel took the letters to Babylon
and told his relatives what had happened.
62 They all praised God, because he was allowing them 63 to go and rebuild Jerusalem
and his temple. Then they held a big celebration for seven days, with music and lots
of food.

The People Leave for Jerusalem

5 After the celebration, the Jews chose
some of the leaders of their clans from
the different tribes to be in charge of the
group going to Jerusalem, and each leader
took along his wife, children, servants, and
livestock. 2-3 King Darius[i] sent a thousand
cavalry troops along for protection, and he
also sent musicians playing drums and
flutes. All the Jews were celebrating as the
group left for Jerusalem.

A List of the People Who Went to Jerusalem

(Ezra 2.1-70; Nehemiah 7.4-73)

4 Here is a list, arranged by families,
clans, and tribes, of those who went to
Jerusalem. 5 First, there was Joshua,[j] the
descendant of Jozadak and Seraiah. He
was one of the priests, the descendants of
Aaron and his son Phinehas.
Joakim the son of Zerubbabel and
grandson of Shealtiel also went. He was
from the family of King David, and so he
was a descendant of Judah and his son
Perez. 6 Zerubbabel was the one who had
showed such great wisdom to King Darius[k]
of Persia, in the month of Nisan[l] of second
year of his rule.
7 King Nebuchadnezzar of Babylonia
had captured many of the people of Judah
and had taken them as prisoners to Babylonia. 8 Now they were on their way back to
Jerusalem and to their own towns everywhere in Judah. Their leaders were Zerubbabel, Joshua, Nehemiah, Seraiah, Resa-
iah, Eneneus, Mordecai, Beelsarus,
Aspharasus, Reeliah, Rehum, and Baanah.
9-17 And here is a list of how many returned
from each family group:[m]

There were 2,172 from the family of Parosh; 472 from the family of Shephatiah; 756 from the family of Arah; 2,812 descendants of Jeshua and Joab from the family of Pahath Moab; 1,254 from the family of Elam; 945 from the family of Zattu; 705 from the family of Chorbe; 648 from the family of Bani; 623 from the family of Bebai; 1,322 from the family of Azgad; 667 from the family of Adonikam; 2,066 from the family of Bigvai; 454 from the family of Adin; 92 from the family of Ater, also called Hezekiah; 67 from the family of Kilan and Azetas; 432 from the family of

[i] **5.2,3** *King Darius*: See the note at 3.1. [j] **5.5** *Joshua*: In this translation the name "Joshua" is used of the descendant of Jehozadak, the last chief priest before the exile (see 1 Chronicles 6.4-15); this Joshua is often mentioned together with Zerubbabel (5.5, 8, 48, 56-58, 68, 70, 71; 6.2; 9.18-20). For other people, the name "Jeshua" is used (5.9-17, 24-28, 58; 8.63; 9.48).
[k] **5.6** *King Darius*: See the note at 3.1. [l] **5.6** *Nisan*: Or Abib, the first month of the Hebrew calendar, from about mid-March to mid-April. [m] **5.9-17** *how many returned from each family group*: The numbers and the forms of the names are different in various manuscripts and ancient translations.

Azaru; 101 from the family of Annias; the family of Arom; 323 from the family of Bezai; 112 from the family of Arsiphurith; and 3,005 from the family of Baiterus.

Here is how many returned, whose ancestors had come from the following towns:

18-23 There were 123 from Bethlehem; 55 from Netophah; 158 from Anathoth; 42 from Beth Azmaveth; 25 from Kiriatharim; 743 from Chephirah and Beeroth; 422 from the villages of the Chadiasans and Ammidians; 621 from Ramah and Geba; 122 from Michmash; 52 from Bethel; 156 from Magbish; 725 from the towns of Elam and Ono; 345 from Jericho; and 3,330 from Senaah.

24-25 Here is a list of how many returned from each family of priests:

There were 972 descendants of Anasib from the family of Jedaiah son of Jeshua; 1,052 from the family of Immer; 1,247 from the family of Pashhur; and 1,017 from the family of Charme.

26-28 Here is a list of how many returned from the families of Levites:

There were 74 from the families of Jeshua, Kadmiel, Bannas, and Sudias; 128 descendants of the temple singers from the family of Asaph; and 139 descendants of the temple guards from the families of Shallum, Ater, Talmon, Akkub, Hatita, and Shobai.

29-32 Here is a list of the families of temple workers whose descendants returned:

Esau, Hasupha, Tabbaoth, Keros, Sua, Padon, Lebanah, Hagabah, Akkub, Uthai, Ketab, Hagab, Subai, Hana, Cathua, Geddur, Jairus, Daisan, Noeba, Chezib, Gazera, Uzza, Phinoe, Hasrah, Basthai, Asnah, Maani, Nephisim, Acuph, Hakupha, Asur, Pharakim, Bazluth, Mehida, Cutha, Charea, Barkos, Serar, Temah, Neziah, Hatipha.

33-34 Here is a list of Solomon's servants whose descendants returned:

Assaphioth, Peruda, Jaalah, Lozon, Isdael, Shephatiah, Agia, Pochereth Hazzebaim, Sarothie, Masiah, Gas, Addus, Subas, Apherra, Barodis, Shaphat, Allon.

35 A total of 372 descendants of temple workers and Solomon's servants returned.

36-37 There were 652 who returned from the families of Nekoda and of Delaiah son of Tobiah, though they could not prove they were Israelites. They had lived in the Babylonian towns of Tel-Melah and Tel-Harsha, and their leaders were Cherub, Addan, and Immer.

38-39 The families of Habaiah, Hakkoz, and Barzillai could not prove that they were priests. Jaddus was the ancestor of the Barzillai family. He had married Agia, one of the daughters of Barzillai from Gilead,[n] and he had taken his wife's family name. But the records of these three families could not be found, and none of them were allowed to serve as priests. 40 In fact, Nehemiah and the governor[o] told them, "You cannot eat the food offered to God, until God tells a high priest that you can."

41-42 There were 42,360 that returned who were age twelve and older, in addition to 7,337 servants and 245 musicians and singers. 43 They brought with them 435 camels; 7,036 horses; 245 mules; and 5,525 donkeys.

44 When the people came to the place in Jerusalem where God's temple had been located, some of the family leaders made a sacred promise to rebuild the temple in the very same place 45 and to give the money to pay for it. They promised to give 1,200 pounds of gold, and 6,000 pounds of silver, and 100 robes for the priests.

46 The priests and Levites and some of the other people settled in Jerusalem and the surrounding villages. The rest of the people, including the temple singers and guards, settled in the towns from which their families had come.

[n]5.38,39 *Barzillai from Gilead*: See 2 Samuel 19.31-39. [o]5.40 *the governor*: Or "Attharias."

5.40 Nu 27.21. **5.46** 1 Ch 9.2; Ne 11.3.

The First Offering on the New Altar
(Ezra 3.1-6)

47 On the first day of the seventh month
of the year,[p] the Israelites who had settled
in their towns went to Jerusalem. They met
to worship together in the open area just
inside the first gate on the eastern side of
the city. 48 The priest Joshua, together with
the other priests, and Zerubbabel son of
Shealtiel and his relatives took their places.
Then they rebuilt the altar of Israel's God,
49 so they could follow the instructions God
gave to Moses and offer sacrifices on it.
50 They built the altar where it had stood
before, because most of the foreigners who
were already living around Jerusalem were
their enemies and were stronger than they
were. However, some of the foreigners were
friendly and helped the Jews. Then the
Jews began burning sacrifices on the altar
at the proper times, including sacrifices
to please the Lord[q] every morning and
evening.

51 The people followed the instructions
in the Law for celebrating the Festival of
Shelters. They also offered the proper sacrifices each day, 52 as well as the special
sacrifices on each Sabbath, at each New
Moon Festival, and at all the other sacred
festivals. 53 Work on the temple itself had
not yet begun. But from that day, the first
day of the seventh month, all those who
made sacred promises offered their sacrifices on the altar to God.[r]

The Rebuilding of the Temple Begins
(Ezra 3.7-13)

54-55 King Cyrus of Persia had said that
the Israelites could have cedar logs from
Lebanon, and so these logs were tied together into rafts and floated by sea to the
harbor at Joppa. The Israelites sent food
and drink and carts[s] to the cities of Tyre
and Sidon as payment for these logs, and
they gave money to the stoneworkers and
carpenters.

56-57 On the first day of the second
month[t] of the second year after the people
had returned to Judea and Jerusalem from
Babylonia, they began laying the foundation for God's temple. Zerubbabel and
Joshua and their relatives started working,
and so did the priests, the Levites, and
everyone else who had returned. 58 Every
Levite over twenty years of age was put in
charge of some part of the building project,
and they worked together to get the job
done. The Levites in charge of the entire
project were Joshua and his sons, his
brother Kadmiel, and his other relatives;
and the sons of Jeshua Emadabun, the
sons of Joda son of Iliadun, and their sons
and other relatives.

While the workers were building the
temple, 59-60 the priests put on their robes
and blew trumpets and played other instruments in honor of the Lord, and the
Levites from the family of Asaph praised
God with cymbals. All of them followed the
instructions given years before by King
David.[u] 61 They praised the Lord and gave
thanks as they sang:

> "Our glorious Lord will be good
> to his people forever."

62 Everyone started blowing trumpets
and shouting praises to the Lord, because
work on the temple had begun. 63 Many of
the older priests and Levites and heads of
families had seen the former temple, and
they cried aloud. 64 Others were happy and
celebrated with trumpet blasts and joyful
shouts. 65 The trumpets could be heard far
away, but up close, the sound of weeping
and crying drowned out the sound of the
trumpets.

[p]**5.47** *On the first day of the seventh month of the year*: The seventh month of the Hebrew calendar is Tishri (also called Ethanim), from about mid-September to mid-October. The Greek has "When the seventh month arrived," but see also verse 53. [q]**5.50** *sacrifices to please the Lord*: See the note at 4.52. [r]**5.53** *made sacred promises . . . to God*: A sacred promise was not completely kept until the person had offered a sacrifice to God (see Leviticus 7.11-18). [s]**5.54,55** *carts*: Some Greek manuscripts; other Greek manuscripts "wine." [t]**5.56,57** *second month*: Ziv (also called Iyyar), the second month of the Hebrew calendar, from about mid-April to mid-May.
[u]**5.59,60** *King David*: Ruled about 1010-970 B.C.

5.52 Nu 28.11—29.39. **5.59,60** 1 Ch 25.1. **5.61** 1 Ch 16.34; 2 Ch 5.11-14; Ps 100.5; 106.1; 118.1; 136.1; Jr 33.11.

Foreigners Want To Help Rebuild the Temple

(Ezra 4.1-5)

66 When the enemies of the tribes of Judah and Benjamin heard the trumpets,
they came to Jerusalem to see what was
happening. 67 They found out that the people who had come back from Babylonia
were rebuilding the temple of the Lord God
of Israel. 68 So they went to Zerubbabel,
Joshua, and the family leaders and said,
"Let us help! 69 Ever since King Esarhaddon[v] of Assyria brought us here, we have
worshiped your Lord and offered sacrifices
to him."
70-71 But Zerubbabel, Joshua, and the
family leaders answered, "You cannot take
part in building a temple for our God, the
Lord of Israel! We will build it ourselves,
just as King Cyrus of Persia[w] has commanded us."
72 But these enemies blocked the roads
and did everything else possible[x] to make
the people of Judah slow down or stop
building. 73 The enemies made secret plans
and public speeches accusing the Jews,
and they even caused riots. And so, the
people of Judah could not work on the
temple for the last two years of Cyrus' rule.

Work on the Temple Starts Again

(Ezra 5.1-17)

6 Two years after Darius[y] became king,
1 the Lord God of Israel told the prophets Haggai and Zechariah[z] to speak in his
name to the people of Judah and Jerusalem.
And they did. 2 Then Zerubbabel the governor and Joshua the priest urged the people
to start working on the temple again, and
God's prophets encouraged them. 3 But
Governor Sisinnes of Southwest Syria
Province[a] and his assistant Sathrabuzanes
got together with some of their officials and
went to Jerusalem. They said to the people,
"Who told you to rebuild this temple?
4 Give us the names of the workers!"
5 But God was kind to the Jewish leaders, because he was looking after the Jews
who had come back from being exiles.
6 And so the governor and his group decided not to make the people stop working
until they could report to Darius and get
his advice.
7 Governor Sisinnes, Sathrabuzanes,
and their advisors sent a report to Darius,
which said:

> 8 Greetings, King Darius! We went
> to Jerusalem in Judah, where the lead-
> ers of the Jews who came from Baby-
> lon now live. 9 The Jews are building a
> large temple for the Lord and are using
> huge stones and expensive wooden
> beams set in the walls. 10 Everyone is
> working carefully but quickly, and this
> beautiful building is going up fast.
> 11 We asked those in charge to tell
> us who gave them permission to re-
> build the temple. 12 We also asked for
> the names of their leaders, so that we
> could write them down for you.
> 13 The leaders claimed that the
> Jews are the servants of the Lord, who
> created heaven and earth. 14 And they
> said they were rebuilding the temple
> that was built many years ago by a fa-
> mous and powerful king of Israel.[b]
> 15 They went on to say that their
> ancestors had sinned and made the
> Lord angry, and so he had let them be
> captured by King Nebuchadnezzar[c] of
> Babylonia,[d] 16 who took them away as
> captives to Babylon. Nebuchadnezzar
> also tore down and burned their tem-
> ple, 17-19 then took its sacred gold and
> silver articles to Babylon and put them
> in the temple of his own god.

[v]**5.69** *King Esarhaddon*: Ruled Assyria 681-669 B.C. These people may have been brought to Palestine in 677 or 676 B.C., when Esarhaddon invaded Syria. [w]**5.70,71** *King Cyrus of Persia*: Ruled Persia 549-529 B.C. [x]**5.72** *did everything else possible*: One possible meaning for the difficult Greek text. [y]**5.73** *Darius*: See the note at 3.1. [z]**6.1** *Zechariah*: Greek "Zechariah son of Iddo." [a]**6.3** *Southwest Syria Province*: See the note at 2.17. [b]**6.14** *a famous and powerful king of Israel*: King Solomon, who ruled about 970-931 B.C. [c]**6.15** *Nebuchadnezzar*: Ruled 605-562 B.C. [d]**6.15** *Babylonia*: The Greek text adds "the king of the Chaldeans," but Chaldea is another name for Babylonia.

5.67,68 2 K 17.24-41. **6.1** Zec 1.1. **6.2** Hg 1.12; Zec 4.6-9. **6.15,16** 2 K 25.8-12; 2 Ch 36.17-20; Jr 52.12-15. **6.17-19** Ezra 1.2-11; 1 Esd 2.3-15.

Tobit hurries to Jerusalem
with offerings. *Tobit 1.6,7*

An Angel of the Lord comes into the fire.
Prayer of Azariah 26-27

Finally, the Jewish leaders said that during the first year that Cyrus was king of Babylonia,[e] he wrote out orders for the Lord's temple to be rebuilt in Jerusalem where it had stood before. Cyrus also gave Zerubbabel and Governor Sheshbazzar the sacred gold and silver articles for them to put back in the temple. 20 Sheshbazzar then went to Jerusalem and laid the foundation for the temple, and the work is still going on.

21 Your Majesty, please have your servants look up the old records in Babylon. 22 Tell them to find out if King Cyrus really did give orders to rebuild the Lord's temple in Jerusalem. Then you can let us know if he did, and whether or not you approve of those orders. Of course, we will do whatever you think we should.

The Order of King Cyrus Is Rediscovered

(Ezra 6.1-5)

23 King Darius[f] ordered someone to go through the old records kept in Babylonia. Finally, a scroll was found in Ecbatana, a fortress city in Media Province, and it said:

24 In the first year Cyrus was king,[g] he gave the following orders. The Lord's temple in Jerusalem is to be rebuilt, so that the Jews can offer sacrifices there on the altar where the fire is always burning. 25 The temple is to be built ninety feet high and ninety feet wide, with one row of new wooden beams for each three rows of large stones. The wood is to come from the region near Jerusalem. The royal treasury will pay for everything.

26 Gather together all the sacred gold and silver things that Nebuchadnezzar took from the temple in Jerusalem and brought to Babylonia. Then return these things to their proper places.

King Darius Orders the Work To Continue

(Ezra 6.6-12)

27 King Darius sent a message to Governor Sisinnes of Southwest Syria Province,[h] to Sathrabuzanes, and to their advisors. He warned them to stay away from the temple in Jerusalem and to let Governor Zerubbabel and the other Jewish leaders rebuild the temple where it stood before. 28 Then he continued:

I want the Jews who returned to Judah to complete the work on this temple, and until they do, I command you to give them all the help you can. 29 Starting right now, you will be very careful to give Zerubbabel part of the tax money you collect from Southwest Syria Province. He will use this money to buy bulls, rams, and lambs for sacrifices. 30 The priests in Jerusalem will tell you how much wheat, salt, wine, and olive oil they need each year to offer the daily sacrifices. And don't argue over how much they need—just give them what they ask for. 31 I want them to be able to offer sacrifices of wine to God Most High and to pray for me and my family.

32 If any of you don't obey the orders written above, or if you try to change what I have said, a wooden beam will be pulled out of your house and sharpened on one end. Then it will be driven through your body.[i] And I will take over everything that belonged to you.

33 I ask the Lord who is worshiped in Jerusalem to destroy any king or nation who tries to harm his temple. 34 I, King Darius, give these orders, and I expect them to be followed carefully.

The Temple Is Dedicated

(Ezra 6.13-18)

7 Governor Sisinnes, Sathrabuzanes, and their advisors obeyed King Darius. 2 They made sure the work on the temple

[e]**6.17-19** *the first year that Cyrus was king of Babylonia*: 539 B.C. (see also the note at 2.1, 2). [f]**6.23** *King Darius*: See the note at 3.1. [g]**6.24** *the first year Cyrus was king*: See the note at verses 17-19. [h]**6.27** *Southwest Syria Province*: See the note at 2.17. [i]**6.32** *driven through your body*: A well-known punishment in the ancient Near East.

was done properly, and they helped the
Jewish leaders and temple officials. 3 The
prophets Haggai and Zechariah encouraged everyone by their preaching, and the
work went along smoothly. 4 So, the temple
was completed at the command of the Lord
God of Israel, and with the approval of
kings Cyrus, Darius, and Artaxerxes[j] of
Persia. 5 On the twenty-third day of the
month of Adar[k] in the sixth year of the rule
of Darius,[l] the temple was finished. 6 The
people of Israel, the priests, the Levites,
and everyone else who had returned from
exile came together and followed all the instructions Moses had written. 7 One hundred bulls, two hundred rams, and four
hundred lambs were offered as sacrifices at
the dedication of the temple. 8 Also twelve
goats were sacrificed as sin offerings for the
nation of Israel, one goat for each of the
leaders of the tribes. 9 Guards were stationed at each gate, and the priests and the
Levites were arranged by families in their
assigned places. They were dressed in their
special robes, and they carried out the instructions that Moses had written about offering sacrifices and gifts to the Lord God
of Israel.

The Passover
(Ezra 6.19-22)

10-11 The people of Israel who had returned from exile celebrated Passover on
the fourteenth day of the first month.[m] The
priests, the Levites, and many of the people
had gone through a ceremony to make
themselves acceptable to worship God.
12 The Levites killed the Passover lambs for
those who had returned, including the
priests and themselves.
13 The sacrifices were eaten by the Israelites who had returned, and also by the
neighboring people who had given up the
sinful customs[n] of other nations in order to
worship the Lord. 14 For seven days they
celebrated the Festival of Thin Bread.
Everyone was happy and praised the Lord,
15 because he had made sure that the king
of Persia[o] would help them build the
temple.

Ezra Comes to Jerusalem
(Ezra 7.1-10)

8 1-3 Much later, when Artaxerxes[p] was
king of Persia, Ezra came to Jerusalem
from Babylonia. Ezra was the son of Seraiah and the grandson of Azariah. His other
ancestors were Hilkiah, Shallum, Zadok,
Ahitub, Amariah, Uzzi, Bukki, Abishua,
Phinehas, Eleazar, and Aaron, the first
priest.

Ezra was an expert in the Law that the
Lord God of Israel had given to Moses.
4 The king respected Ezra and would give
him anything he asked for.

5 Other Jews, including priests, Levites,
musicians, and temple guards and servants, came to Jerusalem with Ezra. 6 They
left Babylonia on the first day of the first
month[q] of the seventh year that Artaxerxes
was king[r] and arrived on the first day of the
fifth month.[s] The Lord had brought Ezra
safely to Jerusalem.

7 Ezra knew everything that the Law of
the Lord commanded. He obeyed it all, and
he taught the people of Israel how to obey
it too.

Why Ezra Came to Jerusalem
(Ezra 7.11-26)

8 One day,[t] King Artaxerxes[u] told a servant to write down some of his commands,

[j]**7.4** *Artaxerxes*: Either Artaxerxes I (ruled 465-425 B.C.) or Artaxerxes II (ruled 405-358 B.C.).
[k]**7.5** *Adar*: The twelfth month of the Hebrew calendar, from about mid-February to mid-March.
[l]**7.5** *sixth year . . . of Darius*: 515 B.C. [m]**7.10,11** *first month*: See the note at 1.1.
[n]**7.13** *the Israelites who had returned, and also by the neighboring people who had given up the sinful customs*: Or "the Israelites who had returned and had rejected the sinful customs."
[o]**7.15** *king of Persia*: The Greek has "king of Assyria," probably meaning the king of Persia, because Assyria was now part of the Persian Empire. [p]**8.1-3** *Artaxerxes*: See the note at 7.4.
[q]**8.6** *first month*: See the note at 1.1. [r]**8.6** *the seventh year that Artaxerxes was king*: See the note at 7.4. [s]**8.6** *fifth month*: Ab, the fifth month of the Hebrew calendar, from about mid-July to mid-August. [t]**8.8** *One day*: The events of verses 8-61 took place before the events of verses 1-7. [u]**8.8** *King Artaxerxes*: See the note at 7.4.
7.3 Hg 1.1. **7.10,11** Ex 12.1-20.

then he gave a copy to Ezra, who was a
priest and an expert in the Law of the
Lord. In this written copy, Artaxerxes said:
9 Greetings from King Artaxerxes to
Ezra the priest, who understands the
Law of the Lord.

10-11 I have decided to show special
kindness to the Jews. And so, any of
the people of Israel or their priests or
Levites in my kingdom may go with
you to Jerusalem if they want to. My
seven trusted friends,[v] who are my
closest advisors, agree with me. You
may go to Jerusalem and Judah 12 to
find out if[w] the laws of your God are
being obeyed.

13 When you go, take the gold and
silver that I and my trusted friends
have promised to give to the Lord, the
God of Israel. Take all the gold and silver that you collect from Babylonia.
14 Also take the gifts that your own
people have given for the temple of the
Lord in Jerusalem. Use the money to
buy bulls, rams, lambs, grain, olive oil,
and wine.[x] 15 Then sacrifice them on
the altar at the Lord's temple in
Jerusalem. 16 After this, you and your
relatives may use the remaining gold
and silver for whatever pleases your
God. 17 Give the Lord your God the sacred things that have been contributed
for use in his temple. 18 And if you
think of anything else that is needed
for the temple, you may have the
money you need from the royal treasury. 19 Ezra, you are a priest and an
expert in the Law of the Most High
God, and I order all the treasurers in
Southwest Syria Province[y] to help you.
20 They will be allowed to give as much
as 7,500 pounds of silver, 500 bushels
of wheat, 550 gallons of wine, 550 gallons of olive oil, and as much salt as is
needed.

21 They must carefully provide
everything God's Law demands for his
temple. He is God Most High, and I
don't want him to be angry with me or
with my descendants, who will rule as
kings after me. 22 I also want you to
know that no priests or Levites, and no
singers, guards, servants, or anyone
else who works in the temple, will
have to pay any kind of taxes. No one
is allowed to change this law!

23 Ezra, use the wisdom God has
given you and choose rulers and
judges to govern the people of Southwest Syria Province[y] according to
God's Law. And you must have God's
Law taught to anyone who doesn't
know it. 24 Everyone who disobeys
God's Law or the king's law will be
punished by a heavy fine or prison or
death.

Ezra Praises God

(Ezra 7.27, 28)

25 Because King Artaxerxes[z] was so
kind, Ezra said:

Give praise to the Lord! He is the
only one who could make the king
want to honor the Lord's temple in
Jerusalem. 26 And because of what the
Lord has done, I am greatly respected
by the king and his advisors, his
trusted friends,[a] and his officials.
27 The Lord has helped me, and I have
been able to bring many people of Israel back to Jerusalem.

The Families Who Came Back with Ezra

(Ezra 8.1-14)

Ezra said:

28 Artaxerxes was king of Persia when I
led the following leaders of the family
groups from Babylonia to Jerusalem:
29-40 Gershom of the Phinehas family;
Gamael of the Ithamar family;

[v]**8.10,11** *trusted friends*: This was a title that kings sometimes gave to their special advisors and highest officials. These friends received many gifts, honors, and privileges. [w]**8.12** *find out if*: Or "make sure that." [x]**8.14** *grain, olive oil, and wine*: Greek "the things that go with them"; when an animal was offered as a sacrifice, grain, olive oil, and wine were offered along with it (see Numbers 15.1-16). [y]**8.19,23** *Southwest Syria Province*: See the note at 2.17. [z]**8.25** *King Artaxerxes*: See the note at 7.4. [a]**8.26** *trusted friends*: See verses 10, 11 and the note there.

Hattush son of Shecaniah from King David's family;
Zechariah and 150 other men from the family of Parosh, who had family records;
Eliehoenai son of Zerahiah with 200 men of the Pahath Moab family;
Shecaniah son of Jahaziel with 300 men of the Zattu family;
Obed son of Jonathan with 250 men of the Adin family;
Jeshaiah son of Gotholiah with 70 men of the Elam family;
Zeraiah son of Michael with 70 men of the Shephatiah family;
Obadiah son of Jehiel with 212 men of the Joab family;
Shelomith son of Josiphiah with 160 men of the Bani family;
Zechariah son of Bebai with 28 men of the Bebai family;
Johanan son of Hakkatan with 110 men of the Azgad family;
Eliphelet, Jeuel, and Shemaiah, who actually returned later with 70 men of the Adonikam family;
Uthai son of Istalcurus with 70 men of the Bigvai family.

Ezra Finds Levites for the Temple

(Ezra 8.15-20)

Ezra said:

41 I brought everyone together by the
Theras River, where we camped for three
days while I talked to the people and found
out who had come. 42 There was not one
priest or Levite in the whole group! 43-44 So
I sent for some wise leaders, whose names
were Eliezar, Iduel, Maasmas, Elnathan,
Shemaiah, Jarib, Nathan, Elnathan,
Zechariah, and Meshullam. 45 Then I sent
them to Iddo, the official in charge of the
treasury. 46 I told them to ask him and his
relatives and the others there to send us
priests to work in the Lord's temple. 47 God
was helping us with his mighty power, and
he had them send us a skillful man named
Sherebiah, who was a Levite from the family of Mahli. Eighteen of his sons and other
relatives came with him. 48 We were also
sent Hashabiah and the two brothers Annunus and Jeshaiah from the family of
Hananiah, along with their twenty sons.
49 In addition, 220 temple servants came
along to help the Levites. The ancestors of
these servants had been chosen years ago
by King David[b] and his officials, and they
were all listed by name.

Ezra Asks the People To Go without Eating and To Pray

(Ezra 8.21-23)

Ezra said:

50 There beside the river I told the
young men to go without eating and to pray
to the Lord, asking him to bring us and our
children and our livestock safely to
Jerusalem. 51 I was ashamed to ask the
king to send foot soldiers and cavalry to
protect us against enemies. 52 After all, we
had told the king, "If people truly worship
the Lord, his mighty power will take care of
them in every way." 53 So we again asked
the Lord for his protection, and he showed
mercy to us.

The Gifts for the Temple

(Ezra 8.24-30)

Ezra said:

54 I chose twelve of the leading priests—
Sherebiah, Hashabiah, and ten of their relatives. 55-57 Then I weighed the gifts that
had been given for the Lord's temple, and I
divided them among the twelve priests I
had chosen. There were gifts of silver and
gold and other things, and they had been
contributed by the king, his advisors, and
the people of Israel. In all there were 25
tons of silver; 100 silver articles weighing
150 pounds; 7,500 pounds of gold; 20 gold
bowls; and twelve bronze objects that were
as shiny as gold.

58 I said to the priests:

You belong to the Lord, the God of
your ancestors, and these things also
belong to him, because his people
made sacred promises to give him this
silver and gold. 59 Be sure to guard
these gifts and keep them safe until
you reach Jerusalem. Then take them
inside the Lord's temple and deliver
them to the leaders of the priests and

[b]**8.49** *King David*: See the note at 5.59, 60.

Levites, and to the heads of the Israelite families.

60 The priests and the Levites then took charge of the gifts, so they could take them to the Lord's temple.

The Return to Jerusalem
(Ezra 8.31-36)

Ezra said:

61 On the twelfth day of the first month,[c] we left the Theras River and started for Jerusalem. Our God watched over us all the way to Jerusalem,[d] and as we traveled along, he rescued us from our enemies. 62 After we had been in Jerusalem for three days, we took the silver and gold to the temple, where it was weighed and turned over to the priest Meremoth son of Uriah. 63 With him were Eleazar son of Phinehas and the Levites Jozabad son of Jeshua and Moeth son of Binnui. 64 Everything was counted, weighed, and recorded.

65-66 Those who had returned from exile offered sacrifices to the Lord, the God of Israel. Twelve bulls were offered for all Israel. Ninety-six rams and seventy-two lambs were offered on the altar. And twelve goats were sacrificed to give thanks to the Lord.

67 Some of those who had returned took the king's orders to the royal officials and governors of Southwest Syria Province.[e] Then these officials gave honor to the Jews and to the temple of God.

Ezra Condemns Mixed Marriages
(Ezra 9.1-4)

Ezra said:

68 Later the Jewish leaders came to me and said:

69 Many of the Israelites, including some of the rulers, the priests, and the Levites, are living just like the people around them. They are even guilty of the same kinds of horrible sins as those committed by the Canaanites, the Hittites, the Perizzites, the Jebusites, the Moabites, the Egyptians, and the Edomites. 70 In addition, Israelite men have married foreign women and have let their sons do the same thing. Some of our own officials and leaders were among the first men to commit this disgusting sin, and now God's holy people are mixed with foreigners.

71 This news made me so angry that I ripped my clothes and my sacred robe and tore hair from my head and beard. Then I just sat down, deeply worried and full of sorrow 72 and grief over this sin. Many of our people really wanted to obey the Lord of Israel, and they gathered around me as I sat there.

Ezra's Prayer
(Ezra 9.5-15)

Ezra said:

At the time of the evening sacrifice 73 I stood up, with my clothing and sacred robe torn. I hadn't eaten anything all day. Then I knelt down, and lifting my arms to the Lord, 74 I prayed:

I am ashamed and confused, Lord.

75-76 Since the time of our ancestors, the sins and mistakes of our people have swept over us like a flood that reaches up to the heavens. And we are still committing terrible sins. 77 That's why we and our relatives, our kings, and our priests have often been defeated by other kings. They have killed some of us and made slaves of others; they have taken our possessions and made us ashamed, just as we are today.

78 And now, Lord, for a short time you have shown kindness to us by letting a few of us settle here and come to your sacred temple, 79 where there is light for our nation once again. All the time we were in slavery, you provided food for us. 80 Even when we were slaves, you never turned your back on us. And because of you, the kings of Persia were kind and gave us food. 81 They have given honor to your temple and are allowing us to rebuild Jerusalem. We can live safely here and in the rest of Judah.

82 Our Lord, what can we say now? Even though you gave us all this, we have disobeyed the commands that

[c]**8.61** *first month*: See the note at 1.1.
[d]**8.61** *all the way to Jerusalem*: They arrived on the first day of the fifth month (see verse 6).
[e]**8.67** *Southwest Syria Province*: See the note at 2.17.

were given to us by your servants the prophets. They said 83 that the land you gave us was full of sinful heathens, who never stop doing disgusting things.[f] 84 And we were warned not to let our daughters and sons marry their sons and daughters.

85 Your prophets also told us never to make peace with those foreigners. You wanted us to become strong and to enjoy the good things in the land, then someday to leave it to our children forever. 86 All of our troubles happened because of our terrible sins, but you did not punish us as much as we deserved, 87 and you have brought some of us back to our homeland. But we rejected your laws and married foreigners who do disgusting things. 88 You were so angry at us before, that you could have destroyed us all! 89 You didn't, though—you were faithful and allowed some of us to survive. 90 But now we admit that we have sinned and are not fit to worship you.

The Plan for Ending Mixed Marriages

(Ezra 10.1-17)

Ezra said:

91 While I was lying face down in front of the temple, praying with tears in my eyes and confessing the sins of the people of Israel, a large number of men, women, and children gathered around me and cried bitterly.

92 Shecaniah son of Jehiel spoke up and said:

Ezra, we have sinned against the Lord by marrying these foreign women. But there is still hope for the people of Israel, 93-94 if we follow your advice and the advice of others who obey the Law of the Lord. We must promise the Lord that we will divorce our foreign wives and send them away, together with their children. 95 Ezra, get up and do something to solve this problem. We will support you, even if you have to be severe with us.

96 So I got up and made the leaders of the priests and Levites and the leaders of Israel swear that they would follow this plan.

9 1 Then I left the courtyard of the temple and went to the living quarters of Jehohanan son of Eliashib, 2 where I spent the night. I continued to mourn over the terrible sins the people had committed, and I did not eat or drink a thing.

3-4 The leaders of the people sent a message to all the men who had returned from Babylonia and were now living in Jerusalem and Judah. It told them to meet in Jerusalem within two days, or three at the most, or else their livestock would be taken and sacrificed to the Lord. In addition, those men would no longer be considered part of the people that had returned from Babylonia.

5 Three days later, on the twentieth day of the ninth month,[g] everyone from Judah and Benjamin came to Jerusalem. 6 They all went to the temple courtyard, where they sat down, shivering in the winter rain.

7 I stood up and said:

You have broken God's Law by marrying foreign women, and you have made the whole nation even more guilty than it already was! 8 Now you must confess your sins to the Lord God of our ancestors. You must give him honor 9 and obey him. Divorce your foreign wives and don't have anything to do with the rest of the foreigners who live around here.

10 Everyone in the crowd shouted:

We will do what you say, 11 but we can't just stand out here in the open. Many of us have sinned, and the matter can't be settled in only a day or two. 12 Why can't our officials stay on in Jerusalem and take care of this for us? Let everyone who has married a foreign woman meet here at a certain time 13 with leaders and judges from their own towns. If we take care of this problem, God will surely stop being so terribly angry with us.

14 Jonathan son of Asahel and Jahzeiah

[f] **8.83** *doing disgusting things*: Probably worshiping idols. [g] **9.5** *ninth month*: Chislev, the ninth month of the Hebrew calendar, from about mid-November to mid-December.

8.84,85 Ex 34.11-16; Dt 7.1-5.

son of Tikvah were put in charge of the plan, and Meshullam, Levi, and Shabbethai were appointed as judges along with them. 15 Everyone who had returned from exile did what the plan required them to do. 16 I myself chose a group of men who were heads of the families, and I listed their names. They started looking into the matter on the first day of the tenth month,[h] 17 and they did not finish until the first day of the first month[i] of the following year.

The Men Who Had Foreign Wives
(Ezra 10.18-44)

18-20 Here is a list of the priests who had agreed to divorce their foreign wives and to sacrifice a ram as a sin offering:

Maaseiah, Eliezar, Jarib, and Jodan from the family of Joshua[j] and his brothers; 21 Hanani, Zebadiah, Maaseiah, Shemaiah, Jehiel, and Azariah from the family of Immer; 22 and Elioenai, Maaseiah, Ishmael, Nathanael, Gedaliah, and Salthas from the family of Pashhur.

23 Those Levites who had foreign wives were Jozabad, Shimei, Kelaiah (also known as Kelita), Pethahiah, Judah, and Jonah.

24 Eliashib and Zaccur were temple singers who had foreign wives.

25 The temple guards Shallum and Telem had foreign wives.

26 Here is a list of the others from Israel who had foreign wives:

Ramiah, Izziah, Malchijah, Mijamin, Eleazar, Asibias, and Benaiah from the family of Parosh;

27 Mattaniah, Zechariah, Jezrielus, Abdi, Jeremoth, and Elijah from the family of Elam;

28 Eliadas, Eliashib, Othoniah, Jeremoth, Zabad, and Zerdaiah from the family of Zamoth;

29 Jehohanan, Hananiah, Zabbai, and Emathis from the family of Bebai;

30 Olamus, Mamuchus, Adaiah, Jashub, Sheal, and Jeremoth from the family of Mani;

31 Naathus, Moossias, Laccunus, Naidus, Bescaspasmys, Sesthel, Belnuus, and Manasseas from the family of Addi;

32 Elionas, Asaias, Melchias, Sabbaias, and Simon Chosamaeus from the family of Annan;

33 Mattenai, Mattattah, Zabad, Eliphelet, Manasseh, and Shimei from the family of Hashum;

34 Jeremai, Momdius, Maerus, Joel, Mamdai, Bedeiah, Vaniah, Carabasion, Eliashib, Mamitanemus, Eliasis, Binnui, Elialis, Shimei, Shelemiah, and Nethaniah from the family of Bani;

Shashai, Azarel, Azael, Samatus, Zambris, and Joseph from the family of Ezora;

35 Mazitias, Zabad, Iddo, Joel, and Benaiah from the family of Nooma.

36 These men divorced their foreign wives, then sent them and their children away.

Ezra Reads God's Law to the People
(Nehemiah 7.73—8.13)

Ezra said:

37 The priests, the Levites, and the other Israelites settled in Jerusalem and in the villages in the country. Then, on the first day of the seventh month,[k] 38 the people came together in the open area in front of the east gate of the temple. 39 Since I was the chief priest and had studied the laws that the Lord God of Israel had given to Moses, the people asked me to bring out the Law and read it to them. 40 This way, the priests and the whole crowd of men and women could hear what it said.

41-47 I stood on a wooden platform that had been built for this occasion. I had been given the place of honor in the center, with Mattathiah, Shema, Ananias, Azariah, Uriah, Hezekiah, and Baalsamus standing to my right, and Pedaiah, Mishael, Malchijah, Lothasubus, Nabariah, and Zechariah to my left.

[h]**9.16** *tenth month*: Tebeth, the tenth month of the Hebrew calendar, from about mid-December to mid-January. [i]**9.17** *first month*: See the note at 1.1. [j]**9.18-20** *Joshua*: Greek "Joshua son of Jehozadak"; see the note at 5.5. [k]**9.37** *seventh month*: See the note at 5.47.

9.37 1 Ch 9.2; Ne 11.3.

Everyone in the crowd stood when I
picked up the book of God's Law and opened
it. And after I gave thanks to the Lord All-
Powerful, the Most High God, everyone
said, "Amen." Then they lifted their hands
and bowed down to worship the Lord.

From early morning till noon, I read the
Law of Moses to them, and they listened
carefully. 48 After this, the Levites Jeshua,
Anniuth, Sherebiah, Jadinus, Akkub, Shabbethai, Hodiah, Maiannas, Kelita, Azariah,
Jozabad, Hanan, and Pelaiah helped teach
the Law to the crowd by reading it and explaining what it meant.

49-50 The people started crying when
God's Law was read to them. Then the governor[l] spoke to me, to the Levites who were
teaching, and to the crowd. He said, "This
is a special day for the Lord! 51-52 So when
you leave the temple, enjoy your good food
and wine, and share some with those who
didn't have anything to bring. Don't be sad.
The Lord will make us strong again."

53 The Levites told the crowd, "This is a
sacred day—don't be sad!"

54-55 Hearing God's Law had encouraged the people, and so when they returned to their homes, they celebrated by
eating and drinking and by sharing their
food with those in need.[m]

[l] **9.49,50** *the governor*: Or "Attharates." [m] **9.54,55** *need*: The Greek text adds "And they came together," which seems to indicate that the book once had a longer ending.

PRAYER OF MANASSEH

ABOUT THIS BOOK

According to 2 Chronicles 33.1-20, Manasseh, the sinful king of Judah, was captured and taken as a prisoner to Babylon. While he was in Babylon, he turned back to the Lord and prayed that the Lord would forgive him. This book shows what kind of prayer Manasseh might have prayed, emphasizing God's mercy and the benefits of giving up sin and turning back to God. As he says to the Lord,

In your great kindness,
you have promised
to forgive and to save
those who stop sinning
and turn to you.
(7b)

A QUICK LOOK AT THIS BOOK

- The Lord God All-Powerful Has Promised To Show Mercy (1-7)
- Manasseh Confesses His Sins (8-10)
- Manasseh Begs for Forgiveness (11-15)

---

1 You, the Lord God All-Powerful,
were worshiped by our ancestors
Abraham, Isaac, and Jacob,
and their faithful descendants.
2 You created the sky, the earth,
and the laws of nature.[a]
3 Your glorious name strikes terror
in the ocean depths,
and at your command
the sea stays in place.
4 Everything trembles with fear
when you show your power.
5 Your tremendous glory
is too much for us,
and we cannot endure your anger
against sinners.
6 Yet you have promised
to show mercy—
more than we can imagine.
7 You, Lord Most High,
are so very patient and kind,
and you punish us much less
than we deserve.
In your great kindness,
you have promised
to forgive and save
those who stop sinning
and turn to you.[b]

8 If I had followed the example
of Abraham, Isaac, and Jacob,
and if I had obeyed your laws,
you would not have told me
to turn from my sins.
9 If each of my sins
were a grain of sand,
they would more than cover
the ocean floor.

[a]**2** *the laws of nature*: Or "all their beauty." [b]**7** *In your great kindness . . . turn to you*: These words do not appear in the two most important manuscripts.
1 2 Ch 33.11-13, 18, 19. **9** 2 K 21.1-18.

I am not worthy
to pray to you.
10 I have sinned too much
for you to accept me.[c]
My sins are a heavy burden—
they are chains of iron
that I cannot remove.
I have disobeyed you
and set up disgusting idols
that made you angry.
11 But now I surrender my pride
and humbly pray for mercy.
12 I admit that I have sinned
and disobeyed you, Lord.
13 Forgive me, I beg you,
please forgive me.
Don't punish me forever;
don't send me down
to the world of the dead.
Yes, Lord, I beg you,
because you accept those
who turn back to you.

14 Although I don't deserve mercy,
save me, and show everyone
how truly good you are.
15 Then I will praise you
every hour of every day,
just as angels in heaven
sing your praises.
And you will be honored forever.
Amen.

[c] **10** *I have sinned . . . accept me*: One possible meaning for the difficult Greek text.

PSALM 151

ABOUT THIS BOOK

This short psalm is numbered 151 because it is included right after Psalm 150 in the ancient Greek translation of the Old Testament. For the most part, Psalm 151 is based on 1 Samuel 16–17.

A QUICK LOOK AT THIS BOOK

- God Chooses David To Be King of Israel (1-5)
- David Fights Goliath (6, 7)

Psalm 151

[This psalm is not included with the others. But it is said to have been written by David after he had fought Goliath by himself.]

1 I was my father's youngest
and smallest son,
and I took care of his sheep.

2 With my own hands,
I made a small harp.

3 And who will tell my Lord?
Will it be the Lord himself?
He is the one who hears.[a]

4 The Lord sent his messenger
to take me from my father's sheep
and show that I would be king.[b]

5 He did not choose my brothers,
though they were tall
and handsome.

6 When I went out to fight
that Philistine giant,
he cursed me in the name
of his idols.

7 But with his own sword,
I cut off his head,
and removed the disgrace
from the people of Israel.

[a]**151.3** *hears*: Some manuscripts have "hears all things"; others have "listens to me."
[b]**151.4** *show that I would be king*: This was done by pouring olive oil on David's head (see 1 Samuel 16.1-13).

151.1 **a**1 S 16.11; **b**1 S 17.15. **151.2** **a**1 S 16.23; **b**2 Ch 29.26. **151.4** **a**2 S 7.8; Ps 78.70, 71; **b**1 S 16.1, 13. **151.5** 1 S 16.7, 10. **151.6** 1 S 17.43. **151.7** 1 S 17.51.

3 MACCABEES

ABOUT THIS BOOK

This book is probably called 3 Maccabees because it follows 1 and 2 Maccabees in the ancient Greek manuscripts. However, it isn't really about the Maccabees at all; rather, it tells about the terrible suffering of the Jews living in Egypt during the rule of King Ptolemy IV Philopator (221-203 B.C.). King Philopator started hating the Jews when they told him that he wasn't allowed to enter the Jerusalem temple. He tried anyway, and after God stopped him, Philopator returned to Egypt, where he started causing trouble for the Jews there. He ordered them to worship an Egyptian god, and when they refused, he brought them together to be trampled by angry elephants. The rest of 3 Maccabees tells how God rescued these Jews three times and how Philopator finally recognized that he could not harm God's people. The Jews were released, and they returned to their homes celebrating and praising God.

Third Maccabees was probably written to comfort the Jews who were suffering under the rule of the Romans in the first century B.C. The author encouraged the Jews to remain faithful to God, who will always protect his people. The book ends with this reminder:

> *God Most High did all the miracles written in this book so that the Jews would be rescued from death. Shout praises forever to the God who saves the people of Israel! Amen.*
>
> *(7.22b, 23)*

A QUICK LOOK AT THIS BOOK

- A Jew Saves King Philopator's Life (1.1-3)
- Philopator Is Kept from Entering the Jerusalem Temple (1.3—2.24)
- Philopator Gives Orders To Kill All the Jews in Egypt (2.25—5.9)
- God Rescues the Jews Three Times (5.10—6.21)
- Philopator Releases the Jews and Promises To Protect Them (6.22—7.9)
- The Jews Return Home Safely (7.10-23)

Dositheus Saves Philopator's Life

1 When King Philopator ruled Egypt,[a] King Antiochus of Syria[b] invaded and took over much of his territory. Some of the Egyptians escaped and told Philopator what had happened. So he immediately called together his entire army, including foot soldiers and cavalry troops. He took along his sister Arsinoe and led the Egyptian troops to the region near Raphia,[c] where Antiochus and his army were camped.

2 That same night a man named
Theodotus decided to murder Philopator to end the war between Egypt and Syria. He took with him many of the best Egyptian

[a]**1.1** *King Philopator . . . Egypt*: Also known as Ptolemy IV (ruled 221-203 B.C.). [b]**1.1** *King Antiochus of Syria*: Antiochus III, later known as Antiochus the Great (ruled 223-187 B.C.).
[c]**1.1** *Raphia*: A town in southern Israel, about three miles from Gaza near the Mediterranean coast.
1.1 Dn 11.11.

weapons that had been assigned to him
years before,[d] and he sneaked into Philopator's tent.
3 But there was a Jewish man by the
name of Dositheus,[e] who had given up the
religion of his ancestors and was now loyal
to the Egyptians. Dositheus somehow
learned what Theodotus planned to do.
And he arranged for Philopator to be away
from his tent that night and for some unimportant man to sleep there in his place.
So Theodotus killed an innocent man.

The Egyptians Defeat the Syrians

4 Not long after the fighting broke out
between the Egyptians and the Syrians,
Philopator realized his troops would be defeated. So his sister Arsinoe went to the
Egyptian troops in tears and with tangled
hair, and she begged them to fight bravely
for their wives and children. She even
promised to pay every soldier four pounds
of gold if the Syrians were defeated. 5 Arsinoe's plan worked. The Egyptians defeated the Syrians and took many of them
prisoners.
6 After that victory, Philopator visited
the nearby cities to meet the people 7 and
donate gifts to their places of worship. The
people felt much safer after his visits, and
they respected him as their ruler.

Philopator Visits Jerusalem and Asks To Enter the Temple

8 The Jews sent some of their religious
leaders to meet King Philopator and to congratulate him on what he had done. Their
visit, together with the gifts, made Philopator even more anxious to visit their
cities.
9 Some time later, Philopator arrived in
Jerusalem and went to the temple, where
he offered the usual sacrifices and gave
thanks to God Most High. The size and
beauty of the temple amazed Philopator
10 so much that he wanted to see what it
looked like inside.
11 The Jews who walked with Philopator
said, "Your Majesty, not even our priests
can enter the most holy place in the temple. Only the high priest is allowed inside,
and he can enter at a certain time just
once a year."
Philopator refused to believe them.
12 Then someone opened a copy of the Law
of Moses and read aloud the part where
God forbids anyone except the high priest
to enter the most holy place in the temple.[f]
The king replied, "Even if others aren't
allowed to enter this temple, why can't I go
in? 13 No one has ever refused to let me
enter a temple before."
14 Without thinking, someone foolishly
answered, "You're wrong to think you can
go into this temple, just because you've
gone into others."
15 Philopator said, "After everything I've
done for this country, I should be allowed
inside whether you say it's all right or not."

The People of Jerusalem Try To Stop Philopator

16 The priests in their priestly robes
bowed down and begged God Most High to
help them stop the evil thing that Philopator was about to do. They cried so loudly
17 that everyone in Jerusalem was scared
and ran to the temple, because they knew
something very unusual was happening.
18 Young women who had never been out
in public[g] sprinkled dust[h] on their heads to
show their sorrow, then rushed outside
with their mothers. The sounds of their
crying and moaning filled the streets of
Jerusalem. 19 Women who were engaged to
be married left their bedrooms and huddled together in the streets, many of them
half-naked. 20 Mothers and the women who

[d]**1.2** *He took with him . . . Egyptian weapons . . . before*: Or "Theodotus took with him many of the best Egyptian soldiers that had been under his command some time ago." According to other ancient writings, Theodotus had been the commander of the Egyptian troops stationed in Syria, but had deserted to join the army of Antiochus III. [e]**1.3** *Dositheus*: Greek "Dositheus, the son of Drimylus." [f]**1.12** *the Law of Moses . . . temple*: See, for example, Leviticus 16.1, 2.
[g]**1.18** *Young women . . . public*: Young women were sometimes kept inside until they were engaged to be married. [h]**1.18** *dust*: Greek; some ancient translations add "and ashes."

1.9 2 Macc 3.36; 3 Macc 1.16; 3.11; 4.16; 5.25; 7.22. **1.11** Ex 30.10; Lv 16.1, 2; He 9.7.
1.16 3 Macc 1.9. **1.18** 3 Macc 3.19. **1.19** Jl 2.16; Ba 2.23; 3 Macc 4.6.

took care of their newborn babies were in such a hurry to get to the holy temple that they completely forgot about the babies and left them behind in houses and in the streets! 21 Everyone ran to the temple, then prayed and begged God to keep Philopator from entering the temple.

22 Meanwhile, a group of brave people had their own plan about how to stop Philopator. 23 They told the soldiers in the city to get their weapons and to be ready to die bravely for the sake of the ancient Law of Moses. These people caused a lot of confusion at the temple, until finally the older men and the respected leaders[i] convinced them to stop and to pray with the others.

24 Everyone prayed sincerely, 25 while the religious leaders tried to talk Philopator out of his arrogant plan. 26 But they were not successful. He stubbornly ignored everything they said and started walking toward the temple. 27 As he did, the people near him, including some of his own officers, began praying and begging God All-Powerful to defend them from the coming disaster and to punish the evil King Philopator. 28 Nothing could be heard except their loud prayers. 29 In fact, it seemed as if the walls of Jerusalem and the earth itself were praying along with them. The people agreed that it would be better for them to die than to watch Philopator make their temple unfit as a place to worship God.

Simon the High Priest Prays

2 Simon the high priest turned toward the temple and kneeled down. Then he raised his arms to heaven and calmly prayed:

2 Our Lord God All-Powerful, you alone are the holy King of heaven and the ruler of all creation. We are in misery and are suffering because of an evil and arrogant man, so hear our prayers. 3 You created all things and rule over them with fairness, and you punish those who depend on their own power.

4 In the past, you destroyed everyone who did what was wrong, including the mighty giants that you wiped out with a raging flood. 5 You sent burning sulphur to kill the proud people of the town of Sodom, making those wicked people an example for anyone who would dare follow their evil ways.

6 Your fearsome power was seen when you punished the king of Egypt for making slaves of your holy people Israel. You punished that arrogant king in terrible ways, 7 and when he chased your people with his troops and chariots, you drowned them in the deep waters of the Red Sea,[j] and you rescued those who trusted you. The whole earth is under your control. 8 After the Israelites saw your amazing victory, they praised you, God All-Powerful.

9 Our King, you created this entire world, and it is too large to measure. You have everything, yet you chose this city of Jerusalem as your own, and you blessed this temple where you are worshiped. You came here in the brightness of your glory and made this temple the one place where you would be praised and honored forever. 10 Your love for Israel is strong, and you promised that if trouble causes any of us to sin, you would listen when we come here to pray. 11 You have always been faithful to keep that promise.

12 Many times in the past you rescued our ancestors when they were being mistreated by wicked enemies. 13 So now, our holy King, look how we are suffering because we have sinned against you! We can do nothing; our enemies are in control. 14 This evil man is taking advantage of our

[i] **1.23** *leaders*: Greek; some ancient translations "priests." [j] **2.7** *Red Sea*: This name comes from the Bible of the early Christians, a translation made into Greek about 200 B.C. It refers to the body of water that the Israelites crossed and was one of the marshes or fresh water lakes near the eastern part of the Nile Delta, where they lived and where the towns of Exodus 13.17—14.9 were located.

1.22 1 Macc 2.39-41; 2 Macc 8.1. **2.1** Ps 105.1-45; 106.1-48; 3 Macc 6.1-15. **2.2** Is 57.15. **2.3** **a**Eph 3.9; Rev 4.11; **b**Ex 18.11; Ps 31.23. **2.4** Gn 6.4-7; 7.22, 23; Ws 14.6, 7; Si 16.7; Ba 3.26-28. **2.5** Gn 19.24; Dt 29.23; 2 P 2.6. **2.6** Ex 9.16; Ro 9.17. **2.7** Ex 14.21-28. **2.8** Ex 15.1-21. **2.9** **a**Ba 3.24, 25; **b**2 Macc 14.35, 36; Acts 17.25; **c**1 K 9.3. **2.10** Dt 4.29, 30; 30.1-6; 1 K 8.33-53. **2.12** 1 S 12.10, 11; Ne 9.28; Ps 22.4, 5; 106.43, 44. **2.14** Jdt 9.8.

distress and is now on his way into the holy
temple built to honor only you. 15 We know
that your home is in the highest heavens
and that no person can ever go there. 16 Yet
you have kindly chosen the people of Israel
as your own and have made this temple the
place where your glory will stay.

17 Please do not punish us for the
wicked things that King Philopator and his
men are doing. If you do, then our enemies
will brag and claim 18 that their strength
destroyed our temple as if it were nothing
but a pagan place of worship.

19 Forgive us for sinning against you and
show us your mercy 20 right now, so that
those who are depressed and hopeless can
sing praises to you. Help us to have peace.

God Punishes Philopator

21-22 The Holy God, who created all things and watches over them, heard Simon's prayer and knocked Philopator down, as easily as wind blows down tall grass. Philopator was paralyzed and unable to speak, because God had punished him for being arrogant and boastful.

23 Philopator's officers and bodyguards were terrified. They panicked and thought he was dying, so they dragged him away from the crowd.

24 Philopator recovered, yet he would not apologize to the Jews, even though he had been severely punished. He left Jerusalem, shouting angry threats at them.

Philopator Mistreats the Jews in Alexandria

25 King Philopator went home to
Alexandria, where he immediately started
mistreating all the Jews. The friends who
drank with him encouraged this, because
they didn't know what it meant to do right.
26 Philopator did more terrible things than
could be counted, but he still wasn't satisfied. He also spread horrible rumors about
the Jews living in the surrounding towns
and villages. Many of his closest friends
agreed to do whatever they could to help
him cause trouble for the Jews 27 and completely disgrace them.

In fact, he set up a memorial stone on the tall tower in the courtyard of the Jewish place of worship, with a sign that read:

> 28 Jews must offer sacrifices to the Greek god Dionysus before they will be allowed to enter this place of worship. The name of every Jew must also be written in a record book to make sure that all taxes are paid and that the Jews remain as slaves. Anyone who refuses to do these things will be arrested and put to death.
>
> 29 The ivy-leaf symbol of the god Dionysus must be tattooed on the skin of all Jews, and their few remaining privileges will be completely stripped away.

30 Philopator did not want people to think he hated everyone, and so he had the following words written on the same sign:

> If any of the Jews decide to start worshiping the god Dionysus, they will be given the full rights of native Alexandrians.

The Jews Respond to Philopator's Threat

31 Some of the Jews in Alexandria did not want to pay the price of remaining faithful to their own religion.[k] So they pledged their loyalty to Philopator and hoped that things would now go better for them.

32 However, most of the Jews would not
abandon their religion and instead bribed
the officials in charge of the record books
to avoid being killed. 33 These faithful Jews
firmly believed that someone would soon
rescue them. They hated the group of rebellious Jews that had chosen to be loyal to
Philopator and considered them enemies,
refusing to have anything to do with them.

[k]2.31 *to pay . . . religion*: One possible meaning for the difficult Greek text.

2.15 **a**1 K 8.27; Is 57.15; 66.1; **b**Pr 30.4; 1 Ti 6.16. **2.18** Is 10.10, 11; 1 Macc 6.7. **2.20** Ps 79.8, 13. **2.21,22** **a**Is 63.16; 4 Macc 5.13; **b**2 Macc 3.22-28; 9.4-10. **2.28** 3 Macc 4.14. **2.29** **a**2 Macc 6.7; **b**Ga 6.17; Rev 7.3; 13.16, 17. **2.31** 3 Macc 3.21. **2.32** 3 Macc 4.19. **2.33** 2 Jn 10, 11.

The Threat against the Jews Living around Alexandria

3 As soon as the evil King Philopator learned what the Jews were doing to avoid being punished, he became terribly angry at the Jews in Alexandria and even more furious at those living in the countryside. He immediately gave orders to bring them together and brutally put every one of them to death.

2 While this was being arranged, some people who wanted to see the Jews suffer started a hateful rumor, saying the Jews were constantly trying to stop others from obeying the king's laws.[l] 3 But in fact, the Jews were always loyal to the king and never caused trouble of any kind. 4 They worshiped their God and obeyed his Law, and they were careful to eat their own food. All this made some people believe the Jews were nothing but troublemakers.

5 Most people respected the Jews and thought they were honest people. 6 Yet there were foreigners who ignored all the good things that the Jews did in Egypt and instead believed every rumor about them. 7 These foreigners gossiped about the Jews and made fun of their worship and their food. They also spread cruel rumors that the Jews opposed the king and disobeyed government leaders.

8 One day, some of the Gentiles who lived in Alexandria saw an angry mob mistreating a group of Jews. These Gentiles were shocked, but because they were ruled by the same cruel leaders, they had no power to do anything except encourage the Jews and tell them things would get better. They knew 9 that the Jews did not deserve to be treated so badly. 10 In fact, some business leaders and friends of the Jews secretly began promising that they would help them in every way possible.

Philopator Orders the Arrest of Every Jew in His Kingdom

11 King Philopator was very proud of what he was accomplishing, and he believed nothing was powerful enough to stop him, including God Most High.

Philopator wrote the following letter:

12 Greetings from King Ptolemy Philopator[m] to my army commanders and soldiers in the surrounding territories. I hope you are well.

13 Our kingdom is strong and secure. 14 In fact, the fighting in Asia was very successful, because the gods were definitely on our side. 15 So we decided to be kind to the people living in the territories of Greater Syria[n] and to treat them as friends instead of enemies. 16 We even gave lots of money to honor their places of worship. Our plan was to do the same for the Jerusalem temple, where those wicked and foolish Jews worship. 17 They said they were glad we were there, but when we asked to enter their holy temple and honor it with expensive offerings, they refused 18 to let us in. They were very arrogant, just as they have always been. We should have punished them right then, but since we are so kind to everyone, we did not harm them. 19 The Jews are the only people who refuse to believe that foreign rulers can be honest and fair. That's why they despise and hate us.

20 When we returned to Egypt after our victories, we treated the Jews very well, just as we treat all foreigners, and we decided to leave them to their own foolish ways. 21 We also told everyone that we would be kind to the Jews, because not only had they signed a treaty with us, but they had often been involved in government matters. We even offered the Jews the opportunity to become full citizens of Alexandria and invited them to participate in our religious ceremonies. 22 But those stubborn Jews were offended by our generous offer, and as always, they chose what is evil 23 and rejected the chance to become Alexandrians. Then

[l]**3.2** *the Jews . . . laws*: One possible meaning for the difficult Greek text. [m]**3.12** *King Ptolemy Philopator*: See the note at 1.1. [n]**3.15** *Greater Syria*: Greek "Coelesyria and Phoenicia."

3.1 3 Macc 4.12. **3.2** Es 3.8. **3.5** Dt 4.5-8; 1 Th 4.12. **3.7** Es 3.8; Gk Est 13.3-5. **3.11** 3 Macc 1.9-15. **3.19** 3 Macc 1.18. **3.21** 3 Macc 2.31; 5.31; 6.25; 7.7, 21.

they completely cut off their own people who chose to accept our offer of
citizenship. They seem to think that
we will soon change our policy toward
them—all of this shows how ignorant
they are.
24 We have concluded that many of
the Jews are simply opposed to us in
every way. And so, to avoid having
these wicked people rebel openly
against us someday, we have come up
with a plan. 25 As soon as you have
read this letter, send us every Jewish
man, woman, and child living in your
territory! Show them no mercy and
bind them in chains to keep them
from escaping. And when they arrive
here, we will be sure they are put to
death as worthless criminals and enemies. 26 Once every Jew is dead, our
kingdom will once again be peaceful.
27 Anyone, whether old or young,
who secretly hides a Jew will be tortured to death, together with every
family member. 28 But any person who
tells us where a Jew is hiding will be
paid two thousand silver coins[o] and
will be honored as a hero.[p] That person will also receive the property of
the criminal who is caught hiding
Jews, 29 and the hiding place will be
completely burned and closed up forever.
30 The above letter was copied and sent
everywhere in Philopator's kingdom.

The Jews Are Brought to Alexandria

4 In every town where Philopator's letter was received, the leaders held
a public feast in honor of the Greek people, who celebrated because they no longer
had to hide their bitter hatred of the
Jews.
2 But the Jews in these towns were extremely frightened and depressed, and they
could not stop mourning and crying about
the king's command to kill them. 3 In the
streets of every city and village in the kingdom, Jews groaned in sorrow 4 as army
commanders prepared to send them to
Alexandria.
The punishment of the Jews was so severe that some of their enemies cried and
felt sorry that they had to face such a horrible death. 5 Old men who could barely walk
were cruelly forced to march out of their
hometowns in straight lines, 6 and young
women who had just been married stopped
singing joyful songs and moaned in sadness. Many of them sprinkled ashes on
their sweet-smelling hair and removed
their wedding veils, and they cried aloud as
the Greek officers severely abused them.[q]
7 The crowds watched as these brides were
dragged in chains to the dock where boats
were waiting to take them to Alexandria.
8 Their new husbands also realized that
they would soon die. They were forced to
wear ropes around their necks instead of
flowers, and they stopped their joyful celebration and moaned in pain. Jewish bride-
grooms were led along the streets with
ropes instead of chains of flowers around
their necks; what should have been a time
for them to celebrate became a time to
mourn, because they knew they were going
to die.
9 The Jews were tied in chains and
dragged on board the boats like wild animals. Some of them were tied to the
benches with ropes around their necks,
while others were held there with chains
around their ankles. 10 They were all
treated like rebels and were put below deck
so they would be in total darkness during
the trip to Alexandria.

The Jews Are Held Prisoner

11 The boats that brought the Jews to
Alexandria docked at Schedia.[r] Then

[o]**3.28** *silver coins*: Drachmas, which weighed between one-fifth and one-fourth of an ounce.
[p]**3.28** *honored as a hero*: One possible meaning for the difficult Greek text. [q]**4.6** *as the Greek officers severely abused them*: Greek; other ancient translations "as if the Greek officers had beaten them with whips." [r]**4.11** *Schedia*: Probably a large, rocky harbor near the city of Alexandria.

3.24 Ex 1.10. **3.25** 3 Macc 4.9; 5.5. **3.30** Gk Est 16.24. **4.2** Es 4.3. **4.6** 1 Macc 1.26, 27; 3 Macc 1.18, 19. **4.9** 3 Macc 3.25; 5.5.

Philopator gave orders to move the Jews at once to the large stadium in front of the city gate. He did this so that everyone leaving or entering Alexandria could see the Jews and make fun of them. Besides that, the Jews would not be close enough to talk to the king's bodyguard, and they would not be in the city itself.[s]

12 Some of the Jews of Alexandria secretly left the city from time to time and went to the stadium, where they mourned the terrible punishment of the Jewish prisoners. Philopator heard about this and was so furious 13 that he commanded his troops to punish every Jew in Alexandria the same way! 14 The name of every Jew was to be written in government records, but this time the Jews would not become slaves—the king planned for them to be violently tortured and then put to death. 15 Although the king's officials worked forty days to register Jews, they still did not finish.

16 Philopator was excited that the Jews were finally going to be punished as he had planned, and he started behaving in odd ways and making no sense when he talked. He held feasts to honor his idols and praised them, even though they could not speak or help anyone. Philopator even dared to curse God Most High!

17 Meanwhile, the officials who were in charge of registering the Jews went to the king and said, "We cannot finish this job. There are simply too many of them. 18 Even if we had every general in Egypt helping us, it would be impossible. There are Jews still being brought to the stadium from their homes in the countryside."

19 Philopator threatened to arrest these officials and accused them of accepting bribes from the Jews. Yet he quickly changed his mind 20 when he saw that the officials had already run out of paper and pens. 21 He did not realize that God All-Powerful had made this happen so that the Jews would be rescued.

Philopator Orders the Death of Every Jew

5 Now King Philopator was more furious than ever, and he sent for Hermon, the man who took care of the elephants that were used in battle. 2 Philopator gave him the following orders: "Tomorrow, give all five hundred elephants large handfuls of frankincense and all the undiluted wine they will drink. Then after the elephants are angry and confused, release them in the stadium so that the Jews will be trampled to death!"

3 After that, the king returned to the feast, where he and his trusted friends[t] and army commanders celebrated the coming death of the Jews. 4 Meanwhile, Hermon left to do what he had been told.

5 The servants at the stadium believed the whole Jewish nation would be wiped out, and they wanted to make sure that none of their prisoners could escape. So that same evening the servants went to the stadium and tied the Jews' hands. 6 All the Gentiles were convinced that nothing could save the Jews now 7 that they couldn't move.

The Jews cried hard and prayed together in loud voices to the Lord God All-Powerful, who rules everything. They called on his mercy, 8 asking him to take revenge on the wicked foreigners and stop their evil plan, and begging him to rescue them from death. 9 God heard their prayers.

God Rescues the Jews

10 Meanwhile, Hermon gave the unsuspecting elephants frankincense and wine until they would eat and drink no more. Then he went to the palace courtyard to tell King Philopator that everything had been done according to plan. 11 But the Lord had caused Philopator to fall into a deep sleep—that was the Lord's way of rescuing the Jews. 12 In fact, Philopator was so

[s]**4.11** *would not be in the city itself*: Or "could not claim they deserved the protection of the city walls." [t]**5.3** *trusted friends*: This was a title that Greek kings gave to special advisors and officials. These friends received gifts, honors, and other privileges.

4.12 3 Macc 3.1. **4.14** 3 Macc 2.28. **4.15** 2 Macc 5.2. **4.16** **a**Ro 1.28; **b**Dn 5.3, 4; **c**3 Macc 1.9. **4.19** 3 Macc 2.32. **5.5** 3 Macc 3.25; 4.9.

sleepy that he wasn't able to give Hermon the orders to carry out the evil plan! 13 The time set aside to kill the Jews had now passed, so they celebrated and praised their holy God for his kindness, then asked him to show the arrogant foreigners his mighty power.

14 By now it was the middle of the afternoon, and the official in charge of the celebration at the palace saw that the guests had started arriving. So he tried to wake Philopator. 15 When he was finally awake, the official told him what had happened and that the feast was ready to begin. 16 Philopator was still confused, and he immediately invited his guests to sit down, then started eating and drinking. 17 He asked everyone there to enjoy themselves and forget about what was going on elsewhere.

18 Some time later, Philopator called for Hermon and demanded to know why the Jews were still alive. 19 Hermon and his officials explained that everything had been done the night before just as the king had ordered. 20 Philopator was angrier than a crazy man[u] and said to Hermon, "The Jews may have been saved today because I overslept, but the first thing tomorrow, make sure the elephants are ready to wipe out those worthless people!"

21 The guests at the feast cheered and approved of the king's plan, then went home. 22 None of them slept well that night; they all lay awake thinking of insults to shout at the doomed Jews.

God Rescues the Jews a Second Time

23 Early the next morning, just after the roosters started crowing, Hermon finished giving the elephants frankincense and wine, and he began leading them down the long passageway that led into the stadium. 24 Along the way, crowds of people were already gathering to see what horrible thing would happen to the Jews at daybreak.

25 The Jews, meanwhile, had lost all hope. They knew they had little time left alive, so they raised their hands to heaven and with loud moaning they cried out to God Most High, begging him to rescue them again.

26 The sun was just coming up as Philopator welcomed his trusted friends[v] to the palace. Hermon finally arrived and told them everything was now ready, and he invited them to go to the stadium. 27 But Philopator suddenly became very confused and had no idea what Hermon was talking about. The king even had to ask Hermon what he was inviting him to do. 28 God, who rules over all things, had made Philopator forget his own plan.

29 Hermon and the king's friends told Philopator that the elephants and the soldiers were ready to kill the Jews, just as the king had ordered. 30 This made the king furious, because God had made him forget everything. Philopator stared at Hermon and the others 31 and said, "I swear that if your parents or children were here, I would let the elephants eat them, instead of eating the Jews. They have done nothing to me and have always been loyal to my ancestors. 32 If it weren't for your usefulness to me and my devotion to you, your lives would have ended long ago."

33 Hermon couldn't believe what he was hearing, and he suddenly became nervous and afraid. 34 The king's friends quietly slipped out one by one and told the crowd of people to go on about their own business.

35 When the Jews heard what the king had said, they knew at once that God had rescued them again. So they praised their Lord God, the king of all rulers.

Philopator Again Tries To Have the Jews Killed

36 King Philopator called his guests back to the celebration and begged them to drink some more. 37 He called for Hermon and shouted in anger, "You worthless fool! How many times do I need to tell you 38 to get those elephants ready? I want the Jews trampled tomorrow!"

[u]**5.20** *a crazy man*: Greek "the cruel Phalaris," a man who was well-known for his anger and violence. He ruled the Greek city of Acragas on the island of Sicily 570-554 B.C. [v]**5.26,44; 6.23** *trusted friends*: See the note at 5.3.

5.25 3 Macc 1.9. **5.28** Pr 21.1. **5.31** 3 Macc 3.21. **5.35** 1 Ti 6.15; Rev 17.14.

39 The officials sitting near Philopator
thought he had gone crazy and asked,
40 "Your Majesty, how long do you think we
will wait for that to happen? We're not
fools! You've said the same thing twice already, and you'll probably change your
mind again. 41 The city of Alexandria is
crowded with people, and they are getting
impatient and angry. We are afraid they
might start a riot."

42 In a violent rage, Philopator forgot
that he had just praised the Jews for their
loyalty. He yelled, "I swear by my own life
that the elephants will trample the Jews to
death immediately! 43 I will attack the
cities of Judea with torches and spears, so
that their cities are nothing but ruins and
the temple in Jerusalem is burned to the
ground. Since I wasn't allowed to enter that
place, then no one will ever offer sacrifices
there again."

44 The king's trusted friends[v] and army
commanders were very excited as they left
and ordered their troops to stand guard at
key places around the city.

The Elephants Are Led into the Stadium

45 Hermon made sure the elephants had
drunk plenty of wine and eaten lots of
frankincense so that they were very angry
and confused. He also tied small swords
and knives to the sides and stomachs of the
elephants. 46 Then he went to the palace
courtyard around dawn and told Philopator
everything was ready. The city was filled
with people crowding their way into the
stadium to watch. 47 Philopator stormed
out of his palace to see the elephants and
to watch the cruel and painful death of the
Jews.

48 The Jews in the stadium saw the dust
that the elephants stirred up as they came
closer to the gate, and they watched as soldiers and other people ran behind the elephants. And when the Jews heard the noisy
crowd, 49 they were convinced that their
terrible wait was over and that they would
soon die. They wept and groaned in sorrow
as they kissed and hugged each other. But
all of them—the parents and the children,
the mothers with babies who were still
nursing—50 all of them remembered that
God had helped them before, so they
bowed down on the ground to pray. Mothers laid aside their babies, 51 while everyone cried out to God in loud voices, asking
him to have mercy on them as they faced
death and for him to show the world that
he is the ruler over everything.

Eleazar Prays

6 Eleazar was a Jewish priest who had
been highly respected for all his long
life, and he was one of the prisoners there
in the stadium. He turned to the leaders
near him and told them to stop praying,
then he prayed the following prayer:

2 God Most High, our All-Powerful
King, you rule your creation with mercy.
3 We are your children, so look down
on us, the descendants of Abraham
and Jacob. Long ago, you chose us to
be your own people, yet now we are dying as foreigners in a strange land.

4 Our ancestors were once slaves
here in Egypt, and the king who ruled
over them proudly boasted about the
strength of his chariots and troops. You
showed the greatness of your mercy for
the people of Israel and drowned that
king and his entire army in the sea.

5 King Sennacherib of Assyria also
boasted about his large number of
troops, and he was able to take control
of every nation in the world. But when
he insulted and attacked Jerusalem,
your holy city, you shattered that cruel
king and showed the world your power.

6 Our Lord, you rescued the three
young men who decided they would
die in a flaming furnace rather than
worship Babylonian idols. Not a hair
on their heads was burned. You cooled
the furnace with dew and burned up
their enemies instead. 7 And you rescued Daniel, who was punished for
lies that others told against him, and

[v]**5.26,44; 6.23** *trusted friends*: See the note at 5.3.

6.1 a2 Macc 6.18; 4 Macc 1.8; 6.5; 7.1; **b**3 Macc 2.1-20. **6.4** Ex 15.1-27. **6.5** 2 K 18.13; 19.35-37. **6.6** Dn 3.21-23, 27; Az/S of 3 H 23-27. **6.7** Dn 6.7, 24.

who was thrown into a pit of lions.
8 When you saw Jonah suffering in the
stomach of a big fish in the ocean, you
rescued him just as he was about to
die, and you let him go safely back to
his family.

9 We are the people of Israel, and
these corrupt foreigners are torturing
and abusing us. You hate pride and
boasting, and you love to show mercy
and protect the weak. So let us see
your power!

10 Though we have turned against
you in our captivity here in Egypt,
please rescue us from our enemies.
Our Lord, if you choose to destroy us,
then do so now in whatever way you
want. 11 That way fools can't praise
their worthless idols when we are
killed or claim that you refused to rescue your own people.

12 You are the Eternal God, and you
are strong and mighty. Protect us and
have mercy on us, because these
wicked people are about to put us to
death as if we were traitors. 13 Make
them tremble with fear at your
strength. We honor you, Lord. You are
always victorious and have the power
to rescue us from death. 14 Hear our
prayers and the prayers of our children, 15 and show all foreigners that
you are on our side and have not rejected us. Keep your promise and be
with us here in this enemy land.

God Appears and Rescues the Jews

16 Just as Eleazar finished praying, King
Philopator arrived at the stadium, along
with the elephants and his proud army.
17 The Jews saw this and began praying so
loudly that the nearby valleys echoed with
their cries, and the noise terrified the soldiers.

18 Just then, the face of God All-Powerful,
the one true God, appeared in the sky! He
opened the gates of heaven, and two angels
came down. Everyone in the stadium
watched in complete horror, yet the Jews
never saw a thing. 19 The two angels fought
the enemy troops and tied them up with
unbreakable chains, leaving them completely shocked and terrified. 20 Philopator
himself began to shake with fear, and he
was no longer puffed-up with pride. 21 Just
then, the elephants turned around and
started trampling the troops who were
marching behind them.

Philopator Orders the Release of the Jews

22 Philopator's anger suddenly turned to
pity, and he cried at the thought of his evil
plan to wipe out these Jews. 23 When he
heard them moaning and saw them bowed
down ready to face death, he screamed in
anger at his own trusted friends:[v]

24 You have rebelled against me and
have acted more cruelly than slave-
masters! I have been kind to you, yet
now you refuse to obey me and instead
are secretly planning things that disgrace my kingdom. 25 You were wrong
and foolish to take these Jews from
their homes and bring them to Alexandria! They have faithfully guarded our
nation for years 26 and are the only
outsiders who have always been kind
to us. I cannot believe that you disobeyed my law and planned to abuse
these brave people. They have suffered
long enough.

27 I order you to release these Jews
and free them from this unfair punishment. Send them back to their own
homes in peace and beg for their forgiveness as they go. 28 These are the
children of God All-Powerful, the living
God of heaven. He has constantly been
a help to our kingdom since the days
of our ancestors, and his children
must be freed!

29 As soon as Philopator had said these
things, the Jews were released, and they
praised their God for rescuing them from
death.

[v] **5.26,44; 6.23** *trusted friends*: See the note at 5.3.

6.8 Jon 2.10. **6.11** Ps 22.8; 115.2; Ws 2.12-20. **6.15** Lv 26.44. **6.18 a**Ws 17.3, 15; 18.14-19; 2 Macc 3.25-29; **b**Dn 10.7; Ac 9.7; 22.6-9; **c**4 Macc 4.10. **6.21** Ps 7.15, 16; 9.15, 16; 35.8; 57.6. **6.25** 3 Macc 3.21. **6.28** Ws 18.13.

The Jews Celebrate

30 Philopator went back to Alexandria and sent for the official who kept track of the kingdom's money. Philopator told him to buy enough wine and food so that the Jews could celebrate seven days. The feast was to be held at the stadium, because that was where they had expected to die.

31 The Jews celebrated with shouts of joy. These same people who had been disgraced and close to death now cheered at the very place where they were supposed to die and be buried. 32 They stopped their songs of mourning and sang praises to God, just like those their ancestors had sung, and they thanked him for saving them with his mighty power. They also arranged for musicians to celebrate by singing joyful songs.[w]

33 Philopator also celebrated at his own feast, and he thanked God for rescuing the Jews. 34 His officials had believed that the Jews would die and be left as food for the birds—now these same officials groaned in disgrace. They had been filled with arrogance and fiery anger as they registered the Jews to die—now they were completely ashamed.

35 While the Jews thanked God and ate at the feast, they listened to the musicians sing their songs of praise. 36 After the Jews had finished celebrating, they decided this rescue should be remembered as a joyful celebration for seven days each year. The festival would not be a time for getting drunk, but a time for them to remember how God had rescued them from death. 37 Then they asked Philopator to let them return to their homes, 38-41 and he agreed.

Philopator's officials had begun registering the Jews on the twenty-fifth day of the month of Pachon[x] and ended on the fourth day of Epeiph[y]—a total of forty days. The Jews were then supposed to have been punished and killed from the fifth day to the seventh day of Epeiph. But the Lord had shown his mercy and rescued every one of them.

So the Jews celebrated seven days, from the eighth day of Epeiph to the fourteenth day, and Philopator himself provided all the wine and food.

Philopator's Letter

Not only did Philopator agree to let the Jews return to their homes, he also wrote a letter about them and sent it to the army commanders in every city of his kingdom. The letter said:

7 Greetings from King Ptolemy Philopator of Egypt[z] to my army commanders and the highest-ranking officials of my kingdom. I hope you are in good health. 2 The people are safe and well, because God Most High has been very kind and has made good things happen to our kingdom.

3 Yet some of my officials here in Alexandria encouraged us to do something evil. They asked us to bring together all the Jews in my kingdom and to severely torture and punish them, as if they were rebels. 4 These wicked officials claimed that the Jews were a constant threat to any nation where they lived, and that our own government would never be completely in control until they were wiped out. 5 The Jews were led to the stadium and treated no better than slaves or traitors. Our own officials were terribly mean and cruel,[a] and they tried their best to put the Jews to death—without asking them a single question!

6 My other officials and I threatened to punish these rebel officials for what they were doing. And then we

[w]**6.32** *by singing joyful songs*: Or "by dancing to joyful songs." [x]**6.38-41** *the twenty-fifth day of the month of Pachon*: A month of the Egyptian calendar; the twenty-fifth day was probably around July 7. [y]**6.38-41** *the fourth day of Epeiph*: A month of the Egyptian calendar; the fourth day was probably around August 15. [z]**7.1** *King Ptolemy Philopator of Egypt*: See the note at 1.1.
[a]**7.5** *terribly mean and cruel*: Greek "meaner than Scythians," a people who were known for their cruelty.

6.32 **a** 1 Ch 16.41, 42; 2 Ch 5.11-13; **b** Ezra 3.11; Ps 136.1-26. **6.34** Gn 40.19; Ez 39.4; 2 Macc 9.15. **6.35** Es 9.18. **6.36** 1 Macc 4.56; 7.48, 49; 13.52; 2 Macc 10.6; 15.36. **7.5** 2 Macc 4.47; 4 Macc 10.7. **7.6** Tob 13.4; Ws 11.10.

rescued the Jews, just as we would rescue any foreigners. We know for certain that the God of heaven defends the Jews and treats them as well as a father treats his own children. 7 The Jews have always been loyal and friendly to us and our ancestors. So we have forgotten every false charge brought against them, 8 and we told them to go back to their own homes. We ordered everyone to leave the Jews alone and not harm them in any way[b] or make fun of them for the awful things that have happened. 9 You know that if we plan to do any evil against the Jews or cause them any trouble at all, we won't have a human ruler as our enemy. God Most High, the ruler over all human powers, will turn against us and avenge them. Good-by.

The Rebellious Jews Are Punished

10 When the faithful Jews read this letter, they did not leave immediately. Instead, they asked Philopator if they could punish the other Jews in Alexandria who had sinned against God and rejected his Law 11 to avoid starving to death.[c] The faithful Jews told Philopator that these rebels would never be truly loyal to him.

12 Philopator agreed and gave the faithful Jews complete authority to wipe out the rebellious Jews who had disobeyed God's commands. 13 The priests and the rest of the Jews clapped and cheered when they heard Philopator's decision, and they shouted praises to God just before they left.

14 As they went through Alexandria, they punished every Jew who had become unacceptable to God by disobeying his commands. These rebels were shamefully put to death where everyone could watch. 15 Three hundred men were killed on that day, and it was remembered as a special day on which many unfaithful Jews were destroyed.

16 After that, the faithful Jews left Alexandria. They wore sweet-smelling flowers around their heads, and they sang beautiful songs of praise in honor of the God their ancestors had worshiped. And as they left, they thanked God for rescuing them, just as he had always rescued the people of Israel.

The Faithful Jews Return Home

17 Some time later, the Jews arrived at Ptolemais,[d] also known as the "City of Roses," where the boats to take them home were docked. The boats waited seven days, because all the Jews agreed 18 to celebrate their rescue once again. They also honored King Philopator, who had provided the supplies they would need until every one of them returned home.

19 The Jews were very thankful when they were safely off the boats, and they decided to remember their travel days as festival days. 20 Before they left for their homes, they found a stone column and carved on it the command to celebrate these sacred festival days each year. Then they dedicated the place as a sacred place for prayer.

Everyone got home safely, because Philopator made sure they were safe all along the way home, whether on land or water. They were very happy that they were free and were no longer abused prisoners. 21 In fact, the enemies of the Jews now respected them and promised to treat them like friends. 22 The people who had taken over the Jews' property were afraid of what God might do, so these people were eager to give it back, according to the government records that told how much the Jews owned.

God Is Praised

God Most High did all the miracles written in this book so that the Jews would be rescued from death. 23 Shout praises forever to the God who saves the people of Israel! Amen.

[b]**7.8** *in any way*: Greek; some ancient translations "anywhere along their way." [c]**7.10,11** *Jews in Alexandria . . . starving to death*: This probably refers to the events of 2.25-31.
[d]**7.17** *Ptolemais*: Possibly a town on the Nile River about twelve miles north of present-day Cairo.
7.7 3 Macc 3.21. **7.10** Dt 13.6-18; Es 8.8-10; Jn 18.30, 31. **7.16** Ba 5.6-9.
7.21 3 Macc 3.21. **7.22** 3 Macc 1.9.

2 ESDRAS

ABOUT THIS BOOK

Esdras is another form of the name Ezra. The book of 2 Esdras is written as a series of seven visions given to Ezra the priest during the rule of King Artaxerxes of Persia, when many of the Jews were forced to live in exile in Media Province of the Persian Empire. The visions were explained by an angel and concerned evil and suffering in the world, God's control of history, the end of time, and God's final judgment.

Second Esdras was probably written in sections by different authors after the Romans destroyed Jerusalem in A.D. 70. Part was written in Hebrew, and part in Greek. But there are no longer any copies of the Hebrew or Greek, and so the *CEV* translates 2 Esdras from Latin.

Second Esdras showed its readers that the problems they faced with the Romans were the same kind that their ancestors had faced with the Babylonians. But the book encouraged the Lord's people to trust him, as he said at the end of the book:

> *So listen to me, my chosen people. The days of misery will soon be here, but I will rescue you. Don't be afraid and don't give up—I am your God, and I will protect you.*
>
> *(16.74, 75)*

A QUICK LOOK AT THIS BOOK

---

1 1-3 I am Ezra the prophet, the son of Seraiah and the grandson of Azariah. I belong to the Levi tribe, because my ancestors go all the way back to Aaron and include Hilkiah, Shallum, Zadok, Ahitub, Ahijah, Phinehas, Eli, Amariah, Azariah, Meraimoth, Arna, Uzzi, Borith, Abishua, Phinehas, and Eleazar son of Aaron.

I wrote this second book[a] during the rule of King Artaxerxes of Persia,[b] while I was a prisoner in Media Province.[c]

---

[a]**1.1-3** *this second book*: Most Latin manuscripts; other Latin manuscripts "this book."
[b]**1.1-3** *King Artaxerxes of Persia*: Either Artaxerxes I (465-425 B.C.) or Artaxerxes II (405-358 B.C.).
[c]**1.1-3** *Media Province*: Part of the Persian Empire.
1.1-3 Ezra 7.1-6; 1 Esd 8.1-3.

The Lord Complains to Ezra

4 One day, the Lord said to me:

5 Ezra, go and remind the people of Israel of the wicked things they have done, and tell them to warn their children and grandchildren how my own people have sinned against me. 6 In fact, they have become more sinful than their ancestors, because they have stopped worshiping me and started offering sacrifices to foreign gods! 7 I rescued the Israelites from Egypt where they were slaves, and now they have made me angry by refusing to listen to my advice.

8 Pull out your hair to show your sorrow, then shout the terrible things that will happen to the Israelites. They deserve to be punished, because they have rebelled against me and refuse to obey my Law. 9 I can't put up with these people any longer—I've done enough for them. 10 I defeated king after king, and I completely destroyed the king of Egypt and his entire army. 11 I conquered every nation that attacked Israel, and even scattered the people of the cities of Tyre and Sidon through the east.[d] I have killed all of Israel's enemies.

The Lord Will Abandon Israel

The Lord said:

12 Ezra, tell these people that I, the Lord, am saying:

13 I am the one who brought you through the Red Sea[e] and who made safe roads where there were no roads at all. I appointed Moses as your leader and Aaron as your priest. 14 I gave you a flaming fire to light your way, and you watched as I did great things for you. But you have still forgotten me. I, the Lord, have spoken.

15 I, the Lord All-Powerful, also sent quails to show that I would take care of you. I provided you with camps where you could be safe, but all you did was complain. 16 I destroyed your enemies, and you refused to celebrate and honor me. All you've ever done is grumble! 17 Have you forgotten how many times I blessed you with good things? And when you were hungry and thirsty in the desert, do you remember that you said to me, 18 "Did you bring us out into the desert to kill us? We would rather have stayed on as slaves in Egypt than to die out here!" 19 I felt sorry for you when I heard your moaning. So I gave you manna, the bread of angels, and you ate it.[f] 20 When you were thirsty, I split open a rock, and all the water you needed flowed out. And I gave you shade trees to protect you from the heat. 21 I divided rich farmland among you, and forced out the Canaanites, the Perizzites, and the Philistines. What else could I have done for you? I, the Lord, have spoken.

22 When you were in the desert at the stream of bitter water, you were thirsty and insulted me. 23 But instead of punishing you with fire for what you said, I threw a piece of wood into the water and made it fit to drink.

24 What should I do with you, people of Israel and Judah? You refused to obey me, and so I will turn to other nations and make them my people. And they will obey my laws. 25 You have abandoned me; now I will abandon you. I won't have pity on you, not even when you beg for it. 26 I will no longer listen to your prayers. Your hands are stained with blood, because you are always eager to murder someone. 27 You haven't just turned against me—you've turned against yourselves! I, the Lord, have spoken.

Israel Will No Longer Be the Lord's People

The Lord said:

28 People of Israel, I, the Lord All-Powerful, have begged you as a parent begs a son or daughter, or as a nursemaid begs a small child. 29 I asked you to be my people, so that I would be your God, and I asked you to be my children, so that I would be

[d]**1.11** *I conquered every nation . . . east*: Most Latin manuscripts; one Latin manuscript "I helped you conquer the town of Bethsaida and even burned down Tyre and Sidon, two cities in the south."
[e]**1.13** *the Red Sea*: Latin "the sea." [f]**1.19** *manna . . . bread . . . you ate it*: Manna was something like a thin wafer (see Exodus 16.1-36).

1.5 Is 58.1. **1.10** Ex 14.28. **1.13** Ex 14.29. **1.14** Ex 13.21, 22. **1.15** Ex 16.13. **1.17,18** Nu 14.3. **1.20** Nu 20.11; Ws 11.4. **1.22,23** Ex 15.22-25.

your father. 30 I gathered you together just as a hen gathers her chicks under her wings. But what should I do with you now? I won't let you be my people any longer. 31 Even when you offer me sacrifices, I will turn away. I have rejected all your religious celebrations, including your New Moon Festivals and the ceremonies where you circumcise men and boys. 32 I sent my servants the prophets to you, but you killed them and cut up their dead bodies. I will make you pay for those murders! I, the Lord, have spoken.

33 Your temple is deserted. Now I, the Lord All-Powerful, will force you out of the land, just as wind blows away straw. 34 Your children will not have children, because like you, they ignored my laws and have done what I hate.

35 A new nation is coming, and I will give your homes to its people. They have not yet heard about me, but they will trust me and obey my laws, even though I have never done great things for them. 36 They have not seen the prophets, yet they follow their teachings that you heard long ago. 37 They will be thankful for what I do, and their children will shout for joy. These people have never seen me, but they will know in their hearts that what I say is true.

38 As for you, Father[g] Ezra,[h] be proud when you see these people coming from the east. 39 I will give them the following leaders: Abraham, Isaac, and Jacob; Hosea, Amos, Micah, Joel, Obadiah, and Jonah; 40 Nahum, Habakkuk, Zephaniah, Haggai, Zechariah, and my messenger Malachi.

Lonely Jerusalem Testifies against God's People

2 The Lord said:

I rescued my people Israel from Egypt where they were slaves, and I sent my servants the prophets to teach them my commands. Yet my people refused to listen to the prophets and ignored everything that I told them.

2 Jerusalem was like a mother who gave birth to my people, and she said to them:

Go away, my children, because I am a lonely widow. 3 I was happy while I raised you, but you sinned against the Lord God even though I told you not to do what was wrong. So you were taken away from me, and I became sad and mournful. 4 I am left completely alone, and there's nothing I can do to help you. So leave me and ask the Lord to have mercy on you.

5 Father Ezra,[h] I, the Lord, want you to be a witness against my people, just as their mother has been, and tell how they rejected my agreement. 6 Cause trouble for them and see that Jerusalem is destroyed, so that my people will never have descendants. 7 My people ignored my agreement with them, and I want them scattered among foreign nations and forgotten forever.

Assyria Is in for Trouble

The Lord said:

8 Assyria, you evil nation, you are in for trouble because you let sinners hide in your land. Do you remember what I did to the towns of Sodom and Gomorrah? 9 Their land is now buried under sulphur and ashes. That is how I punish people who disobey me. I, the Lord All-Powerful have spoken.

Jerusalem Will Be Taken from Israel

10 The Lord said to Ezra:

Tell my new people that I will give them the city of Jerusalem after I take it away from Israel. 11 I will also take from Israel my shining glory and will give my new people the temple where I am worshiped forever. These things will no longer belong to Israel. 12 My people will smell the sweetness of the tree that gives life, and they will no longer work or get tired.

13 Ask,[i] and you will receive. Pray that these things will happen soon, and then get

[g]**1.38** *Father*: Latin; one ancient translation "Brother." [h]**1.38; 2.5** *Father Ezra*: The Lord is probably using this title to show that Ezra was considered the father of the nation.
[i]**2.13** *Ask*: Some Latin manuscripts; other Latin manuscripts "Go."
1.30 Mt 23.37; Lk 13.34. **1.35,36** Ro 10.14-20. **2.2** Is 54.1; Ga 4.26, 27; Ba 4.19.
2.8 Gn 19.24. **2.12** Rev 2.7; 22.2, 14. **2.13** Mt 7.7, 8; 25.34.

ready, because the kingdom has already
been prepared for you. 14 Call the sky and
the earth as witnesses that I have destroyed
wickedness and have created good. I, the
living Lord, have spoken.

Words of Advice for Mother Jerusalem

The Lord said:

15 Jerusalem, I have chosen you to be
Israel's mother. So hold your children close
and keep them safe. Raise them joyfully,
just as a dove raises her young. 16 I, the
Lord, will bring those who have died back to
life and free them from their tombs, because
they are still my people. 17 Mother Jerusalem, don't be afraid—I have chosen you.
18 I will send my servants Isaiah and
Jeremiah to help you. They have already
suggested that I provide you with twelve
trees loaded with all kinds of fruit, 19 twelve
springs that flow with milk and honey, and
seven high mountains covered with roses
and lilies. These will make your children
very happy.

20 Defend widows and protect orphans.
Give to the poor and donate clothes to people who have none. 21 Take care of those
who are injured or weak and don't make
fun of anyone who is lame. Protect the
crippled and help the blind to imagine
what my shining glory looks like. 22 Make
sure that old people and young children are
safe within the city walls. 23 And if you find
a dead body, bury it and mark the grave.
Then I will give you the place of honor
when I raise the dead to life. 24 My people,
you must calm down, because your time of
rest is coming.

25 Be like a good nursemaid—feed your
children well and keep them safe, 26 so that
none of my servants will die. I am holding
you responsible for each of them. 27 Don't
worry when trouble or misery comes, and
when you hear others groan in sadness, be
happy and successful. 28 Foreign nations
will be jealous of you, but you will be safe
29 because I will protect you. I won't let any
of your children end up in the world of the
dead.

30 So be glad, Mother Jerusalem. I, the
Lord, will rescue you and your children.
31 I will show mercy to your children who
are now dead. I will raise them out of their
graves and bring them back to life. 32 Hold
your children close until I come. Tell them
that my mercy and kindness are like
springs of water that never run dry.

Israel Rejects Ezra

Ezra said:

33 I was on Mount Sinai when the Lord
told me to go speak to the people of Israel.
But when I went there, they rejected me
and refused to listen to this message from
the Lord. 34 So I said to the nations that
would listen:

> The end of time is coming soon,
> when your shepherd[j] will come to give
> you rest that will never end. 35 Be
> ready, because you will be blessed with
> the kingdom, and light will shine on
> you forever. 36 Run from the darkness
> of these times and look forward to the
> happiness that is coming to you. And
> as my witness I call on the one who
> saves me. 37 The Lord appointed him,
> so welcome him and give thanks—God
> has invited you into his holy kingdom.
> 38 Stand up and see how many have
> been allowed to share the Lord's ban-
> quet. 39 The Lord gave dazzling white
> robes to those who have died and have
> left this evil world.
>
> 40 Mount Zion,[k] it is time for you to
> accept everyone who has obeyed the
> Law of the Lord and is dressed in
> white. This is the complete number of
> your people. 41 The number of the
> children you wanted is finally known.
> The Lord chose them from the begin-
> ning of time, so pray that the Lord will
> make them completely holy.

Ezra Sees a Large Crowd of People

Ezra said:

42 While I was on Mount Zion, I saw a
crowd of people too large to count, and all
of them were singing praises to the Lord.

[j]**2.34** *your shepherd*: Probably Christ (see the Introduction to this book). [k]**2.40** *Mount Zion*: Probably the Church (see the Introduction to this book).

2.18 Rev 22.2. **2.23** Tb 1.17-19. **2.26** Jn 17.12. **2.42** Rev 7.9.

43 In the middle of this crowd was a young
man who stood much taller than everyone
else, and he was placing a crown on each
person's head. I couldn't believe what I was
seeing, 44 so I asked an angel, "Sir, who are
these people?"

45 The angel answered, "They are the
ones who have died and have been given
everlasting life. They have been completely
loyal to God, and they are now receiving
crowns and palm leaves in honor of their
victory."

46 Then I asked, "Who is the young man
giving them the crowns and the palm
leaves?"

47 The angel replied, "He is the Son of
God, and they worshiped him while they
were still alive."

As I began praising the people for being
brave and honoring the Lord, 48 the angel
said, "Go tell my people about the amazing
things you have seen the Lord God do."

THE FIRST VISION

Ezra Complains to the Lord

3 Thirty years after Jerusalem was destroyed I was in the city of Babylon,
where I was known as Salathiel. As I lay on
my bed, I was very disturbed 2 that
Jerusalem was in complete ruins, while the
Jews of Babylonia were enjoying their
wealth.[l] 3 I was so bothered by my thoughts
that I complained to God Most High 4 and
prayed:

Our Lord God, at your command,
you alone created the world. You told
the dust 5 to form Adam. He was nothing more than a dead body, until you
breathed life into him, and he became
a man. 6 You led him into the garden
that you had planted with your right
hand before you created the earth,
7 and you gave him only one command
to obey.[m] But he disobeyed it, and you
immediately decided that he and his
descendants would not live forever.

Countless nations and tribes, clans
and families descended from Adam,
8 and every one of them did what they
wanted. They ignored your Law and
did what you said was wrong, yet you
did not stop them. 9 But when the
time was right, you flooded the world
and drowned them. 10 Just as Adam
died long ago, everyone else died in
that flood 11 except for one family. You
rescued Noah, his family, and his faithful descendants.

12-13 Soon, a large number of nations covered the earth, and they were
more sinful than their ancestors. But
you chose Abraham to belong to you,
14 and you loved him so much that one
night you told only him what would
happen at the end of time. 15 You
made a solemn agreement and promised Abraham that you would never
abandon his descendants.[n]

You gave him Isaac, and later you
gave Isaac two sons, Jacob and Esau.
16 You chose Jacob as your own, and
his descendants became a powerful
nation. But you rejected Esau. 17 Later,
you rescued Jacob's descendants from
Egypt, and you guided them to Mount
Sinai. 18 There you covered the land
with thick clouds and shook the entire
earth; you made the waters deep in
the earth tremble and caused everyone
to panic. 19 The brightness of your
glory then appeared through the four
fiery gates and also in an earthquake,
in a strong wind, and in hail, so that
you could give your Law to Jacob's descendants, the people of Israel. 20 But
you did not take away their desire to
do evil or make your Law force them
to do right. 21 That's why all of Adam's
descendants sinned and died, just as
Adam died in wickedness. 22 The disease of sin struck everyone, so your
Law and this wickedness became a
part of every person. Soon the bad
forced out the good.

23 Years later, you chose your serv-

[l] **3.2** *while the Jews . . . wealth*: Or "while the Babylonians were enjoying their wealth." [m] **3.7** *one command to obey*: See Genesis 2.15-17. [n] **3.15** *descendants*: See Genesis 15.7-21.

3.1 Ezra 3.2; 5.2; Ne 12.1. **3.7** Ws 1.13, 14; 2.23, 24. **3.8** Gn 6.11, 12. **3.9** Gn 6.9—8.22. **3.20** Si 15.14.

ant David 24 and told him to build a city where you would be worshiped and where sacrifices would be offered to you. 25 The people of Jerusalem did this for a while, but soon they started sinning against you 26 and doing evil, just like their ancestor Adam and his descendants. 27 So you let enemies defeat your own city Jerusalem.

28 It was then that I said to myself, "The Babylonians must be better than we are, or else they couldn't have defeated Jerusalem." 29 But when I got to Babylon, I saw more wickedness than I could have imagined, and for the past thirty years, I have seen a lot of evil people. I was very confused 30 when I saw that you did not punish sinners and attack our enemies, yet you completely wiped out your own people. 31 You didn't even tell us how to make sense of all this. Are the people of Babylonia really that much better than those of Jerusalem? 32 Israel has been the only nation to worship you and accept your agreement. 33 But you have not honored the Israelites or helped them succeed. I have seen many wealthy nations in the world, and none of them obey or worship you. 34 Compare our sins to those of foreigners, and you will see that foreigners are much more wicked. 35 It's true that people have always sinned against you, but Israel has been more loyal to your Law than any other nation on earth. 36 Here and there, you may find one or two people who have completely obeyed your Law, but you will never find an entire nation.

The Angel Uriel Questions Ezra

4 God sent the angel Uriel to me, 2 and Uriel said, "Ezra, you don't understand what happens on earth. Do you really think you could understand what God Most High does?"

3 I said, "Yes sir, I do!"

Uriel continued, "I have been sent to ask you three riddles. 4 If you can answer just one of them correctly, then I will answer your questions about how God treats people, and I will explain why people do evil things."

5 I replied, "I'm ready for you to ask."

Uriel said, "All right. How do you weigh fire? How do you measure a puff of wind? How do you bring back the past?"

6 I answered, "Don't ask me that! No person alive could answer those questions."

7 Uriel replied, "I didn't ask you how many things live at the bottom of the ocean or how many streams run through the middle of the earth or how much water is held in the sky. And I didn't ask you how to leave the world of the dead or enter heaven.[o] 8 Ezra, if I had asked such questions, you would have told me that you had never been to the bottom of the ocean or to the world below or to heaven above. 9 Instead, I asked you about things you already know about, such as fire and wind and the past. But you couldn't answer my questions about those things either. 10 If you don't understand things that have been a part of your life, 11 how do you expect to understand how God Most High works in this world? No one living in this corrupt world will ever be able to understand the holy God."

When I heard Uriel say this, I fell to my knees in agony[p] 12 and cried out, "I wish we humans had never been created! Then we would not have to live in an evil world where we suffer without knowing why."

A Lesson from a Forest and the Sea

13 Uriel said to me:

One time, I went into a forest and heard the trees say 14 to each other, "Let's attack the sea and push it back, so we can have more room for trees."

15 At exactly the same time, the waves of the sea were saying to each other, "Let's flood the forest, so we can have more room."

16 The plan made by the forest was worthless, because a fire burned down every tree. 17 And the plan made by the sea was just as useless, because

[o]4.7 *how to leave the world of the dead or enter heaven*: Most ancient translations; Latin "how to leave heaven." [p]4.11 *agony*: One possible meaning for the difficult Latin text of verse 11.

the sand along the shore blocked its way. 18 Suppose you had to judge the forest and the sea. Which one would be right?

19 I answered, "They both had foolish plans! Trees belong in a forest, while waves belong in the sea."

20 Uriel replied, "Right! So why can't you answer your own questions? 21 Trees belong in the forest, and waves belong in the sea. And so it is with people—they can understand only what happens on earth, and God[q] alone can understand what happens in heaven."

Why Doesn't God Help Us?

22 Then I asked the angel Uriel,

Why was I given the gift of understanding these difficult things?[r] 23 After all, I asked only about what happens on earth, not about what goes on in heaven. I want to know why God allowed foreign nations to defeat and disgrace Israel. Why has he let the people he loves be controlled by wicked nations? Why do people ignore the Law he gave our ancestors? 24 Our lives seem no longer than a breath.[s] Why do we die as suddenly as locusts? We do not deserve to receive God's mercy, 25 but why doesn't God help us for the sake of his own reputation? These are the questions I want answered.

26 Uriel replied:

Even if you live a long time, you will still be amazed at what happens—the end of time will come suddenly! 27 It must come, because the present days are filled with sadness and evil, and faithful people will never be blessed as God has promised until these days end. 28 You asked me about this evil world. I tell you that evil has already been planted, but it hasn't been harvested. 29 Yet it must be harvested soon, so that the world can end and goodness can be planted in its place. 30 Long ago, a small seed of evil was planted in Adam's heart, and since then everyone has constantly sinned against God. Yet that seed will produce even more wickedness before it is harvested. 31 This one small seed has produced so much sin and hatred, 32 that at the end of time, a huge threshing place will be needed to trample all those heads of evil grain!

When Will the End of Time Come?

33 I then asked the angel Uriel, "When will the end of time come? How long must we wait before these things happen? Why are our lives so short and miserable?"

34 He answered:

Don't try to rush what God Most High has planned! You are concerned only about yourself, yet God is concerned about everyone.[t] 35 The souls waiting for the end of time are anxious to receive their reward for being faithful to God, and they have also asked how long they would have to wait. 36 The chief angel Jeremiel told them that when the number of faithful people is complete, their reward will come. He said that God has measured this age; 37 he has counted its years and days and will not let them end until everything happens just as he has planned.

38 "But sir," I said, "those of us who are alive are terrible sinners! 39 Are the souls of the faithful having to wait to be rewarded, just because we are so evil?"

40 He replied, "Can a woman stop her baby from being born after being pregnant for nine months?"

41 "No, sir," I answered. "She cannot."

Then he said, "The place where the souls are waiting in the world below is like a mother's womb. 42 That place is in a hurry to give back these souls that have been there since the beginning of time, just as a pregnant woman is in a hurry to end the pain of childbirth. 43 When these souls

[q]**4.21** *God*: Or "those in heaven." [r]**4.22** *things*: One possible meaning for the difficult Latin text of verse 22. [s]**4.24** *a breath*: Most ancient translations, Latin "fear." [t]**4.34** *everyone*: One possible meaning for the difficult Latin text of verse 34.

4.21 Is 55.8, 9; Jn 3.31; 1 Co 2.14. **4.30** 2 Esd 3.20. **4.36** 2 Esd 2.41; Rev 6.11.

leave the world below, then all your questions will be answered."

Ezra Sees a Vision of Fire and Water

44 I said to the angel Uriel, "If you think
I can understand and am worthy to know,
45 would you please tell me one more
thing? Is the time we have yet to wait for
the end of time longer than the time we
have already waited? 46 I know how long
we've waited in the past, but I don't know
about the future."
47 Uriel replied, "Stand at my right side,
and I will show you a vision and explain
what it means."
48 As I stood there, I saw a fiery furnace
move past me with a trail of smoke following behind. 49 Then I saw a rain cloud float
by, and it brought a heavy rainstorm. And
soon the downpour was just a sprinkle of
rain.
50 Uriel said, "I want you to think about
what you just saw. The downpour was heavier than the sprinkle, and the fire was hotter
than the smoke. The time you must wait for
the end of time is like the sprinkle and the
smoke—the time that has already passed
will be much longer than the time to wait."
51 I asked, "Will I live to see the end of
time? Who will be alive when it comes?"
52 He answered, "I cannot tell you how
long you will live; I don't know. I can only
tell you about some of the signs that show
the end of time is coming."

The Signs of the End of Time

Uriel the angel said to Ezra:

5 I will tell you the signs that show the
end of time is coming soon.
Everyone on earth will be completely
confused.[u] Truth will be impossible to find,
and no one will have the faith to survive.
2 People will become more wicked than
you've ever seen or heard. 3 The nation
now ruling the world will be an empty
wasteland. 4 And if God Most High lets you
live long enough, you will later[v] see that
nation completely confused.
The sun will shine during the night, and
the moon will shine during the day. 5 Blood
will drip from trees while rocks cry out. No
one will understand why the planets and
stars are different from usual.[w] 6 A ruler no
person on earth wants will begin to rule,
and all birds will fly away. 7 The Dead Sea
will even produce fish! People everywhere
will hear an unknown voice at night, 8 and
riots will break out everywhere on earth.
Fires will suddenly start in different places,
and wild animals will freely leave the
forests. Women who are having their period
will give birth to monsters. 9 Fresh water
will become salty, and friends will violently
attack each other.
Then understanding and wisdom will go
into hiding. 10 Everyone will search for wisdom, but never find it. Wickedness will be
so common that people everywhere will do
only what is evil.
11 Nations will ask one another, "Has
anyone honest and good ever come to your
land?" But the answer will certainly
be "No!" 12 This will be a time when people get nothing they hope for and receive
nothing for their hard work.
13 That is all I can tell about the signs of
the end of time. Yet if you pray again and
cry as you have done and go without eating
for seven days, then you will learn even
more things.

Ezra Wakes Up

14 I woke up, and every part of my body
was trembling in fear. I was in so much
agony that I almost fainted. 15 But the angel Uriel who had spoken to me reached
down and helped me to my feet.
16 The next night, a leader named
Phaltiel came to me and said, "Where have
you been? And why do you look sad? 17 You
have been appointed the ruler of the Israelites living in exile. 18 Get up and eat
something! Don't abandon us like a shepherd who lets vicious wolves attack his
sheep."
19 I said to him, "Leave me alone for

[u] **5.1** *confused*: One possible meaning for the difficult Latin text. [v] **5.4** *later*: Latin "after the third." [w] **5.5** *why the planets and stars are different from usual*: One possible meaning for the difficult Latin text.

4.51—5.19 Mt 24.4-31; Mk 13.5-27; Lk 21.8-28. **5.2** Mt 24.12. **5.5** Hb 2.11.

seven days. Then you can come back." So
he left.

THE SECOND VISION

Ezra Again Complains to God

20 I cried and went without eating for
the next seven days, just as the angel Uriel
had commanded.[x] 21 After that, I became
very upset and troubled, just like before.[y]
22 But soon I could think better, and once
again I prayed to God Most High. 23 I said:

Our Lord God, you have chosen
this vine from all the trees in the
world, 24 and you have chosen this
small nation[z] from all those on earth.
You have picked this one lily from all
the flowers, 25 and you have selected
one river from all the water in the
oceans. Out of all the cities on earth,
you have chosen to call only Jerusalem
your own, 26 and from all the birds that
have lived, you have chosen this dove,
and from all the animals, this one
sheep. 27 You have chosen us to be
your special people from all the people
on earth, and you have given us your
Law that is respected by everyone
everywhere.

28 So why have you disgraced[a] your
own people more than all others, by
letting enemy nations defeat and scatter us across the earth? 29 We have
trusted your solemn promises, yet foreigners who reject you have trampled
and beaten us. 30 If you hate us so
much and want us to be punished,
then do it yourself!

The Angel Uriel Answers Ezra

31 After I had finished complaining to
God, he sent the angel Uriel to answer me.
32 Uriel said, "Listen carefully, and I will
tell you more things."

33 I replied, "Please speak, sir."

Then he said, "You seem very upset about
the people of Israel. Do you think you love
them more than God their Creator does?"

34 "No, sir," I answered. "I said these
things because I am worried and constantly
distressed. I don't understand why God
Most High is treating Israel so terribly."

35 Uriel said, "You cannot understand."

I answered, "If not, then I should have
died before I was born. At least I would not
have seen my people suffer so long."

36 He replied, "Tell me how many people will be born in the future. Collect all
the raindrops in one place and make dried
flowers bloom again. 37 Open the rooms
where the wind waits to blow and describe
what a sound looks like. If you can do these
five things, then I will tell you why the people of Israel are suffering."

38 I said, "Sir, I am merely your servant.
No one can do these things except God. 39 I
don't know about such things, so I cannot
answer you."

40 Uriel replied, "Just as you cannot do
even one of these things I asked, you can
never understand why God punishes the
people of Israel or why he promised to love
them forever."

Everyone Will Be Brought Back to Life

41 I asked the Lord God, "I know you
care about the people who are alive at the
end of time. But what about those who
have already died or those of us who are
alive now or those who will be born after
us? Will you care about those as well?"

42 The Lord answered, "My concern for
people at the end of time is like a circle[b]—
it has no beginning and no end. I will care
about all people, whether they arrive first
or last."

43 I said, "You could have shown that
concern sooner if you had created all
people to live at the same time."

44 He replied, "The world and its people
can only be created when I choose. Besides, if everyone had lived at the same
time, there would be no room for all of
them."

45 Then I said, "But you told me that

[x] **5.20** *commanded*: See verse 13. [y] **5.21** *upset and troubled . . . before*: See 3.3.
[z] **5.24** *nation*: One ancient translation; Latin "pit." [a] **5.28** *disgraced*: Most ancient translations; Latin "prepared." [b] **5.42** *circle*: Or "crown."
5.35 Job 3.11.

someday you will bring back to life at the
same time everyone who has ever lived. If
the world could hold everybody then, why
can't it hold everybody now?"
46 The Lord asked, "Could a woman give
birth to ten children at the exact same
time?"
47 "No," I answered. "Only one child
can be born at a time."
48 He said, "That's the way it is with the
world. I have made it so that a certain
number of people live here at a time.
49 Just as neither a very young girl nor an
old woman can give birth, so the world can
be filled with people only when I choose."
50 Then I said, "Since you mentioned a
young girl and an old woman, I want to ask
another question. Is the world young
or old?"
51 The Lord answered:
Find a mother who has many children 52 and ask her why her older children are bigger than her younger ones.
53 She will tell you that the children
born when she was younger are
healthier than those born when she
was older. 54 You are smaller than the
people who lived long ago, 55 and those
who will live after you will be even
smaller. That's because this world is
getting older and isn't as strong as it
used to be.

God Is in Charge of the End of Time

56 I said to the Lord, "If you will, please
tell me who will judge the world at the end
of time."
6 The Lord answered:
I decided that when I created the
world—before the doors of the world
were put in place or the wind started
to blow; 2 before thunder roared or
lightning flashed; before the foundations of heaven[c] were laid; 3 before
beautiful flowers bloomed or stars
moved across the sky or crowds of angels gathered together; 4 before the sky
and heaven were set in the air and
given names; before I chose Mount
Zion as my own or 5 years were
counted; before the evil plans of sinners were destroyed or people who
faithfully worshiped me were counted
as mine. 6 Before all these things happened, I made the decision that since I
alone had created the world and everything in it, I alone would bring it to
an end.
7 I asked, "How much time will pass between the end of the present age and the
beginning of the next?"
8 The Lord answered:
The same amount of time that
passed between Abraham and his son
Isaac, who was the father of the twins
Jacob and Esau. Esau was born first,
but Jacob was holding onto Esau's heel
as they were born. 9-10 Esau's heel is
like the end of this present age, and Jacob's hand is like the beginning of the
next age. There's no space in between
the two, so don't look for any.

More Signs of the End of Time

11 I said to Uriel the angel,[d] "Sir, would
you please 12 show me more signs of the
end of time? You showed me only some of
them the other night."[e]
13 Uriel[f] answered, "Stand up, and you
will hear a loud voice. 14 Don't be afraid if
the place where you are standing begins to
shake back and forth 15 while the voice is
speaking. The message will be about the
end of time, and the foundations of the
earth will know 16 that the message is
about them. They will tremble in fear because they know they will be changed
when the end comes."
17 So I stood up and listened. I heard a
voice as loud as a roaring ocean, 18 and it
said:
Soon I will come to judge all people
on earth 19 and punish everyone who
does evil. Then Jerusalem's time of
disgrace will end, 20 and the present
age will begin to disappear, because I

[c]**6.2** *heaven*: Latin "Paradise." [d]**6.11** *I said to Uriel the angel*: Latin "I said." [e]**6.12** *the other night*: See 5.1-13. [f]**6.13** *Uriel*: Latin "He."

5.52 Gn 6.4; Nu 13.33. **6.17** Rev 1.15; 14.2; 19.6. **6.20** Dn 7.10; 12.1; Ml 3.16; Rev 20.12.

will bring it to a close. I will show the
following signs: the books which list
the names of my people will be opened
in the sky where everyone can see
them. 21 Children a year old will begin
speaking, and pregnant women will
give birth after only three or four
months, yet the babies will live and play.
22 Fields where seeds have been planted
will be bare, and barns that were full
will be empty. 23 A trumpet will be blown,
and everyone will be terrified. 24 Friends
will suddenly become enemies. The
earth and all living things will tremble
with fear. Rivers and springs will stop
flowing for three hours.
25 I will rescue everyone who survives these disasters, and they will live
to see the end of this world. 26 They
will meet those who were taken up
into heaven without dying.[g] The hearts
of everyone on earth will be changed,
27 so that evil will disappear. 28 Faithfulness will increase and overcome
wickedness, and truth will be seen
after being hidden for so long.
29 While this voice was speaking, I felt
the ground under me begin shaking back
and forth.[h]
30 Then Uriel said to me:
I have come tonight to show you
these things.[i] 31 But if you pray and go
without eating for seven more days, I
will show you even greater things,
32 because God Most High has heard
your prayer. Our mighty God has
watched you obey and do right since
you were young. 33 And so he sent me
to show these things and to tell you to
be brave and trust him to keep you
safe. 34 If you waste time worrying and
asking about the past, then you will be
in a rush when the end comes."

THE THIRD VISION

How Long Will Foreign Nations Rule Over Us?

35 Some time later, I cried and went without eating for seven more days, just as I
had done before,[j] and so my three weeks of
sorrow were complete.[k] 36 Then on the very
next night,[l] I once again became upset and
started praying to God Most High. 37 I was
very depressed and nervous, 38 but I prayed:
Our Lord, on the first day of creation, you said, "I command the heavens and the earth[m] to appear." And
they did, just as you commanded.
39 There was a wind blowing, while a
silent darkness covered everything. No
human voice could be heard. 40 Then
you commanded bright light to shine
from the storehouse of light, so that
your creation could be seen.
41 On the second day, you created
the spirit of the dome and commanded
it to separate the water above from the
water below.
42 On the third day, you commanded the water to come together
and cover one-seventh of the world.
You dried up the other six parts to
make them useful for planting and
harvesting crops. 43 As soon as you
commanded these things, they happened. 44 All kinds of fruits and vegetables suddenly appeared, each of them
different and tasty. Colorful, sweet-
smelling flowers began blooming. All of
this happened on the third day.
45 On the fourth day, you commanded the sun, the moon, and the
stars to shine in the sky. 46 And you
gave them orders to serve the humans
you would soon make.
47 On the fifth day, you commanded

[g]**6.26** *those who were taken up into heaven without dying*: Such as Enoch (see Genesis 5.24) and Elijah (see 2 Kings 2.11, 12). [h]**6.29** *forth*: One possible meaning for the difficult Latin text of verse 29. [i]**6.30** *things*: One possible meaning for the difficult Latin text of verse 30.
[j]**6.35** *just as I had done before*: See 5.20. [k]**6.35** *my three weeks of sorrow were complete*: Only two weeks were mentioned in this book. Perhaps the author is remembering another seven-day period that is no longer part of the book. Three weeks of sorrow is a normal period of time (see Daniel 10.2, 3). [l]**6.36** *the very next night*: Latin, "the eighth night." [m]**6.38** *the heavens and the earth*: The entire universe.

6.23 1 Co 15.51, 52; 1 Th 4.16. **6.26** Gn 5.23, 24; 2 K 2.11, 12; Si 44.16; Ml 4.5, 6.
6.38 Ps 33.6; He 11.3; 2 P 3.5.

the ocean to be filled with birds, fishes, and other living creatures. And it happened. 48 The water that had no life of its own produced living creatures, just as you commanded, so that nations would be amazed at your creation.

49 You named two of these living creatures: one was Behemoth, and the other was Leviathan. 50 You put them in different places, because the ocean could not hold them both. 51 Behemoth was sent to live on dry land, in an area covered with thousands of mountains. 52 Leviathan was allowed to live in the ocean. You created them both, so that the people you choose can eat them at the time you have decided.

53 On the sixth day, you commanded the earth to give life to tame animals, wild animals, and reptiles. 54 Then you created Adam and made him the ruler over everything you had created. We, your chosen people, are his descendants.

55 I have told you this, our Lord, because you said that you created the world for our sake alone.[n] 56 And you said that the rest of the nations on earth, even though they are also descendants of Adam, are as worthless as spit. They are no more important to you than a single drop of water in a bucket. 57 But these nations are the ones that have defeated us and are ruling over us. 58 You have called us your first-born child, and we are the only people you have chosen as your own. You honor and love us, although you allowed enemy nations to conquer us. 59 If this world was created for us, then how long must we wait before we can take control?

The Angel Uriel Answers Ezra

7 After I had finished praying, God sent the angel Uriel to me, just as he had done twice before.[o] 2 Uriel said, "Stand up, Ezra, and listen to what I have to say."

3 I said, "Sir, I'm ready to listen."

Uriel replied:

Suppose there is a very large and deep ocean, 4 but the only way into the ocean is through a narrow opening no wider than a stream. 5 Anyone who wants to visit this ocean or take control of it will first have to go through this narrow place. 6 Now suppose that in a large valley, there is a city filled with good things. 7 But the gate of the city is on a narrow and steep place, with fire on the right side and deep water on the left. 8 The path to the gate is so narrow that only one person can walk on it at a time. 9 If someone inherited this city, the only way to get there would be to walk along this dangerous path.

10 I said, "You're right, sir."

Then Uriel said:

That's how it is with the people of Israel. 11 God created this world for them, but when Adam disobeyed him, God punished the entire world. 12 So the ways into this world became narrow and dangerous. There are only a few paths, and they are difficult to walk on and are filled with evil.[p] 13 But the ways into the better world to come are wide and safe, and they lead to everlasting life. 14 People must pass through the difficult and evil ways of this life before they receive the good things waiting for them in the world to come. 15 Now I ask you, Ezra, why are you so upset and worried that you will someday die? 16 Stop thinking about the present and think instead about the age to come."

17 I answered, "Sir, the Lord God said in his Law that people who do right will be blessed with good things, and that people who do evil will die. 18 I understand that good people can suffer difficulties along this narrow way, because they know they will reach the better world. But those who

[n]**6.55** *you said that you created the world for our sake alone*: This idea is not found in the Old Testament. It is a later Jewish interpretation of such verses as Exodus 4.22; Deuteronomy 10.15, and 14.2. [o]**7.1** *God sent the angel Uriel . . . twice before*: See 4.1 and 5.31. [p]**7.12** *There are only a few . . . with evil*: One possible meaning for the difficult Latin text.

6.49-52 Job 7.12; Ps 74.12-15. **7.11** Ro 5.18-20. **7.15,16** 2 Co 4.18.

do evil will suffer the same difficulties and never see any good things."

19 Uriel replied:

Do you think you could treat people fairer than God Most High treats them or understand more than he does? 20 Many of today's evil people would be better off to die than to disobey the Law that God has given them. 21 God clearly told everyone how he wants them to live so they could avoid being punished. 22 But a lot of them refused to listen and disobeyed him. They were fools 23 and did wicked and selfish things. They acted as if God Most High did not exist, and they decided to abandon his ways. 24 They rejected his Law and his solemn promises, and they ignored everything he commanded. 25 Ezra, that's why evil people will receive nothing, and good people will receive much.

The Final Judgment

God said to Ezra:

26 Very soon, you will see all the signs I have told you about. The city[q] and the land that are now hidden will appear, 27 and everyone who survives the disasters I have warned you about will see me do amazing things. 28 I have chosen my Son to be my special servant,[r] and very soon he and others with him will appear, bringing four hundred years of peace to the survivors. 29 After those years of peace, he and every person left alive will die, 30 and the world will be completely empty for seven days, just as it was at the beginning of time.

31 After those seven days, the present evil age will die forever, and a new age will begin. 32 Everyone who is dead and buried will rise from death, and the rooms in the world of the dead will be opened. 33 Then I, God Most High, will start judging all people. I will no longer be kind and gentle to sinners, 34 because I will judge with truth and justice. 35 Everything, good or bad, that people have done will be known, and I will quickly reward or punish them. 36 On one side will be the fiery world of the dead where some are punished forever, and on the other side will be the happy place of eternal blessing and rest.

37 Then I, God Most High, will turn to the nations that have been brought back to life and say, "Listen to me! I am the one you have ignored and disobeyed, and it is my Law you have rejected. 38 Look around. There is happiness and rest on one side, and misery and torment on the other."

I will say those things on the day of final judgment. 39 That will be a day when the sun and moon and stars will not shine. 40 There will be no clouds or thunder and lightning or wind or water or air. Darkness will cover everything, so that evenings and mornings will disappear, 41 and spring, summer, and winter will stop. There will be no heat or cold, no frost or hail, rain or dew. 42 The light of day and the dark of night will be gone—no sunrise, no noon, no sunset. The only light will be the dazzling brightness of my presence, and everyone will see and follow this light 43 that will shine for seven years.

44 Ezra, you are the only one who knows what I have planned for the day of final judgment.

Only A Few People Will Be Saved

45 I said:

Lord God, what I've already said is true—the people who are alive now and can obey your Law are very fortunate. 46 But no one is perfect. Every person alive has sinned against you. So I will keep praying for those people, 47 because now I realize that the world to come will bring happiness to only a few and misery to many. 48 The wickedness in us has become strong enough to make us disobey your Law. We are ruined and hopeless, and we face a terrible death. This wickedness has destroyed almost everyone who has lived.

49 God said, "Listen, Ezra, and I will tell you again exactly what will happen. 50 I

[q] 7.26 *city*: Some ancient translations; Latin "bride." [r] 7.28 *I have chosen . . . servant*: Latin "My Son the Messiah."

7.32 Dn 12.2. **7.36** Lk 16.23, 24; Rev 9.2.

created two worlds[s] instead of just one,
51 and you're right that only a few people
are completely good, while most are evil.
But think about this: 52 If you had a few
precious stones, would you add pieces of
lead and clay to have more?"[t]
53 I answered, "No one would do that."
54 Then God replied, "That's not all.
Humbly ask the earth 55 how much gold,
silver, bronze, iron, lead, and clay it produces. 56 It will tell you that there is more
silver than gold, more bronze than silver,
more iron than bronze, more lead than
iron, and more clay than lead. 57 Then you
decide which ones are more valuable—
those that are common or those that are
rare."
58 I said, "Lord God, common things are
cheap, while the rare ones are expensive."
59 God replied:
That's right. Now think carefully
about what you have said. Whoever
has something that is rare is happier
than someone who has something that
is plentiful. 60 That's how it is with the
final judgment[u] I have planned. I will
celebrate over the few people who will
be saved, because they are the ones
who have faithfully worshiped me and
told others about me. 61 I won't be sad
about the crowds of people who will
die. They are like fog, and they disappear as quickly as smoke or a flame
that blazes up, and then goes out.

Ezra Mourns the Human Mind

62 I said to the earth:
It's your fault that people were
born! After all, every living thing, including the human mind, came from
your dust. 63 It would have been better
if you had never been born, then we
would not have minds to think with.
64 But as we grow older, our minds give
us the ability to think, and they cause
us pain, because we know that we will
someday die! 65 We mourn in sadness
while cattle and wild animals are
happy, 66 not knowing anything about
what happens after death, whether
good or bad. They don't have to face a
final judgment, and so they are much
better off than we are. 67 We will someday survive the horrors of death, but
for now we must suffer the torture of
life. 68 Everyone who has ever lived
has been evil and guilty of sinning
against God. 69 It would be much better for us if God did not judge us at
death.
70 The angel Uriel answered:
When God Most High was creating
the world and Adam and his descendants, God first planned how the final
judgment would take place. 71 Think
carefully about what you have just
said. The mind gives people the ability
to think, 72 and they suffer for doing
what they know is wrong. People have
God's Law, but refuse to obey it, 73 and
so they will have no excuse at the final
judgment. 74 God Most High has always been very patient with people—
not for their sake, but for the sake of
the world to come.

What Happens After We Die?

75 I then said, "Sir, please answer another question for me. What happens to us
after we give up our soul and die? Will God
keep us safe until the new world is created? Or will our torture begin right away?"
76 The angel answered:
I will answer those questions for
you. But don't include yourself among
those who will be tortured. They have
rejected God and religion, 77 while you
have always done what is right. You
have been loyal to God Most High,
though you won't see the record of
these things until the end of time.
78 And now, I will tell you what happens at death. God Most High decides
the exact time you will die, and when
that time comes, your soul leaves the
body and returns to God, the maker of
life. The soul will then immediately
praise God's glory.

[s] **7.50** *two worlds*: The present world and the world to come. [t] **7.52** *would . . . more*: One possible meaning for the difficult Latin text. [u] **7.60** *final judgment*: Most ancient translations; Latin "creation."

79 But it's not that way for people
who have completely ignored God and
hated those who worshiped him.
80 The souls of these rebellious people
won't have a place to rest, but will
wander forever, miserable and distressed. Seven things will make them
sad. 81 First, they have rejected the
Law of God Most High. 82 Second,
they can no longer change their minds
and decide to worship God and have a
good life. 83 Third, they will see the
blessings ready for those who believe
in the promise of God. 84 Fourth, they
must think about the suffering they
will face at the end of time. 85 Fifth,
they will see the safe homes of the
faithful and the angels quietly guarding them. 86 Sixth, they will realize
that they will soon be tortured. 87 And
the seventh thing will trouble them the
most: They will see the bright glory of
God Most High and will be filled with
shame and guilt. They will tremble in
fear because the God they sinned
against in life will judge them at the
end of time.

88 Now let me explain what will
happen at death to those who faithfully obeyed God 89 and his Law during
their lives, even when it was dangerous to do so. 90 Listen to their reward.
91 They will celebrate when they see
the brightness of God's glory, and God
will receive them into heaven. Then
they will have eternal happiness for
seven reasons. 92 First, because they
were able to defeat the evil that was a
part of them and weren't tempted to
follow death instead of life. 93 Second,
because they will see how confused
the souls of the wicked are as they
wander around and what a terrible
punishment is waiting for them at the
end of time. 94 Third, because they will
hear that God their Creator will tell
how faithfully they obeyed his Law
during their lives. 95 Fourth, because
they will know that at the end of time
they will be brought together in one
place and blessed with peace, while
angels guard them in silence. 96 Fifth,
because they will see both the cruel,
harsh world they have escaped and the
comfortable, future world they will
soon inherit forever. 97 Sixth, because
they will see how their faces will always shine as brightly as the sun or the
stars. 98 Seventh and best of all, because they will celebrate without fear
or shame as they hurry to meet God,
the one they obeyed during their lives
and who will reward them in heaven.
99 So now you know the rewards waiting for the people who faithfully worshiped God and the punishments waiting for those who refused to obey him.
These things will happen exactly as I
have said.[v]

100 Then I asked, "When the souls of
the faithful people leave their bodies, will
they have time to see what you have just
described?"

101 He answered, "They will have seven
days to see these things, and then they will
be brought together to the place they will
stay."

No Hope for the Wicked at the Final Judgment

102 I asked:

Would you please answer another
question for me? On the day of final
judgment, will the faithful people of
God Most High be able to ask him to
show mercy to the wicked? 103 For example, will fathers be able to pray for
their children, and children pray for
their parents or brothers and sisters?
What about close relatives or friends
who pray for each other?

104 The angel Uriel said:

Since you are deserving, I will answer your questions. The final judgment will be a hard time, because the
truth about every person will be told.
Parents would never let their child get
sick or go to sleep or eat or get well in
their place. And children would never
let their parents do that. In fact, slave

[v]**7.99** *These things . . . said*: One possible meaning for the difficult Latin text.

7.97 Dn 12.3; Mt 13.43. **7.98** Mt 5.8; He 12.14; 1 Jn 3.2; Rev 22.4.

owners would not ask their slaves to do that, and friends would not ask their friends. If all this is true for the present time, [105] it will certainly be true at the final judgment. No one will be able to pray for another—all people will receive the reward or punishment they deserve.

106 I replied:

If it's true that no person can pray for another, then why was Abraham able to pray for the people of Sodom?[w] Moses prayed for our own ancestors who sinned in the desert,[x] [107] and Joshua prayed for the people of Israel while Achan was alive.[y] [108] During Saul's days as king,[z] Samuel prayed for our people,[a] just as David did for those who were dying from a horrible disease,[b] and Solomon did when he dedicated the temple to God.[c] [109] The prophet Elijah prayed that rain would come and that a dead person would come back to life,[d] [110] and King Hezekiah of Judah prayed during the rule of King Sennacherib of Assyria.[e] Many others have prayed similar prayers. [111] So at the final judgment why won't God's faithful people be able to pray for the wicked, who are even more evil than their ancestors?

112 Uriel answered:

The world you now live in isn't the end. God's bright glory cannot always be seen here. That's why God's most faithful people could pray for those who are weak. [113] But the final judgment will be the end of this present world and will begin the world that will last forever. Then all wickedness will disappear, [114] while selfishness will be wiped out. Faith and right living and truth will take over. [115] So at the final judgment, no one will be able to show mercy to someone guilty of sinning against God, and no one will be able to harm someone who has been faithful.

People Have No Hope

116 I said to Uriel the angel:

I still believe what I told you before—it would have been much better if the world had not produced Adam, or at least if it had not given him the ability to sin. [117] What good is it for us to be sad our entire lives and then have only punishment to face after we die? [118] When Adam sinned, he caused misery not only for himself, but for all of us who are his descendants. [119] So what if we are promised a life that never ends—the sins we have committed will bring only death. [120] We have completely failed and are hopeless, with no chance of eternal life. [121] God has promised us safe homes in heaven, yet our lives are filled with wickedness [122] and sin, even though God Most High has promised to help us be faithful. [123] He has shown us how wonderful heaven will be, where good things will never spoil, and we will have everything we need. But we won't ever get there [124] because our lives here on earth are sinful. [125] You said that the faces of good people will shine brighter than the stars. What good is that for us, whose faces will be blacker than night? [126] We have sinned each day we have lived, not knowing that we will suffer when we die.

127 Uriel replied:

Everyone on earth must struggle to do what is right. [128] If they are defeated by evil, they will suffer, just as

[w]**7.106** *Abraham . . . Sodom*: See Genesis 18.16-33. [x]**7.106** *Moses . . . desert*: See Exodus 32.1-14. [y]**7.107** *Joshua . . . alive*: See Joshua 7.1-18. [z]**7.108** *During Saul's days as king*: Some ancient translations; these words are not in the Latin translation. [a]**7.108** *During Saul's . . . Samuel . . . our people*: See 1 Samuel 7.7-14. [b]**7.108** *David . . . horrible disease*: See 2 Samuel 24.10-17. [c]**7.108** *Solomon . . . temple to God*: See 1 Kings 8.22-53.
[d]**7.109** *Elijah prayed that rain . . . dead person . . . life*: See 1 Kings 18.41-46; 17.17-24.
[e]**7.110** *King Hezekiah . . . King Sennacherib of Assyria*: See 2 Kings 19.14-19.
7.106 Gn 18.23; Ex 32.11. **7.107** Js 7.6, 7. **7.108** 1 S 7.9, 10; 2 S 24.17; 1 K 8.22, 23, 30.
7.109 1 K 18.42, 45, 46; 17.20, 21. **7.110** 2 K 19.15-19. **7.123** Ez 47.12; Rev 22.2.

you have said. But if they win the
fight, they will receive the rewards I
have told you about. 129 That's why
Moses told the people long ago to
choose life, so that they would live a
good and prosperous life.[f] 130 But they
did not believe him or the prophets
who lived after him. They even refused
to believe me! 131 So when they die,
there will be only a little sadness, while
there will be joyful celebration for
those who will be saved.

Will God Show Mercy to the Wicked?

132 I said:
Uriel, I know that God Most High
shows mercy to everyone, even before
they are born, 133 and he shows great
love to those who choose to obey his
Law. 134 He is very patient with sinners, because he created them, 135 and
he likes to answer their prayers.
136 God forgives sinners, whether they
are dead or alive or not yet born. 137 If
he did not forgive sins, everyone in the
entire world would die. 138 He gives us
what is good, so that we can have life.
If he didn't, then not even one person
in ten thousand would live. 139 God is
the judge who accepts sinners and forgives the guilt of the people he created. 140 Otherwise, only very few
would be left alive.

8 Uriel answered:
God Most High created this world
where many people live, but he created the future world for only a few of
them. 2 For example, Ezra, if you ask
the earth, it will tell you that it produces a lot of clay to make pots. But
this same earth has a very small
amount of gold. That's the way it is
with this present world: 3 Many have
been created, but only a few will be
saved.

People Live Only a Short Time

4 I said to myself, "I must try to understand what all this means. 5 I didn't decide
when to be born,[g] and I won't decide when
to die. God will let me live only a few
years."
6 Then I prayed:
Our Lord in heaven, please hear
this prayer from your servant. Plant a
new seed in us, so that our hearts and
minds will obey you, and so that all
humans will stop sinning and live.
7 You alone are God, and you have created each one of us, 8 giving us life before we are born and adding arms and
legs to our unborn bodies. You keep us
safe in fire and water for the nine
months that you shape our bodies.
9 Both the womb that holds the unborn baby and the baby itself are protected until the time of birth arrives.
10 Then, in obedience to you, the
mother's breasts produce milk so her
baby 11 can be fed for a while. After
that, your love helps the baby grow
12 and learn what is right. You teach
the child your Law and guide it with
your wisdom. 13 You are the Creator of
life, and so you can take the life of this
child or let it live. 14 I ask you, Lord, if
you carefully create everyone and then
put them to death, why do you create
them at all?
15 I realize that you care about all
people and know them well, but I am
very sad about the suffering of your
chosen ones. 16 I am mourning the
pain of Israel, the descendants of Jacob. You chose them to be your own,
17 and so I will pray for them and for
all of us on earth who sin against you.
18 The time when you will judge is
coming soon. 19 That's why I am
begging you to listen to my prayer.

Ezra Prays for the People of Israel

Just before I was taken up into heaven
20 I prayed:
Our Lord, you live forever in the
highest heavens, and they belong to
you. 21 Your throne is too large to measure, and your glory is greater than we

[f] **7.129** *Moses . . . life*: See Deuteronomy 30.19.

[g] **8.5** *I didn't decide when to be born*: One possible meaning for the difficult Latin text.

7.129 Dt 30.19. **8.3** Mt 22.14.

can imagine. Angels tremble when
they stand in front of you, 22 and they
change into wind or fire at your command. We believe your laws and everything you say, just as an army believes
its strong leader. 23 One look from you
dries up the deepest ocean, and mountains melt when they see your anger.
Your truth will never be changed. 24 I
am your servant, because you created
me, so please hear my prayer. 25 I will
speak as long as I am alive and can
think.

26 Ignore the sins of your people
and instead look carefully at those who
have faithfully worshiped you. 27 Forget what the wicked do, but remember
how your faithful followers struggled to
obey your laws, even when this caused
them trouble. 28 Don't pay attention to
those who constantly do wrong, but
take care of everyone who listens with
fear to what you command. 29 Don't
wipe out those people who behave like
wild animals; instead, honor those
who enjoy teaching your Law to others. 30 Don't get angry with those you
know are no better than wild beasts.
Instead show your love to everyone
who has trusted your glory.

31 We and our ancestors have done
things that lead to death, yet it is because of our sins that you are called a
God of mercy. 32 We are sinful and
guilty, so if you have pity on us, you
will certainly be called a merciful God.
33 You will bless the people who have
always done what is right.

34 Why are you so angry with people? What good are we anyway? 35 No
one on earth has ever been perfect—
everyone has sinned! 36 If you show
mercy to those who have done nothing
for others, then everyone will know
how kind and good you are.

The Lord Promises a Future Reward for Ezra

37 The Lord answered:

Ezra, some of what you just said is
true, and those things will happen
exactly as you said. 38 It's true that I
won't even think about sinners or their
birth, death, judgment, and everlasting
punishment. 39 Instead, I will celebrate
the birth of good people, their lives on
earth, and how they were saved from
destruction and how they will be rewarded. 40 Things will happen just as I
have told you. 41 A farmer plants a lot
of seeds and small plants, yet not all of
them will take root and grow. It's the
same with people—not everyone on
earth will be saved at the end of time.
42 Then I replied:

Please listen to me again. 43 The
seeds the farmer planted may not grow
because you stopped the rain from
falling. Or maybe there was too much
rain, and they rotted in the ground.
44 People aren't the same as seeds. You
made people to be like you, and then
you created all plants and animals
for them. Are we the same as seeds?
45 Surely not. Save us, Lord, because
you created us to be your very own.
Have mercy on us.
46 The Lord said:

The present time is for those who
are now alive, and the future is for
those who will come later. 47 It's true
that you cannot love my creation more
than I do, but stop thinking of yourself
as wicked. 48 Yet I am pleased that you
49 don't think of yourself as perfect and
that you realize it's wrong to boast.
50 These arrogant people who have
boasted about themselves will suffer
much pain at the end of time.

51 Meanwhile, you should think
about the glorious reward that you and
other faithful followers will receive at
that time. 52 Heaven will be open to all
of you. In fact, the tree that brings life
has been planted, and the future world
is ready. I have built the holy city,
where you will have everything you
need, including perfect rest. All things
that are good and wise are waiting for
you. 53 Things that are evil will be kept
from you, so that you won't ever be
sick or unhappy. You will live forever,

8.22 Ps 104.4; He 1.7. **8.52** 1 P 1.4.

because wickedness and the world of
the dead will be wiped out.[h] 54 All misery will disappear at the end of time,
and everyone will receive the gift of
everlasting life.
55 So stop asking about the large
number of people who will die. 56 After
all, when they had the chance to
choose, they rejected me and refused
to obey my laws and commands.
57 They abused those who were faithful
to me 58 and even said I wasn't real,
knowing they would someday die.
59 That's why the rewards I have described will be given to you, while the
wicked will receive nothing but thirst
and torture. I, the Most High God, do
not like to see people die without
hope. 60 But it's their fault for disgracing me, even though I created them
and offered them a good life. 61 The
time of their judgment is coming soon.
62 No one besides you and a few other
faithful followers know this.

More Signs of the End of Time

I said 63 to the Lord, "You have shown
me a lot of things that will be signs of the
end of time, but you have not told me
when they will take place."

9 The Lord answered:
Think carefully about what I've
told you. And when you see some of
these signs happen, 2 you will know for
certain that the end of time has come,
and that I will soon judge everything
I have created. 3 When earthquakes
shake the earth, and rebellions tear
nations apart, and people no longer
trust their rulers, and leaders lie to
each other, then these things will happen. 4 You will know that the things I
said at the beginning of creation are
coming true. 5 The things that happen
in this world have a clear beginning
and end,[i] 6 and the same is true for
the heavenly world. Miracles show the
beginning of time, and signs point to
the end of time.
7 The people who will be saved
from destruction will escape because
they have done what is right and have
been faithful to me. 8 They will survive
the tortures I have described, and they
will safely reach the land I set aside as
my own for all time. 9 Then those who
have disobeyed me and have ignored
my Law will be shocked when they realize they are to be tormented forever.
10 I'm talking about those who rejected
me in their lifetimes, even though they
accepted the blessings I offered, 11 and
those who ignored my Law when they
had the chance to obey it, and those
who refused to turn to me when they
were able. 12 They must suffer the misery of admitting that I was right from
the beginning. 13 So Ezra, stop asking
questions about how wicked people
will be punished! Instead ask about
how and when the faithful will be
saved. I created the world for them,
and it belongs to them.
14 I replied, 15 "I will repeat again what
I've already said—more people will die than
will be saved. 16 It's like comparing an
ocean wave to a drop of water."
17 The Lord said:
A seed will grow only if the field is
fertile. The colors of a flower will be
bright only if the flower is beautiful. A
job will be done well, only if the workers are skilled. A harvest will be large
only if the farmer works hard. 18 Long
ago when I was creating this world and
its people, no one was there to oppose
what I did. 19 But now the people in
this world constantly sin against me,
even though I have given them plenty
of food and a Law that leads to wisdom. 20 I saw that my world was
ruined, and that the evil plans of people were destroying it. 21 I was angry
enough to wipe out everyone, yet I decided to save a few, like one grape out
of a bunch or one tree out of a forest.
22 The rest will die! But I will keep my
few chosen ones safe, because I have

[h] **8.53** *because wickedness . . . out*: One possible meaning for the difficult Latin text. [i] **9.5** *a clear beginning and end*: One possible meaning for the difficult Latin text.

8.59 Lk 16.24. **9.11** Ws 12.10, 20; He 12.17.

worked hard to show them how to live
right.
23 Ezra, wait seven more days, but
this time you don't have to go without
eating.[j] 24 Go to a deserted field where
only wild flowers grow. Don't eat any
meat or drink any wine, but eat the
flowers 25 and pray to me without stopping. Then I will come and talk with
you again.

THE FOURTH VISION

God's Law Will Never Be Destroyed

26 I obeyed God's command and went to
the field called Ardat, where I sat among
the wild flowers and ate them until I was
full. 27 Seven days later, I was lying on the
grass and was feeling depressed as I had
before.[k] 28 Suddenly, I starting speaking to
God Most High:
29 Our Lord, you appeared to my
ancestors as they crossed the barren
desert after leaving Egypt. 30-31 You
told them you were giving them your
Law because they were the descendants of Jacob, the ancestor of all Israelites. You promised that your Law
would help them live right, just like
a seed that produces healthy fruit.
And you said they would be rewarded
forever if they obeyed it. 32 Though
my ancestors refused to obey the
Law you had given them, its fruit
wasn't destroyed—you had created
it! 33 The people who had the Law
were punished, because they disobeyed it and ignored the seed that
had been planted in them. 34 Usually
when a seed dies after being planted
in the ground, or a ship sinks into
the ocean or food spoils in a dish,
35 the ground and the ocean and the
dish are not destroyed—just the things
they hold. But that isn't what happened to those who disobeyed your
Law. 36 You put it in our hearts, and
when we sinned, we were destroyed—
37 not your Law. It will never be destroyed; your Law will remain glorious
forever.

Ezra Sees a Vision of a Mourning Woman

38 While I was thinking about these
things, I looked to my right and saw a
woman who was crying and very upset. Her
clothes were torn, and she had put ashes
on her head to show her sorrow. 39 I forgot my own troubles and turned 40 to ask
the woman, "Why are you crying and so
upset?"
41 She answered, "Please, sir, just let me
cry and mourn by myself. I am very sad."
42 Then I said, "Tell me what has
happened to you."
43 The woman replied:
Sir, I had been married for thirty
years, but never had a child. 44 Every
hour of every day I prayed to God Most
High, 45 and finally he saw how sad I
had been those thirty years. He gave
me a son, and that made my husband
and me and our friends very happy. We
thanked God for blessing us. 46 We
raised our son right, 47 and after he
had grown up, I found a wife for him
and arranged the wedding celebration.
10 But on their wedding night, as
soon as my son went into the bedroom to be with his bride, he dropped
dead! 2 So we let our oil lamps go out,
and all our neighbors came to comfort
us. I controlled my sadness until the
next evening, 3 and when everyone
had gone home, I got up in the night
and ran to this field. 4 I will never go
back to town. I am going to stay out
here and mourn and go without eating
until I starve to death.
5 After hearing this, I stopped thinking
only of myself and said in anger:
6 You must be the most foolish
woman in the world! Look around and
see how we are suffering. 7 The people
of our holy city Jerusalem are sad and
hopeless. 8 You should be sad and
mourning for Jerusalem along with the

[j]**9.23** *wait seven more days . . . go without eating*: In 5.13 and 6.31, Ezra had been told to go without eating while he waited seven days. [k]**9.27** *as I had before*: See 6.36, 37.
9.29 Ex 19.9; 24.10; Dt 4.12. **10.7** Ga 4.26.

rest of us, instead of grieving for your
son. 9 The earth itself will tell you that
many of its people have died, and
for that reason it deserves to mourn.
10 Many people have been born on this
earth, and many more will be born.
And almost every one of us is doomed
at the end of our lives. 11 So the earth
is mourning the death of most of its
children, while you are mourning the
death of only one child. Who should
be sadder? 12 I know that you think
your pain is greater than the earth's
because you suffered the pain of giving
birth to your child. 13 And you say that
birth and death take place on this
earth every day. 14 But listen to me—
from the beginning of time the earth
has had to suffer the birth of her children, just as you suffered the birth of
your son. 15 So keep your sadness to
yourself, and bravely accept what has
happened to you. 16 Admit that God is
fair in what he does, and you will one
day get your son back. Then other
mothers will praise you. 17 Now return
home to your husband.

18 She answered, "No! I will never go
back. I am going to die out here."

19 I replied:

20 Please don't talk like that. Pay
attention to the sadness and grief of
Jerusalem, and you won't feel so bad
about your own situation. 21 The temple and its altar have been torn down,
22 and our joyful worship and songs of
praise have stopped. The oil lamps
have gone out, and the sacred chest
has been carried away. In fact, all the
sacred things at the temple have been
ruined. Our God has been disgraced,
because the enemy has abused our
children and burned our priests to
death. The priests who survived from
the Levi tribe were taken away as prisoners. The young women of Jerusalem
have been raped, and wives have been
beaten. Even the most faithful men of
our city have been taken captive. The
children have been abandoned, while
the young men have been made slaves,
and the strongest soldiers have been
left with no weapons. 23 Worst of all,
our hated enemies have disgraced
Jerusalem, which was once known as
God's own city, though they now control it. 24 So stop being sad and depressed, and perhaps God All-Powerful
will show you mercy. I pray that he
will keep you safe from any more troubles.

25 While I was talking to the woman,
her face started shining bright as lightning.
I was afraid to go any closer and was
amazed at what was happening. 26 Just
then, she screamed in such a loud and
frightening voice that the whole earth
shook. 27 After that, I couldn't see her any
longer. All I could see was a city being built
on a very large foundation. I was now terrified, and I shouted, 28 "Where is the angel
Uriel who spoke to me earlier? He caused
all my confusion. I will soon die, and so my
prayers are useless."

The Angel Uriel Explains the Vision

29 Before I finished speaking, the angel
Uriel appeared to me again, and when he
saw me 30 lying on the ground as if I were
dead, he grabbed my right hand and helped
me stand up. Then he asked, 31 "What's
wrong, Ezra? Why are you so confused and
upset?"

32 I answered, "It's because you left me
alone. I came out to this field just as you
told me, and now I don't understand what
I'm seeing!"

33 "Stand up and be brave," he ordered,
"and I will explain it to you."

34 I replied, "Please do that, sir. Don't
leave me again, or else I will die not knowing. 35 I cannot understand what I've seen
and heard here. 36 Am I imagining all this?
Is it a nightmare? 37 I beg you to tell me
what this weird vision is all about."

38 Uriel said:

Listen carefully, and I will explain
the vision that frightened you so
much. God Most High has been showing you many secret things, 39 because
he knows you are a good man who has
always worried about Jerusalem and

10.27 He 11.10; Rev 21.9-27.

the people of Israel. 40 So I will tell you
the meaning of the vision.
41 A short time ago, a woman appeared to you, and when you saw that
she was mourning, you tried to comfort her. 42-43 She began telling you
about the death of her son, and when
she suddenly disappeared, you saw a
city being built. Listen to what all this
means.
44 Both the woman and the city
stand for Jerusalem. 45 The thirty years
she lived without having a child are
the three thousand[l] years when no
sacrifice was offered in Jerusalem.
46 Then the woman had a son—this is
the time when King Solomon built the
temple in Jerusalem and began making offerings there. 47 The time the
woman spent taking care of and raising her son is the time when Jerusalem was filled with people. 48 And
the moment her son died stands for
the fall of Jerusalem. 49 You tried to
comfort her when you saw her mourning the death of her son. 50 And when
God Most High saw your deep sadness
over the woman, he showed you the
bright light of her beauty and glory. 51 I
told you to come to this deserted field
52 because I knew God would show you
these things. 53 The reason the field
had to be completely empty, with no
building or foundation of any kind,
54 is that nothing done by humans
could stand in the place where God
would show you his holy city.
55 So, Ezra, stop being afraid! Walk
into the city and look at the beautiful,
large buildings. Look as long as you
want, 56 and listen to everything you
hear. 57 God Most High respects you
much more than he does anyone else,
and so you have been blessed. 58 Stay
there until tomorrow night, 59 and
then he will show you in dreams and
visions what he will do with the people
who are alive at the end of time.

So I stayed in the city two nights, just as
Uriel had told me.

THE FIFTH VISION

Ezra Sees a Vision of an Eagle

11 During the second night that I was
in the city, I dreamed about an eagle flying out of the ocean. It had twelve
wings and three heads, 2 and as I watched,
the eagle spread out its wings over the
whole earth. Wind from every direction
blew in toward it, and clouds gathered
around it. 3 Then from each of the twelve
large wings I saw smaller, weaker wings appear. 4 The middle head of the eagle was
larger than either of the other two, and all
three were asleep. 5 The eagle soared high
in the air and became the ruler of everyone in the world—6 not one living thing
opposed the eagle.
7 The eagle landed, and I watched it
stand on its claws and heard it say to its
wings, 8 "Take turns waking up to stand
guard and be sure to sleep when you have
the chance. 9 The heads will take their
turns last."
10 Then I realized the voice was coming
from the middle of the eagle's body and not
from one of its heads.
11 I counted eight small wings growing
from the larger ones, 12 and then I saw the
large wings on the right side of the eagle
rise up and take control of the whole world.
13 Soon its time to rule was over, and it disappeared without a trace. Then another
wing took its place, and it ruled for a very
long time. 14 But after its rule, it also began
to disappear. 15 All at once, a voice said to
this wing, 16 "You have ruled the earth a
long time. Now before you are gone, I want
you to listen to me. 17 No one after you will
rule as long as you have—not even half as
long."
18 After that, a third wing also took over
and ruled, then soon disappeared like all
the others. 19 Each one had its turn to rule,
and was then gone forever.
20 While I watched, I saw the smaller
wings on the right side of the eagle take
their turns to rule. Some of them ruled
briefly, then disappeared, 21 and some
never ruled at all. 22 I realized that the

[l] **10.45** *three thousand*: Most ancient translations; Latin "three."
11.1 Dn 7.3, 4; Rev 13.1.

twelve large wings and two of the smaller wings were gone, 23 so the only things on the eagle's body were the three heads and six small wings.

24 Suddenly, two of the small wings left their place and moved under the head on the right side of the eagle. The other four wings remained in place, 25 but they started planning to take over the world. 26 The first one rose up to rule, and quickly disappeared. 27 When the second one rose up, it disappeared more quickly than the first. 28 The last two made plans to rule together, 29 but while they were planning, the larger head in the middle woke up. 30 The other two heads also woke up, 31 and together they ate the two small wings. 32 The large, middle head then controlled the entire earth and was cruel to everyone, because it had much more power than any of the wings had ever had. 33 In a short time, however, this head disappeared just as quickly as the wings had, 34 and so only two heads were left. They also ruled the world and its people, 35 but soon the head on the right ate the one on the left.

36 Just then, a voice said, "Ezra, look carefully at what you see in front of you."

37 I saw something that looked like a roaring lion coming from a forest, and I heard it speak in a human voice to the eagle:

> 38 Listen, because this message is from God Most High: 39 I chose four beasts to rule my world and to bring about the end of time. You are the last of these four, 40 and you have defeated them all. During your entire rule, you caused terrible fear, and abused and cheated others. 41 You have judged unfairly 42 and have tortured innocent and kind people. You hate honesty and make friends with liars. You have destroyed innocent people's homes and the walls around them. 43 I am God Most High, and I know that you are proud and arrogant. 44 I have looked at the past, and the time is near when this world will come to an end.
>
> 45 As for you, eagle, you will also disappear—your terrifying large wings, your evil small wings, your hateful heads, your wicked claws, and your worthless body. 46 The whole world will then be free from your violence. It will be refreshed as it looks forward to the final judgment and to the mercy that I will show to my creation.

Ezra continued:

12 While the lion was still speaking to the eagle, I noticed 2 that the last head of the eagle was no longer there. Then the last two small wings that had moved under this head rose up to rule the world. Their rule was very short and weak. 3 As I watched, they also disappeared. Then the body of the eagle burst into flames, and the whole world was shaken with fear.

Ezra Is Told the Meaning of the Vision

I was so afraid and confused by what I had seen that I woke up and said to myself, 4 "I'm to blame for all my distress, because I've tried to understand the ways of God Most High. 5 My mind is exhausted, and my body is completely worn out, because of what I have seen tonight. 6 So I will pray and ask God to give me strength until the end of time."

7 I prayed, "Our Lord God, if you are pleased with me and find me more faithful than others, and if you have heard my prayers, 8 I ask that you give me strength and tell me what this horrible vision means. 9 After all, you have already told me what to expect at the end of time."

10 The angel Uriel[m] answered:

> Here is what the vision means. 11 The eagle you saw stands for the fourth kingdom that your ancestor Daniel also saw long ago.[n] 12 But I will explain it differently. 13 One day, a kingdom will rule the world, and this kingdom will be more oppressive than any before it. 14 Twelve kings will rule this kingdom, one after another, 15 but the second king will rule longer than

[m]**12.10** *The angel Uriel*: Latin "He." [n]**12.11** *the fourth kingdom . . . Daniel . . . ago*: See Daniel 7.7, 23, 24.

12.11 Dn 7.7.

any of the others. 16 That is the meaning of the twelve large wings that
you saw.
17 You heard a voice coming from
the eagle's body instead of from any of
its heads. 18 That voice stands for a rebellion that will take place in the kingdom after the second king has ruled.
That struggle will make the kingdom
weaker, but it will survive and then be
powerful as ever.
19 The eight small wings you saw
growing from the larger ones means
that 20 eight more kings will rule the
kingdom for only a short time. 21 Two
kingdoms will fall at about the mid-
point of their rule; four more will fall
toward the end, and two will remain
until the end of time.
22 The three heads of the eagle that
were sleeping stand for 23 three kings
that will appear near the end of time.
God Most High will make these kings
strong and powerful as they rule the
earth, 24 and they will be meaner than
any of the kings before them. They
represent the heads of the eagle, 25 because the wickedness of the eagle will
be at its height with these three kings.
26 You saw the largest head suddenly
disappear. That's because one of the
kings will die a painful death while
sleeping. 27 The other two will die in
battle. 28 One will kill the other, then
someone will kill him in a battle at the
end of time.
29 The two small wings you saw
moving under the head on the right
side of the eagle 30 are the two kings
that God Most High will keep until the
end of time. Their rule will be very
short and full of trouble, just as you
have seen.
31 You saw a roaring lion coming
from a forest, and you heard it speak to
the eagle and condemn it for being so
wicked. 32 That lion is God's own chosen servant who will appear at the end
of time. He will be one of David's descendants, and he will warn the kings
about their evil ways and condemn
them for disobeying God Most High.
33 He will judge them before they die,
and after he has shown their guilt, he
will put them to death. 34 But he will
have mercy on the rest of God's people
who have survived and are living in his
nation. They will be happy until the final judgment, which I have already
told you about.
35 This was the vision you saw and
what it meant. 36 God Most High has
chosen only you to know this secret,
because you are the only one loyal to
him. 37 So write down in a book everything you've seen and keep it in a safe
place. 38 Teach these things to people
who are wise enough to understand
and will keep them secret. 39 Now wait
here seven more days to see if God
Most High wants to show you anything
else.
Then the angel[o] left.

The People Find Ezra

40 Seven days later, the people living in
the city heard that I had not yet returned.
So they all met together, both young and
old, and came to ask, 41 "Are you angry at
us? Have we done something to make you
leave the city and live out here? 42 You are
the only one of our prophets left to speak to
us. You're as special as the last bunch of
grapes in the vineyard or an oil lamp in a
dark place or a safe harbor for a ship in a
storm. 43 Haven't we suffered enough?
44-45 If you desert us now, we might as well
be dead, just like the others who died in
the fire that destroyed Jerusalem." And
they started crying loudly.
I said, 46 "Listen to me, people of Israel.
Be brave and stop being sad. 47 God Most
High hasn't forgotten you in your misery.
48 I haven't left you, but I have come here
to pray for the lonely city of Jerusalem and
to ask God to show mercy on the ruined
temple. 49 Now all of you go home, and I
will see you in a few days." 50 So they left
and went back to the city.
51 I stayed in the field seven more days,

[o]**12.39** *the angel*: Latin "he."
12.32 Dn 7.13, 14.

as the angel had commanded, and I ate nothing except wild flowers and plants.

THE SIXTH VISION

Ezra Sees a Vision of a Man from the Sea

13 Seven nights later, I dreamed that [2] I saw a storm at sea with rising waves. [3] I saw what looked like a man come up from the middle of the sea and fly with the clouds.[p] Wherever he turned, everything he looked at trembled with fear. [4] And when he spoke, everyone who heard him melted, like wax in a fire.

[5] Then I saw many people from every direction coming together in a crowd too large to count, and they were ready to fight the man from the sea. [6] This man carved out a huge mountain and flew to the top of it. [7] I tried to see from what nation or region he had taken the mountain, but I couldn't see.

[8] I noticed that the people were terrified of the man, yet they still planned to attack and defeat him. [9] When he saw them rushing toward him, he didn't pick up a weapon of any kind. [10] Instead, he opened his mouth, and a stream of fire shot out. Flames came from his lips, and sparks jumped from his tongue. [11] These fiery things came together and fell on the crowd, completely burning up everyone. Nothing was left of the crowd except for smoke and ashes. I was amazed at what I had seen.

[12] I watched as the man from the sea came down from the mountain and called together a different crowd of people—a peaceful crowd. [13] Some of these that came to him were happy, some were sad, while some were tied up and led along by others.[q]

Ezra Asks What the Vision Means

I was terrified when I woke up, and I prayed to God Most High:

[14] Our Lord, you have shown me a lot of amazing things, and you feel I deserve to have my prayers answered. [15] So would you also explain this vision to me? [16] You know that I am terribly concerned about what will happen to those who are alive at the end of time. And what about those who die before that? [17] They will suffer terribly [18] because they won't receive any of the blessings that will come at the end. [19] Yet those alive at that time are also in for trouble. They must face dangerous and troublesome times, just as you have shown me in these visions. [20] I still think that those who survive these troubles will be better off than those who disappear from this world as quickly as a cloud. Those who survive will live until the end of time, yet those who die will never see what takes place.

The angel Uriel[r] answered:

[21] I will explain the meaning of this vision and answer your questions. [22] You have asked about people who will survive until the end of time, and about those who will die before then.[s] So I will tell you [23] that the same one who causes trouble in the last times is the one who will protect those who have been faithful and obedient to God All-Powerful. [24] You can be certain that the people who survive will be much better off than those who are dead.

[25] Now I will tell you what the vision means. The man that you saw coming out of the sea [26] is the one God Most High has kept ready during the history of the world. He will set God's creation free and will keep the faithful safe in the world to come. [27] You saw this man breathe flames and a fiery storm, [28] and you watched him wipe out the crowd of people who were attacking him, without ever reaching for a weapon. This means that [29] God Most High will one day rescue all people who have been faithful to him.

[p] **13.3** *fly with the clouds*: Some ancient translations; Latin "growing stronger with the clouds." [q] **13.13** *while some . . . others*: One possible meaning for the difficult Latin text. [r] **13.20** *The angel Uriel*: See the note at 12.10. [s] **13.22** *and about those who will die before then*: Some ancient translations; these words are not in the Latin translation.

13.3 Dn 7.13; 2 Esd 13.32. **13.6** Dn 2.44, 45. **13.13** Is 66.20.

30 Everyone on earth will be shocked 31 and will plot war against one another—cities will fight against other cities, regions against other regions, nations against other nations, kingdoms against other kingdoms. 32 And when you see these things happen, together with the signs I told you about earlier, then people everywhere will see God's Son, the one you saw as a man coming up out of the sea.

33 When the people of every nation hear his voice, they will stop fighting against one another and will leave their homes 34 and gather together into one crowd too large to count, just as you saw in your vision. They will plot to defeat God's Son, 35 but he will stand on the mountain of Jerusalem, 36 and the new city of Jerusalem will be shown to everyone. This is the mountain you saw carved out, without human hands in the vision. 37 The storm you saw stands for the time when God's Son will judge all godless nations. 38 He will remind them of every wicked and evil plan they had and will tell them of the tortures they must face. These were the flames you saw. Then finally he will easily wipe out the godless nations by using God's holy Law. This was the fire in the vision.

39 You saw God's Son call together a peaceful crowd. 40 These are the nine tribes that King Shalmaneser of Assyria captured during the rule of King Hoshea of Israel and led away to a foreign land across the Euphrates River.[t] 41 But these tribes decided to leave this foreign land and settle in a place where no one had ever lived, 42 and where they could obey God's laws more faithfully than they had in their own country. 43 They chose to cross the Euphrates at the most difficult place, 44 so God Most High had to perform amazing miracles and stop the flow of the river until they had safely crossed. 45 They traveled a year and a half through the region known as Arzareth,[u] 46 where they have lived ever since. Before the end of time, they will come back home, 47 and God Most High will once again stop the flow of the river to let them cross. This was the large and peaceful crowd you saw gathered around God's Son. 48 They are the ones who will be left of your people. They will be found within God's holy nation and will be rescued 49 when his Son destroys the godless nations that gather together to attack him. He will defend your people who survive 50 and work amazing miracles for them.

51 I replied, "Sir, why did I see the man coming up out of the sea?"

52 He said:

Just as no one knows what is at the bottom of the sea, so no one on earth will see God's Son or those with him until the final day comes. 53 That's what your vision means, and only you have been told these things 54 because you care more about studying God's Law than you do about following your own concerns. 55 You have spent your life searching for wisdom, and knowledge has been as dear to you as a mother. 56 That's why God has shown you these things and will one day reward you. Now after three more days, I will explain to you other important and marvelous things.

57 As I walked across the field, I worshiped and praised God Most High for the amazing miracles he had done 58 and for controlling history and all that happens. I stayed there for three days.

THE SEVENTH VISION

Ezra Hears a Voice from a Bush

14 On the third day, while I was sitting under an oak tree, I suddenly heard a voice calling my name from a bush, 2 so I stood up and answered, "Here I am, Lord."

[t] **13.40** *King Shalmaneser . . . Euphrates River*: See 2 Kings 17. [u] **13.45** *Arzareth*: In Latin "Arzareth" means "Another Land."

13.31 Mt 24.7. **13.36** 2 Esd 7.26; Rev 21.2, 9. **13.40** 2 K 17.1-6. **14.2** Ex 3.4.

3 The voice said:

I appeared to Moses and spoke with him from a bush when my people were slaves in Egypt. 4 Then I sent him to bring them out of Egypt and to lead them to Mount Sinai, where I talked with Moses for a long time. 5 I told him a lot of amazing things and secrets about the end of time, and I carefully taught him 6 what to tell openly and what to keep secret. 7 Ezra, I am commanding you 8 to remember all the signs, the visions, and the meanings that I have shown you. 9 Soon you and my other faithful followers will be taken away from this earth to live with my Son until the end of time. 10 This world isn't young any more; it is growing old. 11-12 The history of the world is divided into twelve parts. We are already halfway through the tenth part, so only two and a half parts are left.

13 So get ready to leave! Warn wicked people to change their ways, encourage those who are humble, and teach anyone who can understand.[v] Then give up your earthly body. 14 Stop worrying about everyday matters and leave behind your weak nature. 15 Quickly forget about the things that upset you, and prepare to leave this world. 16 You have seen terrible things happen already, but things worse than these will take place, 17 because as the world gets older and weaker, evil disasters will increase even more. 18 Truth will be forgotten and dishonesty will take over. And the eagle you saw in the vision is now on its way here.

The Lord Commands Ezra To Write Down the Law

19 I answered:

Please listen to me, Lord. 20 I am ready to do what you have commanded. I will warn the people who are alive today. But who will warn those who will be born after I'm gone? This world is a dark and sinful place, and its people need to be shown what is right. 21 Your Law has been destroyed by fire, and so no one knows what you have done in the past or what you plan to do in the future. 22 Please send your Spirit to help me write down everything that has happened in the world since the beginning of time; these things were written in your Law. Then people who desire to be faithful to you can know right from wrong and can live until the end of time.

23 The Lord replied:

Bring everyone together and tell them to leave you alone for the next forty days. 24 Then get a lot of writing tablets, and ask Sarea, Dabria, Selemia, Ethanus, and Asiel to help you—they have been taught to write rapidly. 25 Come back to me, and I will give you the knowledge you need to finish this job. 26 When you have finished, I will tell you what things to announce in public and what things to tell only to the wise. You should start writing tomorrow at this time.

Ezra Begins His Work

27 I did exactly as I had been told and called together the people of the city. Then I said to them:

28 Listen to me, people of Israel. 29 Long ago, our ancestors lived in Egypt as foreigners. Later, they were set free 30 and were given God's Law—the Law that leads to life. Our ancestors disobeyed it, and you have done the same thing. 31 God gave you the land of Israel as your own, yet both you and your ancestors sinned and did not follow his teachings. 32 God Most High judges all people fairly, and so it wasn't long before he took away what he had given you. 33 Now look where you are! You are captives here in this foreign land,[w] while some of your people are held even farther away from your homeland. 34 Control your thoughts and learn from me. God will protect you now and show you mercy at death.

[v] **14.13** *and teach anyone who can understand*: Some ancient translations; these words are not in the Latin translation. [w] **14.33** *this foreign land*: Babylon.

35 Judgment will come after death.
Then we will be brought back to life,
when everyone can see who has been
faithful to God, and who has done evil.
36 For now, leave me completely alone
for forty days!
37 After that, I called together the five
men, and we went to live in the field, just
as I had been told. 38 The very next day, I
heard a voice saying, "Ezra, open your
mouth and drink what I give you."
39 I opened my mouth and was given a
cup filled with something fiery red. 40 I
took it and drank. Immediately I became
wise and could remember everything,
41 and I started talking and could not stop.
42 God Most High also gave understanding
to the five men, and they took turns writing
down what I said, using letters they had
never seen before. They worked forty days,
writing during the day and eating at night.
43 I spoke all day and through the night,
44 and at the end of forty days, ninety-four
books[x] had been written.
45 When the time was up, God Most
High said, "Take to the people the twenty-
four books that you wrote first, so that
everyone, whether worthy or unworthy, can
read them. 46 Keep back the other seventy
books and let only the wisest people read
them. 47 These books are filled with understanding, wisdom, and knowledge that flow
like streams of fresh water."
48 I did what I had been commanded.

ADDITIONAL WORDS FROM EZRA

Disaster Is Coming for the World

15 The Lord said:
Tell my people the messages I
am giving you 2 and have them written
down, because they are true and can be
trusted. 3 Don't be afraid of those who plot
against you or be upset if some don't believe. 4 Those who refuse to believe will die
for their stubbornness.
5 I plan to punish the world cruelly with
war and starvation, with death and destruction, 6 because evil and wickedness
have taken it over. 7 I, the Lord, 8 will no
longer ignore the sins of those godless people, without doing something about them.
They have killed innocent people, and the
blood and the souls of these faithful ones
constantly cry out to me. 9 Know for certain
that I hear them and will take revenge for
the deaths of every innocent person who
has been brutally murdered.
10 My people are being slaughtered like
a flock of sheep, but now I will no longer
let them live in Egypt. 11 I will use my
power to bring them out, then I will punish
the people of Egypt with terrible diseases,
just as before, and I will destroy their land.
12 Their entire nation will groan, and the
cities will fall when I punish it. 13 The
farmers there will mourn when their seeds
die in the ground and when their trees are
ruined by disease, hail, and violent storms.
14 Disaster is coming for this world and
all who live in it. 15 Wars will soon break
out, and nations will fight against one another. 16 Groups of people will plot to rule
others, while ignoring the true leaders.
17 Cities will become too dangerous to visit,
18 because their buildings will be in ruins,
and fearsome riots will be taking place
everywhere. 19 People will be so desperate
that they will beat and rob their friends to
get food and supplies.
20 I am gathering together the kings
from the north, south, east, and west to
make them pay for what they have taken.
21 I will treat them as harshly as they have
treated my chosen people. 22 I will show no
mercy to those who have sinned against
me, and I won't spare anyone who has
killed innocent people. 23 My anger has become hot as fire and has burned the foundations of the earth, wiping out sinners as
if they were straw. 24 Those who refuse to
obey my Law are doomed! 25 I will show
them no mercy. Get away from me, you
worthless rebels, and stop polluting my holy
temple with your unfaithfulness. 26 I know
who you are, and I will condemn you to a
violent death. 27 Horrible disasters have already begun, and there is no way to stop
them. You have sinned against me, and I
will not spare you.

[x] **14.44** *ninety-four books*: One possible meaning for the difficult Latin text.

A Frightening Vision in the East

The Lord said:

28 Ezra, you will see a frightening vision
in the east. 29 The fierce armies of Arabia
will appear in chariots, charging and hiss-
ing like dragons, and their sound will make
everyone tremble with fear. 30 The Carmonians[y] will rush out of a forest as angry as
wild boars, and they will attack the dragons
with their powerful teeth and tusks, wiping
out an entire region of Assyria. 31 But the
armies of Arabia will join forces and fight
bravely side-by-side, and they will win.
They will quickly defeat the Carmonians,
32 who will retreat in fear. 33 Meanwhile, an
Assyrian army will ambush the Carmonians
and kill one of their kings and his soldiers.[z]
The rest of the soldiers and the other kings
will panic and shake with fear.

34 You will then see dark, threatening
storm clouds move in from the east, the
north, and the south. 35 When they crash
into each other, a storm of anger and violence will fall over the earth.[a] Blood will
flow as high as a horse's stomach 36 or a
person's thigh or a camel's knee. 37 People
will be terrified and will shake in horror at
the sight of this violence. 38 Then more
storm clouds will move in from the south,
the north, and the west, 39 but winds from
the east will be stronger and will hold back
these destructive storm clouds.[b] 40 Then
large and dark storm clouds will move in
and destroy the earth and its people. They
will pour down great anger on every hill
and mountain,[c] 41 with lightning and hail
and flying swords, until rivers flood nearby
fields. 42 Walled cities, mountains and hills,
forests and crops will be destroyed.
43-44 The floodwater will flow as far as
Babylon and surround it with violence and
anger. Babylon will be wiped out, and the
dust and smoke will fill the air. Everyone
who sees this happen will mourn, 45 and its
survivors will become slaves to those who
destroyed the city.

Asia Is No Better Than Babylon

Ezra said:

46-47 Asia, you are doomed! You shared
the glorious fame of Babylon, and now
you're just as wicked and arrogant. You
dressed your daughters like prostitutes so
they would satisfy your lovers, yet those
lovers wanted only you. 48 And now, because you have followed the disgusting and
evil ways of that place, God says:

> 49 I plan to punish you with terrible
> disasters. You will soon be a widow,
> and I will send poverty, starvation, war,
> and disease to destroy your houses and
> kill your people. 50 Your proud strength
> will wither away like a flower when my
> fiery anger falls on you. 51 You will be
> weak and helpless, like an abused
> woman, and will no longer attract rich
> lovers. 52-53 If you had spared my cho-
> sen people, I wouldn't punish you so
> severely. But you enjoyed killing them,
> and you cheered and clapped at their
> pain while you were drunk.
>
> 54 Put on your make-up 55 and get
> ready to be rewarded for being a prosti-
> tute! 56 I will pay you back with disas-
> ter for what you have done to my peo-
> ple. 57 Your children will starve, and
> you will be killed, together with your
> people living in the countryside. Your
> cities will be destroyed, 58 while the
> people living in the mountains will get
> so hungry and thirsty that they will eat
> their own flesh and drink their own
> blood. 59 You will suffer more than any-
> one else has ever suffered, but things
> will get even worse. 60 The army that
> wiped out Babylon will come back
> through your land and crush your
> peaceful cities and destroy your beau-
> tiful countryside, leaving your great
> nation in ruins. 61 You will be nothing
> but scorched straw. 62 This army will
> smash every city and make your land
> and mountains empty wastelands.

[y] **15.30** *Carmonians*: A people similar to the Medes and the Persians; they lived on the Persian Gulf, north of the Strait of Hormuz. [z] **15.33** *one of their kings and his soldiers*: Latin "one."
[a] **15.35** *a storm . . . earth*: One possible meaning for the difficult Latin text. [b] **15.39** *clouds*: One possible meaning for the difficult Latin text of verse 39. [c] **15.40** *hill and mountain*: Or "important person."

15.46-48 Rev 14.8; 17.4, 5.

Your forests and fruit trees will be
burned to the ground. 63 This cruel
army will carry away your children and
your wealth, leaving you stripped of
your glory.

The Enemies of Israel Are Doomed

Ezra said:

16 Babylonia, Asia, Egypt, and Syria,
all of you are doomed! 2 Put on
sackcloth and cloth made of goat's hair to
show your sorrow. Cry and mourn for your
children, because the time of your destruction is already here. 3 The Lord is sending
war on your nations, and no one can stop
it. 4 He will set you on fire, and no one can
put it out. 5 Disasters will come to you, and
no one can save you. 6 Can anyone stop the
attack of a hungry lion or put out a grass
fire 7 or turn back an arrow shot by a strong
archer? 8 When the Lord punishes with
disasters, no one can stop them. 9 His
anger is like a fire that no one can put out,
10 and when he sends thunder and lightning, people are terrified. 11 They drop to
their knees in horror when he threatens
destruction. 12 The deepest parts of the
earth and the sea, together with the waves
and fish, tremble at the sight of God's
bright glory. 13 His powerful right arm pulls
back the bow, and his sharp arrows fly
across the earth without missing their target. 14 The troubles he has sent are like
those arrows—they won't stop until they
reach their targets. 15 He has started a fire,
and it will burn until the earth is destroyed.
16 The disasters are coming and cannot be
turned back, just as the arrows cannot be
stopped. 17 Even I am doomed! Who will
rescue me in those terrible days?

Sinners Will Never Change Their Ways

Ezra said:

18 Sorrows will begin, and there will be
much crying. Famine will strike, and many
people will die. Wars will break out, and
powerful armies will be terrified. Disasters
will come, and everyone will tremble with
fear. What will people do when these things
happen? 19 The Lord must send starvation
and disease, pain and disaster to punish
sinners. 20 But they will never change their
ways, and they will forget about their punishment.

21 The time is coming when food and
supplies will be so cheap that people will
think peace is coming. Then suddenly disasters will strike—war and starvation and
constant confusion. 22 People on earth will
starve, and those who survive will be killed
in war. 23 The dead bodies will be thrown
out like garbage, and no one will be left to
comfort those who mourn. The earth will
be an empty wasteland, with all its cities
lying in ruins. 24 No one will be alive to
work the land and plant seeds. 25 Trees
will produce fruit, but no one will gather
it. 26 Grape vines will have grapes, but
no one will make wine. The earth will be
as lonely as a desert. 27 A person will
wish to see another human or just to hear
someone's voice. 28 Only ten people will
survive in a city, and only two will be left in
the countryside, hidden in a forest or a
cave.

29 When olives are picked from their
trees, three or four are left behind. 30 And
when grapes are gathered in a vineyard, a
few bunches are overlooked by even the
most careful pickers. 31 That's how it will
be when these disasters begin. Soldiers
with swords will search each home, ready
to kill any survivors, and only three or four
won't be found. 32 The land will be empty;
its fields will be covered with thorns;[d]
its roads and paths will be overgrown
with weeds, because no sheep will graze
there. 33 Young women will be sad because no one will be left to marry them,
and wives will mourn because their husbands will be dead, and daughters will
groan in sorrow because there will be no
one to help them. 34 Every young man will
die in battle, and every husband will die of
starvation.

The Lord's People Must Be Ready for the Coming Disasters

Ezra said:

35 Listen to me, you people who faithfully worship the Lord. 36 I have a message

[d]**16.32** *covered with thorns*: Some ancient translations; Latin "plowed up."

from him, so pay attention and believe
it. 37 The disasters will begin very soon,
and nothing can stop them. 38 A woman
about to give birth suffers pain for two or
three hours before her baby is born, but
when the right time comes, she cannot
stop it. 39 The same is true for the world
when these disasters strike. It will groan
in pain and will not be able to stop the
troubles.

40 My people, listen to what I am saying.
Prepare for the battles, and act as if you
don't live on this earth. 41 Sellers must run
from a sale, and buyers must expect to be
cheated. 42 Merchants must not expect a
profit, and builders must not expect to live
in a house they've built. 43 Farmers must
not expect to gather their crops or pick
their grapes. 44 You married couples must
not expect to have children, and you unmarried people will live as if you were widows. 45 All your work will have been for
nothing, 46 because foreigners will harvest
your crops and steal your possessions.
These foreigners will rob your homes and
make your children their slaves. Children
will either become slaves or else starve to
death, 47 and whatever money you earn will
be stolen. The more you spend to decorate
your cities and your homes and to make
yourselves attractive, 48 the angrier I, the
Lord, will become with you, because of
your sins. 49 Just as a good woman hates
prostitutes, 50 so right living hates the at-
traction of wickedness. Right living will
show how useless evil is when God comes
to judge this sinful world. 51 So don't follow
the ways of sinners, 52 because very soon
all wickedness will be wiped off the earth,
and goodness will rule us all.

Sins Cannot Be Hidden from God

53 Sinners won't be able to deny their
evil ways. In fact, God will torture them
with burning coals if they say they have not
sinned against him and his glory. 54 The
Lord God knows everything we do and plan
and feel. 55 He created the earth and the
heavens with just a command. 56 With one
word he put the stars in place, and he
knows exactly how many there are. 57 He
knows what treasures lie in the deepest
parts of the sea, and he has carefully
measured it and everything there. 58 He
commanded the sea to stay in its place and
the land to stay above the water. 59 He
stretched out the sky like a dome and made
sure it stays above the ocean. 60 He made
springs of water in the dry desert and lakes
at the tops of mountains, so they could run
down to form rivers and to water the
ground. 61 He made human beings and
gave each of them a heart. He gave them
the breath of life and clear understanding,
62 and he put in them his own powerful
Spirit. God All-Powerful, who created all
things and knows every secret, did these
things!

63 The Lord himself knows what you
plan and what you think. Don't be foolish
enough to imagine that you can hide your
sins from him. 64 He will carefully look at
everything you've done and judge you in
front of everyone. 65 On that day, you will
be ashamed of your evil ways, and they will
prove you guilty. 66 What will you do then?
Will you still try to hide your sins from
God? 67 He is your final judge, so fear him!
Stop sinning once and for all and turn from
your wickedness! Maybe God will rescue
you from the coming disasters.

The Lord Promises To Rescue His People

68 A powerful, angry mob of people is
ready to drag many of you away and force
you to eat food that has been sacrificed to
idols. 69 Anyone who eats this food will be
mocked and insulted and abused. 70 In city
after city, my faithful people will be beaten
and tortured. 71 The attackers will be wild
and will show no mercy to anyone. They
will beat and kill everyone who worships
me. 72 They will steal their possessions and
burn down their homes, leaving my people
with no places to live. 73 But my followers
will prove their faithfulness by surviving
these tortures, just as gold is purified with
fire.

74 So listen to me, my chosen people.
The days of misery will soon be here, but I
will rescue you. 75 Don't be afraid and don't

16.73 Zec 13.9; 1 P 1.7.

give up—I am your God, and I will protect
you. 76 You have always obeyed my laws
and commands, so don't let your sins take
over and control you. 77 You're in for trouble if you let your sins trap you or take over
your thinking. You will be nothing but a
field of weeds, with its paths so covered
with thorns that no one can walk through
it. 78 You will be ignored and left to be completely wiped out by fire.

4 MACCABEES

ABOUT THIS BOOK

Fourth Maccabees was written in the form of a speech. It encourages people to think clearly and have faith in God so that feelings of fear, doubt, selfishness, anger, and hatred cannot stop them from doing what is right. The author uses the examples of nine faithful Jews who gave up their lives rather than disobey God. They died just before the time of the rebellion led by Judas Maccabeus, and so the book is known as 4 Maccabees.

According to the author, their death showed others how to be faithful, but even more importantly, God accepted it as a sacrifice that took away the sin of the entire Jewish nation. God rescued the people of Israel from horrible suffering and gave them his blessing.

The stories in 4 Maccabees also remind all who worship God that if they think clearly and have faith in him and obey his law, he will constantly be with them and give them strength and courage.

A QUICK LOOK AT THIS BOOK

- Why This Book Was Written (1.1-30)
- How Clear Thinking Helped Joseph, Moses, Jacob, and David (1.30—3.19)
- The Jews Are Forced To Live Like Greeks (3.20—4.26)
- The Example of Eleazar the Priest (5.1—7.23)
- The Example of the Seven Brothers (8.1—14.10)
- The Example of Their Mother (14.11—17.6)
- How These Faithful Jews Saved Israel (17.7—18.24)

Why This Book Was Written

1 I am writing this book to discuss clear thinking and faith in God, and whether these together can control emotions. So please read carefully. This question is very important, 2 because everyone who wants to be wise should know the answer. And besides, thinking clearly about difficult questions is one of the most honorable things a person can do.

3 Everyone knows that clear thinking is much better than having strong desires to overeat and to have sex—these two emotions completely take over a person's mind. 4 Clear thinking is also better than hatred and anger and pain and fear—emotions like these stand in the way of courage and doing what is right. 5 You might hear someone ask, "If clear thinking controls my emotions, then why can't I learn more and never forget it?" That is a foolish question, 6 because stupidity and forgetfulness keep a person from thinking clearly. But when people use their minds to think clearly about something, they will be brave and will do what is right and fair.

7 I have lots of examples to prove that our minds can control our emotions. 8 However, the best examples are the stories of the brave people who willingly died rather than do wrong. I am talking especially about nine people: Eleazar, seven brave brothers, and the mother of these

1.5 4 Macc 2.24. **1.7** 4 Macc 17.8. **1.8** 3 Macc 6.1.

seven young men. [9] These nine refused to do evil, even when threatened with death. That surely proves that clear thinking is stronger than emotions!

[10] So on this festival day,[a] I want to praise these people. I know God has certainly blessed and honored them already, because they were put to death for their loyalty and right living. [11] The guards and other people who watched them die were amazed at their courage and patience. In fact, their faithfulness saved our entire nation from being controlled by wicked rulers. [12] I will write more about these brave people later and will give thanks to the God who knows everything. But first, I want to tell you more about clear thinking.

What Is Clear Thinking?

[13] Our question is whether clear thinking can control emotions. [14] We must first ask three questions: What is clear thinking? What are emotions? And how many different kinds of emotions are there? After we answer those questions, then we can ask if clear thinking can control each different feeling.

[15] Clear thinking comes from the mind and leads to wisdom, [16] which is knowledge about God and people, and about why things happen the way they do. [17] We become wise by obeying the Law of Moses, because in it God tells how he wants us to live.

[18] Besides making good decisions, wise people are brave and treat everyone fairly, and they also keep themselves from doing wrong. [19] The ability to make good decisions is most important, because it proves that clear thinking controls emotions.

[20-21] The two most common emotions are happiness and sadness, and these two emotions often determine how people think and act. [22] For example, if people get what they want, they are usually pleased and happy. [23] And if they are afraid, they will usually be sad and miserable. [24] Yet, we all know that people can have angry feelings whether they are happy or sad. [25] Sometimes a happy person can be very mean, and that feeling is the hardest one to understand. [26] It makes people boastful, greedy, selfish, and hateful, [27] and it also causes people to overeat and love food more than anything else.

[28] Happiness and sadness are like two plants that grow out of the same mind and body, and these two plants have lots of branches. [29] Clear thinking is the gardener who takes care of these young plants. All human emotions and actions are controlled by clear thinking, because it makes sure they stay healthy and strong and pure, just as a gardener waters and weeds and ties up the young plants in a garden. [30] Clear thinking leads to right living, but emotions without clear thinking are always out of control.

Clear Thinking Keeps Us from Doing What Is Wrong

I want you to know first that clear thinking controls emotions by keeping us from doing what is wrong. [31] This is what keeps our desires under control, [32] whether or not they are ever strong enough to make us do something evil. [33] For example, I believe clear thinking is more powerful than hunger, and that's why we can turn down delicious-looking food that is forbidden by God's Law. [34] When we think clearly, we are able to refuse fish and bird and any meat that is unclean. [35] The feelings we have when we are hungry are controlled by thinking clearly, just as it controls all the desires of our bodies.

2 You should also know that clear thinking keeps us from always wanting beautiful things. [2] We praise our ancestor Joseph for using his mind to control his desire to have sex. [3] Even though he was young and strong, he refused to give in to sexual desires. [4] That's why I say that the mind keeps us from evil desires, including the wrong kind of sex. [5] The Law of Moses says, "Do not want your neighbor's wife or

[a]**1.10** *this festival day*: Probably a special day to remember those who were put to death for their obedience to God's Law.

1.11 4 Macc 6.29. **1.17** Ps 19.7; Pr 9.10. **1.18** Ws 8.7. **1.20,21** Ro 1.28.
1.34 Lv 11.1-47; Dt 14.3-21; Ac 10.14. **2.2** Gn 39.7-12.

husband or anything that belongs to someone else."[b] 6 The Law clearly forbids us from wanting what isn't ours, and I could give you many more examples of how clear thinking controls those desires.

Clear Thinking Keeps Us from Being Selfish

Clear thinking also keeps us from being selfish and unfair. 7 People who eat or drink too much can control these bad habits because their mind is more powerful than their emotions. 8 Even greedy people who start obeying God's Law will stop their selfish ways. They will agree to lend money to those in need without charging interest[c] and after six years will not ask them to pay it back.[d] 9 Greedy people who start thinking clearly and begin obeying God's Law will leave some of their grain standing along the edges of the fields and will not pick up what falls on the ground.[e]

Clear thinking controls our emotions in every situation, 10 and God's Law is even more important than the love we have for our parents. 11-13 His Law is more important than loving our wives or husbands or children or friends, and so we can warn and punish them when they sin. 14 And don't be surprised when clear thinking and God's Law cause us to be kind to someone we hate.[f] After all, the Law says we are not to cut down the fruit trees of our enemies. Instead, we are to protect their property and not let anyone destroy it.[g]

Clear Thinking Helps Us Control Our Anger

15 Finally, clear thinking helps us control the more fierce emotions, like pride, arrogance, hatred, and the desire for power. 16 The mind is more powerful than these emotions, just as it is more powerful than anger. 17 When our ancestor Moses was angry with Dathan and Abiram, he did not punish them in uncontrolled anger.[h] 18 I have said already that the mind can help us control some of our emotions and destroy others. 19 That's why our wise ancestor Jacob did not punish Simeon and Levi for slaughtering the entire tribe of Shechem. Instead, Jacob placed a curse on them for being so violent.[i] 20 If he had not used his mind to control his anger, he would have punished them severely for their crime.

21 It's true that when God created us, he gave us many different emotions and desires, 22 but he also gave each of us a mind so we could control them. 23 And God gave us his Law to control our minds. The people who obey this Law will always do what is right and will be brave and fair and kind.

24 Some people ask, "If clear thinking controls my emotions, then why can't it keep me from being stupid and forgetful?"

3 That question is foolish! Stupidity and forgetfulness are the two things that keep a person from thinking clearly, and so clear thinking can't control them. But it does have power over our emotions. 2 None of us can ever completely get rid of selfish desires, but our mind helps us control them, 3 just as it helps us control our anger 4 and our hatred. 5 We will always have desires and anger and hatred in our lives, but clear thinking helps us overcome those emotions.

The Example of King David

6 I can explain all this by telling a story about the time when King David was very thirsty. 7 All day long, David and his army had been attacking and killing Philistines. 8 That evening he was hot and tired as he returned and went into his royal tent in the middle of camp. 9 Then, while his soldiers were eating, 10 David became very thirsty, but the spring water he was offered would not satisfy his thirst. 11 David suddenly wanted water from the Philistine territory and couldn't get it off his mind. 12 As his

[b]**2.5** *else*: See Exodus 20.17. [c]**2.8** *to lend money . . . without charging interest*: See Exodus 22.25. [d]**2.8** *after six years . . . pay it back*: See Deuteronomy 15.1-3. [e]**2.9** *leave some of their grain . . . ground*: See Leviticus 19.9, 10. [f]**2.14** *to be kind to someone we hate*: See Exodus 23.4, 5. [g]**2.14** *not to cut down the fruit trees . . . protect their property . . . destroy it*: See Deuteronomy 20.19, 20. [h]**2.17** *Moses . . . Dathan and Abiram . . . anger*: See Numbers 16.1-38. [i]**2.19** *Jacob . . . Simeon and Levi . . . violent*: See Genesis 49.5-7.

2.11-13 Mt 10.37; Lk 14.26. **2.24** 4 Macc 1.5.

guards complained that getting him water
from there was very dangerous, two young
soldiers decided to go and get it anyway. So
they armed themselves with weapons and
took an empty pitcher, then climbed over
the dirt ramps that protected the Philistine
territory. 13 The Philistine guards did not
see David's two soldiers, so they looked
around the enemy camp 14 until they found
a spring of water. They dipped the pitcher
into the water and bravely carried it back to
David.

15 Though David was very thirsty, he
suddenly realized how brave these two soldiers had been to do such a dangerous
thing. He refused to drink the water, because he knew they had risked their lives
to get it. 16 His mind was stronger than
his thirst, so he poured out the water as a
sacrifice to God.[j]

17 Clear thinking can control even our
strongest desires. 18 Our mind can help us
handle pain and our fiercest emotions.

19 Now I want to tell more stories about
how clear thinking can control emotions.

Apollonius Tries To Rob the Temple Treasury

20 At one time, our ancestors in Jerusalem were living in peace and were pros-
pering, because they were faithfully obeying
God's Law.[k] King Seleucus Nicanor of Asia[l]
was kind to them and even gave money to
pay for sacrifices at the temple. 21 But about
the same time, a group of people planned
troubles that would upset the peace of
the city.

4 Onias[m] was high priest of the nation at
the time, and he was honest and respected. However, a man named Simon
was an enemy of Onias and told horrible
lies about him. But the people refused to
believe anything bad about Onias, and
so Simon left Israel, promising to cause
trouble for the entire nation.

2 Simon went to Apollonius, the governor
of Syria, Phoenicia, and Cilicia and said,
3 "Sir, I am a loyal servant of King Seleucus.
I am here to report that a lot of the money
kept in the temple treasury in Jerusalem
has come from people's private accounts.
This money doesn't belong to the temple—
it belongs to King Seleucus himself!"

4 Apollonius immediately thanked Simon for his honesty and loyalty, then went
to tell Seleucus about the money. 5 After
the king had put Apollonius in charge of
getting the money from the Jerusalem temple, Apollonius and Simon left for Jerusalem and took a powerful army with them.

6 When they arrived in Jerusalem, Apollonius told the people that King Seleucus
had ordered him to take all private accounts from the temple treasury. 7 The people became very angry and couldn't believe
that their own money was about to be
stolen. So they did everything they could to
stop Apollonius.

8 He ignored them and began walking
toward the temple, shouting threats at the
crowd, 9 while priests and women and children begged God to protect his holy temple
from being dishonored. 10 Just as Apollonius and his army reached the temple and
started inside to collect the money, angels
appeared in the sky! They were on horses,
and their weapons flashed back and forth
like lightning. Apollonius and his soldiers
were weak from fear, 11 and he fell to his
knees right there in the temple courtyard.
He raised his hands to heaven and started
crying, then begged the Hebrew people to
pray for him and ask God to stop the army
of angels. 12 Apollonius confessed that he
had sinned against God and deserved to
die, and he promised to praise the sacred
temple in front of everyone if God would let
him live.

13 Onias the high priest heard Apollonius and prayed for him, though he didn't

[j]**3.16** *God*: See 2 Samuel 23.13-17; 1 Chronicles 11.15-19. [k]**3.20** *Law*: See 2 Maccabees 3.1. [l]**3.20** *King Seleucus Nicanor of Asia*: The author of this book confused Seleucus I Nicanor (ruled 305-281 B.C.) with Seleucus IV (ruled 187-175 B.C.); see 2 Maccabees 3.3. [m]**4.1** *Onias*: Also known as Onias III. He belonged to the family of priests that descended from Zadok. Members of Zadok's family served as priests and high priests for almost eight hundred years from the time of David (2 Samuel 20.25) and Solomon (1 Kings 1.39-45) down to 171 B.C.

4.3 2 Macc 3.5. **4.10** 3 Macc 6.18.

deserve it. Onias knew that if he didn't ask
God to forgive Apollonius, King Seleucus
would think that the people had killed him.
14 Apollonius lived and went back to tell
Seleucus exactly what had happened to
him in Jerusalem.

The Jews Are Forced To Live Like Greeks

15 After the death of King Seleucus,[n] his
arrogant and dishonest son Antiochus
Epiphanes[o] became king. 16 Antiochus
quickly removed Onias from his position as
high priest and replaced him with Jason,
the brother of Onias. 17 Jason had promised
that if he became high priest, he would pay
the king three thousand six hundred silver
coins each year. 18 So Antiochus appointed
him high priest and ruler of the country.
19 Right away Jason changed the customs of the country and the way it was
run—everything he did was forbidden by
God's Law. 20 Jason built a sports stadium
near the Jerusalem temple, and he ordered
all worship at the temple to stop forever!
21 God became very angry at these things,
and Antiochus himself became even more
determined to attack the Jews. 22 While
Antiochus was at war with King Ptolemy of
Egypt,[p] he heard that a rumor of his death
was going around Jerusalem, and that the
people were celebrating. So Antiochus immediately marched against the city 23 and
carried off everything of value, then gave
orders that anyone worshiping the God of
Israel would be put to death. 24 But the
people ignored his threats and continued to
obey God's Law. 25 Some young mothers
circumcised their sons, even though they
knew that they and their babies would be
thrown to their death from a high place.
26 The people hated Antiochus and his demands, so he tried using torture to force
the Jews to eat food forbidden by God's
Law and to reject their religion.

Eleazar Refuses To Eat the Meat of Pigs

5 The evil King Antiochus held a meeting with his top advisors in an official
building[q] guarded by his armed soldiers.
2 He then ordered his troops to capture all
the Jews in the city and force them to eat
the meat of pigs and the sacrifices that had
been offered to idols.[r] 3 Anyone who refused to eat such unclean food was to be
severely tortured[s] and put to death.
4 After many Jews had been arrested,
Eleazer the priest and leader of the Jews
was taken to Antiochus. Though Eleazar
was old, most of the king's officials knew
him because he was intelligent[t] and an
expert in the Law of Moses. 5 When
Antiochus saw him, he said:

6 Before you are tortured, old man,
I will give you a chance to save yourself by eating the meat of pigs. 7 I certainly respect your old age, but I still
think you're being foolish to remain a
Jew. 8 After all, what's wrong with this
meat? It is one of the best things
nature has given us, 9 and it certainly
isn't unclean, as you say.

While you may be a fool for not enjoying its taste, 10 you are stupid for
not obeying me! Forget what your Law
says about the meat of pigs 11 and
think like a wise old man. Remember
that what you decide to do can save
your life. 12 So be good to yourself and
listen to advice. 13 If God really did
give you this Law, he will forgive you
for doing something you've been
forced to do.

14 After Antiochus had finished speaking, Eleazar asked if he could have a

[n]**4.15** *King Seleucus*: Seleucus IV (ruled 187-175 B.C.). [o]**4.15** *his . . . son Antiochus Epiphanes*: The author is confused once again; Antiochus IV Epiphanes (ruled 175-164 B.C.) was the brother of Seleucus IV, not his son. [p]**4.22** *King Ptolemy of Egypt*: Ptolemy VI Philometor (ruled 180-145 B.C.). [q]**5.1** *in an official building*: Probably in Jerusalem. [r]**5.2** *to eat . . . pigs and the sacrifices . . . idols*: Eating pigs was forbidden by God's Law (see Leviticus 11.4-8; Deuteronomy 14.8) and eating such sacrifices was thought to be worshiping other gods. [s]**5.3** *severely tortured*: Greek "stretched out on the wheel." [t]**5.4** *intelligent*: Greek; other ancient translations "so old."

4.15-26 1 Macc 1.20-63; 2 Macc 5.11—6.11. **4.16** 2 Macc 4.7. **4.20** 2 Macc 4.12. **4.22** 1 Macc 1.16-19. **5.1—7.23** 2 Macc 6.18-31. **5.2** Ac 15.29; 1 Co 10.18-22. **5.13** 3 Macc 2.21, 22.

chance to speak. 15 Antiochus agreed, and Eleazar said in a voice loud enough for the crowd to hear:

16 Your Majesty, we Jews believe that nothing can stop us from obeying the Law that our God has given us. 17 That's why we refuse to do anything his Law forbids. 18 You seem to believe that God did not give it to us. I tell you that we would still follow this sacred custom, even if that were true. 19 It would be terrible for us to eat the meat of pigs, 20 because disobeying God's Law is always wrong, whether the sin is serious or not. 21 We will not insult God or go against his Law.

22 You make fun of our beliefs as if they were crazy, 23 but they teach us to control our emotions and desires. We learn how to be brave and how to suffer without complaining, 24 and our beliefs teach us to be fair to all people in everything we do. Most important, these beliefs teach us to live right and worship the only living God.

25 So we refuse to eat food that our God has said is unclean. He is the Creator of the world, and he gave us this Law out of mercy. 26 God said we could eat food that is good for us, but he has forbidden us to eat what is bad. 27 You cannot force us to break God's Law! Besides, if we eat this unclean food, you might make fun of us for being unfaithful, and that would disgrace us even more!

28 You will not have the chance to laugh at me, 29 because I will not ignore the sacred customs of my ancestors. I refuse to disobey God's Law, 30 even if you poke out my eyes and burn my insides! 31 Though I am old, I think as clearly as a young man, and I will bravely worship God. 32 So get ready to torture me and make that fire even hotter! 33 I don't need your pity. I am completely loyal to the ancient Law of Moses 34 and all its teachings. I have studied them my whole life and will do what they have taught me. 35 As an honored priest and an expert in the Law, I refuse to ignore my own clear thinking and be put to shame. 36 Your Majesty, I will not be disgraced by letting you insult my age and my obedience to the Law. 37 My ancestors will respect and honor me, because I am not afraid to be cruelly punished, even if it kills me. 38 You may be able to control wicked people, yet nothing you say or do will force me to go against the sacred Laws of my God.

The Death of Eleazar

6 After Eleazar had finished his speech to King Antiochus, the guards standing nearby grabbed Eleazar and dragged him to the place of torture. 2 Even after they ripped off Eleazar's clothes, he did not feel disgraced. 3 The guards tied his arms to poles on his left and right, then they whipped him, 4 while one of the king's officials shouted, "You will obey King Antiochus!" 5 But like always,[u] Eleazar was very brave, and he let them whip him, acting as if nothing at all was happening to him. 6 While he looked toward heaven, the whips tore off his skin and cut his sides. Blood flowed down his body, 7 and he fell to the ground in pain, though his mind was still strong, and he continued to think clearly. 8 One of the cruel guards ran over to Eleazar and kicked him in the side to make him get up. 9 Eleazar was tortured and abused, yet he endured the pain 10 and the whipping like a strong athlete who refused to be defeated. 11 Sweat poured down his face, and he could barely breathe, but his courage amazed the guards who were torturing him.

12-13 Just then, some of the king's officials who knew Eleazar began to feel sorry for him. They couldn't believe he was enduring such pain, so they said, 14 "Eleazar, why are you doing this to yourself? You are foolish not to give in to King Antiochus.

[u]**6.5** *always*: Greek "like a true Eleazar"; in Greek, "Eleazar" means "God helps."

5.20 Ga 3.10; Jas 2.10. **5.26** Lv 11.1-23. **5.37** 2 Macc 7.36; 4 Macc 9.22; 17.11, 12. **6.5** 3 Macc 6.1. **6.6** Ac 7.55. **6.10** 4 Macc 9.8; 11.20; 16.16; 17.11, 12; 1 Co 9.24-27; He 12.1.

15 Let us give you some meat from a pig,
and you can save yourself by pretending to
eat it."

16 Eleazar became very upset when he
heard their advice, and he replied in a loud
voice:

> 17 Listen to me, all descendants of
> Abraham! Never let fear make you pre-
> tend to do something so disgusting!
> 18 We would be fools if we disobeyed
> God's Law now, after carefully obeying
> it our entire lives. 19 Every young per-
> son here would follow our wicked ex-
> ample and eat food that God has for-
> bidden. 20 Besides, if we ate this
> unclean meat and lived longer, we
> would be laughed at for being cowards,
> 21 and King Antiochus himself would
> think we are weak for not choosing
> to die for the sake of God's Law. 22 So
> be ready to die bravely for your faith
> in God!
>
> 23 And now, you guards of the evil
> Antiochus, don't wait any longer to
> torture me.

24 The guards realized that Eleazar
would not change his mind, and that he
would bravely face any pain. So they
dragged him to the fire, 25 where they
burned his body with red-hot metal poles.
Then they threw him to the ground and
poured boiling vinegar up his nose. 26 Now
that Eleazar had been burned both inside
and out, he was close to death. But he
looked toward heaven and prayed, 27 "Our
God, you know that I could have saved myself from this pain, yet I am dying for the
sake of your Law. 28 Have pity on your people, so that they will not have to suffer the
pain I have suffered. 29 Let my blood and
my death take away their sin and guilt."

30 After Eleazar had said these things,
he died. This faithful man had been cruelly
tortured, but he refused to reject God's
Law. His clear thinking gave him the
courage to face such pain.

31 This story proves that faith and clear
thinking can control our emotions. 32 If
Eleazar's emotions had taken over his
thinking, then we would have told you.
33 But that didn't happen! Eleazar's mind
was stronger than his emotions 34 and his
painful suffering. You would be foolish to
think that clear thinking has no power over
emotions.[v] 35 I have shown that clear
thinking will always help you endure both
pain and happiness.

The Example of Eleazar

7 Our ancestor Eleazar was like the
skilled captain of a ship, and the Jewish religion was his ship. He was able to
think clearly, and so he steered the ship
through the rough sea of emotions. 2 The
evil King Antiochus was a raging storm that
pounded Eleazar's ship, and the painful
abuse he endured were the waves that almost drowned him. 3 But Eleazar headed
straight into the storm and refused to give
up, and he finally reached the safety of
never-ending victory, which was his death.

4 The faithful man Eleazar was stronger
than a city attacked by powerful weapons.
He was tortured in horrible ways, but he
used the shield of his faith and his mind to
defeat his enemies. 5 Eleazar's mind was
like a rocky cliff, stronger than the mighty
waves of emotions.

6 He was an honored priest whose entire
body was completely sacred and acceptable,
because he never ate anything God had forbidden. 7 Eleazar obeyed God's Law in
everything he did, and he knew how to live
right. 8 All priests[w] should follow Eleazar's
example and be willing to suffer and die for
the sake of the Law.

9 Our ancestor Eleazar showed wonderful patience when he endured such suffering, and he has helped us become more
loyal to God's sacred Law. He never rejected it, but proved that faith and clear
thinking can stand up against anything.
10 Though Eleazar was old, his courage and
strength were more powerful than both the
brutal torture and fire. 11 He was like our
ancestor Aaron who picked up a pan filled

[v] **6.34** *You . . . emotions*: One possible meaning for the difficult Greek text. [w] **7.8** *All priests*: Greek "Those who make the law."

6.15 2 Macc 6.21. **6.29** Is 53.5-12; 4 Macc 1.11; 17.17-22; 18.4; Mk 10.45. **7.1** 4 Macc 13.6, 7; 15.31, 32; 1 P 3.20, 21. **7.11** Ws 18.20-25.

with incense and ran into a crowd of people to defeat the fiery angel of death.[x]
12 Eleazar himself was tortured with fire,
yet he refused to give up his loyalty to the
Law. 13-14 His body and muscles were weak
and flabby from old age, but he amazed the
crowd as if he had the mind of a young
man. Eleazar had a strong mind and was
able to think clearly, just like his ancestor
Isaac, and so the painful torture was useless against him. 15 He obeyed the Law in
everything he did, and God blessed him
with a long life, then made him completely
holy at death.

16 Eleazar was a faithful old man who
endured the painful suffering that led to
his death. His story proves once again that
clear thinking, together with faith in God,
can control emotions. 17 You might be asking, "What if someone cannot think clearly
and carefully? Does that person still have
control over emotions?" 18 Yes, because
people who are completely faithful to God
will be able to control their evil desires.
19 Like our ancestors Abraham, Isaac, and
Jacob, those who have faith in God will always do right. 20 So don't think that someone who seems to be controlled by emotions cannot think clearly. 21 People who
trust in God and think wisely 22 know that
they will be blessed for doing what is right,
and they will be able to use their faith to
control their emotions. 23 Only those who
are wise and brave are the masters of their
emotions.

Seven Brave Brothers

8 Young people who are faithful to God
and who think clearly are also able to
endure painful suffering and torture. 2 For
example, when the evil King Antiochus realized he could not force Eleazar to eat
food that would have made him unacceptable to worship God,[y] Antiochus became
furious. He immediately ordered his guards
to bring other Hebrew prisoners to him,
then said to them, "If any of you choose to
eat this food, you will be set free. But if you
refuse, you will be punished even more
cruelly than Eleazar was."

3 Seven brave brothers and their mother
were soon brought to Antiochus. The
brothers were honest and good-looking,
4 and they proudly stood in a circle around
their mother. Antiochus was surprised to
meet such successful young Jewish men,
and he liked them right away. He smiled
and asked them to come closer. Then he
said:

> 5 Young men, I like every one of
> you, and I think you are handsome
> and lucky to have such a large family. I
> am your friend, so listen to this advice:
> Don't follow the example of the foolish
> old man who was just tortured to
> death. 6 I have the power to punish
> you if you refuse to obey my command.
> But I can also help you if you choose
> to do what I say. 7 Follow my advice
> and reject the ancient customs of your
> religion, and I will give you powerful
> positions in my kingdom.
>
> 8 As young men, you would enjoy
> the Greek way of life if you choose to
> change your ways. 9 But I'm warning
> you, if you make me angry by disobey-
> ing me, I will put every one of you to
> death in brutal and horrible ways!
> 10 Be kind to yourselves. I am your en-
> emy, yet because you're so young and
> handsome I would be sorry to have to
> kill you. 11 Think carefully about your
> decision, because if you refuse to obey
> me, you will die by torture!

12 As soon as the king had finished
speaking, he ordered the guards to bring
everything they used to torture people, so
that the brothers could see them. The king
hoped they would be horrified enough to
eat the disgusting food. 13 So the guards
brought out torture wheels, stretching
frames, hooks,[z] pounding machines, big
pots and pans, iron clamps and wedges,[a] as
well as the blowers to keep the fire hot.

As they carried these things out, the
king shouted, 14 "Now it's time to be afraid,

[x]**7.11** *Aaron . . . fiery angel of death*: See Numbers 16.41-50. [y]**8.2** *food . . . God*: The meat of pigs (see 2 Maccabees 7.1). [z]**8.13** *hooks*: One possible meaning for the difficult Greek text. [a]**8.13** *wedges*: The use of many of the things mentioned in verse 13 isn't certain.

7.13,14 Gn 22.1-14. **7.19** 4 Macc 16.25. **8–13** 2 Macc 7.1-41. **8.6** Jn 19.10.

my young friends. Pray, and your God will
forgive you for being forced to disobey
his Law."
15 But even after the seven brothers
heard the king's threats and saw these horrible things, they were not afraid. In fact,
they stood up to him and would not let him
control their thinking or their faith.
16 Suppose one of the brothers had been
afraid. He might have said something like
this to the others:

> 17 We are fools! King Antiochus has
> said that he would be kind to us if we
> obeyed him. 18 So we should listen to
> him and avoid suffering such pain—it
> will kill us. 19 My brothers, think how
> cruelly we would be tortured with
> these awful things. Let's forget what
> we believe and stop being proud. 20 We
> are young men who respect our
> mother, 21 and we certainly don't de-
> serve to die! Even if we disobeyed
> God's Law, 22 God is kind enough to
> forgive us for being afraid of this king.
> 23 I don't want to die and leave this
> wonderful life behind. 24 There's noth-
> ing to be proud of if we oppose the
> king and are painfully tortured.
> 25 God's Law doesn't condemn a per-
> son to death for fearing such punish-
> ment, 26 so why should we stubbornly
> disobey the king and die, when we can
> obey him and live in peace?

27 But not one of the young brothers
said these things or even asked these questions! They were about to be tortured,
28 yet they refused to think such thoughts.
The brothers controlled their fear of pain,
29 and as soon as Antiochus had stopped
warning them to eat the food, they all
replied at the same time:

> 9 Go ahead and torture us, you evil
> king! We will die rather than disobey
> our ancient law. 2 We will not put our
> ancestors to shame by disobeying the
> law that our teacher Moses gave us.
> 3 You are a wicked ruler, and we know
> you hate us. But we don't feel sorry for
> ourselves, so don't you feel sorry for
> us.[b] 4 We realize you could rescue us if
> we rejected our law, but we don't want
> your pity. That would be worse than
> being killed.
> 5 You keep threatening to put us to
> death and trying to scare us into obey-
> ing you. Didn't you learn anything
> from watching Eleazar's faith just a
> short time ago? 6 And in the past, He-
> brew men much older than we are re-
> mained faithful to God while they en-
> dured painful torture. We are young
> and strong, and if you torture us, as
> you did our teacher Eleazar, we will
> certainly choose to die. 7 Go ahead and
> test us! You can torture us and put us
> to death for remaining true to our reli-
> gion, but you will never destroy our
> faith. 8 After we have endured the
> cruel and painful suffering, we will be
> rewarded for our faith and will be with
> God, because we suffer for his sake
> alone. 9 God will punish you with fire
> for killing us, and your torment will
> never end.

The First Brother Is Tortured

10 After the seven brothers had finished
speaking, King Antiochus was fiercely angry
at them for refusing to obey him and for
not accepting his offer to set them free.
11 So Antiochus ordered his guards to grab
the oldest brother. They tore off his tunic,
then tied his hands and arms together with
ropes. 12 They whipped him until they were
exhausted, yet he still would not give in to
Antiochus. Then they stretched out the
brave young man on the large wheel 13 until all his bones were out of joint. 14 He
shouted to Antiochus, 15 "You are an evil
and cruel king who is opposing God! You
are slaughtering me only for protecting
God's Law, not because I am a murderer or
an ungodly man."
16 The guards said, "Eat the meat of
pigs, and we will release you."
17 The brother replied, "You worthless
servants! This wheel isn't strong enough to
destroy my ability to think clearly. Go ahead
and slash my arms and legs. Burn my skin
and twist my joints. 18 I will show you that

[b]**9.3** *But . . . us*: One possible meaning for the difficult Greek text.
9.7 4 Macc 10.4; Mt 10.28; Lk 12.4, 5. **9.8** 4 Macc 6.10; Jas 1.12.

Hebrews will endure anything rather than do what is wrong."

19 As he was speaking, the guards started a fire underneath him. Some of them fanned the fire to make it hotter, while others tightened the wheel to stretch the young man even more. 20 Soon the wheel was covered with his blood, and his insides dripped down and put out part of the fire. Pieces of his skin fell to the ground, 21 and his muscles ripped apart. Yet the brave young man proved that he was worthy to be called Abraham's descendant. He did not groan, 22 but seemed almost divine as he suffered this pain with no fear.

23 "Do as I have done, my brothers," he shouted. "Do not give in after you've seen me die, but rely on the courage of our family and our Jewish brothers and sisters. 24 Be brave and oppose Antiochus for the sake of our religion. Then the God our ancestors worshiped will have mercy on our nation and will punish this wicked king." 25 After saying that, the oldest brother died.

The Second Brother Is Tortured

26 The crowd was amazed at the courage of the oldest brother. And just then, the guards brought the second brother forward. Each of the guards picked up a heavy iron club with sharp hooks on its end, and they tied him to the place where he would be tortured.

27 They first asked the young man if he wanted to eat the meat of pigs, and after they listened to his answer, 28 the guards tore out his muscles with their iron clubs. They ripped his skin from the neck down, then cut up his scalp. The brother endured the pain, even though the guards were as vicious as leopards.

29 The brother shouted, "I will gladly die for the sake of my ancient religion!" 30 He then turned to Antiochus and said, "You are suffering much more than I am, you evil ruler. You must watch us endure and overcome your cruel punishment. 31 In fact, I can barely feel any pain because my obedience makes me so happy. 32 God will severely punish you for being the most evil ruler in the world."

The Third Brother Is Tortured

10 After the second brother had died a glorious death, the third brother was brought forward. Many people begged him again and again to eat the meat of pigs and save himself from death. 2 But he shouted, "My two older brothers and I have the same mother and father, and they raised us all the same way. 3-4 And so I refuse to ignore the honor and love I share with them."[c]

5 The brother's courage made the guards angry. They pulled the bones of his hands and feet out of joint, 6 then broke his fingers, his arms and elbows, and his legs. 7 When they realized they could not force him to change his mind,[d] they threw down the things they had been using to torture him and dug their fingernails into his scalp, just as the Scythians[e] do. 8 They dragged him to the torture wheel and stretched him out on it. The brother felt his back breaking, and he saw his skin being torn and blood dripping from his insides.

9 Just as he was about to die, he said, 10 "Listen to me, you horrible man. My brothers and I are suffering only because our parents taught us to lead good lives. 11 But you will suffer never-ending pain for your evil and savage ways!"

The Fourth Brother Is Tortured

12 After the third brother had died as bravely as the first two, the guards dragged in the fourth brother. They told him, 13 "Don't be stupid like your three older brothers. Obey King Antiochus and save yourself from such pain."

14 He replied, "You can't make this fire hot enough to scare me! 15 I will never give

[c] **10.3,4** *them*: Greek; other ancient translations add the following verse: "So go ahead and torture me in any way you want. You will never destroy my faith!" [d] **10.7** *they . . . his mind*: One possible meaning for the difficult Greek text. [e] **10.7** *Scythians*: People known for their cruelty.

9.22 Ac 6.15; 2 Co 3.18; Phil 3.21. **9.28** 1 Co 15.32. **10.4** 4 Macc 9.7; Mt 10.28; Lk 12.4, 5. **10.7** 2 Macc 4.47; 3 Macc 7.5.

in to the king or disgrace my family. I swear this by my brothers' sacred death and by the endless torment of the king and by the never-ending lives of faithful Jews. 16 Torture me however you want, then watch me endure all pain, just as my brothers did."

17 The cruel Antiochus was so furious when he heard these words that he ordered his guards to cut out the brother's tongue! This showed what an evil and horrible murderer Antiochus really was.

18 Before they did, the brother said, "Even if you cut out my tongue so that I cannot speak, God will still hear my prayers. 19 And you will never stop any of us from thinking clearly. 20 For the sake of our God, we will gladly let you slaughter our bodies. 21 But know that our God will soon punish you for cutting out a tongue that has sung songs of praise to him."

The Fifth Brother Is Tortured

11 After the fourth brother had been cruelly tortured, he died. Then his younger brother jumped up and said, 2 "Listen, you brutal king. I am willing to be tortured for the sake of my obedience to God's Law. 3 I will let you put me to death, so that you will be guilty of yet another murder! Then God will severely punish you as a criminal. 4 I know that you hate people who do right, and that's why you are killing us. 5 We worship God, the Creator of the entire world, and we obey his sacred Law. 6-8 For this, we should be honored, not punished.[f]

9 Before he finished speaking, the guards tied him up and dragged him to the place where he would be tortured. 10 They forced him to his knees, then tied him to the wheel and placed iron clamps around his legs. They bent his whole body backwards across the wheel[g] until he was curled up like a scorpion, and his bones were out of joint. 11 He could barely breathe because of the pain, 12 yet he said, "Cruel king, thank you for forcing us to suffer in these horrible ways, because you will become very angry when you watch us bravely endure them for the sake of God's Law."

The Sixth Brother Is Tortured

13 The fifth brother then died, and the sixth brother was brought forward. King Antiochus asked, "Are you willing to eat the meat of pigs, so that you will be set free?"

The brother answered, 14 "Though I am younger than my brothers, I can think as clearly as they did. 15 We were taught to do right and to be faithful to God, and we will die doing that! 16 So if you are planning to torture me for not eating this unclean food, then torture me!"

17 After he had finished speaking, the guards led him to the torture wheel. 18 They stretched him tightly across the wheel until his back was broken, then they started a fire under him. 19 They poked his back and sides with fiery hot sticks until his insides were scorched.

20 While they were torturing him, he said, "My brothers and I have been brought to this cruel place to see if our faith can help us stand up to your wickedness. And we have won, 21 because an intelligent smart person with a deep faith can never be defeated. 22 I am an honest and good man, and I will bravely die, just as my brothers have. 23 You proudly think of ways to torture and abuse those who remain faithful to God, yet my death will bring your downfall. 24 My five brothers and I have put an end to your brutal ways, 25 because you have not been able to force us to change our mind or to eat the disgusting meat of pigs. 26 Your fire isn't hot enough to scare us, and none of your cruel ways can destroy our faith. 27 Even your guards have no power over us! God's Law has protected us and helped us hold on to our ability to think clearly."

The Seventh Brother Is Tortured

12 The sixth brother was then thrown into a large pot of boiling oil, where he died a glorious death. The youngest

[f]**11.6** *punished*: Greek; other ancient translations add "You don't know what it's like to have feelings, and you have no hope of forgiveness. In fact, you will never know God, because you torture those who worship him." [g]**11.10** *They bent . . . wheel*: One possible meaning for the difficult Greek text.

10.18 Is 53.7-12; Ro 8.27. **10.21** Is 35.6. **11.20** 4 Macc 6.10. **11.26** He 12.2.

brother was finally brought in. 2 King Antiochus had hated the other six brothers, yet when he saw their youngest brother already tied in chains, he felt sorry for him. The king asked this boy to come closer to him, then begged, 3 "Don't be stupid like your older brothers. They died horrible deaths because they refused to obey me. 4 And if you refuse to obey me, you will also be brutally tortured and will die a young boy. 5 But if you do as I say, then I will treat you as a friend and will make you a leader in my kingdom."

6 After Antiochus had said these things, he ordered his guards to bring in the mother of the seven brothers. He wanted to express his sorrow over the deaths of her six sons and to talk her into making her last son obey him.

7 She talked to her youngest son in Hebrew, and later in the book I will tell you what she said. 8 But after she finished speaking, the boy replied, "Let me go, so that I can talk to the king and his officials myself!" 9 The guards were glad that he had asked to be let go, so they untied him right away.

10 The boy ran to the nearest pot of hot coals 11 and shouted, "You disgusting and evil ruler! God has given you this kingdom and every good thing you have. You should be ashamed that you have tortured and killed his faithful servants. 12 And so, because of your cruel ways, God will punish you with never-ending fire and horrible pain. You will suffer forever! 13 You weren't ashamed to watch your guards abuse my brothers and cut out their tongues, even though my brothers were human beings and had feelings just as you do. You are more like a wild animal than a human, 14 but they proved their courage and loyalty to God. You will soon moan in sorrow for killing such good and innocent men."

15 The boy knew he was about to be killed, so he said, 16 "I will follow the perfect example of my brothers, 17 and I pray that the God of my ancestors will show mercy to our nation.[h] 18 God will surely punish you now and in the life to come!"

19 After he had made these threats, he jumped into the large pot of coals and killed himself.

The Brothers Controlled Their Fear with Clear Thinking

13 The seven brothers willingly endured suffering and death, and so you surely agree now that thinking clearly, together with faith in God, can control emotions. 2 If these seven brothers had listened to their emotions and had eaten the disgusting meat of pigs, then we would agree that fear defeated them. 3 But that didn't happen! The young men never stopped thinking what they needed to do. God blessed them for this, and so they conquered their emotions. 4 The power of the mind must never be forgotten! With their minds, the brothers controlled their fear and pain, 5 and they refused to give in to the cruel and fiery tortures. That's why I am convinced that clear thinking can control emotions.

6 Tall, rocky cliffs protect a harbor from raging waves, so that boats can dock safely in calm water. 7 Just like those strong cliffs, the brothers' clear thinking protected their faith and conquered their raging emotions. 8 The young men encouraged one another and sang like a holy choir, 9 "Dear brothers, let us die together for the sake of God's Law! We will be like the three young men who were thrown into a flaming furnace in Assyria.[i] 10 Be brave and show our enemies how faithful we are to God."

11 They encouraged one another by saying such things as, "Have courage, brothers, and proudly endure this torture. 12 Remember our ancestor Abraham and his son Isaac, who would have let his own father kill him for the sake of religion."

13 The seven brothers were joyful and fearless, and they looked at one another and said:

[h]**12.17** *our nation*: Greek; other ancient translations "my people." [i]**13.9** *the three young men . . . Assyria*: See Daniel 3.

12.13 Ws 7.1-6; Ac 14.15. **12.17** 4 Macc 6.29. **12.19** 4 Macc 17.1. **13.6** 4 Macc 7.1; 15.31. **13.8** 4 Macc 14.7, 8. **13.9** Dn 3.1-30; 4 Macc 16.21. **13.12** Gn 22.1-14; Is 51.1; Ws 10.5; 4 Macc 14.20; 15.28; He 11.17-19.

We dedicated ourselves completely
to God. He gave us our lives and our
bodies, so we could use them to defend his sacred Law. 14 King Antiochus
thinks he is putting us to death, yet we
refuse to fear him. 15 Instead, we fear
the endless struggle and punishment
we will face if we sin against God's
command.

16 So let us have faith and clear
thinking—these will give us self-
control and will protect us, just as armor protects a soldier. 17 We might
die,[j] but when we do, Abraham, Isaac,
and Jacob will welcome us into death,
and all our ancestors will praise us.

18 As each of the brothers was dragged
away to be punished, the people watching
said to each one of them, "Don't make us
ashamed of our Jewish religion, dear
friend. And don't disgrace the faith of our
ancestors."

The Love of the Seven Brothers

19 You know how strong the love of a
family can be. In fact, God was wise in seeing that family love begins even before a
child is born, and that it is carried down
through the child's descendants. 20 Each of
the brothers spent the same amount of
time growing in their mother's womb, and
each one was born into this world in the
same way. 21 Their mother nursed and
hugged them all, and so they grew up in a
loving family. 22 This love helped the brothers grow into strong and intelligent men
who knew a lot about God's Law.

23 Their loving family also taught them
to love each other, 24 and they learned the
same lessons about right living and obeying
God. 25 The brothers gladly helped each
other grow into honest and respected men,
26 and their faith in God made them closer
than most brothers.

27 All of these things—their birth and
close family and lessons about life—helped
the brothers grow up loving each other very
much. But even as Antiochus was cruelly
torturing the brothers to death, the others
who were still alive were able to watch patiently because of their loyalty to the Jewish
religion.

14 The brothers encouraged one another to endure great pain, so they
would be strong enough to overcome the
torture and to control their emotions of
love.

The Courage of the Bothers

2 Clear thinking[k] is more dignified than
kings and cannot be controlled by anyone.
3 The seven brothers agreed to be completely faithful to their religion, 4 and each
one was brave, even when faced with
death. 5 They seemed to be in a hurry to
die and win the prize of never-ending life.
6 Just as hands and feet move when the
mind tells them, the holy young brothers
listened to their undying loyalty to God and
willingly died. 7-8 Praise the seven holy
brothers, because they also remained loyal
to one another. They conquered their fears
by joining together and treating torture as
though it were something to sing about.
The brothers were like the seven days
of creation, dancing together around the
center of religion.[l]

9 We shudder when we hear how these
young brothers were tortured. Not only
were they forced to watch each other suffer
and listen to the angry threats of Antiochus, they also had to endure the pain of
being burned to death 10 by a fire that
quickly destroyed their bodies. No other
death could be that brutal!

The Courage of Their Mother

11 Clear thinking wasn't the only thing
that helped the seven brothers endure the
suffering. The mind of a woman who had
endured her own tortures encouraged
them. 12 The mother of the seven young
men was very brave as she watched her
sons being cruelly put to death.

13 It is difficult to imagine how much a
mother loves her children. She feels that

[j] **13.17** *die*: Greek; other ancient translations "suffer." [k] **14.2** *Clear thinking*: Or "The mind."
[l] **14.7,8** *They conquered . . . religion*: One possible meaning for the difficult Greek text.

13.14 Mt 10.28; Lk 12.4, 5. **13.17** 4 Macc 5.37; Lk 16.22. **14.2** He 12.1.
14.7,8 4 Macc 13.8.

love deep inside. 14 In fact, part of being a parent is having a strong love for your child. That's also true for animals. 15 For example, birds build nests to keep their young safe—tame birds build on the roofs of houses, 16 and wild birds build in the cracks of rocky hills and in the tops of trees. They wait until the eggs hatch, then they protect the baby birds by keeping away dangerous animals. 17 If animals do start to attack, then out of love the parent birds fly in circles over the nest, trying to help the young by calling them to safety.

18 You may wonder why I chose to use animals to show parents' love for their children. 19 After all, when bees are busy making honeycombs, they will risk death and use their iron-like stingers to protect their hive. 20 But though this mother loved her seven sons very much, she did not lose courage as she watched them die. Her mind and her faith were as strong as Abraham's.

15 The clear thinking of these young men conquered their worst fears, while their mother depended upon her faith, which she knew was more important than her own children.

2 She had two choices: She could remain loyal to her Jewish religion, or she could rescue her sons for a little while, just as the evil king promised. 3 She chose to remain loyal to her religion, because she knew it would give her sons never-ending life, just as God had promised.

A Mother's Love

4 As parents, we love our children very much. And one day, they will grow to be very much like us, thinking and acting in ways we have shown them. This is especially true for mothers, who have a deeper understanding of their children than fathers do, because the mothers suffer the pain of giving birth. 5 Though women are not as strong as men, they are much more devoted to their children, because they are the ones who gave birth.

6-7 No mother has ever loved her children more than this mother loved her seven sons. She suffered the pain of childbirth seven times, each birth making her love for them even deeper. 8 However, she feared God and refused to rescue them from danger. 9 Her sons were strong and obeyed God's Law, and so she loved them even more. 10 They loved her and each other, and they bravely obeyed her and remained faithful to God right up to the time of their death.

11 The mother of these brothers suffered along with them, because she loved them very much. Yet their punishment was never brutal enough to make her stop thinking clearly. 12 As each of her sons was tortured, she encouraged him to die for the sake of their religion. 13 The love she had for her sons was strong and unending, and she suffered her own pain 14 as she watched them being tortured and burned to death. Her faith gave her the courage 15 to see their toes and fingers fall to the ground and the skin on their heads peel away like a mask.

16 She suffered more pain as she watched her sons die than she did when she gave birth to them. 17 This woman showed complete loyalty to her religion at all times 18 and remained strong when her three oldest sons died, even when her second son sadly looked up at her. 19 A large crowd had gathered, but she did not cry when she saw the agony in her sons' eyes and heard their last breath. 20 And she refused to moan in sorrow when she saw the pile of their burned skin and hands and heads and bodies. 21 She could not ignore the tortured cries of her children as they called out to her.[m] 22 The woman's distress and pain were tremendous as she watched Antiochus torture her sons on the wheel and with hot irons. 23 But her clear thinking, together with her faith in God, gave

[m] **15.21** *She could not ignore . . . called out to her*: The Greek text states that their voices attracted her attention even more than would two legendary sounds that could not be ignored: First, the singing of the sirens, which were creatures thought to be half bird or fish and half woman, whose beautiful songs cast a spell on sailors and tricked them into ramming their ships onto the rocks; and second, the singing of swans as they die.

14.20 4 Macc 13.12. **15.2** Jr 21.8; He 11.25.

her enough courage to control her love for
them.

The Constant Faith of This Mother

24 This mother's faith in God was so
strong that she was able to endure seeing
the horrible abuse and death of her seven
sons. 25 She was in complete distress as she
watched her own children being tortured.[n]
26 She had two choices: let them die or rescue them so they could live a little while
longer. 27 The woman refused to save any
of her seven sons for even a short time.
28 Instead, with the faith of her ancestor
Abraham, she remained faithful to God.

29 She is the hero of our nation and our
religion, because she proved the strength
of God's Law by winning a great victory.
30 Her courage and endurance were
stronger than those of any man, 31 as she
bravely survived the mighty waves of fear,
just as Noah's boat safely carried his family
through the flood.[o] 32 This woman remained faithful to God's Law, even though
emotions flooded her heart and pounded
inside her as she watched her sons suffer
and die. She defeated the raging storms
that attack our faith.

The Mother's Faith Defeated King Antiochus

16 This older woman was able to
watch her seven sons being tortured to death. This certainly proves that
clear thinking and faith in God can control
emotions.

2 So I have proven that people can rule
over their emotions, and that this mother
defeated the cruelest of tortures. 3 The love
she had for her sons became even stronger
as she saw Antiochus punish them in different ways. Her love was fiercer than the
lions that surrounded Daniel[p] and more
powerful than the flaming furnace where
Mishael was thrown.[q] 4 But she used her
mind to control her strong emotions.

5 Suppose this mother had given up and
mourned her sons' death. She might have
said something like this:

6 I am such a miserable and unhappy woman! I was once the mother
of seven sons, yet now they are dead.
7 I was pregnant and gave birth seven
times for nothing, and the time I spent
nursing and taking care of my babies
was wasted.

8 My sons, I suffered while giving
birth to each of you and raising you to
be young men. Now all of that means
nothing. 9 Some of you were unmarried, and the rest of you had no children, and so I will never know the
happiness of being a grandmother.

10 I was the mother of seven beautiful children. Now I am a very sad and
lonely widow, 11 with no son to bury
me when I die.

12 But the woman feared God and refused to mourn for her sons like that. She
never tried to talk them out of their decision
to die, and she never groaned in sorrow.
13 In fact, she encouraged each of them to
die for the sake of the Jewish religion, because she knew that death would begin
never-ending life for them. 14 She was certainly a faithful and respected leader who
won a victory for God by defeating that evil
King Antiochus! Her words and her actions
prove that she is stronger than any man.

15 When this woman and her sons were
arrested, she watched as Eleazar was tortured, then turned to her sons and said in
Hebrew:

16 My sons, be proud of your
chance to be a witness for our Jewish
nation. Fight hard for God's ancient
Law! 17 This old man is enduring
much pain for the sake of our religion.
You are young men, and so I would be
ashamed if you were terrified of being
tortured. 18 Since God has given you a
happy life in this world, 19 you should
willingly suffer anything for his sake.

20 It was for the sake of our God

[n] **15.25** *tortured*: One possible meaning for the difficult Greek text of verse 25. [o] **15.31** *Noah's boat . . . flood*: See Genesis 6-9. [p] **16.3** *the lions . . . Daniel*: See Daniel 6.1-28. [q] **16.3** *the flaming furnace . . . Mishael . . . thrown*: See Daniel 1.7; 3.1-30.

15.28 4 Macc 13.12; 17.6. **15.31** Ws 14.6, 7; 4 Macc 7.1; 13.6. **16.16** 4 Macc 6.10. **16.20** Gn 22.10; 4 Macc 13.12.

that our ancestor Abraham was willing
to sacrifice his son Isaac.[r] And when
Isaac saw his father raise the knife
over his body, he did not cry or beg
him to stop. 21 Daniel was thrown into
a pit of lions. Hananiah, Azariah, and
Mishael were thrown into a flaming
furnace.[s] They all endured pain for the
sake of our God. 22 So you must have
the same strong faith and stop being
miserable. 23 It is foolish to think that
people who have faith in God cannot
overcome such great pain.
24 With these words, the woman encouraged her seven sons and convinced
them to die rather than disobey God's Law.
25 They realized that anyone who dies for
the sake of God will have done what is
right, just like Abraham, Isaac, Jacob, and
all our ancestors.

17 Some of the guards who arrested
this woman said that when she was
about to be put to death, she threw herself into the fire, so that no one could
touch her.

Praise to This Brave Mother

2 Brave woman, you and your sons defeated King Antiochus by showing courage
and by stopping his cruel and evil plan.
3 You are a strong roof that is set on top of
the columns of your sons, and you never
trembled or fell when their pain shook your
insides. 4 Be brave, faithful mother, and
keep your hope in God strong. 5 The moon
and the stars are not as majestic as you, because you showed your sons what it means
to be holy. God has honored you and has
given you a place in heaven alongside
them, 6 because you gave birth to faithful
descendants of our ancestor Abraham.[t]

These Faithful Jews Saved Israel

7 If I could show you the history of the
Jewish religion by painting a picture, the
first person to look at it would be shocked
to see the mother of the seven sons standing by as they were tortured to death for
the sake of our faith.
8 The people of Israel must never forget
these nine people who willingly died for the
sake of our God. Their tomb should be
honored with the following words:

> 9 Buried in this tomb are a respected
> priest, a dear old woman, and her
> seven sons. The evil King Antiochus
> brutally killed them as he tried to de-
> stroy the Jewish religion. 10 But these
> nine people remained faithful to God
> and bravely endured being tortured to
> death. And so, they proved that their
> nation was innocent of any crime.

11-12 God certainly helped them endure
in the contest which tested their obedience. And the prize they received was
never-ending life! 13 Eleazar was the first
one to oppose Antiochus, then the mother,
and finally her seven sons. 14 King Antiochus was the fierce enemy, and the
crowds stood watching him. 15 But obedience to God won, and he gave the prize to
these nine faithful people. 16 The crowds
were amazed and knew that these who had
died were truly God's people.
17 Antiochus and his officials couldn't
believe these nine had the strength to endure such torture. 18 God rewarded them,
and so they will live forever with God.
19 Moses said, "God protects everyone who
is faithful to him." 20 That's exactly what
happened to these nine persons. They remained faithful to God, and he honored
them with life that never ends.

God has blessed us because of them.
Our enemies no longer have control over
us, 21 King Antiochus was punished, and
our entire country is once again pure.
These nine who willingly died in our place
took away the sin of our nation! 22 They
suffered as a sacrifice to God, and because
of their death, he rescued Israel from
horrible abuse.

[r] **16.20** *Abraham . . . Isaac*: See Genesis 22.1-19.
[s] **16.21** *Daniel . . . Hananiah, Azariah, and Mishael . . . furnace*: See the notes at verse 3.
[t] **17.6** *Abraham*: One possible meaning for the difficult Greek text of verse 6.

16.21 4 Macc 13.9. **16.25** 4 Macc 7.19. **17.1** 2 Macc 7.41; 4 Macc 12.19.
17.6 4 Macc 15.28. **17.11,12** **a** 4 Macc 6.10; **b** 2 Macc 7.36; 4 Macc 5.37; 9.22.
17.17-22 4 Macc 6.29. **17.19** Dt 33.3. **17.21** Ro 3.25, 26; He 9.11-15; 1 P 1.19; 1 Jn 1.7.

23 After Antiochus had seen their courage and strength, he used them as an example and ordered his own soldiers to be as fearless. 24 His soldiers became brave warriors in battle, and so his army attacked and defeated every enemy.

18 Listen to me, you people of Israel. We are the descendants of Abraham, so obey God's Law and always do what is right. 2 Now you know that clear thinking and faith in him will conquer all emotions, both those that make us suffer inside and those that cause pain to our bodies.

3 The nine people who willingly died cruel deaths for the sake of our Jewish religion were respected by others and were also honored with God's blessing. 4 Because they showed us once again how to obey God's Law, our country is at peace and has wiped out our enemy. 5 Antiochus was punished on earth and will be punished forever after his death. He could not force us to worship pagan idols or to reject our ancient customs, so he left Jerusalem and attacked the Persians.

The Mother's Last Words to Her Sons

6 The mother spoke these words to her seven sons just before they were tortured:

> 7 When I was a young woman, I kept myself safe by living in my father's house, and I refused to have sex with any man. 8 No one ever bothered me when I crossed the desert, though it is filled with demons that tried to harm me.[u] 9 When I was older, I married and lived with my husband, and soon we became parents.
>
> Your father died when you were very young. He was a happy man, who loved you and was proud of each of you. 10 He taught you God's Law and about his prophets, 11 about how Cain murdered his brother Abel,[v] about Isaac who was placed on the altar to be sacrificed,[w] and about how Joseph ended up in prison.[x] 12 Your father told you about the faith of Phinehas,[y] and about Hananiah, Azariah, and Mishael in the flaming furnace.[z] 13 He praised and blessed Daniel, who was thrown into a pit of lions.[a] 14 He taught you this promise of God in the book of Isaiah: "When you walk through fire, you won't be scorched by the flames."[b] 15 You learned from him the songs of David, who sang, "The Lord's people will suffer a lot,"[c] 16 and your father made you learn the wise sayings of Solomon, like "The life-giving tree will be given to all who do what God commands."[d] 17 He answered for you the prophet Ezekiel's question: "Can these dried-out bones come back to life?"[e] 18 And your father taught you to sing the song of Moses, where God said, 19 "I am the one who takes life and gives it again; I am the only one who can let you live a long time."[f]

God Is Praised

20 The day this mother died was terrible, but not completely. Antiochus, the brutal king of the Greeks, made the fire under the large pots hotter and hotter, and he tortured the seven sons of this faithful Israelite woman in one way after another. 21 He poked out their eyes and cut out their tongues and put them each to death in horrible ways. 22 God will certainly punish him for these crimes!

23 Yet, because of that terrible day, the seven descendants of Abraham and their famous mother are now with the choir of their ancestors in heaven, where God has already given them pure life that will never end. 24 Give praise to God forever! Amen.

[u] **18.8** *it is filled with demons that tried to harm me*: The desert was believed to be a dangerous place where demons lived. [v] **18.11** *Cain murdered his brother Abel*: See Genesis 4.1-16. [w] **18.11** *Isaac . . . sacrificed*: See Genesis 22.1-19. [x] **18.11** *how Joseph ended up in prison*: See Genesis 39.1-23. [y] **18.12** *the faith of Phinehas*: See Numbers 25.1-13. [z] **18.12** *Hananiah, Azariah, and Mishael . . . flaming furnace*: See Daniel 1.7; 3.1-30. [a] **18.13** *Daniel . . . pit of lions*: See Daniel 6.1-28. [b] **18.14** *When you walk . . . flames*: See Isaiah 43.2. [c] **18.15** *The Lord's people will suffer a lot*: See Psalm 34.19. [d] **18.16** *life-giving tree . . . commands*: See Proverbs 3.18. [e] **18.17** *Can these dried-out bones . . . life*: See Ezekiel 37.1-3. [f] **18.19** *I am the only one . . . a long time*: See Deuteronomy 30.20; 32.39.

18.4 4 Macc 6.29. **18.8** Dt 22.25-27. **18.24** Ro 11.36; 16.27; 2 Ti 4.18; He 13.21.

The
NEW TESTAMENT

About the New Testament

The New Testament is a collection of 27 books and letters written in Greek. They are arranged in four groups:

(1) Gospels and Acts. This group contains the four Gospels, which are Matthew, Mark, Luke, and John. The term "gospel" means "good news," and these four Gospels tell the good news about Jesus Christ. The group also contains the book of Acts, which tells how the good news spread in the years after Jesus died and was raised from death.

(2) Letters of Paul. This group is made up of Romans, 1 and 2 Corinthians, Galatians, Ephesians, Philippians, Colossians, 1 and 2 Thessalonians, 1 and 2 Timothy, Titus, and Philemon. These letters have traditionally been called "epistles," and each one is named for the group or person that it was written to.

(3) Other Letters. This group contains letters written by people other than Paul. It contains Hebrews, James, 1 and 2 Peter, 1, 2, and 3 John, and Jude. The Letter to the Hebrews doesn't give its author's name, but each of the other letters is named for the person who wrote it.

(4) Revelation. This book is quite different from the other New Testament books, because it is a book of visions and prophecies.

MATTHEW

ABOUT THIS BOOK

The Sermon on the Mount (5.1—7.28), the Lord's Prayer (6.9-13), and the Golden Rule (7.12: "Treat others as you want them to treat you") are all in this book. It is perhaps the best known and the most quoted of all the books that have ever been written about Jesus. That is one reason why Matthew was placed first among the four books about Jesus called Gospels.

One of the most important ideas found here is that God expects his people to obey him, and this is what is meant by the Greek word that appears in many translations as *righteousness*. It is used seven times by Matthew, but only once by Luke, and not at all by Mark. So it is an important clue to much of what Matthew wants his readers to understand about the teaching of Jesus.

Jesus first uses this word at his own baptism, when he tells John the Baptist, "We must do all that God wants us to do" (3.15). Then, during his Sermon on the Mount, he speaks five more times of what God's people must do to obey him (5.6, 10, 20; 6.1, 33). And finally, he reminds the chief priests and leaders of the people, "John the Baptist showed you how to do right" (21.32).

Matthew wanted to provide for the people of his time a record of Jesus' message and ministry. It is clear that the Old Testament Scriptures were very important to these people. And Matthew never fails to show when these texts point to the coming of Jesus as the Messiah sent from God. Matthew wrote this book to make sure Christians knew that their faith in Jesus as the Messiah was well anchored in the Old Testament Scriptures, and to help them grow in faith.

Matthew ends his story with the words of Jesus to his followers, which tell what they are to do after he leaves them:

> *"I have been given all authority in heaven and on earth! Go to the people of all nations and make them my disciples. Baptize them in the name of the Father, the Son, and the Holy Spirit, and teach them to do everything I have told you. I will be with you always, even until the end of the world."*
>
> *(28.18b-20)*

A QUICK LOOK AT THIS BOOK

- The Ancestors and Birth of Jesus (1.1—2.23)
- The Message of John the Baptist (3.1-12)
- The Baptism and Temptation of Jesus (3.13—4.11)
- Jesus in Galilee (4.12—18.35)
- Jesus Goes from Galilee to Jerusalem (19.1—20.34)
- Jesus' Last Week: His Trial and Death (21.1—27.66)
- Jesus Is Alive (28.1-20)

The Ancestors of Jesus
(Luke 3.23-38)

1 Jesus Christ came from the family of
King David and also from the family of
Abraham. And this is a list of his ancestors.
2-6a From Abraham to King David, his ancestors were:

Abraham, Isaac, Jacob, Judah and his
brothers (Judah's sons were Perez and
Zerah, and their mother was Tamar),
Hezron;

Ram, Amminadab, Nahshon, Salmon,
Boaz (his mother was Rahab), Obed (his
mother was Ruth), Jesse, and King David.

6b-11 From David to the time of the exile
in Babylonia, the ancestors of Jesus were:

David, Solomon (his mother had been
Uriah's wife), Rehoboam, Abijah, Asa, Jehoshaphat, Jehoram;

Uzziah, Jotham, Ahaz, Hezekiah, Manasseh, Amon, Josiah, and Jehoiachin and
his brothers.

12-16 From the exile to the birth of Jesus,
his ancestors were:

Jehoiachin, Shealtiel, Zerubbabel,
Abiud, Eliakim, Azor, Zadok, Achim;

Eliud, Eleazar, Matthan, Jacob, and
Joseph, the husband of Mary, the mother of
Jesus, who is called the Messiah.

17 There were fourteen generations
from Abraham to David. There were also
fourteen from David to the exile in Babylonia and fourteen more to the birth of the
Messiah.

The Birth of Jesus
(Luke 2.1-7)

18 This is how Jesus Christ was born. A
young woman named Mary was engaged to
Joseph from King David's family. But before
they were married, she learned that she
was going to have a baby by God's Holy
Spirit. 19 Joseph was a good man[a] and did
not want to embarrass Mary in front of
everyone. So he decided to quietly call off
the wedding.

20 While Joseph was thinking about this,
an angel from the Lord came to him in a
dream. The angel said, "Joseph, the baby
that Mary will have is from the Holy Spirit.
Go ahead and marry her. 21 Then after her
baby is born, name him Jesus,[b] because he
will save his people from their sins."

22 So the Lord's promise came true, just
as the prophet had said, 23 "A virgin will
have a baby boy, and he will be called
Immanuel," which means "God is with us."

24 After Joseph woke up, he and Mary
were soon married, just as the Lord's angel
had told him to do. 25 But they did not
sleep together before her baby was born.
Then Joseph named him Jesus.

The Wise Men

2 When Jesus was born in the village of
Bethlehem in Judea, Herod was king.
During this time some wise men[c] from the
east came to Jerusalem 2 and said, "Where
is the child born to be king of the Jews? We
saw his star in the east[d] and have come to
worship him."

3 When King Herod heard about this, he
was worried, and so was everyone else in
Jerusalem. 4 Herod brought together the
chief priests and the teachers of the Law of
Moses and asked them, "Where will the
Messiah be born?"

5 They told him, "He will be born in
Bethlehem, just as the prophet wrote,

6 'Bethlehem in the land
  of Judea,
you are very important
  among the towns of Judea.
From your town
  will come a leader,
who will be like a shepherd
  for my people Israel.' "

7 Herod secretly called in the wise men
and asked them when they had first seen
the star. 8 He told them, "Go to Bethlehem
and search carefully for the child. As soon
as you find him, let me know. I want to go
and worship him too."

[a] **1.19** *good man*: Or "kind man," or "man who always did the right thing." [b] **1.21** *name him Jesus*: In Hebrew the name "Jesus" means "the Lord saves." [c] **2.1** *wise men*: People famous for studying the stars. [d] **2.2** *his star in the east*: Or "his star rise."

1.6b-11 2 K 24.14, 15; 2 Ch 36.10; Jr 27.19-21. **1.18** Lk 1.27. **1.21** Si 46.1; Lk 1.31. **1.23** Is 7.14 (LXX). **1.25** Lk 2.21. **2.6** Mic 5.2.

9 The wise men listened to what the
king said and then left. And the star they
had seen in the east went on ahead of
them until it stopped over the place where
the child was. 10 They were thrilled and excited to see the star.
11 When the men went into the house
and saw the child with Mary, his mother,
they knelt down and worshiped him. They
took out their gifts of gold, frankincense,
and myrrh[e] and gave them to him. 12 Later
they were warned in a dream not to return
to Herod, and they went back home by another road.

The Escape to Egypt

13 After the wise men had gone, an angel from the Lord appeared to Joseph in a
dream and said, "Get up! Hurry and take
the child and his mother to Egypt! Stay there
until I tell you to return, because Herod is
looking for the child and wants to kill him."
14 That night, Joseph got up and took
his wife and the child to Egypt, 15 where
they stayed until Herod died. So the Lord's
promise came true, just as the prophet had
said, "I called my son out of Egypt."

The Killing of the Children

16 When Herod found out that the wise
men from the east had tricked him, he was
very angry. He gave orders for his men to
kill all the boys who lived in or near Bethlehem and were two years old and younger.
This was based on what he had learned
from the wise men.
17 So the Lord's promise came true, just
as the prophet Jeremiah had said,

18 "In Ramah a voice was heard
crying and weeping loudly.
Rachel was mourning
for her children,
and she refused
to be comforted,
because they were dead."

The Return from Egypt

19 After King Herod died, an angel from
the Lord appeared in a dream to Joseph
while he was still in Egypt. 20 The angel
said, "Get up and take the child and his
mother back to Israel. The people who
wanted to kill him are now dead."
21 Joseph got up and left with them for
Israel. 22 But when he heard that Herod's son
Archelaus was now ruler of Judea, he was
afraid to go there. Then in a dream he was
told to go to Galilee, 23 and they went to live
there in the town of Nazareth. So the
Lord's promise came true, just as the prophet
had said, "He will be called a Nazarene."[f]

The Preaching of John the Baptist
(Mark 1.1-8; Luke 3.1-18; John 1.19-28)

3 Years later, John the Baptist started
preaching in the desert of Judea. 2 He
said, "Turn back to God! The kingdom of
heaven[g] will soon be here."[h]
3 John was the one the prophet Isaiah
was talking about, when he said,

"In the desert someone
is shouting,
'Get the road ready
for the Lord!
Make a straight path
for him.' "

4 John wore clothes made of camel's
hair. He had a leather strap around his
waist and ate grasshoppers and wild honey.
5 From Jerusalem and all Judea and
from the Jordan River Valley crowds of people went to John. 6 They told how sorry
they were for their sins, and he baptized
them in the river.
7 Many Pharisees and Sadducees also
came to be baptized. But John said to
them:

You bunch of snakes! Who warned
you to run from the coming judgment?
8 Do something to show that you have

[e]**2.11** *frankincense, and myrrh*: Frankincense was a valuable powder that was burned to make a sweet smell. Myrrh was a valuable sweet-smelling powder often used in perfume. [f]**2.23** *He will be called a Nazarene*: The prophet who said this is not known. [g]**3.2** *kingdom of heaven*: In the Gospel of Matthew "kingdom of heaven" is used with the same meaning as "God's kingdom" in Mark and Luke. [h]**3.2** *will soon be here*: Or "is already here."

2.15 Ho 11.1. **2.18** Jr 31.15. **2.23** Mk 1.24; Lk 2.39; Jn 1.45. **3.2** Mt 4.17; Mk 1.15. **3.3** Is 40.3 (LXX). **3.4** 2 K 1.8. **3.7** Mt 12.34; 23.33.

really given up your sins. 9 And don't
start telling yourselves that you belong
to Abraham's family. I tell you that God
can turn these stones into children for
Abraham. 10 An ax is ready to cut the
trees down at their roots. Any tree
that doesn't produce good fruit will
be chopped down and thrown into a fire.
11 I baptize you with water so that
you will give up your sins.[i] But someone more powerful is going to come,
and I am not good enough even to
carry his sandals.[j] He will baptize you
with the Holy Spirit and with fire.
12 His threshing fork is in his hand,
and he is ready to separate the wheat
from the husks.[k] He will store the
wheat in a barn and burn the husks in
a fire that never goes out.

The Baptism of Jesus
(Mark 1.9-11; Luke 3.21, 22)

13 Jesus left Galilee and went to the Jordan River to be baptized by John. 14 But
John kept objecting and said, "I ought to be
baptized by you. Why have you come
to me?"
15 Jesus answered, "For now this is how
it should be, because we must do all that
God wants us to do." Then John agreed.
16 So Jesus was baptized. And as soon as
he came out of the water, the sky opened,
and he saw the Spirit of God coming down
on him like a dove. 17 Then a voice from
heaven said, "This is my own dear Son,
and I am pleased with him."

Jesus and the Devil
(Mark 1.12, 13; Luke 4.1-13)

4 The Holy Spirit led Jesus into the
desert, so that the devil could test
him. 2 After Jesus had gone without eating[l]
for forty days and nights, he was very hungry. 3 Then the devil came to him and said,
"If you are God's Son, tell these stones to
turn into bread."
4 Jesus answered, "The Scriptures say:

'No one can live only on food.
People need every word
that God has spoken.' "

5 Next, the devil took Jesus to the holy
city and had him stand on the highest part
of the temple. 6 The devil said, "If you are
God's Son, jump off. The Scriptures say:

'God will give his angels
orders about you.
They will catch you
in their arms,
and you won't hurt
your feet on the stones.' "

7 Jesus answered, "The Scriptures also
say, 'Don't try to test the Lord your God!' "
8 Finally, the devil took Jesus up on a
very high mountain and showed him all the
kingdoms on earth and their power. 9 The
devil said to him, "I will give all this to you,
if you will bow down and worship me."
10 Jesus answered, "Go away Satan! The
Scriptures say:

'Worship the Lord your God
and serve only him.' "

11 Then the devil left Jesus, and angels
came to help him.

Jesus Begins His Work
(Mark 1.14, 15; Luke 4.14, 15)

12 When Jesus heard that John had
been put in prison, he went to Galilee.
13 But instead of staying in Nazareth, Jesus
moved to Capernaum. This town was be-

[i]**3.11** *so that you will give up your sins*: Or "because you have given up your sins." [j]**3.11** *carry his sandals*: This was one of the duties of a slave. [k]**3.12** *His threshing fork is in his hand, and he is ready to separate the wheat from the husks*: After Jewish farmers had trampled out the grain, they used a large fork to pitch the grain and the husks into the air. Wind would blow away the light husks, and the grain would fall back to the ground, where it could be gathered up. [l]**4.2** *without eating*: The Jewish people sometimes went without eating (also called "fasting") to show their love for God or to show sorrow for their sins.

3.9 Jn 8.33. **3.10** Mt 7.19. **3.12** Ws 5.14, 23. **3.17** Gn 22.2; Ps 2.7; Is 42.1; Mt 12.18; 17.5; Mk 1.11; Lk 9.35. **4.1** He 2.18; 4.15. **4.4** Dt 8.3. **4.6** Ps 91.11, 12. **4.7** Dt 6.16. **4.10** Dt 6.13. **4.12** Mt 14.3, 4; Mk 6.17; Lk 3.19, 20. **4.13** Jn 2.12.

side Lake Galilee in the territory of Zebulun and Naphtali.[m] 14 So God's promise came
true, just as the prophet Isaiah had said,

15 "Listen, lands of Zebulun
and Naphtali,
lands along the road
to the sea and east
of the Jordan!
Listen Galilee,
land of the Gentiles!
16 Although your people
live in darkness,
they will see
a bright light.
Although they live
in the shadow of death,
a light will shine
on them."

17 Then Jesus started preaching, "Turn
back to God! The kingdom of heaven will
soon be here."[n]

Jesus Chooses Four Fishermen

(Mark 1.16-20; Luke 5.1-11)

18 While Jesus was walking along the
shore of Lake Galilee, he saw two brothers.
One was Simon, also known as Peter, and
the other was Andrew. They were fishermen, and they were casting their net into
the lake. 19 Jesus said to them, "Come with
me! I will teach you how to bring in people
instead of fish." 20 Right then the two
brothers dropped their nets and went with
him.

21 Jesus walked on until he saw James
and John, the sons of Zebedee. They were
in a boat with their father, mending their
nets. Jesus asked them to come with him
too. 22 Right away they left the boat and
their father and went with Jesus.

Jesus Teaches, Preaches, and Heals

(Luke 6.17-19)

23 Jesus went all over Galilee, teaching
in the Jewish meeting places and preaching
the good news about God's kingdom. He
also healed every kind of disease and sickness. 24 News about him spread all over
Syria, and people with every kind of sickness
or disease were brought to him. Some of
them had a lot of demons in them, others
were thought to be crazy,[o] and still others
could not walk. But Jesus healed them all.

25 Large crowds followed Jesus from
Galilee and the region around the ten cities
known as Decapolis.[p] They also came from
Jerusalem, Judea, and from across the Jordan River.

The Sermon on the Mount

5 When Jesus saw the crowds, he went
up on the side of a mountain and sat
down.[q]

Blessings

(Luke 6.20-23)

Jesus' disciples gathered around him,
2 and he taught them:

3 God blesses those people
who depend only on him.
They belong to the kingdom
of heaven![r]
4 God blesses those people
who grieve.
They will find comfort!
5 God blesses those people
who are humble.
The earth will belong
to them!
6 God blesses those people
who want to obey him[s]
more than to eat or drink.

[m]**4.13** *Zebulun and Naphtali*: In Old Testament times these tribes were in northern Palestine, and in New Testament times many Gentiles lived where these tribes had once been. [n]**4.17** *The kingdom of heaven will soon be here*: See the two notes at 3.2. [o]**4.24** *thought to be crazy*: In ancient times people with epilepsy were thought to be crazy. [p]**4.25** *the ten cities known as Decapolis*: A group of ten cities east of Samaria and Galilee, where the people followed the Greek way of life. [q]**5.1** *sat down*: Teachers in the ancient world, including Jewish teachers, usually sat down when they taught. [r]**5.3** *They belong to the kingdom of heaven*: Or "The kingdom of heaven belongs to them." [s]**5.6** *who want to obey him*: Or "who want to do right" or "who want everyone to be treated right."

4.15,16 Is 9.1, 2. **4.17** Mt 3.2. **4.23** Mt 9.35; Mk 1.39. **5.4** Is 61.2. **5.5** Ps 37.11. **5.6** Is 55.1, 2; Si 24.21.

They will be given
what they want!
7 God blesses those people
who are merciful.
They will be treated
with mercy!
8 God blesses those people
whose hearts are pure.
They will see him!
9 God blesses those people
who make peace.
They will be called
his children!
10 God blesses those people
who are treated badly
for doing right.
They belong to the kingdom
of heaven.[t]

11 God will bless you when people
insult you, mistreat you, and tell all
kinds of evil lies about you because of
me. 12 Be happy and excited! You will
have a great reward in heaven. People
did these same things to the prophets
who lived long ago.

Salt and Light

(Mark 9.50; Luke 14.34, 35)

13 You are like salt for everyone on
earth. But if salt no longer tastes like
salt, how can it make food salty? All it
is good for is to be thrown out and
walked on.
14 You are like light for the whole
world. A city built on top of a hill cannot be hidden, 15 and no one would
light a lamp and put it under a clay
pot. A lamp is placed on a lampstand,
where it can give light to everyone in
the house. 16 Make your light shine, so
that others will see the good that you do
and will praise your Father in heaven.

The Law of Moses

17 Don't suppose that I came to do
away with the Law and the Prophets.[u]
I did not come to do away with them,
but to give them their full meaning.
18 Heaven and earth may disappear.
But I promise you that not even a period
or comma will ever disappear from the
Law. Everything written in it must
happen.
19 If you reject even the least important command in the Law and
teach others to do the same, you will
be the least important person in the
kingdom of heaven. But if you obey
and teach others its commands, you
will have an important place in the
kingdom. 20 You must obey God's commands better than the Pharisees and
the teachers of the Law obey them. If
you don't, I promise you that you will
never get into the kingdom of heaven.

Anger

21 You know that our ancestors
were told, "Do not murder" and "A
murderer must be brought to trial."
22 But I promise you that if you are angry with someone,[v] you will have to
stand trial. If you call someone a fool,
you will be taken to court. And if you
say that someone is worthless, you will
be in danger of the fires of hell.
23 So if you are about to place your
gift on the altar and remember that
someone is angry with you, 24 leave
your gift there in front of the altar.
Make peace with that person, then
come back and offer your gift to God.
25 Before you are dragged into
court, make friends with the person
who has accused you of doing wrong.
If you don't, you will be handed over to
the judge and then to the officer who
will put you in jail. 26 I promise you
that you will not get out until you have
paid the last cent you owe.

Marriage

27 You know the commandment
which says, "Be faithful in marriage."

[t] **5.10** *They belong to the kingdom of heaven*: See the note at 5.3. [u] **5.17** *the Law and the Prophets*: The Jewish Scriptures, that is, the Old Testament. [v] **5.22** *someone*: In verses 22-24 the Greek text has "brother," which may refer to people in general or to other followers.

5.8 Ps 24.3, 4; 2 Esd 7.98. **5.10** 1 P 3.14. **5.11** 1 P 4.14. **5.12** 2 Ch 36.16; Si 2.8; Ac 7.52. **5.13** Mk 9.50; Lk 14.34, 35. **5.14** Jn 8.12; 9.5. **5.15** Mk 4.21; Lk 8.16; 11.33. **5.16** 1 P 2.12. **5.18** Lk 16.17. **5.21** Ex 20.13; Dt 5.17. **5.27** Ex 20.14; Dt 5.18.

28 But I tell you that if you look at another woman and want her, you are already unfaithful in your thoughts. 29 If your right eye causes you to sin, poke it out and throw it away. It is better to lose one part of your body, than for your whole body to end up in hell. 30 If your right hand causes you to sin, chop it off and throw it away! It is better to lose one part of your body, than for your whole body to be thrown into hell.

Divorce

(Matthew 19.9; Mark 10.11, 12; Luke 16.18)

31 You have been taught that a man who divorces his wife must write out divorce papers for her.[w] 32 But I tell you not to divorce your wife unless she has committed some terrible sexual sin.[x] If you divorce her, you will cause her to be unfaithful, just as any man who marries her is guilty of taking another man's wife.

Promises

33 You know that our ancestors were told, "Don't use the Lord's name to make a promise unless you are going to keep it." 34 But I tell you not to swear by anything when you make a promise! Heaven is God's throne, so don't swear by heaven. 35 The earth is God's footstool, so don't swear by the earth. Jerusalem is the city of the great king, so don't swear by it. 36 Don't swear by your own head. You cannot make one hair white or black. 37 When you make a promise, say only "Yes" or "No." Anything else comes from the devil.

Revenge

(Luke 6.29, 30)

38 You know that you have been taught, "An eye for an eye and a tooth for a tooth." 39 But I tell you not to try to get even with a person who has done something to you. When someone slaps your right cheek,[y] turn and let that person slap your other cheek. 40 If someone sues you for your shirt, give up your coat as well. 41 If a soldier forces you to carry his pack one mile, carry it two miles.[z] 42 When people ask you for something, give it to them. When they want to borrow money, lend it to them.

Love

(Luke 6.27, 28, 32-36)

43 You have heard people say, "Love your neighbors and hate your enemies." 44 But I tell you to love your enemies and pray for anyone who mistreats you. 45 Then you will be acting like your Father in heaven. He makes the sun rise on both good and bad people. And he sends rain for the ones who do right and for the ones who do wrong. 46 If you love only those people who love you, will God reward you for that? Even tax collectors[a] love their friends. 47 If you greet only your friends, what's so great about that? Don't even unbelievers do that? 48 But you must always act like your Father in heaven.

Giving

6 When you do good deeds, don't try to show off. If you do, you won't get a reward from your Father in heaven.

[w]**5.31** *write out divorce papers for her*: Jewish men could divorce their wives, but the women could not divorce their husbands. The purpose of writing these papers was to make it harder for a man to divorce his wife. Before this law was made, all a man had to do was to send his wife away and say that she was no longer his wife. [x]**5.32** *some terrible sexual sin*: This probably refers to the laws about the wrong kinds of marriages that are forbidden in Leviticus 18.6-18 or to some serious sexual sin. [y]**5.39** *right cheek*: A slap on the right cheek was a bad insult. [z]**5.41** *two miles*: A Roman soldier had the right to force a person to carry his pack as far as one mile. [a]**5.46** *tax collectors*: These were usually Jewish people who paid the Romans for the right to collect taxes. They were hated by other Jews who thought of them as traitors to their country and to their religion.

5.29 Mt 18.9; Mk 9.47. **5.30** Mt 18.8; Mk 9.43, 44. **5.31** Dt 24.1-4; Mt 19.7; Mk 10.4. **5.32** Mt 19.9; Mk 10.11, 12; Lk 16.18; 1 Co 7.10, 11. **5.33** **a** Lv 19.12; **b** Nu 30.2; Dt 23.21. **5.34** **a** Jas 5.12; **b** Is 66.1; Mt 23.22. **5.35** **a** Is 66.1; **b** Ps 48.2. **5.38** Ex 21.24; Lv 24.20; Dt 19.19-21. **5.43** Si 12.4-7. **5.45** Si 4.10. **5.48** Lv 19.2. **6.1** Mt 23.5.

2 When you give to the poor, don't
blow a loud horn. That's what show-
offs do in the meeting places and on
the street corners, because they are always looking for praise. I can assure
you that they already have their
reward.
3 When you give to the poor, don't
let anyone know about it.[b] 4 Then your
gift will be given in secret. Your Father
knows what is done in secret, and he
will reward you.

Prayer

(Luke 11.2-4)

5 When you pray, don't be like those
show-offs who love to stand up and
pray in the meeting places and on the
street corners. They do this just to look
good. I can assure you that they already have their reward.
6 When you pray, go into a room
alone and close the door. Pray to your
Father in private. He knows what
is done in private, and he will reward you.
7 When you pray, don't talk on and
on as people do who don't know God.
They think God likes to hear long
prayers. 8 Don't be like them. Your
Father knows what you need before
you ask.
9 You should pray like this:

Our Father in heaven,
help us to honor
your name.
10 Come and set up
your kingdom,
so that everyone on earth
will obey you,
as you are obeyed
in heaven.
11 Give us our food for today.[c]
12 Forgive us for doing wrong,
as we forgive others.
13 Keep us from being tempted
and protect us from evil.[d]

14 If you forgive others for the
wrongs they do to you, your Father in
heaven will forgive you. 15 But if you
don't forgive others, your Father will
not forgive your sins.

Worshiping God by Going without Eating

16 When you go without eating,[e]
don't try to look gloomy as those show-
offs do when they go without eating. I
can assure you that they already have
their reward. 17 Instead, comb your
hair and wash your face. 18 Then others won't know that you are going
without eating. But your Father sees
what is done in private, and he will reward you.

Treasures in Heaven

(Luke 12.33, 34)

19 Don't store up treasures on
earth! Moths and rust can destroy
them, and thieves can break in and
steal them. 20 Instead, store up your
treasures in heaven, where moths and
rust cannot destroy them, and thieves
cannot break in and steal them.
21 Your heart will always be where your
treasure is.

Light

(Luke 11.34-36)

22 Your eyes are like a window for
your body. When they are good, you
have all the light you need. 23 But
when your eyes are bad, everything is
dark. If the light inside you is dark, you
surely are in the dark.

Money

(Luke 16.13)

24 You cannot be the slave of two
masters! You will like one more than

[b] **6.3** *don't let anyone know about it*: The Greek text has, "Don't let your left hand know what your right hand is doing." [c] **6.11** *our food for today*: Or "the food that we need" or "our food for the coming day." [d] **6.13** *evil*: Or "the evil one," that is, the devil. Some manuscripts add, "The kingdom, the power, and the glory are yours forever. Amen." [e] **6.16** *without eating*: See the note at 4.2.

6.5 Lk 18.10-14. **6.7** Si 7.14. **6.14,15** Mk 11.25, 26. **6.14** Si 28.1-5.
6.17 Jdt 10.3. **6.19** Jas 5.2, 3. **6.20** Si 29.11.

the other or be more loyal to one than the other. You cannot serve both God and money.

Worry
(Luke 12.22-31)

25 I tell you not to worry about your life. Don't worry about having something to eat, drink, or wear. Isn't life more than food or clothing? 26 Look at the birds in the sky! They don't plant or harvest. They don't even store grain in barns. Yet your Father in heaven takes care of them. Aren't you worth more than birds?

27 Can worry make you live longer?[f] 28 Why worry about clothes? Look how the wild flowers grow. They don't work hard to make their clothes. 29 But I tell you that Solomon with all his wealth[g] wasn't as well clothed as one of them. 30 God gives such beauty to everything that grows in the fields, even though it is here today and thrown into a fire tomorrow. He will surely do even more for you! Why do you have such little faith?

31 Don't worry and ask yourselves, "Will we have anything to eat? Will we have anything to drink? Will we have any clothes to wear?" 32 Only people who don't know God are always worrying about such things. Your Father in heaven knows that you need all of these. 33 But more than anything else, put God's work first and do what he wants. Then the other things will be yours as well.

34 Don't worry about tomorrow. It will take care of itself. You have enough to worry about today.

Judging Others
(Luke 6.37, 38, 41, 42)

7 Don't condemn others, and God won't condemn you. 2 God will be as hard on you as you are on others! He will treat you exactly as you treat them.

3 You can see the speck in your friend's eye, but you don't notice the log in your own eye. 4 How can you say, "My friend, let me take the speck out of your eye," when you don't see the log in your own eye? 5 You're nothing but show-offs! First, take the log out of your own eye. Then you can see how to take the speck out of your friend's eye.

6 Don't give to dogs what belongs to God. They will only turn and attack you. Don't throw pearls down in front of pigs. They will trample all over them.

Ask, Search, Knock
(Luke 11.9-13)

7 Ask, and you will receive. Search, and you will find. Knock, and the door will be opened for you. 8 Everyone who asks will receive. Everyone who searches will find. And the door will be opened for everyone who knocks. 9 Would any of you give your hungry child a stone, if the child asked for some bread? 10 Would you give your child a snake if the child asked for a fish? 11 As bad as you are, you still know how to give good gifts to your children. But your heavenly Father is even more ready to give good things to people who ask.

12 Treat others as you want them to treat you. This is what the Law and the Prophets[h] are all about.

The Narrow Gate
(Luke 13.24)

13 Go in through the narrow gate. The gate to destruction is wide, and the road that leads there is easy to follow. A lot of people go through that gate. 14 But the gate to life is very narrow. The road that leads there is so hard to follow that only a few people find it.

[f] **6.27** *live longer*: Or "grow taller." [g] **6.29** *Solomon with all his wealth*: The Jewish people thought that Solomon was the richest person who had ever lived. [h] **7.12** *the Law and the Prophets*: See the note at 5.17.

6.29 1 K 10.4-7; 2 Ch 9.3-6. **7.2** Mk 4.24. **7.7,8** 2 Esd 2.13. **7.12** Tb 4.15; Lk 6.31. **7.13,14** Si 15.16, 17.

A Tree and Its Fruit
(Luke 6.43-45)

15 Watch out for false prophets!
They dress up like sheep, but inside
they are wolves who have come to attack you. 16 You can tell what they are
by what they do. No one picks grapes
or figs from thornbushes. 17 A good
tree produces good fruit, and a bad
tree produces bad fruit. 18 A good tree
cannot produce bad fruit, and a bad
tree cannot produce good fruit.
19 Every tree that produces bad fruit
will be chopped down and burned.
20 You can tell who the false prophets
are by their deeds.

A Warning
(Luke 13.26, 27)

21 Not everyone who calls me their
Lord will get into the kingdom of
heaven. Only the ones who obey my
Father in heaven will get in. 22 On the
day of judgment many will call me
their Lord. They will say, "We
preached in your name, and in your
name we forced out demons and
worked many miracles." 23 But I will
tell them, "I will have nothing to do
with you! Get out of my sight, you evil
people!"

Two Builders
(Luke 6.47-49)

24 Anyone who hears and obeys
these teachings of mine is like a wise
person who built a house on solid rock.
25 Rain poured down, rivers flooded,
and winds beat against that house. But
it did not fall, because it was built on
solid rock.
26 Anyone who hears my teachings
and doesn't obey them is like a foolish
person who built a house on sand. 27 The
rain poured down, the rivers flooded,
and the winds blew and beat against
that house. Finally, it fell with a crash.
28 When Jesus finished speaking, the
crowds were surprised at his teaching.
29 He taught them like someone with authority, and not like their teachers of the
Law of Moses.

Jesus Heals a Man
(Mark 1.40-45; Luke 5.12-16)

8 As Jesus came down the mountain, he
was followed by large crowds. 2 Suddenly a man with leprosy[i] came and knelt
in front of Jesus. He said, "Lord, you have
the power to make me well, if only you
wanted to."
3 Jesus put his hand on the man and
said, "I want to! Now you are well." At once
the man's leprosy disappeared. 4 Jesus told
him, "Don't tell anyone about this, but go
and show the priest that you are well. Then
take a gift to the temple just as Moses commanded, and everyone will know that you
have been healed."[j]

Jesus Heals an Army Officer's Servant
(Luke 7.1-10; John 4.43-54)

5 When Jesus was going into the town of
Capernaum, an army officer came up to
him and said, 6 "Lord, my servant is at
home in such terrible pain that he can't
even move."
7 "I will go and heal him," Jesus replied.
8 But the officer said, "Lord, I'm not
good enough for you to come into my
house. Just give the order, and my servant
will get well. 9 I have officers who give orders to me, and I have soldiers who take orders from me. I can say to one of them,
'Go!' and he goes. I can say to another,
'Come!' and he comes. I can say to my
servant, 'Do this!' and he will do it."
10 When Jesus heard this, he was so
surprised that he turned and said to the
crowd following him, "I tell you that in all

[i] **8.2** *leprosy*: In biblical times the word "leprosy" was used for many different kinds of skin diseases. [j] **8.4** *everyone will know that you have been healed*: People with leprosy had to be examined by a priest and told that they were well (that is "clean") before they could once again live a normal life in the Jewish community. The gift that Moses commanded was the sacrifice of some lambs together with flour mixed with olive oil.

7.16 Si 27.6. **7.19** Mt 3.10; Lk 3.9. **7.20** Mt 12.33. **7.23** Ps 6.8.
7.28,29 Mk 1.22; Lk 4.32. **8.4** Lv 14.1-32. **8.9** Ba 3.33-35.

of Israel I've never found anyone with this
much faith! 11 Many people will come from
everywhere to enjoy the feast in the kingdom of heaven with Abraham, Isaac, and
Jacob. 12 But the ones who should have been in
the kingdom will be thrown out into the dark.
They will cry and grit their teeth in pain."
13 Then Jesus said to the officer, "You
may go home now. Your faith has made it
happen."

Right then his servant was healed.

Jesus Heals Many People

(Mark 1.29-34; Luke 4.38-41)

14 Jesus went to the home of Peter,
where he found that Peter's mother-in-law
was sick in bed with fever. 15 He took her
by the hand, and the fever left her. Then
she got up and served Jesus a meal.
16 That evening many people with
demons in them were brought to Jesus.
And with only a word he forced out the evil
spirits and healed everyone who was sick.
17 So God's promise came true, just as the
prophet Isaiah had said,

> "He healed our diseases
> and made us well."

Some Who Wanted To Go with Jesus

(Luke 9.57-62)

18 When Jesus saw the crowd,[k] he went
across Lake Galilee. 19 A teacher of the
Law of Moses came up to him and said,
"Teacher, I'll go anywhere with you!"
20 Jesus replied, "Foxes have dens, and
birds have nests. But the Son of Man
doesn't have a place to call his own."
21 Another disciple said to Jesus, "Lord,
let me wait till I bury my father."
22 Jesus answered, "Come with me, and
let the dead bury their dead." [l]

A Storm

(Mark 4.35-41; Luke 8.22-25)

23 After Jesus left in a boat with his disciples, 24 a terrible storm suddenly struck
the lake, and waves started splashing into
their boat.

Jesus was sound asleep, 25 so the disciples went over to him and woke him up.
They said, "Lord, save us! We're going to
drown!"
26 But Jesus replied, "Why are you so
afraid? You surely don't have much faith."
Then he got up and ordered the wind and
the waves to calm down. And everything
was calm.
27 The men in the boat were amazed
and said, "Who is this? Even the wind and
the waves obey him."

Two Men with Demons in Them

(Mark 5.1-20; Luke 8.26-39)

28 After Jesus had crossed the lake, he
came to shore near the town of Gadara[m]
and started down the road. Two men with
demons in them came to him from the
tombs.[n] They were so fierce that no one
could travel that way. 29 Suddenly they
shouted, "Jesus, Son of God, what do you
want with us? Have you come to punish us
before our time?"
30 Not far from there a large herd of pigs
was feeding. 31 So the demons begged
Jesus, "If you force us out, please send us
into those pigs!" 32 Jesus told them to go,
and they went out of the men and into the
pigs. All at once the pigs rushed down the
steep bank into the lake and drowned.
33 The people taking care of the pigs
ran to the town and told everything, especially what had happened to the two men.
34 Everyone in town came out to meet Jesus.
When they saw him, they begged him to
leave their part of the country.

Jesus Heals a Crippled Man

(Mark 2.1-12; Luke 5.17-26)

9 Jesus got into a boat and crossed back
over to the town where he lived.[o]
2 Some people soon brought to him a crippled man lying on a mat. When Jesus saw

[k]8.18 *saw the crowd*: Some manuscripts have "large crowd." Others have "large crowds."
[l]8.22 *let the dead bury their dead*: For the Jewish people a proper burial of their dead was a very important duty. But Jesus teaches that following him is even more important. [m]8.28 *Gadara*: Some manuscripts have "Gergesa." Others have "Gerasa." [n]8.28 *tombs*: It was thought that demons and evil spirits lived in tombs and in caves that were used for burying the dead.
[o]9.1 *where he lived*: Capernaum (see 4.13).

8.11 Lk 13.29. **8.12** Mt 22.13; 25.30; Lk 13.28. **8.17** Is 53.5. **8.21** Tb 4.3, 4.

how much faith they had, he said to the
crippled man, "My friend, don't worry!
Your sins are forgiven."
3 Some teachers of the Law of Moses
said to themselves, "Jesus must think he is
God!"
4 But Jesus knew what was in their
minds, and he said, "Why are you thinking
such evil things? 5 Is it easier for me to tell
this crippled man that his sins are forgiven
or to tell him to get up and walk? 6 But I
will show you that the Son of Man has the
right to forgive sins here on earth." So
Jesus said to the man, "Get up! Pick up
your mat and go on home." 7 The man got
up and went home. 8 When the crowds saw
this, they were afraid[p] and praised God for
giving such authority to people.

Jesus Chooses Matthew
(Mark 2.13-17; Luke 5.27-32)

9 As Jesus was leaving, he saw a tax collector[q] named Matthew sitting at the place
for paying taxes. Jesus said to him, "Come
with me." Matthew got up and went with
him.
10 Later, Jesus and his disciples were
having dinner at Matthew's house.[r] Many
tax collectors and other sinners were also
there. 11 Some Pharisees asked Jesus' disciples, "Why does your teacher eat with tax
collectors and other sinners?"
12 Jesus heard them and answered,
"Healthy people don't need a doctor, but
sick people do. 13 Go and learn what the
Scriptures mean when they say, 'Instead of
offering sacrifices to me, I want you to be
merciful to others.' I didn't come to invite
good people to be my followers. I came to
invite sinners."

People Ask about Going without Eating
(Mark 2.18-22; Luke 5.33-39)

14 One day some followers of John the
Baptist came and asked Jesus, "Why do we
and the Pharisees often go without eating,[s]
while your disciples never do?"
15 Jesus answered:
The friends of a bridegroom don't
go without eating while he is still with
them. But the time will come when he
will be taken from them. Then they
will go without eating.
16 No one uses a new piece of cloth
to patch old clothes. The patch would
shrink and tear a bigger hole.
17 No one pours new wine into old
wineskins. The wine would swell and
burst the old skins.[t] Then the wine
would be lost, and the skins would be
ruined. New wine must be put into
new wineskins. Both the skins and the
wine will then be safe.

A Dying Girl and a Sick Woman
(Mark 5.21-43; Luke 8.40-56)

18 While Jesus was still speaking, an official came and knelt in front of him. The
man said, "My daughter has just now died!
Please come and place your hand on her.
Then she will live again."
19 Jesus and his disciples got up and
went with the man.
20 A woman who had been bleeding for
twelve years came up behind Jesus and
barely touched his clothes. 21 She had said
to herself, "If I can just touch his clothes, I
will get well."
22 Jesus turned. He saw the woman and
said, "Don't worry! You are now well because of your faith." At that moment she
was healed.
23 When Jesus went into the home of
the official and saw the musicians and the
crowd of mourners,[u] 24 he said, "Get out of
here! The little girl isn't dead. She is just
asleep." Everyone started laughing at Jesus.
25 But after the crowd had been sent out
of the house, Jesus went to the girl's bed-
side. He took her by the hand and helped
her up.

[p]**9.8** *afraid*: Some manuscripts have "amazed." [q]**9.9** *tax collector*: See the note at 5.46.
[r]**9.10** *Matthew's house*: Or "Jesus' house." [s]**9.14** *without eating*: See the note at 4.2.
[t]**9.17** *swell and burst the old skins*: While the juice from grapes was becoming wine, it would swell and stretch the skins in which it had been stored. If the skins were old and stiff, they would burst. [u]**9.23** *the crowd of mourners*: The Jewish people often hired mourners for funerals.
9.10,11 Lk 15.1, 2. **9.13** **a** Mt 12.7; **b** Ho 6.6.

26 News about this spread all over that part of the country.

Jesus Heals Two Blind Men

27 As Jesus was walking along, two blind men began following him and shouting, "Son of David,[v] have pity on us!"

28 After Jesus had gone indoors, the two blind men came up to him. He asked them, "Do you believe I can make you well?"

"Yes, Lord," they answered.

29 Jesus touched their eyes and said, "Because of your faith, you will be healed." 30 They were able to see, and Jesus strictly warned them not to tell anyone about him. 31 But they left and talked about him to everyone in that part of the country.

Jesus Heals a Man Who Could Not Talk

32 As Jesus and his disciples were on their way, some people brought to him a man who could not talk because a demon was in him. 33 After Jesus had forced the demon out, the man started talking. The crowds were so amazed that they began saying, "Nothing like this has ever happened in Israel!"

34 But the Pharisees said, "The leader of the demons gives him the power to force out demons."

Jesus Has Pity on People

35 Jesus went to every town and village. He taught in their meeting places and preached the good news about God's kingdom. Jesus also healed every kind of disease and sickness. 36 When he saw the crowds, he felt sorry for them. They were confused and helpless, like sheep without a shepherd. 37 He said to his disciples, "A large crop is in the fields, but there are only a few workers. 38 Ask the Lord in charge of the harvest to send out workers to bring it in."

Jesus Chooses His Twelve Apostles
(Mark 3.13-19; Luke 6.12-16)

10 Jesus called together his twelve disciples. He gave them the power to force out evil spirits and to heal every kind of disease and sickness. 2 The first of the twelve apostles was Simon, better known as Peter. His brother Andrew was an apostle, and so were James and John, the two sons of Zebedee. 3 Philip, Bartholomew, Thomas, Matthew the tax collector,[w] James the son of Alphaeus, and Thaddaeus were also apostles. 4 The others were Simon, known as the Eager One,[x] and Judas Iscariot,[y] who later betrayed Jesus.

Instructions for the Twelve Apostles
(Mark 6.7-13; Luke 9.1-6)

5 Jesus sent out the twelve apostles with these instructions:

Stay away from the Gentiles and don't go to any Samaritan town. 6 Go only to the people of Israel, because they are like a flock of lost sheep. 7 As you go, announce that the kingdom of heaven will soon be here.[z] 8 Heal the sick, raise the dead to life, heal people who have leprosy,[a] and force out demons. You received without paying, now give without being paid. 9 Don't take along any gold, silver, or copper coins. 10 And don't carry[b] a traveling bag or an extra shirt or sandals or a walking stick.

Workers deserve their food. 11 So when you go to a town or a village, find

[v] **9.27** *Son of David*: The Jewish people expected the Messiah to be from the family of King David, and for this reason the Messiah was often called the "Son of David." [w] **10.3** *tax collector*: See the note at 5.46. [x] **10.4** *known as the Eager One*: The Greek text has "Cananaean," which probably comes from a Hebrew word meaning "zealous" (see Luke 6.15). "Zealot" was the name later given to the members of a Jewish group that resisted and fought against the Romans. [y] **10.4** *Iscariot*: This may mean "a man from Kerioth" (a place in Judea). But more probably it means "a man who was a liar" or "a man who was a betrayer." [z] **10.7** *will soon be here*: Or "is already here." [a] **10.8** *leprosy*: See the note at 8.2. [b] **10.9,10** *Don't take along . . . don't carry*: Or "Don't accept . . . don't accept."

9.34 Mt 10.25; 12.24; Mk 3.22; Lk 11.15. **9.35** Mt 4.23; Mk 1.39; Lk 4.44. **9.36** Nu 27.17; 1 K 22.17; 2 Ch 18.16; Ez 34.5; Mk 6.34. **9.37,38** Lk 10.2. **10.10** 1 Co 9.14; 1 Ti 5.18.

someone worthy enough to have you
as their guest and stay with them until
you leave. 12 When you go to a home,
give it your blessing of peace. 13 If the
home is deserving, let your blessing remain with them. But if the home isn't
deserving, take back your blessing of
peace. 14 If someone won't welcome
you or listen to your message, leave
their home or town. And shake the
dust from your feet at them.[c] 15 I
promise you that the day of judgment
will be easier for the towns of Sodom
and Gomorrah[d] than for that town.

Warning about Trouble
(Mark 13.9-13; Luke 21.12-17)

16 I am sending you like lambs into
a pack of wolves. So be as wise as
snakes and as innocent as doves.
17 Watch out for people who will take
you to court and have you beaten in
their meeting places. 18 Because of
me, you will be dragged before rulers
and kings to tell them and the Gentiles
about your faith. 19 But when someone
arrests you, don't worry about what
you will say or how you will say it. At
that time you will be given the words
to say. 20 But you will not really be the
one speaking. The Spirit from your
Father will tell you what to say.
21 Brothers and sisters will betray
one another and have each other put
to death. Parents will betray their own
children, and children will turn against
their parents and have them killed.
22 Everyone will hate you because of
me. But if you remain faithful until the
end, you will be saved. 23 When people
mistreat you in one town, hurry to another one. I promise you that before
you have gone to all the towns of Israel, the Son of Man will come.
24 Disciples are not better than
their teacher, and slaves are not better
than their master. 25 It is enough for
disciples to be like their teacher and
for slaves to be like their master. If
people call the head of the family Satan, what will they say about the rest of
the family?

The One To Fear
(Luke 12.2-7)

26 Don't be afraid of anyone! Everything that is hidden will be found out,
and every secret will be known.
27 Whatever I say to you in the dark,
you must tell in the light. And you
must announce from the housetops
whatever I have whispered to you.
28 Don't be afraid of people. They can
kill you, but they cannot harm your
soul. Instead, you should fear God who
can destroy both your body and your
soul in hell. 29 Aren't two sparrows sold
for only a penny? But your Father
knows when any one of them falls to
the ground. 30 Even the hairs on your
head are counted. 31 So don't be
afraid! You are worth much more than
many sparrows.

Telling Others about Christ
(Luke 12.8, 9)

32 If you tell others that you belong
to me, I will tell my Father in heaven
that you are my followers. 33 But if you
reject me, I will tell my Father in
heaven that you don't belong to me.

Not Peace, but Trouble
(Luke 12.51-53; 14.26, 27)

34 Don't think that I came to bring
peace to the earth! I came to bring
trouble, not peace. 35 I came to turn
sons against their fathers, daughters
against their mothers, and daughters-
in-law against their mothers-in-law.

[c] **10.14** *shake the dust from your feet at them*: This was a way of showing rejection (see Acts 13.51). [d] **10.15** *Sodom and Gomorrah*: During the time of Abraham the Lord destroyed these towns because the people there were so evil.

10.14 Ac 13.51. **10.15** **a** Mt 11.24; **b** Gn 19.24-28. **10.7-15** Lk 10.4-12. **10.16** Lk 10.3. **10.17-20** Mk 13.9-11; Lk 12.11, 12; 21.12-15. **10.21** Mk 13.12; Lk 21.16. **10.22** **a** Mt 24.9; Mk 13.13; Lk 21.17; **b** Mt 24.13; Mk 13.13. **10.24** **a** Lk 6.40; **b** Jn 13.16; 15.20. **10.25** Mt 9.34; 12.24; Mk 3.22; Lk 11.15. **10.26** Mk 4.22; Lk 8.17. **10.28** **a** 4 Macc 13.14; **b** 4 Macc 9.7; 10.4. **10.33** 2 Ti 2.12. **10.35,36** Mic 7.6.

36 Your worst enemies will be in your own family.

37 If you love your father or mother or even your sons and daughters more than me, you are not fit to be my disciples. 38 And unless you are willing to take up your cross and come with me, you are not fit to be my disciples. 39 If you try to save your life, you will lose it. But if you give it up for me, you will surely find it.

Rewards
(Mark 9.41)

40 Anyone who welcomes you welcomes me. And anyone who welcomes me also welcomes the one who sent me. 41 Anyone who welcomes a prophet, just because that person is a prophet, will be given the same reward as a prophet. Anyone who welcomes a good person, just because that person is good, will be given the same reward as a good person. 42 And anyone who gives one of my most humble followers a cup of cool water, just because that person is my follower, will surely be rewarded.

John the Baptist
(Luke 7.18-35)

11 After Jesus had finished instructing his twelve disciples, he left and began teaching and preaching in the towns.[e]

2 John was in prison when he heard what Christ was doing. So John sent some of his followers 3 to ask Jesus, "Are you the one we should be looking for? Or must we wait for someone else?"

4 Jesus answered, "Go and tell John what you have heard and seen. 5 The blind are now able to see, and the lame can walk. People with leprosy[f] are being healed, and the deaf can hear. The dead are raised to life, and the poor are hearing the good news. 6 God will bless everyone who doesn't reject me because of what I do."

7 As John's followers were going away, Jesus spoke to the crowds about John:

What sort of person did you go out into the desert to see? Was he like tall grass blown about by the wind? 8 What kind of man did you go out to see? Was he someone dressed in fine clothes? People who dress like that live in the king's palace. 9 What did you really go out to see? Was he a prophet? He certainly was. I tell you that he was more than a prophet. 10 In the Scriptures God says about him, "I am sending my messenger ahead of you to get things ready for you." 11 I tell you that no one ever born on this earth is greater than John the Baptist. But whoever is least in the kingdom of heaven is greater than John.

12 From the time of John the Baptist until now, violent people have been trying to take over the kingdom of heaven by force. 13 All the Books of the Prophets and the Law of Moses[g] told what was going to happen up to the time of John. 14 And if you believe them, John is Elijah, the prophet you are waiting for. 15 If you have ears, pay attention!

16 You people are like children sitting in the market and shouting to each other,

17 "We played the flute,
  but you would not dance!
We sang a funeral song,
  but you would not mourn!"

18 John the Baptist did not go around eating and drinking, and you said, "That man has a demon in him!" 19 But the Son of Man goes around eating and drinking, and you say, "That man eats and drinks too much! He is even a friend of tax collectors[h] and sinners." Yet Wisdom is shown to be right by what it does.

[e] **11.1** *the towns*: The Greek text has "their towns," which may refer to the towns of Galilee or to the towns where Jesus' disciples had lived. [f] **11.5** *leprosy*: See the note at 8.2. [g] **11.13** *the Books of the Prophets and the Law of Moses*: The Jewish Scriptures, that is, the Old Testament. [h] **11.19** *tax collectors*: See the note at 5.46.

10.37 4 Macc 2.11-13. **10.38** Mt 16.24; Mk 8.34; Lk 9.23. **10.39** Mt 16.25; Mk 8.35; Lk 9.24; 17.33; Jn 12.25. **10.40** **a** Lk 10.16; Jn 13.20; **b** Mk 9.37; Lk 9.48. **11.5** **a** Is 35.5, 6; **b** Is 61.1. **11.10** Ml 3.1. **11.12,13** Lk 16.16. **11.14** Ml 4.5; Mt 17.10-13; Mk 9.11-13.

The Unbelieving Towns
(Luke 10.13-15)

20 In the towns where Jesus had worked
most of his miracles, the people refused to
turn to God. So Jesus was upset with them
and said:
21 You people of Chorazin are in for
trouble! You people of Bethsaida are in
for trouble too! If the miracles that
took place in your towns had happened in Tyre and Sidon, the people
there would have turned to God long
ago. They would have dressed in sackcloth and put ashes on their heads.[i]
22 I tell you that on the day of judgment the people of Tyre and Sidon will
get off easier than you will.
23 People of Capernaum, do you
think you will be honored in heaven?
You will go down to hell! If the miracles that took place in your town had
happened in Sodom, that town would
still be standing. 24 So I tell you that on
the day of judgment the people of
Sodom will get off easier than you.

Come to Me and Rest
(Luke 10.21, 22)

25 At that moment Jesus said:
My Father, Lord of heaven and
earth, I am grateful that you hid all
this from wise and educated people
and showed it to ordinary people.
26 Yes, Father, that is what pleased you.
27 My Father has given me everything, and he is the only one who
knows the Son. The only one who truly
knows the Father is the Son. But the
Son wants to tell others about the
Father, so that they can know him too.
28 If you are tired from carrying
heavy burdens, come to me and I will
give you rest. 29 Take the yoke[j] I give
you. Put it on your shoulders and learn
from me. I am gentle and humble, and
you will find rest. 30 This yoke is easy
to bear, and this burden is light.

A Question about the Sabbath
(Mark 2.23-28; Luke 6.1-5)

12 One Sabbath, Jesus and his disciples were walking through some
wheat fields.[k] His disciples were hungry
and began picking and eating grains of
wheat. 2 Some Pharisees noticed this and
said to Jesus, "Why are your disciples picking grain on the Sabbath? They are not
supposed to do that!"
3 Jesus answered:
You surely must have read what
David did when he and his followers
were hungry. 4 He went into the house
of God, and then they ate the sacred
loaves of bread that only priests are
supposed to eat. 5 Haven't you read in
the Law of Moses that the priests are
allowed to work in the temple on the
Sabbath? But no one says that they are
guilty of breaking the law of the Sabbath. 6 I tell you that there is something here greater than the temple.
7 Don't you know what the Scriptures
mean when they say, "Instead of offering sacrifices to me, I want you to
be merciful to others?" If you knew
what this means, you would not condemn these innocent disciples of
mine. 8 So the Son of Man is Lord over
the Sabbath.

A Man with a Crippled Hand
(Mark 3.1-6; Luke 6.6-11)

9 Jesus left and went into one of the
Jewish meeting places, 10 where there was
a man whose hand was crippled. Some
Pharisees wanted to accuse Jesus of doing
something wrong, and they asked him, "Is
it right to heal someone on the Sabbath?"

[i] **11.21** *sackcloth . . . ashes on their heads*: This was one way that people showed how sorry they were for their sins. [j] **11.29** *yoke*: Yokes were put on the necks of animals, so that they could pull a plow or wagon. A yoke was a symbol of obedience and hard work. [k] **12.1** *walking through some wheat fields*: It was the custom to let hungry travelers pick grains of wheat.

11.21 Is 23.1-18; Ez 26.1—28.26; Jl 3.4-8; Am 1.9, 10; Zec 9.2-4. **11.23** **a** Is 14.13-15; **b** Gn 19.24-28. **11.24** Mt 10.15; Lk 10.12. **11.27** **a** Jn 3.35; **b** Jn 1.18; 10.15. **11.28-30** Si 6.24-30; 24.19; 51.23-26. **11.29** Jr 6.16. **12.1** Dt 23.25. **12.3,4** 1 S 21.1-6. **12.4** Lv 24.9. **12.5** Nu 28.9, 10. **12.7** **a** Mt 9.13; **b** Ho 6.6.

11 Jesus answered, "If you had a sheep
that fell into a ditch on the Sabbath,
wouldn't you lift it out? 12 People are worth
much more than sheep, and so it is right to
do good on the Sabbath." 13 Then Jesus told
the man, "Hold out your hand." The man
did, and it became as healthy as the other one.
14 The Pharisees left and started making
plans to kill Jesus.

God's Chosen Servant

15 When Jesus found out what was happening, he left there and large crowds followed him. He healed all of their sick,
16 but warned them not to tell anyone
about him. 17 So God's promise came true,
just as Isaiah the prophet had said,

18 "Here is my chosen servant!
I love him,
and he pleases me.
I will give him my Spirit,
and he will bring justice
to the nations.
19 He won't shout or yell
or call out in the streets.
20 He won't break off a bent reed
or put out a dying flame,
but he will make sure
that justice is done.
21 All nations will place
their hope in him."

Jesus and the Ruler of the Demons

(Mark 3.20-30; Luke 11.14-23; 12.10)

22 Some people brought to Jesus a man
who was blind and could not talk because
he had a demon in him. Jesus healed the
man, and then he was able to talk and see.
23 The crowds were so amazed that they
asked, "Could Jesus be the Son of David?"[l]
24 When the Pharisees heard this, they
said, "He forces out demons by the power
of Beelzebul, the ruler of the demons!"
25 Jesus knew what they were thinking,
and he said to them:

Any kingdom where people fight
each other will end up ruined. And a
town or family that fights will soon destroy itself. 26 So if Satan fights against
himself, how can his kingdom last?
27 If I use the power of Beelzebul to
force out demons, whose power do
your own followers use to force them
out? Your followers are the ones who
will judge you. 28 But when I force out
demons by the power of God's Spirit, it
proves that God's kingdom has already
come to you. 29 How can anyone break
into a strong man's house and steal his
things, unless he first ties up the strong
man? Then he can take everything.

30 If you are not on my side, you are
against me. If you don't gather in the
harvest with me, you scatter it. 31-32 I
tell you that any sinful thing you do or
say can be forgiven. Even if you speak
against the Son of Man, you can be
forgiven. But if you speak against the
Holy Spirit, you can never be forgiven,
either in this life or in the life to come.

A Tree and Its Fruit

(Luke 6.43-45)

33 A good tree produces only good
fruit, and a bad tree produces bad
fruit. You can tell what a tree is like by
the fruit it produces. 34 You are a
bunch of evil snakes, so how can you
say anything good? Your words show
what is in your hearts. 35 Good people
bring good things out of their hearts,
but evil people bring evil things out of
their hearts. 36 I promise you that on
the day of judgment, everyone will
have to account for every careless
word they have spoken. 37 On that day
they will be told that they are either innocent or guilty because of the things
they have said.

A Sign from Heaven

(Mark 8.11, 12; Luke 11.29-32)

38 Some Pharisees and teachers of the
Law of Moses said, "Teacher, we want you
to show us a sign from heaven."

[l] **12.23** *Could Jesus be the Son of David*: Or "Does Jesus think he is the Son of David?" See the note at 9.27.

12.11 Lk 14.5. **12.18-21** Is 42.1-4 (LXX). **12.24** Mt 9.34; 10.25. **12.29** Tb 8.3. **12.30** Mk 9.40. **12.31,32** Lk 12.10. **12.33** Si 27.6; Mt 7.20; Lk 6.44. **12.34** **a** Mt 3.7; 23.33; Lk 3.7; **b** Mt 15.18; Lk 6.45. **12.38** Mt 16.1; Mk 8.11; Lk 11.16.

39 But Jesus replied:
You want a sign because you are evil
and won't believe! But the only sign
you will get is the sign of the prophet
Jonah. 40 He was in the stomach of a
big fish for three days and nights, just
as the Son of Man will be deep in the
earth for three days and nights. 41 On
the day of judgment the people of Nineveh[m] will stand there with you and
condemn you. They turned to God
when Jonah preached, and yet here is
something far greater than Jonah.
42 The Queen of the South[n] will also
stand there with you and condemn you.
She traveled a long way to hear
Solomon's wisdom, and yet here is
something much greater than Solomon.

Return of an Evil Spirit
(Luke 11.24-26)

43 When an evil spirit leaves a person, it travels through the desert, looking for a place to rest. But when the
demon doesn't find a place, 44 it says,
"I will go back to the home I left."
When it gets there and finds the place
empty, clean, and fixed up, 45 it goes
off and finds seven other evil spirits
even worse than itself. They all come
and make their home there, and the
person ends up in worse shape than
before. That's how it will be with you
evil people of today.

Jesus' Mother and Brothers
(Mark 3.31-35; Luke 8.19-21)

46 While Jesus was still speaking to the
crowds, his mother and brothers came and
stood outside because they wanted to talk
with him. 47 Someone told Jesus, "Your
mother and brothers are standing outside
and want to talk with you."[o]
48 Jesus answered, "Who is my mother
and who are my brothers?" 49 Then he
pointed to his disciples and said, "These
are my mother and my brothers! 50 Anyone
who obeys my Father in heaven is my
brother or sister or mother."

A Story about a Farmer
(Mark 4.1-9; Luke 8.4-8)

13 That same day Jesus left the house
and went out beside Lake Galilee,
where he sat down to teach.[p] 2 Such large
crowds gathered around him that he had to
sit in a boat, while the people stood on the
shore. 3 Then he taught them many things
by using stories. He said:
A farmer went out to scatter seed in
a field. 4 While the farmer was scattering the seed, some of it fell along the
road and was eaten by birds. 5 Other
seeds fell on thin, rocky ground and
quickly started growing because the
soil wasn't very deep. 6 But when the
sun came up, the plants were scorched
and dried up, because they did not
have enough roots. 7 Some other seeds
fell where thornbushes grew up and
choked the plants. 8 But a few seeds
did fall on good ground where the
plants produced a hundred or sixty or
thirty times as much as was scattered.
9 If you have ears, pay attention!

Why Jesus Used Stories
(Mark 4.10-12; Luke 8.9, 10)

10 Jesus' disciples came to him and
asked, "Why do you use nothing but stories
when you speak to the people?"
11 Jesus answered:
I have explained the secrets about
the kingdom of heaven to you, but not
to others. 12 Everyone who has something will be given more. But people
who don't have anything will lose even
what little they have. 13 I use stories
when I speak to them because when
they look, they cannot see, and when
they listen, they cannot hear or under-

[m] **12.41** *Nineveh*: During the time of Jonah this city was the capital of the Assyrian Empire, which was Israel's worst enemy. But Jonah was sent there to preach, so that the people would turn to the Lord and be saved. [n] **12.42** *Queen of the South*: Sheba, probably a country in southern Arabia. [o] **12.47** *with you*: Some manuscripts do not have verse 47. [p] **13.1** *sat down to teach*: See the note at 5.1.

12.39 Mt 16.4; Mk 8.12. **12.40** Jon 1.17. **12.41** Jon 3.5. **12.42** 1 K 10.1-10; 2 Ch 9.1-12. **13.2** Lk 5.1-3. **13.12** Mt 25.29; Mk 4.25; Lk 8.18; 19.26.

stand. 14 So God's promise came true,
just as the prophet Isaiah had said,

"These people will listen
and listen,
but never understand.
They will look and look,
but never see.
15 All of them have
stubborn minds!
Their ears are stopped up,
and their eyes are covered.
They cannot see or hear
or understand.
If they could,
they would turn to me,
and I would heal them."

16 But God has blessed you, because your eyes can see and your ears
can hear! 17 Many prophets and good
people were eager to see what you see
and to hear what you hear. But I tell
you that they did not see or hear.

Jesus Explains the Story about the Farmer

(Mark 4.13-20; Luke 8.11-15)

18 Now listen to the meaning of the
story about the farmer:

19 The seeds that fell along the road
are the people who hear the message
about the kingdom, but don't understand it. Then the evil one comes
and snatches the message from their
hearts. 20 The seeds that fell on rocky
ground are the people who gladly hear
the message and accept it right away.
21 But they don't have deep roots, and
they don't last very long. As soon as life
gets hard or the message gets them in
trouble, they give up.

22 The seeds that fell among the
thornbushes are also people who hear
the message. But they start worrying
about the needs of this life and are
fooled by the desire to get rich. So the
message gets choked out, and they
never produce anything. 23 The seeds
that fell on good ground are the people
who hear and understand the message. They produce as much as a hundred or sixty or thirty times what was
planted.

Weeds among the Wheat

24 Jesus then told them this story:

The kingdom of heaven is like what
happened when a farmer scattered
good seed in a field. 25 But while everyone was sleeping, an enemy came and
scattered weed seeds in the field and
then left.

26 When the plants came up and
began to ripen, the farmer's servants
could see the weeds. 27 The servants
came and asked, "Sir, didn't you scatter good seed in your field? Where did
these weeds come from?"

28 "An enemy did this," he replied.

His servants then asked, "Do you
want us to go out and pull up the
weeds?"

29 "No!" he answered. "You might
also pull up the wheat. 30 Leave the
weeds alone until harvest time. Then
I'll tell my workers to gather the weeds
and tie them up and burn them. But
I'll have them store the wheat in my
barn."

Stories about a Mustard Seed and Yeast

(Mark 4.30-32; Luke 13.18-21)

31 Jesus told them another story:

The kingdom of heaven is like what
happens when a farmer plants a mustard seed in a field. 32 Although it is
the smallest of all seeds, it grows larger
than any garden plant and becomes a
tree. Birds even come and nest on its
branches.

33 Jesus also said:

The kingdom of heaven is like what
happens when a woman mixes a little
yeast into three big batches of flour.
Finally, all the dough rises.

The Reason for Teaching with Stories

(Mark 4.33, 34)

34 Jesus used stories when he spoke to
the people. In fact, he did not tell them
anything without using stories. 35 So God's

13.14,15 Is 6.9, 10 (LXX). **13.16,17** Lk 10.23, 24. **13.35** Ps 78.2.

promise came true, just as the prophet[q] had said,

"I will use stories
to speak my message
and to explain things
that have been hidden
since the creation
of the world."

Jesus Explains the Story about the Weeds

36 After Jesus left the crowd and went inside,[r] his disciples came to him and said, "Explain to us the story about the weeds in the wheat field."

37 Jesus answered:

The one who scattered the good seed is the Son of Man. 38 The field is the world, and the good seeds are the people who belong to the kingdom. The weed seeds are those who belong to the evil one, 39 and the one who scattered them is the devil. The harvest is the end of time, and angels are the ones who bring in the harvest.

40 Weeds are gathered and burned. That's how it will be at the end of time. 41 The Son of Man will send out his angels, and they will gather from his kingdom everyone who does wrong or causes others to sin. 42 Then he will throw them into a flaming furnace, where people will cry and grit their teeth in pain. 43 But everyone who has done right will shine like the sun in their Father's kingdom. If you have ears, pay attention!

A Hidden Treasure

44 The kingdom of heaven is like what happens when someone finds treasure hidden in a field and buries it again. A person like that is happy and goes and sells everything in order to buy that field.

A Valuable Pearl

45 The kingdom of heaven is like what happens when a shop owner is looking for fine pearls. 46 After finding a very valuable one, the owner goes and sells everything in order to buy that pearl.

A Fish Net

47 The kingdom of heaven is like what happens when a net is thrown into a lake and catches all kinds of fish. 48 When the net is full, it is dragged to the shore, and the fishermen sit down to separate the fish. They keep the good ones, but throw the bad ones away. 49 That's how it will be at the end of time. Angels will come and separate the evil people from the ones who have done right. 50 Then those evil people will be thrown into a flaming furnace, where they will cry and grit their teeth in pain.

New and Old Treasures

51 Jesus asked his disciples if they understood all these things. They said, "Yes, we do."

52 So he told them, "Every student of the Scriptures who becomes a disciple in the kingdom of heaven is like someone who brings out new and old treasures from the storeroom."

The People of Nazareth Turn against Jesus

(Mark 6.1-6; Luke 4.16-30)

53 When Jesus had finished telling these stories, he left 54 and went to his hometown. He taught in their meeting place, and the people were so amazed that they asked, "Where does he get all this wisdom and the power to work these miracles? 55 Isn't he the son of the carpenter? Isn't Mary his mother, and aren't James, Joseph, Simon, and Judas his brothers? 56 Don't his sisters still live here in our town? How can he do all this?" 57 So the people were very unhappy because of what he was doing.

But Jesus said, "Prophets are honored by everyone, except the people of their hometown and their own family." 58 And because the people did not have any faith, Jesus did not work many miracles there.

[q] **13.35** *the prophet*: Some manuscripts have "the prophet Isaiah." [r] **13.36** *went inside*: Or "went home."

13.43 2 Esd 7.97. **13.57** Jn 4.43, 44.

The birth of Jesus *Luke 2.1-21*

The boy Jesus in the temple *Luke 2.46-50*

The baptism of Jesus *Mark 1.9-11*

Jesus with Jarius' daughter

Mark 5.35-43

The Death of John the Baptist
(Mark 6.14-29; Luke 9.7-9)

14 About this time Herod the ruler[s]
heard the news about Jesus 2 and
told his officials, "This is John the Baptist! He has come back from death, and
that's why he has the power to work these
miracles."

3-4 Herod had earlier arrested John and
had him chained and put in prison. He did
this because John had told him, "It isn't
right for you to take Herodias, the wife of
your brother Philip." 5 Herod wanted to kill
John. But the people thought John was a
prophet, and Herod was afraid of what they
might do.

6 When Herod's birthday came, the
daughter of Herodias danced for the
guests. She pleased Herod 7 so much that
he swore to give her whatever she wanted.
8 But the girl's mother told her to say,
"Here on a platter I want the head of John
the Baptist!"

9 The king was sorry for what he had
said. But he did not want to break the
promise he had made in front of his guests.
So he ordered a guard 10 to go to the prison
and cut off John's head. 11 It was taken on
a platter to the girl, and she gave it to her
mother. 12 John's followers took his body
and buried it. Then they told Jesus what
had happened.

Jesus Feeds Five Thousand
(Mark 6.30-44; Luke 9.10-17; John 6.1-14)

13 After Jesus heard about John, he
crossed Lake Galilee[t] to go to some place
where he could be alone. But the crowds
found out and followed him on foot from
the towns. 14 When Jesus got out of the
boat, he saw the large crowd. He felt sorry
for them and healed everyone who was
sick.

15 That evening the disciples came to
Jesus and said, "This place is like a desert,
and it is already late. Let the crowds leave,
so they can go to the villages and buy some
food."

16 Jesus replied, "They don't have to leave.
Why don't you give them something to eat?"

17 But they said, "We have only five
small loaves of bread[u] and two fish."
18 Jesus asked his disciples to bring the
food to him, 19 and he told the crowd to sit
down on the grass. Jesus took the five
loaves and the two fish. He looked up toward heaven and blessed the food. Then he
broke the bread and handed it to his disciples, and they gave it to the people.

20 After everyone had eaten all they
wanted, Jesus' disciples picked up twelve
large baskets of leftovers.

21 There were about five thousand men
who ate, not counting the women and
children.

Jesus Walks on the Water
(Mark 6.45-52; John 6.15-21)

22 Right away, Jesus made his disciples
get into a boat and start back across the
lake.[v] But he stayed until he had sent the
crowds away. 23 Then he went up on a
mountain where he could be alone and
pray. Later that evening, he was still there.

24 By this time the boat was a long way
from the shore. It was going against the
wind and was being tossed around by the
waves. 25 A little while before morning,
Jesus came walking on the water toward
his disciples. 26 When they saw him,
they thought he was a ghost. They were terrified and started screaming.

27 At once, Jesus said to them, "Don't
worry! I am Jesus. Don't be afraid."

28 Peter replied, "Lord, if it is really you,
tell me to come to you on the water."

29 "Come on!" Jesus said. Peter then got
out of the boat and started walking on the
water toward him.

30 But when Peter saw how strong
the wind was, he was afraid and started
sinking. "Save me, Lord!" he shouted.

31 Right away, Jesus reached out his
hand. He helped Peter up and said, "You
surely don't have much faith. Why do you
doubt?"

[s] **14.1** *Herod the ruler*: Herod Antipas, the son of Herod the Great (see 2.1). [t] **14.13** *crossed Lake Galilee*: To the east side. [u] **14.17** *small loaves of bread*: These would have been flat and round or in the shape of a bun. [v] **14.22** *back across the lake*: To the west side.

14.3,4 **a** Lk 3.19, 20; **b** Lv 18.16; 20.21.

32 When Jesus and Peter got into the
boat, the wind died down. 33 The men in
the boat worshiped Jesus and said, "You really are the Son of God!"

Jesus Heals Sick People in Gennesaret
(Mark 6.53-56)

34 Jesus and his disciples crossed the
lake and came to shore near the town of
Gennesaret. 35 The people found out that
he was there, and they sent word to everyone who lived in that part of the country. So
they brought all the sick people to Jesus.
36 They begged him just to let them touch his
clothes, and everyone who did was healed.

The Teaching of the Ancestors
(Mark 7.1-13)

15 About this time some Pharisees
and teachers of the Law of Moses
came from Jerusalem. They asked Jesus,
2 "Why don't your disciples obey what our
ancestors taught us to do? They don't even
wash their hands[w] before they eat."
3 Jesus answered:
Why do you disobey God and follow
your own teaching? 4 Didn't God command you to respect your father and
mother? Didn't he tell you to put to
death all who curse their parents?
5 But you let people get by without
helping their parents when they
should. You let them say that what
they have has been offered to God.[x]
6 Is this any way to show respect to
your parents? You ignore God's commands in order to follow your own
teaching. 7 And you are nothing but
show-offs! Isaiah the prophet was right
when he wrote that God had said,

8 "All of you praise me
with your words,
but you never really
think about me.
9 It is useless for you
to worship me,
when you teach rules
made up by humans."

What Really Makes People Unclean
(Mark 7.14-23)

10 Jesus called the crowd together and
said, "Pay attention and try to understand
what I mean. 11 The food that you put into
your mouth doesn't make you unclean and
unfit to worship God. The bad words that
come out of your mouth are what make you
unclean."
12 Then his disciples came over to him
and asked, "Do you know that you insulted
the Pharisees by what you said?"
13 Jesus answered, "Every plant that my
Father in heaven did not plant will be
pulled up by the roots. 14 Stay away from
those Pharisees! They are like blind people
leading other blind people, and all of them
will fall into a ditch."
15 Peter replied, "What did you mean
when you talked about the things that
make people unclean?"
16 Jesus then said:
Don't any of you know what I am
talking about by now? 17 Don't you
know that the food you put into your
mouth goes into your stomach and
then out of your body? 18 But the
words that come out of your mouth
come from your heart. And they are
what make you unfit to worship God.
19 Out of your heart come evil
thoughts, murder, unfaithfulness in
marriage, vulgar deeds, stealing, telling
lies, and insulting others. 20 These are
what make you unclean. Eating without washing your hands will not make
you unfit to worship God.

A Woman's Faith
(Mark 7.24-30)

21 Jesus left and went to the territory
near the cities of Tyre and Sidon. 22 Suddenly a Canaanite woman[y] from there

[w] **15.2** *wash their hands*: The Jewish people had strict laws about washing their hands before eating, especially if they had been out in public. [x] **15.5** *has been offered to God*: According to Jewish custom, when people said something was offered to God, it belonged to him and could not be used for anyone else, not even for their own parents. [y] **15.22** *Canaanite woman*: This woman was not Jewish.

15.4 a Ex 20.12; Dt 5.16; **b** Ex 21.17; Lv 20.9. **15.8,9** Is 29.13 (LXX). **15.14** Lk 6.39. **15.18** Mt 12.34.

came out shouting, "Lord and Son of David,[z] have pity on me! My daughter is full of demons." 23 Jesus did not say a word. But the woman kept following along and shouting, so his disciples came up and asked him to send her away.

24 Jesus said, "I was sent only to the people of Israel! They are like a flock of lost sheep."

25 The woman came closer. Then she knelt down and begged, "Please help me, Lord!"

26 Jesus replied, "It isn't right to take food away from children and feed it to dogs."[a]

27 "Lord, that's true," the woman said, "but even dogs get the crumbs that fall from their owner's table."

28 Jesus answered, "Dear woman, you really do have a lot of faith, and you will be given what you want." At that moment her daughter was healed.

Jesus Heals Many People

29 From there, Jesus went along Lake Galilee. Then he climbed a hill and sat down. 30 Large crowds came and brought many people who were crippled or blind or lame or unable to talk. They placed them, and many others, in front of Jesus, and he healed them all. 31 Everyone was amazed at what they saw and heard. People who had never spoken could now speak. The lame were healed, the crippled could walk, and the blind were able to see. Everyone was praising the God of Israel.

Jesus Feeds Four Thousand

(Mark 8.1-10)

32 Jesus called his disciples together and told them, "I feel sorry for these people. They have been with me for three days, and they don't have anything to eat. I don't want to send them away hungry. They might faint on their way home."

33 His disciples said, "This place is like a desert. Where can we find enough food to feed such a crowd?"

34 Jesus asked them how much food they had. They replied, "Seven small loaves of bread[b] and a few little fish."

35 After Jesus had told the people to sit down, 36 he took the seven loaves of bread and the fish and gave thanks. He then broke them and handed them to his disciples, who passed them around to the crowds.

37 Everyone ate all they wanted, and the leftovers filled seven large baskets.

38 There were four thousand men who ate, not counting the women and children.

39 After Jesus had sent the crowds away, he got into a boat and sailed across the lake. He came to shore near the town of Magadan.[c]

A Demand for a Sign from Heaven

(Mark 8.11-13; Luke 12.54-56)

16 The Pharisees and Sadducees came to Jesus and tried to test him by asking for a sign from heaven. 2 He told them:

If the sky is red in the evening, you say the weather will be good. 3 But if the sky is red and gloomy in the morning, you say it is going to rain. You can tell what the weather will be like by looking at the sky. But you don't understand what is happening now.[d] 4 You want a sign because you are evil and won't believe! But the only sign you will be given is what happened to Jonah.[e] Then Jesus left.

The Yeast of the Pharisees and Sadducees

(Mark 8.14-21)

5 The disciples had forgotten to bring any bread when they crossed the lake.[f] 6 Jesus then warned them, "Watch out! Guard against the yeast of the Pharisees and Sadducees."

[z] **15.22** *Son of David*: See the note at 9.27. [a] **15.26** *feed it to dogs*: The Jewish people sometimes referred to Gentiles as dogs. [b] **15.34** *small loaves of bread*: See the note at 14.17. [c] **15.39** *Magadan*: The location is unknown. [d] **16.2,3** *If the sky is red . . . what is happening now*: The words of Jesus in verses 2 and 3 are not in some manuscripts. [e] **16.4** *what happened to Jonah*: Jonah was in the stomach of a big fish for three days and nights (see 12.40). [f] **16.5** *crossed the lake*: To the east side.

16.1 Mt 12.38; Lk 11.16. **16.4** Mt 12.39; Lk 11.29. **16.6** Lk 12.1.

7 The disciples talked this over and said
to each other, "He must be saying this because we didn't bring along any bread."
8 Jesus knew what they were thinking
and said:

You surely don't have much faith!
Why are you talking about not having
any bread? 9 Don't you understand?
Have you forgotten about the five
thousand people and all those baskets
of leftovers from just five loaves of
bread? 10 And what about the four
thousand people and all those baskets
of leftovers from only seven loaves of
bread? 11 Don't you know by now that I
am not talking to you about bread?
Watch out for the yeast of the Pharisees and Sadducees!

12 Finally, the disciples understood that
Jesus wasn't talking about the yeast used to
make bread, but about the teaching of the
Pharisees and Sadducees.

Who Is Jesus?

(Mark 8.27-30; Luke 9.18-21)

13 When Jesus and his disciples were
near the town of Caesarea Philippi, he
asked them, "What do people say about the
Son of Man?"
14 The disciples answered, "Some people say you are John the Baptist or maybe
Elijah[g] or Jeremiah or some other
prophet."
15 Then Jesus asked them, "But who do
you say I am?"
16 Simon Peter spoke up, "You are the
Messiah, the Son of the living God."
17 Jesus told him:

Simon, son of Jonah, you are
blessed! You didn't discover this on
your own. It was shown to you by my
Father in heaven. 18 So I will call you
Peter, which means "a rock." On this
rock I will build my church, and death
itself will not have any power over it.
19 I will give you the keys to the kingdom of heaven, and God in heaven will
allow whatever you allow on earth. But
he will not allow anything that you
don't allow.

20 Jesus told his disciples not to tell anyone that he was the Messiah.

Jesus Speaks about His Suffering and Death

(Mark 8.31—9.1; Luke 9.22-27)

21 From then on, Jesus began telling his
disciples what would happen to him. He
said, "I must go to Jerusalem. There the
nation's leaders, the chief priests, and the
teachers of the Law of Moses will make me
suffer terribly. I will be killed, but three
days later I will rise to life."
22 Peter took Jesus aside and told him to
stop talking like that. He said, "God would
never let this happen to you, Lord!"
23 Jesus turned to Peter and said, "Satan, get away from me! You're in my way
because you think like everyone else and
not like God."
24 Then Jesus said to his disciples:

If any of you want to be my followers, you must forget about yourself.
You must take up your cross and follow
me. 25 If you want to save your life,[h]
you will destroy it. But if you give up
your life for me, you will find it.
26 What will you gain, if you own the
whole world but destroy yourself?
What would you give to get back your
soul?

27 The Son of Man will soon come
in the glory of his Father and with his
angels to reward all people for what
they have done. 28 I promise you that
some of those standing here will not
die before they see the Son of Man
coming with his kingdom.

The True Glory of Jesus

(Mark 9.2-13; Luke 9.28-36)

17 Six days later Jesus took Peter and
the brothers James and John with
him. They went up on a very high moun-

[g] **16.14** *Elijah*: Many of the Jewish people expected the prophet Elijah to come and prepare the way for the Messiah. [h] **16.25** *life*: In verses 25 and 26 the same Greek word is translated "life," "yourself," and "soul."

16.9 Mt 14.17-21. **16.10** Mt 15.34-38. **16.14** Mt 14.1, 2; Mk 6.14, 15; Lk 9.7, 8.
16.16 Jn 6.68, 69. **16.19** Mt 18.18; Jn 20.23. **16.24** Mt 10.38; Lk 14.27.
16.25 Mt 10.39; Lk 17.33; Jn 12.25. **16.27** **a** Mt 25.31; **b** Ps 62.12; Ro 2.6.

tain where they could be alone. 2 There in
front of the disciples, Jesus was completely
changed. His face was shining like the sun,
and his clothes became white as light.
3 All at once Moses and Elijah were
there talking with Jesus. 4 So Peter said to
him, "Lord, it is good for us to be here! Let
us make three shelters, one for you, one for
Moses, and one for Elijah."
5 While Peter was still speaking, the
shadow of a bright cloud passed over them.
From the cloud a voice said, "This is my
own dear Son, and I am pleased with him.
Listen to what he says!" 6 When the disciples heard the voice, they were so afraid
that they fell flat on the ground. 7 But Jesus
came over and touched them. He said,
"Get up and don't be afraid!" 8 When they
opened their eyes, they saw only Jesus.
9 On their way down from the mountain, Jesus warned his disciples not to tell
anyone what they had seen until after the
Son of Man had been raised from death.
10 The disciples asked Jesus, "Don't the
teachers of the Law of Moses say that Elijah must come before the Messiah does?"
11 Jesus told them, "Elijah certainly
will come and get everything ready. 12 In
fact, he has already come. But the people
did not recognize him and treated him just
as they wanted to. They will soon make
the Son of Man suffer in the same way."
13 Then the disciples understood that
Jesus was talking to them about John the
Baptist.

Jesus Heals a Boy
(Mark 9.14-29; Luke 9.37-43a)

14 Jesus and his disciples returned to
the crowd. A man knelt in front of him
15 and said, "Lord, have pity on my son! He
has a bad case of epilepsy and often falls
into a fire or into water. 16 I brought him to
your disciples, but none of them could heal
him."
17 Jesus said, "You people are too stubborn to have any faith! How much longer
must I be with you? Why do I have to put
up with you? Bring the boy here." 18 Then
Jesus spoke sternly to the demon. It went out
of the boy, and right then he was healed.
19 Later the disciples went to Jesus in
private and asked him, "Why couldn't we
force out the demon?"
20-21 Jesus replied:

It is because you don't have enough
faith! But I can promise you this. If
you had faith no larger than a mustard
seed, you could tell this mountain to
move from here to there. And it would.
Everything would be possible for you.[i]

Jesus Again Speaks about His Death
(Mark 9.30-32; Luke 9.43b-45)

22 While Jesus and his disciples were going from place to place in Galilee, he told
them, "The Son of Man will be handed
over to people 23 who will kill him. But
three days later he will rise to life." All of
this made the disciples very sad.

Paying the Temple Tax

24 When Jesus and the others arrived in
Capernaum, the collectors for the temple
tax came to Peter and asked, "Does your
teacher pay the temple tax?"
25 "Yes, he does," Peter answered.
After they had returned home, Jesus
went up to Peter and asked him, "Simon,
what do you think? Do the kings of this
earth collect taxes and fees from their own
people or from foreigners?"[j]
26 Peter answered, "From foreigners."
Jesus replied, "Then their own people[k]
don't have to pay. 27 But we don't want to
cause trouble. So go cast a line into the
lake and pull out the first fish you hook.
Open its mouth, and you will find a coin.
Use it to pay your taxes and mine."

[i] **17.20,21** *for you*: Some manuscripts add, "But the only way to force out that kind of demon is by praying and going without eating." [j] **17.25** *from their own people or from foreigners*: Or "from their children or from others." [k] **17.26** *From foreigners . . . their own people*: Or "From other people . . . their children."

17.5 a Gn 22.2; Ps 2.7; Is 42.1; Mt 3.17; 12.18; Mk 1.11; Lk 3.22; **b** Dt 18.15.
17.1-5 2 P 1.17, 18. **17.10** Ml 4.5. **17.11** Si 48.10. **17.12** Mt 11.14.
17.20,21 Mt 21.21; Mk 11.23; 1 Co 13.2. **17.24** Ex 30.13-15; 38.26.

Who Is the Greatest?
(Mark 9.33-37; Luke 9.46-48)

18 About this time the disciples came
to Jesus and asked him who would
be the greatest in the kingdom of heaven.
2 Jesus called a child over and had the
child stand near him. 3 Then he said:

I promise you this. If you don't
change and become like a child, you
will never get into the kingdom of
heaven. 4 But if you are as humble as
this child, you are the greatest in the
kingdom of heaven. 5 And when you
welcome one of these children because of me, you welcome me.

Temptations To Sin
(Mark 9.42-48; Luke 17.1, 2)

6 It will be terrible for people who
cause even one of my little followers to
sin. Those people would be better off
thrown into the deepest part of the
ocean with a heavy stone tied around
their necks! 7 The world is in for trouble because of the way it causes people
to sin. There will always be something
to cause people to sin, but anyone who
does this will be in for trouble.

8 If your hand or foot causes you to
sin, chop it off and throw it away! You
would be better off to go into life crippled or lame than to have two hands
or two feet and be thrown into the fire
that never goes out. 9 If your eye
causes you to sin, poke it out and get
rid of it. You would be better off to go
into life with only one eye than to have
two eyes and be thrown into the fires
of hell.

The Lost Sheep
(Luke 15.3-7)

10-11 Don't be cruel to any of these
little ones! I promise you that their angels are always with my Father in
heaven.[l] 12 Let me ask you this. What
would you do if you had a hundred
sheep and one of them wandered off?
Wouldn't you leave the ninety-nine on
the hillside and go look for the one
that had wandered away? 13 I am sure
that finding it would make you happier
than having the ninety-nine that never
wandered off. 14 That's how it is with
your Father in heaven. He doesn't
want any of these little ones to be lost.

When Someone Sins
(Luke 17.3)

15 If one of my followers[m] sins
against you, go and point out what was
wrong. But do it in private, just between the two of you. If that person
listens, you have won back a follower.
16 But if that one refuses to listen, take
along one or two others. The Scriptures teach that every complaint must
be proven true by two or more witnesses. 17 If the follower refuses to listen to them, report the matter to the
church. Anyone who refuses to listen
to the church must be treated like an
unbeliever or a tax collector.[n]

Allowing and Not Allowing

18 I promise you that God in heaven
will allow whatever you allow on earth,
but he will not allow anything you
don't allow. 19 I promise that when any
two of you on earth agree about something you are praying for, my Father in
heaven will do it for you. 20 Whenever
two or three of you come together in
my name,[o] I am there with you.

An Official Who Refused To Forgive

21 Peter came up to the Lord and asked,
"How many times should I forgive
someone[p] who does something wrong to
me? Is seven times enough?"

[l] **18.10,11** *in heaven*: Some manuscripts add, "The Son of Man came to save people who are lost." [m] **18.15** *followers*: The Greek text has "brother," which is used here and elsewhere in this chapter to refer to a follower of Christ. [n] **18.17** *tax collector*: See the note at 5.46. [o] **18.20** *in my name*: Or "as my followers." [p] **18.21** *someone*: Or "a follower." See the note at 18.15.

18.1 Lk 22.24. **18.3** Mk 10.15; Lk 18.17. **18.8** Mt 5.30. **18.9** Mt 5.29. **18.10,11** Tb 12.15; Lk 19.10. **18.15** Lk 17.3. **18.16** Dt 19.15. **18.18** Mt 16.19; Jn 20.23. **18.21,22** Lk 17.3, 4.

[22] Jesus answered:

Not just seven times, but seventy-seven times![q] [23] This story will show you what the kingdom of heaven is like:

One day a king decided to call in his officials and ask them to give an account of what they owed him. [24] As he was doing this, one official was brought in who owed him fifty million silver coins. [25] But he didn't have any money to pay what he owed. The king ordered him to be sold, along with his wife and children and all he owned, in order to pay the debt.

[26] The official got down on his knees and began begging, "Have pity on me, and I will pay you every cent I owe!" [27] The king felt sorry for him and let him go free. He even told the official that he did not have to pay back the money.

[28] As the official was leaving, he happened to meet another official, who owed him a hundred silver coins. So he grabbed the man by the throat. He started choking him and said, "Pay me what you owe!"

[29] The man got down on his knees and began begging, "Have pity on me, and I will pay you back." [30] But the first official refused to have pity. Instead, he went and had the other official put in jail until he could pay what he owed.

[31] When some other officials found out what had happened, they felt sorry for the man who had been put in jail. Then they told the king what had happened. [32] The king called the first official back in and said, "You're an evil man! When you begged for mercy, I said you did not have to pay back a cent. [33] Don't you think you should show pity to someone else, as I did to you?" [34] The king was so angry that he ordered the official to be tortured until he could pay back everything he owed. [35] That is how my Father in heaven will treat you, if you don't forgive each of my followers with all your heart.

Teaching about Divorce

(Mark 10.1-12)

19 When Jesus finished teaching, he left Galilee and went to the part of Judea that is east of the Jordan River. [2] Large crowds followed him, and he healed their sick people.

[3] Some Pharisees wanted to test Jesus. They came up to him and asked, "Is it right for a man to divorce his wife for just any reason?"

[4] Jesus answered, "Don't you know that in the beginning the Creator made a man and a woman? [5] That's why a man leaves his father and mother and gets married. He becomes like one person with his wife. [6] Then they are no longer two people, but one. And no one should separate a couple that God has joined together."

[7] The Pharisees asked Jesus, "Why did Moses say that a man could write out divorce papers and send his wife away?"

[8] Jesus replied, "You are so heartless! That's why Moses allowed you to divorce your wife. But from the beginning God did not intend it to be that way. [9] I say that if your wife has not committed some terrible sexual sin,[r] you must not divorce her to marry someone else. If you do, you are unfaithful."

[10] The disciples said, "If that's how it is between a man and a woman, it's better not to get married."

[11] Jesus told them, "Only those people who have been given the gift of staying single can accept this teaching. [12] Some people are unable to marry because of birth defects or because of what someone has done to their bodies. Others stay single for the sake of the kingdom of heaven. Anyone who can accept this teaching should do so."

[q] **18.22** *seventy-seven times*: Or "seventy times seven." The large number means that one follower should never stop forgiving another. [r] **19.9** *some terrible sexual sin*: See the note at 5.32.

18.22 Gn 4.24. **19.4** Gn 1.27; 5.1, 2. **19.5** Gn 2.24. **19.7** Dt 24.1-4; Mt 5.31. **19.9** Mt 5.32; 1 Co 7.10, 11.

Jesus Blesses Little Children
(Mark 10.13-16; Luke 18.15-17)

13 Some people brought their children
to Jesus, so that he could place his hands
on them and pray for them. His disciples
told the people to stop bothering him.
14 But Jesus said, "Let the children come to
me, and don't try to stop them! People who
are like these children belong to God's
kingdom."[s] 15 After Jesus had placed his
hands on the children, he left.

A Rich Young Man
(Mark 10.17-31; Luke 18.18-30)

16 A man came to Jesus and asked,
"Teacher, what good thing must I do to
have eternal life?"
17 Jesus said to him, "Why do you ask
me about what is good? Only God is good.
If you want to have eternal life, you must
obey his commandments."
18 "Which ones?" the man asked.
Jesus answered, "Do not murder. Be
faithful in marriage. Do not steal. Do not
tell lies about others. 19 Respect your father
and mother. And love others as much
as you love yourself." 20 The young man
said, "I have obeyed all of these. What else
must I do?"
21 Jesus replied, "If you want to be perfect, go sell everything you own! Give the
money to the poor, and you will have riches
in heaven. Then come and be my follower."
22 When the young man heard this, he was
sad, because he was very rich.
23 Jesus said to his disciples, "It's terribly hard for rich people to get into the kingdom of heaven! 24 In fact, it's easier for a
camel to go through the eye of a needle than
for a rich person to get into God's kingdom."
25 When the disciples heard this, they
were greatly surprised and asked, "How can
anyone ever be saved?"
26 Jesus looked straight at them and
said, "There are some things that people
cannot do, but God can do anything."
27 Peter replied, "Remember, we have
left everything to be your followers! What
will we get?"
28 Jesus answered:
Yes, all of you have become my followers. And so in the future world,
when the Son of Man sits on his glorious throne, I promise that you will sit
on twelve thrones to judge the twelve
tribes of Israel. 29 All who have given
up home or brothers and sisters or
father and mother or children or land
for me will be given a hundred times
as much. They will also have eternal
life. 30 But many who are now first will
be last, and many who are last will be
first.

Workers in a Vineyard

20 As Jesus was telling what the kingdom of heaven would be like, he
said:
Early one morning a man went out
to hire some workers for his vineyard.
2 After he had agreed to pay them the
usual amount for a day's work, he sent
them off to his vineyard.
3 About nine that morning, the man
saw some other people standing in the
market with nothing to do. 4 He said
he would pay them what was fair, if
they would work in his vineyard. 5 So
they went.
At noon and again about three in
the afternoon he returned to the market. And each time he made the same
agreement with others who were loafing around with nothing to do.
6 Finally, about five in the afternoon
the man went back and found some
others standing there. He asked them,
"Why have you been standing here all
day long doing nothing?"
7 "Because no one has hired us,"
they answered. Then he told them to
go work in his vineyard.

[s] **19.14** *People who are like these children belong to God's kingdom*: Or "God's kingdom belongs to people who are like these children."

19.18 **a** Ex 20.13; Dt 5.17; **b** Ex 20.14; Dt 5.18; **c** Ex 20.15; Dt 5.19; **d** Ex 20.16; Dt 5.20.
19.19 **a** Ex 20.12; Dt 5.16; **b** Lv 19.18. **19.28** **a** Mt 25.31; **b** Lk 22.30. **19.30** Mt 20.16; Lk 13.30.

8 That evening the owner of the
vineyard told the man in charge of the
workers to call them in and give them
their money. He also told the man to
begin with the ones who were hired
last. 9 When the workers arrived, the
ones who had been hired at five in the
afternoon were given a full day's pay.

10 The workers who had been hired
first thought they would be given more
than the others. But when they were
given the same, 11 they began complaining to the owner of the vineyard.
12 They said, "The ones who were
hired last worked for only one hour.
But you paid them the same that you
did us. And we worked in the hot sun
all day long!"

13 The owner answered one of
them, "Friend, I didn't cheat you. I
paid you exactly what we agreed on.
14 Take your money now and go! What
business is it of yours if I want to pay
them the same that I paid you?
15 Don't I have the right to do what I
want with my own money? Why
should you be jealous, if I want to be
generous?"

16 Jesus then said, "So it is. Everyone
who is now first will be last, and everyone
who is last will be first."

Jesus Again Tells about His Death

(Mark 10.32-34; Luke 18.31-34)

17 As Jesus was on his way to Jerusalem,
he took his twelve disciples aside and told
them in private:

18 We are now on our way to Jerusalem, where the Son of Man will be
handed over to the chief priests and
the teachers of the Law of Moses.
They will sentence him to death,
19 and then they will hand him over to
foreigners[t] who will make fun of him.
They will beat him and nail him to a
cross. But on the third day he will rise
from death.

A Mother's Request

(Mark 10.35-45)

20 The mother of James and John[u]
came to Jesus with her two sons. She knelt
down and started begging him to do something for her. 21 Jesus asked her what she
wanted, and she said, "When you come
into your kingdom, please let one of my
sons sit at your right side and the other at
your left."[v]

22 Jesus answered, "Not one of you
knows what you are asking. Are you able to
drink from the cup[w] that I must soon drink
from?"

James and John said, "Yes, we are!"

23 Jesus replied, "You certainly will
drink from my cup! But it isn't for me to
say who will sit at my right side and at my
left. That is for my Father to say."

24 When the ten other disciples heard
this, they were angry with the two brothers.
25 But Jesus called the disciples together
and said:

You know that foreign rulers like to
order their people around. And their
great leaders have full power over
everyone they rule. 26 But don't act like
them. If you want to be great, you
must be the servant of all the others.
27 And if you want to be first, you must
be the slave of the rest. 28 The Son of
Man did not come to be a slave master,
but a slave who will give his life to rescue[x] many people.

Jesus Heals Two Blind Men

(Mark 10.46-52; Luke 18.35-43)

29 Jesus was followed by a large crowd as
he and his disciples were leaving Jericho.
30 Two blind men were sitting beside the
road. And when they heard that Jesus was

[t] **20.19** *foreigners*: The Romans, who ruled Judea at this time. [u] **20.20** *mother of James and John*: The Greek text has "mother of the sons of Zebedee" (see 26.37). [v] **20.21** *right side . . . left*: The most powerful people in a kingdom sat at the right and left side of the king. [w] **20.22** *drink from the cup*: In the Scriptures a cup is sometimes used as a symbol of suffering. To "drink from the cup" is to suffer. [x] **20.28** *rescue*: The Greek word often, though not always, means the payment of a price to free a slave or a prisoner.

20.8 Lv 19.13; Dt 24.15. **20.16** Mt 19.30; Mk 10.31; Lk 13.30. **20.25,26** Lk 22.25, 26. **20.26,27** Mt 23.11; Mk 9.35; Lk 22.26.

coming their way, they shouted, "Lord and Son of David,[y] have pity on us!"

31 The crowd told them to be quiet, but they shouted even louder, "Lord and Son of David, have pity on us!"

32 When Jesus heard them, he stopped and asked, "What do you want me to do for you?"

33 They answered, "Lord, we want to see!"

34 Jesus felt sorry for them and touched their eyes. Right away they could see, and they became his followers.

Jesus Enters Jerusalem

(Mark 11.1-11; Luke 19.28-38; John 12.12-19)

21 When Jesus and his disciples came near Jerusalem, he went to Bethphage on the Mount of Olives and sent two of them on ahead. 2 He told them, "Go into the next village, where you will at once find a donkey and her colt. Untie the two donkeys and bring them to me. 3 If anyone asks why you are doing that, just say, 'The Lord[z] needs them.' Right away he will let you have the donkeys."

4 So God's promise came true, just as the prophet had said,

5 "Announce to the people
of Jerusalem:
'Your king is coming to you!
He is humble
and rides on a donkey.
He comes on the colt
of a donkey.' "

6 The disciples left and did what Jesus had told them to do. 7 They brought the donkey and its colt and laid some clothes on their backs. Then Jesus got on.

8 Many people spread clothes in the road, while others put down branches[a] which they had cut from trees. 9 Some people walked ahead of Jesus and others followed behind. They were all shouting,

"Hooray[b] for the Son of David![c]
God bless the one who comes
in the name of the Lord.
Hooray for God
in heaven above!"

10 When Jesus came to Jerusalem, everyone in the city was excited and asked, "Who can this be?"

11 The crowd answered, "This is Jesus, the prophet from Nazareth in Galilee."

Jesus in the Temple

(Mark 11.15-19; Luke 19.45-48; John 2.13-22)

12 Jesus went into the temple and chased out everyone who was selling or buying. He turned over the tables of the moneychangers and the benches of the ones who were selling doves. 13 He told them, "The Scriptures say, 'My house should be called a place of worship.' But you have turned it into a place where robbers hide."

14 Blind and lame people came to Jesus in the temple, and he healed them. 15 But the chief priests and the teachers of the Law of Moses were angry when they saw his miracles and heard the children shouting praises to the Son of David.[c] 16 The men said to Jesus, "Don't you hear what those children are saying?"

"Yes, I do!" Jesus answered. "Don't you know that the Scriptures say, 'Children and infants will sing praises'?" 17 Then Jesus left the city and went out to the village of Bethany, where he spent the night.

Jesus Puts a Curse on a Fig Tree

(Mark 11.12-14, 20-24)

18 When Jesus got up the next morning, he was hungry. He started out for the city, 19 and along the way he saw a fig tree. But when he came to it, he found only leaves and no figs. So he told the tree, "You will never again grow any fruit!" Right then the fig tree dried up.

20 The disciples were shocked when they saw how quickly the tree had dried up.

[y]**20.30** *Son of David*: See the note at 9.27. [z]**21.3** *The Lord*: Or "The master of the donkeys." [a]**21.8** *spread clothes . . . put down branches*: This was one way that the Jewish people welcomed a famous person. [b]**21.9** *Hooray*: This translates a word that can mean "please save us." But it is most often used as a shout of praise to God. [c]**21.9,15** *Son of David*: See the note at 9.27.

21.5 Zec 9.9. **21.9** Ps 118.25, 26. **21.13** Is 56.7; Jr 7.11. **21.16** Ps 8.2 (LXX).

21 But Jesus said to them, "If you have faith
and don't doubt, I promise that you can do
what I did to this tree. And you will be able
to do even more. You can tell this mountain to get up and jump into the sea, and it
will. 22 If you have faith when you pray, you
will be given whatever you ask for."

A Question about Jesus' Authority

(Mark 11.27-33; Luke 20.1-8)

23 Jesus had gone into the temple
and was teaching when the chief priests
and the leaders of the people came up to
him. They asked, "What right do you have
to do these things? Who gave you this
authority?"
24 Jesus answered, "I have just one
question to ask you. If you answer it, I will
tell you where I got the right to do these
things. 25 Who gave John the right to baptize? Was it God in heaven or merely some
human being?"
They thought it over and said to each
other, "We can't say that God gave John
this right. Jesus will ask us why we didn't
believe John. 26 On the other hand, these
people think that John was a prophet, and
we are afraid of what they might do to us.
That's why we can't say that it was merely
some human who gave John the right to
baptize." 27 So they told Jesus, "We don't
know."
Jesus said, "Then I won't tell you who
gave me the right to do what I do."

A Story about Two Sons

28 Jesus said:
I will tell you a story about a man
who had two sons. Then you can tell
me what you think. The father went to
the older son and said, "Go work in the
vineyard today!" 29 His son told him
that he would not do it, but later he
changed his mind and went. 30 The
man then told his younger son to go
work in the vineyard. The boy said he
would, but he didn't go. 31 Which one
of the sons obeyed his father?
"The older one," the chief priests and
leaders answered.
Then Jesus told them:
You can be sure that tax collectors[d]
and prostitutes will get into the kingdom of God before you ever will!
32 When John the Baptist showed you
how to do right, you would not believe
him. But these evil people did believe.
And even when you saw what they did,
you still would not change your minds
and believe.

Renters of a Vineyard

(Mark 12.1-12; Luke 20.9-19)

33 Jesus told the chief priests and leaders to listen to this story:
A land owner once planted a vineyard. He built a wall around it and dug
a pit to crush the grapes in. He also
built a lookout tower. Then he rented
out his vineyard and left the country.
34 When it was harvest time, the
owner sent some servants to get his
share of the grapes. 35 But the renters
grabbed those servants. They beat up
one, killed one, and stoned one of them
to death. 36 He then sent more servants than he did the first time. But the
renters treated them in the same way.
37 Finally, the owner sent his own
son to the renters, because he thought
they would respect him. 38 But when
they saw the man's son, they said,
"Someday he will own the vineyard.
Let's kill him! Then we can have it all
for ourselves." 39 So they grabbed him,
threw him out of the vineyard, and
killed him.
40 Jesus asked, "When the owner of that
vineyard comes, what do you suppose he
will do to those renters?"
41 The chief priests and leaders answered, "He will kill them in some horrible
way. Then he will rent out his vineyard to
people who will give him his share of
grapes at harvest time."
42 Jesus replied, "You surely know that
the Scriptures say,

'The stone that the builders
tossed aside

[d]**21.31** *tax collectors*: See the note at 5.46.

21.21 Mt 17.20; 1 Co 13.2. **21.32** Lk 3.12; 7.29, 30. **21.33** Is 5.1, 2. **21.42** Ps 118.22, 23.

is now the most important
stone of all.
This is something
the Lord has done,
and it is amazing to us.'

43 I tell you that God's kingdom will be
taken from you and given to people who
will do what he demands. 44 Anyone who
stumbles over this stone will be crushed,
and anyone it falls on will be smashed to
pieces."[e]
45 When the chief priests and the Pharisees heard these stories, they knew that
Jesus was talking about them. 46 So they
looked for a way to arrest Jesus. But they
were afraid to, because the people thought
he was a prophet.

The Great Banquet

(Luke 14.15-24)

22 Once again Jesus used stories to
teach the people:
2 The kingdom of heaven is like
what happened when a king gave a
wedding banquet for his son. 3 The
king sent some servants to tell the invited guests to come to the banquet,
but the guests refused. 4 He sent other
servants to say to the guests, "The banquet is ready! My cattle and prize
calves have all been prepared. Everything is ready. Come to the banquet!"
5 But the guests did not pay any attention. Some of them left for their
farms, and some went to their places
of business. 6 Others grabbed the servants, then beat them up and killed
them.
7 This made the king so furious that
he sent an army to kill those murderers and burn down their city. 8 Then
he said to the servants, "It is time for
the wedding banquet, and the invited
guests don't deserve to come. 9 Go out
to the street corners and tell everyone you meet to come to the banquet."
10 They went out on the streets and
brought in everyone they could find,
good and bad alike. And the banquet
room was filled with guests.
11 When the king went in to meet
the guests, he found that one of them
wasn't wearing the right kind of
clothes for the wedding. 12 The king
asked, "Friend, why didn't you wear
proper clothes for the wedding?" But
the guest had no excuse. 13 So the king
gave orders for that person to be tied
hand and foot and to be thrown outside into the dark. That's where people
will cry and grit their teeth in pain.
14 Many are invited, but only a few are
chosen.

Paying Taxes

(Mark 12.13-17; Luke 20.20-26)

15 The Pharisees got together and
planned how they could trick Jesus into
saying something wrong. 16 They sent some
of their followers and some of Herod's followers[f] to say to him, "Teacher, we know
that you are honest. You teach the truth
about what God wants people to do. And
you treat everyone with the same respect,
no matter who they are. 17 Tell us what you
think! Should we pay taxes to the Emperor
or not?"
18 Jesus knew their evil thoughts and
said, "Why are you trying to test me? You
show-offs! 19 Let me see one of the coins
used for paying taxes." They brought him a
silver coin, 20 and he asked, "Whose picture and name are on it?"
21 "The Emperor's," they answered.
Then Jesus told them, "Give the Emperor what belongs to him and give God
what belongs to God." 22 His answer surprised them so much that they walked away.

Life in the Future World

(Mark 12.18-27; Luke 20.27-40)

23 The Sadducees did not believe that
people would rise to life after death. So
that same day some of the Sadducees came
to Jesus and said:

[e]**21.44** *pieces*: Verse 44 is not in some manuscripts. [f]**22.16** *Herod's followers*: People who were political followers of the family of Herod the Great (see 2.1) and his son Herod Antipas (see 14.1), and who wanted Herod to be king in Jerusalem.

22.13 Mt 8.12; 25.30; Lk 13.28. **22.14** 2 Esd 8.3. **22.23** Ac 23.8.

24 Teacher, Moses wrote that if a
married man dies and has no children,
his brother should marry the widow.
Their first son would then be thought
of as the son of the dead brother.
25 Once there were seven brothers
who lived here. The first one married,
but died without having any children.
So his wife was left to his brother.
26 The same thing happened to the
second and third brothers and finally
to all seven of them. 27 At last the
woman died. 28 When God raises people from death, whose wife will this
woman be? She had been married to
all seven brothers.

29 Jesus answered:

You are completely wrong! You don't
know what the Scriptures teach. And
you don't know anything about the
power of God. 30 When God raises people to life, they won't marry. They will
be like the angels in heaven. 31 And as
for people being raised to life, God was
speaking to you when he said, 32 "I am
the God worshiped by Abraham, Isaac,
and Jacob."[g] He isn't the God of the
dead, but of the living.

33 The crowds were surprised to hear
what Jesus was teaching.

The Most Important Commandment

(Mark 12.28-34; Luke 10.25-28)

34 After Jesus had made the Sadducees
look foolish, the Pharisees heard about
it and got together. 35 One of them was
an expert in the Jewish Law. So he tried
to test Jesus by asking, 36 "Teacher, what
is the most important commandment in
the Law?"

37 Jesus answered:

Love the Lord your God with all
your heart, soul, and mind. 38 This is
the first and most important commandment. 39 The second most important commandment is like this one.
And it is, "Love others as much as you
love yourself." 40 All the Law of Moses
and the Books of the Prophets[h] are
based on these two commandments.

About David's Son

(Mark 12.35-37; Luke 20.41-44)

41 While the Pharisees were still there,
Jesus asked them, 42 "What do you think
about the Messiah? Whose family will he
come from?"

They answered, "He will be a son of
King David."[i]

43 Jesus replied, "How then could the
Spirit lead David to call the Messiah his
Lord? David said,

44 'The Lord said to my Lord:
Sit at my right side[j]
until I make your enemies
into a footstool for you.'

45 If David called the Messiah his Lord,
how can the Messiah be a son of King
David?" 46 No one was able to give Jesus an
answer, and from that day on, no one dared
ask him any more questions.

Jesus Condemns the Pharisees and the Teachers of the Law of Moses

(Mark 12.38-40; Luke 11.37-52; 20.45-47)

23 Jesus said to the crowds and to his
disciples:

2 The Pharisees and the teachers of
the Law are experts in the Law of
Moses. 3 So obey everything they teach
you, but don't do as they do. After all,
they say one thing and do something
else.

4 They pile heavy burdens on people's shoulders and won't lift a finger
to help. 5 Everything they do is just to
show off in front of others. They even
make a big show of wearing Scripture
verses on their foreheads and arms,

[g]22.32 *I am the God worshiped by Abraham, Isaac, and Jacob*: Jesus argues that if God is worshiped by these three, they must still be alive, because he is the God of the living. [h]22.40 *the Law of Moses and the Books of the Prophets*: The Jewish Scriptures, that is, the Old Testament.
[i]22.42 *son of King David*: See the note at 9.27. [j]22.44 *right side*: The place of power and honor.

22.24 Dt 25.5. **22.30** Ws 5.5. **22.32** Ex 3.6. **22.37** Dt 6.5. **22.39** Lv 19.18. **22.35-40** Lk 10.25-28. **22.44** Ps 110.1. **23.5** **a** Mt 6.1; **b** Dt 6.8; **c** Nu 15.38.

and they wear big tassels[k] for everyone
to see. 6 They love the best seats at
banquets and the front seats in the
meeting places. 7 And when they are in
the market, they like to have people
greet them as their teachers.

8 But none of you should be called
a teacher. You have only one teacher,
and all of you are like brothers and sisters. 9 Don't call anyone on earth your
father. All of you have the same Father
in heaven. 10 None of you should be
called the leader. The Messiah is your
only leader. 11 Whoever is the greatest
should be the servant of the others.
12 If you put yourself above others, you
will be put down. But if you humble
yourself, you will be honored.

13-14 You Pharisees and teachers of
the Law of Moses are in for trouble!
You're nothing but show-offs. You lock
people out of the kingdom of heaven.
You won't go in yourselves, and you
keep others from going in.[l]

15 You Pharisees and teachers of
the Law of Moses are in for trouble!
You're nothing but show-offs. You
travel over land and sea to win one follower. And when you have done so,
you make that person twice as fit for
hell as you are.

16 You are in for trouble! You are
supposed to lead others, but you are
blind. You teach that it doesn't matter
if a person swears by the temple. But
you say that it does matter if someone swears by the gold in the temple.
17 You blind fools! Which is greater, the
gold or the temple that makes the gold
sacred?

18 You also teach that it doesn't
matter if a person swears by the altar.
But you say that it does matter if
someone swears by the gift on the altar. 19 Are you blind? Which is more
important, the gift or the altar that
makes the gift sacred? 20 Anyone who
swears by the altar also swears by
everything on it. 21 And anyone who
swears by the temple also swears by
God, who lives there. 22 To swear by
heaven is the same as swearing by
God's throne and by the one who sits
on that throne.

23 You Pharisees and teachers are
show-offs, and you're in for trouble!
You give God a tenth of the spices from
your garden, such as mint, dill, and
cumin. Yet you neglect the more important matters of the Law, such as
justice, mercy, and faithfulness. These
are the important things you should
have done, though you should not
have left the others undone either.
24 You blind leaders! You strain out a
small fly but swallow a camel.

25 You Pharisees and teachers are
show-offs, and you're in for trouble!
You wash the outside of your cups and
dishes, while inside there is nothing
but greed and selfishness. 26 You blind
Pharisee! First clean the inside of a
cup, and then the outside will also be
clean.

27 You Pharisees and teachers are
in for trouble! You're nothing but
show-offs. You're like tombs that have
been whitewashed.[m] On the outside
they are beautiful, but inside they are
full of bones and filth. 28 That's what
you are like. Outside you look good,
but inside you are evil and only pretend to be good.

29 You Pharisees and teachers are

[k] **23.5** *wearing Scripture verses on their foreheads and arms . . . tassels*: As a sign of their love for the Lord and his teachings, the Jewish people had started wearing Scripture verses in small leather boxes. But the Pharisees tried to show off by making the boxes bigger than necessary. The Jewish people were also taught to wear tassels on the four corners of their robes to show their love for God. [l] **23.13,14** *from going in*: Some manuscripts add, "You Pharisees and teachers are in for trouble! And you're nothing but show-offs! You cheat widows out of their homes and then pray long prayers just to show off. So you will be punished most of all." [m] **23.27** *whitewashed*: Tombs were whitewashed to keep anyone from accidentally touching them. A person who touched a dead body or a tomb was considered unclean and could not worship with the rest of the Jewish people.

23.11 Mt 20.26, 27; Mk 9.35; 10.43, 44; Lk 22.26. **23.12** Lk 14.11; 18.14. **23.22** Is 66.1; Mt 5.34. **23.23** Lv 27.30. **23.27** Ac 23.3.

nothing but show-offs, and you're in for trouble! You build monuments for the prophets and decorate the tombs of good people. 30 And you claim that you would not have taken part with your ancestors in killing the prophets. 31 But you prove that you really are the relatives of the ones who killed the prophets. 32 So keep on doing everything they did. 33 You are nothing but snakes and the children of snakes! How can you escape going to hell?

34 I will send prophets and wise people and experts in the Law of Moses to you. But you will kill them or nail them to a cross or beat them in your meeting places or chase them from town to town. 35 That's why you will be held guilty for the murder of every good person, beginning with the good man Abel. This also includes Barachiah's son Zechariah,[n] the man you murdered between the temple and the altar. 36 I can promise that you people living today will be punished for all these things!

Jesus Loves Jerusalem
(Luke 13.34, 35)

37 Jerusalem, Jerusalem! Your people have killed the prophets and have stoned the messengers who were sent to you. I have often wanted to gather your people, as a hen gathers her chicks under her wings. But you wouldn't let me. 38 And now your temple will be deserted. 39 You won't see me again until you say,

"Blessed is the one who comes
in the name of the Lord."

The Temple Will Be Destroyed
(Mark 13.1, 2; Luke 21.5, 6)

24 After Jesus left the temple, his disciples came over and said, "Look at all these buildings!"

2 Jesus replied, "Do you see these buildings? They will certainly be torn down! Not one stone will be left in place."

Warning about Trouble
(Mark 13.3-13; Luke 21.7-19)

3 Later, as Jesus was sitting on the Mount of Olives, his disciples came to him in private and asked, "When will this happen? What will be the sign of your coming and of the end of the world?"

4 Jesus answered:

Don't let anyone fool you. 5 Many will come and claim to be me. They will say that they are the Messiah, and they will fool many people.

6 You will soon hear about wars and threats of wars, but don't be afraid. These things will have to happen first, but that isn't the end. 7 Nations and kingdoms will go to war against each other. People will starve to death, and in some places there will be earthquakes. 8 But this is just the beginning of troubles.

9 You will be arrested, punished, and even killed. Because of me, you will be hated by people of all nations. 10 Many will give up and will betray and hate each other. 11 Many false prophets will come and fool a lot of people. 12 Evil will spread and cause many people to stop loving others. 13 But if you keep on being faithful right to the end, you will be saved. 14 When the good news about the kingdom has been preached all over the world and told to all nations, the end will come.

The Horrible Thing
(Mark 13.14-23; Luke 21.20-24)

15 Someday you will see that "Horrible Thing" in the holy place, just as the prophet Daniel said. Everyone who reads this must try to understand! 16 If you are living in Judea at that time,

[n]**23.35** *Zechariah*: Genesis is the first book in the Jewish Scriptures, and it tells that Abel was the first person to be murdered. Second Chronicles is the last book in the Jewish Scriptures, and the last murder that it tells about is that of Zechariah.

23.33 Mt 3.7; 12.34; Lk 3.7. **23.35** **a** Gn 4.8; **b** 2 Ch 24.20-22. **23.38** Jr 22.5. **23.39** Ps 118.26. **24.3** 2 Esd 4.51—5.19. **24.7** 2 Esd 13.31. **24.9** Mt 10.22. **24.13** Mt 10.22. **24.15** Dn 9.27; 11.31; 12.11; 1 Macc 1.54; 6.7.

run to the mountains. 17 If you are on
the roof[o] of your house, don't go inside
to get anything. 18 If you are out in the
field, don't go back for your coat. 19 It
will be a terrible time for women who
are expecting babies or nursing young
children. 20 And pray that you won't
have to escape in winter or on a Sabbath.[p] 21 This will be the worst time of
suffering since the beginning of the
world, and nothing this terrible will
ever happen again. 22 If God doesn't
make the time shorter, no one will be
left alive. But because of God's chosen
ones, he will make the time shorter.

23 Someone may say, "Here is the
Messiah!" or "There he is!" But don't
believe it. 24 False messiahs and false
prophets will come and work great
miracles and signs. They will even try
to fool God's chosen ones. 25 But I
have warned you ahead of time. 26 If
you are told that the Messiah is out in
the desert, don't go there! And if you
are told that he is in some secret place,
don't believe it! 27 The coming of the
Son of Man will be like lightning that
can be seen from east to west.
28 Where there is a corpse, there will
always be buzzards.[q]

When the Son of Man Appears

(Mark 13.24-27; Luke 21.25-28)

29 Right after those days of suffering,

"The sun will become dark,
and the moon
will no longer shine.
The stars will fall,
and the powers in the sky[r]
will be shaken."

30 Then a sign will appear in the
sky. And there will be the Son of Man.[s]
All nations on earth will weep when
they see the Son of Man coming on
the clouds of heaven with power and
great glory. 31 At the sound of a loud
trumpet, he will send his angels to
bring his chosen ones together from all
over the earth.

A Lesson from a Fig Tree

(Mark 13.28-31; Luke 21.29-33)

32 Learn a lesson from a fig tree.
When its branches sprout and start
putting out leaves, you know that summer is near. 33 So when you see all
these things happening, you will know
that the time has almost come.[t] 34 I
can promise you that some of the people of this generation will still be alive
when all this happens. 35 The sky and
the earth won't last forever, but my
words will.

No One Knows the Day or Time

(Mark 13.32-37; Luke 17.26-30, 34-36)

36 No one knows the day or hour.
The angels in heaven don't know, and
the Son himself doesn't know.[u] Only
the Father knows. 37 When the Son of
Man appears, things will be just as
they were when Noah lived. 38 People
were eating, drinking, and getting married right up to the day that the flood

[o]**24.17** *roof*: In Palestine the houses usually had a flat roof. Stairs on the outside led up to the roof, which was made of beams and boards covered with packed earth. [p]**24.20** *in winter or on a Sabbath*: In Palestine the winters are cold and rainy and make travel difficult. The Jewish people were not allowed to travel much more than half a mile on the Sabbath. For these reasons it was hard for them to escape from their enemies in the winter or on a Sabbath. [q]**24.28** *Where there is a corpse, there will always be buzzards*: This saying may mean that when anything important happens, people soon know about it. Or the saying may mean that whenever something bad happens, curious people gather around and stare. But the word translated "buzzard" also means "eagle" and may refer to the Roman army, which had an eagle as its symbol. [r]**24.29** *the powers in the sky*: In ancient times people thought that the stars were spiritual powers. [s]**24.30** *And there will be the Son of Man*: Or "And it will be the Son of Man." [t]**24.33** *the time has almost come*: Or "he (that is, the Son of Man) will soon be here." [u]**24.36** *and the Son himself doesn't know*: These words are not in some manuscripts.

24.17,18 Lk 17.31. **24.21** Dn 12.1; Rev 7.14. **24.26,27** Lk 17.23, 24. **24.28** Lk 17.37. **24.29** **a** Is 13.10; Jl 2.10, 31; 3.15; Rev 6.12; **b** Is 13.10; Ez 32.7; Jl 2.10; 3.15; **c** Is 34.4; Rev 6.13. **24.30** Dn 7.13; Zec 12.10-14; Rev 1.7. **24.37** Gn 6.5-8.

came and Noah went into the big boat. 39 They didn't know anything was happening until the flood came and swept them all away. That is how it will be when the Son of Man appears.

40 Two men will be in the same field, but only one will be taken. The other will be left. 41 Two women will be together grinding grain, but only one will be taken. The other will be left. 42 So be on your guard! You don't know when your Lord will come. 43 Homeowners never know when a thief is coming, and they are always on guard to keep one from breaking in. 44 Always be ready! You don't know when the Son of Man will come.

Faithful and Unfaithful Servants
(Luke 12.35-48)

45 Who are faithful and wise servants? Who are the ones the master will put in charge of giving the other servants their food supplies at the proper time? 46 Servants are fortunate if their master comes and finds them doing their job. 47 You may be sure that a servant who is always faithful will be put in charge of everything the master owns. 48 But suppose one of the servants thinks that the master won't return until late. 49 Suppose that evil servant starts beating the other servants and eats and drinks with people who are drunk. 50 If that happens, the master will surely come on a day and at a time when the servant least expects him. 51 That servant will then be punished and thrown out with the ones who only pretended to serve their master. There they will cry and grit their teeth in pain.

A Story about Ten Girls

25 The kingdom of heaven is like what happened one night when ten girls took their oil lamps and went to a wedding to meet the groom.[v] 2 Five of the girls were foolish and five were wise. 3 The foolish ones took their lamps, but no extra oil. 4 The ones who were wise took along extra oil for their lamps.

5 The groom was late arriving, and the girls became drowsy and fell asleep. 6 Then in the middle of the night someone shouted, "Here's the groom! Come to meet him!"

7 When the girls got up and started getting their lamps ready, 8 the foolish ones said to the others, "Let us have some of your oil! Our lamps are going out."

9 The girls who were wise answered, "There's not enough oil for all of us! Go and buy some for yourselves."

10 While the foolish girls were on their way to get some oil, the groom arrived. The girls who were ready went into the wedding, and the doors were closed. 11 Later the other girls returned and shouted, "Sir, sir! Open the door for us!"

12 But the groom replied, "I don't even know you!"

13 So, my disciples, always be ready! You don't know the day or the time when all this will happen.

A Story about Three Servants
(Luke 19.11-27)

14 The kingdom is also like what happened when a man went away and put his three servants in charge of all he owned. 15 The man knew what each servant could do. So he handed five thousand coins to the first servant, two thousand to the second, and one thousand to the third. Then he left the country.

16 As soon as the man had gone, the servant with the five thousand coins used them to earn five thousand more. 17 The servant who had two

[v]**25.1** *to meet the groom*: Some manuscripts add "and the bride." It was the custom for the groom to go to the home of the bride's parents to get his bride. Young girls and other guests would then go with them to the home of the groom's parents, where the wedding feast would take place.

24.39 Gn 7.5-24. **24.43,44** Lk 12.39, 40. **25.1** Lk 12.35. **25.11,12** Lk 13.25. **25.14-30** Lk 19.11-27.

thousand coins did the same with his
money and earned two thousand more.
18 But the servant with one thousand
coins dug a hole and hid his master's
money in the ground.

19 Some time later the master of
those servants returned. He called
them in and asked what they had done
with his money. 20 The servant who
had been given five thousand coins
brought them in with the five thousand that he had earned. He said, "Sir,
you gave me five thousand coins, and I
have earned five thousand more."

21 "Wonderful!" his master replied.
"You are a good and faithful servant. I
left you in charge of only a little, but
now I will put you in charge of much
more. Come and share in my happiness!"

22 Next, the servant who had been
given two thousand coins came in and
said, "Sir, you gave me two thousand
coins, and I have earned two thousand
more."

23 "Wonderful!" his master replied.
"You are a good and faithful servant. I
left you in charge of only a little, but
now I will put you in charge of much
more. Come and share in my happiness!"

24 The servant who had been given
one thousand coins then came in and
said, "Sir, I know that you are hard to
get along with. You harvest what you
don't plant and gather crops where you
haven't scattered seed. 25 I was frightened and went out and hid your
money in the ground. Here is every
single coin!"

26 The master of the servant told
him, "You are lazy and good-for-
nothing! You know that I harvest what
I don't plant and gather crops where I
haven't scattered seed. 27 You could
have at least put my money in the
bank, so that I could have earned interest on it."

28 Then the master said, "Now your
money will be taken away and given to
the servant with ten thousand coins!
29 Everyone who has something will be
given more, and they will have more
than enough. But everything will be
taken from those who don't have anything. 30 You are a worthless servant,
and you will be thrown out into the
dark where people will cry and grit
their teeth in pain."

The Final Judgment

31 When the Son of Man comes in
his glory with all of his angels, he will
sit on his royal throne. 32 The people of
all nations will be brought before him,
and he will separate them, as shepherds separate their sheep from their
goats.

33 He will place the sheep on his
right and the goats on his left. 34 Then
the king will say to those on his right,
"My father has blessed you! Come and
receive the kingdom that was prepared
for you before the world was created.
35 When I was hungry, you gave me
something to eat, and when I was
thirsty, you gave me something to
drink. When I was a stranger, you welcomed me, 36 and when I was naked,
you gave me clothes to wear. When I
was sick, you took care of me, and
when I was in jail, you visited me."

37 Then the ones who pleased the
Lord will ask, "When did we give you
something to eat or drink? 38 When
did we welcome you as a stranger or
give you clothes to wear 39 or visit you
while you were sick or in jail?"

40 The king will answer, "Whenever
you did it for any of my people, no
matter how unimportant they seemed,
you did it for me."

41 Then the king will say to those
on his left, "Get away from me! You are
under God's curse. Go into the everlasting fire prepared for the devil and
his angels! 42 I was hungry, but you did
not give me anything to eat, and I was
thirsty, but you did not give me anything to drink. 43 I was a stranger, but

25.29 Mt 13.12; Mk 4.25; Lk 8.18. **25.30** Mt 8.12; 22.13; Lk 13.28. **25.31** **a** Mt 16.27; **b** Mt 19.28. **25.35,36** Si 7.32-36.

you did not welcome me, and I was
naked, but you did not give me any
clothes to wear. I was sick and in jail,
but you did not take care of me."
44 Then the people will ask, "Lord,
when did we fail to help you when you
were hungry or thirsty or a stranger or
naked or sick or in jail?"
45 The king will say to them,
"Whenever you failed to help any of
my people, no matter how unimportant they seemed, you failed to do it
for me."
46 Then Jesus said, "Those people will
be punished forever. But the ones who
pleased God will have eternal life."

The Plot To Kill Jesus

(Mark 14.1, 2; Luke 22.1, 2; John 11.45-53)

26 When Jesus had finished teaching,
he told his disciples, 2 "You know
that two days from now will be Passover.
That is when the Son of Man will be
handed over to his enemies and nailed to a
cross."
3 At that time the chief priests and the
nation's leaders were meeting at the home
of Caiaphas the high priest. 4 They planned
how they could sneak around and have
Jesus arrested and put to death. 5 But they
said, "We must not do it during Passover,
because the people will riot."

At Bethany

(Mark 14.3-9; John 12.1-8)

6 Jesus was in the town of Bethany, eating at the home of Simon, who had
leprosy.[w] 7 A woman came in with a bottle
of expensive perfume and poured it on
Jesus' head. 8 But when his disciples saw
this, they became angry and complained,
"Why such a waste? 9 We could have sold
this perfume for a lot of money and given it
to the poor."
10 Jesus knew what they were thinking,
and he said:

Why are you bothering this woman?
She has done a beautiful thing for me.
11 You will always have the poor with
you, but you won't always have me.
12 She has poured perfume on my
body to prepare it for burial.[x] 13 You
may be sure that wherever the good
news is told all over the world, people
will remember what she has done. And
they will tell others.

Judas and the Chief Priests

(Mark 14.10, 11; Luke 22.3-6)

14 Judas Iscariot[y] was one of the twelve
disciples. He went to the chief priests
15 and asked, "How much will you give me if
I help you arrest Jesus?" They paid Judas
thirty silver coins, 16 and from then on he
started looking for a good chance to betray
Jesus.

Jesus Eats the Passover Meal with His Disciples

(Mark 14.12-21; Luke 22.7-13; John 13.21-30)

17 On the first day of the Festival of
Thin Bread, Jesus' disciples came to him
and asked, "Where do you want us to prepare the Passover meal?"
18 Jesus told them to go to a certain
man in the city and tell him, "Our teacher
says, 'My time has come! I want to eat
the Passover meal with my disciples in
your home.' " 19 They did as Jesus told
them and prepared the meal.
20-21 When Jesus was eating with his
twelve disciples that evening, he said, "One
of you will surely hand me over to my
enemies."
22 The disciples were very sad, and each
one said to Jesus, "Lord, you can't mean me!"
23 He answered, "One of you men who
has eaten with me from this dish will betray me. 24 The Son of Man will die, as the
Scriptures say. But it's going to be terrible
for the one who betrays me! That man
would be better off if he had never been
born."

[w]**26.6** *leprosy*: See the note at 8.2. [x]**26.12** *poured perfume on my body to prepare it for burial*: The Jewish people taught that giving someone a proper burial was even more important than helping the poor. [y]**26.14** *Iscariot*: See the note at 10.4.

25.46 Dn 12.2. **26.2** Ex 12.1-27. **26.7** Lk 7.37, 38. **26.11** Dt 15.11. **26.15** Zec 11.12. **26.23** Ps 41.9.

25 Judas said, "Teacher, you surely don't mean me!"

"That's what you say!" Jesus replied. But later, Judas did betray him.

The Lord's Supper

(Mark 14.22-26; Luke 22.14-23; 1 Corinthians 11.23-25)

26 During the meal Jesus took some bread in his hands. He blessed the bread and broke it. Then he gave it to his disciples and said, "Take this and eat it. This is my body."

27 Jesus picked up a cup of wine and gave thanks to God. He then gave it to his disciples and said, "Take this and drink it. 28 This is my blood, and with it God makes his agreement with you. It will be poured out, so that many people will have their sins forgiven. 29 From now on I am not going to drink any wine, until I drink new wine with you in my Father's kingdom." 30 Then they sang a hymn and went out to the Mount of Olives.

Peter's Promise

(Mark 14.27-31; Luke 22.31-34; John 13.36-38)

31 Jesus said to his disciples, "During this very night, all of you will reject me, as the Scriptures say,

'I will strike down
the shepherd,
and the sheep
will be scattered.'

32 But after I am raised to life, I will go to Galilee ahead of you."

33 Peter spoke up, "Even if all the others reject you, I never will!"

34 Jesus replied, "I promise you that before a rooster crows tonight, you will say three times that you don't know me." 35 But Peter said, "Even if I have to die with you, I will never say I don't know you."

All the others said the same thing.

Jesus Prays

(Mark 14.32-42; Luke 22.39-46)

36 Jesus went with his disciples to a place called Gethsemane. When they got there, he told them, "Sit here while I go over there and pray."

37 Jesus took along Peter and the two brothers, James and John.[z] He was very sad and troubled, 38 and he said to them, "I am so sad that I feel as if I am dying. Stay here and keep awake with me."

39 Jesus walked on a little way. Then he knelt with his face to the ground and prayed, "My Father, if it is possible, don't make me suffer by having me drink from this cup.[a] But do what you want, and not what I want."

40 He came back and found his disciples sleeping. So he said to Peter, "Can't any of you stay awake with me for just one hour? 41 Stay awake and pray that you won't be tested. You want to do what is right, but you are weak."

42 Again Jesus went to pray and said, "My Father, if there is no other way, and I must suffer, I will still do what you want."

43 Jesus came back and found them sleeping again. They simply could not keep their eyes open. 44 He left them and prayed the same prayer once more.

45 Finally, Jesus returned to his disciples and said, "Are you still sleeping and resting?[b] The time has come for the Son of Man to be handed over to sinners. 46 Get up! Let's go. The one who will betray me is already here."

Jesus Is Arrested

(Mark 14.43-50; Luke 22.47-53; John 18.3-12)

47 Jesus was still speaking, when Judas the betrayer came up. He was one of the twelve disciples, and a large mob armed with swords and clubs was with him. They had been sent by the chief priests and the nation's leaders. 48 Judas had told them ahead of time, "Arrest the man I greet with a kiss."[c]

[z]**26.37** *the two brothers, James and John*: The Greek text has "the two sons of Zebedee" (see 27.56). [a]**26.39** *having me drink from this cup*: In the Scriptures "to drink from a cup" sometimes means to suffer (see the note at 20.22). [b]**26.45** *Are you still sleeping and resting*: Or "You may as well keep on sleeping and resting." [c]**26.48** *the man I greet with a kiss*: It was the custom for people to greet each other with a kiss on the cheek.

26.28 **a** Ex 24.8; **b** Jr 31.31-34. **26.31** Zec 13.7. **26.32** Mt 28.16.

49 Judas walked right up to Jesus and said,
"Hello, teacher." Then Judas kissed him.
50 Jesus replied, "My friend, why are you
here?"[d]

The men grabbed Jesus and arrested
him. 51 One of Jesus' followers pulled out a
sword. He struck the servant of the high
priest and cut off his ear.
52 But Jesus told him, "Put your sword
away. Anyone who lives by fighting will die
by fighting. 53 Don't you know that I could
ask my Father, and right away he would
send me more than twelve armies of angels? 54 But then, how could the words of
the Scriptures come true, which say that
this must happen?"
55 Jesus said to the mob, "Why do you
come with swords and clubs to arrest me
like a criminal? Day after day I sat and
taught in the temple, and you didn't arrest
me. 56 But all this happened, so that what
the prophets wrote would come true."

All of Jesus' disciples left him and ran
away.

Jesus Is Questioned by the Council

(Mark 14.53-65; Luke 22.54, 55, 63-71; John 18.13, 14, 19-24)

57 After Jesus had been arrested, he was
led off to the house of Caiaphas the high
priest. The nation's leaders and the teachers of the Law of Moses were meeting
there. 58 But Peter followed along at a distance and came to the courtyard of the
high priest's palace. He went in and sat
down with the guards to see what was going to happen.
59 The chief priests and the whole council wanted to put Jesus to death. So they
tried to find some people who would tell
lies about him in court.[e] 60 But they could
not find any, even though many did come
and tell lies. At last, two men came forward
61 and said, "This man claimed that he
would tear down God's temple and build it
again in three days."
62 The high priest stood up and asked
Jesus, "Why don't you say something in
your own defense? Don't you hear the
charges they are making against you?"
63 But Jesus did not answer. So the high
priest said, "With the living God looking
on, you must tell the truth. Tell us, are you
the Messiah, the Son of God?"[f]
64 "That is what you say!" Jesus answered. "But I tell all of you,

'Soon you will see
the Son of Man
sitting at the right side[g]
of God All-Powerful
and coming on the clouds
of heaven.' "

65 The high priest then tore his robe and
said, "This man claims to be God! We don't
need any more witnesses! You have heard
what he said. 66 What do you think?"

They answered, "He is guilty and deserves to die!" 67 Then they spit in his face
and hit him with their fists. Others slapped
him 68 and said, "You think you are the
Messiah! So tell us who hit you!"

Peter Says He Doesn't Know Jesus

(Mark 14.66-72; Luke 22.56-62; John 18.15-18, 25-27)

69 While Peter was sitting out in the
courtyard, a servant girl came up to him
and said, "You were with Jesus from
Galilee."
70 But in front of everyone Peter said,
"That isn't so! I don't know what you are
talking about!"
71 When Peter had gone out to the gate,
another servant girl saw him and said to
some people there, "This man was with
Jesus from Nazareth."
72 Again Peter denied it, and this time
he swore, "I don't even know that man!"
73 A little while later some people standing there walked over to Peter and said,
"We know that you are one of them. We

[d]**26.50** *why are you here*: Or "do what you came for." [e]**26.59** *some people who would tell lies about him in court*: The Law of Moses taught that two witnesses were necessary before a person could be put to death (see verse 60). [f]**26.63** *Son of God*: One of the titles used for the kings of Israel. [g]**26.64** *right side*: See the note at 22.44.

26.55 Lk 19.47; 21.37. **26.61** Jn 2.19. **26.64** Dn 7.13. **26.65,66** Lv 24.15, 16. **26.67** Is 50.6.

can tell it because you talk like someone
from Galilee."
74 Peter began to curse and swear, "I
don't know that man!"
Right then a rooster crowed, 75 and Peter remembered that Jesus had said, "Before a rooster crows, you will say three
times that you don't know me." Then Peter
went out and cried hard.

Jesus Is Taken to Pilate

(Mark 15.1; Luke 23.1, 2; John 18.28-32)

27 Early the next morning all the
chief priests and the nation's leaders met and decided that Jesus should be
put to death. 2 They tied him up and led
him away to Pilate the governor.

The Death of Judas

(Acts 1.18, 19)

3 Judas had betrayed Jesus, but when he
learned that Jesus had been sentenced to
death, he was sorry for what he had done.
He returned the thirty silver coins to the
chief priests and leaders 4 and said, "I have
sinned by betraying a man who has never
done anything wrong."
"So what? That's your problem," they
replied. 5 Judas threw the money into the
temple and then went out and hanged
himself.
6 The chief priests picked up the money
and said, "This money was paid to have a
man killed. We can't put it in the temple
treasury." 7 Then they had a meeting and
decided to buy a field that belonged to
someone who made clay pots. They wanted
to use it as a graveyard for foreigners.
8 That's why people still call that place
"Field of Blood." 9 So the words of the
prophet Jeremiah came true,

"They took
the thirty silver coins,
the price of a person
among the people of Israel.
10 They paid it
for a potter's field,[h]
as the Lord
had commanded me."

Pilate Questions Jesus

(Mark 15.2-5; Luke 23.3-5; John 18.33-38)

11 Jesus was brought before Pilate the
governor, who asked him, "Are you the king
of the Jews?"
"Those are your words!" Jesus answered. 12 And when the chief priests and
leaders brought their charges against him,
he did not say a thing.
13 Pilate asked him, "Don't you hear
what crimes they say you have done?"
14 But Jesus did not say anything, and the
governor was greatly amazed.

The Death Sentence

*(Mark 15.6-15; Luke 23.13-26;
John 18.39—19.16)*

15 During Passover the governor always
freed a prisoner chosen by the people. 16 At
that time a well-known terrorist named
Jesus Barabbas[i] was in jail. 17 So when the
crowd came together, Pilate asked them,
"Which prisoner do you want me to set
free? Do you want Jesus Barabbas or Jesus
who is called the Messiah?" 18 Pilate knew
that the leaders had brought Jesus to him
because they were jealous.
19 While Pilate was judging the case, his
wife sent him a message. It said, "Don't
have anything to do with that innocent man.
I have had nightmares because of him."
20 But the chief priests and the leaders
convinced the crowds to ask for Barabbas
to be set free and for Jesus to be killed.
21 Pilate asked the crowd again, "Which
of these two men do you want me to set
free?"
"Barabbas!" they replied.
22 Pilate asked them, "What am I to do
with Jesus, who is called the Messiah?"
They all yelled, "Nail him to a cross!"
23 Pilate answered, "But what crime has
he done?"
"Nail him to a cross!" they yelled even
louder.

[h]**27.10** *a potter's field*: Perhaps a field owned by someone who made clay pots. But it may have been a field where potters came to get clay or to make pots or to throw away their broken pieces of pottery. [i]**27.16** *Jesus Barabbas*: Here and in verse 17 many manuscripts have "Barabbas."

27.3-8 Ac 1.18, 19. **27.9,10** Zec 11.12, 13.

24 Pilate saw that there was nothing he
could do and that the people were starting
to riot. So he took some water and washed
his hands[j] in front of them and said, "I
won't have anything to do with killing this
man. You are the ones doing it!"
25 Everyone answered, "We and our own
families will take the blame for his death!"
26 Pilate set Barabbas free. Then he ordered his soldiers to beat Jesus with a whip
and nail him to a cross.

Soldiers Make Fun of Jesus

(Mark 15.16-21; John 19.2, 3)

27 The governor's soldiers led Jesus into
the fortress[k] and brought together the rest
of the troops. 28 They stripped off Jesus'
clothes and put a scarlet robe[l] on him.
29 They made a crown out of thorn
branches and placed it on his head, and
they put a stick in his right hand. The soldiers knelt down and pretended to worship
him. They made fun of him and shouted,
"Hey, you king of the Jews!" 30 Then they
spit on him. They took the stick from him
and beat him on the head with it.

Jesus Is Nailed to a Cross

(Mark 15.22-32; Luke 23.27-43; John 19.17-27)

31 When the soldiers had finished making fun of Jesus, they took off the robe.
They put his own clothes back on him and
led him off to be nailed to a cross. 32 On
the way they met a man from Cyrene
named Simon, and they forced him to
carry Jesus' cross.
33 They came to a place named Golgotha,
which means "Place of a Skull."[m] 34 There
they gave Jesus some wine mixed with a
drug to ease the pain. But when Jesus
tasted what it was, he refused to drink it.
35 The soldiers nailed Jesus to a cross
and gambled to see who would get his
clothes. 36 Then they sat down to guard him.
37 Above his head they put a sign that told
why he was nailed there. It read, "This is
Jesus, the King of the Jews." 38 The soldiers
also nailed two criminals on crosses, one to
the right of Jesus and the other to his left.
39 People who passed by said terrible
things about Jesus. They shook their heads
and 40 shouted, "So you're the one who
claimed you could tear down the temple
and build it again in three days! If you are
God's Son, save yourself and come down
from the cross!"
41 The chief priests, the leaders, and the
teachers of the Law of Moses also made
fun of Jesus. They said, 42 "He saved others, but he can't save himself. If he is the
king of Israel, he should come down from
the cross! Then we will believe him. 43 He
trusted God, so let God save him, if he
wants to. He even said he was God's Son."
44 The two criminals also said cruel things
to Jesus.

The Death of Jesus

(Mark 15.33-41; Luke 23.44-49; John 19.28-30)

45 At noon the sky turned dark and
stayed that way until three o'clock. 46 Then
about that time Jesus shouted, "Eli, Eli,
lema sabachthani?"[n] which means, "My
God, my God, why have you deserted me?"
47 Some of the people standing there
heard Jesus and said, "He's calling for Elijah."[o] 48 One of them at once ran and
grabbed a sponge. He soaked it in wine, then
put it on a stick and held it up to Jesus.
49 Others said, "Wait! Let's see if Elijah
will come[p] and save him." 50 Once again
Jesus shouted, and then he died.

[j]**27.24** *washed his hands*: To show that he was innocent. [k]**27.27** *fortress*: The place where the Roman governor stayed. It was probably at Herod's palace west of Jerusalem, though it may have been Fortress Antonia north of the temple, where the Roman troops were stationed.
[l]**27.28** *scarlet robe*: This was probably a Roman soldier's robe. [m]**27.33** *Place of a Skull*: The place was probably given this name because it was near a large rock in the shape of a human skull. [n]**27.46** *Eli . . . sabachthani*: These words are in Hebrew. [o]**27.47** *Elijah*: In Aramaic the name "Elijah" sounds like "Eli," which means "my God." [p]**27.49** *Elijah will come*: See the note at 16.14.

27.24 Dt 21.6-9. **27.34** Ps 69.21. **27.35** Ps 22.18. **27.39** Ps 22.7; 109.25; Si 12.17, 18; 13.7. **27.40** Mt 26.61; Jn 2.19. **27.43** Ps 22.8; Ws 2.18-20. **27.46** Ps 22.1. **27.48** Ps 69.21.

51 At once the curtain in the temple[q]
was torn in two from top to bottom. The
earth shook, and rocks split apart.
52 Graves opened, and many of God's people were raised to life. 53 Then after Jesus
had risen to life, they came out of their
graves and went into the holy city, where
they were seen by many people.
54 The officer and the soldiers guarding Jesus felt the earthquake and saw
everything else that happened. They were
frightened and said, "This man really was
God's Son!"
55 Many women had come with Jesus
from Galilee to be of help to him, and
they were there, looking on at a distance.
56 Mary Magdalene, Mary the mother of
James and Joseph, and the mother of
James and John[r] were some of these
women.

Jesus Is Buried

(Mark 15.42-47; Luke 23.50-56; John 19.38-42)

57 That evening a rich disciple named
Joseph from the town of Arimathea 58 went
and asked for Jesus' body. Pilate gave orders for it to be given to Joseph, 59 who
took the body and wrapped it in a clean
linen cloth. 60 Then Joseph put the body in
his own tomb that had been cut into solid
rock[s] and had never been used. He rolled a
big stone against the entrance to the tomb
and went away.
61 All this time Mary Magdalene and the
other Mary were sitting across from the
tomb.
62 On the next day, which was a Sabbath, the chief priests and the Pharisees
went together to Pilate. 63 They said, "Sir,
we remember what that liar said while he
was still alive. He claimed that in three
days he would come back from death. 64 So
please order the tomb to be carefully
guarded for three days. If you don't, his disciples may come and steal his body. They
will tell the people that he has been raised
to life, and this last lie will be worse than
the first one."[t]
65 Pilate said to them, "All right, take some
of your soldiers and guard the tomb as well
as you know how." 66 So they sealed it tight
and placed soldiers there to guard it.

Jesus Is Alive

(Mark 16.1-8; Luke 24.1-12; John 20.1-10)

28 The Sabbath was over, and it was
almost daybreak on Sunday when
Mary Magdalene and the other Mary went
to see the tomb. 2 Suddenly a strong earthquake struck, and the Lord's angel came
down from heaven. He rolled away the
stone and sat on it. 3 The angel looked
as bright as lightning, and his clothes
were white as snow. 4 The guards shook
from fear and fell down, as though they
were dead.
5 The angel said to the women, "Don't
be afraid! I know you are looking for Jesus,
who was nailed to a cross. 6 He isn't here!
God has raised him to life, just as Jesus
said he would. Come, see the place where
his body was lying. 7 Now hurry! Tell his
disciples that he has been raised to life and
is on his way to Galilee. Go there, and
you will see him. That is what I came to
tell you."
8 The women were frightened and yet
very happy, as they hurried from the tomb
and ran to tell his disciples. 9 Suddenly
Jesus met them and greeted them. They
went near him, held on to his feet, and
worshiped him. 10 Then Jesus said, "Don't
be afraid! Tell my followers to go to Galilee.
They will see me there."

[q] **27.51** *curtain in the temple*: There were two curtains in the temple. One was at the entrance, and the other separated the holy place from the most holy place that the Jewish people thought of as God's home on earth. The second curtain is probably the one that is meant. [r] **27.56** *of James and John*: The Greek text has "of Zebedee's sons" (see 26.37). [s] **27.60** *tomb . . . solid rock*: Some of the Jewish people buried their dead in rooms carved into solid rock. A heavy stone was rolled against the entrance. [t] **27.64** *the first one*: Probably the belief that Jesus is the Messiah.

27.51 Ex 26.31-33. **27.55,56** Lk 8.2, 3. **27.63** Mt 16.21; 17.23; 20.19; Mk 8.31; 9.31; 10.33, 34; Lk 9.22; 18.31-33.

Report of the Guard

[11] While the women were on their way,
some soldiers who had been guarding the
tomb went into the city. They told the chief
priests everything that had happened. [12] So
the chief priests met with the leaders and
decided to bribe the soldiers with a lot of
money. [13] They said to the soldiers, "Tell
everyone that Jesus' disciples came during
the night and stole his body while you were
asleep. [14] If the governor[u] hears about this,
we will talk to him. You won't have anything to worry about." [15] The soldiers took
the money and did what they were told.
The Jewish people still tell each other this
story.

What Jesus' Followers Must Do

(Mark 16.14-18; Luke 24.36-49; John 20.19-23; Acts 1.6-8)

[16] Jesus' eleven disciples went to a
mountain in Galilee, where Jesus had told
them to meet him. [17] They saw him and
worshiped him, but some of them doubted.
[18] Jesus came to them and said:

I have been given all authority in
heaven and on earth! [19] Go to the people
of all nations and make them my
disciples. Baptize them in the name
of the Father, the Son, and the Holy
Spirit, [20] and teach them to do everything I have told you. I will be with you
always, even until the end of the world.

[u]**28.14** *governor*: Pontius Pilate.

28.16 Mt 26.32; Mk 14.28. **28.19** Ac 1.8.

MARK

ABOUT THIS BOOK

This is the shortest of the four New Testament books that tell about the life and teachings of Jesus, but it is also the most action-packed. From the very beginning of his ministry, Jesus worked mighty wonders. After choosing four followers (1.16-20), he immediately performed many miracles of healing. Among those healed were a man with an evil spirit in him (1.21-28), Simon's mother-in-law (1.30, 31), crowds of sick people (1.32-34), and a man with leprosy (1.40-45). Over and over Mark tells how Jesus healed people, but always in such a way as to show that he did these miracles by the power of God.

The religious leaders refused to accept Jesus. This led to conflicts (2.2—3.6) that finally made them start looking for a way to kill him (11.18). But the demons saw the power of Jesus, and they knew that he was the Son of God, although Jesus would not let them tell anyone.

This book is full of miracles that amazed the crowds and Jesus' followers. But, according to Mark, the most powerful miracle of Jesus is his suffering and death. The first person to understand this miracle was the Roman soldier who saw Jesus die on the cross and said, "This man really was the Son of God!" (15.39).

This Gospel is widely thought to be the first one written. The many explanations of Aramaic words and Jewish customs in Mark suggest that Mark wrote to Gentile or non-Jewish Christians. He wants to tell about Jesus and to encourage readers to believe in the power of Jesus to rescue them from sickness, demons, and death. He also wants to remind them that the new life of faith is not an easy life, and that they must follow Jesus by serving others and being ready to suffer as he did.

The first followers of Jesus to discover the empty tomb were three women, and the angel told them:

> *"Don't be alarmed! You are looking for Jesus from Nazareth, who was nailed to a cross. God has raised him to life, and he isn't here."*
>
> *(16.6)*

A QUICK LOOK AT THIS BOOK

- The Message of John the Baptist (1.1-8)
- The Baptism and Temptation of Jesus (1.9-13)
- Jesus in Galilee (1.14—9.50)
- Jesus Goes from Galilee to Jerusalem (10.1-52)
- Jesus' Last Week: His Trial and Death (11.1—15.47)
- Jesus Is Alive (16.1-8)
- Jesus Appears to His Followers (16.9-20)

The Preaching of John the Baptist
(Matthew 3.1-12; Luke 3.1-18; John 1.19-28)

1 This is the good news about Jesus
Christ, the Son of God.[a] 2 It began just
as God had said in the book written by Isaiah the prophet,

"I am sending my messenger
to get the way ready
for you.
3 In the desert
someone is shouting,
'Get the road ready
for the Lord!
Make a straight path
for him.' "

4 So John the Baptist showed up in the
desert and told everyone, "Turn back to
God and be baptized! Then your sins will
be forgiven."
5 From all Judea and Jerusalem crowds
of people went to John. They told how
sorry they were for their sins, and he baptized them in the Jordan River.
6 John wore clothes made of camel's
hair. He had a leather strap around his
waist and ate grasshoppers and wild
honey.
7 John also told the people, "Someone
more powerful is going to come. And I am
not good enough even to stoop down and
untie his sandals.[b] 8 I baptize you with water, but he will baptize you with the Holy
Spirit!"

The Baptism of Jesus
(Matthew 3.13-17; Luke 3.21, 22)

9 About that time Jesus came from
Nazareth in Galilee, and John baptized him
in the Jordan River. 10 As soon as Jesus
came out of the water, he saw the sky open
and the Holy Spirit coming down to him
like a dove. 11 A voice from heaven said,
"You are my own dear Son, and I am
pleased with you."

Jesus and Satan
(Matthew 4.1-11; Luke 4.1-13)

12 Right away God's Spirit made Jesus
go into the desert. 13 He stayed there for
forty days while Satan tested him. Jesus
was with the wild animals, but angels took
care of him.

Jesus Begins His Work
(Matthew 4.12-17; Luke 4.14, 15)

14 After John was arrested, Jesus went
to Galilee and told the good news that
comes from God.[c] 15 He said, "The time
has come! God's kingdom will soon be
here.[d] Turn back to God and believe the
good news!"

Jesus Chooses Four Fishermen
(Matthew 4.18-22; Luke 5.1-11)

16 As Jesus was walking along the shore
of Lake Galilee, he saw Simon and his
brother Andrew. They were fishermen and
were casting their nets into the lake.
17 Jesus said to them, "Come with me! I
will teach you how to bring in people instead of fish." 18 Right then the two brothers dropped their nets and went with him.
19 Jesus walked on and soon saw James
and John, the sons of Zebedee. They were
in a boat, mending their nets. 20 At once
Jesus asked them to come with him. They
left their father in the boat with the hired
workers and went with him.

A Man with an Evil Spirit
(Luke 4.31-37)

21 Jesus and his disciples went to the
town of Capernaum. Then on the next
Sabbath he went into the Jewish meeting
place and started teaching. 22 Everyone
was amazed at his teaching. He taught with
authority, and not like the teachers of the
Law of Moses. 23 Suddenly a man with an
evil spirit[e] in him entered the meeting
place and yelled, 24 "Jesus from Nazareth,
what do you want with us? Have you come

[a] **1.1** *the Son of God*: These words are not in some manuscripts. [b] **1.7** *untie his sandals*: This was the duty of a slave. [c] **1.14** *that comes from God*: Or "that is about God." [d] **1.15** *will soon be here*: Or "is already here." [e] **1.23** *evil spirit*: A Jewish person who had an evil spirit was considered "unclean" and was not allowed to eat or worship with other Jewish people.

1.2 Ml 3.1. **1.3** Is 40.3 (LXX). **1.6** 2 K 1.8. **1.11** Gn 22.2; Ps 2.7; Is 42.1; Mt 3.17; 12.18; Mk 9.7; Lk 3.22. **1.15** Mt 3.2. **1.22** Mt 7.28, 29.

to destroy us? I know who you are! You are
God's Holy One."
25 Jesus told the evil spirit, "Be quiet
and come out of the man!" 26 The spirit
shook him. Then it gave a loud shout and
left.
27 Everyone was completely surprised
and kept saying to each other, "What is
this? It must be some new kind of powerful
teaching! Even the evil spirits obey him."
28 News about Jesus quickly spread all over
Galilee.

Jesus Heals Many People

(Matthew 8.14-17; Luke 4.38-41)

29 As soon as Jesus left the meeting
place with James and John, they went
home with Simon and Andrew. 30 When
they got there, Jesus was told that Simon's
mother-in-law was sick in bed with fever.
31 Jesus went to her. He took hold of her
hand and helped her up. The fever left her,
and she served them a meal.
32 That evening after sunset,[f] all who
were sick or had demons in them were
brought to Jesus. 33 In fact, the whole town
gathered around the door of the house.
34 Jesus healed all kinds of terrible diseases
and forced out a lot of demons. But the
demons knew who he was, and he did not
let them speak.
35 Very early the next morning, Jesus got
up and went to a place where he could be
alone and pray. 36 Simon and the others
started looking for him. 37 And when they
found him, they said, "Everyone is looking
for you!"
38 Jesus replied, "We must go to the
nearby towns, so that I can tell the good
news to those people. This is why I have
come." 39 Then Jesus went to Jewish meeting places everywhere in Galilee, where he
preached and forced out demons.

Jesus Heals a Man

(Matthew 8.1-4; Luke 5.12-16)

40 A man with leprosy[g] came to Jesus
and knelt down.[h] He begged, "You have
the power to make me well, if only you
wanted to."
41 Jesus felt sorry for[i] the man. So he
put his hand on him and said, "I want to!
Now you are well." 42 At once the man's
leprosy disappeared, and he was well.
43 After Jesus strictly warned the man,
he sent him on his way. 44 He said, "Don't
tell anyone about this. Just go and show the
priest that you are well. Then take a gift to
the temple as Moses commanded, and
everyone will know that you have been
healed."[j]
45 The man talked about it so much and
told so many people, that Jesus could no
longer go openly into a town. He had to
stay away from the towns, but people still
came to him from everywhere.

Jesus Heals a Crippled Man

(Matthew 9.1-8; Luke 5.17-26)

2 Jesus went back to Capernaum, and a
few days later people heard that he
was at home.[k] 2 Then so many of them
came to the house that there wasn't even
standing room left in front of the door.
Jesus was still teaching 3 when four people came up, carrying a crippled man on a
mat. 4 But because of the crowd, they could
not get him to Jesus. So they made a hole
in the roof[l] above him and let the man
down in front of everyone.
5 When Jesus saw how much faith they
had, he said to the crippled man, "My
friend, your sins are forgiven."
6 Some of the teachers of the Law of
Moses were sitting there. They started wondering, 7 "Why would he say such a thing?

[f]**1.32** *after sunset*: The Sabbath was over, and a new day began at sunset. [g]**1.40** *leprosy*: In biblical times the word "leprosy" was used for many different kinds of skin diseases. [h]**1.40** *and knelt down*: These words are not in some manuscripts. [i]**1.41** *felt sorry for*: Some manuscripts have "was angry with." [j]**1.44** *everyone will know that you have been healed*: People with leprosy had to be examined by a priest and told that they were well (that is, "clean") before they could once again live a normal life in the Jewish community. The gift that Moses commanded was the sacrifice of some lambs together with flour mixed with olive oil. [k]**2.1** *at home*: Or "in the house" (perhaps Simon Peter's home). [l]**2.4** *roof*: In Palestine the houses usually had a flat roof. Stairs on the outside led up to the roof that was made of beams and boards covered with packed earth.

1.39 Mt 4.23; 9.35. **1.44** Lv 14.1-32.

He must think he is God! Only God can forgive sins."

8 Right away, Jesus knew what they were thinking, and he said, "Why are you thinking such things? 9 Is it easier for me to tell this crippled man that his sins are forgiven or to tell him to get up and pick up his mat and go on home? 10 I will show you that the Son of Man has the right to forgive sins here on earth." So Jesus said to the man, 11 "Get up! Pick up your mat and go on home."

12 The man got right up. He picked up his mat and went out while everyone watched in amazement. They praised God and said, "We have never seen anything like this!"

Jesus Chooses Levi

(Matthew 9.9-13; Luke 5.27-32)

13 Once again, Jesus went to the shore of Lake Galilee. A large crowd gathered around him, and he taught them. 14 As he walked along, he saw Levi, the son of Alphaeus. Levi was sitting at the place for paying taxes, and Jesus said to him, "Come with me!" So he got up and went with Jesus.

15 Later, Jesus and his disciples were having dinner at Levi's house.[m] Many tax collectors[n] and other sinners had become followers of Jesus, and they were also guests at the dinner.

16 Some of the teachers of the Law of Moses were Pharisees, and they saw that Jesus was eating with sinners and tax collectors. So they asked his disciples, "Why does he eat with tax collectors and sinners?"

17 Jesus heard them and answered, "Healthy people don't need a doctor, but sick people do. I didn't come to invite good people to be my followers. I came to invite sinners."

People Ask about Going without Eating

(Matthew 9.14-17; Luke 5.33-39)

18 The followers of John the Baptist and the Pharisees often went without eating.[o] Some people came and asked Jesus, "Why do the followers of John and those of the Pharisees often go without eating, while your disciples never do?"

19 Jesus answered:

The friends of a bridegroom don't go without eating while he is still with them. 20 But the time will come when he will be taken from them. Then they will go without eating.

21 No one patches old clothes by sewing on a piece of new cloth. The new piece would shrink and tear a bigger hole.

22 No one pours new wine into old wineskins. The wine would swell and burst the old skins.[p] Then the wine would be lost, and the skins would be ruined. New wine must be put into new wineskins.

A Question about the Sabbath

(Matthew 12.1-8; Luke 6.1-5)

23 One Sabbath Jesus and his disciples were walking through some wheat fields. His disciples were picking grains of wheat as they went along.[q] 24 Some Pharisees asked Jesus, "Why are your disciples picking grain on the Sabbath? They are not supposed to do that!"

25 Jesus answered, "Haven't you read what David did when he and his followers were hungry and in need? 26 It was during the time of Abiathar the high priest. David went into the house of God and ate the sacred loaves of bread that only priests are allowed to eat. He also gave some to his followers."

[m] **2.15** *Levi's house*: Or "Jesus' house." [n] **2.15** *tax collectors*: These were usually Jewish people who paid the Romans for the right to collect taxes. They were hated by other Jews who thought of them as traitors to their country and to their religion. [o] **2.18** *without eating*: The Jewish people sometimes went without eating (also called "fasting") to show their love for God or to show sorrow for their sins. [p] **2.22** *swell and burst the old skins*: While the juice from grapes was becoming wine, it would swell and stretch the skins in which it had been stored. If the skins were old and stiff, they would burst. [q] **2.23** *went along*: It was the custom to let hungry travelers pick grains of wheat.

2.23 Dt 23.25. **2.26** Lv 24.9. **2.25,26** 1 S 21.1-6.

27 Jesus finished by saying, "People were not made for the good of the Sabbath. The Sabbath was made for the good of people. 28 So the Son of Man is Lord over the Sabbath."

A Man with a Crippled Hand

(Matthew 12.9-14; Luke 6.6-11)

3 The next time that Jesus went into the meeting place, a man with a crippled hand was there. 2 The Pharisees[r] wanted to accuse Jesus of doing something wrong, and they kept watching to see if Jesus would heal him on the Sabbath.

3 Jesus told the man to stand up where everyone could see him. 4 Then he asked, "On the Sabbath should we do good deeds or evil deeds? Should we save someone's life or destroy it?" But no one said a word.

5 Jesus was angry as he looked around at the people. Yet he felt sorry for them because they were so stubborn. Then he told the man, "Stretch out your hand." He did, and his bad hand was healed.

6 The Pharisees left. And right away they started making plans with Herod's followers[s] to kill Jesus.

Large Crowds Come to Jesus

7 Jesus led his disciples down to the shore of the lake. Large crowds followed him from Galilee, Judea, 8 and Jerusalem. People came from Idumea, as well as other places east of the Jordan River. They also came from the region around the cities of Tyre and Sidon. All of these crowds came because they had heard what Jesus was doing. 9 He even had to tell his disciples to get a boat ready to keep him from being crushed by the crowds.

10 After Jesus had healed many people, the other sick people begged him to let them touch him. 11 And whenever any evil spirits saw Jesus, they would fall to the ground and shout, "You are the Son of God!" 12 But Jesus warned the spirits not to tell who he was.

Jesus Chooses His Twelve Apostles

(Matthew 10.1-4; Luke 6.12-16)

13 Jesus decided to ask some of his disciples to go up on a mountain with him, and they went. 14 Then he chose twelve of them to be his apostles,[t] so that they could be with him. He also wanted to send them out to preach 15 and to force out demons. 16 Simon was one of the twelve, and Jesus named him Peter. 17 There were also James and John, the two sons of Zebedee. Jesus called them Boanerges, which means "Thunderbolts." 18 Andrew, Philip, Bartholomew, Matthew, Thomas, James son of Alphaeus, and Thaddaeus were also apostles. The others were Simon, known as the Eager One,[u] 19 and Judas Iscariot,[v] who later betrayed Jesus.

Jesus and the Ruler of Demons

(Matthew 12.22-32; Luke 11.14-23; 12.10)

20 Jesus went back home,[w] and once again such a large crowd gathered that there was no chance even to eat. 21 When Jesus' family heard what he was doing, they thought he was crazy and went to get him under control.

22 Some teachers of the Law of Moses came from Jerusalem and said, "This man is under the power of Beelzebul, the ruler of demons! He is even forcing out demons with the help of Beelzebul."

23 Jesus told the people to gather around him. Then he spoke to them in riddles and said:

How can Satan force himself out?
24 A nation whose people fight each
other won't last very long. 25 And a
family that fights won't last long either.

[r]**3.2** *Pharisees*: The Greek text has "they" (but see verse 6). [s]**3.6** *Herod's followers*: People who were political followers of the family of Herod the Great and his son Herod Antipas. [t]**3.14** *to be his apostles*: These words are not in some manuscripts. [u]**3.18** *known as the Eager One*: The Greek text has "Cananaean," which probably comes from a Hebrew word meaning "zealous" (see Luke 6.15). "Zealot" was the name later given to the members of a Jewish group that resisted and fought against the Romans. [v]**3.19** *Iscariot*: This may mean "a man from Kerioth" (a place in Judea). But more probably it means "a man who was a liar" or "a man who was a betrayer."
[w]**3.20** *went back home*: Or "entered a house" (perhaps the home of Simon Peter).
3.9,10 Mk 4.1; Lk 5.1-3. **3.22** Mt 9.34; 10.25.

26 So if Satan fights against himself,
that will be the end of him.
27 How can anyone break into the
house of a strong man and steal his
things, unless he first ties up the
strong man? Then he can take everything.
28 I promise you that any of the sinful things you say or do can be forgiven, no matter how terrible those
things are. 29 But if you speak against
the Holy Spirit, you can never be forgiven. That sin will be held against you
forever.
30 Jesus said this because the people
were saying that he had an evil spirit
in him.

Jesus' Mother and Brothers

(Matthew 12.46-50; Luke 8.19-21)

31 Jesus' mother and brothers came and
stood outside. Then they sent someone
with a message for him to come out to
them. 32 The crowd that was sitting around
Jesus told him, "Your mother and your
brothers and sisters[x] are outside and want
to see you."
33 Jesus asked, "Who is my mother and
who are my brothers?" 34 Then he looked
at the people sitting around him and said,
"Here are my mother and my brothers.
35 Anyone who obeys God is my brother or
sister or mother."

A Story about a Farmer

(Matthew 13.1-9; Luke 8.4-8)

4 The next time Jesus taught beside
Lake Galilee, a big crowd gathered. It
was so large that he had to sit in a boat out
on the lake, while the people stood on the
shore. 2 He used stories to teach them
many things, and this is part of what he
taught:
3 Now listen! A farmer went out to
scatter seed in a field. 4 While the
farmer was scattering the seed, some
of it fell along the road and was eaten
by birds. 5 Other seeds fell on thin,
rocky ground and quickly started growing because the soil wasn't very deep.
6 But when the sun came up, the
plants were scorched and dried up, because they did not have enough roots.
7 Some other seeds fell where thornbushes grew up and choked out the
plants. So they did not produce any
grain. 8 But a few seeds did fall on
good ground where the plants grew
and produced thirty or sixty or even a
hundred times as much as was scattered.
9 Then Jesus said, "If you have ears, pay
attention."

Why Jesus Used Stories

(Matthew 13.10-17; Luke 8.9, 10)

10 When Jesus was alone with the twelve
apostles and some others, they asked him
about these stories. 11 He answered:
I have explained the secret about
God's kingdom to you, but for others I
can use only stories. 12 The reason is,

"These people will look
and look, but never see.
They will listen and listen,
but never understand.
If they did,
they would turn to God,
and he would forgive them."

Jesus Explains the Story about the Farmer

(Matthew 13.18-23; Luke 8.11-15)

13 Jesus told them:
If you don't understand this story,
you won't understand any others.
14 What the farmer is spreading is really the message about the kingdom.
15 The seeds that fell along the road
are the people who hear the message.
But Satan soon comes and snatches it
away from them. 16 The seeds that fell
on rocky ground are the people who
gladly hear the message and accept it
right away. 17 But they don't have any
roots, and they don't last very long. As
soon as life gets hard or the message
gets them in trouble, they give up.

[x] **3.32** *and sisters*: These words are not in some manuscripts.
3.29 Lk 12.10. **4.1** Lk 5.1-3. **4.12** Is 6.9, 10 (LXX).

18 The seeds that fell among the
thornbushes are also people who hear
the message. 19 But they start worrying
about the needs of this life. They are
fooled by the desire to get rich and to
have all kinds of other things. So the
message gets choked out, and they
never produce anything. 20 The seeds
that fell on good ground are the people
who hear and welcome the message.
They produce thirty or sixty or even a
hundred times as much as was planted.

Light
(Luke 8.16-18)

21 Jesus also said:
You don't light a lamp and put it
under a clay pot or under a bed. Don't
you put a lamp on a lampstand?
22 There is nothing hidden that will
not be made public. There is no secret
that will not be well known. 23 If you
have ears, pay attention!
24 Listen carefully to what you hear!
The way you treat others will be the
way you will be treated—and even worse.
25 Everyone who has something will be
given more. But people who don't have
anything will lose what little they have.

Another Story about Seeds

26 Again Jesus said:
God's kingdom is like what happens
when a farmer scatters seed in a field.
27 The farmer sleeps at night and is up
and around during the day. Yet the
seeds keep sprouting and growing, and
he doesn't understand how. 28 It is the
ground that makes the seeds sprout
and grow into plants that produce
grain. 29 Then when harvest season
comes and the grain is ripe, the farmer
cuts it with a sickle.[y]

A Mustard Seed
(Matthew 13.31, 32; Luke 13.18, 19)

30 Finally, Jesus said:
What is God's kingdom like? What
story can I use to explain it? 31 It is like
what happens when a mustard seed is
planted in the ground. It is the smallest seed in all the world. 32 But once it
is planted, it grows larger than any garden plant. It even puts out branches
that are big enough for birds to nest in
its shade.

The Reason for Teaching with Stories
(Matthew 13.34, 35)

33 Jesus used many other stories when
he spoke to the people, and he taught them
as much as they could understand. 34 He
did not tell them anything without using
stories. But when he was alone with his
disciples, he explained everything to them.

A Storm
(Matthew 8.23-27; Luke 8.22-25)

35 That evening, Jesus said to his disciples, "Let's cross to the east side." 36 So
they left the crowd, and his disciples
started across the lake with him in the
boat. Some other boats followed along.
37 Suddenly a windstorm struck the lake.
Waves started splashing into the boat, and
it was about to sink.
38 Jesus was in the back of the boat with
his head on a pillow, and he was asleep. His
disciples woke him and said, "Teacher,
don't you care that we're about to drown?"
39 Jesus got up and ordered the wind
and the waves to be quiet. The wind
stopped, and everything was calm.
40 Jesus asked his disciples, "Why were
you afraid? Don't you have any faith?"
41 Now they were more afraid than ever
and said to each other, "Who is this? Even
the wind and the waves obey him!"

A Man with Evil Spirits
(Matthew 8.28-34; Luke 8.26-39)

5 Jesus and his disciples crossed Lake
Galilee and came to shore near the
town of Gerasa.[z] 2 When he was getting out
of the boat, a man with an evil spirit

[y] **4.29** *sickle*: A knife with a long curved blade, used to cut grain and other crops. [z] **5.1** *Gerasa*: Some manuscripts have "Gadara," and others have "Gergesa."

4.21 Mt 5.15; Lk 11.33. **4.22** Mt 10.26; Lk 12.2. **4.24** Mt 7.2; Lk 6.38. **4.25** Mt 13.12; 25.29; Lk 19.26. **4.29** Jl 3.13.

quickly ran to him 3 from the graveyard[a]
where he had been living. No one was able
to tie the man up anymore, not even with a
chain. 4 He had often been put in chains
and leg irons, but he broke the chains and
smashed the leg irons. No one could control him. 5 Night and day he was in the
graveyard or on the hills, yelling and cutting himself with stones.

6 When the man saw Jesus in the distance, he ran up to him and knelt down.
7 He shouted, "Jesus, Son of God in
heaven, what do you want with me?
Promise me in God's name that you won't
torture me!" 8 The man said this because
Jesus had already told the evil spirit to
come out of him.

9 Jesus asked, "What is your name?"

The man answered, "My name is Lots,
because I have 'lots' of evil spirits." 10 He
then begged Jesus not to send them away.

11 Over on the hillside a large herd of
pigs was feeding. 12 So the evil spirits
begged Jesus, "Send us into those pigs! Let
us go into them." 13 Jesus let them go, and
they went out of the man and into the pigs.
The whole herd of about two thousand pigs
rushed down the steep bank into the lake
and drowned.

14 The men taking care of the pigs ran
to the town and the farms to spread the
news. Then the people came out to see
what had happened. 15 When they came to
Jesus, they saw the man who had once
been full of demons. He was sitting there
with his clothes on and in his right mind,
and they were terrified.

16 Everyone who had seen what had
happened told about the man and the pigs.
17 Then the people started begging Jesus to
leave their part of the country.

18 When Jesus was getting into the boat,
the man begged to go with him. 19 But
Jesus would not let him. Instead, he said,
"Go home to your family and tell them how
much the Lord has done for you and how
good he has been to you."

20 The man went away into the region
near the ten cities known as Decapolis[b]
and began telling everyone how much
Jesus had done for him. Everyone who
heard what had happened was amazed.

A Dying Girl and a Sick Woman

(Matthew 9.18-26; Luke 8.40-56)

21 Once again Jesus got into the boat
and crossed Lake Galilee.[c] Then as he
stood on the shore, a large crowd gathered
around him. 22 The person in charge of the
Jewish meeting place was also there. His
name was Jairus, and when he saw Jesus,
he went over to him. He knelt at Jesus' feet
23 and started begging him for help. He
said, "My daughter is about to die! Please
come and touch her, so she will get well and
live." 24 Jesus went with Jairus. Many people followed along and kept crowding around.

25 In the crowd was a woman who had
been bleeding for twelve years. 26 She had
gone to many doctors, and they had not
done anything except cause her a lot of
pain. She had paid them all the money she
had. But instead of getting better, she only
got worse.

27 The woman had heard about Jesus,
so she came up behind him in the crowd
and barely touched his clothes. 28 She had
said to herself, "If I can just touch his
clothes, I will get well." 29 As soon as she
touched them, her bleeding stopped, and
she knew she was well.

30 At that moment Jesus felt power go
out from him. He turned to the crowd and
asked, "Who touched my clothes?"

31 His disciples said to him, "Look at all
these people crowding around you! How
can you ask who touched you?" 32 But
Jesus turned to see who had touched him.

33 The woman knew what had happened to her. She came shaking with fear
and knelt down in front of Jesus. Then she
told him the whole story.

34 Jesus said to the woman, "You are
now well because of your faith. May God
give you peace! You are healed, and you
will no longer be in pain."

[a]**5.3** *graveyard*: It was thought that demons and evil spirits lived in graveyards. [b]**5.20** *the ten cities known as Decapolis*: A group of ten cities east of Samaria and Galilee, where the people followed the Greek way of life. [c]**5.21** *crossed Lake Galilee*: To the west side.

5.26 Tb 2.10.

35 While Jesus was still speaking, some men came from Jairus' home and said, "Your daughter has died! Why bother the teacher anymore?"

36 Jesus heard[d] what they said, and he said to Jairus, "Don't worry. Just have faith!"

37 Jesus did not let anyone go with him except Peter and the two brothers, James and John. 38 They went home with Jairus and saw the people crying and making a lot of noise.[e] 39 Then Jesus went inside and said to them, "Why are you crying and carrying on like this? The child isn't dead. She is just asleep." 40 But the people laughed at him. After Jesus had sent them all out of the house, he took the girl's father and mother and his three disciples and went to where she was. 41-42 He took the twelve-year-old girl by the hand and said, "Talitha, koum!"[f] which means, "Little girl, get up!" The girl got right up and started walking around.

Everyone was greatly surprised. 43 But Jesus ordered them not to tell anyone what had happened. Then he said, "Give her something to eat."

The People of Nazareth Turn against Jesus

(Matthew 13.53-58; Luke 4.16-30)

6 Jesus left and returned to his hometown[g] with his disciples. 2 The next Sabbath he taught in the Jewish meeting place. Many of the people who heard him were amazed and asked, "How can he do all this? Where did he get such wisdom and the power to work these miracles? 3 Isn't he the carpenter,[h] the son of Mary? Aren't James, Joseph, Judas, and Simon his brothers? Don't his sisters still live here in our town?" The people were very unhappy because of what he was doing.

4 But Jesus said, "Prophets are honored by everyone, except the people of their hometown and their relatives and their own family." 5 Jesus could not work any miracles there, except to heal a few sick people by placing his hands on them. 6 He was surprised that the people did not have any faith.

Instructions for the Twelve Apostles

(Matthew 10.5-15; Luke 9.1-6)

Jesus taught in all the neighboring villages. 7 Then he called together his twelve apostles and sent them out two by two with power over evil spirits. 8 He told them, "You may take along a walking stick. But don't carry food or a traveling bag or any money. 9 It's all right to wear sandals, but don't take along a change of clothes. 10 When you are welcomed into a home, stay there until you leave that town. 11 If any place won't welcome you or listen to your message, leave and shake the dust from your feet[i] as a warning to them."

12 The apostles left and started telling everyone to turn to God. 13 They forced out many demons and healed a lot of sick people by putting olive oil[j] on them.

The Death of John the Baptist

(Matthew 14.1-12; Luke 9.7-9)

14 Jesus became so well-known that Herod the ruler[k] heard about him. Some people thought he was John the Baptist, who had come back to life with the power to work miracles. 15 Others thought he was Elijah[l] or some other prophet who had lived long ago. 16 But when Herod heard about Jesus, he said, "This must be John! I had his head cut off, and now he has come back to life."

17-18 Herod had earlier married Herodias, the wife of his brother Philip. But

[d]**5.36** *heard*: Or "ignored." [e]**5.38** *crying and making a lot of noise*: The Jewish people often hired mourners for funerals. [f]**5.41,42** *Talitha, koum*: These words are in Aramaic, a language spoken in Palestine during the time of Jesus. [g]**6.1** *hometown*: Nazareth. [h]**6.3** *carpenter*: The Greek word may also mean someone who builds or works with stone or brick. [i]**6.11** *shake the dust from your feet*: This was a way of showing rejection. [j]**6.13** *olive oil*: The Jewish people used olive oil as a way of healing people. Sometimes olive oil is a symbol for healing by means of a miracle (see James 5.14). [k]**6.14** *Herod the ruler*: Herod Antipas, the son of Herod the Great. [l]**6.15** *Elijah*: Many of the Jewish people expected the prophet Elijah to come and prepare the way for the Messiah.

6.4 Jn 4.43, 44. **6.11** Ac 13.51. **6.8-11** Lk 10.4-11. **6.13** Jas 5.14. **6.14,15** Mt 16.14; Mk 8.28; Lk 9.19. **6.17,18** Lk 3.19, 20.

John had told him, "It isn't right for you to
take your brother's wife!" So, in order to
please Herodias, Herod arrested John and
put him in prison.
19 Herodias had a grudge against John
and wanted to kill him. But she could not
do it 20 because Herod was afraid of John
and protected him. He knew that John was
a good and holy man. Even though Herod
was confused by what John said,[m] he was
glad to listen to him. And he often did.
21 Finally, Herodias got her chance
when Herod gave a great birthday celebration for himself and invited his officials, his
army officers, and the leaders of Galilee.
22 The daughter of Herodias[n] came in and
danced for Herod and his guests. She
pleased them so much that Herod said,
"Ask for anything, and it's yours! 23 I swear
that I will give you as much as half of my
kingdom, if you want it."
24 The girl left and asked her mother,
"What do you think I should ask for?"
Her mother answered, "The head of
John the Baptist!"
25 The girl hurried back and told Herod,
"Right now on a platter I want the head of
John the Baptist!"
26 The king was very sorry for what he
had said. But he did not want to break the
promise he had made in front of his guests.
27 At once he ordered a guard to cut off
John's head there in prison. 28 The guard
put the head on a platter and took it to the
girl. Then she gave it to her mother.
29 When John's followers learned that
he had been killed, they took his body and
put it in a tomb.

Jesus Feeds Five Thousand

(Matthew 14.13-21; Luke 9.10-17; John 6.1-14)

30 After the apostles returned to Jesus,[o]
they told him everything they had done
and taught. 31 But so many people were
coming and going that Jesus and the
apostles did not even have a chance to
eat. Then Jesus said, "Let's go to a place[p]
where we can be alone and get some rest."
32 They left in a boat for a place where they
could be alone. 33 But many people saw
them leave and figured out where they
were going. So people from every town ran
on ahead and got there first.
34 When Jesus got out of the boat, he
saw the large crowd that was like sheep
without a shepherd. He felt sorry for the people and started teaching them many things.
35 That evening the disciples came to
Jesus and said, "This place is like a desert,
and it is already late. 36 Let the crowds
leave, so they can go to the farms and villages near here and buy something to eat."
37 Jesus replied, "You give them something to eat."
But they asked him, "Don't you know
that it would take almost a year's wages[q] to
buy all of these people something to eat?"
38 Then Jesus said, "How much bread
do you have? Go and see!"
They found out and answered, "We have
five small loaves of bread[r] and two fish."
39 Jesus told his disciples to have the people
sit down on the green grass. 40 They sat down
in groups of a hundred and groups of fifty.
41 Jesus took the five loaves and the two
fish. He looked up toward heaven and
blessed the food. Then he broke the bread
and handed it to his disciples to give to the
people. He also divided the two fish, so that
everyone could have some.
42 After everyone had eaten all they
wanted, 43 Jesus' disciples picked up twelve
large baskets of leftover bread and fish.
44 There were five thousand men who
ate the food.

Jesus Walks on the Water

(Matthew 14.22-33; John 6.15-21)

45 Right away, Jesus made his disciples
get into the boat and start back across to
Bethsaida. But he stayed until he had sent

[m] **6.20** *was confused by what John said*: Some manuscripts have "did many things because of what John said." [n] **6.22** *Herodias*: Some manuscripts have "Herod." [o] **6.30** *the apostles returned to Jesus*: From the mission on which he had sent them (see 6.7, 12, 13). [p] **6.31** *a place*: This was probably northeast of Lake Galilee (see verse 45). [q] **6.37** *almost a year's wages*: The Greek text has "two hundred silver coins." Each coin was the average day's wage for a worker.
[r] **6.38** *small loaves of bread*: These would have been flat and round or in the shape of a bun.
6.34 Nu 27.17; 1 K 22.17; 2 Ch 18.16; Ez 34.5; Mt 9.36.

the crowds away. 46 Then he told them
good-by and went up on the side of a
mountain to pray.
47 Later that evening he was still there
by himself, and the boat was somewhere in
the middle of the lake. 48 He could see that
the disciples were struggling hard, because
they were rowing against the wind. Not
long before morning, Jesus came toward
them. He was walking on the water and
was about to pass the boat.
49 When the disciples saw Jesus walking
on the water, they thought he was a ghost,
and they started screaming. 50 All of them
saw him and were terrified. But at that
same time he said, "Don't worry! I am
Jesus. Don't be afraid." 51 He then got into
the boat with them, and the wind died
down. The disciples were completely confused. 52 Their minds were closed, and they
could not understand the true meaning of
the loaves of bread.

Jesus Heals Sick People in Gennesaret
(Matthew 14.34-36)

53 Jesus and his disciples crossed the
lake and brought the boat to shore near the
town of Gennesaret. 54 As soon as they got
out of the boat, the people recognized
Jesus. 55 So they ran all over that part of
the country to bring their sick people to
him on mats. They brought them each
time they heard where he was. 56 In every
village or farm or marketplace where Jesus
went, the people brought their sick to him.
They begged him to let them just touch his
clothes, and everyone who did was healed.

The Teaching of the Ancestors
(Matthew 15.1-9)

7 Some Pharisees and several teachers
of the Law of Moses from Jerusalem
came and gathered around Jesus. 2 They
noticed that some of his disciples ate without first washing their hands.[s]
3 The Pharisees and many other Jewish
people obey the teachings of their ancestors. They always wash their hands in the
proper way[t] before eating. 4 None of them
will eat anything they buy in the market
until it is washed. They also follow a lot of
other teachings, such as washing cups,
pitchers, and bowls.[u]
5 The Pharisees and teachers asked
Jesus, "Why don't your disciples obey what
our ancestors taught us to do? Why do they
eat without washing their hands?"
6 Jesus replied:

You are nothing but show-offs! The
prophet Isaiah was right when he
wrote that God had said,

"All of you praise me
with your words,
but you never really
think about me.
7 It is useless for you
to worship me,
when you teach rules
made up by humans."

8 You disobey God's commands in
order to obey what humans have
taught. 9 You are good at rejecting
God's commands so that you can
follow your own teachings! 10 Didn't
Moses command you to respect your
father and mother? Didn't he tell you
to put to death all who curse their parents? 11 But you let people get by without helping their parents when they
should. You let them say that what
they own has been offered to God.[v]
12 You won't let those people help their
parents. 13 And you ignore God's commands in order to follow your own
teaching. You do a lot of other things
that are just as bad.

What Really Makes People Unclean
(Matthew 15.10-20)

14 Jesus called the crowd together again
and said, "Pay attention and try to under-

[s]**7.2** *without first washing their hands*: The Jewish people had strict laws about washing their hands before eating, especially if they had been out in public. [t]**7.3** *in the proper way*: The Greek text has "with the fist," but the exact meaning is not clear. It could mean "to the wrist" or "to the elbow." [u]**7.4** *bowls*: Some manuscripts add "and sleeping mats." [v]**7.11** *has been offered to God*: According to Jewish custom, when anything was offered to God, it could not be used for anyone else, not even for a person's parents.

7.6,7 Is 29.13 (LXX). **7.10** **a** Ex 20.12; Dt 5.16; **b** Ex 21.17; Lv 20.9.

stand what I mean. 15-16 The food that you put into your mouth doesn't make you unclean and unfit to worship God. The bad words that come out of your mouth are what make you unclean."[w]

17 After Jesus and his disciples had left the crowd and had gone into the house, they asked him what these sayings meant. 18 He answered, "Don't you know what I am talking about by now? You surely know that the food you put into your mouth cannot make you unclean. 19 It doesn't go into your heart, but into your stomach, and then out of your body." By saying this, Jesus meant that all foods were fit to eat.

20 Then Jesus said:

> What comes from your heart is what makes you unclean. 21 Out of your heart come evil thoughts, vulgar deeds, stealing, murder, 22 unfaithfulness in marriage, greed, meanness, deceit, indecency, envy, insults, pride, and foolishness. 23 All of these come from your heart, and they are what make you unfit to worship God.

A Woman's Faith
(Matthew 15.21-28)

24 Jesus left and went to the region near the city of Tyre, where he stayed in someone's home. He did not want people to know he was there, but they found out anyway. 25 A woman whose daughter had an evil spirit in her heard where Jesus was. And right away she came and knelt down at his feet. 26 The woman was Greek and had been born in the part of Syria known as Phoenicia. She begged Jesus to force the demon out of her daughter. 27 But Jesus said, "The children must first be fed! It isn't right to take away their food and feed it to dogs."[x]

28 The woman replied, "Lord, even dogs eat the crumbs that children drop from the table."

29 Jesus answered, "That's true! You may go now. The demon has left your daughter." 30 When the woman got back home, she found her child lying on the bed. The demon had gone.

Jesus Heals a Man Who Was Deaf and Could Hardly Talk

31 Jesus left the region around Tyre and went by way of Sidon toward Lake Galilee. He went through the land near the ten cities known as Decapolis.[y] 32 Some people brought to him a man who was deaf and could hardly talk. They begged Jesus just to touch him.

33 After Jesus had taken him aside from the crowd, he stuck his fingers in the man's ears. Then he spit and put it on the man's tongue. 34 Jesus looked up toward heaven, and with a groan he said, "Effatha!"[z] which means "Open up!" 35 At once the man could hear, and he had no more trouble talking clearly.

36 Jesus told the people not to say anything about what he had done. But the more he told them, the more they talked about it. 37 They were completely amazed and said, "Everything he does is good! He even heals people who cannot hear or talk."

Jesus Feeds Four Thousand
(Matthew 15.32-39)

8 One day another large crowd gathered around Jesus. They had not brought along anything to eat. So Jesus called his disciples together and said, 2 "I feel sorry for these people. They have been with me for three days, and they don't have anything to eat. 3 Some of them live a long way from here. If I send them away hungry, they might faint on their way home."

4 The disciples said, "This place is like a desert. Where can we find enough food to feed such a crowd?"

5 Jesus asked them how much food they had. They replied, "Seven small loaves of bread."[a]

6 After Jesus told the crowd to sit down, he took the seven loaves and blessed them. He then broke the loaves and handed them

[w]**7.15,16** *unclean*: Some manuscripts add, "If you have ears, pay attention." [x]**7.27** *feed it to dogs*: The Jewish people often referred to Gentiles as dogs. [y]**7.31** *the ten cities known as Decapolis*: See the note at 5.20. [z]**7.34** *Effatha*: This word is in Aramaic, a language spoken in Palestine during the time of Jesus. [a]**8.5** *small loaves of bread*: See the note at 6.38.

to his disciples, who passed them out to the
crowd. 7 They also had a few little fish, and
after Jesus had blessed these, he told the
disciples to pass them around.
8-9 The crowd of about four thousand
people ate all they wanted, and the leftovers filled seven large baskets.
As soon as Jesus had sent the people
away, 10 he got into the boat with the disciples and crossed to the territory near Dalmanutha.[b]

A Sign from Heaven
(Matthew 16.1-4)

11 The Pharisees came out and started
an argument with Jesus. They wanted to
test him by asking for a sign from heaven.
12 Jesus groaned and said, "Why are you always looking for a sign? I can promise you
that you will not be given one!" 13 Then he
left them. He again got into a boat and
crossed over to the other side of the lake.

The Yeast of the Pharisees and of Herod
(Matthew 16.5-12)

14 The disciples had forgotten to bring
any bread, and they had only one loaf with
them in the boat. 15 Jesus warned them,
"Watch out! Guard against the yeast of the
Pharisees and of Herod."[c]
16 The disciples talked this over and said
to each other, "He must be saying this because we don't have any bread."
17 Jesus knew what they were thinking
and asked, "Why are you talking about not
having any bread? Don't you understand?
Are your minds still closed? 18 Are your
eyes blind and your ears deaf? Don't you
remember 19 how many baskets of leftovers
you picked up when I fed those five thousand
people with only five small loaves of bread?"
"Yes," the disciples answered. "There
were twelve baskets."
20 Jesus then asked, "And how many
baskets of leftovers did you pick up when I
broke seven small loaves of bread for those
four thousand people?"
"Seven," they answered.
21 "Don't you know what I am talking
about by now?" Jesus asked.

Jesus Heals a Blind Man at Bethsaida

22 As Jesus and his disciples were going
into Bethsaida, some people brought a
blind man to him and begged him to touch
the man. 23 Jesus took him by the hand
and led him out of the village, where he
spit into the man's eyes. He placed his
hands on the blind man and asked him if
he could see anything. 24 The man looked
up and said, "I see people, but they look
like trees walking around."
25 Once again Jesus placed his hands on
the man's eyes, and this time the man
stared. His eyes were healed, and he saw
everything clearly. 26 Jesus said to him,
"You may return home now, but don't go
into the village."

Who Is Jesus?
(Matthew 16.13-20; Luke 9.18-21)

27 Jesus and his disciples went to the
villages near the town of Caesarea Philippi.
As they were walking along, he asked them,
"What do people say about me?"
28 The disciples answered, "Some say
you are John the Baptist or maybe Elijah.[d]
Others say you are one of the prophets."
29 Then Jesus asked them, "But who do
you say I am?"
"You are the Messiah!" Peter replied.
30 Jesus warned the disciples not to tell
anyone about him.

Jesus Speaks about His Suffering and Death
(Matthew 16.21-28; Luke 9.22-27)

31 Jesus began telling his disciples what
would happen to him. He said, "The nation's leaders, the chief priests, and the
teachers of the Law of Moses will make the
Son of Man suffer terribly. He will be rejected and killed, but three days later he
will rise to life." 32 Then Jesus explained
clearly what he meant.

[b] **8.10** *Dalmanutha*: The place is unknown. [c] **8.15** *Herod*: Herod Antipas, the son of Herod the Great. [d] **8.28** *Elijah*: See the note at 6.15.

8.11 Mt 12.38; Lk 11.16. **8.12** Mt 12.39; Lk 11.29. **8.15** Lk 12.1. **8.18** Jr 5.21; Ez 12.2; Mk 4.12. **8.28** Mk 6.14, 15; Lk 9.7, 8. **8.29** Jn 6.68, 69.

Peter took Jesus aside and told him to stop talking like that. 33 But when Jesus turned and saw the disciples, he corrected Peter. He said to him, “Satan, get away from me! You are thinking like everyone else and not like God.”

34 Jesus then told the crowd and the disciples to come closer, and he said:

> If any of you want to be my followers, you must forget about yourself. You must take up your cross and follow me. 35 If you want to save your life,[e] you will destroy it. But if you give up your life for me and for the good news, you will save it. 36 What will you gain, if you own the whole world but destroy yourself? 37 What could you give to get back your soul?
>
> 38 Don’t be ashamed of me and my message among these unfaithful and sinful people! If you are, the Son of Man will be ashamed of you when he comes in the glory of his Father with the holy angels.
>
> 9 I can assure you that some of the people standing here will not die before they see God’s kingdom come with power.

The True Glory of Jesus
(Matthew 17.1-13; Luke 9.28-36)

2 Six days later Jesus took Peter, James, and John with him. They went up on a high mountain, where they could be alone. There in front of the disciples, Jesus was completely changed. 3 And his clothes became much whiter than any bleach on earth could make them. 4 Then Moses and Elijah were there talking with Jesus.

5 Peter said to Jesus, “Teacher, it is good for us to be here! Let us make three shelters, one for you, one for Moses, and one for Elijah.” 6 But Peter and the others were terribly frightened, and he did not know what he was talking about.

7 The shadow of a cloud passed over and covered them. From the cloud a voice said, “This is my Son, and I love him. Listen to what he says!” 8 At once the disciples looked around, but they saw only Jesus.

9 As Jesus and his disciples were coming down the mountain, he told them not to say a word about what they had seen, until the Son of Man had been raised from death. 10 So they kept it to themselves. But they wondered what he meant by the words “raised from death.”

11 The disciples asked Jesus, “Don’t the teachers of the Law of Moses say that Elijah must come before the Messiah does?”

12 Jesus answered:

> Elijah certainly will come[f] to get everything ready. But don’t the Scriptures also say that the Son of Man must suffer terribly and be rejected? 13 I can assure you that Elijah has already come. And people treated him just as they wanted to, as the Scriptures say they would.

Jesus Heals a Boy
(Matthew 17.14-20; Luke 9.37-43a)

14 When Jesus and his three disciples came back down, they saw a large crowd around the other disciples. The teachers of the Law of Moses were arguing with them.

15 The crowd was really surprised to see Jesus, and everyone hurried over to greet him.

16 Jesus asked, “What are you arguing about?”

17 Someone from the crowd answered, “Teacher, I brought my son to you. A demon keeps him from talking. 18 Whenever the demon attacks my son, it throws him to the ground and makes him foam at the mouth and grit his teeth in pain. Then he becomes stiff. I asked your disciples to force out the demon, but they couldn’t do it.”

19 Jesus said, “You people don’t have any faith! How much longer must I be with you? Why do I have to put up with you? Bring the boy to me.”

20 They brought the boy, and as soon as the demon saw Jesus, it made the boy shake all over. He fell down and began rolling on the ground and foaming at the mouth.

[e] **8.35** *life*: In verses 35-37 the same Greek word is translated “life,” “yourself,” and “soul.”
[f] **9.12** *Elijah certainly will come*: See the note at 6.15.

8.34 Mt 10.38; Lk 14.27. **8.35** Mt 10.39; Lk 17.33; Jn 12.25. **9.2-7** 2 P 1.17, 18.
9.7 Mt 3.17; Mk 1.11; Lk 3.22. **9.11** Ml 4.5; Mt 11.14. **9.12** Si 48.10.

21 Jesus asked the boy's father, "How
long has he been like this?"
The man answered, "Ever since he was
a child. 22 The demon has often tried to kill
him by throwing him into a fire or into
water. Please have pity and help us if
you can!"
23 Jesus replied, "Why do you say 'if you
can'? Anything is possible for someone who
has faith!"
24 Right away the boy's father shouted,
"I do have faith! Please help me to have
even more."
25 When Jesus saw that a crowd was
gathering fast, he spoke sternly to the evil
spirit that had kept the boy from speaking or hearing. He said, "I order you to
come out of the boy! Don't ever bother him
again."
26 The spirit screamed and made the
boy shake all over. Then it went out of him.
The boy looked dead, and almost everyone
said he was. 27 But Jesus took hold of his
hand and helped him stand up.
28 After Jesus and the disciples had
gone back home and were alone, they
asked him, "Why couldn't we force out that
demon?"
29 Jesus answered, "Only prayer can
force out that kind of demon."

Jesus Again Speaks about His Death
(Matthew 17.22, 23; Luke 9.43b-45)

30 Jesus left with his disciples and
started through Galilee. He did not want
anyone to know about it, 31 because he was
teaching the disciples that the Son of Man
would be handed over to people who would
kill him. But three days later he would rise
to life. 32 The disciples did not understand
what Jesus meant, and they were afraid
to ask.

Who Is the Greatest?
(Matthew 18.1-5; Luke 9.46-48)

33 Jesus and his disciples went to his
home in Capernaum. After they were inside the house, Jesus asked them, "What
were you arguing about along the way?"
34 They had been arguing about which one
of them was the greatest, and so they did
not answer.
35 After Jesus sat down and told the
twelve disciples to gather around him, he
said, "If you want the place of honor, you
must become a slave and serve others!"
36 Then Jesus had a child stand near
him. He put his arm around the child and
said, 37 "When you welcome even a child
because of me, you welcome me. And
when you welcome me, you welcome the
one who sent me."

For or against Jesus
(Luke 9.49, 50)

38 John said, "Teacher, we saw a man
using your name to force demons out of
people. But he wasn't one of us, and we
told him to stop."
39 Jesus said to his disciples:

Don't stop him! No one who works
miracles in my name will soon turn
and say something bad about me.
40 Anyone who isn't against us is for
us. 41 And anyone who gives you a cup
of water in my name, just because you
belong to me, will surely be rewarded.

Temptations To Sin
(Matthew 18.6-9; Luke 17.1, 2)

42 It will be terrible for people who
cause even one of my little followers to
sin. Those people would be better off
thrown into the ocean with a heavy
stone tied around their necks. 43-44 So
if your hand causes you to sin, cut it
off! You would be better off to go into
life crippled than to have two hands
and be thrown into the fires of hell
that never go out.[g] 45-46 If your foot
causes you to sin, chop it off. You
would be better off to go into life lame
than to have two feet and be thrown
into hell.[h] 47 If your eye causes you to

[g]**9.43,44** *never go out*: Some manuscripts add, "The worms there never die, and the fire never stops burning." [h]**9.45,46** *thrown into hell*: Some manuscripts add, "The worms there never die, and the fire never stops burning."

9.34 Lk 22.24. **9.35** Mt 20.26, 27; 23.11; Mk 10.43, 44; Lk 22.26. **9.37** Mt 10.40; Lk 10.16; Jn 13.20. **9.40** Mt 12.30; Lk 11.23. **9.41** Mt 10.42. **9.43,44** Mt 5.30. **9.47** Mt 5.29.

sin, get rid of it. You would be better
off to go into God's kingdom with only
one eye than to have two eyes and be
thrown into hell. 48 The worms there
never die, and the fire never stops
burning.
49 Everyone must be salted with fire.[i]
50 Salt is good. But if it no longer
tastes like salt, how can it be made
salty again? Have salt among you and
live at peace with each other.[j]

Teaching about Divorce
(Matthew 19.1-12; Luke 16.18)

10 After Jesus left, he went to Judea
and then on to the other side of the
Jordan River. Once again large crowds
came to him, and as usual, he taught them.
2 Some Pharisees wanted to test Jesus.
So they came up to him and asked if it was
right for a man to divorce his wife. 3 Jesus
asked them, "What does the Law of Moses
say about that?"
4 They answered, "Moses allows a man
to write out divorce papers and send his
wife away."
5 Jesus replied, "Moses gave you this law
because you are so heartless. 6 But in the
beginning God made a man and a woman.
7 That's why a man leaves his father and
mother and gets married. 8 He becomes
like one person with his wife. Then they
are no longer two people, but one. 9 And no
one should separate a couple that God has
joined together."
10 When Jesus and his disciples were
back in the house, they asked him about
what he had said. 11 He told them, "A man
who divorces his wife and marries someone
else is unfaithful to his wife. 12 A woman
who divorces her husband[k] and marries
again is also unfaithful."

Jesus Blesses Little Children
(Matthew 19.13-15; Luke 18.15-17)

13 Some people brought their children
to Jesus so that he could bless them by
placing his hands on them. But his disciples told the people to stop bothering him.
14 When Jesus saw this, he became angry and said, "Let the children come to me!
Don't try to stop them. People who are like
these little children belong to the kingdom
of God.[l] 15 I promise you that you cannot
get into God's kingdom, unless you accept
it the way a child does." 16 Then Jesus took
the children in his arms and blessed them
by placing his hands on them.

A Rich Man
(Matthew 19.16-30; Luke 18.18-30)

17 As Jesus was walking down a road, a
man ran up to him. He knelt down, and
asked, "Good teacher, what can I do to
have eternal life?"
18 Jesus replied, "Why do you call me
good? Only God is good. 19 You know the
commandments. 'Do not murder. Be faithful in marriage. Do not steal. Do not tell
lies about others. Do not cheat. Respect
your father and mother.' "
20 The man answered, "Teacher, I have
obeyed all these commandments since I
was a young man."
21 Jesus looked closely at the man. He
liked him and said, "There's one thing
you still need to do. Go sell everything you
own. Give the money to the poor, and you
will have riches in heaven. Then come
with me."
22 When the man heard Jesus say this,
he went away gloomy and sad because he
was very rich.
23 Jesus looked around and said to his
disciples, "It's hard for rich people to get

[i]**9.49** *salted with fire*: Some manuscripts add "and every sacrifice will be seasoned with salt." The verse may mean that Christ's followers must suffer because of their faith. [j]**9.50** *Have salt among you and live at peace with each other*: This may mean that when Christ's followers have to suffer because of their faith, they must still try to live at peace with each other. [k]**10.12** *A woman who divorces her husband*: Roman law let a woman divorce her husband, but Jewish law did not let a woman do this. [l]**10.14** *People who are like these little children belong to the kingdom of God*: Or "The kingdom of God belongs to people who are like these little children."

9.48 Is 66.24. **9.50** Mt 5.13; Lk 14.34, 35. **10.4** Dt 24.1-4; Mt 5.31. **10.6** Gn 1.27; 5.1, 2. **10.7,8** Gn 2.24. **10.11,12** Mt 5.32; 1 Co 7.10, 11. **10.15** Mt 18.3. **10.19** **a** Ex 20.13; Dt 5.17; **b** Ex 20.14; Dt 5.18; **c** Ex 20.15; Dt 5.19; **d** Ex 20.16; Dt 5.20; **e** Ex 20.12; Dt 5.16.

into God's kingdom!" 24 The disciples were
shocked to hear this. So Jesus told them
again, "It's terribly hard[m] to get into God's
kingdom! 25 In fact, it's easier for a camel
to go through the eye of a needle than for a
rich person to get into God's kingdom."

26 Jesus' disciples were even more
amazed. They asked each other, "How can
anyone ever be saved?"

27 Jesus looked at them and said, "There
are some things that people cannot do, but
God can do anything."

28 Peter replied, "Remember, we left
everything to be your followers!"

29 Jesus told him:

> You can be sure that anyone who
> gives up home or brothers or sisters or
> mother or father or children or land
> for me and for the good news 30 will be
> rewarded. In this world they will be
> given a hundred times as many houses
> and brothers and sisters and mothers
> and children and pieces of land,
> though they will also be mistreated.
> And in the world to come, they will
> have eternal life. 31 But many who are
> now first will be last, and many who
> are now last will be first.

Jesus Again Tells about His Death
(Matthew 20.17-19; Luke 18.31-34)

32 The disciples were confused as Jesus
led them toward Jerusalem, and his other
followers were afraid. Once again, Jesus
took the twelve disciples aside and told
them what was going to happen to him. He
said:

> 33 We are now on our way to
> Jerusalem where the Son of Man will
> be handed over to the chief priests and
> the teachers of the Law of Moses.
> They will sentence him to death and
> hand him over to foreigners,[n] 34 who
> will make fun of him and spit on him.
> They will beat him and kill him. But
> three days later he will rise to life.

The Request of James and John
(Matthew 20.20-28)

35 James and John, the sons of Zebedee,
came up to Jesus and asked, "Teacher, will
you do us a favor?"

36 Jesus asked them what they wanted,
37 and they answered, "When you come
into your glory, please let one of us sit at
your right side and the other at your left."[o]

38 Jesus told them, "You don't really know
what you're asking! Are you able to drink
from the cup[p] that I must soon drink from
or be baptized as I must be baptized?"[q]

39 "Yes, we are!" James and John answered.

Then Jesus replied, "You certainly will
drink from the cup from which I must
drink. And you will be baptized just as I
must! 40 But it isn't for me to say who will
sit at my right side and at my left. That is
for God to decide."

41 When the ten other disciples heard
this, they were angry with James and John.
42 But Jesus called the disciples together
and said:

> You know that those foreigners who
> call themselves kings like to order their
> people around. And their great leaders
> have full power over the people they
> rule. 43 But don't act like them. If
> you want to be great, you must be the
> servant of all the others. 44 And if you
> want to be first, you must be everyone's
> slave. 45 The Son of Man did not come
> to be a slave master, but a slave who
> will give his life to rescue[r] many people.

Jesus Heals Blind Bartimaeus
(Matthew 20.29-34; Luke 18.35-43)

46 Jesus and his disciples went to Jericho. And as they were leaving, they were

[m] **10.24** *hard*: Some manuscripts add "for people who trust in their wealth." Others add "for the rich." [n] **10.33** *foreigners*: The Romans who ruled Judea at this time. [o] **10.37** *right side . . . left*: The most powerful people in a kingdom sat at the right and left side of the king. [p] **10.38** *drink from the cup*: In the Scriptures a "cup" is sometimes used as a symbol of suffering. To "drink from the cup" would be to suffer. [q] **10.38** *as I must be baptized*: Baptism is used with the same meaning that "cup" has in this verse. [r] **10.45** *rescue*: The Greek word often, though not always, means the payment of a price to free a slave or a prisoner.

10.31 Mt 20.16; Lk 13.30. **10.38** Lk 12.50. **10.42,43** Lk 22.25, 26.
10.43,44 Mt 23.11; Mk 9.35; Lk 22.26. **10.45** 4 Macc 6.29.

followed by a large crowd. A blind beggar by
the name of Bartimaeus son of Timaeus
was sitting beside the road. 47 When he
heard that it was Jesus from Nazareth, he
shouted, "Jesus, Son of David,[s] have pity
on me!" 48 Many people told the man to
stop, but he shouted even louder, "Son of
David, have pity on me!"

49 Jesus stopped and said, "Call him
over!"

They called out to the blind man and
said, "Don't be afraid! Come on! He is calling for you." 50 The man threw off his coat
as he jumped up and ran to Jesus.

51 Jesus asked, "What do you want me
to do for you?"

The blind man answered, "Master,[t] I
want to see!"

52 Jesus told him, "You may go. Your
eyes are healed because of your faith."

Right away the man could see, and he
went down the road with Jesus.

Jesus Enters Jerusalem

(Matthew 21.1-11; Luke 19.28-40; John 12.12-19)

11 Jesus and his disciples reached
Bethphage and Bethany near the
Mount of Olives. When they were getting
close to Jerusalem, Jesus sent two of them
on ahead. 2 He told them, "Go into the
next village. As soon as you enter it, you
will find a young donkey that has never
been ridden. Untie the donkey and bring it
here. 3 If anyone asks why you are doing
that, say, 'The Lord[u] needs it and will soon
bring it back.' "

4 The disciples left and found the donkey tied near a door that faced the street.
While they were untying it, 5 some of the
people standing there asked, "Why are you
untying the donkey?" 6 They told them
what Jesus had said, and the people let
them take it.

7 The disciples led the donkey to Jesus.
They put some of their clothes on its back,
and Jesus got on. 8 Many people spread
clothes on the road, while others went to
cut branches from the fields.[v]

9 In front of Jesus and behind him, people went along shouting,

"Hooray![w]
God bless the one who comes
in the name of the Lord!
10 God bless the coming kingdom
of our ancestor David.
Hooray for God
in heaven above!"

11 After Jesus had gone to Jerusalem, he
went into the temple and looked around at
everything. But since it was already late in
the day, he went back to Bethany with the
twelve disciples.

Jesus Puts a Curse on a Fig Tree

(Matthew 21.18, 19)

12 When Jesus and his disciples left
Bethany the next morning, he was hungry.
13 From a distance Jesus saw a fig tree covered with leaves, and he went to see if
there were any figs on the tree. But there
were not any, because it wasn't the season
for figs. 14 So Jesus said to the tree, "Never
again will anyone eat fruit from this tree!"
The disciples heard him say this.

Jesus in the Temple

(Matthew 21.12-17; Luke 19.45-48; John 2.13-22)

15 After Jesus and his disciples reached
Jerusalem, he went into the temple and began chasing out everyone who was selling
and buying. He turned over the tables of
the moneychangers and the benches of
those who were selling doves. 16 Jesus
would not let anyone carry things through
the temple. 17 Then he taught the people
and said, "The Scriptures say, 'My house
should be called a place of worship for all
nations.' But you have made it a place
where robbers hide!"

[s] **10.47** *Son of David*: The Jewish people expected the Messiah to be from the family of King David, and for this reason the Messiah was often called the "Son of David." [t] **10.51** *Master*: A Hebrew word that may also mean "Teacher." [u] **11.3** *The Lord*: Or "The master of the donkey." [v] **11.8** *spread . . . branches from the fields*: This was one way that the Jewish people welcomed a famous person. [w] **11.9** *Hooray*: This translates a word that can mean "please save us." But it is most often used as a shout of praise to God.

11.9 Ps 118.25, 26. **11.17** **a** Is 56.7; **b** Jr 7.11.

18 The chief priests and the teachers of
the Law of Moses heard what Jesus said,
and they started looking for a way to kill
him. They were afraid of him, because the
crowds were completely amazed at his
teaching.
19 That evening, Jesus and the disciples
went outside the city.

A Lesson from the Fig Tree
(Matthew 21.20-22)

20 As the disciples walked past the fig
tree the next morning, they noticed that it
was completely dried up, roots and all.
21 Peter remembered what Jesus had said
to the tree. Then Peter said, "Teacher, look!
The tree you put a curse on has dried up."
22 Jesus told his disciples:
Have faith in God! 23 If you have
faith in God and don't doubt, you can
tell this mountain to get up and jump
into the sea, and it will. 24 Everything
you ask for in prayer will be yours, if
you only have faith.
25-26 Whenever you stand up to
pray, you must forgive what others
have done to you. Then your Father in
heaven will forgive your sins.[x]

A Question about Jesus' Authority
(Matthew 21.23-27; Luke 20.1-8)

27 Jesus and his disciples returned to
Jerusalem. And as he was walking through
the temple, the chief priests, the nation's
leaders, and the teachers of the Law of
Moses came over to him. 28 They asked,
"What right do you have to do these
things? Who gave you this authority?"
29 Jesus answered, "I have just one
question to ask you. If you answer it, I will
tell you where I got the right to do these
things. 30 Who gave John the right to baptize? Was it God in heaven or merely some
human being?"
31 They thought it over and said to each
other, "We can't say that God gave John
this right. Jesus will ask us why we didn't
believe John. 32 On the other hand, these
people think that John was a prophet. So
we can't say that it was merely some human who gave John the right to baptize."
They were afraid of the crowd 33 and
told Jesus, "We don't know."
Jesus replied, "Then I won't tell you who
gave me the right to do what I do."

Renters of a Vineyard
(Matthew 21.33-46; Luke 20.9-19)

12 Jesus then told them this story:
A farmer once planted a vineyard. He built a wall around it and dug
a pit to crush the grapes in. He also
built a lookout tower. Then he rented
out his vineyard and left the country.
2 When it was harvest time, he sent
a servant to get his share of the grapes.
3 The renters grabbed the servant.
They beat him up and sent him away
without a thing.
4 The owner sent another servant,
but the renters beat him on the head
and insulted him terribly. 5 Then the
man sent another servant, and they
killed him. He kept sending servant after servant. They beat some of them
and killed others.
6 The owner had a son he loved
very much. Finally, he sent his son to
the renters because he thought they
would respect him. 7 But they said to
themselves, "Someday he will own this
vineyard. Let's kill him! That way we
can have it all for ourselves." 8 So they
grabbed the owner's son and killed
him. Then they threw his body out of
the vineyard.
9 Jesus asked, "What do you think the
owner of the vineyard will do? He will
come and kill those renters and let someone else have his vineyard. 10 You surely
know that the Scriptures say,

'The stone that the builders
tossed aside
is now the most important
stone of all.
11 This is something
the Lord has done,
and it is amazing to us.' "

[x]**11.25,26** *your sins*: Some manuscripts add, "But if you do not forgive others, God will not forgive you."
11.23 Mt 17.20; 1 Co 13.2. **11.25,26** Mt 6.14, 15. **12.1** Is 5.1, 2.
12.10,11 Ps 118.22, 23.

12 The leaders knew that Jesus was really talking about them, and they wanted to
arrest him. But because they were afraid of
the crowd, they let him alone and left.

Paying Taxes
(Matthew 22.15-22; Luke 20.20-26)

13 The Pharisees got together with
Herod's followers.[y] Then they sent some
men to trick Jesus into saying something
wrong. 14 They went to him and said,
"Teacher, we know that you are honest. You
treat everyone with the same respect, no
matter who they are. And you teach the truth
about what God wants people to do. Tell us,
should we pay taxes to the Emperor or not?"
15 Jesus knew what they were up to, and
he said, "Why are you trying to test me?
Show me a coin!"
16 They brought him a silver coin, and
he asked, "Whose picture and name are
on it?"
"The Emperor's," they answered.
17 Then Jesus told them, "Give the Emperor what belongs to him and give God
what belongs to God." The men were
amazed at Jesus.

Life in the Future World
(Matthew 22.23-33; Luke 20.27-40)

18 The Sadducees did not believe that
people would rise to life after death. So
some of them came to Jesus and said:
19 Teacher, Moses wrote that if a
married man dies and has no children,
his brother should marry the widow.
Their first son would then be thought
of as the son of the dead brother.
20 There were once seven brothers.
The first one married, but died without having any children. 21 The second
brother married his brother's widow,
and he also died without having children. The same thing happened to the
third brother, 22 and finally to all seven
brothers. At last the woman died.
23 When God raises people from death,
whose wife will this woman be? After
all, she had been married to all seven
brothers.
24 Jesus answered:
You are completely wrong! You don't
know what the Scriptures teach. And
you don't know anything about the
power of God. 25 When God raises people to life, they won't marry. They will
be like the angels in heaven. 26 You
surely know about people being raised
to life. You know that in the story
about Moses and the burning bush,
God said, "I am the God worshiped by
Abraham, Isaac, and Jacob."[z] 27 He
isn't the God of the dead, but of the
living. You Sadducees are all wrong.

The Most Important Commandment
(Matthew 22.34-40; Luke 10.25-28)

28 One of the teachers of the Law of
Moses came up while Jesus and the Sadducees were arguing. When he heard Jesus
give a good answer, he asked him, "What is
the most important commandment?"
29 Jesus answered, "The most important
one says: 'People of Israel, you have only
one Lord and God. 30 You must love him
with all your heart, soul, mind, and
strength.' 31 The second most important
commandment says: 'Love others as much
as you love yourself.' No other commandment is more important than these."
32 The man replied, "Teacher, you are
certainly right to say there is only one God.
33 It is also true that we must love God with
all our heart, mind, and strength, and that
we must love others as much as we love
ourselves. These commandments are more
important than all the sacrifices and offerings that we could possibly make."
34 When Jesus saw that the man had
given a sensible answer, he told him, "You
are not far from God's kingdom." After this,
no one dared ask Jesus any more questions.

[y] **12.13** *Herod's followers*: People who were political followers of the family of Herod the Great and his son Herod Antipas. [z] **12.26** *"I am the God worshiped by Abraham, Isaac, and Jacob"*: Jesus argues that if God is worshiped by these three, they must still be alive, because he is the God of the living.

12.18 Ac 23.8. **12.19** Dt 25.5, 6. **12.26** Ex 3.6. **12.29,30** Dt 6.4, 5. **12.31** Lv 19.18. **12.32** Dt 4.35, 36. **12.33** Ho 6.6. **12.28-34** Lk 10.25-28.

About David's Son
(Matthew 22.41-46; Luke 20.41-44)

35 As Jesus was teaching in the temple, he said, "How can the teachers of the Law of Moses say that the Messiah will come from the family of King David? 36 The Holy Spirit led David to say,

'The Lord said to my Lord:
Sit at my right side[a]
until I make your enemies
into a footstool for you.'

37 If David called the Messiah his Lord, how can the Messiah be his son?"[b]

The large crowd enjoyed listening to Jesus teach.

Jesus Condemns the Pharisees and the Teachers of the Law of Moses
(Matthew 23.1-36; Luke 20.45-47)

38 As Jesus was teaching, he said:

Guard against the teachers of the Law of Moses! They love to walk around in long robes and be greeted in the market. 39 They like the front seats in the meeting places and the best seats at banquets. 40 But they cheat widows out of their homes and pray long prayers just to show off. They will be punished most of all.

A Widow's Offering
(Luke 21.1-4)

41 Jesus was sitting in the temple near the offering box and watching people put in their gifts. He noticed that many rich people were giving a lot of money. 42 Finally, a poor widow came up and put in two coins that were worth only a few pennies. 43 Jesus told his disciples to gather around him. Then he said:

I tell you that this poor widow has put in more than all the others. 44 Everyone else gave what they didn't need. But she is very poor and gave everything she had. Now she doesn't have a cent to live on.

The Temple Will Be Destroyed
(Matthew 24.1, 2; Luke 21.5, 6)

13 As Jesus was leaving the temple, one of his disciples said to him, "Teacher, look at these beautiful stones and wonderful buildings!"

2 Jesus replied, "Do you see these huge buildings? They will certainly be torn down! Not one stone will be left in place."

Warning about Trouble
(Matthew 24.3-14; Luke 21.7-19)

3 Later, as Jesus was sitting on the Mount of Olives across from the temple, Peter, James, John, and Andrew came to him in private. 4 They asked, "When will these things happen? What will be the sign that they are about to take place?"

5 Jesus answered:

Watch out and don't let anyone fool you! 6 Many will come and claim to be me. They will use my name and fool many people.

7 When you hear about wars and threats of wars, don't be afraid. These things will have to happen first, but that isn't the end. 8 Nations and kingdoms will go to war against each other. There will be earthquakes in many places, and people will starve to death. But this is just the beginning of troubles.

9 Be on your guard! You will be taken to courts and beaten with whips in their meeting places. And because of me, you will have to stand before rulers and kings to tell about your faith. 10 But before the end comes, the good news must be preached to all nations.

11 When you are arrested, don't worry about what you will say. You will be given the right words when the time comes. But you will not really be the ones speaking. Your words will come from the Holy Spirit.

12 Brothers and sisters will betray each other and have each other put to

[a] **12.36** *right side*: The place of power and honor. [b] **12.37** *David . . . his son*: See the note at 10.47.

12.36 Ps 110.1. **13.4** 2 Esd 4.51—5.19. **13.9-11** Mt 10.17-20; Lk 12.11, 12.

death. Parents will betray their own children, and children will turn against their parents and have them killed. 13 Everyone will hate you because of me. But if you keep on being faithful right to the end, you will be saved.

The Horrible Thing
(Matthew 24.15-21; Luke 21.20-24)

14 Someday you will see that "Horrible Thing" where it should not be.[c] Everyone who reads this must try to understand! If you are living in Judea at that time, run to the mountains. 15 If you are on the roof[d] of your house, don't go inside to get anything. 16 If you are out in the field, don't go back for your coat. 17 It will be an awful time for women who are expecting babies or nursing young children. 18 Pray that it won't happen in winter.[e] 19 This will be the worst time of suffering since God created the world, and nothing this terrible will ever happen again. 20 If the Lord doesn't make the time shorter, no one will be left alive. But because of his chosen and special ones, he will make the time shorter.

21 If someone should say, "Here is the Messiah!" or "There he is!" don't believe it. 22 False messiahs and false prophets will come and work miracles and signs. They will even try to fool God's chosen ones. 23 But be on your guard! That's why I am telling you these things now.

When the Son of Man Appears
(Matthew 24.29-31; Luke 21.25-28)

24 In those days, right after that time of suffering,

"The sun will become dark,
and the moon
will no longer shine.
25 The stars will fall,
and the powers in the sky[f]
will be shaken."

26 Then the Son of Man will be seen coming in the clouds with great power and glory. 27 He will send his angels to gather his chosen ones from all over the earth.

A Lesson from a Fig Tree
(Matthew 24.32-35; Luke 21.29-33)

28 Learn a lesson from a fig tree. When its branches sprout and start putting out leaves, you know summer is near. 29 So when you see all these things happening, you will know that the time has almost come.[g] 30 You can be sure that some of the people of this generation will still be alive when all this happens. 31 The sky and the earth will not last forever, but my words will.

No One Knows the Day or Time
(Matthew 24.36-44)

32 No one knows the day or the time. The angels in heaven don't know, and the Son himself doesn't know. Only the Father knows. 33 So watch out and be ready! You don't know when the time will come. 34 It is like what happens when a man goes away for a while and places his servants in charge of everything. He tells each of them what to do, and he orders the guard to keep alert. 35 So be alert! You don't know when the master of the house will come back. It could be in the evening or at midnight or before dawn or in the morning. 36 But if he comes suddenly, don't let him find you asleep. 37 I tell everyone just what I have told you. Be alert!

[c] **13.14** *where it should not be*: Probably the holy place in the temple. [d] **13.15** *roof*: See the note at 2.4. [e] **13.18** *in winter*: In Palestine the winters are cold and rainy and make travel difficult. [f] **13.25** *the powers in the sky*: In ancient times people thought that the stars were spiritual powers. [g] **13.29** *the time has almost come*: Or "he (that is, the Son of Man) will soon be here."

13.13 Mt 10.22. **13.14** Dn 9.27; 11.31; 12.11; 1 Macc 1.54; 6.7. **13.15,16** Lk 17.31. **13.19** Dn 12.1; Rev 7.14. **13.24** **a** Is 13.10; Jl 2.10, 31; 3.15; Rev 6.12; **b** Is 13.10; Ez 32.7. **13.25** **a** Is 34.4; Rev 6.13; **b** Jl 2.10. **13.26** Dn 7.13; Rev 1.7. **13.32** Mt 24.36. **13.34** Lk 12.36-38.

A Plot To Kill Jesus

(Matthew 26.1-5; Luke 22.1, 2; John 11.45-53)

14 It was now two days before Passover and the Festival of Thin Bread. The chief priests and the teachers of the Law of Moses were planning how they could sneak around and have Jesus arrested and put to death. 2 They were saying, "We must not do it during the festival, because the people will riot."

At Bethany

(Matthew 26.6-13; John 12.1-8)

3 Jesus was eating in Bethany at the home of Simon, who once had leprosy,[h] when a woman came in with a very expensive bottle of sweet-smelling perfume.[i] After breaking it open, she poured the perfume on Jesus' head. 4 This made some of the guests angry, and they complained, "Why such a waste? 5 We could have sold this perfume for more than three hundred silver coins and given the money to the poor!" So they started saying cruel things to the woman.

6 But Jesus said:

Leave her alone! Why are you bothering her? She has done a beautiful thing for me. 7 You will always have the poor with you. And whenever you want to, you can give to them. But you won't always have me here with you. 8 She has done all she could by pouring perfume on my body to prepare it for burial. 9 You may be sure that wherever the good news is told all over the world, people will remember what she has done. And they will tell others.

Judas and the Chief Priests

(Matthew 26.14-16; Luke 22.3-6)

10 Judas Iscariot[j] was one of the twelve disciples. He went to the chief priests and offered to help them arrest Jesus. 11 They were glad to hear this, and they promised to pay him. So Judas started looking for a good chance to betray Jesus.

Jesus Eats with His Disciples

(Matthew 26.17-25; Luke 22.7-14, 21-23; John 13.21-30)

12 It was the first day of the Festival of Thin Bread, and the Passover lambs were being killed. Jesus' disciples asked him, "Where do you want us to prepare the Passover meal?"

13 Jesus said to two of the disciples, "Go into the city, where you will meet a man carrying a jar of water.[k] Follow him, 14 and when he goes into a house, say to the owner, 'Our teacher wants to know if you have a room where he can eat the Passover meal with his disciples.' 15 The owner will take you upstairs and show you a large room furnished and ready for you to use. Prepare the meal there."

16 The two disciples went into the city and found everything just as Jesus had told them. So they prepared the Passover meal.

17-18 While Jesus and the twelve disciples were eating together that evening, he said, "The one who will betray me is now eating with me."

19 This made the disciples sad, and one after another they said to Jesus, "You surely don't mean me!"

20 He answered, "It is one of you twelve men who is eating from this dish with me. 21 The Son of Man will die, just as the Scriptures say. But it is going to be terrible for the one who betrays me. That man would be better off if he had never been born."

The Lord's Supper

(Matthew 26.26-30; Luke 22.14-23; 1 Corinthians 11.23-25)

22 During the meal Jesus took some bread in his hands. He blessed the bread and broke it. Then he gave it to his disciples and said, "Take this. It is my body."

23 Jesus picked up a cup of wine and gave thanks to God. He gave it to his disciples, and they all drank some. 24 Then he said, "This is my blood, which is poured

[h] **14.3** *leprosy*: In biblical times the word "leprosy" was used for many different skin diseases.
[i] **14.3** *sweet-smelling perfume*: The Greek text has "perfume made of pure spikenard," a plant used to make perfume. [j] **14.10** *Iscariot*: See the note at 3.19. [k] **14.13** *a man carrying a jar of water*: A male slave carrying water could mean that the family was rich.

14.1 Ex 12.1-27. **14.3** Lk 7.37, 38. **14.7** Dt 15.11. **14.17,18** Ps 41.9.
14.24 **a** Ex 24.8; **b** Jr 31.31-34.

out for many people, and with it God
makes his agreement. 25 From now on I will
not drink any wine, until I drink new wine
in God's kingdom." 26 Then they sang
a hymn and went out to the Mount of
Olives.

Peter's Promise

(Matthew 26.31-35; Luke 22.31-34; John 13.36-38)

27 Jesus said to his disciples, "All of you
will reject me, as the Scriptures say,

'I will strike down
the shepherd,
and the sheep
will be scattered.'

28 But after I am raised to life, I will go
ahead of you to Galilee."
29 Peter spoke up, "Even if all the others
reject you, I never will!"
30 Jesus replied, "This very night before
a rooster crows twice, you will say three
times that you don't know me."
31 But Peter was so sure of himself that
he said, "Even if I have to die with you, I
will never say that I don't know you!"
All the others said the same thing.

Jesus Prays

(Matthew 26.36-46; Luke 22.39-46)

32 Jesus went with his disciples to a
place called Gethsemane, and he told
them, "Sit here while I pray."
33 Jesus took along Peter, James, and
John. He was sad and troubled and 34 told
them, "I am so sad that I feel as if I am dying. Stay here and keep awake with me."
35-36 Jesus walked on a little way. Then
he knelt down on the ground and prayed,
"Father,[l] if it is possible, don't let this happen to me! Father, you can do anything.
Don't make me suffer by having me drink
from this cup.[m] But do what you want, and
not what I want."
37 When Jesus came back and found the
disciples sleeping, he said to Simon Peter,
"Are you asleep? Can't you stay awake for
just one hour? 38 Stay awake and pray that
you won't be tested. You want to do what is
right, but you are weak."
39 Jesus went back and prayed the same
prayer. 40 But when he returned to the disciples, he found them sleeping again. They
simply could not keep their eyes open, and
they did not know what to say.
41 When Jesus returned to the disciples
the third time, he said, "Are you still sleeping and resting?[n] Enough of that! The
time has come for the Son of Man to be
handed over to sinners. 42 Get up! Let's go.
The one who will betray me is already
here."

Jesus Is Arrested

(Matthew 26.47-56; Luke 22.47-53; John 18.3-12)

43 Jesus was still speaking, when Judas
the betrayer came up. He was one of the
twelve disciples, and a mob of men armed
with swords and clubs were with him. They
had been sent by the chief priests, the nation's leaders, and the teachers of the Law
of Moses. 44 Judas had told them ahead of
time, "Arrest the man I greet with a kiss.[o]
Tie him up tight and lead him away."
45 Judas walked right up to Jesus and
said, "Teacher!" Then Judas kissed him,
46 and the men grabbed Jesus and arrested him.
47 Someone standing there pulled out a
sword. He struck the servant of the high
priest and cut off his ear.
48 Jesus said to the mob, "Why do you
come with swords and clubs to arrest me
like a criminal? 49 Day after day I was with
you and taught in the temple, and you
didn't arrest me. But what the Scriptures
say must come true."
50 All of Jesus' disciples ran off and left
him. 51 One of them was a young man who
was wearing only a linen cloth. And when
the men grabbed him, 52 he left the cloth
behind and ran away naked.

[l] **14.35,36** *Father*: The Greek text has "Abba," which is an Aramaic word meaning "father."
[m] **14.35,36** *by having me drink from this cup*: See the note at 10.38. [n] **14.41** *Are you still sleeping and resting*: Or "You may as well keep on sleeping and resting." [o] **14.44** *greet with a kiss*: It was the custom for people to greet each other with a kiss on the cheek.
14.27 Zec 13.7. **14.28** Mt 28.16. **14.49** Lk 19.47; 21.37.

Jesus Is Questioned by the Council

(Matthew 26.57-68; Luke 22.54, 55, 63-71; John 18.13, 14, 19-24)

53 Jesus was led off to the high priest.
Then the chief priests, the nation's leaders, and the teachers of the Law of Moses
all met together. 54 Peter had followed at a
distance. And when he reached the courtyard of the high priest's house, he sat down
with the guards to warm himself beside a
fire.
55 The chief priests and the whole council tried to find someone to accuse Jesus of
a crime, so they could put him to death.
But they could not find anyone to accuse
him. 56 Many people did tell lies against
Jesus, but they did not agree on what they
said. 57 Finally, some men stood up and lied
about him. They said, 58 "We heard him say
he would tear down this temple that we
built. He also claimed that in three days he
would build another one without any help."
59 But even then they did not agree on
what they said.
60 The high priest stood up in the council and asked Jesus, "Why don't you say
something in your own defense? Don't you
hear the charges they are making against
you?" 61 But Jesus kept quiet and did not
say a word. The high priest asked him another question, "Are you the Messiah, the
Son of the glorious God?"[p]
62 "Yes, I am!" Jesus answered.

"Soon you will see
the Son of Man
sitting at the right side[q]
of God All-Powerful,
and coming with the clouds
of heaven."

63 At once the high priest ripped his
robe apart and shouted, "Why do we need
more witnesses? 64 You heard him claim to
be God! What is your decision?" They all
agreed that he should be put to death.
65 Some of the people started spitting on
Jesus. They blindfolded him, hit him with
their fists, and said, "Tell us who hit you!"
Then the guards took charge of Jesus and
beat him.

Peter Says He Doesn't Know Jesus

(Matthew 26.69-75; Luke 22.56-62; John 18.15-18, 25-27)

66 While Peter was still in the courtyard,
a servant girl of the high priest came up
67 and saw Peter warming himself by the
fire. She stared at him and said, "You were
with Jesus from Nazareth!"
68 Peter replied, "That isn't true! I don't
know what you're talking about. I don't
have any idea what you mean." He went
out to the gate, and a rooster crowed.[r]
69 The servant girl saw Peter again and
said to the people standing there, "This
man is one of them!"
70 "No, I'm not!" Peter replied.
A little while later some of the people
said to Peter, "You certainly are one of
them. You're a Galilean!"
71 This time Peter began to curse and
swear, "I don't even know the man you're
talking about!"
72 Right away the rooster crowed a second time. Then Peter remembered that
Jesus had told him, "Before a rooster crows
twice, you will say three times that you
don't know me." So Peter started crying.

Pilate Questions Jesus

(Matthew 27.1, 2, 11-14; Luke 23.1-5; John 18.28-38)

15 Early the next morning the chief
priests, the nation's leaders, and
the teachers of the Law of Moses met together with the whole Jewish council. They
tied up Jesus and led him off to Pilate.
2 He asked Jesus, "Are you the king of
the Jews?"
"Those are your words," Jesus answered.
3 The chief priests brought many
charges against Jesus. 4 Then Pilate questioned him again, "Don't you have anything
to say? Don't you hear what crimes they say
you have done?" 5 But Jesus did not answer, and Pilate was amazed.

[p] **14.61** *Son of the glorious God*: "Son of God" was one of the titles used for the kings of Israel.
[q] **14.62** *right side*: See the note at 12.36. [r] **14.68** *a rooster crowed*: These words are not in some manuscripts.

14.58 Jn 2.19. **14.62** Dn 7.13. **14.64** Lv 24.15, 16.

The Death Sentence

(Matthew 27.15-26; Luke 23.13-25; John 18.39—19.16)

6 During Passover, Pilate always freed one prisoner chosen by the people. 7 And at that time there was a prisoner named Barabbas. He and some others had been arrested for murder during a riot. 8 The crowd now came and asked Pilate to set a prisoner free, just as he usually did.

9 Pilate asked them, "Do you want me to free the king of the Jews?" 10 Pilate knew that the chief priests had brought Jesus to him because they were jealous.

11 But the chief priests told the crowd to ask Pilate to free Barabbas.

12 Then Pilate asked the crowd, "What do you want me to do with this man you say is[s] the king of the Jews?"

13 They yelled, "Nail him to a cross!"

14 Pilate asked, "But what crime has he done?"

"Nail him to a cross!" they yelled even louder.

15 Pilate wanted to please the crowd. So he set Barabbas free. Then he ordered his soldiers to beat Jesus with a whip and nail him to a cross.

Soldiers Make Fun of Jesus

(Matthew 27.27-30; John 19.2, 3)

16 The soldiers led Jesus inside the courtyard of the fortress[t] and called together the rest of the troops. 17 They put a purple robe[u] on him, and on his head they placed a crown that they had made out of thorn branches. 18 They made fun of Jesus and shouted, "Hey, you king of the Jews!" 19 Then they beat him on the head with a stick. They spit on him and knelt down and pretended to worship him.

20 When the soldiers had finished making fun of Jesus, they took off the purple robe. They put his own clothes back on him and led him off to be nailed to a cross. 21 Simon from Cyrene happened to be coming in from a farm, and they forced him to carry Jesus' cross. Simon was the father of Alexander and Rufus.

Jesus Is Nailed to a Cross

(Matthew 27.31-44; Luke 23.27-43; John 19.17-27)

22 The soldiers took Jesus to Golgotha, which means "Place of a Skull."[v] 23 There they gave him some wine mixed with a drug to ease the pain, but he refused to drink it.

24 They nailed Jesus to a cross and gambled to see who would get his clothes. 25 It was about nine o'clock in the morning when they nailed him to the cross. 26 On it was a sign that told why he was nailed there. It read, "This is the King of the Jews." 27-28 The soldiers also nailed two criminals on crosses, one to the right of Jesus and the other to his left.[w]

29 People who passed by said terrible things about Jesus. They shook their heads and shouted, "Ha! So you're the one who claimed you could tear down the temple and build it again in three days. 30 Save yourself and come down from the cross!"

31 The chief priests and the teachers of the Law of Moses also made fun of Jesus. They said to each other, "He saved others, but he can't save himself. 32 If he is the Messiah, the king of Israel, let him come down from the cross! Then we will see and believe." The two criminals also said cruel things to Jesus.

The Death of Jesus

(Matthew 27.45-56; Luke 23.44-49; John 19.28-30)

33 About noon the sky turned dark and stayed that way until around three o'clock.

[s] **15.12** *this man you say is*: These words are not in some manuscripts. [t] **15.16** *fortress*: The place where the Roman governor stayed. It was probably at Herod's palace west of Jerusalem, though it may have been Fortress Antonia, north of the temple, where the Roman troops were stationed. [u] **15.17** *purple robe*: This was probably a Roman soldier's robe. [v] **15.22** *Place of a Skull*: The place was probably given this name because it was near a large rock in the shape of a human skull. [w] **15.27-28** *left*: Some manuscripts add, "So the Scriptures came true which say, 'He was accused of being a criminal.' "

15.21 Ro 16.13. **15.24** Ps 22.18. **15.27,28** Is 53.12. **15.29** **a** Ps 22.7; 109.25; **b** Mk 14.58; Jn 2.19.

34 Then about that time Jesus shouted,
"Eloi, Eloi, lema sabachthani?"[x] which
means, "My God, my God, why have you
deserted me?"
35 Some of the people standing there
heard Jesus and said, "He is calling for Elijah."[y] 36 One of them ran and grabbed a
sponge. After he had soaked it in wine, he
put it on a stick and held it up to Jesus. He
said, "Let's wait and see if Elijah will come[z]
and take him down!" 37 Jesus shouted and
then died.
38 At once the curtain in the temple[a]
tore in two from top to bottom.
39 A Roman army officer was standing in
front of Jesus. When the officer saw how
Jesus died, he said, "This man really was
the Son of God!"
40-41 Some women were looking on from
a distance. They had come with Jesus to
Jerusalem. But even before this they had
been his followers and had helped him
while he was in Galilee. Mary Magdalene
and Mary the mother of the younger James
and of Joseph were two of these women.
Salome was also one of them.

Jesus Is Buried

(Matthew 27.57-61; Luke 23.50-56; John 19.38-42)

42 It was now the evening before the
Sabbath, and the Jewish people were getting ready for that sacred day. 43 A man
named Joseph from Arimathea was brave
enough to ask Pilate for the body of Jesus.
Joseph was a highly respected member of
the Jewish council, and he was also waiting
for God's kingdom to come.
44 Pilate was surprised to hear that
Jesus was already dead, and he called in
the army officer to find out if Jesus had
been dead very long. 45 After the officer
told him, Pilate let Joseph have Jesus' body.
46 Joseph bought a linen cloth and took
the body down from the cross. He had it
wrapped in the cloth, and he put it in a
tomb that had been cut into solid rock.
Then he rolled a big stone against the entrance to the tomb.
47 Mary Magdalene and Mary the
mother of Joseph were watching and saw
where the body was placed.

Jesus Is Alive

(Matthew 28.1-8; Luke 24.1-12; John 20.1-10)

16 After the Sabbath, Mary Magdalene, Salome, and Mary the mother
of James bought some spices to put on
Jesus' body. 2 Very early on Sunday morning,
just as the sun was coming up, they went to
the tomb. 3 On their way, they were asking
one another, "Who will roll the stone away
from the entrance for us?" 4 But when they
looked, they saw that the stone had already
been rolled away. And it was a huge stone!
5 The women went into the tomb, and
on the right side they saw a young man in a
white robe sitting there. They were alarmed.
6 The man said, "Don't be alarmed! You
are looking for Jesus from Nazareth, who
was nailed to a cross. God has raised him to
life, and he isn't here. You can see the
place where they put his body. 7 Now go
and tell his disciples, and especially Peter,
that he will go ahead of you to Galilee. You
will see him there, just as he told you."
8 When the women ran from the tomb,
they were confused and shaking all over.
They were too afraid to tell anyone what
had happened.

ONE OLD ENDING TO MARK'S GOSPEL[b]

Jesus Appears to Mary Magdalene

(Matthew 28.9, 10; John 20.11-18)

9 Very early on the first day of the week,
after Jesus had risen to life, he appeared to

[x] **15.34** *Eloi . . . sabachthani*: These words are in Aramaic, a language spoken in Palestine during the time of Jesus. [y] **15.35** *Elijah*: The name "Elijah" sounds something like "Eloi," which means "my God." [z] **15.36** *see if Elijah will come*: See the note at 6.15. [a] **15.38** *curtain in the temple*: There were two curtains in the temple. One was at the entrance, and the other separated the holy place from the most holy place that the Jewish people thought of as God's home on earth. The second curtain is probably the one which is meant. [b] **16.9** *One Old Ending to Mark's Gospel*: Verses 9-20 are not in some manuscripts.

15.34 Ps 22.1. **15.36** Ps 69.21. **15.38** Ex 26.31-33. **15.40,41** Lk 8.2, 3. **16.7** Mt 26.32; Mk 14.28.

Mary Magdalene. Earlier he had forced
seven demons out of her. 10 She left and
told his friends, who were crying and
mourning. 11 Even though they heard that
Jesus was alive and that Mary had seen
him, they would not believe it.

Jesus Appears to Two Disciples

(Luke 24.13-35)

12 Later, Jesus appeared in another form
to two disciples, as they were on their way
out of the city. 13 But when these disciples
told what had happened, the others would
not believe.

What Jesus' Followers Must Do

(Matthew 28.16-20; Luke 24.36-49; John 20.19-23; Acts 1.6-8)

14 Afterwards, Jesus appeared to his
eleven disciples as they were eating. He
scolded them because they were too stubborn to believe the ones who had seen him
after he had been raised to life. 15 Then he
told them:

> Go and preach the good news to
> everyone in the world. 16 Anyone who
> believes me and is baptized will be
> saved. But anyone who refuses to be-
> lieve me will be condemned. 17 Every-
> one who believes me will be able to do
> wonderful things. By using my name
> they will force out demons, and they
> will speak new languages. 18 They will
> handle snakes and will drink poison
> and not be hurt. They will also heal
> sick people by placing their hands on
> them.

Jesus Returns to Heaven

(Luke 24.50-53; Acts 1.9-11)

19 After the Lord Jesus had said these
things to the disciples, he was taken back
up to heaven where he sat down at the
right side[c] of God. 20 Then the disciples left
and preached everywhere. The Lord was
with them, and the miracles they worked
proved that their message was true.

ANOTHER OLD ENDING TO MARK'S GOSPEL[d]

9-10 The women quickly told Peter and
his friends what had happened. Later,
Jesus sent the disciples to the east and to the
west with his sacred and everlasting message of how people can be saved forever.

[c] **16.19** *right side*: See the note at 12.36. [d] **16.9,10** *Another Old Ending to Mark's Gospel*: Some manuscripts and early translations have both this shorter ending and the longer one (verses 9-20).

16.15 Ac 1.8. **16.19** Ac 1.9-11.

LUKE

ABOUT THIS BOOK

God's love is for everyone! Jesus came into the world to be the Savior of all people! These are two of the main thoughts in this book. Several of the best known stories that Jesus used for teaching about God's love are found only in Luke's Gospel: The Good Samaritan (10.25-37), A Lost Sheep (15.1-7), and A Lost Son (15.11-32). Only Luke tells how Jesus visited in the home of a hated tax collector (19.1-10) and promised life in paradise to a dying criminal (23.39-43).

Luke mentions God's Spirit more than any of the other New Testament writers. For example, the power of the Spirit was with John the Baptist from the time he was born (1.15). And the angel promised Mary, "The Holy Spirit will come down to you . . . So your child will be called the holy Son of God" (1.35). Jesus followed the Spirit (4.1, 14, 18; 10.21) and taught that the Spirit is God's greatest gift (11.13).

Luke shows how important prayer was to Jesus. Jesus prayed often: after being baptized (3.21), before choosing the disciples (6.12), before asking his disciples who they thought he was (9.18), and before giving up his life on the cross (23.34, 46). From Luke we learn of three stories that Jesus told to teach about prayer (11.5-9; 18.1-8, 9-14).

An important part of Luke's story is the way in which he shows the concern of Jesus for the poor: the good news is preached to them (4.18; 7.22), they receive God's blessings (6.20), they are invited to the great feast (14.13, 21), the poor man Lazarus is taken to heaven by angels (16.20, 22), and Jesus commands his disciples to sell what they have and give the money to the poor (12.33).

To make sure that readers would understand that Jesus was raised physically from death, Luke reports that the risen Jesus ate a piece of fish (24.42, 43). There could be no mistake about the risen Jesus: he was not a ghost. His being raised from death was real and not someone's imagination. Luke also wrote another book—the Acts of the Apostles—to show what happened to Jesus' followers after he was raised from death and taken up to heaven. No other Gospel has a second volume that continues the story.

Luke closes this first book that he wrote by telling that Jesus returned to heaven. But right before Jesus leaves, he tells his disciples:

> *"The Scriptures say that the Messiah must suffer, then three days later he will rise from death. They also say that all people of every nation must be told in my name to turn to God, in order to be forgiven. So beginning in Jerusalem, you must tell everything that has happened."*
>
> *(24.46-48)*

A QUICK LOOK AT THIS BOOK

- Why Luke Wrote This Book (1.1-4)
- The Births of John the Baptist and Jesus (1.5—2.52)
- The Message of John the Baptist (3.1-20)
- The Baptism and Temptation of Jesus (3.21—4.13)
- Jesus' Ministry in Galilee (4.14—9.50)

- Jesus Goes from Galilee to Jerusalem (9.51—19.27)
- Jesus' Last Week: His Trial and Death (19.28—23.56)
- Jesus Is Alive (24.1-12)
- Jesus Appears. He Is Taken to Heaven (24.13-53)

---

1 Many people have tried to tell the
story of what God has done among us.
2 They wrote what we had been told by the
ones who were there in the beginning and
saw what happened. 3 So I made a careful
study[a] of everything and then decided to
write and tell you exactly what took place.
Honorable Theophilus, 4 I have done this
to let you know the truth about what you
have heard.

An Angel Tells about the Birth of John

5 When Herod was king of Judea, there
was a priest by the name of Zechariah from
the priestly group of Abijah. His wife Elizabeth was from the family of Aaron.[b] 6 Both
of them were good people and pleased the
Lord God by obeying all that he had commanded. 7 But they did not have children.
Elizabeth could not have any, and both
Zechariah and Elizabeth were already old.
8 One day Zechariah's group of priests
were on duty, and he was serving God as a
priest. 9 According to the custom of the
priests, he had been chosen to go into the
Lord's temple that day and to burn incense,[c] 10 while the people stood outside
praying.

11 All at once an angel from the Lord appeared to Zechariah at the right side of the
altar. 12 Zechariah was confused and afraid
when he saw the angel. 13 But the angel
told him:

> Don't be afraid, Zechariah! God has
> heard your prayers. Your wife Eliza-
> beth will have a son, and you must
> name him John. 14 His birth will make
> you very happy, and many people will
> be glad. 15 Your son will be a great serv-
> ant of the Lord. He must never drink
> wine or beer, and the power of the
> Holy Spirit will be with him from the
> time he is born.
>
> 16 John will lead many people in Is-
> rael to turn back to the Lord their God.
> 17 He will go ahead of the Lord with
> the same power and spirit that Elijah[d]
> had. And because of John, parents will be
> more thoughtful of their children. And
> people who now disobey God will begin
> to think as they ought to. That is how
> John will get people ready for the Lord.

18 Zechariah said to the angel, "How
will I know this is going to happen? My wife
and I are both very old."
19 The angel answered, "I am Gabriel,
God's servant, and I was sent to tell you
this good news. 20 You have not believed
what I have said. So you will not be able to
say a thing until all this happens. But everything will take place when it is supposed to."
21 The crowd was waiting for Zechariah
and kept wondering why he was staying so
long in the temple. 22 When he did come
out, he could not speak, and they knew he
had seen a vision. He motioned to them
with his hands, but did not say a thing.
23 When Zechariah's time of service in
the temple was over, he went home.
24 Soon after that, his wife was expecting a
baby, and for five months she did not leave
the house. She said to herself, 25 "What the
Lord has done for me will keep people from
looking down on me."[e]

An Angel Tells about the Birth of Jesus

26 One month later God sent the angel
Gabriel to the town of Nazareth in Galilee
27 with a message for a virgin named Mary.

---

[a] **1.3** *a careful study*: Or "a study from the beginning." [b] **1.5** *Aaron*: The brother of Moses and the first priest. [c] **1.9** *burn incense*: This was done twice a day, once in the morning and again in the late afternoon. [d] **1.17** *Elijah*: The prophet Elijah was known for his power to work miracles. [e] **1.25** *keep people from looking down on me*: When a married woman could not have children, it was thought that the Lord was punishing her.

1.5 1 Ch 24.7-18. **1.15** Nu 6.3. **1.17** Ml 4.5, 6; Si 48.10, 11. **1.19** Dn 8.16; 9.21; Tb 12.15. **1.27** Mt 1.18.

She was engaged to Joseph from the family
of King David. 28 The angel greeted Mary
and said, "You are truly blessed! The Lord
is with you."
29 Mary was confused by the angel's
words and wondered what they meant.
30 Then the angel told Mary, "Don't be
afraid! God is pleased with you, 31 and you
will have a son. His name will be Jesus.
32 He will be great and will be called the
Son of God Most High. The Lord God will
make him king, as his ancestor David was.
33 He will rule the people of Israel forever,
and his kingdom will never end."
34 Mary asked the angel, "How can this
happen? I am not married!"
35 The angel answered, "The Holy Spirit
will come down to you, and God's power
will come over you. So your child will be
called the holy Son of God. 36 Your relative
Elizabeth is also going to have a son, even
though she is old. No one thought she
could ever have a baby, but in three months
she will have a son. 37 Nothing is impossible for God!"
38 Mary said, "I am the Lord's servant!
Let it happen as you have said." And the
angel left her.

Mary Visits Elizabeth

39 A short time later Mary hurried to a
town in the hill country of Judea. 40 She
went into Zechariah's home, where
she greeted Elizabeth. 41 When Elizabeth
heard Mary's greeting, her baby moved
within her.
The Holy Spirit came upon Elizabeth.
42 Then in a loud voice she said to Mary:

> God has blessed you more than any
> other woman! He has also blessed the
> child you will have. 43 Why should the
> mother of my Lord come to me? 44 As
> soon as I heard your greeting, my baby
> became happy and moved within me.
> 45 The Lord has blessed you because
> you believed that he will keep his
> promise.

Mary's Song of Praise

46 Mary said:

With all my heart
I praise the Lord,
47 and I am glad
because of God my Savior.
48 He cares for me,
his humble servant.
From now on,
all people will say
God has blessed me.
49 God All-Powerful has done
great things for me,
and his name is holy.
50 He always shows mercy
to everyone
who worships him.
51 The Lord has used
his powerful arm
to scatter those
who are proud.
52 He drags strong rulers
from their thrones
and puts humble people
in places of power.
53 God gives the hungry
good things to eat,
and sends the rich away
with nothing.
54 He helps his servant Israel
and is always merciful
to his people.
55 The Lord made this promise
to our ancestors,
to Abraham and his family
forever!

56 Mary stayed with Elizabeth about
three months. Then she went back home.

The Birth of John the Baptist

57 When Elizabeth's son was born,
58 her neighbors and relatives heard how
kind the Lord had been to her, and they too
were glad.
59 Eight days later they did for the child
what the Law of Moses commands.[f] They

[f]**1.59** *what the Law of Moses commands*: This refers to circumcision. It is the cutting off of skin from the private part of Jewish boys eight days after birth to show that they belong to the Lord.

1.31 Mt 1.21. **1.32,33** 2 S 7.12, 13, 16; Is 9.7. **1.37** Gn 18.14. **1.42** Jdt 13.18.
1.52 Job 5.11; 12.19; Si 10.14. **1.55** Gn 17.7. **1.46-55** 1 S 2.1-10. **1.59** Lv 12.3.

were going to name him Zechariah, after
his father. 60 But Elizabeth said, "No! His
name is John."
61 The people argued, "No one in your
family has ever been named John." 62 So
they motioned to Zechariah to find out
what he wanted to name his son.
63 Zechariah asked for a writing tablet.
Then he wrote, "His name is John." Everyone was amazed. 64 Right away, Zechariah
started speaking and praising God.
65 All the neighbors were frightened because of what had happened, and everywhere in the hill country people kept talking about these things. 66 Everyone who
heard about this wondered what this child
would grow up to be. They knew that the
Lord was with him.

Zechariah Praises the Lord

67 The Holy Spirit came upon Zechariah, and he began to speak:

68 Praise the Lord,
the God of Israel!
He has come
to save his people.
69 Our God has given us
a mighty Savior[g]
from the family
of David his servant.
70 Long ago the Lord promised
by the words
of his holy prophets
71 to save us from our enemies
and from everyone
who hates us.
72 God said he would be kind
to our people and keep
his sacred promise.
73 He told our ancestor Abraham
74 that he would rescue us
from our enemies.
Then we could serve him
without fear,
75 by being holy and good
as long as we live.

76 You, my son, will be called
a prophet of God
in heaven above.
You will go ahead of the Lord
to get everything ready
for him.
77 You will tell his people
that they can be saved
when their sins
are forgiven.
78 God's love and kindness
will shine upon us
like the sun that rises
in the sky.[h]
79 On us who live
in the dark shadow
of death
this light will shine
to guide us
into a life of peace.

80 As John grew up, God's Spirit gave him
great power. John lived in the desert until
the time he was sent to the people of Israel.

The Birth of Jesus

(Matthew 1.18-25)

2 About that time Emperor Augustus
gave orders for the names of all the
people to be listed in record books.[i] 2 These
first records were made when Quirinius
was governor of Syria.[j]
3 Everyone had to go to their own hometown to be listed. 4 So Joseph had to leave
Nazareth in Galilee and go to Bethlehem in
Judea. Long ago Bethlehem had been King
David's hometown, and Joseph went there
because he was from David's family.
5 Mary was engaged to Joseph and traveled with him to Bethlehem. She was soon
going to have a baby, 6 and while they were
there, 7 she gave birth to her first-born[k]

[g] **1.69** *a mighty Savior*: The Greek text has "a horn of salvation." In the Scriptures animal horns are often a symbol of great strength. [h] **1.78** *like the sun that rises in the sky*: Or "like the Messiah coming from heaven." [i] **2.1** *names . . . listed in record books*: This was done so that everyone could be made to pay taxes to the Emperor. [j] **2.2** *Quirinius was governor of Syria*: It is known that Quirinius made a record of the people in A.D. 6 or 7. But the exact date of the record taking that Luke mentions is not known. [k] **2.7** *first-born*: The Jewish people said that the first-born son in each of their families belonged to the Lord.

1.76 Ml 3.1. **1.79** Is 9.2.

son. She dressed him in baby clothes[l] and
laid him on a bed of hay, because there was
no room for them in the inn.

The Shepherds

8 That night in the fields near Bethlehem some shepherds were guarding their
sheep. 9 All at once an angel came down to
them from the Lord, and the brightness of
the Lord's glory flashed around them. The
shepherds were frightened. 10 But the angel
said, "Don't be afraid! I have good news for
you, which will make everyone happy.
11 This very day in King David's hometown
a Savior was born for you. He is Christ the
Lord. 12 You will know who he is, because
you will find him dressed in baby clothes
and lying on a bed of hay."
13 Suddenly many other angels came
down from heaven and joined in praising
God. They said:

14 "Praise God in heaven!
Peace on earth to everyone
who pleases God."

15 After the angels had left and gone
back to heaven, the shepherds said to each
other, "Let's go to Bethlehem and see what
the Lord has told us about." 16 They hurried off and found Mary and Joseph, and
they saw the baby lying on a bed of hay.
17 When the shepherds saw Jesus, they
told his parents what the angel had said
about him. 18 Everyone listened and was
surprised. 19 But Mary kept thinking about
all this and wondering what it meant.
20 As the shepherds returned to their
sheep, they were praising God and saying
wonderful things about him. Everything
they had seen and heard was just as the angel had said.
21 Eight days later Jesus' parents did for
him what the Law of Moses commands.[m]
And they named him Jesus, just as the angel had told Mary when he promised she
would have a baby.

Simeon Praises the Lord

22 The time came for Mary and Joseph
to do what the Law of Moses says a mother
is supposed to do after her baby is born.[n]
They took Jesus to the temple in
Jerusalem and presented him to the Lord,
23 just as the Law of the Lord says, "Each
first-born[o] baby boy belongs to the Lord."
24 The Law of the Lord also says that parents have to offer a sacrifice, giving at least
a pair of doves or two young pigeons. So
that is what Mary and Joseph did.
25 At this time a man named Simeon
was living in Jerusalem. Simeon was a good
man. He loved God and was waiting for
God to save the people of Israel. God's
Spirit came to him 26 and told him that he
would not die until he had seen Christ the
Lord.
27 When Mary and Joseph brought Jesus
to the temple to do what the Law of Moses
says should be done for a new baby, the
Spirit told Simeon to go into the temple.
28 Simeon took the baby Jesus in his arms
and praised God,

29 "Lord, I am your servant,
and now I can die in peace,
because you have kept
your promise to me.
30 With my own eyes I have seen
what you have done
to save your people,
31 and foreign nations
will also see this.
32 Your mighty power is a light
for all nations,
and it will bring honor
to your people Israel."

33 Jesus' parents were surprised at what
Simeon had said. 34 Then he blessed them

[l]**2.7** *dressed him in baby clothes*: The Greek text has "wrapped him in wide strips of cloth," which was how young babies were dressed. [m]**2.21** *what the Law of Moses commands*: See the note at 1.59. [n]**2.22** *after her baby is born*: After a Jewish mother gave birth to a son, she was considered "unclean" and had to stay home until he was circumcised (see the note at 1.59). Then she had to stay home for another 33 days, before offering a sacrifice to the Lord. [o]**2.23** *first-born*: See the note at 2.7.

2.9 Tb 5.4. **2.21** **a** Lv 12.3; **b** Lk 1.31. **2.23** Ex 13.2, 12. **2.22-24** Lv 12.6-8. **2.32** Is 42.6; 49.6; 52.10.

and told Mary, "This child of yours will
cause many people in Israel to fall and others to stand. The child will be like a warning sign. Many people will reject him,
35 and you, Mary, will suffer as though you
had been stabbed by a dagger. But all this
will show what people are really thinking."

Anna Speaks about the Child Jesus

36 The prophet Anna was also there in
the temple. She was the daughter of Phanuel
from the tribe of Asher, and she was very
old. In her youth she had been married for
seven years, but her husband died. 37 And
now she was eighty-four years old.[p] Night
and day she served God in the temple by
praying and often going without eating.[q]
38 At that time Anna came in and
praised God. She spoke about the child
Jesus to everyone who hoped for Jerusalem
to be set free.

The Return to Nazareth

39 After Joseph and Mary had done
everything that the Law of the Lord commands, they returned home to Nazareth
in Galilee. 40 The child Jesus grew.
He became strong and wise, and God
blessed him.

The Boy Jesus in the Temple

41 Every year Jesus' parents went to
Jerusalem for Passover. 42 And when Jesus
was twelve years old, they all went there as
usual for the celebration. 43 After Passover
his parents left, but they did not know that
Jesus had stayed on in the city. 44 They
thought he was traveling with some other
people, and they went a whole day before
they started looking for him. 45 When they
could not find him with their relatives and
friends, they went back to Jerusalem and
started looking for him there.
46 Three days later they found Jesus sitting in the temple, listening to the teachers
and asking them questions. 47 Everyone
who heard him was surprised at how much
he knew and at the answers he gave.
48 When his parents found him, they
were amazed. His mother said, "Son, why
have you done this to us? Your father and I
have been very worried, and we have been
searching for you!"
49 Jesus answered, "Why did you have
to look for me? Didn't you know that I
would be in my Father's house?"[r] 50 But
they did not understand what he meant.
51 Jesus went back to Nazareth with his
parents and obeyed them. His mother kept
on thinking about all that had happened.
52 Jesus became wise, and he grew
strong. God was pleased with him and so
were the people.

The Preaching of John the Baptist

(Matthew 3.1-12; Mark 1.1-8; John 1.19-28)

3 For fifteen years[s] Emperor Tiberius
had ruled that part of the world. Pontius Pilate was governor of Judea, and
Herod[t] was the ruler of Galilee. Herod's
brother, Philip, was the ruler in the countries of Iturea and Trachonitis, and Lysa-
nias was the ruler of Abilene. 2 Annas and
Caiaphas were the Jewish high priests.[u]
At that time God spoke to Zechariah's
son John, who was living in the desert. 3 So
John went along the Jordan Valley, telling
the people, "Turn back to God and be baptized! Then your sins will be forgiven."
4 Isaiah the prophet wrote about John
when he said,

"In the desert
    someone is shouting,
'Get the road ready
    for the Lord!

[p]**2.37** *And now she was eighty-four years old*: Or "And now she had been a widow for eighty-four years." [q]**2.37** *without eating*: The Jewish people sometimes went without eating (also called "fasting") to show their love for God or to show sorrow for their sins. [r]**2.49** *in my Father's house*: Or "doing my Father's work." [s]**3.1** *For fifteen years*: This was either A.D. 28 or 29, and Jesus was about thirty years old (see 3.23). [t]**3.1** *Herod*: Herod Antipas, the son of Herod the Great. [u]**3.2** *Annas and Caiaphas . . . high priests*: Annas was high priest from A.D. 6 until 15. His son-in-law Caiaphas was high priest from A.D. 18 until 37.

2.36,37 Jdt 8.4, 5. **2.39** Mt 2.23. **2.41** Ex 12.1-27; Dt 16.1-8. **2.52** 1 S 2.26; Pr 3.4. **3.4-6** Is 40.3-5 (LXX).

Make a straight path
for him.
5 Fill up every valley
and level every mountain
and hill.
Straighten the crooked paths
and smooth out
the rough roads.
6 Then everyone will see
the saving power of God.' "

7 Crowds of people came out to be baptized, but John said to them, "You bunch of
snakes! Who warned you to run from the
coming judgment? 8 Do something to show
that you really have given up your sins.
Don't start saying that you belong to Abraham's family. God can turn these stones
into children for Abraham.[v] 9 An ax is ready
to cut the trees down at their roots. Any
tree that doesn't produce good fruit will be
cut down and thrown into a fire."

10 The crowds asked John, "What
should we do?"

11 John told them, "If you have two
coats, give one to someone who doesn't
have any. If you have food, share it with
someone else."

12 When tax collectors[w] came to be baptized, they asked John, "Teacher, what
should we do?"

13 John told them, "Don't make people
pay more than they owe."

14 Some soldiers asked him, "And what
about us? What do we have to do?"

John told them, "Don't force people to
pay money to make you leave them alone.
Be satisfied with your pay."

15 Everyone became excited and wondered, "Could John be the Messiah?"

16 John said, "I am just baptizing with
water. But someone more powerful is going
to come, and I am not good enough even
to untie his sandals.[x] He will baptize you
with the Holy Spirit and with fire. 17 His
threshing fork[y] is in his hand, and he is
ready to separate the wheat from the
husks. He will store the wheat in his barn
and burn the husks with a fire that never
goes out."

18 In many different ways John
preached the good news to the people.
19 But to Herod the ruler, he said, "It was
wrong for you to take Herodias, your
brother's wife." John also said that Herod
had done many other bad things. 20 Finally,
Herod put John in jail, and this was the
worst thing he had done.

The Baptism of Jesus

(Matthew 3.13-17; Mark 1.9-11)

21 While everyone else was being baptized, Jesus himself was baptized. Then as
he prayed, the sky opened up, 22 and the
Holy Spirit came down upon him in the
form of a dove. A voice from heaven said,
"You are my own dear Son, and I am
pleased with you."

The Ancestors of Jesus

(Matthew 1.1-17)

23 When Jesus began to preach, he was
about thirty years old. Everyone thought he
was the son of Joseph. But his family went
back through Heli, 24 Matthat, Levi,
Melchi, Jannai, Joseph, 25 Mattathias,
Amos, Nahum, Esli, Naggai, 26 Maath, Mattathias, Semein, Josech, Joda;

27 Joanan, Rhesa, Zerubbabel, Shealtiel,
Neri, 28 Melchi, Addi, Cosam, Elmadam,
Er, 29 Joshua, Eliezer, Jorim, Matthat, Levi;

30 Simeon, Judah, Joseph, Jonam, Eli-
akim, 31 Melea, Menna, Mattatha, Nathan,
David, 32 Jesse, Obed, Boaz, Salmon,
Nahshon;

33 Amminadab, Admin, Arni, Hezron,
Perez, Judah, 34 Jacob, Isaac, Abraham,

[v]**3.8** *children for Abraham*: The Jewish people thought they were God's chosen people because of God's promises to their ancestor Abraham. [w]**3.12** *tax collectors*: These were usually Jewish people who paid the Romans for the right to collect taxes. They were hated by other Jews who thought of them as traitors to their country and to their religion. [x]**3.16** *untie his sandals*: This was the duty of a slave. [y]**3.17** *threshing fork*: After Jewish farmers had trampled out the grain, they used a large fork to pitch the grain and the husks into the air. Wind would blow away the light husks, and the grain would fall back to the ground, where it could be gathered up.

3.7 Mt 12.34; 23.33. **3.8** Jn 8.33. **3.9** Mt 7.19. **3.12** Lk 7.29.
3.19,20 Mt 14.3, 4; Mk 6.17, 18. **3.22** Gn 22.2; Ps 2.7; Is 42.1; Mt 3.17; Mk 1.11; Lk 9.35.

Terah, Nahor, 35 Serug, Reu, Peleg, Eber,
Shelah;
36 Cainan, Arphaxad, Shem, Noah,
Lamech, 37 Methuselah, Enoch, Jared,
Mahalaleel, Kenan, 38 Enosh, and Seth.
The family of Jesus went all the way
back to Adam and then to God.

Jesus and the Devil

(Matthew 4.1-11; Mark 1.12, 13)

4 When Jesus returned from the Jordan
River, the power of the Holy Spirit was
with him, and the Spirit led him into the
desert. 2 For forty days Jesus was tested by
the devil, and during that time he went
without eating.[z] When it was all over, he
was hungry.
3 The devil said to Jesus, "If you are
God's Son, tell this stone to turn into
bread."
4 Jesus answered, "The Scriptures say,
'No one can live only on food.' "
5 Then the devil led Jesus up to a high
place and quickly showed him all the nations on earth. 6 The devil said, "I will give
all this power and glory to you. It has been
given to me, and I can give it to anyone I
want to. 7 Just worship me, and you can
have it all."
8 Jesus answered, "The Scriptures say:

'Worship the Lord your God
and serve only him!' "

9 Finally, the devil took Jesus to Jerusalem and had him stand on top of the temple. The devil said, "If you are God's Son,
jump off. 10-11 The Scriptures say:

'God will tell his angels
to take care of you.
They will catch you
in their arms,
and you will not hurt
your feet on the stones.' "

12 Jesus answered, "The Scriptures also
say, 'Don't try to test the Lord your God!' "
13 After the devil had finished testing
Jesus in every way possible, he left him for
a while.

Jesus Begins His Work

(Matthew 4.12-17; Mark 1.14, 15)

14 Jesus returned to Galilee with the
power of the Spirit. News about him spread
everywhere. 15 He taught in the Jewish
meeting places, and everyone praised him.

The People of Nazareth Turn against Jesus

(Matthew 13.53-58; Mark 6.1-6)

16 Jesus went back to Nazareth, where
he had been brought up, and as usual he
went to the meeting place on the Sabbath.
When he stood up to read from the Scriptures, 17 he was given the book of Isaiah the
prophet. He opened it and read,

18 "The Lord's Spirit
has come to me,
because he has chosen me
to tell the good news
to the poor.
The Lord has sent me
to announce freedom
for prisoners,
to give sight to the blind,
to free everyone
who suffers,
19 and to say, 'This is the year
the Lord has chosen.' "

20 Jesus closed the book, then handed it
back to the man in charge and sat down.
Everyone in the meeting place looked
straight at Jesus.
21 Then Jesus said to them, "What you
have just heard me read has come true
today."
22 All the people started talking about
Jesus and were amazed at the wonderful
things he said. They kept on asking, "Isn't
he Joseph's son?"
23 Jesus answered:

You will certainly want to tell me this
saying, "Doctor, first make yourself well."
You will tell me to do the same things
here in my own hometown that you
heard I did in Capernaum. 24 But you
can be sure that no prophets are liked
by the people of their own hometown.

[z] **4.2** *went without eating*: See the note at 2.37.

4.4 Dt 8.3. **4.8** Dt 6.13. **4.10,11** Ps 91.11, 12. **4.12** Dt 6.16. **4.18,19** Is 61.1, 2 (LXX). **4.24** Jn 4.43, 44.

25 Once during the time of Elijah
there was no rain for three and a half
years, and people everywhere were
starving. There were many widows in
Israel, 26 but Elijah was sent only to a
widow in the town of Zarephath near
the city of Sidon. 27 During the time of
the prophet Elisha, many men in
Israel had leprosy.[a] But no one was
healed, except Naaman who lived in
Syria.
28 When the people in the meeting
place heard Jesus say this, they became so
angry 29 that they got up and threw him out
of town. They dragged him to the edge of
the cliff on which the town was built, because they wanted to throw him down from
there. 30 But Jesus slipped through the
crowd and got away.

A Man with an Evil Spirit
(Mark 1.21-28)

31 Jesus went to the town of Capernaum
in Galilee and taught the people on the
Sabbath. 32 His teaching amazed them because he spoke with power. 33 There in the
Jewish meeting place was a man with an
evil spirit. He yelled out, 34 "Hey, Jesus of
Nazareth, what do you want with us? Are
you here to get rid of us? I know who you
are! You are God's Holy One."
35 Jesus ordered the evil spirit to be
quiet and come out. The demon threw the
man to the ground in front of everyone and
left without harming him.
36 They all were amazed and kept saying
to each other, "What kind of teaching is
this? He has power to order evil spirits out
of people!" 37 News about Jesus spread all
over that part of the country.

Jesus Heals Many People
(Matthew 8.14-17; Mark 1.29-34)

38 Jesus left the meeting place and went
to Simon's home. When Jesus got there, he
was told that Simon's mother-in-law was
sick with a high fever. 39 So Jesus went over
to her and ordered the fever to go away.
Right then she was able to get up and serve
them a meal.
40 After the sun had set, people with all
kinds of diseases were brought to Jesus. He
put his hands on each one of them and
healed them. 41 Demons went out of many
people and shouted, "You are the Son of
God!" But Jesus ordered the demons not
to speak because they knew he was the
Messiah.
42 The next morning Jesus went out to a
place where he could be alone, and crowds
came looking for him. When they found
him, they tried to stop him from leaving.
43 But Jesus said, "People in other towns
must hear the good news about God's kingdom. That's why I was sent." 44 So he kept
on preaching in the Jewish meeting places
in Judea.[b]

Jesus Chooses His First Disciples
(Matthew 4.18-22; Mark 1.16-20)

5 Jesus was standing on the shore of
Lake Gennesaret,[c] teaching the people
as they crowded around him to hear God's
message. 2 Near the shore he saw two boats
left there by some fishermen who had gone
to wash their nets. 3 Jesus got into the boat
that belonged to Simon and asked him to
row it out a little way from the shore. Then
Jesus sat down[d] in the boat to teach the
crowd.
4 When Jesus had finished speaking, he
told Simon, "Row the boat out into the
deep water and let your nets down to catch
some fish."
5 "Master," Simon answered, "we have
worked hard all night long and have not
caught a thing. But if you tell me to, I will
let the nets down." 6 They did it and
caught so many fish that their nets began
ripping apart. 7 Then they signaled for their
partners in the other boat to come and
help them. The men came, and together
they filled the two boats so full that they
both began to sink.

[a] **4.27** *leprosy*: In biblical times the word "leprosy" was used for many different kinds of skin diseases. [b] **4.44** *Judea*: Some manuscripts have "Galilee." [c] **5.1** *Lake Gennesaret*: Another name for Lake Galilee. [d] **5.3** *sat down*: Teachers in the ancient world, including Jewish teachers, usually sat down when they taught.

4.25 1 K 17.1. **4.26** 1 K 17.8-16. **4.27** 2 K 5.1-14. **4.32** Mt 7.28, 29.
5.1-3 Mt 13.1, 2; Mk 3.9, 10; 4.1. **5.5** Jn 21.3. **5.6** Jn 21.6.

8 When Simon Peter saw this happen,
he knelt down in front of Jesus and said,
"Lord, don't come near me! I am a sinner."
9 Peter and everyone with him were completely surprised at all the fish they had
caught. 10 His partners James and John,
the sons of Zebedee, were surprised too.

Jesus told Simon, "Don't be afraid! From
now on you will bring in people instead of
fish." 11 The men pulled their boats up on
the shore. Then they left everything and
went with Jesus.

Jesus Heals a Man

(Matthew 8.1-4; Mark 1.40-45)

12 Jesus came to a town where there was
a man who had leprosy.[e] When the man
saw Jesus, he knelt down to the ground in
front of Jesus and begged, "Lord, you have
the power to make me well, if only you
wanted to."

13 Jesus put his hand on him and said,
"I want to! Now you are well." At once the
man's leprosy disappeared. 14 Jesus told
him, "Don't tell anyone about this, but go
and show yourself to the priest. Offer a gift
to the priest, just as Moses commanded,
and everyone will know that you have been
healed."[f]

15 News about Jesus kept spreading.
Large crowds came to listen to him teach
and to be healed of their diseases. 16 But
Jesus would often go to some place where
he could be alone and pray.

Jesus Heals a Crippled Man

(Matthew 9.1-8; Mark 2.1-12)

17 One day some Pharisees and experts
in the Law of Moses sat listening to Jesus
teach. They had come from every village in
Galilee and Judea and from Jerusalem.

God had given Jesus the power to heal
the sick, 18 and some people came carrying
a crippled man on a mat. They tried to take
him inside the house and put him in front
of Jesus. 19 But because of the crowd, they
could not get him to Jesus. So they went up
on the roof,[g] where they removed some
tiles and let the mat down in the middle of
the room.

20 When Jesus saw how much faith they
had, he said to the crippled man, "My
friend, your sins are forgiven."

21 The Pharisees and the experts began
arguing, "Jesus must think he is God! Only
God can forgive sins."

22 Jesus knew what they were thinking,
and he said, "Why are you thinking that?
23 Is it easier for me to tell this crippled
man that his sins are forgiven or to tell him
to get up and walk? 24 But now you will see
that the Son of Man has the right to forgive
sins here on earth." Jesus then said to the
man, "Get up! Pick up your mat and walk
home."

25 At once the man stood up in front of
everyone. He picked up his mat and went
home, giving thanks to God. 26 Everyone
was amazed and praised God. What they
saw surprised them, and they said, "We
have seen a great miracle today!"

Jesus Chooses Levi

(Matthew 9.9-13; Mark 2.13-17)

27 Later, Jesus went out and saw a tax
collector[h] named Levi sitting at the place
for paying taxes. Jesus said to him, "Come
with me." 28 Levi left everything and went
with Jesus.

29 In his home Levi gave a big dinner for
Jesus. Many tax collectors and other guests
were also there.

30 The Pharisees and some of their
teachers of the Law of Moses grumbled to
Jesus' disciples, "Why do you eat and drink
with those tax collectors and other sinners?"

31 Jesus answered, "Healthy people

[e]**5.12** *leprosy*: See the note at 4.27. [f]**5.14** *everyone will know that you have been healed*: People with leprosy had to be examined by a priest and told that they were well (that is, "clean") before they could once again live a normal life in the Jewish community. The gift that Moses commanded was the sacrifice of some lambs together with flour mixed with olive oil. [g]**5.19** *roof*: In Palestine the houses usually had a flat roof. Stairs on the outside led up to the roof, which was made of beams and boards covered with packed earth. Luke says that the roof was made of (clay) tiles, which were also used for making roofs in New Testament times. [h]**5.27** *tax collector*: See the note at 3.12.

5.14 Lv 14.1-32. **5.30** Lk 15.1, 2.

don't need a doctor, but sick people do. 32 I
didn't come to invite good people to turn to
God. I came to invite sinners."

People Ask about Going without Eating

(Matthew 9.14-17; Mark 2.18-22)

33 Some people said to Jesus, "John's
followers often pray and go without eating,[i]
and so do the followers of the Pharisees.
But your disciples never go without eating
or drinking."
34 Jesus told them, "The friends of a
bridegroom don't go without eating while
he is still with them. 35 But the time will
come when he will be taken from them.
Then they will go without eating."
36 Jesus then told them these sayings:
No one uses a new piece of cloth to
patch old clothes. The patch would
shrink and make the hole even bigger.
37 No one pours new wine into old
wineskins. The new wine would swell
and burst the old skins.[j] Then the
wine would be lost, and the skins
would be ruined. 38 New wine must be
put only into new wineskins.
39 No one wants new wine after
drinking old wine. They say, "The old
wine is better."

A Question about the Sabbath

(Matthew 12.1-8; Mark 2.23-28)

6 One Sabbath when Jesus and his disciples were walking through some
wheat fields,[k] the disciples picked some
wheat. They rubbed the husks off with
their hands and started eating the grain.
2 Some Pharisees said, "Why are you
picking grain on the Sabbath? You're not
supposed to do that!"
3 Jesus answered, "You surely have read
what David did when he and his followers
were hungry. 4 He went into the house of
God and took the sacred loaves of bread
that only priests were supposed to eat. He
not only ate some himself, but even gave
some to his followers."
5 Jesus finished by saying, "The Son of
Man is Lord over the Sabbath."

A Man with a Crippled Hand

(Matthew 12.9-14; Mark 3.1-6)

6 On another Sabbath[l] Jesus was teaching in a Jewish meeting place, and a man
with a crippled right hand was there.
7 Some Pharisees and teachers of the Law
of Moses kept watching Jesus to see if he
would heal the man. They did this because
they wanted to accuse Jesus of doing something wrong.
8 Jesus knew what they were thinking.
So he told the man to stand up where
everyone could see him. And the man
stood up. 9 Then Jesus asked, "On the Sabbath should we do good deeds or evil
deeds? Should we save someone's life or
destroy it?"
10 After he had looked around at everyone, he told the man, "Stretch out your
hand." He did, and his bad hand became
completely well.
11 The teachers and the Pharisees were
furious and started saying to each other,
"What can we do about Jesus?"

Jesus Chooses His Twelve Apostles

(Matthew 10.1-4; Mark 3.13-19)

12 About that time Jesus went off to a
mountain to pray, and he spent the whole
night there. 13 The next morning he called
his disciples together and chose twelve of
them to be his apostles. 14 One was Simon,
and Jesus named him Peter. Another was
Andrew, Peter's brother. There were also
James, John, Philip, Bartholomew,
15 Matthew, Thomas, and James the son of
Alphaeus. The rest of the apostles were Simon, known as the Eager One,[m] 16 Jude,

[i] **5.33** *without eating*: See the note at 2.37. [j] **5.37** *swell and burst the old skins*: While the juice from grapes was becoming wine, it would swell and stretch the skins in which it had been stored. If the skins were old and stiff, they would burst. [k] **6.1** *walking through some wheat fields*: It was the custom to let hungry travelers pick grains of wheat. [l] **6.6** *On another Sabbath*: Some manuscripts have a reading which may mean "the Sabbath after the next." [m] **6.15** *known as the Eager One*: The word "eager" translates the Greek word "zealot," which was a name later given to the members of a Jewish group that resisted and fought against the Romans.

6.1 Dt 23.25. **6.4** Lv 24.9. **6.3,4** 1 S 21.1-6.

who was the son of James, and Judas Iscariot,[n] who later betrayed Jesus.

Jesus Teaches, Preaches, and Heals
(Matthew 4.23-25)

17 Jesus and his apostles went down from the mountain and came to some flat, level ground. Many other disciples were there to meet him. Large crowds of people from all over Judea, Jerusalem, and the coastal cities of Tyre and Sidon were there too. 18 These people had come to listen to Jesus and to be healed of their diseases. All who were troubled by evil spirits were also healed. 19 Everyone was trying to touch Jesus, because power was going out from him and healing them all.

Blessings and Troubles
(Matthew 5.1-12)

20 Jesus looked at his disciples and said:

God will bless you people
who are poor.
His kingdom belongs to you!
21 God will bless
you hungry people.
You will have plenty
to eat!
God will bless you people
who are crying.
You will laugh!

22 God will bless you when others hate you and won't have anything to do with you. God will bless you when people insult you and say cruel things about you, all because you are a follower of the Son of Man. 23 Long ago your own people did these same things to the prophets. So when this happens to you, be happy and jump for joy! You will have a great reward in heaven.

24 But you rich people
are in for trouble.
You have already had
an easy life!
25 You well-fed people
are in for trouble.
You will go hungry!
You people
who are laughing now
are in for trouble.
You are going to cry
and weep!

26 You are in for trouble when everyone says good things about you. That is what your own people said about those prophets who told lies.

Love for Enemies
(Matthew 5.38-48; 7.12a)

27 This is what I say to all who will listen to me:

Love your enemies, and be good to everyone who hates you. 28 Ask God to bless anyone who curses you, and pray for everyone who is cruel to you. 29 If someone slaps you on one cheek, don't stop that person from slapping you on the other cheek. If someone wants to take your coat, don't try to keep back your shirt. 30 Give to everyone who asks and don't ask people to return what they have taken from you. 31 Treat others just as you want to be treated.

32 If you love only someone who loves you, will God praise you for that? Even sinners love people who love them. 33 If you are kind only to someone who is kind to you, will God be pleased with you for that? Even sinners are kind to people who are kind to them. 34 If you lend money only to someone you think will pay you back, will God be pleased with you for that? Even sinners lend to sinners because they think they will get it all back.

35 But love your enemies and be good to them. Lend without expecting to be paid back.[o] Then you will get a great reward, and you will be the true children of God in heaven. He is good even to people who are unthankful and cruel. 36 Have pity on others, just as your Father has pity on you.

[n] **6.16** *Iscariot*: This may mean "a man from Kerioth" (a place in Judea). But more probably it means "a man who was a liar" or "a man who was a betrayer." [o] **6.35** *without expecting to be paid back*: Some manuscripts have "without giving up on anyone."

6.22 1 P 4.14. **6.23** 2 Ch 36.16; Ac 7.52. **6.31** Tb 4.15; Mt 7.12. **6.35** Si 4.10, 11.

Judging Others
(Matthew 7.1-5)

37 Jesus said:
Don't judge others, and God won't
judge you. Don't be hard on others,
and God won't be hard on you. Forgive
others, and God will forgive you. 38 If
you give to others, you will be given a
full amount in return. It will be packed
down, shaken together, and spilling
over into your lap. The way you treat
others is the way you will be treated.
39 Jesus also used some sayings as he
spoke to the people. He said:
Can one blind person lead another
blind person? Won't they both fall into
a ditch? 40 Are students better than
their teacher? But when they are fully
trained, they will be like their teacher.
41 You can see the speck in your
friend's eye. But you don't notice the
log in your own eye. 42 How can you
say, "My friend, let me take the speck
out of your eye," when you don't see
the log in your own eye? You show-offs! First, get the log out of your own
eye. Then you can see how to take the
speck out of your friend's eye.

A Tree and Its Fruit
(Matthew 7.17-20; 12.34b, 35)

43 A good tree cannot produce bad
fruit, and a bad tree cannot produce
good fruit. 44 You can tell what a tree is
like by the fruit it produces. You cannot pick figs or grapes from thorn-bushes. 45 Good people do good things
because of the good in their hearts.
Bad people do bad things because of
the evil in their hearts. Your words
show what is in your heart.

Two Builders
(Matthew 7.24-27)

46 Why do you keep on saying that I
am your Lord, when you refuse to do
what I say? 47 Anyone who comes and
listens to me and obeys me 48 is like
someone who dug down deep and built
a house on solid rock. When the flood
came and the river rushed against the
house, it was built so well that it didn't
even shake. 49 But anyone who hears
what I say and doesn't obey me is like
someone whose house wasn't built on
solid rock. As soon as the river rushed
against that house, it was smashed to
pieces!

Jesus Heals an Army Officer's Servant
(Matthew 8.5-13; John 4.43-54)

7 After Jesus had finished teaching the
people, he went to Capernaum. 2 In
that town an army officer's servant was sick
and about to die. The officer liked this
servant very much. 3 And when he heard
about Jesus, he sent some Jewish leaders to
ask him to come and heal the servant.
4 The leaders went to Jesus and begged
him to do something. They said, "This man
deserves your help! 5 He loves our nation
and even built us a meeting place." 6 So
Jesus went with them.
When Jesus wasn't far from the house,
the officer sent some friends to tell him,
"Lord, don't go to any trouble for me! I am
not good enough for you to come into my
house. 7 And I am certainly not worthy to
come to you. Just say the word, and my
servant will get well. 8 I have officers who
give orders to me, and I have soldiers who
take orders from me. I can say to one of
them, 'Go!' and he goes. I can say to another, 'Come!' and he comes. I can say to
my servant, 'Do this!' and he will do it."
9 When Jesus heard this, he was so surprised that he turned and said to the crowd
following him, "In all of Israel I've never
found anyone with this much faith!"
10 The officer's friends returned and
found the servant well.

A Widow's Son

11 Soon Jesus and his disciples were on
their way to the town of Nain, and a big
crowd was going along with them. 12 As
they came near the gate of the town, they
saw people carrying out the body of a
widow's only son. Many people from the
town were walking along with her.
13 When the Lord saw the woman, he
felt sorry for her and said, "Don't cry!"

6.39 Mt 15.14. **6.40** Mt 10.24, 25; Jn 13.16; 15.20. **6.44** Mt 12.33. **6.45** Mt 12.34.

14 Jesus went over and touched the
stretcher on which the people were carrying the dead boy. They stopped, and Jesus
said, "Young man, get up!" 15 The boy sat
up and began to speak. Jesus then gave
him back to his mother.

16 Everyone was frightened and praised
God. They said, "A great prophet is here
with us! God has come to his people."

17 News about Jesus spread all over
Judea and everywhere else in that part of
the country.

John the Baptist

(Matthew 11.1-19)

18-19 John's followers told John everything that was being said about Jesus. So
he sent two of them to ask the Lord, "Are
you the one we should be looking for? Or
must we wait for someone else?"

20 When these messengers came to
Jesus, they said, "John the Baptist sent us
to ask, 'Are you the one we should be looking for? Or are we supposed to wait for
someone else?' "

21 At that time Jesus was healing many
people who were sick or in pain or were
troubled by evil spirits, and he was giving
sight to a lot of blind people. 22 Jesus said
to the messengers sent by John, "Go and
tell John what you have seen and heard.
Blind people are now able to see, and the
lame can walk. People who have leprosy[p]
are being healed, and the deaf can now
hear. The dead are raised to life, and the
poor are hearing the good news. 23 God will
bless everyone who doesn't reject me because of what I do."

24 After John's messengers had gone,
Jesus began speaking to the crowds about
John:

What kind of person did you go out
to the desert to see? Was he like tall
grass blown about by the wind?
25 What kind of man did you really go
out to see? Was he someone dressed in
fine clothes? People who wear expensive clothes and live in luxury are in
the king's palace. 26 What then did you
go out to see? Was he a prophet? He
certainly was! I tell you that he was
more than a prophet. 27 In the Scriptures, God calls John his messenger
and says, "I am sending my messenger
ahead of you to get things ready for
you." 28 No one ever born on this earth
is greater than John. But whoever is
least important in God's kingdom is
greater than John.

29 Everyone had been listening to John.
Even the tax collectors[q] had obeyed God
and had done what was right by letting
John baptize them. 30 But the Pharisees
and the experts in the Law of Moses refused to obey God and be baptized by John.

31 Jesus went on to say:

What are you people like? What
kind of people are you? 32 You are like
children sitting in the market and
shouting to each other,

"We played the flute,
but you would not dance!
We sang a funeral song,
but you would not cry!"

33 John the Baptist did not go around
eating and drinking, and you said,
"John has a demon in him!" 34 But because the Son of Man goes around eating and drinking, you say, "Jesus eats
and drinks too much! He is even a
friend of tax collectors and sinners."
35 Yet Wisdom is shown to be right by
what its followers do.

Simon the Pharisee

36 A Pharisee invited Jesus to have dinner with him. So Jesus went to the Pharisee's home and got ready to eat.[r]

37 When a sinful woman in that town
found out that Jesus was there, she bought
an expensive bottle of perfume. 38 Then
she came and stood behind Jesus. She
cried and started washing his feet with her

[p]**7.22** *leprosy*: See the note at 4.27. [q]**7.29** *tax collectors*: See the note at 3.12. [r]**7.36** *got ready to eat*: On special occasions the Jewish people often followed the Greek and Roman custom of lying down on their left side and leaning on their left elbow, while eating with their right hand. This is how the woman could come up behind Jesus and wash his feet (see verse 38).

7.22 **a** Is 35.5, 6; **b** Is 61.1. **7.27** Ml 3.1. **7.29,30** Mt 21.32; Lk 3.12.
7.37,38 Mt 26.7; Mk 14.3; Jn 12.3.

tears and drying them with her hair. The woman kissed his feet and poured the perfume on them.

39 The Pharisee who had invited Jesus saw this and said to himself, "If this man really were a prophet, he would know what kind of woman is touching him! He would know that she is a sinner."

40 Jesus said to the Pharisee, "Simon, I have something to say to you."

"Teacher, what is it?" Simon replied.

41 Jesus told him, "Two people were in debt to a moneylender. One of them owed him five hundred silver coins, and the other owed him fifty. 42 Since neither of them could pay him back, the moneylender said that they didn't have to pay him anything. Which one of them will like him more?"

43 Simon answered, "I suppose it would be the one who had owed more and didn't have to pay it back."

"You are right," Jesus said.

44 He turned toward the woman and said to Simon, "Have you noticed this woman? When I came into your home, you didn't give me any water so I could wash my feet. But she has washed my feet with her tears and dried them with her hair. 45 You didn't greet me with a kiss, but from the time I came in, she has not stopped kissing my feet. 46 You didn't even pour olive oil on my head,[s] but she has poured expensive perfume on my feet. 47 So I tell you that all her sins are forgiven, and that is why she has shown great love. But anyone who has been forgiven for only a little will show only a little love."

48 Then Jesus said to the woman, "Your sins are forgiven."

49 Some other guests started saying to one another, "Who is this who dares to forgive sins?"

50 But Jesus told the woman, "Because of your faith, you are now saved.[t] May God give you peace!"

Women Who Helped Jesus

8 Soon after this, Jesus was going through towns and villages, telling the good news about God's kingdom. His twelve apostles were with him, 2 and so were some women who had been healed of evil spirits and all sorts of diseases. One of the women was Mary Magdalene,[u] who once had seven demons in her. 3 Joanna, Susanna, and many others had also used what they owned to help Jesus[v] and his disciples. Joanna's husband Chuza was one of Herod's officials.[w]

A Story about a Farmer
(Matthew 13.1-9; Mark 4.1-9)

4 When a large crowd from several towns had gathered around Jesus, he told them this story:

5 A farmer went out to scatter seed in a field. While the farmer was doing it, some of the seeds fell along the road and were stepped on or eaten by birds. 6 Other seeds fell on rocky ground and started growing. But the plants did not have enough water and soon dried up. 7 Some other seeds fell where thornbushes grew up and choked the plants. 8 The rest of the seeds fell on good ground where they grew and produced a hundred times as many seeds.

When Jesus had finished speaking, he said, "If you have ears, pay attention!"

Why Jesus Used Stories
(Matthew 13.10-17; Mark 4.10-12)

9 Jesus' disciples asked him what the story meant. 10 So he answered:

I have explained the secrets about

[s]**7.44-46** *washed my feet . . . greet me with a kiss . . . pour olive oil on my head*: Guests in a home were usually offered water so they could wash their feet, because most people either went barefoot or wore sandals and would come in the house with very dusty feet. Guests were also greeted with a kiss on the cheek, and special ones often had sweet-smelling olive oil poured on their head.

[t]**7.50** *saved*: Or "healed." The Greek word may have either meaning. [u]**8.2** *Magdalene*: Meaning "from Magdala," a small town on the western shore of Lake Galilee. There is no hint that she is the sinful woman in 7.36-50. [v]**8.3** *used what they owned to help Jesus*: Women often helped Jewish teachers by giving them money. [w]**8.3** *Herod's officials*: Herod Antipas, the son of Herod the Great.

8.2,3 Mt 27.55, 56; Mk 15.40, 41; Lk 23.49. **8.10** Is 6.9 (LXX).

God's kingdom to you, but for others I
can only use stories. These people
look, but they don't see, and they hear,
but they don't understand.

Jesus Explains the Story about a Farmer

(Matthew 13.18-23; Mark 4.13-20)

11 This is what the story means:
The seed is God's message, 12 and the
seeds that fell along the road are the
people who hear the message. But
the devil comes and snatches the message out of their hearts, so that they
will not believe and be saved. 13 The
seeds that fell on rocky ground are the
people who gladly hear the message
and accept it. But they don't have deep
roots, and they believe only for a little
while. As soon as life gets hard, they
give up.
14 The seeds that fell among the
thornbushes are also people who hear
the message. But they are so eager for
riches and pleasures that they never
produce anything. 15 Those seeds that
fell on good ground are the people who
listen to the message and keep it in
good and honest hearts. They last and
produce a harvest.

Light

(Mark 4.21-25)

16 No one lights a lamp and puts it
under a bowl or under a bed. A lamp is
always put on a lampstand, so that
people who come into a house will see
the light. 17 There is nothing hidden
that will not be found. There is no secret that will not be well known. 18 Pay
attention to how you listen! Everyone
who has something will be given more,
but people who have nothing will lose
what little they think they have.

Jesus' Mother and Brothers

(Matthew 12.46-50; Mark 3.31-35)

19 Jesus' mother and brothers went to
see him, but because of the crowd they
could not get near him. 20 Someone told
Jesus, "Your mother and brothers are
standing outside and want to see you."
21 Jesus answered, "My mother and my
brothers are those people who hear and
obey God's message."

A Storm

(Matthew 8.23-27; Mark 4.35-41)

22 One day, Jesus and his disciples got
into a boat, and he said, "Let's cross the
lake."[x] They started out, 23 and while they
were sailing across, he went to sleep.

Suddenly a windstorm struck the lake,
and the boat started sinking. They were in
danger. 24 So they went to Jesus and woke
him up, "Master, Master! We are about to
drown!"

Jesus got up and ordered the wind and
waves to stop. They obeyed, and everything
was calm. 25 Then Jesus asked the disciples, "Don't you have any faith?"

But they were frightened and amazed.
They said to each other, "Who is this? He
can give orders to the wind and the waves,
and they obey him!"

A Man with Demons in Him

(Matthew 8.28-34; Mark 5.1-20)

26 Jesus and his disciples sailed across
Lake Galilee and came to shore near the
town of Gerasa.[y] 27 As Jesus was getting out
of the boat, he was met by a man from that
town. The man had demons in him. He had
gone naked for a long time and no longer
lived in a house, but in the graveyard.[z]
28 The man saw Jesus and screamed.
He knelt down in front of him and shouted,
"Jesus, Son of God in heaven, what do you
want with me? I beg you not to torture
me!" 29 He said this because Jesus had already told the evil spirit to go out of him.

The man had often been attacked by the
demon. And even though he had been
bound with chains and leg irons and kept
under guard, he smashed whatever bound
him. Then the demon would force him out
into lonely places.

[x] **8.22** *cross the lake*: To the eastern shore of Lake Galilee, where most of the people were not Jewish. [y] **8.26** *Gerasa*: Some manuscripts have "Gergesa." [z] **8.27** *graveyard*: It was thought that demons and evil spirits lived in graveyards.

8.16 Mt 5.15; Lk 11.33. **8.17** Mt 10.26; Lk 12.2. **8.18** Mt 25.29; Lk 19.26.

30 Jesus asked the man, "What is your name?"

He answered, "My name is Lots." He said this because there were 'lots' of demons in him. 31 They begged Jesus not to send them to the deep pit,[a] where they would be punished.

32 A large herd of pigs was feeding there on the hillside. So the demons begged Jesus to let them go into the pigs, and Jesus let them go. 33 Then the demons left the man and went into the pigs. The whole herd rushed down the steep bank into the lake and drowned.

34 When the men taking care of the pigs saw this, they ran to spread the news in the town and on the farms. 35 The people went out to see what had happened, and when they came to Jesus, they also found the man. The demons had gone out of him, and he was sitting there at the feet of Jesus. He had clothes on and was in his right mind. But the people were terrified.

36 Then all who had seen the man healed told about it. 37 Everyone from around Gerasa[b] begged Jesus to leave, because they were so frightened.

When Jesus got into the boat to start back, 38 the man who had been healed begged to go with him. But Jesus sent him off and said, 39 "Go back home and tell everyone how much God has done for you." The man then went all over town, telling everything that Jesus had done for him.

A Dying Girl and a Sick Woman

(Matthew 9.18-26; Mark 5.21-43)

40 Everyone had been waiting for Jesus, and when he came back, a crowd was there to welcome him. 41 Just then the man in charge of the Jewish meeting place came and knelt down in front of Jesus. His name was Jairus, and he begged Jesus to come to his home 42 because his twelve-year-old child was dying. She was his only daughter.

While Jesus was on his way, people were crowding all around him. 43 In the crowd was a woman who had been bleeding for twelve years. She had spent everything she had on doctors,[c] but none of them could make her well.

44 As soon as she came up behind Jesus and barely touched his clothes, her bleeding stopped.

45 "Who touched me?" Jesus asked.

While everyone was denying it, Peter said, "Master, people are crowding all around and pushing you from every side."[d]

46 But Jesus answered, "Someone touched me, because I felt power going out from me." 47 The woman knew that she could not hide, so she came trembling and knelt down in front of Jesus. She told everyone why she had touched him and that she had been healed right away.

48 Jesus said to the woman, "You are now well because of your faith. May God give you peace!"

49 While Jesus was speaking, someone came from Jairus' home and said, "Your daughter has died! Why bother the teacher anymore?"

50 When Jesus heard this, he told Jairus, "Don't worry! Have faith, and your daughter will get well."

51 Jesus went into the house, but he did not let anyone else go with him, except Peter, John, James, and the girl's father and mother. 52 Everyone was crying and weeping for the girl. But Jesus said, "The child isn't dead. She is just asleep." 53 The people laughed at him because they knew she was dead.

54 Jesus took hold of the girl's hand and said, "Child, get up!" 55 She came back to life and got right up. Jesus told them to give her something to eat. 56 Her parents were surprised, but Jesus ordered them not to tell anyone what had happened.

Instructions for the Twelve Apostles

(Matthew 10.5-15; Mark 6.7-13)

9 Jesus called together his twelve apostles and gave them complete power over all demons and diseases. 2 Then he sent them to tell about God's kingdom and

[a]**8.31** *deep pit*: The place where evil spirits are kept and punished. [b]**8.37** *Gerasa*: See the note at 8.26. [c]**8.43** *She had spent everything she had on doctors*: Some manuscripts do not have these words. [d]**8.45** *from every side*: Some manuscripts add "and you ask, 'Who touched me?' "

to heal the sick. 3 He told them, "Don't
take anything with you! Don't take a walking stick or a traveling bag or food or
money or even a change of clothes. 4 When
you are welcomed into a home, stay there
until you leave that town. 5 If people won't
welcome you, leave the town and shake the
dust from your feet[e] as a warning to them."
6 The apostles left and went from village
to village, telling the good news and healing
people everywhere.

Herod Is Worried
(Matthew 14.1-12; Mark 6.14-29)

7 Herod[f] the ruler heard about all that
was happening, and he was worried. Some
people were saying that John the Baptist
had come back to life. 8 Others were saying
that Elijah had come[g] or that one of the
prophets from long ago had come back to
life. 9 But Herod said, "I had John's head
cut off! Who is this I hear so much about?"
Herod was eager to meet Jesus.

Jesus Feeds Five Thousand
(Matthew 14.13-21; Mark 6.30-44; John 6.1-14)

10 The apostles came back and told
Jesus everything they had done. He then
took them with him to the village of Bethsaida, where they could be alone. 11 But a
lot of people found out about this and followed him. Jesus welcomed them. He
spoke to them about God's kingdom and
healed everyone who was sick.
12 Late in the afternoon the twelve
apostles came to Jesus and said, "Send the
crowd to the villages and farms around
here. They need to find a place to stay and
something to eat. There is nothing in this
place. It is like a desert!"
13 Jesus answered, "You give them
something to eat."
But they replied, "We have only five
small loaves of bread[h] and two fish. If we
are going to feed all these people, we will
have to go and buy food." 14 There were
about five thousand men in the crowd.
Jesus said to his disciples, "Have the
people sit in groups of fifty." 15 They did this,
and all the people sat down. 16 Jesus took the
five loaves and the two fish. He looked up
toward heaven and blessed the food. Then
he broke the bread and fish and handed
them to his disciples to give to the people.
17 Everyone ate all they wanted. What
was left over filled twelve baskets.

Who Is Jesus?
(Matthew 16.13-19; Mark 8.27-29)

18 When Jesus was alone praying, his
disciples came to him, and he asked them,
"What do people say about me?"
19 They answered, "Some say that you
are John the Baptist or Elijah[i] or a prophet
from long ago who has come back to life."
20 Jesus then asked them, "But who do
you say I am?"
Peter answered, "You are the Messiah
sent from God."
21 Jesus strictly warned his disciples not
to tell anyone about this.

Jesus Speaks about His Suffering and Death
(Matthew 16.20-28; Mark 8.30—9.1)

22 Jesus told his disciples, "The nation's
leaders, the chief priests, and the teachers
of the Law of Moses will make the Son of
Man suffer terribly. They will reject him
and kill him, but three days later he will
rise to life."
23 Then Jesus said to all the people:
If any of you want to be my followers, you must forget about yourself.
You must take up your cross each day
and follow me. 24 If you want to save
your life,[j] you will destroy it. But if you

[e]**9.5** *shake the dust from your feet*: This was a way of showing rejection. [f]**9.7** *Herod*: Herod Antipas, the son of Herod the Great. [g]**9.8** *Elijah had come*: Many of the Jewish people expected the prophet Elijah to come and prepare the way for the Messiah. [h]**9.13** *small loaves of bread*: These would have been flat and round or in the shape of a bun. [i]**9.19** *Elijah*: See the note at 9.8. [j]**9.24** *life*: In verses 24, 25 a Greek word which often means "soul" is translated "life" and "yourself."

9.5 Ac 13.51. **9.3-5** Lk 10.4-11. **9.7,8** Mt 16.14; Mk 8.28; Lk 9.19. **9.19** Mt 14.1, 2; Mk 6.14, 15; Lk 9.7, 8. **9.20** Jn 6.68, 69. **9.23** Mt 10.38; Lk 14.27. **9.24** Mt 10.39; Lk 17.33; Jn 12.25.

give up your life for me, you will save
it. 25 What will you gain, if you own the
whole world but destroy yourself or
waste your life? 26 If you are ashamed
of me and my message, the Son of
Man will be ashamed of you when he
comes in his glory and in the glory of
his Father and the holy angels. 27 You
can be sure that some of the people
standing here will not die before they
see God's kingdom.

The True Glory of Jesus

(Matthew 17.1-8; Mark 9.2-8)

28 About eight days later Jesus took Peter, John, and James with him and went up
on a mountain to pray. 29 While he was
praying, his face changed, and his clothes
became shining white. 30 Suddenly Moses
and Elijah were there speaking with him.
31 They appeared in heavenly glory and
talked about all that Jesus' death[k] in Jerusalem would mean.

32 Peter and the other two disciples had
been sound asleep. All at once they woke
up and saw how glorious Jesus was. They
also saw the two men who were with him.

33 Moses and Elijah were about to leave,
when Peter said to Jesus, "Master, it is good
for us to be here! Let us make three shelters, one for you, one for Moses, and one
for Elijah." But Peter did not know what he
was talking about.

34 While Peter was still speaking, a
shadow from a cloud passed over them,
and they were frightened as the cloud covered them. 35 From the cloud a voice spoke,
"This is my chosen Son. Listen to what he
says!"

36 After the voice had spoken, Peter,
John, and James saw only Jesus. For some
time they kept quiet and did not say anything about what they had seen.

Jesus Heals a Boy

(Matthew 17.14-18; Mark 9.14-27)

37 The next day Jesus and his three disciples came down from the mountain and
were met by a large crowd. 38 Just then
someone in the crowd shouted, "Teacher,
please do something for my son! He is my
only child! 39 A demon often attacks him
and makes him scream. It shakes him until
he foams at the mouth, and it won't leave
him until it has completely worn the boy
out. 40 I begged your disciples to force out
the demon, but they couldn't do it."

41 Jesus said to them, "You people are
stubborn and don't have any faith! How
much longer must I be with you? Why do I
have to put up with you?"

Then Jesus said to the man, "Bring your
son to me." 42 While the boy was being
brought, the demon attacked him and
made him shake all over. Jesus ordered the
demon to stop. Then he healed the boy and
gave him back to his father. 43 Everyone
was amazed at God's great power.

Jesus Again Speaks about His Death

(Matthew 17.22, 23; Mark 9.30-32)

While everyone was still amazed at what
Jesus was doing, he said to his disciples,
44 "Pay close attention to what I am telling
you! The Son of Man will be handed over
to his enemies." 45 But the disciples did not
know what he meant. The meaning was
hidden from them. They could not understand it, and they were afraid to ask.

Who Is the Greatest?

(Matthew 18.1-5; Mark 9.33-37)

46 Jesus' disciples were arguing about
which one of them was the greatest. 47 Jesus
knew what they were thinking, and he had
a child stand there beside him. 48 Then he
said to his disciples, "When you welcome
even a child because of me, you welcome
me. And when you welcome me, you welcome the one who sent me. Whichever one
of you is the most humble is the greatest."

For or against Jesus

(Mark 9.38-40)

49 John said, "Master, we saw a man using your name to force demons out of peo-

[k]**9.31** *Jesus' death*: In Greek this is "his departure," which probably includes his rising to life and his return to heaven.

9.35 Is 42.1; Mt 3.17; 12.18; Mk 1.11; Lk 3.22. **9.28-35** 2 P 1.17, 18. **9.46** Lk 22.24.
9.48 Mt 10.40; Lk 10.16; Jn 13.20.

ple. But we told him to stop, because he isn't one of us."

50 "Don't stop him!" Jesus said. "Anyone who isn't against you is for you."

A Samaritan Village Refuses To Receive Jesus

51 Not long before it was time for Jesus to be taken up to heaven, he made up his mind to go to Jerusalem. 52 He sent some messengers on ahead to a Samaritan village to get things ready for him. 53 But he was on his way to Jerusalem, so the people there refused to welcome him. 54 When the disciples James and John saw what was happening, they asked, "Lord, do you want us to call down fire from heaven to destroy these people?"[l]

55 But Jesus turned and corrected them for what they had said.[m] 56 Then they all went on to another village.

Three People Who Wanted To Be Followers

(Matthew 8.19-22)

57 Along the way someone said to Jesus, "I'll go anywhere with you!"

58 Jesus said, "Foxes have dens, and birds have nests, but the Son of Man doesn't have a place to call his own."

59 Jesus told someone else to come with him. But the man said, "Lord, let me wait until I bury my father."[n]

60 Jesus answered, "Let the dead take care of the dead, while you go and tell about God's kingdom."

61 Then someone said to Jesus, "I want to go with you, Lord, but first let me go back and take care of things at home."

62 Jesus answered, "Anyone who starts plowing and keeps looking back isn't worth a thing to God's kingdom!"

The Work of the Seventy-Two Followers

10 Later the Lord chose seventy-two[o] other followers and sent them out two by two to every town and village where he was about to go. 2 He said to them:

A large crop is in the fields, but there are only a few workers. Ask the Lord in charge of the harvest to send out workers to bring it in. 3 Now go, but remember, I am sending you like lambs into a pack of wolves. 4 Don't take along a moneybag or a traveling bag or sandals. And don't waste time greeting people on the road.[p] 5 As soon as you enter a home, say, "God bless this home with peace." 6 If the people living there are peace-loving, your prayer for peace will bless them. But if they are not peace-loving, your prayer will return to you. 7 Stay with the same family, eating and drinking whatever they give you, because workers are worth what they earn. Don't move around from house to house.

8 If the people of a town welcome you, eat whatever they offer. 9 Heal their sick and say, "God's kingdom will soon be here!"[q]

10 But if the people of a town refuse to welcome you, go out into the street and say, 11 "We are shaking the dust from our feet[r] as a warning to you. And you can be sure that God's kingdom will soon be here!"[s] 12 I tell you

[l]**9.54** *to destroy these people*: Some manuscripts add "as Elijah did." [m]**9.55** *what they had said*: Some manuscripts add, "and said, 'Don't you know what spirit you belong to? The Son of Man did not come to destroy people's lives, but to save them.' " [n]**9.59** *bury my father*: The Jewish people taught that giving someone a proper burial was even more important than helping the poor. [o]**10.1** *seventy-two*: Some manuscripts have "seventy." According to Jewish tradition, there were seventy nations on earth. But the ancient Greek translation of the Old Testament has "seventy-two" in place of "seventy." Jesus probably chose this number of followers to show that his message was for everyone in the world. [p]**10.4** *waste time greeting people on the road*: In those days a polite greeting could take a long time. [q]**10.9** *will soon be here*: Or "is already here." [r]**10.11** *shaking the dust from our feet*: This was a way of showing rejection. [s]**10.11** *will soon be here*: Or "is already here."

9.54 2 K 1.9-16. **9.61** 1 K 19.20. **10.2** Mt 9.37, 38. **10.3** Mt 10.16. **10.7** 1 Co 9.14; 1 Ti 5.18. **10.10,11** Ac 13.51. **10.4-11** Mt 10.7-14; Mk 6.8-11; Lk 9.3-5. **10.12** **a** Gn 19.24-28; Mt 11.24; **b** Mt 10.15.

that on the day of judgment the people
of Sodom will get off easier than the
people of that town!

The Unbelieving Towns

(Matthew 11.20-24)

13 You people of Chorazin are in for
trouble! You people of Bethsaida are
also in for trouble! If the miracles that
took place in your towns had happened in Tyre and Sidon, the people
there would have turned to God long
ago. They would have dressed in sackcloth and put ashes on their heads.[t]
14 On the day of judgment the people
of Tyre and Sidon will get off easier
than you will. 15 People of Capernaum,
do you think you will be honored in
heaven? Well, you will go down to hell!
16 My followers, whoever listens to
you is listening to me. Anyone
who says "No" to you is saying "No" to
me. And anyone who says "No" to me
is really saying "No" to the one who
sent me.

The Return of the Seventy-Two

17 When the seventy-two[u] followers returned, they were excited and said, "Lord,
even the demons obeyed when we spoke in
your name!"
18 Jesus told them:
I saw Satan fall from heaven like a
flash of lightning. 19 I have given you
the power to trample on snakes and
scorpions and to defeat the power of
your enemy Satan. Nothing can harm
you. 20 But don't be happy because evil
spirits obey you. Be happy that your
names are written in heaven!

Jesus Thanks His Father

(Matthew 11.25-27; 13.16, 17)

21 At that same time, Jesus felt the joy that
comes from the Holy Spirit,[v] and he said:
My Father, Lord of heaven and
earth, I am grateful that you hid all
this from wise and educated people
and showed it to ordinary people. Yes,
Father, that is what pleased you.
22 My Father has given me everything, and he is the only one who
knows the Son. The only one who really knows the Father is the Son. But
the Son wants to tell others about the
Father, so that they can know him too.
23 Jesus then turned to his disciples and
said to them in private, "You are really
blessed to see what you see! 24 Many
prophets and kings were eager to see what
you see and to hear what you hear. But I
tell you that they did not see or hear."

The Good Samaritan

25 An expert in the Law of Moses stood
up and asked Jesus a question to see what
he would say. "Teacher," he asked, "what
must I do to have eternal life?"
26 Jesus answered, "What is written in
the Scriptures? How do you understand
them?"
27 The man replied, "The Scriptures say,
'Love the Lord your God with all your
heart, soul, strength, and mind.' They also
say, 'Love your neighbors as much as you
love yourself.' "
28 Jesus said, "You have given the right
answer. If you do this, you will have eternal
life."
29 But the man wanted to show that he
knew what he was talking about. So he
asked Jesus, "Who are my neighbors?"
30 Jesus replied:
As a man was going down from
Jerusalem to Jericho, robbers attacked
him and grabbed everything he had.
They beat him up and ran off, leaving
him half dead.
31 A priest happened to be going
down the same road. But when he saw
the man, he walked by on the other
side. 32 Later a temple helper[w] came

[t] **10.13** *dressed in sackcloth . . . ashes on their heads*: This was one way that people showed how sorry they were for their sins. [u] **10.17** *seventy-two*: See the note at 10.1. [v] **10.21** *the Holy Spirit*: Some manuscripts have "his spirit." [w] **10.32** *temple helper*: A man from the tribe of Levi, whose job it was to work around the temple.

10.13 Is 23.1-18; Ez 26.1—28.26; Jl 3.4-8; Am 1.9, 10; Zec 9.2-4. **10.15** Is 14.13-15. **10.16** Mt 10.40; Mk 9.37; Lk 9.48; Jn 13.20. **10.19** Ps 91.13. **10.22 a** Jn 3.35; **b** Jn 10.15. **10.25-28** Mt 22.35-40; Mk 12.28-34. **10.27 a** Dt 6.5; **b** Lv 19.18. **10.28** Lv 18.5.

to the same place. But when he saw
the man who had been beaten up, he
also went by on the other side.
33 A man from Samaria then came
traveling along that road. When he
saw the man, he felt sorry for him
34 and went over to him. He treated
his wounds with olive oil and wine[x]
and bandaged them. Then he put him
on his own donkey and took him to an
inn, where he took care of him. 35 The
next morning he gave the innkeeper
two silver coins and said, "Please take
care of the man. If you spend more
than this on him, I will pay you when I
return."
36 Then Jesus asked, "Which one of
these three people was a real neighbor to
the man who was beaten up by robbers?"
37 The teacher answered, "The one who
showed pity."
Jesus said, "Go and do the same!"

Martha and Mary

38 The Lord and his disciples were traveling along and came to a village. When
they got there, a woman named Martha
welcomed him into her home. 39 She had a
sister named Mary, who sat down in front
of the Lord and was listening to what he
said. 40 Martha was worried about all that
had to be done. Finally, she went to Jesus
and said, "Lord, doesn't it bother you that
my sister has left me to do all the work by
myself? Tell her to come and help me!"
41 The Lord answered, "Martha, Martha! You are worried and upset about
so many things, 42 but only one thing is
necessary. Mary has chosen what is best,
and it will not be taken away from her."

Prayer

(Matthew 6.9-13; 7.7-11)

11 When Jesus had finished praying,
one of his disciples said to him,
"Lord, teach us to pray, just as John taught
his followers to pray."
2 So Jesus told them, "Pray in this way:

'Father, help us
to honor your name.
Come and set up
your kingdom.
3 Give us each day
the food we need.[y]
4 Forgive our sins,
as we forgive everyone
who has done wrong to us.
And keep us
from being tempted.' "

5 Then Jesus went on to say:
Suppose one of you goes to a friend
in the middle of the night and says,
"Let me borrow three loaves of bread.
6 A friend of mine has dropped in, and
I don't have a thing for him to eat."
7 And suppose your friend answers,
"Don't bother me! The door is bolted,
and my children and I are in bed. I
cannot get up to give you something."
8 He may not get up and give you
the bread, just because you are his
friend. But he will get up and give you
as much as you need, simply because
you are not ashamed to keep on
asking.
9 So I tell you to ask and you will receive, search and you will find, knock
and the door will be opened for you.
10 Everyone who asks will receive,
everyone who searches will find, and
the door will be opened for everyone
who knocks. 11 Which one of you
fathers would give your hungry child a
snake if the child asked for a fish?
12 Which one of you would give your
child a scorpion if the child asked for
an egg? 13 As bad as you are, you still
know how to give good gifts to your
children. But your heavenly Father is
even more ready to give the Holy Spirit
to anyone who asks.

Jesus and the Ruler of Demons

(Matthew 12.22-30; Mark 3.20-27)

14 Jesus forced a demon out of a man
who could not talk. And after the demon

[x] **10.34** *olive oil and wine*: In New Testament times these were used as medicine. Sometimes olive oil is a symbol for healing by means of a miracle (see James 5.14). [y] **11.3** *the food we need*: Or "food for today" or "food for the coming day."

10.33,34 2 Ch 28.15. **10.38,39** Jn 11.1, 2.

had gone out, the man started speaking, and the crowds were amazed. 15 But some people said, "He forces out demons by the power of Beelzebul, the ruler of the demons!"

16 Others wanted to put Jesus to the test. So they asked him to show them a sign from God. 17 Jesus knew what they were thinking, and he said:

A kingdom where people fight each other will end up in ruin. And a family that fights will break up. 18 If Satan fights against himself, how can his kingdom last? Yet you say that I force out demons by the power of Beelzebul. 19 If I use his power to force out demons, whose power do your own followers use to force them out? They are the ones who will judge you. 20 But if I use God's power to force out demons, it proves that God's kingdom has already come to you.

21 When a strong man arms himself and guards his home, everything he owns is safe. 22 But if a stronger man comes and defeats him, he will carry off the weapons in which the strong man trusted. Then he will divide with others what he has taken. 23 If you are not on my side, you are against me. If you don't gather in the crop with me, you scatter it.

Return of an Evil Spirit
(Matthew 12.43-45)

24 When an evil spirit leaves a person, it travels through the desert, looking for a place to rest. But when it doesn't find a place, it says, "I will go back to the home I left." 25 When it gets there and finds the place clean and fixed up, 26 it goes off and finds seven other evil spirits even worse than itself. They all come and make their home there, and that person ends up in worse shape than before.

Being Really Blessed

27 While Jesus was still talking, a woman in the crowd spoke up, "The woman who gave birth to you and nursed you is blessed!"

28 Jesus replied, "That's true, but the people who are really blessed are the ones who hear and obey God's message!"[z]

A Sign from God
(Matthew 12.38-42; Mark 8.12)

29 As crowds were gathering around Jesus, he said:

You people of today are evil! You keep looking for a sign from God. But what happened to Jonah[a] is the only sign you will be given. 30 Just as Jonah was a sign to the people of Nineveh, the Son of Man will be a sign to the people of today. 31 When the judgment comes, the Queen of the South[b] will stand there with you and condemn you. She traveled a long way to hear Solomon's wisdom, and yet here is something far greater than Solomon. 32 The people of Nineveh will also stand there with you and condemn you. They turned to God when Jonah preached, and yet here is something far greater than Jonah.

Light
(Matthew 5.15; 6.22, 23)

33 No one lights a lamp and then hides it or puts it under a clay pot. A lamp is put on a lampstand, so that everyone who comes into the house can see the light. 34 Your eyes are the lamp for your body. When your eyes are good, you have all the light you need. But when your eyes are bad, everything is dark. 35 So be sure that your light isn't darkness. 36 If you have light, and nothing is dark, then light will be everywhere, as when a lamp shines brightly on you.

[z] **11.28** *"That's true, but the people who are really blessed . . . message"*: Or "That's not true, the people who are blessed . . . message." [a] **11.29** *what happened to Jonah*: Jonah was in the stomach of a big fish for three days and nights (see Matthew 12.40). [b] **11.31** *Queen of the South*: Sheba, probably a country in southern Arabia.

11.15 Mt 9.34; 10.25. **11.16** Mt 12.38; 16.1; Mk 8.11. **11.23** Mk 9.40. **11.29** Mt 16.4; Mk 8.12. **11.30** Jon 3.4. **11.31** 1 K 10.1-10; 2 Ch 9.1-12. **11.32** Jon 3.5. **11.33** Mt 5.15; Mk 4.21; Lk 8.16.

Jesus Condemns the Pharisees and Teachers of the Law of Moses

(Matthew 23.1-36; Mark 12.38-40; Luke 20.45-47)

37 When Jesus finished speaking, a
Pharisee invited him home for a meal.
Jesus went and sat down to eat.[c] 38 The
Pharisee was surprised that he did not
wash his hands[d] before eating. 39 So the
Lord said to him:

You Pharisees clean the outside of
cups and dishes, but on the inside you
are greedy and evil. 40 You fools! Didn't
God make both the outside and the inside?[e] 41 If you would only give what
you have to the poor, everything you do
would please God.

42 You Pharisees are in for trouble!
You give God a tenth of the spices
from your gardens, such as mint and
rue. But you cheat people, and you
don't love God. You should be fair and
kind to others and still give a tenth
to God.

43 You Pharisees are in for trouble!
You love the front seats in the meeting
places, and you like to be greeted with
honor in the market. 44 But you are in
for trouble! You are like unmarked
graves[f] that people walk on without
even knowing it.

45 A teacher of the Law of Moses
spoke up, "Teacher, you said cruel things
about us."

46 Jesus replied:

You teachers are also in for trouble!
You load people down with heavy burdens, but you won't lift a finger to help
them carry the loads. 47 Yes, you are
really in for trouble. You build monuments to honor the prophets your
own people murdered long ago. 48 You
must think that was the right thing for
your people to do, or else you would
not have built monuments for the
prophets they murdered.

49 Because of your evil deeds, the
Wisdom of God said, "I will send
prophets and apostles to you. But you
will murder some and mistreat others." 50 You people living today will be
punished for all the prophets who have
been murdered since the beginning of
the world. 51 This includes every
prophet from the time of Abel to the
time of Zechariah,[g] who was murdered
between the altar and the temple. You
people will certainly be punished for
all of this.

52 You teachers of the Law of Moses
are really in for trouble! You carry the
keys to the door of knowledge about
God. But you never go in, and you
keep others from going in.

53 Jesus was about to leave, but the
teachers and the Pharisees wanted to get
even with him. They tried to make him say
what he thought about other things, 54 so
that they could catch him saying something
wrong.

Warnings

12 As thousands of people crowded
around Jesus and were stepping on
each other, he told his disciples:

Be sure to guard against the dishonest teaching[h] of the Pharisees! It is
their way of fooling people. 2 Everything that is hidden will be found out,
and every secret will be known.
3 Whatever you say in the dark will be
heard when it is day. Whatever you

[c]**11.37** *sat down to eat*: See the note at 7.36. [d]**11.38** *did not wash his hands*: The Jewish people had strict laws about washing their hands before eating, especially if they had been out in public. [e]**11.40** *Didn't God make both the outside and the inside*: Or "Doesn't the person who washes the outside always wash the inside too?" [f]**11.44** *unmarked graves*: Tombs were whitewashed to keep anyone from accidentally touching them. A person who touched a dead body or a tomb was considered unclean and could not worship with other Jewish people. [g]**11.51** *from the time of Abel . . . Zechariah*: Genesis is the first book in the Jewish Scriptures, and it tells that Abel was the first person to be murdered. Second Chronicles is the last book in the Jewish Scriptures, and the last murder that it tells about is that of Zechariah. [h]**12.1** *dishonest teaching*: The Greek text has "yeast," which is used here of a teaching that is not true (see Matthew 16.6, 12).

11.42 Lv 27.30. **11.51** **a** Gn 4.8; **b** 2 Ch 24.20-22. **12.1** Mt 16.6; Mk 8.15. **12.2** Mk 4.22; Lk 8.17.

whisper in a closed room will be
shouted from the housetops.

The One To Fear
(Matthew 10.28-31)

4 My friends, don't be afraid of people. They can kill you, but after that,
there is nothing else they can do.
5 God is the one you must fear. Not
only can he take your life, but he can
throw you into hell. God is certainly
the one you should fear!
6 Five sparrows are sold for just two
pennies, but God doesn't forget a one
of them. 7 Even the hairs on your head
are counted. So don't be afraid! You
are worth much more than many
sparrows.

Telling Others about Christ
(Matthew 10.32, 33; 12.32; 10.19, 20)

8 If you tell others that you belong
to me, the Son of Man will tell God's
angels that you are my followers. 9 But
if you reject me, you will be rejected in
front of them. 10 If you speak against
the Son of Man, you can be forgiven,
but if you speak against the Holy
Spirit, you cannot be forgiven.
11 When you are brought to trial in
the Jewish meeting places or before
rulers or officials, don't worry about
how you will defend yourselves or what
you will say. 12 At that time the Holy
Spirit will tell you what to say.

A Rich Fool

13 A man in a crowd said to Jesus,
"Teacher, tell my brother to give me my
share of what our father left us when he
died."
14 Jesus answered, "Who gave me the
right to settle arguments between you and
your brother?"
15 Then he said to the crowd, "Don't be
greedy! Owning a lot of things won't make
your life safe."
16 So Jesus told them this story:
A rich man's farm produced a big
crop, 17 and he said to himself, "What
can I do? I don't have a place large
enough to store everything."
18 Later, he said, "Now I know what
I'll do. I'll tear down my barns and build
bigger ones, where I can store all my
grain and other goods. 19 Then I'll say to
myself, 'You have stored up enough
good things to last for years to come. Live
it up! Eat, drink, and enjoy yourself.' "
20 But God said to him, "You fool!
Tonight you will die. Then who will get
what you have stored up?"
21 "This is what happens to people who
store up everything for themselves, but are
poor in the sight of God."

Worry
(Matthew 6.25-34)

22 Jesus said to his disciples:
I tell you not to worry about your
life! Don't worry about having something to eat or wear. 23 Life is more
than food or clothing. 24 Look at the
crows! They don't plant or harvest,
and they don't have storehouses or
barns. But God takes care of them. You
are much more important than any
birds. 25 Can worry make you live
longer?[i] 26 If you don't have power
over small things, why worry about
everything else?
27 Look how the wild flowers grow!
They don't work hard to make their
clothes. But I tell you that Solomon
with all his wealth[j] wasn't as well
clothed as one of these flowers. 28 God
gives such beauty to everything that
grows in the fields, even though it is
here today and thrown into a fire tomorrow. Won't he do even more for
you? You have such little faith!
29 Don't keep worrying about having
something to eat or drink. 30 Only people who don't know God are always
worrying about such things. Your
Father knows what you need. 31 But
put God's work first, and these things
will be yours as well.

[i] **12.25** *live longer*: Or "grow taller." [j] **12.27** *Solomon with all his wealth*: The Jewish people thought that Solomon was the richest person who had ever lived.

12.4,5 **a** 4 Macc 13.14; **b** 4 Macc 9.7; 10.4. **12.10** Mt 12.31, 32; Mk 3.29. **12.11,12** Mt 10.19, 20; Mk 13.11; Lk 21.14, 15. **12.19** Si 11.19. **12.27** 1 K 10.4-7; 2 Ch 9.3-6.

Treasures in Heaven
(Matthew 6.19-21)

32 My little group of disciples, don't
be afraid! Your Father wants to give
you the kingdom. 33 Sell what you have
and give the money to the poor. Make
yourselves moneybags that never wear
out. Make sure your treasure is safe in
heaven, where thieves cannot steal it
and moths cannot destroy it. 34 Your
heart will always be where your treasure is.

Faithful and Unfaithful Servants
(Matthew 24.45-51)

35 Be ready and keep your lamps
burning 36 just like those servants who
wait up for their master to return from
a wedding feast. As soon as he comes
and knocks, they open the door for
him. 37 Servants are fortunate if their
master finds them awake and ready
when he comes! I promise you that he
will get ready and have his servants sit
down so he can serve them. 38 Those
servants are really fortunate if their
master finds them ready, even though
he comes late at night or early in the
morning. 39 You would surely not let a
thief break into your home, if you
knew when the thief was coming. 40 So
always be ready! You don't know when
the Son of Man will come.

41 Peter asked Jesus, "Did you say this
just for us or for everyone?"

42 The Lord answered:

Who are faithful and wise servants?
Who are the ones the master will put
in charge of giving the other servants
their food supplies at the proper time?
43 Servants are fortunate if their master comes and finds them doing their
job. 44 A servant who is always faithful
will surely be put in charge of everything the master owns.

45 But suppose one of the servants
thinks that the master won't return
until late. Suppose that servant starts
beating all the other servants and eats
and drinks and gets drunk. 46 If that
happens, the master will come on a
day and at a time when the servant
least expects him. That servant will
then be punished and thrown out with
the servants who cannot be trusted.

47 If servants are not ready or willing to do what their master wants
them to do, they will be beaten hard.
48 But servants who don't know what
their master wants them to do will not
be beaten so hard for doing wrong. If
God has been generous with you, he
will expect you to serve him well. But
if he has been more than generous,
he will expect you to serve him even
better.

Not Peace, but Trouble
(Matthew 10.34-36)

49 I came to set fire to the earth,
and I wish it were already on fire! 50 I
am going to be put to a hard test. And I
will have to suffer a lot of pain until it
is over. 51 Do you think that I came to
bring peace to earth? No indeed! I
came to make people choose sides.
52 A family of five will be divided, with
two of them against the other three.
53 Fathers and sons will turn against
one another, and mothers and daughters will do the same. Mothers-in-law
and daughters-in-law will also turn
against each other.

Knowing What To Do
(Matthew 16.2, 3; 5.25, 26)

54 Jesus said to all the people:

As soon as you see a cloud coming
up in the west, you say, "It's going to
rain," and it does. 55 When the south
wind blows, you say, "It's going to get
hot," and it does. 56 Are you trying to
fool someone? You can predict the
weather by looking at the earth and
sky, but you don't really know what's
going on right now. 57 Why don't you
understand the right thing to do?
58 When someone accuses you of
something, try to settle things before
you are taken to court. If you don't,

12.35 Mt 25.1-13. **12.36** Mk 13.34-36. **12.39,40** Mt 24.43, 44. **12.50** Mk 10.38. **12.53** Mic 7.6.

you will be dragged before the judge.
Then the judge will hand you over to
the jailer, and you will be locked up.
59 You won't get out until you have
paid the last cent you owe.

Turn Back to God

13 About this same time Jesus was
told that Pilate had given orders for
some people from Galilee to be killed while
they were offering sacrifices. 2 Jesus
replied:

Do you think that these people were
worse sinners than everyone else in
Galilee just because of what happened
to them? 3 Not at all! But you can be
sure that if you don't turn back to God,
every one of you will also be killed.
4 What about those eighteen people who died when the tower in Siloam fell on them? Do you think they
were worse than everyone else in
Jerusalem? 5 Not at all! But you can be
sure that if you don't turn back to God,
every one of you will also die.

A Story about a Fig Tree

6 Jesus then told them this story:

A man had a fig tree growing in his
vineyard. One day he went out to pick
some figs, but he didn't find any. 7 So
he said to the gardener, "For three
years I have come looking for figs on
this tree, and I haven't found any yet.
Chop it down! Why should it take up
space?"

8 The gardener answered, "Master,
leave it for another year. I'll dig around
it and put some manure on it to make
it grow. 9 Maybe it will have figs on it
next year. If it doesn't, you can have it
cut down."

Healing a Woman on the Sabbath

10 One Sabbath, Jesus was teaching in a
Jewish meeting place, 11 and a woman was
there who had been crippled by an evil
spirit for eighteen years. She was completely bent over and could not straighten
up. 12 When Jesus saw the woman, he
called her over and said, "You are now
well." 13 He placed his hands on her, and
right away she stood up straight and
praised God.

14 The man in charge of the meeting
place was angry because Jesus had healed
someone on the Sabbath. So he said to the
people, "Each week has six days when we
can work. Come and be healed on one of
those days, but not on the Sabbath."

15 The Lord replied, "Are you trying to
fool someone? Won't any one of you untie
your ox or donkey and lead it out to drink
on a Sabbath? 16 This woman belongs to
the family of Abraham, but Satan has kept
her bound for eighteen years. Isn't it right
to set her free on the Sabbath?" 17 Jesus'
words made his enemies ashamed. But
everyone else in the crowd was happy
about the wonderful things he was doing.

A Mustard Seed and Yeast

(Matthew 13.31-33; Mark 4.30-32)

18 Jesus said, "What is God's kingdom
like? What can I compare it with? 19 It is
like what happens when someone plants a
mustard seed in a garden. The seed grows
as big as a tree, and birds nest in its
branches."

20 Then Jesus said, "What can I compare God's kingdom with? 21 It is like what
happens when a woman mixes yeast into
three batches of flour. Finally, all the dough
rises."

The Narrow Door

(Matthew 7.13, 14, 21-23)

22 As Jesus was on his way to Jerusalem,
he taught the people in the towns and villages. 23 Someone asked him, "Lord, are
only a few people going to be saved?"

Jesus answered:

24 Do all you can to go in by the
narrow door! A lot of people will try to
get in, but will not be able to. 25 Once
the owner of the house gets up and
locks the door, you will be left standing
outside. You will knock on the door
and say, "Sir, open the door for us!"

But the owner will answer, "I don't
know a thing about you!"

26 Then you will start saying, "We

13.14 Ex 20.9, 10; Dt 5.13, 14.

dined with you, and you taught in our streets."

27 But he will say, "I really don't know who you are! Get away from me, you evil people!"

28 Then when you have been thrown outside, you will weep and grit your teeth because you will see Abraham, Isaac, Jacob, and all the prophets in God's kingdom. 29 People will come from all directions and sit down to feast in God's kingdom. 30 There the ones who are now least important will be the most important, and those who are now most important will be least important.

Jesus and Herod

31 At that time some Pharisees came to Jesus and said, "You had better get away from here! Herod[k] wants to kill you."

32 Jesus said to them:

Go tell that fox, "I am going to force out demons and heal people today and tomorrow, and three days later I'll be through." 33 But I am going on my way today and tomorrow and the next day. After all, Jerusalem is the place where prophets are killed.

Jesus Loves Jerusalem

(Matthew 23.37-39)

34 Jerusalem, Jerusalem! Your people have killed the prophets and have stoned the messengers who were sent to you. I have often wanted to gather your people, as a hen gathers her chicks under her wings. But you wouldn't let me. 35 Now your temple will be deserted. You won't see me again until the time when you say,

"Blessed is the one who comes
in the name of the Lord."

Jesus Heals a Sick Man

14 One Sabbath, Jesus was having dinner in the home of an important Pharisee, and everyone was carefully watching Jesus. 2 All of a sudden a man with swollen legs stood up in front of him. 3 Jesus turned and asked the Pharisees and the teachers of the Law of Moses, "Is it right to heal on the Sabbath?" 4 But they did not say a word.

Jesus took hold of the man. Then he healed him and sent him away. 5 Afterwards, Jesus asked the people, "If your son or ox falls into a well, wouldn't you pull him out right away, even on the Sabbath?" 6 There was nothing they could say.

How To Be a Guest

7 Jesus saw how the guests had tried to take the best seats. So he told them:

8 When you are invited to a wedding feast, don't sit in the best place. Someone more important may have been invited. 9 Then the one who invited you will come and say, "Give your place to this other guest!" You will be embarrassed and will have to sit in the worst place.

10 When you are invited to be a guest, go and sit in the worst place. Then the one who invited you may come and say, "My friend, take a better seat!" You will then be honored in front of all the other guests. 11 If you put yourself above others, you will be put down. But if you humble yourself, you will be honored.

12 Then Jesus said to the man who had invited him:

When you give a dinner or a banquet, don't invite your friends and family and relatives and rich neighbors. If you do, they will invite you in return, and you will be paid back. 13 When you give a feast, invite the poor, the crippled, the lame, and the blind. 14 They cannot pay you back. But God will bless you and reward you when his people rise from death.

The Great Banquet

(Matthew 22.1-10)

15 After Jesus had finished speaking, one of the guests said, "The greatest

[k] **13.31** *Herod*: Herod Antipas, the son of Herod the Great.

13.27 Ps 6.8. **13.28** Mt 22.13; 25.30. **13.28,29** Mt 8.11, 12. **13.30** Mt 19.30; 20.16; Mk 10.31. **13.34** 2 Esd 1.30. **13.35** Ps 118.26. **14.5** Mt 12.11. **14.8-10** Pr 25.6, 7. **14.11** Mt 23.12; Lk 18.14.

blessing of all is to be at the banquet in God's kingdom!"

16 Jesus told him:

A man once gave a great banquet and invited a lot of guests. 17 When the banquet was ready, he sent a servant to tell the guests, "Everything is ready! Please come."

18 One guest after another started making excuses. The first one said, "I bought some land, and I've got to look it over. Please excuse me."

19 Another guest said, "I bought five teams of oxen, and I need to try them out. Please excuse me."

20 Still another guest said, "I have just gotten married, and I can't be there."

21 The servant told his master what happened, and the master became so angry that he said, "Go as fast as you can to every street and alley in town! Bring in everyone who is poor or crippled or blind or lame."

22 When the servant returned, he said, "Master, I've done what you told me, and there is still plenty of room for more people."

23 His master then told him, "Go out along the back roads and fence rows and make people come in, so that my house will be full. 24 Not one of the guests I first invited will get even a bite of my food!"

Being a Disciple

(Matthew 10.37, 38)

25 Large crowds were walking along with Jesus, when he turned and said:

26 You cannot be my disciple, unless you love me more than you love your father and mother, your wife and children, and your brothers and sisters. You cannot come with me unless you love me more than you love your own life.

27 You cannot be my disciple unless you carry your own cross and come with me.

28 Suppose one of you wants to build a tower. What is the first thing you will do? Won't you sit down and figure out how much it will cost and if you have enough money to pay for it? 29 Otherwise, you will start building the tower, but not be able to finish. Then everyone who sees what is happening will laugh at you. 30 They will say, "You started building, but could not finish the job."

31 What will a king do if he has only ten thousand soldiers to defend himself against a king who is about to attack him with twenty thousand soldiers? Before he goes out to battle, won't he first sit down and decide if he can win? 32 If he thinks he won't be able to defend himself, he will send messengers and ask for peace while the other king is still a long way off. 33 So then, you cannot be my disciple unless you give away everything you own.

Salt and Light

(Matthew 5.13; Mark 9.50)

34 Salt is good, but if it no longer tastes like salt, how can it be made to taste salty again? 35 It is no longer good for the soil or even for the manure pile. People simply throw it out. If you have ears, pay attention!

One Sheep

(Matthew 18.12-14)

15 Tax collectors[l] and sinners were all crowding around to listen to Jesus. 2 So the Pharisees and the teachers of the Law of Moses started grumbling, "This man is friendly with sinners. He even eats with them."

3 Then Jesus told them this story:

4 If any of you has a hundred sheep, and one of them gets lost, what will you do? Won't you leave the ninety-nine in the field and go look for the lost sheep until you find it? 5 And when you find it, you will be so glad that you will put it on your shoulder 6 and carry it home. Then you will call

[l]**15.1** *Tax collectors*: See the note at 3.12.

14.26 4 Macc 2.11-13; Mt 10.37. **14.27** Mt 10.38; 16.24; Mk 8.34; Lk 9.23. **15.1,2** Lk 5.29, 30.

in your friends and neighbors and say,
"Let's celebrate! I've found my lost
sheep."
7 Jesus said, "In the same way there is
more happiness in heaven because of one
sinner who turns to God than over ninety-
nine good people who don't need to."

One Coin

8 Jesus told the people another story:
What will a woman do if she has
ten silver coins and loses one of them?
Won't she light a lamp, sweep the floor,
and look carefully until she finds it?
9 Then she will call in her friends and
neighbors and say, "Let's celebrate!
I've found the coin I lost."
10 Jesus said, "In the same way God's
angels are happy when even one person
turns to him."

Two Sons

11 Jesus also told them another story:
Once a man had two sons. 12 The
younger son said to his father, "Give
me my share of the property." So the
father divided his property between his
two sons.
13 Not long after that, the younger
son packed up everything he owned
and left for a foreign country, where he
wasted all his money in wild living.
14 He had spent everything, when a
bad famine spread through that whole
land. Soon he had nothing to eat.
15 He went to work for a man in
that country, and the man sent him
out to take care of his pigs.[m] 16 He
would have been glad to eat what the
pigs were eating,[n] but no one gave him
a thing.
17 Finally, he came to his senses
and said, "My father's workers have
plenty to eat, and here I am, starving
to death! 18 I will go to my father and
say to him, 'Father, I have sinned
against God in heaven and against you.
19 I am no longer good enough to be
called your son. Treat me like one of
your workers.' "
20 The younger son got up and
started back to his father. But when he
was still a long way off, his father saw
him and felt sorry for him. He ran to
his son and hugged and kissed him.
21 The son said, "Father, I have
sinned against God in heaven and
against you. I am no longer good
enough to be called your son."
22 But his father said to the servants, "Hurry and bring the best
clothes and put them on him. Give
him a ring for his finger and sandals[o]
for his feet. 23 Get the best calf and
prepare it, so we can eat and celebrate.
24 This son of mine was dead, but has
now come back to life. He was lost and
has now been found." And they began
to celebrate.
25 The older son had been out in
the field. But when he came near the
house, he heard the music and dancing. 26 So he called one of the servants
over and asked, "What's going on
here?"
27 The servant answered, "Your
brother has come home safe and
sound, and your father ordered us to
kill the best calf." 28 The older brother
got so angry that he would not even go
into the house.
His father came out and begged
him to go in. 29 But he said to his
father, "For years I have worked for you
like a slave and have always obeyed
you. But you have never even given me
a little goat, so that I could give a dinner for my friends. 30 This other son of
yours wasted your money on prostitutes. And now that he has come
home, you ordered the best calf to be
killed for a feast."

[m] **15.15** *pigs*: The Jewish religion taught that pigs were not fit to eat or even to touch. A Jewish man would have felt terribly insulted if he had to feed pigs, much less eat with them. [n] **15.16** *what the pigs were eating*: The Greek text has "(bean) pods," which came from a tree in Palestine. These were used to feed animals. Poor people sometimes ate them too. [o] **15.22** *ring . . . sandals*: These show that the young man's father fully accepted him as his son. A ring was a sign of high position in the family. Sandals showed that he was a son instead of a slave, since slaves did not usually wear sandals.

31 His father replied, "My son, you are always with me, and everything I have is yours. 32 But we should be glad and celebrate! Your brother was dead, but he is now alive. He was lost and has now been found."

A Dishonest Manager

16 Jesus said to his disciples:

A rich man once had a manager to take care of his business. But he was told that his manager was wasting money. 2 So the rich man called him in and said, "What is this I hear about you? Tell me what you have done! You are no longer going to work for me."

3 The manager said to himself, "What shall I do now that my master is going to fire me? I can't dig ditches, and I'm ashamed to beg. 4 I know what I'll do, so that people will welcome me into their homes after I've lost my job."

5 Then one by one he called in the people who were in debt to his master. He asked the first one, "How much do you owe my master?"

6 "A hundred barrels of olive oil," the man answered.

So the manager said, "Take your bill and sit down and quickly write 'fifty'."

7 The manager asked someone else who was in debt to his master, "How much do you owe?"

"A thousand bushels[p] of wheat," the man replied.

The manager said, "Take your bill and write 'eight hundred'."

8 The master praised his dishonest manager for looking out for himself so well. That's how it is! The people of this world look out for themselves better than the people who belong to the light.

9 My disciples, I tell you to use wicked wealth to make friends for yourselves. Then when it is gone, you will be welcomed into an eternal home. 10 Anyone who can be trusted in little matters can also be trusted in important matters. But anyone who is dishonest in little matters will be dishonest in important matters. 11 If you cannot be trusted with this wicked wealth, who will trust you with true wealth? 12 And if you cannot be trusted with what belongs to someone else, who will give you something that will be your own? 13 You cannot be the slave of two masters. You will like one more than the other or be more loyal to one than to the other. You cannot serve God and money.

Some Sayings of Jesus
(Matthew 11.12, 13; 5.31, 32; Mark 10.11, 12)

14 The Pharisees really loved money. So when they heard what Jesus said, they made fun of him. 15 But Jesus told them:

You are always making yourselves look good, but God sees what is in your heart. The things that most people think are important are worthless as far as God is concerned.

16 Until the time of John the Baptist, people had to obey the Law of Moses and the Books of the Prophets.[q] But since God's kingdom has been preached, everyone is trying hard to get in. 17 Heaven and earth will disappear before the smallest letter of the Law does.

18 It is a terrible sin[r] for a man to divorce his wife and marry another woman. It is also a terrible sin for a man to marry a divorced woman.

Lazarus and the Rich Man

19 There was once a rich man who wore expensive clothes and every day ate the best food. 20 But a poor beggar named Lazarus was brought to the gate of the rich man's house. 21 He

[p] **16.7** *A thousand bushels*: The Greek text has "A hundred measures," and each measure is about ten or twelve bushels. [q] **16.16** *the Law of Moses and the Books of the Prophets*: The Jewish Scriptures, that is, the Old Testament. [r] **16.18** *a terrible sin*: The Greek text uses a word that means the sin of being unfaithful in marriage.

16.9 Tb 4.9-11. **16.13** Mt 6.24. **16.16** Mt 11.12, 13. **16.17** Mt 5.18. **16.18** Mt 5.32; 1 Co 7.10, 11.

was happy just to eat the scraps that fell from the rich man's table. His body was covered with sores, and dogs kept coming up to lick them. 22 The poor man died, and angels took him to the place of honor next to Abraham.[s]

The rich man also died and was buried. 23 He went to hell[t] and was suffering terribly. When he looked up and saw Abraham far off and Lazarus at his side, 24 he said to Abraham, "Have pity on me! Send Lazarus to dip his finger in water and touch my tongue. I'm suffering terribly in this fire."

25 Abraham answered, "My friend, remember that while you lived, you had everything good, and Lazarus had everything bad. Now he is happy, and you are in pain. 26 And besides, there is a deep ditch between us, and no one from either side can cross over."

27 But the rich man said, "Abraham, then please send Lazarus to my father's home. 28 Let him warn my five brothers, so they won't come to this horrible place."

29 Abraham answered, "Your brothers can read what Moses and the prophets[u] wrote. They should pay attention to that."

30 Then the rich man said, "No, that's not enough! If only someone from the dead would go to them, they would listen and turn to God."

31 So Abraham said, "If they won't pay attention to Moses and the prophets, they won't listen even to someone who comes back from the dead."

Faith and Service

(Matthew 18.6, 7, 21, 22; Mark 9.42)

17 Jesus said to his disciples:

There will always be something that causes people to sin. But anyone who causes them to sin is in for trouble. A person who causes even one of my little followers to sin 2 would be better off thrown into the ocean with a heavy stone tied around their neck. 3 So be careful what you do.

Correct any followers[v] of mine who sin, and forgive the ones who say they are sorry. 4 Even if one of them mistreats you seven times in one day and says, "I am sorry," you should still forgive that person.

5 The apostles said to the Lord, "Make our faith stronger!"

6 Jesus replied:

If you had faith no bigger than a tiny mustard seed, you could tell this mulberry tree to pull itself up, roots and all, and to plant itself in the ocean. And it would!

7 If your servant comes in from plowing or from taking care of the sheep, would you say, "Welcome! Come on in and have something to eat"? 8 No, you wouldn't say that. You would say, "Fix me something to eat. Get ready to serve me, so I can have my meal. Then later on you can eat and drink." 9 Servants don't deserve special thanks for doing what they are supposed to do. 10 And that's how it should be with you. When you've done all you should, then say, "We are merely servants, and we have simply done our duty."

Ten Men with Leprosy

11 On his way to Jerusalem, Jesus went along the border between Samaria and Galilee. 12 As he was going into a village, ten men with leprosy[w] came toward him. They stood at a distance 13 and shouted, "Jesus, Master, have pity on us!"

14 Jesus looked at them and said, "Go show yourselves to the priests."[x]

[s] **16.22** *the place of honor next to Abraham*: The Jewish people thought that heaven would be a banquet that God would give for them. Abraham would be the most important person there, and the guest of honor would sit next to him. [t] **16.23** *hell*: The Greek text has "hades," which the Jewish people often thought of as the place where the dead wait for the final judgment. [u] **16.29** *Moses and the prophets*: The Jewish Scriptures, that is, the Old Testament. [v] **17.3** *followers*: The Greek text has "brothers," which is often used in the New Testament for followers of Jesus.
[w] **17.12** *leprosy*: See the note at 4.27. [x] **17.14** *show yourselves to the priests*: See the note at 5.14.

16.22 4 Macc 13.17. **16.23,24** 2 Esd 7.36; 8.59. **17.3** Mt 18.15. **17.14** Lv 14.1-32.

On their way they were healed. 15 When
one of them discovered that he was healed,
he came back, shouting praises to God.
16 He bowed down at the feet of Jesus and
thanked him. The man was from the country of Samaria.
17 Jesus asked, "Weren't ten men
healed? Where are the other nine? 18 Why
was this foreigner the only one who came
back to thank God?" 19 Then Jesus told the
man, "You may get up and go. Your faith
has made you well."

God's Kingdom

(Matthew 24.23-28, 37-41)

20 Some Pharisees asked Jesus when
God's kingdom would come. He answered,
"God's kingdom isn't something you can
see. 21 There is no use saying, 'Look! Here
it is' or 'Look! There it is.' God's kingdom is
here with you."[y]
22 Jesus said to his disciples:
The time will come when you will
long to see one of the days of the Son
of Man, but you will not. 23 When people say to you, "Look there," or "Look
here," don't go looking for him. 24 The
day of the Son of Man will be like lightning flashing across the sky. 25 But first
he must suffer terribly and be rejected
by the people of today. 26 When the
Son of Man comes, things will be just
as they were when Noah lived. 27 People were eating, drinking, and getting
married right up to the day when
Noah went into the big boat. Then the
flood came and drowned everyone on
earth.
28 When Lot[z] lived, people were
also eating and drinking. They were
buying, selling, planting, and building.
29 But on the very day Lot left Sodom,
fiery flames poured down from the sky
and killed everyone. 30 The same will
happen on the day when the Son of
Man appears.
31 At that time no one on a rooftop[a]
should go down into the house to get
anything. No one in a field should go
back to the house for anything. 32 Remember what happened to Lot's wife.[b]
33 People who try to save their lives
will lose them, and those who lose
their lives will save them. 34 On that
night two people will be sleeping in the
same bed, but only one will be taken.
The other will be left. 35-36 Two women
will be together grinding wheat, but
only one will be taken. The other will
be left.[c]
37 Then Jesus' disciples spoke up, "But
where will this happen, Lord?"
Jesus said, "Where there is a corpse,
there will always be buzzards."[d]

A Widow and a Judge

18 Jesus told his disciples a story
about how they should keep on
praying and never give up:
2 In a town there was once a judge
who didn't fear God or care about people. 3 In that same town there was a
widow who kept going to the judge and
saying, "Make sure that I get fair treatment in court."
4 For a while the judge refused to do
anything. Finally, he said to himself,
"Even though I don't fear God or care
about people, 5 I will help this widow
because she keeps on bothering me. If
I don't help her, she will wear me out."
6 The Lord said:

[y] **17.21** *here with you*: Or "in your hearts." [z] **17.27,28** *Noah . . . Lot*: When God destroyed the earth by a flood, he saved Noah and his family. And when God destroyed the cities of Sodom and Gomorrah and the evil people who lived there, he rescued Lot and his family (see Genesis 19.1-29). [a] **17.31** *rooftop*: See the note at 5.19. [b] **17.32** *what happened to Lot's wife*: She turned into a block of salt when she disobeyed God (see Genesis 19.26). [c] **17.35,36** *will be left*: Some manuscripts add, "Two men will be in the same field, but only one will be taken. The other will be left." [d] **17.37** *Where there is a corpse, there will always be buzzards*: This saying may mean that when anything important happens, people soon know about it. Or the saying may mean that whenever something bad happens, curious people gather around and stare. But the word translated "buzzard" also means "eagle" and may refer to the Roman army, which had an eagle as its symbol.

17.26 Gn 6.5-8. **17.27** Gn 7.5-24. **17.28,29** Gn 18.20—19.25. **17.31** Mt 24.17, 18; Mk 13.15, 16. **17.32** Gn 19.26. **17.33** Mt 10.39; 16.25; Mk 8.35; Lk 9.24; Jn 12.25.

Think about what that crooked judge said. 7 Won't God protect his chosen ones who pray to him day and night? Won't he be concerned for them? 8 He will surely hurry and help them. But when the Son of Man comes, will he find on this earth anyone with faith?

A Pharisee and a Tax Collector

9 Jesus told a story to some people who thought they were better than others and who looked down on everyone else:

10 Two men went into the temple to pray.[e] One was a Pharisee and the other a tax collector.[f] 11 The Pharisee stood over by himself and prayed,[g] "God, I thank you that I am not greedy, dishonest, and unfaithful in marriage like other people. And I am really glad that I am not like that tax collector over there. 12 I go without eating[h] for two days a week, and I give you one tenth of all I earn."

13 The tax collector stood off at a distance and did not think he was good enough even to look up toward heaven. He was so sorry for what he had done that he pounded his chest and prayed, "God, have pity on me! I am such a sinner."

14 Then Jesus said, "When the two men went home, it was the tax collector and not the Pharisee who was pleasing to God. If you put yourself above others, you will be put down. But if you humble yourself, you will be honored."

Jesus Blesses Little Children

(Matthew 19.13-15; Mark 10.13-16)

15 Some people brought their little children for Jesus to bless. But when his disciples saw them doing this, they told the people to stop bothering him. 16 So Jesus called the children over to him and said, "Let the children come to me! Don't try to stop them. People who are like these children belong to God's kingdom.[i] 17 You will never get into God's kingdom unless you enter it like a child!"

A Rich and Important Man

(Matthew 19.16-30; Mark 10.17-31)

18 An important man asked Jesus, "Good Teacher, what must I do to have eternal life?"

19 Jesus said, "Why do you call me good? Only God is good. 20 You know the commandments: 'Be faithful in marriage. Do not murder. Do not steal. Do not tell lies about others. Respect your father and mother.' "

21 He told Jesus, "I have obeyed all these commandments since I was a young man."

22 When Jesus heard this, he said, "There is one thing you still need to do. Go and sell everything you own! Give the money to the poor, and you will have riches in heaven. Then come and be my follower." 23 When the man heard this, he was sad, because he was very rich.

24 Jesus saw how sad the man was. So he said, "It's terribly hard for rich people to get into God's kingdom! 25 In fact, it's easier for a camel to go through the eye of a needle than for a rich person to get into God's kingdom."

26 When the crowd heard this, they asked, "How can anyone ever be saved?"

27 Jesus replied, "There are some things that people cannot do, but God can do anything."

28 Peter said, "Remember, we left everything to be your followers!"

29 Jesus answered, "You can be sure that anyone who gives up home or wife or brothers or family or children because of God's kingdom 30 will be given much more in this life. And in the future world they will have eternal life."

[e] **18.10** *into the temple to pray*: Jewish people usually prayed there early in the morning and late in the afternoon. [f] **18.10** *tax collector*: See the note at 3.12. [g] **18.11** *stood over by himself and prayed*: Some manuscripts have "stood up and prayed to himself." [h] **18.12** *without eating*: See the note at 2.37. [i] **18.16** *People who are like these children belong to God's kingdom*: Or "God's kingdom belongs to people who are like these children."

18.7 Si 35.19. **18.13** Man 8. **18.14** Mt 23.12; Lk 14.11. **18.20** **a** Ex 20.14; Dt 5.18; **b** Ex 20.13; Dt 5.17; **c** Ex 20.15; Dt 5.19; **d** Ex 20.16; Dt 5.20; **e** Ex 20.12; Dt 5.16.

Jesus Again Tells about His Death

(Matthew 20.17-19; Mark 10.32-34)

31 Jesus took the twelve apostles aside
and said:

We are now on our way to Jerusalem. Everything that the prophets
wrote about the Son of Man will
happen there. 32 He will be handed
over to foreigners,[j] who will make fun
of him, mistreat him, and spit on
him. 33 They will beat him and kill
him, but three days later he will rise to
life.

34 The apostles did not understand
what Jesus was talking about. They
could not understand, because the
meaning of what he said was hidden from
them.

Jesus Heals a Blind Beggar

(Matthew 20.29-34; Mark 10.46-52)

35 When Jesus was coming close to Jericho, a blind man sat begging beside the
road. 36 The man heard the crowd walking
by and asked what was happening. 37 Some
people told him that Jesus from Nazareth
was passing by. 38 So the blind man
shouted, "Jesus, Son of David,[k] have pity
on me!" 39 The people who were going
along with Jesus told the man to be quiet.
But he shouted even louder, "Son of David,
have pity on me!"

40 Jesus stopped and told some people
to bring the blind man over to him. When
the blind man was getting near, Jesus
asked, 41 "What do you want me to do
for you?"

"Lord, I want to see!" he answered.

42 Jesus replied, "Look and you will see!
Your eyes are healed because of your faith."
43 Right away the man could see, and he
went with Jesus and started thanking God.
When the crowds saw what happened, they
praised God.

Zacchaeus

19 Jesus was going through Jericho,
2 where a man named Zacchaeus
lived. He was in charge of collecting taxes[l]
and was very rich. 3-4 Jesus was heading his
way, and Zacchaeus wanted to see what he
was like. But Zacchaeus was a short man
and could not see over the crowd. So he
ran ahead and climbed up into a sycamore
tree.

5 When Jesus got there, he looked up
and said, "Zacchaeus, hurry down! I want
to stay with you today." 6 Zacchaeus hurried down and gladly welcomed Jesus.

7 Everyone who saw this started grumbling, "This man Zacchaeus is a sinner!
And Jesus is going home to eat with him."

8 Later that day Zacchaeus stood up and
said to the Lord, "I will give half of my
property to the poor. And I will now pay
back four times as much[m] to everyone I
have ever cheated."

9 Jesus said to Zacchaeus, "Today you
and your family have been saved,[n] because
you are a true son of Abraham.[o] 10 The Son
of Man came to look for and to save people
who are lost."

A Story about Ten Servants

(Matthew 25.14-30)

11 The crowd was still listening to Jesus
as he was getting close to Jerusalem. Many
of them thought that God's kingdom would
soon appear, 12 and Jesus told them this
story:

A prince once went to a foreign
country to be crowned king and then
to return. 13 But before leaving, he
called in ten servants and gave each of
them some money. He told them, "Use
this to earn more money until I get
back."

14 But the people of his country
hated him, and they sent messengers

[j] **18.32** *foreigners*: The Romans, who ruled Judea at this time. [k] **18.38** *Son of David*: The Jewish people expected the Messiah to be from the family of King David, and for this reason the Messiah was often called the "Son of David." [l] **19.2** *in charge of collecting taxes*: See the note at 3.12. [m] **19.8** *pay back four times as much*: Both Jewish and Roman law said that a person must pay back four times the amount that was taken. [n] **19.9** *saved*: Zacchaeus was Jewish, but it is only now that he is rescued from sin and placed under God's care. [o] **19.9** *son of Abraham*: As used in this verse, the words mean that Zacchaeus is truly one of God's special people.

19.10 Mt 18.10, 11.

to the foreign country to say, "We don't
want this man to be our king."
15 After the prince had been made
king, he returned and called in his servants. He asked them how much they
had earned with the money they had
been given.
16 The first servant came and said,
"Sir, with the money you gave me I
have earned ten times as much."
17 "That's fine, my good servant!"
the king said. "Since you have shown
that you can be trusted with a small
amount, you will be given ten cities to
rule."
18 The second one came and said,
"Sir, with the money you gave me, I
have earned five times as much."
19 The king said, "You will be given
five cities."
20 Another servant came and said,
"Sir, here is your money. I kept it safe
in a handkerchief. 21 You are a hard
man, and I was afraid of you. You take
what isn't yours, and you harvest crops
you didn't plant."
22 "You worthless servant!" the king
told him. "You have condemned yourself by what you have just said. You
knew that I am a hard man, taking
what isn't mine and harvesting what
I've not planted. 23 Why didn't you put
my money in the bank? On my return,
I could have had the money together
with interest."
24 Then he said to some other servants standing there, "Take the money
away from him and give it to the
servant who earned ten times as
much."
25 But they said, "Sir, he already
has ten times as much!"
26 The king replied, "Those who
have something will be given more.
But everything will be taken away from
those who don't have anything. 27 Now
bring me the enemies who didn't want
me to be their king. Kill them while I
watch!"

Jesus Enters Jerusalem

(Matthew 21.1-11; Mark 11.1-11; John 12.12-19)

28 When Jesus had finished saying all
this, he went on toward Jerusalem. 29 As he
was getting near Bethphage and Bethany
on the Mount of Olives, he sent two of his
disciples on ahead. 30 He told them, "Go
into the next village, where you will find a
young donkey that has never been ridden.
Untie the donkey and bring it here. 31 If
anyone asks why you are doing that, just
say, 'The Lord[p] needs it.' "
32 They went off and found everything
just as Jesus had said. 33 While they were
untying the donkey, its owners asked, "Why
are you doing that?"
34 They answered, "The Lord[p] needs it."
35 Then they led the donkey to Jesus.
They put some of their clothes on its back
and helped Jesus get on. 36 And as he rode
along, the people spread clothes on the
road[q] in front of him. 37 When Jesus was
starting down the Mount of Olives, his
large crowd of disciples were happy and
praised God because of all the miracles
they had seen. 38 They shouted,

"Blessed is the king who comes
in the name of the Lord!
Peace in heaven
and glory to God."

39 Some Pharisees in the crowd said to
Jesus, "Teacher, make your disciples stop
shouting!"
40 But Jesus answered, "If they keep
quiet, these stones will start shouting."
41 When Jesus came closer and could
see Jerusalem, he cried 42 and said:
It is too bad that today your people
don't know what will bring them
peace! Now it is hidden from them.
43 Jerusalem, the time will come when
your enemies will build walls around
you to attack you. Armies will surround you and close in on you from
every side. 44 They will level you to the
ground and kill your people. Not one
stone in your buildings will be left on

[p] **19.31,34** *The Lord*: Or "The master of the donkey." [q] **19.36** *spread clothes on the road*: This was one way that the Jewish people welcomed a famous person.

19.26 Mt 13.12; Mk 4.25; Lk 8.18. **19.11-27** Mt 25.14-30. **19.38** Ps 118.26.

top of another. This will happen because you did not see that God had
come to save you.[r]

Jesus in the Temple

(Matthew 21.12-17; Mark 11.15-19;
John 2.13-22)

45 When Jesus entered the temple, he
started chasing out the people who were
selling things. 46 He told them, "The Scriptures say, 'My house should be a place of
worship.' But you have made it a place
where robbers hide!"

47 Each day, Jesus kept on teaching in
the temple. So the chief priests, the teachers of the Law of Moses, and some other
important people tried to have him killed.
48 But they could not find a way to do it,
because everyone else was eager to listen
to him.

A Question about Jesus' Authority

(Matthew 21.23-27; Mark 11.27-33)

20 One day, Jesus was teaching in the
temple and telling the good news.
So the chief priests, the teachers, and the
nation's leaders 2 asked him, "What right
do you have to do these things? Who gave
you this authority?"

3 Jesus replied, "I want to ask you a
question. 4 Who gave John the right to baptize? Was it God in heaven or merely some
human being?"

5 They talked this over and said to each
other, "We can't say that God gave John
this right. Jesus will ask us why we didn't
believe John. 6 And we can't say that it was
merely some human who gave John the
right to baptize. The crowd will stone us to
death, because they think John was a
prophet."

7 So they told Jesus, "We don't know
who gave John the right to baptize."

8 Jesus replied, "Then I won't tell you
who gave me the right to do what I do."

Renters of a Vineyard

(Matthew 21.33-46; Mark 12.1-12)

9 Jesus told the people this story:
A man once planted a vineyard and
rented it out. Then he left the country
for a long time. 10 When it was time to
harvest the crop, he sent a servant to
ask the renters for his share of the
grapes. But they beat up the servant
and sent him away without anything.
11 So the owner sent another servant.
The renters also beat him up. They insulted him terribly and sent him away
without a thing. 12 The owner sent a
third servant. He was also beaten terribly and thrown out of the vineyard.

13 The owner then said to himself,
"What am I going to do? I know what.
I'll send my son, the one I love so
much. They will surely respect him!"

14 When the renters saw the owner's son, they said to one another,
"Someday he will own the vineyard.
Let's kill him! Then we can have it all
for ourselves." 15 So they threw him
out of the vineyard and killed him.

Jesus asked, "What do you think the
owner of the vineyard will do? 16 I'll tell you
what. He will come and kill those renters
and let someone else have his vineyard."

When the people heard this, they said,
"This must never happen!"

17 But Jesus looked straight at them and
said, "Then what do the Scriptures mean
when they say, 'The stone that the builders
tossed aside is now the most important
stone of all'? 18 Anyone who stumbles over
this stone will get hurt, and anyone it falls
on will be smashed to pieces."

19 The chief priests and the teachers of
the Law of Moses knew that Jesus was talking about them when he was telling this
story. They wanted to arrest him right then,
but they were afraid of the people.

Paying Taxes

(Matthew 22.15-22; Mark 12.13-17)

20 Jesus' enemies kept watching him
closely, because they wanted to hand him
over to the Roman governor. So they sent
some men who pretended to be good. But
they were really spies trying to catch Jesus
saying something wrong. 21 The spies said

[r] **19.44** *that God had come to save you*: The Jewish people looked for the time when God would come and rescue them from their enemies. But when Jesus came, many of them refused to obey him.

19.46 Is 56.7; Jr 7.11. **19.47** Lk 21.37. **20.9** Is 5.1. **20.17** Ps 118.22.

to him, "Teacher, we know that you teach
the truth about what God wants people to
do. And you treat everyone with the same
respect, no matter who they are. 22 Tell
us, should we pay taxes to the Emperor
or not?"
23 Jesus knew that they were trying to
trick him. So he told them, 24 "Show me a
coin." Then he asked, "Whose picture and
name are on it?"
"The Emperor's," they answered.
25 Then he told them, "Give the Emperor what belongs to him and give God
what belongs to God." 26 Jesus' enemies
could not catch him saying anything wrong
there in front of the people. They were
amazed at his answer and kept quiet.

Life in the Future World
(Matthew 22.23-33; Mark 12.18-27)

27 The Sadducees did not believe that
people would rise to life after death. So
some of them came to Jesus 28 and said:
Teacher, Moses wrote that if a married man dies and has no children, his
brother should marry the widow. Their
first son would then be thought of as
the son of the dead brother.
29 There were once seven brothers.
The first one married, but died without having any children. 30 The second
one married his brother's widow, and
he also died without having any children. 31 The same thing happened to
the third one. Finally, all seven brothers married that woman and died
without having any children. 32 At last
the woman died. 33 When God raises
people from death, whose wife will this
woman be? All seven brothers had
married her.
34 Jesus answered:
The people in this world get married. 35 But in the future world no one
who is worthy to rise from death will
either marry 36 or die. They will be like
the angels and will be God's children,
because they have been raised to life.
37 In the story about the burning
bush, Moses clearly shows that people
will live again. He said, "The Lord is
the God worshiped by Abraham, Isaac,
and Jacob."[s] 38 So the Lord isn't the
God of the dead, but of the living. This
means that everyone is alive as far as
God is concerned.
39 Some of the teachers of the Law of
Moses said, "Teacher, you have given a
good answer!" 40 From then on, no one
dared to ask Jesus any questions.

About David's Son
(Matthew 22.41-46; Mark 12.35-37)

41 Jesus asked, "Why do people say that
the Messiah will be the son of King David?[t]
42 In the book of Psalms, David himself says,

'The Lord said to my Lord,
Sit at my right side[u]
43 until I make your enemies
into a footstool for you.'

44 David spoke of the Messiah as his Lord,
so how can the Messiah be his son?"

Jesus and the Teachers of the Law of Moses
(Matthew 23.1-36; Mark 12.38-40; Luke 11.37-54)

45 While everyone was listening to
Jesus, he said to his disciples:
46 Guard against the teachers of the
Law of Moses! They love to walk
around in long robes, and they like to
be greeted in the market. They want
the front seats in the meeting places
and the best seats at banquets. 47 But
they cheat widows out of their homes
and then pray long prayers just to
show off. These teachers will be punished most of all.

A Widow's Offering
(Mark 12.41-44)

21 Jesus looked up and saw some rich
people tossing their gifts into the
offering box. 2 He also saw a poor widow

[s]**20.37** *"The Lord is the God worshiped by Abraham, Isaac, and Jacob"*: Jesus argues that if God is worshiped by these three, they must be alive, because he is the God of the living. [t]**20.41** *the son of King David*: See the note at 18.38. [u]**20.42** *right side*: The place of power and honor.

20.27 Ac 23.8. **20.28** Dt 25.5, 6. **20.37** Ex 3.6. **20.42,43** Ps 110.1.

putting in two pennies. 3 And he said, "I
tell you that this poor woman has put in
more than all the others. 4 Everyone else
gave what they didn't need. But she is very
poor and gave everything she had."

The Temple Will Be Destroyed
(Matthew 24.1, 2; Mark 13.1, 2)

5 Some people were talking about the
beautiful stones used to build the temple
and about the gifts that had been placed in
it. Jesus said, 6 "Do you see these stones?
The time is coming when not one of them
will be left in place. They will all be
knocked down."

Warning about Trouble
(Matthew 24.3-14; Mark 13.3-13)

7 Some people asked, "Teacher, when
will all this happen? How can we know
when these things are about to take place?"
8 Jesus replied:

Don't be fooled by those who will
come and claim to be me. They will
say, "I am Christ!" and "Now is the
time!" But don't follow them. 9 When
you hear about wars and riots, don't be
afraid. These things will have to happen first, but that isn't the end.

10 Nations will go to war against
one another, and kingdoms will attack
each other. 11 There will be great
earthquakes, and in many places people will starve to death and suffer terrible diseases. All sorts of frightening
things will be seen in the sky.

12 Before all this happens, you will
be arrested and punished. You will be
tried in your meeting places and put in
jail. Because of me you will be placed
on trial before kings and governors.
13 But this will be your chance to tell
about your faith.

14 Don't worry about what you will
say to defend yourselves. 15 I will give
you the wisdom to know what to say.
None of your enemies will be able
to oppose you or to say that you are
wrong. 16 You will be betrayed by your
own parents, brothers, family, and
friends. Some of you will even be
killed. 17 Because of me, you will be
hated by everyone. 18 But don't worry![v]
19 You will be saved by being faithful
to me.

Jerusalem Will Be Destroyed
(Matthew 24.15-21; Mark 13.14-19)

20 When you see Jerusalem surrounded by soldiers, you will know that
it will soon be destroyed. 21 If you are
living in Judea at that time, run to the
mountains. If you are in the city, leave
it. And if you are out in the country,
don't go back into the city. 22 This time
of punishment is what is written about
in the Scriptures. 23 It will be an awful
time for women who are expecting babies or nursing young children! Everywhere in the land people will suffer
horribly and be punished. 24 Some of
them will be killed by swords. Others
will be carried off to foreign countries.
Jerusalem will be overrun by foreign
nations until their time comes to
an end.

When the Son of Man Appears
(Matthew 24.29-31; Mark 13.24-27)

25 Strange things will happen to the
sun, moon, and stars. The nations on
earth will be afraid of the roaring sea
and tides, and they won't know what to
do. 26 People will be so frightened that
they will faint because of what is happening to the world. Every power in
the sky will be shaken.[w] 27 Then the
Son of Man will be seen, coming in a
cloud with great power and glory.
28 When all of this starts happening,
stand up straight and be brave. You
will soon be set free.

[v] **21.18** *But don't worry*: The Greek text has "Not a hair of your head will be lost," which means, "There's no need to worry." [w] **21.26** *Every power in the sky will be shaken*: In ancient times people thought that the stars were spiritual powers.

21.7 2 Esd 4.51—5.19. **21.14,15** Lk 12.11, 12. **21.22** Ho 9.7. **21.25** Is 13.10; Ez 32.7; Jl 2.31; Rev 6.12, 13. **21.27** Dn 7.13; Rev 1.7.

A Lesson from a Fig Tree
(Matthew 24.32-35; Mark 13.28-31)

29 Then Jesus told them a story:
When you see a fig tree or any
other tree 30 putting out leaves, you
know that summer will soon come.
31 So, when you see these things happening, you know that God's kingdom
will soon be here. 32 You can be sure
that some of the people of this generation will still be alive when all of
this takes place. 33 The sky and the
earth won't last forever, but my words
will.

A Warning

34 Don't spend all of your time
thinking about eating or drinking or
worrying about life. If you do, the final
day will suddenly catch you 35 like a
trap. That day will surprise everyone
on earth. 36 Watch out and keep praying that you can escape all that is going to happen and that the Son of Man
will be pleased with you.
37 Jesus taught in the temple each day,
and he spent each night on the Mount of
Olives. 38 Everyone got up early and came
to the temple to hear him teach.

A Plot To Kill Jesus
(Matthew 26.1-5, 14, 16;
Mark 14.1, 2, 10, 11; John 11.45-53)

22 The Festival of Thin Bread, also
called Passover, was near. 2 The
chief priests and the teachers of the Law of
Moses were looking for a way to get rid of
Jesus, because they were afraid of what the
people might do. 3 Then Satan entered the
heart of Judas Iscariot,[x] who was one of
the twelve apostles.
4 Judas went to talk with the chief
priests and the officers of the temple police
about how he could help them arrest Jesus.
5 They were very pleased and offered to pay
Judas some money. 6 He agreed and started
looking for a good chance to betray Jesus
when the crowds were not around.

Jesus Eats with His Disciples
(Matthew 26.17-25; Mark 14.12-21;
John 13.21-30)

7 The day had come for the Festival of
Thin Bread, and it was time to kill the
Passover lambs. 8 So Jesus said to Peter
and John, "Go and prepare the Passover
meal for us to eat."
9 But they asked, "Where do you want
us to prepare it?"
10 Jesus told them, "As you go into the
city, you will meet a man carrying a jar of
water.[y] Follow him into the house 11 and
say to the owner, 'Our teacher wants to
know where he can eat the Passover meal
with his disciples.' 12 The owner will take
you upstairs and show you a large room
ready for you to use. Prepare the meal
there."
13 Peter and John left. They found everything just as Jesus had told them, and they
prepared the Passover meal.

The Lord's Supper
(Matthew 26.26-30; Mark 14.22-26;
1 Corinthians 11.23-25)

14 When the time came for Jesus and
the apostles to eat, 15 he said to them, "I
have very much wanted to eat this Passover
meal with you before I suffer. 16 I tell you
that I will not eat another Passover meal
until it is finally eaten in God's kingdom."
17 Jesus took a cup of wine in his hands
and gave thanks to God. Then he told the
apostles, "Take this wine and share it with
each other. 18 I tell you that I will not drink
any more wine until God's kingdom
comes."
19 Jesus took some bread in his hands
and gave thanks for it. He broke the bread
and handed it to his apostles. Then he said,
"This is my body, which is given for you.
Eat this as a way of remembering me!"
20 After the meal he took another cup of
wine in his hands. Then he said, "This is
my blood. It is poured out for you, and with
it God makes his new agreement. 21 The
one who will betray me is here at the table
with me! 22 The Son of Man will die in

[x]**22.3** *Iscariot*: See the note at 6.16. [y]**22.10** *a man carrying a jar of water*: A male slave carrying water would probably mean that the family was rich.

21.37 Lk 19.47. **22.1** Ex 12.1-27. **22.20** Jr 31.31-34. **22.21** Ps 41.9.

the way that has been decided for him, but it will be terrible for the one who betrays him!"

23 Then the apostles started arguing about who would ever do such a thing.

An Argument about Greatness

24 The apostles got into an argument about which one of them was the greatest. 25 So Jesus told them:

Foreign kings order their people around, and powerful rulers call themselves everyone's friends.[z] 26 But don't be like them. The most important one of you should be like the least important, and your leader should be like a servant. 27 Who do people think is the greatest, a person who is served or one who serves? Isn't it the one who is served? But I have been with you as a servant.

28 You have stayed with me in all my troubles. 29 So I will give you the right to rule as kings, just as my Father has given me the right to rule as a king. 30 You will eat and drink with me in my kingdom, and you will each sit on a throne to judge the twelve tribes of Israel.

Jesus' Disciples Will Be Tested

(Matthew 26.31-35; Mark 14.27-31; John 13.36-38)

31 Jesus said, "Simon, listen to me! Satan has demanded the right to test each one of you, as a farmer does when he separates wheat from the husks.[a] 32 But Simon, I have prayed that your faith will be strong. And when you have come back to me, help the others."

33 Peter said, "Lord, I am ready to go with you to jail and even to die with you."

34 Jesus replied, "Peter, I tell you that before a rooster crows tomorrow morning, you will say three times that you don't know me."

Moneybags, Traveling Bags, and Swords

35 Jesus asked his disciples, "When I sent you out without a moneybag or a traveling bag or sandals, did you need anything?"

"No!" they answered.

36 Jesus told them, "But now, if you have a moneybag, take it with you. Also take a traveling bag, and if you don't have a sword,[b] sell some of your clothes and buy one. 37 Do this because the Scriptures say, 'He was considered a criminal.' This was written about me, and it will soon come true."

38 The disciples said, "Lord, here are two swords!"

"Enough of that!" Jesus replied.

Jesus Prays

(Matthew 26.36-46; Mark 14.32-42)

39 Jesus went out to the Mount of Olives, as he often did, and his disciples went with him. 40 When they got there, he told them, "Pray that you won't be tested."

41 Jesus walked on a little way before he knelt down and prayed, 42 "Father, if you will, please don't make me suffer by having me drink from this cup.[c] But do what you want, and not what I want."

43 Then an angel from heaven came to help him. 44 Jesus was in great pain and prayed so sincerely that his sweat fell to the ground like drops of blood.[d]

45 Jesus got up from praying and went over to his disciples. They were asleep and worn out from being so sad. 46 He said to them, "Why are you asleep? Wake up and pray that you won't be tested."

[z]**22.25** *everyone's friends*: This translates a Greek word that rulers sometimes used as a title for themselves or for special friends. [a]**22.31** *separates wheat from the husks*: See the note at 3.17. [b]**22.36** *moneybag . . . traveling bag . . . sword*: These were things that someone would take on a dangerous journey. Jesus was telling his disciples to be ready for anything that might happen. They seem to have understood what he meant (see 22.49-51). [c]**22.42** *having me drink from this cup*: In the Scriptures "to drink from a cup" sometimes means to suffer. [d]**22.43,44** *Then an angel . . . like drops of blood*: Verses 43, 44 are not in some manuscripts.

22.24 Mt 18.1; Mk 9.34; Lk 9.46. **22.26** Mt 23.11; Mk 9.35. **22.25,26** Mt 20.25-27; Mk 10.42-44. **22.27** Jn 13.12-15. **22.30** Mt 19.28. **22.35** Mt 10.9, 10; Mk 6.8, 9; Lk 9.3; 10.4. **22.37** Is 53.12.

Jesus Is Arrested

(Matthew 26.47-56; Mark 14.43-50; John 18.3-11)

47 While Jesus was still speaking, a crowd came up. It was led by Judas, one of the twelve apostles. He went over to Jesus and greeted him with a kiss.[e]

48 Jesus asked Judas, "Are you betraying the Son of Man with a kiss?"

49 When Jesus' disciples saw what was about to happen, they asked, "Lord, should we attack them with a sword?" 50 One of the disciples even struck at the high priest's servant with his sword and cut off the servant's right ear.

51 "Enough of that!" Jesus said. Then he touched the servant's ear and healed it.

52 Jesus spoke to the chief priests, the temple police, and the leaders who had come to arrest him. He said, "Why do you come out with swords and clubs and treat me like a criminal? 53 I was with you every day in the temple, and you didn't arrest me. But this is your time, and darkness[f] is in control."

Peter Says He Doesn't Know Jesus

(Matthew 26.57, 58, 67-75; Mark 14.53, 54, 66-72; John 18.12-18, 25-27)

54 Jesus was arrested and led away to the house of the high priest, while Peter followed at a distance. 55 Some people built a fire in the middle of the courtyard and were sitting around it. Peter sat there with them, 56 and a servant girl saw him. Then after she had looked at him carefully, she said, "This man was with Jesus!"

57 Peter said, "Woman, I don't even know that man!"

58 A little later someone else saw Peter and said, "You are one of them!"

"No, I'm not!" Peter replied.

59 About an hour later another man insisted, "This man must have been with Jesus. They both come from Galilee."

60 Peter replied, "I don't know what you are talking about!" Right then, while Peter was still speaking, a rooster crowed.

61 The Lord turned and looked at Peter. And Peter remembered that the Lord had said, "Before a rooster crows tomorrow morning, you will say three times that you don't know me." 62 Then Peter went out and cried hard.

63 The men who were guarding Jesus made fun of him and beat him. 64 They put a blindfold on him and said, "Tell us who struck you!" 65 They kept on insulting Jesus in many other ways.

Jesus Is Questioned by the Council

(Matthew 26.59-66; Mark 14.55-64; John 18.19-24)

66 At daybreak the nation's leaders, the chief priests, and the teachers of the Law of Moses got together and brought Jesus before their council. 67 They said, "Tell us! Are you the Messiah?"

Jesus replied, "If I said so, you wouldn't believe me. 68 And if I asked you a question, you wouldn't answer. 69 But from now on, the Son of Man will be seated at the right side of God All-Powerful."

70 Then they asked, "Are you the Son of God?"[g]

Jesus answered, "You say I am!"[h]

71 They replied, "Why do we need more witnesses? He said it himself!"

Pilate Questions Jesus

(Matthew 27.1, 2, 11-14; Mark 15.1-5; John 18.28-38)

23 Everyone in the council got up and led Jesus off to Pilate. 2 They started accusing him and said, "We caught this man trying to get our people to riot and to stop paying taxes to the Emperor. He also claims that he is the Messiah, our king."

3 Pilate asked Jesus, "Are you the king of the Jews?"

"Those are your words," Jesus answered.

4 Pilate told the chief priests and

[e]**22.47** *greeted him with a kiss*: It was the custom for people to greet each other with a kiss on the cheek. [f]**22.53** *darkness*: Darkness stands for the power of the devil. [g]**22.70** *Son of God*: This was one of the titles used for the kings of Israel. [h]**22.70** *You say I am*: Or "That's what you say."

22.53 Lk 19.47; 21.37.

the crowd, "I don't find him guilty of anything."

5 But they all kept on saying, "He has been teaching and causing trouble all over Judea. He started in Galilee and has now come all the way here."

Jesus Is Brought before Herod

6 When Pilate heard this, he asked, "Is this man from Galilee?" 7 After Pilate learned that Jesus came from the region ruled by Herod,[i] he sent him to Herod, who was in Jerusalem at that time.

8 For a long time Herod had wanted to see Jesus and was very happy because he finally had this chance. He had heard many things about Jesus and hoped to see him work a miracle.

9 Herod asked him a lot of questions, but Jesus did not answer. 10 Then the chief priests and the teachers of the Law of Moses stood up and accused him of all kinds of bad things.

11 Herod and his soldiers made fun of Jesus and insulted him. They put a fine robe on him and sent him back to Pilate. 12 That same day Herod and Pilate became friends, even though they had been enemies before this.

The Death Sentence

(Matthew 27.15-26; Mark 15.6-15; John 18.39—19.16)

13 Pilate called together the chief priests, the leaders, and the people. 14 He told them, "You brought Jesus to me and said he was a troublemaker. But I have questioned him here in front of you, and I have not found him guilty of anything that you say he has done. 15 Herod didn't find him guilty either and sent him back. This man doesn't deserve to be put to death! 16-17 I will just have him beaten with a whip and set free."[j]

18 But the whole crowd shouted, "Kill Jesus! Give us Barabbas!" 19 Now Barabbas was in jail because he had started a riot in the city and had murdered someone.

20 Pilate wanted to set Jesus free, so he spoke again to the crowds. 21 But they kept shouting, "Nail him to a cross! Nail him to a cross!"

22 Pilate spoke to them a third time, "But what crime has he done? I have not found him guilty of anything for which he should be put to death. I will have him beaten with a whip and set free."

23 The people kept on shouting as loud as they could for Jesus to be put to death. 24 Finally, Pilate gave in. 25 He freed the man who was in jail for rioting and murder, because he was the one the crowd wanted to be set free. Then Pilate handed Jesus over for them to do what they wanted with him.

Jesus Is Nailed to a Cross

(Matthew 27.31-44; Mark 15.21-32; John 19.17-27)

26 As Jesus was being led away, some soldiers grabbed hold of a man from Cyrene named Simon. He was coming in from the fields, but they put the cross on him and made him carry it behind Jesus.

27 A large crowd was following Jesus, and in the crowd a lot of women were crying and weeping for him. 28 Jesus turned to the women and said:

> Women of Jerusalem, don't cry for me! Cry for yourselves and for your children. 29 Someday people will say, "Women who never had children are really fortunate!" 30 At that time everyone will say to the mountains, "Fall on us!" They will say to the hills, "Hide us!" 31 If this can happen when the wood is green, what do you think will happen when it is dry?[k]

32 Two criminals were led out to be put to death with Jesus. 33 When the soldiers came to the place called "The Skull,"[l] they nailed Jesus to a cross. They also nailed the

[i] **23.7** *Herod*: Herod Antipas, the son of Herod the Great. [j] **23.16,17** *set free*: Some manuscripts add, "Pilate said this, because at every Passover he was supposed to set one prisoner free for the Jewish people." [k] **23.31** *If this can happen when the wood is green, what do you think will happen when it is dry*: This saying probably means, "If this can happen to an innocent person, what do you think will happen to one who is guilty?" [l] **23.33** *"The Skull"*: The place was probably given this name because it was near a large rock in the shape of a human skull.

23.30 Ho 10.8; Rev 6.16.

Jesus blesses little children *Mark 10.13-16*

Jesus and the Samaritan woman *John 4.3-26*

The miracle of the loaves and fish

John 6.1-15

The Good Samaritan *Luke 10.25-37*

two criminals to crosses, one on each side
of Jesus.
34-35 Jesus said, "Father, forgive these
people! They don't know what they're
doing."[m]
While the crowd stood there watching
Jesus, the soldiers gambled for his clothes.
The leaders insulted him by saying, "He
saved others. Now he should save himself,
if he really is God's chosen Messiah!"
36 The soldiers made fun of Jesus and
brought him some wine. 37 They said, "If
you are the king of the Jews, save yourself!"
38 Above him was a sign that said, "This
is the King of the Jews."
39 One of the criminals hanging there
also insulted Jesus by saying, "Aren't you
the Messiah? Save yourself and save us!"
40 But the other criminal told the first
one off, "Don't you fear God? Aren't you
getting the same punishment as this man?
41 We got what was coming to us, but he
didn't do anything wrong." 42 Then he said
to Jesus, "Remember me when you come
into power!"
43 Jesus replied, "I promise that today
you will be with me in paradise."[n]

The Death of Jesus
(Matthew 27.45-56; Mark 15.33-41; John 19.28-30)

44 Around noon the sky turned dark and
stayed that way until the middle of the afternoon. 45 The sun stopped shining, and
the curtain in the temple[o] split down the
middle. 46 Jesus shouted, "Father, I put myself in your hands!" Then he died.
47 When the Roman officer saw what
had happened, he praised God and said,
"Jesus must really have been a good man!"
48 A crowd had gathered to see the terrible sight. Then after they had seen it, they
felt brokenhearted and went home. 49 All of
Jesus' close friends and the women who
had come with him from Galilee stood at a
distance and watched.

Jesus Is Buried
(Matthew 27.57-61; Mark 15.42-47; John 19.38-42)

50-51 There was a man named Joseph,
who was from Arimathea in Judea. Joseph
was a good and honest man, and he was
eager for God's kingdom to come. He was
also a member of the council, but he did
not agree with what they had decided.
52 Joseph went to Pilate and asked for
Jesus' body. 53 He took the body down from
the cross and wrapped it in fine cloth.
Then he put it in a tomb that had been cut
out of solid rock and had never been used.
54 It was Friday, and the Sabbath was about
to begin.[p]
55 The women who had come with Jesus
from Galilee followed Joseph and watched
how Jesus' body was placed in the tomb.
56 Then they went to prepare some sweet-
smelling spices for his burial. But on the
Sabbath they rested, as the Law of Moses
commands.

Jesus Is Alive
(Matthew 28.1-10; Mark 16.1-8; John 20.1-10)

24 Very early on Sunday morning the
women went to the tomb, carrying
the spices that they had prepared. 2 When
they found the stone rolled away from the
entrance, 3 they went in. But they did not
find the body of the Lord[q] Jesus, 4 and they
did not know what to think.
Suddenly two men in shining white
clothes stood beside them. 5 The women
were afraid and bowed to the ground. But

[m]**23.34,35** *Jesus said, "Father, forgive these people! They don't know what they're doing."*: These words are not in some manuscripts. [n]**23.43** *paradise*: In the Greek translation of the Old Testament, this word is used for the Garden of Eden. In New Testament times it was sometimes used for the place where God's people are happy and at rest, as they wait for the final judgment.

[o]**23.45** *curtain in the temple*: There were two curtains in the temple. One was at the entrance, and the other separated the holy place from the most holy place that the Jewish people thought of as God's home on earth. The second curtain is probably the one which is meant. [p]**23.54** *the Sabbath was about to begin*: The Sabbath begins at sunset on Friday. [q]**24.3** *the Lord*: These words are not in some manuscripts.

23.34,35 **a** Ps 22.18; **b** Ps. 22.7. **23.36** Ps 69.21. **23.45** Ex 26.31-33.
23.46 Ps 31.5. **23.49** Lk 8.2, 3. **23.56** Ex 20.10; Dt 5.14.

the men said, "Why are you looking in the
place of the dead for someone who is alive?
6 Jesus isn't here! He has been raised from
death. Remember that while he was still in
Galilee, he told you, 7 'The Son of Man will
be handed over to sinners who will nail
him to a cross. But three days later he will
rise to life.' " 8 Then they remembered
what Jesus had said.
9-10 Mary Magdalene, Joanna, Mary the
mother of James, and some other women
were the ones who had gone to the tomb.
When they returned, they told the eleven
apostles and the others what had happened. 11 The apostles thought it was all
nonsense, and they would not believe.
12 But Peter ran to the tomb. And when
he stooped down and looked in, he saw
only the burial clothes. Then he returned,
wondering what had happened.[r]

Jesus Appears to Two Disciples
(Mark 16.12, 13)

13 That same day two of Jesus' disciples
were going to the village of Emmaus, which
was about seven miles from Jerusalem.
14 As they were talking and thinking about
what had happened, 15 Jesus came near
and started walking along beside them.
16 But they did not know who he was.
17 Jesus asked them, "What were you
talking about as you walked along?"
The two of them stood there looking
sad and gloomy. 18 Then the one named
Cleopas asked Jesus, "Are you the only person from Jerusalem who didn't know what
was happening there these last few days?"
19 "What do you mean?" Jesus asked.
They answered:
Those things that happened to
Jesus from Nazareth. By what he did
and said he showed that he was a powerful prophet, who pleased God and all
the people. 20 Then the chief priests
and our leaders had him arrested and
sentenced to die on a cross. 21 We had
hoped that he would be the one to set
Israel free! But it has already been
three days since all this happened.
22 Some women in our group surprised us. They had gone to the tomb
early in the morning, 23 but did not
find the body of Jesus. They came
back, saying that they had seen a vision of angels who told them that he is
alive. 24 Some men from our group
went to the tomb and found it just as
the women had said. But they didn't
see Jesus either.
25 Then Jesus asked the two disciples,
"Why can't you understand? How can you
be so slow to believe all that the prophets
said? 26 Didn't you know that the Messiah
would have to suffer before he was given
his glory?" 27 Jesus then explained everything written about himself in the Scriptures, beginning with the Law of Moses and
the Books of the Prophets.[s]
28 When the two of them came near the
village where they were going, Jesus
seemed to be going farther. 29 They begged
him, "Stay with us! It's already late, and
the sun is going down." So Jesus went into
the house to stay with them.
30 After Jesus sat down to eat, he took
some bread. He blessed it and broke it.
Then he gave it to them. 31 At once they
knew who he was, but he disappeared.
32 They said to each other, "When he
talked with us along the road and explained
the Scriptures to us, didn't it warm our
hearts?" 33 So they got right up and returned to Jerusalem.
The two disciples found the eleven
apostles and the others gathered together.
34 And they learned from the group that the
Lord was really alive and had appeared to
Peter. 35 Then the disciples from Emmaus
told what happened on the road and how
they knew he was the Lord when he broke
the bread.

What Jesus' Followers Must Do
(Matthew 28.16-20; Mark 16.14-18; John 20.19-23; Acts 1.6-8)

36 While Jesus' disciples were talking
about what had happened, Jesus appeared
and greeted them. 37 They were frightened

[r] **24.12** *what had happened*: Verse 12 is not in some manuscripts. [s] **24.27** *the Law of Moses and the Books of the Prophets*: See the note at 16.16.

24.6,7 Mt 16.21; 17.22, 23; 20.18, 19; Mk 8.31; 9.31; 10.33, 34; Lk 9.22; 18.31-33.

and terrified because they thought they
were seeing a ghost.
38 But Jesus said, "Why are you so
frightened? Why do you doubt? 39 Look at
my hands and my feet and see who I am!
Touch me and find out for yourselves.
Ghosts don't have flesh and bones as you
see I have."
40 After Jesus said this, he showed them
his hands and his feet. 41 The disciples
were so glad and amazed that they could
not believe it. Jesus then asked them, "Do
you have something to eat?" 42 They gave
him a piece of baked fish. 43 He took it and
ate it as they watched.
44 Jesus said to them, "While I was still
with you, I told you that everything written
about me in the Law of Moses, the Books
of the Prophets, and in the Psalms[t] had to
happen."
45 Then he helped them understand the
Scriptures. 46 He told them:

The Scriptures say that the Messiah
must suffer, then three days later he
will rise from death. 47 They also say
that all people of every nation must be
told in my name to turn to God, in order to be forgiven. So beginning in
Jerusalem, 48 you must tell everything
that has happened. 49 I will send you
the one my Father has promised,[u] but
you must stay in the city until you are
given power from heaven.

Jesus Returns to Heaven
(Mark 16.19, 20; Acts 1.9-11)

50 Jesus led his disciples out to Bethany,
where he raised his hands and blessed
them. 51 As he was doing this, he left and
was taken up to heaven.[v] 52 After his disciples had worshiped him,[w] they returned to
Jerusalem and were very happy. 53 They
spent their time in the temple, praising God.

[t]**24.44** *Psalms*: The Jewish Scriptures were made up of three parts: (1) the Law of Moses, (2) the Books of the Prophets, (3) and the Writings, which included the Psalms. Sometimes the Scriptures were just called the Law or the Law (of Moses) and the Books of the Prophets. [u]**24.49** *the one my Father has promised*: Jesus means the Holy Spirit. [v]**24.51** *and was taken up to heaven*: These words are not in some manuscripts. [w]**24.52** *After his disciples had worshiped him*: These words are not in some manuscripts.

24.49 Ac 1.4. **24.50,51** Si 50.20; Ac 1.9-11.

JOHN

ABOUT THIS BOOK

Who is Jesus Christ? John answers this question in the first chapter of his Gospel. Using the words of an early Christian hymn, he calls Jesus the "Word" by which God created everything and by which he gave life to everyone (1.3, 4). He shows how John the Baptist announced Jesus' coming, "Here is the Lamb of God who takes away the sin of the world" (1.29). When Philip met Jesus he knew Jesus was "the one that Moses and the Prophets wrote about" (1.45). And, in the words of Nathanael, Jesus is "the Son of God and the King of Israel" (1.49).

In John's Gospel we learn a lot about who Jesus is by observing what he said and did when he was with other people. These include a Samaritan woman who received Jesus' offer of life-giving water, a woman who had been caught in sin, his friend Lazarus who was brought back to life by Jesus, and his follower Thomas who doubted that Jesus was raised from death. Jesus also refers to himself as "I am," a phrase which translates the most holy name for God in the Hebrew Scriptures. He uses this name for himself when he makes his claim to be the life-giving bread, the light of the world, the good shepherd, and the true vine.

Jesus performs seven miracles that are more than miracles. Each of them is a "sign" that tells us something about Jesus as the Son of God. For example, by healing a lame man (5.1-8), Jesus shows that he is just like his Father, who never stops working (5.17). This sign also teaches that the Son does only what he sees his Father doing (5.19), and that like the Father "the Son gives life to anyone he wants to" (5.21).

The way John tells the story of Jesus is quite different from the other three Gospels. Here, Jesus has long conversations with people about who he is and what God sent him to do. In these conversations he teaches many important things—for example, that he is the way, the truth and the life.

Why did John write? John himself tells us, "So that you will put your faith in Jesus as the Messiah and the Son of God" (20.31). How is this possible? Jesus answers that question in his words to Nicodemus:

> *"God loved the people of this world so much that he gave his only Son, so that everyone who has faith in him will have eternal life and never really die."*
>
> *(3.16)*

A QUICK LOOK AT THIS BOOK

- A Hymn in Praise of the Word (1.1-18)
- The Message of John the Baptist (1.19-34)
- Jesus Chooses His First Disciples (1.35-51)
- Jesus' Seven Special Miracles (2.1—12.50)
- Jesus' Last Week: His Trial and Death (13.1—19.42)
- Jesus Is Alive (20.1-10)
- Jesus Appears to His Disciples (20.11—21.25)

The Word of Life

1 In the beginning was the one
who is called the Word.
The Word was with God
and was truly God.
2 From the very beginning
the Word was with God.
3 And with this Word,
God created all things.
Nothing was made
without the Word.
Everything that was created
4 received its life from him,
and his life gave light
to everyone.
5 The light keeps shining
in the dark,
and darkness has never
put it out.[a]
6 God sent a man named John,
7 who came to tell
about the light
and to lead all people
to have faith.
8 John wasn't that light.
He came only to tell
about the light.

9 The true light that shines
on everyone
was coming into the world.
10 The Word was in the world,
but no one knew him,
though God had made the world
with his Word.
11 He came into his own world,
but his own nation
did not welcome him.
12 Yet some people accepted him
and put their faith in him.
So he gave them the right
to be the children of God.
13 They were not God's children
by nature or because
of any human desires.
God himself was the one
who made them his children.

14 The Word became
a human being
and lived here with us.
We saw his true glory,
the glory of the only Son
of the Father.
From him all the kindness
and all the truth of God
have come down to us.

15 John spoke about him and shouted,
"This is the one I told you would come! He
is greater than I am, because he was alive
before I was born."
16 Because of all that the Son is, we
have been given one blessing after another.[b]
17 The Law was given by Moses,
but Jesus Christ brought us undeserved
kindness and truth.
18 No one has ever
seen God. The only Son, who is truly God
and is closest to the Father, has shown us
what God is like.

John the Baptist Tells about Jesus

(Matthew 3.1-12; Mark 1.1-8; Luke 3.15-17)

19-20 The Jewish leaders in Jerusalem
sent priests and temple helpers to ask John
who he was. He told them plainly, "I am
not the Messiah."
21 Then when they asked
him if he were Elijah, he said, "No, I am
not!" And when they asked if he were the
Prophet,[c] he also said "No!"
22 Finally, they said, "Who are you then?
We have to give an answer to the ones who
sent us. Tell us who you are!"
23 John answered in the words of the
prophet Isaiah, "I am only someone shouting in the desert, 'Get the road ready for
the Lord!' "
24 Some Pharisees had also been sent to
John.
25 They asked him, "Why are you
baptizing people, if you are not the Messiah
or Elijah or the Prophet?"
26 John told them, "I use water to
baptize people. But here with you is
someone you don't know.
27 Even though I
came first, I am not good enough to untie
his sandals."
28 John said this as he was

[a] **1.5** *put it out*: Or "understood it." [b] **1.16** *one blessing after another*: Or "one blessing in place of another." [c] **1.21** *the Prophet*: Many of the Jewish people expected God to send them a prophet who would be like Moses, but with even greater power (see Deuteronomy 18.15, 18).

1.6 Mt 3.1; Mk 1.4; Lk 3.1, 2. **1.21 a** Ml 4.5; **b** Dt 18.15, 18; Si 48.10, 11. **1.23** Is 40.3 (LXX).

baptizing east of the Jordan River in
Bethany.[d]

The Lamb of God

29 The next day, John saw Jesus coming
toward him and said:

Here is the Lamb of God who takes
away the sin of the world! 30 He is the
one I told you about when I said,
"Someone else will come. He is greater
than I am, because he was alive before
I was born." 31 I didn't know who he
was. But I came to baptize you with
water, so that everyone in Israel would
see him.

32 I was there and saw the Spirit
come down on him like a dove from
heaven. And the Spirit stayed on him.
33 Before this I didn't know who he
was. But the one who sent me to
baptize with water had told me, "You
will see the Spirit come down and
stay on someone. Then you will know
that he is the one who will baptize
with the Holy Spirit." 34 I saw this happen, and I tell you that he is the Son
of God.

The First Disciples of Jesus

35 The next day, John was there again,
and two of his followers were with him.
36 When he saw Jesus walking by, he said,
"Here is the Lamb of God!" 37 John's two
followers heard him, and they went with
Jesus.

38 When Jesus turned and saw them, he
asked, "What do you want?"

They answered, "Rabbi, where do you
live?" The Hebrew word "Rabbi" means
"Teacher."

39 Jesus replied, "Come and see!" It was
already about four o'clock in the afternoon
when they went with him and saw where
he lived. So they stayed on for the rest of
the day.

40 One of the two men who had heard
John and had gone with Jesus was Andrew, the brother of Simon Peter. 41 The
first thing Andrew did was to find his
brother and tell him, "We have found the
Messiah!" The Hebrew word "Messiah"
means the same as the Greek word
"Christ."

42 Andrew brought his brother to Jesus.
And when Jesus saw him, he said, "Simon
son of John, you will be called Cephas."
This name can be translated as "Peter."[e]

Jesus Chooses Philip and Nathanael

43-44 The next day Jesus decided to go to
Galilee. There he met Philip, who was from
Bethsaida, the hometown of Andrew
and Peter. Jesus said to Philip, "Come
with me."

45 Philip then found Nathanael and
said, "We have found the one that Moses
and the Prophets[f] wrote about. He is Jesus,
the son of Joseph from Nazareth."

46 Nathanael asked, "Can anything good
come from Nazareth?"

Philip answered, "Come and see."

47 When Jesus saw Nathanael coming
toward him, he said, "Here is a true descendant of our ancestor Israel. And he
isn't deceitful."[g]

48 "How do you know me?" Nathanael
asked.

Jesus answered, "Before Philip called
you, I saw you under the fig tree."

49 Nathanael said, "Rabbi, you are the
Son of God and the King of Israel!"

50 Jesus answered, "Did you believe me
just because I said that I saw you under the
fig tree? You will see something even
greater. 51 I tell you for certain that you will
see heaven open and God's angels going up
and coming down on the Son of Man."[h]

[d] **1.28** *Bethany*: An unknown village east of the Jordan with the same name as the village near Jerusalem. [e] **1.42** *Peter*: The Aramaic name "Cephas" and the Greek name "Peter" each mean "rock." [f] **1.45** *Moses and the Prophets*: The Jewish Scriptures, that is, the Old Testament. [g] **1.47** *Israel . . . isn't deceitful*: Israel (meaning "a man who wrestled with God" or "a prince of God") was the name that the Lord gave to Jacob (meaning "cheater" or "deceiver"), the famous ancestor of the Jewish people. [h] **1.51** *going up and coming down on the Son of Man*: When Jacob (see the note at verse 47) was running from his brother Esau, he had a dream in which he saw angels going up and down on a ladder from earth to heaven (see Genesis 32.22-32).

1.51 Gn 28.12.

Jesus at a Wedding in Cana

2 Three days later Mary, the mother of
Jesus, was at a wedding feast in the
village of Cana in Galilee. 2 Jesus and his
disciples had also been invited and were
there.
3 When the wine was all gone, Mary said
to Jesus, "They don't have any more wine."
4 Jesus replied, "Mother, my time hasn't
yet come![i] You must not tell me what
to do."
5 Mary then said to the servants, "Do
whatever Jesus tells you to do."
6 At the feast there were six stone water
jars that were used by the people for washing themselves in the way that their religion said they must. Each jar held about
twenty or thirty gallons. 7 Jesus told the
servants to fill them to the top with water.
Then after the jars had been filled, 8 he
said, "Now take some water and give it to
the man in charge of the feast."
The servants did as Jesus told them,
9 and the man in charge drank some of the
water that had now turned into wine. He
did not know where the wine had come
from, but the servants did. He called the
bridegroom over 10 and said, "The best
wine is always served first. Then after the
guests have had plenty, the other wine is
served. But you have kept the best until
last!"
11 This was Jesus' first miracle,[j] and he
did it in the village of Cana in Galilee.
There Jesus showed his glory, and his disciples put their faith in him. 12 After this, he
went with his mother, his brothers, and his
disciples to the town of Capernaum, where
they stayed for a few days.

Jesus in the Temple

*(Matthew 21.12, 13; Mark 11.15-17;
Luke 19.45, 46)*

13 Not long before the Jewish festival of
Passover, Jesus went to Jerusalem. 14 There
he found people selling cattle, sheep, and
doves in the temple. He also saw moneychangers sitting at their tables. 15 So he
took some rope and made a whip. Then he
chased everyone out of the temple, together with their sheep and cattle. He
turned over the tables of the moneychangers and scattered their coins.
16 Jesus said to the people who had
been selling doves, "Get those doves out of
here! Don't make my Father's house a
marketplace."
17 The disciples then remembered that
the Scriptures say, "My love for your house
burns in me like a fire."
18 The Jewish leaders asked Jesus,
"What miracle[j] will you work to show us
why you have done this?"
19 "Destroy this temple," Jesus answered, "and in three days I will build it
again!"
20 The leaders replied, "It took forty-six
years to build this temple. What makes you
think you can rebuild it in three days?"
21 But Jesus was talking about his body
as a temple. 22 And when he was raised
from death, his disciples remembered what
he had told them. Then they believed the
Scriptures and the words of Jesus.

Jesus Knows What People Are Like

23 In Jerusalem during Passover many
people put their faith in Jesus, because
they saw him work miracles.[j] 24 But Jesus
knew what was in their hearts, and he
would not let them have power over him.
25 No one had to tell him what people were
like. He already knew.

Jesus and Nicodemus

3 There was a man named Nicodemus
who was a Pharisee and a Jewish
leader. 2 One night he went to Jesus and
said, "Sir, we know that God has sent you
to teach us. You could not work these miracles, unless God were with you."
3 Jesus replied, "I tell you for certain

[i]**2.4** *my time hasn't yet come*: The time when the true glory of Jesus would be seen, and he would be recognized as God's Son (see 12.23). [j]**2.11,18,23** *miracle*: The Greek text has "sign." In the Gospel of John the word "sign" is used for the miracle itself and as a way of pointing to Jesus as the Son of God.

2.12 Mt 4.13. **2.13** Ex 12.1-27. **2.17** Ps 69.9. **2.19** Mt 26.61; 27.40; Mk 14.58; 15.29.

that you must be born from above[k] before
you can see God's kingdom!"
4 Nicodemus asked, "How can a grown
man ever be born a second time?"
5 Jesus answered:
I tell you for certain that before you
can get into God's kingdom, you must
be born not only by water, but by the
Spirit. 6 Humans give life to their children. Yet only God's Spirit can change
you into a child of God. 7 Don't be surprised when I say that you must be
born from above. 8 Only God's Spirit
gives new life. The Spirit is like the
wind that blows wherever it wants to.
You can hear the wind, but you don't
know where it comes from or where it
is going.
9 "How can this be?" Nicodemus asked.
10 Jesus replied:
How can you be a teacher of Israel
and not know these things? 11 I tell
you for certain that we know what we
are talking about because we have
seen it ourselves. But none of you will
accept what we say. 12 If you don't believe when I talk to you about things
on earth, how can you possibly believe
if I talk to you about things in heaven?
13 No one has gone up to heaven
except the Son of Man, who came
down from there. 14 And the Son of
Man must be lifted up, just as that
metal snake was lifted up by Moses in
the desert.[l] 15 Then everyone who has
faith in the Son of Man will have eternal life.
16 God loved the people of this
world so much that he gave his only
Son, so that everyone who has faith in
him will have eternal life and never really die. 17 God did not send his Son
into the world to condemn its people.
He sent him to save them! 18 No one
who has faith in God's Son will be condemned. But everyone who doesn't
have faith in him has already been
condemned for not having faith in
God's only Son.
19 The light has come into the
world, and people who do evil things
are judged guilty because they love the
dark more than the light. 20 People
who do evil hate the light and won't
come to the light, because it clearly
shows what they have done. 21 But
everyone who lives by the truth will
come to the light, because they want
others to know that God is really the
one doing what they do.

Jesus and John the Baptist

22 Later, Jesus and his disciples went to
Judea, where he stayed with them for a
while and was baptizing people.
23-24 John had not yet been put in jail.
He was at Aenon near Salim, where there
was a lot of water, and people were coming
there for John to baptize them.
25 John's followers got into an argument
with a Jewish man[m] about a ceremony of
washing.[n] 26 They went to John and said,
"Rabbi, you spoke about a man when you
were with him east of the Jordan. He is
now baptizing people, and everyone is going to him."
27 John replied:
No one can do anything unless God
in heaven allows it. 28 You surely remember how I told you that I am not
the Messiah. I am only the one sent
ahead of him.
29 At a wedding the groom is the
one who gets married. The best man is
glad just to be there and to hear the
groom's voice. That's why I am so glad.
30 Jesus must become more important,
while I become less important.

[k]**3.3** *from above*: Or "in a new way." The same Greek word is used in verses 7, 31. [l]**3.14** *just as that metal snake was lifted up by Moses in the desert*: When the Lord punished the people of Israel by sending snakes to bite them, he told Moses to hold a metal snake up on a pole. Everyone who looked at the snake was cured of the snake bites (see Numbers 21.4-9). [m]**3.25** *a Jewish man*: Some manuscripts have "some Jewish men." [n]**3.25** *about a ceremony of washing*: The Jewish people had many rules about washing themselves and their dishes, in order to make themselves fit to worship God.

3.12 Ws 9.16, 17. **3.13** Ba 3.29. **3.14** Nu 21.9; Ws 16.5-7. **3.23,24** Mt 14.3, 4; Mk 6.17, 18; Lk 3.19, 20. **3.28** Jn 1.19, 20.

The One Who Comes from Heaven

31 God's Son comes from heaven and is above all others. Everyone who comes from the earth belongs to the earth and speaks about earthly things. The one who comes from heaven is above all others. 32 He speaks about what he has seen and heard, and yet no one believes him. 33 But everyone who does believe him has shown that God is truthful. 34 The Son was sent to speak God's message, and he has been given the full power of God's Spirit.

35 The Father loves the Son and has given him everything. 36 Everyone who has faith in the Son has eternal life. But no one who rejects him will ever share in that life, and God will be angry with them forever.

4 Jesus knew that the Pharisees had heard that he was winning and baptizing more followers than John was. 2 But Jesus' disciples were really the ones doing the baptizing, and not Jesus himself.

Jesus and the Samaritan Woman

3 Jesus left Judea and started for Galilee again. 4 This time he had to go through Samaria, 5 and on his way he came to the town of Sychar. It was near the field that Jacob had long ago given to his son Joseph. 6-8 The well that Jacob had dug was still there, and Jesus sat down beside it because he was tired from traveling. It was noon, and after Jesus' disciples had gone into town to buy some food, a Samaritan woman came to draw water from the well.

Jesus asked her, "Would you please give me a drink of water?"

9 "You are a Jew," she replied, "and I am a Samaritan woman. How can you ask me for a drink of water when Jews and Samaritans won't have anything to do with each other?"[o]

10 Jesus answered, "You don't know what God wants to give you, and you don't know who is asking you for a drink. If you did, you would ask me for the water that gives life."

11 "Sir," the woman said, "you don't even have a bucket, and the well is deep. Where are you going to get this life-giving water? 12 Our ancestor Jacob dug this well for us, and his family and animals got water from it. Are you greater than Jacob?"

13 Jesus answered, "Everyone who drinks this water will get thirsty again. 14 But no one who drinks the water I give will ever be thirsty again. The water I give is like a flowing fountain that gives eternal life."

15 The woman replied, "Sir, please give me a drink of that water! Then I won't get thirsty and have to come to this well again."

16 Jesus told her, "Go and bring your husband."

17-18 The woman answered, "I don't have a husband."

"That's right," Jesus replied, "you're telling the truth. You don't have a husband. You have already been married five times, and the man you are now living with isn't your husband."

19 The woman said, "Sir, I can see that you are a prophet. 20 My ancestors worshiped on this mountain,[p] but you Jews say Jerusalem is the only place to worship."

21 Jesus said to her:

> Believe me, the time is coming when you won't worship the Father either on this mountain or in Jerusalem. 22 You Samaritans don't really know the one you worship. But we Jews do know the God we worship, and by using us, God will save the world. 23 But a time is coming, and it is already here! Even now the true worshipers are being led by the Spirit to worship the Father according to the truth. These are the ones the Father is seeking to worship him. 24 God is Spirit, and those who worship God must be led by the Spirit to worship him according to the truth.

[o]**4.9** *won't have anything to do with each other*: Or "won't use the same cups." The Samaritans lived in the land between Judea and Galilee. They worshiped God differently from the Jews and did not get along with them. [p]**4.20** *this mountain*: Mount Gerizim, near the city of Shechem.

3.35 Mt 11.27; Lk 10.22. **4.5** Gn 33.19; Js 24.32. **4.9** Ezra 4.1-5; Ne 4.1, 2.

25 The woman said, "I know that the
Messiah will come. He is the one we call
Christ. When he comes, he will explain
everything to us."

26 "I am that one," Jesus told her, "and I
am speaking to you now."

27 The disciples returned about this
time and were surprised to find Jesus talking with a woman. But none of them asked
him what he wanted or why he was talking
with her.

28 The woman left her water jar and ran
back into town. She said to the people,
29 "Come and see a man who told me
everything I have ever done! Could he be
the Messiah?" 30 Everyone in town went
out to see Jesus.

31 While this was happening, Jesus' disciples were saying to him, "Teacher, please
eat something."

32 But Jesus told them, "I have food that
you don't know anything about."

33 His disciples started asking each
other, "Has someone brought him something to eat?"

34 Jesus said:

My food is to do what God wants!
He is the one who sent me, and I must
finish the work that he gave me to do.
35 You may say that there are still four
months until harvest time. But I tell
you to look, and you will see that the
fields are ripe and ready to harvest.

36 Even now the harvest workers
are receiving their reward by gathering
a harvest that brings eternal life. Then
everyone who planted the seed and
everyone who harvests the crop will
celebrate together. 37 So the saying
proves true, "Some plant the seed, and
others harvest the crop." 38 I am sending you to harvest crops in fields where
others have done all the hard work.

39 A lot of Samaritans in that town put
their faith in Jesus because the woman had
said, "This man told me everything I have
ever done." 40 They came and asked him to
stay in their town, and he stayed on for two
days.

41 Many more Samaritans put their faith
in Jesus because of what they heard him
say. 42 They told the woman, "We no longer
have faith in Jesus just because of what you
told us. We have heard him ourselves, and
we are certain that he is the Savior of the
world!"

Jesus Heals an Official's Son

(Matthew 8.5-13; Luke 7.1-10)

43-44 Jesus had said, "Prophets are honored everywhere, except in their own country." Then two days later he left 45 and went
to Galilee. The people there welcomed
him, because they had gone to the festival
in Jerusalem and had seen everything he
had done.

46 While Jesus was in Galilee, he returned to the village of Cana, where he had
turned the water into wine. There was an
official in Capernaum whose son was sick.
47 And when the man heard that Jesus had
come from Judea, he went and begged him
to keep his son from dying.

48 Jesus told the official, "You won't
have faith unless you see miracles and
wonders!"

49 The man replied, "Lord, please come
before my son dies!"

50 Jesus then said, "Your son will live.
Go on home to him." The man believed
Jesus and started back home.

51 Some of the official's servants met
him along the road and told him, "Your son
is better!" 52 He asked them when the boy
got better, and they answered, "The fever
left him yesterday at one o'clock."

53 The boy's father realized that at one
o'clock the day before, Jesus had told him,
"Your son will live!" So the man and everyone in his family put their faith in Jesus.

54 This was the second miracle[q] that
Jesus worked after he left Judea and went
to Galilee.

Jesus Heals a Sick Man

5 Later, Jesus went to Jerusalem for another Jewish festival.[r] 2 In the city
near the sheep gate was a pool with five

[q] **4.54** *miracle*: See the note at 2.11,18,23. [r] **5.1** *another Jewish festival*: Either the Festival of Shelters or Passover.

4.43,44 Mt 13.57; Mk 6.4; Lk 4.24. **4.45** Jn 2.23. **4.46** Jn 2.1-11.

porches, and its name in Hebrew was
Bethzatha.[s]
3-4 Many sick, blind, lame, and crippled
people were lying close to the pool.[t]
5 Beside the pool was a man who had
been sick for thirty-eight years. 6 When
Jesus saw the man and realized that he had
been crippled for a long time, he asked
him, "Do you want to be healed?"
7 The man answered, "Lord, I don't
have anyone to put me in the pool when
the water is stirred up. I try to get in, but
someone else always gets there first."
8 Jesus told him, "Pick up your mat and
walk!" 9 Right then the man was healed.
He picked up his mat and started walking
around. The day on which this happened
was a Sabbath.
10 When the Jewish leaders saw the
man carrying his mat, they said to him,
"This is the Sabbath! No one is allowed to
carry a mat on the Sabbath."
11 But he replied, "The man who healed
me told me to pick up my mat and walk."
12 They asked him, "Who is this man
that told you to pick up your mat and
walk?" 13 But he did not know who Jesus
was, and Jesus had left because of the
crowd.
14 Later, Jesus met the man in the temple and told him, "You are now well. But
don't sin anymore or something worse
might happen to you." 15 The man left and
told the leaders that Jesus was the one who
had healed him. 16 They started making a
lot of trouble for Jesus because he did
things like this on the Sabbath.
17 But Jesus said, "My Father has never
stopped working, and that is why I keep on
working." 18 Now the leaders wanted to kill
Jesus for two reasons. First, he had broken
the law of the Sabbath. But even worse, he
had said that God was his Father, which
made him equal with God.

The Son's Authority

19 Jesus told the people:
I tell you for certain that the Son
cannot do anything on his own. He
can do only what he sees the Father
doing, and he does exactly what he
sees the Father do. 20 The Father loves
the Son and has shown him everything he does. The Father will
show him even greater things, and
you will be amazed. 21 Just as the
Father raises the dead and gives life,
so the Son gives life to anyone he
wants to.
22 The Father doesn't judge anyone,
but he has made his Son the judge of
everyone. 23 The Father wants all people to honor the Son as much as they
honor him. When anyone refuses to
honor the Son, that is the same as refusing to honor the Father who sent
him. 24 I tell you for certain that everyone who hears my message and has
faith in the one who sent me has eternal life and will never be condemned.
They have already gone from death to
life.
25 I tell you for certain that the time
will come, and it is already here, when
all of the dead will hear the voice of
the Son of God. And those who listen
to it will live! 26 The Father has the
power to give life, and he has given
that same power to the Son. 27 And he
has given his Son the right to judge
everyone, because he is the Son
of Man.
28 Don't be surprised! The time will
come when all of the dead will hear
the voice of the Son of Man, 29 and
they will come out of their graves.
Everyone who has done good things
will rise to life, but everyone who has
done evil things will rise and be condemned.
30 I cannot do anything on my
own. The Father sent me, and he is
the one who told me how to judge. I
judge with fairness, because I obey
him, and I don't just try to please myself.

[s]**5.2** *Bethzatha*: Some manuscripts have "Bethesda" and others have "Bethsaida." [t]**5.3,4** *pool*: Some manuscripts add, "They were waiting for the water to be stirred, because an angel from the Lord would sometimes come down and stir it. The first person to get into the pool after that would be healed."

5.10 Ne 13.19; Jr 17.21-24. **5.18** Ws 2.16. **5.29** Dn 12.2.

Witnesses to Jesus

31 If I speak for myself, there is no way to prove I am telling the truth. 32 But there is someone else who speaks for me, and I know what he says is true. 33 You sent messengers to John, and he told them the truth. 34 I don't depend on what people say about me, but I tell you these things so that you may be saved. 35 John was a lamp that gave a lot of light, and you were glad to enjoy his light for a while.

36 But something more important than John speaks for me. I mean the things that the Father has given me to do! All of these speak for me and prove that the Father sent me.

37 The Father who sent me also speaks for me, but you have never heard his voice or seen him face to face. 38 You have not believed his message, because you refused to have faith in the one he sent.

39 You search the Scriptures, because you think you will find eternal life in them. The Scriptures tell about me, 40 but you refuse to come to me for eternal life.

41 I don't care about human praise, 42 but I do know that none of you love God. 43 I have come with my Father's authority, and you have not welcomed me. But you will welcome people who come on their own. 44 How could you possibly believe? You like to have your friends praise you, and you don't care about praise that the only God can give!

45 Don't think that I will be the one to accuse you to the Father. You have put your hope in Moses, yet he is the very one who will accuse you. 46 Moses wrote about me, and if you had believed Moses, you would have believed me. 47 But if you don't believe what Moses wrote, how can you believe what I say?

Feeding Five Thousand

(Matthew 14.13-21; Mark 6.30-44; Luke 9.10-17)

6 Jesus crossed Lake Galilee, which was also known as Lake Tiberias. 2 A large crowd had seen him work miracles to heal the sick, and those people went with him. 3-4 It was almost time for the Jewish festival of Passover, and Jesus went up on a mountain with his disciples and sat down.[u]

5 When Jesus saw the large crowd coming toward him, he asked Philip, "Where will we get enough food to feed all these people?" 6 He said this to test Philip, since he already knew what he was going to do.

7 Philip answered, "Don't you know that it would take almost a year's wages[v] just to buy only a little bread for each of these people?"

8 Andrew, the brother of Simon Peter, was one of the disciples. He spoke up and said, 9 "There is a boy here who has five small loaves[w] of barley bread and two fish. But what good is that with all these people?"

10 The ground was covered with grass, and Jesus told his disciples to have everyone sit down. About five thousand men were in the crowd. 11 Jesus took the bread in his hands and gave thanks to God. Then he passed the bread to the people, and he did the same with the fish, until everyone had plenty to eat.

12 The people ate all they wanted, and Jesus told his disciples to gather up the leftovers, so that nothing would be wasted. 13 The disciples gathered them up and filled twelve large baskets with what was left over from the five barley loaves.

14 After the people had seen Jesus work this miracle,[x] they began saying, "This must be the Prophet[y] who is to come into

[u] **6.3,4** *sat down*: Possibly to teach. Teachers in the ancient world, including Jewish teachers, usually sat down to teach. [v] **6.7** *almost a year's wages*: The Greek text has "two hundred silver coins." Each coin was worth the average day's wages for a worker. [w] **6.9** *small loaves*: These would have been flat and round or in the shape of a bun. [x] **6.14** *miracle*: See the note at 2.11,18,23. [y] **6.14** *the Prophet*: See the note at 1.21.

5.33 Jn 1.19-27; 3.27-30. **5.35** Si 48.1. **5.37** Mt 3.17; Mk 1.11; Lk 3.22. **5.39** Ba 4.1.

the world!" 15 Jesus realized that they would try to force him to be their king. So he went up on a mountain, where he could be alone.

Jesus Walks on the Water
(Matthew 14.22-27; Mark 6.45-52)

16 That evening, Jesus' disciples went down to the lake. 17 They got into a boat and started across for Capernaum. Later that evening Jesus had still not come to them, 18 and a strong wind was making the water rough.

19 When the disciples had rowed for three or four miles, they saw Jesus walking on the water. He kept coming closer to the boat, and they were terrified. 20 But he said, "I am Jesus![z] Don't be afraid!" 21 The disciples wanted to take him into the boat, but suddenly the boat reached the shore where they were headed.

The Bread That Gives Life

22 The people who had stayed on the east side of the lake knew that only one boat had been there. They also knew that Jesus had not left in it with his disciples. But the next day 23 some boats from Tiberias sailed near the place where the crowd had eaten the bread for which the Lord had given thanks. 24 They saw that Jesus and his disciples had left. Then they got into the boats and went to Capernaum to look for Jesus. 25 They found him on the west side of the lake and asked, "Rabbi, when did you get here?"

26 Jesus answered, "I tell you for certain that you are not looking for me because you saw the miracles,[a] but because you ate all the food you wanted. 27 Don't work for food that spoils. Work for food that gives eternal life. The Son of Man will give you this food, because God the Father has given him the right to do so."

28 "What exactly does God want us to do?" the people asked.

29 Jesus answered, "God wants you to have faith in the one he sent."

30 They replied, "What miracle will you work, so that we can have faith in you? What will you do? 31 For example, when our ancestors were in the desert, they were given manna[b] to eat. It happened just as the Scriptures say, 'God gave them bread from heaven to eat.' "

32 Jesus then told them, "I tell you for certain that Moses wasn't the one who gave you bread from heaven. My Father is the one who gives you the true bread from heaven. 33 And the bread that God gives is the one who came down from heaven to give life to the world."

34 The people said, "Lord, give us this bread and don't ever stop!"

35 Jesus replied:

> I am the bread that gives life! No one who comes to me will ever be hungry. No one who has faith in me will ever be thirsty. 36 I have told you already that you have seen me and still do not have faith in me. 37 Everything and everyone that the Father has given me will come to me, and I won't turn any of them away.
>
> 38 I didn't come from heaven to do what I want! I came to do what the Father wants me to do. He sent me, 39 and he wants to make certain that none of the ones he has given me will be lost. Instead, he wants me to raise them to life on the last day.[c] 40 My Father wants everyone who sees the Son to have faith in him and to have eternal life. Then I will raise them to life on the last day.

41 The people started grumbling because Jesus had said he was the bread that had come down from heaven. 42 They were asking each other, "Isn't he Jesus, the son of Joseph? Don't we know his father and mother? How can he say that he has come down from heaven?"

[z]**6.20** *I am Jesus*: The Greek text has "I am" (see the note at 8.24). [a]**6.26** *miracles*: The Greek text has "signs" here and "sign" in verse 30 (see the note at 2.11,18,23). [b]**6.31** *manna*: When the people of Israel were wandering through the desert, the Lord gave them a special kind of food to eat. It tasted like a wafer and was called "manna," which in Hebrew means, "What is this?" [c]**6.39** *the last day*: When God will judge all people.

6.27 Si 24.19-22. **6.31** Ex 16.4, 15; Ps 78.24; Ws 16.20, 21.

43 Jesus told them:
Stop grumbling! 44 No one can
come to me, unless the Father who
sent me makes them want to come.
But if they do come, I will raise them
to life on the last day. 45 One of the
prophets wrote, "God will teach all of
them." And so everyone who listens to
the Father and learns from him will
come to me.
46 The only one who has seen the
Father is the one who has come from
him. No one else has ever seen the
Father. 47 I tell you for certain that
everyone who has faith in me has
eternal life.
48 I am the bread that gives life!
49 Your ancestors ate manna[d] in the
desert, and later they died. 50 But the
bread from heaven has come down, so
that no one who eats it will ever die.
51 I am that bread from heaven! Everyone who eats it will live forever. My
flesh is the life-giving bread that I give
to the people of this world.
52 They started arguing with each other
and asked, "How can he give us his flesh
to eat?"
53 Jesus answered:
I tell you for certain that you won't
live unless you eat the flesh and drink
the blood of the Son of Man. 54 But if
you do eat my flesh and drink my
blood, you will have eternal life, and I
will raise you to life on the last day.
55 My flesh is the true food, and my
blood is the true drink. 56 If you
eat my flesh and drink my blood, you are
one with me, and I am one with you.
57 The living Father sent me, and I
have life because of him. Now everyone who eats my flesh will live because
of me. 58 The bread that comes down
from heaven isn't like what your ancestors ate. They died, but whoever eats
this bread will live forever.
59 Jesus was teaching in a Jewish place
of worship in Capernaum when he said
these things.

The Words of Eternal Life

60 Many of Jesus' disciples heard him
and said, "This is too hard for anyone to
understand."
61 Jesus knew that his disciples were
grumbling. So he asked, "Does this bother
you? 62 What if you should see the Son of
Man go up to heaven where he came from?
63 The Spirit is the one who gives life! Human strength can do nothing. The words
that I have spoken to you are from that life-
giving Spirit. 64 But some of you refuse to
have faith in me." Jesus said this, because
from the beginning he knew who would
have faith in him. He also knew which one
would betray him.
65 Then Jesus said, "You cannot come to
me, unless the Father makes you want to
come. That is why I have told these things
to all of you."
66 Because of what Jesus said, many of
his disciples turned their backs on him and
stopped following him. 67 Jesus then asked
his twelve disciples if they were going to
leave him. 68 Simon Peter answered, "Lord,
there is no one else that we can go to! Your
words give eternal life. 69 We have faith in
you, and we are sure that you are God's
Holy One."
70 Jesus told his disciples, "I chose all
twelve of you, but one of you is a demon!"
71 Jesus was talking about Judas, the son of
Simon Iscariot.[e] He would later betray
Jesus, even though he was one of the
twelve disciples.

Jesus' Brothers Don't Have Faith in Him

7 Jesus decided to leave Judea and to
start going through Galilee because
the Jewish leaders wanted to kill him. 2 It
was almost time for the Festival of Shelters,
3 and Jesus' brothers said to him, "Why
don't you go to Judea? Then your disciples

[d] **6.49** *manna*: See the note at 6.31. [e] **6.71** *Iscariot*: This may mean "a man from Kerioth" (a place in Judea). But more probably it means "a man who was a liar" or "a man who was a betrayer."

6.45 Is 54.13. **6.63** Ws 9.13-18. **6.68,69** Mt 16.16; Mk 8.29; Lk 9.20. **7.2** Lv 23.34; Dt 16.13-15.

can see what you are doing. 4 No one does
anything in secret, if they want others
to know about them. So let the world
know what you are doing!" 5 Even Jesus'
own brothers had not yet become his
followers.
6 Jesus answered, "My time hasn't yet
come,[f] but your time is always here. 7 The
people of this world cannot hate you. They
hate me, because I tell them that they
do evil things. 8 Go on to the festival. My
time hasn't yet come, and I am not going."
9 Jesus said this and stayed on in Galilee.

Jesus at the Festival of Shelters

10 After Jesus' brothers had gone to the
festival, he went secretly, without telling
anyone.
11 During the festival the Jewish leaders
looked for Jesus and asked, "Where is he?"
12 The crowds even got into an argument
about him. Some were saying, "Jesus is a
good man," while others were saying,
"He is lying to everyone." 13 But the people
were afraid of their leaders, and none of
them talked in public about him.
14 When the festival was about half over,
Jesus went into the temple and started
teaching. 15 The leaders were surprised
and said, "How does this man know so
much? He has never been taught!"
16 Jesus replied:

I am not teaching something that I
thought up. What I teach comes from
the one who sent me. 17 If you really
want to obey God, you will know if
what I teach comes from God or from
me. 18 If I wanted to bring honor to
myself, I would speak for myself. But I
want to honor the one who sent me.
That is why I tell the truth and not a
lie. 19 Didn't Moses give you the Law?
Yet none of you obey it! So why do you
want to kill me?

20 The crowd replied, "You're crazy!
What makes you think someone wants to
kill you?"
21 Jesus answered:

I worked one miracle,[g] and it
amazed you. 22 Moses commanded you
to circumcise your sons. But it wasn't
really Moses who gave you this command.
It was your ancestors, and even
on the Sabbath you circumcise your
sons 23 in order to obey the Law of
Moses. Why are you angry with me for
making someone completely well on
the Sabbath? 24 Don't judge by appearances.
Judge by what is right.

25 Some of the people from Jerusalem
were saying, "Isn't this the man they want
to kill? 26 Yet here he is, speaking for everyone
to hear. And no one is arguing with
him. Do you suppose the authorities know
that he is the Messiah? 27 But how could
that be? No one knows where the Messiah
will come from, but we know where this
man comes from."
28 As Jesus was teaching in the temple,
he shouted, "Do you really think you know
me and where I came from? I didn't come
on my own! The one who sent me is truthful,
and you don't know him. 29 But I know
the one who sent me, because I came
from him."
30 Some of the people wanted to arrest
Jesus right then. But no one even laid a
hand on him, because his time had not
yet come.[h] 31 A lot of people in the crowd
put their faith in him and said, "When
the Messiah comes, he surely won't perform
more miracles[i] than this man has
done!"

Officers Sent To Arrest Jesus

32 When the Pharisees heard the crowd
arguing about Jesus, they got together with
the chief priests and sent some temple police
to arrest him. 33 But Jesus told them, "I
will be with you a little while longer, and
then I will return to the one who sent me.
34 You will look for me, but you won't find
me. You cannot go where I am going."
35 The Jewish leaders asked each other,
"Where can he go to keep us from finding

[f]7.6 *My time hasn't yet come*: See the note at 2.4. [g]7.21 *one miracle*: The healing of the lame man (5.1-18; see also the note at 2.11,18,23). [h]7.30 *his time had not yet come*: See the note at 2.4. [i]7.31 *miracles*: See the note at 2.11,18,23.

7.22 a Lv 12.3; **b** Gn 17.10, 11. **7.23** Jn 5.9.

him? Is he going to some foreign country
where our people live? Is he going there to
teach the Greeks?[j] 36 What did he mean by
saying that we will look for him, but won't
find him? Why can't we go where he is
going?"

Streams of Life-Giving Water

37 On the last and most important day of
the festival, Jesus stood up and shouted, "If
you are thirsty, come to me and drink!
38 Have faith in me, and you will have life-
giving water flowing from deep inside you,
just as the Scriptures say." 39 Jesus was
talking about the Holy Spirit, who would be
given to everyone that had faith in him.
The Spirit had not yet been given to anyone, since Jesus had not yet been given his
full glory.[k]

The People Take Sides

40 When the crowd heard Jesus say this,
some of them said, "He must be the
Prophet!"[l] 41 Others said, "He is the
Messiah!" Others even said, "Can the
Messiah come from Galilee? 42 The Scriptures say that the Messiah will come from
the family of King David. Doesn't this
mean that he will be born in David's hometown of Bethlehem?" 43 The people started
taking sides against each other because of
Jesus. 44 Some of them wanted to arrest
him, but no one laid a hand on him.

The Leaders Refuse To Have Faith in Jesus

45 When the temple police returned to
the chief priests and Pharisees, they were
asked, "Why didn't you bring Jesus here?"
46 They answered, "No one has ever
spoken like that man!"
47 The Pharisees said to them, "Have
you also been fooled? 48 Not one of the
chief priests or the Pharisees has faith in
him. 49 And these people who don't know
the Law are under God's curse anyway."
50 Nicodemus was there at the time. He
was a member of the council, and was the
same one who had earlier come to see
Jesus.[m] He said, 51 "Our Law doesn't let us
condemn people before we hear what they
have to say. We cannot judge them before
we know what they have done."
52 Then they said, "Nicodemus, you
must be from Galilee! Read the Scriptures,
and you will find that no prophet is to
come from Galilee."

A Woman Caught in Sin

8 53 Everyone else went home, 1 but
Jesus walked out to the Mount of
Olives. 2 Then early the next morning he
went to the temple. The people came to
him, and he sat down[n] and started teaching them.
3 The Pharisees and the teachers of the
Law of Moses brought in a woman who had
been caught in bed with a man who wasn't
her husband. They made her stand in the
middle of the crowd. 4 Then they said,
"Teacher, this woman was caught sleeping
with a man who isn't her husband. 5 The
Law of Moses teaches that a woman like
this should be stoned to death! What do
you say?"
6 They asked Jesus this question, because they wanted to test him and bring
some charge against him. But Jesus simply
bent over and started writing on the ground
with his finger.
7 They kept on asking Jesus about the
woman. Finally, he stood up and said, "If
any of you have never sinned, then go
ahead and throw the first stone at her!"
8 Once again he bent over and began
writing on the ground. 9 The people left
one by one, beginning with the oldest. Finally, Jesus and the woman were there
alone.
10 Jesus stood up and asked her, "Where
is everyone? Isn't there anyone left to accuse you?"

[j] **7.35** *Greeks*: Perhaps Gentiles or Jews who followed Greek customs. [k] **7.39** *had not yet been given his full glory*: In the Gospel of John, Jesus is given his full glory both when he is nailed to the cross and when he is raised from death to sit beside his Father in heaven. [l] **7.40** *the Prophet*: See the note at 1.21. [m] **7.50** *who had earlier come to see Jesus*: See 3.1-21. [n] **8.2** *sat down*: See the note at 6.3, 4.

7.37 Lv 23.36. **7.38** Ez 47.1; Zec 14.8. **7.42** 2 S 7.12; Mic 5.2. **7.50** Jn 3.1, 2. **8.5** Lv 20.10; Dt 22.22-24. **8.7** Su 34.

11 "No sir," the woman answered.
Then Jesus told her, "I am not going
to accuse you either. You may go now, but
don't sin anymore."[o]

Jesus Is the Light for the World

12 Once again Jesus spoke to the people.
This time he said, "I am the light for the
world! Follow me, and you won't be walking
in the dark. You will have the light that
gives life."
13 The Pharisees objected, "You are the
only one speaking for yourself, and what
you say isn't true!"
14 Jesus replied:
Even if I do speak for myself, what I
say is true! I know where I came from
and where I am going. But you don't
know where I am from or where I am
going. 15 You judge in the same way
that everyone else does, but I don't
judge anyone. 16 If I did judge, I would
judge fairly, because I would not be doing it alone. The Father who sent me is
here with me. 17 Your Law requires two
witnesses to prove that something
is true. 18 I am one of my witnesses,
and the Father who sent me is the
other one.
19 "Where is your Father?" they asked.
"You don't know me or my Father!"
Jesus answered. "If you knew me, you
would know my Father."
20 Jesus said this while he was still
teaching in the place where the temple
treasures were stored. But no one arrested
him, because his time had not yet come.[p]

You Cannot Go Where I Am Going

21 Jesus also told them, "I am going
away, and you will look for me. But you
cannot go where I am going, and you will
die with your sins unforgiven."
22 The Jewish leaders asked, "Does he
intend to kill himself? Is that what he
means by saying we cannot go where he is
going?"
23 Jesus answered, "You are from below,
but I am from above. You belong to this
world, but I don't. 24 That is why I said you
will die with your sins unforgiven. If you
don't have faith in me for who I am,[q] you
will die, and your sins will not be forgiven."
25 "Who are you?" they asked Jesus.
Jesus answered, "I am exactly who I told
you at the beginning. 26 There is a lot more
I could say to condemn you. But the one
who sent me is truthful, and I tell the people of this world only what I have heard
from him."
27 No one understood that Jesus was
talking to them about the Father.
28 Jesus went on to say, "When you have
lifted up the Son of Man,[r] you will know
who I am. You will also know that I don't do
anything on my own. I say only what my
Father taught me. 29 The one who sent me
is with me. I always do what pleases him,
and he will never leave me."
30 After Jesus said this, many of the people put their faith in him.

The Truth Will Set You Free

31 Jesus told the people who had faith in
him, "If you keep on obeying what I have
said, you truly are my disciples. 32 You will
know the truth, and the truth will set you
free."
33 They answered, "We are Abraham's
children! We have never been anyone's
slaves. How can you say we will be set
free?"
34 Jesus replied:
I tell you for certain that anyone
who sins is a slave of sin! 35 And slaves
don't stay in the family forever, though
the Son will always remain in the family. 36 If the Son gives you freedom, you

[o]**8.11** *don't sin anymore*: Verses 1-11 are not in some manuscripts. In other manuscripts these verses are placed after 7.36 or after 21.25 or after Luke 21.38, with some differences in the text.
[p]**8.20** *his time had not yet come*: See the note at 2.4.
[q]**8.24** *I am*: For the Jewish people the most holy name of God is "Yahweh," which may be translated "I am." In the Gospel of John "I am" is sometimes used by Jesus to show that he is that one.
[r]**8.28** *lifted up the Son of Man*: See the note at 7.39.

8.12 Ws 7.26; Mt 5.14; Jn 9.5. **8.13** Jn 5.31. **8.17** Dt 19.15. **8.32** 1 Esd 4.38. **8.33** Mt 3.9; Lk 3.8.

are free! 37 I know that you are from
Abraham's family. Yet you want to kill
me, because my message isn't really in
your hearts. 38 I am telling you what
my Father has shown me, just as
you are doing what your father has
taught you.

Your Father Is the Devil

39 The people said to Jesus, "Abraham is
our father!"
Jesus replied, "If you were Abraham's
children, you would do what Abraham did.
40 Instead, you want to kill me for telling
you the truth that God gave me. Abraham
never did anything like that. 41 But you are
doing exactly what your father does."
"Don't accuse us of having someone else
as our father!" they said. "We just have one
father, and he is God."
42 Jesus answered:
If God were your Father, you would
love me, because I came from God
and only from him. He sent me. I did
not come on my own. 43 Why can't you
understand what I am talking about?
Can't you stand to hear what I am saying? 44 Your father is the devil, and you
do exactly what he wants. He has always been a murderer and a liar. There
is nothing truthful about him. He
speaks on his own, and everything he
says is a lie. Not only is he a liar himself, but he is also the father of all lies.
45 Everything I have told you is
true, and you still refuse to have faith
in me. 46 Can any of you accuse me of
sin? If you cannot, why won't you have
faith in me? After all, I am telling you
the truth. 47 Anyone who belongs to
God will listen to his message. But you
refuse to listen, because you don't belong to God.

Jesus and Abraham

48 The people told Jesus, "We were right
to say that you are a Samaritan[s] and that
you have a demon in you!"
49 Jesus answered, "I don't have a demon in me. I honor my Father, and you
refuse to honor me. 50 I don't want honor
for myself. But there is one who wants me
to be honored, and he is also the one who
judges. 51 I tell you for certain that if you
obey my words, you will never die."
52 Then the people said, "Now we are
sure that you have a demon. Abraham is
dead, and so are the prophets. How can
you say that no one who obeys your words
will ever die? 53 Are you greater than our
father Abraham? He died, and so did the
prophets. Who do you think you are?"
54 Jesus replied, "If I honored myself, it
would mean nothing. My Father is the one
who honors me. You claim that he is your
God, 55 even though you don't really know
him. If I said I didn't know him, I would be
a liar, just like all of you. But I know him,
and I do what he says. 56 Your father Abraham was really glad to see me."
57 "You are not even fifty years old!"
they said. "How could you have seen
Abraham?"
58 Jesus answered, "I tell you for certain
that even before Abraham was, I was, and I
am."[t] 59 The people picked up stones to kill
Jesus, but he hid and left the temple.

Jesus Heals a Man Born Blind

9 As Jesus walked along, he saw a man
who had been blind since birth.
2 Jesus' disciples asked, "Teacher, why was
this man born blind? Was it because he or
his parents sinned?"
3 "No, it wasn't!" Jesus answered. "But
because of his blindness, you will see God
work a miracle for him. 4 As long as it is
day, we must do what the one who sent me
wants me to do. When night comes, no one
can work. 5 While I am in the world, I am
the light for the world."
6 After Jesus said this, he spit on the
ground. He made some mud and smeared
it on the man's eyes. 7 Then he said, "Go
and wash off the mud in Siloam Pool." The
man went and washed in Siloam, which
means "One Who Is Sent." When he had
washed off the mud, he could see.
8 The man's neighbors and the people
who had seen him begging wondered if he

[s] **8.48** *Samaritan*: See 4.9 and the note there.
[t] **8.58** *I am*: See the note at 8.24.

8.44 Ws 1.13; 2.24. **9.5** Mt 5.14; Jn 8.12.

really could be the same man. [9] Some of
them said he was the same beggar, while
others said he only looked like him. But he
told them, "I am that man."
[10] "Then how can you see?" they asked.
[11] He answered, "Someone named
Jesus made some mud and smeared it on
my eyes. He told me to go and wash it off
in Siloam Pool. When I did, I could see."
[12] "Where is he now?" they asked.
"I don't know," he answered.

The Pharisees Try To Find Out What Happened

[13-14] The day when Jesus made the mud
and healed the man was a Sabbath. So the
people took the man to the Pharisees.
[15] They asked him how he was able to see,
and he answered, "Jesus made some mud
and smeared it on my eyes. Then after I
washed it off, I could see."
[16] Some of the Pharisees said, "This
man Jesus doesn't come from God. If he
did, he would not break the law of the Sabbath."
Others asked, "How could someone who
is a sinner work such a miracle?"[u]
Since the Pharisees could not agree
among themselves, [17] they asked the man,
"What do you say about this one who
healed your eyes?"
"He is a prophet!" the man told them.
[18] But the Jewish leaders would not believe that the man had once been blind.
They sent for his parents [19] and asked
them, "Is this the son that you said was
born blind? How can he now see?"
[20] The man's parents answered, "We are
certain that he is our son, and we know
that he was born blind. [21] But we don't
know how he got his sight or who gave it to
him. Ask him! He is old enough to speak
for himself."
[22-23] The man's parents said this because they were afraid of the Jewish leaders. The leaders had already agreed that no
one was to have anything to do with anyone
who said Jesus was the Messiah.
[24] The leaders called the man back and
said, "Swear by God to tell the truth! We
know that Jesus is a sinner."
[25] The man replied, "I don't know if he
is a sinner or not. All I know is that I used
to be blind, but now I can see!"
[26] "What did he do to you?" the Jewish
leaders asked. "How did he heal your
eyes?"
[27] The man answered, "I have already
told you once, and you refused to listen.
Why do you want me to tell you again? Do
you also want to become his disciples?"
[28] The leaders insulted the man and
said, "You are his follower! We are followers
of Moses. [29] We are sure that God spoke
to Moses, but we don't even know where
Jesus comes from."
[30] "How strange!" the man replied. "He
healed my eyes, and yet you don't know
where he comes from. [31] We know that God
listens only to people who love and obey
him. God doesn't listen to sinners. [32] And
this is the first time in history that anyone
has ever given sight to someone born blind.
[33] Jesus could not do anything unless he
came from God."
[34] The leaders told the man, "You
have been a sinner since the day you
were born! Do you think you can teach us
anything?" Then they said, "You can
never come back into any of our meeting
places!"
[35] When Jesus heard what had happened, he went and found the man. Then
Jesus asked, "Do you have faith in the Son
of Man?"
[36] He replied, "Sir, if you will tell me
who he is, I will put my faith in him."
[37] "You have already seen him," Jesus
answered, "and right now he is talking
with you."
[38] The man said, "Lord, I put my faith
in you!" Then he worshiped Jesus.
[39] Jesus told him, "I came to judge the
people of this world. I am here to give sight
to the blind and to make blind everyone
who can see."
[40] When the Pharisees heard Jesus say
this, they asked, "Are we blind?"
[41] Jesus answered, "If you were blind,
you would not be guilty. But now that
you claim to see, you will keep on being
guilty."

[u]**9.16** *miracle*: See the note at 2.11,18,23.

A Story about Sheep

10 Jesus said:

I tell you for certain that only thieves and robbers climb over the fence instead of going in through the gate to the sheep pen. 2-3 But the gatekeeper opens the gate for the shepherd, and he goes in through it. The sheep know their shepherd's voice. He calls each of them by name and leads them out.

4 When he has led out all of his sheep, he walks in front of them, and they follow, because they know his voice. 5 The sheep will not follow strangers. They don't recognize a stranger's voice, and they run away.

6 Jesus told the people this story. But they did not understand what he was talking about.

Jesus Is the Good Shepherd

7 Jesus said:

I tell you for certain that I am the gate for the sheep. 8 Everyone who came before me was a thief or a robber, and the sheep did not listen to any of them. 9 I am the gate. All who come in through me will be saved. Through me they will come and go and find pasture.

10 A thief comes only to rob, kill, and destroy. I came so that everyone would have life, and have it in its fullest. 11 I am the good shepherd, and the good shepherd gives up his life for his sheep. 12 Hired workers are not like the shepherd. They don't own the sheep, and when they see a wolf coming, they run off and leave the sheep. Then the wolf attacks and scatters the flock. 13 Hired workers run away because they don't care about the sheep.

14 I am the good shepherd. I know my sheep, and they know me. 15 Just as the Father knows me, I know the Father, and I give up my life for my sheep. 16 I have other sheep that are not in this sheep pen. I must bring them together too, when they hear my voice. Then there will be one flock of sheep and one shepherd.

17 The Father loves me, because I give up my life, so that I may receive it back again. 18 No one takes my life from me. I give it up willingly! I have the power to give it up and the power to receive it back again, just as my Father commanded me to do.

19 The people took sides because of what Jesus had told them. 20 Many of them said, "He has a demon in him! He is crazy! Why listen to him?"

21 But others said, "How could anyone with a demon in him say these things? No one like that could give sight to a blind person!"

Jesus Is Rejected

22 That winter, Jesus was in Jerusalem for the Temple Festival. 23 One day he was walking in that part of the temple known as Solomon's Porch,[v] 24 and the people gathered all around him. They said, "How long are you going to keep us guessing? If you are the Messiah, tell us plainly!"

25 Jesus answered:

I have told you, and you refused to believe me. The things I do by my Father's authority show who I am. 26 But since you are not my sheep, you don't believe me. 27 My sheep know my voice, and I know them. They follow me, 28 and I give them eternal life, so that they will never be lost. No one can snatch them out of my hand. 29 My Father gave them to me, and he is greater than all others.[w] No one can snatch them from his hands, 30 and I am one with the Father.

31 Once again the Jewish leaders picked up stones in order to kill Jesus. 32 But he said, "I have shown you many good things that my Father sent me to do. Which one are you going to stone me for?"

33 They answered, "We are not stoning you because of any good thing you did. We

[v] **10.23** *Solomon's Porch*: A public place with tall columns along the east side of the temple.

[w] **10.29** *he is greater than all others*: Some manuscripts have "they are greater than all others."

10.11 Si 18.13. **10.15** Mt 11.27; Lk 10.22. **10.22** 1 Macc 4.36, 52-59; 2 Macc 1.18; 10.5. **10.29** Ws 3.1.

are stoning you because you did a terrible
thing. You are just a man, and here you are
claiming to be God!"
34 Jesus replied:
In your Scriptures doesn't God say,
"You are gods"? 35 You can't argue with
the Scriptures, and God spoke to those
people and called them gods. 36 So
why do you accuse me of a terrible sin
for saying that I am the Son of God?
After all, it is the Father who prepared
me for this work. He is also the one
who sent me into the world. 37 If I
don't do as my Father does, you should
not believe me. 38 But if I do what my
Father does, you should believe because of that, even if you don't have
faith in me. Then you will know for
certain that the Father is one with me,
and I am one with the Father.
39 Again they wanted to arrest Jesus.
But he escaped 40 and crossed the Jordan
to the place where John had earlier been
baptizing. While Jesus was there, 41 many
people came to him. They were saying,
"John didn't work any miracles, but everything he said about Jesus is true." 42 A lot
of those people also put their faith in Jesus.

The Death of Lazarus

11 1-2 A man by the name of Lazarus
was sick in the village of Bethany.
He had two sisters, Mary and Martha. This
was the same Mary who later poured perfume on the Lord's head and wiped his feet
with her hair. 3 The sisters sent a message
to the Lord and told him that his good
friend Lazarus was sick.
4 When Jesus heard this, he said, "His
sickness won't end in death. It will bring
glory to God and his Son."
5 Jesus loved Martha and her sister and
brother. 6 But he stayed where he was for
two more days. 7 Then he said to his disciples, "Now we will go back to Judea."
8 "Teacher," they said, "the people there
want to stone you to death! Why do you
want to go back?"
9 Jesus answered, "Aren't there twelve
hours in each day? If you walk during the
day, you will have light from the sun, and
you won't stumble. 10 But if you walk during the night, you will stumble, because
you don't have any light." 11 Then he told
them, "Our friend Lazarus is asleep, and I
am going there to wake him up."
12 They replied, "Lord, if he is asleep, he
will get better." 13 Jesus really meant that
Lazarus was dead, but they thought he was
talking only about sleep.
14 Then Jesus told them plainly,
"Lazarus is dead! 15 I am glad that I wasn't
there, because now you will have a chance
to put your faith in me. Let's go to him."
16 Thomas, whose nickname was
"Twin," said to the other disciples, "Come
on. Let's go, so we can die with him."

Jesus Brings Lazarus to Life

17 When Jesus got to Bethany, he found
that Lazarus had already been in the tomb
four days. 18 Bethany was only about two
miles from Jerusalem, 19 and many people
had come from the city to comfort Martha
and Mary because their brother had
died.
20 When Martha heard that Jesus had
arrived, she went out to meet him, but
Mary stayed in the house. 21 Martha said to
Jesus, "Lord, if you had been here, my
brother would not have died. 22 Yet even
now I know that God will do anything
you ask."
23 Jesus told her, "Your brother will live
again!"
24 Martha answered, "I know that he
will be raised to life on the last day,[x] when
all the dead are raised."
25 Jesus then said, "I am the one who
raises the dead to life! Everyone who has
faith in me will live, even if they die. 26 And
everyone who lives because of faith in me
will never really die. Do you believe this?"
27 "Yes, Lord!" she replied. "I believe
that you are Christ, the Son of God. You are
the one we hoped would come into the
world."
28 After Martha said this, she went and

[x] **11.24** *the last day*: When God will judge all people.

10.34 Ps 82.6. **10.40** Jn 1.28. **11.1,2** **a** Lk 10.38, 39; **b** Jn 12.3.
11.24 2 Macc 7.22, 23; 12.43-45.

privately said to her sister Mary, "The
Teacher is here, and he wants to see you."
29 As soon as Mary heard this, she got up
and went out to Jesus. 30 He was still outside the village where Martha had gone to
meet him. 31 Many people had come to
comfort Mary, and when they saw her
quickly leave the house, they thought she
was going out to the tomb to cry. So they
followed her.

32 Mary went to where Jesus was. Then
as soon as she saw him, she knelt at his
feet and said, "Lord, if you had been here,
my brother would not have died."

33 When Jesus saw that Mary and the
people with her were crying, he was terribly
upset 34 and asked, "Where have you put
his body?"

They replied, "Lord, come and you
will see."

35 Jesus started crying, 36 and the people
said, "See how much he loved Lazarus."

37 Some of them said, "He gives sight to
the blind. Why couldn't he have kept Lazarus from dying?"

38 Jesus was still terribly upset. So he
went to the tomb, which was a cave with a
stone rolled against the entrance. 39 Then
he told the people to roll the stone away.
But Martha said, "Lord, you know that
Lazarus has been dead four days, and there
will be a bad smell."

40 Jesus replied, "Didn't I tell you that
if you had faith, you would see the glory
of God?"

41 After the stone had been rolled aside,
Jesus looked up toward heaven and prayed,
"Father, I thank you for answering
my prayer. 42 I know that you always answer my prayers. But I said this, so that
the people here would believe that you
sent me."

43 When Jesus had finished praying,
he shouted, "Lazarus, come out!" 44 The
man who had been dead came out. His
hands and feet were wrapped with strips
of burial cloth, and a cloth covered his
face.

Jesus then told the people, "Untie him
and let him go."

The Plot To Kill Jesus

(Matthew 26.1-5; Mark 14.1, 2; Luke 22.1, 2)

45 Many of the people who had come to
visit Mary saw the things that Jesus did,
and they put their faith in him. 46 Others
went to the Pharisees and told what Jesus
had done. 47 Then the chief priests and the
Pharisees called the council together
and said, "What should we do? This man
is working a lot of miracles.[y] 48 If we
don't stop him now, everyone will put
their faith in him. Then the Romans will
come and destroy our temple and our
nation."[z]

49 One of the council members was Caiaphas, who was also high priest that year.
He spoke up and said, "You people don't
have any sense at all! 50 Don't you know it
is better for one person to die for the people than for the whole nation to be destroyed?" 51 Caiaphas did not say this on
his own. As high priest that year, he was
prophesying that Jesus would die for the
nation. 52 Yet Jesus would not die just for
the Jewish nation. He would die to bring
together all of God's scattered people.
53 From that day on, the council started
making plans to put Jesus to death.

54 Because of this plot against him,
Jesus stopped going around in public. He
went to the town of Ephraim, which was
near the desert, and he stayed there with
his disciples.

55 It was almost time for Passover. Many
of the Jewish people who lived out in the
country had come to Jerusalem to get
themselves ready[a] for the festival. 56 They
looked around for Jesus. Then when they
were in the temple, they asked each other,
"You don't think he will come here for
Passover, do you?"

57 The chief priests and the Pharisees
told the people to let them know if any of
them saw Jesus. That is how they hoped to
arrest him.

[y] **11.47** *miracles*: See the note at 2.11,18,23. [z] **11.48** *destroy our temple and our nation*: The Jewish leaders were afraid that Jesus would lead his followers to rebel against Rome and that the Roman army would then destroy their nation. [a] **11.55** *get themselves ready*: The Jewish people had to do certain things to prepare themselves to worship God.

At Bethany
(Matthew 26.6-13; Mark 14.3-9)

12 Six days before Passover Jesus went
back to Bethany, where he had
raised Lazarus from death. 2 A meal had
been prepared for Jesus. Martha was doing
the serving, and Lazarus himself was there.
3 Mary took a very expensive bottle of
perfume[b] and poured it on Jesus' feet. She
wiped them with her hair, and the sweet
smell of the perfume filled the house.
4 A disciple named Judas Iscariot[c] was
there. He was the one who was going to betray Jesus, and he asked, 5 "Why wasn't
this perfume sold for three hundred silver
coins and the money given to the poor?"
6 Judas did not really care about the poor.
He asked this because he carried the
moneybag and sometimes would steal
from it.
7 Jesus replied, "Leave her alone! She
has kept this perfume for the day of my
burial. 8 You will always have the poor with
you, but you won't always have me."

A Plot To Kill Lazarus

9 A lot of people came when they heard
that Jesus was there. They also wanted to
see Lazarus, because Jesus had raised him
from death. 10 So the chief priests made
plans to kill Lazarus. 11 He was the reason
that many of the Jewish people were turning from them and putting their faith in
Jesus.

Jesus Enters Jerusalem
(Matthew 21.1-11; Mark 11.1-11; Luke 19.28-40)

12 The next day a large crowd was in
Jerusalem for Passover. When they heard
that Jesus was coming for the festival,
13 they took palm branches and went out to
greet him.[d] They shouted,

"Hooray![e]
God bless the one who comes
in the name of the Lord!
God bless the King
of Israel!"

14 Jesus found a donkey and rode on it,
just as the Scriptures say,

15 "People of Jerusalem,
don't be afraid!
Your King is now coming,
and he is riding
on a donkey."

16 At first, Jesus' disciples did not
understand. But after he had been given
his glory,[f] they remembered all this. Everything had happened exactly as the Scriptures said it would.
17-18 A crowd had come to meet Jesus
because they had seen him call Lazarus
out of the tomb. They kept talking about
him and this miracle.[g] 19 But the Pharisees said to each other, "There is nothing
that can be done! Everyone in the world is
following Jesus."

Some Greeks Want To Meet Jesus

20 Some Greeks[h] had gone to Jerusalem
to worship during Passover. 21 Philip from
Bethsaida in Galilee was there too. So they
went to him and said, "Sir, we would like
to meet Jesus." 22 Philip told Andrew.
Then the two of them went to Jesus and
told him.

The Son of Man Must Be Lifted Up

23 Jesus said:
The time has come for the Son of
Man to be given his glory.[i] 24 I tell you
for certain that a grain of wheat that
falls on the ground will never be more
than one grain unless it dies. But if
it dies, it will produce lots of wheat.

[b] **12.3** *very expensive bottle of perfume*: The Greek text has "expensive perfume made of pure spikenard," a plant used to make perfume. [c] **12.4** *Iscariot*: See the note at 6.71.
[d] **12.13** *took palm branches and went out to greet him*: This was one way that the Jewish people welcomed a famous person. [e] **12.13** *Hooray*: This translates a word that can mean "please save us." But it is most often used as a shout of praise to God. [f] **12.16** *had been given his glory*: See the note at 7.39. [g] **12.17,18** *miracle*: See the note at 2.11,18,23. [h] **12.20** *Greeks*: Perhaps Gentiles who worshiped with the Jews. See the note at 7.35. [i] **12.23** *be given his glory*: See the note at 7.39.

12.3 Lk 7.37, 38. **12.8** Dt 15.11. **12.13** Ps 118.25, 26; 1 Macc 13.51. **12.15** Zec 9.9.

25 If you love your life, you will lose it.
If you give it up in this world, you will
be given eternal life. 26 If you serve
me, you must go with me. My servants
will be with me wherever I am. If you
serve me, my Father will honor you.
27 Now I am deeply troubled, and I
don't know what to say. But I must not
ask my Father to keep me from this
time of suffering. In fact, I came into
the world to suffer. 28 So Father, bring
glory to yourself.
A voice from heaven then said, "I have
already brought glory to myself, and I will
do it again!" 29 When the crowd heard the
voice, some of them thought it was thunder. Others thought an angel had spoken to
Jesus.
30 Then Jesus told the crowd, "That
voice spoke to help you, not me. 31 This
world's people are now being judged, and
the ruler of this world[j] is already being
thrown out! 32 If I am lifted up above the
earth, I will make everyone want to come
to me." 33 Jesus was talking about the way
he would be put to death.
34 The crowd said to Jesus, "The Scriptures teach that the Messiah will live
forever. How can you say that the Son
of Man must be lifted up? Who is this Son
of Man?"
35 Jesus answered, "The light will be
with you for only a little longer. Walk in
the light while you can. Then you won't be
caught walking blindly in the dark. 36 Have
faith in the light while it is with you, and
you will be children of the light."

The People Refuse To Have Faith in Jesus

After Jesus had said these things, he left
and went into hiding. 37 He had worked a
lot of miracles[k] among the people, but they
were still not willing to have faith in him.
38 This happened so that what the prophet
Isaiah had said would come true,

"Lord, who has believed
our message?
And who has seen
your mighty strength?"

39 The people could not have faith in Jesus,
because Isaiah had also said,

40 "The Lord has blinded
the eyes of the people,
and he has made
the people stubborn.
He did this so that they
could not see
or understand,
and so that they
would not turn to the Lord
and be healed."

41 Isaiah said this, because he saw the
glory of Jesus and spoke about him.[l]
42 Even then, many of the leaders put their
faith in Jesus, but they did not tell anyone
about it. The Pharisees had already given
orders for the people not to have anything
to do with anyone who had faith in Jesus.
43 And besides, the leaders liked praise
from others more than they liked praise
from God.

Jesus Came To Save the World

44 In a loud voice Jesus said:
Everyone who has faith in me also
has faith in the one who sent me.
45 And everyone who has seen me has
seen the one who sent me. 46 I am the
light that has come into the world. No
one who has faith in me will stay in
the dark.
47 I am not the one who will judge
those who refuse to obey my teachings.
I came to save the people of this world,
not to be their judge. 48 But everyone
who rejects me and my teachings will
be judged on the last day[m] by what I
have said. 49 I don't speak on my own.
I say only what the Father who sent
me has told me to say. 50 I know that

[j] **12.31** *world*: In the Gospel of John "world" sometimes refers to the people who live in this world and to the evil forces that control their lives. [k] **12.37** *miracles*: See the note at 2.11,18,23.
[l] **12.41** *he saw the glory of Jesus and spoke about him*: Or "he saw the glory of God and spoke about Jesus." [m] **12.48** *the last day*: See the note at 6.39.
12.25 Mt 10.39; 16.25; Mk 8.35; Lk 9.24; 17.33. **12.34** Ps 110.4; Is 9.7; Ez 37.24, 25; Dn 7.14. **12.38** Is 53.1 (LXX). **12.40** Is 6.10 (LXX).

his commands will bring eternal life. That is why I tell you exactly what the Father has told me.

Jesus Washes the Feet of His Disciples

13 It was before Passover, and Jesus knew that the time had come for him to leave this world and to return to the Father. He had always loved his followers in this world, and he loved them to the very end.

2 Even before the evening meal started, the devil had made Judas, the son of Simon Iscariot,[n] decide to betray Jesus.

3 Jesus knew that he had come from God and would go back to God. He also knew that the Father had given him complete power. 4 So during the meal Jesus got up, removed his outer garment, and wrapped a towel around his waist. 5 He put some water into a large bowl. Then he began washing his disciples' feet and drying them with the towel he was wearing.

6 But when he came to Simon Peter, that disciple asked, "Lord, are you going to wash my feet?"

7 Jesus answered, "You don't really know what I am doing, but later you will understand."

8 "You will never wash my feet!" Peter replied.

"If I don't wash you," Jesus told him, "you don't really belong to me."

9 Peter said, "Lord, don't wash just my feet. Wash my hands and my head."

10 Jesus answered, "People who have bathed and are clean all over need to wash just their feet. And you, my disciples, are clean, except for one of you." 11 Jesus knew who would betray him. That is why he said, "except for one of you."

12 After Jesus had washed his disciples' feet and had put his outer garment back on, he sat down again.[o] Then he said:

Do you understand what I have done? 13 You call me your teacher and Lord, and you should, because that is who I am. 14 And if your Lord and teacher has washed your feet, you should do the same for each other. 15 I have set the example, and you should do for each other exactly what I have done for you. 16 I tell you for certain that servants are not greater than their master, and messengers are not greater than the one who sent them. 17 You know these things, and God will bless you, if you do them.

18 I am not talking about all of you. I know the ones I have chosen. But what the Scriptures say must come true. And they say, "The man who ate with me has turned against me!" 19 I am telling you this before it all happens. Then when it does happen, you will believe who I am.[p] 20 I tell you for certain that anyone who welcomes my messengers also welcomes me, and anyone who welcomes me welcomes the one who sent me.

Jesus Tells What Will Happen to Him

(Matthew 26.20-25; Mark 14.17-21; Luke 22.21-23)

21 After Jesus had said these things, he was deeply troubled and told his disciples, "I tell you for certain that one of you will betray me." 22 They were confused about what he meant. And they just stared at each other.

23 Jesus' favorite disciple was sitting next to him at the meal, 24 and Simon motioned for that disciple to find out which one Jesus meant. 25 So the disciple leaned toward Jesus and asked, "Lord, which one of us are you talking about?"

26 Jesus answered, "I will dip this piece of bread in the sauce and give it to the one I was talking about."

Then Jesus dipped the bread and gave it to Judas, the son of Simon Iscariot.[q] 27 Right then Satan took control of Judas.

Jesus said, "Judas, go quickly and do what you have to do." 28 No one at the

[n] **13.2** *Iscariot*: See the note at 6.71. [o] **13.12** *sat down again*: On special occasions the Jewish people followed the Greek and Roman custom of lying down on their left side and leaning on their left elbow, while eating with their right hand. [p] **13.19** *I am*: See the note at 8.24.
[q] **13.26** *Iscariot*: See the note at 6.71.

13.12-15 Lk 22.27. **13.16** Mt 10.24; Lk 6.40; Jn 15.20. **13.18** Ps 41.9.
13.20 Mt 10.40; Mk 9.37; Lk 9.48; 10.16.

meal understood what Jesus meant. 29 But
because Judas was in charge of the money,
some of them thought that Jesus had told
him to buy something they needed for the
festival. Others thought that Jesus had told
him to give some money to the poor. 30 Judas took the piece of bread and went out.
It was already night.

The New Command

31 After Judas had gone, Jesus said:
Now the Son of Man will be given
glory, and he will bring glory to God.
32 Then, after God is given glory because of him, God will bring glory to
him, and God will do it very soon.
33 My children, I will be with you
for a little while longer. Then you will
look for me, but you won't find me. I
tell you just as I told the people, "You
cannot go where I am going." 34 But I
am giving you a new command. You
must love each other, just as I have
loved you. 35 If you love each other,
everyone will know that you are my
disciples.

Peter's Promise

(Matthew 26.31-35; Mark 14.27-31; Luke 22.31-34)

36 Simon Peter asked, "Lord, where are
you going?"
Jesus answered, "You can't go with me
now, but later on you will."
37 Peter asked, "Lord, why can't I go
with you now? I would die for you!"
38 "Would you really die for me?" Jesus
asked. "I tell you for certain that before a
rooster crows, you will say three times that
you don't even know me."

Jesus Is the Way to the Father

14 Jesus said to his disciples, "Don't
be worried! Have faith in God and
have faith in me.[r] 2 There are many rooms
in my Father's house. I wouldn't tell you
this, unless it was true. I am going there to
prepare a place for each of you. 3 After I
have done this, I will come back and take
you with me. Then we will be together.
4 You know the way to where I am going."
5 Thomas said, "Lord, we don't even
know where you are going! How can we
know the way?"
6 "I am the way, the truth, and the life!"
Jesus answered. "Without me, no one can
go to the Father. 7 If you had known me,
you would have known the Father. But
from now on, you do know him, and you
have seen him."
8 Philip said, "Lord, show us the Father.
That is all we need."
9 Jesus replied:
Philip, I have been with you for a
long time. Don't you know who I am?
If you have seen me, you have seen
the Father. How can you ask me to
show you the Father? 10 Don't you believe that I am one with the Father and
that the Father is one with me? What I
say isn't said on my own. The Father
who lives in me does these things.
11 Have faith in me when I say that
the Father is one with me and that I
am one with the Father. Or else have
faith in me simply because of the
things I do. 12 I tell you for certain that
if you have faith in me, you will do the
same things that I am doing. You will
do even greater things, now that I am
going back to the Father. 13 Ask me,
and I will do whatever you ask. This
way the Son will bring honor to the
Father. 14 I will do whatever you ask
me to do.

The Holy Spirit Is Promised

15 Jesus said to his disciples:
If you love me, you will do as I command. 16 Then I will ask the Father to
send you the Holy Spirit who will help[s]
you and always be with you. 17 The
Spirit will show you what is true. The
people of this world cannot accept the
Spirit, because they don't see or know

[r] **14.1** *Have faith in God and have faith in me*: Or "You have faith in God, so have faith in me."
[s] **14.16** *help*: The Greek word may mean "comfort," "encourage," or "defend."

13.33 Jn 7.34. **13.34** Jn 15.12, 17; 1 Jn 3.23; 2 Jn 5. **14.6** Ba 3.13, 14.
14.15 Ws 6.18.

him. But you know the Spirit, who is with you and will keep on living in you.

18 I won't leave you like orphans. I will come back to you. 19 In a little while the people of this world won't be able to see me, but you will see me. And because I live, you will live. 20 Then you will know that I am one with the Father. You will know that you are one with me, and I am one with you. 21 If you love me, you will do what I have said, and my Father will love you. I will also love you and show you what I am like.

22 The other Judas, not Judas Iscariot,[t] then spoke up and asked, "Lord, what do you mean by saying that you will show us what you are like, but you will not show the people of this world?"

23 Jesus replied:

If anyone loves me, they will obey me. Then my Father will love them, and we will come to them and live in them. 24 But anyone who doesn't love me, won't obey me. What they have heard me say doesn't really come from me, but from the Father who sent me.

25 I have told you these things while I am still with you. 26 But the Holy Spirit will come and help[u] you, because the Father will send the Spirit to take my place. The Spirit will teach you everything and will remind you of what I said while I was with you.

27 I give you peace, the kind of peace that only I can give. It isn't like the peace that this world can give. So don't be worried or afraid.

28 You have already heard me say that I am going and that I will also come back to you. If you really love me, you should be glad that I am going back to the Father, because he is greater than I am.

29 I am telling you this before I leave, so that when it does happen, you will have faith in me. 30 I cannot speak with you much longer, because the ruler of this world is coming. But he has no power over me. 31 I obey my Father, so that everyone in the world might know that I love him.

It is time for us to go now.

Jesus Is the True Vine

15 Jesus said to his disciples:

I am the true vine, and my Father is the gardener. 2 He cuts away every branch of mine that doesn't produce fruit. But he trims clean every branch that does produce fruit, so that it will produce even more fruit. 3 You are already clean because of what I have said to you.

4 Stay joined to me, and I will stay joined to you. Just as a branch cannot produce fruit unless it stays joined to the vine, you cannot produce fruit unless you stay joined to me. 5 I am the vine, and you are the branches. If you stay joined to me, and I stay joined to you, then you will produce lots of fruit. But you cannot do anything without me. 6 If you don't stay joined to me, you will be thrown away. You will be like dry branches that are gathered up and burned in a fire.

7 Stay joined to me and let my teachings become part of you. Then you can pray for whatever you want, and your prayer will be answered. 8 When you become fruitful disciples of mine, my Father will be honored. 9 I have loved you, just as my Father has loved me. So remain faithful to my love for you. 10 If you obey me, I will keep loving you, just as my Father keeps loving me, because I have obeyed him.

11 I have told you this to make you as completely happy as I am. 12 Now I tell you to love each other, as I have loved you. 13 The greatest way to show love for friends is to die for them. 14 And you are my friends, if you obey me. 15 Servants don't know what their master is doing, and so I don't speak to you as my servants. I speak to you as my friends, and I have told you everything that my Father has told me.

[t] **14.22** *Iscariot*: See the note at 6.71. [u] **14.26** *help*: See the note at 14.16.

14.21 Ws 6.12, 18; Si 4.14. **15.12** Jn 13.34; 15.17; 1 Jn 3.23; 2 Jn 5.

16 You did not choose me. I chose you and sent you out to produce fruit, the kind of fruit that will last. Then my Father will give you whatever you ask for in my name.[v] 17 So I command you to love each other.

The World's Hatred

18 If the people of this world[w] hate you, just remember that they hated me first. 19 If you belonged to the world, its people would love you. But you don't belong to the world. I have chosen you to leave the world behind, and that is why its people hate you. 20 Remember how I told you that servants are not greater than their master. So if people mistreat me, they will mistreat you. If they do what I say, they will do what you say.

21 People will do to you exactly what they did to me. They will do it because you belong to me, and they don't know the one who sent me. 22 If I had not come and spoken to them, they would not be guilty of sin. But now they have no excuse for their sin.

23 Everyone who hates me also hates my Father. 24 I have done things that no one else has ever done. If they had not seen me do these things, they would not be guilty. But they did see me do these things, and they still hate me and my Father too. 25 That is why the Scriptures are true when they say, "People hated me for no reason."

26 I will send you the Spirit who comes from the Father and shows what is true. The Spirit will help[x] you and will tell you about me. 27 Then you will also tell others about me, because you have been with me from the beginning.

16 I am telling you this to keep you from being afraid. 2 You will be chased out of the Jewish meeting places. And the time will come when people will kill you and think they are doing God a favor. 3 They will do these things because they don't know either the Father or me. 4 I am saying this to you now, so that when the time comes, you will remember what I have said.

The Work of the Holy Spirit

I was with you at the first, and so I didn't tell you these things. 5 But now I am going back to the Father who sent me, and none of you asks me where I am going. 6 You are very sad from hearing all of this. 7 But I tell you that I am going to do what is best for you. That is why I am going away. The Holy Spirit cannot come to help[x] you until I leave. But after I am gone, I will send the Spirit to you.

8 The Spirit will come and show the people of this world the truth about sin and God's justice and the judgment. 9 The Spirit will show them that they are wrong about sin, because they didn't have faith in me. 10 They are wrong about God's justice, because I am going to the Father, and you won't see me again. 11 And they are wrong about the judgment, because God has already judged the ruler of this world.

12 I have much more to say to you, but right now it would be more than you could understand. 13 The Spirit shows what is true and will come and guide you into the full truth. The Spirit doesn't speak on his own. He will tell you only what he has heard from me, and he will let you know what is going to happen. 14 The Spirit will bring glory to me by taking my message and telling it to you. 15 Everything that the Father has is mine. That is why I have said that the Spirit takes my message and tells it to you.

Sorrow Will Turn into Joy

16 Jesus told his disciples, "For a little while you won't see me, but after a while you will see me."

17 They said to each other, "What does Jesus mean by saying that for a little while

[v]**15.16** *in my name*: Or "because you are my followers." [w]**15.18** *world*: See the note at 12.31. [x]**15.26; 16.7** *help*: See the note at 14.16.

15.20 Mt 10.24; Lk 6.40; Jn 13.16. **15.25** Ps 35.19; 69.4. **16.13** Ws 9.11.

we won't see him, but after a while we will see him? What does he mean by saying that he is going to the Father? 18 What is this 'little while' that he is talking about? We don't know what he means."

19 Jesus knew that they had some questions, so he said:

You are wondering what I meant when I said that for a little while you won't see me, but after a while you will see me. 20 I tell you for certain that you will cry and be sad, but the world will be happy. You will be sad, but later you will be happy.

21 When a woman is about to give birth, she is in great pain. But after it is all over, she forgets the pain and is happy, because she has brought a child into the world. 22 You are now very sad. But later I will see you, and you will be so happy that no one will be able to change the way you feel. 23 When that time comes, you won't have to ask me about anything. I tell you for certain that the Father will give you whatever you ask for in my name. 24 You have not asked for anything in this way before, but now you must ask in my name.[y] Then it will be given to you, so that you will be completely happy.

25 I have used examples to explain to you what I have been talking about. But the time will come when I will speak to you plainly about the Father and will no longer use examples like these. 26 You will ask the Father in my name,[z] and I won't have to ask him for you. 27 God the Father loves you because you love me, and you believe that I have come from him. 28 I came from the Father into the world, but I am leaving the world and returning to the Father.

29 The disciples said, "Now you are speaking plainly to us! You are not using examples. 30 At last we know that you understand everything, and we don't have any more questions. Now we believe that you truly have come from God."

31 Jesus replied:

Do you really believe me? 32 The time will come and is already here when all of you will be scattered. Each of you will go back home and leave me by myself. But the Father will be with me, and I won't be alone. 33 I have told you this, so that you might have peace in your hearts because of me. While you are in the world, you will have to suffer. But cheer up! I have defeated the world.[a]

Jesus Prays

17 After Jesus had finished speaking to his disciples, he looked up toward heaven and prayed:

Father, the time has come for you to bring glory to your Son, in order that he may bring glory to you. 2 And you gave him power over all people, so that he would give eternal life to everyone you give him. 3 Eternal life is to know you, the only true God, and to know Jesus Christ, the one you sent. 4 I have brought glory to you here on earth by doing everything you gave me to do. 5 Now, Father, give me back the glory that I had with you before the world was created.

6 You have given me some followers from this world, and I have shown them what you are like. They were yours, but you gave them to me, and they have obeyed you. 7 They know that you gave me everything I have. 8 I told my followers what you told me, and they accepted it. They know that I came from you, and they believe that you are the one who sent me. 9 I am praying for them, but not for those who belong to this world.[a] My followers belong to you, and I am praying for them. 10 All that I have is yours, and all that you have is mine, and they will bring glory to me.

11 Holy Father, I am no longer in the world. I am coming to you, but my followers are still in the world. So keep

[y] **16.23,24** *in my name . . . in my name*: Or "as my disciples . . . as my disciples." [z] **16.26** *in my name*: Or "because you are my followers." [a] **16.33; 17.9** *world*: See the note at 12.31.
17.3 Ws 15.3.

them safe by the power of the name
that you have given me. Then they will
be one with each other, just as you and
I are one. 12 While I was with them, I
kept them safe by the power you have
given me. I guarded them, and not one
of them was lost, except the one who
had to be lost. This happened so that
what the Scriptures say would come
true.

13 I am on my way to you. But I say
these things while I am still in the
world, so that my followers will have
the same complete joy that I do. 14 I
have told them your message. But the
people of this world hate them, because they don't belong to this world,
just as I don't.

15 Father, I don't ask you to take my
followers out of the world, but keep
them safe from the evil one. 16 They
don't belong to this world, and neither
do I. 17 Your word is the truth. So
let this truth make them completely
yours. 18 I am sending them into the
world, just as you sent me. 19 I have
given myself completely for their sake,
so that they may belong completely to
the truth.

20 I am not praying just for these
followers. I am also praying for everyone else who will have faith because of
what my followers will say about me.
21 I want all of them to be one with
each other, just as I am one with you
and you are one with me. I also want
them to be one with us. Then the people of this world will believe that you
sent me.

22 I have honored my followers in
the same way that you honored me, in
order that they may be one with each
other, just as we are one. 23 I am one
with them, and you are one with me,
so that they may become completely
one. Then this world's people will
know that you sent me. They will know
that you love my followers as much as
you love me.

24 Father, I want everyone you have
given me to be with me, wherever
I am. Then they will see the glory
that you have given me, because you
loved me before the world was created.
25 Good Father, the people of this
world don't know you. But I know you,
and my followers know that you sent
me. 26 I told them what you are like,
and I will tell them even more. Then
the love that you have for me will become part of them, and I will be one
with them.

Jesus Is Betrayed and Arrested

(Matthew 26.47-56; Mark 14.43-50;
Luke 22.47-53)

18 When Jesus had finished praying,
he and his disciples crossed the
Kidron Valley and went into a garden.[b]
2 Jesus had often met there with his disciples, and Judas knew where the place was.
3-5 Judas had promised to betray Jesus.
So he went to the garden with some Roman soldiers and temple police, who had
been sent by the chief priests and the Pharisees. They carried torches, lanterns, and
weapons. Jesus already knew everything
that was going to happen, but he asked,
"Who are you looking for?"

They answered, "We are looking for
Jesus from Nazareth!"

Jesus told them, "I am Jesus!"[c] 6 At
once they all backed away and fell to the
ground.

7 Jesus again asked, "Who are you looking for?"

"We are looking for Jesus from
Nazareth," they answered.

8 This time Jesus replied, "I have
already told you that I am Jesus. If I am
the one you are looking for, let these others
go. 9 Then everything will happen, just
as I said, 'I did not lose anyone you
gave me.' "

10 Simon Peter had brought along a
sword. He now pulled it out and struck
at the servant of the high priest. The servant's name was Malchus, and Peter cut off

[b] **18.1** *garden*: The Greek word is usually translated "garden," but probably referred to an olive orchard. [c] **18.3-5** *I am Jesus*: The Greek text has "I am" (see the note at 8.24).
17.12 Ps 41.9; 2 Esd 2.26; Jn 13.18.

his right ear. 11 Jesus told Peter, "Put your sword away. I must drink from the cup[d] that the Father has given me."

Jesus Is Brought to Annas

(Matthew 26.57, 58; Mark 14.53, 54; Luke 22.54)

12 The Roman officer and his men, together with the temple police, arrested Jesus and tied him up. 13 They took him first to Annas, who was the father-in-law of Caiaphas, the high priest that year. 14 This was the same Caiaphas who had told the Jewish leaders, "It is better if one person dies for the people."

Peter Says He Doesn't Know Jesus

(Matthew 26.69, 70; Mark 14.66-68; Luke 22.55-57)

15 Simon Peter and another disciple followed Jesus. That disciple knew the high priest, and he followed Jesus into the courtyard of the high priest's house. 16 Peter stayed outside near the gate. But the other disciple came back out and spoke to the girl at the gate. She let Peter go in, 17 but asked him, "Aren't you one of that man's followers?"

"No, I am not!" Peter answered.

18 It was cold, and the servants and temple police had made a charcoal fire. They were warming themselves around it, when Peter went over and stood near the fire to warm himself.

Jesus Is Questioned by the High Priest

(Matthew 26.59-66; Mark 14.55-64; Luke 22.66-71)

19 The high priest questioned Jesus about his followers and his teaching. 20 But Jesus told him, "I have spoken freely in front of everyone. And I have always taught in our meeting places and in the temple, where all of our people come together. I have not said anything in secret. 21 Why are you questioning me? Why don't you ask the people who heard me? They know what I have said."

22 As soon as Jesus said this, one of the temple police hit him and said, "That's no way to talk to the high priest!"

23 Jesus answered, "If I have done something wrong, say so. But if not, why did you hit me?" 24 Jesus was still tied up, and Annas sent him to Caiaphas the high priest.

Peter Again Denies that He Knows Jesus

(Matthew 26.71-75; Mark 14.69-72; Luke 22.58-62)

25 While Simon Peter was standing there warming himself, someone asked him, "Aren't you one of Jesus' followers?"

Again Peter denied it and said, "No, I am not!"

26 One of the high priest's servants was there. He was a relative of the servant whose ear Peter had cut off, and he asked, "Didn't I see you in the garden with that man?"

27 Once more Peter denied it, and right then a rooster crowed.

Jesus Is Tried by Pilate

(Matthew 27.1, 2, 11-14; Mark 15.1-5; Luke 23.1-5)

28 It was early in the morning when Jesus was taken from Caiaphas to the building where the Roman governor stayed. But the crowd waited outside. Any of them who had gone inside would have become unclean and would not be allowed to eat the Passover meal.[e]

29 Pilate came out and asked, "What charges are you bringing against this man?"

30 They answered, "He is a criminal! That's why we brought him to you."

31 Pilate told them, "Take him and judge him by your own laws."

The crowd replied, "We are not allowed

[d] **18.11** *drink from the cup*: In the Scriptures a cup is sometimes used as a symbol of suffering. To "drink from the cup" is to suffer.

[e] **18.28** *would have become unclean and would not be allowed to eat the Passover meal*: Jewish people who came in close contact with foreigners right before Passover were not allowed to eat the Passover meal.

18.11 Mt 26.39; Mk 14.35, 36; Lk 22.42. **18.14** Jn 11.49, 50. **18.30,31** 3 Macc 7.10.

to put anyone to death." 32 And so what
Jesus said about his death[f] would soon
come true.
33 Pilate then went back inside. He
called Jesus over and asked, "Are you the
king of the Jews?"
34 Jesus answered, "Are you asking this
on your own or did someone tell you
about me?"
35 "You know I'm not a Jew!" Pilate said.
"Your own people and the chief priests
brought you to me. What have you
done?"
36 Jesus answered, "My kingdom doesn't
belong to this world. If it did, my followers
would have fought to keep me from
being handed over to the Jewish leaders.
No, my kingdom doesn't belong to this
world."
37 "So you are a king," Pilate replied.
"You are saying that I am a king," Jesus
told him. "I was born into this world to tell
about the truth. And everyone who belongs
to the truth knows my voice."
38 Pilate asked Jesus, "What is truth?"

Jesus Is Sentenced to Death

(Matthew 27.15-31; Mark 15.6-20; Luke 23.13-25)

Pilate went back out and said, "I don't
find this man guilty of anything! 39 And
since I usually set a prisoner free for you at
Passover, would you like for me to set free
the king of the Jews?"
40 They shouted, "No, not him! We
want Barabbas." Now Barabbas was a terrorist.[g]

19 Pilate gave orders for Jesus to be
beaten with a whip. 2 The soldiers
made a crown out of thorn branches and
put it on Jesus. Then they put a purple
robe on him. 3 They came up to him and
said, "Hey, you king of the Jews!" They also
hit him with their fists.
4 Once again Pilate went out. This time
he said, "I will have Jesus brought out to
you again. Then you can see for yourselves
that I have not found him guilty."
5 Jesus came out, wearing the crown of
thorns and the purple robe. Pilate said,
"Here is the man!"[h]
6 When the chief priests and the temple
police saw him, they yelled, "Nail him to a
cross! Nail him to a cross!"
Pilate told them, "You take him and nail
him to a cross! I don't find him guilty of
anything."
7 The crowd replied, "He claimed to be
the Son of God! Our Jewish Law says that
he must be put to death."
8 When Pilate heard this, he was terrified. 9 He went back inside and asked
Jesus, "Where are you from?" But Jesus did
not answer.
10 "Why won't you answer my question?" Pilate asked. "Don't you know that I
have the power to let you go free or to nail
you to a cross?"
11 Jesus replied, "If God had not given
you the power, you couldn't do anything at
all to me. But the one who handed me over
to you did something even worse."
12 Then Pilate wanted to set Jesus free.
But the crowd again yelled, "If you set this
man free, you are no friend of the Emperor! Anyone who claims to be a king is an
enemy of the Emperor."
13 When Pilate heard this, he brought
Jesus out. Then he sat down on the judge's
bench at the place known as "The Stone
Pavement." In Aramaic this pavement is
called "Gabbatha." 14 It was about noon on
the day before Passover, and Pilate said to
the crowd, "Look at your king!"
15 "Kill him! Kill him!" they yelled. "Nail
him to a cross!"
"So you want me to nail your king to a
cross?" Pilate asked.
The chief priests replied, "The Emperor
is our king!" 16 Then Pilate handed Jesus
over to be nailed to a cross.

[f] **18.32** *about his death*: Jesus had said that he would die by being "lifted up," which meant that he would die on a cross. The Romans killed criminals by nailing them on a cross, but they did not let the Jews kill anyone in this way. [g] **18.40** *terrorist*: Someone who stirred up trouble against the Romans in the hope of gaining freedom for the Jewish people. [h] **19.5** *"Here is the man!"*: Or "Look at the man!"

18.32 Jn 3.14; 12.32. **19.11** Ws 6.3.

Jesus Is Nailed to a Cross
(Matthew 27.32-44; Mark 15.21-32;
Luke 23.26-43)

Jesus was taken away, 17 and he carried
his cross to a place known as "The Skull."[i]
In Aramaic this place is called "Golgotha."
18 There Jesus was nailed to the cross, and
on each side of him a man was also nailed
to a cross.

19 Pilate ordered the charge against
Jesus to be written on a board and put
above the cross. It read, "Jesus of Nazareth,
King of the Jews." 20 The words were written in Hebrew, Latin, and Greek.

The place where Jesus was taken wasn't
far from the city, and many of the Jewish
people read the charge against him. 21 So
the chief priests went to Pilate and said,
"Why did you write that he is King of
the Jews? You should have written, 'He
claimed to be King of the Jews.' "

22 But Pilate told them, "What is written
will not be changed!"

23 After the soldiers had nailed Jesus to
the cross, they divided up his clothes into
four parts, one for each of them. But his
outer garment was made from a single
piece of cloth, and it did not have any
seams. 24 The soldiers said to each other,
"Let's not rip it apart. We will gamble to
see who gets it." This happened so that the
Scriptures would come true, which say,

"They divided up my clothes
and gambled
for my garments."

The soldiers then did what they had
decided.

25 Jesus' mother stood beside his cross
with her sister and Mary the wife of Clopas.
Mary Magdalene was standing there too.[j]
26 When Jesus saw his mother and his
favorite disciple with her, he said to his
mother, "This man is now your son."
27 Then he said to the disciple, "She is now
your mother." From then on, that disciple
took her into his own home.

The Death of Jesus
(Matthew 27.45-56; Mark 15.33-41;
Luke 23.44-49)

28 Jesus knew that he had now finished
his work. And in order to make the Scriptures come true, he said, "I am thirsty!"
29 A jar of cheap wine was there. Someone
then soaked a sponge with the wine and
held it up to Jesus' mouth on the stem of a
hyssop plant. 30 After Jesus drank the wine,
he said, "Everything is done!" He bowed
his head and died.

A Spear Is Stuck in Jesus' Side

31 The next day would be both a Sabbath and the Passover. It was a special day
for the Jewish people,[k] and they did not
want the bodies to stay on the crosses during that day. So they asked Pilate to break
the men's legs[l] and take their bodies down.
32 The soldiers first broke the legs of
the other two men who were nailed there.
33 But when they came to Jesus, they saw
that he was already dead, and they did not
break his legs.

34 One of the soldiers stuck his spear
into Jesus' side, and blood and water came
out. 35 We know this is true, because it was
told by someone who saw it happen. Now
you can have faith too. 36 All this happened
so that the Scriptures would come true,
which say, "No bone of his body will be
broken" 37 and, "They will see the one in
whose side they stuck a spear."

[i] **19.17** *The Skull*: The place was probably given this name because it was near a large rock in the shape of a human skull. [j] **19.25** *Jesus' mother stood beside his cross with her sister and Mary the wife of Clopas. Mary Magdalene was standing there too*: The Greek text may also be understood to include only three women ("Jesus' mother stood beside the cross with her sister, Mary the mother of Clopas. Mary Magdalene was standing there too.") or merely two women ("Jesus' mother was standing there with her sister Mary of Clopas, that is, Mary Magdalene."). "Of Clopas" may mean "daughter of" or "mother of." [k] **19.31** *a special day for the Jewish people*: Passover could be any day of the week. But according to the Gospel of John, Passover was on a Sabbath in the year that Jesus was nailed to a cross. [l] **19.31** *break the men's legs*: This was the way that the Romans sometimes speeded up the death of a person who had been nailed to a cross.

19.24 Ps 22.18. **19.28** Ps 22.15; 69.21. **19.36** Ex 12.46; Nu 9.12; Ps 34.20.
19.37 Zec 12.10; Rev 1.7.

Jesus Is Buried
(Matthew 27.57-61; Mark 15.42-47;
Luke 23.50-56)

38 Joseph from Arimathea was one of
Jesus' disciples. He had kept it secret
though, because he was afraid of the Jewish leaders. But now he asked Pilate to let
him have Jesus' body. Pilate gave him permission, and Joseph took it down from the
cross.
39 Nicodemus also came with about
seventy-five pounds of spices made from
myrrh and aloes. This was the same Nicodemus who had visited Jesus one night.[m]
40 The two men wrapped the body in a linen
cloth, together with the spices, which was
how the Jewish people buried their dead.
41 In the place where Jesus had been nailed
to a cross, there was a garden with a tomb
that had never been used. 42 The tomb
was nearby, and since it was the time to
prepare for the Sabbath, they were in a
hurry to put Jesus' body there.

Jesus Is Alive
(Matthew 28.1-10; Mark 16.1-8;
Luke 24.1-12)

20 On Sunday morning while it was
still dark, Mary Magdalene went to
the tomb and saw that the stone had been
rolled away from the entrance. 2 She ran to
Simon Peter and to Jesus' favorite disciple
and said, "They have taken the Lord from
the tomb! We don't know where they have
put him."
3 Peter and the other disciple started for
the tomb. 4 They ran side by side, until the
other disciple ran faster than Peter and got
there first. 5 He bent over and saw the
strips of linen cloth lying inside the tomb,
but he did not go in.
6 When Simon Peter got there, he went
into the tomb and saw the strips of cloth.
7 He also saw the piece of cloth that had
been used to cover Jesus' face. It was rolled
up and in a place by itself. 8 The disciple
who got there first then went into the
tomb, and when he saw it, he believed. 9 At
that time Peter and the other disciple did
not know that the Scriptures said Jesus
would rise to life. 10 So the two of them
went back to the other disciples.

Jesus Appears to Mary Magdalene
(Mark 16.9-11)

11 Mary Magdalene stood crying outside
the tomb. She was still weeping, when she
stooped down 12 and saw two angels inside.
They were dressed in white and were sitting where Jesus' body had been. One was
at the head and the other was at the foot.
13 The angels asked Mary, "Why are you
crying?"
She answered, "They have taken away
my Lord's body! I don't know where they
have put him."
14 As soon as Mary said this, she turned
around and saw Jesus standing there. But
she did not know who he was. 15 Jesus
asked her, "Why are you crying? Who are
you looking for?"
She thought he was the gardener and
said, "Sir, if you have taken his body away,
please tell me, so I can go and get him."
16 Then Jesus said to her, "Mary!"
She turned and said to him, "Rabboni."
The Aramaic word "Rabboni" means
"Teacher."
17 Jesus told her, "Don't hold on to me! I
have not yet gone to the Father. But tell my
disciples that I am going to the one who is
my Father and my God, as well as your
Father and your God." 18 Mary Magdalene
then went and told the disciples that she
had seen the Lord. She also told them
what he had said to her.

Jesus Appears to His Disciples
(Matthew 28.16-20; Mark 16.14-18;
Luke 24.36-49)

19 The disciples were afraid of the Jewish leaders, and on the evening of that
same Sunday they locked themselves in a
room. Suddenly, Jesus appeared in the
middle of the group. He greeted them
20 and showed them his hands and his side.
When the disciples saw the Lord, they became very happy.
21 After Jesus had greeted them again,
he said, "I am sending you, just as the

[m] **19.39** *Nicodemus who had visited Jesus one night*: See 3.1-21.
19.39 Jn 3.1, 2.

Father has sent me." 22 Then he breathed on them and said, "Receive the Holy Spirit. 23 If you forgive anyone's sins, they will be forgiven. But if you don't forgive their sins, they will not be forgiven."

Jesus and Thomas

24 Although Thomas the Twin was one of the twelve disciples, he wasn't with the others when Jesus appeared to them. 25 So they told him, "We have seen the Lord!"

But Thomas said, "First, I must see the nail scars in his hands and touch them with my finger. I must put my hand where the spear went into his side. I won't believe unless I do this!"

26 A week later the disciples were together again. This time, Thomas was with them. Jesus came in while the doors were still locked and stood in the middle of the group. He greeted his disciples 27 and said to Thomas, "Put your finger here and look at my hands! Put your hand into my side. Stop doubting and have faith!"

28 Thomas replied, "You are my Lord and my God!"

29 Jesus said, "Thomas, do you have faith because you have seen me? The people who have faith in me without seeing me are the ones who are really blessed!"

Why John Wrote His Book

30 Jesus worked many other miracles[n] for his disciples, and not all of them are written in this book. 31 But these are written so that you will put your faith in Jesus as the Messiah and the Son of God. If you have faith in[o] him, you will have true life.

Jesus Appears to Seven Disciples

21 Jesus later appeared to his disciples along the shore of Lake Tiberias. 2 Simon Peter, Thomas the Twin, Nathanael from Cana in Galilee, and the brothers James and John,[p] were there, together with two other disciples. 3 Simon Peter said, "I'm going fishing!"

The others said, "We will go with you." They went out in their boat. But they didn't catch a thing that night.

4 Early the next morning Jesus stood on the shore, but the disciples did not realize who he was. 5 Jesus shouted, "Friends, have you caught anything?"

"No!" they answered.

6 So he told them, "Let your net down on the right side of your boat, and you will catch some fish."

They did, and the net was so full of fish that they could not drag it up into the boat.

7 Jesus' favorite disciple told Peter, "It's the Lord!" When Simon heard that it was the Lord, he put on the clothes that he had taken off while he was working. Then he jumped into the water. 8 The boat was only about a hundred yards from shore. So the other disciples stayed in the boat and dragged in the net full of fish.

9 When the disciples got out of the boat, they saw some bread and a charcoal fire with fish on it. 10 Jesus told his disciples, "Bring some of the fish you just caught." 11 Simon Peter got back into the boat and dragged the net to shore. In it were one hundred fifty-three large fish, but still the net did not rip.

12 Jesus said, "Come and eat!" But none of the disciples dared ask who he was. They knew he was the Lord. 13 Jesus took the bread in his hands and gave some of it to his disciples. He did the same with the fish. 14 This was the third time that Jesus appeared to his disciples after he was raised from death.

Jesus and Peter

15 When Jesus and his disciples had finished eating, he asked, "Simon son of John, do you love me more than the others do?"[q]

Simon Peter answered, "Yes, Lord, you know I do!"

"Then feed my lambs," Jesus said.

[n]**20.30** *miracles*: See the note at 2.11,18,23. [o]**20.31** *put your faith in . . . have faith in*: Some manuscripts have "keep on having faith in . . . keep on having faith in." [p]**21.2** *the brothers James and John*: Greek "the two sons of Zebedee." [q]**21.15** *more than the others do*: Or "more than you love these things?"

20.23 Mt 16.19; 18.18. **21.3** Lk 5.5. **21.6** Lk 5.6.

16 Jesus asked a second time, "Simon
son of John, do you love me?"

Peter answered, "Yes, Lord, you know I love you!"

"Then take care of my sheep," Jesus told him.

17 Jesus asked a third time, "Simon son
of John, do you love me?"

Peter was hurt because Jesus had asked him three times if he loved him. So he told Jesus, "Lord, you know everything. You know I love you."

Jesus replied, "Feed my sheep. 18 I tell
you for certain that when you were a young man, you dressed yourself and went wherever you wanted to go. But when you are old, you will hold out your hands. Then others will wrap your belt around you and lead you where you don't want to go."

19 Jesus said this to tell how Peter would
die and bring honor to God. Then he said to Peter, "Follow me!"

Jesus and His Favorite Disciple

20 Peter turned and saw Jesus' favorite
disciple following them. He was the same one who had sat next to Jesus at the meal and had asked, "Lord, who is going to betray you?"
21 When Peter saw that disciple,
he asked Jesus, "Lord, what about him?"

22 Jesus answered, "What is it to you, if
I want him to live until I return? You must follow me."
23 So the rumor spread among
the other disciples that this disciple would not die. But Jesus did not say he would not die. He simply said, "What is it to you, if I want him to live until I return?"

24 This disciple is the one who told all of
this. He wrote it, and we know he is telling the truth.

25 Jesus did many other things. If they
were all written in books, I don't suppose there would be room enough in the whole world for all the books.

21.20 Jn 13.25.

ACTS

ABOUT THIS BOOK

This is the second book written by Luke. His first one is commonly known as the Gospel of Luke. In it he told "all that Jesus did and taught from the very first until he was taken up to heaven" (1.1, 2). In this book Luke continues the story by describing some of the struggles the disciples faced as they tried to obey the command of Jesus: "You will tell everyone about me in Jerusalem, in all Judea, in Samaria, and everywhere in the world" (1.8).

So many different countries are mentioned in Acts that the book may seem to have been written only to tell about the spread of the Christian message. But that is only part of the story. After Jesus was taken up to heaven, one of the big problems for his followers was deciding who could belong to God's people. And since Jesus and his first followers were Jews, it was only natural for many of them to think that his message was only for Jews. But in Acts, the Spirit is always present to show that Jesus came to save both Jews and Gentiles, and that God wants followers from every nation and race to be part of his people.

The first conflict between Christians and Jews took place when some of the Jewish religious leaders rejected the message about Jesus (4.1-31; 7.1-59). But the most serious problems for the early church happened because the disciples at first failed to understand that anyone could become a follower of Jesus without first becoming a Jew. This began to change when Philip dared to take the message to the Samaritans (8.7-25), and when Peter went to the home of Cornelius, a captain in the Roman army (10.1-48).

Finally, Peter reported to the church in Jerusalem (11.1-18) and a meeting was held there (15.3-35) to discuss the question of who could become followers of Christ. Before the meeting was over, everyone agreed that the Spirit of God was leading them to reach out to Gentiles as well as Jews with the good news of Jesus.

The one who did the most for the spread of the faith was a man named Paul, and much of the book tells about his preaching among the Gentiles. Finally, he took the message to Rome, the world's most important city at that time (28.16-31). One of Luke's main reasons for writing was to show that nothing could keep the Christian message from spreading everywhere:

> *For two years Paul stayed in a rented house and welcomed everyone who came to see him. He bravely preached about God's kingdom and taught about the Lord Jesus Christ, and no one tried to stop him.*
>
> *(28.30, 31)*

A QUICK LOOK AT THIS BOOK

- Telling the Good News in Jerusalem (1.1—8.3)
- The Good News in Judea and Samaria (8.4—12.25)
- Paul's First Journey To Tell the Good News (13.1—14.28)
- An Important Decision in Jerusalem (15.1-35)
- Paul's Second Journey To Tell the Good News (15.36—18.22)
- Paul's Third Journey To Tell the Good News (18.23—21.16)

- Paul's Arrest in Jerusalem (21.17—23.22)
- Paul Is Taken to Caesarea (23.23—26.32)
- Paul Is Taken to Rome (27.1—28.31)

---

1 Theophilus, I first wrote to you[a] about
all that Jesus did and taught from the
very first 2 until he was taken up to heaven.
But before he was taken up, he gave orders
to the apostles he had chosen with the help
of the Holy Spirit.
3 For forty days after Jesus had suffered
and died, he proved in many ways that he
had been raised from death. He appeared
to his apostles and spoke to them about
God's kingdom. 4 While he was still with
them, he said:

> Don't leave Jerusalem yet. Wait
> here for the Father to give you the
> Holy Spirit, just as I told you he has
> promised to do. 5 John baptized with
> water, but in a few days you will be
> baptized with the Holy Spirit.

Jesus Is Taken to Heaven

6 While the apostles were still with
Jesus, they asked him, "Lord, are you
now going to give Israel its own king
again?"[b]
7 Jesus said to them, "You don't need to
know the time of those events that only the
Father controls. 8 But the Holy Spirit will
come upon you and give you power. Then
you will tell everyone about me in Jerusalem, in all Judea, in Samaria, and everywhere in the world." 9 After Jesus had said
this and while they were watching, he was
taken up into a cloud. They could not see
him, 10 but as he went up, they kept looking up into the sky.
Suddenly two men dressed in white
clothes were standing there beside them.
11 They said, "Why are you men from
Galilee standing here and looking up into
the sky? Jesus has been taken to heaven.
But he will come back in the same way that
you have seen him go."

Someone To Take the Place of Judas

12-13 The Mount of Olives was about half
a mile from Jerusalem. The apostles who
had gone there were Peter, John, James,
Andrew, Philip, Thomas, Bartholomew,
Matthew, James the son of Alphaeus, Simon, known as the Eager One,[c] and Judas
the son of James.
After the apostles returned to the city,
they went upstairs to the room where they
had been staying.
14 The apostles often met together and
prayed with a single purpose in mind.[d] The
women and Mary the mother of Jesus
would meet with them, and so would his
brothers. 15 One day there were about one
hundred twenty of the Lord's followers
meeting together, and Peter stood up to
speak to them. 16-17 He said:

> My friends, long ago by the power of
> the Holy Spirit, David said something
> about Judas, and what he said has now
> happened. Judas was one of us and
> had worked with us, but he brought
> the mob to arrest Jesus. 18 Then Judas
> bought some land with the money he
> was given for doing that evil thing. He
> fell headfirst into the field. His body
> burst open, and all his insides came
> out. 19 When the people of Jerusalem
> found out about this, they called the
> place Akeldama, which in the local
> language means "Field of Blood."
> 20 In the book of Psalms it says,
>
> "Leave his house empty,
> and don't let anyone
> live there."

[a]**1.1** *I first wrote to you*: The Gospel of Luke. [b]**1.6** *are you now going to give Israel its own king again*: Or "Are you now going to rule Israel as its king?" [c]**1.12,13** *known as the Eager One*: The Greek text has "Zealot," a name later given to the members of a Jewish group that resisted and fought against the Romans. [d]**1.14** *met together and prayed with a single purpose in mind*: Or "met together in a special place for prayer."

1.1 Lk 1.1-4. **1.4** Lk 24.49. **1.5** Mt 3.11; Mk 1.8; Lk 3.16; Jn 1.33. **1.8** Mt 28.19; Mk 16.15; Lk 24.47, 48. **1.9** Mk 16.19; Lk 24.50, 51. **1.12,13** Mt 10.2-4; Mk 3.16-19; Lk 6.14-16. **1.18,19** Mt 27.3-8. **1.20** **a** Ps 69.25; **b** Ps 109.8.

It also says,

"Let someone else
have his job."

21-22 So we need someone else to
help us tell others that Jesus has been
raised from death. He must also be
one of the men who was with us from
the very beginning. He must have
been with us from the time the Lord
Jesus was baptized by John until the
day he was taken to heaven.
23 Two men were suggested: One of
them was Joseph Barsabbas, known as Justus, and the other was Matthias. 24 Then
they all prayed, "Lord, you know what
everyone is like! Show us the one you have
chosen 25 to be an apostle and to serve in
place of Judas, who got what he deserved."
26 They drew names, and Matthias was
chosen to join the group of the eleven
apostles.

The Coming of the Holy Spirit

2 On the day of Pentecost[e] all the Lord's
followers were together in one place.
2 Suddenly there was a noise from heaven
like the sound of a mighty wind! It filled
the house where they were meeting.
3 Then they saw what looked like fiery
tongues moving in all directions, and a
tongue came and settled on each person
there. 4 The Holy Spirit took control of
everyone, and they began speaking whatever languages the Spirit let them speak.
5 Many religious Jews from every country in the world were living in Jerusalem.
6 And when they heard this noise, a crowd
gathered. But they were surprised, because
they were hearing everything in their own
languages. 7 They were excited and
amazed, and said:
Don't all these who are speaking
come from Galilee? 8 Then why do we
hear them speaking our very own languages? 9 Some of us are from Parthia,
Media, and Elam. Others are from
Mesopotamia, Judea, Cappadocia,
Pontus, Asia, 10 Phrygia, Pamphylia,
Egypt, parts of Libya near Cyrene,
Rome, 11 Crete, and Arabia. Some of
us were born Jews, and others of us
have chosen to be Jews. Yet we all hear
them using our own languages to tell
the wonderful things God has done.
12 Everyone was excited and confused.
Some of them even kept asking each other,
"What does all this mean?"
13 Others made fun of the Lord's followers and said, "They are drunk."

Peter Speaks to the Crowd

14 Peter stood with the eleven apostles and
spoke in a loud and clear voice to the crowd:
Friends and everyone else living in
Jerusalem, listen carefully to what I
have to say! 15 You are wrong to think
that these people are drunk. After all,
it is only nine o'clock in the morning. 16 But this is what God had the
prophet Joel say,

17 "When the last days come,
I will give my Spirit
to everyone.
Your sons and daughters
will prophesy.
Your young men
will see visions,
and your old men
will have dreams.
18 In those days I will give
my Spirit to my servants,
both men and women,
and they will prophesy.

19 I will work miracles
in the sky above
and wonders
on the earth below.
There will be blood and fire
and clouds of smoke.
20 The sun will turn dark,
and the moon
will be as red as blood
before the great

[e]**2.1** *Pentecost*: A Jewish festival that came fifty days after Passover and celebrated the wheat harvest. Jews later celebrated Pentecost as the time when they were given the Law of Moses.
1.21,22 **a** Mt 3.16; Mk 1.9; Lk 3.21; **b** Mk 16.19; Lk 24.51. **2.1** Lv 23.15-21; Dt 16.9-11.
2.17-21 Jl 2.28-32 (LXX).

and wonderful day
of the Lord appears.
21 Then the Lord
will save everyone
who asks for his help."

22 Now, listen to what I have to
say about Jesus from Nazareth. God
proved that he sent Jesus to you by
having him work miracles, wonders,
and signs. All of you know this. 23 God
had already planned and decided that
Jesus would be handed over to you. So
you took him and had evil men put
him to death on a cross. 24 But God set
him free from death and raised him to
life. Death could not hold him in its
power. 25 What David said are really
the words of Jesus,

"I always see the Lord
near me,
and I will not be afraid
with him at my right side.
26 Because of this,
my heart will be glad,
my words will be joyful,
and I will live in hope.
27 The Lord won't leave me
in the grave.
I am his holy one,
and he won't let
my body decay.
28 He has shown me
the path to life,
and he makes me glad
by being near me."

29 My friends, it is right for me to
speak to you about our ancestor David.
He died and was buried, and his tomb
is still here. 30 But David was a
prophet, and he knew that God had
made a promise he would not break.
He had told David that someone from
his own family would someday be king.
31 David knew this would happen,
and so he told us that Christ would be
raised to life. He said that God would
not leave him in the grave or let his
body decay. 32 All of us can tell you
that God has raised Jesus to life!
33 Jesus was taken up to sit at the
right side[f] of God, and he was given
the Holy Spirit, just as the Father had
promised. Jesus is also the one who
has given the Spirit to us, and that is
what you are now seeing and hearing.
34 David didn't go up to heaven. So
he wasn't talking about himself when
he said, "The Lord told my Lord to sit
at his right side, 35 until he made my
Lord's enemies into a footstool for
him." 36 Everyone in Israel should
then know for certain that God has
made Jesus both Lord and Christ, even
though you put him to death on a cross.
37 When the people heard this, they
were very upset. They asked Peter and the
other apostles, "Friends, what shall we do?"
38 Peter said, "Turn back to God! Be
baptized in the name of Jesus Christ,
so that your sins will be forgiven. Then
you will be given the Holy Spirit. 39 This
promise is for you and your children. It is
for everyone our Lord God will choose, no
matter where they live."
40 Peter told them many other things as
well. Then he said, "I beg you to save yourselves from what will happen to all these
evil people." 41 On that day about three
thousand believed his message and were
baptized. 42 They spent their time learning
from the apostles, and they were like family
to each other. They also broke bread[g] and
prayed together.

Life among the Lord's Followers

43 Everyone was amazed by the many
miracles and wonders that the apostles
worked. 44 All the Lord's followers often
met together, and they shared everything
they had. 45 They would sell their property
and possessions and give the money to
whoever needed it. 46 Day after day they
met together in the temple. They broke
bread[g] together in different homes and

[f]**2.33** *right side*: The place of honor and power. [g]**2.42,46** *broke bread*: They ate together and celebrated the Lord's Supper.

2.23 Mt 27.35; Mk 15.24; Lk 23.33; Jn 19.18. **2.24** Mt 28.5, 6; Mk 16.6; Lk 24.5.
2.25-28 Ps 16.8-11 (LXX). **2.30** 2 S 7.12, 13; Ps 132.11. **2.34,35** Ps 110.1.
2.44 Ac 4.32-35.

shared their food happily and freely,
47 while praising God. Everyone liked them,
and each day the Lord added to their group
others who were being saved.

Peter and John Heal a Lame Man

3 The time of prayer[h] was about three
o'clock in the afternoon, and Peter
and John were going into the temple. 2 A
man who had been born lame was being
carried to the temple door. Each day he
was placed beside this door, known as the
Beautiful Gate. He sat there and begged
from the people who were going in.
3 The man saw Peter and John entering
the temple, and he asked them for money.
4 But they looked straight at him and said,
"Look up at us!"
5 The man stared at them and thought
he was going to get something. 6 But Peter
said, "I don't have any silver or gold! But I
will give you what I do have. In the name
of Jesus Christ from Nazareth, get up and
start walking." 7 Peter then took him by the
right hand and helped him up.

At once the man's feet and ankles became strong, 8 and he jumped up and
started walking. He went with Peter and
John into the temple, walking and jumping
and praising God. 9 Everyone saw him
walking around and praising God. 10 They
knew that he was the beggar who had been
lying beside the Beautiful Gate, and they
were completely surprised. They could not
imagine what had happened to the man.

Peter Speaks in the Temple

11 While the man kept holding on to Peter and John, the whole crowd ran to them
in amazement at the place known as Solomon's Porch.[i] 12 Peter saw that a crowd
had gathered, and he said:

Friends, why are you surprised at
what has happened? Why are you staring at us? Do you think we have some
power of our own? Do you think we
were able to make this man walk because we are so religious? 13 The God
that Abraham, Isaac, Jacob, and our
other ancestors worshiped has brought
honor to his Servant[j] Jesus. He is the
one you betrayed. You turned against
him when he was being tried by Pilate,
even though Pilate wanted to set him
free.

14 You rejected Jesus, who was holy
and good. You asked for a murderer to
be set free, 15 and you killed the one
who leads people to life. But God
raised him from death, and all of us
can tell you what he has done. 16 You
see this man, and you know him. He
put his faith in the name of Jesus and
was made strong. Faith in Jesus made
this man completely well while everyone was watching.

17 My friends, I am sure that you
and your leaders didn't know what you
were doing. 18 But God had his
prophets tell that his Messiah would
suffer, and now he has kept that
promise. 19 So turn to God! Give up
your sins, and you will be forgiven.
20 Then that time will come when
the Lord will give you fresh strength.
He will send you Jesus, his chosen
Messiah. 21 But Jesus must stay in
heaven until God makes all things
new, just as his holy prophets promised
long ago.

22 Moses said, "The Lord your God
will choose one of your own people to
be a prophet, just as he chose me. Listen to everything he tells you. 23 No
one who disobeys that prophet will be
one of God's people any longer."

24 Samuel and all the other prophets who came later also spoke about
what is now happening. 25 You are
really the ones God told his prophets to speak to. And you were given
the promise that God made to your
ancestors. He said to Abraham, "All

[h] **3.1** *The time of prayer*: Many of the Jewish people prayed in their homes at regular times each day (see Daniel 6.11), and on special occasions they prayed in the temple. [i] **3.11** *Solomon's Porch*: A public place with tall columns along the east side of the temple. [j] **3.13** *Servant*: Or "Son."

3.13 Ex 3.14-16. **3.14** Mt 27.15-23; Mk 15.6-14; Lk 23.13-23; Jn 19.12-15.
3.22 Dt 18.15, 18 (LXX). **3.23** Dt 18.19. **3.25** Gn 22.18.

nations on earth will be blessed because of someone from your family."
26 God sent his chosen Son[k] to you
first, because God wanted to bless you
and make each one of you turn away
from your sins.

Peter and John Are Brought in Front of the Council

4 The apostles were still talking to the
people, when some priests, the captain
of the temple guard, and some Sadducees
arrived. 2 These men were angry because
the apostles were teaching the people that
the dead would be raised from death, just
as Jesus had been raised from death. 3 It
was already late in the afternoon, and they
arrested Peter and John and put them in
jail for the night. 4 But a lot of people who
had heard the message believed it. So by
now there were about five thousand followers of the Lord.

5 The next morning the leaders, the elders, and the teachers of the Law of Moses
met in Jerusalem. 6 The high priest Annas
was there, as well as Caiaphas, John, Alexander, and other members of the high
priest's family. 7 They brought in Peter and
John and made them stand in the middle
while they questioned them. They asked,
"By what power and in whose name have
you done this?"

8 Peter was filled with the Holy Spirit
and told the nation's leaders and the
elders:

9 You are questioning us today
about a kind deed in which a crippled
man was healed. 10 But there is something we must tell you and everyone
else in Israel. This man is standing
here completely well because of the
power of Jesus Christ from Nazareth.
You put Jesus to death on a cross, but
God raised him to life. 11 He is the
stone that you builders thought was
worthless, and now he is the most important stone of all. 12 Only Jesus has
the power to save! His name is the
only one in all the world that can save
anyone.

13 The officials were amazed to see how
brave Peter and John were, and they knew
that these two apostles were only ordinary
men and not well educated. The officials
were certain that these men had been with
Jesus. 14 But they could not deny what had
happened. The man who had been healed
was standing there with the apostles.

15 The officials commanded them to
leave the council room. Then the officials
said to each other, 16 "What can we do with
these men? Everyone in Jerusalem knows
about this miracle, and we cannot say it
didn't happen. 17 But to keep this thing
from spreading, we will warn them never
again to speak to anyone about the name of
Jesus." 18 So they called the two apostles
back in and told them that they must
never, for any reason, teach anything about
the name of Jesus.

19 Peter and John answered, "Do you
think God wants us to obey you or to obey
him? 20 We cannot keep quiet about what
we have seen and heard."

21-22 The officials could not find any
reason to punish Peter and John. So they
threatened them and let them go. The man
who was healed by this miracle was more
than forty years old, and everyone was
praising God for what had happened.

Peter and Others Pray for Courage

23 As soon as Peter and John had been
set free, they went back and told the others
everything that the chief priests and the
leaders had said to them. 24 When the rest
of the Lord's followers heard this, they
prayed together and said:

Master, you created heaven and
earth, the sea, and everything in them.
25 And by the Holy Spirit you spoke to
our ancestor David. He was your servant, and you told him to say:

"Why are all the Gentiles
so furious?
Why do people
make foolish plans?
26 The kings of earth
prepare for war,

[k]3.26 *Son*: Or "Servant."

4.11 Ps 118.22. **4.24** Ex 20.11; Ne 9.6; Ps 146.6. **4.25,26** Ps 2.1, 2 (LXX).

and the rulers
join together
against the Lord
and his Messiah."

27 Here in Jerusalem, Herod[l] and Pontius Pilate got together with the Gentiles and the people of Israel. Then they turned against your holy Servant[m] Jesus, your chosen Messiah. 28 They did what you in your power and wisdom had already decided would happen.

29 Lord, listen to their threats! We are your servants. So make us brave enough to speak your message. 30 Show your mighty power, as we heal people and work miracles and wonders in the name of your holy Servant[m] Jesus. 31 After they had prayed, the meeting place shook. They were all filled with the Holy Spirit and bravely spoke God's message.

Sharing Possessions

32 The group of followers all felt the same way about everything. None of them claimed that their possessions were their own, and they shared everything they had with each other. 33 In a powerful way the apostles told everyone that the Lord Jesus was now alive. God greatly blessed his followers,[n] 34 and no one went in need of anything. Everyone who owned land or houses would sell them and bring the money 35 to the apostles. Then they would give the money to anyone who needed it.

36-37 Joseph was one of the followers who had sold a piece of property and brought the money to the apostles. He was a Levite from Cyprus, and the apostles called him Barnabas, which means "one who encourages others."

Peter Condemns Ananias and Sapphira

5 Ananias and his wife Sapphira also sold a piece of property. 2 But they agreed to cheat and keep some of the money for themselves.

So when Ananias took the rest of the money to the apostles, 3 Peter said, "Why has Satan made you keep back some of the money from the sale of the property? Why have you lied to the Holy Spirit? 4 The property was yours before you sold it, and even after you sold it, the money was still yours. What made you do such a thing? You didn't lie to people. You lied to God!"

5 As soon as Ananias heard this, he dropped dead, and everyone who heard about it was frightened. 6 Some young men came in and wrapped up his body. Then they took it out and buried it.

7 Three hours later Sapphira came in, but she did not know what had happened to her husband. 8 Peter asked her, "Tell me, did you sell the property for this amount?"

"Yes," she answered, "that's the amount."

9 Then Peter said, "Why did the two of you agree to test the Lord's Spirit? The men who buried Ananias are by the door, and they will carry you out!" 10 At once she fell at Peter's feet and died.

When the young men came back in, they found Sapphira lying there dead. So they carried her out and buried her beside her husband. 11 The church members were afraid, and so was everyone else who heard what had happened.

Peter's Unusual Power

12 The apostles worked many miracles and wonders among the people. All of the Lord's followers often met in the part of the temple known as Solomon's Porch.[o] 13 No one outside their group dared join them, even though everyone liked them very much.

14 Many men and women started having faith in the Lord. 15 Then sick people were brought out to the road and placed on cots and mats. It was hoped that Peter would walk by, and his shadow would fall on them and heal them. 16 A lot of people living in the towns near Jerusalem brought those who were sick or troubled by evil spirits, and they were all healed.

[l] **4.27** *Herod*: Herod Antipas, the son of Herod the Great. [m] **4.27,30** *Servant*: See the note at 3.13. [n] **4.33** *God greatly blessed his followers*: Or "Everyone highly respected his followers." [o] **5.12** *Solomon's Porch*: See the note at 3.11.

4.27 **a** Lk 23.7-11; **b** Mt 27.1, 2; Mk 15.1; Lk 23.1; Jn 18.28, 29. **4.32** Ac 2.44, 45. **5.5** Su 55.

Trouble for the Apostles

[17] The high priest and all the other Sadducees who were with him became jealous.
[18] They arrested the apostles and put them
in the city jail. [19] But that night an angel
from the Lord opened the doors of the jail
and led the apostles out. The angel said,
[20] "Go to the temple and tell the people
everything about this new life." [21] So they
went into the temple before sunrise and
started teaching.

The high priest and his men called together their council, which included all of
Israel's leaders. Then they ordered the
apostles to be brought to them from the
jail. [22] The temple police who were sent
to the jail did not find the apostles. They
returned and said, [23] "We found the jail
locked tight and the guards standing at
the doors. But when we opened the doors
and went in, we didn't find anyone there."
[24] The captain of the temple police and the
chief priests listened to their report, but
they did not know what to think about it.

[25] Just then someone came in and said,
"Right now those men you put in jail are in
the temple, teaching the people!" [26] The
captain went with some of the temple police and brought the apostles back. But
they did not use force. They were afraid
that the people might start throwing stones
at them.

[27] When the apostles were brought before the council, the high priest said to
them, [28] "We told you plainly not to teach
in the name of Jesus. But look what you
have done! You have been teaching all over
Jerusalem, and you are trying to blame us
for his death."

[29] Peter and the apostles replied:

We don't obey people. We obey God.
[30] You killed Jesus by nailing him to a
cross. But the God our ancestors worshiped raised him to life [31] and made
him our Leader and Savior. Then God
gave him a place at his right side,[p] so
that the people of Israel would turn
back to him and be forgiven. [32] We are
here to tell you about all this, and so is
the Holy Spirit, who is God's gift to
everyone who obeys God.

[33] When the council members heard
this, they became so angry that they
wanted to kill the apostles. [34] But one of
the members was the Pharisee Gamaliel, a
highly respected teacher. He ordered the
apostles to be taken out of the room for a
little while. [35] Then he said to the council:

People of Israel, be careful what you
do with these men. [36] Not long ago
Theudas claimed to be someone important, and about four hundred men
joined him. But he was killed. All his
followers were scattered, and that was
the end of that.

[37] Later, when the people of our nation were being counted, Judas from
Galilee showed up. A lot of people followed him, but he was killed, and all
his followers were scattered.

[38] So I advise you to stay away from
these men. Leave them alone. If what
they are planning is something of their
own doing, it will fail. [39] But if God is
behind it, you cannot stop it anyway,
unless you want to fight against God.

The council members agreed with what
he said, [40] and they called the apostles back
in. They had them beaten with a whip and
warned them not to speak in the name of
Jesus. Then they let them go.

[41] The apostles left the council and
were happy, because God had considered
them worthy to suffer for the sake of Jesus.
[42] Every day they spent time in the temple
and in one home after another. They never
stopped teaching and telling the good news
that Jesus is the Messiah.

Seven Leaders for the Church

6 A lot of people were now becoming followers of the Lord. But some of the
ones who spoke Greek started complaining
about the ones who spoke Aramaic. They
complained that the Greek-speaking widows were not given their share when the
food supplies were handed out each day.

[2] The twelve apostles called the whole
group of followers together and said,

[p]**5.31** *right side*: See the note at 2.33.
5.28 Mt 27.25. **5.39** 2 Macc 7.19.

"We should not give up preaching God's message in order to serve at tables.[q] 3 My friends, choose seven men who are respected and wise and filled with God's Spirit. We will put them in charge of these things. 4 We can spend our time praying and serving God by preaching."

5 This suggestion pleased everyone, and they began by choosing Stephen. He had great faith and was filled with the Holy Spirit. Then they chose Philip, Prochorus, Nicanor, Timon, Parmenas, and also Nicolaus, who worshiped with the Jewish people[r] in Antioch. 6 These men were brought to the apostles. Then the apostles prayed and placed their hands on the men to show that they had been chosen to do this work. 7 God's message spread, and many more people in Jerusalem became followers. Even a large number of priests put their faith in the Lord.

Stephen Is Arrested

8 God gave Stephen the power to work great miracles and wonders among the people. 9 But some Jews from Cyrene and Alexandria were members of a group who called themselves "Free Men."[s] They started arguing with Stephen. Some others from Cilicia and Asia also argued with him. 10 But they were no match for Stephen, who spoke with the great wisdom that the Spirit gave him. 11 So they talked some men into saying, "We heard Stephen say terrible things against Moses and God!"

12 They turned the people and their leaders and the teachers of the Law of Moses against Stephen. Then they all grabbed Stephen and dragged him in front of the council.

13 Some men agreed to tell lies about Stephen, and they said, "This man keeps on saying terrible things about this holy temple and the Law of Moses. 14 We have heard him claim that Jesus from Nazareth will destroy this place and change the customs that Moses gave us." 15 Then all the council members stared at Stephen. They saw that his face looked like the face of an angel.

Stephen's Speech

7 The high priest asked Stephen, "Are they telling the truth about you?" 2 Stephen answered:

Friends, listen to me. Our glorious God appeared to our ancestor Abraham while he was still in Mesopotamia, before he had moved to Haran. 3 God told him, "Leave your country and your relatives and go to a land that I will show you." 4 Then Abraham left the land of the Chaldeans and settled in Haran.

After his father died, Abraham came and settled in this land where you now live. 5 God didn't give him any part of it, not even a square foot. But God did promise to give it to him and his family forever, even though Abraham didn't have any children. 6 God said that Abraham's descendants would live for a while in a foreign land. There they would be slaves and would be mistreated four hundred years. 7 But he also said, "I will punish the nation that makes them slaves. Then later they will come and worship me in this place."

8 God said to Abraham, "Every son in each family must be circumcised to show that you have kept your agreement with me." So when Isaac was eight days old, Abraham circumcised him. Later, Isaac circumcised his son Jacob, and Jacob circumcised his twelve sons. 9 These men were our ancestors.

Joseph was also one of our famous ancestors. His brothers were jealous of him and sold him as a slave to be

[q]**6.2** *to serve at tables*: This may mean either that they were in charge of handing out food to the widows or that they were in charge of the money, since the Greek word "table" may also mean "bank."
[r]**6.5** *worshiped with the Jewish people*: This translates the Greek word "proselyte" that means a Gentile who had accepted the Jewish religion.
[s]**6.9** *Free Men*: A group of Jewish men who had once been slaves, but had been freed.

6.15 4 Macc 9.22. **7.2,3** Gn 12.1. **7.4** **a** Gn 11.31; **b** Gn 12.4, 5. **7.5** Gn 12.7; 13.15; 15.18; 17.8. **7.6,7** Gn 15.13-15. **7.7** Ex 3.12. **7.8** **a** Gn 17.10-14; **b** Gn 21.2-4; **c** Gn 25.26; **d** Gn 29.31—35.18. **7.9** **a** Gn 37.11; **b** Gn 37.28; **c** Gn 39.2, 3, 21.

taken to Egypt. But God was with him
10 and rescued him from all his troubles. God made him so wise that the
Egyptian king Pharaoh[t] thought highly
of him. The king even made Joseph
governor over Egypt and put him in
charge of everything he owned.
11 Everywhere in Egypt and Canaan
the grain crops failed. There was terrible suffering, and our ancestors could
not find enough to eat. 12 But when
Jacob heard that there was grain in
Egypt, he sent our ancestors there for
the first time. 13 It was on their second
trip that Joseph told his brothers who
he was, and Pharaoh learned about
Joseph's family.
14 Joseph sent for his father and his
relatives. In all, there were seventy-five
of them. 15 His father went to Egypt
and died there, just as our ancestors
did. 16 Later their bodies were taken
back to Shechem and placed in the
tomb that Abraham had bought from
the sons of Hamor.
17 Finally, the time came for God to
do what he had promised Abraham. By
then the number of our people in
Egypt had greatly increased. 18 Another king was ruling Egypt, and he
didn't know anything about Joseph.
19 He tricked our ancestors and was
cruel to them. He even made them
leave their babies outside, so they
would die.
20 During this time Moses was
born. He was a very beautiful child,
and for three months his parents took
care of him in their home. 21 Then
when they were forced to leave him
outside, the king's daughter found
him and raised him as her own son.
22 Moses was given the best education
in Egypt. He was a strong man and a
powerful speaker.
23 When Moses was forty years old,
he wanted to help the Israelites
because they were his own people.
24 One day he saw an Egyptian mistreating one of them. So he rescued
the man and killed the Egyptian.
25 Moses thought the rest of his people
would realize that God was going
to use him to set them free. But they
didn't understand.
26 The next day Moses saw two of
his own people fighting, and he tried
to make them stop. He said, "Men, you
are both Israelites. Why are you so
cruel to each other?"
27 But the man who had started
the fight pushed Moses aside and
asked, "Who made you our ruler and
judge? 28 Are you going to kill me, just
as you killed that Egyptian yesterday?"
29 When Moses heard this, he ran
away to live in the country of Midian.
His two sons were born there.
30 Forty years later, an angel
appeared to Moses from a burning
bush in the desert near Mount Sinai.
31 Moses was surprised by what he saw.
He went closer to get a better look,
and the Lord said, 32 "I am the God
who was worshiped by your ancestors,
Abraham, Isaac, and Jacob." Moses
started shaking all over and didn't dare
to look at the bush.
33 The Lord said to him, "Take off
your sandals. The place where you are
standing is holy. 34 With my own eyes I
have seen the suffering of my people
in Egypt. I have heard their groans and
have come down to rescue them. Now
I am sending you back to Egypt."
35 This was the same Moses that
the people rejected by saying, "Who
made you our leader and judge?"
God's angel had spoken to Moses from
the bush. And God had even sent the
angel to help Moses rescue the people
and be their leader.

[t] **7.10** *Pharaoh*: A Hebrew word sometimes used for the title of the King of Egypt.

7.10 Gn 41.39-41. **7.11** Gn 42.1, 2. **7.13 a** Gn 45.1; **b** Gn 45.16. **7.14 a** Gn 45.9, 10, 17, 18; **b** Gn 46.27 (LXX). **7.15 a** Gn 46.1-7; **b** Gn 49.33. **7.16** Gn 23.3-18; 33.19; 50.7-13; Js 24.32. **7.17,18** Ex 1.7, 8. **7.19 a** Ex 1.10, 11; **b** Ex 1.22. **7.20** Ex 2.2. **7.21** Ex 2.3-10. **7.23-29** Ex 2.11-15. **7.29** Ex 18.2-4. **7.30-34** Ex 3.1-10. **7.35** Ex 2.14.

36 In Egypt and at the Red Sea[u] and in the desert, Moses rescued the people by working miracles and wonders for forty years. 37 Moses is the one who told the people of Israel, "God will choose one of your people to be a prophet, just as he chose me." 38 Moses brought our people together in the desert, and the angel spoke to him on Mount Sinai. There he was given these life-giving words to pass on to us. 39 But our ancestors refused to obey Moses. They rejected him and wanted to go back to Egypt.

40 The people said to Aaron, "Make some gods to lead us! Moses led us out of Egypt, but we don't know what's happened to him now." 41 Then they made an idol in the shape of a calf. They offered sacrifices to the idol and were pleased with what they had done.

42 God turned his back on his people and left them. Then they worshiped the stars in the sky, just as it says in the Book of the Prophets, "People of Israel, you didn't offer sacrifices and offerings to me during those forty years in the desert. 43 Instead, you carried the tent where the god Molech is worshiped, and you took along the star of your god Rephan. You made those idols and worshiped them. So now I will have you carried off beyond Babylonia."

44 The tent where our ancestors worshiped God was with them in the desert. This was the same tent that God had commanded Moses to make. And it was made like the model that Moses had seen. 45 Later it was given to our ancestors, and they took it with them when they went with Joshua. They carried the tent along as they took over the land from those people that God had chased out for them. Our ancestors used this tent until the time of King David. 46 He pleased God and asked him if he could build a house of worship for the people[v] of Israel. 47 And it was finally King Solomon who built a house for God.[w]

48 But the Most High God doesn't live in houses made by humans. It is just as the prophet said, when he spoke for the Lord,

49 "Heaven is my throne,
and the earth
is my footstool.
What kind of house
will you build for me?
In what place will I rest?
50 I have made everything."

51 You stubborn and hardheaded people! You are always fighting against the Holy Spirit, just as your ancestors did. 52 Is there one prophet that your ancestors didn't mistreat? They killed the prophets who told about the coming of the One Who Obeys God.[x] And now you have turned against him and killed him. 53 Angels gave you God's Law, but you still don't obey it.

Stephen Is Stoned to Death

54 When the council members heard Stephen's speech, they were angry and furious. 55 But Stephen was filled with the Holy Spirit. He looked toward heaven, where he saw our glorious God and Jesus standing at his right side.[y] 56 Then Stephen said, "I see heaven open and the Son of Man standing at the right side of God!"

57 The council members shouted and

[u]**7.36** *Red Sea*: This name comes from the Bible of the early Christians, a translation made into Greek about 200 B.C. It refers to the body of water that the Israelites crossed and was one of the marshes or fresh water lakes near the eastern part of the Nile Delta, where they lived and where the towns of Exodus 13.17—14.9 were located. [v]**7.46** *the people*: Some manuscripts have "God." [w]**7.47** *God*: Or "the people." [x]**7.52** *One Who Obeys God*: That is, Jesus. [y]**7.55** *standing at his right side*: The "right side" is the place of honor and power. "Standing" may mean that Jesus is welcoming Stephen (see verse 59).

7.36 a Ex 7.3, 4; **b** Ex 14.21; **c** Nu 14.33. **7.37** Dt 18.15, 18. **7.38** Ex 19.1—20.17; Dt 5.1-33. **7.40** Ex 32.1. **7.41** Ex 32.2-6. **7.42,43** Am 5.25-27 (LXX). **7.44** Ex 25.9, 40. **7.45** Js 3.14-17. **7.46** 2 S 7.1-16; 1 Ch 17.1-14. **7.47** 1 K 6.1-38; 2 Ch 3.1-17. **7.49,50** Is 66.1, 2. **7.51** Is 63.10. **7.55** 3 Macc 6.6.

covered their ears. At once they all attacked
Stephen 58 and dragged him out of the city.
Then they started throwing stones at him.
The men who had brought charges against
him put their coats at the feet of a young
man named Saul.[z]
59 As Stephen was being stoned to
death, he called out, "Lord Jesus, please
welcome me!" 60 He knelt down and
shouted, "Lord, don't blame them for what
they have done." Then he died.
8 1-2 Saul approved the stoning of
Stephen. Some faithful followers of
the Lord buried Stephen and mourned
very much for him.

Saul Makes Trouble for the Church

At that time the church in Jerusalem
suffered terribly. All of the Lord's followers,
except the apostles, were scattered everywhere in Judea and Samaria. 3 Saul started
making a lot of trouble for the church. He
went from house to house, arresting men
and women and putting them in jail.

The Good News Is Preached in Samaria

4 The Lord's followers who had been
scattered went from place to place, telling
the good news. 5 Philip went to the city of
Samaria and told the people about Christ.
6 They crowded around Philip because they
were eager to hear what he was saying and
to see him work miracles. 7 Many people
with evil spirits were healed, and the spirits
went out of them with a shout. A lot of
crippled and lame people were also healed.
8 Everyone in that city was very glad because of what was happening.
9 For some time a man named Simon
had lived in the city of Samaria and had
amazed the people. He practiced witchcraft and claimed to be somebody great.
10 Everyone, rich and poor, crowded
around him. They said, "This man is the
power of God called 'The Great Power.' "
11 For a long time, Simon had used
witchcraft to amaze the people, and they
kept crowding around him. 12 But when
they believed what Philip was saying about
God's kingdom and about the name of
Jesus Christ, they were all baptized. 13 Even
Simon believed and was baptized. He
stayed close to Philip, because he marveled
at all the miracles and wonders.
14 The apostles in Jerusalem heard that
some people in Samaria had accepted
God's message, and they sent Peter and
John. 15 When the two apostles arrived,
they prayed that the people would be given
the Holy Spirit. 16 Before this, the Holy
Spirit had not been given to anyone in
Samaria, though some of them had been
baptized in the name of the Lord Jesus.
17 Peter and John then placed their hands
on everyone who had faith in the Lord, and
they were given the Holy Spirit.
18 Simon noticed that the Spirit was
given only when the apostles placed their
hands on the people. So he brought money
19 and said to Peter and John, "Let me
have this power too! Then anyone I place
my hands on will also be given the Holy
Spirit."
20 Peter said to him, "You and your
money will both end up in hell if you think
you can buy God's gift! 21 You don't have
any part in this, and God sees that your
heart isn't right. 22 Get rid of these evil
thoughts and ask God to forgive you. 23 I
can see that you are jealous and bound by
your evil ways."
24 Simon said, "Please pray to the Lord,
so that what you said won't happen to me."
25 After Peter and John had preached
about the Lord, they returned to Jerusalem.
On their way they told the good news
in many villages of Samaria.

Philip and an Ethiopian Official

26 The Lord's angel said to Philip, "Go
south[a] along the desert road that leads
from Jerusalem to Gaza."[b] 27 So Philip left.
An important Ethiopian official happened to be going along that road in his
chariot. He was the chief treasurer for

[z] **7.58** *Saul*: Better known as Paul, who became a famous follower of Jesus. [a] **8.26** *Go south*: Or "About noon go." [b] **8.26** *the desert road that leads from Jerusalem to Gaza*: Or "the road that leads from Jerusalem to Gaza in the desert."

8.3 Ac 22.4, 5; 26.9-11.

Candace, the Queen of Ethiopia. The official had gone to Jerusalem to worship
28 and was now on his way home. He was
sitting in his chariot, reading the book of
the prophet Isaiah.
29 The Spirit told Philip to catch up with
the chariot. 30 Philip ran up close and
heard the man reading aloud from the book
of Isaiah. Philip asked him, "Do you understand what you are reading?"
31 The official answered, "How can I
understand unless someone helps me?" He
then invited Philip to come up and sit beside him.
32 The man was reading the passage
that said,

"He was led like a sheep
on its way to be killed.
He was silent as a lamb
whose wool
is being cut off,
and he did not say
a word.
33 He was treated like a nobody
and did not receive
a fair trial.
How can he have children,
if his life
is snatched away?"

34 The official said to Philip, "Tell me,
was the prophet talking about himself or
about someone else?" 35 So Philip began at
this place in the Scriptures and explained
the good news about Jesus.
36-37 As they were going along the road,
they came to a place where there was some
water. The official said, "Look! Here is
some water. Why can't I be baptized?"[c]
38 He ordered the chariot to stop. Then
they both went down into the water, and
Philip baptized him.
39 After they had come out of the water,
the Lord's Spirit took Philip away. The official never saw him again, but he was very
happy as he went on his way.
40 Philip later appeared in Azotus. He
went from town to town, all the way to
Caesarea, telling people about Jesus.

Saul Becomes a Follower of the Lord

(Acts 22.6-16; 26.12-18)

9 Saul kept on threatening to kill the
Lord's followers. He even went to the
high priest 2 and asked for letters to
the Jewish leaders in Damascus. He did this
because he wanted to arrest and take to
Jerusalem any man or woman who had accepted the Lord's Way.[d] 3 When Saul had
almost reached Damascus, a bright light
from heaven suddenly flashed around him.
4 He fell to the ground and heard a voice
that said, "Saul! Saul! Why are you so
cruel to me?"
5 "Who are you?" Saul asked.
"I am Jesus," the Lord answered. "I am
the one you are so cruel to. 6 Now get up
and go into the city, where you will be told
what to do."
7 The men with Saul stood there
speechless. They had heard the voice, but
they had not seen anyone. 8 Saul got up
from the ground, and when he opened his
eyes, he could not see a thing. Someone
then led him by the hand to Damascus,
9 and for three days he was blind and did
not eat or drink.
10 A follower named Ananias lived in
Damascus, and the Lord spoke to him in a
vision. Ananias answered, "Lord, here I am."
11 The Lord said to him, "Get up and go
to the house of Judas on Straight Street.
When you get there, you will find a man
named Saul from the city of Tarsus. Saul is
praying, 12 and he has seen a vision. He
saw a man named Ananias coming to him
and putting his hands on him, so that he
could see again."
13 Ananias replied, "Lord, a lot of people have told me about the terrible things
this man has done to your followers in Jerusalem. 14 Now the chief priests have given
him the power to come here and arrest
anyone who worships in your name."

[c]**8.36,37** *Why can't I be baptized*: Some manuscripts add, "Philip replied, 'You can, if you believe with all your heart.' The official answered, 'I believe that Jesus Christ is the Son of God.' "

[d]**9.2** *accepted the Lord's Way*: In the book of Acts, this means to become a follower of the Lord Jesus.

8.32,33 Is 53.7, 8 (LXX). **9.7** Dn 10.7; 3 Macc 6.18; Ac 22.6-9.

15 The Lord said to Ananias, "Go! I have chosen him to tell foreigners, kings, and the people of Israel about me. 16 I will show him how much he must suffer for worshiping in my name."

17 Ananias left and went into the house where Saul was staying. Ananias placed his hands on him and said, "Saul, the Lord Jesus has sent me. He is the same one who appeared to you along the road. He wants you to be able to see and to be filled with the Holy Spirit."

18 Suddenly something like fish scales fell from Saul's eyes, and he could see. He got up and was baptized. 19 Then he ate and felt much better.

Saul Preaches in Damascus

For several days Saul stayed with the Lord's followers in Damascus. 20 Soon he went to the Jewish meeting places and started telling people that Jesus is the Son of God. 21 Everyone who heard Saul was amazed and said, "Isn't this the man who caused so much trouble for those people in Jerusalem who worship in the name of Jesus? Didn't he come here to arrest them and take them to the chief priests?"

22 Saul preached with such power that he completely confused the Jewish people in Damascus, as he tried to show them that Jesus is the Messiah.

23 Later some of them made plans to kill Saul, 24 but he found out about it. He learned that they were guarding the gates of the city day and night in order to kill him. 25 Then one night his followers let him down over the city wall in a large basket.

Saul in Jerusalem

26 When Saul arrived in Jerusalem, he tried to join the followers. But they were all afraid of him, because they did not believe he was a true follower. 27 Then Barnabas helped him by taking him to the apostles. He explained how Saul had seen the Lord and how the Lord had spoken to him. Barnabas also said that when Saul was in Damascus, he had spoken bravely in the name of Jesus.

28 Saul moved about freely with the followers in Jerusalem and told everyone about the Lord. 29 He was always arguing with the Jews who spoke Greek, and so they tried to kill him. 30 But the followers found out about this and took Saul to Caesarea. From there they sent him to the city of Tarsus.

31 The church in Judea, Galilee, and Samaria now had a time of peace and kept on worshiping the Lord. The church became stronger, as the Holy Spirit encouraged it and helped it grow.

Peter Heals Aeneas

32 While Peter was traveling from place to place, he visited the Lord's followers who lived in the town of Lydda. 33 There he met a man named Aeneas, who for eight years had been sick in bed and could not move. 34 Peter said to Aeneas, "Jesus Christ has healed you! Get up and make up your bed."[e] Right away he stood up.

35 Many people in the towns of Lydda and Sharon saw Aeneas and became followers of the Lord.

Peter Brings Dorcas Back to Life

36 In Joppa there was a follower named Tabitha. Her Greek name was Dorcas, which means "deer." She was always doing good things for people and had given much to the poor. 37 But she got sick and died, and her body was washed and placed in an upstairs room. 38 Joppa wasn't far from Lydda, and the followers heard that Peter was there. They sent two men to say to him, "Please come with us as quickly as you can!" 39 Right away, Peter went with them.

The men took Peter upstairs into the room. Many widows were there crying. They showed him the coats and clothes that Dorcas had made while she was still alive.

40 After Peter had sent everyone out of the room, he knelt down and prayed. Then he turned to the body of Dorcas and said, "Tabitha, get up!" The woman opened her eyes, and when she saw Peter, she sat up. 41 He took her by the hand and helped her to her feet.

[e]**9.34** *and make up your bed*: Or "and fix something to eat."

9.18 Tb 11.13-15. **9.23-25** 2 Co 11.32, 33.

Peter called in the widows and the other
followers and showed them that Dorcas
had been raised from death. 42 Everyone in
Joppa heard what had happened, and many
of them put their faith in the Lord. 43 Peter
stayed on for a while in Joppa in the house
of a man named Simon, who made leather.

Peter and Cornelius

10 In Caesarea there was a man
named Cornelius, who was the
captain of a group of soldiers called "The
Italian Unit." 2 Cornelius was a very religious man. He worshiped God, and so did
everyone else who lived in his house. He
had given a lot of money to the poor and
was always praying to God.
3 One afternoon at about three o'clock,[f]
Cornelius had a vision. He saw an angel
from God coming to him and calling him by
name. 4 Cornelius was surprised and stared
at the angel. Then he asked, "What is this
all about?"
The angel answered, "God has heard
your prayers and knows about your gifts to
the poor. 5 Now send some men to Joppa
for a man named Simon Peter. 6 He is visiting with Simon the leather maker, who
lives in a house near the sea." 7 After saying this, the angel left.
Cornelius called in two of his servants
and one of his soldiers who worshiped God.
8 He explained everything to them and sent
them off to Joppa.
9 The next day about noon these men
were coming near Joppa. Peter went up on
the roof[g] of the house to pray 10 and became very hungry. While the food was being prepared, he fell sound asleep and had
a vision. 11 He saw heaven open, and something came down like a huge sheet held up
by its four corners. 12 In it were all kinds of
animals, snakes, and birds. 13 A voice said
to him, "Peter, get up! Kill these and eat
them."
14 But Peter said, "Lord, I can't do that!
I've never eaten anything that is unclean
and not fit to eat."[h]
15 The voice spoke to him again, "When
God says that something can be used for
food, don't say it isn't fit to eat."
16 This happened three times before the
sheet was suddenly taken back to heaven.
17 Peter was still wondering what all of
this meant, when the men sent by Cornelius came and stood at the gate. They
had found their way to Simon's house
18 and were asking if Simon Peter was staying there.
19 While Peter was still thinking about
the vision, the Holy Spirit said to him,
"Three[i] men are here looking for you.
20 Hurry down and go with them. Don't
worry, I sent them."
21 Peter went down and said to the men,
"I am the one you are looking for. Why
have you come?"
22 They answered, "Captain Cornelius
sent us. He is a good man who worships
God and is liked by the Jewish people. One
of God's holy angels told Cornelius to send
for you, so he could hear what you have to
say." 23 Peter invited them to spend the
night.
The next morning, Peter and some of
the Lord's followers in Joppa left with the
men who had come from Cornelius. 24 The
next day they arrived in Caesarea where
Cornelius was waiting for them. He had
also invited his relatives and close friends.
25 When Peter arrived, Cornelius
greeted him. Then he knelt at Peter's feet
and started worshiping him. 26 But Peter
took hold of him and said, "Stand up! I am
nothing more than a human."
27 As Peter entered the house, he was
still talking with Cornelius. Many people
were there, 28 and Peter said to them, "You
know that we Jews are not allowed to have
anything to do with other people. But God
has shown me that he doesn't think anyone
is unclean or unfit. 29 I agreed to come

[f] **10.3** *at about three o'clock*: Probably while he was praying (see 3.1 and the note there).
[g] **10.9** *roof*: In Palestine the houses usually had a flat roof. Stairs on the outside led up to the roof, which was made of beams and boards covered with packed earth. [h] **10.14** *unclean and not fit to eat*: The Law of Moses taught that some foods were not fit to eat. [i] **10.19** *Three*: One manuscript has "two;" some manuscripts have "some."

10.9 Jdt 8.5. **10.14** 4 Macc 1.34.

here, but I want to know why you sent for me."

30 Cornelius answered:

Four days ago at about three o'clock in the afternoon I was praying at home. Suddenly a man in bright clothes stood in front of me. 31 He said, "Cornelius, God has heard your prayers, and he knows about your gifts to the poor. 32 Now send to Joppa for Simon Peter. He is visiting in the home of Simon the leather maker, who lives near the sea."

33 I sent for you right away, and you have been good enough to come. All of us are here in the presence of the Lord God, so that we can hear what he has to say.

34 Peter then said:

Now I am certain that God treats all people alike. 35 God is pleased with everyone who worships him and does right, no matter what nation they come from. 36 This is the same message that God gave to the people of Israel, when he sent Jesus Christ, the Lord of all, to offer peace to them.

37 You surely know what happened[j] everywhere in Judea. It all began in Galilee after John had told everyone to be baptized. 38 God gave the Holy Spirit and power to Jesus from Nazareth. He was with Jesus, as he went around doing good and healing everyone who was under the power of the devil. 39 We all saw what Jesus did both in Israel and in the city of Jerusalem.

Jesus was put to death on a cross. 40 But three days later, God raised him to life and let him be seen. 41 Not everyone saw him. He was seen only by us, who ate and drank with him after he was raised from death. We were the ones God chose to tell others about him.

42 God told us to announce clearly to the people that Jesus is the one he has chosen to judge the living and the dead. 43 Every one of the prophets has said that all who have faith in Jesus will have their sins forgiven in his name.

44 While Peter was still speaking, the Holy Spirit took control of everyone who was listening. 45 Some Jewish followers of the Lord had come with Peter, and they were surprised that the Holy Spirit had been given to Gentiles. 46 Now they were hearing Gentiles speaking unknown languages and praising God.

Peter said, 47 "These Gentiles have been given the Holy Spirit, just as we have! I am certain that no one would dare stop us from baptizing them." 48 Peter ordered them to be baptized in the name of Jesus Christ, and they asked him to stay on for a few days.

Peter Reports to the Church in Jerusalem

11 The apostles and the followers in Judea heard that Gentiles had accepted God's message. 2 So when Peter came to Jerusalem, some of the Jewish followers started arguing with him. They wanted Gentile followers to be circumcised, and 3 they said, "You stayed in the homes of Gentiles, and you even ate with them!"

4 Then Peter told them exactly what had happened:

5 I was in the town of Joppa and was praying when I fell sound asleep and had a vision. I saw heaven open, and something like a huge sheet held by its four corners came down to me. 6 When I looked in it, I saw animals, wild beasts, snakes, and birds. 7 I heard a voice saying to me, "Peter, get up! Kill these and eat them."

8 But I said, "Lord, I can't do that! I've never taken a bite of anything that is unclean and not fit to eat."[k]

9 The voice from heaven spoke to me again, "When God says that something can be used for food, don't say it isn't fit to eat." 10 This happened three

[j] **10.37** *what happened*: Or "the message that went." [k] **11.8** *unclean and not fit to eat*: See the note at 10.14.

10.34 Dt 10.17.

times before it was all taken back into
heaven.
11 Suddenly three men from Caesarea stood in front of the house where
I was staying. 12 The Holy Spirit told
me to go with them and not to worry.
Then six of the Lord's followers went
with me to the home of a man 13 who
told us that an angel had appeared to
him. The angel had ordered him to
send to Joppa for someone named Simon Peter. 14 Then Peter would tell
him how he and everyone in his house
could be saved.
15 After I started speaking, the Holy
Spirit was given to them, just as the
Spirit had been given to us at the beginning. 16 I remembered that the Lord
had said, "John baptized with water,
but you will be baptized with the Holy
Spirit." 17 God gave those Gentiles the
same gift that he gave us when we put
our faith in the Lord Jesus Christ. So
how could I have gone against God?
18 When they heard Peter say this, they
stopped arguing and started praising God.
They said, "God has now let Gentiles turn
to him, and he has given life to them!"

The Church in Antioch

19 Some of the Lord's followers had
been scattered because of the terrible trouble that started when Stephen was killed.
They went as far as Phoenicia, Cyprus, and
Antioch, but they told the message only to
the Jews.
20 Some of the followers from Cyprus
and Cyrene went to Antioch and started
telling Gentiles[l] the good news about the
Lord Jesus. 21 The Lord's power was with
them, and many people turned to the Lord
and put their faith in him. 22 News of what
was happening reached the church in
Jerusalem. Then they sent Barnabas to
Antioch.
23 When Barnabas got there and saw
what God had been kind enough to do for
them, he was very glad. So he begged them
to remain faithful to the Lord with all their
hearts. 24 Barnabas was a good man of
great faith, and he was filled with the Holy
Spirit. Many more people turned to the
Lord.
25 Barnabas went to Tarsus to look for
Saul. 26 He found Saul and brought him to
Antioch, where they met with the church
for a whole year and taught many of its
people. There in Antioch the Lord's followers were first called Christians.
27 During this time some prophets from
Jerusalem came to Antioch. 28 One of them
was Agabus. Then with the help of the
Spirit, he told that there would be a terrible
famine everywhere in the world. And it
happened when Claudius was Emperor.[m]
29 The followers in Antioch decided to send
whatever help they could to the followers
in Judea. 30 So they had Barnabas and Saul
take their gifts to the church leaders in
Jerusalem.

Herod Causes Trouble for the Church

12 At that time King Herod[n] caused
terrible suffering for some members of the church. 2 He ordered soldiers
to cut off the head of James, the brother
of John. 3 When Herod saw that this
pleased the Jewish people, he had Peter arrested during the Festival of Thin Bread.
4 He put Peter in jail and ordered four
squads of soldiers to guard him. Herod
planned to put him on trial in public after
the festival.
5 While Peter was being kept in jail, the
church never stopped praying to God for him.

Peter Is Rescued

6 The night before Peter was to be put
on trial, he was asleep and bound by two
chains. A soldier was guarding him on each
side, and two other soldiers were guarding
the entrance to the jail. 7 Suddenly an angel from the Lord appeared, and light
flashed around in the cell. The angel poked

[l] **11.20** *Gentiles*: This translates a Greek word that may mean "people who speak Greek" or "people who live as Greeks do." Here the word seems to mean "people who are not Jews." Some manuscripts have "Greeks," which also seems to mean "people who are not Jews." [m] **11.28** *when Claudius was Emperor*: A.D. 41-54. [n] **12.1** *Herod*: Herod Agrippa I, the grandson of Herod the Great.

11.16 Ac 1.5. **11.19** Ac 8.1-4. **11.28** Ac 21.10. **12.3,4** Ex 12.1-27.

Peter in the side and woke him up. Then
he said, "Quick! Get up!"
The chains fell off his hands, 8 and the
angel said, "Get dressed and put on your
sandals." Peter did what he was told. Then
the angel said, "Now put on your coat and
follow me." 9 Peter left with the angel, but
he thought everything was only a dream.
10 They went past the two groups of soldiers, and when they came to the iron gate
to the city, it opened by itself. They went
out and were going along the street, when
all at once the angel disappeared.
11 Peter now realized what had happened, and he said, "I am certain that the
Lord sent his angel to rescue me from
Herod and from everything the Jewish
leaders planned to do to me." 12 Then Peter went to the house of Mary the mother
of John whose other name was Mark. Many
of the Lord's followers had come together
there and were praying.
13 Peter knocked on the gate, and a
servant named Rhoda came to answer.
14 When she heard Peter's voice, she was
too excited to open the gate. She ran back
into the house and said that Peter was
standing there.
15 "You are crazy!" everyone told her.
But she kept saying that it was Peter. Then
they said, "It must be his angel."[o] 16 But
Peter kept on knocking, until finally they
opened the gate. They saw him and were
completely amazed.
17 Peter motioned for them to keep
quiet. Then he told how the Lord had led
him out of jail. He also said, "Tell James[p]
and the others what has happened." After
that, he left and went somewhere else.
18 The next morning the soldiers who
had been on guard were terribly worried
and wondered what had happened to Peter.
19 Herod ordered his own soldiers to search
for him, but they could not find him. Then
he questioned the guards and had them
put to death. After this, Herod left Judea to
stay in Caesarea for a while.

Herod Dies

20 Herod and the people of Tyre and
Sidon were very angry with each other. But
their country got its food supply from the
region that he ruled. So a group of them
went to see Blastus, who was one of
Herod's high officials. They convinced
Blastus that they wanted to make peace between their cities and Herod, 21 and a day
was set for them to meet with him.
Herod came dressed in his royal robes.
He sat down on his throne and made a
speech. 22 The people shouted, "You speak
more like a god than a man!" 23 At once an
angel from the Lord struck him down because he took the honor that belonged to
God. Later, Herod was eaten by worms and
died.
24 God's message kept spreading. 25 And
after Barnabas and Saul had done the work
they were sent to do, they went back to
Jerusalem[q] with John, whose other name
was Mark.

Barnabas and Saul Are Chosen and Sent

13 The church at Antioch had several
prophets and teachers. They were
Barnabas, Simeon, also called Niger,
Lucius from Cyrene, Manaen, who was
Herod's[r] close friend, and Saul. 2 While
they were worshiping the Lord and going
without eating,[s] the Holy Spirit told them,
"Appoint Barnabas and Saul to do the work
for which I have chosen them." 3 Everyone
prayed and went without eating for a while
longer. Next, they placed their hands on
Barnabas and Saul to show that they had
been appointed to do this work. Then
everyone sent them on their way.

Barnabas and Saul in Cyprus

4 After Barnabas and Saul had been
sent by the Holy Spirit, they went to Seleucia. From there they sailed to the island of
Cyprus. 5 They arrived at Salamis and be-

[o] **12.15** *his angel*: Probably meaning "his guardian angel." [p] **12.17** *James*: The brother of the Lord. [q] **12.25** *went back to Jerusalem*: Some manuscripts have "left Jerusalem," and others have "went to Antioch." [r] **13.1** *Herod's*: Herod Antipas, the son of Herod the Great. [s] **13.2** *going without eating*: The Jews often went without eating as a way of showing how much they loved God. This is also called "fasting."

12.20-23 2 Macc 9.5-28.

gan to preach God's message in the Jewish meeting places. They also had John[t] as a helper.

6 Barnabas and Saul went all the way to the city of Paphos on the other end of the island, where they met a Jewish man named Bar-Jesus. He practiced witchcraft and was a false prophet. 7 He also worked for Sergius Paulus, who was very smart and was the governor of the island. Sergius Paulus wanted to hear God's message, and he sent for Barnabas and Saul. 8 But Bar-Jesus, whose other name was Elymas, was against them. He even tried to keep the governor from having faith in the Lord.

9 Then Saul, better known as Paul, was filled with the Holy Spirit. He looked straight at Elymas 10 and said, "You son of the devil! You are a liar, a crook, and an enemy of everything that is right. When will you stop speaking against the true ways of the Lord? 11 The Lord is going to punish you by making you completely blind for a while."

Suddenly the man's eyes were covered by a dark mist, and he went around trying to get someone to lead him by the hand. 12 When the governor saw what had happened, he was amazed at this teaching about the Lord. So he put his faith in the Lord.

Paul and Barnabas in Antioch of Pisidia

13 Paul and the others left Paphos and sailed to Perga in Pamphylia. But John[t] left them and went back to Jerusalem. 14 The rest of them went on from Perga to Antioch in Pisidia. Then on the Sabbath they went to the Jewish meeting place and sat down.

15 After the reading of the Law and the Prophets,[u] the leaders sent someone over to tell Paul and Barnabas, "Friends, if you have anything to say that will help the people, please say it."

16 Paul got up. He motioned with his hand and said:

People of Israel, and everyone else who worships God, listen! 17 The God of Israel chose our ancestors, and he let our people prosper while they were living in Egypt. Then with his mighty power he led them out, 18 and for about forty years he took care of[v] them in the desert. 19 He destroyed seven nations in the land of Canaan and gave their land to our people. 20 All this happened in about 450 years.

Then God gave our people judges until the time of the prophet Samuel, 21 but the people demanded a king. So for forty years God gave them King Saul, the son of Kish from the tribe of Benjamin. 22 Later, God removed Saul and let David rule in his place. God said about him, "David the son of Jesse is the kind of person who pleases me most! He does everything I want him to do."

23 God promised that someone from David's family would come to save the people of Israel, and that one is Jesus. 24 But before Jesus came, John was telling everyone in Israel to turn back to God and be baptized. 25 Then, when John's work was almost done, he said, "Who do you people think I am? Do you think I am the Promised One? He will come later, and I am not good enough to untie his sandals."

26 Now listen, you descendants of Abraham! Pay attention, all of you Gentiles who are here to worship God! Listen to this message about how to be saved, because it is for everyone. 27 The people of Jerusalem and their leaders didn't realize who Jesus was. And they didn't understand the words of the prophets that they read each Sabbath. So they condemned Jesus just as the prophets had said.

28-29 They did exactly what the Scriptures said they would. Even

[t] **13.5,13** *John*: Whose other name was Mark (see 12.12, 25). [u] **13.15** *the Law and the Prophets*: The Jewish Scriptures, that is, the Old Testament. [v] **13.18** *took care of*: Some manuscripts have "put up with."

13.17 **a** Ex 1.7; **b** Ex 12.51. **13.18** Nu 14.34; Dt 1.31. **13.19** **a** Dt 7.1; **b** Js 14.1. **13.20** **a** Jg 2.16; **b** 1 S 3.20. **13.21** **a** 1 S 8.5; **b** 1 S 10.21. **13.22** **a** 1 S 13.14; **b** 1 S 16.12; Ps 89.20. **13.24** Mk 1.4; Lk 3.3. **13.25** **a** Jn 1.19, 20; **b** Mt 3.11; Mk 1.7; Lk 3.16; Jn 1.27. **13.28,29** Mt 27.22, 23; Mk 15.13, 14; Lk 23.21-23; Jn 19.15.

though they couldn't find any reason
to put Jesus to death, they still asked
Pilate to have him killed.
After Jesus had been put to death,
he was taken down from the cross[w]
and placed in a tomb. 30 But God
raised him from death! 31 Then for
many days Jesus appeared to his followers who had gone with him from
Galilee to Jerusalem. Now they are
telling our people about him.
32 God made a promise to our ancestors. And we are here to tell you the
good news 33 that he has kept this
promise to us. It is just as the second
Psalm says about Jesus,

"You are my son because today
I have become your Father."

34 God raised Jesus from death and
will never let his body decay. It is just
as God said,

"I will make to you
the same holy promise
that I made to David."

35 And in another psalm it says, "God
will never let the body of his Holy One
decay."
36 When David was alive, he obeyed
God. Then after he died, he was
buried in the family grave, and his
body decayed. 37 But God raised Jesus
from death, and his body did not decay.
38 My friends, the message is that
Jesus can forgive your sins! The Law
of Moses could not set you free from
all your sins. 39 But everyone who
has faith in Jesus is set free. 40 Make
sure that what the prophets have said
doesn't happen to you. They said,

41 "Look, you people
who make fun of God!
Be amazed
and disappear.
I will do something today
that you won't believe,
even if someone
tells you about it!"

42 As Paul and Barnabas were leaving
the meeting, the people begged them to say
more about these same things on the next
Sabbath. 43 After the service, many Jews
and a lot of Gentiles who worshiped God
went with them. Paul and Barnabas begged
them all to remain faithful to God, who had
been so kind to them.
44 The next Sabbath almost everyone in
town came to hear the message about the
Lord.[x] 45 When the Jewish people saw the
crowds, they were very jealous. They insulted
Paul and spoke against everything he said.
46 But Paul and Barnabas bravely said:
We had to tell God's message to you
before we told it to anyone else. But
you rejected the message! This proves
that you don't deserve eternal life.
Now we are going to the Gentiles.
47 The Lord has given us this command,

"I have placed you here
as a light
for the Gentiles.
You are to take
the saving power of God
to people everywhere on earth."

48 This message made the Gentiles glad,
and they praised what they had heard
about the Lord.[x] Everyone who had been
chosen for eternal life then put their faith
in the Lord.
49 The message about the Lord spread
all over that region. 50 But the Jewish leaders went to some of the important men in
the town and to some respected women
who were religious. They turned them
against Paul and Barnabas and started
making trouble for them. They even chased
them out of that part of the country.
51 Paul and Barnabas shook the dust

[w] **13.28,29** *cross*: This translates a Greek word that means "wood," "pole," or "tree."
[x] **13.44,48** *the Lord*: Some manuscripts have "God."
13.29 Mt 27.57-61; Mk 15.42-47; Lk 23.50-56; Jn 19.38-42. **13.31** Ac 1.3. **13.33** Ps 2.7. **13.34** Is 55.3 (LXX). **13.35** Ps 16.10. **13.41** Hb 1.5 (LXX). **13.47** Is 42.6; 49.6. **13.51** Mt 10.14; Mk 6.11; Lk 9.5; 10.11.

from that place off their feet[y] and went on to the city of Iconium.
52 But the Lord's followers in Antioch were very happy and were filled with the Holy Spirit.

Paul and Barnabas in Iconium

14 Paul and Barnabas spoke in the Jewish meeting place in Iconium, just as they had done at Antioch, and many Jews and Gentiles[z] put their faith in the Lord. 2 But the Jews who did not have faith in him made the other Gentiles angry and turned them against the Lord's followers.
3 Paul and Barnabas stayed there for a while, having faith in the Lord and bravely speaking his message. The Lord gave them the power to work miracles and wonders, and he showed that their message about his great kindness was true.
4 The people of Iconium did not know what to think. Some of them believed the Jewish group, and others believed the apostles. 5 Finally, some Gentiles and Jews, together with their leaders, decided to make trouble for Paul and Barnabas and to stone them to death.
6-7 But when the two apostles found out what was happening, they escaped to the region of Lycaonia. They preached the good news there in the towns of Lystra and Derbe and in the nearby countryside.

Paul and Barnabas in Lystra

8 In Lystra there was a man who had been born with crippled feet and had never been able to walk. 9 The man was listening to Paul speak, when Paul saw that he had faith in Jesus and could be healed. So he looked straight at the man 10 and shouted, "Stand up!" The man jumped up and started walking around.
11 When the crowd saw what Paul had done, they yelled out in the language of Lycaonia, "The gods have turned into humans and have come down to us!" 12 The people then gave Barnabas the name Zeus, and they gave Paul the name Hermes,[a] because he did the talking.
13 The temple of Zeus was near the entrance to the city. Its priest and the crowds wanted to offer a sacrifice to Barnabas and Paul. So the priest brought some bulls and flowers to the city gates. 14 When the two apostles found out about this, they tore their clothes in horror and ran to the crowd, shouting:

> 15 Why are you doing this? We are humans just like you. Please give up all this foolishness. Turn to the living God, who made the sky, the earth, the sea, and everything in them. 16 In times past, God let each nation go its own way. 17 But he showed that he was there by the good things he did. God sends rain from heaven and makes your crops grow. He gives food to you and makes your hearts glad.

18 Even after Paul and Barnabas had said all this, they could hardly keep the people from offering a sacrifice to them.
19 Some Jewish leaders from Antioch and Iconium came and turned the crowds against Paul. They hit him with stones and dragged him out of the city, thinking he was dead. 20 But when the Lord's followers gathered around Paul, he stood up and went back into the city. The next day he and Barnabas went to Derbe.

Paul and Barnabas Return to Antioch in Syria

21 Paul and Barnabas preached the good news in Derbe and won some people to the Lord. Then they went back to Lystra, Iconium, and Antioch in Pisidia. 22 They encouraged the followers and begged them to remain faithful. They told them, "We have to suffer a lot before we can get into God's kingdom." 23 Paul and Barnabas chose some leaders for each of the churches. Then they went without eating[b] and prayed that the Lord would take good care of these leaders.

[y] **13.51** *shook the dust from that place off their feet*: This was a way of showing rejection.
[z] **14.1** *Gentiles*: The Greek text has "Greeks," which probably means people who were not Jews. But it may mean Gentiles who worshiped with the Jews. [a] **14.12** *Hermes*: The Greeks thought of Hermes as the messenger of the other gods, especially of Zeus, their chief god. [b] **14.23** *went without eating*: See the note at 13.2.
14.15 Ex 20.11; Ps 146.6; 4 Macc 12.13.

24 Paul and Barnabas went on through
Pisidia to Pamphylia, 25 where they
preached in the town of Perga. Then they
went down to Attalia 26 and sailed to Antioch in Syria. It was there that they had
been placed in God's care for the work they
had now completed.[c]
27 After arriving in Antioch, they called
the church together. They told the people
what God had helped them do and how he
had made it possible for the Gentiles to believe. 28 Then they stayed there with the
followers for a long time.

15 Some people came from Judea and
started teaching the Lord's followers that they could not be saved, unless
they were circumcised as Moses had
taught. 2 This caused trouble, and Paul
and Barnabas argued with them about
this teaching. So it was decided to send
Paul and Barnabas and a few others to
Jerusalem to discuss this problem with the
apostles and the church leaders.

The Church Leaders Meet in Jerusalem

3 The men who were sent by the church
went through Phoenicia and Samaria,
telling how the Gentiles had turned to
God. This news made the Lord's followers
very happy. 4 When the men arrived in
Jerusalem, they were welcomed by the
church, including the apostles and the
leaders. They told them everything God
had helped them do. 5 But some Pharisees
had become followers of the Lord. They
stood up and said, "Gentiles who have faith
in the Lord must be circumcised and told
to obey the Law of Moses."
6 The apostles and church leaders met
to discuss this problem about Gentiles.
7 They had talked it over for a long time,
when Peter got up and said:
My friends, you know that God decided long ago to let me be the one
from your group to preach the good
news to the Gentiles. God did this so
that they would hear and obey him.
8 He knows what is in everyone's
heart. And he showed that he had chosen the Gentiles, when he gave them
the Holy Spirit, just as he had given
his Spirit to us. 9 God treated them in
the same way that he treated us. They
put their faith in him, and he made
their hearts pure.
10 Now why are you trying to make
God angry by placing a heavy burden
on these followers? This burden was
too heavy for us or our ancestors.
11 But our Lord Jesus was kind to us,
and we are saved by faith in him, just
as the Gentiles are.
12 Everyone kept quiet and listened as
Barnabas and Paul told how God had given
them the power to work a lot of miracles
and wonders for the Gentiles.
13 After they had finished speaking,
James[d] said:
My friends, listen to me! 14 Simon
Peter[e] has told how God first came to
the Gentiles and made some of them
his own people. 15 This agrees with
what the prophets wrote,

16 "I, the Lord, will return
and rebuild
David's fallen house.
I will build it from its ruins
and set it up again.
17 Then other nations
will turn to me
and be my chosen ones.
I, the Lord, say this.
18 I promised it long ago."

19 And so, my friends, I don't think
we should place burdens on the Gentiles who are turning to God. 20 We
should simply write and tell them not
to eat anything that has been offered
to idols. They should be told not to eat
the meat of any animal that has been
strangled or that still has blood in it.

[c] **14.26** *the work they had now completed*: See 13.1-3. [d] **15.13** *James*: The Lord's brother.
[e] **15.14** *Simon Peter*: The Greek text has "Simeon," which is another form of the name "Simon." The apostle Peter is meant.

15.1 Lv 12.3. **15.7** Ac 10.1-43. **15.8** Ac 2.4; 10.44. **15.16-18** Am 9.11, 12 (LXX).
15.20 **a** Ex 34.15-17; **b** Lv 17.10-16; **c** Lv 18.6-23.

They must also not commit any terrible sexual sins.[f]
21 We must remember that the Law
of Moses has been preached in city after city for many years, and every Sabbath it is read when we Jews meet.

A Letter to Gentiles Who Had Faith in the Lord

22 The apostles, the leaders, and all the
church members decided to send some
men to Antioch along with Paul and Barnabas. They chose Silas and Judas Barsabbas,[g] who were two leaders of the Lord's
followers. 23 They wrote a letter that said:
We apostles and leaders send
friendly greetings to all of you Gentiles
who are followers of the Lord in Antioch, Syria, and Cilicia.
24 We have heard that some people
from here have terribly upset you by
what they said. But we did not send
them! 25 So we met together and decided to choose some men and to send
them to you along with our good
friends Barnabas and Paul. 26 These
men have risked their lives for our
Lord Jesus Christ. 27 We are also sending Judas and Silas, who will tell you
in person the same things that we are
writing.
28 The Holy Spirit has shown us
that we should not place any extra
burden on you. 29 But you should not
eat anything offered to idols. You
should not eat any meat that still has
the blood in it or any meat of any animal that has been strangled. You must
also not commit any terrible sexual
sins. If you follow these instructions,
you will do well.
We send our best wishes.
30 The four men left Jerusalem and
went to Antioch. Then they called the
church members together and gave them
the letter. 31 When the letter was read,
everyone was pleased and greatly encouraged. 32 Judas and Silas were prophets, and
they spoke a long time, encouraging and
helping the Lord's followers.
33 The men from Jerusalem stayed on in
Antioch for a while. And when they left to
return to the ones who had sent them, the
followers wished them well. 34-35 But Paul
and Barnabas stayed on in Antioch, where
they and many others taught and preached
about the Lord.[h]

Paul and Barnabas Go Their Separate Ways

36 Sometime later Paul said to Barnabas, "Let's go back and visit the Lord's followers in the cities where we preached his
message. Then we will know how they are
doing." 37 Barnabas wanted to take along
John, whose other name was Mark. 38 But
Paul did not want to, because Mark had left
them in Pamphylia and had stopped working with them.
39 Paul and Barnabas argued, then each
of them went his own way. Barnabas took
Mark and sailed to Cyprus, 40 but Paul took
Silas and left after the followers had placed
them in God's care. 41 They traveled
through Syria and Cilicia, encouraging the
churches.

Timothy Works with Paul and Silas

16 Paul and Silas went back to Derbe
and Lystra, where there was a follower named Timothy. His mother was also
a follower. She was Jewish, and his father
was Greek. 2 The Lord's followers in Lystra
and Iconium said good things about Timothy, 3 and Paul wanted him to go with
them. But Paul first had him circumcised,
because all the Jewish people around there
knew that Timothy's father was Greek.[i]
4 As Paul and the others went from city
to city, they told the followers what the

[f] **15.20** *not commit any terrible sexual sins*: This probably refers to the laws about the wrong kind of marriages that are forbidden in Leviticus 18.6-18 or to some serious sexual sin. [g] **15.22** *Judas Barsabbas*: He may have been a brother of Joseph Barsabbas (see 1.23), but the name "Barsabbas" was often used by the Jewish people. [h] **15.34,35** Verse 34, which says that Silas decided to stay on in Antioch, is not in some manuscripts. [i] **16.3** *had him circumcised . . . Timothy's father was Greek*: Timothy would not have been acceptable to the Jews unless he had been circumcised, and Greeks did not circumcise their sons.

15.29 4 Macc 5.2. **15.38** Ac 13.13.

apostles and leaders in Jerusalem had decided, and they urged them to follow these instructions. 5 The churches became stronger in their faith, and each day more people put their faith in the Lord.

Paul's Vision in Troas

6 Paul and his friends went through Phrygia and Galatia, but the Holy Spirit would not let them preach in Asia. 7 After they arrived in Mysia, they tried to go into Bithynia, but the Spirit of Jesus would not let them. 8 So they went on through[j] Mysia until they came to Troas.

9 During the night, Paul had a vision of someone from Macedonia who was standing there and begging him, "Come over to Macedonia and help us!" 10 After Paul had seen the vision, we began looking for a way to go to Macedonia. We were sure that God had called us to preach the good news there.

Lydia Becomes a Follower of the Lord

11 We sailed straight from Troas to Samothrace, and the next day we arrived in Neapolis. 12 From there we went to Philippi, which is a Roman colony in the first district of Macedonia.[k]

We spent several days in Philippi. 13 Then on the Sabbath we went outside the city gate to a place by the river, where we thought there would be a Jewish meeting place for prayer. We sat down and talked with the women who came. 14 One of them was Lydia, who was from the city of Thyatira and sold expensive purple cloth. She was a worshiper of the Lord God, and he made her willing to accept what Paul was saying. 15 Then after she and her family were baptized, she kept on begging us, "If you think I really do have faith in the Lord, come stay in my home." Finally, we accepted her invitation.

Paul and Silas Are Put in Jail

16 One day on our way to the place of prayer, we were met by a slave girl. She had a spirit in her that gave her the power to tell the future. By doing this she made a lot of money for her owners. 17 The girl followed Paul and the rest of us and kept yelling, "These men are servants of the Most High God! They are telling you how to be saved."

18 This went on for several days. Finally, Paul got so upset that he turned and said to the spirit, "In the name of Jesus Christ, I order you to leave this girl alone!" At once the evil spirit left her.

19 When the girl's owners realized that they had lost all chances for making more money, they grabbed Paul and Silas and dragged them into court. 20 They told the officials, "These Jews are upsetting our city! 21 They are telling us to do things we Romans are not allowed to do."

22 The crowd joined in the attack on Paul and Silas. Then the officials tore the clothes off the two men and ordered them to be beaten with a whip. 23 After they had been badly beaten, they were put in jail, and the jailer was told to guard them carefully. 24 The jailer did as he was told. He put them deep inside the jail and chained their feet to heavy blocks of wood.

25 About midnight Paul and Silas were praying and singing praises to God, while the other prisoners listened. 26 Suddenly a strong earthquake shook the jail to its foundations. The doors opened, and the chains fell from all the prisoners.

27 When the jailer woke up and saw that the doors were open, he thought that the prisoners had escaped. He pulled out his sword and was about to kill himself. 28 But Paul shouted, "Don't harm yourself! No one has escaped."

29 The jailer asked for a torch and went into the jail. He was shaking all over as he knelt down in front of Paul and Silas. 30 After he had led them out of the jail, he asked, "What must I do to be saved?"

31 They replied, "Have faith in the Lord Jesus and you will be saved! This is also true for everyone who lives in your home."

32 Then Paul and Silas told him and everyone else in his house about the Lord. 33 While it was still night, the jailer took them to a place where he could wash their

[j] **16.8** *went on through*: Or "passed by." [k] **16.12** *in the first district of Macedonia*: Some manuscripts have "and the leading city of Macedonia."

cuts and bruises. Then he and everyone in his home were baptized. 34 They were very glad that they had put their faith in God. After this, the jailer took Paul and Silas to his home and gave them something to eat.

35 The next morning the officials sent some police with orders for the jailer to let Paul and Silas go. 36 The jailer told Paul, "The officials have ordered me to set you free. Now you can leave in peace."

37 But Paul told the police, "We are Roman citizens,[l] and the Roman officials had us beaten in public without giving us a trial. They threw us into jail. Now do they think they can secretly send us away? No, they cannot! They will have to come here themselves and let us out."

38 When the police told the officials that Paul and Silas were Roman citizens, the officials were afraid. 39 So they came and apologized. They led them out of the jail and asked them to please leave town. 40 But Paul and Silas went straight to the home of Lydia, where they saw the Lord's followers and encouraged them. Then they left.

Trouble in Thessalonica

17 After Paul and his friends had traveled through Amphipolis and Apollonia, they went on to Thessalonica. A Jewish meeting place was in that city. 2 So as usual, Paul went there to worship, and on three Sabbaths he spoke to the people. He used the Scriptures 3 to show them that the Messiah had to suffer, but that he would rise from death. Paul also told them that Jesus is the Messiah he was preaching about. 4 Some of them believed what Paul had said, and they became followers with Paul and Silas. Some Gentiles[m] and many important women also believed the message.

5 The Jewish leaders were jealous and got some worthless bums who hung around the marketplace to start a riot in the city. They wanted to drag Paul and Silas out to the mob, and so they went straight to Jason's home. 6 But when they did not find them there, they dragged out Jason and some of the Lord's followers. They took them to the city authorities and shouted, "Paul and Silas have been upsetting things everywhere. Now they have come here, 7 and Jason has welcomed them into his home. All of them break the laws of the Roman Emperor by claiming that someone named Jesus is king."

8 The officials and the people were upset when they heard this. 9 So they made Jason and the other followers pay bail before letting them go.

People in Berea Welcome the Message

10 That same night the Lord's followers sent Paul and Silas on to Berea, and after they arrived, they went to the Jewish meeting place. 11 The people in Berea were much nicer than those in Thessalonica, and they gladly accepted the message. Day after day they studied the Scriptures to see if these things were true. 12 Many of them put their faith in the Lord, including some important Greek women and several men.

13 When the Jewish leaders in Thessalonica heard that Paul had been preaching God's message in Berea, they went there and caused trouble by turning the crowds against Paul.

14 Right away the followers sent Paul down to the coast, but Silas and Timothy stayed in Berea. 15 Some men went with Paul as far as Athens, and then returned with instructions for Silas and Timothy to join him as soon as possible.

Paul in Athens

16 While Paul was waiting in Athens, he was upset to see all the idols in the city. 17 He went to the Jewish meeting place to speak to the Jews and to anyone who worshiped with them. Day after day he also spoke to everyone he met in the market. 18 Some of them were Epicureans[n] and some were Stoics,[o] and they started arguing with him.

[l] **16.37** *Roman citizens*: Only a small number of the people living in the Roman Empire were citizens, and they had special rights and privileges. [m] **17.4** *Gentiles*: See the note at 14.1. [n] **17.18** *Epicureans*: People who followed the teaching of a man named Epicurus, who taught that happiness should be the main goal in life. [o] **17.18** *Stoics*: Followers of a man named Zeno, who taught that people should learn self-control and be guided by their consciences.

People were asking, "What is this know-
it-all trying to say?"

Some even said, "Paul must be preaching about foreign gods! That's what he
means when he talks about Jesus and
about people rising from death."[p]

19 They brought Paul before a council
called the Areopagus, and said, "Tell us
what your new teaching is all about. 20 We
have heard you say some strange things,
and we want to know what you mean."

21 More than anything else the people of
Athens and the foreigners living there loved
to hear and to talk about anything new.
22 So Paul stood up in front of the council
and said:

> People of Athens, I see that you are
> very religious. 23 As I was going
> through your city and looking at the
> things you worship, I found an altar
> with the words, "To an Unknown
> God." You worship this God, but you
> don't really know him. So I want to tell
> you about him. 24 This God made the
> world and everything in it. He is Lord
> of heaven and earth, and he doesn't
> live in temples built by human hands.
> 25 He doesn't need help from anyone.
> He gives life, breath, and everything
> else to all people. 26 From one person
> God made all nations who live on
> earth, and he decided when and where
> every nation would be.
>
> 27 God has done all this, so that we
> will look for him and reach out and
> find him. He isn't far from any of us,
> 28 and he gives us the power to live, to
> move, and to be who we are. "We are
> his children," just as some of your po-
> ets have said.
>
> 29 Since we are God's children, we
> must not think that he is like an idol
> made out of gold or silver or stone. He
> isn't like anything that humans have
> thought up and made. 30 In the past,
> God forgave all this because people did
> not know what they were doing. But
> now he says that everyone everywhere
> must turn to him. 31 He has set a day
> when he will judge the world's people
> with fairness. And he has chosen the
> man Jesus to do the judging for him.
> God has given proof of this to all of us
> by raising Jesus from death.

32 As soon as the people heard Paul say
that a man had been raised from death,
some of them started laughing. Others
said, "We will hear you talk about this some
other time." 33 When Paul left the council
meeting, 34 some of the men put their faith
in the Lord and went with Paul. One of
them was a council member named Diony-
sius. A woman named Damaris and several
others also put their faith in the Lord.

Paul in Corinth

18 Paul left Athens and went to
Corinth, 2 where he met Aquila, a
Jewish man from Pontus. Not long before
this, Aquila had come from Italy with his
wife Priscilla, because Emperor Claudius
had ordered the Jewish people to leave
Rome.[q] Paul went to see Aquila and
Priscilla 3 and found out that they were
tent makers. Paul was a tent maker too. So
he stayed with them, and they worked
together.

4 Every Sabbath, Paul went to the Jewish meeting place. He spoke to Jews and
Gentiles[r] and tried to win them over. 5 But
after Silas and Timothy came from Macedonia, he spent all his time preaching to
the Jews about Jesus the Messiah. 6 Finally,
they turned against him and insulted him.
So he shook the dust from his clothes[s]
and told them, "Whatever happens to you
will be your own fault! I am not to blame.
From now on I am going to preach to the
Gentiles."

7 Paul then moved into the house of a
man named Titius Justus, who worshiped
God and lived next door to the Jewish

[p] **17.18** *people rising from death*: Or "a goddess named 'Rising from Death.' " [q] **18.2** *Emperor Claudius had ordered all the Jewish people to leave Rome*: Probably A.D. 49, though it may have been A.D. 41. [r] **18.4** *Gentiles*: Here the word is "Greeks." But see the note at 14.1. [s] **18.6** *shook the dust from his clothes*: This means the same as shaking dust from the feet (see the note at 13.51).

17.23 Ws 13.1. **17.24,25** 1 K 8.27; Is 42.5; Ac 7.48. **17.25** 2 Macc 14.35; 3 Macc 2.9. **17.26** 2 Macc 7.23. **17.27** Ws 13.6-9.

meeting place. 8 Crispus was the leader of
the meeting place. He and everyone in his
family put their faith in the Lord. Many
others in Corinth also heard the message,
and all the people who had faith in the
Lord were baptized.
9 One night, Paul had a vision, and in it
the Lord said, "Don't be afraid to keep on
preaching. Don't stop! 10 I am with you,
and you won't be harmed. Many people in
this city belong to me." 11 Paul stayed on in
Corinth for a year and a half, teaching
God's message to the people.
12 While Gallio was governor of Achaia,
some of the Jewish leaders got together and
grabbed Paul. They brought him into court
13 and said, "This man is trying to make
our people worship God in a way that is
against our Law!"
14 Even before Paul could speak, Gallio
said, "If you were charging this man with a
crime or some other wrong, I would have
to listen to you. 15 But since this concerns
only words, names, and your own law, you
will have to take care of it. I refuse to judge
such matters." 16 Then he sent them out of
the court. 17 The crowd grabbed Sosthenes,
the Jewish leader, and beat him up in front
of the court. But none of this mattered to
Gallio.

Paul Returns to Antioch in Syria

18 After Paul had stayed for a while with
the Lord's followers in Corinth, he told
them good-by and sailed on to Syria with
Aquila and Priscilla. But before he left, he
had his head shaved[t] at Cenchreae because
he had made a promise to God.
19 The three of them arrived in Ephesus, where Paul left Priscilla and Aquila.
He then went into the Jewish meeting
place to talk with the people there. 20 They
asked him to stay longer, but he refused.
21 He told them good-by and said, "If God
lets me, I will come back."
22 Paul sailed to Caesarea, where he
greeted the church. Then he went on to
Antioch. 23 After staying there for a while,
he left and visited several places in Galatia
and Phrygia. He helped the followers there
to become stronger in their faith.

Apollos in Ephesus

24 A Jewish man named Apollos came to
Ephesus. Apollos had been born in the city
of Alexandria. He was a very good speaker
and knew a lot about the Scriptures. 25 He
also knew much about the Lord's Way,[u]
and he spoke about it with great excitement. What he taught about Jesus was
right, but all he knew was John's message
about baptism.
26 Apollos started speaking bravely in
the Jewish meeting place. But when
Priscilla and Aquila heard him, they took
him to their home and helped him understand God's Way even better.
27 Apollos decided to travel through
Achaia. So the Lord's followers wrote
letters, encouraging the followers there
to welcome him. After Apollos arrived in
Achaia, he was a great help to everyone
who had put their faith in the Lord Jesus
because of God's kindness. 28 He got into
fierce arguments with the Jewish people,
and in public he used the Scriptures to
prove that Jesus is the Messiah.

Paul in Ephesus

19 While Apollos was in Corinth, Paul
traveled across the hill country to
Ephesus, where he met some of the Lord's
followers. 2 He asked them, "When you put
your faith in Jesus, were you given the Holy
Spirit?"
"No!" they answered. "We have never
even heard of the Holy Spirit."
3 "Then why were you baptized?" Paul
asked.
They answered, "Because of what John
taught."[v]
4 Paul replied, "John baptized people so

[t] **18.18** *he had his head shaved*: Paul had promised to be a "Nazirite" for a while. This meant that for the time of the promise, he could not cut his hair or drink wine. When the time was over, he would have to cut his hair and offer a sacrifice to God.

[u] **18.25** *the Lord's Way*: See the note at 9.2.

[v] **19.3** *Then why were you baptized? . . . Because of what John taught*: Or "In whose name were you baptized? . . . We were baptized in John's name."

18.18 Nu 6.18. **19.4** Mt 3.11; Mk 1.4, 7, 8; Lk 3.4, 16; Jn 1.26, 27.

that they would turn to God. But he also
told them that someone else was coming,
and that they should put their faith in him.
Jesus is the one that John was talking
about." 5 After the people heard Paul say
this, they were baptized in the name of the
Lord Jesus. 6 Then Paul placed his hands
on them. The Holy Spirit was given to
them, and they spoke unknown languages
and prophesied. 7 There were about twelve
men in this group.

8 For three months Paul went to the
Jewish meeting place and talked bravely
with the people about God's kingdom. He
tried to win them over, 9 but some of them
were stubborn and refused to believe. In
front of everyone they said terrible things
about God's Way. Paul left and took the followers with him to the lecture hall of
Tyrannus. He spoke there every day 10 for
two years, until every Jew and Gentile[w] in
Asia had heard the Lord's message.

The Sons of Sceva

11 God gave Paul the power to work
great miracles. 12 People even took hand-
kerchiefs and aprons that had touched
Paul's body, and they carried them to everyone who was sick. All of the sick people
were healed, and the evil spirits went out.
13 Some Jewish men started going
around trying to force out evil spirits by using the name of the Lord Jesus. They said
to the spirits, "Come out in the name of
that same Jesus that Paul preaches about!"
14 Seven sons of a Jewish high priest
named Sceva were doing this, 15 when an
evil spirit said to them, "I know Jesus! And
I have heard about Paul. But who are you?"
16 Then the man with the evil spirit jumped
on them and beat them up. They ran out of
the house, naked and bruised.

17 When the Jews and Gentiles[w] in Ephesus heard about this, they were so frightened that they praised the name of the
Lord Jesus. 18 Many who were followers
now started telling everyone about the
evil things they had been doing. 19 Some
who had been practicing witchcraft even
brought their books and burned them in
public. These books were worth about fifty
thousand silver coins. 20 So the Lord's
message spread and became even more
powerful.

The Riot in Ephesus

21 After all of this had happened, Paul
decided[x] to visit Macedonia and Achaia on
his way to Jerusalem. Paul had said, "From
there I will go on to Rome." 22 So he sent
his two helpers, Timothy and Erastus, to
Macedonia. But he stayed on in Asia for a
while.

23 At that time there was serious trouble
because of the Lord's Way.[y] 24 A silversmith
named Demetrius had a business that
made silver models of the temple of the
goddess Artemis. Those who worked for
him earned a lot of money. 25 Demetrius
brought together everyone who was in the
same business and said:

> Friends, you know that we make a
> good living at this. 26 But you have
> surely seen and heard how this man
> Paul is upsetting a lot of people, not
> only in Ephesus, but almost every-
> where in Asia. He claims that the gods
> we humans make are not really gods at
> all. 27 Everyone will start saying terri-
> ble things about our business. They
> will stop respecting the temple of the
> goddess Artemis, who is worshiped in
> Asia and all over the world. Our great
> goddess will be forgotten!

28 When the workers heard this, they
got angry and started shouting, "Great is
Artemis, the goddess of the Ephesians!"
29 Soon the whole city was in a riot, and
some men grabbed Gaius and Aristarchus,
who had come from Macedonia with Paul.
Then everyone in the crowd rushed to the
place where the town meetings were
held.

30 Paul wanted to go out and speak to
the people, but the Lord's followers would
not let him. 31 A few of the local officials
were friendly to Paul, and they sent someone to warn him not to go.

32 Some of the people in the meeting
were shouting one thing, and others were

[w] **19.10,17** *Gentile(s)*: The text has "Greek(s)" (see the note at 14.1). [x] **19.21** *Paul decided*: Or "Paul was led by the Holy Spirit." [y] **19.23** *the Lord's Way*: See the note at 9.2.

shouting something else. Everyone was
completely confused, and most of them did
not even know why they were there.
33 Several of the Jewish leaders pushed
a man named Alexander to the front of the
crowd and started telling him what to say.
He motioned with his hand and tried to explain what was going on. 34 But when the
crowd saw that he was Jewish, they all
shouted for two hours, "Great is Artemis,
the goddess of the Ephesians!"
35 Finally, a town official made the
crowd be quiet. Then he said:

People of Ephesus, who in the
world doesn't know that our city is the
center for worshiping the great goddess Artemis? Who doesn't know that
her image which fell from heaven is
right here? 36 No one can deny this,
and so you should calm down and not
do anything foolish. 37 You have
brought men in here who have not
robbed temples or spoken against our
goddess.
38 If Demetrius and his workers
have a case against these men, we
have courts and judges. Let them take
their complaints there. 39 But if you
want to do more than that, the matter
will have to be brought before the city
council. 40 We could easily be accused
of starting a riot today. There is no excuse for it! We cannot even give a reason for this uproar.

41 After saying this, he told the people to
leave.

Paul Goes through Macedonia and Greece

20 When the riot was over, Paul sent
for the followers and encouraged
them. He then told them good-by and left
for Macedonia. 2 As he traveled from place
to place, he encouraged the followers with
many messages. Finally, he went to Greece[z]
3 and stayed there for three months.
Paul was about to sail to Syria. But some
of the Jewish leaders plotted against him,
so he decided to return by way of Macedonia. 4 With him were Sopater, son of Pyr-
rhus from Berea, and Aristarchus and
Secundus from Thessalonica. Gaius from
Derbe was also with him, and so were Timothy and the two Asians, Tychicus and
Trophimus. 5 They went on ahead to Troas
and waited for us there. 6 After the Festival
of Thin Bread, we sailed from Philippi. Five
days later we met them in Troas and stayed
there for a week.

Paul's Last Visit to Troas

7 On the first day of the week[a] we met
to break bread together.[b] Paul spoke to the
people until midnight because he was leaving the next morning. 8 In the upstairs
room where we were meeting, there were a
lot of lamps. 9 A young man by the name of
Eutychus was sitting on a window sill.
While Paul was speaking, the young man
got very sleepy. Finally, he went to sleep
and fell three floors all the way down to the
ground. When they picked him up, he was
dead.
10 Paul went down and bent over Eutychus. He took him in his arms and said,
"Don't worry! He's alive." 11 After Paul had
gone back upstairs, he broke bread, and ate
with us. He then spoke until dawn and left.
12 Then the followers took the young man
home alive and were very happy.

The Voyage from Troas to Miletus

13 Paul decided to travel by land to Assos. The rest of us went on ahead by ship,
and we were to take him aboard there.
14 When he met us in Assos, he came
aboard, and we sailed on to Mitylene.
15 The next day we came to a place near
Chios, and the following day we reached
Samos. The day after that we sailed to
Miletus. 16 Paul had decided to sail on past
Ephesus, because he did not want to spend
too much time in Asia. He was in a hurry
and wanted to be in Jerusalem in time for
Pentecost.[c]

[z]**20.2** *Greece*: Probably Corinth. [a]**20.7** *On the first day of the week*: Since the Jewish day began at sunset, the meeting would have begun in the evening. [b]**20.7** *break bread together*: See the note at 2.46. [c]**20.16** *in time for Pentecost*: The Jewish people liked to be in Jerusalem for this festival (see the note at 2.1).

Paul Says Good-By to the Church Leaders of Ephesus

17 From Miletus, Paul sent a message for
the church leaders at Ephesus to come and
meet with him. 18 When they got there, he
said:

You know everything I did during
the time I was with you when I first
came to Asia. 19 Some of the Jews plotted against me and caused me a lot
of sorrow and trouble. But I served
the Lord and was humble. 20 When I
preached in public or taught in your
homes, I didn't hold back from telling
anything that would help you. 21 I told
Jews and Gentiles to turn to God and
have faith in our Lord Jesus.

22 I don't know what will happen to
me in Jerusalem, but I must obey
God's Spirit and go there. 23 In every
city I visit, I am told by the Holy Spirit
that I will be put in jail and will be in
trouble in Jerusalem. 24 But I don't
care what happens to me, as long as I
finish the work that the Lord Jesus
gave me to do. And that work is to tell
the good news about God's great kindness.

25 I have gone from place to place,
preaching to you about God's kingdom,
but now I know that none of you will
ever see me again. 26 I tell you today
that I am no longer responsible for any
of you! 27 I have told you everything
God wants you to know. 28 Look after
yourselves and everyone the Holy
Spirit has placed in your care. Be like
shepherds to God's church. It is the
flock that he bought with the blood of
his own Son.[d]

29 I know that after I am gone, others will come like fierce wolves to attack you. 30 Some of your own people
will tell lies to win over the Lord's followers. 31 Be on your guard! Remember how day and night for three years I
kept warning you with tears in my
eyes.

32 I now place you in God's care.
Remember the message about his
great kindness! This message can help
you and give you what belongs to you
as God's people. 33 I have never
wanted anyone's money or clothes.
34 You know how I have worked with
my own hands to make a living for myself and my friends. 35 By everything I
did, I showed how you should work to
help everyone who is weak. Remember
that our Lord Jesus said, "More blessings come from giving than from receiving."

36 After Paul had finished speaking, he
knelt down with all of them and prayed.
37 Everyone cried and hugged and kissed
him. 38 They were especially sad because
Paul had told them, "You will never see me
again."

Then they went with him to the ship.

Paul Goes to Jerusalem

21 After saying good-by, we sailed
straight to Cos. The next day we
reached Rhodes and from there sailed on
to Patara. 2 We found a ship going to Phoenicia, so we got on board and sailed off.

3 We came within sight of Cyprus and
then sailed south of it on to the port of Tyre
in Syria, where the ship was going to un-
load its cargo. 4 We looked up the Lord's
followers and stayed with them for a week.
The Holy Spirit had told them to warn
Paul not to go on to Jerusalem. 5 But when
the week was over, we started on our way
again. All the men, together with their
wives and children, walked with us from
the town to the seashore. We knelt on the
beach and prayed. 6 Then after saying
good-by to each other, we got into the ship,
and they went back home.

7 We sailed from Tyre to Ptolemais,
where we greeted the followers and stayed
with them for a day. 8 The next day we
went to Caesarea and stayed with Philip,
the preacher. He was one of the seven men
who helped the apostles, 9 and he had four
unmarried[e] daughters who prophesied.

10 We had been in Caesarea for several
days, when the prophet Agabus came to us
from Judea. 11 He took Paul's belt, and with

[d]**20.28** *the blood of his own Son*: Or "his own blood." [e]**21.9** *unmarried*: Or "virgin."

20.24 2 Ti 4.7. **21.8** Ac 6.5; 8.5. **21.10** Ac 11.28.

it he tied up his own hands and feet. Then
he told us, "The Holy Spirit says that some
of the Jewish leaders in Jerusalem will tie
up the man who owns this belt. They will
also hand him over to the Gentiles." 12 After
Agabus said this, we and the followers living
there begged Paul not to go to Jerusalem.
13 But Paul answered, "Why are you crying and breaking my heart? I am not only
willing to be put in jail for the Lord Jesus. I
am even willing to die for him in Jerusalem!"
14 Since we could not get Paul to change
his mind, we gave up and prayed, "Lord,
please make us willing to do what you want."
15 Then we got ready to go to Jerusalem.
16 Some of the followers from Caesarea
went with us and took us to stay in the
home of Mnason. He was from Cyprus and
had been a follower from the beginning.

Paul Visits James

17 When we arrived in Jerusalem, the
Lord's followers gladly welcomed us.
18 Paul went with us to see James[f] the next
day, and all the church leaders were present. 19 Paul greeted them and told how
God had used him to help the Gentiles.
20 Everyone who heard this praised God
and said to Paul:

My friend, you can see how many
tens of thousands of the Jewish people
have become followers! And all of
them are eager to obey the Law of
Moses. 21 But they have been told that
you are teaching those who live among
the Gentiles to disobey this Law. They
claim that you are telling them not to
circumcise their sons or to follow Jewish customs.

22 What should we do now that our
people have heard that you are here?
23 Please do what we ask, because four
of our men have made special
promises to God. 24 Join with them
and prepare yourself for the ceremony
that goes with the promises. Pay the
cost for their heads to be shaved. Then
everyone will learn that the reports
about you are not true. They will know
that you do obey the Law of Moses.

25 Some while ago we told the Gentile followers what we think they
should do. We instructed them not to
eat anything offered to idols. They
were told not to eat any meat with
blood still in it or the meat of an animal that has been strangled. They
were also told not to commit any terrible sexual sins.[g]

26 The next day Paul took the four men
with him and got himself ready at the same
time they did. Then he went into the temple and told when the final ceremony
would take place and when an offering
would be made for each of them.

Paul Is Arrested

27 When the period of seven days for
the ceremony was almost over, some of the
Jewish people from Asia saw Paul in the
temple. They got a large crowd together
and started attacking him. 28 They were
shouting, "Friends, help us! This man goes
around everywhere, saying bad things
about our nation and about the Law of
Moses and about this temple. He has even
brought shame to this holy temple by bringing in Gentiles." 29 Some of them thought
that Paul had brought Trophimus from
Ephesus into the temple, because they had
seen them together in the city.
30 The whole city was in an uproar, and
the people turned into a mob. They
grabbed Paul and dragged him out of the
temple. Then suddenly the doors were
shut. 31 The people were about to kill Paul
when the Roman army commander heard
that all Jerusalem was starting to riot. 32 So
he quickly took some soldiers and officers
and ran to where the crowd had gathered.

As soon as the mob saw the commander
and soldiers, they stopped beating Paul.
33 The army commander went over and arrested him and had him bound with two
chains. Then he tried to find out who Paul

[f]**21.18** *James*: The Lord's brother. [g]**21.25** *not to commit any terrible sexual sins*: See the note at 15.20.

21.23,24 Nu 6.13-21. **21.25** Ac 15.29. **21.29** Ac 20.4.

was and what he had done. 34 Part of the
crowd shouted one thing, and part of them
shouted something else. But they were
making so much noise that the commander
could not find out a thing. Then he ordered
Paul to be taken into the fortress. 35 As they
reached the steps, the crowd became so
wild that the soldiers had to lift Paul up
and carry him. 36 The crowd followed and
kept shouting, "Kill him! Kill him!"

Paul Speaks to the Crowd

37 When Paul was about to be taken into
the fortress, he asked the commander,
"Can I say something to you?"

"How do you know Greek?" the commander asked. 38 "Aren't you that Egyptian
who started a riot not long ago and led four
thousand terrorists into the desert?"

39 "No!" Paul replied. "I am a Jew from
Tarsus, an important city in Cilicia. Please
let me speak to the crowd."

40 The commander told him he could
speak, so Paul stood on the steps and motioned to the people. When they were
quiet, he spoke to them in Aramaic:

22 "My friends and leaders of our nation, listen as I explain what happened!" 2 When the crowd heard Paul
speak to them in Aramaic, they became
even quieter. Then Paul said:

3 I am a Jew, born and raised in the
city of Tarsus in Cilicia. I was a student of Gamaliel and was taught to follow every single law of our ancestors.
In fact, I was just as eager to obey God
as any of you are today.

4 I made trouble for everyone who
followed the Lord's Way,[h] and I even
had some of them killed. I had others
arrested and put in jail. I didn't care if
they were men or women. 5 The high
priest and all the council members can
tell you that this is true. They even
gave me letters to the Jewish leaders in
Damascus, so that I could arrest people there and bring them to Jerusalem
to be punished.

6 One day about noon I was getting
close to Damascus, when a bright light
from heaven suddenly flashed around
me. 7 I fell to the ground and heard a
voice asking, "Saul, Saul, why are you
so cruel to me?"

8 "Who are you?" I answered.

The Lord replied, "I am Jesus from
Nazareth! I am the one you are so
cruel to." 9 The men who were traveling with me saw the light, but did not
hear the voice.

10 I asked, "Lord, what do you want
me to do?"

Then he told me, "Get up and go to
Damascus. When you get there, you
will be told what to do." 11 The light
had been so bright that I couldn't see.
And the other men had to lead me by
the hand to Damascus.

12 In that city there was a man
named Ananias, who faithfully obeyed
the Law of Moses and was well liked
by all the Jewish people living there.
13 He came to me and said, "Saul, my
friend, you can now see again!"

At once I could see. 14 Then Ananias told me, "The God that our ancestors worshiped has chosen you to
know what he wants done. He has
chosen you to see the One Who Obeys
God[i] and to hear his voice. 15 You
must tell everyone what you have seen
and heard. 16 What are you waiting
for? Get up! Be baptized, and wash
away your sins by praying to the Lord."

17 After this I returned to Jerusalem
and went to the temple to pray. There I
had a vision 18 of the Lord who said to
me, "Hurry and leave Jerusalem! The
people won't listen to what you say
about me."

19 I replied, "Lord, they know that
in many of our meeting places I
arrested and beat people who had
faith in you. 20 Stephen was killed because he spoke for you, and I stood
there and cheered them on. I even

[h]**22.4** *followed the Lord's Way*: See the note at 9.2. [i]**22.14** *One Who Obeys God*: See the note at 7.52.

22.3 Ac 5.34-39. **22.4,5** Ac 8.3; 26.9-11. **22.6-9** Dn 10.7; 3 Macc 6.18; Ac 9.7. **22.20** Ac 7.58.

guarded the clothes of the men who murdered him."

21 But the Lord told me to go, and he promised to send me far away to the Gentiles.

22 The crowd listened until Paul said this. Then they started shouting, "Get rid of this man! He doesn't deserve to live." 23 They kept shouting. They waved their clothes around and threw dust into the air.

Paul and the Roman Army Commander

24 The Roman commander ordered Paul to be taken into the fortress and beaten with a whip. He did this to find out why the people were screaming at Paul.

25 While the soldiers were tying Paul up to be beaten, he asked the officer standing there, "Is it legal to beat a Roman citizen before he has been tried in court?"

26 When the officer heard this, he went to the commander and said, "What are you doing? This man is a Roman citizen!"

27 The commander went to Paul and asked, "Tell me, are you a Roman citizen?"

"Yes," Paul answered.

28 The commander then said, "I paid a lot of money to become a Roman citizen."[j]

But Paul replied, "I was born a Roman citizen."

29 The men who were about to beat and question Paul quickly backed off. And the commander himself was frightened when he realized that he had put a Roman citizen in chains.

Paul Is Tried by the Council

30 The next day the commander wanted to know the real reason why the Jewish leaders had brought charges against Paul. So he had Paul's chains removed, and he ordered the chief priests and the whole council to meet. Then he had Paul led in and made him stand in front of them.

23 Paul looked straight at the council members and said, "My friends, to this day I have served God with a clear conscience!"

2 Then Ananias the high priest ordered the men standing beside Paul to hit him on the mouth. 3 Paul turned to the high priest and said, "You whitewashed wall![k] God will hit you. You sit there to judge me by the Law of Moses. But at the same time you order men to break the Law by hitting me."

4 The men standing beside Paul asked, "Don't you know you are insulting God's high priest?"

5 Paul replied, "Oh! I didn't know he was the high priest. The Scriptures do tell us not to speak evil about a leader of our people."

6 When Paul saw that some of the council members were Sadducees and others were Pharisees, he shouted, "My friends, I am a Pharisee and the son of a Pharisee. I am on trial simply because I believe that the dead will be raised to life."

7 As soon as Paul said this, the Pharisees and the Sadducees got into a big argument, and the council members started taking sides. 8 The Sadducees do not believe in angels or spirits or that the dead will rise to life. But the Pharisees believe in all of these, 9 and so there was a lot of shouting. Some of the teachers of the Law of Moses were Pharisees. Finally, they became angry and said, "We don't find anything wrong with this man. Maybe a spirit or an angel really did speak to him."

10 The argument became fierce, and the commander was afraid that Paul would be pulled apart. So he ordered the soldiers to go in and rescue Paul. Then they took him back into the fortress.

11 That night the Lord stood beside Paul and said, "Don't worry! Just as you have told others about me in Jerusalem, you must also tell about me in Rome."

A Plot To Kill Paul

12-13 The next morning more than forty Jewish men got together and vowed that they would not eat or drink anything until they had killed Paul. 14 Then some of them went to the chief priests and the nation's

[j]**22.28** *Roman citizen*: See the note at 16.37. [k]**23.3** *whitewashed wall*: Someone who pretends to be good, but really isn't.

23.3 Mt 23.27, 28. **23.5** Ex 22.28. **23.6** Ac 26.4, 5; Phil 3.5. **23.8** Mt 22.23; Mk 12.18; Lk 20.27.

leaders and said, "We have promised God that we would not eat a thing until we have killed Paul. 15 You and everyone in the council must go to the commander and pretend that you want to find out more about the charges against Paul. Ask for him to be brought before your court. Meanwhile, we will be waiting to kill him before he gets there."

16 When Paul's nephew heard about the plot, he went to the fortress and told Paul about it. 17 So Paul said to one of the army officers, "Take this young man to the commander. He has something to tell him."

18 The officer took him to the commander and said, "The prisoner named Paul asked me to bring this young man to you, because he has something to tell you."

19 The commander took the young man aside and asked him in private, "What do you want to tell me?"

20 He answered, "Some men are planning to ask you to bring Paul down to the Jewish council tomorrow. They will claim that they want to find out more about him. 21 But please don't do what they say. More than forty men are going to attack Paul. They have made a vow not to eat or drink anything until they have killed him. Even now they are waiting to hear what you decide."

22 The commander sent the young man away after saying to him, "Don't let anyone know that you told me this."

Paul Is Sent to Felix the Governor

23 The commander called in two of his officers and told them, "By nine o'clock tonight have two hundred soldiers ready to go to Caesarea. Take along seventy men on horseback and two hundred foot soldiers with spears. 24 Get a horse ready for Paul and make sure that he gets safely through to Felix the governor."

25 The commander wrote a letter that said:

> 26 Greetings from Claudius Lysias to the Honorable Governor Felix:
>
> 27 Some Jews grabbed this man and were about to kill him. But when I found out that he was a Roman citizen, I took some soldiers and rescued him.
>
> 28 I wanted to find out what they had against him. So I brought him before their council 29 and learned that the charges concern only their religious laws. This man isn't guilty of anything for which he should die or even be put in jail.
>
> 30 As soon as I learned that there was a plot against him, I sent him to you and told their leaders to bring charges against him in your court.

31 The soldiers obeyed the commander's orders, and that same night they took Paul to the city of Antipatris. 32 The next day the foot soldiers returned to the fortress and let the soldiers on horseback take him the rest of the way. 33 When they came to Caesarea, they gave the letter to the governor and handed Paul over to him.

34 The governor read the letter. Then he asked Paul and found out that he was from Cilicia. 35 The governor said, "I will listen to your case as soon as the people come to bring their charges against you." After saying this, he gave orders for Paul to be kept as a prisoner in Herod's palace.[l]

Paul Is Accused in the Court of Felix

24 Five days later Ananias the high priest, together with some of their leaders and a lawyer named Tertullus, went to the governor to present their case against Paul. 2 So Paul was called in, and Tertullus stated the case against him:[m]

> Honorable Felix, you have brought our people a long period of peace, and because of your concern our nation is much better off. 3 All of us are always grateful for what you have done. 4 I don't want to bother you, but please be patient with us and listen to me for just a few minutes.
>
> 5 This man has been found to be a real pest and troublemaker for Jews all over the world. He is also a leader of

[l]**23.35** *Herod's palace*: The palace built by Herod the Great and used by the Roman governors of Palestine. [m]**24.2** *Paul was called in, and Tertullus stated the case against him*: Or "Tertullus was called in and stated the case against Paul."

a group called Nazarenes. 6-8 When
he tried to disgrace the temple, we
arrested him.[n] If you question him,
you will find out for yourself that our
charges are true.
9 The Jewish crowd spoke up and agreed
with what Tertullus had said.

Paul Defends Himself

10 The governor motioned for Paul to
speak, and he began:

I know that you have judged the
people of our nation for many years,
and I am glad to defend myself in your
court.

11 It was no more than twelve days
ago that I went to worship in Jerusalem. You can find this out easily
enough. 12 Never once did the Jews
find me arguing with anyone in the
temple. I didn't cause trouble in the
Jewish meeting places or in the city itself. 13 There is no way that they can
prove these charges that they are now
bringing against me.

14 I admit that their leaders think
that the Lord's Way[o] which I follow is
based on wrong beliefs. But I still worship the same God that my ancestors
worshiped. And I believe everything
written in the Law of Moses and in the
Prophets.[p] 15 I am just as sure as these
people are that God will raise from
death everyone who is good or evil.
16 And because I am sure, I try my best
to have a clear conscience in whatever
I do for God or for people.

17 After being away for several
years, I returned here to bring gifts for
the poor people of my nation and to offer sacrifices. 18 This is what I was doing when I was found going through a
ceremony in the temple. I wasn't with
a crowd, and there was no uproar.

19 Some Jews from Asia were there
at that time, and if they have anything
to say against me, they should be here
now. 20 Or ask the ones who are here.
They can tell you that they didn't find
me guilty of anything when I was tried
by their own council. 21 The only
charge they can bring against me is
what I shouted out in court, when I
said, "I am on trial today because I believe that the dead will be raised to
life!"

22 Felix knew a lot about the Lord's
Way.[q] But he brought the trial to an end
and said, "I will make my decision after
Lysias the commander arrives." 23 He then
ordered the army officer to keep Paul under guard, but not to lock him up or to stop
his friends from helping him.

Paul Is Kept under Guard

24 Several days later Felix and his wife
Drusilla, who was Jewish, went to the place
where Paul was kept under guard. They
sent for Paul and listened while he spoke to
them about having faith in Christ Jesus.
25 But Felix was frightened when Paul
started talking to them about doing right,
about self-control, and about the coming
judgment. So he said to Paul, "That's
enough for now. You may go. But when I
have time I will send for you." 26 After this,
Felix often sent for Paul and talked with
him, because he hoped that Paul would offer him a bribe.

27 Two years later Porcius Festus became governor in place of Felix. But since
Felix wanted to do the Jewish leaders a favor, he kept Paul in jail.

Paul Asks To Be Tried by the Roman Emperor

25 Three days after Festus had
become governor, he went from
Caesarea to Jerusalem. 2 There the chief
priests and some Jewish leaders told him
about their charges against Paul. They also
asked Festus 3 if he would be willing to

[n]**24.6-8** *we arrested him*: Some manuscripts add, "We wanted to judge him by our own laws. But Lysias the commander took him away from us by force. Then Lysias ordered us to bring our charges against this man in your court." [o]**24.14** *the Lord's Way*: See the note at 9.2. [p]**24.14** *Law of Moses . . . the Prophets*: The Jewish Scriptures, that is, the Old Testament. [q]**24.22** *the Lord's Way*: See the note at 9.2.

24.17,18 Ac 21.17-28. **24.21** Ac 23.6.

bring Paul to Jerusalem. They begged him
to do this because they were planning to attack and kill Paul on the way. 4 But Festus
told them, "Paul will be kept in Caesarea,
and I am soon going there myself. 5 If he
has done anything wrong, let your leaders
go with me and bring charges against him
there."
6 Festus stayed in Jerusalem for eight or
ten more days before going to Caesarea.
Then the next day he took his place as
judge and had Paul brought into court. 7 As
soon as Paul came in, the Jewish leaders
from Jerusalem crowded around him and
said he was guilty of many serious crimes.
But they could not prove anything. 8 Then
Paul spoke in his own defense, "I have not
broken the Law of my people. And I have
not done anything against either the temple or the Emperor."
9 Festus wanted to please the leaders.
So he asked Paul, "Are you willing to go to
Jerusalem and be tried by me on these
charges?"
10 Paul replied, "I am on trial in the Emperor's court, and that's where I should be
tried. You know very well that I have not
done anything to harm the Jewish nation.
11 If I had done something deserving death,
I would not ask to escape the death penalty.
But I am not guilty of any of these crimes,
and no one has the right to hand me over
to these people. I now ask to be tried by the
Emperor himself."
12 After Festus had talked this over with
members of his council, he told Paul, "You
have asked to be tried by the Emperor, and
to the Emperor you will go!"

Paul Speaks to Agrippa and Bernice

13 A few days later King Agrippa and
Bernice came to Caesarea to visit Festus.
14 They had been there for several days,
when Festus told the king about the
charges against Paul. He said:

> Felix left a man here in jail, 15 and
> when I went to Jerusalem, the chief
> priests and the Jewish leaders came
> and asked me to find him guilty. 16 I
> told them that it isn't the Roman cus-
> tom to hand a man over to people who
> are bringing charges against him. He
> must first have the chance to meet
> them face to face and to defend him-
> self against their charges.
> 17 So when they came here with
> me, I wasted no time. On the very next
> day I took my place on the judge's
> bench and ordered him to be brought
> in. 18 But when the men stood up to
> make their charges against him, they did
> not accuse him of any of the crimes
> that I thought they would. 19 Instead,
> they argued with him about some of
> their beliefs and about a dead man
> named Jesus, who Paul said was alive.
> 20 Since I did not know how to find
> out the truth about all this, I asked
> Paul if he would be willing to go to
> Jerusalem and be put on trial there.
> 21 But Paul asked to be kept in jail un-
> til the Emperor could decide his case.
> So I ordered him to be kept here until
> I could send him to the Emperor.

22 Then Agrippa said to Festus, "I would
also like to hear what this man has to say."
Festus answered, "You can hear him tomorrow."
23 The next day Agrippa and Bernice
made a big show as they came into the
meeting room. High ranking army officers
and leading citizens of the town were
also there. Festus then ordered Paul to be
brought in 24 and said:

> King Agrippa and other guests, look
> at this man! Every Jew from Jerusalem
> and Caesarea has come to me, de-
> manding for him to be put to death.
> 25 I have not found him guilty of any
> crime deserving death. But because he
> has asked to be judged by the Emperor,
> I have decided to send him to Rome.
> 26 I have to write some facts about
> this man to the Emperor. So I have
> brought him before all of you, but es-
> pecially before you, King Agrippa. After
> we have talked about his case, I will
> then have something to write. 27 It
> makes no sense to send a prisoner to
> the Emperor without stating the
> charges against him.

Paul's Defense before Agrippa

26 Agrippa told Paul, "You may now
speak for yourself."
Paul stretched out his hand and said:

2 King Agrippa, I am glad for this
chance to defend myself before you today on all these charges that my own
people have brought against me. 3 You
know a lot about our religious customs
and the beliefs that divide us. So I ask
you to listen patiently to me.
4-5 All the Jews have known me
since I was a child. They know what
kind of life I have lived in my own
country and in Jerusalem. And if they
were willing, they could tell you that I
was a Pharisee, a member of a group
that is stricter than any other. 6 Now I
am on trial because I believe the promise God made to our people long ago.
7 Day and night our twelve tribes
have earnestly served God, waiting for
his promised blessings. King Agrippa,
because of this hope, the Jewish leaders have brought charges against me.
8 Why should any of you doubt that
God raises the dead to life?
9 I once thought that I should do
everything I could to oppose Jesus
from Nazareth. 10 I did this first in
Jerusalem, and with the authority of
the chief priests I put many of God's
people in jail. I even voted for them to
be killed. 11 I often had them punished
in our meeting places, and I tried to
make them give up their faith. In fact,
I was so angry with them, that I went
looking for them in foreign cities.
12 King Agrippa, one day I was on
my way to Damascus with the authority and permission of the chief priests.
13 About noon I saw a light brighter
than the sun. It flashed from heaven
on me and on everyone traveling with
me. 14 We all fell to the ground. Then I
heard a voice say to me in Aramaic,
"Saul, Saul, why are you so cruel to
me? It's foolish to fight against me!"
15 "Who are you?" I asked.
Then the Lord answered, "I am
Jesus! I am the one you are so cruel to.
16 Now stand up. I have appeared to
you, because I have chosen you to be
my servant. You are to tell others what
you have learned about me and what I
will show you later."
17 The Lord also said, "I will protect
you from the Jews and from the Gentiles that I am sending you to. 18 I want
you to open their eyes, so that they will
turn from darkness to light and from
the power of Satan to God. Then their
sins will be forgiven, and by faith in me
they will become part of God's holy
people."
19 King Agrippa, I obeyed this vision
from heaven. 20 First I preached to the
people in Damascus, and then I went
to Jerusalem and all over Judea. Finally, I went to the Gentiles and said,
"Stop sinning and turn to God! Then
prove what you have done by the way
you live."
21 That is why some men grabbed
me in the temple and tried to kill me.
22 But all this time God has helped me,
and I have preached both to the rich
and to the poor. I have told them only
what the prophets and Moses said
would happen. 23 I told them how the
Messiah would suffer and be the first
to be raised from death, so that he
could bring light to his own people and
to the Gentiles.
24 Before Paul finished defending himself, Festus shouted, "Paul, you're crazy!
Too much learning has driven you out of
your mind."
25 But Paul replied, "Honorable Festus, I
am not crazy. What I am saying is true, and
it makes sense. 26 None of these things
happened off in a corner somewhere. I am
sure that King Agrippa knows what I am
talking about. That's why I can speak so
plainly to him."
27 Then Paul said to Agrippa, "Do
you believe what the prophets said? I know
you do."
28 Agrippa asked Paul, "In such a short
time do you think you can talk me into being a Christian?"
29 Paul answered, "Whether it takes a
short time or a long time, I wish you and
everyone else who hears me today would

26.5 Ac 23.6; Phil 3.5. **26.8** 2 Macc 7.9. **26.9-11** Ac 8.3; 22.4, 5. **26.20** Ac 9.20, 28, 29. **26.23** **a** 1 Co 15.20; **b** Is 42.6; 49.6.

become just like me! Except, of course, for these chains."

30 Then King Agrippa, Governor Festus, Bernice, and everyone who was with them got up. 31 But before they left, they said, "This man isn't guilty of anything. He doesn't deserve to die or to be put in jail."

32 Agrippa told Festus, "Paul could have been set free, if he had not asked to be tried by the Roman Emperor."

Paul Is Taken to Rome

27 When it was time for us to sail to Rome, Captain Julius from the Emperor's special troops was put in charge of Paul and the other prisoners. 2 We went aboard a ship from Adramyttium that was about to sail to some ports along the coast of Asia. Aristarchus from Thessalonica in Macedonia sailed on the ship with us.

3 The next day we came to shore at Sidon. Captain Julius was very kind to Paul. He even let him visit his friends, so they could give him whatever he needed.
4 When we left Sidon, the winds were blowing against us, and we sailed close to the island of Cyprus to be safe from the wind.
5 Then we sailed south of Cilicia and Pamphylia until we came to the port of Myra in
Lycia. 6 There the army captain found a ship from Alexandria that was going to Italy. So he ordered us to board that ship.

7 We sailed along slowly for several days and had a hard time reaching Cnidus. The wind would not let us go any farther in that direction, so we sailed past Cape Salmone, where the island of Crete would protect us
from the wind. 8 We went slowly along the coast and finally reached a place called Fair Havens, not far from the town of Lasea.

9 By now we had already lost a lot of time, and sailing was no longer safe. In fact, even the Great Day of Forgiveness[r]
was past. 10 Then Paul spoke to the crew of the ship, "Men, listen to me! If we sail now, our ship and its cargo will be badly damaged, and many lives will be lost." 11 But Julius listened to the captain of the ship and its owner, rather than to Paul.

12 The harbor at Fair Havens wasn't a good place to spend the winter. Because of this, almost everyone agreed that we should at least try to sail along the coast of Crete as far as Phoenix. It had a harbor that opened toward the southwest and northwest,[s] and we could spend the winter there.

The Storm at Sea

13 When a gentle wind from the south started blowing, the men thought it was a good time to do what they had planned. So they pulled up the anchor, and we sailed
along the coast of Crete. 14 But soon a strong wind called "The Northeaster" blew
against us from the island. 15 The wind struck the ship, and we could not sail against it. So we let the wind carry the ship.

16 We went along the island of Cauda on the side that was protected from the wind. We had a hard time holding the lifeboat in
place, 17 but finally we got it where it belonged. Then the sailors wrapped ropes around the ship to hold it together. They lowered the sail and let the ship drift along, because they were afraid it might hit the sandbanks in the gulf of Syrtis.

18 The storm was so fierce that the next day they threw some of the ship's cargo
overboard. 19 Then on the third day, with their bare hands they threw overboard
some of the ship's gear. 20 For several days we could not see either the sun or the stars. A strong wind kept blowing, and we finally gave up all hope of being saved.

21 Since none of us had eaten anything for a long time, Paul stood up and told the men:

> You should have listened to me! If you had stayed on in Crete, you would not have had this damage and loss.
> 22 But now I beg you to cheer up, because you will be safe. Only the ship will be lost.
>
> 23 I belong to God, and I worship

[r]**27.9** *Great Day of Forgiveness*: This Jewish festival took place near the end of September. The sailing season was dangerous after the middle of September, and it was stopped completely between the middle of November and the middle of March. [s]**27.12** *southwest and northwest*: Or "northeast and southeast."

him. Last night he sent an angel 24 to tell me, "Paul, don't be afraid! You will stand trial before the Emperor. And because of you, God will save the lives of everyone on the ship." 25 Cheer up! I am sure that God will do exactly what he promised. 26 But we will first be shipwrecked on some island.

27 For fourteen days and nights we had been blown around over the Mediterranean Sea. But about midnight the sailors realized that we were getting near land. 28 They measured and found that the water was about one hundred twenty feet deep. A little later they measured again and found it was only about ninety feet. 29 The sailors were afraid that we might hit some rocks, and they let down four anchors from the back of the ship. Then they prayed for daylight.

30 The sailors wanted to escape from the ship. So they lowered the lifeboat into the water, pretending that they were letting down an anchor from the front of the ship. 31 But Paul said to Captain Julius and the soldiers, "If the sailors don't stay on the ship, you won't have any chance to save your lives." 32 The soldiers then cut the ropes that held the lifeboat and let it fall into the sea.

33 Just before daylight Paul begged the people to eat something. He told them, "For fourteen days you have been so worried that you haven't eaten a thing. 34 I beg you to eat something. Your lives depend on it. Do this and not one of you will be hurt." 35 After Paul had said this, he took a piece of bread and gave thanks to God. Then in front of everyone, he broke the bread and ate some. 36 They all felt encouraged, and each of them ate something. 37 There were 276 people on the ship, 38 and after everyone had eaten, they threw the cargo of wheat into the sea to make the ship lighter.

The Shipwreck

39 Morning came, and the ship's crew saw a coast that they did not recognize. But they did see a cove with a beach. So they decided to try to run the ship aground on the beach. 40 They cut the anchors loose and let them sink into the sea. At the same time they untied the ropes that were holding the rudders. Next, they raised the sail at the front of the ship and let the wind carry the ship toward the beach. 41 But it ran aground on a sandbank. The front of the ship stuck firmly in the sand, and the rear was being smashed by the force of the waves.

42 The soldiers decided to kill the prisoners to keep them from swimming away and escaping. 43 But Captain Julius wanted to save Paul's life, and he did not let the soldiers do what they had planned. Instead, he ordered everyone who could swim to dive into the water and head for shore. 44 Then he told the others to hold on to planks of wood or parts of the ship. At last, everyone safely reached shore.

On the Island of Malta

28 When we came ashore, we learned that the island was called Malta. 2 The local people were very friendly, and they welcomed us by building a fire, because it was rainy and cold.

3 After Paul had gathered some wood and had put it on the fire, the heat caused a snake to crawl out, and it bit him on the hand. 4 When the local people saw the snake hanging from Paul's hand, they said to each other, "This man must be a murderer! He didn't drown in the sea, but the goddess of justice will kill him anyway."

5 Paul shook the snake off into the fire and wasn't harmed. 6 The people kept thinking that Paul would either swell up or suddenly drop dead. They watched him for a long time, and when nothing happened to him, they changed their minds and said, "This man is a god."

7 The governor of the island was named Publius, and he owned some of the land around there. Publius was very friendly and welcomed us into his home for three days. 8 His father was in bed, sick with fever and stomach trouble, and Paul went to visit him. Paul healed the man by praying and placing his hands on him.

9 After this happened, everyone on the island brought their sick people to Paul, and they were all healed. 10 The people were very respectful to us, and when we sailed, they gave us everything we needed.

From Malta to Rome

11 Three months later we sailed in a
ship that had been docked at Malta for the
winter. The ship was from Alexandria in
Egypt and was known as "The Twin Gods."[t]
12 We arrived in Syracuse and stayed for
three days. 13 From there we sailed to
Rhegium. The next day a south wind began
to blow, and two days later we arrived in
Puteoli. 14 There we found some of the
Lord's followers, who begged us to stay
with them. A week later we left for the city
of Rome.

15 Some of the followers in Rome heard
about us and came to meet us at the Market of Appius and at the Three Inns. When
Paul saw them, he thanked God and was
encouraged.

Paul in Rome

16 We arrived in Rome, and Paul was allowed to live in a house by himself with a
soldier to guard him.

17 Three days after we got there, Paul
called together some of the Jewish leaders
and said:

> My friends, I have never done any-
> thing to hurt our people, and I have
> never gone against the customs of our
> ancestors. But in Jerusalem I was
> handed over as a prisoner to the Ro-
> mans. 18 They looked into the charges
> against me and wanted to release me.
> They found that I had not done any-
> thing deserving death. 19 The Jewish
> leaders disagreed, so I asked to be tried
> by the Emperor.
>
> But I don't have anything to say
> against my own nation. 20 I am bound
> by these chains because of what we
> people of Israel hope for. That's why I
> have called you here to talk about this
> hope of ours.

21 The leaders replied, "No one from
Judea has written us a letter about you.
And not one of them has come here to report on you or to say anything against you.
22 But we would like to hear what you have
to say. We understand that people everywhere are against this new group."

23 They agreed on a time to meet with
Paul, and many of them came to his house.
From early morning until late in the afternoon, Paul talked to them about God's
kingdom. He used the Law of Moses and
the Books of the Prophets[u] to try to win
them over to Jesus.

24 Some of the leaders agreed with what
Paul said, but others did not. 25 Since they
could not agree among themselves, they
started leaving. But Paul said, "The Holy
Spirit said the right thing when he sent
Isaiah the prophet 26 to tell our ancestors,

'Go to these people
and tell them:
You will listen and listen,
but never understand.
You will look and look,
but never see.
27 All of you
have stubborn hearts.
Your ears are stopped up,
and your eyes are covered.
You cannot see or hear
or understand.
If you could,
you would turn to me,
and I would heal you.' "

28-29 Paul said, "You may be sure that
God wants to save the Gentiles! And they
will listen."[v]

30 For two years Paul stayed in a rented
house and welcomed everyone who came
to see him. 31 He bravely preached about
God's kingdom and taught about the Lord
Jesus Christ, and no one tried to stop him.

[t]**28.11** *known as "The Twin Gods"*: Or "carried on its bow a wooden carving of the Twin Gods." These gods were Castor and Pollux, two of the favorite gods among sailors. [u]**28.23** *Law of Moses and the Books of the Prophets*: The Jewish Bible, that is, the Old Testament. [v]**28.28,29** *And they will listen*: Some manuscripts add, "After Paul said this, the people left, but they got into a fierce argument among themselves."

28.19 Ac 25.11. **28.26,27** Is 6.9, 10 (LXX).

ROMANS

ABOUT THIS LETTER

Paul wrote this letter to introduce himself and his message to the church at Rome. He had never been to this important city, although he knew the names of many Christians there and hoped to visit them soon (15.22—16.21). Paul tells them that he is an apostle, chosen to preach the good news (1.1). And the message he proclaims "is God's powerful way of saving all people who have faith, whether they are Jews or Gentiles" (1.16).

Paul reminds his readers, "All of us have sinned and fallen short of God's glory" (3.23). But how can we be made acceptable to God? This is the main question that Paul answers in this letter. He begins by showing how everyone has failed to do what God requires. The Jews have not obeyed the Law of Moses, and the Gentiles have refused even to think about God, although God has spoken to them in many different ways (1.18—3.20).

> *Now we see how God does make us acceptable to him. . . . He accepts people only because they have faith in Jesus Christ . . . God treats us much better than we deserve, and because of Christ Jesus, he freely accepts us and sets us free from our sins.*
>
> *(3.21a, 22b, 24)*
>
> *God gave Jesus to die for our sins, and he raised him to life, so that we would be made acceptable to God.*
>
> *(4.25)*

A QUICK LOOK AT THIS LETTER

- Paul and His Message of Good News (1.1-17)
- Everyone Is Guilty (1.18—3.20)
- God's Way of Accepting People (3.21—4.25)
- A New Life for God's People (5.1—8.39)
- What about the People of Israel? (9.1—11.36)
- How to Live the New Life of Love (12.1—15.13)
- Paul's Plans and Personal Greetings (15.14—16.27)

---

1 From Paul, a servant of Christ Jesus.
God chose me to be an apostle, and
he appointed me to preach the good news
2 that he promised long ago by what his
prophets said in the holy Scriptures.
3-4 This good news is about his Son, our
Lord Jesus Christ! As a human, he was
from the family of David. But the Holy
Spirit[a] proved that Jesus is the powerful
Son of God,[b] because he was raised from
death.
5 Jesus was kind to me and chose me
to be an apostle,[c] so that people of all nations would obey and have faith. 6 You are
some of those people chosen by Jesus Christ.
7 This letter is to all of you in Rome.

[a]1.4 *the Holy Spirit*: Or "his own spirit of holiness." [b]1.4 *proved that Jesus is the powerful Son of God*: Or "proved in a powerful way that Jesus is the Son of God." [c]1.5 *Jesus was kind to me and chose me to be an apostle*: Or "Jesus was kind to us and chose us to be his apostles."

God loves you and has chosen you to be his
very own people.
I pray that God our Father and our Lord
Jesus Christ will be kind to you and will
bless you with peace!

A Prayer of Thanks

8 First, I thank God in the name of Jesus
Christ for all of you. I do this because people everywhere in the world are talking
about your faith. 9 God has seen how I
never stop praying for you, while I serve
him with all my heart and tell the good
news about his Son.
10 In all my prayers, I ask God to make it
possible for me to visit you. 11 I want to see
you and share with you the same blessings
that God's Spirit has given me. Then you
will grow stronger in your faith. 12 What I
am saying is that we can encourage each
other by the faith that is ours.
13 My friends, I want you to know that I
have often planned to come for a visit. But
something has always kept me from doing it. I want to win followers to Christ in
Rome, as I have done in many other places.
14-15 It doesn't matter if people are civilized
and educated, or if they are uncivilized and
uneducated. I must tell the good news to
everyone. That's why I am eager to visit all
of you in Rome.

The Power of the Good News

16 I am proud of the good news! It is
God's powerful way of saving all people
who have faith, whether they are Jews or
Gentiles. 17 The good news tells how God
accepts everyone who has faith, but only
those who have faith.[d] It is just as the
Scriptures say, "The people God accepts because of their faith will live."[e]

Everyone Is Guilty

18 From heaven God shows how angry
he is with all the wicked and evil things
that sinful people do to crush the truth.
19 They know everything that can be known
about God, because God has shown it all to
them. 20 God's eternal power and character
cannot be seen. But from the beginning of
creation, God has shown what these are
like by all he has made. That's why those
people don't have any excuse. 21 They
know about God, but they don't honor him
or even thank him. Their thoughts are useless, and their stupid minds are in the
dark. 22 They claim to be wise, but they are
fools. 23 They don't worship the glorious
and eternal God. Instead, they worship
idols that are made to look like humans
who cannot live forever, and like birds, animals, and reptiles.
24 So God let these people go their own
way. They did what they wanted to do, and
their filthy thoughts made them do shameful things with their bodies. 25 They gave
up the truth about God for a lie, and they
worshiped God's creation instead of God,
who will be praised forever. Amen.
26 God let them follow their own evil desires. Women no longer wanted to have sex
in a natural way, and they did things with
each other that were not natural. 27 Men
behaved in the same way. They stopped
wanting to have sex with women and had
strong desires for sex with other men. They
did shameful things with each other, and
what has happened to them is punishment
for their foolish deeds.
28 Since these people refused even to
think about God, he let their useless minds
rule over them. That's why they do all sorts
of indecent things. 29 They are evil, wicked,
and greedy, as well as mean in every possible way. They want what others have, and
they murder, argue, cheat, and are hard to
get along with. They gossip, 30 say cruel
things about others, and hate God. They
are proud, conceited, and boastful, always
thinking up new ways to do evil.
These people don't respect their parents. 31 They are stupid, unreliable, and
don't have any love or pity for others.
32 They know God has said that anyone

[d] **1.17** *but only those who have faith*: Or "and faith is all that matters." [e] **1.17** *The people God accepts because of their faith will live*: Or "The people God accepts will live because of their faith."

1.13 Ac 19.21. **1.16** Mk 8.38. **1.17** Hb 2.4. **1.20** Ws 13.1-9; Si 17.8. **1.21** Eph 4.17, 18. **1.23** Dt 4.16-18; Ws 11.15; 12.24; 13.10-19. **1.28** 3 Macc 4.16; 4 Macc 1.20, 21.

who acts this way deserves to die. But they keep on doing evil things, and they even encourage others to do them.

God's Judgment Is Fair

2 Some of you accuse others of doing wrong. But there is no excuse for what you do. When you judge others, you condemn yourselves, because you are guilty of doing the very same things. 2 We know that God is right to judge everyone who behaves in this way. 3 Do you really think God won't punish you, when you behave exactly like the people you accuse? 4 You surely don't think much of God's wonderful goodness or of his patience and willingness to put up with you. Don't you know that the reason God is good to you is because he wants you to turn to him?

5 But you are stubborn and refuse to turn to God. So you are making things even worse for yourselves on that day when he will show how angry he is and will judge the world with fairness. 6 God will reward each of us for what we have done. 7 He will give eternal life to everyone who has patiently done what is good in the hope of receiving glory, honor, and life that lasts forever. 8 But he will show how angry and furious he can be with every selfish person who rejects the truth and wants to do evil. 9 All who are wicked will be punished with trouble and suffering. It doesn't matter if they are Jews or Gentiles. 10 But all who do right will be rewarded with glory, honor, and peace, whether they are Jews or Gentiles. 11 God doesn't have any favorites!

12 Those people who don't know about God's Law will still be punished for what they do wrong. And the Law will be used to judge everyone who knows what it says. 13 God accepts those who obey his Law, but not those who simply hear it.

14 Some people naturally obey the Law's commands, even though they don't have the Law. 15 This proves that the conscience is like a law written in the human heart. And it will show whether we are forgiven or condemned, 16 when God appoints Jesus Christ to judge everyone's secret thoughts, just as my message says.

The Jews and the Law

17 Some of you call yourselves Jews. You trust in the Law and take pride in God. 18 By reading the Scriptures you learn how God wants you to behave, and you discover what is right. 19 You are sure that you are a guide for the blind and a light for all who are in the dark. 20 And since there is knowledge and truth in God's Law, you think you can instruct fools and teach young people.

21 But how can you teach others when you refuse to learn? You preach that it is wrong to steal. But do you steal? 22 You say people should be faithful in marriage. But are you faithful? You hate idols, yet you rob their temples. 23 You take pride in the Law, but you disobey the Law and bring shame to God. 24 It is just as the Scriptures tell us, "You have made foreigners say insulting things about God."

25 Being circumcised is worthwhile, if you obey the Law. But if you don't obey the Law, you are no better off than people who are not circumcised. 26 In fact, if they obey the Law, they are as good as anyone who is circumcised. 27 So everyone who obeys the Law, but has never been circumcised, will condemn you. Even though you are circumcised and have the Law, you still don't obey its teachings.

28 Just because you live like a Jew and are circumcised doesn't make you a real Jew. 29 To be a real Jew you must obey the Law. True circumcision is something that happens deep in your heart, not something done to your body. And besides, you should want praise from God and not from humans.

3 What good is it to be a Jew? What good is it to be circumcised? 2 It is good in a lot of ways! First of all, God's messages were spoken to the Jews. 3 It is true that some of them did not believe the message. But does this mean that God cannot be trusted, just because they did not have faith? 4 No, indeed! God tells the

2.1 Mt 7.1; Lk 6.37. **2.4** Ws 11.23. **2.6** Ps 62.12; Pr 24.12. **2.11** Dt 10.17.
2.24 Is 52.5 (LXX). **2.29** Dt 30.6. **3.4** Ps 51.4 (LXX).

truth, even if everyone else is a liar. The
Scriptures say about God,

"Your words
will be proven true,
and in court
you will win your case."

5 If our evil deeds show how right God
is, then what can we say? Is it wrong for
God to become angry and punish us? What
a foolish thing to ask. 6 But the answer is,
"No." Otherwise, how could God judge the
world? 7 Since your lies bring great honor
to God by showing how truthful he is, you
may ask why God still says you are a sinner.
8 You might as well say, "Let's do something
evil, so that something good will come of
it!" Some people even claim that we are
saying this. But God is fair and will judge
them as well.

No One Is Good

9 What does all this mean? Does it
mean that we Jews are better off[f] than the
Gentiles? No, it doesn't! Jews, as well as
Gentiles, are ruled by sin, just as I have
said. 10 The Scriptures tell us,

"No one is acceptable to God!
11 Not one of them understands
or even searches for God.
12 They have all turned away
and are worthless.
There isn't one person
who does right.
13 Their words are like
an open pit,
and their tongues are good
only for telling lies.
Each word is as deadly
as the fangs of a snake,
14 and they say nothing
but bitter curses.
15 These people quickly
become violent.
16 Wherever they go,
they leave ruin
and destruction.
17 They don't know how
to live in peace.
18 They don't even fear God."

19 We know that everything in the Law
was written for those who are under
its power. The Law says these things to
stop anyone from making excuses and to
let God show that the whole world is
guilty. 20 God doesn't accept people
simply because they obey the Law. No, indeed! All the Law does is to point out
our sin.

God's Way of Accepting People

21 Now we see how God does make us
acceptable to him. The Law and the
Prophets[g] tell how we become acceptable,
and it isn't by obeying the Law of Moses.
22 God treats everyone alike. He accepts
people only because they have faith in
Jesus Christ. 23 All of us have sinned and
fallen short of God's glory. 24 But God treats
us much better than we deserve,[h] and because of Christ Jesus, he freely accepts us
and sets us free from our sins. 25-26 God
sent Christ to be our sacrifice. Christ offered his life's blood, so that by faith in him
we could come to God. And God did this to
show that in the past he was right to be patient and forgive sinners. This also shows
that God is right when he accepts people
who have faith in Jesus.

27 What is left for us to brag about? Not
a thing! Is it because we obeyed some law?
No! It is because of faith. 28 We see that
people are acceptable to God because they
have faith, and not because they obey the
Law. 29 Does God belong only to the Jews?
Isn't he also the God of the Gentiles? Yes,
he is! 30 There is only one God, and he accepts Gentiles as well as Jews, simply be-

[f]**3.9** *better off*: Or "worse off." [g]**3.21** *The Law and the Prophets*: The Jewish Scriptures, that is, the Old Testament. [h]**3.24** *treats us much better than we deserve*: The Greek word *charis*, traditionally rendered "grace," is translated here and other places in the CEV to express the overwhelming kindness of God.

3.10-12 Ps 14.1-3 (LXX); Ps 53.1-3 (LXX). **3.13** **a** Ps 5.9 (LXX); **b** Ps 140.3. **3.14** Ps 10.7 (LXX). **3.15-17** Is 59.7, 8. **3.18** Ps 36.1. **3.20** Ps 143.2; Ga 2.16. **3.22** Ga 2.16. **3.25,26** 4 Macc 17.21. **3.30** Dt 6.4; Ga 3.20.

cause of their faith. 31 Do we destroy the
Law by our faith? Not at all! We make it
even more powerful.

The Example of Abraham

4 Well then, what can we say about our
ancestor Abraham? 2 If he became acceptable to God because of what he did,
then he would have something to brag
about. But he would never be able to brag
about it to God. 3 The Scriptures say, "God
accepted Abraham because Abraham had
faith in him."

4 Money paid to workers isn't a gift. It is
something they earn by working. 5 But you
cannot make God accept you because of
something you do. God accepts sinners
only because they have faith in him. 6 In
the Scriptures David talks about the blessings that come to people who are acceptable to God, even though they don't do anything to deserve these blessings. David
says,

7 "God blesses people
whose sins are forgiven
and whose evil deeds
are forgotten.
8 The Lord blesses people
whose sins are erased
from his book."

9 Are these blessings meant for circumcised people or for those who are not circumcised? Well, the Scriptures say that
God accepted Abraham because Abraham
had faith in him. 10 But when did this happen? Was it before or after Abraham was
circumcised? Of course, it was before.

11 Abraham let himself be circumcised
to show that he had been accepted because
of his faith even before he was circumcised. This makes Abraham the father of all
who are acceptable to God because of their
faith, even though they are not circumcised. 12 This also makes Abraham the
father of everyone who is circumcised and
has faith in God, as Abraham did before he
was circumcised.

The Promise Is for All Who Have Faith

13 God promised Abraham and his descendants that he would give them
the world. This promise wasn't made
because Abraham had obeyed a law, but
because his faith in God made him
acceptable. 14 If Abraham and his descendants were given this promise because they
had obeyed a law, then faith would mean
nothing, and the promise would be worthless.

15 God becomes angry when his Law is
broken. But where there isn't a law, it cannot be broken. 16 Everything depends on
having faith in God, so that God's promise
is assured by his great kindness. This
promise isn't only for Abraham's descendants who have the Law. It is for all who
are Abraham's descendants because they
have faith, just as he did. Abraham is the
ancestor of us all. 17 The Scriptures say
that Abraham would become the ancestor
of many nations. This promise was made to
Abraham because he had faith in God, who
raises the dead to life and creates new
things.

18 God promised Abraham a lot of descendants. And when it all seemed hopeless, Abraham still had faith in God and
became the ancestor of many nations.
19 Abraham's faith never became weak, not
even when he was nearly a hundred years
old. He knew that he was almost dead and
that his wife Sarah could not have children. 20 But Abraham never doubted or
questioned God's promise. His faith made
him strong, and he gave all the credit
to God.

21 Abraham was certain that God could
do what he had promised. 22 So God accepted him, 23 just as we read in the Scriptures. But these words were not written
only for Abraham. 24 They were written for
us, since we will also be accepted because
of our faith in God, who raised our Lord
Jesus to life. 25 God gave Jesus to die for our
sins, and he raised him to life, so that we
would be made acceptable to God.

4.3 Gn 15.6; Ga 3.6. **4.7,8** Ps 32.1, 2. **4.11** Gn 17.10, 11. **4.13** Gn 17.4-6; 22.17, 18; Ga 3.29. **4.14** Ga 3.18. **4.16** Ga 3.7. **4.17** Gn 17.4, 5. **4.18** Gn 15.5. **4.19** Gn 17.17. **4.25** Is 53.4, 5.

What It Means To Be Acceptable to God

5 By faith we have been made acceptable to God. And now, because of our
Lord Jesus Christ, we live at peace[i] with
God. 2 Christ has also introduced us[j] to
God's undeserved kindness on which we
take our stand. So we are happy, as we look
forward to sharing in the glory of God.
3 But that's not all! We gladly suffer,[k] because we know that suffering helps us to
endure. 4 And endurance builds character,
which gives us a hope 5 that will never disappoint us. All of this happens because God
has given us the Holy Spirit, who fills our
hearts with his love.

6 Christ died for us at a time when we
were helpless and sinful. 7 No one is really
willing to die for an honest person, though
someone might be willing to die for a truly
good person. 8 But God showed how much
he loved us by having Christ die for us,
even though we were sinful.

9 But there is more! Now that God has
accepted us because Christ sacrificed his
life's blood, we will also be kept safe from
God's anger. 10 Even when we were God's
enemies, he made peace with us, because
his Son died for us. Yet something even
greater than friendship is ours. Now that
we are at peace with God, we will be saved
by his Son's life. 11 And in addition to
everything else, we are happy because God
sent our Lord Jesus Christ to make peace
with us.

Adam and Christ

12 Adam sinned, and that sin brought
death into the world. Now everyone has
sinned, and so everyone must die. 13 Sin
was in the world before the Law came. But
no record of sin was kept, because there
was no Law. 14 Yet death still had power
over all who lived from the time of Adam to
the time of Moses. This happened, though
not everyone disobeyed a direct command
from God, as Adam did.

In some ways Adam is like Christ who
came later. 15 But the gift that God was
kind enough to give was very different from
Adam's sin. That one sin brought death to
many others. Yet in an even greater way,
Jesus Christ alone brought God's gift of
kindness to many people.

16 There is a lot of difference between
Adam's sin and God's gift. That one sin led
to punishment. But God's gift made it possible for us to be acceptable to him, even
though we have sinned many times.
17 Death ruled like a king because Adam
had sinned. But that cannot compare with
what Jesus Christ has done. God has been
so kind to us, and he has accepted us because of Jesus. And so we will live and rule
like kings.

18 Everyone was going to be punished
because Adam sinned. But because of the
good thing that Christ has done, God accepts us and gives us the gift of life.
19 Adam disobeyed God and caused many
others to be sinners. But Jesus obeyed him
and will make many people acceptable
to God.

20 The Law came, so that the full power
of sin could be seen. Yet where sin was
powerful, God's kindness was even more
powerful. 21 Sin ruled by means of death.
But God's kindness now rules, and God has
accepted us because of Jesus Christ our
Lord. This means that we will have eternal
life.

Dead to Sin but Alive because of Christ

6 What should we say? Should we keep
on sinning, so that God's wonderful
kindness will show up even better? 2 No,
we should not! If we are dead to sin, how
can we go on sinning? 3 Don't you know
that all who share in Christ Jesus by being
baptized also share in his death? 4 When
we were baptized, we died and were buried
with Christ. We were baptized, so that we
would live a new life, as Christ was raised
to life by the glory of God the Father.

5 If we shared in Jesus' death by being
baptized, we will be raised to life with him.
6 We know that the persons we used to be
were nailed to the cross with Jesus. This

[i]**5.1** *we live at peace*: Some manuscripts have "let us live at peace." [j]**5.2** *introduced us*: Some manuscripts add "by faith." [k]**5.3** *We gladly suffer*: Or "Let us gladly suffer."

5.12 Gn 3.6; Ws 2.24. **5.18** 2 Esd 7.11. **6.4** Col 2.12.

was done, so that our sinful bodies would no longer be the slaves of sin. 7 We know that sin doesn't have power over dead people.

8 As surely as we died with Christ, we believe we will also live with him. 9 We know that death no longer has any power over Christ. He died and was raised to life, never again to die. 10 When Christ died, he died for sin once and for all. But now he is alive, and he lives only for God. 11 In the same way, you must think of yourselves as dead to the power of sin. But Christ Jesus has given life to you, and you live for God.

12 Don't let sin rule your body. After all, your body is bound to die, so don't obey its desires 13 or let any part of it become a slave of evil. Give yourselves to God, as people who have been raised from death to life. Make every part of your body a slave that pleases God. 14 Don't let sin keep ruling your lives. You are ruled by God's kindness and not by the Law.

Slaves Who Do What Pleases God

15 What does all this mean? Does it mean we are free to sin, because we are ruled by God's wonderful kindness and not by the Law? Certainly not! 16 Don't you know that you are slaves of anyone you obey? You can be slaves of sin and die, or you can be obedient slaves of God and be acceptable to him. 17 You used to be slaves of sin. But I thank God that with all your heart you obeyed the teaching you received from me. 18 Now you are set free from sin and are slaves who please God.

19 I am using these everyday examples, because in some ways you are still weak. You used to let the different parts of your body be slaves of your evil thoughts. But now you must make every part of your body serve God, so that you will belong completely to him.

20 When you were slaves of sin, you didn't have to please God. 21 But what good did you receive from the things you did? All you have to show for them is your shame, and they lead to death. 22 Now you have been set free from sin, and are you are God's slaves. This will make you holy and will lead you to eternal life. 23 Sin pays off with death. But God's gift is eternal life given by Jesus Christ our Lord.

An Example from Marriage

7 My friends, you surely understand enough about law to know that laws only have power over people who are alive. 2 For example, the Law says that a man's wife must remain his wife as long as he lives. But once her husband is dead, she is free 3 to marry someone else. However, if she goes off with another man while her husband is still alive, she is said to be unfaithful.

4 That is how it is with you, my friends. You are now part of the body of Christ and are dead to the power of the Law. You are free to belong to Christ, who was raised to life so that we could serve God. 5 When we thought only of ourselves, the Law made us have sinful desires. It made every part of our bodies into slaves who are doomed to die. 6 But the Law no longer rules over us. We are like dead people, and it cannot have any power over us. Now we can serve God in a new way by obeying his Spirit, and not in the old way by obeying the written Law.

The Battle with Sin

7 Does this mean that the Law is sinful? Certainly not! But if it had not been for the Law, I would not have known what sin is really like. For example, I would not have known what it means to want something that belongs to someone else, unless the Law had told me not to do that. 8 It was sin that used this command as a way of making me have all kinds of desires. But without the Law, sin is dead.

9 Before I knew about the Law, I was alive. But as soon as I heard that command, sin came to life, 10 and I died. The very command that was supposed to bring life to me, instead brought death. 11 Sin used this command to trick me, and because of it I died. 12 Still, the Law and its commands are holy and correct and good.

13 Am I saying that something good caused my death? Certainly not! It was sin that killed me by using something good.

7.7 Ex 20.17; Dt 5.21. **7.11** Gn 3.13.

Now we can see how terrible and evil sin
really is. 14 We know that the Law is spiritual. But I am merely a human, and I have
been sold as a slave to sin. 15 In fact, I don't
understand why I act the way I do. I don't
do what I know is right. I do the things I
hate. 16 Although I don't do what I know is
right, I agree that the Law is good. 17 So I
am not the one doing these evil things. The
sin that lives in me is what does them.

18 I know that my selfish desires won't
let me do anything that is good. Even when
I want to do right, I cannot. 19 Instead of
doing what I know is right, I do wrong.
20 And so, if I don't do what I know is right,
I am no longer the one doing these evil
things. The sin that lives in me is what
does them.

21 The Law has shown me that something in me keeps me from doing what I
know is right. 22 With my whole heart I
agree with the Law of God. 23 But in every
part of me I discover something fighting
against my mind, and it makes me a prisoner of sin that controls everything I do.
24 What a miserable person I am. Who will
rescue me from this body that is doomed
to die? 25 Thank God! Jesus Christ will rescue me.

So with my mind I serve the Law of
God, although my selfish desires make me
serve the law of sin.

Living by the Power of God's Spirit

8 If you belong to Christ Jesus, you
won't be punished. 2 The Holy Spirit
will give you life that comes from Christ
Jesus and will set you[l] free from sin and
death. 3 The Law of Moses cannot do this,
because our selfish desires make the Law
weak. But God set you free when he sent
his own Son to be like us sinners and to be
a sacrifice for our sin. God used Christ's
body to condemn sin. 4 He did this, so that
we would do what the Law commands by
obeying the Spirit instead of our own desires.

5 People who are ruled by their desires
think only of themselves. Everyone who is
ruled by the Holy Spirit thinks about spiritual things. 6 If our minds are ruled by our
desires, we will die. But if our minds are
ruled by the Spirit, we will have life and
peace. 7 Our desires fight against God, because they do not and cannot obey God's
laws. 8 If we follow our desires, we cannot
please God.

9 You are no longer ruled by your desires, but by God's Spirit, who lives in you.
People who don't have the Spirit of Christ
in them don't belong to him. 10 But Christ
lives in you. So you are alive because God
has accepted you, even though your bodies
must die because of your sins. 11 Yet God
raised Jesus to life! God's Spirit now lives in
you, and he will raise you to life by his Spirit.

12 My dear friends, we must not live to
satisfy our desires. 13 If you do, you will die.
But you will live, if by the help of God's
Spirit you say "No" to your desires. 14 Only
those people who are led by God's Spirit are
his children. 15 God's Spirit doesn't make
us slaves who are afraid of him. Instead, we
become his children and call him our
Father.[m] 16 God's Spirit makes us sure that
we are his children. 17 His Spirit lets us
know that together with Christ we will be
given what God has promised. We will also
share in the glory of Christ, because we
have suffered with him.

A Wonderful Future for God's People

18 I am sure that what we are suffering
now cannot compare with the glory that
will be shown to us. 19 In fact, all creation
is eagerly waiting for God to show who his
children are. 20 Meanwhile, creation is confused, but not because it wants to be confused. God made it this way in the hope
21 that creation would be set free from decay and would share in the glorious freedom of his children. 22 We know that all
creation is still groaning and is in pain, like
a woman about to give birth.

[l] **8.2** *you*: Some manuscripts have "me." [m] **8.15** *our Father*: The Greek text uses the Aramaic word "Abba" (meaning "father"), which shows the close relation between the children and their father.

7.15 Ga 5.17. **8.11** 1 Co 3.16. **8.15-17** Ga 4.5-7. **8.15** Mk 14.35, 36; Ga 4.6.
8.18 Ws 3.5, 6. **8.20** Gn 3.17-19.

23 The Spirit makes us sure about what we will be in the future. But now we groan silently, while we wait for God to show that we are his children.[n] This means that our bodies will also be set free. 24 And this hope is what saves us. But if we already have what we hope for, there is no need to keep on hoping. 25 However, we hope for something we have not yet seen, and we patiently wait for it.

26 In certain ways we are weak, but the Spirit is here to help us. For example, when we don't know what to pray for, the Spirit prays for us in ways that cannot be put into words. 27 All of our thoughts are known to God. He can understand what is in the mind of the Spirit, as the Spirit prays for God's people. 28 We know that God is always at work for the good of everyone who loves him.[o] They are the ones God has chosen for his purpose, 29 and he has always known who his chosen ones would be. He had decided to let them become like his own Son, so that his Son would be the first of many children. 30 God then accepted the people he had already decided to choose, and he has shared his glory with them.

God's Love

31 What can we say about all this? If God is on our side, can anyone be against us? 32 God did not keep back his own Son, but he gave him for us. If God did this, won't he freely give us everything else? 33 If God says his chosen ones are acceptable to him, can anyone bring charges against them? 34 Or can anyone condemn them? No indeed! Christ died and was raised to life, and now he is at God's right side,[p] speaking to him for us. 35 Can anything separate us from the love of Christ? Can trouble, suffering, and hard times, or hunger and nakedness, or danger and death? 36 It is exactly as the Scriptures say,

"For you we face death
all day long.
We are like sheep
on their way
to be butchered."

37 In everything we have won more than a victory because of Christ who loves us. 38 I am sure that nothing can separate us from God's love—not life or death, not angels or spirits, not the present or the future, 39 and not powers above or powers below. Nothing in all creation can separate us from God's love for us in Christ Jesus our Lord!

God's Choice of Israel

9 I am a follower of Christ, and the Holy Spirit is a witness to my conscience. So I tell the truth and I am not lying when I say 2 my heart is broken and I am in great sorrow. 3 I would gladly be placed under God's curse and be separated from Christ for the good of my own people. 4 They are the descendants of Israel, and they are also God's chosen people. God showed them his glory. He made agreements with them and gave them his Law. The temple is theirs and so are the promises that God made to them. 5 They have those famous ancestors, who were also the ancestors of Jesus Christ. I pray that God, who rules over all, will be praised forever![q] Amen.

6 It cannot be said that God broke his promise. After all, not all of the people of Israel are the true people of God. 7-8 In fact, when God made the promise to Abraham, he meant only Abraham's descendants by his son Isaac. God was talking only about Isaac when he promised 9 Sarah, "At this time next year I will return, and you will already have a son."

10 Don't forget what happened to the twin sons of Isaac and Rebekah. 11-12 Even before they were born or had

[n]**8.23** *to show that we are his children*: These words are not in some manuscripts. The translation of the remainder of the verse would then read, "while we wait for God to set our bodies free."
[o]**8.28** *God is always at work for the good of everyone who loves him*: Or "All things work for the good of everyone who loves God" or "God's Spirit always works for the good of everyone who loves God." [p]**8.34** *right side*: The place of power and honor. [q]**9.5** *Christ. I pray that God, who rules over all, will be praised forever*: Or "Christ, who rules over all. I pray that God will be praised forever" or "Christ. And I pray that Christ, who is God and rules over all, will be praised forever."

8.23 2 Co 5.2-4. **8.27** 4 Macc 10.18. **8.36** Ps 44.22. **9.4** Ex 4.22. **9.7,8** Gn 21.12. **9.9** Gn 18.10. **9.11,12** Gn 25.23.

done anything good or bad, the Lord told
Rebekah that her older son would serve the
younger one. The Lord said this to show
that he makes his own choices and that it
wasn't because of anything either of them
had done. 13 That's why the Scriptures
say that the Lord liked Jacob more than
Esau.
14 Are we saying that God is unfair? Certainly not! 15 The Lord told Moses that he
has pity and mercy on anyone he wants to.
16 Everything then depends on God's mercy
and not on what people want or do. 17 In
the Scriptures the Lord says to Pharaoh of
Egypt, "I let you become king, so that I
could show you my power and be praised
by all people on earth." 18 Everything depends on what God decides to do, and he
can either have pity on people or make
them stubborn.

God's Anger and Mercy

19 Someone may ask, "How can God
blame us, if he makes us behave in the way
he wants us to?" 20 But, my friend, I ask,
"Who do you think you are to question
God? Does the clay have the right to ask
the potter why he shaped it the way he
did? 21 Doesn't a potter have the right to
make a fancy bowl and a plain bowl out of
the same lump of clay?"
22 God wanted to show his anger and re-
veal his power against everyone who deserved to be destroyed. But instead, he patiently put up with them. 23 He did this by
showing how glorious he is when he has
pity on the people he has chosen to share
in his glory. 24 Whether Jews or Gentiles,
we are those chosen ones, 25 just as the
Lord says in the book of Hosea,

"Although they are not
my people,
I will make them my people.
I will treat with love
those nations
that have never been loved.

26 "Once they were told,
'You are not my people.'
But in that very place
they will be called
children of the living God."

27 And this is what the prophet Isaiah
said about the people of Israel,

"The people of Israel
are as many
as the grains of sand
along the beach.
But only a few who are left
will be saved.
28 The Lord will be quick
and sure to do on earth
what he has warned
he will do."

29 Isaiah also said,

"If the Lord All-Powerful
had not spared some
of our descendants,
we would have been destroyed
like the cities of Sodom
and Gomorrah."[r]

Israel and the Good News

30 What does all of this mean? It means
that the Gentiles were not trying to be acceptable to God, but they found that he
would accept them if they had faith. 31-32 It
also means that the people of Israel were
not acceptable to God. And why not? It
was because they were trying[s] to be acceptable by obeying the Law instead of by
having faith in God. The people of Israel
fell over the stone that makes people
stumble, 33 just as God says in the Scriptures,

"Look! I am placing in Zion
a stone to make people
stumble and fall.
But those who have faith
in that one will never
be disappointed."

[r] **9.29** *Sodom and Gomorrah*: During the time of Abraham the Lord destroyed these two cities because their people were so sinful. [s] **9.31,32** *because they were trying*: Or "while they were trying" or "even though they were trying."

9.13 Ml 1.2, 3. **9.15** Ex 33.19. **9.17** Ex 9.16 (LXX); 3 Macc 2.6. **9.20** Is 29.16; 45.9; Ws 12.12. **9.21** Ws 15.7; Si 33.13. **9.22** Ws 12.20, 21. **9.25** Ho 2.23. **9.26** Ho 1.10. **9.27,28** Is 10.21-23 (LXX). **9.29** Is 1.9 (LXX). **9.33** Is 28.16 (LXX).

10 Dear friends, my greatest wish and
my prayer to God is for the people
of Israel to be saved. 2 I know they love
God, but they don't understand 3 what
makes people acceptable to him. So they
refuse to trust God, and they try to be acceptable by obeying the Law. 4 But Christ
makes the Law no longer necessary[t] for
those who become acceptable to God by
faith.

Anyone Can Be Saved

5 Moses said that a person could become acceptable to God by obeying the
Law. He did this when he wrote, "If you
want to live, you must do all that the Law
commands."
6 But people whose faith makes them
acceptable to God will never ask, "Who will
go up to heaven to bring Christ down?"
7 Neither will they ask, "Who will go down
into the world of the dead to raise him to
life?"
8 All who are acceptable because of their
faith simply say, "The message is as near as
your mouth or your heart." And this is the
same message we preach about faith. 9 So
you will be saved, if you honestly say, "Jesus
is Lord," and if you believe with all your
heart that God raised him from death.
10 God will accept you and save you, if you
truly believe this and tell it to others.
11 The Scriptures say that no one who
has faith will be disappointed, 12 no matter
if that person is a Jew or a Gentile. There is
only one Lord, and he is generous to everyone who asks for his help. 13 All who call
out to the Lord will be saved.
14 How can people have faith in the
Lord and ask him to save them, if they
have never heard about him? And how can
they hear, unless someone tells them?
15 And how can anyone tell them without
being sent by the Lord? The Scriptures say
it is a beautiful sight to see even the feet of
someone coming to preach the good news.
16 Yet not everyone has believed the message. For example, the prophet Isaiah
asked, "Lord, has anyone believed what we
said?"
17 No one can have faith without hearing the message about Christ. 18 But am I
saying that the people of Israel did not
hear? No, I am not! The Scriptures say,

"The message was told
everywhere on earth.
It was announced
all over the world."

19 Did the people of Israel understand or
not? Moses answered this question when
he told that the Lord had said,

"I will make Israel jealous
of people
who are a nation
of nobodies.
I will make them angry
at people
who don't understand
a thing."

20 Isaiah was fearless enough to tell that
the Lord had said,

"I was found by people
who were not looking
for me.
I appeared to the ones
who were not asking
about me."

21 And Isaiah said about the people of Israel,

"All day long the Lord
has reached out
to people who are stubborn
and refuse to obey."

God Has Not Rejected His People

11 Am I saying that God has turned
his back on his people? Certainly
not! I am one of the people of Israel, and I
myself am a descendant of Abraham from
the tribe of Benjamin. 2 God did not turn

[t] **10.4** *But Christ makes the Law no longer necessary*: Or "But Christ gives the full meaning to the Law."

10.5 Lv 18.5. **10.6-8** Dt 30.12-14. **10.11** Is 28.16 (LXX). **10.13** Jl 2.32.
10.15 Is 52.7. **10.16** Is 53.1 (LXX). **10.18** Ps 19.4 (LXX). **10.19** Dt 32.21.
10.20 Is 65.1 (LXX). **10.21** Is 65.2 (LXX). **11.1** Phil 3.5.

his back on his chosen people. Don't you
remember reading in the Scriptures how
Elijah complained to God about the people
of Israel? 3 He said, "Lord, they killed your
prophets and destroyed your altars. I am the
only one left, and now they want to kill me."
4 But the Lord told Elijah, "I still have
seven thousand followers who have not
worshiped Baal." 5 It is the same way now.
God was kind to the people of Israel, and so
a few of them are still his followers. 6 This
happened because of God's undeserved
kindness and not because of anything they
have done. It could not have happened except for God's kindness.
7 This means that only a chosen few of
the people of Israel found what all of them
were searching for. And the rest of them
were stubborn, 8 just as the Scriptures say,

"God made them so stupid
that their eyes are blind,
and their ears
are still deaf."

9 Then David said,

"Turn their meals
into bait for a trap,
so that they will stumble
and be given
what they deserve.
10 Blindfold their eyes!
Don't let them see.
Bend their backs
beneath a burden
that will never be lifted."

Gentiles Will Be Saved

11 Do I mean that the people of Israel
fell, never to get up again? Certainly not!
Their failure made it possible for the Gentiles to be saved, and this will make the
people of Israel jealous. 12 But if the rest of
the world's people were helped so much by
Israel's sin and loss, they will be helped
even more by their full return.
13 I am now speaking to you Gentiles,
and as long as I am an apostle to you, I will
take pride in my work. 14 I hope in this way
to make some of my own people jealous
enough to be saved. 15 When Israel rejected
God,[u] the rest of the people in the world
were able to turn to him. So when God
makes friends with Israel, it will be like
bringing the dead back to life. 16 If part of a
batch of dough is made holy by being offered to God, then all of the dough is holy.
If the roots of a tree are holy, the rest of the
tree is holy too.
17 You Gentiles are like branches of a
wild olive tree that were made to be part of
a cultivated olive tree. You have taken the
place of some branches that were cut away
from it. And because of this, you enjoy the
blessings that come from being part of that
cultivated tree. 18 But don't think you are
better than the branches that were cut
away. Just remember that you are not supporting the roots of that tree. Its roots are
supporting you.
19 Maybe you think those branches were
cut away, so that you could be put in their
place. 20 That's true enough. But they were
cut away because they did not have faith,
and you are where you are because you do
have faith. So don't be proud, but be afraid.
21 If God cut away those natural branches,
couldn't he do the same to you?
22 Now you see both how kind and how
hard God can be. He was hard on those
who fell, but he was kind to you. And he
will keep on being kind to you, if you keep
on trusting in his kindness. Otherwise, you
will be cut away too.
23 If those other branches will start
having faith, they will be made a part of
that tree again. God has the power to put
them back. 24 After all, it wasn't natural for
branches to be cut from a wild olive tree
and to be made part of a cultivated olive
tree. So it is much more likely that God will
join the natural branches back to the cultivated olive tree.

The People of Israel Will Be Brought Back

25 My friends, I don't want you Gentiles
to be too proud of yourselves. So I will explain the mystery of what has happened to

[u]**11.15** *When Israel rejected God*: Or "When Israel was rejected."
11.3 1 K 19.10, 14. **11.4** 1 K 19.18. **11.8** Dt 29.4-6; Is 29.10. **11.9,10** Ps 69.22, 23 (LXX).

the people of Israel. Some of them have become stubborn, and they will stay like that
until the complete number of you Gentiles
has come in. 26 In this way all of Israel will
be saved, as the Scriptures say,

"From Zion someone will come
to rescue us.
Then Jacob's descendants
will stop being evil.
27 This is what the Lord
has promised to do
when he forgives their sins."

28 The people of Israel are treated as
God's enemies, so that the good news can
come to you Gentiles. But they are still the
chosen ones, and God loves them because
of their famous ancestors. 29 God doesn't
take back the gifts he has given or forget
about the people he has chosen.
30 At one time you Gentiles rejected
God. But now Israel has rejected God, and
you have been shown mercy. 31 And because of the mercy shown to you, they will
also be shown mercy. 32 All people have disobeyed God, and that's why he treats them
as prisoners. But he does this, so that he
can have mercy on all of them.
33 Who can measure the wealth and
wisdom and knowledge of God? Who can
understand his decisions or explain what
he does?

34 "Has anyone known
the thoughts of the Lord
or given him advice?
35 Has anyone loaned
something to the Lord
that must be repaid?"

36 Everything comes from the Lord. All
things were made because of him and will
return to him. Praise the Lord forever! Amen.

Christ Brings New Life

12 Dear friends, God is good. So I beg
you to offer your bodies to him as a
living sacrifice, pure and pleasing. That's
the most sensible way to serve God. 2 Don't
be like the people of this world, but let God
change the way you think. Then you will
know how to do everything that is good and
pleasing to him.
3 I realize how kind God has been to me,
and so I tell each of you not to think you
are better than you really are. Use good
sense and measure yourself by the amount
of faith that God has given you. 4 A body is
made up of many parts, and each of them
has its own use. 5 That's how it is with us.
There are many of us, but we each are part
of the body of Christ, as well as part of one
another.
6 God has also given each of us different
gifts to use. If we can prophesy, we should
do it according to the amount of faith we
have. 7 If we can serve others, we should
serve. If we can teach, we should teach. 8 If
we can encourage others, we should encourage them. If we can give, we should be
generous. If we are leaders, we should do
our best. If we are good to others, we
should do it cheerfully.

Rules for Christian Living

9 Be sincere in your love for others.
Hate everything that is evil and hold tight
to everything that is good. 10 Love each
other as brothers and sisters and honor
others more than you do yourself. 11 Never
give up. Eagerly follow the Holy Spirit and
serve the Lord. 12 Let your hope make you
glad. Be patient in time of trouble and
never stop praying. 13 Take care of God's
needy people and welcome strangers into
your home.
14 Ask God to bless everyone who mistreats you. Ask him to bless them and not
to curse them. 15 When others are happy,
be happy with them, and when they are
sad, be sad. 16 Be friendly with everyone.
Don't be proud and feel that you are
smarter than others. Make friends with ordinary people.[v] 17 Don't mistreat someone
who has mistreated you. But try to earn the
respect of others, 18 and do your best to live
at peace with everyone.

[v] **12.16** *Make friends with ordinary people*: Or "Do ordinary jobs."

11.26 Is 59.20, 21 (LXX). **11.27** Is 27.9 (LXX). **11.33** Is 55.8; Ws 17.1. **11.34** Is 40.13 (LXX). **11.35** Job 41.11. **11.36** 4 Macc 18.24; 1 Co 8.6. **12.4,5** 1 Co 12.12. **12.6-8** 1 Co 12.4-11. **12.14** Mt 5.44; Lk 6.28. **12.15** Si 7.34. **12.16** Pr 3.7.

19 Dear friends, don't try to get even.
Let God take revenge. In the Scriptures the
Lord says,

"I am the one to take revenge
and pay them back."

20 The Scriptures also say,

"If your enemies are hungry,
give them something to eat.
And if they are thirsty,
give them something
to drink.
This will be the same
as piling burning coals
on their heads."

21 Don't let evil defeat you, but defeat evil
with good.

Obey Rulers

13 Obey the rulers who have authority
over you. Only God can give authority to anyone, and he puts these rulers
in their places of power. 2 People who oppose the authorities are opposing what
God has done, and they will be punished.
3 Rulers are a threat to evil people, not to
good people. There is no need to be afraid
of the authorities. Just do right, and they
will praise you for it. 4 After all, they
are God's servants, and it is their duty to
help you.

If you do something wrong, you ought to
be afraid, because these rulers have the
right to punish you. They are God's servants who punish criminals to show how
angry God is. 5 But you should obey the
rulers because you know it is the right
thing to do, and not just because of God's
anger.

6 You must also pay your taxes. The authorities are God's servants, and it is their
duty to take care of these matters. 7 Pay all
that you owe, whether it is taxes and fees
or respect and honor.

Love

8 Let love be your only debt! If you love
others, you have done all that the Law demands. 9 In the Law there are many commands, such as, "Be faithful in marriage.
Do not murder. Do not steal. Do not want
what belongs to others." But all of these are
summed up in the command that says,
"Love others as much as you love yourself."
10 No one who loves others will harm them.
So love is all that the Law demands.

The Day When Christ Returns

11 You know what sort of times we live
in, and so you should live properly. It is
time to wake up. You know that the day
when we will be saved is nearer now than
when we first put our faith in the Lord.
12 Night is almost over, and day will soon
appear. We must stop behaving as people
do in the dark and be ready to live in the
light. 13 So behave properly, as people do
in the day. Don't go to wild parties or
get drunk or be vulgar or indecent. Don't
quarrel or be jealous. 14 Let the Lord Jesus
Christ be as near to you as the clothes you
wear. Then you won't try to satisfy your
selfish desires.

Don't Criticize Others

14 Welcome all the Lord's followers,
even those whose faith is weak.
Don't criticize them for having beliefs that
are different from yours. 2 Some think it is
all right to eat anything, while those whose
faith is weak will eat only vegetables. 3 But
you should not criticize others for eating or
for not eating. After all, God welcomes
everyone. 4 What right do you have to criticize someone else's servants? Only their
Lord can decide if they are doing right, and
the Lord will make sure that they do right.
5 Some of the Lord's followers think one
day is more important than another. Others
think all days are the same. But each of you
should make up your own mind. 6 Any followers who count one day more important
than another day do it to honor their Lord.
And any followers who eat meat give
thanks to God, just like the ones who don't
eat meat.
7 Whether we live or die, it must be for

12.19 Dt 32.35. **12.20** Pr 25.21, 22 (LXX). **13.1** Ws 6.3. **13.6,7** Mt 22.21; Mk 12.17; Lk 20.25. **13.9** **a** Ex 20.14; Dt 5.18; **b** Ex 20.13; Dt 5.17; **c** Ex 20.15; Dt 5.19; **d** Ex 20.17; Dt 5.21; **e** Lv 19.18. **14.1-6** Col 2.16.

God, rather than for ourselves. [8] Whether we live or die, it must be for the Lord. Alive or dead, we still belong to the Lord. [9] This is because Christ died and rose to life, so that he would be the Lord of the dead and of the living. [10] Why do you criticize other followers of the Lord? Why do you look down on them? The day is coming when God will judge all of us. [11] In the Scriptures God says,

"I swear by my very life
that everyone will kneel down
and praise my name!"

[12] And so, each of us must give an account to God for what we do.

Don't Cause Problems for Others

[13] We must stop judging others. We must also make up our minds not to upset anyone's faith. [14] The Lord Jesus has made it clear to me that God considers all foods fit to eat. But if you think some foods are unfit to eat, then for you they are not fit.

[15] If you are hurting others by the foods you eat, you are not guided by love. Don't let your appetite destroy someone Christ died for. [16] Don't let your right to eat bring shame to Christ. [17] God's kingdom isn't about eating and drinking. It is about pleasing God, about living in peace, and about true happiness. All this comes from the Holy Spirit. [18] If you serve Christ in this way, you will please God and be respected by people. [19] We should try[w] to live at peace and help each other have a strong faith.

[20] Don't let your appetite destroy what God has done. All foods are fit to eat, but it is wrong to cause problems for others by what you eat. [21] It is best not to eat meat or drink wine or do anything else that causes problems for other followers of the Lord. [22] What you believe about these things should be kept between you and God. You are fortunate, if your actions don't make you have doubts. [23] But if you do have doubts about what you eat, you are going against your beliefs. And you know that is wrong, because anything you do against your beliefs is sin.

Please Others and Not Yourself

15 If our faith is strong, we should be patient with the Lord's followers whose faith is weak. We should try to please them instead of ourselves. [2] We should think of their good and try to help them by doing what pleases them. [3] Even Christ did not try to please himself. But as the Scriptures say, "The people who insulted you also insulted me." [4] And the Scriptures were written to teach and encourage us by giving us hope. [5] God is the one who makes us patient and cheerful. I pray that he will help you live at peace with each other, as you follow Christ. [6] Then all of you together will praise God, the Father of our Lord Jesus Christ.

The Good News Is for Jews and Gentiles

[7] Honor God by accepting each other, as Christ has accepted you. [8] I tell you that Christ came as a servant of the Jews to show that God has kept the promises he made to their famous ancestors. Christ also came, [9] so that the Gentiles would praise God for being kind to them. It is just as the Scriptures say,

"I will tell the nations
about you,
and I will sing praises
to your name."

[10] The Scriptures also say to the Gentiles, "Come and celebrate with God's people."
[11] Again the Scriptures say,

"Praise the Lord,
all you Gentiles.
All you nations, come
and worship him."

[12] Isaiah says,

"Someone from David's family
will come to power.

[w] **14.19** *We should try*: Some manuscripts have "We try."

14.10 2 Co 5.10. **14.11** Is 45.23 (LXX). **15.3** Ps 69.9. **15.4** 1 Macc 12.9; 2 Macc 15.9. **15.9** 2 S 22.50; Ps 18.49. **15.10** Dt 32.43. **15.11** Ps 117.1. **15.12** Is 11.10 (LXX).

He will rule the nations,
and they will put their hope
in him."

13 I pray that God, who gives hope, will
bless you with complete happiness and
peace because of your faith. And may the
power of the Holy Spirit fill you with hope.

Paul's Work as a Missionary

14 My friends, I am sure that you are
very good and that you have all the knowledge you need to teach each other. 15 But I
have spoken to you plainly and have tried
to remind you of some things. God was so
kind to me! 16 He chose me to be a servant
of Christ Jesus for the Gentiles and to do
the work of a priest in the service of his
good news. God did this so that the Holy
Spirit could make the Gentiles into a holy
offering, pleasing to him.

17 Because of Christ Jesus, I can take
pride in my service for God. 18 In fact, all I
will talk about is how Christ let me speak
and work, so that the Gentiles would obey
him. 19 Indeed, I will tell how Christ
worked miracles and wonders by the power
of the Holy Spirit. I have preached the
good news about him all the way from
Jerusalem to Illyricum. 20 But I have always
tried to preach where people have never
heard about Christ. I am like a builder who
doesn't build on anyone else's foundation.
21 It is just as the Scriptures say,

"All who haven't been told
about him
will see him,
and those who haven't heard
about him
will understand."

Paul's Plan To Visit Rome

22 My work has always kept me from
coming to see you. 23 Now there is nothing
left for me to do in this part of the world,
and for years I have wanted to visit you.
24 So I plan to stop off on my way to Spain.
Then after a short, but refreshing, visit with
you, I hope you will quickly send me on.
25-26 I am now on my way to Jerusalem
to deliver the money that the Lord's followers in Macedonia and Achaia collected for
God's needy people. 27 This is something
they really wanted to do. But sharing their
money with the Jews was also like paying
back a debt, because the Jews had already
shared their spiritual blessings with the
Gentiles. 28 After I have safely delivered
this money, I will visit you and then go on
to Spain. 29 And when I do arrive in Rome,
I know it will be with the full blessings of
Christ.

30 My friends, by the power of the Lord
Jesus Christ and by the love that comes
from the Holy Spirit, I beg you to pray sincerely with me and for me. 31 Pray that God
will protect me from the unbelievers in
Judea, and that his people in Jerusalem
will be pleased with what I am doing. 32 Ask
God to let me come to you and have a
pleasant and refreshing visit. 33 I pray that
God, who gives peace, will be with all of
you. Amen.

Personal Greetings

16 I have good things to say about
Phoebe, who is a leader in the
church at Cenchreae. 2 Welcome her in a
way that is proper for someone who has
faith in the Lord and is one of God's own
people. Help her in any way you can. After
all, she has proved to be a respected leader
for many others, including me.

3 Give my greetings to Priscilla and
Aquila. They have not only served Christ
Jesus together with me, 4 but they have
even risked their lives for me. I am grateful for them and so are all the Gentile
churches. 5 Greet the church that meets in
their home.

Greet my dear friend Epaenetus, who
was the first person in Asia to have faith in
Christ.

6 Greet Mary, who has worked so hard
for you.

7 Greet my relatives[x] Andronicus and
Junias,[y] who were in jail with me. They are

[x] **16.7** *relatives*: Or "Jewish friends." [y] **16.7** *Junias*: Or Junia. Some manuscripts have Julia.

15.21 Is 52.15 (LXX). **15.22** Ro 1.13. **15.25,26** 1 Co 16.1-4. **15.27** 1 Co 9.11. **16.3** Ac 18.2.

highly respected by the apostles and were followers of Christ before I was.

8 Greet Ampliatus, my dear friend whose faith is in the Lord.

9 Greet Urbanus, who serves Christ along with us.

Greet my dear friend Stachys.

10 Greet Apelles, a faithful servant of Christ.

Greet Aristobulus and his family.

11 Greet Herodion, who is a relative[z] of mine.

Greet Narcissus and the others in his family, who have faith in the Lord.

12 Greet Tryphaena and Tryphosa, who work hard for the Lord.

Greet my dear friend Persis. She also works hard for the Lord.

13 Greet Rufus, that special servant of the Lord, and greet his mother, who has been like a mother to me.

14 Greet Asyncritus, Phlegon, Hermes, Patrobas, and Hermas, as well as our friends who are with them.

15 Greet Philologus, Julia, Nereus and his sister, and Olympas, and all of God's people who are with them.

16 Be sure to give each other a warm greeting.

All of Christ's churches greet you.

17 My friends, I beg you to watch out for anyone who causes trouble and divides the church by refusing to do what all of you were taught. Stay away from them! 18 They want to serve themselves and not Christ the Lord. Their flattery and fancy talk fool people who don't know any better. 19 I am glad that everyone knows how well you obey the Lord. But still, I want you to understand what is good and not have anything to do with evil. 20 Then God, who gives peace, will soon crush Satan under your feet. I pray that our Lord Jesus will be kind to you.

21 Timothy, who works with me, sends his greetings, and so do my relatives,[z] Lucius, Jason, and Sosipater.

22 I, Tertius, also send my greetings. I am a follower of the Lord, and I wrote this letter.[a]

23-24 Gaius welcomes me and the whole church into his home, and he sends his greetings.

Erastus, the city treasurer, and our dear friend Quartus send their greetings too.[b]

Paul's Closing Prayer

25 Praise God! He can make you strong by means of my good news, which is the message about[c] Jesus Christ. For ages and ages this message was kept secret, 26 but now at last it has been told. The eternal God commanded his prophets to write about the good news, so that all nations would obey and have faith. 27 And now, because of Jesus Christ, we can praise the only wise God forever! Amen.[d]

[z] **16.11,21** *relative(s)*: See the note at verse 7. [a] **16.22** *I wrote this letter*: Paul probably dictated this letter to Tertius. [b] **16.23,24** *send their greetings too*: Some manuscripts add, "I pray that our Lord Jesus Christ will always be kind to you. Amen." [c] **16.25** *about*: Or "from."
[d] **16.27** *Amen*: Some manuscripts have verses 25-27 after 14.23. Others have the verses here and after 14.23, and one manuscript has them after 15.33.

16.13 Mk 15.21. **16.21** Ac 16.1. **16.23,24** **a** Ac 19.29; 1 Co 1.14; **b** 2 Ti 4.20.
16.27 4 Macc 18.24.

1 CORINTHIANS

ABOUT THIS LETTER

Although this letter is called the First Letter to the Corinthians, it is not really the first one that Paul wrote to this church. We know this because he mentions in this letter that he had written one before (5.9). The Christians in Corinth had also written to him (7.1), and part of First Corinthians contains Paul's answers to questions they had asked.

Corinth is a large port city in southern Greece. Paul began his work there in a Jewish meeting place, but he had to move next door to the home of a Gentile who had become a follower of Jesus (Acts 18.1-17). Most of the followers in Corinth were poor people (1 Corinthians 1.26-29), though some of them were wealthy (1 Corinthians 11.18-21), and one was even the city treasurer (Romans 16.23). While he was in Corinth, Paul worked as a tentmaker to earn a living (Acts 18.3; 1 Corinthians 4.12; 9.1-18).

Paul was especially concerned about the way the Corinthian Christians were always arguing and dividing themselves into groups (1.10—4.21) and about the way they treated one another (5.1—6.20). These are two of Paul's main concerns as he writes this letter. But he also wants to answer the questions they asked him about marriage (7.1-40) and food offered to idols (8.1-13). Paul encourages them to worship God the right way (10.1—14.40) and to be firm in their belief that God has given them victory over death (15.1-58).

Love, Paul tells them, is even more important than faith or hope. All of the problems in the church could be solved, if all the members would love one another, as Christians should:

Love is kind and patient,
never jealous, boastful,
proud, or rude.
Love rejoices in the truth,
but not in evil.
Love is always supportive,
loyal, hopeful,
and trusting.
Love never fails!
(13.4, 5a, 6-8a)

A QUICK LOOK AT THIS LETTER

- Paul's Greeting and Prayer (1.1-9)
- A Call for Unity (1.10—4.21)
- Problems in Relationships (5.1—7.40)
- Honoring God Instead of Idols (8.1—11.1)
- Guidance for Worship and Church Life (11.2—14.40)
- Christ's Victory Over Death (15.1-58)
- An Offering for the Poor (16.1-4)
- Paul's Travel Plans (16.5-12)
- Personal Concerns and Greetings (16.13-24)

1 From Paul, chosen by God to be an
apostle of Christ Jesus, and from Sosthenes, who is also a follower.
2 To God's church in Corinth. Christ
Jesus chose you to be his very own people,
and you worship in his name, as we and all
others do who call him Lord.
3 My prayer is that God our Father and
the Lord Jesus Christ will be kind to you
and will bless you with peace!
4 I never stop thanking my God for being kind enough to give you Christ Jesus,
5 who helps you speak and understand so
well. 6 Now you are certain that everything
we told you about our Lord Christ Jesus is
true. 7 You are not missing out on any
blessings, as you wait for him to return.
8 And until the day Christ does return, he
will keep you completely innocent. 9 God
can be trusted, and he chose you to be
partners with his Son, our Lord Jesus
Christ.

Taking Sides

10 My dear friends, as a follower of our
Lord Jesus Christ, I beg you to get along
with each other. Don't take sides. Always
try to agree in what you think. 11 Several
people from Chloe's family[a] have already
reported to me that you keep arguing with
each other. 12 They have said that some of
you claim to follow me, while others claim
to follow Apollos or Peter[b] or Christ.
13 Has Christ been divided up? Was I
nailed to a cross for you? Were you baptized in my name? 14 I thank God[c] that I
didn't baptize any of you except Crispus
and Gaius. 15 Not one of you can say that
you were baptized in my name. 16 I did
baptize the family[d] of Stephanas, but I
don't remember if I baptized anyone else.
17 Christ did not send me to baptize. He
sent me to tell the good news without using
big words that would make the cross of
Christ lose its power.

Christ Is God's Power and Wisdom

18 The message about the cross doesn't
make any sense to lost people. But for
those of us who are being saved, it is God's
power at work. 19 As God says in the Scriptures,

"I will destroy the wisdom
of all who claim
to be wise.
I will confuse those
who think they know
so much."

20 What happened to those wise people?
What happened to those experts in the
Scriptures? What happened to the ones
who think they have all the answers?
Didn't God show that the wisdom of this
world is foolish? 21 God was wise and decided not to let the people of this world use
their wisdom to learn about him.

Instead, God chose to save only those
who believe the foolish message we preach.
22 Jews ask for miracles, and Greeks want
something that sounds wise. 23 But we
preach that Christ was nailed to a cross.
Most Jews have problems with this, and
most Gentiles think it is foolish. 24 Our
message is God's power and wisdom for the
Jews and the Greeks that he has chosen.
25 Even when God is foolish, he is wiser
than everyone else, and even when God is
weak, he is stronger than everyone else.
26 My dear friends, remember what you
were when God chose you. The people of
this world didn't think that many of you
were wise. Only a few of you were in places
of power, and not many of you came from
important families. 27 But God chose the
foolish things of this world to put the wise
to shame. He chose the weak things of this
world to put the powerful to shame.
28 What the world thinks is worthless,
useless, and nothing at all is what God has
used to destroy what the world considers

[a]**1.11** *family*: Family members and possibly slaves and others who may have lived in the house.
[b]**1.12** *Peter*: The Greek text has "Cephas," which is an Aramaic name meaning "rock." Peter is the Greek name with the same meaning. [c]**1.14** *I thank God*: Some manuscripts have "I thank my God." [d]**1.16** *family*: See the note at 1.11.

1.2 Ac 18.1. **1.12** Ac 18.24. **1.14** **a** Ac 18.8; **b** Ac 19.29; Ro 16.23, 24.
1.16 1 Co 16.15. **1.19** Is 29.14 (LXX). **1.20** **a** Job 12.17; Is 19.12; 33.18; **b** Is 44.25.
1.21 Ws 13.1-9.

important. 29 God did all this to keep anyone from bragging to him. 30 You are God's
children. He sent Christ Jesus to save us
and to make us wise, acceptable, and holy.
31 So if you want to brag, do what the
Scriptures say and brag about the Lord.

Telling about Christ and the Cross

2 Friends, when I came and told you the
mystery[e] that God had shared with us,
I didn't use big words or try to sound wise.
2 In fact, while I was with you, I made up
my mind to speak only about Jesus Christ,
who had been nailed to a cross.
3 At first, I was weak and trembling with
fear. 4 When I talked with you or preached,
I didn't try to prove anything by sounding
wise. I simply let God's Spirit show his
power. 5 That way you would have faith because of God's power and not because of
human wisdom.
6 We do use wisdom when speaking to
people who are mature in their faith. But it
isn't the wisdom of this world or of its
rulers, who will soon disappear. 7 We speak
of God's hidden and mysterious wisdom
that God decided to use for our glory long
before the world began. 8 The rulers of this
world didn't know anything about this wisdom. If they had known about it, they
would not have nailed the glorious Lord to
a cross. 9 But it is just as the Scriptures say,

"What God has planned
for people who love him
is more than eyes have seen
or ears have heard.
It has never even
entered our minds!"

10 God's Spirit has shown you everything. His Spirit finds out everything, even
what is deep in the mind of God. 11 You are
the only one who knows what is in your
own mind, and God's Spirit is the only one
who knows what is in God's mind. 12 But
God has given us his Spirit. That's why we
don't think the same way that the people
of this world think. That's also why we
can recognize the blessings that God has
given us.
13 Every word we speak was taught to us
by God's Spirit, not by human wisdom. And
this same Spirit helps us teach spiritual
things to spiritual people.[f] 14 That's why
only someone who has God's Spirit can
understand spiritual blessings. Anyone who
doesn't have God's Spirit thinks these blessings are foolish. 15 People who are guided
by the Spirit can make all kinds of judgments, but they cannot be judged by others. 16 The Scriptures ask,

"Has anyone ever known
the thoughts of the Lord
or given him advice?"

But we understand what Christ is
thinking.[g]

Working Together for God

3 My friends, you are acting like the people of this world. That's why I could
not speak to you as spiritual people. You are
like babies as far as your faith in Christ is
concerned. 2 So I had to treat you like babies and feed you milk. You could not take
solid food, and you still cannot, 3 because
you are not yet spiritual. You are jealous
and argue with each other. This proves that
you are not spiritual and that you are acting
like the people of this world.
4 Some of you say that you follow me,
and others claim to follow Apollos. Isn't
that how ordinary people behave? 5 Apollos
and I are merely servants who helped you
to have faith. It was the Lord who made it
all happen. 6 I planted the seeds, Apollos
watered them, but God made them sprout
and grow. 7 What matters isn't those who
planted or watered, but God who made the
plants grow. 8 The one who plants is just as
important as the one who waters. And each
one will be paid for what they do. 9 Apollos
and I work together for God, and you are
God's garden and God's building.

[e]**2.1** *mystery*: Some manuscripts have "testimony." [f]**2.13** *teach spiritual things to spiritual people*: Or "compare spiritual things with spiritual things." [g]**2.16** *we understand what Christ is thinking*: Or "we think as Christ does."

1.31 Jr 9.24. **2.3** Ac 18.9. **2.8** Ba 3.14-17. **2.9** Is 64.4; Si 1.9, 10. **2.16** Is 40.13 (LXX). **3.2** He 5.12, 13. **3.4** 1 Co 1.12. **3.6** **a** Ac 18.4-11; **b** Ac 18.24-28.

The last week of Jesus' life *Matthew 21; 26 -- 28*

The coming of the Holy Spirit

Acts 2.1-13

Philip and an Ethiopian official *Acts 8.26-40*

Saul becomes a follower of the Lord *Acts 9.3-7*

Only One Foundation

10 God was kind and let me become an
expert builder. I laid a foundation on which
others have built. But we must each be
careful how we build, 11 because Christ is
the only foundation. 12-13 Whatever we
build on that foundation will be tested by
fire on the day of judgment. Then everyone
will find out if we have used gold, silver,
and precious stones, or wood, hay, and
straw. 14 We will be rewarded if our building
is left standing. 15 But if it is destroyed by
the fire, we will lose everything. Yet we ourselves will be saved, like someone escaping
from flames.

16 All of you surely know that you are
God's temple and that his Spirit lives in
you. 17 Together you are God's holy temple,
and God will destroy anyone who destroys
his temple.

18 Don't fool yourselves! If any of you
think you are wise in the things of this
world, you will have to become foolish before you can be truly wise. 19 This is because God considers the wisdom of this
world to be foolish. It is just as the Scriptures say, "God catches the wise when they
try to outsmart him." 20 The Scriptures also
say, "The Lord knows that the plans made
by wise people are useless." 21-22 So stop
bragging about what anyone has done. Paul
and Apollos and Peter[h] all belong to you. In
fact, everything is yours, including the world,
life, death, the present, and the future.
Everything belongs to you, 23 and you belong to Christ, and Christ belongs to God.

The Work of the Apostles

4 Think of us as servants of Christ who
have been given the work of explaining God's mysterious ways. 2 And since our
first duty is to be faithful to the one we
work for, 3 it doesn't matter to me if I am
judged by you or even by a court of law. In
fact, I don't judge myself. 4 I don't know of
anything against me, but that doesn't prove
that I am right. The Lord is my judge. 5 So
don't judge anyone until the Lord returns.
He will show what is hidden in the dark
and what is in everyone's heart. Then God
will be the one who praises each of us.

6 Friends, I have used Apollos and myself as examples to teach you the meaning
of the saying, "Follow the rules." I want you
to stop saying that one of us is better than
the other. 7 What is so special about you?
What do you have that you were not given?
And if it was given to you, how can you brag?
8 Are you already satisfied? Are you now
rich? Have you become kings while we are
still nobodies? I wish you were kings. Then
we could have a share in your kingdom.

9 It seems to me that God has put us
apostles in the worst possible place. We are
like prisoners on their way to death. Angels
and the people of this world just laugh at
us. 10 Because of Christ we are thought of
as fools, but Christ has made you wise. We
are weak and hated, but you are powerful
and respected. 11 Even today we go hungry
and thirsty and don't have anything to wear
except rags. We are mistreated and don't
have a place to live. 12 We work hard with
our own hands, and when people abuse us,
we wish them well. When we suffer, we are
patient. 13 When someone curses us, we
answer with kind words. Until now we are
thought of as nothing more than the trash
and garbage of this world.

14 I am not writing to embarrass you. I
want to help you, just as parents help their
own dear children. 15 Ten thousand people
may teach you about Christ, but I am your
only father. You became my children when
I told you about Christ Jesus, 16 and I want
you to be like me. 17 That's why I sent Timothy to you. I love him like a son, and he is
a faithful servant of the Lord. Timothy will
tell you what I do to follow Christ and how
it agrees with what I always teach about
Christ in every church.

18 Some of you think I am not coming
for a visit, and so you are bragging. 19 But if
the Lord lets me come, I will soon be there.
Then I will find out if the ones who are doing all this bragging really have any power.
20 God's kingdom isn't just a lot of words. It

[h]**3.21,22** *Peter*: See the note at 1.12.

3.16 1 Co 6.19; 2 Co 6.16. **3.19** Job 5.13. **3.20** Ps 94.11. **4.12** Ac 18.3.
4.16 1 Co 11.1; Phil 3.17.

is power. 21 What do you want me to do
when I arrive? Do you want me to be hard
on you or to be kind and gentle?

Immoral Followers

5 I have heard terrible things about
some of you. In fact, you are behaving
worse than the Gentiles. A man is even
sleeping with his own stepmother.[i] 2 You
are proud, when you ought to feel bad
enough to chase away anyone who acts like
that.

3-4 I am with you only in my thoughts.
But in the name of our Lord Jesus I have
already judged this man, as though I were
with you in person. So when you meet together and the power of the Lord Jesus is
with you, I will be there too. 5 You must
then hand that man over to Satan. His
body will be destroyed, but his spirit will be
saved when the Lord Jesus returns.

6 Stop being proud! Don't you know how
a little yeast can spread through the whole
batch of dough? 7 Get rid of the old yeast!
Then you will be like fresh bread made
without yeast, and that is what you are.
Our Passover lamb is Christ, who has already been sacrificed. 8 So don't celebrate
the festival by being evil and sinful, which
is like serving bread made with yeast. Be
pure and truthful and celebrate by using
bread made without yeast.

9 In my other letter[j] I told you not to
have anything to do with immoral people.
10 But I wasn't talking about the people of
this world. You would have to leave this
world to get away from everyone who is immoral or greedy or who cheats or worships
idols. 11 I was talking about your own people who are immoral or greedy or worship
idols or curse others or get drunk or cheat.
Don't even eat with them! 12 Why should
I judge outsiders? Aren't we supposed to
judge only church members? 13 God judges
everyone else. The Scriptures say, "Chase
away any of your own people who are
evil."

Taking Each Other to Court

6 When one of you has a complaint
against another, do you take your complaint to a court of sinners? Or do you take
it to God's people? 2 Don't you know that
God's people will judge the world? And if
you are going to judge the world, can't you
settle small problems? 3 Don't you know
that we will judge angels? And if that is so,
we can surely judge everyday matters.
4 Why do you take everyday complaints
to judges who are not respected by the
church? 5 I say this to your shame. Aren't
any of you wise enough to act as a judge between one follower and another? 6 Why
should one of you take another to be tried
by unbelievers?

7 When one of you takes another to
court, all of you lose. It would be better to
let yourselves be cheated and robbed. 8 But
instead, you cheat and rob other followers.

9 Don't you know that evil people won't
have a share in the blessings of God's kingdom? Don't fool yourselves! No one who is
immoral or worships idols or is unfaithful
in marriage or is a pervert or behaves like a
homosexual 10 will share in God's kingdom.
Neither will any thief or greedy person or
drunkard or anyone who curses and cheats
others. 11 Some of you used to be like that.
But now the name of our Lord Jesus Christ
and the power of God's Spirit have washed
you and made you holy and acceptable
to God.

Honor God with Your Body

12 Some of you say, "We can do anything
we want to." But I tell you that not everything is good for us. So I refuse to let anything have power over me. 13 You also say,
"Food is meant for our bodies, and our bodies are meant for food." But I tell you that
God will destroy them both. We are not
supposed to do indecent things with our
bodies. We are to use them for the Lord
who is in charge of our bodies. 14 God will

[i] **5.1** *is even sleeping with his own stepmother*: Or "has even married his own stepmother."
[j] **5.9** *other letter*: An unknown letter that Paul wrote to the Christians at Corinth before he wrote this one.

5.1 Dt 22.30. **5.6** Ga 5.9. **5.7** Ex 12.4, 5. **5.8** Ex 13.7; Dt 16.3, 4. **5.13** Dt 13.5; 17.5-7 (LXX). **6.12** 1 Co 10.23.

raise us from death by the same power that he used when he raised our Lord to life.

15 Don't you know that your bodies are part of the body of Christ? Is it right for me to join part of the body of Christ to a prostitute? No, it isn't! 16 Don't you know that a man who does that becomes part of her body? The Scriptures say, "The two of them will be like one person." 17 But anyone who is joined to the Lord is one in spirit with him.

18 Don't be immoral in matters of sex. That is a sin against your own body in a way that no other sin is. 19 You surely know that your body is a temple where the Holy Spirit lives. The Spirit is in you and is a gift from God. You are no longer your own. 20 God paid a great price for you. So use your body to honor God.

Questions about Marriage

7 Now I will answer the questions that you asked in your letter. You asked, "Is it best for people not to marry?"[k] 2 Well, having your own husband or wife should keep you from doing something immoral. 3 Husbands and wives should be fair with each other about having sex. 4 A wife belongs to her husband instead of to herself, and a husband belongs to his wife instead of to himself. 5 So don't refuse sex to each other, unless you agree not to have sex for a little while, in order to spend time in prayer. Then Satan won't be able to tempt you because of your lack of self-control. 6 In my opinion that is what should be done, though I don't know of anything the Lord said about this matter. 7 I wish that all of you were like me, but God has given different gifts to each of us.

8 Here is my advice for people who have never been married and for widows. You should stay single, just as I am. 9 But if you don't have enough self-control, then go ahead and get married. After all, it is better to marry than to burn with desire.[l]

10 I instruct married couples to stay together, and this is exactly what the Lord himself taught. A wife who leaves her husband 11 should either stay single or go back to her husband. And a husband should not leave his wife.

12 I don't know of anything else the Lord said about marriage. All I can do is to give you my own advice. If your wife isn't a follower of the Lord, but is willing to stay with you, don't divorce her. 13 If your husband isn't a follower, but is willing to stay with you, don't divorce him. 14 Your husband or wife who isn't a follower is made holy by having you as a mate. This also makes your children holy and keeps them from being unclean in God's sight.

15 If your husband or wife isn't a follower of the Lord and decides to divorce you, then you should agree to it. You are no longer bound to that person. After all, God chose you and wants you to live at peace. 16 And besides, how do you know if you will be able to save your husband or wife who isn't a follower?

Obeying the Lord at All Times

17 In every church I tell the people to stay as they were when the Lord Jesus chose them and God called them to be his own. Now I say the same thing to you. 18 If you are already circumcised, don't try to change it. If you are not circumcised, don't get circumcised. 19 Being circumcised or uncircumcised isn't really what matters. The important thing is to obey God's commands. 20 So don't try to change what you were when God chose you. 21 Are you a slave? Don't let that bother you. But if you can win your freedom, you should. 22 When the Lord chooses slaves, they become his free people. And when he chooses free people, they become slaves of Christ. 23 God paid a great price for you. So don't become slaves of anyone else. 24 Stay what you were when God chose you.

Unmarried People

25 I don't know of anything that the Lord said about people who have never been married.[m] But I will tell you what I

[k] **7.1** *people not to marry*: Or "married couples not to have sex." [l] **7.9** *with desire*: Or "in the flames of hell." [m] **7.25** *people who have never been married*: Or "virgins."

6.16 Gn 2.24. **6.19** 1 Co 3.16; 2 Co 6.16. **7.10,11** Mt 5.32; 19.9; Mk 10.11, 12; Lk 16.18. **7.18** 1 Macc 1.15.

think. And you can trust me, because the
Lord has treated me with kindness. 26 We
are now going through hard times, and I
think it is best for you to stay as you are.
27 If you are married, stay married. If you
are not married, don't try to get married.
28 It isn't wrong to marry, even if you have
never been married before. But those who
marry will have a lot of trouble, and I want
to protect you from that.

29 My friends, what I mean is that the
Lord will soon come,[n] and it won't matter if
you are married or not. 30 It will be all the
same if you are crying or laughing, or if you
are buying or are completely broke. 31 It
won't make any difference how much good
you are getting from this world or how
much you like it. This world as we know it
is now passing away.

32 I want all of you to be free from worry.
An unmarried man worries about how to
please the Lord. 33 But a married man has
more worries. He must worry about the
things of this world, because he wants to
please his wife. 34 So he is pulled in two directions. Unmarried women and women
who have never been married[o] worry only
about pleasing the Lord, and they keep
their bodies and minds pure. But a married
woman worries about the things of this
world, because she wants to please her
husband. 35 What I am saying is for your
own good—it isn't to limit your freedom. I
want to help you to live right and to love
the Lord above all else.

36 But suppose you are engaged to
someone old enough to be married, and
you want her so much that all you can
think about is getting married. Then go
ahead and marry.[p] There is nothing wrong
with that. 37 But it is better to have self-
control and to make up your mind not to
marry. 38 It is perfectly all right to marry,
but it is better not to get married at all.

39 A wife should stay married to her
husband until he dies. Then she is free to
marry again, but only to a man who is a follower of the Lord. 40 However, I think I am
obeying God's Spirit when I say she would
be happier to stay single.

Food Offered to Idols

8 In your letter you asked me about food
offered to idols. All of us know something about this subject. But knowledge
makes us proud of ourselves, while love
makes us helpful to others. 2 In fact, people
who think they know so much don't know
anything at all. 3 But God has no doubts
about who loves him.

4 Even though food is offered to idols,
we know that none of the idols in this
world are alive. After all, there is only one
God. 5 Many things in heaven and on earth
are called gods and lords, but none of them
really are gods or lords. 6 We have only one
God, and he is the Father. He created
everything, and we live for him. Jesus
Christ is our only Lord. Everything was
made by him, and by him life was given
to us.

7 Not everyone knows these things. In
fact, many people have grown up with the
belief that idols have life in them. So when
they eat meat offered to idols, they are
bothered by a weak conscience. 8 But food
doesn't bring us any closer to God. We are
no worse off if we don't eat, and we are no
better off if we do.

9 Don't cause problems for someone
with a weak conscience, just because you
have the right to eat anything. 10 You know
all this, and so it doesn't bother you to eat
in the temple of an idol. But suppose a person with a weak conscience sees you and
decides to eat food that has been offered to
idols. 11 Then what you know has destroyed
someone Christ died for. 12 When you sin
by hurting a follower with a weak conscience, you sin against Christ. 13 So if I

[n]**7.29** *the Lord will soon come*: Or "there's not much time left" or "the time for decision comes quickly." [o]**7.34** *women who have never been married*: Or "virgins." [p]**7.36** *But suppose you are engaged . . . go ahead and marry*: Verses 36-38 may also be translated: 36"If you feel that you are not treating your grown daughter right by keeping her from getting married, then let her marry. You won't be doing anything wrong. 37But it is better to have self-control and make up your mind not to let your daughter get married. 38It is all right for you to let her marry. But it is better if you don't let her marry at all."

hurt one of the Lord's followers by what I
eat, I will never eat meat as long as I live.

The Rights of an Apostle

9 I am free. I am an apostle. I have seen
the Lord Jesus and have led you to
have faith in him. 2 Others may think that I
am not an apostle, but you are proof that I
am an apostle to you.
3 When people question me, I tell them
4 that Barnabas and I have the right to our
food and drink. 5 We each have the right to
marry one of the Lord's followers and to
take her along with us, just as the other
apostles and the Lord's brothers and Peter[q]
do. 6 Are we the only ones who have to support ourselves by working at another job?
7 Do soldiers pay their own salaries? Don't
people who raise grapes eat some of what
they grow? Don't shepherds get milk from
their own goats?
8-9 I am not saying this on my own authority. The Law of Moses tells us not to
muzzle an ox when it is grinding grain. But
was God concerned only about an ox?
10 No, he wasn't! He was talking about us.
This was written in the Scriptures so that
all who plow and all who grind the grain
will look forward to sharing in the harvest.
11 When we told the message to you, it
was like planting spiritual seed. So we have
the right to accept material things as our
harvest from you. 12 If others have the right
to do this, we have an even greater right.
But we haven't used this right of ours. We are
willing to put up with anything to keep from
causing trouble for the message about Christ.
13 Don't you know that people who work
in the temple make their living from what
is brought to the temple? Don't you know
that a person who serves at the altar is
given part of what is offered? 14 In the
same way, the Lord wants everyone who
preaches the good news to make a living
from preaching this message.
15 But I have never used these privileges
of mine, and I am not writing this because
I want to start now. I would rather die than
have someone rob me of the right to take
pride in this. 16 I don't have any reason to
brag about preaching the good news.
Preaching is something God told me to do,
and if I don't do it, I am doomed. 17 If I
preach because I want to, I will be paid.
But even if I don't want to, it is still something God has sent me to do. 18 What pay
am I given? It is the chance to preach the
good news free of charge and not to use the
privileges that are mine because I am a
preacher.
19 I am not anyone's slave. But I have
become a slave to everyone, so that I can
win as many people as possible. 20 When I
am with the Jews, I live like a Jew to win
Jews. They are ruled by the Law of Moses,
and I am not. But I live by the Law to win
them. 21 And when I am with people who
are not ruled by the Law, I forget about the
Law to win them. Of course, I never really
forget about the law of God. In fact, I am
ruled by the law of Christ. 22 When I am
with people whose faith is weak, I live as
they do to win them. I do everything I can
to win everyone I possibly can. 23 I do all
this for the good news, because I want to
share in its blessings.

A Race and a Fight

24 You know that many runners enter a
race, and only one of them wins the prize.
So run to win! 25 Athletes work hard to win
a crown that cannot last, but we do it for a
crown that will last forever. 26 I don't run
without a goal. And I don't box by beating
my fists in the air. 27 I keep my body under
control and make it my slave, so I won't
lose out after telling the good news to
others.

Don't Worship Idols

10 Friends, I want to remind you that
all of our ancestors walked under
the cloud and went through the sea. 2 This
was like being baptized and becoming followers of Moses. 3 All of them also ate the
same spiritual food 4 and drank the same

[q]**9.5** *Peter*: See the note at 1.12.

9.8,9 Dt 25.4; 1 Ti 5.18. **9.11** Ro 15.27. **9.13** Dt 18.1. **9.14** Mt 10.10; Lk 10.7.
9.24-27 4 Macc 6.10. **9.25** Ws 4.2; 5.16. **10.1 a** Ex 13.21, 22; **b** Ex 14.22-29.
10.3 Ex 16.35, 36. **10.4** Ex 17.6; Nu 20.11.

spiritual drink, which flowed from the spiritual rock that followed them. That rock
was Christ. 5 But most of them did not
please God. So they died, and their bodies
were scattered all over the desert.
6 What happened to them is a warning
to keep us from wanting to do the same evil
things. 7 They worshiped idols, just as the
Scriptures say, "The people sat down to eat
and drink. Then they got up to dance
around." So don't worship idols. 8 Some of
those people did shameful things, and in a
single day about twenty-three thousand of
them died. Don't do shameful things as
they did. 9 And don't try to test Christ,[r] as
some of them did and were later bitten by
poisonous snakes. 10 Don't even grumble,
as some of them did and were killed by the
destroying angel. 11 These things happened
to them as a warning to us. All this was
written in the Scriptures to teach us who
live in these last days.
12 Even if you think you can stand up to
temptation, be careful not to fall. 13 You are
tempted in the same way that everyone
else is tempted. But God can be trusted not
to let you be tempted too much, and he will
show you how to escape from your temptations.
14 My friends, you must keep away from
idols. 15 I am speaking to you as people who
have enough sense to know what I am talking about. 16 When we drink from the cup
that we ask God to bless, isn't that sharing
in the blood of Christ? When we eat the
bread that we break, isn't that sharing in
the body of Christ? 17 By sharing in the
same loaf of bread, we become one body,
even though there are many of us.
18 Aren't the people of Israel sharing in
the worship when they gather around the
altar and eat the sacrifices offered there?
19 Am I saying that either the idols or the
food sacrificed to them is anything at all?
20 No, I am not! That food is really sacrificed to demons and not to God. I don't
want you to have anything to do with
demons. 21 You cannot drink from the cup
of demons and still drink from the Lord's
cup. You cannot eat at the table of demons
and still eat at the Lord's table. 22 We
would make the Lord jealous if we did that.
And we are not stronger than the Lord.

Always Honor God

23 Some of you say, "We can do whatever we want to!" But I tell you that not
everything may be good or helpful. 24 We
should think about others and not about
ourselves. 25 However, when you buy meat
in the market, go ahead and eat it. Keep
your conscience clear by not asking where
the meat came from. 26 The Scriptures say,
"The earth and everything in it belong to
the Lord."
27 If an unbeliever invites you to dinner,
and you want to go, then go. Eat whatever
you are served. Don't cause a problem for
someone's conscience by asking where the
food came from. 28-29 But if you are told
that it has been sacrificed to idols, don't
cause a problem by eating it. I don't mean a
problem for yourself, but for the one who
told you. Why should my freedom be limited by someone else's conscience? 30 If I
give thanks for what I eat, why should anyone accuse me of doing wrong?
31 When you eat or drink or do anything
else, always do it to honor God. 32 Don't
cause problems for Jews or Greeks or anyone else who belongs to God's church. 33 I
always try to please others instead of myself, in the hope that many of them will be
11 saved. 1 You must follow my example, as I follow the example of
Christ.

Rules for Worship

2 I am proud of you, because you always
remember me and obey the teachings I
gave you. 3 Now I want you to know that
Christ is the head over all men, and a man
is the head over a woman. But God is the
head over Christ. 4 This means that any

[r] **10.9** *Christ*: Some manuscripts have "the Lord."

10.5 Nu 14.29, 30. **10.7** Ex 32.6. **10.8** Nu 25.1-18. **10.9** Nu 21.5, 6. **10.10** Nu 16.41-49. **10.13** Jdt 8.25-27; Si 15.11-20. **10.16** Mt 26.26-28; Mk 14.22-24; Lk 22.19, 20. **10.18** Lv 7.6. **10.18-22** 4 Macc 5.2. **10.20** Dt 32.17 (LXX). **10.22** Dt 32.21. **10.23** 1 Co 6.12. **10.26** Ps 24.1. **11.1** 1 Co 4.16; Phil 3.17.

man who prays or prophesies with something on his head brings shame to his head.

5 But any woman who prays or prophesies without something on her head brings shame to her head. In fact, she may as well shave her head.[s] 6 A woman should wear something on her head. It is a disgrace for a woman to shave her head or cut her hair. But if she refuses to wear something on her head, let her cut off her hair.

7 Men were created to be like God and to bring honor to God. This means that a man should not wear anything on his head. Women were created to bring honor to men. 8 It was the woman who was made from a man, and not the man who was made from a woman. 9 He wasn't created for her. She was created for him. 10 And so, because of this, and also because of the angels, a woman ought to wear something on her head, as a sign of her authority.[t]

11 As far as the Lord is concerned, men and women need each other. 12 It is true that the first woman came from a man, but all other men have been given birth by women. Yet God is the one who created everything. 13 Ask yourselves if it is proper for a woman to pray without something on her head. 14 Isn't it unnatural and disgraceful for men to have long hair? 15 But long hair is a beautiful way for a woman to cover her head. 16 This is how things are done in all of God's churches,[u] and that's why none of you should argue about what I have said.

Rules for the Lord's Supper

17 Your worship services do you more harm than good. I am certainly not going to praise you for this. 18 I am told that you can't get along with each other when you worship, and I am sure that some of what I have heard is true. 19 You are bound to argue with each other, but it is easy to see which of you have God's approval.

20 When you meet together, you don't really celebrate the Lord's Supper. 21 You even start eating before everyone gets to the meeting, and some of you go hungry, while others get drunk. 22 Don't you have homes where you can eat and drink? Do you hate God's church? Do you want to embarrass people who don't have anything? What can I say to you? I certainly cannot praise you.

The Lord's Supper

(Matthew 26.26-29; Mark 14.22-25; Luke 22.14-20)

23 I have already told you what the Lord Jesus did on the night he was betrayed. And it came from the Lord himself.

He took some bread in his hands.
24 Then after he had given thanks, he
broke it and said, "This is my body,
which is given for you. Eat this and remember me."
25 After the meal, Jesus took a cup
of wine in his hands and said, "This is
my blood, and with it God makes his
new agreement with you. Drink this
and remember me."

26 The Lord meant that when you eat this bread and drink from this cup, you tell about his death until he comes.

27 But if you eat the bread and drink the wine in a way that isn't worthy of the Lord, you sin against his body and blood. 28 That's why you must examine the way you eat and drink. 29 If you fail to understand that you are the body of the Lord, you will condemn yourselves by the way you eat and drink. 30 That's why many of you are sick and weak and why a lot of others have died. 31 If we carefully judge ourselves, we won't be punished. 32 But when the Lord judges and punishes us, he does it to keep us from being condemned with the rest of the world.

33 My dear friends, you should wait until everyone gets there before you start eating. 34 If you really are hungry, you can eat at home. Then you won't condemn yourselves when you meet together.

After I arrive, I will instruct you about the other matters.

[s]**11.5** *she may as well shave her head*: A woman's hair was a mark of beauty, and it was shameful for a woman to cut her hair short or to shave her head, so that she looked like a man. [t]**11.10** *as a sign of her authority*: Or "as a sign that she is under someone's authority." [u]**11.16** *This is how things are done in all of God's churches*: Or "There is no set rule for this in any of God's churches."

11.7 Gn 1.26, 27. **11.8,9** Gn 2.18-23. **11.25** **a** Ex 24.8; Jr 31.31-34; **b** Ex 24.6-8.

Spiritual Gifts

12 My friends, you asked me about
spiritual gifts. 2 I want you to remember that before you became followers
of the Lord, you were led in all the wrong
ways by idols that cannot even talk. 3 Now I
want you to know that if you are led by
God's Spirit, you will say that Jesus is Lord,
and you will never curse Jesus.
4 There are different kinds of spiritual
gifts, but they all come from the same
Spirit. 5 There are different ways to serve
the same Lord, 6 and we can each do different things. Yet the same God works in all
of us and helps us in everything we do.
7 The Spirit has given each of us a special way of serving others. 8 Some of us can
speak with wisdom, while others can speak
with knowledge, but these gifts come from
the same Spirit. 9 To others the Spirit has
given great faith or the power to heal the
sick 10 or the power to work mighty miracles. Some of us are prophets, and some of
us recognize when God's Spirit is present.[v]
Others can speak different kinds of languages, and still others can tell what these
languages mean. 11 But it is the Spirit who
does all this and decides which gifts to give
to each of us.

One Body with Many Parts

12 The body of Christ has many different
parts, just as any other body does. 13 Some
of us are Jews, and others are Gentiles.
Some of us are slaves, and others are free.
But God's Spirit baptized each of us and
made us part of the body of Christ. Now we
each drink from that same Spirit.[w]
14 Our bodies don't have just one part.
They have many parts. 15 Suppose a foot
says, "I'm not a hand, and so I'm not part
of the body." Wouldn't the foot still belong
to the body? 16 Or suppose an ear says,
"I'm not an eye, and so I'm not part of the
body." Wouldn't the ear still belong to the
body? 17 If our bodies were only an eye, we
couldn't hear a thing. And if they were only
an ear, we couldn't smell a thing. 18 But
God has put all parts of our body together
in the way that he decided is best.
19 A body isn't really a body, unless there
is more than one part. 20 It takes many
parts to make a single body. 21 That's why
the eyes cannot say they don't need the
hands. That's also why the head cannot say
it doesn't need the feet. 22 In fact, we cannot get along without the parts of the body
that seem to be the weakest. 23 We take
special care to dress up some parts of our
bodies. We are modest about our personal
parts, 24 but we don't have to be modest
about other parts.
God put our bodies together in such a
way that even the parts that seem the least
important are valuable. 25 He did this to
make all parts of the body work together
smoothly, with each part caring about the
others. 26 If one part of our body hurts, we
hurt all over. If one part of our body is honored, the whole body will be happy.
27 Together you are the body of Christ.
Each one of you is part of his body. 28 First,
God chose some people to be apostles and
prophets and teachers for the church. But
he also chose some to work miracles or
heal the sick or help others or be leaders or
speak different kinds of languages. 29 Not
everyone is an apostle. Not everyone is a
prophet. Not everyone is a teacher. Not
everyone can work miracles. 30 Not everyone
can heal the sick. Not everyone can speak
different kinds of languages. Not everyone
can tell what these languages mean. 31 I
want you to desire the best gifts.[x] So I will
show you a much better way.

Love

13 What if I could speak
all languages of humans
and of angels?
If I did not love others,
I would be nothing more

[v] **12.10** *and some of us . . . present*: Or "and some of us recognize the difference between God's Spirit and other spirits." [w] **12.13** *Some of us are Jews . . . that same Spirit*: Verse 13 may also be translated, "God's Spirit is inside each of us, and all around us as well. So it doesn't matter that some of us are Jews and others are Gentiles and that some are slaves and others are free. Together we are one body." [x] **12.31** *I want you to desire the best gifts*: Or "You desire the best gifts."

12.4-11 Ro 12.6-8. **12.12** Ro 12.4, 5. **12.28** Eph 4.11.

than a noisy gong
or a clanging cymbal.
2 What if I could prophesy
and understand all secrets
and all knowledge?
And what if I had faith
that moved mountains?
I would be nothing,
unless I loved others.
3 What if I gave away all
that I owned
and let myself
be burned alive?[y]
I would gain nothing,
unless I loved others.
4 Love is kind and patient,
never jealous, boastful,
proud, or 5 rude.
Love isn't selfish
or quick tempered.
It doesn't keep a record
of wrongs that others do.
6 Love rejoices in the truth,
but not in evil.
7 Love is always supportive,
loyal, hopeful,
and trusting.
8 Love never fails!

Everyone who prophesies
will stop,
and unknown languages
will no longer
be spoken.
All that we know
will be forgotten.
9 We don't know everything,
and our prophecies
are not complete.
10 But what is perfect
will someday appear,
and what isn't perfect
will then disappear.

11 When we were children,
we thought and reasoned
as children do.
But when we grew up,
we quit our childish ways.
12 Now all we can see of God
is like a cloudy picture
in a mirror.
Later we will see him
face to face.
We don't know everything,
but then we will,
just as God completely
understands us.
13 For now there are faith,
hope, and love.
But of these three,
the greatest is love.

Speaking Unknown Languages and Prophesying

14 Love should be your guide. Be
eager to have the gifts that come
from the Holy Spirit, especially the gift of
prophecy. 2 If you speak languages that others don't know, God will understand what
you are saying, though no one else will
know what you mean. You will be talking
about mysteries that only the Spirit understands. 3 But when you prophesy, you will
be understood, and others will be helped.
They will be encouraged and made to feel
better.
4 By speaking languages that others
don't know, you help only yourself. But by
prophesying you help everyone in the
church. 5 I am glad for you to speak unknown languages, although I had rather for
you to prophesy. In fact, prophesying does
much more good than speaking unknown
languages, unless someone can help the
church by explaining what you mean.
6 My friends, what good would it do, if I
came and spoke unknown languages to you
and didn't explain what I meant? How
would I help you, unless I told you what God
had shown me or gave you some knowledge
or prophecy or teaching? 7 If all musical instruments sounded alike, how would you
know the difference between a flute and a
harp? 8 If a bugle call isn't clear, how would
you know to get ready for battle?
9 That's how it is when you speak unknown languages. If no one can understand what you are talking about, you will
only be talking to the wind. 10 There are

[y] **13.3** *and let myself be burned alive*: Some manuscripts have "so that I could brag."
13.2 Mt 17.20, 21; 21.21; Mk 11.23.

many different languages in this world, and
all of them make sense. [11] But if I don't
understand the language that someone is
using, we will be like foreigners to each
other. [12] If you really want spiritual gifts,
choose the ones that will be most helpful to
the church.

[13] When we speak languages that others
don't know, we should pray for the power to
explain what we mean. [14] For example, if I
use an unknown language in my prayers,
my spirit prays but my mind is useless.
[15] Then what should I do? There are times
when I should pray with my spirit, and
times when I should pray with my mind.
Sometimes I should sing with my spirit, and
at other times I should sing with my mind.

[16] Suppose some strangers are in your
worship service, when you are praising God
with your spirit. If they don't understand
you, how will they know to say, "Amen"?
[17] You may be worshiping God in a wonderful way, but no one else will be helped. [18] I
thank God that I speak unknown languages
more than any of you. [19] But words that
make sense can help the church. That's
why in church I had rather speak five
words that make sense than to speak ten
thousand words in a language that others
don't know.

[20] My friends, stop thinking like children. Think like mature people and be as
innocent as tiny babies. [21] In the Scriptures
the Lord says,

"I will use strangers
who speak unknown languages
  to talk to my people.
They will speak to them
  in foreign languages,
but still my people
  won't listen to me."

[22] Languages that others don't know
may mean something to unbelievers, but
not to the Lord's followers. Prophecy, on
the other hand, is for followers, not for unbelievers. [23] Suppose everyone in your worship service started speaking unknown
languages, and some outsiders or some
unbelievers come in. Won't they think you
are crazy? [24] But suppose all of you are
prophesying when those unbelievers and
outsiders come in. They will realize that
they are sinners, and they will want to
change their ways because of what you are
saying. [25] They will tell what is hidden in
their hearts. Then they will kneel down
and say to God, "We are certain that you
are with these people."

Worship Must Be Orderly

[26] My friends, when you meet to worship, you must do everything for the good
of everyone there. That's how it should be
when someone sings or teaches or tells
what God has said or speaks an unknown
language or explains what the language
means. [27] No more than two or three of you
should speak unknown languages during
the meeting. You must take turns, and
someone should always be there to explain
what you mean. [28] If no one can explain,
you must keep silent in church and speak
only to yourself and to God.

[29] Two or three persons may prophesy,
and everyone else must listen carefully. [30] If
someone sitting there receives a message
from God, the speaker must stop and let
the other person speak. [31] Let only one
person speak at a time, then all of you will
learn something and be encouraged. [32] A
prophet should be willing to stop and let
someone else speak. [33] God wants everything to be done peacefully and in order.

When God's people meet in church,
[34] the women must not be allowed to speak.
They must keep quiet and listen, as the Law
of Moses teaches. [35] If there is something
they want to know, they can ask their husbands when they get home. It is disgraceful
for women to speak in church. [36] God's
message did not start with you people, and
you are not the only ones it has reached.

[37] If you think of yourself as a prophet
or a spiritual person, you will know that I
am writing only what the Lord has commanded. [38] So don't pay attention to anyone who ignores what I am writing. [39] My
friends, be eager to prophesy and don't stop
anyone from speaking languages that others don't know. [40] But do everything properly and in order.

14.21 Is 28.11, 12.

Christ Was Raised to Life

15 My friends, I want you to remember the message that I preached
and that you believed and trusted. 2 You
will be saved by this message, if you hold
firmly to it. But if you don't, your faith was
all for nothing.
3 I told you the most important part of
the message exactly as it was told to me.
That part is:

Christ died for our sins,
as the Scriptures say.
4 He was buried,
and three days later
he was raised to life,
as the Scriptures say.
5 Christ appeared to Peter,[z]
then to the twelve.
6 After this, he appeared
to more than five hundred
other followers.
Most of them are still alive,
but some have died.
7 He also appeared to James,
and then to all
of the apostles.

8 Finally, he appeared to me, even
though I am like someone who was born at
the wrong time.[a]
9 I am the least important of all the
apostles. In fact, I caused so much trouble
for God's church that I don't even deserve
to be called an apostle. 10 But God was
kind! He made me what I am, and his wonderful kindness wasn't wasted. I worked
much harder than any of the other apostles, although it was really God's kindness
at work and not me. 11 But it doesn't matter if I preached or if they preached. All of
you believed the message just the same.

God's People Will Be Raised to Life

12 If we preach that Christ was raised
from death, how can some of you say that
the dead will not be raised to life? 13 If they
won't be raised to life, Christ himself wasn't
raised to life. 14 And if Christ wasn't raised
to life, our message is worthless, and so is
your faith. 15 If the dead won't be raised to
life, we have told lies about God by saying
that he raised Christ to life, when he really
did not.
16 So if the dead won't be raised to life,
Christ wasn't raised to life. 17 Unless Christ
was raised to life, your faith is useless, and
you are still living in your sins. 18 And those
people who died after putting their faith in
him are completely lost. 19 If our hope in
Christ is good only for this life, we are
worse off than anyone else.
20 But Christ has been raised to life!
And he makes us certain that others will
also be raised to life. 21 Just as we will die
because of Adam, we will be raised to life
because of Christ. 22 Adam brought death
to all of us, and Christ will bring life to all
of us. 23 But we must each wait our turn.
Christ was the first to be raised to life, and
his people will be raised to life when he returns. 24 Then after Christ has destroyed all
powers and forces, the end will come, and
he will give the kingdom to God the Father.
25 Christ will rule until he puts all his
enemies under his power, 26 and the last
enemy he destroys will be death. 27 When
the Scriptures say that he will put everything under his power, they don't include
God. It was God who put everything under
the power of Christ. 28 After everything is
under the power of God's Son, he will put
himself under the power of God, who put
everything under his Son's power. Then
God will mean everything to everyone.
29 If the dead are not going to be raised
to life, what will people do who are being
baptized for them? Why are they being baptized for those dead people? 30 And why do
we always risk our lives 31 and face death
every day? The pride that I have in you because of Christ Jesus our Lord is what
makes me say this. 32 What do you think I
gained by fighting wild animals in Ephesus? If the dead are not raised to life,

[z] **15.5** *Peter*: See the note at 1.12. [a] **15.8** *who was born at the wrong time*: The meaning of these words in Greek is not clear.

15.3 Is 53.5-12. **15.4** Ps 16.8-10; Mt 12.40; Ac 2.24-32. **15.5** **a** Lk 24.34; **b** Mt 28.16, 17; Mk 16.14; Lk 24.36; Jn 20.19. **15.8** Ac 9.3-6. **15.9** Ac 8.3. **15.25** Ps 110.1. **15.27** Ps 8.6. **15.29** 2 Macc 12.44. **15.32** Is 22.13; 4 Macc 9.28.

"Let's eat and drink.
Tomorrow we die."

33 Don't fool yourselves. Bad friends will destroy you. 34 Be sensible and stop sinning. You should be embarrassed that some people still don't know about God.

What Our Bodies Will Be Like

35 Some of you have asked, "How will the dead be raised to life? What kind of bodies will they have?" 36 Don't be foolish. A seed must die before it can sprout from the ground. 37 Wheat seeds and all other seeds look different from the sprouts that come up. 38 This is because God gives everything the kind of body he wants it to have. 39 People, animals, birds, and fish are each made of flesh, but none of them are alike. 40 Everything in the heavens has a body, and so does everything on earth. But each one is very different from all the others. 41 The sun isn't like the moon, the moon isn't like the stars, and each star is different.

42 That's how it will be when our bodies are raised to life. These bodies will die, but the bodies that are raised will live forever. 43 These ugly and weak bodies will become beautiful and strong. 44 As surely as there are physical bodies, there are spiritual bodies. And our physical bodies will be changed into spiritual bodies.

45 The first man was named Adam, and the Scriptures tell us that he was a living person. But Jesus, who may be called the last Adam, is a life-giving spirit. 46 We see that the one with a spiritual body did not come first. He came after the one who had a physical body. 47 The first man was made from the dust of the earth, but the second man came from heaven. 48 Everyone on earth has a body like the body of the one who was made from the dust of the earth. And everyone in heaven has a body like the body of the one who came from heaven. 49 Just as we are like the one who was made out of earth, we will be like the one who came from heaven.

50 My friends, I want you to know that our bodies of flesh and blood will decay. This means that they cannot share in God's kingdom, which lasts forever. 51 I will explain a mystery to you. Not every one of us will die, but we will all be changed. 52 It will happen suddenly, quicker than the blink of an eye. At the sound of the last trumpet the dead will be raised. We will all be changed, so that we will never die again. 53 Our dead and decaying bodies will be changed into bodies that won't die or decay. 54 The bodies we now have are weak and can die. But they will be changed into bodies that are eternal. Then the Scriptures will come true,

"Death has lost the battle!
55 Where is its victory?
Where is its sting?"

56 Sin is what gives death its sting, and the Law is the power behind sin. 57 But thank God for letting our Lord Jesus Christ give us the victory!

58 My dear friends, stand firm and don't be shaken. Always keep busy working for the Lord. You know that everything you do for him is worthwhile.

A Collection for God's People

16 When you collect money for God's people, I want you to do exactly what I told the churches in Galatia to do. 2 That is, each Sunday each of you must put aside part of what you have earned. If you do this, you won't have to take up a collection when I come. 3 Choose some followers to take the money to Jerusalem. I will send them on with the money and with letters which show that you approve of them. 4 If you think I should go along, they can go with me.

Paul's Travel Plans

5 After I have gone through Macedonia, I hope to see you 6 and visit with you for a while. I may even stay all winter, so that you can help me on my way to wherever I will be going next. 7 If the Lord lets me, I would rather come later for a longer visit than to stop off now for only a short visit.

15.45 Gn 2.7. **15.51,52** 2 Esd 6.23; 1 Th 4.15-17. **15.54** Is 25.8. **15.55** Ho 13.14 (LXX). **16.1** Ro 15.25, 26. **16.5** Ac 19.21.

8 I will stay in Ephesus until Pentecost,
9 because there is a wonderful opportunity for me to do some work here. But there are also many people who are against me.

10 When Timothy arrives, give him a friendly welcome. He is doing the Lord's
work, just as I am. 11 Don't let anyone mistreat him. I am looking for him to return to me together with the other followers. So when he leaves, send him off with your blessings.

12 I have tried hard to get our friend Apollos to visit you with the other followers. He doesn't want to come just now, but he will come when he can.

Personal Concerns and Greetings

13 Keep alert. Be firm in your faith. Stay
brave and strong. 14 Show love in everything you do.

15 You know that Stephanas and his family were the first in Achaia to have faith in the Lord. They have done all they can for God's people. My friends, I ask you 16 to
obey leaders like them and to do the same for all others who work hard with you.

17 I was glad to see Stephanas and Fortunatus and Achaicus. Having them here
was like having you. 18 They made me feel much better, just as they made you feel better. You should appreciate people like them.

19 Greetings from the churches in Asia. Aquila and Priscilla, together with the church that meets in their house, send greetings in the name of the Lord.

20 All of the Lord's followers send their greetings.

Give each other a warm greeting.

21 I am signing this letter myself: PAUL.

22 I pray that God will put a curse on everyone who doesn't love the Lord. And may the Lord come soon.

23 I pray that the Lord Jesus will be kind to you.

24 I love everyone who belongs to Christ Jesus.

16.8 Lv 23.15-21; Dt 16.9-11. **16.8,9** Ac 19.8-10. **16.10** 1 Co 4.17. **16.15** 1 Co 1.16. **16.19** Ac 18.2.

2 CORINTHIANS

ABOUT THIS LETTER

In the beginning of this letter Paul answers the concerns of the Christians in Corinth who accused him of not living up to his promise to visit them. Paul had changed his mind for a good reason. He had stayed away from Corinth so that he would not seem to be too hard and demanding (1.23). He also wanted to see if they would follow his instructions about forgiving and comforting people who had sinned (2.5-11).

Paul reminds the Corinthians that God is generous and wants them to be just as generous in their giving to help God's people in Jerusalem and Judea (8.1—9.15).

Paul is a servant of God's new agreement (3.1-17). He is faithful in trying to bring people to God, even if it means terrible suffering for himself (4.1—6.13; 10.1—12.10). And what has God done to make it possible for us to come to him?

> *God has done it all! He sent Christ to make peace between himself and us, and he has given us the work of making peace between himself and others.*
>
> *What we mean is that God was in Christ, offering peace and forgiveness to the people of this world. And he has given us the work of sharing his message about peace.*
>
> *(5.18, 19)*

A QUICK LOOK AT THIS LETTER

- Paul Gives Thanks to God (1.1-11)
- The Work of an Apostle for God's People (1.12—2.17)
- Guided by the Love of Christ (3.1—7.16)
- Gifts for the Poor (8.1—9.15)
- Paul Is a True Apostle (10.1—13.10)
- Final Greetings (13.11-13)

---

1 From Paul, chosen by God to be an
apostle of Jesus Christ, and from Timothy, who is also a follower.
To God's church in Corinth and to all of
God's people in Achaia.
2 I pray that God our Father and the
Lord Jesus Christ will be kind to you and
will bless you with peace!

Paul Gives Thanks

3 Praise God, the Father of our Lord
Jesus Christ! The Father is a merciful God,
who always gives us comfort. 4 He comforts
us when we are in trouble, so that we can
share that same comfort with others in
trouble. 5 We share in the terrible sufferings of Christ, but also in the wonderful
comfort he gives. 6 We suffer in the hope
that you will be comforted and saved. And
because we are comforted, you will also be
comforted, as you patiently endure suffering like ours. 7 You never disappoint us. You
suffered as much as we did, and we know
that you will be comforted as we were.
8 My friends, I want you to know what a
hard time we had in Asia. Our sufferings

1.1 Ac 18.1. **1.8** 1 Co 15.32.

were so horrible and so unbearable that death seemed certain. 9 In fact, we felt sure that we were going to die. But this made us stop trusting in ourselves and start trusting God, who raises the dead to life. 10 God saved us from the threat of death,[a] and we are sure that he will do it again and again. 11 Please help us by praying for us. Then many people will give thanks for the blessings we receive in answer to all these prayers.

Paul's Change of Plans

12 We can be proud of our clear conscience. We have always lived honestly and sincerely, especially when we were with you. And we were guided by God's wonderful kindness instead of by the wisdom of this world. 13 I am not writing anything you cannot read and understand. I hope you will understand it completely, 14 just as you already partly understand us. Then when our Lord Jesus returns, you can be as proud of us as we are of you.

15 I was so sure of your pride in us that I had planned to visit you first of all. In this way you would have the blessing of two visits from me. 16 Once on my way to Macedonia and again on my return from there. Then you could send me on to Judea. 17 Do you think I couldn't make up my mind about what to do? Or do I seem like someone who says "Yes" or "No" simply to please others? 18 God can be trusted, and so can I, when I say that our answer to you has always been "Yes" and never "No." 19 This is because Jesus Christ the Son of God is always "Yes" and never "No." And he is the one that Silas,[b] Timothy, and I told you about.

20 Christ says "Yes" to all of God's promises. That's why we have Christ to say "Amen"[c] for us to the glory of God. 21 And so God makes it possible for you and us to stand firmly together with Christ. God is also the one who chose us 22 and put his Spirit in our hearts to show that we belong only to him.

23 God is my witness that I stayed away from Corinth, just to keep from being hard on you. 24 We are not bosses who tell you what to believe. We are working with you to make you glad, because your faith is strong.

2 I have decided not to make my next visit with you so painful. 2 If I make you feel bad, who would be left to cheer me up, except the people I had made to feel bad? 3 The reason I want to be happy is to make you happy. I wrote as I did because I didn't want to visit you and be made to feel bad, when you should make me feel happy. 4 At the time I wrote, I was suffering terribly. My eyes were full of tears, and my heart was broken. But I didn't want to make you feel bad. I only wanted to let you know how much I cared for you.

Forgiveness

5 I don't want to be hard on you. But if one of you has made someone feel bad, I am not really the one who has been made to feel bad. Some of you are the ones. 6 Most of you have already pointed out the wrong that person did, and that is punishment enough for what was done.

7 When people sin, you should forgive and comfort them, so they won't give up in despair. 8 You should make them sure of your love for them.

9 I also wrote because I wanted to test you and find out if you would follow my instructions. 10 I will forgive anyone you forgive. Yes, for your sake and with Christ as my witness, I have forgiven whatever needed to be forgiven. 11 I have done this to keep Satan from getting the better of us. We all know what goes on in his mind.

12 When I went to Troas to preach the good news about Christ, I found that the Lord had already prepared the way. 13 But I was worried when I didn't find my friend Titus there. So I left the other followers and went on to Macedonia.

14 I am grateful that God always makes it possible for Christ to lead us to victory. God also helps us spread the knowledge

[a] **1.10** *the threat of death*: Some manuscripts have "many threats of death." [b] **1.19** *Silas*: The Greek text has "Silvanus," which is another form of the name Silas. [c] **1.20** *Amen*: The word "amen" is used here with the meaning of "yes."

1.16 Ac 19.21. **1.19** Ac 18.5. **2.12,13** Ac 20.1.

about Christ everywhere, and this knowledge is like the smell of perfume. 15-16 In
fact, God thinks of us as a perfume that
brings Christ to everyone. For people who
are being saved, this perfume has a sweet
smell and leads them to a better life. But
for people who are lost, it has a bad smell
and leads them to a horrible death.

No one really has what it takes to do this
work. 17 A lot of people try to get rich from
preaching God's message. But we are God's
sincere messengers, and by the power of
Christ we speak our message with God as
our witness.

God's New Agreement

3 Are we once again bragging about ourselves? Do we need letters to you or
from you to tell others about us? Some
people do need letters that tell about them.
2 But you are our letter, and you are in our[d]
hearts for everyone to read and understand. 3 You are like a letter written by
Christ and delivered by us. But you are not
written with pen and ink or on tablets
made of stone. You are written in our
hearts by the Spirit of the living God.

4 We are sure about all this. Christ makes
us sure in the very presence of God. 5 We
don't have the right to claim that we have
done anything on our own. God gives us what
it takes to do all that we do. 6 He makes us
worthy to be the servants of his new agreement that comes from the Holy Spirit and
not from a written Law. After all, the Law
brings death, but the Spirit brings life.

7 The Law of Moses brought only the
promise of death, even though it was
carved on stones and given in a wonderful
way. Still the Law made Moses' face shine
so brightly that the people of Israel could
not look at it, even though it was a fading
glory. 8 So won't the agreement that the
Spirit brings to us be even more wonderful? 9 If something that brings the death
sentence is glorious, won't something that
makes us acceptable to God be even more
glorious? 10 In fact, the new agreement is
so wonderful that the Law is no longer glorious at all. 11 The Law was given with a
glory that faded away. But the glory of the
new agreement is much greater, because it
will never fade away.

12 This wonderful hope makes us feel
like speaking freely. 13 We are not like
Moses. His face was shining, but he covered it to keep the people of Israel from
seeing the brightness fade away. 14 The
people were stubborn, and something still
keeps them from seeing the truth when the
Law is read. Only Christ can take away the
covering that keeps them from seeing.

15 When the Law of Moses is read, they
have their minds covered over 16 with a
covering that is removed only for those who
turn to the Lord. 17 The Lord and the
Spirit are one and the same, and the Lord's
Spirit sets us free. 18 So our faces are not
covered. They show the bright glory of the
Lord, as the Lord's Spirit makes us more
and more like our glorious Lord.

Treasure in Clay Jars

4 God has been kind enough to trust us
with this work. That's why we never
give up. 2 We don't do shameful things that
must be kept secret. And we don't try to
fool anyone or twist God's message around.
God is our witness that we speak only the
truth, so others will be sure that we can be
trusted. 3 If there is anything hidden about
our message, it is hidden only to someone
who is lost.

4 The god who rules this world has
blinded the minds of unbelievers. They
cannot see the light, which is the good
news about our glorious Christ, who shows
what God is like. 5 We are not preaching
about ourselves. Our message is that Jesus
Christ is Lord. He also sent us to be your
servants. 6 The Scriptures say, "God commanded light to shine in the dark." Now
God is shining in our hearts to let you
know that his glory is seen in Jesus Christ.

7 We are like clay jars in which this
treasure is stored. The real power comes
from God and not from us. 8 We often suffer,
but we are never crushed. Even when we

[d]**3.2** *our*: Some manuscripts have "your."

3.3 **a** Ex 24.12; **b** Jr 31.33; Ez 11.19; 36.26. **3.6** Jr 31.31. **3.7** Ex 34.29.
3.13 Ex 34.33. **3.16** Ex 34.34. **3.18** 4 Macc 9.22. **4.6** Gn 1.3.

don't know what to do, we never give up.
9 In times of trouble, God is with us, and
when we are knocked down, we get up again.
10-11 We face death every day because of
Jesus. Our bodies show what his death
was like, so that his life can also be seen in
us. 12 This means that death is working in
us, but life is working in you.

13 In the Scriptures it says, "I spoke because I had faith." We have that same kind
of faith. So we speak 14 because we know
that God raised the Lord Jesus to life. And
just as God raised Jesus, he will also raise
us to life. Then he will bring us into his
presence together with you. 15 All of this
has been done for you, so that more and
more people will know how kind God is and
will praise and honor him.

Faith in the Lord

16 We never give up. Our bodies are
gradually dying, but we ourselves are being
made stronger each day. 17 These little
troubles are getting us ready for an eternal
glory that will make all our troubles seem
like nothing. 18 Things that are seen don't
last forever, but things that are not seen are
eternal. That's why we keep our minds on
the things that cannot be seen.

5 Our bodies are like tents that we live
in here on earth. But when these tents
are destroyed, we know that God will give
each of us a place to live. These homes will
not be buildings that someone has made,
but they are in heaven and will last forever.
2 While we are here on earth, we sigh
because we want to live in that heavenly
home. 3 We want to put it on like clothes
and not be naked.

4 These tents we now live in are like a
heavy burden, and we groan. But we don't do
this just because we want to leave these
bodies that will die. It is because we want
to change them for bodies that will never
die. 5 God is the one who makes all of this
possible. He has given us his Spirit to make
us certain that he will do it. 6 So always be
cheerful!

As long as we are in these bodies, we are
away from the Lord. 7 But we live by faith,
not by what we see. 8 We should be cheerful, because we would rather leave these
bodies and be at home with the Lord. 9 But
whether we are at home with the Lord or
away from him, we still try our best to
please him. 10 After all, Christ will judge
each of us for the good or the bad that we
do while living in these bodies.

Bringing People to God

11 We know what it means to respect the
Lord, and we encourage everyone to turn
to him. God himself knows what we are
like, and I hope you also know what kind of
people we are. 12 We are not trying once
more to brag about ourselves. But we want
you to be proud of us, when you are with
those who are not sincere and brag about
what others think of them.

13 If we seem out of our minds, it is between God and us. But if we are in our
right minds, it is for your good. 14 We are
ruled by Christ's love for us. We are certain
that if one person died for everyone else,
then all of us have died. 15 And Christ did
die for all of us. He died so we would no
longer live for ourselves, but for the one
who died and was raised to life for us.

16 We are careful not to judge people by
what they seem to be, though we once
judged Christ in that way. 17 Anyone who
belongs to Christ is a new person. The past
is forgotten, and everything is new. 18 God
has done it all! He sent Christ to make
peace between himself and us, and he has
given us the work of making peace between
himself and others.

19 What we mean is that God was in
Christ, offering peace and forgiveness to
the people of this world. And he has given
us the work of sharing his message about
peace. 20 We were sent to speak for Christ,
and God is begging you to listen to our
message. We speak for Christ and sincerely
ask you to make peace with God. 21 Christ
never sinned! But God treated him as a
sinner, so that Christ could make us acceptable to God.

6 We work together with God, and we
beg you to make good use of God's
kindness to you. 2 In the Scriptures God
says,

5.1 Ws 9.15. **5.10** Ro 14.10. **6.2** Is 49.8 (LXX).

"When the time came,
I listened to you,
and when you needed help,
I came to save you."

That time has come. This is the day for you
to be saved.
3 We don't want anyone to find fault
with our work, and so we try hard not to
cause problems. 4 But in everything and in
every way we show that we truly are God's
servants. We have always been patient,
though we have had a lot of trouble, suffering, and hard times. 5 We have been
beaten, put in jail, and hurt in riots. We
have worked hard and have gone without
sleep or food. 6 But we have kept ourselves
pure and have been understanding, patient, and kind. The Holy Spirit has been
with us, and our love has been real. 7 We
have spoken the truth, and God's power
has worked in us. In all our struggles we
have said and done only what is right.
8 Whether we were honored or dishonored or praised or cursed, we always told
the truth about ourselves. But some people
said we did not. 9 We are unknown to others, but well known to you. We seem to be
dying, and yet we are still alive. We have
been punished, but never killed, 10 and we
are always happy, even in times of suffering. Although we are poor, we have made
many people rich. And though we own
nothing, everything is ours.
11 Friends in Corinth, we are telling the
truth when we say that there is room in
our hearts for you. 12 We are not holding
back on our love for you, but you are holding back on your love for us. 13 I speak to
you as I would speak to my own children.
Please make room in your hearts for us.

The Temple of the Living God

14 Stay away from people who are not
followers of the Lord! Can someone who is
good get along with someone who is evil?
Are light and darkness the same? 15 Is
Christ a friend of Satan?[e] Can people who
follow the Lord have anything in common
with those who don't? 16 Do idols belong in
the temple of God? We are the temple of
the living God, as God himself says,

"I will live with these people
and walk among them.
I will be their God,
and they will be
my people."

17 The Lord also says,

"Leave them and stay away!
Don't touch anything
that isn't clean.
Then I will welcome you
18 and be your Father.
You will be my sons
and my daughters,
as surely as I am God,
the All-Powerful."

7 My friends, God has made us these
promises. So we should stay away from
everything that keeps our bodies and spirits
from being clean. We should honor God
and try to be completely like him.

The Church Makes Paul Happy

2 Make a place for us in your hearts! We
haven't mistreated or hurt anyone. We
haven't cheated anyone. 3 I am not saying
this to be hard on you. But, as I have said
before, you will always be in our thoughts,
whether we live or die. 4 I trust you completely.[f] I am always proud of you, and I am
greatly encouraged. In all my trouble I am
still very happy.
5 After we came to Macedonia, we didn't
have any chance to rest. We were faced
with all kinds of problems. We were troubled by enemies and troubled by fears.
6 But God cheers up people in need, and
that is what he did when he sent Titus to
us. 7 Of course, we were glad to see Titus,
but what really made us glad is the way you
cheered him up. He told how sorry you
were and how concerned you were about
me. And this made me even happier.

[e]**6.15** *Satan*: The Greek text has "Beliar," which is another form of the Hebrew word "Belial," meaning "wicked" or "useless." The Jewish people sometimes used this as a name for Satan.

[f]**7.4** *I trust you completely*: Or "I have always spoken the truth to you" or "I can speak freely to you."

6.5 Ac 16.23. **6.16** **a** 1 Co 3.16; 6.19; **b** Lv 26.12; Ez 37.27. **6.17** Is 52.11.
6.18 2 S 7.14; 1 Ch 17.13; Is 43.6; Jr 31.9. **7.5** 2 Co 2.13.

8 I don't feel bad anymore, even though my letter[g] hurt your feelings. I did feel bad at first, but I don't now. I know that the letter hurt you for a while. 9 Now I am happy, but not because I hurt your feelings. It is because God used your hurt feelings to make you turn back to him, and none of you were harmed by us. 10 When God makes you feel sorry enough to turn to him and be saved, you don't have anything to feel bad about. But when this world makes you feel sorry, it can cause your death.

11 Just look what God has done by making you feel sorry! You sincerely want to prove that you are innocent. You are angry. You are shocked. You are eager to see that justice is done. You have proved that you were completely right in this matter. 12 When I wrote you, it wasn't to accuse the one who was wrong or to take up for the one who was hurt. I wrote, so that God would show you how much you do care for us. 13 And we were greatly encouraged.

Although we were encouraged, we felt even better when we saw how happy Titus was, because you had shown that he had nothing to worry about. 14 We had told him how much we thought of you, and you did not disappoint us. Just as we have always told you the truth, so everything we told him about you has also proved to be true. 15 Titus loves all of you very much, especially when he remembers how you obeyed him and how you trembled with fear when you welcomed him. 16 It makes me really glad to know that I can depend on you.

Generous Giving

8 My friends, we want you to know that the churches in Macedonia[h] have shown others how kind God is. 2 Although they were going through hard times and were very poor, they were glad to give generously. 3 They gave as much as they could afford and even more, simply because they wanted to. 4 They even asked and begged us to let them have the joy of giving their money for God's people. 5 And they did more than we had hoped. They gave themselves first to the Lord and then to us, just as God wanted them to do.

6 Titus was the one who got you started doing this good thing, so we begged him to have you finish what you had begun. 7 You do everything better than anyone else. You have stronger faith. You speak better and know more. You are eager to give, and you love us better.[i] Now you must give more generously than anyone else.

8 I am not ordering you to do this. I am simply testing how real your love is by comparing it with the concern that others have shown. 9 You know that our Lord Jesus Christ was kind enough to give up all his riches and become poor, so that you could become rich.

10 A year ago you were the first ones to give, and you gave because you wanted to. So listen to my advice. 11 I think you should finish what you started. If you give according to what you have, you will prove that you are as eager to give as you were to think about giving. 12 It doesn't matter how much you have. What matters is how much you are willing to give from what you have.

13 I am not trying to make life easier for others by making life harder for you. But it is only fair 14 for you to share with them when you have so much, and they have so little. Later, when they have more than enough, and you are in need, they can share with you. Then everyone will have a fair share, 15 just as the Scriptures say,

"Those who gathered
too much
had nothing left.
Those who gathered
only a little
had all they needed."

Titus and His Friends

16 I am grateful that God made Titus care as much about you as we do. 17 When

[g]**7.8** *my letter*: There is no copy of this letter that Paul wrote to the church at Corinth.
[h]**8.1** *churches in Macedonia*: The churches that Paul had started in Philippi and Thessalonica. The church in Berea is probably also meant. [i]**8.7** *you love us better*: Some manuscripts have "we love you better."

8.1-4 Ro 15.25, 26. **8.15** Ex 16.18.

we begged Titus to visit you, he said he
would. He wanted to because he cared so
much for you. 18 With Titus we are also
sending one of the Lord's followers who is
well known in every church for spreading
the good news. 19 The churches chose this
follower to travel with us while we carry
this gift that will bring praise to the Lord
and show how much we hope to help.
20 We don't want anyone to find fault with
the way we handle your generous gift.
21 But we want to do what pleases the Lord
and what people think is right.

22 We are also sending someone else
with Titus and the other follower. We approve of this man. In fact, he has already
shown us many times that he wants to
help. And now he wants to help even more
than ever, because he trusts you so much.
23 Titus is my partner, who works with me
to serve you. The other two followers are
sent by the churches, and they bring honor
to Christ. 24 Treat them in such a way that
the churches will see your love and will
know why we bragged about you.

The Money for God's People

9 I don't need to write you about the
money you plan to give for God's people. 2 I know how eager you are to give. And
I have proudly told the Lord's followers in
Macedonia that you people in Achaia have
been ready for a whole year. Now your desire to give has made them want to give.
3 That's why I am sending Titus and the
two others to you. I want you to be ready,
just as I promised. This will prove that we
were not wrong to brag about you.

4 Some followers from Macedonia may
come with me, and I want them to find
that you have the money ready. If you don't,
I would be embarrassed for trusting you to
do this. But you would be embarrassed
even more. 5 So I have decided to ask Titus
and the others to spend some time with
you before I arrive. This way they can
arrange to collect the money you have
promised. Then you will have the chance
to give because you want to, and not because you feel forced to.

6 Remember this saying,

"A few seeds make
a small harvest,
but a lot of seeds make
a big harvest."

7 Each of you must make up your own
mind about how much to give. But don't
feel sorry that you must give and don't feel
that you are forced to give. God loves people who love to give. 8 God can bless you
with everything you need, and you will
always have more than enough to do
all kinds of good things for others. 9 The
Scriptures say,

"God freely gives his gifts
to the poor,
and always does right."

10 God gives seed to farmers and provides
everyone with food. He will increase what
you have, so that you can give even more to
those in need. 11 You will be blessed in
every way, and you will be able to keep on
being generous. Then many people will
thank God when we deliver your gift.

12 What you are doing is much more
than a service that supplies God's people
with what they need. It is something that
will make many others thank God. 13 The
way in which you have proved yourselves
by this service will bring honor and praise
to God. You believed the message about
Christ, and you obeyed it by sharing generously with God's people and with everyone
else. 14 Now they are praying for you and
want to see you, because God used you to
bless them so very much. 15 Thank God for
his gift that is too wonderful for words!

Paul Defends His Work for Christ

10 Do you think I am a coward when I
am with you and brave when I am
far away? Well, I ask you to listen, because
Christ himself was humble and gentle.
2 Some people have said that we act like
the people of this world. So when I arrive, I
expect I will have to be firm and forceful in
what I say to them. Please don't make me
treat you that way. 3 We live in this world,
but we don't act like its people 4 or fight our
battles with the weapons of this world.
Instead, we use God's power that can de-

8.21 Pr 3.4 (LXX). **9.7** Si 20.10-15. **9.9** Ps 112.9. **9.10** Is 55.10.

stroy fortresses. We destroy arguments
5 and every bit of pride that keeps anyone
from knowing God. We capture people's
thoughts and make them obey Christ.
6 And when you completely obey him, we
will punish anyone who refuses to obey.
7 You judge by appearances.[j] If any of
you think you are the only ones who belong
to Christ, then think again. We belong to
Christ as much as you do. 8 Maybe I brag a
little too much about the authority that the
Lord gave me to help you and not to hurt
you. Yet I am not embarrassed to brag.
9 And I am not trying to scare you with my
letters. 10 Some of you are saying, "Paul's
letters are harsh and powerful. But in person, he is a weakling and has nothing
worth saying." 11 Those people had better
understand that when I am with you, I will
do exactly what I say in my letters.
12 We won't dare compare ourselves
with those who think so much of themselves. But they are foolish to compare
themselves with themselves. 13 We won't
brag about something we don't have a right
to brag about. We will only brag about the
work that God has sent us to do, and you
are part of that work. 14 We are not bragging more than we should. After all, we did
bring the message about Christ to you.
15 We don't brag about what others have
done, as if we had done those things ourselves. But I hope that as you become
stronger in your faith, we will be able to
reach many more of the people around
you.[k] That has always been our goal.
16 Then we will be able to preach the good
news in other lands where we cannot take
credit for work someone else has already
done. 17 The Scriptures say, "If you want to
brag, then brag about the Lord." 18 You may
brag about yourself, but the only approval
that counts is the Lord's approval.

Paul and the False Apostles

11 Please put up with a little of my
foolishness. 2 I am as concerned
about you as God is. You were like a virgin
bride I had chosen only for Christ. 3 But
now I fear that you will be tricked, just as
Eve was tricked by that lying snake. I am
afraid that you might stop thinking about
Christ in an honest and sincere way. 4 We
told you about Jesus, and you received the
Holy Spirit and accepted our message. But
you let some people tell you about another
Jesus. Now you are ready to receive another spirit and accept a different message.
5 I think I am as good as any of those super
apostles. 6 I may not speak as well as they
do, but I know as much. And this has already been made perfectly clear to you.
7 Was it wrong for me to lower myself
and honor you by preaching God's message
free of charge? 8 I robbed other churches
by taking money from them to serve you.
9 Even when I was in need, I still didn't
bother you. In fact, some of the Lord's followers from Macedonia brought me what I
needed. I have not been a burden to you in
the past, and I will never be a burden. 10 As
surely as I speak the truth about Christ, no
one in Achaia can stop me from bragging
about this. 11 And it isn't because I don't
love you. God himself knows how much I
do love you.
12 I plan to go on doing just what I have
always done. Then those people won't be
able to brag about doing the same things
we are doing. 13 Anyway, they are no more
than false apostles and dishonest workers.
They only pretend to be apostles of Christ.
14 And it is no wonder. Even Satan tries to
make himself look like an angel of light.
15 So why does it seem strange for Satan's
servants to pretend to do what is right?
Someday they will get exactly what they deserve.

Paul's Sufferings for Christ

16 I don't want any of you to think that I
am a fool. But if you do, then let me be a
fool and brag a little. 17 When I do all this
bragging, I do it as a fool and not for the
Lord. 18 Yet if others want to brag about
what they have done, so will I. 19 And since

[j] **10.7** *You judge by appearances*: Or "Take a close look at yourselves." [k] **10.15** *we will be able to reach many more of the people around you*: Or "you will praise us even more because of our work among you."

10.17 Jr 9.24. **11.3** Gn 3.1-5, 13. **11.9** Phil 4.15-18.

you are so smart, you will gladly put up
with a fool. 20 In fact, you let people make
slaves of you and cheat you and steal from
you. Why, you even let them strut around
and slap you in the face. 21 I am ashamed
to say that we are too weak to behave in
such a way.

If they can brag, so can I, but it is a foolish thing to do. 22 Are they Hebrews? So am
I. Are they Jews? So am I. Are they from
the family of Abraham? Well, so am I.
23 Are they servants of Christ? I am a fool
to talk this way, but I serve him better than
they do. I have worked harder and have
been put in jail more times. I have been
beaten with whips more and have been in
danger of death more often.

24 Five times the Jews gave me thirty-
nine lashes with a whip. 25 Three times the
Romans beat me with a big stick, and once
my enemies stoned me. I have been shipwrecked three times, and I even had to
spend a night and a day in the sea. 26 During my many travels, I have been in danger
from rivers, robbers, the Jews, and foreigners. My life has been in danger in cities, in
deserts, at sea, and with people who only
pretended to be the Lord's followers.

27 I have worked and struggled and
spent many sleepless nights. I have gone
hungry and thirsty and often had nothing to eat. I have been cold from not having enough clothes to keep me warm.
28 Besides everything else, each day I am
burdened down, worrying about all the
churches. 29 When others are weak, I am
weak too. When others are tricked into sin,
I get angry.[l]

30 If I have to brag, I will brag about how
weak I am. 31 God, the Father of our Lord
Jesus, knows I am not lying. And God is to
be praised forever! 32 The governor of
Damascus at the time of King Aretas had
the city gates guarded, so that he could
capture me. 33 But I escaped by being let
down in a basket through a window in the
city wall.

Visions from the Lord

12 I have to brag. There is nothing to
be gained by it, but I must brag
about the visions and other things that the
Lord has shown me. 2 I know about one of
Christ's followers who was taken up into
the third heaven fourteen years ago. I don't
know if the man was still in his body when
it happened, but God certainly knows.

3 As I said, only God really knows if this
man was in his body at the time. 4 But he
was taken up into paradise,[m] where he
heard things that are too wonderful to tell.
5 I will brag about that man, but not about
myself, except to say how weak I am.

6 Yet even if I did brag, I would not be
foolish. I would simply be speaking the
truth. But I will try not to say too much.
That way, none of you will think more
highly of me than you should because of
what you have seen me do and say. 7 Of
course, I am now referring to the wonderful things I saw. One of Satan's angels was
sent to make me suffer terribly, so that I
would not feel too proud.[n]

8 Three times I begged the Lord to make
this suffering go away. 9 But he replied, "My
kindness is all you need. My power is
strongest when you are weak." So if Christ
keeps giving me his power, I will gladly brag
about how weak I am. 10 Yes, I am glad to be
weak or insulted or mistreated or to have
troubles and sufferings, if it is for Christ.
Because when I am weak, I am strong.

Paul's Concern for the Lord's Followers at Corinth

11 I have been making a fool of myself.
But you forced me to do it, when you
should have been speaking up for me. I
may be nothing at all, but I am as good as
those super apostles. 12 When I was with

[l] **11.29** *When others are tricked into sin, I get angry*: Or "When others stumble into sin, I hurt for them." [m] **12.4** *paradise*: In the Greek translation of the Old Testament, this word is used for the Garden of Eden. In New Testament times it was sometimes used for the place where God's people are happy and at rest, as they wait for the final judgment. [n] **12.7** *Of course . . . too proud*: Or "Because of the wonderful things that I saw, one of Satan's angels was sent to make me suffer terribly, so that I would not feel too proud."

11.23 Ac 16.23. **11.24** Dt 25.3. **11.25** **a** Ac 16.22; **b** Ac 14.19. **11.26** **a** Ac 9.23; **b** Ac 14.5. **11.32,33** Ac 9.23-25.

you, I was patient and worked all the powerful miracles and signs and wonders of a true apostle. [13] You missed out on only one blessing that the other churches received. That is, you didn't have to support me. Forgive me for doing you wrong.

[14] I am planning to visit you for the third time. But I still won't make a burden of myself. What I really want is you, and not what you have. Children are not supposed to save up for their parents, but parents are supposed to take care of their children. [15] So I will gladly give all that I have and all that I am. Will you love me less for loving you too much? [16] You agree that I wasn't a burden to you. Maybe that's because I was trying to catch you off guard and trick you. [17] Were you cheated by any of those I sent to you? [18] I urged Titus to visit you, and I sent another follower with him. But Titus didn't cheat you, and we felt and behaved the same way he did.

[19] Have you been thinking all along that we have been defending ourselves to you? Actually, we have been speaking to God as followers of Christ. But, my friends, we did it all for your good.

[20] I am afraid that when I come, we won't be pleased with each other. I fear that some of you may be arguing or jealous or angry or selfish or gossiping or insulting each other. I even fear that you may be proud and acting like a mob. [21] I am afraid God will make me ashamed when I visit you again. I will feel like crying because many of you have never given up your old sins. You are still doing things that are immoral, indecent, and shameful.

Final Warnings and Greetings

13 I am on my way to visit you for the third time. And as the Scriptures say, "Any charges must be proved true by at least two or three witnesses." [2] During my second visit I warned you that I would punish you and anyone else who doesn't stop sinning. I am far away from you now, but I give you the same warning. [3] This should prove to you that I am speaking for Christ. When he corrects you, he won't be weak. He will be powerful! [4] Although he was weak when he was nailed to the cross, he now lives by the power of God. We are weak, just as Christ was. But you will see that we will live by the power of God, just as Christ does.

[5] Test yourselves and find out if you really are true to your faith. If you pass the test, you will discover that Christ is living in you. But if Christ isn't living in you, you have failed. [6] I hope you will discover that we have not failed. [7] We pray that you will stop doing evil things. We don't pray like this to make ourselves look good, but to get you to do right, even if we are failures.

[8] All we can do is to follow the truth and not fight against it. [9] Even though we are weak, we are glad that you are strong, and we pray that you will do even better. [10] I am writing these things to you before I arrive. This way I won't have to be hard on you when I use the authority that the Lord has given me. I was given this authority, so that I could help you and not destroy you.

[11] Good-by, my friends. Do better and pay attention to what I have said. Try to get along and live peacefully with each other.

Now I pray that God, who gives love and peace, will be with you. [12] Give each other a warm greeting. All of God's people send their greetings.

[13] I pray that the Lord Jesus Christ will bless you and be kind to you! May God bless you with his love, and may the Holy Spirit join all your hearts together.

13.1 Dt 17.5-7; 19.15.

GALATIANS

ABOUT THIS LETTER

From the very beginning of this letter to the churches in the region of Galatia (in central Asia Minor), Paul makes two things clear to his readers: he is a true apostle, and his message is the only true message (1.1-10). These statements were very important, because some people claimed that Paul was a false apostle with a false message.

Paul was indeed a true apostle, and his mission to the Gentiles was given to him by the Lord and approved by the apostles in Jerusalem (1.18—2.10). Paul had even corrected the apostle Peter, when he had stopped eating with Gentile followers who were not obeying the Law of Moses (2.1-18).

Faith is the only way to be saved. Paul insists that this was true already for Abraham, who had received God's promise by faith. And Paul leaves no doubt about what his own faith means to him:

> *"I have been nailed to the cross with Christ. I have died, but Christ lives in me. And I now live by faith in the Son of God, who loved me and gave his life for me."*
>
> *(2.19b, 20)*

A QUICK LOOK AT THIS LETTER

- A True Apostle and the True Message (1.1-10)
- God Chose Paul To Be an Apostle (1.11-24)
- Paul Defends His Message (2.1-21)
- Faith Is the Only Way To Be Saved (3.1—4.31)
- Guided by the Spirit and Love (5.1—6.10)
- Final Warnings (6.11-18)

---

1 1-2 From the apostle Paul and from all
the Lord's followers with me.
I was chosen to be an apostle by Jesus Christ and by God the Father, who raised him from death. No mere human chose or appointed me to this work.

To the churches in Galatia.

3 I pray that God the Father and our
Lord Jesus Christ will be kind to you and
will bless you with peace! 4 Christ obeyed
God our Father and gave himself as a sacrifice for our sins to rescue us from this evil
world. 5 God will be given glory forever and
ever. Amen.

The Only True Message

6 I am shocked that you have so quickly
turned from God, who chose you because
of his wonderful kindness.[a] You have believed another message, 7 when there is really only one true message. But some people are causing you trouble and want to
make you turn away from the good news
about Christ. 8 I pray that God will punish
anyone who preaches anything different
from our message to you! It doesn't matter
if that person is one of us or an angel from
heaven. 9 I have said it before, and I will
say it again. I hope God will punish anyone

[a] **1.6** *his wonderful kindness*: Some manuscripts have "the wonderful kindness of Christ."

who preaches anything different from what you have already believed.

10 I am not trying to please people. I want to please God. Do you think I am trying to please people? If I were doing that, I would not be a servant of Christ.

How Paul Became an Apostle

11 My friends, I want you to know that no one made up the message I preach. 12 It wasn't given or taught to me by some mere human. My message came directly from Jesus Christ when he appeared to me.

13 You know how I used to live as a Jew. I was cruel to God's church and even tried to destroy it. 14 I was a much better Jew than anyone else my own age, and I obeyed every law that our ancestors had given us. 15 But even before I was born, God had chosen me. He was kind and had decided 16 to show me his Son, so that I would announce his message to the Gentiles. I didn't talk this over with anyone. 17 I didn't say a word, not even to the men in Jerusalem who were apostles before I was. Instead, I went at once to Arabia, and afterwards I returned to Damascus.

18 Three years later I went to visit Peter[b] in Jerusalem and stayed with him for fifteen days. 19 The only other apostle I saw was James, the Lord's brother. 20 And in the presence of God I swear I am telling the truth.

21 Later, I went to the regions of Syria and Cilicia. 22 But no one who belonged to Christ's churches in Judea had ever seen me in person. 23 They had only heard that the one who had been cruel to them was now preaching the message that he had once tried to destroy. 24 And because of me, they praised God.

2 Fourteen years later I went to Jerusalem with Barnabas. I also took along Titus. 2 But I went there because God had told me to go, and I explained the good news that I had been preaching to the Gentiles. Then I met privately with the ones who seemed to be the most important leaders. I wanted to make sure that my work in the past and my future work would not be for nothing.

3 Titus went to Jerusalem with me. He was a Greek, but still he wasn't forced to be circumcised. 4 We went there because of those who pretended to be followers and had sneaked in among us as spies. They had come to take away the freedom that Christ Jesus had given us, and they were trying to make us their slaves. 5 But we wanted you to have the true message. That's why we didn't give in to them, not even for a second.

6 Some of them were supposed to be important leaders, but I didn't care who they were. God doesn't have any favorites! None of these so-called special leaders added anything to my message. 7 They realized that God had sent me with the good news for Gentiles, and that he had sent Peter with the same message for Jews. 8 God, who had sent Peter on a mission to the Jews, was now using me to preach to the Gentiles.

9 James, Peter,[b] and John realized that God had given me the message about his undeserved kindness. And these men are supposed to be the backbone of the church. They even gave Barnabas and me a friendly handshake. This was to show that we would work with Gentiles and that they would work with Jews. 10 They only asked us to remember the poor, and that was something I had always been eager to do.

Paul Corrects Peter at Antioch

11 When Peter came to Antioch, I told him face to face that he was wrong. 12 He used to eat with Gentile followers of the Lord, until James sent some Jewish followers. Peter was afraid of the Jews and soon stopped eating with Gentiles. 13 He and the other Jews hid their true feelings so well that even Barnabas was fooled. 14 But when I saw that they were not really obeying the truth that is in the good news, I corrected Peter in front of everyone and said:

[b] **1.18; 2.9** *Peter*: The Greek text has "Cephas," which is an Aramaic name meaning "rock." Peter is the Greek name with the same meaning.

1.13 Ac 8.3; 22.4, 5; 26.9-11. **1.14** Ac 22.3. **1.15,16** Ac 9.3-6; 22.6-10; 26.13-18. **1.18** Ac 9.26-30. **2.1** Ac 11.30; 15.2. **2.6** Dt 10.17.

Peter, you are a Jew, but you live like a Gentile. So how can you force Gentiles to live like Jews?

15 We are Jews by birth and are not sinners like Gentiles. 16 But we know that God accepts only those who have faith in Jesus Christ. No one can please God by simply obeying the Law. So we put our faith in Christ Jesus, and God accepted us because of our faith.

17 When we Jews started looking for a way to please God, we discovered that we are sinners too. Does this mean that Christ is the one who makes us sinners? No, it doesn't! 18 But if I tear down something and then build it again, I prove that I was wrong at first. 19 It was the Law itself that killed me and freed me from its power, so that I could live for God.

I have been nailed to the cross with Christ. 20 I have died, but Christ lives in me. And I now live by faith in the Son of God, who loved me and gave his life for me. 21 I don't turn my back on God's undeserved kindness. If we can be acceptable to God by obeying the Law, it was useless for Christ to die.

Faith Is the Only Way

3 You stupid Galatians! I told you exactly how Jesus Christ was nailed to a cross. Has someone now put an evil spell on you? 2 I want to know only one thing. How were you given God's Spirit? Was it by obeying the Law of Moses or by hearing about Christ and having faith in him? 3 How can you be so stupid? Do you think that by yourself you can complete what God's Spirit started in you? 4 Have you gone through all of this for nothing? Is it all really for nothing? 5 God gives you his Spirit and works miracles in you. But does he do this because you obey the Law of Moses or because you have heard about Christ and have faith in him?

6 The Scriptures say that God accepted Abraham because Abraham had faith. 7 And so, you should understand that everyone who has faith is a child of Abraham.[c] 8 Long ago the Scriptures said that God would accept the Gentiles because of their faith. That's why God told Abraham the good news that all nations would be blessed because of him. 9 This means that everyone who has faith will share in the blessings that were given to Abraham because of his faith.

10 Anyone who tries to please God by obeying the Law is under a curse. The Scriptures say, "Everyone who doesn't obey everything in the Law is under a curse." 11 No one can please God by obeying the Law. The Scriptures also say, "The people God accepts because of their faith will live."[d]

12 The Law isn't based on faith. It promises life only to people who obey its commands. 13 But Christ rescued us from the Law's curse, when he became a curse in our place. This is because the Scriptures say that anyone who is nailed to a tree is under a curse. 14 And because of what Jesus Christ has done, the blessing that was promised to Abraham was taken to the Gentiles. This happened so that by faith we would be given the promised Holy Spirit.

The Law and the Promise

15 My friends, I will use an everyday example to explain what I mean. Once someone agrees to something, no one else can change or cancel the agreement.[e] 16 That is how it is with the promises God made to Abraham and his descendant.[f] The promises were not made to many descend-

[c] **3.7** *a child of Abraham*: God chose Abraham, and so it was believed that anyone who was a child of Abraham was also a child of God (see the note at 3.29). [d] **3.11** *The people God accepts because of their faith will live*: Or "The people God accepts will live because of their faith." [e] **3.15** *Once someone . . . cancel the agreement*: Or "Once a person makes out a will, no one can change or cancel it." [f] **3.16** *descendant*: The Greek text has "seed," which may mean one or many descendants. In this verse Paul says it means Christ.

2.16 a Ps 143.2; Ro 3.20; **b** Ro 3.22. **3.6** Gn 15.6; Ro 4.3. **3.7** Ro 4.16. **3.8** Gn 12.3. **3.10** Dt 27.14-26 (LXX); 4 Macc 5.20. **3.11** Hb 2.4. **3.12** Lv 18.5. **3.13** Dt 21.23.

ants, but only to one, and that one is
Christ. 17 What I am saying is that the Law
cannot change or cancel God's promise
that was made 430 years before the Law
was given. 18 If we have to obey the Law in
order to receive God's blessings, those
blessings don't really come to us because of
God's promise. But God was kind to Abraham and made him a promise.

19 What is the use of the Law? It was
given later to show that we sin. But it was
only supposed to last until the coming of
that descendant[g] who was given the
promise. In fact, angels gave the Law to
Moses, and he gave it to the people.
20 There is only one God, and the Law did
not come directly from him.

Slaves and Children

21 Does the Law disagree with God's
promises? No, it doesn't! If any law could
give life to us, we could become acceptable
to God by obeying that law. 22 But the
Scriptures say that sin controls everyone,
so that God's promises will be for anyone
who has faith in Jesus Christ.

23 The Law controlled us and kept us
under its power until the time came when
we would have faith. 24 In fact, the Law
was our teacher. It was supposed to teach
us until we had faith and were acceptable
to God. 25 But once a person has learned to
have faith, there is no more need to have
the Law as a teacher.

26 All of you are God's children because
of your faith in Christ Jesus. 27 And when
you were baptized, it was as though you
had put on Christ in the same way you put
on new clothes. 28 Faith in Christ Jesus is
what makes each of you equal with each
other, whether you are a Jew or a Greek, a
slave or a free person, a man or a woman.
29 So if you belong to Christ, you are now
part of Abraham's family,[h] and you will be
4 given what God has promised. 1 Children who are under age are no better
off than slaves, even though everything
their parents own will someday be theirs.
2 This is because children are placed in the
care of guardians and teachers until the
time their parents have set. 3 That is how it
was with us. We were like children ruled by
the powers of this world.

4 But when the time was right, God sent
his Son, and a woman gave birth to him.
His Son obeyed the Law, 5 so he could set
us free from the Law, and we could become
God's children. 6 Now that we are his children, God has sent the Spirit of his Son
into our hearts. And his Spirit tells us that
God is our Father. 7 You are no longer
slaves. You are God's children, and you will
be given what he has promised.

Paul's Concern for the Galatians

8 Before you knew God, you were slaves
of gods that are not real. 9 But now you
know God, or better still, God knows you.
How can you turn back and become the
slaves of those weak and pitiful powers?[i]
10 You even celebrate certain days, months,
seasons, and years. 11 I am afraid I have
wasted my time working with you.

12 My friends, I beg you to be like me,
just as I once tried to be like you. Did you
mistreat me 13 when I first preached to
you? No you didn't, even though you knew
I had come there because I was sick. 14 My
illness must have caused you some trouble,
but you didn't hate me or turn me away because of it. You welcomed me as though I
were one of God's angels or even Christ
Jesus himself. 15 Where is that good feeling
now? I am sure that if it had been possible,
you would have taken out your own eyes
and given them to me. 16 Am I now your
enemy, just because I told you the truth?

17 Those people may be paying you a lot
of attention, but it isn't for your good. They
only want to keep you away from me, so
you will pay them a lot of attention. 18 It is
always good to give your attention to something worthwhile, even when I am not with
you. 19 My children, I am in terrible pain

[g] **3.19** *that descendant*: Jesus. [h] **3.29** *you are now part of Abraham's family*: Paul tells the Galatians that faith in Jesus Christ is what makes someone a true child of Abraham and of God (see the note at 3.7). [i] **4.9** *powers*: Spirits were thought to control human lives and were believed to be connected with the movements of the stars.

3.17 Ex 12.40, 41. **3.18** Ro 4.14. **3.29** Ro 4.13. **4.5-7** Ro 8.15-17. **4.6** 2 Esd 10.7.

until Christ may be seen living in you. [20] I
wish I were with you now. Then I would
not have to talk this way. You really have
me puzzled.

Hagar and Sarah

[21] Some of you would like to be under
the rule of the Law of Moses. But do you
know what the Law says? [22] In the Scriptures we learn that Abraham had two sons.
The mother of one of them was a slave,
while the mother of the other one had always been free. [23] The son of the slave
woman was born in the usual way. But the
son of the free woman was born because of
God's promise.

[24] All of this has another meaning as
well. Each of the two women stands for
one of the agreements God made with his
people. Hagar, the slave woman, stands for
the agreement that was made at Mount
Sinai. Everyone born into her family is a
slave. [25] Hagar also stands for Mount Sinai
in Arabia[j] and for the present city of Jerusalem. She[k] and her children are slaves.

[26] But our mother is the city of Jerusalem in heaven above, and she isn't a slave.
[27] The Scriptures say about her,

"You have never had children,
but now you can be glad.
You have never given birth,
but now you can shout.
Once you had no children,
but now you will have
more children than a woman
who has been married
for a long time."

[28] My friends, you were born because of
this promise, just as Isaac was. [29] But the
child who was born in the natural way
made trouble for the child who was born
because of the Spirit. The same thing is
happening today. [30] The Scriptures say,
"Get rid of the slave woman and her son!
He won't be given anything. The son of the
free woman will receive everything." [31] My
friends, we are children of the free woman
and not of the slave.

Christ Gives Freedom

5 Christ has set us free! This means we
are really free. Now hold on to your
freedom and don't ever become slaves of
the Law again.

[2] I, Paul, promise you that Christ won't
do you any good if you get circumcised. [3] If
you do, you must obey the whole Law.
[4] And if you try to please God by obeying
the Law, you have cut yourself off from
Christ and his wonderful kindness. [5] But
the Spirit makes us sure that God will accept us because of our faith in Christ. [6] If
you are a follower of Christ Jesus, it makes
no difference whether you are circumcised
or not. All that matters is your faith that
makes you love others.

[7] You were doing so well until someone
made you turn from the truth. [8] And that
person was certainly not sent by the one
who chose you. [9] A little yeast can change a
whole batch of dough, [10] but you belong to
the Lord. That makes me certain that you
will do what I say, instead of what someone
else tells you to do. Whoever is causing
trouble for you will be punished.

[11] My friends, if I still preach that people need to be circumcised, why am I in so
much trouble? The message about the
cross would no longer be a problem, if I
told people to be circumcised. [12] I wish that
everyone who is upsetting you would not
only get circumcised, but would cut off
much more!

[13] My friends, you were chosen to be
free. So don't use your freedom as an excuse to do anything you want. Use it as an
opportunity to serve each other with love.
[14] All that the Law says can be summed up
in the command to love others as much as
you love yourself. [15] But if you keep attacking each other like wild animals, you had
better watch out or you will destroy yourselves.

[j]**4.25** *Hagar also stands for Mount Sinai in Arabia*: Some manuscripts have "Sinai is a mountain in Arabia." This sentence would then be translated: "Sinai is a mountain in Arabia, and Hagar stands for the present city of Jerusalem." [k]**4.25** *She*: "Hagar" or "Jerusalem."

4.22 a Gn 16.15, 16; **b** Gn 21.2. **4.26** 2 Esd 2.2; 10.7. **4.27** Is 54.1 (LXX). **4.29** Gn 21.9,10. **4.30** Gn 21.9,10. **5.9** 1 Co 5.6. **5.14** Lv 19.18.

God's Spirit and Our Own Desires

16 If you are guided by the Spirit, you won't obey your selfish desires. 17 The Spirit and your desires are enemies of each other. They are always fighting each other and keeping you from doing what you feel you should. 18 But if you obey the Spirit, the Law of Moses has no control over you.

19 People's desires make them give in to immoral ways, filthy thoughts, and shameful deeds. 20 They worship idols, practice witchcraft, hate others, and are hard to get along with. People become jealous, angry, and selfish. They not only argue and cause trouble, but they are 21 envious. They get drunk, carry on at wild parties, and do other evil things as well. I told you before, and I am telling you again: No one who does these things will share in the blessings of God's kingdom.

22 God's Spirit makes us loving, happy, peaceful, patient, kind, good, faithful, 23 gentle, and self-controlled. There is no law against behaving in any of these ways. 24 And because we belong to Christ Jesus, we have killed our selfish feelings and desires. 25 God's Spirit has given us life, and so we should follow the Spirit. 26 But don't be conceited or make others jealous by claiming to be better than they are.

Help Each Other

6 My friends, you are spiritual. So if someone is trapped in sin, you should gently lead that person back to the right path. But watch out, and don't be tempted yourself. 2 You obey the law of Christ when you offer each other a helping hand.

3 If you think you are better than others, when you really aren't, you are wrong. 4 Do your own work well, and then you will have something to be proud of. But don't compare yourself with others. 5 We each must carry our own load.

6 Share every good thing you have with anyone who teaches you what God has said.

7 You cannot fool God, so don't make a fool of yourself! You will harvest what you plant. 8 If you follow your selfish desires, you will harvest destruction, but if you follow the Spirit, you will harvest eternal life. 9 Don't get tired of helping others. You will be rewarded when the time is right, if you don't give up. 10 We should help people whenever we can, especially if they are followers of the Lord.

Final Warnings

11 You can see what big letters I make when I write with my own hand.

12 Those people who are telling you to get circumcised are only trying to show how important they are. And they don't want to get into trouble for preaching about the cross of Christ. 13 They are circumcised, but they don't obey the Law of Moses. All they want is to brag about having you circumcised. 14 But I will never brag about anything except the cross of our Lord Jesus Christ. Because of his cross, the world is dead as far as I am concerned, and I am dead as far as the world is concerned.

15 It doesn't matter if you are circumcised or not. All that matters is that you are a new person.

16 If you follow this rule, you will belong to God's true people. God will treat you with undeserved kindness and will bless you with peace.

17 On my own body are scars that prove I belong to Christ Jesus. So I don't want anyone to bother me anymore.

18 My friends, I pray that the Lord Jesus Christ will be kind to you! Amen.

5.17 Ro 7.15-23. **6.17** 3 Macc 2.29.

EPHESIANS

ABOUT THIS LETTER

"Praise the God and Father of our Lord Jesus Christ for the spiritual blessings that Christ has brought us from heaven!" (1.3). Paul begins his letter to the Christians in Ephesus with a powerful reminder of the main theme of his message. Christ died on the cross to set us free (1.7, 8). But God raised Christ from death, and he now sits at God's right side in heaven, where he rules over this world. And he will rule over the future world as well (1.20, 21).

Christ brought Jews and Gentiles together by "breaking down the wall of hatred" that separated them (2.14) and he united them all as part of that holy temple where God's Spirit lives (2.22). This was according to God's eternal plan (3.11).

There is only one Lord, one Spirit of God, and one God, who is the Father of all people (4.4, 5). This means that Christians must let the Spirit keep their hearts united, so they can live at peace with each other (4.3). The idea of all Christians being one with Christ is so central to this letter that it occurs twenty times. There is one faith and one baptism by which believers become one body.

Ephesus was a port city on the western shore of Asia Minor (modern-day Turkey). In Paul's time this was the fourth largest city in the Roman Empire. It was also an ancient center of nature religion where the goddess Artemis was widely worshiped (Acts 19).

Paul lets the Ephesians know that much is expected of people who are called to a new life (4.17—5.20). Followers of the Lord are God's dear children, and they must do as God does (5.1). They used to live in the dark, but they must now live in the light and make their light shine (5.8, 9).

Paul then teaches husbands and wives, children and parents, and slaves and masters how to live as Christians (5.21—6.9).

Paul never forgets how kind God is:

> *God was merciful! We were dead because of our sins, but God loved us so much that he made us alive with Christ, and God's wonderful kindness is what saves you. . . . You were saved by faith in God, who treats us much better than we deserve. This is God's gift to you, and not anything you have done on your own.*
>
> *(2.4, 5, 8)*

A QUICK LOOK AT THIS LETTER

- Greetings (1.1, 2)
- Christ Brings Spiritual Blessings (1.3—3.21)
- A New Life in Unity with Christ (4.1—6.20)
- Final Greetings (6.21-24)

1 From Paul, chosen by God to be an
apostle of Christ Jesus.
To God's people who live in Ephesus
and[a] are faithful followers of Christ Jesus.
2 I pray that God our Father and our
Lord Jesus Christ will be kind to you and
will bless you with peace!

Christ Brings Spiritual Blessings

3 Praise the God and Father of our Lord
Jesus Christ for the spiritual blessings that
Christ has brought us from heaven! 4 Before the world was created, God had Christ
choose us to live with him and to be his
holy and innocent and loving people. 5 God
was kind[b] and decided that Christ would
choose us to be God's own adopted children.
6 God was very kind to us because of the Son
he dearly loves, and so we should praise God.
7-8 Christ sacrificed his life's blood to set
us free, which means that our sins are now
forgiven. Christ did this because God was
so kind to us. God has great wisdom and
understanding, 9 and by what Christ has
done, God has shown us his own mysterious ways. 10 Then when the time is right,
God will do all that he has planned, and
Christ will bring together everything in
heaven and on earth.
11 God always does what he plans, and
that's why he appointed Christ to choose
us. 12 He did this so that we Jews would
bring honor to him and be the first ones to
have hope because of him. 13 Christ also
brought you the truth, which is the good
news about how you can be saved. You put
your faith in Christ and were given the
promised Holy Spirit to show that you belong to God. 14 The Spirit also makes us
sure that we will be given what God has
stored up for his people. Then we will be set
free, and God will be honored and praised.

Paul's Prayer

15 I have heard about your faith in the
Lord Jesus and your love for all of God's
people. 16 So I never stop being grateful for
you, as I mention you in my prayers. 17 I
ask the glorious Father and God of our
Lord Jesus Christ to give you his Spirit.
The Spirit will make you wise and let you
understand what it means to know God.
18 My prayer is that light will flood your
hearts and that you will understand the
hope that was given to you when God
chose you. Then you will discover the glorious blessings that will be yours together
with all of God's people.
19 I want you to know about the great
and mighty power that God has for us followers. It is the same wonderful power he
used 20 when he raised Christ from death
and let him sit at his right side[c] in heaven.
21 There Christ rules over all forces, authorities, powers, and rulers. He rules over
all beings in this world and will rule in the
future world as well. 22 God has put all
things under the power of Christ, and for
the good of the church he has made him
the head of everything. 23 The church is
Christ's body and is filled with Christ who
completely fills everything.[d]

From Death to Life

2 In the past you were dead because you
sinned and fought against God. 2 You
followed the ways of this world and obeyed
the devil. He rules the world, and his spirit
has power over everyone who doesn't obey
God. 3 Once we were also ruled by the selfish desires of our bodies and minds. We
had made God angry, and we were going to
be punished like everyone else.
4-5 But God was merciful! We were dead
because of our sins, but God loved us so
much that he made us alive with Christ,
and God's wonderful kindness is what
saves you. 6 God raised us from death to
life with Christ Jesus, and he has given us
a place beside Christ in heaven. 7 God did
this so that in the future world he could
show how truly good and kind he is to us

[a] **1.1** *live in Ephesus and*: Some manuscripts do not have these words. [b] **1.4,5** *holy and innocent and loving people. [5]God was kind*: Or "holy and innocent people. God was loving [5]and kind." [c] **1.20** *right side*: The place of power and honor. [d] **1.23** *and is filled with Christ who completely fills everything*: Or "which completely fills Christ and fully completes his work."

1.1 Ac 18.19-21; 19.1. **1.7,8** Col 1.14. **1.20** Ps 110.1. **1.22** Ps 8.6. **1.22,23** Col 1.18. **2.1-5** Col 2.13.

because of what Christ Jesus has done.
8 You were saved by faith in God, who treats
us much better than we deserve.[e] This is
God's gift to you, and not anything you
have done on your own. 9 It isn't something
you have earned, so there is nothing you
can brag about. 10 God planned for us to do
good things and to live as he has always
wanted us to live. That's why he sent
Christ to make us what we are.

United by Christ

11 Don't forget that you are Gentiles. In
fact, you used to be called "uncircumcised"
by those who take pride in being circumcised. 12 At that time you did not know
about Christ. You were foreigners to the
people of Israel, and you had no part in the
promises that God had made to them. You
were living in this world without hope and
without God, 13 and you were far from God.
But Christ offered his life's blood as a sacrifice and brought you near God.
14 Christ has made peace between Jews
and Gentiles, and he has united us by
breaking down the wall of hatred that separated us. Christ gave his own body 15 to destroy the Law of Moses with all its rules
and commands. He even brought Jews and
Gentiles together as though we were only
one person, when he united us in peace.
16 On the cross Christ did away with our
hatred for each other. He also made peace[f]
between us and God by uniting Jews and
Gentiles in one body. 17 Christ came and
preached peace to you Gentiles, who were
far from God, and peace to us Jews, who
were near God. 18 And because of Christ,
all of us can come to the Father by the
same Spirit.
19 You Gentiles are no longer strangers
and foreigners. You are citizens with everyone else who belongs to the family of God.
20 You are like a building with the apostles and prophets as the foundation and
with Christ as the most important stone.
21 Christ is the one who holds the building
together and makes it grow into a holy temple for the Lord. 22 And you are part of that
building Christ has built as a place for
God's own Spirit to live.

Paul's Mission to the Gentiles

3 Christ Jesus made me his prisoner, so
that I could help you Gentiles. 2 You
have surely heard about God's kindness in
choosing me to help you. 3 In fact, this letter tells you a little about how God has
shown me his mysterious ways. 4 As you
read the letter, you will also find out how
well I really do understand the mystery
about Christ. 5 No one knew about this
mystery until God's Spirit told it to his holy
apostles and prophets. 6 And the mystery is
this: Because of Christ Jesus, the good
news has given the Gentiles a share in the
promises that God gave to the Jews. God
has also let the Gentiles be part of the same
body.
7 God treated me with kindness. His
power worked in me, and it became my job
to spread the good news. 8 I am the least
important of all God's people. But God was
kind and chose me to tell the Gentiles that
because of Christ there are blessings that
cannot be measured. 9 God, who created
everything, wanted me to help everyone
understand the mysterious plan that had
always been hidden in his mind. 10 Then
God would use the church to show the
powers and authorities in the spiritual
world that he has many different kinds of
wisdom.
11 God did this according to his eternal
plan. And he was able to do what he had
planned because of all that Christ Jesus
our Lord had done. 12 Christ now gives us
courage and confidence, so that we can
come to God by faith. 13 That's why you
should not be discouraged when I suffer for
you. After all, it will bring honor to you.

Christ's Love for Us

14 I kneel in prayer to the Father. 15 All
beings in heaven and on earth receive their

[e]**2.8** *treats us much better than we deserve*: The Greek word *charis*, traditionally rendered "grace," is translated here and other places in the CEV to express the overwhelming kindness of God.
[f]**2.16** *He also made peace*: Or "The cross also made peace."
2.15 Col 2.14. **2.16** Col 1.20. **2.17** Is 57.19. **3.4-6** Col 1.26, 27. **3.9** 3 Macc 2.3.

life from him.[g] 16 God is wonderful and glorious. I pray that his Spirit will make you
become strong followers 17 and that Christ
will live in your hearts because of your
faith. Stand firm and be deeply rooted in
his love. 18 I pray that you and all of God's
people will understand what is called wide
or long or high or deep.[h] 19 I want you to
know all about Christ's love, although it is
too wonderful to be measured. Then your
lives will be filled with all that God is.

20-21 I pray that Christ Jesus and the
church will forever bring praise to God. His
power at work in us can do far more than
we dare ask or imagine. Amen.

Unity with Christ

4 As a prisoner of the Lord, I beg you to
live in a way that is worthy of the people God has chosen to be his own. 2 Always
be humble and gentle. Patiently put up
with each other and love each other. 3 Try
your best to let God's Spirit keep your
hearts united. Do this by living at peace.
4 All of you are part of the same body. There
is only one Spirit of God, just as you were
given one hope when you were chosen to
be God's people. 5 We have only one Lord,
one faith, and one baptism. 6 There is one
God who is the Father of all people. Not
only is God above all others, but he works
by using all of us, and he lives in all of us.

7 Christ has generously divided out his
gifts to us. 8 As the Scriptures say,

"When he went up
to the highest place,
he led away many prisoners
and gave gifts to people."

9 When it says, "he went up," it means
that Christ had been deep in the earth.
10 This also means that the one who went
deep into the earth is the same one who
went into the highest heaven, so that he
would fill the whole universe.

11 Christ chose some of us to be apostles, prophets, missionaries, pastors, and
teachers, 12 so that his people would learn to
serve and his body would grow strong. 13 This
will continue until we are united by our faith
and by our understanding of the Son of God.
Then we will be mature, just as Christ is,
and we will be completely like him.[i]

14 We must stop acting like children. We
must not let deceitful people trick us by
their false teachings, which are like winds
that toss us around from place to place.
15 Love should always make us tell the
truth. Then we will grow in every way and
be more like Christ, the head 16 of the body.
Christ holds it together and makes all of its
parts work perfectly, as it grows and becomes strong because of love.

The Old Life and the New Life

17 As a follower of the Lord, I order you
to stop living like stupid, godless people.
18 Their minds are in the dark, and they
are stubborn and ignorant and have missed
out on the life that comes from God. They
no longer have any feelings about what is
right, 19 and they are so greedy that they do
all kinds of indecent things.

20-21 But that isn't what you were taught
about Jesus Christ. He is the truth, and you
heard about him and learned about him.
22 You were told that your foolish desires
will destroy you and that you must give up
your old way of life with all its bad habits.
23 Let the Spirit change your way of thinking 24 and make you into a new person. You
were created to be like God, and so you
must please him and be truly holy.

Rules for the New Life

25 We are part of the same body. Stop lying and start telling each other the truth.
26 Don't get so angry that you sin. Don't go
to bed angry 27 and don't give the devil a
chance.

28 If you are a thief, quit stealing. Be
honest and work hard, so you will have
something to give to people in need.

29 Stop all your dirty talk. Say the right

[g] **3.15** *receive their life from him*: Or "know who they really are because of him." [h] **3.18** *what is called wide or long or high or deep*: This may refer to the heavenly Jerusalem or to God's love or wisdom or to the meaning of the cross. [i] **4.13** *and we will be completely like him*: Or "and he is completely perfect."

3.18 Si 1.3. **4.2** Col 3.12, 13. **4.8** Ps 68.18. **4.16** Col 2.19. **4.22** Col 3.9. **4.24** **a** Col 3.10; **b** Gn 1.26; Ws 9.3. **4.25** Zec 8.16. **4.26** Ps 4.4 (LXX).

thing at the right time and help others by
what you say.
30 Don't make God's Spirit sad. The
Spirit makes you sure that someday you
will be free from your sins.
31 Stop being bitter and angry and mad
at others. Don't yell at one another or curse
each other or ever be rude. 32 Instead, be
kind and merciful, and forgive others, just
as God forgave you because of Christ.

5 Do as God does. After all, you are his
dear children. 2 Let love be your guide.
Christ loved us[j] and offered his life for us
as a sacrifice that pleases God.
3 You are God's people, so don't let it be
said that any of you are immoral or indecent or greedy. 4 Don't use dirty or foolish
or filthy words. Instead, say how thankful
you are. 5 Being greedy, indecent, or immoral is just another way of worshiping
idols. You can be sure that people who behave in this way will never be part of the
kingdom that belongs to Christ and to God.

Living as People of Light

6 Don't let anyone trick you with foolish
talk. God punishes everyone who disobeys
him and says[k] foolish things. 7 So don't
have anything to do with anyone like that.
8 You used to be like people living in the
dark, but now you are people of the light
because you belong to the Lord. So act like
people of the light 9 and make your light
shine. Be good and honest and truthful,
10 as you try to please the Lord. 11 Don't
take part in doing those worthless things
that are done in the dark. Instead, show
how wrong they are. 12 It is disgusting even
to talk about what is done in the dark.
13 But the light will show what these things
are really like. 14 Light shows up everything,[l] just as the Scriptures say,

"Wake up from your sleep
and rise from death.
Then Christ will shine on you."

15 Act like people with good sense and
not like fools. 16 These are evil times, so
make every minute count. 17 Don't be stupid. Instead, find out what the Lord wants
you to do. 18 Don't destroy yourself by getting drunk, but let the Spirit fill your life.
19 When you meet together, sing psalms,
hymns, and spiritual songs, as you praise
the Lord with all your heart. 20 Always use
the name of our Lord Jesus Christ to thank
God the Father for everything.

Wives and Husbands

21 Honor Christ and put others first.
22 A wife should put her husband first, as
she does the Lord. 23 A husband is the
head of his wife, as Christ is the head and
the Savior of the church, which is his own
body. 24 Wives should always put their husbands first, as the church puts Christ first.
25 A husband should love his wife as
much as Christ loved the church and gave
his life for it. 26 He made the church holy
by the power of his word, and he made it
pure by washing it with water. 27 Christ did
this, so that he would have a glorious and
holy church, without faults or spots or
wrinkles or any other flaws.
28 In the same way, a husband should
love his wife as much as he loves himself. A
husband who loves his wife shows that he
loves himself. 29 None of us hate our own
bodies. We provide for them and take good
care of them, just as Christ does for the
church, 30 because we are each part of
his body. 31 As the Scriptures say, "A man
leaves his father and mother to get married, and he becomes like one person with
his wife." 32 This is a great mystery, but
I understand it to mean Christ and his
church. 33 So each husband should love his
wife as much as he loves himself, and each
wife should respect her husband.

Children and Parents

6 Children, you belong to the Lord, and
you do the right thing when you obey
your parents. The first commandment with
a promise says, 2 "Obey your father and

[j]5.2 *us*: Some manuscripts have "you." [k]5.6 *says*: Or "does." [l]5.14 *Light shows up everything*: Or "Everything that is seen in the light becomes light itself."

4.32 Col 3.13. **5.2** Ex 29.18; Ps 40.6. **5.16** Col 4.5. **5.19,20** Col 3.16, 17. **5.22** Col 3.18; 1 P 3.1. **5.25** Col 3.19; 1 P 3.7. **5.31** Gn 2.24. **6.1** Col 3.20. **6.2,3** Ex 20.12; Dt 5.16.

your mother, 3 and you will have a long and
happy life."
4 Parents, don't be hard on your children. Raise them properly. Teach them and
instruct them about the Lord.

Slaves and Masters

5 Slaves, you must obey your earthly
masters. Show them great respect and be
as loyal to them as you are to Christ. 6 Try
to please them at all times, and not just
when you think they are watching. You are
slaves of Christ, so with your whole heart
you must do what God wants you to do.
7 Gladly serve your masters, as though they
were the Lord himself, and not simply people. 8 You know that you will be rewarded
for any good things you do, whether you are
slaves or free.
9 Slave owners, you must treat your
slaves with this same respect. Don't
threaten them. They have the same Master
in heaven that you do, and he doesn't have
any favorites.

The Fight against Evil

10 Finally, let the mighty strength of the
Lord make you strong. 11 Put on all the armor that God gives, so you can defend
yourself against the devil's tricks. 12 We are
not fighting against humans. We are fighting against forces and authorities and
against rulers of darkness and powers in
the spiritual world. 13 So put on all the armor that God gives. Then when that evil
day[m] comes, you will be able to defend
yourself. And when the battle is over, you
will still be standing firm.
14 Be ready! Let the truth be like a belt
around your waist, and let God's justice
protect you like armor. 15 Your desire to tell
the good news about peace should be like
shoes on your feet. 16 Let your faith be like
a shield, and you will be able to stop all the
flaming arrows of the evil one. 17 Let God's
saving power be like a helmet, and for a
sword use God's message that comes from
the Spirit.
18 Never stop praying, especially for others. Always pray by the power of the Spirit.
Stay alert and keep praying for God's people. 19 Pray that I will be given the message
to speak and that I may fearlessly explain
the mystery about the good news. 20 I was
sent to do this work, and that's the reason I
am in jail. So pray that I will be brave and
will speak as I should.

Final Greetings

21-22 I want you to know how I am getting along and what I am doing. That's why
I am sending Tychicus to you. He is a dear
friend, as well as a faithful servant of the
Lord. He will tell you how I am doing, and
he will cheer you up.
23 I pray that God the Father and the
Lord Jesus Christ will give peace, love, and
faith to every follower! 24 May God be kind
to everyone who keeps on loving our Lord
Jesus Christ.

[m]**6.13** *that evil day*: Either the present (see 5.16) or "the day of death" or "the day of judgment."

6.4 Col 3.21. **6.5-8** Col 3.22-25. **6.9** **a** Col 4.1; **b** Dt 10.17; Col 3.25.
6.11 Ws 5.17. **6.14-17** Ws 5.18-23. **6.14** **a** Is 11.5; **b** Is 59.17. **6.15** Is 52.7.
6.17 Is 59.17. **6.21,22** Ac 20.4; 2 Ti 4.12; Col. 4.7, 8.

PHILIPPIANS

ABOUT THIS LETTER

Paul wrote this letter from jail (1.7) to thank the Lord's followers at Philippi for helping him with their gifts and prayers (1.5; 4.10-19). He hopes to be set free, so that he can continue preaching the good news (3.17-19). But he knows that he might be put to death (1.21; 2.17; 3.10).

The city of Philippi is in the part of northern Greece known as Macedonia. It was at Philippi that Paul had entered Europe for the first time, and there he preached the good news and began a church (Acts 16). He now warns the Christians at Philippi that they may have to suffer, just as Christ suffered and Paul is now suffering. If this happens, the Philippians should count it a blessing that comes from having faith in Christ (1.28-30).

There were problems in the church at Philippi, because some of the members claimed that people must obey the law of Moses, or they could not be saved. But Paul has no patience with such members and warns the church, "Watch out for those people who behave like dogs!" (3.2-11). This letter is also filled with joy. Even in jail, Paul is happy because he has discovered how to make the best of a bad situation and because he remembers all the kindness shown to him by the people in the church at Philippi.

Paul reminds them that God's people are to live in harmony (2.2; 4.2, 3) and to think the same way that Christ Jesus did:

Christ was truly God.
But he did not try to remain
equal with God.
Instead he gave up everything
and became a slave,
when he became
like one of us.
(2.6, 7)

A QUICK LOOK AT THIS LETTER

- Greetings and a Prayer (1.1-11)
- What Life Means to Paul (1.12-30)
- Christ's Example of True Humility (2.1-18)
- News about Paul's Friends (2.19-30)
- Being Acceptable to God (3.1—4.9)
- Paul Thanks the Philippians (4.10-20)
- Final Greetings (4.21-23)

1 From Paul and Timothy, servants of Christ Jesus.

To all of God's people who belong to Christ Jesus at Philippi and to all of your church officials and officers.[a]

2 I pray that God our Father and the Lord Jesus Christ will be kind to you and will bless you with peace!

Paul's Prayer for the Church in Philippi

3 Every time I think of you, I thank my God. 4 And whenever I mention you in my prayers, it makes me happy. 5 This is because you have taken part with me in spreading the good news from the first day you heard about it. 6 God is the one who began this good work in you, and I am certain that he won't stop before it is complete on the day that Christ Jesus returns.

7 You have a special place in my heart. So it is only natural for me to feel the way I do. All of you have helped in the work that God has given me, as I defend the good news and tell about it here in jail. 8 God himself knows how much I want to see you. He knows that I care for you in the same way that Christ Jesus does.

9 I pray that your love will keep on growing and that you will fully know and understand 10 how to make the right choices. Then you will still be pure and innocent when Christ returns. And until that day, 11 Jesus Christ will keep you busy doing good deeds that bring glory and praise to God.

What Life Means to Paul

12 My dear friends, I want you to know that what has happened to me has helped to spread the good news. 13 The Roman guards and all the others know that I am here in jail because I serve Christ. 14 Now most of the Lord's followers have become brave and are fearlessly telling the message.[b]

15 Some are preaching about Christ because they are jealous and envious of us. Others are preaching because they want to help. 16 They love Christ and know that I am here to defend the good news about him. 17 But the ones who are jealous of us are not sincere. They just want to cause trouble for me while I am in jail. 18 But that doesn't matter. All that matters is that people are telling about Christ, whether they are sincere or not. That is what makes me glad.

I will keep on being glad, 19 because I know that your prayers and the help that comes from the Spirit of Christ Jesus will keep me safe. 20 I honestly expect and hope that I will never do anything to be ashamed of. Whether I live or die, I always want to be as brave as I am now and bring honor to Christ.

21 If I live, it will be for Christ, and if I die, I will gain even more. 22 I don't know what to choose. I could keep on living and doing something useful. 23 It is a hard choice to make. I want to die and be with Christ, because that would be much better. 24-25 But I know that all of you still need me. That's why I am sure I will stay on to help you grow and be happy in your faith. 26 Then, when I visit you again, you will have good reason to take great pride in Christ Jesus because of me.[c]

27 Above all else, you must live in a way that brings honor to the good news about Christ. Then, whether I visit you or not, I will hear that all of you think alike. I will know that you are working together and that you are struggling side by side to get others to believe the good news.

28 Be brave when you face your enemies. Your courage will show them that they are going to be destroyed, and it will show you that you will be saved. God will make all of this happen, 29 and he has blessed you. Not only do you have faith in Christ, but you suffer for him. 30 You saw me suffer, and you still hear about my troubles. Now you must suffer in the same way.

[a]**1.1** *church officials and officers*: Or "bishops and deacons." [b]**1.14** *the message*: Some manuscripts have "the Lord's message," and others have "God's message." [c]**1.26** *take great pride in Christ Jesus because of me*: Or "take great pride in me because of Christ Jesus."

1.1 Ac 16.12. **1.13** Ac 28.30. **1.30** Ac 16.19-40.

True Humility

2 Christ encourages you, and his love
comforts you. God's Spirit unites you,
and you are concerned for others. 2 Now
make me completely happy! Live in harmony by showing love for each other.
Be united in what you think, as if you
were only one person. 3 Don't be jealous or
proud, but be humble and consider others
more important than yourselves. 4 Care
about them as much as you care about
yourselves 5 and think the same way that
Christ Jesus thought:[d]

6 Christ was truly God.
But he did not try to remain[e]
equal with God.
7 Instead he gave up everything[f]
and became a slave,
when he became
like one of us.

8 Christ was humble.
He obeyed God and even died
on a cross.
9 Then God gave Christ
the highest place
and honored his name
above all others.

10 So at the name of Jesus
everyone will bow down,
those in heaven, on earth,
and under the earth.
11 And to the glory
of God the Father
everyone will openly agree,
"Jesus Christ is Lord!"

Lights in the World

12 My dear friends, you always obeyed
when I was with you. Now that I am away,
you should obey even more. So work with
fear and trembling to discover what it really
means to be saved. 13 God is working in you
to make you willing and able to obey him.

14 Do everything without grumbling or
arguing. 15 Then you will be the pure and
innocent children of God. You live among
people who are crooked and evil, but you
must not do anything that they can say is
wrong. Try to shine as lights among the
people of this world, 16 as you hold firmly
to[g] the message that gives life. Then on the
day when Christ returns, I can take pride
in you. I can also know that my work and
efforts were not useless.

17 Your faith in the Lord and your service are like a sacrifice offered to him. And
my own blood may have to be poured out
with the sacrifice.[h] If this happens, I will
be glad and rejoice with you. 18 In the
same way, you should be glad and rejoice
with me.

Timothy and Epaphroditus

19 I want to be encouraged by news
about you. So I hope the Lord Jesus will
soon let me send Timothy to you. 20 I don't
have anyone else who cares about you as
much as he does. 21 The others think only
about what interests them and not about
what concerns Christ Jesus. 22 But you
know what kind of person Timothy is. He
has worked with me like a son in spreading
the good news. 23 I hope to send him to
you, as soon as I find out what is going to
happen to me. 24 And I feel sure that the
Lord will also let me come soon.

25 I think I ought to send my dear friend
Epaphroditus back to you. He is a follower
and a worker and a soldier of the Lord, just
as I am. You sent him to look after me,
26 but now he is eager to see you. He is
worried, because you heard he was sick.
27 In fact, he was very sick and almost died.
But God was kind to him, and also to me,
and he kept me from being burdened down
with sorrow.

28 Now I am more eager than ever to
send Epaphroditus back again. You will be
glad to see him, and I won't have to worry

[d]**2.5** *think the same way that Christ Jesus thought*: Or "think the way you should because you belong to Christ Jesus." [e]**2.6** *remain*: Or "become." [f]**2.7** *He gave up everything*: Greek, "He emptied himself." [g]**2.16** *hold firmly to*: Or "offer them." [h]**2.17** *my own blood may have to be poured out with the sacrifice*: Offerings of water or wine were sometimes poured out when animals were sacrificed on the altar.

2.10,11 Is 45.23 (LXX). **2.15** Dt 32.5.

any longer. 29 Be sure to give him a cheerful welcome, just as people who serve the
Lord deserve. 30 He almost died working
for Christ, and he risked his own life to do
for me what you could not.

Being Acceptable to God

3 Finally, my dear friends, be glad that
you belong to the Lord. It doesn't
bother me to write the same things to you
that I have written before. In fact, it is for
your own good.

2 Watch out for those people who behave like dogs! They are evil and want to
do more than just circumcise you. 3 But we
are the ones who are truly circumcised, because we worship by the power of God's
Spirit[i] and take pride in Christ Jesus. We
don't brag about what we have done, 4 although I could. Others may brag about
themselves, but I have more reason to brag
than anyone else. 5 I was circumcised
when I was eight days old,[j] and I am from
the nation of Israel and the tribe of Benjamin. I am a true Hebrew. As a Pharisee, I
strictly obeyed the Law of Moses. 6 And I
was so eager that I even made trouble for
the church. I did everything the Law demands in order to please God.

7 But Christ has shown me that what I
once thought was valuable is worthless.
8 Nothing is as wonderful as knowing
Christ Jesus my Lord. I have given up
everything else and count it all as garbage.
All I want is Christ 9 and to know that I belong to him. I could not make myself acceptable to God by obeying the Law of
Moses. God accepted me simply because of
my faith in Christ. 10 All I want is to know
Christ and the power that raised him to
life. I want to suffer and die as he did, 11 so
that somehow I also may be raised to life.

Running toward the Goal

12 I have not yet reached my goal, and I
am not perfect. But Christ has taken hold
of me. So I keep on running and struggling
to take hold of the prize. 13 My friends, I
don't feel that I have already arrived. But I
forget what is behind, and I struggle for
what is ahead. 14 I run toward the goal, so
that I can win the prize of being called to
heaven. This is the prize that God offers
because of what Christ Jesus has done.
15 All of us who are mature should think in
this same way. And if any of you think differently, God will make it clear to you.
16 But we must keep going in the direction
that we are now headed.

17 My friends, I want you to follow my
example and learn from others who closely
follow the example we set for you. 18 I often
warned you that many people are living as
enemies of the cross of Christ. And now
with tears in my eyes, I warn you again
19 that they are headed for hell! They worship their stomachs and brag about the disgusting things they do. All they can think
about are the things of this world.

20 But we are citizens of heaven and are
eagerly waiting for our Savior to come from
there. Our Lord Jesus Christ 21 has power
over everything, and he will make these
poor bodies of ours like his own glorious
body.

4 Dear friends, I love you and long to
see you. Please keep on being faithful
to the Lord. You are my pride and joy.

Paul Encourages the Lord's Followers

2 Euodia and Syntyche, you belong to
the Lord, so I beg you to stop arguing with
each other. 3 And, my true partner,[k] I ask
you to help them. These women have
worked together with me and with Clement
and with the others in spreading the good
news. Their names are now written in the
book of life.[l]

4 Always be glad because of the Lord! I
will say it again: Be glad. 5 Always be gentle
with others. The Lord will soon be here.
6 Don't worry about anything, but pray
about everything. With thankful hearts offer up your prayers and requests to God.

[i] **3.3** *by the power of God's Spirit*: Some manuscripts have "sincerely." [j] **3.5** *when I was eight days old*: Jewish boys are circumcised eight days after birth. [k] **4.3** *partner*: Or "Syzygus," a person's name. [l] **4.3** *the book of life*: A book in which the names of God's people are written.

3.5 a Ro 11.1; **b** Ac 23.6; 26.4, 5. **3.6** Ac 8.3; 22.4; 26.9-11. **3.17** 1 Co 4.16; 11.1. **3.21** 4 Macc 9.22.

7 Then, because you belong to Christ Jesus,
God will bless you with peace that no one
can completely understand. And this peace
will control the way you think and feel.
8 Finally, my friends, keep your minds
on whatever is true, pure, right, holy,
friendly, and proper. Don't ever stop thinking about what is truly worthwhile and worthy of praise. 9 You know the teachings I
gave you, and you know what you heard me
say and saw me do. So follow my example.
And God, who gives peace, will be with you.

Paul Gives Thanks for the Gifts He Was Given

10 The Lord has made me very grateful
that at last you have thought about me
once again. Actually, you were thinking
about me all along, but you didn't have any
chance to show it. 11 I am not complaining
about having too little. I have learned to be
satisfied with[m] whatever I have. 12 I know
what it is to be poor or to have plenty, and I
have lived under all kinds of conditions. I
know what it means to be full or to be hungry, to have too much or too little. 13 Christ
gives me the strength to face anything.
14 It was good of you to help me when I
was having such a hard time. 15 My friends
at Philippi, you remember what it was like
when I started preaching the good news in
Macedonia.[n] After I left there, you were the
only church that became my partner by giving blessings and by receiving them in return. 16 Even when I was in Thessalonica,
you helped me more than once. 17 I am not
trying to get something from you, but I
want you to receive the blessings that come
from giving.
18 I have been paid back everything, and
with interest. I am completely satisfied with
the gifts that you had Epaphroditus bring
me. They are like a sweet-smelling offering
or like the right kind of sacrifice that
pleases God. 19 I pray that God will take
care of all your needs with the wonderful
blessings that come from Christ Jesus!
20 May God our Father be praised forever
and ever. Amen.

Final Greetings

21 Give my greetings to all who are God's
people because of Christ Jesus.
The Lord's followers here with me send
you their greetings.
22 All of God's people send their greetings, especially those in the service of the
Emperor.
23 I pray that our Lord Jesus Christ will
be kind to you and will bless your life!

[m] **4.11** *be satisfied with*: Or "get by on." [n] **4.15** *when I started preaching the good news in Macedonia*: Paul is talking about his first visit to Philippi (see Acts 16.12-40).

4.16 Ac 17.1. **4.15,16** 2 Co 11.9. **4.18** Ex 29.18.

COLOSSIANS

ABOUT THIS LETTER

Colossae was an important city in western Asia Minor, about 100 miles east of the port city of Ephesus. Paul had never been to Colossae, but he was pleased to learn that the Christians there were strong in their faith (1.3-7; 2.6, 7). They had heard the good news from a man named Epaphras who had lived there (1.7; 4.12, 13), but was in jail with Paul (Philemon 23) at the time that Paul wrote this letter (1.14; 4.3, 10, 18).

Many of the church members in Colossae were Gentiles (1.27), and some of them were influenced by strange religious ideas and practices (2.16-23). They thought that to obey God fully they must give up certain physical desires and worship angels and other spiritual powers. But Paul wanted them to know that Christ was with God in heaven, ruling over all powers in the universe (3.1). And so, their worship should be directed to Christ.

Paul quotes a beautiful hymn that explains who Christ is:

Christ is exactly like God,
who cannot be seen.
He is the first-born Son,
superior to all creation.

God himself was pleased
to live fully in his Son.
And God was pleased
for him to make peace
by sacrificing his blood
on the cross.
(1.15, 19, 20a)

A QUICK LOOK AT THIS LETTER

- Greetings (1.1, 2)
- A Prayer of Thanks (1.3-8)
- The Person and Work of Christ (1.9—2.19)
- New Life with Christ (2.20—4.6)
- Final Greetings (4.7-18)

---

1 From Paul, chosen by God to be an
apostle of Christ Jesus, and from Timothy, who is also a follower.
2 To God's people who live in Colossae
and are faithful followers of Christ.

I pray that God our Father will be kind to you and will bless you with peace!

A Prayer of Thanks

3 Each time we pray for you, we thank
God, the Father of our Lord Jesus Christ.
4 We have heard of your faith in Christ and
of your love for all of God's people, 5 because what you hope for is kept safe for you
in heaven. You first heard about this hope

when you believed the true message, which is the good news.
6 The good news is spreading all over the world with great success. It has spread in that same way among you, ever since the first day you learned the truth about God's wonderful kindness
7 from our good friend Epaphras. He works together with us for Christ and is a faithful worker for you.[a]
8 He is also the one who told us about the love that God's Spirit has given you.

The Person and Work of Christ

9 We have not stopped praying for you since the first day we heard about you. In fact, we always pray that God will show you everything he wants you to do and that you may have all the wisdom and understanding that his Spirit gives.
10 Then you will live a life that honors the Lord, and you will always please him by doing good deeds. You will come to know God even better.
11 His glorious power will make you patient and strong enough to endure anything, and you will be truly happy.
12 I pray that you will be grateful to God for letting you[a] have part in what he has promised his people in the kingdom of light.
13 God rescued us from the dark power of Satan and brought us into the kingdom of his dear Son,
14 who forgives our sins and sets us free.

15 Christ is exactly like God,
who cannot be seen.
He is the first-born Son,
superior to all creation.
16 Everything was created by him,
everything in heaven
and on earth,
everything seen and unseen,
including all forces
and powers,
and all rulers
and authorities.
All things were created
by God's Son,
and everything was made
for him.
17 God's Son was before all else,
and by him everything
is held together.
18 He is the head of his body,
which is the church.
He is the very beginning,
the first to be raised
from death,
so that he would be
above all others.

19 God himself was pleased
to live fully in his Son.
20 And God was pleased
for him to make peace
by sacrificing his blood
on the cross,
so that all beings in heaven
and on earth
would be brought back to God.

21 You used to be far from God. Your thoughts made you his enemies, and you did evil things.
22 But his Son became a human and died. So God made peace with you, and now he lets you stand in his presence as people who are holy and faultless and innocent.
23 But you must stay deeply rooted and firm in your faith. You must not give up the hope you received when you heard the good news. It was preached to everyone on earth, and I myself have become a servant of this message.

Paul's Service to the Church

24 I am glad that I can suffer for you. I am pleased also that in my own body I can continue[b] the suffering of Christ for his body, the church.
25 God's plan was to make me a servant of his church and to send me to preach his complete message to you.
26 For ages and ages this message was kept secret from everyone, but now it has been explained to God's people.
27 God did this because he wanted you Gentiles to understand his wonderful and glorious mystery. And the mystery is that Christ lives in you, and he is your hope of sharing in God's glory.

[a] **1.7,12** *you*: Some manuscripts have "us." [b] **1.24** *continue*: Or "complete."
1.7 Col 4.12; Phm 23. **1.14** Eph 1.7, 8. **1.15** Ws 7.26. **1.18** Eph 1.22, 23.
1.20 Eph 2.16.

28 We announce the message about Christ, and we use all our wisdom to warn and teach everyone, so that all of Christ's followers will grow and become mature. 29 That's why I work so hard and use the mighty power he gives me.

2 I want you to know what a struggle I am going through for you, for God's people at Laodicea, and for all of those followers who have never met me. 2 I do it to encourage them. Then as their hearts are joined together in love, they will be wonderfully blessed with complete understanding. And they will truly know Christ. Not only is he the key to God's mystery, 3 but all wisdom and knowledge are hidden away in him. 4 I tell you these things to keep you from being fooled by fancy talk. 5 Even though I am not with you, I keep thinking about you. I am glad to know that you are living as you should and that your faith in Christ is strong.

Christ Brings Real Life

6 You have accepted Christ Jesus as your Lord. Now keep on following him. 7 Plant your roots in Christ and let him be the foundation for your life. Be strong in your faith, just as you were taught. And be grateful.

8 Don't let anyone fool you by using senseless arguments. These arguments may sound wise, but they are only human teachings. They come from the powers of this world[c] and not from Christ.

9 God lives fully in Christ. 10 And you are fully grown because you belong to Christ, who is over every power and authority. 11 Christ has also taken away your selfish desires, just as circumcision removes flesh from the body. 12 And when you were baptized, it was the same as being buried with Christ. Then you were raised to life because you had faith in the power of God, who raised Christ from death. 13 You were dead, because you were sinful and were not God's people. But God let Christ make you[d] alive, when he forgave all our sins.

14 God wiped out the charges that were against us for disobeying the Law of Moses. He took them away and nailed them to the cross. 15 There Christ defeated all powers and forces. He let the whole world see them being led away as prisoners when he celebrated his victory.

16 Don't let anyone tell you what you must eat or drink. Don't let them say that you must celebrate the New Moon festival, the Sabbath, or any other festival. 17 These things are only a shadow of what was to come. But Christ is real!

18 Don't be cheated by people who make a show of acting humble and who worship angels.[e] They brag about seeing visions. But it is all nonsense, because their minds are filled with selfish desires. 19 They are no longer part of Christ, who is the head of the whole body. Christ gives the body its strength, and he uses its joints and muscles to hold it together, as it grows by the power of God.

Christ Brings New Life

20 You died with Christ. Now the forces of the universe[f] don't have any power over you. Why do you live as if you had to obey such rules as, 21 "Don't handle this. Don't taste that. Don't touch this."? 22 After these things are used, they are no longer good for anything. So why be bothered with the rules that humans have made up? 23 Obeying these rules may seem to be the smart thing to do. They appear to make you love God more and to be very humble and to have control over your body. But they don't really have any power over our desires.

3 You have been raised to life with Christ. Now set your heart on what is in heaven, where Christ rules at God's right side.[g] 2 Think about what is up there, not about what is here on earth. 3 You died,

[c]**2.8** *powers of this world*: Spirits and unseen forces were thought to control human lives and were believed to be connected with the movements of the stars. [d]**2.13** *you*: See the note at 1.7. [e]**2.18** *worship angels*: Or "worship with angels (in visions of heaven)." [f]**2.20** *forces of the universe*: See the note at 2.8. [g]**3.1** *right side*: The place of power and honor.

2.12 Ro 6.4. **2.13** Eph 2.1-5. **2.14** Eph 2.15. **2.16** Ro 14.1-6. **2.19** Eph 4.16. **3.1** Ps 110.1.

which means that your life is hidden with Christ, who sits beside God. 4 Christ gives meaning to your[h] life, and when he appears, you will also appear with him in glory.

5 Don't be controlled by your body. Kill every desire for the wrong kind of sex. Don't be immoral or indecent or have evil thoughts. Don't be greedy, which is the same as worshiping idols. 6 God is angry with people who disobey him by doing[i] these things. 7 And that is exactly what you did, when you lived among people who behaved in this way. 8 But now you must stop doing such things. You must quit being angry, hateful, and evil. You must no longer say insulting or cruel things about others. 9 And stop lying to each other. You have given up your old way of life with its habits.

10 Each of you is now a new person. You are becoming more and more like your Creator, and you will understand him better. 11 It doesn't matter if you are a Greek or a Jew, or if you are circumcised or not. You may even be a barbarian or a Scythian,[j] and you may be a slave or a free person. Yet Christ is all that matters, and he lives in all of us.

12 God loves you and has chosen you as his own special people. So be gentle, kind, humble, meek, and patient. 13 Put up with each other, and forgive anyone who does you wrong, just as Christ has forgiven you. 14 Love is more important than anything else. It is what ties everything completely together.

15 Each one of you is part of the body of Christ, and you were chosen to live together in peace. So let the peace that comes from Christ control your thoughts. And be grateful. 16 Let the message about Christ completely fill your lives, while you use all your wisdom to teach and instruct each other. With thankful hearts, sing psalms, hymns, and spiritual songs to God. 17 Whatever you say or do should be done in the name of the Lord Jesus, as you give thanks to God the Father because of him.

Some Rules for Christian Living

18 A wife must put her husband first. This is her duty as a follower of the Lord.

19 A husband must love his wife and not abuse her.

20 Children must always obey their parents. This pleases the Lord.

21 Parents, don't be hard on your children. If you are, they might give up.

22 Slaves, you must always obey your earthly masters. Try to please them at all times, and not just when you think they are watching. Honor the Lord and serve your masters with your whole heart. 23 Do your work willingly, as though you were serving the Lord himself, and not just your earthly master. 24 In fact, the Lord Christ is the one you are really serving, and you know that he will reward you. 25 But Christ has no favorites! He will punish evil people, just as they deserve.

4 Slave owners, be fair and honest with your slaves. Don't forget that you have a Master in heaven.

2 Never give up praying. And when you pray, keep alert and be thankful. 3 Be sure to pray that God will make a way for us to spread his message and explain the mystery about Christ, even though I am in jail for doing this. 4 Please pray that I will make the message as clear as possible.

5 When you are with unbelievers, always make good use of the time. 6 Be pleasant and hold their interest when you speak the message. Choose your words carefully and be ready to give answers to anyone who asks questions.

Final Greetings

7 Tychicus is the dear friend, who faithfully works and serves the Lord with us,

[h]**3.4** *your*: Some manuscripts have "our." [i]**3.6** *people who disobey him by doing*: Some manuscripts do not have these words. [j]**3.11** *a barbarian or a Scythian*: Barbarians were people who could not speak Greek and would be in the lower class of society. Scythians were people who were known for their cruelty.

3.9 Eph 4.22. **3.10** **a** Eph 4.24; **b** Gn 1.26. **3.12,13** Eph 4.2. **3.13** Eph 4.32. **3.16,17** Eph 5.19, 20. **3.18** Eph 5.22; 1 P 3.1. **3.19** Eph 5.25; 1 P 3.7. **3.20** Eph 6.1. **3.21** Eph 6.4. **3.22-25** Eph 6.5-8. **3.25** Dt 10.17; Eph 6.9. **4.1** Eph 6.9. **4.5** Eph 5.16. **4.6** Ws 8.12. **4.7** Ac 20.4; 2 Ti 4.12. **4.7,8** Eph 6.21, 22.

and he will give you the news about me. 8 I am sending him to cheer you up by telling you how we are getting along. 9 Onesimus, that dear and faithful follower from your own group, is coming with him. The two of them will tell you everything that has happened here.

10 Aristarchus is in jail with me. He sends greetings to you, and so does Mark, the cousin of Barnabas. You have already been told to welcome Mark, if he visits you. 11 Jesus, who is known as Justus, sends his greetings. These three men are the only Jewish followers who have worked with me for the kingdom of God. They have given me much comfort.

12 Your own Epaphras, who serves Christ Jesus, sends his greetings. He always prays hard that you may fully know what the Lord wants you to do and that you may do it completely. 13 I have seen how much trouble he has gone through for you and for the followers in Laodicea and Hierapolis.

14 Our dear doctor Luke sends you his greetings, and so does Demas.

15 Give my greetings to the followers at Laodicea, especially to Nympha and the church that meets in her home.

16 After this letter has been read to your people, be sure to have it read in the church at Laodicea. And you should read the letter that I have sent to them.[k]

17 Remind Archippus to do the work that the Lord has given him to do.

18 I am signing this letter myself: PAUL. Don't forget that I am in jail.

I pray that God will be kind to you.

[k]**4.16** *the letter that I have sent to them*: This is the only mention of the letter to the church at Laodicea.

4.9 Phm 10-12. **4.10** **a** Ac 19.29; 27.2; Phm 24; **b** Ac 12.12, 25; 13.13; 15.37-39. **4.12** Col 1.7; Phm 23. **4.14** **a** 2 Ti 4.11; Phm 24; **b** 2 Ti 4.10; Phm 24. **4.17** Phm 2.

1 THESSALONIANS

ABOUT THIS LETTER

Paul started the church in Thessalonica (2.13, 14), while working hard to support himself (2.9). In this important city of northern Greece, many of the followers had worshiped idols before becoming Christians (1.9). But they were faithful to the Lord, and because of them the Lord's message had spread everywhere in that region (1.8). This letter may have been the first one that Paul wrote, and maybe even the first of all the New Testament writings.

Some people in Thessalonica began to oppose Paul, and he had to escape to Athens. But he sent his young friend Timothy to find out how the Christians were doing (3.1-5). When Timothy returned, he gave Paul good reports of their faith and love (3.6-10).

The church itself had problems. Some of its members had quit working, since they thought that the Lord would soon return (4.11, 12). Others were worried because relatives and friends had already died before Christ's return. So Paul tried to explain to them more clearly what would happen when the Lord returns (4.13-15), and then told them how they should live in the meanwhile (5.1-11).

Paul's final instructions are well worth remembering:

> *Always be joyful and never stop praying. Whatever happens, keep thanking God because of Jesus Christ. This is what God wants you to do.*
>
> *(5.16-18)*

A QUICK LOOK AT THIS LETTER

- Greetings (1.1-3)
- The Thessalonians' Faith and Example (1.4—3.13)
- A Life That Pleases God (4.1-12)
- What to Expect When the Lord Returns (4.13—5.11)
- Final Instructions and Greetings (5.12-28)

---

1 From Paul, Silas,[a] and Timothy.
To the church in Thessalonica, the
people of God the Father and of the Lord
Jesus Christ.
I pray that God will be kind to you and
will bless you with peace!
2 We thank God for you and always
mention you in our prayers. Each time we
pray, 3 we tell God our Father about your
faith and loving work and about your firm
hope in our Lord Jesus Christ.

The Thessalonians' Faith and Example

4 My dear friends, God loves you, and
we know he has chosen you to be his people. 5 When we told you the good news, it
was with the power and assurance that
come from the Holy Spirit, and not simply
with words. You knew what kind of people
we were and how we helped you. 6 So,
when you accepted the message, you followed our example and the example of

[a] **1.1** *Silas*: The Greek text has "Silvanus," another form of the name Silas.
1.1 Ac 17.1. **1.6** Ac 17.5-9.

the Lord. You suffered, but the Holy Spirit made you glad.

7 You became an example for all the Lord's followers in Macedonia and Achaia. 8 And because of you, the Lord's message has spread everywhere in those regions. Now the news of your faith in God is known all over the world, and we don't have to say a thing about it. 9 Everyone is talking about how you welcomed us and how you turned away from idols to serve the true and living God. 10 They also tell how you are waiting for his Son Jesus to come from heaven. God raised him from death, and on the day of judgment Jesus will save us from God's anger.

Paul's Work in Thessalonica

2 My friends, you know that our time with you wasn't wasted. 2 As you remember, we had been mistreated and insulted at Philippi. But God gave us the courage to tell you the good news about him, even though many people caused us trouble. 3 We didn't have any hidden motives when we won you over, and we didn't try to fool or trick anyone. 4 God was pleased to trust us with his message. We didn't speak to please people, but to please God who knows our motives.

5 You also know that we didn't try to flatter anyone. God himself knows that what we did wasn't a cover-up for greed. 6 We were not trying to get you or anyone else to praise us. 7 But as apostles, we could have demanded help from you. After all, Christ is the one who sent us. We chose to be like children or like a mother[b] nursing her baby. 8 We cared so much for you, and you became so dear to us, that we were willing to give our lives for you when we gave you God's message.

9 My dear friends, you surely haven't forgotten our hard work and hardships. You remember how night and day we struggled to make a living, so that we could tell you God's message without being a burden to anyone. 10 Both you and God are witnesses that we were pure and honest and innocent in our dealings with you followers of the Lord. 11 You also know we did everything for you that parents would do for their own children. 12 We begged, encouraged, and urged each of you to live in a way that would honor God. He is the one who chose you to share in his own kingdom and glory.

13 We always thank God that you believed the message we preached. It came from him, and it isn't something made up by humans. You accepted it as God's message, and now he is working in you. 14 My friends, you did just like God's churches in Judea and like the other followers of Christ Jesus there. And so, you were mistreated by your own people, in the same way they were mistreated by their people.

15 Those Jews killed the Lord Jesus and the prophets, and they even chased us away. God doesn't like what they do and neither does anyone else. 16 They keep us from speaking his message to the Gentiles and from leading them to be saved. The Jews have always gone too far with their sins. Now God has finally become angry and will punish them.

Paul Wants To Visit the Church Again

17 My friends, we were kept from coming to you for a while, but we never stopped thinking about you. We were eager to see you and tried our best to visit you in person. 18 We really wanted to come. I myself tried several times, but Satan always stopped us. 19 After all, when the Lord Jesus appears, who else but you will give us hope and joy and be like a glorious crown for us? 20 You alone are our glory and joy!

3 Finally, we couldn't stand it any longer. We decided to stay in Athens by ourselves 2 and send our friend Timothy to you. He works with us as God's servant and preaches the good news about Christ. We wanted him to make you strong in your faith and to encourage you. 3 We didn't want any of you to be discouraged by all these troubles. You knew we would have to suffer, 4 because when we were with you, we told you this would happen. And we did

[b]**2.7** *like children or like a mother*: Some manuscripts have "as gentle as a mother."

2.2 **a** Ac 16.19-24; **b** Ac 17.1-9. **2.14** Ac 17.5. **2.15** Ac 9.23, 29; 13.45, 50; 14.2, 5, 19; 17.5, 13; 18.12. **3.1** Ac 17.15.

suffer, as you well know. 5 At last, when I
could not wait any longer, I sent Timothy to
find out about your faith. I hoped that Satan had not tempted you and made all our
work useless.
6 Timothy has come back from his visit
with you and has told us about your faith
and love. He also said that you always have
happy memories of us and that you want to
see us as much as we want to see you.
7 My friends, even though we have a lot
of trouble and suffering, your faith makes
us feel better about you. 8 Your strong faith
in the Lord is like a breath of new life.
9 How can we possibly thank God enough
for all the happiness you have brought us?
10 Day and night we sincerely pray that we
will see you again and help you to have an
even stronger faith.
11 We pray that God our Father and our
Lord Jesus will let us visit you. 12 May the
Lord make your love for each other and for
everyone else grow by leaps and bounds.
That's how our love for you has grown. 13 And
when our Lord comes with all of his people,
I pray that he will make your hearts pure and
innocent in the sight of God the Father.

A Life That Pleases God

4 Finally, my dear friends, since you belong to the Lord Jesus, we beg and
urge you to live as we taught you. Then you
will please God. You are already living that
way, but try even harder. 2 Remember the
instructions we gave you as followers of the
Lord Jesus. 3 God wants you to be holy, so
don't be immoral in matters of sex. 4 Respect and honor your wife.[c] 5 Don't be a
slave of your desires or live like people who
don't know God. 6 You must not cheat any
of the Lord's followers in matters of sex.[d]
Remember, we warned you that he punishes everyone who does such things. 7 God
didn't choose you to be filthy, but to be
pure. 8 So if you don't obey these rules, you
are not really disobeying us. You are disobeying God, who gives you his Holy Spirit.
9 We don't have to write you about the
need to love each other. God has taught
you to do this, 10 and you already have
shown your love for all of his people in
Macedonia. But, my dear friends, we ask
you to do even more. 11 Try your best to live
quietly, to mind your own business, and to
work hard, just as we taught you to do.
12 Then you will be respected by people
who are not followers of the Lord, and you
won't have to depend on anyone.

The Lord's Coming

13 My friends, we want you to understand how it will be for those followers who
have already died. Then you won't grieve
over them and be like people who don't
have any hope. 14 We believe that Jesus
died and was raised to life. We also believe
that when God brings Jesus back again, he
will bring with him all who had faith in
Jesus before they died. 15 Our Lord Jesus
told us that when he comes, we won't go
up to meet him ahead of his followers who
have already died.
16 With a loud command and with the
shout of the chief angel and a blast of
God's trumpet, the Lord will return from
heaven. Then those who had faith in
Christ before they died will be raised to life.
17 Next, all of us who are still alive will be
taken up into the clouds together with
them to meet the Lord in the sky. From
that time on we will all be with the Lord
forever. 18 Encourage each other with these
words.

5 I don't need to write you about the
time or date when all this will happen.
2 You surely know that the Lord's return[e]
will be as a thief coming at night. 3 People
will think they are safe and secure. But destruction will suddenly strike them like the
pains of a woman about to give birth. And
they won't escape.
4 My dear friends, you don't live in darkness, and so that day won't surprise you
like a thief. 5 You belong to the light and
live in the day. We don't live in the night or
belong to the dark. 6 Others may sleep, but

[c] **4.4** *your wife*: Or "your body." [d] **4.6** *in matters of sex*: Or "in business." [e] **5.2** *the Lord's return*: The Greek text has "the day of the Lord."

3.6 Ac 18.5. **4.12** 3 Macc 3.5. **4.15-17** 1 Co 15.51, 52. **4.15** Si 48.11.
4.16 2 Esd 6.23. **5.2** Mt 24.43; Lk 12.39; 2 P 3.10.

we should stay awake and be alert. 7 People
sleep during the night, and some even get
drunk. 8 But we belong to the day. So we
must stay sober and let our faith and love
be like a suit of armor. Our firm hope that
we will be saved is our helmet.

9 God doesn't intend to punish us, but
wants us to be saved by our Lord Jesus
Christ. 10 Christ died for us, so that we
could live with him, whether we are alive
or dead when he comes. 11 That's why you
must encourage and help each other, just
as you are already doing.

Final Instructions and Greetings

12 My friends, we ask you to be thoughtful of your leaders who work hard and tell
you how to live for the Lord. 13 Show them
great respect and love because of their
work. Try to get along with each other.
14 My friends, we beg you to warn anyone
who isn't living right. Encourage anyone
who feels left out, help all who are weak,
and be patient with everyone. 15 Don't be
hateful to people, just because they are
hateful to you. Rather, be good to each
other and to everyone else.

16 Always be joyful 17 and never stop
praying. 18 Whatever happens, keep thanking God because of Jesus Christ. This is
what God wants you to do.

19 Don't turn away God's Spirit 20 or ignore prophecies. 21 Put everything to the
test. Accept what is good 22 and don't have
anything to do with evil.

23 I pray that God, who gives peace, will
make you completely holy. And may your
spirit, soul, and body be kept healthy and
faultless until our Lord Jesus Christ returns. 24 The one who chose you can be
trusted, and he will do this.

25 Friends, please pray for us.

26 Give the Lord's followers a warm
greeting.

27 In the name of the Lord I beg you to
read this letter to all his followers.

28 I pray that our Lord Jesus Christ will
be kind to you!

5.8 Is 59.17; Eph 6.13-17.

2 THESSALONIANS

ABOUT THIS LETTER

In this letter to the believers in Thessalonica, Paul begins by thanking God that their faith and love keep growing all the time (1.3). They were going through a lot of troubles, but Paul insists that this is God's way of testing their faith, not a way of punishing them (1.4, 5).

Someone in Thessalonica claimed to have a letter from Paul, saying that the Lord had already returned (2.2). But Paul warns the church not to be fooled! The Lord will not return until after the "wicked one" has appeared (2.3).

Paul also warns against laziness (3.6-10), and he tells the church to guard against any followers who refuse to obey what he has written in this letter.

The letter closes with a prayer:

I pray that the Lord, who gives peace, will always bless you with peace. May the Lord be with all of you.

(3.16)

A QUICK LOOK AT THIS LETTER

- Greetings (1.1, 2)
- The Lord's Return Will Bring Justice (1.3-12)
- The Lord Has Not Returned Yet (2.1-12)
- Be Faithful (2.13-17)
- Pray and Work (3.1-15)
- A Final Prayer (3.16-18)

---

1 From Paul, Silas,[a] and Timothy.
To the church in Thessalonica, the
people of God our Father and of the Lord
Jesus Christ.
2 I pray that God our Father and the
Lord Jesus Christ will be kind to you and
will bless you with peace!

When Christ Returns

3 My dear friends, we always have good
reason to thank God for you, because your
faith in God and your love for each other
keep growing all the time. 4 That's why we
brag about you to all of God's churches. We
tell them how patient you are and how you
keep on having faith, even though you are
going through a lot of trouble and suffering.
5 All of this shows that God judges fairly
and that he is making you fit to share in his
kingdom for which you are suffering. 6 It is
only right for God to punish everyone who
is causing you trouble, 7 but he will give
you relief from your troubles. He will do
the same for us, when the Lord Jesus
comes from heaven with his powerful angels 8 and with a flaming fire.
Our Lord Jesus will punish anyone who
doesn't know God and won't obey his message. 9 Their punishment will be eternal
destruction, and they will be kept far from

[a] **1.1** *Silas*: The Greek text has "Silvanus," which is another form of the name Silas.
1.1 Ac 17.1. **1.9** Is 2.10.

the presence of our Lord and his glorious strength. 10 This will happen on that day when the Lord returns to be praised and honored by all who have faith in him and belong to him. This includes you, because you believed what we said.

11 God chose you, and we keep praying that God will make you worthy of being his people. We pray for God's power to help you do all the good things that you hope to do and that your faith makes you want to do. 12 Then, because God and our Lord Jesus Christ are so kind, you will bring honor to the name of our Lord Jesus, and he will bring honor to you.

The Lord's Return

2 When our Lord Jesus returns, we will be gathered up to meet him. So I ask you, my friends, 2 not to be easily upset or disturbed by people who claim that the Lord[b] has already come. They may say that they heard this directly from the Holy Spirit, or from someone else, or even that they read it in one of our letters. 3 But don't be fooled! People will rebel against God. Then before the Lord returns, the wicked[c] one who is doomed to be destroyed will appear. 4 He will brag and oppose everything that is holy or sacred. He will even sit in God's temple and claim to be God. 5 Don't you remember that I told you this while I was still with you?

6 You already know what is holding this wicked one back until it is time for him to come. 7 His mysterious power is already at work, but someone is holding him back. And the wicked one won't appear until that someone is out of the way. 8 Then he will appear, but the Lord Jesus will kill him simply by breathing on him. He will be completely destroyed by the Lord's glorious return.

9 When the wicked one appears, Satan will pretend to work all kinds of miracles, wonders, and signs. 10 Lost people will be fooled by his evil deeds. They could be saved, but they will refuse to love the truth and accept it. 11 So God will make sure that they are fooled into believing a lie. 12 All of them will be punished, because they would rather do evil than believe the truth.

Be Faithful

13 My friends, the Lord loves you, and it is only natural for us to thank God for you. God chose you to be the first ones to be saved.[d] His Spirit made you holy, and you put your faith in the truth. 14 God used our preaching as his way of inviting you to share in the glory of our Lord Jesus Christ. 15 My friends, that's why you must remain faithful and follow closely what we taught you in person and by our letters.

16 God our Father loves us. He is kind and has given us eternal comfort and a wonderful hope. We pray that our Lord Jesus Christ and God our Father 17 will encourage you and help you always to do and say the right thing.

Pray for Us

3 Finally, our friends, please pray for us. This will help the message about the Lord to spread quickly, and others will respect it, just as you do. 2 Pray that we may be kept safe from worthless and evil people. After all, not everyone has faith. 3 But the Lord can be trusted to make you strong and protect you from harm. 4 He has made us sure that you are obeying what we taught you and that you will keep on obeying. 5 I pray that the Lord will guide you to be as loving as God and as patient as Christ.

Warnings against Laziness

6 My dear friends, in the name of[e] the Lord Jesus, I beg you not to have anything to do with any of your people who loaf around and refuse to obey the instructions we gave you. 7 You surely know that you should follow our example. We didn't waste our time loafing, 8 and we didn't accept food from anyone without paying for it. We didn't want to be a burden to any of you, so night and day we worked as hard as we could.

[b]**2.2** *Lord*: The Greek text has "day of the Lord." [c]**2.3** *wicked*: Some manuscripts have "sinful." [d]**2.13** *God chose you to be the first ones to be saved*: Some manuscripts have "From the beginning God chose you to be saved." [e]**3.6** *in the name of*: Or "as a follower of."

2.1 1 Th 4.15-17. **2.4** Ez 28.2; Dn 11.36. **2.8** Is 11.4. **2.9** Mt 24.24.

9 We had the right not to work, but we
wanted to set an example for you. 10 We also
gave you the rule that if you don't work,
you don't eat. 11 Now we learn that some of
you just loaf around and won't do any work,
except the work of a busybody. 12 So, for
the sake of our Lord Jesus Christ, we ask
and beg these people to settle down and
start working for a living. 13 Dear friends,
you must never become tired of doing right.
14 Be on your guard against any followers who refuse to obey what we have written in this letter. Put them to shame by not
having anything to do with them. 15 Don't
consider them your enemies, but speak
kindly to them as you would to any other
follower.

Final Prayer

16 I pray that the Lord, who gives peace, will always bless you with peace. May the Lord be with all of you.
17 I always sign my letters as I am now doing: PAUL.
18 I pray that our Lord Jesus Christ will be kind to all of you.

1 TIMOTHY

ABOUT THIS LETTER

Timothy traveled and worked with Paul (Romans 16.21; 1 Corinthians 16.10; Philippians 2.19), and because of their shared faith, Timothy was like a son to Paul (1.2). Timothy became one of Paul's most faithful co-workers, and Paul mentions Timothy in five of his letters.

Although this letter is addressed to Timothy personally, it actually addresses many of the concerns Paul had with the life of the entire church. Guidelines are given for choosing church officials (3.1-7), officers (3.8-13), and leaders (5.17-20).

Christians are to pray for everyone and to remember:

There is only one God,
and Christ Jesus
is the only one
who can bring us
to God.
(2.5a)

A QUICK LOOK AT THIS LETTER

- Greetings (1.1, 2)
- Instructions for Church Life (1.3—3.13)
- The Mystery of Our Religion (3.14—4.5)
- Paul's Advice to Timothy (4.6—6.21)

1 From Paul.
God our Savior and Christ Jesus commanded me to be an apostle of Christ Jesus, who gives us hope.

2 Timothy, because of our faith, you are like a son to me. I pray that God our Father and our Lord Jesus Christ will be kind and merciful to you. May they bless you with peace!

Warning against False Teaching

3 When I was leaving for Macedonia, I asked you to stay on in Ephesus and warn certain people there to stop spreading their false teachings. 4 You needed to warn them to stop wasting their time on senseless stories and endless lists of ancestors. Such things only cause arguments. They don't help anyone to do God's work that can only be done by faith.

5 You must teach people to have genuine love, as well as a good conscience and true faith. 6 There are some who have given up these for nothing but empty talk. 7 They want to be teachers of the Law of Moses. But they don't know what they are talking about, even though they think they do.

8 We know that the Law is good, if it is used in the right way. 9 We also understand that it wasn't given to control people who please God, but to control lawbreakers, criminals, godless people, and sinners. It is for wicked and evil people, and for murderers, who would even kill their own parents. 10 The Law was written for people who are sexual perverts or who live as homosexuals

1.2 Ac 16.1.

or are kidnappers or liars or won't tell the truth in court. It is for anything else that opposes the correct teaching 11 of the good news that the glorious and wonderful God has given me.

Being Thankful for God's Kindness

12 I thank Christ Jesus our Lord. He has given me the strength for my work because he knew that he could trust me. 13 I used to say terrible and insulting things about him, and I was cruel. But he had mercy on me because I didn't know what I was doing, and I had not yet put my faith in him. 14 Christ Jesus our Lord was very kind to me. He has greatly blessed my life with faith and love just like his own.

15 "Christ Jesus came into the world to save sinners." This saying is true, and it can be trusted. I was the worst sinner of all! 16 But since I was worse than anyone else, God had mercy on me and let me be an example of the endless patience of Christ Jesus. He did this so that others would put their faith in Christ and have eternal life. 17 I pray that honor and glory will always be given to the only God, who lives forever and is the invisible and eternal King! Amen.

18 Timothy, my son, the instructions I am giving you are based on what some prophets[a] once said about you. If you follow these instructions, you will fight like a good soldier. 19 You will be faithful and have a clear conscience. Some people have made a mess of their faith because they didn't listen to their consciences. 20 Two of them are Hymenaeus and Alexander. I have given these men over to the power of Satan, so they will learn not to oppose God.

How To Pray

2 First of all, I ask you to pray for everyone. Ask God to help and bless them all, and tell God how thankful you are for each of them. 2 Pray for kings and others in power, so that we may live quiet and peaceful lives as we worship and honor God. 3 This kind of prayer is good, and it pleases God our Savior. 4 God wants everyone to be saved and to know the whole truth, which is,

5 There is only one God,
and Christ Jesus
is the only one
who can bring us
to God.
Jesus was truly human,
and he gave himself
to rescue all of us.
6 God showed us this
at the right time.

7 This is why God chose me to be a preacher and an apostle of the good news. I am telling the truth. I am not lying. God sent me to teach the Gentiles about faith and truth.

8 I want everyone everywhere to lift innocent hands toward heaven and pray, without being angry or arguing with each other.

9 I would like for women to wear modest and sensible clothes. They should not have fancy hairdos, or wear expensive clothes, or put on jewelry made of gold or pearls. 10 Women who claim to love God should do helpful things for others, 11 and they should learn by being quiet and paying attention. 12 They should be silent and not be allowed to teach or to tell men what to do. 13 After all, Adam was created before Eve, 14 and the man Adam wasn't the one who was fooled. It was the woman Eve who was completely fooled and sinned. 15 But women will be saved by having children,[b] if they stay faithful, loving, holy, and modest.

Church Officials

3 It is true that[c] anyone who desires to be a church official[d] wants to be something worthwhile. 2 That's why officials

[a] **1.18** *prophets*: Probably the Christian prophets referred to in 4.14. [b] **2.15** *saved by having children*: Or "brought safely through childbirth" or "saved by the birth of a child" (that is, by the birth of Jesus) or "saved by being good mothers." [c] **3.1** *It is true that*: These words may be taken with 2.15. If so, that verse would be translated: "It is true that women will be saved . . . holy, and modest." And 3.1 would be translated, "Anyone who desires . . . something worthwhile." [d] **3.1** *church official*: Or "bishop."

1.13 Ac 8.3; 9.4, 5. **2.7** 2 Ti 1.11. **2.9** 1 P 3.3. **2.13** **a** Gn 2.7; **b** Gn 2.21, 22. **2.14** Gn 3.1-6. **3.2-7** Titus 1.6-9.

must have a good reputation and be faithful in marriage.[e] They must be self-controlled, sensible, well-behaved, friendly to strangers, and able to teach. 3 They must not be heavy drinkers or troublemakers. Instead, they must be kind and gentle and not love money.

4 Church officials must be in control of their own families, and they must see that their children are obedient and always respectful. 5 If they don't know how to control their own families, how can they look after God's people?

6 They must not be new followers of the Lord. If they are, they might become proud and be doomed along with the devil. 7 Finally, they must be well-respected by people who are not followers. Then they won't be trapped and disgraced by the devil.

Church Officers

8 Church officers[f] should be serious. They must not be liars, heavy drinkers, or greedy for money. 9 And they must have a clear conscience and hold firmly to what God has shown us about our faith. 10 They must first prove themselves. Then if no one has anything against them, they can serve as officers.

11 Women[g] must also be serious. They must not gossip or be heavy drinkers, and they must be faithful in everything they do.

12 Church officers must be faithful in marriage.[h] They must be in full control of their children and everyone else in their home. 13 Those who serve well as officers will earn a good reputation and will be highly respected for their faith in Christ Jesus.

The Mystery of Our Religion

14 I hope to visit you soon. But I am writing these instructions, 15 so that if I am delayed, you will know how everyone who belongs to God's family ought to behave. After all, the church of the living God is the strong foundation of truth.

16 Here is the great mystery of our religion:

Christ[i] came as a human.
The Spirit proved
  that he pleased God,
and he was seen by angels.

Christ was preached
  to the nations.
People in this world
  put their faith in him,
and he was taken up to glory.

People Will Turn from Their Faith

4 God's Spirit clearly says that in the last days many people will turn from their faith. They will be fooled by evil spirits and by teachings that come from demons. 2 They will also be fooled by the false claims of liars whose consciences have lost all feeling. These liars 3 will forbid people to marry or to eat certain foods. But God created these foods to be eaten with thankful hearts by his followers who know the truth. 4 Everything God created is good. And if you give thanks, you may eat anything. 5 What God has said and your prayer will make it fit to eat.

Paul's Advice to Timothy

6 If you teach these things to other followers, you will be a good servant of Christ Jesus. You will show that you have grown up on the teachings about our faith and on the good instructions you have obeyed. 7 Don't have anything to do with worthless, senseless stories. Work hard to be truly religious. 8-9 As the saying goes,

"Exercise is good
  for your body,
but religion helps you
  in every way.
It promises life
  now and forever."

These words are worthwhile and should not be forgotten. 10 We have put our hope in the living God, who is the Savior of everyone, but especially of those who have

[e]**3.2** *be faithful in marriage*: Or "be the husband of only one wife" or "have never been divorced." [f]**3.8** *Church officers*: Or "Deacons." [g]**3.11** *Women*: Either church officers or the wives of church officers. [h]**3.12** *be faithful in marriage*: See the note at 3.2. [i]**3.16** *Christ*: The Greek text has "he," probably meaning "Christ." Some manuscripts have "God."

faith. That's why we work and struggle so hard.[j]

11 Teach these things and tell everyone to do what you say. 12 Don't let anyone make fun of you, just because you are young. Set an example for other followers by what you say and do, as well as by your love, faith, and purity.

13 Until I arrive, be sure to keep on reading the Scriptures in worship, and don't stop preaching and teaching. 14 Use the gift you were given when the prophets spoke and the group of church leaders[k] blessed you by placing their hands on you. 15 Remember these things and think about them, so everyone can see how well you are doing. 16 Be careful about the way you live and about what you teach. Keep on doing this, and you will save not only yourself, but the people who hear you.

How To Act toward Others

5 Don't correct an older man. Encourage him, as you would your own father. Treat younger men as you would your own brother, 2 and treat older women as you would your own mother. Show the same respect to younger women that you would to your sister.

3 Take care of any widow who is really in need. 4 But if a widow has children or grandchildren, they should learn to serve God by taking care of her, as she once took care of them. This is what God wants them to do. 5 A widow who is really in need is one who doesn't have any relatives. She has faith in God, and she keeps praying to him night and day, asking for his help.

6 A widow who thinks only about having a good time is already dead, even though she is still alive.

7 Tell all of this to everyone, so they will do the right thing. 8 People who don't take care of their relatives, and especially their own families, have given up their faith. They are worse than someone who doesn't have faith in the Lord.

9 For a widow to be put on the list of widows, she must be at least sixty years old, and she must have been faithful in marriage.[l] 10 She must also be well-known for doing all sorts of good things, such as raising children, giving food to strangers, welcoming God's people into her home,[m] helping people in need, and always making herself useful.

11 Don't put young widows on the list. They may later have a strong desire to get married. Then they will turn away from Christ 12 and become guilty of breaking their promise to him. 13 Besides, they will become lazy and get into the habit of going from house to house. Next, they will start gossiping and become busybodies, talking about things that are none of their business.

14 I would prefer that young widows get married, have children, and look after their families. Then the enemy won't have any reason to say insulting things about us. 15 Look what's already happened to some of the young widows! They have turned away to follow Satan.

16 If a woman who is a follower has any widows in her family, she[n] should help them. This will keep the church from having that burden, and then the church can help widows who are really in need.

Church Leaders

17 Church leaders[o] who do their job well deserve to be paid[p] twice as much, especially if they work hard at preaching and teaching. 18 It is just as the Scriptures say, "Don't muzzle an ox when you are using it to grind grain." You also know the saying, "Workers are worth their pay."

19 Don't listen to any charge against a

[j]**4.10** *struggle so hard*: Some manuscripts have "are treated so badly." [k]**4.14** *group of church leaders*: Or "group of elders" or "group of presbyters" or "group of priests." This translates one Greek word, and it is related to the one used in 5.17, 19. [l]**5.9** *been faithful in marriage*: Or "been the wife of only one husband" or "never been divorced." [m]**5.10** *welcoming God's people into her home*: The Greek text has "washing the feet of God's people." In New Testament times most people either went barefoot or wore sandals, and a host would often wash the feet of special guests. [n]**5.16** *woman . . . she*: Some manuscripts have "man or woman . . . that person." [o]**5.17** *leaders*: Or "elders" or "presbyters" or "priests." [p]**5.17** *paid*: Or "honored" or "respected."

5.5 Jdt 8.4-6. **5.18** **a** Dt 25.4; **b** Mt 10.10; Lk 10.7. **5.19** Dt 17.5-7; 19.15.

church leader, unless at least two or three
people bring the same charges. 20 But if
any of the leaders should keep on sinning,
they must be corrected in front of the
whole group, as a warning to everyone else.
21 In the presence of God and Christ
Jesus and their chosen angels, I order you
to follow my instructions! Be fair with
everyone, and don't have any favorites.
22 Don't be too quick to accept people
into the service of the Lord[q] by placing
your hands on them.

Don't sin because others do, but stay
close to God.
23 Stop drinking only water. Take a little
wine to help your stomach trouble and the
other illnesses you always have.
24 Some people get caught in their sins
right away, even before the time of judgment. But other people's sins don't show
up until later. 25 It is the same with good
deeds. Some are easily seen, but none of
them can be hidden.

6 If you are a slave, you should respect
and honor your owner. This will keep
people from saying bad things about God
and about our teaching. 2 If any of you
slaves have owners who are followers, you
should show them respect. After all, they
are also followers of Christ, and he loves
them. So you should serve and help them
the best you can.

False Teaching and True Wealth

These are the things you must teach
and tell the people to do. 3 Anyone who
teaches something different disagrees with
the correct and godly teaching of our Lord
Jesus Christ. 4 Those people who disagree
are proud of themselves, but they don't really know a thing. Their minds are sick,
and they like to argue over words. They
cause jealousy, disagreements, unkind
words, evil suspicions, 5 and nasty quarrels.
They have wicked minds and have missed
out on the truth.

These people think religion is supposed
to make you rich. 6 And religion does make
your life rich, by making you content with
what you have. 7 We didn't bring anything
into this world, and we won't[r] take anything with us when we leave. 8 So we
should be satisfied just to have food and
clothes. 9 People who want to be rich fall
into all sorts of temptations and traps. They
are caught by foolish and harmful desires
that drag them down and destroy them.
10 The love of money causes all kinds of
trouble. Some people want money so much
that they have given up their faith and
caused themselves a lot of pain.

Fighting a Good Fight for the Faith

11 Timothy, you belong to God, so keep
away from all these evil things. Try your
best to please God and to be like him. Be
faithful, loving, dependable, and gentle.
12 Fight a good fight for the faith and claim
eternal life. God offered it to you when you
clearly told about your faith, while so many
people listened. 13 Now I ask you to make a
promise. Make it in the presence of God,
who gives life to all, and in the presence of
Jesus Christ, who openly told Pontius Pilate
about his faith. 14 Promise to obey completely and fully all that you have been told
until our Lord Jesus Christ returns.

15 The glorious God
is the only Ruler,
the King of kings
and Lord of lords.
At the time that God
has already decided,
he will send Jesus Christ
back again.

16 Only God lives forever!
And he lives in light
that no one can come near.
No human has ever seen God
or ever can see him.
God will be honored,
and his power
will last forever. Amen.

17 Warn the rich people of this world not
to be proud or to trust in wealth that is easily lost. Tell them to have faith in God, who

[q]**5.22** *to accept people into the service of the Lord*: Or "to forgive people." [r]**6.7** *we won't*: Some manuscripts have "we surely won't."

6.13 Jn 18.37. **6.15** 3 Macc 5.35. **6.16** 3 Macc 2.15.

is rich and blesses us with everything we
need to enjoy life. 18 Instruct them to do as
many good deeds as they can and to help
everyone. Remind the rich to be generous
and share what they have. 19 This will lay a
solid foundation for the future, so that they
will know what true life is like.

20 Timothy, guard what God has placed
in your care! Don't pay any attention to
that godless and stupid talk that sounds
smart but really isn't. 21 Some people have
even lost their faith by believing this talk.

I pray that the Lord will be kind to all
of you!

2 TIMOTHY

ABOUT THIS LETTER

In his second letter to Timothy, Paul is more personal than in his first one. Timothy is like a "dear child" to Paul, and Paul always mentions him in his prayers (1.2, 3) because he wants Timothy to be a "good soldier" of Christ Jesus and to learn to endure suffering (2.1, 3). Paul mentions Timothy's mother and grandmother by name in this letter and reminds Timothy how he had placed his hands on him as a special sign that the Spirit was guiding his work.

Some who claimed to be followers of the Lord had already been trapped by the devil, and Paul warns Timothy to run from those temptations that often catch young people (2.20-26; 3.1-9). He tells Timothy to keep preaching God's message, even if it is not the popular thing to do (4.2). He should also beware of false teachers.

Paul knows that he will soon die for his faith, but he will be rewarded for his faithfulness (4.6-8), and he reminds Timothy of the true message:

"If we died with Christ,
we will live with him.
If we don't give up,
we will rule with him."
(2.11, 12a)

A QUICK LOOK AT THIS LETTER

- Greetings and Prayer for Timothy (1.1, 2)
- Do Not Be Ashamed of the Lord (1.3-18)
- How To Be a Good Soldier of Christ (2.1-26)
- What People Will Be Like in the Last Days (3.1-9)
- Keep Being Faithful (3.10—4.8)
- Personal Instructions and Final Greetings (4.9-22)

1 From Paul, an apostle of Christ Jesus.
God himself chose me to be an
apostle, and he gave me the promised life
that Jesus Christ makes possible.
2 Timothy, you are like a dear child to
me. I pray that God our Father and our
Lord Christ Jesus will be kind and merciful
to you and will bless you with peace!

Do Not Be Ashamed of the Lord

3 Night and day I mention you in my
prayers. I am always grateful for you, as I
pray to the God my ancestors and I have
served with a clear conscience. 4 I remember
how you cried, and I want to see you,
because that will make me truly happy. 5 I
also remember the genuine faith of your
mother Eunice. Your grandmother Lois
had the same sort of faith, and I am sure
that you have it as well. 6 So I ask you to
make full use of the gift that God gave you
when I placed my hands on you.[a] Use it
well. 7 God's Spirit[b] doesn't make cowards
out of us. The Spirit gives us power, love,
and self-control.

[a] **1.6** *when I placed my hands on you*: Church leaders placed their hands on people who were being appointed to preach or teach (see 1 Timothy 4.14). [b] **1.7** *God's Spirit*: Or "God."

1.2 Ac 16.1. **1.5** Ac 16.1.

8 Don't be ashamed to speak for our
Lord. And don't be ashamed of me, just
because I am in jail for serving him. Use
the power that comes from God and join
with me in suffering for telling the good
news.

9 God saved us and chose us
to be his holy people.
We did nothing
to deserve this,
but God planned it
because he is so kind.
Even before time began
God planned for Christ Jesus
to show kindness to us.

10 Now Christ Jesus has come
to show us the kindness
of God.
Christ our Savior defeated death
and brought us
the good news.
It shines like a light
and offers life
that never ends.

11 My work is to be a preacher, an apostle, and a teacher.[c] 12 That's why I am
suffering now. But I am not ashamed! I
know the one I have faith in, and I am
sure that he can guard until the last day
what he has trusted me with.[d] 13 Now follow
the example of the correct teaching I gave
you, and let the faith and love of Christ
Jesus be your model. 14 You have been
trusted with a wonderful treasure. Guard
it with the help of the Holy Spirit, who
lives within you.
15 You know that everyone in Asia has
turned against me, especially Phygelus and
Hermogenes.
16 I pray that the Lord will be kind to
the family of Onesiphorus. He often
cheered me up and wasn't ashamed of me
when I was put in jail. 17 Then after he arrived in Rome, he searched everywhere until he found me. 18 I pray that the Lord
Jesus will ask God to show mercy to Onesiphorus on the day of judgment. You know
how much he helped me in Ephesus.

A Good Soldier of Christ Jesus

2 Timothy, my child, Christ Jesus is
kind, and you must let him make you
strong. 2 You have often heard me teach.
Now I want you to tell these same things to
followers who can be trusted to tell others.
3 As a good soldier of Christ Jesus you
must endure your share of suffering. 4 Soldiers on duty don't work at outside jobs.
They try only to please their commanding
officer. 5 No one wins an athletic contest
without obeying the rules. 6 And farmers
who work hard are the first to eat what
grows in their field. 7 If you keep in mind
what I have told you, the Lord will help you
understand completely.
8 Keep your mind on Jesus Christ! He
was from the family of David and was
raised from death, just as my good news
says. 9 And because of this message, I am
locked up in jail and treated like a criminal.
But God's good news isn't locked in jail,
10 and so I am willing to put up with anything. Then God's special people will be
saved. They will be given eternal glory because they belong to Christ Jesus. 11 Here
is a true message:

"If we died with Christ,
we will live with him.
12 If we don't give up,
we will rule with him.
If we deny
that we know him,
he will deny
that he knows us.
13 If we are not faithful,
he will still be faithful.
Christ cannot deny
who he is."

An Approved Worker

14 Don't let anyone forget these things.
And with God[e] as your witness, you must
warn them not to argue about words. These

[c] **1.11** *teacher*: Some manuscripts add "of the Gentiles." [d] **1.12** *what he has trusted me with*: Or "what I have trusted him with." [e] **2.14** *God*: Some manuscripts have "the Lord," and others have "Christ."

1.11 1 Ti 2.7. **2.12** Mt 10.33; Lk 12.9.

arguments don't help anyone. In fact, they
ruin everyone who listens to them. 15 Do
your best to win God's approval as a worker
who doesn't need to be ashamed and who
teaches only the true message.
16 Keep away from worthless and useless
talk. It only leads people farther away from
God. 17 That sort of talk is like a sore that
won't heal. And Hymenaeus and Philetus
have been talking this way 18 by teaching
that the dead have already been raised to
life. This is far from the truth, and it is destroying the faith of some people.
19 But the foundation that God has laid
is solid. On it is written, "The Lord knows
who his people are. So everyone who worships the Lord must turn away from evil."
20 In a large house some dishes are
made of gold or silver, while others are
made of wood or clay. Some of these are
special, and others are not. 21 That's also
how it is with people. The ones who stop
doing evil and make themselves pure will
become special. Their lives will be holy and
pleasing to their Master, and they will be
able to do all kinds of good deeds.
22 Run from temptations that capture
young people. Always do the right thing. Be
faithful, loving, and easy to get along with.
Worship with people whose hearts are
pure. 23 Stay away from stupid and senseless arguments. These only lead to trouble,
24 and God's servants must not be troublemakers. They must be kind to everyone,
and they must be good teachers and very
patient.
25 Be humble when you correct people
who oppose you. Maybe God will lead them
to turn to him and learn the truth. 26 They
have been trapped by the devil, and he
makes them obey him, but God may help
them escape.

What People Will Be Like in the Last Days

3 You can be certain that in the last days
there will be some very hard times.
2 People will love only themselves and
money. They will be proud, stuck-up, rude,
and disobedient to their parents. They will
also be ungrateful, godless, 3 heartless, and
hateful. Their words will be cruel, and they
will have no self-control or pity. These people will hate everything that is good. 4 They
will be sneaky, reckless, and puffed up with
pride. Instead of loving God, they will love
pleasure. 5 Even though they will make a
show of being religious, their religion won't
be real. Don't have anything to do with
such people.
6 Some men fool whole families, just to
get power over those women who are slaves
of sin and are controlled by all sorts of desires. 7 These women always want to learn
something new, but they never can discover the truth. 8 Just as Jannes and Jambres[f] opposed Moses, these people are enemies of the truth. Their minds are sick,
and their faith isn't real. 9 But they won't
get very far with their foolishness. Soon
everyone will know the truth about them,
just as Jannes and Jambres were found out.

Paul's Last Instructions to Timothy

10 Timothy, you know what I teach and
how I live. You know what I want to do and
what I believe. You have seen how patient
and loving I am, and how in the past I put
up with 11 trouble and suffering in the
cities of Antioch, Iconium, and Lystra. Yet
the Lord rescued me from all those terrible
troubles. 12 Anyone who belongs to Christ
Jesus and wants to live right will have trouble from others. 13 But evil people who pretend to be what they are not will become
worse than ever, as they fool others and are
fooled themselves.
14 Keep on being faithful to what you
were taught and to what you believed. After
all, you know who taught you these things.
15 Since childhood, you have known the
Holy Scriptures that are able to make you
wise enough to have faith in Christ Jesus
and be saved. 16 Everything in the Scriptures is God's Word. All of it is useful for
teaching and helping people and for

[f]**3.8** *Jannes and Jambres*: These names are not found in the Old Testament. But many believe these were the names of the two Egyptian magicians who opposed Moses when he wanted to lead the people of Israel out of Egypt (see Exodus 7.11, 22).

3.8 Ex 7.11. **3.11** **a** Ac 13.14-52; **b** Ac 14.1-7; **c** Ac 14.8-20.

correcting them and showing them how to
live. 17 The Scriptures train God's servants
to do all kinds of good deeds.

4 When Christ Jesus comes as king, he
will be the judge of everyone, whether
they are living or dead. So with God and
Christ as witnesses, I command you 2 to
preach God's message. Do it willingly, even
if it isn't the popular thing to do. You must
correct people and point out their sins. But
also cheer them up, and when you instruct
them, always be patient. 3 The time is coming when people won't listen to good teaching. Instead, they will look for teachers
who will please them by telling them only
what they are itching to hear. 4 They will
turn from the truth and eagerly listen to
senseless stories. 5 But you must stay calm
and be willing to suffer. You must work
hard to tell the good news and to do your
job well.

6 Now the time has come for me to die.
My life is like a drink offering[g] being
poured out on the altar. 7 I have fought
well. I have finished the race, and I have
been faithful. 8 So a crown will be given
to me for pleasing the Lord. He judges
fairly, and on the day of judgment he
will give a crown to me and to everyone
else who wants him to appear with
power.

Personal Instructions

9 Come to see me as soon as you can.
10 Demas loves the things of this world so
much that he left me and went to Thessalonica. Crescens has gone to Galatia, and
Titus has gone to Dalmatia. 11 Only Luke
has stayed with me.

Mark can be very helpful to me, so
please find him and bring him with you.
12 I sent Tychicus to Ephesus.

13 When you come, bring the coat I left
at Troas with Carpus. Don't forget to bring
the scrolls, especially the ones made of
leather.[h]

14 Alexander, the metalworker, has hurt
me in many ways. But the Lord will pay
him back for what he has done. 15 Alexander opposes what we preach. You had better watch out for him.

16 When I was first put on trial, no one
helped me. In fact, everyone deserted me. I
hope it won't be held against them. 17 But
the Lord stood beside me. He gave me the
strength to tell his full message, so that all
Gentiles would hear it. And I was kept safe
from hungry lions. 18 The Lord will always
keep me from being harmed by evil, and he
will bring me safely into his heavenly kingdom. Praise him forever and ever! Amen.

Final Greetings

19 Give my greetings to Priscilla and
Aquila and to the family of Onesiphorus.
20 Erastus stayed at Corinth.

Trophimus was sick when I left him at
Miletus.
21 Do your best to come before winter.

Eubulus, Pudens, Linus, and Claudia
send you their greetings, and so do the rest
of the Lord's followers.

22 I pray that the Lord will bless your life
and will be kind to you.

[g] **4.6** *drink offering*: Water or wine was sometimes poured out as an offering when an animal sacrifice was made. [h] **4.13** *the ones made of leather*: A scroll was a kind of rolled up book, and it could be made out of paper (called "papyrus") or leather (that is, animal skin) or even copper.

4.10 a Col 4.14; Phm 24; **b** 2 Co 8.23; Ga 2.3; Titus 1.4. **4.11 a** Col 4.14; Phm 24; **b** Ac 12.12, 25; 13.13; 15.37-39; Col 4.10; Phm 24. **4.12** Ac 20.4; Eph 6.21, 22; Col 4.7, 8. **4.13** Ac 20.6. **4.14 a** 1 Ti 1.20; **b** Ps 62.12; Ro 2.6. **4.18** 4 Macc 18.24. **4.19 a** Ac 18.2; **b** 2 Ti 1.16, 17. **4.20 a** Ac 19.22; Ro 16.23; **b** Ac 20.4; 21.29.

TITUS

ABOUT THIS LETTER

Paul mentions Titus several times in his letters as someone who worked with him in Asia Minor and Greece (2 Corinthians 2.13; 7.6, 13; 8.6, 16, 23; 12.18; Galatians 2.3). He is told by Paul to appoint church leaders and officials in Crete.

Paul instructs Titus to make sure that church leaders and officials have good reputations (1.5-9) and that all of the Lord's followers keep themselves pure and avoid arguments (1.10—2.9).

Paul includes special instructions for the different groups within the church in Crete. He reminds Titus that a new way of life is possible because of what God has done by sending Jesus Christ: God has saved them, washed them by the power of the Holy Spirit, and given them a fresh start and the hope of eternal life.

Paul also tells how we are saved:

God our Savior showed us
how good and kind he is.
He saved us because
of his mercy,
and not because
of any good things
that we have done.
(3.4, 5a)

A QUICK LOOK AT THIS LETTER

- Greetings and a Prayer for Titus (1.1-4)
- Instructions for Church Officials (1.5-16)
- Instructions for Church People (2.1—3.11)
- Personal Advice and Final Greetings (3.12-15)

---

1 From Paul, a servant of God and an
apostle of Jesus Christ.
I encourage God's own people to have
more faith and to understand the truth
about religion. 2 Then they will have the hope
of eternal life that God promised long ago.
And God never tells a lie! 3 So, at the proper
time, God our Savior gave this message and
told me to announce what he had said.
4 Titus, because of our faith, you are like
a son to me. I pray that God our Father and
Christ Jesus our Savior will be kind to you
and will bless you with peace!

What Titus Was To Do in Crete

5 I left you in Crete to do what had been
left undone and to appoint leaders[a] for the
churches in each town. As I told you, 6 they
must have a good reputation and be faithful in marriage.[b] Their children must be
followers of the Lord and not have a reputation for being wild and disobedient.

[a] **1.5** *leaders*: Or "elders" or "presbyters" or "priests." [b] **1.6** *be faithful in marriage*: Or "be the husband of only one wife" or "have never been divorced."

1.4 2 Co 8.23; Ga 2.3; 2 Ti 4.10. **1.6-9** 1 Ti 3.2-7.

7 Church officials[c] are in charge of God's work, and so they must also have a good reputation. They must not be bossy, quick-tempered, heavy drinkers, bullies, or dishonest in business. 8 Instead, they must be friendly to strangers and enjoy doing good things. They must also be sensible, fair, pure, and self-controlled. 9 They must stick to the true message they were taught, so that their good teaching can help others and correct everyone who opposes it.

10 There are many who don't respect authority, and they fool others by talking nonsense. This is especially true of some Jewish followers. 11 But you must make them be quiet. They are after money, and they upset whole families by teaching what they should not. 12 It is like one of their own prophets once said,

"The people of Crete
always tell lies.
They are greedy and lazy
like wild animals."

13 That surely is a true saying. And you should be hard on such people, so you can help them grow stronger in their faith. 14 Don't pay any attention to any of those senseless Jewish stories and human commands. These are made up by people who won't obey the truth.

15 Everything is pure for someone whose heart is pure. But nothing is pure for an unbeliever with a dirty mind. That person's mind and conscience are destroyed. 16 Such people claim to know God, but their actions prove that they really don't. They are disgusting. They won't obey God, and they are too worthless to do anything good.

Instructions for Different Groups of People

2 Titus, you must teach only what is correct. 2 Tell the older men to have self-control and to be serious and sensible. Their faith, love, and patience must never fail.

3 Tell the older women to behave as those who love the Lord should. They must not gossip about others or be slaves of wine. They must teach what is proper, 4 so the younger women will be loving wives and mothers. 5 Each of the younger women must be sensible and kind, as well as a good homemaker, who puts her own husband first. Then no one can say insulting things about God's message.

6 Tell the young men to have self-control in everything.

7 Always set a good example for others. Be sincere and serious when you teach. 8 Use clean language that no one can criticize. Do this, and your enemies will be too ashamed to say anything against you.

9 Tell slaves always to please their owners by obeying them in everything. Slaves must not talk back to their owners 10 or steal from them. They must be completely honest and trustworthy. Then everyone will show great respect for what is taught about God our Savior.

God's Kindness and the New Life

11 God has shown us how kind he is by coming to save all people. 12 He taught us to give up our wicked ways and our worldly desires and to live decent and honest lives in this world. 13 We are filled with hope, as we wait for the glorious return of our great God and Savior Jesus Christ.[d] 14 He gave himself to rescue us from everything that is evil and to make our hearts pure. He wanted us to be his own people and to be eager to do right.

15 Teach these things, as you use your full authority to encourage and correct people. Make sure you earn everyone's respect.

Doing Helpful Things

3 Remind your people to obey the rulers and authorities and not to be rebellious. They must always be ready to do something helpful 2 and not say cruel things or argue. They should be gentle and

[c]**1.7** *Church officials*: Or "Bishops." [d]**2.13** *the glorious return of our great God and Savior Jesus Christ*: Or "the glorious return of our great God and our Savior Jesus Christ" or "the return of Jesus Christ, who is the glory of our great God and Savior."

2.14 **a** Ps 130.8; **b** Ex 19.5; Dt 4.20; 7.6; 14.2; 1 P 2.9.

kind to everyone. 3 We used to be stupid, disobedient, and foolish, as well as slaves of all sorts of desires and pleasures. We were evil and jealous. Everyone hated us, and we hated everyone.

4 God our Savior showed us
how good and kind he is.
5 He saved us because
of his mercy,
and not because
of any good things
that we have done.

God washed us by the power
of the Holy Spirit.
He gave us new birth
and a fresh beginning.
6 God sent Jesus Christ
our Savior
to give us his Spirit.

7 Jesus treated us much better
than we deserve.
He made us acceptable to God
and gave us the hope
of eternal life.

8 This message is certainly true.

These teachings are useful and helpful for everyone. I want you to insist that the people follow them, so that all who have faith in God will be sure to do good deeds. 9 But don't have anything to do with stupid arguments about ancestors. And stay away from disagreements and quarrels about the Law of Moses. Such arguments are useless and senseless.

10 Warn troublemakers once or twice. Then don't have anything else to do with them. 11 You know that their minds are twisted, and their own sins show how guilty they are.

Personal Instructions and Greetings

12 I plan to send Artemas or Tychicus to you. After he arrives, please try your best to meet me at Nicopolis. I have decided to spend the winter there.

13 When Zenas the lawyer and Apollos get ready to leave, help them as much as you can, so they won't have need of anything.

14 Our people should learn to spend their time doing something useful and worthwhile.

15 Greetings to you from everyone here. Greet all of our friends who share in our faith.

I pray that the Lord will be kind to all of you!

3.12 Ac 20.4; Eph 6.21, 22; Col 4.7, 8; 2 Ti 4.12.

3.13 Ac 18.24; 1 Co 16.12.

PHILEMON

ABOUT THIS LETTER

Philemon was a wealthy man who owned slaves and who used his large house for church meetings (2). He probably lived in Colossae, since Paul's letter to the Colossians mentions Onesimus, a slave of Philemon, and Archippus (Colossians 4.9, 17).

Paul is writing from jail on behalf of Onesimus, a runaway slave owned by Philemon. Onesimus had become a follower of the Lord and a valuable friend to Paul, and Paul is writing to encourage Philemon to accept Onesimus also as a friend and follower of the Lord.

This letter is an excellent example of the art of letter-writing in the Roman world, and it is the most personal of all Paul's letters. The way the letter is written suggests that Paul and Philemon were close friends.

A QUICK LOOK AT THIS LETTER

- Greetings to Philemon (1-3)
- Paul Speaks to Philemon about Onesimus (4-22)
- Final Greetings and a Prayer (23-25)

---

1 From Paul, who is in jail for serving Christ Jesus, and from Timothy, who is like a brother because of our faith.

Philemon, you work with us and are very dear to us. This letter is to you
2 and to the church that meets in your home. It is also to our dear friend Apphia and to Archippus, who serves the Lord as we do.

3 I pray that God our Father and our Lord Jesus Christ will be kind to you and will bless you with peace!

Philemon's Love and Faith

4 Philemon, each time I mention you in
my prayers, I thank God. 5 I hear about
your faith in our Lord Jesus and about your
love for all of God's people. 6 As you share
your faith with others, I pray that they may
come to know all the blessings Christ has
given us. 7 My friend, your love has made
me happy and has greatly encouraged me. It has also cheered the hearts of God's people.

Paul Speaks to Philemon about Onesimus

8 Christ gives me the courage to tell you
what to do. 9 But I would rather ask you to
do it simply because of love. Yes, as someone[a] in jail for Christ, 10 I beg you to help
Onesimus![b] He is like a son to me because
I led him to Christ here in jail. 11 Before
this, he was useless to you, but now he is
useful both to you and to me.

12 Sending Onesimus back to you makes
me very sad. 13 I would like to keep him
here with me, where he could take your
place in helping me while I am here in
prison for preaching the good news. 14 But
I won't do anything unless you agree to it
first. I want your act of kindness to come

[a]9 *someone*: Greek "a messenger" or "an old man." [b]10 *Onesimus*: In Greek this name means "useful."

2 Col 4.17. **10** Col 4.9.

from your heart, and not be something you
feel forced to do.
[15] Perhaps Onesimus was taken from
you for a little while so that you could have
him back for good, [16] but not as a slave.
Onesimus is much more than a slave. To
me he is a dear friend, but to you he is
even more, both as a person and as a follower of the Lord.
[17] If you consider me a friend because
of Christ, then welcome Onesimus as you
would welcome me. [18] If he has cheated
you or owes you anything, charge it to my
account. [19] With my own hand I write:
I, PAUL, WILL PAY YOU BACK. But
don't forget that you owe me your life.
[20] My dear friend and follower of Christ
our Lord, please cheer me up by doing this
for me.
[21] I am sure you will do all I have asked,
and even more. [22] Please get a room ready
for me. I hope your prayers will be answered, and I can visit you.
[23] Epaphras is also here in jail for being
a follower of Christ Jesus. He sends his
greetings, [24] and so do Mark, Aristarchus,
Demas, and Luke, who work together with
me.
[25] I pray that the Lord Jesus Christ will
be kind to you!

23 Col 1.7; 4.12. **24** **a** Ac 12.12, 25; 13.13; 15.37-39; Col 4.10; **b** Ac 19.29; 27.2; Col 4.10; **c** Col 4.14; 2 Ti 4.10; **d** Col 4.14; 2 Ti 4.11.

HEBREWS

ABOUT THIS LETTER

Many religious people in the first century after Jesus' birth, both Jews and Gentiles, had questions about the religion of the early Christians. They were looking for evidence that this new faith was genuine. Jews had the miracle of crossing the Red Sea and the agreement made with God at Mount Sinai to support their faith. But what miracles did Christians have? Jews had beautiful worship ceremonies and a high priest who offered sacrifices in the temple so that the people would be forgiven. But what did Christians have? How could this new Christian faith, centered in Jesus, offer forgiveness of sins and friendship with God?

The letter to the Hebrews was written to answer exactly these kinds of questions. In it the author tells the readers how important Jesus really is. He is greater than any of God's angels (1.5-14), greater than any prophet, and greater even than Moses and Joshua (2.1—4.14). Jesus is the perfect high priest because he never sinned, and by offering his own life he has made the perfect sacrifice for sin once for all time (9.23—10.18). By his death and return from death he has opened the way for all people to come to God (4.14—5.10; 7.1—8.13).

This letter has much to say about the importance of faith. The writer points out that what Jesus offers comes only by faith. And this faith makes his followers sure of what they hope for and gives them proof of things that cannot be seen. The writer praises God's faithful people of the past (11.1-40) and encourages those who follow Jesus now to keep their eyes on him as they run the race (12.1-3).

What does it mean to have a high priest like Jesus?

> *Jesus understands every weakness of ours, because he was tempted in every way that we are. But he did not sin! So whenever we are in need, we should come bravely before the throne of our merciful God. There we will be treated with undeserved kindness, and we will find help.*
>
> *(4.15, 16)*

A QUICK LOOK AT THIS LETTER

- The Greatness of God's Son (1.1-4)
- Jesus Is Greater than Angels (1.5—2.18)
- Jesus Is Greater than Moses and Joshua (3.1—4.13)
- Jesus Is the Great High Priest (4.14—7.28)
- Jesus Brings a Better Agreement (8.1—9.22)
- Jesus' Sacrifice Is Once and for All (9.23—10.31)
- Some of God's People Who Had Great Faith (11.1-40)
- Follow the Example of Jesus (12.1—13.19)
- Final Prayers and Greetings (13.20-25)

1 Long ago in many ways and at many
times God's prophets spoke his message to our ancestors. 2 But now at last,
God sent his Son to bring his message to
us. God created the universe by his Son,
and everything will someday belong to the
Son. 3 God's Son has all the brightness of
God's own glory and is like him in every
way. By his own mighty word, he holds the
universe together.
After the Son had washed away our
sins, he sat down at the right side[a] of the
glorious God in heaven. 4 He had become
much greater than the angels, and the
name he was given is far greater than any
of theirs.

God's Son Is Greater than Angels

5 God has never said
to any of the angels,
"You are my Son, because today
I have become your Father!"
Neither has God said
to any of them,
"I will be his Father,
and he will be my Son!"

6 When God brings his first-born Son[b]
into the world, he commands all of his angels to worship him.
7 And when God speaks about the angels, he says,

"I change my angels into wind
and my servants
into flaming fire."

8 But God says about his Son,

"You are God,
and you will rule
as King forever!
Your[c] royal power
brings about justice.
9 You loved justice
and hated evil,
and so I, your God,
have chosen you.
I appointed you
and made you happier
than any of your friends."

10 The Scriptures also say,

"In the beginning, Lord,
you were the one
who laid the foundation
of the earth
and created the heavens.
11 They will all disappear
and wear out like clothes,
but you will last forever.
12 You will roll them up
like a robe
and change them
like a garment.
But you are always the same,
and you will live forever."

13 God never said to any
of the angels,
"Sit at my right side
until I make your enemies
into a footstool for you!"

14 Angels are merely spirits sent to serve
people who are going to be saved.

This Great Way of Being Saved

2 We must give our full attention to what
we were told, so that we won't drift away.
2 The message spoken by angels proved to
be true, and all who disobeyed or rejected it
were punished as they deserved. 3 So if we
refuse this great way of being saved, how
can we hope to escape? The Lord himself
was the first to tell about it, and people
who heard the message proved to us that it
was true. 4 God himself showed that his
message was true by working all kinds of
powerful miracles and wonders. He also
gave his Holy Spirit to anyone he chose to.

The One Who Leads Us To Be Saved

5 We know that God did not put the future world under the power of angels.

[a] **1.3** *right side*: The place of honor and power. [b] **1.6** *first-born Son*: The first son born into a family had certain privileges that the other children did not have. In 12.23 "first-born" refers to God's special people. [c] **1.8** *Your*: Some manuscripts have "His."

1.2 Ws 7.22. **1.3** Ws 7.25, 26; 8.1. **1.5** **a** Ps 2.7; **b** 2 S 7.14; 1 Ch 17.13. **1.6** Dt 32.43 (LXX). **1.7** Ps 104.4 (LXX). **1.8,9** Ps 45.6, 7. **1.10-12** Ps 102.25-27 (LXX). **1.13** Ps 110.1. **1.14** Tb 12.14, 15.

6 Somewhere in the Scriptures someone
says to God,

"What makes you care
about us humans?
Why are you concerned
for weaklings such as we?
7 You made us lower
than the angels
for a while.
Yet you have crowned us
with glory and honor.[d]
8 And you have put everything
under our power!"

God has put everything under our power
and has not left anything out of our power.
But we still don't see it all under our power.
9 What we do see is Jesus, who for a little
while was made lower than the angels. Because of God's wonderful kindness, Jesus
died for everyone. And now that Jesus has
suffered and died, he is crowned with glory
and honor!

10 Everything belongs to God, and all
things were created by his power. So God
did the right thing when he made Jesus
perfect by suffering, as Jesus led many of
God's children to be saved and to share
in his glory. 11 Jesus and the people he
makes holy all belong to the same family.
That is why he isn't ashamed to call them
his brothers and sisters. 12 He even said
to God,

"I will tell them your name
and sing your praises
when they come together
to worship."

13 He also said,

"I will trust God."

Then he said,

"Here I am with the children
God has given me."

14 We are people of flesh and blood.
That is why Jesus became one of us. He
died to destroy the devil, who had power
over death. 15 But he also died to rescue all
of us who live each day in fear of dying.
16 Jesus clearly did not come to help angels, but he did come to help Abraham's
descendants. 17 He had to be one of us, so
that he could serve God as our merciful
and faithful high priest and sacrifice himself for the forgiveness of our sins. 18 And
now that Jesus has suffered and was
tempted, he can help anyone else who is
tempted.

Jesus Is Greater than Moses

3 My friends, God has chosen you to be
his holy people. So think about Jesus,
the one we call our apostle and high priest!
2 Jesus was faithful to God, who appointed
him, just as Moses was faithful in serving
all of[e] God's people. 3 But Jesus deserves
more honor than Moses, just as the builder
of a house deserves more honor than the
house. 4 Of course, every house is built by
someone, and God is really the one who
built everything.

5 Moses was a faithful servant and told
God's people what would be said in the future. 6 But Christ is the Son in charge of
God's people. And we are those people, if
we keep on being brave and don't lose
hope.

A Rest for God's People

7 It is just as the Holy Spirit says,

"If you hear God's voice today,
8 don't be stubborn!
Don't rebel like those people
who were tested
in the desert.
*9 For forty years your ancestors
tested God and saw
the things he did.

10 "Then God got tired of them
and said,
'You people never
show good sense,
and you don't understand
what I want you to do.'

[d]**2.7** *and honor*: Some manuscripts add "and you have placed us in charge of all you created."
[e]**3.2** *all of*: Some manuscripts do not have these words.
2.6-8 Ps 8.4-6. **2.12** Ps 22.22. **2.13** **a** Is 8.17 (LXX); **b** Is 8.18. **2.16** Is 41.8, 9.
3.2 Nu 12.7. **3.7-11** Ps 95.7-11 (LXX).

[11] God became angry
and told the people,
'You will never enter
my place of rest!' "

[12] My friends, watch out! Don't let evil
thoughts or doubts make any of you turn
from the living God. [13] You must encourage
one another each day. And you must keep
on while there is still a time that can be
called "today." If you don't, then sin may
fool some of you and make you stubborn.
[14] We were sure about Christ when we first
became his people. So let's hold tightly
to our faith until the end. [15] The Scriptures say,

"If you hear his voice today,
don't be stubborn
like those who rebelled."

[16] Who were those people that heard
God's voice and rebelled? Weren't they the
same ones that came out of Egypt with
Moses? [17] Who were the people that made
God angry for forty years? Weren't they the
ones that sinned and died in the desert?
[18] And who did God say would never enter
his place of rest? Weren't they the ones
that disobeyed him? [19] We see that those
people did not enter the place of rest because they did not have faith.

4 The promise to enter the place of rest
is still good, and we must take care
that none of you miss out. [2] We have heard
the message, just as they did. But they
failed to believe what they heard, and the
message did not do them any good. [3] Only
people who have faith will enter the place
of rest. It is just as the Scriptures say,

"God became angry
and told the people,
'You will never enter
my place of rest!' "

God said this, even though everything
has been ready from the time of creation.
[4] In fact, somewhere the Scriptures say
that by the seventh day, God had finished
his work, and so he rested. [5] We also read
that he later said, "You people will never
enter my place of rest!" [6] This means that
the promise to enter is still good, because
those who first heard about it disobeyed
and did not enter. [7] Much later God told
David to make the promise again, just as I
have already said,

"If you hear his voice today,
don't be stubborn!"

[8] If Joshua had really given the people
rest, there would not be any need for God
to talk about another day of rest. [9] But
God has promised us a Sabbath when we
will rest, even though it has not yet come.
[10] On that day God's people will rest from
their work, just as God rested from his
work.

[11] We should do our best to enter that
place of rest, so that none of us will disobey
and miss going there, as they did. [12] What
God has said isn't only alive and active! It is
sharper than any double-edged sword. His
word can cut through our spirits and souls
and through our joints and marrow, until it
discovers the desires and thoughts of our
hearts. [13] Nothing is hidden from God! He
sees through everything, and we will have
to tell him the truth.

Jesus Is the Great High Priest

[14] We have a great high priest, who has
gone into heaven, and he is Jesus the Son
of God. That is why we must hold on to
what we have said about him. [15] Jesus understands every weakness of ours, because
he was tempted in every way that we are.
But he did not sin! [16] So whenever we are
in need, we should come bravely before the
throne of our merciful God. There we will
be treated with undeserved kindness, and
we will find help.

5 Every high priest is appointed to help
others by offering gifts and sacrifices
to God because of their sins. [2] A high priest
has weaknesses of his own, and he feels
sorry for foolish and sinful people. [3] That is
why he must offer sacrifices for his own
sins and for the sins of others. [4] But no one

3.15 Ps 95.7, 8 (LXX). **3.16-18** Nu 14.1-35. **4.3** Ps 95.11. **4.4** Gn 2.2. **4.5** Ps 95.11. **4.7** Ps 95.7, 8 (LXX). **4.8** Dt 31.7; Js 22.4. **4.10** Gn 2.2. **4.13** Ws 1.6. **5.3** Lv 9.7. **5.4** Ex 28.1.

can have the honor of being a high priest
simply by wanting to be one. Only God can
choose a priest, and God is the one who
chose Aaron.
5 That is how it was with Christ. He became a high priest, but not just because he
wanted the honor of being one. It was God
who told him,

"You are my Son, because today
I have become your Father!"

6 In another place, God says,

"You are a priest forever
just like Melchizedek."[f]

7 God had the power to save Jesus from
death. And while Jesus was on earth, he
begged God with loud crying and tears to
save him. He truly worshiped God, and
God listened to his prayers. 8 Jesus is God's
own Son, but still he had to suffer before
he could learn what it really means to obey
God. 9 Suffering made Jesus perfect, and
now he can save forever all who obey him.
10 This is because God chose him to be a
high priest like Melchizedek.

Warning against Turning Away

11 Much more could be said about this
subject. But it is hard to explain, and all of
you are slow to understand. 12 By now you
should have been teachers, but once again
you need to be taught the simplest things
about what God has said. You need milk instead of solid food. 13 People who live on
milk are like babies who don't really know
what is right. 14 Solid food is for mature
people who have been trained to know
right from wrong.

6 We must try to become mature and
start thinking about more than just the
basic things we were taught about Christ.
We shouldn't need to keep talking about
why we ought to turn from deeds that bring
death and why we ought to have faith in
God. 2 And we shouldn't need to keep
teaching about baptisms[g] or about the laying on of hands[h] or about people being
raised from death and the future judgment.
3 Let's grow up, if God is willing.
4-6 But what about people who turn
away after they have already seen the light
and have received the gift from heaven and
have shared in the Holy Spirit? What about
those who turn away after they have received the good message of God and the
powers of the future world? There is no
way to bring them back. What they are doing is the same as nailing the Son of God to
a cross and insulting him in public!
7 A field is useful to farmers, if there is
enough rain to make good crops grow. In
fact, God will bless that field. 8 But land
that produces only thornbushes is worthless. It is likely to fall under God's curse,
and in the end it will be set on fire.
9 My friends, we are talking this way.
But we are sure that you are doing those really good things that people do when they
are being saved. 10 God is always fair. He
will remember how you helped his people
in the past and how you are still helping
them. You belong to God, and he won't forget the love you have shown his people.
11 We wish that each of you would always
be eager to show how strong and lasting
your hope really is. 12 Then you would
never be lazy. You would be following the
example of those who had faith and were
patient until God kept his promise to them.

God's Promise Is Sure

13 No one is greater than God. So he
made a promise in his own name when he
said to Abraham, 14 "I, the Lord, will bless
you with many descendants!" 15 Then after
Abraham had been very patient, he was
given what God had promised. 16 When
anyone wants to settle an argument, they
make a vow by using the name of someone
or something greater than themselves.
17 So when God wanted to prove for certain

[f]**5.6** *Melchizedek*: When Melchizedek is mentioned in the Old Testament, he is described as a priest who lived before Aaron. Nothing is said about his ancestors or his death (see 7.3 and Genesis 14.17-20). [g]**6.2** *baptisms*: Or "ceremonies of washing." [h]**6.2** *laying on of hands*: This was a ceremony in which church leaders and others put their hands on people to show that those people were chosen to do some special kind of work.

5.5 Ps 2.7. **5.6** Ps 110.4. **5.7** Mt 26.36-46; Mk 14.32-42; Lk 22.39-46.
5.12,13 1 Co 3.2. **6.8** Gn 3.17, 18. **6.14** Gn 22.16, 17.

that his promise to his people could not be broken, he made a vow. 18 God cannot tell lies! And so his promises and vows are two things that can never be changed.

We have run to God for safety. Now his promises should greatly encourage us to take hold of the hope that is right in front of us. 19 This hope is like a firm and steady anchor for our souls. In fact, hope reaches behind the curtain[i] and into the most holy place. 20 Jesus has gone there ahead of us, and he is our high priest forever, just like Melchizedek.[j]

The Priestly Family of Melchizedek

7 Melchizedek was both king of Salem and priest of God Most High. He was the one who went out and gave Abraham his blessing, when Abraham returned from killing the kings. 2 Then Abraham gave him a tenth of everything he had.

The meaning of the name Melchizedek is "King of Justice." But since Salem means "peace," he is also "King of Peace." 3 We are not told that he had a father or mother or ancestors or beginning or end. He is like the Son of God and will be a priest forever.[k]

4 Notice how great Melchizedek is! Our famous ancestor Abraham gave him a tenth of what he had taken from his enemies. 5 The Law teaches that even Abraham's descendants must give a tenth of what they possess. And they are to give this to their own relatives, who are the descendants of Levi and are priests. 6 Although Melchizedek wasn't a descendant of Levi, Abraham gave him a tenth of what he had. Then Melchizedek blessed Abraham, who had been given God's promise. 7 Everyone agrees that a person who gives a blessing is greater than the one who receives the blessing.

8 Priests are given a tenth of what people earn. But all priests die, except Melchizedek, and the Scriptures teach that he is alive. 9 Levi's descendants are now the ones who receive a tenth from people. We could even say that when Abraham gave Melchizedek a tenth, Levi also gave him a tenth. 10 This is because Levi was born later into the family of Abraham, who gave a tenth to Melchizedek.

11 Even though the Law of Moses says that the priests must be descendants of Levi, those priests cannot make anyone perfect. So there needs to be a priest like Melchizedek, rather than one from the priestly family of Aaron.[l] 12 And when the rules for selecting a priest are changed, the Law must also be changed.

13 The person we are talking about is our Lord, who came from a tribe that had never had anyone to serve as a priest at the altar. 14 Everyone knows he came from the tribe of Judah, and Moses never said that priests would come from that tribe.

15 All of this becomes clearer, when someone who is like Melchizedek is appointed to be a priest. 16 That person wasn't appointed because of his ancestors, but because his life can never end. 17 The Scriptures say about him,

"You are a priest forever,
just like Melchizedek."

18 In this way a weak and useless command was put aside, 19 because the Law cannot make anything perfect. At the same time, we are given a much better hope, and it can bring us close to God.

20-21 God himself made a promise when this priest was appointed. But he did not make a promise like this when the other priests were appointed. The promise he made is,

"I, the Lord, promise that you
will be a priest forever!
And I will never
change my mind!"

22 This means that Jesus guarantees us a better agreement with God. 23 There have

[i]**6.19** *behind the curtain*: In the tent that was used for worship, a curtain separated the "holy place" from the "most holy place," which only the high priest could enter. [j]**6.20** *Melchizedek*: See the note at 5.6. [k]**7.3** *will be a priest forever*: See the note at 5.6. [l]**7.11** *descendants of Levi . . . from the priestly family of Aaron*: Levi was the ancestor of the tribe from which priests and their helpers (called "Levites") were chosen. Aaron was the first high priest.

6.19 Lv 16.1, 2. **6.20** Ps 110.4. **7.1,2** Gn 14.17-20. **7.5** Nu 18.21. **7.17** Ps 110.4. **7.20,21** Ps 110.4.

been a lot of other priests, and all of them
have died. 24 But Jesus will never die, and
so he will be a priest forever! 25 He is forever able to save[m] the people he leads to
God, because he always lives to speak to
God for them.
26 Jesus is the high priest we need. He is
holy and innocent and faultless, and not at
all like us sinners. Jesus is honored above
all beings in heaven, 27 and he is better
than any other high priest. Jesus doesn't
need to offer sacrifices each day for his
own sins and then for the sins of the people. He offered a sacrifice once for all,
when he gave himself. 28 The Law appoints
priests who have weaknesses. But God's
promise, which came later than the Law,
appoints his Son. And he is the perfect
high priest forever.

A Better Promise

8 What I mean is that we have a high
priest who sits at the right side[n] of
God's great throne in heaven. 2 He also
serves as the priest in the most holy place[o]
inside the real tent there in heaven. This
tent of worship was set up by the Lord, not
by humans.
3 Since all priests must offer gifts and
sacrifices, Christ also needed to have
something to offer. 4 If he were here on
earth, he would not be a priest at all, because here the Law appoints other priests
to offer sacrifices. 5 But the tent where they
serve is just a copy and a shadow of the real
one in heaven. Before Moses made the
tent, he was told, "Be sure to make it exactly like the pattern you were shown on
the mountain!" 6 Now Christ has been appointed to serve as a priest in a much better way, and he has given us much assurance of a better agreement.
7 If the first agreement with God had
been all right, there would not have been
any need for another one. 8 But the Lord
found fault with it and said,

"I tell you the time will come,
when I will make
a new agreement
with the people of Israel
and the people of Judah.
9 It won't be like the agreement
that I made
with their ancestors,
when I took them by the hand
and led them out of Egypt.
They broke their agreement
with me,
and I stopped caring
about them!

10 "But now I tell the people
of Israel
this is my new agreement:
'The time will come
when I, the Lord,
will write my laws
on their minds and hearts.
I will be their God,
and they will be
my people.
11 Not one of them
will have to teach another
to know me, their Lord.'

"All of them will know me,
no matter who they are.
12 I will treat them with kindness,
even though they are wicked.
I will forget their sins."

13 When the Lord talks about a new
agreement, he means that the first one is
out of date. And anything that is old and
useless will soon disappear.

The Tent in Heaven

9 The first promise that was made included rules for worship and a tent for
worship here on earth. 2 The first part of
the tent was called the holy place, and a
lampstand, a table, and the sacred loaves of
bread were kept there.
3 Behind the curtain was the most holy
place. 4 The gold altar that was used for

[m]**7.25** *forever able to save*: Or "able to save forever." [n]**8.1** *right side*: See the note at 1.3.
[o]**8.2** *most holy place*: See the note at 6.19.

7.27 Lv 9.7. **8.1** Ps 110.1. **8.5** Ex 25.40. **8.8-12** Jr 31.31-34 (LXX).
9.2 **a** Ex 26.1-30; **b** Ex 25.31-40; **c** Ex 25.23-30. **9.3** Ex 26.31-33. **9.4** **a** Ex 30.1-6;
b Ex 25.10-16; **c** Ex 16.33; **d** Nu 17.8-10; **e** Ex 25.16; Dt 10.3-5.

burning incense was in this holy place. The
gold-covered sacred chest was also there,
and inside it were three things. First, there
was a gold jar filled with manna.[p] Then
there was Aaron's walking stick that
sprouted.[q] Finally, there were the flat
stones with the Ten Commandments written on them. 5 On top of the chest were the
glorious creatures with wings[r] opened out
above the place of mercy.[s]

Now isn't the time to go into detail
about these things. 6 But this is how everything was when the priests went each day
into the first part of the tent to do their duties. 7 However, only the high priest could
go into the second part of the tent, and he
went in only once a year. Each time he carried blood to offer for his sins and for any
sins that the people had committed without meaning to.

8 All of this is the Holy Spirit's way of
saying that no one could enter the most
holy place while the tent was still the place
of worship. 9 This also has a meaning for
today. It shows that we cannot make our
consciences clear by offering gifts and sacrifices. 10 These rules are merely about such
things as eating and drinking and ceremonies
for washing ourselves. And rules about
physical things will last only until the time
comes to change them for something better.

11 Christ came as the high priest of the
good things that are now here.[t] He also
went into a much better tent that wasn't
made by humans and that doesn't belong to
this world. 12 Then Christ went once for all
into the most holy place and freed us from
sin forever. He did this by offering his own
blood instead of the blood of goats and
bulls.

13 According to the Law of Moses, those
people who become unclean are not fit to
worship God. Yet they will be considered
clean, if they are sprinkled with the blood
of goats and bulls and with the ashes of a
sacrificed calf. 14 But Christ was sinless,
and he offered himself as an eternal and
spiritual sacrifice to God. That's why his
blood is much more powerful and makes
our[u] consciences clear. Now we can serve
the living God and no longer do things that
lead to death.

15 Christ died to rescue those who had
sinned and broken the old agreement. Now
he brings his chosen ones a new agreement
with its guarantee of God's eternal blessings! 16 In fact, making an agreement of
this kind is like writing a will. This is because the one who makes the will must die
before it is of any use. 17 In other words, a
will doesn't go into effect as long as the one
who made it is still alive.

18 Blood was also used[v] to put the first
agreement into effect. 19 Moses told the
people all that the Law said they must do.
Then he used red wool and a hyssop plant
to sprinkle the people and the book of the
Law with the blood of bulls and goats[w] and
with water. 20 He told the people, "With this
blood God makes his agreement with you."
21 Moses also sprinkled blood on the tent
and on everything else that was used in
worship. 22 The Law says that almost everything must be sprinkled with blood, and no
sins can be forgiven unless blood is offered.

Christ's Great Sacrifice

23 These things are only copies of what
is in heaven, and so they had to be made
holy by these ceremonies. But the real

[p]**9.4** *manna*: When the people of Israel were wandering through the desert, the Lord provided them with food that could be made into thin wafers. This food was called manna, which in Hebrew means "What is it?" [q]**9.4** *Aaron's walking stick that sprouted*: According to Numbers 17.1-11, Aaron's walking stick sprouted and produced almonds to show that the Lord was pleased with him and Moses. [r]**9.5** *glorious creatures with wings*: Two of these creatures (called "cherubim" in Hebrew and Greek) with outspread wings were on top of the sacred chest and were symbols of God's throne. [s]**9.5** *place of mercy*: The lid of the sacred chest, which was thought to be God's throne on earth. [t]**9.11** *that are now here*: Some manuscripts have "that were coming." [u]**9.14** *our*: Some manuscripts have "your," and others have "their." [v]**9.18** *Blood was also used*: Or "There also had to be a death." [w]**9.19** *blood of bulls and goats*: Some manuscripts do not have "and goats."

9.5 Ex 25.18-22. **9.6** Nu 18.2-6. **9.7** Lv 16.1, 2-34; 3 Macc 1.11. **9.11-15** 4 Macc 17.21. **9.13** **a** Lv 16.15, 16; **b** Nu 19.9, 17-19. **9.19,20** Ex 24.6-8. **9.21** Lv 8.15. **9.22** Lv 17.11.

things in heaven must be made holy by something better. 24 This is why Christ did not go into a tent that had been made by humans and was only a copy of the real one. Instead, he went into heaven and is now there with God to help us.

25 Christ did not have to offer himself many times. He wasn't like a high priest who goes into the most holy place each year to offer the blood of an animal. 26 If he had offered himself every year, he would have suffered many times since the creation of the world. But instead, near the end of time he offered himself once and for all, so that he could be a sacrifice that does away with sin.

27 We die only once, and then we are judged. 28 So Christ died only once to take away the sins of many people. But when he comes again, it will not be to take away sin. He will come to save everyone who is waiting for him.

10 The Law of Moses is like a shadow of the good things to come. This shadow isn't the good things themselves, because it cannot free people from sin by the sacrifices that are offered year after year. 2 If there were worshipers who already have their sins washed away and their consciences made clear, there would not be any need to go on offering sacrifices. 3-4 But the blood of bulls and goats cannot take away sins. It only reminds people of their sins from one year to the next.

5 When Christ came into the world, he said to God,

"Sacrifices and offerings
are not what you want,
but you have given me
my body.
6 No, you are not pleased
with animal sacrifices
and offerings for sin."

7 Then Christ said,

"And so, my God,
I have come to do
what you want,
as the Scriptures say."

8 The Law teaches that offerings and sacrifices must be made because of sin. But why did Christ mention these things and say that God did not want them? 9 Well, it was to do away with offerings and sacrifices and to replace them. That is what he meant by saying to God, "I have come to do what you want." 10 So we are made holy because Christ obeyed God and offered himself once for all.

11 The priests do their work each day, and they keep on offering sacrifices that can never take away sins. 12 But Christ offered himself as a sacrifice that is good forever. Now he is sitting at God's right side,[x] 13 and he will stay there until his enemies are put under his power. 14 By his one sacrifice he has forever set free from sin the people he brings to God.

15 The Holy Spirit also speaks of this by telling us that the Lord said,

16 "When the time comes,
I will make an agreement
with them.
I will write my laws
on their minds and hearts.
17 Then I will forget
about their sins
and no longer remember
their evil deeds."

18 When sins are forgiven, there is no more need to offer sacrifices.

Encouragement and Warning

19 My friends, the blood of Jesus gives us courage to enter the most holy place 20 by a new way that leads to life! And this way takes us through the curtain that is Christ himself.

21 We have a great high priest who is in charge of God's house. 22 So let's come near God with pure hearts and a confidence that comes from having faith. Let's keep our hearts pure, our consciences free from evil, and our bodies washed with

[x] **10.12** *right side*: See the note at 1.3.

9.28 Is 53.12. **10.5-7** Ps 40.6-8 (LXX). **10.11** Ex 29.38. **10.12,13** Ps 110.1. **10.16** Jr 31.33. **10.17** Jr 31.34. **10.22** Lv 8.30; Ez 36.25.

clean water. 23 We must hold tightly to the
hope that we say is ours. After all, we can
trust the one who made the agreement with
us. 24 We should keep on encouraging each
other to be thoughtful and to do helpful
things. 25 Some people have gotten out of the
habit of meeting for worship, but we must
not do that. We should keep on encouraging
each other, especially since you know that
the day of the Lord's coming is getting
closer.

26 No sacrifices can be made for people
who decide to sin after they find out about
the truth. 27 They are God's enemies, and
all they can look forward to is a terrible
judgment and a furious fire. 28 If two or
more witnesses accused someone of breaking
the Law of Moses, that person could be
put to death. 29 But it is much worse to dishonor
God's Son and to disgrace the blood
of the promise that made us holy. And it is
just as bad to insult the Holy Spirit, who
shows us mercy. 30 We know that God has
said he will punish and take revenge. We
also know that the Scriptures say the Lord
will judge his people. 31 It is a terrible thing
to fall into the hands of the living God!

32 Don't forget all the hard times you
went through when you first received the
light. 33 Sometimes you were abused and
mistreated in public, and at other times
you shared in the sufferings of others.
34 You were kind to people in jail. And you
gladly let your possessions be taken away,
because you knew you had something better,
something that would last forever.

35 Keep on being brave! It will bring you
great rewards. 36 Learn to be patient, so
that you will please God and be given what
he has promised. 37 As the Scriptures say,

"God is coming soon!
It won't be very long.
38 The people God accepts
will live because
of their faith.[y]
But he isn't pleased
with anyone
who turns back."

39 We are not like those people who turn
back and get destroyed. We will keep on
having faith until we are saved.

The Great Faith of God's People

11 Faith makes us sure of what we
hope for and gives us proof of what
we cannot see. 2 It was their faith that
made our ancestors pleasing to God.

3 Because of our faith, we know that the
world was made at God's command. We
also know that what can be seen was made
out of what cannot be seen.

4 Because Abel had faith, he offered God
a better sacrifice than Cain did. God was
pleased with him and his gift, and even
though Abel is now dead, his faith still
speaks for him.

5 Enoch had faith and did not die. He
pleased God, and God took him up to heaven.
That's why his body was never found.
6 But without faith no one can please
God. We must believe that God is real and
that he rewards everyone who searches
for him.

7 Because Noah had faith, he was
warned about something that had not yet
happened. He obeyed and built a boat that
saved him and his family. In this way the
people of the world were judged, and Noah
was given the blessings that come to everyone
who pleases God.

8 Abraham had faith and obeyed God.
He was told to go to the land that God had
said would be his, and he left for a country
he had never seen. 9 Because Abraham had
faith, he lived as a stranger in the promised
land. He lived there in a tent, and so did
Isaac and Jacob, who were later given the
same promise. 10 Abraham did this, because
he was waiting for the eternal city
that God had planned and built.

[y] **10.38** *The people God accepts will live because of their faith*: Or "The people God accepts because of their faith will live."

10.27 Is 26.11 (LXX). **10.28** Dt 17.5-7; 19.15. **10.29** Ex 24.8. **10.30** **a** Dt 32.35; **b** Dt 32.36. **10.37,38** Hb 2.3, 4 (LXX). **11.2** Si 44.10—50.21; 1 Macc 2.51-64. **11.3** Gn 1.1; Ps 33.6, 9; Jn 1.3. **11.4** Gn 4.3-10. **11.5** Gn 5.21-24 (LXX); Si 44.16. **11.7** Gn 6.13-22. **11.8** Gn 12.1-5. **11.9** Gn 35.27.

11 Even when Sarah was too old to have
children, she had faith that God would do
what he had promised, and she had a son.
12 Her husband Abraham was almost dead,
but he became the ancestor of many people. In fact, there are as many of them as
there are stars in the sky or grains of sand
along the beach.

13 Every one of those people died. But
they still had faith, even though they had
not received what they had been promised.
They were glad just to see these things
from far away, and they agreed that they
were only strangers and foreigners on this
earth. 14 When people talk this way, it
is clear that they are looking for a place
to call their own. 15 If they had been
talking about the land where they had once
lived, they could have gone back at
any time. 16 But they were looking forward
to a better home in heaven. That's
why God wasn't ashamed for them to call
him their God. He even built a city for
them.

17-18 Abraham had been promised that
Isaac, his only son,[z] would continue his
family. But when Abraham was tested, he
had faith and was willing to sacrifice Isaac,
19 because he was sure that God could raise
people to life. This was just like getting
Isaac back from death.

20 Isaac had faith, and he promised
blessings to Jacob and Esau. 21 Later, when
Jacob was about to die, he leaned on his
walking stick and worshiped. Then because
of his faith he blessed each of Joseph's
sons. 22 And right before Joseph died, he
had faith that God would lead the people of
Israel out of Egypt. So he told them to take
his bones with them.

23 Because Moses' parents had faith,
they kept him hidden until he was three
months old. They saw that he was a beautiful child, and they were not afraid to disobey the king's orders.[a] 24 Then after
Moses grew up, his faith made him refuse
to be called Pharaoh's grandson. 25 He
chose to be mistreated with God's people
instead of having the good time that sin
could bring for a little while. 26 Moses knew
that the treasures of Egypt were not as
wonderful as what he would receive from
suffering for the Messiah,[b] and he looked
forward to his reward.

27 Because of his faith, Moses left Egypt.
Moses had seen the invisible God and wasn't
afraid of the king's anger. 28 His faith also
made him celebrate Passover. He sprinkled
the blood of animals on the doorposts, so that
the first-born sons of the people of Israel
would not be killed by the destroying angel.
29 Because of their faith, the people
walked through the Red Sea[c] on dry land.
But when the Egyptians tried to do it, they
were drowned.

30 God's people had faith, and when
they had walked around the city of Jericho
for seven days, its walls fell down.

31 Rahab had been a prostitute, but she
had faith and welcomed the spies. So
she wasn't killed with the people who disobeyed.

32 What else can I say? There isn't
enough time to tell about Gideon, Barak,
Samson, Jephthah, David, Samuel, and the
prophets. 33 Their faith helped them con-

[z] **11.17,18** *his only son*: Although Abraham had a son by a slave woman, his son Isaac was considered his only son, because he was born as a result of God's promise to Abraham.
[a] **11.23** *the king's orders*: The king of Egypt ordered all Israelite baby boys to be left outside of their homes, so they would die or be killed. [b] **11.26** *the Messiah*: Or "Christ." [c] **11.29** *Red Sea*: This name comes from the Bible of the early Christians, a translation made into Greek about 200 B.C. It refers to the body of water that the Israelites crossed and was one of the marshes or fresh water lakes near the eastern part of the Nile Delta, where they lived and where the towns of Exodus 13.17—14.9 were located.

11.11 Gn 18.11-14; 21.2. **11.12** Gn 15.5; 22.17; 32.12. **11.13** Gn 23.4; 1 Ch 29.15; Ps 39.12. **11.17,18** Gn 21.12; 22.1-14. **11.17-19** 4 Macc 13.12. **11.20** Gn 27.27-29, 39, 40. **11.21** **a** Gn 48.1-20; **b** Gn 47.31 (LXX). **11.22** Gn 50.24, 25; Ex 13.19. **11.23** **a** Ex 2.2; **b** Ex 1.22. **11.24** Ex 2.10-12. **11.25** 4 Macc 15.2. **11.28** Ex 12.21-30. **11.29** Ex 14.21-31. **11.30** Js 6.12-25. **11.31** **a** Js 6.21-25; **b** Js 2.1-21. **11.32** **a** Jg 6.11—8.32; **b** Jg 4.6—5.31; **c** Jg 13.2—16.31; **d** Jg 11.1—12.7; **e** 1 S 16.1—1 K 2.11; **f** 1 S 1.1—25.1. **11.33** Dn 6.1-27.

quer kingdoms, and because they did right,
God made promises to them. They closed
the jaws of lions 34 and put out raging fires
and escaped from the swords of their enemies. Although they were weak, they were
given the strength and power to chase foreign armies away.
35 Some women received their loved
ones back from death. Many of these people were tortured, but they refused to be released. They were sure that they would get
a better reward when the dead are raised to
life. 36 Others were made fun of and beaten
with whips, and some were chained in jail.
37 Still others were stoned to death or
sawed in two[d] or killed with swords. Some
had nothing but sheep skins or goat skins
to wear. They were poor, mistreated, and
tortured. 38 The world did not deserve
these good people, who had to wander in
deserts and on mountains and had to live
in caves and holes in the ground.
39 All of them pleased God because of
their faith! But still they died without being
given what had been promised. 40 This was
because God had something better in store
for us. And he did not want them to reach
the goal of their faith without us.

A Large Crowd of Witnesses

12 Such a large crowd of witnesses is
all around us! So we must get rid of
everything that slows us down, especially
the sin that just won't let go. And we must
be determined to run the race that is ahead
of us. 2 We must keep our eyes on Jesus,
who leads us and makes our faith complete. He endured the shame of being
nailed to a cross, because he knew that
later on he would be glad he did. Now he is
seated at the right side[e] of God's throne!
3 So keep your mind on Jesus, who put up
with many insults from sinners. Then you
won't get discouraged and give up.
4 None of you have yet been hurt[f] in your
battle against sin. 5 But you have fogotten
that the Scriptures say to God's children,

"When the Lord punishes you,
don't make light of it,
and when he corrects you,
don't be discouraged.
6 The Lord corrects the people
he loves
and disciplines those
he calls his own."

7 Be patient when you are being corrected! This is how God treats his children.
Don't all parents correct their children?
8 God corrects all of his children, and if he
doesn't correct you, then you don't really
belong to him. 9 Our earthly fathers correct
us, and we still respect them. Isn't it even
better to be given true life by letting our
spiritual Father correct us?
10 Our human fathers correct us for a
short time, and they do it as they think
best. But God corrects us for our own good,
because he wants us to be holy, as he is.
11 It is never fun to be corrected. In fact, at
the time it is always painful. But if we learn
to obey by being corrected, we will do right
and live at peace.
12 Now stand up straight! Stop your
knees from shaking 13 and walk a straight
path. Then lame people will be healed, instead of getting worse.

Warning against Turning from God

14 Try to live at peace with everyone!
Live a clean life. If you don't, you will never
see the Lord. 15 Make sure that no one
misses out on God's wonderful kindness.
Don't let anyone become bitter and cause
trouble for the rest of you. 16 Watch out for
immoral and ungodly people like Esau,
who sold his future blessing[g] for only one
meal. 17 You know how he later wanted it
back. But there was nothing he could do to

[d] **11.37** *sawed in two*: Some manuscripts have "tested" or "tempted." [e] **12.2** *right side*: See the note at 1.3. [f] **12.4** *hurt*: Or "killed." [g] **12.16** *sold his future blessing*: As the first-born son, Esau had certain privileges that were known as a "birthright."

11.34 Dn 3.1-30. **11.35** 1 K 17.17-24; 2 K 4.25-37; 2 Macc 6.18—7.42. **11.36** 1 K 22.26, 27; 2 Ch 18.25, 26; Jr 20.2; 37.15, 16; 38.6. **11.37** 2 Ch 24.21, 22. **12.1 a** 4 Macc 6.10; **b**.4 Macc 14.2. **12.2** 4 Macc 11.26. **12.5,6** Job 5.17; Pr 3.11, 12 (LXX). **12.12** Is 35.3 (LXX). **12.13** Pr 4.26 (LXX). **12.15** Dt 29.18 (LXX). **12.16** Gn 25.29-34. **12.17** Gn 27.30-40.

change things, even though he begged his
father and cried.
18 You have not come to a place like
Mount Sinai[h] that can be seen and
touched. There is no flaming fire or dark
cloud or storm 19 or trumpet sound. The
people of Israel heard a voice speak. But
they begged it to stop, 20 because they
could not obey its commands. They
were even told to kill any animal that
touched the mountain. 21 The sight was so
frightening that Moses said he shook with
fear.
22 You have now come to Mount Zion
and to the heavenly Jerusalem. This is the
city of the living God, where thousands
and thousands of angels have come
to celebrate. 23 Here you will find all of
God's dearest children,[i] whose names are
written in heaven. And you will find God
himself, who judges everyone. Here also
are the spirits of those good people who
have been made perfect. 24 And Jesus is
here! He is the one who makes God's new
agreement with us, and his sprinkled blood
says much better things than the blood of
Abel.[j]
25 Make sure that you obey the one
who speaks to you. The people did not
escape, when they refused to obey the
one who spoke to them at Mount Sinai.
Do you think you can possibly escape,
if you refuse to obey the one who speaks
to you from heaven? 26 When God spoke
the first time, his voice shook only the
earth. This time he has promised to shake
the earth once again, and heaven too.
27 The words "once again" mean that
these created things will someday be
shaken and removed. Then what cannot be
shaken will last. 28 We should be grateful
that we were given a kingdom that cannot
be shaken. And in this kingdom we please
God by worshiping him and by showing
him great honor and respect. 29 Our God is
like a destructive fire!

Service That Pleases God

13 Keep being concerned about each
other as the Lord's followers should.
2 Be sure to welcome strangers into your
home. By doing this, some people have
welcomed angels as guests, without even
knowing it.
3 Remember the Lord's people who are
in jail and be concerned for them. Don't
forget those who are suffering, but imagine
that you are there with them.
4 Have respect for marriage. Always be
faithful to your partner, because God will
punish anyone who is immoral or unfaithful in marriage.
5 Don't fall in love with money. Be satisfied with what you have. The Lord has
promised that he will not leave us or
desert us. 6 That should make you feel like
saying,

"The Lord helps me!
Why should I be afraid
of what people
can do to me?"

7 Don't forget about your leaders who
taught you God's message. Remember what
kind of lives they lived and try to have faith
like theirs.
8 Jesus Christ never changes! He is the
same yesterday, today, and forever. 9 Don't
be fooled by any kind of strange teachings. It
is better to receive strength from God's undeserved kindness than to depend on certain
foods. After all, these foods don't really help
the people who eat them. 10 But we have
an altar where even the priests who
serve in the place of worship have no right
to eat.
11 After the high priest offers the blood

[h] **12.18** *a place like Mount Sinai*: The Greek text has "a place," but the writer is referring to the time that the Lord spoke to the people of Israel from Mount Sinai (see Exodus 19.16-25). [i] **12.23** *all of God's dearest children*: The Greek text has "the gathering of the first-born children" (see the note at 1.6). [j] **12.24** *blood of Abel*: Cain and Abel were the two sons of Adam and Eve. Cain murdered Abel (see Genesis 4.1-16).

12.18,19 Ex 19.16-22; 20.18-21; Dt 4.11, 12; 5.22-27. **12.20** Ex 19.12, 13. **12.24** Gn 4.10. **12.25** Ex 20.22. **12.26** Hg 2.6 (LXX). **12.29** Dt 4.24. **13.2** Gn 18.1-8; 19.1-3; Tb 5.4, 5. **13.4** Ws 3.13. **13.5** Dt 31.6, 8; Js 1.5. **13.6** Ps 118.6 (LXX). **13.11** Lv 16.27.

Paul and Silas in prison
Acts 16.25, 26

Runners racing for the prize
1 Corinthians 9.24-27

Young Timothy with his mother
and grandmother
2 Timothy 1.5

"They were from every race, tribe, nation . . ." *Revelation 7.9*

of animals as a sin offering, the bodies of those animals are burned outside the camp.
12 Jesus himself suffered outside the city
gate, so that his blood would make people
holy. 13 That's why we should go outside
the camp to Jesus and share in his disgrace.
14 On this earth we don't have a city
that lasts forever, but we are waiting for
such a city.

15 Our sacrifice is to keep offering praise
to God in the name of Jesus. 16 But don't
forget to help others and to share your possessions with them. This too is like offering a sacrifice that pleases God.

17 Obey your leaders and do what they say. They are watching over you, and they must answer to God. So don't make them sad as they do their work. Make them happy. Otherwise, they won't be able to help you at all.

18 Pray for us. Our consciences are
clear, and we always try to live right. 19 I especially want you to pray that I can visit
you again soon.

Final Prayers and Greetings

20 God gives peace, and he raised our Lord Jesus Christ from death. Now Jesus is like a Great Shepherd whose blood was used to make God's eternal agreement with
his flock.[k] 21 I pray that God will make you
ready to obey him and that you will always be eager to do right. May Jesus help you do what pleases God. To Jesus Christ be glory forever and ever! Amen.

22 My friends, I have written only a short letter to encourage you, and I beg you to pay close attention to what I have said.

23 By now you surely must know that our friend Timothy is out of jail. If he gets here in time, I will bring him with me when I come to visit you.

24 Please give my greetings to your leaders and to the rest of the Lord's people.

His followers from Italy send you their greetings.

25 I pray that God will be kind to all of you![l]

[k] **13.20** *whose blood was used to make God's eternal agreement with his flock*: See 9.18-22.
[l] **13.25** *to all of you*: Some manuscripts add "Amen."
13.21 4 Macc 18.24.

JAMES

ABOUT THIS LETTER

This is a good example of a general letter, because it is addressed to Christians scattered throughout the Roman Empire. Though written as a letter, it is more like a short book of instructions for daily living.

For James faith means action! In fact, the entire book is a series of examples that show faith in action in wise and practical ways.

His advice was clear and to the point: If you are poor, don't despair! Don't give up when your faith is being tested. Don't get angry quickly. Don't favor the rich over the poor. Do good things for others. Control your tongue and desires. Surrender to God and rely on his wisdom. Resist the devil. Don't brag about what you are going to do. If you are rich, use your money to help the poor. Be patient and kind, and pray for those who need God's help.

A QUICK LOOK AT THIS LETTER

---

1 From James, a servant of God and of
our Lord Jesus Christ.
Greetings to the twelve tribes scattered
all over the world.[a]

Faith and Wisdom

2 My friends, be glad, even if you have a
lot of trouble. 3 You know that you learn to
endure by having your faith tested. 4 But
you must learn to endure everything, so
that you will be completely mature and not
lacking in anything.
5 If any of you need wisdom, you should
ask God, and it will be given to you. God is
generous and won't correct you for asking.
6 But when you ask for something, you
must have faith and not doubt. Anyone
who doubts is like an ocean wave tossed
around in a storm. 7-8 If you are that kind
of person, you can't make up your mind,
and you surely can't be trusted. So don't
expect the Lord to give you anything at all.

Poor People and Rich People

9 Any of God's people who are poor
should be glad that he thinks so highly of
them. 10 But any who are rich should be
glad when God makes them humble. Rich
people will disappear like wild flowers
11 scorched by the burning heat of the sun.
The flowers lose their blossoms, and their
beauty is destroyed. That is how the rich

---

[a]**1.1** *twelve tribes scattered all over the world*: James is saying that the Lord's followers are like the tribes of Israel that were scattered everywhere by their enemies.

1.1 Mt 13.55; Mk 6.3; Ac 15.13; Ga 1.19. **1.2** Ws 3.5, 6. **1.5** Ws 8.21; Si 51.13, 14. **1.10,11** Is 40.6, 7 (LXX).

will disappear, as they go about their
business.

Trials and Temptations

12 God will bless you, if you don't give up
when your faith is being tested. He will reward you with a glorious life,[b] just as he rewards everyone who loves him.
13 Don't blame God when you are
tempted! God cannot be tempted by evil,
and he doesn't use evil to tempt others.
14 We are tempted by our own desires that
drag us off and trap us. 15 Our desires
make us sin, and when sin is finished with
us, it leaves us dead.
16 Don't be fooled, my dear friends.
17 Every good and perfect gift comes down
from the Father who created all the lights
in the heavens. He is always the same and
never makes dark shadows by changing.
18 He wanted us to be his own special people,[c] and so he sent the true message to
give us new birth.

Hearing and Obeying

19 My dear friends, you should be quick
to listen and slow to speak or to get angry.
20 If you are angry, you cannot do any of the
good things that God wants done. 21 You
must stop doing anything immoral or evil.
Instead be humble and accept the message
that is planted in you to save you.
22 Obey God's message! Don't fool yourselves by just listening to it. 23 If you hear
the message and don't obey it, you are like
people who stare at themselves in a mirror
24 and forget what they look like as soon as
they leave. 25 But you must never stop looking at the perfect law that sets you free. God
will bless you in everything you do, if you
listen and obey, and don't just hear and
forget.
26 If you think you are being religious,
but can't control your tongue, you are fooling yourself, and everything you do is useless. 27 Religion that pleases God the Father
must be pure and spotless. You must help
needy orphans and widows and not let this
world make you evil.

Warning against Having Favorites

2 My friends, if you have faith in our
glorious Lord Jesus Christ, you won't
treat some people better than others.
2 Suppose a rich person wearing fancy
clothes and a gold ring comes to one of
your meetings. And suppose a poor person
dressed in worn-out clothes also comes.
3 You must not give the best seat to the one
in fancy clothes and tell the one who is
poor to stand at the side or sit on the floor.
4 That is the same as saying that some people are better than others, and you would
be acting like a crooked judge.
5 My dear friends, pay attention. God
has given a lot of faith to the poor people in
this world. He has also promised them a
share in his kingdom that he will give to
everyone who loves him. 6 You mistreat
the poor. But isn't it the rich who boss you
around and drag you off to court? 7 Aren't
they the ones who make fun of your
Lord?
8 You will do all right, if you obey the
most important law[d] in the Scriptures. It is
the law that commands us to love others as
much as we love ourselves. 9 But if you
treat some people better than others, you
have done wrong, and the Scriptures teach
that you have sinned.
10 If you obey every law except one, you
are still guilty of breaking them all.
11 The same God who told us to be faithful
in marriage also told us not to murder.
So even if you are faithful in marriage,
but murder someone, you still have broken
God's Law.
12 Speak and act like people who will be
judged by the law that sets us free. 13 Do this,

[b] **1.12** *a glorious life*: The Greek text has "the crown of life." In ancient times an athlete who had won a contest was rewarded with a crown of flowers as a sign of victory. [c] **1.18** *his own special people*: The Greek text has "the first of his creatures." The Law of Moses taught that the first-born of all animals and the first part of the harvest were special and belonged to the Lord. [d] **2.8** *most important law*: The Greek text has "royal law," meaning the one given by the king (that is, God).

1.12 4 Macc 9.8. **1.13** Si 15.11-20. **1.19** Si 5.11. **2.8** Lv 19.18. **2.10** 4 Macc 5.20. **2.11** **a** Ex 20.14; Dt 5.18; **b** Ex 20.13; Dt 5.17.

because on the day of judgment there will be no pity for those who have not had pity on others. But even in judgment, God is merciful![e]

Faith and Works

14 My friends, what good is it to say you have faith, when you don't do anything to show that you really do have faith? Can that kind of faith save you? 15 If you know someone who doesn't have any clothes or food, 16 you shouldn't just say, "I hope all goes well for you. I hope you will be warm and have plenty to eat." What good is it to say this, unless you do something to help? 17 Faith that doesn't lead us to do good deeds is all alone and dead!

18 Suppose someone disagrees and says, "It is possible to have faith without doing kind deeds."

I would answer, "Prove that you have faith without doing kind deeds, and I will prove that I have faith by doing them." 19 You surely believe there is only one God. That's fine. Even demons believe this, and it makes them shake with fear.

20 Does some stupid person want proof that faith without deeds is useless? 21 Well, our ancestor Abraham pleased God by putting his son Isaac on the altar to sacrifice him. 22 Now you see how Abraham's faith and deeds worked together. He proved that his faith was real by what he did. 23 This is what the Scriptures mean by saying, "Abraham had faith in God, and God was pleased with him." That's how Abraham became God's friend.

24 You can now see that we please God by what we do and not only by what we believe. 25 For example, Rahab had been a prostitute. But she pleased God when she welcomed the spies and sent them home by another way.

26 Anyone who doesn't breathe is dead, and faith that doesn't do anything is just as dead!

The Tongue

3 My friends, we should not all try to become teachers. In fact, teachers will be judged more strictly than others. 2 All of us do many wrong things. But if you can control your tongue, you are mature and able to control your whole body.

3 By putting a bit into the mouth of a horse, we can turn the horse in different directions. 4 It takes strong winds to move a large sailing ship, but the captain uses only a small rudder to make it go in any direction. 5 Our tongues are small too, and yet they brag about big things.

It takes only a spark to start a forest fire! 6 The tongue is like a spark. It is an evil power that dirties the rest of the body and sets a person's entire life on fire with flames that come from hell itself. 7 All kinds of animals, birds, reptiles, and sea creatures can be tamed and have been tamed. 8 But our tongues get out of control. They are restless and evil, and always spreading deadly poison.

9-10 My dear friends, with our tongues we speak both praises and curses. We praise our Lord and Father, and we curse people who were created to be like God, and this isn't right. 11 Can clean water and dirty water both flow from the same spring? 12 Can a fig tree produce olives or a grapevine produce figs? Does fresh water come from a well full of salt water?

Wisdom from Above

13 Are any of you wise or sensible? Then show it by living right and by being humble and wise in everything you do. 14 But if your heart is full of bitter jealousy and selfishness, don't brag or lie to cover up the truth. 15 That kind of wisdom doesn't come from above. It is earthly and selfish and comes from the devil himself. 16 Whenever people are jealous or selfish, they cause trouble and do all sorts of cruel things. 17 But the wisdom that comes from above

[e]**2.13** *But even in judgment, God is merciful*: Or "So be merciful, and you will be shown mercy on the day of judgment."

2.21 Gn 22.1-14; Si 44.19-21; 1 Macc 2.52. **2.23** **a** Gn 15.6; **b** 2 Ch 20.7; Is 41.8. **2.25** Js 2.1-21. **3.2** Si 5.9-15; 14.1; 28.13-26. **3.6** Si 5.13; 28.21, 22. **3.9,10** Gn 1.26. **3.13** Si 19.20-30.

leads us to be pure, friendly, gentle, sensible, kind, helpful, genuine, and sincere.
18 When peacemakers plant seeds of peace,
they will harvest justice.

Friendship with the World

4 Why do you fight and argue with each
other? Isn't it because you are full of
selfish desires that fight to control your
body? 2 You want something you don't
have, and you will do anything to get it. You
will even kill! But you still cannot get what
you want, and you won't get it by fighting
and arguing. You should pray for it. 3 Yet
even when you do pray, your prayers are
not answered, because you pray just for
selfish reasons.
4 You people aren't faithful to God!
Don't you know that if you love the world,
you are God's enemies? And if you decide
to be a friend of the world, you make yourself an enemy of God. 5 Do you doubt the
Scriptures that say, "God truly cares about
the Spirit he has put in us"?[f] 6 In fact, God
treats us with even greater kindness, just as
the Scriptures say,

"God opposes everyone
who is proud,
but he is kind to everyone
who is humble."

7 Surrender to God! Resist the devil,
and he will run from you. 8 Come near to
God, and he will come near to you. Clean
up your lives, you sinners. Purify your
hearts, you people who can't make up your
mind. 9 Be sad and sorry and weep. Stop
laughing and start crying. Be gloomy instead of glad. 10 Be humble in the Lord's
presence, and he will honor you.

Saying Cruel Things about Others

11 My friends, don't say cruel things
about others! If you do, or if you condemn
others, you are condemning God's Law.
And if you condemn the Law, you put yourself above the Law and refuse to obey either it 12 or God who gave it. God is our
judge, and he can save or destroy us. What
right do you have to condemn anyone?

Warning against Bragging

13 You should know better than to say,
"Today or tomorrow we will go to the city.
We will do business there for a year and
make a lot of money!" 14 What do you know
about tomorrow? How can you be so sure
about your life? It is nothing more than
mist that appears for only a little while before it disappears. 15 You should say, "If the
Lord lets us live, we will do these things."
16 Yet you are stupid enough to brag, and it
is wrong to be so proud. 17 If you don't do
what you know is right, you have sinned.

Warning to the Rich

5 You rich people should cry and weep!
Terrible things are going to happen to
you. 2 Your treasures have already rotted,
and moths have eaten your clothes. 3 Your
money has rusted, and the rust will be evidence against you, as it burns your body
like fire. Yet you keep on storing up wealth
in these last days. 4 You refused to pay the
people who worked in your fields, and now
their unpaid wages are shouting out against
you. The Lord All-Powerful has surely
heard the cries of the workers who harvested your crops.
5 While here on earth, you have thought
only of filling your own stomachs and having a good time. But now you are like fat
cattle on their way to be butchered. 6 You
have condemned and murdered innocent
people, who couldn't even fight back.

Be Patient and Kind

7 My friends, be patient until the Lord
returns. Think of farmers who wait patiently for the spring and summer rains to
make their valuable crops grow. 8 Be patient like those farmers and don't give up.
The Lord will soon be here! 9 Don't grumble about each other or you will be judged,
and the judge is right outside the door.
10 My friends, follow the example of the

[f]**4.5** *God truly cares about the Spirit he has put in us*: One possible meaning for the difficult Greek text; other translations are possible, such as, "the Spirit that God put in us truly cares."

4.6 Pr 3.34 (LXX). **4.13,14** Pr 27.1. **4.13** Ws 2.4; 5.9-13. **5.2,3** Mt 6.19.
5.3 Si 29.10-12. **5.4** Dt 24.14, 15. **5.6** Ws 2.10-20.

prophets who spoke for the Lord. They
were patient, even when they had to suffer.
11 In fact, we praise the ones who endured
the most. You remember how patient Job
was and how the Lord finally helped him.
The Lord did this because he is so merciful
and kind.

12 My friends, above all else, don't take
an oath. You must not swear by heaven or
by earth or by anything else. "Yes" or "No"
is all you need to say. If you say anything
more, you will be condemned.

13 If you are having trouble, you should
pray. And if you are feeling good, you
should sing praises. 14 If you are sick, ask
the church leaders[g] to come and pray for
you. Ask them to put olive oil[h] on you in
the name of the Lord. 15 If you have faith
when you pray for sick people, they will get
well. The Lord will heal them, and if they
have sinned, he will forgive them.

16 If you have sinned, you should tell
each other what you have done. Then you
can pray for one another and be healed.
The prayer of an innocent person is powerful, and it can help a lot. 17 Elijah was just
as human as we are, and for three and a
half years his prayers kept the rain from
falling. 18 But when he did pray for rain, it
fell from the skies and made the crops
grow.

19 My friends, if any followers have wandered away from the truth, you should try
to lead them back. 20 If you turn sinners from
the wrong way, you will save them from
death, and many of their sins will be forgiven.

[g]**5.14** *church leaders*: Or "elders" or "presbyters" or "priests." [h]**5.14** *olive oil*: The Jewish people used olive oil for healing.

5.11 a Job 1.21, 22; 2.10; **b** Ps 103.8. **5.12** Mt 5.34-37. **5.14** Mk 6.13. **5.16** Si 4.26. **5.17** 1 K 17.1; 18.1, 2; Si 48.2, 3. **5.18** 1 K 18.42-46. **5.20** Pr 10.12; Tb 12.9; 1 P 4.8.

1 PETER

ABOUT THIS LETTER

In this letter Peter has much to say about suffering. He shows how it can be a way of serving the Lord, of sharing the faith, and of being tested. The letter was written to Christians scattered all over the northern part of Asia Minor. In this part of the Roman Empire many Christians had already suffered unfair treatment from people who did not believe in Jesus. And they could expect to suffer even more.

Peter was quick to offer encouragement. His letter reminds the readers that some of the Lord's followers may have to go through times of hard testing. But this should make them glad, Peter declares, because it will strengthen their faith and bring them honor on the day when Jesus Christ returns (1.6, 7).

Peter reminds them that Christ suffered here on earth, and when his followers suffer for doing right they are sharing his sufferings (2.18-25; 4.12-17). In fact, Christians should expect to suffer for their faith (3.8—4.19).

But because of who God is and because of what God has done by raising Jesus Christ from death, Christians can have hope in the future. Just as Christ suffered before he received honor from God, so will Christians be tested by suffering before they receive honor when the Lord returns. Peter uses poetic language to remind his readers of what Christ has done:

Christ died once for our sins.
An innocent person died
for those who are guilty.
Christ did this
to bring you to God,
when his body
was put to death
and his spirit
was made alive.
(3.18)

A QUICK LOOK AT THIS LETTER

- Greetings and Prayer (1.1, 2)
- A Real Reason for Hope (1.3-12)
- Living as God's Holy People (1.13—2.17)
- The Example of Christ's Suffering (2.18-25)
- Being a Christian and Suffering (3.1—4.19)
- Advice for Church Leaders (5.1-11)
- Final Greetings (5.12-14)

1 From Peter, an apostle of Jesus Christ.
To God's people who are scattered
like foreigners in Pontus, Galatia, Cappadocia, Asia, and Bithynia.
2 God the Father decided to choose you
as his people, and his Spirit has made you
holy. You have obeyed Jesus Christ and are
sprinkled with his blood.[a]
I pray that God will be kind to you and
will keep on giving you peace!

A Real Reason for Hope

3 Praise God, the Father of our Lord
Jesus Christ. God is so good, and by raising
Jesus from death, he has given us new life
and a hope that lives on. 4 God has something stored up for you in heaven, where it
will never decay or be ruined or disappear.
5 You have faith in God, whose power
will protect you until the last day.[b] Then he
will save you, just as he has always planned
to do. 6 On that day you will be glad, even if
you have to go through many hard trials for
a while. 7 Your faith will be like gold that
has been tested in a fire. And these trials
will prove that your faith is worth much
more than gold that can be destroyed. They
will show that you will be given praise and
honor and glory when Jesus Christ returns.
8 You have never seen Jesus, and you
don't see him now. But still you love him
and have faith in him, and no words can
tell how glad and happy 9 you are to be
saved. That's why you have faith.
10 Some prophets told how kind God
would be to you, and they searched hard to
find out more about the way you would be
saved. 11 The Spirit of Christ was in them
and was telling them how Christ would suffer and would then be given great honor. So
they searched to find out exactly who
Christ would be and when this would happen. 12 But they were told that they were
serving you and not themselves. They
preached to you by the power of the Holy
Spirit, who was sent from heaven. And
their message was only for you, even
though angels would like to know more
about it.

Chosen To Live a Holy Life

13 Be alert and think straight. Put all
your hope in how kind God will be to you
when Jesus Christ appears. 14 Behave like
obedient children. Don't let your lives be
controlled by your desires, as they used to
be. 15 Always live as God's holy people
should, because God is the one who chose
you, and he is holy. 16 That's why the Scriptures say, "I am the holy God, and you must
be holy too."
17 You say that God is your Father, but
God doesn't have favorites! He judges all
people by what they do. So you must honor
God while you live as strangers here on
earth. 18 You were rescued[c] from the useless way of life that you learned from your
ancestors. But you know that you were not
rescued by such things as silver or gold that
don't last forever. 19 You were rescued by
the precious blood of Christ, that spotless
and innocent lamb. 20 Christ was chosen
even before the world was created, but because of you, he did not come until these
last days. 21 And when he did come, it was
to lead you to have faith in God, who raised
him from death and honored him in a glorious way. That's why you have put your
faith and hope in God.
22 You obeyed the truth,[d] and your souls
were made pure. Now you sincerely love
each other. But you must keep on loving
with all your heart. 23 Do this because God
has given you new birth by his message
that lives on forever. 24 The Scriptures say,

"Humans wither like grass,
and their glory fades
like wild flowers.
Grass dries up,

[a] **1.2** *sprinkled with his blood*: According to Exodus 24.3-8 the people of Israel were sprinkled with the blood of cows to show they would keep their agreement with God. Peter says that it is the blood of Jesus that seals the agreement between God and his people (see Hebrews 9.18-21). [b] **1.5** *the last day*: When God will judge all people. [c] **1.18** *rescued*: The Greek word often, though not always, means payment of a price to free a slave or prisoner. [d] **1.22** *You obeyed the truth*: Some manuscripts add "by the power of the Spirit."

1.4 2 Esd 8.52. **1.7** 2 Esd 16.73. **1.16** Lv 11.44, 45; 19.2. **1.19** 4 Macc 17.21. **1.24,25** Is 40.6-8 (LXX).

and flowers fall
to the ground.
25 But what the Lord has said
will stand forever."

Our good news to you is what the Lord
has said.

A Living Stone and a Holy Nation

2 Stop being hateful! Quit trying to fool
people, and start being sincere. Don't
be jealous or say cruel things about others.
2 Be like newborn babies who are thirsty for
the pure spiritual milk that will help you
grow and be saved. 3 You have already
found out how good the Lord really is.
4 Come to Jesus Christ. He is the living
stone that people have rejected, but which
God has chosen and highly honored. 5 And
now you are living stones that are being
used to build a spiritual house. You are also
a group of holy priests, and with the help of
Jesus Christ you will offer sacrifices that
please God. 6 It is just as God says in the
Scriptures,

"Look! I am placing in Zion
a choice and precious
cornerstone.
No one who has faith
in that one
will be disappointed."

7 You are followers of the Lord, and that
stone is precious to you. But it isn't precious to those who refuse to follow him.
They are the builders who tossed aside the
stone that turned out to be the most important one of all. 8 They disobeyed the message and stumbled and fell over that stone,
because they were doomed.
9 But you are God's chosen and special
people. You are a group of royal priests and
a holy nation. God has brought you out of
darkness into his marvelous light. Now you
must tell all the wonderful things that he
has done. The Scriptures say,

10 "Once you were nobody.
Now you are God's people.
At one time no one
had pity on you.
Now God has treated you
with kindness.

Live as God's Servants Should

11 Dear friends, you are foreigners and
strangers on this earth. So I beg you not to
surrender to those desires that fight against
you. 12 Always let others see you behaving
properly, even though they may still accuse
you of doing wrong. Then on the day of
judgment, they will honor God by telling
the good things they saw you do.
13 The Lord wants you to obey all human authorities, especially the Emperor,
who rules over everyone. 14 You must also
obey governors, because they are sent by
the Emperor to punish criminals and to
praise good citizens. 15 God wants you to silence stupid and ignorant people by doing
right. 16 You are free, but still you are God's
servants, and you must not use your freedom as an excuse for doing wrong. 17 Respect everyone and show special love for
God's people. Honor God and respect the
Emperor.

The Example of Christ's Suffering

18 Servants, you must obey your masters
and always show respect to them. Do this,
not only to those who are kind and
thoughtful, but also to those who are cruel.
19 God will bless you, even if others treat
you unfairly for being loyal to him. 20 You
don't gain anything by being punished for
some wrong you have done. But God will
bless you, if you have to suffer for doing
something good. 21 After all, God chose you
to suffer as you follow in the footsteps of
Christ, who set an example by suffering
for you.

22 Christ did not sin
or ever tell a lie.
23 Although he was abused,
he never tried to get even.
And when he suffered,
he made no threats.

2.3 Ps 34.8. **2.6** Is 28.16 (LXX). **2.7** Ps 118.22. **2.8** Is 8.14, 15.
2.9 **a** Ex 19.5, 6; Is 43.20 (LXX); **b** Ex 19.5; Dt 4.20; 7.6; 14.2; Titus 2.14; **c** Is 43.21; **d** Is 9.2.
2.10 Ho 2.23. **2.22** Is 53.9. **2.23** Is 53.7.

Instead, he had faith in God,
who judges fairly.
24 Christ carried the burden
of our sins.
He was nailed to the cross,
so that we would stop sinning
and start living right.
By his cuts and bruises
you are healed.
25 You had wandered away
like sheep.
Now you have returned
to the one
who is your shepherd
and protector.

Wives and Husbands

3 If you are a wife, you must put your
husband first. Even if he opposes our
message, you will win him over by what you
do. No one else will have to say anything to
him, 2 because he will see how you honor
God and live a pure life. 3 Don't depend on
things like fancy hairdos or gold jewelry or
expensive clothes to make you look beautiful. 4 Be beautiful in your heart by being
gentle and quiet. This kind of beauty will
last, and God considers it very special.
5 Long ago those women who worshiped
God and put their hope in him made themselves beautiful by putting their husbands
first. 6 For example, Sarah obeyed Abraham
and called him her master. You are her true
children, if you do right and don't let anything frighten you.
7 If you are a husband, you should be
thoughtful of your wife. Treat her with
honor, because she isn't as strong as you
are, and she shares with you in the gift of
life. Then nothing will stand in the way of
your prayers.

Suffering for Doing Right

8 Finally, all of you should agree and
have concern and love for each other. You
should also be kind and humble. 9 Don't be
hateful and insult people just because they
are hateful and insult you. Instead, treat
everyone with kindness. You are God's chosen ones, and he will bless you. The Scriptures say,

10 "Do you really love life?
Do you want to be happy?
Then stop saying cruel things
and quit telling lies.
11 Give up your evil ways
and do right,
as you find and follow
the road that leads
to peace.
12 The Lord watches over
everyone who obeys him,
and he listens
to their prayers.
But he opposes everyone
who does evil."

13 Can anyone really harm you for being
eager to do good deeds? 14 Even if you have
to suffer for doing good things, God will
bless you. So stop being afraid and don't
worry about what people might do.
15 Honor Christ and let him be the Lord of
your life.
Always be ready to give an answer when
someone asks you about your hope. 16 Give
a kind and respectful answer and keep your
conscience clear. This way you will make
people ashamed for saying bad things about
your good conduct as a follower of Christ.
17 You are better off to obey God and suffer
for doing right than to suffer for doing
wrong.

18 Christ died once for our sins.
An innocent person died
for those who are guilty.
Christ did this
to bring you to God,
when his body
was put to death
and his spirit
was made alive.

19 Christ then preached to the spirits
that were being kept in prison. 20 They had
disobeyed God while Noah was building the
boat, but God had been patient with them.

2.24,25 Is 53.5, 6 (LXX). **3.1** Eph 5.22; Col 3.18. **3.3** 1 Ti 2.9. **3.7** Eph 5.25; Col 3.19. **3.10-12** Ps 34.12-16 (LXX). **3.14** Mt 5.10. **3.14,15** Is 8.12, 13. **3.20** Gn 6.1—7.24. **3.20,21** 4 Macc 7.1.

Eight people went into that boat and were
brought safely through the flood.
21 Those flood waters were like baptism
that now saves you. But baptism is more
than just washing your body. It means
turning to God with a clear conscience,
because Jesus Christ was raised from
death. 22 Christ is now in heaven, where
he sits at the right side[e] of God. All angels,
authorities, and powers are under his
control.

Being Faithful to God

4 Christ suffered here on earth. Now
you must be ready to suffer as he did,
because suffering shows that you have
stopped sinning. 2 It means you have
turned from your own desires and want to
obey God for the rest of your life. 3 You
have already lived long enough like people
who don't know God. You were immoral
and followed your evil desires. You went
around drinking and partying and carrying
on. In fact, you even worshiped disgusting
idols. 4 Now your former friends wonder
why you have stopped running around with
them, and they curse you for it. 5 But they
will have to answer to God, who judges the
living and the dead. 6 The good news has
even been preached to the dead,[f] so that
after they have been judged for what they
have done in this life, their spirits will live
with God.
7 Everything will soon come to an end.
So be serious and be sensible enough to
pray.
8 Most important of all, you must sincerely love each other, because love wipes
away many sins.
9 Welcome people into your home and
don't grumble about it.
10 Each of you has been blessed with
one of God's many wonderful gifts to be
used in the service of others. So use your
gift well. 11 If you have the gift of speaking,
preach God's message. If you have the gift
of helping others, do it with the strength
that God supplies. Everything should be
done in a way that will bring honor to God
because of Jesus Christ, who is glorious
and powerful forever. Amen.

Suffering for Being a Christian

12 Dear friends, don't be surprised or
shocked that you are going through testing
that is like walking through fire. 13 Be glad
for the chance to suffer as Christ suffered.
It will prepare you for even greater happiness when he makes his glorious return.
14 Count it a blessing when you suffer
for being a Christian. This shows that
God's glorious Spirit is with you. 15 But you
deserve to suffer if you are a murderer, a
thief, a crook, or a busybody. 16 Don't be
ashamed to suffer for being a Christian.
Praise God that you belong to him. 17 God
has already begun judging his own people.
And if his judgment begins with us, imagine how terrible it will be for those who
refuse to obey his message. The Scriptures say,

18 "If good people barely escape,
what will happen to sinners
and to others
who don't respect God?"

19 If you suffer for obeying God, you
must have complete faith in your faithful
Creator and keep on doing right.

Helping Christian Leaders

5 Church leaders,[g] I am writing to encourage you. I too am a leader, as well
as a witness to Christ's suffering, and I will
share in his glory when it is shown to us.
2 Just as shepherds watch over their
sheep, you must watch over everyone God
has placed in your care. Do it willingly in
order to please God, and not simply because you think you must. Let it be something you want to do, instead of something
you do merely to make money. 3 Don't be
bossy to those people who are in your care,
but set an example for them. 4 Then when

[e] **3.22** *right side*: The place of honor and power. [f] **4.6** *the dead*: Either people who died after becoming followers of Christ or the people of Noah's day (see 3.19). [g] **5.1** *Church leaders*: Or "Elders" or "Presbyters" or "Priests."

4.8 Pr 10.12; Tb 12.9. **4.18** Pr 11.31 (LXX). **5.2** Jn 21.15-17.

Christ the Chief Shepherd returns, you will be given a crown that will never lose its glory.

5 All of you young people should obey your elders. In fact, everyone should be humble toward everyone else. The Scriptures say,

"God opposes proud people,
but he helps everyone
who is humble."

6 Be humble in the presence of God's mighty power, and he will honor you when the time comes. 7 God cares for you, so turn all your worries over to him.
8 Be on your guard and stay awake. Your enemy, the devil, is like a roaring lion, sneaking around to find someone to attack.
9 But you must resist the devil and stay strong in your faith. You know that all over the world the Lord's followers are suffering just as you are. 10 But God shows undeserved kindness to everyone. That's why he appointed Christ Jesus to choose you to share in his eternal glory. You will suffer for a while, but God will make you complete, steady, strong, and firm. 11 God will be in control forever! Amen.

Final Greetings

12 Silvanus helped me write this short letter, and I consider him a faithful follower of the Lord. I wanted to encourage you and tell you how kind God really is, so that you will keep on having faith in him.
13 Greetings from the Lord's followers in Babylon.[h] They are God's chosen ones.

Mark, who is like a son to me, sends his greetings too.

14 Give each other a warm greeting. I pray that God will give peace to everyone who belongs to Christ.[i]

[h] **5.13** *Babylon*: This may be a secret name for the city of Rome. [i] **5.14** *Christ*: Some manuscripts add "Amen."

5.5 Pr 3.34 (LXX). **5.6** Mt 23.12; Lk 14.11; 18.14. **5.7** Si 2.1-18. **5.12** Ac 15.22, 40. **5.13** Ac 12.12, 25; 13.13; 15.37-39; Col 4.10; Phm 24.

2 PETER

ABOUT THIS LETTER

The writer of this letter wants the readers to know that Christians must live in a way that pleases God (1.3) and hold firmly to the truth they were given (1.12).

He warns them that false prophets and teachers had entered the Christian community and were trying to lead the Lord's followers away from the truth. But they will be punished for their evil deeds (2.1-22). When false teachers are at work, Christians must stick to their faith and be examples for others of right living. They must have understanding, self-control and patience, and they should show love for God and all people.

The readers must never forget that the Lord's return is certain, no matter what others may say (3.1-18):

Don't forget that for the Lord one day is the same as a thousand years, and a thousand years is the same as one day. The Lord isn't slow about keeping his promises, as some people think he is. In fact, God is patient, because he wants everyone to turn from sin and no one to be lost.

(3.8, 9)

A QUICK LOOK AT THIS LETTER

- Greetings and Prayer (1.1, 2)
- How the Lord's Followers Should Live (1.3-15)
- The Glory of Christ (1.16-21)
- False Prophets and Teachers (2.1-22)
- The Lord's Return Is Certain (3.1-18)

---

1 From Simon Peter, a servant and an
apostle of Jesus Christ.
To everyone who shares with us in the
privilege of believing that our God and
Savior Jesus Christ will do what is just
and fair.[a]
2 I pray that God will be kind to you and
will let you live in perfect peace! May you
keep learning more and more about God
and our Lord Jesus.

Living as the Lord's Followers

3 We have everything we need to live a
life that pleases God. It was all given to us
by God's own power, when we learned that
he had invited us to share in his wonderful
goodness. 4 God made great and marvelous
promises, so that his nature would become
part of us. Then we could escape our evil
desires and the corrupt influences of this
world.
5 Do your best to improve your faith.
You can do this by adding goodness, understanding, 6 self-control, patience, devotion
to God, 7 concern for others, and love. 8 If
you keep growing in this way, it will show
that what you know about our Lord Jesus
Christ has made your lives useful and
meaningful. 9 But if you don't grow, you are
like someone who is nearsighted or blind,
and you have forgotten that your past sins
are forgiven.
10 My friends, you must do all you can
to show that God has really chosen and

[a] **1.1** *To everyone who . . . just and fair*: Or "To everyone whose faith in the justice and fairness of our God and Savior Jesus Christ is as precious as our own faith."

selected you. If you keep on doing this, you
won't stumble and fall. 11 Then our Lord
and Savior Jesus Christ will give you a glorious welcome into his kingdom that will
last forever.

12 You are holding firmly to the truth
that you were given. But I am still going to
remind you of these things. 13 In fact, I
think I should keep on reminding you until
I leave this body. 14 And our Lord Jesus
Christ has already told me that I will soon
leave it behind. 15 That is why I am doing
my best to make sure that each of you remembers all of this after I am gone.

The Message about the Glory of Christ

16 When we told you about the power
and the return of our Lord Jesus Christ, we
were not telling clever stories that someone
had made up. But with our own eyes we
saw his true greatness. 17 God, our great
and wonderful Father, truly honored him
by saying, "This is my own dear Son, and I
am pleased with him." 18 We were there
with Jesus on the holy mountain and heard
this voice speak from heaven.

19 All of this makes us even more certain that what the prophets said is true. So
you should pay close attention to their
message, as you would to a lamp shining in
some dark place. You must keep on paying
attention until daylight comes and the
morning star rises in your hearts. 20 But
you need to realize that no one alone can
understand any of the prophecies in the
Scriptures. 21 The prophets did not think
these things up on their own, but they were
guided by the Spirit of God.

False Prophets and Teachers

2 Sometimes false prophets spoke to the
people of Israel. False teachers will
also sneak in and speak harmful lies to you.
But these teachers don't really belong to
the Master who paid a great price for them,
and they will quickly destroy themselves.
2 Many people will follow their evil ways
and cause others to tell lies about the true
way. 3 They will be greedy and cheat you
with smooth talk. But long ago God decided
to punish them, and God doesn't sleep.

4 God did not have pity on the angels
that sinned. He had them tied up and
thrown into the dark pits of hell until the
time of judgment. 5 And during Noah's
time, God did not have pity on the ungodly
people of the world. He destroyed them
with a flood, though he did save eight people, including Noah, who preached the
truth.

6 God punished the cities of Sodom and
Gomorrah[b] by burning them to ashes, and
this is a warning to anyone else who wants
to sin.

7-8 Lot lived right and was greatly troubled by the terrible way those wicked people were living. He was a good man, and
day after day he suffered because of the
evil things he saw and heard. So the Lord
rescued him. 9 This shows that the Lord
knows how to rescue godly people from
their sufferings and to punish evil people
while they wait for the day of judgment.

10 The Lord is especially hard on people
who disobey him and don't think of anything except their own filthy desires. They
are reckless and proud and are not afraid of
cursing the glorious beings in heaven.
11 Although angels are more powerful than
these evil beings,[c] even the angels don't
dare to accuse them to the Lord.

12 These people are no better than
senseless animals that live by their feelings
and are born to be caught and killed. They
speak evil of things they don't know anything about. But their own corrupt deeds
will destroy them. 13 They have done evil,
and they will be rewarded with evil.

They think it is fun to have wild parties
during the day. They are immoral, and the
meals they eat with you are spoiled by the
shameful and selfish way they carry on.[d]

[b]**2.6** *Sodom and Gomorrah*: During the time of Abraham the Lord destroyed these cities because the people there were so evil (see Genesis 19.24). [c]**2.11** *evil beings*: Or "evil teachers."
[d]**2.13** *and the meals they eat with you are spoiled by the shameful and selfish way they carry on*: Some manuscripts have "and the meals they eat with you are spoiled by the shameful way they carry on during your feasts of Christian love."

1.17,18 Mt 17.1-5; Mk 9.2-7; Lk 9.28-35. **2.5** Gn 6.1—7.24; Ws 10.4. **2.6** Gn 19.24; 3 Macc 2.5. **2.7,8** Gn 19.1-16; Ws 10.6-8.

14 All they think about is having sex with someone else's husband or wife. There is no end to their wicked deeds. They trick people who are easily fooled, and their minds are filled with greedy thoughts. But they are headed for trouble!

15 They have left the true road and have gone down the wrong path by following the example of the prophet Balaam. He was the son of Beor and loved what he got from being a crook. 16 But a donkey corrected him for this evil deed. It spoke to him with a human voice and made him stop his foolishness.

17 These people are like dried up water holes and clouds blown by a windstorm. The darkest part of hell is waiting for them. 18 They brag out loud about their stupid nonsense. And by being vulgar and crude, they trap people who have barely escaped from living the wrong kind of life. 19 They promise freedom to everyone. But they are merely slaves of filthy living, because people are slaves of whatever controls them.

20 When they learned about our Lord and Savior Jesus Christ, they escaped from the filthy things of this world. But they are again caught up and controlled by these filthy things, and now they are in worse shape than they were at first. 21 They would have been better off if they had never known about the right way. Even after they knew what was right, they turned their backs on the holy commandments that they were given. 22 What happened to them is just like the true saying,

"A dog will come back
to lick up its own vomit.
A pig that has been washed
will roll in the mud."

The Lord Will Return

3 My dear friends, this is the second letter I have written to encourage you to do some honest thinking. I don't want you to forget 2 what God's prophets said would happen. You must never forget what the holy prophets taught in the past. And you must remember what the apostles told you our Lord and Savior has commanded us to do.

3 But first you must realize that in the last days some people won't think about anything except their own selfish desires. They will make fun of you 4 and say, "Didn't your Lord promise to come back? Yet the first leaders have already died, and the world hasn't changed a bit."

5 They will say this because they want to forget that long ago the heavens and the earth were made at God's command. The earth came out of water and was made from water. 6 Later it was destroyed by the waters of a mighty flood. 7 But God has commanded the present heavens and earth to remain until the day of judgment. Then they will be set on fire, and ungodly people will be destroyed.

8 Dear friends, don't forget that for the Lord one day is the same as a thousand years, and a thousand years is the same as one day. 9 The Lord isn't slow about keeping his promises, as some people think he is. In fact, God is patient, because he wants everyone to turn from sin and no one to be lost.

10 The day of the Lord's return will surprise us like a thief. The heavens will disappear with a loud noise, and the heat will melt the whole universe.[e] Then the earth and everything on it will be seen for what they are.[f]

11 Everything will be destroyed. So you should serve and honor God by the way you live. 12 You should look forward to the day when God judges everyone, and you should try to make it come soon.[g] On that day the heavens will be destroyed by fire, and everything else will melt in the heat. 13 But God has promised us a new heaven and a new earth, where justice will rule. We are really looking forward to that!

[e] **3.10** *the whole universe*: Probably the sun, moon, and stars, or the elements that everything in the universe is made of. [f] **3.10** *will be seen for what they are*: Some manuscripts have "will go up in flames." [g] **3.12** *and you should try to make it come soon*: Or "and you should eagerly desire for that day to come."

2.15,16 Nu 22.4-35. **2.22** Pr 26.11. **3.3** Jd 18. **3.5** Gn 1.6-9. **3.6** Gn 7.11, 12. **3.8** Ps 90.4. **3.10** Mt 24.43; Lk 12.39; 1 Th 5.2; Rev 16.15. **3.13** Is 65.17; 66.22; Rev 21.1.

14 My friends, while you are waiting, you
should make certain that the Lord finds
you pure, spotless, and living at peace.
15 Don't forget that the Lord is patient because he wants people to be saved. This is
also what our dear friend Paul said when
he wrote you with the wisdom that God
had given him. 16 Paul talks about these
same things in all his letters, but part of
what he says is hard to understand. Some
ignorant and unsteady people even destroy themselves by twisting what he said.
They do the same thing with other Scriptures too.
17 My dear friends, you have been
warned ahead of time! So don't let the er-
rors of evil people lead you down the wrong
path and make you lose your balance.
18 Let the wonderful kindness and the understanding that come from our Lord and
Savior Jesus Christ help you to keep on growing. Praise Jesus now and forever! Amen.[h]

[h]**3.18** *Amen*: Some manuscripts do not have "Amen."

1 JOHN

ABOUT THIS LETTER

John wants Christian believers to know that when we tell God about our sins, God will forgive us and take them away (1.9).

The true test of faith is love for each other (3.11-24). Because God is love, his people must be like him (4.1-21). For a complete victory over sin, we must not only love others, but we must believe that Jesus, the Son of God, is truly Christ, and that his death for us was real (5.1-12).

Remember:

The Word that gives life
was from the beginning,
and this is the one
our message is about.
(1.1a)

A QUICK LOOK AT THIS LETTER

- The Word that Gives Life (1.1-4)
- God Is Light and Christ Is Our Example (1.5—2.6)
- The New Commandment (2.7-17)
- The Enemies of Christ and God's Children (2.18—3.10)
- God's Love and Our Love (3.11—4.21)
- Victory Over the World (5.1-21)

---

1 The Word that gives life
was from the beginning,
and this is the one
our message is about.

Our ears have heard,
our own eyes have seen,
and our hands touched
this Word.

2 The one who gives life appeared! We
saw it happen, and we are witnesses to
what we have seen. Now we are telling you
about this eternal life that was with the
Father and appeared to us. 3 We are telling
you what we have seen and heard, so that
you may share in this life with us. And we
share in it with the Father and with his Son
Jesus Christ. 4 We are writing to tell you these
things, because this makes us[a] truly
happy.

God Is Light

5 Jesus told us that God is light and
doesn't have any darkness in him. Now we
are telling you.

6 If we say that we share in life with God
and keep on living in the dark, we are lying
and are not living by the truth. 7 But if we
live in the light, as God does, we share in
life with each other. And the blood of his
Son Jesus washes all our sins away. 8 If we
say that we have not sinned, we are fooling
ourselves, and the truth isn't in our hearts.
9 But if we confess our sins to God, he can

[a]**1.4** *us*: Some manuscripts have "you."
1.1 Jn 1.1. **1.2** Jn 1.14. **1.7** 4 Macc 17.21.

always be trusted to forgive us and take our
sins away.
10 If we say that we have not sinned, we
make God a liar, and his message isn't in
our hearts.[b]

Christ Helps Us

2 My children, I am writing this so that
you won't sin. But if you do sin, Jesus
Christ always does the right thing, and he
will speak to the Father for us. 2 Christ is
the sacrifice that takes away our sins and
the sins of all the world's people.
3 When we obey God, we are sure that
we know him. 4 But if we claim to know
him and don't obey him, we are lying and
the truth isn't in our hearts. 5 We truly love
God only when we obey him as we should,
and then we know that we belong to him.
6 If we say we are his, we must follow the
example of Christ.

The New Commandment

7 My dear friends, I am not writing to
give you a new commandment. It is the
same one that you were first given, and it is
the message you heard. 8 But it really is a
new commandment, and you know its true
meaning, just as Christ does. You can see
the darkness fading away and the true light
already shining.
9 If we claim to be in the light and hate
someone, we are still in the dark. 10 But if
we love others, we are in the light, and we
don't cause problems for them.[c] 11 If we
hate others, we are living and walking in
the dark. We don't know where we are going,
because we can't see in the dark.

12 Children, I am writing you,
because your sins
have been forgiven
in the name of Christ.
13 Parents, I am writing you,
because you have known
the one who was there
from the beginning.
Young people, I am writing you,
because you have defeated
the evil one.
14 Children, I am writing you,
because you have known
the Father.
Parents, I am writing you,
because you have known
the one who was there
from the beginning.
Young people, I am writing you,
because you are strong.
God's message is firm
in your hearts,
and you have defeated
the evil one.

15 Don't love the world or anything that
belongs to the world. If you love the world,
you cannot love the Father. 16 Our foolish
pride comes from this world, and so do our
selfish desires and our desire to have everything
we see. None of this comes from the
Father. 17 The world and the desires it
causes are disappearing. But if we obey
God, we will live forever.

The Enemy of Christ

18 Children, this is the last hour. You
heard that the enemy of Christ would appear
at this time, and many of Christ's enemies
have already appeared. So we know
that the last hour is here. 19 These people
came from our own group, yet they were
not part of us. If they had been part of us,
they would have stayed with us. But they
left, which proves that they did not belong
to our group.
20 Christ, the Holy One,[d] has blessed[e]
you, and now all of you understand.[f] 21 I

[b] **1.10** *and his message isn't in our hearts*: Or "because we have not accepted his message."
[c] **2.10** *and we don't cause problems for them*: Or "and we can see anything that might make us fall."
[d] **2.20** *Christ, the Holy One*: The Greek text has "the Holy One" which may refer either to Christ or to God the Father. [e] **2.20** *blessed*: This translates a word which means "to pour olive oil on (someone's head)." In Old Testament times it was the custom to pour olive oil on a person's head when that person was chosen to be a priest or a king. Here the meaning is not clear. It may refer to the ceremony of pouring olive oil on the followers of the Lord right before they were baptized or it may refer to the gift of the Holy Spirit which they were given at baptism (see verse 27). [f] **2.20** *now all of you understand*: Some manuscripts have "you understand all things."
2.7 Jn 13.34.

did not need to write you about the truth, since you already know it. You also know that liars do not belong to the truth. 22 And a liar is anyone who says that Jesus isn't truly Christ. Anyone who says this is an enemy of Christ and rejects both the Father and the Son. 23 If we reject the Son, we reject the Father. But if we say that we accept the Son, we have the Father. 24 Keep thinking about the message you first heard, and you will always be one in your heart with the Son and with the Father. 25 The Son[g] has promised us[h] eternal life.

26 I am writing to warn you about those people who are misleading you. 27 But Christ has blessed you with the Holy Spirit.[i] Now the Spirit stays in you, and you don't need any teachers. The Spirit is truthful and teaches you everything. So stay one in your heart with Christ, just as the Spirit has taught you to do.

Children of God

28 Children, stay one in your hearts with Christ. Then when he returns, we will have confidence and won't have to hide in shame. 29 You know that Christ always does right and that everyone who does right is a child of God.

3 Think how much the Father loves us. He loves us so much that he lets us be called his children, as we truly are. But since the people of this world did not know who Christ[j] is, they don't know who we are. 2 My dear friends, we are already God's children, though what we will be hasn't yet been seen. But we do know that when Christ returns, we will be like him, because we will see him as he truly is. 3 This hope makes us keep ourselves holy, just as Christ[k] is holy.

4 Everyone who sins breaks God's law, because sin is the same as breaking God's law. 5 You know that Christ came to take away sins. He isn't sinful, 6 and people who stay one in their hearts with him won't keep on sinning. If they do keep on sinning, they don't know Christ, and they have never seen him.

7 Children, don't be fooled. Anyone who does right is good, just like Christ himself. 8 Anyone who keeps on sinning belongs to the devil. He has sinned from the beginning, but the Son of God came to destroy all that he has done. 9 God's children cannot keep on being sinful. His life-giving power[l] lives in them and makes them his children, so that they cannot keep on sinning. 10 You can tell God's children from the devil's children, because those who belong to the devil refuse to do right or to love each other.

Love Each Other

11 From the beginning you were told that we must love each other. 12 Don't be like Cain, who belonged to the devil and murdered his own brother. Why did he murder him? He did it because his brother was good, and he was evil. 13 My friends, don't be surprised if the people of this world hate you. 14 Our love for each other proves that we have gone from death to life. But if you don't love each other, you are still under the power of death.

15 If you hate each other, you are murderers, and we know that murderers do not have eternal life. 16 We know what love is because Jesus gave his life for us. That's why we must give our lives for each other. 17 If we have all we need and see one of our own people in need, we must have pity on that person, or else we cannot say we love God. 18 Children, you show love for others by truly helping them, and not merely by talking about it.

19 When we love others, we know that we belong to the truth, and we feel at ease in the presence of God. 20 But even if we don't feel at ease, God is greater than our

[g]**2.25** *The Son*: The Greek text has "he" and may refer to God the Father. [h]**2.25** *us*: Some manuscripts have "you." [i]**2.27** *Christ has blessed you with the Holy Spirit*: The Greek text has "You received a pouring on of olive oil from him" (see verse 20). The "pouring on of olive oil" is here taken to refer to the gift of the Holy Spirit, and "he" may refer either to Christ or to the Father. [j]**3.1** *Christ*: The Greek text has "he" and may refer to God. [k]**3.3** *Christ*: The Greek text has "that one" and may refer to God. [l]**3.9** *His life-giving power*: The Greek text has "his seed."

3.1 Jn 1.12. **3.5** Jn 1.29. **3.11** Jn 13.34. **3.12** Gn 4.8. **3.14** Jn 5.24.

feelings, and he knows everything. 21 Dear
friends, if we feel at ease in the presence of
God, we will have the courage to come
near him. 22 He will give us whatever we
ask, because we obey him and do what
pleases him. 23 God wants us to have faith
in his Son Jesus Christ and to love each
other. This is also what Jesus taught us
to do. 24 If we obey God's commandments,
we will stay one in our hearts with him,
and he will stay one with us. The Spirit
that he has given us is proof that we are
one with him.

God Is Love

4 Dear friends, don't believe everyone
who claims to have the Spirit of God.
Test them all to find out if they really do
come from God. Many false prophets have
already gone out into the world, 2 and you
can know which ones come from God. His
Spirit says that Jesus Christ had a truly human body. 3 But when someone doesn't say
this about Jesus, you know that person has
a spirit that doesn't come from God and is
the enemy of Christ. You knew that this enemy was coming into the world and now is
already here.

4 Children, you belong to God, and you
have defeated these enemies. God's Spirit[m]
is in you and is more powerful than the one
that is in the world. 5 These enemies belong to this world, and the world listens to
them, because they speak its language.
6 We belong to God, and everyone who
knows God will listen to us. But the people
who don't know God won't listen to us.
That is how we can tell the Spirit that
speaks the truth from the one that tells
lies.

7 My dear friends, we must love each
other. Love comes from God, and when we
love each other, it shows that we have been
given new life. We are now God's children,
and we know him. 8 God is love, and anyone who doesn't love others has never
known him. 9 God showed his love for us
when he sent his only Son into the world to
give us life. 10 Real love isn't our love for
God, but his love for us. God sent his Son
to be the sacrifice by which our sins are
forgiven. 11 Dear friends, since God loved
us this much, we must love each other.

12 No one has ever seen God. But if we
love each other, God lives in us, and his
love is truly in our hearts.

13 God has given us his Spirit. That is
how we know that we are one with him,
just as he is one with us. 14 God sent his
Son to be the Savior of the world. We saw
his Son and are now telling others about
him. 15 God stays one with everyone who
openly says that Jesus is the Son of God.
That's how we stay one with God 16 and are
sure that God loves us.

God is love. If we keep on loving others,
we will stay one in our hearts with God,
and he will stay one with us. 17 If we truly
love others and live as Christ did in this
world, we won't be worried about the day of
judgment. 18 A real love for others will
chase those worries away. The thought of
being punished is what makes us afraid. It
shows that we have not really learned to
love.

19 We love because God loved us first.
20 But if we say we love God and don't love
each other, we are liars. We cannot see
God. So how can we love God, if we don't
love the people we can see? 21 The commandment that God has given us is: "Love
God and love each other!"

Victory over the World

5 If we believe that Jesus is truly Christ,
we are God's children. Everyone who
loves the Father will also love his children.
2 If we love and obey God, we know that we
will love his children. 3 We show our love
for God by obeying his commandments,
and they are not hard to follow.

4 Every child of God can defeat the
world, and our faith is what gives us this
victory. 5 No one can defeat the world without having faith in Jesus as the Son of God.

Who Jesus Is

6 Water and blood came out from the
side of Jesus Christ. It wasn't just water, but

[m] **4.4** *God's Spirit*: The Greek text has "he" and may refer to the Spirit or to God or to Jesus.

3.23 Jn 13.34; 15.12, 17. **4.12** Jn 1.18. **5.3** Jn 14.15.

water and blood.[n] The Spirit tells about
this, because the Spirit is truthful. 7 In fact,
there are three who tell about it. 8 They are
the Spirit, the water, and the blood, and
they all agree.

9 We believe what people tell us. But we
can trust what God says even more, and
God is the one who has spoken about his
Son. 10 If we have faith in God's Son, we
have believed what God has said. But if we
don't believe what God has said about his
Son, it is the same as calling God a liar.
11 God has also said that he gave us eternal
life and that this life comes to us from his
Son. 12 And so, if we have God's Son, we
have this life. But if we don't have the Son,
we don't have this life.

Knowing about Eternal Life

13 All of you have faith in the Son of
God, and I have written to let you know
that you have eternal life. 14 We are certain
that God will hear our prayers when we ask
for what pleases him. 15 And if we know
that God listens when we pray, we are sure
that our prayers have already been answered.

16 Suppose you see one of our people
commit a sin that isn't a deadly sin. You
can pray, and that person will be given eternal
life. But the sin must not be one that is
deadly. 17 Everything that is wrong is sin,
but not all sins are deadly.

18 We are sure that God's children do
not keep on sinning. God's own Son protects
them, and the devil cannot harm
them.

19 We are certain that we come from
God and that the rest of the world is under
the power of the devil.

20 We know that Jesus Christ the Son of
God has come and has shown us the true
God. And because of Jesus, we now belong
to the true God who gives eternal life.

21 Children, you must stay away from
idols.

[n]**5.6** *Water and blood came out from the side of Jesus Christ. It wasn't just water, but water and blood*: See John 19.34. It is also possible to translate, "Jesus Christ came by the water of baptism and by the blood of his death! He was not only baptized, but he bled and died." The purpose of the verse is to tell that Jesus was truly human and that he really died.

5.11 Jn 3.36.

2 JOHN

ABOUT THIS LETTER

John writes again about the importance of love in a Christian's life. He points out that truth and love must go together. We must also believe that Christ was truly human, and we must love each other.

A QUICK LOOK AT THIS LETTER

- Greetings and Prayer (1-3)
- Truth and Love (4-11)
- Final Greetings (12, 13)

1 From the church leader.[a]

To a very special woman and her children.[b] I truly love all of you, and so does everyone else who knows the truth. 2 We love you because the truth is now in our hearts, and it will be there forever.

3 I pray that God the Father and Jesus Christ his Son will be kind and merciful to us! May they give us peace and truth and love.

Truth and Love

4 I was very glad to learn that some of your children are obeying the truth, as the Father told us to do. 5 Dear friend, I am not writing to tell you and your children to do something you have not done before. I am writing to tell you to love each other, which is the first thing you were told to do. 6 Love means that we do what God tells us. And from the beginning, he told you to love him.

7 Many liars have gone out into the world. These deceitful liars are saying that Jesus Christ did not have a truly human body. But they are liars and the enemies of Christ. 8 So be sure not to lose what we[c] have worked for. If you do, you won't be given your full reward. 9 Don't keep changing what you were taught about Christ, or else God will no longer be with you. But if you hold firmly to what you were taught, both the Father and the Son will be with you. 10 If people won't agree to this teaching, don't welcome them into your home or even greet them. 11 Greeting them is the same as taking part in their evil deeds.

Final Greetings

12 I have much more to tell you, but I don't want to write it with pen and ink. I want to come and talk to you in person, because that will make us[d] really happy.

13 Greetings from the children of your very special sister.[e]

[a]**1** *church leader*: Or "elder" or "presbyter" or "priest." [b]**1** *very special woman and her children*: A group of the Lord's followers who met together for worship. "The children of your . . . sister" (see verse 13) is another group of followers. "Very special" (here and verse 13) probably means "chosen (by the Lord)." [c]**8** *we*: Some manuscripts have "you." [d]**12** *us*: Some manuscripts have "you." [e]**13** *sister*: See the note at verse 1.

5 Jn 13.34; 15.12, 17. **10,11** 3 Macc 2.33.

3 JOHN

ABOUT THIS LETTER

In this letter the writer reminds Christian readers that they should help support those who go to other parts of the world to tell others about the Lord. The letter is written to an important church member named Gaius, who had been very helpful to Christians who traveled around and preached the good news.

A QUICK LOOK AT THIS LETTER

- Greetings to Gaius (1-4)
- The Importance of Working Together (5-12)
- Final Greetings (13-15)

---

1 From the church leader.[a]
To my dear friend Gaius.
I love you because we follow the truth,
2 dear friend, and I pray that all goes well
for you. I hope that you are as strong in
body, as I know you are in spirit. 3 It makes
me very happy when the Lord's followers
come by and speak openly of how you obey
the truth. 4 Nothing brings me greater happiness than to hear that my children[b] are
obeying the truth.

Working Together

5 Dear friend, you have always been
faithful in helping other followers of the
Lord, even the ones you didn't know before. 6 They have told the church about
your love. They say you were good enough
to welcome them and to send them on
their mission in a way that God's servants
deserve. 7 When they left to tell others
about the Lord, they decided not to accept
help from anyone who wasn't a follower.
8 We must support people like them, so
that we can take part in what they are doing to spread the truth.
9 I wrote to the church. But Diotrephes
likes to be the number-one leader, and he
won't pay any attention to us. 10 So if I
come, I will remind him of how he has
been attacking us with gossip. Not only has
he been doing this, but he refuses to welcome any of the Lord's followers who come
by. And when other church members want
to welcome them, he puts them out of the
church.
11 Dear friend, don't copy the evil deeds
of others! Follow the example of people
who do kind deeds. They are God's children, but those who are always doing evil
have never seen God.
12 Everyone speaks well of Demetrius,
and so does the true message that he
teaches. I also speak well of him, and you
know what I say is true.

Final Greetings

13 I have much more to say to you, but I
don't want to write it with pen and ink. 14 I
hope to see you soon, and then we can talk
in person.
15 I pray that God will bless you with
peace!
Your friends send their greetings. Please
give a personal greeting to each of our
friends.

---

[a]**1** *church leader*: Or "elder" or "presbyter" or "priest."

[b]**4** *children*: Probably persons that the leader had led to be followers of the Lord.

1 Ac 19.29; Ro 16.23, 24; 1 Co 1.14.

JUDE

ABOUT THIS LETTER

Jude has much to say about false teachers. They are evil! God will punish them, and Christians should not follow their teaching or imitate the way they live.

Jude ends with a beautiful prayer-like blessing:

Offer praise to God our Savior because of our Lord Jesus Christ! Only God can keep you from falling and make you pure and joyful in his glorious presence. Before time began and now and forevermore, God is worthy of glory, honor, power, and authority. Amen.

(24, 25)

A QUICK LOOK AT THIS LETTER

- Greetings (1, 2)
- Defending the Faith against False Teachers (3-23)
- Final Prayer (24, 25)

1 From Jude, a servant of Jesus Christ
and the brother of James.
To all who are chosen and loved by God
the Father and are kept safe by Jesus Christ.
2 I pray that God will greatly bless you
with kindness, peace, and love!

False Teachers

3 My dear friends, I really wanted to
write you about God's saving power at work
in our lives. But instead, I must write and
ask you to defend the faith that God has
once for all given to his people. 4 Some
godless people have sneaked in among us
and are saying, "God treats us much better
than we deserve, and so it is all right to be
immoral." They even deny that we must
obey Jesus Christ as our only Master and
Lord. But long ago the Scriptures warned
that these godless people were doomed.
5 Don't forget what happened to those
people that the Lord rescued from Egypt.
Some of them did not have faith, and he
later destroyed them. 6 You also know about
the angels[a] who didn't do their work and
left their proper places. God chained them
with everlasting chains and is now keeping
them in dark pits until the great day of
judgment. 7 We should also be warned by
what happened to the cities of Sodom and
Gomorrah[b] and the nearby towns. Their
people became immoral and did all sorts of
sexual sins. Then God made an example of
them and punished them with eternal fire.
8 The people I am talking about are behaving just like those dreamers who destroyed their own bodies. They reject all authority and insult angels. 9 Even Michael,
the chief angel, didn't dare to insult the
devil, when the two of them were arguing
about the body of Moses.[c] All Michael said
was, "The Lord will punish you!"

[a]**6** *angels*: This may refer to the angels who liked the women on earth so much that they came down and married them (see Genesis 6.2). [b]**7** *Sodom and Gomorrah*: During the time of Abraham the Lord destroyed these cities because the people there were so evil. [c]**9** *Michael . . . the body of Moses*: This refers to what was said in an ancient Jewish book about Moses.

1 Mt 13.55; Mk 6.3. **5** **a** Ex 12.51; **b** Nu 14.29, 30. **7** Gn 19.1-24. **9** **a** Dn 10.13, 21; 12.1; Rev 12.7; **b** Dt 34.6; **c** Zec 3.2.

10 But these people insult powers they
don't know anything about. They are like
senseless animals that end up getting destroyed, because they live only by their feelings. 11 Now they are in for real trouble.
They have followed Cain's example[d] and
have made the same mistake that Balaam[e]
did by caring only for money. They have
also rebelled against God, just as Korah
did.[f] Because of all this, they will be destroyed.
12 These people are filthy minded, and
by their shameful and selfish actions they
spoil the meals you eat together. They are
like clouds blown along by the wind, but
never bringing any rain. They are like leaf-
less trees, uprooted and dead, and unable
to produce fruit. 13 Their shameful deeds
show up like foam on wild ocean waves.
They are like wandering stars forever
doomed to the darkest pits of hell.
14 Enoch was the seventh person after
Adam, and he was talking about these people when he said:

> Look! The Lord is coming with
> thousands and thousands of holy an-
> gels 15 to judge everyone. He will pun-
> ish all those ungodly people for all the
> evil things they have done. The Lord
> will surely punish those ungodly sin-
> ners for every evil thing they have ever
> said about him.

16 These people grumble and complain
and live by their own selfish desires. They
brag about themselves and flatter others to
get what they want.

More Warnings

17 My dear friends, remember the warning you were given by the apostles of our
Lord Jesus Christ. 18 They told you that
near the end of time, selfish and godless
people would start making fun of God.
19 And now these people are already making you turn against each other. They think
only about this life, and they don't have
God's Spirit.
20 Dear friends, keep building on the
foundation of your most holy faith, as the
Holy Spirit helps you to pray. 21 And keep
in step with God's love, as you wait for our
Lord Jesus Christ to show how kind he is by
giving you eternal life. 22 Be helpful to[g] all
who may have doubts. 23 Rescue any who
need to be saved, as you would rescue someone from a fire. Then with fear in your own
hearts, have mercy on everyone who needs
it. But hate even the clothes of those who
have been made dirty by their filthy deeds.

Final Prayer

24-25 Offer praise to God our Savior because of our Lord Jesus Christ! Only God
can keep you from falling and make you
pure and joyful in his glorious presence.
Before time began and now and forevermore, God is worthy of glory, honor, power,
and authority. Amen.

[d]**11** *Cain's example*: Cain murdered his brother Abel. [e]**11** *Balaam*: According to the biblical account, Balaam refused to curse the people of Israel for profit (see Numbers 22.18; 24.13), though he led them to be unfaithful to the Lord (see Numbers 25.1-3; 31.16). But by New Testament times, some Jewish teachers taught that Balaam was greedy and did accept money to curse them.
[f]**11** *just as Korah did*: Together with Dathan and Abiram, Korah led a rebellion against Moses and Aaron (see Numbers 16.1-35; 26.9, 10). [g]**22** *Be helpful to*: Some manuscripts have "Correct."
11 **a** Gn 4.3-8; **b** Nu 22.1-35; **c** Nu 16.1-35. **14** Gn 5.18, 21-24. **18** 2 P 3.3.

REVELATION

ABOUT THIS BOOK

This book tells what John had seen in a vision about God's message and about what Jesus Christ had said and done (1.2). The message has three main parts: (1) There are evil forces at work in the world, and Christians may have to suffer and die; (2) Jesus is Lord, and he will conquer all people and powers who oppose God; and (3) God has wonderful rewards in store for his faithful people, who remain faithful to him, especially for those who lose their lives in his service.

This was a powerful message of hope for those early Christians who had to suffer or die for their faith. In this book they learned that, in spite of the cruel power of the Roman Empire, the Lamb of God would win the final victory. And this gave them the courage to be faithful.

Because this book is so full of visions that use ideas and word pictures from the Old Testament, it was like a book with secret messages for the early Christians. The book could be passed around and be understood by Christians, but an official of the Roman Empire would not be able to understand it. For example, when the fall of Babylon is described (chapter 18), the early Christians knew that this pointed to the fall of the Roman Empire. This knowledge gave them hope.

At the beginning of this book there are seven letters to seven churches. These letters show what different groups of the Lord's followers will do in times of persecution (2.1—3.22).

The author uses many powerful images to describe God's power and judgment. The vision of God's throne (4.1-11) and of the scroll and the Lamb (5.1-14) show that God and Christ are in control of all human and supernatural events. Opening seven seals (6.1—8.5), blowing the seven trumpets (8.6—11.19), and emptying the seven bowls (16.1-21) are among the visions that show God's fierce judgment on the world.

After the suffering has ended, God's faithful people will receive the greatest blessing of all:

> *"God's home is now with his people. He will live with them, and they will be his own. Yes, God will make his home among his people. He will wipe all tears from their eyes, and there will be no more death, suffering, crying, or pain. These things of the past are gone forever."*
>
> *(21.3b, 4)*

A QUICK LOOK AT THIS BOOK

- A Prophecy from John (1.1-8)
- A Vision of the Living Lord (1.9-20)
- Letters to the Seven Churches (2.1—3.22)
- A Vision of Worship in Heaven (4.1-11)
- A Scroll with Seven Seals (5.1—6.17)
- Worship in Front of God's Throne (7.1-17)
- Seven Trumpets (8.1—11.19)
- A Dragon and Two Beasts (12.1—13.18)

- Visions of God's Judgment and Protection (14.1—15.8)
- Seven Bowls of God's Anger (16.1-21)
- God's Enemies Are Defeated (17.1—20.10)
- The Final Judgment (20.11-15)
- A New Heaven and a New Earth (21.1-8)
- New Jerusalem (21.9—22.5)
- Christ Will Soon Return (22.6-21)

---

1 This is what God showed to Jesus
Christ, so that he could tell his servants what must happen soon. Christ then
sent his angel with the message to his servant John. 2 And John told everything that
he had seen about God's message and
about what Jesus Christ had said and done.
3 God will bless everyone who reads this
prophecy to others,[a] and he will bless
everyone who hears and obeys it. The time
is almost here.
4 From John to the seven churches in
Asia.[b]

I pray that you
will be blessed
with kindness and peace
from God, who is and was
and is coming.
May you receive
kindness and peace
from the seven spirits
before the throne of God.
5 May kindness and peace
be yours
from Jesus Christ,
the faithful witness.

Jesus was the first
to conquer death,
and he is the ruler
of all earthly kings.
Christ loves us,
and by his blood
he set us free
from our sins.
6 He lets us rule as kings
and serve God his Father
as priests.
To him be glory and power
forever and ever! Amen.
7 Look! He is coming
with the clouds.
Everyone will see him,
even the ones who stuck
a sword through him.
All people on earth
will weep because of him.
Yes, it will happen! Amen.

8 The Lord God says, "I am Alpha and
Omega,[c] the one who is and was and is
coming. I am God All-Powerful!"

A Vision of the Risen Lord

9 I am John, a follower together with all
of you. We suffer because Jesus is our king,
but he gives us the strength to endure.
I was sent to Patmos Island,[d] because I
had preached God's message and had
told about Jesus. 10 On the Lord's day the
Spirit took control of me, and behind me
I heard a loud voice that sounded like a
trumpet. 11 The voice said, "Write in a
book what you see. Then send it to the
seven churches in Ephesus, Smyrna, Pergamum, Thyatira, Sardis, Philadelphia, and
Laodicea."[e]
12 When I turned to see who was speaking to me, I saw seven gold lampstands.
13 There with the lampstands was someone
who seemed to be the Son of Man.[f] He was

[a] **1.3** *who reads this prophecy to others*: A public reading, in a worship service. [b] **1.4** *Asia*: The section 1.4—3.22 is in the form of a letter. Asia was in the eastern part of the Roman Empire and is present day Turkey. [c] **1.8** *Alpha and Omega*: The first and last letters of the Greek alphabet, which sometimes mean "first" and "last." [d] **1.9** *Patmos Island*: A small island where prisoners were sometimes kept by the Romans. [e] **1.11** *Ephesus . . . Laodicea*: Ephesus was in the center with the six other cities forming a half-circle around it. [f] **1.13** *Son of Man*: That is, Jesus.

1.4 a Ex 3.14; **b** Rev 4.5. **1.5 a** Is 55.4; **b** Ps 89.27. **1.6** Ex 19.6; Rev 5.10.
1.7 a Dn 7.13; Mt 24.30; Mk 13.26; Lk 21.27; 1 Th 4.17; **b** Zec 12.10; Jn 19.34, 37; **c** Zec 12.10; Mt 24.30. **1.8 a** Rev 22.13; **b** Ex 3.14. **1.13 a** Dn 7.13; **b** Dn 10.5.

wearing a robe that reached down to his
feet, and a gold cloth was wrapped around
his chest. 14 His head and his hair were
white as wool or snow, and his eyes looked
like flames of fire. 15 His feet were glowing
like bronze being heated in a furnace, and
his voice sounded like the roar of a waterfall. 16 He held seven stars in his right
hand, and a sharp double-edged sword was
coming from his mouth. His face was shining as bright as the sun at noon.

17 When I saw him, I fell at his feet like
a dead person. But he put his right hand
on me and said:

Don't be afraid! I am the first, the
last, 18 and the living one. I died, but
now I am alive forevermore, and I have
the keys to death and the world of the
dead.[g] 19 Write what you have seen
and what is and what will happen after
these things. 20 I will explain the mystery of the seven stars that you saw at
my right side and the seven gold lampstands. The seven stars are the angels[h]
of the seven churches, and the lampstands are the seven churches.

The Letter to Ephesus

2 This is what you must write to the angel of the church in Ephesus:

I am the one who holds the seven
stars in my right hand, and I walk
among the seven gold lampstands. Listen to what I say.

2 I know everything you have done,
including your hard work and how you
have endured. I know you won't put up
with anyone who is evil. When some
people pretended to be apostles, you
tested them and found out that they
were liars. 3 You have endured and
gone through hard times because of
me, and you have not given up.

4 But I do have something against
you! And it is this: You don't have as
much love as you used to. 5 Think
about where you have fallen from, and
then turn back and do as you did at
first. If you don't turn back, I will come
and take away your lampstand. 6 But
there is one thing you are doing right.
You hate what the Nicolaitans[i] are doing, and so do I.

7 If you have ears, listen to what the
Spirit says to the churches. I will let
everyone who wins the victory eat from
the life-giving tree in God's wonderful
garden.

The Letter to Smyrna

8 This is what you must write to the angel of the church in Smyrna:

I am the first and the last. I died,
but now I am alive! Listen to what
I say.

9 I know how much you suffer and
how poor you are, but you are rich. I
also know the cruel things being said
about you by people who claim to be
Jews. But they are not really Jews. They
are a group that belongs to Satan.

10 Don't worry about what you will
suffer. The devil will throw some of
you into jail, and you will be tested and
made to suffer for ten days. But if you
are faithful until you die, I will reward
you with a glorious life.[j]

11 If you have ears, listen to what
the Spirit says to the churches. Whoever wins the victory will not be hurt
by the second death.[k]

The Letter to Pergamum

12 This is what you must write to the angel of the church in Pergamum:

I am the one who has the sharp

[g] **1.18** *keys to death and the world of the dead*: That is, power over death and the world of the dead. [h] **1.20** *angels*: Perhaps guardian angels that represent the churches, or they may be church leaders or messengers sent to the churches. [i] **2.6** *Nicolaitans*: Nothing else is known about these people, though it is possible that they claimed to be followers of Nicolaus from Antioch (see Acts 6.5). [j] **2.10** *a glorious life*: The Greek text has "a crown of life." In ancient times an athlete who had won a contest was rewarded with a crown of flowers as a sign of victory.
[k] **2.11** *second death*: The first death is physical death, and the "second death" is eternal death.
1.14 Dn 7.9. **1.14,15** Dn 10.6. **1.15** Ez 1.24; 43.2; 2 Esd 6.17. **1.17** Is 44.6; 48.12; 2 Esd 10.30; Rev 2.8; 22.13. **2.7** **a** Gn 2.9; 2 Esd 2.12; Rev 22.2; **b** Ez 28.13; 31.8 (LXX).
2.8 Is 44.6; 48.12; Rev 1.17; 22.13. **2.11** Rev 20.14; 21.8.

double-edged sword! Listen to what
I say.
13 I know that you live where Satan
has his throne.[l] But you have kept true
to my name. Right there where Satan
lives, my faithful witness Antipas[m] was
taken from you and put to death. Even
then you did not give up your faith
in me.
14 I do have a few things against
you. Some of you are following the
teaching of Balaam.[n] Long ago he told
Balak to teach the people of Israel to
eat food that had been offered to idols
and to be immoral. 15 Now some of you
are following the teaching of the Nicolaitans.[o] 16 Turn back! If you don't, I
will come quickly and fight against
these people. And my words will cut
like a sword.
17 If you have ears, listen to what
the Spirit says to the churches. To
everyone who wins the victory, I will
give some of the hidden food.[p] I will
also give each one a white stone[q] with
a new name[r] written on it. No one will
know that name except the one who is
given the stone.

The Letter to Thyatira

18 This is what you must write to the angel of the church in Thyatira:
I am the Son of God! My eyes are
like flames of fire, and my feet are like
bronze. Listen to what I say.
19 I know everything about you, including your love, your faith, your
service, and how you have endured. I
know that you are doing more now
than you have ever done before. 20 But
I still have something against you because of that woman Jezebel.[s] She
calls herself a prophet, and you let her
teach and mislead my servants to do
immoral things and to eat food offered
to idols. 21 I gave her a chance to turn
from her sins, but she did not want to
stop doing these immoral things.
22 I am going to strike down
Jezebel. Everyone who does these immoral things with her will also be punished, if they don't stop. 23 I will even
kill her followers.[t] Then all the
churches will see that I know everyone's thoughts and feelings. I will treat
each of you as you deserve.
24 Some of you in Thyatira don't
follow Jezebel's teaching. You don't
know anything about what her followers call the "deep secrets of Satan." So
I won't burden you down with any
other commands. 25 But until I come,
you must hold firmly to the teaching
you have.
26 I will give power over the nations
to everyone who wins the victory and
keeps on obeying me until the end.
27-28 I will give each of them the same
power that my Father has given me.
They will rule the nations with an iron

[l] **2.13** *where Satan has his throne*: The meaning is uncertain, but it may refer to the city as a center of pagan worship or of Emperor worship. [m] **2.13** *Antipas*: Nothing else is known about this man, who is mentioned only here in the New Testament. [n] **2.14** *Balaam*: According to Numbers 22–24, Balaam refused to disobey the Lord. But in other books of the Old Testament, he is spoken of as evil (see Deuteronomy 23.4, 5; Joshua 13.22; 24.9, 10; Nehemiah 13.2). [o] **2.15** *Nicolaitans*: See the note at 2.6. [p] **2.17** *hidden food*: When the people of Israel were going through the desert, the Lord provided a special food for them. Some of this was placed in a jar and stored in the sacred chest (see Exodus 16). According to later Jewish teaching, the prophet Jeremiah rescued the sacred chest when the temple was destroyed by the Babylonians. He hid the chest in a cave, where it would stay until God came to save his people. [q] **2.17** *white stone*: The meaning of this is uncertain, though it may be the same as a ticket that lets a person into God's banquet where the "hidden food" is eaten. Or it may be a symbol of victory. [r] **2.17** *a new name*: Either the name of Christ or God or the name of the follower who is given the stone. [s] **2.20** *Jezebel*: Nothing else is known about her. This may have been her real name or a name that was given to her because she was like Queen Jezebel, who opposed the Lord (see 1 Kings 19.1, 2; 21.1-26). [t] **2.23** *her followers*: Or "her children."

2.14 a Nu 22.5, 7; 31.16; Dt 23.4; **b** Nu 25.1-3. **2.17 a** Ex 16.14, 15; 16.33, 34; Jn 6.48-50; **b** Is 62.2; 65.15. **2.20** 1 K 16.31; 2 K 9.22, 30. **2.23 a** Ps 7.9; Jr 17.10; **b** Ps 62.12. **2.26-28** Ps 2.8, 9 (LXX).

rod and smash those nations to pieces
like clay pots. I will also give them the
morning star.[u]
29 If you have ears, listen to what
the Spirit says to the churches.

The Letter to Sardis

3 This is what you must write to the angel of the church in Sardis:
I have the seven spirits of God and
the seven stars. Listen to what I say.
I know what you are doing. Everyone may think you are alive, but you
are dead. 2 Wake up! You have only a
little strength left, and it is almost
gone. So try to become stronger. I have
found that you are not completely
obeying God. 3 Remember the teaching that you were given and that you
heard. Hold firmly to it and turn from
your sins. If you don't wake up, I will
come when you least expect it, just as
a thief does.
4 A few of you in Sardis have not
dirtied your clothes with sin. You will
walk with me in white clothes, because
you are worthy. 5 Everyone who wins
the victory will wear white clothes.
Their names will not be erased from
the book of life,[v] and I will tell my
Father and his angels that they are my
followers.
6 If you have ears, listen to what the
Spirit says to the churches.

The Letter to Philadelphia

7 This is what you must write to the angel of the church in Philadelphia:
I am the one who is holy and true,
and I have the keys that belonged to
David.[w] When I open a door, no one
can close it. And when I close a door,
no one can open it. Listen to what
I say.
8 I know everything you have done.
And I have placed before you an open
door that no one can close. You were
not very strong, but you obeyed my
message and did not deny that you are
my followers.[x] 9 Now you will see what
I will do with those people who belong
to Satan's group. They claim to be
Jews, but they are liars. I will make
them come and kneel down at your
feet. Then they will know that I
love you.
10 You obeyed my message and endured. So I will protect you from the
time of testing that everyone in all the
world must go through. 11 I am coming soon. So hold firmly to what you
have, and no one will take away the
crown that you will be given as your
reward.
12 Everyone who wins the victory
will be made into a pillar in the temple
of my God, and they will stay there forever. I will write on each of them the
name of my God and the name of his
city. It is the new Jerusalem that my
God will send down from heaven. I will
also write on them my own new name.
13 If you have ears, listen to what
the Spirit says to the churches.

The Letter to Laodicea

14 This is what you must write to the angel of the church in Laodicea:
I am the one called Amen![y] I am
the faithful and true witness and the
source[z] of God's creation. Listen to
what I say.
15 I know everything you have done,
and you are not cold or hot. I wish you
were either one or the other. 16 But
since you are lukewarm and neither
cold nor hot, I will spit you out of my
mouth. 17 You claim to be rich and

[u] **2.27,28** *the morning star*: Probably thought of as the star that signals the end of night and the beginning of day. In 22.16 Christ is called the "morning star." [v] **3.5** *book of life*: The book in which the names of God's people are written. [w] **3.7** *the keys that belonged to David*: The keys stand for authority over David's kingdom. [x] **3.8** *did not deny that you are my followers*: Or "did not say evil things about me." [y] **3.14** *Amen*: Meaning "Trustworthy." [z] **3.14** *source*: Or "beginning."

3.3 Mt 24.43, 44; Lk 12.39, 40; Rev 16.15. **3.5** **a** Ex 32.32, 33; Ps 69.28; Rev 20.12; **b** Mt 10.32; Lk 12.8. **3.7** Is 22.22; Job 12.14. **3.9** **a** Is 49.23; 60.14; **b** Is 43.4. **3.12** **a** Rev 21.2; **b** Is 62.2; 65.15. **3.14** Pr 8.22.

successful and to have everything you
need. But you don't know how bad off
you are. You are pitiful, poor, blind,
and naked.
18 Buy your gold from me. It has
been refined in a fire, and it will make
you rich. Buy white clothes from me.
Wear them and you can cover up your
shameful nakedness. Buy medicine for
your eyes, so that you will be able to see.
19 I correct and punish everyone I
love. So make up your minds to turn
away from your sins. 20 Listen! I am
standing and knocking at your door. If
you hear my voice and open the door, I
will come in and we will eat together.
21 Everyone who wins the victory will
sit with me on my throne, just as I won
the victory and sat with my Father on
his throne.
22 If you have ears, listen to what
the Spirit says to the churches.

Worship in Heaven

4 After this, I looked and saw a door that
opened into heaven. Then the voice
that had spoken to me at first and that
sounded like a trumpet said, "Come up
here! I will show you what must happen
next." 2 Right then the Spirit took control
of me, and there in heaven I saw a throne
and someone sitting on it. 3 The one who
was sitting there sparkled like precious
stones of jasper[a] and carnelian.[b] A rainbow
that looked like an emerald[c] surrounded
the throne.
4 Twenty-four other thrones were in a
circle around that throne. And on each of
these thrones there was an elder dressed in
white clothes and wearing a gold crown.
5 Flashes of lightning and roars of thunder
came out from the throne in the center of
the circle. Seven torches, which are the
seven spirits of God, were burning in front
of the throne. 6 Also in front of the throne
was something that looked like a glass sea,
clear as crystal.
Around the throne in the center were
four living creatures covered front and back
with eyes. 7 The first creature was like a
lion, the second one was like a bull, the
third one had the face of a human, and
the fourth was like a flying eagle. 8 Each of
the four living creatures had six wings, and
their bodies were covered with eyes. Day
and night they never stopped singing,

"Holy, holy, holy is the Lord,
  the all-powerful God,
who was and is
  and is coming!"

9 The living creatures kept praising,
honoring, and thanking the one who sits on
the throne and who lives forever and ever.
10 At the same time the twenty-four elders
knelt down before the one sitting on the
throne. And as they worshiped the one who
lives forever, they placed their crowns in
front of the throne and said,

11 "Our Lord and God,
  you are worthy
to receive glory,
  honor, and power.
You created all things,
and by your decision they are
  and were created."

The Scroll and the Lamb

5 In the right hand of the one sitting on
the throne I saw a scroll[d] that had
writing on the inside and on the outside.
And it was sealed in seven places. 2 I saw a
mighty angel ask with a loud voice, "Who is
worthy to open the scroll and break its
seals?" 3 No one in heaven or on earth or
under the earth was able to open the scroll
or see inside it.
4 I cried hard because no one was found
worthy to open the scroll or see inside it.
5 Then one of the elders said to me, "Stop

[a] **4.3** *jasper*: Usually green or clear. [b] **4.3** *carnelian*: Usually deep-red or reddish-white.
[c] **4.3** *emerald*: A precious stone, usually green. [d] **5.1** *scroll*: A roll of paper or special leather used for writing on. Sometimes a scroll would be sealed on the outside with one or more pieces of wax.

3.19 Pr 3.12; He 12.6. **4.2,3** Ez 1.26-28; 10.1. **4.5** **a** Ex 19.16; Tb 12.15; Rev 8.5; 11.19; 16.18; **b** Ez 1.13; **c** Rev 1.4; Zec 4.2. **4.6** Ez 1.22, 23. **4.6,7** Ez 1.5-10; 10.14. **4.8** **a** Ez 1.18; 10.12; **b** Is 6.2, 3. **4.11** 3 Macc 2.3. **5.1** **a** Ez 2.9, 10; **b** Is 29.11. **5.5** **a** Gn 49.9; **b** Is 11.1, 10.

crying and look! The one who is called both
the 'Lion from the Tribe of Judah'[e] and
'King David's Great Descendant'[f] has won
the victory. He will open the book and its
seven seals."
6 Then I looked and saw a Lamb standing in the center of the throne that was
surrounded by the four living creatures and
the elders. The Lamb looked as if it had
once been killed. It had seven horns and
seven eyes, which are the seven spirits[g] of
God, sent out to all the earth.
7 The Lamb went over and took the
scroll from the right hand of the one who
sat on the throne. 8 After he had taken it,
the four living creatures and the twenty-
four elders knelt down before him. Each of
them had a harp and a gold bowl full of
incense,[h] which are the prayers of God's
people. 9 Then they sang a new song,

"You are worthy
to receive the scroll
and open its seals,
because you were killed.
And with your own blood
you bought for God
people from every tribe,
language, nation, and race.
10 You let them become kings
and serve God as priests,
and they will rule on earth."

11 As I looked, I heard the voices of a lot
of angels around the throne and the voices
of the living creatures and of the elders.
There were millions and millions of them,
12 and they were saying in a loud voice,

"The Lamb who was killed
is worthy to receive power,
riches, wisdom, strength,
honor, glory, and praise."

13 Then I heard all beings in heaven and
on the earth and under the earth and in
the sea offer praise. Together, all of them
were saying,

"Praise, honor, glory,
and strength
forever and ever
to the one who sits
on the throne
and to the Lamb!"

14 The four living creatures said
"Amen," while the elders knelt down and
worshiped.

Opening the Seven Seals

6 At the same time that I saw the Lamb
open the first of the seven seals, I
heard one of the four living creatures shout
with a voice like thunder. It said, "Come
out!" 2 Then I saw a white horse. Its rider
carried a bow and was given a crown. He
had already won some victories, and he
went out to win more.
3 When the Lamb opened the second
seal, I heard the second living creature say,
"Come out!" 4 Then another horse came
out. It was fiery red. And its rider was given
the power to take away all peace from the
earth, so that people would slaughter one
another. He was also given a big sword.
5 When the Lamb opened the third seal,
I heard the third living creature say, "Come
out!" Then I saw a black horse, and its
rider had a balance scale in one hand. 6 I
heard what sounded like a voice from
somewhere among the four living creatures. It said, "A quart of wheat will cost
you a whole day's wages! Three quarts of
barley will cost you a day's wages too. But
don't ruin the olive oil or the wine."
7 When the Lamb opened the fourth
seal, I heard the voice of the fourth living
creature say, "Come out!" 8 Then I saw a
pale green horse. Its rider was named
Death, and Death's Kingdom followed be-

[e]**5.5** *'Lion from the Tribe of Judah'*: In Genesis 49.9 the tribe of Judah is called a young lion, and King David was from Judah. [f]**5.5** *'King David's Great Descendant'*: The Greek text has "the root of David" which is a title for the Messiah based on Isaiah 11.1, 10. [g]**5.6** *the seven spirits*: Some manuscripts have "the spirits." [h]**5.8** *incense*: A material that produces a sweet smell when burned. Sometimes it is a symbol for the prayers of God's people.

5.6 **a** Is 53.7; **b** Zec 4.10. **5.8** Ps 141.2. **5.9** Ps 33.3; 98.1; Is 42.10. **5.10** Ex 19.6; Rev 1.6. **5.11** Dn 7.10. **6.2** Zec 1.7, 8; 6.3, 6. **6.4** Zec 1.7, 8; 6.2. **6.5** Zec 6.2, 6. **6.8** Ez 14.21.

hind. They were given power over one fourth of the earth, and they could kill its people with swords, famines, diseases, and wild animals.

9 When the Lamb opened the fifth seal, I saw under the altar the souls of everyone who had been killed for speaking God's message and telling about their faith. 10 They shouted, "Master, you are holy and faithful! How long will it be before you judge and punish the people of this earth who killed us?"

11 Then each of those who had been killed was given a white robe and told to rest for a little while. They had to wait until the complete number of the Lord's other servants and followers would be killed.

12 When I saw the Lamb open the sixth seal, I looked and saw a great earthquake. The sun turned as dark as sackcloth,[i] and the moon became as red as blood. 13 The stars in the sky fell to earth, just like figs shaken loose by a windstorm. 14 Then the sky was rolled up like a scroll,[j] and all mountains and islands were moved from their places.

15 The kings of the earth, its famous people, and its military leaders hid in caves or behind rocks on the mountains. They hid there together with the rich and the powerful and with all the slaves and free people. 16 Then they shouted to the mountains and the rocks, "Fall on us! Hide us from the one who sits on the throne and from the anger of the Lamb. 17 That terrible day has come! God and the Lamb will show their anger, and who can face it?"

The 144,000 Are Marked for God

7 1-2 After this I saw four angels. Each one was standing on one of the earth's four corners. The angels held back the four winds, so that no wind would blow on the earth or on the sea or on any tree. These angels had also been given the power to harm the earth and the sea. Then I saw another angel come up from where the sun rises in the east, and he was ready to put the mark of the living God on people. He shouted to the four angels, 3 "Don't harm the earth or the sea or any tree! Wait until I have marked the foreheads of the servants of our God."

4 Then I heard how many people had been marked on the forehead. There were one hundred forty-four thousand, and they came from every tribe of Israel:

5 12,000 from Judah,
12,000 from Reuben,
12,000 from Gad,
6 12,000 from Asher,
12,000 from Naphtali,
12,000 from Manasseh,
7 12,000 from Simeon,
12,000 from Levi,
12,000 from Issachar,
8 12,000 from Zebulun,
12,000 from Joseph, and
12,000 from Benjamin.

People from Every Nation

9 After this, I saw a large crowd with more people than could be counted. They were from every race, tribe, nation, and language, and they stood before the throne and before the Lamb. They wore white robes and held palm branches in their hands, 10 as they shouted,

"Our God, who sits
upon the throne,
has the power
to save his people,
and so does the Lamb."

11 The angels who stood around the throne knelt in front of it with their faces to the ground. The elders and the four living creatures knelt there with them. Then they all worshiped God 12 and said,

"Amen! Praise, glory, wisdom,
thanks, honor, power,
and strength belong to our God
forever and ever! Amen!"

[i]**6.12** *sackcloth*: A rough, dark-colored cloth made from goat or camel hair and used to make grain sacks. It was worn in times of trouble or sorrow. [j]**6.14** *scroll*: See the note at 5.1.

6.11 2 Esd 4.36. **6.12** **a** Rev 11.13; 16.18; **b** Is 13.10; Jl 2.10, 31; 3.15; Mt 24.29; Mk 13.24, 25; Lk 21.25. **6.13,14** Is 34.4. **6.14** Rev 16.20. **6.15** Is 2.19, 21. **6.16** Ho 10.8; Lk 23.30. **6.17** Jl 2.11; Ml 3.2. **7.1,2** Jr 49.36; Dn 7.2; Zec 6.5. **7.3** Ez 9.4-6; 3 Macc 2.29. **7.9** 2 Esd 2.42.

13 One of the elders asked me, "Do you know who these people are that are dressed in white robes? Do you know where they come from?"

14 "Sir," I answered, "you must know."

Then he told me:

"These are the ones
who have gone through
the great suffering.
They have washed their robes
in the blood of the Lamb
and have made them white.
15 And so they stand
before the throne of God
and worship him in his temple
day and night.
The one who sits on the throne
will spread his tent
over them.
16 They will never hunger
or thirst again,
and they won't be troubled
by the sun
or any scorching heat.

17 The Lamb in the center
of the throne
will be their shepherd.
He will lead them to streams
of life-giving water,
and God will wipe all tears
from their eyes."

The Seventh Seal Is Opened

8 When the Lamb opened the seventh seal, there was silence in heaven for about half an hour. 2 I noticed that the seven angels who stood before God were each given a trumpet.

3 Another angel, who had a gold container for incense,[k] came and stood at the altar. This one was given a lot of incense to offer with the prayers of God's people on the gold altar in front of the throne. 4 Then
the smoke of the incense, together with the prayers of God's people, went up to God from the hand of the angel.

5 After this, the angel filled the incense container with fire from the altar and threw it on the earth. Thunder roared, lightning flashed, and the earth shook.

The Trumpets

6 The seven angels now got ready to blow their trumpets.

7 When the first angel blew his trumpet, hail and fire mixed with blood were thrown down on the earth. A third of the earth, a third of the trees, and a third of all green plants were burned.

8 When the second angel blew his trumpet, something like a great fiery mountain was thrown into the sea. A third of the sea
turned to blood, 9 a third of the living creatures in the sea died, and a third of the ships were destroyed.

10 When the third angel blew his trumpet, a great star fell from heaven. It was burning like a torch, and it fell on a third of the rivers and on a third of the springs of
water. 11 The name of the star was Bitter, and a third of the water turned bitter. Many people died because the water was so bitter.

12 When the fourth angel blew his trumpet, a third of the sun, a third of the moon, and a third of the stars were struck. They each lost a third of their light. So during a third of the day there was no light, and a third of the night was also without light.

13 Then I looked and saw a lone eagle flying across the sky. It was shouting, "Trouble, trouble, trouble to everyone who lives on earth! The other three angels are now going to blow their trumpets."

9 When the fifth angel blew his trumpet, I saw a star[l] fall from the sky to earth. It was given the key to the tunnel that leads
down to the deep pit. 2 As it opened the tunnel, smoke poured out like the smoke of a great furnace. The sun and the air turned

[k] **8.3** *incense*: See the note at 5.8. [l] **9.1** *star*: In the ancient world, stars were often thought of as living beings, such as angels.

7.14 Dn 12.1; Mt 24.21; Mk 13.19. **7.16** Is 49.10. **7.17 a** Ps 23.1; Ez 34.23; **b** Ps 23.2; Is 49.10; **c** Is 25.8. **8.3 a** Am 9.1; **b** Ex 30.1, 3. **8.5 a** Lv 16.12; Ez 10.2; **b** Ex 19.16; Rev 11.19; 16.18. **8.6,7** Ws 11.5—12.2. **8.7** Ex 9.23-25; Ez 38.22. **8.10** Is 14.12. **8.11** Jr 9.15. **8.12** Is 13.10; Ez 32.7; Jl 2.10, 31; 3.15. **9.2** Gn 19.28; 2 Esd 7.36.

dark because of the smoke. 3 Locusts[m] came out of the smoke and covered the earth. They were given the same power that scorpions have.

4 The locusts were told not to harm the grass on the earth or any plant or any tree. They were to punish only those people who did not have God's mark on their foreheads. 5 The locusts were allowed to make them suffer for five months, but not to kill them. The suffering they caused was like the sting of a scorpion. 6 In those days people will want to die, but they will not be able to. They will hope for death, but it will escape from them.

7 These locusts looked like horses ready for battle. On their heads they wore something like gold crowns, and they had human faces. 8 Their hair was like a woman's long hair, and their teeth were like those of a lion. 9 On their chests they wore armor made of iron. Their wings roared like an army of horse-drawn chariots rushing into battle. 10 Their tails were like a scorpion's tail with a stinger that had the power to hurt someone for five months. 11 Their king was the angel in charge of the deep pit. In Hebrew his name was Abaddon, and in Greek it was Apollyon.[n]

12 The first horrible thing has now happened! But wait. Two more horrible things will happen soon.

13 Then the sixth angel blew his trumpet. I heard a voice speak from the four corners of the gold altar that stands in the presence of God. 14 The voice spoke to this angel and said, "Release the four angels who are tied up beside the great Euphrates River." 15 The four angels had been prepared for this very hour and day and month and year. Now they were set free to kill a third of all people.

16 By listening, I could tell there were more than two hundred million of these war horses. 17 In my vision their riders wore fiery-red, dark-blue, and yellow armor on their chests. The heads of the horses looked like lions, with fire and smoke and sulfur coming out of their mouths. 18 One-third of all people were killed by the three terrible troubles caused by the fire, the smoke, and the sulfur. 19 The horses had powerful mouths, and their tails were like poisonous snakes that bite and hurt.

20 The people who lived through these terrible troubles did not turn away from the idols they had made, and they did not stop worshiping demons. They kept on worshiping idols that were made of gold, silver, bronze, stone, and wood. Not one of these idols could see, hear, or walk. 21 No one stopped murdering or practicing witchcraft or being immoral or stealing.

The Angel and the Little Scroll

10 I saw another powerful angel come down from heaven. This one was covered with a cloud, and a rainbow was over his head. His face was like the sun, his legs were like columns of fire, 2 and with his hand he held a little scroll[o] that had been unrolled. He stood there with his right foot on the sea and his left foot on the land. 3 Then he shouted with a voice that sounded like a growling lion. Thunder roared seven times.

4 After the thunder stopped, I was about to write what it had said. But a voice from heaven shouted, "Keep it secret! Don't write these things."

5 The angel I had seen standing on the sea and the land then held his right hand up toward heaven. 6 He made a promise in the name of God who lives forever and who created heaven, earth, the sea, and every living creature. The angel said, "You won't have to wait any longer. 7 God told his secret plans to his servants the prophets, and it will all happen by the time the seventh angel sounds his trumpet."

8 Once again the voice from heaven spoke to me. It said, "Go and take the open

[m]**9.3** *Locusts*: A type of grasshopper that comes in swarms and causes great damage to crops.
[n]**9.11** *Abaddon . . . Apollyon*: The Hebrew word "Abaddon" and the Greek word "Apollyon" each mean "destruction." [o]**10.2** *scroll*: See the note at 5.1.

9.3 Ex 10.12-15; Ws 16.9. **9.4** Ez 9.4. **9.6** Job 3.21; Jr 8.3. **9.7** Jl 2.4. **9.8** Jl 1.6. **9.9** Jl 2.5. **9.13** Ex 30.1-3. **9.17** Ws 11.17, 18. **9.20** Ps 115.4-7; 135.15-17; Dn 5.23. **10.5-7** Ex 20.11; Dt 32.40; Dn 12.7; Am 3.7. **10.8-10** Ez 2.8—3.3.

scroll from the hand of the angel standing on the sea and the land."

9 When I went over to ask the angel for the little scroll, the angel said, "Take the scroll and eat it! Your stomach will turn sour, but the taste in your mouth will be as sweet as honey." 10 I took the little scroll from the hand of the angel and ate it. The taste was as sweet as honey, but my stomach turned sour.

11 Then some voices said, "Keep on telling what will happen to the people of many nations, races, and languages, and also to kings."

The Two Witnesses

11 An angel gave me a measuring stick and said:

> Measure around God's temple. Be sure to include the altar and everyone worshiping there. 2 But don't measure the courtyard outside the temple building. Leave it out. It has been given to those people who don't know God, and they will trample all over the holy city for forty-two months. 3 My two witnesses will wear sackcloth,[p] while I let them preach for one thousand two hundred sixty days.

4 These two witnesses are the two olive trees and the two lampstands that stand in the presence of the Lord who rules the earth. 5 Any enemy who tries to harm them will be destroyed by the fire that comes out of their mouths. 6 They have the power to lock up the sky and to keep rain from falling while they are prophesying. And whenever they want to, they can turn water to blood and cause all kinds of terrible troubles on earth.

7 After the two witnesses have finished preaching God's message, the beast that lives in the deep pit will come up and fight against them. It will win the battle and kill them. 8 Their bodies will be left lying in the streets of the same great city where their Lord was nailed to a cross. And that city is spiritually like the city of Sodom or the country of Egypt.

9 For three and a half days the people of every nation, tribe, language, and race will stare at the bodies of these two witnesses and refuse to let them be buried. 10 Everyone on earth will celebrate and be happy. They will give gifts to each other, because of what happened to the two prophets who caused them so much trouble. 11 But three and a half days later, God will breathe life into their bodies. They will stand up, and everyone who sees them will be terrified.

12 The witnesses then heard a loud voice from heaven, saying, "Come up here." And while their enemies were watching, they were taken up to heaven in a cloud. 13 At that same moment there was a terrible earthquake that destroyed a tenth of the city. Seven thousand people were killed, and the rest were frightened and praised the God who rules in heaven.

14 The second horrible thing has now happened! But the third one will be here soon!

The Seventh Trumpet

15 At the sound of the seventh trumpet, loud voices were heard in heaven. They said,

"Now the kingdom
of this world
belongs to our Lord
and to his Chosen One!
And he will rule
forever and ever!"

16 Then the twenty-four elders, who were seated on thrones in God's presence, knelt down and worshiped him. 17 They said,

"Lord God All-Powerful,
you are and you were,
and we thank you.
You used your great power
and started ruling.
18 When the nations got angry,
you became angry too!

[p] **11.3** *sackcloth*: See the note at 6.12.

11.1 Ez 40.3; Zec 2.1, 2. **11.2** Lk 21.24. **11.4** Zec 4.3, 11-14. **11.6 a** 1 K 17.1; **b** Ex 7.17-19; **c** 1 S 4.8. **11.7 a** Dn 7.7; Rev 13.5-7; 17.8; **b** Dn 7.21. **11.8** Is 1.9, 10. **11.11** Ez 37.10. **11.12** 2 K 2.11. **11.13** Rev 6.12; 16.18. **11.15** Ex 15.18; Dn 2.44; 7.14, 27. **11.18 a** Ps 2.5; 110.5; **b** Ps 115.13.

Now the time has come
for the dead
to be judged.
It is time for you to reward
your servants the prophets
and all of your people
who honor your name,
no matter who they are.
It is time to destroy everyone
who has destroyed
the earth."

19 The door to God's temple in heaven
was then opened, and the sacred chest[q]
could be seen inside the temple. I saw
lightning and heard roars of thunder. The
earth trembled and huge hailstones fell to
the ground.

The Woman and the Dragon

12 Something important appeared in
the sky. It was a woman whose
clothes were the sun. The moon was under
her feet, and a crown made of twelve stars
was on her head. 2 She was about to give
birth, and she was crying because of the
great pain.
3 Something else appeared in the sky. It
was a huge red dragon with seven heads
and ten horns, and a crown on each of its
seven heads. 4 With its tail, it dragged a
third of the stars from the sky and threw them
down to the earth. Then the dragon turned
toward the woman, because it wanted to
eat her child as soon as it was born.
5 The woman gave birth to a son, who
would rule all nations with an iron rod.
The boy was snatched away. He was taken
to God and placed on his throne. 6 The
woman ran into the desert to a place that
God had prepared for her. There she would
be taken care of for one thousand two hundred sixty days.

Michael Fights the Dragon

7 A war broke out in heaven. Michael
and his angels were fighting against the
dragon and its angels. 8 But the dragon lost
the battle. It and its angels were forced out
of their places in heaven 9 and were thrown
down to the earth. Yes, that old snake and
his angels were thrown out of heaven! That
snake, who fools everyone on earth, is
known as the devil and Satan. 10 Then I
heard a voice from heaven shout,

"Our God has shown
his saving power,
and his kingdom has come!
God's own Chosen One
has shown his authority.
Satan accused our people
in the presence of God
day and night.
Now he has been thrown out!

11 Our people defeated Satan
because of the blood[r]
of the Lamb
and the message of God.
They were willing
to give up their lives.

12 The heavens should rejoice,
together with everyone
who lives there.
But pity the earth
and the sea,
because the devil
was thrown down
to the earth.
He knows his time is short,
and he is very angry."

13 When the dragon realized that it had
been thrown down to the earth, it tried to
make trouble for the woman who had given
birth to a son. 14 But the woman was given
two wings like those of a huge eagle, so that
she could fly into the desert. There she
would escape from the snake and be taken
care of for a time, two times, and half a
time.
15 The snake then spewed out water like

[q]**11.19** *sacred chest*: In Old Testament times the sacred chest was kept in the tent used for worship. It was the symbol of God's presence with his people and also of his agreement with them.
[r]**12.11** *blood*: Or "death."

11.19 2 Macc 2.4-8; **a** Rev 8.5; 16.18; **b** Rev 16.21. **12.3** Dn 7.7. **12.4** Dn 8.10.
12.5 **a** Is 66.7; **b** Ps 2.9. **12.7** Dn 10.13, 21; 12.1; Jd 9. **12.9** **a** Gn 3.1; **b** Lk 10.18.
12.10 Job 1.9-11; Zec 3.1. **12.14** Dn 7.25; 12.7.

a river to sweep the woman away. 16 But the earth helped her and swallowed the water that had come from the dragon's mouth. 17 This made the dragon terribly angry with the woman. So it started a war against the rest of her children. They are the people who obey God and are faithful to what Jesus did and taught. 18 The dragon[s] stood on the beach beside the sea.

The Two Beasts

13 I looked and saw a beast coming up from the sea. This one had ten horns and seven heads, and a crown was on each of its ten horns. On each of its heads were names that were an insult to God. 2 The beast that I saw had the body of a leopard, the feet of a bear, and the mouth of a lion. The dragon handed over its own power and throne and great authority to this beast. 3 One of its heads seemed to have been fatally wounded, but now it was well. Everyone on earth marveled at this beast, 4 and they worshiped the dragon who had given its authority to the beast. They also worshiped the beast and said, "No one is like this beast! No one can fight against it."

5 The beast was allowed to brag and claim to be God, and for forty-two months it was allowed to rule. 6 The beast cursed God, and it cursed the name of God. It even cursed the place where God lives, as well as everyone who lives in heaven with God. 7 It was allowed to fight against God's people and defeat them. It was also given authority over the people of every tribe, nation, language, and race. 8 The beast was worshiped by everyone whose name wasn't written before the time of creation in the book of the Lamb who was killed.[t]

9 If you have ears,
then listen!
10 If you are doomed
to be captured,
you will be captured.
If you are doomed
to be killed by a sword,
you will be killed
by a sword.

This means that God's people must learn to endure and be faithful!

11 I now saw another beast. This one came out of the ground. It had two horns like a lamb, but spoke like a dragon. 12 It worked for the beast whose fatal wound had been healed. And it used all its authority to force the earth and its people to worship that beast. 13 It worked mighty miracles, and while people watched, it even made fire come down from the sky.

14 This second beast fooled people on earth by working miracles for the first one. Then it talked them into making an idol in the form of the beast that did not die after being wounded by a sword. 15 It was allowed to put breath into the idol, so that it could speak. Everyone who refused to worship the idol of the beast was put to death. 16 All people were forced to put a mark on their right hand or forehead. Whether they were powerful or weak, rich or poor, free people or slaves, 17 they all had to have this mark, or else they could not buy or sell anything. This mark stood for the name of the beast and for the number of its name.

18 You need wisdom to understand the number of the beast! But if you are smart enough, you can figure this out. Its number is six hundred sixty-six, and it stands for a person.

The Lamb and His 144,000 Followers

14 I looked and saw the Lamb standing on Mount Zion![u] With him were a hundred forty-four thousand, who had his name and his Father's name written on their foreheads. 2 Then I heard a sound from heaven that was like a roaring flood or loud thunder or even like the music of harps. 3 And a new song was being sung in front of God's throne and in front

[s] **12.18** *The dragon*: The text has "he," and some manuscripts have "I." [t] **13.8** *wasn't written . . . was killed*: Or "not written in the book of the Lamb who was killed before the time of creation." [u] **14.1** *Mount Zion*: Another name for Jerusalem.

13.1 a Dn 7.3; 2 Esd 11.1; **b** Rev 17.3, 7-12. **13.2** Dn 7.4-6. **13.5,6** Dn 7.8, 25; 11.36. **13.7** Dn 7.21. **13.8** Ps 69.28. **13.10** Jr 15.2; 43.11. **13.16,17** 3 Macc 2.29. **14.1** Ez 9.4; Rev 7.3. **14.2** 1 Esd 6.17.

of the four living creatures and the elders. No one could learn that song, except the one hundred forty-four thousand who had been rescued from the earth. 4 All of these are pure virgins, and they follow the Lamb wherever he leads. They have been rescued to be presented to God and the Lamb as the most precious people[v] on earth. 5 They never tell lies, and they are innocent.

The Messages of the Three Angels

6 I saw another angel. This one was flying across the sky and had the eternal good news to announce to the people of every race, tribe, language, and nation on earth. 7 The angel shouted, "Worship and honor God! The time has come for him to judge everyone. Kneel down before the one who created heaven and earth, the oceans, and every stream."

8 A second angel followed and said, "The great city of Babylon has fallen! This is the city that made all nations drunk and immoral. Now God is angry, and Babylon has fallen."

9 Finally, a third angel came and shouted:

> Here is what will happen if you worship the beast and the idol and have the mark of the beast on your hand or forehead. 10 You will have to drink the wine that God gives to everyone who makes him angry. You will feel his mighty anger, and you will be tortured with fire and burning sulfur, while the holy angels and the Lamb look on.
>
> 11 If you worship the beast and the idol and accept the mark of its name, you will be tortured day and night. The smoke from your torture will go up forever and ever, and you will never be able to rest.

12 God's people must learn to endure. They must also obey his commands and have faith in Jesus.

13 Then I heard a voice from heaven say, "Put this in writing. From now on, the Lord will bless everyone who has faith in him when they die."

The Spirit answered, "Yes, they will rest from their hard work, and they will be rewarded for what they have done."

The Earth Is Harvested

14 I looked and saw a bright cloud, and someone who seemed to be the Son of Man[w] was sitting on the cloud. He wore a gold crown on his head and held a sharp sickle[x] in his hand. 15 An angel came out of the temple and shouted, "Start cutting with your sickle! Harvest season is here, and all crops on earth are ripe." 16 The one on the cloud swung his sickle and harvested the crops.

17 Another angel with a sharp sickle then came out of the temple in heaven. 18 After this, an angel with power over fire came from the altar and shouted to the angel who had the sickle. He said, "All grapes on earth are ripe! Harvest them with your sharp sickle." 19 The angel swung his sickle on earth and cut off its grapes. He threw them into a pit[y] where they were trampled on as a sign of God's anger. 20 The pit was outside the city, and when the grapes were mashed, blood flowed out. The blood turned into a river that was about two hundred miles long and almost deep enough to cover a horse.

The Last of the Terrible Troubles

15 After this, I looked at the sky and saw something else that was strange and important. Seven angels were bringing the last seven terrible troubles. When these are ended, God will no longer be angry.

2 Then I saw something that looked like a glass sea mixed with fire, and people were standing on it. They were the ones who had defeated the beast and the idol and the

[v]**14.4** *the most precious people*: The Greek text has "the first people." The Law of Moses taught that the first-born of all animals and the first part of the harvest were special and belonged to the Lord. [w]**14.14** *Son of Man*: See the note at 1.13. [x]**14.14** *sickle*: A knife with a long curved blade, used to cut grain and other crops. [y]**14.19** *pit*: It was the custom to put grapes in a pit (called a wine press) and stomp on them to make juice that would later turn to wine.

14.5 Zep 3.13. **14.8** Is 21.9; Jr 51.8; Rev 18.2. **14.10** **a** Is 51.17; **b** Gn 19.24; Ez 38.22. **14.11** Is 34.10. **14.14** Dn 7.13. **14.15** Jl 3.13. **14.20** Is 63.3; Lm 1.15; Rev 19.15.

number that tells the name of the beast.
God had given them harps, 3 and they were
singing the song that his servant Moses and
the Lamb had sung. They were singing,

"Lord God All-Powerful,
you have done great
and marvelous things.
You are the ruler
of all nations,
and you do what is
right and fair.
4 Lord, who doesn't honor
and praise your name?
You alone are holy,
and all nations will come
and worship you,
because you have shown
that you judge
with fairness."

5 After this, I noticed something else in
heaven. The sacred tent used for a temple
was open. 6 And the seven angels who were
bringing the terrible troubles were coming
out of it. They were dressed in robes of
pure white linen and wore belts made of
pure gold. 7 One of the four living creatures
gave each of the seven angels a bowl made
of gold. These bowls were filled with the
anger of God who lives forever and ever.
8 The temple quickly filled with smoke
from the glory and power of God. No one
could enter it until the seven angels had
finished pouring out the seven last troubles.

The Bowls of God's Anger

16 From the temple I heard a voice
shout to the seven angels, "Go and
empty the seven bowls of God's anger on
the earth."
2 The first angel emptied his bowl on
the earth. At once ugly and painful sores
broke out on everyone who had the mark of
the beast and worshiped the idol.
3 The second angel emptied his bowl on
the sea. Right away the sea turned into
blood like that of a dead person, and every
living thing in the sea died.
4 The third angel emptied his bowl into
the rivers and streams. At once they turned
to blood. 5 Then I heard the angel, who has
power over water, say,

"You have always been,
and you always will be
the holy God.
You had the right
to judge in this way.
6 They poured out the blood[z]
of your people
and your prophets.
So you gave them blood
to drink,as they deserve!"
7 After this, I heard
the altar shout,
"Yes, Lord God All-Powerful,
your judgments are honest
and fair."

8 The fourth angel emptied his bowl on
the sun, and it began to scorch people like
fire. 9 Everyone was scorched by its great
heat, and all of them cursed the name of
God who had power over these terrible
troubles. But no one turned to God and
praised him.
10 The fifth angel emptied his bowl on
the throne of the beast. At once darkness
covered its kingdom, and its people began
biting their tongues in pain. 11 And because
of their painful sores, they cursed the God
who rules in heaven. But still they did not
stop doing evil things.
12 The sixth angel emptied his bowl on
the great Euphrates River, and it completely dried up to make a road for the
kings from the east. 13 An evil spirit that
looked like a frog came out of the mouth of
the dragon. One also came out of the
mouth of the beast, and another out of the
mouth of the false prophet. 14 These evil
spirits had the power to work miracles.
They went to every king on earth, to bring
them together for a war against God All-
Powerful. But that will be the day of God's
great victory.

[z] **16.6** *They poured out the blood*: A way of saying, "They murdered."
15.3 Ex 15.1. **15.4** **a** Jr 10.7; **b** Ps 86.9. **15.5** Ex 38.21-23. **15.8** Ex 40.34; 1 K 8.10, 11; 2 Ch 5.11-14; Is 6.4. **16.2** Ex 9.10. **16.4** Ex 7.17-21; Ps 78.44. **16.10** Ex 10.21. **16.12** Is 11.15.

15 Remember that Christ says, "When I
come, it will surprise you like a thief! But
God will bless you, if you are awake and
ready. Then you won't have to walk around
naked and be ashamed."
16 Those armies came together in a
place that in Hebrew is called Armagedon.[a]
17 As soon as the seventh angel emptied
his bowl in the air, a loud voice from the
throne in the temple shouted, "It's done!"
18 There were flashes of lightning, roars of
thunder, and the worst earthquake in all
history. 19 The great city of Babylon split
into three parts, and the cities of other nations fell. So God made Babylon drink from
the wine cup that was filled with his anger.
20 Every island ran away, and the mountains disappeared. 21 Hailstones, weighing
about a hundred pounds each, fell from the
sky on people. Finally, the people cursed
God, because the hail was so terrible.

The Prostitute and the Beast

17 One of the seven angels who had
emptied the bowls came over and
said to me, "Come on! I will show you how
God will punish that shameless prostitute
who sits on many oceans. 2 Every king on
earth has slept with her, and her shameless
ways are like wine that has made everyone
on earth drunk."
3 With the help of the Spirit, the angel
took me into the desert, where I saw a
woman sitting on a red beast. The beast
was covered with names that were an insult
to God, and it had seven heads and ten
horns. 4 The woman was dressed in purple
and scarlet robes, and she wore jewelry
made of gold, precious stones, and pearls.
In her hand she held a gold cup filled with
the filthy and nasty things she had done.
5 On her forehead a mysterious name was
written:

I AM THE GREAT CITY OF BABYLON,
THE MOTHER OF EVERY IMMORAL
AND FILTHY THING ON EARTH.

6 I could tell that the woman was drunk on
the blood of God's people who had given
their lives for Jesus. This surprising sight
amazed me, 7 and the angel said:
Why are you so amazed? I will explain the mystery about this woman
and about the beast she is sitting on,
with its seven heads and ten horns.
8 The beast you saw is one that used to
be and no longer is. It will come back
from the deep pit, but only to be destroyed. Everyone on earth whose
names were not written in the book of
life[b] before the time of creation will be
amazed. They will see this beast that
used to be and no longer is, but will be
once more.
9 Anyone with wisdom can figure
this out. The seven heads that the
woman is sitting on stand for seven
hills. These heads are also seven kings.
10 Five of the kings are dead. One is
ruling now, and the other one has not
yet come. But when he does, he will
rule for only a little while.
11 You also saw a beast that used to
be and no longer is. That beast is one
of the seven kings who will return as
the eighth king, but only to be destroyed.
12 The ten horns that you saw are
ten more kings, who have not yet come
into power, and they will rule with the
beast for only a short time. 13 They all
think alike and will give their power
and authority to the beast. 14 These
kings will go to war against the Lamb.
But he will defeat them, because he is
Lord over all lords and King over all
kings. His followers are chosen and
special and faithful.
15 The oceans that you saw the
prostitute sitting on are crowds of people from all races and languages.
16 The ten horns and the beast will
start hating the shameless woman.

[a] **16.16** *Armagedon*: The Hebrew form of the name would be "Har Megiddo," meaning "Hill of Megiddo," where many battles were fought in ancient times (see Judges 5.19; 2 Kings 23.29, 30). [b] **17.8** *book of life*: See the note at 3.5.

16.15 Mt 24.43, 44; Lk 12.39, 40; Rev 3.3. **16.16** 2 K 23.29; Zec 12.11. **16.18** Rev 8.5; 11.13, 19. **16.19** Is 51.17. **16.20** Rev 6.14. **16.21** Ex 9.23, 24; Rev 11.19. **17.1** Jr 51.13. **17.2** Is 23.17; Jr 51.7. **17.3** Rev 13.1. **17.4** Jr 51.7. **17.8** **a** Dn 7.7; Rev 11.7; **b** Ps 69.28. **17.12** Dn 7.24. **17.14** 3 Macc 5.35.

They will strip off her clothes and leave her naked. Then they will eat her flesh and throw the rest of her body into a fire.
17 God is the one who made these kings all think alike and decide to give their power to the beast. And they will do this until what God has said comes true.
18 The woman you saw is the great city that rules over all kings on earth.

The Fall of Babylon

18 I saw another angel come from heaven. This one had great power, and the earth was bright because of his glory.
2 The angel shouted,

"Fallen! Powerful Babylon
has fallen
and is now the home
of demons.
It is the den
of every filthy spirit
and of all unclean birds,
and every dirty
and hated animal.
3 Babylon's evil and immoral wine
has made all nations drunk.
Every king on earth
has slept with her,
and every merchant on earth
is rich because of
her evil desires."

4 Then I heard another voice
from heaven shout,
"My people, you must escape
from Babylon.
Don't take part in her sins
and share her punishment.
5 Her sins are piled
as high as heaven.
God has remembered the evil
she has done.
6 Treat her as she
has treated others.
Make her pay double
for what she has done.
Make her drink twice as much
of what she mixed
for others.
7 That woman honored herself
with a life of luxury.
Reward her now
with suffering and pain.

"Deep in her heart
Babylon said,
'I am the queen!
Never will I be a widow
or know what it means
to be sad.'
8 And so, in a single day
she will suffer the pain
of sorrow, hunger, and death.
Fire will destroy
her dead body,
because her judge
is the powerful Lord God."

9 Every king on earth who slept with her and shared in her luxury will mourn. They will weep, when they see the smoke from that fire.
10 Her sufferings will frighten them, and they will stand at a distance and say,

"Pity that great
and powerful city!
Pity Babylon!
In a single hour
her judgment has come."

11 Every merchant on earth will mourn, because there is no one to buy their goods.
12 There won't be anyone to buy their gold, silver, jewels, pearls, fine linen, purple cloth, silk, scarlet cloth, sweet-smelling wood, fancy carvings of ivory and wood, as well as things made of bronze, iron, or marble.
13 No one will buy their cinnamon, spices, incense, myrrh, frankincense,[c] wine, olive oil, fine flour, wheat, cattle, sheep, horses, chariots, slaves, and other humans.

14 Babylon, the things
your heart desired

[c] **18.13** *myrrh, frankincense*: Myrrh was a valuable sweet-smelling powder often used in perfume. Frankincense was a valuable powder that was burned to make a sweet smell.

18.2 **a** Is 21.9; Jr 51.8; Rev 14.8; **b** Is 13.21; Jr 50.39. **18.3** Is 23.17; Jr 51.7. **18.4** Is 48.20; Jr 50.8; 51.6, 45. **18.5** Gn 18.20, 21; Jr 51.9. **18.6** Ps 137.8; Jr 50.29. **18.7,8** Is 47.7-9. **18.9,10** Ez 26.16, 17. **18.11** Ez 27.31, 36. **18.12,13** Ez 27.12, 13, 22.

have all escaped
from you.
Every luxury
and all your glory
will be lost forever.
You will never
get them back.

15 The merchants had become rich because of her. But when they saw her sufferings, they were terrified. They stood at a distance, crying and mourning. 16 Then they shouted,

"Pity the great city
of Babylon!
She dressed in fine linen
and wore purple
and scarlet cloth.
She had jewelry
made of gold
and precious stones
and pearls.
17 Yet in a single hour
her riches disappeared."

Every ship captain and passenger and sailor stood at a distance, together with everyone who does business by traveling on the sea. 18 When they saw the smoke from her fire, they shouted, "This was the greatest city ever!"

19 They cried loudly, and in their sorrow they threw dust on their heads, as they said,

"Pity the great city
of Babylon!
Everyone who sailed the seas
became rich
from her treasures.
But in a single hour
the city was destroyed.
20 The heavens should be happy
with God's people
and apostles and prophets.
God has punished her
for them."

21 A powerful angel then picked up a huge stone and threw it into the sea. The angel said,

"This is how the great city
of Babylon
will be thrown down,
never to rise again.
22 The music of harps and singers
and of flutes and trumpets
will no longer be heard.
No workers will ever
set up shop in that city,
and the sound
of grinding grain
will be silenced forever.
23 Lamps will no longer shine
anywhere in Babylon,
and couples will never again
say wedding vows there.
Her merchants ruled
the earth,
and by her witchcraft
she fooled all nations.
24 On the streets of Babylon
is found the blood
of God's people
and of his prophets,
and everyone else."

19 After this, I heard what sounded like a lot of voices in heaven, and they were shouting,

"Praise the Lord!
To our God belongs
the glorious power to save,
2 because his judgments
are honest and fair.
That filthy prostitute
ruined the earth
with shameful deeds.
But God has judged her
and made her pay
the price for murdering
his servants."

3 Then the crowd shouted,

"Praise the Lord!
Smoke will never stop rising
from her burning body."

4 After this, the twenty-four elders and the four living creatures all knelt before the

18.15 Ez 27.31, 36. **18.17** Is 23.14; Ez 27.26-30. **18.18** Ez 27.32. **18.19** Ez 27.30-34. **18.20** Dt 32.43; Jr 51.48. **18.21** **a** Jr 51.63, 64; **b** Ez 26.21. **18.22** Is 24.8; Ez 26.13. **18.22,23** Jr 7.34; 25.10. **18.24** Jr 51.49. **19.2** Dt 32.43; 2 K 9.7. **19.3** Is 34.10.

throne of God and worshiped him. They said, "Amen! Praise the Lord!"

The Marriage Supper of the Lamb

5 From the throne a voice said,

"If you worship
and fear our God,
give praise to him,
no matter who you are."

6 Then I heard what seemed to be a large crowd that sounded like a roaring flood and loud thunder all mixed together. They were saying,

"Praise the Lord!
Our Lord God All-Powerful
now rules as king.
7 So we will be glad and happy
and give him praise.
The wedding day of the Lamb
is here,
and his bride is ready.
8 She will be given
a wedding dress
made of pure
and shining linen.
This linen stands for
the good things
God's people have done."

9 Then the angel told me, "Put this in writing. God will bless everyone who is invited to the wedding feast of the Lamb." The angel also said, "These things that God has said are true."

10 I knelt at the feet of the angel and began to worship him. But the angel said, "Don't do that! I am a servant, just like you and everyone else who tells about Jesus. Don't worship anyone but God. Everyone who tells about Jesus does it by the power of the Spirit."

The Rider on the White Horse

11 I looked and saw that heaven was open, and a white horse was there. Its rider was called Faithful and True, and he is always fair when he judges or goes to war. 12 He had eyes like flames of fire, and he was wearing a lot of crowns. His name was written on him, but he was the only one who knew what the name meant.

13 The rider wore a robe that was covered with[d] blood, and he was known as "The Word of God." 14 He was followed by armies from heaven that rode on horses and were dressed in pure white linen. 15 From his mouth a sharp sword went out to attack the nations. He will rule them with an iron rod and will show the fierce anger of God All-Powerful by trampling the grapes in the pit where wine is made. 16 On the part of the robe that covered his thigh was written, "KING OF KINGS AND LORD OF LORDS."

17 I then saw an angel standing on the sun, and he shouted to all the birds flying in the sky, "Come and join in God's great feast! 18 You can eat the flesh of kings, rulers, leaders, horses, riders, free people, slaves, important people, and everyone else."

19 I also saw the beast and all kings of the earth come together. They fought against the rider on the white horse and against his army. 20 But the beast was captured and so was the false prophet. This is the same prophet who had worked miracles for the beast, so that he could fool everyone who had the mark of the beast and worshiped the idol. The beast and the false prophet were thrown alive into a lake of burning sulfur. 21 But the rest of their army was killed by the sword that came from the mouth of the rider on the horse. Then birds stuffed themselves on the dead bodies.

The Thousand Years

20 I saw an angel come down from heaven, carrying the key to the deep pit and a big chain. 2 He chained the dragon for a thousand years. It is that old snake, who is also known as the devil and Satan. 3 Then the angel threw the dragon into the pit. He locked and sealed it, so that

[d]**19.13** *covered with*: Some manuscripts have "sprinkled with."

19.5 Ps 115.13. **19.6** **a** Ez 1.24; 2 Esd 6.17; **b** Ps 93.1; 97.1; 99.1. **19.9** Mt 22.2, 3.
19.11 **a** Ez 1.1-3; **b** Ps 96.13; Is 11.4. **19.12** Dn 10.6. **19.13** Ws 18.14-19.
19.15 **a** Ps 2.9; **b** Is 63.3; Jl 3.13; Rev 14.20. **19.17,18** Ez 39.17-20.
19.20 Rev 13.1-18. **20.2** Gn 3.1.

a thousand years would go by before the
dragon could fool the nations again. But after that, it would have to be set free for a
little while.
4 I saw thrones, and sitting on those
thrones were the ones who had been given
the right to judge. I also saw the souls of
the people who had their heads cut off because they had told about Jesus and
preached God's message. They were the
same ones who had not worshiped the
beast or the idol, and they had refused to
let its mark be put on their hands or foreheads. They will come to life and rule with
Christ for a thousand years.
5-6 These people are the first to be
raised to life, and they are especially
blessed and holy. The second death[e] has no
power over them. They will be priests for
God and Christ and will rule with them for
a thousand years.

No other dead people were raised to life
until a thousand years later.

Satan Is Defeated

7 At the end of the thousand years, Satan will be set free. 8 He will fool the countries of Gog and Magog, which are at the
far ends of the earth, and their people will
follow him into battle. They will have as
many followers as there are grains of sand
along the beach, 9 and they will march all
the way across the earth. They will surround the camp of God's people and the
city that his people love. But fire will come
down from heaven and destroy the whole
army. 10 Then the devil who fooled them
will be thrown into the lake of fire and
burning sulfur. He will be there with the
beast and the false prophet, and they will
be in pain day and night forever and ever.

The Judgment at the Great White Throne

11 I saw a great white throne with someone sitting on it. Earth and heaven tried to
run away, but there was no place for them
to go. 12 I also saw all the dead people
standing in front of that throne. Every one
of them was there, no matter who they had
once been. Several books were opened, and
then the book of life[f] was opened. The
dead were judged by what those books said
they had done.
13 The sea gave up the dead people who
were in it, and death and its kingdom also
gave up their dead. Then everyone was
judged by what they had done. 14 Afterwards, death and its kingdom were thrown
into the lake of fire. This is the second
death.[g] 15 Anyone whose name wasn't written in the book of life was thrown into the
lake of fire.

The New Heaven and the New Earth

21 I saw a new heaven and a new
earth. The first heaven and the
first earth had disappeared, and so had the
sea. 2 Then I saw New Jerusalem, that holy
city, coming down from God in heaven. It
was like a bride dressed in her wedding
gown and ready to meet her husband.
3 I heard a loud voice shout from the
throne:

> God's home is now with his people.
> He will live with them, and they will be
> his own. Yes, God will make his home
> among his people. 4 He will wipe all
> tears from their eyes, and there will be
> no more death, suffering, crying, or
> pain. These things of the past are gone
> forever.

5 Then the one sitting on the throne
said:

> I am making everything new. Write
> down what I have said. My words are
> true and can be trusted. 6 Everything
> is finished! I am Alpha and Omega,[h]
> the beginning and the end. I will freely
> give water from the life-giving fountain
> to everyone who is thirsty. 7 All who
> win the victory will be given these

[e]**20.5,6** *second death*: See the note at 2.11. [f]**20.12** *book of life*: See the note at 3.5.
[g]**20.14** *second death*: See the note at 2.11. [h]**21.6** *Alpha and Omega*: See the note at 1.8.
20.4 Dn 7.9, 22. **20.8** Ez 38.2, 9, 15. **20.11,12** Dn 7.9, 10. **20.12** 2 Esd 6.20.
21.1 Is 65.17; 66.22; 2 P 3.13. **21.2** **a** Is 52.1; **b** 2 Esd 13.36; **c** Rev 3.12; **d** Is 61.10.
21.3 Ez 37.27; Lv 26.11, 12. **21.4** **a** Is 25.8; **b** Is 35.10; 65.19. **21.6** Is 55.1.
21.7 2 S 7.14; Ps 89.26, 27.

blessings. I will be their God, and they
will be my people.
8 But I will tell you what will happen to cowards and to everyone who is
unfaithful or dirty-minded or who
murders or is sexually immoral or uses
witchcraft or worships idols or tells
lies. They will be thrown into that lake
of fire and burning sulfur. This is the
second death.[i]

The New Jerusalem

9 I saw one of the seven angels who had
the bowls filled with the seven last terrible
troubles. The angel came to me and said,
"Come on! I will show you the one who will
be the bride and wife of the Lamb." 10 Then
with the help of the Spirit, he took me to
the top of a very high mountain. There he
showed me the holy city of Jerusalem coming down from God in heaven.
11 The glory of God made the city bright.
It was dazzling and crystal clear like a precious jasper stone. 12 The city had a high
and thick wall with twelve gates, and each
one of them was guarded by an angel. On
each of the gates was written the name of
one of the twelve tribes of Israel. 13 Three
of these gates were on the east, three were
on the north, three more were on the
south, and the other three were on the
west. 14 The city was built on twelve foundation stones. On each of the stones was
written the name of one of the Lamb's
twelve apostles.
15 The angel who spoke to me had a
gold measuring stick to measure the city
and its gates and its walls. 16 The city was
shaped like a cube, because it was just as
high as it was wide. When the angel measured the city, it was about fifteen hundred
miles high and fifteen hundred miles wide.
17 Then the angel measured the wall, and
by our measurements it was about two
hundred sixteen feet high.
18 The wall was built of jasper, and the
city was made of pure gold, clear as crystal.
19 Each of the twelve foundations was a
precious stone. The first was jasper,[j] the
second was sapphire, the third was agate,
the fourth was emerald, 20 the fifth was
onyx, the sixth was carnelian, the seventh
was chrysolite, the eighth was beryl, the
ninth was topaz, the tenth was chrysoprase, the eleventh was jacinth, and the
twelfth was amethyst. 21 Each of the twelve
gates was a solid pearl. The streets of the
city were made of pure gold, clear as crystal.
22 I did not see a temple there. The
Lord God All-Powerful and the Lamb were
its temple. 23 And the city did not need the
sun or the moon. The glory of God was
shining on it, and the Lamb was its light.
24 Nations will walk by the light of that
city, and kings will bring their riches there.
25 Its gates are always open during the day,
and night never comes. 26 The glorious
treasures of nations will be brought into the
city. 27 But nothing unworthy will be allowed to enter. No one who is dirty-minded
or who tells lies will be there. Only those
whose names are written in the Lamb's
book of life[k] will be in the city.

22 The angel showed me a river that
was crystal clear, and its waters
gave life. The river came from the throne
where God and the Lamb were seated.
2 Then it flowed down the middle of the
city's main street. On each side of the river
are trees[l] that grow a different kind of fruit
each month of the year. The fruit gives life,
and the leaves are used as medicine to heal
the nations.
3 God's curse will no longer be on the

[i] **21.8** *second death*: See the note at 2.11. [j] **21.19** *jasper*: The precious and semi-precious stones mentioned in verses 19, 20 are of different colors. *Jasper* is usually green or clear; *sapphire* is blue; *agate* has circles of brown and white; *emerald* is green; *onyx* has different bands of color; *carnelian* is deep-red or reddish-white; *chrysolite* is olive-green; *beryl* is green or bluish-green; *topaz* is yellow; *chrysoprase* is apple-green; *jacinth* is reddish-orange; and *amethyst* is deep purple. [k] **21.27** *book of life*: See the note at 3.5. [l] **22.2** *trees*: The Greek has "tree," which is used in a collective sense of trees on both sides of the heavenly river.

21.10 Ez 40.1, 2; 2 Esd 10.27. **21.12,13** Ez 48.30-35. **21.15** Ez 40.3. **21.18-21** Is 54.11, 12. **21.18** Tb 13.16, 17. **21.23** Is 60.19, 20. **21.24** Is 60.3. **21.25,26** Is 60.11. **21.27** Is 52.1; Ez 44.9. **22.1** Ez 47.1; Zec 14.8. **22.2** Gn 2.9; 2 Esd 2.12; 7.123. **22.3** Zec 14.10, 11 (cp. Gn 3.17).

people of that city. He and the Lamb will be
seated there on their thrones, and its people will worship God 4 and will see him face
to face. God's name will be written on the
foreheads of the people. 5 Never again will
night appear, and no one who lives there will
ever need a lamp or the sun. The Lord God
will be their light, and they will rule forever.

The Coming of Christ

6 Then I was told:

These words are true and can be
trusted. The Lord God controls the
spirits of his prophets, and he is the
one who sent his angel to show his
servants what must happen right away.
7 Remember, I am coming soon! God
will bless everyone who pays attention
to the message of this book.

8 My name is John, and I am the one
who heard and saw these things. Then after I had heard and seen all this, I knelt
down and began to worship at the feet of
the angel who had shown it to me.

9 But the angel said,

Don't do that! I am a servant, just
like you. I am the same as a follower or
a prophet or anyone else who obeys
what is written in this book. God is the
one you should worship.

10 Don't keep the prophecies in this
book a secret. These things will happen soon.

11 Evil people will keep on being
evil, and everyone who is dirty-minded
will still be dirty-minded. But good
people will keep on doing right, and
God's people will always be holy.

12 Then I was told:

I am coming soon! And when I
come, I will reward everyone for what
they have done. 13 I am Alpha and
Omega,[m] the first and the last, the beginning and the end.

14 God will bless all who have
washed their robes. They will each
have the right to eat fruit from the tree
that gives life, and they can enter the
gates of the city. 15 But outside the city
will be dogs, witches, immoral people,
murderers, idol worshipers, and everyone who loves to tell lies and do wrong.

16 I am Jesus! And I am the one
who sent my angel to tell all of you
these things for the churches. I am
David's Great Descendant,[n] and I am
also the bright morning star.[o]

17 The Spirit and the bride say, "Come!"

Everyone who hears this[p] should say,
"Come!"

If you are thirsty, come! If you want life-
giving water, come and take it. It's free!

18 Here is my warning for everyone who
hears the prophecies in this book:

If you add anything to them, God
will make you suffer all the terrible
troubles written in this book. 19 If you
take anything away from these prophecies, God will not let you have part in
the life-giving tree and in the holy city
described in this book.

20 The one who has spoken these things
says, "I am coming soon!"

So, Lord Jesus, please come soon!

21 I pray that the Lord Jesus will be kind
to all of you.

[m]**22.13** *Alpha and Omega*: See the note at 1.8. [n]**22.16** *David's Great Descendant*: See the note at 5.5. [o]**22.16** *the bright morning star*: Probably thought of as the brightest star (see 2.27, 28). [p]**22.17** *who hears this*: The reading of the book of Revelation in a service of worship.

22.4 2 Esd 7.98. **22.5** **a** Is 60.19; **b** Dn 7.18. **22.11** Dn 12.10. **22.12** **a** Is 40.10; 62.11; **b** Ps 28.4; Is 40.10; Jr 17.10. **22.13** **a** Rev 1.8; **b** Is 44.6; 48.12; Rev 1.17; 2.8. **22.14** Gn 2.9; 3.22. **22.16** Is 11.1, 10. **22.17** Is 55.1. **22.18,19** Dt 4.2; 12.32.

A MINI DICTIONARY FOR THE BIBLE

A Mini Dictionary for the Bible

This dictionary is divided into 21 sections. The indexes below list all of the sections, and all of the entries in alphabetical order, so that you can find what you are looking for more easily.

Section Index

Alphabetical Index

1. A Few Basics

CEV The *Contemporary English Version* of the Bible.

Old Testament This first part of the Bible is made up of the 39 books from Genesis through Malachi. They were written mostly in Hebrew, with a few passages in Aramaic.

New Testament This second part of the Bible is made up of the 27 books from Matthew through Revelation. They were written in Greek.

Chapter and Verse Numbers These numbers were not part of the original books, but were added hundreds of years later as a way to refer to specific parts of the books of Scripture. For example, Genesis 1.3 means "the book of Genesis, chapter 1, verse 3." Genesis 2.4,5 means "the book of Genesis, chapter 2, verses 4 through 5." And Genesis 1–2 means, "the book of Genesis, chapters 1 through 2." A few books are so short that they were not divided into chapters, and so these books only have verse numbers. In the text of the CEV, sometimes verse numbers have been combined, for example, [3-4] . One reason verse numbers might be combined is that contemporary English says things in a different order than ancient Greek and Hebrew, and so two or more verses are sometimes blended together in the CEV translation. And in lists, the verse numbers are sometimes combined into a single heading to avoid confusion. But all the meaning from the original Greek and Hebrew has been carefully included in the CEV text.

2. Scriptures, Manuscripts

Ancient Translations The Old Testament was translated into Greek over the period 250-150 B.C. Later, the whole Bible was translated into Latin, Syriac, and some other languages. These ancient translations can sometimes show what the Hebrew or Greek text said at the time they were translated, and so the CEV notes will sometimes refer to them.

Commandments God's rules for his people to live by. The most famous are the Ten Commandments (see Exodus 20.1-17; Deuteronomy 5.6-21).

Dead Sea Scrolls Manuscripts found near the Dead Sea from 1947-1954. They date from about 250 B.C. to A.D. 68. These manuscripts include at least some parts of nearly all Old Testament books.

God's Law God's rules for his people to live by. They are found in the Old Testament, especially in the first five books.

Law and the Prophets A term used in New Testament times to refer to the sacred writings of the Jews. The Law and the Prophets were two of the three sections of the Old Testament, but the expression sometimes refers to the entire Old Testament.

Law of Moses and **Law of the Lord** Usually refers to the first five books of the Old Testament, but sometimes to the entire Old Testament.

Manuscript In ancient times, all books were copied by hand. A copy made this way is called "a manuscript."

Proverb A wise saying that is short and easy to remember.

Psalm A Hebrew poem. Psalms were often written in such a way that they could be prayed or sung by an individual or a group. Some of the psalms thank and praise God, while others ask God to take away sins or to give protection, comfort, vengeance, or mercy.

Samaritan Hebrew Text The Hebrew text of Genesis through Deuteronomy used and preserved by the Samaritans (see also "Samaria"). This text uses forms of letters and many spellings that are different from the Standard Hebrew Text. It has traditionally been called "the Samaritan Pentateuch."

Scriptures Although this term now refers to the whole Bible, in the New Testament it refers to the Old Testament.

Standard Hebrew Text The Hebrew text that is found in most Hebrew manuscripts of the Old Testament. Almost all of these manuscripts were copied after A.D. 900 (but see also "Dead Sea Scrolls").

Wisdom Often refers to the common sense and practical skill needed to solve everyday problems, but sometimes involves trying to find answers to the hard questions about the meaning of life.

3. Languages

Aramaic A language closely related to Hebrew. In New Testament times Aramaic was spoken by many Jews including Jesus. Ezra 4.8—6.18; 7.12-26; and Daniel 2.4b—7.28 were written in Aramaic.

Greek The language used throughout the Mediterranean world in New Testament times, and the language in which the New Testament was written.

Hebrew The language used by most of the people of Israel until the Exile. But after the people returned, more and more people spoke Aramaic instead. Most of the Old Testament was written in Hebrew.

4. People

Aaron The brother of Moses. Only he and his descendants were to serve as priests and offer sacrifices for the people of Israel (see Exodus 4.14-16; 28.1; Numbers 16.1—18.7).

Abel The second son of Adam and Eve and the younger brother of Cain. Abel was killed by Cain after God accepted Abel's offering and refused to accept Cain's (see Genesis 4.1-11).

Abraham The first of the three great ancestors of the people of Israel. Abraham was the husband of Sarah and the father of Isaac. At first Abraham's name was Abram, meaning "Great Father." Then, when Abram was ninety-nine years old, God changed Abram's name to Abraham, which means "Father of a Crowd." Abraham trusted God, and so God promised that Abraham and his wife Sarah would have a son and more descendants than could be counted. God also promised that Abraham would be a blessing to everyone on earth (see Genesis 12.1-7; 17.1—18.15).

Abram See "Abraham."

Adam The first man and the husband of Eve (see Genesis 1.26—3.21).

Agrippa (1) Herod Agrippa was king of Judea A.D. 41–44 and mistreated Christians (see Acts 12.1-5). (2) Agrippa II was the son of Herod Agrippa and ruled parts of Palestine from A.D. 53 to A.D. 93 or later. He and his sister Bernice listened to Paul defend himself (see Acts 25.13—26.32).

Antipas (1) Herod Antipas, son of Herod the Great (see "Herod"). (2) An otherwise unknown Christian at Pergamum, who was killed because he was a follower of Christ (see Revelation 2.13).

Augustus A title meaning "honored," which was given to Octavian by the Romans when he began ruling the Roman world in 27 B.C. He was the Roman Emperor when Jesus was born.

Cain The first son of Adam and Eve; Cain killed his brother Abel after God accepted Abel's offering and refused to accept Cain's (see Genesis 4.1-17).

David King of Israel from about 1010–970 B.C. David was the most famous king Israel ever had, and many of the people of Israel hoped that one of his descendants would always be their king (see 1 Samuel 16–30; 2 Samuel; 1 Kings 12).

Esau The older son of Isaac and Rebekah, and the brother of Jacob. Esau was also known as Edom and as the ancestor of the Edomites (see Genesis 25.20-34; 26.34-46; 32.1—33.16).

Eve The first woman and the wife of Adam (see Genesis 1.26—3.21).

Felix The Roman governor of Palestine A.D. 52–60, who listened to Paul speak and kept him in jail (see Acts 23.24—24.27).

Festus The Roman governor after Felix, who sent Paul to stand trial in Rome (see Acts 24.27—26.32).

Hagar A slave of Sarah, the wife of Abraham. When Sarah could not have any children, she followed the ancient custom of letting her husband have a child by Hagar, her slave. The boy's name was Ishmael (see Genesis 16; 21.8-21).

Herod (1) Herod the Great was the king of all Palestine 37–4 B.C., and so he was king at the time Jesus was born (see the note at "A.D."). (2) Herod Antipas was the son of Herod the Great and was the ruler of Galilee 4 B.C.–A.D. 39. (3) Herod Agrippa I, the grandson of Herod the Great, ruled Palestine A.D. 41–44.

Isaac The second of the three great ancestors of the people of Israel. He was the son of Abraham and Sarah, and he was the father of Esau and Jacob.

Ishmael The son of Abraham and Hagar.

Israel See "Jacob."

Jacob The third great ancestor of the people of Israel. Jacob was the son of Isaac and Rebekah, and his name was changed to Israel when he struggled with God at Peniel near the Jabbok River (see Genesis 32.22-32).

Joseph A son of Jacob and Rachel. Joseph was sold as a slave by his brothers, but later he became governor of Egypt (see Genesis 37.12-36; 41.1-57).

Lot A nephew of Abraham and the ancestor of the Moabites and Ammonites (see Genesis 11.27; 13.1-13; 18.16—19.38).

Noah When God destroyed the world by a flood, Noah and his family were kept safe in a big boat that God had told him to build (see Genesis 6–8).

Rebekah The wife of Isaac, and the mother of Jacob and Esau (see Genesis 24.1-67; 25.19-28).

Sarah The wife of Abraham and the mother of Isaac. At first her name was Sarai, but when she was old, God promised her that she would have a son, and he changed her name to Sarah. Both names mean "princess" (see Genesis 11.29,30; 17.15-19; 18.9-15; 21.1-7).

Solomon A son of King David and Bathsheba. After David's death, Solomon ruled Israel about 970–931 B.C. Solomon built the temple in Jerusalem and was widely known for his wisdom. The Hebrew text indicates that he wrote many of the proverbs and two of the psalms.

5. Prophets

Anna A woman prophet who stayed in the temple night and day. Soon after Jesus was born, Mary and Joseph took him to the temple and presented him to the Lord, and Anna talked about the child Jesus to everyone who hoped for Jerusalem to be set free (see Luke 2.36-38).

Balaam A foreign prophet. Balaam was hired by the king of Moab to put a curse on Israel, but instead Balaam blessed Israel (see Numbers 22–24).

Deborah A prophet and judge who helped lead Israel to defeat King Jabin of Hazor (see Judges 4–5).

Elijah A prophet who spoke for God in the early ninth century B.C. and who opposed the evil King Ahab and Queen Jezebel of the northern kingdom. Many Jews in later centuries thought Elijah would return to get everything ready for the day of judgment or for the coming of the Messiah (see 1 Kings 17–21; 2 Kings 1–2; Malachi 4.1-6; Matthew 17.10,11; Mark 9.11,12).

Elisha A prophet who assisted Elijah and later took his place. Elisha spoke for God in the late ninth century B.C., and was the prophet who healed Naaman (see 1 Kings 19.19-21; 2 Kings 2–9; 13.14-21).

Huldah A prophet who spoke for God during the late seventh century B.C. After *The Book of God's Law* was found in the temple, King Josiah asked her what the Lord wanted him to do (see 2 Kings 22.14-20).

Micaiah The prophet who told King Ahab that he would die in battle against the Syrian army (see 1 Kings 22.5-38).

Moses The prophet who led the people of Israel when God rescued them from slavery in Egypt. Moses also received laws from God and gave them to Israel (see Exodus 2–12; 19–24; Numbers 12.68).

Prophesy To speak as a prophet (see "Prophet").

Prophet Someone who speaks God's message, which at times included telling what would happen in the future. Sometimes when the Spirit of God took control of prophets, they lost some or all control over their speech and actions or were not aware of what was happening around them.

6. Twelve Tribes of Israel

The Bible speaks of all the people in a tribe as having descended from one of the twelve sons of Jacob. The tribes of Ephraim and Manasseh were a little different, because the people in those tribes descended from the two sons of Joseph, who was one of Jacob's sons. That would make a total of thirteen tribes, but the Bible always counts only twelve. In some passages Ephraim and Manasseh are counted as one tribe, and in other passages the Levi tribe is left out, probably because they were designated for priestly service to all the tribes, and as such, were scattered throughout the land belonging to the other tribes. People from other nations were sometimes allowed to become Israelites (see Exodus 12.38; Deuteronomy 23.1-8; and the book of Ruth), and these people would then belong to one of the tribes.

Asher Occupied land along the Mediterranean coast from Mount Carmel to the border with the city of Tyre.

Benjamin Occupied land between Bethel and Jerusalem. When the northern tribes of Israel broke away following the death of Solomon, only the tribes of Benjamin and Judah were left to form the southern kingdom.

Dan First occupied land west of Judah, Benjamin, and Ephraim. But after the Philistines took control of this area, part of the tribe then moved to the northernmost area of Israel.

Ephraim One of the largest tribes. Ephraim occupied the land north of Benjamin and south of West Manasseh.

Gad Occupied land east of the Jordan River from the northern end of the Dead Sea north to the Jabbok River.

Issachar Occupied land southwest of Lake Galilee.

Judah Occupied the hill country west of the Dead Sea. When the ten northern tribes of Israel broke away following the death of Solomon, only the tribes of Judah and Benjamin were left to form the southern kingdom, and it was also called "Judah."

Levi The men of this tribe were to be the special servants of the Lord at the sacred tent and later at the temple, and so the people of this tribe were not given tribal land. Instead, they were given towns scattered throughout the other twelve tribes (see also "Levite").

Manasseh Occupied two areas of land: (1) East Manasseh lived east of the Jordan River and north of the Jabbok River in the areas of Bashan and northern Gilead. (2) West Manasseh lived west of the Jordan River and to the north of Ephraim.

Naphtali Occupied land north and west of Lake Galilee.

Reuben Occupied land east of the Dead Sea, from the Arnon River in the south to the northern end of the Dead Sea.

Simeon Occupied land southwest of Judah, and was later practically absorbed into Judah.

Zebulun Occupied land north of Manasseh from the eastern end of Mount Carmel to Mount Tabor.

7. Christ's Twelve Apostles

Apostle A person chosen and sent by Christ to take his message to others. Lists of the names of Christ's twelve apostles can be found in Matthew 10.2-4; Mark 3.16-19; Luke 6.14-16; Acts 1.12,13. Later, others such as Paul and James the brother of Jesus also became known as apostles.

Simon also known as Peter or Cephas

Andrew Simon Peter's brother

James the son of Zebedee

John the son of Zebedee (James and John were also known as "Thunderbolts")

Philip from Bethsaida, the hometown of Simon and Andrew

Bartholomew mentioned in all New Testament lists of the apostles, but nowhere else

Thomas also known as "The Twin"

Matthew also known as Levi

James the son of Alphaeus

Thaddeus also known as Judas or Jude the son of James

Simon also known as "the Eager One"

Judas Iscariot who betrayed Jesus

Matthias who was chosen to replace Judas Iscariot

8. Cities, Nations, and Groups of People

Amalekites A nomadic nation living mostly in the area south and east of the Dead Sea. They were enemies of Israel.

Ammon A nation that lived east of Israel. According to Genesis 19.30-38, the people of Ammon descended from Lot, a nephew of Abraham.

Amorites Usually a name for all the non-Israelite nations who lived in Canaan, but in some passages it may refer to one nation scattered in several areas of Canaan.

Anakim Perhaps a group of very large people who lived in Palestine before the Israelites (see Numbers 13.33 and Deuteronomy 2.10,11,20,21).

Asia A Roman province in what is today the nation of Turkey.

Assyria An empire of Old Testament times, whose capital city Nineveh was located in what is today northern Iraq. In 722 B.C. Assyria conquered the kingdom of Israel and took many Israelites as captives. The Assyrians then forced people from other parts of its empire to settle on Israel's land (see 2 Kings 18.9-12).

Avvites A nation that lived along the Mediterranean seacoast before the Philistines came and took their land. The Avvites who survived lived south of the Philistines.

Babylonia A large empire of Old Testament times, whose capital city Babylon was located in south-central Mesopotamia. The Babylonians defeated the southern kingdom of Judah in 586 B.C. and forced many of its people to live in Babylonia (see 2 Kings 25.1-12).

Canaanites The nations who lived in Canaan before the Israelites. Many Canaanites continued to live there even after the Israelites came.

Cush The Hebrew form for Ethiopia (see "Ethiopia" below).

Disciples Those who were followers of Jesus and learned from him. The term often refers to his twelve apostles.

Edomites A nation living in Edom or Seir, an area south and southeast of the Dead Sea. According to Genesis 36.1-43, the Edomites descended from Esau, Jacob's brother.

Empire A number of kingdoms ruled by one strong military power.

Epicureans People who followed the teachings of a man named Epicurus, who taught that happiness should be the main goal in life.

Ethiopia A region south of Egypt that included parts of the present countries of Ethiopia and Sudan.

Exiles Israelites who were taken away as prisoners to Babylonia (see also "Exile").

Gentiles Those people who are not Jews.

Girgashites One of the nations that lived in Canaan before the Israelites.

Hebrew An older term for "Israelite" or "Jewish."

Hittites A nation whose capital city was located in what is now Turkey. The Hittites had an empire that at times controlled some kingdoms in Canaan before 1200 B.C., and many Hittites remained in Canaan even after the Israelites came.

Hivites A nation that lived in Canaan before the Israelites, probably related to the Horites.

Horites A nation that lived in Canaan before the Israelites. The Horites were also known as "Hurrians."

Israel (1) The nation made up of the twelve tribes descended from Jacob (see Section 6, "Twelve Tribes of Israel"). (2) The northern kingdom, after the northern tribes broke away following the death of Solomon (see 1 Kings 12.1-20).

Jebusites A group of Canaanite people who lived at Jebus, also known as Jerusalem (see 2 Samuel 5.6-10).

Jews A name first used in referring to someone belonging to the tribe of Judah. Later, the term came to be used of any Israelite.

Kadesh A town in the desert of Paran southwest of the Dead Sea, near the southern border of Israel and the western border of Edom. Israel camped at Kadesh while the twelve tribal leaders explored Canaan (see Numbers 13–14).

Levites Those Israelites who belonged to the tribe of Levi. God chose the men of one Levite family, the descendants of Aaron, to be Israel's priests. The other men from this tribe helped with the work in the sacred tent and later in the temple (see Numbers 3.5-10).

Medes A nation that lived in what is today northwest Iran. Their kingdom, called "Media," later became one of the most important provinces of the Persian Empire, and Persian laws were referred to as the laws of the Medes and Persians (see Esther 1.19; Daniel 6.8,12,15).

Midianites A nomadic nation who lived mainly in the desert along the eastern shore of the Gulf of Aqaba.

Moab A nation that lived east of the Dead Sea. According to Genesis 19.30-38, the people of Moab descended from Lot, the nephew of Abraham.

Nazarenes A name that was sometimes used for the followers of Jesus, who came from the small town of Nazareth (see Acts 24.5).

Perizzites A nation that lived in the central hill country of Canaan, before the Israelites.

Persia A large empire of Old Testament times, whose capital was located in what is now southern Iran. It is sometimes called "the Medo-Persian Empire," because of the importance of the province of Media.

Pharisees A group of Jews who thought they could best serve God by strictly obeying the laws of the Old Testament as well as their own rules, traditions, and teachings.

Philistines The land along the Mediterranean coast controlled by the Philistine people was called "Philistia." There were five main cities, each with its own ruler: Ashdod, Ashkelon, Ekron, Gath, and Gaza. The Philistines were often at war with Israel.

Phoenicia The territory along the Mediterranean Sea controlled by the cities of Tyre, Sidon, Arvad, and Byblos. The coast of modern Lebanon covers about the same area.

Rapha Perhaps a group of very large people who lived in Palestine before the Israelites (see Deuteronomy 2.11,20).

Roman Empire Controlled the area around the Mediterranean Sea in New Testament times. Its capital was Rome.

Sadducees A small and powerful group of Jews in New Testament times. They were closely connected with the high priests and accepted only the first five books of the Old Testament as their Bible. They also did not believe in life after death.

Samaria (1) The capital city of the northern kingdom of Israel beginning with the rule of King Omri (ruled 885–874 B.C.). (2) In New Testament times, a district between Judea and Galilee, named for the city of Samaria. The people of this district, called "Samaritans," worshiped God differently from the Jews, and these two groups refused to have anything to do with one another.

Sidon See "Phoenicia."

Stoics Followers of a man named Zeno, who taught that people should learn self-control and be guided by their consciences.

Tyre See "Phoenicia."

9. Places

Bashan The flat highlands and wooded hills of southern Syria. Bashan was just north of the region of Gilead and was known for its fat cattle and fine grain.

Canaan The area now covered by Israel plus Gaza, the West Bank of Jordan, Lebanon, and southern Syria (see Numbers 34.1-12). Many passages use the term to refer only to the area south of Lebanon.

Gethsemane A garden or olive orchard on the Mount of Olives (see "Mount of Olives").

Gilead A region east of the Jordan River. Moab lay to the south of Gilead, and Bashan was to the north.

Hinnom Valley A valley west and south of Jerusalem, where human sacrifice was sometimes made in Old Testament times (see "Molech").

Mount of Olives A mountain just east of Jerusalem, across Kidron Valley from the temple. Gethsemane, a place where Jesus and his disciples often went to pray, was on this mountain, and so were the villages of Bethany, Bethphage, and Bahurim (see Matthew 26.36; Mark 14.32; Luke 22.39; John 18.1,2).

Palestine The area now covered by Israel, Gaza, and Jordan.

Peniel A place near the Jabbok River where Jacob wrestled with God. Then God changed Jacob's name to Israel (see Genesis 32.22-32).

Zion Another name for Jerusalem. Zion can also refer to the hill in Jerusalem where the temple was built.

10. Objects

Chariot A two-wheeled cart that was open at the back and that was pulled by horses.

Cistern A hole or pit used for storing rainwater. Cisterns were sometimes dug in the ground and lined with stones and plaster, and at other times they were cut into the rock. The CEV sometimes translates "cistern" as "well."

Cross A device used by the Romans to put people to death. It was made of two pieces of lumber crossed in a **"T," "†,"** or **"X"** shape.

Piece of Silver In the Old Testament, this usually refers to an amount of silver weighing about 0.4 oz. Coins were not invented until late Old Testament times, so when silver or gold was used to buy things, it was weighed. In traditional translations this amount is called "a shekel." Silver and gold were worth more in biblical times than they are today.

Sackcloth A rough, dark-colored cloth made from goat or camel hair. Sackcloth was usually used to make grain sacks, but clothing made from it was worn in times of trouble or sorrow.

Scroll A roll of paper or special thin leather used for writing on.

Scepter A decorated rod, often made of gold, that a king held in his hand as a symbol of royal power.

Sling A weapon used to throw rocks a little smaller than a tennis ball. A sling was made of a piece of leather that wrapped almost around the rock and had a leather strap at each end. The person would hold the ends of the straps and swing the sling around and around. When the person let go of one strap, the rock would fly out of the sling.

Tomb A burial place, often made by cutting a small room out of the rock.

11. Festivals and Holy Days

Many of these festivals are still celebrated by Jewish people.

Festival of Shelters A festival in the early fall celebrating the period of forty years when the people of Israel walked through the desert and lived in small shelters. This happy celebration began on the fifteenth day of Tishri, and for the next seven days, the people lived in small shelters made of tree branches. The name of this festival in Hebrew is "Sukkoth."

Festival of Thin Bread A seven-day festival right after Passover. During this festival the Israelites ate a thin, flat bread made without yeast to remind themselves how God freed the people of Israel from slavery in Egypt and made them into a nation. The name of this festival in Hebrew is "Mazzoth."

Festival of Trumpets See "New Moon Festival."

Great Day of Forgiveness The tenth day of Tishri in the early fall. On this one day of the year, the high priest was allowed to go into the most holy part of the temple and sprinkle some of the blood of a sacrificed bull on the sacred chest. This was done so that the people's sins would be forgiven. In English this holy day has traditionally been called "the Day of Atonement," and its name in Hebrew is "Yom Kippur."

Harvest Festival See "Pentecost."

New Moon Festival A religious festival held on the day of the new moon, the day when only a thin edge of the moon can be seen. This day was always the first day of the month for the Hebrew calendar. The New Moon Festival was a time for rest from work, and a time for worship, sacrifices, celebration, and eating. The New Moon Festival in the month of Tishri in the early fall was also called "the Festival of Trumpets," and it involved even more sacrifices.

Passover A festival held on the fourteenth day of Abib in the early spring. At Passover the Israelites celebrated the time God rescued them from slavery in Egypt. The name of this festival in Hebrew is "Pesach."

Pentecost A Jewish festival held in mid-spring, fifty days after Passover. At this festival Israelites celebrated the wheat harvest. Pentecost was also known as "the Harvest Festival" and has traditionally been called "the Feast of Weeks"; in Hebrew, its name is "Shavuoth."

Festival of Purim A Jewish festival on the fourteenth and fifteenth of Adar, near the end of winter, when the Jews celebrated how they were saved from Haman, the evil prime minister of Persia who wanted to have them killed (see Esther 9.20-32).

Sabbath The seventh day of the week, from sunset on Friday to sunset on Saturday. Israelites worshiped on the Sabbath and rested from their work in obedience to the Lord's command (Exodus 20.8; Deuteronomy 5.12-15).

Temple Festival In 165 B.C. the Jewish people recaptured the temple in Jerusalem from their enemies and made it fit for worship again. They celebrated this event each year by an eight-day festival that began on the twenty-fifth day of the month of Chislev in the late fall. This festival is traditionally called "the Festival of Dedication," or in Hebrew, "Hanukkah."

12. Sacrifice, Temple, Worship

Altar A raised structure where sacrifices and offerings were presented to God or to pagan gods. Altars could be made of rocks, packed earth, metal, or pottery.

Amen A Hebrew word used after a prayer or a blessing and meaning that what had been said was right and true.

Fire Pan A metal pan used for burning incense or carrying hot coals from the altar.

God's Tent See "Sacred Tent."

High Priest See "Priest."

Holy Place The main room of the sacred tent and of the temple. This room contained the sacred bread, the golden incense altar, and the golden lamp stand. A curtain or wall separated the holy place from the most holy place. A priest would go into the holy place once each morning and evening to burn incense on the golden altar (see also "Most Holy Place").

Incense A material that makes a sweet smell when burned. It was used in the worship of God.

Local Shrine See "Place of Worship."

Most Holy Place The inner room of the sacred tent and of the temple. In the sacred tent this room contained only the sacred chest; in Solomon's temple, the most holy place also held statues of winged creatures. Only the high priest could enter the most holy place, and even he could enter it only once a year on the Great Day of Forgiveness. The most holy place has traditionally been called "the holy of holies."

Offerings See "Sacrifices."

Place of Worship A place to worship God or pagan gods. These places were often on a hill outside of a town and have traditionally been called "high places." In the CEV they are sometimes called "local shrines."

Priest A man who led the worship in the sacred tent or in the temple and who offered sacrifices. Some of the more important priests were called "chief priests," and the most important priest was called the "high priest."

Sacred Chest The chest or box that contained the two flat stones with the Ten Commandments written on them. The chest was covered with gold, and two golden statues of winged creatures were on the lid of the chest. These winged creatures and the chest represented God's throne on earth. Two wooden poles, one on each side, were put through rings at the corners of the chest, so that the Levites could carry the chest without touching it. The chest was kept in the most holy place (see Exodus 25.10-22).

Sacred Tent The tent where the people of Israel worshiped God before the temple was built. It has traditionally been called "the tabernacle" (see Exodus 26).

Sacrifices These gifts to God included certain animals, grains, fruits, and sweet-smelling spices. Israelites offered sacrifices to give thanks to God, to ask for his forgiveness and his blessing, and to make a payment for a wrong. Some sacrifices were completely burned on the altar. In the case of other sacrifices, a portion was given to the Lord and burned on the altar, then the rest was eaten by the priests or the worshipers who had offered the sacrifice.

Sacrifices To Ask the LORD's Blessing Traditionally called "peace offerings" or "offerings of well-being." A main purpose was to ask for the LORD's blessing, and so in the CEV they are sometimes called "sacrifices to ask the LORD's blessing" (see Leviticus 3).

Sacrifices To Give Thanks to the LORD Traditionally called "grain offerings." A main purpose of such sacrifices was to thank the LORD with a gift of grain, and so in the CEV they are sometimes called "sacrifices to give thanks to the LORD" (see Leviticus 2).

Sacrifices To Make Things Right Traditionally called "guilt offerings." A main purpose was to make things right when a person had cheated someone or the LORD. These sacrifices were also made when a person had broken certain religious rules (see Leviticus 5.14—6.7).

Sacrifices To Please the LORD Traditionally called "whole burnt offerings" because the whole animal was burned on the altar. While these sacrifices did involve forgiveness for sin, a main purpose was to please the LORD with the smell of the smoke from the sacrifice, and so in the CEV they are often called "sacrifices to please the LORD" (see Leviticus 1).

Snuffer A small tool used for putting out the flame of an oil lamp, or for trimming off the charred part of the wick.

Temple A building used as a place of worship. The god that was worshiped in a particular temple was believed to be present there in a special way. The LORD's temple was in Jerusalem.

13. Customs

Ashes People put ashes, dust, or dirt on their heads, or they rolled in ash piles or dust or dirt, as a way of showing sorrow.

Circumcise To cut off the foreskin from the male organ. This was done for Israelite boys eight days after they were born. God commanded that all newborn Israelite boys be circumcised to show that they belonged to his people (see Genesis 17.9-14).

Clean and **Unclean** (1) In Old Testament times, a person who was acceptable to worship God was called "clean." A person who had certain kinds of diseases, who had touched a dead body, or who had broken certain laws became "unclean," and was unacceptable to worship God. If a person was unclean because of disease, the disease would have to be cured before the person could be clean again. And becoming clean involved performing certain ceremonies that sometimes included sacrifices. (2) Animals that were acceptable as food were called "clean." Those that were not acceptable were called "unclean" (see Leviticus 11.1-47; Deuteronomy 14.3-21). (3) Many things including tools, dishes, houses, and land could also become unclean and unusable, especially if they were touched by something unclean. Some unclean objects had to be destroyed, but others could be made clean by being washed or placed in a fire for a short time.

Going without Eating This was a way of showing sorrow, or of asking for God's help. It is also called "fasting."

Tearing Clothes A way of showing sorrow or anger, or of asking for God's help.

14. God, Jesus, Angels

Angel A supernatural being who tells God's messages to people or protects those who belong to God.

Christ A Greek word meaning "the Chosen One" and used to translate the Hebrew word "Messiah." In New Testament times, many of the Jews believed that God was going to send the Messiah to set them free from the power of their enemies. The term "Christ" is used in the New Testament both as a title and as a name for Jesus.

Eternal Life Life that is the gift of God and that never ends.

Glory Something seen, heard, or felt that shows a person or thing is important, wonderful, or powerful. When God appeared to people, his glory was often seen as a bright light or as fire and smoke. Jesus' glory was seen when he performed miracles, when he was lifted up on the cross, and when he was raised from death.

God's Kingdom God's rule over people, both in this life and in the next.

Holy One A name for the Savior that God had promised to send (see "Savior").

Kingdom of Heaven See "God's kingdom."

LORD In the Old Testament the word "LORD" in capital letters stands for the Hebrew consonants *YHWH*, the personal name of God. Ancient Hebrew did not have vowel letters, and so anyone reading Hebrew would have to know what vowels to put with the consonants. It is not known for certain what vowel sounds were originally used with the consonants *YHWH*. The word "Lord" represents the Hebrew term *Adonai*, the usual word for "lord." By late Old Testament times, Jews considered God's personal name too holy to be pronounced. So they said *Adonai*, "Lord," whenever they read *YHWH*. When the Jewish scribes first translated the Hebrew Scriptures into ancient Greek, they translated the personal name of God as *Kurios*, "Lord." Since that time, most translations, including the *Contemporary English Version*, have followed their example and have avoided using the personal name of God.

Messiah See "Christ."

Promised One A title for the Savior that God promised to send (see "Savior").

Save To rescue people from the power of their enemies or from the power of evil, and to give them new life and place them under God's care (see also "Savior").

Savior The one that God has chosen to rescue or save his people (see also "Save").

Sin Turning away from God and disobeying the teachings or commandments of God.

Son of Man A title often used by Jesus to refer to himself. This title is also found in the Hebrew text of Daniel 7.13 and Psalm 8.4, and God uses it numerous times in the book of Ezekiel to refer to Ezekiel.

Way In the book of Acts the Christian life is sometimes called "the Way" or "the Way of the Lord" or "God's Way."

Winged Creature These supernatural beings represented the presence of God and supported his throne in Ezekiel 1.4-25; 10.1-22. Statues of winged creatures were on top of the sacred chest, and larger ones were in the most holy place in the temple built by Solomon. Wood carvings of winged creatures decorated the inside walls and doors of the temple, and figures of winged creatures were woven into the curtain separating the holy place from the most holy place in the sacred tent. The traditional term for winged creature is "cherub" (or "cherubim" for more than one).

15. Foreign Gods, Fortunetellers, Evil Spirits

Astarte A Canaanite goddess. Those who worshiped her believed that she gave them fertile land and many children, and that she helped their animals give birth to lots of young.

Baal A Canaanite god. The Canaanites believed that Baal was the most powerful of all the gods.

Dagon The chief god of the Philistines.

Demons and **Evil Spirits** Supernatural beings that do harmful things to people and sometimes cause them to do bad things. In the New Testament they are sometimes called "unclean spirits," because people under their power were thought to be unclean and unfit to worship God.

Devil The chief of the demons and evil spirits, also known as "Satan."

Evil Spirits See "Demons."

Fortuneteller Fortunetellers thought they could learn secrets or learn about the future by doing such things as watching the flight of birds, looking at the livers of animals, and rolling dice.

Hermes The Greek god of skillful speaking and the messenger of the other Greek gods.

Molech or **Milcom** The national god of the Ammonites. Some Israelites offered human sacrifices to Molech in Hinnom Valley near Jerusalem.

Satan See "Devil."

Zeus The chief god of the Greeks.

16. Plants, Animals, and Farming

Acacia A flowering tree that produces a hard, durable wood. The sacred chest, the altars, and certain other wooden objects in the sacred tent were made of acacia wood.

Aloes A sweet-smelling spice that was mixed with myrrh and used as a perfume.

Barley A grain that was used to make bread.

Cedar A tall tree once common in the Lebanon mountains and used for many of the royal building projects in Jerusalem.

Cumin A plant with small seeds used for seasoning food.

Flax The stalks of flax plants were harvested, soaked in water, and dried. Then their fibers were separated and spun into thread, which was woven to make linen cloth.

Hyssop A bush with clusters of small branches. In religious ceremonies, hyssop was sometimes dipped in a liquid and then used to sprinkle people or objects.

Jackal A wild desert animal related to wolves, but smaller.

Leviathan A legendary sea monster representing revolt and evil, also known from Canaanite writings.

Locust A type of grasshopper that comes in huge swarms and causes great damage to plant life.

Mint A garden plant used for seasoning and medicine.

Mustard A large plant with very small seeds, which were ground up and used as a spice.

Myrrh A valuable sweet-smelling powder used in perfume.

Pomegranate A reddish fruit with a hard rind. Figures of pomegranates were used as decorations on the high priest's robe and in the temple.

Reed Several kinds of tall plants related to the grass family can be called "reeds." Some varieties are hollow, and some grow in shallow water. The stems were strong and could be up to 18 feet long and 3 inches across at the base.

Rue A garden plant used for seasoning and medicine.

Threshing The process of separating grain from its husks. Grain was spread out at a "threshing place," a flat area of stone or packed earth. People or animals walked on the grain or dragged heavy boards across it to remove the husks. Then the grain and husks were tossed into the air with a special shovel called a "threshing fork." The wind would blow the light husks away, but the heavy grain would fall back to the surface of the threshing place.

Wine-pit A hollow place cut into the rock where the juice was squeezed from grapes to make wine.

Yoke A strong, heavy, wooden collar that fit around the neck of an ox, so that the ox could pull a plow or a cart.

17. Society and Its Leaders

Citizen A person who is given special rights and privileges by a nation or state. In return, a citizen was expected to be loyal to that nation or state.

Council (1) A group of leaders who meet and make decisions for their people. (2) The Old Testament refers to God's council as a group of angels who meet and talk with God in heaven.

Elders Men whose age and wisdom made them respected leaders.

Emperor The person who ruled an empire.

Generation One way of describing a group of people who live during the same period of time. In the Bible the time of one generation is often understood to be about forty years.

Judges Leaders chosen by the Lord for the people of Israel after the time of Joshua and before the time of the kings.

Tax Collectors See "Taxes."

Taxes Special fees collected by rulers. Taxes are usually part of the value of crops, property, or income. Taxes were collected at markets, city gates, ports, and border crossings. In New Testament times, Jews were hired by the Roman government to collect taxes from other Jews, and these tax collectors were hated by their own people.

18. Families, Relatives

Ancestor Someone born earlier in a family line, especially several generations earlier.

Clan A group of families who were related to each other and who often lived close to each other. A group of clans made up a tribe.

Descendant Someone born one or more generations later in a family line.

Tribe A large group of people descended from a common ancestor (see also "Clan" and Section 6, "Twelve Tribes of Israel").

19. Events

Exile The time in Israel's history (597–539 B.C.) when the Babylonians took away many of the people of Jerusalem and Judah as prisoners of war and made them live in Babylonia. The northern tribes had been taken away by Assyria in 722 B.C.

Exodus The people of Israel leaving Egypt, led by Moses and Aaron. This event is celebrated each year as Passover.

20. Dates

B.C. Before Christ. Used to date events that happened before Christ's birth. "B.C." is used after the number of the year.

A.D. *Anno Domini,* Latin for "In the year of the Lord." Used to date events that happened after Christ's birth. "A.D." is often used before the number of the year.[a]

931 B.C. The nation of Israel split into two parts, Israel, the northern kingdom, and Judah, the southern kingdom.

722 B.C. Samaria, the capital of the northern kingdom, was captured by the Assyrian army.

[a]**Note:** The numbering system now in use was developed about A.D. 525. The plan was that the year of Christ's birth would be A.D. 1, and then the years would be numbered before and after. But an error was made in assigning A.D. 1, and by the time the error was discovered, the numbering system could not be changed. And so, the correct year of Christ's birth according to the numbering system is probably about 6 B.C.

586 B.C. Jerusalem, the capital of the southern kingdom, was captured by the Babylonian army.

538 B.C. Cyrus of Persia allowed the Jews to return to Judah.

333 B.C. Alexander the Great took control of Palestine.

323 B.C. Palestine was taken over by the Ptolemy, who was one of Alexander's generals and who became the ruler of Egypt after Alexander's death.

198 B.C. Palestine was taken over by the Seleucids, the descendants of one of Alexander's generals. They had been the rulers of Syria since Alexander's death.

166 B.C. The Jews revolted, led by Judas Maccabeus and his brothers.

63 B.C. Rome took control of Palestine.

37 B.C. Herod the Great was appointed king of the Jews by the Roman government.

6 B.C. Jesus was born. (See the note following "A.D." above.)

A.D. 30 (Or possibly A.D. 33) Jesus died and was raised to life.

21. The Hebrew Calendar

Nisan or **Abib** first month, about mid-March to mid-April.

Iyyar or **Ziv** second month about mid-April to mid-May.

Sivan third month, about mid-May to mid-June.

Tammuz fourth month, about mid-June to mid-July.

Ab fifth month, about mid-July to mid-August.

Elul sixth month, about mid-August to mid-September.

Tishri or **Ethanim** seventh month, about mid-September to mid-October.

Marchesvan or **Bul** eighth month, about mid-October to mid-November.

Chislev ninth month, about mid-November to mid-December.

Tebeth tenth month, about mid-December to mid-January.

Shebat eleventh month, about mid-January to mid-February.

Adar twelfth month, about mid-February to mid-March.

CHRONOLOGY OF THE BIBLE

MAPS

CHRONOLOGY OF THE BIBLE

B.C. = Before Christ
c. = circa (around)*

DATE	Time scales represent varied number of years.
PREHISTORY	**THE BEGINNINGS: EVENTS IN PREHISTORY** Creation Adam and Eve in the Garden Cain and Abel Noah and the Flood The Tower of Babel
2000 B.C.	**THE ANCESTORS OF THE ISRAELITES** Abraham comes to Palestine. *c.* 1900 Isaac is born to Abraham. Jacob is born to Isaac.
1800 B.C.	Jacob has twelve sons, who become the ancestors of the twelve tribes of Israel. The most prominent of these sons is Joseph, who becomes adviser to the King of Egypt. **THE ISRAELITES IN EGYPT** The descendants of Jacob are enslaved in Egypt. *c.* 1700 — *c.* 1290
1600 B.C.	
1250 B.C.	Moses leads the Israelites out of Egypt. *c.* 1290 The Israelites wander in the wilderness. During this time Moses receives the Law on Mount Sinai. *c.* 1290 — *c.* 1250 **THE CONQUEST AND SETTLEMENT OF CANAAN** Joshua leads the first stage of the invasion of Canaan. *c.* 1250 Israel remains a loose confederation of tribes, and leadership is exercised by heroic figures known as the Judges.
1000 B.C.	**THE UNITED ISRAELITE KINGDOM** Reign of Saul *c.* 1030 — *c.* 1010 Reign of David *c.* 1010 — *c.* 970 Reign of Solomon *c.* 970 — 931

*A circa date is only an approximation. Generally speaking, the earlier the time, the less precise is the dating. From the time of the death of Solomon in 931 B.C. to the Edict of Cyrus in 538 B.C., the dates given are fairly accurate, but even in this epoch a possible error of a year or two must be allowed for.

CHRONOLOGY OF THE BIBLE

THE TWO ISRAELITE KINGDOMS

DATE	JUDAH (Southern Kingdom) *Kings*	*Prophets*	ISRAEL (Northern Kingdom) *Kings*
950 B.C.	Rehoboam 931-913		Jeroboam 931-910
	Abijah 913-911		Nadab 910-909
900 B.C.	Asa 911-870		Baasha 909-886
			Elah 886-885
	Jehoshaphat 870-848	Elijah	Zimri 7 days in 885
			Omri 885-874
			Ahab 874-853
850 B.C.	Jehoram 848-841		Ahaziah 853-852
	Ahaziah 841		Joram 852-841
	Queen Athaliah 841-835		Jehu 841-814
	Joash 835-796	Elisha	Jehoahaz 814-798
800 B.C.	Amaziah 796-781		Jehoash 798-783
	Uzziah 781-740	Jonah	Jeroboam II 783-743
		Amos	Zechariah 6 mo. in 743
			Shallum 1 mo. in 743
750 B.C.	Jotham 740-736	Hosea	Menahem 743-738
	Ahaz 736-716	Micah	Pekahiah 738-737
		Isaiah	Pekah 737-732
	Hezekiah 716-687		Hoshea 732-723
			Fall of Samaria 722

THE LAST YEARS OF THE KINGDOM OF JUDAH

DATE	Kings	*Prophets*
700 B.C.	Manasseh 687-642	
650 B.C.	Amon 642-640	
	Josiah 640-609	Zephaniah
	Joahaz 3 mo. in 609	Nahum
	Jehoiakim 609-598	Jeremiah
600 B.C.	Jehoiachin 3 mo. in 598	Habakkuk?
	Zedekiah 598-587	Ezekiel
	Fall of Jerusalem July 587 or 586	

CHRONOLOGY OF THE BIBLE

DATE

550 B.C.

THE EXILE AND THE RESTORATION

The Judeans taken into exile in Babylonia after the fall of Jerusalem

	Prophets	
Persian rule begins. 539		
Edict of Cyrus allows Jews to return. 538	Haggai	Zechariah
Foundations of New Temple laid. 520	Obadiah	Daniel
Restoration of the walls of Jerusalem 445-443	Malachi Joel?	

400 B.C.

THE TIME BETWEEN THE TESTAMENTS

Alexander the Great establishes Greek rule in Palestine. 333

Palestine is ruled by the Ptolemies, descendants of one of Alexander's generals, who had been given the position of ruler over Egypt. 323 to 198

200 B.C.

Palestine is ruled by the Seleucids, descendants of one of Alexander's generals, who had acquired the rule of Syria. 198 to 166

Jewish revolt under Judas Maccabeus reestablishes Jewish independence. Palestine is ruled by Judas' family and descendants, the Hasmoneans. 166 to 63

The Roman general Pompey takes Jerusalem 63 B.C. Palestine is ruled by puppet kings appointed by Rome. One of these is Herod the Great, who rules from 37 B.C. to 4 B.C.

THE TIME OF THE NEW TESTAMENT

A.D. 1

Birth of Jesus*

Ministry of John the Baptist; baptism of Jesus and beginning of his public ministry

A.D. 30

Death and resurrection of Jesus

Conversion of Paul (Saul of Tarsus) *c.* A.D. 37

Ministry of Paul *c.* A.D. 41 to A.D. 65

Final imprisonment of Paul *c.* A.D. 65

*The present era was calculated to begin with the birth of Jesus Christ, that is, in A.D. 1 (A.D. standing for *Anno Domini* 'in the year of the Lord'). However, the original calculation was later found to be wrong by a few years, so that the birth of Christ took place perhaps about 6 B.C.

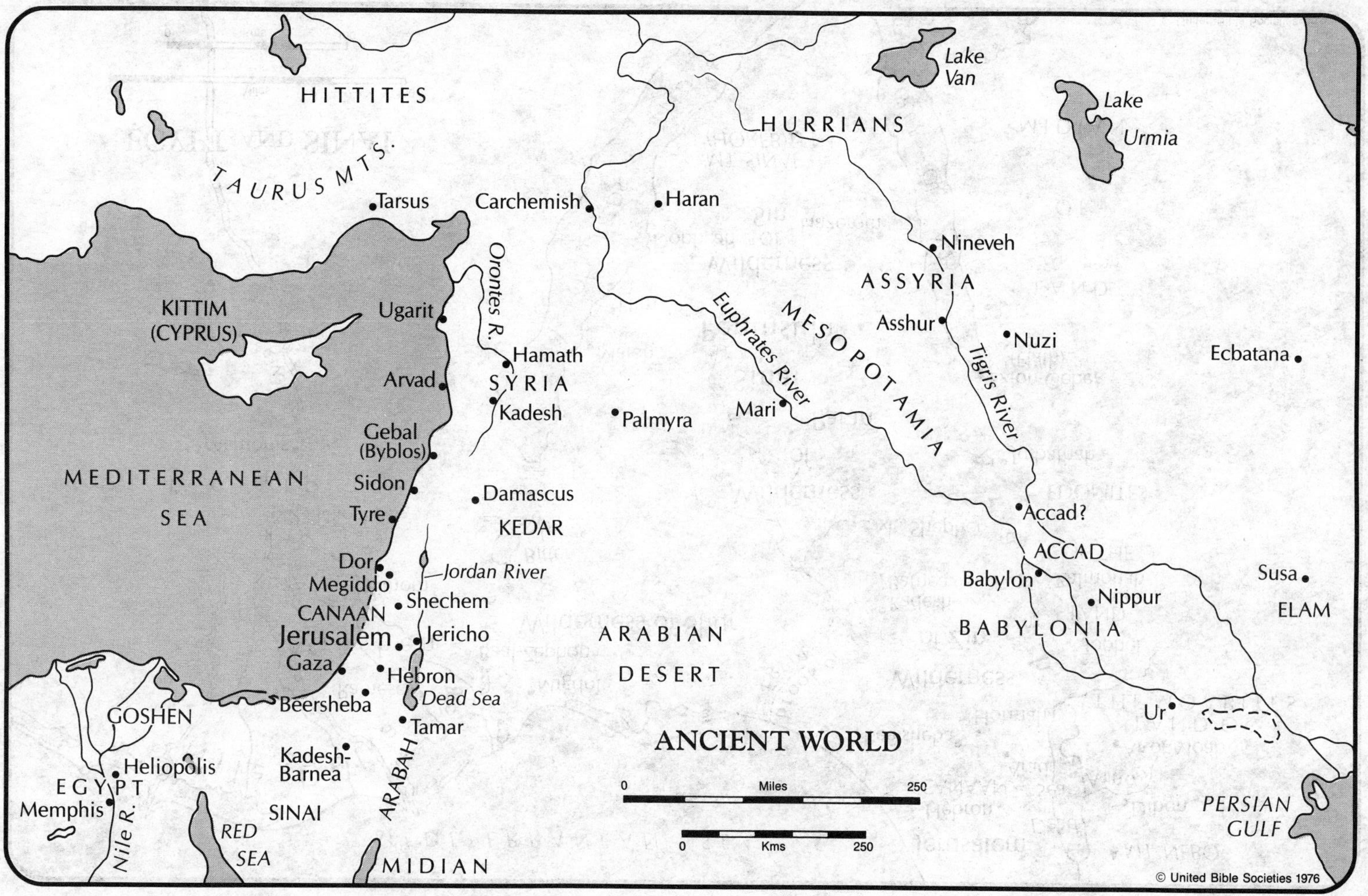

ANCIENT WORLD
HITTITES
TAURUS MTS.
Tarsus
Carchemish
Haran
HURRIANS
Lake Van
Lake Urmia
Nineveh
ASSYRIA
Asshur
Nuzi
Ecbatana
MESOPOTAMIA
Euphrates River
Tigris River
Mari
Palmyra
KITTIM (CYPRUS)
Ugarit
Orontes R.
Hamath
SYRIA
Arvad
Kadesh
Gebal (Byblos)
MEDITERRANEAN SEA
Sidon
Damascus
Tyre
KEDAR
Accad?
ACCAD
Babylon
Nippur
BABYLONIA
Susa
ELAM
Dor
Megiddo
Jordan River
Shechem
CANAAN
Jerusalem
Jericho
ARABIAN DESERT
Gaza
Hebron
Dead Sea
Beersheba
GOSHEN
Tamar
Ur
Kadesh-Barnea
Heliopolis
EGYPT
Memphis
Nile R.
SINAI
RED SEA
ARABAH
MIDIAN
0 Miles 250
0 Kms 250
PERSIAN GULF

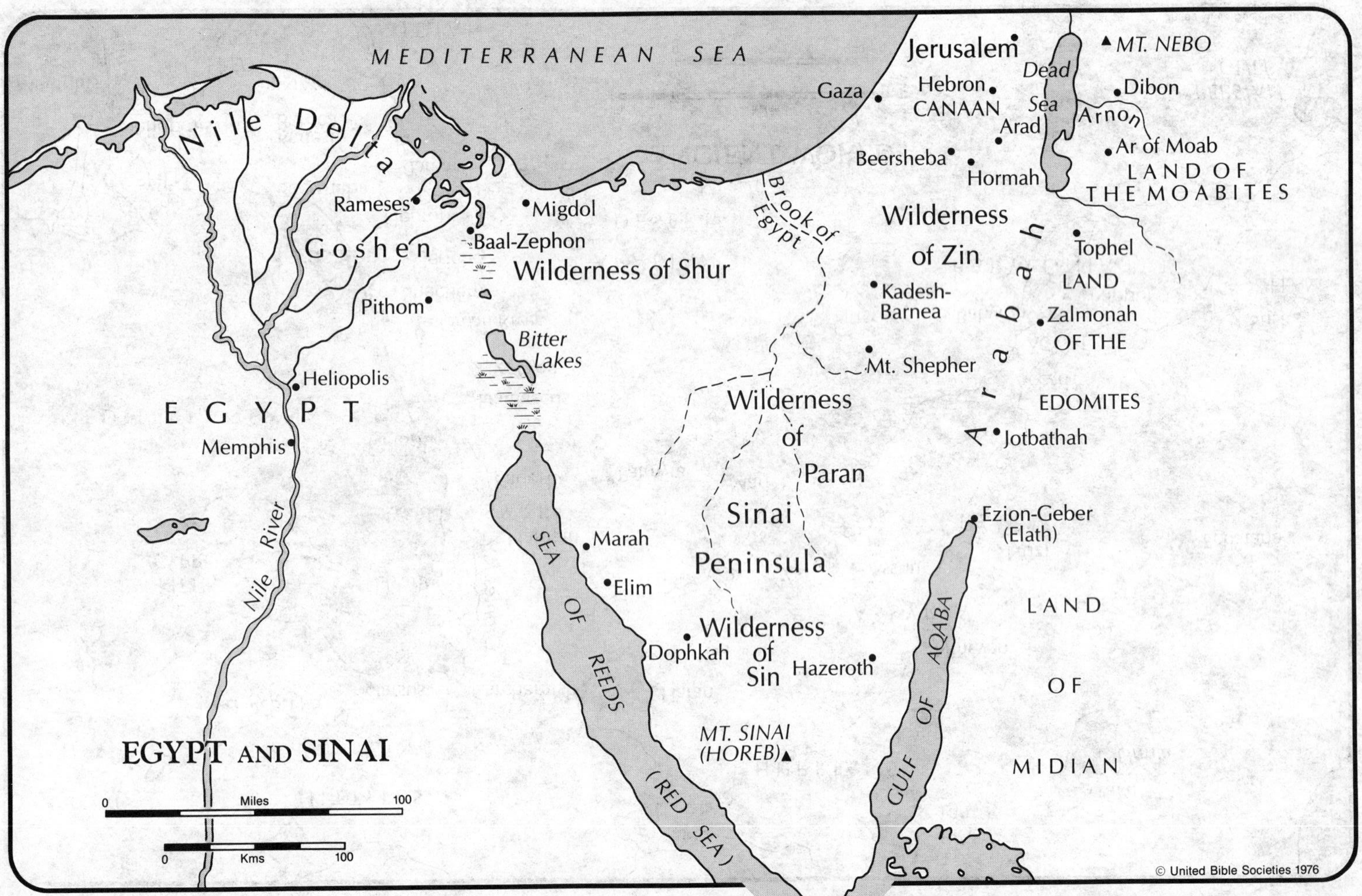
EGYPT AND SINAI
MEDITERRANEAN SEA
Nile Delta
Rameses
Goshen
Pithom
Heliopolis
EGYPT
Memphis
Nile River
Migdol
Baal-Zephon
Wilderness of Shur
Bitter Lakes
SEA OF REEDS (RED SEA)
Marah
Elim
Dophkah
Wilderness of Sin
MT. SINAI (HOREB)
Hazeroth
Sinai Peninsula
Wilderness of Paran
Brook of Egypt
Gaza
Jerusalem
Hebron
CANAAN
Beersheba
Arad
Hormah
Dead Sea
Arnon
MT. NEBO
Dibon
Ar of Moab
LAND OF THE MOABITES
Wilderness of Zin
Kadesh-Barnea
Mt. Shepher
Arabah
Tophel
Zalmonah
LAND OF THE EDOMITES
Jotbathah
Ezion-Geber (Elath)
GULF OF AQABA
LAND OF MIDIAN
Miles
Kms
0
100

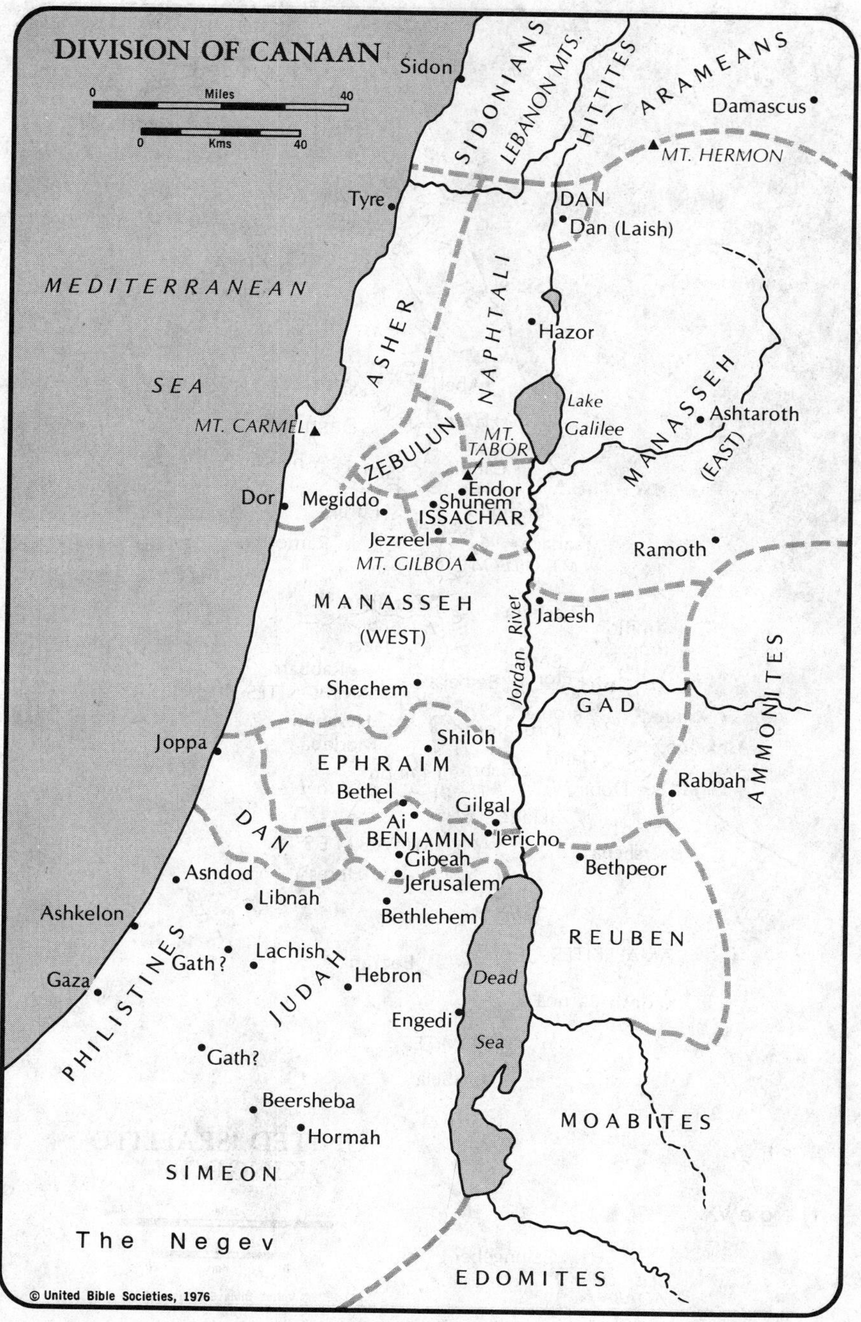
DIVISION OF CANAAN
0 Miles 40
0 Kms 40
Sidon
SIDONIANS
LEBANON MTS.
HITTITES
ARAMEANS
Damascus
MT. HERMON
Tyre
DAN
Dan (Laish)
MEDITERRANEAN
SEA
ASHER
NAPHTALI
Hazor
Lake
Galilee
MANASSEH
(EAST)
Ashtaroth
MT. CARMEL
ZEBULUN
MT.
TABOR
Endor
Dor
Megiddo
Shunem
ISSACHAR
Jezreel
MT. GILBOA
Ramoth
MANASSEH
(WEST)
Jordan River
Jabesh
AMMONITES
Shechem
GAD
Joppa
Shiloh
EPHRAIM
Rabbah
Bethel
Gilgal
Ai
DAN
BENJAMIN
Jericho
Gibeah
Bethpeor
Ashdod
Jerusalem
Libnah
Bethlehem
Ashkelon
REUBEN
Gath ?
Lachish
Hebron
Dead
Sea
Gaza
PHILISTINES
JUDAH
Engedi
Gath?
Beersheba
MOABITES
Hormah
SIMEON
The Negev
EDOMITES

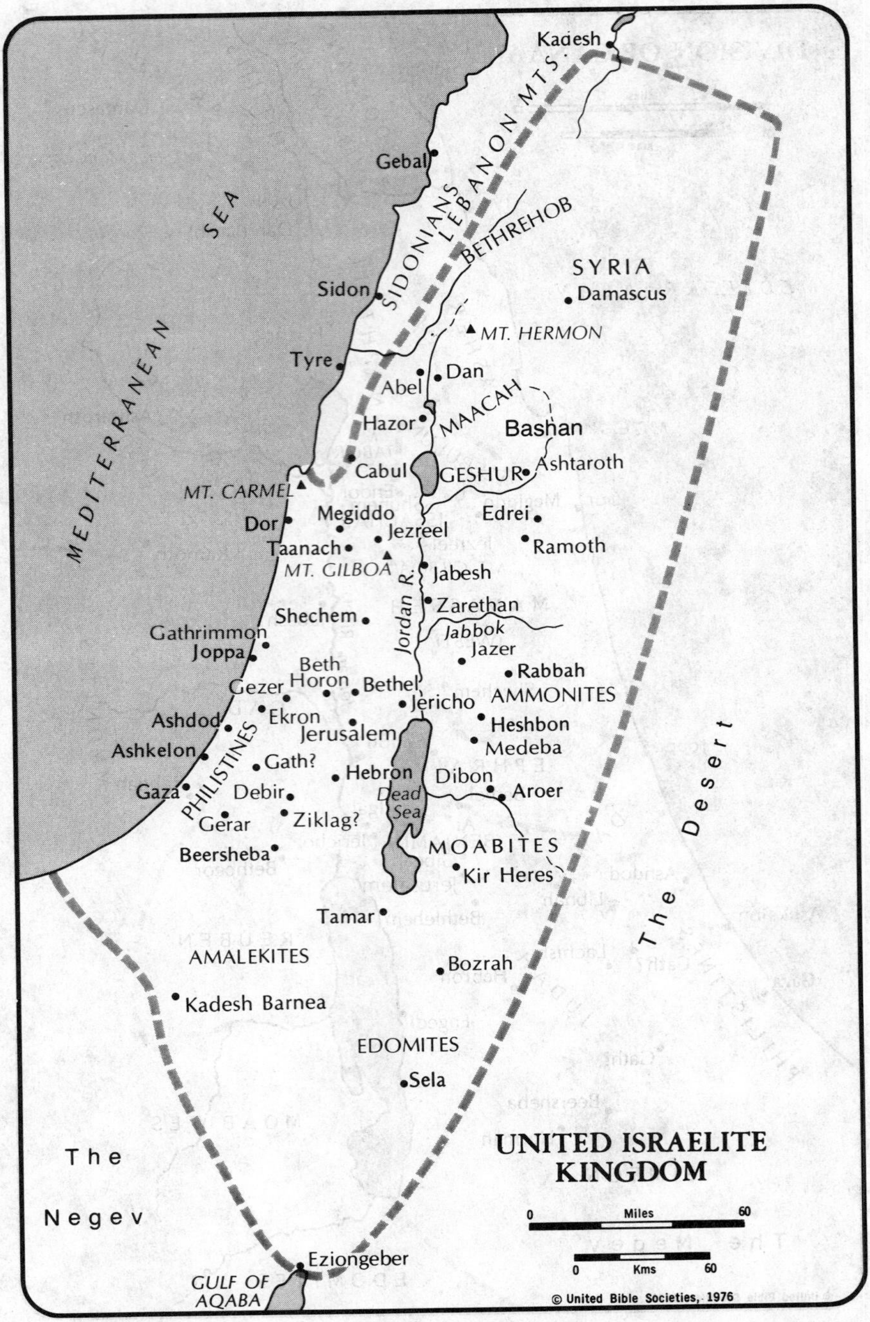

Kadesh
LEBANON MTS.
Gebal
SEA
SIDONIANS
BETHREHOB
SYRIA
Sidon
Damascus
MT. HERMON
MEDITERRANEAN
Tyre
Dan
Abel
MAACAH
Hazor
Bashan
Cabul
GESHUR
Ashtaroth
MT. CARMEL
Dor
Megiddo
Edrei
Jezreel
Taanach
Ramoth
MT. GILBOA
Jabesh
Jordan R.
Zarethan
Shechem
Jabbok
Gathrimmon
Jazer
Joppa
Beth Horon
Rabbah
Gezer
Bethel
Jericho
AMMONITES
Ashdod
Ekron
Heshbon
Jerusalem
Medeba
Ashkelon
PHILISTINES
Gath?
Hebron
Dibon
Gaza
Debir
Dead Sea
Aroer
Gerar
Ziklag?
MOABITES
Beersheba
Kir Heres
The Desert
Tamar
AMALEKITES
Bozrah
Kadesh Barnea
EDOMITES
Sela
The Negev
UNITED ISRAELITE KINGDOM
0 Miles 60
0 Kms 60
Eziongeber
GULF OF AQABA
© United Bible Societies, 1976

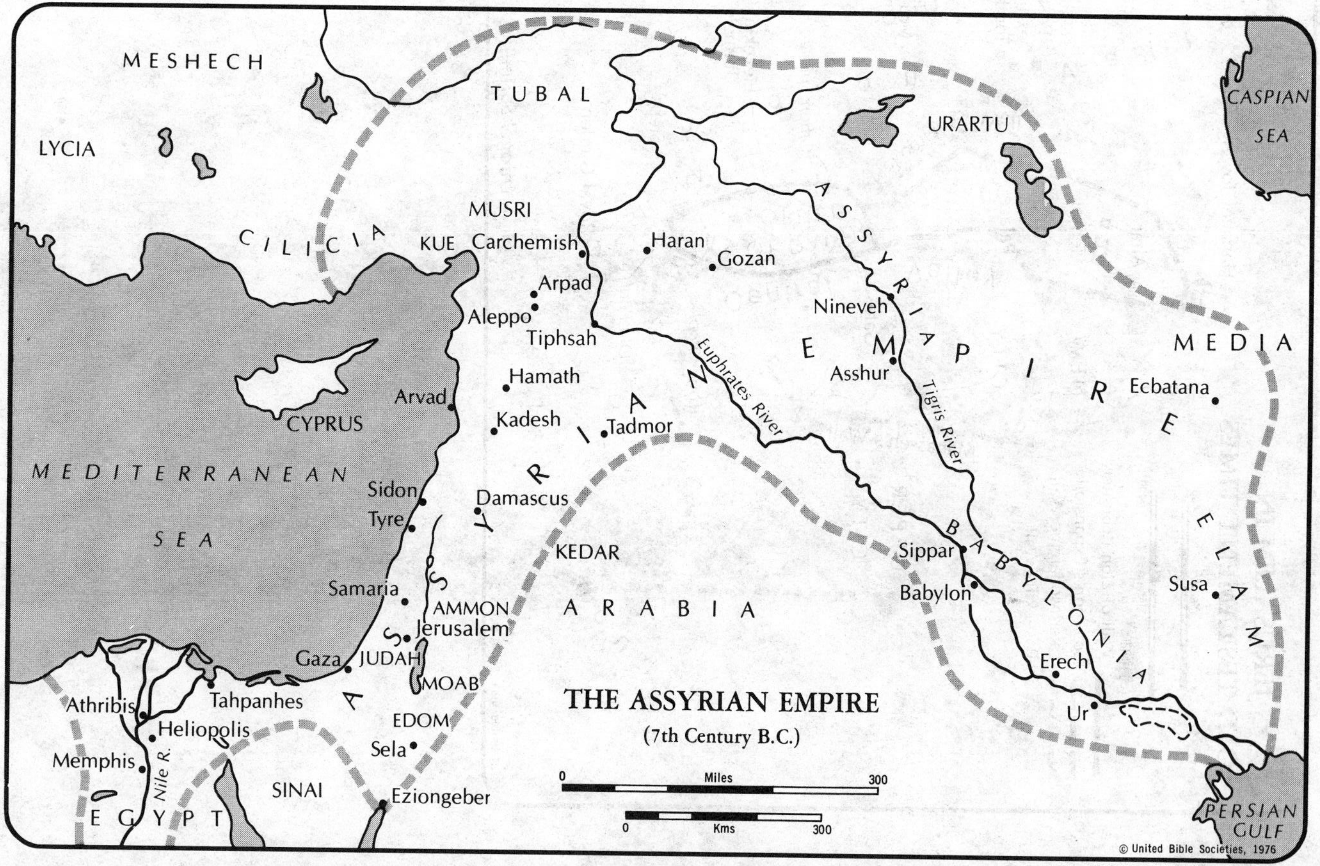

THE ASSYRIAN EMPIRE
(7th Century B.C.)
MESHECH
LYCIA
TUBAL
CILICIA
MUSRI
KUE
Carchemish
Haran
Gozan
Arpad
Aleppo
Tiphsah
URARTU
CASPIAN SEA
ASSYRIA
Nineveh
Asshur
MEDIA
Ecbatana
ASSYRIAN EMPIRE
Euphrates River
Tigris River
CYPRUS
Arvad
Hamath
Kadesh
Tadmor
MEDITERRANEAN SEA
Sidon
Tyre
Damascus
KEDAR
Samaria
AMMON
Jerusalem
JUDAH
MOAB
EDOM
Sela
Gaza
ARABIA
BABYLONIA
Sippar
Babylon
Erech
Ur
ELAM
Susa
PERSIAN GULF
Athribis
Tahpanhes
Heliopolis
Memphis
Nile R.
SINAI
Eziongeber
EGYPT
0 Miles 300
0 Kms 300
© United Bible Societies, 1976

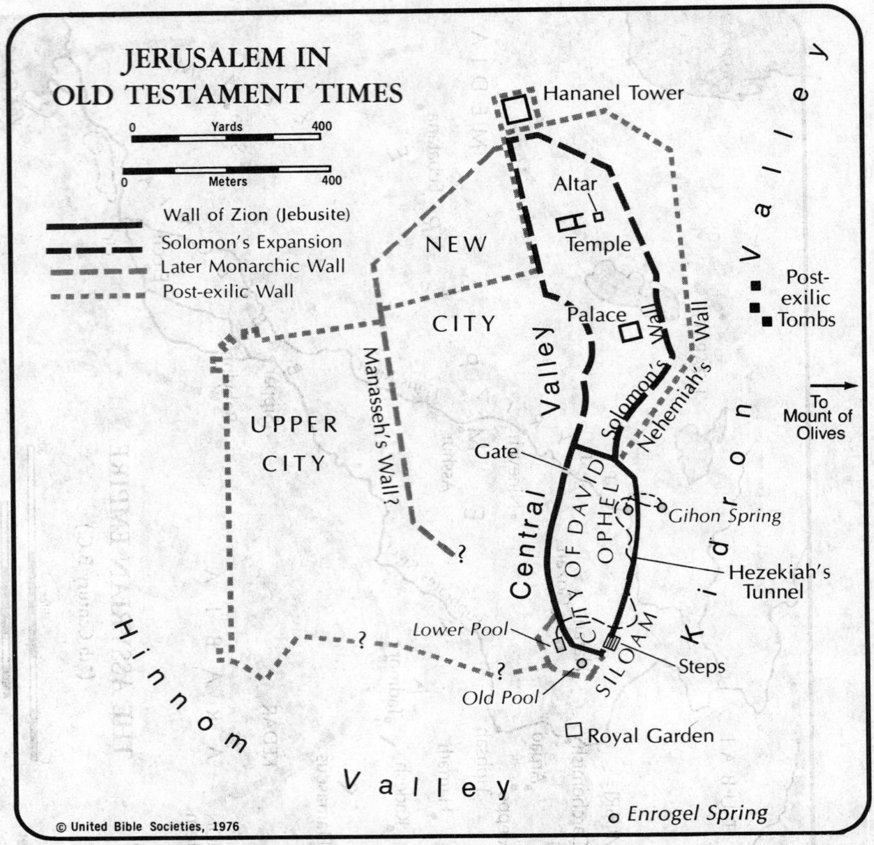
JERUSALEM IN OLD TESTAMENT TIMES
0 Yards 400
0 Meters 400
Wall of Zion (Jebusite)
Solomon's Expansion
Later Monarchic Wall
Post-exilic Wall
Hananel Tower
Altar
Temple
NEW CITY
Palace
UPPER CITY
Manasseh's Wall?
Central Valley
Solomon's Wall
Nehemiah's Wall
Post-exilic Tombs
To Mount of Olives
Gate
CITY OF DAVID
OPHEL
Gihon Spring
Hezekiah's Tunnel
Lower Pool
SILOAM
Steps
Old Pool
Royal Garden
Hinnom Valley
Kidron Valley
Enrogel Spring

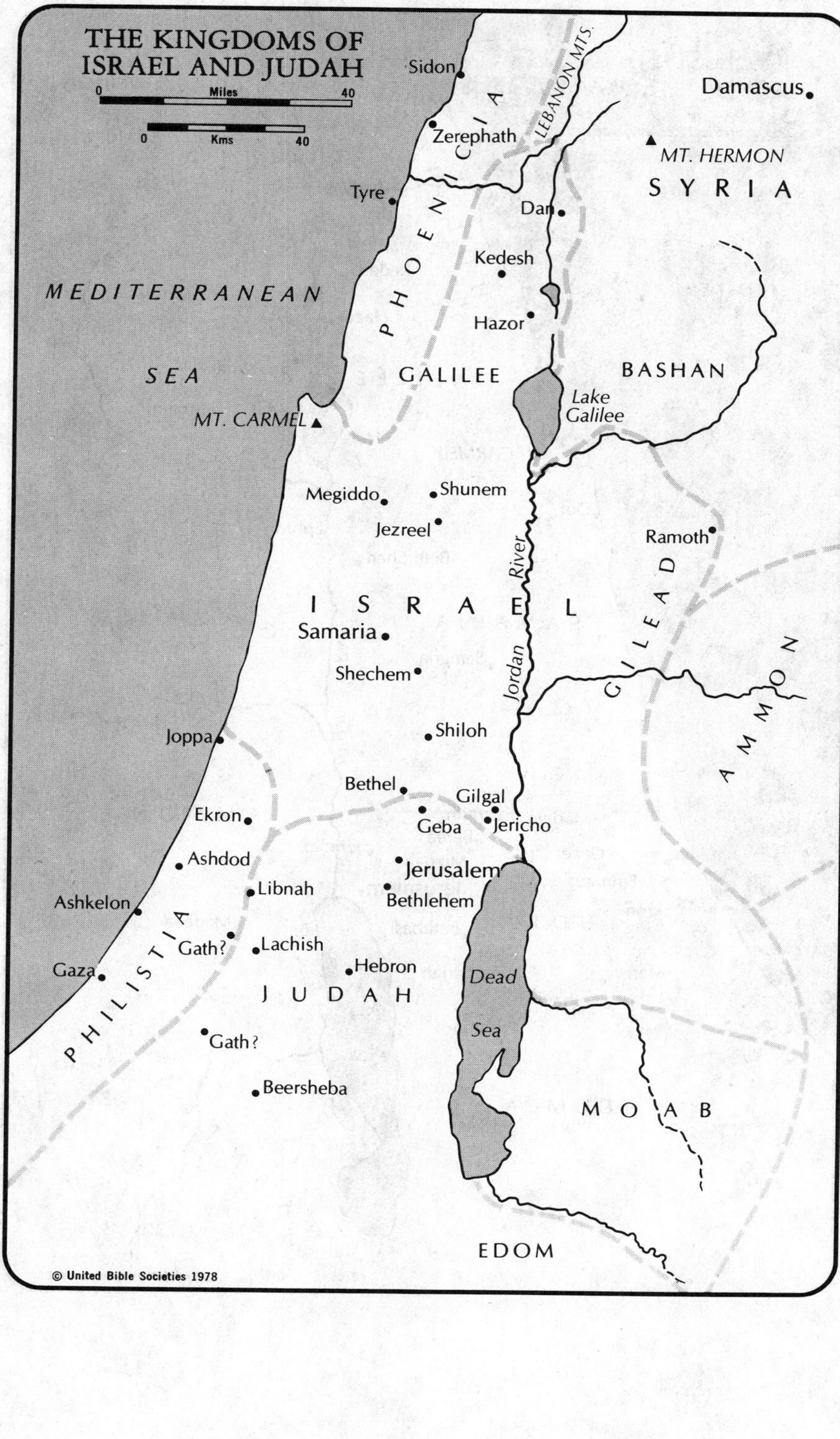

THE KINGDOMS OF ISRAEL AND JUDAH
0 Miles 40
0 Kms 40
Sidon
Zerephath
Tyre
PHOENICIA
LEBANON MTS.
Damascus
MT. HERMON
SYRIA
Dan
Kedesh
Hazor
MEDITERRANEAN
SEA
GALILEE
BASHAN
Lake Galilee
MT. CARMEL
Megiddo
Shunem
Jezreel
Jordan River
Ramoth
ISRAEL
GILEAD
Samaria
Shechem
AMMON
Joppa
Shiloh
Bethel
Gilgal
Geba
Jericho
Ekron
Ashdod
Jerusalem
Libnah
Bethlehem
Ashkelon
Gath?
Lachish
Gaza
Hebron
Dead Sea
PHILISTIA
JUDAH
Gath?
Beersheba
MOAB
EDOM

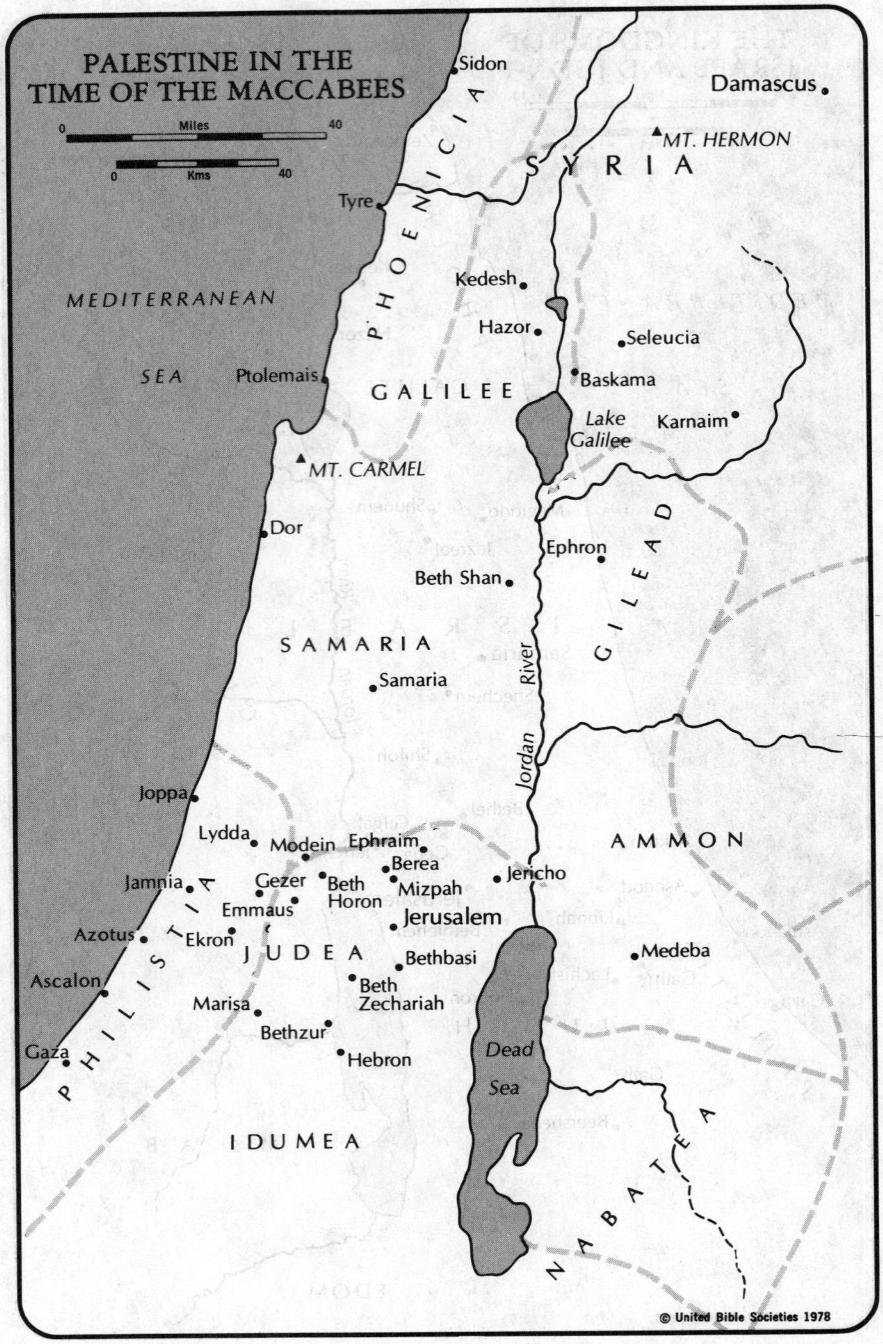
PALESTINE IN THE TIME OF THE MACCABEES
0 Miles 40
0 Kms 40
MEDITERRANEAN SEA
Sidon
Damascus
MT. HERMON
SYRIA
PHOENICIA
Tyre
Kedesh
Hazor
Seleucia
Ptolemais
Baskama
GALILEE
Lake Galilee
Karnaim
MT. CARMEL
Dor
Ephron
GILEAD
Beth Shan
SAMARIA
Samaria
Jordan River
Joppa
Lydda
Modein
Ephraim
Berea
Jamnia
Gezer
Beth Horon
Mizpah
Jericho
AMMON
Emmaus
Jerusalem
Azotus
Ekron
JUDEA
Bethbasi
Medeba
Ascalon
Beth Zechariah
Marisa
Bethzur
Gaza
Hebron
Dead Sea
PHILISTIA
IDUMEA
NABATEA

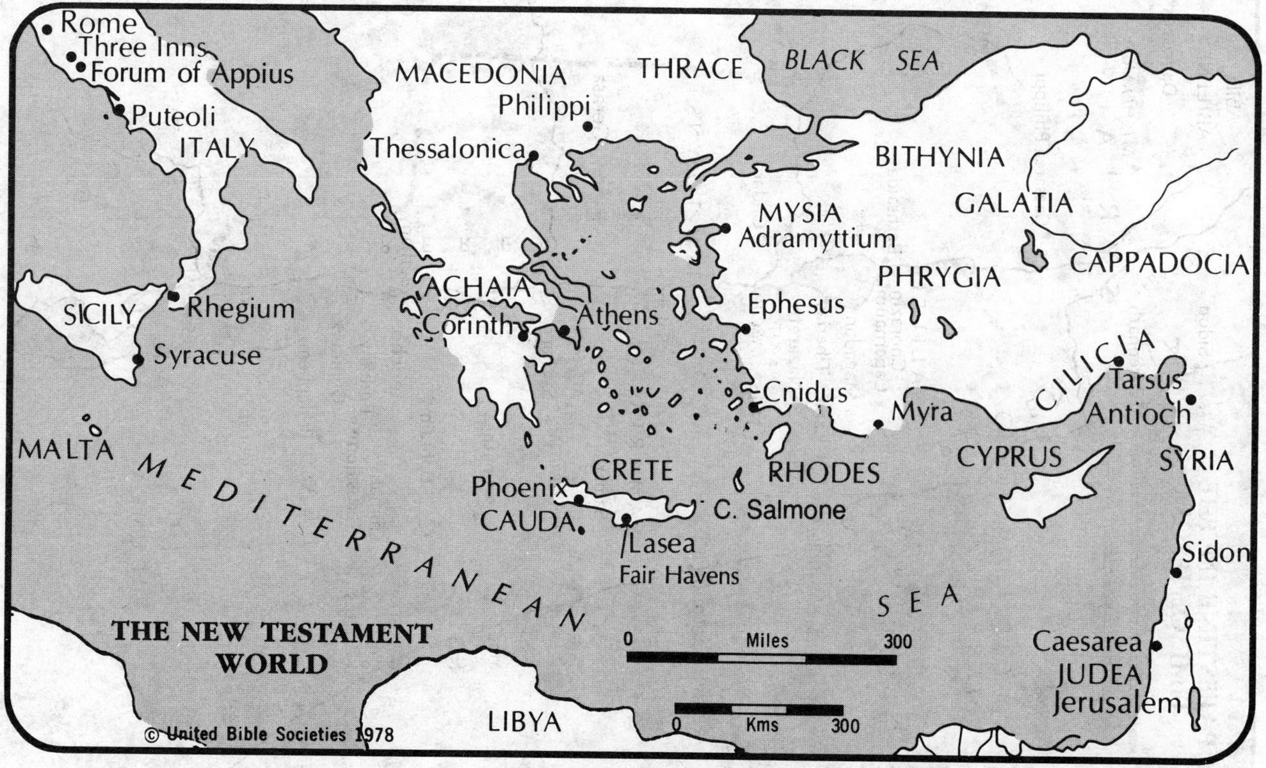
THE NEW TESTAMENT WORLD
Rome
Three Inns
Forum of Appius
Puteoli
ITALY
SICILY
Rhegium
Syracuse
MALTA
MACEDONIA
Philippi
Thessalonica
THRACE
BLACK SEA
ACHAIA
Corinth
Athens
MYSIA
Adramyttium
BITHYNIA
GALATIA
PHRYGIA
CAPPADOCIA
Ephesus
Cnidus
Myra
CILICIA
Tarsus
Antioch
SYRIA
CYPRUS
RHODES
CRETE
Phoenix
CAUDA
Lasea
Fair Havens
C. Salmone
MEDITERRANEAN SEA
Sidon
Caesarea
JUDEA
Jerusalem
LIBYA
0 Miles 300
0 Kms 300
© United Bible Societies 1978

PALESTINE IN THE TIME OF JESUS
0 Miles 40
0 Kms 40
Sidon
Zarephath
LEBANON MTS.
Abila
ABILENE
Damascus
MT. HERMON
SYRIA
PHOENICIA
Tyre
Caesarea Philippi
MEDITERRANEAN
SEA
Ptolemais
GALILEE
Chorazin
Capernaum
Bethsaida
Lake
Galilee
Magadan
Cana
Tiberias
MT. CARMEL
Nazareth
MT. TABOR
Nain
Gadara
Caesarea
TEN TOWNS
Salim
Aenon
SAMARIA
Samaria
Gerasa
MT. EBAL
MT. GERIZIM
Sychar
Jordan River
PEREA
Joppa
Arimathea?
Ephraim
Jericho
Bethany
Emmaus
Bethany
Jerusalem
Qumran
Azotus
Ascalon
JUDEA
Bethlehem
Gaza
Hebron
Dead Sea
IDUMEA
NABATEA

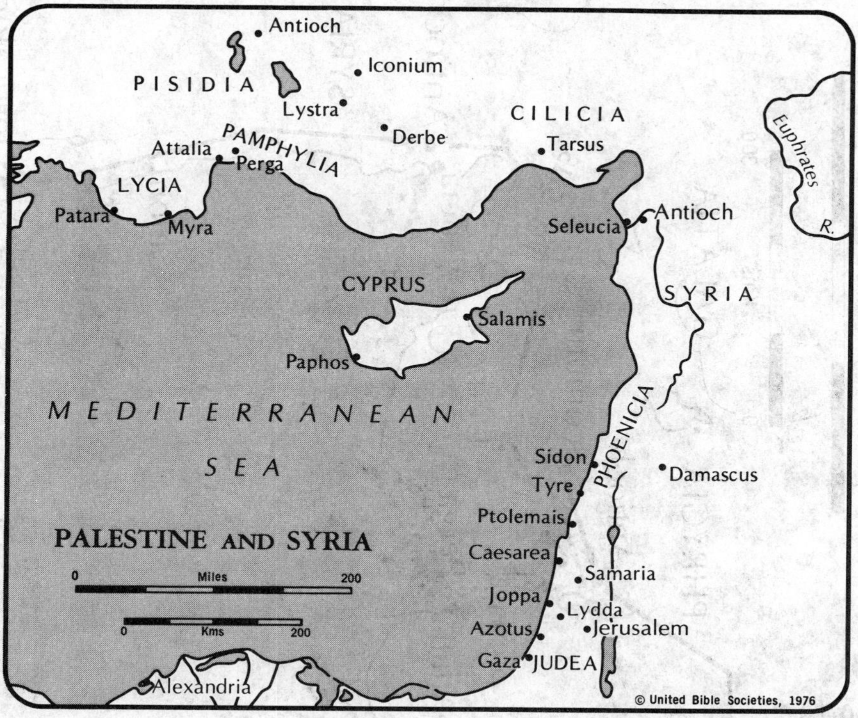

PALESTINE AND SYRIA

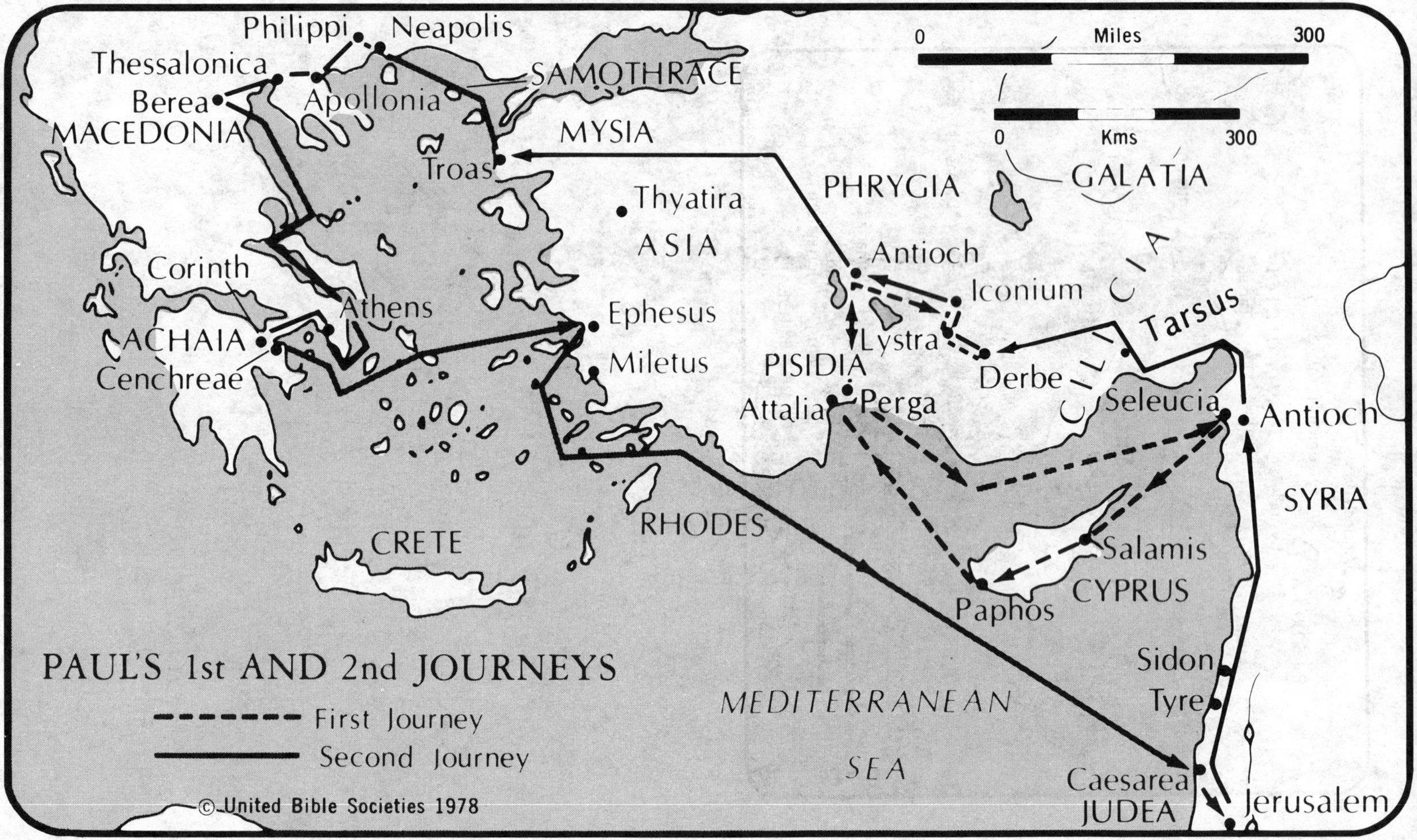
PAUL'S 1st AND 2nd JOURNEYS
First Journey
Second Journey
© United Bible Societies 1978
0
Miles
300
0
Kms
300
Philippi
Neapolis
Thessalonica
Apollonia
Berea
MACEDONIA
SAMOTHRACE
MYSIA
Troas
Thyatira
ASIA
Corinth
Athens
ACHAIA
Cenchreae
Ephesus
Miletus
CRETE
RHODES
PHRYGIA
GALATIA
Antioch
Iconium
Lystra
PISIDIA
Derbe
Attalia
Perga
CILICIA
Tarsus
Seleucia
Antioch
SYRIA
Salamis
CYPRUS
Paphos
MEDITERRANEAN
SEA
Sidon
Tyre
Caesarea
JUDEA
Jerusalem

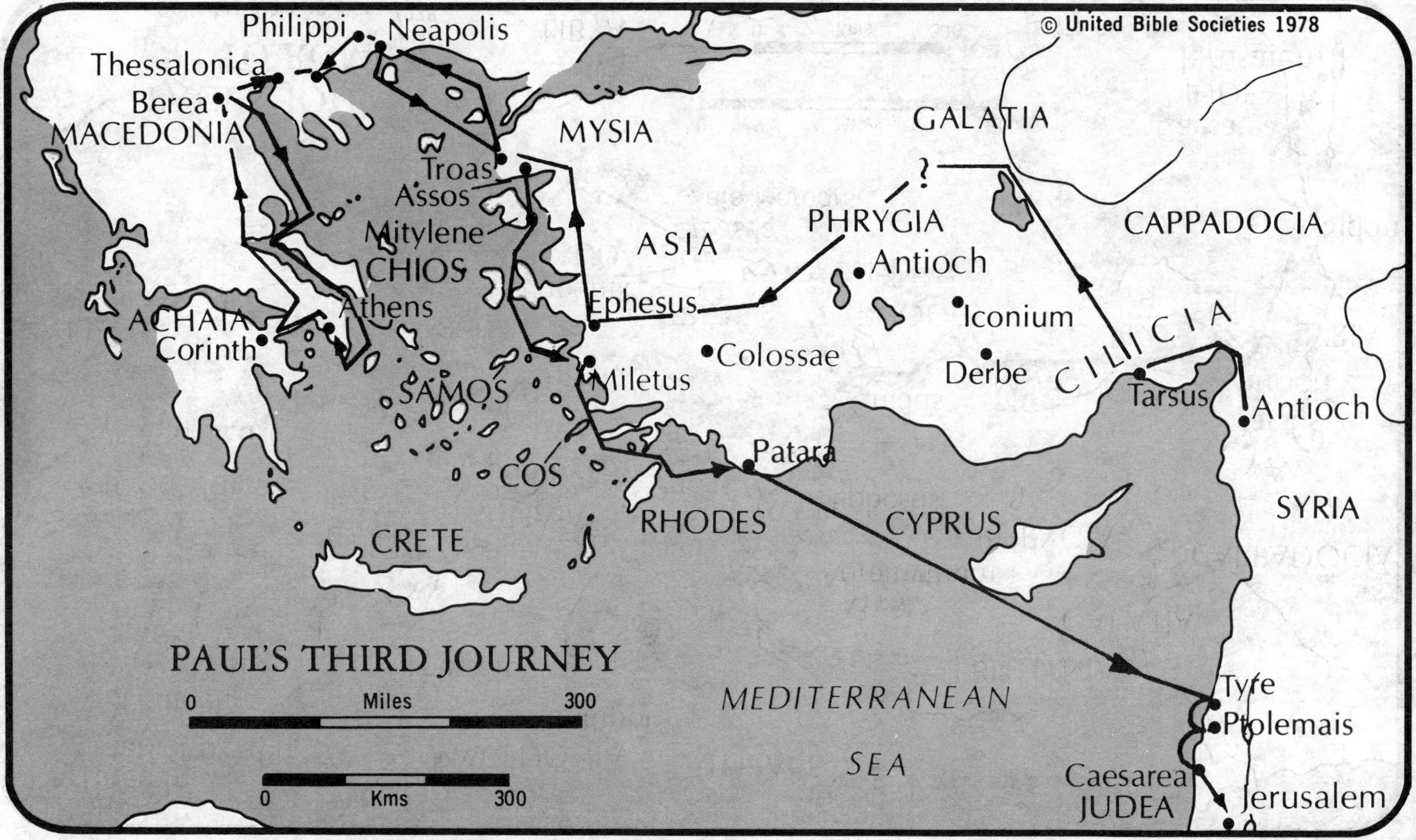
PAUL'S THIRD JOURNEY
© United Bible Societies 1978
Philippi
Neapolis
Thessalonica
Berea
MACEDONIA
MYSIA
GALATIA
?
Troas
Assos
Mitylene
CHIOS
PHRYGIA
CAPPADOCIA
ASIA
Antioch
Athens
ACHAIA
Corinth
Ephesus
Iconium
CILICIA
Colossae
Derbe
Miletus
SAMOS
Tarsus
Antioch
Patara
COS
RHODES
CYPRUS
SYRIA
CRETE
MEDITERRANEAN
SEA
0
Miles
300
0
Kms
300
Tyre
Ptolemais
Caesarea
JUDEA
Jerusalem

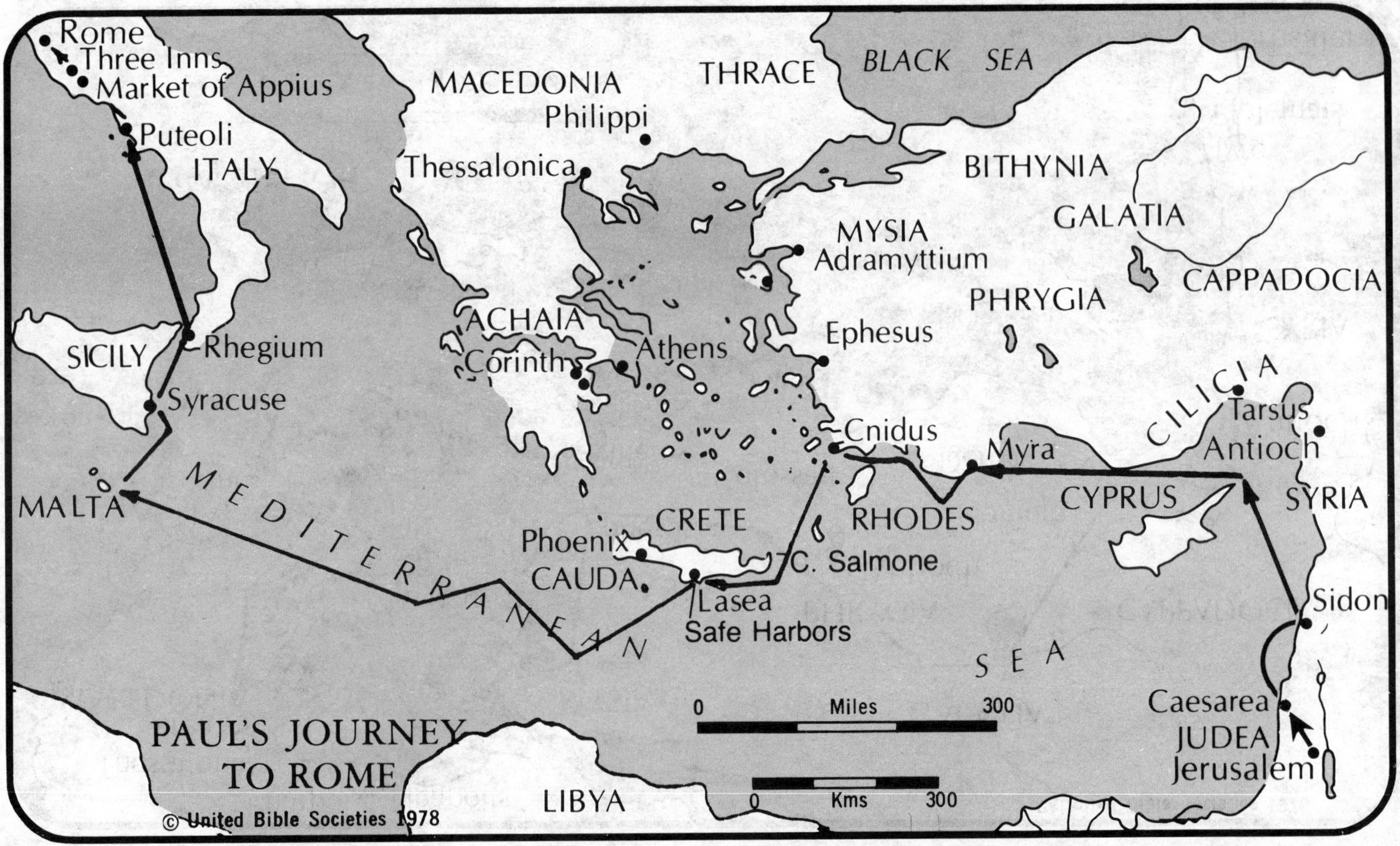
PAUL'S JOURNEY TO ROME
Rome
Three Inns
Market of Appius
Puteoli
ITALY
MACEDONIA
Philippi
Thessalonica
THRACE
BLACK SEA
BITHYNIA
GALATIA
MYSIA
Adramyttium
CAPPADOCIA
PHRYGIA
ACHAIA
Corinth
Athens
Ephesus
SICILY
Rhegium
Syracuse
CILICIA
Tarsus
Antioch
Cnidus
Myra
MALTA
MEDITERRANEAN
CYPRUS
SYRIA
CRETE
RHODES
Phoenix
CAUDA
C. Salmone
Lasea
Safe Harbors
Sidon
SEA
Caesarea
JUDEA
Jerusalem
0 Miles 300
0 Kms 300
LIBYA
© United Bible Societies 1978

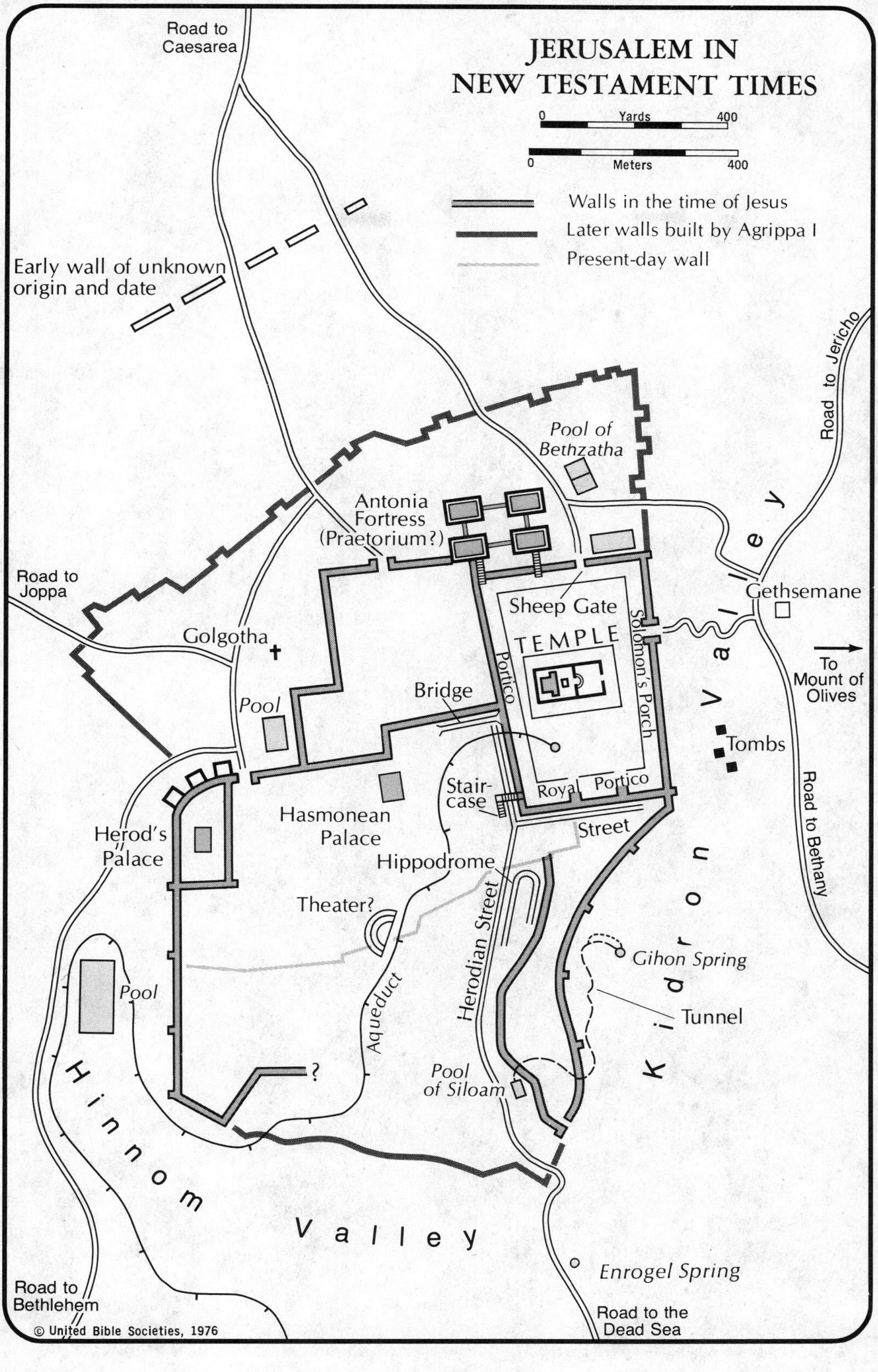
JERUSALEM IN
NEW TESTAMENT TIMES
0 Yards 400
0 Meters 400
Walls in the time of Jesus
Later walls built by Agrippa I
Present-day wall
Road to Caesarea
Early wall of unknown origin and date
Road to Jericho
Pool of Bethzatha
Antonia Fortress (Praetorium?)
Road to Joppa
Sheep Gate
Gethsemane
Solomon's Porch
TEMPLE
Golgotha
Portico
To Mount of Olives
Bridge
Pool
Tombs
Stair-case
Royal Portico
Herod's Palace
Hasmonean Palace
Street
Hippodrome
Road to Bethany
Theater?
Herodian Street
Gihon Spring
Pool
Aqueduct
Tunnel
Kidron Valley
?
Pool of Siloam
Hinnom Valley
Enrogel Spring
Road to Bethlehem
Road to the Dead Sea

SHARING GOD'S WORD WITH THE WORLD

This Bible represents a legacy of translating God's Word into the language of the people – into languages that will bring the Scriptures to life in the hearts of readers and hearers. The American Bible Society works with scholars from many countries to faithfully translate the Scriptures into languages and formats that speak clearly to both mind and heart. We encourage people everywhere to engage with the inspired Word of God – to embody its message and to experience a relationship with God through its reading.

To this end the American Bible Society, a not-for-profit Christian organization, offers programs to churches, other Bible-centered organizations, and individuals that connect people with God's living Word, and support the work of more than 100 other Bible Societies worldwide. Since our founding in 1816, people have generously supported the American Bible Society in its global mission to translate, publish, and provide Scriptures that are easily understood and affordable.

In many areas of the world, and even within the United States, the cost of a Bible often represents a hardship for many who thirst for God's Word. Thanks to the faithful support of many individuals, churches, and ministry partners, the American Bible Society continues to respond to the Scripture needs of the underserved and under engaged through effective programs and ministry partnerships.

We invite you to participate with us as we share God's Word with the world. To find how, please contact us at:

American Bible Society
1865 Broadway
New York, New York 10023-7505
1-888-227-8262